Western
Civilization
▼▼▼▼▼

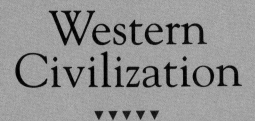

Western Civilization
▼▼▼▼▼

Jackson J. Spielvogel
The Pennsylvania State University

West Publishing Company
St. Paul   New York   Los Angeles   San Francisco

Production Credits

▼ ▼ ▼

Copyediting:	Patricia Lewis
Design:	David Farr, Imagesmythe Inc. & Tech Arts
Composition:	Carlisle Communications, Joan Weber, Coordinator.
Cover Illustration:	Pierre Deni-Martin, *Procession After Louis XV's Coronation at Rheims*, Musée National des Chateau de Versailles, © Photo R. M. N.

▼ ▼ ▼

COPYRIGHT © 1991   BY WEST PUBLISHING COMPANY
50 W. Kellogg Boulevard
P.O. Box 64526
St. Paul, MN 55164–0526

Printed in the United States of America

98 97 96 95 94 93 92 91   8 7 6 5 4 3 2 1 0

Library of Congress Cataloging-in-Publication Data

Spielvogel, Jackson J., 1939–
    Western civilization / Jackson J. Spielvogel.
       p.   cm.
    Includes bibliographical references.
    ISBN 0-314-82894-X (hardcover : comprehensive). — ISBN
0-314-82893-1 (volume I : softcover). — ISBN 0-314-82895-8 (volume
II : softcover). — ISBN 0-314-82896-6 (volume A : softcover). —
ISBN 0-314-82897-4 (volume B : softcover). — ISBN 0-314-82898-2
(volume C : softcover). — ISBN 0-314-82899-0 (since 1300 :
softcover)
    1. Civilization, Occidental—History: I. Title.
    CB245.S63 1990
    909′.09821—dc20   90–21772
                                         CIP ∞

Illustration Credits

▼ ▼ ▼

Chapter 1

Page 0 Egyptian Museum, Cairo; **5** Akkad, *Stele of Naram-Sin*, Musée du Louvre, © Photo R. M. N.; **6** Reproduced by Courtesy of the Trustees of the British Museum; **8** Robert Harding Picture Library; **9** Samuel Kramer, *The Sumerians*, University of Chicago Press, 1963, © University of Chicago Press; **12** Babylonian, *Stele of Hammurabi*, Musée du Louvre, © Photo R. M. N.; **17** Pair Statue of King Mycerinus and His Queen; From Giza, Dynasty IV, 2599–1571 B.C., Slate Schist, 54 1/2 in.; Harvard MFA Expedition. Courtesy, Museum of Fine Arts, Boston; **20** A. F. Kersting; **21** Courtesy of Jackson Spielvogel; **23** Egyptian Museum, Cairo; **25** Rene Burri/Magnum Photos, Inc.; **26** Reproduced by Courtesy of the Trustees of the British Museum; **27** Scala/Art Resource, N.Y.; **29** Courtesy of Karen Harvey.

Chapter 2

Page 32 Archers of the Persian Guard, Musée du Louvre, © Photo R. M. N.; **33** Phoenician Galleys, Musée du Louvre, © Photo R. M. N.; **35** Ronald Sheridan/Ancient Art and Architecture; **36** Marcello Bertinetti, Photo Researchers, Inc.; **42** Reproduced by Courtesy of the Trustees of the British Museum; **46** Reproduced by Courtesy of the Trustees of the British Museum; **47** Hirmer Fotoarchiv, Munich; **49** Popperfoto; **50** Archers of the Persian Guard, Musée du Louvre, © Photo R. M. N.; **52** Giraudon/Art Resource, N.Y.

Chapter 3

Page 56 The Metropolitan Museum of Art, Fletcher Fund, 1931 (31.11.10); **58** Minatallah/Art Resource, N.Y.; **59** Walter S. Clark/Photo Researchers, Inc.; **61** Black Figure Hydria: *Achilles Dragging the Body of Hector around the Walls of Troy*, William Francis Warden Fund; Courtesy, Museum of Fine Arts, Boston; **65** The Granger Collection, New York; **70** Minatallah/Art Resource, N.Y.; **76** Reproduced by Courtesy of the Trustees of the British Museum; **80** Courtesy of William M. Murray; **82** Sonia Halliday Photographs; **85** Courtesy of Jackson Spielvogel; **86** Scala/Art Resource, N.Y.; **89** The Metropolitan Museum of Art, Fletcher Fund, 1931(31.11.10).

Chapter 4

Page 96 The Granger Collection, New York; **98** American Numismatic Society, New York; **102** Scala/Art Resource, N.Y.; **103** The Granger Collection, New York; **105** Giraudon/Art Resource, N.Y.; **106** East Berlin, Staatliche Museen, Antikensammlung; **110** Reproduced by Courtesy of the Trustees of the British Museum; **115** The Metropolitan Museum of Art, Rogers Fund, 1909(09.39); **116** *Venus de Milo*, Musée du Louvre, © Photo R. M. N.; **117** The Metropolitan Museum of Art, Rogers Fund, 1911(11.90); **120** Yale University Art Gallery, Dura-Europos Collection.

(continued following Index)

About the Author

▼ ▼ ▼

Jackson J. Spielvogel is associate professor of history at The Pennsylvania State University. He received his Ph.D. from The Ohio State University, where he specialized in Reformation history under Harold J. Grimm. His articles and reviews have appeared in such journals as *Moreana, Journal of General Education, Catholic Historical Review, Archiv für Reformationsgeschichte,* and *American Historical Review.* He has also contributed chapters or articles to *The Social History of the Reformation, The Holy Roman Empire: A Dictionary Handbook, Simon Wiesenthal Center Annual of Holocaust Studies,* and *Utopian Studies.* His work has been supported by fellowships from the Fulbright Foundation and the Foundation for Reformation Research. At Penn State, he helped inaugurate the Western civilization courses as well as a popular course on Nazi Germany. His book, *Hitler and Nazi Germany,* was published in 1987. He has won three major university-wide teaching awards. During the year 1988–1989, he held the Penn State Teaching Fellowship, the University's most prestigious teaching award.

To Diane, whose love and support made it all possible

Contents

▼▼▼▼▼

Chapter 3

▼ The Civilization of the Greeks   56

Chapter 4

▼ The Hellenistic World   96

Chapter 5

▼ The Roman Republic   124

Chapter 6

▼ The Roman Empire   160

Chapter 7

▼ The Passing of the Roman World and the Emergence of Medieval Civilization (400–750)   198

Chapter 8

▼ European Civilization in the Early Middle Ages, 750–1000   232

Chapter 15

▼ Discovery and Crisis in the Sixteenth and Seventeenth Centuries   482

Chapter 16

▼ Response to Crisis: Absolute and Limited Monarchy in the Seventeenth and Early Eighteenth Centuries (to 1715)   522

Chapter 17

▼ Toward a New Heaven and a New Earth: The Scientific Revolution and the Emergence of Modern Science   562

Chapter 28

▼ The Deepening of the European Crisis: World War II 970

Chapter 29

▼ The Postwar Western World 1002

Chapter 30

▼ Epilogue–Toward a Global Civilization 1046

Documents

▼▼▼▼▼

Maps

▼▼▼▼▼

Chronologies

▼▼▼▼▼

Preface

▼ ▼ ▼

We are often reminded how important it is to understand today's world if we are to deal with our growing number of challenges. And yet that understanding will be incomplete if we in the Western world do not comprehend the meaning of Western civilization and the role Western civilization has played in the world. For all of our modern progress, we still greatly reflect our religious traditions, our political systems and theories, our economic and social structures, and our cultural heritage. I have written this history of Western civilization to assist a new generation of students in learning more about the past that has helped create them and the world in which they live.

As a teacher of Western civilization courses at a major university, I have become aware of the tendency of many textbooks to simplify the content of Western civilization courses by emphasizing an intellectual perspective or political perspective or, most recently, a social perspective, often at the expense of sufficient details in a chronological framework. This approach is confusing to students whose high school social studies programs have often neglected a systematic study of Western civilization. I have attempted to write a well-balanced work in which the political, economic, social, religious, intellectual, cultural, and military aspects of Western civilization have been integrated into a chronologically-ordered synthesis. I have been especially aware of the need to integrate the latest research on social history and women's history into each chapter of the book rather than isolating it either in lengthy topical chapters, which confuse the student by interrupting the chronological narrative, or in separate sections that appear at periodic intervals between chapters. If the results of the new social and women's history are to be taken seriously, they must be fully integrated into the basic narrative itself.

Another purpose in writing this history of Western civilization has been to put the story back in history. That story is an exciting one, yet many textbooks, often the product of several authors with different writing styles, fail to capture the imagination of their readers. Narrative history effectively transmits the knowledge of the past and is the form that best aids remembrance. At the same time, I have not overlooked the need for the kind of historical analysis that makes students aware that historians often disagree in their interpretations of the past.

To enliven the past and let readers see for themselves the materials that historians use to create their pictures of the past, I have included primary sources (boxed documents) in each chapter that are keyed to the discussion in the text. The documents include examples of the religious, artistic, intellectual, social, economic, and political aspects of Western life. Such varied sources as a Roman banquet menu, a student fight song in twentieth-century Britain, letters exchanged between a husband on the battle front and his wife in World War I, the Declaration of the Rights of Woman and the Citizen in the French Revolution, and a debate in the Reformation era, all reveal in a vivid fashion what Western civilization meant to the individual men and women who shaped it by their activities.

Each chapter has a lengthy introduction and conclusion to help maintain the continuity of the narrative and to provide a synthesis of important themes. Timelines enable students to see at a glance the major developments of an era, while the more detailed chronologies reinforce the events discussed in the text. An annotated bibliography at the end of each chapter reviews the most recent literature on each period and also gives references to some of the older, "classic" works in each field. Extensive maps and illustrations serve to deepen the readers' understanding of the text. In order to facilitate understanding of cultural movements, illustrations of artistic works discussed in the text are placed next to the discussions.

Because courses in Western civilization at American colleges and universities follow different chronological divisions, a one-volume edition, two two-volume editions, and a three-volume edition of this text are being made available to fit the needs of instructors. Teaching and learning ancillaries include an Instructor's Manual with Test Items (written by the author of the book), a Study Guide, Computerized Test Items, and Map Transparencies.

▼ Acknowledgements

I began to teach at age five in my family's grape arbor. By the age of ten, I wanted to know and understand everything in the world so I set out to memorize our entire set of encyclopedia volumes. At seventeen, as editor of the high school yearbook, I chose "Patterns" as its theme. With that as my early history, followed by twenty rich years of teaching, writing, and family nurturing, it seemed quite natural to accept the challenge of writing a history of Western civilization as I approached that period in life often described as the age of wisdom. Although I see this writing adventure as part of the natural unfolding of my life, I gratefully acknowledge that without the generosity of many others, it would not have been possible.

David Redles gave generously of his time and ideas, especially for chapter 29. Additional research and editorial assistance were provided by Laurie Batitto, Alex Spencer, Stephen Maloney, Shaun Mason, Peter Angelos, and Fred Schooley. I deeply appreciate the valuable technical assistance provided by Dayton Coles. I am thankful to the thousands of students whose questions and responses have caused me to see many aspects of Western civilization in new ways.

My ability to undertake a project of this magnitude was in part due to the outstanding European history teachers that I had both as an undergraduate and graduate student. These included: Kent Forster (modern Europe) and Robert W. Green (early modern Europe) at The Pennsylvania State University; and Franklin Pegues (medieval), Andreas Dorpalen (modern Germany), William McDonald (ancient), and Harold J. Grimm (Renaissance and Reformation) at The Ohio State University. These teachers provided me with profound insights into Western civilization and also taught me by their examples that learning only becomes true understanding when it is accompanied by compassion, gentleness, and openness.

Thanks to West Publishing Company's comprehensive review process, many historians were asked to evaluate my manuscript. I am grateful to the following for the innumerable suggestions that have greatly improved my work:

Roy A. Austensen
Illinois State University

James T. Baker
Western Kentucky University

John F. Battick
University of Maine

Fredric J. Baumgartner
Virginia Polytechnic Institute

Phillip N. Bebb
Ohio University

Leonard R. Berlanstein
University of Virginia

Werner Braatz
University of Wisconsin-Oshkosh

Alfred S. Bradford
University of Missouri

Hugh S. Bonar
California State University

Maryann E. Brink
College of William & Mary

Elizabeth Carney
Clemson University

Marc Cooper
Southwest Missouri State

Richard A. Cosgrove
University of Arizona

Porter Ewing
Los Angeles City College

Steven Fanning
University of Illinois at Chicago

Ellsworth Faris
California State University-Chico

Gary B. Ferngren
Oregon State University

A.Z. Freeman
Robinson College

Frank J. Frost
University of California, Santa Barbara

Richard M. Golden
Clemson University

Amy G. Gordon
Denison University

Hanns Gross
Loyola University

Jeffrey S. Hamilton
Old Dominion University

A.J. Heisserer
University of Oklahoma

Boyd H. Hill, Jr.
University of Colorado at Boulder

Frank L. Holt
University of Houston

Richard A. Jackson
University of Houston

Jenny M. Jochens
Towson State University

William M. Johnston
University of Massachusetts

James M. Kittelson
Ohio State University

Mavis Mate
University of Oregon

Eugene W. Miller, Jr.
The Pennsylvania State University-Hazleton

William M. Murray
University of South Florida

Otto M. Nelson
Texas Tech. University

Donald Ostrowski
Harvard University

James O. Overfield
University of Vermont

Linda J. Piper
University of Georgia

Janet Polasky
University of New Hampshire

Charles A. Povlovich
California State University-Fullerton

Jerome V. Reel, Jr.
Clemson University

Julius R. Ruff
Marquette University

Richard Saller
University of Chicago

Magdalena Sanchez
Texas Christian University

Jack Schanfield
Suffolk County Community College

Roger Schlesinger
Washington State University

Kyle C. Sessions
Illinois State University

Paul W. Strait
Florida State University

James E. Straukamp
Cal. State Univ.-Sacramento

Fred Suppe
Ball State University

Donna L. VanRapphorst
Cuyahoga Community College

Allen M. Ward
University of Connecticut

Walter J. Wussow
University of Wisconsin-Eau Claire

Edwin M. Yamauchi
Miami University

The editors at West Publishing Company have been both helpful and congenial at all times. Their flexible policies allowed the creative freedom that a writer cherishes. I especially wish to thank Clark Baxter, whose faith in my ability to do this project was inspiring. Developmental editor Nancy Crochiere was always helpful with many practical details. My production editor, Tamborah Moore, was a pillar of strength through a very lengthy process. Pat Lewis, my copy editor, taught me much about the fine points of the English language. Kara ZumBahlen and Lynn Reichel provided valuable assistance in obtaining illustrations and permissions for the boxed documents. I appreciate the professional and personal relationships that I have shared with the West "family."

Above all, I thank my family for their support. My daughters Jennifer and Kathryn, my sons Eric and Christian, and my daughter-in-law Liz were patient and tolerant of my time in the study. My wife and best friend Diane provided me with editorial assistance and the loving support that made it possible for me to complete a project of this magnitude. I could not have written the book without her.

JACKSON J. SPIELVOGEL

Introduction to Western Civilization

▼ ▼ ▼

Civilization, as historians identify it, first emerged between 5000 and 6000 years ago when people began to live in organized communities with distinct political, military, economic, and social structures. Religious, intellectual, and artistic activities also assumed important functions in these early societies. The focus of this book is on Western civilization, a civilization that for most of its history has been identified with the continent of Europe. Its origins, however, go back to the Mediterranean basin, including lands in North Africa and the Near East as well as Europe itself. Moreover, the spread of Europeans abroad led to the development of offshoots of Western civilization in other parts of the world.

Because civilized life includes all of the activities and experiences of people dwelling together in organized communities, the history of a civilization must encompass a series of studies. Examination of a society's economic structure reveals how it grew its food, how it made its goods, how it furnished the services it needed for the life of its people, and how private individuals and public authorities employed the material assets of their community. Although the way private individuals spend their money reflects individual goals, it also affects the larger society of which those individuals are a part. How governing authorities use public resources reveals much about the nature of a society. Huge expenditures on the military sector of a society, for example, decreases the availability of resources for the domestic welfare of its citizens.

From a study of social structure, we learn about the relationships that existed among the various social groups, how the wealth of the community was distributed, and how each social group lived. Political structure reveals how society was governed and which social group or groups controlled power. An investigation of the political structure also discloses the existence of mechanisms for change, or without such mechanisms, how revolutions arose and were justified by their leaders.

Also crucial to the understanding of a civilization is its culture, or the ideas, beliefs, and achievements of its people. This includes what historians now call high culture, which consists of the writings of a society's thinkers and the works of its artists. Frequently, the ideas and achievements of the intellectuals and artists have been used to define the ideals of a civilization. But historians now write as well of a civilization's popular culture, the world of ideas and experiences of the masses who constituted most of the people. Less privileged and less educated, however, they were often unable to express their ideas in writing, and until the recent work of social historians and anthropologists, were often considered less important to the story of a civilization.

The history of a civilization is also explained by how people in a society interpret their relationship to a spiritual reality. The definition of that relationship creates a society's religion and its system of values. In fact, religious values and perspectives have played crucial roles in the development of civilization.

The study of Western civilization, then, requires us to examine the political, economic, social, military, cultural, intellectual, and religious aspects that make up the life of that civilization and show how they are interrelated. In so doing, we need also at times to focus on some of the unique features of Western civilization. Certainly, science played a crucial role in the development of modern Western civilization. Although such societies as those of the Greeks, the Romans, and medieval Europeans were based largely on a belief in the existence of a spiritual order, Western civilization experienced a dramatic departure to a natural or material view of the universe in the seventeenth-century Scientific Revolution. Science and technology have been important in the growth of a modern and largely secular Western civilization, although antecedents to scientific development also existed in Greek, Islamic, and medieval thought and practice. By the twentieth century, science and technology had created the instruments that made possible incredible material and physical benefits as well as a threat of ecological catastrophe and physical annihilation.

For many historians, the concept of political liberty, the fundamental value of every individual, and the creation of a rational outlook, based on a system of logical, analytical thought, have also been viewed as unique aspects of Western civilization. Of course, Western civilization has also witnessed the frightening negation of liberty, individualism, and reason. Racism, violence, world wars, totalitarianism—these, too, must form part of the story. Finally, regardless of our concentration on Western civilization and its characteristics, we need to take into account that Western civilization was influenced by other civilizations and it, in turn, has affected the course of other civilizations.

Western Civilization

▼▼▼▼▼

Chapter 1

The Ancient Near East: Early Civilizations

▼ ▼ ▼ ▼ ▼

The development of civilized communities was a worldwide phenomenon. In the fertile valleys of the Tigris and Euphrates, the Nile, the Indus, and the Yellow River, in Mesopotamia, Egypt, India, and China, intensive agriculture became capable of supporting large groups of people. In these regions the first cities and states were born. The beginnings of Western civilization can be traced back to the ancient Near East, where people in Mesopotamia and Egypt developed organized societies and created the ideas and institutions that we associate with civilization. The later Greeks and Romans, who played such a crucial role in the development of Western civilization, were themselves nourished and influenced by these older societies in the Near East. It is appro-

priate, therefore, to begin our story of Western civilization in the ancient Near East with the early civilizations of Mesopotamia and Egypt. Before considering them, however, we must briefly examine humankind's prehistory and observe how human beings made the shift from hunting and gathering to agricultural communities and finally to cities and civilization.

▼ Early Human Beings

Historians use documents to create their pictures of the past. Such written records, however, do not exist for the prehistory of humankind. Consequently, the story of early humanity depends upon archaeological and, more recently, biological information, which anthropologists and archaeologists use to create theories about our early past. Although modern science has fostered the devel-

End of Neolithic Era	Sumerian Cities	Old Kingdom of Egypt	Middle Kingdom of Egypt	New Kingdom of Egypt
▼	▼	▼	▼	▼

•••••••• 4000 •••••••••• 3300 ••••••••••• 2600 •••••••••• 1900 •••••••••• 1200 ••••••••••

Sumerian Cuneiform	Epic of Gilgamesh	Great Pyramids	Code of Hammurabi
▲	▲	▲	▲

opment of more precise methods, much of our understanding of early humans relies upon considerable conjecture. Many archaeologists now believe that the earliest recognizable form of human being was *Homo habilis* (or "skilled human being"), who lived in Africa about 2.5 million years ago. However, the first anatomically modern humans, known as *Homo sapiens* (or "thinking human beings"), emerged in southern and eastern Africa around 100,000 years ago and eventually moved outward from there.

The Old Stone Age, c. 800,000–10,000 B.C.

One of the basic distinguishing features of the human species is the ability to make tools. The earliest tools were made of stone, and the term *Paleolithic* (or Old Stone Age) is used to designate this early period of human history. The archaeological record contains evidence of gradual changes in the human species during the Paleolithic period. Utilization of the opposable thumb made it possible to manipulate the hands and make tools. The development of the human brain encouraged the growth of abstract thought. At the same time, changing physical conditions during the ice ages posed a considerable threat to human existence.

There is no doubt that human adaptability was crucial to human survival. Paleolithic peoples gradually learned to employ their tools to alter their physical environment. The power to speak and think enabled humans to create a human culture that embodied a set of common ideas or beliefs, institutions, and material products that could be passed on to later generations.

The acquisition of food by hunting, fishing, and gathering was a major characteristic of the Paleolithic Age. Notably absent was any regular production of food. Fire came to be used for both cooking and heating. Paleolithic life may well have featured a social division grounded in gender. Women played an important role in gathering berries, nuts, and grains as well as making utensils, clothing, and baskets. Most importantly,

women bore and raised children, necessitating a more sedentary role. Men probably hunted, fished, made weapons, and undertook the fighting needed to protect their band from wild animals and fellow human beings.

The hunting of animals and the gathering of wild food undoubtedly necessitated certain patterns of living. Paleolithic groups were nomadic since they had no choice but to follow animal migrations and vegetation cycles. Hunting depended upon careful observation of animal behavior patterns and demanded group effort for any real chance of success. Over the years, tools became more refined and more useful. The invention of the spear, and later the bow and arrow, made hunting considerably easier while bone harpoons and fishhooks increased the catch of fish.

The Agricultural Revolution, c. 10,000–4000 B.C.

The end of the ice age around 10,000 B.C. was followed by what some historians call the Neolithic Revolution; that is, the revolution that occurred in the New Stone Age. This dramatic change involved the shift from the hunting of animals and the gathering of food to the production of food by systematic agriculture. The domestication of plants and food-producing animals created a new relationship between humans and nature. Although requiring great effort, this conscious production of food gave humans greater control over their environment. It also led them to organize in settled communities.

The shift to food producing from hunting and gathering was not, however, as sudden as was once believed. The Mesolithic period ("Middle Stone Age," c. 10,000–7000 B.C.) saw a gradual transition from the old food-gathering and hunting economy to a food-producing one and witnessed a gradual domestication of animals as well. Likewise, the movement toward the use of plants and their seeds as an important source of nourishment was also not sudden. Evidence seems to support the pos-

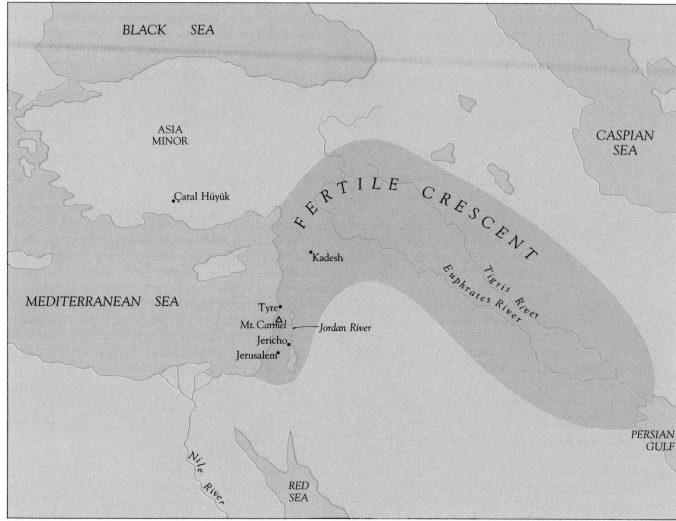

▼ **Map 1.1** The Ancient Near East

sibility that Paleolithic hunters and gatherers had already grown crops to supplement their traditional sources of food.

In fact, there is little certainty as to where systematic agriculture first began. It probably developed independently between 8000 and 7000 B.C. in four different areas of the world. In each of these areas, different plants were cultivated: wheat, barley, and lentils in the Near East, rice and millet in southern Asia, millet and yams in western Africa, and beans, potatoes, and corn in the middle Americas. In the Near East as elsewhere, the Neolithic agricultural revolution needed a favorable environment. For that reason, the upland areas above the Fertile Crescent (present-day northern Iraq and southern Turkey) were initially more conducive to systematic

farming than the river valleys. This region had the necessary rainfall and contained two wild plant (barley, wheat) and four wild animal (pigs, cows, goats, sheep) species that came to be domesticated for human use.

The growing of crops on a regular basis gave rise to more permanent settlements, which historians refer to as Neolithic farming villages or towns. One of the oldest known agricultural villages was Jericho, in Palestine near the Dead Sea. Jericho existed by 8000 B.C. and by 7000 B.C. covered several acres. It had a wall several feet thick that enclosed houses made of sun-dried bricks. Çatal Hüyük, located in modern-day Turkey, was an even larger community. Its walls enclosed thirty-two acres, and its population probably reached several thousand inhabitants during its high point from 6700 to 5700 B.C.

Archaeologists have discovered twelve cultivated products there including fruits, nuts, and three kinds of wheat. Çatal Hüyük contained buildings used exclusively for religious purposes. Female statuettes have also been found there. Molded with noticeably large breasts and buttocks, these "earth mothers" perhaps symbolically represented the fertility of both "our mother" earth and human mothers. In Çatal Hüyük as well as in other Neolithic towns, social roles were probably grounded in gender. While males continued to hunt, women took on greater importance by their active involvement in the early development of agriculture.

The Neolithic agricultural revolution had far-reaching consequences. The organized villages allowed a surplus of food and goods to be produced. Trade developed throughout the Near East. Individuals also began to specialize in certain crafts, and a division of labor developed. Pottery was made from clay and fired. The pots were used as containers and for cooking. Thread was made from vegetable and animal fibers, and the resulting flax and wool were woven into cloth by 6000 B.C. Baskets were also produced. Finally, stone tools were refined as flint blades were turned into microliths that could be used in sickles and hoes, both useful to agriculture.

Between 4000 and 3000 B.C., significant technical developments began to transform the Neolithic towns. The invention of writing (see Writing below) made possible the keeping of records while the emergence of bronze metallurgy marked a new level of human control over the environment and its resources. Already, before 4000 B.C., specialist craftsmen had discovered that metal-bearing rocks could be melted down in high-temperature kilns to produce liquid metal that could then be cast in molds to produce metal hoes, axes, knives, and swords that were much more effective than stone instruments. The smelting of gold to produce jewelry had already preceded the casting of metal for tools. Copper, which has a low melting point, was the first metal to be used for making tools. But after 4000 B.C., craftsmen in western Asia discovered that a combination of copper and tin produced bronze, a far harder and sturdier metal than copper. Its widespread use has led historians to speak of a Bronze Age from around 3000 to 1200 B.C., when bronze was increasingly replaced by iron. By the beginning of the Bronze Age, the concentration of larger numbers of people in the river valleys of Mesopotamia and Egypt was leading to a new phenomenon—the urban revolution. With it came civilization.

▼ The Emergence of Civilization

Historians have identified a number of basic characteristics of civilization, most of which are evident in the Mesopotamian and Egyptian civilizations. These include (1) an urban revolution: cities and city-states became the focal points for political, economic, social, and religious development; (2) a distinct religious structure: the gods were deemed crucial to the community's success, and professional priestly classes, as stewards of the gods' property, regulated relations with the gods; (3) new political and military structures: an organized government bureaucracy arose to meet the administrative demands of the growing population while armies were organized to gain land and power; (4) a new social structure based on economic power: while kings and an upper class of priests, political leaders, and warriors dominated, there also existed a large group of free men (farmers, artisans, craftsmen) and at the very bottom, socially, a class of slaves; (5) the development of writing: kings, priests, merchants, and artisans used writing to keep records; (6) new forms of significant artistic and intellectual activity, such as monumental architectural structures, usually religious, occupied a prominent place in urban environments; and (7) the development of more complexity in a material sense: capital was accumulated and metals smelted to produce a variety of material objects.

What caused the development of early civilizations remains difficult to explain. Since early civilizations developed independently in India, China, Mesopotamia, and Egypt, were there general causes that would explain the emergence of all of these civilizations? A number of possibilities have been suggested to explain the beginnings of civilization. In his famous A Study of History, historian Arnold Toynbee suggested a theory of challenge and response. Challenges forced human beings to make efforts that resulted in the rise of civilization. Some scholars have adhered to a material explanation. Material forces, such as the growth of food surpluses, made possible the specialization of labor and development of large communities with bureaucratic organization. But the area of the Fertile Crescent, in which Mesopotamian civilization occurred, was not naturally conducive to agriculture. It required massive human effort for careful management of water to produce abundant food, an effort that created the need for organization and bureaucratic control and led to civilized cities. Some historians have argued that nonmaterial forces, primarily religious, provided the sense of unity and purpose that made such organized activities possible. Finally, some scholars doubt that we are capable of ever discovering the actual causes of early civilization.

▼ Mesopotamian Civilization

The Greeks spoke of the river valley between the Tigris and Euphrates rivers as Mesopotamia, the land "between the rivers." Mesopotamia is a region of little rain, but the soil of the plain of southern Mesopotamia was enlarged and enriched over the years by layers of silt deposited by the two rivers. In late spring, the Tigris and Euphrates overflow their banks and deposit their fertile silt, but since this flooding depends upon the melting of snows in the upland mountains where the rivers begin, it is irregular and sometimes catastrophic. Therefore, farming could be accomplished only with human intervention in the form of irrigation and drainage ditches. A complex system was required to control the flow of the rivers and produce the crops. Large-scale irrigation made possible the expansion of agriculture in this region, and the abundant food provided the material base for the emergence of civilization in Mesopotamia.

Political Structures

The creators of Mesopotamian civilization were the Sumerians, whose origins are not clear. By 3000 B.C., the Sumerians had established a number of independent city-states consisting of walled cities and the surrounding countrysides. The earliest was Eridu, but Ur, Uruk, Umma, and Lagash were also well known. To the north of the Sumerians, a Semitic-speaking people known as the Akkadians had settled.

Sumerian history in the Early Dynastic Age (3000–2340 B.C.) witnessed three major political developments: the evolution of kingship, endemic warfare among the city-states, and a move toward larger territorial states. Although Sumerian myths have led some historians to believe that early Sumerian city-states practiced a form of "primitive democracy" in which political power resided in the hands of free citizens, it is more likely that control was in the hands of a priest-ruler (en, later ensi) or a king (lugal). It is possible that early kings were elected and initially served for a limited period of time, but kingship gradually became permanent and kings came to rival the priests for control of a community. Eventually, after kingship was institutionalized, Sumerians came to view it as divine in origin. Kings derived their power from the gods and were considered agents of the gods. The actual powers of kings included command of the armies, the initiation of legislation, the building of public works, the provision of a court of last resort, and the organization of labor to carry out the irrigation projects upon which Mesopotamian agriculture depended. Three institutions, loyal to the king, aided his execution of governmental power, the army, the government bureaucracy, and the priesthood, although the lat-

▼ **Map 1.2** Ancient Mesopotamia

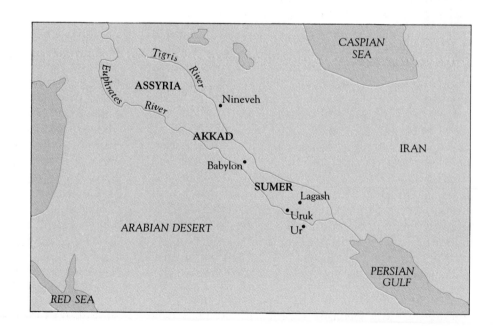

ter was sometimes equal to the kings in power and in some instances even dominated the state.

Constant rivalry over land and water rights dominated the relations between the Sumerian city-states. The fortunes of different cities rose and fell over the centuries, but attempts to dominate all of Sumer tended to fail until the king of Umma, Lugalzaggisi, succeeded in defeating Lagash, Uruk, and Ur and became ruler of all Sumer. But his success proved short-lived.

Around 2340 B.C., Sargon, leader of the Akkadians, defeated the army of Lugalzaggisi and established a new dynastic empire with Akkad as his capital city. Sargon's empire included all of Mesopotamia as well as lands westward to the Mediterranean and inspired generations of Near Eastern leaders to do what he had done. Despite a period of economic growth, prosperity, and cultural flowering, however, Sargon's successors were ultimately unable to preserve his empire. Domestic dissension, overexpansion, and pressure from new peoples caused the fall of Akkad by 2100 B.C.

One of Sargon's claims was that he had conquered a prosperous state called Ebla. In the 1960s and 1970s, archaeologists uncovered ancient Ebla in modern Syria. Excavations indicated that Ebla had been a well-organized city-state possessing a rich and complex urban culture. With a large population, it flourished from 2600 to 2250 B.C. and seemed to control an extensive area northwest of Mesopotamia. The discovery of 20,000 clay tablets written in a version of Sumerian cuneiform (see Writing below) provided important sources of information about this hitherto unknown community. The Ebla tablets revealed a Semitic civilization that had borrowed a great deal from Mesopotamian culture, a clear indication that Mesopotamian culture itself had spread far outside its own boundaries.

HAMMURABI AND THE BABYLONIAN EMPIRE   The end of the Akkadian empire brought a return to independent city-states in Mesopotamia until Ur-Nammu of Ur succeeded in reunifying much of Mesopotamia. The Third Dynasty of Ur (c. 2113–2000 B.C.) that he established witnessed a final flowering of Sumerian culture. New temples and canals were built. In addition to promulgating the first known comprehensive law code in Sumer, Ur-Nammu developed an efficient system of monthly obligations levied on major Sumerian and Akkadian provinces. A perennial problem in Mesopotamian history, invasion by nomadic tribes, proved disastrous for the Third Dynasty of Ur, however. After a lengthy period of fighting and confusion, the sixth king of the Amorite dynasty managed to establish power. Under

▼ **Stele of Naram-Sin, King of Akkad.** This sculpture in pink sandstone is from the period of Akkadian hegemony in Mesopotamia. The Akkadians were a Semitic-speaking people who had settled to the north of the Sumerians. Under their king Sargon, the Akkadians eventually came to dominate all of Mesopotamia. Internal disorder, overexpansion, and pressure from other peoples led to the end of Akkadian hegemony by 2100 B.C. The sculpture depicts the Akkadians attacking a hill tribe.

Hammurabi, the Amorites or Old Babylonians, a large group of Semitic-speaking seminomads, created a new empire.

Hammurabi (1792–1750 B.C.) was a competent king who learned to divide his opponents and subdue them one by one. He gained control of Sumer and Akkad and reunified Mesopotamia almost to the old borders created by Sargon of Akkad. A new capital was established at

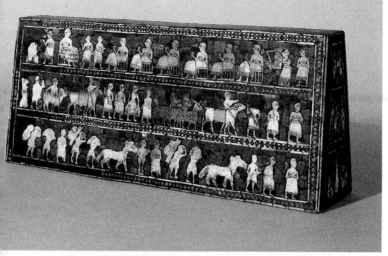

▼ **Standard of Ur.** For over a century after the disintegration of the Akkadian empire, Mesopotamia was dominated by warring city-states. It was not until Ur-Nammu of Ur succeeded in establishing another Sumerian empire that the greater part of Mesopotamia was reunited. While its actual use is not really known, this work, composed of shells, red limestone, and lapis-lazuli, may have been set on a pole to serve as a processional standard.

Babylon, north of Akkad. Hammurabi followed in the footsteps of previous conquerors by assimilating Mesopotamian culture with the result that Sumerian ways continued to exist despite the end of the Sumerians as a political entity. Hammurabi is best known for his law code, which provides considerable insight into social conditions in Mesopotamia (see Daily Life in Mesopotamia below). Hammurabi managed to strengthen a dynasty that lasted until the Kassites from the northeast took over in the 1550s B.C.

Economic and Social Structures

City-states were the basic units of Sumerian civilization. They were generally composed of three areas: an inner city consisting of dwellings, an outer city containing fields and unfortified villages, and a harbor area where merchants lived and carried on commercial activities. These cities were surrounded by walls. Uruk, for example, occupied an area of approximately a thousand acres encircled by a wall six miles long with defense towers located along the wall at intervals of thirty to thirty-five feet. City dwellings, built of sun-dried bricks, included both the small flats of peasants and the larger dwellings of the civic and priestly officials. The most prominent architectural feature was the temple dedicated to the patron god or goddess of the city and built adjacent to a massive stepped tower called a ziggurat.

Although its primary purpose was religious, the temple owned much of the city's land and livestock and served as the political, economic, and social center of the city. The Mesopotamian economy was primarily agricultural, but commerce and industry became important as well. Industry consisted of the production of woolen textiles and metal work for which the Mesopotamians became especially well known. As revealed in the documents of the Third Dynasty of Ur, foreign trade, which was primarily a royal monopoly, could be extensive. Royal officials imported luxury items, such as copper and tin, aromatic woods, and fruit trees, by land and sea in exchange for dried fish, wool, barley, wheat, and the metal goods produced by Mesopotamian craftsmen. Although goods were bartered, silver was also used for monetary payments. Besides the royal trade, temple agents and private individuals participated in commercial activity. Although it is sometimes difficult to draw a line between public and private economies in Mesopotamia, the public sector was usually more important with the palaces and temples amassing the greatest concentration of wealth. Taxes and tithes were paid to both complexes and then invested in independent commercial and agricultural enterprises.

Mesopotamian society came to be structured along very specific lines. There were three major social groups—nobles, commoners, and slaves. Nobles included royal and priestly officials and their families. Commoners consisted of clients who worked for palace and temple estates and other free citizens who worked as farmers, merchants, fishermen, scribes, and craftsmen. Probably 90 percent or more of the population were involved in agricultural pursuits. Crops could be exchanged for the goods of artisans in free town markets. Slaves belonged to palace officials, who used them mostly in building projects, temple officials, who used mostly female slaves to weave cloth and grind grain, and rich landowners, who used them for farming and domestic work.

Mesopotamian Culture

A spiritual worldview was of fundamental importance to Mesopotamian culture. In Mesopotamia, the gods were living realities who affected all aspects of life. It was crucial, therefore, that the correct hierarchies be observed. Leaders could prepare armies for war, but success really depended on a favorable relationship with the gods. This helps to explain the importance of the priestly class and the reason why even the kings took great care to dedicate offerings and monuments to the gods. The records of these dedications are among our earliest historical documents.

THE IMPORTANCE OF RELIGION The Mesopotamians viewed their city-states as earthly copies of a divine model and order. Each city-state was sacred since it was linked to a god or goddess. Hence, Nippur, the earliest center of Sumerian religion, was dedicated to Enlil, enforcer of the Sumerian gods, and Babylon to Marduk, who supplanted Enlil in Babylonian myth. Nannar, a moon god, was the owner of Ur. Moreover, located at the heart of each city-state was a temple complex. Occupying several acres, this sacred area consisted of a ziggurat with a temple at the top and bottom dedicated to the god or goddess who owned the city. The temple complex was the true center of the community. The main god or goddess dwelt there symbolically in the form of a statue, although the ceremony of dedication included a ritual that linked the statue to the god or goddess and thus supposedly harnessed the power of the deity for the city's benefit. Considerable wealth was poured into the construction of temples as well as other buildings used for the residences of priests and priestesses who helped the gods. Although the gods literally owned the city, the temple complex used only part of the land and rented out the remainder. Essentially, the temples dominated individual and commercial life, indicating the close relationship of religion to Mesopotamian culture.

The physical environment had an obvious impact on the Mesopotamian view of the universe. Ferocious floods, heavy downpours, scorching winds, and oppressive humidity were all part of the Mesopotamian climate. These conditions and resulting famines easily convinced Mesopotamians that this world was controlled by supernatural forces and that the days of human beings "are numbered; whatever he may do, he is but wind," as *The Epic of Gilgamesh* relates (see Mesopotamian Literature below). In the presence of nature, Mesopotamians could easily feel helpless, as this poem relates:

The rampant flood which no man can oppose,
Which shakes the heavens and causes earth to tremble,
In an appalling blanket folds mother and child,
Beats down the canebrake's full luxuriant greenery,
And drowns the harvest in its time of ripeness.

Rising waters, grievous to eyes of man,
All-powerful flood, which forces the embankments
And mows down mighty trees,

Sumerian City-States: Early Dynastic Age	c. 3000–2340 B.C.
Sargon's Empire	c. 2340–2100 B.C.
The Third Dynasty of Ur	c. 2113–2000 B.C.
Hammurabi's Reign	1792–1750 B.C.
Invasion by Kassites	c. 1550 B.C.

Frenzied storm, tearing all things in massed confusion
With it in hurtling speed.[1]

The Mesopotamians discerned cosmic rhythms in the universe and accepted its order, but perceived that it was not completely safe because of the presence of willful, powerful cosmic forces that they identified with gods and goddesses.

With its numerous gods and goddesses animating all aspects of the universe, Mesopotamian religion was polytheistic in nature. The four most important deities were An, Enlil, Enki, and Ninhursaga. An was the god of the sky and hence the most important force in the universe. Since his basic essence was authority, he was also viewed as the source or active principle of all authority, including the earthly power of rulers and fathers alike. In one myth, the gods address him thus:

What you have ordered comes true!
The utterance of prince and lord is but
*   what you have ordered, do agree with.*
O An! your great command takes precedence,
*   who could gainsay it?*
O father of the gods, your command,
*   the very foundations of heaven and earth,*
*   what god could spurn it?*[2]

Enlil, god of wind, was considered the second greatest power of the visible universe. In charge of the wind and thus an expression of the legitimate use of force, Enlil became the symbol of the proper use of force on earth as well. But the wind included not only the moist winds of spring that brought fertility to the soil, but also the destructive storms. This other side of Enlil created a justifiable fear of him, as this Mesopotamian hymn reveals:

What has he planned? . . .
What is in my father's heart?

▼ **Ziggurat at Ur.** This ziggurat, located at Ur, is rectangular in shape, not square like later ones. The ziggurat was located in the temple complex, which was at the heart of the city and occupied several acres. The ziggurat had a temple at both the top and the bottom dedicated to the god believed to own the city. The god was thought to dwell symbolically in the form of a statue at the temple complex, and a ritual performed during the ceremony of dedication supposedly linked the statue to the god, thus harnessing the god's power for the city.

What is in Enlil's holy mind?
What has he planned against me in his holy mind?
A net he spread: the net of an enemy;
* a snare he set: the snare of an enemy.*
He has stirred up the waters and will catch the fishes,
* he has cast his net, and will bring down the birds*
* too.*[3]

Enki was god of the earth. Since the earth was the source of life-giving waters, Enki was also god of rivers, wells, and canals. More generally, he represented the waters of creativity and was responsible for inventions and crafts. Ninhursaga began as a goddess associated with soil, mountains, and vegetation. Eventually, however, she was worshiped as a mother goddess, a "mother of all children," who manifested her power by giving birth to kings and conferring their insignia of officialdom upon them.

Although these four deities ranked supreme, there were numerous gods and goddesses below them. One group included astral deities, the powers in the lesser cosmic elements, who were all grandchildren and great-grandchildren of An. These included Utu, god of the sun, the moon god Nannar, and Inanna, goddess of the morning and evening star as well as of war and rain. Unlike humans, these and the various other gods and goddesses were divine and immortal. But it is important to remember that they were not all-powerful, since no one god had control over the entire universe. Moreover, humans were capable of devising ways to discover the will of the gods and to influence them as well.

The relationship of human beings to the gods was based on subservience since, according to Sumerian myth, humans had been created from the blood of a beast to serve the gods. Humans were consequently insecure since they could never be sure of the gods' actions. But humans did make attempts to circumvent or relieve their anxiety by discovering the intentions of the gods; these efforts gave rise to the development of the arts of divination. Their importance can be seen in the fact that texts on divination are the largest single category of Akkadian literature.

Divination took a variety of forms. A common form, at least for kings and priests who could afford it, involved killing animals, such as sheep or goats, and examining their livers or other organs. Supposedly, features seen in the organs of the sacrificed animals foretold events to come. Thus, one handbook states that if the animal organ has shape x, then the outcome of the military campaign will be y. Private individuals relied on cheaper divinatory techniques. These included interpreting patterns of smoke from burning incense or the pattern formed when oil was poured into water. Even the throw of dice could be used to foretell events. These methods of divination were based on the principle that a human request would evoke a divine response.

These methods were eventually superseded by intuitive ones that were based on the belief that divine purpose was everywhere and hence accessible. The new intuitive techniques included the interpretation of dreams and the examination of facial and bodily characteristics for omens. Rulers used more elaborate intuitive methods, primarily astrological ones, to read the skies to see what was coming. Horoscopic astrology, based on determining the specific heavenly influences at the time of one's birth, also came to be used.

The Mesopotamian arts of divination arose out of the desire to discover the purposes of the gods. If people could decipher the signs that foretold events, the events would be predictable and humans could act wisely. But the Mesopotamians also developed cultic arts to influence good powers (gods and goddesses) whose decisions could determine human destiny and to ward off evil powers (demons). These cultic arts included ritualistic formulas, such as spells against evil spirits, and prayers or hymns to the gods to gain their positive influence. Since only the priests knew the precise rituals, it is not hard to explain the important role they exercised in a society dominated by a belief in the reality of spiritual powers.

WRITING The realization of writing's great potential was another aspect of Mesopotamian culture. The oldest written Mesopotamian texts date to around 3000 B.C.

The Sumerians used a cuneiform ("wedge-shaped") system of writing. Using a reed stylus, they made wedge-shaped impressions on clay tablets, which were then baked or dried in the sun. Once dried, these tablets were virtually indestructible, and the several hundred thousand that have been found so far have provided a valuable source of information for modern scholars. Originally, Sumerian writing was pictographic. Scribes drew pictures or representations of concrete objects. Each sign represented a word identical in meaning to the object pictured, although pictures could also represent more than the actual object. Hence, the pictograph for boomerang meant not only boomerang, but also to throw and to throw down. The pictographic system proved cumbersome, however, and the characters were gradually simplified and stylized, and their pictographic nature gave way to conventionalized signs that symbolized ideas. The sign for star could be used to mean heaven, sky, or god. The next major step in simplification was the development of phonetization in which characters or signs were used to represent sounds. Thus, the character for water was also used to mean "in," since the Sumerian words for "water" and "in" sounded similar. With a phonetic system, the scribes could now represent words for which there were no pictographs, making possible the written expression of abstract ideas. Eventually, this led to a simplified system containing fundamental groups of symbols, creating a phonetic system with a number of symbols standing for a syllable.

Sumerian was the chief spoken and written language of Mesopotamia and the surrounding areas in the third millennium, but was replaced in the second millennium by Akkadian. After 2500 B.C., Sumerian cuneiform was adapted by Semitic-speaking peoples (as seen in Old Akkadian) for their own written languages. Eventually, two dialects of Old Akkadian were used in Mesopotamia, Assyrian in the north and Babylonian in the south.

Writing was used in Mesopotamian society primarily for record keeping. The most common cuneiform tablets record transactions of daily life: tallies of cattle kept by

▼ **The Development of the Cuneiform System of Writing.** This table shows the evolution of eighteen representative signs from c. 3000 B.C. to 600 B.C. Examples: No. 1 is a picture of a star. The sign for star also meant heaven, sky, or god. No. 11 is a picture of a water stream. The sign for water was also used for the word "in" since the Sumerian words for both "water" and "in" sounded alike. No. 12 is a picture of a head emphasizing the mouth and water. The compound sign represents a Sumerian word meaning to eat.

A Sumerian Schoolboy

▼ ▼ ▼

This document is a Sumerian essay narrating the daily activities of a schoolboy, written by a teacher as a copying exercise for pupils. The schoolboy experiences numerous trials and tribulations, including being beaten ("caned") for improper behavior. Scribal schools came into being in Sumer around 2500 B.C.

A Sumerian Essay for Schoolboys

"Schoolboy, where did you go from earliest day?"

"I went to school."

"What did you do in school?"

"I read my tablet, wrote it, finished it; then my prepared lines were prepared for me and in the afternoon, my hand copies were prepared for me."

Upon the school's dismissal, I went home, entered the house, there was my father sitting. I spoke to my father of my hand copies, then read the tablet to him, and my father was pleased; truly I found favor with my father.

"I am thirsty, give me drink, I am hungry, give me bread, wash my feet, set up the bed, I want to go to sleep; wake me early in the morning, I must not be late, or my teacher will cane me."

When I awoke early in the morning, I faced my mother, and said to her: "Give me my lunch, I want to go to school. . . ."

My mother gave me two "rolls," I went to school.

In the tablet-house, the monitor said to me: "Why are you late?" I was afraid, my heart beat fast. I entered before my teacher, took my place.

My "school-father" read my tablet to me, said "The . . . is cut off," caned me. . . .

Who was in charge of drawing said "Why when I was not here did you stand up?" caned me.

Who was in charge of the gate said "Why when I was not here did you go out?" caned me. . . .

My teacher said "Your hand is not good," caned me.

[At this point, the student decides he needs help and suggests to his father that he invite his teacher and give him some presents. The father does so, thanks the teacher, and treats him to a feast and gifts. The teacher now responds to the student.]

Young man, because you did not neglect my word, did not forsake it,

May you reach the pinnacle of the scribal art, achieve it completely

Because you gave me that which you were by no means obliged to give,

You presented me with a gift over and above my earnings, have shown me great honor, may Nidaba, the queen of the guardian deities, be your guardian deity.

May she show favor to your fashioned reed,

May she take all evil from your hand copies.

Of your brothers, may you be their leader,

Of your companions, may you be their chief,

May you rank the highest of all the schoolboys.

---

herdsmen for their owners; production figures; lists of taxes and wage payments; accounts; contracts; and court decisions affecting business life. There are also monumental texts, documents that were intended to last forever, such as inscriptions etched in stone on statues and royal buildings.

Still another category of cuneiform inscriptions includes a large body of basic texts produced for teaching purposes (see the box above). Schools for scribes were in operation by 2500 B.C. They were necessary because of the time needed to master the cuneiform system of writing. The primary goal of scribal education was to produce professionally trained scribes for careers in the temples and palaces, the military, and government service. Pupils were male and primarily from wealthy families. Gradually, the schools became important centers for culture since Mesopotamian literature was utilized for instructional purposes. Moreover, new literary productions came out of the scribal schools.

MESOPOTAMIAN LITERATURE   Although many fragments of Mesopotamian literary works remain, the most famous piece of Mesopotamian literature was *The Epic of Gilgamesh*. This epic poem, Sumerian in origin but preserved in Akkadian, records the exploits of a legendary

The Great Flood
▼ ▼ ▼

The great epic poem of Mesopotamian literature, The Epic of Gilgamesh, *includes an account by Utnapishtim (a Mesopotamian version of the later biblical Noah), who had built a ship and survived the flood unleashed by the gods to destroy humankind. This selection recounts how the god Ea advised Utnapishtim to build a boat and how he came to land his boat at the end of the flood. In this section, Utnapishtim is narrating his tale to Gilgamesh.*

The Epic of Gilgamesh

"In those days the world teemed, the people multiplied, the world bellowed like a wild bull, and the great god was aroused by the clamour. Enlil heard the clamour and he said to the gods in council, 'The uproar of mankind is intolerable and sleep is no longer possible by reason of the babel.' So the gods agreed to exterminate mankind. Enlil did this, but Ea [Sumerian Enki, god of the waters] because of his oath warned me in a dream. . . . 'tear down your house and build a boat, abandon possessions and look for life, despise worldly goods and save your soul alive. Tear down your house, I say, and build a boat. . . . then take up into the boat the seed of all living creatures. . . .' [Utnapishtim did as he was told and then the destruction came.]

"For six days and six nights the winds blew, torrent and tempest and flood overwhelmed the world, tempest and flood raged together like warring hosts. When the seventh day dawned the storm from the south subsided, the sea grew calm, the flood was stilled; I looked at the face of the world and there was silence, all mankind was turned to clay. The surface of the sea stretched as flat as a roof-top; I opened a hatch and the light fell on my face. Then I bowed low, I sat down and I wept, the tears streamed down my face, for on every side was the waste of water. I looked for land in vain, but fourteen leagues distant there appeared a mountain, and there the boat grounded; on the mountain of Nisir the boat held fast, she held fast and did not budge. . . . When the seventh day dawned I loosed a dove and let her go. She flew away, but finding no resting-place she returned. Then I loosed a swallow, and she flew away but finding no resting-place she returned. I loosed a raven, she saw that the waters had retreated, she ate, she flew around, she cawed, and she did not come back. Then I threw everything open to the four winds, I made a sacrifice and poured out a libation on the mountain top."

---

king of Uruk. Gilgamesh, wise, strong, and perfect in body, part man, part god, came to be disliked by the citizens of Uruk because of his constant activities. The citizens requested the gods to send a competitor to oppose him and keep him busy. The gods comply and send a hairy, barbaric beast named Enkidu whom Gilgamesh tries to weaken by having a prostitute seduce him. When Enkidu finally comes to Uruk, he and Gilgamesh engage in a fierce struggle that neither can win. The two become fast friends and set off in pursuit of heroic deeds. Ishtar (Sumerian Inanna), goddess of love, attempts to seduce Gilgamesh, but he refuses her advances. In anger, she convinces her father Anu (Sumerian An) to send a Bull of Heaven to kill Gilgamesh and Enkidu. They, however, manage to kill the bull instead, and the gods now decide that in return one of them must die. Enlil, god of wind, rules for Enkidu, and he falls ill and dies,

much to the prolonged grief of Gilgamesh. Gilgamesh experiences the pain of mortality and enters upon a search for the secret of immortality. He finds the man who had been granted "everlasting life" by the gods, Utnapishtim. The latter tells him the story of how he survived the Great Flood sent by the gods to destroy humankind (see the box above). Regretting what they had done, the gods bestowed immortality upon Utnapishtim. The latter now passes the secret on to Gilgamesh and instructs him to dive to the bottom of a river and find a certain plant that gives the power to grow younger. Although Gilgamesh finds the plant, a snake snatches it away before he can eat it. Gilgamesh remains mortal. The desire for immortality, one of humankind's great searches, ends in complete frustration. "Everlasting life," as this Mesopotamian epic makes clear, is only for the gods.

MATHEMATICS AND ASTRONOMY   The Mesopotamians made outstanding achievements in mathematics and astronomy. In math, they devised a number system based on 60, using combinations of 6 and 10 for practical solutions. They used the processes of multiplication and division and compiled tables for the computation of interest. The Mesopotamians also developed a sense of place value; that is, the value of a number depends on where it stands relative to other numbers. Geometry was utilized for practical purposes, such as measuring fields and building projects. In astronomy, the Mesopotamians made use of units of 60 and charted the chief heavenly constellations. Their calendar was based on twelve lunar months and was brought into harmony with the solar year by adding an extra month from time to time.

Daily Life in Mesopotamia

Remarkable insight into the daily life of Mesopotamia, at least for its later period, is provided in a famous document from the Babylonia of Hammurabi. As we have seen, people in Mesopotamian society viewed themselves as subservient to the gods. Unsure of the gods' actions because of their arbitrary decisions, the Mesopotamians manifested much insecurity. To counter it, they not only developed the arts of divination to fathom the wishes of the gods, but also relieved some anxiety by establishing codes that regulated their relationships with each other. These law codes became an integral part of Mesopotamian society. Although there were early Sumerian law codes, the best-preserved Mesopotamian compilation was that of Hammurabi (see the box on p. 13).

Since Babylonian society had no public prosecutors, private individuals were responsible for bringing charges before a court of law. To ensure that accusations of wrongdoing were not brought lightly, the accuser in cases of murder was responsible for proving his case against the defendant. If the accuser could not, he was put to death. Providing false testimony in a murder case was also punished by death. Similarly, since witchcraft was viewed as a serious social problem, the accused was subjected to an ordeal by water. He was pitched into the Euphrates River, and if he sank, his estate was given to the accuser. If he floated, the gods had declared his innocence, and he received the estate of the accuser who would in turn be put to death.

The Code of Hammurabi reveals a society with a system of strict justice. Penalties for criminal offenses were severe and varied by class. According to Hammurabi's code, there were three social classes in Babylonia: an upper class of nobles, which included government officials, priests, and warriors; a class of freemen comprised of merchants, artisans, professionals, and wealthier

▼ **Stele of Hammurabi (Code of Hammurabi, King of Babylonia).** Although there were earlier Sumerian law codes, Hammurabi's was the most famous in early Mesopotamian history. The code recognized three social classes in Babylonia (nobles, freemen, and slaves), and contained laws dealing with marriage and divorce, job performance, punishments for crime, and even sexual relations. The upper section of the stele depicts Hammurabi standing in front of a seated god, raising his right hand as a sign of devotion, while the lower section contains the actual code.

The Code of Hammurabi
▼ ▼ ▼

Although there were earlier Mesopotamian law codes, Hammurabi's is the most complete. It was inscribed on a stone stele topped by a bas-relief picturing Hammurabi receiving the inspiration for the law code from the sun god Shamash, who was also the god of justice. The law code emphasizes the principle of retribution ("an eye for an eye") and punishments that vary according to social status. Punishments could be severe. Marriage and family affairs also play a large role in the code. The following examples illustrate these concerns.

The Code of Hammurabi

25. If fire broke out in a seignior's [the translator used the word *seignior* to designate any free man of the upper class] house and a seignior, who went to extinguish it, cast his eye on the goods of the owner of the house and has appropriated the goods of the owner of the house, that seignior shall be thrown into that fire.

129. If the wife of a seignior has been caught while lying with another man, they shall bind them and throw them into the water. If the husband of the woman wishes to spare his wife, then the king in turn may spare his subject.

131. If a seignior's wife was accused by her husband, but she was not caught while lying with another man, she shall make affirmation by god and return to her house.

196. If a seignior has destroyed the eye of a member of the aristocracy, they shall destroy his eye.

198. If he has destroyed the eye of a commoner or broken the bone of a commoner, he shall pay one mina of silver.

199. If he has destroyed the eye of a seignior's slave or broken the bone of a seignior's slave, he shall pay one-half his value.

209. If a seignior struck another seignior's daughter and has caused her to have a miscarriage, he shall pay ten shekels of silver for her fetus.

210. If that woman has died, they shall put his daughter to death.

211. If by a blow he has caused a commoner's daughter to have a miscarriage, he shall pay five shekels of silver.

212. If that woman has died, he shall pay one-half mina of silver.

213. If he struck a seignior's female slave and has caused her to have a miscarriage, he shall pay two shekels of silver.

---

farmers; and a lower class of slaves, who, though oppressed, did possess some rights. An offense against a member of the upper class was punished with considerably more severity than the same offense against a member of a lower class. Moreover, the principle of retaliation ("an eye for an eye, a tooth for a tooth") was fundamental to this system of justice. It was applied in cases where members of the upper class committed criminal offenses against their own social equals. But for offenses against members of the lower classes, a money payment was made instead. Hence, "If a seignior has knocked out the tooth of a seignior of his own rank, they shall knock out his tooth. If he has knocked out a commoner's tooth, he shall pay one-third mina of silver."

It appears that Mesopotamian society, like all others, had its share of crime. Burglary was common and punishments were stern. If a person stole goods belonging to the temples or the state, he was put to death and so was the person receiving the stolen goods. If the private property of citizens was stolen, the thief had to make a tenfold restitution. If he could not afford to, he was put to death. Since the mudbrick construction of Mesopotamian homes made them easily vulnerable to robbery by digging holes in the walls, robbers, if caught in the act, "shall be put to death in front of that breach" and walled in. An offender caught attempting to loot a burning house was to be "thrown into that fire." These practices gave legal support to what people would ordinarily do anyway under those circumstances.

Hammurabi took seriously the responsibilities of his officials. The governor of an area and city officials were expected to catch burglars. If they failed to do so, officials in the district where the crime was committed had to replace the lost property. If murderers were not found, the officials had to pay a fine to the relatives of the murdered person. Soldiers were likewise expected to fulfill their duties and responsibilities for the order and maintenance of the state. If a soldier hired a substitute to fight for him, he was put to death, and the substitute was given control of his estate. Laws also sheltered ordinary soldiers from the wrongful actions of their officers. An officer who forced someone to join his army, took the goods of his soldiers, or wronged them seriously was executed.

Proper performance of work was also furthered by the law code, in what virtually amount to consumer protection laws. Builders were held responsible for the buildings they constructed. If a house collapsed and caused the death of the owner, the builder was put to death. If the collapse caused the death of the son of the owner, the son of the builder was put to death. If goods were destroyed by the collapse, they must be replaced and the house itself reconstructed at the builder's expense. While doctors were rewarded for successful operations, they could be severely punished for unsuccessful ones. If a doctor performed a major operation and his patient died, his hand would be cut off. If the patient was a slave, however, the doctor merely had to compensate the owner for the loss of a slave.

Slavery was a common feature of Mesopotamian society. Slaves were obtained from numerous sources. Some were war captives; others came from within the society itself. Crimes, such as striking one's older brother and kicking one's mother, were punished by condemnation to slavery. The head of a household could pay his debts by selling both his children and wife into slavery, although usually only for a specified period of years. He himself could be condemned to slavery if he defaulted on his loans. Slaves were used in temples, in the royal buildings, and in the homes of private citizens. In the temples, most slaves were women who did domestic chores, such as cooking and weaving. Royal slaves were used to construct buildings and fortifications. The slaves of private citizens mostly performed domestic duties. Laws were harsh for slaves who tried to escape or disobeyed. Hence, "If a male slave has said to his master, 'You are not my master,' his master shall prove him to be his slave and cut off his ear." Despite such harshness, slaves in Mesopotamia also possessed a number of privileges (at least, for slaves), such as being able to hold property, participate in business, marry free men or women (the children of such unions were free), and purchase their freedom.

The number of laws in Hammurabi's code dedicated to land tenure and commerce reveal the importance of agriculture and trade in the Mesopotamian economy. Numerous laws dealt with questions of landholding, such as the establishment of conditions for the renting of farmland and the division of produce between tenants and their landlords. Tenant farming was the basis of Mesopotamian agriculture. Tenant farmers paid their annual rent in crops rather than money. Laws concerning land use and irrigation were especially strict, an indication of the importance of agriculture to this society and the danger of declining crop yields if the land were used incompetently. If landowners and tenants failed to keep dikes in good repair or to control water flow properly and thus caused damage to others' crops, they were required to pay for the grain that was destroyed. If they could not pay, they were sold into slavery and their goods sold and the proceeds divided among the injured parties.

Commercial activity was carefully regulated. Rates of interest on loans were closely watched. If the lender raised his rate of interest after a loan was made, he lost the entire amount of the loan. The Code of Hammurabi even specified the precise wages of laborers and artisans, such as brickmakers and jewelers. Taverns were closely watched, and tavern operators (usually women) were drowned if they were caught watering down drinks to make greater profits.

The largest number of laws in the Code of Hammurabi were dedicated to marriage and the family. Parents arranged marriages for their children. After marriage, the parties involved signed a marriage contract; without it, no one was considered legally married. While the husband provided a bridal payment, the woman's parents were responsible for a dowry to the new husband. Dowries were carefully monitored and were governed by specific regulations.

As in many patriarchal societies, women possessed far fewer privileges and rights in the married relationship than men. A woman's place was in the home, and failure to fulfill her expected duties was grounds for divorce. If she was not able to bear children, her husband could divorce her, but he did have to return the dowry to the woman's family. If his wife tried to leave home to engage in business, thus neglecting her house, her husband could divorce her and did not have to repay the dowry. Furthermore, if his wife was a "gadabout, . . . neglecting her house [and] humiliating her husband," she could be drowned. We do know that in practice not all women remained at home. Some worked in business and were especially prominent in the running of taverns.

Women were guaranteed some rights, however. If a woman was divorced without good reason, she received the dowry back. A woman could seek divorce and get her dowry back if her husband was unable to show that she had done anything wrong. In theory, a wife was guaranteed the use of her husband's legal property in the event of his death. The mother also chose to which son an inheritance would be passed. Specific regulations were laid down in the event a husband was captured in war. If a warrior was taken captive, his wife was responsible for taking care of the household if her husband had been financially sound. Refusal to do so by leaving the estate resulted in drowning. If her husband's estate was not financially sound, his wife could remarry. But if the first husband returned from captivity, the woman had to return to him. If she had had children by both husbands, each father took his own children.

Sexual relations were strictly regulated as well. Husbands, but not wives, were permitted sexual activity outside marriage. A wife caught committing adultery was pitched into the river, although her husband could ask the king to pardon her. Incest was strictly forbidden. If a father committed incestuous relations with his daughter, he would be banished. Incest between a son and his mother resulted in both being burned.

Fathers ruled their children as well as their wives. Obedience was duly expected: "If a son has struck his father, they shall cut off his hand." If a son committed a serious enough offense, his father could disinherit him, although fathers were not permitted to disinherit their sons arbitrarily. Obviously, Hammurabi's law code covered virtually every aspect of people's lives. Recently, however, some legal scholars have questioned the extent to which these laws were actually employed in Babylonian jurisprudence.

▼ Egyptian Civilization

Although contemporaneous with Mesopotamia, civilization in Egypt evolved along somewhat different lines. Of central importance to the development of Egyptian civilization was the Nile River. That the Egyptian people recognized its significance is seen in this Hymn to the Nile (see the box on p. 18): "The bringer of food, rich in provisions, creator of all good, lord of majesty, sweet of fragrance. . . . He who . . . fills the magazines, makes the granaries wide, and gives things to the poor. He who makes every beloved tree to grow. . . ."[4] Egypt, like Mesopotamia, was a river civilization.

The Nile was responsible for creating an area several miles wide on both banks of the river that was fertile and capable of producing abundant harvests. The "miracle"

Chronology

▼ ▼ ▼

The Egyptians

Thinite Period or Early Dynastic (Dynasties 1–2)	c. 3100–2700 B.C.
Old Kingdom (Dynasties 3–6)	c. 2700–2200 B.C.
First Intermediate Period (Dynasties 7–10)	c. 2200–2060 B.C.
Middle Kingdom (Dynasties 11–12)	c. 2060–1785 B.C.
Second Intermediate Period (Dynasties 13–17)	c. 1785–1575 B.C.
New Kingdom (Dynasties 18–20)	c. 1575–1086 B.C.
Post-Empire (Dynasties 21–31)	1086–30 B.C.

of the Nile was its annual flooding. It rose in the summer from rains in central Africa, crested in Egypt in September and October, and left a deposit of silt that created an ever-renewable belt of cultivable soil. Unlike Mesopotamia's rivers, the flooding of the Nile was gradual and usually predictable, and the river itself was seen as life enhancing, not life threatening. Although a system of organized irrigation was still necessary, the small villages along the Nile could make the effort without the massive state intervention that was required in Mesopotamia. Egyptian civilization, consequently, tended to remain more rural with many small population centers congregated along a narrow band on both sides of the Nile.

The Nile enhanced other aspects of Egyptian civilization as well. In addition to providing food, it promoted easy transportation and encouraged communication. The Nile served as a unifying factor in Egyptian history. About one hundred miles from the Mediterranean, the river splits into two major branches before emptying into the sea, thus forming the delta, a triangular-shaped territory called Lower Egypt to distinguish it from Upper Egypt, the land of higher elevation to the south. Egypt's important cities developed at the apex of the delta.

Unlike Mesopotamia, which was subject to constant invasion, Egypt was blessed by natural barriers that fostered isolation, protected it from invasion, and gave it a sense of security. These barriers included the deserts to the west and east, the cataracts (rapids) on the southern part of the Nile, which made defense relatively easy, and the Mediterranean Sea to the north. The latter, of course, could and did serve later as an invasion route. These barriers, however, did not prevent the development of trade. Indeed, there is evidence of very early trade between Egypt and Mesopotamia itself.

In essence, Egyptian geography and topography played important roles in the early history of the country. The regularity of the Nile floods and the relative isolation of the Egyptians created a sense of security that was accompanied by a feeling of changelessness. Egyptian civilization was characterized by a remarkable degree of continuity over thousands of years. It was certainly no accident that Egyptians believed in cyclical rather than linear progress. Like the daily cycles of the sun and the annual overflow of the Nile, Egyptian kings too reaffirmed the basic, unchanging principles of justice at the beginning of each new cycle of rule.

Political Structures: The Old and Middle Kingdoms

The basic framework for the study of Egyptian history was provided by an Egyptian priest and historian, Manetho, who lived in the early third century B.C. He divided Egyptian history into thirty dynasties of kings. Based on Manetho and other king lists, modern historians have divided Egyptian history into three major periods known as the Old Kingdom, Middle Kingdom, and New Kingdom. These were periods of long-term stability characterized by strong monarchical authority, competent bureaucracy, freedom from invasion, much construction of temples and pyramids, and considerable in-

▼ **Map 1.3** Ancient Egypt

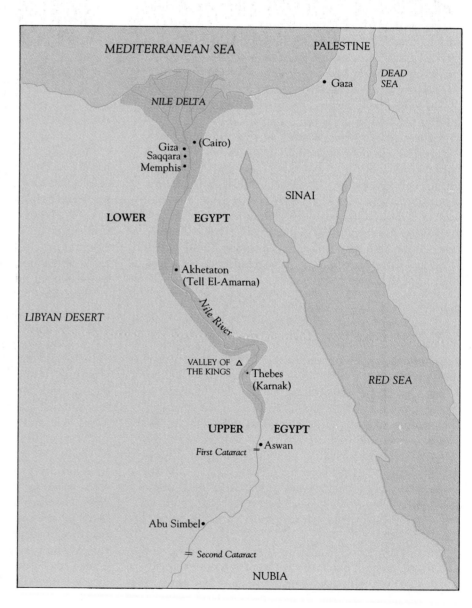

tellectual and cultural activity. But between the periods of stability were ages of political chaos known as the Intermediate periods, which were characterized by weak political structures and rivalry for leadership, invasions, a decline in building activity, and a restructuring of society.

THE OLD KINGDOM According to the Egyptians' own tradition, their land consisted initially of numerous populated areas ruled by tribal chieftains. Around 3100 B.C., during the Thinite or Early Dynastic period, the first Egyptian royal dynasty, under a king called Menes, united both Upper and Lower Egypt into a single kingdom. Henceforth, the king would be called "King of Upper and King of Lower Egypt," and the royal crown would be a double diadem, signifying the unification of all Egypt. Just as the Nile served to unite Upper and Lower Egypt physically, kingship served to unite the two areas politically.

The Old Kingdom encompassed the third through sixth dynasties of Egyptian kings, lasting from around 2700 to 2200 B.C. It was an age of prosperity and splendor, made visible in the construction of the greatest and largest pyramids in Egypt's history. The capital of the Old Kingdom was located at Memphis, south of the delta.

Kingship was a divine institution in ancient Egypt and formed part of a universal cosmic scheme (see the box on p. 18): "What is the king of Upper and Lower Egypt? He is a god by whose dealings one lives, the father and mother of all men, alone by himself, without an equal."[5] In obeying their king, subjects helped to maintain the cosmic order. A breakdown in royal power could only mean that citizens were offending divinity and weakening the universal structure. Among their various titles, that of pharaoh (originally meaning "great house" or "palace") became most common for the Egyptian kings during the period of the New Kingdom (see Chaos and a New Order below).

Although they possessed absolute power, Egyptian kings were not supposed to rule arbitrarily, but according to set principles. The chief one was called *Ma'at*, a spiritual precept that conveyed the idea of truth and justice, but especially right order and harmony. To ancient Egyptians, this fundamental order and harmony had existed throughout the universe since the beginning of time. Pharaohs were the divine instruments who maintained it and were themselves subject to it.

Although theoretically absolute in their power, in practice Egyptian kings did not rule alone. Initially, administrative tasks were performed by members of the

▼ **Pair Statue of King Menkaure and His Queen.** The period designated as the Old Kingdom began approximately four centuries after Egypt's unification (c. 3100 B.C.) and lasted until approximately 2200 B.C. This was the period in which Egypt's greatest and largest pyramids were constructed. The kings (eventually called "pharaohs") were understood to be gods, divine instruments who maintained the fundamental order and harmony of the universe and who wielded absolute power. This statue depicts King Menkaure and his queen (Dynasty IV).

king's family, but by the fourth dynasty a bureaucracy with regular procedures had developed. Especially important was the office of vizier, "steward of the whole land." Directly responsible to the king, the vizier was in charge of the bureaucracy with its numerous departments, such as police, justice, river transport, and public

Significance of the Nile River and the Pharaoh
▼ ▼ ▼

Two of the most important sources of life for the ancient Egyptians were the Nile River and the pharaoh. Egyptians perceived that the Nile River made possible the abundant food that was a major source of their well-being. This Hymn to the Nile, probably from the nineteenth and twentieth dynasties in the New Kingdom, expresses the gratitude Egyptians felt for the Nile.

Hymn to the Nile

Hail to you, O Nile, that issues from the earth
and comes to keep Egypt alive! . . .
He that waters the meadows which Re created,
in order to keep every kid alive.
He that makes to drink the desert and the place distant
from water:
that is his dew coming down from heaven. . . .
The lord of fishes, he who makes the marsh-birds to go
upstream. . . .
He who makes barley and brings emmer into being,
that he may make the temples festive.
If he is sluggish, then nostrils are stopped up, and
everybody is poor. . . .
When he rises, then the land is in jubilation, then every
belly is in joy,
every backbone takes on laughter, and every tooth is
exposed.
The bringer of good, rich in provisions, creator of all
good,
lord of majesty, sweet of fragrance. . . .
He who makes every beloved tree to grow, without lack
of them.

The Egyptian king, or pharaoh, was viewed as a god and the absolute ruler of Egypt. His significance and the gratitude of the Egyptian people for his existence are evident in this hymn from the reign of Sesotris III (c. 1880–1840 B.C.).

Hymn to the Pharaoh

He has come unto us that he may carry away Upper
Egypt;
the double diadem [crown of Upper and Lower
Egypt] has rested on his head.
He has come unto us and has united the Two Lands;
he has mingled the reed with the bee [symbols of
Lower and Upper Egypt].
He has come unto us and has brought the Black Land
under his sway;
he has apportioned to himself the Red Land.
He has come unto us and has taken the Two Lands
under his protection;
he has given peace to the Two Riverbanks.
He has come unto us and has made Egypt to live;
he has banished its suffering.
He has come unto us and has made the people to live;
he has caused the throat of the subjects to
breathe. . . .
He has come unto us and has done battle for his
boundaries;
he has delivered them that were robbed.

---

works. Agriculture and the treasury were the most important departments. Agriculture was, of course, the backbone of Egyptian prosperity, and the treasury collected the taxes that were paid in kind. A careful assessment of land and tenants was undertaken to establish the tax base.

For administrative purposes, Egypt was divided into provinces or nomes, as they were later called by the Greeks—twenty-two in Upper and twenty in Lower Egypt. A governor, called by the Greeks a nomarch, was head of each nome and was responsible to the king and vizier. Nomarchs, however, tended to build up large holdings of land and power within their nomes, creating a potential rivalry with the pharaohs. Of special importance to the administration of the state was a vast bureaucracy of scribes who kept records of everything. Armed with the knowledge of writing and reading, they were highly regarded and considered themselves a superior class of men. Their high standard of living reflected their exalted status.

THE MIDDLE KINGDOM Despite the theory of divine order, the Old Kingdom eventually collapsed, ushering in an Intermediate period of chaos (c. 2200–2060 B.C.). A so-called prophet named Nefer-Rohu (Neferti) described the scene:

This land is so damaged that there is no one who is concerned with it, no one who speaks, no one who weeps. . . . The sun disc is covered over. It will not shine so that people may see. . . . The rivers of Egypt are empty, so that the water is crossed on foot. Men seek for water for the ships to sail on it. . . . Foes have arisen in the east, and Asiatics have come down into Egypt. . . . This land is helter-skelter, and no one knows the result that will come about, which is hidden from speech, sight, or hearing.[6]

Several problems overwhelmed the Old Kingdom. Nomarchs grew in power as their positions became virtually hereditary over time. Consequently, the nomes became more independent and central authority was weakened. Loyalty to the nome replaced loyalty to the pharaoh. Famines, stemming from crop failures as a result of low Nile flooding, caused economic decline. During this first Intermediate period of chaos, new centers of importance even established rival dynasties, such as those at Heracleopolis near Lower Egypt and Thebes in Upper Egypt. Finally, the king of Thebes, Mentuhotep, defeated the ruler of Heracleopolis and achieved the reunification of all Egypt, thus beginning the Middle Kingdom, a new period of stability lasting from 2060 to 1785 B.C.

Much of the Middle Kingdom's history centered around the twelfth dynasty founded by Amenemhet I, a vizier who established himself and his successors as pharaohs. Egyptians later portrayed the Middle Kingdom as a golden age, a clear indication of its stability. Several factors contributed to its vitality. The nome structure was reorganized. The boundaries of each nome were now settled precisely, and the obligations of the nomes to the state were clearly delineated. Nomarchs were confirmed as hereditary officeholders but with the understanding that their duties must be performed faithfully. These included the collection of taxes for the state and the recruitment of labor forces for royal projects, such as stone quarrying. A new system of co-regency, in which the pharaoh took his son as a co-ruler to prepare him for governing and preclude succession problems, added to the vigor of the Middle Kingdom.

The Middle Kingdom was characterized by a new concern of the pharaohs for the people. In the Old Kingdom, the pharaoh had been viewed as an inaccessible god-king. Now he was portrayed as the shepherd of his people with the responsibility to build public works and provide for the public welfare. As one pharaoh expressed it: "He [a particular god] created me as one who should do that which he had done, and to carry out that which he commanded should be done. He appointed me herdsman of this land, for he knew who would keep it in order for him."[7]

As confirmation of its newfound strength, Egypt embarked upon a period of expansion. Lower Nubia was conquered, and fortresses were built to protect the new southern frontier. The government also sent military expeditions into Palestine and Syria. Although they did not remain there, this campaign marks the beginning of Egyptian imperialism in those areas.

Social and Economic Structures

Egyptian society had a simple structure in the Old and Middle Kingdoms; basically, it was organized along hierarchical lines with the god-king at the top. The king was surrounded by an upper class of nobles and priests who participated in the elaborate rituals of life that surrounded the pharaoh. This ruling class ran the government and managed its own landed estates, which provided much of its wealth.

Below the upper classes were merchants and artisans. Within Egypt, merchants engaged in an active trade up and down the Nile as well as in town and village markets. Barter was the primary means by which goods were exchanged. Some merchants also engaged in international trade; they were sent by the king to Crete and Syria where they obtained wood and other products. Expeditions traveled into Nubia for ivory and down the Red Sea to Punt for incense and spices. Egyptian artisans displayed unusually high standards of craftsmanship and physical beauty, while producing an incredible variety of goods: stone dishes; beautifully painted boxes made of clay; wooden furniture, especially of Lebanon cedar; gold, silver, and copper tools and containers; paper and rope made of papyrus; and linen clothes.

By far, the largest number of people in Egypt simply worked the land. In theory, the king owned all the land, but granted out portions of it to his subjects. Large sections were in the possession of nobles and the temple complexes. Moreover, although free farmers who owned their own land had once existed, by the end of the Old Kingdom, this group had disappeared. Most of the lower classes were serfs or common people bound to the land who cultivated the estates. They paid taxes in the form of crops to the king, nobles, and priests, lived in small villages or towns, and provided military service and labor for building projects.

The Culture of Egypt

Egypt produced a culture that dazzled and overawed its later conquerors. The Egyptians' technical achievements alone, especially visible in the construction of the pyramids, demonstrated a measure of skill unique to the

▼ **Temple of Hatshepsut.** This temple was built during the New Kingdom for Hatshepsut, who served as regent for her stepson Thutmoses III. Later she assumed the throne for herself and remained in power until her death. Although her claim to the throne was doubtful, she justified this move by claiming that her father had named her as his successor, that the God Amon named her pharaoh in an oracle, and that she was in fact the daughter of Amon.

world of that time. To the Egyptians, all of these achievements were part of a cosmic order suffused with the presence of the divine.

SPIRITUAL LIFE IN EGYPTIAN SOCIETY   It is misleading to speak of religion in Egyptian society. The Egyptians had no word for religion, since it was an inseparable element of the entire world order to which Egyptian society belonged. In the Old Kingdom, a document called the Memphite Theology portrayed Ptah as the creator-god who had held an image of the universe in his mind and

brought the entire universe into being by speaking the word. Ptah was embodied in every fiber of that universe, including Egypt. Egypt, then, belonged to the universal cosmic scheme, and the pharaoh was the divine being whose function was to maintain its stability within that cosmic order.

The Egyptians possessed a remarkable number of gods associated with heavenly bodies and natural forces. Two groups, sun gods and land gods, came to have special prominence, hardly unusual in view of the importance of the sun, the river, and the fertile land along its banks to Egypt's well-being. The sun was the source of life and hence worthy of worship. A sun cult developed, especially at Heliopolis, now a suburb of modern Cairo. The sun god took on different forms and names, depending on his specific function. He was worshiped as Atum in human form, as Khepra in the form of a scarab beetle, since it was believed that the sun, like the scarab, came forth out of its own substance, and as Re, who had a human body but the head of a falcon. In this last embodiment, he was also identified with the god Horus. Later, in the New Kingdom, Re became associated with Amon, an air god of Thebes, as Amon-Re. The pharaoh took the title of "Son of Re," since he was regarded as the earthly embodiment of Re.

River and land deities included Osiris and Isis with their child Horus, who was related to the Nile and to the sun as well. Osiris became especially important as a symbol of resurrection. A famous Egyptian myth related the struggle between Osiris, who brought civilization to Egypt, and his evil brother Seth, who killed him. The dead Osiris was found by his wife Isis who received the cooperation of other gods in resurrecting Osiris to new life. Their son Horus avenged his father by castrating Seth. As a symbol of resurrection and judge of the dead, Osiris took on an important role for the Egyptians. By identifying with Osiris, one could hope to gain new life, just as Osiris had done. The dead, embalmed and mummified, were placed in tombs (in the case of kings, in pyramidal tombs), given the name of Osiris, and, by a process of magical identification, became Osiris. Like Osiris, they could then be resurrected. The story of Osiris is one of the earliest accounts of a reborn god who helped humans to achieve immortality.

Later Egyptian spiritual practice developed an emphasis on morality by stressing Osiris's role as judge of the dead. The dead were asked to give an account of their earthly deeds to show whether they deserved a reward. Other means were also employed to gain immortality. As seen in the *Book of the Dead*, magical incantations were used to ensure a favorable journey to a happy afterlife.

Specific instructions were given on what to do when confronted with the judge of the dead. These instructions had two aspects. The negative confession gave a detailed list of what one had not done:

> What is said on reaching the Broad-Hall of the Two Justices [the place of the next-world judgment], absolving X [the name and title of the deceased] of every sin which he had committed, . . .
>
> I have not committed evil against men.
> I have not mistreated cattle.
> I have not committed sin in the place of truth [temple or burial place].
> I have not blasphemed a god. . . .
> I have not done violence to a poor man.
> I have not done that which the gods abominate.
> I have not defamed a slave to his superior.
> I have not made anyone sick.
> I have not made anyone weep.
> I have not killed. . . .
> I have not caused anyone suffering. . . .
> I have not had sexual relations with a boy.
> I have not defiled myself. . . .
> I have not driven cattle away from their pasturage. . . .
> I have not built a dam against running water. . . .
> I have not driven away the cattle of the god's property.[8]

Later the supplicant made a speech listing his good actions: "I have done that which men said and that with which gods are content. . . . I have given bread to the hungry, water to the thirsty, clothing to the naked, and a ferry-boat to him who was marooned. I have provided divine offerings for the gods and mortuary offerings for the dead."[9]

During the Middle Kingdom, the Osiris cult became "democratized"—extended to all Egyptians who aspired to an afterlife. This is particularly evident in the magical formulas called Coffin Texts that were inscribed on the wooden coffins of less wealthy Egyptians to ensure that the deceased would pass to a blessed afterlife.

THE PYRAMIDS   One of the great achievements of Egyptian civilization, the building of pyramids, occurred in the time of the Old Kingdom. Pyramids were not built in isolation but as part of a larger complex dedicated to the dead, in effect, a city of the dead. The area included a large pyramid for the king's burial, smaller pyramids for his family, and mastabas, rectangular structures with flat roofs as tombs for the pharaoh's noble officials. In order to hold services for the dead, a mortuary temple was built at the eastern base of the pyramid. From this temple, a causeway led to a valley chapel about a quarter of a mile away near the river bank. This causeway served as a processional avenue for the spirits of the dead. The tombs were well prepared for their residents. The rooms were furnished and stocked with numerous supplies, including chairs, boats, chests, weapons, games, dishes, and a variety of food. The Egyptians believed that the physical body had an etheric counterpart or vital force,

▼ **Sphinx and the Great Pyramid.** Both the Sphinx and the Great Pyramid were built during the Old Kingdom under the direction of King Khufu. Pyramids served as tombs for both the king and his immediate family, and were filled with the objects of everyday life, for it was believed that the *ka* (or spirit) would return after the death of the body and continue the life it had enjoyed on earth.

which they called the *ka*. If the physical body was properly preserved (hence mummification) and the tomb furnished with all the various objects of regular life, the *ka* could return and continue its life despite the death of the physical body. The pyramid, then, served a dual purpose. It was the king's tomb, but it could also be seen for miles away as a visible reminder of the glory and might of the ruler who was a living god on earth.

The first of the great pyramids was built in the third dynasty during the reign of King Djoser. The architect Imhotep, a priest of Heliopolis, the center dedicated to the sun cult, was responsible for the step pyramid at Saqqara. Beginning with Djoser, wives and immediate families of the kings were buried in pyramids, nobles and officials in mastabas.

The first real pyramid, in which each side was filled in to make an even surface, was constructed in the fourth dynasty around 2600 B.C. by King Snefru who built three pyramids. But the largest and most magnificent of all was built under Snefru's son Khufu. Constructed at Giza around 2540 B.C., the famous Great Pyramid covers thirteen acres, measures 756 feet at each side of its base, and stands 481 feet high. Its four sides are almost precisely oriented to the four points of the compass.

The building of the Great Pyramid was an enormous construction project that used limestone blocks as well as granite from Upper Egypt. The Greek historian Herodotus (see Chapter 3) reported the tradition that it took 100,000 Egyptians twenty years to build the great pyramid. But Herodotus wrote two thousand years after the event, and considerable controversy and speculation still surround the construction of the Great Pyramid, especially in view of the precision with which it was built. The interior included a grand gallery to the burial chamber, which was built of granite with a lidless sarcophagus for the pharaoh's body. The Great Pyramid still stands as a visible symbol of the power of Egyptian kings and the spiritual conviction that underlay Egyptian society. No pyramid built later in the Middle and New Kingdoms ever matched its size or splendor.

ART AND WRITING   Egyptian art was largely functional. Commissioned by kings or nobles, Egyptian art was used in either temples or tombs. In neither case was it intended to beautify or decorate its surroundings. Mural scenes and sculptured images of gods and kings in temples served a strictly spiritual purpose. They were an integral part of the performance of ritual, which was thought necessary to maintain the proper order of things and the well-being of Egypt. Likewise, the wall paintings and sculptured figures found in the tombs had a specific function. They were supposed to assist the passage of the deceased into the next world and secure his well-being once he was there. Although placed there to aid the dead, these works of art have proved valuable to us by providing glimpses of Egyptian daily life. Peasants are shown plowing the fields and harvesting their abundant crops. Nobles hunt and fish, and their banquets are pictured in graphic detail.

Egyptian art was also formulaic. Artists and sculptors were expected to observe strict canons that governed every aspect of form and presentation. These canons gave Egyptian art a distinctive appearance for thousands of years. Especially characteristic was the convention of combining the profile, semiprofile, and frontal views of the human body in relief work and painting in order to present accurately the true form of each part of the body. This fashion created an art that was highly stylized, yet still allowed distinctive features to be displayed.

Writing in Egypt emerged during the first two dynasties. It was the Greeks who later labeled Egyptian writing hieroglyphics, meaning "priest-carvings" or "sacred writings." Hieroglyphs were sacred characters used as picture signs that depicted objects and had a sacred value at the same time. Although hieroglyphs were later simplified for writing purposes into two scripts, they never developed into an alphabet. Egyptian hieroglyphs were initially carved in stone, but later the two simplified scripts were written on papyrus, a paper made from the papyrus reed that grew along the Nile. Most of the ancient Egyptian literature that has come down to us was written on papyrus rolls and wooden tablets. The most popular literature consisted of adventure stories about the actions of historical kings and famous men. The so-called Wisdom Texts were the most highly regarded pieces of literature. Written in the form of instructions from a father to his son, they provided sound advice based on tradition and worldly experience.

Chaos and a New Order

In contrast to the twelfth dynasty, the thirteenth exhibited considerable instability, foreshadowing the Second Intermediate period (c. 1785–1575 B.C.). This second age of chaos was initiated by an incursion into the delta region by a people known as the Hyksos. The Hyksos were part of a larger group of peoples who spoke Semitic languages and originally lived in the Arabian peninsula. Some of these Semitic-speaking peoples had moved into northern Mesopotamia as well as Syria and Palestine. The Hyksos began to infiltrate Egypt at the beginning of the eighteenth century B.C. and came to dominate much of Egypt from 1720 to 1575. Other peoples, such as the Nubians in the south, took advantage of Egypt's problems to free themselves from Egyptian control. However, the presence of the Hyksos was not entirely negative for Egypt. They introduced Egypt to Bronze Age technology by teaching the Egyptians how to make bronze for use in new agricultural tools and weapons. More significantly, the Hyksos introduced new aspects of warfare to Egypt, including the horse-drawn war chariot, a heavier sword, and the compound bow. Eventually, the Egyptians made use of their new weapons to throw off Hyksos domination.

It was the pharaoh Ahmose I who managed to defeat and expel the Hyksos from Egypt. He reunited Egypt, founded the eighteenth dynasty, established the New Kingdom (c. 1575–1086 B.C.), and launched the Egyptians along a new militaristic and imperialistic path. A more professional army was developed. Viziers, who were in charge of the state bureaucracy, were now chosen only from the ranks of military commanders.

During the period of the New Kingdom, Egypt became the most powerful state in the ancient Near East. Thutmose III (c. 1480–c. 1450 B.C.) led seventeen military campaigns into Syria and Palestine and even reached the Euphrates. Palestine and Syria were occupied, and local native princes were permitted to rule, but under Egyptian suzerainty. The sons of these princes were brought to Egypt as hostages to ensure cooperation. Thutmose also led his armies westward into Libya. Egypt was no longer content to remain in isolation but pursued an active political and diplomatic policy.

The height in power of the new Egyptian imperial state was reached during the reign of Amenhotep III (c. 1412–1375 B.C.), the great-grandson of Thutmose III. The achievements of the empire were made visible in the construction of magnificent new buildings and temples. Especially famous were the temple centers at Karnak and Luxor and the seventy-foot high statues of Amenhotep III in front of the mortuary temples along the Nile.

Egyptian conquests in its imperialistic age brought significant changes to the government of Egypt. Although the pharaoh was still viewed as a god, he lost a significant amount of real power to three strong institutions—the army, the royal bureaucracy, and the priesthoods. Conquests had greatly strengthened army commanders who had grown accustomed to acting autonomously while abroad. With the pharaohs frequently absent on military campaigns, the royal bureaucracy experienced a tremendous growth in independent power. Finally, the priesthoods, such as those of Re at Heliop-

▼ **Amenhotep IV (Akhnaton).** During the New Kingdom, the reign of Amenhotep IV was one of religious revolution. In place of the various deities worshiped by the Egyptians, Amenhotep introduced Aton, god of the sun disk, as the sole god. He closed temples dedicated to their gods, and strove to eliminate the cult of Amon-Re. For whatever reasons he might have had for beginning his revolution, Amenhotep failed, and Egypt remained polytheistic.

olis, Ptah at Memphis, and especially Amon-Re at Thebes, became rich and powerful. Gifts of conquered lands enabled the temples to accumulate vast estates and numerous slaves. The priesthood at Amon-Re had, in fact, became the chief land and capital owner in Egypt.

Akhnaton's Hymn to Aton

▼ ▼ ▼

Amenhotep IV, more commonly known as Akhnaton, created a religious revolution in Egypt by introducing the worship of Aton, god of the sun disk, as the sole god. Akhnaton's attitude to Aton is seen in this hymn. Some authorities have noted a similarity in spirit and wording to the 104th Psalm of the Old Testament.

Hymn to Aton

Your rays suckle every meadow.
When you rise, they live, they grow for you.
You make the seasons in order to rear all that you have
    made,
The winter to cool them,
And the heat that they may taste you.
You have made the distant sky in order to rise therein,
In order to see all that you do make.
While you were alone,
Rising in your form as the living Aton,
Appearing, shining, withdrawing or approaching,
You made millions of forms of yourself alone.
Cities, towns, fields, road, and river—

Every eye beholds you over against them,
For you are the Aton of the day over the earth. . . .
The world came into being by your hand,
According as you have made them.
When you have risen they live,
When you set they die.
You are lifetime your own self,
For one lives only through you.
Eyes are fixed on beauty until you set.
All work is laid aside when you set in the west.
But when you rise again,
Everything is made to flourish for the king, . . .
Since you did found the earth
And raise them up for your son,
Who came forth from your body:
the King of Upper and Lower Egypt, . . .
    Akh-en-Aton, . . . and the
Chief Wife of the King . . . Nefert-iti, living and
    youthful forever and ever.

By the end of his reign, Amenhotep III faced a growing military challenge from a people known as the Hittites (see The Hittites below). His son, Amenhotep IV (c. 1364–1347 B.C.), proved even less able to deal with this threat and even lost Syria and Palestine to the Hittites. In large part, Amenhotep's failure to respond favorably to foreign challenges was due to his preoccupation with a religious revolution that he had initiated in Egypt.

Amenhotep introduced the worship of Aton, god of the sun disk, as the sole god (see the box above). Some historians see this as the introduction of monotheism in a society that had always been polytheistic and consequently tolerant of many gods. Amenhotep pursued the worship of Aton with great enthusiasm, changing his own name to Akhnaton ("It is well with Aton"). He closed the temples of other gods and especially endeavored to lessen the power of Amon-Re and his priesthood at Thebes. Akhnaton strove to reduce their influence by replacing Thebes as the capital of Egypt with Akhetaton ("dedicated to Aton"), a new city located near modern Tell-el-Amarna, two hundred miles north of Thebes.

Historians are undecided about the significance of Akhnaton's revolution. Was it done for religious reasons? Was Amon-Re rejected by the pharaoh because he was deeply religious and believed in a single creator god? Or did the pharaoh create a religious revolution for political reasons, since reducing the power of the rich and powerful Amon-Re priesthood was certainly a necessity if Akhnaton wished to reassert royal power? Regardless of his reasons, Akhnaton's attempt at religious revolution proved to be a failure. It was too much to ask Egyptians to ignore their traditional ways and beliefs, especially since they saw the destruction of the old gods as subversive of the very cosmic order upon which Egypt's survival and continuing prosperity depended. Moreover, the priesthood at Thebes was unalterably opposed to the changes because of the implications for their position. Akhnaton's changes were soon undone after his death by those who influenced the boy-pharaoh Tutankhamon (1347–1338 B.C.). Tutankhamon returned the government to Thebes and restored the old gods. The Aton experiment had failed to take hold, and the eighteenth dynasty itself came to an end with the rise to power of a military officer and vizier, Horemhab, who assumed the kingship in 1333.

The nineteenth dynasty managed to restore Egyptian power one more time. Under Rameses II (c. 1279–1213 B.C.), the Egyptians regained control of Palestine but were unable to reestablish the borders of their earlier empire. New invasions in the thirteenth century by the "Sea Peoples," as the Egyptians called them, destroyed Egyptian power in Palestine and drove the Egyptians back within their old frontiers. The days of Egyptian empire were ended, and the New Kingdom itself expired with the end of the twentieth dynasty in 1086. For the next thousand years, despite periodic revivals of strength, Egypt was dominated by Libyans, Nubians, Persians, and finally Macedonians after the conquest of Alexander the Great (see Chapter 4). In the first century B.C., Egypt became a province in Rome's mighty empire. Egypt continued, however, to influence its conquerors by the richness of its heritage and the awesome magnificence of its physical remains.

Daily Life in Ancient Egypt

The spiritual preoccupations of the Egyptians did not lead them to practice asceticism in the hope of a better life in the next world. Ancient Egyptians had a very positive attitude toward daily life on earth. The Egyptian's home was his castle, and he followed the wise man who advised people to marry young and establish a home and family. Monogamy was the general rule, although a husband was allowed to keep additional wives if his first wife was childless. Pharaohs, of course, were entitled to harems. The queen was acknowledged, however, as the Great Wife with a status higher than that of the other wives. The husband was master in the house, but wives were very much respected and in charge of the household and education of the children. From a book of wise sayings (which the Egyptians called "instructions") came this advice:

> If you are a man of standing, you should found your household and love your wife at home as is fitting. Fill her belly; clothe her back. Ointment is the prescription for her body. Make her heart glad as long as you live. She is a profitable field for her lord. You should not contend with her at law, and keep her far from gaining control. . . . Let her heart be soothed through what may accrue to you; it means keeping her long in your house.[10]

Women did have equal legal rights with men. Their property and inheritance remained in their hands, even in marriage. Although most careers and public offices were closed to women, some did operate businesses. Peasant women worked long hours in the fields and at numerous domestic tasks. Upper-class women could function as priestesses, and a queen even became pha-

▼ **Temple of Rameses II at Abu Simbel.** After being driven out of Palestine and Syria by the Hittites during the reign of Amenhotep IV, Egypt grew to power one final time under Rameses II (c. 1279–1213). He succeeded in reconquering Palestine, but was unable to restore the boundaries of the previous empire. The massive Temple of Rameses II, located at Abu Simbel, was carved out of a cliff of Nubian sandstone. The giant statues represent Rameses II.

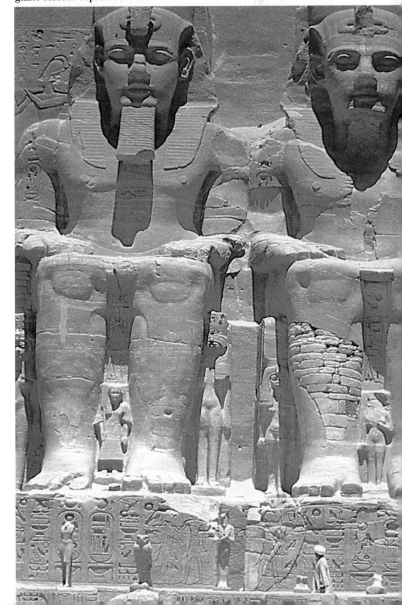

▼ **Banquet Scene.** The upper classes of Egypt indulged themselves with numerous banquets where an abundance of food and a variety of entertainments were provided for the guests. Although dancing girls were common at such gatherings, music was perhaps the primary form of entertainment. Many different instruments, ranging from flutes and trumpets to drums and harps, were used, and the generosity of the host was often praised in song. The detail is taken from a wall painting in a tomb found near Thebes.

raoh in her own right. This was Hatshepsut in the New Kingdom. Statues portray her with a flat chest, adorned with the pharaoh's traditional false beard.

Little is known about marital arrangements and ceremonies although it does appear that marriages were arranged by parents. The primary concerns were family and property, and the chief purpose of marriage was clearly to produce children, especially sons. From the New Kingdom came this piece of wisdom: "Take to yourself a wife while you are [still] a youth, that she may produce a son for you."[11] Only sons could carry on the family name. Daughters were not slighted, however. Numerous tomb paintings show the close and affectionate relationship parents had with both sons and daughters. Although marriages were arranged, some of the surviving love poems from ancient Egypt would indicate an element of romance in some marriages. Here is the lament of a lovesick boy for his "sister" (lovers referred to each other as "brother" and "sister"):

Seven days to yesterday I have not seen the sister,
  and a sickness has invaded me;

My body has become heavy,
  And I am forgetful of my own self.
If the chief physicians come to me,
  My heart is not content with their remedies . . . .
What will revive me is to say to me: "Here she is!"
  Her name is what will lift me up. . . .
My health is her coming in from outside:
  When I see her, then I am well.[12]

Marriages could and did end in divorce, which was allowed, apparently with compensation for the wife. Adultery, however, was strictly prohibited with stiff punishments, especially for women who could have their noses cut off or be burned at the stake.

Under normal circumstances, Egypt was blessed by a material abundance that not only kept its entire population fed, but also enabled its upper classes to lead a life of gracious leisure. These wealthy families had attractive homes located on estates surrounded by walls. Much energy was devoted to the garden, which contained space for fruit trees and vegetables, as well as tree-lined paths and pools for the family's leisure time.

Tomb paintings indicate that the upper classes participated in numerous banquets where guests were lavishly fed and entertained. Although some people obviously got drunk, a collection of "instructions" advises more circumspect behavior:

> If you are one of those sitting at the table of one greater than yourself, take what he may give, when it is set before your nose. You should gaze at what is before you. . . . Let your face be cast down until he addresses you, and you should speak only when he addresses you. Laugh after he laughs, and it will be very pleasing to his heart and what you may do will be pleasing to the heart.[13]

The same collection of "instructions" warns that when one has been invited to a party, "beware of approaching the women. It does not go well with the place where that is done."[14]

Entertainment, especially music, was a regular feature of parties. The Egyptians used an astonishing variety of instruments: drums, tambourines, flutes, trumpets, and a variety of stringed instruments that were plucked rather than played with a bow. Singers, accompanying themselves on lute or harp, presented songs in praise of the host's generosity and, judging from the words of this Middle Kingdom song, of dedication to enjoying life while one could: "Follow your desire, as long as you shall live. Put myrrh upon your head and clothing of fine linen upon you, ... Set an increase to your good things; let not your heart flag. Follow your desire and your good. Fulfill your needs upon earth, after the command of your heart, ..."[15]

Judging from the paintings in their tombs, the upper classes found a myriad of ways to entertain themselves as well. Fowling in the stands of papyrus reeds that grew along the riverbanks was a favorite pastime. Using a reed skiff, the huntsman used a boomerang to bring down his prey, much to the delight of his family who accompanied him. The hunting of animals was only for the men. The hunters rode in chariots using dogs to pursue antelope, gazelles, and other creatures who were shot with bows and arrows. Indoor activities consisted, among other things, of board games. The earliest known board games in the world have been found in Egyptian tombs. Many are made of wood decorated with ivory or ebony. The games played on them involved moving pieces on the boards according to the roll of the dice. We know considerably less about the activities of the lower classes, but we can be sure that they did not have the leisurely lifestyle of their social superiors.

▼ The Hittites

Our story of civilization in the ancient Near East has been dominated so far by Mesopotamia and Egypt. These two civilizations had at times expanded beyond their own frontiers and made contact with each other before 1500 B.C. By that time, however, new groups of peoples had established themselves in the Near East. The Hurrians created a new Kingdom of Mitanni, which reached its height around 1500 B.C. in the upper Euphrates valley. The Kassites seized Babylonia and established a Third Babylonian Dynasty (c. 1600–1100 B.C.).

▼ **Lion Gate at Hattusha.** The Hittites were an Indo-European people from Asia Minor and Anatolia (modern Turkey). They began expanding from this area in the thirteenth century B.C., moving into Mesopotamia and conquering Syria. The Hittites borrowed from the cultures of the peoples they conquered, as is evident from their law code and their religion, both of which reflect the influence of Mesopotamian culture. The sculpture is believed to have been part of a sacred well, although its true purpose is not known.

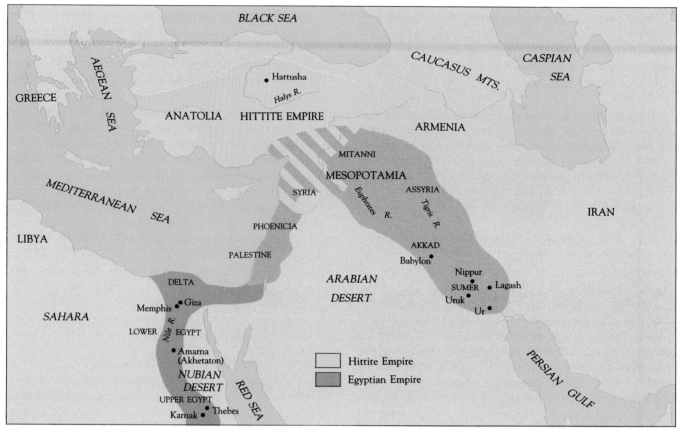

▼ **Map 1.4** Egyptian and Hittite Empires

Most important of all were an Indo-European people known as the Hittites.

The phrase *Indo-European* refers to people who used a language derived from a single parent tongue. Indo-European languages include Greek, Latin, Persian, Sanskrit, and the Germanic languages (see Table 1.1). As far as is currently known, the original Indo-European–speaking peoples were based somewhere in central Europe or southern Russia. Although there had been earlier migrations, around 2000 B.C. they began major nomadic movements into Europe (including present-day Italy and Greece), India, and the Near East. The Indo-Europeans who moved into Asia Minor and Anatolia (modern Turkey) coalesced with the native peoples to form the Hittite kingdom around 1750 B.C. with its capital at Hattusha (Bogazköy in modern Turkey).

The Hittites began to spread outward around 1600 B.C., but it was not until the reign of Suppiluliumas (c. 1380–1340 B.C.) that the Hittites established a real empire. He destroyed the power of the Hurrian Mitanni kingdom, which was allied with the Egyptians, and then conquered Syria. For the next hundred years, the Hittites were in conflict with Egypt until the Egyptian pharaoh Rameses II made a remarkable nonaggression treaty that stabilized relations between Egypt and the Hittites. The end of Hittite power came around 1200 when the Sea Peoples struck at both Egypt and the Hittite Empire. Egypt managed to keep the invaders out but remained weakened thereafter. The Hittite Empire was destroyed, however. By 1190, Hittite power was at an end.

Table 1.1 ▼ Some Indo-European Languages

Subfamily	Languages
Indo-Iranian	*Sanskrit*; Persian
Balto-Slavic	Russian; Serbo-Croatian; Czech; Polish; Lithuanian
Hellenic	Greek
Italic	*Latin*; Romance Languages (French, Italian, Spanish)
Celtic	Irish; Gaelic
Germanic	Swedish, Danish, Norwegian, German, Dutch, English

[Languages in italics are dead languages]

During its height, the Hittite Empire demonstrated an interesting ability to assimilate other cultures to create its own. In languages, literature, art, law, and religion, the Hittites borrowed much from Mesopotamia as well as the native peoples that they had subdued. Their law code, for example, though less harsh, reflected the influence of Mesopotamia. Hittite religion combined Indo-European deities and Mesopotamian gods, such as An and Ishtar. Recent scholarship has stressed the important role of the Hittites in transmitting Mesopotamian culture, as they transformed it, to later Western civilization in the Mediterranean area, especially to the Mycenaean Greeks.

The foundation stones for the building of Western civilization were laid by the Mesopotamians and the Egyptians. They developed cities and struggled with the problems of organized states. They developed writing to keep records and created literature. They constructed monumental architecture to please their gods, symbolize their power, and preserve their culture for all time. They developed new political, military, social, and religious structures to deal with the basic problems of human existence and organization. These first literate civilizations left detailed records that allow us to view how they grappled with three of the fundamental problems that humans have pondered: the nature of human relationships,

▼ **Stonehenge.** The Bronze Age in northwestern Europe is known for its "megaliths," or large standing stones. Between 3200 and 1500 B.C., standing stones that were placed in circles or lined up in rows were constructed throughout the British Isles and northwestern France. Some archaeologists have demonstrated that the stone circles were used as observatories to detect not only such simple astronomical phenomena as midwinter and midsummer sunrises, but also such sophisticated observations as the major and minor standstills of the moon. By far, the most famous of these megalithic constructions was Stonehenge in Great Britain. Stonehenge consists of a series of concentric rings of standing stones. Its construction was no small accomplishment. The eighty bluestones used at Stonehenge, for example, weighed four tons each and were transported to the site from their original source, a distance of 135 miles away.

the nature of the universe, and the role of divine forces in that cosmos. Although later peoples in Western civilization would provide different answers from those of the Mesopotamians and Egyptians, it was they who first posed the questions, gave answers, and wrote them down. Human memory begins with these two civilizations.

By the middle of the second millennium B.C., much of the creative impulse of the Mesopotamian and Egyptian civilizations was beginning to wane. The invasion of the Sea Peoples around 1200 B.C. ushered in a whole new pattern of petty states and new kingdoms that created the largest empires the ancient Near East had seen.

Notes
▼ ▼ ▼

1. Quoted in Thorkild Jacobsen, "Mesopotamia," in Henri Frankfort et al., *Before Philosophy* (Baltimore, 1949), p. 139.

2. Quoted in Thorkild Jacobsen, *The Treasures of Darkness: A History of Mesopotamian Religion* (New Haven, Conn., 1976), p. 97.

3. Ibid., pp. 101–2.

4. James B. Pritchard, *Ancient Near Eastern Texts*, 3d ed. (Princeton, N.J., 1969), p. 372.

5. Quoted in Milton Covensky, *The Ancient Near Eastern Tradition* (New York, 1966), p. 51.

6. Pritchard, *Ancient Near Eastern Texts*, p. 445.

7. Quoted in B. G. Trigger, B. J. Kemp, D. O'Connor, and A. B. Lloyd, *Ancient Egypt: A Social History* (Cambridge, 1983), p. 74.

8. Pritchard, *Ancient Near Eastern Texts*, p. 34.

9. Ibid., p. 36.

10. Ibid., p. 413.

11. Ibid., p. 420.

12. Quoted in John A. Wilson, *The Culture of Ancient Egypt* (Chicago, 1956), p. 264.

13. Pritchard, *Ancient Near Eastern Texts*, p. 412.

14. Ibid., p. 413.

15. Ibid., p. 467.

Suggestions for Further Reading
▼ ▼ ▼

For a beautifully illustrated introduction to the ancient world, see *Past Worlds: The Times Atlas of Archaeology* (Maplewood, N.J., 1988), written by an international group of scholars. A similar kind of guide with more elaborate historical discussions is provided by A. Cotterell, ed., *The Penguin Encyclopedia of Ancient Civilization* (London, 1980). A detailed history of the ancient world with chapters written by different specialists is available in the twelve volumes of *The Cambridge Ancient History*, now in its third edition. The following works are of considerable value in examining the prehistory of humankind: G. Clark, *World History in New Perspective* (Cambridge, 1977); M. N. Cohen, *The Food Crisis in Prehistory: Overpopulation and the Origins of Agriculture* (New Haven, Conn., 1977); R. Leakey, *The Making of Mankind* (London, 1981); J. Mellaert, *The Neolithic of the Near East* (New York, 1976); T. Champion, C. Gamble, S. Shennan, and A. Whittle, *Prehistoric Europe* (London, 1984); A. Whittle, *Neolithic*

Europe: A Survey (Cambridge, 1985); B. Bender, *Farming in Prehistory: From Hunter-Gatherer to Food Producer* (London and New York, 1975); C. Renfrew, *Before Civilization: The Radiocarbon Revolution and Prehistoric Europe* (London, 1973); and C. Redman, *The Rise of Civilization* (San Francisco, 1978). For a specialized study of the role of women in early human society, see F. Dahlberg, ed., *Woman the Gatherer* (New Haven, Conn., 1981).

A fascinating introduction to the world of ancient Near Eastern studies can be found in W. D. Jones, *Venus and Sothis: How the Ancient Near East Was Rediscovered* (Chicago, 1982). A very competent general survey primarily of the political history of Mesopotamia and Egypt is W. W. Hallo and W. K. Simpson, *The Ancient Near East: A History* (New York, 1971). Also valuable are C. Burney, *The Ancient Near East* (Ithaca, N.Y., 1977); J. N. Postgate, *The First Empires* (Oxford, 1977); and H. J. Nissen, *The Early History of the Ancient Near*

East, 9000–2000 B.C. (Chicago, 1988). Specialized studies on cultural aspects of the ancient Near East include S. N. Kramer, ed., *Mythologies of the Ancient World* (Garden City, N.Y., 1961); and H. Frankfort, *Art and Architecture of the Ancient Orient* (London, 1970). The fundamental collection of translated documents from the ancient Near East is J. B. Pritchard, *Ancient Near Eastern Texts,* 3d ed. with supplement (Princeton, N.J., 1969).

General works on ancient Mesopotamia include A. L. Oppenheim, *Ancient Mesopotamia,* 2d ed. (Chicago, 1977); S. Lloyd, *The Archaeology of Mesopotamia,* rev. ed. (London, 1984); G. Roux, *Ancient Iraq* (Harmondsworth, 1966); and M. E. Mallowan, *Early Mesopotamia and Iran* (New York, 1965). The world of the Sumerians has been well described in S. N. Kramer, *The Sumerians* (Chicago, 1963) and *History Begins at Sumer* (New York, 1959). Kramer's book *Sumerian Mythology* (New York, 1961) is a study of Sumer's spiritual and literary achievement in the third millenium B.C. On the recently discovered Ebla, see C. Bermant and M. Weitzmann, *Ebla: A Revelation in Archaeology* (New York, 1979); and P. Matthiae, *Ebla: An Empire Rediscovered* (London, 1980). The fundamental work on the spiritual perspective of ancient Mesopotamia is T. Jacobsen, *The Treasures of Darkness: A History of Mesopotamian Religion* (New Haven, Conn., 1976). On art, see S. Lloyd, *The Art of the Ancient Near East* (New York, 1961).

A. Gardiner, *Egypt of the Pharaohs* (Oxford, 1961) is a good narrative of political and military events in ancient Egypt. For an interesting introduction to Egyptian history, see B. J. Kemp, *Ancient Egypt* (London, 1989). A new approach is attempted in B. G. Trigger, B. J.

Kemp, D. O'Connor, and A. B. Lloyd, *Ancient Egypt: A Social History* (Cambridge, 1983). On Akhnaton and his religious revolution, see C. Aldred, *Akhenaten, Pharaoh of Egypt: A New Study* (New York, 1968); and D. Redford, *Akhenaten; the Heretic King* (Princeton, N.J., 1984). Egyptian religion is covered in H. Frankfurt, *Ancient Egyptian Religion* (New York, 1948), a brief but superb study; and S. Morenz, *Egyptian Religion* (London, 1973). The importance of the afterlife in Egyptian civilization is examined in A. Spencer, *Death in Ancient Egypt* (Harmondsworth, 1982). On culture in general, see J. A. Wilson, *The Culture of Ancient Egypt* (Chicago, 1956). The leading authority on the pyramids is I. E. S. Edwards, *The Pyramids of Egypt,* rev. ed. (Harmondsworth, 1976). On art, see E. Otto, *Ancient Egyptian Art* (New York, 1968); and H. Schäfer, *The Principles of Egyptian Art* (Oxford, 1974). There are many examples of Egyptian literature in M. Lichtheim, *Ancient Egyptian Literature,* 3 vols. (Berkeley, 1973–80). Daily life in ancient Egypt can be examined in J. White, *Everyday Life in Ancient Egypt* (London, 1963); P. Montet, *Everyday Life in Egypt in the Days of Ramses the Great,* trans. A. R. Maxwell-Hyslop (New York, 1974); and T. G. H. James, *Pharaoh's People: Scenes from Life in Imperial Egypt* (London, 1984).

On the Sea Peoples, see the standard work by N. Sandars, *The Sea Peoples: Warriors of the Ancient Mediterranean* (London, 1978). A good introductory survey on the Hittites can be found in O. R. Gurney, *The Hittites,* 2d ed. (Harmondsworth, 1981). See also J. Macqueen, *The Hittites and Their Contemporaries in Asia Minor* (Boulder, Col., 1975). On the Hyksos, see J. Van Seters, *The Hyksos: A New Investigation* (New Haven, 1966).

Chapter 2

The Ancient Near East: Peoples and Empires

▼ ▼ ▼ ▼ ▼

The destruction of the Hittite kingdom and the weakening of Egypt around 1200 B.C. temporarily left no dominant powers in the Near East, allowing a patchwork of petty kingdoms and city-states to emerge, especially in the area of Syria and Palestine. One of these small states, the Hebrew nation, has played a role in Western civilization completely disproportionate to its size. The Hebrews were a minor factor in the politics of the ancient Near East, but their spiritual heritage —in the form of the Judaeo-Christian view of life—is one of the basic pillars of Western civilization.

The small states did not last, however. Ever since the first city-states had arisen in the Near East around 3000 B.C., there had been an ongoing movement toward the creation of larger territorial states with more sophisticated systems of control. This process reached a high point in the first millennium B.C. with the appearance of empires that embraced the entire Near East. Between 1000 and 500 B.C., the Assyrians, Chaldeans, and Persians all created empires that encompassed either large areas or all of the ancient Near East. Each had impressive and grandiose capital cities that emphasized the power and wealth of its rulers. Each brought peace and order for a period of time by employing new administrative techniques. Each eventually fell to other conquerors. In the long run, these large empires had less impact on Western civilization than the Hebrew people. In human history, the power of ideas is often more significant than the power of empires.

▼ The Neighbors of the Hebrews

The Hebrews were not the only people who settled in the area of Palestine. The Philistines were probably part of the Sea Peoples who established five towns on the coastal plain of Palestine. They settled down as farmers and eventually entered into conflict with the Hebrews. While the Philistines were newcomers to the area, the Phoenicians had resided there for some time, but now found themselves with a new independence. A Semitic-speaking people, the Phoenicians resided along the Mediterranean coast on a narrow band of land 120 miles long. Their major cities, Byblos, Tyre, and Sidon, were rebuilt after destruction by the Sea Peoples. Their new-found political independence helped the Phoenicians expand the trade that was already the foundation of their prosperity. In fact, Byblos had been the principal distribution center for Egyptian papyrus outside Egypt (the Greek word for book, *biblos,* is derived from the name Byblos).

The chief cities of Phoenicia—Byblos, Tyre, and Sidon—were ports on the eastern Mediterranean, but they also served as distribution centers for the lands to the east in Mesopotamia. The Phoenicians themselves produced a number of goods for foreign markets, including purple dye, glass, wine, and lumber from the famous cedars of Lebanon. In addition, the Phoenicians improved their ships and became the great international sea traders of the ancient Near East. They chartered new routes, not only in the Mediterranean, but also in the Atlantic Ocean where they reached Britain and sailed south along the west coast of Africa. The Phoenicians established a number of colonies in the western Mediterranean, including settlements in southern Spain, Sicily, and Sardinia. Most of the Phoenician colonies were trading stations, not places where Phoenicians brought their families and settled permanently. A major exception was Carthage, the Phoenicians' most famous colony, located on the north African coast.

Culturally, the Phoenicians are best known as transmitters. Instead of using pictographs or signs to represent whole words and syllables as the Mesopotamians and Egyptians did, the Phoenicians simplified their writing by using twenty-two different signs to represent the sounds of their speech. These twenty-two characters or letters could be used to spell out all the words in the

▼ **Phoenician Galley.** The Phoenicians were a Semitic-speaking people dwelling in ancient Palestine. After gaining their independence with the fall of the Egyptian and Hittite empires, they became the predominant sea trading nation of the ancient Near East. The Phoenicians also established a number of colonies in the western Mediterranean. A Phoenician-type galley is depicted here.

Phoenician language. Although the Phoenicians were not the only people to invent an alphabet, they developed one that was eventually passed on to the Greeks. From the Greek alphabet was derived the Roman alphabet that we still use today. The Phoenicians achieved much while independent, but they ultimately fell subject to the Assyrians, Chaldeans, and Persians.

▼ The Hebrews

To the south of the Phoenicians existed another group of Semitic-speaking people known as the Hebrews. They had a tradition concerning their origins that was eventually written down as part of the Jewish Bible, known to Christians as the Old Testament. Historians do not agree on the extent to which the early books of the Jewish Bible reflect a true history of the early Hebrews. The Hebrews' own tradition states that

▼ **Map 2.1** Ancient Palestine

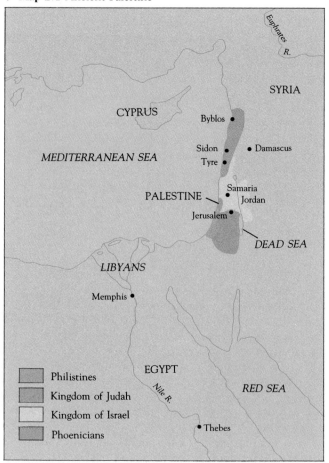

they were descendants of the patriarch Abraham who had migrated from Mesopotamia to the land of Palestine, where they became identified as the "Children of Israel." The Hebrews were a nomadic people, organized along tribal lines, who followed a lifestyle based on grazing flocks and herds rather than farming. According to tradition, because of drought the Hebrews migrated to Egypt where they lived peacefully until a pharaoh enslaved them. Thereafter, they remained in bondage until Moses led his people out of Egypt in the well-known "exodus." Some historians believe this would have occurred in the first half of the thirteenth century B.C. The Hebrews then wandered for many years in the desert until they entered Palestine (possibly around 1220 B.C.). Organized in tribes, they entered into conflict with the Philistines, who had settled in the coastal area of Palestine but were beginning to move into the inland areas. Leaders called judges assumed the leadership of the Hebrews in these conflicts. Around 1000 B.C., under the pressure of the ongoing struggle with the Philistines, the Hebrews embarked upon the establishment of a monarchy.

Political Aspirations and Frustrations

The creation of a monarchy, first accomplished by Saul (c. 1020–1000 B.C.), was not an easy task because many Hebrews were still accustomed to tribal life and tribal organization. Saul achieved some success in the ongoing struggle with the Philistines but committed suicide after a defeat by his enemies. After a brief period of anarchy, one of Saul's lieutenants, David (c. 1000–971 B.C.), reunited the Hebrews, defeated the Philistines, and established control over all of Palestine. The city of Jerusalem was conquered and made into the capital of a united kingdom. David's conquests accelerated the integration of the formerly nomadic Hebrews into a more settled community based on farming and urban life. Centralized political organization was replacing the independent ways of the twelve Hebrew tribes.

David's son Solomon (c. 971–931 B.C.) did even more to strengthen royal power. He expanded the political and military establishments and was especially active in extending the trading activities of the Hebrews. Solomon is best known for his building projects, including a large palace with state offices and forts for the protection of trade routes. Of all his new construction projects, the most famous was the Temple in the city of Jerusalem. The Hebrews viewed the Temple as the symbolic center of their religion, and hence of the Hebrew kingdom itself. The Temple now housed the Ark of the

Covenant, the holy chest containing the sacred relics of the Hebrew religion and, symbolically, the throne of the invisible God of Israel. Under Solomon, ancient Israel was at the height of its power, but his efforts to centralize royal power along the lines of Mesopotamian despotism led to dissatisfaction among his subjects, who believed that his actions threatened the old Hebrew tribal ties.

After Solomon's death, the tension between the northern and southern Hebrew tribes led to the establishment of two separate kingdoms—a Kingdom of Israel, composed of the ten northern tribes with its capital at Samaria, and a southern Kingdom of Judah, consisting of two tribes with its capital at Jerusalem. The northern Kingdom of Israel, especially under King Ahab (869–850 B.C.), joined other petty Syrian states to stop temporarily the onslaught of the Assyrians, who had consolidated their kingdom to the northeast (see The Assyrian Empire below). But the power of Israel declined after Ahab and by the end of the ninth century, the Kingdom of Israel was forced to pay tribute to powerful Assyria. In the next century, the kingdom itself was destroyed. The Assyrians overran it, destroyed the capital of Samaria in 722 B.C., and deported many Hebrews to other parts of the Assyrian empire. These dispersed Hebrews (the "ten lost tribes") merged with neighboring peoples and gradually lost their identity.

The southern Kingdom of Judah was also forced to pay tribute to Assyria but managed to survive as an independent state because of declining Assyrian power. A new enemy, however, appeared on the horizon. The Chaldeans, allied with the Medes from Iran, brought the final destruction of Assyria. Under King Nebuchadnezzar, the Chaldeans then conquered the Kingdom of Judah and completely destroyed Jerusalem in 586 B.C. Many upper-class Hebrews were sent into exile to Babylonia, the memory of which is still evoked in the stirring words of Psalm 137:

> By the rivers of Babylon, we sat and wept when we
>   remembered Zion. . . .
> How can we sing the songs of the Lord while in a
>   foreign land?
> If I forgot you, O Jerusalem, may my right hand forget
>   its skill.
> May my tongue cling to the roof of my mouth if I do
>   not remember you, if I do not consider Jerusalem my
>   highest joy.[1]

But the Babylonian captivity of the Hebrew people did not last. Upon the destruction of the Chaldean kingdom by a new set of conquerors, the Persians, the Jews were

▼ **A Representation of the Ark of the Covenant.** The most famous project carried out under King Solomon was the building of the Temple in Jerusalem. Within the Temple, the Israelites placed the Ark of the Covenant, the holy chest that contained the sacred relics of the Hebrew faith. The Ark was also considered to be the throne of the invisible God on earth. This representation of the Ark, believed to be one of the earliest, is from the second century A.D. synagogue at Capernaum.

allowed to return to Jerusalem and rebuild their city and temple. The revived Kingdom of Judah remained under Persian control until the conquests of Alexander the Great in the fourth century B.C. The people of Judah survived, eventually becoming known as the Jews and giving their name to Judaism, the religion of Yahweh, the Jewish god. The Babylonian captivity had served to transform Judaism. It became a stateless religion, based on the conviction that God was not fixed to one particular land, but was both creator and lord of the whole world.

Spiritual Dimensions of Israel

The great empires of the Assyrians, Chaldeans, and Persians obliterated many small communities of peoples. For the majority of these states, destruction and exile meant the end of these peoples on the historical scene. Although the Hebrews suffered both defeat and exile, they did not disappear from history, primarily due to their religious strength. The Hebrews believed that their god Yahweh had saved them from obliteration. Obviously, historians are not capable of confirming such a claim, but they are aware that often in history what people believe about themselves is more important than the actual events themselves. The Hebrews "knew" they were the chosen people, and their conviction secured their survival. Their religion, then, is crucial to an understanding of the Hebrews.

The spiritual dimensions of the Hebrews evolved over a period of time. The earliest ancestors of the Hebrews were polytheistic in their spiritual outlook, but by the

▼ **Mount Sinai.** According to their tradition, the Hebrews entered into a covenant with God while wandering in the desert after leaving Egypt. They promised to worship only Yahweh and to obey his laws. A part of these laws is the Decalogue (the Ten Commandments), received by the prophet Moses on Mount Sinai. Both the law and the covenant with Yahweh became crucial elements of the Hebrew faith. Mount Sinai is pictured in the photograph.

time they had returned to Palestine after their captivity in Egypt, the Hebrew version of monotheism had begun to emerge. It was centuries, however, before pure monotheism, or the belief that there is only one God for all peoples, became standard. Clearly, the Hebrew religion was rooted in historical experience, and our examination of it must begin with how the Hebrews viewed God after a long period of evolution.

THE CONCEPTION OF GOD   The Hebrew conception of God is monotheistic. There is but one God, whom the Hebrews called YHWH, which by convention is written Yahweh. God is the creator of the world and everything in it. Indeed, Yahweh means "he causes to be." All the gods of all other peoples were simply idols, whose worship constituted acts of idolatry. The Hebrew God was totally sovereign and ruled the world; he was subject to nothing. All peoples were his servants, whether they knew it or not. This God was also transcendent. He had created nature, but was not in nature. The stars, moon, rivers, wind, and other natural phenomena were not divinities or suffused with divinity, as other peoples of the ancient Near East believed, but God's handiwork. All of God's creations could be admired for their awesome beauty, but not worshiped as god.

This omnipotent creator of the universe was not removed from the life he had created, however, but was a just and good God who expected goodness from his people. If they did not obey his will, they would be punished. But he was also a God of mercy and love: "The Lord is gracious and compassionate, slow to anger and rich in love. The Lord is good to all; he has compassion on all he has made."[2] The God of the Hebrews was a loving father who bore the Hebrews an "everlasting love" despite their disobedience.

The Hebrew conception of God directly affected their conception of human beings. The Hebrew spiritual perspective emphasized individual worth. Each person, possessed of moral freedom, had the ability to choose between good and evil. But an important condition was attached to this freedom. People could not simply establish their own ethical standards. Through Moses and other holy men, God had made known his commandments, his ideals of behavior. True freedom consisted of accepting God's ethical norms voluntarily. If people chose to ignore the good, then suffering and evil would follow. Each individual ultimately bore responsibility for his or her decisions. Despite the powerful dimensions of God as creator and sustainer of the universe, the Hebrew message also emphasized that each person could have a personal relationship with this powerful being. As the

The Covenant and the Law: The Book of *Exodus*
▼▼▼

During the exodus from Egypt, the Hebrews supposedly made their covenant with Yahweh. They agreed to obey their God and follow his law. In return, Yahweh promised to take special care of his chosen people. This selection from the book of Exodus describes the making of the covenant and God's commandments to the Hebrews.

Exodus 19: 1–8

In the third month after the Israelites left Egypt—on the very day—they came to the Desert of Sinai. After they set out from Rephidim, they entered the desert of Sinai, and Israel camped there in the desert in front of the mountain. Then Moses went up to God, and the Lord called to him from the mountain, and said, "This is what you are to say to the house of Jacob and what you are to tell the people of Israel: 'You yourselves have seen what I did to Egypt, and how I carried you on eagles' wings and brought you to myself. Now if you obey me fully and keep my covenant, then out of all nations you will be my treasured possession. Although the whole earth is mine, you will be for me a kingdom of priests and a holy nation.' These are the words you are to speak to the Israelites." So Moses went back and summoned the elders of the people and set before them all the words the Lord had commanded him to speak. The people all responded together, "We will do everything the Lord has said." So Moses brought their answer back to the Lord.

Exodus 20: 1–3, 7–17

And God spoke all these words, "I am the lord your God, who brought you out of Egypt, out of the land of slavery. You shall have no other gods before me. . . . You shall not misuse the name of the Lord your God, for the Lord will not hold anyone guiltless who misuses his name. Remember the Sabbath day by keeping it holy. Six days you shall labor and do all your work, but the seventh day is a Sabbath to the Lord your God. On it you shall not do any work, neither you, nor your son or daughter, nor your man-servant or maidservant, nor your animals, nor the alien within your gates. For in six days the Lord made the heavens and the earth, the sea, and all that is in them, but he rested on the seventh day. Therefore the Lord blessed the Sabbath day and made it holy. Honor your father and your mother, so that you may live long in the land the Lord your God is giving you. You shall not murder. You shall not commit adultery. You shall not steal. You shall not give false testimony against your neighbor. You shall not covet your neighbor's house. You shall not covet your neighbor's wife, or his manservant or maidservant, his ox or donkey, or anything that belongs to your neighbor.

psalmist sang: "My help comes from the Lord, the Maker of heaven and earth. He will not let your foot slip—he who watches over you will not slumber."[3]

The Hebrew conception of God was closely related to three aspects of the Hebrew religious tradition that have special significance: the covenant, the law, and the prophets.

THE COVENANT AND THE LAW During the exodus from Egypt, when Moses led his people out of bondage into the promised land, a special event supposedly occurred that determined the Hebrew experience for all time. According to tradition, God entered into a covenant or contract with the tribes of Israel who believed that Yahweh had spoken to them through Moses (see the box above). The Hebrews promised to obey Yahweh and follow his law. In return, Yahweh promised to take special care of his chosen people, "a peculiar treasure unto me above all people."

This covenant between Yahweh and his chosen people could be fulfilled, however, only by Hebrew obedience to the law of God. Law became a crucial element of the Hebrew world. This law stemmed from three sources: the customs of the originally nomadic Hebrews, the law of Palestine, which was similar to the law codes of Mesopotamia, and the laws given by God to Moses for the Hebrews, as seen in the Ten Commandments. Consequently, Hebrew law had a number of different dimensions. In some instances, it set forth specific requirements, such as payments for offenses. Most important, since the major characteristic of God was his goodness, ethical concerns stood at the center of the law. Sometimes these took the form of specific standards of moral behavior: "You shall not murder. You shall not commit adultery. You shall not steal."[4] But these concerns were also expressed in decrees that regulated the economic, social, and political life of the community since God's laws of morality applied to all areas of life. These laws made no class distinctions and emphasized the protection of the poor, widows, orphans, and slaves.

THE PROPHETS   The prophets were "holy men" who supposedly had special communion with God and felt called upon to serve as his voice to his people. Since the prophets were believed to be able to foretell the future, even the kings sometimes sought their advice and guidance. The prophets, however, had little interest in power and possessions. They preached, whether invited to or not, and had no hesitation in saying whatever pleased them, even if it displeased the established authorities. In the ninth century B.C., the prophets were particularly vociferous about the tendency of the Hebrews to accept other gods, chiefly the fertility and earth gods of other peoples in Palestine. They warned of the terrible retribution that God would exact from the Hebrews if they did not keep the covenant and remain faithful to him alone (see the box on p. 39).

The golden age of prophecy began in the mid-eighth century and continued during the time when the Hebrews were threatened by Assyrian and Chaldean conquerors. The words of these reforming prophets were written down and are part of the Hebrew Bible. These "men of God" went through the land warning the Hebrews that they had failed to keep God's commandments and would be punished for breaking the covenant: "I will punish you for all your iniquities." Amos prophesied the fall of the northern kingdom of Israel to Assyria; twenty years later Isaiah said the kingdom of Judah too would fall; and two hundred years later, Jeremiah said that Jerusalem would be crushed by the Babylonians.

But the prophets did not just spread doom and gloom. Once the disasters had occurred as they foretold and many Hebrews had been sent into exile, the prophets offered a new message of hope. Fearful that the Hebrew exiles might accept the conqueror's gods out of desperation and despair, the prophets tried to kindle optimism by changing their basic message. Since the Hebrews had been punished for their sins and had repented of their evil ways, God would forgive them and express his kindness again toward his chosen people. Israel, they proclaimed, would be reborn out of the ashes, a prophecy seemingly fulfilled in 538 B.C. when the Persians allowed the Hebrews to return to the Kingdom of Judah and reestablish the Temple in the city of Jerusalem.

Out of words of the prophets came new concepts that enriched the Hebrew tradition and Western civilization, including a notion of universalism and a yearning for social justice. Although Hebrew religious practices gave Jews a sense of separateness from other peoples, the prophets transcended this by embracing a concern for all humanity. All nations would someday come to the God of Israel: "all the earth shall worship you." A universal community of all people under God would someday be established by Israel's effort. This vision encompassed the elimination of war and the establishment of peace for all the nations of the world. In the words of the prophet Isaiah: "He will judge between the nations and will settle disputes for many people. They will beat their swords into plowshares and their spears into pruning hooks. Nation will not take up sword against nation, nor will they train for war anymore."[5]

The change in Israel's social structure from a classless tribal society to a monarchical state with class differences produced outcries by the prophets against social injustice. They condemned the rich for causing the poor to suffer, denounced luxuries as worthless, and threatened Israel with prophecies of dire punishments for these sins. God's command was to live justly, share with one's neighbors, care for the poor and the unfortunate, and to act with compassion. By not following God's command, the social fabric of the community was threatened. These proclamations by Israel's prophets became a source for Western ideals of social justice, even if they have never been very perfectly realized.

THE HEBREW BIBLE   The chief source of information about Israel's spiritual conceptions is contained in the Hebrew Bible or the Old Testament of the Christian Bible. Its purpose was to teach the Hebrews the essential beliefs about the God of Israel after the Babylonian captivity of the Jews and their dispersal. But it also provides an unusual collection of Hebrew literature, since it contains hymns (the Psalms), adages (Proverbs), folk tales, literary romances, love lyrics (Book of Solomon), and, of course, a great deal of history.

The basic core of the Hebrew Bible consists of works written before the Babylonian captivity of the Jews. The first five books (known as the Pentateuch), which range from the beginning of the world until the Hebrews arrived in Palestine, constitute the Torah, or law code, governing the lives of worshipers and their relations to one another and to the non-Jewish population. The Hebrew Bible also includes historical books, which describe Jewish attempts to develop institutions by which they could observe the law properly, and the words of the prophets. The Hebrew Bible focuses on one basic theme—the necessity for the Hebrews to obey their God.

The Hebrew Prophets: Isaiah and Amos
▼ ▼ ▼

The Hebrew prophets warned the Hebrew people of the need to obey God's commandments or face being punished for breaking their covenant with God. These selections from the prophets Isaiah and Amos make clear that God's punishment would fall upon the Hebrews for their sins. Even the Assyrians, as Isaiah indicated, would be used as God's instrument to punish them.

Isaiah 3: 14–17, 24–26

The Lord enters into judgment against the elders and leaders of his people: "It is you who have ruined my vineyard; the plunder from the poor is in your houses. What do you mean by crushing my people and grinding the faces of the poor?" declares the Lord, the Lord Almighty. The Lord says, "The women of Zion are haughty, walking along with outstretched necks, flirting with their eyes, tripping along with mincing steps, with ornaments jingling on their ankles. Therefore the Lord will bring sores on the heads of the women of Zion; the Lord will make their scalps bald. . . ." Instead of fragrance there will be a stench; instead of a sash, a rope; instead of well-dressed hair, baldness; instead of fine clothing, sackcloth; instead of beauty, branding. Your men will fall by the sword, your warriors in battle. The gates of Zion will lament and mourn; destitute, she will sit on the ground.

Isaiah 10: 1–6

Woe to those who make unjust laws, to those who issue oppressive decrees, to deprive the poor of their rights and withhold justice from the oppressed of my people, making their prey and robbing the fatherless. What will you do on the day of reckoning, when disaster comes from afar? To whom will you run for help? Where will you leave your riches? Nothing will remain but to cringe among the captives or fall among the slain. Yet for all this, his anger is not turned away, his hand is still upraised. "Woe to the Assyrian, the rod of my anger, in whose hand is the club of my wrath! I send him against a godless nation, I dispatch him against a people who anger me, to seize loot and snatch plunder, and to trample them down like mud in the streets."

Amos 3: 1–2

Hear this word the Lord has spoken against you, O people of Israel—against the whole family I brought up out of Egypt: "You only have I chosen of all the families of the earth; therefore I will punish you for all your sins."

UNIQUENESS OF THE HEBREW RELIGION IN THE NEAR EAST The Hebrew religion was unique compared to the religions of other people in the ancient Near East. The Hebrews' belief that there is only one God for all peoples (a true monotheism) most dramatically separates them from all the others. But the Hebrews also differed in other significant ways. In virtually every religion in the ancient Near East, priests alone (and occasionally rulers) had access to the gods and their desires. In the Hebrew tradition, God's wishes, although communicated to the people through a series of special holy men, had all been written down. No Jewish spiritual leader could claim that he alone knew God's will. It was accessible to anyone who could read Hebrew. Judaism was a religion initially of the spoken word and eventually of the written word. Finally, although the Hebrew prophets eventually developed a sense of universalism, the demands of the Hebrew religion (the need to obey their God) encouraged a separation between Jews and their non-Jewish neighbors. Unlike most other peoples of the Near East, Jews could not simply be amalgamated into a community by accepting the gods of their conquerors and their neighbors. To remain faithful to the demands of their God, they would even have to refuse loyalty to political leaders.

Social Structures

Originally, the Hebrews had been organized along tribal lines with no division into social groups. As they settled in Palestine, tribal organization broke down, and a new social structure had evolved by the time of the monarchy as the Hebrews settled in towns and villages. Although historians warn that the Hebrews did not develop social classes in the modern sense of self-conscious

Exodus from Egypt	Between 1300 and 1200 B.C.
Saul—First King	c. 1020–1000 B.C.
King David	c. 1000–971 B.C.
King Solomon	c. 971–931 B.C.
Northern Kingdom of Israel Destroyed by Assyria	722 B.C.
Fall of Southern Kingdom of Judah to Chaldeans; Destruction of Jerusalem	586 B.C.
Return of Exiles to Jerusalem	538 B.C.

groups opposed to one another, there were conspicuous "divisions of the population."

The "men of rank and influence" formed a special group of considerable importance in Hebrew society. This group included officials of the king, military officers, civil officials, and governors. Although simply servants to the kings, they held a privileged position in the society at large. These men of position, who were often synonymous with the heads of the great families, were most numerous in the capital cities, Samaria and Jerusalem. The common people, sometimes called "people of the land," remained a body of free people having basic civil rights. Their livelihood came mostly from the land and from various crafts. These peasants and craftsmen sold their own produce and products directly to buyers in markets in their local town or village squares, thus eliminating middlemen or traders. There was no real merchant class in ancient Israel. Commerce was carried on by foreigners, such as the Phoenicians. Not until the Diaspora, when Jews became scattered throughout the ancient world after their exile to Babylon, did they become merchants.

Hebrew society included other groups of people as well. There existed a category known as resident aliens, such as the Canaanites in Palestine after the Hebrews established their control. Although considered free men, they lacked full civic rights and were not regarded as citizens. Since landed property was in the hands of Hebrews, the resident aliens had to sell their services to survive and were usually poor as a result.

As was customary in the ancient Near East, Hebrews possessed slaves. Hebrew law permitted Hebrews to buy both male and female slaves of foreign birth or children of resident aliens. Hebrews themselves could be enslaved to other Hebrews, but only temporarily: "If you buy a Hebrew servant, he is to serve you for six years. But in the seventh year, he shall go free, without paying anything."[6] When Hebrews were enslaved, it was usually because they or a relative had been too poor to repay a debt. Thieves who could not repay what they had stolen were also sold as slaves to recoup the loss.

The number of domestic slaves in ancient Israel seems small, especially in comparison to later Greece and Rome. A family of substance might have one or two. Although slaves belonged to their masters and could be used as they wished, Hebrew law afforded slaves some protection. If the owner caused bodily injury, the slave would be freed. If a slave was beaten to death, the owner would be punished. Domestic slaves were usually regarded as part of the family and were protected and cared for accordingly. There are even examples of slaves inheriting their master's estate or marrying into a family and gaining freedom as a result. Hebrew slaves were marked out for especially favorable treatment. Masters were advised to treat them as wage earners and not have them do degrading tasks, such as washing the master's feet. Female slaves were usually treated differently. Girls were sold as slaves to become concubines of their masters or their masters' sons. They were not freed after six years. A master had the power to free his slaves, although this applied more to Hebrew slaves than to foreign slaves. But emancipation could be a mixed blessing. If a master had allowed his slave to marry and have a family, the wife and children remained the master's property after the slave was freed. If a slave then refused his freedom, he became a slave for life.

The state also possessed slaves, who were obtained primarily as prisoners of war. These slaves either worked in the temples or for the kings. Solomon, for example, used slaves in mines, his building projects, and the big commercial and industrial enterprises run by the royal authority.

The family was the central social institution in Hebrew life and consisted of those connected by common blood and a common living place. A family living in one house could comprise husband and wife, married sons and their wives, and their children. The Hebrew family was patriarchal. The husband-father was master of his wife and possessed absolute authority over his children, including the power of life and death. This encompassed married sons and their wives if they lived in his house. The closeness of family ties was a remnant of tribal life, but the shift to a settled life in towns and villages affected the family. The old patriarchal system broke down. Fewer people could remain in one small house.

Married sons now moved out of their father's house and into their own. Moreover, by the eighth century B.C., wage earners replaced domestic slaves and servants, and the old extended family with master, children, grandchildren, and servants living in one house passed away. These changes also weakened the authority of the head of the family. Fathers no longer had the power of life and death over their children, and the right of judgment for children's misdeeds was put in the hands of the town elders. As family bonds disintegrated, the individual was liberated from family control. The weakening of family solidarity created new problems, however. Relatives began to neglect their duty of mutual assistance to family members. As the plight of orphans and widows worsened, the prophets, as we have seen, arose to plead their case.

Marriage was an important aspect of Hebrew family life. In ancient Israel, under the judges and the monarchy, polygamy was an accepted form of marriage, especially for kings and wealthier citizens. Hebrew law limited kings to eighteen wives and subjects to four. In practice, only kings could afford a large harem. When others had more than one wife, it was usually because they desired more children; the first wife, for example, might be unable to have children or have produced only daughters.

It is clear, however, that most Hebrews believed that monogamy was the preferred form of marriage. Wives were honored for their faithfulness and dedication to their husbands. The book of Proverbs in the Hebrew Bible provides a picture of what Hebrews considered a perfect wife:

> A wife of noble character who can find? She is worth
>   far more than rubies.
> Her husband has full confidence in her and lacks
>   nothing of value.
> She brings him good, not harm, all the days of her life.
> She selects wool and flax and works with eager hands.
> She is like the merchant ships, bringing her food from
>   afar.
> She gets up while it is still dark; she provides food for
>   her family and portions for her servant girls.
> She considers a field and buys it; out of her earnings she
>   plants a vineyard.
> She sets about her work vigorously; her arms are strong
>   for her tasks.
> She sees that her trading is profitable, and her lamp does
>   not go out at night.
> In her hand she holds the distaff and grasps the spindle
>   with her fingers.

> She opens her arms to the poor and extends her hands
>   to the needy. . . .
> She makes linen garments and sells them, and supplies
>   the merchants with sashes.
> She is clothed with strength and dignity; she can laugh
>   at the days to come.
> She speaks with wisdom, and faithful instruction is on
>   her tongue.
> She watches over the affairs of her household, and does
>   not eat the bread of idleness.
> Her children arise and call her blessed; her husband
>   also, and he praises her.[7]

Women were greatly valued, but their work was obviously never done.

It should not surprise us to learn that a married woman was subject to her husband's authority. The Hebrews, unlike the Mesopotamians, did not develop the custom of a dowry from the bride's parents. They did, however, have a practice whereby the bridegroom's family paid a sum of money to the bride's family, not as a purchase price as such, but apparently as compensation to the family for the loss of their daughter. A married woman left her parents' home, lived with her husband's family, and became a member of their clan. Her children also belonged to the husband's clan.

Since boys and girls were married at a relatively young age, parents took the responsibility for matchmaking. Although there were marriages between persons of different families and even with foreign women, it was customary to find marriage partners within one's own clan or extended family. Indeed, marriages between first cousins were frequently arranged.

Since marriage was a civil contract, it did not involve a religious ceremony. The primary marriage ceremony, instead, was the formal entry of the bride into the house of the groom. This was treated as a festive occasion and cause for much celebration. The bridegroom and friends went to the bride's house and escorted her and her friends to the bridegroom's house. The bride was magnificently dressed, bedecked with jewels, and wore a veil, which was not taken off until the couple was in their bridal chamber. After the bride arrived at the groom's house, a feast took place that usually lasted seven days. The couple, however, consummated their marriage on the first night of the feasting.

In ancient Israel, divorce was readily available for the husband, but not for the wife. Although opinions differed on the legitimate grounds for divorce, there were few restrictions on the husband's right to do so. If a man used the excuse that his wife was not a virgin at the time of the marriage and the accusation proved incorrect, the husband could not divorce his wife at all. Likewise, a man who had been forced to marry a girl because of having premarital sex with her could never divorce her. Although divorce was easy—a husband simply drew up a divorce writ—there is no evidence to suggest that it was very common. Infidelity, in any case, could be costly. A man committed no crime by having sex with prostitutes, but adultery with a married woman was punishable by death. Wives were expected to remain faithful to their husbands.

The primary goal of marriage was to produce children. They were the "crown of man," and sons, in particular, were desired. Daughters would eventually leave the family house, but sons carried on the family line. The eldest son possessed special prerogatives. Upon the father's death, he became head of the family and was given a double portion of his father's estate. The rights of an elder son were protected by law, although committing a grave offense, such as incest, could cost him those rights. A father's inheritance passed only to his sons. The family house and property were probably given intact to the eldest son only.

Children were named immediately after birth since it was believed that one's name defined one's essence and disclosed the destiny and character of the child. The early education of children was placed in the hands of the mother, especially in regard to basic moral principles. As boys matured, their fathers took over responsibility for their education, which remained largely informal. This included religious instruction as well as general education for life. The rod was not spared as a matter of principle. Since trades were usually hereditary, fathers also provided their sons' occupational education. As one rabbi stated, "He who does not teach his son a useful trade is bringing him up to be a thief."[8] Additional education for boys came from priests, whose sacred mission was to instruct people in the Torah, or law code of ancient Israel. An organized school system was not established until much later, possibly in the second century B.C. The only education girls received was from their mothers who taught them the basic fundamentals of how to be good wives, mothers, and housekeepers.

▼ The Assyrian Empire

The existence of an independent Hebrew state was only possible because of the power vacuum existing in the ancient Near East after the destruction of the Hittite kingdom and the weakening of the Egyptian empire. But this condition did not last, as new empires soon arose and came to dominate vast stretches of the ancient Near East. The first of these empires was formed in Assyria, located on the upper Tigris River, an area that brought it into both cultural and political contact with Mesopotamia. The Assyrians were a Semitic-speaking people, akin to the Akkadians in Mesopotamia. For much of their early history, the Assyrians were vassals of foreign rulers, including Sargon of Akkad, the Third Dynasty of Ur, and the Babylonian king Hammurabi. From about 1650 to 1360 B.C., the Hurrian Kingdom of Mitanni dominated Assyria (see Chapter 1). The Assyrians finally became independent when the Hittites destroyed the Kingdom of Mitanni; we read in Hittite documents from about 1360 B.C. of the emergence of the "king of

▼ **War Relief of Ashurbanipal.** Assyria was the first great empire to gain control over the ancient Near East in the first millennium B.C. The empire was established under Tiglath-pileser I, who also introduced the use of terror both to rule and to conquer. The Assyrians had a highly efficient and well-organized military machine, capable of fighting under a variety of conditions. This relief depicts King Ashurbanipal laying siege to an Egyptian city (667 B.C.).

▼ **Map 2.2** The Assyrian Empire

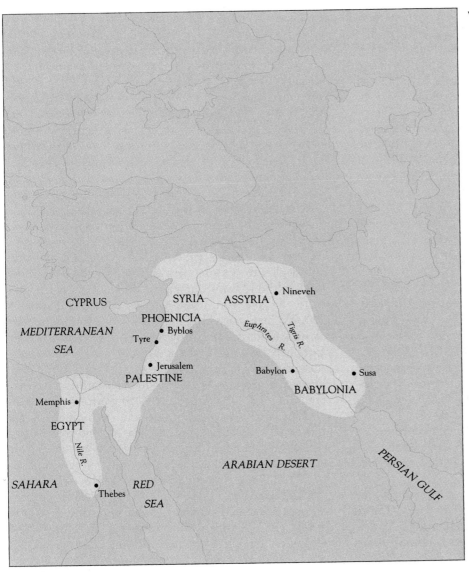

the land of Assyria." For the next 250 years, the Assyrians experienced alternate expansion and decline until the reassertion of Assyrian power under Tiglath-pileser I (c. 1115–1077 B.C.). He was a brutal conqueror whose policy of deliberate terror set a pattern for later Assyrian rulers.

The Assyrian empire created by Tiglath-pileser was unable to maintain its strength after his death. A new phase of expansion did not begin until the ninth century with the conquests of Shalmaneser III (858–824 B.C.), who marched westward into Palestine and southward into Babylonia. Yet Assyrian power did not go unchallenged. Almost continuous warfare on these new frontiers was not ended until Sargon II (721–705 B.C.) re-

established control over Babylonia and completely subdued Palestine. By 700 B.C., the Assyrian Empire had reached the height of its power and included Mesopotamia, Elam, parts of the Iranian plateau, sections of Asia Minor, Syria, Palestine, and Egypt down to Thebes.

Ashurbanipal (669–626 B.C.) was one of the strongest Assyrian rulers, but it was already becoming apparent during his reign that the Assyrian Empire was greatly overextended. Other problems plagued the empire as well. Internal strife intensified as powerful Assyrian nobles gained control of vast territories and waged their own private military campaigns. The importation of large numbers of conquered foreigners into Assyria led over generations to the infiltration of foreign peoples into the Assyrian civil service and army. Moreover, the subject peoples greatly resented Assyrian rule. The hatred that the Babylonians felt after the brutal Assyrian sack of the city of Babylon in 689 B.C., for example, led them to rebel during the reign of Ashurbanipal. As Ashurbanipal became mired in Babylonian affairs, Egypt freed itself from Assyrian control. Soon after Ashurbanipal's reign, the Assyrian Empire began to disintegrate rapidly. The capital city of Nineveh fell to a coalition of Chaldeans and Medes (see The Chaldean Empire below) in 612 B.C., and in 605 B.C., the rest of the empire was finally divided between the coalition powers.

At its height, the Assyrian empire was ruled by kings whose power was considered absolute. Officially, kings served as viceregents of the god Ashur, the chief Assyrian deity. But it is clear that by the first millennium B.C. Assyrian kings viewed themselves as sole rulers in their own right. Although the king was considered absolute, certain taboos conditioned the exercise of royal power. Normally, only the superintendent of the palace had direct access to his exalted majesty. Others could approach the king, but only if the astrological omens were favorable. Basically, omens, whether favorable or unfavorable, determined when government business could be carried on and international affairs pursued.

During its period of expansion, the Assyrian Empire came to be well organized. Especially by the eighth century, greater control over the resources of the empire had been put in the hands of the king by the development of new provincial arrangements. Governorships held by nobles on a hereditary basis were eliminated, and a new hierarchy of local officials, directly responsible to the king, was instituted. The Assyrians also developed an efficient system of communication to administer their empire more effectively. A network of posting stages was established throughout the empire that used relays of horses (mules or donkeys in mountainous terrain) to carry messages. The system was so effective that a provincial governor anywhere in the empire (except Egypt) could send a question and receive an answer from the king in his palace within a week. Although the Assyrians did not pave the roads, except in their capital cities, they did keep their highways clear to facilitate rapid transit. The Assyrians were also known for developing an efficient intelligence network. By using spies, they were able to gain inside information about places they planned to attack.

At the beginning of the first millennium B.C., the Assyrians had a reputation as a mighty military machine.

In large part, this was because of their topography. Assyria had no natural boundaries; its pasture lands lay open to invaders. After their experiences in the third and second millennia, the Assyrians felt the need for a strong military to protect themselves. In order to prevent invasions, they decided to expand into areas from which they traditionally had been attacked. That expansion, of course, led to a need for further expansion to protect the newly occupied territories. We could say that their quest for security led the Assyrians to a large empire. The Assyrian rulers claimed that their expansion was a divine mission; it was the will of their god Ashur.

The ability of the Assyrians to conquer and maintain an empire was due to a combination of factors. Over many years of practice, the Assyrians developed good military leaders and fighters. They were able to enlist and deploy troops numbering in the hundreds of thousands, although most campaigns were not on such a large scale. In 845 B.C., Shalmaneser III led an army of 120,000 men across the Euphrates on a campaign. Size alone was not decisive, however. The Assyrian army was extremely well organized and disciplined. It included a standing army of infantrymen as its core, accompanied by cavalrymen and horse-drawn war chariots that were used as mobile platforms for shooting arrows. The army also included specialized units, such as a pioneer corps that made smooth tracks for the wagons and chariots and constructed pontoon bridges over rivers for the movement of troops. Other specialized military personnel included language interpreters, intelligence officers, and scribes who kept a record of the booty. Moreover, the Assyrians had the advantage of having the first large armies equipped with iron weapons. The Hittites (see Chapter 1) had been the first to develop iron metallurgy after the introduction of iron around 1200 B.C.

Another factor in the army's success was its ability to use different kinds of military tactics (see the box on p. 45). The Assyrian army was capable of fighting guerrilla warfare in the mountains and set battles on open ground as well as laying siege to cities. The Assyrians were especially renowned for their siege warfare. They made efficient use of heavy siege engines, which were wheeled, and armored battering rams. Sappers were organized to dig tunnels to undermine the foundations of walls and cause them to collapse. The besieging Assyrian armies learned to cut off supplies so effectively that if a city did not fall to them, the inhabitants could be starved into submission. The Assyrians themselves had no difficulty obtaining supplies because in addition to the supply wagons that accompanied the army, regular bases were main-

The Assyrian Military Machine
▼ ▼ ▼

The Assyrians achieved a reputation for possessing a mighty military machine. They were able to use a variety of military tactics and were successful whether they were fighting guerrilla warfare and set battles or laying siege to cities. These three selections contain accounts by Assyrian kings of their military conquests.

King Sennacherib (704–681 B.C.) Describes a Battle with the Elamites in 691

At the command of the god Ashur, the great Lord, I rushed upon the enemy like the approach of a hurricane. . . . I put them to rout and turned them back. I transfixed the troops of the enemy with javelins and arrows. . . . I cut their throats like sheep. . . . My prancing steeds, trained to harness, plunged into their welling blood as into a river; the wheels of my battle chariot were bespattered with blood and filth. I filled the plain with the corpses of their warriors like herbage. . . . As to the sheikhs of the Chaldeans, panic from my onslaught overwhelmed them like a demon. They abandoned their tents and fled for their lives, crushing the corpses of their troops as they went. . . . In their terror they passed scalding urine and voided their excrement into their chariots.

King Sennacherib Describes His Siege of Jerusalem (701 B.C.)

As to Hezekiah, the Jew, he did not submit to my yoke, I laid siege to 46 of his strong cities, walled forts and to the countless small villages in their vicinity, and conquered them by means of well-stamped earth-ramps, and battering-rams brought thus near to the walls combined with the attack by foot soldiers, using mines, breeches as well as sapper work. I drove out of them 200,150 people, young and old, male and female, horses, mules, donkeys, camels, big and small cattle beyond counting, and considered them booty. Himself I made a prisoner in Jerusalem, his royal residence, like a bird in a cage. I surrounded him with earthwork in order to molest those who were leaving his city's gate.

King Ashurbanipal (669–626 B.C.) Describes His Treatment of Conquered Babylon

I tore out the tongues of those whose slanderous mouths had uttered blasphemies against my god Ashur and had plotted against me, his god-fearing prince; I defeated them completely. The others, I smashed alive with the very same statues of protective deities with which they had smashed my own grandfather Sennacherib—now finally as a belated burial sacrifice for his soul. I fed their corpses, cut into small pieces, to dogs, pigs, . . . vultures, the birds of the sky and also to the fish of the ocean. After I had performed this and thus made quiet again the hearts of the great gods, my lords, I removed the corpses of those whom the pestilence had felled, whose leftovers after the dogs and pigs had fed on them were obstructing the streets, filling the places of Babylon, and of those who had lost their lives through the terrible famine.

---

tained in major Assyrian cities and in occupied lands to store provisions for men and animals.

A final factor in the effectiveness of the Assyrian military machine was its ability to create a climate of terror as an instrument of warfare. The Assyrians became famous for their terror tactics, although some historians believe their policies were no worse than other Near Eastern conquerors. As a matter of regular policy, the Assyrians laid waste the land in which they were fighting, smashing dams, looting and destroying towns, setting crops on fire, and cutting down trees, particularly fruit trees. The Assyrians were especially known for committing atrocities on their captives. King Ashurnasirpal recorded this account of his treatment of prisoners:

> 3000 of their combat troops I felled with weapons. . . . Many of the captives taken from them I burned in a fire. Many I took alive; from some of these I cut off their hands to the wrist, from others I cut off their noses, ears, and fingers; I put out the eyes of many of the soldiers. . . . I burned their young men and women to death.

After conquering another city, the same king wrote: "I fixed up a pile of corpses in front of the city's gate. I flayed the nobles, as many as had rebelled, and spread their skins out on the piles. . . . I flayed many within my land and spread their skins out on the walls."[9] (Obviously, not a king to play games with!) It should be noted that this policy of extreme cruelty to prisoners was not used against all enemies, but was primarily reserved for those who were already part of the empire and then rebelled against Assyrian rule.

Many prisoners of newly conquered territories were deported from their native lands to Assyria. They were generally well treated, since they were useful to Assyria. Usually, communities and families were deported en masse. They were sent to work as skilled labor in cities, to farm in rural areas, and to repopulate sections that had been decimated by warfare. It has been estimated that over a period of three centuries between four and five million people were deported to Assyria, resulting in a population that was very racially and linguistically mixed. In fact, in some major Assyrian cities, ethnic Assyrians were a minority, overwhelmed by Aramaeans (a Semitic-speaking people who lived in what is now eastern Syria), Egyptians, Hebrews, Phoenicians, Medes, and others.

Assyrian Society and Culture

Unlike the Hebrews, the Assyrians were not fearful of mixing with other peoples. In fact, Assyrian deportation policies created a polyglot society in which ethnic differences were not very important. What gave identity to the Assyrians themselves was their language, although

even that was akin to that of their southern neighbors in Babylonia who also spoke a Semitic language. Religion was also a cohesive force. Assyria was literally, "the land of Ashur," a reference to its chief god. The king, as the human representative of the god Ashur, provided a final unifying focus.

Little is certain about Assyrian social stratification. By the end of the second millennium B.C., society was composed of two distinct groups, the free and nonfree (slave) with gradations of status among the free men. By the first millennium, however, it appears that royal officials, who owed their position to the favor of the king, made up the leading group of free men. Moreover, at the bottom of the social scale, the distinction between free and slave had become blurred because large numbers of peasants had lost their old land rights and had been reduced to serfdom.

Agriculture formed the principal basis of Assyrian life. Assyria was a land of farming villages with relatively few significant cities, especially in comparison to Mesopotamia. Unlike Mesopotamia, where farming required the minute organization of large numbers of people to control irrigation, Assyrian farming received sufficient moisture from regular rainfall. Irrigation was used in Assyria but only for auxiliary purposes.

Trade was second to agriculture in economic importance. Internal trade depended on a system that used metals, such as gold, silver, copper, and bronze, as a medium of exchange. Various agricultural products also served as a form of payment or exchange. Because of their geographical location, the Assyrians served as middlemen and participated in an international trade in which they

▼ **King Ashurbanipal's Lion Hunt.** This relief, sculptured on alabaster as a decoration for the northern palace in Nineveh, depicts King Ashurbanipal engaged in a lion hunt. The relief sculpture, one of the best known forms of Assyrian art, ironically reached its high point under Ashurbanipal at the same time that the Assyrian empire began to disintegrate. The loss of Egypt and the resistance of the Chaldeans to Assyrian rule both occurred during the reign of this king.

imported timber, wine, and precious metals and stones while they exported textiles produced in palaces, temples, and private villas. However, the levying of tribute from various parts of the empire in the first millennium diminished the need for international trade.

The culture of the Assyrian Empire was essentially hybrid in nature. The Assyrians assimilated much of Mesopotamian civilization and saw themselves as guardians of Sumerian and Babylonian culture. Ashurbanipal, for example, created a large library at Nineveh that included the available works of Mesopotamian history. Assyrian kings also tried to maintain old traditions when they rebuilt damaged temples by ensuring that the new buildings were constructed on the original foundations, not in new locations. Assyrian religion reflected this assimilation of other cultures as well. Although the Assyrians had their own national god Ashur as their chief deity, virtually all of their remaining gods and goddesses were Mesopotamian.

Among the best-known objects of Assyrian art are the relief sculptures found in the royal palaces in three of the Assyrian capital cities, Nimrud, Nineveh, and Khorsabad. These reliefs, which were begun during the reign of Ashurnasirpal in the ninth century and reached their high point in the reign of Ashurbanipal in the seventh century, depicted two different kinds of subject matter: ritual or ceremonial scenes revolving around the person of the king and scenes of hunting and war. The latter reliefs show realistic action scenes of the king and his warriors engaged in battle or hunting animals, especially lions. These pictures depict a strongly masculine world where discipline, brute force, and toughness are the enduring values, indeed, the very values of the Assyrian military monarchy.

▼ The Chaldean Empire

The Chaldeans, a Semitic-speaking people, had gained ascendancy in Babylonia by the seventh century and came to form the chief resistance to Assyrian control of Mesopotamia. The Chaldean king Nabopolassar (625–605 B.C.), who joined forces with the Medes to capture the Assyrian capital Nineveh in 612 B.C., was responsible for establishing a new Babylonian monarchy. But it was his son Nebuchadnezzar II (605–562 B.C.) who achieved the final defeat of the Assyrian Empire. Under his rule, the Chaldeans defeated Egypt to gain control of Syria and Palestine, destroyed Jerusalem, carried the Jews into exile in Babylon and in the process regained for Babylonia a position as the leading power in the ancient Near East.

▼ **Ishtar Gate of Babylon.** The Chaldeans formed the chief resistance to Assyrian control of Mesopotamia. Under Nebuchadnezzar II, the Chaldeans finally succeeded in destroying the Assyrian Empire. Nebuchadnezzar II had Babylon rebuilt as the center of his empire, and adorned it with such architectural wonders as the Ishtar gate that opened onto the Triumphal Way. The picture shows the west wall of the inner gatehouse of the Ishtar Gate.

During Nebuchadnezzar's reign, Babylonia was renowned for a prosperity based upon lush agricultural lands, lucrative trade routes running through Mesopotamia, and industries, especially its much-desired textiles and metals. Nebuchadnezzar rebuilt Babylon as the center of his empire, giving it a reputation as one of the great cities of the ancient world. Babylon was surrounded by great walls, eight miles in length, encircled by a moat filled by the Euphrates River. The Ishtar Gate opened onto a Triumphal Way that led to the sacred precincts of Marduk, the chief Babylonian god. Babylon was adorned with temples and palaces; most famous of all were the Hanging Gardens, known as one of the Seven Wonders of the ancient world. These were supposedly built to satisfy Nebuchadnezzar's wife, a princess from the land of Media, who missed the mountains of her homeland. A series of terraces led to a plateau, an artificial mountain, at the top of which grew the lush gardens irrigated by water piped to the top. From a distance the gardens appeared to be suspended in air.

The splendor of Chaldean Babylonia proved to be short-lived. Nabonidus (555–539 B.C.) was the last of the Chaldean dynasty. He had a great interest in history and encouraged scholars to collect Sumerian texts and study the Sumerian language. But his policies created considerable internal dissent. Among other things, Nabonidus tried to replace Marduk with the moon god Sin, an insult to the Babylonians. When Babylon fell to the

Persian conqueror Cyrus in 539 B.C., the Babylonians welcomed him as a liberator, clearly indicating their disaffection with Nabonidus's rule.

▼ The Persian Empire

The Persians were an Indo-European–speaking people related to the Medes. Both peoples are first mentioned in Assyrian documents in the ninth century B.C. and probably formed part of the great waves of Indo-European migrations from central Europe into the Mediterranean, the Near East, and India. The Persians lived to the southeast of the Medes, who occupied the western Iranian plateau south of the Caspian Sea. Although crops were grown, lack of moisture made the lands of these people more suitable for pasture. The Medes, in particular, were famous throughout the Near East for the quality of the horses they bred. Primarily nomadic, both Medes and Persians were organized in tribes or clans. Leaders of both peoples were petty kings assisted by a group of warriors who formed a class of nobles. Their populations also included both free and unfree people who worked the land, craftsmen, and slaves.

By 735 B.C., the Medes had begun to form a confederation of the various tribes, and sometime at the beginning of the seventh century, they became unified under a monarchy. The Persians did likewise under the so-called Achaemenid dynasty established in Persis in southern Iran. About fifty years later, the Persians were made subject to the Medes. The Medes now constituted a powerful state and joined the Babylonians in attacking the Assyrians. After the capture of Nineveh in 612 B.C., King Cyaxares established a Median empire, the first Iranian empire known to the ancient Near East.

Cyrus the Great (559–530 B.C.)

In 559 B.C., Cyrus became the leader of the Persians, united them under his rule, and went on the offensive against the Medes. In 550 B.C., he overcame the Median king Astyages and established Persian control over Media, making it the first Persian satrapy or province. The conquest of Media brought Cyrus into confrontation

▼ **Map 2.3** The Persian Empire

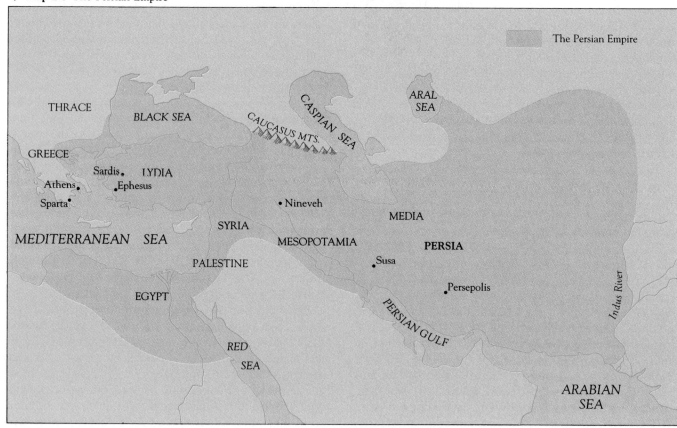

with the three surviving powers of the ancient Near East—Lydia, Babylonia, and Egypt. Only the last would escape his conquest.

In the northwest, the Halys River formed the boundary between the old Median empire Cyrus had subdued and the Kingdom of Lydia under King Croesus, whose wealth was legendary. The defeat of the Medes by Cyrus led Croesus to attempt to recover his former lands east of the Halys River. Cyrus marched west to meet this challenge, defeated Croesus decisively in 547 B.C., and occupied the Lydian capital of Sardis. Lydia was made into another Persian satrapy. The conquest of Lydia in western Asia Minor brought the Persians into their first contact with the Greeks settled on the Ionian coast. The Greek city-states had been subjects of Lydia, but had been allowed to keep their own institutions and had grown rich from the commercial opportunities in Lydia. Cyrus's forces easily conquered the Ionian Greek city-states, which were then placed under the control of local tyrants loyal to Cyrus.

While a Persian army took care of the Ionian Greeks, Cyrus turned his attention eastward where he felt his power threatened by barbaric nomadic tribes. He subdued the eastern part of the Iranian plateau and then moved into Sogdia, a territory between the Oxus and Jaxartes rivers. He even advanced into the western part of India. His eastern conquests doubled the territory, but not the wealth or population, of the growing Persian Empire. He did gain more soldiers, however, and was now able to turn on the powerful state to his south, the Chaldean Empire.

In 539 B.C., he entered Mesopotamia and easily captured Babylon. The disgust of the Babylonians with their king Nabonidus led them to welcome Cyrus as a hero. Cyrus showed remarkable restraint and wisdom in his conquest of Babylonia. Babylonia was made into a Persian province under a Persian satrap, but many government officials were kept in their positions. Cyrus took the title "King of All, Great King, Mighty King, King of Babylon, King of the Land of Sumer and Akkad, King of the Four Rims (of the Earth), the Son of Cambyses the Great King, King of Anshan,"[10] and insisted that he stood in the ancient, unbroken line of Babylonian kings. By flattering the vanity of the Babylonians, he won their loyalty. Cyrus also undid the destructive work of Nabonidus. He restored the statues of gods that the Babylonian ruler had brought to Babylon from various cities and temples throughout Babylonia. Temples were restored and the rightful worship of Marduk was reestablished. Cyrus also issued an edict permitting the Jews, who had been brought to Babylon in the reign of Neb-

▼ **Tomb of Cyrus at Murgab.** Cyrus became leader of the Persians in 559 B.C., freeing them from the rule of the Medes and establishing Persian control over Media. While Cyrus was unquestionably a great military commander, he was also well loved by the Persians and even regarded by those he conquered as their legitimate ruler and a great leader. Cyrus led the Persians to control most of the ancient Near East, Egypt alone remaining free of his rule.

uchadnezzar, to return to Jerusalem with their sacred temple objects and to rebuild their Temple as well.

From 538 to 530 B.C., Cyrus consolidated his empire. Among other things, he constructed forts, especially in the northeastern part of his empire, to protect against nomadic incursions. It was to the northeast that he undertook his last campaign. In 530 B.C., he marched into the territory of the Massagetae where he was killed in battle.

To his contemporaries, Cyrus the Great was deserving of his epithet. The Greek historian Herodotus recounted that the Persians viewed him as a "father," a ruler who was "gentle, and procured them all manner of goods."[11] Certainly, Cyrus must have been an unusual ruler for his time, a man who demonstrated considerable wisdom and compassion in the conquest and organization of his empire. Cyrus attempted—successfully—to obtain the favor of the priesthoods in his conquered lands by restoring temples and permitting a wide degree of religious toleration. He won approval by using not only Persians, but also native peoples as government officials in their own states. He allowed Medes to be military commanders.

Unlike the Assyrian rulers of a previous empire, he had a reputation for mercy. Medes, Babylonians, and Jews all accepted him as their legitimate ruler. Some peoples, such as the Greeks and Jews, portrayed him as a great leader and peacemaker. Indeed, the Jews regarded him as the anointed one of God: "I am the Lord who says of Cyrus, 'He is my shepherd and will accomplish all that I please'; he will say of Jerusalem, 'Let it be rebuilt'; and of the temple, 'Let its foundations be laid.' This is what the Lord says to his anointed, to Cyrus, whose right hand I take hold of to subdue nations before him."[12] Cyrus had a genuine respect for ancient civilizations—in building his palaces, he made use of Assyrian, Babylonian, Egyptian, and Lydian practices. Indeed, Cyrus had a

▼ **Archers of the Persian Guard.** One of the main pillars supporting the Persian Empire was the military. Recruited from the various subject peoples of the empire, the actual size of the forces sent on a campaign could be enormous. This frieze, composed of enamel brick, depicts members of the famous infantry force known as the Immortals, so-called because their number was never allowed to drop below 10,000. Those killed would be replaced immediately. They carry the standard lance and bow and arrow of the infantry.

sense that he was creating a "world empire" that included peoples who had ancient and venerable traditions and institutions.

A "World Empire"

In 538 B.C., Cyrus had installed his son Cambyses as king in Babylon while he returned to the Persian homeland. Upon his father's death in 530 B.C., Cambyses took over power as the Great King. Four years later, he undertook the invasion of Egypt, the only kingdom in the Near East not yet brought under Persian control. Aided by the Phoenician fleet, he defeated and captured the pharoah and the Egyptian forces. Egypt was made into a satrapy with Memphis as its capital. In the summer of 525 B.C., Cambyses took the title of pharoah.

After the death of Cambyses in 522, Darius, a young member of a collateral branch of the Achaemenid ruling family, emerged as Great King after a year of intense civil war. Once in charge, Darius (521–486 B.C.) turned to the task of strengthening the empire. He codified Egyptian law and built a canal to link the Red Sea and the Mediterranean. A campaign into western India led to the creation of a new Persian province that extended to the Indus River. Darius also moved into Europe proper conquering Thrace and making the Macedonian king a vassal. A revolt of the Ionian Greek cities in 499 B.C. resulted in temporary freedom for these communities in western Asia Minor. Aid from the Greek mainland, most notably from Athens, led to a brief invasion of Lydia by the Ionians and the burning of Sardis, center of the Lydian satrapy. This event led to Darius's involvement with the mainland Greeks. After reestablishing control of the Ionian Greek cities, Darius undertook an invasion of the Greek mainland, which culminated in the famous Athenian victory in the Battle of Marathon in 490 B.C. (see Chapter 3).

Civil Administration and the Military

Although the Greeks viewed their struggle with the Persians as crucial to their survival, the Persians saw it as a minor episode on their western frontier. By the reign of Darius, the Persians had created the largest empire the world had yet seen. It included not only all the old centers of power in the Near East, Egypt, Mesopotamia, and Assyria, but also extended into Thrace and Asia Minor in the west and into India in the east.

For administrative purposes, the empire had been divided into approximately twenty provinces called satrapies. Each province was ruled by a governor or satrap, literally a "protector of the Kingdom." Although Darius had not introduced the system of satrapies, he did see that it was organized more rationally. He also created a sensible system for calculating the tribute that each satrapy owed to the central government. Instead of contributions based on local practices, Darius determined the levies on the basis of the productive capacity of each satrapy, resulting in a fixed annual sum. Satrapies also provided soldiers for the royal army. Satraps had both civil and military duties. They collected tributes, were responsible for justice and security, raised military levies, and normally commanded the military forces within their satrapies. In terms of real power, the satraps were miniature kings who established courts imitative of the Great King's.

From the time of Darius on, satraps were men of Persian descent. The major satrapies were given to princes of the king's family, and their position became essentially hereditary. The minor satrapies were placed in the hands of Persian nobles. Their offices, too, tended to pass from father to son. The hereditary nature of the governors' offices made it necessary to provide some checks to their power. Consequently, some historians think that there were officials at the satrapal courts, such as secretaries and generals in charge of the garrison, who reported directly to the Great King, keeping him informed of what was going on within the various satrapal governments. It is also possible that an official known as the "king's eye," or "king's messenger" made annual inspections of each satrapy.

An efficient system of communication was considered crucial to sustain the Persian Empire. Roads were maintained to facilitate the rapid transit of military and government personnel. One in particular, the so-called Royal Road, stretched from Sardis, the center of Lydia in Asia Minor, to Susa, the chief capital of the Persian Empire. Like the Assyrians, the Persians established staging posts equipped with fresh horses for the king's messengers. Moreover, trunk roads off the Royal Road linked important cities like Memphis to the capital at Susa.

In this vast administrative system, the Persian king occupied an exalted position. Although not considered to be a god as was the Egyptian pharaoh, he was nevertheless the elect one or regent of the Persian god Ahuramazda (see Persian Religion below). All subjects were the king's servants, and he was the source of all justice, possessing the power of life and death over everyone. Persian kings were largely secluded and not easily available. They resided in a series of splendid palaces. Darius especially was a palace builder on a grand scale. His

Chronology
The Empires

The Assyrians	
Domination of Assyria by Kingdom of Mitanni	c. 1650–1360 B.C.
Assyrian Independence	c. 1360 B.C.
Tiglath-pileser I	c. 1115–1077 B.C.
Conquests of Shalmaneser III	858–824 B.C.
Sargon II	721–705 B.C.
Height of Power	700 B.C.
Ashurbanipal	669–626 B.C.
Capture of Nineveh	612 B.C.
Assyrian Empire Destroyed	605 B.C.
The Chaldeans	
Ascendancy in Babylonia	600s B.C.
Nabopolassar Establishes New Babylonian Monarchy	625–605 B.C.
Height of Empire under King Nebuchadnezzar II	605–562 B.C.
Fall of Babylon	539 B.C.
The Persians	
Unification under Achaemenid Dynasty	600s B.C.
Persian Control over Medes	550 B.C.
Conquests of Cyrus the Great	559–530 B.C.
Cambyses and Conquest of Egypt	530–522 B.C.
Reign of Darius	521–486 B.C.

description of the construction of a palace in the chief Persian capital of Susa demonstrated what a truly international empire Persia was:

This is the . . . palace which at Susa I built. From afar its ornamentation was brought. . . . The cedar timber was brought from a mountain named Lebanon; the Assyrians brought it to Babylon, and from Babylon the Carians and Ionians brought it to Susa. Teakwood was brought from Gandara and from Carmania. The gold which was used here was brought from Sardis and from Bactria. The stone—lapis lazuli and carnelian—was brought from Sogdiana. . . . The silver and copper were brought from Egypt. The ornamentation with which the wall was adorned was brought from Ionia. The ivory was brought from Ethiopia, from India, and from Arachosia. The stone pillars were brought from . . . Elam. The artisans who dressed the stone were Ionians and Sardians. The goldsmiths who wrought the gold were Medes and Egyptians. . . . Those who worked the baked brick (with figures) were Babylonians. The men who adorned the wall were Medes and Egyptians. At Susa here a splendid work was ordered; very splendid did it turn out.[13]

But Darius was unhappy with Susa. He did not really consider it his homeland, and it was oppressively hot in the summer months. Darius built another residence at Persepolis, a new capital located to the east of the old one and at a higher elevation.

The policies of Darius also tended to widen the gap between the king and his subjects. As the Great King himself said of all his subjects: "what was said to them by me, night and day it was done."[14] Over a period of time, the Great Kings in their greed came to hoard immense quantities of gold and silver in the various treasuries located in the capital cities. Both their hoarding of wealth and their later overtaxation of their subjects are seen as crucial factors in the ultimate weakening of the Persian Empire (see the box on p. 53).

In its heyday, however, the empire stood supreme, and much of its power depended upon the military. By the time of Darius, the Persian monarchs had created a standing army of professional soldiers. This army was truly international in character, composed of contingents from the various peoples who made up the empire.

At its core was a cavalry force of 10,000 and an elite infantry force of 10,000 Medes and Persians known as the Immortals because they were never allowed to fall below 10,000 in number. When one was killed, he was immediately replaced. These Immortals enjoyed special privileges. When out on a campaign, they were accompanied by their concubines and servants in wagons. Their own special food was brought along on camels, which were used by the Persians as pack animals. On a major campaign, the size of the Persian army could be enormous.

The Persians made effective use of their cavalry, especially for operating behind enemy lines and breaking up lines of communication. When the army fought on level ground, the cavalry would ride up near the enemy lines, shoot their arrows, throw their spears, and then wheel away before they could be harmed. The infantry were armed with wicker shields, spears, and bows and arrows. Generally, the infantry advanced on the enemy, set up their wicker shields as a protective barrier, and then fired arrows at the enemy from behind them. Not until the arrows were used up did they engage in hand-to-hand combat. The Persian navy consisted of ships from subject states, including the Phoenicians, Egyptians, Anatolians, and Ionian Greeks.

Persian Religion

Of all the Persians' cultural contributions, the most original was their religion. The popular religion of the

▼ **The Palace at Persepolis.** The chief Persian capital was Susa, the capital of ancient Elam, located in present-day Iran. The great king Darius, however, disliked Susa, and so moved his residence to Persepolis, a city located in the heart of the Persian Empire. This new capital served not only as a residence for the king, however. It also became a religious center and contained administrative offices and the chief treasury of the empire.

A Dinner of the Persian King
▼ ▼ ▼

The Persian kings lived in luxury as a result of their conquests and ability to levy taxes from their conquered subjects. In this selection we read a description of how a Persian king dined with his numerous guests.

Athenaeus, *The Deipnosophists*, IV: 145–46

Heracleides of Cumae, author of the *Persian History*, writes, in the second book of the work entitled *Equipment:* "All who attend upon the Persian kings when they dine first bathe themselves and then serve in white clothes, and spend nearly half the day on preparations for the dinner. Of those who are invited to eat with the king, some dine outdoors, in full sight of anyone who wishes to look on; others dine indoors in the king's company. Yet even these do not eat in his presence, for there are two rooms opposite each other, in one of which the king has his meal, in the other the invited guests. The king can see them through the curtain at the door, but they cannot see him. Sometimes, however, on the occasion of a public holiday, all dine in a single room with the king, in the great hall. And whenever the king commands a symposium [drinking-bout following the dinner] which he does often, he has about a dozen companions at the drinking. When they have finished dinner, that is the king by himself, the guests in the other room, these fellow-drinkers are summoned by one of the eunuchs; and entering they drink with him, though even they do not have the same wine; moreover, they sit on the floor, while he reclines on a couch supported by feet of gold, and they depart after having drunk to excess. In most cases the king breakfasts and dines alone, but sometimes his wife and some of his sons dine with him. And throughout the dinner his concubines sing and play the lyre; one of them is the soloist, the others sing in chorus. And so, Heracleides continues, the 'king's dinner,' as it is called, will appear prodigal to one who merely hears about it, but when one examines it carefully it will be found to have been got up with economy and even with parsimony; and the same is true of the dinners among other Persians in high station. For one thousand animals are slaughtered daily for the king; these comprise horses, camels, oxen, asses, deer, and most of the small animals; many birds also are consumed, including Arabian ostriches—and the creature is large—geese, and cocks. And of all these only moderate portions are served to each of the king's guests, and each of them may carry home whatever he leaves untouched at the meal. But the greater part of these meats and other foods are taken out into the courtyard for the body-guard and light-armed troopers maintained by the king; there they divide all the half-eaten remnants of meat and bread and share them in equal portions. . . ."

Iranians before the advent of Zoroastrianism in the sixth century focused on the worship of the powers of nature, such as the sun, moon, fire, and winds. Mithra was an especially popular god of light and war who came to be viewed as a sun god. These powers of nature were worshiped and sacrificed to with the aid of priests, known as Magi.

Zoroaster was a semi-legendary figure who, according to Persian tradition, was born in 660 B.C. After a period of wandering and solitude, he experienced revelations that caused him to be revered as a prophet of the "true religion." It is difficult to know what Zoroaster's original teachings were since the sacred book of Zoroastrianism, the *Zend Avesta,* was not written down until the third century A.D. Scholars believe, however, that the earliest section of the *Zend Avesta,* known as the *Yasna,* consisting of seventeen hymns or gathas, contains the actual writings of Zoroaster. This enables us to piece together his message.

That spiritual message was grounded in a monotheistic framework. Although Ahuramazda was not a new god to the Iranians, to Zoroaster he was the only god and the religion he preached was the only perfect one. Ahuramazda (the "Wise Lord") was the supreme deity who brought all things into being:

This I ask of You, O Ahuramazda; answer me well:
Who at the Creation was the first father of Justice?—
Who assigned their path to the sun and the stars?—
Who decreed the waxing and waning of the moon, if it
was not You?— . . .

Who has fixed the earth below, and the heaven above
with its clouds that it might not be moved?—
Who has appointed the waters and the green things
upon the earth?—
Who has harnessed to the wind and the clouds their
steeds?— . . .
Thus do I strive to recognize in You, O Wise One,
Together with the Holy Spirit, the Creator of all
things.[15]

According to Zoroaster, Ahuramazda also possessed abstract qualities or states that all humans should aspire to, such as Good Thought, Right, and Piety. Although Ahuramazda was supreme, he was not unopposed. Right is opposed by the Lie, Truth by Falsehood, Life by Death. At the beginning of the world, the good spirit of Ahuramazda was opposed by the evil spirit (in later Zoroastrianism, the evil spirit is identified with Ahriman). Although it appears that Zoroaster saw it as simply natural that where there is good, there will be evil, later followers had a tendency to make these abstractions concrete and overemphasize the reality of an evil spirit. Humans also played a role in this cosmic struggle between good and evil. Ahuramazda, the creator, gave all humans free will and the power to choose between right and wrong. The good man chooses the right way of Ahuramazda. Zoroaster taught that there would be an end to the struggle between good and evil. Ahuramazda would eventually triumph, and at the last judgment at the end of the world, the final separation of good and evil would occur. Zoroaster also provided for individual judgment as well. Each soul faced a final evaluation of its actions. If a person had performed good deeds, he or she would achieve paradise, the "House of Song" or the "Kingdom of Good Thought"; if evil deeds, then the soul would be thrown into an abyss, the "House of Worst Thought," where it would experience future ages of darkness, torment, and misery.

What brought about the spread of Zoroastrianism was its acceptance by the Great Kings of Persia. The inscriptions of Darius make clear that he believed Ahuramazda was the only god. Although he mentions "other gods that are," he gives them no role whatever in the scheme of things. Although Darius may have been a monotheist, as the kings and Magi or priests of Persia propagated Zoroaster's teachings on Ahuramazda, dramatic changes occurred. Zoroastrianism lost its monotheistic emphasis, and the old nature worship resurfaced. Hence, Persian religion returned to polytheism with Ahuramazda becoming only the chief of a number of gods of light. Mithra, the sun god, became a helper of Ahuramazda and later, in Roman times, the source of another religion. Persian kings were also very tolerant of other religions, and gods and goddesses of those religions tended to make their way into the Persian pantheon. Moreover, Zoroaster's teachings, as frequently happens to the ideas of founders of religions, acquired concrete forms that he had never originally intended. The struggle between good and evil was taken beyond the abstractions of Zoroaster into a strong ethical dualism. The spirit of evil became an actual being who had to be warded off by the use of spells and incantations. Descriptions of the last judgment came to be filled with minute physical details. Some historians believe that Zoroastrianism, with its emphasis on good and evil, a final judgment, and individual judgment of souls, had an impact on Christianity, a religion that eventually surpassed it in significance.

Around 1200 B.C., the decline of the Hittites and Egyptians had created a power vacuum that allowed a number of small states to emerge and flourish temporarily. All of them were eventually overshadowed by the rise of the great empires of the Assyrians, Chaldeans, and Persians. The Assyrian Empire had been the first to unite almost all of the ancient Near East. Even larger, however, was the empire of the Great Kings of Persia. Although it owed much to the administrative organization created by the Assyrians, the Persian Empire had its own peculiar strengths. Persian rule was not only efficient, but also tolerant. Conquered peoples were allowed to keep their own religions, customs, and methods of doing business. The many years of peace that the Persian Empire brought to the Near East facilitated trade and the general well-being of its peoples. It is no wonder that many Near Eastern peoples expressed their gratitude for being subjects of the Great Kings of Persia.

One of these peoples was the Hebrews. They created no empire and were dominated by the Assyrians, Chaldeans, and Persians. Nevertheless, they left a spiritual legacy that influenced much of the later development of Western civilization. The evolution of Hebrew monotheism created in Judaism one of the world's greatest religions; it influenced the development of both Christianity and Islam. When we speak of the Judaeo-Christian heritage of Western civilization, we refer not only to the concept of monotheism, but also to ideas of law, morality, and social justice that have become important parts of Western culture.

On the western fringes of the Persian Empire, another relatively small group of people, the Greeks, were creating cultural and political ideals that would also have an important impact on Western civilization. It is to the Greeks that we must now turn.

Notes
▼ ▼ ▼

1. Psalms 137: 1, 4–6.
2. Psalms 145: 8–9.
3. Psalms 121: 2–3.
4. Exodus 20: 13–15.
5. Isaiah 2: 4.
6. Exodus 21: 2.
7. Proverbs 31: 10–20, 24–28.
8. Quoted in Roland de Vaux, *Ancient Israel: Its Life and Institutions* (New York, 1961), p. 49.
9. Quoted in H. W. F. Saggs, *The Might That Was Assyria* (London, 1984), pp. 261–262.

10. Quoted in J. M. Cook, *The Persian Empire* (New York, 1983), p. 32.
11. Herodotus, *The Persian Wars*, trans. George Rawlinson (New York, 1942), p. 257.
12. Isaiah, 44: 28;45: 1.
13. Quoted in A. T. Olmstead, *History of the Persian Empire* (Chicago, 1948), p. 168.
14. Quoted in Cook, *The Persian Empire*, p. 76.
15. Yasna 44: 3–4, 7, as quoted in A. C. Bouquet, *Sacred Books of the World* (Harmondsworth, 1954), pp. 111–12.

Suggestions for Further Reading
▼ ▼ ▼

For a good account of Phoenician domestic and overseas expansion, see D. Harden, *The Phoenicians*, rev. ed. (Harmondsworth, 1980). On the development of the alphabet, see D. Diringer, *The Alphabet* (London, 1975). There is an enormous literature on ancient Israel. Two good studies on the archaeological aspects are Y. Aharoni, *The Archaeology of the Land of Israel* (Philadelphia, 1982); and W. F. Albright, *The Archaeology of Palestine* (Harmondsworth, 1949). For historical narratives, see especially J. Bright, *A History of Israel,* 3d ed. (Philadelphia, 1981), a fundamental study; W. F. Albright, *The Biblical Period from Abraham to Ezra* (New York, 1963), a concise summary; G. W. Anderson, *The History and Religion of Israel* (London, 1966); the recent, well-done survey by M. Grant, *The History of Ancient Israel* (New York, 1984); and H. Shanks, *Ancient Israel: A Short History from Abraham to the Roman Destruction of the Temple* (Englewood Cliffs, N.J., 1988). R. de Vaux, *Ancient Israel: Its Life and Institutions* (New York, 1961) is especially good on the social institutions of ancient Israel.

For general studies on the religion of the Hebrews, see Y. Kaufmann, *The Religion of Israel* (Chicago, 1960); and H. Ringgren, *Israelite Religion* (London, 1966). On the covenant and law, see D. R. Hillers, *Covenant: The History of a Biblical Idea* (Baltimore, 1969). The role of the prophets is examined in J. Lindblom, *Prophecy in Ancient Israel* (Oxford, 1962); and R. B. Y. Scott, *The Relevance of the Prophets* (New York, 1968).

A recent detailed account of Assyrian political, economic, social, military, and cultural history is H. W. F. Saggs, *The Might That Was Assyria* (London, 1984). The same author has also written an account of daily life entitled *Everyday Life in Babylonia and Assyria* (London, 1965). Information from the Assyrians themselves can be found in A. Grayson, *Assyrian and Babylonian Chronicles* (New York, 1975); and J. Laessoe, *People of Ancient Assyria: Their Inscriptions and Correspondence*, trans. F. S. Leigh-Browne (London, 1963). On different aspects of Assyrian culture, see R. D. Barnett, *Assyrian Sculpture* (Toronto, 1975); and P. Albenda, *The Palace of Sargon King of Assyria* (Paris, 1986). The Chaldean empire can be examined in J. Oates, *Babylon* (London, 1979).

The classic work on the Persian Empire is A. T. Olmstead, *History of the Persian Empire* (Chicago, 1948), but a recent work by J. M. Cook, *The Persian Empire* (New York, 1983) provides new material and fresh interpretations. Also of value are B. Dicks, *The Ancient Persians* (Newton Abbott, 1979); R. Frye, *The Heritage of Persia* (Cleveland, 1963); and W. Cullican, *The Medes and the Persians* (New York, 1965). On the history of Zoroastrianism, see especially R. C. Zaehner, *The Dawn and Twilight of Zoroastrianism* (London, 1961). Also helpful is M. Boyce, *Zoroastrians: Their Religious Beliefs and Practices* (London, 1979).

Chapter 3

The Civilization of the Greeks

▼ ▼ ▼ ▼ ▼

I t was the Greeks who created the intellectual foundations of our Western heritage. They asked some basic questions about human life that still dominate our own intellectual pursuits: What is the nature of the universe? What is the purpose of human existence? What is our relationship to divine forces? What constitutes a community? What constitutes a state? What is true education? What are the true sources of law? What is truth itself and how do we realize it? The Greeks not only gave answers to these questions; they proceeded to create a system of logical, analytical thought in order to examine them. This rational outlook has remained an important feature of Western civilization.

The story of ancient Greek civilization is a remarkable one that begins with the first arrival of the Greeks around 2000 B.C. By the eighth century B.C., the characteristic institution of ancient Greek life, the *polis* or city-state, had emerged. Greek civilization flourished and reached its height in the classical era of the fifth century B.C., which has come to be closely identified with the achievements of Athenian democracy. But the inability of the Greek states to end their fratricidal warfare eventually helped to lead to the conquest of Greece by the Macedonian king Philip II and to bring an end to the Greek world of independent city-states.

▼ Early Greece

Geography played an important role in the evolution of Greek history. Compared to the landmasses of Mesopotamia and Egypt, Greece occupied a small area. It was

Mycenaean Greece	Dark Age	Archaic Age	Classical Age
▼	▼	▼	▼

• • • • • • • • • 1600 • • • • • • • • • • 1275 • • • • • • • • • • • 950 • • • • • • • • • • 625 • • • • • • • • • • 300 • • • • • • • • • •

▲	▲	▲	▲ ▲
Mycenaean *Tholos* Tombs	Homer	Greek Drama	Greek Philosophy Parthenon

a mountainous peninsula that encompassed only 45,000 square miles of territory, about the size of the state of Louisiana. The mountains and the sea played especially significant roles in the development of Greek history. Much of Greece consists of small plains and river valleys surrounded by mountain ranges 8,000–10,000 feet high. The valleys were fertile and the hillsides could be used for pasture, but the mountainous terrain had the effect of isolating Greeks from one another. Consequently, Greek communities tended to follow their own separate paths and develop their own way of life. Over a period of time, these Greek communities became so fiercely attached to their independence that they were unwilling to join into larger units of organization and only too willing to fight one another to gain advantage. No doubt the small size of these independent Greek communities fostered participation in political affairs and unique cultural expressions, but the rivalry among these communities also led to the internecine warfare that ultimately devastated Greek society.

The sea also influenced the evolution of Greek society. Greece had a long seacoast, dotted by bays and inlets that provided numerous harbors. The Greeks also inhabited a number of islands to the west, south, and particularly to the east of the Greek mainland. It is no accident that the Greeks became seafarers who sailed out into the Aegean and the Mediterranean seas first to make contact with the outside world and later to establish colonies that would spread Greek civilization throughout the Mediterranean world.

Greek topography helped to determine the major territories into which Greece was ultimately divided. South of the Gulf of Corinth was the Peloponnesus, virtually an island as seen on a map. Consisting mostly of hills, mountains, and small valleys, the Peloponnesus was the location of Sparta, as well as the site of Olympia where the famous athletic games were held. Northeast of the Peloponnesus was the Attic peninsula (or Attica), the home of Athens, hemmed in by mountains to the north and west and surrounded by the sea to the south and

▼ **Map 3.1** Ancient Greece.

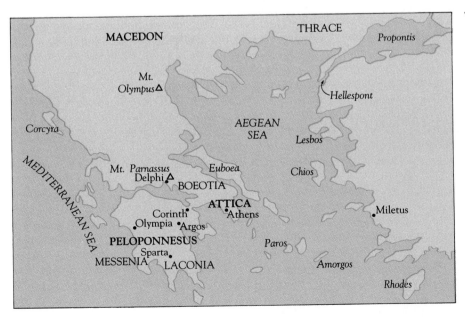

east. Northwest of Attica was Boeotia in central Greece with its chief city of Thebes. To the north of Boeotia was Thessaly, which contained the largest plains and became a great producer of grain and horses. To the north of Thessaly lay Macedonia, which was not of much importance in Greek history until the Greeks, by their own fratricidal warfare, opened the door to invasion by the Macedonian king Philip II in 338 B.C.

Minoan Crete

By 2800 B.C., a Bronze Age civilization that used metals, especially bronze, in the construction of its weapons had been established in the area of the Aegean Sea. The early Bronze Age settlements on the Greek mainland, created by non-Greek-speaking peoples, were overshadowed by another Aegean Bronze Age civilization on the large island of Crete, southeast of the Greek mainland.

The civilization of Minoan Crete was first discovered by the English archaeologist, Arthur Evans, who named it *Minoan* after Minos, the legendary king of Crete. Evans's excavations on Crete at the beginning of the twentieth century led to the discovery of an enormous palace complex at Cnossus near modern Heracleion. The remains revealed a rich and prosperous culture with Cnossus as the probable center of a far-ranging "sea empire," probably largely commercial in nature. Since Evans found few military fortifications for the defense of Cnossus itself, he assumed that Minoan Crete had a strong navy. We do know from archaeological remains that the people of Minoan Crete were accustomed to sea travel and had made contact with the more advanced civilization of Egypt. Egyptian products have been found in Crete and Cretan products in Egypt. Indeed, some

historians have argued that Crete served as a cultural link between the Greeks and the great civilizations to the east.

The Minoan Cretans were non-Greek-speaking peoples, whose civilization reached its height between 2000 and 1450 B.C. The palace at Cnossus, the royal seat of the kings, demonstrates the obvious prosperity and power of this civilization. It was an elaborate structure built around a central courtyard. Since it was constructed on the slope of a hill, some parts of the palace were several stories high. It included numerous private living rooms for the royal family and workshops for making decorated vases, small sculptures, such as ivory figurines, and jewelry. Even bathrooms, with elaborate drains, formed part of the complex. The rooms were decorated with frescoes in bright colors showing sporting events and naturalistic scenes that have led some to assume that the Cretans had a great love of nature. Storerooms in the palace held enormous jars of oil, wine, and grain, presumably paid as taxes in kind to the king. The kings were apparently assisted by a large bureaucracy that kept detailed records of the payments.

The centers of Minoan civilization on Crete suffered a sudden and catastrophic collapse around 1450 B.C. Although the cause of this destruction has been vigorously debated, many historians believe that it was the result of invasion and pillage by mainland Greeks known as the Mycenaeans.

The Mycenaeans

The term *Mycenaean* is derived from Mycenae, a remarkable fortified site first excavated by the amateur German archaeologist, Heinrich Schliemann. In a series of shaft graves, Schliemann discovered an incredible col-

▼ **Mural Painting from Thera.** This detail is taken from a larger mural found in the remains of the wealthy Minoan colony on Thera. Many of the murals found at Thera, like the frescoes of Cnossus, depict nature scenes, while this detail is taken from a painting that celebrates a naval battle. The colony at Thera was destroyed in the fifteenth century B.C. by a massive volcanic eruption, which ironically helped to preserve this and other artifacts by covering the island in a thick layer of ash.

lection of gold masks, cups, jewelry, bronze weapons, and pottery, all belonging to the Mycenaean Greek civilization, which flourished between 1600 and 1100 B.C.

The Mycenaean Greeks were part of the Indo-European family of peoples (see Chapter 1) who spread from their original location in central Europe into southern and western Europe, India, and Iran. One group entered the territory of Greece from the north around 1900 B.C. From the evidence of pottery, archaeologists have argued that, over a period of time, these Indo-European–speaking invaders managed to gain control of the Greek mainland and develop a civilization.

Mycenaean culture reached its high point between 1400 and 1200 B.C. It is especially noted for its fortified palace-centers, which were built on hills surrounded by gigantic stone walls. While the royal families lived within the walls of these complexes, the civilian populations lived in scattered locations outside the walls. Among the noticeable features of these Mycenaean centers were the tombs where members of the royal families were buried. Known as *tholos* tombs, they were built into hillsides. An entryway led into a circular tomb chamber constructed of cut stone blocks in a domed shape that resembled a beehive in appearance.

Mycenaean Greek civilization consisted of a number of powerful monarchies centered in the palace complexes, such as those found at Mycenae, Tiryns, Pylos, Thebes, and Orchomenos. These various centers of power probably formed a loose confederacy of independent states with Mycenae the strongest. According to tablets written in an early form of Greek script called Linear B, a Mycenaean king used the title of *wanax*. Next in importance to the king were commanders of the army, priests, and bureaucrats who kept careful records. The free citizenry included peasants, soldiers, and artisans with the lowest rung of the social ladder consisting of serfs and slaves. The latter were often victims of war, such as the five hundred women listed as slaves from Asia who worked at Pylos collecting and preparing flax for weaving clothes.

The Mycenaean Greeks were, above all, a warrior people who prided themselves on their heroic deeds in battle. Unlike Cretan frescoes, Mycenaean wall murals often show war and hunting scenes, the natural occupations of a warrior aristocracy. Archaeological evidence also indicates that the Mycenaean monarchies developed an extensive commercial network. Mycenaean pottery has been found throughout the Mediterranean basin, in Syria and Egypt to the east and Sicily and southern Italy to the west. But some scholars also believe that the Mycenaean Greeks, led by Mycenae itself,

▼ **Lion Gate, Mycenae.** The Mycenaean civilization reached its height between 1400 and 1200 B.C. Evidence suggests that the Mycenaean Greeks conducted trade throughout the Mediterranean and also expanded militarily. While the reasons for the eventual decline of this civilization are debated, it is clear that its collapse by 1100 B.C. ushered in the Greek Dark Age. The photo shows the Lion Gate to the citadel at Mycenae.

spread outward militarily, conquering Crete and making it part of the Mycenaean world. Some of the Aegean islands also fell subject to Mycenaean control. The archives of the Hittites (see Chapter 1) in Asia Minor contain references that apparently allude to military expeditions of the Mycenaean Greeks. They may also be mentioned in Egyptian records as pirates in the Nile delta. The most famous of all their supposed military adventures has come down to us in the epic poetry of

Homer (see the discussion of Homer in the next section). Did the Mycenaean Greeks, led by Agamemnon, king of Mycenae, sack the city of Troy on the northwestern coast of Asia Minor around 1250 B.C.? Since the excavations of Heinrich Schliemann, begun in 1870, scholars have debated this question. Many do believe in the basic authenticity of the Homerian legend, even if the details have become shrouded in mystery.

By the late thirteenth century, Mycenaean Greece was showing signs of serious trouble. Mycenae itself was torched around 1190 B.C., reinhabited, and finally abandoned around 1125 B.C. Other Mycenaean centers show similar patterns of destruction. By 1100 B.C., the Mycenaean culture was coming to an end.

Modern scholars have proposed a number of theories to explain the collapse of Mycenaean civilization. According to the Greeks' own legend, their mainland was invaded from the north by another Greek-speaking people who were less civilized than the Mycenaean Greeks. Called the Dorians, these invaders supposedly destroyed the old centers of Mycenaean power and ultimately established themselves in the Peloponnesus. Some historians believe that the Dorians destroyed the Mycenaean civilization. One theory, not generally accepted, holds that a long drought depopulated Greece and so weakened the Mycenaean monarchies that the Dorians simply moved in and assumed power. Other historians argue that internal conflict among the Mycenaean kings was a major factor in the Mycenaean decline. Perhaps all these factors played some role in the destruction of Mycenaean Greek civilization. What is certain is that by 1100 B.C., the Greek world had entered a new period of considerable insecurity.

▼ The Greek Dark Age (c. 1100–c. 750 B.C.)

With the collapse of Mycenaean Greek civilization, a veil of considerable darkness descends upon Greek history as there are few touchstones to help us reconstruct what happened in this period. No writing is known until the eighth century, and few significant intellectual or artistic products appear for three hundred years.

But upon close examination, so-called Dark Ages are rarely all that dark, and it is obvious that during the period from 1100 to 750 B.C. significant underlying developments were occurring that established the contours of later Greek civilization. This was a period of migrations. After 1200, large numbers of Greeks left the mainland and migrated across the Aegean Sea to various islands, and especially to the western shores of Asia Minor, a strip of territory that came to be called Ionia. Based on their dialect, the Greeks who resided there were called Ionians. Two other major groups of Greeks settled in established parts of Greece. The Aeolian Greeks who were located in northern and central Greece colonized the large island of Lesbos and the adjacent territory of the mainland. The Dorians established themselves in southwest Greece, especially in the Peloponnesus, as well as on some of the islands in the south Aegean sea, including Crete.

Other important activities occurred in this Dark Age as well. After 1000 B.C., a new type of geometric pottery emerged in Greece. There was a revival of some trade and some economic activity besides agriculture. Iron came into use for the construction of weapons. And at some point in the eighth century B.C., the Greeks adopted the Phoenician alphabet to give themselves a new system of writing. Near the very end of this so-called Dark Age appeared the work of Homer, who has come to be viewed as one of the truly great poets of all time.

Homer

The origins of the *Iliad* and the *Odyssey*, the first two great epics of early Greece, are to be found in the oral tradition of reciting poems recounting the deeds of heroes of the Mycenaean age. It is generally assumed that early in the eighth century B.C., Homer made use of these oral traditions to compose the *Iliad*, his epic of the Trojan War. But the *Iliad* is not so much the story of the war itself as it is the tale of the Greek hero Achilles and how the "wrath of Achilles" led to disaster. As is true of all great literature, the *Iliad* abounds in universal lessons. Underlying them all is the clear message, as one commentator has observed, that "men will still come and go like the generations of leaves in the forest; that he will still be weak, and the gods strong and incalculable; that the quality of a man matters more than his achievement; that violence and recklessness will still lead to disaster, and that this will fall on the innocent as well as on the guilty."[1]

Although the *Odyssey* has long been considered Homer's other masterpiece, some scholars believe that it was composed later than the *Iliad* and was probably not the work of Homer. The *Odyssey* is an epic romance that recounts the journeys of one of the Greek heroes, Odysseus, after the fall of Troy and his ultimate return to his wife. But there is a larger vision here as well: the testing of the heroic stature of Odysseus until, by both cunning and patience, he prevails. In the course of this testing, the underlying moral message is "that virtue is a better policy than vice."[2]

The *Iliad* and the *Odyssey* supposedly describe the heroes of the Mycenaean age of the thirteenth century B.C. However, there is considerable debate about their usefulness as historical documents. Since the epics were probably composed in the eighth century B.C., some historians believe that they really describe social conditions of that century, while others believe that they reveal the circumstances of the Dark Age itself in the tenth and ninth centuries. Still others have argued that the epics may incorporate elements from different periods. If we do accept these works as indicative of the Dark Age, what kind of society do they describe?

Homeric Greece was a society based on agriculture in which a landed warrior-aristocracy controlled much wealth and exercised considerable power. Kings were regarded as simply first among equals and ruled kingdoms petty in size and power compared to the Mycenaean Greek monarchies. Homer's kings were assisted in ruling by a council of nobles who were free to give advice contrary to the king and even to disobey his commands. There was also an assembly of commoners, consisting in wartime of all soldiers and in peacetime of all who lived near the king's residence. The king and the council of nobles brought only major questions to the assembly, which did not debate but simply made decisions by acclamation. There is no doubt that Homer's society was divided along class lines with the warrior-aristocrats as the dominant group. Homer's world reflects the values of aristocratic heroes.

This, of course, explains the importance of Homer to later generations of Greeks. Homer did not so much record history; he made it. The Greeks regarded the *Iliad* and the *Odyssey* as authentic history and as the work of one poet, Homer. These masterpieces gave to the Greeks an ideal past with a legendary age of heroes and came to be used as standard texts for the education of generations of Greek males. As one Athenian stated, "My father was anxious to see me develop into a good man . . . and as a means to this end he compelled me to memorize all of Homer."[3] The values Homer inculcated were essentially the aristocratic values of courage and honor (see the box on p. 62). It was important to strive for the excellence befitting a hero, which the Greeks called *arete*. In the warrior-aristocratic world of Homer, *arete* is won in a struggle or contest. In his willingness to fight, the hero protects his family and friends, preserves and expands his own honor and that of his family, and earns his reputa-

▼ **The Dragging of Hector's Body by Achilles.** This late sixth-century Athenian vase depicts Achilles' dragging of Hector's body around the city of Troy, a scene taken from Homer's *Iliad*. The *Iliad* is Homer's masterpiece, and while many scholars doubt its historical accuracy, this work (and the *Odyssey*) gained importance in the eyes of later Greeks as a means of teaching the aristocratic values of courage and honor.

tion. It is important to remember, however, that in Homer this presentation of heroic values is never straightforward and consistent. The *Iliad* contains many debates about these very values. But there is no doubt that to a later generation of Greek males, these heroic values formed the core of aristocratic virtue, a fact that explains the tremendous popularity of Homer as an educational tool. Homer gave to the Greeks one universally known model of heroism, honor, and nobility. It proved to be a source of great strength—and also of weakness, as we shall see.

The Civilization of the Greeks ▼ 61

Homer's Ideal of Excellence

▼ ▼ ▼

The Iliad *and the* Odyssey, *which the Greeks believed were both written by Homer, were used as basic texts for the education of Greeks in antiquity for hundreds of years. This passage from the* Iliad, *describing the encounter between Hector, prince of Troy, and his wife Andromache, illustrates the Greek ideal of gaining honor through combat. At the end of the passage, Homer also reveals the Greek attitude toward women.*

Homer, *Iliad*

Hector looked at his son and smiled, but said nothing. Andromache, bursting into tears, went up to him and put her hand in his. "Hector," she said, "you are possessed. This bravery of yours will be your end. You do not think of your little boy or your unhappy wife, whom you will make a widow soon. Some day the Achaeans [Greeks] are bound to kill you in a massed attack. And when I lose you I might as well be dead. . . . I have no father, no mother, now. . . . I had seven brothers too at home. In one day all of them went down to Hades' House. The great Achilles of the swift feet killed them all. . . ."

"So you, Hector, are father and mother and brother to me, as well as my beloved husband. Have pity on me now; stay here on the tower; and do not make your boy an orphan and your wife a widow. . . ."

"All that, my dear," said the great Hector of the glittering helmet, "is surely my concern. But if I hid myself like a coward and refused to fight, I could never face the Trojans and the Trojan ladies in their trailing gowns. Besides, it would go against the grain, for I have trained myself always, like a good soldier, to take my place in the front line and win glory for my father and myself. . . ."

As he finished, glorious Hector held out his arms to take his boy. But the child shrank back with a cry to the bosom of his girdled nurse, alarmed by his father's appearance. He was frightened by the bronze of the helmet and the horsehair plume that he saw nodding grimly down at him. His father and his lady mother had to laugh. But noble Hector quickly took his helmet off and put the dazzling thing on the ground. Then he kissed his son, dandled him in his arms, and prayed to Zeus and the other gods: "Zeus, and you other gods, grant that this boy of mine may be, like me, pre-eminent in Troy; as strong and brave as I; a mighty king of Ilium. May people say, when he comes back from battle, 'Here is a better man than his father.' Let him bring home the bloodstained armour of the enemy he has killed, and make his mother happy."

Hector handed the boy to his wife, who took him to her fragrant breast. She was smiling through her tears, and when her husband saw this he was moved. He stroked her with his hand and said: "My dear, I beg you not to be too much distressed. No one is going to send me down to Hades before my proper time. But Fate is a thing that no man born of woman, coward or hero, can escape. Go home now, and attend to your own work, the loom and the spindle, and see that the maidservants get on with theirs. War is men's business; and this war is the business of every man in Ilium, myself above all."

▼ Archaic Greece
(c. 750–c. 500 B.C.)

In the eighth century B.C., Greek civilization burst forth with new energies, beginning the period that historians have called the Archaic Age of Greece. Two major developments stand out in this era: the evolution of the *polis* as the central institution in Greek life and the Greeks' colonization of the Mediterranean and Black seas.

The Polis

The origins of the Greek *polis* (plural *poleis*) are not very clear. It developed slowly during the Dark Age following the upheavals that brought a close to the Mycenaean age and by the eighth century B.C. had emerged as a truly unique and fundamental institution in Greek society. In the most basic sense, a *polis* could be defined as a small but sovereign political unit in which all major political, social, and religious activities were carried out at one central location.

In a physical sense, the *polis* encompassed a town or city or even a village and its surrounding countryside. But the town or city or village served as the focus or central point where the citizens of the *polis* could assemble for political, social, and religious activities. In some *poleis*, this central meeting point was a hill, like the Acropolis at Athens, which could serve as a place of refuge during an attack and later in some sites came to be the religious center on which temples and public monuments were erected. Below the acropolis would be an agora, an open space that served both as a place where citizens could assemble and as a market. Citizens resided alike in town and country, but the town remained the center of political activity.

Poleis could vary greatly in size, from a few square miles to a few hundred square miles. The larger ones were the product of consolidation. The territory of Attica, for example, had once had twelve *poleis*, but eventually became a single *polis* (Athens) through a process of amalgamation. Although the Greek philosopher Plato considered 5,000 citizens an ideal size for a *polis*, Athens grew to have a population of more than 300,000, with an adult male citizen body of about 43,000. Most *poleis* were considerably smaller than Athens, however, and were closer to Plato's ideal.

The *polis* was much more than just a political institution. It was, above all, a community of citizens in which all political, economic, social, cultural, and religious activities were focused. To some Greeks, it was simply inconceivable that civilized people could live in any other way. The Greek philosopher Aristotle (see Greek Philosophy later in this chapter) stated in his *Politics* that the *polis* "belongs among the things that exist by nature, and that man is by nature a being of the *polis*." As a community, the *polis* consisted of citizens with political rights (adult males), citizens with no political rights (women and children), and noncitizens (slaves and resident aliens).

Crucial to the *polis* were the sense of community that generated cooperation and the great strength that came from that cooperation. All citizens of a *polis* were equal in the sense that they possessed the same fundamental rights. The *polis* rested upon a respect for law. As one Greek poet proclaimed, "The law-abiding town, though small and set on a lofty rock, outranks senseless Nineveh" (the capital city of the Assyrian Empire). Rights, however, were coupled with responsibilities. Aristotle argued that the citizen did not just belong to himself; "we must rather regard every citizen as belonging to the state." The unity of citizens was important and often meant that states would take an active role in directing the patterns of life.

The system of the *polis* also relied on local patriotism, which was encouraged by the veneration of a god or goddess as patron of the community. But there was also a negative side to local patriotism. It tended to foster mutual suspicion and divide Greece into a large number of tiny sovereign units. In times of emergency, some of the Greek states managed to shed their rivalries and cooperate against an outside enemy. But freedom of the *polis* often came first, and in the long run, the division of Greece into fiercely patriotic sovereign units helped to bring about its ruin. "Greece" was not a united country, but a geographical expression. The cultural unity of the Greeks, reinforced by a common language and common gods, did not mean much politically.

The development of the *polis* was paralleled by the emergence of a new military system. Greek fighting had previously been dominated by aristocratic cavalrymen, who reveled in individual duels with enemy soldiers. But by the end of the eighth century and beginning of the seventh century B.C., the hoplite infantry formation—the phalanx—came into being. Hoplites were heavily armed infantrymen, who wore bronze helmets, breastplates, and greaves (shin guards). Each carried a round shield, short sword, and a thrusting spear about nine feet long. Hoplites advanced into battle as a unit, forming a phalanx in tight order, usually eight ranks deep. As long as the hoplites kept their order, were not outflanked, and did not break, they either secured victory or, at the very least, suffered no harm. The phalanx was easily routed, however, if it broke its order.

The hoplite force, which apparently developed first in the Peloponnesus, had political as well as military repercussions. The aristocratic cavalry was now outdated. Since each hoplite provided his own armor, men of property, both aristocrats and small farmers, made up the new phalanx. Initially, this created a bond between the aristocrats and peasants, which minimized class conflict and enabled the aristocrats to dominate their societies as monarchical institutions began to disappear. In the long run, however, those who could become hoplites and fight for the state could also challenge aristocratic control.

Colonization

Greek expansion overseas was another major development of the Archaic Age. Between 750 and 550 B.C., the Greek people left their homeland in large numbers to settle in distant lands. One reason for the exodus was the poverty and land hunger created by the growing gulf between rich and poor, between wealthy landed aristocrats who seized more and more land and the peasants who lost their land. The land problem was intensified by overpopulation. The growing division in some Greek communities caused the ruling classes to look with favor upon the migration of discontented elements to new lands. Throughout history, colonization has always been a safety valve to release potentially revolutionary pressures. Trade, too, was a factor in the development of colonization. By the eighth century B.C., Greeks were producing dyed woolen fabrics and pottery, and these goods, along with olive oil and wine, were playing important roles in a growing commerce. Some colonies were established in places ideal for trade and at locations where important raw materials, such as metals, could be obtained. Greek tyrants (see Tyranny in the Greek Polis later in the chapter) proved especially eager to win the approval of merchants and traders by establishing new colonies.

Greek colonies varied in purpose and organization. Some were simply trading posts or centers for the transshipment of goods to Greece. Most were larger settlements that included good agricultural land taken from the native populations found in those areas. Each colony was founded as a *polis* and was usually independent of the mother *polis* (hence, the word *metropolis*) that had established it. Indeed, the use of the word *colony* is misleading in describing Greek expansion. Although the mother *polis* created a colony to further its interests, invariably the colony saw itself as an independent entity. Its links to the mother city were not political, but were based on sharing common social, economic, and especially religious practices.

In the western Mediterranean, new Greek settlements were established along the coastline of southern Italy, such as the cities of Tarentum and Neapolis (Naples). So many Greek communities were established in southern Italy that the Romans later called it *Magna Graecia* ("Great Greece"). An important city was founded at Syracuse in eastern Sicily in 734 B.C. by the city-state of Corinth, one of the most active Greek states in establishing colonies. Greek settlements were also established in southern France (Massilia; modern Marseilles), eastern Spain, and northern Africa west of Egypt.

▼ **Map 3.2** The Greek Colonies.

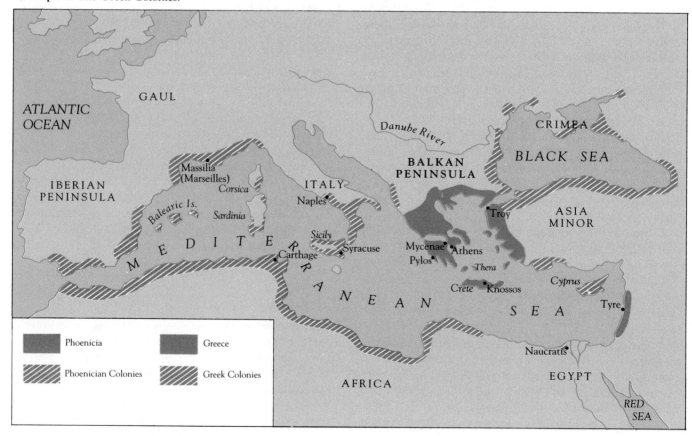

To the north, the Greeks set up colonies in Thrace, where they sought good agricultural lands to grow grains. Greeks also settled along the shores of the Black Sea and secured the approaches to it with cities on the Hellespont and Bosphorus, most notably Byzantium, site of the later Constantinople (Istanbul). A trading post was established in Egypt, giving the Greeks access to both the products and the advanced culture of the east.

These settlements by the Greeks over such a wide area had important effects. For one thing, they contributed to the diffusion of culture. In addition to gaining new ideas, the Greeks also established their own culture throughout the Mediterranean basin. The later Romans, after all, made their first contact with the Greeks through the settlements in southern Italy. In addition, colonization led to increased trade and industry. The Greeks sent their pottery, wine, and olive oil to these areas; in return, they received grains and metals from the west and fish, timber, wheat, metals, and slaves from the Black Sea region. The expansion of trade and industry created a new group of rich men in many *poleis* who desired political privileges commensurate with their wealth, but found them impossible to gain because of the power of the ruling aristocrats. The desire for change on the part of this group soon led to political crisis in many Greek states.

Tyranny in the Greek Polis

When the *polis* emerged as an important institution in Greece in the eighth century, the power of kings waned, and kings virtually disappeared in most Greek states or survived only as ceremonial figures with no real power. Instead, political power passed into the hands of local aristocracies. But increasing divisions in Greek *poleis* between rich and poor and the aspirations of newly rising industrial and commercial groups opened the door to the rise of tyrants in the seventh and sixth centuries B.C. They were not necessarily oppressive or wicked as our word *tyrant* connotes. Greek tyrants were rulers who came to power in an unconstitutional way; a tyrant was not subject to the law. Many who became tyrants were actually aristocrats who opposed the control of the ruling aristocratic factions in their cities. The support for the tyrants, however, came from the new rich who had made their money in trade and industry and the poor peasants. Both groups were opposed to the domination of political power by aristocratic oligarchies.

Tyrants usually achieved power by a local coup d'etat and maintained it by using mercenary soldiers. Once in power, they promoted public works projects, such as the

▼ **A Spartan Warrior.** The Greek hoplites were infantrymen equipped with large round shields and long thrusting spears. In battle they advanced in a tight phalanx formation and were dangerous opponents as long as this formation remained unbroken. The dedication of the Spartan state to military ideals gave to a Spartan male his chief ambition: to achieve glory as a warrior. Spartan soldiers were famous for their fighting abilities.

construction of new marketplaces, temples, and walls, that not only glorified the city but also enhanced their own popularity. Tyrants also favored the interests of merchants and traders by encouraging the founding of new colonies, developing new coinage, and establishing new systems of weights and measures. In many instances, they added to the prosperity of their cities. By their patronage of the arts, they encouraged cultural development.

Despite these achievements, tyranny was largely extinguished by the end of the sixth century B.C. The children and grandchildren of tyrants, who tended to be corrupted by their inherited power and wealth, often became cruel and unjust rulers, making tyranny no longer seem such a desirable institution. Its very nature as a system outside the law seemed contradictory to the ideal of law in a Greek community. Tyranny did not last, but it played a significant role in the evolution of Greek history. The rule of narrow aristocratic oligarchies was destroyed. Once the tyrants were eliminated, the door was opened to the participation of new and more people in the affairs of the community. Although this trend culminated in the development of democracy in some communities, in other states expanded oligarchies of one kind or another managed to remain in power. Greek states exhibited considerable variety in their governmental structures; this can perhaps best be seen by examining the two most famous and most powerful Greek city-states, Sparta and Athens.

Sparta

The Greeks of Sparta and Athens spoke different dialects and developed different political systems. The Spartans sought stability and conformity and emphasized order. The Athenians allowed for individual differences and stressed freedom. Although they shared a common heritage, their differences grew so large in their own minds that they were ultimately willing to engage in a life-and-death struggle to support their separate realities. When they did so, the entire Greek world was the real loser.

Sparta had been a monarchy in Mycenaean and Homeric times. After emerging out of the Dark Age, it remained a monarchy, but one that possessed two kings with their powers limited by a strong council and assembly. The Spartan constitution underwent dramatic changes, however, as a result of Sparta's imperialism.

Located in the southeastern Peloponnesus, Sparta, like other Greek states, was faced with a problem of land hunger. Rather than solving this problem by colonization, Sparta looked for land nearby and, beginning around 740 B.C., undertook the conquest of neighboring Messenia despite its larger size and population. Messenia possessed a large, fertile plain ideal for growing grain. After its conquest, Sparta subjected the Messenians, although greatly outnumbered by them (7 to 1), to serfdom. Known as helots, they were bound to the land for Sparta's benefit. Initially, this imperialistic venture had little apparent effect on Sparta. In the eighth and even seventh centuries B.C., Sparta still appears to have been

a culturally vibrant state. But in the seventh century, the Messenians revolted. Although Sparta succeeded in quelling the revolt, the struggle was so long and hard that the Spartans made a conscious decision to renounce the amenities of civilized life and create a military state so that they could dominate Messenia for ages to come.

After 600 B.C., the Spartans instituted a series of reforms that are associated with the name of the lawgiver Lycurgus (see the box on p. 67). Although historians are not sure of his historicity, there is no doubt about the results of these reforms. By the end of the sixth century B.C., Sparta had been transformed into a perpetual military camp.

The lives of Spartans were now rigidly organized. At birth, each child was examined by state officials who decided whether it was fit to live. Those judged unfit were exposed to die. Boys were taken from their mothers at the age of seven and put under control of the state. They lived in military-like barracks, where they were subjected to harsh discipline to make them tough and given an education that stressed military training and obedience to authority. At twenty, Spartan males were enrolled in the army for regular military service. Although allowed to marry, they continued to live in the military barracks. All meals were eaten in public dining halls with fellow soldiers. Meals were simple; the famous Spartan black broth consisted of a piece of pork boiled in blood, salt, and vinegar, causing a visitor who ate in a public mess to remark that he now understood why Spartans were not afraid to die. At thirty, Spartan males were recognized as mature and allowed to vote in the assembly and live at home, but they remained in military service until the age of sixty. Spartan females were subjected to similar training but only until they married. While their husbands remained in military barracks until age thirty, women lived at home. Spartan women had greater freedom of movement than was common elsewhere in Greece.

The Spartan social structure was rigidly organized. At the summit were the *Spartiates*—full Spartan citizens. Each Spartan citizen owned a piece of land, worked by the Messenian helots, to provide economic sustenance. With their material needs provided for them, Spartan citizens could dedicate themselves to their duties as a ruling class. Below the *Spartiates* were the *perioeci*. Though free, they did not possess the privileges of citizenship and served as small merchants and craftsmen. They were subject to military duty, however. At the bottom of the social scale were the helots, perpetually bound to the land. They were assigned to the lands of the Spartan citizens. The helots farmed the land and

The Lycurgan Reforms

▼ ▼ ▼

In order to maintain their control over the conquered Messenians, the Spartans instituted the reforms that created their military state. In this account of the supposed lawgiver Lycurgus, the Greek historian Plutarch discusses the effect of these reforms on the treatment and education of boys.

Plutarch, *Lycurgus*

Lycurgus was of another mind; he would not have masters bought out of the market for his young Spartans, . . . nor was it lawful, indeed, for the father himself to breed up the children after his own fancy; but as soon as they were seven years old they were to be enrolled in certain companies and classes, where they all lived under the same order and discipline, doing their exercises and taking their play together. Of these, he who showed the most conduct and courage was made captain; they had their eyes always upon him, obeyed his orders, and underwent patiently whatsoever punishment he inflicted; so that the whole course of their education was one continued exercise of a ready and perfect obedience. The old men, too, were spectators of their performances, and often raised quarrels and disputes among them, to have a good opportunity of finding out their different characters, and of seeing which would be valiant, which a coward, when they should come to more dangerous encounters. Reading and writing they gave them, just enough to serve their turn; their chief care was to make them good subjects, and to teach them to endure pain and conquer in battle. To this end, as they grew in years, their discipline was proportionately increased; their heads were close-clipped, they

were accustomed to go barefoot, and for the most part to play naked.

After they were twelve years old, they were no longer allowed to wear any undergarments, they had one coat to serve them a year; their bodies were hard and dry, with but little acquaintance of baths and unguents; these human indulgences they were allowed only on some few particular days in the year. They lodged together in little bands upon beds made of the rushes which grew by the banks of the river Eurotas, which they were to break off with their hands with a knife; if it were winter, they mingled some thistle-down with their rushes, which it was thought had the property of giving warmth. By the time they were come to this age there was not any of the more hopeful boys who had not a lover to bear him company. The old men, too, had an eye upon them, coming often to the grounds to hear and see them contend either in wit or strength with one another, and this as seriously . . . as if they were their fathers, their tutors, or their magistrates; so that there scarcely was any time or place without some one present to put them in mind of their duty, and punish them if they had neglected it.

[Spartan boys were also encouraged to steal their food.] They stole, too, all other meat they could lay their hands on, looking out and watching all opportunities, when people were asleep or more careless than usual. If they were caught, they were not only punished with whipping, but hunger, too, being reduced to their ordinary allowance, which was but very slender, and so contrived on purpose, that they might set about to help themselves, and be forced to exercise their energy and address. This was the principal design of their hard fare.

gave their masters one-half of the produce. A secret police force lived among them and was permitted to kill any helot considered dangerous. To legalize this murder, the state officially declared war on the helots at the beginning of each year.

The so-called Lycurgan reforms also reorganized the Spartan government. The political structure combined monarchical, aristocratic, and democratic elements.

The executive branch of the Spartan state originally consisted of two kings from different families. They were primarily responsible for military affairs and served as the leaders of the Spartan army on its campaigns. Moreover, the kings served as the supreme priests within the state religion and had some role in foreign policy. Probably in the early eighth century, the domestic role of the kings was superseded by a college of five *ephors*. Elected annually, their duties included supervising the education of youth and the conduct of all citizens. They also served as judges in all civil cases.

The Spartan constitution contained an aristocratic element in the form of a body called the *gerousia*, a council of old men. It consisted of twenty-eight citizens over the age of sixty, who were elected for life, and the two kings. Although the *gerousia* helped the *ephors* manage public affairs, its primary task was to determine the issues that would be presented to the assembly of citizens. It also acted as a judicial body, primarily in criminal cases. The democratic element of the state was in an assembly of all male citizens called the *apella*. The *apella* did not debate, but only voted on the issues put before it by the *gerousia*. The assembly also elected the *ephors* and *gerousia*.

To guarantee the continuity of their new military state, the Spartans deliberately turned their backs on outside society and cultural amenities. Foreigners were discouraged from visiting Sparta to prevent the importation of novel ideas. Nor were Spartans, except for military reasons, encouraged to travel abroad where they might pick up new ideas. Trade and commerce were likewise minimized. Spartan citizens were discouraged from pursuing philosophy, literature, the arts, or any subject that might foster novel thoughts dangerous to the stability of the state. Eventually, however, for reasons of security, the Spartans were forced to wage war outside the Peloponnesus. When they did go abroad, Spartan leaders often seemed to justify the wisdom of these restrictions by not following the Spartan ideal and succumbing to the allurement of wealth and power.

In the sixth century, Sparta used her military might and the fear it inspired to gain greater control of the Peloponnesus by organizing an alliance of almost all the Peloponnesian states. Sparta's strength enabled it to dominate this Peloponnesian League and determine its policies.

By 500 B.C., the Spartans had organized a powerful military state that maintained order and stability in the Peloponnesus. Of course, this was achieved at great cost, especially the loss of freedom, not only for the Messenians, their subject peoples, but also for the Spartans themselves. It is doubtful that the Spartans saw it that way, however. Raised from early childhood to believe that total loyalty to the Spartan state was the basic reason for existence, the Spartans viewed their strength as justification for their militaristic ideals and regimented society. In the struggle to come with the Persians, the Spartan military machine would be much appreciated by all Greeks.

Athens

By 700 B.C., Athens had established a unified *polis* on the peninsula of Attica. Although early Athens had been ruled by a monarchy, by the seventh century B.C., it had fallen under the control of its aristocrats. They possessed the best land and controlled political and religious life by means of a council of nobles called the Areopagus, assisted by a board of nine archons. Since the archons served only one year and entered the Areopagus afterward, it was the latter body that held the real power. Although there was an *ecclesia* or assembly of full citizens, it possessed few powers.

Near the end of the seventh century B.C., Athens was experiencing political and social discontent stemming from the development of rival factions within the aristocracy and serious economic problems. A codification of the laws about 621 B.C. by the archon Draco failed to stop the unrest. Increasing numbers of Athenian farmers found themselves sold into slavery when they were unable to repay the loans they had borrowed from their aristocratic neighbors, pledging themselves as collateral. Repeatedly, revolutionary cries for cancellation of debts and a redistribution of land were heard. As we have seen, it was precisely this kind of economic and social crisis that produced tyrannies in other *poleis*.

Hoping to avoid tyranny, the ruling Athenian aristocrats responded to this crisis by choosing Solon, a liberally minded aristocrat, as sole archon in 594 B.C. and giving him full power to make reforms. Solon's reforms dealt with both the economic and political problems. He canceled all current land debts, outlawed new loans based on humans as collateral, and freed people who had fallen into slavery for debt. He refused, however, to carry out the redistribution of the land and hence failed to deal with the basic cause of the economic crisis. This failure, however, was overshadowed by other economic steps that ultimately led to increased prosperity for Athens. These included devising new weights and measures, enacting a less severe law code, encouraging the growth of olive trees and the export of olive oil, and attracting foreign artisans by offering them citizenship—all steps that helped Athens achieve increased commercial and industrial prosperity in the following decades.

Like his economic reforms, Solon's political measures were also a compromise. While by no means eliminating the power of the aristocracy, they opened the door to the participation of new people, especially the nonaristocratic wealthy, into the government. Solon now divided all Athenian citizens into four classes on the basis of wealth. Only men in the first two classes (the wealthiest classes) could hold the archonship and be members of the Areopagus. Men in the third class could be elected to a new council of 400 called the *boule*, whose function it was to prepare the agenda for the assembly. The fourth (and poorest) class, though not allowed to hold any political offices, could now vote in the assembly. All four classes could also sit in the new popular court (the *heliaea*) instituted by Solon to hear appeals from cases tried before the archons.

Solon's reforms, while popular, did not truly solve Athens' problems. Aristocratic factions continued to vie for power, and the poorer peasants resented Solon's failure to institute land redistribution. Internal strife finally led to the very institution Solon had hoped to avoid—tyranny. Pisistratus, an aristocrat and a distant relative of Solon, seized power in 560 B.C. and made himself a tyrant. Although driven into exile twice after his initial coup d'etat, he used mercenary soldiers to reestablish his tyranny in 546 B.C. and remained in power until his death in 527 B.C.

Pisistratus did not tamper very much with the constitution. The assembly, councils, and courts continued to function while he made sure that his supporters were elected as magistrates and to the councils. Pisistratus curried favor by an ambitious building program, aimed at beautifying the city. To encourage patriotic unity, he introduced new public festivals, such as the one to Dionysus, god of wine, while old festivals, such as the Panathenaia, celebrated in honor of the patron goddess Athena, were expanded and made more appealing to the public. Pursuing a foreign policy that aided Athenian trade, Pisistratus remained popular with the mercantile and industrial classes.

Pisistratus's mild tyranny had been popular with many Athenians, but the ruthless policies of his son Hippias (527–510 B.C.) produced a reaction. With the help of Spartan troops under their ambitious and active King Cleomenes I, the Athenians sent Hippias into exile and ended the tyranny. Although the aristocrats attempted, with Spartan help, to reestablish an aristocratic oligarchy, Cleisthenes, a liberal aristocrat, opposed this plan and, with the backing of the Athenian people, gained the upper hand in 508 B.C. The reforms of Cleisthenes now established the basis for Athenian democracy.

A major aim of Cleisthenes' reforms was to weaken the power of traditional localities and regions, which had provided the foundation for aristocratic strength. He made the deme the basic unit of Athenian political life. Citizens were now those people who were enrolled in the demes, which ultimately numbered about 170. The residents of the demes were grouped into ten new

Chronology
▼ ▼ ▼
Archaic Greece: Athens and Sparta

Athens	
Draco's laws	c. 621 B.C.
Solon's reforms	594 B.C.
Tyranny of Pisistratus	c. 560–556 and 546–527 B.C.
Deposition of Hippias— end of tyranny	510 B.C.
Cleisthenes' reforms	c. 508–501 B.C.
Sparta	
Conquest of Messenia	c. 740–710 B.C.
Messenian revolt	c. 650–625 B.C.
Beginning of Peloponnesian League	c. 560–550 B.C.

tribes instead of the traditional four. Each tribe contained demes located in the country districts of Attica, the coastal areas, and Athens. The new tribes thus contained a cross section of the population and reflected all of Attica, a move that diminished local interests and increased loyalty to the *polis*. Cleisthenes' ten new tribes were then linked to a new council of 500 that replaced Solon's council of 400. Each of the ten tribes chose fifty members by lot each year for the new council. No one was allowed to serve more than two years (and then not in succession) on the council. It prepared the business that would be handled by the assembly and was responsible for the administration of both foreign and financial affairs. The assembly of all the citizens had final authority in the passing of laws after debate; thus, Cleisthenes' reforms had reinforced the assembly's central role in the Athenian political system.

The reforms of Cleisthenes created the foundations for Athenian democracy. More changes would come in the fifth century when the Athenians themselves would begin to use the word *democracy* to describe their system. By 500 B.C., Athens was more united than it had been and was on the verge of playing a more important role in Greek affairs.

Archaic Greek Culture

The period after the Dark Age, as we have seen, was one of economic growth, social upheaval, and political change. It witnessed a revitalization of Greek life that is also evident in Greek art and literature. Some aspects of archaic Greek culture, such as pottery and sculpture, were especially influenced by the East. Greek sculpture, particularly that of the Ionian Greek settlements in western Asia Minor, demonstrates the impact of the considerably older Egyptian civilization. There we first see the life-size stone statues of young male nudes known as the *kouros* figures. The *kouros* bears considerable re-

▼ **Kouros of Sounion.** Found at Cape Sounion, this statue of a young male nude dates back to the end of the seventh century B.C., thus making it the earliest example of *kouros* sculpture. The role these statues played in the Greek world is not known. The most common belief is that since they were placed in temples (along with companion figures of young women, known as *korai*), they were meant to be representations of the faithful dedicated to the gods.

semblance to Egyptian statues of the New Kingdom. The figures are not realistic, but stiff, with a slight smile; one leg is advanced ahead of the other, and the arms are held rigidly at the sides of the body.

Greek literature of the seventh century is perhaps best known for its lyric poetry. Unlike epic poetry (such as Homer's), the lyric is considerably shorter and centers on personal emotions, usually the power of love and its impact on human lives. Later Greeks acknowledged Sappho as their greatest female lyric poet (see the box on p. 71). Born in the seventh century, Sappho lived on the island of Lesbos in the Aegean Sea, where she taught music and poetry to her young charges. Many of her poems are love songs to her female students. Our word *lesbian* is derived from Sappho's island of Lesbos. Sappho, like many upper-class Greeks, accepted that homosexual and heterosexual feelings could exist in the same individual. Sappho was both a wife and mother who also wrote poems about love between men and women.

Archaic Greece is also known for poets who reflected the lifestyles of the two major groups of people of the period. Although trade and industry were growing, most people still lived off the land. A wide gulf, however, separated the wealthy aristocrat with his large landed estates from the poor peasants and small farmers who eked out their existence as best they could. Hesiod, a poet from Boeotia in central Greece who lived around 700 B.C, wrote a lengthy epic poem entitled *Works and Days*. Himself a farmer, Hesiod reflected the values of his nonaristocratic society. He distrusted aristocrats and looked down upon what he considered the aristocratic emphasis on pride and war. One of his aims was to show that the gods punished injustice:

> *But there are some who till the fields of pride*
> *And work at evil deeds; Zeus marks them out,*
> *And often, all the city suffers for*
> *Their wicked schemes, and on these men, from heaven*
> *The son of Kronos [Zeus] sends great punishments,*
> *Both plague and famine, and the people die.*
> *Their wives are barren, and their villages*
> *Dwindle, according to the plan of Zeus.*
> *At other times the son of Kronos will*
> *Destroy their army, or will snatch away*
> *Their city wall, or all their ships at sea.*
> *You lords, take notice of this punishment.*
> *The deathless gods are never far away;*
> *They mark the crooked judges who grind down*
> *Their fellow-men and do not fear the gods.*

The way to success was to work: "Famine and blight do not beset the just, who till their well-worked fields and

The Lyric Poetry of Sappho

▼ ▼ ▼

These love poems are examples of the work of Sappho of Lesbos, regarded as one of Greece's greatest lyric poets. She wrote directly about her personal world of emotions. She is an unusual figure, an independent woman in a world dominated by males. Her attitude toward the Trojan War, as seen in the poem, To Anaktoria, is quite different from that found in Homer's Iliad.

Sappho, To Anaktoria, Now a Soldier's Wife in Lydia

Some say cavalry and some would claim
infantry or a fleet of long oars
is the supreme sight on the black earth.
   I say it is

the girl you love. And easily proved.
Did not Helen, who was queen of mortal
beauty, choose as first among mankind
   the very scourge

of Trojan honor? Haunted by Love
she forgot kinsmen, her own dear child,
and wandered off to a remote country.
   O weak and fitful

woman bending before any man:
so Anaktoria, although you are
far, do not forget your loving friends.
   And I for one

would rather listen to your soft step
and see your radiant face—than watch
all the dazzling horsemen and armored
   hoplites of Lydia.

To Atthis

So I shall never see Atthis again,
and really I long to be dead,
although she too cried bitterly

when she left, and she said to me,
"Ah, what a nightmare we've suffered.
Sappho, I swear I go unwillingly."

And I answered, "Go, and be happy.
But remember me, for surely you
know how I worshipped you. If not,

then I want you to remember all
the exquisite days we two shared;
how when near me you would adorn

your hanging locks with violets and
tiny roses and your sapling throat
with necklets of a hundred blossoms;

how your young flesh was rich with kingly
myrrh as you leaned near my breasts on
the soft couch where delicate girls

served us all an Ionian could desire;
how we went to every hill, brook,
and holy place, and when early spring

filled the woods with noises of birds
and a choir of nightingales—we two
in solitude were wandering there."

---

feast. The earth supports them lavishly." *Works and Days* is the first paean to work in Western literature.

In his poem, Hesiod gave a calendar for the farmer's work. In fall, one ploughs and plants the main crop of grain. In fall and winter, he builds wagons, cuts wood, and makes ploughs and other tools. In early May, he harvests the grain and threshes and stores it in July. In the heat of summer comes time to relax: "Exhausting summertime has come. The goats are very fat, and wine is very good. . . . Then may I sit in shade and drink the shining wine, and eat my fill." But soon it is time to harvest the grapes and make the wine for next year. No sooner is that done, than it is time to begin the cycle anew and plough and plant. Hesiod emphasized the importance of two things to the farmer's success. It depended, first of all, on proper respect for and treatment of divine forces: "Please the gods with incense and libations, when you go to bed, and when the holy light returns, that they may favour you, with gracious hearts and spirits, so that you may buy the lands of other men, and they may not buy yours." But success depended on more than prayer; therefore:

. . . you must learn to organize your work
So you may have full barns at harvest time.
From working, men grow rich in flocks and gold
And dearer to the deathless gods. In work
There is no shame; shame is in idleness.
And if you work, the lazy man will soon
Envy your wealth: a rich man can become
Famous and good. No matter what your luck,
To work is better; turn your foolish mind
From other men's possessions to your own,
And earn your living, as I tell you to.[4]

To Hesiod, hard work and honesty were the keys to success.

Theognis of Megara presented a way of life considerably different from Hesiod's. He was an aristocrat who lived and wrote primarily in the sixth century B.C. Because of revolutionary upheaval, he, like other aristocrats in sixth-century *poleis*, lost his position and probably his wealth. Sent into exile, he became a bitter man. In his poetry, he portrayed aristocrats as the only good people who are distinguished from others by their natural intelligence, virtue, honor, and moderation. The lower classes or common people were by nature bad and debased:

Only a fool does favours for the base;
You'd do as well to sow the grey salt sea.
No crop of corn would come up from the deep,
No gratitude, no favours from the base.
The scum are never sated. If you slip,
Just once, their former friendship melts away.
But put a gentleman once in your debt,
You have a friend for life; he won't forget.

Aristocrats, then, should associate only with other aristocrats: "avoid low company, mix only with the better sort of men. . . . from them you will learn goodness. Men of little worth will spoil the natural virtue of your birth."

The poems of Theognis show clearly the political views and biases of a typical sixth-century aristocrat. It should not surprise us to learn that some of his poems were used to extol the aristocratic perspective. Some of his poems were also used as drinking songs, especially at symposia. The symposium (*symposion*) was an important part of aristocratic social life. The participants (men only) ate, drank wine, played games, enjoyed such entertainments as dancing and singing, and participated in contests to see who could compose the best poetry or even the best philosophical argument. Drunkenness was

not the goal of the party, as Theognis makes clear in one of his poems: "To drink too much is bad, but if you would drink wisely, you'd find wine not bad, but good." Pleasure was acceptable: "Let's give our hearts to banqueting, while we can still find pleasure in delightful things. For glorious youth goes by as fast as thought."[5] These last lines catch the air of delight, of enjoying life to the full that made the symposium important to the aristocratic class.

▼ Classical Greece

Classical Greece is the name given to the period of Greek history from around 500 B.C. to the conquest of Greece by the Macedonian king Philip II in 338 B.C. It was a period of brilliant achievement, much of it associated with the flowering of democracy in Athens under the leadership of Pericles. Many of the lasting contributions of the Greeks to Western civilization occurred during this period. The age began with a mighty confrontation between the Greek states and the mammoth Persian Empire.

The Challenge of Persia

Archaic Greece had the luxury of developing its civilization without an external threat to its freedom of action. But as Greek civilization grew and expanded throughout the Mediterranean, it was inevitable that it would come into contact with the Persian Empire to the east. In his play *The Persians*, the Greek playwright Aeschylus reflected what some Greeks perceived to be the essential difference between themselves and the Persians. The Persian queen, curious to find out more about the Athenians, asks: "Who commands them? Who is shepherd of their host?" The chorus responds: "They are slaves to none, nor are they subject."[6] Thus, at least some Greeks saw the struggle with the Persians as a contest between freedom and slavery.

The Ionian Greek cities in western Asia Minor had already fallen subject to the Persian Empire by the mid-sixth century B.C. (see Chapter 2). But the Greek cities were restless under Persian tyranny, and a revolt of the Ionian cities, led by the tyrant Aristagoras of Miletus, broke out against the Persians in 499 B.C. Aristagoras sought aid from the mainland Greeks. The Spartans refused, but the Athenians sent twenty ships and helped the Milesians capture and burn Sardis, the Persian capital of the Lydian satrapy. The success was temporary, however, and the Persians managed to sack Miletus and reestablish control. By 494 B.C., the rebellion had been

The Battle of Marathon
▼ ▼ ▼

The Battle of Marathon (490 B.C.) was an important event in the struggle between the Greeks and Persians. The defeat of the mighty Persians gave Athenian confidence a tremendous boost. In his History of the Persian Wars, the Greek historian Herodotus gave an account of this momentous battle.

Herodotus, *History of the Persian Wars*

So when the battle was set in array, and the victims showed themselves favourable, instantly the Athenians, so soon as they were let go, charged the barbarians at a run. Now the distance between the two armies was little short of a mile. The Persians, therefore, when they saw the Greeks coming on at speed, made ready to receive them, although it seemed to them that the Athenians were bereft of their senses, and bent upon their own destruction; for they saw a mere handful of men coming on at a run without either horsemen or archers. Such was the opinion of the barbarians; but the Athenians in close array fell upon them, and fought in a manner worthy of being recorded. They were the first of the Greeks, so far as I know, who introduced the custom of charging the enemy at a run, and they were likewise the first who dared to look upon the Median garb, and to face men

clad in that fashion. Until this time the very name of the Medes had been a terror to the Greeks to hear.

The two armies fought together on the plain of Marathon for a length of time; and in the mid battle, where the Persians themselves and the Sacae had their place, the barbarians were victorious, and broke and pursued the Greeks into the inner country; but on the two wings the Athenians and the Plataeans defeated the enemy. Having so done, they suffered the routed barbarians to fly at their ease, and joining the two wings in one, fell upon those who had broken their own centre, and fought and conquered them. These likewise fled, and now the Athenians hung upon the runaways and cut them down, chasing them all the way to the shore, on reaching which they laid hold of the ships and called for fire. . . .

After the full of the moon 2,000 Lacedaemonians [Spartans] came to Athens. So eager had they been to arrive in time, that they took but three days to reach Attica from Sparta. They came, however, too late for the battle; yet, as they had a longing to behold the Medes, they continued their march to Marathon and there viewed the slain. Then, after giving the Athenians all praise for their achievement, they departed and returned home.

---

suppressed. The Persian ruler Darius now decided to attack the mainland Greeks, in part, no doubt, to gain revenge for the Athenian action, but also to expand his empire westward. In 490 B.C., a Persian expedition was sent to Greece.

The Persians sailed across the Aegean, established a base on the island of Euboea across from Attica, and then transferred their army to the plain of Marathon, only twenty-six miles from Athens. The Athenians requested aid from the Spartans, who complied, but arrived too late for the decisive battle at Marathon. The Athenians, aided by the Plataeans (from a neighboring town in Boeotia), confronted the Persians without additional assistance. The two armies were quite different. The Persians were more mobile and flexible with their light-armed troops and relied heavily on missiles; the Greek hoplites were armed with heavy shields and relied on spear thrusts at close range. The Athenians and Plataeans were clearly outnumbered, probably mustering

10,000 troops compared to the 20,000 Persians. Nevertheless, the Greeks went on the attack and defeated the Persians decisively (see the box above). The Persians did not mount another attack against mainland Greece for ten years. Although a minor defeat to the Persians, the Battle of Marathon was of great importance to the Athenians, who had proven that the Persians could be beaten.

In the meantime, Athens had acquired a new leader, Themistocles, who persuaded his fellow citizens to pursue a new military policy, namely, the development of a navy. The Athenians used a new vein of silver from Laurium to construct ships and new port facilities. By 480 B.C., Athens had produced a navy of about 200 vessels, primarily triremes (ships with three banks of oars).

A revolt in Egypt, compounded by the death of Darius in 486, kept the Persians from mounting another attack on Greece. Xerxes, the new Persian monarch, was bent on revenge and expansion, however. After first securing Egypt and then spending several years in preparation, he renewed the invasion of Greece. Some of the Greeks prepared by forming a defensive league under Spartan leadership, although many Greek states remained neutral; some even fought on the Persian side.

Xerxes and the Persians undertook their invasion in 480 B.C. Their military forces were massive: close to 150,000 troops, almost 700 naval ships, and hundreds of supply ships to keep their large army fed. The Persians crossed the Hellespont by a bridge of ships and then moved through Thrace and Macedonia on their way into Greece. The Greek plan, as it evolved, was to fight a delaying action at the pass of Thermopylae along the main road from Thessaly into Boeotia, probably to give the Greek fleet of 300 ships at Artemisium, off northern Euboea, the chance to fight the Persian fleet. The Greeks knew that the Persian army was dependent on the fleet for supplies to maintain its army. A Greek force numbering close to 9,000, under the leadership of the Spartan King Leonidas and his contingent of 300 Spartans, managed to hold the Persian army for two days until a Greek traitor told the Persians how to use a mountain path to outflank the Greek force. Although some of the Greeks retreated when they became aware of the Persian movement, King Leonidas and the 300 Spartans fought to the last man.

The Athenians, now threatened by the onslaught of the Persian forces, decided to abandon Athens and evacuated the population of Attica to the offshore island of Salamis. Meanwhile the Greek fleet remained in the straits off Salamis while the Persians sacked and burned

▼ **Map 3.3** The Persian and Peloponnesian Wars.

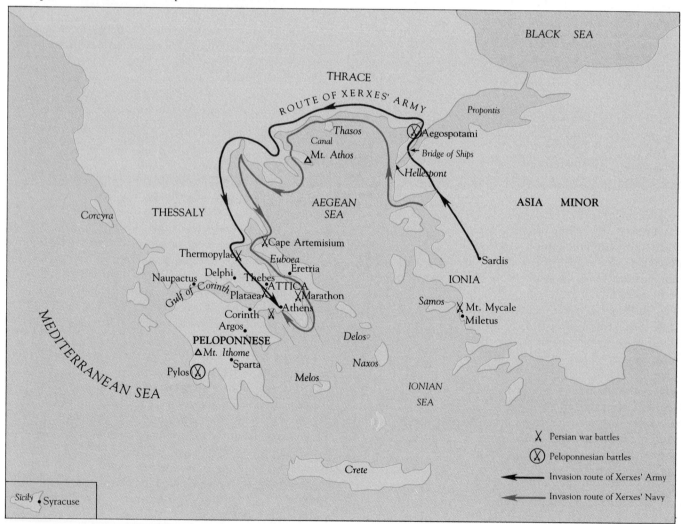

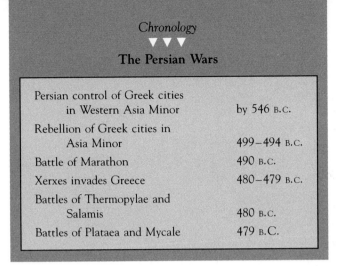

Chronology
▼ ▼ ▼
The Persian Wars

Persian control of Greek cities in Western Asia Minor	by 546 B.C.
Rebellion of Greek cities in Asia Minor	499–494 B.C.
Battle of Marathon	490 B.C.
Xerxes invades Greece	480–479 B.C.
Battles of Thermopylae and Salamis	480 B.C.
Battles of Plataea and Mycale	479 B.C.

Athens. The Peloponnesians wanted the Greeks to retreat to the Peloponnesus and the Greek ships to move to the isthmus as well. Themistocles' refusal and his threat to withdraw the Athenian ships altogether if a fight was not made forced the ships to remain and set up the naval Battle of Salamis. Although the Greeks were outnumbered, they managed to outmaneuver the Persian fleet (mostly Phoenicians and Ionians) and decisively defeated them. The Persians still had their army and much of their fleet intact, but Xerxes, frightened at the prospect of another Ionian revolt, decided to return to Asia. He left a Persian force in Thessaly under his general Mardonius.

Early in 479 B.C., the Greeks formed the largest Greek army seen up to that time. The Athenians forced the Spartans to move north of the Peloponnesus and take on the Persians at Plataea, northwest of Attica, where the Greek forces decisively defeated the Persian army. The remnants of the Persian forces returned to Asia. At the same time, in a naval battle at Mycale in Ionia, the Greeks destroyed much of the Persian fleet. The Greeks had won the war decisively and were now free to pursue their own destiny.

The Growth of an Athenian Empire

After the defeat of the Persians, some Greeks perceived the need for an offensive policy that would free the Ionian Greek cities in Asia Minor and push the Persians out of the Aegean Sea. The Spartans, always fearful of foreign entanglements, withdrew from the leadership role they had assumed in Greek affairs. Athens stepped in to provide new leadership against the Persians by forming a confederation called the Delian League.

Organized in the winter of 478/477 B.C., the Delian League was dominated by the Athenians from the beginning. Its main headquarters was the island of Delos, sacred to the Ionian Greeks, but its chief officials, including the treasurers and commanders of the fleet, were Athenians. Athens also provided most of the ships. While the larger states in the league, such as Lesbos, Samos, and Chios, contributed ships, the smaller communities made payments in money.

Under the leadership of the Athenians, the Delian League pursued the attack against the Persian Empire. Virtually all of the Greek states in the Aegean were liberated from Persian control, and the Persian fleet and army were decisively defeated in 469 B.C. in southern Asia Minor. Arguing that the Persian threat was now over, some members of the Delian League wished to withdraw. Naxos did so in 470 and Thasos in 465 B.C. The Athenians responded vigorously. They attacked both states, destroyed their walls, took over their fleets, eliminated their liberty, and forced them to pay tribute. "No secession" became Athenian policy. The Delian League was rapidly becoming an instrument of Athenian imperialism and the nucleus of an Athenian Empire.

THE AGE OF PERICLES   At home, Athenians favored the new imperial policy. One of the chief benefits, a prosperous economy, was only too apparent. Although they were agreed on the new empire, considerable squabbling on other issues divided conservative and liberal factions in domestic Athenian politics. The conservative party, led by Cimon, favored more privileges for the property-owning classes and a pro-Spartan foreign policy. The liberal faction was led by Ephialtes, the successor to Themistocles, and a newcomer, a young aristocrat named Pericles. The liberals favored further changes in the direction of democracy and severing the ties with Sparta in order to expand Athenian power in Greece. In 461 B.C., the liberal faction triumphed. Cimon was sent into exile, and the powers of the council of the Areopagus were curtailed. Athens embarked upon both the expansion of democracy at home and the extension of its new empire abroad. Both policies were guided by Pericles, who was a dominant figure in Athenian politics until 429 B.C. This period of Athenian and Greek history, which historians have subsequently labeled the age of Pericles, witnessed the height of Athenian power and the culmination of its brilliance as a civilization.

In the age of Pericles, the Athenians became deeply attached to their democratic system. The sovereignty of the people was embodied in the assembly (*ecclesia*), which consisted of all male citizens over eighteen years of age. In the 440s, that was probably a group of about 43,000; women, slaves, and foreigners, who made up a majority of Attica's approximately 300,000 residents, were excluded from participation in government. Meetings of the assembly were held every ten days on the hillside of the Pnyx, east of the Acropolis. Not all attended, and the number present seldom reached 6,000. The assembly passed all laws and made final decisions on war and foreign policy. Although anyone could speak, usually only respected leaders did so, a feat that required considerable speaking ability in such a large crowd. Per-

▼ **Pericles: Roman Copy of Fifth Century Bronze Original.**
Pericles dominated Athenian politics from 461 B.C. until 429 B.C. In addition to increasing the Athenians' participation in their own democratic system, he also pursued an imperialistic policy, expanding the Athenian empire both on the Greek mainland and abroad. Largely with funds taken from the treasury of the Delian League, Pericles initiated a number of beautification projects for Athens. Under his leadership, Athens was brought into a struggle against Sparta that had dire consequences for all that Pericles had built.

Chronology
▼ ▼ ▼
Events between the Persian Wars and the Great Peloponnesian War

Delian League is created	478–477 B.C.
Victory over Persians in southern Asia Minor	469 B.C.
Ostracism of Cimon	461 B.C.
Curtailment of Areopagus	461 B.C.
Beginning of First Peloponnesian War	c. 460 B.C.
Treasury of Delian League moved to Athens	454 B.C.
Peace with Persia	449 B.C.
Thirty Years' Peace and end of First Peloponnesian War	445 B.C.

icles expanded the involvement of Athenians in their democracy (see the box on p. 77). Lower-class citizens were now eligible for public offices formerly closed to them. Pericles also introduced state pay for officeholders, including the widely held jury duty. This meant that poor citizens could now participate in public affairs.

The reforms of Cleisthenes had introduced the council of 500 elected by lot from the ten tribes. It prepared the agenda for the assembly and made recommendations for action. Thus the council served as a control on the assembly. The council was divided into ten smaller groups of fifty called prytanies. Each prytany held office for one-tenth of the year to supervise the execution of the laws passed by the assembly.

Routine administration of public affairs was maintained by a large body of city magistrates, usually chosen by lot without regard to class. The general directors of policy, a board of ten officials known as generals (*strategoi*), were elected by public vote and were usually wealthy aristocrats, even though the people were free to select otherwise. The generals could be reelected, enabling individual leaders to play an important political role. Pericles, for example, was elected to the generalship thirty times between 461 and 429 B.C. But all public officials were subject to scrutiny and could be deposed from office if they lost the people's confidence. After 488 B.C., the Athenians had also devised a way to protect themselves against overly ambitious politicians. Called ostracism, this practice enabled the members of the assembly to write on a broken pottery fragment (*ostrakon*) the name of the person they most disliked or considered most harmful to the polis. A person who received a

Athenian Democracy: The Funeral Oration of Pericles
▼ ▼ ▼

In *his* History of the Peloponnesian War, *the Greek historian Thucydides presented his reconstruction of the eulogy given by Pericles in the winter of 431/430 B.C. to honor the Athenians killed in the first campaigns of the Great Peloponnesian War. It is a magnificent, idealized description of the Athenian democracy at its height.*

Thucydides, *History of the Peloponnesian War*

Our constitution is called a democracy because power is in the hands not of a minority but of the whole people. When it is a question of settling private disputes, everyone is equal before the law; when it is a question of putting one person before another in positions of public responsibility, what counts is not membership of a particular class, but the actual ability which the man possesses. No one, so long as he has it in him to be of service to the state, is kept in political obscurity because of poverty. And, just as our political life is free and open, so is our day-to-day life in our relations with each other. We do not get into a state with our next-door neighbour if he enjoys himself in his own way, nor do we give him the kind of black looks which, though they do no real harm, still do hurt people's feeling. We are free and tolerant in our private lives; but in public affairs we keep to the law. This is because it commands our deep respect.

We give our obedience to those whom we put in positions of authority, and we obey the laws themselves, especially those which are for the protection of the oppressed, and those unwritten laws which it is an acknowledged shame to break. . . . Here each individual is interested not only in his own affairs but in the affairs of the state as well: even those who are mostly occupied with their own business are extremely well-informed on general politics—this is a peculiarity of ours: we do not say that a man who takes no interest in politics is a man who minds his own business; we say that he has no business here at all. We Athenians, in our own persons, take our decisions on policy or submit them to proper discussions: for we do not think that there is an incompatibility between words and deeds; the worst thing is to rush into action before the consequences have been properly debated. . . . Taking everything together then, I declare that our city is an education to Greece, and I declare that in my opinion each single one of our citizens, in all the manifold aspects of life, is able to show himself the rightful lord and owner of his own person, and do this, moreover, with exceptional grace and exceptional versatility. And to show that this is no empty boasting for the present occasion, but real tangible fact, you have only to consider the power which our city possesses and which has been won by those very qualities which I have mentioned.

---

majority (if at least 6,000 votes were cast) was exiled for ten years.

The Athenian pursuit of democracy at home was coupled with increasing imperialism abroad as Athens attempted to create both a land empire in Greece and a maritime empire in the Aegean. As we have seen, after 470 B.C., Athenian policies had the effect of converting the voluntary allies of the Delian League into the involuntary subjects of an Athenian naval empire. After 462 B.C., Athens attempted to expand its empire on the Greek mainland as well. The creation of a land empire, however, overextended the Athenians and involved them in a series of skirmishes with Sparta and its allies called the First Peloponnesian War (c. 460–445 B.C.). After a series of defeats in 445 B.C., the land empire of

Athens disintegrated, and Athens agreed to a Thirty Years' Peace with the Spartans in the following year. Athens consented to give up most of its land empire, and in return, Sparta recognized the existence of Athens' maritime empire.

While building its land empire, Athens continued its offensive against Persia and at the same time tightened its control over the Delian League. Citing the threat of the Persian fleet in the Aegean, the Athenians moved the treasury of the league from the island of Delos to Athens itself in 454 B.C. Members were, in effect, charged a fee (tribute) for the Athenian claim of protection. Pericles also used the treasury money of the league, without the approval of its members, to build new temples in Athens, a clear indication that the Delian League had become the Athenian Empire. Henceforth, any protest by a league state against the tribute imposed by Athens could be heard only before an Athenian court. However, Athenian imperialism, pursued both in Greece and abroad, took its toll. Pericles recognized the dangers of Athenian exhaustion and sought a lull; peace was made with Persia in 449 B.C. and, as we have seen, with Sparta in 445 B.C. After 445 B.C., the Athenians had a breathing space in which to beautify Athens and enjoy the fruits of empire, but it was not long before all Greece was confronted with a new and prolonged struggle.

The Great Peloponnesian War (431–404 B.C.)

After the Thirty Years' Peace in 445 B.C., the Greek world seemed to accept that it was divided into two major camps: Sparta and its Peloponnesian League and the Athenian maritime empire. It was not long before the rivalry between the two erupted again into war.

In his classic *History of the Peloponnesian War*, the great Greek historian Thucydides pointed out that the fundamental, long-range cause of the Peloponnesian War was the fear that Athens and its empire inspired in Sparta and its allies (see the box on p. 79). The immediate causes of the war involved petty disputes that might have been handled amicably if the two great powers had been so inclined. The conflicts between Corinth and Athens over Corcyra and Potidaea, and between Athens and Megara, were the sources of appeals to

(see the box on p. 79)

Sparta for aid against the imperialistic Athenians, appeals that convinced the Spartans to send an ultimatum to Athens. Athens refused to compromise, perhaps because Pericles believed war was unavoidable and Athens was as strong militarily as it would ever be.

At the beginning of the war in 431 B.C., both sides believed they had winning strategies. The Athenian plan was based on its navy. The citizens in Attica would be brought in behind the protective walls of Athens and the port of Piraeus. It would use its overseas empire and its navy to keep it supplied. Pericles knew perfectly well that the Spartans and their allies could beat the Athenians in pitched battles, which, of course, formed the focus of the Spartan strategy. The Spartans and their allies invaded Attica and ravaged the fields and orchards, hoping that the Athenians would send out their army to fight beyond the walls. But Pericles was convinced that Athens was secure behind its walls and retaliated by sending out naval excursions to ravage the

Chronology
▼ ▼ ▼
The Great Peloponnesian War

Invasion of Attica	431 B.C.
Peace of Nicias	421 B.C.
Athenian invasion of Sicily	415–413 B.C.
Battle of Aegospotami	405 B.C.
Surrender of Athens	404 B.C.

▼ **Map 3.4** Long Walls Connecting Athens and Piraeus.

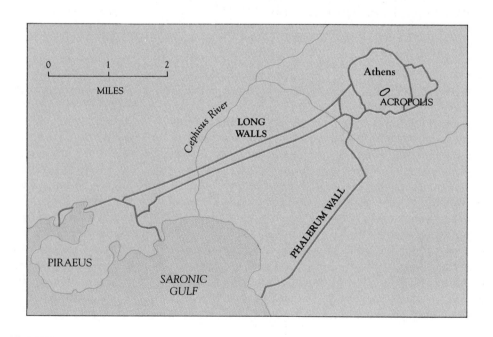

The Significance of the Great Peloponnesian War
▼ ▼ ▼

In his History of the Peloponnesian War, *Thucydides gave a detailed account of the origins, course, and effects of the Great Peloponnesian War. Thucydides was an Athenian general who was banished from Athens for failure to win an important battle against the Spartans. Near the beginning of his history, he discussed the significance of this war to the Greeks and its underlying cause.*

Thucydides, *History of the Peloponnesian War*

The greatest war in the past was the Persian War; yet in this war the decision was reached quickly as a result of two naval battles and two battles on land. The Peloponnesian War, on the other hand, not only lasted for a long time, but throughout its course brought with it unprecedented suffering for Hellas. Never before had so many cities been captured and then devastated, whether by foreign armies or by the Hellenic Powers themselves; never had there been so many exiles; never such loss of life—both in the actual warfare and in internal revolutions. Old stories of past prodigies, which had not found much confirmation in recent experience, now became credible. Wide areas, for instance, were affected by violent earthquakes; there were more frequent eclipses of the sun than had ever been recorded before; in various parts of the country there were extensive droughts followed by famine; and there was the plague which did more harm and destroyed more life than almost any other single factor. All of these calamities fell together upon the Hellenes after the outbreak of war.

War began when the Athenians and the Peloponnesians broke the Thirty Years Truce which had been made after the capture of Euboea. As to the reasons why they broke the truce, I propose first to give an account of the causes of complaint which they had against each other and of the specific instances where their interests clashed: this is in order that there should be no doubt in anyone's mind about what led to this great war falling upon the Hellenes. But the real reason for the war is, in my opinion, most likely to be disguised by such an argument. What made war inevitable was the growth of Athenian power and the fear which this caused in Sparta.

seacoast of the Peloponnesus. In the second year of the war, however, plague devastated the crowded city of Athens and wiped out possibly one-third of the Athenian population. Pericles himself died the following year (429 B.C.), a severe loss to Athens. Dominance now passed to Cleon, leader of the war party, who was opposed by Nicias, head of a conservative faction that favored peace. Despite the losses from the plague, the Athenians fought on in a struggle that witnessed numerous instances of futile destruction. Cleon achieved some successes for the Athenians; Brasidas came to be a dynamic general for the Spartans. At the battle of Amphipolis in 422 B.C., both generals were killed and the new Athenian leader Nicias negotiated the Peace of Nicias (421 B.C.). Although both parties agreed to keep the peace for fifty years, the truce did not really solve the problems that had caused the war in the first place.

A second phase of the war began only six years after the fifty-year truce began. This phase was initiated by Alcibiades, a nephew of Pericles. Elected to the generalship in 420 B.C., he proved to be a poor choice because of his recklessness and his self-seeking. In 415 B.C., he convinced the Athenians to invade the island of Sicily, arguing that its conquest would give the Athenians a strong source of support to carry on a lengthy war. But the expedition was ill-fated. Alcibiades himself was removed from leadership of the expedition on a charge of profaning the religious mysteries. Rather than stand trial, he fled to Sparta and advised them how to defeat Athens by getting help from Persia and establishing a navy with ships and money supplied by the Persians. The Spartans later followed his advice.

In the meantime, the Athenians pursued the Sicilian policy. A "great expedition" consisting of 5,000 Athenian hoplites was sent out in 415 B.C. and reinforced in 413 B.C. by an even larger army of Athenians and allies. All was in vain. The Athenians failed to take Syracuse and were captured during their retreat. All of the Athenians were killed or sold into slavery. These heavy losses at Syracuse had immediate domestic repercussions. The democracy was weakened and an aristocatic oligarchy was temporarily established (411–10 B.C.).

Despite the disaster, the Athenians refused to give up, but raised new armies and sent out new fleets. The final

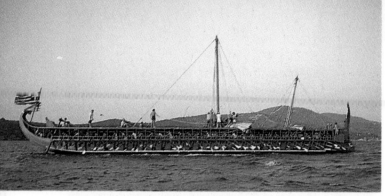

▼ **Greek Trireme.** The trireme became the standard warship of ancient Greece. Highly maneuverable, fast, and outfitted with metal prows, Greek triremes were especially effective in ramming enemy ships. The photo shows the *Olympias*, a trireme recently reconstructed by the Greek navy.

crushing blow came, however, in 405 B.C., when the Athenian fleet was destroyed at Aegospotami on the Hellespont. Athens was besieged and surrendered in 404 B.C. Its walls were torn down, the navy disbanded, and the Athenian Empire destroyed. The great war was finally over.

THE DECLINE OF THE GREEK STATES (404–338 B.C.)   The next seventy years of Greek history are a tale of continuing warfare among the Greeks with the leading roles shifting between Sparta, Athens, and a new Greek power, the city-state of Thebes. After the defeat of Athens in 404 B.C., the Spartans established their own control over Greece. The Athenian Empire was dissolved. Oligarchies, headed by local *decarchies* (ten-man boards) in cooperation with Spartan garrisons, were placed in control of the states "liberated" from Athenian imperialism. But oligarchical control proved ineffective, especially in Athens where the ruling oligarchical faction of thirty, set up by the Spartans, earned their nickname of "Thirty Tyrants" by executing about 1,500 of their democratic opponents. This led to a reaction in which the Athenians were able to reestablish their democracy in 403 B.C. But the golden years of Athens were long past. Its population was only half of what it had been, and both its empire and its navy were gone.

To maintain its newly organized leadership in Greek affairs, Sparta encouraged a Panhellenic crusade against the Persians as a common enemy. The Persians had taken advantage of the Greeks' internal struggle to reimpose their control over the Greek states in western Asia Minor. The Spartans, under King Agesilaus, led a Greek expedition into Asia Minor in 396 B.C. But the Persians had learned the lessons of Greek politics and offered financial support to Athens, Thebes, and other Greek states to oppose Spartan power within Greece itself, thus beginning a new war, the Corinthian War (395–387 B.C.). The war ended when the Greek states, weary of the struggles, accepted the King's Peace dictated by the Great King of Persia.

The city-state of Thebes, in Boeotia, north of Athens, now began to exert its influence. Under its leader Epaminondas, the Thebans dramatically defeated the Spartan army at the Battle of Leuctra in 371 B.C. Spartan power declined, to be replaced by the ascendancy of the Thebans. But it was short-lived. After the death of Epaminondas in the Battle of Mantinea in 362 B.C., the Thebans could no longer dominate Greek politics. And yet the Greek states continued their petty wars, seemingly oblivious to the growing danger to their north in Macedonia where King Philip II was developing a unified state that would finally end the destructive fratricide of the Greek states by conquest.

The Culture of Classical Greece

Classical Greece saw a period of remarkable intellectual and cultural growth throughout the Greek world. Historians agree, however, that Periclean Athens was the most important center of classical Greek culture. Indeed, the eighteenth-century French philosopher and writer Voltaire listed the Athens of Pericles as one of four happy ages "when the arts were brought to perfection and which, marking an era of the greatness of the human mind, are an example to posterity."[7]

THE BIRTH OF HISTORY   History as we know it, as the systematic analysis of past events, was a Greek creation. Herodotus (c. 484–c. 425 B.C.), an Ionian Greek from Asia Minor, has rightly been called the "father of history" since his *History of the Persian Wars* is usually regarded as the first real history in Western civilization. It is indeed the earliest lengthy Greek prose work to have survived intact. The Greek word *historia* (from which we derive our word *history*) means "research" or "investigation," and it is in the opening line of Herodotus's *History* that we find the first recorded use of the word:

> These are the researches [*historia*] of Herodotus of Halicarnassus, which he publishes, in the hope of thereby preserving from decay the remembrance of what men have done, and of preventing the great and wonderful actions of the Greeks and the Barbarians from losing their due meed of glory; and withal to put on record what were their ground of feud.[8]

The central theme of Herodotus's work is the conflict between the Greeks and the Persians, which he viewed as a struggle between Greek freedom and oriental despotism. Herodotus felt it important, however, to discuss the histories of all the peoples involved in the Persian Wars and thus provides considerable background information. All of book two, for example (there are nine books in the *History*), is devoted to a discussion of Egyptian history, customs, traditions, and geography. His account demonstrates a remarkable range of interests, including geography, politics, social structures, economics, religion, and even psychology. Herodotus traveled extensively for his information and was dependent for his sources on what we today would call oral history. Although he was a master storyteller and sometimes included considerable fanciful material, Herodotus was also capable of exhibiting a critical attitude toward the materials he used. Regardless of its weaknesses, Herodotus's *History* is an important source of information on the Persians and certainly our chief source on the Persian Wars themselves.

Thucydides (c. 460–c. 400 B.C.) was, by far, the better historian; in fact, historians consider him the greatest historian of the ancient world. Thucydides was an Athenian and a participant in the Peloponnesian War. He had been elected a general, but a defeat in battle led the fickle Athenian assembly to send him into exile, which gave him the opportunity to write his *History of the Peloponnesian War*. In the book, he described his own activities in the war:

> I lived through the whole of it, being of an age to understand what was happening, and I put my mind to the subject so as to get an accurate view of it. It happened, too, that I was banished from my country for twenty years after my command at Amphipolis [424 B.C.]; I saw what was being done on both sides, particularly on the Peloponnesian side, because of my exile, and this leisure gave me rather exceptional facilities for looking into things.[9]

Some scholars regard Thucydides as the first modern historian. Unlike Herodotus, Thucydides was not concerned with underlying divine forces or gods as explanatory causal factors in history. He saw war and politics in purely rational terms, as the activities of human beings. He examined the long-range and immediate causes of the Peloponnesian War in a clear, methodical, objective fashion. Thucydides placed much emphasis on accuracy and the precision of his facts. As he stated:

> And with regard to my factual reporting of the events of the war I have made it a principle not to write down the first story that came my way, and not even to be guided by my own general impressions; either I was present myself at the events which I have described or else I heard of them from eyewitnesses whose reports I have checked with as much thoroughness as possible.[10]

Thucydides also provided remarkable insight into the human condition. He believed that human nature was a constant: "It will be enough for me, however, if these words of mine are judged useful by those who want to understand clearly the events which happened in the past and which (human nature being what it is) will, at some time or other and in much the same ways, be repeated in the future."[11] He was not so naive as to believe in an exact repetition of events, but felt that political situations recur in similar fashion and that the study of history is of great value in understanding the present.

GREEK DRAMA Drama, as we know it, was created by the Greeks. Tragedy was clearly intended to do more than entertain. It was used to educate citizens and was supported by the state for that reason. Its origins, however, are unclear. Many historians assume that it developed out of religious ritual, and its performance was certainly connected to religious festivals. In Athens, tragedy was given its initial form by Thespis, who wrote tragedies that had one actor and a chorus and were performed at the festival of the City Dionysia (see Greek Religion later in this chapter) instituted by the tyrant Pisistratus in the 530s B.C. The form of Greek tragedy remained rather stable; the chorus spoke the important lines, but eventually a second and later a third actor were added, creating more dialogue with the chorus as background. Action was very limited. Content was generally based on myths or legends that the audience already knew. In fact, early Greek tragedy derived many of its themes and its basic preoccupation with the sufferings of the tragic hero from Homer.

Aeschylus (525–456 B.C.) is the first tragedian whose plays are known to us. He had fought at the battles of Marathon and Salamis and considered his participation there a greater achievement than his plays. Although he wrote ninety tragedies, only seven have survived. As was customary in Greek tragedy, his plots are simple, and the characters are primarily embodiments of a single passion. The entire drama focuses on a single tragic event and its meaning. At the City Dionysia, Greek tragedies were supposed to be presented in a trilogy (a set of three plays) built around a common theme. The only complete trilogy we possess, called the *Oresteia*, was composed by

▼ **The Theater at Epidaurus.** Drama in ancient Greece was designed to do more than simply entertain. Tragedy generally had an educational function, while comedy featured contemporary issues and was used to attack or satirize prominent individuals. The photo shows the theater at Epidaurus in the eastern Peloponnesus. It held eighteen thousand onlookers for the theatrical presentations and athletic games that were part of the religious festivals dedicated to Asclepius, the god of healing.

Aeschylus. The theme of this trilogy is derived from Homer. Agamemnon, the king of Mycenae, returns a hero from the defeat of Troy. His wife Clytemnestra revenges the sacrificial death of her daughter Iphigenia by murdering Agamemnon, who had been responsible for Iphigenia's death. In the second play of the trilogy, Agamemnon's son Orestes avenges his father by killing his mother. Orestes is now pursued by the avenging furies who torment him for killing his mother. Evil acts breed evil acts and suffering is one's lot, suggests Aeschylus. But Orestes is put on trial and acquitted by Athena, the patron goddess of Athens. Personal vendetta has been eliminated and law has prevailed. Reason has triumphed over the forces of evil.

Sophocles (c. 496–406 B.C.) added a third actor to his plays and diminished the role of the chorus. Only 7 of his 123 plays have survived. Probably his most famous play, considered by the Greek philosopher Aristotle to be the best example of tragedy, was *Oedipus the King.*

The oracle of Apollo foretells how a man (Oedipus) will kill his own father and marry his mother. Despite all attempts to prevent it, the tragic events occur. Although it appears that Oedipus suffered the fate determined by the gods, Oedipus also accepts that he himself as a free man must bear responsibility for his actions: "It was Apollo, friends, Apollo, that brought this bitter bitterness, my sorrows to completion. But the hand that struck me was none but my own."[12]

The third outstanding Athenian tragedian, Euripides (c. 485–406 B.C.) moved beyond his predecessors in creating more realistic characters. His plots also became more complex with a greater interest in real-life situations. Perhaps the greatest of all his plays was *The Bacchae,* which dealt with the introduction of the hysterical rites caused by Dionysus, god of wine. Euripides is often seen as a skeptic, who questioned traditional moral and religious values. Was *The Bacchae* a criticism of the gods' traditional behavior? Euripides was also critical of the traditional view that war was glorious. He portrayed war as brutal and barbaric and expressed deep compassion for the women and children who suffered from it.

Greek tragedies dealt with universal themes still relevant to our day. They probed such problems as the nature of good and evil, the conflict between spiritual values and the demands of the state or family, the rights of the individual, the nature of divine forces, and the nature of human beings. Over and over again, the tragic lesson was repeated: humankind was free and yet could operate only within limitations imposed by the gods. The real task was to cultivate the balance and moderation that made one aware of one's true position. But the pride in human accomplishment and independence is real. As the chorus chants in Sophocles' *Antigone:* "Is there anything more wonderful on earth, our marvellous planet, than the miracle of man?"[13]

Competitions for Greek comedy developed later than those for tragedy. We first see comedies organized at the festival of Dionysus in Athens in 488/487 B.C. The plays of Aristophanes (c. 450–c. 385 B.C.), who used both grotesque masks and obscene jokes to entertain the Athenian audience, are examples of Old Comedy. But comedy in Athens was also more clearly political than tragedy. It was used to attack or savagely satirize both politicians and intellectuals. In *The Clouds,* for example, Aristophanes characterized the philosopher Socrates as the operator of a thought factory where people could learn deceitful ways to handle other people. Later plays gave up the element of personal attack and featured contemporary issues. Of special importance to Aristophanes was his opposition to the Peloponnesian War. *Lysistrata,*

Athenian Comedy: Sex as an Antiwar Instrument
▼ ▼ ▼

Greek comedy became a regular feature of the dramatic presentations at the festival of Dionysus in Athens beginning in 488/487 B.C. Aristophanes used his comedies to present political messages, especially to express his antiwar sentiments. The plot of Lysistrata centers on a sex strike by wives in order to get their husbands to end the Peloponnesian War. In this scene from the play, Lysistrata (whose name means "she who dissolves the armies") has the women take a special oath.

Aristophanes, Lysistrata

Lysistrata: *Lampito: all of you women: come, touch the bowl, and repeat after me:* I WILL HAVE NOTHING TO DO WITH MY HUSBAND OR MY LOVER

Kalonike: *I will have nothing to do with my husband or my lover*

Lysistrata: THOUGH HE COME TO ME IN PITIABLE CONDITION

Kalonike: *Though he come to me in pitiable condition (Oh, Lysistrata! This is killing me!)*

Lysistrata: I WILL STAY IN MY HOUSE UNTOUCHABLE

Kalonike: *I will stay in my house untouchable*

Lysistrata: IN MY THINNEST SAFFRON SILK

Kalonike: *In my thinnest saffron silk*

Lysistrata: AND MAKE HIM LONG FOR ME.

Kalonike: *And make him long for me.*

Lysistrata: I WILL NOT GIVE MYSELF

Kalonike: *I will not give myself*

Lysistrata: AND IF HE CONSTRAINS ME

Kalonike: *And if he constrains me*

Lysistrata: I WILL BE AS COLD AS ICE AND NEVER MOVE

Kalonike: *I will be as cold as ice and never move*

Lysistrata: I WILL NOT LIFT MY SLIPPERS TOWARD THE CEILING

Kalonike: *I will not lift my slippers toward the ceiling*

Lysistrata: OR CROUCH ON ALL FOURS LIKE THE LIONESS IN THE CARVING

Kalonike: *Or crouch on all fours like the lioness in the carving*

Lysistrata: AND IF I KEEP THIS OATH LET ME DRINK FROM THIS BOWL

Kalonike: *And if I keep this oath let me drink from this bowl*

Lysistrata: IF NOT, LET MY OWN BOWL BE FILLED WITH WATER.

Kalonike: *If not, let my own bowl be filled with water.*

Lysistrata: *You have all sworn?*

Myrrhine: *We have.*

---

performed in 411 B.C., at a time when Athens was in serious danger of losing the war, had a comic but effective message against the war (see the box above).

THE ARTS The arts of the Western world have been largely dominated by the artistic standards established by the Greeks of the classical period. Classical Greek art did not aim at experimentation for experiment's sake, but was concerned with expressing eternally true ideals. Its subject matter was basically the human being, but expressed harmoniously as an object of great beauty. The classic style, based on the ideals of reason, moderation, symmetry, balance, and harmony in all things, was meant to civilize the emotions.

In architecture the most important form was the temple dedicated to a god or goddess. Since Greek religious ceremonies were held at altars in the open air, temples were not used, as modern churches are, to enclose the faithful. At the center of Greek temples were walled rooms that housed the statues of deities and treasuries in which gifts to the gods and goddesses were safeguarded. These central rooms were surrounded, however, by a screen of columns that make Greek temples open structures rather than closed ones. The columns were originally made of wood, but changed to limestone in the seventh century and to marble in the fifth century B.C. The most significant formal element in Greek temples was the shape and size of the columns in combination with the features above and below the column. The Doric order, evolved first in the Dorian Peloponnesus, consisted of thick, fluted columns with simple capitals resting directly on a platform without a base. Above the capitals was a fairly complex entablature. The Greeks considered the Doric order grave, dignified, and masculine. The Ionic style was first developed in western Asia Minor and consisted of slender columns with a more elaborate base and volute or spiral-shaped capitals. The Greeks characterized the Ionic order as slender, elegant, and feminine in principle. Corinthian columns, with their more detailed capitals modeled after acanthus leaves, came later, near the end of the fifth century B.C.

It is in fifth-century Athens that some of the finest examples of Greek classical architecture were built. The development of Athenian architecture was aided tremendously by the massive rebuilding program funded from the treasury of the Delian League and instituted almost a half-century after the Persians destroyed Athens in the Persian Wars. New buildings were erected in the agora, but especially important was a series of constructions on the Acropolis begun in 448 B.C., which included a monumental entrance gate, a temple to Athena Nike (the Bringer of Victory), and the Erechtheum, a multilevel temple. These temples honored the gods and heroes who protected Athens. The most famous building, regarded as the greatest example of the classical Greek temple, was the Parthenon, built between 447 and 432 B.C. The master builders Ictinus and Callicrates directed the construction of this temple consecrated to Athena, the patron goddess of Athens. We could say, however, that the Parthenon, an expression of Athenian enthusiasm, was also dedicated to the glory of Athens and the Athenians. Greek architects knew that from a distance straight lines appear curved. Consequently, every line of the Parthenon was gently curved to create the illusion of straight lines when seen from a distance. The Parthenon typifies the principles of classical architecture: the search for calmness, clarity, and freedom from superfluous detail. The individual parts of the temple were constructed in accordance with certain mathematical ratios also found in natural phenomena. The concern of the architects with these laws of proportion is paralleled by the attempt of Greek philosophers to understand the general laws underlying nature.

Greek sculpture also developed a classic style that differed significantly from the artificial stiffness of the *kouros* figure of the archaic period. Statues of the male nude, the favorite subject of Greek sculptors, now possessed more relaxed attitudes; their faces were self-assured; their bodies flexible and smooth-muscled. Although the figures possessed natural features that made them lifelike, Greek sculptors sought to achieve not realism, but a standard of ideal beauty. Polyclitus, a fifth-century sculptor, authored a treatise (now lost) on a canon of proportions that he illustrated in a work known as the *Doryphoros*. His theory maintained that the use of ideal proportions, based on mathematical ratios found in nature, could produce an ideal human form, beautiful in its perfected and refined features. This search for ideal beauty was the dominant feature of the classical standard in sculpture.

▼ **Doric and Ionic Orders.** The illustration depicts the Doric and Ionic orders of columns. The size and shape of a column constituted one of the most important aspects of Greek temple architecture. The Doric order, with plain capitals and no base, developed first in the Dorian Peloponnesus, and was rather simple in comparison to the slender Ionic column, which had an elaborate base and spiral-shaped capitals.

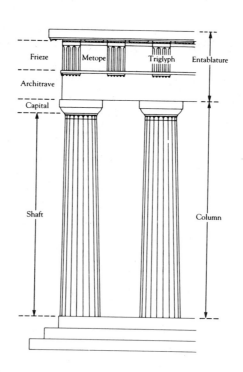
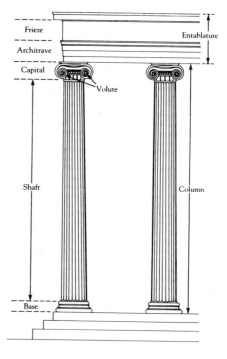

GREEK PHILOSOPHY Philosophy is a Greek word that originally meant "love of wisdom." Although influenced by the cosmology and theology of the Near East, early Greek philosophers went their own way in seeking "wisdom." They were concerned with the development of critical or rational thought about the nature of the universe and the place of divine forces and souls in it.

Much of early Greek philosophy focused on the attempt to explain the universe on the basis of unifying principles. Thales of Miletus, an Ionian Greek who lived around 600 B.C., postulated the unity of the universe. All things were linked by water as the basic substance. Another Ionian Greek, Pythagoras (c. 580–c. 490 B.C.), taught that the essence of the universe could be found in music and number. These early Greek philosophers may have eliminated the role of the gods as they were portrayed in Greek myths, but they did not eliminate divinity itself from the world, tending instead to identify it with the underlying, unchanging forces that govern the universe.

Another major preoccupation of the so-called pre-Socratic philosophers (Greek philosophers before Socrates) was the nature of reality. Some philosophers saw change as the only reality, while others took the opposite view that all change is merely an illusion of the senses. Empedocles (c. 493–c. 433 B.C.) arrived at a compromise, believing that there are four basic substances: earth, air, fire, and water. They are unchanging, but their interaction makes up the physical universe and produces the appearance of change.

Many Greeks, however, were simply not interested in speculations on the nature of the universe or reality. The Sophists were a group of philosophical teachers in the fifth century who rejected such speculation as foolish; they argued that to understand the universe was simply beyond the reach of the human mind. It was more important for individuals to improve themselves, so the only worthwhile object of study was human behavior. The Sophists were wandering scholars who sold their services as professional teachers to the young men of Greece, especially those of Athens. The Sophists stressed the importance of rhetoric (the art of persuasive oratory) in winning debates and swaying an audience, a skill that was especially valuable in democratic Athens. The Sophists tended to be skeptics who questioned the traditional values of their societies. Their skepticism was often intertwined with relativism, the idea that there are no absolute values or beliefs. There was, for example, no absolute right or wrong—what was right for one individual might be wrong for another. Consequently, true wisdom consisted of being able to perceive one's own

▼ **The Parthenon.** The arts in classical Greece were designed to express the eternal ideals of reason, moderation, symmetry, balance, and harmony. In architecture, the most important form was the temple, and the classical example of this kind of architecture is the Parthenon, built between 447 and 432 B.C. While the Parthenon, located on the Acropolis, was dedicated to Athena, the patron goddess of the city, it also served as a shining example of the power and wealth of the Athenian empire.

good and to pursue its acquisition. Many people, however, viewed the Sophists as harmful to the traditional values of society and especially dangerous to the values of young people.

In classical Greece, Athens became the foremost intellectual and artistic center. Its reputation is perhaps strongest of all in philosophy. After all, Socrates, Plato, and Aristotle raised basic questions that have been debated for two thousand years; these are still largely the same philosophical questions we wrestle with today.

Socrates (469–399 B.C.) left no writings, but we know about him from his pupils, especially his most famous one, Plato. By occupation, Socrates was a stonemason, but his true love was philosophy. He taught a number of pupils, but not for pay, since he believed that the goal of education was only to improve the individual. He made use of a teaching method that has become known by his name. The "Socratic method" utilizes a question-and-answer technique to lead pupils to see things for themselves by using their own reason. Socrates believed that all real knowledge is within each person; only critical examination was needed to call it forth. This was the real task of philosophy since "the unexamined life is not worth living."

Socrates' questioning of authority and public demonstration of others' lack of knowledge led him into trouble. Athens had had a tradition of free thought and inquiry, but defeat in the Peloponnesian War had created

▼ **Doryphoros.** This statue, known as the *Doryphoros,* or spear-carrier, is by the fifth-century sculptor Polyclitus, and was believed by him to illustrate the ideal proportions of the human figure. Classical Greek sculpture moved away from the stiffness of the *kouros* figure, but retained the young male nude as the favorite subject matter. The statues became more life-like, possessing relaxed figures and flexible, smooth-muscled bodies. The aim of sculpture, however, was not simply realism, but rather the expression of ideal beauty.

an environment intolerant of open debate and soul-searching. Socrates was accused and convicted of corrupting the youth of Athens by his teaching. An Athenian jury sentenced him to death (see the box on p. 87).

One of Socrates' disciples was Plato (c. 429–347 B.C.), considered by many the greatest philosopher of Western civilization. Unlike his master Socrates, who

wrote nothing, Plato wrote a great deal. In his dialogues, he used Socrates as his chief philosophical debater.

Plato's philosophical thought focused on the essence of reality and was centered in the concept of Ideas or ideal Forms. According to Plato, there has always existed a higher world of eternal, unchanging Ideas or Forms. To know these Forms is to know truth. These ideal Forms constitute reality and can only be apprehended by a trained mind, which, of course, is the goal of philosophy. The objects that we perceive with our senses are simply reflections of the ideal Forms. Hence, they are shadows while reality is found in the Forms themselves.

Plato's ideas of government were set out in his dialogue entitled *The Republic.* Based on his experience in Athens, Plato had come to distrust the workings of democracy. It was obvious to Plato that individuals could not attain an ethical life unless they lived in a just and rational state. Plato's search for the just state led him to construct an ideal state. *The Republic* is often considered the first major work of utopian literature. In his ideal state, the population was divided into three basic groups. At the top was an upper class, a ruling elite, the famous philosopher-kings: "Unless either philosophers become kings in their countries or those who are now called kings and rulers come to be sufficiently inspired with a genuine desire for wisdom; unless, that is to say, political power and philosophy meet together . . . there can be no rest from troubles . . . for states, nor yet, as I believe, for all mankind."[14] The second group were those who showed courage; they would be the warriors who protected the society. All the rest made up the masses, essentially people driven, not by wisdom or courage, but by desire. They would be the producers of society—the artisans, tradesmen, and farmers. Contrary to common Greek custom, Plato also stressed that men and women should have the same education and equal access to all positions.

Plato established a school at Athens known as the Academy. One of his pupils, who studied there for twenty years, was Aristotle (384–322 B.C.), who later became a tutor to Alexander the Great. Aristotle differed significantly from his teacher in that he did not accept Plato's theory of ideal Forms. He, like Plato, believed in universal principles or forms, but he believed that form and matter were inseparable. By examining individual objects, we can perceive their form and arrive at universal principles, but they do not exist as a separate higher world of reality beyond material things, but are a part of things themselves. Aristotle's interests, then, lay in analyzing and classifying things based on thorough

The Death of Socrates
▼ ▼ ▼

In his dialogue entitled the Phaedo, Plato gave an account of the death of his teacher. Socrates had been charged with corrupting the youth of Athens and was sentenced to death by an Athenian jury. He died by drinking poison (hemlock) as described in this scene. Some historians however, have questioned whether the effects of hemlock are as gentle as portrayed here.

Plato, Phaedo

At this Crito made a sign to his servant, who was standing near by. The servant went out and after spending a considerable time returned with the man who was to administer the poison; he was carrying it ready prepared in a cup. When Socrates saw him he said: "Well, my good fellow, you understand these things; what ought I to do?"

"Just drink it," he said, "and then walk about until you feel a weight in your legs, and then lie down. Then it will act of its own accord. . . ."

Up till this time most of us had been fairly successful in keeping back our tears; but when we saw that he was drinking, that he had actually drunk it, we could do so no longer; in spite of myself the tears came pouring out, so that I covered my face and wept broken-heartedly—not for him, but for my own calamity in losing such a friend. . . . Socrates . . . said:

"Really, my friends, what a way to behave! Why, that was my main reason for sending away the women, to prevent this sort of disturbance; because I am told that one should make one's end in a tranquil frame of mind. Calm yourselves and try to be brave."

This made us feel ashamed, and we controlled our tears. Socrates walked about, and presently, saying that his legs were heavy, lay down on his back—that was what the man recommended. The man . . . kept his hand upon Socrates, and after a little while examined his feet and legs; then pinched his foot hard and asked if he felt it. Socrates said no. Then he did the same to his legs; and moving gradually upwards in this way let us see that he was getting cold and numb. Presently he felt him again and said that when it reached the heart, Socrates would be gone.

The coldness was spreading about as far as his waist when Socrates uncovered his face—for he had covered it up—and said (they were his last words): "Crito, we ought to offer a cock to Asclepius [the god of healing]. See to it, and don't forget."

"No, it shall be done," said Crito. "Are you sure that there is nothing else?"

Socrates made no reply to this question, but after a little while he stirred; and when the man uncovered him, his eyes were fixed. When Crito saw this, he closed the mouth and eyes.

Such . . . was the end of our comrade, who was, we may fairly say, of all those whom we knew in our time, the bravest and also the wisest and most upright man.

---

research and investigation. His interests were wide-ranging, and he wrote treatises on an enormous number of subjects: ethics, logic, politics, poetry, astronomy, geology, biology, and physics.

Like Plato, Aristotle wished for an effective form of government that would rationally direct human affairs. Unlike Plato, he did not seek an ideal state based on embodiment of an ideal Form of justice, but tried to find the best form of government by a rational examination of existing governments. For his Politics, Aristotle examined the constitutions of 158 states and arrived at general categories for organizing governments. He identified three good forms of government: monarchy, aristocracy, and constitutional government. But based on his examination, he warned that monarchy can easily turn into tyranny, aristocracy into oligarchy, and constitutional government into radical democracy or anarchy. He favored constitutional government as the best form for most people.

With Aristotle's death, the great age of classical Greek philosophy came to an end. By 322 B.C., the world of the small city-state was also coming to a close, and a time for new empires had arrived. Philosophical thought began to move into channels more appropriate for the age.

Greek Religion

The emphasis on rationalism and the role of human beings in Greek literature and thought might lead some to believe that a spiritual perspective was not important to the Greeks. This is simply not true. Even Plato, the greatest of the philosophers, though skeptical of popular religious manifestations, believed in a divine principle. Greek religion was intricately connected to every aspect of daily life; it was both social and practical. Public festivals, which originated from religious practices, served specific functions: boys were prepared to be warriors, girls to be mothers. Especially dangerous activities, such as seafaring, required numerous rituals since the people involved needed special protection. Since religion was related to every aspect of life, citizens had to have a proper attitude to the gods. Religion was a civic cult necessary for the well-being of the state. Temples dedicated to a god or goddess were the major buildings of Greek society. Much misunderstanding about the role of Greek religion arises from the fact that, unlike Christianity, Greek religion did not require belief in a body of doctrine. There were no sacred books, such as the Bible. Proper ritual rather than belief formed the crucial part of Greek religion. It had no official body of priests enunciating dogma and controlling religious matters. Although there were priests and priestesses to care for certain religious shrines, most religious ceremonies were led by civilians serving as priests, and priesthoods were civic offices.

The epic poetry of Homer contained a coherent theogony or genealogy of the gods that served to give a definite structure to Greek religion. Over a period of time, all Greeks accepted a common Olympian religion. There were twelve chief gods who supposedly lived on Mount Olympus, the highest mountain in Greece. Among the twelve were Zeus, the chief deity and father of the gods; Athena, goddess of wisdom and crafts; Apollo, god of the sun and poetry; Aphrodite, goddess of love; and Poseidon, brother of Zeus and god of the seas and earthquakes.

Greek mythology was closely related to the gods and goddesses of Greek religion, although it also included stories of heroes and heroines. Through the works of Homer and Hesiod, gods were seen as human in their activities, but also superhuman in that they were immortal. While the mythic stories were often entertaining, they also served a number of purposes: they could explain phenomena, such as thunderbolts (from Zeus); they could serve a political function, such as legitimizing control of a particular territory; they could define relationships, such as those between men and women, or between humans and gods; and they could preserve the history of names and great events. They could also be very confusing since the many variants of the stories often conflicted with each other.

The twelve Olympian gods were common to all Greeks, who thus shared a basic polytheistic religion. Each *polis* usually singled out one of the twelve Olympians as a guardian deity of its community. Athena was the patron goddess of Athens, for example. But each *polis* also had its own local deities who remained important to the community as a whole, and each family had patron gods as well. Since it was desirable to have the gods look favorably upon one's activities, ritual assumed enormous proportions in Greek religion. Prayers were often combined with gifts to the gods based on the principle, "I give so that you [the gods] will give [in return]." Some prayers directly reflected this mutual benefit: "Protect our city. I believe that what I say is in our common interest. For a flourishing city honours the gods." Ritual meant sacrifices, whether of animals or agricultural products. Animal victims were burned on an altar in front of a temple or on a small altar in front of a home. The Greeks maintained religious calendars (lists of sacrifices) specifying what a god or goddess should receive and on what day it should be offered. The father made sacrifices for the family, officials did so for the state.

Festivals were also developed as a way to honor the gods and goddesses. Some of these (the Panhellenic celebrations) came to have international significance and were held at special locations, such as those dedicated to the worship of Zeus at Olympia; to Poseidon at the Isthmus of Corinth; and to Apollo at Delphi. Numerous events were held in honor of the gods at the great festivals, including athletic competitions to which all Greeks were invited. The first such games were held at the Olympic festival in 776 B.C. and then held every four years thereafter to honor Zeus. Initially, the Olympic contests consisted of foot races and wrestling, but later, boxing, javelin throwing, and various other contests were added. Competitions were always between individuals, not groups.

Individual *poleis* also held religious festivals on a regular basis. At Athens, the most splendid was the Great Panathenaia, begun in the early sixth century and held every four years in July. Dedicated to the patron goddess Athena, the highlight of the festival was a great procession of the entire community through the city. But as with all great religious festivals, the Great Panathenaia also included dancing and singing, choruses of men and women, torch races, and athletic and musical contests. At the festival of Dionysus, known as the City Dionysia, tragedies and comedies were presented as part of the festival.

As another practical side of Greek religion, Greeks wanted to know the will of the gods. There were seers who obtained omens from dreams, the flight of birds, or the entrails of sacrificial animals. But perhaps the most famous method to divine the will of the gods was the use of the oracle, a sacred shrine dedicated to a god or goddess who revealed the future. The most famous was the oracle of Apollo at Delphi, located on the side of Mount Parnassus, overlooking the Gulf of Corinth. At Delphi, a priestess listened to questions while in a state of ecstasy that was believed to be induced by Apollo. Her responses were interpreted by the priests and given in verse form to the person asking questions. Both states and individuals traveled to Delphi to consult the oracle of Apollo. States might inquire whether they should undertake a military expedition; individuals might raise such questions as, "Heracleidas asks the god whether he will have offspring from the wife he has now." Responses were often enigmatic and at times even politically motivated. Oracles tended to favor one side against another in the great struggles that wracked Greece.

Greek religion, centered in ritual and a formal relationship with the gods, tended to lack a strong emotional component. It also gave little or no certain hope of life after death for most people. As a result, the Greeks sometimes turned to mystery religions, which included initiation into secret rites that promised a more emotional involvement with spiritual forces and a greater hope of immortality. The most important mysteries were those of the Eleusinian cult connected with the myth of Demeter. This was a fertility cult in which participants felt reborn and gained some hope for life after death. The Orphic cultists, who considered themselves followers of the legendary singer Orpheus, believed in cycles of reincarnation since the human soul had become trapped in the physical body. Their aim was to liberate the soul from its confinement.

Daily Life in Classical Athens

The picture of Athenian society presented by looking at the arts, philosophy, and theater can be misleading. It gives us an impression of a city where all was rational discourse, vigorous and constant debate, and admiration of beauty and artistic pleasures. Athenian society had a dark side as well, and nowhere is this more evident than in certain aspects of daily life in Athens in the fifth century.

The *polis* was, above all, a male community: only adult male citizens took part in public life. In Athens, this meant the exclusion of women, slaves, and foreign residents, or roughly, 85 percent of the total population in the area of Attica. In the fifth century, Athens had the largest population of all the Greek *poleis*. There were

▼ **Women in the Loom Room.** This painting shows two women weaving, a task carried out in the Athenian home where rooms were set aside for such work. In Athens, women were considered to be citizens and could participate in religious cults and festivals, but had no rights and were barred from any political activity. They were thought to belong in the house, caring for the children and the needs of the household.

probably 150,000 citizens, of whom about 43,000 were adult males who exercised political power. Resident foreigners, known as metics, numbered about 35,000. In return for registering with the authorities and paying a small tax, metics received the protection of the laws. They were also subject, however, to some of the responsibilities of citizens, namely, military service and the funding of festivals. Metics were usually loyal to Athens, and some, in fact, became prosperous through industry, trade, or banking. A few even became citizens. The remaining social group, the slaves, numbered around 100,000.

Slavery was a common institution in the ancient world. Owners of slaves in Athens were permitted to treat their slaves as they wished, although it was obviously not to their advantage to be overly harsh. Economic necessity dictated the desirability of owning at least one slave, although the very poor in Athens did not own any. A soldier on campaign usually took along one slave to carry his armor. The really wealthy might own large numbers, but those who did usually employed them in industry. Most often, slaves in Athens performed domestic tasks, such as being tutors, cooks, and maids, or worked in the fields. Few peasants could afford more than one or two. Other slaves worked as unskilled and skilled labor. Those who worked in public construction were paid the same as metics or citizens. For some slaves, this created the possibility of eventually buying their freedom. In many ways, as some historians have argued, although Athens was a slave-owning society, the economy was not dependent on the use of slaves. Slavery in most instances was a substitute for wage labor, which was frowned upon by most freedom-loving Athenians. Only in one area of economic life did the Athenians have a real slave economy, and that was in the silver mines of Laurium.

The Athenian economy was largely agricultural, but highly diversified as well. Agriculture consisted of growing grains, vegetables, and fruit trees for local consumption, vines and olive trees for wine and olive oil, which were exportable products, and the grazing of sheep and goats for wool and milk products. Given the size of the population in Attica and the lack of abundant fertile land, Athens had to import between 50 and 80 percent of its grain, a staple in the Athenian diet. Trade thus took on much importance to the Athenian economy. The building of the port at Piraeus and the Long Walls (a series of defensive walls four and one-half miles long connecting Athens and Piraeus) created the physical conditions that made Athens the leading trade center in the fifth-century Greek world.

Craftsmen did not exist in large numbers in Athens, but they were important to the economy. Athens was the chief producer of high-quality painted pottery in the fifth century. Other crafts had moved beyond the small workshop into the factory through the use of slave labor. The shield factory of Lysias, for example, employed 120 slaves. Public works projects also provided considerable livelihood for Athenians. The building program of Pericles, financed from the Delian League treasury, made possible the hiring of both skilled and unskilled labor. This labor force was mixed, consisting of free Athenians, foreign residents, and slaves. All were paid the same wages. The mining of silver was also important to the Athenian economy, especially the new vein discovered at Laurium early in the fifth century. The state leased concessions to private entrepreneurs who used gangs of slaves in the mines. Profits were enormous, both for the state and the individuals who bought the concessions, as well as for the suppliers of labor. Nicias, who provided a labor force of 1,000 slaves, made a 33 percent return on his capital investment. In fact, given the pitiful working conditions, many slaves did not survive more than three years working in the mines. Even at that, an investor could still make money by simply buying new slaves rather than caring for the old ones.

The Athenian lifestyle was basically simple. Athenian houses were furnished with necessities bought from craftsmen, such as beds, couches, tables, chests, pottery, stools, baskets, and cooking utensils. Clothes and blankets were made at home by wives and slaves. The Athenian diet was rather plain. Basic foods consisted of barley, wheat, millet, lentils, grapes, figs, olives, almonds, bread made at home, vegetables, eggs, fish, cheese, and chicken. Olive oil was widely used, not only for eating, but for lighting lamps, and rubbing on the body after washing and exercise. Although country houses kept animals, they were used for reasons other than their flesh: oxen for ploughing, sheep for wool, and goats for milk and cheese. Meat was consumed only on special occasions, such as festivals when animals were sacrificed and the cooked meat then eaten.

The family was an important institution in ancient Athens. It was composed of husband, wife, and children (a nuclear family), although other dependent relatives and slaves were regarded as part of the family because of its economic unity. The family's primary social function was to produce new citizens. Strict laws of the fifth century had stipulated that a citizen must be the offspring of a legally acknowledged marriage between two Athenian citizens whose parents were also citizens. By law, property was divided by lot among all the surviving sons; as a result, marriages were usually sought within a close circle of relatives so as to preserve the family property. The family also served to protect and enclose women.

Women were citizens who could participate in most religious cults and festivals, but were otherwise excluded from public life. They could not own property beyond personal items and always had a male guardian: if unmarried, a father or male relative; if married, a husband; if widowed, a son or male relative.

Household Management and the Role of the Athenian Wife
▼ ▼ ▼

In fifth-century Athens, a woman's place was in the home. She had two major responsibilities: the bearing and raising of children and the management of the household. In his dialogue on estate management, Xenophon relates the advice of an Attican gentleman on how to train a wife.

Xenophon, Oeconomicus

[Ischomachus addresses his new wife] For it seems to me, dear, that the gods with great discernment have coupled together male and female, as they are called, chiefly in order that they may form a perfect partnership in mutual service. For, in the first place, that the various species of living creatures may not fail, they are joined in wedlock for the production of children. Secondly, offspring to support them in old age is provided by this union, to human beings, at any rate. Thirdly, human beings live not in the open air, like beasts, but obviously need shelter. Nevertheless, those who mean to win stores to fill the covered place, have need of someone to work at the open-air occupations; since ploughing, sowing, planting and grazing are all such open-air employments; and these supply the needful food. . . . For he made the man's

body and mind more capable of enduring cold and heat, and journeys and campaigns; and therefore imposed on him the outdoor tasks. To the woman, since he had made her body less capable of such endurance, I take it that God has assigned the indoor tasks. And knowing that he had created in the woman and had imposed on her the nourishment of the infants, he meted out to her a larger portion of affection for new-born babes than to the man. . . . Now since we know, dear, what duties have been assigned to each of us by God, we must endeavor, each of us, to do the duties allotted to us as well as possible. . . .

Your duty will be to remain indoors and send out those servants whose work is outside, and superintend those who are to work indoors, and to receive the incomings, and distribute so much of them as must be spent, and watch over so much as is to be kept in store, and take care that the sum laid by for a year be not spent in a month. And when wool is brought to you, you must see that cloaks are made for those that want them. You must see too that the dry corn is in good condition for making food. One of the duties that fall to you, however, will perhaps seem rather thankless: you will have to see that any servant who is ill is cared for.

Women were involved in the transfer of property in two ways. Both demonstrate their subservient position. The guardian provided a dowry for a woman to marry. Once the husband received the dowry, the marriage was completed. The dowry was controlled by the husband. If he died or obtained a divorce, the dowry (plus 18 percent interest) along with the wife were returned to the guardian. This was a strong incentive for a man to avoid divorce. The other occasion in which a woman could be involved in the transfer of property occurred when a man died leaving no male heirs, but only a daughter to inherit his property. If this happened, then she was married to the closest male relative, often to her paternal uncle. A claimant could even be forced to divorce his wife to marry the heiress, and a wife could be forced to divorce her husband to marry the claimant. The goal was to keep the wealth in the family regardless of the woman's (or man's) wishes.

The function of the Athenian woman as wife was very clear. Her foremost obligation was to bear children, especially male children who would preserve the family line. The marriage formula that Athenians used put it succinctly: "I give this woman for the procreation of legitimate children." Secondly, a wife was to take care of her family and her house, either doing the household work herself or supervising the slaves who did the actual work (see the box above).

Women were kept under strict control. Since they were married at fourteen or fifteen, it was easier to teach them early about their responsibilities. Although many managed to learn to read and play musical instruments, they were often cut off from any formal education. And women were expected to remain at home out of sight unless they attended funerals or festivals, such as the women's festival of Thesmophoria. If they left the house, they were to be accompanied. A woman working alone in public was either poverty-stricken or not a citizen.

Women in Athens served males in other ways as well. Prostitution (both male and female) flourished in classical Athens. Most female prostitutes were slaves in brothels run as a business or trade by an Athenian citizen. Another class of prostitutes in Athenian society occupied a more favorable position; these more refined courtesans were known as *hetairai*, literally "female companions." Usually ex-slaves or foreign residents, these women were more sophisticated than ordinary prostitutes and were known for their intellectual and musical achievements as well as their physical ones. Athenian males continued the aristocratic practice of the symposium, the sophisticated drinking party, where *hetairai* were often present. Symposia were held in the men's dining rooms and wives were not present. *Hetairai* danced, played musical instruments, and provided entertainment, including sex. Some *hetairai* achieved fortune and considerable renown. Aspasia was certainly the most famous. A friend of Socrates and known for her learning, she was the mistress of Pericles and eventually became his common-law wife.

It perhaps comes as little surprise to learn that in a society where males spent most of their time with other males, male homosexuality was a prominent feature. Male homosexuality was widely practiced in classical Athens and certainly tolerated. Athenian law disfranchised a citizen who had prostituted his body to another male, but nothing was done to males who engaged in homosexual love with male prostitutes or other adult males for love or pleasure. The law did not eliminate male prostitution, but assured that male prostitutes would be foreigners, not Athenian citizens.

The Greek homosexual ideal was a relationship between a mature man and a young male. It is most likely that this was an aristocratic ideal and not one practiced by the common people. As we have seen, the ties between husband and wife were not strong in Athenian society; the same could be said of the relationship between fathers and children. Some historians have argued that the older man–young boy relationship was a substitute for the failure of these relationships. While the homosexual relationship was frequently physical, the Greeks also viewed it as educational. The older male (the "lover") won the love of his "beloved" (usually an adolescent twelve to nineteen years old) by his value as a teacher and by the devotion he demonstrated in training his charge. In a sense, this love relationship was seen as a way of initiating young males into the male world of political and military dominance. When he became an adult, the young man became a friend, and the erotic element of the relationship was expected to end. The Greeks did not feel that the coexistence of homosexual and heterosexual predilections created any special problems for individuals or their society.

The civilization of the ancient Greeks was the fountainhead of Western culture. Socrates, Plato, and Aristotle established the foundations of Western philosophy. Herodotus and Thucydides created the discipline of history. Our literary forms are largely derived from Greek poetry and drama. Greek notions of harmony, proportion, and beauty have remained the touchstones for all subsequent Western art. A rational method of inquiry, so important to modern science, was conceived in ancient Greece. Many of our political terms are Greek in origin, and so too are our concepts of the rights and duties of citizenship, especially as they were conceived in Athens, the first great democracy the world had seen. Especially during their classical period, the Greeks raised and debated the fundamental questions about the purpose of human existence, the structure of human society, and the nature of the universe that have concerned Western thinkers ever since.

All of these achievements came from a group of small city-states in ancient Greece. And yet there remains an element of tragedy about Greek civilization. For all of their brilliant accomplishments, the Greeks were unable to rise above the divisions and rivalries that caused them to fight each other and undermine their own civilization. Of course, their contributions to Western civilization have outlived their political struggles, but in studying the Greeks and seeing what went wrong, we can come to appreciate one of the remaining challenges of Western civilization.

Notes
▼ ▼ ▼

1. H. D. F. Kitto, *The Greeks* (Harmondsworth, 1951), p. 64.
2. Homer, *Odyssey*, trans. E. V. Rieu (Harmondsworth, 1946), p. 337.
3. Xenophon, *Symposium*, trans. O. J. Todd (Cambridge, Mass., 1968), III, 5.
4. Hesiod, *Works and Days*, trans. Dorothea Wender (Harmondsworth, 1973), pp. (in order of quotations) 66, 77, 69, 73, 71, 68.
5. Theognis, *Elegies*, trans. Dorothea Wender (Harmondsworth, 1973), pp. (in order of quotations), 118, 100, 98, 114, 131.
6. Aeschylus, *The Persians*, in *The Complete Greek Tragedies*, vol. 1, ed. David Grene and Richmond Lattimore (Chicago, 1959), p. 229.

7. Voltaire, *The Age of Louis XIV*, trans. Martyn Pollack (London, 1926), p. 1.
8. Herodotus, *The Persian Wars*, trans. George Rawlinson (New York, 1942), p. 3.
9. Thucydides, *The Peloponnesian War*, trans. Rex Warner (Harmondsworth, 1954). p. 324.
10. Ibid., p. 24.
11. Ibid.
12. Sophocles, *Oedipus the King*, trans. David Grene (Chicago, 1959), pp. 68–69.
13. Sophocles, *Antigone*, trans. Don Taylor (London, 1986), p. 146.
14. Plato, *The Republic*, trans. F. M. Cornford (New York, 1945), pp. 178–79.

Suggestions for Further Reading
▼ ▼ ▼

The standard one-volume reference work for Greek history remains J. B. Bury and R. Meiggs, *A History of Greece to the Death of Alexander the Great*, 4th ed. (New York, 1975). Other good, general introductions to Greek history include *The Oxford History of the Classical World*, ed. J. Boardman, J. Griffin, and O. Murray (Oxford, 1986), pp. 19–314; N. G. L. Hammond, *A History of Greece to 322* B.C., 3d ed. (Oxford, 1986); A. Andrewes, *Greek Society* (Harmondsworth, 1975); H. D. F. Kitto, *The Greeks* (Harmondsworth, 1951); and M. I. Finley, *The Legacy of Greece: A New Appraisal* (Oxford, 1981). For a general survey of economic and social aspects, see P. Naquet, *Economic and Social History of Ancient Greece: An Introduction* (Berkeley, 1978). Warfare is covered in F. Adcock, *The Greek and Macedonian Art of War* (Berkeley, 1957).

Early Greek history is examined in O. Murray, *Early Greece* (London, 1980); E. Vermeule, *Greece in the Bronze Age* (Chicago, 1964); and L. W. Taylor, *The Mycenaeans*, rev. ed. (London, 1983). For Dark Age Greece, see A. M. Snodgrass, *The Dark Age of Greece* (Edinburgh, 1971). For good introductions to Homer and the Homeric problem, see J. Griffin, *Homer* (Oxford, 1980); and D. Page, *History and the Homeric Iliad* (Berkeley, 1959). On Homer and his world, see the modern classic by M. I. Finley, *The World of Odysseus*, 2d ed. (New York, 1979).

The best general works on Archaic Greece include A. M. Snodgrass, *Archaic Greece* (London, 1980); W. G. Forrest, *The Emergence of Greek Democracy* (London, 1966); and A. R. Burn, *The Lyric Age of Greece* (London, 1960). Economic and social history of the period is covered in C. Starr, *The Economic and Social Growth of Early Greece, 800–500* B.C. (Oxford, 1977). On colonization, see J. Boardman, *The Greeks Overseas*, rev. ed. (Baltimore, 1980). The best work on tyranny is A. Andrewes, *The Greek Tyrants* (New York, 1963). On the culture of Archaic Greece, see A. R. Burn, *The World of Hesiod* (London, 1936); and A. J. Podlecki, *The Early Greek Poets and Their Themes* (Vancouver, 1984). See also the work of translation by W. Barnstone, *Greek Lyric Poetry* (New York, 1962). The best histories of Sparta are W. Forrest, *A History of Sparta, 950–121* B.C., 2d ed. (London, 1980); and P. A. Cartledge, *Sparta and Laconia: A Regional History, 1300–362* B.C. (London, 1979). On early Athens, see the still valuable A. Jones, *Athenian Democracy* (London, 1957); and R. Osborne, *Demos* (New York, 1985). The Persian Wars are examined in A. Burn, *Persia and the Greeks: The Defense of the West*, rev. ed. (Stanford, 1984); and C. Hignett, *Xerxes' Invasion of Greece* (Oxford, 1963).

A general history of classical Greece can be found in S. Hornblower, *The Greek World, 479–323* B.C. (London, 1983); and J. K. Davies, *Democracy and*

Classical Greece (London, 1978). Economic aspects are examined in R. Hopper, *Trade and Industry in Classical Greece* (London, 1979). Recent, important works on Athens include W. R. Connor, *The New Politicians of Fifth-Century Athens* (Princeton, 1971); and P. J. Rhodes, *The Athenian Boule* (Oxford, 1972). On the development of the Athenian empire, see R. Meiggs, *The Athenian Empire* (Oxford, 1975); and the recent work by M. F. McGregor, *The Athenians and Their Empire* (Vancouver, 1987). A provocative view of male politics in fifth-century Athens can be found in E. C. Keuls, *The Reign of the Phallus: Sexual Politics in Ancient Athens* (New York, 1985). The best way to examine the Great Peloponnesian War is to read the work of Thucydides, *History of the Peloponnesian War,* trans. Rex Warner (Harmondsworth, 1954). A detailed study has been done in the three books by D. Kagan, *Outbreak of the Peloponnesian War* (Ithaca, N.Y., 1969); *The Archidamian War* (Ithaca, N.Y., 1974); and *The Peace of Nicias and the Sicilian Expedition* (Ithaca, N.Y., 1981). A study of an important aspect of fourth-century Greek history can be found in J. Buckler, *The Theban Hegemony, 371–362* B.C. (Cambridge, Mass., 1980).

For a comprehensive history of Greek art, see M. Robertson, *A History of Greek Art,* 2 vols. (Cambridge, 1975). A good, brief study is J. Boardman, *Greek Art* (London, 1985). On sculpture, see G. M. A. Richter, *Sculpture and Sculptors of the Greeks* (Oxford, 1971). A basic survey of architecture is H. W. Lawrence, *Greek Architecture,* rev. ed. (Harmondsworth, 1983). For another aspect of Greek architecture, see J. Coulton, *Greek Architects at Work* (London, 1977). On Greek drama, see the general work by A. Lesky, *History of Greek Literature* (London, 1966). More specialized studies include K. Dover, *Aristophanic Comedy* (London, 1972); K. Reinhardt, *Sophocles* (Oxford, 1978); the classic *Euripides and His Age* (Oxford, 1965) by G. Murray; and A. W. Pickard-Cambridge, *The Dramatic Festivals of Athens,* 2d ed. (Oxford, 1968). For a sound study of Greek history writing, see A. Momigliano, *Essays in Ancient and Modern Historiography* (Oxford, 1977). Individual studies include J. A. S. Evans, *Herodotus* (Boston, Mass., 1982); K. Dover, *Thucydides* (Oxford, 1973); and F. M. Cornford, *Thucydides Mythistoricus* (Philadelphia, 1970). On Greek philosophy, a detailed study is available in W. K. C. Guthrie, *A History of Greek Philosophy,* 6 vols. (Cambridge, 1962–81). Individual works include J. Barnes, *Aristotle* (Oxford, 1982), primarily on his scientific and logical works; J. Findlay, *Plato and Platonism* (New York, 1978); and A. Taylor, *Socrates* (New York, 1933).

A short, general study of Greek religion is W. Guthrie, *The Greeks and Their Gods* (Boston, 1965). Other works of value are W. Burkert, *Greek Religion,* trans. J. Raffan (Cambridge, Mass., 1985); C. Seltman, *The Twelve Olympians* (New York, 1960); M. P. Nilsson, *Greek Popular Religion* (New York, 1940); J. D. Mikalson, *Athenian Popular Religion* (Chapel Hill, N.C., 1983); and H. W. Parke, *Greek Oracles* (London, 1967). On the special character of Greek mythology, see G. S. Kirk, *The Nature of Greek Myths* (Harmondsworth, 1974). E. R. Dodds, *The Greeks and the Irrational* (Berkeley, 1951), examines the role of the supernatural in Greek life.

For general accounts of daily life in classical Athens, see T. B. L. Webster, *Everyday Life in Classical Athens* (London, 1969); and M. and C. Quennell, *Everyday Things in Ancient Greece* (London, 1954). On the family and women, see W. K. Lacey, *The Family in Classical Greece* (London, 1968); S. C. Humphreys, *The Family, Women and Death* (London, 1983); and S. B. Pomeroy, *Goddesses, Whores, Wives, and Slaves* (New York, 1975), the best general book on women. On slavery, see M. I. Finley, ed., *Slavery in Classical Antiquity* (Cambridge, 1960). The fundamental study of homosexuality is K. J. Dover, *Greek Homosexuality* (London, 1978).

Chapter 4

The Hellenistic World

▼▼▼▼▼

I n 338 B.C., King Philip II defeated the Greeks and established his control over the Greek peninsula. The Greek city-states were never the same after their defeat by the Macedonian monarch. Philip's son Alexander led the Macedonians and Greeks on a spectacular conquest of the Persian Empire and opened the door to the spread of Greek culture throughout the ancient Near East. Greek settlers poured into the lands of the ancient Near East as bureaucrats, traders, soldiers, and scholars. Alexander's triumph created a new series of kingdoms that blended together the achievements of the eastern world with the cultural outlook and attitudes of the Greeks. We use the term *Hellenistic* to designate this new order. The Hellenistic world was the world of Greeks and non-Greek easterners, and it resulted, in its own way, in a remarkable series of accomplishments that form the story of this chapter.

▼ The Rise of Macedonia and the End of Hellenic Civilization

While the Greek city-states were continuing their fratricidal warfare, to their north a new and ultimately powerful kingdom was emerging in its own right. Although a Greek-speaking people, the Macedonians were viewed as barbarians by their southern neighbors, the Greeks. The Macedonians were mostly rural folk and were organized in tribes, not city-states. Not until the end of the fifth century B.C., during the reign of King Archelaus (c. 413–399 B.C.) did Macedonia emerge as an important kingdom. But his reign was followed by decades of repeated foreign invasions and internal strife until King Philip II (359–336 B.C.) took control and

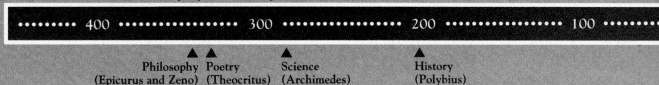

Phillip II conquers Greece	Conquests of Alexander the Great ▼	The Hellenistic Monarchies ▼		Roman Conquests in the East ▼

•••••••• 400 •••••••••• 300 •••••••••••• 200 •••••••••••• 100 ••••••••

Philosophy (Epicurus and Zeno) ▲   Poetry (Theocritus) ▲   Science (Archimedes) ▲   History (Polybius) ▲

turned Macedonia into the chief power of the Greek world.

Philip had spent three years as a hostage in Thebes, where he had gained a great admiration for Greek culture and absorbed the latest Greek military developments from Epaminondas, who had been the military leader behind Thebes' brief ascendancy over the Greek city-states (see Chapter 3). Philip understood the importance of having an efficient army if Macedonia was to be a strong state. He was aware that the Greek states, in the course of their struggles with each other, had come to rely too much on mercenaries. Philip used Macedonian countrymen, sturdy peasants and shepherds, as the core of his phalanx of infantrymen. From the gold mines of Mount Pangaeus, he obtained the wealth to pay these soldiers and establish a standing professional army. The Macedonian phalanx was also armed with longer thrusting spears and supported by strong cavalry contingents that served to break the opposing line of battle and create disorder in the enemy's ranks. Philip's new army

defeated the Illyrians to the west and the Thracians to the north and east, took Amphipolis from the Athenians, and was then drawn into the Greeks' interstate conflicts.

The reactions within the Greek world to Philip's growing strength and expansion were mixed. Many Athenians, especially the orator Demosthenes, came to have a strong distrust of the Macedonian leader's intentions. Demosthenes delivered a series of orations, known as the Philippics, in which he portrayed Philip as ruthless, deceitful, treacherous, and barbaric, and called upon the Athenians to undertake a struggle against him (see the box on p. 99). Athenians, such as the philosopher Isocrates, viewed Philip as a savior who would rescue the Greeks from themselves by uniting them and organizing the entire Greek world in a crusade against the common enemy, the Persians.

Demosthenes' repeated calls for action, combined with Philip's rapid expansion, finally spurred Athens into action. Allied with Thebes and some other smaller

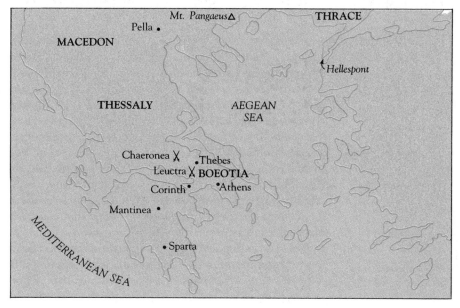

▼ Map 4.1 Macedonia and Mainland Greece.

states, Athens fought the Macedonians at the Battle of Chaeronea, near Thebes, in 338 B.C. The Macedonian army crushed the Greek allies, and Philip was now free to consolidate his control over the Greek peninsula. While Thebes was punished severely, Athens, out of respect for its past and expected cooperation in the future, was treated leniently. The Greek states were joined together in an alliance that we call the Corinthian League because they met at Corinth. While based on the principle of self-governing, independent states, the league did have an army and a council. Philip of Macedon was recognized as *hegemon* (leader) of the league and its army. Moreover, Macedonian garrisons were stationed at strategic locations in Greece. Although Philip allowed the Greek city-states autonomy in domestic affairs, he retained the general direction of their foreign affairs. Many Greeks still objected to being subject to the less civilized master from the north, but Philip in-

Chronology
▼ ▼ ▼
The Rise of Macedonia and the Conquests of Alexander

Reign of Philip II	359–336 B.C.
Battle of Chaeronea; Philip II conquers Greece	338 B.C.
Reign of Alexander the Great	336–323 B.C.
Alexander invades Asia; Battle of Granicus River	334 B.C.
Battle of Issus	333 B.C.
Battle of Gaugamela	331 B.C.
Fall of Persepolis, the Persian Capital	330 B.C.
Alexander enters India	327 B.C.
Death of Alexander	323 B.C.

▼ **Philip II.** While often overshadowed by the exploits of his son Alexander, the achievements of Philip II were what made Alexander's conquests possible. Having unified Macedonia, Philip built a powerful standing army from his Macedonian subjects and defeated the Greek city-states allied against him in 338 B.C. He then imposed order on the Greek peninsula and demanded that the Greek states aid him in his planned invasion of Persia. Before he could move against the Persians, however, Philip was assassinated. This silver coin depicts the Macedonian king.

sisted that the Greek states end their bitter rivalries and cooperate with him in a war against Persia.

Before Philip could undertake his invasion of Asia, however, he was assassinated, leaving the task to his son Alexander. Although Alexander justly deserves credit for the destruction of the Persian Empire, it was Philip who really paved the way for the conquest. It was he who had unified Macedonia, created a powerful military machine, and subdued the Greeks. He did for the Greeks what the Greeks had not been able to do for themselves.

▼ The Conquests of Alexander the Great

Alexander was only twenty and not yet great when he became king of Macedonia. In only twelve years, he achieved so much that he has since been called Alexander the Great. The illustrious conqueror was, in many ways, prepared for kingship by his father. Philip had allowed Alexander to act as regent while he was away, had taken him along on military campaigns, and indeed, at the important Battle of Chaeronea, had given him control of the cavalry. After his father's assassination, Alexander moved quickly to assert his authority, securing the Macedonian frontiers and smothering a rebellion in Greece. He then turned to his father's dream, the invasion of the Persian Empire.

There is no doubt that Alexander was taking a chance in attacking the Persian Empire. Although weakened in some respects, it was still a strong state. Alexander's fleet was inferior to the Persians, and his finances were shaky

Demosthenes Condemns Philip of Macedonia
▼ ▼ ▼

Among the Greeks, Demosthenes, above all, reacted strongly to the growing strength and expansionary policies of the Macedonian king Philip II. Demosthenes delivered a series of orations to the Athenian assembly in which he pictured Philip as a ruthless and barbaric man. This excerpt is from the Third Philippic, probably delivered in 341 B.C.

Demosthenes, *The Third Philippic*

I observe, however, that all men, and you first of all, have conceded to him something which has been the occasion of every war that the Greeks have ever waged. And what is that? The power of doing what he likes, of calmly plundering and stripping the Greeks one by one, and of attacking their cities and reducing them to slavery. Yet your hegemony in Greece lasted seventy-three years, that of Sparta twenty-nine, and in these later times Thebes too gained some sort of authority after the battle of Leuctra. But neither to you nor to the Thebans nor to the Lacedaemonians [Spartans] did the Greeks ever yet, men of Athens, concede the right of unrestricted action, or anything like it. On the contrary, when you, or rather the Athenians of that day, were thought to be showing a want of consideration in dealing with others, all felt it their duty, even those who had no grievance against them, to go to war in support of those who had been injured. . . . Yet all the faults committed by the Lacedaemonians in those thirty years, and by our ancestors in their seventy years of supremacy, are fewer, men of Athens, than the wrongs which Philip has done to the Greeks in the thirteen incomplete years in which he has been coming to the top—or rather, they are not a fraction of them. . . . Ay, and you know this also, that the wrongs which the Greeks suffered from the Lacedaemonians or from us, they suffered at all events at the hands of true-born sons of Greece, and they might have been regarded as the acts of a legitimate son, born to great possessions, who should be guilty of some fault or error in the management of his estate: so far he would deserve blame and reproach, yet it could not be said that it was not one of the blood, not the lawful heir who was acting thus. But if some slave or supposititious bastard had wasted and squandered what he had no right to, heavens! how much more monstrous and exasperating all would have called it! Yet they have no such qualms about Philip and his present conduct, though he is not only no Greek, nor related to the Greeks, but not even a barbarian from any place that can be named with honour, but a pestilent knave from Macedonia, whence it was never yet possible to buy a decent slave.

at best. His army would have to live off the countryside and win quick victories to gain the resources needed to continue the struggle. In the spring of 334 B.C., Alexander entered Asia Minor with an army of some 37,000 men. About half were Macedonians, the rest being Greeks and other allies. The cavalry, which would play an important role as a striking force, numbered about 5,000. The army was accompanied by architects, engineers, historians, and scientists, a clear indication of Alexander's grand vision and positive expectations at the beginning of his campaign.

His first confrontation with the Persians, at the battle at the Granicus River in 334 B.C., almost cost him his life, but resulted in a major victory. By the spring of 333 B.C., the entire western half of Asia Minor was in Alexander's hands, and the Ionian Greek cities of western Asia Minor had been "liberated" from the Persian oppressor. Not all

of them wished to be liberated, regarding Alexander simply as their new master. There is evidence that they were hardly "free and autonomous" as Alexander claimed.

Meanwhile, the Persian king Darius III mobilized his forces to stop Alexander's army. Although the Persian troops outnumbered Alexander's, the Battle of Issus was fought on a narrow field that canceled the advantage of superior numbers and resulted in another Macedonian success. It certainly did not help the Persian cause when Darius made a spectacular exit from the battlefield before it was even clear who would be victorious. After his victory at Issus in 333 B.C., Alexander laid siege to the port cities of Tyre and Gaza to prevent Persian control of the sea. Egypt surrendered without a fight, and by the winter of 332, Syria, Palestine, and Egypt were under Alexander's domination. He took the traditional title of pharaoh of Egypt and was hailed as the "son of Amon," to the Greeks the equivalent of being called the son of Zeus. Alexander also built the first of a series of cities named after him (Alexandria) as the Greek administrative capital of Egypt. It became (and remains today) one of Egypt's and the Mediterranean world's most important cities.

In the meantime, Darius indicated his willingness to make a peace settlement, offering to cede all land west of the Euphrates River to Alexander. Alexander refused and renewed the offensive. He moved now into the territory of the ancient Near Eastern kingdoms and fought the decisive battle with the Persians at Gaugamela, not far from Babylon, in the summer of 331. At Gaugamela, Alexander encountered clearly superior Persian forces, which had established the battle site on a broad, open plain where their war chariots could be maneuvered to best advantage. Alexander was able to break through the center of the Persian line with his heavy cavalry, followed by the infantry. The battle turned into a rout, although Darius managed to escape. After his victory at Gaugamela, Alexander entered Babylon and then pro-ceeded to the Persian capitals at Susa and Persepolis where he acquired the Persian treasuries and took possession of vast quantities of gold and silver (see the box on p. 101). By 330, Alexander was again on the march, pursuing Darius. After Darius was killed by one of his own men, Alexander took the title and office of the Great King of the Persians. But he was not content to rest with the spoils of the Persian Empire. Over the next three years he moved east and northeast, as far as modern Pakistan. By the summer of 327 B.C., he had entered India, where he experienced a number of difficult campaigns. Weary of campaigning year after year, his soldiers mutinied and refused to go further. Alexander surrendered to their demands and agreed to return, leading his troops through southern Iran across the Gedrosian Desert, where they suffered heavy losses from appalling desert conditions. Alexander and the remnant of his army went to Susa and then Babylon, where he planned more campaigns. But in June 323 B.C., weakened from wounds, fever, and probably excessive alcohol, he died at the young age of thirty-three.

▼ **Map 4.2** Conquests of Alexander the Great.

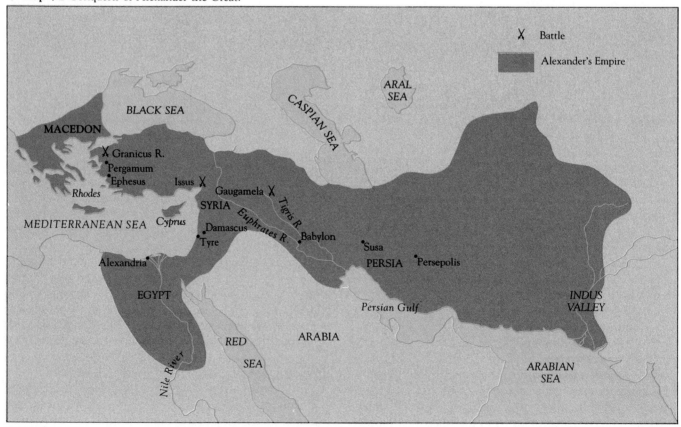

The Destruction of the Persian Palace at Persepolis

▼ ▼ ▼

After Alexander's decisive victory at Gaugamela, he moved into Persia where he captured the chief Persian cities. At Persepolis, he burned the Persian grand palace to the ground. The ancient historians Arrian and Diodorus of Sicily gave different explanations of this act: one argues that it was a deliberate act of revenge for the Persian invasion of Greece in the fifth century; the other that the burning resulted from a wild drinking party. Modern historians do not agree on which version is more plausible. Arrian was a Greek-speaking Roman senator of the second century A.D. Diodorus of Sicily lived in the first century B.C.

Arrian, The Life of Alexander the Great

Thence he marched to Persepolis with such rapidity that the garrison had no time to plunder the city's treasure before his arrival. He also captured the treasure of Cyrus the First at Pasargadae. . . . He burnt the palace of the Persian kings, though this act was against the advice of Parmenio, who urged him to spare it for various reasons, chiefly because it was hardly wise to destroy what was now his own property, and because the Asians would, in his opinion, be less willing to support him if he seemed bent merely upon passing through their country as a conqueror rather than upon ruling it securely as a king. Alexander's answer was that he wished to punish the Persians for their invasion of Greece; his present act was retribution for the destruction of Athens, the burning of the temples, and all the other crimes they had committed against the Greeks.

Diodorus of Sicily, Library of History

Alexander held games in honour of his victories. He performed costly sacrifices to the gods and entertained his friends bountifully. While they were feasting and the drinking was far advanced, as they began to be drunken a madness took possession of the minds of the intoxicated guests. At this point one of the women present, Thaïs by name and Attic by origin, said that for Alexander it would be the finest of all his feats in Asia if he joined them in a triumphal procession, set fire to the palaces, and permitted women's hands in a minute to extinguish the famed accomplishments of the Persians. This was said to men who were still young and giddy with wine, and so, as would be expected someone shouted out to form the procession and light torches, and urged all to take vengeance for the destruction of the Greek temples. Others took up the cry and said that this was a deed worthy of Alexander alone. When the king had caught fire at their words, all leaped up from their couches and passed the word along to form a victory procession in honour of Dionysus [god of wine and religious ecstasy].

Promptly many torches were gathered. Female musicians were present at the banquet, so the king led them all out for the procession to the sound of voices and flutes and pipes, Thaïs the courtesan leading the whole performance. She was the first, after the king, to hurl her blazing torch into the palace. As the others all did the same, immediately the entire palace area was consumed, so great was the conflagration. It was most remarkable that the impious act of Xerxes, king of the Persians, against the acropolis at Athens should have been repaid in kind after many years by one woman, a citizen of the land which had suffered it, and in sport.

Alexander's Ideals

Alexander is one of the most puzzling great figures in history. Although they use the same sources, historians give vastly different pictures of him. Some portray him as an idealistic visionary and others as a ruthless Machiavellian. How did Alexander the Great view himself? We know that he sought to imitate Achilles, the hero of Homer's *Iliad,* destroyer of Hector and Troy. He also claimed to be descended from Heracles, the Greek hero who came to be worshiped as a god. No doubt, Alexander aspired to divine honors; as pharaoh of Egypt, he became a living god according to Egyptian tradition and at one point even sent instructions to the Greek cities to "vote him a god."

Some historians have argued that Alexander believed in an ideal of universal humanity. As evidence they cite the fact that he urged his soldiers to marry native women, and at Susa in 324 B.C. he celebrated the marriages of 10,000 of them en masse to native women. Alexander himself married easterners—Stateira, daughter of Darius, and Roxane, the daughter of a Bactrian baron. Was Alexander pursuing a lofty ideal or was he simply looking for a realistic way to unify his newly won domains? Early on in his conquests, he adopted features of Persian rule. He called himself the Great King and asked his subjects to bow before him in the Persian fashion. He wore Persian dress, used Persians as administrators, and trained native youths in Macedonian military methods. His fellow Macedonians objected to these trappings of oriental despotism and the equal treatment he accorded Persians. Some even went so far as to attempt his assassination. But Alexander must have felt a need to fuse the Macedonian-Greeks and the Persians into a ruling class that would enable him to control such an extensive empire. One is left with the impression that he aspired to autocratic monarchy rather than a lofty vision of the unity of humankind.

Alexander's Legacy

Regardless of his ideals, motives, or views about himself, one fact stands out: Alexander truly created a new age, the Hellenistic era. The word *Hellenistic* is derived from a Greek word meaning "to imitate Greeks." It is an appropriate way, then, to describe an age that saw the extension of the Greek language and ideas to the non-Greek world of the ancient Near East. Alexander's destruction of the Persian monarchy had extended Greco-Macedonian rule over an enormous area. It created opportunities for Greek engineers, intellectuals, merchants, soldiers, and administrators. While the Greeks on the mainland might remain committed to the ideals of their city-states, those who followed Alexander and his successors participated in a new political unity based on the principle of monarchy. Alexander had transformed his army from a Macedonian force into an international one, owing loyalty only to himself. His successors used force to establish military monarchies that dominated the Hellenistic world after his death. Autocratic power, based on military strength and pretensions of divine rule, became a regular feature of those Hellenistic monarchies and was part of Alexander's political legacy to the Hellenistic world.

But Alexander also left a cultural legacy. As a result of his conquests, Greek language, art, architecture, and literature spread throughout the Near East. The urban centers of the Hellenistic age, many founded by Alexander and his successors, became springboards for the diffusion of Greek culture. Alexander had established a

▼ **Alexander and Darius at the Battle of Issus.** This late Hellenistic mosaic from Pompeii depicts the battle between Alexander and Darius III, King of Persia, at Issus in 333 B.C. Alexander landed his forces in western Asia Minor in 334 B.C. to begin his Persian campaign, and first met Darius at Issus where the narrow field made the greater numbers of the Persians useless. Darius was eventually murdered by one of his own men, whereupon Alexander assumed the title and office of the Persian monarch.

number of cities and military colonies named Alexandria to guard strategic points and supervise wide areas. Most of the settlers were Greek mercenaries. It has been estimated that, in the course of his campaigns, Alexander summoned some 60,000 to 65,000 additional mercenaries from Greece, at least 36,000 of whom took residence in the garrisons and new cities. While the Greeks spread their culture in the East, they were also inevitably influenced by eastern ways. Thus, Alexander's legacy included one of the basic characteristics of the Hellenistic world: the clash and fusion of different cultures.

Some historians have suggested that Alexander overextended the Greco-Macedonian world by his conquests. They argue that the Greeks and Macedonians did not possess the resources to govern either efficiently or for the long run and that in trying to do so they weakened the Greek world and opened the door to Roman conquest. Perhaps so. It is always easier to be wise after the event, but none of Alexander's Greek and Macedonian contemporaries would have questioned the capacity of Greeks to be masters over barbarians. In any case, the creation of an empire was part of Alexander's chief legacy. His vision of empire no doubt inspired the Romans, who were, of course, the real heirs of Alexander's legacy.

▼ **Portrait of Deified Alexander.** This silver tetradrachm (four-drachma coin), dating back to the third century B.C., depicts a deified Alexander. While aspiring to be another Achilles, the tragic hero of Homer's *Iliad*, Alexander also sought more divine honors. He claimed to be descended from Heracles, a Greek hero worshipped as a god, and as pharaoh of Egypt, he gained recognition as a living deity.

▼ The World of the Hellenistic Kingdoms

The united empire that Alexander created by his conquests disintegrated soon after his death. An attempt to create a system of joint rule by Alexander's weak-minded half brother and infant son under a regency of the most important Macedonian generals failed. All too soon, these military leaders were engaged in a struggle for power. By 301 B.C., after the Battle of Ipsus, any hope of unity was dead, and eventually four Hellenistic kingdoms emerged as the successors to Alexander: Macedonia under the Antigonid dynasty, Syria and the East under the Seleucids, the Attalid kingdom of Pergamum, and Egypt under the Ptolemies.

In Macedonia, the struggles for power led to the extermination of Alexander the Great's dynasty. Not until 276 B.C. did Antigonus Gonatus, the grandson of one of Alexander's generals, succeed in establishing the Antigonid dynasty as rulers of Macedonia. The Antigonids viewed control of Greece as essential to their power, but did not see outright conquest as necessary. Macedonia was, of course, also important to the Greeks. As one ancient commentator noted, "It is in the interest of the Greeks that the Macedonian dominion should be hum-

bled for long, but by no means that it should be destroyed. For in that case . . . they would very soon experience the lawless violence of the Thracians and Gauls, as they had on more than one occasion."[1] But the Greeks, like the Macedonians, eventually fell subject to Roman power.

Another Hellenistic monarchy was founded by the Alexandrian general Seleucus, who established the Seleucid dynasty of Syria. This was the largest of the Hellenistic kingdoms and controlled much of the old Persian Empire from Turkey in the west to India in the east, although the Seleucids found it increasingly difficult to maintain control of the eastern territories. Moreover, a third Hellenistic kingdom came into being by freeing itself from the Seleucids. This was the kingdom of Pergamum in western Asia Minor under the Attalid dynasty. It was Pergamum that brought the Romans into the area by seeking their aid first against the Antigonids and then against the Seleucids. This led to the Roman defeat of Antiochus III, probably the strongest of the Seleucid monarchs, in 191 B.C. The Seleucids declined thereafter until their small remaining territory was made a Roman province in 63 B.C. Seventy years before that, the last of the Attalid dynasty had bequeathed his kingdom to Rome in his will.

The fourth Hellenistic monarchy was Egypt, which had come under the control of Ptolemy, another Macedonian general. Named governor of Egypt after Alexander's death, Ptolemy had established himself as king by 305 B.C., creating the Ptolemaic dynasty of pharaohs. Hellenistic Egypt lasted longer than all the other Hellenistic monarchies; it was not until the reign of Cleopatra VII, who allied herself with the wrong side in the Roman civil wars (see Chapter 5), that Egypt fell to the Romans in 30 B.C.

Hellenistic Monarchies

The Hellenistic monarchies created a semblance of stability for several centuries, even though Hellenistic kings refused to accept the new status quo and periodically engaged in wars to alter it. At the same time, an underlying strain always existed between the new Greco-Macedonian ruling class and the native populations. To-

gether these factors created a certain degree of tension that was never truly ended until the vibrant Roman state to the west stepped in and imposed a new order.

The Hellenistic kingdoms shared a common political system that represented a break with their Greek past. With the exception of the Spartan kings, monarchy had not been a regular feature of classical Greek life. To the Greeks, monarchy was an institution for barbarians, associated in their minds with people like the Persians. While they retained democratic forms of government in their cities, at the same time the Greeks of the Hellenistic world were forced to accept monarchy as a new fact of political life.

The power of Hellenistic kings was despotic. "The king's will is right" formed a basic operating principle. Only in Macedonia were there remnants of old constitutional forms that might have placed limits on the

▼ **Map 4.3** The World of the Hellenistic Monarchies.

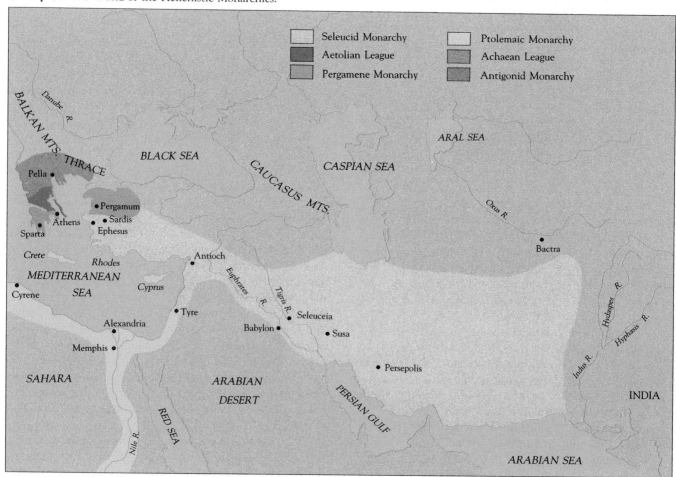

king's power, but even there they failed to be important. In addition to a council to assist the king personally, Hellenistic monarchs had a government bureaucracy to execute their wishes. Both the Seleucids and Ptolemies utilized previous administrative frameworks. The Seleucid kingdom was divided into provinces similar to the Persians' satrapies (see Chapter 2), and the Ptolemies used the system of the pharaohs (see Chapter 1), which came to be called "nomes" (from the Greek word for district).

Both the Seleucid and Ptolemaic dynasties excluded natives from important administrative positions. Contrary to Alexander the Great's plan to fuse Greeks and easterners, Hellenistic monarchs relied only on Greeks and Macedonians to form the new ruling class. It has been estimated that in the Seleucid kingdom, for example, only 2.5 percent of the people in authority were non-Greek and most of them were commanders of local military units. Those who did advance to important administrative posts had learned Greek (all government business was transacted in Greek) and had become hellenized in a cultural sense. The policy of excluding non-Greeks from leadership positions, it should be added, was not due to the incompetence of the natives, but to the determination of the Greek ruling class to maintain its privileged position. It was the Greco-Macedonian ruling class that provided the only unity in the Hellenistic world.

Since the Hellenistic monarchs created and maintained their kingdoms by military force, warfare continued to be an integral part of the Hellenistic world. The size of armies increased dramatically with some Hellenistic kings raising forces of 68,000 troops or more for a single encounter. Unable to recruit adequate forces from their cities, the Hellenistic monarchs frequently made use of mercenaries. The phalanx or heavily armed infantry with long spears (lengthened from thirteen to eighteen feet) and the cavalry still formed the core of the Hellenistic forces.

Along with the familiar phalanx, Hellenistic armies employed some innovative practices. Most noticeable was the utilization of elephants, "the tanks of ancient warfare," especially in the army of the Seleucids who procured theirs from India and the Ptolemies who obtained them from northern Africa. But even more important, since armies quickly learned tricks that neutralized the role of elephants, was the development of new siege techniques, especially the catapult and siege towers. In classical times, cities with good walls were virtually impregnable; Alexander and later Hellenistic rulers could capture cities by using their new equipment.

▼ **Gaul and His Wife: Monument to the Victory of a Hellenistic King.** After the death of Alexander, the empire he had created collapsed and four Hellenistic kingdoms arose in its place. Warfare continued to be of importance to these kingdoms, as it was through warfare that they were created, maintained, and expanded. They did not, however, merely fight among themselves; they also faced foreign enemies, such as the Gauls, who first entered the Hellenistic world in 279 B.C. This statue of a Gaulish chieftain and his wife was part of a larger monument erected to commemorate the victory of Attalus I of Pergamum over the Gauls, a victory that gave Pergamum control over much of Asia Minor.

Hellenistic Cities

Since the hellenizing process was largely an urban phenomenon, the creation of new Greek cities is an especially important topic. In his conquests, Alexander had created a series of new cities and military settlements, and

Hellenistic kings did likewise. The Seleucids, in particular, created more than sixty. The new population centers varied considerably in size and importance. Military settlements were meant to maintain order and might consist of only a few hundred men strongly dependent upon the king. But there were also new independent cities with thousands of inhabitants. Alexandria in Egypt was the largest city in the Mediterranean region by the first century B.C.

Hellenistic rulers encouraged this massive spread of Greek colonists to the Near East because of their intrinsic value to the new monarchies. Greeks (and Macedonians) provided not only a recruiting ground for the army, but also a pool of civilian administrators and workers who would contribute to economic development. Even architects, engineers, dramatists, and actors were in demand in the new Greek cities. Many Greeks and Macedonians were quick to see the advantages of moving to the new urban centers and gladly sought their fortunes in the Near East. Greeks of all backgrounds joined the exodus, at least until around 250 B.C. when the outpouring began to slow significantly.

Within the Hellenistic cities, the culture was primarily Greek. A common Greek language called *koiné* ("common tongue") developed that transcended all the old Greek dialects. Moreover, the political institutions of the cities were modeled after those of the Greek *polis.* Greeks of the classical period would easily have recog-

nized the councils, magistracies, assemblies, and codes of law. The physical layout of the new cities was likewise modeled after those of the Greek homeland. Using the traditional rectilinear grid, cities were laid out with stoas (porticoes), temples, altars (some were quite elaborate), and stone theaters. Many amenities, such as a regular water supply and public lavatories, were also available.

Many of the new urban centers were completely dominated by Greeks while the native populations remained cut off from all civic institutions. The Greeks commissioned purely Greek sculpture, read literature of the classical period, and had separate law courts for themselves. Complaints caused by racial resentment have been recorded. An Egyptian camel-driver, for example, complained bitterly that he was not paid regularly because he did "not know how to behave like a Greek." Not only was it difficult for easterners to enter the ranks of the ruling class, but those who did so had to become thoroughly hellenized. This often required alienation from one's own culture and led to humiliating experiences.

The Greeks easily rationalized their political domination of easterners by believing in their own cultural superiority. But this control was also important because the kings frequently used the cities as instruments of government, enabling them to rule considerable territory without an extensive bureaucracy. At the same time, for security reasons, the Greeks needed the support of the kings. After all, the Hellenistic cities were islands of Greek culture in a sea of non-Greeks. The relationship between rulers and cities, therefore, was a symbiotic one that bore serious consequences for the cities.

In their political system, religious practices, and city architecture, the Greeks tried to recreate the *polis* of their homeland in their new cities. But it was no longer possible to do so. The new cities were not autonomous entities and soon found themselves dependent upon the power of the Hellenistic monarchies. Although the kings did not rule the cities directly, they restricted their freedom in other ways. Cities knew they could not conduct an independent foreign policy and did not try to do so. The kings also demanded tribute, which could be a heavy burden.

A noticeable feature of the Hellenistic cities was the increasing control of the rich over urban affairs. Alexander and his successors had encouraged the practice of democracy in both old and new Greek cities: all had a council, magistrates, and, most important, a popular assembly that enabled the people to exercise control over political life. But by 300 B.C., the wealthy citizens in Greek communities were using their money to ingratiate themselves with their communities and to make their

▼ **Model of the Acropolis at Pergamum.** The chief vehicle used for the spread of Greek culture throughout the Near East was the city. Both Alexander and the Hellenistic kings created a number of new cities and military settlements. These cities were dominated by Greeks and Macedonians, and their physical appearance was modeled on the Greek *poleis,* as is evident in this model of the Acropolis at Pergamum.

Athens Honors a Wealthy Citizen
▼ ▼ ▼

By 300 B.C., *wealthy citizens in Hellenistic cities were spending enormous sums of money on various contributions to their local communities. This patronage opened the door to increased political control by the rich over their communities. In this decree of 283/282 B.C., Athens bestows honors upon the poet Philippides for his beneficence.*

Decree of Athens in Honor of the Poet Philippides

Since Philippides has on every occasion continued to show his goodwill towards the people, and having gone abroad to King Lysimachus and having previously discussed the matter with the king, he brought back to the people a gift of 10,000 Attic measures of wheat for distribution to all the Athenians . . . for those who wished to serve in the army he obtained the right to enrol in separate formations with their own commanders, while to those who chose to leave he provided clothes and supplies from his own resources and sent them each to their chosen destination, more than 300 men altogether; and he also appealed for the release of all the Athenian citizens who had been placed in custody by Demetrius and Antigonus and were captured in Asia, and has constantly shown himself helpful to any Athenian who meets him and calls on his assistance; and after the people recovered its freedom [287 or 286] he has constantly spoken and acted in the interests of the city's safety, and urged the king to help with money and corn, so that the people may continue to be free and recover the Piraeus and the forts as soon as possible; . . . and when he was appointed agonothete [official who organized the city's competitions] in the archonship of Isaeus [284/283], he complied with the will of the people voluntarily from his own funds, offered the ancestral sacrifices to the gods on behalf of the people, . . . and supervised the other contests and sacrifices on behalf of the city and for all this he spent much money from his own private resources and rendered his accounts according to the laws, and he has never said or done anything contrary to the interests of the democracy. Therefore, so that it may be manifest to all that the people knows how to return adequate thanks to benefactors for the services they have performed, . . . the council resolves to praise Philippides . . . for his merits and the goodwill he constantly shows towards the people of Athens, and to crown him with a gold crown according to the law, and proclaim the crown at the tragic contest of the Great Dionysia; and to set up a bronze statue of him in the theatre, and to grant to him and for all time to the eldest of his descendants free meals in the prytaneum and a seat of honour in all the contests organised by the city.

---

communities dependent upon them (see the box above on page). Patronage by the wealthy was, of course, not a new practice in Greek cities, but it increased in both volume and frequency. Furthermore, it enabled the rich to dominate the magistracies with the acquiescence of the citizenry who expected further beneficence from the wealthy in exchange. By the third century B.C., the power of the magistrates and councils was surpassing that of the popular assemblies, a clear indication of a shift from democracy to oligarchy or the rule of a wealthy elite.

But the increasing power of the wealthy and the growing gap between rich and poor gave rise to class conflict and even calls for social revolution, usually couched in the familiar demands for the redistribution of land and the cancellation of debts. Such appeals were heard more frequently on the Greek mainland than in the rest of the Hellenistic world. But such appeals rarely led to successful revolutions, and Roman entry into the Hellenistic world put an end to them altogether. The Romans made it clear that they supported wealthy oligarchies at the expense of the poor.

The Greek cities of the Hellenistic era were the chief agents for the spread of Hellenic culture in the Near East, as far, in fact, as modern Afghanistan and India. These Greek cities were also remarkably vibrant despite their subordination to the Hellenistic monarchies and persisted in being a focal point for the loyalty of their citizens. Their continuing vitality is perhaps most evident on the Greek mainland where the Greek cities formed two important leagues, the Aetolian League in central Greece and the Achaean League in the Peloponnese. Both leagues concentrated their efforts on foreign policy, and neither was dominated by a single city as the Delian League had been by Athens and the Peloponnesian League by Sparta in the fifth century B.C. (see Chapter 3). One of the goals of the Achaean League, however, was to expel the Macedonians and restore the Greeks' "ancestral freedom." It succeeded only briefly, for time was running out on the viability of small cities. The Hellenistic monarchies had already demonstrated that they were more powerful than the cities, and the Romans were, after all, waiting in the wings.

Economic Trends

Agriculture was still of primary importance to both the native populations and the new Greek cities of the Hellenistic world. The Greek cities continued their old agrarian patterns. A well-defined citizen body owned land and worked it with the assistance of slaves. But these were isolated units in a vast area of land ultimately owned by the king or assigned to large estate owners and worked by native peasants dwelling in villages. There was little change, then, in agricultural patterns and no significant changes in methods of production.

There were some improvements, however. New irrigation canals were constructed, especially in Egypt where the Ptolemies were active in land reclamation. The irrigation of the Fayum in Egypt created a large expanse of land that was used primarily by the Greek settlers. Fully 50 percent of the villages that developed there had Greek names. New fruits and crops were also introduced. The Greeks were especially active in introducing grapevines and olive trees wherever they could.

Similarly, few new products or manufacturing methods were introduced in the Hellenistic world. The most famous invention was the "Archimedean screw," which was a mechanism used to pump water out of mines or into irrigation trenches. Many historians believe that the availability of cheap labor (especially slaves) worked against the invention of labor-saving machines. Most articles were produced by individual craftsmen or small-scale operations consisting of an owner and a few slaves. It should be noted, however, that both royal and city governments in the Hellenistic era also became involved in manufacturing as a state enterprise. In Egypt, the Ptolemies experimented with state factories for the production of oil and textiles. State factories at Pergamum produced textiles and parchment. Slaves were used as the chief source of labor in these factories. The city of Miletus owned textile factories worked by slaves and

became the center of the woolen industry in the Hellenistic world.

But although products and methods of production were much the same, the centers of manufacturing shifted significantly in the Hellenistic era. Industry spread from Greece to the East—especially to Asia Minor, Rhodes, and Egypt. New textile centers were set up at Pergamum, while glass and silver crafts were developed in Syria. And busiest of all cities in manufacturing was Alexandria in Egypt, which became the center for the production of parchment, textiles, linens, oil, metalwork, and glass.

Commerce experienced considerable expansion in the Hellenistic era. Indeed, it was trade that tied much of the Hellenistic world together. Increased commercial traffic was furthered by fewer political barriers. Although Hellenistic monarchs still fought wars, the conquests of Alexander and the policies of his successors made possible greater trade between east and west. Technical improvements were minor, but still helpful. Extensive work was done on harbors, especially the building of breakwaters to protect them. Manuals, such as On Harbors by Timosthenes, provided aid in navigation. While real improvements in roads would await the Romans, trade routes between east and west were facilitated by the Hellenistic kingdoms. Two major trade routes were used to connect the east with the Mediterranean world. The central route was the major one and led by sea from India to the Persian Gulf, up the Tigris River to Seleucia on the Tigris, which replaced Babylon as the center for waterborne traffic from the Persian Gulf and overland caravan routes as well. Overland routes from Seleucia then led to Antioch and Ephesus. A southern route wound its way from India by sea but went around Arabia and up the Red Sea to Petra or later Berenice. Caravan routes then led overland to Coptos on the Nile, thence to Alexandria and the Mediterranean.

An incredible variety of products were traded: gold and silver from Spain; tin from Cornwall and Brittany; iron from northern Armenia; salt from Asia Minor; balsam from Jericho; timber from Macedonia; purple dye from Tyre; ebony, gems, ivory, and spices from India; frankincense (used on altars) from Arabia; slaves from Thrace, Syria, and Asia Minor; silk from Cos; fine wines from Syria and western Asia Minor; olive oil from Athens; and numerous exquisite foodstuffs, such as the famous prunes of Damascus. The greatest trade, however, was in the basic staple of life—grain. The great exporting areas were Egypt, Sicily, and the Black Sea region, while Rhodes and Delos served as the major depots for the international grain trade.

Trade in the Hellenistic world was greatly facilitated by the development of a money economy in the East, a product of Alexander's conquests and the Greek colonization encouraged by the Seleucid dynasty. Alexander had confiscated enormous quantities of gold and silver from the Persian treasuries, much of which was coined or recoined in Greek mints for further circulation. The Alexander drachma was based on the Attic standard and came to be used in Macedonia, parts of Greece, Asia Minor, and the Seleucid kingdom. Although Egypt continued to use a Phoenician standard, the simplification of coinage to two basic international standards facilitated commercial activity. So too did the development of banks by states, cities, and private individuals, which took in money on deposit and provided loans for commercial enterprises.

▼ Hellenistic Society

One of the more noticeable features of social life in the Hellenistic world was the creation of new opportunities for women—at least, for upper-class women. No doubt this was related to the changes in Hellenistic society itself, since the subordination of the cities to the kings altered the way men related to their *polis* and to each other. Some historians maintain that the visible role of Hellenistic queens may also have created a different model for upper-class women.

New Opportunities for Upper-Class Women

The creation of the Hellenistic monarchies, which represented a considerable departure from the world of the city-state, gave new scope to the role played by the monarchs' wives, the Hellenistic queens. In Macedonia, a pattern of alliances between mothers and sons provided openings for women to take an active role in politics, especially in political intrigue. In Egypt, opportunities for royal women were even greater since the Ptolemaic rulers reverted back to an Egyptian custom of kings marrying their own sisters. Of the first eight Ptolemaic rulers, four wed their sisters. Ptolemy II and his sister-wife Arsinoë II were both worshiped as gods in their lifetimes. Arsinoë played an energetic role in government and was involved in the expansion of the Egyptian navy. She was also the first Egyptian queen whose portrait appeared on coins with her husband. Hellenistic queens also showed an intense interest in culture. They wrote poems, collected art, and corresponded with intellectuals.

But it is important to remember the limitations on the power of Hellenistic queens. In the final analysis, they were still largely dependent upon a male world for their status. Their power was usually derived from their position as regents for underage sons or as wives or mothers, especially if their husbands or sons were weak rulers. Moreover, the traditional pattern in which male guardians arranged marriages to further diplomatic and military alliances still continued. If it suited them, kings were not averse to ousting their queens for political reasons.

Of course, Hellenistic queens constituted only a very small number of women, but their status undoubtedly had some impact on the prestige of upper-class women in general. The most notable gains for upper-class women came in the economic area. Documents show increasing numbers of women involved in the management of slaves, the sale of property, and even the making of loans. Even then, legal contracts in which women were involved had to include their official male guardians, although in numerous instances these men no longer played an important function but were only listed to satisfy legal requirements. Only in Sparta were women completely free to control their own economic affairs. Many Spartan women were noticeably wealthy. It has been estimated that 40 percent of the Spartan land was owned by females. Some Spartan women even entered their racehorses in the competitions at the Olympic games, in part perhaps to make others aware of their affluence.

Spartan women, however, were an exception, especially on the Greek mainland. Women in Athens, for example, still remained highly restricted and supervised. Although a few philosophers, especially among the Epicureans, welcomed female participation in men's affairs, many philosophers rejected equality between men and women and asserted that the traditional roles of wives and mothers were most satisfying for women.

But the opinions of philosophers did not prevent upper-class women from making gains in areas other than the economic sphere. New possibilities for females arose when women in some areas of the Hellenistic world were allowed to pursue education in the traditional fields of literature, music, and even athletics. Education, then, provided new opportunities for women: female poets appeared again in the third century, and there are instances of women involved in both scholarly and artistic pursuits.

Some wealthy aristocratic women even became politically active in the running of their cities. In the second century B.C., a number of cities passed degrees honoring women for their services to their communities. Cyme, in Asia Minor, for example, paid homage to Archippe for her enormous financial contributions. In return, some women were given political rights and in a few instances were even allowed to hold office as city magistrates. But often economic motives were attached to this generosity. When Phile of Priene was made a magistrate of her city, it was probably with the understanding that she would donate funds for public works. Once in office, she did build an aqueduct and reservoir for the community.

In some areas of the Hellenistic world, especially outside Greece, gradual improvements were made in the legal status of Greek women, although one could hardly describe the changes as dramatic. In Egypt, for example, Greek women could petition the government or police without a guardian but still needed guardians for everything else. Married women's rights were expanded by contractual limitations on a husband's freedom for sexual activity outside the marriage. Some marriage contracts even provided equal opportunities for husbands and wives to divorce each other.

These improvements in the position of females were, of course, largely restricted to upper-class women. A harsher reality existed for a large group of women condemned to the practice of prostitution. The practice of infanticide or exposing unwanted children to die was one source of prostitutes. Inscriptional evidence indicates that small families were common in the Hellenistic world; boys were preferred and rarely was more than one daughter raised. Hence girls were more commonly subjected to infanticide. Some of these infants exposed to die were gathered up by eager entrepreneurs and raised to be slave prostitutes. Only the more beautiful and lucky prostitutes came to be the companions (the *hetairai*) of upper-class men.

Slavery

The Hellenistic world witnessed the migration of large numbers of people from one area to another. Greeks and Macedonians, of course, went into the Hellenistic kingdoms of the East as administrators, mercenaries, engineers, scholars, artists, teachers, and merchants. Moreover, significantly large numbers of non-Greeks moved around for economic and military purposes. But the largest number of uprooted people were slaves. Although statistics on slavery in antiquity are almost completely lacking, we do know that the number of slaves was significantly large while slavery itself was viewed as a normal part of life in the Hellenistic world and in antiquity in general.

Slaves were obtained from four chief sources: the children of slaves; children who were sold by their parents or abandoned to perish; persons kidnapped by pirates; and, perhaps the largest source of all, prisoners of war. Delos, a major trade center, could handle 10,000 slaves a day in

▼ **Two Women in Conversation.** This small statue, dating back to the second century B.C., depicts two women engaged in conversation. Many upper-class women became involved in managing their own economic affairs during the Hellenistic age, such as the handling of slaves and the sale of property. Some cities also offered education to women and allowed them to participate in the political activities of the city. These new privileges, however, were most often restricted to the women of the upper-class.

Treatment of Slaves in the Egyptian Gold Mines
▼▼▼

Slavery was a common practice throughout antiquity. In both classical Greece and the Hellenistic world, the worst-treated slaves were those who worked in the mines. The Egyptians were especially notorious for their treatment of slaves in the gold mines in Nubia, described in this account by Diodorus of Sicily who lived in the first century B.C. *His account was based on the now lost work of the second-century writer Agatharchides.*

Diodorus of Sicily, *Library of History*

And those who have been condemned in this way—and they are a great multitude and are all bound in chains—work at their task unceasingly both by day and throughout the entire night, enjoying no respite and being carefully cut off from any means of escape; since guards of foreign soldiers who speak a language different from theirs stand watch over them, so that not a man, either by conversation or by some contact of a friendly nature, is able to corrupt one of his keepers. . . . And the entire operations are in charge of a skilled worker who distinguishes the stone and points it out to the labourers; and of those who are assigned to this unfortunate task the physically strongest break the quartz-rock with iron hammers, applying no skill to the task, but only force, and cutting tunnels through the stone, not in a straight line but wherever the seam of gleaming rock may lead. Now these men, working in darkness as they do because of the bending and winding of the passages, carry lamps bound on their foreheads; and since much of the time they change the position of their bodies to follow the particular character of the stone they throw the blocks, as they cut them out, on the ground; and at this task they labour without ceasing beneath the sternness and blows of an overseer.

The boys there who have not yet come to maturity, entering through the tunnels into the galleries formed by the removal of the rock, laboriously gather up the rock as it is cast down piece by piece and carry it out into the open to the place outside the entrance. Then those who are above thirty years of age take this quarried stone from them and with iron pestles pound a specified amount of it in stone mortars, until they have worked it down to the size of a vetch. Thereupon the women and older men receive from them the rock of this size and cast it into mills of which a number stand there in a row, and taking their places in groups of two or three at the spoke or handle of each mill they grind it until they have worked down the amount given them to the consistency of the finest flour. And since no opportunity is afforded any of them to care for his body and they have no garment to cover their shame, no man can look upon the unfortunate wretches without feeling pity for them because of the exceeding hardships they suffer. For no leniency or respite of any kind is given to any man who is sick, or maimed, or aged, or in the case of a woman for her weakness, but all without exception are compelled by blows to persevere in their labours, until through ill-treatment they die in the midst of their tortures. Consequently the poor unfortunates believe, because their punishment is so excessively severe, that the future will always be more terrible than the present and therefore look forward to death as more to be desired than life.

its markets. Although slaves came from everywhere, Thracians and Syrians were most numerous. Slaves varied in price; Macedonians, Thracians, and Italians drew the highest prices.

Slaves were put to work in numerous ways in the Hellenistic world. States employed slaves as servants for government officials and in government-run industries, such as weaving. Most slaves were used in domestic service, farming, and mines, but the situation could vary from state to state. Egypt had no slave class in the countryside, nor was there much domestic slavery, except in Alexandria. But the Egyptians did use slave labor in state-run textile factories and made especially brutal use of them in mining operations (see the box above). Women were also sold as slaves to be concubines for Greek and Macedonian soldiers and civilians.

The effects of slavery could also be important. The employment of large numbers of slaves in the Hellenistic kingdoms added to the hellenizing process. Working in homes, farms, or factories created opportunities for slaves to absorb Greek ways. This is especially evident in the case of the slave-wives of Hellenistic soldiers.

Education

In the Hellenistic world, education underwent a significant transformation. In the classical period of Greek history, education had been largely left to private enterprise. Greek cities now began to supervise education in new ways. The Greek gymnasium, which had been primarily an athletic institution, evolved into a secondary school. The curriculum centered on music, physical exercise, and literature, especially the poetry of Homer. Wealthy individuals often provided the money for the schools and also specified how it should be spent. An inscription from the city of Teos in Asia Minor specified that Polythroos "gave 34,000 drachmas, . . . for there to be appointed each year . . . three grammar-masters to teach the boys and the girls; . . . for two gymnastics-masters to be appointed, . . . for a lyre—or harp—player to be appointed . . . he will teach music and lyre—or harp—playing to the children. . . ."[2]

Education was usually for upper-class male children, although as the above inscription makes clear, in some cities, such as Teos, schools were established for both boys and girls. An official known as a gymnasiarch served as the actual head of a gymnasium. Essentially, this was a civic position of considerable prestige. He was not paid and was expected to provide money for sacrifices, competitions, entertainment, and even school repairs. Many cities passed decrees awarding praise and a "gold crown" to the gymnasiarch for his "munificence towards the people." The educational year culminated with various musical, academic, and athletic contests in which students competed for the honor of having their names inscribed on a victory column.

Hellenistic kings also served as patrons of gymnasia, recognizing their importance in training youths who might serve later as administrators of the state. The institution of the gymnasium played a significant role in the diffusion of Greek culture throughout the Hellenistic world. Whether an upper-class Greek youth lived on the Greek mainland, in Alexandria, or in another city in the East, he could imbibe Greek culture and maintain that sense of superiority that characterized the Greek overlords of the Hellenistic kingdoms.

Medicine

The scientific foundations of medicine made considerable strides in the Hellenistic period, especially at Alexandria. This represents a continuation from the fifth century when Hippocrates, a contemporary of Socrates, is credited with having been the "first to separate medicine from philosophy" by stressing natural explanations and natural cures for disease. Herophilus and Erasistratus, both well-known physicians, were active in Alexandria in the first half of the third century B.C. Both were interested in anatomy and used dissection and vivisection (the dissection of living bodies) to expand their knowledge, or so the Roman author Celsus claimed:

> Moreover, as pains, and also various kinds of diseases, arise in the more internal parts, they hold that no one can apply remedies for these who is ignorant about the parts themselves; hence it becomes necessary to lay open the bodies of the dead and to scrutinize their viscera and intestines. They hold that Herophilus and Erasistratus did this in the best way by far, when they laid open men whilst alive—criminals received out of prison from the kings—and whilst these were still breathing, observed parts which beforehand nature had concealed, their position, color, shape, size, arrangement, hardness, softness, smoothness, relation, processes and depressions of each, and whether any part is inserted into or is received into another.[3]

Herophilus added significantly to the understanding of the brain, eye, liver, and the reproductive and nervous systems. Erasistratus made discoveries in the process of digestion, clarified the distinction between sensory and motor nerves, and theorized on the flow of blood through the veins without, however, arriving at an understanding of the circulation of the blood through the body. After these two, the reputation of Alexandrian doctors began to decline, and by the second century B.C., according to the historian Polybius, they were no longer to be trusted: "Not a few invalids indeed who had nothing serious the matter with them have before now come very near losing their lives by entrusting themselves to these physicians, impressed by their rhetorical powers."[4]

It would be misleading to think of medicine in the Hellenistic world only in terms of scientific advances. Alongside these developments, a wide range of alternative methods of healing continued to exist. These included magical practices, such as the use of amulets to cast off evil spirits, herbal remedies, and the healing powers of deities, especially those of Asclepius, the god of healing (see the box on p. 113).

▼ Hellenistic Culture

Although the Hellenistic kingdoms encompassed tremendous territorial areas and many diverse peoples, the Greeks provided a sense of unity as a result of the diffu-

Miraculous Cures

▼ ▼ ▼

Although all gods and goddesses were believed to have healing powers, special curative powers were attributed to Asclepius, the god of healing. A cult of supernatural healing came to be associated with him. Dreams that people experienced when they slept in a sanctuary dedicated to Asclepius supposedly had curative powers, as these texts demonstrate.

Texts on the Miraculous Cures at Epidaurus

A man with the fingers of his hand paralysed except for one came as a suppliant to the god, and when he saw the tablets in the sanctuary he would not believe the cures and was rather contemptuous of the inscriptions, but when he went to sleep he saw a vision: he thought that as he was playing dice below the sanctuary and was about to throw the dice, the god appeared, sprang on his hand and stretched out his fingers, and when the god moved away, the man thought he bent his hand and stretched out the fingers one by one, and when he had straightened them all out, the god asked him whether he still did not believe the inscriptions on the tablets in the sanctuary, and the man said he did. The god said: "Since previously you would not believe them, although they are not incredible, in future let [your name] be 'Incredulous.' " When day came he went away cured.

Ambrosia from Athens, blind in one eye. She came as a suppliant to the god, and as she walked about the sanctuary she ridiculed some of the cures as being incredible and impossible, that persons who were lame and blind should be restored to health merely by seeing a dream. But when she went to sleep she saw a vision: she thought the god was standing next to her and saying that he would restore her to health, but she must dedicate in the sanctuary as a reward a silver pig, as a memorial of her stupidity. Having said this he split open the diseased eye and poured in a medicine. When day came she went away cured.

---

sion of Greek culture throughout the Hellenistic world. The Hellenistic era was a period of considerable cultural accomplishment in many areas—literature, art, science, and philosophy. Although these achievements occurred throughout the Hellenistic world, certain centers, especially the great Hellenistic cities of Alexandria and Pergamum, stood out. In both cities, cultural developments were encouraged by the rulers themselves. Of course, the patronage of culture was not a new phenomenon, as the cities of classical Greece illustrate, but rich Hellenistic kings had considerably greater resources with which to make contributions to cultural life.

The Ptolemies in Egypt made Alexandria an especially important cultural center. The library became the largest in ancient times with over 500,000 scrolls. The museum (literally, "temple of the Muses") created a desirable environment for scholarly research. Alexandria became home to poets, writers, philosophers, and scientists—scholars of all kinds. The library encouraged the systematic study of language and literature. As a result of patronage from the Attalid dynasty, Pergamum, the greatest city in Asia Minor, also became a leading cultural center, which attracted both scholars and artists. Its library was second only to that of Alexandria.

Literature

The Hellenistic age produced an enormous quantity of literature, most of which has not survived. Literary talent was held in high esteem by Hellenistic monarchs who were inclined to subsidize literary people on a grand scale. The Ptolemaic rulers of Egypt were particularly lavish. The combination of their largess and the famous library drew a host of scholars and authors to Alexandria, including a circle of poets. Theocritus (c. 315–250 B.C.) was originally a native of the island of Sicily. He wrote "little poems" or idylls dealing with erotic themes, lovers' complaints, and, above all, pastoral themes expressing his love of nature and his appreciation of nature's beauties (see the box on p. 114). In writing short poems, Theocritus was following the advice of Greek literary scholars who argued that Homer could never by superseded and urged writers to stick to well-composed, short poems instead. But Apollonius of Rhodes (born c. 295 B.C.) ignored this advice and wrote an epic called the *Argonautica*, which recounts the story of Jason's search for the Golden Fleece. Although he was not a particularly good storyteller, Apollonius did write a remarkably sympathetic portrait of Medea's love for Jason: "Time and again

Little is known of the poet Theocritus (c. 315–250 B.C.). Born in Syracuse on the island of Sicily, he also lived in Miletus, Cos, and Alexandria. He is best known as the creator of pastoral idylls that portray his great love of nature. This selection is from the famous Seventh Idyll (called the "queen of pastorals"), which describes a delightful day on the island of Cos.

Theocritus, The Seventh Idyll

This I sang, and Lykidas laughed
again pleasantly, and gave me his stick
in fellowship of the Muses,
and turned left, taking the road
to Pyxa, but Eukritos
and handsome Amyntas and I
turned off at Phrasidamos's
and happily laid ourselves down
on beds of sweet grass and vine-leaves,
freshly picked. Overhead, many elms
and poplars rustled, and nearby
the sacred waters splashed down
from the Nymphs' cave. Brown cicadas
shrilled from the shady branches,
and far off the tree-frog whined
in the heavy underbrush.

Larks and finches sang, doves crooned,
and bees hummed about the spring.
Everything smelled of rich summer
and rich fruits. Pears lay at our feet,
apples in plenty rolled beside us,
and branches loaded down with plums
bent to the ground. And we broke
the four-year seals on the wine-jars.
Nymphs of Kastalia that live
on the slopes of Parnassos, tell me,
was it such a cup old Chiron
offered Herakles in Pholos'
rocky cave? Was it a drink like this
set Polyphemos dancing,
that mighty shepherd who grazed
his flocks beside the Anapos
and pelted ships with mountains—
such nectar as you mixed for us,
you Nymphs, that day by the altar
of Demeter of the Harvest?
May I plant the great winnowing-fan
another time in her grain-heaps,
while she stands and smiles at us
with wheat-sheaves and poppies in her hands.

she darted a bright glance at Jason. All else was forgotten. Her heart, brimful of this new agony, throbbed within her and overflowed with the sweetness of the pain. . . . Such was the fire of Love, stealthy but all-consuming, that swept through Medea's heart."[5]

In the Hellenistic era, Athens remained the theatrical center of the Greek world. While little remained of tragedy, a New Comedy developed, which completely rejected political themes and sought only to entertain and amuse. The Athenian playwright Menander (c. 342–291 B.C.) was perhaps the best representative of New Comedy. Plots were simple: typically, a hero falls in love with a not-really-so-bad prostitute who turns out eventually to be the long-lost daughter of a rich neighbor. The hero marries her and they live happily ever after. The strongest criticism of New Comedy was that it was not always very funny.

The Hellenistic period saw a great outpouring of historical and biographical literature. Much of it had a narrow focus, such as histories of Greek cities or districts. The chief historian of the Hellenistic age was Polybius (c. 203–c. 120 B.C.), a Greek who lived for some years in Rome. He is regarded by many historians as second only to Thucydides among Greek historians. His major work consisted of forty books narrating the history of the "inhabited Mediterranean world" from 221 to 146 B.C. Only the first five books are extant although long extracts from the rest of the books survive. His history focuses on the growth of Rome from a city-state to a world empire. It is apparent that Polybius understood the significance of the Romans' achievement. He followed Thucydides in seeking rational motives for historical events. He also had a well-developed critical sense in the use of sources and used firsthand accounts. In his eagerness to write accurately, he even undertook journeys to visit the sites of battles personally.

Another characteristic of the Hellenistic literary world was its interest in preserving the classical Greek authors. As we have seen, libraries were established to preserve manuscripts, but Hellenistic scholars also developed methods of scholarship for evaluating different versions of the same works in order to establish a standard text. At Alexandria, scholars established critical editions of the classical Greek poets, but the work that preoccupied them the most was the scholarly examination of Homer. Scholars also wrote detailed commentaries on the thought and language of older authors. All in all, Hellenistic scholars established basic guidelines for the systematic study of language and literature.

Art

The founding of new cities and the rebuilding of old ones provided numerous opportunities for Greek architects and sculptors. The Hellenistic monarchs were particularly eager to spend their money to beautify and adorn the cities within their states. Hellenistic architects laid out their new cities on the rectilinear grid model first used by Hippodamus of Miletus in the fifth century B.C. The buildings of the Greek homeland—gymnasia, baths, theaters, and, of course, temples—lined the streets of these cities. Most noticeable in the construction of temples was the use of the more ornate Corinthian order (see Chapter 3), which became especially popular during the Hellenistic era.

Sculptors were patronized by Hellenistic kings and rich citizens. Thousands of statues, many paid for by the people honored, were erected in towns and cities all over the Hellenistic world. Hellenistic sculptors traveled throughout this world, attracted by the material rewards offered by wealthy patrons. As a result, although distinct styles developed in Alexandria, Rhodes, and Pergamum, Hellenistic sculpture was characterized by a considerable degree of uniformity. While maintaining the technical skill of the classical period, Hellenistic sculptors moved away from the idealism of fifth-century classicism to a more emotional and realistic art, seen in numerous statues of old women, drunks, and little children at play. The interest in realism also produced excellent portraits, especially of rulers on coins.

Science

The Hellenistic era witnessed a more conscious separation of science from philosophy. In classical Greece, what we would call the physical and life sciences had been divisions of philosophical inquiry. Nevertheless, the Greeks, by the time of Aristotle, had already estab-

▼ **Old Market Woman.** Greek architects and sculptors were highly valued throughout the Hellenistic world, as kings undertook projects to beautify the cities within their lands. The sculptors of this period no longer tried to capture ideal beauty in their sculpture, a quest that characterized Greek classicism, but moved towards a more emotional and realistic art. This statue of an old market woman is typical of this new trend in art, a trend that also immortalized wealthy citizens and children at play.

lished an important principle of scientific investigation, empirical research or systematic observation as the basis for generalization. In the Hellenistic age, the sciences tended to be studied in their own right. While Athens remained the philosophical center, Alexandria and Pergamum, the two leading cultural centers of the Hellenistic world, played a significant role in the development of Hellenistic science. Alexandria, in particular, with its library and museum, provided a focus for these activities.

One of the traditional areas of Greek science was astronomy, and two Alexandrian scholars continued this exploration. Aristarchus of Samos (c. 310–230 B.C.) authored a work on the sizes and distances from earth of

▼ **Aphrodite of Milos (Venus de Milo).** Discovered in 1820 on the island of Milos, this statue represents the Greek goddess Aphrodite (the Roman Venus) and is modeled after a type of Greek female nude that goes back to the fourth century B.C. However, this second or first century B.C. statue, with its soft body and stylized elegance, reflects the emphasis on sensuality found in the sculpture of the late Hellenistic period.

the sun and moon and also presented a heliocentric view of the universe; that is, that the sun and the fixed stars remain stationary while the earth rotates around the sun in a circular orbit. He also argued that the earth rotates around its own axis. This view was not widely accepted, and most scholars clung to the earlier geocentric view of the Greeks, which held that the earth was at the center of the universe. Some Hellenistic theorists developed complicated schemes of epicycles (circular orbits within circular orbits) and eccentric circles to make the geocentric theory work.

Another Alexandrian astronomical scholar was Eratosthenes (c. 275–194 B.C.). Eratosthenes became head of the library at Alexandria and was active in many disciplines, writing works on poetry, philosophy, mathematics, and the history of comedy. His most interesting achievement, however, was his calculation of the earth's circumference by the use of simple geometry. He arrived at a figure of 24,675 miles, an estimate that was within 200 miles of the actual figure. Eratosthenes also proposed that the oceans constituted a single body of water and that Europe, Asia, and Africa formed a single large island. He wrote a handbook of geography that one historian has labeled "the first scientific description of the world."

A third Alexandrian scholar was Euclid, who lived around 300 B.C. He established a school in Alexandria but is primarily known for his work entitled the *Elements.* This was a systematic organization of the fundamental elements of geometry as they had already been worked out and became the standard textbook of plane geometry, used up to modern times.

By far the most famous of the scientists of the Hellenistic period, Archimedes of Syracuse (287–212 B.C.), came from the western Mediterranean region. Archimedes was especially important for his work on the geometry of spheres and cylinders, for establishing the value of the mathematical constant pi, and for creating the science of hydrostatics. Archimedes was also a practical inventor. It was he who may have devised the so-called Archimedean screw used to pump water out of mines and to lift irrigation water as well as a compound pulley for transporting heavy weights. During the Roman siege of his native city of Syracuse, he constructed a number of devices to thwart the attackers. According to Plutarch's account, the Romans became so frightened "that if they did but see a little rope or a piece of wood from the wall, instantly crying out, that there it was again, Archimedes was about to let fly some engine at them, they turned their backs and fled."[6] Archimedes' accomplishments inspired a wealth of semilegendary stories. Supposedly, he discovered specific gravity by observing the water he displaced in his bath and became so excited by his realization that he jumped out of the water and ran home naked, shouting, "Eureka" ("I have found it"). He is said to have emphasized the importance of levers by proclaiming to the king of Syracuse: "Give me a place to stand on and I will move the earth." The king was so impressed that he encouraged Archimedes to lower his sights and build defensive weapons instead.

Historians have observed that most Hellenistic scientists made little effort to translate their abstract scientific knowledge into applied technology or the creation of labor-saving devices. Many have argued that cheap labor, whether slave or low-paid free men and women, provided no incentive for creating labor-saving devices. Others have pointed to the contempt that upper-class Greeks (who, after all, had the leisure to be scientists and philosophers) had for manual labor and crafts. The ancient author Plutarch expressed the belief that even Archimedes himself shared this attitude:

> Yet Archimedes possessed so high a spirit, so profound a soul, and such treasures of scientific knowledge, that though these inventions had now obtained him the renown of more than human sagacity, he yet would not deign to leave behind him any commentary or writing on such subjects; but, repudiating as sordid and ignoble the whole trade of engineering, and every sort of art that lends itself to mere use and profit, he placed his whole affection and ambition in those purer speculations where there can be no reference to the vulgar needs of life. . . .[7]

Regardless of the reasons for the failure to develop a technological revolution, there was one field in which practical applications of scientific knowledge were encouraged: military science. The Hellenistic kings were quite ready to employ military technicians to work on siege towers, grappling-engines, and new forms of catapults.

Philosophy

While Alexandria and Pergamum became the renowned cultural centers of the Hellenistic world, Athens remained the prime center for philosophy. After Alexander the Great, the home of Socrates, Plato, and Aristotle continued to attract the most illustrious philosophers from the Greek world who chose to establish their schools there. While Plato's Academy and Aristotle's Lyceum continued to exist and attract some students, new schools of philosophical thought (the Epicureans and Stoics) reinforced Athens' reputation as a philosophical center.

Epicurus (341–270 B.C.), the founder of Epicureanism, established a school in Athens near the end of the fourth century B.C. Epicurus's famous belief in a doctrine of "pleasure" began with his view of the world. While he did not eliminate the gods from existence, he did not believe they played any active role in the world. The universe ran on its own. This left human beings free to follow self-interest as a basic motivating force. Happiness was the goal of life, and the means to achieve it was the pursuit of pleasure, the only true good. But the pursuit of pleasure was not meant in a physical, hedonistic sense:

> When, therefore, we maintain that pleasure is the end, we do not mean the pleasures of profligates and those that consist in sensuality, as is supposed by some who are either ignorant or disagree with us or do not understand, but freedom from pain in the body and from trouble in the mind. For it is not continuous drinkings and revellings, nor the satisfaction of lusts, nor the enjoyment of fish and other luxuries of the wealthy table, which produce a pleasant life, but sober reasoning, searching out the motives for all choice and avoidance, and banishing mere opinions, to which are due the greatest disturbance of the spirit.

▼ **Portrait of Epicurus.** Epicurus was the founder of the Epicurean school of philosophy, which grew very popular during the Hellenistic period. He maintained an "atomic" theory of the universe—that the only things that exist are atoms moving through the void—and an ethical theory based upon the pursuit of pleasure. By pleasure, Epicurus understood the absence of physical and mental pain and discomfort. By pursuing such pleasure, the Epicureans believed, happiness could be attained.

Pleasure was not satisfying one's desire in an active, gluttonous fashion. Luxury and self-indulgence, after all, led to physical discomfort and to additional desires that disturbed one's peace. Pleasure was freedom from emotional turmoil, freedom from worry, the freedom that came from a mind at rest. To achieve this passive pleasure, one had to free oneself from public activity: "We must release ourselves from the prison of affairs and politics." They were too strenuous to give peace of mind. But this was not a renunciation of all social life, for to Epicurus, a complete life could only exist when it was centered on the basic ideal of friendship: "Of all the things which wisdom acquires to produce the blessedness of the complete life, far the greatest is the possession of friendship."[8] Epicurus's own life in Athens was an embodiment of his teachings. He and his family created their own private community where they could pursue their ideal of true happiness.

Epicureanism was eventually overshadowed by another school of thought known as Stoicism, which became the most popular philosophy of the Hellenistic world and later flourished in the Roman Empire as well. It was the product of a teacher named Zeno (335–263 B.C.), who came to Athens and began to teach in a public colonnade known as the Painted Portico (the *Stoa Poikile*—hence Stoicism). Like Epicureanism, Stoicism was concerned with how individuals find happiness. But Stoics took a radically different approach to the problem. To them, happiness, the supreme good, could be found only in virtue, which meant essentially living in harmony with the will of God: "And this very thing constitutes the virtue of the happy man and the smooth current of life, when all actions promote the harmony of the spirit dwelling in the individual man with the will of him who orders the universe."[9] One achieved happiness by choosing to follow the will of God through the free exercise of one's own will. To the Stoics, the will of God was the same thing as the will of nature since nature was simply a manifestation or expression of God. "Living according to nature," therefore, meant following the will of God or the natural laws that God established to run the universe.

Virtuous living, then, was living in accordance with the laws of nature or submitting to the will of God (see the box on p. 119). This led to the acceptance of whatever one received in life since God's will for us was by its very nature good. By accepting God's law, people mastered themselves and gained inner peace. Life's problems could not disturb such individuals, and they could bear whatever life offered (hence our word "stoic"). The Stoics did not believe that it was difficult to know the will

of God. This knowledge could be derived through the senses, or what the Stoics called the "perception conveying direct apprehension." Sense perceptions of overwhelming strength had to be a revelation of God's standards.

Unlike Epicureans, Stoics did not believe in the need to separate oneself from the world and politics. Public service was regarded as noble. The real Stoic was a good citizen and could even be a good government official. Since Stoics believed that a divine principle was present throughout the universe, each human being also contained a divine spark. This led to a belief in the oneness of humanity. The world constituted a single society of equal human beings. Although not equal in the outer world, the divine spark in each meant that all were free to follow God's will (what was best for each individual). All persons then, even slaves, though unfree in body, were equal at the level of the soul.

Epicureanism and especially Stoicism appealed to large numbers of people in the Hellenistic world. Both of these philosophies focused primarily on the problem of human happiness. Their popularity would suggest a fundamental change in the character of the Greek lifestyle. In the classical Greek world, the happiness of individuals and the meaning of life were closely associated with the life of the *polis*. One found fulfillment within the community. In the Hellenistic kingdoms, although the *polis* continued to exist, the sense that one could find satisfaction and fulfillment through life in the *polis* had weakened. Not only did individuals seek new philosophies that offered personal happiness, but in the cosmopolitan world of the Hellenistic states with their mixtures of peoples, a new openness to thoughts of universality could also emerge. For some people, Stoicism embodied this larger sense of community. The appeal of new philosophies in the Hellenistic era can also be explained by the apparent decline in certain aspects of traditional religion, which we can see by examining the status of Hellenistic religion.

▼ Religion in the Hellenistic World

The spread of Greek civilization to the Hellenistic kingdoms of the Near East made an impact on Greek religion, but not necessarily to the advantage of the Greeks. In religious life, the Greeks took more from the Near East than they gave. When the Greeks spread throughout the Hellenistic kingdoms, they took their gods with them. While the construction of temples may have been less important than in classical times, there

The Stoic Ideal of Harmony with God
▼ ▼ ▼

The Stoic Cleanthes (331–232 B.C.) succeeded Zeno as head of this school of philosophy. One historian of Hellenistic civilization has called this work by Cleanthes the greatest religious hymn in Greek literature. Certainly, it demonstrates that Stoicism, unlike Epicureanism, did have an underlying spiritual foundation. This poem has been compared to the great psalms of the Hebrews.

Cleanthes, Hymn to Zeus

Nothing occurs on the earth apart from you, O God,
nor in the heavenly regions nor on the sea,
except what bad men do in their folly;
but you know to make the odd even,
and to harmonize what is dissonant; to you the alien is akin.
And so you have wrought together into one all things that are good and bad,
So that there arises one eternal logos [rationale] of all things,
Which all bad mortals shun and ignore,
Unhappy wretches, ever seeking the possession of good things
They neither see nor hear the universal law of God,
By obeying which they might enjoy a happy life.

were still many demonstrations of a lively religious faith. Hellenistic cities increased the number of public festivals and celebrated them with great magnificence. The priesthoods tied to the civic cults were still desirable to the leading citizens who competed to purchase these offices. But over a period of time, there was a noticeable decline in the vitality of the traditional Greek Olympian religion. Much of Greek religion had always revolved around ritual, but the civic cults based on the traditional gods no longer seemed sufficient to satisfy people's emotional needs. Then, too, the breakdown of the old commitment to the *polis* brought insecurity and changes that the civic cults, tied to the traditional Greek *polis*, seemed unable to meet. The spread of ruler cults was yet another sign of the weakening of the traditional Greek civic cults.

The Hellenistic kings who established themselves after Alexander were eager to buttress their power by religious support. The new royal families all embraced a traditional Greek Olympian god or goddess as a protector. The Antigonid dynasty of Macedonia asserted that they were descendants of the demigod Heracles. While the Seleucids of Syria adopted Apollo and the Attalids Athena as their "ancestors," the Egyptian Ptolemies dedicated themselves to the cult of Dionysus.

But the cults of these patron gods were soon overshadowed by ruler cults devoted to the worship of the Hellenistic kings themselves, both dead and living, as gods. Although there are earlier isolated examples of such a practice among the Greeks, Alexander's success, combined with the traditions of the Near East where god

kings were not unknown, inspired the widespread institution of such cults in the Hellenistic kingdoms. Ptolemy I of Egypt had created a cult of Alexander by 285 B.C. and was himself proclaimed a god by his son upon his death in 283 B.C. Later, the Ptolemies added their own names to the official cult while still alive. The divinization of living Seleucids did not take place until the end of the third century, while the Attalids of Pergamum were never acknowledged as divine while alive. The Antigonids refused to be gods, whether dead or alive. As their founders intended, the ruler cults added to the authority and legitimacy of the Hellenistic dynasties.

Greek cities on the mainland likewise instituted religious cults dedicated to living rulers. In fact, they seemed particularly eager to pay homage to rulers who could affect their lives, thus demonstrating the close relationship between political and religious motivations in the establishment of ruler cults. Indeed, the Athenians sang the following hymn to honor Demetrius, the king of Macedonia:

> Something august he seems, all his friends about him, and he himself in their midst, his friends the stars, even as he is the sun. O son of the most mighty god Poseidon and of Aphrodite, hail! For other gods are either far away, or have not ears, or are not, or heed us not at all; but you we can see in very presence, not in wood and not in stone, but in truth. And so we pray to you.[10]

One wonders what the hymn really meant to people since it expresses doubts about the efficacy of the traditional gods.

▼ **Seleucus Relief from Dura-Europa.** This relief was found at the small town of Dura-Europa located near the Euphrates River, a town founded by Seleucus Nicator, first ruler of the Seleucid empire. Seleucus was worshiped as a god by the people of this town, an instance of the growth of ruler-cults in the Hellenistic world. The ruler-cults centered around the worship of the Hellenistic kings themselves, proclaimed gods either during their life or after death. The ruler-cults had a distinct political effect, adding both authority and legitimacy to the ruling dynasties of the Hellenistic world. This relief depicts Seleucus Nicator.

The decline in traditional Greek religion left the Greeks receptive to the numerous religious cults of the eastern world. The Greeks were always tolerant of other existing religious institutions. Hence in the Hellenistic cities of the Near East, the traditional civic cults of their own gods, ruler cults, and foreign cults existed side by side. Alexandria had cults of the traditional Greek gods, Alexander and the Ptolemies, Egyptian deities, such as Isis and Horus, the Babylonian Astarte, and the Syrian Atargatis. This medley of cults existed in Greek cities everywhere, whether large or small. While the Greeks maintained their own cults out of pride, at the same time there was a movement toward syncretism or the fusing of one god with another as a manifestation of different forms of the same underlying divine force. Moreover, the strongest appeal of eastern religions to the Greeks came from the mystery religions. What was the source of their attraction?

The normal forms of religious worship in Hellenistic communities had lost some of their appeal. Ruler cults and patron gods could obviously be viewed as politically motivated. The practices of traditional, ritualized Greek religion in the civic cults seemed increasingly meaningless. For many people, the search for personal meaning remained unfulfilled. People sought alternatives. Among educated Greeks, the philosophies of Epicureanism and especially Stoicism offered help. Another source of solace came in the form of mystery religions. Their popularity speaks volumes about the spiritual needs of Hellenistic Greeks.

Mystery cults, with their secret initiations and promises of individual salvation, were, of course, not new to the Greek world; we have already seen the Eleusinian mysteries in Attica, for example (see Chapter 3). But the Greeks were also strongly influenced by eastern mystery cults, such as those of Egypt, which offered a distinct advantage over the Greek mystery religions. The latter had usually been connected to specific locations (such as Eleusis), which meant that a would-be initiate had to undertake a pilgrimage in order to participate in the rites. In contrast, the eastern mystery religions were readily available since temples to their gods and goddesses were located throughout the Greek cities of the east.

All of the mystery religions were based on the same fundamental premises. Individuals could pursue a path to salvation and the achievement of eternal life by being initiated into a union with a savior god or goddess who had died and risen again. The ritual of initiation, by which the seeker identified with the god or goddess, was, no doubt, a highly emotional experience.

The Egyptian cults of Isis and Serapis were the most popular of the mystery religions. The cult of Isis was very ancient, but became truly universal in Hellenistic times, as seen in this inscription from one of her Egyptian temples: "The Syrians call her Astarte, Artemis, and Anaia; . . . the Thracians, the Mother of the Gods; the Greeks, Hera of the mighty throne, and Aphrodite, good Hestia, Rheia, and Demeter; the Egyptians Thiouis, for you alone are all the other goddesses named by the nations."[11] Isis was the goddess of women, marriage, and children, as one of her hymns states: "I am she whom women call goddess. I ordained that women should be loved by men: I brought wife and husband together, and invented the marriage contract. I ordained that women should bear children. . . ."[12] Isis was portrayed as the giver of civilization who had brought laws and letters to all humankind. The cult of Serapis emerged during the reign of the first Ptolemaic rulers of Egypt. The worship of Serapis was centered in Alexandria, but he also became a universal deity whose worship spread throughout the Hellenistic world. The cults of both Isis and Serapis offered a precious commodity to their initiates—the promise of eternal life. In many ways, the mystery religions of the Hellenistic era helped to pave the way for the coming and the success of Christianity (see Chapter 6).

There were other spiritual manifestations in the Hellenistic era as well. Some people spoke of *Tyche* or Fortune as a deified force that affected lives. Others became involved in the practice of astrology, which proved to be highly popular in the Hellenistic era. Although influenced by Babylonian astronomy, astrology as an organized system was a product of Hellenistic times. The first astrological handbooks appeared in Ptolemaic Egypt in the second century B.C. Astrology was considered a spiritual science by its practitioners, who adhered to the Greek belief that the heavens operated in a regular and predictable fashion. Future events could be foretold by an understanding of heavenly movements ("as above, so below"), and the lives of individuals were affected by the position of the planets and heavenly constellations at the time of their birth. Since astrologers believed their system was a product of divine wisdom, astrology could and did serve as a substitute for religion. The Stoics found much value in astrology, and some of the Alexandrian scientists, such as Hipparchus and Poseidonius, found nothing incompatible in their interests in both astrology and astronomy.

The Jews in the Hellenistic World

In observing the similarities among their gods and goddesses, Greeks and easterners tended to assume they were the same beings with different names, giving rise to a process of syncretism. But a special position was occupied in the Hellenistic world by the Hebrews, whose monotheistic religion was exclusive and did not permit this kind of fusion of spiritual beings.

The Jewish kingdom of Judaea was ruled by the Ptolemies until it fell under the control of the Seleucids by 200 B.C. Initially, this led to little change. There was some inclination to hellenization, but also a strong reaction against it that led to greater Jewish orthodoxy. In the reign of the Seleucid king Antiochus IV (175–163 B.C.), conflict erupted in Judaea. Hellenistic monarchs were generally tolerant of all religions, but problems with Rome caused Antiochus to seek a kingdom more unified in culture and religion. When he sent troops to Jerusalem and seized the Temple, an uprising led by Judas Maccabaeus took place (164 B.C.) that led to the recapture of the Temple. Although the conflict continued, the Seleucids ultimately made concessions and allowed the Jews considerable freedom.

But since the Diaspora (see Chapter 2), large numbers of Jews no longer lived in Judaea. There was a large Jewish population in Egypt, particularly in Alexandria, as well as Jewish settlements throughout the cities of Asia Minor and Syria. In each city, Jews generally set up a synagogue and formed a private association for worship as other foreigners did. But Jews were also allowed by some city authorities to form a *politeuma* or political corporation that gave them greater rights than other resident aliens. Most importantly, they gained the privilege to live by their own laws and their own judicial system. The Jews were not really interested in citizenship in the cities in which they resided since full citizenship meant worship of the city's gods, an anathema to Jews who believed only in Yahweh.

Residence in Greek cities did lead to some hellenization of the Jews. Some abandoned Hebrew for the Greek language. In Alexandria, this led to the translation of the Old Testament from Hebrew to Greek (this Greek version is known as the Septuagint). Services in some synagogues were held in Greek. A number of Jews also took Greek names. However, most Jews accepted only the forms, not the substance of Greek life. They clung to their Hebrew religion and were never really integrated into the hellenized world.

Although historians used to view the Hellenistic era as a period of stagnation after the brilliant Greek civilization of the fifth century B.C., our survey of the Hellenistic world has shown the weakness of that position. The Hellenistic period was, in its own way, a vibrant one. New cities arose and flourished. New philosophical ideas captured the minds of many. Significant achievements were made in art, literature, and science. Greek culture spread throughout the Near East and made an impact wherever it was carried. But serious problems remained. Hellenistic kings continued to engage in inconclusive wars. The gulf between rich and poor was indeed great. Much of the formal culture was the special preserve of the Greek conquerors whose attitude of superiority kept them largely separated from the native masses of the Hellenistic kingdoms. Although the Hellenistic world achieved a degree of political stability, by the late third century B.C. signs of decline were beginning to multiply. Some of the more farsighted perhaps realized the danger presented to the Hellenistic world by the growing power of Rome. The Romans would ultimately inherit Alexander's empire, and we must now turn to them and try to understand what made them such successful conquerors.

Notes

1. Polybius, *The Histories*, trans. W. R. Paton (Cambridge, Mass., 1960), XVIII, 37, 8–10.

2. Roger S. Bagnall and Peter Derow, *Greek Historical Documents: The Hellenistic Period* (Chico, Calif., 1981), p. 113.

3. Celsus, *De Medicina*, trans. W. G. Spencer (Cambridge, Mass., 1935), Prooemium 23–24.

4. Polybius, *The Histories*, XII, 25d, 5.

5. Apollonius of Rhodes, *The Voyage of Argo*, trans. E. V. Rieu (Baltimore, 1959), p. 117.

6. Plutarch, *Life of Marcellus*, trans. John Dryden (New York, n.d.), p. 378.

7. Ibid.

8. *Epicurus: The Extant Remains*, trans. Cyril Bailey (Oxford, 1926), pp. (in order of quotations) 89–91, 115, 101.

9. Diogenes Laertius, *Life of Zeno*, vol. 2, trans. R. D. Hicks (London, 1925), p. 195.

10. Athenaeus, *The Deipnosophistae*, trans. Charles B. Gulick (Cambridge, Mass., 1929), VI, 253d–e.

11. Quoted in C. Bradford Welles, *Alexander and the Hellenistic World* (Toronto, 1970), p. 197.

12. Quoted in W. W. Tarn, *Hellenistic Civilization* (London, 1930), p. 324.

Suggestions for Further Reading

For a general introduction to the Hellenistic era, see J. Boardman, J. Griffin, and O. Murray, eds., *The Oxford History of the Classical World* (Oxford, 1986), pp. 315–85. A brief, but excellent guide to recent trends in scholarship on the Hellenistic era can be found in C. Starr, *Past and Future in Ancient History* (Lanham, Md., 1987), pp. 19–32. The best general survey is F. W. Walbank, *The Hellenistic World* (London, 1981). A solid study is C. B. Welles, *Alexander and the Hellenistic World* (Toronto, 1970). Older, but substantial works include M. Cary, *A History of the Greek World from 323 to 146 B.C.*, 2d ed. (London, 1963), heavily political in its coverage; and W. W. Tarn and G. T. Griffith, *Hellenistic Civilisation*, 3d ed. (London, 1952). There are good collections of sources in translation in M. M. Austin, *The Hellenistic World from Alexander to the Roman Conquest* (Cambridge, 1981); R. S. Bagnall and P. Derow, *Greek Historical Documents: The Hellenistic Period* (Chico, Calif., 1981); and S. M. Burstein, *The Hellenistic Age from the Battle of Ipsos to the Death of Kleopatra VII* (Cambridge, 1985).

For a good introduction to the early history of Macedonia, see E. N. Borza, *In the Shadow of Olympus: The Emergence of Macedon* (Princeton, N.J., 1990). Philip of Macedon is covered well in G. L. Cawkwell, *Philip of Macedon* (London, 1978); and N. Hammond and G. Griffith, *A History of Macedonia*, vol. 2, 550–336 B.C. (Oxford, 1979). There are considerable differences of opinion on Alexander the Great. The best biographies

include R. L. Fox, *Alexander the Great* (London, 1973); and J. R. Hamilton, *Alexander the Great* (London, 1973). See also P. Green, *Alexander the Great* (London, 1970); G. T. Griffith, *Alexander the Great, the Main Problems* (Cambridge, 1966), for a collection of articles on Alexander by different authors; and the older biographies by W. W. Tarn, *Alexander the Great* (Cambridge, 1948); and U. Wilcken, *Alexander the Great*, intro. and notes by E. N. Borza (New York, 1967).

Studies on the different Hellenistic monarchies include N. G. L. Hammond and F. W. Walbank, *A History of Macedonia*, vol. 3, 336–167 B.C. (Oxford, 1988); H. I. Bell, *Egypt from Alexander the Great to the Arab Conquest* (Oxford, 1948); G. M. Cohen, *The Seleucid Colonies* (Wiesbaden, 1978); E. V. Hansen, *The Attalids of Pergamum*, 2d ed. (Ithaca, N.Y., 1971); R. E. Allen, *The Attalid Kingdom* (Oxford, 1983); and O. Morkholm, *Antiochus IV of Syria* (Copenhagen, 1966) on one of the Seleucid rulers. On the theory of Hellenistic kingship, see G. J. D. Aalders, *Political Thought in Hellenistic Times* (Amsterdam, 1975). The limits of Hellenization are discussed in A. D. Momigliano, *Alien Wisdom: The Limits of Hellenization* (Cambridge, 1975); S. K. Eddy, *The King Is Dead: Studies in the Near Eastern Resistance to Hellenism 334–31 B.C.* (Lincoln, Neb., 1961); M. Hengel, *Judaism and Hellenism* (London, 1974); and V. Tcherikover, *Hellenistic Civilization and the Jews* (Philadelphia, 1959). On Hellenistic military developments, see W. W. Tarn, *Hellenistic Military and Naval Developments* (Cambridge,

1930); G. T. Griffith, *Mercenaries of the Hellenistic World* (Cambridge, 1935); and B. Bar-Kochva, *The Seleucid Army* (Cambridge, 1976). The problems of piracy is covered in H. A. Ormerod, *Piracy in the Ancient World* (Liverpool, 1924).

A good survey of Hellenistic cities can be found in A. H. M. Jones, *The Greek City from Alexander to Justinian* (Oxford, 1940). Alexandria is covered in P. M. Fraser, *Ptolemaic Alexandria* (Oxford, 1972). On the contributions of the rich to their cities, see A. R. Hands, *Charities and Social Aid in Greece and Rome* (London, 1968). On economic and social trends, see M. I. Finley, *The Ancient Economy*, 2d ed. (London, 1985); and the classic and still indispensable M. I. Rostovtzeff, *Social and Economic History of the Hellenistic World*, 3 vols., 2d ed. (Oxford, 1953).

Hellenistic women are examined in two works by S. B. Pomeroy, *Goddesses, Whores, Wives, and Slaves* (New York, 1975), pp. 120–48, and *Women in Hellenistic Egypt* (New York, 1984). Slavery is examined in W. L. Westermann, *The Slave-Systems of Greek and Roman Antiquity* (Philadelphia, 1955). The classic work on education is H. I. Marrou, *A History of Education in Antiquity* (London, 1956).

For a general introduction to Hellenistic culture, see M. Hadas, *Hellenistic Culture: Fusion and Diffusion* (New York, 1959). The best general survey of Hellenistic philosophy is A. A. Long, *Hellenistic Philosophy: Stoics, Epicureans, Skeptics*, 2d ed. (London, 1986). A superb work on Hellenistic science is G. E. R. Lloyd, *Greek Science after Aristotle* (London, 1973). A good survey of Hellenistic literature is A. Lesky, *A History of Greek Literature* (London, 1966), pp. 642–806.

On various facets of Hellenistic religion, see H. I. Bell, *Cults and Creeds in Graeco-Roman Egypt* (Liverpool, 1954); A. D. Nock, *Conversion* (Oxford, 1933); and R. E. Witt, *Isis in the Graeco-Roman World* (London, 1971). There is a collection of sources in translation in F. C. Grant, *Hellenistic Religions: The Age of Syncretism* (New York, 1953). The best introduction to astrology is now S. J. Tester, *A History of Western Astrology* (Wolfeboro, N.H., 1987).

On the entry of Rome into the Hellenistic world, see the basic work by E. S. Gruen, *The Hellenistic World and the Coming of Rome*, 2 vols. (Berkeley, 1984).

Chapter 5

The Roman Republic

▼▼▼▼▼

I n the first millennium B.C., a group of Latin-speaking people known as the Romans established a small community on a plain called Latium on the Italian peninsula. Rome was merely one of numerous Latin-speaking communities in Latium, and these, in turn, constituted only some of the many peoples in Italy. Roman history is basically the story of the Romans' conquest of the plain of Latium, then Italy, and finally the entire Mediterranean world. Why were the Romans able to do this? Scholars do not really know all the answers. The Romans made the right decisions at the right time, which is to say, the Romans were a people distinguished by a high degree of political wisdom.

The Romans were also a practical people. Unlike the Greeks, who reserved their citizenship for small, select groups, the Romans offered their citizenship to the peoples they conquered, thus laying the basis for a strong, integrated empire. The Romans knew that they were inferior to the Greeks in the intellectual sphere and did not hesitate to borrow ideas and culture from them. Roman strength lay in government, law, and engineering. The Romans knew how to govern people, establish legal structures, and construct the roads that took them to the ends of the known world. Throughout their empire, they carried their law, their political institutions, their engineering skills, and their Latin language. And even after the Romans were gone, those same gifts continued to play an important role in the continuing saga of Western civilization.

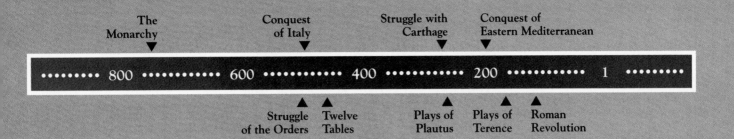

The Monarchy

Conquest of Italy

Struggle with Carthage

Conquest of Eastern Mediterranean

800 • 600 • 400 • 200 • 1

Struggle of the Orders

Twelve Tables

Plays of Plautus

Plays of Terence

Roman Revolution

▼ Early Rome and the Etruscans

There is still considerable uncertainty about the nature of the prehistoric peoples who lived in Italy. We do know that Indo-European peoples moved into Italy during the second half of the second millennium B.C. By the first millennium B.C., other peoples had also settled in Italy—the two most notable being the Greeks and the Etruscans. Before examining these peoples, however, we need to consider the influence geography had on the historical development of the peoples on the Italian peninsula.

Geography of the Italian Peninsula

Italy is a peninsula extending about 750 miles from north to south. It is not very wide, however, averaging about 120 miles across. The Alps in the north form a natural barrier although numerous passes did permit peoples to cross into northern Italy. The Apennines are not as high as the Alps, but connect with the Alps in northwest Italy and then traverse the peninsula from north to south, providing a ridge down the middle that divides west from east. Nevertheless, Italy is left with some fairly large fertile plains ideal for farming. Most important were the Po valley in the north, probably the most fertile agricultural area, the plain of Latium, on which Rome was located, and Campania to the south of Latium. To the east of the Italian peninsula is the Adriatic Sea and to the west the Tyrrhenian Sea with the nearby large islands of Corsica and Sardinia. Sicily lies just west of the toe of the boot-shaped peninsula.

While geography alone did not determine the course of Roman development, it did have an impact on Roman history. Although the Apennines bisected Italy, they were less rugged than the mountain ranges of Greece and did not divide the peninsula into many small isolated communities. Italy also possessed considerably more productive agricultural land than Greece, enabling it to support a large population. Rome's location was favorable from a geographical point of view. Located eighteen miles inland on the Tiber River, Rome had access to the sea and was yet far enough inland to be safe from pirates. Built on the famous seven hills of Rome, it was easily defended. Situated where the Tiber could be readily forded, Rome became a natural crossing point for north-south traffic in western Italy. All in all, Rome had a good central location in Italy from which to expand.

Moreover, the Italian peninsula juts into the Mediterranean, making it an important crossroads between the western and eastern Mediterranean. Once Rome had unified Italy, involvement in Mediterranean affairs was probably inevitable. And after the Romans had conquered their Mediterranean empire, Italy's central location made their task of governing that empire considerably less difficult.

The Greeks

The Greeks arrived on the Italian peninsula in large numbers during the age of Greek colonization (750–550 B.C.—see Chapter 3). Initially, the Greeks settled in southern Italy. They founded Cumae in the Bay of Naples, Naples itself (Neapolis), and Tarentum and then crept around the coast and up the peninsula as far as Brindisi (Brundisium). The eastern two-thirds of Sicily was also occupied by the Greeks. In establishing their colonies, the Greeks displayed certain uniform characteristics. They planned permanent communities, secured the coastal plains for agriculture, and built walled cities with harbors to carry on trade. Ultimately, the Greeks had considerable influence on Italy, particularly the Etruscan cities and Rome. They cultivated the olive and the vine, passed on their alphabetic system of writing, and provided artistic and cultural models through their sculpture, architecture, and literature. Indeed, many historians view Roman culture as a continuation of Greek culture. While Greek influence initially touched Rome indirectly through the Etruscans, the Roman conquest of southern Italy and Sicily brought them into direct contact with the Greeks. Later, in the second century B.C., the Roman conquest of Greece completed the Greek cultural domination of Rome.

The Etruscans

The initial development of Rome was influenced most by a mysterious people known as the Etruscans. The Etruscans were located north of Rome in Etruria. They were a city-dwelling people who established their towns in commanding positions and fortified them with walls. Their pottery reflected considerable Greek influence. Numerous inscriptions in tombs show that the Etruscans adopted alphabetic writing from the Greeks before 600 B.C.

The origins of the Etruscans are not clear. Were they native Italians or, like the Greeks in Italy, were they immigrants from the east? The debate about their ancestry began in the ancient world. One Greek historian, Herodotus, maintained that the Etruscans stemmed from Asia Minor, while another, Dionysius of Halicarnassus, argued for Italian origins. The most obvious arguments for a non-Italic origin include their language, which is non-Indo-European, and their use of Near Eastern reli-gious customs, such as divination (see Chapter 1). Many scholars now believe that the archaeological evidence is best interpreted as showing an unbroken evolution from earlier native, non-Indo-European–speaking peoples known as the Villanovans.

After 650 B.C., the Etruscans expanded in Italy and became the dominant cultural and economic force in a number of areas. To the north, they moved into north-central Italy, including the Po valley. To the south, according to Roman tradition and archaeological evidence, they controlled Rome and possibly all of Latium. From Latium they moved south into Campania, founded a settlement at Capua, and came into direct contact with Greek colonists in southern Italy. They also encountered the Greeks in naval conflicts. Around 535 B.C., the Etruscans joined with the Carthaginians to defeat the Greeks in a battle off the island of Corsica, but were later routed by the Greeks in a naval battle off Cumae around 480 B.C. By this time, Etruscan power was on the decline. By 400 B.C., they had been limited to Etruria itself and later were invaded by the Gauls and then conquered by the Romans. The Etruscans, then, reached the height of their power in the sixth century B.C. Nevertheless, they had had an impact. By their transformation of villages into towns and cities, they brought urbanization to northern and central Italy (the Greeks brought urbanization to southern Italy). Rome was, of course, the Etruscans' most famous product, and it is time now to examine that city's early history.

Early Rome

According to Roman legend, Rome was founded by the twin brothers, Romulus and Remus, in 753 B.C. Of course, the Romans invented this story to provide a noble ancestry for their city. After all, the twins' father was supposed to have been the god Mars, the most important deity in early Roman religion. Archaeologists have found, however, that by the eighth century there was a settlement consisting of huts on the tops of Rome's hills. The early Romans, basically a pastoral people, spoke Latin, which, like Greek, belongs to the Indo-European family of languages (see the chart in Chapter 1). The Roman historical tradition also maintained that early Rome (753–509 B.C.) had been under the control of seven kings and that two of the last three had been Etruscans. Some historians believe that the king list, with the exception of Romulus as the first, may have some historical accuracy. What is certain is that Rome did fall under the influence of the Etruscans for about a hundred years during the period of the kings. The Etr-

▼ **Etruscan Married Couple.** This sculpture, dating from 550 B.C., depicts an Etruscan married couple. The Etruscans were a mysterious people who greatly influenced the early development of Rome. At first a farming community, Rome was transformed into a city through Etruscan influence. The Etruscans had an impact on Roman religion, Roman sporting events, and the development of the Roman military.

uscans found Rome a pastoral community but left it a city.

Etruscan influence on Rome appears to have begun around 625 B.C. The Etruscans were responsible for draining the area of the Forum and inaugurating its use as a public arena. By the beginning of the sixth century, under Etruscan influence, Rome began to emerge as an actual city. The Etruscans were responsible for an outstanding building program. They constructed the first roadbed of the chief street through Rome—the Sacred Way—before 575 B.C. and oversaw the development of temples, markets, shops, streets, and houses. By 509 B.C., supposedly when the monarchy was overthrown, a new Rome had emerged, essentially a product of the fusion of Etruscan and native Roman elements.

The Etruscans had an impact on Roman civilization in numerous ways—both small and large. Etruscan dress—the toga and short cloak—was adopted by the Romans. The insignia of the Etruscan kings became the insignia of Roman magistrates in the Republic. Most impressive was the *fasces,* an axe surrounded by a bundle of rods used as a symbol for the power to scourge and execute, hence to rule. In the Republic, the consuls as chief magistrates were preceded by twelve lictors bearing the *fasces.* The Romans were also indebted to the Etruscans for the alphabet. The Etruscan alphabet was derived from the Greeks although historians are unsure whether it was from the Greek settlements in Italy or the mainland Greeks. The Latin alphabet was a modification of the Greek-derived Etruscan one.

▼ **Map 5.1** Ancient Italy and City of Rome (inset).

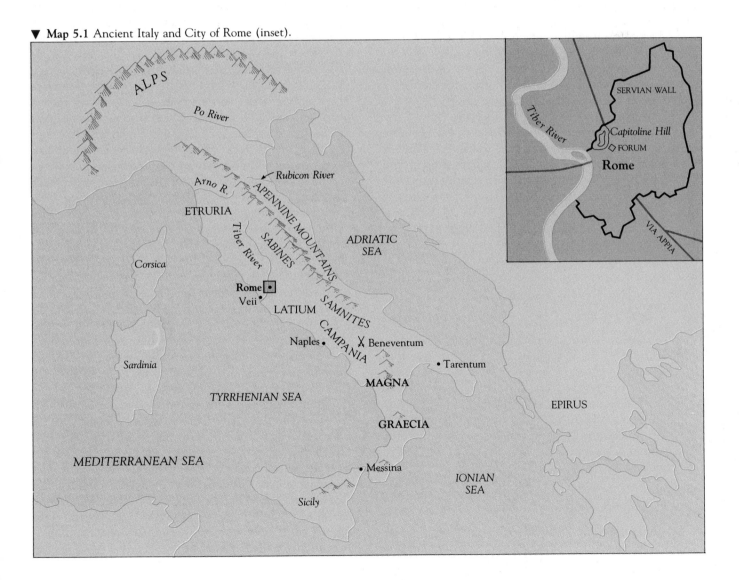

The Etruscans are also thought to have had an impact on the Romans in military matters. Rome's greatness, of course, was based on military power, and it was an Etruscan innovation that probably made it possible. The Etruscans adopted the Greek hoplite shield, body armor, and weapons and made them standard equipment by the sixth century B.C. This meant a shift from reliance on cavalry, normally the preserve of aristocrats, to the hoplite infantry.

The Romans traditionally associated the end of both monarchy and Etruscan domination with the rape of Lucretia, a Roman noblewoman of great virtue. Forcibly seduced by a son of the king, Lucretia informed her father, husband, and their friends what had happened and then committed suicide. In revenge, the Roman nobles drove the king and his family from Rome and established a republican form of government, which ushered in the era of the Republic. According to the Romans of the late Republic, all this occurred in 509 B.C. Though interesting, the story has little historical foundation. It is more likely that the overthrow of the monarchy was accomplished by nobles who experienced a loss of power because of the shift from cavalry to heavy-armed infantry during the reign of Servius Tullius, the next-to-last King. The overthrow was not a patriotic uprising, but an attempt by Roman nobles to maintain their position of power. Some scholars have even argued that the continuation of Etruscan influence at Rome into the fifth century necessitates dating the beginning of the Roman Republic to around 475 B.C., but most historians remain committed to a date close to the traditional one of 509 B.C.

▼ The Roman Republic (c. 509–264 B.C.)

The transition from monarchy to a republican government was not as smooth as Latin writers assert in their accounts. Historians now believe that Rome experienced a considerable economic setback at this time that might have lasted fifty years. Moreover, it is apparent that Rome felt threatened by enemies from every direction. In the process of meeting these threats, Rome embarked on a course of military expansion that led to the conquest of the entire Italian peninsula.

The Roman Conquest of Italy

At the beginning of the Republic, Rome was surrounded by enemies, including the Etruscans to the north and the Sabines, Volscians, and Aequi to the east and south. A more immediate threat was posed by the Latin communities on the plain of Latium. They had been allies of Rome during the period of the monarchy, but after the expulsion of the Etruscan kings, a new league of Latin allies had formed that separated itself from Rome and challenged Roman leadership in Latium. But supposedly in 496 B.C., after an inconclusive battle, the Romans established a new alliance with the Latin communities, which provided for a common defense of Latium.

Rome was under constant pressure for the next hundred years from its neighbors. If we are to believe Livy, one of the chief ancient sources for the history of the early Roman Republic, Rome was engaged in almost continuous warfare with the Volscians, Sabines, Aequi, and others. One of Rome's important victories came in 396 B.C., when, according to the traditional version, the Etruscan city of Veii fell to the Romans, supposedly after a ten-year siege.

In his account of these years, the historian Livy provided a detailed narrative of Roman efforts. Many of Livy's stories were legendary in character and indeed were modeled after events in Greek history. The account of the 306 members of the Fabii clan who were ambushed by the Etruscans but stood their ground and died to the last man fulfilling their duty is very reminiscent of the stand of the 300 Spartans at Thermopylae (see Chapter 3). The ten-year siege of Veii corresponds to Homer's account of Troy. But Livy, writing in the first century B.C., used such stories to teach Romans the moral values and virtues that had made Rome great. These included tenacity, duty, courage, and especially discipline (see the box on p. 129). Indeed, Livy recounted stories of military leaders who executed their own sons for leaving their place in battle, a serious offense since the success of the hoplite infantry depended on maintaining a precise order. These stories had little basis in fact, but like the story of George Washington and the cherry tree in American history, they provided mythical images to reinforce Roman patriotism.

The Roman success at Veii proved to be short-lived. In 387 B.C., the Celts, known to the Romans as the Gauls, a people from north of the Alps who had previously moved into northern Italy, defeated the Romans in a battle outside Rome. The Gauls conquered Rome, sacked large parts of the city, and probably left only after the Romans had paid an indemnity. Rome was left in shambles. But Roman tenacity won out. The city was rebuilt, although haphazardly, and with new determination the Romans began again.

Cincinnatus Saves Rome: A Roman Morality Tale
▼ ▼ ▼

There is perhaps no better account of how the virtues of duty and simplicity enabled good Roman citizens to prevail during the travails of the fifth century B.C. than Livy's account of Cincinnatus. He was chosen dictator, supposedly in 457 B.C., to defend Rome against the attacks of the Aequi. The position of dictator was a temporary expedient used only in emergencies; the consuls would resign and a leader with unlimited power would be appointed for a limited period (usually six months). In this account, Cincinnatus did his duty, defeated the Aequi, and returned to his simple farm in just fifteen days.

Livy, *The Early History of Rome*

The city was thrown into a state of turmoil, and the general alarm was as great as if Rome herself were surrounded. Nautius was sent for, but it was quickly decided that he was not the man to inspire full confidence; the situation evidently called for a dictator, and, with no dissentient voice, Lucius Quinctius Cincinnatus was named for the post.

Now I would solicit the particular attention of those numerous people who imagine that money is everything in this world, and that rank and ability are inseparable from wealth: let them observe that Cincinnatus, the one man in whom Rome reposed all her hope of survival, was at that moment working a little three-acre farm . . . west of the Tiber, just opposite the spot where the shipyards are today. A mission from the city found him at work on his land—digging a ditch, maybe, or ploughing. Greetings were exchanged, and he was asked—with a prayer for divine blessing on himself and his country—to put on his toga and hear the Senate's instructions. This naturally surprised him, and, asking if all were well, he told his wife Racilia to run to their cottage and fetch his toga. The toga was brought, and wiping the grimy sweat from his hands and face he put it on; at once the envoys from the city saluted him, with congratulations, as Dictator, invited him to enter Rome, and informed him of the terrible danger of Municius's army. A state vessel was waiting for him on the river, and on the city bank he was welcomed by his three sons who had come to meet him, then by other kinsmen and friends, and finally by nearly the whole body of senators. Closely attended by all these people and preceded by his lictors he was then escorted to his residence through streets lined with great crowds of common folk who, be it said, were by no means so pleased to see the new Dictator, as they thought his power excessive and dreaded the way in which he was likely to use it.

[Cincinnatus proceeds to raise an army, march out, and defeat the Aequi.]

In Rome the Senate was convened by Quintus Fabius the City Perfect, and a decree was passed inviting Cincinnatus to enter in triumph with his troops. The chariot he rode in was preceded by the enemy commanders and the military standards, and followed by his army loaded with its spoils . . . . Cincinnatus finally resigned after holding office for fifteen days, having originally accepted it for a period of six months.

In 340 B.C., however, Rome had to deal with a revolt of the Latin states in Latium, which had come to resent Rome's increasing domination of their alliance. The Romans crushed the revolt and established complete supremacy in Latium, inaugurating a new system that ultimately became the basis for organizing the entire Italian peninsula: the Roman confederation, formed in 338 B.C. Under this system, Rome established treaties with the defeated members of the Latin League whereby these communities were related to Rome in one of three ways. The first category included only five or six privileged states in which all the citizens were given full Roman citizenship. A second category of communities acquired municipal status, which entitled them to make legal contracts and intermarry with Romans, but not to vote or hold office in Rome. The remaining communities were made allies and bound to Rome by special treaties specifying their relations with Rome. All three categories of states remained largely autonomous in their domestic affairs, but were required to provide soldiers for Rome. In the Roman confederation, Rome created a system that could be expanded, as it eventually was, to the rest of Italy. Moreover, the Romans did not regard the status of the conquered states as permanent. Loyal

Defeat of the Latin League	496 B.C.
Fall of Veii	396 B.C.
Sack of Rome by the Gauls	387 B.C.
Latin revolt	340–338 B.C.
Creation of the Roman Confederation	338 B.C.
First Samnite War	343–341 B.C.
Second Samnite War	326–304 B.C.
Third Samnite War	298–290 B.C.
Pyrrhic War	281–275 B.C.

allies could improve their status and even have hopes of becoming Roman citizens. Thus, Rome had found a way to give conquered states a stake in Rome's success.

Even before they had crushed the Latin League, the Romans had entered into renewed conflict with a very stubborn opponent, the Samnites, resulting in the three Samnite Wars (343–290 B.C.). The Samnites were a hill people from the central Apennines. In the fifth century, some of them had moved into Campania where they had forced out the Etruscans and settled down, becoming known as the Oscans. But in the fourth century B.C., the position of the Oscans was threatened by a second wave of Samnites. The Oscans asked Rome for help, and in the first two Samnite Wars (343–341 and 326–304 B.C.), the Romans fought only to protect Campania and, of course, themselves. Although successful, the Romans made a critical change in policy when they concluded that the only sure way to protect themselves was to control the Samnites; therefore, a Third Samnite War (298–290 B.C.) broke out. Rome was victorious and incorporated Campania and the Samnite states of central Italy into an expanded Roman confederation as Italian allies. These communities agreed to provide military aid (cavalry and infantry soldiers) to Rome and to allow Rome to control their foreign policy. Otherwise, they were free to govern themselves and maintain their own laws and political institutions. Though internally free, the "allies" were ringed with colonies of Roman veterans settled on confiscated land and knew that if they showed any signs of disloyalty to Rome, a Roman army would quickly appear to show them the error of their ways.

The conquest of the Samnites gave Rome considerable control over a large part of Italy and also brought it

into direct contact with the Greek communities of southern Italy. While the Greek cities had occupied the coastal plains, they did not control the interior so attacks by the native populations were rather frequent. In 282 B.C., the Greek city of Thurii, attacked by the Bruttians, asked Rome for help. Rome agreed knowing full well the possible consequences of becoming involved in hostilities in southern Italy. Rome's aid to Thurii caused anxiety among the other Greek cities, especially Tarentum, the most powerful of the Greek states on the southern Italian peninsula. Consequently, when a Roman fleet appeared off Tarentum, the Tarentines attacked and sank it. The result was the Pyrrhic War (281–275 B.C.).

Tarentum and the other Greek communities were primarily commercial cities and possessed no standing armies. They were accustomed to hiring mercenaries to fight their battles for them. Consequently, they bought the aid of King Pyrrhus of Epirus (approximately modern-day Epirus in Greece), who crossed the Adriatic with 20,000 troops and defeated the Romans twice. In both battles, however, Pyrrhus experienced heavy losses,

▼ **King Pyrrhus.** By sinking a Roman fleet off its coast, the Greek city of Tarentum initiated the Pyrrhic war. The Tarentines bought the aid of King Pyrrhus of Epirus, who defeated the Romans in their first two encounters, but not without suffering heavy losses. In their third battle, in which the Romans stampeded Pyrrhus' war elephants into his own troops, Rome was victorious. Pictured is a marble bust of Pyrrhus found at Herculaneum.

leading him to comment that one more victory would ruin him (hence our phrase "Pyrrhic victory"). After a diversion to Sicily, Pyrrhus came back for one more battle with the Romans, and this time was decisively defeated in 275 B.C. The Romans completed their conquest of southern Italy and added the Greek states to the Roman confederation. Their relationship to Rome, also determined by treaties, was the same as the Italian allies, except that the Greeks were required to furnish naval assistance—warships and sailors—instead of infantry and cavalry. After crushing the remaining Etruscan states to the north, Rome had conquered all of Italy, except the extreme north, by 264 B.C.

In the course of their expansion throughout Italy, the Romans had pursued consistent policies that help to explain their success. The Romans excelled in making the correct diplomatic decisions; they were superb diplomats. While firm and even cruel when necessary—rebellions were crushed without mercy—they were also shrewd in extending their citizenship and allowing autonomy in domestic affairs. Their conquest of Italy could hardly be said to be the result of a direct policy of expansion. Much of it was opportunistic. The Romans did not hesitate to act once they felt their security threatened. And surrounded by potential enemies, Rome in a sense never felt secure. The Romans were not only good soldiers, but persistent ones. The loss of an army or a fleet did not cause them to quit, but spurred them on to build new armies and new fleets. Finally, the Romans had a practical sense of strategy. As they conquered, they settled Romans and Latins in new communities outside Latium. By 264 B.C., the Romans had established colonies—fortified towns—at all strategic locations. By building roads to these settlements and connecting them, the Romans assured themselves of an impressive military and communications network that enabled them to rule effectively and efficiently. By insisting upon military service from the allies in the Roman confederation, Rome essentially mobilized the entire military manpower of all Italy for her wars.

Thus, by 264 B.C., Rome had united all of Italy, except for the Po valley, into the Roman confederation. Each city and its inhabitants were bound to Rome by a treaty, which specified the terms of the alliance. While all communities owed military service to Rome and had their foreign policy determined for them, they were still allowed to have their own municipal freedom with their own magistrates. The Roman confederation brought unity to Italy on the eve of Rome's struggle with Carthage. It proved to be an important factor in the Romans' victory over this powerful enemy.

The Roman State (c. 509–264 B.C.)

During the period of Roman expansion in Italy, the Roman Republic developed a set of political institutions that were, in many ways, determined by the social divisions that existed within the community. In law and politics, as in conquest, the Romans took a practical approach. They did not concern themselves with the construction of an ideal government, but instead fashioned political institutions in response to problems as they arose. Hence it is important to remember that the political institutions we will discuss evolved over a period of centuries.

POLITICAL INSTITUTIONS   The Romans had a clear concept of executive authority that was embodied in their word *imperium,* or "the right to command." Invested with *imperium,* the chief magistrates of the Roman state exercised a supreme power that was circumscribed only by extraneous means—officials held office for a limited term and could be tried for offenses committed in office once their term ended. While political institutions changed, the concept of *imperium* did not, and it is the one factor that gives Roman constitutional history continuity and unity.

The chief executive officers of the Roman Republic who possessed *imperium* were the consuls and praetors. Two consuls who were chosen annually administered the government and led the Roman army into battle. In 366 B.C., a new office, that of the praetor, was created. The praetor also possessed *imperium* and could govern Rome when the consuls were away from the city and could also lead armies. The praetor's primary function, however, was the execution of justice. He was in charge of the *ius civile,* or the civil law as it applied to Roman citizens. In 242 B.C., reflecting Rome's growth, another praetor was added to judge cases in which one or both parties were noncitizens. The praetors' decisions in these cases eventually came to form the basis of a body of international law that the Romans called the *ius gentium* (see Law later in this chapter).

As Rome expanded into the Mediterranean, additional praetors were established to govern the newly conquered provinces (two in 227, two more in 197 B.C.). But as the number of provinces continued to grow, the Romans devised a new system in which exconsuls and expraetors who had served their one-year terms were given the title of proconsul and propraetor, respectively, and sent out as provincial governors. This demonstrates once again the Romans' practical solution to an immediate problem. It was reasonable to assume that officials with governmental experience would make good provincial administrators, although this was not always true in practice due to the opportunities for financial corruption in the provinces.

Periodically, the Republic also created an extraordinary executive. In an emergency the consuls would resign, and a dictator with unlimited power would be chosen to run the state. This office was supposed to last only for the duration of the emergency, the usual limit being six months. In the last century of the Republic, this practice was badly abused, a sure sign of the Republic's disintegration at that time.

The Roman state also had administrative officials who handled specialized duties. Quaestors were assigned to assist consuls and praetors in the administration of financial affairs. Aediles supervised the public games and watched over the grain supply of the city, a major problem for a rapidly growing urban community that came to rely on the importation of grain to feed its population. Censors were chosen every five years whose chief responsibility was to make an assessment of the population on the basis of age and property for purposes of taxes, military service, and officeholding.

▼ **Lictors with *Fasces*.** Pictured are lictors bearing the *fasces*, an axe surrounded by a bundle of rods tied with a red thong, an insignia borrowed from the Etruscan kings. The *fasces* was a symbol for the power to rule, and the consuls, the chief executives of the Roman Republic, were always preceded by twelve lictors bearing the *fasces*.

The Roman senate came to hold an especially important position in the Roman Republic. The senate or council of elders was a select group of about 300 men who served for life. The senate was not a legislative body, but could only advise the magistrates. This advice of the senate (called *senatus consultum*) was not taken lightly, however, and by the third century B.C. had virtually the force of law. No doubt the prestige of the senate's members furthered this development. But it also helped that the senate met continuously, while the chief magistrates changed annually and the popular assemblies were slow in operation and met only periodically.

The Roman Republic possessed a number of popular assemblies. The earliest assembly, known as the *comitia curiata*, went back to the monarchical period and fell into disuse during the Republic. By far the most important was the *comitia centuriata* (the centuriate assembly), essentially the Roman army functioning in its political role. Organized by classes based on wealth, it was structured in such a way that the wealthiest citizens always had a majority. The centuriate assembly elected the chief magistrates and passed laws. It is important to remember, however, that the Romans passed few statutory laws, since much activity was simply left to magisterial authority. As a result of the struggle between the orders, a third assembly, the *concilium plebis* or plebeian assembly, came into being in 471 B.C. (see The Struggle of the Orders later in this chapter).

SOCIAL ORGANIZATION　The family was the basis of Roman society. At its head was the *paterfamilias* who theoretically had unlimited power over his family. In the early Republic, for example, it is claimed that he had the right to put his children to death, although there are very few instances in which this actually occurred. With the *paterfamilias* at the head, the family resembled a kind of miniature state within the state. When a father died, his sons became heads of their own families. Since many families had the same name, a new social unit was instituted known as the *gens* or clan. The clan became very important later in Roman history.

Closely associated with the clan and family was the practice of clientage. Clients constituted a dependent class, people who did not have the means to protect themselves or their families without the assistance of a patron. The patron, usually a wealthy member of the upper classes, gave protection and especially legal assistance to his clients. In return, clients performed certain services, such as field labor, military assistance, and, especially important in the Republic, providing votes for their patrons. The mutual obligations between patrons and clients were not sanctioned by law, but by custom and religion, and even become hereditary in nature.

The most noticeable element in the social organization of early Rome was the division between two groups—the patricians and the plebeians. The word *patrician* is derived from *patres*—the fathers—as the members of the Roman senate were called. The patrician class in Rome consisted of those families who were descended from the original senators appointed during the period of the kings. Their initial emergence was probably due to their wealth as great landowners. Thus, patricians constituted an aristocratic governing class. What particularly distinguished the patricians was their possession of certain religious privileges that enabled them to control the government. They alone had mastery of the religious calendar and knew on what days legal or political business could be conducted. Only they could be consuls, other magistrates, and senators. By being patrons of large numbers of dependent clients, they could control the centuriate assembly and many other facets of Roman life. The plebeians constituted the considerably larger group of "independent, unprivileged, poorer and vulnerable men" as well as nonpatrician large landowners, less wealthy landholders, craftsmen, merchants, and small farmers. While citizens, they did not possess the same rights as the patricians and at the beginning of the fifth century B.C. began a struggle to rectify that situation. The plebeians who led the struggle for plebeian rights were large landowners who were equal in wealth to many patricians and, therefore, considered themselves equally qualified to enjoy their privileges.

THE STRUGGLE OF THE ORDERS   As we have seen, the Roman republican constitution had evolved through the necessity to differentiate functions, especially at the executive level. But the constitutional struggle between the orders also resulted in innovations in Roman political institutions. Although we do not know the specific grievances, two major problems existed in the fifth century that probably fueled the struggle between the patricians and the plebeians. No doubt the chief issue was power and specifically the patrician monopoly and the plebeian lack of it. Both patricians and plebeians could vote, but only the patricians could be elected to governmental offices. Both had the right to make legal contracts and marriages, but intermarriage between patricians and plebeians was forbidden. The wealthy plebeians wanted political equality with the patricians, namely, the right to hold office, and social equality in the form of the right of intermarriage. To the political and social issues was probably added an economic issue

Chronology
▼ ▼ ▼
The Struggle of the Orders

First secession of the plebeians; creation of tribunes of the plebs	494 B.C.
Creation of *concilium plebis* (plebeian council)	471 B.C.
Publication of the Twelve Tables of Law	451–450 B.C.
Lex Canuleia: Right of plebeians to marry patricians	445 B.C.
Licinian-Sextian laws: One counsul may be a plebeian	367 B.C.
Both consuls may be plebeians; one must be	342 B.C.
Chief priesthoods opened to the plebeians	300 B.C.
Lex Hortensia: Laws passed by plebeian council are binding on all Romans	287 B.C.

that was of greater concern to the less wealthy. No doubt the economic problems of the fifth century, heavy debts and food shortages, exacerbated the sense of crisis.

The plebeians used their numerical strength and military importance to force the issue by withdrawing physically from the state. This first secession of the plebs (the traditional date is 494 B.C.) would be imitated later. It was a successful tactic that forced the patricians, who by themselves could not defend Rome, to make compromises. Two new officials known as tribunes of the plebs were instituted (later raised to five and then ten in number) who were given the power to protect plebeians against arrest by patrician magistrates. Moreover, after a new popular assembly for plebeians only, called the *concilium plebis* (council of the plebs), was created in 471 B.C., the tribunes became responsible for convoking and placing proposals before it. If adopted, they became *plebiscita* ("it is the opinion of the plebs"), but they were binding only on the plebeians, not the patricians. Nevertheless, the plebeian council gave the plebeians political leverage and virtually made them a legal corporation or a state within the state.

The next step for the plebeians involved the law. The plebeians came to realize that if they were to make advances for themselves, they needed knowledge of the law and the legal and governmental procedures carefully guarded by the patricians. Due to plebeian pressure, a special commission of ten officials known as the *decemviri* ("ten men") was created with the task of regularizing and publishing the laws. This action resulted in the publication of the Twelve Tables of Law in 450 B.C., which included, among other things, the legal procedures for going to court; provisions on family, women, and divorce; regulations concerning private property; rules governing relationships and injuries to others; and a provision prohibiting intermarriage between patricians and plebeians (see the box on p. 135). This publication of the laws produced further agitation from the plebeians between 450 and 445 since they could now see how disadvantaged they were. In particular, they demanded the right of intermarriage and admission to the chief magistracies, especially the consulship. In 445 B.C., the *lex Canuleia* allowed patricians and plebeians to intermarry. Once this was permitted, the division between the two groups became less important. The solidarity of the patrician class against plebeian gains began to falter. But it was not until 367 B.C. that the consulship was opened to plebeians. The Licinian-Sextian laws stipulated that one consul could now be a plebeian. From 366 to 361 B.C., however, only two plebeians were elected to the consulship, and from 361 to 340, only three, a clear indication that only the most prominent plebeian families could obtain the office. In 342 B.C., another law stipulated that both consuls could be plebeians, while one had to be. In 300 B.C., all religious offices were opened to the plebeians as well, so that patrician monopoly over the Roman state religion was eliminated.

The chief landmark in Roman constitutional history—and the climax of the struggle between the orders—came in 287 B.C. with the *lex Hortensia*. Henceforth, all *plebiscita* passed by the plebeian council had the force of law and were binding on the entire community, both plebeians and patricians. Moreover, unlike the laws passed by the centuriate assembly, these *plebiscita* did not need the approval of the senate.

The struggle between the orders, then, had a significant impact on the development of the Roman constitution. Plebeians could hold the highest offices of state, they could intermarry with the patricians, and their council, like the regular assemblies, could pass laws binding on the entire Roman community. Although the struggle had been long, the Romans had handled it by compromise, not violent revolution. Theoretically, by 287 B.C. all Roman citizens were equal under the law, and all could strive for political office. But in reality, as a result of the right of intermarriage, a select number of

patrician and plebeian families formed a new senatorial aristocracy called the *nobiles,* which came to dominate the political offices. The Roman Republic had not become a democracy.

▼ The Roman Conquest of the Mediterranean (264–133 B.C.)

After their conquest of the Italian peninsula, the Romans found themselves face-to-face with a formidable Mediterranean power—Carthage. Founded around 800 B.C. by Phoenicians from Tyre, Carthage was located in a favorable position for commanding Mediterranean trade routes and had become an important commercial center. It had become politically and militarily strong as well. Around 600 B.C. Carthage took the lead in heading off Greek colonists in the western Mediterranean and in a series of wars lasting about three centuries had ejected the Greeks from most of the Spanish coast, reducing them for the most part to Sicily and southern Italy. By the third century B.C., the Carthaginian empire included the coast of northern Africa, southern Spain, Sardinia, Corsica, and western Sicily. With its monopoly of western Mediterranean trade, Carthage was the largest and richest state in the area. Although it possessed a fine navy, its army was not as formidable, usually being made up of mercenaries or men drafted from the local area. Both were hard to control. The officers, however, constituted a professional military class and were experienced, especially in comparison to the Romans who relied on annually appointed magistrates as commanders.

In its relations with Italy, Carthage had relied on diplomacy rather than warfare. In the fourth century B.C., when the Romans had acquired a fairly large seafront, Carthage had offered them two successive treaties and supplemented these with a military alliance against Pyrrhus in 279 B.C., although it appears that neither Carthage nor Rome provided military help to the other. Yet Rome was apparently apprehensive about Carthaginian encroachment on the Italian coast for the Romans had stipulated in each of the three treaties with Carthage that the latter must not establish a permanent foothold on Italian soil. As late as 264 B.C., a war between Rome and Carthage seemed to be far away, and it took a number of circumstances to bring it on.

The First Punic War (264–241 B.C.)

The treaties between Rome and Carthage had made no attempt to define precisely the spheres of influence of

The Twelve Tables
▼▼▼

In 451 B.C., *plebeian pressure led to the creation of a special commission of ten men who were responsible for codifying Rome's laws and making them public. In so doing, the plebeians hoped that they could restrict the arbitrary power of the patrician magistrates who alone had access to the laws. The Twelve Tables represent the first formal codification of Roman laws and customs. The laws dealt with litigation procedures, debt, family relations, property, and other matters of public and sacred law. The Twelve Tables were considered a landmark in the development of Roman law and until the time of Cicero remained one of the fundamental texts memorized by Roman schoolboys. The code was inscribed on bronze plaques, which eventually were destroyed. These selections are taken from reconstructions of the code preserved in later writers.*

Selections from the Twelve Tables

Table III: Execution; Law of Debt

When a debt has been acknowledged, or judgment about the matter has been pronounced in court, thirty days must be the legitimate time of grace. After that, the debtor may be arrested by laying on of hands. Bring him into court. If he does not satisfy the judgment, or no one in court offers himself as surety in his behalf, the creditor may take the defaulter with him. He may bind him either in stocks or in fetters . . . .

Unless they make a settlement, debtors shall be held in bonds for sixty days. During that time they shall be brought before the praetor's court in the meeting place on three successive market days, and the amount for which they are judged liable shall be announced; on the third market day they shall suffer capital punishment or be delivered up for sale abroad, across the Tiber.

Table IV: Rights of Head of Family

Quickly kill . . . a dreadfully deformed child.

If a father thrice surrender a son for sale, the son shall be free from the father.

A child born ten months after the father's death will not be admitted into a legal inheritance.

Table V: Guardianship; Succession

Females shall remain in guardianship even when they have attained their majority.

If a man is raving mad, rightful authority over his person and chattels shall belong to his agnates [nearest male relatives] or to his clansmen.

A spendthrift is forbidden to exercise administration over his own goods . . . . A person who, being insane or a spendthrift, is prohibited from administering his own goods shall be under trusteeship of agnates.

Table VII: Rights concerning Land

Branches of a tree may be lopped off all round to a height of more than 15 feet . . . . Should a tree on a neighbor's farm be bent crooked by a wind and lean over your farm, action may be taken for removal of that tree.

It is permitted to gather up fruit falling down on another man's farm.

Table VIII: Torts or Delicts

If any person has sung or composed against another person a song such as was causing slander or insult to another, he shall be clubbed to death.

If a person has maimed another's limb, let there be retaliation in kind unless he makes agreement for settlement with him.

Any person who destroys by burning any building or heap of corn deposited alongside a house shall be bound, scourged, and put to death by burning at the stake, provided that he has committed the said misdeed with malice aforethought; but if he shall have committed it by accident, that is, by negligence, it is ordained that he repair the damage, or, if he be too poor to be competent for such punishment, he shall receive a lighter chastisement.

Table IX: Public Law

The penalty shall be capital punishment for a judge or arbiter legally appointed who has been found guilty of receiving a bribe for giving a decision.

Table XI: Supplementary Laws

Intermarriage shall not take place between plebeians and patricians.

both powers on Sicily since the Romans at that time had no important interest in the island. But an unforeseen situation arose at Messana (modern Messina)—a city that commanded the straits between Italy and Sicily—that became the immediate cause of war. Since 289 B.C., Messana had been controlled by a group of mercenaries from Campania called the Mamertines. In 264 B.C., Messana was besieged by Hiero, the king of Syracuse. The Mamertines sought help first from Carthage and then from the Romans. The Romans hesitated, knowing this was their first commitment outside Italy and was likely to involve them in a struggle with Carthage. But the Romans also perceived the strategic importance of Messana and Sicily to the security of southern Italy and sent a detachment of troops to Messana. The Carthaginians, who had also sent an army there, fled, but considered this just cause for war. Both states shipped reinforcements to Sicily and the First Punic War began.

Both sides sought to conquer Sicily. The Romans perceived that the war would be long and drawn out if they could not supplement their land operations with a navy. But building ships and finding admirals to sail them proved to be difficult. The Roman fleet suffered severe losses in both battles and storms, but Rome showed its tenacity once again. In 253 B.C., Rome lost 284 ships out of a fleet of 364 in a storm. Within three months, the Romans had constructed 220 new ships. The Carthaginian problem, on the other hand, lay in finding enough mercenaries to continue the fight. After a long struggle in which both sides lost battles in northern Africa and

Sicily, a Roman fleet defeated the Carthaginian navy off Drepana near Sicily in 242 B.C. The Sicilian cities controlled by Carthage on the western part of the island capitulated. Carthage sued for peace and the war ended in 241 B.C. Carthage gave up all rights to Sicily and had to pay an indemnity. Three years later, Rome took advantage of Carthage's problems with its mercenaries to seize the islands of Sardinia and Corsica. This act so angered the Carthaginians that, according to one story, their leading general, Hamilcar Barca, made his nine-year-old son swear that he would hate Rome ever after. The son's name was Hannibal.

The Second Punic War (218–201 B.C.)

Between the wars, Carthage made an unexpected recovery under the leadership of the general who had been briefly successful in Sicily in the First Punic War—Hamilcar Barca. Hamilcar extended Carthage's domains in Spain to compensate for the territory lost to Rome. The primary objective of this new empire was to find fresh sources of revenue to make up for the recent war losses. Carthage was especially successful in this regard, benefiting tremendously from the copper and silver mines in southern Spain. Another purpose in creating the Spanish empire was to get manpower for Carthage. The Spanish natives made great soldiers, being physically strong and possessing excellent swords. Hamilcar and his successors proceeded to build up a formidable

▼ **Map 5.2** The Western Mediterranean.

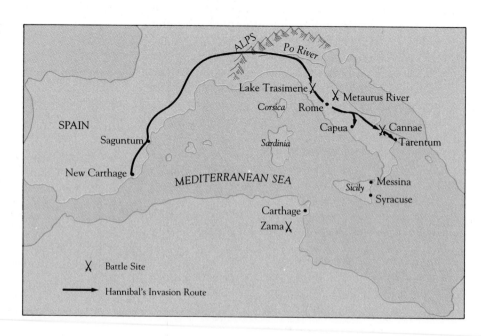

land army in the event of a second war with Rome, because they realized that Carthage's success depended upon defeating Rome on land. In 221 B.C., Hannibal, Hamilcar Barca's twenty-five-year-old son, took over direction of Carthaginian policy. Within three years, Rome and Carthage were again at war.

Carthage and Rome had agreed to divide Spain into respective spheres of influence. Although Saguntum was located in the Carthaginian sphere, Rome made an alliance with the city and encouraged its inhabitants in anti-Carthaginian activities. Thoroughly provoked by the Roman action, Hannibal attacked Saguntum, and the Romans declared war on Carthage in 218 B.C. This time the Carthaginian strategy aimed at bringing the war home to the Romans and defeating them in their own backyard. In an amazing march, Hannibal crossed the Alps with an army of 30,000–40,000 men and advanced into northern Italy. After defeating the Romans at the Trebia River, he added thousands of Gauls to his army and proceeded into central Italy. At Lake Trasimene in Etruria he again defeated the Romans. In desperation, the Romans elected as consul Quintus Fabius Maximus who became known as the "Delayer" because of his tactics of following and delaying Hannibal's army without risking a pitched battle. Hannibal hoped to destroy the Roman confederation and win Italian cities away from Rome. The policy failed initially; virtually all remained loyal to Rome.

In 216 B.C., the Romans decided to meet Hannibal head on. It was a serious mistake. At Cannae, Hannibal's forces decimated a Roman army, killing as many as 40,000. Now at last, some of the southern Italian cities rebelled against Roman rule and went over to Hannibal. Rome seemed on the brink of disaster but refused to give up and raised yet another army.

Rome gradually recovered. While Hannibal remained free to roam in Italy, he had neither the men nor the equipment to lay siege to the major cities, including Rome itself. The Romans began to reconquer some of the rebellious Italian cities. More important, the Romans pursued a Spanish strategy that aimed at undermining the Carthaginian empire in Spain. Publius Cornelius Scipio, later known as Scipio Africanus, was given command of the Roman forces in Spain despite the fact that he was too young to hold the position. But he was a brilliant general who learned from Hannibal's tactics and by 206 B.C. had pushed the Carthaginians out of Spain.

The Romans then took the war directly to Carthage. Late in 204 B.C., Scipio led a Roman army from Sicily into northern Africa and forced the Carthaginians to

▼ **Frieze Showing a Roman Warship.** After years of avoiding war through the art of diplomacy, Rome became embroiled in the first of three struggles with the chief power of the western Mediterranean, Carthage. With problems in Sicily finally drawing the two states into battle, the First Punic War (264–241 B.C.) ended with the destruction of the Carthaginian fleet in 241 B.C. In 238 B.C., Rome further injured the Carthaginian empire by seizings its islands of Sardinia and Corsica. This first-century B.C. relief depicts Roman soldiers preparing to leave a galley.

recall Hannibal from Italy. At the Battle of Zama in 202 B.C., Scipio decisively defeated Hannibal and the Carthaginian forces, and the war was over. By the peace treaty signed in 201, Carthage lost Spain, agreed to pay an indemnity, and promised not to go to war without Rome's permission. Spain, like Sicily, Corsica, and Sardinia earlier, was made into a Roman province ruled by a governor who possessed full *imperium*. The inhabitants were now Roman subjects required to pay tribute to their new masters. By 201 B.C., Carthage was no longer a great state, and Rome had become the dominant power in the western Mediterranean.

The Eastern Mediterranean

Roman involvement with the Hellenistic states of the eastern Mediterranean began indirectly in 219 B.C. when Rome sent soldiers across the Adriatic into Illyria to suppress pirates who were harassing commercial ships in the Adriatic. Philip V, king of Macedonia (221–179 B.C.), was disturbed by Roman entry into an area he considered his own sphere of influence. In revenge, Philip made an alliance with Hannibal after the Roman loss at Cannae, although he did not provide any real

Military alliance with Carthage	279 B.C.
First Punic War	264–241 B.C.
Rome seizes Corsica and Sardinia	238 B.C.
Second Punic War	218–201 B.C.
Battle of Cannae	216 B.C.
Scipio completes seizure of Spain	206 B.C.
Battle of Zama	202 B.C.
Third Punic War	149–146 B.C.
Destruction of Carthage	146 B.C.

itics. But Rome was preoccupied with the Carthaginians and agreed to a separate peace with Philip of Macedonia in 205 B.C., thus ending the so-called First Macedonian War.

After the defeat of Carthage, some Romans advocated punishing Macedonia for its alliance with Hannibal. Despite their war weariness, the Romans undertook the Second Macedonian War (200–197 B.C.) in alliance with both the Achaean and Aetolian Leagues of Greek states. At Cynoscephalae in Thessaly in 197 B.C., the Roman legions met and defeated the Macedonian phalanx. Philip was forced to pay a small indemnity, and in 196 B.C. the Romans announced the freedom of all the Greek states. The Romans, however, expected the Greeks to behave as if they were clients in the domestic system of clientage. When they did not, Roman policy changed.

The Aetolian League was especially unhappy with the Roman peace. Although an ally of Rome, it felt that it had achieved no real gains from fighting on Rome's side

assistance to the Carthaginians. The Romans, in turn, made an alliance with the Greek Aetolian League, a move that pulled Rome into the world of Hellenistic pol-

▼ **Map 5.3** The Eastern Mediterranean.

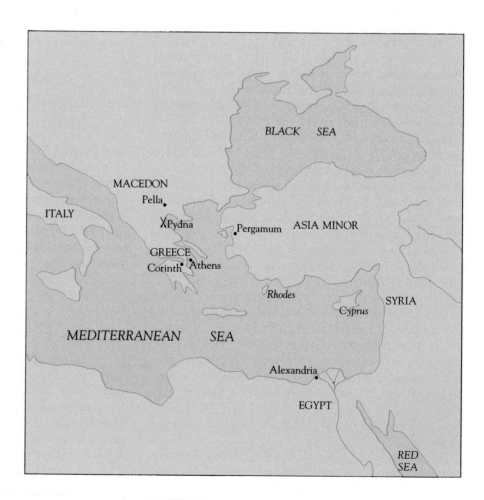

against the Macedonian king. Consequently, the league allied itself with the Seleucid ruler, Antiochus III (223–187 B.C.). Antiochus had far-flung ambitions that included control of Thrace to gain a foothold in Europe. The Romans had no intention of allowing Antiochus to become established in Greece and again went to war—the Syrian War (192–189 B.C.). Rome first defeated an army of the Aetolians and Antiochus in 191 B.C. and in 189 routed the forces of Antiochus at the Battle of Magnesia. Antiochus was forced to pay a large indemnity and to transfer his lands in Asia Minor to the Roman ally, the kingdom of Pergamum. The Romans took no lands for themselves.

Meanwhile, the Romans found it impossible to extricate themselves from Greek affairs. Greek states were constantly appealing to Rome against the encroachment of the Macedonians. When Philip's son Perseus continued what the Romans considered to be anti-Roman policies, Rome again declared war on Macedonia and inaugurated the Third Macedonian War (171–167 B.C.). At Pydna in 168 B.C., Perseus and the Macedonians were decisively defeated. Macedonia was not annexed but split into four republics. The Romans confiscated the Macedonian treasury and enslaved many people. Imperialism could be profitable; in 167 B.C., the Romans eliminated the payment of direct property taxes by Roman citizens. The spoils of war had made them unnecessary.

The Roman settlement after the Third Macedonian War failed to last, however. After a revolt, the Romans fought a brief and final Fourth Macedonian War (149–148 B.C.). Macedonia was now made a Roman province. The Greeks, especially the Achaean League, also rose in revolt against Rome's restrictive policies and were decisively defeated. The city of Corinth, leader of the revolt, was destroyed in 146 B.C. to teach the Greeks a lesson. Greece was not made a province but placed under the control of the provincial governor of Macedonia.

In the midst of these final struggles with the Macedonians and Greeks, Rome, led by Scipio Aemilianus, the younger Africanus, also undertook its third and last war with Carthage (149–146 B.C.). The Carthaginians had technically broken their peace treaty with Rome by going to war against one of Rome's north African allies who had been encroaching on Carthage's home territory. The Romans used this opportunity to carry out the complete destruction of Carthage in 146 B.C., a policy advocated by a number of Romans, especially the conservative politician Cato, who ended every speech he made to the senate with the words, "And I think

First Macedonian War	215–205 B.C.
Second Macedonian War	200–197 B.C.
Battle of Cynoscephalae	197 B.C.
Proclamation of Greek freedom	196 B.C.
Syrian War	192–189 B.C.
Battle of Magnesia—defeat of Antiochus III	189 B.C.
Third Macedonian War	171–167 B.C.
Battle of Pydna	168 B.C.
Fourth Macedonian War	149–148 B.C.

Carthage must be destroyed" (see the box on p. 140). The territory of Carthage was made a province called Africa. Rome was now master of the Mediterranean Sea.

The Nature of Roman Imperialism

Rome's empire was built in three stages: the conquest of Italy, the conflict with Carthage and expansion into the western Mediterranean, and the involvement with and domination of the Hellenistic kingdoms in the eastern Mediterranean. The Romans did not possess a master plan for the creation of an empire. Much of their expansion was opportunistic; once involved in a situation that threatened their security, the Romans did not hesitate to act. And the more they expanded, the more threats to their security appeared on the horizon, involving them in yet more conflicts. Indeed, the Romans liked to portray themselves as declaring war only for defensive reasons or to protect allies. That is only part of the story, however. It is likely, as some historians have recently suggested, that at some point a group of Roman aristocratic leaders emerged who favored expansion both for the glory it offered and for the economic benefits it provided. Certainly, by the second century B.C., aristocratic senators perceived new opportunities for lucrative foreign commands, enormous spoils of war, and an abundant supply of slave labor for their growing landed estates. By that same time, the destruction of Corinth and Carthage indicate Roman imperialism had become more arrogant and brutal as well. Rome's foreign success also had enormous repercussions for the internal development of the Roman Republic.

The Destruction of Carthage
▼ ▼ ▼

The Romans used a technical breach of Carthage's peace treaty with Rome to undertake a third and final war with Carthage (149–146 B.C.). Although Carthage posed no real threat to Rome's security, the Romans still remembered the traumatic experiences of the Second Punic War when Hannibal had ravaged much of their homeland. The hardliners gained the upper hand in the senate and called for the complete destruction of Carthage. The city was razed, the survivors sold into slavery, and the land turned into a province. In this passage, the historian Appian of Alexandria describes the final destruction of Carthage by the Romans under the command of Scipio Aemilianus.

Appian, *Roman History*

Then came new scenes of horror. The fire spread and carried everything down, and the soldiers did not wait to destroy the buildings little by little, but pulled them all down together. So the crashing grew louder, and many fell with the stones into the midst dead. Others were seen still living, especially old men, women, and young children who had hidden in the inmost nooks of the houses, some of them wounded, some more or less burned, and uttering horrible cries. Still others, thrust out and falling from such a height with the stones, timbers, and fire, were torn asunder into all kinds of horrible shapes, crushed and mangled. Nor was this the end of their miseries, for the street cleaners, who were removing the rubbish with axes, mattocks, and boathooks, and making the roads passable, tossed with these instruments the dead and the living together into holes in the ground, sweeping them along like sticks and stones or turning them over with their iron tools, and man was used for filling up a ditch. Some were thrown in head foremost, while their legs, sticking out of the ground, writhed a long time. Others fell with their feet downward and their heads above the ground. Horses ran over them, crushing their faces and skulls, not purposely on the part of the riders, but in their headlong haste. Nor did the street cleaners either do these things on purpose; but the press of war, the glory of approaching victory, the rush of the soldiery, the confused noise of heralds and trumpeters all round, the tribunes and centurions changing guard and marching the cohorts hither and thither—all together made everybody frantic and heedless of the spectacle before their eyes.

Six days and nights were consumed in this kind of turmoil, the soldiers being changed so that they might not be worn out with toil, slaughter, want of sleep, and these horrid sights. . . .

Scipio, beholding this city, which had flourished 700 years from its foundation and had ruled over so many lands, islands, and seas, as rich in arms and fleets, elephants, and money as the mightiest empires, but far surpassing them in hardihood and high spirit . . . now come to its end in total destruction—Scipio, beholding this spectacle, is said to have shed tears and publicly lamented the fortune of the enemy. After meditating by himself a long time and reflecting on the inevitable fall of cities, nations, and empires, as well as of individuals, upon the fate of Troy, that once proud city, upon the fate of the Assyrian, the Median, and afterwards of the great Persian empire, and, most recently of all, of the splendid empire of Macedon, either voluntarily or otherwise the words of the poet [Homer, *Illiad*] escaped his lips:

The day shall come in which our sacred Troy
And Priam, and the people over whom
Spear-bearing Priam rules, shall perish all.

Being asked by Polybius in familiar conversation (for Polybius had been his tutor) what he meant by using these words, Polybius says that he did not hesitate frankly to name his own country, for whose fate he feared when he considered the mutability of human affairs. And Polybius wrote this down just as he heard it.

▼ Society and Culture in the Roman Republic

One of the most noticeable characteristics of Roman society and culture is the impact of the Greeks. The Romans had experienced Greek influence early on, indirectly through the Etruscans and directly through the Greek cities in southern Italy. By the end of the third century B.C., however, Greek civilization played an ever-increasing role in Roman culture. Greek ambassadors, merchants, and artists traveled to Rome and spread Greek thought and practices. After their conquest of the Hellenistic kingdoms, Roman military commanders shipped Greek manuscripts and art back to Rome. Multitudes of educated Greek slaves were used in Roman households. Virtually every area of Roman life, from literature and philosophy to religion and education, was affected by Greek models. Rich Romans hired Greek tutors and sent their sons to Athens to study. As the Roman poet Horace said, "captive Greece took captive her rude conqueror." Greek thought captivated the less sophisticated Roman minds, and the Romans became willing transmitters of Greek culture—not, however, without some resistance from Romans who had nothing but contempt for Greek politics and who feared the end of old Roman values. Even those who favored Greek culture, such as Scipio Aemilianus, blamed the Greeks for Rome's new vices, including luxury and homosexual practices.

Roman Religion

Every aspect of Roman society was permeated with religion. The main feature of early Roman religion was its animism or the belief that spirits or living forces dwell in all the objects of the natural world. Gradually, the Romans came to identify such spiritual forces with gods, but worshiped them without images or temples. The early triad of chief divinities consisted of Mars, Jupiter, and Quirinus worshiped at open-air altars on the hill called the Quirinal.

The Etruscans made a major impact on Roman religion. They introduced the personalization of the gods, so that Roman deities were now presented in human form with statues or visual images housed in temples. The Etruscans introduced a sky god, similar to the Greek Zeus and, during the period of Etruscan kingship, built a huge temple to this Jupiter. A new triad of chief deities emerged consisting of Jupiter, Juno, the patron goddess of women, and Minerva, the goddess of craftsmen. Jupiter Optimus Maximus (best and greatest) became the

▼ **A Roman Soothsayer.** Roman religion revolved around ritual, for it was by ritual, the Romans believed, that a right relationship could be established between the gods and themselves. Augurs, or soothsayers, interpreted signs revealed to people by the gods, and therefore held important positions in the state. The state magistrates would consult the augurs before every important act, and their reading of the signs either validated or condemned the proposed act. This engraving pictures a Roman soothsayer examining a liver.

patron deity of Rome and assumed central significance in the religious life of the city. As Rome developed and came into contact with other peoples and gods, the community simply adopted new deities. Hence, the Greek Hermes became the Roman Mercury and the Greek Demeter, Ceres. Apollo and Asclepius, both gods of healing, were added directly to the Roman pantheon. The Romans also took over the enormous body of Greek mythology as well. By the end of the third century B.C., a rather complete amalgamation of Greek and Roman religion had occurred. In general, the Romans were very tolerant of new religious cults and only occasionally outlawed them. The most prominent example occurred in 186 B.C. when

authorities curtailed the orgiastic cult of Bacchus (Dionysus) because of its danger to public morals and because its secret societies seemed to be fomenting anti-Roman conspiracies.

Roman religion focused on the worship of the gods for a very practical reason—human beings were thought to be totally dependent upon them. The Romans expressed this dependency in contractual terms. If a man followed the correct ritual in worship, then the gods would act favorably toward him; if they granted his request, he must make an offering in gratitude; if a man failed to observe proper ritual, he could expect to be punished. Not morality, but the exact performance of ritual was crucial to establishing a right relationship with the gods. What was true for individuals was also valid for the state. It also had to observe correct ritual in order to receive its reward. Accurate performance of ritual was consequently important, and the Romans established a college of priests or pontiffs to carry out that responsibility. Initially three in number, by the first century B.C., they had increased to sixteen. The pontiffs were in charge of what the Romans called the *ius divinum* (divine law) or, in other words, of maintaining the right relationship between the state and the gods. The pontiffs then were really officials of the state; in effect, they were the heads of the religious department of state. They performed all public religious acts and supervised magistrates in the correct ritual for public political acts. If the rituals were performed correctly, then the Romans would obtain the "peace of the gods." No doubt, the Roman success in creating an empire was a visible confirmation of divine favor. As Cicero, the first-century politician and writer claimed, "We have overcome all the nations of the world, because we have realized that the world is directed and governed by the gods."[1] Religion and politics obviously went hand in hand to the Romans, despite the abuses of the late Republic in the first century B.C. when politicians frequently manipulated religion in the interests of politics.

In addition to the college of pontiffs, a college of augurs existed whose responsibility was to interpret the signs (auspices) or warnings that the gods gave to men. Before every important act of state, a magistrate with *imperium* took the auspices to make sure the gods approved. The Romans attributed great importance to this—if the omens were unfavorable, then the act was invalid or the planned action was not auspicious. As Cicero later commented, the augurs had "the highest and most important authority in the State" because "no act of any magistrate at home or in the field can have any validity for any person without their authority."[2] Aus-

pices were taken by observing the flights of birds, lightning and other natural phenomena, and the behavior of certain animals.

Just as the state had an official cult, so too did families. Because the family was regarded as a small state within the state, it had its own household cults, which included Janus, the spirit of the doorway; Vesta, goddess of the hearth; and the Penates, the spirits of the storehouse. Here, too, proper ritual was important, and it was the responsibility of the *paterfamilias* as head of the family to ensure proper fulfillment of religious obligations. One of the most important ceremonies involved purification. In his manual *On Agriculture*, Marcus Cato the Elder spelled out the proper ritual for purification of a landed estate. The ceremony included these words:

> Father Mars [god of vegetation as well as war], I beg and entreat you to be of good will and favorable to me and to our house and household, for which purpose I have ordered the swine-sheep-bull procession to be led around my land and fields and farm. And [I beg] that you will check, thrust back, and avert diseases seen and unseen, crop failure and crop destruction, sudden losses and storms, and that you will permit the annual crops, the grain crops, the vineyards, and tree and vine slips to grow and turn out well. And [that you] keep safe the shepherds and the flocks and give good health and strength to me and to our house and household: with these purposes in view . . . receive the honor of this suckling swine–sheep–bull sacrifice.[3]

Proper observance of the ritual was so crucial that any error necessitated a repetition of the entire ritual.

Religious festivals were an important part of Roman religious practice. There were two kinds: public festivals ordained and paid for by the state and private festivals celebrated by individuals and families. Public festivals included annual ones, such as the Lupercalia, and irregular ones that were held upon the occasion of a victory or emergency of some kind. By the mid-second century B.C., six public festivals were celebrated annually, each lasting several days.

The holding of games also grew out of religious festivals. They were inaugurated in honor of Jupiter Optimus Maximus, but became annual events by 366 B.C. In the late Republic both the number of games and the number of days they lasted were increased. Consequently, state funds became inadequate for the magnificence expected, and the aediles, who were in charge of the games and hoped to use their office as a stepping-stone to higher political offices, paid additional expenses out of their own pockets. Originally, the games consisted of chariot racing in the Circus Maximus; later, animal hunts and

theatrical performances were added. In the Empire, gladiatorial contests would become the primary focus.

Education

The Romans did not possess a system of public education. In the early Republic, education consisted of training in the various skills needed by a Roman citizen and was done within the context of the family. Such training would include mastering the basic elements of farming; developing physical skills needed for soldiering; learning the traditions of the state through the legends of heroic Roman ancestors; and becoming acquainted with public affairs.

Through contact with the Greek world, Roman education took on new ideals in the third and second centuries B.C. The wealthy classes wanted their children exposed to Greek studies and were especially attracted to the training in rhetoric and philosophy that would prepare their sons for a successful public career. This training, of course, accorded well with Roman practicality. The new educational ideal emphasized the concept of *humanitas*—essentially, an education in the liberal arts that would avoid overspecialization, develop sound character, and prepare one for a public career.

Since knowledge of Greek was a crucial ingredient in education, schools taught by professional teachers emerged to supply this need. Those who could afford to might provide Greek tutors for their children. But private schools with instruction provided mostly by educated slaves or freedmen, who were usually Greeks, also developed for less well endowed families. After several years of primary instruction, whose aim was simply to teach the basics of reading, writing, and arithmetic, the pupil went to a secondary school run by a *grammaticus* or grammarian. These schools had a standard curriculum based on the liberal arts: literature, dialectic, arithmetic, geometry, astronomy, and music. The core of the liberal arts and the curriculum, however, was Greek literature. As a result, by the second and first centuries B.C., educated Romans had become increasingly bilingual. Higher education in Rome consisted of special schools of oratory run by Greeks of high social standing. Romans seriously interested in the pursuit of philosophy rounded off their education by going to school in Greece, especially Athens, which was still considered the primary center for philosophical study.

Slavery

While slavery was a common institution throughout the ancient world, no people possessed more slaves or relied so much on slave labor as the Romans eventually did. Before the third century B.C., a small Roman farmer might possess one or two slaves who would help farm his few acres and perform domestic chores. Only the very rich would have large numbers of slaves. These slaves would most likely be from Italy and be regarded as part of the family household.

The Roman conquest of the Mediterranean brought a drastic change in the use of slaves. Large numbers of foreign slaves were brought back to Italy. During the Republic, then, the chief source of slaves was from capture in war, followed by piracy. Of course, the children of slaves also became slaves. While some Roman generals brought back slaves to be sold to benefit the public treasury, ambitious generals of the first century, such as Pompey and Caesar, made personal fortunes by treating slaves captured by their armies as private property.

Slaves were used in many ways in Roman society. The rich, of course, owned the most and the best. In the late Republic it became a badge of prestige to be attended by many slaves. Greeks were in much demand in households as tutors, musicians, doctors, and artists. Roman businessmen would employ them as shop assistants or craftsmen. Slaves were also used as farm laborers; in fact, huge gangs of slaves worked the large landed estates known as *latifundia* under pitiful conditions. Cato the Elder argued that it was cheaper to work them to death and then replace them than to treat them favorably. Many slaves of all nationalities were used as menial household workers, such as cooks, valets, waiters, cleaners, and gardeners. The building of roads and aqueducts and other public buildings was done by contractors utilizing slave labor. The total number of slaves is difficult to judge—estimates vary from two to four free men to every slave.

It is also difficult to generalize about the treatment of Roman slaves. There are numerous instances of humane treatment by masters and situations where slaves even protected their owners from danger out of gratitude and esteem. But slaves were also subject to severe punishments, torture, abuse, and hard labor that drove some to run away or even revolt against their owners. The Republic had stringent laws against aiding a runaway slave. The murder of a master by a slave might mean the execution of all the other household slaves. Near the end of the second century B.C., large-scale slave revolts occurred in Sicily where enormous gangs of slaves were subjected to horrible working conditions on large landed estates. Slaves were branded, beaten, fed inadequately, worked in chains, and housed at night in underground prisons. It took three years (from 135 to 132 B.C.) to

Cato the Elder on Women
▼ ▼ ▼

During the Second Punic War, the Romans enacted the Oppian Law, which limited the amount of gold women could possess and restricted their dress and use of carriages. In 195 B.C., an attempt to repeal the law was made, and women demonstrated in the streets on behalf of this effort. According to the Roman historian Livy, the conservative Roman official Cato the Elder spoke against repeal and against the women favoring it. Although the words are probably not Cato's own, they do reflect a traditional male Roman attitude toward women.

Livy, *The History of Rome*

"If each of us, citizens, had determined to assert his rights and dignity as a husband with respect to his own spouse, we should have less trouble with the sex as a whole; as it is, our liberty, destroyed at home by female violence, even here in the Forum is crushed and trodden underfoot, and because we have not kept them individually under control, we dread them collectively. . . . But from no class is there not the greatest danger if you permit them meetings and gatherings and secret consultations. . . ."

"Our ancestors permitted no women to conduct even personal business without a guardian to intervene in her behalf; they wished them to be under the control of fathers, brothers, husbands; we (Heaven help us!) allow them now even to interfere in public affairs, yes, and to visit the Forum and our informal and formal sessions. What else are they doing now on the streets and at the corners except urging the bill of the tribunes and voting for the repeal of the law? Give loose rein to their uncontrollable nature and to this untamed creature and expect that they will themselves set bounds to their licence; unless you act, this is the least of the things enjoined upon women by custom or law and to which they submit with a feeling of injustice. It is complete liberty or, rather, if we wish to speak the truth, complete licence that they desire."

"If they win in this, what will they not attempt? Review all the laws with which your forefathers restrained their licence and made them subject to their husbands; even with all these bonds you can scarcely control them. What of this? If you suffer them to seize these bonds one by one and wrench themselves free and finally to be placed on a parity with their husbands, do you think that you will be able to endure them? The moment they begin to be your equals, they will be your superiors. . . ."

"Now they publicly address other women's husbands, and, what is more serious, they beg for a law and votes, and from sundry men they get what they ask. In matters affecting yourself, your property, your children, you, Sir, can be importuned; once the law has ceased to set a limit to your wife's expenditures you will never set it yourself. Do not think, citizens, that the situation which existed before the law was passed will ever return. . . ."

---

crush a revolt of 70,000 slaves, and the great revolt on Sicily (104–101 B.C.) involved most of the island and took a Roman army of 17,000 men to suppress it. The most famous revolt on the Italian peninsula occurred in 73 B.C. Led by a Thracian gladiator named Spartacus, the revolt broke out in southern Italy and involved 70,000 slaves. Spartacus managed to defeat several Roman armies before he was finally trapped and killed in southern Italy in 71 B.C. Six thousand of his followers were crucified, the traditional form of execution for slaves.

The Roman Family

At the heart of the Roman social structure stood the family, headed by the *paterfamilias*—the dominant male.

The household also included the wife, sons with their wives and children, unmarried daughters, and slaves. As we have seen, a family was virtually a small state within the state, and the power of the *paterfamilias* was parallel to that of the state magistrates over citizens. Like the Greeks, Roman males believed that the weakness of the female sex necessitated male guardians (see the box above). The *paterfamilias* exercised that authority; upon his death, sons or the nearest male relatives assumed the role of guardians. By the late Republic, however, although the rights of male guardians remained legally in effect, upper-class women found numerous ways to circumvent the power of their guardians.

Fathers arranged the marriages of daughters, although there are instances of mothers and daughters having influence on the choice. In the Republic women married

cum manu, "with legal control" passing from father to husband. By the mid-first century B.C., the dominant practice had changed to *sine manu*, "without legal control," which meant that married daughters officially remained within the father's legal power. Since the fathers of most married women were dead, not being in the "legal control" of a husband entailed independent property rights that forceful women could translate into considerable power within the household and outside it. Traditionally, Roman marriages were intended to be for life, but divorce was introduced in the third century and became relatively easy to obtain since either party could initiate it and no one needed to prove the breakdown of the marriage. Divorce became especially prevalent in the first century B.C.—a period of political turmoil—when marriages were used to cement political alliances.

Some parents in upper-class families provided education for their daughters. Some had private tutors and others may have gone to primary schools. But, at the age when boys were entering secondary schools, girls were pushed into marriage. The legal minimum age was twelve, although fourteen was a more common age in practice. Although some Roman doctors warned that early pregnancies could be dangerous to young girls, early marriages persisted due to the desire to benefit from dowries as soon as possible and the reality of early mortality. A good example is Tullia, Cicero's beloved daughter. She was married at sixteen, widowed at twenty-two, remarried one year later, divorced at twenty-eight, remarried at twenty-nine, and divorced at thirty-three. She died at thirty-four, not unusual for females in Roman society.

In contrast to upper-class Athenian women, Roman upper-class women were not segregated from males in the home. Wives were appreciated as enjoyable company and were at the center of household social life. Women talked to visitors and were free to shop, visit friends, and go to games, temples, and theaters. Nevertheless, they were not allowed to participate in public life, although there are examples of women exerting considerable political influence through their husbands.

Law

One of Rome's chief gifts to the Mediterranean world of its day and to succeeding generations of Western civilization was its development of law. After the Twelve Tables of 450 B.C., there was no complete codification of Roman law until that of the Byzantine Emperor Justinian in the sixth century A.D. (see Chapter 7). The Twelve Tables, although inappropriate for later times, were

▼ **A Roman Lady.** Roman women, mainly those of the upper class, developed comparatively more freedom than women in classical Athens despite the persistent male belief that women required guardianship. While usually pushed into early marriages, some upper-class Roman women received an education, and many were not segregated from males in the household. They could visit friends, temples, and the theater, and were, in general, the center of the social life of a household. This mural decoration was found in the remains of a villa destroyed by the eruption of Mount Vesuvius.

never officially abrogated and were still memorized by schoolboys in the first century B.C. Civil law (*ius civile*) derived from the Twelve Tables proved inadequate for later Roman needs, however, and gave way to corrections and additions by the praetors. Upon taking office, a praetor issued an edict listing his guidelines for dealing with different kinds of legal cases. Although as a member of the Roman ruling class the praetor was knowledgeable in law, he also relied on Roman jurists for advice in preparing his edicts. These jurists were not professional lawyers, but amateur law experts, who helped to determine the law through the use of precedents, not theory. Their interpretations, often embodied in the edicts of the praetors, created a body of legal principles.

In 242 B.C., the Romans appointed a second praetor responsible for examining suits involving non-Romans. The Romans found that although some of their rules of law could be used in these cases, special rules were often needed. These rules gave rise to a body of law known as the *ius gentium*—the law of nations—defined by the Romans as "that part of the law which we apply both to ourselves and to foreigners." But the influence of Greek philosophy, primarily Stoicism, led Romans in the late Republic to develop the idea of *ius naturale*—the law of nature—or universal divine law derived from right reason. The Romans came to view their *ius gentium* as derived from or identical to this *ius naturale*, thus giving Roman jurists a philosophical justification for systematizing Roman law according to basic principles.

Literature and Art

The Romans produced little literature before the third century B.C. The Latin literature that emerged in that century was strongly influenced by Greek models. In drama, for example, Latin translations of Greek plays for presentation at the public festivals in Rome introduced Romans to the world of Greek theater. The demand for plays at public festivals eventually led to a growing number of native playwrights. The best-known were Plautus and Terence.

Plautus (c. 254–184 B.C.) used plots from Greek New Comedy (see Chapter 4) for his own plays (see the box on p. 147). The actors wore Greek costumes and Greek masks and portrayed the same stock characters: the dirty old men, the skillful slaves, the prostitutes, and the young men in love, whose pains are recounted in this brief excerpt:

Not the throes of all mankind
Equal my distracted mind.
I strain and I toss
On a passionate cross;
Love's goad makes me reel,
I whirl on Love's wheel,
In a swoon of despair
Hurried here, hurried there—
Torn asunder, I am blind
With a cloud upon my mind.[4]

While indebted to the Greeks, Plautus managed to infuse his plays with his own earthy Latin quality, incorporating elements that appealed to the Romans: drunkenness, gluttony, and womanizing. Plautus wrote for the masses and became a very popular playwright in Rome.

A second playwright of distinction was Terence (185–159 B.C.), who was born in Carthage and brought to Rome as a slave by a Roman senator who freed him. Terence died at an early age after he had written six plays. He also used plots from Greek New Comedy, but his plays contained less slapstick than those of Plautus. Terence was more concerned with the subtle portrayal of character and the artistry of his language. His refined Latin style appealed more to a cultivated audience than to the masses. In the prologue to *The Brothers*, he stated:

The author . . . takes it as a high compliment if he can win the approval of men who themselves find favor with you all

▼ **Roman Theater—A Comedy Scene.** Early Latin works in the realms of poetry and playwriting tended to be copies of Greek originals. With a growing demand for plays at public festivals, however, more and more Latin playwrights emerged. Many, such as Plautus, continued to borrow from the Greeks. The actors wore Greek masks, dressed as Greeks, and represented the stock characters developed in Greek theater. Distinctly Roman elements, however, such as gluttony and womanizing, were sometimes added. This marble relief depicts a scene from a New Comedy play.

Roman Comedy
▼ ▼ ▼

This excerpt is a scene from one of the plays of Plautus. While Plautus made use of Greek New Comedy, his devious plots and earthiness were original. His farcical humor and buffoonery made his plays exceedingly popular, especially with the masses. This excerpt is from Miles Gloriosus ("The Swaggering Soldier"). This opening scene features a pompous general and a parasitical bootlicker. Plautus loved to create fantastic names for his characters. Pyrgopolynices means "Often victorious over fortresses" and Artotrogus means "Bread eater."

Plautus, *The Swaggering Soldier*

Pyrgopolynices: My shield, there—have it burnished brighter than the bright splendour of the sun on any summer's day. Next time I have occasion to use it in the press of battle, it must flash defiance into the eyes of the opposing foe. My sword, too, I see, is pining for attention; poor chap, he's quite disheartened and cast down, hanging idly at my side so long; he's simply itching to get at an enemy and carve him into little pieces. . . . Where's Artotrogus?

Artotrogus: Here, at his master's heels, close to his hero, his brave, his blessed, his royal, his doughty warrior—whose valor Mars himself could hardly challenge or outshine.

Pyrgopolynices [reminiscent]: Ay—what of the man whose life I saved on the Curculionean field, where the enemy was led by Bumbomachides Clytomestoridysarchides, a grandson of Neptune?

Artotrogus: I remember it well. I remember his golden armor, and how you scattered his legions with a puff of breath, like a wind sweeping up leaves or lifting the thatch from a roof.

Pyrgopolynices [modestly]: It was nothing much, after all.

Artotrogus: Oh, to be sure, nothing to the many more famous deeds you did—[aside] or never did. [He comes down, leaving the captain attending to his men.] If anyone ever saw a bigger liar or more conceited braggart than this one, he can have me for keeps. . . . The only thing to be said for him is, his cook makes a marvellous olive salad. . . .

Pyrgopolynices [missing him]: Where have you got to, Artotrogus?

Artotrogus [obsequiously]: Here I am sir. I was thinking about that elephant in India, and how you broke his ulna with a single blow of your fist.

Pyrgopolynices: His ulna, was it?

Artotrogus: His femur, I should have said.

Pyrgopolynices: It was only a light blow, too.

Artotrogus: By Jove, yes, if you had really hit him, your arm would have smashed through the animal's hide, bones, and guts.

Pyrgopolynices [modestly]: I'd rather not talk about it, really.

---

and with the general public, men whose services in war, in peace, and in your private affairs, are given at the right moment, without ostentation, to be available for each one of you.[5]

As this quotation indicates, Terence really wrote for Rome's aristocracy.

Latin prose works developed later than poetry and playwriting and were often the products of Rome's ruling elite. These upper classes were interested in history because it could be a means of exalting their ideals and in oratory because it could be an important instrument for effective statecraft. Hence, their emphasis in writing prose was on works of a practical value. This is a prominent feature of the oldest existing work of Latin prose, Cato the Elder's treatise *On Agriculture*. In effect, this was a technical manual reminiscent of the practical handbooks produced in the Hellenistic world.

Despite their attraction to the Greek world, Romans were generally repelled by much of Greek philosophy with the exception of Stoicism. The latter's emphasis on virtuous conduct and performance of duty (see Chapter 4) fit well with Roman ideals and the practical bent of the Roman character. Panaetius of Rhodes (c. 180–111 B.C.), whose works helped introduce Stoicism to the Romans, proved especially popular.

The Romans were also dependent on the Greeks for artistic inspiration. During the third and second centuries B.C., they adopted many features of the Hellenistic style of art (see Chapter 4). The Romans excelled in architecture, a highly practical art. In addition to their justly famous highways, they built bridges and aqueducts

▼ **Appian Way.** The Romans were a practical-minded people. Because of this, they excelled in certain arts, one of which was architecture. In addition to aqueducts, amphitheaters, and tenement buildings, the Romans constructed a series of highways that traversed and linked together the Roman world. Pictured here is one such highway, the Appian Way, created by the censor Appius Claudius in 312 B.C. The Appian Way connected Rome to Capua through the Pontine plain.

making use of the arch. They also developed a new technique by using concrete in construction projects. Its utilization made possible the erection of giant amphitheaters, public baths, and the high-rise tenement buildings that housed Rome's exploding population in the late second and first centuries B.C.

The Romans developed a taste for Greek statues, which they placed not only in public buildings, but in their private houses. Once demand outstripped the supply of original works, reproductions of Greek statues became fashionable. The Romans' own portrait sculpture was characterized by an intense realism that included even unpleasant physical details.

Values and Attitudes

By their very nature, the Romans were a conservative people. They were very concerned about maintaining the *mos maiorum,* the customs or traditions of their ancestors. The Romans emphasized parental authority and,

above all, their obligations to the state. The highest virtue was *pietas*—the dutiful execution of one's obligations to one's fellow citizens, to the gods, and to the state.

By the second century B.C., however, the creation of an empire had begun to weaken the old values. The Romans began to place greater stress on affluence, status, and material possessions. There was also more emphasis on individualism and less on collective well-being, on the old public spirit that had served Rome so well. Those who worried about the decline of the old values blamed it on different causes. Some felt that after the destruction of Carthage, the Romans no longer had any strong enemies to challenge them. Others believed that the Romans had simply been overwhelmed by the affluence created by the new empire. And finally, there were those who blamed everything on the Greeks for importing ideas and practices baneful to the Romans.

Of course, Romans responded differently to the changes brought by the creation of an empire. Two examples from the second century demonstrate this well. Marcus Cato the Elder (234–149 B.C.) was a Roman praetor, consul, and member of the ruling class who became censor in 184. Cato scorned the "Greeklings"—people who followed Greek ways and read Greek philosophy and literature. He even introduced a decree to force all Greek philosophers to leave Rome. He wrote to his son:

> I shall speak about those Greek fellows in their proper place, son Marcus, and point out the results of my enquiries at Athens, and convince you what benefit comes from dipping into their literature, and not making a close study of it. They are a quite worthless people, and an intractable one, and you must consider my words prophetic. When that race gives us literature it will corrupt all things. . . .[6]

But Cato was not stupid. He not only learned Greek himself but also allowed his own son to study in Athens. He knew only too well that, like it or not, Greek was becoming a necessity for Roman political life.

Scipio Aemilianus (185–129 B.C.) was a member of a patrician family and a brilliant general who easily achieved the top offices of the Roman state. Scipio was also concerned about the traditional Roman values, but he was much more inclined to accept Rome's growing urbanization as it became the center of the Mediterranean world and was consequently more open to the Greeks as well. He was a philhellene—an admirer of Greek philosophy and literature. He created the so-called Scipionic circle, a group of intellectuals dedicated to Greek thought, which included Polybius, Terence, and Panaetius. While desirous of maintaining old Ro-

The Decline of the Roman Republic
▼ ▼ ▼

*A*lthough Rome stood supreme over the Mediterranean world by 133 B.C., the internal structure of the Republic began to disintegrate. Over the next hundred years, the Republic was afflicted with mob violence, assassinations, civil wars, and unscrupulous politicians who seized every opportunity to advance their own interests. The Roman historian Sallust (86–35 B.C.), who lived through many of these crises, reflected upon the causes of Rome's problems. In this selection, he discusses the moral decline that set in after the destruction of Carthage in 146 B.C.

Sallust, *The War with Catiline*

Accordingly, good morals were cultivated at home and in the field; [in the early Republic] there was the greatest harmony and little or no avarice; justice and probity prevailed among them, thanks not so much to laws as to nature. Quarrels, discord, and strife were reserved for their enemies; citizen vied with citizen only for the prize of merit. They were lavish in their offerings to the gods, frugal in the home, loyal to their friends. By practicing these two qualities, boldness in warfare and justice when peace came, they watched over themselves and their country. In proof of these statements, I present this convincing evidence; firstly, in time of war punishment was more often inflicted for attacking the enemy contrary to orders, or for withdrawing too tardily when recalled from the field, than for venturing to abandon the standards or to give ground under stress; and sec-

ondly, in time of peace they ruled by kindness rather than fear, and when wronged preferred forgiveness to vengeance.

But when our country had grown great through toil and the practice of justice, when great kings had been vanquished in war, savage tribes and mighty peoples subdued by force of arms, when Carthage, the rival of Rome's sway, had perished root and branch, and all seas and lands were open, then Fortune began to grow cruel and to bring confusion into all our affairs. Those who had found it easy to bear hardships and dangers, anxiety and adversity, found leisure and wealth, desirable under other circumstances, a burden and a curse. Hence the lust for power first, then for money, grew upon them; these were, I may say, the root of all evils. For avarice destroyed honor, integrity, and all other noble qualities; taught in their place insolence, cruelty, to neglect the gods, to set a price on everything. Ambition drove many men to become false; to have one thought locked in the breast, another ready on the tongue; to value friendships and enmities not on their merits but by the standard of self-interest, and to show a good front rather than a good heart. At first these vices grew slowly, from time to time they were punished; finally, when the disease had spread like a deadly plague, the state was changed and a government second to none in equity and excellence became cruel and intolerable.

man virtues, Scipio was well aware that the acquisition of an empire had created a new world with new demands and values.

▼ The Decline and Fall of the Roman Republic (133–31 B.C.)

By the mid-second century B.C., Roman domination of the Mediterranean Sea was well established. The process of creating an empire had weakened and threatened the internal stability of Rome. To paraphrase a Christian injunction: what did it profit Rome to gain the whole world and lose its soul? This internal instability characterizes the period of Roman history from 133 until 31 B.C., when the armies of Octavian defeated Mark Antony and stood supreme over the Roman world. By that time, the constitution of the Roman Republic was in shambles (see the box above).

Background: Social, Economic, and Political Problems

By the second century B.C., the senate had become the effective governing body of the Roman state. It had achieved this position not by constitutional enactment but through its own initiative–not through law, but by custom. It comprised some 300 men, drawn primarily from the landed aristocracy; they remained senators for life and held the chief magistracies of the Republic. During the wars of the third and second centuries, the senate came to exercise enormous power. It directed the wars and took control of both foreign and domestic policy, including financial affairs. The *senatus consultum*, or advice of the senate to the consuls, had come to have the force of law.

Moreover, the magistracies and senate were increasingly controlled by a relatively select circle of wealthy and powerful families—both patrician and plebeian—called the *nobiles* ("nobles") The *nobiles* were essentially the men whose families were elected to the more important political offices of the Republic. In the hundred years from 233 to 133 B.C., 80 percent of the consuls came from twenty-six families; moreover, 50 percent came from only ten families. Hence, the *nobiles* constituted a governing oligarchy that managed, through its landed wealth, patronage, and intimidation, to maintain its hold over the magistracies and senate and thus guide the destiny of Rome while running the state in its own interests. When a new man—called a *novus homo*—did win a consulship, he and his descendants became members of this select oligarchy. The *nobiles* and other aristocrats also tended to split into various allied groups, strengthened by intermarriage, for the political advantage of the *familiea.*

By the end of the second century B.C., two types of aristocratic leaders called the *optimates* ("the best men") and the *populares* ("favoring the people") became prominent. These were not political parties or even individual cliques, but leaders who followed two different approaches to politics. *Optimates* and *populares* were terms of political rhetoric that were used by individuals within the aristocracy against fellow aristocratic rivals to distinguish one set of tactics from another. The *optimates* tended to be the *nobiles* who currently controlled the senate and wished to maintain their oligarchical privileges, while the *populares* were usually other ambitious aristocrats who used the peoples' assemblies, especially

▼ **Map 5.4** Roman Empire in the Late Republic.

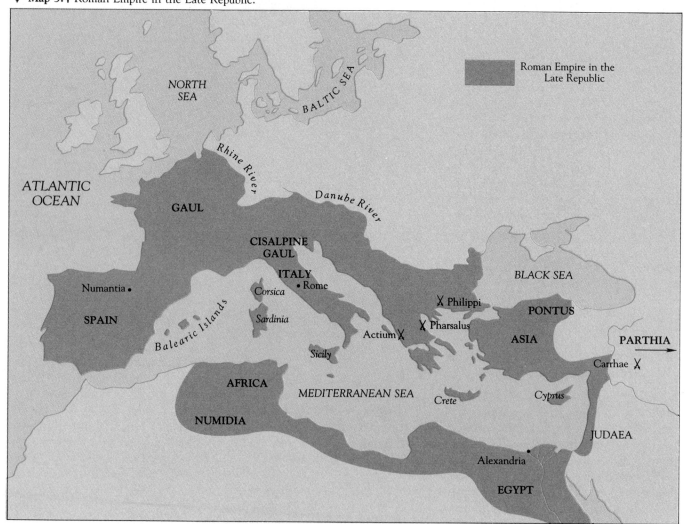

the *concilium plebis* as instruments to break the domination of the *optimates*. Although politicians of both types pursued their own political ambitions, they may also have believed some of their own rhetoric—that a traditional oligarchy on the one hand or a leadership more concerned with the desires of nonaristocrats on the other was best for Rome. In any case, the conflicts between these two types of aristocratic leaders and their supporters engulfed the first century in political turmoil.

Another social group in Rome also became entangled in this political turmoil—the *equites* or equestrians, a name derived from the fact that they had once formed Rome's cavalry. The equestrians had become extremely wealthy through a variety of means, many of which were related to the creation of the empire. Some, for example, were private contractors who derived their wealth from government contracts for the collection of taxes, the outfitting of armies, and the construction of fleets and public works. In 218 B.C., the senate had effectively barred these people from high political office by enacting a law that forbade senators to bid for state contracts or engage in commerce. By the end of the second century B.C., the equestrians were seeking real political power commensurate with their financial stake in the empire. They would play an important role in the political turmoil that brought an end to the Republic.

Of course, both equestrians and *nobiles* formed only a tiny minority of the Roman people. The backbone of the Roman state and army had traditionally been the small farmer class. But economic changes that began in the period of the Punic Wars increasingly undermined the position of that group. This occurred for several reasons. Their lands had been severely damaged during the second Punic War when Hannibal invaded Italy. Moreover, in order to win the wars, Rome had to increase the term of military service from two to six years. When they returned to their lands, many farmers found them so deteriorated that they chose to sell out instead of restoring them. By this time, capitalistic agriculture was also increasing rapidly. Landed aristocrats had been able to develop large estates (called *latifundia*) by taking over state-owned land and by buying out small peasant owners. These large estates relied on slave and tenant labor and frequently concentrated on cash crops, such as vines for wine, olives, and sheep for wool, which small farmers could not afford to do. Thus, the rise of *latifundia* contributed to the decline in the number of small citizen farmers. Since the latter group traditionally formed the backbone of the Roman army—Romans only conscripted people with a financial stake in the community—the number of men available for military service declined. Moreover, many of these small farmers

drifted to the cities, especially Rome, forming a large class of day laborers who possessed no property. This new class of urban proletariat formed a highly unstable mass with the potential for much trouble in depressed times. Thus, Rome's economic, social, and political problems were serious and needed attention. In 133 B.C., a member of the aristocracy proposed a solution that infuriated his fellow aristocrats.

The Reforms of Tiberius and Gaius Gracchus (133–121 B.C.)

Tiberius Gracchus (163–133 B.C.) was a member of the *nobiles* who ruled Rome. Although concerned with the immediate problem of a shortage of military recruits, Tiberius believed that the underlying cause of Rome's problems was the decline of the small farmer, the traditional backbone of the army and state. Tiberius was not a revolutionary, and his proposals for reform, drafted with the help of several prominent senators, were essentially conservative; he was looking backward to what had constituted the foundation of Rome's greatness.

Tiberius Gracchus was elected one of the tribunes of the plebs for 133 B.C. Without consulting the senate, where he knew his rivals would oppose his proposal, Tiberius took his legislation directly to the *concilium plebis* or plebeian council. After some effort, his land-reform bill was passed. It placed limits on the amount of state-owned land (*ager publicus* or "public land") that could be held by any Roman and stipulated that the public land reclaimed in this fashion should be given to landless Romans on a permanent lease at low rent. Tiberius believed this would restore the small farmer and reinvigorate the traditional system. His law also established a land commission to redistribute the land. Many senators, themselves large landowners whose estates included large tracts of public land, opposed this reform, which would also have created a large mass of clients loyal to Tiberius among the rural voters. When Tiberius decided to run again for the office of tribune, a group of senators, fearful that his appeal to such a large bloc of voters would make him and his supporters even more powerful, took the law into their own hands and assassinated him. The land commission continued to divide the large estates, although its work was slowed after 129 B.C., when the senate deprived the commission of its judicial power. The land reform of Tiberius had not failed (thousands of small allotments had been made), but the use of political violence—the breaking of the law by the people sworn to uphold it—to prevent Tiberius from reaping the political rewards of his reform created an ominous omen for the Republic.

Reforms of Tiberius Gracchus	133 B.C.
Reforms of Gaius Gracchus	123–122 B.C.
Jugurthine War	111–105 B.C.
Marius: First consulship	107 B.C.
Marius: Consecutive consulships	104–100 B.C.
Italian or Social War	90–88 B.C.
Sulla's march on Rome	88 B.C.
Sulla as dictator	82–79 B.C.
Pompey's command in Spain	77–71 B.C.
Campaign of Crassus against Spartacus	73–71 B.C.
Consulship of Crassus and Pompey	70 B.C.
First Triumvirate (Caesar, Pompey, Crassus)	60 B.C.
Caesar in Gaul	59–49 B.C.
Crassus and Pompey as consuls	55 B.C.
Crassus killed by Parthians	53 B.C.
Caesar crosses the Rubicon	49 B.C.
Battle of Pharsalus; Pompey is killed in Egypt	48 B.C.
End of civil war	45 B.C.
Caesar as dictator	47–44 B.C.
Second Triumvirate (Octavian, Antony, Marcus Lepidus) is formed; Cicero is killed	43 B.C.
Defeat of Caesar's assassins at Philippi	42 B.C.
Octavian defeats Antony at Actium	31 B.C.

lectors. Thus, Gaius gave the *equites* two instruments of public power: control over the jury courts that often tried provincial governors, and provincial taxation. Another law appealed to the Roman proletariat by establishing government subsidies that enabled grain to be sold at below market prices. Finally, Gaius proposed legislation that would have made all Latin allies Roman citizens. Although this legislation probably failed to pass, this offer of Roman citizenship was widely popular throughout Italy, but not among Romans who feared that their privileges would be diluted by such a large influx of new citizens.

Despite his efforts, Gaius was not reelected to the tribuneship for a third year. Fellow senators, hostile to his reforms and fearful of his growing popularity, made use of a constitutional innovation, a *senatus consultum ultimum* (a final decree of the senate), which virtually gave the consuls the right to use martial law against Gaius and his followers. As a result, the reformer and many of his friends were killed in 121 B.C.

The attempts of the Gracchi brothers to bring reforms by using the tribuneship and *concilium plebis* created a popular alternative to the power of the *optimates* in the magistracies and senate. No doubt both sides felt justified in their positions: the *populares* believed they needed to bypass the senate to break the domination of their rivals within the senatorial aristocracy, while the *optimates* thought that the popular leaders were aspirants to tyranny who were using the masses to further their own ambitions. Although there may have been an element of truth on both sides, the unwillingness to compromise and the willingness to use assassination and constitutionally dubious expedients simply opened the door to more instability and further violence.

Marius and the New Roman Army

In the closing years of the second century B.C., a series of military disasters gave rise to a fresh outburst of popular anger against the old leaders of the senate and resulted in the rise of Marius (157–86 B.C.).

Marius came to prominence during the war in northern Africa against Jugurtha and the Numidians. The senate had badly bungled the war effort. Marius had served as legate to the senatorial-appointed commanding general Metellus, but quarreled with his superior, returned to Rome, and ran for the consulship on a "win the war" campaign slogan. Despite being a *novus homo*—a "new man"—from the equestrian order, Marius won and became a consul for 107 B.C. The plebeian council then voted to give Marius command of the army

The efforts of Tiberius Gracchus were continued by his brother Gaius, elected tribune for both 123 and 122 B.C. Gaius broadened his reform program to appeal to more people disenchanted with the current senatorial leadership. He restored the old judicial powers in the land commission and appealed to the small farmers by quickening the pace of land redistribution. To win the support of the *equites*, he replaced the senators on the jury courts that tried provincial governors accused of extortion with members of the equestrian order and opened the new province of Asia to equestrian tax col-in Africa, a definite encroachment on the senate's right to conduct wars. Generals no longer needed to be loyal to the senate.

Marius brought the Jugurthine War to a successful conclusion and was then called upon to defeat the Celtic tribes (or Gauls, as the Romans called them), who had annihilated a Roman army and threatened an invasion of Italy. Marius was made consul for five years, from 104 to 100 B.C., raised a new army, and decisively defeated the Celts, leaving him in a position of personal ascendancy in Rome.

In raising a new army, Marius initiated military reforms that proved to have drastic consequences. The Roman army had traditionally been a conscript army of small landholders. Marius recruited volunteers from both the urban and rural proletariat who possessed no property. These volunteers swore an oath of loyalty to the general, not the senate, and thus inaugurated a professional-type army that might no longer be subject to the state. Moreover, to recruit these men, a general would promise them land, so generals had to play politics in order to get legislation passed that would provide the land for their veterans. In 100 B.C., for example, while still consul, Marius entered into an alliance with a tribune, Saturninus, to gain land for his soldiers through legislation in the plebeian council. However, complications arose, and the senate passed a final decree requesting Marius as consul to put down Saturninus. Marius did so, apparently putting the senate's call for order ahead of his previous alliance with the tribune. Soon after, Marius retired from politics. But he left a powerful legacy. He had created a new system of military recruitment that placed much power in the hands of the individual generals. By using his army to crush Saturninus, he had shown how this army could be used to save the Republic. His action had another implication as well—such an army could also be used to destroy the Republic. Roman republican politics was entering a new and potentially dangerous stage.

The Role of Sulla

After almost a decade of relative quiet, the Roman Republic was threatened with another crisis—the Italian War (90–88 B.C.). This war resulted from Rome's unwillingness to deal constructively with the complaints of its Italian allies. These allies had fought loyally on Rome's side but felt they had not shared sufficiently in the lands and bonuses given to Roman veterans. In 90 B.C., the Italians rebelled and formed their own confederation. After a two-year struggle, the Romans managed

to end the rebellion, but only by granting full rights of Roman citizenship to all free Italians. "Rome was now Italy, and Italy Rome."[7] This influx of new voters drastically altered the voting power structure in favor of the *populares* who had earlier favored enfranchisement of the Italians.

During this war, a new figure began to emerge into prominence—Lucius Cornelius Sulla (138–78 B.C.). Sulla had been made consul for 88 B.C. and been given command by the senate of the war against Mithridates, the king of Pontus in Asia Minor, who had rebelled against Roman power. However, Marius, who had retired from Roman politics, now returned to the scene. The plebeian council, contradicting the senate's wishes, transferred command of the war against Mithridates to Marius. Considering this action illegal, Sulla marched on Rome with his army. Marius fled and Sulla reestablished his command. It was the first time a Roman consul had used his forces against fellow Roman citizens. After Sulla left again for the east, Marius joined forces with the consul Cinna, marched on Rome, seized control of the government, outlawed Sulla, and killed many of Sulla's supporters. Civil war had become a fact of life in Roman politics.

Marius soon died, but Cinna continued to use his forces to remain as consul. His control, however, really depended upon the fortunes of Sulla and his army. After defeating Mithridates in the east, Sulla returned to Rome, crushed the armies opposing him in Italy, and seized Rome itself in 82 B.C. He forced the senate to grant him the title of dictator to "reconstitute the Republic." After conducting a reign of terror to wipe out all opposition, Sulla revised the constitution to restore power to the hands of the senate. He eliminated most of the powers of the popular assemblies and the tribunes of the plebs and restored the senators to the jury courts. He also enlarged the senate by adding men of the equestrian order. In 79 B.C., believing that he had restored the traditional Republic governed by a powerful senate, he resigned his office of dictator and retired. But his real legacy was quite different from what he had intended. His example of how an army could be used to seize power would prove most attractive to ambitious men.

The Collapse of the Republic

For the next fifty years, Roman history would be characterized by two important features: the jostling for power by a number of powerful individuals and the civil wars generated by their conflicts. Not long after Sulla's attempts to revive senatorial power, the senate made two extraordinary military appointments that raised to prominence two very strong personalities—Crassus (c. 112–53 B.C.) and Pompey (106–48 B.C.) Crassus had fought for Sulla and had also become extremely rich—he was known as the richest man in Rome. In 73 B.C., the senate gave Crassus a military command against the slave rebellion led by Spartacus, which he successfully completed. Pompey had also fought for Sulla and was given an important military command in Spain in 77 B.C. When he returned in 71 B.C., he was hailed as a military hero.

Despite their jealousy of one another, Pompey and Crassus joined forces and were elected consuls for 70 B.C. Although both men had been Sulla's supporters, they undid the work of Sulla. They restored the power of the tribunes and helped put *equites* back on the jury courts, thereby reviving the *populares* as a path to political power.

With their power reestablished by this action, friendly plebeian tribunes now proposed legislation that gave two important military commands to Pompey. In 67

▼ **Cicero.** The great orator Marcus Tullius Cicero, whose writings provide much information about politics and upper-class life during his time, rose to the highest offices in the Republic due to his oratorical skills. He was a supporter of the senate and wished to establish a "concord of the orders," or a cooperation between the equestrians and the senators in ruling the state.

▼ **Pompey.** A popular and powerful figure of the late Republic, Pompey was a successful general who joined with Caesar and Crassus in a coalition known as the First Triumvirate in order to secure his reorganization of the east and to obtain lands for his veterans. Later, he opposed Caesar during the civil war of 49–45 B.C. Pictured is a marble copy of the head of Pompey.

B.C., he cleared the Mediterranean Sea of the pirates who were harassing Roman commerce. After this success, he was put in charge of the campaign against Mithridates, who felt he could take advantage of Rome's internal troubles to pursue his plans of conquest. Pompey defeated Mithridates and reorganized the East, winning immense success and prestige as well as enormous wealth. When he returned to Rome, he disbanded his army, expecting the senate would automatically ratify his eastern settlement and give land to his veterans. But new forces and new personalities had risen to prominence during his absence, and complications developed over his requests.

Marcus Tullius Cicero (106–43 B.C.) was one of these new personalities. A "new man" from the equestrian order and the first of his family to achieve the consulship, Cicero rose to prominence through his oratorical skills (see the box on p. 155). He became consul in 63

Exploitation of the Provinces

▼ ▼ ▼

As the Romans expanded their territory outside Italy, conquered lands were made provinces. These possessions were clearly distinguished from Italy by the fact that their inhabitants were forced to pay tribute to the Roman state. Eventually, the senate came to control the appointment of governors who administered the provinces. By the first century B.C., many provincial governors used their provinces to amass enormous fortunes through extortion, confiscation of property, and bribery. Although governors could be prosecuted after their term of office, the senators who served as judges often protected the accused who were members of their own class. Cicero successfully prosecuted Verres, the corrupt governor of Sicily, and thereby gained prominence as a politician. This excerpt is taken from one of his speeches against Verres.

Cicero, *Against Verres*

But nowhere did he multiply and magnify the memorials and the proofs of all his evil qualities so thoroughly as in his governorship of Sicily; which island for the space of three years he devastated and ruined so effectually that nothing can restore it to its former condition, and it hardly seems possible that a long lapse of years and a succession of upright governors can in time bring it a partial revival of prosperity. So long as Verres was governing it, its people were protected neither by their own laws, nor by the decrees of the Roman Senate, nor by the rights that belong to all nations alike. . . .

For the space of three years, the law awarded nothing to anybody unless Verres chose to agree; and nothing was so undoubtedly inherited from a man's father or grandfather that the courts would not cancel his right to it, if Verres bade them do so. Countless sums of money, under a new and unprincipled regulation, were wrung from the purses of the farmers; our most loyal allies were treated as if they were national enemies; Roman citizens were tortured and executed like slaves; the guiltiest criminals bought their legal acquittal, while the most honourable, and honest men would be prosecuted in absence, and condemned and banished unheard; strongly fortified harbours, mighty and well-defended cities, were left open to the assaults of pirates and buccaneers; Sicilian soldiers and sailors, our allies and our friends, were starved to death; fine fleets, spendidly equipped, were to the great disgrace of our nation destroyed and lost to us. Famous and ancient works of art, some of them the gifts of wealthy kings, who intended them to adorn the cities where they stood, others the gifts of Roman generals, who gave or restored them to the communities of Sicily in the hour of victory—this same governor stripped and despoiled every one of them. Nor was it only the civic statues and works of art that he treated thus; he also pillaged the holiest and most venerated sanctuaries . . . . As to his adulteries and the like vile offences, a sense of decency makes me afraid to repeat the tale of his acts of wanton wickedness: and besides, I would not wish, by repeating it, to add to the calamities of those who have not been suffered to save their children and their wives from outrage at the hands of this lecherous scoundrel. Is it alleged that he did these things so secretly that they were not known everywhere? I do not believe that one human being lives, who has heard the name of Verres spoken and cannot also repeat the tale of his evil doings.

B.C. and upheld the interests of the senate. While consul, he added to his reputation by acting forcefully to suppress a political conspiracy led by a desperate and bankrupt aristocrat named Catiline. Cicero was one of the few prominent politicians who attempted to analyze the problems of the Republic systematically. He believed in a "concord of the orders," meaning the cooperation of the equestrians and senators. In effect, Cicero harkened back to the days of collective rule, a time when working together for the good of the Roman state motivated political leaders. But collective rule was no longer meaningful to ambitious men seeking personal power. Cicero realized that the senate needed the support of a powerful general if the concord of the orders were to be made a reality. In 62 B.C., he saw Pompey as that man. But a large element in the senate felt Pompey had become too powerful, and they now refused to grant his wishes after his return from the East. This same element in the senate treated Julius Caesar in a similar fashion when he returned from Spain. It turned out to be a big mistake.

Julius Caesar (100–44 B.C.) had been a spokesman for the *populares* from the beginning of his political career, an alliance that ran in the family—Marius was his uncle by marriage. Caesar pursued political power by appealing to many of the same groups who had supported Marius. After serving as aedile and praetor, he sought a military command and was sent to Spain. He returned from Spain in 60 B.C. and requested a special dispensation so that he could both celebrate a triumph with his troops and run for the consulship, which would place him in the highest rank within the senate. Rival senators blocked his request. Consequently, Caesar joined with two fellow senators, Crassus and Pompey, who were being stymied by the same men. Historians call their coalition the First Triumvirate. Though others had made political deals before, the combined wealth and power of these three men was enormous, enabling them to dominate the political scene. Caesar was elected consul for 59 B.C. and used the popular assemblies to achieve the

▼ **Caesar.** Conqueror of Gaul and member of the First Triumvirate, Julius Caesar is perhaps the best known figure of the late Republic. Caesar became dictator of Rome in 47 B.C., and after his victories in the Civil War, was made dictator for life. Some members of the senate who resented his power assassinated him in 44 B.C. Pictured is a marble copy of the bust of Caesar.

basic aims of the triumvirs: Pompey received his eastern settlement and lands for his veterans; equestrian allies of Crassus were given a reduction on tax contracts for which they had overbid; and Caesar was granted a special military command in Gaul (modern France) for five years.

Caesar did so well in Gaul that Crassus and Pompey realized anew the value of military command. They became consuls again for 55 B.C. and garnered more benefits for the coalition: Caesar was given a five-year extension in Gaul; Crassus a command in Syria; and Pompey one in Spain. When Crassus was killed in battle in 53 B.C., it left two powerful men with armies in direct competition. Caesar had used his time in Gaul wisely. He had conquered all of Gaul and gained fame, wealth, and military experience as well as an army of seasoned veterans who were loyal to him. No doubt, most senators would have preferred both Pompey and Caesar to lay down their commands and give up their armies. Since both refused, the leading senators fastened on Pompey as the least harmful to their cause and voted for Caesar to lay down his command and return as a private citizen to Rome. Such a step was intolerable to Caesar since it would leave him totally vulnerable to his enemies. He chose to keep his army and crossed the Rubicon, the river that formed the southern boundary of his province on January 10, 49 B.C. In bringing his army into Italy, he guaranteed a civil war between his forces and those of Pompey and his allies. At the Battle of Pharsalus in 48 B.C., Caesar's veterans carried the day against Pompey's forces. The defeated Pompey fled to Egypt where the king was one of his foreign clients, but one of the king's advisers had Pompey killed. The war continued, however, since some of the senators on his side, including Cato the Younger, had recruited new troops. After victories in North Africa and Spain, Caesar returned triumphant to Rome in 45 B.C.

Caesar had officially been made dictator in 47 B.C. and in 44 B.C. was made dictator for life. No doubt he realized that the old order of unfettered political competition could not be saved. While his ultimate intentions are a matter of speculation, he did institute a number of reforms designed to solve problems that ambitious senators like himself had previously exploited. In this way he hoped to ensure his continued control unchallenged. He increased the senate to 900 members by filling it with many of his supporters. He granted citizenship to a number of people in the provinces who had provided assistance to him. By establishing colonies of Roman citizens in North Africa, Gaul, and Spain, he initiated a process of romanization in those areas. He

The Assassination of Julius Caesar
▼ ▼ ▼

When it quickly became apparent that Julius Caesar had no intention of restoring the Republic as they conceived it, about sixty senators, many of them friends or pardoned enemies, formed a conspiracy to assassinate the dictator. It was led by Gaius Cassius and Marcus Brutus, who naively imagined that this act would restore the traditional Republic. The conspirators set the Ides of March (March 15) 44 B.C. as the date for the assassination. Caesar was in the midst of preparations for a campaign in the eastern part of the empire. Although warned about a plot against his life, he chose to disregard it. This account of Caesar's death is taken from his biography by the Greek writer Plutarch.

Plutarch, *Life of Caesar*

Fate, however, is to all appearance more unavoidable than unexpected. For many strange prodigies and apparitions are said to have been observed shortly before this event. . . . One finds it also related by many that a soothsayer bade him [Caesar] prepare for some great danger on the Ides of March. When this day was come, Caesar, as he went to the senate, met this soothsayer, and said to him by way of raillery, "The Ides of March are come," who answered him calmly, "Yes, they are come, but they are not past. . . ."

All these things might happen by chance. But the place which was destined for the scene of this murder, in which the senate met that day, was the same in which Pompey's statue stood, and was one of the edifices which Pompey had raised and dedicated with his theatre to the use of the public, plainly showing that there was something of a supernatural influence which guided the action and ordered it to that particular place. Cassius, just before the act, is said to have looked towards Pompey's statue, and silently implored his assistance. . . . When Caesar entered, the senate stood up to show their respect to him, and of Brutus's confederates, some came about his chair and stood behind it, others met him, pretending to add their petitions to those of Tillius Cimber, in behalf of his brother, who was in exile; and they followed him with their joint applications till he came to his seat. When he sat down, he refused to comply with their requests, and upon their urging him further began to reproach them severely for their importunities, when Tillius, laying hold of his robe with both his hands, pulled it down from his neck, which was the signal for the assault. Casca gave him the first cut in the neck, which was not mortal nor dangerous, as coming from one who at the beginning of such a bold action was probably very much disturbed; Caesar immediately turned about, and laid his hand upon the dagger and kept hold of it. And both of them at the same time cried out, he that received the blow, in Latin, "Vile Casca, what does this mean?" and he that gave it, in Greek to his brother, "Brother, help!" Upon this first onset, those who were not privy to the design were astonished, and their horror and amazement at what they saw were so great that they dared not fly nor assist Caesar, nor so much as speak a word. But those who came prepared for the business enclosed him on every side, with their naked daggers in their hands. Which way soever he turned he met with blows, and saw their swords levelled at his face and eyes, and was encompassed like a wild beast in the toils on every side. For it had been agreed they should each of them make a thrust at him, and flesh themselves with his blood: for which reason Brutus also gave him one stab in the groin. Some say that he fought and resisted all the rest, shifting his body to avoid the blows, and calling out for help, but that when he saw Brutus's sword drawn, he covered his face with his robe and submitted, letting himself fall, whether it were by chance or that he was pushed in that direction by his murderers, at the foot of the pedestal on which Pompey's statue stood, and which was thus wetted with his blood. So that Pompey himself seemed to have presided, as it were, over the revenge done upon his adversary, who lay here at his feet, and breathed out his soul through his multitude of wounds, for they say he received three-and-twenty. And the conspirators themselves were many of them wounded by each other, whilst they all levelled their blows at the same person.

tried to reorganize the administrative structures of cities in Italy in order to create some sense of rational order in their government. He planned much more in the way of building projects and military adventures in the East, but was not able to carry them out. In 44 B.C., a group of leading senators who resented his domination assassinated him in the belief that they had struck a blow for republican liberty (see the box on p. 157). In truth, they had set the stage for another civil war that delivered the death blow to the Republic.

Civil War, 43–31 B.C.

A new struggle for power soon ensued. Caesar's heir, his grandnephew Octavian, though only eighteen, took command of some of Caesar's legions and made himself into a player of substantial importance. After forcing the senate to name him consul, he joined forces with Mark Antony, Caesar's ally and assistant, and Marcus Lepidus, who had been commander of Caesar's cavalry. Together, the three formed the Second Triumvirate, which was legally empowered to rule Rome. In addition to proscribing their enemies at home (Cicero was one of those killed), the three commanders pursued Caesar's assassins, who had meanwhile formed an army, and defeated them at Philippi in Macedonia. Lepidus was soon shunted aside, and Octavian and Antony then divided the Roman world between them—Octavian taking the west and Antony the east. But the empire of the Romans, large as it was, was still too small for two masters.

Octavian and Antony eventually came into conflict. Antony allied himself closely with the Egyptian Queen Cleopatra VII. Octavian accused Antony of catering to Cleopatra and giving away Roman territory to the Egyptian queen. Finally, at the Battle of Actium in Greece in 31 B.C., Octavian's forces smashed the army and navy of Antony and Cleopatra. Both fled to Egypt where they committed suicide a year later. Octavian, at the age of thirty-two, stood supreme over the Roman world. The civil wars were ended. And so was the Republic.

In the eighth and seventh centuries B.C., the pastoral community of Rome emerged as an actual city. Between 509 and 264 B.C., the expansion of this city led to the union of almost all of Italy under Rome's control. Even more dramatically, between 264 and 133 B.C., Rome expanded to the west and east and became master of the Mediterranean Sea.

After 133 B.C., however, Rome's republican institutions proved inadequate for the task of ruling an empire. In the breakdown that ensued, ambitious individuals saw opportunities for power unparalleled in Roman history and succumbed to the temptations. After a series of bloody civil wars, peace was finally achieved when Octavian defeated Antony and Cleopatra. Octavian's real task was at hand: to create a new system of government that seemed to preserve the Republic while establishing the basis for a new order that would rule the empire in an orderly fashion. Octavian proved equal to the task of establishing a Roman imperial state.

Notes
▼ ▼ ▼

1. Quoted in Chester Starr, *Past and Future in Ancient History* (Lanham, Md., 1987), pp. 38–39.
2. Cicero, *Laws*, trans. C. W. Keyes (Cambridge, Mass., 1966), II, xii, 31.
3. Cato the Censor, *On Farming*, trans. Ernest Brehaut (New York, 1933), CXLI.
4. Quoted in J. Wright Duff, *A Literary History of Rome* (London, 1960), pp. 136–137.

5. Terence, *The Comedies*, trans. Betty Radice (Harmondsworth, 1976), p. 339.
6. Pliny, *Natural History*, trans. W. H. S. Jones (Cambridge, Mass., 1963), XXIX, vii.
7. Mary Beard and Michael Crawford, *Rome in the Late Republic* (London, 1985), p. 3.

Suggestions for Further Reading
▼ ▼ ▼

For a recent general account of the Roman Republic, see J. Boardman, J. Griffin, and O. Murray, eds., *The Oxford History of the Classical World* (Oxford, 1986), pp.

384–523. A brief, but excellent guide to recent trends in scholarship on the Roman Republic can be found in C. Starr, *Past and Future in Ancient History* (Lanham,

Md., 1987), pp. 33–45. A standard one-volume reference is M. Cary and H. H. Scullard, *A History of Rome down to the Reign of Constantine*, 3d ed. (New York, 1975). Good surveys of Roman history include M. H. Crawford, *The Roman Republic* (London, 1978); H. H. Scullard, *History of the Roman World 753–146 B.C.*, 4th ed. (London, 1978) and *From the Gracchi to Nero*, 4th ed. (London, 1976); and K. Christ, *The Romans*, trans. C. Holme (London, 1984). A good collection of source materials in translation is contained in N. Lewis and M. Reinhold, eds., *Roman Civilization*, vol. 1 (New York, 1951). The history of early Rome is well covered in R. M. Ogilvie, *Early Rome and the Etruscans* (London, 1976). Good works on the Etruscans include M. Pallottino, *The Etruscans*, rev. ed. (Bloomington, Ind., 1975); and M. Grant, *The Etruscans* (New York, 1980).

A general work, heavily political, on Rome's impact on Italy is E. T. Salmon, *The Making of Roman Italy* (London, 1983). Other aspects of the impact of Roman expansion on Italy are examined in P. A. Brunt, *Italian Manpower* (Oxford, 1971); and E. Gabba, *Republican Rome, the Army and the Allies* (Oxford, 1976).

Aspects of the Roman political structure can be studied in A. N. Sherwin-White, *The Roman Citizenship*, 2d ed. (Oxford, 1973); T. P. Wiseman, *New Men in the Roman Senate* (Oxford, 1971); and M. Gelzer, *The Roman Nobility* (Oxford, 1969). On Roman military practices, see F. Adcock, *The Roman Art of War under the Republic*, rev. ed. (Cambridge, Mass., 1963). Changes in Rome's economic life can be examined in K. Hopkins, *Conquerors and Slaves* (Cambridge, 1978); and J. H. D'Arms, *Commerce and Social Standing in Ancient Rome* (Cambridge, Mass., 1981). On the Roman social structure, see G. Alfoeldy, *The Social History of Rome* (London, 1985).

General accounts of Rome's expansion in the Mediterranean world are provided by R. M. Errington, *The Dawn of Empire: Rome's Rise to World Power* (Ithaca, N.Y., 1971); and J. Heurgon, *The Rise of Rome to 264 B.C.*, trans. J. Willis (Berkeley, 1973). The best work on Carthage is B. H. Warmington, *Carthage*, rev. ed. (London, 1969). On one aspect of Rome's struggle with Carthage, see the detailed study by J. Lazenby, *Hannibal's War: A Military History of the Second Punic War* (Warminster, 1978). Especially important works on Roman expansion and imperialism include W. V. Harris, *War and Imperialism in Republican Rome* (Oxford, 1979); and E. Badian, *Foreign Clientelae* (Oxford, 1958), which examines the application of the Roman client-patron relationship in foreign affairs, and *Roman Imperialism in the Late Republic* (Oxford, 1968). On Roman expansion in the eastern Mediterranean, see the fundamental works by A. N. Sherwin-White, *Roman Foreign Policy in the Greek East* (London, 1984); and E. S. Gruen, *The Hellenistic World and the Coming of Rome*, 2 vols. (Berkeley, 1984).

Roman religion can be examined in J. Liebeschuetz, *Continuity and Change in Roman Religion* (Oxford, 1979); and H. H. Scullard, *Festivals and Ceremonies of the Roman Republic* (Ithaca, N.Y., 1981). General studies of daily life in Rome include F. R. Cowell, *Everyday Life in Ancient Rome* (London, 1961); and J. Balsdon, *Life and Leisure in Ancient Rome* (New York, 1969). Roman women are examined in J. Balsdon, *Roman Women*, rev. ed., (London, 1974); S. Pomeroy, *Goddesses, Whores, Wives, and Slaves: Women in Classical Antiquity* (New York, 1976), pp. 149–189; J. F. Gardner, *Women in Roman Law and Society* (Bloomington, Ind., 1986); and J. P. Hallett, *Fathers and Daughters in Roman Society* (Princeton, N.J., 1984). On different aspects of Roman law, see H. F. Jolowicz and B. Nicholas, *Historical Introduction to Roman Law* (Cambridge, 1972); and J. Crook, *Law and Life in Rome* (London, 1977). For a brief and readable survey of Latin literature, see R. M. Ogilvie, *Roman Literature and Society* (Harmondsworth, 1980). There are good translations of Terence by B. Radice and Plautus by E. F. Watling in the Penguin Classics series. On Roman art and architecture, see A. Boethius, *Etruscan and Early Roman Architecture* (Harmondsworth, 1978); and G. Richter, *Ancient Italy* (Ann Arbor, 1955). For studies of Cato and Scipio Aemilianus, see the two works by A. Astin, *Cato the Censor* (Oxford, 1978) and *Scipio Aemilianus* (Oxford, 1967).

An excellent account of basic problems in the history of the late Republic can be found in M. Beard and M. H. Crawford, *Rome in the Late Republic* (London, 1985). The classic work on the fall of the Republic is R. Syme, *The Roman Revolution* (Oxford, 1960). A more recent work is E. S. Gruen, *The Last Generation of the Roman Republic* (Berkeley, 1974). Also valuable are P. A. Brunt, *Social Conflicts in the Roman Republic* (London, 1971); and C. Nicolet, *The World of the Citizen in Republican Rome* (London, 1980). Numerous biographies provide many details on the politics of the period. Especially worthwhile are A. H. Bernstein, *Tiberius Sempronius Gracchus: Tradition and Apostasy* (Ithaca, N.Y., 1978); D. Stockton, *The Gracchi* (Oxford, 1979); M. Gelzer, *Caesar: Politician and Statesman* (London, 1968); R. Seager, *Pompey: A Political Biography* (Berkeley, 1980); A. Ward, *Marcus Crassus and the Late Roman Republic* (Columbia, Mo., 1977); and D. Stockton, *Cicero: A Political Biography* (London, 1971).

Chapter 6

The Roman Empire

▼▼▼▼▼

With the victories of Octavian, peace finally settled upon the Roman world. Although there would still be occasional civil conflict, the new imperial state constructed by Octavian experienced a period of remarkable stability for the next two hundred years. The Romans imposed their peace upon the largest empire established in antiquity. Indeed, Rome's writers proclaimed that "by heaven's will my Rome shall be capital of the world."[1] To the Romans, their divine mission was clearly to rule nations and peoples.

By the third century A.D., however, the Roman Empire began to experience renewed civil war, economic chaos, and invasions. Although order was reestablished by the end of the third and beginning of the fourth centuries, Rome's decline was halted only temporarily. In the meantime, the growth of Christianity, one of the remarkable success stories of Western civilization, led to the emergence of a vibrant and powerful institution that picked up the pieces left by Roman collapse and provided the civilizing core for a new medieval civilization.

▼ The Age of Augustus (31 B.C.–A.D. 14)

In 27 B.C., Octavian proclaimed the "restoration of the Republic." He understood the need to appease the senatorial ruling class and realized from the experience of Julius Caesar that he could not exercise power too openly. Only traditional republican forms would satisfy the senatorial aristocracy. At the same time, Octavian was aware that the Republic could not be fully restored and managed to arrive at a compromise that worked at least during his lifetime. In 27 B.C., the senate awarded

him the title of Augustus—"the revered one." He preferred the title *princeps*, meaning chief citizen or first among equals. The system of rule that Augustus established is sometimes called the principate, conveying the idea of a constitutional monarch as co-ruler with the senate. But while Augustus worked to maintain this appearance, in reality, power was heavily weighted in favor of the *princeps*. After the devastating political chaos of the late Republic, it should come as no surprise that the position of *princeps* eventually became that of an absolute monarch.

The New Constitutional Order

In the new constitutional order that Augustus created, the basic governmental structure consisted of a *princeps* (Augustus) and an aristocratic senate. Augustus retained the senate as the chief deliberative body of the Roman state. Its decrees, screened in advance by the *princeps*, now had the effect of law. The senate officially controlled disbursements from the public treasury and served as a high court of justice. Despite its powers, however, the senate was not a full and equal partner with the *princeps*.

The title of *princeps*—first citizen of the state—carried no power in itself. While Augustus wished to avoid the appearance of absolute authority, at the same time, he had no intention of giving up his control. Initially, the legal foundation for Augustus's power came from holding the office of consul each year beginning in 31 B.C., thus giving him *imperium* or the right to command (see Chapter 5). This lasted until 23 B.C., when Augustus gave up the consulship and was granted a greater proconsular or *maius imperium*—a greater *imperium* than all others. The consulship was now unnecessary. Moreover, very probably in 23 B.C., Augustus was accorded the *tribunicia potestas*, the power of a tribune without actually holding the office itself. This power enabled him to propose laws and veto any item of public business. Periodically, he also assumed the power of *censor*, which permitted him to revise the citizenship lists and the roll of senators. In 12 B.C., Augustus was also elected *pontifex maximus* or chief pontiff, head of the official state religion. While the election of officials continued, Augustus's authority was such that his candidates for offices usually won. This situation caused a decline of participation in elections. Consequently, the popular assemblies, shorn of any real role in elections and increasingly overshadowed by the senate's decrees, gradually declined in importance.

By observing proper legal forms for his power, Augustus proved to be highly popular. At times he even refused public offices that the people and senate wished to confer upon him. As the Roman historian Tacitus commented, "Indeed, he attracted everybody's goodwill by the enjoyable gift of peace. . . . Opposition did not exist."[2] No doubt, the ending of the civil wars had greatly bolstered Augustus's popularity (see the box on p. 163). At the same time, his continuing control of the army, while making possible the Roman peace, was a crucial source of his power.

The Army

The peace of the Roman Empire depended on the army and so did the security of the *princeps*. While primarily responsible for guarding the frontiers of the empire, the army was also used to maintain domestic order within the provinces. Moreover, the army played an important social role. It was an agent of upward mobility for both officers and recruits and provided impetus for romanization wherever the legions were stationed. The colonies of veterans established by Augustus throughout the empire proved especially valuable in romanizing the provinces.

After the Battle of Actium in 31 B.C., Augustus reorganized the army. He maintained a standing army of twenty-eight legions. Since each legion at full strength numbered 5,400 soldiers, the Roman Empire had an army of about 150,000 men, certainly not large either by modern standards or when one considers the size of the

▼ **Augustus.** Octavian, Caesar's adopted son, emerged victorious from the civil conflict that rocked the Republic after Caesar's assassination. While claiming to have restored the Republic and while allowing a measure of power to the senate, Augustus operated through a number of legal formalities to insure that control of the Roman state rested firmly in his hands. This marble status from Prima Porta depicts the *princeps* Augustus.

empire itself. Roman legionaries served twenty years and were recruited only from the citizenry and, under Augustus, largely from Italy. Augustus also maintained a large contingent of auxiliary forces enlisted from the subject peoples. They served as both light-armed troops and cavalry and were commanded by Roman officers as well as tribal leaders. The German Arminius, who de-

feated the Romans in Germany in A.D. 9 (see Roman Provinces and Frontiers later in this chapter), had, in fact, once commanded a cohort of German tribesmen as Roman auxiliaries. During the reign of Augustus, the auxiliaries numbered around 130,000. They were recruited only from noncitizens, served for twenty-four years, and along with their families received citizenship after their terms of service.

Augustus was responsible for establishing the praetorian guard. Although nominally a military reserve, these "9 cohorts of elite troops," roughly 9,000 men, had the important task of guarding the person of the *princeps*. They were recruited from Roman citizens in Italy and served for sixteen years. Eventually, the praetorian guard would play an important role in making and unmaking emperors.

The role of the *princeps* as military commander gave rise to a title by which this ruler eventually came to be known. When victorious, a military commander was acclaimed by his troops as *imperator*. Augustus was so acclaimed on a number of occasions. *Imperator* is our word emperor. Although such a title was applied to Augustus and his successors, Augustus still preferred to use the title of *princeps*. Not until the reign of Vespasian (69–79) did emperor become the common title for the Roman ruler.

Roman Provinces and Frontiers

During the Republic, as we have seen, the Romans had established control over a number of overseas possessions, which were called provinces. Two praetors were chosen in 227 B.C. to govern the first provinces of Sicily and Sardinia, and two more beginning in 197 for the two Spanish provinces. Eventually, a new system developed in which ex-consuls and ex-praetors had their *imperium* extended (as proconsuls and propraetors) and were then sent out as governors. Under the Republic, the senate supervised the allocation of the provinces.

Augustus inaugurated a new system for governing the provinces. Certain provinces were allotted to the *princeps*, who assigned deputies known as legates to govern them. These legates were from the senatorial class and held office as long as the emperor chose. The remaining provinces were designated as senatorial provinces. They continued to be ruled by proconsuls and propraetors as governors who were appointed annually by lot for one year and reported directly to the senate. Although this practice seemed to create a system of dual administration for the provinces, in fact the greater proconsular *imperium* that had been granted to Augustus gave him the power to overrule the senatorial governors and hence to

The Achievements of Augustus

▼ ▼ ▼

This excerpt is taken from a text written by Augustus and inscribed on a bronze tablet at Rome. Copies of the text were displayed in stone in many provincial capitals. Called "the most famous ancient inscription," the Res Gestae *of Augustus summarizes his accomplishments in three major areas: his offices; his private expenditures on behalf of the state; and his exploits in war and peace. While factual in approach, it is a highly subjective account. Although Augustus proclaimed the restoration of the Republic, the content of the inscription is in some ways similar to those of oriental monarchs.*

Augustus, *Res Gestae*

Below is a copy of the accomplishments of the deified Augustus by which he brought the whole world under the empire of the Roman people, and of the moneys expended by him on the state and the Roman people, as inscribed on two bronze pillars set up in Rome.

1. At the age of nineteen, on my own initiative and at my own expense, I raised an army by means of which I liberated the Republic, which was oppressed by the tyranny of a faction [Mark Antony and his supporters]. . . .

2. Those who assassinated my father [Julius Caesar, his adoptive father] I drove into exile, avenging their crime by due process of law; and afterwards when they waged war against the state, I conquered them twice on the battlefield.

3. I waged many wars throughout the whole world by land and by sea, both civil and foreign, and when victorious I spared all citizens who sought pardon. . . .

5. The dictatorship offered to me . . . by the people and the senate, both in my absence and in my presence, I refused to accept. . . .

9. The senate decreed that vows for my health should be offered up every fifth year by the consuls and priests. In fulfillment of these vows, games were often celebrated during my lifetime, sometimes by the four most distinguished colleges of priests, sometimes by the consuls. Moreover, the whole citizen body, with one accord, both individually and as members of municipalities, prayed continuously for my health at all the shrines. . . .

17. Four times I came to the assistance of the treasury with my own money, transferring to those in charge of the treasury 150,000,000 sesterces. And in the consulship of Marcus Lepidus and Lucius Arruntius I transferred out of my own patrimony 170,000,000 sesterces to the soldiers' bonus fund, which was established on my advice for the purpose of providing bonuses for soldiers who had completed twenty or more years of service. . . .

20. I repaired the Capitol and the theater of Pompey with enormous expenditures on both works, without having my name inscribed on them. I repaired the conduits of the aqueducts which were falling into ruin in many places because of age, and I doubled the capacity of the aqueduct called Marcia by admitting a new spring into its conduit. . . .

22. I gave a gladiatorial show three times in my own name, and five times in the names of my sons or grandsons; at these shows about 10,000 fought. . . .

25. I brought peace to the sea by suppressing the pirates. In that war I turned over to their masters for punishment nearly 30,000 slaves who had run away from their owners and taken up arms against the state. . . .

26. I extended the frontiers of all the provinces of the Roman people on whose boundaries were peoples not subject to our empire. . . .

27. I added Egypt to the empire of the Roman people. . . .

28. I established colonies of soldiers in Africa, Sicily, Macedonia, in both Spanish provinces, in Achaea, Asia, Syria, Narbonese Gaul, and Pisidia. Italy, moreover, has twenty-eight colonies established by me, which in my lifetime have grown to be famous and populous. . . .

35. When I held my thirteenth consulship, the senate, the equestrian order, and the entire Roman people gave me the title of "father of the country" and decreed that this title should be inscribed in the vestibule of my house, in the Julian senate house, and in the Augustan Forum on the pedestal of the chariot which was set up in my honor by decree of the senate. At the time I wrote this document I was in my seventy-sixth year.

establish unity in imperial policy. Egypt was treated differently from the other provinces since the emperor considered it a personal possession and governed it through an equestrian prefect. Because all provincial governors, whether of imperial or senatorial provinces, now received regular salaries, there was less need for the kind of extortion that had characterized provincial administration in the late Republic. In general, although there were still instances of abuses, especially in the area of tax collection, provincial administration under Augustus was more efficient and provided better protection of provincials against abuse of power than under the Republic.

Since a governor had relatively few administrative officials to assist him, effective government of the provinces necessitated considerable cooperation from local authorities. By supporting the power of local elites in return for their cooperation, Roman policy encouraged a substantial degree of self-government and local autonomy in the cities. By fostering municipal life, Rome essentially made cities and city-states the basic units of imperial administration. City councils of leading citizens made for stable local government, and leading city officials were rewarded for their administrative services with Roman citizenship.

Augustus's frontier policy was not wholly defensive as it is sometimes portrayed. He was not immune to the glories of military conquest and, in fact, added more territory to the Roman Empire than any other single Roman. He did, however, use diplomacy rather than force to retrieve the Roman battle standards seized by the Parthians when they destroyed a Roman force under Crassus in the first century B.C. Augustus also encouraged the establishment of client kingdoms in the east instead of creating new provinces. In effect, Augustus minimized the Roman military presence in the east so that he could use his forces elsewhere. After the final pacification of Spain in 19 B.C., the *princeps* expended his greatest military efforts along the northern frontiers of the Roman Empire. He conquered the central and maritime Alps and then expanded Roman control of the Balkan peninsula up to the Danube River.

The extension of Roman power to the Danube now opened the door for Augustus's major military project—expansion into Germany. After 15 B.C., Roman forces advanced across the Rhine and by 9 B.C. had reached the Elbe River in eastern Germany. By 6 A.D., plans were coordinated for another advance between the Elbe and the Danube. This time, however, the Romans encountered a series of difficulties, including the great catastrophe of 9 A.D. when three Roman legions under Varus were massacred in the Teutoburg Forest by a coalition of German tribes led by Arminius, a German tribal leader who had served in the Roman auxiliary forces and had even received Roman citizenship. Roman historians blamed Varus for the disaster: "He [Varus] entertained the notion that the Germans were a people who were men only in voice and limbs. . . . With this purpose in mind, he entered the heart of Germany as though he were going among a people enjoying the blessings of peace. . . ."[3] The defeat severely dampened Augustus's enthusiasm for limitless expansion in central Europe. Thereafter, the Romans were content to use the Rhine as the frontier between the Roman province of Gaul and the German tribes to the east. In fact, Augustus's difficulties had convinced him that "the empire should not be extended beyond its present frontiers."[4] Although Augustus had not practiced what he later preached, his defeats in Germany taught him that Rome's power was not unlimited.

Augustan Society

Roman society in the Early Empire was characterized by a system of social stratification, inherited from the Republic, in which Roman citizens were divided into three basic classes: the senatorial, equestrian, and lower classes. Although the differences between the classes were more precisely defined during the Early Empire, with each class having its own functions and opportunities, the system was not completely rigid. There were possibilities for mobility from one group to another.

Augustus had accepted the senatorial order as a ruling class for the empire. Senators filled the chief magistracies of the Roman government, held the most important military posts, and governed the provinces. An order of ranks was established by which a member of the senatorial order advanced from minor military and magisterial posts to the most important offices in the state. One needed to possess property worth 1,000,000 sesterces (an unskilled laborer in Rome received 3 sesterces a day; a Roman legionary 900 sesterces a year in pay) to belong to the senatorial order. When Augustus took charge, the senate had over a thousand members. Augustus revised the senatorial list and reduced its size to six hundred, but also added new men from wealthy families throughout Italy. Overall, Augustus was successful in winning the support of the senatorial class for his new order.

The equestrian order, which had played an important role in the conflicts of the first century B.C., was expanded under Augustus and given a share of power in the new imperial state. The equestrian order was open to all Roman citizens of good standing who possessed property valued at 400,000 sesterces. They, too, could now hold military and governmental offices, but the positions open to them were less important than those held by the senatorial order. Like the senators, the equestrians had an order of ranks by which they could proceed from lesser military appointments to administrative positions in the civil service, and finally to one of the chief prefectures, such as commander of the imperial guards, administrator of the grain supply of Rome, or governor of Egypt. At the end of his career, an equestrian might be rewarded by membership in the senatorial order.

Those citizens not of the senatorial or equestrian orders belonged to the lower classes, who obviously constituted the overwhelming majority of the free citizens. The diminution of the power of the Roman assemblies ended whatever political power they may have possessed earlier in the Republic. Many of these people were provided with free grain and public spectacles to keep them from creating disturbances. Nevertheless, by gaining wealth and serving as lower officers in the Roman legions, it was sometimes possible for them to advance to the equestrian order.

Augustus was very concerned about certain aspects of Rome's social health, especially the customs and traditions of the Roman state. One area of great concern was religion. Augustus believed that the civil strife of the first century B.C. had sapped the strength of public religion, which he considered the cornerstone of a strong state. Therefore, he restored traditional priesthoods that had fallen into disuse in the late Republic, rebuilt many ruined temples and shrines, and constructed new ones to honor the Roman gods. Moreover, he insisted upon the careful observance of traditional festivals.

Augustus also created a new religious cult that would serve to strengthen the empire. Since the Roman state was intimately tied to Roman religion, the creation of an imperial cult served as a unifying instrument for the Roman world. Augustus did not claim to be a god, but he did permit the construction of temples to his deified adoptive father, Julius Caesar. Augustus also permitted the building of temples to Augustus and Roma, the personification of the Roman state. The cult of Augustus and Roma became the foundation stone for the development of an imperial cult. This process was furthered when Augustus was acclaimed as a god upon his death.

Augustus's belief that Roman morals had been corrupted during the late Republic led him to initiate social legislation to arrest the decline. He thought that increased luxury had undermined traditional Roman frugality and simplicity and caused a decline in morals, evidenced by easy divorce, a falling birthrate among the upper classes, and lax behavior manifested in hedonistic parties and the love affairs of prominent Romans with fashionable women and elegant boys.

Through his new social legislation, Augustus hoped to restore respectability to the upper classes and reverse the declining birthrate as well. Sumptuary legislation limited expenditures for feasts. Other laws made adultery a criminal offense. Augustus's own daughter Julia, in fact, was exiled for adultery. The tax laws were revised to penalize bachelors, widowers, and married persons who had fewer than three children. While the laws were enforced, there is little evidence that they had much effect.

Literature in the Late Republic and Augustan Age

The last century of the Roman Republic had witnessed the completion of the union of Greek and Roman culture in a truly Greco-Roman civilization. After all, Greek was the language not only of Greece but of the entire eastern Mediterranean Hellenistic world, which Rome had conquered. Moreover, educated Romans of the upper classes spoke Greek fluently. The influence of Greece would continue to be felt in the development of Latin literature.

THE LATE REPUBLIC In the last century of the Republic, the Romans began to produce a new poetry, less dependent on epic themes, and more inclined to personal expressions. Latin poets were now able to use various Greek forms to express their own feelings about people, social and political life, and love. The finest example of this can be seen in the work of Catullus (c. 87–54 B.C.), the "best lyric poet" Rome produced and one of the greatest in world literature.

Like most of the great Roman writers of the first century B.C., Catullus was not from Rome. He grew up in northern Italy, but came to Rome where he belonged to a group of carefree, youthful aristocrats. He became a master at adapting and refining Greek forms of poetry to express his emotions. He wrote a variety of poems on, among other things, political figures, social customs, the use of language, the death of his brother, and the travails of love. Catullus became infatuated with Clodia, the promiscuous sister of a tribune and wife of a provincial governor, and addressed a number of poems to her (he called her Lesbia), describing his passionate love and hatred for her (Clodia had many other lovers besides Catullus):

Lesbia for ever on me rails;
To talk of me, she never fails.
Now, hang me, but for all her art
I find that I have gained her heart.
My proof is this: I plainly see
The case is just the same with me;
I curse her every hour sincerely,
Yet, hang me, but I love her dearly.[5]

The ability of Catullus to express in simple fashion his intense feelings and curiosity about himself and his world had a noticeable impact on later Latin poets.

Another important poet of the late Republic was Lucretius (c. 94–55 B.C.), who followed an old Greek tradition of expounding philosophy in the form of poetry. Although Stoicism was the Greek school of philosophy that the Romans found most congenial, the philosophy of Epicurus also enjoyed a period of intense popularity between 60 and 40 B.C. No doubt, Lucretius's lengthy poem, *On the Nature of the Universe*, played an important role in furthering that philosophy. This work was an attempt by Lucretius to set out poetically Epicurus's idea that the world and all its creatures had been created by an accidental combination of atoms and not by the operation of divine forces. Two themes are repeated: divine forces have no effect on us, and death is of no real consequence since the soul like the body is material and after death also dissolves into atoms. Lucretius was especially adept at using vivid imagery. Describing the movement of atoms in the void, he said:

> Observe what happens when sunbeams are admitted into a building and shed light on its shadowy places. You will see a multitude of tiny particles mingling in a multitude of ways in the empty space within the light of the beam, as though contending in everlasting conflict, rushing into battle rank upon rank with never a moment's pause in a rapid sequence of unions and disunions.[6]

If the gods and death are of no significance, how then are we to lead our lives? Lucretius's Epicurean argument that a simple life free of political worries was the highest good ran counter to Roman ideals, but had an obvious appeal to Romans sick of the civil discord of the first century B.C.

The development of Roman prose was greatly aided by the practice of oratory. Romans had great respect for oratory since the ability to persuade people in public debate meant success in politics. Oratory was brought to perfection in a literary fashion by Cicero (106–43 B.C.), the best exemplar of the literary and intellectual interests of the senatorial elite of the late Republic and, indeed, the greatest prose writer of that period. For Cicero, oratory was not simply skillful speaking. An orator was a statesman, a man who achieved his highest goal by pursuing an active life in public affairs.

Later, when the turmoil of the late Republic forced him into semiretirement politically, Cicero became more interested in the writing of philosophical treatises. He was not an original thinker, but served a most valuable purpose for Roman society by popularizing and making understandable the works of Greek philosophers. In his philosophical works, Cicero, more than anyone else, transmitted the classical intellectual heritage to the Western world.

Cicero's original contributions to Western thought came in the field of politics. His works *On the Laws* and *On the Republic* provided fresh insights into political thought. His emphasis on the need to pursue an active life to benefit and improve humankind would greatly influence the later Italian Renaissance. Cicero's correspondence, especially his letters to his friend and adviser Atticus, are a font of information about politics and society in the last century of the Republic.

Rome's upper classes continued to have a strong interest in history. The best-known historian of the late Republic is Sallust (86–35 B.C.), who established an approach to historical studies that influenced later Roman historians. Sallust, who served as governor of the province of Africa, was on Caesar's side in the civil war and after Caesar's death went into retirement and turned to the writing of history. His two extant works are the *War with Jugurtha*, which discusses the Roman war with the African king from 112–105 B.C., and the *War with Catiline*, an account of the conspiracy of the disaffected aristocrat Catiline, whom Cicero had opposed during his consulship in 63 B.C.

Sallust modeled his style after that of the Greek historian Thucydides, whose historical work experienced a sudden wave of popularity in the later 50s and 40s B.C. Sallust's works expressed his belief that the most important causative factor in Roman history was the moral degeneration of Roman society, which he attributed to the lack of a strong enemy after Carthage and the corrupting influence of the Greeks (see the box on p. 149 in Chapter 5).

Brief mention should also be made of Julius Caesar's (100–44 B.C.) historical writing. His most famous is the *Commentaries on the Gallic War*, an account of his conquest of Gaul (modern France) between 58 and 51 B.C. The work was published in 51 B.C., at a time when Caesar was afraid that his political enemies would take advantage of his absence from the Roman scene. Although the *Commentaries* served a partisan purpose by defending his actions in Gaul, Caesar presented his material in straightforward, concise prose with objective detachment. He referred to himself in the third person and, as the following passage indicates, was not averse to extolling his own bravery:

> Caesar saw that the situation was critical, and there was no reserve to throw in. He snatched a shield from a soldier in the rear—he had not brought one himself—and moved to the front line; he called upon the centurions by name, encouraged the men to advance, and directed them to open their lines out to give freer play to their swords. His coming inspired the men with hope and gave them new heart. Even in a desperate situation each man was anxious to do his utmost when his general was looking on, and the enemy's onset was somewhat slowed down.[7]

Caesar's work reminds us that some of the best prose works of the late Republic were written by politicians who needed to enhance their own position in a world of civil conflict.

THE AUGUSTAN AGE   From a cultural point of view, the Augustan Age is closely tied to the late Republic. Some of the great literary talents matured during the final phases of the Republic. Traditionally, Roman aristocrats had provided financial support for artists and poets in order to gain prestige and enhance their own reputations. Augustus continued this tradition. He perceived the publicity value of literature and art and became the most important patron of the arts during his principate. The literary accomplishments of the Augustan Age were such that the period has been called the "golden age" of Latin literature.

The most distinguished poet of the Augustan Age was Virgil (70–19 B.C.). The son of a small landholder in northern Italy, he proved to be only the first of a series of literary figures in the Augustan Age who welcomed the rule of Augustus. Virgil's first poems were the *Eclogues*, a series of pastoral poems inspired by the Hellenistic poet, Theocritus of Cos (see Chapter 4). The pastoral images in these poems are a combination of natural observation and imaginary, idealized landscapes. His second major work, the *Georgics*, was a didactic poem on farming modeled after the Greek Hesiod's *Works and Days* (see Chapter 3). The *Georgics* showed Virgil's love of the country, but not without pointing out two other realities—the potential harshness of nature and the destruction wrought by humans, especially in wartime. Therefore, he also extolled Augustus for restor-

ing peace and promised to write an even greater work in his honor. Both the *Eclogues* and *Georgics* used Greek models, but increasingly Virgil infused those models with a distinctly Latin spirit. His poetry sang of the beauties of Italy: "Add thereto all her illustrious cities and the labors wrought in her, all her towns piled high by men's hands on their sheer rocks, and her rivers that glide beneath immemorial walls" and "But neither those Median forests where earth is richest, nor fair Ganges and Hermus turbid with gold, may vie with the praise of Italy. . . . Here is perpetual spring and summer in months not her own."[8]

Virgil's masterpiece was the epic poem, the *Aeneid*, clearly meant to rival the work of Homer and fulfill the promise made to Augustus in the *Georgics*. The connection between Troy and Rome is made explicitly. Aeneas, the son of Anchises of Troy, survives the destruction of Troy and eventually settles in Latium; hence, Roman civilization is linked to Greek history. The character of Aeneas is portrayed in terms that remind us of the ideal Roman—his virtues are duty, piety, and faithfulness. Virgil's overall purpose was to show that Aeneas had fulfilled his mission to establish the Romans in Italy and thereby start Rome on her divine mission to rule the world:

> Let others fashion from bronze more lifelike, breathing
>   images—
> For so they shall—and evoke living faces from marble;
> Others excel as orators, others track with their
>   instruments
> The planets circling in heaven and predict when stars
>   will appear.
> But, Romans, never forget that government is your
>   medium!
> Be this your art:—to practise men in the habit of peace,
> Generosity to the conquered, and firmness against
>   aggressors.[9]

As Virgil expressed it, ruling was Rome's gift.

Another prominent Augustan poet was Horace (65–8 B.C.), a friend of Virgil. Horace was the son of a freedman from southern Italy, whose land had been confiscated for being on the wrong side of the civil war. Like Virgil, however, Horace was later provided a farm for his livelihood. He was also close to Augustus and had a strong sense of identification with Italy.

Horace was a very sophisticated writer whose overriding concern seems to have been to point out to his contemporaries the "follies and vices of his age." In the *Satires*, a medley of poems on a variety of subjects, Horace is revealed as a detached observer of human weaknesses. He directed his attacks against movements, not living people, and took on such subjects as sexual immorality, greed, and job dissatisfaction ("How does it happen, Maecenas, that no man alone is content with his lot?"[10]). Horace mostly laughs at the weaknesses of humankind and calls for forbearance: "Supposing my friend has got liquored and wetted my couch . . . is he for such a lapse to be deemed less dear as a friend, or because when hungry he snatched up before me a chicken from my side of the dish?"[11] In his final work, the *Epistles*, Horace used another Greek form—the imaginary letter in verse—to provide a portrait of his friends and society and those things he held most dear: a simple life, good friends, and his beloved countryside.

Ovid (43 B.C.–A.D. 18) was the last of the great poets of the golden age. He came from a wealthy equestrian family and, contrary to his father's wishes, decided to pursue literary studies: "Often my father told me: 'Why this useless endeavor? Homer himself left nothing behind him of worldly wealth.' "[12] Ovid belonged to a youthful, privileged social group in Rome that liked to ridicule old Roman values. In keeping with the spirit of this group, Ovid wrote a frivolous series of love poems known as the *Amores*. Intended to entertain and shock, they achieved their goal. Ovid's most popular work was the *Metamorphoses*, a series of fifteen complex mythological tales involving transformations of shapes, such as the change of chaos into order. A storehouse of mythological information, the *Metamorphoses* inspired many Western painters, sculptors, and writers, including Shakespeare.

Another of Ovid's works was *The Art of Love*. This was essentially a takeoff on didactic poems. Whereas authors of earlier didactic poems had written guides to farming, hunting, or some such subject, Ovid's work was a handbook on the seduction of females (see the box on p. 169). *The Art of Love* appeared to applaud the loose sexual morals of the Roman upper classes at a time when Augustus was trying to clean up the sexual scene in upper-class Rome. The *princeps* was not pleased. Ovid chose to ignore the wishes of Augustus and paid a price for it. In A.D. 8, he was implicated in a sexual scandal, possibly involving the emperor's daughter Julia. He was banished to a small town on the coast of the Black Sea. Despite appeals, he was never permitted to return to Rome and died in exile.

The most famous Latin prose work of the golden age was written by the historian Livy (59 B.C.–A.D. 17) Livy's masterpiece was the *History of Rome* from the foundation of the city to 9 B.C., written in 142 books. Only 35 of the books have survived, although we do possess brief summaries of the whole work from other authors. Livy was born in northern Italy but also came to live in Rome. He was not involved in public affairs and though not patronized like Virgil and Horace, did become close to the family of Augustus.

Livy perceived history in terms of moral lessons. He stated in the preface that

> The study of history is the best medicine for a sick mind; for in history you have a record of the infinite variety of human experience plainly set out for all to see; and in that record you can find for yourself and your country both examples and warnings: fine things to take as models, base things, rotten through and through, to avoid.[13]

For Livy, human character was the determining factor in history.

Livy's history celebrated Rome's greatness. He built scene upon scene that not only revealed the character of the chief figures but also demonstrated the virtues that had made Rome great. Of course, he had serious weaknesses as a historian. He was not always concerned about the factual accuracy of his myriad stories and was not overly critical of his sources. But he did tell a good story, and his work became the standard history of Rome for a long time.

The Augustan Age was a lengthy one. Augustus died in A.D. 14 after dominating the Roman world for forty-five years. He had created a new order while placating the old by restoring and maintaining traditional values, a fitting combination for a leader whose favorite maxim was "make haste slowly." By the time of his death, his new order was so well established that few agitated for an alternative. Indeed, as the Roman historian Tacitus pointed out, "Actium had been won before the younger men were born. Even most of the older generation had come into a world of civil wars. Practically no one had ever seen truly Republican government. . . . Political equality was a thing of the past; all eyes watched for imperial commands."[14] The Republic was now only a memory and, given its last century of warfare, an unpleasant one at that. The new order was here to stay.

▼ The Early Empire (14–180)

There was no serious opposition to Augustus's choice of his stepson Tiberius as his successor. Although Tiberius was not Augustus's first choice, he had managed to outlive the other relatives whom Augustus would have preferred. The designation of a family member as *princeps* was tantamount to accepting the principle of dynas-

Ovid and the Art of Love
▼ ▼ ▼

Ovid has been called the last great poet of the Augustan golden age of literature. One of his most famous works was The Art of Love, a guidebook on the seduction of women. Unfortunately for Ovid, the work appeared at a time when Augustus was anxious to improve the morals of the Roman upper class. Augustus considered the poem offensive, and Ovid soon found himself in exile.

Ovid, The Art of Love

Now I'll teach you how to captivate and hold the woman of your choice. This is the most important part of all my lessons. Lovers of every land, lend an attentive ear to my discourse; let goodwill warm your hearts, for I am going to fulfil the promises I made you.

First of all, be quite sure that there isn't a woman who cannot be won, and make up your mind that you will win her. Only you must prepare the ground. Sooner would the birds cease their song in the springtime, or the grasshopper be silent in the summer . . . than a woman resist the tender wooing of a youthful lover. . . .

Now the first thing you have to do is to get on good terms with the fair one's maid. She can make things easy for you. Find out whether she is fully in her mistress's confidence, and if she knows all about her secret dissipations. Leave no stone unturned to win her over. Once you have her on your side, the rest is easy. . . .

In the first place, it's best to send her a letter, just to pave the way. In it you should tell her how you dote on her; pay her pretty compliments and say all the nice things lovers always say. . . . Even the gods are moved by the voice of entreaty. And promise, promise, promise. Promises will cost you nothing. Everyone's a millionaire where promises are concerned. . . .

If she refuses your letter and sends it back unread, don't give up; hope for the best and try again. . . .

Don't let your hair stick up in tufts on your head; see that your hair and your beard are decently trimmed. See also that your nails are clean and nicely filed; don't have any hair growing out of your nostrils; take care that your breath is sweet, and don't go about reeking like a billy-goat. All other toilet refinements leave to the women or to perverts. . . .

When you find yourself at a feast where the wine is flowing freely, and where a woman shares the same couch with you, pray to that god whose mysteries are celebrated during the night, that the wine may not overcloud your brain. 'Tis then you may easily hold converse with your mistress in hidden words whereof she will easily divine the meaning. . . .

By subtle flatteries you may be able to steal into her heart, even as the river insensibly overflows the banks which fringe it. Never cease to sing the praises of her face, her hair, her taper fingers and her dainty foot. . . .

Tears, too, are a mighty useful resource in the matter of love. They would melt a diamond. Make a point, therefore, of letting your mistress see your face all wet with tears. Howbeit, if you can manage to squeeze out any tears—and they won't always flow just when you want them to—put your finger in your eyes.

---

tic rule, hardly appropriate to the image Augustus had tried to create of the *princeps* as only the "first citizen of the state." By his actions, Augustus established the Julio-Claudian dynasty; the next four successors of Augustus were related either to the family of Augustus or that of his wife Livia.

The Julio-Claudians (14–69) and Flavians (69–96)

The Julio-Claudian rulers varied greatly in ability. Tiberius (14–37) was a competent general and able administrator who tried initially to involve the senate in government. Caligula (37–41) was a grandnephew of Tiberius and great-grandson of Augustus. He exhibited tyrannical behavior and was excessively erratic, probably due to mental instability. Claudius (41–54) had been mistreated by his family because of a physical disability due to partial paralysis, but he was intelligent, well educated, and proved to be a competent administrator. He was followed by Nero (54–68), who was only sixteen when he came to power. Nero's interest in the arts caused him to neglect affairs of state, especially the military, and proved to be his undoing.

Augustus	31 B.C.–A.D. 14
Julio-Claudian Dynasty	
Tiberius	14–37
Caligula	37–41
Claudius	41–54
Nero	54–68
Flavian Dynasty	
Vespasian	69–79
Titus	79–81
Domitian	81–96
Good Emperors	
Nerva	96–98
Trajan	98–117
Hadrian	117–138
Antoninus Pius	138–161
Marcus Aurelius	161–180

Several major tendencies emerged during the reigns of the four Julio-Claudians. In general, more and more of the responsibilities that Augustus had given to the senate tended to be taken over by the emperors. It is interesting to observe that both Tiberius and Claudius initially encouraged senators to act more independently but wound up undermining the senate's authority in the long run. Moreover, an imperial bureaucracy was instituted under Claudius. He rationalized the central government by developing bureaucratic departments with talented freedmen as their chiefs. This practice further undermined the authority of the senators since they had previously shared in these responsibilities.

As the Julio-Claudian successors of Augustus acted more openly like real rulers rather than "first citizens of the state," the opportunity for arbitrary and corrupt acts also increased. In the last years of his reign, Tiberius had scores of people executed on a charge of treason. Caligula, who was mentally unstable, declared that he would make his horse a consul and wanted to be hailed as a god. Nero freely eliminated people he wanted out of the way, including his own mother, whom he had murdered. Without troops, the senators proved unable to oppose these excesses. Only the praetorian guard established by Augustus seemed capable of interfering with these rulers, but did so in a manner that did not bode well for future stability. Caligula proved so capricious

that the officers of the praetorian guard hatched a plot and assassinated him before he had even ruled for four complete years. Afterward, they chose Claudius, uncle of Caligula, as the next emperor and forced the senate to confirm their act, thereby demonstrating the power of the military units stationed around Rome.

The downfall of the Julio-Claudian dynasty came with the mistakes of Nero. He failed to take an adequate interest in the army and lost its loyalty. At the same time, he created animosity by executing a popular general on a charge of treason. His extravagance caused economic difficulties, leading to a conspiracy, not by the praetorian guard, but by the Roman legions themselves. In 68, Galba, governor of one of the Spanish provinces, rose in revolt and secured the principate for himself, but was not readily accepted by the other provincial armies. The result was a free-for-all in 69, known as the year of the four emperors (see the box on p. 171). Finally, Vespasian, commander of the legions in the east, established himself as sole ruler and his family as a new dynasty known as the Flavians. The significance of the year 69 was summed up precisely by Tacitus when he stated that "a well-hidden secret of the principate had been revealed: it was possible, it seemed, for an emperor to be chosen outside Rome."[15]

The accession of Vespasian to the imperial power demonstrated that it was no longer necessary to be descended from an ancient aristocratic family to be emperor. In fact, Vespasian (69–79) was from the equestrian order. Once in control, he managed to reestablish the economy on a sound basis after the extravagances of Nero and the destruction wrought by the civil wars of 69. More importantly, Vespasian had no compunctions whatever about establishing the principle of dynastic succession for the principate. He was followed by his sons Titus (79–81) and Domitian (81–96). The Flavians, especially Domitian, dropped the pretense of the word *princeps* and began to use the title of *imperator*, emperor, freely. While the emperor was rapidly becoming an absolute monarch, the Flavian dynasty itself came to an abrupt end with the assassination of Domitian in 96.

The Five "Good Emperors" (96–180)

Many historians see the *Pax Romana* (the Roman peace) and the prosperity it engendered as the chief benefits of Roman rule during the first and second centuries A.D. The *Pax Romana* is especially associated with the five so-called good emperors. These rulers treated

The Fate of Cremona in the Year of the Four Emperors
▼▼▼

After the death of Nero in A.D. 68, a power struggle ensued that resulted in a year of confusion with four different emperors, each the leader of a field army. Galba replaced Nero and was succeeded, in turn, by Otho who was then defeated by Vitellius. Finally, Vespasian established a new dynasty. Some of the Italian cities suffered greatly in these struggles between Roman legions loyal to their commanders. This excerpt is from Tacitus's account of the destruction of Cremona by the forces that had declared for Vespasian.

Tacitus, *The Histories*

Forty thousand armed men forced their way into the city. . . . Neither rank nor years saved the victims from an indiscriminate orgy in which rape alternated with murder and murder with rape. Greybeards and frail old women, who had no value as loot, were dragged off to raise a laugh. But any full-grown girl or good-looking lad who crossed their path was pulled this way and that in a violent tug-of-war between the would-be captors, and finally drove them to destroy each other. A single looter trailing a hoard of money or temple-offerings of massive gold was often cut to pieces by others who were stronger. Some few turned up their noses at the obvious finds and inflicted flogging and torture on the owners in order to rummage after hidden valuables and dig for buried treasure. In their hands they held firebrands, which, once they had got their spoil away, they wantonly flung into the empty houses and rifled temples. It is not surprising that, in an army of varied tongues and conventions, including Romans, allies and foreigners [auxiliaries], there was a diversity of wild desires, differing conceptions of what was lawful, and nothing barred. Cremona lasted them four days. While all its buildings, sacred and secular, collapsed in flames, only the temple of Mefitis [goddess of pestilential vapors] outside the walls remained standing, defended by its position or the power of the divinity.

---

the ruling classes with respect, cooperated with the senate, ended arbitrary executions, maintained peace in the empire, and supported domestic policies generally beneficial to the empire. While absolute monarchs, they were known for their tolerance and diplomacy.

The first of the good emperors was Nerva (96–98), who was chosen by the senate after the assassination of Domitian. By chance, Nerva and his next three successors had no sons and had to resort to adoption to obtain heirs. As his successor, Nerva chose Trajan, a capable man who was also acceptable to the army, an increasingly important requirement. Trajan (98–117) had been born in Spain to an old Roman family and was the first emperor of provincial origin. Trajan was succeeded by his second cousin Hadrian (117–138), who also came from a Roman family that had settled in Spain. Hadrian adopted as his successor Antoninus Pius (138–161), who achieved a reputation as the most beneficent of all the good emperors. Unlike Hadrian, who traveled extensively in the provinces, Antoninus Pius stayed in Rome and made even greater use of the senate. In turn, he adopted Marcus Aurelius (161–180), who has been viewed as a philosopher-king of the sort Plato envisioned (see Chapter 3). Marcus Aurelius was highly influenced by Stoicism and wrote his *Meditations*, reflecting the ideal of Stoic duty as a religious concept.

Under the five good emperors, the powers of the emperor continued to be extended at the expense of the senate. Increasingly, imperial officials appointed and directed by the emperor took over the running of the government. This development of an imperial civil service, staffed primarily by members of the equestrian order, was greatly aided by the efforts of Hadrian. It was he who regularized the appointment of equestrians to the important secretaryships in the imperial bureaucracy.

The good emperors extended the scope of imperial administration to areas previously untouched by the imperial government. Nerva introduced and Trajan implemented the establishment of institutions called *alimenta*. The alimentary program provided state funds to assist poor parents in raising and educating their children. The program was not motivated simply by benevolence since it was thought that such assistance would materially aid in creating a larger pool of young men in Italy eligible for military service.

The good emperors were widely praised by their subjects for their extensive building programs. Trajan and Hadrian were especially active in constructing public

▼ **Hadrian.** The rule of the five "good emperors" brought a period of peace and prosperity to the Early Empire. While continuing to limit the power of the senate, all five treated the ruling classes with respect and implemented beneficial domestic policies. Moreover, they were able to maintain peace within the empire itself while also strengthening and even expanding the borders of the state. This bronze head represents Hadrian, the third of the "good emperors."

works—aqueducts, bridges, roads, and harbor facilities—throughout the provinces and in Rome. Trajan built a new forum in Rome to contain his celebrated victory column. Hadrian is best remembered for his mausoleum, which is now the Castel Sant' Angelo.

Frontiers, the Army, and the Provinces

With the exception of Claudius' annexation of Britain, the first-century successors of Augustus had largely followed his advice to curb expansion and remain within the natural frontiers of the empire—the ocean to the west, the rivers in the north, and the desert in the east and south. Two areas prompted special concern. The

Rhine-Danube frontier in the north became the most heavily fortified frontier area because of the threat from restless barbarian tribes. In the east, the Romans used a system of client states to serve as a buffer against the troublesome Parthian Empire.

Although Trajan broke with Augustus's policy of defensive imperialism by extending Roman rule into Dacia (modern Romania), Mesopotamia, and the Sinai peninsula, his conquests represent the high-water mark of Roman expansion. His successors recognized that the empire was overextended and pursued a policy of re-

▼ **Trajan's Column.** Trajan was the first of the "good emperors" to conduct wars of expansion. Trajan established new Roman provinces in both the north and the east. Although he added territory to the empire, Trajan also left it overextended, and his successor Hadrian introduced a defensive policy of retrenchment. Pictured here is Trajan's column, decorated with spiral reliefs that illustrate events from Trajan's military campaigns in Dacia (modern Romania).

trenchment. Hadrian withdrew Roman forces from much of Mesopotamia. Although he retained Dacia and Arabia, he went on the defensive in his frontier policy by reinforcing the fortifications along a line connecting the Rhine and Danube rivers and building a defensive wall eighty miles long across northern Britain. By the reign of Marcus Aurelius, the vulnerability of the empire had become apparent. Frontiers were stabilized and the Roman forces were established in permanent bases behind the frontiers. But when one frontier was attacked, troops had to be drawn from other frontiers, leaving them vulnerable to attack. The empire lacked a real strategic reserve, and in the next century its weakness would be ever more apparent.

The Roman army was the primary instrument for the defense of the Roman frontiers. In A.D. 14, it numbered twenty-five legions, but had increased to thirty by the time of Trajan. The auxiliaries were increased correspondingly, making a Roman army of about 400,000 by the end of the second century. Since legionaries had to be Roman citizens, most recruits in Augustus's time were from Italy. But in the course of the first century, the Italians' reluctance to serve in the military led to the recruitment of citizens from the provinces. By the time of Vespasian, 50 percent of the legionaries were non-Italian; by 100, only one in five was Italian. Increasingly, in the second century, more and more recruits came from the frontier provinces rather than from the more romanized ones.

This process was encouraged by the defensive nature of the military forces. The Roman army had become primarily a garrison force, ensconced in large fortified camps behind the frontier's defensive lines. The camps functioned as bases of operations from which military roads were built to favorable locations on the frontier to allow swift troop movement for defensive or offensive means. The roads were, in turn, protected by forts staffed by auxiliary units. It became easier and cheaper to recruit soldiers from territories close to these defensive positions. But this policy meant that Roman legions were increasingly less and less Roman and would lead to dire consequences for the Roman army in the third and fourth centuries.

In addition to defense and protection, the Roman army served two other important functions: it was an avenue for social mobility and an agent of romanization. Auxiliary units recruited noncitizens who then became Roman citizens after being discharged. Moreover, an army career brought many rewards, especially for those who achieved the rank of centurion. Retired senior centurions, in particular, were viewed as high-ranking citi-

▼ **A Rome in Africa.** While serving mostly as a defensive force in the first and second centuries A.D., the Roman army also helped to bring Roman culture and institutions to the provinces. Local production and trade grew up around the military camps to meet the soldiers' needs, and cities often developed from the bases themselves or from colonies located nearby. Pictured are the ruins of Timgad, a Roman city built in the mountains of Algeria.

zens upon return to their cities and often served in important municipal posts.

The army also served as an important instrument for romanizing the provinces. Roman military camps became centers for the spread of the Latin language and Roman institutions and ways of thought and conduct. The presence of large numbers of troops and their dependent women and slaves encouraged the development of trade and local production to meet the army's need for supplies. Urban centers developed around army bases or colonies nearby. Many cities along the Rhine had their roots in legionary bases or auxiliary forts. The city of Cologne, for example, grew out of the military colony the Romans called Colonia Agrippinensis.

At its height in the second century, the Roman Empire was the greatest state the world had seen, surpassing both the Persian Empire and the Hellenistic Empire of Alexander the Great. It covered about three and a half million square miles and had a population that has been estimated at more than 50 million. While the emperors and the imperial administration provided a degree of unity, considerable leeway was given to local customs, and the privileges of Roman citizenship were extended to many people throughout the empire. In A.D. 212, the emperor Caracalla completed the process by giving Roman citizenship to every free inhabitant of the empire. Latin was the language of the western part of the empire while Greek was used in the east. Although Roman culture spread to all parts of the empire, there were limits to romanization since local languages persisted and many of the empire's residents spoke neither Latin nor Greek.

The administration and cultural life of the Roman Empire depended greatly upon cities and towns. Cities were important to the administration of the empire. A provincial governor's staff was not large, so it was left to local city officials to act as Roman agents in carrying out many government functions, especially those related to taxes. Most towns and cities were not large by modern standards. The largest was Rome, but there were also some large cities in the east: Alexandria in Egypt numbered over 300,000 inhabitants, Ephesus in Asia Minor had 200,000, Antioch in Syria around 150,000. In the west cities were usually small, with only a few thousand inhabitants. Cities were important in the spread of Ro-

▼ **Map 6.1** The Roman Empire

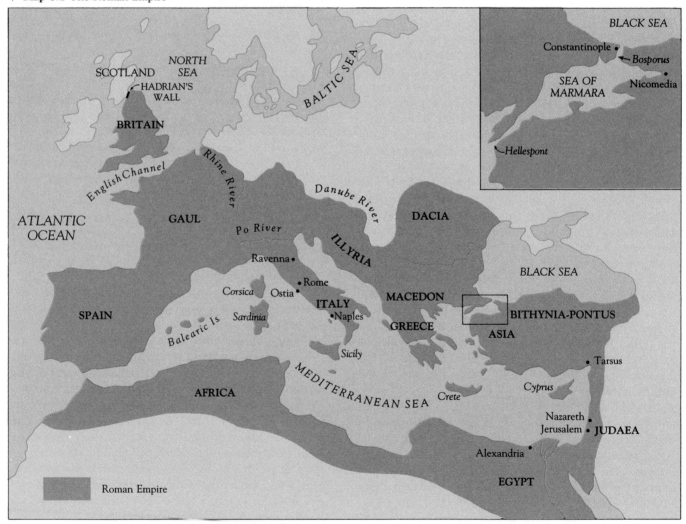

man culture, law, and the Latin language. They were also uniform in physical appearance with similar temples, markets, amphitheaters, and other public buildings.

Magistrates and town councillors chosen from the ranks of the wealthy upper classes directed municipal administration. These municipal offices were unsalaried, but were nevertheless desired by wealthy citizens since they received prestige and power at the local level as well as Roman citizenship. Roman municipal policy effectively tied the upper classes to Roman rule and ensured control by these classes over the rest of the population.

The process of romanization in the provinces was reflected in significant changes in the governing classes of the empire. In the course of the first century, there was a noticeable decline in the number of senators from Italian families. By the end of the second century, Italian senators made up less than 50 percent of the total. Only one senatorial family, that of the Acilii Glabriones, went back to republican times. Increasingly, the Roman senate was being recruited from wealthy provincial equestrian families. The provinces also provided many of the equestrian officials for important administrative positions, as well as legionaries for the Roman army. And beginning with Trajan, the provinces also supplied many of the emperors.

Economic and Social Conditions

Although serious economic problems began to occur in the Roman Empire in the second century, historians agree that the Early Empire was a period of considerable prosperity. Internal peace and the use of a single currency throughout all the provinces resulted in unprecedented levels of trade. Merchants from all over the empire came to the chief Italian ports of Puteoli on the Bay of Naples and Ostia at the mouth of the Tiber. Trade, however, extended beyond the Roman boundaries and included even silk goods from China. Already in the first century, the balance of trade tilted heavily against the city of Rome and the western half of the empire. The importation of large quantities of grain to feed the populace of Rome and an incredible quantity of luxury items for the wealthy upper classes in the west led to a steady drainage of gold and silver coins from Italy and the west to the eastern part of the empire.

Increased trade helped to stimulate manufacturing. The cities of the east still produced the items made in Hellenistic times (see Chapter 4). The first two centuries of the empire also witnessed the high point of industrial development in Italy. Some industries became concentrated in certain areas, such as bronze work in Capua and pottery in Arretium in Etruria. Other industries, such as brickmaking, were pursued in rural areas as by-products of large landed estates. Much industrial production remained small scale and was done by individual craftsmen, usually freedmen or slaves. In the course of the first century, Italian centers of industry experienced increasing competition from the provinces. Pottery produced in Gaul, for example, began to outsell Italian pottery from Arretium.

Despite the prosperity from trade and commerce, agriculture remained the chief occupation of most people and the underlying basis of Roman prosperity. While the large landed estates called *latifundia* still dominated agriculture, especially in southern and central Italy, small peasant farms remained in existence, particularly in Etruria and the Po valley. Although large estates concentrating on sheep and cattle raising used slaves, the lands of some *latifundia* were also worked by free tenant farmers called *coloni*. The *colonus* was essentially a sharecropper who paid rent in labor, produce, or sometimes cash.

In considering the prosperity of the Roman world, it is important to remember the enormous gulf between rich and poor underlying it (see the box on p. 175). The development of towns and cities, so important to the creation of any civilization, is based in large degree upon the agricultural surpluses of the countryside. In ancient times, the margin of surplus produced by each farmer was relatively small. Therefore, the upper classes and urban populations had to be supported by the labor of a large number of agricultural producers who never found

it easy to produce much more than enough for their own subsistence. In lean years, when there were no surpluses, the townspeople often took what they wanted, leaving little for the peasants.

Roman Culture and Society in the Early Empire

LITERATURE   In the history of Latin literature, the century and a half after Augustus is often labeled the "silver age" to indicate that the literary efforts of the period, while good, were not equal to the high standards of the Augustan "golden age." The popularity of rhetorical training encouraged the use of clever and ornate literary expressions at the expense of original and meaningful content. A good example of this trend can be found in the works of Seneca.

Educated in Rome, Seneca (c. 4 B.C.–A.D. 65) became strongly attached to the philosophy of Stoicism (see Chapter 4). After serving as tutor to Nero, he and Burrus, prefect of the praetorian guard, helped to run the government during the first five years of Nero's reign. Seneca began to withdraw from politics after Nero took a more active role in government. In 65, he was charged with involvement in a conspiracy against Nero and committed suicide at Nero's command.

Seneca was a prolific writer, producing nine tragedies, 124 philosophical letters, seven books of *Natural Questions*, and a number of philosophical dialogues. In letters written to a young friend, he expressed the basic tenets of Stoicism: living according to nature, accepting events dispassionately as part of the divine plan, and a universal love for all humanity. Thus, "The first thing philosophy promises us is the feeling of fellowship, of belonging to mankind and being members of a community. . . . Philosophy calls for simple living, not for doing penance, and the simple way of life need not be a crude one."[16] Viewed in retrospect, Seneca displays some glaring inconsistencies. While preaching the virtues of simplicity, he amassed a fortune and was ruthless at times in protecting it. His letters show humanity, benevolence, and fortitude, but his sentiments are often undermined by an attempt to be clever with words.

The silver age also produced a work called the *Satyricon*, described by some literary historians as the first picaresque novel in Western literature. It was written by Petronius (?–A.D. 66), probably a former governor of Bithynia who had joined Nero's inner circle as "arbiter of taste": "to the blasé emperor smartness and elegance were restricted to what Petronius had approved."[17] The *Satyricon* is a humorous satire on the excesses of the

Roman social scene. Basically, it is the story of a young man and his two male companions who engage in a series of madcap escapades and homosexual antics. The longest surviving episode contains a description of an elaborate and vulgar dinner party given by Trimalchio, a freedman who had become a millionaire through an inheritance from his former master. In Trimalchio, Petronius gave a hilarious, satirical portrait of Rome's new rich (see the box above).

The greatest historian of the silver age was Tacitus (c. 56–120). His main works included the *Annals* and *Histories*, which presented a narrative account of Roman history from the reign of Tiberius through the assassination of Domitian (14–96). Tacitus believed that history had a moral purpose: "It seems to me a historian's foremost duty to ensure that merit is recorded, and to confront evil deeds and words with the fear of posterity's denunciations."[18] As a member of the senatorial class, Tacitus was disgusted with the abuses of power perpetrated by the emperors. Forced to be silent in the reign of Domitian, he was determined that the "evil deeds" of wicked men would not be forgotten. Many historians believe he went too far in projecting back into his account of the past the evils of his own day. Much of what he ascribes to Tiberius, for example, parallels what happened in the reign of Domitian. His work *Germania* is especially important as a source of information about the early Germans. But it too is colored by Tacitus's attempt to show the Germans as noble savages in comparison to the decadent Romans.

By the second century A.D., Latin writers were beginning to look back to Latin models. While familiar with and still influenced by the Greeks, they tended to follow in the footsteps of the great Latin writers. This practice was true of Tacitus who looked more to Livy and Sallust than to Thucydides and was also evident in the work of Juvenal, the best poet of the silver age.

Juvenal (c. 55–c. 128) wrote five books of *Satires* in which he pilloried the manners and vices of his generation. He attacked the affectations of Roman women, the abuse of slaves, the excesses of emperors, the eastern and Greek immigrants, his own poverty, and the inequities of Roman society. For example: "They demand that the teacher shall mould these tender minds, . . . 'See to it,' you're told, and when the school year's ended, you'll get as much as a jockey makes from a single race."[19] But Juvenal was not a reformer. Though he attacked many vices, he offered no basic critique of his society. He criticized the abuse of slaves, but he did not object to the system of slavery itself.

▼ The Roman Aqueduct. As engineers and architects, the Romans not only followed Greek models, but also made significant innovations, such as their extensive use of concrete and curvilinear forms. Their engineering skills enabled them to erect the massive Colosseum in Rome, the public baths built under Caracalla, approximately 50,000 miles of roads, and aqueducts.

After Juvenal, there is a noticeable decline in both the quantity and quality of Latin literature. Christian writers would revive it, but their concerns would be worlds removed from the Latin authors of the Early Empire.

ART   The Romans contributed little that was original to painting and sculpture. Much work was done by Greek artists and craftsmen who adhered to the Roman desire for realism and attention to details. Wall paintings and frescoes in the houses of the rich realistically depicted landscapes, portraits, and scenes from mythological stories.

In architecture, the Romans continued to utilize Greek styles and made use of colonnades, rectangular structures, and post and lintel construction. But the Romans were also innovative. They made considerable use of curvilinear forms: the arch, vault, and dome. While they borrowed the arch and vault from the Etruscans, they achieved better results through their use of concrete. The Romans were indeed the first people in antiquity to develop the use of concrete on a massive scale. By combining concrete and curvilinear forms, they were able to construct massive buildings—public baths, such as those of Caracalla, and amphitheaters, the most famous of which was the Colosseum in Rome, built by the Flavian emperors and capable of seating 50,000 spectators. These large buildings were made possible by Roman engineering skills. These same skills were put to use in constructing roads (the Romans built a network of 50,000 miles of roads throughout their empire), aque-

▼ Roman Fresco. In the realms of painting and sculpture, the Romans contributed little that was original. Much of their work was done for them by Greek artists. Pictured here is a Roman fresco depicting the Greek Ulysses among the Laestrygones. Such frescoes were popular wall decorations in the houses of the rich and reflected the Roman desire for realism and attention to details.

ducts (in Rome, almost a dozen aqueducts kept a population of one million supplied with water), and bridges.

IMPERIAL ROME   At the center of the colossal Roman Empire was the ancient city of Rome. Truly a capital city, Rome had the largest population of any city in the empire. It is estimated that its population was close to one million by the time of Augustus and may have increased even more in the second century A.D. For anyone with ambitions, Rome was the place to be. Literary figures came there to seek their fortunes, for, despite its poverty and discomforts, Rome was regarded as the cultural center of the western part of the empire. A magnet to many people, Rome was extremely cosmopolitan. Nationalities from all over the empire resided there with entire sections inhabited by specific groups, such as Greeks and Syrians.

Rome was, no doubt, an overcrowded and noisy city. Because of the congestion, cart and wagon traffic was banned from the streets during the day. The noise from the resulting vehicular movement at night often made sleep difficult. Evening pedestrian travel was dangerous. Although Augustus had organized a police force, lone travelers could be assaulted, robbed, and soaked by filth thrown out of the upper-story windows of Rome's massive apartment buildings.

An enormous gulf existed between rich and poor in the city of Rome. While the rich had comfortable villas, the poor lived in apartment blocks called *insulae*, which might be six stories high. Constructed of concrete, they were often poorly built and not infrequently collapsed. The use of wooden beams in the floors and movable stoves, torches, candles, and lamps within the rooms for heat and light made the danger of fire a constant companion. Once started, fires were extremely difficult to put out. The famous conflagration of 64, which Nero was unjustly accused of starting, devastated a good part of the city. Besides the hazards of collapse and fire, living conditions were also poor. High rents forced entire families into one room. The absence of plumbing, central heating, and open fireplaces created uncomfortable living conditions, with the result that poorer Romans spent most of their time outdoors in the streets.

Fortunately for these people, Rome boasted public buildings unequaled anywhere in the empire. Its temples, fora, markets, baths, theaters, triumphal arches, governmental buildings, and amphitheaters gave parts of the city an appearance of grandeur and magnificence (see the box on p. 180).

While the center of a great empire, Rome was also a great parasite. Beginning with Augustus, the emperors

▼ **The Baths of Caracalla.** The public baths, founded in Rome by the second century B.C., became quite popular among both rich and poor. While used for cleanliness, the baths also became places for socializing and entertainment. Pictured here are the ruins of the baths built by the Emperor Caracalla at the beginning of the third century A.D. This construction covered thirty-three acres and housed not only the baths, but also rooms for exercise and games, shops, libraries, and gardens.

accepted responsibility for providing food for the urban populace, with about 200,000 people receiving free grain. Rome needed about six million sacks of grain a year and imported large quantities from its African and Egyptian provinces to meet these requirements. Even with the free grain, conditions were grim for the poor. Early in the second century A.D., a Roman doctor claimed that rickets was common among children in the city.

In addition to food, entertainment was also provided on a grand scale for the inhabitants of Rome. The poet Juvenal said of the Roman masses: "But nowadays, with no vote to sell, their motto is 'Couldn't care less.' Time was when their plebiscite elected generals, heads of state, commanders of legions: but now they've pulled in their horns, there's only two things that concern them: Bread and Circuses."[20] Public spectacles were provided by the emperor and other state officials as part of the great festivals—most of them religious in origin—celebrated by the state. Over one hundred days a year were given over to these public holidays. The festivals included three major types of entertainment. At the Circus Maximus, horse and chariot races attracted hundreds of thousands, while dramatic and other perfor-

The Public Baths of the Roman Empire

▼ ▼ ▼

The public baths in Rome and other cities played an important role in urban life. Introduced to Rome in the second century B.C. as a result of Greek influence, the number of public baths grew at a rapid pace in the Early Empire as the emperors contributed funds for their construction. The public baths were especially noisy near the end of the afternoon when Romans stopped in after work to use the baths before dinner. The following description is by Lucian, a traveling lecturer who lived in the second century and wrote satirical dialogues in Greek. This selection is taken from Hippias, or the Bath.

Lucian, Hippias, or the Bath

The building suits the magnitude of the site, accords well with the accepted idea of such an establishment, and shows regard for the principles of lighting. The entrance is high, with a flight of broad steps of which the tread is greater than the pitch, to make them easy to ascend. On entering, one is received into a public hall of good size, with ample accommodations for servants and attendants. On the left are the lounging rooms, also of just the right sort for a bath, attractive, brightly lighted retreats. Then, besides them, a hall, larger than need be for the purposes of a bath, but necessary for the reception of richer persons. Next, capacious locker rooms to undress in, on each side, with a very high and brilliantly lighted hall between

them, in which are three swimming pools of cold water; it is finished in Laconian marble, and has two statues of white marble in the ancient style. . . .

On leaving this hall, you come into another which is slightly warmed instead of meeting you at once with fierce heat; it is oblong, and has an apse on each side. Next to it, on the right, is a very bright hall, nicely fitted up for massage. . . . Then near this is another hall, the most beautiful in the world, in which one can stand or sit with comfort, linger without danger, and stroll about with profit. It also is refulgent with Phrygian marble clear to the roof. Next comes the hot corridor, faced with Numidian marble. The hall beyond it is very beautiful, full of abundant light and aglow with color like that of purple hangings. It contains three hot tubs.

When you have bathed, you need not go back through the same rooms, but can go directly to the cold room through a slightly warmed chamber. Everywhere there is copious illumination and full indoor daylight. . . . Why should I go on to tell you of the exercising floor and of the cloak rooms? . . . Moreover, it is beautified with all other marks of thoughtfulness—with two toilets, many exits, and two devices for telling time, a water clock that makes a bellowing sound and a sundial.

---

mances were held in theaters. But the most famous of all the public spectacles were the gladiatorial shows.

THE GLADIATORIAL SHOWS The gladiatorial shows were an integral part of Roman society. They took place in amphitheaters, with the first permanent one having been constructed at Rome in 29 B.C. Perhaps the most famous was the Flavian amphitheater, called the Colosseum, constructed at Rome under Vespasian and his son Titus to seat 50,000 spectators. Amphitheaters were not limited to the city of Rome but were constructed throughout the empire. In Tunisia alone, which was but a part of the Roman province of Africa, there were over twenty. They varied greatly in size with capacities ranging from a few thousand to tens of thousands. Considerable resources and ingenuity went into building them, especially in the arrangements for moving wild beasts

efficiently into the arena. In most cities and towns, amphitheaters came to be the biggest buildings, rivaled only by the circuses for races and the public baths. As we shall see repeatedly in the course of Western civilization, where a society invests its money gives an idea of its priorities. Since the amphitheater was the primary location for the gladiatorial games, it is fair to say that public slaughter was an important part of Roman culture.

Gladiatorial games were held from dawn to dusk. Contests to the death between trained fighters formed the central focus of these games. Most gladiators were slaves or condemned criminals, although some free men lured by the hope of popularity and patronage by wealthy fans participated voluntarily. They were trained for combat in special gladiatorial schools.

Gladiatorial games included other forms of entertainment as well. Criminals of all ages and both sexes were sent into the arena without weapons to face certain death from wild animals who would tear them to pieces. Numerous kinds of animal contests were also held: wild beasts against each other, such as bears against buffalo; staged hunts with men shooting safely from behind iron bars; and gladiators in the arena with bulls, tigers, and lions. It is recorded that five thousand beasts were killed in one day of games when the Emperor Titus inaugurated the Colosseum in 80 A.D. Enormous resources were invested in the capture and shipment of wild animals for slaughter, while whole species were hunted to extinction in parts of the empire.

There is no doubt that these bloodthirsty spectacles were popular with the Roman people. The Roman historian Tacitus said, "Few indeed are to be found who talk of any other subjects in their homes, and whenever we enter a classroom, what else is the conversation of the youths."[21] The Romans justified their gladiatorial games in a number of ways. They were apparently inherited from the Etruscans (see Chapter 5) and arose in the context of human sacrifice. The shades of the dead and the anger of the gods were supposedly appeased by the sacrifice of human beings. The masses of the empire, of course, knew nothing of these origins; what had once been sacred rapidly became secularized. The aristocratic statesman Pliny argued that the contests inspired a contempt for pain and death, since even slaves and criminals displayed a love of praise and desire for victory in the arena. Most importantly, the gladiatorial games, as well as the other forms of public entertainment, fulfilled

▼ **Interior of the Colosseum of Rome.** The Colosseum was a large amphitheater constructed under the emperor Vespasian and his son Titus. The amphitheaters in which the gladiatorial contests were held varied in size throughout the empire. The Roman emperors understood that gladiatorial shows and other forms of entertainment helped to divert the poor and destitute from any political unrest.

both a political and a social function. Certainly, the games served to divert the idle masses from any political unrest. It was said of the Emperor Trajan that he understood that although the distribution of grain and money satisfied the individual, spectacles were necessary for the "contentment of the masses." But the games performed in the amphitheaters also served to remind the masses of what happens to those who fail to please their masters. While the masses became accustomed to violence, it was

▼ **Gladiators.** The gladiators were often condemned criminals, slaves, prisoners of war, or even free men enticed by the possibility of rewards. The more bizarre an event, the more popular it was with the spectators. Trained in special schools, a great gladiator could win his freedom through the games. The fresco pictured here depicts a battle of gladiators.

the rulers who institutionalized it to strengthen their own position. It is significant that it was not until the emperors became Christians that the public bloodbaths of the Roman Empire were finally outlawed.

MEDICINE   Although early Romans had no professional physicians, they still possessed an art of medicine. Early Roman medicine was essentially herbal. The *paterfamilias* would prepare various remedies to heal wounds and cure illnesses. Knowledge of the healing qualities of plants was passed down from generation to generation. This traditional herbal medicine continued to be used in the Early Empire. Of course, numerous recipes for nonillnesses, such as remedies to prevent baldness, were also passed on. One such formula consisted of wine, saffron, pepper, vinegar, *laserpicium* (the queen of Roman medicinal plants), and rat dung.

As in other areas of Roman life, Greek influence was also felt in medicine. At the end of the third century B.C., scientific medicine entered the Roman world through professional practitioners from the Hellenistic world. Doctors became fashionable in Rome, although prejudice against them was never completely abandoned. Many were Greek slaves who belonged to the households of large aristocratic families. The first public doctors in Rome were attached to the Roman army. Military practices were then extended to imperial officials and their families in the provinces and included the establishment of public hospitals. Gladiatorial schools had their own resident doctors as well. In fact, one of the most famous physicians, the Greek Galen (129–199), emerged from the ranks of gladiatorial doctors to become court physician to the Emperor Marcus Aurelius. Roman scientific medicine also witnessed the development of numerous specialists. For example, Alcon, the famous surgeon of the Flavian age, specialized in bone diseases and hernia operations.

LAW   The Early Empire experienced great progress in the study and codification of law. The second and early third centuries A.D. witnessed the "classical age of Roman law," a period in which a number of great jurists classified and compiled basic legal principles that have proved invaluable to the Western world. Ulpian (d. 228) was one of these jurists. Like others, he emphasized the emperor as the source of law: "What has pleased the emperor has the force of law."

As we saw in Chapter 5, civil law in Rome developed through the edicts of urban praetors and the opinions of jurisconsults. This process was aided by the Emperor Hadrian who had the praetors' edicts edited and published. In a similar manner, a body of fundamental law for the provinces developed from the edicts of Roman governors.

In the "classical age of Roman law," the identification of the *ius gentium* (law of nations) with *ius naturale* (natural law) led to a concept of natural rights. According to the jurist Ulpian, natural rights implied that all men are born equal and should therefore be equal before the law. In practice, however, such a principle was not applied, particularly in the third and later centuries.

SLAVERY   The number of slaves had increased dramatically in the Roman Republic as the empire was expanded through warfare. As a result of this increase, slaves were highly visible in the Early Empire. The households of the rich were filled with slaves. Possessing a large number of slaves was a status symbol; a single residence might include dozens of slaves, serving as hairdressers, footmen, messengers, accountants, secretaries, carpenters, plumbers, librarians, goldsmiths, and doctors as well as ordinary domestic servants. The reliance on slaves, especially as skilled craftsmen, undoubtedly created unemployment among the free population. Some slaves possessed high-status jobs as accountants, architects, and managers of businesses, while some imperial slaves held positions in the government bureaucracy. Slaves were also used on landed estates.

But the number of slaves probably peaked in the Early Empire. The defensive imperial policies pursued after Augustus led to a decline in the supply of slaves from foreign conquest. Manumission also contributed to the decline in the number of slaves. It had been customary in Rome for "good masters" to free their slaves, especially well-educated ones or good workers. While freedmen became Roman citizens, they were not given full rights of citizenship. They could vote but not run for office.

Many authors have commented on the supposed advance in humanitarian attitudes toward slaves in the Early Empire, especially in the second century. They argue that the philosophy of Stoicism, with its emphasis on the universality of humanity, had an influence in this direction. Certainly, Seneca stressed the need for kindness to slaves. Very likely, however, the practical Romans were as much, if not more, concerned about the usefulness of their slaves than about any humanitarian attitudes. New laws in the second century did more to moralize than actually improve the condition of slaves. Hadrian, for example, forbade the sale of slaves for immoral or gladiatorial purposes. Such laws had little impact, however, on how masters actually treated their

The Roman Fear of Slaves
▼ ▼ ▼

The lowest stratum of the Roman population consisted of slaves. They were used extensively in households, at the court, as craftsmen in industrial enterprises, as business managers, and in numerous other ways. Although some historians have argued that slaves were treated more humanely during the Early Empire, these selections by the Roman historian Tacitus and the Roman statesman Pliny indicate that slaves still rebelled against their masters because of mistreatment. Many masters continued to live in fear of their slaves as witnessed by the saying, "As many enemies as you have slaves."

Tacitus, *The Annals of Imperial Rome*

Soon afterwards the City Prefect, Lucius Pedanius Secundus, was murdered by one of his slaves [A.D. 61]. Either Pedanius had refused to free the murderer after agreeing to a price, or the slave, in a homosexual infatuation, found competition from his master intolerable. After the murder, ancient custom required that every slave residing under the same roof must be executed. But a crowd gathered, eager to save so many innocent lives; and rioting began. The senate-house was besieged. Inside, there was feeling against excessive severity, but the majority opposed any change. Among the latter was Gaius Cassius Longinus, who when his turn came spoke as follows. . . .

'An ex-consul has been deliberately murdered by a slave in his own home. None of his fellow-slaves prevented or betrayed the murderer, though the senatorial decree threatening the whole household with execution still stands. Exempt them from the penalty if you like. But then, if the City Prefect was not important enough to be immune, who will be? Who will have enough slaves to protect him if Pedanius' four hundred were too few? Who can rely on his household's help if even fear for their own lives does not make them shield us?' [The sentence of death was carried out.]

Pliny the Younger to Acilius

This horrible affair demands more publicity than a letter—Larcius Macedo, a senator and ex-praetor, has fallen a victim to his own slaves. Admittedly he was a cruel and overbearing master, too ready to forget that his father had been a slave, or perhaps too keenly conscious of it. He was taking a bath in his house at Formiae when suddenly he found himself surrounded; one slave seized him by the throat while the others struck his face and hit him in the chest and stomach and—shocking to say—in his private parts. When they thought he was dead they threw him on to the hot pavement, to make sure he was not still alive. Whether unconscious or feigning to be so, he lay there motionless, thus making them believe that he was quite dead. Only then was he carried out, as if he had fainted with the heat, and received by his slaves who had remained faithful, while his concubines ran up, screaming frantically. Roused by their cries and revived by the cooler air he opened his eyes and made some movement to show that he was alive, it being now safe to do so. The guilty slaves fled, but most of them have been arrested and a search is being made for the others. Macedo was brought back to life with difficulty, but only for a few days; at least he died with the satisfaction of having revenged himself, for he lived to see the same punishment meted out as for murder. There you see the dangers, outrages, and insults to which we are exposed. No master can feel safe because he is kind and considerate; for it is their brutality, not their reasoning capacity, which leads slaves to murder masters.

---

slaves. Despite the changes, there were still instances of slaves murdering their owners, and Romans continued to live in unspoken fear of their slaves (see the box above).

THE UPPER-CLASS ROMAN FAMILY   By the second century A.D., significant changes were occurring in the Roman family. The foundations of the authority of the *paterfa-* milias over his family, which had already begun to weaken in the late Republic, were further undermined. The *paterfamilias* no longer had absolute authority over his children; he could no longer sell his children into slavery or have them put to death. Moreover, the husband's absolute authority over his wife also disappeared, a practice that had also begun in the late Republic with the shift to marriage *sine manu* ("without legal control") by which a married daughter remained within the father's legal power (see Chapter 5). In the Early Empire, the idea of male guardianship continued to weaken significantly. Augustus had exempted mothers of three children from such a practice, although he had done so to encourage more prolific marriages. In Hadrian's reign, a married woman no longer needed a guardian to draft her will. By the late second century, though guardianships had not been abolished, they had become a formality.

Roman upper-class women in the Early Empire had considerable freedom and independence. They had acquired the right to own, inherit, and dispose of property. Upper-class women could attend races, the theater, and events in the amphitheater, although in the latter two places they were forced to sit in separate female sections. Moreover, ladies of rank were still accompanied by maids and companions when they went out. Some women operated businesses, such as shipping firms. Women still could not participate in politics, but the Early Empire saw a number of important women who influenced politics through their husbands, including Livia, the wife of Augustus, Agrippina, the mother of Nero, and Plotina, the wife of Trajan.

Divorce had already become common among the upper classes in the last century of the Republic. This practice continued and could be initiated by either the husband or the wife. Under Augustus wives were given the right to demand the return of their dowry. Some husbands divorced their wives for blatant adultery.

At the end of the first century and beginning of the second, there was a noticeable decline in the number of children among the upper classes, a trend that had already begun in the late Republic. Especially evident was an increase in childless marriages. Despite imperial laws aimed at increasing the number of children, the low birthrate persisted. While infanticide continued to be practiced, upper-class Romans used both contraception and abortion to limit their families. There were numerous techniques for contraception. Though highly touted, amulets, magical formulas, and potions to induce temporary sterility proved ineffective, as did the rhythm method, since Roman medical writers believed that the most fertile time for a woman occurred just when menstruation was ending. A more dependable practice involved the use of oils, ointments, and soft wool to obstruct the opening of the uterus. Contraceptive techniques for males were also advocated. An early version of a condom involved using the bladder of a goat, but it was prohibitively expensive. Although the medical sources do not mention it, it is possible that the Romans also used the ubiquitous coitus interruptus. Abortion was practiced, either by the use of drugs or by surgical instruments. Ovid chastises Corinna: "Ah, women, why will you thrust and pierce with the instrument, and give dire poisons to your children yet unborn?"[22]

▼ Religion in the Early Empire: The Rise of Christianity

The rise of Christianity marks a fundamental break with the dominant values of the Greco-Roman world. Christian views of God, human beings, and the world were quite different from those of the Greeks and Romans. Nevertheless, Christianity also had much in common with its contemporary religions. Consequently, to understand the rise of Christianity, we must first examine both the religious environment of the Roman world and the Jewish background from which Christianity emerged.

The Religious World of the Roman Empire

Augustus had taken a number of steps to revive the Roman state religion, which had declined during the turmoil of the late Republic. The official state religion focused on the worship of a pantheon of Greco-Roman gods and goddesses, including Jupiter, Juno, Minerva, and Mars. Observance of proper ritual by state priests theoretically brought the Romans into proper relationship with the gods and guaranteed security, peace, and prosperity. The polytheistic Romans were extremely tolerant of other religions. The Romans allowed the worship of native gods and goddesses throughout their provinces and even adopted some of the local gods. Caligula, for example, approved the cult of the Egyptian Isis (see Chapter 4). In addition, the imperial cult of Roma and Augustus was developed to bolster support for the emperors. After Augustus, those dead emperors deified by the Roman senate were included in the official imperial cult.

In addition to the formal, official religion, the Romans had cults of household and countryside spirits whose worship appealed especially to the common people. While these cults gave the Romans a more immediate sense of spiritual contact than they found in the official religion, these cults too failed to satisfy many people. Consequently, some turned to astrology and occult practices to achieve greater understanding of the supernatural world.

The desire for a more emotional spiritual experience also led many people to the mystery religions of the

Hellenistic east, which flooded into the western Roman world during the Early Empire. The mystery religions offered secret teachings that supposedly brought special benefits. They promised their followers advantages unavailable through Roman religion: an entry into a higher world of reality and the promise of a future life superior to the present one. They also featured elaborate rituals with deep emotional appeal. By participating in their ceremonies and performing their rites, an adherent could achieve communion with spiritual beings and undergo purification that opened the door to life after death.

Many mystery cults were vying for the attention of the Roman world. While the cults of Cybele or the Great Mother and the Egyptian Isis and Serapis had many followers, perhaps the most important mystery cult was Mithraism. Mithras was the chief agent of Ahuramazda, the supreme god of light in Persian Zoroastrianism (see Chapter 2). In the Roman world, Mithra came to be identified with the sun god and was known by his Roman title of the Unconquered Sun. Mithraism had spread rapidly in Rome and the western provinces by the second century A.D. and was especially favored by soldiers who viewed Mithras as their patron deity. It was a religion for men only and featured an initiation ceremony in which devotees were baptized in the blood of a sacrificed bull. Mithraists paid homage to the sun on the first day of the week (Sunday), commemorated the sun's birthday around December 25, and celebrated ceremonial meals. All of these practices had parallels in Christianity.

The Jewish Background

Jesus of Nazareth was a Palestinian Jew who was condemned to death by Pontius Pilate, the procurator of the Roman province of Judaea, which embraced the lands of the old Jewish kingdom of Judah (see Chapter 2). Christianity emerged out of Judaism, and it is to the Jewish political-religious world that we must turn to find the beginnings of Christianity.

In Hellenistic times, the Jewish people had enjoyed considerable independence under their Seleucid rulers (see Chapter 4). Roman involvement with the Jews began in 63 B.C., and by A.D. 6, Judaea had been made a province and placed under the direction of a Roman procurator. But unrest continued, augmented by divisions among the Jews themselves. The Sadducees favored a rigid adherence to Hebrew law, rejected the possibility of personal immortality, and favored cooperation with the Romans. The Pharisees took a more liberal approach to Jewish law, believed in an afterlife, and

wanted to liberate Judaea from Roman control. The Essenes, as revealed in the Dead Sea Scrolls, a collection of documents first discovered in 1947, constituted a Jewish sect that lived in a religious community near the Dead Sea. They, like many other Jews, awaited a Messiah who would save Israel from oppression, usher in the kingdom of God, and establish a true paradise on earth. A fourth group, the Zealots, were militant extremists who advocated the violent overthrow of Roman rule. A Jewish revolt in 66 was crushed by the Romans four years later. The Jewish Temple in Jerusalem was destroyed, and Roman power once more stood supreme in Judaea.

The Rise of Christianity

In the midst of the confusion and conflict in Judaea, Jesus of Nazareth (c. 6 B.C.–A.D. 29) began his public preaching. Jesus grew up in Galilee, an important center of the militant Zealots. Jesus' message was basically simple. He reassured his fellow Jews that he did not plan to undermine their traditional religion: "Do not think that I have come to abolish the Law or the Prophets; I have not come to abolish them but to fulfill them."[23] According to Jesus, what was important was not strict adherence to the letter of the law and attention to rules and prohibitions, but the transformation of the inner person: "So in everything, do to others what you would have them do to you, for this sums up the Law and the Prophets."[24] God's command was a simple one: to love God and one another: "Love the Lord your God with all your heart and with all your soul and with all your mind and with all your strength. The second is this: Love your neighbor as yourself."[25] In the Sermon on the Mount (see the box on p. 186), Jesus presented the ethical concepts—humility, charity, and brotherly love—that would form the basis for the value system of medieval Western civilization. As we have seen, these were not the values of classical Greco-Roman civilization.

While some people welcomed Jesus as the Messsiah who would save Israel from oppression and establish God's kingdom on earth, Jesus spoke of a heavenly kingdom, not an earthly one: "My kingdom is not of this world."[26] Consequently, he disappointed the radicals. On the other hand, conservative religious leaders believed Jesus was undermining respect for traditional Jewish religion. To the Roman authorities of Palestine and their local allies, the Nazarene was a potential revolutionary who might transform Jewish expectations of a messianic kingdom into a revolt against Rome. Therefore, Jesus found himself denounced on many sides and

Christian Ideals: The Sermon on the Mount

▼ ▼ ▼

Christianity was simply one of many religions competing for attention in the Roman Empire during the first and second centuries. The rise of Christianity marked a fundamental break with the value system of the upper-class elites who dominated the world of classical antiquity. As these excerpts from the Sermon on the Mount in the Gospel of Matthew illustrate, Christians emphasized humility, charity, brotherly love, and a belief in the inner being and a spiritual kingdom superior to this material world. These values and principles were not those of classical Greco-Roman civilization as exemplified in the words and deeds of its leaders.

The Gospel According to Matthew

Now when he saw the crowds, he went up on a mountainside and sat down. His disciples came to him, and he began to teach them saying:

Blessed are the poor in spirit: for theirs is the kingdom of heaven.
Blessed are those who mourn: for they will be comforted.
Blessed are the meek: for they will inherit the earth.
Blessed are those who hunger and thirst for righteousness: for they will be filled.
Blessed are the merciful: for they will be shown mercy.
Blessed are the pure in heart: for they will see God.
Blessed are the peacemakers: for they will be called sons of God.
Blessed are those who are persecuted because of righteousness for theirs is the kingdom of heaven. . . .

You have heard that it was said, 'Eye for eye, and tooth for tooth.' But I tell you, Do not resist an evil person. If someone strikes you on the right cheek, turn to him the other also. . . .

You have heard that it was said, 'Love your neighbor, and hate your enemy.' But I tell you, Love your enemies and pray for those who persecute you. . . .

Do not store up for yourselves treasures on earth, where moth and rust destroy, and where thieves break in and steal. But store up for yourselves treasures in heaven, where moth and rust do not destroy, and where thieves do not break in and steal. For where your treasure is, there your heart will be also. . . .

No one can serve two masters. Either he will hate the one and love the other, or he will be devoted to the one and despise the other. You cannot serve both God and Money.

Therefore I tell you, do not worry about your life, what you will eat or drink; or about your body, what you will wear. Is not life more important than food, and the body more important than clothes? Look at the birds of the air; they do not sow or reap to store away in barns, and yet your heavenly Father feeds them. Are you not much more valuable than they? . . . So do not worry, saying, What shall we eat? or What shall we drink? or What shall we wear? For the pagans run after all these things, and your heavenly Father knows that you need them. But seek first his kingdom and his righteousness, and all these things will be given to you as well.

---

was given over to the Roman authorities. The procurator Pontius Pilate ordered his crucifixion. But that did not solve the problem. A few loyal followers of Jesus spread the story that Jesus had overcome death and had been resurrected. He was then labeled *Christos* ("the anointed one") and hailed as the savior-God who had come to reveal the secrets of salvation and personal immortality.

Christianity began, then, as a religious movement within Judaism and was viewed that way by Roman authorities for many decades. Although tradition holds that one of Christ's disciples, Peter, founded the Christian church at Rome, the most important figure in early Christianity after Christ was Paul of Tarsus (c. 5– c. 67). Paul reached out to non-Jews and transformed Christianity from a Jewish sect into a world religion.

Called the "second founder of Christianity," Paul was a Jewish Roman citizen who had been strongly influenced by Hellenistic Greek culture. He believed that the message of Christ should be preached not only to Jews but to Gentiles (non-Jews) as well. Paul was responsible for founding Christian communities throughout Asia Minor and along the shores of the Aegean.

It was Paul who provided a universal foundation for the spread of Christ's ideas. He taught that Christ was, in effect, a savior-God, the son of God, who had come to earth to save all humans who were basically sinners as a result of Adam's original sin of disobedience against God. By his death, Christ had atoned for the sins of all humans and made possible their reconciliation with God and hence their salvation. By accepting Christ as their savior, they too could be saved.

At first, Christianity spread slowly. Although the teachings of early Christianity were mostly disseminated by the preaching of convinced Christians, written materials also appeared. Paul had written a series of letters or epistles to different Christian communities that outlined Christian beliefs. Some of Christ's disciples may also have preserved some of the sayings of the master in writing and would have passed on personal memories that became the basis of the written gospels—the "good news" concerning Christ—which attempted to give a record of Christ's life and teachings and formed the core of the New Testament. Although Jerusalem was the first center of Christianity, its destruction by the Romans in A.D. 70 dispersed the Christians and left individual Christian churches with considerable independence. By 100, Christian churches had been established in most of the major cities of the east and in some places in the western part of the empire. Many early Christians came from the ranks of Hellenized Jews and the Greek-speaking populations of the east. But in the second and third centuries, an increasing number of followers would come from Latin-speaking people. A Latin translation of the Greek New Testament that appeared soon after 200 aided this process.

Early Christian groups met in private homes in the evening to share a common meal called an *agape* or love feast and to celebrate what became known as the sacrament of the eucharist or Lord's Supper—the communal celebration of Christ's Last Supper:

> While they were eating, Jesus took bread, gave thanks and broke it, and gave it to the disciples, saying, Take and eat; this is my body. Then he took the cup, gave thanks, and offered it to them, saying, Drink from it, all of you. This is my blood of the covenant, which is poured out for many for the forgiveness of sins.[27]

These early Christian churches were organized along democratic lines. Each Christian community was directed by a board of elders (presbyters) assisted by deacons. Both elders and deacons were elected from and by the community.

Although some of the fundamental values of Christianity differed markedly from those of the Greco-Roman world, the Romans initially did not pay much attention to the Christians, whom they regarded at first as simply another sect of Judaism. The structure of the Roman Empire itself aided the growth of Christianity. Christian missionaries, including some of Christ's original twelve

▼ **Christ and His Apostles.** Pictured is a fresco from a Roman catacomb depicting Christ and the apostles. Under the leadership of individuals such as Paul of Tarsus, Christianity grew from a small sect within Judaism to a powerful religious force within the empire. Christianity eventually became the official state religion.

disciples or apostles, used Roman roads to travel throughout the empire spreading their "good news." Thus, the universalism of the Roman Empire paved the way for the universalism of the Christian church.

As time passed, however, the Roman attitude toward Christianity began to change. As we have seen, the Romans were tolerant of other religions except when they threatened public order or public morals. Many Romans came to view Christians as harmful to the order of the Roman state. These views were often based on misperceptions. The practice of the Lord's Supper, for example, led to rumors that Christians practiced horrible crimes, such as the ritualistic murder of children. While obviously untrue, such rumors could be used to incite people against the Christians during times of crisis and then to accuse them of creating popular disturbances. Moreover, since Christians held their meetings in secret and seemed to be connected to Christian groups in other areas, the government could view them as potentially dangerous to the state.

Some Romans felt that Christians were overly exclusive and hence harmful to the community and public order. The refusal of Christians to recognize other gods meant abstention from public festivals that were tied to these divinities. Finally, Christians refused to participate in the worship of the state gods and imperial cult. Since the Romans regarded these as important to the state, the Christians' refusal undermined the security of the state and hence constituted an act of treason, punishable by death. It was also proof of atheism (disbelief in the gods) and subject to punishment on those grounds. But to the Christians, who believed there was only one real God, the worship of state gods and the emperors meant committing idolatry and endangering their own salvation.

Roman persecution of Christians in the first and second centuries was never systematic, but only sporadic and local. Persecution began during the reign of Nero. After the fire that destroyed much of Rome, the emperor used the Christians as scapegoats, accusing them of arson and hatred of the human race and subjecting them to cruel deaths in Rome. In the second century, Christians were largely ignored as harmless.

By the end of the reigns of the five good emperors, Christians still represented a small minority, but one of considerable strength. That strength lay in their conviction of the rightness of their path, a conviction that had been reinforced by the willingness of the first Christians to become martyrs for their faith. As the empire disintegrated in the next three centuries, it would be the Christians who literally picked up the pieces and became the dominant force.

▼ The Terrible Third Century

During the reign of Marcus Aurelius, the last good emperor, a number of natural catastrophes struck Rome. Floods of the Tiber, famine, and plague brought back from the east by the army led to considerable population loss and a shortage of military manpower. To many Romans, these natural disasters seemed to portend an ominous future for Rome. New problems arose soon after the death of Marcus Aurelius.

The failures of Commodus (180–192), the incompetent son of Marcus Aurelius, led to a brief renewal of civil war until Septimius Severus (193–211), who was born in north Africa and spoke Latin with an accent, used his legions to establish a new dynasty. These Severan rulers (193–235) began to create a military monarchy. The army was expanded, soldiers' pay was increased, and military officers were appointed to important government positions.

Military monarchy was followed by military anarchy. For a period of almost fifty years, from 235 to 284, the Roman Empire was mired in the chaos of continual civil war. The Roman imperial throne was occupied by anyone who had the military strength to seize it. In these almost fifty years, there were twenty-two emperors, only two of whom did not meet a violent death. At the same time, the empire was beset by a series of invasions, no doubt exacerbated by the civil wars. In the east, the Sassanid Persians made inroads into Roman territory. A fitting symbol of Rome's decline was the capture of the Roman emperor Valerian (253–260) by the Persians and his death in captivity, an event previously unheard of in Roman history. Germanic tribes also poured into the empire. The Goths overran the Balkans and moved into Greece and Asia Minor. The Franks advanced into Gaul and Spain. The Alemanni even invaded Italy. Moreover, a number of provinces were seized by military commanders who took advantage of the chaotic conditions. It was not until the reign of Aurelian (270–275) that most of the boundaries were restored. Although he abandoned the Danubian province of Dacia, he reconquered Gaul and reestablished order in the east and along the Danube. Grateful citizens hailed him as "restorer of the world."

Invasions, civil wars, and recurrence of the plague came close to causing an economic collapse of the Roman Empire in the third century. There was a noticeable decline in trade and small industry. The manpower shortage created by the plague affected both military recruiting and the economy. Farm production deteriorated significantly. Fields were ravaged by barbarians, but even more often by the defending Roman armies. Many farmers complained that Roman commanders and their soldiers were confiscating produce and livestock. Provincial governors seemed powerless to stop these depredations, and some even joined in the extortion.

The monetary system began to show signs of collapse as a result of debased coinage and the beginnings of serious inflation. Gold coins disappeared from circulation and silver coins were diluted. The standard coin—the denarius—was now worth less than 50 percent of its first-century value. After further decline, it was replaced by new coins of even less value. Goods began to replace money as a medium of exchange.

Armies were needed more than ever, but financial strains made it difficult to pay and enlist the necessary soldiers. Whereas in the second century, the Roman army had been recruited among the inhabitants of frontier provinces, by the mid-third century, the state had to rely on hiring barbarians to fight under Roman commanders. These soldiers had no understanding of Roman traditions and no real attachment to either the empire or the emperors.

Map 6.2 Divisions of the Restored Roman Empire.

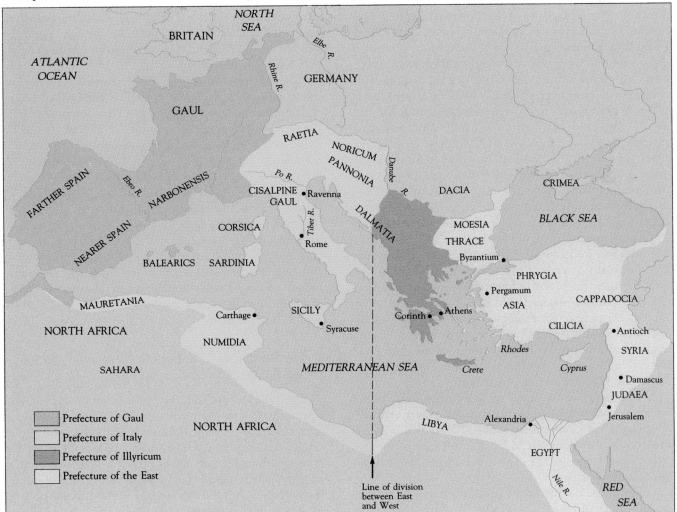

▼ The Restored Empire of the Fourth Century

In the course of the third century, the Roman Empire came near to collapse. At the end of the third and beginning of the fourth centuries, it gained a new lease on life through the efforts of two strong emperors, Diocletian and Constantine, who restored order and stability. This restoration, however, was largely accomplished at the expense of freedom. The Roman Empire was virtually transformed into a new state: the so-called Late Empire, which included a new governmental structure, a rigid economic and social system, and a new state religion—Christianity.

Diocletian and Constantine: Political and Military Reforms

The Emperor Diocletian (284–305) created a new administrative system for a restructured empire. The number of provinces was increased to over one hundred by creating smaller districts superintended by more officials. In turn, the provinces were grouped into twelve dioceses, each headed by an official called a vicar. The twelve dioceses were grouped into four prefectures, each led by a praetorian prefect. The entire Roman Empire was divided into two parts: each part contained two prefectures and was ruled by an "Augustus." Diocletian ruled the east and Maximian, a strong military commander, the west. Each Augustus was assisted by a chief lieutenant or "vice-emperor" called a "Caesar," who theoretically would eventually succeed to the position of Augustus. This new system was called the tetrarchy (rule by four). Diocletian had obviously come to believe that one man was incapable of ruling such an enormous empire, especially in view of the barbarian invasions of the third century. Each of the four tetrarchs—two Augusti and two Caesars—resided in a different administrative capital. Diocletian, for example, established his base at Nicomedia in Bithynia. Despite the appearance of four-man rule, however, it is important to note that Diocletian's military seniority enabled him to claim a higher status and hold the ultimate authority.

Diocletian's system failed to work very well. Soon after his retirement, a new struggle for power ensued. The victory of Constantine (306–337) at the Milvian Bridge north of Rome in 312 led to his control of the entire west. Later, in 324, he managed to establish himself as the sole ruler.

Constantine continued and even expanded the autocratic policies of Diocletian. Under these two rulers, the Roman Empire was transformed into an autocratic monarchy of the Persian type. The emperor, now clothed in jewel-bedecked robes of gold and blue, was seen as a divinely sanctioned monarch whose will was law. Government officials were humble servants required to kneel before the emperor and kiss his robe. The Roman senate was stripped of any power and became simply the city council for Rome.

Diocletian and Constantine greatly strengthened and enlarged the administrative bureaucracies of the Roman Empire. Henceforth, civil and military bureaucracies were sharply separated. Each contained a hierarchy of officials who exercised control at the various levels. The emperor presided over both hierarchies and served as the only link between them. New titles of nobility—such as *illustres* ("illustrious ones") and *illustrissimi* ("most illustrious ones")—were instituted to dignify the holders of positions in the civil and military bureaucracies.

Additional military reforms were also instituted. The army was enlarged to 500,000 men, including barbarian units. Mobile units were established that could be quickly moved to support frontier troops where the borders were threatened.

Constantine was especially interested in building programs despite the strain placed on the budget. Much of the construction took place in the provinces since Rome had become merely a symbolic capital. It was no longer an imperial administrative center since it was considered too far from the frontiers. Constantine's biggest project was the construction of a new capital city in the east on the site of the Greek city of Byzantium on the shores of the Bosporus. Eventually renamed Constantinople (modern Istanbul), it was developed for defensive reasons; it had an excellent strategic location. Calling it his "New Rome," Constantine endowed the city with a forum, large palaces, and a vast amphitheater. Constantinople would become the center of the Eastern Roman or Byzantine Empire (see Chapter 7) and one of the great cities of the world.

Diocletian and Constantine: Economic, Social, and Cultural Trends

The political and military reforms of Diocletian and Constantine created two enormous institutions—the army and civil service—that drained most of the public funds. While more revenues were needed to pay for the army and bureaucracy, the population was not growing, so the tax base could not be expanded. Diocletian and Constantine devised new economic and social policies to deal with these financial burdens. Like their political

Compulsory Services in the Late Empire
▼ ▼ ▼

The political, economic, and social policies of the restored empire under Diocletian and Constantine were based on coercion. This is especially evident in the use of edicts to force people to remain in their occupations and the magistracies in the cities. These excerpts are taken from the Theodosian Code of 438, a compilation of imperial edicts going back to the reign of Constantine. These examples illustrate the plight of city councillors, shipmasters, bakers, and peasants.

Decrees from the Theodosian Code

Since we have learned that the municipal councils are being left deserted by persons who, though subject to them through origin, are requesting military service for themselves through supplications [to the emperor] and are running away to the legions and the various government offices, we order all municipal councils to be advised that if they catch any persons in government service less than twenty years who have either fled from [the duties of] their origin or, rejecting nomination [to municipal office], have enrolled themselves in the military service, they shall drag such persons back to the municipal councils.

If any shipmaster by birth becomes captain of a lighter, he shall nonetheless continue right along to remain in the same group in which his parents appear to have been.

No breadmaker or any of his descendants shall be allowed to pass from his service by the union of marriage with private persons or with persons of the stage or with persons held bound by the profession of charioteer, even if the assent of all the breadmakers should agree to such action, or even if our edicts should be surreptitiously elicited in any way.

Any person whatsoever in whose possession a *colonus* belonging to another is found not only shall restore the said *colonus* to his place of origin but shall also assume the capitation tax on him for the time [that he had him]. And as for *coloni* themselves, it will be proper for such as contemplate flight to be bound with chains to a servile status, so that by virtue of such condemnation to servitude they may be compelled to fulfill the duties that befit free men.

---

policies, these economic and social policies were all based on coercion and loss of individual freedom (see the box above).

To fight inflation, in 301 Diocletian resorted to issuing a price edict that established maximum wages and prices for the entire empire. It was applied mostly in the east, but despite severe penalties, like most wage and price controls, it was unenforceable and failed to work. The decline in circulation of coins led Diocletian to collect taxes and make government payments in produce. Constantine, however, managed to introduce a new gold coin—the solidus—and new silver coins that remained in circulation during his reign.

In the third century, the city councils, which had formed one of the most important administrative units of the empire, had begun to decline. Since the *curiales* (the city councillors) were forced to pay out of their own pockets when they collected insufficient taxes, the wealthy no longer wanted to serve in these positions. Diocletian and Constantine responded by issuing edicts that forced the rich to continue in their posts as *curiales*,

virtually making the positions hereditary. Some *curiales* realized that their fortunes would be wiped out and fled the cities to escape the clutches of the imperial bureaucracy. If caught, however, they were returned to their cities like runaway slaves and forced to assume their duties.

Coercion came to form the underlying basis for numerous occupations in the Late Roman Empire. In order to ensure the tax base and keep the empire going despite the shortage of manpower, the emperors issued edicts that forced people to remain in their designated vocations. Hence, basic jobs, such as bakers and shippers, became hereditary.

Free tenant farmers—the *coloni*—continued to decline and soon found themselves bound to the land as well. Large landowners took advantage of depressed agricultural conditions to enlarge their landed estates, which became the forerunners of the manors of the Middle Ages. Free tenant farmers, unable to survive, became dependent on these large estates and soon found that landlords, in order to guarantee their supply of labor, gained government cooperation in attaching them to their estates. By the time of Constantine, many of the formerly free tenant farmers were becoming a class of serfs, peasants bound to the land.

In addition to increased restrictions on their freedom, the lower classes found themselves with enormous tax burdens since the wealthiest classes in the Late Roman Empire were either exempt from paying taxes or evaded them by bribing the tax collectors. These tax pressures undermined lower-class support for the regime. A fifth-century writer reported that the Roman peasants welcomed the Visigothic invaders of southern Gaul as liberators since the enemy was more lenient to them than the tax collectors.

In general, the economic and social policies of Diocletian and Constantine were based on an unprecedented degree of control and coercion. While temporarily successful, such authoritarian policies in the long run stifled the very vitality the Late Empire needed to revive its sagging fortunes.

The pagan culture of the Late Empire revealed a decline of vitality as well. The books that have survived are textbooks and manuals that were primarily summaries of past knowledge. There were no figures to compare with the writers of the golden and silver ages of Latin litera-

ture. Yet Latin literature did not die. Latin remained the language of the representatives of a Christian culture that was dynamically surging to the forefront of a decaying civilization.

The Triumph of Christianity

The sporadic persecution of Christians by the Romans in the first and second centuries had done nothing to stop the growth of Christianity. It had, in fact, served to strengthen Christianity as an institution in the second and third centuries by causing it to shed the loose structure of the first century and move toward a more centralized organization of its various church communities. Crucial to this change was the emerging role of the bishops. While still chosen by the community, bishops began to assume more control with the bishop serving as leader and the presbyters emerging as priests subject to the bishop's authority. By the third century, bishops were nominated by the clergy, simply approved by the congregation, and then officially ordained into office. The Christian church was creating a well-defined hierarchical structure in which the bishops and clergy were salaried officers separate from the laity or regular church members.

Christianity grew slowly in the first century, took root in the second, and by the third had spread widely. Why was Christianity able to attract so many followers? Historians are not really sure, but have offered several answers to this question. Certainly, the Christian message had much to offer the Roman world. The promise of salvation, made possible by Christ's death and resurrection, made a resounding impact on a world full of suffering and injustice. Christianity seemed to imbue life with a meaning and purpose beyond the simple material things of everyday reality. Secondly, Christianity was not entirely unfamiliar. It could be viewed as simply another eastern mystery religion, offering immortality as the result of the sacrificial death of a savior-god. At the same time, it offered advantages that the other mystery religions lacked. Christ had been a human figure, not a mythological one, such as Isis or Mithras. Moreover, Christianity had universal appeal. Unlike Mithraism, it was not restricted to men. Furthermore, it did not require a painful or expensive initiation rite as other mystery religions did. Initiation was accomplished simply by baptism—a purification by water—by which one entered into a personal relationship with Christ. In addition, Christianity gave new meaning to life and offered what the Roman state religions could not—a personal relationship with God and connection to higher worlds.

Finally, Christianity fulfilled the human need to belong. Christians formed communities bound to one another in which people could express their love by helping each other and offering assistance to the poor, sick, widows, and orphans. Christianity satisfied the need to belong in a way that the huge, impersonal, and remote Roman Empire could never do.

Christianity proved attractive to all classes. The promise of eternal life was for all—rich, poor, aristocrats, slaves, men, and women. As Paul stated in his Epistle to the Colossians: "And [you] have put on the new self, which is being renewed in knowledge in the image of its Creator. Here there is no Greek nor Jew, circumcised or uncircumcised, barbarian, Scythian, slave or free, but Christ is all, and is in all."[28] Although it did not call for revolution or social upheaval, Christianity emphasized a sense of spiritual equality for all people.

As the Christian church became more organized, some emperors in the third century responded with more systematic persecutions. The Emperor Decius (249–251) blamed the Christians for the disasters befalling the Roman Empire in the terrible third century: it was they who had failed to acknowledge the state gods and consequently brought on the gods' retribution against the Romans. Moreover, as the administrative organization of the church grew, Christianity appeared to Decius even more like a state within a state that was undermining the empire. Accordingly, he initiated the first systematic persecution of Christians. All citizens were required to appear before their local magistrates and offer sacrifices to the Roman gods. Christians, of course, refused to do so. Decius's scheme, however, failed to work. Local officials did not cooperate, and Decius's reign was also not that long. The last great persecution was by Diocletian at the beginning of the fourth century. But even he had to admit what had become apparent in the course of the third century—Christianity had become too strong to be eradicated by force. Most pagans had come to accept the existence of Christianity.

In the fourth century, Christianity prospered as never before after the Emperor Constantine became the first Christian emperor. Historians are unsure about when and how he was converted as well as his motives in doing so. According to the traditional story, before a crucial battle, he saw a vision of a Christian cross with the writing, "In this sign you will conquer." Having won the battle, the story goes, Constantine was convinced of the power of the Christian God. Although he was not baptized until the end of his life, in 313 he issued the famous Edict of Milan officially tolerating the existence of Christianity. After Constantine, the emperors were Christian with the exception of Julian (360–363) who tried briefly to restore the traditional Greco-Roman polytheistic religion. But he died in battle, and his reign was too short to make a difference. Under Theodosius "the Great" (378–395), Christianity was made the official religion of the Roman Empire. Ironically, once in control, Christian leaders used their influence and power to outlaw pagan religious practices. Christianity had triumphed.

▼ The Fall of the Roman Empire

The restored empire of Diocletian and Constantine limped along for over another hundred years. Only one institution—the Christian church—grew and expanded as Roman society itself was being transformed. After Constantine, the empire continued to divide into western and eastern parts. The west came under increasing pressure from invading barbarian forces. The major breakthrough into the Roman Empire came in the second half of the fourth century. Ferocious warriors from Asia, known as Huns, moved into eastern Europe and put pressure on the Germanic Visigoths and Ostrogoths who in turn moved south and west crossing the Danube into Roman territory. The Roman attempt to stop them at Adrianople in 378 led to a crushing defeat and the death of the Emperor Valens (364–378).

Adrianople proved to be a turning point. Increasing numbers of German barbarians crossed the frontiers. In 410, the Visigoths under Alaric seized and sacked Rome and frightened many people in the western Empire. The floodgates were now opened. Vandals poured into southern Spain and Africa; Visigoths into Spain and Gaul. The Vandals crossed into Italy from northern Africa and sacked Rome in 455. Twenty-one years later, the western emperor Romulus Augustulus (475–476) was deposed by the barbarian Odoacer. A series of German successor states replaced the Roman Empire in the west while an Eastern Roman Empire continued with its center at Constantinople.

The end of the Roman Empire has given rise to numerous theories that purport to explain the "decline and fall of the Roman Empire": Christianity's emphasis on a spiritual kingdom undermined Roman military virtues and patriotism; traditional Roman values declined as non-Italians gained prominence in the empire; lead poisoning through leaden water pipes and cups caused a mental decline; plague decimated the population; Rome failed to advance technologically because of slavery; and Rome was unable to achieve a workable political system. All of these theories have been challenged, especially by the observation that the same conditions existed in the

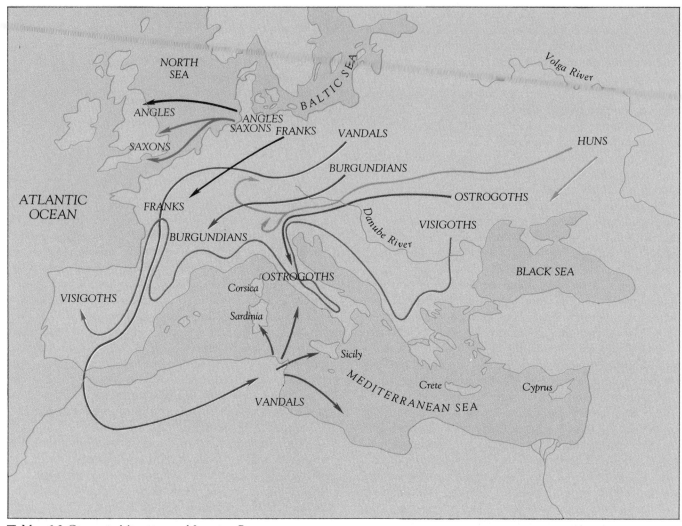

▼ **Map 6.3** Germanic Migration and Invasion Routes.

eastern part of the empire, which did not collapse for another thousand years. History is an intricate web of relationships, causes, and effects. No single explanation will ever suffice to explain historical events. As the famous eighteenth-century historian Edward Gibbon noted in his masterpiece, *The Decline and Fall of the Roman Empire*, perhaps the really important question is not why the empire fell, but why it did not fall earlier.

The Roman Empire was the largest empire in antiquity. Using their practical skills, the Romans made achievements in law, government, language, and engineering that were bequeathed to the future. They also preserved the intellectual heritage of the ancient world. While we are justified in praising the empire, it is also important to remember its dark side: the enormous gulf

between rich and poor, the dependence upon enslaved or otherwise subject human beings, the bloodthirsty spectacles in the amphitheaters, and the use of institutionalized terror to maintain the order for which the empire is so often praised. As the British chieftain Calgacus is supposed to have said, "To robbery, slaughter, plunder, they [the Romans] give the lying name of empire; they make a solitude and call it peace."[29] In its last two hundred years, as Christianity with its new ideals of spiritual equality and respect for human life grew, a slow transformation of the Roman world took place. The Germanic invasions greatly accelerated this process. While many aspects of the Roman world would continue, a new civilization was emerging that would carry on yet another stage in the development of Western civilization.

Notes
▼ ▼ ▼

1. Livy, *The Early History of Rome*, trans. Aubrey de Sélincourt (Harmondsworth, 1960), p. 35.

2. Tacitus, *The Annals of Imperial Rome*, trans. Michael Grant (Harmondsworth, 1956), p. 30.

3. Velleius Paterculus, *Compendium of Roman History*, trans. Frederick Shipley (Cambridge, Mass., 1967), 2: 117, p. 297.

4. Tacitus, *The Annals of Imperial Rome*, p. 37.

5. Michael Grant, ed., *Roman Readings* (Harmondsworth, 1958), p. 86.

6. Lucretius, *On the Nature of the Universe*, trans. Ronald Latham (Harmondsworth, 1951), p. 63.

7. Julius Caesar, *The Gallic War and Other Writings*, trans. Moses Hadas (New York, 1957), 2:25, pp. 52–53.

8. Virgil, *Georgics*, in *Virgil's Works*, trans. J. W. Mackail (New York, 1950), pp. 312–13.

9. Virgil, *The Aeneid*, trans. C. Day Lewis (Garden City, N.Y., 1952), p. 154.

10. Horace, *Satires*, in *The Complete Works of Horace*, trans. Lord Dunsany and Michael Oakley (London, 1961), 1.1, p. 139.

11. Ibid., 1.3, p. 151.

12. Ovid, *Tristia*, trans. L. R. Lind (Athens, Ga., 1975), 4.10: 21–22, p. 112.

13. Livy, *The Early History of Rome*, p. 18.

14. Tacitus, *The Annals of Imperial Rome*, p. 31.

15. Tacitus, *The Histories*, trans. Kenneth Wallesley (Harmondsworth, 1964), p. 23.

16. Seneca, *Letters from a Stoic*, trans. Robin Campbell (Harmondsworth, 1969), Letter 5.

17. Tacitus, *The Annals of Imperial Rome*, p. 377.

18. Ibid., p. 147.

19. Juvenal, *The Sixteen Satires*, trans. Peter Green (Harmondsworth, 1967), Satire 7, p. 171.

20. Ibid., Satire 10, p. 207.

21 Tacitus, *A Dialogue on Oratory*, in *The Complete Works of Tacitus*, trans. Alfred Church and William Brodribb (New York, 1942), 29, p. 758.

22. Ovid, *The Amores*, trans. Grant Showerman (Cambridge, Mass., 1963), 2.14: 26–27.

23. Matthew 5: 17.

24. Matthew 7: 12.

25. Mark 12: 30–31.

26. John 18: 36.

27. Matthew 26: 26–28.

28. Colossians 3: 10–11.

29. Tacitus, *The Life of Cnaeus Julius Agricola*, in *The Complete Works of Tacitus*, p. 695.

Suggestions for Further Reading

For a general account of the Roman Empire, see J. Boardman, J. Griffin, and O. Murray, eds., *The Oxford History of the Classical World* (Oxford, 1986), pp. 531–828. A brief and reliable guide to recent trends in scholarship on the Roman Empire can be found in C. Starr, *Past and Future in Ancient History* (Lanham, Md., 1987), pp. 47–57. There is an excellent collection of essays on numerous aspects of imperial Rome in J. Wacher, *The Roman World*, 2 vols. (London and New York, 1987). Good surveys of the Early Empire include P. Garnsey and R. P. Saller, *The Roman Empire: Economy, Society and Culture* (London, 1987); C. Wells, *The Roman Empire* (Stanford, 1984); A. Garzetti, *From Tiberius to the Antonines* (London, 1974); J. Wacher, *The Roman Empire* (London, 1987); and F. Millar, *Roman Empire and Its Neighbors*, 2d ed. (London, 1981). An excellent collection of source materials in translation can be found in N. Lewis and M. Reinhold, eds., *Roman Civilization*, vol. 2 (New York, 1955).

Studies of Roman emperors of the first and second centuries include F. Millar and E. Segal, eds., *Caesar Augustus* (Oxford, 1984); R. Seager, *Tiberius* (London, 1972); A. Barrett, *Caligula, The Corruption of Power* (New Haven, Conn., 1990), a new appraisal of Caligula; A. Momigliano, *Claudius, the Emperor and His Achievement*, trans. W. D. Hogarth (Cambridge, 1961); M. Griffin, *Nero: The End of a Dynasty* (London, 1984); and M. Hammond, *The Antonine Monarchy* (Rome, 1959). A fundamental work on Roman government and the role of the emperor is F. Millar, *The Emperor in the Roman World* (London, 1977).

There are many specialized studies on various aspects of the administrative, economic, and social conditions in the Early Empire. R. P. Saller's *Personal Patronage under the Early Empire* (Cambridge, 1982) deals with reasons for promotion within the Roman administrative system. On the Greek cities in the empire, see A. H. M. Jones, *The Cities of the Eastern Roman Provinces* (Oxford, 1971). On the growth of cities in Italy and the spread of Roman citizenship outside Italy, see A. N. Sherwin White, *The Roman Citizenship*, 2d ed. (Oxford, 1973). A detailed examination of economic matters is T. Frank, *An Economic Survey of Ancient Rome*, vols. 2–5 (Baltimore, 1933–40). See also M. I. Rostovtzeff, *Social and Economic History of the Roman Empire*, 2d ed., 2 vols. (Oxford, 1957). G. E. M. de Ste. Croix, *The Class Struggle in the Ancient Greek World* (London, 1981), deals with the wide gulf between rich and poor in the empire from a Marxist perspective. On social relations in general, see R. MacMullen, *Enemies of the Roman Order: Treason, Unrest and Alienation in the Empire* (Cambridge, Mass., 1967) and *Roman Social Relations, 56 B.C. to A.D. 284* (New Haven, Conn., 1974).

The Roman army is examined in G. Webster, *The Roman Imperial Army of the First and Second Centuries AD*, 2d ed. (London, 1979); L. Keppie, *The Making of the Roman Army* (London, 1984); and J. B. Campbell, *The Emperor and the Roman Army* (Oxford, 1984). On the provinces and Roman foreign policy, see E. N. Luttwak, *The Grand Strategy of the Roman Empire from the First Century A.D. to the Third* (Baltimore, 1976); and S. L. Dyson, *The Creation of the Roman Frontier* (Princeton, 1985).

A good survey of Roman literature can be found in R. M. Ogilvie, *Roman Literature and Society* (Harmondsworth, 1980). More specialized studies include G. Williams, *Change and Decline: Roman Literature in the Early Empire* (Berkeley, 1978); R. O. Lyne, *The Latin Love Poets from Catullus to Horace* (Oxford, 1980); M. L. W. Laistner, *The Greater Roman Historians* (Berkeley, 1947); and A. Momigliano, *Essays in Ancient and Modern Historiography* (Oxford, 1977), especially chapters 4, 5, 7.

A brief survey of Roman art can be found in J. M. C. Toynbee, *Art of the Romans* (London and New York, 1965). D. E. Strong, *Roman Art* (Harmondsworth, 1976), presents a more detailed account. Architecture is covered in the standard work by J. B. Ward-Perkins, *Roman Imperial Architecture* (Harmondsworth, 1981) and domestic architecture in A. G. McKay, *Houses, Villas and Palaces in the Roman World* (London, 1975).

Various aspects of Roman society are covered in J. Carcopino, *Daily Life in Ancient Rome* (New Haven, 1940); and J. P. V. D. Balsdon, *Life and Leisure in Ancient Rome* (London, 1969). See also the essay by P. Veyne on "The Roman Empire" in P. Veyne, ed., *A History of Private Life*, vol. 1 (Cambridge, Mass., 1987). Studies on Roman women include J. P. V. D. Balsdon, *Roman Women: Their History and Habits* (London, 1969); and S. B. Pomeroy, *Goddesses, Whores, Wives and Slaves: Women in Classical Antiquity* (New York, 1975), pp. 149–226. On Roman law, see H. F. Jolowicz and B. Nicholas, *Historical Introduction to the Study of Roman Law*, 3d ed. (Cambridge, 1972); and J. Crook, *Law and Life of Rome* (London, 1967). On slavery, see T. Wiedemann, *Greek and Roman Slavery* (Baltimore, 1981).

An introduction to the problems relating to the religious history of the imperial period is E. R. Dodds, *Pagan and Christian in an Age of Anxiety* (Cambridge, 1965). Useful works on early Christianity include W. A. Meeks, *The First Urban Christians* (New Haven, 1983); W. H. C. Frend, *Martyrdom and Persecution in the Early Church* (Oxford, 1965) and *The Rise of Christianity* (Philadelphia, 1984); and R. MacMullen, *Christianizing the Roman Empire* (New Haven, Conn., 1984).

The classic work on the "decline and fall" of the Roman Empire is Edward Gibbon, *Decline and Fall of the Roman Empire*, J. B. Bury edition (London, 1909–14). An excellent survey is P. Brown, *The World of Late Antiquity* (London, 1971). Also valuable is R. MacMullen, *Roman Government's Response to Crisis A.D. 235–337* (New Haven, Conn., 1976). On the fourth century, see D. Bowder, *The Age of Constantine and Julian* (London, 1978); T. D. Barnes, *The New Empire of Diocletian and Constantine* (Cambridge, Mass., 1982); and S. Williams, *Diocletian and the Roman Recovery* (London, 1985). On economic and social history, including the bureaucracy, see A. H. M. Jones, *The Later Roman Empire*, (Oxford, 1964). The barbarians are covered in J. M. Wallace-Hadrill, *The Barbarian West*, 3d ed. (London, 1967). Recent studies analyzing the aristocratic circles, the barbarian invasions, and the military problem include J. Matthews, *Western Aristocracies and Imperial Court, A.D. 364–425* (Oxford, 1975); E. A. Thompson, *Romans and Barbarians* (Madison, 1982); A. Ferrill, *The Fall of the Roman Empire: The Military Explanation* (London, 1986); and J. M. O'Flynn, *Generalissimos of the Western Roman Empire* (Edmonton, 1983).

Chapter 7

The Passing of the Roman World and the Emergence of Medieval Civilization (400–750)

▼ ▼ ▼ ▼ ▼

The period that saw the disintegration of the Roman Empire also witnessed the emergence of medieval civilization. Scholars know that major historical transitions are never tidy; chaos is often the ground out of which new civilizations are born. The early medieval civilization that arose out of the dissolution of the Roman Empire was formed by the coalescence of three major elements: the Germanic peoples who moved in and settled the western empire; the continuing attraction of the Greco-Roman cultural legacy; and the Christian church. Christianity was the most distinctive and powerful component of the new medieval civilization. The church assimilated the classical tradition and through its clergy, especially the monks, brought Christianized civilization to the Germanic tribes.

During the time when the Germanic successor states were establishing their roots in the west, the eastern part of the old Roman Empire, increasingly Greek in culture, continued to survive as the Byzantine Empire. While serving as a buffer between Europe and the peoples to the east, the Byzantine or Eastern Roman Empire also preserved the intellectual and legal accomplishments of Greek and Roman antiquity. At the same time, a new world of Islam emerged in the east that occupied large parts of the old Roman Empire, preserved much of Greek culture, and created its own flourishing civilization. This chapter, then, largely concerns the heirs of Rome and the new world they created.

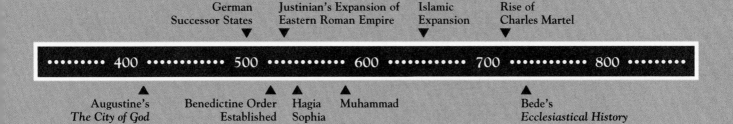

German
Successor States ▼

Justinian's Expansion of
Eastern Roman Empire ▼

Islamic
Expansion ▼

Rise of
Charles Martel ▼

•••••••• 400 ••••••••••• 500 •••••••••• 600 •••••••••• 700 ••••••••• 800 •••••••••

Augustine's ▲
The City of God

Benedictine Order ▲
Established

Hagia ▲
Sophia

Muhammad ▲

Bede's ▲
Ecclesiastical History

▼ The Role and Development of the Christian Church

First officially tolerated in 313 by Emperor Constantine, Christianity had become the predominant religion of the Roman state by the end of the fourth century (see Chapter 6). As the official Roman state disintegrated, the Christian church played an increasingly important role in the new civilization built upon the ruins of the old Roman Empire. We must therefore examine the role and development of the Christian church in order to understand the emergence of medieval civilization.

Organization of the Church

During the course of the fourth century, the Christian church had undergone significant organizational and structural changes. Church government was based on a territorial plan borrowed from Roman administration. For some time, the Christian community in each city had been headed by a bishop (see Chapter 6), whose area of jurisdiction was known as a bishopric. The Christian bishopric was roughly synonymous with the Roman city-state. Moreover, the bishoprics of each Roman province were clustered together under the direction of an archbishop, although the Christian church had not yet developed a centralized administrative system comparable to the Roman imperial bureaucracy. Nevertheless, the bishops of four great cities, Rome, Jerusalem, Alexandria, and Antioch, held positions of special power in church affairs since the churches in these cities all asserted that they had been founded by the original apostles sent out by Christ. Eventually, the bishop of Rome claimed a position of preeminence above all the other bishops (see Papal Primacy later in this chapter).

Heresy

One reason the church needed a more formal organization was the problem of heresy. As Christianity developed and spread, contradictory interpretations of important doctrines emerged. Heresy came to be viewed as a teaching different from the official catholic or universal beliefs of the church. In a world where people were concerned about salvation, the question of whether Christ's nature is divine or human took on great significance. Moreover, heresies had political repercussions. By creating disunity, they undermined imperial authority.

The two major heresies of the fourth century were Donatism and Arianism. The name Donatist is derived from Donatus, a priest in northern Africa, who taught that the sacraments of the church, the channels by which a Christian received God's grace, were not valid if administered by an immoral priest or one who had denied his faith under persecution. Donatus's deviation from traditional teaching on the subject created so much dissension that it came to the attention of the Emperor Constantine, who convened a council of western bishops to denounce it. It was not until 411, however, that the church declared authoritatively that the efficacy of the sacraments was not dependent upon the moral state of the priest administering them as long as the priest had been properly ordained.

Arianism was a product of the followers of Arius, a priest from Alexandria in Egypt. Arius postulated that if Jesus Christ had been human, he must have been created by God and was thus inferior to God the Father. Arius was opposed by Athanasius who argued that Christ was human, but also truly God. Emperor Constantine, disturbed by the controversy, called the first ecumenical council of the church, a meeting composed of representatives from the entire Christian community. The Council of Nicaea, held in 325, condemned Arianism and stated that Christ was of "the same substance" as God: "We believe in one God the Father All-sovereign, maker of all things visible and invisible; And in one Lord Jesus Christ, the Son of God, begotten of the Father, only-begotten, that is, of the substance of the Father, God of God, Light of Light, true God of true God, begotten not made, of one substance with the Father. . . ."[1] The Council of Nicaea did not end the controversy, however; not only did Arianism persist in some parts of the Roman Empire for many years, but more importantly, many of the Germanic Goths who would eventually establish successor states in the west converted to Arian Christianity, with important implications for those kingdoms (see The German Successor States later in this chapter).

As a result of these fourth-century theological controversies, the Roman emperor came to play an increasingly important role in church affairs. At the same time, such divisions also created a need for leadership within the church and soon led to the elevation of the bishop of Rome to a preeminent position in the affairs of the Christian or Catholic church.

Papal Primacy

In the early centuries of Christianity, the churches in the larger cities came to have great influence in the administration of the church. It was only natural, then, that the bishops of those cities would also exercise considerable power. One of the far-reaching developments in the history of the Christian church was the emergence of one bishop—that of Rome—as the recognized leader of the western Christian church. This was, by no means, as inevitable as it may seem in retrospect.

The doctrine of Petrine supremacy, based on the belief that the bishops of Rome occupied a preeminent position in the church, was grounded in Scripture. According to the Gospel of Matthew:

> But what about you? he [Jesus] asked. Who do you say I am? Simon Peter answered, You are the Christ, the Son of the living God. Jesus replied, Blessed are you, Simon, Simon son of Jonah, for this was not revealed by man, but by my Father in heaven. And I tell you that you are Peter, and on this rock I will build my church, and the gates of hell will not overcome it. I will give you the keys of the kingdom of heaven; whatever you bind on earth will be bound in heaven: and whatever you loose on earth will be loosed in heaven.[2]

According to church tradition, Christ had given the keys to the kingdom of heaven to Peter, who was considered the chief apostle and the first bishop of Rome. Subsequent bishops of Rome were considered Peter's successors and later the "vicars of Christ" on earth. While this exalted view of the bishops of Rome was by no means accepted by all early Christians, Rome's position as the traditional capital of the Roman Empire served to buttress this claim.

In the fourth and fifth centuries, a series of Roman bishops sought to establish the preeminence of the see of Rome. Damasus, bishop of Rome from 366 to 384, began to address other bishops as "sons" rather than "brothers" in his correspondence with them. By the end of the fourth century, the bishops of Rome were using the title of *papa* or father (our word *pope*). Leo I (440–461) was especially energetic in expounding systematically the doctrine of Petrine supremacy. He portrayed himself as the heir of Peter, whom Christ had chosen to be head of the Christian church. Although western Christians came to accept the bishop of Rome as head of the church, there was certainly no unanimity on the extent of the powers the pope possessed as a result of this position. Nevertheless, the establishment by the fifth century of the superiority of the Roman bishop laid the foundation for later medieval popes, who would claim a direct, centralized control over all Christians based on this primacy.

Church-State Relations

Once the Roman emperors became Christians, beginning with Constantine in the early fourth century, they came to play a significant role in the affairs of the church. Christian emperors viewed themselves as God's representatives on earth. They not only built churches and influenced the structure of the church's organization, but also became involved in church government and doctrinal controversies. As we have seen, their unwillingness to countenance disunity quickly involved them in the struggles over heresies.

While emperors were busying themselves in church affairs, bishops were playing a more active role in imperial government. Increasingly, they served as advisers to Christian Roman emperors. Moreover, as imperial authority declined, bishops often played a noticeably independent political role. A number of powerful bishops had sufficient authority to weather the collapse of the Roman imperial government in the west. Ambrose (c. 339–397) of Milan was an early example of a strong and independent bishop. As a young man, Ambrose entered the Roman imperial service and became governor of the northern Italian province of Emilia with its administrative capital in the city of Milan. In 374, the Christian population of the city proclaimed Ambrose the bishop of Milan. Through his activities and writings, such as his manual on a bishop's administrative responsibilities, Ambrose created an image of the ideal Christian bishop. Among other things, this ideal bishop would defend the independence of the church against the tendency of imperial officials to oversee church policy: "Exalt not yourself, but if you would reign the longer, be subject to God. It is written, God's to God and Caesar's to Caesar. The palace is the Emperor's, the Churches are the Bishop's."[3] When Emperor Theodosius I ordered the massacre of many citizens in Thessalonica for refusing to obey his commands, Ambrose denounced the massacre and refused to allow the emperor to take part in church ceremonies. Theodosius finally agreed to do public penance for his dastardly deed in the cathedral of Milan. Ambrose proved himself a formidable advocate of the position that spiritual authority should take precedence over temporal power, at least in spiritual matters. This emphasis on an independent role for the church made possible the emergence of a dual power structure between church and state that formed one of the most important elements of medieval civilization.

The weakness of the political authorities on the Italian peninsula also contributed to the church's independence in that area. In the German successor states (see The German Successor States later in this chapter), the kings controlled both churches and bishops. But in Italy a different tradition prevailed, fed by semilegendary accounts of papal deeds. Pope Leo I, for example, supposedly caused Attila the Hun to turn away from Rome in 452. While plague rather than papal persuasion was probably more conducive to Attila's withdrawal, the pope got the credit. Popes, then, played significant political roles in Italy, which only added to their claims of power vis-à-vis the secular authorities. Pope Gelasius I (492–496) could write to the emperor at Constantinople:

> There are two powers, august Emperor, by which this world is ruled from the beginning: the consecrated authority of the bishops, and the royal power. In these matters the priests bear the heavier burden because they will render account, even for rulers of men, at the divine judgment. Besides, most gracious son, you are aware that, although you in your office are the ruler of the human race, nevertheless you devoutly bow your head before those who are leaders in things divine and look to them for the means of your salvation; and in the reception and proper administration of the heavenly sacraments you know that you ought to submit to Christian order rather than take the lead, and in those matters follow their judgment without wanting to subject them to your will.[4]

According to Gelasius, while there were two ruling powers, spiritual and temporal, with different functions, the church was ultimately the higher authority since all men, including emperors, must look to the church "for the means of . . . salvation." Church-state relations would prove to be one of the most important issues of the Middle Ages.

Cultural Attitudes

Many early Christians expressed considerable hostility toward the pagan culture of the classical world. Tertullian (c. 160–c. 225), a Christian writer from Carthage, had proclaimed: "What has Jerusalem to do with Athens, the Church with the Academy, the Christian with the heretic? . . . After Jesus Christ we have no need of speculation, after the Gospel no need of research."[5] To many early Christians, the Bible contained all the knowledge anyone needed.

Others, however, thought it was not possible to separate Christian theological thought from classical traditions and education and encouraged Christians to absorb the classical heritage. As it spread in the eastern Roman world, Christianity adopted Greek as its language. The New Testament (see Chapter 6) was written in Greek. Christians also turned to Greek thought for help in expressing complicated theological concepts. An especially important influence was Neoplatonism, a revival of Platonic thought that reached its high point in the third century A.D. Neoplatonism emphasized rigorous thought as an instrument in understanding the links between the invisible spiritual and visible material worlds. Christian theologians used Neoplatonic concepts to explain doctrines on Christ, especially the distinction between his human and divine natures. In many ways, then, Christianity served to preserve Greco-Roman culture and to keep alive a vision of a golden age that would later prove useful in generating a series of revivals of classical thought in an attempt to recapture that earlier world.

The work of Augustine (354–430) provides one of the best examples of how Christianity absorbed pagan culture in the service of Christianity. Born in north Africa, he was reared by his mother, an ardent Christian. Augustine eventually became a teacher of rhetoric. He went to Rome to teach and then became a professor of rhetoric at Milan in 384.

Augustine's success opened the door to a lucrative career in the imperial bureaucracy if he had wished to pursue it. However, throughout his rapid ascent, although he had turned his back on Christianity, he had continued to explore spiritual alternatives, including Neoplatonism and a dualist heresy known as Manicheanism. While in Milan, he came under the influ-

The Confessions of Augustine

▼ ▼ ▼

Augustine's spiritual and intellectual autobiography is a revealing self-portrait of the inner struggles of one of the intellectual giants of early Christianity. The first excerpt is taken from Book VIII, in which Augustine describes how he heard a voice from heaven and was converted from his old habits. In the second excerpt from Book IX, Augustine expresses joy and gratitude for his conversion.

Augustine, The Confessions

So was I speaking and weeping in the most bitter contrition of my heart, when, lo! I heard from a neighboring house a voice, as of boy or girl, I know not, chanting, and oft repeating, "Take up and read; Take up and read." Instantly, my countenance altered, I began to think most intently whether children were wont in any kind of play to sing such words: nor could I remember ever to have heard the like. So checking the torrent of my tears, I arose; interpreting it to be no other than a command from God to open the book, and read the first chapter I should find. For I had heard of Antony, that coming in during the reading of the Gospel, he received the admonition, as if what was being read was spoken to him: Go, sell all that thou hast, and give to the poor, and thou shalt have treasure in heaven, and come and

follow me: and by such oracle he was forthwith converted unto Thee. Eagerly then I returned to the place where Alypius was sitting; for there had I laid the volume of the Apostle when I arose thence. I seized, opened, and in silence read that section on which my eyes first fell: Not in rioting and drunkenness, not in chambering and wantonness, not in strife and envying; but put ye on the Lord Jesus Christ, and make not provision for the flesh, in concupiscence. No further would I read; nor needed I: for instantly at the end of this sentence, by a light as it were of serenity infused into my heart, all the darkness of doubt vanished away. . . .

O Lord I am thy servant; I am thy servant, and the son of Thy handmaid: Thou hast broken my bonds in sunder. I will offer to Thee the sacrifice of praise. Let my heart and my tongue praise Thee; yea, let all my bones say, O Lord, who is like unto Thee? Let them say, and answer Thou me, and say unto my soul, I am thy salvation. Who am I, and what am I? What evil have not been either my deeds, or if not my deeds, my words, or if not my words, my will? But Thou, O Lord, art good and merciful, and Thy right hand had respect unto the depth of my death, and from the bottom of my heart emptied that abyss of corruption.

---

ence of the popular bishop Ambrose who encouraged Augustine to return to his mother's religion. After experiencing a profound and moving religious experience (see the box above), he gave up his teaching position in 386 and went back to northern Africa, where he became bishop of Hippo from 396 until his death in 430.

As bishop of Hippo, Augustine did not become an adviser to emperors like his contemporary Ambrose, but produced an enormous outpouring of Christian literature. In his sermons, letters, treatises on dogma, and commentaries on Scripture, Augustine gave reasoned opinions on virtually every aspect of Christian thought. He stressed that while philosophy could bring some understanding, divine revelation was a necessity for perceiving complete truth, an approach to knowledge that became standard in the education of the Middle Ages. Augustine's ideas on free will, grace, and predestination helped shape the contours of medieval theology and later had a profound impact on the reformers of the

Protestant Reformation of the sixteenth century. In fact, many historians feel that Augustine was the primary intellectual shaper of western Christianity and the most important formative theologian of Christianity, both Catholic and Protestant, for the next thousand years.

His two most famous works are the *Confessions* and *The City of God*. Written in 397, the *Confessions* was a self-portrait not of Augustine's worldly activities, but of the "history of a heart," an account of his own personal and spiritual experiences, written to help others with their search: "To whom do I tell this? not to You, my God; but before You to my own kind, even to that small portion of mankind as may light upon these writings of mine. And to what purpose? that whosoever reads this, may think out of what depths we are to cry unto You. For what is nearer to Your ears than a confessing heart, and a life of faith.?"[6] Augustine describes how he struggled throughout his early life to find God until in his thirty-second year he "hears a voice from heaven, opens Scripture, and is converted." This portrait of an inner journey became a model for an entire genre of autobiographical literature in Western society for generations to come.

The City of God, Augustine's other major work, was a profound expression of a Christian philosophy of government and history. It was written in response to a line of argument that arose soon after the sack of Rome in 410. Some pagan philosophers maintained that Rome's problems stemmed from the Roman state's recognition of Christianity and abandonment of the old, traditional gods. In his book, Augustine theorized on the ideal relations between two kinds of societies existing throughout time—the City of God and the City of the World. The fundamental loyalty of those who loved God was to the City of God, whose ultimate location was the kingdom of heaven. Earthly society would always be insecure and subject to change because of human beings' fallen nature and inclination to sin. Nevertheless, the City of the World was still necessary for it was the duty of rulers to curb the depraved instincts of sinful humans and maintain the peace necessary for Christians to live in the world. Hence, Augustine posited that secular government and authority were necessary for the pursuit of the true Christian life on earth; in doing so, he provided a justification for secular political authority that would play an important role in medieval thought.

Augustine and Ambrose came to be seen as the first of the Latin Fathers of the Catholic church, intellectuals who wrote in Latin and profoundly influenced the development of Christian thought in the west. Another Latin Father was Jerome (345–420), who was born in what is now Yugoslavia. He pursued literary studies in Rome and became a master of Latin prose. Jerome had mixed feelings about his love for liberal studies, however, and, like Augustine, experienced a spiritual conversion after which he tried to dedicate himself more fully to Christ. He had a dream in which Christ appeared as his judge: "Asked who and what I was, I replied: 'I am a Christian.' But He who presided said: 'You lie, you are a follower of Cicero, not of Christ. For where your treasure is, there will your heart be also.' Instantly, I became dumb. . . . Accordingly I made oath and called upon His name, saying: 'Lord, if ever again I possess worldly books [the classics], or if ever again I read such, I have denied You.' " After this dream, Jerome determined to "read the books of God with a zeal greater than I had previously given to the books of men."[7]

Ultimately, Jerome found a compromise by purifying the literature of the pagan world and then using it to further the Christian faith. Eventually, he moved to Palestine and settled in Bethlehem, where he spent the rest of his life settling doctrinal disputes and translating Scripture. Jerome was the greatest scholar among the Latin Fathers, and his extensive knowledge of both Hebrew and Greek enabled him to translate the Old and New Testaments into Latin. In the process, he created the so-called Latin Vulgate or common text of the Scriptures that became the standard edition for the Catholic church in the Middle Ages.

Monasticism

The spread of Christianity was greatly fostered by the development of monasticism. Although Christian monasticism had its beginnings in the third century, historians have labeled the fourth century the "century of monasticism." A monk (Latin *monachus,* meaning "someone who lives alone") was a person who sought to live a solitary life, divorced from the world, in order to pursue an ideal of godliness or total dedication to the will of God.

Christian monasticism developed first in Egypt in a form called eremitical monasticism, since it was based on the model of the solitary hermit who forsakes all civilized society to pursue spirituality. Saint Anthony (c. 250–350) has been called the "father of eremitical monasticism." He was a relatively prosperous peasant in Egypt who decided to follow Christ's injunction in the Gospel of Mark: "Go your way, sell whatsoever you have, and give to the poor, and you shall have treasure in heaven: and come, take up the cross, and follow me."[8] Anthony gave away his three hundred acres of land to the poor and went into the desert to pursue his ideal of holiness (see the box on p. 204). Others did likewise, often to extremes. St. Simeon the Stylite lived in a basket atop a pillar over sixty feet high for three decades. These spiritual gymnastics established a new ideal for Christianity. While the early Christian model had been the martyr who died for the faith and achieved eternal life in the process, the new ideal was the monk who died to the world and achieved spiritual life through denial, asceticism, and mystical experience of God.

These early monks, however, soon found themselves unable to live in solitude. Their feats of holiness attracted followers on a wide scale, and as the monastic ideal spread throughout the east, cenobitic monasticism, based upon the practice of communal life, soon became the dominant form. Saint Pachomius (c. 290–346), regarded as the founder of cenobitic monasticism, organized communities of monks and wrote the first monastic rule for living in communities. He emphasized the need for obedience and manual labor. It was Saint Basil (329–

The Life of Saint Anthony

▼ ▼ ▼

In the third and early fourth centuries, the lives of martyrs had provided important models for early Christianity. But in the course of the fourth century, monks or desert fathers, who attempted to achieve spiritual perfection through asceticism, the denial of earthly life, and the struggle with demons became the new spiritual ideal for Christians. Consequently, spiritual biographies of early monks became a significant new form of Christian literature. Especially noteworthy was The Life of Saint Anthony by Saint Athanasius, the defender of Catholic orthodoxy against the Arians. His work had been translated into Latin before 386. This excerpt demonstrates how Anthony fought off the temptations of Satan.

Athanasius, *The Life of Saint Anthony*

Now when the Enemy [Satan] saw that his craftiness in this matter was without profit, and that the more he brought temptation unto Saint Anthony, the more strenuous the saint was in protecting himself against him with the armor of righteousness, he attacked him by means of the vigor of early manhood which is bound up in the nature of our humanity. With the goadings of passion he used to trouble him by night, and in the daytime also he would vex him and pain him with the same to such an extent that even those who saw him knew from his appearance that he was waging war against the Adversary. But the more the Evil One brought unto him filthy and maddening thoughts, the more Saint Anthony took refuge in prayer and in abundant supplication, and amid them all he remained wholly chaste. And the Evil One was working upon him every shameful deed according to his wont, and at length he even appeared unto Saint Anthony in the form of a woman; and other things which resembled this he performed with each, for such things are a subject of boasting to him.

But the blessed Anthony knelt down upon his knees on the ground, and prayed before Him who said, "Before thou criest unto Me, I will answer thee," and said, "O my Lord, this I entreat Thee: let not Thy love be blotted out from my mind, and behold, I am, by Thy grace, innocent before Thee." And again the Enemy multiplied in him the thoughts of lust, until Saint Anthony became as one who was being burned up, not through the Evil One, but through his own lusts; but he girded himself about with the threat of the thought of the Judgment, and of the torture of Gehenna, and of the worm which dieth not. And whilst meditating on the thoughts which could be directed against the Evil One, he prayed for thoughts which would be hostile to him. Thus, to the reproach and shame of the Enemy, these things could not be performed; for he who imagined that he could be God was made a mock of by a young man, and he who boasted over flesh and blood was vanquished by a man who was clothed with flesh. . . .

379), however, who was the true founder of Christian monasticism in the eastern world. Born in Palestine, he visited Egypt and established a community of monks under one roof since he believed they needed fellowship and work. Monastic communities soon came to be seen as the ideal Christian society that could provide a moral example to the wider society around them.

The fundamental form of monastic life in the western Christian church was established by Saint Benedict of Nursia (c. 480–c. 543). He belonged to a noble Roman family and received an excellent education. After a religious experience, he sought hermitic solitude south of Rome but soon found himself surrounded by followers. Benedict then went to Monte Cassino where he founded a monastic house, for which he wrote his famous rule, sometime between 520 and 530. The Benedictine rule came to be used by other monastic groups and was crucial to the growth of monasticism in the western Christian world.

Benedict's rule largely rejected the ascetic ideals of eastern monasticism, which had tended to emphasize such practices as fasting and self-inflicted torments (such as living atop pillars for thirty years), in favor of an ideal of moderation. In Chapter 40 of the rule, on the amount of drink a monk should imbibe, this sense of moderation becomes apparent:

'Every man has his proper gift from God, one after this manner, another after that.' And therefore it is with some misgiving that we determine the amount of food for someone else. Still, having regard for the weakness of some brothers, we believe that a hemina of wine per day will suffice for all. Let those, however, to whom God gives the gift of abstinence, know that they shall have their proper reward. But if either the circumstances of the place, the work, or the heat of summer necessitates more, let it lie in the discretion of the abbot to grant it. But let him take care in all things lest satiety or drunkenness supervene.

At the same time, moderation did not preclude a hard and disciplined existence based on the ideals of poverty, chastity, and obedience.

According to Benedict's rule, each day was divided into a series of activities with primary emphasis upon prayer and manual labor. Physical work of some kind was required of all monks for several hours a day: "Idleness is the enemy of the soul. The brothers, therefore, ought to be engaged at certain times in manual labor. . . ." Peasants, however, were hired to do heavy farm work. At the very heart of community practice was prayer, the proper "Work of God." While this included private meditation and reading, all monks gathered together seven times during the day for common prayer and chanting of psalms. A Benedictine life was a communal one; monks ate, worked, slept, and worshiped together.

Each Benedictine monastery was strictly ruled by an abbot, or "father" of the monastery. Although chosen by his fellow monks, the abbot possessed complete authority over them; unquestioning obedience to the will of the abbot was expected of each monk. However, Benedict urged that the abbot take care "not to teach, ordain, or command anything which is against the law of the Lord" and cautioned him to be moderate: "He should be

▼ **Map 7.1** The Spread of Christianity, 400–750.

prudent and considerate in all his commands; and whether the task he enjoins concerns God or the world, let him be discreet and temperate . . ." Each Benedictine monastery possessed lands that enabled it to be a self-sustaining community, isolated from and independent of the world surrounding it. Within the monastery, however, monks were to fulfill their vow of poverty: "Let all things be common to all, as it is written, lest anyone should say that anything is his own or arrogate it to himself."[9] By the eighth century, Benedictine monasticism had spread throughout the west, where it remained the primary monastic form until the High Middle Ages (see Chapters 9 and 10).

Although the original monks were men, women soon followed suit in attempting to withdraw from the world to dedicate themselves to God. Around 320, Saint Pachomius began organizing cenobitic communities that included convents of women. In fact, Pachomius governed a community founded by his sister. The brothers took care of the material needs of the convent but were not permitted to eat there. Relations with the nuns were carefully regulated. The first monastic rule for western women was produced by Caesarius of Arles for his sister in the fifth century. It strongly emphasized a rigid cloistering of female religious to preserve them from dangers. Later in the west, in the seventh and eighth centuries, the growth of double monasteries allowed monks and nuns to reside close by and follow a common rule, often the Benedictine rule, under a common head.

Monasticism played an indispensable role in early medieval civilization. Monks became the new heroes of Christian civilization. Their dedication to God became the highest ideal of Christian life and acted as a countervailing force against the secularization of the church. Moreover, as we shall see later, the monks played an increasingly significant role not only in spreading Christianity to the entire medieval European world, but also in the economy, education, and government of that civilization. Indeed, as one cultural historian has noted, the monks formed the "seed centers" for the new medieval Christian civilization that came to replace the Roman world.

▼ The Germanic Peoples and Their Kingdoms

The third major component of the new medieval civilization came from the contributions of the Germanic peoples. Although our knowledge of early Germanic tribes is scanty, we do know that around 500 B.C., the Germans began to migrate from their northern Scandinavian homeland south into the Baltic states and Germany and east into the fertile lands of the Ukraine. While the Romans had established a series of political frontiers in the western empire, Romans and Germans often came into contact across those boundaries. Many Germans served in Roman military units and received Roman citizenship. In general, throughout the third and fourth centuries, a gradual Germanization of the western Roman provinces had occurred and, correspondingly, a slow romanization of the Germans. But at the end of the fourth century, new circumstances, especially pressure from the east by the Huns, "a race savage beyond all parallel," forced some of the German tribes, especially the Goths, westward, bringing them across the boundaries of the Roman Empire.

Invasions or Migrations?

The end of the Roman Empire in the west was characterized by vast movements of Germanic peoples. Historians have debated whether these movements constituted "migrations" or "invasions." Northern Europe was probably settled by migrations since Germanic-speaking tribes entered areas where Roman armies had already begun to pull out. Elsewhere in the Roman Empire, the movements of Germanic-speaking peoples were closer to invasions, at least at times. In any event, whether through migration or invasion, at the end of the fourth and beginning of the fifth centuries, a number of Germanic peoples moved into the Roman world.

After the Visigoths defeated the Romans at the Battle of Adrianople in 378 (see Chapter 6), they wandered through the Balkans and northern Greece and into Italy. They sacked Rome in 410 and then continued on into Gaul and finally Spain, where they eventually established a Visigothic kingdom. The Burgundians settled themselves in much of eastern Gaul, just south of another Germanic tribe called the Alemanni. The Vandals sacked parts of Gaul, crossed the Pyrenees Mountains into Spain, and began to establish a Vandal kingdom there. Defeated by incoming Visigoths, the Vandals crossed the Straits of Gibraltar and moved into Roman North Africa by 429. Under King Gaiseric, the Vandals conquered the whole province of Africa. Gaiseric built a fleet and began to harass Sicily and southern Italy. In 455, the Vandals even attacked Rome and sacked it more ferociously than the Visigoths had in 410.

Increasingly, German military leaders were dominating the imperial courts of the western empire. One such leader finally ended the charade of Roman imperial rule. Odoacer, who had served as master of soldiers, deposed the Roman emperor, Romulus Augustulus, returned the imperial regalia to Zeno, emperor of the eastern empire at Constantinople, and began to function as the emperor's regent. Zeno was unable to undo Odoacer's actions, but, in his desire to act against the German leader, brought another German tribe, the Ostrogoths, into Italy.

The Ostrogoths were another branch of the Goths who had recovered from a defeat by the Huns in the fourth century. Under their king Theodoric (453–526), they had attacked Constantinople. To divert them, Emperor Zeno had invited Theodoric to act as his deputy to defeat Odoacer and bring Italy back into the empire. Theodoric accepted the challenge, marched into Italy, killed Odoacer, and then, contrary to Zeno's wishes, established himself as ruler of Italy in 493.

The German Successor States

By 500, the Western Roman Empire was being replaced politically by a series of so-called successor states that were ruled by German kings. The pattern of settlement and the fusion of the Romans and Germans took different forms in the various successor states.

THE OSTROGOTHIC KINGDOM OF ITALY   More than any other successor state, the Ostrogothic kingdom of Italy managed to maintain the Roman tradition of government. The Ostrogothic king Theodoric had received a Roman education while a hostage in Constantinople. After establishing control of Italy, he was eager to create a synthesis of Ostrogothic and Roman practices (see the box on p. 209). In addition to maintaining the entire structure of imperial Roman government, he used separate systems of rule for the Ostrogoths and Romans. The Italian population lived under Roman law administered by Roman officials. The Ostrogoths were governed by their own customs and their own officials. However, while the Roman administrative system was kept intact, it was the Goths alone who controlled the army. Despite the apparent success of this "dual approach," Theodoric's system was unable to keep friction from developing between the Italian population and their Germanic overlords.

Religion proved to be a major source of trouble between Ostrogoths and Romans. The Ostrogoths had been converted earlier to Christianity, but to Arian Christianity, and consequently were viewed by western Christians and the Italians as heretics. Theodoric's rule

▼ **A Vandal Noble Leaves His Villa.** This mosaic from about 500 A.D. depicts a Vandal noble. The Vandals were one of a number of Germanic tribes that moved into the declining western Roman Empire and established Germanic kingdoms. The Vandals had originally settled in Spain, but were pushed into Roman North Africa by the Visigoths. Although they sacked Rome in 455, the Vandals were rapidly conquered by Byzantine forces under the emperor Justinian in 533.

grew ever harsher as discontent with Ostrogothic rule deepened. After Theodoric's death in 526, it quickly became apparent that much of his success had been due to the force of his own personality. His successors soon found themselves face-to-face with opposition from the imperial forces of the Byzantine or Eastern Roman Empire. Under Emperor Justinian (527–565) (see The Reign of Justinian later in this chapter), Byzantine armies reconquered Italy between 535 and 554, devastating much of the peninsula and destroying Rome as one of the great urban centers of the Mediterranean world in the process. The Byzantine reconquest proved ephemeral, however. Another German tribe, the Lombards, invaded Italy in 568 and conquered much of northern and central Italy. Unlike the Ostrogoths, the Lombards were harsh rulers and cared little for Roman structures and traditions. The Lombards' fondness for fighting each other enabled the Byzantines to retain control of some parts of Italy, especially the area around Ravenna, which became the capital of imperial government.

THE VISIGOTHIC KINGDOM OF SPAIN   The Visigothic kingdom in Spain, while surviving longer, demonstrated a number of parallels to the Ostrogothic kingdom of Italy. Both favored coexistence between the Roman and

German populations; both featured a warrior caste dominating a considerably larger native population; and both inherited and continued to maintain much of the Roman structure of government while largely excluding Romans from power. There were also noticeable differences, however. Perceiving that their Arianism was a stumbling block to good relations, the Visigothic rulers in the late sixth century converted to Catholic Christianity and ended the tension caused by this heresy. Laws preventing intermarriage were dropped, and the Visigothic and Hispano-Roman peoples began to fuse together. A new body of law common to both peoples also developed.

The Visigothic kingdom possessed one fatal weakness, however, a constant fighting over the kingship. The Visigoths had no law of hereditary kingship and no established procedure for choosing new rulers. Church officials tried to help develop a sense of order, as this canon from the Fourth Council of Toledo in 633 illustrates: "No one of us shall dare to seize the kingdom; no one shall arouse sedition among the citizenry; no one shall think of killing the king. . . ." Church decrees failed to stop the feuds, and assassinations remained a way of life in Visigothic Spain. In 711, the Visigothic kingdom itself was defeated by Muslim invaders (see The Rise of Islam later in this chapter).

▼ **Map 7.2** German Successor States.

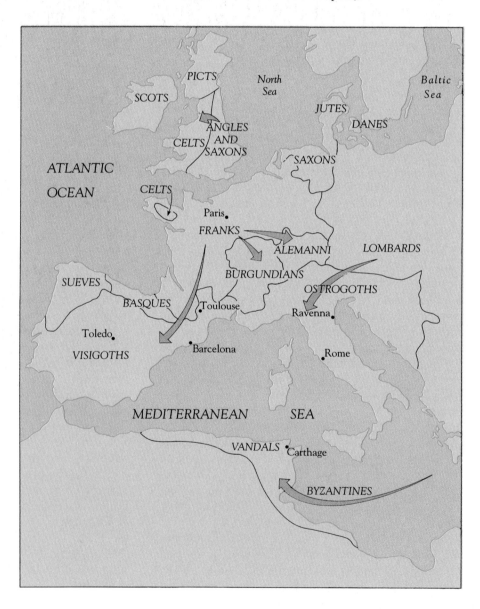

Theodoric and Ostrogothic Italy
▼ ▼ ▼

T he Ostrogothic king Theodoric (493–526), who had been educated in Constantinople, was determined to maintain Roman culture rather than destroy it. His attempt to preserve civilitas *or the traditional Roman civic culture was well expressed in the official letters written in his name by Cassiodorus, who succeeded Boethius as master of offices in 525. Theodoric's efforts were largely undone by opposition from the Roman nobility and especially by Justinian's reconquest of the Italian peninsula shortly after Theodoric's death.*

Letters of Cassiodorus

King Theodoric to Colossaeus

We delight to entrust our mandates to persons of approved character. . . .

Show forth the justice of the Goths, a nation happily situated for praise, since it is theirs to unite the forethought of the Romans and the virtue of the Barbarians. Remove all ill-planted customs, and impress upon all your subordinates that we would rather that our Treasury lost a suit than that it gained one wrongfully, rather that we lost money than the taxpayer was driven to suicide.

King Theodoric to Unigis, the Sword-Bearer

We delight to live after the law of the Romans, whom we seek to defend with our arms; and we are as much interested in the maintenance of morality as we can possibly be in war. For what profit is there in having removed the turmoil of the Barbarians, unless we live

according to law? . . . Let other kings desire the glory of battles won, of cities taken, of ruins made; our purpose is, God helping us, so to rule that our subjects shall grieve that they did not earlier acquire the blessing of our dominion.

King Theodoric to All the Jews of Genoa

The true mark of *civilitas* is the observance of law. It is this which makes life in communities possible, and which separates man from the brutes. We therefore gladly accede to your request that all the privileges which the foresight of antiquity conferred upon the Jewish customs shall be renewed to you, for in truth it is our great desire that the laws of the ancients shall be kept in force to secure the reverence due to us. Everything which has been found to conduce to *civilitas* should be held fast with enduring devotion.

King Theodoric to All the Goths Settled in Picenum and Samnium

The presence of the Sovereign doubles the sweetness of his gifts, and that man is like one dead whose face is not known to his lord. Come therefore by God's assistance, come all into our presence on the eighth day before the Ides of June [June 6], there solemnly to receive our royal largesse. But let there be no excesses by the way, no plundering the harvest of the cultivators nor trampling down their meadows, since for this cause do we gladly defray the expense of our armies that *civilitas* may be kept intact by armed men.

THE FRANKISH KINGDOM   Only one of the German successor states on the European continent proved long-lasting—the kingdom of the Franks. The establishment of a Frankish kingdom was closely associated with Clovis (c. 482–511), the leader of one group of Franks who eventually became king of them all.

It is highly significant that Clovis became a Catholic Christian around 500. Unlike many other Germanic peoples who had been converted to Arian Christianity, Clovis found that his conversion from paganism directly to Catholic Christianity (see the box on p. 210) furthered the development of a society based on the fusion

of Gallo-Romans and Germans. Clovis's action had other repercussions as well. He gained the support of the western church and the Roman popes who were only too eager to obtain the friendship of a major ruler in the successor states who was a Catholic Christian. The conversion of the king also paved the way for the conversion of the Frankish peoples. Finally, Clovis could pose as a defender of the orthodox Christian faith in order to justify his expansionary tendencies at the beginning of the sixth century. He defeated the Alemanni in southwest Germany and the Visigoths in southern Gaul. By 510, Clovis had established a powerful new Frankish kingdom

The Conversion of Clovis, King of the Franks
▼ ▼ ▼

Perhaps the most important event in the reign of Clovis, king of the Franks, was his conversion to Catholic Christianity. Clovis and the Franks then became acceptable to the Gallo-Roman aristocracy in a manner that the Arian Goths never could. Clovis's conversion experience, as recounted by the historian of the Franks, Gregory of Tours (c. 538–593), is strikingly parallel to the conversion of the first Christian emperor, Constantine.

Gregory of Tours, *The History of the Franks*

The queen [Clotilda] did not cease to urge him [Clovis] to recognize the true God and cease worshiping idols. [Clovis's wife was a baptized Christian.] But he could not be influenced in any way to this belief, until at last a war arose with the Alemanni, in which he was driven by necessity to confess what before he had of his free will denied. It came about that as the two armies were fighting fiercely, there was much slaughter, and Clovis's army began to be in danger of destruction. He saw it and raised his eyes to heaven, and with remorse in his heart he burst into tears and cried: "Jesus Christ, whom Clotilda asserts to be the son of the living God, who art said to give aid to those in distress, and to bestow victory on those who

hope in thee, I beseech the glory of thy aid, with the vow that if thou wilt grant me victory over these enemies, and I shall know that power which she says that people dedicated in thy name have had from thee, I will believe in thee and be baptized in thy name. For I have invoked my own gods, but, as I find, they have withdrawn from aiding me; and therefore I believe that they possess no power, since they do not help those who obey them. I now call upon thee, I desire to believe thee, only let me be rescued from my adversaries." And when he said this, the Alemanni turned their backs, and began to disperse in flight. And when they saw that their king was killed, they submitted to the dominion of Clovis, saying, "Let not the people perish further, we pray; we are yours now." And he stopped the fighting, and after encouraging his men, retired in peace and told the queen how he had had merit to win the victory by calling on the name of Christ. . . .

And so the king confessed all-powerful God in the Trinity, and was baptized in the name of the Father, Son and holy Spirit, and was anointed with the holy ointment with the sign of the cross of Christ. And of his army more than 3000 were baptized.

---

stretching from the Pyrenees in the west to the German lands in the east. Its relative isolation from the Mediterranean world helped it maintain its independence.

Clovis was responsible, then, for establishing a Frankish kingdom under the Merovingian dynasty, a name derived from Merovech, their semilegendary ancestor. Clovis came to rely on his Frankish followers to rule in the old Roman city-states under the title of count. Often these officials were forced to share power with the Gallo-Roman Catholic bishops, producing a gradual fusion of Latin and German cultures with the church serving to preserve the Latin culture. Clovis spent the last years of his life ensuring the survival of his dynasty by killing off relatives who were leaders of other groups of Franks.

After the death of Clovis, his sons divided the newly created Frankish kingdom. During the sixth and seventh centuries, the once-united Frankish kingdom came to be partitioned into three major areas: Neustria in northern Gaul; Austrasia, consisting of the ancient Frankish lands on both sides of the Rhine; and the former kingdom of

Burgundy. All three were ruled by members of the Merovingian dynasty. Within the three territories, members of the Merovingian dynasty were assisted by powerful nobles. Frankish society possessed a ruling class that gradually intermarried with the old Gallo-Roman senatorial class to form a new nobility. These noble families took advantage of their position to strengthen their own lands and wealth at the expense of the monarchy. Within the royal household, the position of *major domus* or mayor of the palace, the chief officer of the king's household, began to overshadow the king. Essentially, both nobles and mayors of the palace were expanding their power at the expense of the kings. In other words, private power was replacing public power.

At the beginning of the eighth century, the most important political development in the Frankish kingdom was the rise of Charles Martel, who served as mayor of the palace of Austrasia beginning in 714. Charles Martel defeated the Muslims near Poitiers in 732 and by the time of his death in 741 had become virtual ruler of the three Merovingian kingdoms. Though he was not king, the dynamic efforts of Charles Martel put his family on the verge of creating a new dynasty—the Carolingians—who would establish an even more powerful Frankish state (see Chapter 8).

During the sixth and seventh centuries, the Frankish kingdom witnessed a process of fusion between Gallo-Roman and Frankish cultures and peoples, a process accompanied by a significant decline in Roman standards of civilization and commercial activity. The Franks were warriors and did little to encourage either urban life or trade. Commerce declined in the interior, while seacoast towns maintained some activity. By 750, Frankish Gaul was basically an agricultural society in which the old Roman villa system of the late empire had continued unimpeded. Institutionally, however, the Roman governmental structure had been replaced by Germanic concepts of kingship and customary law. While the kingdom had become Catholic Christian, Frankish Christianity was often corrupt and at times bore little resemblance to the ideals of early Christianity. Important church offices, such as those of bishops, came to be controlled by Frankish nobles. In retrospect, we can see that this fusion of Franks, Gallo-Romans, and Christianity in the Frankish kingdom was producing a new culture and a new state. Eventually, as we shall see in the next chapter, it would become a new European civilization.

ANGLO-SAXON ENGLAND The barbarian pressures on the Western Roman Empire had forced the emperors to withdraw the Roman armies and abandon Britain by the beginning of the fifth century. This opened the door to a series of invasions by the Angles and Saxons, Germanic tribes from Denmark and northern Germany. While these same peoples had made plundering raids for the past century, the withdrawal of the Roman armies enabled them to make settlements instead. They met with resistance from the Celtic Britons, however, who still controlled the western regions of Cornwall, Wales, and Cumberland at the beginning of the seventh century. The German invaders eventually succeeded in carving out small kingdoms throughout the island, Kent in southeast England being one of them. This wave of German invaders would eventually be converted to Christianity by new groups of Christian missionaries.

The Society of the Germanic Peoples in the Successor Kingdoms

As the Germans infiltrated the Roman Empire, they were influenced by the Roman society they encountered. Consequently, the Germanic peoples of the fifth, sixth, and seventh centuries were probably quite different from the Germans that the forces of Augustus encountered in the first century A.D. Moreover, there was a meaningful fusion of Roman and German upper classes in the successor kingdoms. In Merovingian Frankish lands, upper-class Gallo-Romans intermarried with Frankish nobles to produce a new ruling class. Each influenced the other. Franks constructed Roman-style villas; Gallo-Romans adapted Frankish weapons.

The crucial social bond among the Germanic peoples was the family, especially the extended or patriarchal family of husbands, wives, children, brothers, sisters, cousins, and grandparents. In addition to working the land together and passing it down to succeeding generations, the extended family provided protection, which was sorely needed in the violent atmosphere of Merovingian times.

The German conception of family and kinship affected the way Germanic law treated the problem of crime and punishment. In the Roman system, as in our own, a crime such as murder was considered an offense against society or the state and was handled by a court that heard evidence and arrived at a decision. Germanic law tended to be personal. An injury by one person against another could mean a blood feud in which the family of the injured party took revenge on the kin of the wrongdoer. Feuds could lead to savage acts of revenge, such as hacking off hands or feet, gouging out eyes, or slicing off ears and noses. Since this system had a tendency to get out of control and allow mayhem to multiply, an alternative system arose that made use of a fine called *wergeld*. This was the amount paid by a wrongdoer to the family of the person he had injured or killed. *Wergeld*, which means "money for a man," was the value of a person in monetary terms. That value varied considerably according to social status. The law of the Salic Franks, which was first written down under Roman influence at the beginning of the sixth century, stated:

> If any one shall have killed a free Frank, or a barbarian living under the Salic law, and it have been proved on him, he shall be sentenced to 8,000 denars. . . .
> But if any one has slain a man who is in the service of the king, he shall be sentenced to 24,000 denars. . . .[10]

An offence against a nobleman obviously cost considerably more than one against a freeman or a slave.

German customary law also provided a different approach for determining guilt. Two forms were most commonly used: compurgation and the ordeal. Compurgation was the swearing of an oath by the accused person, backed up by a group of "oathhelpers," numbering 12 or 25, who would also swear that the accused person should be believed. The ordeal functioned in a variety of ways, all of which were based on the principle of divine intervention; divine forces (whether pagan or Christian) would not allow an innocent person to be harmed (see the box on p. 213). The ordeal continued to be used in parts of Europe until the thirteenth century, when the Catholic church finally withdrew its sanction.

THE FRANKISH FAMILY AND MARRIAGE For the Franks, like other Germanic peoples of the early Middle Ages, the extended family was at the center of social organization. The Frankish family structure was quite simple. Males were dominant and made all the important decisions. A woman obeyed her father until she married and then fell under the legal domination of her husband. A widow, however, could hold property without a male guardian. In Frankish law, the *wergeld* of a wife of childbearing age, of value because she could bear children, was considerably higher than that of a man. The Salic Law stated: "If any one killed a free woman after she had begun bearing children, he shall be sentenced to 24,000 denars. . . . After she can have no more children, he who kills her shall be sentenced to 8,000 denars. . . ."[11]

Since marriage affected the extended family group, fathers or uncles could arrange marriages for the good of the family without considering their children's wishes. Most important was the engagement ceremony in which a prospective son-in-law made a payment symbolizing the purchase of paternal authority over the bride. The essential feature of the marriage itself involved placing the married couple in bed to achieve their physical union. In first marriages, it was considered important that the wife be a virgin so as to ensure that any children would be the husband's. A virgin symbolized the ability of the bloodline to continue. For this reason, adultery was viewed as pollution of the woman and her offspring, hence poisoning the future. Adulterous wives were severely punished (an adulterous woman could be strangled or even burned alive); adulterous husbands were not. Frankish men were, in fact, accustomed to keeping concubines. Divorce was relatively simple and primarily was initiated by the husband. Divorced wives simply returned to their families. Christianity would eventually make an impact on marriage as well as sexual attitudes (see Chapter 8).

▼ The Development of the Latin Christian Church

The western Christian church, led by the Roman popes, underwent a period of considerable uncertainty in the sixth century. The rulers of the Eastern Roman Empire (see The Byzantine Empire later in this chapter) treated the Roman popes as mere instruments of their imperial policy. While the invasion of the Lombards saved the popes from Byzantine control, Lombard domination seemed a poor alternative. The emergence of a strong pope, Gregory I, known as Gregory the Great and called "the father of the medieval papacy," set the papacy and the Roman Catholic church, as the Christian church of the west came to be called, on an energetic path that enabled the church in the seventh and eighth centuries to play an increasingly prominent role in civilizing the Germans and aiding the emergence of a distinctly new European civilization.

Pope Gregory the Great

As pope, Gregory I (590–604) assumed direction of Rome and its surrounding territories, which had suffered enormously from the Ostrogothic-Byzantine struggle and Lombard invasion of the sixth century. Gregory described the conditions in a sermon to the people of Rome:

> What Rome herself, once deemed the Mistress of the World, has now become, we see—wasted away with afflictions grievous and many, with the loss of citizens, the assaults of ene-

Germanic Customary Law: The Ordeal
▼ ▼ ▼

In Germanic customary law, the ordeal came to be used as a means by which accused persons might purge themselves. Although the ordeal took different forms, all involved a physical trial of some sort, such as holding a red-hot iron. It was believed God would protect the innocent and allow them to come through the ordeal unharmed. This sixth-century account by Gregory of Tours describes an ordeal by hot water.

Gregory of Tours: An Ordeal of Hot Water (c. 580)

An Arian presbyter disputing with a deacon of our religion made venomous assertions against the Son of God and the Holy Ghost, as is the habit of that sect [the Arians]. But when the deacon had discoursed a long time concerning the reasonableness of our faith and the heretic, blinded by the fog of unbelief, continued to reject the truth, . . . the former said: "Why weary ourselves with long discussions? Let acts approve the truth; let a kettle be heated over the fire and someone's ring be thrown into the boiling water. Let him who shall take it from the heated liquid be approved as a follower of the truth, and afterwards let the other party be converted to the knowledge of the truth. And do thou also understand, O heretic, that this our party will fulfil the conditions with the aid of the Holy Ghost; thou shalt confess that there is no discordance, no dissimilarity in the Holy Trinity." The heretic consented to the proposition and they separated after appointing the next morning for the trial. But the fervor of faith in which the deacon had first made this suggestion began to cool through the instigation of the enemy. Rising with the dawn he bathed his arm in oil and smeared it with ointment.

But nevertheless he made the round of the sacred places and called in prayer on the Lord. . . . About the third hour they met in the market place. The people came together to see the show. A fire was lighted, the kettle was placed upon it, and when it grew very hot the ring was thrown into the boiling water. The deacon invited the heretic to take it out of the water first. But he promptly refused, saying, "Thou who didst propose this trial art the one to take it out." The deacon all of a tremble bared his arm. And when the heretic presbyter saw it besmeared with ointment he cried out: "With magic arts thou hast thought to protect thyself, that thou hast made use of these salves, but what thou hast done will not avail." While they were thus quarreling there came up a deacon from Ravenna named Iacinthus and inquired what the trouble was about. When he learned the truth he drew his arm out from under his robe at once and plunged his right hand into the kettle. Now the ring that had been thrown in was a little thing and very light so that it was thrown about by the water as chaff would be blown about by the wind; and searching for it a long time he found it after about an hour. Meanwhile the flame beneath the kettle blazed up mightily so that the greater heat might make it difficult for the ring to be followed by the hand; but the deacon extracted it at length and suffered no harm, protesting rather that at the bottom the kettle was cold while at the top is was just pleasantly warm. When the heretic beheld this he was greatly confused and audaciously thrust his hand into the kettle saying, "My faith will aid me." As soon as his hand had been thrust in all the flesh was boiled off the bones clear up to the elbow. And so the dispute ended.

---

mies, the frequent fall of ruined buildings. . . . Where is the Senate? Where is the people? The bones are all dissolved, the flesh is consumed, all the pomp of the dignities of this world is gone.[12]

Gregory took charge and made Rome and its surrounding area into an administrative unit that eventually came to be known as the Papal States. While historians disagree about Gregory's motives in establishing papal temporal power, it is important to remember that Gre-

gory was probably only doing what he felt needed to be done: to provide for the defense of Rome against the Lombards, to establish a government for Rome, and to feed the people. Gregory remained loyal to the empire and continued to address the Byzantine emperor as the rightful ruler of Italy.

Gregory also pursued a policy of extending papal authority over the Christian church in the west. He intervened in ecclesiastical conflicts throughout Italy and corresponded with the Frankish rulers, urging them to

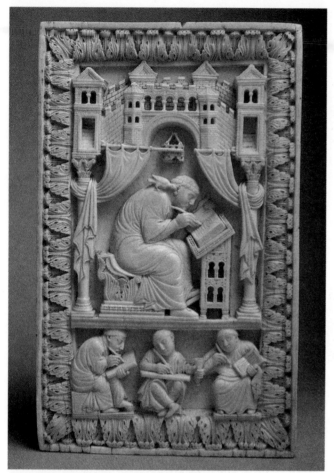

▼ **Pope Gregory I.** Pope Gregory the Great became one of the most important popes of the early Middle Ages. After the devastation Rome suffered in the sixth century, Gregory assumed control of the city and its surrounding territories. He also attempted to extend papal control over the western churches and worked both to reform the churches of Gaul and to convert England. This ivory sculpture presents Gregory at his desk.

reform the church in Gaul. He successfully initiated the efforts of missionaries to convert England to Christianity.

While medieval Christians regarded Gregory as the fourth Latin Father of the church, along with Jerome, Augustine, and Ambrose, few scholars doubt that Gregory's theological work was considerably inferior to theirs. Rather than producing original work, Gregory was primarily important in passing on a simplified version of Augustine's ideas. His *Dialogues* are simply a compilation of saints' lives in which the pope underscored the numerous miracles performed by these holy men and in the process advanced a belief that dominated the medieval world: spiritual forces intervened in everyday life. The most important of his writings, however, was *The Book of Pastoral Care*. This treatise gave detailed advice on how a good bishop should care for his flock and became a basic medieval guide for running the episcopal office.

The Monks and Their Missions

Pope Gregory the Great was especially active in converting the pagan peoples of Germanic Europe. His primary instrument was the monastic movement. Monks turned pagans to the ideals of orthodox Christianity. They also copied Latin works and passed on the legacy of the ancient world to Western civilization in its European stage. Monasticism proved to be the most important "spiritual and cultural force" in medieval Europe.

Moreover, in the fifth, sixth, and seventh centuries, monks turned their conversion efforts to areas not previously part of either the Roman or German world. The British Isles, in particular, became an important center of Christian culture and missionary fervor. After their conversion, the Celts of Ireland and Anglo-Saxons of England created new centers of Christian learning and, in turn, themselves became enthusiastic missionaries. Through these efforts, the monks of Ireland and England made important contributions to the development of Christianity in the Middle Ages.

Ireland had remained a Celtic world outside the boundaries of the Roman Empire and the world of the Germanic invaders. Certainly, the most famous of the Christian missionaries to Ireland in the fifth century was Saint Patrick (c. 390–461). Son of a Romano-British Christian, Patrick was kidnapped as a young man by Irish raiders and kept as a slave in Ireland. After his escape, he became a monk and chose to return to Ireland to convert the Irish to Christianity. Irish tradition ascribes to Patrick the title of "founder of Irish Christianity," a testament to his apparent success.

Since Ireland had not been part of the Roman world and was fairly isolated from the European continent after its conversion, Irish Christianity tended to develop along lines somewhat different from Roman Christianity. While Catholic ecclesiastical structure had followed Roman government models, the absence of these models in Ireland made possible a different pattern of church organization. Rather than bishoprics, monasteries became the fundamental units of church organization, and abbots, the heads of the monasteries, exercised far more control over the Irish church than bishops.

By the sixth century, Irish monasticism was a flourishing institution with its own striking characteristics. It was strongly ascetic. Monks performed strenuous fasts, prayed and meditated frequently under extreme privations, and confessed their sins on a regular basis to their superiors. In fact, Irish monasticism gave rise to the use of penitentials or manuals that provided a guide for examining one's life to see what sins, or offenses against the will of God, one had committed (see the box on p. 216).

A great love of learning also characterized Irish monasticism. The Irish eagerly absorbed both Latin and Greek culture and fostered education as a major part of their monastic life. Irish monks were preserving classical Latin at the same time spoken Latin was being corrupted on the continent into new dialects that eventually became the Romance languages, such as Italian, French, and Spanish. Since their interest in education encouraged writing, Irish monasteries produced extraordinary illuminated manuscripts illustrated with abstract geometrical patterns combined with Oriental elements.

Their emphasis on asceticism led many Irish monks to go into voluntary exile. This "exile for the love of God" was not into isolation, however, but into missionary activity. In the Roman Empire, monasteries had been centers where people could withdraw from the world; in contrast, Irish monks became fervid missionaries. Saint Columba (521–597) left Ireland in 565 as a "pilgrim for Christ" and founded a highly influential monastic community off the coast of Scotland on the island of Iona. From there Irish missionaries went to northern England to begin the process of converting the Angles and Saxons. Aidan of Iona, for example, founded the island monastery of Lindisfarne in the Anglo-Saxon kingdom of Northumbria. Lindisfarne, in turn, became a training center for monks who spread out to different parts of Anglo-Saxon England. Meanwhile, other Irish monks traveled to the European continent. Saint Columbanus (c. 530–615) proceeded to Gaul, then Switzerland, and wound up in northern Italy where he established a monastery at Bobbio. New monasteries founded by the Irish became centers of learning wherever they were located.

At the same time the Irish monks were busy bringing their version of Christianity to the Anglo-Saxons of Britain, Pope Gregory the Great had also set in motion his own effort to convert England to Roman Christianity. His most important agent was Augustine, a monk from Saint Andrew's monastery in Rome, who arrived in England in 597. England at that time had a number of Germanic kingdoms. Augustine went first to Kent where he converted King Ethelbert; thereupon most of the king's subjects followed suit. Pope Gregory's techniques of conversion included the use of persuasion rather than force and, as seen in this excerpt from one of his letters, the willingness to assimilate old pagan practices in order to coax the pagans into the new faith:

> We wish you [Abbot Mellitus] to inform him [Augustine] that we have been giving careful thought to the affairs of the English, and have come to the conclusion that the temples of the idols among that people should on no account be destroyed. The idols are to be destroyed, but the temples themselves are to be aspersed with holy water, altars set up in them, and relics deposited there. For if these temples are

▼ **The Book of Kells.** While Ireland remained free of both Rome and the Germanic invasions, it did not remain beyond the reach of Christian missionaries. Irish Christianity revolved around the monastery, and the monks stressed the importance of education. This emphasis on education led to the production of beautiful manuscripts elaborately illustrated. Pictured here is the opening page of the Gospel of St. Mark in the Book of Kells, a text believed to have been made by the monks of Iona.

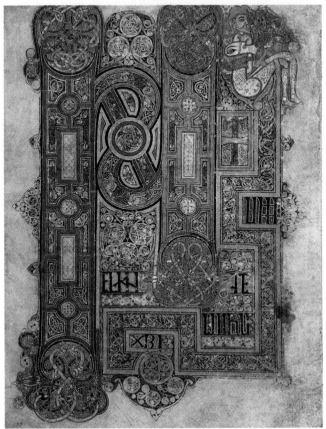

Irish Monasticism and the Penitential
▼ ▼ ▼

I rish monasticism became well known for its ascetic practices. Much emphasis was placed on careful examination of conscience to determine if one had committed a sin against God. To facilitate this examination, penitentials were developed in which descriptions of possible sins were listed with appropriate penances attached to them. Penance usually meant fasting a number of days per week on bread and water. Although these penitentials were eventually used throughout Christendom, they were especially important in Irish Christianity. This excerpt from the Penitential of Cummean, an Irish abbot, was written about 650 and demonstrates a distinctive feature of the penitentials, an acute preoccupation with sexual sins.

The Penitential of Cummean

A bishop who commits fornication shall be degraded and shall do penance for twelve years.

A presbyter or a deacon who commits natural fornication, having previously taken the vow of a monk, shall do penance for seven years. He shall ask pardon every hour; he shall perform a special fast during every week except in the days between Easter and Pentecost.

He who defiles his mother shall do penance for three years, with perpetual pilgrimage.

So shall those who commit sodomy do penance for seven years.

He who merely desires in his mind to commit fornication, but is not able, shall do penance for one year, especially in the three forty-day periods.

He who is willingly polluted during sleep shall arise and sing nine psalms in order, kneeling. On the following day, he shall live on bread and water.

A cleric who commits fornication once shall do penance for one year on bread and water; if he begets a son he shall do penance for seven years as an exile; so also a virgin.

He who loves any woman, but is unaware of any evil beyond a few conversations, shall do penance for forty days.

He who is in a state of matrimony ought to be continent during the three forty-day periods and on Saturday and on Sunday, night and day, and in the two appointed week days [Wednesday and Friday], and after conception, and during the entire menstrual period.

After a birth he shall abstain, if it is a son, for thirty-three [days]; if a daughter, for sixty-six [days].

Boys talking alone and trangressing the regulations of the elders [in the monastery], shall be corrected by three special fasts.

Children who imitate acts of fornication, twenty days; if frequently, forty.

But boys of twenty years who practice masturbation together and confess [shall do penance] twenty or forty days before they take communion.

---

well-built, they must be purified from the worship of demons and dedicated to the service of the true God. In this way, we hope that the people, seeing that their temples are not destroyed, may abandon their error and, flocking more readily to their accustomed resorts, may come to know and adore the true God.[13]

Likewise, old pagan feasts were to be given new names and incorporated into the Christian calendar: "And since they have a custom of sacrificing many oxen to demons, let some other solemnity be substituted in its place, such as a day of Dedication or the Festivals of the holy martyrs whose relics are enshrined there."[14] No doubt, Gregory was aware that early Christians had done likewise, transforming, for example, Lupercalia day, a Roman invocation of fertility celebrated in mid-February, to Saint Valentine's day in honor of a Christian martyr.

As Roman Christianity spread northward in Britain, it encountered Irish Christianity moving southward. Soon, arguments arose over the differences between Celtic and Roman Christianity, especially over different calendar days for feasts and matters of discipline. The conflict was settled at the Synod of Whitby held in the kingdom of Northumbria in 664. When the king of Northumbria accepted the arguments of the representatives of Roman Christianity, the issue was decided in favor of Roman practices. There now ensued a gradual fusion of Celtic and Roman Christianity within a framework of Roman ecclesiastical organization. The archbishop of Canterbury was made the highest ranking church official and various bishops were subordinated to him. Despite its newfound unity and loyalty to Rome, the English church retained some Celtic features. Most important was the concentration on monastic culture with special emphasis on learning and missionary work. As a result, by 700 the English church had become the best trained and most learned in western Europe.

Following the Irish example, English monastic missionaries spread to the European continent to carry on the work of conversion. The most important monk was from Wessex and used the name Boniface (c. 680–755). He undertook the conversion of pagan Germans in Frisia, Bavaria, and Saxony. Boniface was also a gifted administrator, and his missionary work soon took on a reforming dimension. He cooperated with the Frankish leader Charles Martel and later his son in undertaking the regeneration of the Frankish higher clergy. Despite bitter opposition, Boniface managed to convene a reform council. His efforts also led to closer cooperation between the Franks and the leaders of the Catholic church at Rome. By 740, Saint Boniface, the "Apostle of the Germans," had become the most famous churchman in Europe. Thirteen years later he was killed while trying to convert the pagan Frisians. Boniface was a brilliant example of the numerous Irish and English monks whose tireless efforts made Europe the bastion of the Roman Catholic faith.

The role of women has frequently been overlooked in the monastic missionary movement and the conversion of the Germanic kingdoms. In both the English and Frankish kingdoms, the most common form of monastic establishment was the so-called double monastery in which both monks and nuns resided and followed a common rule under a common head. Frequently, this leader was an abbess rather than an abbot. Many of these abbesses belonged to royal houses, especially in Anglo-Saxon England. Some of them ruled over thousands of men and women and vast territories. In the double monastery, monks were frequently subordinate to a female leader and were used for heavy labor and to lead church services, since only males could be priests in the Catholic church.

Nuns of the seventh and eight centuries were not always as heavily cloistered as they had once been and were therefore able to play an important role in the spread of Christianity. The great English missionary Boniface relied on nuns in England for books and money. He also asked the abbess of Wimborne to send groups of nuns to establish convents in newly converted German lands. A nun named Leoba established the first convent in Germany at Bischofsheim.

It is difficult to assess what Christianity meant to the converted pagans, especially the peasants upon whom the Irish and English monks had expended their greatest efforts. As Pope Gregory had recommended, Christian

▼ **Celtic Cross.** Due to Ireland's isolation from the European continent, Irish Christianity developed some unique characteristics. Abbots exercised more power than bishops and Irish monasticism was strongly ascetic. Instead of withdrawing from the world, Irish monks became dedicated missionaries. The Celtic cross, as pictured here at the monastery of Clonmacnois, was a widespread symbol of Irish Christianity.

beliefs and values were usually superimposed upon older pagan customs. While effective in producing quick conversions, it is an open question how much people actually understood of Christian theology. Popular belief tended to focus on God as a judge who needed to be appeased to avert disasters in daily life and gain salvation. Except for the promise of salvation, such an image of God was not all that different from Roman religious practices.

Christianity and Intellectual Life

Invasions, wars, and devastation destroyed much of the physical foundation of the classical world and its intellectual life. Although the Christian church came to accept classical culture, it was not easy to do so in the world of the German successor states. Nevertheless, a number of Christian scholars managed to keep learning alive, even if it meant only preserving a heritage rather than creating new bodies of knowledge.

Boethius and Cassiodorus, two important Christian intellectuals, both served as officials of the Ostrogothic king Theodoric. Boethius (c. 480–524) received the traditional education typical of the Roman aristocracy. He met King Theodoric in 505, became his adviser, and eventually rose to be the highest civil official in Italy. As an example of Roman talent serving a German king, he stands as a symbol of that process of fusion by which the Roman world was transformed to the medieval. Boethius was also a scholar. He translated some of the works of Aristotle into Latin, especially his works on logic, and left an important legacy to the medieval world by providing a systematic Latin vocabulary for the analysis of logic. Boethius's most famous work was written in prison, where he was kept for a year by Theodoric on a charge of treason before being executed. This work, *On the Consolation of Philosophy,* is a dialogue between Boethius and philosophy personified as a woman. Philosophy leads Boethius to a clear understanding of true happiness and the highest good, which she equates with God. These are not achieved by outward conditions, since the man who lives virtuously finds his happiness within. Basically, Boethius was restating Stoic philosophy rather than a Christian theology; nevertheless, he presented it eloquently.

Cassiodorus (c. 490–c. 585) also came from an aristocratic Roman family. Whereas Boethius had been concerned with philosophy and theology, Cassiodorus was more interested in history, which he used to reconcile the Romans and Goths by demonstrating how the Goths were attempting to preserve Roman tradition. After the execution of Boethius, Cassiodorus held the position of master of offices to Theodoric. His letters, written while he was secretary to Theodoric, provide us with a major source of information about this period (see the box on p. 209).

The conflicts that erupted after the death of Theodoric led Cassiodorus to withdraw from public life and retire to his landed estates in southern Italy, where he wrote his final work, *Divine and Human Readings.* This was a compendium of the literature of both Christian and pagan antiquity. Cassiodorus accepted the advice of earlier Christian intellectuals to make use of classical works while treasuring the Scriptures above all else: "And therefore, as the blessed Augustine and other very learned Fathers say, secular writings should not be spurned. It is proper, however, . . . to 'meditate in the (divine) law day and night,' for, though a worthy knowledge of some matters is occasionally obtained from secular writings, this law is the source of eternal life."[15]

Cassiodorus continued the tradition of late antiquity of classifying knowledge according to certain subjects. In assembling his compendium of authors, he followed the works of Boethius and other late ancient authors in placing all secular knowledge into the categories of the seven liberal arts, which were divided into two major groups: the *trivium,* consisting of grammar, rhetoric, and dialectic or logic; and the *quadrivium,* consisting of the mathematical subjects of arithmetic, geometry, astronomy, and music. The seven liberal arts would become the cornerstone of education until the seventeenth century.

Isidore of Seville (c. 570–636) was a product of Visigothic Spain. While not an original thinker, he was especially good at compiling existing knowledge, as his well-known *Etymologiae (Etymologies)* illustrates. This was a twenty-volume compendium of knowledge organized through explanations of the etymology of Latin words. While simplistic at times ("Man (homo) is so called because he was made out of earth (ex humo) as is recounted in Genesis."), Isidore still passed on a considerable body of knowledge to medieval people.

The Venerable Bede (c. 672–735) was a scholar and product of Christian Anglo-Saxon England. He entered a monastery at Jarrow as a small boy and remained there most of the rest of his life. Many historians consider Bede the first major historian of the Middle Ages. His *Ecclesiastical History of the English People,* completed in 731, was a product of the remarkable flowering of English ecclesiastical and monastic culture in the eighth century. His work is a history of England that begins with the coming of Christianity to Britain. Although Bede shared the credulity of his age in regard to stories of miracles, he had a remarkable sense of history. He used his sources judiciously to give us our chief source of information about early Anglo-Saxon England. His work was a remarkable accomplishment for a monk from a small corner of England and reflects the high degree of intellectual achievement of England in the eighth century.

▼ The Byzantine Empire

In the fourth century, a noticeable separation between the western and eastern parts of the Roman Empire began to develop (see Chapter 6). In the course of the fifth century, while the Germans moved into the western part of the empire and established their successor states, the Roman Empire in the east, centered on Constantinople, continued to exist. While the eastern Roman emperors treated German rulers, such as Odoacer and Theodoric, as their regents, it was not until the reign of Justinian that an attempt was made to restore Roman institutions and civilization to the entire Mediterranean world.

The Reign of Justinian (527–565)

As the nephew and heir of the previous emperor, Justinian had been well trained in imperial administration. He married Theodora, daughter of a lower-class circus trainer who was herself said to have been an actress and prostitute. She proved to be a remarkably strong-willed and intelligent woman, who played a crucial role in giving Justinian the determination to crush a revolt against his rule in 532. Justinian was determined to reestablish the Roman Empire in the entire Mediterranean world and began his attempt to reconquer the west within a year after the revolt had failed.

Justinian's army under Belisarius, probably the best general of the late Roman world, presented a formidable

▼ **The Emperor Justinian Surrounded by His Court.** This mosaic from Ravenna depicts the Byzantine emperor Justinian and his court. Justinian wanted to restore the Roman Empire in the Mediterranean world, and although he managed to recapture most of the lost territories, Spain and Gaul could not be conquered and the Lombards took Italy shortly after his death. Justinian was also responsible for a codification of Roman law, which eventually became the basis of the legal system of continental Europe.

force. It marched into north Africa and quickly destroyed the Vandals in two major battles. From north Africa Belisarius led his forces onto the Italian peninsula after occupying Sicily in 535. Although he had conquered Italy south of the Po River by 540, the Ostrogoths were given a reprieve when Belisarius had to return east to defend the empire against the Persians. Consequently, the struggle in Italy continued for another twelve years until 552, when the Ostrogoths were defeated and, like the Vandals, became extinct as a separate people. This struggle devastated Italy, which suffered more from Justinian's reconquest than from all of the previous barbarian invasions.

Justinian has been criticized for overextending his resources and bankrupting the empire. Historians now think, however, that a devastating plague in 542 and long-term economic factors were far more damaging to the Eastern Roman Empire than Justinian's conquests. Before he died, Justinian appeared to have achieved his goals. He had restored the imperial Mediterranean world; his empire included Italy, part of Spain, north Africa, Asia Minor, Palestine, and Syria. But the conquest of the western empire proved ephemeral. Only three years after Justinian's death, the Lombards entered Italy. Although the eastern empire maintained the fiction of Italy as a province, its forces were limited to southern and central Italy, Sicily, and coastal areas, such as the territory around Ravenna.

THE CODIFICATION OF ROMAN LAW Though his conquests proved short-lived, Justinian's most important contribution to Western civilization was his codification of Roman law. The eastern empire was heir to a vast quantity of materials connected to the development of Roman law. These included laws passed by the senate and assemblies; legal comments of jurists; decisions of praetors; and the edicts of emperors. Justinian had been well trained in imperial government and was well acquainted with Roman law. He wished to codify and simplify this mass of materials, as he explained:

> Therefore, since there is nothing to be found in all things so worthy of attention as the authority of the law, which properly regulates all affairs both divine and human, and expels all injustice; We have found the entire arrangement of the law which has come down to us from the foundation of the City of Rome and the times of Romulus, to be so confused that it is extended to an infinite length and is not within the grasp of human capacity; and hence We were first induced to begin by examining what had been enacted by former most venerated princes, to correct their constitutions, and make them more easily understood; to the end that being included

in a single Code, and having had removed all that is superfluous in resemblance and all iniquitous discord, they may afford to all men the ready assistance of their true meaning.[16]

To accomplish his goal, Justinian authorized the jurist Trebonian to make a systematic compilation of imperial edicts. The result was the Code of Law, the first part of the *Corpus Iuris Civilis* (*The Body of Civil Law*), completed in 529. Four years later, two other parts of the *Corpus* appeared: the *Digest*, a compendium of writings of Roman jurists, and the *Institutes*, a brief summary of the chief principles of Roman law that could be used as a textbook on Roman law. The fourth part of the *Corpus* was the *Novels*, a compilation of the most important new edicts issued during Justinian's reign.

Justinian's codification of Roman law became the basis of imperial law in the Byzantine Empire until its end in 1453. More importantly, however, since it was written in Latin (it was, in fact, the last product of eastern Roman culture to be written in Latin, which was soon replaced by Greek), it was also eventually used in the west and, in fact, became the basis of the legal system of all of continental Europe.

From Eastern Roman to Byzantine Empire

Although the accomplishments of Justinian's reign had been spectacular, the Eastern Roman Empire was left with serious problems: an empty treasury, a decline in population after the plague, and renewed threats to its frontiers. The seventh century proved to be an important turning point in the history of the Eastern Roman Empire. In the first half of the century, during the reign of Heraclius (610–641), the empire was faced with attacks from the Persians to the east and the Slavs to the north.

The empire was left exhausted by these struggles. In the midst of them, it had developed a new system of defense by combining civil and military offices into one. While this innovation helped the empire survive, it also fostered an increased militarization of the empire. By the mid-seventh century, it had become apparent that a restored Mediterranean empire was simply beyond the resources of the eastern empire, which now increasingly turned its back upon the Latin west. A renewed series of external threats in the second half of the seventh century only strengthened this development.

The most serious challenge to the eastern empire was presented by the rise of Islam, which unified the Arab tribes and created a powerful new force that swept through the east (see The Rise of Islam later in this chapter). The defeat of an eastern Roman army at Yarmuk in 636 meant the loss of the provinces of Syria and Palestine. The Arabs also moved into the old Persian Empire and conquered it. Although the Islamic attempt to besiege Constantinople failed, Arabs and eastern Roman forces faced each other along a frontier in southern Asia Minor.

There were, however, problems along the northern frontier as well, especially in the Balkans, where an Asiatic people known as the Bulgars had arrived earlier in the sixth century. In 679, the Bulgars defeated the eastern Roman forces and took possession of the lower Danube valley, creating a strong Bulgarian kingdom.

By the beginning of the eighth century, the Eastern Roman Empire was greatly diminished in size, consisting only of the eastern Balkans and Asia Minor. It was now an eastern Mediterranean state. These external challenges had important internal repercussions as well. By the eighth century, the Eastern Roman Empire had been transformed into what historians call the Byzantine Empire, a civilization with its own unique character that would last until 1453. What were the characteristics of this Byzantine Empire in the eighth century?

The Byzantine Empire was a Greek state. Justinian's *Body of Civil Law* had been the last official work published in Latin. Increasingly, Latin fell into disuse as Greek became not only the common language of the Byzantine Empire, but its official language as well.

The Byzantine Empire was an orthodox Christian state. Christianity, in fact, had become the foundation stone of the Byzantine state. The empire possessed a single faith that was shared in a profound way by all its citizens. An enormous amount of artistic talent was poured into the construction of churches, church ceremonies, and church decoration. Byzantine art was deeply permeated by spiritual principles. The importance of orthodox Christianity to the Byzantines explains why theological controversies took on an exaggerated form. The most famous of these controversies, the so-called iconoclastic controversy, threatened the stability of the empire in the first half of the eighth century.

Beginning in the sixth century, the use of religious images, especially in the form of icons or pictures of sacred figures, grew so widespread that charges of idolatry, or the worship of images, began to be heard. The use of images or icons had been justified by the argument that icons were not worshiped, but were simply used to help illiterate people understand their religion. This rationalization failed to stop the movement against icons.

Chronology
▼ ▼ ▼
The Byzantine Empire

Protective Walls of Theodosius II	408–450
Justinian Codifies Roman Law	529–533
Reconquest of Italy by the Byzantines	535–554
Completion of Hagia Sophia	537
Attacks on the Empire in Reign of Heraclius	610–641
Arab Defeat of Byzantines at Yarmuk	636
Defeat by the Bulgars; Losses in the Balkans	679

Beginning in 730, the Byzantine Emperor Leo III (717–741) outlawed the use of icons as worship of images. Severe resistance ensued, especially from monks. Leo III also used the iconoclastic controversy to add to the prestige of the patriarch of Constantinople, the highest church official in the east and second in dignity only to the bishop of Rome. The Roman popes were opposed to the iconoclastic edicts, and their opposition created considerable dissension between the popes and the Byzantine emperors. Late in the eighth century, the Byzantine rulers reversed their stand on the use of images, but not until considerable damage had been done to the unity of the Christian church. Although the separation between Roman Catholicism and Greek Orthodoxy did not occur until the eleventh century, the iconoclastic controversy was important in moving both sides in that direction.

The Byzantine Empire was characterized by what might be called a permanent war economy. Byzantine emperors maintained the late Roman policy of state regulation of economic affairs. Of course, it was easy to justify; the survival of the empire was dependent upon careful shepherding of economic resources and the maintenance of the army. Thus, the state encouraged agricultural production, regulated the guilds or corporations responsible for industrial production and the various stages of manufacturing, and controlled commerce by making trade in grain and silk, the two most valuable products, government monopolies.

The emperor occupied a crucial position in the Byzantine state. Portrayed as chosen by God, the Byzantine emperor was crowned in sacred ceremonies, and his subjects were expected to prostrate themselves in his presence. His power was considered absolute and limited in practice only by deposition or assassination. The emperor was assisted in his rule by a rather unusual ruling class. Civil servants and high churchmen essentially stemmed from the same ranks of the urban society of Constantinople. They received the same education and often followed the same careers in civil service until they went their separate ways into ecclesiastical and government offices. Their education combined Greek classics with Christian theology, with special emphasis on the importance of Neoplatonic philosophy in Greek Christian theology. This educated class of clerical and civil officials was an important element of Byzantine civilization.

The similar background of the ruling classes, whether clerical or civil, meant that there was no real division between church and state in the Byzantine Empire, a condition symbolized by the divinely chosen emperor,

▼ **Oldest Surviving Map of Constantinople.** Constantinople was the largest city in Europe during the Middle Ages. It also served as medieval Europe's greatest center of commerce until the twelfth century. Its strategic location on the Bosphorus allowed the city to dominate the trade routes between the Black Sea and the Mediterranean.

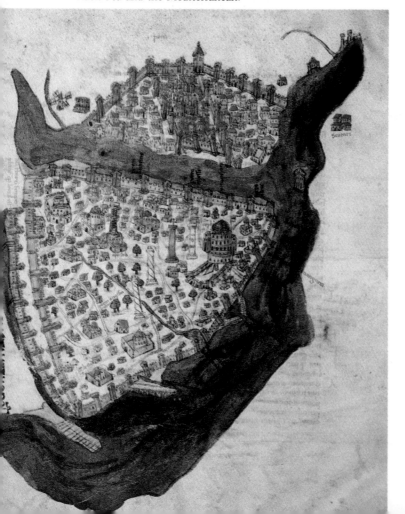

who appointed the patriarch of the church and exercised control over both church and state. The Byzantines believed that God had commanded their state to preserve the true faith—Orthodox Christianity. Emperor, churchmen, and civic officials were all bound together in service to this ideal. It can be said that spiritual values truly held the Byzantine state together.

Intellectual and Social Life

The intellectual life of Byzantium was highly influenced by the tradition of classical civilization. Byzantine scholars sought actively to preserve the works of the ancient Greeks while a great deal of Byzantine literature itself was based on classical models. Although the Byzantines produced a substantial body of literature, much of it was very practical in nature, focusing on legal, military, and administrative treatises. The most outstanding literary achievements of the early Byzantine Empire, however, were historical and religious works. The latter were sometimes of an extremely combative nature because of the intense theological controversies.

The best known of the early Byzantine historians was Procopius (c. 500–c. 562), court historian during the reign of Justinian. Procopius served as legal assistant and secretary to the great general Belisarius and accompanied him on his wars on behalf of Justinian. Procopius's best historical work, the *Wars,* is a firsthand account of Justinian's wars of reconquest in the western Mediterranean and his wars against the Persians in the east. Deliberately modeled after the work of his hero, the Greek historian Thucydides (see Chapter 3), Procopius's narrative contains vivid descriptions of battle scenes, clear judgment, and noteworthy objectivity. Procopius also wrote a work that many historians consider mostly scandalous gossip, his infamous *Secret History.* At the beginning of this work, Procopius informed his readers that "What I shall write now follows a different plan, supplementing the previous formal chronicle with a disclosure of what really happened throughout the Roman Empire."[17] What he revealed constituted a scathing attack upon Justinian and his wife Theodora for their alleged misdeeds.

In natural science, the early Byzantines made few contributions except for practical inventions. By far the most famous was Greek fire, used against the Arab fleets attempting to besiege Constantinople. Greek fire was a petroleum-based compound containing quicklime and sulfur. Since it would burn under water, the Byzantines created the equivalent of modern flamethrowers by blowing Greek fire from tubes upon wooden ships with frightening effect. Understandably, the formula for Greek fire was closely guarded by the government and remains a matter of debate even today.

LIFE IN CONSTANTINOPLE   After the destruction caused by the riots of 532, Justinian rebuilt Constantinople and gave it the appearance it would keep until its sack by the crusaders in 1204 and its capture by the Turks in 1453 (see Chapter 13). With a population estimated in the hundreds of thousands, Constantinople was the largest city in Europe during the Middle Ages. It viewed itself as center of an empire and a special Christian city. After all, its founder Constantine had dedicated the city with these words: "Oh Christ, ruler and master of the world. To you now I dedicate this subject city, and these scepters and the might of Rome. Protect her; save her from all harm."

Until the twelfth century, Constantinople was the medieval world's greatest center of commerce. The city was the chief entrepot for the exchange of products between west and east. Highly desired in Europe were the products of the east: silk from China; spices from southeast Asia and India; jewelry and ivory from India (the latter used by Byzantine craftsmen for church items); wheat and furs from southern Russia; and flax and honey from the Balkans. Many of these eastern goods were then shipped to the Mediterranean area and northern Europe. Despite the Germanic incursions, European trade did not entirely end.

Moreover, imported raw materials were used in Constantinople for local industries. Justinian was the first ruler to smuggle silkworms from China and begin a Byzantine silk industry. The state had a monopoly on the production of silk cloth, and the workshops themselves were housed in Constantinople's royal palace complex. European demand for silk cloth made it the city's most lucrative product. It is interesting to note that the upper classes, including emperors and empresses, were not discouraged from participating in trade and manufacturing to make money. Indeed, one empress even manufactured perfumes in her bedroom.

Much of Constantinople's appearance in the Early Middle Ages was due to Justinian's program of rebuilding in the sixth century. Earlier, in the mid-fifth century, Emperor Theodosius II (408–450) had constructed an enormous defensive wall to protect the city on its land side. The city was dominated by an immense palace complex, a huge arena known as the Hippodrome, and hundreds of churches. No residential district was particularly fashionable; palaces, tenements, and slums ranged alongside one another. Justinian added many new buildings. His public works projects included roads, bridges,

▼ **Walls of Constantinople.** Pictured here are the ruins of the walls of Constantinople. From a military perspective, Constantinople was in an ideal strategic location. On two sides it was surrounded by water, and on the third side the city was protected by massive walls. The defensive walls were built by Theodosius II and until the city was taken in 1453 by Muslim invaders, Constantinople remained impregnable.

walls, public baths, law courts, and colossal underground reservoirs to hold the city's water supply. He also built hospitals, schools, monasteries, and churches. The latter was his special passion, and in Constantinople alone he built or rebuilt thirty-four of them. His greatest achievement was the famous Hagia Sophia—the church of the Holy Wisdom.

Completed in 537, Hagia Sophia was designed by a Greek architect who did not use the simple, flat-roofed basilica of western architecture. The center of Hagia Sophia consisted of four enormous piers crowned by an enormous dome, which seemed to be floating in space. This effect was emphasized by Procopius, the court historian, who, at Justinian's request, wrote a treatise on the emperor's building projects: "From the lightness of the building, it does not appear to rest upon a solid foundation, but to cover the place beneath as though it were suspended from heaven by the fabled golden chain." In part, this impression was created by putting forty-two windows around the base of the dome, which allowed an incredible play of light within the cathedral. Light served to remind the worshipers of God; as Procopius commented:

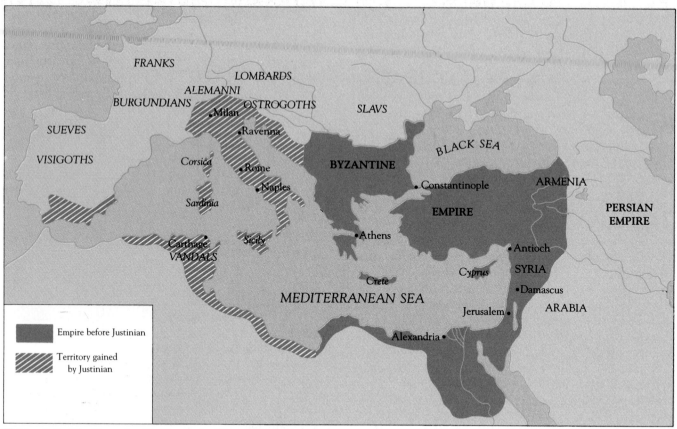

▼ **Map 7.3a** The Byzantine Empire in the Time of Justinian.

▼ **Map 7.3b** Constantinople.

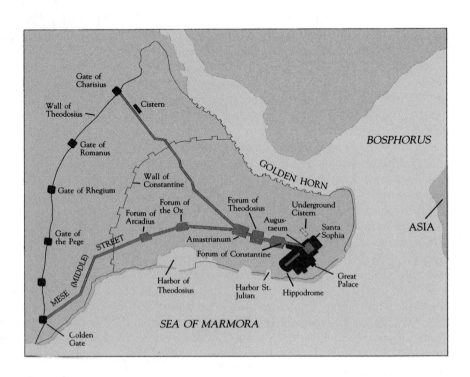

Whoever enters there to worship perceives at once that it is not by any human strength or skill, but by the favor of God that this work has been perfected; his mind rises sublime to commune with God, feeling that He cannot be far off, but must especially love to dwell in the place which He has chosen; and this takes place not only when a man sees it for the first time, but it always makes the same impression upon him, as though he had never beheld it before.[18]

As darkness is illumined by invisible light, so too it was believed the world is illumined by invisible spirit.

The royal palace complex, Hagia Sophia, and the Hippodrome were the three dominant buildings in Constantinople. The latter was a huge amphitheater, constructed of brick covered by marble, holding between 40,000 and 60,000 spectators. Although gladiator fights were held there, the main events were the chariot races; twenty-four would usually be presented in one day. The citizens of Constantinople were passionate fans of chariot racing. Successful charioteers were acclaimed as heroes and honored with public statues. Crowds in the Hippodrome also took on political significance. Being a member of the two chief factions of charioteers—the Blues or Greens—was the only real outlet for political expression. Even emperors had to be aware of their demands and attitudes since rioting could threaten even their power. The loss of a race in the Hippodrome frequently resulted in bloody riots.

By 750, it was apparent that two of Rome's heirs, the Germanic successor states and the Byzantine Empire, were moving in different directions. Nevertheless, Byzantine influence on the medieval Western world was significant. The images of a Roman imperial state that continued to haunt the west had a living reality in the Byzantine state. The legal system of the west came to owe much to Justinian's codification of Roman law. In addition, the Byzantine Empire served in part as a buffer state, protecting the west for a long time from incursions from the east. Although the Byzantine Empire would continue to influence the west until its demise in 1453, it went its own unique way. One of its most bitter enemies was the new power of Islam that erupted out of Arabia in the name of the holy man Muhammad. This third heir of Rome soon controlled large areas of the old Roman Mediterranean area.

▼ The Rise of Islam

The Arabs were a Semitic-speaking people of the Near East who had a long history. They had been mentioned by the Greeks in the fifth century B.C. and even

earlier in the Old Testament. In Roman times, the Arabian peninsula seemed less prosperous than previously and came to be dominated by Bedouins, tribes of nomads originally from the northern part of the peninsula. Although some Arabs prospered from trading activities, especially in the north, the majority of the Arabs consisted of poor Bedouins, whose tribes were known for their independence, their warlike qualities, their dedication to their tribal gods, and their dislike for the urban-dwelling Arabs.

In the fifth and sixth centuries A.D., urban Arabs became more important as new trade routes appeared along the western fringes of the Arabian peninsula. Especially important was Mecca. Though known for its trade, it was more important as a growing pilgrimage town since it possessed important shrines, especially the

▼ **Interior View of Hagia Sophia.** Pictured here is the interior of the Church of the Holy Wisdom, constructed under Justinian by Anthemius of Tralles and Isidore of Milan. In Constantinople alone, Justinian had thirty-four churches either built or re-built, but the Hagia Sophia is undoubtedly his greatest achievement. The pulpits and the great plaques bearing inscriptions from the Koran were introduced when the Turks converted this church into a mosque in the fifteenth century.

Birth of Muhammad	c. 570
Muhammad's Flight from Mecca (Hegira)	622
Death of Muhammad	632
Defeat of Byzantines at Yarmuk	636
Seizure of Byzantine Provinces of Syria and Egypt	640–642
Defeat of Persians	637–650
Invasion of Spain	710
Arab Failure to Capture Constantinople	717–718
Defeat of Muslims near Poitiers	732

Ka'ba, the sanctuary that held the sacred black meteorite. Mecca attracted Bedouins as well, which created conflicts between the independent tribespeople and the increasingly wealthy commercial class. Into this tense world stepped Muhammad, whose spiritual visions would unify the Arab world with a speed no one would have suspected possible.

Muhammad (c. 570–632) was born in Mecca and orphaned at the age of six. He became a caravan manager and eventually married a rich widow who was also his employer. Despite a background of Arabic polytheism, Muhammed arrived at a monotheistic perspective, owing much to the Hebrew and Christian traditions. In his middle years, he began to experience visions inspired by Allah. Muhammad believed that while Allah had already revealed himself in part through Moses and Jesus—and thus through the Hebrew and Christian traditions—the final revelations were now being given to him. Out of his revelations, which were eventually dictated to secretaries, came the *Qu'ran* or *Koran,* the holy scriptures, which contained the guidelines by which a follower of Allah was to live. Like the Christians and Jews, Muslims were a "People of the Book." Muhammad's teachings formed the basis for the religion known as Islam, which means "submission to the will of Allah." Allah was the all-powerful being who had created the universe and everything in it. Humans must subject themselves to Allah if they wished to achieve everlasting life. Those who became his followers were called Muslims, meaning those who practiced Islam.

Muhammad's first followers came from his own family and clan. The Meccan aristocracy opposed him, fearful of his impact on the traditional idol worship of Arab society. He and his followers were forced to flee from Mecca in 622, a flight known as the Hegira (the date of the flight—September 24, 622—is the first date of the official calendar of Islam). Muhammad and his supporters fled to the rival city of Medina, where they gained additional supporters and managed to unite the townspeople with Bedouin tribes from the surrounding countryside.

Muslims saw no separation between political and religious authority. Submission to the will of God meant submission to his Prophet Muhammad. Consequently, Muhammad's political skills enabled him to put together a significant force with which he returned to Mecca. From there, Muhammad's ideas spread quickly in the Arabian peninsula and within a relatively short time had resulted in both the religious and political union of Arab society.

The rapid spread of Islam to the Arabs was a remarkable phenomenon that has not been fully explained by historians. In a true religious revolution, the Arabs moved from a polytheistic dedication to their tribal gods to a single vision and system in which individuals were tied directly to a monotheistic God. Islam emphasized Allah as an absolute authority. It made a simple, yet apparently powerful appeal to people at all social levels.

▼ **Muhammad on a Camel.** This scene is taken from a medieval manuscript of the *Universal History* by Rashid al-Din, a Persian historian. Here Jesus Christ is shown riding on a donkey beside the prophet Muhammad who rides on a camel. This was done to indicate that while Jesus was accepted as a forerunner of the prophet, his own teachings were superseded by the message of Muhammad.

The *Koran* and the Spread of the Muslim Faith
▼ ▼ ▼

*T*he Koran *contains the revelations that God suppos-edly made to his Prophet Muhammad after they were systematically written down in 114 suras or chapters. The* Koran *is the sacred book of the Muslims, comparable to the Bible in Christianity. In this selection from Chapter 47, entitled "Muhammad, Revealed at Medina," it is apparent that Islam encourages the spreading of the faith. For believers who died for Allah, there awaited a garden of paradise quite unlike the arid desert homeland of the Arab warriors.*

The *Koran*: Chapter 47, "Muhammad, Revealed at Medina"

Allah will bring to nothing the deeds of those who disbelieve and debar others from His path. As for the faithful who do good works and believe in what is revealed to Muhammad—which is the truth from their Lord—He will forgive them their sins and en-noble their state.

This, because the unbelievers follow falsehood, while the faithful follow the truth from their Lord. Thus Allah coins their sayings for mankind.

When you meet the unbelievers in the battlefield strike off their heads and, when you have laid them low, bind your captives firmly. Then grant them their freedom or take ransom from them, until War shall lay down her armour.

Thus shall you do. Had Allah willed, He could Himself have punished them; but He has ordained it thus that He might test you, the one by the other. As for those who are slain in the cause of Allah, He will not allow their works to perish. He will vouchsafe them guidance and ennoble their state; He will admit them to the Paradise He has made known to them.

Believers, if you help Allah, Allah will help you and make you strong. But the unbelievers shall be consigned to perdition. He will bring their deeds to nothing. Because they have opposed His revelations, He will frustrate their works.

Have they never journeyed through the land and seen what was the end of those who have gone before them? Allah destroyed them utterly. A similar fate awaits the unbelievers, because Allah is the protector of the faithful; because the unbelievers have no pro-tector.

Allah will admit those who embrace the true faith and do good works to gardens watered by running streams. The unbelievers take their fill of pleasure and eat as the beasts eat: but Hell shall be their home. . . .

This is the Paradise which the righteous have been promised. There shall flow in it rivers of unpolluted water, and rivers of milk forever fresh; rivers of de-lectable wine and rivers of clearest honey. They shall eat therein of every fruit and receive forgiveness from their Lord. Is this like the lot of those who shall abide in Hell for ever and drink scalding water which will tear their bowels? . . .

Know that there is no god but Allah. Implore Him to forgive your sins and to forgive the true believers, men and women. Allah knows your busy haunts and resting-places.

Both extremes of Arabic society—the independent fierce tribes and the practical-minded merchants—were caught up by the message of Muhammad.

At the heart of Islam was the *Koran* with its basic message that there is no God but Allah and Muhammad is his Prophet (see the box above). Essentially, the Ko-ran contains Muhammad's revelations of a heavenly book narrated to him by an angelic messenger and writ-ten down by secretaries. It comprised 114 suras or chap-ters. The *Koran* was not only a "Holy Bible" of Islam, but an ethical guidebook and a code of law and political theory combined.

Islam was a direct and simple faith, emphasizing the need to obey the will of Allah. This meant following a basic ethical code that demanded belief in Allah and Muhammad as his Prophet; standard prayer five times a day and public prayer on Friday at midday to worship Allah; observation of the holy month of Ramadan with fasting from dawn to sunset; making a pilgrimage, if pos-sible, to Mecca in one's lifetime; and giving alms to the poor and unfortunate. The faithful who observed the law were guaranteed a place in an eternal paradise that con-tained sensuous delights obviously lacking in the midst of the Arabian desert.

After Muhammad's death in 632, a new institution called the caliphate was created to provide leadership. Muhammad and the early caliphs who succeeded him took up the Arabic tribal custom of the *razzia* or raid against their persecutors. The *Koran* called this activity "striving in the way of the Lord" or a *jihad.* Although misleadingly called a Holy War, the *jihad* grew out of the Arabic tradition of tribal raids, which were permitted as a way to channel the warlike energies of the Arab tribes. Such aggression was not carried out to convert others since conversion to Islam was purely voluntary. Those who did not convert were required only to submit to Muslim rule and pay taxes.

Once the Arabs had become unified under Muhammad's successor, they began to direct the warlike energy formerly expended upon each other outward against neighboring peoples, thus undertaking a *jihad* on a large scale. The Byzantines and Persians were the first to feel the strength of the newly united Arabs. At Yarmuk in 636, the Muslims defeated the Byzantine army, and by 640 they had taken possession of the province of Syria. To the east, the Arabs defeated the Persian forces in 637 and then went on to conquer the entire Persian Empire by 650. In the meantime, by 642, Egypt and additional parts of northern Africa had been added to the new Muslim empire. It has been argued that the earlier Byzantine-Persian conflict had weakened both powers

and made their defeats by the Arabs substantially easier. Although there is some truth in this assertion, one should not overlook the power of the Arab armies. Led by the caliphs and a series of brilliant generals, the Arabs had put together a large and fundamentally fanatical army, whose valor was enhanced by the belief that Muslim warriors were guaranteed a place in paradise if they died in battle.

Early caliphs, ruling from Medina, organized their newly conquered territories into taxpaying provinces. By the mid-seventh century, problems arose over the succession to the Prophet until Ali, son-in-law of Muhammad, was assassinated and the general Muawiyah reestablished the Umayyad dynasty in 661. This dynasty would rule until it, in turn, was overthrown in 750. As one of its first actions, the Umayyad dynasty moved the capital of the Muslim empire from Medina to Damascus in Syria. This internal dissension over the caliphate created a split in Islam between the Shiítes, or those who accepted only the descendants of Ali, Muhammad's son-in-law, as the true rulers, and the Sunnites, who claimed that the descendants of the Umayyads were the true caliphs. This seventh-century split in Islam has lasted until the present day.

The internal crisis did not stop the Islamic expansion, however. At the beginning of the eighth century, new attacks were made at both the western and eastern ends

▼ **Muslims Celebrate the End of Ramadan.** Ramadan is the holy month of Islam during which all Muslims must fast from dawn to sunset. Observance of this holy month is regarded as one of the "five pillars" of Islam. Muhammad created the fast during his stay at Medina. It was designed to replace the single Jewish Day of Atonement. This Persian miniature depicts Muslims on horseback celebrating the end of Ramadan.

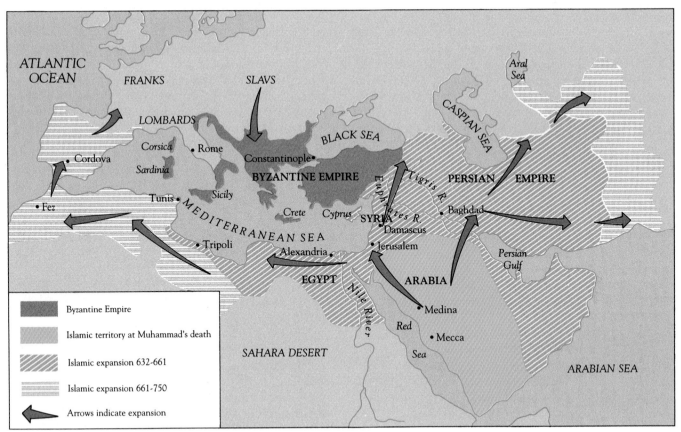

▼ **Map 7.4** The Expansion of Islam.

of the Mediterranean world. After sweeping across northern Africa and adding the Berbers, a north African people, to their army after their conversion to Islam, the Muslims invaded Germanic Europe by moving into Spain around 710. The Visigothic kingdom, already weakened by internecine warfare, collapsed, and by 725 most of Spain had become a Muslim state with its center at Córdoba. By 730, a Muslim army, making a foray into southern France, was defeated by the army of Charles Martel near Poitiers in 732. Some historians feel that internal exhaustion would have forced the Muslims to retreat anyway. Meanwhile, in 717, another Muslim force was launching an attack on Constantinople with the hope of destroying the Byzantine Empire. In the spring of 718, the Byzantines' use of Greek fire destroyed the Muslim fleet and saved the Byzantine Empire and indirectly Christian Europe, since the fall of Constantinople would no doubt have opened the door to Muslim invasion of eastern Europe. The Byzantine Empire and Islam now established an uneasy frontier in southern Asia Minor.

Islamic expansion had finally been stopped, but not before the southern and eastern Mediterranean parts of the old Roman Empire had been conquered. Islam had truly become heir to the lion's share of the old Roman Empire. The Umayyad dynasty at Damascus now ruled an enormous empire. While expansion had conveyed untold wealth and new ethnic groups into the fold of Islam, it also brought contact with Byzantine and Persian civilization. As a result, the new Arab empire would be influenced by Greek culture as well as the older civilizations of the ancient Near East. The children of the conquerors would be educated in new ways and produce a brilliant culture that would eventually influence western Europe intellectually.

The period from 400 to 750 was both chaotic and creative. Three new entities fell heir to Roman civilization: the German successor states, the Byzantine Empire, and the world of Islam. In the west, Roman elements combined with German and Celtic influences; in the east, Greek and eastern elements of late antiquity were of more consequence. Although the successor states of the west and the Byzantine civilization of the east came to share a common bond in Christianity, it proved incapable of keeping them in harmony politically as the two civilizations continued to move apart. Christianity, however, remained a dominant influence in both civilizations and in the west was especially important as a civilizing agent that brought pagan peoples into a new European civilization that was slowly being born. The rise of Islam, Rome's third heir, resulted in the loss of the southern and eastern Mediterranean worlds of the old Roman Empire to a religious power hostile to Christianity. The new Islamic empire forced Europe proper back upon itself, and slowly, a new civilization emerged that became the heart of what we know as Western civilization.

Notes

▼ ▼ ▼

1. The Creed of Nicaea, in Henry Bettenson, ed., *Documents of the Christian Church* (London, 1963), p. 35.
2. Matthew, 16: 15–19.
3. R. C. Petry, ed., *A History of Christianity: Readings in the History of Early and Medieval Christianity* (Englewood Cliffs, N.J., 1962), p. 70.
4. Brian Pullan, ed., *Sources for the History of Medieval Europe* (Oxford, 1966), p. 46.
5. Tertullian, "The Prescriptions against the Heretics," in *The Library of Christian Classics*, vol. 5, *Early Latin Theology*, ed. and trans. S. L. Greenslade (Philadelphia, 1956), p. 36.
6. Saint Augustine, *The Confessions*, trans. Edward B. Pusey (New York, 1957), p. 22.
7. Anne Fremantle, ed., *A Treasury of Early Christianity* (New York, 1953), p. 91.
8. Mark, 10: 21.
9. Norman F. Cantor, ed., *The Medieval World: 300–1300* (New York, 1963), pp. (in order of quotations) 104, 101, 108, 103.

10. Ernest F. Henderson, *Select Historical Documents of the Middle Ages* (London, 1892), p. 182.
11. Ibid., p. 181.
12. Quoted in Sidney Painter and Brian Tierney, *Western Europe in the Middle Ages, 300–1475* (New York, 1983), p. 106.
13. Bede, *A History of the English Church and People*, trans. Leo Sherley-Price (Harmondsworth, 1968), pp. 86–87.
14. Ibid., p. 87.
15. Cassiodorus, *An Introduction to Divine and Human Readings*, trans. Leslie Jones (New York, 1969), p. 205.
16. Quoted in Cantor, *The Medieval World, 300–1300*, pp. 84–85.
17. Procopius, *Secret History*, trans. Richard Atwater (Ann Arbor, Mich., 1963), p. 3.
18. Procopius, *Buildings of Justinian* (Palestine Pilgrims' Text Society, 1897), pp. (in order of quotations) 9, 6–7, 11.

Suggestions for Further Reading

▼ ▼ ▼

Good general histories of the entire medieval period can be found in S. Painter and B. Tierney, *Western Europe in the Middle Ages, 1300–1475* (New York, 1983); E. Peters, *Europe and the Middle Ages*, 2d ed. (Englewood Cliffs, N.J., 1989); and G. Holmes, ed., *The Oxford Illustrated History of Medieval Europe* (Oxford, 1988). For a superb illustrated introduction to medieval civilization, see D. Rice, ed., *The Dark Ages: The Making of European Civilization* (London, 1965); and J. Evans, *The Flowering of the Middle Ages* (London, 1966).

Brief histories of the period covered in this chapter include M. Grant, *Dawn of the Middle Ages* (New York, 1981), which contains a lively text and excellent illustrations; and H. St. L. B. Moss, *The Birth of the Middle Ages, 395–814* (Oxford, 1935).

For brief, general works on the Christian church, see H. Chadwick, *The Early Church* (Baltimore, 1967); and R. W. Southern, *Western Society and the Church in the Middle Ages* (Baltimore, 1970). On church dogma, see J. Pelikan, *The Spirit of Eastern Christendom* (Chicago,

1974), and *The Growth of Medieval Theology* (Chicago, 1978). Aspects of Christianity in the Roman Empire are covered in E. R. Dodds, *Pagan and Christian in an Age of Anxiety* (New York, 1965); and R. A. Markus, *Christianity in the Roman World* (London, 1974). On the relationship of Christian thought to the classical tradition, see H. Chadwick, *Early Christian Thought and the Classical Tradition* (Oxford, 1966); C. N. Cochrane, *Christianity and Classical Culture* (New York, 1957); and R. A. Markus, *Christianity in the Roman World* (London, 1974). On Augustine and Jerome, see P. Brown, *Augustine of Hippo* (Berkeley and Los Angeles, 1969); and J. N. D. Kelly, *Saint Jerome* (London, 1975). A brief, illustrated history of monasticism is G. Zarnecki, *The Monastic Achievement* (New York, 1972). For a more detailed account, see C. H. Lawrence, *Medieval Monasticism* (London, 1984). On Saint Benedict and the Benedictine ideal, see L. von Matt, *Saint Benedict* (London, 1961); and O. Chadwick, *The Making of the Benedictine Ideal* (London, 1981). For women in monastic life, see S. F. Wemple, *Women in Frankish Society: Marriage and the Cloister, 500–900* (Philadelphia, 1981).

For good surveys on the German tribes and their migrations, see L. Musset, *The German Invasions* (University Park, Pa., 1975); J. M. Wallace-Hadrill, *The Barbarian West*, 3d ed. (London, 1967); T. S. Burns, *A History of the Ostrogoths* (Bloomington, Ind., 1984); E. A. Thompson, *The Goths in Spain* (Oxford, 1969); E. James, *The Franks* (Oxford, 1988); and especially H. Wolfram, *The Goths*, trans. T. J. Dunlop (Berkeley, 1988). Also valuable is the revisionist work of W. Goffart, *Barbarians and Romans*, A.D. *418–554: The Techniques of Accommodation* (Princeton, N.J., 1980); and P. Geary, *Before France and Germany* (Oxford, 1988).

A brief survey of the development of the papacy can be found in G. Barraclough, *The Medieval Papacy* (New York, 1968). J. Richards, *The Popes and the Papacy in the Early Middle Ages, 476–752* (Boston, 1979) is a more detailed study of the early papacy. On Pope Gregory the Great, see the biography by J. Richards, *Consul of God: The Life and Times of Gregory the Great* (Boston, 1980). The conversion of Ireland and the significance of Celtic Christianity can be examined in K. Hughes, The *Church in Early Irish Society* (Ithaca, N.Y., 1965). On

Christianity and intellectual life, see the earlier, but still sound work of E. K. Rand, *Founders of the Middle Ages*, reprint ed. (New York, 1957); J. J. O'Donnell, *Cassiodorus* (Berkeley and Los Angeles, 1979); and P. H. Blair, *The World of Bede* (London, 1970). An important aspect of Christian culture is discussed in P. Brown, *The Cult of Saints* (Chicago, 1981).

Brief but good introductions to Byzantine history can be found in H. W. Haussig, *A History of Byzantine Civilization* (New York, 1971); J. M. Hussey, *The Byzantine World* (New York, 1961); and C. Mango, *Byzantium: The Empire of New Rome* (London, 1980). The best single political history is G. Ostrogorsky, *A History of the Byzantine State*, 2d ed. (New Brunswick, N.J., 1968). Specialized studies include J. W. Barker, *Justinian and the Later Roman Empire* (Madison, Wis., 1966); D. J. Geanakoplos, *Interaction of the Sibling Byzantine and Western Cultures in the Middle Ages and Italian Renaissance (300–1600)* (New Haven, Conn., 1976); and W. Kaegi, *Byzantium and the Decline of Rome* (Princeton, N.J., 1968) on the impact of the barbarian invasions on the Eastern Roman Empire. On Justinian, see R. Browning, *Justinian and Theodora*, 2d ed. (London, 1987). On Constantinople and daily life, see D. T. Rice, *Constantinople: From Byzantium to Istanbul* (New York, 1965); P. Sherrard, *Constantinople: Iconography of a Sacred City* (New York, 1965); and T. T. Rice, *Everyday Life in Byzantium* (New York, 1967). The role of the Christian church is discussed in J. Hussey, *The Orthodox Church in the Byzantine Empire* (Oxford, 1986).

Good brief surveys of the Islamic Middle East include A. Goldschmidt, Jr., *A Concise History of the Middle East*, 3d ed. (Boulder, Colo., 1988); and S. N. Fisher, *The Middle East: A History*, rev. ed. (New York, 1978). On the rise of Islam, see W. M. Watt, *Muhammad: Prophet and Statesman* (London, 1961); M. Lings, *Muhammad: His Life Based on the Earliest Sources* (New York, 1983); G. E. von Grunebaum, *Classical Islam: A History, 600–1258*, trans. Katherine Watson (London, 1970); F. Gabrieli, *Muhammad and the Conquests of Islam* (London, 1968); P. Crone and M. Hinds, *God's Caliph: Religious Authority in the First Centuries of Islam* (New York, 1986); and F. Donner, *The Early Islamic Conquests* (Princeton, N.J., 1980).

Chapter 8

European Civilization in the Early Middle Ages, 750–1000

▼▼▼▼▼

By the late eighth century, the contours of a new European civilization were beginning to emerge in western Europe. Increasingly, Europe would become the focus and center of Western civilization. Building upon a fusion of Germanic, classical, and Christian elements, the first visible beginnings of that medieval European world emerged in the Carolingian Empire of Charlemagne. The agrarian foundations of the eighth and ninth centuries, however, proved inadequate for the maintenance of a large monarchical system, and a new political and military order based on the decentralization of political power subsequently evolved to become an integral part of the political world of the Middle Ages.

European civilization began on a shaky and uncertain foundation, however. In the ninth century, Vikings, Magyars, and Muslims posed threats that could easily have stifled the new society. But a vibrant civilization can absorb such challenges, and European civilization did just that. The Vikings and Magyars were assimilated, and recovery slowly began to set in. By 1000, European civilization was ready to embark upon a period of dazzling vitality and expansion.

▼ Population and Environment

There exists little certainty about the precise number of people in early medieval Europe. In all probability, the losses caused by the plagues of the sixth and seventh centuries had not been compensated for by the eighth century. Historians generally believe that in the Early Middle Ages Europe was a sparsely populated landscape

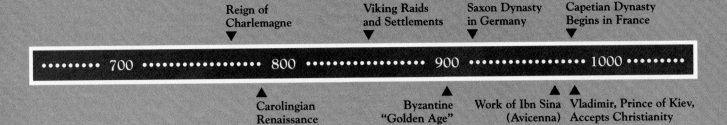

Reign of
Charlemagne
▼

Viking Raids
and Settlements
▼

Saxon Dynasty
in Germany
▼

Capetian Dynasty
Begins in France
▼

•••••••• 700 ••••••••••• 800 •••••••••••••••• 900 ••••••••••••••• 1000 ••••••••

▲
Carolingian
Renaissance

▲
Byzantine
"Golden Age"

▲
Work of Ibn Sina
(Avicenna)

▲
Vladimir, Prince of Kiev,
Accepts Christianity

dotted with villages and groups of villages of farmers and warriors. Although rivers, such as the Loire, Seine, Rhine, Elbe, and Oder, served as major arteries of communication, villages were still separated from one another by forests, swamps, and mountain ridges. Forests, which provided building and heating materials as well as game, continued to dominate the European landscape. In fact, it has been estimated that less than 10 percent of the land was cultivated, a figure so small that some economic historians believe that Europe had difficulty feeding even its small population. Thus, hunting and fishing were necessary to supplement the European diet.

The cultivation of new land proved especially difficult in the Early Middle Ages. Given the crude implements of the time, it was not easy to clear forests and cultivate new land. Moreover, German tribes had for centuries considered trees sacred and resisted cutting them down to clear land for farming. Even their conversion to Christianity did not entirely change these attitudes. In addition, the heavy soils of northern Europe were not easily plowed. The methods of agriculture also worked against significant crop yields. Land was allowed to lie fallow (idle) every other year to regain its fertility, but even so it produced low yields. Evidence shows that Frankish estates yielded incredibly low ratios of two measures of grain to one measure of seed. Although climatic patterns show that around 700 European weather began to improve after a centuries-long period of wetter and colder conditions, natural disasters were still a threat, especially since the low yields meant little surplus could be saved for bad times. Drought or too much rain could mean bad harvests, famine, and dietary deficiencies that made people particularly susceptible to a wide range of diseases. This was a period of low life expectancy. One study of Hungarian graves found that of every five skeletons, one was a child below the age of one, and two were children between one and fourteen; more than one in five was a woman below the age of twenty. Overall then, the picture of early medieval Europe is of a relatively small population subsisting on the basis of a lim-

ited agricultural economy and leading, in most cases, a precarious existence.

▼ The World of the Carolingians

During the seventh and eighth centuries, within the Frankish kingdom of western Europe, the Carolingian mayors of the palace of Neustria and Austrasia had expanded their power at the expense of the Merovingian dynasty (see Chapter 7). One of these mayors, Charles Martel, provided the military leadership to defend the Frankish kingdom against the Muslims. Pepin, the son of Charles Martel, finally took the logical step of deposing the decadent Merovingians and assuming the kingship of the Frankish state for himself and his family.

Emergence of the Carolingian Dynasty

Pepin had hesitated to usurp the throne since the Merovingian rulers had a blood right to be kings. To justify his action, he sought the advice of Pope Zacharias I (741–752), who, for his own political reasons, reassured Pepin:

> Burchard, bishop of Würzburg, and Fulrad, priest and chaplain, were sent [by Pepin] to pope Zacharias to ask his advice in regard to the kings who were then ruling in France, who had the title of king but no real royal authority. The pope replied by these ambassadors that it would be better that he who actually had the power should be called king.[1]

Pepin's actions constituted a papal-approved revolution that created a new form of Frankish kingship. Pepin was crowned king and formally anointed by a representative of the pope with holy oil in imitation of an Old Testament practice. As it was said of David, "Then Samuel took the horn of oil, and anointed him in the midst of his brethren: and the Spirit of the Lord came upon David from that day forward."[2] Whereas only priests had been anointed before, so now were Frankish kings; the anointing not only symbolized that the kings had been entrusted with a sacred office but also provides yet another example of how a Germanic institution fused with a Christian practice in the Early Middle Ages.

As Pope Zacharias had hoped, the anointing of Pepin (751–768) as the new king of the Franks led to practical benefits for the papacy, including an alliance between the new Frankish king and the Roman popes. The latter were being seriously threatened by the Lombards, who had captured Ravenna, one of the chief remaining centers of Byzantine power in Italy, and now menaced Rome itself. The popes had relied on the Byzantine presence in Italy for military protection. However, because of the Muslim threat and the disagreement between the Roman pontiffs and the Byzantine emperors over the iconoclastic controversy (see Chapter 7), the Byzantines refused papal

requests for assistance. Pope Stephen II (752–757) turned to the Franks instead and received promises of aid from the newly crowned Pepin. Pepin made a number of expeditions to Italy, defeated the Lombards, and granted to the papacy conquered lands (the so-called Donation of Pepin) in central Italy that added to church holdings around Rome. This area became known as the Papal States, the papacy's own territorial state in central Italy, which the popes managed to retain until 1870.

Charlemagne and the Carolingian Empire (768–814)

Pepin's death in 768 brought to the throne of the Frankish kingdom a dynamic and powerful ruler known to history as Charles the Great or Charlemagne (from *Carolus magnus* in Latin). Charlemagne was a determined and decisive man, highly intelligent and inquisitive. A fierce warrior, he was also a resolute statesman and a wise patron of learning (see the box on p. 235). He greatly expanded the territory of the Carolingian Empire during his lengthy rule.

EXPANSION OF THE CAROLINGIAN EMPIRE In the tradition of the Germanic kings, Charlemagne was a determined warrior who undertook fifty-four military campaigns. Even though the Frankish army was relatively small—only 8,000 men gathered each spring for campaigning—supplying it and transporting it to distant areas could still present serious problems. The Frankish army comprised mostly infantry with some cavalry armed with swords and spears.

After ascending the Frankish throne, it soon became evident to Charlemagne that Pepin's arrangements in Italy would not last. In 773, Charlemagne led his army into Italy, crushed the Lombards, and took control of the Lombard state. Although his son was crowned as king of Italy, Charlemagne was its real ruler.

Four years after his invasion of Italy, Charlemagne moved his forces into northern Spain. This campaign proved to be disappointing; his army was harassed by the Basques while crossing the Pyrenees to return home, and his rear guard was ambushed. Later Charlemagne established the Spanish March, a stretch of territory south of the Pyrenees that was strongly fortified and served as a defensive bulwark against the Muslim forces in Spain.

Charlemagne was considerably more successful in his eastern campaigns into Germany, especially against the Saxons located between the Elbe River and the North Sea. As Einhard, Charlemagne's biographer, recounted it:

▼ **Gold Equestrian Statue of Charlemagne.** This statue is believed to represent the emperor Charles the Great. While he was an able warrior and greatly increased the size of the Frankish kingdom, Charlemagne also worked to organize his state, to reform the church, and to foster education. Charlemagne's empire was held together by the charisma of its ruler, and when he died, his vast state eventually disintegrated.

A Description of Charlemagne
▼ ▼ ▼

E inhard, the biographer of Charlemagne, was born in the valley of the Main River in Germany about 775. Raised and educated in the monastery of Fulda, an important center of learning, he arrived at the court of Charlemagne in 791 or 792. Einhard was an important addition to Charlemagne's palace school headed by Alcuin. Although he did not achieve high office under Charlemagne, he served as private secretary to Louis the Pious, Charlemagne's son and successor. Einhard's Life of Charlemagne was modeled on Suetonius's Lives of the Caesars, especially his biography of Augustus. Einhard's work, written between 817 and 830, was the "first medieval biography of a lay figure." In this selection, he describes the person and character of Charlemagne.

Einhard, *Life of Charlemagne*

Charles was large and strong, and of lofty stature, though not disproportionately tall . . . ; the upper part of his head was round, his eyes very large and animated, nose a little long, hair fair, and face laughing and merry. Thus his appearance was always stately and dignified, whether he was standing or sitting; although his neck was thick and somewhat short, and his belly rather prominent; but the symmetry of the rest of his body concealed these defects. His gait was firm, his whole carriage manly, and his voice clear, but not so strong as his size led one to expect. His health was excellent, except during the four years preceding his death, when he was subject to frequent fevers; at the last he even limped a little with one foot. Even in those years he consulted rather his own inclinations than the advice of physicians, who were almost hateful to him, because they wanted him to give up roasts, to which he was accustomed, and to eat boiled meat instead. In accordance with the national custom, he took frequent exercise on horseback and in the chase, accomplishments in which scarcely any people in the world can equal the Franks. He enjoyed the exhalations from natural warm springs, and often practiced swimming, in which he was such an adept that none could surpass him; and hence it was that he built his palace at Aachen, and lived there constantly during his latter years until his death. He used not only to invite his sons to his bath, but his nobles and friends, and now and then a troop of his retinue or bodyguard, so that a hundred or more persons sometimes bathed with him. . . .

Charles was temperate in eating, and particularly so in drinking, for he abominated drunkenness in anybody, much more in himself and those of his household; but he could not easily abstain from food, and often complained that fasts injured his health. He very rarely gave entertainments, only on great feast days, and then to large numbers of people. His meals ordinarily consisted of four courses, not counting the roast, which his huntsmen used to bring in on the spit; he was more fond of this than of any other dish. While at the table, he listened to reading or music. The subjects of the readings were the stories and deeds of olden time: he was fond, too, of St. Augustine's books, and especially of the one entitled "The City of God." He was so moderate in the use of wine and all sorts of drink that he rarely allowed himself more than three cups in the course of a meal. In summer, after the midday meal, he would eat some fruit, drain a single cup, put off his clothes and shoes, just as he did for the night, and rest for two or three hours. He was in the habit of awaking and rising from bed four or five times during the night. While he was dressing and putting on his shoes, he not only gave audience to his friends, but if the Count of the Palace told him of any suit in which judgment was necessary, he had the parties brought before him forthwith, took cognizance of the case, and gave his decision, just as if he were sitting on the judgment seat. This was not the only business that he transacted at this time, but he performed any duty of the day whatever, whether he had to attend to the matter himself, or to give commands concerning it to his officers.

No war ever undertaken by the Frank nation was carried on with such persistence and bitterness, or cost so much labor, because the Saxons, like almost all the tribes of Germany, were a fierce people, given to the worship of devils, and hostile to our religion, and did not consider it dishonorable to transgress and violate all law, human and divine.[3]

Charlemagne's insistence that the Saxons convert to Christianity simply fueled their resistance. Not until 804, after eighteen campaigns, was Saxony finally pacified and added to the Carolingian domain.

In southeastern Germany, Charlemagne invaded the land of the Bavarians in 787 and brought them into his empire by the following year, an expansion that brought him into contact with the southern Slavs and the Avars. The latter disappeared from history after their utter devastation at the hands of Charlemagne's army. Now at its height, Charlemagne's empire covered much of western and central Europe; not until the time of Napoleon in the nineteenth and Hitler in the twentieth century would an empire its size be seen again in Europe.

ADMINISTRATION OF THE EMPIRE   Charlemagne continued the efforts of his father in organizing the Carolingian kingdom. Since there was no system of public taxation, Charlemagne was highly dependent upon the royal estates for the resources he needed to govern his empire. Food and goods derived from these lands provided support for the king, his household staff, and officials. To keep the nobles in his service, Charlemagne granted part of the royal lands as lifetime holdings to nobles who assisted him.

Besides the household staff, the administration of the empire depended upon the utilization of counts as the king's chief representatives in local areas, although in dangerous border districts officials known as margraves (literally, *mark graf*, count of the border district) were used. Counts were part of the nobility that had already existed under the Merovingians. They had come to control public services in their own lands and thus acted as judges, military leaders, and agents of the king. Gradually, as the rule of the Merovingian kings weakened, many counts had simply attached the royal lands and

▼ **Map 8.1** The Carolingian Empire.

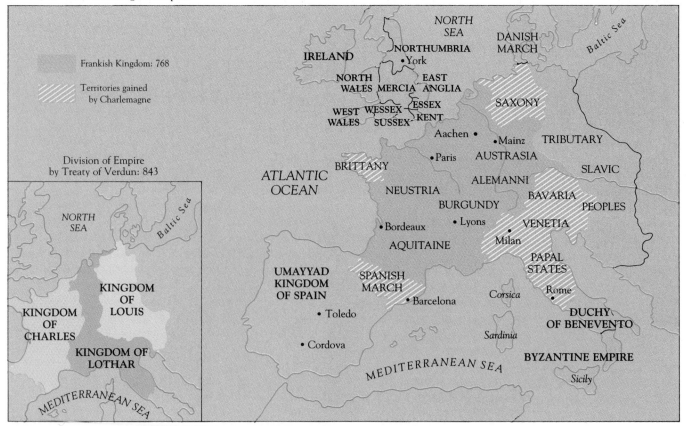

services performed on behalf of the king to their own family possessions.

In an effort to gain greater control over his kingdom, Charlemagne attempted to limit the power of the counts. They were required to serve outside their own family lands and were moved about periodically rather than being permitted to remain in a county for life. By making the offices appointive, Charlemagne tried to prevent the counts' children from automatically inheriting their offices. Moreover, as another check on the counts, Charlemagne instituted the *missi dominici* ("messengers of the lord king"), two men, one lay lord and one church official, who were sent out to local districts to ensure that the counts were executing the king's wishes. The counts also has assistants, but they were members of their households, not part of a bureaucratic office.

The last point is an important reminder that we should not think of Carolingian government in the modern sense of government offices run by officials committed to an impersonal ideal of state service. The Carolingian system was glaringly inefficient. Great distances had to be covered on horseback, making it impossible for Charlemagne and his household staff to exercise much supervision over local affairs. What held the system together was personal loyalty to the king. Since disloyalty meant the breakdown of government order, an act of treason consisted of disloyalty to the lord to whom one had taken an oath of allegiance.

Charlemagne also realized that the Catholic church could provide invaluable assistance in governing his kingdom. By the late seventh century, the system of ecclesiastical government within the Christian church that had been created in the late Roman Empire had largely disintegrated. Church offices were not filled or were often held by grossly unqualified relatives of the royal family. After an impetus for regeneration had come from Saint Boniface (See Chapter 7), both Pepin and his son Charlemagne took up the cause of church reform by creating new bishoprics and archbishoprics, restoring old ones, and seeing to it that the clergy accepted the orders of their superiors and executed their duties. Although the church failed at times to appreciate the degree to which Charlemagne saw himself as its caretaker, the king did gain significant support from the church in return for his efforts.

In examining the governmental machinery of the Carolingian Empire, it is important to realize that Charlemagne's kingdom was held together not by the Christianity that was common to the entire kingdom or by any powerful administrative system, but largely by

▼ **Charlemagne's Palace at Aachen.** Construction of the palace chapel at Aachen pictured here began in the early 790s. Charlemagne's throne is located on the first floor, directly over the main altar. To govern his kingdom better, Charlemagne worked to limit the power of his representatives, the counts, and to gain the loyalty of the nobility by granting them parts of the royal lands.

loyalty to a single ruler who was strong enough to ensure loyalty by force when necessary. The Carolingian system worked as long as it had a powerful and energetic ruler like Charlemagne. But even during the last years of Charlemagne's reign, as his energy began to wane, the Carolingian Empire itself began to disintegrate, a process that would continue after his death.

CHARLEMAGNE AS EMPEROR   As Charlemagne's power grew, so too did his prestige as the most powerful Christian ruler; one monk even wrote of his empire as the "kingdom of Europe." Charlemagne acquired a new title in 800, but there is substantial controversy surrounding this event, and it can only be understood within the context of the relationship between the papacy and the Frankish monarchs.

We have seen in Pepin's reign the growing alliance between the kingdom of the Franks and the papacy. As a result of this alliance and the Donation of Pepin that grew out of it, papal claims to temporal power increased dramatically. In the late eighth century, the pope first brandished a document known as the Donation of Constantine, in which the Emperor Constantine in 313 supposedly gave political control of the western parts of the Roman Empire to the bishop of Rome. The document was not frequently cited, but its very appearance in the eighth century demonstrates that the popes were already interested in boosting their claims to temporal power. Although the document was a forgery, the fact was known to few people, and the Donation of Constantine was periodically cited by popes throughout the Middle Ages to bolster papal power (see the box on p. 239).

Meanwhile, in the course of the second half of the eighth century, the popes increasingly severed their ties with the Byzantine Empire and drew closer to the Frankish kingdom. Charlemagne encouraged this development. In 799, after a rebellion against his authority, Pope Leo III (795–816) managed to escape from Rome and flee to safety at Charlemagne's court. Charlemagne assisted him, and when he went to Rome in November 800 to settle affairs, he was received by the pope like an emperor. On Christmas Day 800, after mass, Pope Leo placed a crown on Charlemagne's head and proclaimed him emperor of the Romans.

The significance of this imperial coronation has been much debated by historians. We are not even sure whether it was the pope or Charlemagne who initiated the idea or whether Charlemagne was pleased or displeased. His biographer Einhard claimed that "at first [he] had such an aversion that he declared that he would not have set foot in the Church the day that they were conferred, although it was a great feastday, if he could have foreseen the design of the Pope."[4] But Charlemagne also perceived the usefulness of the imperial title; after all, he was now on a level of equality with the Byzantine emperor, a status he did not reject. Moreover, the papacy now had a defender of great stature, even though later popes in the Middle Ages became involved in fierce struggles with emperors over who possessed the higher power.

In any case, Charlemagne's coronation as Roman emperor certainly demonstrated the strength, even after 300 years, of the concept of an enduring Roman Empire. More importantly, it symbolized the fusion of those Roman, Christian, and Germanic elements that constituted the foundation of European civilization. A Germanic king had been crowned emperor of the Romans by the spiritual leader of Western Christendom. A new civilization had emerged.

▼ **The Crowning of Charlemagne.** A rebellion in 799 against his authority forced Pope Leo III to seek safety at Charlemagne's court. On Christmas Day 800, after having gone to Rome to settle the affair, Charlemagne was crowned emperor of the Romans by the pope. While the motives behind this coronation are still debated, it clearly symbolized the fusion of the Roman, Christian, and Germanic elements that formed the basis of European civilization.

The Carolingian Intellectual Renewal

Charlemagne had a strong desire to revive learning in his kingdom, an attitude that stemmed from his own intellectual curiosity as well as the need to provide educated clergy for the church and literate officials for the government. His efforts led to a revival of learning and culture that some historians have labeled a Carolingian Renaissance or "rebirth" of learning.

The term is only partly appropriate, since the Carolingian era is hardly known for outstanding creativity and originality of ideas. There did occur, however, a true revival of classical studies and an attempt to assimilate and preserve Latin and early Christian culture. This goal

The Donation of Constantine
▼ ▼ ▼

O ne of the major documents used by the popes to bolster their claim to temporal power was the Donation of Constantine. Purportedly, this was a fourth-century document in which the Emperor Constantine, in gratitude for being cured of leprosy by Pope Sylvester, had granted complete political supremacy over the western empire to the popes. The document was actually a forgery, probably created in the second half of the eighth century, although it was not until the fifteenth century that the scholar Lorenzo Valla decisively proved its lack of authenticity.

The Donation of Constantine

And when, the blessed Sylvester preaching them, I perceived these things, and learned that by the kindness of St. Peter himself I had been entirely restored to health: I . . . considered it advisable that, as on earth he [Peter] is seen to have been constituted vicar of the Son of God, so the pontiffs, who are the representatives of that same chief of the apostles, should obtain from us and our empire the power of a supremacy greater than the earthly clemency of our imperial serenity is seen to have had conceded to it—we choosing that same prince of the apostles, or his vicars, to be our constant intercessors with God. And, to the extent of our earthly imperial power, we decree that his holy Roman church shall be honored with veneration; and that, more than our empire and earthly throne, the most sacred seat of St. Peter shall be gloriously exalted; we giving to it the imperial power, and dignity of glory, and vigor and honor.

And we ordain and decree that he shall have the supremacy as well over the four chief seats Antioch, Alexandria, Constantinople and Jerusalem, as also over all the churches of God in the whole world. And he who for the time being shall be pontiff of that holy Roman church shall be more exalted than, and chief over, all the priests of the whole world; and, according to his judgment, everything which is to be provided for the service of God or the stability of the faith of the Christians is to be administered. . . .

In imitation of our own power, in order that for that cause the supreme pontificate may not deteriorate, but may rather be adorned with power and glory even more than is the dignity of an earthly rule: behold we—giving over to the oft-mentioned most blessed pontiff, our father Sylvester the universal pope, as well our palace, as has been said, as also the city of Rome and all the provinces, districts and cities of Italy or of the western regions; and relinquishing them, by our inviolable gift, to the power and sway of himself or the pontiffs his successors—do decree, by this our godlike charter and imperial constitution, that it shall be (so) arranged; and do concede that they (the palaces, provinces, etc.) shall lawfully remain with the holy Roman church.

Wherefore we have perceived it to be fitting that our empire and the power of our kingdom should be transferred and changed to the regions of the East; and that, in the province of Byzantium, in a most fitting place, a city should be built in our name; and that our empire should there be established. For, where the supremacy of priests and the head of the Christian religion has been established by a heavenly Ruler, it is not just that there an earthly ruler should have jurisdiction.

---

became a major task of the monasteries, many of which had been established by the Irish and English missionaries of the seventh and eighth centuries (see Chapter 7). By the ninth century, the "work" required of Benedictine monks was the copying of manuscripts. Monasteries established *scriptoria* or writing rooms, where monks copied not only the works of early Christianity, such as the Bible and the treatises of the Church Fathers, but also the works of Latin classical authors. The head of the *scriptorium* became one of the important offices of the monastery.

Following the example of Irish and English monks, their Carolingian counterparts developed new ways of producing books. Their texts were written on pages made of parchment or sheepskin rather than papyrus and then bound in covers decorated with jewels and precious metals. Carolingian monastic scribes also developed a new writing style called the Carolingian minuscule. This was really printing rather than cursive writing and was far easier to read than the Merovingian cursive script.

The production of illuminated manuscripts in Carolingian monastic *scriptoria* was a crucial factor in the preservation of the ancient legacy. About 8,000 manuscripts, many of them in Carolingian minuscule script, survive from Carolingian times. Virtually 90 percent of the ancient Roman works that we have today exist because they were copied by Carolingian monks. Without the work of the medieval monks, there would not have been any later Renaissance or "rebirth" of learning such as occurred in the twelfth and especially fourteenth and fifteenth centuries.

Charlemagne personally encouraged learning by establishing a palace school and encouraging scholars from all over Europe to come to the Carolingian court. These included men of letters from Italy, Spain, Germany, and Ireland. Most well known was Alcuin, called by Einhard the "greatest scholar of that day." He was from the famous school at York that was a product of the great revival of learning in the Anglo-Saxon kingdom of Northumbria. From 782 to 796, while serving at Charle-

magne's court as an adviser on ecclesiastical affairs, Alcuin also provided the leadership for Charlemagne's palace school. He concentrated on the teaching of classical Latin and adopted Cassiodorus's sevenfold division of knowledge known as the liberal arts (see Chapter 7), which became the basis for all later medieval education. All in all, the Carolingian Renaissance played a crucial role in keeping the classical heritage alive as well as maintaining the intellectual life of the Catholic church.

Life in the Carolingian World

In daily life as well as intellectual life, the newly emerging European world of the Carolingian era witnessed a fusion of Gallo-Roman, Germanic, and Christian practices. The latter in particular seems to have exercised an ever-increasing influence.

▼ **Bible Manuscript Made at Tours.** Charlemagne's attempts to revive learning led to what has been called the Carolingian Renaissance. In trying to renew classical art, the king commissioned a number of artists and scholars to create new manuscripts. This miniature of Moses presenting the Ten Commandments comes from a Bible manuscript made at Tours after Charlemagne's death. Those receiving the law are depicted as Charlemagne and his court.

THE FAMILY AND MARRIAGE   By Carolingian times, the Catholic church had begun to make a significant impact upon Frankish family life and marital and sexual attitudes. As we have seen, in Frankish society marriages were arranged by fathers or uncles to meet the needs of the extended family. Although wives were expected to be faithful to their husbands, Frankish aristocrats often possessed concubines, either slave girls or free women from their estates. Even the "most Christian king" Charlemagne kept a number of concubines.

To limit such sexual license, the church increasingly emphasized its role in marriage and attempted to Christianize it. Although marriage was a civil arrangement, priests tried to add their blessings and strengthen the concept of a special marriage ceremony. A local church council in 755 stated that all "lay folks . . . should celebrate their nuptials publicly." Moreover, the church tried to serve as the caretaker of marriage by stipulating that a girl over fifteen must give her consent to her guardian's choice of a husband or her marriage was not valid in the eyes of the church. Slowly, the church was moving toward the institutionalization of marriage as a sacrament, a goal not achieved until the twelfth century.

To stabilize marriages, the church also began to emphasize monogamy and permanence. A Frankish church council in 789 stipulated that marriage was an "indissoluble sacrament" and condemned the practice of concubinage and easy divorce. At first, the church tried to restrict divorce by limiting it for the most part to two cases: the flagrant adultery of the wife or the impotence of the husband. But during the reign of Emperor Louis the Pious (814–840), the church finally won the right to prohibit divorce. It was now expected that the man who married must remain with his wife "even though she were sterile, deformed, old, dirty, drunken, a frequenter of bad company, lascivious, vain, greedy, unfaithful, quarrelsome, abusive . . . for when that man was free, he freely engaged himself."[5] This was not easily accepted since monogamy and indissoluble marriages were viewed as obstacles to the well-established practice of concubinage. It was not until the tenth century that divorce was largely stamped out among both the common people and the nobility.

The acceptance and spread of the Catholic church's marital views on the indissolubility of marriage encouraged the development of the nuclear family at the expense of the extended family. Although the kin was still an influential social and political force, the conjugal unit came to be seen as the basic unit of society. The new practice of young couples establishing their own households brought a dynamic element to European society and contributed to the growth of urban life in the eleventh and twelfth centuries. It also had a significant impact on women. In the extended family, the eldest woman controlled all the other female members; in the nuclear family, the wife was still dominated by her husband, but at least she now had control of her own household and children (see the box on p. 242).

CHRISTIANITY AND SEXUALITY   The early church fathers had stressed that celibacy and a complete abstinence from sexual activity constituted an ideal state superior to marriage. Subsequently, the early church gradually developed a case for clerical celibacy although it proved impossible to enforce in the Early Middle Ages. Not until the Gregorian reform movement of the eleventh century would the Catholic church attempt to enforce its standard of clerical celibacy (see Chapter 10).

The early fathers had also emphasized, however, that not all people had the self-discipline to remain celibate. It was thus permissible to marry, as Paul had indicated in his first epistle to the Corinthians: "It is good for a man not to touch a woman. Nevertheless, to avoid fornication, let every man have his own wife, and let every woman have her own husband. . . . I say therefore to the unmarried and widows, It is good for them if they abide even as I. But if they cannot contain, let them marry: for it is better to marry than to burn [with desire]."[6] The church then viewed marriage as the lesser of two evils; it was a concession to human weakness and fulfilled the need for companionship, sex, and children. Although there was much debate within the church about marriage in the Early Middle Ages, it was generally agreed that marriage gave the right to indulge in sexual intercourse. Sex, then, was permissible within marriage, but only so long as it was used for the sole purpose of procreation or the begetting of children, not for pleasure.

Since the church developed the tradition that sexual relations between man and wife were only legitimate if done for purposes of procreation, it condemned all forms of contraception. The church also strongly condemned abortion, although its prohibition failed to stop the practice. Various herbal potions, whose formulas were included in writings from Roman and Byzantine doctors, were available to prevent conception or cause abortion. These concoctions included such substances as fern roots, rue, willow leaves, pepper, and saffron. The Catholic church accepted only one way to limit children, by either periodic or total abstinence from intercourse.

The Catholic church's condemnation of sexual activity outside marriage also included homosexuality. Nei-

The Responsibilities of a Carolingian Aristocratic Wife
▼ ▼ ▼

The wife of a Carolingian aristocrat bore numerous responsibilities. She was entrusted with the management of the household and even the administration of extensive landed estates while her husband was absent in the royal service or on a military campaign. A wife was also expected to bear large numbers of children and to supervise their upbringing. This selection by Dhouda, wife of Bernard, marquis of Septimania (in southern France), is taken from a manual written by her to instruct her son on his duties to his new lord, King Charles the Bald (840–877).

Dhouda of Septimania, *Manual*

An admonition relating to your lord.

Since God, as I believe, and your father Bernard have chosen you, in the flower of your youth, to serve Charles as your lord, I urge you ever to remember the record of your family, illustrious on both sides, and not to serve your master simply to satisfy him outwardly, but to maintain towards him and his service in all things a devoted and certain fealty both of body and soul. . . . This is why, my son, I exhort you to maintain faithfully all that is in your charge, with all your strength of body and soul, as long as your life shall last. . . . May the madness of infidelity be ever far from you; may evil never find such a place in your heart as to render you unfaithful to your lord in any manner whatsoever. . . . But I do not fear this on your part or on the part of those who serve with you. . . . Therefore, my son William, you who are of our blood, show yourself towards your lord, as I have already urged, true, vigilant, useful and most prompt to his service. In every matter which concerns the power and welfare of the king, both within the kingdom and without, show that wisdom with which God has plentifully endowed you. . . . And when you receive his commands, apply yourself faithfully to execute them. Observe also and regard carefully those who show the greatest fidelity and assiduity in his service, and learn of them the way in which to act.

---

ther Roman religion nor Roman law had recognized any real difference between homosexual and heterosexual eroticism, and the Roman Empire had taken no legal measures against the practice of homosexuality between adults. Later, in the Byzantine Empire, the Emperor Justinian in 538 condemned homosexuality, emphasizing that such practices brought down the wrath of God ("we have provoked Him to anger") and endangered the welfare of the state:

> For because of such crimes, there are famines, earthquakes, and pestilences; wherefore we admonish men to abstain from the aforesaid unlawful acts, that they may not lose their souls. . . . We order the most illustrious prefect of the capital to arrest those who persist in the aforesaid lawless and impious acts after they have been warned by us, and to inflict on them the extreme punishments, so that the city and the state may not come to harm by reason of such wicked deeds.[7]

Justinian recommended that the guilty parties be punished by castration. Although the church in the Early Middle Ages viewed homosexuality similarly and condemned it, it also pursued a flexible policy in its treatment of homosexuals. In the Early Middle Ages, homosexuals were treated less harshly than married couples who practiced contraception. Between the seventh and tenth centuries, the Catholic hierarchy did not seem overly concerned with homosexual behavior. A fundamental change in the church's policy would not come until the eleventh century.

CHILDREN   The Catholic church also had an impact upon another aspect of family life—children. The ancient Romans had limited their family size by the practice of infanticide or the exposure of unwanted children, which was accepted in classical society. Romans had then paid much attention to the children chosen to survive, as is especially evident in the education of upper-class children. In the emerging early medieval world, barbarian practices of child rearing became influential. Although the Germans had large families, it is questionable how much they valued their children. As we saw in Chapter 7, the Germanic law codes listed *wergelds*, whose size represented a crude evaluation of a person's importance. According to the Visigothic code of the mid-seventh century, for example, male children were valued at 60 solidi. At the age of twenty, when they had become warriors, the *wergeld* increased fivefold to 300 solidi, where it remained until the adult male

buildings. In addition, there was a separate guest house for travelers of high rank with two heated rooms, servants' bedrooms, and stables for horses. It was customary for monasteries to have two guest houses, one for the rich and another for the poor. In the Early Middle Ages, however, one could not always be sure of hospitality. The famous English missionary to Germany, Saint Boniface, reported that female pilgrims to Rome had been forced to become prostitutes in every town along their route in order to obtain their sustenance and reach their goal. The church responded by forbidding females to go on such pilgrimages.

DIET AND HEALTH   The basic staple in the Carolingian diet for both rich and poor was bread. The aristocratic classes, as well as the monks, favored white bread and

reached fifty, after which it again declined. Female children were valued at only one-half that of males, although their value also jumped tremendously (to 250 solidi) between the ages of fifteen and forty because of their importance as bearers of children.

Although the Christian church condemned infanticide, it was not able to eliminate its practice, especially among the poor and those who had been seduced and did not want to keep their illegitimate offspring. Nevertheless, priests tried to discourage such practices by encouraging people to abandon their children in churches. Oftentimes, such children were taken in by monasteries and raised to be monks. Following the example of Christ's love for children, monks tended to respect and preserve the virtues of childhood. As children grew older, however, the "master of the boys," who was responsible for their education, considered it necessary to use strict discipline to control what was considered the natural inclination of children to sin, especially by disobeying their elders.

TRAVEL   Monasteries served another important function in the early medieval world as providers of hospitality. Both monasteries and aristocratic households were expected to provide a place to stay for weary travelers who were ever at risk from thieves or violence of many kinds. Indeed, Burgundian law stipulated that "anyone who refused to offer a visitor shelter and warmth shall pay a fine of three solidi."[8] Hospitality, then, was a sacred duty, and monasteries were especially active in providing it. The plan for the monastery of Saint Gall, for example, provided pilgrims and paupers with a separate house containing benches, two dormitories, and out-

▼ **Pilgrim Souvenirs.** This sixth-century metal flask depicting the Ascension of Christ is a souvenir brought back from the Holy Land to Rome by pilgrims. Pilgrimages were common in the Early Middle Ages. Since the pilgrim was subject to thievery and violence, both monasteries and noble houses were expected to offer hospitality and shelter to travelers.

consumed it in large quantities. Ovens at the monastery of Saint Gall were able to bake 1,000 loaves of bread. Carolingian white bread was quite different, however, from modern white bread, for it was made of pure wheat flour with only the hulls and chaff removed. The lower classes ate a much coarser bread made of whole wheat flour with rye, barley, or oats added. Sometimes, a gruel made of barley and oats was substituted for bread in the peasant diet. Besides bread, peasants supplemented their diet with vegetables, such as lettuce, onions, peas, beans, and turnips, grown in their own small garden plots.

The upper classes in Carolingian society had a substantially more varied diet. They ate little beef and mutton since cattle were raised for dairy cows and oxen to pull plows while sheep were kept for wool. Pork served as the major red meat. Domestic pigs, allowed to run wild in forested areas to find their own food, were rounded up and slaughtered in the fall, then smoked and salted to last the winter. Since Carolingian aristocrats were especially fond of roasted meat, hunting wild game became one of their favorite activities. In place of meats, Carolingians also ate fish caught in streams or rivers or kept in well-stocked fish ponds, which enabled people to eat it fresh. Fish were also salted or smoked for longer use.

Dairy products became common in the Carolingian diet. Chickens were kept not as a regular source of meat, but for their eggs. Since milk spoiled quickly, it was made into cheese and butter. While the Greeks and Romans had used olive oil for cooking, the harsher northern climate did not permit the growth of olive trees, and butter was used for cooking instead. Finally, vegetables also formed a crucial part of Carolingian diets, whether of the rich or poor. These included legumes, such as beans, peas, and lentils, and roots, such as garlic, onions, and carrots.

The Carolingian diet, especially of the upper classes, was also heavily dependent on honey and spices. Honey was used as a sweetener, both for foods and for many drinks, including wine and ale. Spices included domestic varieties, such as thyme, sage, and chives that were grown in home gardens, and more exotic—and outrageously expensive—varieties imported from the east, such as pepper, cumin, cloves, and cinnamon. Aristocrats were especially fond of spicy dishes, not only for their taste, but as a sign of prestige and wealth; spices were also believed to aid the digestion.

Everyone in Carolingian society, including abbots and monks, drank heavily and often to excess. Taverns became a regular feature of life and were found everywhere: in marketplaces, pilgrimage centers, and on royal, episcopal, and monastic estates. Drinking contests were not unusual; one penitential stated: "Does drunken bravado encourage you to attempt to out-drink your friends? If so, thirty days fast."

Both gluttony and drunkenness were vices shared by many people in Carolingian society. Monastic rations were greatly enlarged in the eighth century to include a daily allotment of 3.7 pounds of bread (nuns were only permitted 3 pounds), one and one-half quarts of wine or ale, 2 or 3 ounces of cheese, and 8 ounces of vegetables (4 for nuns). These rations totaled 6,000 calories a day, and since only heavy and fatty foods—bread, milk, and cheese—were considered nourishing, we begin to understand why some Carolingians were known for their potbellies. Malnutrition, however, remained a widespread problem for common people in this period.

Wine was favored above all other beverages by the aristocrats and monks. Much care was lavished on its production, especially by monasteries. Some monks even tried to take their full wine casks with them when fleeing from the invasions of the Vikings (see The Vikings later in this chapter). Although ale was considered inferior in some quarters, it was especially popular in the northern and eastern parts of the Carolingian world. Water was also drunk as a beverage, but much care had to be taken to obtain pure sources from wells or clear streams. Monasteries were particularly active in going to the sources of water and building conduits to bring it to the cloister or kitchen fountains.

Water was also used for bathing. While standards of personal hygiene were not high, medieval people did not ignore cleanliness. A royal palace, such as Charlemagne's, possessed both hot and cold baths. Carolingian aristocrats changed clothes and bathed at least once a week, on Saturdays. The Saturday bath was a regular monastic practice as well, as indeed it was for many people in the Carolingian world. To monks, bathing more than once a week seemed an unnecessary luxury; to aristocrats, it often seemed desirable.

Bathing was only one of a number of practices used by Carolingian people to avoid and cure illness. Medical practice in Carolingian times stressed the use of medicinal herbs (see the box on p. 245) and bleeding. Although the latter was practiced regularly, moderation was frequently recommended. Some advised carefulness as well: "Who dares to undertake a bleeding should see to it that his hand does not tremble."

Physicians were also available when people faced serious illnesses. Many were clerics and monasteries trained their own. Monastic libraries kept medical manuscripts copied from ancient works and grew herbs

Medical Practices in the Early Middle Ages
▼ ▼ ▼

A number of medical manuscripts written in Old English have survived from Anglo-Saxon England. Although most of the medical texts date from the tenth to twelfth centuries, scholars believe that they include copies of earlier works and contain older influences as well. As the following selections from three of these treatises illustrate, herbs were the basic materials of the Anglo-Saxon physician (or leech as he was known), and his treatments consequently focused almost entirely on botanical remedies.

The Anglo-Saxon Herbal

Cress (Nasturtium)

1. In case a man's hair falls out, take juice of the wort which one names nasturtium and by another name cress, put it on the nose, the hair shall grow.
2. This wort is not sown but it is produced of itself in springs and in brooks; also it is written that in some lands it will grow against walls.
3. For a sore head, that is for scurf and for itch, take the seed of this same wort and goose grease, pound together, it draws from off the head the whiteness of the scurf.
4. For soreness of the body [indigestion], take this same wort nasturtium and pennyroyal, soak them in water and give to drink; the soreness and the evil departs.

The Leechbook of Bald

Here are wound salves for all wounds and drinks and cleansings of every sort, whether internally or externally. Waybroad beaten and mixed with old lard, the fresh is of no use. Again, a wound salve: take waybroad seed, crush it small, shed it on the wound and soon it will be better.

For a burn, if a man be burned with fire only, take woodruff and lily and brooklime; boil in butter and smear therewith. If a man be burned with a liquid, let him take elm rind and roots of the lily, boil them in milk, smear thereon three times a day. For sunburn, boil in butter tender ivy twigs and smear thereon.

The Peri-Didaxeon

For a Broken Head

For a broken or wounded head which is caused by the humours of the head. Take betony and pound it and lay it on the wound and it will relieve all the pain.

For Sleep

Thus must one do for the man who cannot sleep; take wormwood and rub it into wine or warm water and let the man drink it and soon it will be better with him.

For Sore Hands

This leechcraft is good for sore hands and for sore fingers which is called chilblains. Take white frankincense and silver cinders and brimstone and mingle together, then take oil and add it into this mixture, then warm the hands and smear them with the mixture thus made. Wrap up the hands in a linen cloth.

to provide stocks of medicinal plants. Carolingian medical manuscripts, while deficient in comparison to those of the Byzantines and Arabs, did contain scientific descriptions of illnesses, recipes for medical potions, and even gynecological advice, although monks in particular expended little effort on female medical needs. Some manuals even included instructions for operations, especially for soldiers injured in battle. Some sources clearly demonstrate that there were accurate techniques for amputating gangrenous limbs:

> If you must cut off an unhealthy limb from a healthy body, then do not cut to the limit of the healthy flesh, but cut further into the whole and quick flesh, so that a better and quicker cure may be obtained. When you set fire on the man [ie., cauterize], take leaves of tender leek and grated salt, overlay the places so that the heat of the fire be more quickly drawn away.[9]

Although scholars are not sure whether such operations were performed without anesthesia, poppy, mandrake, and henbane were recommended in medieval manuals for their narcotic properties.

Physicians of the Early Middle Ages supplemented their medicines and natural practices with appeals for otherworldly help. Magical rites and influences were carried over from pagan times since Germanic tribes had used magical medicine for centuries. Physicians recommended that patients wear amulets and charms around their bodies to ward off diseases:

> Procure a little bit of the dung of a wolf, preferably some which contains small bits of bone, and pack it in a tube which the patient may easily wear as an amulet.
>
> For epilepsy take a nail of a wrecked ship, make it into a bracelet and set therein the bone of a stag's heart taken from its body whilst alive; put it on the left arm; you will be astonished at the result.[10]

But as pagans were converted to Christianity, miraculous healing through the intervention of God, Christ, or the saints soon replaced pagan practices. Medieval chronicles abound with accounts of people healed by touching a saint's body. The use of Christian prayers, written down and used as amulets, however, reminds us that for centuries Christian and pagan medical practices survived side by side.

▼ The Disintegration of the Carolingian Empire: Internal Dissension and New Invasions

The Carolingian Empire began to disintegrate soon after Charlemagne's death. Although Christianity was common to the entire empire, the ideal of Christian unity preached by clerics was not necessarily shared by a Frankish aristocracy inured to violence. Even Charlemagne, near the end of his life, questioned whether the Franks were "truly Christian." Charlemagne's absence from the scene soon made it apparent that he alone had held the empire together. The internal dissension that ensued after his death was a prime factor in the disintegration of the empire.

Internal Dissension

Charlemagne was survived by his son Louis the Pious (814–840). Though a decent man, he was not a strong ruler and was unable to control either the Frankish ar-

▼ **Map 8.2** Invasions of the Ninth and Tenth Centuries.

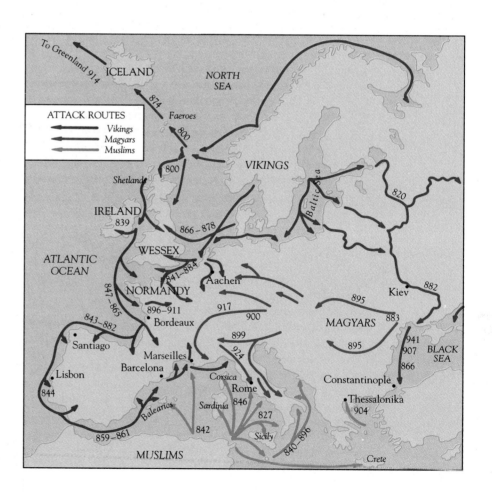

istocracy or his own four sons who fought continually. In 843, after their father's death, the three surviving brothers signed the Treaty of Verdun, which has been called by some historians the "most important treaty of medieval Europe." This agreement divided the Carolingian Empire among them into three major sections: Charles the Bald (843–877) obtained the west Frankish lands, which formed the core of the eventual kingdom of France; Louis the German (843–876) took the eastern lands, which became Germany; and Lothair (840–855) received the title of emperor and a "Middle Kingdom" extending from the North Sea to Italy, including the Netherlands, the Rhineland, and northern Italy. The territories of the Middle Kingdom became a source of incessant struggle between the other two Frankish rulers and their heirs. Indeed, France and Germany would fight over the territories of this Middle Kingdom for centuries.

Although this division of the Carolingian Empire was made for political and not nationalistic reasons, it is apparent that two different cultures were beginning to emerge. By the ninth century, inhabitants of the west Frankish area were speaking a Romance language derived from Latin that became French. Eastern Franks spoke a Germanic dialect. The later kingdoms of France and Germany, however, did not yet exist. In the ninth century, the frequent struggles among the numerous heirs of the sons of Louis the Pious led to further disintegration of the Carolingian Empire. In the meantime, while powerful aristocrats acquired even more power in their own local territories at the expense of the squabbling Carolingian rulers, the process of disintegration was further abetted by external attacks on different parts of the old Carolingian world.

Invasions of the Ninth and Tenth Centuries

Invasions and migrations of peoples were a regular experience for western Europe. The incursion of Germanic peoples had been part of the dissolution of the Western Roman Empire. The sixth-century Byzantine invasion of Italy had not produced a renewed empire, but more chaos. Later, the *jihad* of the Muslims had ended any Mediterranean unity for Christian peoples. In the ninth and tenth centuries, western Europe was beset by a new wave of invasions of several non-Christian peoples—one old enemy, the Muslims, and two new ones, the Magyars and Vikings. Although battered by these onslaughts, Christian Europe hung on and, with the exception of the Muslims, wound up assimilating the other two peoples into Christian European civilization.

MUSLIMS AND MAGYARS The first great wave of Muslim expansion had ended at the beginning of the eighth century (see Chapter 7). Gradually, the Muslims built up a series of sea bases in their occupied territories in north Africa, Spain, and southern Gaul and began a new series of attacks in the Mediterranean in the ninth century. They raided the southern coasts of Europe, especially Italy, and even threatened Rome in 843. Their invasion of Sicily in 827 eventually led to a successful occupation of the entire island. Muslim forces also destroyed the Carolingian defenses in northern Spain and conducted forays into southern France. Marauding Muslim bands then set up camps from which they could prey on pilgrims and merchants crossing the Alps.

The Magyars were a Finno-Ugrian people from western Asia. When the Byzantine emperors encouraged them to attack the troublesome Bulgars, the latter in turn encouraged a people known as the Pechenegs to attack the Magyars instead. Consequently, the Magyars, under severe Pecheneg pressure, had moved west into eastern and central Europe by the end of the ninth century. They established themselves on the plains of Hungary and from there made raids into Germany, France, and even Italy, especially between 898 and 920. The Magyars were finally crushed at the Battle of Lechfeld in Germany in 955 and, by the end of the tenth century, were converted to Christianity and settled down to establish the kingdom of Hungary.

THE VIKINGS By far, the most devastating and far-reaching attacks of the time came from the Northmen or Norsemen of Scandinavia, also known to us as the Vikings. The Vikings were a Germanic people based in Scandinavia and constitute, in a sense, the "last great wave of Germanic migration." Why they did so is not very clear to historians. The most common explanations focus on the limited resources created by overpopulation and the emergence of more effective monarchs in Denmark, Norway, and Sweden, which caused some of the freedom-loving Scandinavians to seek escape from the growing order. Others have offered more prosaic reasons: the Vikings' great love of adventure and their search for booty and new avenues of trade. Indeed, it has recently been suggested that the end of the silver trade between the Islamic Abbasid Empire and the Carolingians encouraged the Vikings to turn to piracy.

Two features of Viking society help to explain what the Vikings accomplished. First of all, they were warriors. Secondly, they were superb shipbuilders and sailors. Their ships were the best of the period. Long and narrow with beautifully carved arched prows, the Viking

▼ **Marauding Vikings.** The most devastating invasions that Europe suffered in the ninth and tenth centuries were those of the Norsemen or Vikings. Fierce warriors, the Vikings originated in the lands of Scandinavia and, through their skills as shipbuilders and sailors, reached areas as far away as Russia, the Byzantine Empire, and even Newfoundland. Carved in c. 900, this stone from Lindisfarne depicts marauding Vikings.

dragon ships carried about fifty men. They had both banks of oars and a single great sail. Their shallow draft enabled them to sail up European rivers and attack places at some distance inland. Although Viking raids in the eighth century tended to be small-scale and sporadic, they became more regular and devastating in the ninth. Vikings sacked villages and towns, destroyed churches, and easily defeated small local armies. They were mobile enough that, when threatened by a larger force, they simply fled the scene rather then engage in a pitched battle.

Since there were different groups of Scandinavians, Viking expansion varied a great deal. Norwegian Vikings moved into Ireland and western England, while the Danes attacked eastern England, Frisia, and the Rhineland and navigated rivers to enter western Frankish lands. Swedish Vikings dominated the Baltic Sea and progressed into the Slavic areas to the east. Moving into northwest Russia, they went down the rivers of Russia to Novgorod and Kiev and established fortified ports throughout these territories. There they made contact with the Byzantine Empire, either as traders or invaders. They also made contact with Arab traders on the Volga River and Sea of Azov.

Early Viking raids had been carried out largely in the summer; by the mid-ninth century, however, the Northmen had begun to build winter settlements in Europe from which they could make expeditions to conquer and settle new lands. By 850, groups of Norsemen had settled in Ireland, while the Danes occupied an area known as the Danelaw in northeast England by 878. Agreeing to accept Christianity, the Danes were eventually assimilated into a larger Anglo-Saxon kingdom. Beginning in 911, the ruler of the western Frankish lands gave one band of Vikings land at the mouth of the Seine River, forming a section of France that ultimately came to be known as Normandy. This policy of settling the Vikings and converting them to Christianity was a deliberate one, since the new inhabitants served as protectors against additional Norsemen attacks.

The Vikings were also daring explorers. After 860, they sailed westward in their long ships across the north Atlantic, reaching Iceland in 874. Erik the Red, a Viking exiled from Iceland, traveled even further west and in 985 discovered Greenland. The only known Viking site in North America was found in Newfoundland.

By the tenth century, however, Viking expansion was already drawing to a close. Greater control by the monarchs of Denmark, Norway, and Sweden over their inhabitants and the increasing Christianization of both the Scandinavian kings and peoples tended to inhibit Viking expansion, but not before Viking settlements had been established throughout many parts of Europe. Like the Magyars, the Vikings were also assimilated into European civilization. Once again, Christianity proved a decisive civilizing force in Western civilization in its European form. Europe and Christianity were virtually becoming synonymous.

The Viking raids and settlements also had important political repercussions. The inability of royal authorities to protect their peoples against these incursions caused local populations to turn to the local aristocrats who provided security for them instead. In the process, the landed aristocrats not only increased their strength and prestige but also assumed even more of the functions of local government that had previously belonged to the kings; over time these developments led to a new political and military order.

▼ The Emerging World of Fief-holding

The effects of the invasions on the disintegration of the Carolingian world can only be understood by examining the system of relationships that developed among the ruling class during the Carolingian period and looking at how these relationships influenced the structure of government. In short, we need to investigate the political, social, and military order that later generations of historians called feudalism and its beginnings in the eighth century.

Feudalism contained two component parts: a personal element called vassalage and a property element called the benefice. The practice of vassalage was derived from Germanic society and was based upon a lord attracting followers to himself on certain conditions, primarily military. It was grounded in the practice of the *comitatus*, the following of a great chief, which was described in the Roman author Tacitus's *Germania*:

> When they go into battle it is a disgrace for the chief to be surpassed in valor, a disgrace for his followers (*comitatus*) not to equal the valor of the chief. And it is an infamy and a reproach for life to have survived the chief, and returned from the field. To defend, to protect him, to ascribe one's own brave deeds to his renown, is the height of loyalty. The chief fights for victory; his vassals fight for their chief.[11]

In Germanic practice, this relationship between chief and followers was a perfectly honorable one, a relationship between social equals. By the eighth century, one who served a lord in a military capacity was known as a vassal.

Feudalism also contained a property element that was ultimately fused with the personal element of vassalage. In the late Roman Empire, it became customary for great landowners to hire retainers. To provide for the latter's maintenance, the lord provided a grant of land that was known as a benefice (Latin *beneficium*). Under the Carolingian mayors of the palace of the eighth century, the personal element of vassalage developed to the point where vassals were holding benefices. This emerged out of a king's or lord's need for fighting men, especially the newly developing cavalry. The Frankish army had originally consisted of foot soldiers, dressed in coats of mail and armed with swords. But in the eighth century, a military change began to occur when larger horses were introduced. Earlier, horsemen had been mobile archers and throwers of spears. Eventually they were armored in coats of mail and wielded long lances that enabled them to act as battering rams. For almost five hundred years, warfare in Europe would be dominated by heavily armored cavalry or knights as they came to be called. They came to have the greatest social prestige and formed the backbone of the European aristocracy.

Of course, ample resources were necessary to supply a horse, armor, and weapons. Moreover, it took time and much practice to learn to wield these weapons skillfully from a horse. Consequently, lords who wanted military retainers to fight for them had to grant each vassal a benefice, a piece of land that provided the vassal's economic support. In return for the grant of land, the vassal provided his lord with one major service, his fighting skills. In the society of early medieval Europe, where there was little commerce and wealth was based primarily on land, land became the fundamental gift a lord could give to a vassal in return for military service. Hence, what historians later came to call feudalism meant essentially the linking together of the personal element of vassalage with the property element of the benefice.

As the relationship between lord and vassal became more formal, the ceremonial commitment of a man to become a vassal to his lord also emerged. To become a vassal, a man performed an act of homage to his lord, as described in this passage from a medieval digest of law and practice:

> The man should put his hands together as a sign of humility, and place them between the two hands of his lord as a token that he vows everything to him and promises faith to him;

▼ **Knight's Equipment Showing Saddle and Stirrups.** In return for his fighting skills, a knight received a piece of land from his lord that provided for his economic support. Pictured here is a charging knight with his equipment. The introduction of the high saddle, the stirrup, and larger horses allowed horsemen to wear heavier armor and to wield long lances, thereby increasing the military importance of the cavalry.

The Loyalty of a Vassal

▼ ▼ ▼

The loyalty that a vassal owed to his lord was a crucial ingredient of fief-holding and rested on the older Germanic traditions of lordship and loyalty. To Germanic warriors, loyalty, especially to one's lord in battle, was the chief male virtue. To desert one's leader was an act of cowardice and dishonor. Although this excerpt is taken from a poem written before fief-holding developed, it demonstrates very well the German sense of loyalty that survived as a crucial element of the lord-vassal relationship. The excerpt is taken from the Anglo-Saxon epic poem *Beowulf*, probably written around 700. This selection describes the disgrace of Beowulf's followers who had deserted their leader at a crucial time: "Not one of them stood by him . . . of his band of comrades, with battle-efforts and acts of valor, but they fled into the forest and looked after their lives."

Beowulf

It was soon after this
That the battle-shirkers came out from the wood,
Ten men together, cowards and vow-breakers
Who had shrunk from throwing a spear in fight
At the hour of their liege lord's heavy need;
But they came in shame carrying their shields,
Their armour of battle where the old man was lying;
Their eyes were on Wiglaf. He in his weariness,
Foot-soldier, sat by the shoulders of his lord,
Tried water to waken him: vain was his work.
Nothing in all the world, though his yearning impelled him,
Could help him to keep that leader alive,
Nor could he prevent what the Lord approved;
Every man's life must lie under the mastery

Of God's decree, as it still lies today.
Grim condemnation from that young man now
Could he quickly expect who had cast away his courage.
Wiglaf spoke, Weohstan's son,
The man vexed at heart scanned hated friends:
'O what but this could the speaker of truth
Say, that the liege lord who gave you those treasures
Of battle—adornment you stand up there—
And often it was that he proffered at the ale-board
To men sitting in hall chain-mail and helmet,
A prince to his retainers, things as he might find
Of the most magnificent from both far and near—
That he, I say, had utterly, vexatiously wasted
Those war-forged arms, when fighting became his?
Scant cause had he, the king of his people,
To be proud of his campaigners; yet God granted him,
The Lord of all victories, to be able to avenge himself
By his sword alone, when strength was his need.
It was little support that I could give him
For his life in that conflict; nevertheless I plunged
Beyond my own ability to my kinsman's aid;
Our deadly enemy when my sword struck him
Grew feebler and feebler, and the flaming from his head
Poured out less furiously. Too few defenders
Crowded round the prince when that hour assailed him.
Now the treasures received and the swords presented,
Amity and concord, happiness of homeland
Shall perish from your people: and every man
Of that kith and kin shall go dispossessed
Of his lawful lands, where hero and nobleman
Hear from afar the story of your flight
And inglorious action. Death is worthier
For every warrior than days of dishonour!'

---

and the lord should receive him and promise to keep faith with him. Then the man should say: "Sir, I enter your homage and faith and become your man by mouth and hands [i.e., by taking the oath and placing his hands between those of the lord], and I swear and promise to keep faith and loyalty to you against all others, and to guard your rights with all my strength.[12]

As in the earlier Germanic band, loyalty to one's lord was a preeminent virtue (see the box above).

By the ninth century, the benefice had become known as a fief as it acquired a new characteristic involving the exercise of political power. While a fief was a landed estate held from the lord by a vassal in return for military service, vassals holding such grants of land came to exercise rights of jurisdiction or political and legal authority within these fiefs. In other words, they held public power rather than simply private power in the lands that constituted their fiefs. As the Carolingian world disintegrated politically under the impact of internal dissension and invasions, an increasing number of powerful lords arose (see the box on p. 252).

Fief-holding also became increasingly complicated with the development of subinfeudation. The vassals of a king, who were themselves great lords, might also have vassals who would owe them military service in return for a grant of land taken from their estates. Those vassals, in turn, might likewise have vassals, who at such a level would be simple knights with barely enough land to provide their equipment. The lord-vassal relationship, then, bound together both greater and lesser landowners. Historians used to speak of a hierarchy with the king at the top, greater lords on the next level, lesser lords on the next, and simple knights at the bottom; however, this was only a model and rarely reflected reality. Such a hierarchy implies a king at the top. The reality in the tenth-century west Frankish kingdom was that the Capetian kings (see New Political Configurations in the Tenth Century later in this chapter) actually controlled no more land than the Ile-de-France, the territory around the city of Paris. They possessed little real power over the great lords who held fiefs throughout France.

The lord-vassal relationship at all levels always constituted an honorable relationship between free men and did not imply any sense of servitude. Since kings could no longer provide security in the midst of the breakdown created by the invasions of the ninth century, the system of subinfeudation became ever more widespread. With their rights of jurisdiction, fiefs gave lords virtual possession of the rights of government.

Fief-holding was essentially Carolingian; its heartland remained the Frankish lands between the Loire and the Rhine rivers. But it also spread to England, Germany, the Slavic kingdoms of central Europe, and in some form to Italy. It was noticeably weak in Spain and Scandinavia. Fief-holding came to be characterized by a set of practices worked out in the course of the tenth century, although they became more prominent after 1000. While we speak of fief-holding as a system based on a series of mutual obligations of lord toward vassal and vassal toward lord, it is crucial to remember that such obligations varied considerably from place to place and even from fief to fief. As usual, practice almost always varied from theory, and the system was far from systematic.

Since the basic objective of fief-holding was to provide military support, it is no surprise to learn that the major obligation of a vassal to his lord was to perform military service. In addition to his own personal service, a great lord was also responsible for providing a group of

knights for the king's army. Moreover, vassals had to furnish suit at court; this meant a vassal was obliged to appear at his lord's court when summoned, either to give advice to the lord or to sit in judgment in a legal case since the important vassals of a lord were peers and only they could judge each other. Many vassals were also obliged to provide hospitality when a lord stayed at his vassal's castle. This obligation was especially important to medieval kings since they tended to be highly itinerant. Finally, vassals were responsible for aids or financial payments to the lord upon a number of occasions, among them the knighting of the lord's eldest son, the marriage of his eldest daughter, and the ransom of the lord's person if the lord had been captured (see the box on p. 252).

In turn, a lord had responsibilities toward his vassals. His major task was to protect his vassal, either by defending him militarily or by taking his side in a court of law if necessary. The lord was also responsible for the maintenance of the vassal, usually by granting him a fief.

As this system of mutual obligations between lord and vassal evolved, certain practices became common. If a lord acted improperly toward his vassal, the bond between them could be dissolved. Likewise, if a vassal failed to fulfill his vow of loyalty, he was subject to forfeiture of his fief. Upon a vassal's death, his fief theoretically reverted back to the lord since it had been granted to him to use, not to own as a possession. In practice, however, by the tenth century fiefs tended to become hereditary. Following the principle of primogeniture, the eldest son inherited the father's fief. If a man died without heirs, the lord could once again reclaim the fief.

New Political Configurations in the Tenth Century

In the tenth century, Europe began to recover from the great invasions of the ninth century. The disintegration of the Carolingian Empire and the emergence of great and powerful lords soon produced new political configurations.

In the eastern Frankish kingdom, the last Carolingian king died in 911. Whereupon, local rulers, especially the powerful dukes of the Saxons, Swabians, Bavarians, Thuringians, and Franconians, who exercised much power in their large dukedoms, elected one of their own number, Conrad of Franconia as king of Germany (as we think of it) or of the eastern Franks (as contemporaries thought of it.) But Conrad did not last long and after his death, the German dukes chose Henry the Fowler, duke of Saxony, as the new king of Germany (919–936). The

Lords, Vassals, and Fiefs

▼ ▼ ▼

The upheavals of the Early Middle Ages produced a number of new institutions—lordship, vassalage, fiefs. The following selections illustrate two facets of fief-holding. The first records the granting of a fief by a lord to a vassal. The second is the classic statement by Bishop Fulbert of Chartres in 1020 on the mutual obligations between lord and vassal.

Record of a Grant Made by Abbot Faritius to Robert, a Knight

Abbot Faritius also granted to Robert, son of William Mauduit, the land of four hides in Weston which his father had held from the former's predecessor, to be held as a fief. And he should do this service for it, to wit: that whenever the church of Abingdon should perform its knight's service he should do the service of half a knight for the same church; that is to say, in castle ward, in military service beyond and on this side the sea, in giving money in proportion to the knights on the capture of the king, and in the rest of the services which the other knights of the church perform.

Bishop Fulbert of Chartres

Asked to write something concerning the form of fealty, I have noted briefly for you, on the authority of the books, the things which follow. He who swears fealty to his lord ought always to have these six things in memory: what is harmless, safe, honorable, useful, easy, practicable. *Harmless*, that is to say, that he should not injure his lord in his body; *safe*, that he should not injure him by betraying his secrets or the defenses upon which he relies for safety; *honorable*, that he should not injure him in his justice or in other matters that pertain to his honor; *useful*, that he should not injure him in his possessions; *easy* and *practicable*, that that good which his lord is able to do easily he make not difficult, nor that which is practicable he make not impossible to him.

That the faithful vassal should avoid these injuries is certainly proper, but not for this alone does he deserve his holding; for it is not sufficient to abstain from evil, unless what is good is done also. It remains, therefore, that in the same six things mentioned above he should faithfully counsel and aid his lord, if he wishes to be looked upon as worthy of his benefice and to be safe concerning the fealty which he has sworn.

The lord also ought to act toward his faithful vassal reciprocally in all these things. And if he does not do this, he will be justly considered guilty of bad faith, just as the former, if he should be detected in avoiding or consenting to the avoidance of his duties, would be perfidious and perjured.

---

first of the Saxon dynasty of German kings, Henry was not overly successful in creating a unified eastern Frankish kingdom. He possessed inadequate resources to impose effective rule over the entire area, although he did begin a practice continued by his successors of using high church officials as administrators.

The best known of the Saxon kings of Germany was Otto I (936–973). He defeated the Magyars at the Battle of Lechfeld in 955 and encouraged an ongoing program of Christianization of both the Slavic and Scandinavian peoples. Even more than his father, he relied on bishops and abbots in governing his kingdom. This practice was in part a response to the tendency of the lay lords to build up their power at the expense of the king. Since the clergy were theoretically celibate, bishops and abbots could not make their offices hereditary, thus al-

lowing the king to maintain more control over them. In the tenth century, Otto's employment of these high church officials as administrators seemed to be a clever move. In the next century, however, it gave rise to a tremendous conflict between the church and emperors over the issue of who should control the clergy.

Otto I also intervened in Italian politics and for his efforts was crowned by the pope in 962 as emperor of the Romans, reviving a title that had fallen into abeyance with the disintegration of Charlemagne's Carolingian Empire. Once again a pope had conferred the Roman imperial title on a king of the Franks, even though he was a Saxon king of the eastern Franks. Otto's creation of a new "Roman Empire" in the hands of the eastern Franks, or Germans as they came to be called, added a tremendous burden to the kingship of Germany. To the

difficulties of governing Germany was appended the onerous task of ruling Italy as well. It proved a formidable and ultimately discouraging task in the centuries to come.

In the ninth and tenth centuries, the Carolingian kings had little success in controlling the great lords of the west Frankish kingdom. The counts, who were supposed to serve as the chief administrative officials, often paid little attention to the wishes of the Carolingian kings. Some of the counts, such as those of Flanders and Autun (northern Burgundy) regarded themselves as quasi-sovereign hereditary princes. In 987, when the Carolingian king died, the west Frankish nobles and chief prelates of the church chose Hugh Capet, count of Orleans and Paris, as the new king (987–996).

The nobles who elected Hugh Capet did not intend to establish a new royal dynasty. After all, although Hugh was officially king of the west Franks and overlord

▼ **Imperial Crown of Otto I.** The last Carolingian king of the eastern Frankish kingdom died in 911 and in 919 the Saxon dynasty came into power. One of the most important Saxon rulers was Otto I. Otto defeated the invading Magyars and worked for the Christianization of the Scandinavian and Slavic peoples. Otto was crowned emperor by the pope in 962, thereby reviving a title that had fallen into disuse in the west.

of the great nobles of the kingdom, his own family controlled only the Ile-de-France, a territory consisting of lands surrounding Paris. Other French nobles possessed lands equal to or greater than those of the Capetians and assumed that the royal crown would simply pass from one family to another. Hugh Capet determined otherwise, however. He asked the nobles, and they agreed, to choose his eldest son Robert as his anointed associate in case Hugh died on a campaign to Spain in 987. And although Hugh Capet could not know it then, the Capetian dynasty would rule the west Frankish kingdom, or France as it came to be known, for centuries. In the late tenth century, however, what became France was not a unified kingdom, but a loose alliance of powerful lords who treated the king of France as one of themselves. They assisted him only when it was in their own interests to do so.

England's development in the ninth and tenth centuries took a course somewhat different from the western and eastern Frankish kingdoms. The long struggle of Anglo-Saxon England against the Danish invasions ultimately produced a unified kingdom. Alfred the Great, king of Wessex (871–899), played a crucial role. He defeated a Danish army in 879 and made peace with the Danes in 885. His successors reconquered the areas occupied by the Danes and established a unified Anglo-Saxon monarchy.

By the time of King Edgar (959–975), Anglo-Saxon England had a well-developed and strong monarchical government. Although the kingship was elective, only the descendants of Alfred were chosen for the position.

In the counties or shires, the administrative units into which England was divided, the king was assisted by an agent appointed and controlled by him, the shire-reeve or sheriff. An efficient chancery or writing office was responsible for issuing writs (or royal letters) conveying the king's orders to the sheriffs.

Economic Structure: Manorialism and Trade

Fief-holding was closely dependent upon the economic system of manorialism. The landholding class of nobles and knights comprised a military elite whose ability to function as warriors depended upon having the leisure time to pursue the arts of war. Landed estates, worked by a dependent peasant class, provided the economic sustenance that made possible this way of life. A manor was simply an agrarian estate operated by a lord and worked by peasants. Lords provided protection; peasants gave up their freedom, became tied to the lord's land, and provided labor services for him. The existence of fief-holding, then, depended upon manorialism and was, in fact, imposed upon an already existing manorial system that had emerged in the sixth and seventh centuries.

Economically speaking, Europe was an overwhelmingly agricultural society in the Early Middle Ages. The basic agricultural unit was the large estate, which to a large extent continued the Roman practices of the late empire. After the Germanic invasions and the establishment of the successor states, estate owners continued to rely on slaves to work the land. But there was a gradual decline in their use from the fifth to seventh centuries. Although the Christian church did not try to prohibit slavery, it did encourage the freeing of slaves. Economic considerations were even more important in ending slavery, however. Landlords found it easier and cheaper to establish slaves on small parcels of land, where they could feed themselves and their families, and to require in exchange that the slaves work the demesne or lord's land. This decline in the utilization of slaves on large estates (they were still used in households) meant some upward movement for the lowest classes in society.

At the same time, there was a general tendency working in the opposite direction. Freemen were losing their freedom. There were still substantial numbers of free farmers in the late Roman Empire whose numbers were actually augmented by the influx of free German peasants. All too soon, however, these free peasants found themselves in a vulnerable position. In the unsettled circumstances of the Early Middle Ages, small farmers often needed protection or food in a time of bad harvests. Free peasants gave up their freedom to the lords of large landed estates in return for protection and sustenance. While a large class of free peasants continued to exist, increasing numbers of free peasants became serfs. It has been estimated that by the ninth century, 60 percent of the population of western Europe had been reduced to serfdom.

Basically, serfs were peasants bound to the land. Technically, they were not slaves since they could not be bought or sold, but they could not leave the lord's land without permission and owed servile obligations as well. These included the payment of a fixed rent, whether in food and/or money, and the duty to work the lord's land or demesne a few days a week. Serfs had to pay "servile dues" or fees for the right to inherit property and to marry a person from outside the manor. Contrary to modern Hollywood notions of medieval peasants, a lord did not have the "right of the first night" with his virginal female serfs.

In the Early Middle Ages, whether free or unfree, a vast majority of men and women, possibly as high as 90 percent, worked the land. It was not an easy existence. This period had certainly witnessed a precipitous decline in trade. Coins and jewelry were often hoarded, and at the local level, goods were frequently bartered since there were so few coins in circulation. It is important to note, however, that, contrary to older historical views of this period, trade was not entirely extinguished but continued to persist. Even in an agrarian society, surplus products could be exchanged at local markets. More significantly, however, both aristocrats and wealthy clerics desired merchandise not produced locally, such as spices, silk cloth, wine, gold, and silver jewelry. It took trade to obtain these items.

Much trade in luxury goods, especially beginning in the ninth century, was with the Byzantine Empire, particularly the city of Constantinople and the Islamic caliphs of Baghdad. Products from the west included iron, timber, furs, and slaves (many from eastern Europe, including captured Slavs, from whom the modern word *slave* is derived). Traders, often Jews, carried goods by boat on European rivers or on caravans with horses or mules. An Arab geographer of the ninth century left this account of Jewish traders from southern France:

> [They] speak Arabic, Persian, Greek, Frankish, Spanish, and Slavonic. They travel from west to east and from east to west, by land and by sea. From the west they bring eunuchs, slave-girls, boys, brocade, castor-skins, marten and other furs, and swords. They take ship from Frank-land in the western Mediterranean sea and land at Farama, whence they take their merchandise on camel-back to Qulzum. . . . Then they sail

on the eastern [Red] Sea from Qulzum, to Al-Jar and Jedda, and onward to Sind, India and China. From China they bring back musk, aloes, camphor, cinnamon, and other products of those parts, and return to Qulzum. Then they transport them to Farama and sail again on the western sea. Some sail with their goods to Constantinople and sell them to the Greeks, and some take them to the king of the Franks and sell them there.[13]

Of course, such caravans were prime targets for thieves and were often plundered. Towns were not needed for such trade, although some ports were frequently utilized. By 900, Italian merchants, especially the Venetians, were entering the trade picture, particularly with the Muslims and Byzantines. Overall, however, western Europe in the Early Middle Ages, compared to the Byzantine Empire or Muslim caliphates, was an underdeveloped, predominantly agrarian society and could not begin to match the splendor of either of the other heirs of the Roman Empire.

▼ The Zenith of Byzantine Civilization

In the seventh and eighth centuries, the Byzantine Empire had lost much of its territory to Slavs, Bulgars, and Muslims. By 750, the empire consisted only of Asia Minor, some lands in the Balkans, and the southern coast of Italy. Although Byzantium was beset with internal dissension and invasions in the ninth century, it was able to deal with them and not only endured, but even expanded, reaching its high point in the tenth century, which some historians have called "the golden age of Byzantine civilization."

During the reign of Michael III (842–867), the Byzantine Empire began to experience a revival. Iconoclasm was finally abolished in 843, and reforms were made in education, church life, the military, and peasant economy. There was a noticeable intellectual renewal. But the Byzantine Empire under Michael was still plagued by persistent problems. The Bulgars mounted new attacks, and the Arabs continued to harass the empire. Moreover, a new church problem with political repercussions erupted over differences between the pope as leader of the western Christian church and the patriarch of Constantinople as leader of the eastern (or Orthodox) Christian church. Patriarch Photius condemned the pope as a heretic for accepting a revised form of the Nicene Creed stating that the Holy Spirit proceeded from the Father and the Son instead of "The Holy Spirit, who proceeds from the Father." A council of eastern bishops followed Photius's wishes and excommunicated the pope, creat-

ing the so-called Photian schism. While the differences were later papered over, this controversy served to further the division between the eastern and western Christian churches.

The problems of Michael's reign were effectively dealt with by a new dynasty of Byzantine emperors, known as the Macedonians (867–1081). In general, this dynastic line managed to beat off the external enemies, go over to the offensive, and reestablish domestic order. Supported by the church, the emperors continued to think of the Byzantine Empire as a continuation of the Christian Roman Empire of late antiquity. Although for diplomatic reasons they occasionally recognized the imperial title of western emperors, such as Charlemagne and Otto I, they still regarded them as little more than barbarian parvenus.

The Macedonian emperors could boast of a remarkable number of achievements in the late ninth and tenth centuries. To bolster the military machine, they created new *themes*. Instituted in the early seventh century as a new administrative unit, the *theme* combined civilian and military offices in the hands of same person. The civil governor was the military leader of the area; the civilian population, consisting primarily of free farmers, served as soldiers. The Macedonian emperors worked to strengthen the farmer-soldiers vis-à-vis the landed aristocrats, who were trying to expand their estates at the expense of the former. The emperors were well aware that the free farmers made up the rank and file of the Byzantine cavalry and provided the military strength of the empire.

The Macedonian emperors fostered a burst of economic prosperity by expanding trade relations with western Europe, especially by selling silks and metalworks. Thanks to this prosperity, the city of Constantinople flourished. Foreign visitors continued to be astounded by its size, wealth, and physical surroundings. To western Europeans, it was the stuff of legends and fables (see the box on p. 256).

In the midst of this prosperity, Byzantine intellectual activity persisted in focusing on historical chronicles and spiritual works, including hymns and tracts of profound mystical devotion. Nevertheless, Byzantine cultural influence expanded during this period due to the active missionary efforts of eastern Byzantine Christians. Eastern Orthodox Christianity was spread to eastern European peoples, such as the Bulgars and Serbs. Perhaps the greatest missionary success occurred when the prince of Kiev in Russia converted to Christianity in 987 (see The Slavic Peoples of Central and Eastern Europe later in this chapter).

A Western View of the Byzantine Empire
▼ ▼ ▼

Bishop Liudprand of Cremona undertook diplomatic missions to Constantinople on behalf of two western kings, Berengar of Italy and Otto I of Germany. This selection is taken from his description of his mission to the Byzantine emperor Constantine VII in 949 as an envoy for Berengar, king of Italy from 950 until his overthrow by Otto I of Germany in 964. Liudprand had mixed feelings about Byzantium: admiration, yet also envy and hostility because of its superior wealth.

Liudprand of Cremona, *Antapodosis*

Next to the imperial residence at Constantinople there is a palace of remarkable size and beauty which the Greeks call Magnavra . . . the name being equivalent to "Fresh breeze." In order to receive some Spanish envoys, who had recently arrived, as well as myself . . . , Constantine gave orders that his palace should be got ready. . . .

Before the emperor's seat stood a tree, made of bronze gilded over, whose branches were filled with birds, also made of gilded bronze, which uttered different cries, each according to its varying species. The throne itself was so marvelously fashioned that at one moment it seemed a low structure, and at another it rose high into the air. It was of immense size and was guarded by lions, made either of bronze or of wood covered over with gold, who beat the ground with their tails and gave a dreadful roar with open mouth and quivering tongue. Leaning upon the shoulders of two eunuchs I was brought into the emperor's presence. At my approach the lions began to roar and the birds to cry out, each according to its kind; but I was neither terrified nor surprised, for I had previously made enquiry about all these things

from people who were well acquainted with them. So after I had three times made obeisance to the emperor with my face upon the ground, I lifted my head, and behold! The man whom just before I had seen sitting on a moderately elevated seat had now changed his raiment and was sitting on the level of the ceiling. How it was done I could not imagine, unless perhaps he was lifted up by some such sort of device as we use for raising the timbers of a wine press. On that occasion he did not address me personally . . . but by the intermediary of a secretary he enquired about Berengar's doings and asked after his health. I made a fitting reply and then, at a nod from the interpreter, left his presence and retired to my lodging.

It would give me some pleasure also to record here what I did then for Berengar. . . . The Spanish envoys . . . had brought handsome gifts from their masters to the emperor Constantine. I for my part had brought nothing from Berengar except a letter and that was full of lies. I was very greatly disturbed and shamed at this and began to consider anxiously what I had better do. In my doubt and perplexity it finally occurred to me that I might offer the gifts, which on my account I had brought for the emperor, as coming from Berengar, and trick out my humble present with fine words. I therefore presented him with nine excellent curaisses, seven excellent shields with gilded bosses, two silver gift cauldrons, some swords, spears and spits, and what was more precious to the emperor than anything, four carzimasia; that being the Greek name for young eunuchs who have had both their testicles and their penis removed. This operation is performed by traders at Verdun, who take the boys into Spain and make a hugh profit.

Under the Macedonian rulers, Byzantium enjoyed a strong civil service, talented emperors, and military advances. The Byzantine civil service was staffed by well-educated, competent aristocrats from Constantinople who oversaw the collection of taxes, domestic administration, and foreign policy. At the same time, the Macedonian dynasty produced some truly outstanding emperors skilled in administration and law, such as Leo VI (886–912) and Basil II (976–1025). In the tenth century, competent emperors combined with a number of

talented generals to mobilize the empire's military resources and take the offensive. The Bulgars were defeated, and both the eastern and western parts of Bulgaria were annexed to the empire. The Byzantines went on to add the islands of Crete and Cyprus to the empire and defeat the Muslim forces in Syria, expanding the empire to the upper Euphrates. By the end of the reign of Basil II in 1025, the Byzantine Empire was the largest it had been since the beginning of the seventh century. After Basil's death, however, a new series of dynastic

struggles ensued that seriously weakened the state internally and inaugurated a fatal decline.

▼ The Slavic Peoples of Central and Eastern Europe

North of Byzantium and east of the Carolingian Empire lay a spacious plain through which a number of Asiatic nomads, such as the Huns, Bulgars, Avars, and Magyars, had pushed their way westward, terrorizing and plundering the settled peasant communities. Eastern Europe was ravaged by these successive waves of invaders who found it relatively easy to create large empires that, in turn, were overthrown by the next invaders. Over a period of time, the invaders themselves were largely assimilated with the native Slavic peoples of the area.

The Slavic peoples were originally a single people in central Europe who, through mass migrations and nomadic invaders, were gradually divided into three major groups: the western, southern, and eastern Slavs. In the region east of the eastern Frankish or Germanic kingdom emerged the Polish and Bohemian kingdoms of the western Slavs. The Germans assumed responsibility for the conversion of these Slavic peoples since German emperors, such as Otto I, considered it their duty to spread Christianity to the barbarians. Of course, it also gave them the opportunity to extend their political authority as well. German missionaries had converted the Czechs in Bohemia by the end of the ninth century, and a bishopric eventually occupied by a Czech bishop was established at Prague in the tenth century. The Slavs in Poland were not converted until the reign of Prince Mieszko (c. 960–992). In 1000, an independent Polish archbishopric was set up at Gniezno by the pope. The non-Slavic kingdom of Hungary, which emerged after the Magyars settled down after their defeat at Lechfeld in 955, was also converted to Christianity by German missionaries. Saint Stephen, king of Hungary from 997 to 1038, facilitated the acceptance of Christianity by his people. The Poles, Czechs, and Hungarians all accepted Catholic or western Christianity and became closely tied to the Roman Catholic church and its Latin culture.

The southern and eastern Slavic populations largely took a different path because of their proximity to the Byzantine Empire. The Slavic peoples of Moravia were converted to the Eastern Orthodox Christianity of the Byzantine Empire by two Byzantine missionary brothers, Cyril and Methodius, who began their activities in 863. They created a Slavonic (Cyrillic) alphabet, translated the Bible into Slavonic, and developed Slavonic church services. While the southern Slavic peoples accepted Christianity, there was an eventual split between the Croats who accepted the Roman church and the Serbs who remained loyal to eastern Christianity.

Although the Bulgars were originally an Asiatic people who conquered much of the Balkan peninsula, they were eventually absorbed by the larger native south

▼ **Emperor Leo VI.** After suffering tremendous defeats in the seventh and eighth centuries, the Byzantine Empire began to experience a revival that culminated in its "golden age" in the tenth century. Under the Macedonian dynasty, the empire achieved economic prosperity through expanded trade, gained new territories from military victories, and sent missionaries among the east European peoples. This mosaic depicts the Macedonian emperor Leo VI prostrating himself before Christ.

Slavic population. Together, by the ninth century, they formed a largely Slavic Bulgarian kingdom. Although the conversion to Christianity of this state was complicated by the rivalry between the Roman Catholic and Eastern Orthodox churches, the Bulgarians eventually accepted the latter. By the end of the ninth century, they embraced the Slavonic church services earlier developed by Cyril and Methodius. The acceptance of Eastern Orthodoxy by the southern Slavic peoples, the Serbs and Bulgarians, meant that their cultural life was also linked to the Byzantine state.

The eastern Slavic peoples, from whom the modern Russians, White (or Byelo-) Russians, and Ukrainians are descended, had settled in the territory of present-day Ukraine and European Russia. There, beginning in the late eighth century, they began to encounter Viking invaders. Swedish Vikings, known to the eastern Slavs as Varangians, moved down the extensive network of rivers into the lands of the eastern Slavs in search of booty and new trade routes. After establishing trading links with the Byzantine state, the Varangians built trading settlements, became involved in the civil wars among the Slavic peoples, and eventually came to dominate the

▼ **Map 8.3** The World of the Slavs

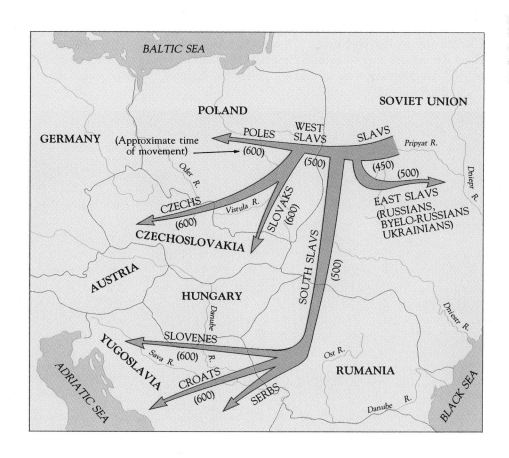

A Muslim's Description of the Rus
▼ ▼ ▼

Despite the difficulties that travel presented, early medieval civilization did witness some contact among the various cultures. This might occur through trade, diplomacy, or the conquest and migration of peoples. This document is a description of the Swedish Rus who eventually merged with the native Slavic peoples to form the principality of Kiev, commonly regarded as the first Russian state. It is written by Ibn Fadlan, a Muslim diplomat sent from Baghdad in 921 to a settlement on the Volga River. His comments on the filthiness of the Rus reflect the Muslim preoccupation with cleanliness.

Ibn Fadlan: Description of the Rus

I saw the Rus folk when they arrived on their trading-mission and settled at the river Atul (Volga). Never had I seen people of more perfect physique. They are tall as date-palms, and reddish in colour. They wear neither coat nor kaftan, but each man carried a cape which covers one half of his body, leaving one hand free. No one is ever parted from his axe, sword, and knife. Their swords are Frankish in design, broad, flat, and fluted. Each man has a number of trees, figures, and the like from the finger-nails to the neck. Each woman carried on her bosom a container made of iron, silver, copper or gold—its size and substance depending on her man's wealth. . . .

They [the Rus] are the filthiest of God's creatures. They do not wash after discharging their natural functions, neither do they wash their hands after meals. They are as lousy as donkeys. They arrive from their distant river, and there they build big houses on its shores. Ten or twenty of them may live together in one house, and each of them has a couch of his own where he sits and diverts himself with the pretty slave girls whom he had brought along for sale. He will make love with one of them while a comrade looks on; sometimes they indulge in a communal orgy, and, if a customer should turn up to buy a girl, the Rus man will not let her go till he has finished with her.

They wash their hands and faces every day in incredibly filthy water. Every morning the girl brings her master a large bowl of water in which he washes his hands and face and hair, then blows his nose into it and spits into it. When he has finished the girl takes the bowl to his neighbour—who repeats the performance. Thus the bowl goes the rounds of the entire household. . . .

If one of the Rus folk falls sick they put him in a tent by himself and leave bread and water for him. They do not visit him, however, or speak to him, especially if he is a serf. Should he recover he rejoins the others; if he dies they burn him. But if he happens to be a serf they leave him for the dogs and vultures to devour. If they catch a robber they hang him to a tree until he is torn to shreds by wind and weather. . . .

native peoples, just as their fellow Vikings were doing in parts of western Europe. According to the traditional version of the story, the semilegendary Rurik secured his ruling dynasty in the Slavic settlement of Novgorod in 862. Rurik and his fellow Vikings were called "the Rus," from which the name Russia is derived; eventually, that name became attached to the state they founded (see the box above). Although much about Rurik is unclear, it is certain that his follower Oleg (c. 873–913) took up residence in Kiev and created the Rus state or union of east Slavic territories known as the principality of Kiev. Oleg's successors extended their control over the eastern Slavs and expanded the territory of Kiev until it encompassed the territory between the Baltic and Black seas and the Danube and Volga rivers. By marrying Slavic wives, the Viking ruling class was gradually assimilated into the Slavic population, a process confirmed by their assumption of Slavic names.

The growth of the principality of Kiev attracted religious missionaries, especially from the Byzantine Empire. One Rus ruler, Vladimir (c. 980–1015) married the Byzantine emperor's sister and officially accepted Christianity for himself and his people in 987. His primary motive was probably not a spiritual one. By all accounts, Vladimir was a cruel and vicious man who believed an established church would be helpful in the development of an organized state. From the end of the tenth century on, Byzantine Christianity became the model for Russian religious life, just as Byzantine imperial ideals came to influence the outward forms of Russian political life.

▼ The World of Islam

The Umayyad dynasty of caliphs had established Damascus as the center of an Islamic empire created by Muslim expansion in the seventh and eighth centuries. A revolt led by Abu al-Abbas, a descendant of the uncle of Muhammad, led to the end of the Umayyad dynasty in 750 and the establishment of the Abbasid dynasty that lasted until 1258. The Abbasid caliphs brought political, economic, and cultural change to the world of Islam. While stressing religious fundamentalism, at the same time they broke down the distinctions between Arab and non-Arab Muslims. All could now hold both

▼ **Mosque at Córdoba.** The first Great Mosque of Córdoba pictured here was built by Abd al-Rahman, founder of the Umayyad dynasty of Spain. Once rulers of the extensive Muslim empire created in the seventh and eighth centuries, the Umayyads were overthrown and replaced by the Abbasid dynasty. Under the Abbasids, the great Muslim empire began to break apart as provincial rulers established independent dynasties. Amid political disunity, the Muslim world was held together by the *Koran* and the spread of Arabic.

civil and military offices. This helped to open Muslim life to the influences of the civilizations they had conquered. In 762, the Abbasids built a new capital city, Baghdad, on the Tigris River far to the east of Damascus. The move eastward allowed Persian influence to come to the fore, encouraging a new cultural orientation. Under the Abbasids, judges, merchants, and government officials, rather than warriors, were viewed as the ideal citizens.

The new Abbasid caliphate experienced a period of splendid rule well into the ninth century. Some of these caliphs were well known, even in the west. Harun-al-Rashed (786–809) was known through the exotic tales of the *Arabian Nights,* which accurately portray the luxurious life at Baghdad during his reign. His son al-Mamun (813–833) was a patron of learning who founded an astronomical observatory and created a foundation for translations of classical works. This was also a period of tremendous economic prosperity. After all, the Arabs had conquered many of the richest provinces of the Roman Empire. Baghdad now became the center of an enormous trade empire that extended into Europe, Asia, and Africa, greatly adding to the wealth of the Islamic world.

The late ninth and tenth centuries were a period of political disunity for the Abbasid caliphs, however. By awarding important positions to court favorites, the Abbasids began to undermine the foundations of their own power and become figureheads. Provincial rulers broke away from their control and established independent dynasties. Spain had already established its own caliphate when a prince of the Umayyad dynasty had escaped execution and fled across north Africa to Spain in 750. A caliphate of the Fatimid family was established in Egypt in 973, and an independent dynasty also operated in north Africa. Despite the political disunity of the Islamic world, however, there was an underlying Islamic civilization based on two common bonds, the *Koran* and the spread of Arabic.

Islamic Civilization

From the beginning of their empire, Muslim Arabs had demonstrated a willingness to absorb the culture of their conquered territories. The Arabs were truly heirs to the remaining Greco-Roman culture of the Roman Empire. Just as readily, they assimilated Byzantine and Persian culture. In the eighth and ninth centuries, numerous Greek, Syrian, and Persian scientific and philosophical works were translated into Arabic. As the chief language in the southern Mediterranean and the Near East, Arabic became a truly international language.

The Muslims created a brilliant urban culture at a time when western Europe was predominantly a rural world of petty villages. This can be seen in such new cities as Baghdad and Cairo, but also in Córdoba, the capital of the Umayyad caliphate in Spain. With a population of possibly 100,000, Córdoba was "second only to Constantinople among the cities of Europe." Islamic cities had a distinctive physical appearance due to their common use of certain architectural features, such as the pointed arch and traceried windows, and specific kinds of buildings. The latter included palaces and public buildings with fountains and secluded courtyards, mosques for worship, public baths, and bazaars or marketplaces. Muslims embellished their buildings with a unique decorative art that avoided representation of living things.

Although Islamic scholars are justly praised for preserving much of classical knowledge for the west, they also made considerable advances of their own. Nowhere is this more true than in their contributions to mathematics and the natural sciences, although early Muslims would have regarded these fields as simply part of the study of philosophy. The list of Muslim achievements in mathematics and astronomy alone is impressive; they adopted and passed on the numerical system of India, added the use of the zero, and created the mathematical discipline of algebra (al-jebr). In astronomy, Muslims discussed the possibility of the earth's axial rotation, named many stars and constellations, and perfected the astrolabe, an instrument used by navigators to observe the positions of heavenly bodies. Muslims also made many new discoveries in optics and chemistry and developed medicine as a field of scientific study. Especially well known was Ibn Sina (Avicenna to the west, 980–1037), who authored a medical encyclopedia that, among other things, emphasized the contagious nature of certain diseases and showed how such diseases could be spread by contaminated water supplies. After its translation into Latin, Avicenna's work became a basic medical textbook for medieval European university students. The achievements of the tenth century were merely a prelude to the great accomplishments of the eleventh and twelfth centuries. Fortunately for Western civilization, the intellectual and scientific work of the Islamic world was eventually translated and passed on to the underdeveloped and certainly less knowledgeable world of European civilization.

After the turmoil of the disintegration of the Roman Empire and the establishment of the Germanic successor states, a new European civilization began to emerge slowly in the Early Middle Ages. The coronation of Charlemagne, descendant of a Germanic tribe converted to Christianity, as Roman emperor in 800 symbolized the fusion of the three chief components of the new European civilization: the German tribes, the classical tradition, and Christianity. In the long run, the creation of a western empire fostered the idea of a distinct European identity and marked the shift of power from the south to the north. Italy and the Mediterranean had been the center of the Roman Empire. The lands north of the Alps now became the political center of Europe.

With the disintegration of the Carolingian Empire, new forms of political institutions began to develop in Europe. These were characterized by a decentralization of political power, in which lords exercised legal, administrative, and military power. The practice of fief-holding transferred public power into many private hands and seemed to provide the security sorely lacking in a time of weak central government and new invasions by Muslims, Magyars, and Vikings. While Europe struggled, the Byzantine and Islamic worlds continued to prosper and flourish, the brilliance of their urban cultures standing in marked contrast to the underdeveloped rural world of Europe. By 1000, however, that rural world had not only recovered, but was beginning to expand in ways undreamed of by previous generations. Europe stood poised for a giant leap.

Notes
▼ ▼ ▼

1. Oliver Thatcher and Edgar McNeal, eds., *A Source Book for Medieval History* (New York, 1905), pp. 37–38.
2. 1 Samuel 16: 13.
3. Einhard, *The Life of Charlemagne*, trans. Samuel Turner (Ann Arbor, Mich., 1960), p. 30.
4. Ibid., p. 57.

5. Quoted in Pierre Riché, *Daily Life in the World of Charlemagne,* trans. Jo Ann McNamara (Philadelphia, 1978), p. 56.

6. 1 Corinthians 7: 1–2, 8–9.

7. Quoted in Derrick Bailey, *Homosexuality and the Western Christian Tradition* (London, 1955), p. 73.

8. Quoted in Paul Veyne, ed., *A History of Private Life,* vol. 1, *From Pagan Rome to Byzantium,* trans. Arthur Goldhammer (Cambridge, Mass., 1987), p. 440.

9. Stanley Rubin, *Medieval English Medicine* (New York, 1974), p. 136.

10. Quoted in Brian Inglis, *A History of Medicine* (New York, 1965), p. 51.

11. Tacitus, *Germany and Its Tribes,* in *The Complete Works of Tacitus,* trans. Alfred Church and William Brodribb (New York, 1942), pp. 715–16.

12. Quoted in Thatcher and McNeal, *A Source Book for Medieval History,* p. 363.

13. Quoted in Bernard Lewis, *The Arabs in History* (London, 1958), p. 90.

Suggestions for Further Reading

▼ ▼ ▼

Surveys of Carolingian Europe include H. Fichtenau, *The Carolingian Empire* (Oxford, 1957); D. Bullough, *The Age of Charlemagne* (New York, 1966); J. Boussard, *The Civilization of Charlemagne,* trans. Frances Partridge (New York, 1971); and R. McKitterick, *The Frankish Kingdoms under the Carolingians, 751–987* (London, 1983). On Charlemagne, see H. R. Loyn and J. Percival, *The Reign of Charlemagne* (New York, 1976); the popular biography by R. Winston, *Charlemagne: From the Hammer to the Cross* (Indianapolis, 1954); and R. Folz, *The Coronation of Charlemagne: 25 December 800* (London, 1974). Carolingian political institutions are examined in F. L. Ganshof, *Frankish Institutions under Charlemagne* (Providence, R.I., 1968). On Carolingian culture, see E. S. Duckett, *Alcuin, Friend of Charlemagne* (New York, 1951); and M. L. W. Laistner, *Thought and Letters in Western Europe, 500–900,* rev. ed. (London, 1957).

Various aspects of social life in the Carolingian world are examined in P. Riché, *Daily Life in the World of Charlemagne,* trans. J. A. McNamara (Philadelphia, 1978); M. Rouche, "The Early Middle Ages in the West," in P. Veyne, ed., *A History of Private Life,* (Cambridge, Mass., 1987), 1: 411–549; S. F. Wemple, *Women in Frankish Society: Marriage and the Cloister* (Philadelphia, 1981); and S. Rubin, *Medieval English Medicine* (New York, 1974). On the attitudes toward sexuality in the early Christian church, see the important works by P. Brown, *The Body and Society* (New York, 1988); and E. Pagels, *Adam, Eve, and the Serpent* (New York, 1988).

A good introduction to the problems of the late ninth and tenth centuries can be found in G. Barraclough, *The Crucible of Europe* (Berkeley and Los Angeles, 1976). The Vikings are examined in P. Sawyer, *The Age of the Vikings* (London, 1962) and *Kings and Vikings* (London, 1982); J. Brøndsted, *The Vikings* (Harmondsworth, 1960); and G. Jones, *A History of the Vikings,* rev. ed. (Oxford, 1984). On the Magyar invasions, see C. A. Macartney, *The Magyars in the Ninth Century* (Cambridge, 1930).

Two important introductory works on feudalism are F. L. Ganshof, *Feudalism,* trans. P. Grierson (London, 1952); and the classic work by M. Bloch, *Feudal Society,* trans. L. A. Manyon (London, 1961). Military aspects of feudalism are examined in J. Beeler, *Warfare in Feudal Europe* (Ithaca, N.Y., 1954). There are good studies on early feudalism in the collections by R. S. Hoyt, ed., *Life and Thought in the Early Middle Ages* (Minneapolis, 1965); and R. F. Cheyette, ed., *Lordship and Community in Medieval Europe* (New York, 1968). Works on the new political configurations that emerged in the tenth century are cited in Chapter 9.

For the economic history of the Early Middle Ages, see G. Duby, *The Early Growth of the European Economy: Warriors and Peasants from the Seventh to the Twelfth Century* (Ithaca, N.Y., 1974). An important work on medieval agriculture is G. Duby, *Rural Economy and Country Life in the Medieval West,* trans. C. Postan (London, 1968). Also worthwhile is B. H. Slicher Van Bath, *The Agrarian History of Western Europe: A.D. 500–1850,* trans. O. Ordish (London, 1963). On population and environment, see E. L. Ladurie, *Times of Feast, Times of Famine* (New York, 1971); and J. C. Russell, *Late Ancient and Medieval Population* (Philadelphia, 1958).

Byzantine civilization in this period is examined in R. Jenkins, *Byzantium: The Imperial Centuries, 610–1071* (New York, 1969). D. Obolensky, *The Byzantine*

Commonwealth (New York, 1971) examines the impact of the Byzantine Empire upon its neighbors. On the Slavic peoples of central and eastern Europe, see F. Dvornik, *The Making of Central and Eastern Europe* (London, 1949) and *The Slavs in European History and Civilization* (New Brunswick, N.J., 1962); A. P. Vlasto, *The Entry of the Slavs into Christendom* (Cambridge, 1970); and Z. Vana, *The World of the Ancient Slavs* (London, 1983). The world of Islam in this period is discussed in H. Kennedy, *The Prophet and the Age of the Caliphates: The Islamic Near East from the Sixth to the Eleventh Century* (London, 1986); J. Lassner, *The Shaping of Abbasid Rule* (Princeton, N.J. 1980); G. Wiet, *Baghdad: Metropolis of the Abbasid Caliphate,* trans. S. Feiler (Norman, Okla., 1971); and O. Grabar, *The Formation of Islamic Art* (New Haven, Conn., 1971).

Chapter 9

The Recovery and Growth of European Society, 1000–1200

▼▼▼▼▼

The new European civilization that had emerged in the ninth and tenth centuries began to come into its own in the eleventh and twelfth centuries. This was a period of recovery and growth for Western civilization, characterized by a greater sense of security and a burst of energy and enthusiasm. Both the Catholic church and the feudal states recovered from the invasions and internal dissension of the Early Middle Ages. New agricultural practices, the revival of commerce, and the growth of towns and cities, all accompanied by a rising population, created new dynamic elements in a formerly static society. The recovery of the church produced a reform movement that led to exalted claims of papal authority and subsequent conflict with state authorities. Nobles built innumerable castles and gave a distinctive look to the countryside of the High Middle Ages. Although lords and vassals seemed forever mired in endless petty conflicts, some medieval kings began to exert a centralizing authority and inaugurated the process of developing new kinds of monarchical states.

▼ Climate, Population, and Food Supply

Although the change probably started before 1000, the period from 1000 to 1200 and possibly beyond witnessed an improvement in climate. A small but nevertheless significant rise in temperature made for longer and better growing seasons, especially in areas such as Scandinavia that were affected by cold weather. Some regions even saw the introduction of crops not previously grown there, such as grape vines in southern England.

Norman Conquest of England ▼	Pope Gregory VII and Investiture Controversy ▼		Henry II ▼	Frederick I and the Hohenstaufen Dynasty ▼

•••••••• 1000 •••••••••••• 1050 ••••••••••• 1100 •••••••••• 1150 ••••••••••• 1200 •••••••••

▲ Growth of Trade and Towns	▲ Concordat of Worms	▲ Spread of Windmills	▲ Murder of Thomas Becket

Although concrete figures are lacking, reasonable calculations exist to warrant one major generalization: Europe experienced a dramatic increase in population after 1000. It has been estimated that the European population virtually doubled between 1000 and 1300, from 38 to 74 million people. As Table 1 indicates, the rate of growth tended to vary from region to region. This rise in population was physically evident in the growth of agricultural villages, towns, and cities and the increase in arable land.

Why this dramatic increase in population? Obviously, fertility rates increased sufficiently to gradually outstrip the relatively high mortality rates of medieval society, which were especially acute in infancy and the childhood years. Recent estimates assume a 15 to 20 percent mortality rate for the first year of life and 30 percent before the age of 20. Male mortality rates were highest in the age group 40–59; female mortality rates were highest between 20 and 39. The latter statistic reflects the travails of pregnancy combined with hard work and greater susceptibility to diseases due to childbearing. The greater mortality rate for women in their twenties and thirties, which was even higher than for males engaged in warfare in the same years, led to a population with 20 to 30 percent more men than women.

Traditionally, historians have tried to explain the population increase by a number of factors. For one, they attribute it to increased security stemming from more settled and peaceful conditions after the invasions of the Early Middle Ages had stopped. Vikings and Magyars were assimilated and Saracen attacks halted. Although the development of fief-holding had created more security, as some have argued, it was still a violent age where feuds and petty wars were a way of life. The decline of slavery may also have been a factor. As it became economically more sound to have people as tenants rather than as slaves, former slaves could marry, have families, and increase the population. Moreover, the change from the extended to nuclear family (see Chapter 8) may also have affected population levels. Finally, there was a dramatic increase in agricultural production after 1000. Although historians are not sure whether it was a cause or effect of the population increase, there is no question about its importance. Without such a significant rise in food supplies, the expansion in population could never have been sustained.

The New Agriculture

In the Early Middle Ages, Europe was overwhelmingly an agricultural society. It continued to be so, more or less, for centuries, even though the eleventh and twelfth centuries witnessed an upswing in commerce and a revival of town and city life that eventually produced a different kind of Western society. This commercial and urban revival was, of course, dependent upon the food

Table 1 ▼ Population Estimates (in millions): 1000 and 1340

Area	1000	1340
Mediterranean		
Greece and Balkans	5	6
Italy	5	10
Iberia	7	9
Total	17	25
Western and Central Europe		
France and Low Countries	6	19
British Isles	2	5
Germany and Scandinavia	4	11.5
Total	12	35.5
Eastern Europe		
Russia	6	8
Poland	2	3
Hungary	1.5	2
Total	9.5	13
Total	38.5	73.5

Source: J. C. Russell, *The Control of Late Ancient and Medieval Population* (Philadelphia: The American Philosophical Society, 1985), p. 36. Demographic specialists admit that these are merely estimates. Some figures, especially those for eastern Europe, could be radically revised by new research.

The Recovery and Growth of European Society, 1000–1200 ▼ 265

The Destruction of Medieval Forests
▼ ▼ ▼

One of the startling environmental changes of the Middle Ages was the virtual destruction of millions of acres of forest to create new areas of arable land and to meet the demand for timber, the chief raw material of the High Middle Ages. Timber was used as fuel and to build houses, mills of all kinds, bridges, fortresses, and ships. Incredible quantities of wood were burned to make charcoal for the iron forges. In addition to environmental damage, the price of wood had skyrocketed by the thirteenth century. This document from 1140 illustrates this destructive process. Suger, the abbot of Saint-Denis, needed thirty-five-foot beams for the construction of a new church. His master carpenters told him that there were no longer any trees big enough in the area around Paris and he would have to go far afield to find such tall trees. This selection recounts his efforts.

Suger's Search for Wooden Beams

On a certain night, when I had returned from celebrating Matins, I began to think in bed that I myself should go through all the forests of these parts. . . . Quickly disposing of other duties and hurrying up in the early morning, we hastened with our carpenters, and with the measurements of the beams, to the forest called Iveline. When we traversed our possession in the Valley of Chevreuse we summoned . . . the keepers of our own forests as well as men who knew about the other woods, and questioned them under oath whether we would find there, no matter with how much trouble, any timbers of that measure. At this they smiled, or rather would have laughed at us if they had dared; they wondered whether we were quite ignorant of the fact that nothing of the kind could be found in the entire region, especially since Milon, the Castellan of Chevreuse . . . had left nothing unimpaired or untouched that could be used for palisades and bulwarks while he was long subjected to wars both by our Lord the King and Amaury de Montfort. We however—scorning whatever they might say—began, with the courage of our faith as it were, to search through the woods; and towards the first hour we found one timber adequate to the measure. Why say more? By the ninth hour or sooner, we had, through the thickets, the depths of the forest and the dense, thorny tangles, marked down twelve timbers (for so many were necessary) to the astonishment of all. . . .

supply, which was dramatically increased by what some have called the "agricultural revolution" of the High Middle Ages, comparable to the agricultural revolution of the eighteenth century that also preceded and accompanied population explosion. Although some historians have questioned whether the medieval developments deserve to be called a "revolution," significant changes did occur in the way Europeans farmed.

Although the improvement in climate played an underlying role by producing better growing conditions, another important factor in increasing the production of food was the expansion of cultivated or arable land. This was done primarily by clearing forested areas for cultivation. We should also note that millions of acres of forests were also cut down to provide timber for fuel, houses, mills, bridges, fortresses, ships, and charcoal for the iron industry (see the box above). Eager for land, peasants of the eleventh and twelfth centuries cut down trees, drained swamps, and, in the area of the Netherlands, even began the reclamation of land from the sea. Monks were especially important in expanding the cul-

tivable land. The Cistercians, founded in 1098 (see Chapter 10), proved particularly ambitious in clearing forests, draining marshes, and plowing new land. By the thirteenth century, Europeans had available a total acreage for farming greater than any used before or since. Once settlers had fully cultivated a given area in western Europe, they tended to move eastward in search of new lands. German settlers crossed the Elbe, Oder, and Vistula rivers to colonize eastern Europe. They called it a civilizing mission; the native Slavs saw it as an invasion.

Technological changes also furthered the development of agriculture. The Middle Ages witnessed an explosion of labor-saving devices, many of which depended upon the use of iron, which was mined in different areas of Europe and traded to places where it was not found. Iron was in demand to make swords and armor as well as scythes, axeheads, new types of farming implements, such as hoes, and saws, hammers, and nails for building purposes. It was crucial to the development of the heavy-wheeled plow, the *carruca*, which made an enormous impact on medieval agriculture north of the Alps.

The plow of the Mediterranean and Near Eastern worlds had been the *aratum*, a nonwheeled light plow made mostly of wood that was sufficient to break the top layer of the light soils of those areas. It could be pulled by a donkey or single animal. South of the Alps, the organization of fields continued along the traditional lines of square fields since they facilitated cross plowing with the light wheelless plow. Since a single family could afford its own light plow, the family farm rather than the village remained the basic social unit in the Mediterranean world.

But such a light plow was totally ineffective in the heavy clay soils north of the Alps. The *carruca*, a new heavy-wheeled plow with an iron ploughshare, came into widespread use by the tenth century. It could turn over heavy soils and allow for their drainage. Because of its weight, six or eight oxen were needed to pull it. Oxen were slow, however, and two new inventions for the horse made greater productivity possible. A new horse collar appeared in the tenth century. Although horses were faster than oxen, they were limited in the amount they could pull because of the traditional harness, which tended to choke the horse if it pulled too much weight. The new horse collar distributed the weight around the shoulders and chest rather than the throat and could be used to hitch up a series of horses, enabling them to pull the new heavy plow faster and cultivate more land. The use of the horseshoe, an iron shoe nailed to the horse's hooves, spread in the eleventh and twelfth centuries and produced greater traction and better protection against the rocky and heavy clay soils of northern Europe.

The use of the heavy-wheeled plow also led to cooperative agricultural villages. Since iron was expensive, a heavy-wheeled plow had to be purchased by the entire community. Likewise an individual family could not afford a team of animals so villagers shared their beasts. Moreover, the size and weight of the plow determined that land would be cultivated in long strips to minimize the amount of turning that would have to be done.

Besides using horsepower, the High Middle Ages harnessed the power of water and wind to do jobs formerly done by human or animal power. The watermill, although invented as early as the second century B.C., was not used much in the Roman Empire since it was considered disruptive to the labor of slaves and free wage earners. Not until the High Middle Ages, when the spread of metals made it easier to build, did the watermill become widespread. In 1086, the survey of English land known as the Domesday Book listed 6,000 of them in England. Located along streams, they were used to grind grains for flour. Even dams were constructed to increase waterpower. The development of the cam enabled millwrights to mechanize entire industries; waterpower was used in certain phases of cloth production and to power triphammers for the working of metals.

Where rivers were unavailable or not easily dammed, Europeans developed windmills to yoke the power of the wind. Historians are unsure if windmills were imported into Europe (they were invented in Persia) or designed independently by Europeans. In either case, by the end of the twelfth century, they were beginning to dot the European landscape. The watermill and windmill were the most important devices for the harnessing of power before the invention of the steam engine in the eighteenth century; their spread had revolutionary consequences in enabling Europeans to produce more food.

The shift from a two-field to a three-field system also contributed to the increase in agricultural production. In the Early Middle Ages, it was common to plant one field while allowing another of equal size to lie fallow to regain its fertility. Now estates were divided into three parts. One field was planted in the fall with winter grains, such as rye and wheat, while spring grains, such as oats and barley, and vegetables, such as peas, beans, or lentils, were planted in the second field. The third was allowed to lie fallow. By rotating their use, only one-third rather than one-half of the land lay fallow at any time. The rotation of crops also prevented the soil from being exhausted so quickly. Grain yields increased, and those of the High Middle Ages remained the highest until the agricultural revolution of the eighteenth century. The three-field system was not adopted everywhere, however. It was not used in Mediterranean lands, and even in northern Europe the two-field and three-field systems existed side by side for centuries.

The Manorial System

As we saw in the last chapter, fief-holding rested upon an economic system known as manorialism. Although there were still free peasants, many peasants in northern Europe lived in agricultural villages as serfs subject to lords. These lords gained their economic sustenance from the labor of this subservient peasantry. In return, the peasants gained protection. The manor, as the agricultural estate with its dependent tenants was called, was the fundamental unit of rural organization in the Middle Ages. Oftentimes, a manor and village were synonymous; one agricultural village constituted the estate of a lord. Or a manor might consist of two or more villages. There was no single formula. Manorialism grew out of earlier practices and was especially encouraged by

The Manorial Court

▼ ▼ ▼

T he way of life of the medieval lord was made possible by the labors of the serfs on his manor. In addition to his right to collect rents, labor services, and fees from his serfs, the lord also possessed political authority over his serfs, including the right to hold a manorial court to try peasants for crimes and infractions of the manor's rules. This selection, taken from the records of an English manorial court from 1246 to 1249, lists the cases heard, the decisions of the jurors, and the subsequent penalties.

Select Pleas in Manorial Courts

John Sperling complains that Richard of Newmere on the Sunday next before S. Bartholomew's day [August 24] last past with his cattle, horses, and pigs wrongfully destroyed the corn on his (John's) land to his damage to the extent of one thrave of wheat, and to his dishonour to the extent of two shillings; and of this he produces suit. And Richard comes and defends all of it. Therefore let him go to the law six handed [with six companions who will swear to his innocence]. His pledges, Simon Combe and Hugh Frith [like bail bondsmen, pledges stood surety for a person ordered to show up in court or pay a fine].

Hugh Free in mercy [fined] for his beast caught in the lord's garden. Pledges, Walter Hill and William Slipper. Fine 6d. [sixpence].

(The) twelve jurors say that Hugh Cross has right in the bank and hedge about which there was a dispute between him and William White. Therefore let him hold in peace and let William be distrained [forced to comply by seizing his property] for his many trespasses. (Afterwards he made fine for 12d.)

From the whole township of Little Ogbourne, except seven, for not coming to wash the lord's sheep, 6s. 8d. [six shillings, eight pence].

Gilbert Richard's son gives 5s. for licence to marry a wife. Pledge, Seaman. Term (for payment), the Purification [February 2].

William Jordan in mercy for bad ploughing on the lord's land. Pledge, Arthur. Fine, 6d.

The parson of the Church is in mercy for his cow caught in the lord's meadow. Pledges, Thomas Ymer and William Coke.

From Martin Shepherd 6d. for the wound that he gave Pekin.

Ragenhilda of Bec gives 2s. for having married without licence. Pledge, William of Primer.

Walter Hull gives 13s. 4d. for licence to dwell on the land of the Prior of Harmondsworth so long as he shall live and as a condition finds pledges, to wit, William Slipper, John Bisuthe, Gilbert Bisuthe, Hugh Tree, William Johnson, John Hulle, who undertake that the said Walter shall do to the lord all the services and customs which he would do if he dwelt on the lord's land. . . .

It was presented that Robert Carter's son by night invaded the house of Peter Burgess and in felony threw stones at his door so that the said Peter raised the hue [alarm]. Therefore let the said Robert be committed to prison. Afterwards he made fine with 2s.

All the ploughmen of Great Ogbourne are convicted by the oath of twelve men . . . because by reason of their default (the land) of the lord is damaged to the amount of 9s. . . . And Walter Reaper is in mercy for concealing (i.e., not giving information as to) the said bad ploughing. Afterwards he made fine with the lord with 1 mark [13 shillings, fourpence].

the unsettled conditions of the Early Middle Ages, when many peasants gave up their freedom in return for protection.

The supervision of manors varied considerably. If the lord of a manor was a simple knight, he would probably live on the estate and supervise it in person. Great lords possessed many manors and relied on a steward or bailiff to run each estate. Lords controlled the lives of their serfs in a number of ways. Peasants were required to

provide labor services, pay rents, and be subject to the lord's jurisdiction.

Labor services consisted of working the lord's demesne, the land retained by the lord, which might consist of one-third to one-half of the cultivated lands scattered throughout the manor (the rest would have been allotted to the peasants for their maintenance), as well as building barns and digging ditches. Although labor requirements varied from manor to manor and person to person, a common work obligation was three days a week.

Many rents were paid in kind and included a share of every product raised by the serfs. Moreover, peasants paid the lord for the use of the manor's common pasturelands, streams, ponds, and surrounding woodlands. For example, if a peasant tenant fished in the pond or stream on a manor, he turned over part of the catch to his lord. If his cow grazed in the common pasture, he paid a rent in cheese produced from the cow's milk. Peasants were also obliged to pay a tithe (a tenth of their produce) to their local village church.

Lords possessed a variety of legal rights over their serfs as a result of their unfree status. Serfs were legally bound to the lord's land; they could not leave without his permission. Although free to marry, serfs could not marry anyone outside their manor without the lord's approval. Moreover, due to the decentralization of public power that was part of fief-holding, lords sometimes exercised public rights or political authority on their lands. This gave the lord the right to try peasants in his own court, although only for lesser crimes (called "low justice"). In fact, the lord's manorial court provided the only law that most peasants knew (see the box on p. 268). Finally, the lord's political authority enabled him to establish monopolies on certain services that provided additional revenues. Peasants could be required to bring their grain to the lord's mill and pay a fee to have it ground into flour. Thus, the rights a lord possessed on his manor gave him virtual control over both the lives and property of his serfs.

We should note that manors were controlled not only by lay lords, but also by monasteries and cathedral churches. Monasteries tended to be far more conscientious about keeping accurate records of their manorial estates than lay lords, and their surveys provide some of the best sources for medieval village life.

Daily Life of the Peasantry

Since conditions varied from manor to manor and region to region, it is impossible to generalize about the way all European peasants lived in the eleventh and twelfth centuries. Based on recent studies, however, we can make some generalizations about peasant life on the manors of Europe north of the Alps.

Peasant activities were largely determined by the seasons of the year. Each season brought a new round of tasks appropriate for the time, although some periods were considerably more hectic than others, especially August and September. The basic staple of the peasant diet was bread, so an adequate harvest of grains was crucial to survival in the winter months. A new cycle began in October when peasants prepared the ground for the planting of winter crops. In November came the slaughter of excess livestock since there was usually insufficient fodder to keep animals all winter. The meat would be salted to preserve it for winter use. In February and March, the land was plowed for spring crops—oats, barley, peas, beans, and lentils. Early summer was a comparatively relaxed time, although there was still weeding and sheepshearing to be done. In every season, the peas-

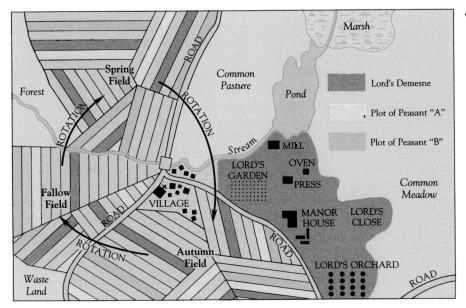

▼ Map 9.1 A Manor.

▼ **Peasant Activities.** The life of the European peasant was to a great degree determined by the seasons of the year. The peasants' primary function was labor, and the kind of work they did was regulated by the month and the season. In June, for example, hay was cut and thistles uprooted while in July the peasant worked at the harvest.

ants worked not only their own land, but also the lord's demesne. They also tended the small gardens attached to their dwellings where they grew the vegetables that made up part of their diet.

But peasants did not face a life of totally unrelieved labor thanks to the feast days or holidays of the Catholic church. Sunday mass, religious feast days, baptisms, marriages, and funerals all were important in peasant lives and brought them into contact with the village church, a crucial part of manorial life. The patron saint of the church was also the patron saint of the village.

THE VILLAGE CHURCH AND FEAST DAYS The village priest was responsible for the peasant's soul. In the village church, the peasant was baptized as an infant, con-

firmed in his or her faith, sometimes married, and given the sacrament of Holy Communion as well as the last rites of the church before death (on the sacraments of the church, see Chapter 10). It was the task of the village priest to instruct the peasants in the basic elements of Christianity so that they would gain the Christian's ultimate goal, salvation. But village priests were often barely literate peasants themselves, and it is hard to know how much church doctrine the peasants actually understood. Very likely, they regarded God as an all-powerful force who needed to be appeased by prayer to bring good harvests.

Special events in the peasant's calendar were the feast days commemorating the great events of the Christian faith or the lives of Christian saints or holy persons. The three great feasts of the Catholic church were Christmas (celebrating the birth of Christ), Easter (celebrating the resurrection of Christ), and Pentecost (celebrating the descent of the Holy Spirit on Christ's disciples fifty days after his resurrection). Numerous other feasts dedicated to saints or the Virgin Mary, the mother of Christ, were also celebrated, making a total of over fifty days that were essentially holidays. The most elaborate celebrations were often reserved for the feast day of the saint of the local church.

A number of the holidays provided a curious blend of paganism and Christianity, which is especially evident in Halloween. In pre-Christian northern Europe, November 1 had been a traditional day for celebrating a feast of the dead. The church made November 1 All Saints' (or Hallows') Day and November 2 All Souls' Day. Although both were feast days, the real celebration came on All Hallows' Eve, the night before November 1, when people lit bonfires and danced around them, frequently disguised in masks. Even Christmas, the most special of the Christian feasts, was held on the pagan celebration of the winter solstice. Feasting and drinking began on Christmas Day itself and continued for twelve days until the feast of the Epiphany on January 6. Of course, December and January were also the least busy months in the work cycle of the peasants and offered time for such gaiety and levity.

The village church was not just a religious center. Royal judges held court there and dispensed justice in both civil and criminal cases. Here also petty merchants peddled their goods, and the parish priest made public announcements of messages from both civil and ecclesiastical authorities.

THE PEASANT HOUSEHOLD AND FAMILY Peasant dwellings were very simple. Peasant cottages had wood frames surrounded by sticks with the space between them filled with straw and rubble and then plastered over with clay. Roofs were simply thatched. The houses of poorer peasants consisted of a single room, but others had at least two rooms—a main room for cooking, eating, and other activities and another room for sleeping. By the thirteenth century, richer peasants began building their houses out of stone. There was little privacy in a medieval household. Floors were simply dirt, which, after repeated sweepings, was gradually worn down. A hearth was located in the main room for heating and cooking, but since there were few or no windows and no chimney, the smoke created by fires in the hearth went out through cracks in the walls or more likely the thatched roof.

Households in medieval villages were based on the nuclear rather than the extended family. Surveys of monastic holdings reveal that the typical peasant household consisted of a husband and wife with two or three children. Due to the high infant mortality rates, more children were born than survived infancy. Males also tended to outnumber females due to the higher mortality rate for females, especially during childbearing years.

Peasant women occupied both an important and difficult position in manorial society. They were expected to carry and bear children and at the same time fulfill their obligation to labor in the fields. Their ability to manage the household might determine whether a peasant family would starve or survive in difficult times.

While simple, a peasant's daily diet was potentially nutritious when food was available. The basic staple of the peasant diet, and the medieval diet in general, was bread. While women made the dough for the bread, the loaves were usually baked in community ovens, which were a monopoly of the lord of the manor. Peasant bread was highly nutritious because it contained not only wheat and rye, but also barley, millet, and oats, giving it its dark appearance and very heavy, hard texture. Bread was supplemented by numerous vegetables from the household gardens, cheese from cow's or goat's milk, and, where available, wild game and fish from hunting and fishing. Manorial lords tended, however, to regulate fishing and were especially reluctant to allow peasants to hunt so that game could be reserved for the nobility. Woodlands also provided nuts, berries, and a foraging area for pigs. Fruits, such as apples, pears, and cherries, were also available. Chickens provided eggs and occasionally meat. Peasants usually ate meat only on the great feast days, such as Christmas, Easter, and Pentecost.

Grains were important not only for bread, but also for making ale. In northern European countries, ale was the most common drink of the poor. If records are accurate, enormous quantities of ale were consumed. A monastery in the twelfth century records a daily allotment to the monks of three gallons a day, far above the weekend consumption of many present-day college students. Peasants in the field undoubtedly consumed even more. This high consumption of alcohol might help to explain the large number of accidental deaths recorded in medieval court records.

▼ The New World of Trade and Cities

Medieval Europe was an overwhelmingly agrarian society with most people living in small villages. In the eleventh and twelfth centuries, however, new elements were introduced that began to transform the economic foundation of Western civilization: a revival of trade, considerable expansion in the circulation of money, a restoration of specialized craftsmen and artisans, and the growth and development of towns. These changes were made possible by the new agricultural practices and subsequent increase in food production, which freed part of the European population from producing their own food, leading to diversification in economic functions. Merchants and craftsmen could now buy their necessities.

▼ **Tasks of Peasant Women.** The peasant woman had a difficult life. While entrusted with such an important task as the management of the household, she was expected both to work in the fields and bear children. So much of her time was spent working with wool, spinning, carding, and weaving it into clothing, that the distaff became a symbol of feminity.

The Medieval Merchant
▼ ▼ ▼

The origins of the merchant class are clouded in uncertainty. Perhaps an occasional runaway serf acquired enough goods to become a wandering peddler and possibly even made enough money to be a flourishing merchant. More likely, however, the merchants' origins are to be found among the younger sons of prosperous farmers who had the capital to set themselves up in business. This exception is taken from the life of Godric, a twelfth-century merchant who became a hermit and a saint.

Life of Saint Godric

When the boy had passed his childish years quietly at home; then, as he began to grow to manhood, he began to follow more prudent ways of life, and to learn carefully and persistently the teachings of worldly forethought. Wherefore he chose not to follow the life of a husbandman, but rather to study, learn and exercise the rudiment of more subtle conceptions. For this reason, aspiring to the merchant's trade, he began to follow the chapman's way of life, first learning how to gain in small bargains and things of insignificant price; and thence, while yet a youth, his mind advanced little by little to buy and sell and gain from things of greater expense. For, in his beginnings, he was wont to wander with small wares around the villages and farmsteads of his own neighborhood; but, in process of time, he gradually associated himself by compact with city merchants. Hence, within a brief space of time, the youth who had trudged for many weary hours from village to village, from farm to farm, did so profit by his increase of age and wisdom as to travel with associates of his own age through towns and boroughs, fortresses and cities, to fairs and to all the various booths of the market-place, in pursuit of his public chaffer. He went along the high-way, neither puffed up by the good testimony of his conscience nor downcast in the nobler part of his soul by the reproach of poverty. . . .

At first, he lived as a chapman for four years in Lincolnshire, going on foot and carrying the smallest wares; then he travelled abroad, first to St. Andrews in Scotland and then for the first time to Rome. On his return, having formed a familiar friendship with certain other young men who were eager for merchandise, he began to launch upon bolder courses, and to coast frequently by sea to the foreign lands that lay around him. Thus, sailing often to and fro between Scotland and Britain, he traded in many divers wares and, amid these occupations, learned much worldly wisdom. . . .

Thus aspiring ever higher and higher, and yearning upward with his whole heart, at length his great labours and cares bore much fruit of worldly gain. For he laboured not only as a merchant but also as a shipman . . . to Denmark and to Flanders and Scotland; in all which lands he found certain rare, and therefore more precious, wares, which he carried to other parts wherein he knew them to be least familiar, and coveted by the inhabitants beyond the price of gold itself; wherefore he exchanged these wares for others coveted by men of other lands; and thus he chaffered most freely and assiduously. Hence he made great profit in all his bargains, and gathered much wealth in the sweat of his brow; for he sold dear in one place the wares which he had bought elsewhere at a small price.

The Revival of Trade

The revival of commercial activity was a gradual process. Although trade had never completely disappeared in western Europe, the uncertainties and chaotic conditions of the Early Middle Ages caused large-scale trade to decline except for Byzantine contacts with Italy and the Jewish traders who moved back and forth between the Muslim and Christian worlds.

By the end of the tenth century, however, men were emerging in Europe with both the skills and products for commercial activity (see the box above). Although most villages produced what they needed locally, other items were made that were unique to their region and could be sold elsewhere. This included a wide range of goods, such as flax and wool for clothes, wine for drinking and for use at the Catholic mass, salt for preserving food, furs for clothing, hemp for rope, and metals for weapons or tools. Some areas became particularly well known for certain products: England for raw wool, Scandinavia and Germany for iron, and Germany for silver.

Cities in Italy assumed a leading role in the revival of commercial activity. Venice, on the northeastern coast, had emerged as a town by the end of the eighth century with close commercial connections to the Byzantine Empire. It developed a commercial fleet and by the end of the tenth century had become the chief western trading center for Byzantine and Islamic commerce. Venice sent wine, grain, and timber to Constantinople in exchange for silk cloth, which was then peddled to other communities in northern Italy. Other coastal communities in western Italy also opened new commercial routes; Genoa and Pisa, for example, ventured into the western Mediterranean despite harassment by Muslim pirates. In the course of the eleventh century, Sardinia, Corsica, and Sicily were liberated from Muslim control; by 1100 the western Mediterranean was relatively safe for Italian commerce.

During the same period, the west had also begun a series of crusades for the "liberation" of the Holy Land from the Muslims (see Chapter 10). Italian merchants benefited from the crusaders' eastern conquests and were able to establish new mercantile settlements in eastern ports. There they obtained silks, sugar, and spices, which they subsequently carried back to Italy and the west. Although these items were not entirely new to western Europe, they were now traded in increasingly larger quantities. At the same time, northern Italy began to experience rapid economic growth from the production of high-quality cloth, which was also being traded.

While the north Italian cities were busy enlarging the scope of commercial activity in the Mediterranean, the towns of Flanders were doing likewise in northern Europe. Flanders, the area along the coast of present-day Belgium and northeastern France, was known for the production of a much desired high-quality woolen cloth. Flanders's location made it a logical entrepot for the traders of northern Europe. Merchants from England, Scandinavia, France, and Germany converged there to trade their wares for woolen cloth. England, in particular, became the chief supplier of raw wool for the Flemish woolen industry. Flanders prospered in the eleventh and twelfth centuries, and such Flemish towns as Bruges and Ghent became centers for the trade and manufacture of woolen cloth.

By the twelfth century, both Italy and Flanders had become centers of a revived trade, making it almost inevitable that a regular exchange of goods would eventually develop between these two major centers of north-

ern and southern European trade. The dangers and difficulties of sea travel around western Europe and the expense of overland journeys, however, made such a project seem unlikely. Lords also felt free to charge tolls to merchants going through their lands and did not hesitate to plunder their caravans when they needed money.

As trade contacts increased, however, even lords began to see the advantages of encouraging trade. The best example comes form the counts of Champagne in northern France who devised a series of six fairs held annually in the chief towns of their territory. They guaranteed the safety of visiting merchants, supervised the trading activities, and, of course, collected a sales tax on all goods exchanged at the fairs. The fairs of Champagne became the largest commercial marketplace in western Europe where the goods of northern Europe could be exchanged for the goods of southern Europe and the east. Northern merchants brought the furs, woolen cloth, tin, hemp, and honey of northern Europe and exchanged them for the cloth and swords of northern Italy and the silks,

▼ **The Medieval Fair.** This fifteenth-century illustration depicts the fair of Lendit, which was held in June of every year outside of Paris. The medieval fairs were places where merchants from northern and southern Europe and from the east could meet and exchange their goods. First created by the Counts of Champagne, the fairs attracted merchants of such wealth that both the nobility and the church accorded them special privileges and special protection.

sugar, and spices of the east. The prosperity of the Champagne fairs caused lords everywhere, both lay and ecclesiastical, to follow their example and establish trading fairs.

Long-distance trade, in turn, was paralleled by the development of local trade throughout Europe's rural world by 1200. Since excess grain could be sold and necessities bought, manors no longer had to be self-sufficient. Rivers made it possible to transport some bulky items, such as wine, considerable distances. After their conquest of England in 1066 (see The European Kingdoms: England later in this chapter), the Norman nobility insisted upon importing wine from their native France. Barges brought the barrels of new wine down the Seine to Rouen where they were transferred to ships that transported them to England across the Channel. New avenues for short-distance trade drastically affected the local economy. Vineyards replaced grain fields in areas favorable to grape growing when both lords and peasants realized the profits that could be made.

As trade increased, the demand for coins arose at fairs and trading markets of all kinds. Without gold mines of its own, western Europe had little gold coinage in circulation before the thirteenth century. Silver and copper coins were most frequently used. Many of the silver coins were made from silver mined in the Harz Mountains of central Germany, where silver had first been discovered at the end of the tenth century. The pound sterling of England and the pounds of Paris, Tours, and Anjou became the most important coins in circulation in France and England in the twelfth century.

Medieval Cities

Most importantly, the revival of commerce fostered the development of urban life. Merchants could not function in a society that emphasized the exaction of labor services and attachment to the land. They needed places where they could build warehouses to store their goods for transshipment and dwelling places that could serve as permanent bases. Medieval cities did not develop just anywhere. To meet merchants' needs, they were located near sources of protection and alongside rivers or major arteries of some kind that provided favorable routes of transportation.

Towns in the economic sense, as centers of population where merchants and artisans practiced their trades and purchased their food from surrounding territories, had greatly declined in the Early Middle Ages, especially in Europe north of the Alps. Old Roman cities continued to exist but had greatly declined in size and popu-

lation. Many had become the sees or seats of bishops and archbishops or the locations of counts and functioned as administrative centers for both church and state. With the revival of trade, merchants began to settle in these old cities, followed by craftsmen or artisans, men who on manors or elsewhere had developed skills and who perceived the opportunity to ply their trade and produce objects that could be sold by the merchants. In the course of the eleventh and twelfth centuries, the old Roman cities came alive with new populations and growth. By 1100, people had expanded into the old areas of the city; after 1100, they moved outside the old walls, necessitating the construction of new city walls.

In the Mediterranean world, cities had survived in a more visible fashion. Spain's Islamic cities had a flourishing urban life, and southern Italy still possessed such thriving cities as Bari, Salerno, Naples, and Amalfi. Although greatly reduced in size, Rome, the old capital of the Roman world, had survived as the center of papal administration. In northern Italy, Venice had already emerged by the end of the eighth century as a town because of its commercial connections to Byzantium.

Beginning in the late tenth century, many new cities or towns were founded, particularly in northern Europe. Usually, a group of merchants established a settlement near some fortified stronghold, such as a castle or monastery. Castles were particularly favored since they were usually located along major routes of transportation or at the intersection of two such trade routes; the lords of the castle also offered protection. If the settlement prospered and expanded, new walls were built to protect it.

The town was a unique phenomenon in medieval society. Most were closely tied to their surrounding territories since they were dependent on the countryside for their food supplies. In addition, they were often part of the territory belonging to a lord and were subject to his jurisdiction. Although lords wanted to treat towns and townspeople as they would their vassals and serfs, cities had totally different needs and a different perspective.

The new class of townspeople did not really fit into the traditional society of the Middle Ages. Since they were not lords, they were not subject to the body of customs that applied to lords. They were not really serfs or peasants either and were reluctant to accommodate themselves to manorial service, although many may originally have come from the ranks of the peasantry of the surrounding countryside. Townspeople needed mobility to trade. Consequently, these townspeople (the merchants and artisans who came to be called burghers or bourgeoisie from the word *burgus*, a Latinized version of the German word *burg* meaning a walled enclosure) constituted a revolutionary group who needed their own unique laws to meet their requirements. Since the townspeople were profiting from the growth of trade and sale of their products, they were willing to pay to make their own laws and govern themselves. In many instances, lords and kings saw the potential for vast new sources of revenues and were willing to grant (or, more accurately, sell) the liberties the townspeople were beginning to demand.

By 1100, townspeople were obtaining charters from their territorial lords, either lay or ecclesiastical, that granted them the privileges they wanted. In most cases, they obtained their goal simply by offering some kind of money payment or regular revenue. Most towns gained at least four basic liberties in their charters. These included a testamentary right, the right to bequeath goods and sell property; the freedom from military obligation to the lord; written urban law that guaranteed the freedom of the townspeople; and the right to become a free person after residing a year and a day in the town. The last provision made it possible for a runaway serf who could avoid capture to become a free man in a city. While almost all new urban communities gained these elementary liberties, not all obtained the right to govern themselves. Some communities received only partial self-government; the town's charter provided for a provost to serve as the king's (or lord's) agent and collect taxes and administer justice in the community. Other communities, however, were granted many rights of self-government. In 1130, King Henry I granted London a charter in which the citizens received the right to choose their own officials, essentially granting them self-government. Moreover, they had the right to administer their own courts of law. While taxes were still paid to the king, they were collected by the city's officials, not the king's.

Often urban communities experienced an unwillingness on the part of their lords to grant them all the liberties they wanted, especially self-government. Bishops in cathedral cities were particularly tenacious of their privileges. In these cities, merchants and serfs lived in the same community; to grant freedom meant the loss of the services of the serfs who tilled the fields outside the city. Thus, for a bishop to grant self-government to local officials within his city meant the end of his own authority. Where townspeople experienced difficulty in obtaining privileges, they often swore an oath, forming an association called a commune, and resorted to force against their lay or ecclesiastical lords.

Communes made their first appearance in Italy where, even in the Early Middle Ages, urban communities continued to exist. In northern Italy, in the regions called Tuscany and Lombardy, towns were governed by their bishops, but the nobles whose lands surrounded the cities took an active interest in the towns, whether they lived there or not. Bishops were usually supported by the emperors, who used them as their chief administrators. In the eleventh century, city residents rebelled against the rule of the bishops, swore communal associations with the noble vassals of the bishops, and used force to overthrow the authority of the bishops. The alliance between town residents and rural nobles was overwhelming, and in the course of the eleventh and twelfth centuries bishops were shorn of their authority. Communes took over the rights of government and created new offices, such as consuls and city councils, for self-rule. Pisa, Milan, Arezzo, and Genoa all had gained self-government by the end of the eleventh century. The major towns of Italy eventually developed into independent city-states, free of any overriding authority.

Although communes were also sworn in northern Europe, especially in France and Flanders, townspeople did not have the support of rural nobles. Revolts against lay lords were usually brutally suppressed; those against bishops, as in Laon at the beginning of the twelfth century (see the box on p. 276), were more frequently successful. When they succeeded, communes received the right to choose their own officials, hold their own courts, and run their own cities. Unlike the Italian towns, however, towns in France and England did not become independent city-states, but remained ultimately subject to royal authority.

Whatever their condition or degree of independence, medieval cities remained relatively small in comparison to either ancient or modern cities. By the twelfth century, a large trading city would number about 5,000 inhabitants. By 1200, London was the largest city in England with 30,000 people. Otherwise, north of the Alps, only a few great centers of commerce, such as Bruges and Ghent, had a population close to 40,000. Italian cities tended to be larger, with Venice, Florence, Genoa, Milan, and Naples numbering almost 100,000. Even the largest European city, however, seemed insignificant alongside the Byzantine capital of Constantinople or the Arab cities of Damascus, Baghdad, and Cairo. For a long time to come, Europe remained predominantly rural. However, the wealth of the cities guaranteed that they would have a significantly disproportionate influence on the political and economic life of Europe. In the long run, the rise of towns and the development of commerce laid the foundations for the eventual transformation of

A Communal Revolt

▼ ▼ ▼

The growth of towns and cities was a major aspect of economic life in the High Middle Ages. When townspeople were unable to gain basic liberties for themselves from the lord in whose territory their town was located, they sometimes swore a "commune" to gain these privileges by force. This selection by a contemporary abbot describes the violence that accompanied a commune formed at Laon in France in 1116. The bishop of Laon, lord of the town, had granted privileges to the townspeople in return for a large payment. Later he rescinded his grant, thereby angering the citizens.

The Autobiography of Guibert, Abbot of Nogent-sous-Coucy

All the efforts of the prelate and nobles in these days were reserved for fleecing their inferiors. But those inferiors were no longer moved by mere anger, but goaded into a murderous lust for the death of the Bishop and his accomplices and bound themselves by oath to effect their purpose. Now they say that four hundred took the oath. Such a mob could not be secret and when it came to the ears of Anselm towards evening of the holy Sabbath, he sent word to the Bishop, as he was retiring to rest, not to go out to the early morning service, knowing that if he did he must certainly be killed. But he, infatuated with excessive pride said, "Fie, surely I shall not perish at the hands of such. . . ."

The next day, that is, the fifth in Easter week, after midday, as he was engaged in business with Archdeacon Walter about the getting of money, behold there arose a disorderly noise throughout the city, men shouting "Commune!" and again through the middle of the chapel of the Blessed Mary through that door by which the murderers of Gerard had come and gone, there citizens now entered the Bishop's court with swords, battle-axes, bows and hatchets, and carrying clubs and spears, a very great company. As soon as this sudden attack was discovered, the nobles rallied from all sides to the Bishop, having sworn to give him aid against such an onset, if it should occur. . . . [Despite the assistance of the nobles, the commoners were victorious.]

Next the outrageous mob attacking the Bishop and howling before the walls of his palace, he with some who were succouring him fought them off by hurling of stones and shooting of arrows. For he now, as at all times, showed great spirit as a fighter; but because he had wrongly and in vain taken up another sword, by the sword he perished. Therefore, being unable to stand against the reckless assaults of the people, he put on the clothes of one of his servants and flying to the vaults of the church hid himself in a cask, shut up in which with the head fastened on by a faithful follower he thought himself safely hidden. And as they ran hither and thither demanding where, not the Bishop, but the hangdog, was, they seized one of his pages, but through his faithfulness could not get what they wanted. Laying hands on another, they learned from the traitor's nod where to look for him. Entering the vaults therefore, and searching everywhere, at last they found [him]. . . .

[The bishop] therefore, sinner though he was, yet the Lord's anointed, was dragged forth from the cask by the hair, beaten with many blows and brought out into the open air in the narrow lane of the clergy's cloister before the house of the chaplain Godfrey. And as he piteously implored them, ready to take oath that he would henceforth cease to be their Bishop, that he would leave the country, and as they with hardened hearts jeered at him, one named Bernard . . . lifting his battle-axe brutally dashed out the brains of that sacred, though sinner's, head, and he slipping between the hands of those who held him, was dead before he reached the ground stricken by another thwart blow under the eye-sockets and across the middle of the nose. There brought to his end, his legs were cut off and many another wound inflicted. But Thibaut seeing the ring on the finger of the erstwhile prelate and not being able to draw it off, cut off the dead man's finger and took it. And so stripped to his skin he was thrown into a corner in front of his chaplain's house. My God, who shall recount the mocking words that were thrown at him by passersby, as he lay there, and with what clods and stones and dirt his corpse was covered?

Europe from a rural agricultural society to an urban industrial one.

Medieval towns and cities represented unique corporative bodies within their larger civilization, quite unlike either ancient or modern cities where laws were (and are) the same for city and rural inhabitants. Medieval cities were bastions of relatively free men and women, but they were by no means democracies where inhabitants were considered equal. The control of cities tended to fall into the hands of patricians, a ruling elite stemming in many cases from families who had made fortunes in long-distance trade. But cities did possess freedoms not found elsewhere in medieval society. Their separation from the rest of their world was symbolized in a sense by their own town walls, which protected them but also separated them from the outside world. Cities were a new world in the midst of kings, serfs, and lords.

▼ The Recovery and Reform of the Catholic Church

In the Early Middle Ages, the Catholic church had played a leading role in converting and civilizing first the Germanic invaders and later the Vikings and Magyars. Although highly successful, this had not been accomplished without challenges that undermined the spiritual life of the church itself.

The Problems of Decline

Since the fourth century, the popes of the Catholic church had operated on the basis of their supremacy over the affairs of the church. After their agreement with Pepin in the eighth century (see Chapter 8), the popes had also come to exercise more control over the territories in central Italy that came to be known as the Papal States. From the eighth through the tenth century, the papacy was faced with serious problems resulting from Italy's political fragmentation. Byzantine possessions, threats from the Muslims, and the attempts of German emperors to rule northern and central Italy menaced the papacy's own interests in central Italy. As the civil rulers of Rome, the popes came to rely on the powerful noble families of the area for protection. As a result, Roman aristocratic families came to view the papacy as an office worth controlling, and it was not unusual in the ninth and tenth centuries for the heads of aristocratic factions to become popes despite their obvious lack of spiritual qualities. Perhaps the most notorious was Pope John XII,

who was made pope in 956 at the age of sixteen and deposed at the age of twenty-three by Emperor Otto I for a series of scandalous crimes and sexual excesses.

The monastic ideal had also suffered during the Early Middle Ages. Benedictine monasteries had sometimes been exemplary centers of Christian living and learning, but the invasions of Vikings, Magyars, and Muslims wreaked havoc with many monastic establishments. Many were obliterated in Ireland, Britain, and France, and many that survived had suffered considerable damage. Discipline declined, as did the monastic reputation for learning and holiness. At the same time, a growing number of monasteries fell under the control of local lords, as did much of the church.

The domination of lay people over the clergy was perhaps inevitable given the chaotic conditions of the Early Middle Ages. The church became increasingly entangled in the evolving fief-holding system. Chief officials of the church, such as bishops and abbots, came to hold their offices as fiefs from nobles. As vassals, they were obliged to carry out the usual services, including military obligations. For some, this meant taking up arms, even though a prelate of the church was forbidden to kill; for others, it involved providing a contingent of knights to fight for the lord. Of course, lords assumed the right to appoint their choices as vassals, even when their vassals included bishops and abbots. Since the lords often selected their vassals from other noble families and chose them for political reasons, it could be expected that this secularization of bishops and abbots would lead to a serious decline in the execution of their spiritual responsibilities. An abbot, for example, chosen for political reasons by a lay lord, might care little about monastic discipline. Bishops, in turn, who were responsible for supervising the monasteries in their districts, might pay scant attention to what the monks were doing. These practices spread to local levels as well where parish priests were simply chosen by local lords to serve their purposes.

It should come as no surprise then that the standards of clerical behavior declined precipitously. Two problems were especially troublesome: clerical marriage and simony. From early on, the Catholic church had encouraged celibacy as the norm for its clergy. In the Early Middle Ages, however, this prohibition had become virtually impossible to enforce and was largely ignored. Simony, the sale of church offices, was a logical outcome of a system that had come to view church offices as secular positions and important sources of revenue. Both simony and clerical marriage were increasingly singled out as the symbols of the church's decline stemming from excessive involvement in worldly affairs. A number of people felt the time had come to reform this situation.

The Cluniac Reform Movement

The reform of the Catholic church began in Burgundy in eastern France in 910 when Duke William of Aquitaine founded the abbey of Cluny. This was the greatest single religious event of the tenth century. The monastery began with a renewed dedication to the highest spiritual ideals of the Benedictine rule and was fortunate in possessing a series of abbots in the tenth century who exemplified and maintained these ideals. Cluny was deliberately kept independent from any secular control. As Duke William stipulated in his original charter: "It has pleased us also to insert in this document that, from this day, those same monks there congregated shall be subject neither to our yoke, nor to that of our relatives, nor to the sway of the royal might, nor to that of any earthly power."[1] Finally, the new monastery at Cluny tried to eliminate some of the abuses that had crept into religious communities by stressing the need for work, replacing manual labor with the copying of manuscripts, and demanding more community worship and less private prayer.

The Cluniac reform movement struck an enthusiastic response, first in France and eventually in all of western and central Europe. New monasteries were founded based on Cluniac ideals, and previously existing monasteries rededicated themselves by adopting the Cluniac program. To avoid the lack of supervision that had allowed so much corruption into the monastic movement, all monasteries that became part of the Cluniac system placed themselves under the supervision of Cluny itself.

The abbot of Cluny was the only abbot for the hundreds of Cluniac religious houses. Each establishment was headed by a prior who was subordinate to the abbot of Cluny. The latter spent considerable time visiting the various houses to ensure their compliance with the Cluniac regulations. This centralization of control guaranteed rigid discipline and the maintenance of the highest standards in every Cluniac monastery. By the eleventh century, the movement was also beginning to reach beyond monasticism and into the papacy itself, which was in dire need of help.

The Reform of the Papacy

By the eleventh century, two different approaches to the reform of the church had emerged. The first, which stemmed from the Carolingian period, was based on the assumption that emperors, and particularly the emperor in the west, had received their power from God. As Conrad II of Germany (1024–1039) was informed by the archbishop of Mainz at his coronation: "Divine Piety has been unwilling for you to be without preparatory discipline, so that after this instruction from Heaven you might take up the Christian Empire. You have come to the highest dignity: you are the vicar of Christ."[2] It was incumbent upon the most holy emperor to lead the way for reform, and from his perspective this meant removing unworthy clerics and even popes from office if necessary.

A different approach to reform focused on the church's freedom. It was argued that no lay authority, including the emperor, should hold power over the church. To expedite reforms, the church needed to be free from lay interference. These two alternative ap-

▼ **Cluny Reconstructed.** Pictured here is a reconstruction of the monastery of Cluny as it appeared in approximately 1157. Founded in 910 by Duke William of Aquitaine, Cluny attempted to eliminate many of the abuses that had arisen within the monastic community. Eventually, the Cluniac program spread throughout Europe, and all those monasteries that became part of the movement were placed under the authority of the abbot of Cluny.

proaches to reform could and did overlap in the first half of the eleventh century. In a very real sense, we could say that the first approach was responsible for creating the second since it was an emperor, Henry III, who took personal responsibility for appointing a reforming line of popes.

In 1046, Emperor Henry III (1039–1056) became outraged when three rival popes claimed to be the rightful one. Following what he believed to be his prerogatives as a Christian emperor, he deposed all three and eventually appointed his cousin as Pope Leo IX (1049–54). Leo IX was the first of a series of reforming popes who brought reform ideals to their leadership of the church and aspired to a universal reform of Christendom.

To ensure the effectiveness of the reform movement, Leo IX instituted structural changes in the government of the church by making regular use of a group of church officials known as cardinals. The word *cardinal* had been used as a title of honor for some of the more important priests in the great churches of Rome. Leo now began to appoint reforming clerics from all over Europe as cardinals and then to use them as his major advisers and administrators. From this time on, cardinals played a major role in the administration of the church. In fact, in 1059, a reform church council at Rome tried to eliminate both Roman aristocratic factions and emperors from interfering in the choice of popes by decreeing that popes should be elected only by the cardinals. The election of popes by the college of cardinals has been Catholic practice ever since.

Strengthening the control of the papacy over the church was only one goal of the reform movement. The reformers also wanted to outlaw simony and eliminate violations of clerical celibacy. As a reform decree of the church stated: "Those who have been advanced to any grade of holy orders, or to any office, through simony, that is, by the payment of money, shall hereafter have no

right to officiate in the holy church. . . . Nor shall clergymen who are married say mass or serve the altar in any way."[3] At the same time, papal reformers called for the church's freedom from lay interference in the appointment of church officials. This issue of lay investiture was dramatically taken up by the greatest of the reform popes of the eleventh century, Gregory VII.

Pope Gregory VII (1073–1085) and the Investiture Controversy

One of the reformers named as a cardinal by Leo IX was a monk named Hildebrand. He was a strong personality, who held a passionate conviction about the need for church reform and papal leadership to accomplish it. Elected pope in 1073, he was absolutely certain that he had been chosen by God to reform the church. In pursuit of those aims, Gregory vigorously restated claims of papal power. His dedication to his ideals led him into the Investiture Conflict, one of the great church-state confrontations of the Middle Ages.

There is no doubt that Gregory VII believed that he was truly God's "vicar on earth." While previous popes had been content to accept their authority over the affairs of the church, Gregory asserted that the pope's authority extended over all of Christendom and included the right to depose emperors if they disobeyed his wishes. Gregory's program of reform was directed toward the "freedom of the church." He perceived that a true reform of the church was not possible if secular rulers controlled the appointment of clerical officials. He sought nothing less than the elimination of lay investiture or the practice by which secular rulers both chose and invested their nominees to church offices with the symbols of their office. Only in this way could the church regain its freedom, by which Gregory meant the right of the church to appoint clergy and run its own affairs. If rulers did not accept these "divine" commands, then they could be deposed by the pope acting in his capacity as the vicar of Christ (see the box on p. 280). Gregory VII soon found himself in conflict with the king of Germany over these claims. (The king of Germany was also the emperor-designate since it had been accepted by this time that only kings of Germany could be emperors, but they did not officially use the title "emperor" until they were crowned by the pope.)

King Henry IV (1056–1106) of Germany was also a determined personality. For many years, German kings had depended upon appointing high-ranking clerics, especially bishops, as their vassals in order to use them as administrators. While to the popes this might seem an infringement on the freedom of the church, it was a

The "Gregorian Revolution:" Papal Claims

▼ ▼ ▼

In the eleventh century, a dynamic group of cardinals and popes pushed for the "freedom of the church." This came to mean not only papal control over the affairs of the church, but also the elimination of lay investiture. The reformers saw the latter as the chief issue at the heart of lay control of the church. In trying to eliminate it, the reforming popes, especially Gregory VII, extended papal claims to include the right to oversee the secular authorities, and, in particular, to depose rulers under certain circumstances. The following selection is from a document that was entered in the papal register in 1075. It consisted of twenty-seven assertions that probably served as headings, or a table of contents, for a collection of ecclesiastical writings that supported the pope's claims.

The Dictates of the Pope

1. That the Roman church was founded by God alone.
2. That the Roman pontiff alone can with right be called universal.
3. That he alone can depose or reinstate bishops.
4. That, in a council, his legate, even if a lower grade, is above all bishops, and can pass sentence of deposition against them.
5. That the pope may depose the absent.
6. That, among other things, we ought not to remain in the same house with those excommunicated by him. . . .
8. That he alone may use the imperial insignia.
9. That of the pope alone all princes shall kiss the feet.
10. That his name alone shall be spoken in the churches.
11. That this is the only name in the world.
12. That it may be permitted to him to depose emperors.
13. That he may be permitted to transfer bishops if need be. . . .
17. That no chapter and no book shall be considered canonical without his authority.
18. That a sentence passed by him may be retracted by no one; and that he himself, alone of all, may retract it.
19. That he himself may be judged by no one.
20. That no one shall dare to condemn one who appeals to the apostolic chair.
21. That to the latter should be referred the more important cases of every church.
22. That the Roman church has never erred; nor will it err to all eternity, the Scripture bearing witness.
23. That the Roman pontiff, if he have been canonically ordained, is undoubtedly made a saint by the merits of St. Peter. . . .
25. That he may depose and reinstate bishops without assembling a synod.
26. That he who is not at peace with the Roman church shall not be considered catholic.
27. That he may absolve subjects from their fealty to wicked men.

---

simple matter of political expediency to the German king; without the bishops, he could not hope to maintain his own power vis-à-vis the powerful German nobles. At the time they entered their offices, bishops in Germany were invested with two symbols: the *regalia,* or the symbols of temporal office (a scepter), and the *spiritualia,* or the symbols of spiritual office (the ring and crozier or staff). The kings of Germany had grown accustomed to investing their nominees as bishop with both symbols of office, the temporal and spiritual. In 1075, Pope Gregory issued a decree forbidding important clerics from receiving their spiritual investiture from lay leaders: "We decree that no one of the clergy shall receive the investiture with a bishopric or abbey or church from the hand of an emperor or king or of any lay person. . . ."[4] Henry had no intention of obeying a decree that challenged the very heart of his administration.

The immediate cause of the so-called Investiture Controversy was a disputed election to the important position of the bishopric of Milan. The bishop was also the lay ruler of the city. Control of such an important Italian bishopric was crucial if the king wished to reestablish German power in northern Italy. Since Milan was considered second only to Rome in importance as a bishopric, papal interest in the office was also keen. Pope and king backed competing candidates for the position.

To gain acceptance of his candidate, the pope threatened the king with excommunication. Excommunication is a censure by which a person is deprived of receiving the sacraments of the church. To counter this threat, the king called a synod or assembly of German bishops, all of whom he had appointed, and had them depose the pope:

> Henry, king not through usurpation but through the holy ordination of God, to Hildebrand, at present not pope but false monk. . . . you . . . have not shunned to rise up against the royal power conferred upon us by God, daring to threaten to divest us of it. As if we have received our kingdom from you! As if the kingdom and the empire were in your and not in God's hand! . . . You, therefore, damned by this curse and by the judgment of all our bishops and by our own, descend and relinquish the apostolic chair which you have usurped . . . I Henry, king by the grace of God, do say unto you, together with all our bishops: Descend, descend, to be damned throughout the ages.[5]

Pope Gregory VII responded by excommunicating the king and freeing his subjects from their allegiance to him. The latter was a clever move. The German nobles were only too eager to diminish the power of a centralized monarchy because of the threat it posed to their own power, and they welcomed this opportunity to rebel against the king. Both the nobles and bishops of Germany agreed to hold a meeting in Germany with the pope to solve the problem, possibly by choosing a new king. Gregory set out for Germany. Henry, realizing the threat to his power, forestalled the pope by traveling to northern Italy, where he met the pope at Canossa in January 1077, admitted his transgressions, and begged for forgiveness and absolution (see the box on p. 282). Although he made the king wait three days, the pope had no choice but to grant absolution to the penitent sinner and lift the ban of excommunication. This did not end the problem however. Henry IV returned to Germany, engaged in a fierce struggle to crush the nobles who had rebelled against him, and returned to his old practices. Within three years, pope and king were again locked in combat. This time, Henry responded to the pope's second excommunication by leading an army into Italy. Gregory was forced to leave Rome and died in exile, convinced he had failed.

The struggle continued until a new German king and a new pope achieved a compromise in 1122 known as the Concordat of Worms. Under this agreement, a bishop in Germany was first elected by the cathedral canons, although the king had the right to be present at the election, a clear indication that the king could still influence the final outcome. After election, the nominee paid homage to the king as his lord, who in turn invested him with the symbols of temporal office. A representative of the pope, however, then invested the new bishop with the symbols of his spiritual office.

This struggle between church and state was an important element in the history of Europe in the High Middle Ages. In the Early Middle Ages, popes had been dependent on emperors and had allowed them to exercise considerable authority over church affairs. But a set of new ideals championed by activist cardinals and popes in the eleventh century now supported the "freedom of the church," which meant not only the freedom of the church to control its own affairs, but also extreme claims of papal authority. Not only was the pope superior to all other bishops, but popes now claimed the right to depose kings under certain circumstances. Such papal claims ensured further church-state confrontations.

▼ The Emergence and Growth of European Kingdoms, 1000–1200

The political organization of Europe had been severely tested by the internal disintegration of the Carolingian Empire and the invasions of the ninth and tenth centuries. The attempts of German kings to reestablish the empire based on Germany and Italy had been largely unsuccessful. Although the development of new economic and social forces, the money economy, commerce, and rise of cities, would eventually undermine feudalism, the period from 1000 to 1200 witnessed the high point of feudal institutions.

The Significance of the Aristocracy

In the High Middle Ages, European society was dominated by a group of men whose primary preoccupation was warfare. King Alfred of England had said that a "well-peopled land" must have "men of prayer, men of war, and men of work," and medieval ideals held to a tripartite division of society into these three basic groups. The "men of war" were the lords and vassals of medieval society.

The lords were the kings, dukes, counts, and viscounts (and even bishops and archbishops) who held extensive lands and considerable political power. They and others formed an aristocracy or nobility that since Carolingian times consisted of people who exercised real political, economic, and social power. Nobles were distinguished by three major criteria: birth, wealth, and

The Investiture Controversy: The Encounter at Canossa
▼ ▼ ▼

Perhaps there is no more dramatic event in the Investiture Controversy than the encounter between Pope Gregory VII and King Henry IV at Canossa in January 1077. To forestall Gregory's meeting with the German prelates and nobles in Germany, Henry traveled to northern Italy and begged the pope for absolution. The pope granted it since he was bound not to refuse absolution to a penitent sinner. This description is from Gregory's own account.

The Correspondence of Pope Gregory VII: To the German Princes

Meanwhile we received certain information that the king was on the way to us. Before he entered Italy he sent us word that he would make satisfaction to God and St. Peter and offered to amend his way of life and to continue obedient to us, provided only that he should obtain from us absolution and the apostolic blessing. For a long time we delayed our reply and held long consultations, reproaching him bitterly through messengers back and forth for his outrageous conduct, until finally, of his own accord and without any show of hostility or defiance, he came with a few followers to the fortress of Canossa where we were staying. There, on three successive days, standing before the castle gate, laying aside all royal insignia, barefooted and in coarse attire, he ceased not with many tears to beseech the apostolic help and comfort until all who were present or who had heard the story were so moved by pity and compassion that they pleaded his cause with prayers and tears. All marveled at our unwonted severity, and some even cried out that we were showing, not the seriousness of apostolic authority, but rather the cruelty of a savage tyrant.

At last, overcome by his persistent show of penitence and the urgency of all present, we released him from the bonds of anathema and received him into the grace of Holy Mother Church, accepting from him the guarantees described below, confirmed by the signatures of the abbot of Cluny, of our daughters, the Countess Matilda [countess of Tuscany] and the Countess Adelaide [marchioness of Turin], and other princes, bishops and laymen who seemed to be of service to us.

---

power. Originally, the ability to fight had been esteemed, but was not considered the crucial characteristic of a noble. In the late tenth century, as lords sought retainers, a group of ordinary knights emerged who expanded in number in the eleventh century. Initially, they were not considered aristocrats, but simply retainers, who fought for their lord in return for weapons and daily sustenance. But in the course of the twelfth and thirteenth centuries, knights and nobles fused together into the social class of the aristocracy. In the process, noble and knight came to mean much the same thing, and warfare likewise tended to become a distinguishing characteristic of a nobleman. The great lords and knights came to form a common caste; they were warriors and the institution of knighthood united them. Nevertheless, there were also social divisions among them based on extremes of wealth and landholdings.

Medieval theory maintained that the warlike qualities of the nobility were justified by their role as defenders of society. Knights, however, were also notoriously known for fighting each other. The Catholic church intervened and while it could not stop the incessant bloodletting, did at least try to limit it by instituting the Peace of God. Beginning in the eleventh century, the church encouraged knights to take an oath to respect churches and pilgrimage centers and to cease from attacking noncombatants, such as clergy, poor people, merchants, and women. It was, of course, permissible to continue killing each other. At the same time, the church initiated the Truce of God, which forbade fighting on Sundays and the primary feast days.

These peace movements did not depend solely upon the pious pronouncements of church leaders and councils. By the end of the eleventh century, Europeans were forming peace associations at the local level in which members took oaths to enforce the Peace and Truce of God; even armies were created to enforce them. In some territories, rulers themselves realized how important it was to minimize private warfare if they were to strengthen their own power. The duke of Normandy, for example, transformed the Peace of God into the Peace of the Duke.

As the church moved to diminish fighting, it also worked to redirect the nobility's warlike energy into different channels, such as crusades against the Muslims (see Chapter 10), and was quite willing to justify violence when used against peace-breakers and especially against the infidel. Hence, being a warrior on behalf of God easily vindicated the nobility's love of war and, in fact, justified their high social status as the defenders of Christian society. The church even furthered this process by steeping knighthood in Christian values. The formal reception of one's arms became a religious ceremony, and weapons were blessed by a priest for Christian service. Throughout the Middle Ages, there remained a constant tension between the ideals of a religion founded on the ideal of peace and the ethos of a nobility based on the love of war.

The Daily Life of the European Nobility in the High Middle Ages

The growth of the European nobility in the High Middle Ages was made visible by an increasing number of castles scattered across the landscape. Although there were enormous variations in castle architecture, castles did possess two common features: they were permanent residences for the noble family, its retainers, and servants, and they were defensible fortifications. The earliest castles were built of wood, but by the eleventh century, they were beginning to be constructed of the more common fieldstone held together by mortar. Initially, the basic castle plan consisted of two parts: a motte, which was an artificial or natural hill, and a bailey, or large open area surrounding the motte. Both motte and bailey were then surrounded by large stone walls. Built on the motte was the keep, the heart of the castle. Constructed of massively thick stone walls, the keep was a large, multistoried building. On the ground floor were the kitchens and stables; the basement housed storerooms for equipment and foodstuffs. Above the ground floor was the great hall, a very large room that served a number of important functions. Here the lord of the castle administered justice and received visitors; here too the inhabitants of the castle ate and even slept. Smaller rooms might open off the great hall: some bedrooms with huge curtained beds with straw mattresses, latrines, and possibly a chapel. The growing wealth of the High Middle Ages made it possible for the European nobility to increase their standard of living. As nobles sought to buy more luxury goods, such as better clothes, jewelry, and exotic spices, so too did they build more elaborate castles with thicker walls and more stone buildings and towers with interiors better furnished and decorated.

▼ **Castles and Peasants.** This illustration depicts the castle and lands belonging to the duke of Berry at Saumur, France. As the European aristocracy grew, the number of castles that dotted the countryside increased. The castle served not only as the permanent home of the noble, his family, servants, and retainers, but also as a defensive construction. In exchange for working the lord's land, the peasants who lived on the manor received shelter within the castle in times of war.

As castles became more elaborate and securely built, they proved to be more easily defended and harder to seize by force. Mining techniques could be used to wreck a section of the walls or undermine a tower. Battering rams, catapults for hurling large stones, and scaling ladders were also used, but defenders often had an advantage, especially against the ladders, by shooting at the attackers with arrows or showering them with stones, molten pitch, or boiling water. More often, attackers simply besieged a castle by camping outside and waiting until the inhabitants starved. But with its own wells for water and a large supply of foodstuffs stored in the basement of the keep, a castle was not easily starved into submission. Overall, capturing castles was a difficult enterprise; so difficult, in fact, that treason from within more often than not proved to be the chief means for successfully overcoming them.

WOMEN IN THE CASTLE   The lady of the castle was responsible for ensuring the food supply of the castle and closely supervising the activities of the servants. Since lords were often away at war, aristocratic wives were often called upon to supervise the estate and even defend the castle, if necessary. Girls were brought up at home and trained from an early age in the principles of castle and estate management. Since aristocratic girls were married in their teens (at the age of fifteen or

▼ **Aristocratic Lady.** This tapestry depicts a French lady sitting in a garden with her sewing basket. Aristocratic wives were expected to oversee the food supply of the castle and supervise the activities of the servants. Also, they were at times responsible for managing estate lands.

▼ **Great Hall of the Castle.** Pictured here is the great hall at Penshurst Place in Kent. The great hall, a room within the keep of a castle, was used for a variety of purposes. Here the lord received visitors and administered justice; here lords, friends, or vassals were assembled and grand banquets were held. The inhabitants sometimes slept in this large room, although smaller rooms, such as bedrooms, latrines, and chapels, often existed off the great hall.

sixteen) and were expected by their husbands to assume their responsibilities immediately, the training of girls in a large body of practical knowledge could never start too early. Girls were also taught a little reading and writing and enough arithmetic to handle household accounts. Although women were expected to be subservient to their husbands (see the box on p. 285), medieval chronicles contain numerous accounts of strong women who advised and sometimes even dominated their husbands.

THE TRAINING OF THE WARRIOR   Although the boys of the nobility spent infancy and early childhood at home, when they reached the age of seven or eight, their parents made a major decision that determined their future lives. At the time, a choice was made either to send a boy into a clerical career, in which case he was sent to a

The Subservience of Women in Medieval Thought
▼ ▼ ▼

Whether a nun or wife of an aristocrat, townsman, or peasant, a woman in the Middle Ages was considered inferior to a man and by nature subject to a man's authority. Although there are a number of examples of strong women who flew in the face of such an attitude, church teachings also reinforced these notions. These two selections are from Gratian, the twelfth-century jurist who authored the first systematic work on canon law, and Thomas Aquinas, the well-known scholastic theologian of the thirteenth century.

Gratian, *Decretum*

Women should be subject to their men. The natural order for mankind is that women should serve men and children their parents, for it is just that the lesser serve the greater.

The image of God is in man and it is one. Women were drawn from man, who has God's jurisdiction as if he were God's vicar, because he has the image of the one God. Therefore woman is not made in God's image.

Woman's authority is nil; let her in all things be subject to the rule of man. . . . And neither can she teach, nor be a witness, nor give a guarantee, nor sit in judgment.

Adam was beguiled by Eve, not she by him. It is right that he whom woman led into wrongdoing should have her under his direction, so that he may not fail a second time through female levity.

Thomas Aquinas, *Summa Theologica*

As regards the individual nature, woman is defective and misbegotten, for the active force in the male seed tends to the production of a perfect likeness in the masculine sex; while the production of woman comes from a defect in the active force or from some material indisposition, or even from some external influence. . . .

The image of God, in its principal signification, namely the intellectual nature, is found both in man and in woman. Hence after the words, "To the image of God He created him," it is added, "Male and female He created them." Moreover it is said "them" in the plural . . . lest it should be thought that both sexes were united in one individual. But in a secondary sense the image of God is found in man, and not in woman: for man is the beginning and end of woman; as God is the beginning and end of every creature.

---

monastic or cathedral school, or to allow him to remain in the secular world. If the latter, he was sent to the castle of a relative or friend for his training in the arts of war to prepare him for the life of a noble. Here, boys learned to ride horses properly and to handle weapons skillfully, at first by using wooden swords and shields. They also engaged in sporting activities that were useful to the military arts, hunting being the most prominent. Occasionally, aristocrats' sons might also learn the basic rudiments of reading and writing, although this began to be more widespread in the thirteenth century.

After his apprenticeship in knighthood, at about the age of twenty-one, a young man formally entered the adult world in a ceremony of "knighting." What had been a simple ceremony in the tenth century had grown to elaborate proportions by the twelfth, including a high degree of Christian symbolism. The day before the ceremony, the prospective knight took a bath of purification, was dressed in white, and passed the night in prayer. On the next day, mass was heard before the actual ceremony, in which the sponsor put a sword on the young candidate and struck him on the cheek or neck with an open hand (or later touched him three times on the shoulder with the blade of a sword), possibly signifying the passing of the sponsor's military valor to the new knight. Other Christian elements included the blessing of the knight's sword and the knight's sacred oath to defend the church, widows, orphans, and the weak and to uphold good and pursue evil. This ceremony, like the noble's life itself, managed to combine God and war without any great discomfort or apparent contradiction.

In the eleventh and twelfth centuries, under the influence of the church, there gradually evolved among the nobility an ideal of civilized courtliness called chivalry. Chivalry represented a more civilized code of ethics that knights were supposed to uphold. In addition to their oath to defend the church and the defenseless, knights were expected to treat captives as honored guests instead of putting them in dungeons. Knightly honor also demanded that unarmed knights should not be attacked. Chivalry also implied that knights should fight only for glory, but this account of a group of English knights by a medieval chronicler reveals another motive for battle: "The whole city was plundered to the last farthing, and then they proceeded to rob all the churches throughout the city, . . . and seizing gold and silver, cloth of all colors, women's ornaments, gold rings, goblets, and precious stones. . . . they all returned to their own lords rich men."[6] Apparently not all chivalric ideals were taken seriously.

After his formal initiation into the world of warriors, a young man returned home to find himself once again subject to his parents' authority. Since it was widely believed that a castle should have only one married couple as the symbolic parents of the entire household, young men were discouraged from marrying until their fathers died, at which time they could marry and become lords of the castle. A special name, *juvenes*, (Latin for youths), was given to these young men who had to wait for their fathers to die before they could come into their inheritance and establish their own households. Sometimes, these "young men" were in their thirties or even forties before they were able to do so.

The *juvenes* were left in an awkward position. They were adults with no adult responsibilities. Since they had been trained to be warriors, they naturally gravitated toward military activities and often furthered the private warfare endemic to the noble class. In the twelfth century, tournaments began to appear as an alternative to the socially destructive fighting that the church was increasingly trying to curb. Initially, tournaments consisted of the "melee," in which warriors on horseback fought with blunted weapons in free-for-all combat. The goal was to take prisoners who would then be ransomed, making success in tournaments a path to considerable gain. Within an eight-month span, the English knight William Marshall made a tour of the tournament circuit, defeated 203 knights, and made enough money that he had to hire two clerks to take care of it. By the late twelfth century, the "melee" was preceded by the joust or individual combat between two knights. Gradually, the joust became the main part of the tournament. No matter how much the church condemned tournaments, knights themselves continued to see them as an excellent way to train for war. As one knight explained: "a knight cannot distinguish himself in that [war] if he has not trained for it in tourneys. He must have seen his blood flow, heard his teeth crack under fist blows, felt his opponent's weight bear down upon him as he lay on the ground and, after being twenty times unhorsed, have risen twenty times to fight."[7]

Tournaments alone, however, did not satisfy the cravings of young men to participate in the one major activity they had been trained for. The best training for war was battle itself. Bertran de Born, a French nobleman and poet, captured the nobles' love of war:

Not so much joy in sleep have I,
Eating and drinking pleases me less

▼ **The Tournament.** Trained for war, many young knights with few responsibilities willingly furthered the private warfare that plagued the nobility. The tournament arose as a socially acceptable alternative to such destructive conflicts. Although the tournament at first consisted of the "melee" alone, the joust, or individual combat between two knights, eventually came to be the central feature of the tournament. Despite the church's condemnation, knights continued to see the tournament as an important way to train for war.

Than hearing on all sides the cry
"At them!" and horses riderless
Among the woodlands neighing.
And well I like to hear the call
Of "Help!" and see the wounded fall,
Loudly for mercy praying,
And see the dead, both great and small,
Pierced by sharp spearheads one and all.[8]

It is this eagerness to do battle that helps to explain the enthusiasm of the young knights for pursuing their destinies in the crusades of the twelfth and thirteenth centuries. What better opportunity to gain glory, rewards, and possibly even salvation itself.

MARRIAGE PATTERNS OF THE ARISTOCRACY   Marriages among the nobility were largely arranged by families, not by personal attraction. Of course, it was expected that a member of the aristocracy would marry within his or her social class. One of the most noticeable features of aristocratic marriage patterns was the usually wide discrepancy in the ages of the marital partners. Daughters of nobles married when they were in their teens—usually at fifteen or sixteen. But their husbands might be in their thirties or even forties since *juvenes* did not marry until they came into their inheritances.

By the twelfth century, marriage had become sufficiently Christianized to be accepted as a sacrament of the church. That did not mean, however, that it was administered by a priest, as other sacraments were (see Chapter 10); instead, the bride and groom married themselves by swearing a mutual oath to be faithful to each other. The marriage ceremony took place outside the church on the church porch. After taking their oath to each other, the couple exchanged rings as a symbol of their commitment. This brief ceremony was usually performed in front of witnesses, but the taking of the mutual oath, even without witnesses, still constituted a valid marriage in the eyes of the church. Only after the ceremony did the couple enter the church to be blessed by a priest and to hear mass. One additional step, however, was needed to complete the marriage sacrament, the physical consummation. The final task of the wedding party was to put the married couple to bed with much encouragement for a successful union.

By the twelfth century, the efforts of the church since Carolingian times to end divorce (see Chapter 8) had borne much fruit. As a sacrament, marriage could not be dissolved; a couple's vow to remain faithful to each other was meant to last for life. In certain cases, however, the church accepted the right of married persons to separate by granting them an annulment or official recognition that their marriage had not been valid in the first place. If it could be established that the couple had not taken their oaths properly or had failed to consummate their marriage physically, then the church would approve their separation. These conditions were often hard to prove, however, especially if one partner wanted the separation and the other did not. The church's definition of incest based on the principle of consanguinity or the degree of blood relationship proved to be the most common foundation for the annulment of marriages. Christians had been forbidden to marry partners related to each other more closely than sixth cousins. By the twelfth century, nobles tended to ignore this proscription by marrying third or fourth cousins even though they knew it was contrary to church law. If the marriage was unsuccessful, which usually meant that it did not produce the expected heirs, then the couple belatedly "remembered" that they had broken the church's law of consanguinity and subsequently gained an annulment. When this practice began to be overused, the Fourth Lateran Council in 1215 reduced the degree of consanguinity to third cousins or less.

The European Kingdoms

The domination of society by the nobility reached its apex in the High Middle Ages. At the same time, however, kings began, however slowly, the process of extending their power in more effective ways. Out of this growth in the monarchies would eventually come the European kingdoms that dominated much of later European history.

In theory kings were regarded as the heads of their kingdoms and expected to lead their vassals and subjects into battle. The king's power, however, was strictly limited. He had to honor the rights and privileges of his vassals and in the case of disputes had to solve them by principles of established law. If he failed to observe his vassals' rights, they could and did rebel. Weak kings were overthrown or, like later Carolingians, replaced by another ruling dynasty.

In retrospect, however, one can see that kings did possess some sources of power that other influential lords did not. Kings were anointed by holy oil in ceremonies reminiscent of Old Testament precedents; thus, their positions seemed sanctioned by divine favor. War and marriage alliances enabled them to increase their power, and their conquests enabled them to reward their followers with grants of land and bind powerful nobles to them. In the eleventh and twelfth centuries, kings found ways to strengthen governmental institutions and consequently to extend their powers. The rewards for their efforts depended on local conditions within their kingdoms and, quite frankly, luck. We can best see the results of early kingdom making by looking at events in western and central Europe.

ENGLAND   At the beginning of the eleventh century, Anglo-Saxon England had fallen subject to Scandinavian control after the successful invasion of the Danes in 1016. King Canute (1016–1035), however, continued English institutions and laws and even supported the Catholic church. His dynastic line proved unable to maintain itself, and in 1042, the Anglo-Saxon line of kings was restored in the person of Edward the Confessor (1042–1066). After his death, the kingship was taken by Harold Godwinson who belonged to one of England's greatest noble families. The king defeated an invasion by the king of Norway in the north but was then forced to move south immediately to face an even greater threat from William, duke of Normandy.

A cousin of Edward the Confessor, William of Normandy laid claim to the throne of England and invaded England in the fall of 1066. The forces of Harold Godwinson and Duke William met at Hastings on October 14, 1066. The Saxon infantry was soundly defeated by the heavily armed Norman knights. Although it was another five years before the Anglo-Saxons were finally pacified, William was crowned king of England at Christmas time in London.

After his conquest, William (1066–1087) treated all of England as a royal possession. Based on the Domesday Book, which William commissioned in 1086 by sending out royal officials to ascertain who owned or held land in tenancy, modern historians have estimated that the Norman royal family took possession of about one-fifth of the land in England as the royal demesne. The remaining English land was held by nobles or the church as fiefs of the king; each of these vassals in turn was responsible for supplying a quota of knights for the royal army. The great landed nobles were allowed to divide their lands among their subvassals however they wished. Thus, the Norman conquest of England had brought a dramatic change. In Anglo-Saxon England, the king had held limited lands while great families controlled large stretches of land and acted rather independently of the king. In contrast, the Normans established a hierarchy of nobles holding land as fiefs from the king. William of Normandy had manipulated the fief-holding system to create a strong, centralized monarchy. To further strengthen his position, William constructed castles throughout his new lands, most notably the Tower of London.

There has been much debate about whether the institutions that developed in England after the conquest owed more to the victorious Normans or to the defeated Anglo-Saxons; certainly, each played a role in the gradual process of fusion that created a new England. While the Norman ruling class spoke French, the intermarriage of the Norman-French with the Anglo-Saxon nobility gradually merged Anglo-Saxon

▼ **Norman Conquest of England from the Bayeaux Tapestry.** This detail from the Bayeaux tapestry depicts the Norman invasion of England. William, the duke of Normandy, was a cousin of Edward the Confessor, who had restored the Anglo-Saxon line of kings in England. When Edward died, Harold Godwinson took the throne. In 1066, William invaded England to take by force what he considered legally his, and at Hastings on October 14, the Normans defeated Harold's army.

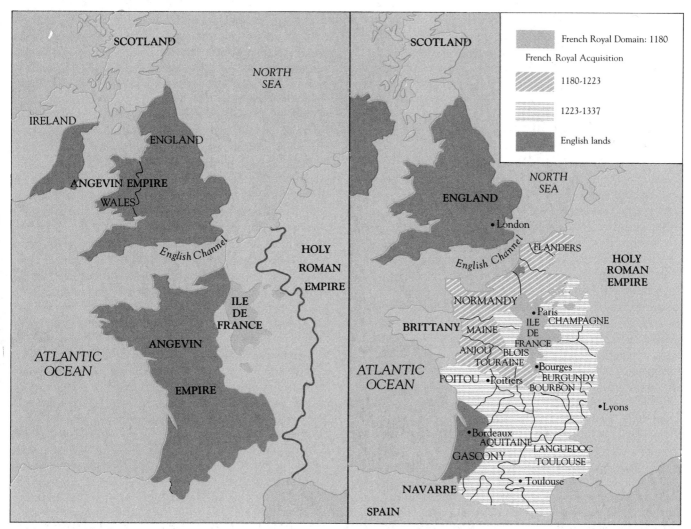

▼ **Map 9.2** England and France.

and French into a new English language. Political amalgamation also occurred as the Normans adapted existing Anglo-Saxon institutions.

William maintained the Anglo-Saxon administrative system in which counties or shires were divided into hundreds or groups of villages. Within each shire, the sheriff (or shire-reeve) was the chief royal officer responsible for leading the military forces of the county and presiding over the county court. William retained the office but replaced the Anglo-Saxon sheriffs with Normans. William also more fully developed the system of taxation and royal courts begun by the Anglo-Saxon and Danish kings of the tenth and eleventh centuries. Henry I (1100–1135), the last son of William the Conqueror, built on his father's foundation and recruited an efficient group of royal servants who excelled at finding ways to

use the courts and tax system to profit the king. Thus, by combining Anglo-Saxon and Norman institutions, the first Norman rulers managed to establish a kingship more powerful than any other monarchy in its time.

The Norman conquest of England had repercussions in France as well. Since the new king of England was still the duke of Normandy, he was both a king (of England) and at the same time a vassal to a king (of France), but a vassal who was now far more powerful than his lord. This connection with France kept England heavily involved in continental affairs throughout the eleventh and twelfth centuries.

In the twelfth century, the power of the English monarchy was greatly enlarged during the reign of Henry II (1154–1189), the first of the Plantagenet dynasty, who reestablished strong rule after a period of civil war following the death of Henry I. Henry II, however, was not only king of England and lord of Ireland, but had sizable possessions in France. He was count of Anjou, duke of Normandy, and, through marriage to Eleanor of Aquitaine, duke of Aquitaine as well. Indeed, while theoretically a vassal of the French king, Henry's Angevin kingdom, as it is called, gave him control of England, Ireland, and all of western France. He was incomparably more powerful than the king of France.

The reign of Henry II was an important one for the development of the English monarchy. During the period of civil war following the death of Henry I, the royal income had declined, and the great nobles had become more independent of royal authority. Henry dealt with these problems and was particularly successful in developing administrative and legal institutions that strengthened the royal government.

First of all, Henry continued the development of the exchequer or permanent royal treasury. Royal officials, known as "barons of the exchequer," received taxes collected by the sheriffs while seated around a table covered by a checkered cloth (hence exchequer table), which served as a counting device. The barons gave receipts to the sheriffs, while clerks recorded the accounts on sheets of parchment that were then rolled up. These so-called pipe rolls have served as an important source of economic and social information for later historians.

▼ **King Henry II and Becket.** Henry II is shown here with Thomas Becket. While adding new territories to his kingdom and increasing the strength of the monarchy, Henry II was forced to accept the freedom of the church from his authority after four of his knights murdered Thomas Becket, the archbishop of Canterbury.

Perhaps even more significant than Henry's financial reforms were his efforts to strengthen the royal courts and his contributions to the development of English common law. Justice had been administered in England by local courts in the counties and hundreds and also in the courts of the various lords. The king's court had been concerned primarily with affairs germane to the king's rights as feudal lord. As overlords of the entire kingdom, however, English kings, beginning with Henry I, had begun to expand matters subject to the king's jurisdiction. In 1166, Henry II issued the *Assizes of Clarendon*, instructions for his royal justices about to tour England. The *Assizes* expanded the number of cases to be tried in the king's court by establishing a finding-jury, which was a group of landholders in each hundred who swore an oath to reveal any criminal acts that had taken place in their territory or declare the true owner of disputed or stolen property. Those accused were then brought before the king's justices. The finding-jury was the ancestor of our modern grand jury. Henry also devised means for taking property cases from feudal and county courts to the royal courts, as well as allowing knights to appeal from the courts of their lords to the royal courts. Henry's goals were clear: expanding the jurisdiction of the royal courts extended the king's power and, of course, brought revenues into his coffers. Moreover, since the royal justices were administering law throughout England, a body of common law (law that was common to the whole kingdom) began to develop to replace the customary law used in county and feudal courts, which often varied from place to place. Thus, Henry's systematic approach to law played an important role in developing royal institutions common to the entire kingdom.

Like his continental counterparts, Henry II was also forced to confront the problem of the relationship between church and state. Indeed, the most famous church-state controversy in medieval England arose between Henry and Thomas Becket, archbishop of Canterbury, the highest ranking English cleric. Conflict erupted over the issue of whether the king had the right to punish clerics in royal courts. Becket claimed that was an infringement of the church's right to try clerics in church courts. Becket had been Henry's chancellor and a very worldly figure indeed. Although Henry had appointed Becket as his archbishop expecting complete loyalty, Becket went through a considerable transformation as archbishop and began to atone for his past worldliness by upholding the rights of the church. Attempts at compromise between the two intense men failed, and after Becket excommunicated some bishops who had supported Henry, the king in exasperation publicly ex-

Murder in the Cathedral

▼ ▼ ▼

The conflict between King Henry II and Thomas Becket, archbishop of Canterbury, was the most dramatic confrontation between church and state in English medieval history. Although Henry did not order the archbishop's murder, he certainly caused it by his reckless public words expressing his desire to be free of Thomas Becket. This excerpt is from a letter by John of Salisbury who served as secretary to Theobald, archbishop of Canterbury, and his successor, Thomas Becket. John was present at the murder of the archbishop in 1170.

John of Salisbury to John of Canterbury, Bishop of Poitiers

The martyr [Becket] stood in the cathedral, before Christ's altar, as we have said, ready to suffer; the hour of slaughter was at hand. When he heard that he was sought—heard the knights who had come for him shouting in the throng of clerks and monks "Where is the archbishop?"—he turned to meet them on the steps which he had almost climbed, and said with steady countenance: "Here am I! What do you want?" One of the knight-assassins flung at him in fury: "That you die now! That you should live longer is impossible." No martyr seems ever to have been more steadfast in his agony than he, . . . and thus, steadfast in speech as in spirit, he replied: "And I am prepared to die for my God, to preserve justice and my church's liberty. If you seek my head, I forbid you on behalf of God almighty and on pain of anathema to do any hurt to any other man, monk, clerk or layman, of high or low degree. Do not involve them

in the punishment, for they have not been involved in the cause: on my head not on theirs be it if any of them have supported the Church in its troubles. I embrace death readily, so long as peace and liberty for the Church follow from the shedding of my blood. . . ." He spoke, and saw that the assassins had drawn their swords; and bowed his head like one in prayer. His last words were "To God and St. Mary and the saints who protect and defend this church, and to the blessed Denis, I commend myself and the church's cause." No one could dwell on what followed without deep sorrow and choking tears. A son's affection forbids me to describe each blow the savage assassins struck, spurning all fear of God, forgetful of all fealty and any human feeling. They defiled the cathedral and the holy season [Christmas] with a bishop's blood and with slaughter; but that was not enough. They sliced off the crown of his head, which had been specially dedicated to God by anointing with holy chrism—a fearful thing even to describe; then they used their evil swords, when he was dead, to spill his brain and cruelly scattered it, mixed with blood and bones, over the pavement. . . . Through all the agony the martyr's spirit was unconquered, his steadfastness marvellous to observe; he spoke not a word, uttered no cry, let slip no groan, raised no arm nor garment to protect himself from an assailant, but bent his head, which he had laid bare to their swords with wonderful courage, till all might be fulfilled. Motionless he held it, and when at last he fell his body lay straight; and he moved neither hand nor foot.

---

pressed the desire to be rid of Becket. Four knights who had heard the king's words took him literally, went to Canterbury, and murdered the archbishop in the cathedral (see the box above) on December 29, 1170. Henry was forced to do public penance for the act. Becket the martyr was made a saint three years later, and his tomb at Canterbury became one of the most famous pilgrimage centers of the Middle Ages (see Chapter 10). Henry was forced to compromise with the church by allowing the right of appeal from English church courts to the papal court. Despite the compromise, Henry had succeeded overall in building a strong English monarchy.

FRANCE   The Capetian dynasty of French kings emerged at the end of the tenth century. Although they carried the title of kings, there was little reason to believe that the Capetians would ever consolidate their control over the West Frankish kingdom (or France as we will now call it). The Capetians controlled as the royal domain only the lands around Paris known as the Ile-de-France. Even that was not entirely under their control; in the eleventh century the Capetians struggled unsuccessfully to restrain the nobility in their own territory. As kings of France, the Capetians were formally the overlords of the great lords of France, such as the dukes of Normandy,

Brittany, Burgundy, and Aquitaine and the counts of Flanders, Maine, Anjou, Blois, and Toulouse. In reality, however, many were considerably more powerful than the Capetian kings. There was, then, no certainty that the Capetians would be successful in establishing a French monarchy.

The Capetians, however, possessed some advantages. As kings anointed of God in a sacred ceremony, the Catholic church supported them tirelessly. We should also note the incredible luck of the Capetians. Their royal domain was so small and insignificant that most of the great lords were not really tempted to attack it, especially since it was ruled by the divinely anointed king of France. Moreover, the Capetians proved to be a very fertile dynasty. While the Capetian monarchy of France did not officially become hereditary until 1223, for generation after generation, Capetian kings succeeded in producing sons who could share in ruling and then be elected kings before their fathers died.

In the twelfth century, two Capetian kings, Louis VI the Fat (1108–1137) and Louis VII (1137–1180) managed to reverse the trend toward loss of control in the royal domain and complete the work of pacifying the Ile-de-France. By establishing a close alliance with the papacy and gaining church support, the Capetians strengthened the royal dynasty. Elsewhere they were less successful. Louis VII sought to enlarge royal support outside the Ile-de-France, but never posed any real threat to the more powerful French lords. All in all, in the eleventh and most of the twelfth centuries, the Capetians did little beyond consolidating their territory in the Ile-de-France. But in doing so, they kept the monarchical principle alive, and in the thirteenth century, the Capetian dynasty began to realize the fruits of its labors.

SPAIN   Much of Spain had been part of the Islamic world since the eighth century. Muslim Spain had flourished in the Early Middle Ages. Córdoba became a major urban center with a population exceeding 300,000 people. Agriculture prospered, and Spain became known as well for excellent leather, steel, wool, silk, and paper. Beginning in the tenth century, however, the most noticeable feature of Spanish history was the weakening of Muslim power and the beginning of a Christian reconquest that lasted until the end of the fifteenth century with the final expulsion of the Muslims.

By the eleventh century, a number of small Christian kingdoms had become established in northern Spain, namely, Leon, Castile, Navarre, Aragon, and Barcelona. Muslim disunity and the support of French nobles, who were eager to battle the infidel, enabled these Spanish Christian states to take the offensive against the Muslims. Rodrigo Díaz, known as El Cid, was the most famous military adventurer of the time. Unlike the Christian warriors of France, El Cid fought under either Christian or Muslim rulers. He carved out his own kingdom of Valencia in 1094, but failed to create a dynasty when it was reconquered by the Muslims after his death.

By the end of the twelfth century, the Christian reconquest of Spain had slowed considerably. The north-

▼ **Map 9.3** Christian Reconquests in the Western Mediterranean.

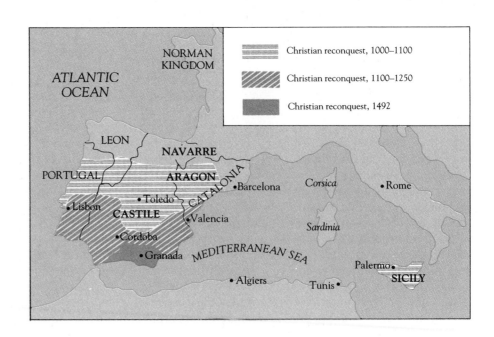

ern half had been consolidated into the Christian kingdoms of Castile, Navarre, Aragon, and Portugal, which had first emerged in 1139 as a separate kingdom. The southern half of Spain remained under the control of the Muslims.

GERMANY AND THE EMPIRE The Saxon kings of the tenth century had strengthened their hold over the German kingdom and revived the empire of Charlemagne. The last of the Saxon dynasty was Henry II (1002–1024), who possessed inadequate resources to maintain his kingship over Germany. A new dynasty, known as the Salian kings, began in 1024 with the election of Conrad II (1024–1039) of Franconia. Both Conrad and his successors, Henry III (1039–1056) and Henry IV (1056–1106), managed to create a strong German monarchy and a powerful empire by leading armies into Italy. But they also experienced the frustrating difficulties inherent in the position of the German kings.

Over a period of time, German kings had become dependent upon the wealth of their own private landed estates to meet the expenses of governing the German kingdom. Moreover, they had grown dependent on the willingness of the great nobles to accept and support them. But these same nobles had little real incentive to do so; strengthening the monarchy only weakened their own position. Consequently, instead of supporting the monarchy, they consciously worked to undermine its authority. For example, the great lords of Germany took advantage of the early death of Henry III and the minority of Henry IV to extend their own power at the expense of the latter. The elective nature of the German monarchy posed an additional problem for the German kings. While some dynasties were strong enough for their members to be elected regularly, the great lords who were the electors did at times deliberately choose otherwise. It was to their advantage to select a weak king.

To compensate for their weaknesses, German kings had come to rely upon their ability to control the church and select bishops and abbots whom they could then use as their royal administrators. The Investiture Controversy, however, had weakened the king's ability to use church officials in this way. The German kings also tried to bolster their power by using their position as emperors to exploit the resources of Italy. But this tended to backfire; many a German king lost armies in Italy in pursuit of the imperial dream. No German dynasty proved more susceptible to the allure of this dream than the Hohenstaufens.

In 1152, Frederick I (1152–1190), known as Barbarossa or Redbeard to the Italians, a powerful lord from

Chronology
▼ ▼ ▼
The European Kingdoms

England	
King Canute	1016–1035
Battle of Hastings	1066
William the Conqueror	1066–1087
Henry II, First Plantagenet Dynasty	1154–1189
Murder of Thomas Becket	1170
France	
Louis VI the Fat	1108–1137
Louis VII	1137–1180
Spain	
El Cid Creates Kingdom of Valencia	1094
Establishment of Portugal	1139
Germany and the Empire	
Conrad II Begins Salian Dynasty	1024–1039
Henry III	1039–1056
Henry IV	1056–1106
Frederick I Barbarossa	1152–1190
Lombard League Defeats Frederick	1176
Henry VI	1190–1197

the Swabian house of Hohenstaufen, was chosen as king. In need of adequate resources to reestablish his control over the German princes, Frederick chose to pursue an Italian policy to build a base for regular revenues. Frederick's plan was to create a new kind of empire. Previous German kings had focused on building a strong German kingdom, to which Italy might be added as an appendage. To Frederick, Germany was simply a feudal monarchy; his chief revenues would come from Italy as the center of a "holy empire," as he called it (hence the term Holy Roman Empire). Consequently, Frederick permitted his cousin Henry the Lion, duke of Saxony and Bavaria, to expand and act independently in much of Germany. Frederick's only request of the princes was that they recognize him as their overlord. In compensation, Frederick turned his efforts toward the south by marching an army into northern Italy, where he was immediately victorious. His victory proved short-lived, however. The papacy was opposed to imperial expansion, fearful that the emperor intended to include Rome and the Papal States as part of his empire. The cities of northern Italy, which had virtually become independent entities after overthrowing the rule of their bishops, were quite unwilling to submit to Frederick's authority as well. An alliance of these northern Italian cities, known as the Lombard League, with the support of the papacy, defeated the forces of Emperor Frederick at Legnano in 1176. Frederick had no alternative but to negotiate a truce and return to Germany, a time he spent profitably by breaking the power of his cousin Henry the Lion. Later, he returned to Italy and arranged a settlement with the northern Italian cities in which they were left independent, in return for an annual payment to the emperor. Frederick now had the financial base he had sought. Moreover, by marrying his son (who became Henry VI, 1190–1197) to the heiress of the Norman kingdom of southern Italy (see Chapter 11), Frederick seemed to be creating the foundation for a Holy Roman Empire. After Frederick's death, Henry VI's control of Germany and both northern and southern Italy made him the strongest European ruler since Charlemagne. The longevity of medieval empires, however, was always highly dependent upon the strength of the ruler. When

Henry VI died prematurely, his son was only two; Henry's empire soon collapsed.

We have seen how Italian affairs were strongly affected by the policies of the German kings and emperors. The German king and emperor Otto III (983–1002) had spent much of his time pursuing an imperial ideal by residing in Rome and attempting to make it the capital of his empire. After his death in 1002, there was no central political authority in Italy. While important nobles struggled to dominate northern Italy, central Italy remained under the control of the Papal States, even though Roman aristocratic families competed for the papacy. In southern Italy, there seemed to be constant conflict between Lombard dukes, Muslims, and the Byzantines.

A group of Norman adventurers dramatically altered the Italian political scene by their invasion of southern Italy. Robert the Guiscard (the cunning), his brothers, and a band of fellow Norman knights conquered much of southern Italy, and Robert was recognized by the pope as

▼ **Map 9.4** The Holy Roman Empire.

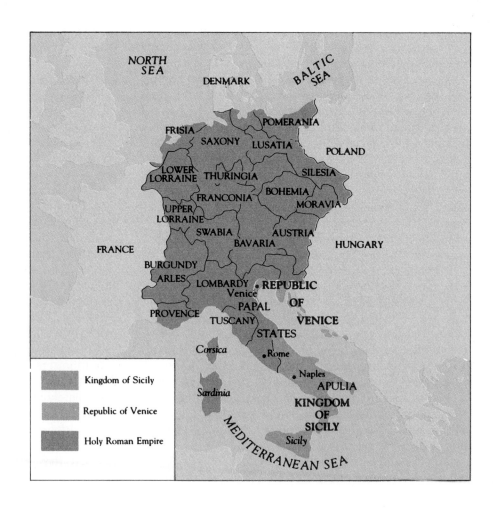

duke of Apulia and Calabria. His brother Roger was given the task of subduing Muslim Sicily, which he accomplished in 1091 after a thirty-year struggle. The Normans in southern Italy demonstrated astute diplomatic and military abilities. They adapted existing institutions to their benefit and developed well-organized and centralized states in southern Italy and Sicily. When Roger II, the son of Roger of Sicily, was crowned king of Sicily by the pope in 1130, the Normans had proved how lordship could be transformed into kingship. By the end of the twelfth century, the Norman kingdom was one of the most powerful in Europe, as well as one of the most fascinating. A melting pot of Christian, Jewish, and Muslim culture, the state's official documents were issued in Latin, Greek, and Arabic.

NORTHERN AND EASTERN EUROPE   The Scandinavian countries of northern Europe had little political organization before 1000. Although monks traveled as missionaries to the northern lands as early as 826, it was not

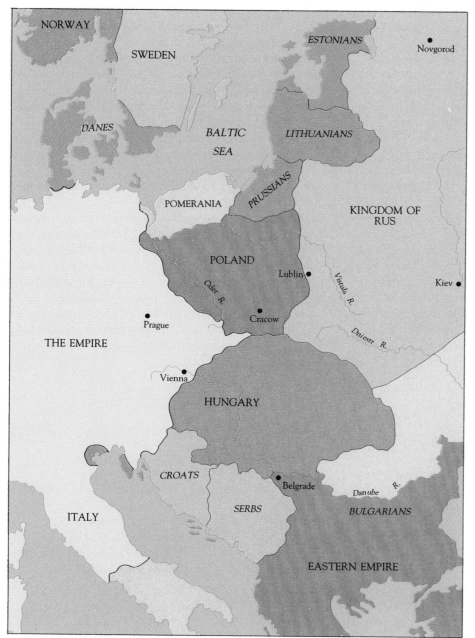

▼ **Map 9.5** Northern and Eastern Europe.

until the second half of the tenth and the first half of the eleventh centuries that the three Scandinavian kingdoms—Denmark, Norway, and Sweden—emerged with a noticeable political structure. At the same time, the three kingdoms were converted to Christianity by kings who believed that an organized church was a necessary accompaniment to an organized state. Although the old pagan religion held on, especially in Sweden, by the twelfth century Christianity had been widely accepted. Its adoption, however, did not eliminate the warlike tendencies of the Scandinavians. Not only did the three kingdoms fight each other in the eleventh and twelfth centuries, but rival families were in regular conflict over the throne in each state. This period also witnessed the growth of a powerful noble landowning class.

While larger states were also created in eastern Europe, there was considerable shuffling of boundaries in this region. Hungary, which had been a Christian state since 1000, remained relatively stable. Poland, however, experienced much change. The Polish ruler, Boleslav the Brave (992–1025), constructed a larger kingdom by extending his authority across the Oder in the west, down into Bohemia, and eastward to Kiev. After his death, the kingdom fell apart, leaving the central part of Boleslav's state to continue as a separate state but without any natural frontiers. Consequently, German settlers encroached on its territory on a regular basis, leading to considerable intermarriage between Slavs and Germans. The Oder River became a crucial dividing line. West of the Oder the Germanic language predominated; east of it the Slavic language did. Instability and shifting boundaries remained a fundamental characteristic of Polish history well into the twentieth century.

The new European civilization that had emerged in the Early Middle Ages began to flourish in the High Middle Ages. The revival of trade, the expansion of towns and cities, and the development of a money economy did not mean the end of a predominantly rural European society, but they did open the door to new ways to make a living and new opportunities for people to expand and enrich their lives. The Catholic church shared in the challenge of new growth by reforming itself and striking out on a path toward greater papal power, both within the church and over European society. While Christianity still continued its missionary activity to convert pagans on the fringes of the European world, it also continued to act as a civilizing agent in other ways. Although it could not eliminate warfare, it tried to mitigate its worst effects. It did not, however, always succeed in the way it intended. The Peace and Truce of God did cut down on the amount of warfare; at the same time, they put Christianity in the awkward position of condoning the warfare that remained, contrary to its founder's message of peace. Perhaps people of the eleventh and twelfth centuries were grateful for the weekend respite from bloodshed and cared not to see the paradox that the fusion of God and warrior created.

The nobles, whose warlike attitudes were rationalized by their label as the defenders of Christian society, continued to dominate the medieval world politically, economically, and socially. But quietly and surely, within this world of castles and private power, kings gradually began to extend their public powers. While they could not know it then, their actions laid the foundation for the European kingdoms that in one form or another have dominated the European political scene ever since.

Notes
▼ ▼ ▼

1.   Ernest F. Henderson, ed., *Select Historical Documents of the Middle Ages* (London, 1892), p.332.
2.   "The Deeds of Conrad II," in *Imperial Lives and Letters of the Eleventh Century*, trans. T. E. Mommsen and K. F. Morrison (New York, 1962), p. 67.
3.   Oliver J. Thatcher and Edgar H. McNeal, eds., *A Source Book for Medieval History* (New York, 1905), pp. 134–135.
4.   Henderson, *Select Historical Documents of the Middle Ages*, p. 365.

5.   Ibid., pp. 372–373.
6.   Quoted in Joseph and Frances Gies, *Life in a Medieval Castle* (New York, 1974), p. 175.
7.   Quoted in Robert Delort, *Life in the Middle Ages*, trans. Robert Allen (New York, 1972), p. 218.
8.   Quoted in Marvin Perry, Joseph Peden, and Theodore Von Laue, *Sources of the Western Tradition* (Boston, 1987), 1: 218.

Suggestions for Further Reading
▼ ▼ ▼

A good introduction to this period is C. N. L. Brooke, *Europe in the Central Middle Ages, 962–1154*, rev. ed. (New York, 1988). On economic conditions, see N. J. G. Pounds, *An Economic History of Medieval Europe* (New York, 1974); *The Fontana Economic History of Europe*, vol. 1, *The Middle Ages*, ed. C. M. Cipolla (London, 1972); and R. S. Lopez, *The Commercial Revolution of the Middle Ages: 950–1350* (Englewood Cliffs, N. J., 1971). Urban history is covered in E. Ennen, *The Medieval Town* (Amsterdam, 1978); H. A. Miskimin, D. Herlihy, and A. L. Udovich, eds., *The Medieval City* (New Haven, Conn., 1977); and the classic work of H. Pirenne, *Medieval Cities* (Princeton, N. J., 1925). A good short introduction to medieval society is C. Brooke, *The Structure of Medieval Society* (London, 1971). On peasant life, see R. Fossier, *Peasant Life in the Medieval West* (New York, 1988); and J. A. Raftis, ed., *Pathways to Medieval Peasants* (Toronto, 1981). Technological changes are discussed in L. White, *Medieval Technology and Social Change* (Oxford, 1962); and J. Gimpel, *The Medieval Machine* (Harmondsworth, 1976). See also J. Langdon, *Horses, Oxen and Technological Innovation* (New York, 1986).

A good work on the problem of reform in the Catholic church is G. Ladner, *The Idea of Reform* (Cambridge, Mass., 1959). On the Cluniac reform movement, see H. E. J. Cowdrey, *The Cluniacs and the Gregorian Reform* (Oxford, 1970); G. Constable, *Cluniac Studies* (London, 1980); and J. Evans, *Monastic Life at Cluny, 910–1157* (Oxford, 1931). On Europe during the time of the Investiture Controversy, see G. Tellenbach, *Church, State and Christian Society at the Time of the Investiture Controversy* (Oxford, 1948). Also valuable are K. F. Morrison, *Tradition and Authority in the Western Church, 300–1140* (Princeton, N. J., 1969); B. Tierney, *The Crisis of Church and State: 1050–1300* (Englewood Cliffs, N. J., 1964); and W. Ullmann, *The Growth of Papal Government in the Middle Ages*, 3d ed. (London, 1970). On the evolution of papal ideology, see W. Ullmann, *A Short History of the Papacy in the Middle Ages* (London, 1974). For a general survey of church life, see R. W. Southern, *Western Society and the Church in the Middle Ages* (Baltimore, 1970).

Works on the function and activities of the nobility in the High Middle Ages include S. Reynolds, *Kingdoms and Communities in Western Europe 900–1300* (Oxford, 1984); T. A. Reuter, ed., *The Medieval Nobility* (Amsterdam and Oxford, 1978); M. Keen, *Chivalry* (London, 1984); P. Contamine, *War in the Middle Ages* (Oxford, 1984); G. Duby, *The Chivalrous Society* (Berkeley, 1977); and the classic work by M. Bloch, *Feudal Society* (London, 1961). G. Duby discusses the theory of medieval social order in *The Three Orders* (Chicago, 1980). Various aspects of the social history of the nobility can be found in G. Duby, *The Knight, the Lady, and the Priest* (London, 1984) on noble marriages; W. Anderson, *Castles of Europe* (London, 1970); and Robert Delort, *Life in the Middle Ages*, trans. Robert Allen (New York, 1972). On women, see R. T. Morewedge, ed., *The Role of Women in the Middle Ages* (Albany, N. Y., 1975); and S. M. Stuard, ed., *Women in Medieval Society* (Philadelphia, 1976).

There are numerous works on the different feudal principalities: On England, see F. Barlow, *The Feudal Kingdom of England, 1042–1216*, 3d ed. (New York, 1972); D. C. Douglas, *William the Conqueror: The Norman Impact upon England* (Berkeley, 1964); and W. L. Warren, *Henry II* (Berkeley, 1973). On Germany, see B. Arnold, *German Knighthood 1050–1300* (Oxford, 1985); H. Fuhrmann, *Germany in the High Middle Ages c. 1050–1250* (Cambridge, 1986), an excellent account; and P. Munz's biography, *Frederick Barbarossa* (London, 1969). On France, see J. Dunbabib, *France in the Making 843–1180* (Oxford, 1985); and E. M. Hallam, *Capetian France 987–1328* (London, 1980), a well-done general account. On the Normans, see J. le Patourel, *The Norman Empire* (Oxford, 1976); R. H. C. Davis, *The Normans and Their Myth* (London, 1976); and D. C. Douglas, *The Norman Achievement* (London, 1969), and *The Norman Fate* (Berkeley, 1977). On Spain, see G. Jackson, *The Making of Medieval Spain* (London, 1972); and A. Mackay, *Spain in the Middle Ages* (London, 1977). On Italy, see D. J. Herlihy, *Cities and Society in Medieval Italy* (London, 1980); and J. K. Hyde, *Society and Politics in Medieval Italy* (London, 1973). On Eastern Europe and Scandinavia, see N. Davies, *God's Playground: A History of Poland*, vol. 1 (Oxford, 1981); T. K. Derry, *A History of Scandinavia* (London, 1979); and the books listed for Chapter 8.

Chapter 10

Crusades, Christianity, and Culture in the High Middle Ages, 1000–1200

▼▼▼▼▼

The economic, political, and religious growth of the eleventh and twelfth centuries gave medieval European society a new confidence. Only a confident Europe could have undertaken the crusades, the military effort to recover the Holy Land of the Near East from the Muslims. Western assurance and energy were also evident in a burst of intellectual and artistic activity that produced a renaissance of classical learning, new educational institutions known as universities, and the beginnings of a religious building spree that left the landscape bedecked with churches that were the visible symbols of Christian Europe's vitality. At the same time, vigorous papal leadership combined with new dimensions of religious life to make the Catholic church a forceful presence in every area of life.

▼ The Eastern World

Although European civilization developed in relative isolation, it had never entirely lost contact with the lands and empires of the east. At the end of the eleventh century, that contact increased in part because developments in the Byzantine and Islamic worlds prompted the first major attempt of that new European civilization to expand beyond Europe proper. Before examining those developments and how they contributed to the crusades, we must briefly look at what was happening in the lands that eventually formed Russia.

The Principality of Kiev

The Kiev Rus state, which had become formally Christian in 987, prospered considerably afterward, reaching its high point in the first half of the eleventh century. The city of Kiev was fairly populous, numbering perhaps 20,000–30,000 inhabitants, making it larger than any contemporary European Christian city. The principality of Kiev also maintained rather close contact with the states of western Europe. Indeed, the ruling dynasty of Kiev arranged marriages with the royal families of France, Germany, and Norway, among others.

Kievan society was dominated by a noble class of landowners known as the boyars, who represented a mixture of Scandinavian (Rus) descendants and chiefs of the old Slavonic tribes. Though mostly free, the peasants worked hard and long hours. Kievan merchants maintained regular trade with Scandinavia to the north and the Islamic and Byzantine worlds to the south.

After the mid-eleventh century, the principality of Kiev began to experience serious problems. The members of the ruling dynasty seemed unwilling and unable to work together, which led to constant fighting and destructive civil wars. New invasions by Asiatic nomadic tribes caused political disruption and increasingly cut off Rus traders from the Black Sea, their major outlet to the Byzantine and Islamic worlds. Competition from Italian merchants, especially in the luxury trade of the Black Sea, hurt commercial prosperity as well. By the twelfth century, the principality of Kiev began to disintegrate into a number of constituent parts. One of these was Novgorod, which freed itself from Kiev's control in 1136 and established a prosperous city republic based on trade with German merchants, especially from the north German city of Lübeck. Other cities also emerged in their own right. Moscow, for example, is first mentioned in a chronicle in 1147. The sack of Kiev by north Russian princes in 1169 brought an inglorious end to the first Russian state.

IMPORTANCE OF THE RUSSIAN CHURCH   The Christian church served as the fundamental civilizing and unifying force of early Russia. The Russian church imitated the liturgy and organization of the Byzantine Empire, whose Eastern Orthodox priests had converted the Kievan Rus to Christianity at the end of the tenth century. Until 1037, when the principality of Kiev established self-government for the Russian church, the metropolitan or head of the Russian church was obedient to the patriarch of Constantinople, the leading authority of the Eastern Christian church.

The Russian church became known for its rigid religious orthodoxy. Only a few basic religious works had been translated into Slavonic for use in Russia, which meant that the Kievan Rus had little awareness of the controversial religious literature of the west and the ancient works on which it was based. Perhaps as a result, the Russian church tended to view religious issues as matters of faith and rarely questioned the few religious authorities that had been translated into Slavonic. Although Christianity provided a common bond between Russian and European civilization, Russia's religious development guaranteed an even closer affinity between Russian and Byzantine civilization. Later in the Middle Ages, new Asiatic conquests would cut Russia off even more from the west.

The Islamic Empire

By the mid-tenth century, the Islamic empire led by the Abbasid caliphate in Baghdad was in the process of disintegration. An attempt was made in the tenth century to unify the Islamic world under the direction of a Shi'ite dynasty known as the Fatimids. Their origins lay in northern Africa, but with the help of the Berbers, they managed to conquer Egypt and establish the new city of Cairo as their capital. In establishing a Shi'ite caliphate, they became rivals to the Sunni caliphate of Baghdad. While the Fatimids did move into Syria and Arabia, they were unable to overcome the Abbasids in Mesopotamia, and the Islamic world remained divided.

As Egypt grew into an important center of eastern trade, the Fatimid dynasty prospered and surpassed the Abbasid caliphate as the dynamic center of the Islamic world. Centered in a luxurious court in Cairo, the Fatimids pursued a religious policy based on toleration and created a strong military by using nonnative peoples as mercenaries. One of them, the Seljuk Turks, soon posed a threat to the Fatimids themselves.

The Seljuk Turks were a nomadic people from central Asia who had been converted to Islam and flourished as military mercenaries for the Abbasid caliphate. Moving gradually into Iran and Armenia, they grew in number until by the eleventh century they were able to take over the eastern provinces of the Abbasid empire. In 1055, a Turkish leader captured Baghdad and assumed command of the Abbasid empire with the title of sultan. While the Abbasid caliph remained as the chief Sunni religious authority, the real military and political power of the state was in the hands of the Seljuk Turks. By the last quarter of the eleventh century, the Seljuk Turks were exerting military pressure on Egypt and the Byzantine Empire. When the Byzantine emperor foolishly challenged the Turks, the latter routed the Byzantine army at Manzikert in 1071. In dire straits, the Byzantine Empire turned to the west for help, setting in motion the papal pleas that led to the crusades. To understand the complexities of the situation, however, we need to look first at the Byzantine Empire.

The Byzantine Empire

The Macedonian dynasty of the tenth and eleventh centuries had restored much of the power of the Byzantine Empire; its incompetent successors, however, reversed most of the gains. After the Macedonian dynasty was extinguished in 1056, internal struggles for power between ambitious military leaders and aristocratic families led these various factions to buy the support of the great landowners of Anatolia by allowing them greater control over their peasants. This policy was self-destructive, however, since the peasant-warrior was the traditional backbone of the Byzantine state.

The Byzantine Empire had also been weakened by the growing split between the Catholic church of the west and the Eastern Orthodox church of the Byzantine Empire. Although theological issues were an important cause of this rift, the question of authority came to overshadow all others. The Eastern Orthodox church was unwilling to accept the pope's claim that he was the sole head of the church. In the mid-eleventh century, this issue reached a climax. To resolve it, Pope Leo IX sent Cardinal Humbert, a dedicated reformer, as his legate to Constantinople. The envoy was not a wise choice. Closed-minded and intense, he was a great champion of papal rights and did not believe that the issue could be

compromised or even negotiated. His opponent in Constantinople was the head of the Byzantine church, the Patriarch Michael Cerularius, who was equally dogmatic and unwilling to come to terms. Unable to agree whatsoever, the two church leaders formally excommunicated each other in 1054, initiating a schism between the two great branches of Christianity that has not been completely healed to this day.

The Byzantine Empire faced external threats to its security as well. The establishment of the Normans in southern Italy had eliminated Byzantine influence from that region; now the Normans invaded Greece, threatening Byzantine control of the Balkans. The greatest challenge to Byzantium, however, came from the advance of the Seljuk Turks who had moved into Asia Minor—the heartland of the empire and its main source of food and manpower. In 1071, the Byzantine forces under Emperor Romanus IV Diogenes were disastrously defeated at Manzikert by a Turkish army. The Turks then advanced into Anatolia where many peasants, already disgusted by their exploitation at the hands of Byzantine landowners, readily accepted Turkish control.

A new dynasty, however, soon breathed new life into the Byzantine Empire. The Comneni, under Alexius I Comnenus (1081–1118), were victorious on the Greek Adriatic coast against the Normans, defeated the Pechenegs in the Balkans, and stopped the Turks in Anatolia. Lacking the resources to undertake additional campaigns against the Turks, Emperor Alexius I turned to the west for military assistance. It was the positive response of the west to the emperor's request that led to the crusades. The Byzantine Empire lived to regret it.

▼ The Crusades

The crusades were based upon the idea of a holy war against the infidel or unbelievers. Although the concept of unbeliever was eventually broadened to include other groups, Christendom's wrath was directed initially against the Muslims. It had already found some expression in the attempt to reconquer Spain from the Muslims and the success of the Normans in reclaiming Sicily (see Chapter 9). At the end of the eleventh century, Christian Europe found itself with a glorious opportunity to attack the Muslims.

The immediate impetus for the crusades came when the Byzantine emperor Alexius I asked Pope Urban II (1088–1099) for help against the Seljuk Turks. Alexius's request was for financial aid to assist him in recruiting mercenaries, but Urban II took a different perspective. Christian forces had recently captured Toledo in

Pope Urban II Proclaims a Crusade

▼ ▼ ▼

Toward the end of the eleventh century, the Byzantine emperor Alexius I sent Pope Urban II a request for aid against the Seljuk Turks. At the Council of Clermont, Urban II appealed to a large crowd to take up weapons and recover Palestine from the Muslims. This description of Urban's appeal is taken from an account by Fulcher of Chartres.

Pope Urban II

Pope Urban II . . . addressed them [the French] in a very persuasive speech, as follows: "O race of the Franks, O people who live beyond the mountains [that is, reckoned from Rome], O people loved and chosen of God, as is clear from your many deeds, distinguished over all other nations by the situation of your land, your catholic faith, and your regard for the holy church, we have a special message and exhortation for you. For we wish you to know what a grave matter has brought us to your country. The sad news has come from Jerusalem and Constantinople that the people of Persia, an accursed and foreign race [the Seljuk Turks], enemies of God, . . . have invaded the lands of those Christians and devastated them with the sword, rapine, and fire. Some of the Christians they have carried away as slaves, others they have put to death. The churches they have either destroyed or turned into mosques. They desecrate and overthrow the altars. They circumcise the Christians and pour the blood from the circumcision on the altars or in the baptismal fonts. Some they kill in a horrible way by cutting open the abdomen, taking out a part of the entrails and tying them to a stake; they then beat them and compel them to walk until all their entrails are drawn out and they fall to the ground. Some they use as targets for their arrows. They compel some to stretch out their necks and then they try to see whether they can cut off their heads with one strike of the sword. It is better to say nothing of their horrible treatment of the women.

They have taken from the Greek empire a tract of land so large that it takes more than two months to walk through it. Whose duty is to avenge this and recover that land, if not yours? For to you more than to any other nations the Lord has given the military spirit, courage, agile bodies, and the bravery to strike down those who resist you. Let your minds be stirred to bravery by the deeds of your forefathers, and by the efficiency and greatness of Karl the Great [Charlemagne], . . . and of the other kings who have destroyed Turkish kingdoms, and established Christianity in their lands. You should be moved especially by the holy grave of our Lord and Saviour which is now held by unclean peoples, and by the holy places which are treated with dishonor and irreverently befouled with their uncleanness. . . ."

When Pope Urban had said this and much more of the same sort, all who were present were moved to cry out with one accord, "It is the will of God, it is the will of God." When the pope heard this he raised his eyes to heaven and gave thanks to God, and commanding silence with a gesture of his hand, he said: "My dear brethren, today there is fulfilled in you that which the Lord says in the Gospel, 'Where two or three are gathered together in my name, there am I in the midst.' For unless the Lord God had been in your minds you would not all have said the same thing. . . . So I say unto you, God, who put those words into your hearts, has caused you to utter them. Therefore let these words be your battle cry, because God caused you to speak them. Whenever you meet the enemy in battle, you shall all cry out, 'It is the will of God, it is the will of God. . . .' Whoever therefore shall determine to make this journey and shall make a vow to God and shall offer himself as a living sacrifice, holy, acceptable to God, shall wear a cross on his brow or on his breast. And when he returns after having fulfilled his vow he shall wear the cross on his back."

Spain, and the Normans had completed their conquest of Sicily. The pope saw a golden opportunity to provide papal leadership for a great cause: to rally the warriors of Europe for the liberation of Jerusalem and the Holy Land from the infidel. At the Council of Clermont in southern France near the end of 1095, Urban challenged Christians to take up their weapons against the infidel and participate in a holy war to recover the Holy Land (see the box above). The pope promised remission of sins: "All who die by the way, whether by land or by sea,

▼ **Peasant's Crusade.** Before the aristocracy could organize itself in answer to the call of Pope Urban II, a large group of peasants joined the fanatical Peter the Hermit in an attempt to free the Holy Land. When they could not buy food, the poorly armed peasants ravaged the countryside and looted towns. Trusting in God to grant them victory, the peasants eagerly went to Asia Minor where the Turks brought a swift and devastating end to the crusade of the peasants.

or in battle against the pagans, shall have immediate remission of sins. This I grant them through the power of God with which I am invested."[1]

The initial response to Urban's speech reveals how appealing many people found this combined call to military arms and religious fervor. The first crusade was preceded by an exercise in religious fanaticism and futility. A self-appointed leader Peter the Hermit, who preached of his visions of the Holy City of Jerusalem, convinced a large mob, most of them poor and many of them peasants, to undertake a crusade to the east. This "Peasant's Crusade" or "Crusade of the Poor" comprised a ragtag rabble that moved through the Balkans, terrorizing natives and looting for their food and supplies. Their misplaced religious enthusiasm led to another tragic by-product as well, the persecution of the Jews, long pictured by the church as the murderers of Christ. As a contemporary chronicler described it, ". . . while passing through the cities along the Rhine, Main, and Danube, led by their zeal for Christianity, they persecuted the hated race of the Jews wherever they were found, and strove either to destroy them completely or

to compel them to become Christians."[2] Two bands of peasant crusaders, led by Peter the Hermit, managed to reach Constantinople. Emperor Alexius I wisely shipped them over to Asia Minor where the undisciplined and poorly armed rabble was massacred by the Turks.

The First Crusade

Pope Urban II did not share the wishful thinking of the peasant crusaders but was more inclined to trust knights who had been well trained in the art of war. The first crusading armies were recruited from the warrior class of western Europe, particularly France. Urban also appointed a bishop, Adhemar of Le Puy, to lead the crusading host. Although the knights who made up this first serious crusading host were motivated by religious fervor, there were other attractions as well. Some sought adventure and welcomed a legitimate opportunity to pursue their favorite pastime—fighting. Others saw an opportunity to gain territory, riches, status, and possibly a title. From the perspective of the pope and the European monarchs, the crusades offered an opening to free Europe of contentious young nobles who disturbed the peace and wasted lives and energy fighting each other.

Three organized crusading bands of noble warriors, most of them French, made their way to Constantinople by 1097. Emperor Alexius was not pleased with their arrival and greatly distrusted their motives. Bohemund, for example, the son of Robert Guiscard, had been one of the invaders of the Greek lands of the Byzantine Empire. The emperor's daughter was acutely suspicious of the true designs of the crusaders: ". . . in their dreams of capturing the capital [they] had come to the same decision . . . that while in appearance making the journey to Jerusalem, in reality their object was to dethrone the Emperor and to capture the capital [Constantinople.]"[3] Instead of a band of mercenaries that he could pay to fight on his behalf, Alexius got a group of French nobles who wanted to conquer the Holy Land for their own purposes. The emperor entered into negotiations with the crusaders who eventually agreed to take an oath of allegiance to him.

The crusading army probably numbered several thousand cavalry and as many as 10,000 infantry. After the capture of Antioch in 1098, much of the crusading host proceeded down the Palestinian coast, evading the garrisoned coastal cities, and reached Jerusalem in June 1099. After a five-week siege, the Holy City was taken amidst a horrible massacre of the inhabitants, men, women, and children. As executed by the crusaders,

"God's judgment" on the infidel was indeed a frightful one (see the box on p. 304).

After further conquest of Palestinian lands, the crusaders largely ignored their promises to the Byzantine emperor and proceeded to organize four crusader states: the principality of Antioch under Bohemund, son of Robert Guiscard of Sicily; the county of Edessa under Baldwin, the brother of Godfrey de Bouillon; the county of Tripoli under Count Raymond of Toulouse; and the kingdom of Jerusalem under Godfrey de Bouillon, but he died within a year and was succeeded by his brother, Baldwin of Edessa (1100–1118). In keeping with their own traditional practices, the crusading leaders created organized feudal states.

Since the Latin kingdoms existed in a world surrounded by Muslims, they grew increasingly dependent upon the Italian commercial cities for supplies from Europe. Some Italian cities, such as Genoa, Pisa, and above all, Venice, waxed rich and powerful in the process. The role of supplier might logically have fallen to the Byzantine Empire, but relations between Byzantium and the Latin kingdoms deteriorated steadily. The presence of the Latin kingdoms in territory that the Byzantines believed belonged to them added to the hostility generated by religious differences. Moreover, commercial competition from the Italian cities hurt deeply at a time when Byzantium was experiencing a loss of lands and manpower and a shrinking tax base.

The Military Religious Orders

An important part of the military force available to defend the Latin kingdoms of the east came from a new institution that was a product of the religious enthusiasm that accompanied the crusades. The military monastic orders combined the two greatest ideals of the High Middle Ages—the monk and the warrior—into a single person. Two such orders arose to defend the Latin kingdoms. The Knights of the Temple came into existence when a group of French knights took a religious oath and began to serve as escorts for pilgrims to the Holy City of Jerusalem. They settled in a house near the Temple of Solomon and soon became known as the Templars. In 1128, they were officially recognized by the pope as a monastic order. In addition to the regular monastic vows of poverty, chastity, and obedience, the brothers took a fourth vow to help and defend people making pilgrimages to Jerusalem. The Knights of St. John of Jerusalem made their debut when they organized a hospital to help sick pilgrims in the Holy Land. Their fourth vow was to take care of the sick, and they were soon acknowledged as a military religious order called the Hospitallers. Both of these monastic orders were given tracts of land in Palestine by the kings of Jerusalem, which they guarded with formidable fortresses. Since both orders also came to possess territories throughout Europe as a result of bequests, their great wealth provided additional support for their missions in the Holy Land. Many of their recruits stemmed from the nobility. At their high point, the Templars and Hospitallers together provided almost one thousand knights to defend the kingdom of Jerusalem.

The ideals of these two monastic orders spread from the east to the rest of Europe. The Templars served as models for three Spanish military orders as well as an order of Teutonic Knights founded in Germany in 1198. The Teutonic Knights conquered territory along the eastern coasts of the Baltic from the pagan Lithuanians, Livonians, and Prussians. From their conquests eventu-

▼ **Siege of Antioch.** Recruited from the noble class of western Europe, the first crusading army reached Constantinople by 1097. By 1098, the crusaders had taken Antioch. Working down the coast of Palestine, they captured Jerusalem in 1099. During the five-week siege, thousands of Jews and Muslims were massacred. Pictured here is a thirteenth-century illustration portraying the siege of Antioch.

ally came the duchy of Prussia, which played an important role in European history.

The Second Crusade

It was not easy for the Latin kingdoms to maintain themselves in the east. Already by the 1120s, the Muslims had begun to strike back. In 1144, Edessa became the first of the four Latin kingdoms to be recaptured. Its fall led to renewed calls for another crusade. This time, the moral exhortations to destroy the infidel came not from the pope, but from the monastic firebrand Saint Bernard of Clairvaux (see New Monastic Orders and New Spiritual Ideals later in the chapter), who exclaimed: "now, on account of our sins, the sacrilegious enemies of the cross have begun to show their faces. . . . What are you doing, you servants of the cross? Will you throw to the dogs that which is most holy? Will you cast pearls before swine?" But it was not beneath even the holy man to mix spiritual injunction with the language of commerce to encourage the enlistment of crusaders:

Or are you a shrewd businessman, a man quick to see the profits of this world? If you are, I can offer you a splendid bargain. . . . Take the sign of the cross. At once you will have indulgence for all the sins which you confess with a contrite heart. It does not cost you much to buy and if you wear it with humility you will find that it is the kingdom of heaven.[4]

Bernard aimed his message at knights and even managed to enlist two powerful rulers, King Louis VII of France and Emperor Conrad III of Germany.

The second crusade seemed destined for failure. The two crusading armies of king and emperor were not well organized and failed to cooperate in coordinating their efforts against the Muslims. They were even incapable of cooperating with the Byzantines. The French knights contemplated an attack on Constantinople, but the French king dissuaded them from such a dastardly act against a Christian city. Finally, the new crusading hosts found little cooperation from the crusader lords of the kingdom of Jerusalem. These local lords had found ways to live with local Muslim leaders and were quite unwilling to destroy the symbiotic relationship they had developed. They, too, undermined the efforts of the two crusading monarchs. The second crusade proved to be a total failure. Saint Bernard attributed its lack of success to the loss of God's favor because of human sinfulness; the French king simply blamed the wickedness of the people involved.

The Third Crusade

The third crusade was a reaction to the renewal of Muslim energies and the fall of the Holy City of Jerusalem. In 1169, the Sunni Muslims of Syria invaded Egypt and, under the leadership of the Kurdish warrior known to the west as Saladin, demolished the Fatimid caliphate. Eventually, Saladin established control over Syria, and the Latin kingdoms faced a unified Muslim power on two frontiers. Saladin's forces invaded the kingdom of Jerusalem and at the Battle of Hattin in 1187 destroyed the Latin forces gathered there. Saladin now began the reconquest of Palestine, and while Tripoli, Antioch, and Tyre were able to resist, Jerusalem fell in October 1187. Unlike the Christians, Saladin did not permit a massacre of the civilian population and even tolerated the continuation of Christian religious ser-

vices. His enlightened policies, however, were overshadowed by the actual fall of Jerusalem to the Muslims.

Now all of Christendom was ablaze with calls for a new crusade in the east. Rulers levied special taxes to raise troops, and three major monarchs agreed to lead their forces in person: Emperor Frederick Barbarossa of Germany (1152–1190), Richard I the Lionhearted of

▼ **Map 10.1** The Crusades.

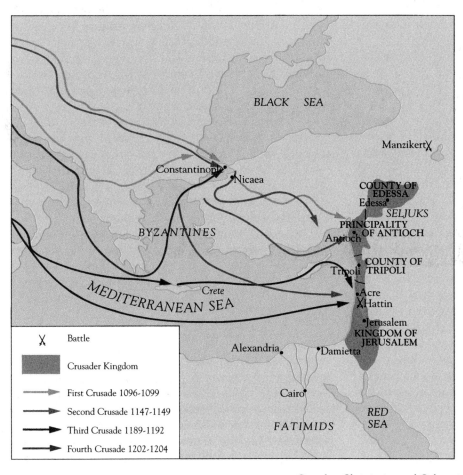

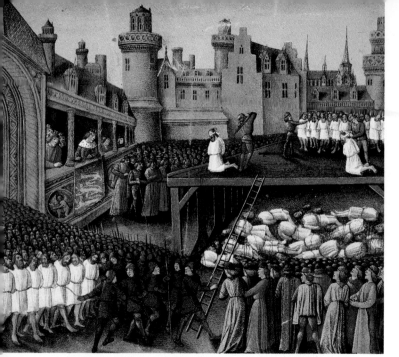

▼ **Richard the Lion-Hearted Executes Muslims at Acre.** The third crusade was organized in response to the capture of the Kingdom of Jerusalem by the Sunni Muslims under the leadership of Saladin. While Saladin was a fair ruler who forbade the massacre of Christians and allowed Christian services to continue, his Christian foes were more harsh, as this illustration shows. Richard the Lion-Hearted (at left with crown) is pictured watching the execution of 2700 Muslims at Acre.

England (1189–1199), and Philip II Augustus, king of France (1180–1223). This overwhelming response seemed auspicious for the successful recovery of the Holy Land.

The crusaders, however, soon encountered the problems that had plagued their predecessors: the difficulties and expenses of either overland or sea travel to the east; conflict with the Byzantines and the leaders of the remaining crusader states; constant infighting (kings were notoriously unwilling to accept advice from anyone, especially fellow kings); and debilitating sickness for large numbers of the crusaders in a hostile climate.

After overcoming the initial difficulties, some of the crusaders finally arrived in the east by 1189 only to encounter more problems. Frederick Barbarossa experienced stunning successes in Asia Minor, but then drowned accidentally while swimming in a local river. Without his strong leadership, his army quickly disintegrated. The English and French arrived by sea and met with success against the coastal cities where they had the support of their fleets. When they moved inland, they failed miserably. Eventually, after Philip went home, Ri-

chard the Lionhearted without more fighting negotiated a settlement whereby Saladin agreed to allow Christian pilgrims free access to Jerusalem.

Effects of the Crusades

Whether the crusades had much effect on European civilization is widely debated. The crusaders made little long-term impact on the east where the only visible remnants of their conquests were their castles. There may have been some broadening of perspective that comes from the exchange between two cultures, but the interaction of Christian Europe with the Muslim world was actually both more intense and more meaningful in Spain and Sicily than in the Holy Land.

Did the crusades help to stabilize European society by removing large numbers of young warriors who would have fought each other in Europe? Some historians think so and believe that western monarchs established their control more easily as a result. There is no doubt that the crusades did benefit the economic growth of the Italian port cities, especially Genoa, Pisa, and Venice. But it is important to remember that it had been the growing wealth and population of eleventh-century Europe that had made the crusades possible in the first place. The crusades may have enhanced the revival of trade, but they certainly did not cause it. Even without the crusades, Italian merchants would have pursued new trade contacts with the eastern world.

The crusades did have side effects that were unfortunate for European society for generations. The first widespread attacks on the Jews began in the crusades. As some Christians argued, to undertake holy wars against infidel Muslims while the "murderers of Christ" ran free at home was unthinkable. The massacre of Jews became a regular feature of medieval European life (see Chapter 11). This intolerance of another civilization, as well as the urge to expand and dominate other peoples that was manifested in the crusades, proved a lasting legacy for Western civilization, as the imperialistic adventures and colonization of much of the rest of the world later demonstrated.

▼ Intellectual and Artistic Renewal in the Eleventh and Twelfth Centuries

The eleventh and twelfth centuries were a time of tremendous intellectual and artistic vitality. They witnessed the growth of educational institutions, the quickening of theological thought, the revival of law, a rebirth of interest in ancient culture, the development of a vernacular literature, and a burst of activity in art and architecture. While monks continued to play an important role in intellectual life, increasingly the secular clergy, cities, and courts, whether of kings, princes, or high church officials, began to exert a newfound influence.

The Rise of Universities

The university as we know it with faculty, students, and degrees was a product not of ancient Greece or Rome, but of the High Middle Ages. The word *university* is derived from the Latin word *universitas* meaning a corporation or guild and referred to either a corporation of teachers or a corporation of students. Medieval universities were educational guilds or corporations that produced educated and trained individuals. Since a guild of students or a guild of teachers was formed without official sanction, there is no clear date for the founding of Europe's oldest universities.

ORIGINS Education in the Early Middle Ages rested primarily with the clergy, especially the monks. Although monastic schools were the centers of learning from the ninth to the early eleventh century, they were surpassed in the course of the eleventh century by the cathedral schools organized by the secular clergy. The great cathedrals were managed by legal corporations called chapters, which were composed of canons who were priests or candidates for the priesthood. Canons assisted bishops in the administration of their dioceses and bore responsibility for their educational establishments.

Cathedral schools expanded rapidly in the eleventh century. There were twenty of them in 900, but by 1100 the number had grown to at least two hundred since every cathedral city felt compelled to establish one. The most famous were Chartres, Reims, Paris, Laon, and Soissons, all located in France, which was truly the intellectual center of Europe by the twelfth century. The primary purpose of the cathedral school was to educate priests to be more literate men of God, especially those aspiring to play an important role in the cathedral chapter and perhaps even become bishops. Cathedral schools also attracted other individuals who desired some education but did not want to become priests. Many university administrators today carry titles, such as chancellor, provost, and dean, that were used to designate the officials of cathedral chapters. Yet universities represented a novel development that moved beyond the sphere of cathedral schools.

The first European university appeared in Bologna, Italy (unless one attributes this distinction to the first medical school established earlier at Salerno, Italy). The emergence of the University of Bologna coincided with the revival of interest in Roman law, especially the rediscovery of Justinian's *Body of Civil Law.* In the twelfth century, a great teacher, such as Irnerius (1088–1125), attracted students from all over Europe. Most of them were laymen, usually older individuals who served as administrators to kings and princes and were particularly eager to learn more about law to apply it in their own jobs. To protect themselves, students at Bologna formed a guild or *universitas,* which was recognized by Emperor Frederick Barbarossa and given a charter in 1158. Although the faculty also organized itself as a group, the *universitas* of students at Bologna was far more influential. It obtained a promise of freedom for students from local authorities, regulated the price of books and lodging, and determined the curriculum, fees, and standards for the masters. Teachers were fined if they missed a class, began their lectures late, or failed to complete their scheduled program for the term. The University of Bologna remained the greatest law school in Europe throughout the Middle Ages.

In northern Europe, the University of Paris became the first recognized university. A number of teachers or masters who had received licenses to teach from the cathedral school of Notre Dame in Paris began to take on extra students for a fee. By the end of the twelfth century, these masters teaching at Paris had formed a *universitas* or guild of masters. By 1200, the king of France, Philip Augustus, officially acknowledged the existence of the University of Paris. In the meantime, in the second half of the twelfth century, a number of students and masters had left Paris and started their own university at Oxford, England. A similar migration from Oxford led to the establishment of Cambridge University. In the Late Middle Ages, kings, popes, and princes vied to found new universities. By the end of the Middle Ages, there were eighty universities in Europe with most of them located in England, France, Italy, and Germany.

Despite variations, most early universities shared similar characteristics. Almost all universities sought to gain independence from both church and lay authorities. All masters and students were regarded as clerics of a "lower order" and wore clerical garb. This is why academic gowns, even today, still look like priests' robes. Since women were not allowed to be priests, they were also excluded from universities. As clerics in minor orders, students and their masters were not subject to arrest by the secular authorities, but could be tried only in ecclesiastical courts. As a result, university authorities sought and obtained widespread secular authority for themselves. The chancellor of Oxford, for example, received from the king of England complete authority over teachers and students, including the granting of degrees, which became a regular feature of most universities.

CURRICULUM AND INSTRUCTION   To gain admission to a medieval university, students were expected to read and write Latin although apparently exams were not rigorous and some students were not all that well prepared. Nevertheless, all classes were conducted in Latin, and it provided a common means of communication for students, regardless of their country of origin.

A student's initial studies at a medieval university centered around the traditional liberal arts curriculum. The trivium consisted of grammar, rhetoric, and logic, and the quadrivium was comprised of arithmetic, geometry, astronomy, and music. Basically, medieval university instruction was done by a lecture method. The word *lecture* is derived from the Latin and means "to read."

Before the development of the printing press in the fifteenth century, books were expensive, and few students could afford them, so masters read from a text (such as a collection of law if the subject were law or a textbook such as the *Sentences* of Peter the Lombard if the subject were theology) and then added commentaries, which came to be known as glosses. A law professor at Bologna described his method, which was not unlike those followed in other fields at other universities:

> Concerning the method of teaching the following order was kept by ancient and modern doctors and especially by my own master, which method I shall observe: First, I shall give you summaries of each title before I proceed to the text; second, I shall give you as clear and explicit a statement as I can of the purport of each law; third, I shall read the text with a view to correcting it; fourth, I shall briefly repeat the contents of the law; fifth, I shall solve apparent contradictions, adding any general principles of law . . . and any distinctions or subtle and useful problems . . . arising out of the law with their solutions, as far as the Divine Providence shall enable me. . . .[5]

▼ **Map 10.2** Intellectual Centers of Medieval Europe.

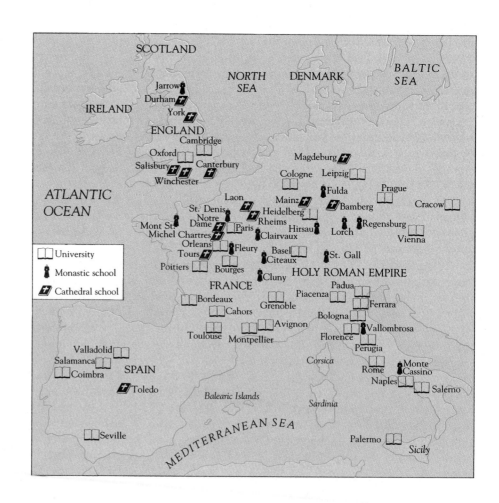

No exams were given after a series of lectures, but when a student applied for a degree, he was a given a comprehensive oral examination by a committee of teachers. These were taken after a four- or six-year period of study. The first degree a student could earn was an A.B., the *artium baccalarius,* or bachelor of arts; later, he might receive an A.M., *artium magister,* a master of arts. All degrees were technically licenses to teach, although most students receiving them did not become teachers.

After completing the liberal arts curriculum, a student could go on to study law, medicine, or theology. As we have seen, Bologna was known for the study of law. Salerno, in southern Italy, specialized in medical studies, although it was eventually overshadowed by French centers, such as Montpellier. The University of Paris was most famous for the study of theology, the most highly regarded subject of the medieval curriculum. The study of law, medicine, or theology was a long process that could take a decade or more. A student who passed his final oral examinations was granted a doctor's degree, which officially enabled him to teach his subject. Most students who pursued advanced degrees received their master's degrees first and taught the arts curriculum while continuing to pursue their advanced degrees.

The development of residence halls known as colleges was another feature of medieval universities. Wealthy benefactors provided these houses where poor students could live and be fed for modest fees. Eventually, masters also took up residence there to provide guidance for the students. The most famous college at the University of Paris was the Sorbonne, founded by Robert de Sorbon, chaplain of King Louis IX in 1258. The colleges of Merton and Balliol were founded at Oxford a few years later. Students who received degrees from medieval universities could pursue other careers besides teaching that proved to be much more lucrative. A law degree was deemed essential for those who wished to serve as advisers to kings and princes. The growing administrative bureaucracies of popes and kings also demanded a supply of clerks with a university education who could keep records and draw up official documents.

STUDENTS IN THE MEDIEVAL UNIVERSITY   Students at medieval universities stemmed predominantly from the middle groups of medieval society, the families of lesser knights, merchants, and artisans. All were male; many were poor, but ambitious and upwardly mobile. Many medieval students started when they were fourteen to eighteen years old and received their bachelor's or master's degrees by their early twenties. Study for a doctorate in one of the specialized schools of law, medicine, or

theology entailed at least another ten years. It was not unusual for men to receive their doctorates in their late thirties or early forties.

There are obvious similarities between medieval and modern students. Then, as now, many students took their studies seriously and worked hard. Then, as now, alcohol, sex, and appeals for spending money were all too common. In medieval universities, handbooks provided form letters that students could use in requesting money from their fathers, guardians, or patrons. This is an example from Oxford:

> B. to his venerable master A., greeting. This is to inform you that I am studying at Oxford with the greatest diligence, but the matter of money stands greatly in the way of my promotion, as it is now two months since I spent the last of what you sent me. The city is expensive and makes many demands; I have to rent lodgings, buy necessaries, and provide for many other things which I cannot now specify. Wherefore I respectfully beg your paternity that by the promptings of divine pity you may assist me, so that I may be able to complete what I have well begun.[6]

Lack of studiousness is not just a modern phenomenon as this letter from a medieval father to his son illustrates:

> To his son G. residing at Orleans, P. of Besançon sends greetings with paternal zeal. It is written, 'He also that is slothful in his work is brother to him that is a great waster.' I have recently discovered that you live dissolutely and slothfully, preferring license to restraint and play to work and strumming a guitar while the others are at their studies, whence it happens that you have read but one volume of law while your more industrious companions have read several. Wherefore I have decided to exhort you herewith to repent utterly of your dissolute and careless ways, that you may no longer be called a waster and your shame may be turned to good repute.[7]

We have no idea whether the letter convinced the student to change his ways.

Medieval universities shared in the violent atmosphere of the age (see the box on p. 310). Records from courts of law reveal numerous instances of disturbances that occurred throughout European universities. One German professor was finally dismissed for stabbing one too many of his colleagues in faculty meetings. A student in Bologna was attacked in the classroom by another student armed with a sword. Oxford regulations attempted to dampen the violence by forbidding students to bring weapons to class. The University of Leipzig initiated a series of graded penalties for students who picked up objects to throw at professors, those who

University Students and Violence in Paris

▼ ▼ ▼

Medieval universities shared in the violent atmosphere of their age. Town and gown quarrels often resulted in bloody conflicts, especially during the universities' formative period. This selection is a proclamation by the episcopal court of Paris against students who went about the city committing crimes.

Proclamation of the Episcopal Court of Paris, 1269

The official of the court of Paris to all the rectors of churches, masters and scholars residing in the city and suburb of Paris, to whom the present letters may come, greeting in the Lord. A frequent and continual complaint has gone the rounds that there are in Paris some clerks and scholars, likewise their servants, trusting in the folly of the same clerks, unmindful of their salvation, not having God before their eyes, who, under pretense of leading the scholastic life, more and more often perpetrate unlawful and criminal acts, relying on their arms: namely, that by day and night they atrociously wound or kill many persons, rape women, oppress virgins, break into inns, also repeatedly committing robberies and many other enormities hateful to God. And since they attempt these and other crimes relying on their arms, we, having in mind the decree of the superior pontiff in which it is warned that clerks bearing arms will be excommunicated, also having in mind that our predecessors sometimes excommunicated those who went about thus, and in view of the fact that this is so notorious and manifest that it cannot be concealed by any evasion and that their proclamation was not revoked, wishing to meet so great evils and to provide for the peace and tranquillity of students and others who wish to live at peace, at the instance of many good men and by their advice do excommunicate in writing clerks and scholars and their servants who go about Paris by day or night armed, unless by permission of the reverend bishop of Paris or ourself. We also excommunicate in writing those who rape women, break into inns, oppress virgins, likewise all those who have banded together for this purpose.

threw and missed, and those who threw and hit their target. Bloody riots between townspeople and students were also not uncommon.

Despite the violence, universities proved important to medieval civilization, not only for the growth of learning, which, after all, is the main task of the university, but also in providing the trained personnel who served as teachers, administrators, lawyers, and doctors in an increasingly specialized society.

Theology and Philosophy

Medieval intellectuals were strongly influenced by a propensity for order. Their desire to introduce a systematic approach to knowledge greatly affected the formal study of religion that we call theology. Christianity's importance in medieval society probably made inevitable theology's central role in the European intellectual world. Whether in monastic or cathedral schools or the new universities, theology reigned as "queen of the sciences."

Beginning in the eleventh century, the effort to apply reason or logical analysis to the church's basic theological doctrines had a significant impact on the study of theology. The word *scholasticism* is used to refer to the philosophical and theological system of the medieval schools. A primary preoccupation of scholasticism was the attempt to reconcile faith and reason, to demonstrate that what was accepted on faith was in harmony with what could be learned by reason. While scholasticism reached its high point in the thirteenth century, it had its beginnings in the theological world of the eleventh and twelfth centuries, especially in the work of two theologians, Anselm and Abelard.

Anselm (c. 1033–1109) was born in northern Italy but became a monk in France. Serving first as schoolmaster and then as abbot of the monastery of Bec in Normandy, he eventually left the monastery to become a bishop and then archbishop of Canterbury in England. Fundamentally, Anselm was a monastic theologian and has, in fact, been called the "last great intellectual of the monastic centuries of education." Anselm began his theological inquiry by stressing the importance of faith as the starting point of all wisdom: "Nor do I seek to understand that I may believe, but I believe that I may understand. For this too I believe, that unless I first believe, I shall not understand."[8] For Anselm the stress on faith did not diminish the significance of reason or the use of logic. Although subordinate to faith, reason could, he thought, be used to further illuminate the truth already known by faith. In his major work, the *Proslogion*, Anselm tried to demonstrate how the truths of faith are compatible with reason. Indeed, it was Anselm who provided an ontological argument to prove by reason the existence of God.

Peter Abelard was even more responsible than Anselm for applying logic in a systematic fashion to church doctrines, greatly furthering the development of scholasticism. Between the time of Anselm and Abelard, however, was the important transformative period during which learning passed from isolated monasteries to the new schools of the urban world.

Abelard (1079–1142) studied in northern France with Anselm of Laon, a pupil of Anselm of Bec. He scorned his teachers as insignificant, however, and took up the teaching of theology in Paris. Possessed of a colorful personality, Abelard was a very popular teacher who attracted many students. A man with a strong ego, he became known for the zest with which he entered into arguments with fellow scholars as well as for his affair with Heloise (see the box on p. 312).

Above all others, Peter Abelard was responsible for furthering the new scholastic approach to theology. In his most famous work, *Sic et Non (Yes and No)*, he listed passages from Scripture and the church fathers that stood in direct contradiction to one another and stressed the need to use logic or dialectical reasoning to reconcile the apparent differences systematically. He summed up his method with the words, "By doubting we come to enquiry, through enquiry to the truth."

Abelard became one of the best-known thinkers in Europe, although his method of applying logic to church doctrine was not highly regarded by all churchmen. He was, in fact, persecuted for a while on the charge of failing to adhere to church teachings. But Abelard was not a skeptic hungering to overthrow established teachings. He, too, accepted church doctrines, yet felt that reason or "dialectical method" must be used to defend them since church authorities could and did disagree on fundamental points of theology.

Both Anselm and Abelard took positions in a major scholastic controversy of the twelfth and succeeding centuries involving the problem of universals. The basic issue dealt with the nature of reality itself: what constitutes what is real? Theologians were divided into two major schools of thought reflecting the earlier traditions of Greek thought, especially the divergent schools of Plato and Aristotle.

Following Plato, the scholastic realists took the position that the individual objects that we perceive with our senses, such as trees, are not real but merely manifestations of exemplifications of universal ideas (hence treeness) that exist in the mind of God. All knowledge, then, is based on the ideas implanted in human reason by the Creator. Truth, according to the realists, can only be discovered by contemplating universals.

The other school, the nominalists, were adherents of Aristotle's ideas and believed that only individual objects are real. Universal ideas or concepts to them were simply names (Latin *nomina*—hence nominalism) created by humans. Truth could be discovered only by examining individual objects. Peter Abelard attempted to reconcile the two positions by maintaining that while universal ideas are real, they cannot be separated from the individual objects in which they inhere; universal ideas do not exist separately from individual objects. The struggle between realists and nominalists remained a fundamental issue in Western philosophical and theological studies until the new scientific categories of thought in the seventeenth century.

The first successful attempt to apply the new dialectical method of Abelard was made by Peter the Lombard, a teacher at Paris and later bishop of the same city. Peter authored the *Four Books of Sentences* around 1150. In this work, he divided theological problems into topical areas, such as the Creation, Trinity, and Incarnation, and then proceeded to summarize and reconcile systematically scriptural passages and the works of church fathers on these topics. The *Sentences* became a fundamental textbook for the study of theology.

The study of theology, now highly influenced by the dialectical method or the tools of logic, became more and more an exercise in systematic explanation and definition. This gave rise to attempts to formulate precise definitions of the sacraments, grace, sin, and salvation; it also led to the firm entrenchment of the scholastic system in the schools. In the thirteenth century, scholasticism reached its high point in the brilliant synthesis of Thomas Aquinas (see Chapter 11).

Law

The development of a systematic approach to knowledge was also expressed in the area of law. Of special importance was the rediscovery of the great legal work of Justinian, the *Corpus Iuris Civilis (Body of Civil Law)*, known to the medieval west before 1100 only in second-hand fashion. At first, famous teachers of law, such as Irnerius at Bologna, were content simply to explain the meaning of Roman legal terms to their students. Grad-

The Misfortunes of Peter Abelard

▼ ▼ ▼

Peter Abelard was a dynamic teacher at Paris and one of the founders of scholasticism. He was also one of the first persons in the Middle Ages to write an autobiographical account of his life, entitled History of My Misfortunes, that revealed much of his personality. In this excerpt, he describes the unfortunate consequences of his affair with Heloise, the niece of Fulbert, a canon of the cathedral of Notre Dame and Abelard's landlord. Heloise bore a child by Abelard and secretly married him, but Fulbert, feeling betrayed by his tenant's behavior, sought revenge.

Peter Abelard, *History of My Misfortunes*

At once we secretly parted [Abelard and Heloise after their secret marriage], nor did we see each other more, unless rarely and hiddenly, greatly concealing what we had done. But her uncle and his servants, seeking solace for their shame, began to divulge the marriage we had entered, and to violate the faith they had given me in this regard. She, on the other hand, denied it and swore that it was most false. From this the uncle was violently moved, and attacked her with frequent abuse. When I learned this, I sent her to a certain abbey of nuns near Paris, which is called Argenteuil, where she herself once as a young girl had been brought up and instructed. I had prepared for her the habit of a religious, suitable to the convent life, and had her wear it, except the veil. When they heard this, her uncle and his relatives and friends thought that I had now very much deceived them, and had conveniently rid myself of her, by making her a nun. They were greatly disturbed by this, and

conspired against me. They bribed one of my servants with money, and one night they took from me a most cruel and shameful vengeance, as I was resting and sleeping in the inner room of my lodging. This punishment the world has learned with the greatest astonishment. For they cut off those parts of my body, by which I had committed the deed which sorrowed them. They turned at once in flight, but two who could be caught lost their eyes and genitals. . . .

At morning, the entire city turned out about me. What shock the populace experienced, what sorrow it suffered, with what shouts they annoyed me, . . . it is difficult, or rather impossible, to express. The clerics above all, and especially our students, tormented me with unbearable laments and groans, so that I suffered more for their compassion than from the pain of the cut. I felt the embarrassment more than the wound, and was more afflicted by shame than by suffering. It occurred to my mind how great my glory once had been, how easily and in a brief incident it had been cast down, or rather entirely extinguished. How I had by the just judgment of God been punished in that part of my body in which I had sinned. . . .

The confusion, I admit, of my shame, rather than the devotion of my life compelled me, caught up in so wretched a sorrow, to the recesses of the monastic cloisters. She, who had taken the veil willingly at our command, had first entered a monastery. We thus received at the same time the sacred habit, I in the abbey of Saint-Denis, and she in the monastery of Argenteuil we have mentioned.

---

ually, they became more sophisticated so that by the mid-twelfth century, "doctors of law" had developed commentaries and systematic treatises on the legal texts. Since these medieval teachers believed that Roman law was still applicable to Italy and the Holy Roman Empire, Italian cities, above all Pavia and Bologna, became prominent centers for the study of Roman law. By the thirteenth century, Italian jurists were systematizing the various professional commentaries on Roman law into a single commentary known as the ordinary gloss (*glossa ordinaria*). Study of Roman law at the universities came to consist of learning both the text of the law along with this gloss.

This revival of Roman law occurred in a world dominated by a body of law quite different from that of the Romans. European law comprised a hodgepodge of Germanic law codes, feudal customs, and urban regulations. The desire to know a more orderly world, already evident in the study of theology, perhaps made it inevitable that Europeans would enthusiastically welcome the more systematic approach of Roman law.

Indeed, while elements of Roman law were incorporated into the various legal systems of western Europe, even more significant was the indirect impact Roman law made on these traditional legal practices. Medieval jurists attempted to systematize and codify their traditional law in imitation of the Roman system. In England, Ranulf de Glanvill wrote a treatise *On the Laws and Customs of the Realm of England* (1189), explaining how English law could be explained in a rational fashion. In practice, King Henry II was attempting the same thing by imposing the law of the royal courts upon all of England as the common law. Moreover, Roman law made it possible again for Europeans to think of the state as a public authority possessing the right to create new legislation. In feudal law, governmental functions had become largely vested in private hands (see Chapter 9).

The training of students in Roman law at medieval universities led to further application of its principles as these students became judges, lawyers, scribes, and councillors for the towns and monarchies of western Europe. By the beginning of the thirteenth century, the old system of ordeal was being replaced by a rational, decision-making process based on a systematic collection and analysis of evidence, a clear indication of the impact of Roman law on the European legal system.

The application of a systematic approach to a body of materials was also evident in the growth of canon law in the twelfth century. The Catholic church possessed a large number of canons or ecclesiastical laws and decrees relating to church affairs, but no authoritative collection of them. A Bolognese monk named Gratian began to right this lack. Around 1140 he authored a book called *A Concord of Discordant Canons*, known informally as the *Decretum*, in which he attempted a systematic codification of church canons, including a reconciliation of those that seemed to be in conflict. His *Decretum* became a model for later officially authorized collections of canon law. After Gratian, popes and scholars created a body of canon law affecting all clerical matters, church property, and lay people. Church law came to regulate numerous aspects of the latter's lives, including contracts, wills, marriages, education, and heresy. Eventually, learned canonists, known as "Decretists" added glosses to Gratian's *Decretum* and tried to reconcile his body of canons with new church laws decreed by contemporary popes and councils.

The Renaissance of the Twelfth Century

Another aspect of the intellectual revival of the High Middle Ages was a resurgence of interest in the works of classical antiquity. The renaissance (or rebirth) of classical antiquity in the twelfth century has been compared to the more famous Renaissance in Italy in the fifteenth century. While the renaissance of the twelfth century was not as deep or far-reaching as the latter, it was a significant step forward in the European recovery and understanding of the classical heritage, and it generated tremendous intellectual optimism. Western Europe and particularly France became the center of this intellectual renewal. The Latin language served as an international language for both speaking and writing.

In the twelfth century, western Europe was introduced to a large number of Greek scientific and philosophical works, including those of Galen and Hippocrates on medicine, Ptolemy on geography and astronomy, and Archimedes and Euclid on mathematics. Above all, the west now had available the complete works of Aristotle. (Greek drama and poetry, however, would not be recovered until the Italian Renaissance of the fifteenth century.) Before the twelfth century, only Aristotle's elementary works on logic (known as the "Old Logic") were available through the earlier translation of Boethius (see Chapter 7). By 1160, Aristotle's remaining works on logic (known as the "New Logic") were in use in European universities, especially at Paris. During the second half of the twelfth century, all the scientific works of Aristotle were translated into Latin. This great influx into the west of Aristotle's works was overwhelming. He came to be viewed as the "master of those who know," the man who seemed to have understood every field of knowledge. Scholastic philosophers and theologians of the thirteenth century would expend much energy trying to assimilate and reconcile Aristotelian thought with Christian doctrines.

The recovery of Greek scientific and philosophical works was not, however, a simple process. Little knowledge of Greek had survived in Europe. It was through the Muslim world that the west recovered Aristotle and other Greek authors. The translation of Greek works into Arabic had formed but one aspect of a brilliant Muslim civilization. In the twelfth century, these writings were now translated from Arabic into Latin, making them available to the west. No doubt, much became garbled in this roundabout recovery of the Greek works (Greek to Arabic to Latin). Wherever Muslim and Christian cultures met—in the Norman kingdom of Sicily, southern Italy, and above all Spain—the work of translation was carried on by both Arabic and Jewish scholars. Some Christian scholars also learned Arabic and made their own translations.

The Islamic world had more to contribute intellectually to the west than translations, however. Scientific work in the ninth and tenth centuries had enabled it to forge far ahead of the western world, and in the twelfth and thirteenth centuries, Arabic works in physics, mathematics, medicine, and optics were made available to the west in Latin translations. In addition, when Aristotle's works were brought into the west in the second half of the twelfth century, they were accompanied by commentaries written by outstanding Arabic and Jewish philosophers. Their works proved highly influential to western intellectuals.

Especially important was Ibn-Rushd or Averroës (1126–1198), a jurist and physician who lived in Córdoba. He studied virtually all of Aristotle's surviving works and composed a systematic commentary on them. There was no doubt in his mind that Aristotle had been the master of all knowledge:

> I consider that the man [Aristotle] was a rule and exemplar which nature devised to show that final perfection of man. . . . The teaching of Aristotle is the supreme truth, because his mind was the final expression of the human mind. Wherefore it has been well said that he was created and given to us by divine providence that we might know all there is to be known. Let us praise God, who sat this man apart from all others in perfection, and made him approach very near to the highest dignity humanity can attain.[9]

Translated into Latin, the work of Averroës, with its concern for the problem of faith versus reason had a noteworthy impact on western scholars of the thirteenth century.

The west was also receptive to the works of Jewish scholars living in the Islamic world. Perhaps the best known is Moses ben Maimon or Maimonides (1135–1204), who also lived in Córdoba. He was conversant with Greek and Arabic traditions and interested in the problem of reconciling faith and reason. In his *Guide for the Perplexed*, written in Arabic, Maimonides attempted to harmonize the rational and natural philosophy of Aristotle with the basic truths of Judaism (see the box on p. 315). Although attacked by some orthodox Jews, western scholars in the thirteenth century paid close attention to it after its translation into Latin.

The great influx of Greek and Arabic works in the twelfth century brought a formidable challenge to western intellectuals. Although the application of reason to Catholic doctrine advanced the development of a systematic theology, it also raised questions and new uncertainties. Aristotle's works, for example, questioned the soul's immortality and God's role in the universe, both direct challenges to Catholic thought. It was left to thirteenth-century theologians to reconcile the Aristotelian corpus with Christian doctrines.

Latin and Vernacular Literature

Latin was the universal language of medieval civilization. Used in the church and schools, it enabled learned men to communicate anywhere in Europe. The intellectual revival of the eleventh and twelfth centuries included an outpouring of Latin literature. The cathedral school at Chartres, where masters used literary models from Roman antiquity, became the literary center of western Europe.

Much of medieval Latin poetry was religious verse that did not follow classical models, but used rhyme and a meter based on accent. *Dies Irae (Day of Wrath)*, whose theme is the Last Judgment, illustrates these characteristics as well as the profound religious feeling of the Middle Ages:

> *Day of wrath, that day of burning!*
> *Earth shall end, to ashes turning:*
> *Thus sing saint and seer, discerning.*
>
> *Ah, the dread beyond expression*
> *When the Judge in awful session*
> *Searcheth out the world's transgression.*
>
> *Then is heard a sound of wonder:*
> *Mighty blasts of trumpet-thunder*
> *Rend the sepulchers asunder. . . .*
>
> *On his throne the Judge is seated,*
> *And our sins are loud repeated,*
> *And to each is vengeance meted.*[10]

There was also a large body of Latin verse dedicated to themes of love and nature. Many of these poems constitute the so-called Goliardic poetry and were written by vagabond students and teachers. Goliardic poetry was highly irreverent and focused on wine, women, and song:

> *My intention is to die*
> *In the tavern drinking;*
> *Wine must be at hand, for I*
> *Want it when I'm sinking.*
> *Angels when they come shall cry,*
> *At my frailties winking:*
> *"Spare this drunkard, God, he's high,*
> *Absolutely stinking!*[11]

The writing of history was yet another aspect of medieval Latin literature. Until the twelfth century, much historical writing had been done in the form of monastic annals, basically records of events pertinent to the monastery. Often narrow in scope and confined to local events, these annals can hardly be called histories. But

The Guide for the Perplexed
▼ ▼ ▼

Maimonides (1135–1204) was the most famous Jewish philosopher of the Middle Ages. Born in Córdoba, Spain, he studied Aristotle and Greek medicine under the best Arab teachers. He and his family migrated to Egypt where he became a physician to the sultan's palace in Cairo. Maimonides' philosophical works were highly regarded by western scholars in the thirteenth century, especially his greatest work, The Guide for the Perplexed. In this selection, Maimonides discusses a problem still debated by modern thinkers—the role of free will versus divine determinism.

Maimonides, *The Guide for the Perplexed*

There are five different theories concerning Divine Providence; they are all ancient, known since the time of the Prophets, when the true Law was revealed to enlighten these dark regions.

First Theory—There is no Providence at all for anything in the Universe; all parts of the Universe, the heavens and what they contain, owe their origin to accident and chance; there exists no being that rules and governs them or provides for them. This is the theory of Epicurus, who assumes also that the Universe consists of atoms, that these have combined by chance, and have received their various forms by mere accident. . . .

Second Theory—Whilst one part of the Universe owes its existence to Providence, and is under the control of a ruler and governor, another part is abandoned and left to chance. This is the view of Aristotle about Providence. . . .

Third Theory—This theory is the reverse of the second. According to this theory, there is nothing in the whole Universe, neither a class nor an individual being, that is due to chance; everything is the result of will, intention, and rule. It is a matter of course

that he who rules must know [that which is under his control]. . . .

Fourth Theory—Man has free will; it is therefore intelligible that the Law contains commands and prohibitions, with announcements of reward and punishment. All acts of God are due to wisdom; no injustice is found in Him, and He does not afflict the good.

Fifth Theory—This is our theory, or that of our Law [Hebrew Law]. . . . The theory of man's perfectly free will is one of the fundamental principles of the Law of our Teacher Moses, and of those who follow the Law. According to this principle man does what is in his power to do, by his nature, his choice, and his will; and his action is not due to any faculty created for the purpose. All species of irrational animals likewise move by their own free will. This is the Will of God; that is to say, it is due to the external divine will that all living beings should move freely, and that man should have power to act according to his will or choice within the limits of his capacity. . . .

My opinion on this principle of Divine Providence I will now explain to you. . . . It is this: In the lower . . . portion of the Universe Divine Providence does not extend to the individual members of species except in the case of mankind. It is only in this species that the incidents in the existence of the individual beings, their good and evil fortunes, are the result of justice, in accordance with the words, "For all His ways are judgment." But I agree with Aristotle as regards all other living beings, . . . plants and all the rest of earthly creatures. For I do not believe that it is through the interference of Divine Providence that a certain leaf drops [from a tree], nor do I hold that when a certain spider catches a certain fly, that this is the direct result of a special decree and will of God in that moment. . . .

in the twelfth century, some sound historical narratives appeared that transcended the monastic annals. Orderic Vitalis, a Norman monk of the early twelfth century, wrote an *Ecclesiastical History* that provided a rather unsystematic, yet considerably detailed account of Normandy in the eleventh and twelfth centuries. William of

Malmesbury's *History of the Kings of England*, although still in the tradition of the monastic annals, presented a skillful narrative and relatively balanced evaluation of historical events.

While Latin continued to be used for literary purposes, by the twelfth century much of the creative literature was being written in the vernacular tongues. There had been a popular vernacular literature throughout the Middle Ages, especially manifest in the Germanic, Celtic, Old Icelandic, and Slavonic sagas. But a new market for vernacular literature appeared in the twelfth century when educated lay people at courts and in the new urban society sought fresh avenues of entertainment.

Perhaps the most popular vernacular literature of the twelfth century was troubadour poetry, chiefly the product of nobles and knights. This poetry focused on themes

▼ **Love Scene-Troubadour Poetry.** The twelfth century was a period of intellectual revival in western Europe. Aristotle was recovered by way of Muslim scholars, classical works on medicine and science were made available, and vernacular literature flourished. Troubadour poetry, which had courtly love as its theme, was the most popular form of vernacular literature. It focused on the love of a knight for a lady, usually one who was married. Pictured here is a love scene taken from a collection of lyrics sung by the troubadours.

of courtly love, the love of a knight for a lady, primarily a married noble lady, who inspires him to become a braver knight and a better poet. A good example is found in the laments of the crusading noble Jaufré Rudel, who cherished a dream lady from afar whom he feared he would never meet, but would always love:

> Most sad, most joyous shall I go away,
> Let me have seen her for a single day,
> My love afar,
> I shall not see her, for her land and mine
> Are sundered, and the ways are hard to find,
> So many ways, and I shall lose my way,
> So wills it God.
>
> Yet shall I know no other love but hers,
> And if not hers, no other love at all.
> She hath surpassed all.
> So fair she is, so noble, I would be
> A captive with the hosts of paynimrie [the Muslims]
> In a far land, if so be upon me
> Her eyes might fall. [12]

Troubadour poetry reached its high point by the midtwelfth century and declined in originality thereafter. Though it originated in southern France, it also spread to northern France, Italy, and Germany.

Another type of vernacular literature appeared at the end of the eleventh century known as the *chanson de geste* or the heroic epic. The earliest and finest example is the *Chanson de Roland (The Song of Roland)*, which appeared around 1100 and was written in a dialect of French, a Romance language derived from Latin (see the box on p. 317).

The *chansons de geste* were written for a maledominated society. The chief events described in these poems, as in *The Song of Roland*, are battles and political contests. Their world is one of combat in which knights fight courageously for their kings and lords. Women play little or no role in this literary genre.

Although *chansons de geste* were still written in the twelfth century, a different kind of long poem, known as the courtly romance also became popular. It was composed in rhymed couplets and dwelt on a romantic subject matter: brave knights, virtuous ladies, evil magicians, bewitched palaces, fairies, talking animals, and strange forests. The story of King Arthur, the legendary king of the fifth-century Britons, became a popular subject for the courtly romance. The best versions of the Arthurian legends survive in the works of Chrétien de Troyes, whose courtly romances in the second half of the twelfth century were viewed by contemporaries as the works of a master storyteller.

The Song of Roland
▼ ▼ ▼

The Song of Roland *is one of the best examples of the medieval chanson de geste or heroic epic. Inspired by an historical event, it recounts the ambush of the rear guard of Charlemagne's Frankish army in the Pyrenees Mountains. It was written three hundred years after the event it supposedly describes, however, and reveals more about the eleventh century than about the age of Charlemagne. The Basques who ambushed Charlemagne's army have been transformed into Muslims; the Frankish soldiers into French knights. This selection describes the death of Roland, Charlemagne's nephew, who was the commander of the decimated rear guard.*

The Song of Roland

Now Roland feels that he is at death's door;
Out of his ears the brain is running forth.
Now for his peers he prays God call them all,
And for himself St. Gabriel's aid implores;
Then in each hand he takes, lest shame befal,
His Olifant and Durendal his sword.
Far as a quarrel flies from a cross-bow drawn,
Toward land of Spain he goes, to a wide lawn,
And climbs a mound where grows a fair tree tall,
And marble stones beneath it stand by four.

Face downward there on the green grass he falls,
And swoons away, for he is at death's door. . . .
Now Roland feels death press upon him hard;
It's creeping down from his head to his heart.
Under a pine-tree he hastens him apart,
There stretches him face down on the green grass,
And lays beneath him his sword and Olifant.
He's turned his head to where the Paynims [Muslims] are,
And this he doth for the French and for Charles,
Since fain is he that they should say, brave heart,
That he has died a conqueror at the last.
He beats his breast full many a time and fast,
Gives, with his glove, his sins into God's charge.

Now Roland feels his time is at an end;
On the steep hill-side, toward Spain he's turned his head,
And with one hand he beats upon his breast;
Saith: "Mea culpa; Thy mercy, Lord, I beg
For all the sins, both the great and the less,
That e'er I did since first I drew my breath
Unto this day when I'm struck down by death."
His right-hand glove he unto God extends;
Angels from Heaven now to his side descend.

Fabliaux or fables were short stories written in rhymed verse concentrating on wandering clerks who outsmarted nobles, merchants and clergy. Priests and monks, in particular, are portrayed as fools and hypocrites. Usually crude, the *fabliaux* had much popular appeal for both knights and the urban middle classes. One of the best known is the story of *Aucassin et Nicolette,* which pokes fun at feudal warfare and religion. At one point, when warned of the dangers of going to hell instead of heaven, Aucassin replies:

In Paradise what have I to do? I care not to enter, but only to have Nicolette, my very sweet friend, whom I love so dearly well. For into Paradise go none but such people as I will tell you of. There go those aged priests, and those old cripples, and the maimed, who all day long and all night cough before the altars, and in the crypts beneath the churches; those who go in worn old mantles and old tattered habits; who are naked, and barefoot, and full of sores; who are dying of hunger and thirst, of cold and of wretchedness. Such as these enter in Paradise, and with them I have nought to do. But in Hell will I go. For to Hell go the fair clerks and the fair knights who are slain in the tourney and the great wars, and the stout archer and the loyal man. With them will I go. And there go the fair and courteous ladies, . . . together with their wedded lords. And there pass the gold and the silver, the ermine and all rich furs, harpers and minstrels, and the happy of the world. With these will I go, so only that I have Nicolette, my very sweet friend, by my side.[13]

Written at the beginning of the thirteenth century, this story makes clear the shift to a growing secular literature.

Romanesque Architecture: "A White Mantle of Churches"

The eleventh and twelfth centuries witnessed an explosion of building, both private and public. The construction of castles and churches absorbed most of the surplus resources of medieval society and at the same time reflected its basic preoccupations, God and warfare. The churches were by far the most conspicuous of the

▼ **Barrel Vaulting, Vienne.** A central feature of the eleventh and twelfth centuries was the enormous amount of attention paid to the construction and reconstruction of churches. Utilizing the basilica shape, master builders replaced the flat wooden roofs that had been used with long, round stone vaults, known as barrel vaults. As this illustration of a Romanesque church indicates, the barrel vault limited the size of a church and left little room for windows.

public buildings. As a chronicler of the eleventh century commented:

> As the year 1003 approached, people all over the world, but especially in Italy and France began to rebuild their churches. Although most of them were well built and in little need of alterations, Christian nations were rivalling each other to have the most beautiful edifices. One might say the world was shaking herself, throwing off her old garments, and robing herself with a white mantle of churches. Then nearly all the cathedrals, the monasteries dedicated to different saints, and even the small village chapels were reconstructed more beautifully by the faithful.[14]

Hundreds of new cathedrals, abbey and pilgrimage churches, as well as thousands of parish churches in rural

villages were built in the eleventh and twelfth centuries. There was not only a dramatic increase in the number of churches but also in their size. The building spree was a direct reflection of a revived religious culture and the increased wealth of the period produced by agriculture, trade, and the growth of cities.

The cathedrals of the eleventh and twelfth centuries were built in the Romanesque style, a truly international style. The construction of churches required the services of professional master builders, whose employment throughout Europe guaranteed an international unity in basic style. Prominent examples of Romanesque churches can be found in Germany (no church of the eleventh century is more massive or impressive than the cathedral at Speyer); France (the church of the Madeleine at Vézelay, dedicated to Saint Mary Magdalene, is certainly one of the most exquisite Romanesque churches); and Spain (where the Romanesque cathedral of Saint James in Santiago de Compostela was a favorite goal of pilgrims).

Romanesque churches were normally built in the basilica shape utilized in the construction of churches in the late Roman Empire. Basilicas were simply rectangular buildings with flat wooden roofs. While using this basic plan, Romanesque builders made a significant innovation by replacing the flat wooden roof with a long, round stone vault called a barrel vault or a cross vault where two barrel vaults intersected. The latter was used when a transept was added to create a church plan in the shape of a cross. Although barrel and cross vaults were

▼ **Grotesque Figures.** While there was a revival of sculpture during the eleventh and twelfth centuries, it was always subordinate to architecture. Sculpture was used primarily for the adornment of churches and cathedrals, and, as these figures indicate, it was seldom realistic. With the emphasis placed on generating an emotional response and depicting stories from the Bible for the illiterate, realism was not stressed.

technically difficult to construct, they were considered aesthetically more pleasing and technically more proficient and were also less apt to catch fire.

Since stone roofs were extremely heavy, Romanesque churches required massive pillars and walls to hold them up. This left little space for windows, and Romanesque churches were correspondingly dark on the inside. Their massive walls and pillars gave Romanesque churches a sense of solidity and almost the impression of a fortress. Indeed, massive walls and slit windows were also characteristic of the castle architecture of the period.

This age also witnessed a revival of sculpture, especially ornamental sculpture in stone used primarily to adorn the exteriors of cathedrals and churches. Entranceways and the spaces above them were filled with figures of men and animals to illustrate scenes from the Bible. There was little attempt at naturalism since the goal of such sculpture was didactic: to teach illiterate people the biblical stories.

▼ Christianity and Medieval Civilization

No matter what topics we have discussed in our survey of medieval civilization, it is apparent that Christianity was an integral part of the fabric of European society and the consciousness of Europe. The tremendous expansion in size and number of churches throughout Europe was only the most obvious visible manifestation of the fundamental role played by Christianity in all levels of European society. Papal directives affected the actions of kings and princes alike while Christian teaching and practices touched the economic, social, intellectual, cultural, and daily lives of all Europeans.

Papal Authority and Church Administration

The popes of the twelfth century did not abandon the reform ideals of Gregory VII (see Chapter 9), but they were less dogmatic and more inclined to consolidate their power and build a strong administrative system. In fact, they were so successful at the latter that they outstripped contemporary monarchs in developing the machinery of centralized administration. Although earlier popes had always claimed great powers, the novelty of the twelfth century was the development of administrative machinery that transformed aspirations into reality.

What made the papal centralization of power possible was the maturation of a highly efficient papal curia or papal court, largely the work of Pope Urban II (1088–1099). The papal curia of the twelfth century has been called the "most sophisticated administrative staff" of its time in Europe. It was divided into a number of specialized divisions, such as a chancery or writing office for documents, a papal chapel, and a treasury. The Roman curia also functioned as a high court of law formulating canon law and serving as a court of final appeal for all cases touching the church's vast ecclesiastical court system, especially matters dealing with church property, marriages, and oaths. The church's interest in systematizing canon law was, as we have seen, crucial in making these changes possible. It is no accident that many of the popes in the twelfth and thirteenth centuries had backgrounds as canon lawyers.

By the twelfth century, the Catholic church possessed a clearly organized hierarchical structure. The pope and papal curia were at the center of the administrative structure. Below them were the bishops since all of Christendom was divided into dioceses under their direction. To be sure, archbishops had larger sees than bishops and were in principle more powerful than the bishops, but at this time they were unable to exercise any real control over the internal matters of the bishops' dioceses. Theoretically, the bishop chose all priests in his diocese, administered his diocese, and was responsible only to the pope. According to church law, bishops were to be elected by the clergy and laity of their dioceses. In fact, the elections of bishops were controlled by the most important clerics in a bishop's cathedral, the cathedral canons, although with close royal supervision in England and Germany. The canons chose the new bishop and served as his diocesan administrators.

The development of efficient, centralized administrative machinery supported by an orderly system of canon law was a major foundation for papal authority in the twelfth century. Other factors also contributed to the growing recognition of papal prestige and power. By assuming leadership of the crusades, Pope Urban II had thrust the papacy into the center of both the spiritual and temporal affairs of Christendom. Moreover, popes exercised their leadership by holding both local and European-wide church councils. Councils promulgated reform decrees that brought the new organizational structure and new developments in theology and canon law to dioceses throughout Europe.

This growth in the institutional power of the papacy was not without some detrimental consequences. In particular, some critics began to assert that the popes were abandoning their moral role in favor of being good administrators. The satirical "Gospel According to Marks of Silver" is a stunning example of this criticism. In this Goliardic tale, a poor man seeks help at the papal court but is refused even though he gives all he has to the cardinals and chamberlains. A murderer who gives rich gifts is well received, however. On receiving an exceptionally splendid gift, the pope summons the cardinals and tells them, "For I have given you an example, that even as much as I have taken, you also should take."

New Monastic Orders and New Spiritual Ideals: Saint Bernard of Clairvaux

In the second half of the eleventh century and the first half of the twelfth century, still another wave of religious enthusiasm seized Europe. One of its manifestations was the crusades, but another appeared in the development of new monastic orders and a spectacular growth in monastic institutions. In England, for example, in the mid-eleventh century, there were 48 Benedictine houses, 36 for monks and 12 for nuns. By the mid-twelfth century, England had 317 monastic houses belonging to six different orders, 245 for monks and 72 for females. Even more significant, from these new monastic orders came new spiritual ideals for the twelfth century.

▼ **Saint Bernard.** The eleventh and twelfth centuries were marked by the development of new monastic orders. One of the most important of these new orders was the Cistercian order, and it was from the Cistercian house at Clairvaux that one of the most famous figures of the twelfth century, Saint Bernard, arose. Bernard advocated a militant expression of Christianity's ideals while at the same time favoring a more personalized understanding of the relationship between humans and God. Pictured here is St. Bernard preaching a sermon to his fellow Cistercians.

One of the most important manifestations of this revival was the emergence of the Cistercian order. In 1098, a group of monks, dissatisfied with the lack of strict discipline at their Benedictine monastery, founded a new monastery at Cîteaux in Burgundy (Cistercium in Latin—hence the name of the new order). Cistercian monasticism spread rapidly from southern France into Italy, Spain, England, Germany, and eastern Europe. In 1115, there were five Cistercian houses; by 1150, there were over three hundred.

The Cistercians emphasized a strict austerity. They ate a simple diet and possessed only a single robe. All decorations were eliminated from their churches and monastic buildings, and no gold or silver ornaments were permitted. More time for private prayer and manual labor was provided by shortening the number of hours spent in liturgical services. Unlike Benedictine and Cluniac houses, Cistercian monasteries were not supported by peasant labor. To escape from the world, many Cistercians had located their monasteries on uninhabited lands, usually wastelands or virgin forests. Since their own manual labor was insufficient to meet the demands of these lands, the Cistercians initiated a separate monastic track for lay brothers from the peasant class. They took monastic vows and participated in common worship, but lived separately from the regular monks and spent most of their time working in the fields and in the industries established by the monks. The Cistercians' attempt to live independently of the world had an ironic result. Cistercians opened up hundreds of thousands of acres of unproductive land for agriculture. They exported wool and wine from their farms and vineyards. They made ample use of the technology of their age, using machines powered by water. As a result, the Cistercians were incredibly successful in creating a widespread "economic empire."

The organization of the Cistercian order followed a principle of close supervision between the original monastery and its daughter houses. An abbot of the mother house inspected daughter houses while abbots of the first four daughter houses were expected to visit and examine Cîteaux; they were, in fact, empowered to remove the abbot for misconduct if necessary. Moreover, all Cistercian abbots met at Cîteaux annually to arrive at communal decisions affecting the order. Unlike Cluny (see Chapter 9), then, the Cistercian order was effectively decentralized; at the same time, unlike the Benedictines, the Cistercian houses were not autonomous.

The Cistercians played a major role in developing a new, activistic spiritual model for twelfth-century Europe. Monasticism had originally been established to iso-

A Miracle of Saint Bernard

▼ ▼ ▼

Saint Bernard of Clairvaux has been called "the most widely respected holy man of the twelfth century." He was an outstanding preacher, wholly dedicated to the service of God. His reputation reportedly influenced many young men to join the Cistercian order. He also inspired a myriad of stories dealing with his miracles.

A Miracle of Saint Bernard

A certain monk, departing from his monastery . . . threw off his habit, and returned to the world at the persuasion of the Devil. And he took a certain parish living; for he was a priest. Because sin is punished with sin, the deserter from his Order lapsed into the vice of lechery. He took a concubine to live with him, as in fact is done by many, and by her he had children.

But as God is merciful and does not wish anyone to perish, it happened that many years after, the blessed abbot [Saint Bernard] was passing through the village in which this same monk was living, and went to stay at his house. The renegade monk recognized him, and received him very reverently, and waited on him devoutly . . . but as yet the abbot did not recognize him.

On the morrow, the holy man said Matins and prepared to be off. But as he could not speak to the priest, since he had got up and gone to the church for Matins, he said to the priest's son "Go, give this message to your master." Now the boy had been born dumb. He obeyed the command and feeling in himself the power of him who had given it, he ran to his father and uttered the words of the Holy Father clearly and exactly. His father, on hearing his son's voice for the first time, wept for joy, and made him repeat the same words . . . and he asked what the abbot had done to him. "He did nothing to me," said the boy, "except to say 'Go and say this to your father.'"

At so evident a miracle the priest repented, and hastened after the holy man and fell at his feet saying "My Lord and Father, I was your monk so-and-so, and at such-and-such a time I ran away from your monastery. I ask your Paternity to allow me to return with you to the monastery, for in your coming God has visited my heart." The saint replied unto him, "Wait for me here, and I will come back quickly when I have done my business, and I will take you with me." But the priest, fearing death (which he had not done before), answered, "Lord, I am afraid of dying before then." But the saint replied, "Know this for certain, that if you die in this condition, and in this resolve, you will find yourself a monk before God."

The saint [eventually] returned and heard that the priest had recently died and been buried. He ordered the tomb to be opened. And when they asked him what he wanted to do, he said, "I want to see if he is lying as a monk or a clerk in his tomb." "As a clerk," they said; "we buried him in his secular habit." But when they had dug up the earth, they found that he was not in the clothes in which they had buried him; but he appeared in all points, tonsure and habit, as a monk. And they all praised God.

---

late a select group of dedicated Christians from the world. A monk often spent hours in ritual prayer to honor God. The Cistercian ideal had a different emphasis: "Arise, soldier of Christ, arise! Get up off the ground and return to the battle from which you have fled! Fight more boldly after your flight, and triumph in glory!"[15] These were the words of Saint Bernard of Clairvaux, the most famous Cistercian of the twelfth century, who more than any other person embodied the new spiritual ideal of Cistercian monasticism.

Bernard of Clairvaux (1090–1153) was the most famous religious figure of the twelfth century (see the box above). A mystic and religious enthusiast, Bernard has been called one of the last of the holy men, an ideal that had emerged in the Christianity of late antiquity. Of noble birth, Bernard joined the Cistercians in 1113 and became abbot of the third daughter house of Citeaux located at Clairvaux. Although well known for his complete dedication to the ascetic ideals of the Cistercians, he also became an active voice outside the monastery. He attacked Peter Abelard for supposed theological errors. He helped to settle a disputed papal election. He called for a new crusade (the second crusade) and even went to Germany to persuade the emperor to join it. He assisted in the foundation of the military monastic order of the Knights Templars. In all of these ways, Bernard encouraged the militant expression of religious ideals in worldly activities. At the same time, Bernard's influence created a spiritual ideal that was both more mystical and more personal than the spirituality of the Early Middle Ages.

Bernard wrote a number of works on prayer and devotion in which he set out a path to God that consisted of four stages of love by which an individual could seek to attain a mystical union with God. His works gave hope that ordinary humans could follow a spiritual path and gain salvation.

Bernard also gave religious piety a more personal touch when he portrayed Christ, the Virgin Mary, and the saints in more human fashion. In the Early Middle Ages, these holy figures were most often presented in a majestic, triumphant manner and viewed as remote from people's lives. Achieving salvation seemed difficult since Christ was portrayed as a stern judge. In his sermons and writings, Bernard pictured these sacred figures as living human beings to whom people could relate directly. He encouraged an emotional love for Jesus and for the mother of Christ, the Virgin Mary, whom he portrayed as a gentle, loving, kindly intercessor with her Son. The new sentiment is apparent in contemporary depictions of the crucified Christ. He is no longer the majestic, triumphant judge, but the suffering son of man. The mystical and personalized approaches of the twelfth century implied a new relationship between humans and God: God had become a loving father who cared for humanity and created new avenues for salvation.

The Women Religious: Hildegard of Bingen

Not only men were susceptible to the religious fervor of the twelfth century; women were also active participants in the spiritual movements of the age. The image of women, in fact, was steadily changing in both religious thought and secular imagery. The cult of the Virgin Mary spread dramatically throughout Europe while the poetry of courtly love made women objects of adoration. At the same time, the number of women joining religious houses grew perceptibly with the growth of the new orders of the twelfth century.

By that time, female monasticism was already hundreds of years old. The first convent had been founded in 512 by a French bishop, and the practice soon spread throughout Europe. Medieval monasticism, however, always remained an overwhelmingly male phenomenon. Even in 1200, after a century of growth, there were only about 3,000 nuns in England compared to 14,000 monks. Moreover, male monasteries were larger and better supported financially. The nuns' secondary role stemmed from the church's view of women as subordinate to men. Not allowed to exercise priestly powers,

▼ **Christ as Judge. Christ as Suffering Servant.** In the Early Middle Ages, Christ was often depicted in a majestic, distant manner that seemed to place him beyond the ordinary person. Saint Bernard, however, worked to change this image by presenting Christ as more of a human being, as the suffering man who died for the sins of the human race. Pictured here are a mosaic depicting Christ as judge and a bas-relief representing him as the suffering servant being taken down from the cross.

women were dependent on male priests for the sacraments and liturgical services of the church.

In the Early Middle Ages, religious houses for females were frequently founded by queens and governed by abbesses of royal or noble blood, a practice that continued into the High Middle Ages. In tenth- and eleventh-century Germany, for example, there were abbesses who ruled vast areas of land and summoned knights to war as vassals of the king. One abbess of Quedlinburg minted her own coins, and another, Matilda, served unofficially as regent for her nephew Otto Ill.

German nuns also possessed a strong intellectual tradition, beginning with Leoba, an eighth-century abbess of Bischofsheim. According to a contemporary monk, she "was so bent on reading that she never laid aside her book except to pray or to strengthen her slight frame with food and sleep." Moreover, "from childhood upwards she had studied grammar and the other liberal arts. . . . She zealously read the books of the Old and New Testaments and . . . further added to the rich store of her knowledge by reading the writings of the holy Fathers, the canonical decrees, and the laws of the Church."[16] Better known than Leoba was Hroswitha of Gandersheim from the tenth century. She wrote a number of literary works including six plays using Terence (see Chapter 6) as her model and a contemporary history in verse form.

In the High Middle Ages, most nuns were from the ranks of the landed aristocracy. Convents were convenient for families unable or unwilling to find husbands for their daughters and for aristocratic women who did not wish to marry. Female intellectuals found them a haven for their activities. Most of the learned women of the Middle Ages, especially in Germany, were nuns. This was certainly true of Hildegard of Bingen, one of the most distinguished figures of the twelfth century.

Hildegard of Bingen (1098–1179) entered a religious house for females at Disibodenberg in western Germany at the age of eight. She took her vows at fourteen. An abbess of the order, a sister of the local count, saw to her education. After twenty-four years as an ordinary nun, Hildegard was chosen abbess of her house in 1136. Eleven years later, she and her charges left Disibodenberg and founded a new convent at Rupertsberg near Bingen.

Hildegard shared in the religious enthusiasm of the twelfth century. Soon after becoming abbess, she began to write down an account of the mystical visions she had experienced for years. "A great flash of light from heaven pierced my brain and . . . in that instant my mind was imbued with the meaning of the sacred books," she

▼ **Group of Nuns.** Although still viewed by the medieval church as inferior to men, women were as susceptible to the spiritual fervor of the twelfth century as men, and female monasticism grew accordingly. The majority of nuns came from the aristocracy during the High Middle Ages and most female intellectuals found a haven in the convent. The miniature pictured here shows a group of nuns listening to the preaching of an abbot.

wrote in a description typical of the world's greatest mystical literature. As part of her vision, she was commanded to write down what she had seen. Eventually she did so and produced three books based on her visions. The most important were *Scivias* (*Scito Vias Domini*—"Know the Ways of the Lord") and the *Book of Divine Works* (see the box on p. 324). In the latter, Hildegard presented the universe as a living cosmology in which nature, humanity, divinity, and the cosmos were all interconnected in a harmonious whole. The macrocosm (universe) was one with the microcosm (humankind). Humans, she wrote, were "completely the image of God," and she urged them to be "co-creators with God."

Hildegard gained considerable renown as a mystic and prophet, and popes, emperors, kings, dukes, bishops, abbots, and abbesses eagerly sought her advice. Her correspondents included Saint Bernard of Clairvaux, Pope Anastasius IV, Emperor Frederick Barbarossa, and King Henry II of England. She wrote to them all as an equal and did not hesitate to be critical. To Henry II of England, she warned, "Look then with fervent zeal at the

The Mystical Visions of Hildegard of Bingen
▼ ▼ ▼

Hildegard of Bingen has been called "one of the greatest intellectuals and mystics of the west." She was incredibly prolific. She wrote books on science, theology, philosophy, and medicine; painted a series of images to render her mystical visions in visible form; and composed over seventy songs. She wrote three books on her visions. This selection is from her third work called The Book of Divine Works. It provides a good example of the spiritual intensity of the twelfth century.

Hildegard of Bingen, *The Book of Divine Works*

First Vision: On the Origin of Life

Vision One: 1

And I saw within the mystery of God, in the midst of the southern breezes, a wondrously beautiful image. It had a human form, and its countenance was of such beauty and radiance that I could have more easily gazed at the sun than at that face. A broad golden ring circled its head. . . . The figure was wrapped in a garment that shone like the sun. . . . [This "spirit of the macrocosm" then spoke to her:]

I, the highest and fiery power, have kindled every spark of life, and I emit nothing that is deadly. I decide on all reality. With my lofty wings I fly above the globe: With wisdom I have rightly put the universe in order. I, the fiery life of divine essence, am aflame beyond the beauty of the meadows, I gleam in the waters, and I burn in the sun, moon, and stars. With every breeze, as with invisible life that contains everything, I awaken everything to life. The air lives by turning green and being in bloom. The waters flow as if they were alive. The sun lives in its light, and the moon is enkindled, after its disappearance, once again by the light of the sun so that the moon is again revived. The stars, too, give a clear light with their beaming. I have established pillars that bear the entire globe as well as the power of the winds which, once again, have subordinate wings—so to speak, weaker winds—which through their gentle power resist the mighty winds so that they do not become dangerous. In the same way, too, the body envelops the soul and maintains it so that the soul does not blow away. For just as the breath of the soul strengthens and fortifies the body so that it does not disappear, the more powerful winds, too, revive the surrounding winds so that they can provide their appropriate service.

And thus I remain hidden in every kind of reality as a fiery power. Everything burns because of me in such a way as our breath constantly moves us, like the wind-tossed flame in a fire. All of this lives in its essence, and there is no death in it. For I am life. I am also Reason, which bears within itself the breath of the resounding Word, through which the whole of creation is made. I breathe life into everything so that nothing is mortal in respect to its species. For I am life. . . .

Vision One: 3

And again I heard a voice from heaven saying to me:

God, who created everything, has formed humanity according to the divine image and likeness, and marked in human beings both the higher and the lower creatures. God loved humanity so much that God designated for it the place from which the fallen angel was ejected,, intending for human beings all the splendor and honor which that angel lost along with his bliss. The countenance you are gazing at is an indication of this fact.

God who created you. For your heart is full of goodwill to do gladly what is good, except when the filthy habits of humankind rush at you and for a time you became entangled in them. Be resolute and flee those entanglements, beloved son of God, and call out to God!"[17] Hildegard of Bingen's last years were clouded by a conflict with the archbishop of Mainz. She died after vindication at the age of eighty-one.

Popular Religion in the High Middle Ages

We have witnessed the actions of popes, cardinals, bishops, and monks. We have seen how the church created a papal monarchy in which the pope, assisted by his curia, ran and directed the hierarchical organization of the Catholic church. But what of ordinary clergy and lay people? What were their religious hopes and fears? What were their spiritual aspirations? It is, of course, not easy to answer these questions with great certainty. Many of these people were illiterate and left few records of their thoughts and feelings. Moreover, there were enormous differences in perspective not only between the educated clergy and the illiterate clergy and laity, but also among the laity themselves with their different social classes and different levels of education.

SAINTS, RELICS, AND PILGRIMAGES   In the early church, saints were men and women who displayed eminent holiness and achieved a special position in the spiritual hierarchy, enabling them to act as intercessors before the throne of God. Their intercessionary powers and ability to protect poor souls enabled them to take on great importance at the popular level. Christ's apostles were, of course, universally recognized throughout Europe as saints, but there were also numerous local saints that were of especial significance to a single area, such as Saint Swithun in Winchester, England. New cults developed rapidly, particularly in the intense religious atmosphere of the eleventh and twelfth centuries. The English introduced Saint Nicholas, the patron saint of children, who remains instantly recognizable today through his identification with Santa Claus. Contemporaries could also be the source of new cults. Thomas Becket, "martyred" by the henchmen of Henry II in 1170, was proclaimed a saint only three years later. He was entombed in a crypt at Canterbury, where his shrine became the scene of many miracles: "the palsied are cured, the blind see, the deaf hear, the dumb speak, the lame walk, folk suffering from fevers are cured, the lepers are cleansed, those possessed of a devil are freed, and the sick are made whole from all manner of disease."[18]

Of all the saints, the Virgin Mary, the mother of Christ, occupied the foremost position in the High Middle Ages. The cult of Mary took on two important aspects. Mary was viewed as the most important mediator with her son Christ, the judge of all sinners. Moreover, from the eleventh century on, with the heightened interest in Jesus as infant, boy, and man, a fascination with Mary as Jesus' human mother became more evident. A sign of Mary's importance is the growing number of churches all over Europe that were dedicated to her in the twelfth and thirteenth centuries. Many monastic houses, especially the Cistercians, made Mary the patron saint of their churches.

As Mary became more popular, the number of stories about miracles occurring through her intercession also increased dramatically. Since medieval society viewed life in hierarchical terms, Mary held a definite place as Queen of Heaven, and numerous prayers were directed to her for intercession. Most widespread was the "Salve Regina," which expresses well the hopes medieval people had in Mary:

> Hail, holy Queen, Mother of Mercy! Our life, our sweetness, and our hope. To thee we cry, poor banished children of Eve; to thee we send up our sighs, mourning and weeping in this valley of tears. Turn, then, most gracious advocate, thy merciful eyes upon us; and after this our exile show us the blessed fruit of thy womb, Jesus. O merciful, O loving, O sweet Virgin Mary!

In the warlike society of the Middle Ages, it was no doubt reassuring to have the comforting and healing presence of such a powerful female figure.

Emphasis on the role of the saints was closely tied to the use of relics, which also increased significantly in the High Middle Ages. Relics were usually the bones of saints or objects intimately connected to saints that were considered worthy of veneration by the faithful. A twelfth-century English monk began his description of the abbey's relics by saying that "There is kept there a thing more precious than gold, . . . the right arm of St. Oswald. . . . This we have seen with our own eyes and have kissed, and have handled with our own hands. . . . There are kept here also part of his ribs and of the soil on which he fell."[19] The monk went on to list additional relics possessed by the abbey, which included two pieces of Christ's swaddling clothes, pieces of Christ's manger and part of the five loaves of bread with which Christ fed 5,000 people. Since the holiness of the saint was considered to be inherent in his relics, these objects were believed to be capable of healing people or producing other miracles.

In the High Middle Ages, it became a regular practice of the church to attach indulgences to these relics. An indulgence brought a remission of the temporal punishment due to sin after the sinner had been absolved by a priest. Indulgences were, in turn, closely connected to the church's doctrine of purgatory, which was first clearly defined in the eleventh and twelfth centuries. Purgatory was believed to be a place of punishment in which the soul of the departed could be purified before ascending into heaven. The living could ease that suffering by masses and prayers offered on behalf of the deceased and, of course, by indulgences. Indulgences were granted for charitable contributions and viewing the relics of saints. Although it was not to be taken literally, the church attached a number of years and days to each indulgence, making possible a lessening of the time spent by the soul in purgatory.

The pilgrimage has been called the "most characteristic mode of travel" in the High Middle Ages. Medieval Christians believed it was of particular spiritual benefit to make a pilgrimage to a holy shrine. The greatest shrine but the most difficult to reach was the Holy City of Jerusalem. On the continent two pilgrim centers were especially popular in the eleventh and twelfth centuries: Rome, which contained the relics of Saints Peter and Paul, and the town of Santiago de Compostela, supposedly the site of the tomb of the Apostle James. Local attractions, such as shrines dedicated to the Blessed Virgin Mary or Canterbury after the murder of Thomas Becket, also became pilgrimage centers.

Travel of this kind was often dangerous, and the pilgrim had to be strongly committed to undertake it. But a social factor was also involved. Making a pilgrimage was a form of entertainment in which men and women from different backgrounds experienced considerable companionship. Indeed, one historian has recently argued that medieval pilgrimages represented the beginning of tourism. Like modern tourists, prospective pilgrims could obtain guidebooks that made their journeys easier.

Pilgrimages, like relics, involved economic considerations as well. Pilgrims, again like modern tourists, bought souvenirs. At Santiago de Compostela, for example, visitors could buy little scallop shells, the symbols of Saint James. Stalls next to pilgrimage churches sold wine, medicine, and shoes, and moneychangers could count on making a profit in the exchange of currencies that would be required for any lengthy journey. The economic importance of pilgrimage churches that housed saints' relics is evident in the flourishing market in relics in the High Middle Ages. Saints' bones not only brought protection to a church, but also attracted pilgrims praying for miracles. These pilgrims brought contributions to the church and business to the local economy. Consequently, relics were in great demand and brought good prices. Finally, there is little doubt that the close interrelationship among saints, relics, and pilgrimages contributed to the dramatic increase in the construction of churches. Certainly, a large number were pilgrimage churches.

THE BIBLE AND PREACHING   The Bible was the most important book in the medieval European world. The task of theology in the schools and universities was to expound the Bible. Preachers were supposed to use its stories to teach the people the basic messages of Christian-

ity. Those same stories were illustrated on walls and in sculpture. Thus, in many ways, the Bible could be found everywhere.

Yet it is noteworthy that there were few translations of the Bible into the vernacular, the language of the people. Although some vernacular translations were made in the Early Middle Ages, they were rarely used in the eleventh and twelfth centuries and, in fact, came to be viewed as dangerous because of their connection to heretical movements (see Chapter 11). Some scholars feel that the story of the Catholic church's opposition to vernacular translations is exaggerated, but it remains true that the church discouraged the use of the Bible in the vernacular and encouraged the clergy to make the Bible available in oral and visual form.

Since preaching was one of the clergy's most important tasks, manuals were written to aid priests in composing their sermons. An examination of medieval sermons has revealed a remarkable change in their content in the High Middle Ages. Sermons of the tenth and eleventh centuries stressed the themes of judgment and fear of hell; those of the twelfth and thirteenth centuries manifested greater optimism, underscoring the need for a good Christian life and practical morality. Preaching did present problems, however, because of the ignorance and illiteracy of many of the clergy. It was not unusual for a bishop's investigation to find that many priests were "thoroughly illiterate," ignorant both of Latin and the Latin church services.

THE SACRAMENTAL SYSTEM   The sacramental system of the Catholic church ensured that the church was an integral part of people's lives, from birth to death. It was not until the twelfth century that the church finally defined the seven sacraments administered by the clergy. Sacraments were viewed as outward symbols of an inward grace and were considered imperative for a Christian's salvation.

The five sacraments that most directly affected the lives of medieval Christians were baptism, marriage, the eucharist, confession, and extreme unction. Holy orders was reserved for the clergy, and confirmation of older children by a bishop did not become a regular practice until the thirteenth century.

Baptism signified membership in the church proper. By the High Middle Ages, it was generally believed that the unbaptized could not be saved. This created pressure to have infants baptized as soon as possible. Although midwives and parents baptized their infants in an informal ceremony, the church tried to minimize this practice and by the eleventh century emphasized the need to baptize infants rather than adults or grown children as had been the custom in the past. Baptism was now done in a cathedral or local parish church where the infant was anointed with holy oil and sprinkled with water by a priest.

Marriage was not viewed as a sacrament by the church until the twelfth century. Since the church had previously emphasized the supremacy of the celibate state, making marriage a sacrament gave it a new dignity and sanctioned the practice of sexual intercourse for the begetting of children. It also meant that legal problems concerning marriage would be tried in church courts.

The eucharist was the highest sacrament of the Catholic church because of its close connection with Christ. In the early Christian church, it was celebrated by the community's partaking of bread and wine as symbols of Christ's body and blood. By the eleventh and twelfth centuries, the eucharist was increasingly viewed as containing the actual body and blood of Christ, and the laity's role in receiving the sacrament had drastically changed. The mass, as the official common worship of the Catholic church came to be called, was dominated by the clergy with lay people in attendance. This made the reception of the eucharist, or Holy Communion, a rare experience—so rare, in fact, that the Fourth Lateran Council in 1215 decreed it necessary for all Christians to partake of the eucharist at least once a year. Attendance at mass was made mandatory on Sundays and at important festivals of the church. Since the liturgy of the mass was in Latin, it was difficult for most lay people to know what was going on.

The confession of sins and their absolution had been a communal practice in the early church. Sins were confessed publicly to one's local community of Christians. In the course of the Middle Ages, however, this practice was replaced by private personal confession to both one's fellow laymen and to priests. By the twelfth century, the right to hear confessions belonged exclusively to priests along with a new ritual of absolution and penance. In 1215, the Fourth Lateran Council prescribed annual confession as well as annual communion. The trend toward private confession was part of the general movement toward a more personal or individual approach to Christian life in the eleventh and twelfth centuries. Gradually, however, confession and penance also became more mechanical in nature. By being penitent and given absolution by a priest, it was believed that a sinner could free his or her soul from the danger of hell. Nevertheless, the punishment of sin remained to be expunged in purgatory where the soul would remain after death till purged of these penalties. The use of indul-

▼ **The Gate to Hell.** This twelfth-century miniature depicts the gate of hell as the jaws of a monster filled with sinners and demons. Despite the undeniable importance of the Bible during the Middle Ages, vernacular translations were seldom used and came to be viewed by some as dangerous. Biblical stories were instead expressed through narrative art and sermons, which were considered less dangerous ways to convey the basic messages of Christianity for the uneducated.

gences to shorten this time opened the door to considerable abuse and the popular belief that indulgences offered a sure way to salvation.

Finally, the church had a sacrament for death. If possible, a priest administered extreme unction or the last rites of the church for the dying. It was commonly believed that regardless of one's sins, proper remorse at the moment of death could still mean salvation. Given medieval life expectancies, the ceremonies connected with burial were probably a very common Christian experience.

The period from 1000 to 1200 was a very dynamic one in the development of Western civilization. It witnessed economic, social, and political changes that some historians believe oot European civilization on a path that lasted until the eighteenth century when the Industrial Revolution created a new pattern. Just as important, however, these two centuries gave birth to an intellectual and spiritual revival that transformed European society. The intellectual revival led to a rediscovery of important aspects of the classical heritage, to new centers of learning in the cathedral schools and universities, and to the use of reason to systematize the study of theology and law and to develop whole new ways of thought. Spiritual renewal in the High Middle Ages led to numerous and even divergent paths: revived papal leadership, the crusading "holy warrior" who killed for God, a dramatic increase in the number and size of churches, and new dimensions to the religious life of the clergy and laity. The theology of Saint Bernard, new forms of monasticism, the doctrine of purgatory, and the emergence of a clearly defined sacramental system all seemed to reflect a greater concern for salvation and a greater possibility of achieving it. In the midst of what must have seemed invincible growth and vitality, the twelfth century also bore witness to the first stirrings of dissent from church teachings. In the thirteenth century, the church would respond with a use of force that to some seemed to conflict with its original message.

Notes

1. Oliver J. Thatcher and Edgar H. McNeal, eds., *A Source Book for Medieval History* (New York, 1905), p. 517.

2. Thatcher and McNeal, *A Source Book for Medieval History*, p. 523.

3. Anna Comnena, *Alexiad*, trans. E. A. S. Dawes (London, 1928), p. 252.

4. Quoted in Hans E. Mayer, *The Crusades*, trans. John Gillingham (New York, 1972), pp. 99–100.

5. Quoted in John W. Baldwin, *The Scholastic Culture of the Middle Ages, 1000–1300* (Lexington, Mass., 1971), p. 60.

6. Quoted in Charles H. Haskins, *The Rise of Universities* (Ithaca, N.Y., 1957), pp. 77–78.

7. Ibid., pp. 79–80.

8. Quoted in Henry O. Taylor, *The Medieval Mind* (Cambridge, Mass., 1949), 1:278.

9. Quoted in David Knowles, *The Evolution of Medieval Thought* (New York, 1964), p. 200.

10. David Herlihy, ed., *Medieval Culture and Society* (New York, 1968), p. 306.

11. *The Goliard Poets*, trans. George Whicher (Cambridge, Mass., 1949), p. 111.

12. Helen Waddell, *The Wandering Scholars* (New York, 1961), p. 222.

13. *Aucassin and Nicolette*, trans. Eugene Mason (New York, 1958), p. 6.

14. Quoted in Baldwin, *The Scholastic Culture of the Middle Ages, 1000–1300*, p. 15.

15. Quoted in R. H. C. Davis, *A History of Medieval Europe from Constantine to Saint Louis*, 2d ed. (London and New York, 1988), p. 252.

16. Quoted in Lina Eckenstein, *Woman under Monasticism* (Cambridge, 1896), pp. 136–37.

17. Matthew Fox, ed., *Hildegard of Bingen's Book of Divine Works with Letters and Songs* (Santa Fe, N.M., 1987), p. 293.

18. W. J. Millor and C. N. L. Brooke, eds., *The Letters of John of Salisbury* (Oxford, 1979), 2:737.

19. Quoted in Rosalind and Christopher Brooke, *Popular Religion in the Middle Ages* (London, 1984), p. 19.

Suggestions for Further Reading

For a general introduction to the history of the High Middle Ages, see the books listed at the end of Chapter 9 and also R. W. Southern, *The Making of the Middle Ages* (London, 1953). For works on the Byzantine and Islamic Empires, see the bibliography at the end of Chapter 8 and M. Angold, *The Byzantine Empire: 1025–1204* (London, 1984); C. M. Brand, *Byzantium Confronts the West* (Cambridge, Mass., 1968); and P. M. Holt, *The Age of the Crusades* (London, 1986).

The best general survey of the crusades is H. E. Mayer, *The Crusades* (New York, 1972). Other works of value are C. Erdmann, *The Origin of the Idea of Crusade*, trans.

M. W. Baldwin and W. Goffart (Princeton, 1977); J. Riley-Smith, *The First Crusade and the Idea of Crusading* (London, 1986), and *What Were the Crusades?* (London, 1977); and J. Prawer, *The Latin Kingdom of Jerusalem* (London, 1972). On the background to the crusades, see B. Z. Kedar, *Crusade and Mission: European Approaches towards the Muslim* (Princeton, 1984).

General works on medieval intellectual life are A. Murray, *Reason and Society in the Middle Ages* (Oxford, 1978); and D. Knowles, *The Evolution of Medieval Thought* (New York, 1962). For a good general introduction to the intellectual and artistic renewal of the eleventh and twelfth centuries, see C. N. L. Brooke, *The Twelfth Century Renaissance* (London, 1969); see also the classic work by C. H. Haskins, *The Renaissance of the Twelfth Century* (Cleveland, 1957). The development of universities is covered in the classic work by H. Rashdall, *The Universities of Europe in the Middle Ages*, 3 vols. (Oxford, 1936); S. Ferruolo, *The Origin of the University* (Stanford, 1985); A. B. Cobban, *The Medieval Universities* (London, 1975); and the brief, older work by C. H. Haskins, *The Rise of Universities* (Ithaca, N.Y., 1957). Various aspects of the intellectual and literary developments of the High Middle Ages are examined in J. W. Baldwin, *The Scholastic Culture of the Middle Ages, 1000–1300* (Lexington, Mass., 1971); C. Morris, *The Discovery of the Individual, 1060–1200* (London, 1972);

R. W. Southern, *St. Anselm and His Biographer* (Cambridge, 1963); D. E. Luscombe, *The School of Peter Abelard* (Cambridge, 1969); B. Smalley, *Historians in the Middle Ages* (London, 1974); and H. Waddell, *The Wandering Scholars* (London, 1934). A good introduction to Romanesque style is G. Künstler, *Romanesque Art in Europe* (New York, 1973).

On the papacy in the High Middle Ages, see the works listed in the bibliography for Chapter 9 and the general survey by G. Barraclough, *The Medieval Papacy* (New York, 1968). Good works on monasticism include B. Bolton, *The Medieval Reformation* (London, 1983); C. H. Lawrence, *Medieval Monasticism* (London, 1984), a good general account; and H. Leyser, *Hermits and the New Monasticism* (London, 1984). On the Cistercians, see W. Braunfels, *Monasteries of Western Europe* (Princeton, 1972). For a good introduction to popular religion in the eleventh and twelfth centuries, see R. and C. N. L. Brooke, *Popular Religion in the Middle Ages* (London, 1984). On the relationship between clerical and popular religion, see A. Gurevich, *Medieval Popular Culture: Problems of Belief and Perception* (Cambridge, 1988). On miracles and the Bible, see B. Ward, *Miracles and the Medieval Mind* (London, 1982); and B. Smalley, *The Study of the Bible in the Middle Ages* (Notre Dame, Ind., 1964).

Chapter 11

The Summit of Medieval Civilization: The Thirteenth Century

▼▼▼▼▼

In the eleventh and twelfth centuries, European civilization established new patterns that reached their zenith in the thirteenth century. While earlier generations of historians have characterized that century as an "age of faith," it might best be characterized as an age of synthesis and expansion in which Europeans built upon the accomplishments of the previous two centuries.

The emergence of trade and cities became a commercial revolution that affected most of Europe. The monarchies solidified their governmental institutions in pursuit of greater power. The papal monarchy of the Catholic church reached the apogee of its power when popes dictated to rulers in a way they would never do again. Intellectually, it was a century of summas or attempts to summarize all of human knowledge in a single book. The dark side of the age was its intolerance. The church's attempt to define its doctrine was paralleled by a desire to keep people faithful to it. Force was used against dissenters and heretics as well as the Muslims and Jews. Religious revival and religious intolerance seemed to be but two sides of the same impulse.

▼ Climate and Population

The "climatic optimum" or favorable climate that Europe experienced in the eleventh and twelfth centuries began to change in the late thirteenth although climatologists are unsure about the degree of change that occurred. It is possible that weather patterns had already begun to alter, resulting in too much rain in some parts of Europe.

The Last Crusades   Magna Carta   Frederick II   Spread of the Mongols   "Saint" Louis IX

▼   ▼   ▼   ▼   ▼

• • • • • • • • 1200 • • • • • • • • • • • 1225 • • • • • • • • • • 1250 • • • • • • • • • • • 1275 • • • • • • • • • • • 1300 • • • • • • • • •

▲   ▲   ▲   ▲

Innocent III and Papal Power   Emergence of Franciscans and Dominicans   Thomas Aquinas   Gothic Cathedrals

Demographers do not agree on the growth of the European population in the thirteenth century. Some believe that there was a steady increase in population with a peak occurring in the late thirteenth century, followed by an ongoing increase at a slower rate until the great plague of 1349. Others have argued that the peak was reached around 1280, followed by a steady decline thereafter. In either case, there is no doubt that European population overall experienced a dramatic increase over the three hundred years between 1000 and 1300.

Although it is virtually impossible to arrive at precise population statistics, sufficiently reasonable estimates exist to justify two observations about thirteenth-century population. European society, first of all, was still overwhelmingly agricultural. Even in the most heavily urbanized areas, Flanders and northern Italy, three out of four people lived in the countryside; in the rest of Europe, nine out of ten did so. Secondly, the size of European towns and cities can be gauged fairly well. Most urban settlements remained small by modern standards with the overwhelming majority containing no more than several thousand inhabitants. Two areas had particularly large urban concentrations. Cities in Flanders, such as Bruges and Ghent, averaged around 40,000-50,000 inhabitants. Italian cities were even larger. By 1300, Florence had 90,000 people; Milan, Venice, and Genoa each numbered around 100,000. Some large cities also existed in areas outside Italy and Flanders. London's population approached 40,000, Paris had close to 100,000, and Cologne in Germany counted 30,000.

Although the lands that could be reclaimed for agriculture reached a limit in the thirteenth century (see Agriculture later in this chapter), the demand for land continued to increase, creating an inner migration or movement of people from the country into urban areas and also into sparsely inhabited lands. This was a European-wide phenomenon. Anglo-Normans moved into Scotland and Ireland while the French moved into Spain to help the native Christians settle the lands

taken from the Muslims. By the mid-thirteenth century, all of Spain except for the small principality of Granada was under Christian control (see Spain later in this chapter).

By far, the most important migration was the movement of Germans and inhabitants of the Low Countries into central and eastern Europe (see the box on p. 332). The *Drang nach Osten*, the push to the east of Germanic-speaking peoples, progressed in two major directions. To the north, they followed the shores of the Baltic Sea, and to the south, they moved down the Danube valley. By 1300, the area of German settlement was three times larger than it had been at the time of Carolingian expansion to the east. Eventually, two major German states, Austria and Brandenburg-Prussia, which would dominate much of European history, were formed out of these territories. Local princes in other eastern areas, such as Poland and Hungary, invited Germanic settlers to their lands because of the need for labor in their relatively underpopulated territory. It has been estimated that Poland, for example, possessed two to three inhabitants per square mile at a time when France possessed eleven to twelve and Italy nine to ten.

It does not appear, however, that "inner migration" solved the problem of overpopulation. Some historians have argued that by the end of the thirteenth century, Europe's population had reached an upper limit. The amount of cultivated land and the technology available to farm it efficiently could not provide enough food for any more people. Although it is difficult to prove or disprove this assumption, the drastic reduction of the population by famine and plague in the fourteenth century (see Chapter 12) solved any existing problem.

▼ Economic and Social Developments

The thirteenth century witnessed a significant extension of the economic and social trends begun in the eleventh and twelfth centuries: the expansion of agri-

Migration to the East

▼ ▼ ▼

There was a considerable migration of people from one part of Europe to another during the High Middle Ages. Perhaps the most important was the movement of Germanic-speaking peoples to the east. The need for labor in underpopulated areas often caused local princes in the east to invite settlers to their lands. New cities also came into existence in this fashion. This excerpt from the chronicle of Helmold of Bosau describes how the territories of Count Adolf II of Holstein, especially the city of Lübeck, came to be populated in the twelfth century. Lübeck became one of the most important trade centers in northern Germany.

German Colonization in the East

Adolf, the count of Holstein, began to rebuild the castle of Segeberg and he encircled it with a wall. But because the land was deserted, he sent messengers to all regions, that is, Flanders and Holland, Utrecht, Westphalia and Frisia, so that whoever might be in difficult straits because of a shortage of fields should come with their families to accept land which was excellent, spacious, fertile with fruits, abounding in fish and meat, and favorable to pastures.

At this invitation, an uncounted multitude arose from the various nations. Taking their families and possessions, they came to the land of the Wagri [the Slavic people conquered by Adolf II] to Count Adolf, in order to take possession of the land which he had promised them. First of all, the people from Holstein accepted settlements in protected places in the region west of Segeberg, around the Trave river, and the fields of Schwentinefeld, and the lands which extend from the river Schwale to Tensfleder and Lake Plön. The Westphalians settled in the land of Dargun, the Hollanders in that of Eutin, the Frisians in the country of Süsel. But the region of Plön has remained deserted to this day. The count gave Oldenburg and Lütjenburg and other lands near to the sea to the Slavs to colonize, who thus became his tributaries.

After this, Count Adolf came to the place known as Bucu and he found there the fortifications of a deserted town, which Cruto, the tyrant of God [that is, a heathen], had erected. He also found a wide island surrounded by two rivers. On one side the river Trave flowed past, and on the other the Wakenitz, and both had a swampy and impassable bank. But on the side where the land road passes is a small hill, next to the fortifications of the castle. Discerning the suitability of the place for the erection of an excellent port, the industrious man began to build a city. He called it Lübeck. . . .He sent messengers to Niclot, prince of the Obotrites [a Slavic people], to make with him a treaty of friendship. He won over all the nobles with gifts, so that they would rival one another in loyalty to him and in the cultivation of his land. Thus, the deserted land of the province of the Wagri began to gain inhabitants, and the number of its settlers multiplied.

---

culture, the revival of trade, the development of a money economy, and the rise of cities. And yet, by the end of the thirteenth century, new problems were emerging that brought dramatic repercussions in the fourteenth century.

Agriculture

The increase in the population of the thirteenth century depended upon a parallel expansion of agriculture to feed more mouths. New methods of reclaiming land, including the draining of river valley swamps and building dikes against the sea as the Dutch did, provided additional land for grazing and farming. Furthermore, the spread of the three-field system of farming resulted in larger agricultural yields. But both large-scale reclamation and increases in productivity seemed to reach their limits during the thirteenth century, making it doubtful that food production could keep pace with the growth of the population.

Some areas proved much more fertile than others, especially some river valleys, such as those of the Po in Italy, the Seine in France, the Rhine in Germany, and the Thames in England. It was no accident that some of the biggest cities developed near these agriculturally rich areas since a surplus food supply was crucial to meeting the needs of growing urban populations.

European agriculture became increasingly specialized. The Rhineland and the areas of Burgundy, Bordeaux, and Champagne in France were well known for their production of wine. Other areas were recognized for growing flax for linen and hemp for rope. Sheep farming was widespread since wool was the most common textile in the High Middle Ages. Although the poor used coarse wool woven locally, the rich demanded the finer products of Flanders and northern Italy, whose woolen industries consumed enormous quantities of raw wool from England.

The increasing demand of towns and cities for agricultural produce led to higher food prices in the thirteenth century and created new possibilities for growing food for profit. This had a serious impact upon the manorial system of the High Middle Ages and the status of the medieval serf.

Owners of landed estates reacted to the development of new markets for agricultural produce in different ways. Some lords expanded their land holdings but worked the land with free peasants hired for wages. This occurred in the Netherlands as well as in some areas of England, France, and Germany.

Most commonly, however, lords reacted to the new conditions by leasing their land to their serfs. Servile labor services were transformed into money payments or fixed rents. In some places, such as northern Italy and southern France, landlords used a system of sharecropping instead of rents. Peasants worked the land of the lord and shared the crops they grew with him. In either case, the introduction of money payments or sharecropping initiated a process that eventually undermined serfdom. The removal of servile labor conditions converted many unfree serfs into free peasants. Although many peasants still remained economically dependent on their lords, they were no longer legally tied to the land. Naturally, this change also affected the lord's position. The commutation of labor services to money payments transformed peasants into tenants and altered the lord's position from the operator of a manor in control of both political and legal privileges to simply a lessor or collector of rents. The political and legal powers formerly exercised by lords were increasingly reclaimed by the monarchical states.

Overall, then, the old manorial system based on unfree peasants was slowly being transformed in the High Middle Ages into a more flexible system. The new relationships between lords and peasants, however, created social tensions that oftentimes led to local peasant uprisings in the late thirteenth century. These proved merely a prelude to the large-scale peasant revolts of the fourteenth century.

Industry and Trade

Although peasants in rural villages continued to make many of the items they needed, the revival of trade enabled cities and towns to become important centers for manufacturing a wide range of goods, such as cloth, metalwork, shoes, and leather goods. A host of crafts was carried on in houses located in the narrow streets of the medieval cities. From the twelfth century on, craftsmen began to organize themselves into guilds, which came to play a leading role in the economic life of the cities.

Originally, guilds were community organizations created by townspeople to meet their common needs and functioned primarily as social and religious fraternities. They gave members a sense of security and companionship, provided financial assistance to the elderly, widows, and orphans, financed religious festivals, and contributed to the building and maintenance of local

▼ **The Dyeing of Cloth.** The revival of trade encouraged the manufacture of a wide range of goods in towns and cities. During the High Middle Ages, the production of woolen cloth was especially prominent in Flanders and northern Italy. The transformation of raw wool into finished cloth required a large number of different activities. This illustration shows workers in a dyehouse laboring over a hot vat in which pieces of cloth are being dyed.

churches. By acquiring a monopoly on a community's business for the guild's members, they provided economic protection. Since medieval towns were relatively small, there might be only one guild for all merchants and artisans. Gradually, however, merchants separated themselves from the craftsmen, and by the middle of the thirteenth century, there were individual craft guilds for virtually every craft, such as tanners, carpenters, and bakers, as well as separate guilds for specialized groups of merchants, such as dealers in silk, spices, wool, or banking. Some communities were so comprehensive in covering all trades that they even had guilds for prostitutes.

In addition to their social and religious functions, guilds gradually came to organize and direct almost every aspect of the production process. They established standards for the articles produced, specified the actual methods of production to be used, and even fixed the price at which the finished goods could be sold; the latter in many instances was set in accordance with the church's doctrine of a "just price" based on equitable bargaining in an open market. Guilds also established the conditions of labor by determining the number of men who could enter a specific trade and the procedure they must follow to do so. A person aspiring to learn a trade first became an apprentice to a master craftsman. After a specified term of service, an apprentice was expected to produce a "masterpiece," a finished piece in his craft that allowed the master craftsmen of the guild to judge whether he was qualified to become a master and join the guild. Even if he passed this test, the apprentice might still have to serve as a journeyman or paid assistant to a master craftsman until he accumulated sufficient capital to open his own shop and become a master himself.

Opinions vary on the effectiveness and importance of the guilds. No doubt, guilds established high standards of quality that are still reflected in the artifacts of the age. Moreover, guilds provided the protection merchants and artisans needed to survive in a hostile world. Indeed, some authorities have questioned whether the new commercial and industrial sectors of the medieval economy would have become established without them. At the same time, guilds could also be harmful to the community. Because they established monopolies, the lack of competition could lead to higher prices and possibly even the rejection of technological innovation. Of course, from the members' point of view, their guilds gave them a sense of security and an assurance of a decent livelihood.

Craft guilds continued to dominate manufacturing in those industries where raw materials could be acquired locally and the products sold locally. But in those industries that required raw materials from outside the local area to produce high-quality products for growing markets abroad, a new form of industry dependent on large concentrations of capital and unskilled labor began to emerge. Viewed by some observers as the beginning of commercial capitalism, it was particularly evident in the "putting-out" system used in the production of woolen cloth in both Flanders and northern Italy. An entrepreneur, whose initial capital outlay probably came from commercial activities, bought raw wool and distributed it to workers who carried out the various stages of carding, spinning, weaving, and dyeing to produce a finished piece of woolen cloth. These laborers worked in their own homes and were paid wages. As wage earners, they were dependent upon their employers and the fluctuations in prices that occurred periodically in the international market for the finished goods. The entrepreneur collected the final products and sold the finished cloth, earning a profit that could then be invested in more production. Woolen industries operated by capitalist entrepreneurs in seventeen principal centers in Flanders and northern Europe produced most of the woolen cloth used in northern Europe. An Italian chronicler at the beginning of the fourteenth century estimated that the woolen industry in Florence produced 80,000 pieces of cloth a year and employed 30,000 men, women, and children, usually at pitiful wages.

The thirteenth century also witnessed an enormous expansion of trade. Historians speak of a commercial revolution to indicate not only the increased volume of goods traded, but also the development of new commercial practices and institutions, many of which were pioneered by Italian merchants. Those of Venice, Genoa, and Pisa, in particular, prospered in the trade of the Mediterranean area.

The goods of thirteenth-century Italian merchants were shipped in galleys, sailing ships with pointed bows using sails and/or oars. Because of the need to enter small harbors, they were not large and usually hugged the shoreline to avoid the dangers of the open sea. Galleys could also navigate by the sun and stars using the astrolabe, which was first developed in the twelfth century and measured the angle of the sun and stars from the horizon, enabling sailors to figure out their latitude. The most daring trade routes of the thirteenth century took a path through the Straits of Gibraltar along the coast of Portugal and France to England and the Low Countries.

The Italian merchants soon discovered that their growing trade required new ways of raising capital and new commercial practices. They created partnerships in

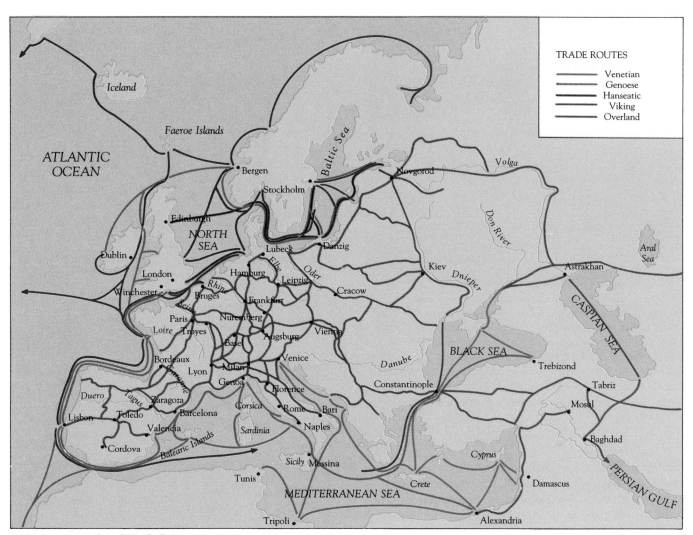

▼ **Map 11.1** Medieval Trade Routes.

order to raise capital for ships and goods in overseas journeys. The most common form of partnership was the *commenda*, a temporary company in which a number of investors put up capital for a merchant ship or trade caravan. If successful, the profits were shared and the group disbanded. The Italians also developed insurance to protect their investments, although rates were prohibitively high. New methods of credit, such as bills of exchange or notes on credit, were utilized to circumvent the problem of insufficient reserves of money or the inconvenience of exchanging coins for large transactions. It should be noted, however, that the Italians also minted new gold coins that became standards in western Europe. The gold florin of Florence was first struck in 1252; the Venetian gold ducat in 1284.

Matters of finance were complicated by the problem of usury. The church regarded economic activity as an ethical matter and disapproved of usury, which was defined as pure interest on a loan. The church had condemned usury at the Second Lateran Council in 1139 as "detestable and disgraceful rapacity" and damned usurers as infamous and unworthy of Christian burial. The church's attitude was troublesome, since the lending of money for productive purposes was crucial in the development of commerce, industry, and banking. Consequently, theologians "discovered" rationalizations and merchants found ways to circumvent the church's ban. Most economic historians doubt that usury laws retarded Europe's economic growth, although they may have caused much grief to individual merchants. One mer-

▼ **The Fortified Town of Carcassone.** The expansion of commerce and industry led to an ongoing growth of towns and cities in the High Middle Ages. As seen in this picture of the French town of Carcassone, medieval towns were surrounded by walls strengthened by defensive towers and punctuated by gates. As is evident here, medieval urban skylines were dominated by towers of all kinds. Because of limited space within the town walls, houses were narrow, multistoried, and closely crowded together.

chant set aside money in his will for the church "for goods wrongfully acquired; for it seems to me, having been a merchant, impossible that I should not have acquired something by wrong means."

Finally, we should note that banking also grew out of mercantile activity. The existence of many different coinages necessitated professional moneychangers who knew their values and could exchange them. Soon, moneychangers became involved in lending money as well. The accumulation of wealth by merchants enabled them to hold large deposits of money and function as bankers. The richest and most prominent early banking houses were Italian. All in all, it was the Italians who took the lead in developing the institutions and methods of the new capitalist system. When it came to making money, northern Europeans looked to the Italians as their teachers.

Towns and Cities

The expansion of industry and commerce was closely tied to the growth of towns and cities. While castles continued to dominate the political landscapes of medi-

eval Europe, cities were rapidly emerging as the new economic centers.

GOVERNMENT IN THE MEDIEVAL CITY Medieval cities possessed varying degrees of self-government depending upon the amount of control retained over them by the lord or king in whose territory they were located (see Chapter 9). In Italy, for example, the decline of the emperor's authority ensured that the northern Italian cities could function as self-governing republics. Nevertheless, all towns, regardless of the degree of outside control, evolved institutions of government for running the affairs of the community.

Medieval cities defined citizenship narrowly and accorded it only to those males born in the city or who had lived there for some time. In many cities, citizens elected members of a city council that bore primary responsibility for running the affairs of the city. City councillors (known as consuls in Italy) not only enacted legislation

▼ **Patricians in Procession.** In most medieval cities, members of the richest and most powerful families, known as the patricians, came to dominate their cities despite periodic protests from lesser merchants and artisans. Pictured here is a procession on Candlemas Day in Perugia, Italy. A drummer and trumpeters precede the proud patricians who carry lighted candles.

but also served as judges and city magistrates. Election of city councillors was by no means democratic. The electoral process was carefully engineered to ensure that only members of the wealthiest and most powerful families, who came to be called the patricians, were elected. They kept the reins of government in their hands despite periodic protests from lesser merchants and artisans.

In the twelfth and thirteenth centuries, cities added some kind of sole executive leader, even if he was only a figurehead. Although it varied from town to town, the title of mayor was frequently used to refer to this executive officer. Mayors could be appointed by the lord or king or elected by the councillors or citizens. In Italy, the executive came to be known as a *podestá*, literally meaning a person with power. Because of the bitter internal feuds within their cities, Italians frequently brought in an outsider to be *podestá*. He was supposed to rule only for one year, but occasionally tried to prolong his tenure. City councils and mayors also had to compete with other authorities, especially ecclesiastical ones. In episcopal cities, for example, bishops continued to exercise control over the city's priests. In some areas, especially Italy, guilds also became closely involved in government. In some cities, such as Florence, each of the major guilds supplied a set number of representatives to the city council.

City governments kept close watch over the activities of their community; some historians have used the phrase "municipal socialism" to describe the all-encompassing role played by medieval city governments. To care for the welfare and safety of the community, a government might regulate air and water pollution; provide water barrels and delegate responsibility to people in every section of the town to fight fires, which were an ever-present danger; construct warehouses to stockpile grain in the event of food emergencies; and establish and supervise the standards of weights and measures used in the various local goods and industries. Although violence was a way of life in the Middle Ages, urban crime was not a major problem in the towns of the High Middle Ages. The relatively small size of communities made it difficult for criminals to operate openly. Medieval urban governments did not have regular police forces, but guards were hired to patrol the streets at night to break up fights and prevent robberies.

People caught committing criminal acts were quickly tried for their offenses. Serious offenses, such as murder, were punished by execution, usually by hanging on a public gallows at the edge of the city. Multiple offenses, such as repeated robbery, could also merit execution or bodily mutilation. Cities without rights of complete self-government did not have the authority to impose capital punishment, however; the right to "high justice," for capital crimes, was reserved for higher territorial courts. These cities would still have jurisdiction over "low justice," or the right to punish lesser crimes by fines or placing the guilty party in a pillory to be scorned by fellow citizens.

DAILY LIFE IN THE MEDIEVAL CITY   By our standards, medieval cities were small. One could traverse the length of the entire city in a fifteen- or twenty-minute walk. Towns were surrounded by walls that were expensive to construct, so the space within was precious and tightly filled. This gave medieval cities their characteristic appearance of narrow, winding streets with houses crowded against each other and the second and third stories of the dwellings built out over the streets. Since dwellings were constructed mostly of wood before the fourteenth century and candles and wood fires were used for light and heat, the danger of fire was great. Medieval cities burned rapidly once a fire started.

▼ **Shops in a Medieval Town.** Most urban residents were merchants involved in trade and artisans who manufactured a wide variety of products. Merchants and artisans usually had their own sections within a town. Master craftsmen had their workshops in the ground-level rooms of their houses. In this scene from a French town, tailors, furriers, a barber, and a grocer are seen at work in their shops. The rooms above the shops provided living quarters for the master and his family.

A medieval urban skyline was dominated by the towers of castles and town halls, but especially of churches, whose number was often staggering. At the beginning of the thirteenth century, London had 120 churches. If the city was the center of a bishop's see, a large cathedral would dominate the other buildings and be visible for miles outside the city. Monastic and parish churches added to the number of churches.

Castles were second in importance to churches, but their number varied depending on the location of the cities. Since the Italian landed nobles established their residences in towns near their estates and were not even adverse to engaging in mercantile activities, the towers of their castles dotted the Italian urban skyscape. Although less common, the castles of kings, lords, and bishops were also found in northern cities. Paris, for example, was dominated by two royal castles, the Louvre and Bastille, as well as a small castle for the king's agent.

Churches and castles had a certain number of people attached to them, but the majority of urban residents consisted of merchants involved in trade and artisans active in manufacturing of some kind. Generally, merchants and artisans had their own sections within a city. The merchant area included warehouses, inns, and taverns. Artisan sections were usually divided along craft lines, and each craft had its own street where its activity was pursued.

Collectively, the merchants and artisans came to be known as the bourgeoisie, the people of a town living within a walled enclosure (*burgus*). There were, of course, enormous differences within their ranks. Wealthy merchants and struggling artisans were widely separated economically and socially. As townspeople, they were all legally free, lived under a common town government, and faced the common opposition of the nobles, who, outside Italy, feared that the bourgeoisie were serious rivals for their position at the top of society. These men of money with their freedom to come and go seemed in many ways to threaten the closely ordered rural world of the Middle Ages where everything was supposed to have a fixed place. Kings shared this hostility initially, but quickly perceived the potential for new tax revenues from townspeople that helped the monarchies free themselves from feudal ties and create new systems of government.

The physical environment of medieval cities was not pleasant. They were often dirty and rife with smells from animal and human waste deposited in backyard privies or on the streets (see the box on p. 339). In some places, city governments required citizens to make periodic collections of garbage and waste and cart it outside the walls. Atmospheric pollution was also a fact of life, not only from the ubiquitous wood fires, but also from the use of a cheaper fuel, coal, used industrially by lime-burners, brewers, and dyers, as well as poor people who could not afford to purchase wood. The coal most frequently used, surface-mined and "sea" coal, produced ill-smelling, noxious fumes. Although the use of sea coal was prohibited under pain of fine, the laws do not seem to have been enforced.

Cities were also unable to prevent industrial water pollution, especially from the tanning and animal-slaughtering industries. Both industries were forced, however, to locate downstream to avoid polluting the water used by the city upstream. Butchers dumped blood and all remaining waste products from their butchered animals into the river while tanners unloaded tannic acids, dried blood, fat, hair, and the other waste products of their operations. Since tanneries and slaughterhouses existed in virtually every medieval town, rivers rapidly became polluted.

Because of the pollution, cities were not inclined to use the rivers for drinking water but relied instead on wells. Occasionally, communities repaired the system of aqueducts left over from Roman times and sometimes even constructed new ones. Private and public baths also existed in medieval towns, and it is fair to say that standards of hygiene were rather high in the twelfth and thirteenth centuries. Paris, for example, had thirty-two public baths for men and women. City statutes forbade lepers and people with "bad reputations" from using them. This did not, however, prevent public baths from gaining a reputation for permissiveness due to public nudity. One contemporary commented on what occurred in public bathhouses: "Shameful things. Men make a point of staying all night in the public baths and women at the break of day come in and through 'ignorance' find themselves in the men's rooms."[1] Authorities came under increasing pressure to close them down, and the great plague of the fourteenth century sealed their fate. The standards of medieval hygiene broke down, and late medieval and early modern European society would prove to be remarkably dirty.

Because of limited space, urban dwellings were narrow and usually multistoried. Beginning in the thirteenth century, most city dwellers were fortunate to have fireplaces in their houses. In the dwellings of craftsmen and lesser merchants, a large room on the ground floor functioned as workshop and retail store. Living quarters were located on the floors above the ground level. Medieval urban houses were difficult to keep clean. Although streets began to be paved in the twelfth century,

The Medieval City
▼ ▼ ▼

Environmental pollution is not new to the twentieth century. Medieval cities and towns had their own problems with filthy living conditions. This excerpt is taken from an order sent by the king of England to the town of Boutham. It demands rectification of the town's pitiful physical conditions. There is little evidence to indicate that the king's order changed the situation dramatically.

The King's Command to Boutham

To the bailiffs of the abbot of St. Mary's, York, at Boutham. Whereas it is sufficiently evident that the pavement of the said town of Boutham is so very greatly broke up that all and singular passing and going through that town sustain immoderate damages and grievances, and in addition the air is so corrupted and infected by the pigsties situated in the king's highways and in the lanes of that town and by the swine feeding and frequently wandering about in the streets and lanes and by dung and dunghills and many other foul things placed in the streets and lanes, that great repugnance overtakes the king's ministers staying in that town and also others there dwelling and passing through, the advantage of more wholesome air is impeded, the state of men is grievously injured, and other unbearable inconveniences and many other injuries are known to proceed from such corruption, to the nuisance of the king's ministers aforesaid and of others there dwelling and passing through, and to the peril of their lives . . . the king, being unwilling longer to tolerate such great and unbearable defects there, orders the bailiffs to cause the pavement to be suitably repaired within their liberty before All Saints next, and to cause the pigsties, aforesaid streets and lanes to be cleansed from all dung and dunghills, and to cause proclamation to be made throughout their bailiwick forbidding any one, under pain of grievous forfeiture, to cause or permit their swine to feed or wander outside his house in the king's streets or the lanes aforesaid.

---

they were often covered with filth, which inevitably made its way inside houses. Floors were covered with rushes, which usually made a wonderful hiding place for a plethora of insects and rodents. Soot from candles, oil lamps, and open fires produced grimy walls.

Men easily outnumbered women in medieval cities. Although many women played important roles in city life, they were denied citizenship. Like their country counterparts, the wives of the middle class were expected to run their households and manage the family finances. Some women, usually the widows of masters, became guild masters themselves. There were numerous jobs that enabled single women to survive, albeit barely since wages for cooks, waitresses, laundresses, and servants were poor. Being a servant for a well-to-do family at least provided food and lodging. Although preachers thundered against it, prostitution enabled some women to earn a living.

▼ The Growth of National Monarchy

By 1200, medieval Europe had experienced the emergence of a number of monarchical states that had begun to develop the administrative machinery of centralized government. In the thirteenth century, this process accelerated in France and England, but slowed noticeably in Germany, which had had the most powerful monarchy in the eleventh century. The growth of cities, the revival of commerce, and the emergence of a money economy enabled monarchs to hire soldiers and officials and to rely less on their vassals.

England

Toward the end of Henry II's successful reign (1154–1189, see Chapter 9), a number of important nobles had begun to resist the centralizing policies of the English king. Although Henry had crushed them, baronial discontent could not be as easily contained in the thirteenth century, and open rebellion broke out in the reign of King John (1199–1216). Following in his father's footsteps, John continued the effort to strengthen royal power and proved particularly ingenious at finding novel ways to levy taxes. The barons of England came to resent him deeply. In 1204, John had lost Normandy to the French king, Philip Augustus; when John's attempt

Magna Carta

▼ ▼ ▼

After the dismal failure of King John to reconquer Normandy from the French king, some of the English barons rebelled against their king. At Runnymeade in 1215, King John agreed to seal the Magna Carta, the Great Charter of liberties regulating the relationship between the king and his vassals. What made Magna Carta an important historical document was its more general clauses defining right and liberties. These were later interpreted in broader terms to make them applicable to all the English people.

Magna Carta

John, by the Grace of God, king of England, lord of Ireland, duke of Normandy and Aquitaine, count of Anjou, to the archbishops, bishops, abbots, earls, barons, justiciars, foresters, sheriffs, reeves, servants, and all bailiffs and his faithful people greeting.

1. In the first place we have granted to God, and by this our present charter confirmed, for us and our heirs forever, that the English church shall be free, and shall hold its rights entire and its liberties uninjured. . . . We have granted moreover to all free men of our kingdom for us and our heirs forever all the liberties written below, to be had and holden by themselves and their heirs from us and our heirs.

2. If any of our earls or barons, or others holding from us in chief by military service shall have died, and when he had died his heir shall be of full age and owe relief, he shall have his inheritance by the ancient relief; that is to say, the heir or heirs of an earl for the whole barony of an earl a hundred pounds; the heir or heirs of a baron for a whole barony a hundred pounds; the heir or heirs of a knight, for a whole knight's fee, a hundred shillings at most; and who owes less let him give less according to the ancient custom of fiefs.

3. If moreover the heir of any one of such shall be under age, and shall be in wardship, when he comes of age he shall have his inheritance without relief and without a fine. . . .

12. No scutage or aid shall be imposed in our kingdom except by the common council of our kingdom, except for the ransoming of our body, for the making of our oldest son a knight, and for once marrying our oldest daughter, and for these purposes it shall be only a reasonable aid. . . .

13. And the city of London shall have all its ancient liberties and free customs, as well by land as by water. Moreover, we will and grant that all other cities and boroughs and villages and ports shall have all their liberties and free customs.

14. And for holding a common council of the kingdom concerning the assessment of an aid otherwise than in the three cases mentioned above, or concerning the assessment of a scutage we shall cause to be summoned the archbishops, bishops, abbots, earls, and greater barons by our letters under seal; and besides we shall cause to be summoned generally, by our sheriffs and bailiffs all those who hold from us in chief, for a certain day, that is at the end of forty days at least, and for a certain place; and in all the letters of that summons, we will express the cause of the summons, and when the summons has thus been given the business shall proceed on the appointed day, on the advice of those who shall be present, even if not all of those who were summoned have come. . . .

39. No free man shall be taken or imprisoned or dispossessed, or outlawed, or banished, or in any way destroyed, nor will we go upon him, nor send upon him, except by the legal judgment of his peers or by the law of the land. . . .

60. Moreover, all those customs and franchises mentioned above which we have conceded in our kingdom, and which are to be fulfilled, as far as pertains to us, in respect to our men; all men of our kingdom as well as clergy as laymen, shall observe as far as pertains to them, in respect to their men.

to reconquer the duchy ended in a devastating defeat, many of the English barons rose in rebellion in 1215. At Runnymeade, John was forced to seal the Magna Carta (the Great Charter) of feudal liberties.

Much of the Magna Carta was aimed at limiting government practices that affected the relations between the king and his vassals on the one hand and between the king and the church on the other (see the box on p. 340). Some provisions, however, came to have greater significance because of the way they were subsequently interpreted. One in particular stood out; chapter 39 read: "No free man shall be taken or imprisoned or dispossessed, or outlawed, or banished, or in any way destroyed, nor will we go upon him, nor send upon him, except by the legal judgment of his peers or by the law of the land."[2] In 1215, the status of "free man" applied to less than half of the English population, but later this statement was applied to all and in the fourteenth century gave rise to trial by jury. Its emphasis on the need to abide by the "law of the land" in proceeding against a free person also came to be interpreted as a guarantee of "due process of law" and a protection against arbitrary judgments.

Despite later interpretations and efforts to broaden its principles, Magna Carta remains, above all, a quintessential feudal document. Feudal custom had always recognized that the relationship between king and vassals was based on mutual rights and obligations. The Magna Carta gave written recognition to that fact and was used in subsequent years to underscore the concept that the monarch should be limited rather than absolute.

John's successor, Henry III (1216–1272), was weak and unable to control the barons of his realm. The nobles were incapable of cooperating, however, and were crushed by Henry's son, Edward I (1271–1307), who proved to be a very talented and powerful monarch. Edward began the process of uniting all of the British Isles into a single kingdom. Although Wales was finally conquered and pacified, the attempt to subdue Scotland failed. Edward managed merely to begin a lengthy conflict between England and Scotland that lasted for centuries.

Edward was successful in reestablishing monarchical rights after a period of baronial control. At the same time, the various branches of the administrative machinery of government, which had evolved out of the king's household staff, became increasingly specialized. The barons and chancellor of the exchequer supervised the treasury and financial affairs. Two royal courts emerged: the court of common pleas took responsibility for civil cases, and the court of king's bench heard either civil or criminal cases relevant to the king's interest. Finally, during Edward's reign, the role of the English Parliament, an institution of great importance in the development of representative government, also began to be defined.

Parliament in England arose out of the king's need to secure the consent of his barons for extraordinary aids (in effect, new taxes) and to "treat" over important matters of state. Originally, the word *parliament* was applied to meetings of the king's Great Council in which the greater barons and chief prelates of the church met with the king's judges and principal advisers. The Great Council was primarily occupied with judicial affairs. The demand for special subsidies to meet the rising cost of government, however, necessitated placing a uniform levy on the personal property of all classes. It was easier to collect such levies if these classes gave their consent. This led to the summoning of greater parliaments, which were called by the king in 1295 and 1297. For them he ordered sheriffs to "cause two knights from the aforesaid county, two citizens from each city in the same county, and two burgesses from each borough . . . to be elected without delay, and to cause them to come to us at the aforesaid time and place."[3] A parliament, then, came to be composed of two knights from every county and two burgesses from every borough as well as the barons and ecclesiastical lords. Eventually, barons and church lords formed the House of Lords; knights and burgesses, the House of Commons. The parliaments of Edward I granted taxes, discussed politics, enacted legislation, and handled judicial business. Although still not the important body it would eventually become, the English Parliament had clearly emerged as an institution by the end of the thirteenth century.

The formation of parliaments was not unique to England, however. Spain and Hungary witnessed their development in the thirteenth century, and the practice soon spread to all of Europe in the fourteenth century. Only the English Parliament, however, eventually grew into a powerful institution capable of controlling the power of the king.

By the beginning of the fourteenth century, England had begun to develop a unique system of national monarchy. The king and his subjects constituted a "community of the realm" in the words of contemporary English jurists. The law of the realm was beginning to be determined not by the king alone, but by the king in consultation with representatives of different groups that constituted the community.

France

In the eleventh and twelfth centuries, the Capetian dynasty of France had managed to consolidate its control over its own royal domain, the Ile-de-France. In the thirteenth century, this dynasty greatly enlarged its royal domain and its power, truly creating a centralized monarchical authority in France.

King Philip II Augustus (1180–1223) perceived that the power of the French monarch would never be extended until the Plantagenet power was defeated (see Chapter 9). After all, Henry II was not only king of England, but ruler of the French territories of Normandy, Maine, Anjou, and Aquitaine. Accordingly, Philip II waged war against the Plantagenets, but not until he defeated King John (1199–1216) was he successful in wresting control of Normandy, Main, Anjou, and Touraine. Through these conquests, Philip quadrupled the income of the French monarchy and greatly enlarged its power.

Philip understood the need to develop centralized institutions of government to rule his new lands. The territories added to the royal domain were divided into bailiwicks, each of which was placed under the jurisdiction of a bailiff or seneschal. Bailiffs were appointed to provinces close to the original royal domain; seneschals to remote provinces. Both royal officials administered justice, collected royal revenues, and served as the king's agents in other matters. Although bailiffs were usually middle-class administrators, seneschals were barons or knights who were able to command royal troops if necessary. Bailiffs, seneschals, and their assistants comprised the beginnings of a French royal bureaucracy in the thirteenth century.

Capetian rulers after Philip II continued to add lands to the royal domain. Although Philip had used military force, other kings used both purchase and marriage to achieve the same end. Much of the thirteenth century was dominated by the man, whom many consider the greatest of the medieval French kings, Louis IX (1226–1270). A deeply religious man, he was later canonized as a saint by the church, an unusual action regardless of the century. "This saintly man loved our lord with all his heart and in all his actions followed His example,"[4] said his contemporary biographer who accompanied the king on a crusade in 1248. Louis was known for his attempts to bring justice to his people and ensure their rights. He sent out royal agents to check on the activities of the bailiffs and seneschals after hearing complaints that they were abusing their power. He was not above hearing complaints personally in a very informal fashion:

Chronology
▼ ▼ ▼
The Growth of National Monarchy

England	
John	1199–1216
Magna Carta	1215
Edward I	1271–1307
The "Greater Parliaments"	1295 and 1297
France	
Philip II Augustus	1180–1223
Louis IX	1226–1270
Philip IV	1285–1314
First Estates-General	1302
Spain	
Alfonso X of Castile	1252–1284
Germany, Italy, and the Empire	
Frederick II	1212–1250
Election of Rudolf of Habsburg as King of Germany	1273
Charles of Anjou Invades Southern Italy	1266
Sicilian Vespers	1282
The Eastern World	
East Prussia Given to the Teutonic Knights	1226
Genghis Khan and the Rise of the Mongols	c. 1162–1227
Mongol Conquest of Russia	1230s
Alexander Nevsky, Prince of Novgorod	c. 1220–1263
Defeat of Germans	1242
Mongol Destruction of Islamic Abbasid Caliphate	1258

In summer, after hearing mass, the king often went to the wood of Vincennes, where he would sit down with his back against an oak, and make us all sit round him. Those who had any suit to present could come to speak to him without hindrance from an usher or any other person. The king would address them directly, and ask "Is there anyone here who has a case to be settled?" Those who had one would stand up. Then he would say, "Keep silent all of you, and you shall be heard in turn, one after the other." Then he would call Pierre de Fontaines and Geoffroi de Villette, and say to one or other of them: "Settle this case for me." If he saw anything needing correction in what was said by those who spoke on his behalf or on behalf of any other person, he would himself intervene to make the necessary adjustment.[5]

Louis was also responsible for establishing a permanent royal court of justice in Paris whose work was carried on by a regular staff of professional jurists. This court came to be known as the *parlement* of Paris. Louis made it increasingly difficult for nobles to wage private wars with each other and eventually outlawed the practice. Sharing in the religious sentiments of his age, he played a major role in two of the later crusades (see The Last Crusades of the Thirteenth Century later in this chapter). Both were failures, and he met his death during an invasion of northern Africa.

Although the successors of Saint Louis were more worldly and less saintly, they continued his centralizing policies. Philip IV (1285–1314) was particularly effective in strengthening the French monarchy. The machinery of government became even more specialized. French kings going back to the early Capetians had possessed a household staff for running their affairs. In effect, it was the division and enlargement of this household staff that produced the three major branches of royal administration: a council for advice; a *chambre des comptes* or chamber of accounts for finances; and a *parlement* or royal court. By the beginning of the fourteenth century, the Capetians had created the firm foundations for a royal bureaucracy.

Philip IV was also responsible for bringing a French parliament into being. When he became involved in a struggle with the pope (see Chapter 12), Philip summoned representatives of the church, nobility, and towns to meet with him in 1302, inaugurating the Estates-General, the first parliament. The Estates-General proved invaluable to the king since feudal custom had limited the power of kings to make changes contrary to that custom. The Estates-General came to function as an instrument to bolster the king's power since he could ask representatives of the major social classes to change the laws or grant new taxes. Only later did the Estates-General develop the idea that it might control the actions of kings.

Philip's reign was also significant for the growing impact of Roman law. Philip's advisers were trained in Roman law and began to view the monarchy not as a feudal monarchy limited in power but in a new way: "The king of France is emperor in his own kingdom, for he recognizes no superior in temporal affairs." In these words, Philip's advisers exalted an ideal of increased monarchical authority.

In the course of the thirteenth century, the Capetian dynasty had acquired new lands to add to the French royal domain, whether by conquest, purchase, marriage, or inheritance. Although the monarchs tried to impose

their authority upon these lands, they also allowed them to keep their own laws and institutions. Not until the French Revolution of the eighteenth century would the French move toward a common pattern for all of France. Despite the lack of institutional uniformity, by the end of the thirteenth century, France was the largest, wealthiest, and best-governed monarchical state in Europe.

Spain

In the thirteenth century, Spain was a major success story at least in terms of the Christian reconquest of Muslim territory. Aragon and Castile had become the two strongest Spanish kingdoms while Portugal reached its modern boundaries. All three states made significant conquests of Muslim territory. Castile subdued most of Andalusia in the south, down to the Atlantic and Mediterranean; at the same time, Aragon conquered Valencia. The Muslims remained ensconced only in the kingdom of Granada in the southeast of the Iberian peninsula, which remained an independent Muslim state.

The Christian conquest of Andalusia meant economic disaster for that region. Hitherto highly urbanized and prosperous, the land became depopulated when skilled workers were driven out of the urban areas. A small group of nobles and knights of the military orders took possession of vast estates that they used for cattle grazing.

The Spanish kingdoms followed no consistent policy in the treatment of the conquered Muslim population. Muslim farmers continued to work the land but were forced to pay very high rents in Aragon. In Castile King Alfonso X (1252–1284), who called himself the "King of Three Religions," encouraged the continued development of a cosmopolitan culture shared by Christians, Jews, and Muslims. Toledo still flourished as an important center of intellectual life.

Germany, Italy, and the Empire

In the twelfth century, the kings of Germany had attempted to maintain control of Germany while claiming to be emperors by including Italy in a wider Christian Roman Empire, the so-called Holy Roman Empire. It was a delicate balancing act, and in the thirteenth century, it unraveled and destroyed the chances for a strong monarchy in Germany.

The premature death of Henry VI (see Chapter 9) brought to the throne his son, Frederick II, the most brilliant of the Hohenstaufen rulers. King of Sicily in

The Deeds of Emperor Frederick II
▼ ▼ ▼

Frederick II, king of Germany and Sicily and would-be ruler of all Italy, was viewed even by contemporaries as one of the most unusual rulers of his time. This account of his "idiosyncracies" is by Salimbene de Adam, a Franciscan friar, who has left in his Chronicle *one of the "richest sources of information" about medieval life in thirteenth-century Italy. He was, however, also known to be notoriously biased against Frederick II.*

Salimbene de Adam, *Chronicle*

Note that Frederick almost always enjoyed having discord with the Church and fighting her on all sides, although she had nourished him, defended him, and raised him up. He held the true faith to be worthless. He was a cunning, crafty man, avaricious, lecherous, and malicious, easily given to wrath.

At times, however, Frederick was a worthy man, and when he wished to show his good, courtly side, he could be witty, charming, urbane, and industrious. He was adept at writing and singing, and was well-versed in the art of writing lyrics and songs. He was a handsome, well-formed man of medium height. I myself saw him and, at one time, loved him. For he once wrote Brother Elias, Minister General of the Friars Minor, on my behalf asking him to return me to my father. He also could speak many and various languages. In short, if he had been a good Catholic and had loved God, the Church, and his own soul, he would scarcely have had an equal as an emperor in the world. . . .

Now, it is necessary to speak of Frederick's idiosyncracies.

His first idiosyncracy is that he had the thumb of a certain notary cut off because he had written his name in a way different from the way the Emperor desired. . . .

His second idiosyncracy was that he wanted to discover what language a child would use when he grew up if he had never heard anyone speak. Therefore, he placed some infants in the care of wet-nurses, commanding them to bathe and suckle the children, but by no means ever to speak to or fondle them. For he wanted to discover whether they would speak Hebrew, the first language, or Greek, Latin, Arabic, or the language of their parents. But he labored in vain, because all of the infants died. . . .

Furthermore, Frederick had many other idiosyncracies: idle curiosity, lack of faith, perversity, tyranny, and accursedness, some of which I have written about in another chronicle. Once, for example, he sealed up a live man in a cask and kept him there until he died in order to prove that the soul totally perished with the body. . . . For Frederick was an Epicurean, and so he and the learned men of his court searched out whatever Biblical passage they could find to prove that there is no life after death. . . .

The sixth example of Frederick's idiosyncracy and idle curiosity . . . was that he fed two men a fine meal, and he sent one to bed to sleep, the other out hunting. And that evening he had both men disemboweled in his presence, in order to determine which one had digested his food the best. The decision by his doctors went to the man who had slept after the meal. . . .

I have heard and known many other idiosyncracies of Frederick, but I keep quiet for the sake of brevity, and because reporting so many of the Emperor's foolish notions is tedious to me.

1198, king of Germany in 1212, and crowned emperor in 1220, Frederick II was a truly remarkable man who awed his contemporaries (see the box above). Frederick had been raised in Sicily with its diverse peoples, languages, and religions. His court brought together a brilliant array of lawyers, poets, artists, and scientists, and he himself took a deep interest in their work. He was by no means a devout Christian by contemporary standards but had no fear of papal threats and proved extremely tolerant of Muslim rulers. He was not adverse to

using Muslim mercenaries, and it was said that he kept a harem of Muslim women for his enjoyment.

Until 1220, Frederick spent much time in Germany; once he left in 1220, he rarely returned. He basically gave the German princes full control of their territories, voluntarily surrendering any real power over Germany to keep it quiet while he pursued his main goal, the establishment of a strong centralized state in Italy dominated by his kingdom in Sicily. He turned Sicily into the best-organized state in Europe, establishing a strong central-

ized government staffed by bureaucrats under his absolute authority as "supreme legislator and judge." Frederick's major task was to gain control of northern Italy. In reaching to extend his power in Italy, he became involved in a deadly struggle with the popes, who realized that a single ruler of northern and southern Italy meant the end of papal secular power in central Italy. The northern Italian cities were also unwilling to give up their freedom. The pope logically allied himself with the northern Italian cities, which recreated the Lombard League that had defeated Frederick Barbarossa a century earlier (see Chapter 9). While popes were intermittently excommunicating him, Frederick waged a bitter struggle in northern Italy, winning many battles but ultimately losing the war. After his death in 1250, the remaining Hohenstaufens were obliterated, and the papacy stood supreme over the ashes of a failed Hohenstaufen empire.

Frederick's preoccupation with the creation of an empire in Italy left Germany in confusion and chaos until 1273 when the major German princes, serving as electors, chose an insignificant German noble, Rudolf of Habsburg, as the new German king. This ended the political chaos in Germany; but in choosing a weak king, the princes were ensuring that the German monarchy would remain impotent and incapable of reestablishing a centralized monarchical state. Rudolf realized the weakness of his position and reacted by taking advantage of his office to acquire territory for his own family. He perceived that in the long run this was the only way to strengthen his standing. Through his efforts, the Habsburgs acquired the duchies of Austria, which eventually became the chief foundation for the power of the Habsburg dynasty.

The German electoral princes, however, saw the dangers of allowing any one family to become overly strong and deliberately elected kings from other families, thus ensuring that the German kings would remain feeble. Some of these kings marched into Italy to be crowned emperor, but in truth, the failure of the Hohenstaufens had led to a situation where his exalted majesty, the German king and Holy Roman emperor, had no real power over either Germany or Italy. Unlike France, England, and even Spain, neither Germany nor Italy created a unified national monarchy in the Middle Ages. Both became geographical designations for loose confederations of hundreds of petty, independent states under the vague direction of king or emperor.

Following the death of Frederick II, Italy fell into considerable political confusion. While the papacy remained in control of much of central Italy, the defeat of imperial power left the cities and towns of northern Italy

independent of any other authority. Gradually, the larger ones began to emerge as strong city-states. After defeating Pisa in 1284, Genoa came to dominate its immediate region. Florence assumed the leadership of Tuscany while Milan, under the guidance of the Visconti family, took control of the Lombard region. With its great commercial wealth, the republic of Venice dominated the northeastern part of the peninsula.

The papacy was determined to crush Hohenstaufen rule in southern Italy. Eventually, the popes turned to France and offered the kingdom of Sicily to the brother of King Louis IX, Charles of Anjou, who invaded southern Italy in 1266 and defeated two Hohenstaufen claimants to become king of Sicily. But he did not last long. As a result of the uprising known as the Sicilian Vespers in 1282, the king of Aragon seized the island of Sicily while the Angevins remained in control of a kingdom in southern Italy, now known as the kingdom of Naples.

Eastern Europe

Two major invasions, altogether different in character, played important roles in the history of eastern Europe in the thirteenth century. The Teutonic Knights had been founded near the end of the twelfth century to protect the Christian Holy Land. In the early thirteenth century, however, these Christian knights found greater opportunity to the east of Germany where they attacked the pagan Slavs. East Prussia was given to the military order in 1226, and five years later, the Teutonic Knights moved beyond the Vistula and waged war against the Slavs for another thirty years. By the end of the thirteenth century, Prussia had become German and Christian, as the pagan Slavs were forced to convert.

The Mongols were invaders of a different kind. As we have seen, central and eastern Europe had periodically been subject to invasions from fierce Asiatic nomads, such as the Huns, Avars, Bulgars, and Magyars. The last to enter the scene, the Mongols were at the same time the most effective and affected a larger area than any of the earlier groups.

The Mongols were a nomadic people living in the mountains of central Asia. They were illiterate, but tough fighters. In the early thirteenth century, under the leadership of Genghis Khan (c. 1162–1227), the Mongol tribes became united and created a powerful military force. Genghis Khan was succeeded by equally competent sons and grandsons.

The Mongols exploded upon the scene in the thirteenth century. They advanced eastward, conquering China and eventually Korea. They moved westward

against the Islamic empire as well. Persia fell by 1233, and by 1258 they had conquered Baghdad and destroyed the Abbasid caliphate. But the Mongols were not invincible as seen by their defeat in Palestine in 1260 by the Mamluks.

Beginning in the 1230s, the Mongols had moved into Europe. They conquered Russia, advanced into Poland and Hungary, and destroyed a force of Poles and Teutonic Knights in Silesia in 1241. Europe then seemingly got lucky when the Mongol hordes turned back because of internal fighting over the succession to the Great Khan. While it appears that western and southern Europe were fortunate in escaping the wrath of the Mongols, it is also possible that the Mongols had reached the limits of their expansion. In the east they were having problems in the jungles of Vietnam and Cambodia. It is doubtful that their cavalry, even with the aid of acquired siege techniques, could have toppled the fortified castles and cities of Europe. Moreover, the Mongol conquests were motivated by little more than plunder and the wish to conquer. To rule their new possessions, they borrowed administrative techniques and administrators from the conquered people. Over the long run, the Mongols left little of any real importance, although their occupation of Russia certainly had some negative effect on that land.

RUSSIA UNDER MONGOL DOMINATION The Mongols, who occupied the territories known as Russia, were part of an immense empire stretching back across Asia. They were not numerous enough to settle the vast Russian lands, but were content to rule directly an area along the lower Volga and north of the Caspian and Black seas to Kiev and rule indirectly elsewhere. In the latter territories, Russian princes were required to pay tribute to the Mongol overlords.

One Russian prince soon emerged as more visible and powerful than the others. Alexander Nevsky (c. 1220–1263), prince of Novgorod, defeated a German invading army at Lake Peipus in northwestern Russia in 1242. His cooperation with the Mongols, which included denouncing his own brother and crushing native tax revolts, won him their favor. The khan, the acknowledged leader of the western part of the Mongol empire, rewarded Alexander Nevsky with the title of grand-prince, enabling his descendants to become the princes of Moscow and eventually leaders of all Russia. The Russian church also proved itself a loyal supporter of the Mongols. The Mongols, who later adhered to Islam, were usually tolerant of Christianity and welcomed the Russian Orthodox church as an ally.

There is considerable historical debate over the effect Mongol rule had on the Russian people. No doubt the Mongols had some impact, especially in passing on to the Russian princes some very practical skills, such as how to make use of an enemy's military practices, how to secure lines of communication over great distances, and how to siphon off heavy taxes. But it is questionable whether the Mongols had a serious impact on the Russian character since the Russian church remained the dominant influence on that aspect of Russian culture.

The Growth of National Monarchies

Our political survey of Europe has revealed that in the thirteenth century the national monarchies reversed the decentralizing tendencies of fief-holding in favor of an increased centralization of power in the hands of kings and princes. By extending the power of the royal courts at the expense of feudal courts, by expanding royal treasuries, and by forming a chancery or secretariat to handle the increased volume of business, rulers became more and more capable of providing the central focus of public power. At the same time, the universities were producing trained lawyers and officials who staffed the new administrative offices. Frederick II even established his own university at Naples just to supply lawyers for the bureaucracy in his southern Italian kingdom. The strength of these new monarchical institutions meant that while medieval Europe might still think of itself as an international body of Christendom, regional patterns were becoming increasingly important. It also made it more difficult for rulers to conquer other territories and integrate them into their own lands.

Moreover, as governments became more centralized and kings extended their authority beyond the vassalage of the fief-holding system, both vassals and new subjects attempted to limit the authority of kings by law to avoid the arbitrary exercise of power. In order to maintain internal stability and gain support for foreign wars, kings acceded to these demands by granting charters to cities and nobles that stipulated limits to the royal power. The Magna Carta of 1215 was the most famous example, but there are others as well. Parliaments, too, brought more subjects into the affairs of kings.

▼ The Decline and Fall of the Crusading Ideal

Once again, in the thirteenth century, the papacy, now at the height of its power, took the initiative in

calling for a crusade. Although it may be apparent in retrospect that the crusading energy of the twelfth century had largely dissipated by the beginning of the thirteenth, at the time, both monarchs and nobles felt compelled to take up the crusading cross. The fourth crusade quickly indicated, however, that greed was beginning to supplant religious motives.

The Fourth Crusade

It was the great pope Innocent III (1198–1216, see The Reign of Innocent III later in this chapter) who inaugurated the fourth crusade. The death of Saladin in 1193 (see Chapter 10) had created new opportunities once his empire began to disintegrate. Innocent judged the moment auspicious and encouraged the nobility of Europe to put on the crusaders' mantle. The nobles of France and the Netherlands responded in great numbers. The Venetians agreed to ship the crusading army to the east, but subverted it from its goal by using it first to capture Zara, a port on the Dalmatian coast and a Christian city. The crusading army now became involved in Byzantine politics, which soon led to a tragic conclusion.

At the beginning of the thirteenth century, the Byzantine Empire was experiencing yet another struggle for the imperial throne. One contender, Alexius, son of the overthrown Emperor Isaac II, appealed to the crusaders in Zara for assistance, offering them 200,000 marks in silver (the Venetians were getting 85,000 as a transport fee) and reconciliation of the Greek church with the Roman Catholic church. The leaders of the crusaders now diverted their forces to Constantinople. When the crusading army arrived, the deposed Isaac II was reestablished with his son Alexius IV as co-emperor. Unfortunately, the co-emperors were unable to pay the promised sum. Relations between the crusaders and the Byzantines deteriorated leading to an attack on Constantinople by the crusaders in the spring of 1204. On April 12, they stormed and sacked the city (see the box on p. 348). Christian crusaders took gold, silver, jewelry, and precious furs while the Catholic clergy accompanying the crusaders stole as many relics as they could find.

The Byzantine Empire now disintegrated into a series of petty states ruled by crusading barons and Byzantine princes. The chief one was the new Latin Empire of Constantinople led by Count Baldwin of Flanders as emperor. The Venetians seized the island of Crete and secured domination of Constantinople's trade. Why had the western crusaders succeeded so easily when Persians,

Chronology
▼ ▼ ▼
The Last Crusades

The Fourth Crusade—Sack of Constantinople	1204
Latin Empire of Constantinople	1204–1261
Fifth Crusade	1219–1221
Frederick II Occupies Jerusalem (Sixth Crusade)	1228
First Crusade of Louis IX (Seventh Crusade)	1248–1254
Second Crusade of Louis IX (Eighth Crusade)	1270
Surrender of Acre and End of Christian Presence in the Holy Land	1291

Bulgars, and Arabs had failed for centuries to conquer Constantinople? Although the crusaders were no doubt motivated by greed and a lust for conquest, they were also convinced that they were acting on behalf of God's cause. After all, a Catholic patriarch (a Venetian) had now been installed in Constantinople and the reconciliation of Eastern Orthodoxy with Catholic Christianity had been put in force. Nor should we overlook the military superiority of the French warriors and the superb organizational skills of the Venetians; together, they formed a union of great effectiveness and power. Conviction, military prowess, and the organizational skill of the mercantile element comprised a combination that eventually enabled Europe to make conquests around the world.

Although he protested the diversion of the crusade from the Holy Land, Pope Innocent III belatedly accepted as "God's work" the conversion of Greek Byzantium to Latin Christianity. Some have argued that Innocent did realize, however, that the use of force to reunite the churches virtually guaranteed the failure of any permanent reunion. All too soon, this proved correct. The west was unable to maintain its Latin empire for the western rulers of the newly created principalities were soon involved in fighting each other. Some parts of the Byzantine Empire had managed to survive under Byzantine princes. In 1259, Michael Paleologus, a Greek military leader, took control of the kingdom of Nicaea in Western Asia Minor, led a Byzantine army in recapturing Constantinople two years later, and then established a new Byzantine dynasty, the Paleologi.

Christian Crusaders Capture Constantinople
▼ ▼ ▼

Pope Innocent III inaugurated the fourth crusade after Saladin's empire began to disintegrate. Tragically, however, the crusading army of mostly French nobles was diverted to Constantinople to intervene in Byzantine politics. In 1204, the Christian crusaders stormed and sacked one of Christendom's greatest cities. This description of the conquest of Constantinople is taken from a contemporary account by a participant in the struggle.

Villehardouin, *The Conquest of Constantinople*

The moment the knights aboard the transports saw this happen, they landed, and raising their ladders against the wall, climbed to the top, and took four more towers. Then all the rest of the troops started to leap out of warships, galleys, and transports, helter-skelter, each as fast as he could. They broke down about three of the gates and entered the city. The horses were then taken out of the transports; the knights mounted and rode straight towards the place where the Emperor had his camp. He had his battalions drawn up in front of the tents; but as soon as his men saw the knights charging towards them on horseback, they retreated in disorder. The Emperor himself fled through the streets of the city to the castle of Bucoleon.

Then followed a scene of massacre and pillage: on every hand the Greeks [Byzantines] were cut down, their horses, palfreys, mules, and other possessions snatched as booty. So great was the number of killed and wounded that no man could count them. A great part of the Greek nobles had fled towards the gate of Blachernae; but by this time it was past six o'clock, and our men had grown weary of fighting and slaughtering. The troops began to assemble in a great square inside Constantinople . . . [and] decided to settle down near the walls and towers they had already captured. . . .

That night passed, and the next day came. . . . Early that morning all the troops, knights and sergeants alike, armed themselves, and each man went to join his division. They left their quarters thinking to meet with stronger resistance than they had encountered the day before, since they did not know that the Emperor had fled during the night. But they found no one to oppose them.

The Marquis de Montferrat rode straight along the shore to the palace of Bucoleon. As soon as he arrived there the place was surrendered to him, on condition that the lives of all the people in it should be spared. Among these were very many ladies of the highest rank who had taken refuge there. . . .Words fail me when it comes to describing the treasures found in the palace, for there was such a store of precious things that one could not possibly count them. . . .

The rest of the army, scattered throughout the city, also gained much booty; so much, indeed, that no one could estimate its amount or its value. It included gold and silver, table-services and precious stones, satin and silk, mantles of squirrel fur, ermine and miniver, and every choicest thing to be found on this earth. Geoffrey de Villehardouin here declares that, to his knowledge, so much booty had never been gained in any city since the creation of the world.

Everyone took quarters where he pleased, and there was no lack of fine dwellings in that city. So the troops of the Crusaders and the Venetians were duly housed. They all rejoiced and gave thanks to our Lord for the honor and the victory He had granted them, so that those who had been poor now lived in wealth and luxury. Thus they celebrated Palm Sunday and the Easter Day following, with hearts full of joy for the benefits our Lord and Saviour had bestowed on them. And well might they praise Him; since the whole of their army numbered no more than twenty thousand men, and with His help they had conquered four hundred thousand, or more, and that in the greatest, most powerful, and most strongly fortified city in the world.

The Byzantine Empire had been saved, but it was no longer a great Mediterranean power. The restored empire was a badly truncated one comprising the city of Constantinople and its surrounding territory, some lands in Asia Minor, and part of Thessalonica. Even in its reduced size, however, the empire limped along for another 190 years until the Ottoman Turks brought about its final capitulation in 1453.

The Last Crusades of the Thirteenth Century

Despite the cynical diversion of the fourth crusade to Constantinople, the crusading ideal was soon restored. The fifth crusade (1219–1221) was directed against Egypt, a powerful Muslim state. In spite of some early successes, its failure marked an end to papal leadership of the western crusaders.

The sixth crusade was directed by the German emperor Frederick II who undertook it without papal support since he had been excommunicated by the pope for starting late. In 1228, Frederick sailed to Palestine where his army paraded around while the emperor undertook negotiations with the sultan of Egypt who finally caved in and agreed to return Jerusalem to the crusaders. Frederick marched into Jerusalem and accepted the crown as king of Jerusalem. The Holy City had been taken without a fight and without papal support. Although he was denounced for his agreement with the Muslims, Frederick had at least achieved the crusaders' major goal. Once Frederick left, the Christian barons regained control, and the city fell once again, this time to a group of Turks allied with the sultan of Egypt.

The last two major crusades were organized by the saintly king of France, Louis IX. In 1248, Louis attacked Egypt, pursuing a plan to regain Palestine by first seizing Egypt. The idea might have been sound, but its execution was pitiful. Although possessed of considerable daring and piety, Louis was an abysmal planner. He and his army were defeated, taken prisoner, and forced to pay an enormous ransom to gain their freedom.

Not content with his failure, Louis tried again in 1270, leading a contingent of troops on an ill-planned and ill-fated expedition to Tunis in northern Africa. Louis's contemporary and noble friend, Jean de Joinville, expressed his contempt for the effort:

> I considered that all those who had advised the king to go on this expedition committed mortal sin. For at that time the state of the country was such that there was perfect peace throughout the kingdom, and between France and her neighbours, while ever since King Louis went away the state of the kingdom has done nothing but go from bad to worse.[6]

Louis and much of his army died from plague without achieving any conquests.

Slowly, the Christian possessions in the east were retaken. Acre, the last foothold of the crusaders, surrendered in 1291. All in all, the crusades had failed to accomplish their primary goal of holding the Holy Land for the Christian west.

▼ **Louis IX Sets Out for a Crusade.** Although new crusades arose in the thirteenth century, they were largely ineffective in achieving their goals. The pious French king Louis IX organized the last two major crusades of the thirteenth century. Both failed miserably. This illustration shows Louis IX setting out from Paris while a procession of monks blesses the king and his fellow crusaders.

▼ The Church Supreme: Popes, Monks, and Heresy

In the thirteenth century, the Catholic church reached the height of its political, intellectual, and secular power. The papal monarchy strengthened its administrative system and extended its sway over both ecclesiastical and temporal affairs. New monastic orders dedicated to papal interests brought a revived spiritual message to the growing number of townspeople. At the same time the organized church stood supreme, however, forces of opposition emerged to challenge both the church's spiritual and secular authority. Although the papacy defeated the Hohenstaufen emperors in the first half of the thirteenth century, by the end of that century national rulers were presenting an even greater threat to papal power. Dissent and heresy also became widespread as Christians challenged the materialism and spiritual authority of the church.

The Reign of Innocent III (1198–1216)

Many historians believe that the medieval papacy reached its high point during the pontificate of Pope Innocent III and that he was "the busiest if not the greatest" medieval pope. He was extremely well trained in both theology and canon law. At the beginning of his pontificate, in a letter to a Tuscan cleric, Innocent made a clear statement of his views on papal supremacy:

> As God, the creator of the universe, set two great lights in the firmament of heaven, the greater light to rule the day, and the lesser light to rule the night so He set two great dignities in the firmament of the universal church, . . . the

greater to rule the day, that is, souls, and the lesser to rule the night, that is, bodies. These dignities are the papal authority and the royal power. And just as the moon gets her light from the sun, and is inferior to the sun . . . so the royal power gets the splendor of its dignity from the papal authority.[7]

While historians do not agree on Innocent's motives, it is apparent that he did, at times, attempt to put this theory into practice by intervening freely in the political affairs of European rulers.

Innocent's actions were those of a man who believed that he, the pope, was the supreme judge of European politics. He forced the king of France, Philip Augustus, to take back his wife and queen after Philip had coerced a group of French prelates into annulling his marriage. Innocent did not consider the annulment valid. The pope intervened in German affairs and established his candidate as emperor. He compelled King John of England to accept his choice for the position of archbishop of Canterbury. In this letter to the new king of Bohemia, Innocent left no doubt as to his role:

> Although there have been many in Bohemia who have worn a royal crown, yet they never received the papal permission to call themselves king in their documents. Nor have we hitherto been willing to call you king, because you were crowned king by Philip, duke of Swabia, who himself had not been legally crowned, and therefore could not legally crown either you or anyone else. But since you have obeyed us, and, deserting the duke of Swabia, have gone over to the illustrious king, Otto, emperor elect, and he regards you as king, we, at his request and out of consideration of your obedience, are willing hereafter to call you king. Now that you know

why this favor has been granted you, strive to shun the vice of ingratitude.[8]

The rulers of Aragon and Portugal officially recognized Innocent as their lord. To achieve his political ends, the pope did not hesitate to use the spiritual weapons at his command, especially excommunication and the interdict. In excommunication, an individual is cut off from the sacraments and deprived of communion with the church. A ruler such as Frederick II might ignore excommunication, but an interdict potentially had more serious consequences. An interdict forbade priests to dispense the sacraments of the church in the hope that the people, deprived of the comforts of religion, would exert pressure against their ruler. It was Pope Innocent's interdict that caused Philip to restore his Danish wife to her rightful place as queen of France. The frequent use of these spiritual weapons by thirteenth-century popes to fight political battles seemed appropriate at the time but gradually undermined their value and the moral authority of the popes. When Innocent's successors chose to utilize the same weapons and pursue his claims of papal supremacy, they had less success.

Pope Innocent III then was a consummate politician in his handling of papal power. He was also concerned about church organization, moral reform, and the purity of the Christian faith. It was Innocent III who called the Fourth Lateran Council of 1215, which defined the sacrament of the Eucharist, decreed annual confession for all Christians, eliminated clerical participation in the judicial ordeal, and established detailed regulations for the moral behavior of the clergy. It was also Innocent who approved the foundation of the Franciscans and Dominicans (see The New Soldiers of Christ later in the chapter), encouraged the nobility of France to massacre the heretical Albigensians of southern France (see Dissent, Heresy, Inquisition, and Intolerance later in the chapter), and proclaimed the fourth crusade.

The Papal Monarchy

In the first half of the thirteenth century, the popes were heavily involved in their struggle with the Holy Roman emperors. To support their position, these popes elaborated upon the theory of papal supremacy enunciated so clearly by Innocent III. Papal destruction of the Hohenstaufen monarchy by 1254 seemed to vindicate their position. During the same time it was pushing its claims to secular power, the papacy perfected the centralized administrative system it had created in the eleventh and twelfth centuries. Canon law was refined and

▼ **Pope Innocent III.** Innocent III was an active and powerful pope during the High Middle Ages. Considering himself the supreme judge of European politics, Innocent III intervened in the affairs of a number of European states. He also approved the creation of the Francsican and Dominican orders and inaugurated the fourth crusade.

defined to underline even more clearly the pope's supremacy over the church. The number of legal cases appealed to the papal court increased dramatically, enhancing the importance of papal administration. The number of papal legates or agents of the pope expanded noticeably, enabling the pope to extend his voice into every area of Europe.

As papal administration expanded, the church required ever-larger revenues. A major source of income came from the Papal States, the territories of the church in central Italy. As temporal lords of these lands, the popes had access to rents, tolls, and other fees assessed on the inhabitants. In the thirteenth century, when other traditional sources of income, such as Peter's Pence, an annual tax of a penny a year on every homestead (hearth), proved inadequate, the popes began to tax the clergy on a regular basis. Since monarchs were reluctant to let such large sums of money out of their kingdoms, the popes wisely shared these revenues with them.

The New Soldiers of Christ

In the revival of religious sentiment in the twelfth century, two contradictory impulses manifested themselves. There was a move toward the contemplative life achieved by withdrawal from the world and at the same time a desire to work in the secular arena of villages and towns. The two impulses were not mutually exclusive, however. In the thirteenth century, two religious leaders, Saint Francis and Saint Dominic, initiated a new synthesis of these impulses and created two new monastic orders that had a profound impact on the lives of ordinary people. The new religious orders were particularly active in the cities, where, by their example, they strove to provide a more personal religious experience for ordinary people.

Saint Francis of Assisi (1182–1226) was born to a wealthy Italian merchant family. He enjoyed fighting in the petty local wars typical of the Italian political scene in the thirteenth century. After having been captured and imprisoned during one of these struggles, he had a series of dramatic spiritual experiences that led him to abandon all worldly goods and material pursuits and to live and preach in poverty, working and begging for his food. His simplicity, joyful nature, and love for others (see the box on p. 352) soon attracted a band of followers, all of whom took vows of absolute poverty, agreeing to reject all property and live by working and begging for their food. Francis drew up a simple rule for his followers that consisted

▼ **Saint Francis Renounces the World.** The religious impulse of the thirteenth century led to the creation of new religious orders. Francis of Assisi was responsible for founding an order of begging friars who ministered to the poor and downtrodden. This illustration is taken from a series of frescoes done by Giotto in a church in Assisi. Pictured here is that dramatic moment in the life of Saint Francis when he abandoned all earthly goods to live in poverty.

merely of biblical precepts focusing on the need to preach and the importance of poverty. He sought approval for his new rule from Pope Innocent III, who confirmed the new order as the Order of Friars Minor, more commonly known as the Franciscans.

The Franciscans struck a responsive chord in the thirteenth century and became very popular. Many people were obviously disgusted with the worldliness and luxurious living of church prelates, including the heads of monastic houses. The Franciscans lived among the people, preaching repentance and aiding the poor. Their calls for a return to the simplicity and poverty of the early church, reinforced by their own example, were especially effective.

Saint Francis: In Praise of Nature

▼ ▼ ▼

The Canticle of the Sun, *which has been called one of the "first masterpieces of Italian vernacular poetry," was written by Saint Francis of Assisi. It reveals an aspect of Francis's personality that was revered by his contemporaries, his great love of nature. Francis envisioned the world of nature as a mirror in which one could see the reflection of God; hence it was important to treat the natural world with great respect as God's handiwork.*

Francis of Assisi, Canticle of the Sun

Most High, Almighty, good Lord,
Thine be the praise, the glory, the honor,
And all blessing.
To Thee alone, Most High, are they due,
And no man is worthy
To speak Thy Name.

Praise to Thee, my Lord, for all Thy creatures,
Above all Brother Sun
Who brings us the day and lends us his light.
Lovely is he, radiant with great splendor,
And speaks to us of Thee,
O Most High.

Praise to Thee, my Lord, for Sister Moon and the stars
Which Thou hast set in the heavens,
Clear, precious, and fair.

Praise to Thee, my Lord, for Brother Wind,
For air and cloud, for calm and all weather,
By which Thou supportest life in all Thy creatures.

Praise to Thee, my Lord, for Sister Water,
Who is so useful and humble,
Precious and pure.

Praise to Thee, my Lord, for Brother Fire,
By whom Thou lightest the night;
He is lovely and pleasant, mighty and strong.

Praise to Thee, my Lord, for our sister Mother Earth
Who sustains and directs us,
And brings forth varied fruits, and colored flowers, and
    plants.

Praise to Thee, my Lord, for those who pardon one
    another
For love of Thee, and endure
Sickness and tribulation.
Blessed are they who shall endure it in peace,
For they shall be crowned by Thee,
O Most High.

Praise to Thee, my Lord, for our Sister bodily Death
From whom no man living may escape:
Woe to those who die in mortal sin.
Blessed are they who are found in Thy most holy will,
For the second death cannot harm them.

Praise and bless my Lord,
Thank Him and serve Him
With great humility.

Unlike other religious orders, the Franciscans lived in the world. They undertook missionary work, at first throughout Italy, and then to all parts of Europe and even to the Muslim world. The Franciscans had a female component as well, known as the Poor Clares, which was founded by Saint Clare, an aristocratic lady of Assisi who was a great admirer of Francis.

As the Franciscan order grew, it ran into the usual dilemmas of the monastic orders dedicated to poverty. Before his death, Francis had written a new rule confirming absolute poverty but allowing for some governmental structure. Wealthy donors, deeply moved by the Franciscans' apparent holiness, donated buildings to the order. After Francis's death, the popes allowed friends to hold property for the order so that the Franciscans could establish communities. Soon Francis's goal of absolute poverty was being superseded by new demands that caused a split in the order itself. The "Spiritual Franciscans" favored absolute poverty while the "Conventuals" believed that some communal property was necessary in order to carry on their study and preaching. At the beginning of the fourteenth century, the Spirituals would be condemned by the pope, demonstrating that the line between orthodoxy and heresy was a thin one.

The second new monastic order of the thirteenth century arose out of the desire to defend orthodox church teachings from heresy (see the next section). The Order of Preachers, popularly known as the Dominicans or the Black Friars (the Franciscans were the Grey Friars from the color of their robes), was created through the efforts of a Spanish priest, Dominic de Guzmán (1170–1221). Unlike Francis, Dominic was an intellectual who was particularly appalled by the growth of heretical movements within the church. He came to believe that a new religious order of men who lived lives of apostolic poverty but were learned and capable of preaching effectively would best be able to attack and eliminate heresy. With the approval of Pope Innocent III, the Dominicans became an order of mendicant (begging) friars in 1215.

Like the Franciscans, the Dominicans took a vow of poverty, but did not emphasize it in the same way. Since their chief function was preaching, the Dominicans established schools to provide their friars with training in theology. The Dominicans also created an elaborate system of representative government for their order. As head of the order, the master-general was elected for life but could be deposed for malfeasance in office. The order was divided into provinces, each administered by a provincial prior chosen by all the members. Each prior was assisted by a council of friars composed of the heads of the provincial monastic houses and elected delegates. These councils were active in framing legislation for the order. This system of representative assemblies paralleled the development of parliaments in the secular states of the thirteenth century.

The Franciscans and Dominicans played a significant role in the spiritual life of the thirteenth century, particularly among ordinary Christians. By their poverty, the friars reached people critical of the church's growing wealth. By their effective preaching, they could be heard above the voices of the heretics who had found preaching in the vernacular an avenue to attract followers.

The emphasis of the friars on preaching led them to stress the importance of education. Although the Dominicans took the lead, after the death of Saint Francis, the Franciscans quickly followed suit. Already by the mid-thirteenth century, both Franciscans and Dominicans were prominent professors of theology in European universities.

In addition to the friars, the thirteenth century witnessed the development of yet another kind of religious order. Known as Beguines, these were communities of women dwelling together in poverty. They were devout and dedicated to prayer. They begged for their daily support or worked as laundresses in hospitals or at other menial tasks. They did not take religious vows and were free to leave the community at will. Although they originated in the Low Countries, they eventually became quite strong in the Rhineland area of Germany as well. The church was never quite sure what to do with them, and in the fourteenth century the Beguines ran into serious difficulty with church officials.

Dissent, Heresy, Inquisition, and Intolerance

The desire for more personal and deeper religious experience, which characterized the spiritual revival of the High Middle Ages, also led people into directions hostile to the institutional church. From the twelfth century on, religious dissent became a serious problem for the Catholic church.

One form of dissent was anticlericalism. Although some people were orthodox in their religious beliefs, they condemned bishops and priests who failed to live up to the moral standards expected of them. In the mid-twelfth century, Arnold of Brescia, an Italian abbot, abandoned his order to become a popular preacher. A contemporary chronicler observed that "he said things that were entirely consistent with the law accepted by Christian people, but not at all with the life they led."[9] His criticism of the bishop of Brescia's behavior so angered the bishop that Arnold was forced to flee for his life. He went to France where he continued to preach against the excessive wealth and corruption of the church hierarchy. Although such criticism was not heretical, it was considered harmful to the church and the social fabric. Arnold of Brescia was caught and executed by the Emperor Frederick Barbarossa.

Other Christians, however, moved beyond anticlericalism or incorporated it into a larger framework of dissenting thought. Their desire for meaningful religious experience could and did lead to heresy or the holding of religious doctrines different from the orthodox teachings of the church. Since even contemporaries observed that heresies seemed to expand as cities grew in number and size, it may be that the concentration of people in urban areas encouraged the spread of heresy.

The two best-known heresies of the twelfth and thirteenth centuries were Catharism and Waldensianism. The Cathars (the word Cathar means "pure") were also called Albigensians after the city of Albi, one of their strongholds in southern France. They believed in a dualist system in which good and evil were separate and distinct (see the box on p. 354). The things of the spirit were good since they were created by a God of light; the things of the world were evil since they were

The Albigensians
▼ ▼ ▼

The Cathars or Albigensians were heretics who were located primarily in southern France. In his determination to eradicate their heresy, Pope Innocent III authorized a crusade by the nobility of northern France against them. Thousands of people were slaughtered, including men, women, and children. One of the crusaders was a young Cistercian monk from the abbey of Vaux-de-Cernay who accompanied the army of Simon of Montfort and wrote a history of the crusade against the Albigensians. This excerpt from his account makes clear his intense feelings against the heretics.

Peter of Vaux-de-Cernay, A History of the Albigensians

It should first be understood that the heretics postulated two creators, to wit, one of the invisible world, whom they called the benign God, and one of the visible world, or the malign god. They ascribed the New Testament to the benign God, the Old Testament to the malign one; the latter book they wholly rejected, except for a few passages which have found their way into the New Testament and which on this account they esteemed worthy of acceptance. . . .

The heretics even affirmed in their secret assemblies that the Christ who was born in terrestrial and visible Bethlehem and crucified in Jerusalem was evil, and that Mary Magdalen was his concubine and the very woman taken in adultery of whom we read in the Gospel; for the good Christ, they said, never ate nor drank nor took on real flesh, and was never of this world, except in a spiritual sense in the body of Paul. . . .

All of these limbs of Antichrist, the first born of Satan, "wicked seed, ungracious children," "speaking lies in hypocrisy," "seducing the hearts of the innocent," corrupted almost the whole province of Narbonne with the poison of their perfidy. They called the Roman Church a "den of thieves" and that harlot of whom we read in Apocalypse. They held as naught the sacraments of the Church to the point of teaching publicly that the water of holy baptism differs not at all from water of a river; that the consecrated bread of the most holy body of Christ is no different from ordinary bread; instilling into the ears of simple folk the blasphemy that the body of Christ, even were it as great as the Alps, would long since have been completely consumed by communicants who partook of it; that confirmation, extreme unction, and confession are trifling and silly matters; and that holy matrimony is nothing else than harlotry, nor can anyone fathering sons and daughters in that state achieve salvation. . . .

Now, it must be understood that certain of the heretics were called the Perfect or the God Men; the others were called the believers of heretics. Those who were called Perfect wore a black mantle; they falsely claimed that they kept themselves chaste; they wholly refused to eat meat, eggs, or cheese; they sought to give the impression of never telling a lie, when they lied constantly, especially concerning God; and they held that one should never for any reason take an oath. Those were called believers of heretics who, while living in the world, did not strive to attain the life of the perfected, but hoped nonetheless to achieve salvation in their faith; they differed, indeed, in their manner of life, but in faith they were at one. Those who were called believers were absorbed in usuries, robberies, murders, sins of the flesh, perjuries, and all sorts of perversities.

created by Satan, the prince of darkness. Humans, too, were enmeshed in dualism. Their souls, which were good, were trapped in material bodies, which were evil. Jesus had not been God since the human body was evil, but an emissary of God who was sent to show people the way out of the soul's entrapment. According to the Cathars, the Catholic church, itself a materialistic institution, had nothing to do with God and was essentially evil. There was no need to follow its teachings or recognize its authority. Catharism also advocated strict asceticism, including fasting and abstention from sexual relations. Since the spirit had become entrapped in the flesh, the procreation of more children simply forced more souls into evil physical bodies. The Cathars, however, had two levels of practitioners. Only a tiny priestly caste, the "perfect ones," adhered to these rigid puritan-ical standards. The majority of Cathars, the "believers," married and led more relaxed lives.

In its dualistic principles, Catharism resembled the Manichean heresy of the early centuries of Christianity. Contemporary theologians, who knew of the Manichees from the writings of Augustine, immediately called these heretics Manicheans, and scholars ever since have debated whether the Cathars were simply carrying on an older heretical tradition or developed their beliefs "spontaneously" in reaction to the corruption in the Catholic church. In any case, the Cathar movement gained valuable support from important nobles in southern France and northern Italy, especially Raymond IV, count of Toulouse, the chief lord of southern France.

Southern France was home to another heretical sect known as the Waldensians, named after their founder Peter Waldo. He was a wealthy French merchant whose background was quite similar to that of Saint Francis. He, too, experienced moments of religious enlightenment in which he decided to give up all of his material possessions, adopt a life of poverty, and preach to the people in the vernacular. In his sermons, he used biblical texts that emphasized the rejection of material goods and the pursuit of the ideal of apostolic poverty. When the archbishop of Lyons ordered Waldo to stop preaching in public because he had no license to preach, he appealed to the pope. The pope accepted Waldo and his followers' wish to dedicate their lives to poverty, but forbade them to preach without their bishop's consent. The Waldensians refused to give up preaching, however, and defied the church authorities. Their message had a strong appeal in southern France where Catharism had also spread. It is interesting to note that this region was notorious for inept clerical leadership. The unwillingness of the Waldensians to accept the church's authority led to their public condemnation as heretics in 1183.

As the parallels and divergences between Waldo and Francis of Assisi suggest, the line between saint and heretic in the High Middle Ages was often a narrow one. Both Francis and Waldo rejected the world and material possessions. Francis became a devoted papal follower and conformed to church authority. Waldo preached the same message of poverty but refused to accept church authority and consequently became a heretic.

The spread of heretical movements in southern France alarmed the church authorities. Pope Innocent III determined to solve the problem, initially by sending preachers to convince the heretics to return to the orthodox Catholic faith. But they achieved little, and when the leaders of southern France refused to help, the pope decided to use force. His appeal to the nobles of northern France for a crusade against the heretics fell on receptive ears, especially by nobles eager for adventure, plunder, and gain.

The crusade against the Albigensians, which began in the summer of 1209 and lasted for almost two decades, was a bloody one. Thousands of heretics (and the innocent) were slaughtered, including entire populations of some towns. In Béziers, for example, seven thousand men, women, and children were massacred when they took refuge in the local church. The count of Toulouse and other lords were stripped of their lands.

Southern France was devastated, but Catharism remained. Over a period of years, the church's attempt to devise a method for discovering and dealing with heretics led to the emergence of the papal inquisition. By 1233, Pope Gregory IX (1227–1241) had entrusted both Dominicans and Franciscans with inquisitorial powers that had formerly belonged only to bishops. The Holy Office, as the Inquisition was called, became a formal court whose job it was to ferret out and try heretics. The Dominicans became especially notorious for their roles as inquisitor-generals.

Gradually, the Holy Office developed its infamous inquisitorial procedure. Anyone could be accused of heresy since the identity of the accuser was not revealed to the indicted heretic. If the accused heretic confessed, he or she was forced to perform public penance and was subjected to punishment, such as flogging; the heretic's property was then confiscated and divided between the secular authorities and the church. Beginning in 1252, those not confessing voluntarily were subjected to torture. Those who refused to confess and were still considered guilty were turned over to the secular authorities for execution. So also were relapsed heretics—those who confessed, did penance, and then reverted to heresy again. The underlying rationale of the Inquisition was quite simple: if possible, save the heretic's soul; if not, stop the heretic from endangering the souls of others. To the Christians of the thirteenth century who believed that there was only one path to salvation, heresy was a crime against God and against humanity, and force was justified to save souls from damnation.

The fanaticism, fear, and greed unleashed in the struggle against heretics was used against others, especially the most well known outgroup of western society, the Jews, and even against a religious order. The Knights Templars (see Chapter 10), a military order established to guard Christian pilgrims in the Holy Land, had built up enormous property holdings and functioned as international bankers. In the process, no small number of people had come to view them as enemies. King Philip

IV of France saw an opportunity to take advantage of this hostility to destroy the order and profit thereby. In 1307, he ordered the Templars arrested and subjected to torture by the Inquisition. They "confessed" to homosexual practices, ritual murder, and heresies. Philip IV bullied Pope Clement V into condemning the order, and the king confiscated their property. The charges were largely fabricated, but it is apparent that Philip had learned how to use the mass fears against heretics to his own benefit. Others perceived that similar benefits could be obtained by persecuting the Jews.

THE JEWS   The Jews constituted the only religious minority in medieval Europe that was allowed to practice a non-Christian religion. In the Early Middle Ages, Jews were actively involved in trade and crafts. Later, after being excluded from both property holding and trades by the feudal and guild systems, some Jews turned to moneylending as a way to survive, although this was probably true only of a minority. Many historians believe that until the eleventh and twelfth centuries, with some exceptions, Jews were still tolerated relatively well by their Christian neighbors.

There is little certainty about the number of Jews in Europe. England had a relatively small population, probably 2,500–3,000, or one-thousandth of the population. There were larger numbers in southern Italy, Spain, France, and Germany. In southern Europe, Jews served an important function as cultural and intellectual intermediaries between the Muslim and Christian worlds. Jewish philosophers, such as Maimonides, were notable influences on Christian scholastic philosophy.

The religious enthusiasm of the High Middle Ages produced an outburst of intolerance against the supposed enemies of Christianity. Although this was evident in the crusades against the Muslims, Christians also took up the search for enemies at home, persecuting Jews in France and the Rhineland at the time of the first crusades. Jews in Speyer, Worms, Mainz, and Cologne were all set upon by bands of Christian crusaders. A contemporary chronicler described how an English band of crusaders at Lisbon, Portugal, en route to the Holy Land "drove away the pagans and Jews, servants of the king, who dwelt in the city and plundered their property and possessions, and burned their houses; and they then stripped their vineyards, not leaving them so much as a grape or a cluster."[10] Even those who tried to protect them were in danger. When the archbishop of Mainz provided shelter for the Jews, his palace was stormed and he was forced to flee. Prominent Christians came to the Jews' defense. Saint Bernard rushed to Germany in 1144 to halt the attacks on Jews, but even the revered holy man was almost lynched by a mob in Mainz when he tried to stop preachers from attacking the Jews. Popes also came to the Jews' defense by issuing decrees reminding Christians that Jews were not to be persecuted.

By the early twelfth century, kings began to establish the principle that Jews were without legal rights unless granted to them by the king. However, by the late twelfth century, while issuing decrees of protection, kings were exploiting the Jews in their territories as well as using various expedients to gain possession of their wealth. For example, in England, when a Jew died, the king confiscated one-third of his wealth. Popes also proved to be dubious protectors. Although they condemned the persecutions, they demonstrated their contempt for Jews by punitive legislation. The Fourth Lateran Council in 1215 decreed that Jews must wear distinguishing marks, such as ribbons, yellow badges, and special veils and cloaks to separate themselves from Christians. The same council encouraged the development of Jewish ghettos, not as walled enclosures to protect them, but to isolate Jews from Christians. Hence, the provincial council of Breslau in 1267 stated:

> The Polish country is still a young plantation in the body of Christendom [pagans had only recently been converted], in order that the Christian populace be not the more easily infected by the superstitions and the depraved mores of the Jews dwelling among them . . . the Jews . . . shall have their houses either contiguous or adjoining in some segregated location of a city or village, in such manner that the quarter of the Jews be separated from the dwellings of the Christians by a fence, a wall or a moat.[11]

Increasingly, the balance between contempt and toleration tilted toward intolerance and persecution of the Jews.

In the thirteenth century, in the supercharged atmosphere of fear created by the struggle with the heretics, Jews were more and more persecuted (see the box on p. 357). Friars urged action against these "murderers of Christ," referring to the traditional Christian view of the Jews as responsible for the death of Christ, and organized public burnings of Jewish books. Especially prevalent among the masses were the charges that the Jews carried out the ritual murder of small children. The persecutions and the new image of the hated Jew stimulated a tradition of anti-Semitism that proved to be one of Christian Europe's most insidious contributions to the Western heritage.

Treatment of the Jews
▼ ▼ ▼

The development of new religious sensibilities in the High Middle Ages also had a negative side, the turning of Christians against their supposed enemies. Although the crusades provide the most obvious example, Christians also turned on their supposed enemies, the "murderers of Christ," the Jews. As a result, Jews suffered increased persecution. These three documents show different sides of the picture. The first is Canon 68 of the decrees of the Fourth Lateran Council called by Pope Innocent III in 1215. The decree specifies the need for special dress, one of the ways Christians tried to separate Jews from their community. The second excerpt is a chronicler's account of the most absurd charge levied against the Jews—that they were guilty of the ritual murder of Christian children to obtain Christian blood for the passover service. This charge led to the murder of many Jews. The third document, taken from a list of regulations issued by the city of Avignon, France, illustrates the contempt Christian society held for the Jews.

Canon 68

In some provinces a difference in dress distinguishes the Jews or Saracens from the Christians, but in certain others such a confusion has grown up that they cannot be distinguished by any difference. Thus it happens at times that through error Christians have relations with the women of Jews or Saracens, and Jews or Saracens with Christian women. Therefore, that they may not, under pretext of error of this sort, excuse themselves in the future for the excesses of such prohibited intercourse, we decree that such Jews and Saracens of both sexes in every Christian province and at all times shall be marked off in the eyes of the public from other peoples through the character of their dress. . . .

Moreover, during the last three days before Easter and especially on Good Friday, they shall not go forth in public at all, for the reason that some of them on these very days, as we hear, do not blush to go forth better dressed and are not afraid to mock the Christians who maintain the memory of the most holy Passion by wearing signs of mourning.

The Jews and Ritual Murder of Christian Children

[. . . The eight-year-old boy] Harold, who is buried in the Church of St. Peter the Apostle, at Gloucester] . . . is said to have been carried away secretly by Jews, in the opinion of many, on Feb. 21, and by them hidden till March 16. On that night, on the sixth of the preceding feast, the Jews of all England coming together as if to circumcise a certain boy, pretend deceitfully that they are about to celebrate the feast [Passover] appointed by law in such case, and deceiving the citizens of Gloucester with that fraud, they tortured the lad placed before them with immense tortures. It is true no Christian was present, or saw or heard the deed, nor have we found that anything was betrayed by any Jew. But a little while after when the whole convent of monks of Gloucester and almost all the citizens of that city, and innumerable persons coming to the spectacle, saw the wounds of the dead body, scars of fire, the thorns fixed on his head, and liquid wax poured into the eyes and face, and touched it with the diligent examination of their hands, those tortures were believed or guessed to have been inflicted on him in that manner. It was clear that they had made him a glorious martyr to Christ, being slain without sin, and having bound his feet with his own girdle, threw him into the river Severn.

The Regulations of Avignon, 1243

Likewise, we declare that Jews or whores shall not dare to touch with their hands either bread or fruit put out for sale, and that if they should do this they must buy what they have touched.

European kings, who had portrayed themselves as protectors, had so fleeced the Jewish communities of their money by the end of the thirteenth century that they too gave in to the mob fury. Edward I expelled all Jews from England in 1290. The French followed suit in 1306, readmitted them in 1315, and expelled them again in 1322. As this policy spread into central Europe, most northern European Jews were forced to move into Poland as a last refuge.

INTOLERANCE AND HOMOSEXUALITY The climate of intolerance that characterized thirteenth-century attitudes toward Muslims, heretics, and Jews was also evident toward another minority group, homosexuals. Although the church had condemned homosexuality in the Early Middle Ages, it had not been overly concerned with homosexual behavior, an attitude also prevalent in the secular world. Before the thirteenth century, few laws had been enacted against homosexual activity. Nor did this approach change initially in the High Middle Ages. Prominent figures, both ecclesiastical and lay, were publicly known and accepted as homosexuals. Between 1050 and 1150, especially among the clergy, there developed a whole subculture of men who produced a literature dwelling on male homosexual love.

By the thirteenth century, however, these tolerant attitudes had altered drastically. Some historians connect this change to the century's climate of fear and intolerance against any minority group that deviated from the standards of the majority. A favorite approach of the critics was to identify homosexuals with other detested groups. Homosexuality was portrayed as a regular practice of Muslims and such notorious heretics as the Albigensians. These hostile attitudes became increasingly evident in legislation enacted throughout Europe in the second half of the thirteenth century. As an example, one Spanish edict stated:

> Although we are reluctant to speak of something which is reckless to consider and reckless to perform, terrible sins are nevertheless sometimes committed, and it happens that one man desires to sin against nature with another. We therefore command that if any commit this sin, once it is proven, both be castrated before the whole populace and on the third day after be hung by the legs until dead, and that their bodies never be taken down.[12]

This law reflected a basic transformation between 1250 and 1300; what had been tolerated in most of Europe was now a criminal act deserving of death.

The legislation against homosexuality commonly referred to it as a "sin against nature." This is precisely the argument developed by Thomas Aquinas (see Scholasticism later in this chapter) who formed Catholic opinion on the subject for centuries to come. In his *Summa Theologica*, Aquinas argued that since the purpose of sex was procreation, it could only be used legitimately in ways that did not exclude this possibility. Hence, homosexuality was "contrary to nature" and a deviation from the natural order established by God. This argument and laws prohibiting homosexual activity on pain of death remained the norm in Europe until the twentieth century.

▼ Summas and Cathedrals: Intellectual and Cultural Life

After the barbarian invasions of the ninth and tenth centuries, the Carolingian renaissance had been unable to sustain itself. The twelfth-century renaissance was more fortunate since the following century was a period of great achievement in philosophy, architecture, and literature. Thirteenth-century thinkers were particularly preoccupied with the creation of summas or compendiums of knowledge that attempted to bring together all the received learning of the preceding centuries on a given subject into a single whole. The most famous of the summas was the *Summa Theologica* of Thomas Aquinas.

Scholasticism

By the thirteenth century, universities had achieved a monopoly on higher education. The chief subjects of instruction were logic, Aristotelian philosophy and science, mathematics, medicine, canon and Roman law, and, above all others, theology. University professors of the Middle Ages were known as the schoolmen or scholastics. Scholasticism, then, in the broadest sense referred simply to the educational system of the medieval schools, but it came to be viewed more narrowly as a philosophical and theological system grounded upon the reconciliation of faith and reason. The scholastic method continued to be the basic instructional mode of the universities. Its emphasis on posing a question, presenting contradictory authorities on that question, and then arriving at conclusions demanded rigorous analytical thought. In the hands of the best professors, it became an intellectual discipline that led to educational growth; in the hands of mediocre professors, it became an exercise in logic chopping and futile argument over nonessentials.

The overriding task of scholasticism in the thirteenth century was to harmonize Christian revelation with the work of Aristotle. The great influx of Aristotle's works into the west in the High Middle Ages threw many theologians into consternation. Aristotle was so highly regarded that he was called "the philosopher," yet he had arrived at his conclusions by rational thought—not revelation—and some of his doctrines, such as the mortality of the individual soul, contradicted the teachings of the church. Many of the attempts of Muslim and Jewish scholars to reconcile their religious traditions with Aristotle had been rejected by Muslim and Jewish fundamentalists who clung rigidly to their spiritual traditions. The initial reaction in the west had also been one of repression. In 1210, Aristotle's books on natural science had been banned from the University of Paris. Fortunately for the west, papal bans were largely ignored. Different approaches were used to reconcile Aristotle and the doctrines of Christianity; the most famous was that of Saint Thomas Aquinas.

Thomas Aquinas (1225–1274) came from the aristocratic class of southern Italy. He began his studies at the University of Naples and became a Dominican monk in 1244. He studied theology at Cologne and Paris under Albertus Magnus (1193–1280), one of the most prominent theologians of the age, who tried to assimilate Aristotle's works on natural philosophy into the body of Christian education. Aquinas taught at both Naples and Paris, and it was at the latter that he finished his famous *Summa Theologica* (*A Summa of Theology*).

This masterpiece was organized according to the dialectical method of the scholastics. Aquinas first posed a question, cited sources that offered opposing opinions on the question, and then resolved them by arriving at his own conclusions. In this fashion, Aquinas raised and discussed some six hundred articles or issues.

Aquinas's reputation derives from his masterful attempt to reconcile faith and reason. He took it for granted that there were truths derived by reason and truths derived by faith. He was certain, however, that the two truths could not be in conflict with each other:

> The light of faith that is freely infused into us does not destroy the light of natural knowledge [reason] implanted in us naturally. For although the natural light of the human mind is insufficient to show us these things made manifest by faith, it is nevertheless impossible that these things which the divine principle gives us by faith are contrary to these implanted in us by nature [reason]. Indeed, were that the case, one or the other would have to be false, and, since both are given to us by God, God would have to the author of untruth, which is impossible . . . it is impossible that those things which are of philosophy can be contrary to those things which are of faith.[13]

The natural mind, unaided by faith, could arrive at truths concerning the physical universe. Without the help of God's grace, however, unaided reason alone could not grasp spiritual truths.

It is important to remember that Aquinas was a thoroughgoing rationalist who viewed human reason as the connecting point betwen the natural and spiritual worlds. He is well known for his attempts to argue five propositions for the existence of God from sense experience. For example, in his fourth argument, he reasoned

that the existence of various levels of perfection in material things meant that there must be an absolute standard of perfection. Therefore, "there is something which is to all beings the cause of their being, and their goodness, and any other perfection. And this being we call God."[14]

The theological system that Aquinas created eventually came to be viewed by the Catholic church as its official philosophy and used as the basis for theological education in its schools, but not in the thirteenth century. Aquinas's work was subjected to close examination and found wanting by other theologians, notably the Franciscans, who supported the Platonic traditions of Augustine against what they considered the fervent Aristotelianism of the Dominicans. Although they did not accept their failure, thirteenth-century theologians, like twentieth-century scientists, seemed incapable of providing a harmonious synthesis of all knowledge that satisfied everyone.

Medieval Science and Technology

In the area of science as in many others, medieval intellectuals considered Aristotle the master of all knowledge. Aristotle had taught that natural science should be based on observations that could then lead to generalizations. In following Aristotle as their master, most medieval philosophers were content to accept his results without question. Even when new empirical observations were made, people were reluctant to question Aristotle's conclusions.

Some natural philosophers, however, furthered the scientific methodology of their day. The Englishman Robert Grosseteste (1168–1253), the chancellor of Oxford University, stressed the need for students to observe the world of nature and was especially interested in the study of light or the science of optics. He was persuaded that a deeper knowledge of physical light would serve to penetrate the nature of the universe. Believing that physical laws could be expressed mathematically, he attempted to show how the radiation of light could be demonstrated geometrically.

Grosseteste's pupil, Roger Bacon (1220–1292), carried on his master's work. Although Bacon achieved no scientific breakthroughs of his own, he is still remembered for his imaginative visions of flying machines, submarines, and powered ships and for emphasizing the importance of mathematics for the study of both "natural" and "divine" philosophy.

What modern authors call the pseudosciences seemed to hold considerably more attraction than the sciences in the High Middle Ages. Especially popular were astrology and alchemy. Despite the church's attempt to downplay it, astrology was widely studied and used by many people. Many rulers including Frederick II would not think of being without their court astrologers. This interest in the movement of planetary bodies, which was of great importance in the construction of astrological charts, did have the side effect of furthering interest in astronomy as well. The increased spread of Arabic mathematics also promoted astronomical studies.

Alchemy was a "spiritual science," commonly regarded as an attempt to transmute base metals into pure ones, such as gold. While alchemists devised elaborate chemical devices to achieve their goal—and are therefore credited with being the first chemists—the more knowledgeable alchemists had a rather different goal,

▼ **Mechanical Clock.** The Middle Ages was an era of technological advances. Machines powered by wind and water were used in a variety of ways to lessen the need for human labor. The inventiveness of the High Middle Ages was especially evident in the creation of the mechanical clock, one of which is shown here in this illustration from a medieval manuscript. Although the mechanical clock was invented at the end of the thirteenth century, it was not perfected until the fourteenth.

the transmutation of the soul from its baseness into pure spirit. Alchemists devised an elaborate system of symbols to disguise their true aims.

Despite what some historians regard as a lack of growth in science in the Middle Ages, it is important to remember that this was a period of many technological advances. Medieval machines, powered by wind and water, were used in such diverse areas as textile production, the grinding of grains, and iron-smelting forges. The development of machines eliminated many tasks previously done by hand. The medieval period was also highly inventive. Both eyeglasses and the first mechanical clocks were invented near the end of the thirteenth century.

Literature

The thirteenth century witnessed the continuation of the *chansons de geste,* the love songs of the troubadours, and the final written versions of old sagas. Of the latter, the most famous was the *Nibelungenlied* (*Song of the Nibelungs*), an epic poem written by an unknown author between 1190 and 1205. Although based on stories from as far back as the sixth century, it was highly popular in thirteenth-century Germany. The story revolves around the deeds of the warrior Siegfried: "Goodly was this knight, . . . his body without blemish, a strong and valiant man of great worship; abroad, through the whole earth, went his fame . . . he rode boldly into many lands."[15] The main motif of the poem is loyalty, not the simple loyalty of a knight like Roland to Charlemagne, but the divided loyalties and the attendant human choices that lead to tragedy.

The best known of the French medieval poems of the thirteenth century focused on one of the deep and abiding interests of courtly society, love. The *Romance of the Rose* was an allegory on courtly love written by two different authors. Guillaume de Lorris wrote the first part around 1240. In it, he presented the dream-vision of a lover who embarks upon winning his lady. His quest ensues in a garden filled with personifications of human traits; Sir Mirth and Lady Gladness are the lord and lady of the garden. The lover is attracted to a rose, symbol of a young woman, and is aided by Courtesy, Gladness, Wealth, and other qualities personified as allegorical figures, but is hindered by Shame, Jealousy, and Danger. Guillaume had an idealistic view of love and reflected the courtly manners of polite society. When the god of Love instructs the lover on the manners he must develop if his lady is to find him desirable, Guillame has him say:

Then, take care that you never say
Those vulgar words or smutty jokes.
To name a vulgar thing,
Never let your mouth be opened.
I don't call that man courteous,
Who mentions what's nasty and bad.
All women serve and honor,
Spare no pain and effort in their service;
And if you hear one speaking ill,
Who mouths contempt for women,
Rebuke him, and bid him be quiet.[16]

The second part was written by Jean de Meun around 1280. Jeun was deeply versed in university learning and makes his work virtually a summa of contemporary learned opinion and knowledge. Although he continues the theme of love begun earlier by Guillaume de Lorris, he approaches it in a new way with a new intensity. Jean held a low opinion of women and his advice on love is more sexually oriented. As this selection on how a woman can win a man demonstrates, gone is the innocence that dominated courtly love:

If her neck be lovely and white her throat,
See to it that her seamstress so cuts her dress,
And so reveals a décolletage,
That her skin appears white and clear,
Six inches in back and front,
If she would be the more seductive.[17]

Both the *Song of the Nibelungs* and the *Romance of the Rose* found favor in courtly life.

Although Latin remained the the universal language for intellectual debate, theological treatises, and state and church documents, the vernacular became popular not only for poetry, but also for the writing of history. Two major historical works were written in French in the thirteenth century. Geoffrey de Villehardouin (c. 1150–1213), a French nobleman, wrote an eyewitness narrative account of the fourth crusade and the capture of Constantinople (see the box on p. 348). Called the "first great monument of French prose," Geoffrey's work was used as a model for other chronicles and histories.

Another French nobleman, Jean de Joinville (1225–1317), wrote a biography of Saint Louis. Written toward the end of the thirteenth century, it was not completed until 1309. Joinville's account of Louis was responsible for creating a positive image of the pious French ruler that lasted in France for centuries.

▼ **Interior of a Gothic Cathedral.** The use of ribbed vaults and pointed arches gave the Gothic cathedral an impression of upward movement. Moreover, the flying buttress, a heavy pier of stone built onto the outside of church walls in order to bear the brunt of the weight of the church's vaulted ceiling, made it possible to build the Gothic cathedral with thin walls and enabled medieval architects to fill church walls with stained glass windows.

The Gothic Cathedral

Begun in the twelfth century and brought to perfection in the thirteenth, the Gothic cathedral remains one of the greatest artistic triumphs of the High Middle Ages. Soaring skyward, almost as if to reach God, it was a fitting symbol for medieval people's preoccupation with God.

Two fundamental innovations of the twelfth century made Gothic cathedrals possible. The combination of ribbed vaults and pointed arches replaced the barrel vault of Romanesque churches (see Chapter 10) and enabled builders to make Gothic churches higher than their Romanesque counterparts. The use of pointed

▼ **The Gothic Cathedral: Notre Dame of Paris.** The Gothic cathedral was one of the great artistic triumphs of the High Middle Ages. Soaring skyward and towering above all other buildings in the medieval city, the Gothic cathedral was an appropriate symbol for the medieval preoccupation with God. Pictured here is the cathedral of Notre Dame in Paris. Begun in 1163, it was not completed until the beginning of the fourteenth century.

arches and ribbed vaults created an impression of upward movement, a sense of weightless upward thrust that implied the energy of God. Another technical innovation was also important. The flying buttress, basically a heavy arched pier of stone built onto the outside of the walls, made it possible to distribute the weight of the church's vaulted ceilings outward and down and thus eliminate the heavy walls used in Romanesque churches to hold the weight of the massive barrel vaults. Gothic cathedrals were built, then, with thin walls that were filled with magnificent stained glass windows, which created a play of light inside that varied with the sun at different times of the day.

Medieval craftsmen of the twelfth and thirteenth centuries perfected the art of stained glass. Small pieces of glass were stained in glowing colors that craftsmen to this day have been unable to duplicate. This preoccupation with colored light in Gothic cathedrals was not accidental, but was executed by people inspired by the belief that light was a metaphor for God. Light is invisible but enables people to see; so too is God invisible, but the existence of God allows the world of matter to

be. Those impressed by the mystical significance of light were also impressed by the mystical significance of number. The proportions of Gothic cathedrals were based on mathematical ratios that their builders believed were derived from the ancient Greek school of Pythagoras and expressed the "inherent harmony of the universe."

▼ **Chartres Cathedral: Stained Glass Window.** The stained glass of Gothic cathedrals is remarkable for the beauty and variety of its colors. Medieval craftsmen brought the technique of making colored glass to a high level of perfection. Stained glass windows illustrated a remarkable variety of scenes. The windows of Chartres cathedral, for example, present Christ and the saints, scenes from the Bible, and views of the everyday activities of ordinary men and women.

The first fully Gothic church was the abbey church of Saint-Denis near Paris, inspired by its famous abbot Suger (1122–1151) and built between 1140 and 1150. Although the Gothic style was a product of northern France, by the mid-thirteenth century, French Gothic architecture had spread to England, Spain, Germany, virtually all of Europe. By the mid-thirteenth century, French Gothic architecture was seen most brilliantly in cathedrals in Paris (Notre Dame), Reims, Amiens, and Chartres.

The facades of Gothic cathedrals were covered with a mass of sculpture that served didactic as well as decorative purposes. Visual images, it was believed, helped ordinary people understand religious truths. The style of human figures was much more lifelike than the sculpture on Romanesque churches. Other objects, such as animals and flowers, were all carved with remarkable naturalism. An element of fantasy also crept in, with sculptures of mythical monsters, such as dragons, unicorns, and griffins.

A Gothic cathedral was the work of an entire community. Bishops and cathedral clergy made the decision to build, but all classes contributed to its construction. Money was raised from wealthy townspeople who had profited from the new trade and industries as well as kings and nobles. The cathedrals were designed by master masons who were both architects and engineers. They drew up the plans and supervised the work of construction. Skilled stonemasons and other craftsmen were paid a daily wage and provided the skilled labor to build the cathedrals. The building of cathedrals often became highly competitive as communities vied with one another to build the highest tower, a rivalry that sometimes ended in disaster. The choir of the cathedral of Beauvais in northern France collapsed in 1284 after reaching an astounding height. Gothic cathedrals also depended on a community's faith. After all, it often took two or more generations to complete a cathedral, and the first generation of builders must have begun with the knowledge that they would not live to see the completed project. Most importantly, a Gothic cathedral symbolized the chief preoccupation of a medieval Christian community, its dedication to a spiritual ideal. As we have observed before, the largest buildings of an era reflect the values of its society. The Gothic cathedral with its towers soaring toward heaven gave witness to an age when a spiritual impulse still underlay most of existence.

In the thirteenth century, the civilization of the High Middle Ages reached its peak. It was a period of tremendous growth in population, cities and towns, trade, and

▼ **Construction of a Cathedral.** A Gothic cathedral was the work of an entire urban community and gave rise to the creation of an enormous building industry. Massive amounts of labor, money, and materials were required to complete them. This illustration from a medieval manuscript shows some of the steps involved in constructing a cathedral. At right, two masons lay stone while other workers heighten the scaffold. At left, workmen building a tower raise a block of stone by means of a primitive crane.

agricultural production. The popes sometimes treated rulers as if they were their servants while monarchs themselves were developing the machinery of government that would eventually enable them to challenge these exalted claims of papal power. The religious enthusiasm of the twelfth century continued well into the thirteenth as Gothic cathedrals and new orders of friars alike gave witness to spiritual growth and passion.

Growth and optimism seemed to characterize the thirteenth century, but underneath the calm exterior lay seeds of discontent and change. Dissent from church teaching and practices grew, leading to a climate of fear and intolerance as the church responded with inquisitorial procedures to enforce conformity to its teachings. Minorities of all kinds suffered intolerance and, worse still, persecution at the hands of people who worked to maintain the image of an ideal Christian society. The breakdown of the old manorial system and the creation of new relationships between lords and peasants led to local peasant uprisings in the late thirteenth century. The crusades ended ignominiously with the fall of the last crusading foothold in the east in 1291. By that time, more and more signs of ominous troubles were appearing. The fourteenth century would prove to be a time of real crisis for European civilization.

Notes
▼ ▼ ▼

1. Quoted in Jean Gimpel, *The Medieval Machine* (Harmondsworth, 1977), p. 92.

2. Quoted in Brian Tierney and Joan Scott, eds., *Western Societies: A Documentary History* (New York, 1984), 1: 277.

3. Ibid., p. 278.

4. Jean de Joinville, *The Life of Saint Louis*, trans. M. R. B. Shaw (Harmondsworth, 1963), p. 167.

5. Ibid., p. 177.

6. Ibid., p. 346.

7. Oliver Thatcher and Edgar McNeal, eds., *A Source Book for Medieval History* (New York, 1905), p. 208.

8. Ibid., p. 218.

9. Quoted in Rosalind and Christopher Brooke, *Popular Religion in the Middle Ages* (London, 1984), p. 94.

10. Henry T. Riley, ed. and trans., *Memorials of London and London Life in the Thirteenth, Fourteenth and Fifteenth Centuries* (London, 1868), 2: 148–49.

11. Quoted in Guido Kisch, *The Jews in Medieval Germany* (Chicago, 1949), p. 293.

12. Quoted in John Boswell, *Christianity, Social Tolerance, and Homosexuality* (Chicago, 1980), p. 288.

13. Quoted in John Mundy, *Europe in the High Middle Ages, 1150–1309* (New York, 1973), pp. 474–75.

14. Quoted in David Herlihy, ed., *Medieval Culture and Society* (New York, 1968), p. 227.

15. Charles W. Jones, ed., *Medieval Literature in Translation* (New York, 1950), p. 438.

16. Herlihy, *Medieval Culture and Society*, p. 237.

17. Ibid., p. 242.

Suggestions for Further Reading
▼ ▼ ▼

An excellent survey of the thirteenth century can be found in J. Mundy, *Europe in the High Middle Ages, 1150–1309* (New York, 1973). Also useful is F. Heer, *The Medieval World: Europe, 1100–1350*, trans. J. Sondheimer (New York, 1962). For books on economic and social developments, see the bibliographies for Chapters 9 and 10. Also valuable is A. Sapori, *The Italian Merchant in the Middle Ages* (New York, 1970). There is an extensive section on medieval cities in M. Girouard, *Cities and People: A Social and Architectural History* (New Haven, Conn., 1985). A popular, readable study is J. and F. Gies, *Life in a Medieval City* (New York, 1969).

For specialized studies in the political history of the thirteenth century, see J. C. Holt, *Magna Carta* (Cambridge, 1965); T. C. Van Cleve, *The Emperor Frederick the Second of Hohenstaufen* (Oxford, 1973); M. W. Labarge, *St. Louis: The Life of Louis IX of France* (London, 1968); J. R. Strayer, *The Reign of Philip the Fair* (Princeton, 1980); J. K. Hyde, *Society and Politics in Medieval Italy* (London, 1973); and J. F. O'Callaghan, *A History of Medieval Spain* (Ithaca, N.Y., 1975).

The disastrous fourth crusade is examined in J. Godfrey, *1204: The Unholy Crusade* (Oxford, 1980); and D. Queller, *The Fourth Crusade* (Philadelphia, 1977).

The papacy of Innocent III is covered in H. Tillmann, *Innocent III* (Amsterdam, 1980). On the church, see P. Partner, *The Lands of St. Peter* (Berkeley, 1972); and D. P. Waley, *The Papal State in the Thirteenth Century* (London, 1961). The new religious orders of the thirteenth century are examined in R. B. Brooke, *The Coming of the Friars* (New York, 1975). L. K. Little,

Religious Poverty and the Profit Economy in Medieval Europe (London, 1979) stresses the social context of the development of the mendicant orders. On dissent and heresy, see M. Lambert, *Medieval Heresy* (New York, 1977); R. I. Moore, *The Origins of European Dissent* (New York, 1977); W. L. Wakefield, *Heresy, Crusade and Inquisition in Southern France, 1100–1250* (Berkeley, 1974); J. Sumption, *The Albigensian Crusade* (London, 1978); and J. Strayer, *The Albigensian Crusades* (New York, 1971). On the Inquisition, see B. Hamilton, *The Medieval Inquisition* (New York, 1981). The persecution of Jews in the thirteenth century can be examined in E. A. Synan, *The Popes and the Jews in the Middle Ages* (New York, 1965); J. Marcus, *The Jew in the Medieval World* (New York, 1972); J. Cohn, *The Friars and the Jews* (Oxford, 1985); and S. Grayzel, *The Church and the Jews in the Thirteenth Century* (Philadelphia, 1933). The basic study on intolerance and homosexuality is J. Boswell, *Christianity, Social Tolerance, and Homosexuality* (Chicago, 1980).

A good general introduction to the philosophy and theology of the thirteenth century is J. W. Baldwin, *The Scholastic Culture of the Middle Ages, 1000–1300* (Lexington, Mass., 1971). A valuable guide to Thomas Aquinas and the scholasticism of the age is M. D. Chenu, *Toward Understanding St. Thomas*, trans. A. M. Landry and D. Hughes (Chicago, 1964). A good biography of Thomas Aquinas is J. Weisheipl, *Friar Thomas d'Aquino: His Life, His Thought and Work* (New York, 1974). Aspects of medieval science are examined in R. C. Dales, *The Scientific Achievement of the Middle Ages* (Philadelphia, 1973); and S. E. Easton, *Roger Bacon* (Oxford, 1952). On the Gothic movement, see G. Henderson, *Gothic* (Baltimore, 1967); O. von Simson, *The Gothic Cathedral* (New York, 1964); E. Panofsky, *Gothic Architecture and Scholasticism* (New York, 1957); and J. Bony, *French Gothic Architecture of the Twelfth and Thirteenth Centuries* (Berkeley, 1983). A good book on the construction of Gothic cathedrals is J. Gimpel, *The Cathedral Builders* (New York, 1961).

Chapter 12

The Late Middle Ages: Disintegration of the Medieval Synthesis in the Fourteenth Century

▼▼▼▼▼

The High Middle Ages of the eleventh and twelfth centuries had been a period of great innovation that had reached its high point in the age of synthesis in the thirteenth century. By 1300, the energy of medieval civilization seemed to be dissipating, and even works of synthesis proved inherently unstable. Aquinas's *Summa Theologica*, for example, regarded by some as a masterful reconciliation of Greek philosophy and Christian revelation, appeared to others as a mixture of incompatible elements. The fourteenth century was a period of significant disintegration, visible in famine, plague, economic depression, war, social upheaval, increased crime and violence, and a decline in the power of the universal Catholic church. Periods of disintegration, however, are often fertile grounds for change and new developments. Out of the dissolution of medieval civilization came a new civilization, a rebirth of culture that many historians have labeled the Renaissance. This process was not unlike the earlier emergence of the Christian civilization of the Middle Ages out of the disintegration of the Roman Empire.

▼ Economic and Social Disintegration

Well into the thirteenth century, Europe had experienced good harvests and an ever-expanding population. By the end of the thirteenth century, however, a period of disastrous changes had begun.

The Popes
at Avignon

Hundred Years' War

Outbreak of
Black Death

Peasant
Revolts

The Great Schism

•••••••• 1300 •••••••••••• 1325 ••••••••••• 1350 •••••••••••• 1375 •••••••••••• 1400 •••••••••

Giotto William
of Occam

Dante,
The Divine Comedy

Chaucer,
The Canterbury Tales

Famine and Population

There were noticeable changes in weather patterns by the end of the thirteenth and beginning of the fourteenth centuries as Europe entered a period that has been called a "little ice age." Although this involved a relatively small shift in overall temperature patterns, even that small variation resulted in shortened growing seasons and disastrous weather conditions including heavy storms and constant rain. Between 1315 and 1317, northern Europe experienced heavy rains that destroyed harvests and caused serious food shortages, resulting in extreme hunger and starvation. The great famine of 1315–1317 in northern Europe became an all-too-familiar pattern. Southern Europe, for example, seems to have been struck by similar conditions, especially in the 1330s and 1340s. Hunger became widespread, and the scene described by this chronicler became common:

> We saw a larger number of both sexes, not only from nearby places but from as much as five leagues away, barefooted and maybe even, except for women, in a completely nude state, together with their priests coming in procession at the Church of the Holy Martyrs, their bones bulging out, devoutly carrying bodies of saints and other relics to be adorned hoping to get relief.[1]

Famine in the first half of the fourteenth century may have caused some decline in the European population.

Europe had experienced a great increase in population in the High Middle Ages. By 1300, however, indications are that Europe had reached the upper limit of its population, not in an absolute sense, but in the number of people who could be supported by existing agricultural production and technology. Virtually all productive land was being farmed, including many marginal lands that needed intensive cultivation and proved easily susceptible to changing weather patterns. We know that there was also a distinct movement from overpopulated rural areas to urban locations. Eighteen percent of the people in the village of Broughton in England, for example, migrated between 1288 and 1340. There is no certainty that these migrants found better economic opportunities in urban areas. We might, in fact, conclude the opposite based on the reports of increasingly larger numbers of poor people in the cities. In 1330, for example, one chronicler estimated that Florence numbered 17,000 paupers among its 100,000 inhabitants, almost 20 percent of the entire population. Moreover, evidence suggests that because of the increase in population, individual peasant holdings by 1300 were shrinking in size to an acreage that could no longer support a peasant family. Clearly then, Europe seemed to have reached an upper limit to population growth. The concept of poverty itself took on new dimensions. Earlier, in the twelfth century, poverty had been seen as a condition voluntarily pursued to achieve holiness. The wandering poor of the twelfth century had deliberately renounced material goods to achieve salvation; the beggars of the fourteenth century hoped merely to survive.

Although the extent to which famine contributed to the decline of population in the early fourteenth century is unclear, some historians have pointed out that it could have had other effects on the surviving population. Famine may have led to chronic malnutrition, which in turn contributed to increased infant mortality, lower birth rates, and higher susceptibility to disease since malnourished people are less able to resist infection. This, they argue, helps to explain the virulence of the great plague known as the Black Death.

The Black Death

The Black Death of the mid-fourteenth century was the most devastating natural disaster in European history. It ravaged Europe, wiping out 25 to 50 percent of the population and causing economic, social, political, and cultural upheaval. A Sienese chronicler wrote that "father abandoned child, wife husband, one brother another, for the plague seemed to strike through breath and sight. And so they died. And no one could be found to bury the dead, for money or friendship."[2] People were horrified by an evil force they could not understand and by the subsequent breakdown of all normal human relations.

Epidemic disease had occurred earlier in Western history. Athens was struck by plague in the early years of the Peloponnesian War (431–404 B.C.); the Roman Empire had been devastated when the troops of Marcus Aurelius brought smallpox back to Italy toward the end of the second century A.D. and then from 251 to 260 by the "Antonine Plague," believed to be a virulent form of measles. Moreover, a great plague had caused considerable loss of life in Justinian's empire in the sixth century and recurred in the seventh century. From the eighth to the mid-fourteenth century, European civilization was mostly free from epidemic diseases. The lack of major epidemic diseases undoubtedly aided medieval Europe's remarkable demographic expansion after 900.

The Black Death, then, struck Europe after a period of considerable freedom from epidemic diseases. The origins of this great plague are found in central Asia. It was spread, it is believed, both by the Mongols as they expanded across Asia and by ecological changes that caused central Asian rodents to move westward. These rodents, especially the Asian black rat, became the most active carriers of the plague bacillus known as *Yersinia pestis*.

The Black Death was actually a mixture of bubonic, pneumonic, and septicaemic plague strains. Bubonic plague was the most common and most important form of plague in the diffusion of the Black Death. It was spread by black rats infested with fleas who were host to the deadly bacterium *Yersinia pestis*. Symptoms of bubonic plague include high fever, aching joints, swelling of the lymph nodes, and dark blotches caused by bleeding beneath the skin. Bubonic plague was actually the least toxic of the three forms of plague, but nevertheless killed 50 to 60 percent of its victims. In pneumonic plague, the bacterial infection spreads to the lungs, resulting in severe coughing, bloody sputum, and the relatively easy spread of the bacillus from human to human by coughing. Fortunately, since it was more deadly, this form of the plague occurred less frequently than bubonic plague. Ninety-five to 100 percent of the people with pneumonic plague died. Very rare was septicaemic plague, which was carried by insects. It was extremely lethal—a victim usually died within one day of the initial infection.

There is general agreement that the plague began in Europe when Genoese merchants brought it from the Middle East to the island of Sicily off the coast of southern Italy in October of 1347. It quickly spread to southern Italy and southern France and Spain by the end of 1347. Generally, the diffusion of the Black Death followed commercial trade routes. In 1348, the plague spread through France and the Low Countries and into Germany. By the end of that year, it had moved to England, which it ravaged in 1349. By the end of 1349,

▼ **Mass Burial of Plague Victims.** The High Middle Ages was a period of prosperity and population growth. With changes in weather patterns, the famine that such changes generated, and the arrival of the infamous Black Death in Europe, many lived in poverty and 25 to 50 percent of the European population was wiped out. Arriving from the Middle East with Genoese merchants, the plague spread rapidly throughout Europe, following the paths of commercial trade routes.

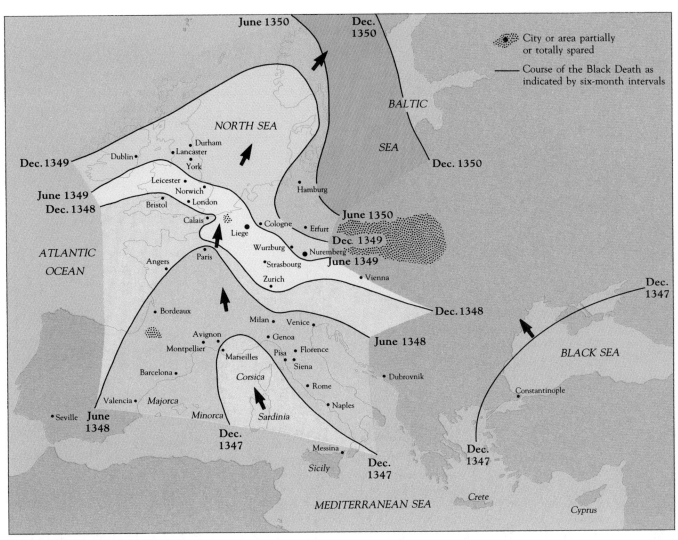

▼ **Map 12.1** Spread of the Black Death.

it had expanded to northern Europe and Scandinavia. Eastern Europe and Russia were affected by 1351, although mortality rates were never as high in eastern Europe as they were in western and central Europe.

Overall, mortality figures for the Black Death were incredibly high. Italy was especially hard hit. As the commercial center of the Mediterranean, Italy possessed scores of ports where the plague could be introduced. Italy's crowded cities, whether large, such as Florence, Genoa, and Venice with populations near 100,000, or small, such as Orvieto and Pistoia, suffered losses of 50 to 60 percent. Only the northern Italian city of Milan miraculously escaped such devastation, suffering only a loss of 15 percent. France and England were also particularly devastated. In northern France, farming villages suffered mortality rates of 30 percent, while cities such as Rouen were more severely affected and experienced losses of 30 to 40 percent. In England and Germany, entire villages simply disappeared from history. In Germany, of approximately 170,000 inhabited locations, only 130,000 were left by the end of the fourteenth century. Overall, however, Germany suffered less than France and England (see the box on p. 370).

Overall, it has been estimated that the European population declined by 25 to 50 percent between 1347 and 1351. If we accept the recent scholarly assessment of a European population of 75 million in the early fourteenth century, this means a death toll in four years of 19 to 38 million people. Moreover, it is important to remember that the plague did not end in 1351. There were

The Black Death
▼ ▼ ▼

The Black Death was the most terrifying natural calamity of the entire Middle Ages. It has been estimated that 25 to 50 percent of the European population died as the plague spread throughout the continent and England between 1347 and 1351. This contemporary account of the great plague by Henry Knighton, a canon of Saint Mary-of-the-Meadow Abbey in Leicester, England, shows the extent of the disaster. In some places entire communities were wiped out. Moreover, the plague had devastating effects on the economy and social order.

Henry Knighton, *The Impact of the Black Death*

In this year [1348] and in the following one there was a general mortality of men throughout the whole world. . . . There died in Avignon in one day one thousand three hundred and twelve persons, according to a count made for the pope, and another day, four hundred persons and more. Three hundred and fifty-eight of the Friars Preachers in the region of Provence died during Lent. At Montpellier, there remained out of a hundred and forty friars only seven. There were left at Magdalena only seven friars out of a hundred and sixty. . . .

At this same time the pestilence became prevalent in England, beginning in the autumn in certain places. It spread throughout the land, ending in the same season of the following year. . . . Then that most grievous pestilence penetrated the coastal regions [of England] by way of Southampton, and came to Bristol, and people died as if the whole strength of the city were seized by sudden death. For there were few who lay in their beds more than three days or two and a half days; then that savage death snatched them about the second day. In Leicester, in the little parish of St. Leonard, more than three hundred and eighty died; in the parish of the Holy Cross, more than four hundred, and in the parish of St. Margaret in Leicester, more than seven hundred. . . .

During this same year, there was a great mortality of sheep everywhere in the kingdom; in one place and in one pasture, more than five thousand sheep died and became so putrefied that neither beast nor bird wanted to touch them. And the price of everything was cheap, because of the fear of death; there were very few who took any care for their wealth, or for anything else. . . . And the sheep and cattle wandered about through the fields and among the crops, and there was no one to go after them or to collect them. They perished in countless numbers everywhere, in secluded ditches and hedges, for lack of watching, since there was such a lack of serfs and servants, that no one knew what he should do. . . . In the following autumn, one could not hire a reaper at a lower wage than eight pence with food, or a mower at less than twelve pence with food. Because of this, much grain rotted in the fields for lack of harvesting, but in the year of the plague, as was said above, among other things there was so great an abundance of all kinds of grain that no one seemed to have concerned himself about it. . . .

After the aforesaid pestilence, many buildings, both large and small, in all cities, towns, and villages had collapsed, and had completely fallen to the ground in the absence of inhabitants. Likewise, many small villages and hamlets were completely deserted; there was not one house left in them, but all those who had lived in them were dead. It is likely that many such hamlets will never again be inhabited.

---

major outbreaks again in 1361–1362 and 1369 and then recurrences every five or six to ten or twelve years depending on climatic and ecological conditions during the remainder of the fourteenth century and all of the fifteenth century. Recent estimates are that the European population declined between 60 and 75 percent between 1347 and 1450 and did not begin to recover until the end of the fifteenth century; not until the mid-sixteenth century did Europe begin to regain its thirteenth-century population levels. Even then, recurrences of the plague did not end until the beginning of the eighteenth century when a new species of brown rat began to replace the black rat.

LIFE AND DEATH IN AN AGE OF PLAGUE: PSYCHOLOGICAL REACTIONS Natural disasters of the magnitude of the great plague produce extreme psychological reactions. There were acts of heroism and great courage. Stories abound of monks and nuns who stayed with the suffering until they themselves died of the plague. Equally large numbers of clergymen fled for their lives as fast as they could. Living for the moment, some people threw themselves with abandon into sexual and alcoholic orgies. The fourteenth-century Italian writer Giovanni Boccaccio gave a classic description of this kind of reaction to the plague in the preface to his famous work *The Decameron:*

> Others, arriving at a contrary conclusion, held that plenty of drinking and enjoyment, singing and free living and the gratification of the appetite in every possible way, letting the devil take the hindmost, was the best preventative of such a malady; and as far as they could, they suited the action to the word. Day and night they went from one tavern to another drinking and carousing unrestrainedly. At the least inkling of something that suited them, they ran wild in other people's houses, and there was no one to prevent them, for everyone had abandoned all responsibility for his belongings as well as for himself, considering his days numbered.[3]

Wealthy and powerful people fled to their country estates, as Boccaccio recounted: "Still others . . . maintained that no remedy against plagues was better than to leave them miles behind. Men and women without number . . . caring for nobody but themselves, abandoned the city, their houses and estates, their own flesh and blood even, and their effects, in search of a country place."[4]

The attempt to explain the Black Death and mitigate its harshness led to extreme sorts of behavior. To many, the plague had either been sent by God as a punishment for humans' sins or caused by the evil one, the devil. Some resorted to extreme asceticism to cleanse themselves of sin and gain God's forgiveness. Such were the flagellants who became a popular movement in 1348,

especially in Germany. Flagellants were not a new phenomenon, but had appeared already in large numbers amidst the intense religious atmosphere of the thirteenth century. The Black Death gave them a new urgency, however, and a new frequency. Groups of flagellants, both men and women, wandered from town to town, flogging each other with whips to win the forgiveness of a God whom they felt had sent the plague to punish humans for their sinful ways. One contemporary chronicler described a flagellant procession:

> The penitents went about, coming first out of Germany. They were men who did public penance and scourged themselves with whips of hard knotted leather with little iron spikes. Some made themselves bleed very badly between the shoulder blades and some foolish women had cloths ready to catch the blood and smear it on their eyes, saying it was miraculous blood. While they were doing penance, they sang very mournful songs about nativity and the passion of Our Lord. The object of this penance was to put a stop to the mortality, for in that time...at least a third of all the people in the world died.[5]

The flagellants attracted attention and created mass hysteria wherever they went. The Catholic church, however, became alarmed when flagellant groups began to kill Jews and attack the clergy who opposed them. Some groups also developed a millenarian aspect, placing their emphasis on the coming end of the world, the return of Christ, and the establishment of a 1000-year kingdom under Christ's governance. Pope Clement VI condemned the flagellants in October 1349 and urged the public authorities to crush them. By the end of 1350, most of the flagellant movements had been destroyed.

▼ **The Flagellants.** Reactions to the plague were diverse and, at times, extreme. For many, the Black Death seemed a punishment from God. Believing that extreme asceticism could atone for humankind's sins and gain God's forgiveness, the flagellants wandered from town to town flogging themselves with whips. Condemned by Pope Clement VI, most of the flagellant movements were eventually crushed.

A Medieval Holocaust: The Cremation of the Strasbourg Jews
▼ ▼ ▼

In their attempt to explain the widespread horrors of the Black Death, medieval Christian communities looked for scapegoats. As at the time of the crusades, the Jews were blamed for poisoning wells and hence spreading the plague. This selection by a contemporary chronicler, written in 1349, gives an account of how Christians in the town of Strasbourg in the Holy Roman Empire dealt with their Jewish community. It is apparent that financial gain was also an important factor in killing the Jews.

Jacob von Königshofen, "The Cremation of the Strasbourg Jews"

In the year 1349 there occurred the greatest epidemic that ever happened. Death went from one end of the earth to the other. . . . And from what this epidemic came, all wise teachers and physicians could only say that it was God's will. . . . This epidemic also came to Strasbourg in the summer of the above-mentioned year, and it is estimated that about sixteen thousand people died.

In the matter of this plague the Jews throughout the world were reviled and accused in all lands of having caused it through the poison which they are said to have put into the water and the wells—that is what they were accused of—and for this reason the Jews were burnt all the way from the Mediterranean into Germany. . . .

[The account then goes on to discuss the situation of the Jews in the city of Strasbourg.]

On Saturday . . . they burnt the Jews on a wooden platform in their cemetery. There were about two thousand people of them. Those who wanted to baptize themselves were spared. [Some say that about a thousand accepted baptism.] Many small children were taken out of the fire and baptized against the will of their fathers and mothers. And everything that was owed to the Jews was cancelled, and the Jews had to surrender all pledges and notes that they had taken for debts. The council, however, took the cash that the Jews possessed and divided it among the working-men proportionately. The money was indeed the thing that killed the Jews. If they had been poor and if the feudal lords had not been in debt to them, they would not have been burnt. . . .

Thus were the Jews burnt at Strasbourg, and in the same year in all the cities of the Rhine, whether Free Cities or Imperial Cities or cities belonging to the lords. In some towns they burnt the Jews after a trial, in others, without a trial. In some cities the Jews themselves set fire to their houses and cremated themselves.

It was decided in Strasbourg that no Jew should enter the city for a hundred years, but before twenty years had passed, the council and magistrates agreed that they ought to admit the Jews again into the city for twenty years. And so the Jews came back again to Strasbourg in the year 1368 after the birth of our Lord.

An outbreak of virulent anti-Semitism also accompanied the Black Death. Jews were accused of causing the plague by poisoning town wells. Although Jews were persecuted in Spain, the worst pogroms against this helpless minority were carried out in Germany; over sixty major Jewish communities in Germany had been exterminated by 1351 (see the box above). Many Jews fled eastward to Russia and especially to Poland where the king offered them protection. Eastern Europe became home to large Jewish communities.

The prevalence of so much death because of the plague and its recurrences affected people in profound ways. Some survivors apparently came to treat life as something cheap and passing. Modern research has confirmed the impression of contemporary chroniclers: there seemed to be a greater degree of violence and violent death after the plague than before. In England, despite the drastic decline in population, the number of murders apparently doubled in the decade of the 1350s.

Postplague Europe also demonstrated a morbid preoccupation with death. In their sermons, priests reminded parishioners that each night's sleep might be their last. Greater emphasis came to be placed on elaborate funerals and detailed funerary monuments. Tombstones were decorated with macabre scenes of naked corpses in various stages of decomposition with snakes entwined in their bones and their innards filled with worms. This morbid preoccupation with death can also be found in art and literature.

Economic Dislocation and Social Upheaval

The population collapse of the fourteenth century had dire economic and social consequences. Economic dislocation was accompanied by social upheaval. Between 1000 and 1300, Europe had been relatively stable. The tripartite division of society into the three estates of clergy (those who pray), nobility (those who fight), and laborers (those who work) had begun to disintegrate in the thirteenth century, however, and was no longer so easily accepted. In the fourteenth century, a series of urban and rural revolts by the lower classes against the oppression of the privileged classes rocked European society.

NOBLE LANDLORDS AND PEASANTS Both peasants and landlords were affected by the demographic crisis of the fourteenth century. Most noticeably, Europe experienced a serious labor shortage that caused a dramatic rise in the price of labor. At Cuxham manor in England, for example, a farm laborer who had received two shillings a week in 1347 was paid seven in 1349 and almost eleven by 1350. At the same time, the decline in population depressed or held stable the demand for agricultural produce, resulting in stable or falling prices for output (although in England prices remained high until the 1380s). The chronicler Henry Knighton observed: "And the price of everything was cheap. . . . For a man could buy a horse for half a mark [six shillings], which before was worth forty shillings. . . ."[6] Since landlords were having to pay more for labor at the same time that their rents or income was declining, they began to experience considerable adversity and lower standards of living. In England, aristocratic incomes dropped more than 20 percent between 1347 and 1353. The wealthiest aristocrats could still afford their privileged lifestyle, but lesser lords faced impoverishment and some even fell out of the ranks of the aristocracy.

Aristocrats responded to adversity in a variety of ways. Some shifted their estates from labor-intensive to land-intensive products. In England, sheepraising increased as landowners perceived that there was still a relatively good market for both raw wool and mutton. Moreover, lords found that certain products had greater elasticity of demand than basic foodstuffs. Instead of growing wheat, they converted to vines for making wine and barley for producing ale. Then, as now, wine and ale remained in constant demand.

Another response to adversity was to seek assistance from the monarchy and their fellow aristocrats by enacting legislation to lower the wage rate artificially. The English Parliament passed the Statute of Laborers (1351), which attempted to limit wages to preplague levels and forbid the mobility of peasants as well. Although such laws proved largely unworkable, they did keep wages from rising as high as they might have in a free market. Overall, the position of noble landlords continued to deteriorate during the late fourteenth and early fifteenth centuries. At the same time, the position of peasants improved, though not uniformly throughout Europe.

The decline in the number of peasants after the Black Death accelerated the process of converting labor services to rents, freeing peasants from the obligations of servile tenure. But there were limits to how much the peasants could advance. They faced the same economic hurdles as the lords. Moreover, peasants were faced with the attempts of lords to impose wage restrictions, reinstate old forms of labor service, and create new obligations. New governmental taxes also hurt. Peasant complaints became widespread and soon gave rise to rural revolts that were largely socioeconomic in character.

PEASANT REVOLTS In 1358, a peasant revolt, known as the *Jacquerie*, broke out in northern France. The de-

▼ **Peasant Rebellion.** The fourteenth century witnessed a number of revolts of the peasantry against noble landowners. Although the plague had in some way improved the economic position of the peasants, the Hundred Years' War and attempts by aristocrats to maintain their standard of living brought the peasants to arms. While initially successful, the revolts were quickly crushed. This illustration shows the destruction of the *Jacquerie.*

A Revolt of French Peasants

▼ ▼ ▼

In 1358, French peasants rose up in a revolt known as the Jacquerie. The relationship between aristocrats and peasants had degenerated as a result of the social upheavals and privations caused by the Black Death and the Hundred Years' War. This excerpt from the chronicle of an aristocrat paints a horrifying picture of the barbarities that occurred during the revolt.

Jean Froissart, *Chronicles*

Not long after the King of Navarre had been set free, there were very strange and terrible happenings in several parts of the kingdom of France. . . . They began when some of the men from the country towns came together in the Beauvais region. They had no leaders and at first they numbered scarcely a hundred. One of them got up and said that the nobility of France, knights and squires, were disgracing and betraying the realm, and that it would be a good thing if they were all destroyed. At this they all shouted: "He's right! He's right! Shame on any man who saves the gentry from being wiped out!"

They banded together and went off, without further deliberation and unarmed except for pikes and knives, to the house of a knight who lived near by. They broke in and killed the knight, with his lady and his children, big and small, and set fire to the house. Next they went to another castle and did much worse; for, having seized the knight and bound him securely to a post, several of them violated his wife and daughter before his eyes. Then they killed the wife, who was pregnant, and the daughter and all the other children, and finally put the knight to death with great cruelty and burned and razed the castle.

They did similar things in a number of castles and big houses, and their ranks swelled until there were a good six thousand of them. Wherever they went their numbers grew, for all the men of the same sort joined them. The knights and squires fled before them with their families. They took their wives and daughters many miles away to put them in safety, leaving their houses open with their possessions inside. And those evil men, who had come together without leaders or arms, pillaged and burned everything and violated and killed all the ladies and girls without mercy, like mad dogs. Their barbarous acts were worse than anything that ever took place between Christians and Saracens. Never did men commit such vile deeds. They were such that no living creature ought to see, or even imagine or think of, and the men who committed the most were admired and had the highest places among them. I could never bring myself to write down the horrible and shameful things which they did to the ladies. But, among other brutal excesses, they killed a knight, put him on a spit, and turned him at the fire and roasted him before the lady and her children. After about a dozen of them had violated the lady, they tried to force her and the children to eat the knight's flesh before putting them cruelly to death.

struction of normal order by the Black Death and the subsequent economic dislocation were important factors in causing the revolt, but the situation of the French peasantry was complicated by the ravages created by the Hundred Years' War (see "War and Political Instability" later in the chapter). Both sides followed a deliberate policy of laying waste to peasants' lands while bands of mercenaries lived off the land by taking peasants' produce as well. Thus, the *Jacquerie* was a revolt of desperation; it was linked to the political ambitions of townspeople in Paris who were also upset with the conduct of the war and wished to limit monarchical power. The leader of the peasants was actually a bourgeois draper, Etienne Marcel.

Peasant anger was also exacerbated by growing class tensions. Landed nobles were eager to hold onto their politically privileged position and felt increasingly threatened in the new postplague world of higher wages and lower prices. Aristocrats looked upon peasants with utter contempt. A French tale narrated to upper-class audiences contained this remarkable passage:

Tell me, Lord, if you please, by what right or title does a villein [peasant] eat beef? . . . Should they eat fish? Rather let them eat thistles and briars, thorns and straw and hay on Sunday and peapods on weekdays. They should keep watch without sleep and have trouble always; that is how villeins should live. Yet each day they are full and drunk on the best wines, and in fine clothes. The great expenditures of villeins comes as a high cost, for it is this that destroys and ruins the world. It is they who spoil the common welfare. From the villein comes all unhappiness. Should they eat meat? Rather should they chew grass on the heath with the horned cattle and go naked on all fours.[7]

The peasants reciprocated this contempt for their so-called social superiors.

The outburst of peasant anger led to savage confrontations. Castles were burned and nobles murdered (see the box on p. 374). Such atrocities did not go unanswered, however. The *Jacquerie* soon failed as the privileged classes closed ranks, savagely massacred the rebels, and ended the revolt.

The English Peasants' Revolt of 1381 was the most famous of all. It was not a revolt caused by desperation but was a product of rising expectations. After the Black Death, the English peasants had enjoyed an improved position with greater freedom and higher wages or lower rents. Aristocratic landlords had fought back with legislation to depress wages and an attempt to reimpose old feudal dues. The most immediate cause of the revolt, however, was the monarchy's attempt to raise revenues by imposing a poll tax or a flat charge on each adult member of the population. Three such poll taxes were levied between 1377 and 1381. The last one was met by a revolt of peasants in eastern England, the wealthiest part of the country. They refused to pay the tax and expelled the collectors forcibly from their villages.

This action produced a widespread rebellion of both peasants and townspeople led by a well-to-do peasant called Wat Tyler and a preacher named John Ball. The latter preached an effective message against the noble class, as recounted by the chronicler Froissart:

> Good people, things cannot go right in England and never will, until goods are held in common and there are no more villeins and gentlefolk, but we are all one and the same. In what way are those whom we call lords greater masters than ourselves? How have they deserved it? Why do they hold us in bondage? If we all spring from a single father and mother, Adam and Eve, how can they claim or prove that they are lords more than us, except by making us produce and grow the wealth which they spend?[8]

The movement developed a famous jingle based on Ball's preaching: "When Adam delved and Eve span, who was then a gentleman?"

The revolt was initially successful. The manor houses of aristocrats, lawyers, and government officials were burned down, and several important officials, including the archbishop of Canterbury, were murdered. After the

peasants marched on London, the young king Richard II promised to accept the rebels' demands if they returned to their homes. They accepted the king's word and began to disperse, but the king reneged and with the assistance of the aristocrats brutally crushed the rebels. The poll tax was eliminated, however.

TRADE, INDUSTRY, AND URBAN CONFLICT   The economic effects of the Black Death varied from sector to sector and region to region. Most economic historians believe that in the areas of trade and industry Europe experienced a severe economic recession. Some, indeed, have spoken of an economic depression, at least in certain regions of Europe.

Commercial and industrial activity suffered almost immediately from the Black Death. An oversupply of goods and an immediate drop in demand led to a decline in trade after 1350. Some industries suffered greatly. Florence's woolen industry, one of the giants, produced 70,000–80,000 pieces of cloth in 1338; in 1378, it was yielding only 24,000 pieces. In Ypres, Flanders, cloth production fell an incredible 85 percent. Bordeaux wine exports fell by 50 percent.

Statistics can be misleading, however. The production of woolen cloth in England rose after the Black

▼ **Italian Bankers.** The aristocracy was not the only class to suffer from the plague. Bourgeois merchants and manufacturers also faced economic difficulties and, like the aristocrats, took steps to protect themselves. The Bardi and Peruzzi, the two most prominent banking houses of the fourteenth century, collapsed when the king of England repudiated his loans.

Death at the same time that production was falling elsewhere. England now exported woolen cloth abroad. In addition, luxury industries flourished temporarily after the Black Death since depopulation produced an initial rise in per capita wealth through inheritance and created demand for luxury goods. Prices rose as did the wages of skilled artisans whose products were much desired. Cities with luxury industries enjoyed a temporary affluence.

Bourgeois merchants and manufacturers responded to adversity in ways similar to landlords, namely, by attempts to restrict competition and resist the demands of the lower classes. Some sought protection from monarchs. In England, for example, the government granted the Merchants of the Staple, a group of wool exporters, a monopoly on the wool trade in return for loans. In the cities, wealthy bourgeoisie tried to eliminate competition by imposing greater restrictions on guild membership.

In urban areas where capitalist industrialists paid low wages and managed to prevent workers from forming organizations to help themselves, industrial revolts broke out throughout Europe. Ghent experienced one in 1381, Rouen in 1382. Most famous, however, was the revolt of the *ciompi* in Florence in 1378. The *ciompi* were wool workers, basically proletarian laborers in Florence's most prominent industry. In the 1370s, the woolen industry was depressed, and wool workers saw their real wages decline as a result of a debasement of the coinage in which they were paid. Their revolt won them some concessions from the communal government, including the right to form guilds and be represented in the government. But their newly won rights were short-lived. A counterrevolution by government authorities brought an end to *ciompi* participation in the government by 1382.

Both the urban and rural revolts of the fourteenth century contained some common elements. As a result of the Black Death, both workers and peasants had sustained some basic improvements in wages and living conditions. The privileged classes, whether noble landlords or wealthy bourgeoisie, wished to retain their old advantages and deny workers and peasants their newfound gains. Peasants and workers simply fought back. They did so at a time when normal law and order were breaking down anyway as a result of the upheaval fostered by the Black Death.

Although the revolts sometimes resulted in short-term gains for the participants, it is also true that the uprisings were relatively easily crushed and their gains quickly lost. Geographically dispersed, rural and urban revolters were not united and had no long-range goals. Immediate gains were uppermost in their minds. Accustomed to ruling, the established classes easily combined and crushed dissent when faced with social uprisings. But after the fourteenth century, the harmony theoretically implicit in the medieval hierarchy of the classes was never the same again. The rural and urban revolts of the fourteenth century ushered in an age of class conflict that characterized much of later European history.

▼ War and Political Instability

Famine, plague, economic turmoil, social upheaval, and violence were not the only problems of the fourteenth century. War and political instability must also be added to the list. Of all the struggles that ensued in the fourteenth century, the Hundred Years' War was the most famous and the most violent. It was not a single war between England and France, but a protracted series of conflicts with interludes of peace. Although its origins lay in a typical feudal dispute, the Hundred Years' War marked a transition from the use of feudal armies to mercenary levies hired by monarchs. The lengthy struggle also resulted in a growth of cultural nationalism that enabled the French monarchy to consolidate its position in France.

Causes of the Hundred Years' War

In 1259, the English king, Henry III, had relinquished his claims to all the French territories previously held by the English monarchy except for one relatively small possession known as the duchy of Gascony. As duke of Gascony, the English king pledged loyalty as a vassal to the French king. But this territory gave rise to numerous disputes between the kings of England and France. By the thirteenth century, the Capetian monarchs had greatly increased their power over their more important vassals, the great lords of France. Royal officials interfered regularly in the affairs of the vassals' fiefs, especially in regard to matters of justice. Although this policy irritated all the vassals, it especially annoyed the king of England who considered himself the peer of the French king.

An economic problem involving the county of Flanders was a second factor contributing to the Hundred Years' War. Urban revolts in Flanders pitted artisans against wealthy merchants and threatened to disrupt the lucrative shipments of English wool to Flanders. Flanders was England's chief market for raw wool, and the English king received huge revenues from export duties on wool. When the French monarchy began to intervene in Flanders on the side of the merchants, the English felt threatened. If the French were to gain control of Flanders, they could play havoc with the wool trade. Accordingly, the English king began to support the Flemish artisans.

A dispute over the right of succession to the French throne also complicated the struggle between the French and English. In the fourteenth century, the Capetian dynasty failed for the first time in almost four hundred years to produce a male heir. In 1328, the senior branch of the Capetian dynasty became extinct in the male line with the death of Charles IV. As the son of the daughter of King Philip IV, King Edward III of England laid claim to the French throne as a close male relative. French practice, however, emphasized descent through the male line, and a cousin of the Capetians, Philip, duke of Valois, became king as Philip VI (1328–1350).

The immediate cause of the war between France and England was the seizure of Gascony by Philip VI in 1337. This action prompted the duke of Gascony, King

Chronology

▼ ▼ ▼

The Hundred Years' War in the Fourteenth Century

Outbreak of Hostilities	1337
Battle of Crécy	1346
Battle of Poitiers	1356
Peace of Brétigny	1359
Death of Edward III	1377
Twenty-Year Truce	1396

Edward III of England (1327–1377), to declare war on Philip, the "so-called King of France." There is no doubt that the personalities of the two monarchs also had much to do with the outbreak of the Hundred Years' War. Both Edward and Philip loved luxury and shared a desire for the glory and prestige that came from military engagements. Both were only too willing to squander their nation's resources to satisfy their own desires. Moreover, for many nobles, the promise of plunder and territorial gain was an incentive to follow the disruptive path of their rulers.

Conduct and Course of the War

The Hundred Years' War began in a burst of knightly enthusiasm. Knights were trained to be warriors; they viewed the clash of battle as the ultimate opportunity to demonstrate their chivalric qualities. The Hundred Years' War proved to be an important watershed, however, since the feudal way of life was on the decline. This would become most evident when peasant infantrymen instead of knights determined the chief battles of the Hundred Years' War.

It was the English, more than the French, who moved beyond the traditional feudal levy. The French army of 1337 with its heavily armed noble cavalry resembled its twelfth- and thirteenth-century forebears. The noble cavalry considered themselves the fighting elite and looked with contempt upon the infantry and crossbowmen since they were peasants or other social inferiors. Such attitudes cost the French dearly in the early battles.

The English army had evolved differently in making use of paid infantrymen. Armed with pikes, many of these infantrymen had also adopted the longbow, invented by the Welsh. The longbow had greater striking power, longer range, and more rapid speed of fire than

▼ Map 12.2 The Hundred Years' War.

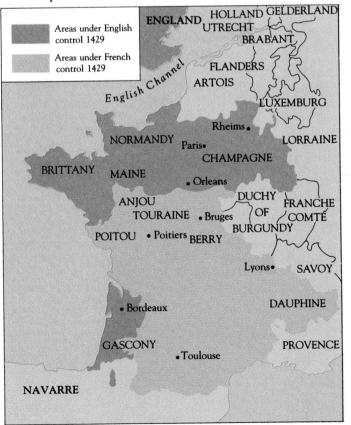

■	Areas under English control 1429
▨	Areas under French control 1429

the crossbow. Although the English made use of heavily armed cavalry, the English army relied even more on large numbers of infantrymen.

Edward III's early campaigns in France were indecisive, costly, and achieved nothing. When Edward renewed his efforts in 1346 with an invasion of Normandy, Philip responded by raising a large force to crush the English army. While Edward tried to flee to Flanders to find allies, he was cut off and forced to fight at Crécy, just south of Flanders. Although historians disagree on the numbers involved, the undoubtedly larger French army followed no battle plan but simply attacked the English lines in a disorderly fashion. The arrows of the English archers decimated the French cavalry. As the chronicler Froissart described it, "[with their longbows] the English continued to shoot into the thickest part of the crowd, wasting none of their arrows. They impaled or wounded horses and riders, who fell to the ground in great distress, unable to get up again without the help of several men."[9] It was a stunning victory for the English.

Edward followed up his victory by capturing the French port of Calais to serve as a staging ground for future invasions. Calais would remain an English fortress until 1558.

The Battle of Crécy was not decisive, however. The English simply did not possess the resources to subjugate all France. Truces, small-scale hostilities, and some major operations were combined in an orgy of seemingly incessant struggle. The English campaigns were waged by Edward III and his son Edward, the prince of Wales, known as the Black Prince. The Black Prince's campaigns in France were devastating (see the box on p. 379). Deliberately avoiding pitched battles, his forces ravaged the land, burned crops and entire unfortified villages and towns, and stole anything of value. For the English, such campaigns were profitable and even enjoyable; for the French people, they meant hunger, deprivation, and death. When the army of the Black Prince was finally forced to do battle, the French, under their king John II (1350–1364), were once again defeated.

▼ **Battle of Crecy.** This miniature depicts the Battle of Crecy, the first of a number of military disasters suffered by the French in the Hundred Years' War. Although the French had superior numbers and had succeeded in preventing Edward III from reaching Flanders, their reliance on their heavily armed cavalry proved to be their undoing. The English longbowmen simply continued to shoot into their ranks, killing the knights or rendering them ineffective.

The Hundred Years' War

▼ ▼ ▼

In his account of the Hundred Years' War, the fourteenth-century chronicler Jean Froissart described the sack of the fortified French town of Limoges by the Black Prince, Edward, the prince of Wales. It presents a vivid example of how noncombatants fared during the war.

Jean Froissart, *Chronicles*

For about a month, certainly not longer, the Prince of Wales remained before Limoges. During that time he allowed no assaults or skirmishes, but pushed on steadily with the mining. The knights inside and the townspeople, who knew what was going on, started a countermine in the hope of killing the English miners, but it was a failure. When the Prince's miners who, as they dug, were continually shoring up their tunnel, had completed their work, they said to the Prince: "My lord, whenever you like now we can bring a big piece of wall down into the moat, so that you can get into the city quite easily and safely."

The Prince was very pleased to hear this. "Excellent," he said. "At six o'clock tomorrow morning show me what you can do."

When they knew it was the right time for it, the miners started a fire in their mine. In the morning, just as the Prince had specified, a great section of the wall collapsed, filling the moat at the place where it fell. For the English, who were armed and ready wait-ing, it was a welcome sight. Those on foot could enter as they liked, and did so. They rushed to the gate, cut through the bars holding it and knocked it down. They did the same with the barriers outside, meeting with no resistance. It was all done so quickly that the people in the town were taken unawares. Then the Prince, the Duke of Lancaster, the Earl of Cambridge, Sir Guichard d'Angle, with all the others and their men burst into the city, followed by pillagers on foot, all in a mood to wreak havoc and do murder, killing indiscriminately, for those were their orders. There were pitiful scenes. Men, women and children flung themselves on their knees before the Prince, crying: "Have mercy on us, gentle sir!" But he was so inflamed with anger that he would not listen. Neither man nor woman was heeded, but all who could be found were put to the sword, including many who were in no way to blame. I do not understand how they could have failed to take pity on people who were too unimportant to have committed treason. Yet they paid for it, and paid more dearly than the leaders who had committed it.

There is no man so hard-hearted that, if he had been in Limoges on that day, and had remembered God, he would not have wept bitterly at the fearful slaughter which took place. More than three thousand persons, men, women and children, were dragged out to have their throats cut. May God receive their souls, for they were true martyrs.

This time even the king was captured. This Battle of Poitiers (1356) ended the first phase of the Hundred Years' War. Under the Peace of Brétigny (1359), the French agreed to pay a large ransom for King John, the English territories in Gascony were enlarged, and Edward renounced his claims to the throne of France in return for John's promise to give up any feudal control over English lands in France. This first phase of the war made it clear that, despite their victories, the English were not really strong enough to subdue all of France and make Edward III's claim to the French monarchy a reality.

Monarchs, however, could be slow learners. The Treaty of Brétigny was never really executed. In the next phase of the war, under the capable hands of John's son Charles V (1364–1380), the French recovered what they had previously lost. The English returned to plundering the French countryside and avoiding pitched battles. That pleased Charles, who did not want to engage in set battles, preferring to use armed bands, especially one led by Bertrand Du Guesclin, to reduce the English fortresses systematically. By 1374, the French had recovered their lost lands, although France itself continued to be plagued by "free companies" of mercenaries, who, no longer paid by the English, simply lived off the land by plunder and ransom. Nevertheless, for the time being, the war seemed over, especially when a twenty-year truce was negotiated in 1396. As we shall see in Chapter 13, the war would break out again in the fifteenth century.

Political Instability

The fourteenth century was a period of adversity for the internal political stability of European governments. Although government bureaucracies grew ever larger, at the same time the question of who should control the bureaucracies led to internal conflict and instability. This instability was part of a general breakdown of the customary fief-holding system. Traditional feudal loyalties were disintegrating rapidly and had not yet been replaced by the national loyalties of the future. Like the lord and serf relationship, the lord and vassal relationship based on land and military service was being replaced by a contract based on money. Especially after the Black Death, money payments were increasingly substituted for military service. Monarchs welcomed this development since they could now hire professional soldiers who tended to be more reliable anyway. As lord and vassal relationships became less personal and less important, new relationships based on political advantage began to be formed, opening up new avenues for political influence—and for corruption as well. Especially noticeable, as the landed aristocrats suffered declining rents and social uncertainties with the new relationships, was the formation of factions of nobles who looked for opportunities to advance their power and wealth at the expense of each other and of their monarchs. At the same time, two other factors, related to the rise of factions, added to the instability of governments in the fourteenth century.

There was an obvious inability of dynasties to perpetuate themselves. By the mid-fifteenth century, reigning monarchs in many European countries were actually not the direct male descendants of those ruling in 1300. The founders of these new dynasties had to struggle for their positions as factions of nobles vied to gain material advantages for themselves. At the end of the fourteenth century and beginning of the fifteenth, there were two claimants to the throne of France, and two aristocratic factions fought for control of England; in Germany, three princes struggled to be recognized as emperor.

Fourteenth-century monarchs, whether of old or new dynasties, found themselves with financial problems as well. The shift to using mercenary soldiers left monarchs perennially short on cash. Traditional revenues, especially rents from property, increasingly proved insufficient to meet their needs. Monarchs attempted to generate new sources of revenues, especially through taxes, which often meant going through parliaments. This opened the door for parliamentary bodies to gain more power by asking for a redress of grievances first. Although unsuccessful in most cases, the parliaments simply added another element of uncertainty and confusion to fourteenth-century politics. By turning now to a survey of western and central European states (eastern Europe will be examined in Chapter 13), we can see how these disruptive factors worked in each country.

England

In the fourteenth century, the lengthy reign of Edward III (1327–1377) was an important one for the evolution of English political institutions. Parliament increased in prominence and developed its basic structure and functions during Edward's reign. Due to his constant need for money to fight the Hundred Years' War, Edward came to rely upon Parliament to levy new taxes. In return for regular grants, Edward made several concessions, including a commitment to levy no direct tax without Parliament's consent and to allow committees of Parliament to examine the government accounts to ensure that the money was being spent properly. By the end of Edward's reign, Parliament had become an important component of the English governmental system. Indeed, Parliament even impeached and condemned several royal ministers for acting contrary to its wishes.

During this same period, Parliament began to assume the organizational structure it has retained to this day. The Great Council of barons became the House of Lords and evolved into a body composed of the chief bishops and abbots of the realm and aristocratic peers whose position in Parliament was hereditary. The representatives of the shires and boroughs, who were considered less important than the lay and ecclesiastical lords, held collective meetings to decide policy and soon came to be regarded as the House of Commons. Together, the House of Lords and House of Commons constituted Parliament. Although the House of Commons did little beyond approving measures proposed by the Lords, during Edward's reign, the Commons did begin the practice of drawing up petitions, which, if accepted by the Lords and king, became law. Although the king and the Lords could amend or reject these petitions, this new procedure represented the beginning of the Commons' role in initiating legislation.

Edward's reign also saw the establishment of justices of the peace, officials appointed by the king from the members of the nobility and lesser aristocracy, who came to control the administration of justice in their counties and to be the chief powers of local government. Since they were appointed by the king, they were royal offi-

cials, but they were not paid and were primarily concerned with their own class interests.

After Edward III's death, England began to experience the internal instability of aristocratic factionalism that was wracking other European countries. The early years of the reign of Edward's grandson, Richard II (1377–1399), began inauspiciously with the Peasants' Revolt that was only ended when the king made concessions. Richard's reign was riven by competing factions of aristocrats who managed for a while to establish a balance of power. But, when Richard began to aspire to absolute power by persuading Parliament to grant him taxes for life and to delegate its authority to a committee established by the king, a baronial revolt ensued.

After the barons had defeated the king's forces, a session of Parliament was convened. Richard II was deposed and soon killed, and the leader of the baronial revolt, Henry of Lancaster, was made king. Although Henry IV (1399–1413) proved to be a competent ruler, factions of nobles soon rose to take advantage of the new situation. In the fifteenth century, this factional conflict led to a devastating series of civil wars known as the War of the Roses.

France

At the beginning of the fourteenth century, France was the "largest, wealthiest, and best governed monarchical state in Europe." By the end of the fourteenth century, much of its wealth had been dissipated, and rival factions of aristocrats had made effective monarchical rule a virtual impossibility.

The French monarchical state had always had an underlying, inherent weakness that proved its undoing in difficult times. Although Capetian monarchs had found ways to enlarge their royal domain and extend their control by developing a large and effective bureaucracy, the various feudal territories that made up France still maintained their own princes, customs, and laws. The parliamentary institutions of France provide a good example of France's basic lack of unity. The French parliament, known as the Estates-General and composed of representatives of the clergy, nobility, and the Third Estate (everyone else), usually represented only the north of France, not the entire kingdom. The southern provinces had their own estates while local estates existed throughout other parts of France. Unlike the English Parliament, which was evolving into a crucial part of the English government, the French Estates-General was simply one of many such institutions.

When Philip VI (1328–1350) became involved in the Hundred Years' War with England, he found it necessary to devise new sources of revenue, including a tax on salt known as the *gabelle* and a hearth tax eventually called the *taille*. These taxes weighed heavily upon the French peasantry and middle class. Consequently, when additional taxes had to be raised to pay for the ransom of King John II after the fiasco at the Battle of Poitiers, the middle-class inhabitants of the towns tried to use the Estates-General to reform the French government and tax structure.

At the meeting of the Estates-General in 1357, under the leadership of the Parisian provost Etienne Marcel, representatives of the Third Estate, in return for granting taxes, gained a promise from King John's son Charles (the successor to the throne known as the dauphin) not to tax without the Estates-General's permission and to allow the Estates-General to meet on a regular basis and participate in important political decisions. After Marcel's movement was crushed in 1358, this attempt to make the Estates-General a functioning part of the French government collapsed. The dauphin became King Charles V (1364–1380) and went on to recover much of the land lost to the English. His military successes underscored his efforts to reestablish strong monarchical powers. He undermined the role of the Estates-General by getting them to grant him taxes with no fixed time limit. Charles's death in 1380 soon led to a new time of troubles for the French monarchy, however.

The insanity of Charles VI (1380–1422), which first became apparent in 1392, opened the door to rival factions of French nobles aspiring to power and wealth. The dukes of Burgundy and Orleans competed to control Charles and the French monarchy. Their struggles created chaos for the French government and the French people. Many nobles supported the Orleanist faction while Paris and other towns favored the Burgundians. By the beginning of the fifteenth century, France seemed hopelessly mired in a civil war. When the English renewed the Hundred Years' War in 1415, the bitter rivalries seemed to guarantee English success, since one French faction took up the English cause and the English monarch's claim to the throne of France.

The German Monarchy

England and France had developed strong national monarchies in the High Middle Ages. By the end of the fourteenth century, they seemed in danger of disintegrat-

ing due to dynastic problems and the pressures generated by the Hundred Years' War. In contrast, the Holy Roman Empire, whose core consisted of the lands of Germany, had already begun to fall apart in the High Middle Ages. Northern Italy, which the German emperors had tried to include in their medieval empire, had been free from any real imperial control since the end of the Hohenstaufen dynasty in the thirteenth century. In Germany itself, the failure of the Hohenstaufens ended any chance of centralized monarchical authority, and Germany became a land of hundreds of virtually independent states. These varied in size and power and included princely states, such as the duchies of Bavaria and Saxony; free imperial city-states, such as Nuremberg; modest territories of petty imperial knights; and ecclesiastical states, such as the archbishopric of Cologne. In the latter states, an ecclesiastical official, such as a bishop, archbishop, or abbot, served in a dual capacity as an administrative official of the Catholic church and secular lord over the territories of his ecclesiastical state. Although all of the rulers of these different states had some obligations to the German king and Holy Roman emperor, increasingly they acted independently of the German ruler.

Because of its unique pattern of development in the High Middle Ages, the German monarchy had become established on an elective rather than hereditary basis. This principle of election was standardized in 1356 by the Golden Bull issued by Emperor Charles IV (1346–1378). This document stated that four lay princes (the count palatine of the Rhine, the duke of Saxony, the margrave of Brandenburg, and the king of Bohemia) and three ecclesiastical rulers (the archbishops of Mainz, Trier, and Cologne) would serve as electors with the legal power to elect the "king of the Romans and future emperor, to be ruler of the world and of the Christian people."[10] "King of the Romans" was the official title of the German king; after his imperial coronation, he would also have the title emperor. The Golden Bull effectively eliminated any papal influence from the election of an emperor.

In the fourteenth century, the electoral principle further ensured that kings of Germany were generally weak. Their ability to exercise effective power depended upon the extent of their own family possessions. Two different families held the title of emperor in the fourteenth century; at the beginning of the fifteenth century, three emperors claimed the throne. Although the dispute was quickly settled, Germany entered the fifteenth century in a condition that verged on anarchy. Princes fought princes and leagues of cities. The emperors were virtually powerless to control any of it.

Italy

By the fourteenth century, Italy, too, had failed to develop a centralized monarchical state. Papal opposition to the Hohenstaufens in the thirteenth century had virtually guaranteed that. Moreover, the kingdom of Naples in the south was dominated by the house of Anjou (Sicily was ruled by the Spanish house of Aragon) while the papacy remained in shaky control of much of central Italy as rulers of the Papal States. Lack of centralized authority had enabled numerous city-states in northern Italy to remain independent of any political authority.

In the fourteenth century, then, Italy was divided into a host of petty states operating independently of one another. The numerous northern city-states engaged in constant quarrels and petty wars as cities fought each other for control of trade routes or other commercial advantages. Within the cities, classes and parties fought for control of the government. In the midst of this confusion, two general tendencies can be discerned in the fourteenth century: the replacement of republican governments by tyrants and the expansion of the larger city-states at the expense of the less powerful ones.

Nearly all the cities of northern Italy began their existence as free communes with republican governments. But in the fourteenth century, they were subjected to intense internal strife, often caused by rivalry among socioeconomic groups, such as the wealthier merchant-industrialists, the lesser artisans and shopkeepers, and a growing body of hired laborers, an incipient proletariat. In their desperation to maintain law and order, city-states resorted to temporary expedients, allowing rule by one man with dictatorial powers, known either as a *podestá* or *capitano del popolo* (captain of the people), for a limited time. Limited rule, however, soon became long-term despotism, as tyrants proved willing to use whatever force and cunning were necessary to maintain themselves in power. Eventually, such tyrants tried to legitimize their power by purchasing titles from the emperor (still nominally ruler of northern Italy as Holy Roman emperor). In this fashion, the Visconti became the dukes of Milan, the Gonzaga the marquises of Mantua, and the d'Este the dukes of Ferrara. With the major exceptions of Florence and Venice, most of the northern Italian city-states lost their republicanism to the rule of the *signore* (lords or despots).

Another change of great significance was the development of larger, regional states as the larger states expanded at the expense of the smaller ones. To fight their battles, city-states came to rely on mercenary soldiers directed by leaders called *condottieri*, who sold the ser-

vices of their bands to the highest bidder. Like the bands of "free companies" in the Hundred Years' War, these mercenaries wreaked havoc on the countryside, living by blackmail and looting when they were not actively engaged in battles. Many were foreigners who flocked to Italy during the periods of truce of the Hundred Years' War. Sir John Hawkwood, called Giovanni Acuto by the Italians, was the most respectable of the fourteenth-century *condottieri*. By the end of the fourteenth century and beginning of the fifteenth, three major states came to dominate northern Italy, the despotic state of Milan and the republican states of Florence and Venice.

Milan had been the chief center of opposition to the Holy Roman emperors in the twelfth and thirteenth centuries. Located in the rich land of the Po valley at the junction of the chief trade routes from Italian coastal cities to the Alpine passes, Milan was one of the richest city-states in Italy. Politically, it was also one of the most agitated. Constant rivalry between the nobles who possessed rich estates in the surrounding countryside and the wealthy merchant class within the city enabled a family known as the Visconti to enhance their own power. Already by 1322, the Visconti had established themselves as hereditary despots of Milan. Giangaleazzo Visconti, who ruled from 1385 to 1402, transformed this despotism into an hereditary duchy by purchasing the title of duke from the emperor in 1395. Under Giangaleazzo's direction, the duchy of Milan extended its power over all of Lombardy and even threatened to conquer much of northern Italy until the duke's untimely death before the gates of Florence in 1402.

Florence, like the other Italian towns, was initially a free commune dominated by a patrician class of nobles known as the *grandi*. But the rapid expansion of Florence's economy made possible the development of a wealthy merchant-industrialist class known as the *popolo grasso*—literally the "fat people." In 1293, the *popolo grasso* assumed a dominant role in government by establishing a new constitution known as the Ordinances of Justice. With some alterations, it remained Florence's basic constitution. It provided for a republican government controlled by the seven major guilds of the city, which represented the interests of the wealthier classes. Executive power was vested in the hands of a council of elected priors (the *signoria*) and a standard-bearer of justice called the *gonfaloniere*, assisted by a number of councils with advisory and overlapping powers. Near the mid-fourteenth century, revolutionary activity by the *popolo minuto*, the small shopkeepers and artisans, won them a share in the government. Even greater expansion occurred briefly when the *ciompi*, or industrial wool

Chronology

▼ ▼ ▼

The States of Western and Central Europe

England	
Edward III	1327–1377
Richard II	1377–1399
Henry IV	1399–1413
France	
Philip VI	1328–1350
John II	1350–1364
Capture at Poitiers	1356
Crushing of the *Jacquerie* and Etienne Marcel	1358
Charles V	1364–1380
Charles VI	1380–1422
The German Monarchy	
The Golden Bull	1356
Italy	
Milan	
Visconti Establish Themselves as Rulers of Milan	1322
Giangaleazzo Visconti Purchases Title of Duke	1395
Florence	
Ordinances of Justice	1293
Venice	
Closing of Great Council	1297

workers, were allowed to be represented in the government after their revolt in 1378. Only four years later, however, a counterrevolution brought the "fat people" back into virtual control of the government. After 1382, the Florentine government was controlled by a small merchant oligarchy that manipulated the supposedly republican government. By that time, Florence had also been successful in a series of wars against its neighbors and had conquered most of Tuscany and established itself as a major territorial state in northern Italy.

The other major northern Italian state was the republic of Venice, which had grown rich from commercial activity throughout the eastern Mediterranean and into northern Europe. A large number of merchant families became extremely wealthy. In the constitution of 1297, these patricians took control of the republic. In this year, the Great Council, the source of all political power, was closed to all but the members of about two hundred families who had been represented there in the past.

Since all other magistrates of the city were either chosen from or by this council, these families now formed an hereditary patriciate that completely dominated the city. Although the doge (or duke) had been the executive head of the republic since the Early Middle Ages, by 1300 he had become largely a figurehead. Actual power was vested in the hands of the Great Council and the legislative body known as the Senate while an extraordinary body known as the Council of Ten, first formed in 1310, came to be the real executive power of the state. Venetian government was respected by contemporaries for its stability. A sixteenth-century Italian historian noted that Venice had "the best government of any city not only in our own times but also in the classical world."[11] It should be noted, however, that the relative secrecy in which the government of Venice was run gave an impression of harmony that sometimes belied the intense rivalry for power and subsequent discord that existed within the patrician class itself.

In the fourteenth century, Venice also embarked on a policy of expansion. By the end of the fourteenth century, it had created a commercial empire by establishing colonies and trading posts in the eastern Mediterranean and Black Sea as well as continuing its commercial monopolies in the Byzantine Empire. At the same time, Venice embarked upon the conquest of a territorial state in northern Italy.

▼ The Decline of the Church

The papacy of the Roman Catholic church reached the height of its power in the thirteenth century. Theories of papal supremacy included a doctrine of "fullness of power" as the spiritual head of Christendom and claims to universal temporal authority over all secular rulers. But the growing secular monarchies of Europe presented a challenge to papal claims of temporal supremacy. The papacy competed with these states by centralizing its administration, developing a competent bureaucracy, and creating a system of taxation to support the bureaucracy. Its repeated claims of temporal authority, however, led the papacy into a conflict with these territorial states that it was unable to win. Papal defeat, in turn, led to other crises that brought into question and undermined not only the pope's temporal authority over all Christendom, but his spiritual authority as well.

Boniface VIII and the Conflict with the State

The struggle between the papacy and the secular monarchies began during the reign of Pope Boniface VIII (1294–1303). On the surface, two issues appeared to be at stake between the pope and King Philip IV (1285–1314) of France and Edward I (1272–1307) of England. The kings, in their desire to acquire new rev-

▼ **Pope Boniface VIII.** Although the papacy claimed temporal supremacy as well as spiritual supremacy, its claims were challenged by the developing secular monarchies of Europe. This conflict between church and state reached its height in the struggle between Pope Boniface VIII and Philip IV of France. Boniface VIII is pictured here presiding over a gathering of cardinals.

Boniface VIII's Defense of Papal Supremacy
▼ ▼ ▼

One of the more remarkable documents of the fourteenth century was the exaggerated statement of papal supremacy issued by Pope Boniface VIII in 1302 in the heat of his conflict with the French king Philip IV. Ironically, this strongest statement ever made of papal supremacy was issued at a time when the rising power of the secular monarchies made it increasingly difficult for the premises to be accepted. Not long after issuing it, Boniface was taken prisoner by the French. Although freed by his fellow Italians, the humiliation of his defeat led to his death a short time later.

Pope Boniface VIII, *Unam Sanctam*

We are compelled, our faith urging us, to believe and to hold—and we do firmly believe and simply confess—that there is one holy catholic and apostolic church, outside of which there is neither salvation nor remission of sins . . . . In this church there is one Lord, one faith and one baptism. . . . Therefore, of this one and only church there is one body and one head . . . Christ, namely, and the vicar of Christ, St. Peter, and the successor of Peter. For the Lord himself said to Peter, feed my sheep. . . .

We are told by the word of the gospel that in this His fold there are two swords—a spiritual, namely, and a temporal. . . . Both swords, the spiritual and the material, therefore, are in the power of the church; the one, indeed, to be wielded for the church, the other by the church; the one by the hand of the priest, the other by the hand of kings and knights, but at the will and sufferance of the priest. One sword, moreover, ought to be under the other, and the temporal authority to be subjected to the spiritual. . . .

Therefore if the earthly power err it shall be judged by the spiritual power; but if the lesser spiritual power err, by the greater. But if the greatest, it can be judged by God alone, not by man, the apostle bearing witness. A spiritual man judges all things, but he himself is judged by no one. This authority, moreover, even though it is given to man and exercised through man, is not human but rather divine, being given by divine lips to Peter and founded on a rock for him and his successors through Christ himself whom he has confessed; the Lord himself saying to Peter: "Whatsoever thou shalt bind, etc." Whoever, therefore, resists this power thus ordained by God, resists the ordination of God. . . .

Indeed, we declare, announce and define, that it is altogether necessary to salvation for every human creature to be subject to the Roman pontiff.

---

enues for war, expressed the right to tax the clergy of their countries. Boniface VIII claimed that the clergy of any state could not pay taxes to their secular ruler without the pope's consent. A second issue arose over the clergy's claim of immunity from royal (or secular) courts. The kings claimed that they had a right to judge clerics in royal courts on certain crimes, such as treason against the king.

These two issues were secondary, however. Underlying them was a basic conflict between the claims of the papacy to universal authority over both church and state, which necessitated complete control over the clergy, and the claims of the monarchs that all subjects, including ecclesiastics, were under the jurisdiction of the crown and subject to the king's authority on matters of taxation and justice. In short, the fundamental issue was the universal sovereignty of the papacy versus the royal sovereignty of the monarchs.

Boniface VIII attempted to assert his position by issuing a series of papal bulls or letters, the most important of which was *Unam Sanctam*, issued in 1302. It was the strongest statement ever made by a pope on the supremacy of the spiritual authority over the temporal authority (see the box above). Its statements, such as "The temporal authority ought to be subject to the spiritual power," and "If the earthly power errs it shall be judged by the spiritual power," made clear papal claims to temporal supremacy. When it became apparent that the pope had decided to act upon these principles by excommunicating Philip IV of France, the latter decided to preempt the pope's action.

To resolve the conflict, Philip IV had the French clergy issue a summons for Boniface VIII to appear on charges of heresy. A small contingent of French forces under the royal lawyer William de Nogaret was sent to capture Boniface and bring him back to France for trial.

The pope was captured in Anagni, although Italian nobles from the surrounding countryside soon rescued the pope from Nogaret's clutches. The shock of this experience, however, soon led to the pope's death. Philip's strong-arm tactics had produced a clear victory for the national monarchy over the papacy since no later pope dared renew the extravagant claims of Boniface VIII. To ensure his position and avoid any future papal threat, Philip IV brought enough pressure to bear on the college of cardinals to achieve the election of a Frenchman as pope in 1305, Clement V (1305–1314). Using the excuse of turbulence in the city of Rome, the new pope took up residence in Avignon on the east bank of the Rhone River. Although Avignon was located in the Holy Roman Empire and was not a French possession, it lay just across the river from the possessions of King Philip IV. Clement may have intended to return to Rome, but he and his successors remained in Avignon for the next seventy-five years, which created yet another crisis for the church.

The Papacy at Avignon (1305–1378)

The residency of the popes in Avignon for almost three-quarters of the fourteenth century led to a decline in papal prestige and a growing antipapal sentiment. The city of Rome was the traditional capital of the universal church. The pope was the bishop of Rome, and his position was based upon being the successor to the apostle Peter, the first bishop of Rome. It was quite unseemly that the head of the Catholic church should reside in Avignon instead of Rome. Although the Avignonese popes frequently announced their intention to return to Rome, the political turmoil in the Papal States in central Italy always gave them an excuse to postpone their departure. In the decades of the 1330s, the popes began to construct a stately palace in Avignon, a clear indication that they intended to stay for some time.

Other factors also led to a decline in papal prestige during the Avignonese residency. It was widely believed that the popes at Avignon were captives of the French monarchy. Although questionable, since Avignon did not belong to the French monarchy, it was easy to believe in view of Avignon's proximity to French lands. Moreover, during the seventy-three years of the Avignonese papacy, of the 134 new cardinals created by the popes, 113 of them were French. Understandably, then, others viewed the papacy as captive to French interests. It would appear, however, that papal policy in the fourteenth century was consistent in itself and not simply an instrument of the kings of France.

The papal residency at Avignon was also an important turning point in the church's attempt to adapt itself to the changing economic and political conditions of Europe. Like the growing monarchical states, the popes centralized their administration by developing a specialized bureaucracy. In fact, the papal bureaucracy in the fourteenth century became the most sophisticated administrative system in the medieval world. Under the leadership of the pope and college of cardinals, it was divided into four major units: the papal penitentiary oversaw ecclesiastical discipline and issued papal pardons; the chancery prepared and sent out papal letters and documents; the Roman rota was responsible for judicial affairs and served as a court of appeals for cases referred to it by the pope; and the papal chamber or treasury encompassed the various departments dealing with the collection and dispersal of the vast revenues of the church. Together, these administrative units constituted an increasingly specialized and efficient bureaucratic machine.

At the same time, the popes extended their right of provision, or the power to appoint incumbents to vacant benefices. A benefice was an ecclesiastical foundation that consisted of a sacred office and the right of the holder to the annual revenues from the endowment. The Avignonese popes extended the categories of benefices reserved for papal provision until they included most major elective offices (archbishops, bishops, abbots) as well as a large number of lesser offices (canons and parish rectors). This right of provision came to be used in a manipulative way and led to serious abuses. Popes rewarded cardinals by giving them a number of benefices (a practice known as pluralism). Since pluralists were frequently absent and simply paid substitutes to perform their duties, the practice led to low levels of performance. Widespread pluralism and absenteeism caused a decline in effective pastoral work.

The right of papal provision was closely related to the raising of new revenues. Popes streamlined tax collection by dividing Christendom into districts. They created new taxes as well. Benefices acquired by papal provision were subject to services, a tax of one-third of the annual revenues of benefices above 100 florins in value held by archbishops, bishops, and abbots. Annates were a tax of the first year's revenue from benefices under 100 florins in value. When benefices were temporarily vacant, popes claimed the right to collect all revenues. Although steady revenues from ecclesiastical offices meant a drastic increase in papal income, such taxes and payments were often hard on the clergy, especially in light of fourteenth-century economic conditions. The failure to pay such taxes was enforced by the use of excommunication.

The use of excommunication to force clerics to pay taxes did not improve people's opinion of the pope's use of his spiritual authority. Furthermore, the splendor in which the pope and cardinals were living in Avignon led to a highly vocal criticism of both clergy and papacy in the fourteenth century. Avignon had become a powerful symbol of abuses within the church. At last, Pope Gregory XI, perceiving the disastrous decline in papal prestige, returned to Rome in 1377. His untimely death shortly afterward, however, soon gave rise to an even greater crisis for the Catholic church.

Chronology
▼ ▼ ▼
The Decline of the Church

Pope Boniface VIII	1294–1303
Unam Sanctam	1302
The Papacy at Avignon	1305–1378
Pope Gregory XI Returns to Rome	1377
The Great Schism Begins	1378
Pope Urban VI	1378–1389
Failure of Council of Pisa to End Schism	1409

The Great Schism

Gregory XI (1370–1378) died in Rome in the spring of 1378. When the college of cardinals met in conclave to elect a new pope, the citizens of Rome, fearful that the French majority would choose another Frenchman who would return the papacy to Avignon, threatened that the cardinals would not leave Rome alive unless a Roman or Italian were elected pope. Indeed, the guards of the conclave warned the cardinals that they "ran the risk of being torn in pieces" if they did not choose an Italian. Wisely, the terrified cardinals duly elected the Italian archbishop of Bari as Pope Urban VI (1378–1389), who was subsequently crowned on Easter Sunday. Following his election, Urban VI made clear his plans to reform the papal curia and even to swamp the college of cardinals with enough new Italian cardinals to eliminate the French majority. After many of the cardinals (the French ones) withdrew from Rome in late summer and were finally free of the Roman mob, they issued a manifesto, saying that they had been coerced by the mob and that Urban's election was therefore null and void. The dissenting cardinals thereupon chose one of their number, a Frenchman, who took the title of Clement VII and promptly returned to Avignon. Since Urban remained in Rome, there were now two popes, initiating what has been called the Great Schism of the church. Europe became divided in its loyalties: France, Spain, Scotland, and southern Italy supported Clement, while England, Germany, Scandinavia, and most of Italy supported Urban. These divisions generally followed political lines. Since the French supported the Avignonese, so did their allies; their enemies, particularly England and its allies, supported the Roman pope. The need for political support caused both popes to subordinate their policies to the policies of these states.

The Great Schism lasted for nearly forty years and had a baleful effect upon the Catholic church and Christendom in general. The schism greatly aggravated the financial abuses that had developed within the church during the Avignonese papacy. Two papal administrative systems (with only one-half the accustomed revenues) worked to increase taxation. At the same time, the schism badly damaged the faith of Christian believers. The pope was widely believed to be the leader of Christendom and, as Boniface VIII had pointed out, held the keys to the kingdom of heaven. Since both lines of popes denounced the other as the antichrist, such a spectacle could not help but undermine the institution that had become the very foundation of the church. The Great Schism introduced doctrinal uncertainty into the daily lives of ordinary Christians.

New Thoughts on Church and State and the Rise of Conciliarism

The conflict between church and state in the reign of Boniface VIII and the crises caused by the Avignonese papacy and Great Schism led to radical critiques of papal power and revolutionary approaches to solving the church's institutional problems. One of the earliest and certainly the most systematic was provided by Marsiglio of Padua (1270?–1342), rector of the University of Paris and author of the remarkable book, *Defender of the Peace*.

This book argued for a radical reversal of the roles traditionally allotted by papal theorists to the spiritual and temporal powers. Marsiglio championed the autonomy of the secular state and not only denied that the temporal authority was subject to the spiritual as popes from Innocent III to Boniface VIII had argued, but went so far as to make the church, which he viewed as only one element of society, part of the secular state with respect to temporal affairs. In effect, the church is subject to the state in secular matters. The church, then, must confine itself solely to spiritual functions. Furthermore, Marsiglio argued that the church was a community of the faithful in which all authority is ultimately derived from the entire community. The church, therefore, comprised all Christians, both lay people and clergy. The only difference between them was not of divine origin, but human, namely, that the authority of the clergy was simply a delegated authority for administrative ends. Final authority in spiritual matters must reside not with the pope but with a general church council representing all members. As Marsiglio stated it: "Doubtful sentences of divine law, especially on those matters which are called articles of the Christian faith, . . . must be defined only by the general council of the believers, . . . no partial group or individual person of whatever status [the pope], has the authority to make such definitions."[12]

As dissatisfaction with the papacy grew, so also did the number of people who espoused the conciliar idea. It was the Great Schism, however, that led large numbers of serious churchmen to take up the theory of conciliarism in the belief that only a general council of the church could end the schism and bring reform to the church in its "head and members." The only serious issue left to be decided was who should call the council. Canon law held that only a pope could convene a council. Professors of theology and canon law argued, however, that since the competing popes would not do so, either members of the church hierarchy or even secular princes, especially the Holy Roman emperor, could convene a council to settle all relevant issues.

In desperation, a group of cardinals from both lines of popes finally heeded these theoretical formulations and convened a general council on their own. This Council of Pisa, which met in 1409, deposed the two popes and eventually elected a new but sorry choice, Pope John XXIII, viewed by one contemporary as a man "great in temporal things, but a zero in spiritual ones." The council's action proved disastrous when the two deposed popes refused to step down. There were now three popes, and the church seemed more hopelessly divided than ever.

Popular Religion in an Age of Adversity

The concern of popes and leading clerics with finances and power in the struggles of Boniface VIII, the Avignonese papacy, and the Great Schism could not help but lead to a decline in prestige and respect for the institutional church, especially the papacy. At the same time, in the fourteenth century, the Black Death and its recurrences made an important impact on the religious life of ordinary Christians by heightening their preoccupation with death and salvation. The church often failed to provide sufficient spiritual comfort as many parish priests fled from the plague. In certain English dioceses, for example, as many as 20 percent of the parish clergy abandoned their parishes.

Christians responded in different ways to the adversities of the fourteenth century. First of all, there was a tendency to stress the performance of good works, including acts of charity, as a means of assuring salvation. This was visible in the increase of bequests in wills to hospitals and other charitable foundations. In London, before 1348, 5 percent of the wills registered in court left a bequest to hospitals. From 1350 to 1360, 15 percent did so while the average bequest increased by 40 percent. Another sign of the heightened concern for salvation was the creation of family chapels served by chantry priests whose primary responsibility was to say masses for the good of the deceased's soul. These became even more significant as the importance of purgatory rose. Purgatory came to be defined by the church as the state in which souls existed after death so that they could be purged of the punishment due to the consequences of sin. In effect, the soul was purified in purgatory before it ascended into heaven. It was believed that, like indulgences, prayers and private masses for the dead could shorten the amount of time souls spent in purgatory.

All of these developments are part of a larger trend—a new emphasis in late medieval Christianity on a mechanical path to salvation. Chalking up good deeds to ensure salvation was done in numerous ways, but was nowhere more evident than in the growing emphasis in the decade of the 1350s on indulgences made possible by the "treasury of merits" or the good deeds of Christ and the saints (see Chapter 10). We should also note that pilgrimages, which became increasingly popular, and charitable contributions were good works that could be accomplished without the involvement of clerics, a reflection of the loss of faith in the institutional church and its clergy and another noticeable feature of popular religious life. But while there was an evident loss of faith in the hierarchical or institutional church, there was not a decline in interest in Christianity itself. This is particularly evident in the popularity of mysticism and lay piety in the fourteenth century.

MYSTICISM AND LAY PIETY   The mysticism of the fourteenth century was certainly not new, for Christians

A Mystical Visionary of the Fourteenth Century
▼ ▼ ▼

The fourteenth century witnessed a significant outpouring of mystical literature which, in turn, sparked a popular movement of lay piety, especially in the Low Countries and along the Rhine River. This selection is taken from the work of Richard Rolle, probably the most influential of the fourteenth-century English mystics. Rolle taught that the soul is capable of achieving a mystical union with God by surrendering to the Divine Being, which he called pure love.

Richard Rolle, *The Fire of Love*

Chapter 5

In all our actions and thoughts let us give greater weight to divine love than to learning and argument. For love delights the soul and sweetens the conscience, drawing it away from the attraction of lesser delights and the appetite for personal distinction. Learning without charity contributes nothing to eternal salvation but blows a man up to miserable perdition. May our spirit therefore be strong in taking upon itself hard labours for God; may it yearn to glow with wisdom eternal and to burn with that sweet flame which excites man to love and desire solely his Maker and be given powerful strength to despise all transitory things. Thus [the soul] puts away trust in the solace of things which do not endure, as one having there no dwelling place, but incessantly seeks that place to come which is not made by hands, and cries "For to me to live is Christ and to die is gain."

Chapter 13

There have been some men, and perhaps they still exist, who altogether prefer the communal to the solitary life; they hold that we must run in crowds if we desire to reach the highest perfection. One cannot seriously argue with such men because they praise only that kind of life which they would wish to follow or at least have known a little. They fail to praise the solitary life simply because they do not know it. For it is a life which no one living in the flesh can know except he to whom God grants that he live it, and no one assuredly judges rightly of this matter who remains uncertain what it is and how it works. I know beyond doubt that if they knew it they would praise it more to others. Others err more dangerously by unceasingly denouncing and slandering the solitary life. They say, "Woe to the solitary," meaning not only "man without God" but "man without fellows." For he is alone with whom God is not. When he shall fall into death he shall at once be taken to the torments and shall for ever be cut off from the sight of God's glory and the saints'. Indeed, he who chooses the solitary life for God and lives it rightly shall be full not of "Woe" but of "Wonderful Virtue" and shall continuously delight in thinking of the name of Jesus.

throughout the Middle Ages had claimed to have had mystical experiences. Mysticism did have a particularly strong impact in the fourteenth century, however, especially along the Rhine River in Germany and in the Low Countries.

Simply defined, mysticism is the immediate experience of oneness with God (see the box above). It is this experience that characterized the teaching of Meister Eckhart (1260–1327), who sparked a mystical movement in western Germany. Eckhart was a well educated Dominican theologian who wrote learned Latin works filled with speculative theology. He was also a popular preacher whose message on the union of the soul with God was typical of mysticism. According to Eckhart, such a union was attainable for those who pursued it wholeheartedly. He referred to this spiritual encounter as the "birth of Christ" in the soul.

Eckhart's mystical teachings were carried on by his disciples and pupils. One in particular, Johannes Tauler (c. 1300–1361), was significant in channeling German mysticism into a practical direction as an inspiration to inner piety or an inwardness of religious feeling. Tauler's sermons concentrated on the same idea of the union of the soul with God, but they also focused on the need to prepare the soul for the mystical encounter by expressing the love of God in the ordinary activities of everyday life. Tauler's ideas deepened the religious life of clerics and lay folk and connected mysticism to the development of the lay piety that became more visible as Eckhart's and Tauler's movement spread from Germany into the Low Countries.

In the Low Countries, German mysticism was transformed into a new form called the Modern Devotion, whose founder was Gerard Groote (1340–1384). Groote was a canon lawyer, but after a religious conversion, he entered a monastery for several years of contemplation before reentering the world. Although he never became a priest, he was ordained as a deacon, entitling him to preach. His messages were typical of a practical mysticism. To achieve true spiritual communion with God, people must imitate Christ and lead lives dedicated to serving the needs of their fellow human beings.

Eventually, Groote attracted a group of followers who came to be known as the Brothers of the Common Life. From this small beginning, a movement developed that spread through the Netherlands and back into Germany. Houses of the Brothers, as well as separate houses for women (Sisters of the Common Life), were founded in one city after another. The Sisters and Brothers of the Common Life did not constitute regular religious orders. They were lay people who took no formal monastic vows, but were nevertheless regulated by quasi-monastic rules that they imposed on their own communities. They also established schools throughout Germany and the Netherlands in which they stressed their message of imitating the life of Christ by serving others. The Brothers and Sisters of the Common Life attest to the vitality of spiritual life among lay Christians in the fourteenth century. It is interesting to note, however, that popes feared the movement since it was not closely controlled by the ecclesiastical establishment.

▼ The Intellectual and Cultural World of the Fourteenth Century

The intellectual world of the fourteenth century was also characterized by ferment and disintegration, especially evidenced in the breakdown of the grand synthesis attempted by Thomas Aquinas.

Late Medieval Scholasticism

In the thirteenth century, Thomas Aquinas's grand synthesis of faith and reason was not widely accepted outside his own Dominican order. At the same time, differences with Aquinas were kept within a framework of commonly accepted scholastic thought. In the fourteenth century, however, the philosopher William of Occam (1285–1329) posed a severe challenge to the scholastic achievements of the High Middle Ages.

Occam posited a radical interpretation of nominalism. He asserted that all universals or general concepts were simply names and that only individual objects perceived by the senses were real. Although the mind was capable of analyzing individual objects or observable phenomena, it could not establish any truths about the nature of external, higher reality. Reason could not be used to substantiate spiritual truths. It could not, for example, prove the statement that "God exists." For William of Occam as a Christian believer, this did not mean that God did not exist, however. It simply indicated that the truths of religion were not demonstrable by reason, but could only be known by an act of faith. At the same time, Occam believed that an unbounded will allowed God infinite freedom to act. The acceptance of Occam's nominalist philosophy at the University of Paris brought an element of uncertainty to late medieval theology by seriously weakening the synthesis of faith and reason that had characterized the theological thought of the High Middle Ages. Nevertheless, Occam's emphasis on using reason to analyze the observable phenomena of the world had an important impact on the development of physical science by creating support for rational and scientific analysis. Some late medieval theologians came to accept the compatibility of rational analysis of the material world with mystical acceptance of spiritual truths.

Vernacular Literature

Although the fourteenth century witnessed severe political problems and even disintegration of some of the evolving national monarchical states, a sense of national consciousness continued to develop in the form of vernacular literature. The spoken vernacular tongues had been used in Europe for centuries, while a written vernacular literature had produced some notable works in early versions of French and German. Although Latin remained the language of the church liturgy and the official documents of both church and state, national languages, the vernaculars, came to be used widely in the fourteenth century. This was particularly evident in Italy where a vernacular literature had been largely lacking until the second half of the thirteenth century.

The development of an Italian vernacular literature was mostly the result of the efforts of three writers in the fourteenth century, Dante, Petrarch and Boccaccio. Their use of the Tuscan dialect common in Florence and its surrounding countryside ensured that it would become the basis of the modern Italian language.

Dante(1265–1321) came from an old Florentine noble family that had fallen upon hard times. Although he

Dante's Vision of Hell
▼ ▼ ▼

The Divine Comedy of Dante Alighieri is regarded as one of the greatest literary works of all time. Many consider it the supreme summary of medieval thought. It combines allegory with a remarkable amount of contemporary history. Indeed, forty-three of the seventy-nine people consigned to hell in the "Inferno" were Florentines. This excerpt is taken from Canto XVIII of the "Inferno," in which Dante and Virgil visit the eighth circle of hell, which is divided into ten trenches containing those who had committed malicious frauds upon their fellow human beings.

Dante, "Inferno," The Divine Comedy

We had already come to where the walk
crosses the second bank, from which it lifts
another arch, spanning from rock to rock.

Hear we heard people whine in the next chasm,
and knock and thump themselves with open palms,
and blubber through their snouts as if in a spasm.

Steaming from that pit, a vapor rose
over the banks, crusting them with a slime
that sickened my eyes and hammered at my nose.

That chasm sinks so deep we could not sight
its bottom anywhere until we climbed
along the rock arch to its greatest height.

Once there, I peered down; and I saw long lines
of people in a river of excrement
that seemed the overflow of the world's latrines.

I saw among the felons of that pit
one wraith who might or might not have been
   tonsured—
one could not tell, he was so smeared with shit.

He bellowed: "You there, why do you stare at me
more than at all the others in this stew?"
And I to him: "Because if memory

serves me, I knew you when your hair was dry.
You are Alessio Interminelli da Lucca.
That's why I pick you from this filthy fry."

And he then, beating himself on his clown's head:
"Down to this have the flatteries I sold
the living sunk me here among the dead."

And my Guide prompted then: "Lean forward a bit
and look beyond him, there—do you see that one
scratching herself with dungy nails, the strumpet

who fidgets to her feet, then to a crouch?
It is the whore Thäis who told her lover
when he sent to ask her, 'Do you thank me much?'

'Much? Nay, past all believing!' And with this
Let us turn from the sight of this abyss."

---

had held high political office in republican Florence, factional conflict led to his exile from the city in 1302. Until the end of his life, Dante hoped to return to his beloved Florence; his wish remained unfulfilled.

Dante's masterpiece in the Italian vernacular was his *Divine Comedy*, written between 1313 and 1321. Cast in a typical medieval framework, the *Divine Comedy* is basically the story of the soul's progression to salvation, a fundamental medieval preoccupation. The lengthy poem was divided into three major sections corresponding to the realms of the afterworld: hell, purgatory, and heaven or paradise. In the "Inferno," Dante is led on an imaginary journey through hell by his guide, the classical author Virgil. Allegorically, the "Inferno" reflects despair, while "Purgatory," the second stage of his journey, reflects hope. In "Paradise," Dante is eventually guided by Saint Bernard, a symbol of mystical contemplation. The saint turns Dante over to the Virgin Mary since grace is necessary to achieve the final step of entering the presence of God, where one beholds "The love that moves the sun and the other stars."[13] Allegorically, "Paradise" reflects perfection or salvation (see the box above).

Some scholars have considered the *Divine Comedy* a synthesis of medieval Christian thought. Like the Gothic cathedrals and the *Summa Theologica*, it reminds

▼ **Dante, *The Divine Comedy*.** Italian vernacular literature was developed largely through the efforts of three fourteenth-century writers, Dante, Petrarch, and Boccaccio. Dante's chief work is the *Divine Comedy*, a lengthy poem that describes a journey through Hell, Purgatory, and finally Heaven. Dante's work is often considered to be a synthesis of medieval Christian thought. Pictured here is an early frontispiece from a manuscript of the *Divine Comedy*.

us that Christian faith was, after all, the basic foundation of medieval culture. The theology of the *Divine Comedy* is that of Saint Thomas Aquinas; its science is that of Aristotle; and its politics centers on the Holy Roman emperor as the savior of Italy. At the same time, some observers believe elements of Dante's work foreshadow the coming new age of the Renaissance. Dante, after all, is a layman describing theology in the vernac-

ular, not Latin. The popes who turn up in hell have been consigned there by a layman. Dante, for example, put his old enemy, Boniface VIII, in a special corner of hell. Moreover, using Virgil as his guide emphasizes the role of the classical tradition in providing wisdom, a theme that became increasingly important in the Renaissance. In addressing Virgil, Dante says, "Canst thou be Virgil? . . . Thou art my master. . . . From thee alone I learned the singing strain, The noble style, that does me honor now."[14]

Like Dante, Petrarch was a Florentine who spent much of his life outside his native city. Petrarch's role in the revival of the classics made him a seminal figure in the literary Italian Renaissance (see Chapter 13). His primary contribution to the development of the Italian vernacular was made in his sonnets. He is considered to be one of the greatest European lyric poets. His sonnets were inspired by his love for a married lady named Laura, whom he had met in 1327. While honoring an idealized female figure was a longstanding medieval tradition, Laura was very human and not just an ideal. She was a real woman with whom Petrarch was involved for a long time. He poured forth his lamentations in sonnet after sonnet:

> *I am as tired of thinking as my thought*
> *Is never tired to find itself in you,*
> *And of not yet leaving this life that brought*
> *Me the too heavy weight of signs and rue;*
>
> *And because to describe your hair and face*
> *And the fair eyes of which I always speak,*
> *Language and sound have not become too weak*
> *And day and night your name they still embrace.*
>
> *And tired because my feet do not yet fail*
> *After following you in every part,*
> *Wasting so many steps without avail,*
>
> *From whence derive the paper and the ink*
> *That I have filled with you; if I should sink,*
> *It is the fault of Love, not of my art.*[15]

Petrarch's lamentations over his inability to gain his lady's love were in the medieval tradition. Yet in analyzing every aspect of the unrequited lover's feelings, he appeared less concerned to sing his lady's praise than to immortalize his own thoughts. This "psychology of love" and interest in his own personality reveal a sense of individuality stronger than in any previous medieval literature.

Although he too wrote poetry, Boccaccio (1313–1375) is primarily known for his contributions to the development of Italian prose. Another Florentine, he also used the Tuscan dialect. While working for the Bardi banking house in Naples, he fell in love with a noble lady whom he called his Fiammetta, his Little Flame. Under her inspiration, Boccaccio began to write prose romances. His best-known work, *The Decameron*, however, was not written until after he had returned to Florence. *The Decameron* is set at the time of the Black Death. Ten young people flee to a villa outside Florence to escape the plague and decide to while away the time by telling stories. Although the stories are not new and still reflect the acceptance of basic Christian values, Boccaccio does present the society of his time from a secular point of view. Boccaccio stresses cleverness and wit rather than piety and devotion. It is the seducer of women, not the knight or philosopher or pious monk, who is the real hero. Perhaps, as some historians have argued, *The Decameron* reflects the immediate easygoing, cynical postplague values. Boccaccio's later work cer-

tainly became gloomier and more pessimistic; as he grew older, he even rejected his earlier work as irrelevant. He commented in a 1373 letter that "I am certainly not pleased that you have allowed the illustrious women in your house to read my trifles. . . . You know how much in them is less than decent and opposed to modesty, how much stimulation to wanton lust, how many things that drive to lust even those most fortified against it."[16]

In the fourteenth century, one of the world's truly gifted poets, Geoffrey Chaucer (c. 1340–1400), brought a new level of sophistication to the English vernacular language in his famous work *The Canterbury Tales*. His beauty of expression and clear, forceful language were important in transforming his East Midland dialect into the chief ancestor of the modern English language. Although Chaucer's materials were taken from a typically medieval literary tradition, he placed much emphasis on individual characters.

The Canterbury Tales constitute a group of stories told by a group of twenty-nine pilgrims journeying from Southwark to the tomb of Saint Thomas at Canterbury. This format gave Chaucer the chance to portray an entire range of English society, both high and low born.

▼ **Giotto, *Pieta*.** In addition to work influenced by the plague, fourteenth-century art moved away from medieval traditions in various ways. The work of Giotto marked the first clear innovation, transcending the Byzantine school from which he arose by his desire to imitate nature. Considered by many as a forerunner of the Renaissance, later artists identified his naturalism as the fundamental element in classical art. In this fresco, the solidity of Giotto's human figures give them a sense of three-dimensionality.

Among others, he presented the Knight, the Squire, the Yeoman, the Prioress, the Monk, the Merchant, the Student, the Lawyer, the Carpenter, the Cook, the Doctor, the Plowman, and, of course, "A Good Wife was there from beside the city of Bath—a little deaf, which was a pity." The stories these pilgrims told to while away the time on the journey were just as varied as the storytellers themselves: knightly romances, fairy tales, saints' lives, sophisticated satires, and crude stories.

Dante, Petrarch, Boccaccio, and Chaucer all contributed to the growth of written vernacular languages in the fourteenth century. Despite the revival of classical languages in the Renaissance of the fifteenth century, the future belonged not to Latin and Greek, but to the vernacular languages of the emerging European states.

Art

The fourteenth century produced an artistic outburst in new directions as well as a large body of morbid work influenced by the Black Death and the recurrence of the plague. The city of Florence witnessed the first dramatic break with medieval tradition in the work of Giotto (1266–1337), often considered a forerunner of Italian Renaissance painting. Coming out of the formal Byzantine school, Giotto transcended it with a new kind of naturalism, a desire to imitate nature that Renaissance artists later identified as the basic component of classical art. Giotto's figures are solid and rounded and provide a sense of three-dimensional depth. Although Giotto had no immediate successors, Florentine painting in the early fifteenth century pursued even more dramatically the new direction his work represents.

The Black Death made a visible impact on art. For one thing, it wiped out entire guilds of artists. At the same time, survivors, including the newly rich who patronized artists, were no longer so optimistic. Some were more guilty about enjoying life and more concerned about gaining salvation. Postplague art began to concentrate on pain and death. A fairly large number of artistic works came to be based on the *ars moriendi*, the art of dying. A morbid concern with death is particularly evident in Francesco Traini's fresco, *The Triumph of Death* in Pisa. The scene on the left where three young nobles encounter three coffins containing decomposing bodies contrasts vividly with the scene on the right where young aristocrats engage in pleasant pursuits but are threatened by a grim figure of Death in the form of a witch flying through the air swinging a large scythe. Beneath her lie piles of dead citizens and clergy cut down in the prime of life.

▼ Society in an Age of Adversity

In the midst of disaster, the fourteenth century proved creative in its own way. New inventions made an impact

▼ **Francesco Traini, *Triumph of Death.*** The plague produced a morbid fascination with death, a fascination that is visible in the art of the period. Death became an important theme in postplague art and is evident in this fresco by Francesco Traini. Even when the rich are presented as enjoying pleasant pursuits, their joy is overshadowed by the spectre of death that flies through the air holding a large scythe.

on daily life at the same time that the effects of plague were felt in many areas of medieval urban life.

Changes in Urban Life

A greater regulation of urban activities was an immediate by-product of the Black Death. Authorities tried to keep cities cleaner by new regulations against filth in the streets. Viewed as unhealthy places, bathhouses were shut down, leading to a decline in regular bathing. In fact, by the end of the fourteenth century, a new pride in not bathing had developed, especially on the part of the upper classes. In the fifteenth century, Queen Isabella of Castile boasted that she had bathed but twice, once at birth and the other the day before her marriage to Ferdinand.

Efforts at regulation also affected the practice of female prostitution. Prostitution had always been tolerated in cities during the High Middle Ages since it was considered better to allow single males to have sex with prostitutes than for them to corrupt virgins or commit adultery with other men's wives. The church attempted to discourage female prostitution by urging such women to amend their lives and built "Mary Magdalene houses" (the biblical Mary Magdalene had been a reformed prostitute) to provide shelter and food for them. Prostitution was often a profession for poor girls from the country who found it the only way to survive in the urban world.

In the late fourteenth century, cities began to regulate prostitution, licensing brothels and forcing prostitutes off the streets. Officially licensed brothels were shunted off to isolated urban areas that became known as "hot streets." It was assumed that the regulation of prostitution made it easier to supervise and hence maintain public order. Brothels were required to establish set prices for services rendered and basic guidelines for wages. City authorities inspected them on a regular basis for health reasons.

FAMILY LIFE AND GENDER ROLES IN LATE MEDIEVAL CITIES The basic unit of the late medieval urban environment was the nuclear family of husband, wife, and children. Especially in wealthier families, there might also be servants, apprentices, and other relatives, including widowed mothers and the husband's illegitimate children.

Before the Black Death, late marriages were common for urban couples. It was not unusual for husbands to be in their late thirties or forties and wives in their early twenties. The expense of beginning a household probably necessitated the delay in marriage. But the situation changed dramatically after the plague, reflecting new economic opportunities for the survivors and a new reluctance to postpone living in the presence of so much death. The economic difficulties of the fourteenth century also had a tendency to strengthen the development of gender roles created by thirteenth-century scholastic theologians and to set new limits on employment oppor-

tunities for women. Thomas Aquinas and others had offered strict polar notions about men and women that were unthinkable in earlier centuries when some women had played important roles (see Chapter 10). Based on the authority of Aristotle, Aquinas had advanced the belief that according to the natural order, men were active and domineering while women were passive and submissive. As more and more lawyers, doctors, and priests, who had been trained in universities where these notions were taught, entered society, these ideas of man's and woman's different natures became widely accepted. Increasingly, women were expected to eschew any active functions in society and remain subject to direction from males. A fourteenth-century Parisian provost commented on glass cutters that "no master's widow who keeps working at his craft after her husband's death may take on apprentices, for the men of the craft do not believe that a woman can master it well enough to teach a child to master it, for the craft is a very delicate one."[17] Although this statement suggests that some women were, in fact, running businesses, it also reveals that they were viewed as incapable of undertaking all of men's activities. Based on a pattern of gender, Europeans created a division of labor roles between men and women that continued until the Industrial Revolution of the eighteenth and nineteenth centuries.

MEDIEVAL CHILDREN   Although historians disagree in their interpretations, there seems to be sufficient evidence to indicate that medieval parents of both the High and Later Middle Ages invested considerable resources and affection in the rearing of their children. The dramatic increase in specialized roles that accompanied the spread of commerce and the growth of cities demanded a commitment to educating children in the marketable skills needed for the new occupations. Philip of Navarre noted in the twelfth century that boys ought to be taught a trade "as soon as possible. Those who early become and long remain apprentices ought to be the best masters."[18] Some cities provided schools to educate the young. A Florentine chronicler related that between eight and ten thousand boys and girls between the ages of six and twelve attended the city's grammar schools, a figure that probably represented one-half of school-aged children. Although grammar school completed education for girls, around 1,100 boys proceeded into six secondary schools that prepared them for business careers while another 600 studied Latin and logic in four other schools that readied them for university training and a career in medicine, law, or the church. In the High Middle Ages,

then, urban communities demonstrated a commitment to the training of the young.

These same communities became concerned about investing in the survival and health of children as a result of the devastating effects of the plague and its recurrences. Although a number of hospitals existed in both Florence and Rome in the fourteenth century, it was not until the 1420s and 1430s that hospitals were founded that catered only to the needs of foundlings, supporting them until boys could be taught a trade and girls could marry.

Medicine

The Black Death made a significant impact upon the existing medieval medical system, and some authorities think it created "the stirrings of modern medicine." The medical community comprised a number of different functionaries. At the top of the medical hierarchy were the physicians, usually clergymen, who received their education in the medieval universities where they studied ancient authorities, such as Hippocrates and Galen. As a result, physicians were highly trained in theory, but had little or no clinical practice. They were educated in six chief medical schools by the fourteenth century, Salerno, Montpellier, Bologna, Oxford, Padua, and Paris. The latter was regarded as the most prestigious by the time of the Black Death.

The preplague medicine of university-trained physicians was theoretically grounded in the classical theory of the "four humors," each connected to a particular organ: blood (from the heart), phlegm (from the brain), yellow bile (from the liver), and black bile (from the spleen). The four humors, in turn, corresponded to the four elemental qualities of the universe, earth (black bile), air (blood), fire (yellow bile), and water (phlegm), making a human being a microcosm of the cosmos. Good health resulted from a perfect balance of the four humors; sickness meant that the humors were out of balance. The task of the medieval physician was to restore proper order by a number of cures, such as rest, diet, herbal medicines, or bloodletting.

Beneath the physicians in the hierarchy of the medical profession stood the surgeons, whose activities included performing operations, setting broken bones, and bleeding patients. Their knowledge was largely based on practical experience. Below surgeons were the barbersurgeons, who were less trained and performed menial tasks such as bloodletting and setting simple bone fractures. They supplemented their incomes by shaving and cutting hair. Apothecaries also constituted part of the medical establishment. Although they filled herbal prescriptions recommended by physicians, they prescribed drugs on their own authority, making them similar in function to physicians.

All of these medical practitioners proved unable to deal with the plague. When King Philip VI of France requested the opinion of the medical faculty of the University of Paris on the plague, their advice proved worthless. This failure to understand the Black Death, however, produced a crisis in medieval medicine that resulted in some new approaches to health care.

One result was the rise of surgeons to greater prominence because of their practical knowledge. Surgeons were now recruited by universities, which placed them on an equal level with physicians and introduced a greater emphasis on practical anatomy into the university curriculum. Connected to this was a rise in medical textbooks, often written in the vernacular and stressing practical, "how to" approaches to medical and surgical problems. Hospitals also took on a new role. Before the plague, they were designed to isolate the sick from the rest of the population. After the Black Death, hospitals expressed a desire in curing patients. New techniques in organization and management provided better facilities. Many hospitals developed associations with doctors or medical students from nearby universities to encourage them to practice there.

Finally, as a result of the plague, cities gave increased attention to public health and sanitation. Public health laws were instituted, and municipal boards of health came into being. The primary concern of the latter was to prevent plague, but gradually they came to control almost every aspect of health and sanitation. Boards of public health, consisting of medical practitioners and public officials, were empowered to enforce sanitary conditions, report on and attempt to isolate epidemics by quarantine (rarely successful), and regulate the activities of doctors. Some communities even began to hire "plague doctors," or municipal physicians and surgeons who were paid to treat victims.

Inventions

Despite its problems, the fourteenth century witnessed a continuation of the technological innovations that had characterized the High Middle Ages. The most extraordinary of these inventions and one that made a visible impact on European cities was the clock. There had been earlier experiments with waterpowered clocks,

▼ **Medical Textbook.** While the medical theories and practices of the day proved unable to deal with the plague, the Black Death did generate new approaches to health care. Surgeons with their practical knowledge were placed on an equal level in medical faculties with physicians after the plague, and medical textbooks that stressed a more "how-to" approach to medical problems were also produced. This illustration is taken from a fourteenth-century medical textbook.

but they had obvious limitations, particularly in northern Europe where they froze in winter. The mechanical clock was invented at the end of the thirteenth century, but not perfected until the fourteenth. The time-telling clock was actually a by-product of a larger astronomical clock. The most accomplished one was constructed by Giovanni di Dondi in the mid-fourteenth century. Dondi's clock contained the signs of the zodiac, but also struck on the hour. Since clocks were expensive, they were usually installed only in the towers of churches or municipal buildings. The first clock striking equal hours was in a church in Milan, which a chronicler described in 1335 as "a wonderful clock, with a very large clapper which strikes a bell twenty-four times according to the twenty-four hours of the day and night and thus at the first hour of the night gives one sound, at the second two strikes . . . and so distinguishes one hour from another, which is of greatest use to men of every degree."[19]

Clocks introduced a wholly new conception of time into the lives of Europeans; they revolutionized how people thought about and used time. Throughout most of the Middle Ages, time was determined by natural rhythms (daybreak and nightfall) or church bells that were rung at more or less regular three-hour intervals, corresponding to the ecclesiastical offices of the church. Clocks made it possible to plan one's day and organize one's activities around the regular striking of bells. This brought a new regularity into the life of workers and merchants, defining urban existence and enabling merchants and bankers to see the value of time in a new way. Indeed, it was a conception that ultimately led them to believe that "time is money."

Like clocks, eyeglasses were introduced in the thirteenth century, but not refined until the fourteenth. Even then they were not overly effective by modern standards and were extremely expensive besides. The high cost of parchment forced people to write in extremely small script; doubtlessly, eyeglasses made it more readable. At the same time, a significant change in writing materials occurred in the fourteenth century when parchment was supplemented by much cheaper paper made from cotton rags. Although it was more subject to insect and water damage than parchment, medieval paper was actually superior to modern papers made of high-acid wood pulp.

Although invented earlier by the Chinese, gunpowder also made its appearance in the west in the fourteenth century. Its primary use was in cannons, but cannon technology was not well developed, and cannons were prone to blow up, making them as dangerous to those firing them as to the enemy.

In the eleventh, twelfth, and thirteenth centuries, European civilization developed many of its fundamental features. Territorial states, parliaments, capitalist trade and industry, banks, cities, the nuclear family, and vernacular literatures were all products of that fertile period. During the same time, the Catholic church under the direction of the papacy reached its apogee. Fourteenth-century European society, however, was challenged by an overwhelming number of disintegrative forces. Devastating plague, decline in trade and industry, bank failures, peasant revolts pitting lower classes against the upper classes, seemingly constant warfare, aristocratic factional conflict that undermined political stability, the absence of the popes from Rome, and even the spectacle of two popes condemning each other as the antichrist all seemed to overpower Europeans in this "calamitous century." Not surprisingly, much of the art of the period depicted the Four Horsemen of the Apocalypse described in the New Testament book of Revelation: Death, Famine, Pestilence, and War. No doubt, to some people it appeared that the last days of the world were at hand.

The new European society, however, proved remarkably resilient. Periods of disintegration are usually paralleled by the emergence of new ideas and new practices. Intellectuals of the period saw themselves as standing on the threshold of a new age or rebirth of the best features of classical civilization. It is their perspective that led historians to speak of a Renaissance in the fifteenth century.

Notes

▼ ▼ ▼

1. Quoted in H. S. Lucas, "The Great European Famine of 1315, 1316, and 1317," *Speculum* 5 (1930): 359.

2. Quoted in Robert Gottfried, *The Black Death: Natural and Human Disaster in Medieval Europe* (New York, 1983), p. xiii.

3. Giovanni Boccaccio, *The Decameron*, trans. Frances Winwar (New York, 1955), p. xxv.

4. Ibid., p. xxvi.

5. Jean Froissart, *Chronicles*, ed. and trans. Geoffrey Brereton (Harmondsworth, 1968), p. 111.

6. Quoted in James B. Ross and Mary M. McLaughlin, *The Portable Medieval Reader* (New York, 1949), pp. 218–19.

7. Quoted in Barbara W. Tuchman, *A Distant Mirror* (New York, 1978), p. 175.

8. Froissart, *Chronicles*, p. 212.

9. Ibid., p. 89.

10. Oliver J. Thatcher and Edgar H. McNeal, eds., *A Source Book for Medieval History* (New York, 1905), p. 288.

11. Quoted in D. S. Chambers, *The Imperial Age of Venice, 1380–1580* (London, 1970), p. 30.

12. Marsiglio of Padua, *The Defender of the Peace*, trans. Alan Gewirth (New York, 1956), 2: 426.

13. Dante Alighieri, *The Divine Comedy*, trans. Dorothy Sayers (New York, 1962), "Paradise," Canto XXXIII, line 145.

14. Ibid., "Hell," Canto I, lines 79–87.

15. Petrarch, *Sonnets and Songs*, trans. Anna Maria Armi (New York, 1968), No. LXXIV, p. 127.

16. Quoted in Millard Meiss, *Painting in Florence and Siena after the Black Death* (Princeton, N.J., 1951), p. 161.

17. Quoted in Susan Stuard, "Dominion of Gender: Women's Fortunes in the High Middle Ages," in Renate Bridenthal, Claudia Koonz, and Susan Stuard, eds., *Becoming Visible: Women in European History*, 2d ed. (Boston, 1987), p. 169.

18. Quoted in David Herlihy, "Medieval Children," in Bede K. Lackner and Kenneth R. Philp, eds., *Essays on Medieval Civilization* (Austin, 1978), p. 121.

19. Quoted in Jean Gimpel, *The Medieval Machine* (New York, 1976), p. 168.

Suggestions for Further Reading

▼ ▼ ▼

For a general introduction to the fourteenth century, see D. Hay, *Europe in the Fourteenth and Fifteenth Centuries* (New York, 1966); G. Holmes, *Europe: Hierarchy and Revolt, 1320–1450* (New York, 1975); and the well-written popular history by B. Tuchman, *A Distant Mirror* (New York, 1978).

Perhaps the best work on the Black Death is R. S. Gottfried, *The Black Death: Natural and Human Disaster in Medieval Europe* (New York, 1983). Also valuable are P. Ziegler, *The Black Death* (New York, 1969); and W. H. McNeill, *Plagues and People* (New York, 1976). On the peasant and urban revolts of the fourteenth century, see M. Mollat and P. Wolff, *The Popular Revolutions of the Late Middle Ages* (Winchester, Mass., 1973). For a vivid portrait of the world of a fourteenth-century merchant, see I. Origo, *The Merchant of Prato* (London, 1957).

The classic work on the Hundred Years' War is E. Perroy, *The Hundred Years War* (New York, 1951). The social impact of the war is described in J. Barnie, *War in Medieval English Society* (Ithaca, N.Y., 1974). On the political history of the period, see B. Guenée, *States and Rulers in Later Medieval Europe*, trans. J. Vale (Oxford, 1985); and D. Waley, *Later Medieval Europe* (New York, 1964). Works on individual countries include P. S. Lewis, *Later Medieval France: The Polity* (London, 1968); F. Pegues, *The Lawyers of the Last Capetians* (Princeton, N.J., 1962); A. R. Myers, *England in the Late Middle Ages* (Harmondsworth, 1952); and F. R. H. Du Boulay, *Germany in the Later Middle Ages* (London, 1983). On the Italian political scene, see D. P. Waley, *The Italian City-Republics* (London, 1978); and

J. Larner, *Italy in the Age of Dante and Petrarch, 1216–1380* (London, 1980). Some good specialized studies include D. G. Bueno de Mesquita, *Giangaleazzo Visconti, Duke of Milan* (Cambridge, 1944); M. Mallet, *Mercenaries and Their Masters* (London, 1974); and F. C. Lane, *Venice: A Maritime Republic* (Baltimore, 1973).

Good general studies of the church in the fourteenth century can be found in F. P. Oakley, *The Western Church in the Later Middle Ages* (Ithaca, N.Y., 1980); and S. Ozment, *The Age of Reform, 1250–1550: An Intellectual and Religious History of Late Medieval and Reformation Europe* (New Haven, Conn., 1980). A good, readable biography is T. S. R. Boase, *Boniface VIII* (London, 1933). On the Avigonese papacy, see Y. Renouard, *The Avignon Papacy, 1305–1403* (London, 1970); and G. Mollat, *The Popes at Avignon* (New York, 1965). Other facets of the religious scene are examined in M. Reeves, *The Influence of Prophecy in the Later Middle Ages* (Oxford, 1969); L. E. Boyle, *Pastoral Care, Clerical Education and Canon Law, 1200–1400* (London, 1981); J. M. Clark, *The Great German Mystics* (Oxford, 1949); and A. Hyma, *The Christian Renaissance: A History of the Devotio Moderna* (Hamden, Conn., 1965). On the ideas of Marsiglio of Padua, see A. Gewirth, *Marsilius of Padua*, 2 vols. (New York, 1951–56).

A classic work on the life and thought of the Later Middle Ages is J. Huizinga, *The Waning of the Middle Ages* (New York, 1949). On the impact of the plague on culture, see the brilliant study by M. Meiss, *Painting in Florence and Siena after the Black Death* (New York, 1964).

A wealth of material on everyday life is provided in the second volume of *A History of Private Life* edited by G. Duby, *Revelations of the Medieval World* (Cambridge, Mass., 1988). On women in the Middle Ages, especially the later period, see S. Shahar, *The Fourth Estate: A History of Women in the Middle Ages*, trans. C. Galai (London, 1983). On childhood, see the work by P. Ariés, *Centuries of Childhood*, trans. R. Baldick (New York, 1962); and the article by D. Herlihy cited in the notes. The subject of medieval prostitution is examined in L. L. Otis, *Prostitution in Medieval Society* (Chicago, 1984). For late medieval townspeople, see J. F. C. Harrison, *The Common People of Great Britain* (Bloomington, Ind., 1985). Poor people are discussed in M. Mollat, *The Poor in the Middle Ages* (New Haven, Conn., 1986). For a general introduction to the changes in medicine, see T. McKeown, *The Role of Medicine* (Princeton, N.J., 1979). The importance of inventions is discussed in J. Gimpel, *The Medieval Machine* (New York, 1976). Another valuable discussion of medieval technology can be found in J. Le Goff, *Time, Work and Culture in the Middle Ages* (Chicago, 1980).

Recovery and Rebirth: The Age of the Renaissance

▼▼▼▼▼

Medieval and Renaissance historians have argued interminably over the significance of the fourteenth and fifteenth centuries. Did they witness a continuation of the Middle Ages or the beginning of a new era? Obviously, both positions contain a modicum of truth. Although the disintegrative patterns of the fourteenth century continued into the fifteenth, there were at the same time elements of recovery that made the fifteenth century a period of significant political, economic, artistic, and intellectual change. The humanists or intellectuals of the age called their period (from the mid-fourteenth to the mid-sixteenth century) an age of rebirth, believing that they had restored arts and letters to new glory after they had been "neglected" or "dead" for centuries. The humanists' view of their age as a rebirth of the classical civilization of the Greeks and Romans ultimately led historians to use the word *Renaissance* to identify this age. Although recent historians have emphasized the many elements of continuity between the Middle Ages and Renaissance, the latter age was also distinguished by its own unique characteristics.

▼ Meaning and Characteristics of the Italian Renaissance

The word *Renaissance* means "rebirth." A number of people who lived in Italy between c. 1350 and c. 1550 believed that they had witnessed a rebirth of antiquity or Greco-Roman civilization, which marked a new age. To them, the approximately thousand years between the end of the Roman Empire and their own era was a middle period (hence the "Middle Ages"), characterized by

Joan of Arc	Medici Rule in Florence	Fall of Constantinople	War of the Roses	Ferdinand and Isabella
▼	▼	▼	▼	▼

•••••••• 1400 •••••••••••• 1430 ••••••••••• 1460 •••••••••••• 1490 ••••••••••• 1520 ••••••••••

▲	▲	▲	▲	▲
Council of Constance	Masaccio's Frescoes	Invention of Printing	High Renaissance (Leonardo, Raphael, Michelangelo)	Machiavelli's *The Prince*

darkness because of its lack of classical culture. Historians of the nineteenth century later used similar terminology to describe this period in Italy. The Swiss historian and art critic, Jacob Burckhardt, created the modern concept of the Renaissance in his celebrated work, *Civilization of the Renaissance in Italy,* published in 1860. He portrayed Italy in the fourteenth and fifteenth centuries as the birthplace of the modern world (the Italians were "the firstborn among the sons of modern Europe") and saw the revival of antiquity, the "perfecting of the individual," and secularism ("worldliness of the Italians") as its distinguishing features. No doubt, Burckhardt exaggerated the individuality and secularism of the Renaissance and failed to recognize the depths of its religious sentiment. Nevertheless, he established the framework for all modern interpretations of the Renaissance. Although contemporary scholars do not believe that the Renaissance represents a sudden or dramatic cultural break with the Middle Ages (as Burckhardt argued)—there was after all much continuity between the two periods in economic, political, and social life— yet the Renaissance can still be viewed as a distinct period of European history that manifested itself first in Italy and then spread to the rest of Europe. What, then, are the characteristics of the Italian Renaissance?

Renaissance Italy was largely an urban society. As a result of its commercial preeminence and political evolution, northern Italy by the mid-fourteenth century was mostly a land of independent cities that dominated the country districts around them. These city-states became the centers of Italian political, economic, and social life. Within this new urban society, a secular spirit emerged as increasing wealth created new possibilities for the enjoyment of worldly things.

Above all, the Renaissance was an age of recovery from the "calamitous fourteenth century." Italy and Europe began a slow process of recuperation from the effects of the Black Death, political disorder, and economic recession. By the end of the fourteenth and beginning of the fifteenth centuries, Italians were using the words *recovery* and *revival* and were actively involved in a rebuilding process.

Recovery was accompanied by rebirth, specifically, a rebirth of classical antiquity. Increasingly aware of their own historical past, Italian intellectuals became intensely interested in the Greco-Roman culture that had informed the ancient Mediterranean world. This new revival of classical antiquity (the Middle Ages, after all, had preserved much of ancient Latin culture) affected activities as diverse as politics and art and led to new attempts to reconcile the pagan philosophy of antiquity with Christian thought as well as new ways of viewing human beings.

Though not entirely new, a revived emphasis on individual ability became characteristic of the Italian Renaissance. As the fifteenth-century Florentine architect, Leon Battista Alberti, expressed it, "Men can do all things if they will."[1] A high regard for human dignity and worth and a realization of individual potentiality created a new social ideal of the well-rounded personality or universal person (*l'uomo universale*) who was capable of achievements in many areas of life.

These general features of the Italian Renaissance were not characteristic of all Italians, but were primarily the preserve of the wealthy upper classes who constituted a small percentage of the total population. The Italian Renaissance was an elitist, not a mass, movement, although indirectly it did have some impact on ordinary people, especially in the cities where so many of the intellectual and artistic accomplishments of the period were most apparent and visible.

▼ The Intellectual Renaissance in Italy

The emergence and growth of individualism and secularism as characteristics of the Italian Renaissance are most noticeable in the intellectual and artistic realms. Italian culture had come of age by the fourteenth century. For the next two centuries, Italy became the cultural leader of Europe. This new Italian culture was largely the product of a relatively wealthy, urban lay society. The most important literary movement we associate with the Renaissance is humanism.

Italian Renaissance Humanism

The word *humanism* has many meanings. It can refer to a tradition of classical scholarship, anything humanitarian, or a philosophy focusing on the significance of human activity. Renaissance humanism encompassed those definitions but above all was a form of education and culture based upon the study of the classics. Humanism was not so much a philosophy of life as it was an educational program that contained a philosophy of life and revolved around a clearly defined group of intellectual disciplines or "liberal arts"—grammar, rhetoric, poetry, moral philosophy or ethics, and history—all based upon the study of classical authors.

But why did the Italian literary world turn to such assiduous study and imitation of classical Latin and Greek? The basic cause can be found in Italy's social development. In developing a new urban society and culture, Italians found little to emulate in either the chivalric or clerical literary traditions of the High Middle Ages. After all, what could the knightly exploits of *The Song of Roland* or the scholastic arguments of a Thomas Aquinas teach the urban, worldly sophisticates of the Italian cities? Greco-Roman society, which had also been urban and secular, held far more interest for these Italian urbanites. Then too, the Italians, living in the heart of the old Roman Empire, were surrounded by the remains of Latin civilization.

The central importance of literary preoccupations in Renaissance humanism is evident in the professional status or occupations of the humanists. Some of them were teachers of the humanities in secondary schools and universities, where they either gave occasional lectures or held permanent positions, often as professors of rhetoric. Others served as secretaries in the chancelleries of Italian city-states or at the courts of princes or popes. All of these occupations were largely secular, and many humanists were laymen rather than members of the clergy.

THE EMERGENCE OF HUMANISM   Petrarch (1304–1374) has often been called the father of Italian Renaissance humanism (see Chapter 12 on Petrarch's use of the Italian vernacular). Petrarch had rejected his father's desire that he become a lawyer and took up a literary career instead. Crowned poet laureate at Rome in 1341, he

spent most of his remaining years in Italy as the guest of various princes and city governments. With his usual lack of modesty, Petrarch once exclaimed, "Some of the greatest kings of our time have loved me and cultivated my friendship. . . . When I was their guest it was more as if they were mine."[2]

Petrarch did more than any other individual in the fourteenth century to foster the development of Renaissance humanism. He was the first intellectual to characterize the Middle Ages as a period of darkness, promoting the mistaken belief that medieval culture was ignorant of classical antiquity. Petrarch condemned the scholastic philosophy of the Middle Ages for its "barbarous" Latin and use of logic rather than rhetoric to harmonize faith and reason. Philosophy, he argued, should be the "art of virtuous living," not a science of logic chopping. Petrarch's interest in the classics led him on a passionate search for forgotten Latin manuscripts and set in motion a ransacking of monastic libraries throughout Europe. In his preoccupation with the classics and their secular content, Petrarch doubted at times whether he was sufficiently attentive to spiritual ideals (see the box on p. 405). His qualms, however, did not prevent him from inaugurating the humanist emphasis on the use of pure classical Latin, making it fashionable for humanists to use Cicero as a model for prose and Virgil for poetry. Humanists would always have the tendency to emphasize style, often at the expense of content.

The humanistic pursuits of Petrarch were best received in Florence. By the end of the fourteenth century, a whole circle of humanistic scholars had emerged in that city. Although some were connected to monastic orders, many were simply laymen. In fact, the latter were responsible for humanism gaining a powerful momentum at the beginning of the fifteenth century when it became closely tied to Florentine civic spirit and pride, giving rise to what one modern scholar has labeled "civic humanism."

HUMANISM IN FIFTEENTH-CENTURY ITALY   Fourteenth-century humanists such as Petrarch had glorified intellectual activity pursued in a life of solitude and had rejected a life of action in the community and family. In the busy civic world of Florence, Florentine intellectuals began to take a new view of the role of intellectuals, a trend that intensified when the city's liberty was threatened at the beginning of the fifteenth century by the Milanese tyrant, Giangaleazzo Visconti. The Roman statesman and intellectual Cicero became their model. Leonardo Bruni (1370–1444), a humanist, Florentine patriot, and chancellor of the city, wrote a biography of

Petrarch: Mountain Climbing and the Search for Spiritual Contentment

▼ ▼ ▼

Petrarch has long been regarded as the father of Italian Renaissance humanism. One of his literary master-pieces was The Ascent of Mt. Ventoux. Its colorful description of an attempt to climb a mountain and survey the world from its top has unwisely led some to see it as a vivid example of the humanists' rediscovery of nature after the medieval period's concentration on the afterlife. Of course, medieval people had been aware of the natural world. Moreover, Petrarch's primary interest is in presenting an allegory of his own soul's struggle to achieve a higher spiritual state. The work is addressed to a professor of theology in Paris who had initially led Petrarch to read Augustine. The latter had experienced a vivid conversion to Christianity almost a thousand years earlier.

Petrarch, The Ascent of Mt. Ventoux

Today I ascended the highest mountain in this region, which, not without cause, they call the Windy Peak. Nothing but the desire to see its conspicuous height was the reason for this undertaking. For many years I have been intending to make this expedition. You know that since my early childhood, as fate tossed around human affairs, I have been tossed around in these parts, and this mountain, visible far and wide from everywhere, is always in your view. So I was at last seized by the impulse to accomplish what I had always wanted to do. . . .

[After some false starts, Petrarch finally achieves his goal and arrives at the top of Mt. Ventoux.]

I was glad of the progress I had made, but I wept over my imperfection and was grieved by the fickleness of all that men do. In this manner I seemed to have somehow forgotten the place I had come to and why, until I was warned to throw off such sorrows, for which another place would be more appropriate. I had better look around and see what I had intended to see in coming here. The time to leave was approaching, they said. . . . Like a man aroused from sleep, I turned back and looked toward the west. . . . one could see most distinctly the mountains of the province of Lyons to the right and, to the left, the sea near Marseilles as well as the waves that break against Aigues Mortes, . . . The Rhone River was directly under our eyes.

I admired every detail, now relishing earthly enjoyment, now lifting up my mind to higher spheres after the example of my body, and I thought it fit to look in the volume of Augustine's Confessions which I owe to your loving kindness and preserve carefully, keeping it always in my hands, in remembrance of the author as well as the donor. It is a little book of smallest size but full of infinite sweetness. I opened it with the intention of reading whatever might occur to me first: nothing, indeed, but pious and devout sentences could come to hand. I happened to hit upon the tenth book of the work. . . . Where I fixed my eyes first, it was written: "And men go to admire the high mountains, the vast floods of the sea, the huge streams of the rivers, the circumference of the ocean, and the revolutions of the stars—and desert themselves." I was stunned, I confess. I bade my brother [who had accompanied him], who wanted to hear more, not to molest me, and closed the book, angry with myself that I still admired earthly things. Long since I ought to have learned, even from pagan philosophers, that "nothing is admirable besides the soul; compared to its greatness nothing is great."

I was completely satisfied with what I had seen of the mountain and turned my inner eye toward myself. From this hour nobody heard me say a word until we arrived at the bottom. These words occupied me sufficiently. I could not imagine that this had happened to me by chance: I was convinced that whatever I had read there was said to me and to nobody else. I remembered that Augustine once suspected the same regarding himself, when, while he was reading the Apostolic Epistles, the first passage that occurred to him was, as he himself relates: "Not in banqueting and drunkenness, not in chambering and wantonness, not in strife and envying; but put ye on the Lord Jesus Christ, and make no provision for the flesh to fulfil your lusts."

Cicero entitled the *New Cicero,* in which he waxed enthusiastically about the fusion of political action and literary achievement in Cicero's life: "No one seeing Cicero's literary legacy would believe that he had any time for dealing with men; anyone reviewing his political deeds, his speeches, his occupations and his struggles both in public and private life, would imagine he could ever have had leisure for reading and writing." How could this be? The answer was that Cicero's literary and political activities were simply two sides of the same task, the work of a Roman citizen on behalf of his state. In the words of Bruni, Cicero became capable "in spite of the great claims made on him by a state which ruled the world, of writing more than philosophers whose lives are spent in leisure and in study; and on the other hand, in spite of intense preoccupation with his studies and his literary work, he was capable of accomplishing more practical work than people unburdened with interest in literary matters."[3] From Bruni's time on, Cicero served as the inspiration for the Renaissance ideal that one must live an active life for one's state, and everything, including riches, must be considered good that increases one's power of action. An active civic life does not distract from, but actually stimulates the highest intellectual energies. An individual only "grows to maturity—both intellectually and morally—through participation" in the life of the state.

Civic humanism emerged in Florence but soon spread to other Italian cities and beyond. It reflected the values of the urban society of the Italian Renaissance. Civic humanism intensified the involvement of humanist intellectuals in government and guaranteed that the rhetorical discipline they praised would be put to the service of the state. It is no accident that humanists served the state as chancellors, councillors, and advisers. Rhetoricians had become diplomats.

Also evident in the humanism of the first half of the fifteenth century was a growing interest in Greek. One of the first Italian humanists to gain a thorough knowledge of Greek was Leonardo Bruni, who became an enthusiastic pupil of the Byzantine scholar Manuel Chrysoloras, who taught in Florence from 1396 to 1400 (see the box on p. 407). Humanists eagerly perused the works of Plato as well as Greek poets, dramatists, historians, and orators, such as Thucydides, Euripides, and Sophocles, all of whom had been neglected by the scholastics of the High Middle Ages.

By the fifteenth century, a consciousness of being humanists had emerged, especially evident in the career of Lorenzo Valla (1407–1457). Valla was brought up in Rome and educated in both Latin and Greek. Eventually, during the pontificate of Nicholas V (1447–1455),

he achieved his chief ambition of becoming a papal secretary. It was Valla, above all others, who turned his attention to the philological and literary criticism of ancient texts. His most famous work was his demonstration that the Donation of Constantine, a document used by the popes, especially in the ninth and tenth centuries (see Chapter 8), to claim temporal sovereignty over all the west, was a forgery written in the eighth century. Valla's other major work, *The Elegances of the Latin Language,* was an effort to purify medieval Latin and restore Latin to its proper position over the vernacular. The treatise surveyed the proper use of classical Latin and created a new literary standard. Early humanists had tended to accept as classical models any author (including Christians) who had written prior to the seventh century A.D. Valla distinguished periods in the development of the Latin language and gave his complete approval only to the Latin of the last century of the Roman Republic and the first century of the empire.

Another significant humanist of this period was Poggio Bracciolini (1380–1459), who reflected the cult of humanism at its best. Born and educated in Florence, he went on to serve as a papal secretary for fifty years, a position that enabled him to become an avid collector of classical manuscripts. In finding all of the writings of fifteen different authors, he became the greatest discoverer of forgotten Latin manuscripts. Poggio's best-known literary work was the *Facetiae,* a lighthearted collection of jokes, which included a rather cynical criticism of the clergy:

> Tale 43: A friar of Tivoli, who was not very considerate of the people, was once thundering away with many words about the detestability of adultery. Among other things, he declared that this sin was so grave that he would prefer to lie with ten virgins than with one married woman. And many of those present shared his opinion.[4]

Poggio and other Italian humanists were very critical of the Catholic church at times, but fundamentally they accepted the church and above all wished only to restore a simpler, purer, and more ethical Christianity. To the humanists, the study of the classics was perfectly compatible with Christianity.

HUMANISM AND PHILOSOPHY   In the second half of the fifteenth century, a new generation of thinkers became preoccupied with philosophies derived from the Greeks. This shift was particularly apparent in Florence. As the Medici family strengthened its rule over the city (see The Italian City-States later in the chapter), the hu-

One of the first humanists to have a thorough knowledge of both Latin and Greek was the Florentine chancellor Leonardo Bruni. Bruni was fortunate to be instructed by the Greek scholar Manuel Chrysoloras, who was persuaded by the Florentines to come to Florence to teach Greek. As this selection illustrates, Bruni seized the opportunity to pursue his passion for Greek letters.

Leonardo Bruni, *History of His Own Times in Italy*

Then first came the knowledge of Greek letters, which for seven hundred years had been lost among us. It was the Byzantine, Chrysoloras, a nobleman in his own country and most skilled in literature, who brought Greek learning back to us. Because his country was invaded by the Turks, he came by sea to Venice; but as soon as his fame went abroad, he was cordially invited and eagerly besought to come to Florence on a public salary to spread his abundant riches before the youth of the city [1396]. At that time I was studying Civil Law. But my nature was afire with the love of learning and I had already given no little time to dialectic and rhetoric. Therefore at the coming of Chrysoloras I was divided in my mind,

feeling that it was a shame to desert the Law and no less wrong to let slip such an occasion for learning Greek. And often with youthful impulsiveness I addressed myself thus: "When you are privileged to gaze upon and have converse with Homer, Plato, and Demosthenes as well as the other poets, philosophers, and orators of whom such wonderful things are reported, and when you might saturate yourself with their admirable teachings, will you turn your back and flee? Will you permit this opportunity, divinely offered you, to slip by? For seven hundred years now no one in Italy has been in possession of Greek and yet we agree that all knowledge comes from that source. What great advancement of knowledge, enlargement of fame, and increase of pleasure will come to you from an acquaintance with this tongue! There are everywhere quantities of doctors of the Civil Law and the opportunity of completing your study in this field will not fail you. However, should the one and only doctor of Greek letters disappear, there will be no one from whom to acquire them."

Overcome at last by these arguments, I gave myself to Chrysoloras and developed such ardor that whatever I learned by day, I revolved with myself in the night while asleep.

manists' interest in civic life waned. At the same time, there appeared a renewed concern for Greek letters, especially the writings of Plato and a series of arcane works known as the *Corpus Hermeticum.* These interests gave rise to the development of two new philosophies called Neoplatonism and Hermeticism.

By the mid-fifteenth century, there had been a dramatic upsurge of interest in the works of Plato, especially evident in the development of the Florentine Platonic Academy, begun not as a formal school, but as an informal discussion group. Cosimo de' Medici, the de facto ruler of Florence, took it under his protection and became its patron. He commissioned a translation of Plato's dialogues by Marsilio Ficino (1433–1499), who was given a life endowment so that he could devote himself to the translation of Plato and the exposition of the Platonic philosophy known as Neoplatonism. Although Neoplatonism became an influential intellectual system, the Platonic Academy itself never became a formal educational institution.

In two major works, Marsilio Ficino undertook the synthesis of Christianity and Platonism into a single system. His Neoplatonism was based upon two primary ideas, the Neoplatonic hierarchy of substances and a theory of spiritual love. The former postulated a hierarchy of substances or great chain of being from the lowest form of physical matter (plants) to the purest spirit (God), in which humans occupied a central or middle position. They were the link between the material world (through the body) and the spiritual world (through the soul), and their highest duty was to apprehend higher things and ascend toward that union with God that was the true end of human existence. Ficino's theory of spiritual or Platonic love maintained that just as all people are bound together in their common humanity by love, so too are all parts of the universe held together by bonds of sympathetic love. Ficino's theory of spiritual love has had a great influence on Western literature.

Renaissance Hermeticism was another product of the Florentine intellectual environment of the late fifteenth century. Upon the request of Cosimo de' Medici, Marsilio Ficino translated into Latin a Greek manuscript entitled the *Corpus Hermeticum*. Although the *Corpus* was actually written between A.D. 100 and 300, Ficino and his contemporaries believed mistakenly that the core of these Hermetic treatises was the work of Hermes Trismegistus, an ancient Egyptian priest.

The Hermetic manuscripts contained two kinds of writings. One type stressed the occult sciences with emphasis on astrology, alchemy, and magic. The other focused on theological and philosophical beliefs and speculations. Some parts of the Hermetic writings were distinctly pantheistic, seeing divinity embodied in all aspects of nature, in the heavenly bodies as well as in earthly objects. As Giordano Bruno, one of the most prominent of the sixteenth-century Hermeticists stated, "God as a whole is in all things."[5] Other sections of the *Corpus Hermeticum* portrayed the universe in organic and animistic terms. Here the world was a living entity, full of life and constant movement. For Renaissance intellectuals, the Hermetic revival offered a new view of humankind. They believed that human beings had been created as divine beings endowed with divine creative power, but had freely chosen to enter the material world (nature). Thus, humans had a dual nature—mortal through their bodies, but immortal through their essential being. They could recover their divinity, however, through a regenerative experience or purification of the soul. Thus regenerated, they became true sages or magi, as the Renaissance called them, who had knowledge of God and of truth. In regaining their original divinity, they reacquired an intimate knowledge of nature and the ability to employ the powers of nature for beneficial purposes. The serious Renaissance magus believed in humans' ability to control nature and became involved in the practice of magic as a means of organizing and controlling experience. Hermetic magic was basically a natural magic that sought to work with the normal powers of the cosmos.

Renaissance magic was the preserve of an intellectual elite from all of Europe. In Italy, the most prominent magi in the late fifteenth century were Ficino and Giovanni Pico della Mirandola (1463–1494), a friend and pupil of Ficino. Pico produced one of the most famous writings of the Renaissance, the *Oration on the Dignity of Man*, a preface to his *900 Conclusions*, which were meant to be a summation of all learning and offered as theses for a public debate. Pico combed diligently through the writings of many philosophers of different backgrounds for the common "nuggets of universal truth" that he believed were all part of God's revelation to humanity. In the *Oration* (see the box on p. 409), Pico offered a ringing statement of unlimited human potential. "To him it is granted to have whatever he chooses, to be whatever he wills."[6] Like Ficino, Pico took an avid interest in Hermetic magic, accepting it as the "science of the Divine," which "embraces the deepest contemplation of the most secret things, and at last the knowledge of all nature."[7]

THE DECLINE OF HUMANISM   Italian Renaissance humanism began to decline and lose its vitality in the first half of the sixteenth century. For example, by then many humanists had begun to adhere rigidly to classical style or insist on an exclusive Ciceronianism, meaning that they would use only Latin words or phrases found in the great Latin writers. A major reason for this loss of vitality was that the humanists had accomplished most of their objectives. By 1520, most classical Latin and Greek texts had been examined and printed in scholarly editions (see The Impact of Printing later in the chapter). At the same time, the content of the classics had become common knowledge to many members of Italy's upper classes. Now, with printed books, there tended to be more and more concentration on the use of the vernacular, including translations of classical works done by the humanists themselves. Essentially, the task of humanism was complete.

Education in the Renaissance

The humanist movement had a profound effect on education. Genuinely optimistic about the educability of human beings, Renaissance humanists produced treatises on educational theory and developed secondary schools based on their educational philosophy. Most famous was the one founded in 1423 by Vittorino da Feltre (1378–1446) at Mantua, where the ruler of that small Italian state, Gian Francesco I Gonzaga, wished to provide a humanist school for his children. Vittorino based much of his educational system on the ideas of classical authors, particularly Cicero and Quintilian.

At the core of the academic training Vittorino offered were the "liberal studies." In the Middle Ages, the liberal arts had provided the foundation for later professional study in law, medicine, or theology, although by the thirteenth century the importance of Aristotle had led to an emphasis on the study of logic at the expense of grammar, rhetoric, and the other liberal arts. Little emphasis was placed on the intrinsic value of the liberal arts in producing individuals of character.

Pico della Mirandola and the Dignity of Man
▼ ▼ ▼

Giovanni Pico della Mirandola was one of the foremost intellects of the Italian Renaissance. Pico boasted that he had studied all schools of philosophy, which he tried to demonstrate by drawing up nine hundred theses for public disputation at the age of twenty-four. As a preface to his theses, he wrote his famous oration, On the Dignity of Man, in which he proclaimed the unlimited potentiality of human beings.

Pico della Mirandola, *Oration of the Dignity of Man*

At last the best of artisans [God] ordained that that creature to whom He had been able to give nothing proper to himself should have joint possession of whatever had been peculiar to each of the different kinds of being. He therefore took man as a creature of indeterminate nature, and assigning him a place in the middle of the world, addressed him thus: "Neither a fixed abode nor a form that is thine alone nor any function peculiar to thyself have we given thee, Adam, to the end that according to thy longing and according to thy judgment thou mayest have and possess what abode, what form, and what functions thou thyself shalt desire. The nature of all other beings is limited and constrained within the bounds of laws prescribed by Us. Thou, constrained by no limits, in accordance with thine own free will, in whose hand We have placed thee, shalt ordain for thyself the limits of thy nature. We have set thee at the world's center that thou mayest from thence more easily observe whatever is in the world. We have made thee neither of heaven nor of earth, neither mortal nor immortal, so that with freedom of choice and with honor, as though the maker and molder of thyself, thou mayest fashion thyself in whatever shape thou shalt prefer. Thou shalt have the power to degenerate into the lower forms of life, which are brutish. Thou shalt have the power, out of thy soul's judgment, to be reborn into the higher forms, which are divine."

O supreme generosity of God the Father, O highest and most marvelous felicity of man! To him it is granted to have whatever he chooses, to be whatever he wills. Beasts as soon as they are born bring with them from their mother's womb all they will ever possess. Spiritual beings, either from the beginning or soon thereafter, become what they are to be for ever and ever. On man when he came into life the Father conferred the seeds of all kinds and the germs of every way of life. Whatever seeds each man cultivates will grow to maturity and bear in him their own fruit. If they be vegetative, he will be like a plant. If sensitive, he will become brutish. If rational, he will grow into a heavenly being. If intellectual, he will be an angel and the son of God.

The Renaissance view of the value of the liberal arts was most strongly influenced by a treatise on education called *Concerning Character* by Pietro Paolo Vergerio (1370–1444). This work stressed the importance of the liberal arts as the key to true freedom, enabling individuals to reach their full potential. According to Vergerio, "we call those studies liberal which are worthy of a free man; those studies by which we attain and practice virtue and wisdom; that education which calls forth, trains, and develops those highest gifts of body and mind which ennoble men, and which are rightly judged to rank next in dignity to virtue only. . . ."[8] What, then, are the "liberal studies?":

Amongst these I accord the first place to History, on grounds both of its attractiveness and of its utility, qualities which appeal equally to the scholar and to the statesman. Next in importance ranks Moral Philosophy, which indeed is, in a peculiar sense, a "Liberal Art," in that its purpose is to teach men the secret of true freedom. History, then, gives us the concrete examples of the precepts inculcated by Philosophy. The one shows what men should do, the other what men have said and done in the past, and what practical lessons we may draw therefrom for the present day. I would indicate as the third main branch of study, Eloquence. . . . By philosophy we learn the essential truth of things, which by eloquence we so exhibit in orderly adornment as to bring conviction to differing minds.[9]

The remaining liberal studies included letters (grammar and logic), poetry, mathematics, astronomy, and music ("as to Music," said Vergerio, "the Greeks refused the title of 'Educated' to anyone who could not sing or play.") Crucial to all liberal studies was the mastery of Greek and Latin since it enabled students to read the great classical authors who were the foundation stones of the liberal arts. In short, the purpose of a liberal education was to produce individuals who followed a path of virtue and wisdom and possessed the rhetorical skills to persuade others to take it.

Following the Greek precept of a sound mind in a sound body, Vittorino's school at Mantua stressed the need for physical education. Pupils were taught the arts of javelin throwing, archery, and dancing and encouraged frequently to run, wrestle, hunt, and swim. Nor was Christianity excluded from Vittorino's school. His students were taught the Scriptures and the works of the church fathers, especially Augustine. A devout Christian, Vittorino required his pupils to attend mass daily and be reverent in word and deed.

Although a small number of children from the lower classes were provided free educations, humanist schools such as Vittorino's were primarily geared for the education of an elite, the ruling classes of their communities. Also largely absent from such schools were females. Vittorino's only female pupils were the two daughters of the Gonzaga ruler of Mantua. While these few female students studied the classics and were encouraged to know some history and to ride, dance, sing, play the lute, and appreciate poetry, they were discouraged from learning mathematics and rhetoric. In the educational treatises of the time, religion and morals were thought to "hold the first place in the education of a Christian lady."

The humanist schools of the Renaissance aimed to develop the human personality to the fullest extent and underscored the new social ideal of the Renaissance, the creation of the universal being known to us as the "Renaissance man." We should also note that Vittorino and other humanist educators considered a humanist education to be a practical preparation for life. The aim of humanist education was not the creation of a great scholar but a complete citizen. As Vittorino said, "Not everyone is obliged to excel in philosophy, medicine, or the law, nor are all equally favored by nature; but all are destined to live in society and to practice virtue."[10] Humanist schools, combining the classics and Christianity, provided the model for the basic education of the European ruling classes until the twentieth century.

Humanism and History

Humanism had a strong impact on the writing of history. Influenced by Roman and Greek historians, the humanists approached the writing of history differently from the chroniclers of the Middle Ages. The humanists' belief that classical civilization had been followed by an age of barbarism (the Middle Ages), which, in turn, had been succeeded by their own age of the rebirth of the classics enabled them to think in terms of the passage of time, of the past as past. Their division of the past into ancient world, dark ages, and their own age provided a new sense of chronology or periodization in history.

The humanists were also responsible for secularizing the writing of history. Humanist historians reduced or eliminated the role of miracles in historical interpretation, not because they were anti-Christian, but because they took a new approach to sources. They wanted to use documents and exercised their newly developed critical and philological skills in examining them. Greater attention was paid to the political events and forces that affected their city-states or larger territorial units. Thus, Leonardo Bruni wrote a *History of the Florentine People;* the German scholar Jacob Wimpheling penned *On the Excellence and Magnificence of the Germans.* The new emphasis on secularization was also evident in the humanists' conception of causation in history. In much medieval historical literature, historical events were often portrayed as being caused by God's active involvement in human affairs. Humanists deemphasized divine intervention in favor of human motives, stressing political forces or the role of individuals in history.

The high point of Renaissance historiography was achieved at the beginning of the sixteenth century in the works of Francesco Guicciardini (1483–1540). He has been called by some Renaissance scholars the greatest historian between Tacitus in the first century A.D. (see Chapter 6) and Voltaire and Gibbon in the eighteenth century (see Chapter 18). His *History of Italy* and *History of Florence* represent the beginning of "modern analytical historiography." To Guicciardini, the purpose of writing history was to teach lessons, but he was so impressed by the complexity of historical events that he felt those lessons were not always obvious. From his extensive background in government and diplomatic affairs, he developed the political skills that enabled him to do precise and critical analyses of political situations. Emphasizing political and military history, his works relied heavily on personal examples and documentary sources.

Vernacular Literature

The humanist emphasis on classical Latin led to its widespread use in the fifteenth and sixteenth centuries, especially among scholars, lawyers, and theologians. Vernacular languages had already developed in the Middle Ages, but in the late fifteenth and early sixteenth centuries, they became broad enough in scope to create national literary forms that could compete with Latin. This was important to the spread of the Reformation in the sixteenth century but was also true in secular literature, especially in the satirical novels of the Frenchman François Rabelais (1483–1553).

Educated in the Latin and Greek classics while a monk, Rabelais believed that education was the key to reforming church and society. His masterpieces in French were *Pantagruel,* which appeared in 1532, and *Gargantua,* published two years later. Both were comic romances detailing the lusty escapades of the giant Pantagruel and his father Gargantua. Interspersed among the hilarious encounters were serious discussions of religion and philosophy. Permeating all, however, was the sense of humor of a man who simultaneously portrayed his own lust for life and pointed out the follies of the turbulent society of his day. His outlook on people was optimistic. He believed that if they could be freed from the tyranny of society's political and religious institutions, people were by nature good; so was life since all came from God. As Rabelais described the ideal monastery of Théleme established by Gargantua as a young man:

> In their rules there was only one clause: DO WHAT YOU WILL because people who are free, well-born, well-bred, and easy in honest company have a natural spur and instinct which drives them to virtuous deeds and deflects them from vice; and this they called honor. When these same men are depressed and enslaved by vile constraint and subjection, they use this noble quality which once impelled them freely towards virtue, to throw off and break this yoke of slavery. For we always strive after things forbidden and covet what is denied us.[11]

Although a convinced Roman Catholic, the Christian concept of original sin meant little to Rabelais. Humans must bear life, with all its sorrows and joy, with as much humor as possible and never lose faith in God or love for their fellow human beings.

The Impact of Printing

The period of the Renaissance witnessed the invention of printing, one of the most important technological innovations of Western civilization. The art of printing made an immediate impact on European intellectual life and thought.

Strictly speaking, printing was not invented in fifteenth-century Europe. Printing from hand-carved wooden blocks had been present in the west since the twelfth century and in China even before that. What was new was multiple printing with reusable, movable

▼ **A Printing Shop.** One of the more crucial innovations in the history of Western civilization, printing had a deep and lasting impact on the intellectual life of Europe. The printing press facilitated the development of a lay reading public and made the rapid spread of ideas possible. Pictured here is a production line where the printers (left) set type and an apprentice (center) stacks sheets.

type. The development of printing from movable type was a slow, evolutionary process that culminated some time between 1445 and 1450; Johannes Gutenberg of Mainz played a leading role in perfecting the process. The first substantial book printed from movable type was the so-called Gutenberg Bible, completed in 1455 or 1456.

The new printing spread rapidly throughout Europe in the last half of the fifteenth century. Printing presses were established throughout the Holy Roman Empire in the 1460s and within ten years had spread to Italy, France, the Low Countries, Spain, and eastern Europe. Especially well known as a printing center was Venice, home by 1500 to almost one hundred printers who had produced almost two million volumes.

By 1500, there were over a thousand printers in Europe who had published almost 40,000 titles (between eight and ten million copies). Probably 50 percent of these books were religious in character—Bibles and biblical commentaries, books of devotion, and sermons. Next in importance were the Latin and Greek classics, medieval grammars, legal handbooks, works on philosophy, and an ever-growing number of popular romances.

Printing became one of the largest industries in Europe, and its effects were soon felt in many areas of European life. Although some humanists condemned printing because they believed that it vulgarized learning, the printing of books actually encouraged the development of scholarly research and the desire to attain knowledge. Moreover, printing facilitated cooperation among scholars and helped produce standardized and definitive texts. Printing also stimulated the development of an ever-expanding lay reading public, a development that had an enormous impact on European society. Indeed, already in the sixteenth century, the new religious ideas of the Reformation would never have spread as rapidly as they did without the printing press.

▼ The Artistic Renaissance

Many Italians in the fourteenth century believed that classical artists had used nature as their model, and it was the imitation of nature that Renaissance painters sought to attain. As Leonardo da Vinci explained: "Hence the painter will produce pictures of small merit if he takes for his standard the pictures of others, but if he will study from natural objects he will bear good fruit . . . those who take for their standard any one but nature . . . weary themselves in vain."[12] Leonardo and other Italians maintained that it was Giotto in the fourteenth century (see Chapter 12) who initiated a rebirth of painting by attempting to portray nature accurately. The desire to imitate nature and the ability to do it are, of course, not the same thing, and Leonardo himself maintained that the imitation of nature begun by Giotto was not taken

up again until the work of Masaccio (1401–1428) in Florence.

Masaccio's cycle of frescoes in the Brancacci Chapel have long been regarded as the first masterpieces of Early Renaissance art. With his use of monumental figures, the demonstration of a more realistic relationship between figures and landscape, and the visual representation of the laws of perspective, a new realistic style of painting was born. This new or Renaissance style was then absorbed and modified by other Florentine painters in the fifteenth century. Especially important was the development of an experimental trend that took two directions. One emphasized the mathematical side of painting, the working out of the laws of perspective and the organization of outdoor space and light by geometry and perspective. In the work of Paolo Uccello (1397–1475), figures became merely stage props to show off his mastery of the laws of perspective. The other aspect of the experimental trend involved the investigation of movement and anatomical structure. *The Martyrdom of St. Sebastian* by Antonio Pollaiuolo (c. 1432–1498) revels in classical motifs and attempts to portray the human body under stress. Indeed, the realistic portrayal of the human nude became one of the foremost preoccupations of Italian Renaissance art. The fifteenth century, then, was a period of experimentation and technical mastery. By the end of the century, Italian artists felt that they had mastered the art of

▼ **Masaccio,** *Tribute Money.* With the frescoes of Masaccio, regarded by many as the first great works of Early Renaissance art, a new realistic style of painting was born. The *Tribute Money,* pictured here, was one of a series of frescoes that Masaccio painted in the Brancacci chapel in the church of Santa Maria del Carmine in Florence. Masaccio used a rational system of perspective to create a realistic relationship between the figures and their background. His massive, three-dimensional human figures provided a model for later generations of Florentine artists.

▼ **Leonardo da Vinci, *The Last Supper*.** Leonardo da Vinci was one of the three great figures who dominated High Renaissance art. He was the impetus behind the High Renaissance's preoccupation with the idealization of nature, moving from a realistic portrayal of the human figure to an idealized form. Evident in Leonardo's *The Last Supper* is his effort to depict a person's character and inner nature by the use of gesture and movement.

depicting nature three dimensionally in their two-dimensional medium and began to search for new forms of expression. This shift to the High Renaissance was marked by Rome's replacing Florence as the cultural center of the Italian Renaissance.

The High Renaissance was dominated by the work of three artistic giants, Leonardo da Vinci (1452–1519), Raphael (1483–1520), and Michelangelo (1475–1564). Leonardo represents a transitional figure in the shift to High Renaissance principles. He carried on the fifteenth-century experimental tradition by studying everything and even dissecting human bodies in order to better see how nature worked. He said, "The summit of art is to draw well the body of a nude man and a nude woman." But Leonardo stressed the need to advance beyond such realism: "On winter evenings, all the drawings from the nude which you have made in the summer should be brought together, and you should make a choice from among them of the best limbs and bodies, and practice these and learn them by heart." Leonardo began the High Renaissance's preoccupation with the idealization of nature, or the attempt to generalize from realistic portrayal to an ideal form. Leonardo's *Last Supper* is a brilliant summary of fifteenth-century trends in its organization of space and use of one-point perspective, but it is also more. The figure of Philip is idealized, and there are profound psychological dimensions to the work. The words of Christ that "one of you shall betray me" are experienced directly as each of the apostles reveals his personality and his relationship to the Savior. In one of his notebooks, Leonardo wrote that the highest and most difficult aim of painting is to depict "the intention of man's soul." Through gestures and movement, Leonardo hoped to reveal a person's inner life.

In his idealized madonnas, Raphael sought a beauty greater than what could be found in nature. At the same time, as his *Alba Madonna* reveals, he demonstrated the basic principles of High Renaissance art when he incorporated the classical principles of balance, harmony, and rational composition into his paintings.

Michelangelo was influenced by Neoplatonism, especially evident in his figures on the ceiling of the Sistine Chapel. These muscular figures reveal an ideal type of human being with perfect proportions. Their beauty is meant to be, in good Neoplatonic fashion, a reflection of divine beauty; the more beautiful the body, the more God-like the figure. In his later work, Michelangelo began to abandon classical principles, leading to a new movement called mannerism.

▼ **Michelangelo, The Sistine Chapel Ceiling.** In 1508, Pope Julius II recalled Michelangelo to Rome and commissioned him to decorate the ceiling of the Sistine Chapel. This colossal project was not completed until 1512. Although Michelangelo attempted to tell the story of the Fall of Man by portraying nine scenes from the biblical book of Genesis, his real artistic focus was on the perfectability of the human figure. The beauty of his well-proportioned and muscular figures are meant to be a reflection of divine beauty.

The Artist and Social Status

In the course of the fifteenth century, the Renaissance artist experienced a change in social position. In the medieval tradition, artists were viewed primarily as artisans who were members of a craft guild. They were certainly not considered the social equals of the wealthy patricians or upper classes. They had little formal edu-

cation, and the subjects for their paintings were usually chosen by their patrons.

During the fifteenth century, the artist emerged as a figure of creative genius. He was welcome in the houses of the upper classes and participated in conversations with humanists and philosophers. Consequently, artists had a greater awareness of the intellectual currents of their day and incorporated them into their art. The Platonic Academy and Renaissance Neoplatonism had an especially important impact upon Florentine painters.

The Northern Artistic Renaissance

In trying to solve the problem of how to portray nature accurately, the artists of the north (especially the Low Countries) and Italy took different approaches. In Italy, the human form became the primary vehicle of expression as Italian artists sought to master the technical skills that allowed them to portray humans in realistic settings. The large wall spaces of Italian churches had given rise to the art of fresco painting, but in the north, the prevalence of Gothic cathedrals with their stained glass windows resulted in more emphasis on illuminated manuscripts and wooden panel painting for altarpieces. The space available in these works was limited, and great care was required to depict each object, leading northern painters to become masters at rendering details.

The most influential northern school of art in the fifteenth century was centered in Flanders. Jan van Eyck (1380?–1441) was among the first to use oil paint and concentrate on details. In the famous *Giovanni Arnolfini and Bride*, his attention to detail is staggering: accurate portraits, glittering jewels, mirrors reflecting the objects in the room, and towns and castles with every window clearly visible. Although each detail was rendered as observed, it is evident that van Eyck did not fully comprehend the laws of perspective. His work is truly indicative of northern Renaissance painters, who, in their effort to imitate nature, did so not by mastery of the laws of perspective and proportion, but by empirical observation of visual reality and the accurate portrayal of details. Moreover, northern painters placed great emphasis on the emotional intensity of religious feeling. Michelangelo summarized the difference between northern and Italian Renaissance painting in these words:

> In Flanders, they paint, before all things, to render exactly and deceptively the outward appearance of things. The

▼ **Raphael, *Alba Madonna*.** Although he died at the age of thirty-seven, Raphael achieved in his own lifetime a fame comparable to that of Michelangelo and Leonardo da Vinci. In his madonnas, Raphael sought an idealized beauty that was typical of the High Renaissance. His *Alba Madonna* illustrates his mastery of the classical principles of balance, harmony, clarity, and rational composition.

painters choose, by preference, subjects provoking transports of piety, like the figures of saints or of prophets. But most of the time they paint what are called landscapes with plenty of figures. Though the eye is agreeably impressed, these pictures have neither choice of values nor grandeur. In short, this art is without power and without distinction; it aims at rendering minutely many things at the same time, of which a single one would have sufficed to call forth a man's whole application.[13]

▼ **Jan van Eyck, *Giovanni Arnolfini and His Bride*.** Northern painters differed from the painters of Italy in their attempt to depict nature accurately. Working in a more limited space, they took great care in depicting each object and became masters in the rendering of details. This emphasis on a realistic portrayal is clearly evident in *Giovanni Arnolfini and His Bride*. The use of oil paint enabled van Eyck to use a more dramatic range of color. In addition to an incredible attention to tiny details, van Eyck showed a remarkable ability to illustrate with remarkable realism the effects of light coming in from the window.

▼ **Albrecht Dürer, *Adoration of the Magi*.** By the end of the fifteenth century, Northern artists began studying in Italy and adopting many of the techniques used by Italian painters. Albrecht Dürer masterfully incorporated the laws of perspective and the ideals of proportion into his works. At the same time, he did not abandon the preoccupation of Northern artists with details. His *Adoration of the Magi* clearly shows how he unified the scientific principles of Italian painting with the attention to detail characteristic of the North.

By the end of the fifteenth century, however, artists from the north began to study in Italy and were visually influenced by what artists were doing there.

No northern artist of this later period was more affected by the Italians than Albrecht Dürer (1471–1528) from Nuremberg. Dürer visited Italy twice and absorbed most of what the Italians could teach, evident in his mastery of the laws of perspective and Renaissance theories of proportion. He wrote detailed treatises on both subjects. At the same time, as in his famous *Adoration of the Magi*, Dürer did not reject the use of minute details characteristic of northern artists. He did try, however, to integrate those details more harmoniously into his works and, like the Italian artists of the High Renaissance, sought ideal beauty by a careful examination of the human form.

▼ Economic and Social Changes

The cultural flowering that we associate with the Italian Renaissance actually began in an era of severe economic difficulties. The commercial revolution of the twelfth, thirteenth, and early fourteenth centuries had produced great wealth and given rise to a money economy and the development of a system of capitalism in which the capital or liquid wealth accumulated by private entrepreneurs was used to make further profits in trade, industry, and banking. After three centuries of economic expansion, in the second half of the fourteenth century, Europeans experienced severe economic reversals and social upheavals (see Chapter 12). By the middle of the fifteenth century, Europe had begun a gradual economic recovery with an increase in the volume of manufacturing and trade. Economic growth varied from area to area, however, and despite the recovery Europe did not experience the economic boom of the High Middle Ages. Also evident in the fifteenth century was the growing contrast between great wealth and abject poverty. Indeed, the rich were getting richer, and the poor poorer.

Trade, Industry, and Banking

By the fourteenth century, Italian merchants were carrying on a flourishing commerce throughout the Mediterranean and had also expanded their lines of trade north along the Atlantic seaboard. The great galleys of the Venetian Flanders Fleet maintained a direct sea route from Venice to England and the Netherlands, where Italian merchants were brought into contact with the increasingly powerful Hanseatic League of merchants. Hard hit by the plague, the Italians lost their commercial preeminence while the Hanseatic League continued to prosper.

As early as the thirteenth century, some north German coastal towns, such as Lübeck, Hamburg, and Bremen, cooperated to gain favorable trading rights in Flemish cities. To protect themselves from pirates and competition from Scandinavian merchants, these and other northern towns formed a commercial and military league known as the Hansa or Hanseatic League. By 1500, over eighty cities belonged to the league, which gained full navigational rights between the Baltic and North seas and established settlements and commercial bases in northern Europe and England. For almost two hundred years, the Hansa had a monopoly on northern European trade in timber, fish, grain, metals, honey, and wines. Its southern outlet in Flanders, the city of Bruges, became the economic crossroads of Europe in the fourteenth century since it served as the meeting place between Hanseatic merchants and the Flanders Fleet of Venice. In the fifteenth century, however, Bruges slowly began to decline, paralleling the decline of the Hanseatic League itself as it proved increasingly unable to compete with the developing larger territorial states.

Overall, trade recovered dramatically from the economic contraction of the fourteenth century. Some have even argued that shipping itself increased in the century after the Black Death. In any case, the Italians and especially the Venetians, despite the new restrictive pressures on their eastern Mediterranean trade from the Ottoman Turks (see The Ottoman Turks and the End of Byzantium later in the chapter), continued to maintain a wealthy commercial empire. Not until the sixteenth century, when the overseas discoveries gave new importance to the states facing the Atlantic, did the petty Italian city-states begin to suffer from the competitive advantages of the ever-growing and more powerful national territorial states.

The economic depression of the fourteenth century also affected patterns of industrial development. The woolen industries of Flanders and the northern Italian cities had been particularly devastated. By the beginning of the fifteenth century, however, the Florentine woolen industry was experiencing a recovery. At the same time, the Italian cities began to develop and expand luxury industries, especially lace and silk, glassware, and hand-worked items in metal and precious stones. Unfortunately, these luxury industries employed fewer people than the woolen industry and contributed less to overall prosperity. Indeed, the concentration of wealth in the hands of fewer people seems to characterize the prosperity of the fifteenth century. It has even been suggested that the wealthy in the fifteenth century, with fewer chances to invest capital in economic enterprises, spent more of their money on works of culture, thereby fostering the cultural flowering of the Renaissance.

The Renaissance witnessed the development of other new industries, especially printing, mining, and metallurgy, that began to rival the textile industry in importance. New machinery and techniques for digging deeper mines and for separating metals from ore and purifying them were put into operation. When rulers began to transfer their titles to underground mineral rights to financiers as collateral for loans, these entrepreneurs quickly developed large mining operations to produce copper, iron, and silver. Especially valuable were the rich mineral deposits in central Europe, Hun-

Florence, "Queen City of the Renaissance"
▼ ▼ ▼

Florence has long been regarded by many historians as the "queen city of the Renaissance." It was the intellectual and cultural center of Italy in the fifteenth century. In a letter written to a Venetian in 1472, Benedetto Dei, a Florentine merchant, gave a proud and boastful description of Florence's economy under the guidance of Lorenzo de' Medici.

Benedetto Dei, Florence

Florence is more beautiful and five hundred years older than your Venice. We spring from triply noble blood. We are one-third Roman, one-third Frankish, and one-third Fiesolan [an ancient Etruscan town three miles northeast of Florence]. . . . We have round about us thirty thousand estates, owned by noblemen and merchants, citizens and craftsmen, yielding us yearly bread and meat, wine and oil, vegetables and cheese, hay and wood, to the value of nine hundred thousand ducats in cash, as you Venetians, Genoese, Chians, and Rhoadians who come to buy them know well enough. We have two trades greater than any four of yours in Venice put together—the trades of wool and silk. . . .

Our beautiful Florence contains within the city in this present year two hundred seventy shops belonging to the wool merchants' guild, from whence their wares are sent to Rome and the Marches, Naples and Sicily, Constantinople and Pera, Adrianople, . . . and the whole of Turkey. It contains also eighty-three rich and splendid warehouses of the silk merchants' guild, and furnishes gold and silver stuffs, velvet, brocade, damask, taffeta, and satin to Rome, Naples, Catalonia, and the whole of Spain, especially Seville, and to Turkey and Barbary. The principal fairs to which these wares go are those of Genoa, the Marches, Ferrara, Mantua, and the whole of Italy; Lyons, Avignon, Montpellier, Antwerp, and London. The number of banks amount to thirty-three; the shops of the cabinetmakers, whose business is carving and inlaid work, to eighty-four; and the workshops of the stonecutters and marble workers in the city and its immediate neighborhood, to fifty-four. There are forty-four goldsmiths' and jewelers' shops, thirty gold-beaters, silver wire-drawers, and a wax-figure maker [wax images were used in all churches]. . . . Go through all the cities of the world, nowhere will you ever be able to find artists in wax equal to those we now have in Florence. . . . Another flourishing industry is the making of light and elegant gold and silver wreaths and garlands, which are worn by young maidens of high degree, and which have given their names to the artist family of Ghirlandaio. Sixty-six is the number of the apothecaries' and grocer shops; seventy that of the butchers, besides eight large shops in which are sold fowls of all kinds, as well as game and also the native wine called Trebbiano, from San Giovanni in the upper Arno Valley; it would awaken the dead in its praise.

---

gary, the Tyrol, Bohemia, and Saxony. Expanding iron production and new skills in metal working, in turn, contributed to the development of firearms that were more effective than the crude weapons of the fourteenth century.

The city of Florence regained its preeminence in banking in the fifteenth century, primarily due to the Medici family (see the box above). The Medici had expanded from cloth production into commerce, real estate, and banking. In its best days (in the fifteenth century), the House of Medici was the greatest banking house in Europe with branches in Venice, Milan, Rome, Avignon, Bruges, London, and Lyons. Moreover, the family had controlling interests in industrial enterprises for wool, silk, and the mining of alum, used in the dyeing of textiles. Except for a brief interruption, the Medici were also the principal bankers for the papacy, a position that produced big profits and influence at the papal court. Despite the preeminence of the Medici bank, however, there was a significant difference between its wealth and that of its fourteenth-century predecessors. The aggregate capital of the main house and seven of the eight Medici branches in 1458 stood at 30,000 florins, while that of the Peruzzi bank in the early fourteenth century stood at 100,000. These figures clearly indicate the extent of the economic downswing of the fourteenth century.

Despite its great success in the early and middle part of the fifteenth century, the Medici bank began a rather sudden decline at the end of the fifteenth century, in part because of the lack of interest and financial ability of Lorenzo de' Medici, the head of the family from 1469 to 1492. A series of bad loans, especially uncollectible loans to rulers, put the entire structure in jeopardy. The final blow came in 1494 when the French expelled the Medici from Florence (see The Italian City-States later in the chapter) and confiscated their property, bringing about the complete collapse of the Medicean financial edifice.

Social Changes in the Renaissance

The Renaissance inherited from the Middle Ages a hierarchic and organic conception of society. Society was fundamentally divided into three estates: the clergy, whose preeminence was grounded in the belief that society should be directed to a spiritual end; the nobility, whose privileged position rested on the theory that it provided protection and justice for society; and the third estate, which consisted of the peasants and inhabitants of the towns and cities. This social order experienced certain adaptations in the Renaissance, which we can see by examining the second and third estates (the clergy will be examined in Chapter 14).

THE SOCIAL CLASSES: THE NOBILITY   Almost everywhere in western Europe, the landholding nobles were faced with declining real incomes during the greater part of the fourteenth and fifteenth centuries, while the expense of maintaining noble status was rising. It was once assumed that this decline of the nobility in the Late Middle Ages led to the triumph of the middle class, whose fortunes were made in trade, banking, and industry. But, in fact, members of the old nobility survived, while new blood infused its ranks. A reconstruction of the aristocracy was well underway by 1500.

As a result of this reconstruction, the nobles, old and new, managed to dominate society as they had done in the Middle Ages, holding important political posts and serving as advisers to the king. Increasingly in the sixteenth century, members of the aristocracy pursued education as the means to maintain their role in government. One noble in the Low Countries, in a letter outlining how his son should be formally educated, stated that, due to his own lack of learning, he dared not express his opinions in the king's council and often "felt deep shame and humiliation" at his ignorance.

In northern Europe, the fifteenth century also saw the final flourishing of chivalry. Nobles played at being great warriors, but their tournaments were now characterized less by bloodshed than by flamboyance and a display of brilliant costumes that showed off an individual's social status.

THE DEVELOPMENT OF A COURTLY SOCIETY IN ITALY   One of the more interesting social developments during the Renaissance was the change that occurred in Italian society. In the Early Renaissance, old noble families had moved into the cities and generally merged with the merchant middle classes to form the upper classes in these new urban societies. Consequently, Italy seemed to lose the very concept of nobility or aristocracy. In the fifteenth century, this began to change as the tenor of upper-class urban, Italian social life became increasingly aristocratic. Although this was especially evident in the princely states, such as the duchy of Milan where a courtly society emerged around the duke, even in the Italian republics the behavior of the upper class was more in keeping with the ideals of a courtly aristocracy than the old middle class (see the box on p. 420).

By 1500, certain ideals came to be expected of the noble or aristocrat, best expressed in the work of the Italian Baldassare Castiglione (1478–1529). *The Book of the Courtier,* first published in 1528, spread to all of Europe and remained a fundamental handbook for European aristocrats well into the twentieth century.

In *The Book of the Courtier,* Castiglione described the three basic attributes of the perfect courtier. First, nobles should possess fundamental native endowments, such as impeccable character, grace, talents, and noble birth. The perfect courtier must also cultivate certain achievements. Primarily, he should participate in military and bodily exercises since the principal profession of a courtier was arms. Whereas military skill was the only requirement for a medieval knight, this was not true of the Renaissance courtier who must seek a humanist or classical education and adorn his life with the arts by playing a musical instrument, drawing, and painting. In Castiglione's hands, the Renaissance ideal of the well-developed personality became a social ideal of the aristocracy. Finally, the aristocrat was expected to follow a certain standard of conduct. Nobles were expected to make good impressions; while being modest, they should not hide their accomplishments, but show them with grace.

But what was the purpose of these courtly standards? Castiglione said:

> Therefore, I think that the aim of the perfect Courtier, which we have not spoken of up to now, is so to win for himself, by means of the accomplishments ascribed to him by these gentlemen, the favor and mind of the prince whom he

A Renaissance Banquet
▼ ▼ ▼

As in Greek and Roman society, the Renaissance banquet was an occasion for good food, interesting conversation, music, and dancing. In Renaissance society, it was also a symbol of status and an opportunity to impress people with the power and wealth of one's family. Banquets were held to celebrate public and religious festivals, official visits, anniversaries, and weddings. The following menu lists the foods served at a grand banquet given by Pope Pius V in the sixteenth century.

A Sixteenth-Century Banquet

First Course: Cold Delicacies from the Sideboard
Pieces of marzipan and marzipan balls
Neapolitan spice cakes
Malaga wine and Pisan biscuits
Fresh grapes
Prosciutto cooked in wine, served with capers and grape pulp
Salted pork tongues cooked in wine, sliced
Spit-roasted songbirds, cold, with their tongues sliced over them
Sweet mustard

Second Course: Hot Foods from the Kitchen, Roasts
Fried veal sweetbreads and liver
Spit-roasted skylarks with lemon sauce
Spit-roasted quails with sliced aubergines
Stuffed spit-roasted pigeons with capers sprinkled over them
Spit-roasted rabbits, with sauce and crushed pine nuts
Partridges larded and spit-roasted, served with lemon
Heavily seasoned poultry with lemon slices
Slices of veal, spit-roasted, with a sauce made from the juices

Leg of goat, spit-roasted with a sauce made from the juices
Soup of almond paste, with the flesh of three pigeons to each serving

Third Course: Hot Foods from the Kitchen, Boiled Meats and Stews
Stuffed fat geese, boiled Lombard style and covered with sliced almonds
Stuffed breast of veal, boiled, garnished with flowers
Very young calf, boiled, garnished with parsley
Almonds in garlic sauce
Turkish-style rice with milk, sprinkled with cinnamon
Stewed pigeons with mortadella sausage and whole onions
Cabbage soup with sausages
Poultry pie, two chickens to each pie
Fricasseed breast of goat dressed with fried onions
Pies filled with custard cream
Boiled calves' feet with cheese and egg

Fourth Course: Delicacies from the Sideboard
Bean tarts
Quince pastries
Pear tarts, the pears wrapped in marzipan
Parmesan cheese and Riviera cheese
Fresh almonds on vine leaves
Chestnuts roasted over the coals and served with salt and pepper
Milk curds
Ring-shaped cakes
Wafers made from ground corn

---

serves that he may be able to tell him, and always will tell him, the truth about everything he needs to know, without fear or risk of displeasing him; and that when he sees the mind of his prince inclined to a wrong action, he may dare to oppose him . . . so as to dissuade him of every evil intent and bring him to the path of virtue.[14]

This ideal of service to the prince reflected the secular ethic of the active life espoused by the earlier civic humanists. Castiglione put the new moral values of the Renaissance into a courtly, aristocratic form that was now acceptable to the nobility throughout Europe. Nobles would adhere to his principles for hundreds of years while they continued to dominate European life socially and politically.

THE SOCIAL CLASSES: THE THIRD ESTATE OF PEASANTS AND TOWNSPEOPLE Traditionally, peasants made up the overwhelming mass of the third estate and indeed continued to constitute as much as 85 to 90 percent of the total European population, except in the highly urbanized areas of northern Italy and Flanders. The most noticeable trend produced by the economic crisis of the fourteenth century was the decline of the manorial system and the continuing elimination of serfdom. This process had already begun in the twelfth century when the introduction of a money economy made possible the conversion of servile labor dues into rents paid in money, although they also continued to be paid in kind or labor. The contraction of the peasantry after the Black Death simply accelerated this process since lords found it easier to deal with the peasants by granting freedom and accepting rents. Demesne lands were then tilled by hired workers or rented out. By the end of the fifteenth century, serfdom was declining, and more and more peasants were becoming legally free, although in many places lords were able to retain many of the fees they charged their peasants. Lords, then, became rentiers, and the old manorial system was replaced by a new arrangement based on cash. It is interesting to note that while serfdom was declining in western Europe, eastern Europe experienced the reverse trend. The weakness of eastern rulers enabled nobles to tie their peasants to the land and use cheap unfree labor in the large-scale production of grain for an ever-growing export market.

The remainder of the third estate centered around the inhabitants of towns and cities, originally the merchants and artisans who formed the so-called middle class. The Renaissance town or city of the fifteenth century actually possessed a multitude of townspeople widely separated socially and economically.

At the top of urban society were the patricians, whose wealth from capitalistic enterprises in trade, industry, and banking, enabled them to dominate their urban communities economically, socially, and politically. Below them were the petty burghers, the shopkeepers, artisans, guildmasters, and guildsmen who were largely concerned with providing goods and services for local consumption. Below these two groups were the propertyless workers earning pitiful wages and the unemployed, living squalid and miserable lives. These people constituted as much as 30 or 40 percent of the urban population. Everywhere in Europe in the late fourteenth and fifteenth centuries, urban poverty had increased dramatically. One rich merchant of Florence wrote:

> Those that are lazy and indolent in a way that does harm to the city, and who can offer no just reason for their condition, should either be forced to work or expelled from the Commune. The city would thus rid itself of that most harmful part of the poorest class. . . . If the lowest order of society earn enough food to keep them going from day to day, then they have enough.[15]

But even this large group was not at the bottom of the social scale; beneath them stood a significantly large group of slaves, especially in the urban world of the Italian Renaissance.

SLAVERY IN THE RENAISSANCE   Agricultural slavery had continued to exist in the Early Middle Ages, but had declined for economic reasons and been replaced by serfdom by the ninth century. Although some domestic slaves remained, slavery in European society had largely disappeared by the eleventh century. It reappeared first in Spain, where both Christians and Muslims used captured prisoners as slaves during the lengthy *reconquista*. In the second half of the fourteenth century, after the Black Death, the shortage of workers led Italians to introduce slavery on a fairly large scale. In 1363, for example, the government of Florence decreed an unlimited importation of foreign slaves.

In the Italian cities, slaves were used as skilled workers, making handcrafted goods for their masters, or as household workers. Girls served as nursemaids and boys as playmates. Fiammetta Adimari wrote to her husband in 1469: "I must remind you that when Alfonso is weaned we ought to get a little slave-girl to look after him, or else one of the black boys to keep him company."[16] In Florence, wealthy merchants might possess two or three slaves; even small shopkeepers had one.

Slaves for the Italian market were obtained primarily from the eastern Mediterranean and the Black Sea region and included Tartars, Russians, Albanians, and Dalmatians. There were also slaves from Africa, either Moors or Ethiopians, and Muslims from Spain. Because of the lucrative nature of the slave trade, Italian merchants became involved in the transportation of slaves. Between 1414 and 1423, 10,000 slaves were sold on the Venetian market. Most slaves were females, many of them young girls.

The Catholic church's attitude toward slavery was ambiguous. While urging Christian masters to be merciful, the church did nothing to eliminate it. The church did insist that slaves be baptized upon their arrival in Italy and then urged that baptized slaves be treated more leniently. The act of baptism, however, did not free a person from slavery. Slaves were simply viewed as things rather than persons and were classed with the owner's livestock. An inventory of goods compiled in Pisa in 1401 stated that "He says that he has a female slave and a horse and two donkeys and three fifths of an ox. Let us put them down at seventy florins."[17]

By the end of the fifteenth century, slavery had declined dramatically in the Italian cities. Many slaves had

Marriage Negotiations

▼ ▼ ▼

Marriages were so important in maintaining families in Renaissance Italy that much energy was put into arranging them. Parents made the choices for their children, most often for considerations that had little to do with the modern notion of love. This selection is taken from the letters of a Florentine matron of the illustrious Strozzi family to her son Filippo in Naples. The family's considerations were complicated by the fact that the son was in exile.

Alessandra Strozzi to Her Son Filippo in Naples

[April 20, 1464] . . . Concerning the matter of a wife [for Filippo], it appears to me that if Francesco di Messer Tanagli wishes to give his daughter, that it would be a fine marriage. . . . Now I will speak with Marco [Parenti, Alessandra's son-in-law], to see if there are other prospects that would be better, and if there are none, then we will learn if he wishes to give her [in marriage]. . . . Francesco Tanagli has a good reputation, and he has held office, not the highest, but still he has been in office. You may ask: "Why should he give her to someone in exile?" There are three reasons. First, there aren't many young men of good family who have both virtue and property. Secondly, she has only a small dowry, 1,000 florins, which is the dowry of an artisan [although not a small sum, either—senior officials in the government bureaucracy earned 300 florins a year]. . . . Third, I believe that he will give her away, because he has a large family and he will need help to settle them. . . .

[July 26, 1465] . . . Francesco is a good friend of Marco and he trusts him. On S. Jacopo's day, he spoke to him discreetly and persuasively, saying that for several months he had heard that we were interested in the girl and . . . that when we had made up our minds, she will come to us willingly. [He said that] you were a worthy man, and that his family had always made good marriages, but that he had only a small dowry to give her, and so he would prefer to send her outside of Florence to someone of worth, rather than to give her to someone here, from among those who were available, with little money. . . . We have information that she is affable and competent. She is responsible for a large family (there are twelve children, six boys and six girls), and the mother is always pregnant and isn't very competent. . . .

[August 31, 1465] . . . I have recently received some very favorable information [about the Tanagli girl] from two individuals. . . . They are in agreement that whoever gets her will be content. . . . Concerning her beauty, they told me what I had already seen, that she is attractive and well-proportioned. Her face is long, but I couldn't look directly into her face, since she appeared to be aware that I was examining her . . . and so she turned away from me like the wind. . . . She reads quite well . . . and she can dance and sing. . . .

So yesterday I sent for Marco and told him what I had learned. And we talked about the matter for a while, and decided that he should say something to the father and give him a little hope, but not so much that we couldn't withdraw, and find out from him the amount of the dowry. . . . May God help us to choose what will contribute to our tranquility and to the consolation of us all.

[September 13, 1465] . . . Marco came to me and said that he had met with Francesco Tanagli, who had spoken very coldly, so that I understand that he had changed his mind. . . .

[Filippo Strozzi eventually married Fiametta di Donato Adimari in 1466.]

---

been freed by their owners for humanitarian reasons while the major source of slaves dried up as the Black Sea slave markets were closed to Italian traders after the Turks conquered the Byzantine Empire. Although some other sources remained, prices rose dramatically, further cutting demand. Moreover, a general feeling had arisen that slaves—the "domestic enemy" as they were called—were dangerous and not worth the effort. By the six-teenth century, slaves were in evidence only at princely courts where they were kept as curious ornaments; this was especially true of black slaves.

In the fifteenth century, the Portuguese had imported increasing numbers of African slaves for southern European markets. It has been estimated that between 1444 and 1505, 140,000 slaves were shipped from Africa. The presence of blacks in European society was not entirely new. Saint Maurice, a Christian martyr of the fourth century, was portrayed by medieval artists as a black knight and became the center of a popular cult in the twelfth and thirteenth centuries. The number of blacks in Europe, however, was small until their importation as slaves.

Black slaves were most often used as domestic servants. They were viewed, however, as rarities and desired for their exotic qualities. Italian nobles liked to have their portraits painted with black servants as symbols of their wealth.

FAMILY AND MARRIAGE IN RENAISSANCE ITALY Family histories and baptismal, tax, and court records have enabled historians to piece together considerable information about the importance of family ties and traditions in Renaissance Italy. The word family (*famiglia*) had two meanings. There was the nuclear family of father, mother, children, and servants in a wealthy household, which could also include grandparents, widowed mothers, and unmarried sisters. Family also had the meaning of "house," a group of men sharing the same surname since they were descended from a common male ancestor. Although the nuclear family had its own household as a basic economic unit, the households of close male relatives were often located nearby. Cousins of the same name frequently organized joint business ventures and formed a bloc in political affairs. Several important extended families might dominate an entire urban district and act as patrons to many inhabitants of that district. Old family names, such as the Strozzi, Rucellai, and Medici, conferred great status and prestige. The family bond, then, was a source of great security in a dangerous and violent world, and its importance helps explain the vendetta in the Italian Renaissance. A crime committed by one family member fell on the entire family, ensuring that retaliation by the offended family would result in bloody affairs involving large numbers of people.

To maintain the family, careful attention was given to marriages that were arranged by parents, often to solidify business or family ties. Details were worked out well in advance, sometimes when children were only two or three, and reinforced by a legally binding marriage contract (see the box on p. 422). The important aspect of the contract was the size of the dowry, a sum of money given by the wife's family to the husband upon marriage. This money was controlled by the husband. If he died, the amount of the dowry was taken out of his estate to support the widow. The dowry could involve large sums of money and was expected of all families. Since poor families often had difficulty providing a dowry, wealthy families established societies to provide dowries for poor girls. In 1425, the government of Florence stepped in to establish the *Monte della Doti* or Dowry Fund. A *Monte* was a city investment fund; the *Monte della Doti* was exclusively for dowries. Fathers paid a small sum to the *Monte*, usually around the second birthday of a daughter, and received a larger sum as a dowry from the fund when the daughter married, usually in her teens. In the meantime, the city used and invested the *Monte* funds. If the daughter died or did not get married, the father did not receive his money back, giving the *Monte* the potential of accumulating large sums. The *Monte* became a very important financial institution in Florence and, in fact, played a crucial role in the Florentine economy. The city grew accustomed to borrowing from it to pay expenses, virtually running the government from the Dowry Fund. Overuse of its capital eventually caused the fund to collapse in the mid-sixteenth century.

In the cities of Renaissance Italy, girls (but not boys) were closely chaperoned and expected to be virgins when they married. In fact, a husband could repudiate

▼ **Wedding Banquet.** Marriages in Renaissance Italy were arranged by parents in order to strengthen business or family ties. A legally binding marriage contract was considered a necessary part of the marital arrangements. So too was a wedding feast. This painting by Botticelli shows a wedding banquet in Florence to celebrate the marriage of Nastagio degli Onesti and the daughter of Paulo Traversaro.

his wife and keep her dowry if he discovered on his wedding night that she was not a virgin. Since marriage was a sacrament, it was difficult to dissolve. Only an annulment could break the bonds of marriage by declaring a marriage invalid due to sexual impotence or deceit. Since such claims were difficult to prove, only the rich could afford the lengthy trials that resulted.

The father-husband was the center of the Italian family. He represented the family legally, gave it his name, administered all finances (wives had no share in his wealth), and made all decisions concerning the children. A father's authority over his children was absolute until he died or formally freed his children. In Renaissance Italy, reaching a certain age did not make children adults since a father had to go to a judge and formally emancipate them. The age of emancipation varied from early teens to late twenties.

The mother managed the household, a position that gave women a certain degree of autonomy in their daily lives. Considering that marriages had been arranged, marital relationships ran the gamut from deep emotional attachments to purely formal ties. The lack of emotional attachment from arranged marriages did encourage extramarital relationships, especially for those groups whose lifestyle offered special temptations. While sexual license for males was the norm for princes and their courts, women were supposed to follow different guidelines. The first wife of Duke Filippo Maria Visconti of Milan had an affair with the court musician and was executed for it.

The great age difference between husbands and wives that was noticeable in Italian Renaissance marriage patterns also heightened the need for sexual outlets outside marriage. In Florence in 1427–1428, that difference was thirteen years. While females married before the age of twenty, factors of environment, wealth, and demographic trends favored relatively late ages for the first marriages of males, usually in their thirties or even early forties. The existence of large numbers of young, unmarried males encouraged extramarital sex as well as prostitution. In Venice, where prostitutes were regarded as incomparable in skill and in price, charges were carefully cataloged. Prostitution was viewed as a necessary vice; since it could not be eliminated, it should be regulated. In Florence in 1415, the city fathers established communal brothels:

> Desiring to eliminate a worse evil by means of a lesser one, the lord priors . . . have decreed that the priors . . . may authorize the establishment of two public brothels in the city of Florence, in addition to the one which already exists. . . .

> [They are to be located] in suitable places or in places where the exercise of such scandalous activity can best be concealed, for the honor of the city and of those who live in the neighborhood in which these prostitutes must stay to hire their bodies for lucre. . . .[19]

A prostitute in Florence was required to wear a traditional garb of "gloves on her hands and a bell on her head."

▼ The State in the Renaissance

The High Middle Ages had witnessed the emergence of territorial states that began to develop the administrative machinery of centralized government. Professional bureaucracies, royal courts, and parliamentary assemblies were all products of the twelfth and thirteenth centuries. Strong monarchy had provided the organizing power for the development of these states, but in the fourteenth century the internal stability of European governments had been threatened by financial and dynastic problems as well as challenges from their nobilities. By the fifteenth century, rulers began to rebuild their governments by restraining turbulent nobles, curbing violence, and maintaining internal order. Some territorial units, such as the Holy Roman Empire and Italy, failed to develop strong national monarchies, but even in these areas, strong princes and city councils managed to centralize their authority within their smaller territorial states. In Italy, Milan, Venice, and Florence managed to become fairly well centralized territorial states. Some historians view the Italian Renaissance states, in their preoccupation with political power, as the first true examples of the modern secular state.

The Italian City-States

In the fourteenth century, Italy had experienced two major developments: the rise of despots in place of republican governments and the expansion of the larger city-states at the expense of the less powerful ones. By the fifteenth century, five major powers dominated the Italian peninsula—the duchy of Milan, Venice, Florence, the Papal States and the kingdom of Naples.

Northern Italy was divided between the duchy of Milan and Venice. After the death of the last Visconti ruler of Milan in 1447, Francesco Sforza, one of the leading *condottieri* (see Chapter 12) of the time, turned on his Milanese employers, conquered the city, and became its new duke. Both the Visconti and Sforza rulers worked to create a highly centralized territorial state. They were especially successful in creating systems of taxation that generated enormous revenues for the government. The maritime republic of Venice remained an extremely stable political entity governed by a small oligarchy of merchant-aristocrats. Its commercial empire brought in enormous revenues and gave it the status of an international power. At the end of the fourteenth century, Venice embarked upon the conquest of a territorial state in northern Italy to protect its food supply and its overland trade routes. Although expansion on the mainland made sense to the Venetians, it frightened Milan and Florence who worked to curb what they perceived as the expansionary designs of the Venetians.

The republic of Florence dominated the region of Tuscany. By the beginning of the fifteenth century, Florence was governed by a small merchant oligarchy that manipulated the apparently republican government. In 1434, Cosimo de' Medici took control of this oligarchy. Although the wealthy Medici family maintained republican forms of government for appearance sake, it ran the government from behind the scenes. Through their lavish patronage and careful courting of political allies, Cosimo (1434–1464) and later his grandson Lorenzo the Magnificent (1469–1492) were successful in dominating the city at a time when Florence was the center of the cultural Renaissance.

The Papal States lay in central Italy. Nominally under the political control of the popes, papal residence in Avignon and the Great Schism had enabled individual cities and territories, such as Urbino, Bologna, and Ferrara, to become independent of papal authority. The Renaissance popes of the fifteenth century directed much of their energy toward reestablishing their control over the Papal States (see The Renaissance Papacy later in the chapter).

The kingdom of Naples, which encompassed most of southern Italy and usually the island of Sicily, was fought over by the French and the Aragonese until the latter established their domination in the mid-fifteenth century. Throughout the Renaissance, the kingdom of Naples remained a largely feudal monarchy with an enormous class of poverty-stricken peasants dominated by unruly barons and shared little in the cultural glories of the Renaissance.

Besides the five major states, there were a number of independent city-states under the control of powerful ruling families that became brilliant centers of Renaissance culture in the fifteenth century. Such were Mantua under the enlightened rule of the Gonzaga lords, Ferrara governed by the flamboyant d'Este family, and perhaps most famous, Urbino, ruled by the Montefeltro dynasty.

Federigo da Montefeltro, who ruled Urbino from 1444 to 1482, received a classical education typical of the famous humanist school in Mantua run by Vittorino da Feltre. He had also learned the skills of fighting, since the Montefeltro family compensated for the poverty of Urbino by hiring themselves out as *condottieri*. Federigo was not only a good ruler, but a rather unusual *condottiere* by fifteenth-century standards. Although not a brilliant general, he was reliable and honest. He did not break his promises, even when urged to do so by a papal legate. His employers included two kings of Naples, three popes, and two dukes of Milan. At the same time, Duke Federigo was one of the greatest patrons of Renaissance culture. Under his direction, Urbino became a well-

▼ **A Renaissance City: Venice.** By the fifteenth century, northern Italy was dominated by the duchy of Milan and the maritime republic of Venice. Venice controlled a vast commercial empire, and although its wealth raised it to the status of an international power, the Venetians felt the need to expand on the mainland in order to protect their trade routes and food supply. This picture shows the Cathedral of Saint Mark and the Doge's Palace in Saint Mark's Square.

known cultural and intellectual center. While despotic, he was also benevolent. It was said of him that he could walk safely through the streets of Urbino, unaccompanied by a bodyguard, a feat few Renaissance rulers dared to emulate (see the box on p. 427).

A noticeable feature of these smaller Renaissance courts was the important role played by women. Battista Sforza, niece of the ruler of Milan, was the wife of Federigo da Montefeltro. The duke called his wife "the delight of both my public and my private hours." An intelligent woman, she was well versed in both Greek and Latin and did much to promote art and letters in Urbino. As a prominent *condottiere*, Federigo was frequently absent, and like earlier feudal wives, Battista Sforza was respected for governing the state "with firmness and good sense."

The most famous of the Renaissance ruling women was Isabella d'Este (1474–1539), daughter of the duke of Ferrara, who married Francesco Gonzaga, marquis of Mantua. Their court was another important center of art and learning in the Renaissance. Educated at the bril-liant court of Ferrara, Isabella was known for her intelligence and political wisdom. Called the "first lady of the world," she attracted artists and intellectuals to the Mantuan court and was responsible for amassing one of the finest libraries in all of Italy. Her numerous letters to friends, family, princes, and artists all over Europe disclose her political acumen as well as a good sense of humor. Both before and after the death of her husband Francesco, she effectively ruled Mantua and won a reputation as a clever negotiator.

The frenzied world of the Italian territorial states gave rise to a political practice that was later used on a larger scale by competing European states. This was the concept of a balance of power, designed to prevent the aggrandizement of any one state at the expense of the others. This system was especially evident after 1454 when the Italian states signed the Peace of Lodi, which ended almost a half-century of war and inaugurated a relatively peaceful era in Italy until 1494. An alliance system (Milan, Florence and Naples versus Venice and the papacy) was then created that led to a workable

▼ **Map 13.1** Renaissance Italy

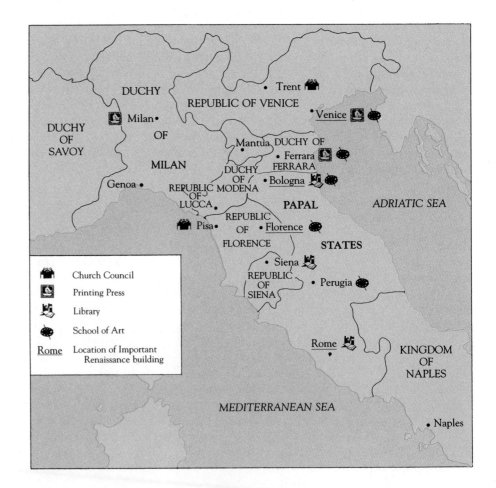

A Renaissance Prince

▼ ▼ ▼

Widely regarded as one of the truly outstanding princes of the Italian Renaissance, Federigo da Montefeltro, duke of Urbino (1422–1482), was a leading condottiere, an astute ruler, and a patron of humanist culture and Renaissance art. Vespasiano da Bisticci, an Italian book dealer, included an account of Federigo in his collection of biographies (known as The Vespasiano Memoirs) of the famous men he had known. In this selection, Vespasiano gives an example of the duke's eagerness to settle dissension among his subjects.

Vespasiano da Bisticci, *The Vespasiano Memoirs*

He gave himself entirely to his state that the people might be content, and one of the greatest of his merits was that when he heard of a quarrel he would send for the parties, and give his wits no rest till peace should be made. Amongst his many kind actions in mitigating dissension was the case of one of his subjects of honest birth who chose as wife a girl of a station similar to his own with numerous kinsfolk, betwixt whom and the husband arose bad feeling, so that he was in no way inclined towards the wife whom he had taken. The affair came to the point at which he might have to defend his honour, which meant that he would probably be cut in pieces by one or other of the kinsfolk. The Duke, knowing the scandal which would follow, by way of avoiding it, ordered the parties to settle their quarrel on a certain day; and when they had come before him he began with those who had the girl in charge; and, speaking in kindly eloquent words, gave them many and good reasons for what he advised them to do. As is the case with ignorant people, the more he said the more firmly they resisted. When he saw their disposition he turned to the young man and said, "If I desired you to become a relative of mine, would you not consent, having regard for my station? Would it not seem to you a desirable relationship?" The young man replied that in this case it would not be fitting, between so great a man as the Duke and one like himself. Then the Duke said, "But will you not pay regard to something which satisfies me?" The young man, persuaded by the Duke, affirmed that he was content, whereupon the Duke said, "I think very highly of this young woman for her virtue and goodness, as if she were my own daughter; so you are becoming a relative of me, and not of her family." By these words the Duke bound him, so that he was forced to consent, and he took her with the good wishes of all. The Duke took them both by the hand, wishing them good luck, and saying that their relationship with him began from that hour, that he wished them always to bear this in mind, and in all their needs to make use of him. He gave them a noble marriage-feast and they both went away highly pleased, and hereafter the husband and wife maintained an admirable carriage one towards the other. Acts like these, the bringing of peace to his subjects, are worthy of a prince.

---

balance of power within Italy. It failed, however, to create a lasting cooperation of the major powers or a common foreign policy.

The growth of powerful national monarchical states (see The New Monarchies later in the chapter) led to trouble for the Italians. Italy soon became a battlefield for the great power struggle between the French and Spanish monarchies. Italian wealth and splendor would probably have been inviting to its northern neighbors under any circumstances, but it was actually the breakdown of the Italian balance of power that encouraged the invasions and began the Italian wars. Feeling isolated, Ludovico Sforza, the duke of Milan, foolishly invited the French to intervene in Italian politics. The French king Charles VIII (1483–1498) was eager to do so and in 1494, with an army of 30,000 men, advanced through Italy and occupied the kingdom of Naples. Other Italian states turned to the Spanish for help, and Ferdinand of Aragon indicated his willingness to intervene. For the next fifteen years, the French and Spanish competed to dominate Italy. Beginning in the decade of the 1510s, the war was continued by a new generation of rulers, Francis I of France and Charles I of Spain (see Chapter 14). This involved a larger struggle for power in Europe between the Valois and Habsburg dynasties. Italy was only a pawn for the two great powers, a convenient arena for fighting battles. The terrible sack of Rome in 1527 by the armies of the Spanish king Charles I brought a temporary end to the Italian wars. Hereafter, the Spaniards dominated Italy; the Renaissance in Italy was at an end.

Although some Italians had developed a sense of national consciousness and differentiated between Italians and "barbarians" (all foreigners), few Italians conceived of creating an alliance or confederation of city-states that could repel foreign invaders. Italians remained fiercely loyal to their own petty states, making invasion a fact of life in Italian history for all too long. Italy would not achieve unification and nationhood until 1870.

The "New Monarchies"

In the first half of the fifteenth century, European states continued the disintegrative patterns of the previous century. In the second half of the fifteenth century, however, recovery set in, and attempts were made to reestablish the centralized power of monarchical governments. To characterize the results, some historians have used the label "Renaissance states"; others have spoken of the "new monarchies," especially those of France, England, and Spain at the end of the fifteenth century. Although appropriate, the term "new monarch" can also be misleading. These Renaissance monarchs were new in their concentration of royal authority, their attempts to suppress the nobility, their efforts to control the church in their lands, and their insistence upon having the loyalty of people living within definite territorial boundaries. Like the rulers of fifteenth-century Italian states, the "new monarchs" were often crafty men obsessed with the acquisition and expansion of political power. Of course, none of these characteristics was entirely new since a number of medieval monarchs, espe-

cially in the thirteenth century, had also exhibited them. Nevertheless, the Renaissance period does mark the further extension of royal centralized authority. There were, of course, variations from area to area in the degree to which monarchs were successful in extending their political authority. In central and eastern Europe, decentralization rather than centralization of political authority remained a fact of life.

END OF THE HUNDRED YEARS' WAR   In the first half of the fifteenth century, the histories of England and France were largely determined by the continuation of the Hundred Years' War (see Chapter 12). This protracted series of struggles between the French and English seemed at an end in 1396 when a twenty-year truce was arranged. Due to his love of fighting, however, the English king, Henry V (1413–1422), found an excuse to renew the war in 1415. At the Battle of Agincourt (1415), the

▼ **Joan of Arc.** A crucial element in the ending of the Hundred Years' War was the influence of Joan of Arc. Born to a peasant family, Joan believed that visions of her favorite saints commanded her to free France and have the dauphin crowned as king. Her presence seemingly inspired the French to victory in 1429. The crowning of the dauphin fulfilled Joan's second task. Captured by allies of the English, Joan was burned at the stake in 1431.

attempt of the heavy, armor-plated French knights to attack across a field turned to mud by heavy rain led to a disastrous French defeat and the death of 1,500 French nobles. Henry went on to reconquer Normandy and forge an alliance with the duke of Burgundy, making the English masters of northern France.

The French cause, seemingly hopeless, fell into the hands of the dauphin Charles, the heir to the throne, who governed the southern two-thirds of French lands from Bourges. Charles was weak and timid, unwilling and unable to rally France against the English, who, in 1428, had turned south and were besieging the city of Orleans to gain access to the valley of the Loire. The French monarch was saved, quite unexpectedly, by a French peasant woman.

Joan of Arc was born in 1412, the daughter of well-to-do peasants from the village of Domrémy in Champagne. Deeply religious, Joan experienced visions and came to believe that her favorite saints had commanded her to free France and have the dauphin crowned as king. In February 1429, Joan made her way to the dauphin's court, where her sincerity and simplicity persuaded Charles to allow her to accompany a French army to Orleans. Apparently inspired by the faith of the peasant woman who called herself "the Maid," the French armies found new confidence in themselves and liberated Orleans. Within a few weeks, the entire Loire valley had been freed of the English. In July 1429, fulfilling Joan's other task, the dauphin was crowned king of France and became Charles VII (1422–1461). In accomplishing the two commands of her angelic voices, Joan had brought the war to a decisive turning point.

Joan, however, did not live to see the war concluded. She was captured by the Burgundian allies of the English in 1430. Wishing to eliminate the "Maid" for obvious political reasons, the English turned Joan over to the Inquisition on charges of witchcraft (see the box above). In the fifteenth century, spiritual visions were thought to be inspired either by God or the devil. Since Joan dressed in men's clothing, it was relatively easy to convince others that she was in league with the "prince of darkness." She was condemned to death as a heretic and burned at the stake in 1431. To the end, as the flames rose up around her, she declared "that her voices came from God and had not deceived her." Twenty-five years later, a new ecclesiastical court exonerated her of these charges. In 1920, she was made a saint of the Roman Catholic church.

Joan of Arc's accomplishments proved decisive. Although the war dragged on in desultory fashion for another two decades, defeats of English armies in Normandy and Aquitaine led to French victory by 1453. All that remained in England's hands was its coastal town of Calais, which remained English for another century.

FRANCE   The Hundred Years' War left France prostrate. Depopulation, desolate farmlands, ruined commerce, and independent and unruly nobles made it difficult for the kings to assert their authority. But the war had also developed a strong degree of French national feeling toward a common enemy that the kings could use to reestablish monarchical power. The need to prosecute the war provided an excuse to strengthen the authority of the king, already evident in the policies of Charles VII (1422–1461) after he was crowned king at Reims. With the consent of the Estates-General, Charles established a royal army composed of cavalrymen and archers. He received from the Estates-General the right to levy the *taille*, an annual direct tax usually on land or property, without any need for further approval from the Estates-General. Losing control of the purse meant less power for this parliamentary body. Charles VII also secured the Pragmatic Sanction of Bourges (1438), an agreement with the papacy that strengthened the liberties of the French church administratively at the expense of the papacy and enabled the king to begin to assume control over the church in France.

The process of developing a French territorial state was greatly advanced by King Louis XI (1461–1483), known as the Spider because of his wily and devious ways. Some historians have called this "new monarch" the founder of the French national state. Louis retained the *taille* as a permanent tax imposed by royal authority, giving him a sound, regular source of income. Louis was not completely successful in repressing the French nobility whose independence posed a threat to his own state building. A major problem was his supposed vassal, the duke of Burgundy. Charles the Bold, duke of Burgundy (1467–1477), tried to create a middle kingdom between France and Germany, stretching from the Low Countries in the north to Switzerland. Louis opposed his action, and when Charles was killed in 1477 fighting the Swiss, Louis added part of Charles's possessions, the duchy of Burgundy, to his own lands. Three years later, the provinces of Anjou, Maine, Bar, and Provence were

brought under royal control. Louis the Spider also encouraged the growth of industry and commerce in an attempt to bolster the French economy. He introduced new industries, such as the silk industry to Lyons.

Many historians believe that Louis created a base for the later development of a strong French monarchy. In any case, the monarchy was at least well enough established to weather the policies of the next two monarchs, Charles VIII (1483–1498) and Louis XII (1498–1515), whose attempts to subdue parts of Italy initiated a series of Italian wars. Internally, France survived these wars without too much difficulty.

ENGLAND   The Hundred Years' War had also strongly affected the other protagonist in that conflict. The cost of the war in its final years and the losses in manpower strained the English economy. Moreover, the end of the war brought even greater domestic turmoil to England when the War of the Roses broke out in the 1450s. This civil war pitted the ducal house of Lancaster, whose symbol was a red rose, against the ducal house of York, whose symbol was a white rose. Many aristocratic families of England were drawn into the conflict. Finally, in 1485, Henry Tudor, duke of Richmond, defeated the last Yorkist king, Richard III (1483–1485), at Bosworth Field and established the new Tudor dynasty.

As the first Tudor king, Henry VII (1485–1509) worked to reduce internal dissension and establish a strong monarchical government. The English aristocracy had been much weakened by the war of the Roses since many nobles had been killed. Henry eliminated the private wars of the nobility by abolishing "livery and maintenance," the practice by which wealthy aristocrats maintained private armies of followers dedicated to the service of their lord. Since England, unlike France and Spain, did not possess a standing army, the king relied on special commissions to trusted nobles to raise troops for a specific campaign, after which the troops were disbanded. Henry also controlled the irresponsible activity of the nobles by establishing the Court of Star Chamber, which did not use juries and allowed the practice of torture to extract confessions.

Henry VII was particularly successful in obtaining sufficient income from the traditional financial resources of the English monarch, such as the crown lands, judicial fees and fines, and customs duties. By using diplomacy to avoid wars, which are always expensive, the king avoided having to call Parliament on any regular basis to grant him funds. By not overburdening the landed gentry and middle class with taxes, Henry won their favor, and they provided much support for his monarchy.

Henry also encouraged commercial activity. By increasing wool exports, royal export taxes on wool rose. Henry's thriftiness as well as his domestic and foreign policies enabled him to leave England with a stable and prosperous government and an enhanced status for the monarchy itself.

SPAIN During the Middle Ages, several independent Christian kingdoms had emerged in the course of the long reconquest of the Iberian peninsula from the Muslims. Aragon and Castile were the strongest Spanish kingdoms; in the west was the independent monarchy of Portugal; in the north the small kingdom of Navarre, oriented toward France; and in the south the Muslim kingdom of Granada. Few people at the beginning of the fifteenth century could have predicted the national unification of Spain.

A major step in that direction was taken with the marriage of Isabella of Castile (1474–1504) and Ferdinand of Aragon (1479–1516) in 1469. This marriage was a dynastic union of two rulers, not a political union. Both kingdoms maintained their own parliaments (Cortes), courts, laws, coinage, speech, customs, and political organs. Nevertheless, the two rulers worked to strengthen royal control of government, especially in Castile. The royal council, which was supposed to supervise local administration and oversee the implementation of government policies, was stripped of aristocrats and filled primarily with middle-class lawyers. Trained in the principles of Roman law, these officials operated on

the belief that the monarchy embodied the power of the state.

The towns were also enlisted in the policy of state building. Medieval town organizations known as *hermandades* ("brotherhoods"), which had been organized to maintain law and order, were revived. Ferdinand and Isabella transformed them into a kind of national militia whose primary goal was to stop the wealthy landed aristocrats from disturbing the peace, a goal also favored by the middle class. The *hermandades* were disbanded by 1498 when the royal administration became strong enough to deal with lawlessness. The appointment of *corregidores* by the crown to replace corrupt municipal officials enabled the monarchs to extend the central authority of royal government into the towns.

Ferdinand and Isabella reorganized the military forces of Spain, seeking to replace the undisciplined feudal levies they had inherited with a more professional royal army. The development of a strong infantry force as the heart of the new Spanish army made it the best in Europe by the sixteenth century.

Because of its vast power and wealth, Ferdinand and Isabella recognized the importance of controlling the Catholic church. They secured from the pope the right to select the most important church officials in Spain, virtually guaranteeing the foundation of a Spanish Catholic church in which the clergy became an instrument for the extension of royal power. The monarchs also used their authority over the church to institute reform. Isabella's chief minister, the able and astute Cardinal

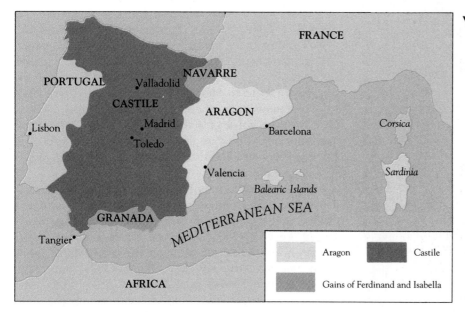

▼ **Map 13.2** Iberian Peninsula.

Ximenes, restored discipline and eliminated immorality among the monks and secular clergy.

The religious zeal exhibited in Cardinal Ximenes's reform program was also evident in the policy of strict religious uniformity pursued by Ferdinand and Isabella. Of course, it served a political purpose as well: to create national unity and further bolster royal power. Spain possessed two large religious minorities, the Jews and Muslims, both of which had been largely tolerated in medieval Spain. Although anti-Semitism had become a fact of life in medieval Europe, Spain had remained tolerant. In some areas of Spain, Jews exercised much influence in economic and intellectual affairs. Increased

▼ **Emperor Maximilian I.** While the Holy Roman emperor possessed little real power in Germany, the Habsburg dynasty, which gained the position of emperor after 1438, steadily increased its wealth and landholdings through dynastic marriages. Although Emperor Maximilian I, pictured here in a portrait by Albrecht Dürer, failed in his attempts to centralize the administration of the empire, his marriage alliances produced one of the most powerful monarchs of the period, namely Charles I, who became heir to the Habsburg, Burgundian, and Spanish royal lines.

persecution in the fourteenth century, however, led the majority of Spanish Jews to convert to Christianity. Although many of these *conversos* came to play important roles in Spanish society, complaints that they were secretly reverting to Judaism prompted Ferdinand and Isabella to ask the pope to introduce the Inquisition into Spain in 1478. Under royal control, the Inquisition worked with cruel efficiency to guarantee the orthodoxy of the *conversos,* but had no authority over practicing Jews. Consequently, in 1492, flush with the success of the conquest of Muslim Granada, Ferdinand and Isabella took the drastic step of expelling all professed Jews from Spain. It is estimated that 150,000 out of possibly 200,000 Jews fled.

Muslims, too, were "encouraged" to convert to Christianity after the conquest of Granada. In 1502, Isabella issued a decree expelling all professed Muslims from her kingdom. To a very large degree, the "Most Catholic" monarchs had achieved their goal of absolute religious orthodoxy as a basic ingredient of the Spanish national state. To be Spanish was to be Catholic, a policy of uniformity enforced by the Inquisition.

During the reigns of Ferdinand and Isabella, Spain (or the union of Castile and Aragon) began to emerge as an important power in European affairs. Both Granada and Navarre had been conquered and incorporated into the royal realms. Nevertheless, Spain remained divided in many ways. Only the royal dynasty provided the centralizing force, and when a single individual, the grandson of Ferdinand and Isabella, succeeded both rulers as Charles I in 1516, he inherited lands that made him the most powerful monarch of his age.

THE HOLY ROMAN EMPIRE   Unlike France, England, and Spain, the Holy Roman Empire failed to develop a strong monarchical authority. After 1438, the position of Holy Roman emperor was held in the hands of the Habsburg dynasty. Having gradually acquired a number of possessions along the Danube, known collectively as Austria, the house of Habsburg had become one of the wealthiest landholders in the empire and by the mid-fifteenth century began to play an important role in European affairs.

Much of the Habsburg success in the fifteenth century was due not to military success, but to a well-executed policy of dynastic marriages. As the old Habsburg motto said: "Leave the waging of wars to others! But thou, happy Austria, marry; for the realms which Mars [god of war] awards to others, Venus [goddess of love] transfers to thee." Although Frederick III (1440–1493) lost the traditional Habsburg possessions of Bohemia and Hungary, he gained Franche-Comté in east central France, Luxembourg, and a large part of the Low Countries by marrying his son Maximilian to Mary, the daughter of Duke Charles the Bold of Burgundy. The addition of these territories made the Habsburg dynasty an international power and brought them the undying opposition of the French monarchy.

Much was expected of the flamboyant Maximilian I (1493–1519) when he became emperor. Through the Reichstag, the imperial diet, Maximilian attempted to centralize the administration by creating new institutions common to the entire empire. Opposition from the German princes doomed these efforts, however. Maximilian's only real success lay in his marriage alliances. Philip of Burgundy, the son of Maximilian's marriage to Mary, was married to Joanna, the daughter of Ferdinand and Isabella. Philip and Joanna produced a son, Charles, who, through a series of unexpected deaths, became heir to all three lines, the Habsburg, Burgundian, and Spanish, making him the leading monarch of his age (see Chapter 14).

Although the Holy Roman Empire did not develop along the lines of a centralized monarchical state, within the empire the power of the independent princes and electors increased steadily. In numerous German states, such as Bavaria, Hesse, Brandenburg, and the Palatinate, princes built up bureaucracies, developed standing armies, created fiscal systems, and introduced Roman law, just like the national monarchs of France, England, and Spain. They proved a real threat to the church, the emperor, and other smaller independent bodies in the Holy Roman Empire, especially the free imperial cities.

EASTERN EUROPE   In eastern Europe, rulers struggled to achieve the centralization of their territorial states but faced insuperable obstacles. Although the population was mostly Slavic, there were islands of other ethnic groups that caused untold difficulties. Religious differences also troubled the area, as Roman Catholics, Greek Orthodox Christians, and pagans confronted each other. Finally, conflict arose between eastern and western institutions and ideas, leading to a relatively strong Slavic nationalism toward the end of the Middle Ages.

Much of Polish history revolved around the bitter struggle between the crown and the landed nobility. The dynastic union of Jagiello, grand prince of Lithuania, with the Polish queen Jadwiga resulted in a large Lithuanian-Polish state in 1386. He and his more immediate successors were able to control the landed magnates, but by the end of the fifteenth century, Jagellonian preoccupation with problems in Bohemia and

Chronology

▼ ▼ ▼

The "New Monarchies"

End of the Hundred Years' War	
Henry V (1413–1422) Renews the War	1415
Battle of Agincourt	1415
French Recovery under Joan of Arc	1429–1431
End of the War	1453
France	
Charles VII	1422–1461
Pragmatic Sanction of Bourges	1438
Louis XI the Spider	1461–1483
Charles VIII	1483–1498
Louis XII	1498–1515
England	
War of the Roses	1450s–1485
Richard III	1483–1485
Henry VII	1485–1509
Spain	
Isabella of Castile	1474–1504
Ferdinand of Aragon	1479–1516
Marriage of Ferdinand and Isabella	1469
Introduction of Inquisition	1478
Expulsion of the Jews	1492
Expulsion of the Muslims	1502
Holy Roman Empire	
Frederick III	1440–1493
Maximilian I	1493–1519
Eastern Europe	
Creation of Lithuanian-Polish State	1386
Hungary: Matthias Corvinus	1458–1490
Russia: Ivan III	1462–1505
Fall of Constantinople and Byzantine Empire	1453

Hungary as well as war with the Russians and Turks enabled the aristocrats to reestablish their power. Through their control of the *Sejm* or national diet, the magnates reduced the peasantry to serfdom by 1511 and established the right to elect their kings. The Polish kings proved unable to establish a strong royal authority.

Recovery and Rebirth: The Age of the Renaissance   ▼   433

Bohemia, Poland's neighbor, was part of the Holy Roman Empire, but Czech distrust of the Germans and their close ethnic ties to the Poles and Slovaks encouraged them to associate with their northeastern Slavic neighbors. The Hussite wars (see The Problems of Heresy and Reform later in the chapter) led to further dissension and civil war. Because of a weak monarchy, the Bohemian nobles increased their authority and wealth at the expense of both crown and church.

The history of Hungary had been closely tied to that of central and western Europe by its conversion to Roman Catholicism by German missionaries. The church became a large and prosperous institution. Wealthy bishops, along with the great territorial lords, became powerful, independent political figures. For a brief while, however, Hungary developed into an important European state, the dominant power in eastern Europe. King Matthias Corvinus (1458–1490) broke the power of the wealthy lords and created a well-organized government bureaucracy. Like a typical Renaissance prince, he patronized the new humanist culture, brought Italian scholars and artists to his capital at Buda, and made his court one of the most brilliant outside Italy. After his death, Hungary returned to weak rule and the work of Corvinus was largely undone.

Since the thirteenth century, Russia had been under the domination of the Mongols. Gradually, the princes of Moscow rose to prominence by using their close relationship to the Mongol khans to increase their wealth and expand their possessions. In the reign of the great prince Ivan III (1462–1505), a new Russian state was born. Ivan III annexed other Russian principalities and took advantage of dissension among the Mongols to throw off their yoke by 1480. He invaded the lands of the Lithuanian-Polish dynasty and added the territories around Kiev, Smolensk, and Chernigov to his new Muscovite state.

THE OTTOMAN TURKS AND THE END OF BYZANTIUM Eastern Europe was increasingly threatened by the steadily advancing Ottoman Turks. The Byzantine Empire had, of course, served as a buffer between the Mus-

▼ **Map 13.3** Southeastern Europe.

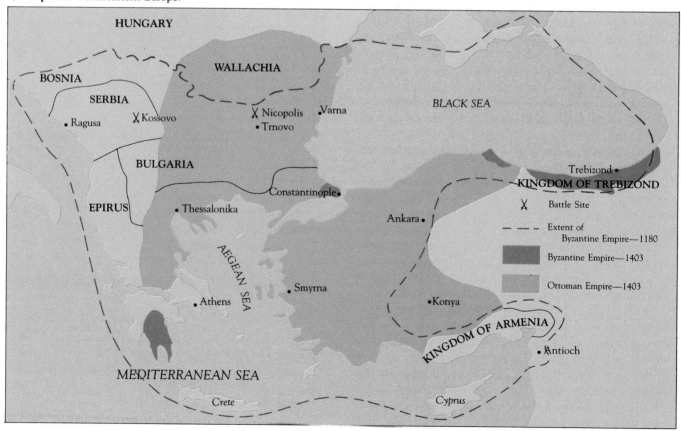

lim Middle East and the Latin West for centuries. It was severely weakened by the sack of Constantinople in 1204 and its occupation by the west. Although the Palaeologus dynasty (1260–1453) had tried to reestablish Byzantine power in the Balkans after the overthrow of the Latin Empire, the threat from the Turks finally doomed the long-lasting empire.

Beginning in northeastern Asia Minor in the thirteenth century, the Ottoman Turks spread rapidly, seizing the lands of the Seljuk Turks and the Byzantine Empire. In 1345, they bypassed Constantinople and moved into the Balkans, which they conquered by the end of the century. Finally in 1453, the great city of Constantinople fell to the Turks after a siege of several months. After consolidating their power, the Turks prepared to exert renewed pressure on the west, both in the Mediterranean and up the Danube valley toward Vienna, and by the end of the fifteenth century were threatening Hungary, Austria, Bohemia, and Poland. The Holy Roman emperor, Charles V, became their bitter enemy in the sixteenth century.

Our survey of European political developments makes it clear that although individual German or especially Italian princes had developed culturally brilliant states, the future belonged to territorial states organized by national monarchies. They possessed superior resources and were developing institutions that represented the interests of much of the population. The Renaissance states were not yet nation-states, but dynastic-states. The interests of the states were the interests of their ruling dynasties. Loyalty was owed to the ruler, not the state. A resident of France considered himself a subject of the French king, not a citizen of France. Moreover, although Renaissance monarchs were strong rulers centralizing their authority, they were by no means absolute monarchs. Some chance of representative government still remained in the form of Parliament, Estates-General, Cortes, or Reichstag. Kings were strongest in the west and, with the exception of the Russian rulers, weakest in the east.

The Birth of Modern Diplomacy

The modern diplomatic system was a product of the Italian Renaissance. There were ambassadors in the Middle Ages, but they were used only on a temporary basis. Moreover, an ambassador, regardless of whose subject he was, regarded himself as the servant of all Christendom, not just his particular employer. As a treatise on diplomacy stated: "An ambassador is sacred because he acts for the general welfare." Since he was the servant of all Christendom, "the business of an ambassador is peace."[19]

This concept of an ambassador changed in the Italian Renaissance because of the political situation in Italy. A large number of states existed, many small enough that their security was easily threatened by their neighbors. To survive, the Italian states began to send resident diplomatic agents to each other to ferret out useful information. During the Italian wars, the practice of resident diplomats spread to the rest of Europe, and in the course of the sixteenth and seventeenth centuries, Europeans developed the diplomatic machinery still in use today, such as the rights of ambassadors in host countries and the proper procedures for conducting diplomatic business.

▼ **Departure of the Ambassadors.** In the Middle Ages, ambassadors were regarded as the servants of all Christendom, not just of their particular states. This changed during the Italian Renaissance, however, when ambassadors began to take up permanent residence in their host states and worked to discover information useful to their home country. The role of the ambassador had thus changed; he no longer served all Christendom, but the interests of his own state. As illustrated in Carpaccio's *The Departure of the Ambassadors*, standard procedures for ambassadorial behavior also came into existence in the Renaissance.

With the use of permanent resident agents or ambassadors, the conception of the purpose of the ambassador also changed. A Venetian diplomat attempted to define the function of an ambassador in a treatise written at the end of the fifteenth century. He wrote: "The first duty of an ambassador is exactly the same as that of any other servant of a government, that is, to do, say, advise and think whatever may best serve the preservation and aggrandizement of his own state."[20] An ambassador was now simply an agent of the territorial state that sent him, not the larger body of Christendom. He could use any methods that were beneficial to the political interests of his own state. We are at the beginning of modern politics when the interests of the state supersede all other considerations.

Machiavelli and the New Statecraft

No one gave better expression to the Renaissance preoccupation with political power than Niccolò Machiavelli (1469–1527). He entered the service of the Florentine republic in 1498, four years after the Medici family had been expelled from the city. As a secretary to the Florentine Council of Ten, he made numerous diplomatic missions, including trips to France and Germany, and saw the workings of statecraft firsthand. Since Italy had been invaded in 1494, Machiavelli was active during a period of Italian tribulation and devastation. In 1512, French defeat and Spanish victory led to the reestablishment of Medici power in Florence. Staunch republicans, including Machiavelli, were sent into exile. Forced to give up politics, the great love of his life, Machiavelli now reflected on political power and wrote books, including *The Prince* (1513), one of the most famous treatises on political power in the Western world.

Machiavelli's ideas on politics stemmed from two major sources, his preoccupation with Italy's political problems and his knowledge of ancient Rome. His major concerns in *The Prince* were the acquisition, maintenance, and expansion of political power. Machiavelli was aware that his own approach to political power was different from previous political theorists. Late medieval political theory conceived of the state as a necessary creation for humankind's spiritual, material, and social well-being. A ruler was justified in his exercise of political power only if it contributed to the common good of the people he served. The ethical side of a prince's activity—how a ruler ought to behave based on Christian moral principles—was the focus of many late medieval treatises on politics. Machiavelli bluntly contradicted this approach:

But since my intention is to say something that will prove of practical use to the inquirer, I have thought it proper to represent things as they are in real truth, rather than as they are imagined . . . the gulf between how one should live and how one does live is so wide that a man who neglects what is actually done for what should be done learns the way to self-destruction rather than self-preservation.[21]

Machiavelli considered his approach far more realistic than that of his medieval forebears.

From Machiavelli's point of view, a prince's attitude toward power must be based on an understanding of human nature, which he perceived as basically self-centered. He said, "One can make this generalization about men: they are ungrateful, fickle, liars, and deceivers, they shun danger and are greedy for profit. . . ." Political activity, therefore, could not be restricted by moral considerations. The prince acts on behalf of the state and for the sake of the state must be willing to let his conscience sleep. As Machiavelli put it:

A prince . . . cannot observe all those things which give men a reputation for virtue, because in order to maintain his state he is often forced to act in defiance of good faith, of charity, of kindness, of religion. And so he should have a flexible disposition, varying as fortune and circumstances dictate. As I said above, he should not deviate from what is good, if that is possible, but he should know how to do evil, if that is necessary.[22]

Machiavelli was among the first to abandon morality as the basis for the analysis of political activity.

Because of the ideas in *The Prince*, Machiavelli is often considered the founder of modern, secular power politics, but we should note that Machiavelli himself was primarily concerned with Italy's tragic political condition. If it hoped to free itself from the "barbarous cruelties and outrages" perpetrated by the monarchical territorial states to the north, Italy needed a prince "to heal her wounds . . . and cleanse those sores which have now been festering for so long." If any person undertook the task, "What Italian would refuse him allegiance?"[23] If he followed the principles enunciated in *The Prince*, he would succeed. Machiavelli's own predilection for a republican form of government was clearly evident in *The Discourses*, a political treatise written a few years after *The Prince*. And yet, Machiavelli doubted whether it was possible, in the turbulent politics of his age, to establish a republic. He said in *The Discourses*: "If any one wanted to establish a republic at the present time, he would find it much easier with the simple mountaineers, who are almost without any civilization, than with such as are

accustomed to live in cities, where civilization is already corrupt."[24]

▼ The Church in the Renaissance

The Great Schism of the Catholic church had encouraged the development of a conciliar movement whose aim was to end the schism and, secondarily, to reform the church. After the Council of Pisa had only worsened the schism (see Chapter 12), leadership in convening a new council passed to the Holy Roman emperor Sigismund. As a result of his efforts, a new ecumenical church council met at Constance from 1414 to 1418. It had three major objectives: to end the schism, to eradicate heresy, and to reform the church in "head and members."

The ending of the schism proved to be the Council of Constance's easiest task. After the three competing popes either resigned or were deposed, a new conclave elected a Roman cardinal Oddone Colonna, a member of a prominent Roman family, as Pope Martin V (1417–1431). The council was much less successful in dealing with the problems of heresy and reform.

The Problems of Heresy and Reform

Heresy was, of course, not a new problem, and in the thirteenth century, the church had developed inquisitorial machinery to deal with it. But two widespread movements in the fourteenth and early fifteenth centuries—Lollardy and Hussitism—posed new threats to the church.

English Lollardy was a product of the Oxford theologian John Wyclif (c. 1328–1384), whose disgust with clerical corruption led him to a far-ranging attack on papal authority and medieval Christian beliefs and practices. Wyclif alleged that there was no basis in Scripture for papal claims of temporal authority and advocated that the popes should be stripped of both their authority and property. At one point, he even denounced the pope as the Antichrist. Believing that the Bible should be a Christian's sole authority, Wyclif urged that it be made available in the vernacular languages so that every Christian could read it. Rejecting all practices not mentioned in Scripture, Wyclif condemned transubstantiation (see Chapter 10), pilgrimages, the veneration of saints, and a whole series of rituals and rites that had developed in the medieval church.

Wyclif has often been viewed as a forerunner of the Reformation of the sixteenth century because his argu-

ments attacked the foundations of the medieval Catholic church's organization and practices. His attacks on church property were especially popular, and he attracted a number of followers who came to be known as Lollards. Persecution by royal and church authorities who feared the socioeconomic consequences of Wyclif's ideas forced the Lollards to go underground after 1400.

A connection between the royal families of England and Bohemia enabled Lollard ideas to spread to Bohemia, where they reinforced the ideas of a group of Czech reformers led by the chancellor of the university at Prague, John Hus (1374–1415). In his call for reform, Hus urged the elimination of the worldliness and corruption of the clergy, criticized the sale of indulgences, and attacked the excessive power of the papacy within the Catholic church. Hus's objections fell on receptive ears, since there was already widespread criticism of the Catholic church as one of the largest landowners in Bohemia. Moreover, many clergymen were German, and the native Czechs' strong resentment of the Germans who dominated Bohemia also contributed to Hus's movement.

The Council of Constance attempted to deal with the growing problem of heresy by summoning John Hus to the council. Granted a safe conduct by Emperor Sigismund, Hus went in the hope of a free hearing of his ideas. Instead he was arrested, condemned as a heretic (by a narrow vote), and burned at the stake in 1415. This action turned the unrest in Bohemia into revolutionary upheaval. The resulting Hussite wars combined religious, social, and national issues and wracked the Holy Roman Empire until a truce was arranged in 1436.

The reform of the church in "head and members" was even less successful than the attempt to eradicate heresy. Two startling reform decrees were passed by the Council of Constance. *Sacrosancta* boldly stated that a general council of the church received its authority from God; hence, every Christian, including the pope, was subject to its authority. The decree *Frequens* provided for the regular holding of general councils in order to maintain an ongoing reform of the church. *Sacrosancta* and *Frequens* were bold and even revolutionary since together they provided for an ecclesiastical legislative system within the church superior to the popes.

Decrees alone, however, proved insufficient to reform the church. Councils could issue decrees, but popes had to execute them and popes would not cooperate with councils that diminished their authority. Beginning as early as Martin V in 1417, successive popes worked steadfastly for the next thirty years to defeat the conciliar movement. The victory of the popes and the final blow

to the conciliar movement came when Pope Pius II issued the papal bull *Execrabilis* in 1460, condemning appeals to a council over the head of a pope as a heretical act.

By the mid-fifteenth century, the popes had reasserted their supremacy over the Catholic church. No longer, however, did they have any possibility of asserting supremacy over temporal governments as the medieval papacy had. Furthermore, in order to gain support during their struggles with the councils, some popes had granted the rulers of territorial states the right to appoint high ecclesiastical officials and tax the clergy. Although these were practical concessions, in truth they limited the pope's exercise of spiritual supremacy. Nevertheless, through all its adversities, the papal monarchy had been maintained, although it had lost much moral prestige. By the mid-fifteenth century, it was incumbent upon the popes to try to regain that prestige by fostering the reforms the church badly needed. Instead, the papacy turned, almost as if in compensation for the loss of its temporal supremacy in Europe, to regaining secular authority in central Italy. The Renaissance papacy provided little spiritual leadership and contributed to a further decline in the moral leadership of the popes.

The Renaissance Papacy

Historians use the phrase "Renaissance papacy" to refer to the line of popes from the end of the Great Schism (1417) to the beginnings of the Reformation in the early sixteenth century. The papacy is, of course, an ecclesiastical institution whose primary concern is governing the Catholic church as its spiritual leader. As heads of the church, popes had temporal preoccupations as well, and the story of the Renaissance papacy is really an account of how the latter came to overshadow the popes' spiritual functions. In the process, the Renaissance papacy and the Catholic church became noticeably secularized.

The preoccupation of the popes with the territory of the Papal States and Italian politics was not new to the Renaissance. Popes had been temporal as well as spiritual rulers for centuries. The manner in which Renaissance popes pursued their temporal interests, however, especially their use of intrigue, deceit, and open bloodshed, was shocking. Undoubtedly, the popes were motivated in part by the desire to maintain their independence. One papal supporter expressed it this way: "I used to think that it would be well to separate completely religious authority from temporal power, but now I see

---

Chronology
▼ ▼ ▼
The Church in the Renaissance

Council of Constance	1414–1418
End of the Great Schism	1417
Pius II Issues the Papal Bull *Execrabilis*	1460
The Renaissance Papacy	
Sixtus IV	1471–1484
Alexander VI	1492–1503
Julius II	1503–1513
Leo X	1513–1521

---

that virtue without power is only ridiculous. The Pope of Rome, without the papal realm, could only be the lackey of kings and princes."[25] In the world of Renaissance politics, maintaining a political state was not easy. It demanded a ruthlessness unbecoming to the spiritual leader of Christendom. Of all the Renaissance popes, Julius II (1503–1513) was most involved in war and politics. The fiery "warrior-pope" personally led armies against his enemies, much to the disgust of pious Christians who viewed the pope as a spiritual leader. The great humanist Erasmus (see Chapter 14) witnessed the triumphant entry of Julius II into Bologna at the head of his troops and later wrote scathing indictments of the papal proclivity for warfare. With Julius II in mind, he proclaimed in *The Complaint of Peace*: "How, O bishop standing in the room of the Apostles, dare you teach the people the things that pertain to war?"

To further their territorial aims in the Papal States, the popes needed financial resources and loyal servants. Preoccupation with finances was not new, but its grossness received considerable comment: "Whenever I entered the chambers of the ecclesiastics of the Papal court, I found brokers and clergy engaged and reckoning money which lay in heaps before them."[26] Since they were not hereditary monarchs, popes could not build dynasties over several generations and came to rely on the practice of nepotism to promote their families' interests. Pope Sixtus IV (1471–1484), for example, made five of his nephews (the word *nepotism* is, in fact, derived from *nepos,* meaning nephew) cardinals and gave them an abundance of church offices to build up their finances. The infamous Borgia pope, Alexander VI (1492–1503), known for his debauchery and sensuality, raised one son, one nephew, and the brother of one mistress to the cardinalate. A Venetian envoy stated that Alexander, "joyous by nature, thought of nothing

but the aggrandizement of his children." Alexander scandalized the church by encouraging his son Cesare to carve a territorial state in central Italy out of the territories of the Papal States.

The Renaissance popes were great patrons of Renaissance culture, and their efforts made Rome the focal point of the High Renaissance at the beginning of the sixteenth century. For the warrior-pope Julius II, the patronage of Renaissance culture was mostly a matter of policy as he endeavored to add to the splendor of his pontificate by tearing down the basilica of Saint Peter and beginning construction of the greatest building in Christendom, Saint Peter's Cathedral. Julius's successor, Leo X (1513–1521), was also a patron of Renaissance culture, not as a matter of policy, but as a deeply involved participant. Such might be expected of the son of Lorenzo de' Medici. Made an archbishop at the age of eight and a cardinal at thirteen, he was raised in the lap of Renaissance luxury. He acquired a refined taste in art, manners, and social life among the Florentine Renaissance elite. He became pope at the age of thirty-seven, supposedly remarking to the Venetian ambassador, "Let us enjoy the papacy, since God has given it to us." Humanists were made papal secretaries, Raphael was commissioned to do paintings, and the construction of Saint Peter's was accelerated as Rome became the literary and artistic center of the Renaissance.

Of course, the popes' cultivation of Renaissance culture was not reprehensible in itself. Tourists today would have much less to see in Rome without it. But it did have adverse effects. It was expensive and led to ever more questionable methods of raising revenue. It is no secret

▼ **A Renaissance Pope: Sixtus IV.** The Renaissance popes allowed secular concerns to overshadow their spiritual duties. They became overly concerned with territorial expansion, finances, and the growth of Renaissance culture in Rome. Pope Sixtus IV, pictured here, had the Sistine Chapel built and later had it decorated by some of the leading artists of his day.

that to raise money to build the new Saint Peter's, Leo X authorized the sale of a special jubilee indulgence in Germany, an indulgence that led indirectly to Luther's Ninety-Five Theses and his challenge to the Catholic church. With all of his political skills and refined taste, Leo X, the acknowledged spiritual leader of Christendom, was unable to comprehend the depth of Luther's religious feeling.

Whether the Renaissance represents the end of the Middle Ages or the beginning of a new era, a frequently debated topic among medieval and Renaissance historians, is perhaps an irrelevant question. The Renaissance was a period of transition that witnessed a continuation of the economic, political, and social trends that had begun in the High Middle Ages. It was also a new age in which intellectuals and artists proclaimed a new vision of humankind and raised fundamental questions about the value and importance of the individual. Of course, intellectuals and artists wrote and painted for the upper classes, and the brilliant intellectual, cultural, and artistic accomplishments of the Renaissance were really products of and for the elite. The ideas of the Renaissance did not have a broad base among the masses of the people. As Lorenzo the Magnificent, ruler of Florence, once commented, "Only men of noble birth can obtain perfection. The poor, who work with their hands and have no time to cultivate their minds, are incapable of it."

The Renaissance did, however, raise new questions about medieval traditions. In advocating a return to the early sources of Christianity and criticizing current religious practices, the humanists raised fundamental issues about the Catholic church, which was still an important institution. In the sixteenth century, the intellectual revolution of the fifteenth century gave way to a religious renaissance that touched the lives of people, including the masses, in new and profound ways. After the Reformation, Europe would never again be the unified Christian commonwealth it once believed it was.

Notes

1. Quoted in Jacob Burckhardt, *The Civilization of the Renaissance in Italy,* trans. S. G. C. Middlemore (London, 1960), p. 81.
2. Petrarch, "Epistle to Posterity," *Letters from Petrarch,* trans. Morris Bishop (Bloomington, Ind., 1966), pp. 6–7.
3. Quoted in Hans Baron, "Cicero and the Roman Civic Spirit in the Middle Ages and Early Renaissance," *Bulletin of the John Rylands Library* 22 (1938): 90.
4. Bernhardt J. Hurwood, trans., *The Facetiae of Giovanni Francesco Poggio Bracciolini* (New York, 1968), p. 57.
5. Quoted in Frances Yates, *Giordano Bruno and the Hermetic Tradition* (Chicago, 1964), p. 211.
6. Giovanni Pico della Mirandola, *Oration on the Dignity of Man,* in E. Cassirer, P. O. Kristeller, J. H. Randall, Jr., eds., *The Renaissance Philosophy of Man* (Chicago, 1948), p. 225.
7. Ibid., pp. 247–9.
8. W. H. Woodward, *Vittorino da Feltre and Other Humanist Educators* (Cambridge, 1897), p. 102.
9. Ibid., pp. 106–7.
10. Quoted in Iris Origo, "The Education of Renaissance Man," *The Light of the Past* (New York, 1959), p. 136.
11. François Rabelais, *The Histories of Gargantua and Pantagruel,* trans. J. M. Cohen (Harmondsworth, 1955), p. 159.
12. Quoted in Elizabeth G. Holt, ed., *A Documentary History of Art* (Garden City, N.Y., 1957), 1: 286.
13. Quoted in Johan Huizinga, *The Waning of the Middle Ages* (Garden City, N.Y., 1956), p. 265.
14. Baldassare Castiglione, *The Book of the Courtier,* trans. Charles S. Singleton (Garden City, N.Y., 1959), pp. 288–9.
15. Quoted in De Lamar Jensen, *Renaissance Europe* (Lexington, Mass., 1981), p. 94.
16. Quoted in Iris Origo, "The Domestic Enemy: The Eastern Slaves in Tuscany in the Fourteenth and Fifteenth Centuries," *Speculum* 30 (1955): 333.
17. Quoted in ibid., p. 334.
18. Gene Brucker, ed., *The Society of Renaissance Florence* (New York, 1971), p. 190.
19. Quoted in Garrett Mattingly, *Renaissance Diplomacy* (Baltimore, 1964), p. 42.
20. Ibid., p. 95.
21. Niccolò Machiavelli, *The Prince,* trans. George Bull (Harmondsworth, 1961), pp. 90–91.
22. Ibid., pp. 100–101.
23. Ibid., pp. 134, 138.

24. Niccolò Machiavelli, *The Discourses*, trans. Christian Detmold (New York, 1950), p. 148.

25. Quoted in Emil Lucki, *History of the Renaissance* (Salt Lake City, 1964), 2: 46.

26. Quoted in Alexander C. Flick, *The Decline of the Medieval Church* (London, 1930), 1: 180.

Suggestions for Further Reading
▼ ▼ ▼

The classic study of the Italian Renaissance is J. Burckhardt, *The Civilization of the Renaissance in Italy*, trans. S. G. C. Middlemore (London, 1960), first published in 1860. The standard work on the historical interpretation of the Renaissance is W. Ferguson, *The Renaissance in Historical Thought* (Boston, 1948). General works on the Renaissance in Europe include De Lamar Jensen, *Renaissance Europe* (Lexington, Mass., 1981); and E. Breisach, *Renaissance Europe, 1300–1517* (New York, 1973).

A brief introduction to Renaissance humanism can be found in F. B. Artz, *Renaissance Humanism, 1300–1550* (Oberlin, Ohio, 1966). A more detailed analysis of various aspects of Renaissance humanism is contained in C. Trinkaus, *The Scope of Renaissance Humanism* (Ann Arbor, Mich., 1983). An important collection of essays can be found in P. O. Kristeller, *Renaissance Thought: The Classic, Scholastic and Humanist Strains* (New York, 1961). On the importance of rhetoric, see J. E. Seigel, *Rhetoric and Philosophy in Renaissance Humanism* (Princeton, N.J., 1968). Also of value is J. F. D'Amico, *Renaissance Humanism in Papal Rome* (Baltimore, 1983). The fundamental work on fifteenth-century civic humanism is H. Baron, *The Crisis of the Early Italian Renaissance*, 2d ed. (Princeton, N.J., 1966). The classic work on humanist education is W. H. Woodward, *Vittorino da Feltre and Other Humanist Educators* (New York, 1963), first published in 1897. A basic work on the writing of history in the Italian Renaissance is E. Cochrane, *Historians and Historiography in the Italian Renaissance* (Chicago, 1981). On Guicciardini, see M. Philips *Francesco Guicciardini: The Historian's Craft* (Toronto, 1977). The impact of printing is exhaustively examined in E. Eisenstein, *The Printing Press as an Agent of Change*, 2 vols. (New York, 1978).

Brief, but basic works on Renaissance economic matters are H. A. Miskimin, *The Economy of Early Renaissance Europe, 1300–1460* (New York, 1975) and *The Economy of Later Renaissance Europe, 1460–1600* (New York, 1978). The fundamental work on the Medici family enterprises is R. de Roover, *The Rise and Decline of the Medici Bank, 1397–1494* (New York, 1966). Numerous facets of social life in the Renaissance are examined in J. R. Hale, *Renaissance Europe: The Individual and Society* (London, 1971); J. Gage, *Life in Italy at the Time of the Medici* (New York, 1968); B. Pullan, *Rich and Poor in Renaissance Venice* (Cambridge, Mass., 1971); J. H. Langbein, *Prosecuting Crime in the Renaissance* (Cambridge, Mass., 1974); and G. Ruggiero, *The Boundaries of Eros: Sex Crime and Sexuality in Renaissance Venice* (Oxford, 1985). On family and marriage, see D. Herlihy, *The Family in Renaissance Italy* (St. Louis, 1974); R. Kelso, *Doctrine of the Lady of the Renaissance*, 2d ed. (Urbana, Ill., 1978); and the valuable C. Klapisch-Zuber, *Women, Family, and Ritual in Renaissance Italy* (Chicago, 1985).

The best overall study of the Italian city-states is L. Martines, *Power and Imagination: City-States in Renaissance Italy* (New York, 1979), although D. Hay and J. Law, *Italy in the Age of the Renaissance* (London, 1989) is also a good, up-to-date survey. A new approach to the culture of Renaissance Italy can be found in P. Burke, *The Italian Renaissance* (Princeton, N.J., 1986). There is an enormous literature on Renaissance Florence. The best introduction is G. A. Brucker, *Renaissance Florence*, rev. ed. (New York, 1983). On the Medici period, see J. R. Hale, *Florence and the Medici: The Pattern of Control* (London, 1977). Works on other Italian states and rulers include D. S. Chambers, *The Imperial Age of Venice, 1380–1580* (New York, 1970); W. L. Gundersheimer, *Ferrara: The Style of a Renaissance Despotism* (Princeton, N.J., 1973); and A. Ryder, *The Kingdom of Naples under Alfonso the Magnanimous* (Oxford, 1976). A popular biography of Isabella d'Este is G. Marek, *The Bed and the Throne* (New York, 1976). On the *condottieri*, see M. Mallett, *Mercenaries and Their Masters: Warfare in Renaissance Italy* (Totowa, 1974).

For a general work on the political development of Europe in the Renaissance, see J. H. Shennan, *The Origins of the Modern European State, 1450–1725*

(London, 1974). On France, see J. R. Major, *Representative Institutions in Renaissance France, 1421–1559* (Madison, Wis., 1960); and P. M. Kendall's biography, *Louis XI: The Universal Spider* (New York, 1971). Early Renaissance England is examined in J. R. Lander, *Crown and Nobility, 1450–1509* (London, 1976). On the first Tudor king, see S. B. Chrimes, *Henry VII* (Berkeley, 1972). Good coverage of Renaissance Spain can be found in J. N. Hillgarth, *The Spanish Kingdoms, 1250–1516,* vol. 2, *Castilian Hegemony, 1410–1516* (New York, 1978). Some good works on eastern Europe include P. W. Knoll, *The Rise of the Polish Monarchy* (Chicago, 1972); and C. A. Macartney, *Hungary: A Short History* (Edinburgh, 1962). On the Ottomans and their expansion, see H. Inalcik, *The Ottoman Empire: The Classical Age, 1300–1600* (London, 1973); and the classic work by S. Runciman, *The Fall of Constantinople, 1453* (Cambridge, 1965). The work by G. Mattingly, *Renaissance Diplomacy* (Boston, 1955) remains the basic one on the subject. Machiavelli's life can be examined in J. R. Hale, *Machiavelli and Renaissance Italy* (New York, 1960); and his thought in F. Gilbert, *Machiavelli and Guicciardini: Politics and History in Sixteenth-Century Florence* (Princeton, N.J., 1965).

On problems of heresy and reform, see C. Crowder, *Unity, Heresy and Reform, 1378–1460* (London, 1977). Aspects of the Renaissance papacy can be examined in E. Lee, *Sixtus IV and Men of Letters* (Rome, 1978); D. Hay, *The Church in Italy in the Fifteenth Century* (Cambridge, 1977); and M. Mallett, *The Borgias* (New York, 1969). On Rome, see especially P. Partner, *Renaissance Rome, 1500–1559: A Portrait of a Society* (Berkeley, 1976).

Good surveys of Renaissance art include M. Levy, *Early Renaissance* (Harmondsworth, 1967); A. Smith, *The Renaissance and Mannerism in Italy* (New York, 1971); and L. Murray, *The High Renaissance* (New York, 1967). For studies of individual artists, see R. Jones and N. Penny, *Raphael* (New Haven, 1983); M. Kemp, *Leonardo da Vinci: the Marvellous Works of Nature and of Man* (London, 1981); and D. Summers, *Michelangelo and the Language of Art* (Princeton, N.J., 1981). Also of value is B. Cole, *The Renaissance Artist at Work from Pisano to Titian* (London, 1983).

Chapter 14

The Age of Reformation

▼▼▼▼▼

Throughout the Middle Ages, the Catholic church continued to assert its primacy of position. It had overcome defiance of its temporal authority by emperors while challenges to its doctrines had been crushed by the Inquisition and combated by new religious orders that carried its message of salvation to all the towns and villages of medieval Europe. The growth of the papacy had parallelled the growth of the church, but by the end of the Middle Ages challenges to papal authority from the rising power of monarchical states had resulted in a loss of papal temporal authority. An even greater threat to papal authority and church unity arose in the sixteenth century when the unity of medieval Christendom was irretrievably shattered by the Reformation.

The movement begun by Martin Luther when he challenged the church's blatant hawking of indulgences quickly spread across Europe, a clear indication of dissatisfaction with Catholic practices. Within a short time, new forms of religious practices, doctrines, and organizations, including Zwinglianism, Calvinism, Anabaptism, and Anglicanism, were attracting adherents all over Europe. Although seemingly helpless to stop the new Protestant churches, the Catholic church also underwent a religious renaissance and managed by the mid-sixteenth century to revive its fortunes. Those historians who speak of the Reformation as the beginning of the modern world exaggerate its importance, but there is no doubt that the splintering of Christendom had consequences that ushered in new ways of thinking and at least prepared the ground for modern avenues of growth.

•••••••••• 1500 •••••••••••• 1515 •••••••••••• 1530 •••••••••••• 1545 •••••••••••• 1560 ••••••••••

| ▲ | ▲ | ▲ | ▲ | ▲ |
| Erasmus, *The Praise of Folly* | Ignatius Loyola, *Spiritual Exercises* | Anabaptists at Münster | Johannes Sturm's Gymnasium | Council of Trent |

▼ Prelude to Reformation: The Northern Renaissance

Martin Luther's reform movement was not the first in sixteenth-century Europe. Christian or northern Renaissance humanism, which evolved as Italian Renaissance humanism spread to northern Europe, had as one of its major goals the reform of Christendom. The new classical learning of the Italian Renaissance did not spread to the European countries north of the Alps until the second half of the fifteenth century. Northern Europe had fewer ties to the classical past than Italy. A deep and profound religious sentiment pervaded northern European society and made it less open than Italy to Greco-Roman secular culture. Gradually, however, intellectuals and artists from the cities north of the Alps flocked to Italy and returned home enthusiastic about the new education and the recovery of ancient thought and literature that we associate with Italian Renaissance humanism. In this manner, Italian humanism spread to the north, but with some noticeable differences. What, then, are the distinguishing characteristics of northern Renaissance humanism, a movement that flourished from the late fifteenth century until it was overwhelmed by the Reformation in the 1520s?

Christian or Northern Renaissance Humanism

Like their Italian counterparts, northern humanists cultivated a knowledge of the classics, the one common bond that united all humanists into a kind of international sodality. Although the northern humanists brought out translations or scholarly editions of the classics for the printing press, they tended to place less emphasis on the secular and more on the ethical content of those works, especially to the extent that this ethical content was reconcilable with Christian ethics. In the classics, northern humanists felt they had found a morality more humane than that in the writings of the medieval scholastics.

In returning to the writings of antiquity, northern humanists (who have been called Christian humanists by historians because of their profound preoccupation with religion) also focused on the sources of early Christianity, the Holy Scriptures and the writings of such church fathers as Augustine, Ambrose, and Jerome. In these early Christian writings, they discovered a simple, vivid religion that they came to feel had been distorted by the complicated theological arguments of the Middle Ages. Their interest in Christian writings also led them to master Greek for the express purpose of reading the Greek New Testament and such early Greek church fathers as John Chrysostom, Basil, and Gregory of Nazianzus. Some northern humanists even mastered Hebrew to study the Old Testament in its original language.

Although Christian humanists sought positions as teachers and scholars, the influence of scholastic theologians in the universities often made it difficult for them to do so. So long as they stuck to the classics, Christian humanists coexisted amicably with the scholastic theologians, but when they began to call for radical change in the methods and aims of theological study, they ran into bitter opposition. Northern Renaissance humanists also had opportunities to serve as secretaries to kings, princes, and cities, where their ability to write good prose and deliver orations made them useful. Support for humanism came from other directions as well, especially from patricians, lawyers, and civic officials, especially in the south German cities.

The most important characteristic of northern humanism was its reform program. With their belief in the ability of human beings to reason and improve themselves, the northern humanists felt that through education in the sources of classical, and especially Christian, antiquity, they could instill a true inner piety or an inward religious feeling that would bring about a reform of the church and society. For this reason, Christian humanists supported schools, brought out new editions of the classics, and prepared new editions of the Bible and writings of the church fathers. In the preface to his edition of the Greek New Testament, the famous humanist Erasmus wrote:

> Indeed, I disagree very much with those who are unwilling that Holy Scripture, translated into the vulgar tongue, be read by the uneducated, as if Christ taught such intricate doctrines that they could scarcely be understood by very few theologians, or as if the strength of the Christian religion consisted in men's ignorance of it . . . I would that even the lowliest women read the Gospels and the Pauline Epistles. And I would that they were translated into all languages so that they could be read and understood not only by Scots and Irish but also by Turks and Saracens. . . .Would that, as a result, the farmer sing some portion of them at the plow, the weaver hum some parts of them to the movement of his shuttle, the traveler lighten the weariness of the journey with stories of this kind![1]

▼ **Erasmus.** Desiderius Erasmus was the most influential of the Northern Renaissance humanists. He sought to restore Christianity to its early simplicity as found in the teachings of Christ and his apostles. The reform program of Erasmus stressed inner piety over dogma and ritual, and called for a clear understanding of the sources of Christianity. Pictured here is a painting of Erasmus by Holbein the Younger.

This belief in the power of education would remain an important characteristic of European civilization. Like later intellectuals, Christian humanists believed that to change society they must first change the human beings who compose it. While some have viewed the Christian humanists as naive, they themselves were very optimistic. And well they might be, for they had no past history of disillusionment with such a program. Erasmus proclaimed in a letter to Pope Leo X: "I congratulate this our age—which bids fair to be an age of gold, if ever such there was—wherein I see . . . three of the chief blessings of humanity are about to be restored to her. I mean, first, that truly Christian piety, . . . secondly, learning of the best sort, . . . and thirdly, the public and lasting concord of Christendom. . . ."[2] This belief that a golden age could be achieved by applying the new learning to the reform of church and society proved to be a common bond among the Christian humanists. The turmoil of the Reformation shattered much of this intellectual optimism, as the lives and careers of two of the most prominent Christian humanists, Desiderius Erasmus and Thomas More, illustrate.

ERASMUS   The most influential of all the Christian humanists, and in a way the symbol of the movement itself, was Desiderius Erasmus (1466–1536), who formulated and popularized the reform program of Christian humanism. Born in Holland, Erasmus was educated at one of the schools of the Brothers of the Common Life. He entered a monastery, but withdrew in 1492 when he became dissatisfied with the opportunities for intellectual life there. He then wandered to France, England, Italy, Germany, and Switzerland, conversing everywhere in the classical Latin that might be called his mother tongue. By 1500, he had turned seriously toward religious studies where he concentrated on reconciling the classics and Christianity through their common ethical focus.

His reputation began to grow when he published the *Adages* (1500), a collection of proverbs from ancient authors that showed his ability in the classics. The *Handbook of the Christian Knight*, published in 1503, reflected his preoccupation with religion. His chief goal was the restoration of Christianity to its early simplicity as taught by Christ and his disciples. He called his conception of religion "the philosophy of Christ," by which he meant that Christianity should be a guiding philosophy for the direction of daily life rather than the system of dogmatic beliefs and practices that the medieval church seemed to stress. In other words, he emphasized inner piety and deemphasized the external forms of re-

Erasmus: In Praise of Folly
▼ ▼ ▼

The Praise of Folly is one of the most famous pieces of literature of the sixteenth century. Written in a short period of time during a visit to the home of Thomas More, Erasmus considered it a "little diversion" from his "serious work." Yet both contemporaries and later generations have appreciated "this laughing parody of every form and rank of human life." In this selection, Erasmus belittles one of his favorite objects of scorn—the monks.

Erasmus, *The Praise of Folly*

Those who are the closest to these [the theologians] in happiness are generally called "the religious" or "monks," both of which are deceiving names, since for the most part they stay as far away from religion as possible and frequent every sort of place. I cannot, however, see how any life could be more gloomy than the life of these monks if I [Folly] did not assist them in many ways. Though most people detest these men so much that accidentally meeting one is considered to be bad luck, the monks themselves believe that they are magnificent creatures. One of their chief beliefs is that to be illiterate is to be of a high state of sanctity, and so they make sure that they are not able to read. Another is that when braying out their gospels in church they are making themselves very pleasing and satisfying to God, when in fact they are uttering these psalms as a matter of repetition rather than from their hearts. . . .

Moreover, it is amusing to find that they insist that everything be done in fastidious detail, as if employing the orderliness of mathematics, a small mistake in which would be a great crime. Just so many knots must be on each shoe and the shoelace may be of only one specified color; just so much lace is allowed on each habit; the girdle must be of just the right material and width; the hood of a certain shape and capacity; their hair of just so many fingers' length; and finally they can sleep only the specified number of hours per day. Can they not understand that, because of a variety of bodies and temperaments, all this equality of restrictions is in fact very unequal? Nevertheless, because of all this detail that they employ they think that they are superior to all other people. And what is more, amid all their pretense of Apostolic charity, the members of one order will denounce the members of another order clamorously because of the way in which the habit has been belted or the slightly darker color of it. . . .

Many of them work so hard at protocol and at traditional fastidiousness that they think one heaven hardly a suitable reward for their labors; never recalling, however, that the time will come when Christ will demand a reckoning of that which he had prescribed, namely charity, and that he will hold their deeds of little account. One monk will then exhibit his belly filled with every kind of fish; another will profess a knowledge of over a hundred hymns. Still another will reveal a countless number of fasts that he has made, and will account for his large belly by explaining that his fasts have always been broken by a single large meal. Another will show a list of church ceremonies over which he has officiated so large that it would fill seven ships.

---

ligion (such as the sacraments, pilgrimages, fasts, veneration of saints, and relics). To return to the simplicity of the early church, people needed to understand the original meaning of the Scriptures and early church fathers. Since Erasmus felt that the standard Latin edition of the Bible known as the Vulgate contained errors, he edited the Greek text of the New Testament from the earliest available manuscripts and published it in 1516.

To Erasmus, the reform of the church meant spreading an understanding of the philosophy of Christ, providing enlightened education in the sources of early Christianity, and making commonsense criticism of the abuses in the church. The latter is especially evident in his work, *The Praise of Folly*, written in 1511. It is a satirical view of his contemporary society in which folly personified as a woman shows how strong her rule is in the affairs of humankind. Through this device, Erasmus was able to engage in a humorous, yet effective criticism of the aspects of contemporary society that he believed were most in need of reform. He was especially harsh on the abuses of the church (see the box above).

Erasmus's reform program was not destined to effect the reform of the church that he so desired. His moderation and his emphasis on education were quickly overwhelmed by the violence unleashed by the passions of the Reformation. Undoubtedly, his work helped to prepare the way for the Reformation; as contemporaries proclaimed, "Erasmus laid the egg that Luther hatched." Yet Erasmus eventually disapproved of Luther and the Protestant reformers. He had no intention of destroying the unity of the medieval Christian church since his whole program was based on reform within the church.

THOMAS MORE   Born the son of a London lawyer, Thomas More (1478–1535) received the benefits of a good education. Although trained as a lawyer, he took an avid interest in the new classical learning and became proficient in both Latin and Greek. Like the Italian humanists who believed in putting their learning at the service of the state, More entered upon a public career that ultimately took him to the highest reaches of power as lord chancellor of England.

His career in government service, however, did not keep More from the intellectual and spiritual interests that were so dear to him. He was well acquainted with other English humanists and became an intimate friend of Erasmus. He made translations from Greek authors and wrote both Latin prose and poetry. A deeply devout man, he spent many hours in prayer and private devotions. Many praised his household as a shining model of Christian family life.

More's most famous work, and one of the most controversial of his age, was *Utopia*, written in 1516. This literary masterpiece is an account of the idealistic life and institutions of the community of Utopia (literally "nowhere"), an imaginary island in the vicinity of the New World, and reflects More's own concerns with the economic, social, and political problems of his day. He presented a revolutionary new social order in which reason, cooperation, and tolerance have replaced power, wealth, and prestige as the proper motivating forces for human society. Utopian society, therefore, is based on communal ownership rather than private property. All persons work but six hours a day, regardless of occupation, and are compensated based on their needs. Possessing abundant leisure time and relieved of competition and greed, Utopians are free to grow intellectually and artistically. Thus, just laws and efficient institutions have created a society where individuals lead good and satisfying lives.

In serving King Henry VIII, More came face to face with the abuses and corruption he had criticized in *Utopia*. But he did not allow the idealism of Utopia to out-

weigh his own ultimate realism, and in *Utopia* itself he justified his service to the king:

> If you can't completely eradicate wrong ideas, or deal with inveterate vices as effectively as you could wish, that's no reason for turning your back on public life altogether. You wouldn't abandon ship in a storm just because you couldn't control the winds. On the other hand, it's no use attempting to put across entirely new ideas, which will obviously carry no weight with people who are prejudiced against them. You must go to work indirectly. You must handle everything as tactfully as you can, and what you can't put right you must try to make as little wrong as possible. For things will never be perfect, until human beings are perfect—which I don't expect them to be for quite a number of years.[3]

More's religious devotion and belief in the universal Catholic church proved even more important than his service to the king, however. Always the man of conscience, More willingly gave up his life opposing England's break with the Roman Catholic church over the divorce of King Henry VIII.

▼ Prelude to Reformation: Church and Religion on the Eve of the Reformation

The institutional problems of the Catholic church in the fourteenth and fifteenth centuries, especially the failure of the Renaissance popes to provide spiritual leadership, were bound to affect the spiritual life of all Christendom. If we were to accept what satirists and reforming preachers were telling their audiences in 1500, the picture is a bleak one. But satirical literature, by its very nature, is exaggerated, and reforming preachers have always tended to convey the impression that the end of the world is near. Nevertheless, allowing for exaggerations, the general impression of the tenor of religious life on the eve of the Reformation is one of much deterioration, coupled with abundant evidence of a continuing desire for valid religious experience from millions of devout lay people.

The Clergy

The economic changes of the Late Middle Ages and Renaissance and the continuing preoccupation of the papal court with finances (see Chapter 13) had an especially strong impact upon the clergy. One need only read the names of the cardinals in the fifteenth century to realize that the highest positions of the clergy were increasingly held by either the nobility or the wealthier members of the bourgeoisie. At the same time, to enhance their revenues, high church officials accumulated church offices in ever-larger numbers. This practice of pluralism (the holding of many church offices) led, in turn, to the problem of absenteeism as church officeholders neglected their episcopal duties and delegated the entire administration of a diocese to an underling, who was often underpaid and little interested in performing his duties.

At the same time, these same economic forces led to an increasing separation between the higher and lower clergy. While cardinals, archbishops, bishops, and abbots vied for church offices and accumulated great wealth, many members of the lower clergy—the parish priests—tended to exist at the same economic level as their parishioners. Social discontent grew, especially among those able and conscientious priests whose path to advancement was blocked by the nobles' domination of higher church offices. By the same token, pluralism on the lower levels left many parishes without episcopal direction of any kind, resulting in a poor quality of lower clergy. The fifteenth century was rife with complaints about the ignorance and incapacity of parish priests, as well as their greed and sexual peccadilloes.

Popular Religion

The atmosphere of the Late Middle Ages and Renaissance, with its uncertainty of life and immediacy of death, brought a craving for meaningful religious expression and certainty of salvation. This impulse, especially strong in Germany, expressed itself in two ways that often seemed contradictory.

One manifestation of religious piety in the fifteenth century was the almost mechanical view of the process of salvation. Collections of relics grew as more and more people sought certainty of salvation through their veneration. By 1509, Frederick the Wise, elector of Saxony and Luther's prince, had amassed over 5,000 relics to which were attached indulgences that could reduce one's time in purgatory officially by 1,443 years (see Chapter 10 on indulgences). Despite the physical dangers, increasing numbers of Christians made pilgrimages to such holy centers as Rome and Jerusalem to gain spiritual benefits.

Another form of religious piety, the quest for a tranquil spirituality, was evident in the popular mystical movement known as the Modern Devotion (see Chapter 12), which spawned the lay religious order, the Brothers and Sisters of the Common Life, and a reform of monastic life in Germany and the Low Countries. The best-known member of the Brothers of the Common Life in the fifteenth century was Thomas à Kempis (1380–1471), to whom most scholars ascribe the writing of the great mystical classic of the Modern Devotion, *The Imitation of Christ*.

One notable feature of *The Imitation of Christ* was its disregard for religious dogma. A life of inner piety, with its total dedication to the moral and ethical precepts of Christ, was not to be achieved by intellectual speculation but by following the life of Christ. As stated by Thomas à Kempis, "Truly, at the day of judgment we shall not be examined by what we have read, but what we have done; not how well we have spoken, but how religiously we have lived." This repudiation of formal theology as unnecessary to the Christian life had deep roots in an emphasis on the Bible as a Christian's primary guide to the true Christian life. In the New Testament, one could find models for the imitation of Christ that even the uneducated could understand. The copying and dissemination of the Bible, as well as its exposition, played an important role in the work of the Brothers of the Common Life.

Popular mysticism, then, as seen in the Modern Devotion, bears an important relationship to the Reformation. Although adherents of the Modern Devotion did not question the traditional beliefs or practices of the church, their deemphasis of them in favor of the inner life of the spirit and direct communion with God minimized the importance of the formal church and undermined the position of the church and its clergy in Christians' lives. At the same time, the movement gained its strength through its appeal to lay people, especially townspeople who liked its direct personal approach to religion.

What is striking about the revival of religious piety in the fifteenth century—whether expressed through such external forces as the veneration of relics and the buying of indulgences or the mystical path—was its adherence to the orthodox beliefs and practices of the Catholic church. The agitation for certainty of salvation and spiritual peace was done within the framework of the "holy mother Church." But disillusionment grew as the devout experienced the clergy's inability to live up to their expectations. The deepening of religious life, especially in the second half of the fifteenth century, found little echo among the worldly-wise clergy, and it is this environment that helps to explain the tremendous and immediate impact of Luther's ideas.

▼ Martin Luther and the Reformation in Germany

The Protestant Reformation had its beginning in a typical medieval question—what must I do to be saved? Martin Luther, a deeply religious man, found an answer in his rediscovery of an earlier Pauline, Augustinian theology. Since his solution did not fit within the traditional teachings of the late medieval church, ultimately he split with that church, destroying the religious unity of western Christendom. That other people were concerned with the same question is evident in the rapid spread of the Reformation. But religion was so entangled in the social, economic, and political forces of the period that the hope of the Protestant reformers to transform the church quickly proved illusory.

The Early Luther

Martin Luther was born on November 10, 1483, into a peasant family, although his father raised himself into the ranks of the lower bourgeoisie by going into mining. His father wanted him to become a lawyer, so Luther enrolled at the University of Erfurt where he received his bachelor's degree in 1502. In 1505, after becoming a master in the liberal arts, the young Martin began to study law. Luther was not content with the study of law and all along had shown religious inclinations. In the summer of 1505, en route back to Erfurt after a brief visit home, he was caught in a ferocious thunderstorm and vowed that if he were spared, he would become a monk. He then entered the monastic order of the Augustinian Hermits in Erfurt, much to his father's disgust. While in the monastery, Luther focused on his major concern, the assurance of salvation. The traditional beliefs and practices of the church seemed unable to assuage his obsession with this question, especially evident in his struggle with the sacrament of penance or confession. The sacraments were a Catholic's chief means of receiving God's grace; that of confession offered the opportunity to have one's sins forgiven. Luther spent hours confessing his sins, but he was always doubtful. Had he remembered all of his sins? Even more, how could a hopeless sinner be acceptable to a totally just and all-powerful God? Luther threw himself into his monastic routine with a vengeance:

I was indeed a good monk and kept my order so strictly that I could say that if ever a monk could get to heaven through monastic discipline, I was that monk. . . .And yet my conscience would not give me certainty, but I always doubted and said, "You didn't do that right. You weren't contrite enough. You left that out of your confession." The more I tried to remedy an uncertain, weak and troubled conscience with human traditions, the more I daily found it more uncertain, weaker and more troubled.[4]

Despite his herculean efforts, Luther achieved no certainty and even came, as he once expressed it, to hate "this just God who punishes sinners."

To help overcome his difficulties, his superiors recommended that the intelligent, yet disturbed monk study theology. He received his doctorate in 1512 and then became a professor in the theological faculty at the University of Wittenberg, lecturing on the Bible. Probably sometime between 1513 and 1516, through his study of the Bible, he arrived at an answer to his problem.

Luther's dilemma had derived from his concept of the "justice of God," which he interpreted as a punitive justice in which God weighs the merits or good works performed by humans as a necessary precondition for salvation. To Luther it appeared that the church was saying that one must earn salvation by good works. In Luther's eye, human beings, weak and powerless in the sight of an almighty God, could never do enough to justify salvation in these terms. Through his study of the Bible, especially his work on Paul's Epistle to the Romans, Luther rediscovered another way of viewing the justice of God:

Night and day I pondered until I saw the connection between the justice of God and the statement that "the just shall live by his faith." Then I grasped that the justice of God is that righteousness by which through grace and sheer mercy God justifies us through faith. Thereupon I felt myself to be reborn and to have gone through open doors into paradise.[5]

To Luther, the "justice of God" was now not a punitive justice but the grace of God that bestows salvation freely to humans, not through their good works, but through the sacrifice of Christ on the cross. Even faith or the power of belief is a product of divine grace or a gift of God. The doctrine of justification by grace through faith alone became the primary doctrine of the Protestant Reformation. Since Luther had arrived at this doctrine from his study of the Bible, it became for Luther as for all other Protestants the chief guide to religious truth. Justification by faith and the Bible as the sole authority in

Luther and the Ninety-Five Theses
▼ ▼ ▼

To most historians, the publication of Luther's Ninety-Five Theses marks the beginning of the Reformation. To Luther, they were simply a response to what he considered to be the blatant abuses of Johann Tetzel's selling of indulgences. Although written in Latin, the theses were soon translated into German and scattered widely across Germany. They made an immense impression on Germans already dissatisfied with the ecclesiastical and financial policies of the papacy.

Martin Luther, Selections from the Ninety-Five Theses

5. The Pope has neither the will nor the power to remit any penalties beyond those he has imposed either at his own discretion or by canon law.

20. Therefore the Pope, by his plenary remission of all penalties, does not mean "all" in the absolute sense, but only those imposed by himself.

21. Hence those preachers of Indulgences are wrong when they say that a man is absolved and saved from every penalty by the Pope's Indulgences.

27. It is mere human talk to preach that the soul flies out [of purgatory] immediately the money clinks in the collection-box.

28. It is certainly possible that when the money clinks in the collection-box greed and avarice can increase; but the intercession of the Church depends on the will of God alone.

45. Christians should be taught that he who sees a needy person and passes him by, although he gives money for pardons, wins for himself not Papal Indulgences but the wrath of God.

50. Christians should be taught that, if the Pope knew the exactions of the preachers of Indulgences,

he would rather have the basilica of St. Peter reduced to ashes than built with the skin, flesh and bones of his sheep.

81. This wanton preaching of pardons makes it difficult even for learned men to redeem respect due to the Pope from the slanders or at least the shrewd questionings of the laity.

82. For example: "Why does not the Pope empty purgatory for the sake of most holy love and the supreme need of souls? This would be the most righteous of reasons, if he can redeem innumerable souls for sordid money with which to build a basilica, the most trivial of reasons."

86. Again: "Since the Pope's wealth is larger than that of the crassest Crassi of our time, why does he not build this one basilica of St. Peter with his own money, rather than with that of the faithful poor?"

88. Again: "What greater good would be done to the Church if the Pope were to bestow these remissions and dispensations, not once, as now, but a hundred times a day, on any believer whatever."

90. To suppress these most conscientious questionings of the laity by authority only, instead of refuting them by reason, is to expose the Church and the Pope to the ridicule of their enemies, and to make Christian people unhappy.

91. If, therefore, pardons were preached in accordance with the spirit and mind of the Pope, all these difficulties would be easily overcome, or rather would never have arisen.

94. Christians should be exhorted to seek earnestly to follow Christ, their Head, through penalties, deaths, and hells.

95. And let them thus be more confident of entering heaven through many tribulations rather than through a false assurance of peace.

---

religious affairs were the twin pillars of the Protestant Reformation.

The event that propelled Luther into an open confrontation with church officials and forced him to see the theological implications of justification by faith alone was the indulgence controversy. In 1517, Pope Leo X had issued a special jubilee indulgence to finance the ongoing construction of the new Saint Peter's Cathedral

(see Chapter 13). This special indulgence, however, was connected to political and ecclesiastical affairs in Germany. Albert of Brandenburg was already a bishop and archbishop, but purchased a special dispensation from Pope Leo X to obtain yet another church office, the archbishopric of Mainz. To get the money, Albert borrowed from the Fugger banking firm, which paid the pope. Albert was then given the rights to sell the special jubilee indulgence in Germany for ten years with half of the proceeds going to the Fuggers to pay off his debt and the other half to Rome to rebuild Saint Peter's. Johann Tetzel, a rambunctious Dominican, hawked the indul-

▼ **Luther and the Wittenberg Reformers.** This painting by Lucas Cranach the Younger shows the reformers of Wittenberg with their prince, Elector John Frederick of Saxony. Luther is at the far left; Philip Melanchthon is at the far right. The powerful presence of John Frederick in the center foreground reminds us of how much Luther's reform movement depended upon the support of German rulers.

gences with a slick slogan: "As soon as the coin in the coffer rings, the soul from purgatory springs."

Luther was greatly distressed by the sale of indulgences, certain that people were simply guaranteeing their eternal damnation by relying on these pieces of paper to assure themselves of salvation. In response, he issued his Ninety-Five Theses, although scholars are unsure whether he nailed them to a church door in Wittenberg, as is traditionally alleged, or mailed them to his ecclesiastical superior. In either case, his theses were a stunning indictment of the abuses in the sale of indulgences (see the box on p. 451). If the pope had the power to grant indulgences, "Why does not the Pope empty purgatory for the sake of most holy love and the supreme need of souls?" It is doubtful that Luther intended any break with the church over the issue of indulgences. If the pope had clarified the use of indulgences, as Luther wished, then he would probably have been satisfied and the controversy closed. But the Renaissance pope Leo X did not take the issue seriously and is even reported to have said that Luther was simply "some drunken German who will amend his ways when he sobers up." But the development of printing prevented such a speedy resolution. A German translation of the Ninety-Five Theses was quickly printed in thousands of copies and received sympathetically in a Germany that had a long tradition of dissatisfaction with papal policies and power.

The controversy reached an important turning point with the Leipzig Debate in July 1519. There Luther's opponent, the clever and capable Catholic theologian Johann Eck, forced Luther to move beyond indulgences and question the authority of popes and councils. In effect, Luther was compelled to see the consequences of his new theology. At the beginning of 1520, he proclaimed: "Farewell, unhappy, hopeless, blasphemous Rome! The Wrath of God has come upon you, as you deserve. We have cared for Babylon, and she is not healed: let us then, leave her, that she may be the habitation of dragons, spectres, and witches."[6] At the same time, Luther was convinced that he was doing God's work and had to proceed regardless of the consequences. To a friend who had urged moderation, he exclaimed: "Let there be a new and great conflagration, who can resist the counsel of God? Who knows whether these insensate men are not predestined by Him as the means of revealing the truth? . . . God alone is in this business. We are carried away by Him. We are led rather than lead."[7]

In three pamphlets published in 1520, Luther moved toward a more definite break with the Catholic church.

The *Address to the Nobility of the German Nation* was a political tract written in German. The papacy, Luther averred, had used three claims to prevent reform: that the church is superior to the state, that only the pope can interpret Scripture, and that only the pope can call a council. All three were false, and he called upon the German princes to overthrow the papacy in Germany and establish a reformed German church. *The Babylonian Captivity of the Church,* written in Latin for theologians, attacked the sacramental system as the means by which the pope and church had held the real meaning of the Gospel in captivity for a thousand years. He called for the reform of monasticism and for the clergy to marry. While virginity is good, Luther argued, marriage is better, and freedom of choice is best. *On the Freedom of a Christian Man* was a short treatise on the doctrine of salvation. It is faith alone, not good works, which justifies, frees, and brings salvation through Christ. But the Christian, saved and freed by his faith in Christ, is not free from good works, but performs good works out of gratitude to God. "Good works do not make a good man, but a good man does good works." From faith flows love and from love a free spirit that is disposed to serve one's neighbor voluntarily. Hence, "a Christian man is the most free lord of all, and subject to none; a Christian man is the most dutiful servant of all, and subject to everyone."[8]

Unable to countenance Luther's forcefully worded dissent from traditional Catholic teachings, the church excommunicated him in January 1521. He was also summoned to appear before the imperial diet or Reichstag of the Holy Roman Empire, convened by the newly elected emperor Charles V (1519–1556). Expected to recant the heretical doctrines he had espoused, Luther refused and made the famous reply that became the battle cry of the Reformation:

> Since then Your Majesty and your lordships desire a simple reply, I will answer without horns and without teeth. Unless I am convicted by Scripture and plain reason—I do not accept the authority of popes and councils, for they have contradicted each other—my conscience is captive to the Word of God. I cannot and I will not recant anything, for to go against conscience is neither right nor safe. Here I stand, I cannot do otherwise. God help me. Amen.[9]

Luther's heroic stand at Worms was once viewed as a step in the development of religious freedom, but that interpretation overlooked an important consideration. While Luther clearly placed his conscience above the authority of the church, he also believed that he had arrived at the truth, from which others were not allowed to deviate. As Luther once expressed it: "I have neither the power nor the will to deny the Word of God. If any man has a different opinion concerning me, he does not think straight or understand what I have actually said."

The young emperor Charles was outraged at Luther's audacity and gave his opinion that "a single friar who goes counter to all Christianity for a thousand years must be wrong." By the Edict of Worms, Martin Luther was made an outlaw within the empire. His works were to be burned and Luther himself captured and delivered to the emperor. Because of his religious conviction, Luther had been forced to defy both the church and emperor. Now deprived of help from these two great medieval authorities, Luther was forced to turn to the German princes and people. In doing so, his religious movement became a revolution.

The Development of Lutheranism

After a brief period of hiding, Luther returned to Wittenberg at the beginning of 1522 and began to organize a reformed church. In the decade of the 1520s, Lutheranism had much appeal and spread rapidly. The University of Wittenberg served as a center for the diffusion of Luther's ideas. Between 1520 and 1560, 16,000 students from all over Germany matriculated at the university and returned home to spread Luther's teachings. The preaching of evangelical sermons, based on a return to the original message of the Bible, found favor throughout Germany. In city after city, the arrival of preachers presenting Luther's teachings was soon followed by a public debate in which the new preachers proved victorious. A reformation was then instituted by state authorities. Also useful to the spread of the Reformation were pamphlets illustrated with vivid woodcuts portraying the enemy as a hideous Antichrist and titled with catchy phrases, such as "I Wonder Why There Is No Money in the Land" (the latter, of course, was an attack on papal greed). Luther also insisted on the use of music as a means to teach the Gospel, and his own "A Mighty Fortress Is Our God" became the Battle Hymn of the Reformation. Lutheranism spread to both princely and ecclesiastical states in northern and central Germany as well as to two-thirds of the free imperial cities, especially those of southern Germany, where prosperous burghers became committed to Luther's cause. Nuremberg, where an active city council led by the dynamic city secretary Lazarus Spengler brought a conversion as early as 1525, was the first imperial city to convert to

Lutheranism. At its outset, the Reformation in Germany was largely an urban phenomenon.

A series of crises in the mid-1520s made it apparent, however, that spreading the word of God was not as easy as Luther had originally envisioned, the usual plight of most reformers. Luther experienced dissent within his own ranks in Wittenberg from people such as Andreas Carlstadt who wished to initiate a more radical reformation by abolishing all relics, images, and the mass. Luther had no sooner dealt with them when he was faced with defection from the Christian humanists. Many had initially supported Luther, believing that he shared their goal of reforming the abuses within the church. But after 1521, when it became apparent that Luther's movement threatened the unity of Christendom, the older generation of Christian humanists, including Erasmus, broke with the reformer. A younger generation of Christian humanists, however, played a significant role in Lutheranism. Philip Melanchthon (1497–1560) arrived in Wittenberg in 1518 (at the age of twenty-one) to teach Greek and Hebrew, was immediately attracted to Luther's ideas, and became his staunch supporter.

It was the Peasants' War that constituted Luther's greatest challenge in the mid-1520s. Peasant dissatisfaction in Germany stemmed from several sources. Many peasants had not been touched by the gradual economic improvement of the early sixteenth century, creating a "revolt of rising expectations." In some areas, especially southwestern Germany, influential local lords continued to abuse their peasants while new demands for taxes and other services caused them to wish for a return to "the good old days." Social discontent soon became entangled with religious revolt as peasants looked to Martin Luther for support. It was not Luther, however, but one of his ex-followers, the radical Thomas Müntzer, who inflamed the peasants against their rulers with his fiery language: "Strike while the iron is hot!" Revolt first erupted in southwestern Germany in June 1524 and spread northward and eastward.

Luther reacted quickly and vehemently against the peasants. In his vitriolic pamphlet, *Against the Robbing and Murdering Hordes of Peasants*, he called upon the German princes to "stab, smite, and slay" the stupid and stubborn peasantry (see the box on p. 455). The issue was clear to Luther. Although compelled in his mind by the word of God to rebel against church authorities, he did not believe in social revolution. To Luther, the state and its rulers were ordained by God and given the authority to maintain the peace and order necessary for the spread of the Gospel. It was the responsibility of subjects to obey these authorities, and it was the duty of princes to suppress all revolt. But Luther was no political thinker, and he certainly knew how much his reformation of the church depended upon the full support of the German princes and magistrates. Luther was fully prepared to lend religious dignity to the rulers in return for their ongoing support. In May 1525, the German princes ruthlessly massacred the remaining peasant hordes in a bloodbath at Frankenhausen. By this time,

▼ **Woodcut: Luther vs. the Pope.** Condemned by both the Catholic church and the Holy Roman Empire, Luther turned to the German princes and people for assistance. In the 1520s, after his return to Wittenberg, Luther's teachings spread rapidly, ending ultimately with a reform movement instituted by state authorities. Pictured here is a woodcut used in spreading the message of the Reformation. The woodcut depicts the crucified Jesus attending Luther's church service while the pope is shown hawking indulgences.

Luther and the "Robbing and Murdering Hordes of Peasants"
▼ ▼ ▼

The Peasants' War of 1524–1525 encompassed a series of risings by German peasants who were suffering from economic changes they did not comprehend. In a sense, it was part of a century of peasant discontent. Led by radical religious leaders, the revolts quickly became entangled with the religious revolt set in motion by Luther's defiance of the church. But it was soon clear that Luther himself did not believe in any way in social revolution. This excerpt is taken from Luther's vitriolic pamphlet written in May 1525 at the height of the peasants' power, but not published until after their defeat.

Martin Luther, *Against the Robbing and Murdering Hordes of Peasants*

The peasants have taken on themselves the burden of three terrible sins against God and man, by which they have abundantly merited death in body and soul. In the first place they have sworn to be true and faithful, submissive and obedient, to their rulers, as Christ commands, when he says, "Render unto Caesar the things that are Caesar's," and in *Romans* XIII, "Let everyone be subject unto the higher powers." Because they are breaking this obedience, and are setting themselves against the higher powers, willfully and with violence, they have forfeited body and soul, as faithless, perjured, lying, disobedient knaves and scoundrels are wont to do. . . .

In the second place, they are starting a rebellion, and violently robbing and plundering monasteries and castles which are not theirs, by which they have a second time deserved death in body and soul, if only as highwaymen and murderers. . . .For rebellion is not simple murder, but is like a great fire, which attacks and lays waste a whole land. . . .Therefore, let everyone who can, smite, slay and stab, secretly or openly, remembering that nothing can be more poisonous, hurtful or devilish than a rebel. . . .

In the third place, they cloak this terrible and horrible sin with the Gospel, call themselves "Christian brothers," receive oaths and homage, and compel people to hold with them to these abominations. Thus they become the greatest of all blasphemers of God and slanderers of his holy Name, serving the devil, under the outward appearance of the Gospel, thus earning death in body and soul ten times over. . . .It does not help the peasants, when they pretend that, according to Genesis I and II, all things were created free and common, and that all of us alike have been baptized. . . .For baptism does not make men free in body and property, but in soul; and the Gospel does not make goods common. . . .Since the peasants, then, have brought both God and man down upon them and are already so many times guilty of death in body and soul, . . .I must instruct the worldly governors how they are to act in the matter with a clear conscience.

First, I will not oppose a ruler who, even though he does not tolerate the Gospel, will smite and punish these peasants without offering to submit the case to judgement. For he is within his rights, since the peasants are not contending any longer for the Gospel, but have become faithless, perjured, disobedient, rebellious murderers, robbers and blasphemers, whom even heathen rulers have the right and power to punish; nay, it is their duty to punish them, for it is just for this purpose that they bear the sword, and are "the ministers of God upon him that doeth evil. . . ."

Luther found himself ever more dependent on state authorities for the growth and maintenance of his reformed church.

Church and State

Justification by faith alone was the starting point for most of Protestantism's major doctrines. Since Luther downplayed the role of good works in salvation, the sacraments also had to be redefined. No longer were they merit-earning works, but divinely established signs signifying the promise of salvation. Based on his interpretation of scriptural authority, Luther kept only two of the Catholic church's seven sacraments, baptism and the Lord's Supper. Baptism signified rebirth through grace. As to the sacrament of the Lord's Supper, Luther denied the Catholic doctrine of transubstantiation, which taught that the substance of the bread and wine is miraculously transformed into the body and blood of Christ. Yet he continued to insist upon the real presence of Christ's body and blood in the bread and wine given as a testament to God's forgiveness of sin.

Luther's emphasis on the importance of Scripture led him to reject the Catholic belief that the authority of Scripture must be supplemented by the traditions and decrees of the church. The word of God as revealed in the Bible was sufficient authority in religious affairs. A hierarchical priesthood was thus unnecessary since all Christians who followed the word of God were their own priests ("priesthood of all believers"). While Luther thus considered the true church to be an invisible one, the difficulties of actually creating a reformed church led him to believe in the need for a visible, organized church. Since the Catholic ecclesiastical hierarchy had been scrapped, Luther came to rely increasingly on the princes or state authorities to organize and guide the new Lutheran reformed churches. He had little choice. By the sixteenth century, secular authorities in Germany as elsewhere were already playing an important role in church affairs. By 1530, in the German states that had converted to Lutheranism, both princes and city councils appointed officials who visited churches in their territories and regulated matters of worship. The Lutheran churches in Germany (and later in Scandinavia) quickly became territorial or state churches in which the state supervised and disciplined church members.

As part of the development of these state-dominated churches, Luther also instituted new religious services to replace the mass. These featured a worship service consisting of a German liturgy that focused on Bible reading, preaching of the word of God, and song. Following his own denunciation of clerical celibacy, Luther married a former nun, Katherina von Bora, in 1525. His union provided a model of married and family life for the new Protestant minister.

▼ Germany and the Reformation: Religion and Politics

From its very beginning, the development of Lutheranism was closely tied to political affairs. In 1519, Charles I, king of Spain and the grandson of the Emperor Maximilian, was elected Holy Roman emperor as Charles V (1519–1556). Charles V ruled over an immense empire, consisting of Spain and its overseas possessions, the traditional Austrian Habsburg lands, Bohemia, Hungary, the Low Countries, and the kingdom of Naples in southern Italy. The extent of his possessions was reflected in the languages he used: "I speak Spanish to God, Italian to women, French to men, and German to my horse." Politically, Charles wanted to

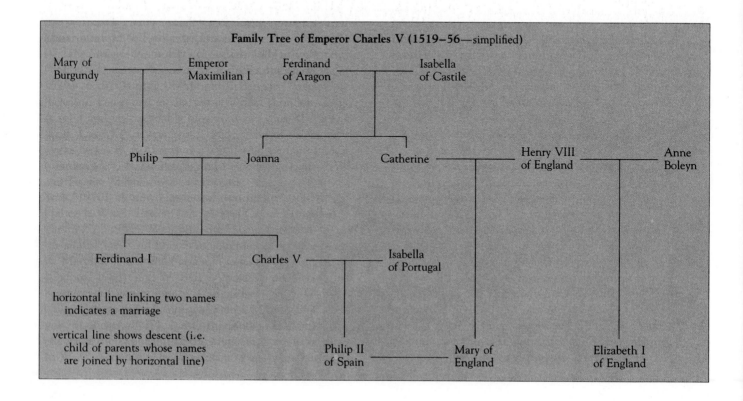

Family Tree of Emperor Charles V (1519–56—simplified)

Mary of Burgundy —— Emperor Maximilian I   Ferdinand of Aragon —— Isabella of Castile

Philip —— Joanna   Catherine —— Henry VIII of England —— Anne Boleyn

Ferdinand I   Charles V —— Isabella of Portugal

horizontal line linking two names indicates a marriage

vertical line shows descent (i.e. child of parents whose names are joined by horizontal line)

Philip II of Spain —— Mary of England   Elizabeth I of England

maintain his dynasty's control over his enormous empire; religiously, he hoped to preserve the unity of his empire in the Catholic faith. Despite his strengths, Charles spent a lifetime in futile pursuit of his goals. Four major problems—the French, the Turks, the papacy, and Germany's internal situation—cost him both his dream and his health.

The chief political concern of Charles V was his rivalry with the king of France. Francis I (1515–1547), the benevolent despot of the Valois dynasty, proved a worthwhile adversary. Encircled by the possessions of the Habsburg empire, Francis entered into conflict with Charles over disputed territories in southern France, the Netherlands, the Rhineland, northern Spain, and Italy. These conflicts, known as the Habsburg-Valois Wars, were fought intermittently over a twenty-five year period

▼ **Francis I.** The conflict between Francis I and Charles V prevented Charles from effectively dealing with the Lutheran problem in Germany. Feeling surrounded by the possessions of Charles V, Francis I of France initiated a series of intermittent wars, known as the Habsburg-Valois Wars, which were fought over a period of twenty-five years. Peace between the two monarchs was finally reached in 1544. Pictured here is a portrait of Francis I by Jean Clouet.

▼ **Charles V.** Charles V ruled over a vast empire. He sought to create religious unity throughout his lands by keeping them within the bounds of the Catholic faith. Unfortunately, due to his conflict with Francis I as well as difficulties with the Turks, the papacy, and the German princes, Charles was never able to check the spread of Lutheranism. This is a portrait of Charles V by the Venetian painter Titian.

(1521–1544), preventing Charles from concentrating his attention on the Lutheran problem in Germany.

Meanwhile, Charles was faced with two other enemies. The Habsburg emperor expected papal cooperation in dealing with the Lutheran heresy. Papal policy, however, was guided by political considerations, not religious ones. Fearful of Charles's growing power in Italy, Pope Clement VII (1523–1534) joined the side of Francis I in the second Habsburg–Valois War (1527–1529), but with catastrophic results. In April 1527, the

Spanish-imperial army of Charles V went berserk in its attack on Rome and subjected the capital of Catholicism to a fearful and bloody sack. Sobered by the experience, Clement came to terms with the emperor, and by 1530 Charles V stood supreme over much of Italy.

In the meantime, a new threat to the emperor's power had erupted in the eastern part of his empire. The Ottoman Turks, under the competent Suleiman the Magnificent (1520–1566), had defeated and killed King Louis of Hungary, Charles's brother-in-law, at the Battle of Mohács in 1526. Subsequently, the Turks overran most of Hungary, moved into Austria, and advanced as far as Vienna, where they were finally repulsed in 1529 (see Chapter 16).

By the end of 1529, Charles was ready to deal with Germany. The second Habsburg-Valois War had ended,

the Turks had been defeated temporarily, and the pope subdued. The internal political situation in the Holy Roman Empire was not in his favor, however. Germany was a land of several hundred territorial states: princely states, ecclesiastical principalities, and free imperial cities (see Chapter 13). While all owed loyalty to the emperor, Germany's medieval development had enabled these states to become quite independent of imperial authority. They had no desire to have a strong emperor. Although those states that had become Lutheran were especially concerned about that possibility, even Catholic authorities that might approve of the emperor's anti-Lutheran policies had no real desire to strengthen the emperor's hand politically.

Charles's attempt to settle the Lutheran problem at the Diet of Augsburg in 1530 proved completely inade-

▼ **Map 14.1** The Empire of Charles V.

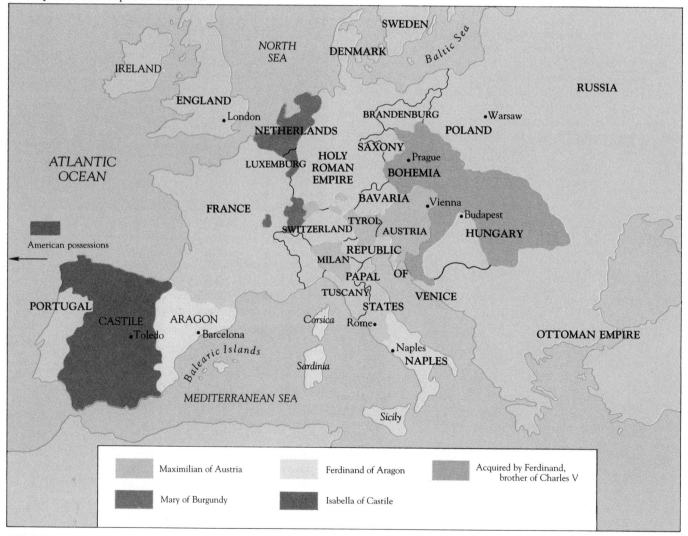

quate, and the emperor wound up demanding that the Lutherans return to the Catholic church by April 15, 1531. In February 1531, fearful of Charles's intentions, eight princes and eleven imperial cities—all Lutheran—formed a defensive alliance known as the Schmalkaldic League. These Protestant German states vowed to assist each other "whenever any one of us is attacked on account of the Word of God and the doctrine of the Gospel." Religion was dividing the empire into two armed camps.

The renewed threat of the Turks against Vienna forced Charles once again to seek compromise instead of war with the Protestant authorities. From 1532 to 1535, Charles was forced to fight off a Turkish, Arab, and Barbary attack on the Mediterranean coasts of Italy and Spain. Two additional Habsburg-Valois Wars (1535–1538 and 1542–1544) soon followed and kept Charles preoccupied with military campaigns in southern France and the Low Counties. Finally, Charles made peace with Francis in 1544 and the Turks in 1545. Fifteen years after the Diet of Augsburg, Charles was finally free to resolve his problem in Germany.

By the time of Luther's death in February 1546, all hopes of a peaceful compromise had faded. Charles brought a sizable imperial army of Germans, Dutch, Italian, and Spanish troops to do battle with the Protestants. In the first phase of the Schmalkaldic Wars (1546–1547), the emperor's forces decisively defeated the Lutherans at the Battle of Mühlberg. Charles V was at the zenith of his power, and the Protestant cause seemed doomed.

Appearances proved misleading, however. The Schmalkaldic League was soon reestablished, and the German Protestant princes allied themselves with the new French king, Henry II (1547–1559), to revive the war in 1552. This time, Charles was less fortunate and was forced to negotiate a truce. Exhausted by his efforts to maintain religious orthodoxy and the unity of his empire, Charles abandoned German affairs to his brother Ferdinand, abdicated all of his titles in 1556, and retired to his country estate in Spain to spend the remaining two years of his life in solitude.

An end to religious warfare in Germany came in 1555 with the Peace of Augsburg, which marks an important turning point in the history of the Reformation. The division of Christianity was formally acknowledged when Lutheranism was granted the same legal rights as Catholicism. Although the German states were now free to choose between Catholicism and Lutheranism, the peace settlement did not recognize the principle of religious toleration, even though it

accepted the right of each German ruler to determine the religion of his subjects.

The Peace of Augsburg was a victory for the German princes. The independence of the numerous German territorial states guaranteed the weakness of the Holy Roman Empire and the continued decentralization of Germany. Charles's hope for a united empire had been completely dashed. At the same time, what had at first been merely feared was now confirmed: the ideal of medieval Christian unity was irretrievably lost. The rapid proliferation of new Protestant groups served to underscore the new reality.

▼ The Spread of the Protestant Reformation

To Catholic critics, Luther's heresy had opened the door to more extreme forms of religious and social upheaval. For both Catholics and Protestant reformers, it also raised the question of how to determine what constituted the correct interpretation of the Bible. The inability to agree on this issue led not only to theological confrontations but also to bloody warfare as each Christian group found itself unwilling to admit that it could be wrong.

Lutheranism in Scandinavia

In 1397, the Union of Kalmar had brought about the unification of Denmark, Norway, and Sweden under the rule of one monarch, the king of Denmark. This union, however, failed to achieve any real social or political unification of the three states, particularly since the independent-minded, landed nobles worked to frustrate any increase in monarchical centralization. By the beginning of the sixteenth century, the union was on the brink of disintegration. In 1520, Christian II (1513–1523) of Denmark, ruler of the three Scandinavian kingdoms, was overthrown by Swedish barons led by Gustavus Vasa. Three years later, Vasa became king of an independent Sweden (1523–1560) and took the lead in establishing a Lutheran Reformation in his country. Swedish nobles supported his efforts, while Olavus Petri, who had studied at Wittenberg, wrote treatises based on Luther's writings and published the first Swedish New Testament in 1526. By the 1530s, a Swedish Lutheran National Church had been created.

Meanwhile, Christian II had also been deposed as the king of Denmark by the Danish nobility and succeeded by his uncle, who became Frederick I (1523–1533). Frederick encouraged Lutheran preachers to spread their evangelical doctrines and to introduce a Lutheran liturgy into the Danish church service. In the 1530s, under Frederick's successor Christian III (1534–1559), a Lutheran state church was installed with the king as the supreme authority in all ecclesiastical affairs. Christian was also instrumental in spreading Lutheranism to Norway. By the 1540s, Scandinavia had become a Lutheran stronghold. Like the German princes, the Scandinavian monarchs had been the dominant force in establishing state-run churches.

The Zwinglian Reformation

Switzerland, which has played little role in our history to date, was home to two major Reformation movements, Zwinglianism and Calvinism. In the sixteenth century, the Swiss Confederation was a loose association of thirteen self-governing states called cantons. Theoretically part of the Holy Roman Empire, they had become virtually independent after the Swiss defeated the forces of Emperor Maximilian in 1499. The six forest cantons were democratic republics while the seven urban cantons, which included Zürich, Bern, and Basel, were mostly governed by city councils controlled by narrow oligarchies of wealthy citizens. Possessed of a weak economy, the Swiss had grown accustomed to selling their warriors as mercenary soldiers and had become the principal exporters of mercenaries in the sixteenth century. All in all, the Swiss Confederation was a loose conglomeration of states that possessed no common institutions and worked together only for survival and gain.

Ulrich Zwingli (1484–1531) was a product of the Swiss rural cantons. The precocious son of a relatively prosperous peasant, the young Zwingli eventually obtained both the bachelor of arts and master of arts degrees. During his university education at Vienna and Basel, Zwingli was strongly influenced by Christian humanism. Ordained a priest in 1506, he accepted a parish post in rural Switzerland until his appointment as a cathedral priest in the Great Minster of Zürich in 1518. Through his preaching there, Zwingli began the Reformation in Switzerland.

Zwingli always asserted that he arrived at his evangelical theology independently of Luther: "I began to preach the Gospel of Christ in 1516, long before anyone in our region had ever heard of Luther. . . . Why don't you call me a Paulinian since I am preaching as St. Paul preached. . . . If Luther preaches Christ, he does just what I do." Modern scholars doubt Zwingli's protestation, believing that he was influenced by Luther's writings, beginning at least in 1519. In any case, Zwingli's evangelical preaching caused such unrest that the city council in 1523 held a public disputation or debate in the town hall. The disputation became a standard practice for the spread of the Reformation to many cities. It gave an advantage to reformers since they had the power of new ideas and Catholics were not used to defending their teachings. Zwingli's party was accorded the victory and the council declared that "Mayor, Council and Great Council of Zürich, in order to do away with disturbance and discord, have upon due deliberation and consultation decided and resolved that Master Zwingli should continue as heretofore to proclaim the Gospel and the pure sacred Scripture."[10]

Over the next two years, evangelical reforms were promulgated in Zürich by a city council strongly influenced by Zwingli. Zwingli looked to the state to supervise the church. "A church without the magistrate is mutilated and incomplete," he declared. Relics and images were abolished; all paintings and decorations were removed from the churches and replaced by whitewashed walls. The mass was replaced by a new liturgy consisting of Scripture reading, prayer, and sermons. Music was eliminated from the service as a distraction from the pure word of God. Monasticism, pilgrimages, the veneration of saints, clerical celibacy, and the pope's authority were all abolished as remnants of papal Christianity. Zwingli's movement soon spread to other cities in Switzerland, including Bern in 1528 and Basel in 1529.

By 1528, Zwingli's reform movement was faced with a serious political problem as the forest cantons remained staunchly Catholic. Zürich feared an alliance between them and the Habsburgs. To counteract this danger, Zwingli attempted to build a league of evangelical cities by seeking an agreement with Luther and the German reformers. An alliance between them seemed possible since the Reformation had spread to the south German cities, especially Strasbourg, where a moderate reform movement containing characteristics of both Luther's and Zwingli's movements had been instituted by Martin Bucer (1491–1551). Both the German and Swiss reformers realized the need for unity to defend against the imperial and conservative opposition. But theological differences divided the two reform movements, and one in particular proved impossible to bridge—the sacrament of the Lord's Supper. Protestant political leaders, especially Landgrave Philip of Hesse, fearful of Charles V's ability to take advantage of the division among the reformers, attempted to promote an alliance of the Swiss and German reformed churches by persuading the leaders of both groups to attend a meeting at Marburg to resolve their differences. Able to agree on virtually everything else, the gathering splintered over the interpretation of the Lord's Supper (see the box on p. 462). Zwingli believed that the scriptural words "This is by Body, This is my blood" should be taken figuratively, not literally, and refused to accept Luther's insistence on the real presence of the body and blood of Christ "in, with, and under the bread and wine." The Marburg Colloquy of 1529 produced no agreement and no evangelical alliance. While harmful to Lutheranism and Philip of Hesse, it proved even more harmful to Zwingli.

In October 1531, war erupted between the Swiss Protestant and Catholic cantons. Zürich's army was routed and Zwingli was killed on the battlefield. Although Zwingli was succeeded by the able Heinrich Büllinger, the momentum of the Zwinglian reform movement was slowed. This Swiss civil war of 1531 provided an early indication of what religious passions would lead to in the sixteenth century. Unable to find peaceful ways to agree on the meaning of the Gospel, the disciples of Christianity resorted to violence and decision by force. When he heard of Zwingli's death, Martin Luther, who had not forgotten the confrontation at Marburg, is supposed to have remarked that Zwingli got what he deserved.

The Radical Reformation: The Anabaptists

Since the Reformation had broken down traditional standards and relationships, reformers such as Luther

▼ **Zwingli.** Ulrich Zwingli began the Reformation in Switzerland through his preaching in Zürich. Zwingli's theology was accepted by Zürich and soon spread to other Swiss cities. Fearing an alliance between the Catholic Swiss cantons and Charles V, Zwingli made an attempt to unite the German and Swiss reform movements. Theological questions, however, kept them divided.

sought a new authority by allowing the state to play an important, if not dominant, role in church affairs. But some people rejected this kind of magisterial reformation and favored a far more radical approach. They believed that Luther and Zwingli had not carried their ideas to their logical conclusion and regarded Lutheranism and Zwinglianism as almost as bad as medieval Catholicism. Collectively called the Anabaptists, these radicals actually formed a large variety of different groups who, nevertheless, shared some common characteristics. Although some middle-class intellectuals participated in this movement, Anabaptism was especially attractive to those peasants, weavers, miners, and artisans who had been adversely affected by the economic changes of the

A Reformation Debate: The Marburg Colloquy
▼▼▼

Debates played a crucial role in the Reformation period. They were a primary instrument in introducing the Reformation into innumerable cities as well as a means of resolving differences among like-minded Protestant groups. This selection contains an excerpt from Luther's and Zwingli's vivacious and often brutal debate over the sacrament of the Lord's Supper at Marburg in 1529. The two protagonists failed to reach agreement.

The Marburg Colloquy, 1529

THE HESSIAN CHANCELLOR FEIGE: My gracious prince and lord [Landgrave Philip of Hesse] has summoned you for the express and urgent purpose of settling the dispute over the sacrament of the Lord's Supper. . . .And let everyone on both sides present his arguments in a spirit of moderation, as becomes such matters. . . .Now then, Doctor Luther, you may proceed.

LUTHER: Noble prince, gracious lord! Undoubtedly the colloquy is well intentioned. . . .Although I have no intention of changing my mind, which is firmly made up, I will nevertheless present the grounds of my belief and show where the others are in error. . . .Your basic contentions are these: In the last analysis you wish to prove that a body cannot be in two places at once, and you produce arguments about the unlimited body which are based on natural reason. I do not question how Christ can be God and man and how the two natures can be joined. For God is more powerful than all our ideas, and we must submit to his word.

Prove that Christ's body is not there where the Scripture says, "This is my body!" Rational proofs I will not listen to. . . .God is beyond all mathematics and the words of God are to be revered and carried out in awe. It is God who commands, "Take, eat, this is my body." I request, therefore, valid scriptural proof to the contrary.

Luther writes on the table in chalk, "This is my body," and covers the words with a velvet cloth.

OECOLAMPADIUS [leader of the reform movement in Basel and a Zwinglian partisan]: The sixth chapter of John clarifies the other scriptural passages. Christ is not speaking there about a local presence. "The flesh is of no avail," he says [John 6:63]. It is not my intention to employ rational, or geometrical, arguments—neither am I denying the power of God—but as long as I have the complete faith I will speak from that. For Christ is risen; he sits at the right hand of God; and so he cannot be present in the bread. Our view is neither new nor sacrilegious, but is based on faith and Scripture. . . .

ZWINGLI: I insist that the words of the Lord's Supper must be figurative. This is ever apparent, and even required by the article of faith: "taken up into heaven, seated at the right hand of the Father." Otherwise, it would be absurd to look for him in the Lord's Supper at the same time that Christ is telling us that he is in heaven. One and the same body cannot possibly be in different places. . . .

LUTHER: I call upon you as before: your basic contentions are shaky. Give way, and give glory to God!

ZWINGLI: And we call upon you to give glory to God and to quit begging the question! The issue at stake is this: Where is the proof of your position? I am willing to consider your words carefully—no harm meant! You're trying to outwit me. I stand by this passage in the sixth chapter of John, verse 63 and shall not be shaken from it. You'll have to sing another tune.

LUTHER: You're being obnoxious.

ZWINGLI (*excitedly*): Don't you believe that Christ was attempting in John 6 to help those who did not understand?

LUTHER: You're trying to dominate things! You insist on passing judgment! Leave that to someone else! . . .It is your point that must be proved, not mine. But let us stop this sort of thing. It serves no purpose.

ZWINGLI: It certainly does! It is for you to prove that the passage in John 6 speaks of a physical repast.

LUTHER: You express yourself poorly and make about as much progress as a cane standing in a corner. You're going nowhere.

ZWINGLI: No, no, no! This is the passage that will break your neck!

LUTHER: Don't be so sure of yourself. Necks don't break this way. You're in Hesse, not Switzerland. . . .

age. The upper classes were aware of the obvious link between social dissatisfaction and religious radicalism, which was particularly evident in commercial and industrial cities like Zürich, Strasbourg, Nuremberg, and Augsburg. All of these cities initiated a Lutheran or Zwinglian Reformation early on but, thanks to their relatively large lower classes affected by economic upheavals, also became centers for radical religious groups.

Anabaptists everywhere shared some common ideas. To them, the true Christian church was a voluntary association of believers who had undergone spiritual rebirth and had then been baptized into the church. Anabaptists advocated adult rather than infant baptism. They also took seriously a return to the practices and spirit of early Christianity. Adhering to the accounts of early Christian communities in the New Testament, they followed a strict sort of democracy in which all believers were considered equal. Each church chose its own minister, who might be any member of the community since all Christians were considered priests (though women were often excluded). Those chosen as ministers had the duty to lead services, which were very simple and contained nothing not found in the early church. Anabaptists rejected theological speculation in favor of simple Christian living according to the pure word of God. The Lord's Supper was interpreted as a remembrance, a meal of fellowship celebrated in the evening in private houses according to Christ's example. Finally, unlike the Catholics and other Protestants, most

Anabaptists believed in the complete separation of church and state. Not only was government to be excluded from the realm of religion, it was not even supposed to exercise political jurisdiction over real Christians. A ruler might be ordained by God, but not among true Christians. Anabaptists refused to hold political office or bear arms since many took literally the commandment "Thou shall not kill," although some Anabaptist groups did become quite violent. Their political beliefs as much as their religious beliefs caused the Anabaptists to be regarded as dangerous radicals who threatened the very fabric of sixteenth-century society. Indeed, the chief thing Protestants and Catholics could agree on was the need to persecute Anabaptists.

One early group of Anabaptists arose in Zürich. Called the Swiss Brethren, they were led by Conrad Grebel (1498–1526), an early supporter of Zwingli who came to believe that the Bible provided no evidence for infant baptism. His teachings frightened Zwingli, and the Swiss Brethren were soon expelled from the city. As their teachings spread into southern Germany, the Austrian Habsburg lands, and Switzerland, Anabaptists suffered ruthless persecution, especially after the Peasants' War of 1524–1525 when the upper classes resorted to repression. To Catholics and Lutherans alike, the Anabaptists threatened not only religious peace but also secular authority because of their political ideas (see the box on p. 464). Virtually stamped out in Germany, Anabaptist survivors emerged in Moravia, Poland, and

▼ **An Anabaptist Execution in the Netherlands.** The Anabaptists were the true radicals of the Reformation. They advocated adult baptism over infant baptism, and believed that the true Christian should not actively participate in or be governed by the secular state. Due to their radical ideas, the Anabaptists were persecuted and put to death by both Catholics and Protestants. This sixteenth-century woodcut depicts the execution of Anabaptist reformers.

The Trial of Michael Sattler

▼ ▼ ▼

Michael Sattler had been prior of a Benedictine monastery before abandoning Catholicism for Lutheranism and then Anabaptism. He was responsible for drawing up a set of seven articles (the Schleitheim Articles) in 1527, which constituted the "first formal Anabaptist confession of faith." Both Catholics and other Protestant sects viewed Anabaptists as dangerous radicals, subversive of both church and state. This excerpt, taken from a contemporary account of Sattler's trial for heresy, begins after Sattler has given a speech detailing his beliefs. As his sentence indicates, Anabaptists were subjected to cruel and unusual punishments.

The Trial of Michael Sattler

Upon this speech the judges laughed and put their heads together, and the town clerk of Ensisheim said, "Yes, you infamous, desperate rascal of a monk, should we dispute with you? The hangman will dispute with you, I assure you!"

Michael said: "God's will be done."

The town clerk said: "It were well if you had never been born."

Michael replied: "God knows what is good."

The town clerk: "You archheretic, you have seduced pious people. If they would only now forsake their error and commit themselves to grace!"

Michael: "Grace is with God alone."

The town clerk: "Yes, you desperate villain, you archheretic, I say, if there were no hangman here, I would hang you myself and be doing God a good service thereby."

Michael: "God will judge aright."

The town clerk then admonished the judges and said: "He will not cease from this chatter anyway. Therefore, my Lord Judge, you may proceed with the sentence. I call for a decision of the court."

The judge asked Michael Sattler whether he too committed it to the court. He replied: "Ministers of God, I am not sent to judge the Word of God. We are sent to testify and hence cannot consent to any adjudication, since we have no command from God concerning it. But we are not for that reason removed from being judged and we are ready to suffer and to await what God is planning to do with us. We will continue in our faith in Christ so long as we have breath in us, unless we be dissuaded from it by the Scriptures."

The town clerk said: "The hangman will instruct you, he will dispute with you, archheretic."

Michael: "I appeal to the Scriptures."

Then the judges arose and went into another room where they . . . determined on the sentence. . . .

The judges having returned to the room, the sentence was read. It was as follows: "In the case of the attorney of His Imperial Majesty [Holy Roman Emperor] vs. Michael Sattler, judgment is passed that Michael Sattler shall be delivered to the executioner, who shall lead him to the place of execution and cut out his tongue, then forge him fast to a wagon and thereon with red-hot tongs twice tear pieces from his body; and after he has been brought outside the gate, he shall be plied five times more in the same manner. . . ."

---

the Netherlands. In the latter, Anabaptism took on a strange form.

In the 1530s, the city of Münster in Westphalia in northwest Germany near the Dutch border was the site of an Anabaptist uprising that determined the fate of Dutch Anabaptism. Seat of a powerful Catholic prince-bishop, Münster had experienced severe economic disasters, including crop failure and plague. Although converted to Lutheranism in 1532, Münster experienced a more radical mass religious hysteria that led to legal recognition for the Anabaptists. Soon, Münster became a haven for Anabaptists from the surrounding neighbor-

hood, especially the more wild-eyed variety known as Melchiorites who believed in a vivid millenarianism focusing on the end of the world and the ushering in of the Kingdom of God with Münster as the New Jerusalem. By the end of February 1534, these millenarian Anabaptists had taken control of the city, driven out the godless or unbelievers, burned all books except the Bible, and proclaimed communal ownership of all property. Eventually, the leadership of this New Jerusalem fell into the hands of one man, John of Leiden, who proclaimed himself king of the New Jerusalem. As king, he would lead out the elect from Münster to cover the entire world and purify it of evil by the sword in preparation for Christ's Second Coming and the creation of a millennial New Age. In this new kingdom, all goods would be held in common and the saints would live without suffering.

But it was not to be. As the Catholic prince-bishop of Münster gathered numerous forces and laid siege to the city, the new king repeatedly had to postpone the ushering forth from Münster. Finally, after many inhabitants had starved, the Catholics recaptured the city in June 1535 and executed the radical Anabaptist leaders in a gruesome fashion. The New Jerusalem had ceased to exist.

Purged of its fantasies and more extreme elements, Dutch Anabaptism reverted to its pacifist tendencies, especially evident in the work of Menno Simons (1496–1561), the man most responsible for rejuvenating Dutch Anabaptism. A popular leader, Menno dedicated his life to the spread of a peaceful, evangelical Anabaptism based on separation from the world in order to live fully a Christ-like life. The Mennonites, as his followers were called, spread from the Netherlands into northwestern Germany and eventually eastward into Poland and Lithuania.

The Reformation in England

The English Reformation was initiated by an act of state. King Henry VIII (1509–1547), with the approval of Parliament, severed the ties of allegiance that bound the church of England to the Roman Catholic church, establishing a national church and proclaiming himself to be the "supreme head" of the church in place of the pope. Henry, however, made few doctrinal changes and believed that he had simply restored the independent authority of the English church illegally taken over centuries before by the pope. Nevertheless, his action added to the ongoing disintegration of Christian unity, and after his death, growing religious protest moved the Church of England in a more definite Protestant direction.

At one time, such a Reformation in England would have been unthinkable. Had not Henry VIII penned an attack against Martin Luther in defense of the seven sacraments and been rewarded for it by the pope with the title "Defender of the Faith"? Nevertheless, there were elements of discontent in England. Antipapal feeling ran high since many Englishmen resented papal influence in English affairs, especially in matters of taxation and justice. Anticlericalism was rife as people denounced greedy clerics who flaunted their great wealth in ostentatious extravagance. One layman charged that "These [the clergy] are not the shepherds, but the ravenous wolves going in shepherds' clothing, devouring the flock."

Anticlericalism and antipapal feelings were not the only manifestations of religious sentiment in early sixteenth-century England. A deep craving for spiritual expression fostered the spread of Lutheran ideas, encouraged in part by two different traditions of dissent. Heretical Lollardy, stressing the use of the Bible in the vernacular and the rejection of papal supremacy, continued to exert influence among the lower classes, while Christian humanism with its calls for reform influenced the English middle and upper classes. People influenced by Lollardy and Christian humanism were among the first to embrace Lutheran writings when they began to arrive in England in the 1520s.

Despite these factors, there might not have been a Reformation in England if it had not been for the king and his consuming desire to divorce his first wife Catherine of Aragon. Henry VIII's reasons were twofold. Catherine had produced no male heir, a *sine qua non* if his Tudor dynasty were to flourish. At the same time, Henry had fallen in love with Anne Boleyn, a lady-in-waiting to Queen Catherine. Her unwillingness to be only the king's mistress as well as the king's desire to have a legitimate male heir made a new marriage imperative. The king's first marriage stood in the way, however.

Henry relied upon Cardinal Wolsey, the highest ranking English church official and lord chancellor to the king, to obtain an annulment of his marriage from Pope Clement VII. Normally, the pope might have been willing to oblige, but the sack of Rome in 1527 had made the pope dependent upon the Holy Roman emperor Charles V, who happened to be the nephew of Queen Catherine. Discretion dictated delay in granting the English king's request. Impatient with the process, Henry dismissed Wolsey in 1529.

Two new advisers now became the king's agents in fulfilling his wishes. These were Thomas Cranmer (1489–1540), who became archbishop of Canterbury in 1532, and Thomas Cromwell (1485–1540), the king's principal secretary after the fall of Wolsey. They advised the king to obtain an annulment of his marriage in England's own ecclesiastical courts. The most important step toward this goal was the promulgation by Parliament of an act cutting off all appeals from English church courts to Rome, a piece of legislation that essentially abolished papal authority in England. Henry no longer needed the pope to attain his annulment. He was now in a hurry, since Anne Boleyn had become pregnant and he had secretly married her in January 1533 to legitimize the expected heir. Now, as archbishop of Canterbury and head of the highest ecclesiastical court in England, Thomas Cranmer held official hearings on the king's case, ruled in May that the king's marriage to Catherine was "null and absolutely void," and then validated Henry's marriage to Anne. At the beginning of June, Anne was crowned queen. Three months later a child was born. Much to the king's disappointment, the baby was a girl, the future Queen Elizabeth.

In 1534, Parliament moved to finalize the break of the Church of England with Rome. An Act of Supremacy of 1534 declared that the king was "taken, accepted, and reputed the only supreme head on earth of the Church of England," a position that gave him control of doctrine, clerical appointments, and discipline. Parliament also passed a Treason Act making it punishable by death to deny that the king was the supreme head of the church. These additional enactments by the Reformation Parliament not only legalized Henry's actions and repudiated papal authority but created the "autonomous sovereignty of the English government." Few challenged the new order. One who did was Thomas More, the humanist and former lord chancellor, who saw clearly to the heart of the issue. To accept the new settlement meant that "therefore am I not bound . . . to conform my conscience to the Council of one realm [England] against the general Council of Christendom,"[11] as he proclaimed at his trial. More's conscience refused to accept the victory of the national state over the church; a Christian could not bow his head to a secular ruler in matters of faith. More was beheaded in London on July 6, 1535.

Above all others, Thomas Cromwell worked out the details of the Tudor government's new role in church affairs based on the centralized power exercised by the king and Parliament. Cromwell came to the extravagant king's financial rescue with a daring plan for the dissolution of the monasteries. About four hundred religious houses were closed in 1536 and their land and possessions confiscated by the king. Many were sold to nobles, gentry, and some merchants. The king received a great boost to his treasury as well as creating a group of supporters who now had a stake in the new Tudor order.

Although Henry VIII had broken with the papacy, little change occurred in matters of doctrine, theology, and ceremony. Some, such as Archbishop Thomas Cranmer, wished to have a religious reformation as well as an administrative one, but Henry was unyielding. To counteract a growing Protestant sentiment, the king had Parliament pass the Six Articles Act of 1539, which

reaffirmed transubstantiation, clerical celibacy, and other aspects of Catholic doctrine. No doubt, Henry's conservatism helped the English accept the basic changes he had made; since religious doctrine and worship had changed very little, most people were indifferent to the transformation that had occurred. Popular acceptance was also furthered by Henry's strategy of involving Parliament in all the changes.

The last decade of Henry's reign was preoccupied with foreign affairs, factional intrigue, and a continued effort to find the perfect wife (he ended up with six). In religious affairs, Henry managed to hold the Church of England in line with Catholic doctrine, but after his death the movement toward Protestantism grew much stronger under his successor, the son of his third wife, Jane Seymour, the underage and sickly Edward VI (1547–1553).

THE EDWARDIAN REFORMATION   Since the new king was only nine years old at the time of his accession to the throne, real control of England passed to a council of regency guided by Edward's uncle, the duke of Somerset. Rather incompetent and incapable of handling the intricacies of royal administration complicated by conflicting aristocratic factions, Somerset was outmaneuvered by his archrival, the duke of Northumberland, and executed in 1551. Northumberland now assumed the leadership of the council of regency and became the virtual ruler of England.

During Edward's reign, Archbishop Cranmer and others inclined toward Protestant doctrines were able to move the Church of England in more of a Protestant direction. Martin Bucer, the reformer of Strasbourg, played an especially important role. Forced out of Europe by the victories of Charles V, Bucer came to England, taught at Cambridge, and influenced the English with his own moderate Protestant beliefs. The Edwardian Reformation, like the Henrician, was largely put into effect by acts of Parliament and included the right of the clergy to marry, the elimination of images, and the creation of a revised Protestant liturgy that was elaborated in a new prayer book and liturgical guide known as the Book of Common Prayer. First published in 1549, it was revised during Northumberland's regency in an even more Protestant direction, particularly apparent in the sentences pronounced at the time of receiving the sacrament of the Lord's Supper. In the 1549 edition, this read: "The Body of our Lord Jesus Christ which was given for thee, preserve thy body and soul unto everlasting life," reflecting a Lutheran conception. But in the 1552 edition, it stated: "Take and eat this in remembrance that Christ died for thee, and feed on him in thy heart by faith, with thanksgiving," an indication of Zwinglian influence. These rapid changes in doctrine and liturgy, enforced by an Act of Uniformity, aroused much opposition and prepared the way for the reaction that occurred when Mary, Henry's first daughter by Catherine of Aragon, came to the throne.

QUEEN MARY AND THE CATHOLIC REVIVAL   There was no doubt that Mary (1553–1558) was a Catholic who intended to restore England to Roman Catholicism. If she had been content to eliminate the more extreme measures taken during Edward's reign, she might have been successful. But, dedicated to Catholicism, she understood little about the practical nature of politics and even less about the changes that had swept over England in the past thirty years.

Mary's restoration of Catholicism, achieved by joint action of the monarch and Parliament, aroused much opposition. Although the new owners of monastic lands were assured otherwise, many feared that the lands confiscated by Henry would be restored to the church. Moreover, there was widespread antipathy to Mary's unfortunate marriage to Philip II, the son of Charles V and the future king of Spain. Philip was strongly disliked in England, and Mary's foreign policy of alliance with Spain simply aroused further hostility, especially when her forces lost Calais, the last English possession from the Hundred Years' War. The burning of over three hundred Protestant heretics roused further ire against "bloody Mary." As a result of her policies, Mary managed to achieve the opposite of what she had intended: England was more Protestant by the end of her reign than it had been at the beginning. When she came to power, Protestantism had become identified with church destruction and religious anarchy. Now people identified it with honesty and English resistance to Spanish interference. The death of Mary in 1558 ended the restoration of Catholicism in England, ironically at the same time that the Catholic Reformation in Europe was taking a more positive approach and rapidly gaining momentum.

John Calvin and the Development of Calvinism

Of the second generation of Protestant reformers, one stands out as the systematic theologian and organizer of the Protestant movement—John Calvin (1509–1564). Born a generation later than Luther, Calvin reached manhood when Christian unity had for all intents and purposes already disappeared. Although his basic doctrinal positions were similar to Luther's, their different backgrounds resulted in significant differences as well.

John Calvin began his academic training in 1523 at the University of Paris, but switched to the study of law at Orléans and Bourges from 1528 to 1531, while simultaneously studying Greek. In 1531, he returned to Paris to concentrate on his humanistic pursuits. In his early development, Calvin was also influenced by Luther's writings, which were being circulated and read by French intellectuals as early as 1523. Up to 1533, then, Calvin had received a remarkably diverse education. In that same year, he experienced a religious crisis that determined the rest of his life's work. He described it in these words:

> God, by a sudden conversion, subdued and brought my mind to a teachable frame, which was more hardened in such matters than might have been expected from one at my early period of life. Having thus received some taste and knowledge of true godliness, I was immediately inflamed with so intense a desire to make progress therein, although I did not leave off other studies, I yet pursued them with less ardor.[12]

Calvin's conversion was solemn and straightforward. He was so convinced of the inner guidance of God that he became the most determined of all the Protestant reformers.

After his conversion and newfound conviction, Calvin was no longer safe in Paris since King Francis I periodically persecuted Protestants. Eventually, Calvin made his way to Basel, where in 1536, he published the first edition of the Institutes of the Christian Religion, a masterful synthesis of Protestant thought, a manual for ecclesiastical organization, and a work that immediately secured Calvin's reputation as one of the new leaders of Protestantism. Although the Institutes were originally written in Latin, Calvin published a French edition in 1541, facilitating the spread of his ideas in French-speaking lands.

On most important doctrines, Calvin stood very close to Luther. He adhered to the doctrine of justification by faith alone to explain how humans achieved salvation. But Calvin also placed much emphasis on the absolute sovereignty of God or the "power, grace, and glory of God." Thus, "God asserts his possession of omnipotence, and claims our acknowledgment of this attribute; not such as is imagined by sophists, vain, idle, and almost asleep, but vigilant, efficacious, operative and engaged in continual action."[13] Certain ideas derived from his emphasis on the absolute sovereignty of God gave a unique cast to Calvin's teachings.

Like other reformers, Calvin believed in predestination. Although it was but one aspect of his doctrine of salvation, predestination became the central focus of succeeding generations of Calvinists. This "eternal decree," as Calvin called it, meant that God had predestined some people to be saved (the elect) and others to be damned (the reprobate). According to Calvin, "He has once for all determined, both whom he would admit to salvation, and whom he would condemn to destruction."[14] If this appeared unjust by human standards, Calvin reminded his listeners that "the will of God is the highest rule of justice, so that what he wills must be considered just, for this very reason, because he wills it."[15]

Calvin identified three presumptive tests to assure his followers of their possible salvation: an open profession of faith, a "decent and godly life," and participation in

▼ **John Calvin Preaching.** After a conversion experience, John Calvin abandoned his life as a humanist in favor of life as a reformer. His theology stressed the omnipotence of God. In 1536, Calvin began working to reform the city of Geneva, a struggle that produced its first major success in the adoption of Calvin's Ecclesiastical Ordinances in 1541. Calvin remained in Geneva until his death in 1564.

the sacraments of baptism and communion. In no instance did Calvin ever suggest that worldly success or material wealth was a sign of election. Most importantly, although Calvin stressed that there could be no absolute certainty of salvation, his followers did not always make this distinction. The practical psychological effect of predestination was to give later Calvinists an unshakable conviction that they were doing God's work on earth. Thus, Calvinism became a dynamic and activist faith. It is no accident that Calvinism became the militant international form of Protestantism.

The absolute sovereignty of God had another implication as well. If only God is sovereign, then no human being, even a king, can lay claim to absolute power. Calvin separated church and state and gave to the state the duty to maintain peace and order, including the prevention of public offenses against religion. Calvin followed Luther in calling for obedience to legally constituted governments. Even if the ruler was an "unbridled despot," his subjects must "obey and suffer." Yet, Calvin foresaw instances in which obedience to a ruler might mean disobedience to God. In that case, he argued, we must follow the biblical injunction to "obey God rather than men." This resistance, however, was not to be undertaken by private individuals but by representative assemblies (parliaments or Estates-Generals). Over the next seventy-five years, Calvinist minorities would use this suggestion by Calvin to justify armed rebellion in France, Scotland, the Netherlands, and England against "licentious kings" who persecuted their faith (see Chapter 15).

A third corollary of Calvin's emphasis on the absolute sovereignty of God was that God exerted his sovereignty through his church. The church, then, was a divine institution largely independent of state power. It had two primary functions: to preach the pure word of God and administer the sacraments. Calvin kept only two sacraments, baptism and the Lord's Supper. Baptism was a sign of the remission of sins. Calvin believed in the real presence of Christ in the sacrament of the Lord's Supper, but only in a spiritual sense. Christ is at the right hand of God, but to the believer, Christ is spiritually present in the Lord's Supper. Finally, Calvin agreed with other reformers that the church had the power to discipline its members. This element seemed to get out of control at times when Calvin finally had the opportunity to establish his church in Geneva.

CALVIN'S REFORMATION IN GENEVA (1536–1564) Up to 1536, John Calvin had essentially been a scholar. In that year, however, he found himself temporarily in Geneva

The Role of Discipline in the "Most Perfect School of Christ on Earth"

▼ ▼ ▼

To John Calvin's followers, the church that the French reformer had created in Geneva was, in the words of John Knox, "the most perfect school of Christ on earth." Calvin had emphasized in his reform movement that the church should have the ability to enforce proper behavior. Consequently, the Ecclesiastical Ordinances of 1541, the constitution of the church in Geneva, provided for an order of elders whose function was to cooperate with the pastors in maintaining discipline, "to have oversight of the life of everyone," as Calvin expressed it. These selections from the official records of the Consistory show the nature of its work.

Reports of the Genevan Consistory

Donna Jane Peterman is questioned concerning her faith and why she does not receive communion and attend worship. She confesses her faith and believes in one God and wants to come to God and the holy Church and has no other faith. She recited the Lord's Prayer in the vernacular. She said that she believes what the Church believes. Is questioned why she never participates in communion when it is celebrated in this town, but goes to other places. She answers that she goes where it seems good to her. Is placed outside the faith.

The sister of Sr. Curtet, Lucresse, to whom remonstrances have been made on account of her going with certain monies to have masses said at Nessy by the monks of St. Claire. Questioned whether she has no scruples as to what she says. Replied that her father and mother have brought her up to obey a different law from the one now in force here. However, she does not desire the present law. Asked as to when was the festival of St. Felix, she replied that it was yesterday. Asked if she had not fasted, she replied that she fasted when it pleased her. Asked if she did not desire to pray to a single God; said that she did. Asked if she did not pray to St. Felix; said that she prayed to St. Felix and other saints who interceded for her. She is very obstinate. Decision that she be sent to some minister of her choice every sermon day and that the Lord's Supper be withheld from her.

At about this time, by resolution of the Consistory . . . the marriage contracted between the widow of Jean Achard, aged more than 70, and a servant of hers, aged about 27 or 28, was dissolved because of the too great inequality of age. The Consistory resolved further that Messieurs should be requested to make a ruling on this matter for the future.

where the local Protestant reformer, William Farel, asked him to stay and assist in reforming the city. Calvin was reluctant to do so, wishing instead to pursue the quiet life of a scholar. But Farel's warning that it was God's will persuaded Calvin to take up a ministry in Geneva that lasted until his death in 1564.

Calvin achieved his first major success when the city council accepted his new church constitution known as the Ecclesiastical Ordinances in 1541. This document established four orders or offices: pastors, teachers, elders, and deacons. The duties of the pastors or ministers were to preach the Gospel, administer the sacraments, and correct un-Christian behavior. To the teachers or doctors was given the responsibility to "instruct the faithful in sound doctrine, in order that the purity of the Gospel may not be corrupted." The elders or presbyters were laymen, chosen from and by the city magistrates,

whose function was to maintain discipline: "to have oversight of the life of everyone, to admonish amicably those whom they see to be erring or to be living a disordered life, and . . . to enjoin fraternal corrections." The deacons were also laymen who were responsible for the care of the poor, widows, and orphans and the administration of the city's hospitals.

The Ecclesiastical Ordinances created a special body for enforcing moral discipline. Consisting of five pastors and twelve elders, the Consistory functioned as a court to oversee the moral life, daily behavior, and doctrinal orthodoxy of Genevans and to admonish and correct deviants (see the box above). As its power increased, the Consistory went from "fraternal corrections" to the use of public penance and excommunication. More serious cases could be turned over to the city council for punishments greater than excommunication.

After his initial success in 1541, Calvin found his existence in Geneva to be burdened by almost continual conflict. On his deathbed, Calvin recounted: "Thus I have been in the midst of battle, and you [the other pastors] will experience ones not less, but greater. For you are in a perverse and unhappy nation, and although she has some honorable men, the nation is perverse and wicked. You will have your hands full after God has taken me away."[16] He faced two kinds of opposition. Calvin demanded complete conformity to his religious reforms, giving rise to opposition to his teachings, especially his emphasis on predestination. Moreover, many opposed his moral discipline, among them Genevan nationalists (the "old Genevans") who attacked Calvin and his supporters as French emigrants. At times his opponents came close to gaining a majority in the councils and expelling him from the city. But in 1553, Calvin became a hero when the notorious heretic Michael Servetus was captured, put on trial, and executed for his anti-Trinitarian beliefs. Calvin's prestige increased, not only in Geneva, but also throughout Europe where he was viewed as the mighty defender of Protestantism. During Calvin's last years, stricter laws against blasphemy were enacted and enforced with banishment and public whippings. Although Calvin's detractors felt that Geneva was an example of religious fanaticism, to visitors of similar inclination, it presented a glorious sight. John Knox, the Calvinist reformer of Scotland, called it "the most perfect school of Christ on earth." By the 1550s Calvinism was the most militant, vibrant, and expansionistic of all forms of Protestantism.

THE SPREAD OF CALVINISM   John Calvin did not restrict his interests to Geneva but hoped that France might also someday became a truly Christian commonwealth. By the 1540s Calvin's reputation and influence were beginning to spread not only in France but elsewhere in Europe as well.

In France, Calvinism replaced an earlier attachment to Lutheranism and Christian humanistic reform. Followers of Calvin in France came from many levels of society, including artisans, merchants, and lawyers in provincial towns, especially those in southern and western France that became Calvinist strongholds. Most helpful to Calvinism in France, however, was support from the members of the nobility.

Calvinism entered the Netherlands, especially the French-speaking provinces in the 1550s. In 1561, the first confession of faith (Belgic Confession) was drafted by a French-speaking minister. England, too, began to experience the impact of Calvinist reformers during the reign of Edward VI (1547–1553). But the more direct influence of Calvinism came after the reign of Mary when a number of religious figures who had fled England during the Catholic restoration and spent time in Geneva returned to England. Calvinism was also established in Scotland due to the efforts of "God's trumpeter," John Knox, and owed its victory primarily to support from the landed nobility.

Calvinism spread into central and eastern Europe as well. In Germany, it was aided by the conversion of the elector and count palatine of the Rhine, Frederick III (1559–1576), who sponsored an influential confession of faith for the German Reformed Church (as Calvinism was known in German-speaking lands) known as the Heidelberg Catechism in 1563. In the 1550s, Calvinism also superseded Lutheranism among the Polish, Hungarian, and Bohemian nobility.

The spread of Calvinism was aided by the militancy of Calvin's followers, who believed that they were chosen by God and operated with the sense of conviction that comes to those who are convinced they are right. At the same time, Calvinist church government, with its combination of lay and clerical participation, provided channels for vigorous demonstrations of this faith. Calvin himself played an important role in the spread of his teachings to many parts of Europe. Calvin was the true leader who sent out his men to carry on the movement. Missionaries trained in Geneva were sent to France, the Netherlands, and other parts of Europe. From 1555 to 1562, Calvin sent 120 missions involving some hundred different preachers to all parts of Europe. Several were even sent to a new French colony in Brazil. The Genevan Academy, founded in 1559, provided the training ground for the leaders of the Reformed Protestant movement of Europe. By the mid-sixteenth century, Calvinism had replaced Lutheranism as the militant international form of Protestantism while Calvin's Geneva stood as the fortress of the Reformation.

▼ The Social Impact of the Protestant Reformation

Since Christianity was such an integral part of European life, it was inevitable that the Reformation would have an impact on the family, education, and popular religious practices.

The Family

For centuries, Catholicism had praised the family and sanctified its existence by making marriage a sacrament. But the church's high regard for abstinence from sex as

A Protestant Woman
▼ ▼ ▼

In the initial zeal of the Protestant Reformation, women were frequently allowed to play unusual roles. Catherine Zell of Germany (c. 1497–1562) first preached beside her husband in 1527. After the death of her two children, she devoted the rest of her life to helping her husband and their Anabaptist faith. This selection is taken from one of her letters to a young Lutheran minister who had criticized her activities.

Catherine Zell to Ludwig Rabus of Memmingen

I, Catherine Zell, wife of the late lamented Mathew Zell, who served in Strassburg, where I was born and reared and still live, wish you peace and enhancement in God's grace. . . .

From my earliest years I turned to the Lord, who taught and guided me, and I have at all times, in accordance with my understanding and His grace, embraced the interests of His church and earnestly sought Jesus. Even in youth this brought me the regard and affection of clergymen and others much concerned with the church, which is why the pious Mathew Zell wanted me as a companion in marriage; and I, in turn, to serve the glory of Christ, gave devotion and help to my husband, both in his ministry and in keeping his house. . . .Ever since I was ten years old I have been a student and a sort of church mother, much given to attending sermons. I have loved and frequented the company of learned men, and I conversed much with them, not about dancing, masquerades, and worldly pleasures but about the kingdom of God. . . .

Consider the poor Anabaptists, who are so furiously and ferociously persecuted. Must the authorities everywhere be incited against them, as the hunter drives his dog against wild animals? Against those who acknowledge Christ the Lord in very much the same way we do and over which we broke with the papacy? Just because they cannot agree with us on lesser things, is this any reason to persecute them and in them Christ, in whom they fervently believe and have often professed in misery, in prison, and under the torments of fire and water?

Governments may punish criminals, but they should not force and govern belief, which is a matter for the heart and conscience not for temporal authorities. . . .When the authorities pursue one, they soon bring forth tears, and towns and villages are emptied.

---

the surest way to holiness made the celibate state of the clergy preferable to marriage. Nevertheless, since not all men could remain chaste, marriage offered the best means to control sexual intercourse and give it a purpose, the procreation of children. To some extent, this attitude persisted among the Protestant reformers; Luther, for example, argued that sex in marriage allowed one to "make use of this sex in order to avoid sin," and Calvin advised that every man should "abstain from marriage only so long as he is fit to observe celibacy." If "his power to tame lust fails him," then he must marry.

But the Reformation did bring some change to the conception of the family. Both Catholic and Protestant clergy preached sermons advocating a more positive side to family relationships. The Protestants were especially important in developing this new view of the family. Since Protestantism had eliminated any idea of special holiness for celibacy, abolishing both monasticism and a celibate clergy, the family could be placed at the center of human life, and a new stress on "mutual love between man and wife" could be extolled. But were doctrine and reality the same? For more radical religious groups, at times they were (see the box above). One Anabaptist wrote to his wife before his execution: "My faithful helper, my loyal friend. I praise God that he gave you to me, you who have sustained me in all my trial."[17] But more often reality reflected the traditional roles of husband as the ruler and wife as the obedient servant whose chief duty was to please her husband. Luther stated it clearly:

> The rule remains with the husband, and the wife is compelled to obey him by God's command. He rules the home and the state, wages war, defends his possessions, tills the soil, builds, plants, etc. The woman on the other hand is like a nail driven into the wall . . . so the wife should stay at home and look after the affairs of the household, as one who has been deprived of the ability of administering those affairs that are outside and that concern the state. She does not go beyond her most personal duties.[18]

But obedience to her husband was not her only role; her other important duty was to bear children. To Calvin and Luther, this function of women was part of the divine plan. God punishes women for the sins of Eve by the burdens of procreation and feeding and nurturing their children, but "it is a gladsome punishment if you consider the hope of eternal life and the honor of motherhood which had been left to her."[19] Although Protestantism sanctified this role of woman as mother and wife, viewing it as a holy vocation, it also left few alternatives for women. Since monasticism had been destroyed, that career avenue was no longer available; for most Protestant women, family life was their only destiny. At the same time, by emphasizing the father as "ruler" and hence the center of household religion, Protestantism even removed the woman from her traditional role as controller of religion in the home.

Protestant reformers called upon men and women to read the Bible and participate in religious services together. In this way, the reformers provided a stimulus for the education of girls so they could read the Bible and other religious literature. The city council of Zwickau, for example, established a girls' school in 1525. But these schools were designed to encourage proper moral values rather than intellectual development and really did little to improve the position of women in society. Likewise, when women attempted to take more active roles in religious life, reformers—Lutheran and Calvinist alike—shrank back in horror. To them, the equality of the Gospel did not mean overthrowing the inequality of social classes or the sexes. Overall, the Protestant Reformation did not noticeably transform women's subordinate place in society.

Education

The Reformation had an important effect upon the development of education in Europe. Renaissance humanism had significantly altered the content of education (see Chapter 13), and Protestant educators were very successful in implementing and using humanist methods in Protestant secondary schools and universities. Unlike the humanist schools, however, which had been mostly for an elite, the sons and a few daughters of the nobility and wealthier bourgeoisie, Protestant schools were aimed at a much wider audience.

While adopting the classical emphasis of humanist schools, Protestant reformers broadened the base of those being educated. Convinced of the need to provide the church with good Christians and good pastors as well as the state with good administrators and citizens, Martin Luther advocated that all children should have the opportunity of an education provided by the state. To that end, he urged the cities and villages of Saxony to establish schools paid for by the public. Luther's ideas were shared by his Wittenberg co-worker, Philip Melanchthon, whose educational efforts earned him the title of *Praecepter Germaniae*, the Teacher of Germany.

▼ **A Sixteenth-Century Classroom.** Protestants in Germany developed secondary schools where instruction in the liberal arts was combined with an education in religion. Oftentimes, however, the classical education took a secondary place to the religious, and both Catholic and Protestant schools concentrated on producing zealous adherents to the faith. This scene from a painting by Hans Holbein shows a schoolmaster instructing a pupil in the alphabet while his wife helps a little girl.

In his scheme for education in Saxony, Melanchthon divided students into three classes or divisions based on their age or capabilities.

Following Melanchthon's example, the Protestants in Germany were responsible for introducing the gymnasium or secondary school where humanist emphasis on the liberal arts based on instruction in Greek and Latin was combined with religious instruction. Most famous was the one in Strasbourg founded by Johannes Sturm in 1538, which served as a model for other Protestant schools. John Calvin's Genevan Academy, for example, founded in 1559, was organized in two distinct parts. The "private school" or gymnasium was divided into seven classes for young people who were taught Latin and Greek grammar and literature as well as logic. In the "public school," students were taught philosophy, Hebrew, Greek, and, most importantly, theology. The Genevan Academy, which eventually became a university, came to concentrate on preparing ministers to spread the Calvinist view of the Gospel.

Catholics also perceived the importance of secondary schools and universities in educating people to their spiritual perspectives. The Jesuits were especially proficient in combining humanist pedagogy with religious instruction. Although both Catholic and Protestant secondary schools and universities were influenced by humanism, some humanists attacked them for misusing their methods. No doubt, as the Reformation progressed, confessional struggles made education increasingly serve the religious goal of producing zealous Protestants or Catholics. Virtually everywhere, teachers and professors were expected to follow the creeds of their ruling authorities.

Religious Practices and Popular Culture

Although Protestant reformers were conservative in their political and social attitudes, their attacks on the Catholic church created radical changes in religious practices. The Protestant Reformation abolished or severely curtailed such customary practices as indulgences, the veneration of relics and saints, pilgrimages, monasticism, and clerical celibacy. In Protestant cities, attacks on the veneration of saints brought an end to popular religious processions that had been an important focus of religious devotion and often served as rituals to placate nature. The elimination of saints put an end to the numerous celebrations of religious holy days and changed a community's sense of time. Thus, in Protestant communities, religious ceremonies and imagery, such as processions and statues, tended to be replaced with individual private prayer, family worship, and collective prayer and worship at the same time each week on Sunday.

Many popular religious practices that had played an important role in popular culture were criticized by Protestant reformers as superstitious or remnants of pagan culture. Smarting under pressure from these Protestant attacks, even Catholic leaders sought to eliminate the more frivolous aspects of popular practices, although they never went as far as the Protestants. In addition to abolishing saints' days and religious carnivals, some Protestant reformers even tried to eliminate traditional games and plays altogether. English Puritans (as English Calvinists were known), for example, attempted to ban card playing, drinking in taverns, dramatic performances, and dancing. One Elizabethan Puritan lamented that dances made possible "filthy groping and unclean handling" and thus served as "an introduction to whoredom." Dutch Calvinists attacked the tradition of giving small presents to children on the feast of Saint Nicholas, near Christmas. Some of these Protestant attacks on popular culture failed outright. The importance of taverns in English social life made it impossible to eradicate them while gift giving and feasting at Christmas time persisted in the Dutch Netherlands.

▼ The Catholic Reformation

By the mid-sixteenth century, Lutheranism had become established in Germany and Scandinavia, and Calvinism in Switzerland, France, the Netherlands, and eastern Europe. In England, the split from Rome had resulted in the creation of a national church. The situation in Europe did not look particularly favorable for the Roman Catholic church. But even at the beginning of the sixteenth century, constructive, positive forces were at work for reform within the Catholic church, and by the mid-sixteenth century, they came to be directed by a revived and reformed papacy, giving the Catholic church new strength. By the second half of the sixteenth century, Catholicism had regained much that it had lost, especially in Germany and eastern Europe, and was able to make new conversions as well, particularly in the New World. We call the story of the revival of Roman Catholicism the Catholic Reformation, although some historians prefer to use the term Counter-Reformation, especially for those elements of the Catholic Reformation that were directly aimed at stopping the spread of the Protestant Reformation.

Although the revival of mysticism and humanism played an important role in Catholic reform, historians focus on three chief pillars of the Catholic Reformation: the development of the Jesuits, the creation of a reformed and revived papacy, and the Council of Trent.

The Society of Jesus

The Catholic Reformation was a mixture of old and new elements. The best features of medieval Catholicism were revived and then adjusted to meet new conditions, a situation most apparent in the revival of monasticism. Virtually all the old monastic orders were reformed and imbued with new vigor to minister to the poor, the dispossessed, and the sick, thereby keeping many common people loyal to the Catholic church.

Moreover, new religious orders were also created, the most important of which was the Society of Jesus, known as the Jesuits. Highly practical in their approach, the Jesuits became the chief instrument of the Catholic Reformation.

The Society of Jesus was founded by a Spanish nobleman, Ignatius of Loyola (1491–1556). Although desirous of being a soldier, battle injuries prevented him from pursuing a military career. Loyola experienced a spiritual torment similar to Luther's but, unlike Luther, resolved his problems not by a new doctrine, but by a decision to submit his will to the will of the church. Unable to be a real soldier, he vowed to be a soldier of God. Over the next twelve years, Loyola prepared for his

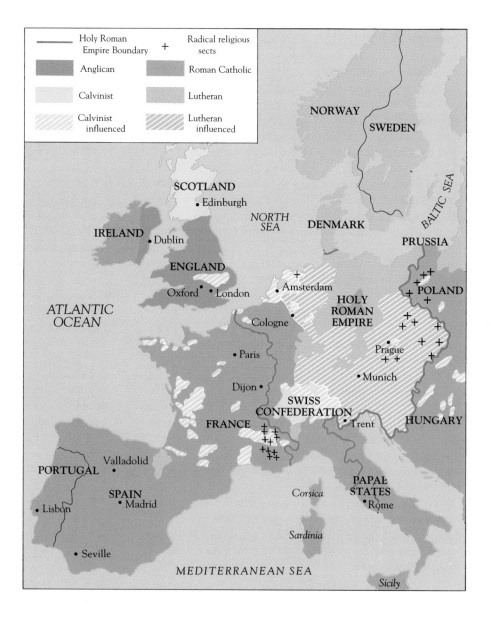

▼ **Map 14.2** Catholics and Protestants in Europe by 1550.

Loyola and Obedience to "Our Holy Mother, the Hierarchical Church"

▼ ▼ ▼

In his Spiritual Exercises, *Ignatius Loyola developed a systematic program for "the conquest of self and the regulation of one's life" for service to the hierarchical Catholic church. Ignatius's supreme goal was the commitment of the Christian to active service under Christ's banner in the Church of Christ (the Catholic church). In the final section of the* Spiritual Exercises, *Loyola explained the nature of that commitment in a series of "Rules for Thinking with the Church."*

Ignatius Loyola, "Rules for Thinking with the Church"

The following rules should be observed to foster the true attitude of mind we ought to have in the Church militant.

1. We must put aside all judgment of our own, and keep the mind ever ready and prompt to obey in all things the true Spouse of Jesus Christ, our holy Mother, the hierarchical Church.
2. We should praise sacramental confession, the yearly reception of the Most Blessed Sacrament [the Lord's Supper], and praise more highly monthly reception, and still more weekly Communion. . . .
3. We ought to praise the frequent hearing of Mass, the singing of hymns, psalmody, and long prayers whether in the church or outside. . . .
4. We must praise highly religious life, virginity, and continency; and matrimony ought not be praised as much as any of these.
5. We should praise vows of religion, obedience, poverty, chastity, and vows to perform other works of supererogation conducive to perfection. . . .
6. We should show our esteem for the relics of the saints by venerating them and praying to the saints. We should praise visits to the Station Churches, pilgrimages, indulgences, jubilees, the lighting of candles in churches.
7. We must praise the regulations of the Church, with regard to fast and abstinence, for example, in Lent, on Ember Days, Vigils, Fridays, and Saturdays.
8. We ought to praise not only the building and adornment of churches, but also images and veneration of them according to the subject they represent.
9. Finally, we must praise all the commandments of the Church, and be on the alert to find reasons to defend them, and by no means in order to criticize them.
10. We should be more ready to approve and praise the orders, recommendations, and way of acting of our superiors than to find fault with them. Though some of the orders, etc., may not have been praiseworthy, yet to speak against them, either when preaching in public or in speaking before the people, would rather be the cause of murmuring and scandal than of profit. As a consequence, the people would become angry with their superiors, whether secular or spiritual. But while it does harm in the absence of our superiors to speak evil of them before the people, it may be profitable to discuss their bad conduct with those who can apply a remedy.
13. If we wish to proceed securely in all things, we must hold fast to the following principle: What seems to me white, I will believe black if the hierarchical Church so defines. For I must be convinced that in Christ our Lord, the bridegroom, and in His spouse the Church, only one Spirit holds sway, which governs and rules for the salvation of souls.

---

life work by mortification, prayer, pilgrimages, going to school, and working out a spiritual program in his brief, but powerful book, *The Spiritual Exercises.* This was a training manual for spiritual development emphasizing exercises by which the human will could be strengthened and made to follow the will of God as manifested through his instrument, the Catholic church (see the box above).

Gradually, Loyola gathered together a small group of individuals who shared his single-minded devotion and were eventually recognized as a religious order, the Society of Jesus, by a papal bull in 1540. The new order was grounded on the principles of absolute obedience to the papacy, a strict hierarchical order for the society, the use of education to achieve its goals, and a dedication to engage in "conflict for God." Jesuit organization came to resemble the hierarchical structure of a military command. A two-year novitiate weeded out all but the most dedicated. Executive leadership was put in the hands of a general, who nominated all important positions in the order and was to be revered as the absolute head of the order. Loyola served as the first general of the order until his death in 1556. A special vow of absolute obedience to the pope made the Jesuits an important instrument for papal policy.

The Jesuits pursued three major activities. They established highly disciplined schools, borrowing freely from humanist schools for their pedagogy. To the Jesuits, the thorough education of young people was crucial to combat the advance of Protestantism. In the course of the sixteenth century, the Jesuits took over the premier academic posts in Catholic universities, and by 1600, they were the most famous educators in Europe. Another prominent Jesuit activity was the propagation of the Catholic faith among the heathen. Francis Xavier (1506–1552), one of the original members of the Society of Jesus, carried the message of Catholic Christianity to the Far East, ministering to India and Japan before dying of fever. Although conversion efforts in Japan proved short-lived, Jesuit activity in China, especially that of the Italian Matteo Ricci, was more long lasting. Finally, the Jesuits were determined to carry the Catholic banner and fight Protestantism. Jesuit missionaries proved singularly successful in restoring Catholicism to parts of Germany and eastern Europe. Poland was, in fact, largely won back for the Catholic church through Jesuit efforts.

In all of these activities, the Jesuits manifested a remarkable emphasis on efficiency and practicality. Jesuits found it worthwhile to subordinate means to ends and were often criticized by other Catholic groups for achieving their goals by somewhat shady practices. The Dominicans, for example, who envied the Jesuits' special relationship to the papacy, attacked the Jesuit policy of including the Chinese rite of ancestor worship in their religious practices. As the "shock troops of the papacy," the Jesuits proved invaluable allies of papal policies.

A Revived Papacy

The involvement of the Renaissance papacy in dubious finances and Italian political and military affairs had created numerous sources of corruption. The meager steps taken to control corruption left the papacy still in need of serious reform, and it took the jolt of the Protestant Reformation to bring it about. Indeed, the change in the papacy in the course of the sixteenth century was one of the more remarkable aspects of the Catholic Reformation.

The pontificate of Pope Paul III (1534–1549) proved to be a turning point in the reform of the papacy. Raised in the lap of Renaissance luxury, Paul III protracted Renaissance papal practices by appointing his nephews as cardinals, involving himself in politics, and patronizing arts and letters on a lavish scale. Nevertheless, he perceived the need for change and expressed it decisively. Advocates of reform, such as Gasparo Contarini and Gian Pietro Caraffa, were made cardinals. In 1535, Paul took the audacious step of appointing a Reform Commission to ascertain the church's ills. The commission's report in 1537, which blamed the church's problems on the corrupt policies of popes and cardinals, was used even by Protestants to demonstrate that their criticisms of Catholic corruption had been justified. It was also Paul III who formally recognized the Jesuits and began the Council of Trent.

A decisive turning point in the direction of the Catholic Reformation and the nature of papal reform came in the 1540s. In 1541, a colloquy had been held at Regensburg in a final attempt to settle the religious division peacefully. Here Catholic moderates, such as Cardinal Contarini, who favored concessions to Protestants in the hope of restoring Christian unity, reached a compromise with Protestant moderates on a number of doctrinal issues. When Contarini returned to Rome with these proposals, Cardinal Caraffa and other hardliners, who regarded all compromise with Protestant innovations as heresy, accused him of selling out to the heretics. It soon became apparent that the conservative reformers were in the ascendancy when Caraffa was able to get Paul III to establish a Roman Inquisition or Holy Office in 1542 to ferret out doctrinal errors. There was to be no compromise with Protestantism.

When Cardinal Caraffa was chosen pope as Paul IV (1555–1559), he so increased the power of the Inquisition that even liberal cardinals were silenced. This "first true pope of the Catholic Counter-Reformation," as he has been called, also created an Index of Forbidden Books, a list of books that Catholics were not allowed to read. It included all the works of Protestant theologians as well as authors considered "unwholesome," a category general enough to include the works of Erasmus and the *Pantagruel* of Rabelais. Rome, the capital of Catholic Christianity, was rapidly becoming fortress Rome; any hope of restoring Christian unity by compromise was fast fading. The activities of the Council of Trent, the third major pillar of the Catholic Reformation, made compromise virtually impossible.

The Council of Trent

Although appeals for a general council of Christendom were frequently advanced as a way to resolve religious differences, herculean obstacles seemed to doom its coming into existence. Following the advice of his humanist chancellor Gattinara, the Holy Roman emperor Charles V believed that religious unity could be reestablished if moderate Catholics and moderate Protestants joined together in a general council to discuss their differences and agree on basic reforms. The popes were fearful of councils, however, aware that historically they had posed a threat to papal power.

It was Pope Paul III who finally capitulated to the emperor's demand for a general church council. In March 1545, a group of cardinals, archbishops, bishops, abbots, and theologians met in the city of Trent on the border between Germany and Italy and initiated a council. This Council of Trent met intermittently from 1545 to 1563 in three major sessions. Two fundamental struggles determined its outcome. While the pope hoped to focus on doctrinal issues, the emperor wanted church reform to be the chief order of business since he realized that defining doctrine first would only make the split in

the church permanent. A second conflict focused on the division between Catholic moderates and conservatives. While the former believed that compromises would have to be made in formulating doctrinal definitions, the latter favored an uncompromising restatement of Catholic doctrines in strict opposition to Protestant positions. The latter group won, although not without a struggle. The Protestants were invited to attend the council, but since they were not permitted to participate, refused the meaningless invitation. By and large, the popes controlled the council.

The final doctrinal decrees of the Council of Trent reaffirmed traditional Catholic teachings in opposition to Protestant beliefs. Scripture and tradition were affirmed as equal authorities in religious matters; only the church could interpret Scripture. Both faith and good works were declared necessary for salvation. The seven sacraments, the Catholic doctrine of transubstantiation, and clerical celibacy were all upheld. Belief in purgatory and in the efficacy of indulgences was affirmed, although indulgence hawkers were abolished. Of the reforming decrees that were passed, the most important established theological seminaries in every diocese for the training of priests.

After the Council of Trent, the Roman Catholic church possessed a clear body of doctrine and a unified church under the acknowledged supremacy of the popes who had triumphed over bishops and councils. The Roman Catholic church had become one Christian denom-

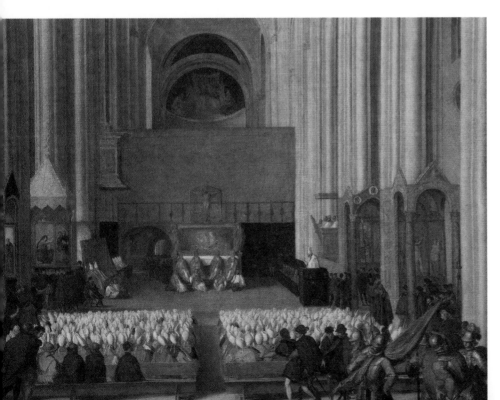

▼ **The Council of Trent: Final Session.** The Council of Trent, organized by Pope Paul III, met intermittently in three major sessions beginning in 1545. While Catholic moderates struggled to achieve a compromise with Protestant reformers, the conservatives were ultimately victorious, and the council, which ended in 1563, reaffirmed traditional Catholic teachings. Providing a clear body of doctrine and an acknowledged leader in the pope, the council prepared the Catholic church for an era of religious warfare.

ination among many with an organizational framework and doctrinal pattern that would not be significantly altered until Vatican Council II four hundred years later. With a new spirit of confidence, the post-Tridentine church entered a militant phase, as well prepared as the Calvinists to do battle for the Lord. An era of religious warfare was about to unfold.

When the Augustinian monk Martin Luther entered the public scene with a series of theses on indulgences, few people in Europe, or Germany for that matter, ever suspected that they would eventually topple the ecclesiastical supremacy of the papacy and produce a division of Europe along religious lines. But the yearning for reform of the church and meaningful religious experience caused a seemingly simple affair between monks of different orders to escalate into a powerful movement. Clearly, the papacy and other elements in the Catholic church underestimated the strength of Martin Luther and the desire for religious change.

While Luther felt that his revival of Christianity based on his interpretation of the Bible should be ac-
ceptable to all, others soon appeared who also read the Bible but interpreted it in different ways. Protestantism split into different sects, which, though united in their dislike of Catholicism, were themselves divided over the interpretation of the sacraments and religious practices. As reform ideas spread, religion and politics became ever more intertwined. Political support played a crucial role in the spread of the Reformation.

Although Lutheranism was legally acknowledged in 1555 by the Peace of Augsburg, it had lost much of its momentum and outside of Scandinavia had scant ability to attract new supporters. Its energy was largely replaced by the new Protestant form of Calvinism, which had a clarity of doctrine and a fervor that made it attractive to a whole new generation of Europeans. But while Calvinism's militancy enabled it to expand into all of Europe, Catholicism was also experiencing its own revival and emerged as a militant faith, prepared to do combat for the souls of the faithful. An age of religious passion would tragically be followed by an age of religious warfare.

Notes

1. Erasmus, *The Paraclesis,* in John Olin, ed., *Christian Humanism and the Reformation: Selected Writings of Erasmus,* 3d ed. (New York, 1987).

2. Quoted in James B. Ross and Mary M. McLaughlin, eds., *The Portable Renaissance Reader* (New York, 1953), p. 83.

3. Thomas More, *Utopia,* trans. Paul Turner (Harmondsworth, 1965), pp. 63–64.

4. Quoted in Alister E. McGrath, *Reformation Thought: An Introduction* (Oxford, 1988), p. 72.

5. Quoted in Roland Bainton, *Here I Stand: A Life of Martin Luther* (New York, 1950), pp. 49–50.

6. Quoted in Gordon Rupp, *Luther's Progress to the Diet of Worms* (New York, 1964), p. 82.

7. Quoted in ibid., p. 81.

8. *On the Freedom of a Christian Man,* quoted in E. G. Rupp and Benjamin Drewery, eds., *Martin Luther* (New York, 1970), p. 50.

9. Quoted in Bainton, *Here I Stand: A Life of Martin Luther,* p. 144.

10. Quoted in De Lamar Jensen, *Reformation Europe* (Lexington, Mass., 1981), p. 83.

11. Quoted in A. G. Dickens and Dorothy Carr, eds., *The Reformation in England to the Accession of Elizabeth I* (New York, 1968), p. 72.

12. Quoted in Lewis W. Spitz, *The Renaissance and Reformation Movements* (Chicago, 1971), p. 414.

13. John Calvin, *Institutes of the Christian Religion,* trans. John Allen (Philadelphia, 1936), 1: 220.

14. Ibid., 1: 228; 2: 181.

15. Ibid., 2: 201.

16. Quoted in William Monter, *Calvin's Geneva* (New York, 1967), p. 96.

17. Quoted in Roland Bainton, *Women of the Reformation in Germany and Italy* (Minneapolis, 1971), p. 154.

18. Quoted in Bonnie S. Anderson and Judith P. Zinsser, *A History of Their Own: Women in Europe from Prehistory to the Present* (New York, 1988), 1: 259.

19. Quoted in John A. Phillips, *Eve: The History of an Idea* (New York, 1984), p. 105.

Suggestions for Further Reading
▼ ▼ ▼

Basic surveys of the Reformation period include H. J. Grimm, *The Reformation Era, 1500–1650*, 2d ed. (New York, 1973); P. J. Klassen, *Europe in the Reformation* (Englewood Cliffs, N.J., 1979); and D. L. Jensen, *Reformation Europe* (Lexington, Mass., 1981). L. W. Spitz, *The Protestant Reformation, 1517–1559* (New York, 1985), is a sound and up-to-date history. A brief but very useful introduction to the theology of the Reformation can be found in A. McGrath, *Reformation Thought: An Introduction* (Oxford, 1988). For an overview of how European religious life in the Late Middles Ages affected the Reformation, see J. Bossy, *Christianity in the West: 1400–1700* (Oxford, 1987).

The development of humanism outside Italy is examined in R. Weiss, *The Spread of Italian Humanism* (London, 1964). For a comprehensive overview, see R. Mandrou, *From Humanism to Science, 1480–1700*, trans. B. Pearce (Harmondsworth, 1978). For studies on Christian humanism in some European countries, see W. L. Gundersheimer, ed., *French Humanism, 1470–1600* (New York, 1969); L. W. Spitz, *The Religious Renaissance of the German Humanists* (Cambridge, Mass., 1963); and C. G. Norena, *Studies in Spanish Renaissance Thought* (The Hague, 1975). On Thomas More, see R. Marius, *Thomas More: A Biography* (New York, 1984); and E. E. Reynolds, *The Life and Death of St. Thomas More* (New York, 1978). The best general biography of Erasmus is still R. Bainton, *Erasmus of Christendom* (New York, 1969), although the shorter work by J. K. Sowards, *Desiderius Erasmus* (Boston, 1975), is also good.

On religious conditions in Europe on the eve of the Reformation, see T. N. Tentler, *Sin and Confession on the Eve of the Reformation* (Princeton, N.J., 1977); and on Germany, G. Strauss, *Manifestations of Discontent in Germany on the Eve of the Reformation* (Bloomington, Ind., 1971).

The Reformation in Germany can be examined in H. Holborn, *A History of Modern Germany: The Reformation* (New York, 1959), still an outstanding survey of the entire Reformation period in Germany; and J. Lortz, *The Reformation in Germany*, trans. R. Walls, 2 vols. (New York, 1968), a detailed Catholic account. The classic account of Martin Luther's life is R. Bainton, *Here I Stand: A Life of Martin Luther* (New York and Nashville, 1950). More recent works include W. von Loewenich, *Martin Luther: The Man and His Work* (Minneapolis,

1986); J. M. Kittelson, *Luther the Reformer: The Story of the Man and His Career* (Minneapolis, Minn., 1986); and H. G. Haile, *Luther: An Experiment in Biography* (Garden City, N.Y., 1980). An interesting psychoanalytical approach to Luther can be found in E. H. Erikson, *Young Man Luther: A Study in Psychoanalysis and History* (New York, 1962). E. Iserloh raised the much debated question of whether Luther mailed his theses to his ecclesiastical superior or nailed them to the door of the Castle Church in Wittenberg in *The Theses Were Not Posted: Luther between Reform and Reformation*, trans. J. Wicks (Boston, 1968). Luther's relations with early Protestant dissenters from his ideas can be examined in M. Edwards, Jr., *Luther and the False Brethren* (Stanford, 1975); and E. G. Rupp, *Patterns of Reformation* (London, 1969). On the Peasants' War, see H. Kirchner, *Luther and the Peasants' War*, trans. D. Jodock (Philadelphia, 1972); R. N. Crossley, *Luther and the Peasants' War: Luther's Actions and Reactions* (New York, 1974); and especially P. Blickle, *The Revolution of 1525: The German Peasants' War from a New Perspective* (Baltimore, Md., 1981). The spread of Luther's ideas in Germany can be examined in M. Hannemann, *The Diffusion of the Reformation in Southwestern Germany, 1518–1534* (Chicago, 1975); B. Moeller, *Imperial Cities and the Reformation* (Durham, N.C., 1982); S. Ozment, *The Reformation in the Cities* (New Haven, Conn., 1975); G. Strauss, *Nuremberg in the Sixteenth Century* (Bloomington, Ind., 1978); H. J. Grimm, *Lazarus Spengler: A Lay Leader of the Reformation* (Columbus, Ohio, 1978); T. Brady, *Ruling Class, Regime and Reformation at Strassburg* (Leiden, 1978); and R. Po-Chia Hsia, ed., *The German People and the Reformation* (Ithaca, N.Y., 1988).

The best account of Ulrich Zwingli is G. R. Potter, *Zwingli* (Cambridge, 1976). Two specialized studies include R. C. Walton, *Zwingli's Theocracy* (Toronto, 1971), on the reformer's ideas on Christian community; and C. Garside, *Zwingli and the Fine Arts* (New Haven, Conn., 1966), on culture. One aspect of the spread of the Reformation in Switzerland is examined in J. M. Kittelson, *Wolfgang Capito: From Humanist to Reformer* (Leiden, 1975).

The most comprehensive account of the various groups and individuals who are called Anabaptists is G. H. Williams, *The Radical Reformation* (Philadelphia, 1962). Other valuable studies include C.-P. Clasen, *Anabaptism:*

A Social History, 1525–1618 (Ithaca, N.Y., 1972); and C. Krahn, *Dutch Anabaptism: Origin, Spread, Life and Thought, 1450–1600* (The Hague, 1968). Also see R. Po-Chia Hsia, *Society and Reformation in Munster, 1535–1618* (New Haven, Conn., 1984).

Two worthwhile surveys of the English Reformation are A. G. Dickens, *The English Reformation* (New York, 1964); and G. R. Elton, *Reform and Reformation: England, 1509–1558* (Cambridge, Mass., 1977). Good biographies of the leading personalities of the age include J. J. Scarisbrick, *Henry VIII* (Berkeley, 1968); B. W. Beckensgale, *Thomas Cromwell, Tudor Minister* (Totowa, 1978); J. Ridley, *Thomas Cranmer* (Oxford, 1962); W. K. Jordan, *Edward VI, the Young King* (Cambridge, Mass., 1968), and *Edward VI, the Threshold of Power* (Cambridge, Mass., 1970); and D.M. Loades, *The Reign of Mary Tudor* (London, 1979). Other specialized works on the period include S. E. Lehmberg, *The Reformation Parliament, 1529–1536* (Cambridge, 1970); the controversial classic by G. R. Elton, *The Tudor Revolution in Government*, 2d ed. (Cambridge, 1973); D. Knowles, *Bare Ruined Choirs: The Dissolution of the English Monasteries* (New York, 1976); and W. R. D. Jones, *The Mid-Tudor Crisis, 1539–1563* (New York, 1973).

For a good biography of Calvin, see the recent work by W. J. Bouwsma, *John Calvin* (New York, 1988). Of value on his theology is F. Wendel, *Calvin: The Origins and Development of His Religious Thought*, trans. P. Mairet (New York, 1963). The best work on Calvin's work in the city of Geneva is W. Monter, *Calvin's Geneva* (New York, 1967). On the spread of Calvinism in France, see above all the basic works by R. Kingdon, *Geneva and the Coming of the Wars of Religion in France* (Geneva, 1956), and *Geneva and the Consolidation of the French Protestant Movement* (Madison, Wis., 1967). On Calvinism's expansion elsewhere, see W. S. Reid, *Trumpeter of God: A Biography of John Knox* (New York, 1974).

The best overall account of the impact of the Reformation on the family is S. Ozment, *When Fathers Ruled: Family Life in Reformation Europe* (Cambridge, Mass., 1983). M. E. Wiesner's *Working Women in Renaissance Germany* (New Brunswick, N.J., 1986), covers primarily the sixteenth century. Also of value is R. Bainton, *Women of the Reformation in Germany and Italy* (Minneapolis, 1971). Broader perspectives are available in L. Stone, *The Family, Sex and Marriage in England: 1500–1800* (New York, 1979); and N. Z. Davis, *Society and Culture in Early Modern France* (Stanford, 1975). On education, see G. Strauss, *Luther's House of Learning* (Baltimore, 1978). R. W. Scribner's *For the Sake of Simple Folk* (Cambridge, 1981) deals with a number of issues on the popular culture of the German Reformation.

A good introduction to the Catholic Reformation can be found in the beautifully illustrated brief study by A. G. Dickens, *The Counter Reformation* (New York, 1969). Also valuable is M. R. O'Connell, *The Counter Reformation, 1559–1610* (New York, 1974). The work by J. Brodrick, *The Origin of the Jesuits* (Garden City, N.Y., 1960) offers a clear discussion of the founding of the Jesuits. A more critical approach is available in R. Fülöp-Miller, *The Jesuits: A History of the Society of Jesus* (New York, 1963). The most detailed study of the Council of Trent is H. Jedin, *History of the Council of Trent*, trans. E. Graf, 2 vols. (London, 1957–61).

Chapter 15

Discovery and Crisis in the Sixteenth and Seventeenth Centuries

▼▼▼▼▼

A lthough the Reformations of the sixteenth century made religion a central focus of people's lives, by the middle of the sixteenth century this renewal of religious passion had been accomplished at a great cost—the breakup of the religious unity of medieval Europe. This religious division (Catholics versus Protestants) was instrumental in beginning a series of wars that dominated much of European history from 1560 to 1650 and, in turn, exacerbated the economic and social crises that were besetting Europe. Wars, revolutions and constitutional crises, economic depression, social disintegration, the witchcraft craze, and demographic crisis all afflicted Europe and have led some historians to speak of the almost hundred wars from 1560 to 1650 as an age of crisis in European life.

Periods of crisis, however, are frequently ages of opportunities, nowhere more apparent than in the geographical discoveries that made this an era of European expansion into new worlds. While the discovery of new territories began before the sixteenth century, it was not until the sixteenth and seventeenth centuries that Europeans began to comprehend the significance of their discoveries and to exploit them for their material gain.

▼ An Age of Discovery and Expansion

Nowhere has the dynamic and even ruthless energy of Western civilization been more apparent than in its expansion into the rest of the world. By the sixteenth century, the Atlantic seaboard had become the center of a commercial activity that raised Portugal and Spain and

Columbus Discovers the Americas ▼	Cortés Conquers Mexico ▼	French Religious Wars ▼	Jesuit Church of Il Gesù ▼	The Thirty Years' War ▼	Puritan Revolution ▼

······· 1500 ··········· 1540 ············ 1580 ············ 1620 ············ 1660 ··········

El Greco ▲	William Shakespeare ▲	Montaigne, *Essays* ▲	Bank of Amsterdam ▲	

later the Dutch Republic, England, and France to prominence. The age of expansion was a crucial factor in the European transition from the agrarian economy of the Middle Ages to a commercial and industrial capitalistic system.

The Motives

For almost a millennium, Catholic Europe had been confined to one area. Its one major attempt to expand beyond those frontiers, the crusades, had largely failed. Of course, Europe had never completely lost contact with the outside world: the goods of Asia and Africa made their way into medieval castles; the works of Muslim philosophers were read in medieval universities; and the Vikings in the ninth and tenth centuries had even made their way to the eastern fringes of North America. But all of these represented limited contacts with non-European civilizations until the end of the fifteenth century, when Europeans embarked upon a remarkable series of overseas journeys. What caused Europeans to undertake such dangerous voyages to the ends of the earth?

Europeans had long had an attraction to the Far East. In the Middle Ages, myths and legends of an exotic Far East of great riches and magic were widespread. Although Muslim control of central Asia cut Europe off from the east, Mongol conquests in the thirteenth century reopened the doors. The most famous medieval travelers to the east were the Polos of Venice. Niccolò and Maffeo, merchants from Venice, accompanied by Niccolò's son Marco, undertook the lengthy journey to the court of the great Mongol ruler Kublai Khan (1259–1294) in 1271. As one of the great Khan's ambassadors, Marco traveled to Japan as well and did not return to Italy until 1295. An account of his experiences, the *Travels*, proved to be the most informative of all the descriptions of Asia by medieval European travelers. Others followed the Polos, but in the fourteenth century

the conquests of the Ottoman Turks and then the overthrow of the Mongols by the first of the Ming Chinese emperors halted Western traffic to the east. The closing of the eastern routes to the Far East now caused a number of people to become interested in the possibility of reaching Asia by sea to gain access to the spices and other precious items of the region.

An economic motive thus looms large in Renaissance European expansion. There were high hopes of finding precious metals and expanding the areas of trade, especially for the spices of the east. The latter continued to come to Europe via Arab middlemen but were outrageously expensive. Many European explorers and conquerors did not hesitate to express their desire for material gain. One Spanish conquistador explained that he and his kind went to the New World to "serve God and His Majesty, to give light to those who were in darkness, and to grow rich, as all men desire to do."[1]

This statement expresses another major reason for the overseas voyages—religious zeal. A crusading mentality was particularly strong in Portugal and Spain where the Muslims had largely been driven out in the Middle Ages. It was said by contemporaries of Prince Henry the Navigator of Portugal (see the next section) that he was motivated by "his great desire to make increase in the faith of our Lord Jesus Christ and to bring him all the souls that should be saved." While most scholars believe the religious motive was secondary to economic considerations, it would be foolish to overlook the genuine desire on the part of both explorers and conquistadores, let alone missionaries, to convert the heathen to Christianity. Hernando Cortés, the conqueror of Mexico, asked his Spanish rulers if it was not their duty to ensure that the native Mexicans "are introduced into and instructed in the holy Catholic faith," and predicted that if "the devotion, trust and hope which they now have in their idols turned so as to repose with the divine power of the true God . . . they would work many miracles."[2] Spiritual and secular affairs were closely intertwined in the sixteenth century. No doubt, grandeur and glory as

Discovery and Crisis in the Sixteenth and Seventeenth Centuries ▼ 483 well as plain intellectual curiosity and spirit of adventure also played some role in European expansion.

If "God, glory, and gold" were the motives, what made the voyages possible? First of all, the expansion of Europe was tied to the growth of centralized monarchies during the Renaissance. While the degree of that centralization is still debated by historians, the reality is that Renaissance expansion was a state enterprise. By the second half of the fifteenth century, European monarchies had increased both their authority and resources and were in a position to turn their energies beyond their borders. That meant the invasion of Italy for France, but for Portugal, a state not strong enough to pursue power in Europe, it meant going abroad. The Spanish scene was more complex since the strength of the Spanish monarchy by the sixteenth century enabled it to pursue power on both the continent and beyond.

At the same time, by the end of the fifteenth century, European states had a level of wealth and technology that enabled them to achieve a regular series of voyages beyond Europe. Although the highly schematic and symbolic medieval maps were of little help to sailors, the portolani or detailed charts made by medieval navigators and mathematicians in the thirteenth and fourteenth centuries, featuring details on coastal contours, distances between ports, and compass readings, proved of great value. By the end of the fifteenth century, cartography had developed to the point that Europeans possessed fairly accurate maps of the known world. Moreover, Europeans had developed remarkably seaworthy ships as well as navigational aids, such as the compass and astrolabe. Much of the geographical knowledge learned in the early phase of expansion was passed on to succeeding generations. Indeed, one of the most immediate results of the age of expansion was an enormous increase in knowledge of the physical proportions of the world.

The Development of a Portuguese Maritime Empire

Portugal took the lead in exploring the coast of Africa under the leadership of Prince Henry the "Navigator" (1394–1460), whose motives were a blend of seeking a Christian kingdom as an ally against the Muslims, acquiring trade opportunities for Portugal, and extending Christianity. Beginning in 1419, Prince Henry founded a school for navigators on the southwestern coast of Portugal and began to send out annual expeditions along the west African coast. After Henry's death in 1460,

there was a hiatus in Portuguese exploration until the 1470s and 1480s. Through regular expeditions, the Portuguese gradually crept down the African coast until Bartholomew Diaz finally rounded the Cape of Good Hope on the southern tip of Africa in 1487. Vasco da Gama surpassed that accomplishment by rounding the cape, skirting the eastern coast of Africa, and cutting across the Indian Ocean to the southwestern coast of India. At the port of Calicut, he took on a cargo of pepper and precious stones and then returned to Portugal, where he made a handsome profit on his valuable goods. Da Gama's successful voyage marked the beginning of an all-water route to India.

After da Gama's return, Portugal sent a larger fleet to the east. Despite opposition from Muslim traders in west India, it managed to return to Portugal with valuable cargo. One contemporary described its contents: "Cinnamon, fresh and dried ginger, much pepper, cloves, nutmegs, mace, musk, porcelains, incense, myrrh, red and white sandalwood, opium, India paper, and a great variety of drugs. . . . I saw many diamonds, rubies, and pearls." By 1501, annual Portuguese fleets to India were making serious inroads into the Mediterranean trade of the Venetians and Turks.

Under the direction of officials known as viceroys, Portugal now created an overseas empire. Most important was Alfonso d'Albuquerque (c. 1462–1515), a tough nobleman who took the lead in establishing a ring of commercial-military bases centered at Goa, an island off the Malabar Coast of India. The Portuguese also reached beyond India by taking the island of Macao at the mouth of the Pearl River in China. The Portuguese empire remained a limited empire of enclaves or trading posts on the coasts of India and China. The Portuguese simply did not possess the power to colonize the Asian regions. Moreover, although they invested heavily in ships and manpower for this empire (hundreds of ships and hundreds of thousands of workers in shipyards and overseas bases), it was very costly. Only one-half of the ships involved in the India trade survived for a second journey. Disease, shipwreck, and battles took a heavy toll of life. Portugal's empire was too large and Portugal too small to maintain it, and by the seventeenth century the Portuguese were being severely challenged in the Far East by the English, Dutch, and French.

Voyages to the New World

Although the Spanish came to overseas discovery and exploration after the initial efforts of Henry the Navigator, their resources enabled them to establish a far grander overseas empire of a quite different nature from the Portuguese.

An important figure in the history of Spanish exploration was an Italian, Cristoforo Colombo, more commonly known as Christopher Columbus (1451–1506). Convinced that the circumference of the earth was less than contemporaries believed and that Asia was larger than people thought, Columbus felt that Asia could be reached by sailing west instead of around Africa. Queen Isabella of Spain was finally persuaded to finance Columbus's exploratory expedition, which reached the Americas in October 1492, exploring the coastline of Cuba and the northern shores of Haiti (Hispaniola). Columbus believed that he had reached Asia and in three subsequent voyages (1493, 1498, 1502) sought in vain to find a route through the outer lands to the Asian mainland. In his four voyages, Columbus reached all the major islands of the Caribbean and Honduras in Central America.

Although Columbus clung to his belief till his death, other explorers soon realized that Columbus had discovered a new frontier altogether. State-sponsored explorers joined the race to the New World. A Venetian seaman, John Cabot, explored the New England coastline of the Americas under a license from King Henry VII of England. Amerigo Vespucci, a Florentine, accompanied several voyages and wrote a series of letters describing the geography of the New World. The publication of these letters led to the use of the name "America" (after Amerigo) for these new lands.

The first two decades of the sixteenth century witnessed numerous overseas voyages that explored the eastern coasts of both North and South America. Perhaps the most dramatic of all these expeditions was the journey of Ferdinand Magellan (1480–1521) in 1519. After passing through the Straits named after him at the bottom of South America, he sailed across the Pacific Ocean and reached the Philippines where he met his death at the hands of the natives. Although only one of his original fleet of five ships survived and returned to Spain, Magellan's name is still associated with the first known circumnavigation of the earth.

The Spanish Empire

The New World was a misnomer since the Western Hemisphere possessed flourishing civilizations populated by millions of people when the Europeans arrived. It was, of course, new to the Europeans who quickly saw

▼ **Two-Masted Ocean-Going Ship.** The Americas were first reached in the fifteenth century by Christopher Columbus, an Italian in the service of the Spanish monarchs. While Columbus believed that he had found a western route to Asia, others realized that he had actually discovered new lands. Explorers such as John Cabot and Amerigo Vespucci rushed to investigate the new world, and numerous overseas voyages to both North and South America were made in the first two decades of the sixteenth century. This detail from a larger work by Pieter Brueghel depicts a two-masted ocean-going ship of the type used in the voyages of sixteenth-century explorers.

opportunities for conquest and exploitation. The Spanish conquistadores were a hardy lot of mostly upper-class individuals motivated by a typical sixteenth-century blend of glory, greed, and religious crusading zeal. Although sanctioned by the Castilian crown, these groups were financed and outfitted privately, not by the government.

Their superior weapons, organizational skills, and determination brought the conquistadores incredible success. Beginning in 1519 with a small band of men, Hernando Cortés took three years to overthrow the mighty

The Spanish Conquistador: Cortés and the Conquest of Mexico
▼ ▼ ▼

Hernando Cortés was a Spanish nobleman who came to the New World in 1504 to seek his fortune. Contrary to his superior's orders, Cortés waged an independent campaign of conquest and overthrew the Aztec Empire of Mexico (1519–1521). Cortés wrote a series of five reports to Emperor Charles V to justify his action. The second report includes a description of Tenochtitlán, an Aztec city he had captured. The Spanish conquistador and his men were obviously impressed by this city, awesome in its architecture yet built by people who lacked European technology, such as wheeled vehicles and tools of hard metal.

Cortés's Description of an Aztec City

The great city Tenochtitlán is built in the midst of this salt lake, and it is two leagues from the heart of the city to any point on the mainland. Four causeways lead to it, all made by hand and some twelve feet wide. The city itself is as large as Seville or Córdova. The principal streets are very broad and straight, the majority of them being of beaten earth, but a few and at least half the smaller thoroughfares are waterways along which they pass in their canoes. Moreover, even the principal streets have openings at regular distances so that the water can freely pass from one to another, and these openings which are very broad are spanned by great bridges of huge beams, very stoutly put together, so firm indeed that over many of them ten horsemen can ride at once. Seeing that if the natives intended any treachery against us they would have every opportunity from the way in which the city is built, for by removing the bridges from the entrances and exits they could leave us to die of hunger with no possibility of getting to the mainland, I immediately set to work as soon as we entered the city on the building of four brigs, and in a short space of time had them finished, so that we could ship three hundred men and the horses to the mainland whenever we so desired.

The city has many open squares in which markets are continuously held and the general business of buying and selling proceeds. One square in particular is twice as big as that of Salamanca and completely surrounded by arcades where there are daily more than sixty thousand folk buying and selling. Every kind of merchandise such as may be met with in every land is for sale there, whether of food and victuals, or ornaments of gold and silver, or lead, brass, copper, tin, precious stones, bones, shells, snails and feathers; limestone for building is likewise sold there, stone both rough and polished, bricks burnt and unburnt, wood of all kinds and in all stages of preparation. . . . There is a street of herb-sellers where there are all manner of roots and medicinal plants that are found in the land. There are houses as it were of apothecaries where they sell medicines made from these herbs, both for drinking and for use as ointments and salves. There are barbers' shops where you may have your hair washed and cut. There are other shops where you may obtain food and drink. . . .

Finally, to avoid prolixity in telling all the wonders of this city, I will simply say that the manner of living among the people is very similar to that in Spain, and considering that this is a barbarous nation shut off from a knowledge of the true God or communication with enlightened nations, one may well marvel at the orderliness and good government which is everywhere maintained.

The actual service of Montezuma and those things which call for admiration by their greatness and state would take so long to describe that I assure your Majesty I do not know where to begin with any hope of ending. For as I have already said, what could there be more astonishing than that a barbarous monarch such as he should have reproductions made in gold, silver, precious stones, and feathers of all things to be found in his land, and so perfectly reproduced that there is no goldsmith or silversmith in the world who could better them, nor can one understand what instrument could have been used for fashioning the jewels; as for the featherwork its like is not to be seen in either wax or embroidery, it is so marvellously delicate.

Aztec Empire on mainland Mexico led by the chieftain Montezuma (see the box on p. 486). Between 1531 and 1550, the Spanish gained control of northern Mexico. Between 1531 and 1536, another expedition led by a hardened and somewhat corrupt soldier, Francesco Pizarro (1470–1541), took control of the Inca Empire high in the Peruvian Andes. Although it took another three decades before the western part of Latin America was brought under Spanish control (the Portuguese took over Brazil), already by 1535, the Spanish had created a system of colonial administration that made the New World an extension of the old.

ADMINISTRATION OF THE SPANISH EMPIRE IN THE NEW WORLD Spanish policy toward the Indians of the New World was a combination of confusion, misguided paternalism, and cruel exploitation. Confusion arose over the nature of the Indians. Unsure whether these strange creatures were "full men" or not, Spanish doctors of law debated how to fit them into currently existing European

▼ **Map 15.1** Discoveries and Possessions in the Sixteenth and Early Seventeenth Centuries.

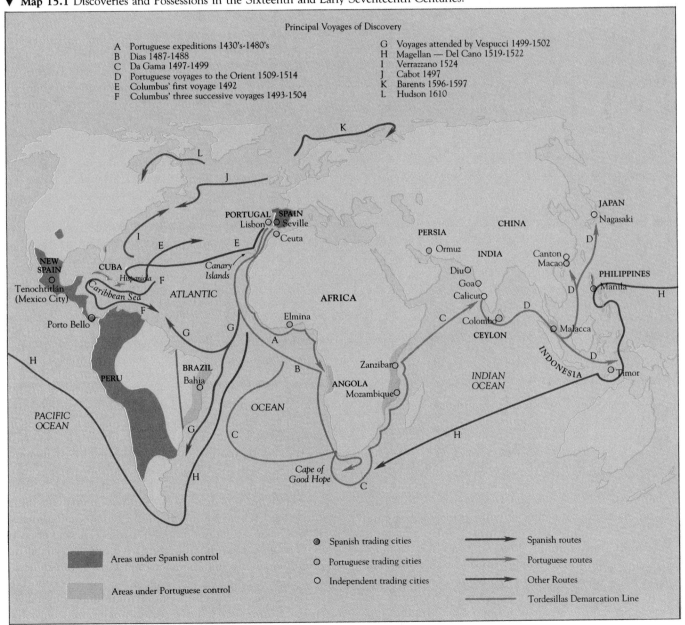

Principal Voyages of Discovery

A   Portuguese expeditions 1430's–1480's
B   Dias 1487–1488
C   Da Gama 1497–1499
D   Portuguese voyages to the Orient 1509–1514
E   Columbus' first voyage 1492
F   Columbus' three successive voyages 1493–1504

G   Voyages attended by Vespucci 1499–1502
H   Magellan — Del Cano 1519–1522
I   Verrazzano 1524
J   Cabot 1497
K   Barents 1596–1597
L   Hudson 1610

Areas under Spanish control

Areas under Portuguese control

● Spanish trading cities
○ Portuguese trading cities
○ Independent trading cities

→ Spanish routes
→ Portuguese routes
→ Other Routes
— Tordesillas Demarcation Line

Las Casas and the Spanish Treatment of the American Natives

▼▼▼

Bartolomé de Las Casas (1474–1566) was a Dominican monk who participated in the conquest of Cuba and received land and Indians in return for his efforts. But in 1514 he underwent a radical transformation that led him to believe that the Indians had been cruelly mistreated by his fellow Spaniards. He spent the remaining years of his life (he lived to the age of ninety-two) fighting for the Indians. This selection is taken from his most influential work, Brevísima Relación de la Destrucción de las Indias, *known to English readers as* The Tears of the Indians. *This work was particularly responsible for the legend of the Spanish as inherently "cruel and murderous fanatics." Most scholars feel that Las Casas may have exaggerated his account in order to shock his contemporaries into action.*

Bartolomé de Las Casas, *The Tears of the Indians*

There is nothing more detestable or more cruel, then the tyranny which the Spaniards use toward the Indians for the getting of pearl. Surely the infernal torments cannot much exceed the anguish that they endure, by reason of that way of cruelty; for they put them under water some four or five ells deep, where they are forced without any liberty of respiration, to gather up the shells wherein the Pearls are; sometimes they come up again with nets full of shells to take breath, but if they stay any while to rest themselves, immediately comes a hangman row'd in a little boat, who as soon as he hath well beaten them, drags them again to their labour. Their food is nothing but filth, and the very same that contains the Pearl, with a small portion of that bread which that Country affords; in the first whereof there is little nourishment; and as for the latter, it is made with great difficulty, besides that they have not enough of that neither for sustenance; they lye upon the ground in fetters, lest they should run away; and many times they are drown'd in this labour, and are never seen again till they swim upon the top of the waves: oftentimes they also are devoured by certain sea monsters, that are frequent in those seas. Consider whether this hard usage of the poor creatures be consistent with the precepts which God commands concerning charity to our neighbour, by those that cast them so undeservedly into the dangers of a cruel death, causing them to perish without any remorse or pity, or allowing them the benefit of the Sacraments, or the knowledge of Religion; it being impossible for them to live any time under the water; and this death is so much the more painful, by reason that by the coarctation of the breast, while the lungs strive to do their office, the vital parts are so afflicted that they die vomiting the blood out of their mouths. Their hair also, which is by nature black, is hereby changed and made of the same color with that of the sea Wolves; their bodies are also so besprinkled with the froth of the sea, that they appear rather like monsters than men.

---

legal patterns. While the conquistadores made decisions based on expediency and their own interests, Queen Isabella declared the natives to be subjects of Castile and instituted the Spanish *encomienda*, a system that permitted the conquering Spaniards to collect tribute from the natives and use them as laborers. In return, the holders of an *encomienda* were supposed to protect the Indians and supervise their spiritual and material needs. In practice, this meant that the settlers were free to implement the paternalistic system of the government as they pleased. Three thousand miles from Spain, Spanish settlers largely ignored their government and brutally used the Indians to pursue their own economic interests. Indians were put to work on plantations and in the lucrative gold and silver mines. Forced labor, starvation, and especially disease took a fearful toll of Indian lives. With little or no natural resistance to European diseases, the Indians of America were ravaged by smallpox, measles, and typhus. These "killers" came with the explorers and the conquistadores. Although scholarly estimates on native population figures vary drastically, a reasonable guess is that 30 to 40 percent of the natives died. On Hispaniola (Haiti) alone, out of an initial population of 100,000 natives when Columbus arrived in 1493, only 300 Indians survived by 1570. In 1542, largely in response to the publications of Bartolomé de Las Casas, a Dominican monk who championed the Indians (see the box above), the government abolished the *encomienda* system and provided more protection for the natives.

The Spanish created a formal administrative system for their new empire. While a board of trade known as the *Casa de Contratación* supervised all economic matters related to the New World, the Council of the Indies became the chief organ of colonial administration. The council suggested the names of colonial officials, oversaw their New World activities, and kept an eye on ecclesiastical affairs in the colonies.

In the New World, the Spanish developed an administrative system based on viceroys. Spanish possessions were initially divided into two major administrative units: New Spain (Mexico, Central America, and the Caribbean islands) with its center in Mexico City and Peru (western South America), governed by a viceroy in Lima. Each viceroy served as the king's chief civil and military officer and was aided by advisory groups called *audiencias*, which also functioned as supreme judicial bodies.

By papal agreement, the Catholic monarchs of Spain were given extensive rights over ecclesiastical affairs in the New World. They could nominate church officials, build churches, collect fees, and supervise the affairs of the various religious orders who sought to Christianize the heathen. Catholic monks had remarkable success in converting and baptizing hundreds of thousands of Indians in the early years of the conquest. Soon after there followed the establishment of dioceses, parishes,

schools, and hospitals—all the trappings of civilized European society.

The Impact of Expansion

European expansion made an enormous impact on both the conquerors and the conquered. The native American civilizations, which had their own unique qualities and a degree of sophistication not much appreciated by Europeans, were virtually destroyed. Ancient social and political structures were ripped up and replaced by European institutions, religion, language, and culture. The Portuguese trading posts in the Far East, on the other hand, had much less impact on native Asian civilizations.

European expansion also affected the conquerors, perhaps most notably in the economic arena. Wherever they went in the New World, Europeans sought to find sources of gold and silver. One Aztec commented that the Spanish conquerors "longed and lusted for gold. Their bodies swelled with greed, and their hunger was ravenous; they hungered like pigs for that gold."[3] Rich silver deposits were found and exploited in Mexico and southern Peru (modern Bolivia). When the mines at Potosí in Peru were opened in 1545, the value of precious metals imported into Europe quadrupled. It has been estimated that between 1503 and 1650 sixteen mil-

▼ **World Map of the Early Sixteenth Century.** Overseas expansion affected not only the inhabitants of the "New World," but also their European conquerors. New sources of gold and silver were discovered and tensions grew between the European states as they competed for trading products. Psychologically, belief in their own superiority was strengthened by the relative ease with which the Europeans dominated the native people. Pictured here is a world map showing the coastlines that had been charted by 1540.

lion kilograms of silver and 185,000 kilograms of gold entered the port of Seville and helped to create a price revolution that affected the Spanish economy.

But gold and silver were only two of the products sent to Europe from the New World. Into Seville flowed sugar, dyes, cotton, vanilla, and hides from livestock raised in the South American pampas. New agricultural products such as potatoes, coffee, corn, and tobacco were also imported. Because of its trading posts in Asia, Portugal soon challenged the Italian states as the chief entry point of the eastern trade in spices, jewels, silk, carpets, ivory, leather, and perfumes, although the Venetians clung tenaciously to the spice trade until they lost out to the Dutch in the seventeenth century. Economic historians believe that the increase in the volume and area of European trade as well as the rise in fluid capital due to this expansion were crucial factors in producing a new era of commercial capitalism that represented the first step toward the world economy that has characterized the modern historical era.

European expansion, which was in part a product of European rivalries, also deepened those rivalries and increased the tensions among European states. Bitter conflicts arose over the cargoes coming from the New World and Asia. Although the Spanish and Portuguese were first in the competition, the Dutch, French, and English soon became involved on a large scale and by the seventeenth century were challenging the Portuguese and Spanish monopolies.

Finally, how does one evaluate the psychological impact of colonization on the colonizers? The relatively easy European success in dominating native peoples reinforced Christian Europe's belief in the inherent superiority of European civilization. The Scientific Revolution of the seventeenth century (see Chapter 17), the Enlightenment of the eighteenth (see Chapter 18), and the imperialism of the nineteenth (see Chapter 26) would all strengthen this Eurocentric perspective that has caused Western civilization so much trouble in its relationship with the rest of the world.

▼ Politics and the Wars of Religion in the Sixteenth Century

The so-called wars of religion were a product of Reformation ideologies that allowed little room for compromise or toleration of differing opinions. By the middle years of the sixteenth century, Calvinism and Catholicism had become highly militant religions dedicated to spreading the word of God as they interpreted it. While

their struggle for the minds and hearts of Europeans is at the heart of the religious wars of the sixteenth century, economic, social, and political forces also played an important role in these conflicts. Of the sixteenth-century religious wars, none was more momentous or shattering than the French civil wars known as the French Wars of Religion.

The French Wars of Religion (1562–1598)

Of all the European countries, France seemed least likely to be the scene of a religious war. The Valois monarchy had proven itself robust and capable in the sixteenth century. Francis I (1515–1547) and Henry II (1547–1559) had been strong rulers aided by royal officials, a permanent mercenary army, the power to tax, and the ability to control the church by nominating French bishops. It soon became apparent, however, that the power of these sixteenth-century monarchs to control France depended upon the forcefulness of their own personalities. When Henry II was killed accidentally in a tournament in 1559 and was succeeded by a series of weak, feeble, and neurotic sons, two of whom were dominated by their mother, Catherine de' Medici, as regent, the forces held in check by the strong monarchy broke loose, beginning a series of intermittent and confused civil wars. Religious, political, economic, and social forces all contributed to these wars.

The religious forces were the most important. The growth of Calvinism led to persecution by Francis I that intensified under Henry II but did little to stop the spread of Calvinism. Huguenots (as the French Calvinists were called) came from all levels of society: artisans and shopkeepers hurt by rising prices and a rigid guild system; merchants and lawyers in provincial towns whose local privileges were tenuous; and members of the nobility. Possibly 40 to 50 percent of the French nobility became Huguenots, including the house of Bourbon, which stood next to the Valois in the royal line of succession and ruled the southern French kingdom of Navarre. The conversion of so many nobles made the Huguenots a potentially dangerous political threat to monarchical power. While the Calvinists constituted only about 7 percent of the population, they were a dedicated, determined, and well-organized minority. Local congregations governed by consistories of ministers and elders sent representatives to district assemblies, which chose delegates for provincial assemblies. The latter sent representatives to a national synod that served as the ultimate authority for all Huguenots in matters of doctrine and discipline. This system of church organization allowed for spontaneity at the local level while guaranteeing the cohesion of a national church. The first national synod met in Paris in 1559 and represented 72 local churches. Only two years later, the national synod represented 2,150 congregations containing 1 to 1.5 million Calvinists. The national synods even mustered troops from local churches or congregations and served as recruiting agents. When civil war came in 1562, the Calvinists were ready for combat.

The Calvinist minority was greatly outnumbered by the Catholic majority. The Valois monarchy was staunchly Catholic, and its control of the Catholic church gave it little incentive to look favorably upon Protestantism. As regent for her sons, the moderate Catholic Catherine de' Medici (1519–1589) looked to religious compromise as a way to defuse the political tensions, but found to her consternation that both sides possessed their share of religious fanatics unwilling to make concessions. The extreme Catholic party—known as the ultra-Catholics—favored strict opposition to the Huguenots and were led by the Guise family. Possessing the loyalty of Paris and large sections of northern and northwestern France through their client-patronage system, they could recruit and pay for large armies and received support abroad from the papacy and Jesuits who favored their noncompromising Catholic position. Ironically, the allegiance of the Catholic Guises to their own dynasty and international Catholicism posed a strong threat to the Catholic Valois monarchy.

The religious issue was not the only factor that contributed to the French civil wars. Towns and provinces, which had long resisted the growing power of monarchical centralization, were only too willing to join a revolt against the monarchy. This was also true of the nobility, and the fact that so many of them were Calvinists created an important base of opposition to the crown. The French Wars of Religion, then, constituted a major constitutional crisis for France. At the same time, they were complicated by foreign intervention. The devout Catholic king of Spain, Philip II, supported the policies of the ultra-Catholic Guise family while Elizabeth I of England supported the Huguenots for political reasons.

The French Wars of Religion temporarily halted the development of the French centralized territorial state. The claim of the ruling dynasty of the state to a person's loyalties was temporarily superseded by loyalty to one's religious belief. The remark of a close friend of the Guises to the Spanish ambassador in 1565 went to the heart of the problem:

Nowadays Catholic princes must not proceed as they once did. At one time friends and enemies were distinguished by the frontiers of provinces and kingdoms, and were called Italians, Germans, French, Spaniards, English, and the like; now we must say Catholics and heretics, and a Catholic prince must consider all Catholics of all countries as his friends, just as the heretics consider all heretics as friends and subjects, whether they are their own vassals or not.[4]

▼ **The St. Bartholomew's Day Massacre.** Although the outbreak of religious war seemed unlikely in France, the collapse of a strong monarchy with the death of Henry II unleashed forces that created a series of civil wars. While religious ideology was the strongest force at work in the outbreak of war, political and social considerations also played a role. Pictured here is the St. Bartholomew's Day massacre of 1572. This contemporary painting of the massacre depicts a number of the incidents of that day when approximately three thousand Huguenots were murdered in Paris.

For some people, the unity of France was less important than religious truth. But there also emerged in France a group of politiques who placed politics before religion and believed that no religious truth was worth the ravages of civil war. The politiques ultimately prevailed, but not until both sides were exhausted by bloodshed.

The wars erupted in 1562 when the powerful duke of Guise massacred a peaceful congregation of Huguenots at Vassy. In the decade of the 1560s, the Huguenots held their own. Too small a group to conquer France, their armies were so good at defensive campaigns that they could not be defeated either, even with the infamous Saint Bartholomew's Day massacre.

This massacre of Huguenots on August 24, 1572, occurred at a time when the Catholic and Calvinist parties had apparently been reconciled through the marriage of Henry of Navarre, the Bourbon ruler of Navarre and acknowledged political leader of the Huguenots, to the sister of the reigning Valois king Charles IX (1560–1574). Many Huguenots traveled to Paris for the wedding. But the Guise family persuaded the king that this gathering of Huguenots was a threat to him. The subsequent massacre on the night of August 24 left three thousand Huguenots dead, although not Henry of Navarre who saved his life by promising to turn Catholic. Thousands more were killed in provincial towns. The massacre boomeranged, however, since it discredited the Valois dynasty without ending the conflict.

The fighting continued. The Huguenots rebuilt their strength while the ultra-Catholics formed a Holy League in 1576, vowing to exterminate heresy and seat a true Catholic champion—Henry, duke of Guise—on the French throne in place of the ruling king, Henry III (1574–1589), who had succeeded his brother Charles IX in 1574. The turning point in the conflict came in the War of the Three Henries in 1588–1589. Henry, duke of Guise, in the pay of Philip II of Spain, seized Paris and forced King Henry III to make him his chief minister. To rid himself of Guise influence, Henry III assassinated the duke of Guise and then joined with Henry of Navarre (who had once again returned to Calvinism), who was next in line to the throne, to crush the Catholic Holy League and retake the city of Paris. Although successful, Henry III in turn was assassinated in 1589 by a monk who was repelled by the spectacle of a Catholic king cooperating with a Protestant. Henry of Navarre now claimed the throne. Realizing, however, that he would never be accepted by Catholic France, Henry took the logical way out and converted once again to Catholicism, issuing his famous aphorism, "Paris is worth a mass." With his coronation in 1594, the Wars of Religion had finally come to an end. It remained only to solve the religious problem, which was accomplished by the Edict of Nantes in 1598. While Catholicism was acknowledged as the official religion of France, the Huguenots were guaranteed their right to worship in selected places in every district and were allowed to retain a number of fortified towns for their protection. In addition, Huguenots were allowed to enjoy all political privileges, including the holding of public offices. Although the Edict of Nantes recognized the rights of the Protestant minority and ostensibly the principle of religious toleration, it did so only out of political necessity, not out of conviction. The French Wars of Religion also demonstrated once again to many Frenchmen the necessity for strong government, laying a foundation for the growth of monarchy in the seventeenth century.

Philip II and the Cause of Militant Catholicism

The greatest advocate of militant Catholicism and the most important political figure in the second half of the sixteenth century was King Philip II of Spain (1556–1598), the son and heir of Charles V (see the box on p. 493). Philip's reign ushered in an age of Spanish greatness, both politically and culturally. A tremendous price was paid, however, for the political and military commitments that Philip made, and we can see in retrospect that the Golden Age of Spain was also the period in which Spain's decline began.

The first major goal of Philip II was to consolidate and secure the lands he had inherited from his father, Charles V. These included Spain, the Netherlands, and

Philip II, the Most Catholic King of Spain

▼ ▼ ▼

After the abdication of Charles V in 1556, his son Philip II became king of Spain at the age of twenty-nine. Modern historical opinions of Philip II have varied widely. Some Protestant historians have viewed him as a moral monster while Catholic apologists have commended him for his sincerity and sense of responsibility. These selections include an assessment of Philip II by a contemporary, the Venetian ambassador to Spain, and a section from a letter by Philip II to his daughters, revealing the more loving side of the king.

Suriano, An Estimate of Philip II

The Catholic king was born in Spain, in the month of May, 1527, and spent a great part of his youth in that kingdom. Here, in accordance with the customs of the country and the wishes of his father and mother, . . . he was treated with all the deference and respect which seemed due to the son of the greatest emperor whom Christendom had ever had, and to the heir to such a number of realms and to such grandeur. As a result of this education, when the king left Spain for the first time and visited Flanders, passing on his way through Italy and Germany, he everywhere made an impression of haughtiness and severity, so that the Italians liked him but little, the Flemings were quite disgusted with him, and the Germans hated him heartily. But when he had been warned by the cardinal of Trent and his aunt, and above all by his father, that this haughtiness was not in place in a prince destined to rule over a number of nations so different in manners and sentiment, he altered his manner so completely that on his second journey, when he went to England, he everywhere exhibited such distinguished mildness and affability that no prince has ever surpassed him in these traits. . . .

In the king's eyes no nation is superior to the Spaniards. It is among them that he lives, it is they that he consults, and it is they that direct his policy; in all this he is acting quite contrary to the habit of his father. He thinks little of the Italians and Flemish and still less of the Germans. Although he may employ the chief men of all the countries over which he rules, he admits none of them to his secret counsels, but utilizes their services only in military affairs, and then perhaps not so much because he really esteems them, as in the hope that he will in this way prevent his enemies from making use of them.

A Letter of Philip II to His Daughters

It is good news for me to learn that you are so well. It seems to me that your little sister is getting her eye teeth pretty early. Perhaps they are in place of the two which I am on the point of losing and which I shall probably no longer have when I get back. But if I had nothing worse to trouble me, that might pass. . . .

I am sending you also some roses and an orange flower, just to let you see that we have them here [Lisbon]. Calabrés brings me bunches of both these flowers every day, and we have had violets for a long time. . . . After this rainy time I imagine that you will be having flowers, too, by the time my sister arrives, or soon after. God keep you as I would have him!

---

the possessions in Italy and the New World. For Philip this meant a strict conformity to Catholicism, enforced by aggressive use of the Spanish Inquisition, and the establishment of strong, monarchical authority. The latter was not an easy task since Philip inherited a structure of government in which each of the various states and territories of his empire stood in an individual relationship to the king. Even in Spain, there was no really deep sense of nationhood. Philip did manage, however, to expand royal power by making the monarchy less dependent on the traditional landed aristocracy, especially in the higher echelons of government. He enlarged the system of administrative councils first developed by Ferdinand and Isabella and broadened by his father. Although Philip found that his ability to enforce his will was limited by local legal traditions, lack of rapid communication, and an inadequate bureaucracy, he tried to be the center of the whole system and supervised the work of all departments, even down to the smallest details. His meticulousness was tragic for both Philip and Spain. Unwilling to delegate authority, he failed to distinguish between important and trivial matters and fell weeks behind on state correspondence, especially since he was inclined to make marginal notes and even correct

spelling. One Spanish official said, "If God used the Escorial [the royal palace where Philip worked] to deliver my death sentence, I would be immortal." Philip's administrative machinery enabled him to do little more than maintain the status quo.

One of Philip's aims was to make Spain a dominant power in Europe. To a great extent, Spain's preeminence depended upon a prosperous economy fueled by its importation of gold and silver from its New World possessions, its agriculture, its commerce, and its industry, especially in textiles, silk, and leather goods. The importation of silver had detrimental effects as well, however, as it helped to lead to a spiraling inflation that disrupted the Spanish economy, eventually hurting both textile production and agriculture. Moreover, the expenses of war, especially after 1580, proved devastating to the Spanish economy. American gold and silver never constituted more than 20 percent of the royal revenue, leading the government to impose a crushing burden of direct and indirect taxes, especially on the people of Castile. Even then the government was forced to borrow. Philip repudiated his debts seven times; still two-thirds of state income went to pay interest on the debt by the end of his reign. The attempt to make Spain a great power led to the decline of Spain after Philip's reign.

Crucial to an understanding of Philip II is the importance of Catholicism to the Spanish people and their ruler. Driven by a heritage of crusading fervor, it was not difficult for Spain to see itself as a nation of people divinely chosen to save Catholic Christianity from the Protestant heretics. Philip II, the "Most Catholic King," became the champion of Catholicism throughout Europe. In Philip's mind, church and state were inextricably intertwined, a fact beautifully symbolized in Philip's new palace known as the Escorial, which served as a seat of government, church, and mausoleum for Charles V. Philip's activities on behalf of Catholicism were not done to please the popes, however. Despite his devotion to Catholicism, Philip allowed them little say in the Spanish Catholic church and did not hesitate to disagree with papal religious and political policies.

Philip's role as the champion of Catholicism led to spectacular victories and equally spectacular defeats for the Spanish king. Spain's leadership of a Holy League against Turkish encroachments in the Mediterranean, especially the Muslim attack on the island of Cyprus, led to a stunning victory over the Turkish fleet in the Battle of Lepanto in 1571. But Philip was to experience few other such successes. His intervention in France in the decade of the 1580s on behalf of the ultra-Catholics led only to failure. But the major thrust of his foreign policy lay in the Netherlands and England. Philip's attempt to crush the revolt in the Netherlands and his tortured policy with the English queen Elizabeth led to his greatest misfortunes.

THE REVOLT OF THE NETHERLANDS   One of the richest parts of Philip's empire, the Spanish Netherlands was of great importance to the "Most Catholic King." The Netherlands consisted of seventeen provinces (modern Netherlands and Belgium). The seven northern provinces were largely Germanic in culture and Dutch speaking, while the French- and Flemish-speaking southern provinces were closely tied to France. Situated at the commercial crossroads of northwestern Europe, the Netherlands had become prosperous through commerce and a flourishing textile industry. Because of its location,

▼ **Philip II of Spain.** This portrait depicts Philip II of Spain at the age of fifty-two. While Spain entered an era of greatness with Philip's rule, the seeds for its eventual decline were also planted. Philip wished to make Spain a dominant power in Europe and perceived himself as a great defender of Catholicism. His attempts to make Spain a great power led to large financial debts and crushing taxes, and his military actions in defense of Catholicism brought him failure and misfortune in both France and the Netherlands.

the Netherlands was open to the religious influences of the age. While both Lutheranism and Anabaptism had been adopted by some inhabitants, by the time of Philip II, Calvinism was also making inroads. There was no real political bond holding these provinces together except for a common ruler, and that ruler was Philip II, a foreigner who was out of touch with the situation in the Netherlands.

Philip II hoped to strengthen his control in the Netherlands, regardless of the traditional privileges of the separate provinces. This was strongly opposed by the nobles who stood to lose the most politically if their jealously guarded privileges and freedoms were weakened. Resentment against Philip was also aroused by the collection of taxes when the residents of the Netherlands realized that these revenues were being used for Spanish interests. Finally, religion became a major catalyst for rebellion when Philip attempted both to reorganize the ecclesiastical structure of the Dutch Catholic church and to crush heresy. Calvinism continued to spread, especially among the nobility and artisans in the towns. Philip's policy of repression served simply to alienate the Calvinists without halting the spread of the movement. Resistance against the king's policies increased, especially from the aristocrats led by William of Nassau, the prince of Orange, also known as William the Silent. Violence erupted in 1566 when Calvinists—especially nobles—began to destroy statues and stained glass windows in Catholic churches. Philip responded by sending the duke of Alva with 10,000 veteran Spanish and Italian troops to crush the rebellion.

The repressive policies of the duke proved counterproductive. The levying of a permanent sales tax alienated many merchants and commoners who now joined the nobles and Calvinists in the struggle against Spanish rule. A special tribunal, known as the Council of Troubles (nicknamed the Council of Blood), inaugurated a reign of terror in which even powerful aristocrats were executed. As a result, the revolt now became organized, especially in the northern provinces where William of Orange and daring Dutch privateers known as the "Sea Beggars" offered growing resistance. In 1573, Philip removed the duke of Alva and shifted to a more conciliatory policy to bring an end to the costly revolt.

William of Orange wished to unify all seventeen provinces, a goal seemingly realized in 1576 with the Pacification of Ghent. This agreement stipulated that all the provinces would stand together under William's leadership, respect religious differences, and demand that Spanish troops be withdrawn. But religious differences proved too strong for any lasting union. When the

duke of Parma, the next Spanish leader, arrived in the Netherlands, he astutely played upon the religious differences of the provinces and split their united front. The southern provinces formed a Catholic union—the Union of Arras—in 1579 and accepted Spanish control. To counter this, William of Orange organized the northern, Dutch-speaking states into a Protestant union—the Union of Utrecht—determined to oppose Spanish rule. The Netherlands was now divided along religious, geographical, and political lines into two hostile camps. Unwilling to rule themselves, the northern provinces sought to place themselves under the French king and then the English queen Elizabeth. Both refused, although Elizabeth further antagonized Philip II by continuing military assistance. The struggle went on after the death of both Philip and Elizabeth until 1609 when a twelve-year truce ended the war, virtually recognizing the independence of the northern provinces. These "United Provinces" soon emerged as the Dutch Republic, although they were not formally recognized as independent by the Spanish until 1648. The southern provinces remained a Spanish possession.

The England of Elizabeth

When Elizabeth Tudor, the daughter of Henry VIII and Anne Boleyn, ascended the throne in 1558, England possessed fewer than four million people. During her reign, England rose to prominence as the relatively small island kingdom became the leader of the Protestant nations of Europe, laid the foundations for a world empire, and experienced a cultural renaissance.

Elizabeth was a complex ruler who was careful to hide her feelings from both private and public sight. While appearing irresolute in avoiding confrontation as long as

possible, she was capable of decisive action when it was finally forced upon her. Shrewd, calculating, and self-confident, she moved quickly to solve the difficult and intractable religious problem she inherited from her half-sister, "Bloody" Mary.

Elizabeth's religious policy was based on moderation and compromise. Although she had some deep religious feelings and a sentimental appreciation for religious rites and ceremonies, the changes she had experienced had taught her caution and tolerance. As a ruler, she wished to prevent England from being torn apart over matters of religion. Interests of state and personal choice combined to favor a temperate approach to religious affairs. As the Scottish Calvinist reformer John Knox remarked, "Elizabeth was neither a good Protestant nor yet a resolute Papist." Nor did she care what her subjects believed privately as long as they did not threaten the state's power.

Parliament cooperated with the queen in initiating the Elizabethan religious settlement in 1559. The Catholic legislation of Mary's reign was repealed, and a new Act of Supremacy designated Elizabeth as "the only supreme governor of this realm, as well in all spiritual or ecclesiastical things or causes, as temporal." An Act of Uniformity restored the church service of the Book of Common Prayer from the reign of Edward VI with some revisions to make it more acceptable to Catholics. Elizabeth's religious settlement was basically Protestant but a moderate Protestantism that avoided overly subtle distinctions and extremes. Theologically, it represented a position close to Lutheranism.

The new religious settlement worked, at least to the extent that it smothered religious differences in England in the second half of the sixteenth century. Two groups, however, the Catholics and Puritans, continued to oppose the new religious settlement. The Catholics dwindled to a tiny minority by the end of Elizabeth's reign, a process aided by the identification of Catholicism in English minds with the Spanish King Philip II. The English were made well aware that Elizabeth's immediate heir was Mary, queen of Scots, a Catholic supported by the Spaniards. The attack on England by the Spanish Armada in 1588 sealed the fate of Catholicism and made it virtually a traitorous activity. Potentially more dangerous to Anglicanism in the long run were the Puritans. The term *Puritanism* first appeared in 1564 when it was applied to those Protestants within the Anglican church who, inspired by Calvinist theology, wished to eliminate any trace of popery from the Church of England. Elizabeth managed to contain the Puritans during her reign, but the indefatigible Puritans would dominate the English scene in the first half of the seventeenth century.

Elizabeth proved as adept in government and foreign policy as in religious affairs. She was well served administratively by the principal secretary of state, an office created by Thomas Cromwell (see Chapter 14). The talents of Sir William Cecil and Sir Francis Walsingham, who together held the office for thirty-two years, ensured much of Elizabeth's success in foreign and domestic affairs. Elizabeth also handled Parliament with much skill; it met only thirteen times during her entire reign (see the box on p. 497).

Elizabeth's foreign policy was also dictated by caution, moderation, and expediency. Fearful of other countries' motives, Elizabeth realized that war could be disastrous for her island kingdom and her own rule. While encouraging English piracy and providing clandestine aid to

▼ **Procession of Queen Elizabeth I.** Intelligent and learned, Elizabeth Tudor was familiar with Latin and Greek and spoke several European languages. She repealed the Catholic legislation of her sister Mary in favor of a more moderate Protestant religious settlement. Served by able administrators, Elizabeth ruled for nearly forty-five years and avoided open military action against any real power. Her participation in the revolt of the Netherlands, however, brought England into conflict with Spain. This picture painted near the end of her reign shows the queen on a ceremonial procession.

Queen Elizabeth Addresses Parliament (1601)

▼ ▼ ▼

Queen Elizabeth I ruled England from 1558 to 1603 with a consummate skill that contemporaries considered unusual in a woman. Though shrewd, calculating, and paternalistic, Elizabeth, like other sixteenth-century monarchs, depended for her power upon the favor of her people. This selection is taken from her speech to Parliament in 1601, when she had been forced to retreat on the issue of monopolies after violent protests by members of Parliament. Although the speech was designed to make peace with Parliament, some historians also feel that it was a sincere expression of the existing rapport between the queen and her subjects.

Queen Elizabeth I, "The Golden Speech"

I do assure you there is no prince that loves his subjects better, or whose love can countervail our love. There is no jewel, be it of never so rich a price, which I set before this jewel: I mean your love. For I do esteem it more than any treasure or riches. . . . And, though God has raised me high, yet this I count the glory of my crown, that I have reigned with your loves. This makes me that I do not so much rejoice that God has made me to be a Queen, as to be a Queen over so thankful a people. . . .

Of myself I must say this: I never was any greedy, scraping grasper, nor a strait, fast-holding Prince, nor yet a waster. My heart was never set on any worldly goods, but only for my subjects' good. What you bestow on me, I will not hoard it up, but receive it to bestow on you again. Yea, mine own properties I account yours, to be expended for your good. . . .

I have ever used to set the Last-Judgment Day before mine eyes, and so to rule as I shall be judged to answer before a higher Judge, to whose judgment seat I do appeal, that never thought was cherished in my heart that tended not unto my people's good. And now, if my kingly bounties have been abused, and my grants turned to the hurt of my people, contrary to my will and meaning, and if any in authority under me neglected or perverted what I have committed to them, I hope God will not lay their culps [crimes] and offences to my charge; who, though there were danger in repealing our grants, yet what danger would I not rather incur for your good, than I would suffer them still to continue?

There will never Queen sit in my seat with more zeal to my country, care for my subjects, and that will sooner with willingness venture her life for your good and safety, than myself. For it is my desire to live nor reign no longer than my life and reign shall be for your good. And though you have had and may have many princes more mighty and wise sitting in this seat, yet you never had nor shall have any that will be more careful and loving. . . .

French Huguenots and Dutch Calvinists to weaken France and Spain, she pretended complete aloofness and avoided alliances that would force her into war with any major power. Gradually, however, Elizabeth was drawn into more active involvement in the Netherlands and by 1585 had reluctantly settled upon a policy of active military intervention there. This move accelerated the already mounting friction between Spain and England. After resisting for years the idea of invading England as too impractical, Philip II of Spain was finally persuaded to do so by advisers who assured him that the people of England would rise against their queen when the Spaniards arrived. Moreover, Philip was easily convinced that the revolt in the Netherlands would never be crushed as long as England provided support for it. In any case, a successful invasion of England would mean the overthrow of heresy and the return of England to Catholicism, surely an act in accordance with the will of God. Accordingly, Philip ordered preparations for an Armada that would rendezvous with the army of the duke of Parma in Flanders and escort his troops across the English Channel for the invasion.

The Armada proved to be a disaster. The Spanish fleet that finally set sail had neither the ships nor the manpower that Philip had planned to send. A conversation between a papal emissary and an officer of the Spanish fleet before the Armada departed reveals the fundamental flaw:

"And if you meet the English armada in the Channel, do you expect to win the battle?" "Of course," replied the Spaniard.

"How can you be sure?" [asked the emissary]

"It's very simple. It is well known that we fight in God's cause. So, when we meet the English, God will surely arrange matters so that we can grapple and board them, either by sending some strange freak of weather or, more likely, just by depriving the English of their wits. If we can come to close quarters, Spanish valor and Spanish steel (and the great masses of soldiers we shall have on board) will make our victory certain. But unless God helps us by a miracle the English, who have faster and handier ships than ours, and many more long-range guns, and who know their advantage just as well as we do, will never close with us at all, but stand aloof and knock us to pieces with their culverins, without our being able to do them any serious hurt. So," concluded the captain, and one fancies a grim smile, "we are sailing against England in the confident hope of a miracle."[5]

The hoped-for miracle never materialized. The Spanish fleet, battered by a number of encounters with the English, sailed back to Spain by a northward route around Scotland and Ireland where it was further battered by storms. Although the English and Spanish would continue their war for another sixteen years, the defeat of the Armada guaranteed for the time being that England would remain a Protestant country. Although Spain made up for its losses within a year and a half, the defeat was a psychological blow to the Spaniards.

▼ Economic and Social Crises

The period of European history from 1560 to 1650 witnessed severe economic and social crises as well as political upheaval. Economic uncertainties, intensified by wildly fluctuating boom and bust cycles, were accompanied by social uncertainties and stark contrasts between the living standards of the rich and the poor. Although historians commonly refer to a sixteenth-century price revolution and a seventeenth-century economic crisis, the lack of concrete data has made it difficult to be precise in these areas, leading to numerous historical controversies.

Inflation and Economic Stagnation

Inflation was a major economic problem in the sixteenth and early seventeenth centuries. This so-called price revolution was a Europeanwide phenomenon, although different areas were affected at different times. While the inflation rate was probably a relatively low 2 to 3 percent a year, it was noticeable in a Europe accustomed to stable prices. Foodstuffs were most subject to high prices, especially evident in the price of wheat. An upward surge in wheat prices was first noticed in the Mediterranean area—in Spain, southern France, and

Italy—and reached its peak there in the 1590s. By the 1620s and 1630s, the same price increases for wheat had become obvious in northern Europe.

Although precise data are lacking, economic historians believe that as a result of the price revolution, wages failed to keep up with price increases. Wage earners, especially agricultural laborers and salaried workers in urban areas, began to experience a lower standard of living. At the same time, landed aristocrats who could raise rents managed to prosper. To contemporaries, in fact, the rent increases imposed by the landed nobility were responsible for the problem, as the English Bishop Latimer proclaimed in a sermon preached before King Edward VI in 1549:

> You landlords, you rent-raisers, I may say you step-lords, you have for your possessions yearly too much. For what here before went for twenty or forty pound by year (which is an honest portion to be had gratis in one lordship of another man's sweat and labor), now is let for fifty or an hundred pound by year. Of this "too much" comes this monstrous and portentous dearth made by man . . . that poor men, which live by their labour cannot with the sweat of their face have a living, all kinds of victuals is so dear. . . .[6]

Wealthy commercial and industrial entrepreneurs also benefited from the price revolution because of rising prices, expanding markets, and relatively cheaper labor costs. Some historians regard this profit inflation as a valuable stimulus to investment and the growth of capitalism, helping to explain the economic expansion and prosperity of the sixteenth century. Governments were likewise affected by inflation. They borrowed heavily from bankers and placed new burdens of taxation on their subjects, often creating additional discontent.

The causes of the price revolution are a subject of much historical debate. Already in the 1560s European intellectuals had associated the rise in prices with the great influx of precious metals from the New World. Although this view was accepted for a long time, many economic historians now believe that the increase in population in the sixteenth century played an important role in creating inflationary pressures. A growing population increased the demand for land and food and drove up prices for both.

But the inflation-fueled prosperity of the sixteenth century showed signs of slackening by the beginning of the seventeenth century. Economic contraction began to be evident in some parts of Europe by the 1620s. In the 1630s and 1640s, as imports of silver declined, economic recession intensified, especially in the Mediterranean area. The industrial and financial center of Europe in the age of the Renaissance, Italy was now becoming an economic backwater. Spain's economy was also seriously failing by the decade of the 1640s.

Trade, Industry, Banking, and Agriculture

The flourishing European trade of the sixteenth century revolved around three major areas: the Mediterranean in the south, the Low Countries and the Baltic region in the north, and central Europe, whose inland trade depended on the Rhine and Danube rivers. Because of the expanding overseas trade, however, the Atlantic seaboard began to play an even more important role, linking the Mediterranean, Baltic, and central European trading areas together and making the whole of Europe into a more integrated market that was all the more vulnerable to price shifts. With their cheaper and faster ships, the Dutch came to monopolize both European and world trade, although they were increasingly challenged by the English and French in the seventeenth century.

The commercial expansion of the sixteenth and seventeenth centuries was made easier by new forms of commercial organization, especially the joint-stock trading company. Individuals bought shares in a company and received dividends on their investment while a board of directors ran the company and made the important business decisions. The return on investments could be spectacular. During its first ten years, investors received 30 percent on their money from the Dutch East India Company, which opened the Spice Islands and southeast Asia to Dutch activity. The joint-stock company made it easier to raise large amounts of capital for world trading ventures.

Enormous profits were also being made in shipbuilding and in mining and metallurgy, where technological innovations, such as the use of pumps and new methods of extracting metals from ores, proved highly successful. The mining industry was closely tied to sixteenth-century family banking firms. In exchange for arranging large loans to Charles V, Jacob Fugger was given a monopoly over silver, copper, and mercury mines in the Habsburg possessions of central Europe that produced profits in excess of 50 percent per year. While these close relationships between governments and entrepreneurs could lead to stunning successes, they could also be precarious. The House of Fugger went bankrupt at the end of the sixteenth century when the Habsburgs defaulted on their loans.

By the seventeenth century, the traditional family banking firms were no longer able to provide the multi-

ple services needed for the commercial capitalism of the seventeenth century. New institutions arose to take their place. The city of Amsterdam created the Bank of Amsterdam in 1609 as both a deposit and transfer institution and the Amsterdam Bourse or Exchange where the trading of stocks replaced the exchange of goods. By 1620, the Amsterdam Exchange had become the center of the international business world, just as Amsterdam itself had replaced Antwerp as the greatest commercial and banking center of Europe.

▼ **Jacob Fugger the Rich.** One of the more profitable industries of the sixteenth century was mining, which was closely tied to family banking firms. Jacob Fugger, pictured here with his secretary, was given a monopoly over the silver, copper, and mercury mines in the Habsburg lands in exchange for giving large loans to Charles V. Such dealings could be dangerous, however, as is shown by the fact that the house of Fugger went bankrupt when the Habsburgs defaulted on their loans.

Despite the growth of commercial capitalism, most of the European economy still depended on an agricultural system that had experienced few changes since the thirteenth century. At least 80 to 90 percent of Europeans still worked on the land. Most of the peasants of western Europe were free of serfdom, although many still owed a variety of feudal dues to the nobility. Despite expanding markets and rising prices, increased rents, fees, and higher taxes imposed by the state meant little or no improvement in the lot of the European peasants. In eastern Europe, their position had even worsened as peasants were increasingly tied to the land in a new serfdom enforced by powerful landowners (see Chapter 16).

Population Trends

The sixteenth century was a period of expanding population, possibly related to a warmer climate and increased food supplies. It has been estimated that the population of Europe increased from 60 million in 1500 to 85 million by 1600, the first major recovery of European population since the devastation of the Black Death in the mid-fourteenth century. However, records also indicate a leveling off of the population by 1620 and even a decline by 1650, especially in central and southern Europe. Only the Dutch, English, and, to a lesser degree, the French grew in number in the first half of the seventeenth century. Europe's longtime adversaries, war, famine, and plague, continued to affect population levels. In 1630, for example, northern Italy was hit by the worst outbreak of bubonic plague since the Black Death; Verona and Mantua lost 60 to 70 percent of their populations. Europe's entry into another "little ice age" after the middle of the sixteenth century, when average temperatures fell and glaciers even engulfed small Alpine villages, affected harvests and gave rise to famines. Historians have noted the parallels between population increase and economic prosperity in the sixteenth century and population decline and economic recession in the seventeenth century.

The rise in population was reflected in the growth of cities. In 1500, Paris, Constantinople, and four cities in Italy (Naples, Venice, Milan, Genoa) had populations above 100,000 people. By 1600, Naples had grown to 300,000, while Rome, Palermo, and Messina reached 100,000. Cities along coasts and well-traveled trade routes grew the most, reflecting the close ties between commerce and urban growth. Naples became the largest port in Italy while Seville in Spain, the port of entry for the wealth of the New World, and Lisbon in Portugal had populations over 100,000 by 1600. Across the English Channel, London's domination of the commercial and financial life of England pushed its population to 250,000 by 1600. By that year, Europe's greatest and most populous city was Paris with its 500,000 people.

Seventeenth-century cities visibly reflected the remarkable disparity in wealth during the seventeenth century. The beautiful houses and palaces of rich nobles and wealthy merchants contrasted sharply with the crowded tenements and dirty hovels of the lower classes. Crime, pollution, filth, and lack of sanitation, fresh water, and food were accompanied by the social tensions between landed nobles who moved into the cities and the native wealthy merchants who resented their presence.

▼ Seventeenth-Century Crises: War, Rebellions, and Revolution

Although many Europeans responded to the upheavals of the second half of the sixteenth century with a desire for peace and order, the first fifty years of the seventeenth century continued to be a period of crisis. A devastating war that affected much of Europe, a revolution in England that led to the beheading of a king, and rebellions seemingly everywhere protracted an atmosphere of disorder and violence.

The Thirty Years' War

Religion, especially the struggle between a militant Catholicism and a militant Calvinism, certainly played an important role in the outbreak of the Thirty Years' War, often called the "last of the religious wars." As the war progressed, however, it became increasingly clear that secular, dynastic-nationalist considerations were far more important.

Although much of the fighting in the Thirty Years' War (1618–1648) was done in the Germanic lands of the Holy Roman Empire, the war became a European-wide struggle. In fact, some historians view it as part of a larger conflict between the Bourbon dynasty of France and the Habsburg dynasties of Spain and the Holy Roman Empire for European leadership and date it from 1609 to 1659. A brief look at the motives of the European states and the situation in Germany provides the background necessary to understand the war.

Since the beginning of the sixteenth century, France had worked to break out of what it perceived as its encirclement by the house of Habsburg (see Chapter 14).

The situation had eased in 1556 when Charles V abdicated and divided his empire. His son Philip inherited Spain, the Netherlands, Italy, and the New World while his brother Ferdinand became Holy Roman emperor and received the Habsburg possessions in Austria and eastern Europe. France felt threatened by the Spanish Habsburgs and feared the consolidation of Germany by the Habsburg emperor.

Spain, which viewed the twelve-year truce negotiated with the Dutch in 1609 as only temporary, was determined to regain control of the Netherlands, specifically, the northern Dutch provinces. English and Dutch control of the seas, however, forced the Spanish to seek an alternative route for shipping supplies and men to the Dutch provinces by way of Italy and western Germany. While in retrospect it might be easy to recognize that Spain's economic decline made it foolish to undertake the reconquest of the Dutch, to contemporaries, Spain remained the greatest power in the Christian world.

The Austrian Habsburgs wished to consolidate their holdings in Austria and Bohemia by eliminating Protestantism and establishing stronger central authority. At the same time, as Holy Roman emperors, they remained frustrated by their lack of real authority over the lands of Germany where hundreds of individual states still provided the real basis of political power. It was among these German states that the Thirty Years' War had its immediate beginnings.

The Peace of Augsburg had brought an end to the religious warfare between Catholics and Lutherans in 1555. Religion, however, continued to play a divisive role in German life as Lutherans and Catholics persisted in vying for control of different principalities. In addition, although the treaty had not recognized the rights of Calvinists, a number of German states had adopted Calvinism as their state church. At the beginning of the seventeenth century, the Calvinist ruler of the Palatinate, the Elector Palatine Frederick IV, assumed the leadership in forming a league of German Protestant states called the Protestant Union. To counteract it, a Catholic League of German states was organized by Duke Maximilian of the south German state of Bavaria. What made this division of Germany into two armed camps even more dangerous was the involvement of foreign states. The Protestant Union gained the support of the Dutch, English, and French, while Spain and the Holy Roman emperor aided the Catholic League. By 1609, then, Germany was dividing into two armed camps in anticipation of a religious war.

The religious division was exacerbated by a constitutional issue. The desire of the Habsburg emperors to consolidate their authority in Germany was resisted by the princes who fought for their "German liberties," their constitutional rights and prerogatives as individual rulers. To pursue their policies, the Habsburg emperors looked to Spain for assistance while the princes turned to the enemies of Spain, especially France, for help against the emperor. The divisions in Germany and Europe made it almost inevitable that if war did erupt, it would be widespread and difficult to stop. Events in Bohemia in 1617 and 1618 finally brought the outbreak of the war everyone dreaded.

Historians have traditionally divided the Thirty Years' War into four major phases. The Bohemian phase (1618–1625) began in one of the Habsburgs' own territories. In 1617, the Bohemian Estates (primarily the nobles) accepted the Habsburg Archduke Ferdinand as their king but soon found themselves unhappy with their choice. While many of the nobles were Calvinists, Ferdinand was a devout Catholic who began a process of re-Catholicizing Bohemia and strengthening the royal power. The Protestant nobles rebelled against Ferdinand in May 1618 and proclaimed their resistance by throwing two of the Habsburg governors and a secretary out of the window of the royal castle in Prague, the seat of Bohemian government. The Catholic side claimed that their seemingly miraculous escape from death in the seventy-foot fall from the castle was due to the intercession of the Virgin Mary, while Protestants pointed out that they fell into a manure pile. The Bohemian rebels now seized control of Bohemia, deposed Ferdinand, and elected as his replacement the Protestant ruler of the Palatinate, Elector Frederick V, who was also head of the Protestant Union.

Ferdinand, who in the meantime had been elected as Holy Roman emperor, refused to accept his deposition. Aided by the imposing forces of Maximilian of Bavaria and the Catholic League, the imperial forces defeated Frederick and the Bohemian nobles at the Battle of White Mountain outside Prague on November 8, 1620. Spanish troops meanwhile took advantage of Frederick's predicament by invading the Palatinate and conquering it by the end of 1622. The unfortunate Frederick who had lost two crowns—Bohemia and the Palatinate—fled into exile in Holland. The Spanish took control of the western part of the Palatinate (to gain the access route from Italy to the Netherlands that they had wanted), and Duke Maximilian of Bavaria took the rest of the territory. Reestablished as king of Bohemia, Emperor Ferdinand declared Bohemia a hereditary Habsburg possession, confiscated the land of the Protestant nobles, and established Catholicism as the sole religion. Some

30,000 Protestant families emigrated to Saxony and Hungary. The Spanish renewed their attack on the Dutch, and the forces of Catholicism seemed on the road to victory. But the war was far from over.

The second phase of the war, the Danish phase (1625–1629), began when King Christian IV of Denmark (1588–1648), a Lutheran, intervened on behalf of the Protestant cause by taking an army into northern Germany. Most likely, he also wished to annex territories in northern Germany that would give him control of the southern Baltic. His campaign turned out to be a complete fiasco.

The imperial forces were now led by a brilliant and enigmatic commander, Albrecht von Wallenstein, a Bohemian nobleman who had taken advantage of Ferdinand's victory to become the country's wealthiest landowner. Wallenstein marched the imperial army north, utterly defeated the Danes, and occupied parts of northern Germany, including the Baltic ports of Hamburg, Lübeck, and Bremen. Christian IV's total defeat ended Danish involvement in the Thirty Years' War and even meant the end of Danish supremacy in the Baltic.

After the success of the imperial armies, the emperor Ferdinand II was at the height of his power and took this opportunity to issue the Edict of Restitution in March 1629. His proclamation prohibited Calvinist worship and restored to the Catholic church all property taken by Protestant princes or cities during the past seventy-five years. But this sudden growth in the power of the Habsburg emperor frightened many German princes who feared for their independent status and reacted by forcing the emperor to dismiss Wallenstein. At the same time, Ferdinand was faced with another intervention by foreign powers as the war entered its third phase.

The Swedish phase (1630–1635) marked the entry of Gustavus Adolphus, king of Sweden (1611–1635), into the war. Gustavus Adolphus was responsible for reviving Sweden and making it into a great Baltic power. The French, disturbed by the Habsburg consolidation of power, provided financial support to Gustavus, a military

▼ **Gustavus Adolphus at the Battle of Lützen.** Both religious and dynastic considerations played roles in the beginning of the Thirty Years' War. Pictured here is Gustavus Adolphus, king of Sweden, leading a cavalry charge just before he was killed in the Battle of Lützen. Beginning the third phase of the war, the Swedes entered the conflict for both political and religious reasons. Gustavus wanted the Baltic to become a Swedish lake. As a Lutheran, he also felt obligated to aid his fellow co-religionists.

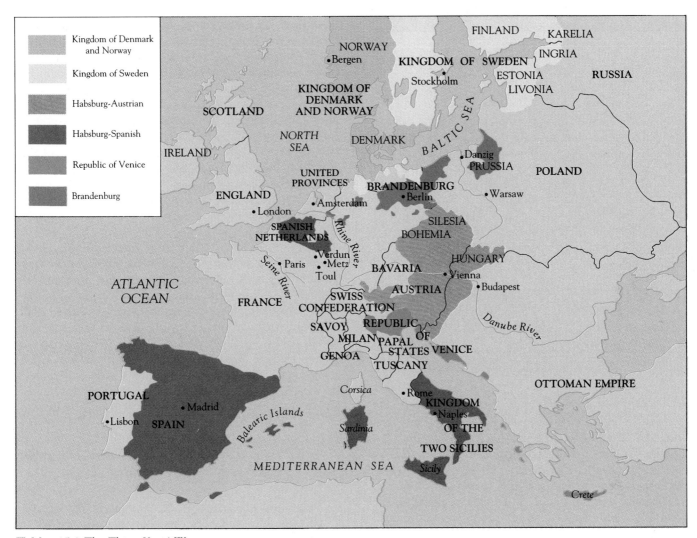

▼ **Map 15.2** The Thirty Years' War.

genius who brought a disciplined and well-equipped Swedish army to northern Germany. Gustavus had no desire to see the Habsburgs in northern Germany since he wanted the Baltic Sea to be a Swedish lake. At the same time, Gustavus Adolphus was a devout Lutheran who felt compelled to aid his coreligionists in Germany.

Gustavus's army swept the imperial forces out of northern Germany and moved into the heart of Germany. In desperation, the imperial side recalled Wallenstein, who was given command of the imperial army that met Gustavus Adolphus's troops near Leipzig. At the Battle of Lützen (1632), the Swedish forces prevailed but paid a high price for the victory when the Swedish king was killed in the battle. Although the Swedish forces remained in Germany, they proved much less effective. Despite the loss of Wallenstein,

who was assassinated in 1634 by one of his own captains, the imperial army decisively defeated the Swedes at the Battle of Nördlingen at the end of 1634 and drove them out of southern Germany. This imperial victory guaranteed that southern Germany would remain Catholic. The emperor used this opportunity to make peace with the German princes by agreeing to annul the Edict of Restitution of 1629. But peace failed to come to war-weary Germany. The Swedes wished to continue while the French, under the direction of Cardinal Richelieu, the chief minister of King Louis XIII (see Chapter 16), entered the war directly, beginning the fourth and final phase of the war, the Franco-Swedish phase (1635–1648).

By this time, religious issues were losing their significance as dynastic power politics came to the fore. The

The Protestant Union	1608
The Catholic League	1609
Election of Habsburg Archduke Ferdinand as King of Bohemia	1617
Bohemian Revolt against Ferdinand	1618
The Bohemian Phase	1618–1625
Battle of White Mountain	1620
Spanish Conquest of Palatinate	1622
The Danish Phase	1625–1629
Edict of Restitution	1629
The Swedish Phase	1630–1635
Battle of Lützen	1632
Battle of Nördlingen	1634
The Franco-Swedish Phase	1635–1648
Battle of Rocroi	1643
Peace of Westphalia	1648
Peace of the Pyrenees	1659

Catholic French, after all, were now supporting the Protestant Swedes against the Catholic Habsburgs of Germany and Spain. This phase of the war was fought by Sweden in northern Germany and by France in the Netherlands and along the Rhine in western Germany. The Battle of Rocroi in 1643 proved decisive as the French beat the Spanish and brought an end to Spanish military greatness. The French then moved on to victories over the imperialist-Bavarian armies in southern Germany. By this time all parties were ready for peace, and after five years of protracted negotiations, the war in Germany was officially ended by the Peace of Westphalia in 1648. The war between France and Spain, however, continued until the Peace of the Pyrenees in 1659. By that time, Spain had become a second-class power, and France had emerged as the dominant nation in Europe.

What were the results of this "basically meaningless conflict," as one historian has called it? The Peace of Westphalia ensured that all German states, including the Calvinist ones, were free to determine their own religion. Territorially, France gained parts of western Germany, part of Alsace and the three cities of Metz, Toul, and Verdun, giving the French control of the Franco-German border area. While Sweden and the German states of Brandenburg and Bavaria gained some territory in Germany, the Austrian Habsburgs did not

really lose any, but did see their authority as rulers of Germany further diminished. The over three hundred states that made up the Holy Roman Empire were virtually recognized as independent states, since each received the power to conduct its own foreign policy; this brought an end to the Holy Roman Empire as a political entity and ensured German disunity for another two hundred years. The Peace of Westphalia made it clear that religion and politics were now separate worlds. The pope was completely ignored in all decisions at Westphalia, and political motives became the guiding forces in public affairs as religion was in the process of becoming primarily a matter of personal conviction and individual choice.

Economically and socially, the effects of the Thirty Years' War on Germany are still debated. An older view pictured a ruined German economy and a decline in German population from 21 to 13 million from 1600 to 1650, but more recent opinions have estimated that Germany's population grew from 16 to 17 million while a redistribution of economic activity rather than an overall decline was taking place. Both views contain some truth. Some areas of Germany were completely devastated while others remained relatively untouched and even experienced economic growth. While historians can debate the figures, many people in Germany would have agreed with this comment by Otto von Guericke, a councillor in the city of Magdeburg, which was sacked ten times (see also the box on p. 505):

> Then there was nothing but beating and burning, plundering, torture, and murder. Most especially was every one of the enemy bent on securing much booty. . . . In this frenzied rage, the great and splendid city . . . was now . . . given over to the flames, and thousands of innocent men, women and children, in the midst of a horrible din of heartrending shrieks and cries, were tortured and put to death in so cruel and shameful a manner that no words would suffice to describe . . . . Thus in a single day this noble and famous city, the pride of the whole country, went up in fire and smoke.[7]

The Thirty Years' War was undoubtedly the most destructive conflict Europeans had yet experienced. Unfortunately, it was not the last.

A Military Revolution?

By the seventeenth century, war played an increasingly important role in European affairs. One historian has calculated that between 1562 and 1721 there were

The Face of War in the Seventeenth Century
▼▼▼

The Thirty Years' War was the most devastating war Europeans had experienced since the Hundred Years' War. Due to the number of nations involved and battles fought, some historians have even called it "the first world war." Destruction was especially severe in Germany. We have a firsthand account of the face of war in Germany from a picaresque novel called Simplicius Simplicissimus, written by Jakob von Grimmelshausen. The author's experiences as a soldier in the Thirty Years' War give his descriptions of the effect of the war on ordinary people a certain vividness and reality. This selection describes the fate of a peasant farm, an experience all too familiar to thousands of German peasants between 1618 and 1648.

Jakob von Grimmelshausen, *Simplicius Simplicissimus*

The first thing these horsemen did in the nice back rooms of the house was to put in their horses. Then everyone took up a special job, one having to do with death and destruction. Although some began butchering, heating water, and rendering lard, as if to prepare for a banquet, others raced through the house, ransacking upstairs and down; not even the privy chamber was safe, as if the golden fleece of Jason might be hidden there. Still others bundled up big packs of cloth, household goods, and clothes, as if they wanted to hold a rummage sale somewhere. What they did not intend to take along they broke and spoiled. Some ran their swords into the hay and straw, as if there hadn't been hogs enough to stick. Some shook the feathers out of beds and put bacon slabs, hams, and other stuff in the ticking, as if they might sleep better on these. Others knocked down the hearth and broke the windows, as if announcing an everlasting summer. They flattened out copper and pewter dishes and baled the ruined goods. They burned up bedsteads, tables, chairs, and benches, though there were yards and yards of dry firewood outside the kitchen. Jars and crocks, pots and casseroles all were broken, either because they preferred their meat broiled or because they thought they'd eat only one meal with us. In the barn, the hired girl was handled so roughly that she was unable to walk away, I am ashamed to report. They stretched the hired man out flat on the ground, stuck a wooden wedge in his mouth to keep it open, and emptied a milk bucket full of stinking manure drippings down his throat; they called it a Swedish cocktail. He didn't relish it and made a very wry face. By this means they forced him to take a raiding party to some other place where they carried off men and cattle and brought them to our farm. Among these were my father, mother, and Ursula [sister].

Then they used thumbscrews, which they cleverly made out of their pistols, to torture the peasants, as if they wanted to burn witches. Though he had confessed to nothing as yet, they put one of the captured hayseeds in the bake-oven and lighted a fire in it. They put a rope around someone else's head and tightened it like a tourniquet until blood came out of his mouth, nose, and ears. In short, every soldier had his favorite method of making life miserable for peasants, and every peasant had his own misery. My father was, as I thought, particularly lucky because he confessed with a laugh what others were forced to say in pain and martyrdom. No doubt because he was the head of the household, he was shown special consideration; they put him close to a fire, tied him by his hands and legs, and rubbed damp salt on the bottoms of his feet. Our old nanny goat had to lick it off and this so tickled my knan [father] that he could have burst laughing. This seemed so clever and entertaining to me—I had never seen or heard my knan laugh so long—that I joined him in laughter, to keep him company or perhaps to cover up my ignorance. In the midst of such glee he told them the whereabouts of hidden treasure much richer in gold, pearls, and jewelry than might have been expected on a farm.

I can't say much about the captured wives, hired girls, and daughters because the soldiers didn't let me watch their doings. But I do remember hearing pitiful screams from various dark corners and I guess that my mother and our Ursula had it no better than the rest.

only four years in which all of Europe was at peace. Military power was considered essential to a ruler's reputation and power, intensifying the pressure to build an effective military machine. Although some would disagree, some historians believe that the changes that occurred in the science of warfare between 1560 and 1650 warrant the title of military revolution.

Medieval warfare, with its mounted knights and auxiliary archers, had been transformed in the Renaissance by the employment of massed infantry squares using pikes and halberds in both offensive and defensive actions. The infantry square of pikemen became a crucial element in sixteenth-century armies and helps to explain the success of the Spanish who perfected its use. The utilization of firearms required adjustments to the size of the infantry square while the cavalry began to substitute pistols for lances.

It was Gustavus Adolphus, the king of Sweden, who developed the first standing army of conscripts, notable for the flexibility of its tactics. The infantry brigades of Gustavus's army, six men deep, were composed of equal numbers of musketeers and pikemen. They employed the salvo in which all rows of the infantry fired at once instead of row by row. These salvos of fire, which cut up the massed ranks of the opposing infantry squares, were followed by a pike charge, giving the infantry a primarily offensive deployment. Gustavus also used the cavalry in a more mobile fashion. After shooting a pistol volley, they charged the enemy with their swords. Additional mobility was created by utilizing smaller pieces of artillery that were more easily moved during battle. All of these changes required coordination, careful training, and better discipline, forcing rulers to move away from undisciplined mercenary forces. Naturally, the success of Gustavus Adolphus led to imitation. Perhaps the best example was the New Model Army of Oliver Cromwell (see The Puritan Revolution later in the chapter). His army consisted of infantry (two-thirds musketeers and one-third pikemen), cavalry, mounted infantry known as dragoons, and artillery units. A well-integrated and disciplined army, it was known for its mobility and flexibility.

The military changes from 1560 to 1650 included an increased use of firearms and cannon, greater flexibility and mobility in tactics, and better disciplined and trained armies. These innovations necessitated standing armies, which grew ever larger and more expensive as the seventeenth century progressed. Such armies could only be maintained by levying greater taxes, making war an economic burden and an ever more important part of the early modern European state.

Rebellions

Before, during, and after the Thirty Years' War, a series of rebellions and civil wars stemming from the discontent of both nobles and commoners rocked the domestic stability of many European governments. To strengthen their power, monarchs attempted to extend their authority at the expense of traditional powerful elements who resisted their rulers' efforts. At the same time, to fight their battles, governments increased taxes and created such hardships that common people also rose in opposition. The resulting widespread revolts of subjects against their ruling princes have caused some historians to speak of a general crisis of authority in the first half of the seventeenth century.

Peasant and lower-class revolts occurred in central and southern France in 1593–1597, 1636–1637, and 1639; in Austria in 1595–1597, 1626–1627, and 1632–1636; and in Hungary in 1597, 1604–1607, and 1631–1632. In the decades of the 1640s and 1650s, even greater upheavals occurred. Portugal and Catalonia rebelled against the Spanish government in 1640. The common people in Naples and Sicily revolted against both the government and landed nobility in 1647. Russia, too, was rocked by urban uprisings in 1641, 1645, and 1648. Nobles rebelled in France from 1648 to 1652 to halt the growth of royal power (see Chapter 16). The northern states of Sweden, Denmark, and Holland were also not immune from upheavals involving clergy, nobles, and mercantile groups. Even relatively stable Switzerland had a peasant rebellion in 1656. By far the most famous and wide-ranging struggle, however, was the civil war and rebellion in England, commonly known as the Puritan Revolution. In many ways, it can also be seen as one of the last religious conflicts spawned by the religious Reformation of the sixteenth century.

The Puritan Revolution

The Puritan Revolution or the English Civil War of the seventeenth century is a highly controversial topic. Historians have approached it from a variety of positions, and contradictions abound in its interpretation. At its core was a struggle between king and Parliament, which evolved into an armed conflict to determine the roles king and Parliament should play in governing England. But the struggle over this political issue was complicated by economic problems and most of all by a deep and profound religious controversy.

During the last decade of Elizabeth's reign, serious problems between crown and Parliament began to arise, but did not come to a head, largely out of deference to the aged queen. Two of the Tudor monarchs, Henry VIII and Elizabeth I, had been strong rulers who had worked through Parliament to achieve their goals. Parliament seemed then little more than a rubber stamp for Tudor actions, but all the same the belief emerged that the crown's authority was expressed by means of an act of Parliament and that monarch and Parliament together formed a "balanced polity." With the death of Queen Elizabeth I in 1603, the Tudors became extinct, and the Stuart line of rulers was inaugurated with the accession to the throne of Elizabeth's cousin, King James VI of Scotland (son of Mary, queen of Scots), who became James I of England.

James I (1603–1625) was ill suited to meet the problems that had arisen but been postponed during the last years of Good Queen Bess. Although used to royal power as king of Scotland, he understood little about the laws, institutions, and customs of the English. As he admitted: "When I came into this land, though I were an old king (having governed a kingdom since I was 12 years old), yet I came here a stranger in government though not in blood." All too soon, a serious strain in the relationship between king and Parliament began to develop.

In 1598, King James had written a book called the *True Law of Free Monarchy* in which he defended the divine right of kings, the belief that kings receive their power directly from God and are responsible to no one except God. In the face of James's claims, Parliament responded in its first session in 1603 with its own claims to legislative and financial supremacy. The latter, in fact, proved to be Parliament's trump card in its relationship with the king. The rise in prices and the increased cost of government made the traditional sources of royal revenue used by Queen Elizabeth insufficient for James. And yet Parliament rejected his requests for additional monies because of his strong views on divine-right monarchy.

The king's relationship with the two major dissenting religious groups in England, the Catholics and Calvinists, also proved divisive. James inherited a strong Anglican church structure from the reign of Queen Elizabeth, who had papered over religious differences to create peace. Catholics were optimistic that James would be more sympathetic to them because his mother Mary, queen of Scots, had been a devout Catholic. His failure to appease them by 1605 led to the infamous Gunpowder Plot in which some fanatical Catholics planned to blow up the houses of Parliament while in session. The plot was quickly crushed, but its discovery led to an intensification of the anti-Catholic feeling that

had first been aroused in the late sixteenth century by the Spanish Armada of 1588.

The Puritans were optimistic about James because he had been king of Scotland, long a Calvinist nation with a Presbyterian church organization, modeled after Calvin's church organization in Geneva, in which ministers and elders (also called presbyters) played an important governing role. When the Puritans met with the king in 1604 and requested the elimination of the episcopal system of organization used in the Church of England (in which the bishop or *episcopos* played the major administrative role) in favor of the Presbyterian model, James lost his temper and threatened to "harry them out of the land" if they did not conform to the Anglican church. He realized that the Anglican church, in which the bishops were appointed by the crown, was a major support of monarchical authority. But the Puritans were not easily cowed and added to the rising chorus of opposition to the king. Many of England's lesser landed nobility, the gentry, had become Puritans, and these Puritan gentry formed not only an important and substantial part of the House of Commons, the lower house of Parliament, but also held important positions locally as justices of the peace and sheriffs. It was not wise to alienate them.

The conflict that had begun during the reign of James came to a head during the reign of his son Charles I (1625–1649). Charles was intelligent and perhaps well-meaning, but stubborn and uncompromising and believed as strongly in divine-right monarchy as his father had. From the first stormy session of Parliament, it became apparent that the issues between this king and Parliament would not be easily resolved.

The skirmishing between Charles and Parliament during the first several years of his reign pointed, first of all, to a serious political issue. While the king demanded grants of money to fight the war with Spain begun by his father, Parliament demanded constitutional reforms and especially a redress of grievances before making the grants. In 1628, for example, Parliament passed a Petition of Right that the king was supposed to accept before being granted any taxes. This petition prohibited taxes without Parliament's consent, arbitrary imprisonment, the quartering of soldiers in private houses, and the declaration of martial law in peacetime. Although he initially accepted it, Charles later reneged on the agreement because of its limitations on royal power. In 1629, Charles decided that since he could not work with Parliament, he would not have it meet. From 1629 to 1640, Charles pursued a course of "personal rule," which to outsiders might have appeared as though England was simply following the common European trend in which central representative bodies were fading away while monarchs extended their authority. Successful at first, Charles was forced at last by his need for money to resort to what members of Parliament regarded as illegal taxation. For example, in 1634, Charles extended the tax called Ship Money, which was a levy on seacoast towns to finance coastal defense, to inland towns and counties as well and then used the money to finance other government operations, rather than just defense. Such expedients simply aroused additional opposition from both middle-class merchants and the landed gentry who interpreted the king's actions as an attempt to tax without Parliament's consent.

The king's religious policy also proved disastrous. His marriage to Henrietta Maria, the Catholic sister of King Louis XIII of France, aroused suspicions about the king's own religious inclinations. Even more important, however, the policy of high Anglicanism pursued by William Laud, the archbishop of Canterbury, with the king's approval, struck the Puritans as a return to Catholic popery. Charles's attempt to force them to conform to his religious policies infuriated the Puritans, thousands of whom went to the "howling wildernesses" of America rather than be forced to conform their consciences to the king's supposed pro-popery nonsense.

Grievances mounted, yet Charles might have survived unscathed if he could have avoided calling Parliament, which alone could provide a focus for the many cries of discontent throughout the land. But the foolish attempt of the king and Archbishop Laud to impose the Anglican Book of Common Prayer upon the fanatical Scottish Presbyterian church led to a rebellion of the Scots against the king. Financially strapped and unable to raise troops to defend against the Scots, the king was forced to call Parliament into session. Eleven years of frustration welled up to create a Parliament determined to deal with the king.

In its first session from November 1640 to September 1641, the so-called Long Parliament (since it lasted in one form or another from 1640 to 1660) took a series of steps that placed severe limitations upon royal authority. These included the abolition of arbitrary courts, such as the Star Chamber; the abolition of taxes that the king had collected without Parliament's consent, such as Ship Money; and the passage of the revolutionary Triennial Act, which specified that Parliament must meet at least once every three years, with or without the king's consent. By the end of 1641, one group within Parliament was prepared to go no further, but a group of more radical parliamentarians pushed for more change, including the

elimination of bishops in the Anglican church. When the king tried to take advantage of the split by arresting some members of the more radical faction in Parliament, a large group in Parliament led by John Pym and his fellow Puritans decided that the king had gone too far. England now slipped into civil war (1642).

Some generalizations can be made about the division of English society in the civil war. It is usually argued that support for the Cavaliers (the Royalists) came from the higher nobility, the Anglican clergy, and many peasants, while the Roundheads, as the parliamentary supporters were known, relied upon some of the great nobles, the landed gentry, middle-class merchants, and, above all, the Puritans. Recent studies have shown, however, that local and regional interests often determined sides. The gentry, for example, appear to have divided fairly evenly between the parliamentary and royal parties. What seems most apparent is that religion was the single greatest catalyst, justifying the use of the term Puritan Revolution to describe what perhaps constituted "the last and grandest episode in Europe's age of religious wars." Oliver Cromwell, who eventually emerged as the leader of Parliament's army, stated it in these words: "Religion was not the thing at first contested for, but God brought it to that issue at last, . . . and at last it proved that which was most dear to us."[8] Cromwell neither forgot nor forgave the king's oppression of the Puritans. And in good Calvinist fashion, he and his religious compatriots saw their cause as lawful resistance to an ungodly ruler.

Parliament proved victorious in the first phase of the English Civil War (1642–1646), aided by two significant factors. The Scots came into the war on Parliament's side when Parliament agreed in 1643 to consider a Presbyterian church organization for England. Even more important, however, was the creation of the New Model Army by Oliver Cromwell, the only real military genius of the war. The New Model Army was composed primarily of more extreme Puritans known as the Independents, recruited by Cromwell on the basis that "I think that he that prays and preaches best will fight best." Consequently, Cromwell raised an army of men who had "the fear of God before their eyes," and who, in typical Calvinist fashion, believed they were doing battle for the Lord. It is striking to read in Cromwell's military reports such statements as "Sir, this is none other but the hand of God; and to Him alone belongs the glory." We might also attribute some of the credit to Cromwell himself since his crusaders were well disciplined and trained in the new continental military tactics. Supported by the New Model Army, Parliament ended the first phase of the civil war with the capture of King Charles I in 1646.

A split now occurred in the parliamentary forces. A Presbyterian majority wanted to disband the army and restore Charles I with a Presbyterian state church. The army, composed mostly of Independents, more radical Puritans who favored religious toleration for most Protestant groups and opposed an established Presbyterian church, marched on London in 1647 and began negotiations with the king. Charles took advantage of this division by fleeing and seeking help from the Scots. Enraged by the king's treachery, Cromwell and the army engaged in a second civil war (1648) that ended with Cromwell's victory and the capture of the king. This time Cromwell was determined to achieve a victory for the army's point of view. The Presbyterian members of Parliament were purged, leaving a Rump Parliament of fifty-three members of the House of Commons who then tried and condemned the king on an act of treason and adjudged that "he, the said Charles Stuart, as a tyrant, traitor, murderer, and public enemy to the good people of this nation, shall be put to death by the severing of his head from his body." Charles was executed on January 30, 1649 (see the box on p. 510). The revolution had triumphed, and the monarchy in England had been destroyed, at least for the moment.

After the death of the king, the Rump Parliament abolished the monarchy and the House of Lords and proclaimed England a republic or Commonwealth (1649–1653). This was not an easy period for Cromwell. As commander-in-chief of the army, he had to

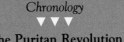

Chronology
▼ ▼ ▼

The Puritan Revolution

James I	1603–1625
Charles I	1625–1649
Petition of Right	1628
Ship Money Controversy	1634
First Session of the Long Parliament	1640–1641
First Civil War	1642–1646
Second Civil War	1648
Execution of Charles I	1649
Commonwealth	1649–1653
Rule by Military Governors	1655
Death of Cromwell	1658
Restoration of Monarchy—Charles II	1660

crush a Catholic uprising in Ireland, which he did with a brutality that earned him the eternal enmity of the Irish people, as well as an uprising in Scotland on behalf of the son of Charles I. He also faced opposition at home, especially from more radically minded groups who took advantage of the upheaval in England to push their agendas. The Levellers, for example, advocated such advanced ideas as freedom of speech, religious toleration, and a democratic republic. Cromwell, a country gentleman, defender of property and the ruling classes, smashed the radicals by force. At the same time, Cromwell found it difficult to work with the Rump Parliament

▼ **Execution of Charles I.** The Puritan Revolution involved political and economic as well as religious considerations. James I and his son Charles I attempted to assert their divine right to rule while limiting the power of Parliament. Moreover, both failed to deal adequately with the religious problems that divided England. When Charles attempted to arrest radical members of Parliament, a civil war erupted that eventually led to the rise of Oliver Cromwell and the execution of Charles I.

The Execution of a King

▼ ▼ ▼

After winning the civil wars (1642–1648), the Rump Parliament, acting as a "High Court of Justice," condemned King Charles I as a "tyrant, murderer, and public enemy," and ordered that he "be put to death by the severing of his head from his body." This excerpt is taken from a contemporary account of the king's execution, an act that was most uncommon in the seventeenth century.

An Account of the Execution of Charles I

And to the executioner he said, "I shall say but very short prayers, and when I thrust out my hands—"

Then he called to the bishop for his cap, and having put it on, asked the executioner, "Does my hair trouble you?" who desired him to put it all under his cap; which, as he was doing by the help of the bishop and the executioner, he turned to the bishop, and said, "I have a good cause, and a gracious God on my side."

The bishop said, "There is but one stage more, which, though turbulent and troublesome, yet is a very short one. You may consider it will soon carry you a very great way; it will carry you from earth to heaven; and there you shall find to your great joy the prize you hasten to, a crown of glory."

The king adjoins, "I go from a corruptible to an incorruptible crown; where no disturbance can be, no disturbance in the world. . . ."

Then the king asked the executioner, "Is my hair well?"

Then putting off his doublet and being in his waistcoat, he put on his cloak again, and looking upon the block, said to the executioner, "You must set it fast."

The executioner. "It is fast, sir."

King. "It might have been a little higher."

Executioner. "It can be no higher, sir."

King. "When I put out my hands this way, then—"

Then having said a few words to himself, as he stood, with hands and eyes lift up, immediately stooping down he laid his neck upon the block; and the executioner, again putting his hair under his cap, his Majesty, thinking he had been going to strike, bade him, "Stay for the sign."

Executioner. "Yes, I will, as it please your Majesty."

After a very short pause, his Majesty stretching forth his hands, the executioner at one blow severed his head from his body; which being held up and showed to the people, was with his body put into a coffin covered with black velvet and carried into his lodging.

His blood was taken up by divers persons for different ends: by some as trophies of their villainy; by others as relics of a martyr; and in some hath had the same effect, by the blessing of God, which was often found in his sacred touch when living.

---

and finally dispersed it by force. As the members of Parliament departed (April 1653), he shouted after them: "It's you that have forced me to do this, for I have sought the Lord night and day that He would slay me rather than put upon me the doing of this work." With the certainty of one who is convinced he is right, Cromwell had destroyed both king and Parliament.

The army provided a new government when it drew up the Instrument of Government, England's first and last written constitution. Executive power was vested in the Lord Protector (a position held by Cromwell) and legislative power in a Parliament. But the new system also failed to work. Cromwell found it difficult to work with the Parliament, especially when its members debated his authority and advocated once again the cre-

ation of a Presbyterian state church. In 1655, Cromwell dissolved Parliament and divided the country into eleven regions, each ruled by a major general who served virtually as a military governor. To meet the cost of military government, Cromwell levied a 10 percent land tax on all former Royalists. Unable to establish a constitutional basis for a working government, Cromwell had resorted to military force to maintain the rule of the Independents, ironically using even more arbitrary policies than those of Charles I.

Oliver Cromwell died in 1658. After floundering for eighteen months, the military establishment decided that arbitrary rule by the army was no longer feasible and reestablished the monarchy in the person of Charles II, the son of Charles I. The restoration of the Stuart monarchy ended England's time of troubles, but it would not be long before England would experience yet another constitutional crisis (see Chapter 16).

▼ The Witchcraft Craze

Hysteria over witchcraft affected the lives of many Europeans in the sixteenth and seventeenth centuries. Witchcraft trials were prevalent in England, Scotland, Switzerland, Germany, some parts of France and the Low Countries, and even New England in America.

Witchcraft was not a new phenomenon in the sixteenth and seventeenth centuries. Although its practice had been part of traditional village culture for centuries, the medieval church made it both sinister and dangerous when it began to connect witches to the activities of the Devil, thereby transforming witchcraft into a heresy that had to be extirpated. By the thirteenth century, after the creation of the Inquisition, people were being accused of a variety of witchcraft practices and, following the biblical injunction, "Thou shalt not suffer a witch to live," were turned over to secular authorities for burning at the stake or hanging (in England).

The search for scapegoats to explain the disaster of the Black Death in the fourteenth century led to a rise in the persecution of people accused of sorcery. In a papal bull of 1484, Pope Innocent VIII made official the belief of the Catholic church in such pernicious practices:

It has recently come to our ears, not without great pain to us, that in some parts of upper Germany, . . . many persons of both sexes, heedless of their own salvation and forsaking the catholic faith, give themselves over to devils male and female, and by their incantations, charms, and conjurings, . . . ruin and cause to perish the offspring of women, the foal of animals, the products of the earth, the grapes of vines, and the fruits of trees, as well as men and women, cattle and flocks and herds and animals of every kind . . .; that they afflict and torture with dire pains and anguish, both internal and external, these men, women, cattle, flocks, herds, and animals, and hinder men from begetting and women from conceiving, and prevent all consummation of marriage; . . . that, moreover, at the instigation of the enemy of mankind [Satan], they do not fear to commit and perpetrate many other abominable offences and crimes.[9]

To combat these dangers, Innocent sent two Dominican monks, Jacob Sprenger and Heinrich Krämer, to Germany to investigate and root out the witches. Based on their findings, they wrote the *Malleus Maleficarum (The Hammer of the Witches)*, which until the eighteenth century remained the standard handbook on the practices of witchcraft and the methods that could be used to discover and try witches.

What distinguished witchcraft in the sixteenth and seventeenth centuries from these previous developments was the high level of hysteria at which neighbors accused neighbors of witchcraft, leading to widespread trials of witches. Although estimates have varied widely, the

▼ **The Persecution of Witches.** A witchcraft hysteria dominated the daily lives of many Europeans in the sixteenth and seventeenth centuries. The medieval church associated witchcraft with devil worship and the secular authorities approved burning at the stake and hanging as punishments for witchcraft. Pictured here is the witches' sabbat or the infamous gathering where witches supposedly feasted, danced, and participated in orgies.

A Witchcraft Trial in Germany

▼ ▼ ▼

Prosecutions for witchcraft reached their high point in the sixteenth and seventeenth centuries when tens of thousands of people were brought to trial. In this excerpt from the minutes of a trial at Bamberg in 1628, we can see how the trial proceeded and why the accused witch stood little chance of exonerating himself.

The Prosecution of a Witch at Bamberg

On Wednesday, June 28, 1628, was examined without torture Johannes Junius, Burgomaster at Bamberg, on the charge of witchcraft: how and in what fashion he had fallen into that vice. Is fifty-years old . . . . Says he is wholly innocent, knows nothing of the crime, has never in his life renounced God; says that he is wronged before God and the world, would like to hear of a single human being who has seen him at such gatherings [as the witch sabbats].

Confrontation of Dr. Georg Adam Haan. Tells him to his face he will stake his life on it, that he saw him, Junius, a year and a half ago at a witchgathering in the electoral council-room, where they ate and drank. Accused denies the same wholly.

Confronted with Hopffens Elsse. Tells him likewise that he was on Haupts-moor at a witch-dance; but first the holy wafer was desecrated. Junius denies. Hereupon he was told that his accomplices had confessed against him and was given time for thought.

On Friday, June 30, 1628, the aforesaid Junius was again without torture exhorted to confess, but again confessed nothing, whereupon . . . since he would confess nothing, he was put to the torture, and first the *Thumb-screws* were applied. Says he has never denied God his Saviour nor suffered himself to be otherwise baptized [by the devil]; will again stake his life on it; feels no pain in the thumb-screws.

Leg-screws. Will confess absolutely nothing; knows nothing about it. He has never renounced God; will never do such a thing; has never been guilty of this vice; feels likewise no pain.

Strappado. He has never renounced God; God will not forsake him; if he were such a wretch he would not let himself be so tortured; God must show some token of his innocence. He knows nothing about witchcraft.

On July 5, the above named Junius is without torture, but with urgent persuasions, exhorted to confess, and at last begins and confesses:

When in the year 1624 his law-suit at Rothweil cost him some six hundred florins, he had gone out, in the month of August, into his orchard at Friedricsbronnen; and, as he sat there in thought, there had come to him a woman like a grass-maid, who had asked him why he sat there so sorrowful; he had answered that he was not despondent, but she had led him by seductive speeches to yield him to her will. . . . And thereafter this wench had changed into the form of a goat, which bleated and said, "Now you see with whom you have had to do. You must be mine or I will forthwith break your neck." Thereupon he had been frightened, and trembled all over for fear. . . . he was obliged to speak this formula: "I renounce God in Heaven and his host, and will henceforward recognize the Devil as my God."

He was then named Krix. His paramour he had to call Vixen. Those present had congratulated him in Beelzebub's name and said that they were now all alike. . . . At this time his paramour had promised to provide him with money, and from time to time to take him to other witch-gatherings.

Whenever he wished to ride forth [to the witch-sabbat] a black dog had come before his bed, which said to him that he must go with him, whereupon he had seated himself upon the dog and the dog had raised himself in the Devil's name and so had fared forth.

---

most recent figures indicate that more than 100,000 people were prosecuted throughout Europe on charges of witchcraft. As more and more people were brought to trial, the fear of witches as well as the fear of being accused of witchcraft escalated to frightening proportions. Approximately 25 percent of the villages in the English county of Essex, for example, had at least one witchcraft trial in the sixteenth and seventeenth centuries. Although larger cities were affected first, the trials also spread to smaller towns and rural areas as the hysteria persisted well into the seventeenth century (see the box above).

From an account of witch persecution in the German city of Trier, we get some glimpse of who the accused were: "Scarcely any of those who were accused escaped punishment. Nor were there spared even the leading men in the city of Trier." Although this statement makes it clear that the witchcraft trials had gone so far that even city officeholders were not immune from persecution, it also implies what is borne out in most witchcraft trials—that the common people were more likely to be accused of witchcraft. Indeed, where lists are given, those mentioned most often are milkmaids, peasant women, and servant girls. In the witchcraft trials of the sixteenth and seventeenth centuries, over 75 percent of those accused were women, most of them single or widowed and many over fifty years old. Moreover, almost all victims belonged to the lower classes, the poor and propertyless.

The accused witches usually confessed to a number of practices. Many of their confessions were extracted by torture, greatly adding to the number and intensity of activities mentioned. But even when people confessed voluntarily, certain practices stand out. Many said that they had sworn allegiance to the devil and attended sabbats or nocturnal gatherings where they feasted, danced, and even copulated with the devil in sexual orgies. More common, however, were admissions of using evil incantations and special ointments and powders to wreak havoc on neighbors by killing their livestock, injuring their children, or raising storms to destroy their crops.

A number of contributing factors have been suggested to explain why the witchcraft craze became so widespread in the sixteenth and seventeenth centuries. Religious uncertainties clearly played some part. Many witchcraft trials occurred in areas where Protestantism had been recently victorious or in regions, such as southwestern Germany, where Protestant-Catholic controversies still raged. As religious passions became inflamed, accusations of being in league with the devil became common on both sides.

Recently, however, historians have emphasized the importance of social conditions, especially the problems of a society in turmoil, in explaining the witchcraft hysteria. At a time when the old communal values that stressed working together for the good of the community were disintegrating before the onslaught of a new economic ethic that emphasized that each person should look out for himself or herself, property owners became more fearful of the growing numbers of poor among them and transformed them psychologically into agents of the devil. Old women were particularly susceptible to suspi-

cion. Many of them, no longer the recipients of the local charity found in traditional society, may even have tried to survive by selling herbs, potions, or secret remedies for healing. When problems arose, and there were many in this crisis-laden period, these same people were the most likely scapegoats at hand.

By the mid-seventeenth century, the witchcraft hysteria began to subside. The destruction of the religious wars had at least forced people to accept a grudging toleration, causing religious passions to subside. Moreover, as governments began to stabilize after the period of crisis, fewer magistrates were willing to accept the unsettling and divisive conditions generated by the trials of witches. Finally, by the end of the seventeenth and beginning of the eighteenth centuries, more and more people were questioning altogether their old attitudes towards religion and found it especially contrary to reason to believe in the old view of a world haunted by evil spirits.

▼ Culture in a Turbulent World

Art and literature passed through two major stylistic stages between the Renaissance and 1650. These changes were closely linked to the religious, political, and intellectual developments of the period.

Art

The artistic Renaissance came to an end when a new movement called Mannerism emerged in Italy in the decades of the 1520s and 1530s. The age of the Reformation had brought a revival of religious values accompanied by much political turmoil. Especially in Italy, the worldly enthusiasm of the Renaissance gave way to anxiety, uncertainty, suffering, and a yearning for spiritual experience. Mannerism reflected this environment in its deliberate attempt to break down the High Renaissance principles of balance, harmony, and moderation. In the *Deposition of Christ* by Jacopo da Pontormo (1494–1557), the rules of proportion are deliberately ignored as elongated figures are used to convey suffering, heightened emotions, and religious ecstasy. A sense of the bizarre is strengthened by the use of strange colors, such as pinkish hues for the color of human skin. Mannerism attempted to substitute a "realistic presentation of emotion" for a "realistic presentation of nature."

Mannerism spread from Italy to other parts of Europe and perhaps reached its apogee in the work of El Greco (1541–1614). Doménikos Theotocópoulos (called "the

Greek"—El Greco) was from Crete, but after studying in Venice and Rome, he moved to Spain in the 1570s where he became a church painter in Toledo. El Greco's use of elongated and contorted figures, portrayed in unusual shades of yellow and green against an eerie background of turbulent grays, reflect well the unresolved tensions created by the religious upheavals of the Reformation.

Mannerism was eventually replaced by a new movement—the Baroque—that dominated the artistic world for another century and a half. The Baroque originated

▼ **Jacopo da Pontormo, *Deposition of Christ.*** The artistic Renaissance came to a close with the rise of Mannerism, which reflected a breakdown of the High Renaissance principles of balance, harmony, and moderation. In Jacopo da Pontormo's *Deposition of Christ*, elongated figures and strange colors ranging from flaming red to icy blue create a world of suffering and strong emotions.

▼ **Peter Paul Rubens, *The Landing of Marie de' Medici at Marseilles.*** In the realm of Baroque painting, Peter Paul Rubens was an important figure. He played a key role in the spreading of the Baroque style from Italy to other parts of Europe. In *The Landing of Marie de' Medici at Marseilles*, Rubens makes a dramatic use of light and color, bodies in motion, and luxurious nudes to heighten the emotional intensity of the scene.

in Italy in the last quarter of the sixteenth century and spread to the rest of Europe. Baroque artists sought to harmonize the classical traditions of Renaissance art with the spiritual dimensions of the sixteenth-century religious revival in a new search for order and unity. The Baroque first appeared in Rome in the Jesuit church of Il Gesù, whose facade was completed in 1575. Although Protestants were also influenced, it was the Catholic reform movement that most wholeheartedly adopted the Baroque, as is evident at Catholic courts, especially those of the Habsburgs in Madrid, Prague, Vienna, and Brussels. Although it was resisted in France, England, and Holland, eventually the Baroque style spread to all of Europe and even Latin America.

In large part, Baroque art and architecture reflected the search for power that was characteristic of much of the seventeenth century (see Chapter 16). Baroque churches and palaces were built with richly ornamented facades, sweeping staircases, and a display and ostentation "exhibited in ornamentation and piling on of material."

The Baroque painting style was known for its use of dramatic effects to heighten emotional intensity, especially evident in the works of Peter Paul Rubens (1577–1640), a prolific artist and an important figure in the spread of the Baroque from Italy to other parts of Europe. In his artistic masterpieces, bodies in violent motion, heavily fleshed nudes, a dramatic use of light and shadow, and rich sensuous pigments converge to show intense emotions. The restless forms and constant movement blend together into a dynamic unity.

Perhaps the greatest figure of the Baroque was the Italian architect and sculptor Gian Lorenzo Bernini (1598–1680), who completed Saint Peter's Basilica and designed the vast colonnade enclosing the piazza in front of it. Action, exuberance, profusion, and dramatic effects mark the work of Bernini in the interior of Saint Peter's, where Bernini's *Throne of St. Peter* hovers in mid-air, held by the hands of the four great doctors of the Catholic church. Above the chair, rays of heavenly

▼ **El Greco,** *Laocöon.* Mannerism reached one of its highest expressions in the work of El Greco. Born in Crete, trained in Venice and Rome, and settling finally in Spain, El Greco worked as a church painter in Toledo. Pictured here is his version of the *Laocöon*, a famous piece of Hellenistic sculpture that had been discovered in Rome in 1506. The elongated, contorted bodies project a world of suffering while the somber background scene of the city of Toledo adds a sense of terror and doom.

▼ **Gian Lorenzo Bernini,** *Throne of St. Peter.* One of the greatest figures of the Baroque period was the Italian sculptor and architect Gian Lorenzo Bernini. Bernini was responsible for the completion of St. Peter's Cathedral and for the designing of the colonnade that surrounds the piazza in front of it. Pictured here is Bernini's *Throne of St. Peter* in the interior of St. Peter's Cathedral.

light drive a mass of clouds and angels toward the spectator. In his most striking sculptural work, the *Ecstasy of St. Theresa,* Bernini depicts a moment of mystical experience in the life of the sixteenth-century Spanish saint; the result is a sensuously real portrayal of physical ecstasy.

Thought: The World of Montaigne

The crises of the century from 1550 to 1650 produced challenges to the optimistic moral and intellectual postulates of the Renaissance. The humanist emphasis on the dignity of man and the role of education in producing moral virtue seemed questionable in view of the often violent and irrational passions of dynastic and religious warfare. Intellectuals and writers began to adopt new approaches in criticizing tradition and authority. The concept of a positive skepticism is closely associated with the work of Michel de Montaigne (1533–1592).

Son of a prosperous French merchant, Montaigne received the kind of classical education advocated by Renaissance humanists. Montaigne served as a lawyer and magistrate in the Parlement of Bordeaux, but the religious wars so disgusted him that he withdrew to his country estate to think and write his *Essays,* the first two books of which were published in 1580. His aim was to "disclose himself," or to use self-knowledge as an instrument to understand the world. Montaigne approached his subjects with an ironic skepticism, questioning inherited tradition and authority with special criticism aimed at moral absolutists. He was especially critical of the Huguenot and ultra-Catholic fanatics of the French Wars of Religion who deluded themselves and took the easy way out of life's complexities by trying to kill each other: "instead of transforming themselves into angels, they transform themselves into beasts."

To counteract fanaticism, Montaigne preached moderation and toleration or the "middle way." In his *Essay on Experience,* he wrote: "It is much easier to go along the sides, where the outer edge serves as a limit and a guide, than by the middle way, wide and open, and to go by art than by nature; but it is also much less noble and less commendable. Greatness of soul is not so much pressing upward and forward as knowing how to set oneself in order."[10] Montaigne also brought his middle way and skeptical mind to bear on other subjects of the day. He wondered, for example, whether "civilized" Europeans were superior to the "savages" of the New World.

Montaigne was secular minded and discussed moral issues without reference to Christian truths. He was, in many ways, out of step with his own age of passionate religious truths and hatreds, but his ideas would be welcomed by many Europeans once Europe passed through this stage of intense intolerance. His maturity, experience, gentleness, and openness all made Montaigne one of the timeless writers of Western civilization.

A Golden Age of Literature: England and Spain

Periods of crisis often produce great writing, and so it was of this age, which was characterized by epic poetry, experimental verse, the first great chivalric novel, and, above all, a golden age of theater. In both England and

William Shakespeare: In Praise of England
▼ ▼ ▼

William Shakespeare is one of the most famous play-wrights in the Western world. He was a universal genius, outclassing all others in his psychological insights, depth of characterization, imaginative skills, and versatility. His historical plays reflected the patriotic enthusiasm of the English in the Elizabethan era, as this excerpt from Richard II illustrates.

William Shakespeare, Richard II

This royal throne of kings, this sceptered isle,
This earth of majesty, this seat of Mars,
This other Eden, demi-Paradise,
This fortress built by Nature for herself
Against infection and the hand of war,
This happy breed of men, this little world,
This precious stone set in the silver sea,
Which serves it in the office of a wall
Or as a moat defensive to a house
Against the envy of less happier lands—

This blessed plot, this earth, this realm, this England,
This nurse, this teeming womb of royal kings,
Feared by their breed and famous by their birth,
Renowned for their deeds as far from home,
For Christian service and true chivalry,
As is the sepulcher in stubborn Jewry [the Holy
    Sepulcher in Jerusalem]
Of the world's ransom, blessed Mary's Son—
This land of such dear souls, this dear dear land,
Dear for her reputation through the world,
Is now leased out, I die pronouncing it,
Like a tenement or pelting farm.
England, bound in with the triumphant sea,
Whose rocky shore beats back the envious siege
Of watery Neptune, is now bound in with shame,
With inky blots and rotten parchment bonds.
That England, that was wont to conquer others,
Hath made a shameful conquest of itself.
Ah, would the scandal vanish with my life,
How happy then were my ensuing death!

Spain, writing for the stage reached new heights between 1580 and 1640. All of this impressive literature was written in the vernacular. Except for academic fields, such as theology, philosophy, jurisprudence, and the sciences, Latin was no longer a universal literary language.

The golden age of English literature is often called the Elizabethan Era because much of the English cultural flowering of the late sixteenth and early seventeenth centuries occurred during her reign. Elizabethan literature exhibits the exuberance and pride associated with English exploits under Queen Elizabeth (see the box above). Of all the forms of Elizabethan literature, none expressed the energy and intellectual versatility of the era better than drama. Of all the dramatists, none is more famous than William Shakespeare (1564–1614).

Shakespeare was the son of a prosperous glovemaker from Stratford-upon-Avon. When he appeared in London in 1592, Elizabethans were already addicted to the stage. By 1576, two professional theaters run by actors' companies were in existence. Elizabethan theater became a tremendously successful business. In or near London, at least four to six theaters were open six afternoons

a week. London theaters ranged from the Globe, which was a circular unroofed structure holding 3,000, to the Blackfriars, which was roofed and held only 500. In the former, an admission charge of one or two pennies enabled even the lower classes to attend, while the higher prices in the latter ensured an audience of the well-to-do. Elizabethan audiences varied greatly, putting pressure on playwrights to write works that pleased nobles, lawyers, merchants, and even vagabonds. When the Puritans, who had long criticized the wickedness of the London stage, assumed power in 1642, one of their first actions was to close the theaters. They did not reopen until the monarchy was restored, eighteen years later.

William Shakespeare was a "complete man of the theater." Although best known for writing plays, he was also an actor and shareholder in the chief company of the time, the Lord Chamberlain's Company, which played in theaters as diverse as the Globe and the Blackfriars. Shakespeare has long been recognized as a universal genius. A master of the English language, he was instrumental in transforming a language that was still in a period of transition. His technical proficiency, however, was matched by an incredible insight into human

▼ **William Shakespeare.** The golden age of English literature is identified with the Elizabethan era. Drama flourished during this period, and the greatest dramatist of the age was William Shakespeare. An actor and shareholder in a theatrical company as well as a playwright, Shakespeare wrote a number of tragedies, comedies, romances, and histories. Regardless of the kind of play he wrote, Shakespeare always exhibited a keen understanding of the human condition.

psychology. Whether in his tragedies or comedies, Shakespeare exhibited a remarkable understanding of the human condition.

The theater was one of the most creative forms of expression during Spain's golden century. In the course of the sixteenth century, Spanish theater made the transition from religious morality plays to a popular form of dramatic art. The first professional theaters established in Seville and Madrid in the 1570s were run by actors' companies as in England. Soon, every large town had a public playhouse, including Mexico City in the New World. Touring companies brought the latest Spanish plays to all parts of the Spanish empire.

Beginning in the 1580s, the agenda for playwrights was set by Lope de Vega (1562–1635). Like Shakespeare, he was from a middle-class background. He was an incredibly prolific writer; almost 500 of his 1,500 plays survive. They have been characterized as witty, charming, action-packed, and realistic. Lope de Vega made no apologies for the fact that he wrote his plays to please his audiences. In a treatise on drama written in 1609, he stated that the foremost duty of the playwright was to satisfy public demand. Shakespeare undoubtedly believed the same thing since his livelihood depended on public approval, but Lope de Vega was considerably more cynical about it: he remarked that if anyone thought he had written his plays for fame, "undeceive him and tell him that I wrote them for money."

One of the crowning achievements of the Golden Age of Spanish literature was the work of Miguel de Cervantes (1547–1616), whose *Don Quixote* has been acclaimed as one of the greatest literary works of all time. While satirizing medieval chivalric literature, Cervantes also perfected the chivalric novel and reconciled it with literary realism. In the two main figures of his famous work, Cervantes presented the dual nature of Spanish character. The knight Don Quixote from La Mancha is the visionary who is so involved in his lofty ideals that he is oblivious to the hard realities around him. To him, for example, windmills appear as four-armed giants. In contrast, the knight's fat and earthy squire, Sancho Panza, is the realist who cannot get his master to see the realities in front of him. But after adventures that took them to all parts of Spain, each came to see the value of the other's perspective. We are left with Cervantes's conviction that idealism and realism, visionary dreams and the hard work of reality, are both necessary to the human condition.

The period from 1560 to 1650 witnessed Europe's attempt to adjust to a whole range of change-laden forces. Population contracted as economic expansion gave way to economic recession. The discovery of new trade routes to the Far East and the "accidental" discovery of the Americas led Europeans to plunge outside the medieval world in which they had been enclosed for virtually a thousand years. The conquest of the Americas brought out the worst and some of the best of European civilization. The greedy plundering of resources and the brutal repression, enslavement, and virtual annihilation of millions of native Americans were hardly balanced by

attempts to create new institutions, convert the natives to Christianity, and foster the rights of the indigenous peoples.

In the sixteenth century, the discoveries made little impact on Europeans preoccupied with the problems of dynastic expansion and, above all, religious division. It took one hundred years of religious warfare complicated by serious political, economic and social issues—the worst series of wars and civil wars since the collapse of the Roman Empire in the west—before Europeans finally admitted that they would have to tolerate different ways to worship God. That men who were disciples of the Apostle of Peace would kill each other—often in brutal and painful fashion—aroused skepticism about Christianity itself. As one German writer put it in 1650, "Lutheran, popish, and Calvinistic, we've got all these beliefs here; but there is some doubt about where Christianity has got to."[11] It is surely no accident that the search for a stable, secular order of politics and for order in the universe through natural laws played such important roles in the seventeenth century. The religious wars of the sixteenth and seventeenth centuries opened the door to the secular perspectives that have characterized modern Western civilization.

Notes
▼ ▼ ▼

1. Quoted in J. H. Parry, *The Age of Reconnaissance: Discovery, Exploration and Settlement, 1450 to 1650* (New York, 1963), p. 33.

2. Quoted in Richard B. Reed, "The Expansion of Europe," in Richard DeMolen, ed., *The Meaning of the Renaissance and Reformation* (Boston, 1974), p. 308.

3. Miguel Leon-Portilla, ed., *The Broken Spears: The Aztec Account of the Conquest of Mexico* (Boston, 1969), p. 51.

4. Quoted in E. Harris Harbison, *The Age of Reformation* (Ithaca, N.Y., 1955), p. 109.

5. Quoted in Garrett Mattingly, *The Armada* (Boston, 1959), pp. 216–17.

6. Quoted in H. G. Koenigsberger, *Early Modern Europe: 1500–1789* (London, 1987), pp. 29–30.

7. Quoted in James Harvey Robinson, *Readings in European History* (Boston, 1934), 2: 211–12.

8. Quoted in Maurice Ashley, *The Greatness of Oliver Cromwell* (New York, 1962), p. 65.

9. Quoted in Alan Kors and Edward Peters, eds., *Witchcraft in Europe, 1100–1700* (Philadelphia, 1972), p. 112.

10. *The Complete Essays of Montaigne*, trans. Donald Frame (Stanford, 1958), p. 852.

11. Quoted in Theodore Schieder, *Handbuch der Europäischen Geschichte*, (Stuttgart, 1979), 3: 579.

Suggestions for Further Reading
▼ ▼ ▼

General works on the period from 1560 to 1650 include C. Wilson, *The Transformation of Europe, 1558–1648* (Berkeley, 1976); and H. Kamen, *The Iron Century: Social Change in Europe, 1550–1660* (New York, 1971). For an extremely detailed account of all aspects of life in the Mediterranean basin in the second half of the sixteenth century, see F. Braudel, *The Mediterranean and the Mediterranean World in the Age of Philip II*, trans. S. Reynolds, 2 vols. (New York, 1972–73).

The best general accounts of European discovery and expansion are J. H. Parry, *The Age of Reconnaissance: Discovery, Exploration and Settlement, 1450 to 1650* (New York, 1963); B. Penrose, *Travel and Discovery in the Renaissance, 1420–1620* (New York, 1962); and the brief work by J. H. Parry, *The Establishment of the European Hegemony, 1415–1715* (New York, 1961). On the technological aspects of the subject, see C. M. Cipolla, *Guns, Sails, and Empires: Technological Innovation and the Early Phases of European Expansion, 1400–1700* (New York, 1965). On the Portuguese expansion, the fundamental work is C. R. Boxer, *The Portuguese Seaborne Empire: 1415–1825* (New York, 1969); but see also W. B. Diffie and G. D. Winius, *Foundations of the Portuguese Empire, 1415–1580* (Minneapolis, 1979). The story of the discovery and settlement of America is engagingly portrayed in S. E. Morison, *The European*

Discovery of America: The Northern Voyages, A.D. 500–1600 (New York, 1971) and The Southern Voyages, A.D. 1492–1616 (New York, 1974). On Columbus, see the brief biography by J. S. Collis, Christopher Columbus (London, 1976). For a fundamental work on Spanish colonization, see J. H. Parry, The Spanish Seaborne Empire (New York, 1966). The standard work on the conquistadores is F. A. Kirkpatrick, The Spanish Conquistadores (Cleveland, 1968). Cortés is examined in W. W. Johnson, Cortés (Boston, 1975). The impact of expansion on European consciousness is explored in J. H. Elliott, The Old World and the New, 1492–1650 (Cambridge, 1970). The human and ecological effects of the interaction of New World and Old World cultures is examined thoughtfully in A. W. Crosby, The Columbian Exchange, Biological and Cultural Consequences of 1492 (Westport, Conn., 1972).

Two works by J. H. M. Salmon provide the best studies on the French Wars of Religion. They are Society in Crisis: France in the Sixteenth Century (New York, 1975) and French Government and Society in the Wars of Religion (St. Louis, 1976). For specialized studies on different aspects of the French religious wars, see N. M. Sutherland, The Massacre of St. Bartholomew and the European Conflict, 1559–1572 (New York, 1973); and F. J. Baumgartner, Radical Reactionaries: The Political Thought of the French Catholic League (Geneva, 1976). An adequate popular biography of Henry of Navarre can be found in D. Seward, The First Bourbon: Henry IV, King of France and Navarre (Boston, 1971).

Two good histories of Spain in the sixteenth century are J. H. Elliott, Imperial Spain, 1469–1716 (New York, 1964); and J. Lynch, Spain under the Habsburgs, vol. 1, Empire and Absolutism, 1516–1598 (New York, 1964). The best biographies of Philip II are P. Pierson, Philip II of Spain (London, 1975); and G. Parker, Philip II (Boston and London, 1978). Economic aspects of sixteenth-century Spain are well discussed in the classic account of J. V. Vives, An Economic History of Spain (Berkeley, 1969). On the revolt of the Netherlands, see the classic work by P. Geyl, The Revolt of the Netherlands, 1555–1609 (London, 1962); and the more recent work of G. Parker, The Dutch Revolt (London, 1977). The latter has also written an interesting account of how the Spanish army was supplied and maintained in the Low Countries in The Army of Flanders and the Spanish Road, 1567–1659 (New York, 1972).

Elizabeth's reign can be examined in three good biographies, J. Ridley, Elizabeth I (New York, 1988); P. Johnson, Elizabeth I, A Biography (New York, 1974); and L. B. Smith, Elizabeth Tudor: Portrait of a Queen (London, 1976). The Elizabethan religious settlement has been examined in C. S. Meyer, Elizabeth I and the Religious Settlement of 1559 (St. Louis, 1960). The role of the Catholic and Puritan minorities is discussed in A. Morey, The Catholic Subjects of Elizabeth I (Totowa, N.J., 1978); and P. Collinson, The Elizabethan Puritan Movement (Berkeley, 1967). Works on Elizabethan foreign policy include P. S. Crowson, Tudor Foreign Policy (London, 1973); and C. Wilson, Queen Elizabeth and the Revolt of the Netherlands (Berkeley, 1970). The classic work on the Armada is the beautifully written The Armada by G. Mattingly (Boston, 1959).

The classic study on the Thirty Years' War is C. V. Wedgwood, The Thirty Years War (Garden City, N.Y., 1961), but needs to be supplemented by the more recent works by S. H. Steinberg, The Thirty Years' War and the Conflict for European Hegemony, 1600–1660 (New York, 1966), which emphasizes the wider context of the struggle; and G. Parker, The Thirty Years War (London, 1984). The best biography of Wallenstein is G. Mann, Wallenstein: His Life Narrated, trans. C. Kessler (New York, 1976). The idea of a military revolution in the sixteenth and seventeenth centuries was first presented forcefully in M. Roberts, The Military Revolution, 1560–1660 (London, 1956), although it has not gone unchallenged; see G. Parker, Spain and the Netherlands (London, 1979), pp. 86–103.

Good general works on the period of the Puritan Revolution include G. E. Aylmer, Rebellion or Revolution? England, 1640–1660 (New York, 1986); L. Stone, Causes of the English Revolution, 1529–1642 (New York, 1972); and the brief study by R. Howell, Jr. The Origins of the English Revolution (St. Louis, 1975). Biographies of the first two Stuart monarchs include W. L. McElwee, The Wisest Fool in Christendom: The Reign of King James I and VI (New York, 1974); and J. Bowle, Charles I: A Biography (Boston, 1976). On the war itself, see C. Hill, God's Englishman: Oliver Cromwell and the English Revolution (New York, 1970); and R. Ashton, The English Civil War: Conservatism and Revolution, 1604–1649 (London, 1976). On Oliver Cromwell, see R. Howell, Jr., Cromwell (Boston, 1977); and the beautifully written popular account by A. Fraser, Cromwell: The Lord Protector (New York, 1974).

The story of the witchcraft craze can be examined in two recent works, J. B. Russell, A History of Witchcraft (London, 1980); and B. P. Levack, The Witch-Hunt in Early Modern Europe (London, 1987). Although more narrow in scope, also of great value is C. Larner, Enemies of God: The Witch-hunt in Scotland (London, 1981).

For a brief, readable guide to mannerism, see L. Murray, The Late Renaissance and Mannerism (New York, 1967). For a general survey of baroque culture, see J. S.

Held, *Seventeenth and Eighteenth Century Art: Baroque Painting, Sculpture, Architecture* (New York, 1971). The best biography of Montaigne remains D. M. Frame, *Montaigne: A Biography* (New York, 1965). On the Spanish golden century of literature, see R. O. Jones, *The Golden Age: Prose and Poetry,* which is volume 2 of *The Literary History of Spain* (London, 1971). The literature on Shakespeare is enormous. For a biography, see A. L. Rowse, *The Life of Shakespeare* (New York, 1963). A new way of viewing Shakespeare, showing the influence of the Hermetic tradition, can be found in F. A. Yates, *Shakespeare's Last Plays: A New Approach* (London, 1975).

Response to Crisis: Absolute and Limited Monarchy in the Seventeenth and Early Eighteenth Centuries (to 1715)

▼▼▼▼▼

The age of crisis from 1560 to 1650 was accompanied by a decline in religious orientation and a growing secularization that affected both the political and intellectual worlds of Europe (on the intellectual effect, see the Scientific Revolution in Chapter 17). Some historians like to speak of the seventeenth century as a turning point in the evolution of Europe to a modern state system. The idea of a united Christian Europe (the practice of a united Christendom had actually been moribund for some time) gave way to the practical realities of a system of secular states in which reason of state took precedence over the salvation of subjects' souls. Of course, these states had emerged and begun their development during the Middle Ages, but medieval ideas about statehood had still been couched in religious terms. By the seventeenth century, Christianity had so weakened its credibility in the religious wars that more and more Europeans could think of politics in secular terms.

One of the responses to the crises of the seventeenth century was a search for order and harmony. As the internal social and political rebellions and revolts died down, it became apparent that the privileged classes of society—the aristocrats—remained in control, although the various states exhibited important differences in political forms. The most general trend saw an extension of monarchical power as a stabilizing force. This development, which historians have called absolutism or absolute monarchy, was most evident in France during the flamboyant reign of

Cardinal Richelieu ▼
Frederick William
the Great Elector ▼
Louis XIV ▼
Glorious
Revolution ▼
Peter the Great ▼

•••••••• 1600 •••••••• 1625 ••••••••• 1650 •••••••••• 1675 ••••••••• 1700 •••••••••

▲ Rembrandt
▲ English, French, Dutch
Settle North America
▲ Racine
▲ Thomas Hobbes,
Leviathan
▲ John Locke, *Two Treatises
of Civil Government*

Louis XIV. But other states, such as England, responded differently to domestic crisis, and another very different system emerged where monarchs were limited by the power of their representative assemblies. Absolute and limited monarchy were the two poles of seventeenth-century state building.

▼ The Theory of Absolutism

Absolute monarchy or absolutism meant that the sovereign power or ultimate authority in the state rested in the hands of a king who claimed to rule by divine right. But what did sovereignty mean? Late sixteenth-century political theorists believed that sovereign power consisted of the authority to make laws, tax, administer justice, control the state's administrative system, and determine foreign policy. These powers made a ruler sovereign.

One of the chief theorists of divine-right monarchy in the seventeenth century was the French theologian and court preacher Bishop Jacques Bossuet (1627–1704), who expressed his ideas in a book entitled *Politics Drawn from the Very Words of Holy Scripture*. Bossuet argued first that government was divinely ordained so that humans could live in an organized society. Of all forms of government, monarchy, he averred, was the most general, most ancient, most natural, and the best, since God established kings and through them reigned over all the peoples of the world. Since kings received their power from God, their authority was absolute. They were responsible to no one (including parliaments) except God. Nevertheless, Bossuet cautioned, although a king's authority was absolute, his power was not since he was limited by the law of God. Bossuet believed there was a difference between absolute monarchy and arbitrary monarchy. The latter contradicted the rule of law and the sanctity of property and was simply lawless tyranny.

Bossuet's distinction between absolute and arbitrary government was not always easy to maintain. There was also a large gulf between the theory of absolutism as expressed by Bossuet and the practice of absolutism. As we shall see in our survey of seventeenth-century states, a monarch's absolute power was often very limited by practical realities.

▼ Absolutism in Western Europe

An examination of seventeenth-century absolutism must begin with western Europe since France during the reign of Louis XIV (1661–1715) has traditionally been regarded as the best example of the practice of absolute monarchy in the seventeenth century.

France

Although historians have recently challenged the more grandiose assumptions about the absolute power of Louis XIV, there is no doubt that France played a dominant role in European affairs by the end of the seventeenth century. French culture, language, and manners reached into all levels of European society. French diplomacy and wars overwhelmed the political affairs of western and central Europe. The court of Louis XIV seemed to be imitated everywhere in Europe. In his desire to emulate Louis XIV, the elector of Brandenburg, although a happily married German prince, added to his court "a lady who had the title and court functions, though not the pleasures, of being his mistress." Of course, French greatness depended upon a treasury filled by imposing ever-increasing tax burdens on the people while the stability of Louis's reign was magnified by the instability that had preceded it.

FOUNDATIONS OF FRENCH ABSOLUTISM The history of France before the reign of Louis XIV was hardly the story of steady, unbroken progress toward the ideal of absolute monarchy that many historians have tended to portray. The fifty years or so before Louis were a period of struggle by royal and ministerial governments to avoid the breakdown of the state. The line between order and anarchy was often a narrow one. Nevertheless, the French monarchy gradually succeeded in overcoming the threats to its power and establishing a strong monarchical authority that lasted until the French Revolution.

Thirty years of bloody civil war had ceased at the end of the sixteenth century when Henry IV established the Bourbon dynasty (see Chapter 15). Henry began the task of reconstructing a badly shattered France, aided by a forceful group of ministers, including the astute minister of finances, the duke of Sully. The accumulation of debts from the wars and a lack of sufficient revenue constituted the government's most serious problems. Sully took steps to remedy them. Tax collectors, who paid the government a lump sum of the taxes they collected in their districts, were forced to take smaller amounts for themselves. More efficiently administered direct taxes were imposed. The *gabelle*, the much-hated tax on salt, a crucial necessity for preserving food in the seventeenth century, was raised to even higher levels. Furthermore, the sale of government offices was increased by the end of Henry's reign. By 1608, half of the government's debt had been paid, and a reservoir of funds had even been accumulated in the state treasury. Sully's expenditures on roads, land drainage, and agricultural improvements helped to stimulate and improve economic growth.

Another major problem was the government's need to restore the central authority of the monarchical government in France after thirty years of civil war. Henry IV began the process by taking numerous trips through the provinces and exercising more control over the appointment of officials in the town governments. While these steps hardly constituted a "master plan for creating absolute monarchy," they did boost the role of the central government in the life of the country. But monarchical authority was still precarious when the king was unexpectedly assassinated in 1610 and succeeded by his nine-year-old son, Louis XIII. Could the new royal government survive under the regency of Henry's wife, the Italian Marie de' Medici?

At first the issue proved problematic. Marie's policy of bribing the great nobles into submission failed to prevent them from rebelling against her authority, to which she responded—successfully—by giving them more money and new positions of power. Marie's palace clique managed to remain in power until her son, Louis XIII, took personal charge of the government in 1617. Louis's problems seemed only to mount, however, until the king's council fell under the control of the cunning, competent, and clever Cardinal Richelieu in 1624. As leader of the royal council and hence the king's chief minister, Richelieu initiated policies that eventually strengthened the power of the monarchy.

It has usually been assumed that Cardinal Richelieu had a clear plan to create an absolute monarchy and a strong state abroad. In his *Political Testament,* he claimed to have promised the king to "use all my industry and all the authority it has pleased you to give me to ruin the Huguenot party, to humble the pride of the great men, to bring your subjects to their duty and to raise your name abroad to the place that is its due."[1] But recent questions about the *Testament's* authenticity make it more likely that Richelieu's primary aims were to keep himself in power and to extend the central government's authority by any means possible.

One of the dangers to royal authority came from the Huguenots. Richelieu's policy toward them was dictated by political, not religious motives, despite his being a cardinal of the Catholic church. Richelieu realized the potential danger of the fortified cities of the Huguenots to the authority of the king, especially if the Huguenots attracted foreign support as they had in the sixteenth century. Just such a situation occurred in 1627, when the Huguenot city of La Rochelle, with English aid, rebelled against the crown. One year after the rebellion was finally crushed and the city occupied by French troops, Richelieu capitalized on his success by issuing the Peace of Alais (1629), which allowed the Huguenots to keep their religious and civil rights from the Edict of Nantes, but stripped them of their private armies and fortified cities. By eliminating their political and military rights while preserving their religious ones, the Peace of Alais helped transform the Huguenots into more reliable subjects.

Richelieu acted more cautiously in "humbling the pride of the great men," the important French nobility. He understood the influential role played by the nobles in the French state. The dangerous ones were those who asserted their territorial independence when they were excluded from participating in the central government. Proceeding slowly but determinedly, Richelieu developed an efficient network of spies to uncover noble plots and then crushed the conspiracies and executed the conspirators, thereby eliminating a major threat to royal authority. Richelieu even issued edicts against dueling as a remnant of the private warfare reminiscent of medieval nobles. To Richelieu, private warfare was as bad as armed rebellion; both repudiated central state authority.

To reform and strengthen the central administration, initially for financial reasons, Richelieu sent out royal officials called intendants to the provinces to execute the orders of the central government. As the functions of the intendants grew, they came into conflict with provincial governors. Since the intendants were victorious in most of these disputes, they further strengthened the power of the crown. Richelieu proved less capable in financial matters, however. Not only was the basic system of state finances corrupt, but so many people benefited from the system's inefficiency and injustice that the government faced strong resistance when it tried to reform it. The *taille* was increased—in 1643 it was two and a half times what it had been in 1610—and crown lands were mortgaged again. Expenditures, especially the cost of war preparations, soon outstripped the additional revenues, however, and French debt continued its upward spiral under Richelieu.

The general success of Richelieu's domestic policy in strengthening the central role of the monarchy was mirrored by a successful foreign policy. That policy was dictated, first of all, by opposition to Spain, which led in turn to further anti-Habsburg activity in the Holy Roman Empire to France's east. Eventually, the Catholic cardinal of France was led to subsidize Protestant Sweden and then in 1635 to intervene directly with French troops to support the Protestant cause against the Habsburgs (see Chapter 15). Although both Richelieu and Louis XIII died before the Thirty Years' War ended, French policy had proved successful at one level since France emerged as Europe's leading power by 1648.

Richelieu died in 1642, followed five months later by King Louis XIII, who was succeeded by his son Louis XIV, then but four years old. This necessitated a regency under Anne of Austria, wife of the dead king. But she allowed Cardinal Mazarin, the trained successor of Cardinal Richelieu and her lover, to dominate the government. An Italian who had come to France as a papal legate and then become naturalized, Mazarin attempted to carry on Richelieu's policies until his death in 1661.

The most important event during Mazarin's rule was a revolt known as the Fronde, which can be viewed as the last serious attempt to limit the growing power of the crown until the French Revolution. As a foreigner, Mazarin was greatly disliked by all elements of the French population. The nobility, who particularly resented the centralized administrative power being built up at the expense of the provincial nobility, temporarily allied with the members of the Parlement in Paris, the central court of justice, which opposed the new taxes levied by the government to pay the costs of the Thirty Years' War,

and the masses of Paris, who were also dissatisfied with the additional taxes. The first Fronde (1648–1649) broke out in Paris, led by the Parlement of Paris, whose members were nobles of the robe, the service nobility of lawyers and administrators. The first revolt was ended by compromise. The second Fronde, begun in 1650, was led by the nobles of the sword, whose ancestors were medieval nobles. They were interested in overthrowing Mazarin for their own purposes: to secure their positions and increase their own power. The second Fronde was

▼ **Cardinal Richelieu.** A key figure in the emergence of a strong monarchy in France was Cardinal Richelieu, pictured here in a portrait by Philippe de Champagne. Chief minister to Louis XIII, Richelieu strengthened royal authority by eliminating the private armies and fortified cities of the Huguenots and by crushing aristocratic conspiracies. His foreign policy elevated France to the position of Europe's leading power by the close of the Thirty Years' War.

Louis XIV: Kingly Advice

▼ ▼ ▼

*T*hroughout his reign, Louis XIV was always on stage, acting the role of the wise "Grand Monarch." In his Memoirs for the Dauphin, Louis presented a frank collection of precepts for the education of his oldest son and heir to the throne. These Memoirs were begun in 1661, after Louis became a father, and were added to over the next twenty years.

Louis XIV, *Memoirs for the Dauphin*

Kings are often obliged to do things which go against their inclinations and offend their natural goodness. They should love to give pleasure and yet they must often punish and destroy persons on whom by nature they wish to confer benefits. The interest of the state must come first. One must constrain one's inclinations and not put oneself in the position of berating oneself because one could have done better in some important affair but did not because of some private interest, because one was distracted from the attention one should have for the greatness, the good and the power of the state. Often there are troublesome places where is it is difficult to make out what one should do. One's ideas are confused. As long as this lasts, one can refrain form making a decision. But as soon as one has fixed one's mind upon something which seems best to do, it must be acted upon. This is what enabled me to succeed so often in what I have done. The mistakes which I made, and which gave me infinite trouble, were the result of the desire to please or of allowing myself to accept too carelessly the opinions of others. Nothing is more dangerous than weakness of any kind whatsoever. In order to command others, one must raise oneself above them and once one has heard the reports from every side one must come to a decision upon the basis of one's own judgment, without anxiety but always with the concern not to command anything which is of itself unworthy either of one's place in the world or of the greatness of the state. Princes with good intentions and some knowledge of their affairs, either from experience or from study and great diligence in making themselves capable, find numerous cases which instruct them that they must give special care and total application to everything. One must be on guard against oneself, resist one's own tendencies, and always by on guard against one's own natural bent. The craft of a king is great, noble and delightful when one feels worthy of doing well whatever one promises to do. But it is not exempt from troubles, weariness and worries. Sometimes uncertainty causes despair, and when one has spent a reasonable time in examining an affair, one must make a decision and take the step which one believes to be best. When one has the state in view, one works for one's self. The good of the one constitutes the glory of the other. When the former is fortunate, eminent and powerful, he who is the cause thereof becomes glorious and consequently should find more enjoyment than his subjects in all the pleasant things of life for himself and for them. When one has made a mistake, it must be corrected as soon as possible, and no other consideration must stand in the way, not even kindness.

---

crushed by 1652, a task made easier when the nobles began fighting each other instead of Mazarin. With the end of the Fronde, a vast number of Frenchmen concluded that the best hope for stability in France lay in the crown. When Mazarin died in 1661, the greatest of the seventeenth-century monarchs, Louis XIV, took over supreme power.

THE REIGN OF LOUIS XIV (1661–1715) The day after Cardinal Mazarin's death, Louis XIV, at the age of twenty-three, expressed his determination to be a real king and the sole ruler of France:

Up to this moment I have been pleased to entrust the government of my affairs to the late Cardinal. It is now time that I govern them myself. You [secretaries and ministers of state] will assist me with your counsels when I ask for them. I request and order you to seal no orders except by my command, . . . I order you not to sign anything, not even a passport . . . without my command; to render account to me personally each day and to favor no one.[2]

His mother, who was well aware of Louis's proclivity for fun and games and getting into the beds of the maids in the royal palace, laughed aloud at these words. But Louis was quite serious.

Louis proved willing to pay the price of being a strong ruler (see the box on p. 526). He established a conscientious routine from which he seldom deviated, but he did not look upon his duties as drudgery since he judged his royal profession to be "grand, noble, and delightful." Eager for glory, Louis created a grand and majestic spectacle at the court of Versailles (see Daily Life at the Court of Versailles later in the chapter). Consequently, Louis and his court came to set the standard for monarchies and aristocracies all over Europe. Less than fifty years after his death, the great French writer Voltaire used the title "Age of Louis XIV" to describe his history of Europe from 1661 to 1715. Historians have tended to use it ever since.

Although Louis may have believed in the theory of absolute monarchy and consciously fostered the myth of himself as the Sun King, the source of light for all of his people, historians are quick to point out that the realities fell far short of the aspirations. Despite the centralizing efforts of Cardinals Richelieu and Mazarin, France still possessed a bewildering system of overlapping authorities in the seventeenth century. Provinces had their own regional parlements, their own local Estates, their own sets of laws. Members of the high nobility with their huge estates and clients among the lesser nobility still exercised much authority. Both towns and provinces possessed privileges and powers seemingly from time immemorial that they would not easily relinquish. Much of Louis's success rested less on the modernization of administrative machinery, as is frequently claimed, than on his clever and adroit manipulation of the traditional priorities and values of French society.

One of the keys to Louis's power was that he was able to restructure the central policy-making machinery of government because it was part of his own court and household. The royal court was an elaborate structure that served three purposes simultaneously: it was the personal household of the king, the location of central governmental machinery, and the place where powerful subjects came to find favors and offices for themselves and their clients as well as the main arena where rival aristocratic factions jostled for power. The greatest danger to Louis's personal rule came from the very high nobles and princes of the blood (the royal princes) who considered it their natural function to assert the policy-making role of royal ministers. Louis eliminated this threat by removing them from the royal council, the chief administrative body of the king and overseer of the central machinery of government, and enticing them to his court where he could keep them preoccupied with court life and out of politics.

Instead of the high nobility and royal princes, Louis relied for his ministers on nobles who came from relatively new aristocratic families. Such were Michel Le Tellier, secretary of state for war; Hugues de Lionne, secretary for foreign affairs; and Nicholas Fouquet, superintendent of finances. His ministers were expected to be subservient; said Louis, "I had no intention of sharing my authority with them." When Fouquet began to flaunt the enormous wealth and power he had amassed in the King's service, Louis ordered his arrest and imprisoned

▼ **Louis XIV.** Louis XIV was determined to be the sole ruler of France. Louis eliminated the threat of the high nobility by removing them from the royal council and replacing them with relatively new aristocrats whose lives he could dominate. He was successful in converting many Protestants and created a standing army under the rule of the king. His reign was troubled by ever-increasing financial problems. This portrait by Hyacinth Rigaud captures the king's sense of royal dignity and grandeur.

him for life. Fouquet was replaced in the king's council by Colbert, another noble of bourgeois origin. Louis's domination of his ministers and secretaries gave him control of the central policy-making machinery of government and thus authority over the traditional areas of monarchical power: the formulation of foreign policy, the making of war and peace, the assertion of the secular power of crown against any religious authority, and the ability to levy taxes to fulfill these functions.

According to recent historical scholarship, however, Louis had considerably less success with the internal administration of the kingdom. The traditional groups and institutions of French society—the nobles, officials, town councils, guilds, and representative Estates in some provinces—were simply too powerful for the king to have direct control over the lives of his subjects. Louis had three ways to rule the provinces. Officially, he worked through hereditary officeholders, usually aristocrats, who were untrustworthy since they were always inclined to balance the king's wishes against their own interests. The king also had his intendants as direct royal agents, but they also proved unreliable and often provoked disturbances in the provinces by their actions. They were not so much the instruments by which the central government carried out decisions, but simply the "eyes and ears of the ministers" in the provinces. Finally, the king had an informal system of royal patronage, which Louis used successfully. The king and his ministers enlisted the aid of nobles and senior churchmen and their clients by granting them offices and pensions. The control of the central government over the provinces and the people, then, was carried out by the careful bribery of the important people to see that the king's policies were executed. Local officials could still obstruct the execution of policies they disliked, indicating clearly that a so-called absolute monarch was not always that absolute.

The maintenance of religious harmony had long been considered an area of monarchical power. The desire to keep it led Louis into conflict with the French Huguenots and the papacy. Louis XIV did not want to allow Protestants to practice their faith in largely Catholic France. Perhaps he was motivated by religion, but it is more likely that Louis, who believed in the motto, "one king, one law, one faith," felt that the existence of this minority undermined his own political authority. His anti-Protestant policy, aimed at converting the Huguenots to Catholicism, began mildly by offering rewards, but escalated by 1681 to a policy of forced conversions. The most favored method was to quarter French soldiers in Huguenot communities and homes with the freedom to misbehave so that their hosts would "see the light quickly." This approach did produce thousands of immediate conversions. In October 1685, Louis issued the Edict of Fontainebleau. In addition to revoking the Edict of Nantes, the new edict provided for the destruction of Huguenot churches and the closing of their schools. Although they were forbidden to leave France, it is estimated that 200,000 Huguenots left for shelter in England, the United Provinces, and the German states. Through their exodus, France lost people who had commercial and industrial skills, although some modern scholars have argued this had only a minor impact on the French economy. Perhaps a more important effect of the Huguenot dispersal was the increased hatred of France that the Huguenot émigrés stirred up in their adopted Protestant countries.

Whatever his motives, Louis's anti-Protestant policy was not aimed at currying papal favor. Louis was a defender of Gallicanism, the belief that the monarchy possessed certain rights over the Catholic church in France, irrespective of papal powers. In the 1670s, Louis claimed the *régale* or the right of the French king to appoint the lower clergy and collect the revenues of a diocese when it was vacant. Pope Innocent XI condemned Louis's actions, threatening him with reprisals. Louis responded by calling a special assembly of French clergy and directing them to draw up a Declaration of Gallican Liberties. This document claimed that the pope's authority in France was limited to spiritual matters and that even in spiritual matters, the pope was subject to the decisions of a general council. The pope protested this challenge to papal authority and the possibility of a schism loomed large. But neither side wanted to go that far. After Innocent's death, a compromise was arranged, and by 1693 the Gallican articles had been retracted.

The cost of building Versailles and other palaces, maintaining his court, and pursuing his wars made finances a crucial issue for Louis XIV. He was most fortunate in having the services of Jean-Baptiste Colbert (1619–1683) as controller-general of finances. Colbert sought to increase the wealth and power of France through general adherence to that loose collection of economic policies called mercantilism, which stressed government regulation of economic activities to benefit the state (see Mercantilism later in the chapter). To decrease the need for imports and increase exports, Colbert attempted to expand the quantity and improve the quality of French manufactured goods. He founded new luxury industries, such as the royal tapestry works at Beauvais; invited Venetian glassmakers and Flemish clothmakers to France; drew up instructions regulating the quality of goods produced; oversaw the training of the workers' and granted special privileges, including tax exemptions, loans, and subsidies to those who established new industries. To improve communications and the transportation of goods internally, he built roads and canals. To decrease imports directly, he raised tariffs on foreign manufactured goods, especially English and Dutch cloth, and created a merchant marine to facilitate the conveyance of French goods.

Colbert was not really much of an innovator, especially in his financial policies. France still depended on the system of tax farming. Moreover, the sale of offices, which remained a common practice, absorbed huge revenues as officeholders sought to take financial advantage of their positions. As one judge expressed it: "The ministry of the judges, their jurisdiction and distribution of justice are nothing but a shop where the offices they have purchased wholesale are sold at retail." Vast exemptions for clergy and nobility as well as towns and provinces made the collection of revenue highly irrational. Colbert was unable or unwilling to change the basic system, although he attempted to correct the most obvious abuses and eliminate some of the tax exemptions. While Colbert's policies are given much credit for fostering the development of manufacturing, some historians are dubious about the usefulness of many of his mercantilistic policies. Regulations were often evaded, and the imposition of high tariffs brought foreign retaliation. French trading companies entered the scene too late to be really competitive with the British and the Dutch. And above all, Colbert's economic policies, which were geared to making his king more powerful, were ultimately self-defeating. As Colbert collected the finances with which Louis could make war, Louis depleted the treasury faster than Colbert could fill it. At the same time, the burden of taxes fell increasingly upon the peasants who still constituted the overwhelming majority of the French population.

The increase in royal power that Louis pursued as well as his desire for military glory had an effect on the development of the military. During Louis's reign, the French army was transformed from a host of small armies dominated by provincial nobles to a state activity, a standing army subject to the monarch's command. Since the first real standing armies had been organized by Venice and the United Provinces, it was neither new nor a product of absolute monarchy. But French resources enabled Louis to develop one larger than Europe had ever seen.

Under the secretary of war, François le Tellier, the marquis of Louvois, France developed a professional army numbering 100,000 men in peacetime and 400,000 in time of war. Unable to fill the ranks with volunteers, the French resorted to conscription, although this practice created a major problem as unwilling soldiers were eager to desert. But the new standing armies did not exist to be admired. Louis and other monarchs used them to make war an almost incessant activity of the seventeenth and eighteenth centuries.

THE WARS OF LOUIS XIV   Louis XIV had a great proclivity for war. Historians have debated the assertion that Louis pursued war to expand his kingdom to its "natural frontiers"—the Alps, Pyrenees, and Rhine River. But few doubt his desire to achieve the prestige and military glory befitting a Sun King as well as his dynastic ambition, his desire to ensure the domination of his Bourbon dynasty over European affairs. His ends soon outstripped his means, however, as his ambitions roused much of Europe to form coalitions that even he could not overcome.

In 1667, Louis began his first war (called the War of Devolution after a legal term in Louis's preliminary demands) by invading the Spanish Netherlands to his north and Franche-Comté to the east. Despite initial successes, a Triple Alliance of the Dutch, English, and Swedes caused him to sue for peace in 1668 and accept a few towns in the Spanish Netherlands for his efforts. He never forgave the Dutch for arranging the Triple Alliance while Colbert, for economic reasons, became obsessed with defeating the Dutch. In 1672, after isolating the Dutch and paying huge subsidies to Charles II of England to declare war on them, France invaded the United Provinces. Initial successes caused internal dissension in the Netherlands, allowing William III, the prince of Orange, to gain the upper hand and create a new coalition of Brandenburg, Spain, and the Holy Roman emperor. Louis was forced to negotiate and ended the Dutch War by making peace at Nimwegen in 1678. While Dutch territory remained intact, France received Franche-Comté from Spain, serving merely to stimulate Louis's appetite for even more land.

This time, Louis moved eastward against the Holy Roman Empire, which he perceived from his previous war as feeble and unable to resist. The piecemeal and pseudo-legal annexation of the provinces of Alsace and Lorraine was followed by the occupation of the city of Strasbourg, a move that led to widespread protest and the formation of a new coalition. The creation of this League of Augsburg, consisting of Spain, the Holy Roman emperor, the United Provinces, Sweden, and England led to Louis's third war, the War of the League of

Augsburg (1689–1697). This bitterly contested eight-year struggle brought economic depression and famine to France. The Treaty of Ryswick ending the war forced Louis to give up most of his conquests in the empire, although he was allowed to keep Strasbourg and part of Alsace. It was hardly worth the bloodshed and misery he had caused the French people.

Louis's fourth war, the War of the Spanish Succession (1702–1713), was over bigger stakes, the succession to the Spanish throne. Charles II, the sickly and childless Habsburg ruler, left the throne of Spain in his will to a grandson of Louis XIV. When the latter became King Philip V of Spain after Charles's death, the suspicion that Spain and France would eventually be united in the

same dynastic family caused the formation of a new coalition, determined to prevent the certain destruction of the European balance of power by a Bourbon hegemony. This coalition of England, Holland, Habsburg Austria, and German states opposed France and Spain in a war that dragged on in Europe and the colonial empires in North America until the Peaces of Utrecht in 1713 and Rastatt in 1714. Although these peace treaties confirmed Philip V as the Spanish ruler, initiating a Spanish Bourbon dynasty that would last into the twentieth century, they also affirmed that the thrones of Spain and France were to remain separated. The Spanish Netherlands, Milan, and Naples were given to Austria while the newly emerging Brandenburg-Prussia gained addi-

▼ **Map 16.1** The Wars of Louis XIV.

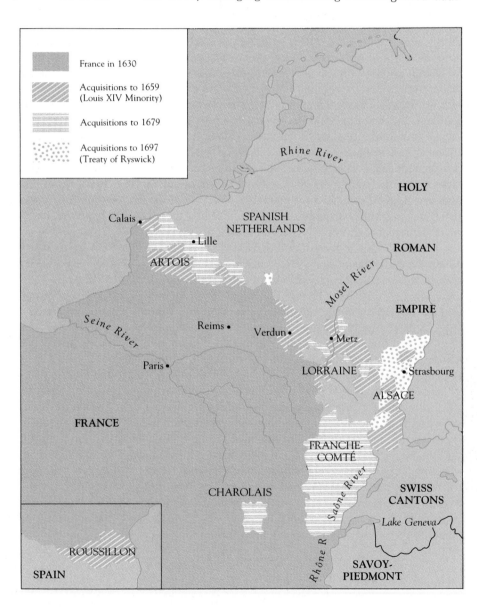

tional territories. The real winner at Utrecht, however, was England, which received Gibraltar as well as the French possessions in America of Newfoundland, Hudson's Bay Territory, and Nova Scotia. While France, by its sheer size and position, remained a great power, England had emerged as a formidable naval power.

Only two years after the treaty, the Sun King was dead, leaving France impoverished and surrounded by enemies. The seventy-six-year-old monarch seemed remorseful when he said to his successor on his deathbed:

> Soon you will be King of a great kingdom. I urge you not to forget your duty to God; remember that you owe everything to Him. Try to remain at peace with your neighbors. I loved war too much. Do not follow me in that or in overspending. Take advice in everything; try to find the best course and follow it. Lighten your people's burden as soon as possible, and do what I have had the misfortune not to do myself.[3]

Did Louis mean it? Did Louis ever realize how tarnished the glory he had sought had become? One of his subjects wrote ten years before the end of his reign: "Even the people . . . who have so much loved you, and have placed such trust in you, begin to lose their love, their trust, and even their respect. . . . They believe you have no pity for their sorrows, that you are devoted only to your power and your glory."[4] In any event, the advice to his successor was probably not remembered; his great-grandson was only five years old.

DAILY LIFE AT THE COURT OF VERSAILLES   The court of Louis XIV at Versailles set a standard that was soon followed by other European rulers. A decision was made in 1669 to convert a hunting lodge at Versailles, located near Paris, into a chateau that made splendor "a permanent and brilliantly organized form of public service." Not until 1688, after untold sums of money had been spent and tens of thousands of workers had labored incessantly, was most of the construction completed on the enormous palace that housed thousands of people.

Versailles served many purposes. It was the residence of the king; a reception hall for state affairs; an office building for the members of the king's government; and home for thousands of royal officials and aristocratic courtiers. Versailles became a symbol for the French absolutist state and the power of the Sun King, Louis XIV. This lavish court was intended to overawe subjects and impress foreign powers as a visible demonstration of France's superiority and wealth. If an age's largest buildings reflect its values, then Versailles is a reminder of the seventeenth-century preoccupation with monarchical authority and magnificence.

Versailles also served a practical political purpose. It became home to the high nobility and princes of the blood (the royal princes), those powerful figures who had aspired to hold the policy-making role of royal ministers. By keeping them involved in the myriad activities that made up daily life at the court of Versailles, Louis excluded them from real power while allowing them to share in the mystique of power as companions of the king.

Life at Versailles became a court ceremony with Louis XIV at the center of it all. The king had little privacy;

▼ **Palace of Versailles.** Between 1669 and 1688, Louis XIV spent untold sums of money in the construction of a new royal residence at Versailles. The palace of Versailles also housed the members of the king's government and served as home for thousands of French nobles. As the largest royal residence in Europe, Versailles impressed foreigners and became a source of envy for other rulers.

only when he visited his wife or mother or mistress or met with ministers was he free of the noble courtiers who swarmed about the palace. Most daily ceremonies were carefully staged, such as those attending Louis's rising from bed, dining, praying, attending mass, and going to bed. A mob of nobles aspired to assist the king in carrying out these solemn activities. It was considered a great honor for a noble to be chosen to hand the king his shirt while dressing. But why did nobles participate in so many ceremonies, some of which were so obviously demeaning? Active involvement in the activities at Versailles was the king's prerequisite for obtaining the offices, titles, and pensions that only he could grant. This policy reduced great nobles and ecclesiastics, the "people of quality," to a plane of equality, allowing Louis to exercise control over them and prevent them from interfering in the real lines of power. To maintain their social prestige, the "people of quality" were expected to adhere to rigid standards of court etiquette appropriate to their rank.

Indeed, court etiquette became so complex that it was virtually a life study. Nobles and royal princes were arranged in an elaborate order of seniority and expected to follow certain rules of precedence. Who could sit down and on what kind of chair was a subject of much debate. Who could sit where at meals with the king was also carefully regulated. On one occasion, when the wife of a minister sat closer to the king than a duchess at dinner, Louis XIV became so angry that he did not eat for the rest of the evening. Another time, Louis reproached his talkative brother for the sin of helping himself to a dish before Louis had touched it with the biting words: "I perceive that you are no better able to control your hands than your tongue."

Besides the daily and occasional ceremonies that made up the regular side of court life at Versailles and the many hours a day Louis spent with his ministers on affairs of state, daily life at Versailles included numerous forms of entertainment. While he was healthy, Louis and his courtiers hunted at least once a week; members of the royal family nearly every day. Walks through the Versailles gardens, boating trips, the performance of tragedies and comedies, ballets, and concerts all provided sources of pleasure (see the box on p. 533). Louis also held an *appartement* three evenings a week when the king was "at home" to his court from seven to ten. The *appartement* was characterized by a formal informality. Relaxed rules of etiquette even allowed people to sit down in the presence of their superiors. The evening's entertainment began with a concert, followed by games of billiards or cards, and ended with a sumptuous buffet.

One form of entertainment—gambling—became an obsession at Versailles. Although a few of the courtiers made a living by their gambling skill, many others were simply amateurs. This did not stop them from playing regularly and losing enormous sums of money. One princess described the scene: "Here in France as soon as people get together they do nothing but play [cards]; they play for frightful sums, and the players seem bereft of their senses. . . . One shouts at the top of his voice, another strikes the table with his fist, a third blasphemes. . . . it is horrible to watch them."[5] Louis did not share the princess's sensibilities; he was not horrified by an activity that kept the Versailles nobles busy and out of mischief.

This obsession with gambling should not surprise us. The lack of really meaningful activities in a world geared to formal and routine ceremonies led inevitably to bore-

▼ **Interior of Versailles: Hall of Mirrors.** Pictured here is the exquisite Hall of Mirrors at Versailles. A number of daily and occasional ceremonies dominated the lives of the residents of Versailles. Rules of etiquette became so complex that they guided every aspect of behavior. Various forms of entertainment were also available to the residents, chief of which was gambling.

Travels with the King
▼ ▼ ▼

The duc de Saint-Simon was one of many noble court-iers who lived at Versailles and had firsthand experi-ence of court life there. In his Memoirs, *he left a contro-versial and critical account of Louis XIV and his court. In this selection, he describes the price court ladies paid for the "privilege" of riding with the great king.*

Duc de Saint-Simon, Memoirs

The King always traveled with his carriage full of women: His mistresses, his bastard daughters, his daughters-in-law, sometimes Madame [the wife of the king's brother], and the other ladies of the court when there was room. This was the case for hunts, and trips to Fontainebleau, Chantilly, Compiègne, and the like. . . . In his carriage during these trips there was always an abundance and variety of things to eat: meats, pastries, and fruit. Before the carriage had gone a quarter league the King would ask who was hungry. He never ate between meals, not even a fruit, but he enjoyed watching others stuff them-selves. It was mandatory to eat, with appetite and good grace, and to be gay; otherwise, he showed his displeasure by telling the guilty party she was putting on airs and trying to be coy. The same ladies or prin-cesses who had eaten that day at the King's table were obliged to eat again as though they were weak from hunger. What is more, the women were forbidden to mention their personal needs, which in any case they could not have relieved without embarrassment, since there were guards and members of the King's household in front and in back of the carriage, and officers and equerries riding alongside the doors. The dust they kicked up choked everyone in the carriage, but the King, who loved fresh air, insisted that all the windows remain open. He would have been ex-tremely displeased if one of the ladies had pulled a curtain to protect herself from the sun, the wind, or the cold.

He pretended not to notice his passengers' discom-fort, and always traveled very fast, with the usual number of relays. Sickness in the carriage was a de-merit which ruled out further invitations. . . . When the king had to relieve himself he did not hesitate to stop the carriage and get out; but the ladies were not allowed to budge.

---

dom and hence gambling, as well as sexual intrigues, gossip, and backbiting. One participant related that at "the Court the least circumstances made for much talk; all there is futile and of little use." How could it have been otherwise? When people engage for hours in petty quarrels over insignificant matters of precedence, we can be sure that we are witnessing the tragedy of people desperate to find some meaning in their empty lives.

Spain

At the beginning of the seventeenth century, Spain possessed the most populous empire in the world, con-trolling almost all of South America and a number of settlements in Asia and Africa. To most Europeans, Spain still seemed the greatest power of the age, but the reality was quite different. The rich provinces of the Netherlands would soon be lost. The treasury was empty; Philip II went bankrupt in 1596 from excessive expenditures on the Armada while his successor Philip III did the same in 1607 by spending a fortune on his court. The armed forces were out-of-date; the govern-ment inefficient; and the commercial class weak in the midst of a suppressed peasantry, a luxury-loving class of nobles, and an oversupply of priests and monks. Spain continued to play the role of a great power, but appear-ances were deceiving.

During the reign of Philip III (1598–1621), many of Spain's weaknesses became only too apparent. Interested only in court luxury or miracle-working relics, Philip III allowed his first minister, the greedy duke of Lerma, to run the country. The aristocratic Lerma's primary inter-est was amassing power and wealth for himself and his family. While important offices were filled with his rel-atives, crucial problems went unsolved. His most drastic decision was to expel all remaining Moriscos (see Chap-ter 13) from Spain, a spectacular blunder in view of their importance to Spain's economy. The loss of labor and rents in the province of Valencia, for example, brought immediate economic disaster there. During Lerma's mis-rule, the gap between privileged and unprivileged grew wider. Notably absent was a prosperous urban middle class, as an astute public official observed in 1600. Spain, he said, had come "to be an extreme contrast of rich and poor, . . . we have rich who loll at ease, or poor who beg, and we lack people of the middling sort, whom neither wealth nor poverty prevents from pursuing the rightful king of business enjoined by natural law."[6] An apparent factor in this imbalance was the dominant role played by the Catholic church. While maintaining strict orthodoxy by efficient inquisitorial courts, the church prospered and attracted ever-larger numbers of clerics to its ranks. The Castilian Cortes (parliament) was informed in 1626 that Castile alone possessed 9,000 monasteries for men. The existence of so many official celibates offered little help to Spain's declining economy or its declining population.

The early reign of Philip IV (1621–1665) seemed to offer hope for a revival of Spain's energies, especially in the capable hands of his chief minister, Gaspar de Guz-

man, the count of Olivares. This clever, hard-working, and power-hungry statesman dominated the king's every move and worked to revive the interests of the monarchy. A flurry of domestic reform decrees, aimed at curtailing the power of the church and the landed aristocracy, was soon followed by a political reform program whose purpose was to further centralize the government of all Spain and its possessions in monarchical hands. All of these efforts met with little real success, however, since both the number (estimated at one-fifth of the population) and power of the Spanish aristocracy made them too strong to curtail in any significant fashion. At the same time, most of the efforts of Olivares and Philip were undermined by their desire to pursue Spain's imperial glory and a series of internal revolts.

Participation in the Thirty Years' War led Spain to become involved in the 1620s, 1630s, and 1640s in a series of frightfully expensive military campaigns that produced more economic misery for overtaxed Spanish subjects. Unfortunately for Spain, they also failed to produce victory. As Olivares wrote to King Philip IV, "God wants us to make peace; for He is depriving us visibly and absolutely of all the means of war."[7] At the same time, increasingly heavy financial exactions to fight the wars led to internal revolts, first in Catalonia, the northeastern province, in 1640, then in the same year in Portugal, which had been joined to Spain in 1580 by Philip II, and finally in the Italian dependency of Naples in 1647. Despite years of civil war, the Spanish government regained control of all these territories except for Portugal, which successfully reestablished the monarchy of the old ruling house of Braganza when Duke John was made King John IV in 1640.

The defeats in Europe and the internal revolts of the 1640s ended any illusions about Spain's greatness. The actual extent of Spain's economic difficulties is still a much debated historical topic, but there is no question about Spain's foreign losses. Dutch independence was formally recognized by the Peace of Westphalia in 1648, and the Peace of the Pyrenees with France in 1659 meant the surrender of Artois and the outlying defenses of the Spanish Netherlands as well as certain border regions, such as the Catalan province of Roussillon, which went to France. It did not augur well for the future of Spain that the king who followed Philip IV, Charles II (1665–1700), perhaps unfairly characterized by historians as a "moribund half-wit," was only of interest to the rest of Europe because he had no heirs. The French and Austrians anxiously awaited his death in the hope of placing a member of their royal houses on the Spanish throne. When he died in 1700, the War of the Spanish Succession soon followed.

▼ Absolutism in Central, Eastern, and Northern Europe

During the seventeenth century, a development of great importance for the modern Western world took place in central and eastern Europe, the appearance of three new powers: Prussia, Austria, and Russia.

The German States

The Peace of Westphalia, which officially ended the Thirty Years' War in 1648, left each of the three hundred or more German states comprising the Holy Roman Empire virtually autonomous and sovereign. After 1648, the Holy Roman Empire was largely a diplomatic fiction; as the French intellectual Voltaire said in the eighteenth century, the Holy Roman Empire was neither holy, nor Roman, nor an empire. Properly speaking, there was no German state, but over three hundred "Germanies." Of these states, two emerged in the seventeenth and eighteenth centuries as great European powers.

BRANDENBURG-PRUSSIA   For much of the seventeenth century, there was little about the German state of Brandenburg that would lead one to think it would ever be a prosperous and powerful state. Indeed, the German states of Bavaria and Saxony would have seemed better candidates for a brilliant future. The development of Brandenburg as a state was largely the story of the Hohenzollern dynasty, which in 1417 had come to rule the rather insignificant principality in northeastern Germany. In 1609, the Hohenzollerns inherited some lands in the Rhine valley in western Germany; nine years later, they received the duchy of Prussia (or east Prussia). By the seventeenth century, then, the dominions of the house of Hohenzollern, now called Brandenburg-Prussia, consisted of three disconnected masses in western, central, and eastern Germany. Although it would appear that Hohenzollern long-range policy would seek to connect the three lands, the Hohenzollerns' more immediate concern was to establish their power in these diverse territories. Each had its own privileges, customs, and loyalties; only the person of the Hohenzollern ruler connected them. Unlike France, an old kingdom possessing a reasonably common culture based on almost a thousand years of history, Brandenburg-Prussia was an artificial creation, highly vulnerable and dependent upon its ruling dynasty to create a state where one simply did not exist.

The first important Hohenzollern ruler and the one who laid the foundation for the Prussian state was Frederick William the Great Elector (1640–1688), who came to power in the midst of the Thirty Years' War. Realizing that Brandenburg-Prussia as a small, open territory with no natural frontiers for defense was vulnerable to the powerful and unscrupulous neighbors that surrounded it, he came to the conclusion that his only hope for survival was a competent and efficient standing army with which he could force stronger states to take him into their calculations. He was adverse to actually using the army, however, preferring diplomatic maneuver to war to gain his ends. Although largely successful, his emphasis on a standing army also made Brandenburg-Prussia into a basically militaristic state.

In 1648, at the end of the Thirty Years' War in Germany, Frederick William had amassed an army of 8,000 men, sufficiently large to get a hearing at the peace gathering at Westphalia and to receive the territories of Magdeburg and eastern Pomerania. After 1648, he continued to enlarge the army so that by 1678, he possessed a force of 40,000 men that absorbed over 50 percent of the state's revenues. To sustain the army and his own power, Frederick William realized the need for a regular source of income. The Estates of old Brandenburg and the new territories jealously guarded their prerogatives, especially their right to raise taxes. The Great Elector broke the power of the Estates and freed himself to raise money by establishing the General War Commissariat to levy taxes for the army and oversee its growth and training. The Commissariat soon evolved into an agency for civil government as well, collecting the new excise tax in the towns and overseeing the foundation of new industrial and commercial enterprises. Directly responsible to the elector, the new bureaucratic machine became his chief instrument for governing the state. Many of its officials were members of the Prussian landed aristocracy, the Junkers, who also served as officers in the all-important army.

The loyalty of the nobles to Frederick William's policies was derived from the tacit agreement that he made with them. In order to eliminate the power that the members of the nobility could exercise in their provincial Estates-General, Frederick William made a deal with the nobles. In return for a free hand in running the government (in other words, for depriving the provincial Estates of their power), nobles were given almost unlimited power over their peasants, exempted from taxation, and awarded the highest ranks in the army and the Commissariat with the understanding that they would not challenge the elector's political control. As far as the peasants were concerned, the nobles were allowed to appropriate their land and bind them to the soil as serfs.

To build Brandenburg-Prussia's economy, Frederick William followed the fashionable mercantilist policies, using high tariffs, subsidies, and monopolies to manufacturers to stimulate domestic industry and building roads and canals. Wisely, Frederick William invited people from other countries to settle in Brandenburg-Prussia and, in 1685, issued an edict encouraging the dispossessed Huguenots from Louis XIV's France to come to Prussia. Almost 20,000 did. Frederick William continued, however, to favor the interests of the nobility at the expense of the commercial and industrial middle classes in the towns.

In these ways, Frederick William the Great Elector laid the foundations for the Prussian state, although it would be misleading to think that he had a modern conception of that state. He thought nothing of amending his will to give pieces of his supposedly unified state as independent principalities to his younger sons. He was succeeded by his son Frederick III (1688–1713), who, less rigid and militaristic than his father, spent much of the treasury building palaces, creating a university, and imitating the splendors of the court of Louis XIV. He did make one significant contribution to the development of Prussia. In return for aiding the Holy Roman emperor in the War of the Spanish Succession, he received officially the title of king in Prussia. Elector Frederick III was transformed into King Frederick I, and Brandenburg-Prussia became simply Prussia. In the eighteenth century, Prussia emerged as a great power on the European stage.

THE EMERGENCE OF AUSTRIA The Austrian Habsburgs had long played a significant role in European politics.

They were Holy Roman emperors and had important family connections with the wealthier Habsburgs of Spain. In the seventeenth century, these two bastions of their power collapsed. By the end of the Thirty Years' War, the Habsburg hopes of creating an empire in Germany had been dashed. At the same time, Spain's decline made that relationship less rewarding, and it ended completely at the beginning of the eighteenth century when Spain came into the hands of the French house of Bourbon. In the seventeenth century, then, the house of Austria made an important transition; the German empire was lost, but a new empire was created in eastern and southeastern Europe.

The nucleus of the new Austrian Empire remained the traditional Austrian hereditary possessions: Lower and Upper Austria, Carinthia, Carniola, Styria, and Tyrol. To these had been added the kingdom of Bohemia, which had been reclaimed by the Habsburgs during the Thirty Years' War. Since 1526, the Habsburg ruler had also been king of Hungary, although he exercised little real power except in northwest Hungary. The eastern Hungarian principality of Transylvania remained independent while the central parts of Hungary were controlled by the Ottoman Turks.

Leopold I (1658–1705) encouraged the movement of the Austrian Empire eastward. He was sorely challenged by the revival of Turkish power in the seventeenth century. Having moved into Transylvania, the Turks eventually pushed westward and laid siege to Vienna in 1683. Only a dramatic rescue by a combined army of Austrians, Saxons, Bavarians, and Poles saved the Austrian

▼ **Map 16.2** Brandenburg-Prussia.

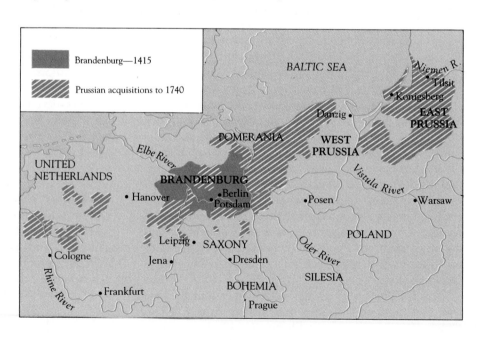

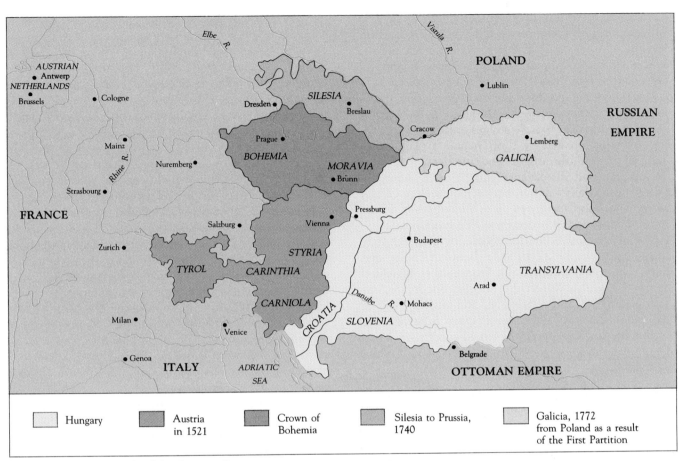

▼ **Map 16.3** The Growth of the Austrian Empire.

city. A European army, led by the Austrians, counterattacked and decisively defeated the Turks in 1687. Austria took control of Hungary, Transylvania, Croatia, and Slovenia, thus establishing an Austrian Empire in southeastern Europe. At the end of the War of the Spanish Succession, Austria gained possession of the Spanish Netherlands and received formal recognition of its occupation of the Spanish possessions in Italy, namely Milan, Mantua, Sardinia, and Naples. By the beginning of the eighteenth century, the house of Austria had acquired a new empire of considerable size.

The Austrian monarchy, however, never become a highly centralized, absolutist state, primarily because it contained so many different national groups. The Austrian Empire remained a collection of territories held together by a personal union. The Hapburg emperor was archduke of Austria, king of Bohemia, and king of Hungary. Each of these areas, however, had its own laws, Estates-General, and political life. There was no common sentiment to tie the regions together; only the landed aristocracies everywhere provided a common bond of service to the house of Habsburg, whether as military officers or government bureaucrats. The nobles in the Austrian Empire remained quite strong and were also allowed to impose serfdom on their peasants. By the beginning of the eighteenth century, Austria was a populous empire in central Europe of great potential military strength.

Italy

By 1530, Emperor Charles V had managed to defeat the French armies in Italy and become the arbiter of Italy. Initially, he was content to establish close ties with many native Italian rulers and allow them to rule provided that they recognize his dominant role. But in 1540, he gave the duchy of Milan to his son Philip II and transferred all imperial rights over Italy to the Spanish monarchy.

From the beginning of Philip II's reign in 1559 to 1713, the Spanish presence was felt everywhere in Italy. Only the major states of Florence, the Papal States, and Venice managed to maintain relatively independent policies. At the same time, the influence of the papacy became oppressive in Italy as the machinery of the Catholic Counter-Reformation—the Inquisition, Index, and the Jesuits—was used to stifle any resistance to the Catholic orthodoxy created by the Council of Trent (see Chapter 14). While artistic and intellectual activity continued in post-Renaissance Italy it often exacted a grievous cost. Many a daring intellectual, such as Galilei Galileo and Giordano Bruno (see Chapter 17), found himself imprisoned or executed by the Inquisition.

At the beginning of the eighteenth century, Italy suffered further from the struggles between France and Spain. But it was Austria, not France, that benefited the most from the War of the Spanish Succession. By gaining Milan, Mantua, Sardinia, and Naples, Austria supplanted Spain as the dominant power in Italy. It was a mixed blessing. Austrian rule would eventually galvanize Italians into a desire for freedom from all foreign domination.

From Muscovy to Russia

Beginning in the Middle Ages, Russia had existed only on the fringes of European society, remote and isolated from the western mainstream. But in the seventeenth century, the energetic Peter the Great pushed Russia westward and to the status of a great power.

A new Russian state had emerged in the fifteenth century under the leadership of the principality of Muscovy and its grand dukes (see Chapter 13). In the sixteenth century, Ivan IV the Stern (1533–1584), who was the first ruler to take the title of tsar, expanded the territories of Russia eastward, after finding westward expansion blocked by the powerful Swedish and Polish states. Ivan also extended the autocracy of the tsar by crushing the power of the Russian nobility, known as the boyars.

Ivan's dynasty came to an end in 1598 and was followed by a resurgence of aristocratic power in a period of anarchy known as the Time of Troubles. It was not ended until the Zemsky Sobor or national assembly chose Michael Romanov as the new tsar, beginning a dynasty that lasted until 1917.

In the seventeenth century, Muscovite society was highly stratified. At the top was the tsar, who claimed to be a divinely ordained autocratic ruler, assisted by two consultative bodies, a Duma or council of boyars and the

Zemsky Sobor, a parliamentary body of sorts begun in 1550 by Ivan IV to facilitate support for his programs. Russian society was dominated by an upper class of landed aristocrats who, in the course of the seventeenth century, managed to bind their peasants to the land. An abundance of land and a shortage of peasants made serfdom desirable to the landowners, who sustained a highly oppressive system. A law of 1625 stipulated that anyone who killed another's serf simply had to replace him. By the end of the seventeenth century, serfs could even be bought and sold. Only peasants on the personal estates of the tsar (the crown peasants) enjoyed a more favorable position. Townspeople were also stratified and controlled. Artisans were sharply separated from merchants, and many of the latter were not allowed to move from their cities without government permission or to sell their businesses to anyone not of their class. Government restrictions on peasants and merchants, however, led to a series of insurrections. Merchant revolts in Moscow and Novgorod were only ended by mass arrests, deportations, and executions. The most serious peasant revolt erupted in 1670, led by Don Cossacks under the leadership of Stenka Razin. It took the government two years to crush the uprising.

Religious schism added to the turmoil of seventeenth-century Muscovy. Illiteracy and ignorance were not only widespread, but often a matter of pride in a land accustomed to cultural isolation. This chauvinism was encouraged by the Russian Orthodox church, which had become independent of its Greek Orthodox mother church in 1589 when the head of the Russian Orthodox church was recognized as a patriarch in his own right. In the mid-seventeenth century, an attempt was made to reform the Russian church by Patriarch Nikon with the support of Tsar Alexis (1645–1676), the second Romanov ruler. The reforms were not profound; they corrected editions of the Bible and attempted a return to the ritualistic practices of Greek orthodoxy. A group of fundamentalists, however, known as the Old Believers, saw any reform as tampering with the received faith of their fathers and started a serious and persistent schism. The state and ecclesiastical hierarchy took up the struggle against the Old Believers in a sometimes fierce and bloody fashion. Thousands of Old Believers burned themselves in mass holocausts to protest the reforms, but in vain.

In the midst of these political and religious upheavals, seventeenth-century Muscovy was experiencing more frequent contacts with the West while Western ideas also began to penetrate a few Russian circles. When Peter the Great arrived on the scene, Muscovy was already under-

Peter the Great Deals with a Rebellion
▼ ▼ ▼

During his first visit to the West in 1697–1698, Peter received word that the streltsy, an elite military unit stationed in Moscow, had revolted against his authority. Peter hurried home and crushed the revolt in a very savage fashion. This selection is taken from an Austrian account of how Peter dealt with the rebels.

Peter and the Streltsy

How sharp was the pain, how great the indignation, to which the tsar's Majesty was mightily moved, when he knew of the rebellion of the Streltsy, betraying openly a mind panting for vengeance! He was still tarrying at Vienna, quite full of the desire of setting out for Italy; but, fervid as was his curiosity of rambling abroad, it was, nevertheless, speedily extinguished on the announcement of the troubles that had broken out in the bowels of his realm. Going immediately to Lefort . . . , he thus indignantly broke out: "Tell me, Francis, how I can reach Moscow by the shortest way, in a brief space, so that I may wreak vengeance on this great perfidy of my people, with punishments worthy of their abominable crime. Not one of them shall escape with impunity. Around my royal city, which, with their impious efforts, they planned to destroy, I will have gibbets and gallows set upon the walls and ramparts, and each and every one of them will I put to a direful death." Nor did he long delay the plan for his justly excited wrath; he took the quick post, as his ambassador suggested, and in four weeks' time he had got over about three hundred miles without accident, and arrived the 4th of September, 1698,—a monarch for the well deposed, but an avenger for the wicked.

His first anxiety after his arrival was about the rebellion—in what it consisted, what the insurgents meant, who dared to instigate such a crime. And as nobody could answer accurately upon all points, and some pleaded their own ignorance, others the obstinacy of the Streltsy, he began to have suspicions of everybody's loyalty. . . . No day, holy or profane, were the inquisitors idle; every day was deemed fit and lawful for torturing. There were as many scourges as there were accused, and every inquisitor was a butcher. . . . The whole month of October was spent in lacerating the backs of culprits with the knout and with flames; no day were those that were left alive exempt from scourging or scorching; or else they were broken upon the wheel, or driven to the gibbet, or slain with the ax. . . .

To prove to all people how holy and inviolable are those walls of the city which the Streltsy rashly meditated scaling in a sudden assault, beams were run out from all the embrasures in the walls near the gates, in each of which two rebels were hanged. This day beheld about two hundred and fifty die that death. There are few cities fortified with as many palisades as Moscow has given gibbets to her guardian Streltsy.

---

going changes. While neither his aims nor his solutions were new, Peter did accelerate the process with a ruthlessness that accomplished much, but at a great price.

THE REIGN OF PETER THE GREAT (1689–1725) Peter was only four years old when his father died so his sister Sophia acted as regent for him and his feeble-minded brother as joint tsars. At the age of seventeen (in 1689), Peter seized power from his sister. Peter the Great was an unusual character. A towering, strong man, six feet, nine inches tall, Peter was coarse in his tastes and rude in his behavior. He enjoyed a low kind of humor—belching contests, crude jokes, comical funerals—and vicious punishments—floggings, impalings, roastings, and beard burnings (see the box above). At the same time, he was capable of tender feelings, especially toward his family.

Peter gained his initial knowledge of Western ideas in the "German suburb," a section of Moscow where Europeans of different nationalities resided. He received a firsthand view of the West when he made a trip there in 1697–1698 and returned to Russia with a firm determination to westernize or Europeanize Russia. Perhaps too much has been made of Peter's desire to westernize a "backward country." Peter's policy of Europeanization was largely technical. He admired European technology and gadgets and desired to transplant these to Russia. Only this kind of modernization could give him the army and navy he needed to make Russia a great power. His only consistent purpose was to win military victories.

▼ **Peter the Great.** Peter the Great wished to westernize Russia, especially in the realm of technical skills. His foremost goal was the creation of a strong army and navy in order to make Russia a great power. He reorganized the central government and adopted mercantilist economic policies to produce revenue for his military expenditures. Peter achieved his goal of making Russia a great European power, although an aristocratic reaction undid much of his work after his death in 1725.

As could be expected, one of his fist priorities was the reorganization of the army and the creation of a navy. Employing both Russians and Europeans as officers, he conscripted peasants for twenty-five year stints of service to build a standing army of 210,000 men. Peter has also been given credit for forming the first Russian navy.

Peter reorganized the central government, partly along Western lines. What remained of the consultative

bodies disappeared; neither the Duma of boyars nor the Zemsky Sobor was ever summoned. In 1711, Peter created a Senate to supervise the administrative machinery of the state while he was away on military campaigns. In time the Senate became something like a ruling council, but its ineffectiveness caused Peter to borrow the Western institution of "colleges," or boards of administrators entrusted with specific functions, such as foreign affairs, war, and justice. To impose the rule of the central government more effectively throughout the land, Peter divided Russia into eight provinces and, later in 1719, into fifty. Although he hoped to create a "police state," by which he meant a well-ordered community governed in accordance with law, few of his bureaucrats shared his concept of honest service and duty to the state. One of his highest officials even stated: "Would your Majesty like to be a ruler without any subjects? We all steal, only some do it on a bigger scale, and in a more conspicuous way, than others."[8] Peter hoped for a sense of civic duty, but his own forceful personality created an atmosphere of fear that prevented it. He wrote to one administrator, "According to these orders act, act, act. I won't write more, but you will pay with your head if you interpret orders again." But when others were understandably cautious in interpreting his written instructions, he stated: "This is as if a servant, seeing his master drowning, would not save him until he had satisfied himself as to whether it was written down in his contract that he should pull him out of the water."[9] Peter wanted his administrators to be slaves and free men at the same time, and it did not occur to him that the task was impossible.

To satisfy his insatiable need of money for an army and navy that absorbed as much as four-fifths of the state revenue, Peter adopted Western mercantilistic policies to stimulate economic growth. He tried to increase exports and develop new industries while exploiting domestic resources like the iron mines in the Urals. But his military needs were endless, and he came to rely on the old expedient of simply raising taxes, placing additional burdens upon the hapless peasants whose position in Peter's Russia grew ever more oppressed.

Peter also sought to gain state control of the Russian Orthodox church. In 1721, he abolished the position of patriarch and created a body called the Holy Synod to make decisions for the church. At its head stood a procurator, a layman who represented the interests of the tsar and assured Peter of effective domination of the church.

Already after his first trip to the West in 1697–1698, Peter began to introduce Western customs, practices, and manners into Russia. He ordered the preparation of the first Russian book of etiquette to teach Western manners. Among other things, it pointed out that it was not polite to spit on the floor or scratch oneself at dinner. Since westerners did not wear beards or the traditional long-skirted coat, Russian beards had to be shaved and coats shortened, a reform Peter personally enforced at court by shaving off his nobles' beards and cutting their coats at the knees with his own hands. Outside the court, the edicts were enforced by barbers and tailors planted at town gates with orders to cut the beards and cloaks of those who entered or left. Anyone who failed to conform was to be "beaten without mercy." For the nobles, who were already partly westernized, these changes were hardly earth-shattering. But to many others who believed that shaving the beard was a "defacement of the image of God," the attack was actually blasphemous.

One group of Russians benefited greatly from Peter's cultural reforms—women. Having watched women mixing freely with men in Western courts, Peter shattered the seclusion of upper-class Russian women and demanded that they remove the traditional veils that covered their faces. Peter also encouraged gatherings in which both sexes could mix for conversation and dancing, which Peter had learned in the West. Women were also now allowed to marry of their own free will.

The object of Peter's domestic reforms was to make Russia into a great state and military power; an examination of his foreign policy reveals how well he succeeded. His primary goal was to "open a window to the west," meaning an ice-free port easily accessible to Europe. This could only be achieved on the Baltic, but at that time the Baltic coast was controlled by Sweden, the most important power in northern Europe. Desirous of these lands, Peter, with the support of Poland and Denmark, attacked Sweden in the summer of 1700, believing that the young king of Sweden, Charles XII, could easily be defeated. Charles, however, proved to be a brilliant general. He smashed the Danes, flattened the Poles, and, with a well-disciplined force of only 8,000 men, routed the Russian army of 40,000 at the Battle of Narva (1700). The Great Northern War (1701–1721) had begun.

While Charles wasted valuable time in an inconclusive war in Poland, Peter took the opportunity to reorganize his army along Western lines. In 1702, he overran

▼ **Map 16.4** From Muscovy to Russia.

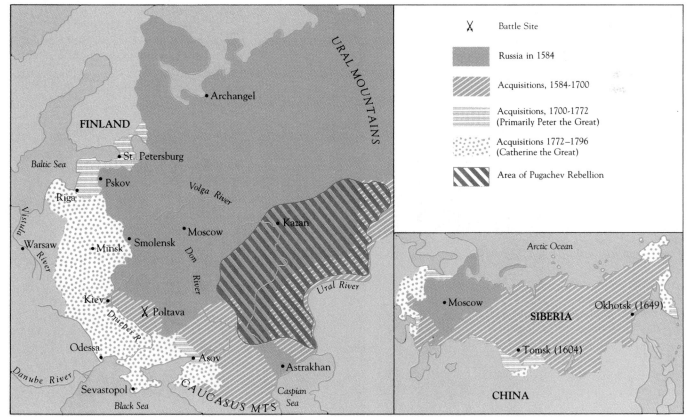

the Swedish Baltic provinces while Charles was preoccupied elsewhere. When the Swedish king turned his attention to Peter again in 1708, he decided to invade Russia and capture Moscow, the capital, but Russian weather and scorched-earth tactics devastated his army. In July 1709, at the Battle of Poltava, Peter's forces defeated Charles's army decisively. Although the war dragged on for another twelve years, the Peace of Nystadt in 1721 gave formal recognition to what Peter had already achieved: the acquisition of Estonia, Livonia, and Karelia. Sweden became a second-rate power while Russia was now the great European state Peter had wanted.

Already in 1703, in these northern lands on the Baltic, Peter had begun the construction of a new city, St. Petersburg, his window on the west and a symbol that Russia was looking westward to Europe. Built on marshland, its construction cost the lives of thousands of peasants. Finished during Peter's lifetime, St. Petersburg remained the Russian capital until 1917.

It is difficult to assess the work of Peter the Great. He modernized and westernized Russia to the extent that it became a great military power and, by his death in 1725, an important member of the European state system. But his policies were also detrimental to Russia. Westernization was a bit of a sham, since Western culture reached only the upper classes while the real object of the reforms, the creation of a strong military, only added more burdens to the masses of the Russian people. The forceful way in which Peter the Great imposed westernization led to a distrust of Europe and Western civilization. Russia was so strained by Peter the Great that after his death an aristocratic reaction undid much of his work.

Scandinavia

As the economic link between the products of eastern Europe and the West, the Baltic Sea bestowed special importance on the lands surrounding it. In the sixteenth century, Sweden had broken its ties with Denmark and emerged as an independent state (see Chapter 14). Despite their common Lutheran religion, Denmark's and Sweden's territorial ambitions in northern Europe in the seventeenth century kept them in rather constant rivalry.

Under Christian IV (1588–1648), Denmark seemed the likely candidate for expansion, but it met with little success. The system of electing monarchs forced the kings to share their power with the Danish nobility who exercised strict control over the peasants who worked their lands. Danish ambitions for ruling the Baltic were severely curtailed by the losses they sustained in the Thirty Years' War and later in the so-called Northern War (1655–1660) with Sweden. Danish military losses led to a constitutional crisis in which a meeting of Denmark's Estates brought to pass a bloodless revolution in 1660. The power of the nobility was curtailed, a hereditary monarchy reestablished, and a new, absolutist constitution proclaimed in 1665. Under Christian V (1670–1699), a centralized administration was instituted with the nobility as the chief officeholders.

▼ **Queen Christina of Sweden.** In the sixteenth century, Sweden emerged as an independent state and came to play a significant role in European affairs during the seventeenth century. Queen Christina, daughter of Gustavus Adolphus, had little interest in political matters. Focusing more on philosophy and religion, she corresponded with French philosopher René Descartes, who eventually came to reside at her court. Her support of the nobility turned the other estates against her, and only her abdication prevented a peasant revolt against the aristocracy.

Compared to Denmark, Sweden seemed a relatively poor country, and historians have found it difficult to explain why Sweden played such a large role in European affairs in the seventeenth century. Its economy was weak while the monarchy was still locked in conflict with the powerful Swedish nobility. During the reign of Gustavus Adolphus (1611–1632), his wise and dedicated chief minister, Axel Oxenstierna, persuaded the king to adopt a new policy in which the nobility formed a "first estate" occupying the bureaucratic positions of an expanded central government. This created a stable monarchy and freed the king to raise a formidable army and participate in the Thirty Years' War, only to be killed in battle in 1632.

Sweden experienced a severe political crisis after the death of Gustavus Adolphus. His daughter Christina (1633–1654) proved to be far more interested in philosophy and religion than ruling. By favoring the interests of the nobility, she caused the other estates of the Riksdag, Sweden's parliament—the burghers, clergy, and peasants—to protest. Her abdication in favor of her cousin, who became King Charles X (1654–1660), defused a potentially explosive peasant revolt against the nobility.

Charles X reestablished domestic order, but it was his successor, Charles XI (1660–1697), who did the painstaking work of building the Swedish monarchy along the lines of an absolute monarchy. By resuming control of the crown lands and the revenues attached to them from the nobility, Charles managed to weaken the independent power of the nobility. He built up a bureaucracy, subdued both the Riksdag and church, improved the army and navy, and left to his son, Charles XII (1697–1718), a well-organized Swedish state that dominated northern Europe. In 1693, he and his heirs were acclaimed as "absolute, sovereign kings, responsible for their actions to no man on earth."

Charles XII was primarily interested in military affairs. Energetic and regarded as a brilliant general, his grandiose plans and strategies, which involved Sweden in conflicts with Poland, Denmark, and Russia, proved to be Sweden's undoing. By the time he died in 1718, Charles XII had lost much of Sweden's northern empire to Russia, and Sweden's status as a first-class northern power had proved to be short-lived.

The Ottoman Empire

After their conquest of Constantinople in 1453, the Ottoman Turks tried to complete their conquest of the Balkans, where they had been established since the four-

Brandenburg-Prussia	
Hohenzollerns Established in Brandenburg	1417
Hohenzollerns Acquire Lands along the Rhine	1609
Hohenzollerns Acquire East Prussia	1618
Frederick William the Great Elector	1640–1688
Elector Frederick III (King Frederick I)	1688–1713
The Austrian Empire	
Leopold I	1658–1705
Turkish Siege of Vienna	1683
Russia	
Ivan IV the Stern	1533–1584
Time of Troubles	1598–1613
Michael Romanov	1613–1645
Alexis	1645–1676
Peter the Great	1689–1725
First Trip to the West	1697–1698
Construction of St. Petersburg Begins	1703
Holy Synod	1721
Great Northern War	1701–1721
Battle of Poltava	1709
Denmark	
Christian IV	1588–1648
"Bloodless Revolution"	1660
Christian V	1670–1699
Sweden	
Gustavus Adolphus	1611–1632
Christina	1633–1654
Charles X	1654–1660
Charles XI	1660–1697
Charles XII	1697–1718
The Ottoman Empire	
Suleiman I the Magnificent	1520–1566
Battle of Lepanto	1571
Turkish Defeat at Vienna	1683

teenth century. Although they were successful in taking the Romanian territory of Wallachia in 1476, the resistance of the Hungarians kept them from advancing up the Danube valley. From 1480 to 1520, internal problems and the need to consolidate their eastern frontiers kept the Turks from any further attacks on Europe.

The reign of Sultan Suleiman I the Magnificent (1520–1566), however, brought the Turks back to Europe's attention. Advancing up the Danube, the Turks seized Belgrade in 1521 and Hungary by 1526, although their attempts to conquer Vienna in 1529 were repulsed. At the same time, Turkish power was extended into the western Mediterranean, which they threatened to turn into a Turkish lake until a large Turkish fleet was destroyed by the Spanish at Lepanto in 1571. Despite the defeat, the Turks continued to hold nominal suzerainty over the southern shores of the Mediterranean.

Although Europeans frequently spoke of new Christian crusades against the infidel Turks, by the beginning of the seventeenth century the Ottoman Empire was being treated like another European power by European rulers seeking alliances and trade concessions. The Ottoman Empire possessed a highly effective governmental system, especially when it was led by strong sultans or powerful grand viziers (prime ministers). The splendid capital Constantinople possessed a population far larger than any European city. Nevertheless, Ottoman politics periodically degenerated into bloody intrigues as factions fought each other for influence and the throne. In one particularly gruesome practice, a ruling sultan would murder his brothers to avoid challenges to his rule. Despite the periodic bouts of civil chaos, a well-trained bureaucracy of civil servants continued to administer state affairs efficiently.

▼ **Map 16.5** The Ottoman Empire.

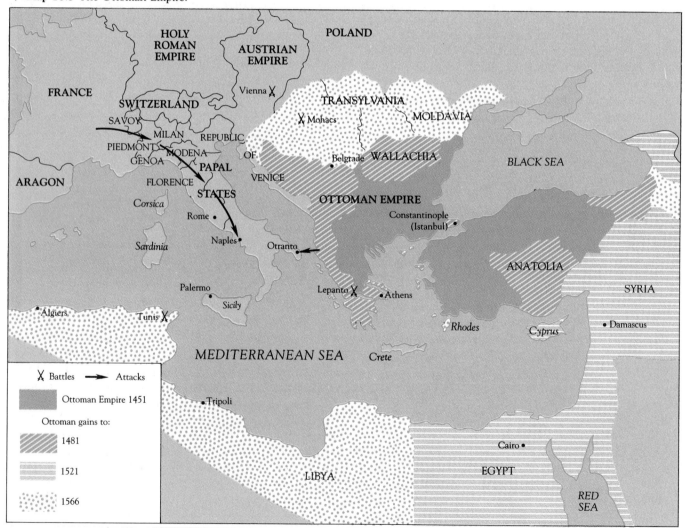

A well-organized military system also added to the strength of the Ottoman Empire. Especially outstanding were the Janissaries, composed of Christian boys who had been taken from their parents, converted to the Muslim faith, and subjected to rigid military discipline to form an elite core of 8,000 troops personally loyal to the sultan. Like other praetorian guards, however, the Janissaries came to play an important role in making and unmaking sultans.

In the first half of the seventeenth century, the Ottoman Empire was a "sleeping giant." Involved in domestic bloodletting and heavily threatened by a challenge from Persia, the Ottomans were content with the status quo in eastern Europe. But under a new line of grand viziers in the second half of the seventeenth century, the Ottoman Empire again took the offensive. By mid-1683, the Ottomans had marched through the Hungarian plain and laid siege to Vienna. Repulsed by a mixed army of Austrians, Poles, Bavarians, and Saxons, the Turks retreated and were pushed out of Hungary by a new European coalition. Although they retained the core of their empire, the Ottoman Turks would never again be a threat to Europe. Although the Ottoman Empire held together for the rest of the seventeenth and eighteenth centuries, it would be faced with new challenges from the ever-growing Austrian Empire in southeastern Europe and the new Russian giant to the north.

The Limits of Absolutism

In recent decades, historical studies of local institutions have challenged the traditional picture of absolute monarchs as powerful rulers whose control of the administrative machinery of state enabled them to dominate the everyday lives of their subjects. The centralization of power was an important element in the growth of the seventeenth-century state, however, and the most successful monarchs were those who managed to restructure the central policy-making machinery of government to give them a certain amount of control over the traditional areas of monarchical power: formulation of foreign policy, making of war and peace, the church, and taxation. Seventeenth-century governments also intervened in economic affairs to strengthen their warmaking capacities. In all of these areas, absolute monarchy meant rulers extending their power or at least resisting challenges to their authority.

It is misleading, however, to think that so-called absolute monarchs actually controlled the lives of their subjects. In 1700, government for most people still

meant the local institutions that affected their lives: local courts, local tax collectors, and local organizers of armed forces. Kings and ministers might determine policies and issue guidelines, but they still had to function through local agents and had no guarantee whatever that their wishes would be carried out. A mass of urban and provincial privileges, liberties, and exemptions (including from taxation) and a whole host of corporate bodies and interest groups—provincial and national Estates, clerical officials, officeholders who had bought or inherited their positions, and provincial nobles—limited what monarchs could achieve. Really successful rulers were not those who tried to destroy the old system, but those like Louis XIV who knew how to use the old system to their advantage. Above all other considerations stood the landholding nobility. Everywhere in the seventeenth century, the landed aristocracy played an important role in the European monarchical system. As military officers, judges, officeholders, and landowners in control of vast, untaxed estates, their power remained immense. In some places, their strength even severely limited how effectively monarchs could rule.

▼ Limited Monarchy and Republics

Almost everywhere in Europe in the seventeenth century, kings and their ministers were in control of central governments. But not all European states followed the pattern of absolute monarchy. In eastern Europe, the Polish aristocracy controlled a virtually powerless king. In western Europe, two great states—England and the Dutch Republic—successfully resisted the power of hereditary monarchs.

Poland

Poland had played a major role in eastern Europe in the fifteenth century and had ruled over Lithuania and much of the Ukraine by the end of the sixteenth. After the elective throne of Poland had been won by the Swede Sigismund III (1587–1631), Poland had a king who even thought seriously of creating a vast Polish empire that would include at least Russia and possibly Finland and Sweden. Poland not only failed to achieve this goal, but became a weak, decentralized state by the end of the seventeenth century.

It was the elective nature of the Polish monarchy that reduced it to impotence. The *Seym* or Polish diet was a two-chamber assembly in which landowners completely dominated the few townsmen and lawyers who were also members. To be elected to the kingship, prospective monarchs (who were mostly foreigners) made agreements with the *Seym* (in effect with the nobles), by which the latter was to share power in matters of taxation, foreign and military policy, and the appointment of state officials and judges. The power of the *Seym* had disastrous results for central monarchical authority since the real aim of most of its members was to ensure that central authority would not affect local interests. The acceptance of the liberum veto in 1652, whereby the meetings of the *Seym* could be stopped by a single dissenting member, reduced government to virtual chaos.

Poland, then, was basically a confederation of semi-independent estates of landed nobles. By the late seventeenth century, it also became a battleground for foreign powers who found it easy to invade, but difficult to rule. The continuation of Polish weakness into the eighteenth century eventually encouraged its more powerful neighbors—Prussia, Austria, and Russia—to dismember it.

The United Provinces

The seventeenth century has often been called the "Golden Age" of the Dutch Republic as the United Provinces held center stage as one of Europe's great powers. Like France and England, the United Provinces was an Atlantic power, underlining the importance of the shift of political and economic power from the Mediterranean basin to the countries on the Atlantic seaboard. As a result of the sixteenth-century revolt of the Netherlands, the seven northern provinces, which began to call themselves the United Provinces of the Netherlands in 1581, became the core of the modern Dutch state. The new state was officially recognized by the Peace of Westphalia in 1648.

With independence came internal dissension. There were two chief centers of political power in the new state. Each province had an official known as a stadholder who was responsible for leading the army and maintaining order. Beginning with William of Orange and his heirs, the house of Orange occupied the stadholderate in most of the seven provinces and favored the development of a centralized government with themselves as hereditary monarchs. The States General, an assembly of representatives from every province, opposed the Orangist ambitions and advocated a decentralized or republican form of government. A requirement of complete unanimity of the delegates served to weaken the effectiveness of this body, however, causing

the States General to refer all issues back to the provincial assemblies and permitting the latter to retain much power. Moreover, as the largest and richest province, Holland exercised the greatest influence in the States General; in fact, an oligarchy of wealthy merchants and financiers, especially from Amsterdam, tended to control this representative body.

The political rivalry between the monarchical and republican blocs was intensified by religious division within the Calvinist church. Orthodox Calvinists, known as the Counter-Remonstrants, favored a strict interpretation of the Calvinist doctrine of predestination and were supported by the Orangists. The Remonstrants, on the other hand, believed that humans participated to some extent in the process of gaining salvation and favored a generally tolerant position on religious differences. Supported by the republican forces, the latter position ultimately prevailed. Although the Calvinist church remained the official church, other religious groups were tolerated as long as they worshiped in private. Catholics, other Protestants, and even Jewish communities felt relatively free in Holland, especially in Amsterdam. The Dutch were truly unique in the seventeenth century for their religious toleration.

During the first half of the seventeenth century, the Orangist stadholders continued to pursue one fundamental aim—the conversion of the Dutch Netherlands into a monarchy under the house of Orange—but met with little success. Indeed, for twenty-two years after 1650, the seven Dutch provinces became accustomed to their republican existence without a stadholder. But in 1672, burdened with war against both France and England, the United Provinces turned once again to the house of Orange and restored it to the stadholderate in the person of William III (1672–1702). Seventeenth-century Dutch history is remarkable for the relative ease with which the Dutch shifted from one power base to the other in accordance with their external and internal needs. From that year on, William III worked consciously to build up his pseudo-royal power. When he succeeded to the throne of England in 1688 (see England and the Emergence of Constitutional Monarchy later in the chapter), it strengthened his position in the Netherlands as well. However, his death in 1702, without direct heirs, enabled the republican forces to gain control once more. The Dutch Republic would not be seriously threatened again by the monarchical forces.

Underlying Dutch prominence in the seventeenth century was its economic prosperity, fueled by the Dutch role as carriers of European trade. But war proved disastrous to the Dutch Republic. The two Anglo-Dutch wars of the 1650s and 1660s, the war with France and England in the 1670s, and their support of England against France in the War of the Spanish Succession placed heavy burdens on Dutch finances and manpower. English shipping began to challenge what had been Dutch commercial supremacy, and by 1715, the Dutch were experiencing a serious economic decline.

DAILY LIFE IN SEVENTEENTH-CENTURY AMSTERDAM By the beginning of the seventeenth century, Amsterdam had replaced Antwerp as the financial and commercial capital of Europe. In 1570, Amsterdam had 30,000 inhabitants; by 1610, that number had doubled as refugees poured in, especially from the Spanish Netherlands. Intellectuals and Jews drawn by the city's reputation for toleration, as well as merchants and workers attracted by the city's prosperity, added to the number of new inhabitants. This rapid growth caused the city government to approve an "urban expansion plan" in 1613, by which the construction of three large concentric canals expanded the city's territory from 500 to 1,800 acres. Building plots were formed by hammering wooden piles through the mud to the hard sand below, while the canals made it possible for businessmen to use their newly built houses for warehouses. Goods carried by small boats were lifted to the upper stories of these dwellings by block and tackle fastened to the gables of the roofs. Amsterdam's physical expansion was soon matched by its population as the city grew to 100,000 people in 1610 and then to 200,000 by 1660.

The exuberant expansion of Amsterdam in the seventeenth century was based upon the city's new role as the commercial and financial center of Europe (see the box on p. 548). But what had made this possible? For one thing, Amsterdam had an excellent merchant marine. Amsterdam merchants possessed vast fleets of ships, many of which were used for the lucrative North Sea herring catch. Amsterdam ships were also important carriers for the products of other countries. The Dutch invention of the fluyt, a shallow-draft ship of large capacity, enabled them to transport enormous quantities of cereals, timber, and iron. Finally, the Dutch produced large ships for oceanic voyages and, by 1650, owned 50 percent of the merchant ships in Europe.

By making available an enormous variety of goods, Amsterdam merchants induced foreigners to buy and sell in Amsterdam, thus making the city a crossroads for many of Europe's chief products. Amsterdam was, of course, the chief port for the Dutch West and East Indian trading companies (see Overseas Trade and Colonies later in the chapter). Moreover, city industries turned imported raw materials into finished goods, making Amsterdam an important producer of cloth, refined sugar and tobacco products, glass, beer, paper, books, jewelry, and leather goods.

A third factor in Amsterdam's prosperity was its importance as a financial center. Large quantities of capital were available for investment from profits in trade. As a haven for religious minorities, Amsterdam housed a number of wealthy refugees with money to invest. Its financial role was greatly facilitated by the foundation in 1609 of the Exchange Bank of Amsterdam, long the greatest public bank in northern Europe. As an English gentleman noted, the reputation of the bank was "another invitation for People to come, and lodge here what part of their Money they could transport, and knew no way of securing at home."[10] The city also founded the Amsterdam Stock Exchange for trading in commodities. Some of the city's great wealth came from war profits; by 1700, Amsterdam was the principal supplier for military goods in Europe.

Amsterdam's prosperity (it possessed the highest per capita income in Europe) did not prevent it from having enormous social differences. At the bottom of the social ladder was the *grauw* or rabble consisting of beggars, unskilled day laborers, and immigrants attracted by Am-

▼ **View of Amsterdam.** Much of Amsterdam's wealth and prestige as a commercial center was due to its excellent merchant marine. Amsterdam was also a major producer of finished products as well as an important European financial center. As seen in this photograph of Amsterdam, the city's charm stemmed from its small streets crisscrossed by a series of canals.

The Economic Superiority of the Dutch
▼ ▼ ▼

Europeans were astonished by the apparent prosperity of the Dutch in the first half of the seventeenth century. This selection is taken from a treatise entitled Observations Touching Trade and Commerce with the Hollanders, and Other Nations. It was written by an Englishman named John Keymer who believed that the Dutch economy could serve as a guide for the English.

John Keymer, *Observations Touching Trade and Commerce with the Hollanders, and Other Nations*

I have diligently in my travels, observed how the countries herein mentioned [mainly Holland] do grow potent with abundance of all thing to serve themselves and other nations, where nothing groweth; and that their never dried fountains of wealth, by which they raise their estate to such an admirable height, [so] that they are . . . [now] a wonder to the world, [come] from your Majesty's seas and lands.

I thus moved, began to dive into the depth of their policies and circumventing practices, whereby they drain, and still covet to exhaust, the wealth and coin of this kingdom, and so with our own commodities to weaken us, and finally beat us quite out of trading in other countries. I found that they more fully obtained these their purposes by their convenient privileges, and settled constitutions, than England with all the laws, and superabundance of home-bred commodities which God hath vouchsafed your sea and land. . . .

To bring this to pass they have many advantages of us; the one is, by their fashioned ships . . . that are made to hold great bulk of merchandise, and to sail with a few men for profit. For example . . . . [Dutch ships] do serve the merchant better cheap by one hundred pounds [English money] in his freight than we can, by reason he hath but nine or ten mariners, and we near thirty; thus he saveth twenty men's meat and wages in a voyage; and so in all other their ships according to their burden, by which means they are freighted wheresoever they come, to great profit, whilst our ships lie still and decay. . . .

Thus they and others glean this wealth and strength from us to themselves; and these reasons following procure them this advantage to us.

1. The merchants . . . which maketh all things in abundance, by reason of their store-houses continually replenished with all kind of commodities.
2. The liberty of free traffic for strangers to buy and sell in Holland, and other countries and states, as if they were free-born, maketh great intercourse.
3. The small duties levied upon merchants, draws all nations to trade with them.
4. Their fashioned ships continually freighted before ours, by reason of their few mariners and great bulk, serving the merchant cheap.
5. Their forwardness to further all manner of trading.
6. Their wonderful employment of their busses [herring boats] for fishing, and the great returns they make.
7. Their giving free custom inward and outwards, for any new-erected trade, by means whereof they have gotten already almost the sole trade into their hands.

sterdam's riches. The upper classes disliked and feared them, which created much ambivalence in the way city authorities treated them. Militia companies made up of upper-class volunteers stood ready to crush lower-class revolts, while wealthy individuals created orphanages and almshouses to care for their needs. Many of the rabble were forcefully recruited as ordinary sailors, especially for dangerous overseas voyages. Above the rabble stood the artisans and manual laborers known as the *kleine man* (little man). These were members of guilds or people who labored for guild members. Since a wife could continue to operate a business after her husband's death, Amsterdam was known for its high number of businesswomen. The *kleine man* lived in an area called the Jordaan, built outside the three new canals. Its closely crowded quarters and small streets crisscrossed by canals created a quaintness and sense of solidarity that appealed to many of Amsterdam's artists.

Above the *kleine man* stood a professional class of lawyers, teachers, bureaucrats, and wealthier guildsmen, but above them were the landed nobles who intermarried with the wealthier burghers and built more elaborate town houses. At the very top of Amsterdam's society stood a small group of very wealthy manufacturers, shipyard owners, and merchants, whose wealth enabled them to control the city government of Amsterdam as well as the Dutch Republic's States General.

In the first half of the seventeenth century, the Calvinist background of the wealthy Amsterdam burghers led them to adopt a simple lifestyle. They wore dark clothes and lived in substantial, but simply furnished houses, known for their narrow and steep stairways. The oft-quoted phrase that "cleanliness is next to Godliness" was literally true for these self-confident Dutch burghers. But in the second half of the seventeenth century, the wealthy burghers began to reject their Calvinist heritage in favor of French styles, a transformation that is especially evident in their more elaborate and colorful clothes.

England and the Emergence of Constitutional Monarchy

The inability of the Puritans to rule England on a long-term basis (see Chapter 15) led to the restoration of the Stuart monarchy in 1660. After eleven years of exile, Charles II (1660–1685) returned to England and entered London amid the acclaim of the people, remarking sardonically, "I never knew that I was so popular in England." The restoration of the monarchy and the House of Lords did not mean, however, that the work of the Puritan Revolution was undone. Parliament kept much of the power it had won: arbitary courts were still abolished; Parliament's role in government was acknowledged; and the necessity for its consent to taxation was accepted.

This did not mean that Charles was content with these limitations on his monarchical authority, but he had lived through the civil wars and eleven years of exile and he was resolved toward moderation. "I am too old to go again on my travels," as he wisely expressed it. Yet Charles utilized adroit and devious political maneuverings to push his own ideas, some of which were clearly out of step with many of the English people.

A serious religious problem disturbed the tranquillity of Charles II's reign. After the restoration of the monarchy, a new Parliament (the Cavalier Parliament) met in 1661 and restored the Anglican church as the official church of England. In addition, laws were passed to force everyone, particularly Catholics and Puritan Dissenters, to conform to the Anglican church and even to exclude these people from holding positions in local government.

Charles was not pleased with this legislation. He was sympathetic to and perhaps even inclined to Catholicism. By the secret Treaty of Dover of 1670 with King Louis XIV of France, Charles had promised, in return for a substantial subsidy, to become Catholic and make England a Catholic commonwealth at the appropriate opportunity. Moreover, Charles's brother James, heir to the throne, did not hide the fact that he was a Catholic. Parliament's suspicions were therefore aroused in 1672 when Charles took the audacious step of issuing a Declaration of Indulgence that suspended the laws that Parliament had passed against Catholics and Puritans. By linking Catholics to Puritan Dissenters, Charles hoped to succeed with his religious policy, but Parliament would have none of it and induced the king to suspend the declaration. Propelled by a strong anti-Catholic sentiment, Parliament then passed a Test Act in 1673, specifying that only Anglicans could hold military and civil offices.

A supposed Catholic plot to assassinate King Charles and place his brother James on the throne, although shown to be imaginary, inflamed Parliament to attempt to pass an Exclusion Bill between 1678 and 1681 that would have barred James from the throne as a professed Catholic. Although these attempts failed, the debate over the bill created two political groupings: the Whigs, who wanted to exclude James and establish a Protestant king with toleration of Dissenters; and the Tories, who supported the king, despite their dislike of James as a Catholic, because they did not believe Parliament should tamper with the lawful succession to the throne. To foil these efforts, Charles dismissed Parliament in 1681, relying on French subsidies to rule alone. When he died in 1685, his Catholic brother came to the throne.

The accession of James II (1685–1688) to the crown virtually guaranteed a new constitutional crisis for England, for the stubborn and uncompromising James II was more reminiscent of his father, Charles I, than his brother. An open and devout Catholic, his attempt to further Catholic interests made religion once more a primary cause of conflict between king and Parliament.

After some initial successes, James took advantage of his newfound popularity to seek advantages for his fellow Catholics. Contrary to the Test Act, he named Catholics to high positions in the government, army, navy, and universities. In 1687, he issued a Declaration of Indulgence, which suspended all laws barring Catholics and Dissenters from office. Parliamentary outcries against

The Bill of Rights

▼ ▼ ▼

In 1688, the English experienced yet another revolution, a rather bloodless one in which the Stuart king James II was replaced by Mary, James's daughter, and her husband, William of Orange. After William and Mary had assumed power, Parliament passed a Bill of Rights that specified the rights of Parliament and laid the foundation for a constitutional monarchy.

The Bill of Rights

Whereas the said late King James II having abdicated the government, and the throne being thereby vacant, his Highness the prince of Orange (whom it hath pleased Almighty God to make the glorious instrument of delivering this kingdom from popery and arbitrary power) did (by the device of the lords spiritual and temporal, and diverse principal persons of the Commons) cause letters to be written to the lords spiritual and temporal, being Protestants, and other letters to the several counties, cities, universities, boroughs, and Cinque Ports, for the choosing of such persons to represent them, as were of right to be sent to parliament, to meet and sit at Westminster upon the two and twentieth day of January, in this year 1689, in order to such an establishment as that their religion, laws, and liberties might not again be in danger of being subverted; upon which letters elections have been accordingly made.

And thereupon the said lords spiritual and temporal and Commons, pursuant to their respective letters and elections, being now assembled in a full and free representation of this nation, taking into their most serious consideration the best means for attaining the ends aforesaid, do in the first place (as their ancestors in like case have usually done), for the vindication and assertion of their ancient rights and liberties, declare:

1. That the pretended power of suspending laws, or the execution of laws, by regal authority, without consent of parliament is illegal.

2. That the pretended power of dispensing with the laws, or the execution of law by regal authority, as it hath been assumed and exercised of late, is illegal.

3. That the commission for erecting the late court of commissioners for ecclesiastical causes, and all other commissions and courts of like nature, are illegal and pernicious.

4. That levying money for or to the use of the crown by pretense of prerogative, without grant of parliament, for longer time or in other manner than the same is or shall be granted, is illegal.

5. That it is the right of the subjects to petition the king, and all commitments and prosecutions for such petitioning are illegal.

6. That the raising or keeping a standing army within the kingdom in time of peace, unless it be with consent of parliament, is against law.

7. That the subjects which are Protestants may have arms for their defense suitable to their conditions, and as allowed by law.

8. That election of members of parliament ought to be free.

9. That the freedom of speech, and debates or proceedings in parliament, ought not to be impeached or questioned in any court or place out of parliament.

10. That excessive bail ought not to be required, nor excessive fines imposed, nor cruel and unusual punishments inflicted.

11. That jurors ought to be duly impaneled and returned, and jurors which pass upon men in trials for high treason ought to be freeholders.

12. That all grants and promises of fines and forfeitures of particular persons before conviction are illegal and void.

13. And that for redress of all grievances, and for the amending, strengthening, and preserving of the laws, parliament ought to be held frequently.

James's policies stopped short of rebellion since members knew that he was an old man and his successors were his Protestant daughters Mary and Anne, born to his first wife. But on June 10, 1688, a son was born to James II's second wife, also a Catholic. Suddenly the specter of a Catholic hereditary monarchy loomed large. A group of seven prominent English noblemen invited William of Orange, husband of James's daughter Mary, to invade

England. An inveterate foe of Louis XIV, William welcomed this opportunity to fight France with England's resources. William and Mary raised an army and invaded England while James, his wife, and infant son fled to France. With almost no bloodshed, England had undergone a "Glorious Revolution," not over the issue of whether there would be a monarchy, but rather over who would be monarch.

The events of late 1688 constituted only the initial stage of the Glorious Revolution. The second, and far more important part, was the Revolution Settlement which confirmed William and Mary as monarchs. In January 1689, a Convention Parliament asserted that James had tried to subvert the constitution "by breaking the original contract between king and people," and declared the throne of England vacant. It then offered the throne to William and Mary, who accepted it along with the provisions of a Declaration of Rights, later enacted into law as a Bill of Rights in 1689 (see the box on p. 550). The Bill of Rights affirmed Parliament's right to make laws and levy taxes and made it impossible for kings to oppose or do without Parliament by stipulating that standing armies could be raised only with the consent of Parliament. Both elections and debates of Parliament had to be free, meaning that the king could not interfere. The rights of citizens to petition the sovereign, keep arms, have a jury trial, and not be subject to excessive bail were also confirmed. The Bill of Rights helped to fashion a system of government based on the rule of law and a freely elected Parliament, thus laying the foundation for a constitutional monarchy.

The Bill of Rights did not settle the religious questions that had played such a large role in England's troubles in the seventeenth century. The Toleration Act of 1689 granted Puritan Dissenters the right of free public worship (Catholics were still excluded), although they did not yet have full civil and political equality since the Test Act was not repealed. Although the Toleration Act did not mean complete religious freedom and equality, it marked a departure in English history since few people would ever again be persecuted for religious reasons.

Many historians have viewed the Glorious Revolution as the end of the seventeenth-century struggle between king and Parliament. By deposing one king and establishing another, Parliament had destroyed the divine-right theory of kingship (William was, after all, king by grace of Parliament, not God) and confirmed its right to participate in the government. Parliament did not have complete control of the government, but it now had an unquestioned right to participate in affairs of state. Over the next century, it would gradually

Chronology
▼ ▼ ▼
Limited Monarchy and Republics

Poland	
Sigismund III	1587–1631
Beginning of Liberum Veto	1652
The United Provinces	
Official Recognition of United Provinces	1648
House of Orange	
William III	1672–1702
England	
Charles II	1660–1685
Cavalier Parliament	1661
Treaty of Dover	1670
Declaration of Indulgence	1672
Test Act	1673
James II	1685–1688
Declaration of Indulgence	1687
Glorious Revolution	1688
Bill of Rights	1689

prove to be the real authority in the English system of constitutional monarchy. This, of course, would not make it a democracy or representative system of government. The members of Parliament, specifically the House of Commons, were elected by a very limited portion of the population, primarily members of the aristocratic landowning class. Indeed, England from 1688 to 1832 was one of the best examples in modern times of rule by an aristocratic oligarchy.

▼ Economic Trends: Mercantilism and European Colonies in the Seventeenth Century

The sixteenth century had witnessed a rising population, severely escalating prices, and a growing economy. The seventeenth century, however, as recent economic studies have demonstrated, was characterized more by economic contraction, if not depression, although variations existed depending on the country or region. Trade, industry, and agriculture all felt the pinch of a depression, which some historians believe bottomed out between 1640 and 1680, while others argue that the decade of the 1690s was still bad, especially in France.

Translated into everyday life, for many people the economic contraction of the seventeenth century meant scarce food, uncertain employment, and high rates of taxation.

Climate, too, played a factor in this economic reversal as Europeans experienced worsening weather patterns. In this "little ice age," extending from the sixteenth well into the eighteenth century, average temperatures fell, winters were colder, summers were wetter, and devastating storms seemed more frequent. Although the exact impact of climatic changes is uncertain, there were numerous reports of crop failures, the worst in 1649, 1660–1661, and the 1690s.

Population was also affected. Based on the birth rate of the seventeenth century, demographers would expect the European population to have doubled every twenty-five years. In reality, Europe experienced either a decline or no steady increase in population, as a result of a variety of factors. Infant mortality rates were high, 30 percent in the first year of life and 50 percent before the age of ten. Epidemics and famines were again common experiences in European life. The last great epidemic of bubonic plague spread across Europe in the middle and late years of the seventeenth century. The Mediterranean region suffered from 1646 to 1657, when the plague killed off 130,000 persons in Naples alone. In 1665, it struck England and devastated London, killing 20 percent of its population. France and Spain experienced outbreaks in the 1690s. The last major outburst of bubonic plague struck Poland, Germany, and Scandinavia between 1708 and 1713.

Mercantilism

Mercantilism is the name historians use to identify a set of economic principles that dominated economic thought in the seventeenth century. Fundamental to mercantilism was the belief that the total volume of trade was unchangeable. Therefore, as Colbert, the French practitioner of mercantilism, stated: "trade causes perpetual conflict, both in war and in peace, among the nations of Europe, as to who should carry off the greatest part. The Dutch, the English and the French are the actors in this conflict."[11] Since one nation could expand its trade and hence its prosperity only at the expense of others, to mercantilists, economic activity was war carried on by peaceful means.

According to the mercantilists, the prosperity of a nation depended upon a plentiful supply of bullion or gold and silver. For this reason, it was desirable to achieve a favorable balance of trade in which goods exported were of greater value than those imported, promoting an influx of gold and silver payments that would increase the quantity of bullion. Furthermore, to encourage exports, governments should stimulate and protect export industries and trade by granting trade monopolies, encouraging investment in new industries through subsidies, importing foreign artisans, and improving transportation systems by building roads, bridges, and canals. By placing high tariffs on foreign goods, they could be kept out of the country and prevented from competing with domestic industries. Colonies were also deemed valuable as sources of raw materials and markets for finished goods.

As a system of economic principles, mercantilism focused on the role of the state, believing that state intervention in some aspects of the economy was desirable for the sake of the national good. Government regulations to ensure the superiority of export goods, the construction of roads and canals, and the granting of subsidies to create trade companies were all predicated on government involvement in economic affairs.

Overseas Trade and Colonies

Mercantilist theory on the role of colonies was matched in practice by Europe's overseas expansion. With the development of colonies and trading posts in the Americas and Far East, Europeans entered into an age of international commerce in the seventeenth century. While some historians speak of a world economy, we should remember that local, regional, and intra-European trade still dominated the scene. At the end of the seventeenth century, for example, English imports totaled 360,000 tons, but only 5,000 tons came from the East Indies. About one-tenth of English and Dutch exports were shipped across the Atlantic; slightly more went to the Far East. What made the transoceanic trade rewarding, however, was not the volume, but the value of its goods. Dutch, English, and French merchants were bringing back products that were still consumed largely by the wealthy, but at the same time were making their way into the lives of artisans and merchants. Pepper and spices from the Indies, West Indian and Brazilian sugar, and Asian coffee and tea were becoming more common for European consumers. The first coffee and tea houses opened in London in the 1650s and spread rapidly to other parts of Europe.

In 1600, much overseas trade was still carried by the Spanish and Portuguese, who alone possessed colonies of any significant size. But war and steady pressure from their Dutch and English rivals eroded Portuguese trade in both the west and east, although Portugal continued to profit from its large colonial empire in Brazil. The Spanish also maintained an enormous South American empire, but Spain's importance as a commercial power declined rapidly in the seventeenth century because of a drop in the output of the silver mines, the poverty of the Spanish monarchy, and the stifling hand of the Spanish aristocracy as well as the pressure of its English rivals.

Although the Dutch became the leading carriers of European products within Europe, they had more severe competition when they moved into Asian and American markets. The Dutch East India Company was formed in 1602 to consolidate the gains made at the expense of the Portuguese and exploit the riches of the Far East. Since the wealthy oligarchy that controlled the company also dominated the Dutch government, this joint-stock company not only had a monopoly on all Asian trade but also possessed the right to make war, sign treaties, establish military and trading bases, and appoint governing officials. Gradually, the Dutch East India Company took control of most of the Portuguese bases in the Far East and opened trade with China and Japan. Its profits were spectacular in the first ten years.

Although the Dutch West India Company was created in 1621 along lines similar to its eastern counterpart, it was less successful. Its efforts were aimed against Portuguese and Spanish trade and possessions, and though it made some inroads in Portuguese Brazil and the Caribbean, they were not enough to compensate for its expenditures. Dutch settlements were also established on the North American continent. The mainland colony of New Netherlands stretched from the mouth of the Hudson as far north as Albany, New York. Present-day names, such as Manhattan, Staten Island, Harlem, and the Catskills remind us that it was the Dutch who

initially settled the Hudson River valley. In the second half of the seventeenth century, rivalry and years of warfare with the English and French brought the decline of the Dutch commercial empire. In 1664, the English seized the colony of New Netherlands and renamed it New York while the Dutch West India Company soon went bankrupt. By the end of the seventeenth century, the Dutch Golden Age was beginning to tarnish.

The Dutch overseas trade and commercial empire faced two major rivals in the seventeenth century—the English and French. The English had founded their own East India Company in 1601 and proceeded to create a colonial empire in the New World along the Atlantic seaboard of North America. The failure of the Virginia Company made it evident that the colonizing of American lands was not necessarily conducive to quick profits. But the desire to escape from religious oppression combined with economic interests did make successful colonization possible, as the Massachusetts Bay Company demonstrated (see the box on p. 554). The Massachusetts colony had 4,000 settlers in its early years, but by 1660 had swelled to 40,000. Although the English had established control over most of the eastern seaboard by the end of the seventeenth century, the North American colonies still remained of minor significance to the English economy.

French commercial companies in the Far East experienced much difficulty. While due in part to a late start, French problems also demonstrated the weakness of a commerce dependent on political rather than economic impetus. The East Indian companies set up by Henry IV and Richelieu all failed. Colbert instituted a new East India Company in 1664 that only barely managed to survive. The French had greater success in North America where in 1663 Canada was made the property of the

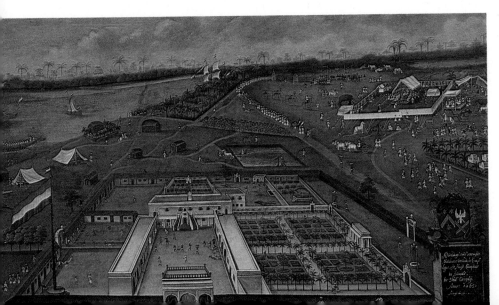

▼ **The Dutch East India Company in India.** Pictured here is the Dutch trading post known as Hugly, founded in Bengal in 1610. While being the leading carriers of European products within Europe, the Dutch faced more difficult challenges when they began to deal with Asian and American markets. The Dutch East India Company eventually came to dominate most of the Portuguese bases in the east, but were less successful in the west and ultimately lost ground to the English.

The Pilgrims at Plymouth

▼ ▼ ▼

British colonization of the eastern seacoast of North America was a slow and often painful process. Unlike the Virginia colony, which had quick profits as its primary aim, the settlers in Massachusetts intended to establish permanent homes. This description of the early colonists at Plymouth is taken from the classic account of Governor William Bradford.

William Bradford, *History of the Plymouth Settlement*

Having now come to the 25th of March, I will begin the year 1621. . . .

They began now to gather in the small harvest they had, and to prepare their houses for the winter, being well recovered in health and strength, and plentifully provisioned; for while some had been thus employed in affairs away from home, others were occupied in fishing for cod, bass, and other fish, of which they caught a good quantity, every family having their portion. All the summer there was no want. And now, as winter approached, wild fowl began to arrive, of which there were plenty when they came here first, though afterwards, they became more scarce. As well as wild fowl, they got abundance of wild turkeys, besides venison, etc. Each person had about a peck of meal a week, or now, since harvest, Indian corn in that proportion; and afterwards many wrote at length about their plenty to their friends in England—not feigned but true reports. . . .

Soon after this ship's departure, the great Narragansett tribe, in a braving manner, sent a messenger to them with a bundle of arrows tied about with a great snake skin, which their interpreters told them was a threatening challenge. Upon which the Governor, with the advice of the others, sent them a round answer, that if they would rather have war than peace, they might begin when they would; they had done them no wrong, neither did they fear them, nor would they find them unprepared. They sent the snake skin back by another messenger with bullets in it; but they would not receive it, and returned it again. . . .

But this made the settlers more careful to look to themselves. They agreed to enclose their dwellings in a good strong stockade and make flankers in convenient places, with gates to shut. These they locked every night and a watch was kept, and when need required there were also outposts in the daytime. The colonists, at the Captain's and Governor's advice, were divided into four squadrons, and everyone had his quarter appointed, to which to repair at any sudden alarm; and in case of fire, a company with muskets was appointed as a guard, to prevent Indian treachery, whilst the others quenched. This was accomplished very cheerfully, and the town was enclosed by the beginning of March, every family having a pretty garden plot.

---

crown and administered like a French province. But the French failed to provide adequate men or money, allowing their continental wars to take precedence over the conquest of the North American continent. Already in 1713, by the Treaty of Utrecht, the French began to cede some of their American possessions to their English rival.

▼ The World of Seventeenth-Century Culture

The seventeenth century was a remarkably talented one. In addition to the intellectuals responsible for the Scientific Revolution (see Chapter 17), the era was blessed with a number of prominent thinkers, artists, and writers. Some historians have even labeled it a century of genius.

Art

In the second half of the seventeenth century, France replaced Italy as the cultural leader of Europe. Rejecting the Baroque style as overly showy and passionate, the French remained committed to the classical values of the High Renaissance. French late classicism with its emphasis on clarity, simplicity, balance, and harmony of design was, however, a rather "frigid" version of the High Renaissance style. Its triumph reflected the shift in seventeenth-century French society from chaos to order.

The nature of French classicism was evident in the principles of the French Academy of Painting and Sculpture. These included an imitation of the artists of antiquity, an emphasis on geometric shapes and the use of definite lines to clearly delineate objects, a deemphasis on color because of its sensuousness, and the idealization of nature. While French classicism rejected the emotionalism and high drama of the Baroque, the latter's conception of grandeur was continued in the portrayal of noble subjects, especially those from classical antiquity. Nicholas Poussin (1594–1665) exemplified these principles in his paintings. His choice of scenes from classical mythology, the calmness of his vistas, the postures of his figures copied from the sculptures of antiquity, and his use of brown tones all reflect the classical principles of the French Academy.

THE GOLDEN AGE OF DUTCH PAINTING   The supremacy of Dutch commerce in the seventeenth century was parallelled by a brilliant flowering of Dutch painting. Since the Dutch possessed no real royal court or rich aristocracy, it was the wealthy patricians and burghers of Dutch urban society who commissioned works of art for their guild halls, town halls, and private dwellings. The interests of this burgher society were reflected in the subject matter of many Dutch paintings: portraits of themselves, group portraits of their military companies and guilds, landscapes, seascapes, genre scenes, still lifes, and the interiors of their residences. Neither classical nor Baroque, Dutch painters were primarily interested in the realistic portrayal of secular, everyday life. To a great extent, they turned away from the religious themes that had dominated art for so long.

The finest example of the Golden Age of Dutch painting was Rembrandt van Rijn (1606–1669). Rembrandt's early career was reminiscent of Rubens since he painted opulent portraits and grandiose scenes in often colorful fashion. Like Rubens, he was prolific and successful; unlike Rubens, he turned away from materialistic success and public approval to follow his own artistic path. In the process, he lost public support and died bankrupt.

Although Rembrandt shared the Dutch preoccupation for realistic portraits, he became more introspective as he grew older. He refused to follow his contemporaries who produced pictures largely secular in subject matter; half of his paintings focused on scenes from biblical tales. Since the Protestant tradition of hostility to religious pictures had discouraged artistic expression, Rembrandt stands out as the one great Protestant painter of the seventeenth century. Rembrandt's religious pictures, however, avoided the monumental subjects, such as the Creation and Last Judgment, that were typical of Catholic artists. Instead, he favored pictures that focused on the individual's relationship with God and depicted people's inward suffering in quiet, evocative scenes.

The Theater: The Triumph of French Neoclassicism

As the great age of theater in England and Spain was drawing to a close around 1630, a new dramatic era began to dawn in France that lasted into the 1680s. Unlike Shakespeare in England and Lope de Vega in Spain, French playwrights wrote more for an elite audience and were forced to depend upon royal patronage.

▼ Nicholas Poussin, *Landscape with the Burial of Phocian.* France became the new cultural leader of Europe in the second half of the seventeenth century. French classicism upheld the values of High Renaissance style, but produced a more static version of it. In Nicholas Poussin's work, we see the emphasis of French classicism on the use of scenes from classical sources and the creation of a sense of grandeur and noble strength in both human figures and landscape.

Louis XIV used theater as he did art and architecture—to attract attention to his monarchy.

French dramatists cultivated a classical style in which the Aristotelian rules for dramatic composition, observing the three unities of time, place, and action, were closely followed. French neoclassicism emphasized the clever, polished, and correct over the emotional and imaginative. Many of the French works of the period derived both their themes and their plots from Greek and Roman sources, especially evident in the works of Jean-Baptiste Racine (1639–1699). In *Phédre*, which has been called his best play, Racine followed closely the plot of the Greek tragedian Euripides' *Hippolytus*. Like the ancient tragedians, Racine, who perfected the French neoclassical tragic style, focused on conflicts, such as between love and honor or inclination and duty, that characterized and revealed the tragic dimensions of life.

Jean-Baptiste Molière (1622–1673) enjoyed the favor of the French court and benefited from the patronage of the Sun King. He wrote, produced, and acted in a series of comedies that often satirized the religious and social world of his time (see the box on p. 557). In *The Misanthrope*, he mocked the corruption of court society,

while in *Tartuffe*, he ridiculed the bigotry of the clergy. Molière's satires, however, sometimes got him into trouble. The Paris clergy did not find *Tartuffe* funny and had it banned for five years. Only the protection of Louis XIV saved Molière from more severe harassment.

International Law and Political Thought

The seventeenth-century search for order and harmony, a response to the disorder generated by wars and internal crises, is apparent in the development of international law. This subject had been of much importance to Italian jurists of the Renaissance. Influenced by the revival of Greco-Roman thought and living in Europe's first secular states, they had deliberated upon the problems of diplomatic relations among states.

It was a seventeenth-century Dutch lawyer with a humanist education, Hugo Grotius (1583–1645), who provided a synthesis of previous doctrine on international law. In his work, *On the Law of War and Peace*, which appeared in 1625, he stated that his goal was to treat "of that law that exists between peoples or between the rulers or peoples." International law, Grotius

▼ **Rembrandt von Rijn,** *Syndics of the Cloth Guild.* The Dutch experienced a Golden Age of painting during the seventeenth century. The burghers and patricians of Dutch urban society commissioned works of art, and these quite naturally reflected the worldly interests of burgher society, as this painting by Rembrandt illustrates. Rembrandt eventually abandoned the largely secular matter with which other artists dealt and turned to more introspective religious works.

French Comedy

▼ ▼ ▼

The comedy writer Jean-Baptiste Molière has long been regarded as one of the best playwrights of the age of Louis XIV. Like Shakespeare, Molière was a complete man of the theater. He wrote, directed, produced, and acted in a series of comedies that satirized the social and religious foibles of his age. This selection from The Would-Be Gentleman comes from a scene in Act II in which Molière ridicules the pretensions of the tutors hired by Monsieur Jourdain, a wealthy, but vain and pretentious Parisian merchant.

Jean-Baptiste Molière, *The Would-Be Gentleman*

(Enter a Philosophy Master.)

M. JOURDAIN: Hola, Monsieur Philosopher, you are come in the nick of time with your philosophy. Come, and make peace a little amongst these people here.

PHILOSOPHY MASTER: What's to do? What's the matter, gentlemen?

M. JOURDAIN: They have put themselves into such a passion about the preference of their professions as to call names, and would come to blows.

PHILOSOPHY MASTER: O fie, gentlemen, what need was there of all this fury? Have you not read the learned treatise upon anger, composed by Seneca? Is there anything more base and shameful than this passion which makes a savage beast of a man? And should not reason be master of all our commotions?

DANCING MASTER: How, sir? Why he has just now been abusing us both, in despising character dancing which is my employment, and music which is his profession.

PHILOSOPHY MASTER: A wise man is above all foul language that can be given him, and the grand answer one should make to all affronts is moderation and patience.

FENCING MASTER: They had both the assurance to compare their professions to mine.

PHILOSOPHY MASTER: Should this disturb you? Men should not dispute about vainglory and rank; that which perfectly distinguishes one from another is wisdom and virtue.

DANCING MASTER: I maintained to him that dancing was a science to which one cannot do sufficient honour.

MUSIC MASTER: And I, that music is one of those that all ages have revered.

FENCING MASTER: And I maintained against 'em both that the science of defence is the finest and most necessary of all sciences.

PHILOSOPHY MASTER: And what becomes of philosophy, then? You are all three very impertinent fellows, methinks, to speak with this arrogance before me; and impudently to give the name of science to things that one ought not to honour even with the name of art, that can't be comprised but under the name of a pitiful trade of gladiator, ballad-singer, and morris-dancer.

FENCING MASTER: Out, ye dog of a philosopher.

MUSIC MASTER: Hence, ye scoundrel of a pedant.

DANCING MASTER: Begone, ye arrant pedagogue.

(The Philosopher falls upon them, they all three lay him on.)

PHILOSOPHY MASTER: How? Varlets as you are—

M. JOURDAIN: Monsieur Philosopher!

PHILOSOPHY MASTER: Infamous dogs! Rogues! Insolent curs!

M. JOURDAIN: Monsieur Philosopher!

FENCING MASTER: Plague on the animal!

M. JOURDAIN: Gentlemen!

PHILOSOPHY MASTER: Impudent villains!

M. JOURDAIN: Monsieur Philosopher!

DANCING MASTER: Deuce take the pack-saddled ass!

M. JOURDAIN: Gentlemen!

PHILOSOPHY MASTER: Profligate vermin!

M. JOURDAIN: Monsieur Philosopher!

MUSIC MASTER: The devil take the impertinent puppy!

PHILOSOPHY MASTER: Knaves! Ragamuffins! Traitors! Imposters!

M. JOURDAIN: Monsieur Philosopher! Gentlemen! Monsieur Philosopher! Gentlemen!

Monsieur Philosopher!

(The four masters beat each other.)

Nay, beat your hearts out if you will, I shall neither meddle nor make with you, I shan't spoil my gown to part you. I should be a great fool to thrust myself among them, and receive some blow that might do me a mischief.

contended, was derived from the natural law instituted by God that was common to all humanity. Natural law included the human need to live in society, the rationality of human nature, and the central role of the family in human society. While war was undesirable, it was unavoidable. What was needed then, according to Grotius, was a system of rules to govern it, just as there was a rational system that ordered the relationship between states and between rulers and their subjects in peacetime.

Grotius and other theorists on international law seemed to realize that the religious divisions created by the Reformation had destroyed what remained of the medieval tradition of Europe as a *corpus Christianum*, a common community of Christians. They accepted the newfound sovereignty of separate European states, but worried about the morality of living in an international jungle. The doctrine of international law gave European states a "secularized moral code" without restricting their freedom to play the game of power politics.

POLITICAL THOUGHT   The preoccupations with order and power, two significant characteristics of the seventeenth century, were reflected in political thought. Thomas Hobbes was an Englishman who was alarmed by the revolutionary upheavals in seventeenth-century England: "The state of man," he wrote, "can never be without some incommodity or other"; nevertheless, "the greatest, that in any form of government can possibly happen to the people in general, is scarce sensible in respect of the miseries, and horrible calamities, that accompany a civil war, or that dissolute condition of masterless men, without subject to laws, and a coercive power to tie their hands from rapine and revenge." Hobbes's name has since been associated with the state's claim to absolute authority over its subjects, which he elaborated in his major treatise on political thought known as the *Leviathan*, published in 1651.

Hobbes viewed human nature in materialistic and mechanistic terms. He claimed that in the theoretical state of nature, before society was organized, human life was "solitary, poor, nasty, brutish, and short." Humans were guided not by reason and moral ideals, but by animalistic instincts and a ruthless struggle for self-preservation (see the box on p. 559). To save themselves from destroying each other (the "war of every man against every man"), people contracted to form a commonwealth, which Hobbes called "that great Leviathan (or rather, to speak more reverently, that mortal god) to which we owe our peace and defense." This common-

wealth placed its collective power into the hands of a sovereign authority, preferably a single ruler, who served as executor, legislator, and judge. This absolute ruler possessed unlimited power. Subjects may not rebel; if they do, they must be suppressed. If the ruler became incapable of effectively exercising his power, he gave up his sovereignty, and his subjects transferred their loyalty to another ruler who would preserve their peace.

Thomas Hobbes's rational analysis of political authority stunned many of his contemporaries. His acceptance of power politics without recourse to spiritual foundations offended many of them. Later, when the secular nation-state became the standard political unit of Western civilization, Hobbes, like Machiavelli, would be acclaimed as a political theorist of great genius.

Other intellectuals in the seventeenth century viewed the exercise of political power quite differently from Hobbes and argued against the absolute rule of one man. The most famous was another Englishman, John Locke (1623–1704), whose experience of English politics was transformed into a political work called *Two Treatises of Government*.

Like Hobbes, Locke argued from the theoretical condition of the state of nature before human existence became organized socially. But, unlike Hobbes, Locke believed humans lived then in a state of equality and freedom rather than a state of war. In this state of nature, humans had certain inalienable natural rights—to life, liberty, and property. Like Hobbes, Locke did not believe all was well in the state of nature. Since there was no impartial judge in the state of nature, people found it difficult to protect these natural rights. So they made a contract and mutually agreed to establish a government to ensure the protection of their rights. This was a contract of mutual obligations: government would protect the rights of the people while the people would act reasonably toward government. But if a government broke this contract—if a monarch, for example, failed to live up to his obligation to protect the natural rights or claimed absolute authority and made laws without the consent of the community—the people might form a new government. "The community perpetually retains a supreme power," Locke claimed. For Locke, however, the community of people was primarily the landholding aristocracy who were represented in Parliament, not the landless masses. Locke was hardly an advocate of political democracy, but his ideas proved important to both Americans and French in the eighteenth century and were used to support demands for constitutional government, the rule of law, and the protection of rights.

Hobbes and the War of "Every Man against Every Man"
▼ ▼ ▼

The seventeenth-century obsession with order and power was well reflected in the political thought of the Englishman Thomas Hobbes. In his Leviathan, *Hobbes presented the case for the state's claim to absolute authority over its subjects. In this selection from his famous work, he describes human life in its original "state of nature."*

Thomas Hobbes, *Leviathan*

Hereby it is manifest, that during the time men live without a common Power to keep them all in awe, they are in that condition which is called War; and such a War, as is of every man, against every man. For War, consists not of Battle only, or the act of fighting; but in a tract of time, wherein the Will to contend by Battle is sufficiently known: and therefore the notion of Time, is to be considered in the nature of War; as it is in the nature of Weather. For as the nature of Foul weather, lieth not in a shower or two of rain; but in an inclination thereto of many days together; So the nature of War, consists not in actual fighting; but in the known disposition thereto, during all the time there is no assurance to the contrary. All other time is PEACE.

Whatsoever therefore is consequent to a time of War, where every man is Enemy to every man; the same is consequent to the time, wherein men live without other security, than what their own strength, and their own invention shall furnish them withall. In such condition, there is no place for Industry; because the fruit thereof is uncertain: and consequently no Culture of the Earth; no Navigation, nor use of the commodities that may by imported by Sea; no commodious Building; no Instruments of moving, and removing such things as require much force; no Knowledge of the face of the Earth; no account of Time; no Arts; no Letters; no Society; and which is worst of all, continual fear, and anger of violent death; And the life of man, solitary, poor, nasty, brutish, and short.

To many historians, the seventeenth century has assumed extraordinary proportions. The divisive effects of the Reformation had been assimilated and the concept of a united Christendom, held as an ideal since the Middle Ages, had been irrevocably destroyed by the religious wars, making possible the emergence of a system of nation-states in which power politics took on an increasing significance. The growth of international law and political thought focusing on the secular origins of state power reflected the changes that were going on in seventeenth-century society.

Within those states, there slowly emerged some of the machinery that made possible a growing centralization of power. In those states called absolutist, strong monarchs with the assistance of their aristocracies took the lead in providing the leadership for greater centralization. But in England, where the landed aristocracy gained power at the expense of the monarchs, the foundations were laid for a constitutional government in which Parliament provided the focus for the institutions of central-ized power. In all the major European states, a growing concern for power and dynastic expansion led to larger armies and greater conflict. The growth of international law represented an attempt to create a rational system for this conflict, but it did nothing to achieve a peaceful solution to human problems. War remained an endemic feature of Western civilization.

But the search for order and harmony continued, evident in art and literature. At the same time, while it would be misleading to state that Europe had become a secular world, we would have to say that religious preoccupations and values were losing ground to secular considerations. The seventeenth century was a transitional period to a more secular spirit that has characterized modern Western civilization until the present time. No stronger foundation for this spirit could be found than in the new view of the universe that was created by the Scientific Revolution of the seventeenth century, and it is to that story that we must now turn.

Notes
▼ ▼ ▼

1. Quoted in D. H. Pennington, *Europe in the Seventeenth Century*, 2d ed. (London and New York, 1989), p. 313.
2. Quoted in John B. Wolf, *Louis XIV* (New York, 1968), p. 134.
3. Quoted in ibid., p. 618.
4. Quoted in Pennington, *Europe in the Seventeenth Century*, p. 494.
5. Quoted in Wolf, *Louis XIV*, p. 284.
6. Quoted in J. H. Elliott, *Imperial Spain, 1469–1716* (New York, 1963), p. 306.

7. Quoted in ibid., p. 338.
8. Quoted in Vasili Klyuchevsky, *Peter the Great*, trans. Liliana Archibald (New York, 1958), p. 244.
9. Quoted in B. H. Sumner, *Peter the Great and the Emergence of Russia* (New York, 1962), p. 122.
10. Quoted in Violet Barbour, *Capitalism in Amsterdam in the 17th Century* (Ann Arbor, Mich., 1963), p. 46.
11. Quoted in H. G. Koenigsberger, *Early Modern Europe: 1500–1798* (London, 1987), p. 172.

Suggestions for Further Reading
▼ ▼ ▼

In addition to the general works listed in Chapter 15, see also D. H. Pennington, *Europe in the Seventeenth Century*, 2d ed. (London and New York, 1989); and R. S. Dunn, *The Age of Religious Wars, 1559–1715*, 2d ed. (New York, 1979).

For a brief account of seventeenth-century French history, see R. Briggs, *Early Modern France, 1560–1715* (Oxford, 1977). More detailed studies on France during the periods of Henry IV and Cardinals Richelieu and Mazarin are M. Greengrass, *France in the Age of Henri IV: The Struggle for Stability* (London, 1984); R. Bonney, *Political Change in France under Richelieu and Mazarin, 1624–1661* (Oxford, 1978); and J. Bergin, *Cardinal Richelieu: Power and the Pursuit of Wealth* (London, 1985). A solid and very readable biography of Louis XIV is J. B. Wolf, *Louis XIV* (New York, 1968). Also of value are the works by G. R. R. Treasure, *Seventeenth Century France* (Garden City, N.Y., 1967); and P. Goubert, *Louis XIV and Twenty Million Frenchmen*, trans. A. Carter (New York, 1970). A now classic work on life in Louis XIV's France is W. H. Lewis, *The Splendid Century* (Garden City, N.Y., 1953). Well-presented summaries of revisionist views on Louis's monarchical power are R. Mettam, *Power and Faction in Louis XIV's France* (Oxford, 1988); and W. Beik, *Absolutism and Society in Seventeenth-Century France* (Cambridge, 1985). C. W. Cole, *Colbert and a Century of French Mercantilism*, 2 vols. (London, 1939), is still the fundamental study. The effects of the expulsion of the Huguenots are examined in W. C. Scoville, *The Persecution of the Huguenots and*

French Economic Development, 1680–1720 (Berkeley, 1960). A specialized study of Louis's last war is H. Kamen, *The War of the Succession in Spain* (London, 1969).

Good general works on seventeenth-century Spanish history include the relevant sections of J. H. Elliott, *Imperial Spain, 1469–1716* (New York, 1963; rev. ed. 1977); H. Kamen, *Spain 1469–1716: A Society of Conflict* (London, 1983); and R. A. Stradling, *Europe and the Decline of Spain, 1580–1720* (London, 1981). On the last half of the seventeenth century, see the more detailed work by H. Kamen, *Spain in the Later Seventeenth Century, 1665–1700* (London, 1980). The important minister Olivares is examined in J. H. Elliott, *The Count-Duke of Olivares: The Statesman in an Age of Decline* (London, 1986).

An older, but still valuable survey of the German states in the seventeenth century can be found in H. Holborn, *A History of Modern Germany, 1648–1840* (London, 1965). On the creation of an Austrian state, see R. J. W. Evans, *The Making of the Habsburg Monarchy, 1550–1700* (Oxford, 1979). The older work by F. L. Carsten, *The Origins of Prussia* (Oxford, 1954), remains an outstanding study of early Prussian history. On aspects of seventeenth-century Swedish history, see the works by M. Roberts, *Gustavus Adolphus: A History of Sweden, 1611–1632*, 2 vols. (London, 1953–58); and *Sweden's Age of Greatness* (London, 1973). A good biography of the dynamic Charles XII is R. Hatton, *Charles XII of Sweden* (London, 1968). For an introduction to Polish history, see N. Davies, *God's Playground: A History of Poland*, vol. 1, *The Origins to 1795* (Oxford, 1981).

On Russian history before Peter the Great, see the classic work by V. O. Klyuchevsky, *A Course in Russian History: The Seventeenth Century* (Chicago, 1968); and R. Nellie, *Enserfment and Military Change in Muscovy* (Chicago, 1971). Works on Peter the Great include V. O. Klyuchevsky, *Peter the Great*, trans. L. Archibald (New York, 1958); M. S. Anderson, *Peter the Great* (London, 1978); B. H. Sumner, *Peter the Great and the Emergence of Russia* (New York, 1962); and the massive popular biography by R. K. Massie, *Peter the Great* (New York, 1980). For an introduction to Ottoman history, see P. Coles, *The Ottoman Impact on Europe, 1350–1699* (London, 1968). J. Stoye, *The Siege of Vienna* (London, 1964), is a fascinating account of the Turkish empire's last great assault on Europe.

In addition to the works listed in Chapter 15 on the seventeenth century in England, see also J. P. Kenyon, *Stuart England* (London, 1978); and C. Hill, *The Century of Revolution* (Edinburgh, 1961). For a general survey of the post-Cromwellian era, see J. R. Jones, *Country and Court: England, 1658–1714* (London, 1978). A more specialized study is J. R. Jones, *The Revolution of 1688 in England* (London, 1972). On Charles II, see the scholarly biography by R. Hutton, *Charles II* (Oxford, 1989).

On the United Provinces, see two short, but sound introductions, K. H. D. Haley, *The Dutch in the Seventeenth Century* (London, 1972); and C. Wilson, *The Dutch Republic and the Civilisation of the Seventeenth Century* (London, 1968). Works on Amsterdam include J. J. Murray, *Amsterdam in the Age of Rembrandt* (Norman, Okla., 1967); and D. Regin, *Traders, Artists, Burghers: A Cultural History of Amsterdam in the 17th Century* (Assen, 1976). Of much value is S. Schama, *The Embarrassment of Riches: An Interpretation of Dutch Culture in the Golden Age* (New York, 1987).

On the economic side of the seventeenth century, there are the three volumes by F. Braudel, *Civilization and Capitalism in the 15th to 18th Century*, which obviously cover much more than just the seventeenth century: *The Structures of Everyday Life* (London, 1981); *The Wheels of Commerce* (London, 1982); and *The Perspective of the World* (London, 1984). Two single-volume comprehensive surveys are J. de Vries, *The Economy of Europe in an Age of Crisis* (Cambridge, 1976); and H. Kellenbenz, *The Rise of the European Economy: An Economic History of Continental Europe from the Fifteenth to the Eighteenth Century* (London, 1976). On overseas trade and colonial empires, see C. R. Boxer, *The Dutch Seaborne Empire, 1600–1800* (New York, 1965); and R. Davis, *English Overseas Trade, 1500–1700* (London, 1973). Although frequently criticized, the standard work on mercantilism remains E. Hecksher, *Mercantilism*, 2 vols. (London, 1935).

A brief survey of the cultural aspects of the seventeenth century can be found in F. B. Artz, *From the Renaissance to Romanticism* (Chicago, 1962). French theater and literature are examined in M. Turnell, *The Classical Moment* (London, 1964); and A. Adam, *Grandeur and Illusion: French Literature and Society, 1600–1715*, trans. J. Tint (New York, 1972). For an examination of French and Dutch art, see A. Blunt, *Art and Architecture in France, 1500–1700* (London, 1953); J. Rosenberg, S. Silve, and E. H. ter Kuele, *Dutch Art and Architecture, 1600–1800* (London, 1966); and C. White, *Rembrandt and His World* (London, 1964). Locke's political ideas are examined in J. H. Franklin, *John Locke and the Theory of Sovereignty* (London, 1978). On Thomas Hobbes, see D. D. Raphael, *Hobbes* (London, 1977).

Toward a New Heaven and a New Earth: The Scientific Revolution and the Emergence of Modern Science

▼▼▼▼▼

In addition to the constitutional, demographic, political, economic, and international crises of the seventeenth century, we need to add an intellectual one. The Scientific Revolution questioned and ultimately challenged conceptions and beliefs about the nature of the external world and reality that had crystallized into a rather strict orthodoxy by the Late Middle Ages. Derived from the works of ancient Greeks and Romans and grounded in Christian thought, the medieval worldview had become a formidable one. No doubt, the breakdown of Christian unity during the Reformation and the subsequent religious wars had created an environment in which Europeans had become accustomed to challenging both the ecclesiastical and political realms. Should it surprise us that a challenge to intellectual authority soon followed?

The Scientific Revolution brought Europeans a new way of viewing the universe and their place in it. The shift from an earth-centered to a sun-centered cosmos had an emotional as well as an intellectual effect upon those who understood it. Thus the Scientific Revolution, popularized in the eighteenth-century Enlightenment, stands as the major force in the transition to the largely secular, rational, and materialistic perspective that has defined the modern Western mentality since its full acceptance in the nineteenth and twentieth centuries.

In one sense, the Scientific Revolution was not a revolution. It was not characterized by the explosive change and rapid overthrow of traditional authority that we normally associate with the

Copernicus, *On the Revolution of the Heavenly Spheres*

Kepler's Laws

Galileo, *The Starry Messenger*

Newton, *Principia*

▼ ▼ ▼ ▼

•••••••• 1500 •••••••••••• 1550 •••••••••••• 1600 •••••••••••• 1650 •••••••••••• 1700 •••••••••

▲ ▲ ▲ ▲ ▲

Vesalius, *On the Fabric of the Human Body*

Harvey's Theory of Circulation

Descartes, *Discourse on Method*

Cavendish, *Grounds of Natural Philosophy*

word *revolution.* The Scientific Revolution did overturn centuries of authority, but only in a gradual and piecemeal fashion. Nevertheless, its results were truly revolutionary. While the Renaissance and Reformation might be viewed, as one historian of science has argued, as "a mere internal displacement within the system of medieval Christendom," the Scientific Revolution was the key factor in setting Western civilization along its modern secular and material path.

▼ Background to the Scientific Revolution

To say that the Scientific Revolution brought about a dissolution of the medieval worldview is not to say that the Middle Ages was a period of scientific ignorance. Many educated Europeans took an intense interest in the world around them since it was, after all, "God's handiwork" and therefore an appropriate subject for study. Late medieval scholastic philosophers from Roger Bacon on had advanced mathematical and physical thinking in many ways, but the subjection of these thinkers to a strict theological framework and their unquestioning reliance on a few ancient authorities, especially Aristotle and Galen, limited where they could go. Many "natural philosophers," as medieval scientists were called, preferred refined logical analysis to systematic observations of the natural world. A number of historians have argued, however, that some of the natural philosophers developed ideas that came to fruition in the seventeenth century. These historians have pointed out, for example, that Galileo's development of the science of mechanics was grounded upon the work of fourteenth-century scholastics. And yet, as other scholars have noted, there was still a great contrast between the "the-

oretical" approach of the scholastics and the "practical" experiments of Galileo that enabled him to make his case.

The historical debate over the issue of late medieval influence on the Scientific Revolution reminds us that historians have had a difficult time explaining the causes of the Scientific Revolution. They have pointed out, however, that a number of changes and advances in the fifteenth and sixteenth centuries may have played a major role in helping natural philosophers abandon their old views and develop new ones.

While medieval scholars had made use of Aristotle, Galen, and Ptolemy in Latin translations to develop many of their positions in the fields of physics, medicine, and astronomy, it was the Renaissance humanists who mastered Greek as well as Latin and made available new works of Galen, Ptolemy, and Archimedes as well as Plato and the pre-Socratics. These writings made it apparent that even the unquestioned authorities of the Middle Ages, Aristotle and Galen, had been contradicted by other thinkers. The desire to discover which school of thought was correct stimulated new scientific work that sometimes led to a complete rejection of the classical authorities. We know that Copernicus, for example, founder of the heliocentric theory, had read in Plutarch (discovered by the Renaissance) that Philolaus and a number of other ancients had believed that it was the earth and not the sun that moved.

Renaissance artists have also been credited with making an impact on scientific study. Their desire to imitate nature led them to rely upon a close observation of nature. Their accurate renderings of rocks, plants, animals, and human anatomy established new standards for the study of natural phenomena. At the same time, the "scientific" study of the problems of perspective and correct anatomical proportions led to new insights. "No painter," one Renaissance artist declared, "can paint well without a thorough knowledge of geometry."[1] Renaissance artists were frequently called upon to be practicing mathematicians as well. Leonardo da Vinci devised "war machines" while Albrecht Dürer made designs for the fortifications of cities.

Although these artistic designs for technical innovations were done primarily on paper, mathematicians, military engineers, naval architects, and navigators were being asked to solve such practical problems as how to navigate in unknown seas, how to compute the trajectories of cannon balls for more effective impact, and how to calculate the tonnage of ships accurately. These technical problems served to stimulate scientific activity since all of them required careful observation and accurate measurements. The fifteenth and sixteenth centuries witnessed a proliferation of books dedicated to machines and technology, all of which espoused the belief that innovation in techniques was necessary. The relationship between technology and the Scientific Revolution, however, is not a simple one since many technological experts did not believe in abstract or academic learning. Indeed, many of the technical innovations of the Middle Ages and Renaissance were accomplished by people outside the universities, where the emphasis was on theoretical rather than practical knowledge. In any case, the invention of new instruments and machines, such as the telescope and microscope, often made new scientific discoveries possible. Above all, the printing press had an indirect, but crucial role in spreading innovative ideas quickly and easily.

Mathematics, which played such a fundamental role in the scientific achievements of the sixteenth and seventeenth centuries, was promoted in the Renaissance by the rediscovery of the works of ancient mathematicians and the influence of Plato (see Chapter 13), who had emphasized the importance of mathematics in explaining the universe. While mathematics was applauded as the key to navigation, military science, and geography, the Renaissance also held the widespread belief that mathematics was the key to understanding the nature of things. According to Leonardo da Vinci, since God eternally geometrizes, nature is inherently mathematical: "Proportion is not only found in numbers and measurements but also in sounds, weights, times, positions, and in whatsoever power there may."[2] Moreover, mathematical reasoning was seen as promoting a degree of certainty that was otherwise impossible. In the words of Leonardo da Vinci: "There is no certainty where one can neither apply any of the mathematical sciences nor any of those which are based upon the mathematical sciences."[3] Copernicus, Kepler, Galileo, and Newton were all great mathematicians who believed that the secrets of nature were written in the language of mathematics.

A final factor in the origins of the Scientific Revolution, the role of magic, has been the object of heated scholarly debate. Renaissance magic was the preserve of an intellectual elite from all of Europe (see the box on p. 565). By the end of the sixteenth century, Hermetic and cabalist magic had become fused with alchemical thought into a single intellectual framework. This tradition believed that the world was a living embodiment of divinity. Humans, who it was believed also had that spark of divinity within, could use magic, especially mathematical magic, to understand and dominate the world of nature or employ the powers of nature for beneficial purposes. Was it Hermeticism, then, that inaugurated the shift in consciousness that made the Scientific Revolution possible, since the desire to control and dominate the natural world was a crucial motivating force in the Scientific Revolution? One scholar has argued:

> It is a movement of the will which really originates an intellectual movement. A new centre of interest arises, surrounded by emotional excitement; the mind turns where the will has directed it and new attitudes, new discoveries follow. Behind the emergence of modern science there was a new direction of the will towards the world, its marvels, and mysterious workings, a new longing and determination to understand those workings and to operate with them.[4]

"This time," the author continues, "the return to the occult [Hermetic-cabalist tradition] stimulates the genuine science."[5] Histories of the Scientific Revolution frequently overlook the fact that the great names we associate with the revolution in cosmology—Copernicus, Kepler, Galileo, and Newton—all had a serious interest in Hermetic ideas and the fields of astrology and alchemy. The mention of these names also reminds us of one final consideration in the origins of the Scientific Revolution: it largely resulted from the work of a handful of great intellectuals.

▼ Toward a New Heaven: A Revolution in Astronomy

The greatest achievements in the Scientific Revolution of the sixteenth and seventeenth centuries came in those fields most dominated by the ideas of the Greeks—astronomy, mechanics, and medicine. The cosmological views of the Late Middle Ages had been built upon a synthesis of the ideas of Aristotle, Claudius Ptolemy (the greatest astronomer of antiquity who lived in the second century A.D.), and Christian theology. In the resulting

Magic and Science: The Case of Girolamo Cardano

▼ ▼ ▼

Girolamo Cardano or Jerome Cardan (1501–1576) was a very important figure in the history of mathematics. He also became a physician and professor of medicine at Pavia in 1547. Like many other intellectuals of the sixteenth century, Cardano was a pupil of magic and astrology. In this selection taken from his autobiography, The Book of My Life, Cardano discusses the presence in his life of what we would call paranormal powers, including prescient dreams, extrasensory perception, and intuitive flashes of direct understanding.

Girolamo Cardano, The Book of My Life

I am conscious that some influence from without seems to bring a murmuring sound to my ear from precisely that direction or region where some one is discussing me. If this discussion be fair, the sound seems to come to rest on the right side; or, if perchance it approaches from the left, it penetrates to the right and becomes a steady hum. If, however, the talk be contentious, strangely conflicting sounds are heard; when evil is spoken, the noise rests in the left ear, and comes from the quarter exactly whence the voices of my detractors are making disturbance, and, accordingly, may approach from any side of my head. . . . Very often when the discussion about me has taken place in the same city, it has happened that the vibration has scarcely ceased before a messenger has appeared who addresses me in the name of my detractors. But if the conversation has taken place in another state and the messenger should appear, one has but to compute the space of time which had elapsed between the discussion and the beginning of the messenger's journey, and the moment I heard the voices and the time of the discussion itself will fall out the same. . . .

A few years later, eight perhaps, that is, about 1534, I began to see in my dreams the events shortly to come to pass. If these events were due to happen on the day following the dream, I used to have clear and defined visions of them just after sunrise, so that even on occasion I saw the motion for my admission to the College of Physicians straightway brought to vote, to a decision, and the motion lost. I dreamed, as well, that I was about to obtain my appointment to the professorship at Bologna. This manifestation by dreams ceased in the year just preceding the cessation of the former manifestation, that is, about 1567. . . . And so it had lasted about thirty-three years.

A third peculiarity is an intuitive flash of direct knowledge. This I employed with gradually increasing advantage. It originated about the year 1529; its effectiveness was increased but it could never be rendered infallible, except toward the close of 1573. For a period between the end of August of that year and the beginning of September 1574, and particularly, as it seems to me, now in this year 1575, I have considered it infallible. It is, moreover, a gift which has not deserted me, and it replaces the powers of those two latter faculties which did; it prepares me to meet my adversaries, and for any pressing necessity. Its component parts are an ingeniously exercised employment of the intuitive faculty, and an accompanying lucidity of understanding.

Ptolemaic or geocentric conception, the universe was seen as a series of concentric spheres with a fixed or motionless earth as its center. Composed of material substance, the earth was imperfect and constantly changing. The spheres that surrounded the earth were made of a crystalline, transparent substance and moved in circular orbits around the earth. Circular movement, according to Aristotle, was the most "perfect" kind of motion and hence appropriate for the "perfect" heavenly bodies thought to consist of a nonmaterial, incorruptible "quintessence." These heavenly bodies, pure orbs of light, were embedded in the moving, concentric spheres and in 1500 numbered ten. Working outward from the earth, eight spheres contained the moon, Mercury, Venus, the sun, Mars, Jupiter, Saturn, and the fixed stars. The ninth sphere imparted to the eighth sphere of the fixed stars its diurnal motion while the tenth sphere was frequently described as the prime mover that moved itself and imparted motion to the other spheres. Beyond the tenth sphere was the Empyrean Heaven—the location of God and all the saved souls. This Christianized Ptolemaic universe, then, was a finite one. It had a fixed end in harmony with Christian thought and expectations.

This medieval, geocentric conception of the universe was one that accorded well with both Christianity and common sense at that time. God and the saved souls were at one end of the universe while humans were at the center. They had been given power over the earth, but their real purpose was to achieve salvation. To ordinary people, this conception of the universe also appeared sensible as they looked up at the night sky. The huge earth could easily be seen as motionless and surrounded by ethereal heavenly bodies circling around it.

This conception, however, did not satisfy professional astronomers who wished to ascertain exactly the paths of the heavenly bodies across the sky. Since observation did not always correspond to the accepted scheme, an elaborate system of devices was developed by astronomers who tried to "save the appearances." They hoped, for example, that epicycles, concentric spheres within spheres as carriers of the planetary bodies, would explain the paths of the planets more precisely while adhering to Aristotle's ideas of circular planetary movement.

Copernicus

Although Nicolaus Copernicus (1473–1543) received a doctorate in canon law and spent the last thirty years of his life as canon of a cathedral, mathematics and astronomy occupied most of his time. He had studied both subjects first at Cracow in his native Poland and later at the Italian universities of Bologna and Padua. Before he left Italy in 1506, he had become aware of ancient views that contradicted the Ptolemaic, earth-centered conception of the universe. Between 1506 and 1530, he completed the manuscript of his famous book, *On the Revolutions of the Heavenly Spheres*, but his own timidity and fear of ridicule from fellow astronomers kept

▼ **Medieval Conception of the Universe.** One of the areas most affected by the Scientific Revolution was astronomy, dominated in the Late Middle Ages by the ideas of Aristotle, Ptolemy, and Christian theology. As this illustration shows, the medieval cosmological view placed earth at the center of the universe, surrounded by a series of concentric spheres. The earth was imperfect and constantly changing while the heavenly bodies that surrounded it were perfect and incorruptible. Beyond the tenth and final sphere was heaven where God and all the saved souls were located.

him from publishing it until May 1543, shortly before his death.

Copernicus was not an accomplished observational astronomer and relied for his data on the records of his predecessors. But he was a mathematician who felt that Ptolemy's geocentric system of epicycles, equants, and eccentrics was too complicated and failed to accord with the observed motions of the heavenly bodies (see the box on p. 568). Copernicus hoped that his heliocentric or sun-centered conception would offer a more accurate explanation.

Using elaborate astronomical and mathematical calculations, Copernicus argued that the universe consisted of eight spheres with the sun motionless at the center and the sphere of the fixed stars at rest in the eighth sphere. The planets revolved around the sun in the order of Mercury, Venus, the earth, Mars, Jupiter, and Saturn. The moon, however, revolved around the earth. More-

over, according to Copernicus, what appeared to be the movement of the sun and the fixed stars around the earth was really explained by the daily rotation of the earth on its axis and the journey of the earth around the sun each year.

Copernicus, however, was basically conservative. He did not reject Aristotle's principle of the existence of heavenly spheres moving in circular orbits. As a result, when he put forth the calculations to prove his new theory, he retained Ptolemy's epicycles and wound up with a system barely less complicated than that of the Alexandrian astronomer.

Nevertheless, the shift from an earth-centered to a sun-centered system was significant and raised, despite Copernicus's own adherence to Aristotle, serious questions about Aristotle's astronomy and physics. It also seemed to create uncertainty about the human role in the universe as well as God's location. Protestant re-

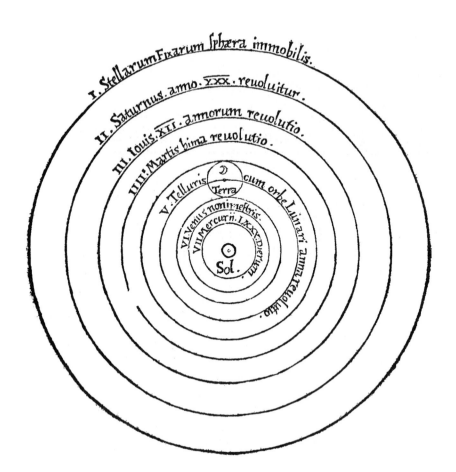

▼ **The Copernican System.** The Copernican system was presented in *On the Revolutions of the Heavenly Spheres*, published shortly before Copernicus's death. As shown in this illustration, Copernicus maintained that the sun was the center of the universe while the planets, including the earth, revolved around it. Moreover, the earth rotated daily on its axis. Copernicus's ideas were condemned by the Catholic church as well as various Protestant reformers.

On the Revolutions of the Heavenly Spheres
▼ ▼ ▼

Nicolaus Copernicus began a revolution in astronomy when he argued that it was the sun and not the earth that was at the center of the universe. Expecting controversy and scorn, Copernicus hesitated to publish the work in which he put forth his heliocentric theory. He finally relented, however, and managed to see a copy of it just before he died.

Nicolaus Copernicus, On the Revolutions of the Heavenly Spheres

For a long time, then, I reflected on this confusion in the astronomical traditions concerning the derivation of the motions of the universe's spheres. I began to be annoyed that the movements of the world machine, created for our sake by the best and most systematic Artisan of all, were not understood with greater certainty by the philosophers, who otherwise examined so precisely the most insignificant trifles of this world. For this reason I undertook the task of rereading the works of all the philosophers which I could obtain to learn whether anyone had ever proposed other motions of the universe's spheres than those expounded by the teachers of astronomy in the schools. And in fact first I found in Cicero that Hicetas supposed the earth to move. Later I also discovered in Plutarch that certain others were of this opinion. I have decided to set his words down here, so that they may be available to everybody:

> Some think that the earth remains at rest. But Philolaus the Pythagorean believes that, like the sun and moon, it revolves around the fire in an oblique circle. Heraclides of Pontus and Ecphantus the Pythagorean make the

earth move, not in a progressive motion, but like a wheel in a rotation from the west to east about its own center.

Therefore, having obtained the opportunity from these sources, I too began to consider the mobility of the earth. And even though the idea seemed absurd, nevertheless I knew that others before me had been granted the freedom to imagine any circles whatever for the purpose of explaining the heavenly phenomena. Hence I thought that I too would be readily permitted to ascertain whether explanations sounder than those of my predecessors could be found for the revolution of the celestial spheres on the assumption of some motion of the earth.

Having thus assumed the motions which I ascribe to the earth later on in the volume, by long and intense study I finally found that if the motions of the other planets are correlated with the orbiting of the earth, and are computed for the revolution of each planet, not only do their phenomena follow therefrom but also the order and size of all the planets and spheres, and heaven itself is so linked together that in no portion of it can anything be shifted without disrupting the remaining parts and the universe as a whole. . . .

Hence I feel no shame in asserting that this whole region engirdled by the moon, and the center of the earth, traverse this grand circle amid the rest of the planets in an annual revolution around the sun. Near the sun is the center of the universe. Moreover, since the sun remains stationary, whatever appears as a motion of the sun is really due rather to the motion of the earth.

---

formers, adhering to a literal interpretation of Scripture, were the first to attack his ideas. Martin Luther thundered against "the new astrologer who wants to prove that the earth moves and goes round. . . . The fool wants to turn the whole art of astronomy upside down. As Holy Scripture tells us, so did Joshua bid the sun stand still and not the earth." Luther's cohort at Wittenberg, Philip Melanchthon condemned him as well:

> The eyes are witness that the heavens revolve in the space of twenty-four hours. But certain men, either from the love of

novelty, or to make a display of ingenuity, have concluded that the earth moves, and they maintain that neither the eighth sphere [of the fixed stars] nor the sun revolves. . . . Now it is a want of honesty and decency to assert such notions publicly, and the example is pernicious. It is the part of a good mind to accept the truth as revealed by God and to acquiesce in it.[6]

The Catholic church remained silent for the time being; it was not until the work of Galileo appeared that Copernicus was denounced. The denunciation came at a

time when an increasing number of astronomers were being attracted to Copernicus's ideas.

Brahe and Kepler

The immediate impact of Copernicus, however, was not momentous—no revolution occurred overnight. Nevertheless, although most people were not yet ready to accept the theory of Copernicus, there were growing doubts about the Ptolemaic system. The next step in destroying the geocentric conception and supporting the Copernican system was taken by Johannes Kepler. It has been argued, however, that Kepler's work would not have occurred without the material provided by Tycho Brahe.

While Tycho Brahe (1546–1601) advanced a new model of the solar system based on a compromise between Copernicus and Ptolemy—the sun and planets revolved around the earth while the other planets revolved around the sun—his real fame rests on a less spectacular contribution. A Danish nobleman, Brahe was granted possession of an island near Copenhagen by King Frederick II. Here Brahe built the elaborate Uraniborg castle, which he outfitted with a library, observatories, and instruments he had designed for more precise astronomical observations. For twenty years, Brahe patiently concentrated on building up a detailed record of his observations of the positions and movements of the stars and planets, a series of observations that have been described as the most accurate up to that time. This body of data led him to reject the Aristotelian-Ptolemaic system, but at the same time he was unable to accept Copernicus's suggestion that the earth actually moved. Brahe's last years were spent in Prague as imperial mathematician to Emperor Rudolf II, who took a keen interest in astronomy, astrology, and the entire Hermetic-cabalist tradition. It was in Prague that Brahe took on an assistant by the name of Johannes Kepler.

Johannes Kepler (1571–1630) had been destined by his parents for a career as a Lutheran minister. While studying theology at the university at Tübingen, however, he fell under the influence of Michael Mästlin, Germany's best-known astronomer, and spent much time pursuing his real interests, mathematics and astronomy. He abandoned theology and became a teacher of mathematics and astronomy at Graz in Austria.

Kepler's work illustrates well the narrow line that often separated magic and science in the early Scientific Revolution. An avid astrologer, Kepler possessed a keen interest in Hermetic thought and Neoplatonic mathematical magic. In a book written in 1596, he elaborated

upon his theory that the universe was constructed on the basis of geometric figures, such as the pyramid and the cube (see the box on p. 570). Believing that the harmony of the human soul (a divine attribute) was mirrored in the numerical relationships existing between the planets, he focused much of his attention upon discovering the "music of the spheres." Kepler was also a brilliant mathematician and astronomer and, after Brahe's death, succeeded him as imperial mathematician to Rudolf II. There he gained possession of Brahe's detailed astronomical data and, using them, arrived at his three laws of planetary motion. These laws may have confirmed Kepler's interest in the "music of the spheres," but more importantly, they confirmed Copernicus's helio-

▼ **Johannes Kepler.** Abandoning theology in favor of mathematics and astrology, Kepler was a key figure in the rise of the new astronomy. Building upon Tycho Brahe's vast astronomical data, Kepler discovered the three laws of planetary motion that both confirmed and modified the Copernican theory. They also eliminated the Ptolemaic-Aristotelian ideas of uniform circular motion and crystalline spheres moving in circular orbits.

Kepler and the Emerging Scientific Community

▼ ▼ ▼

An important avenue for scientific communication involved the exchange of letters between intellectuals who sought to provide practical assistance to each other as well as encouragement in light of the negative reactions to their innovative work. After receiving a copy of Johannes Kepler's first major work, the Italian Galileo Galilei wrote to Kepler, inaugurating a correspondence between them. This selection contains samples of their letters to each other as well as Kepler's letter to his teacher at Tübingen.

Galileo to Kepler, Padua, August 4, 1597

Your book, highly learned gentleman, which you sent me through Paulus Amberger, reached me not days ago but only a few hours ago, and as this Paulus just informed me of his return to Germany, I should think myself indeed ungrateful if I should not express to you my thanks by this letter. I thank you especially for having deemed me worthy of such a proof of your friendship. . . . So far I have read only the introduction, but have learned from it in some measure your intentions and congratulate myself on the good fortune of having found such a man as a companion in the exploration of truth. For it is deplorable that there are so few who seek the truth and do not pursue a wrong method of philosophizing. But this is not the place to mourn about the misery of our century but to rejoice with you about such beautiful ideas proving the truth. . . . I would certainly dare to approach the public with my ways of thinking if there were more people of your mind. As this is not the case, I shall refrain from doing so. . . . I shall always be at your service. Farewell, and do not neglect to give me further good news of yourself.

Yours in sincere friendship,
Galilaeus Galilaeus
Mathematician at the Academy of Padua

Kepler to Michael Mästlin, Graz, September 1597

. . . Lately I have sent two copies of my little book to Italy. They were received with gladness by a mathematician named Galileo Galilei, as he signs himself. He has also been attached for many years to the Copernican heresy.

Kepler to Galileo, Graz, October 13, 1597

I received your letter of August 4 on September 1. It was a double pleasure to me. First because I became friends with you, the Italian, and second because of the agreement in which we find ourselves concerning Copernican cosmography. As you invite me kindly at the end of your letter to enter into correspondence with you, and I myself feel greatly tempted to do so, I will not let pass the occasion of sending you a letter with the present young nobleman. For I am sure, if your time has allowed it, you have meanwhile obtained a closer knowledge of my book. And so a great desire has taken hold of me, to learn your judgment. For this is my way, to urge all those to whom I have written to express their candid opinion. Believe me, the sharpest criticism of one single understanding man means much more to me than the thoughtless applause of the great masses.

I would, however, have wished that you who have such a keen insight into everything would choose another way to reach your practical aims. By the strength of your personal example you advise us, in a cleverly veiled manner, to go out of the way of general ignorance and warn us against exposing ourselves to the furious attacks of the scholarly crowd. (In this you are following the lead of Plato and Pythagoras, our true masters.) But after the beginning of a tremendous enterprise has been made in our time, and furthered by so many learned mathematicians, and after the statement that the earth moves can no longer be regarded as something new, would it not be better to pull the rolling wagon to its destination with united effort. . . . For it is not only you Italians who do not believe that they move unless they feel it, but we in Germany, too, in no way make ourselves popular with this idea. Yet there are ways in which we protect ourselves against these difficulties. . . . Be of good cheer, Galileo, and appear in public. If I am not mistaken there are only a few among the distinguished mathematicians of Europe who would dissociate themselves from us. So great is the power of truth. If Italy seems less suitable for your publication and if you have to expect difficulties there, perhaps Germany will offer us more freedom. But enough of this. Please let me know, at least privately if you do not want to do so publicly, what you have discovered in favor of Copernicus.

centric theory while modifying it in some ways. Above all, they drove another nail into the coffin of the Aristotelian-Ptolemaic system.

Kepler published his first two laws of planetary motion in 1609. Although at Tübingen he had accepted Copernicus's heliocentric ideas, in his first law he contradicted Copernicus by showing that the orbits of the planets around the sun were not circular but elliptical in shape with the sun at one focus of the ellipse rather than at the center. In his second law, he demonstrated that the speed of a planet is greater when it is closer to the sun and decreases as its distance from the sun increases. This proposition destroyed a fundamental Aristotelian tenet that Copernicus had shared—that the motion of the planets was steady and unchanging. Published ten years later, Kepler's third law established that the square of a planet's period of revolution is proportional to the cube of its average distance from the sun. In other words, planets with larger orbits revolve at a slower average velocity than those with smaller orbits.

Kepler's three laws effectively eliminated the idea of uniform circular motion as well as the idea of crystalline spheres revolving in circular orbits. The basic structure of the traditional Ptolemaic system had been destroyed, and people had been freed to think in new terms of the actual paths of planets revolving around the sun in elliptical orbits. By the end of Kepler's life, the Ptolemaic system was rapidly losing ground to the new ideas. Important questions remained unanswered, however: What were the planets made of? And how does one explain motion in the universe? It was an Italian scientist who achieved the next important breakthrough to a new cosmology by answering the first question and making important strides toward answering the second.

Galileo

Galileo Galilei (1564–1642) was the son of a lesser noble Pisan family. Knowing that his son was obviously gifted, his father encouraged him to study medicine, which at that time was a financially rewarding career. Before long Galileo abandoned medicine for his true love, mathematics, and was soon teaching this subject, first at Pisa and later at Padua, one of the most prestigious universities in Europe.

Galileo was the first European to make systematic observations of the heavens by means of a telescope, thereby inaugurating a new age in astronomy. He had heard of a Flemish lens grinder who had created a "spyglass" that magnified objects seen at a distance and soon constructed his own after reading about it. Instead of

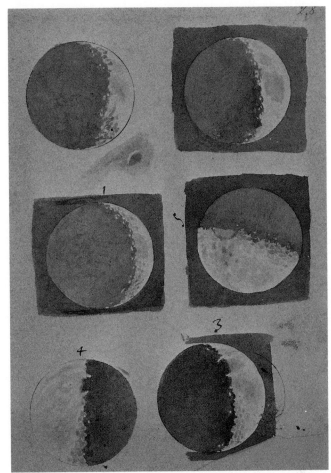

▼ **Galileo's Sketch of the Phases of the Moon.** Galileo Galilei was the first European scientist to use the telescope in making systematic observations of the heavens. Galileo discovered mountains on the moon, sunspots, and the phases of Venus. Pictured here are drawings of the moon from Galileo's notes for one of his books. Galileo was a firm supporter of Copernicus's heliocentric theory, and his defense of this theory brought him into conflict with the Catholic church. Forced to recant his errors in 1633, Galileo spent the remaining eight years of his life in house arrest on his estate.

peering at terrestrial objects, Galileo turned his telescope to the skies and made a remarkable series of discoveries: mountains on the moon, four moons revolving around Jupiter, the phases of Venus, and sun spots. Galileo's observations seemed to destroy yet another aspect of the traditional cosmology in that the universe seemed to be composed of material substance similar to that of the earth rather than ethereal or perfect and unchanging substance.

The Starry Messenger
▼ ▼ ▼

The Italian Galileo Galilei was the first European to use a telescope to make systematic observations of the heavens. His observations, as reported in The Starry Messenger in 1610, stunned European intellectuals by revealing that the celestial bodies were not perfect and immutable, as had been believed, but were apparently composed of material substance similar to the earth. In this selection, Galileo describes how he devised a telescope and what he saw with it.

Galileo Galilei, *The Starry Messenger*

About ten months ago a report reached my ears that a certain Fleming had constructed a spyglass by means of which visible objects, though very distant from the eye of the observer, were distinctly seen as if nearby. Of this truly remarkable effect several experiences were related, to which some persons gave credence while others denied them. A few days later the report was confirmed to me in a letter from a noble Frenchman at Paris, Jacques Badovere, which caused me to apply myself wholeheartedly to inquire into the means by which I might arrive at the invention of a similar instrument. This I did shortly afterwards, my basis being the theory of refraction. First I prepared a tube of lead, at the ends of which I fitted two glass lenses, both plane on one side while on the other side one was spherically convex and the other concave. Then placing my eye near the concave lens I perceived objects satisfactorily large and near, for they appeared three times closer and nine times larger than when seen with the naked eye alone. Next I constructed another one, more accurate, which represented objects as enlarged more than sixty times. Finally, sparing neither labor nor expense, I suc-

ceeded in constructing for myself so excellent an instrument that objects seen by means of it appeared nearly one thousand times larger and over thirty times closer than when regarded with our natural vision.

It would be superfluous to enumerate the number and importance of the advantages of such an instrument at sea as well as on land. But forsaking terrestrial observations, I turned to celestial ones, and first I saw the moon from as near at hand as if it were scarcely two terrestrial radii. After that I observed often with wondering delight both the planets and the fixed stars, and since I saw these latter to be very crowded, I began to seek (and eventually found) a method by which I might measure their distances apart. . . .

Now let us review the observations made during the past two months, once more inviting the attention of all who are eager for true philosophy to the first steps of such important contemplations. Let us speak first of that surface of the moon which faces us. For greater clarity I distinguish two parts of this surface, a lighter and a darker; the lighter part seems to surround and to pervade the whole hemisphere, while the darker part discolors the moon's surface like a kind of cloud, and makes it appear covered with spots. . . . From observation of these spots repeated many times I have been led to the opinion and conviction that the surface of the moon is not smooth, uniform, and precisely spherical as a great number of philosophers believe it (and the other heavenly bodies) to be, but is uneven, rough, and full of cavities and prominences, being not unlike the face of the earth, relieved by chains of mountains and deep valleys.

Galileo's revelations, published in the *The Starry Messenger* in 1610, stunned his contemporaries and probably did more to make Europeans aware of the new picture of the universe than the mathematical theories of Copernicus and Kepler (see the box above). The English ambassador in Venice wrote to the chief minister of King James I in 1610:

> I send herewith unto His Majesty the strangest piece of news . . . that he has ever yet received from any part of the world; which is the annexed book of the Mathematical Professor at

Padua [Galileo], who by the help of an optical instrument . . . has discovered four new planets rolling about the sphere of Jupiter. . . . So upon the whole subject he has first overthrown all former astronomy. . . . By the next ship your Lordship shall receive from me one of the above instruments [a telescope], as it is bettered by this man.[7]

During a trip to Rome, Galileo was received by cardinals and scholars as a conquering hero. Grand Duke Cosimo II of Florence offered him a new position as his court mathematician, which Galileo readily accepted. But even in the midst of his newfound acclaim, Galileo found himself increasingly suspect by the authorities of the Catholic church.

In *The Starry Messenger*, Galileo had revealed himself as a firm proponent of Copernicus's heliocentric system. Encouraged by the Dominicans, who held strongly to Aristotelian ideas, and Cardinal Robert Bellarmine, head of the Jesuit College in Rome, who like other officials feared any dissension that would weaken Catholicism in its struggle with Protestantism, the Roman Inquisition (or Holy Office) of the Catholic church condemned Copernicanism and ordered Galileo to abandon the Copernican thesis. As one cardinal commented, "the intention of the Holy Spirit is to teach us not how the heavens go, but how to go to heaven." The report of the Inquisition ran: "That the doctrine that the sun was the center of the world and immovable was false and absurd, formally heretical and contrary to Scripture, whereas the doctrine that the earth was not the center of the world but moved, and has further a daily motion, was philosophically false and absurd and theologically at least erroneous."[8] Galileo was told, however, that he could continue to discuss Copernicanism as long as he maintained that it was not a fact but a mathematical supposition. It is apparent from the Inquisition's response that the church attacked the Copernican system because it threatened not only Scripture, but also an entire conception of the universe. The heavens were no longer a spiritual world, but a world of matter. Humans were no longer at the center and God was no longer in a specific place. The new system raised such uncertainties that it seemed prudent simply to condemn it.

Galileo, however, never really accepted his condemnation. In 1632, he published his most famous work, *Dialogue on the Two Chief World Systems: Ptolemaic and Copernican*. Unlike most scholarly treatises, it was written in Italian rather than Latin, making it more widely available to the public, which no doubt alarmed the church authorities. The work took the form of a dialogue between Simplicio, a congenial but somewhat stupid supporter of Aristotle and Ptolemy; Sagredo, an openminded layman; and Salviati, a proponent of Copernicus's ideas. There is no question who wins the argument, and the *Dialogue* was quickly perceived as a defense of the Copernican system. Galileo was dragged once more before the Inquisition in 1633, found guilty of teaching the condemned Copernican system, and forced to recant his errors. Placed under house arrest on his estate near Florence, he spent the remaining eight years of his life studying mechanics, a field in which he made significant contributions.

One of the problems that fell under the heading of mechanics was the principle of motion. The Aristotelian conception, which dominated the late medieval world, held that an object remained at rest unless a force was applied against it. If a force was constantly exerted, then the object moved at a constant rate, but if it was removed, then the object stopped. This created some difficulties, especially with a projectile thrown out of a cannon. Late medieval theorists had solved this problem by arguing that the rush of air behind it kept the projectile in motion. The Aristotelian principle of motion also raised problems in the new Copernican system. In the Ptolemaic system, the concentric spheres surrounding the earth were weightless, but in the Copernican system, if a constant force had to be applied to objects to cause movement, then what power or force kept the heavy earth and other planets in motion?

Galileo made two contributions to the problem of motion. First, he demonstrated by experiments that if a uniform force was applied to an object, it would move at an accelerated speed rather than a constant speed. Moreover, Galileo discovered the principle of inertia when he argued that a body in motion continues in motion forever unless deflected by an external force. Thus, a state of uniform motion is just as natural as a state of rest. Before Galileo, natural philosophers had tried to explain motion; now their task was to explain changes in motion. Historians agree that Galileo's work on inertia was important, but differ on whether his work was merely the culmination of the medieval tradition or pointed the way to Newton's law of dynamics.

The condemnation of Galileo by the Inquisition seriously hampered further scientific work in Italy, which had been at the forefront of scientific innovation. Leadership in science now passed to the northern countries, especially England, France, and the Dutch Netherlands. By the 1630s and 1640s, no reasonable astronomer could overlook that Galileo's discoveries combined with Kepler's mathematical laws had made nonsense of the Ptolemaic-Aristotelian world system and clearly established the reasonableness of the Copernican model. Despite Galileo's theories of dynamics, the problem of explaining motion in the universe and tying together the ideas of Copernicus, Galileo, and Kepler had not yet been done. This would be the work of an Englishman who has long been considered the greatest genius of the Scientific Revolution.

Newton

Born in the little English village of Woolsthorpe in 1642, the young Isaac Newton showed little brilliance until he attended Cambridge University and fell under the influence of the mathematician Isaac Barrow. New-

Newton's Rules of Reasoning

▼ ▼ ▼

In 1687, Isaac Newton published his masterpiece, the *Mathematical Principles of Natural Philosophy. In this work, Newton demonstrated the mathematical proofs for his universal law of gravitation and completed the new cosmology begun by Copernicus, Kepler, and Galileo. Newton's work demonstrated that the universe was one huge, regulated, and uniform machine operating according to natural laws. He also described the rules of reasoning by which he arrived at his universal law.*

Isaac Newton, Rules of Reasoning in Philosophy

Rule 1

We are to admit no more causes of natural things than such as are both true and sufficient to explain their appearances.

To this purpose the philosophers say that Nature does nothing in vain, and more is in vain when less will serve; for Nature is pleased with simplicity, and affects not the pomp of superfluous causes.

Rule 2

Therefore to the same natural effects we must, as far as possible, assign the same causes.

As to respiration in a man and in a beast; the descent of stones in Europe and in America; the light of our culinary fire and of the sun; the reflection of light in the earth, and in the planets.

Rule 3

The qualities of bodies, which admit neither intensification nor remission of degrees, and which are found to belong to all bodies within the reach of our experiments, are to be esteemed the universal qualities of all bodies whatsoever.

For since qualities of bodies are only known to us by experiments, we are to hold for universal all such as universally agree with experiments; and such as are not liable to diminution can never be quite taken away.

Rule 4

In experimental philosophy we are to look upon propositions inferred by general induction from phenomena as accurately or very nearly true, notwithstanding any contrary hypotheses that may be imagined, till such time as other phenomena occur, by which they may either be made more accurate, or liable to exceptions.

This rule we must follow, that the argument of induction may not be evaded by hypotheses.

---

ton experienced his first great burst of creative energy in 1666 when the fear of plague closed Cambridge and forced him to return to Woolsthorpe for eighteen months. There Newton discovered his creative talents: "In those days I was in the prime of my life for invention and minded mathematics and philosophy more than at any time since."[9] During this period he invented the calculus, a mathematical means of calculating rates of change, began his investigations into the composition of light, and inaugurated his work on the law of universal gravitation. Two years after his return to Cambridge, in 1669, he accepted a chair of mathematics at the university. During a second intense period of creativity from 1684 to 1686, he wrote his famous *Principia* (see the box above). After a nervous breakdown in 1693, he sought and received an administrative post as warden of the royal mint and was advanced to master of the mint by 1699, a post he held until his death in 1727. Made president of the Royal Society (see The Scientific Societies later in the chapter) in 1703 and knighted in 1705

for his great achievements, Sir Isaac Newton wound up the only English scientist to be buried in Westminster Abbey.

Although Isaac Newton occupies a very special place in the history of modern science, we need to remember that he, too, remained extremely interested in aspects of the occult world. He left behind hundreds of manuscript pages of his studies of alchemy, and, in fact, his alchemical experiments were a major feature of his life until he moved to London in 1696 to become warden of the royal mint. The British economist John Maynard Keynes said of Newton after examining his manuscripts in 1936:

> Newton was not the first of the age of reason. He was the last of the magicians. . . . He looked on the whole universe and all that is in it as a riddle, as a secret which could be read by applying pure thought to certain evidence, certain mystic clues which God had laid about the world to allow a sort of philosopher's treasure hunt to the esoteric brotherhood. He believed that these clues were to be found partly in the ev-

idence of the heavens and in the constitution of elements, . . . but also partly in certain papers and traditions handed down by the brethren in an unknown chain back to the original cryptic revelation in Babylonia.[10]

Although Newton may have considered himself a representative of the Hermetic tradition, he chose, it has been recently argued, for both political and psychological reasons to repress that part of his being, and it is as the "symbol of Western science" that Newton came to be viewed.

Newton's major work, the "hinge point of modern scientific thought," was the *Mathematical Principles of Natural Philosophy*, known simply as the *Principia* by the first word of its Latin title. In this work, the last, highly influential book in Europe to be written in Latin, Newton spelled out the mathematical proofs demonstrating his universal law of gravitation. Newton's work was the culmination of the theories of Copernicus, Kepler, and Galileo. While each had undermined some part of the Ptolemaic-Aristotelian cosmology, no one until Newton had pieced together a coherent synthesis for a new cosmology.

In the first book of the *Principia*, Newton defined the basis concepts of mechanics by elaborating the three laws of motion: the law of inertia that every object continues in a state of rest or uniform motion in a straight line unless deflected by a force; the rate of change of motion of an object is proportional to the force acting upon it; and to every action there is always an equal and opposite reaction. In Book Three, Newton applied his theories of mechanics to the problems of astronomy by demonstrating that these three laws of motion govern the planetary bodies as well as terrestrial objects. Integral to his whole argument was the universal law of gravitation to explain why the planetary bodies did not go off in straight lines but continued in elliptical orbits about the sun. In mathematical terms, Newton explained that every object in the universe was attracted to every other object with a force (that is, gravity) that is directly proportional to the product of their masses and inversely proportional to the square of the distances between them.

The implications of Newton's universal law of gravitation were enormous, even if it took another century before they were widely recognized. Newton had demonstrated that one universal law mathematically proved could explain all motion in the universe. The secrets of the natural world could be known by human investigations. At the same time, the Newtonian synthesis created a new cosmology in which the world was seen

largely in mechanistic terms. The universe was one huge, regulated, and uniform machine that operated according to natural laws in absolute time, space, and motion. Although Newton believed that God was "everywhere present" and acted as the force that moved all bodies on the basis of the laws he had discovered, later generations dropped his spiritual assumptions. Newton's world-machine, conceived as operating absolutely in space, time, and motion, dominated the western worldview until the twentieth century, when the Einsteinian revolution based on a concept of relativity superseded the Newtonian mechanistic concept.

Newton's ideas were soon accepted in England, possibly out of national pride, conviction, and, as has been argued recently, for political reasons (see Science and Society later in the chapter). Natural philosophers on the continent resisted Newton's ideas, and it took much

▼ **Isaac Newton.** Pictured here is a portrait of Isaac Newton by Sir Godfrey Kneller. With a single law, that of universal gravitation, Newton was able to explain all motion in the universe. His great synthesis of the work of his predecessors created a new picture of the universe, one in which the universe was viewed as a great machine operating according to natural laws. Despite his reputation as an eminent scientist, Newton also maintained a keen interest in alchemy.

of the eighteenth century before they were generally accepted everywhere in Europe. They were also reinforced by developments in other fields, especially medicine.

▼ The Breakthrough in Medicine

Although the Scientific Revolution of the sixteenth and seventeenth centuries is associated primarily with the dramatic changes in astronomy and mechanics that precipitated a new perception of the universe, a third field that had been dominated by Greek thought in the Late Middle Ages, that of medicine, also experienced a transformation. Late medieval medicine was dominated not by the teachings of Aristotle, but by those of the Greek physician Galen who had lived in the second century A.D.

Galen's impact on the medieval medical world was pervasive in anatomy, physiology, and disease. Galen had relied on animal, rather than human dissection to arrive at a picture of human anatomy that was quite inaccurate in many instances. Even when Europeans began to practice human dissection in the Late Middle Ages, instruction in anatomy still relied on Galen. While a professor read a text of Galen, an assistant dissected a cadaver for illustrative purposes. Physiology or the functioning of the body was also dominated by Galenic hypotheses, including the belief that there were two separate blood systems. One controlled muscular activities and contained bright red blood moving upward and downward through the arteries; the other governed the digestive functions and contained dark red blood that ebbed and flowed in the veins.

Treatment of disease was highly influenced by Galen's doctrine of four bodily humors: blood, considered warm and moist; yellow bile, warm and dry; phlegm, cold and moist; and black bile, cold and dry. Since disease was supposedly the result of an imbalance of humors that could be discerned from the quantity and color of urine, the examination of a patient's urine became the chief diagnostic tool. Although purging and bleeding to remedy the imbalance were often harmful to patients, the use of traditional herbal medicines frequently proved beneficial.

Three figures are associated with the changes in medicine in the sixteenth and seventeenth centuries: Paracelsus, Andreas Vesalius, and William Harvey. Philippus Aureolus von Hohenheim (1493–1541), who renamed himself Paracelsus (or greater than Celsus, the ancient physician), was born in a small town near Zürich, the son of a country physician who dabbled in astrology. After leaving home at the age of fourteen, Paracelsus traveled widely and may have been awarded a medical degree from the University of Ferrara. He achieved a moment of glory when he was appointed city physician and professor of medicine at Basel in 1527. But this, like so many other appointments, proved short-lived due to his vanity, cantankerous nature, and quick temper. He could never disguise his contempt for universities and physicians who did not agree with his new ideas:

> I am *monarcha medicorum*, monarch of physicians, and I can prove to you what you cannot prove. . . . It was not the constellations that made me a physician: God made me . . . I need not don a coat of mail or a buckler against you, for you are not learned or experienced enough to refute even one word of mine. I wish I could protect my bald head against the flies as effectively as I can defend my monarchy. . . . Let me tell you this: every little hair on my neck knows more than you and all your scribes, and my shoebuckles are more learned than your Galen and Avicenna, and my beard has more experience than all your high colleges.[11]

It was not easy to get along with Paracelsus, and he was forced to wander from one town to another until his death in 1541.

Paracelsus rejected the work of both Aristotle and Galen and attacked the universities as centers of their moribund philosophy. He and his followers hoped to replace the traditional system with a new Christian chemical philosophy that was derived from Neoplatonic, Hermetic, and alchemical foundations and was based upon a new understanding of nature derived from fresh observation and experiment. This chemical philosophy was, in turn, closely connected to a vitalistic universe based on the macrocosm-microcosm analogy. According to this system, a human being was a small replica of the larger world about him. All parts of the universe were represented within each person. As Paracelsus said: "For the sun and the moon and all planets, as well as the stars and the whole chaos, are in man. . . . For what is outside is also inside; and what is not outside man is not inside. The outer and the inner are one thing."[12]

The chemical philosophy of Paracelsus began with his belief that creation had been a "divine chemical separation" in which the four Aristotelian elements—earth, water, air, and fire—were constituted, together with a new triad of elements or "principles," sulfur, mercury, and salt. In accordance with the macrocosmic-microcosmic principle, he believed that the chemical reactions of the universe as a whole were reproduced in human beings on a smaller scale. Disease, then, was not caused by the Galenic imbalance of the four humors, but was due to chemical influences that were localized in specific organs and treated by chemical remedies. Having rejected the humoral theory of Galenic medicine, Paracelsus also rejected the traditional Galenic remedies prepared from herbs. He has since been viewed as the founder of modern chemical medicine.

Although others had used chemical remedies, Paracelsus and his followers differed from them in their careful attention to the proper dosage of their chemically prepared metals and minerals. Gauging the proper amount was especially important in view of the fact that Paracelsus had turned against the Galenic principle that "contraries cure" in favor of the ancient Germanic folk principle that "like cures like." The poison that caused a disease would be its cure if used in proper form and quantity. This use of toxic substances to cure patients was, despite its apparent effectiveness (Paracelsus did have a strong reputation for actually curing his patients), viewed by his opponents as the practice of a "homicide Physician." Later generations came to view Paracelsus more favorably, and historians who have stressed Paracelsus's concept of disease and recognition of "new drugs" for medicine have viewed him as a father of modern medicine. Others have argued that his macrocosmic-microcosmic philosophy and use of "like cures like" drugs make him the forerunner of both homeopathy and the holistic medicine of the postmodern era.

Historians usually associate the name of Paracelsus with the diagnosis and treatment of disease. The new anatomy of the sixteenth century, however, was the work of Andreas Vesalius (1514–1564). His study of medicine at Paris involved him in the works of Galen, the great ancient authority. Especially important to him was a recently discovered text of Galen, *On Anatomical Procedures*, that led Vesalius to emphasize practical research as the principal avenue for understanding human anatomy. After receiving a doctorate in medicine at the University of Padua in 1536, he accepted a position there as professor of surgery. In 1543, he published his masterpiece, *On the Fabric of the Human Body*.

This book was based on his Paduan lectures, in which he deviated from traditional practice by personally dissecting a body to illustrate what he was discussing. Vesalius's anatomical treatise presented a careful examination of the individual organs and general structure of the human body. The book would not have been feasible without either the artistic advances of the Renaissance or technical developments in the art of printing. Together, they made possible the creation of illustrations superior to any hitherto produced.

▼ **Paracelsus.** An extremely arrogant man, Paracelsus was one of the chief figures in the revision of late medieval medicine, which had been dominated by the ideas of the Greek physician Galen. Paracelus embraced a chemical philosophy in which disease, viewed as the result of chemical influences, could be treated by chemical remedies.

Vesalius's "hands-on" approach to teaching anatomy enabled him to overthrow some of Galen's most glaring errors. He did not hesitate, for example, to correct Galen's assertion that the great blood vessels originated from the liver since his own observations made it apparent that they came from the heart. Nevertheless, Vesalius still clung to a number of Galen's erroneous assertions, including the Greek physician's ideas on the ebb and flow of two kinds of blood in the veins and arteries. It was not until William Harvey's work on the circulation of the blood that this Galenic misperception was corrected.

William Harvey (1578–1657) attended Cambridge University and later Padua where he received a doctor-

texts. The daughters and sisters of prominent Christian humanists, for example, were known for their learning. In northern Italy, a number of educated families allowed their young women to pursue a life of scholarship. The ideal of a humanist education for some of the daughters of Europe's elite persisted into the seventeenth century, but only for some privileged women.

In the same fashion as they were drawn to humanism, women were also attracted to the Scientific Revolution. Unlike females educated formally in humanist schools, women attracted to science had to obtain a largely informal education. Female contributions to science were even more remarkable when we consider that women

ate of medicine in 1602. Appointed physician to St. Bartholomew's Hospital in 1609, he later became physician to King James I and Charles I. His reputation, however, rests upon his book, *On the Motion of the Heart and Blood,* published in 1628.

Although questions had been raised in the sixteenth century about Galen's physiological principles, no major break from his system had occurred. Harvey's work, which was based upon meticulous observations and experiments, led him to demolish the ancient Greek's work. Harvey demonstrated that the heart and not the liver was the beginning point of the circulation of blood in the body, that the same blood flows in both veins and arteries, and, most importantly, that the blood makes a complete circuit as it passes through the body. Although Harvey's work dealt a severe blow to Galen's theories, his ideas did not begin to achieve general recognition until the 1660s, when the capillaries, which explained the passing of the body's blood from the arteries to the veins, were discovered. Harvey's theory of the circulation of the blood laid the foundation for modern physiology.

▼ Women in the Origins of Modern Science

During the Middle Ages, except for members of religious orders, women who sought a life of learning were severely hampered by the traditional attitude that a woman's proper role was as a daughter, wife, and mother. But in the late fourteenth and early fifteenth centuries, new opportunities for elite women emerged as enthusiasm for the new secular learning called humanism encouraged Europe's privileged and learned men to encourage women to read and study classical and Christian

▼ **Vesalius Dissecting a Corpse.** The revision of Galenic anatomy was done in part by Andreas Vesalius, shown here dissecting a corpse. In his lectures on human anatomy, he often dissected a human cadaver to illustrate his point. While correcting many of Galen's faulty conclusions, Vesalius still upheld some of the Greek's mistaken observations, such as the ebb and flow of the two kinds of blood.

were largely excluded from universities and the new scientific societies. This was not quite the handicap that it would be today, however. Since science in the seventeenth century was not the preserve of universities, there was often no real dividing line between popular science and professional science, creating chances for women to enter scientific circles. Aristocratic and princely courts as well as artisan workshops presented two such major opportunities for women.

European nobles had the leisure and resources that gave them easy access to the world of learning. This door was also open to noblewomen who could participate in the informal scientific networks of their fathers and brothers. One of the most prominent female scientists of the seventeenth century, Margaret Cavendish (1623–1673), came from an aristocratic background. Cavendish was not a popularizer of science for women but a participant in the crucial scientific debates of her time. She also corresponded with important people on these issues. Despite her achievements, however, she was excluded from membership in the Royal Society (see The Scientific Societies later in the chapter), although she was once allowed to attend a meeting. She wrote a number of works on scientific matters including *Observations upon Experimental Philosophy* and *Grounds of Natural Philosophy*. In these works she did not hesitate to attack what she considered the defects of the rationalist and empiricist approaches to scientific knowledge and was especially critical of the growing belief that humans through science were the masters of nature: "We have no power at all over natural causes and effects. . . . for man is but a small part, . . . his powers are but particular actions of Nature, and he cannot have a supreme and absolute power."[13]

As an aristocrat, the duchess of Cavendish was a good example of the women in France and England who worked in science. Women interested in science who lived in Germany came from a different background. There the tradition of female participation in craft production enabled some women to become involved in observational science, especially entomology and astronomy. Between 1650 and 1710, women constituted 14 percent of all German astronomers.

A good example of female involvement in the Scientific Revolution stemming from the craft tradition was Maria Sibylla Merian (1647–1717), who had established a reputation as an important entomologist by the beginning of the eighteenth century. Merian's training came from working in her father's workshop where she learned the art of illustration, a training of great importance since her exact observation of insects and plants was only demonstrated through the superb illustrations she made. Her first work was the *Wonderful Metamorphosis and Special Nourishment of Caterpillars*, an illustrated study of caterpillars showing every stage in their development, which she had carefully observed and rendered in her drawings. In 1699, she undertook an expedition into the wilds of the Dutch colony of Surinam to collect and draw samples of plants and insect life. This led to her major scientific work, the *Metamorphosis of the Insects of Surinam*, in which she used sixty illustrations to show the reproductive and developmental cycles of Surinam's insect life.

The craft organization of astronomy also gave women opportunities to become involved in science. Those who did worked in family observatories; hence daughters and wives received training as apprentices to fathers or husbands. The most famous of the female astronomers in Germany was Maria Winkelmann (1670–1720). She was educated by her father and uncle and received advanced training in astronomy from a nearby self-taught astronomer. Her opportunity to be a practicing astronomer came when she married Gottfried Kirch, Germany's foremost astronomer. She became his assistant at the astronomical observatory operated in Berlin by the Academy of Science. She made some original contributions, including a hitherto undiscovered comet as her husband related:

> Early in the morning (about 2:00 A.M.) the sky was clear and starry. Some nights before, I had observed a variable star, and my wife (as I slept) wanted to find and see it for herself. In so doing, she found a comet in the sky. At which time she woke me, and I found that it was indeed a comet . . . I was surprised that I had not seen it the night before.[14]

Moreover, Winkelmann corresponded with the famous scientist Leibniz (who invented the calculus independently of Newton), who was effusive in his praise of her as "a most learned woman who could pass as a rarity." When her husband died in 1710, she submitted herself as a candidate for a position as assistant astronomer for which she was highly qualified. As a woman—with no university degree—she was denied the post by the Berlin Academy, which feared that it would establish a precedent by hiring a woman ("mouths would gape"). Winkelmann managed, nevertheless, to continue her astronomical work a while longer at the private observatory of Baron Friederich von Krosigk in Berlin.

Winkelmann's difficulties with the Berlin Academy reflect the obstacles women faced in being accepted in scientific work, which was considered a male preserve.

Although there were no formal statutes excluding women from membership in the new scientific societies, no woman was invited to join either the Royal Society of England or the French Academy of Sciences until the twentieth century. All of these women scientists were exceptional women since a life devoted to any kind of scholarship was still viewed as being at odds with the domestic duties women were expected to perform.

The nature and value of women had been the subject of an ongoing, centuries-long debate known as the *querelles des femmes*—arguments about women. Male opinions in the debate were largely a carryover from medieval times and were not favorable. Women were portrayed as inherently base, prone to vice, easily swayed, and "sexually insatiable." Hence, men needed to control them. Learned women were viewed as having overcome female liabilities to become like men. One man in praise of a woman scholar remarked that her writings were so good that you "would hardly believe they were done by a woman at all."

In the early modern era, women joined this debate by arguing against the distorted images of women held by men. They argued that women also had rational minds and could grow from education. Further, since most women were pious, chaste, and temperate, there was no need for male authority over them. These female defenders of women in the *querelles des femmes* emphasized education as the key to women's ability to move into the world. How, then, did the era of the Scientific Revolution affect this debate over the nature of women? As an era of intellectual revolution in which traditional authorities were being overthrown, we might expect significant change in men's views of women. But by and large, instead of becoming an instrument for liberation, science was used to find new support for the old, traditional views about a woman's place in the scheme of things. This was done in a variety of ways.

One approach is evident in the work of William Harvey who was renowned for his work on the circulation of the blood. In his 1651 book on human reproduction, he argued that a woman provided "matter" but it was the man who gave it life and form from his semen. Harvey regarded semen as the active agent, and in his view it was so powerful that it was "vivifying, endowed with force and spirit and generative influence." By the end of the century, however, some scientists were arguing that males and females influenced the generative process equally. Likewise, new views on anatomy also appeared, but interestingly enough were used to perpetuate old stereotypes about women.

From the work of Galen until late in the sixteenth century, the male and female genitals had been portrayed as not significantly different. The uterus, for example, had been pictured as an internal and inadequate penis. According to Galen, "All parts that men have, women have too . . . the difference between them lies in only one thing . . . that in women the parts are within the body, whereas in men they are outside."[15] But this perspective was radically reevaluated in the seventeenth century, and the uterus was now presented as a perfect instrument for childbearing. It was not long before this view was used to reinforce the traditional argument that women were designed for their role as bearer of their husband's children.

An important project in the new anatomy of the sixteenth centuries was the attempt to illustrate the human body and skeleton. For Vesalius, the portrayal of physical differences between males and females was limited to external bodily form (the outlines of the body) and the sexual organs. Vesalius saw no difference in skeletons and portrayed them as the same for men and women. It was not until the eighteenth century, in fact, that a new anatomy finally prevailed. Drawings of female skeletons between 1730 and 1790 varied, but females tended to have a larger pelvic area, and, in some instances, female skulls were portrayed as smaller than those of males. Eighteenth-century studies on the anatomy and physiology of sexual differences provided "scientific evidence" to reaffirm the traditional inferiority of women. The larger pelvic area "proved" that women were meant to be childbearers while the larger skull "demonstrated" the superiority of the male mind. Male-dominated science had been used to "prove" male social dominance.

At the same time, during the seventeenth and eighteenth centuries, women even lost the traditional spheres of influence they had possessed, especially in the science-related art of midwifery. Women serving as midwives had traditionally been responsible for birthing. Similar to barber-surgeons or apothecaries (see Chapter 18), midwives had acquired their skills through apprenticeship. But the impact of the Scientific Revolution caused traditional crafts to be upgraded and then even professionalized as males took over. When medical men entered this arena, they also began to use devices and techniques derived from the study of anatomy. These were increasingly used to justify the male takeover of the traditional role of midwives. By the end of the eighteenth century, midwives were simply accessories to the art they had once controlled, except for the poor. Since little money was to be made in serving them, midwives were allowed to continue to practice their traditional art for the lower classes.

Overall the Scientific Revolution reaffirmed traditional ideas about women's nature. Male scientists used

The "Natural" Inferiority of Women
▼▼▼

Despite the shattering of old views and the emergence of a new worldview in the Scientific Revolution of the seventeenth century, attitudes toward women remained tied to traditional perspectives. In this selection, the philosopher Benedict de Spinoza argues for the "natural" inferiority of women to men.

Benedict de Spinoza, A Political Treatise

But, perhaps, someone will ask, whether women are under men's authority by nature or institution? For if it has been by mere institution, then we had no reason compelling us to exclude women from government. But if we consult experience itself, we shall find that the origin of it is in their weakness. For there has never been a case of men and women reigning together, but wherever on the earth men are found, there we see that men rule, and women are ruled, and that on this plan, both sexes live in harmony. But on the other hand, the Amazons, who are reported to have held rule of old, did not suffer men to stop in their country, but reared only their female children, killing the males to whom they gave birth. But if by nature women were equal to men, and were equally distinguished by force of character and ability, in which human power and therefore human right chiefly consist; surely among nations so many and different some would be found, where both sexes rule alike, and others, where men are ruled by women, and so brought up, that they can make less use of their abilities. And since this is nowhere the case, one may assert with perfect propriety, that women have not by nature equal right with men: but that they necessarily give way to men, and that thus it cannot happen, that both sexes should rule alike, much less that men should be ruled by women. But if we further reflect upon human passions, how men, in fact, generally love women merely from the passion of lust, and esteem their cleverness and wisdom in proportion to the excellence of their beauty, and also how very ill-disposed men are to suffer the women they love to show any sort of favour to others, and other facts of this kind, we shall easily see that men and women cannot rule alike without great hurt to peace.

the new science to spread the view that women were inferior by nature, subordinate to men, and suited by nature to play a domestic role as nurturing mothers. The widespread distribution of books ensured the continuation of these ideas (see the box above). Jean de La Bruyère, the seventeenth-century French moralist, was typical when he remarked that an educated woman was like a gun that was a collector's item "which one shows to the curious, but which has no use at all, any more than a carousel horse."[16]

▼ Toward a New Earth: Descartes, Rationalism, and a New View of Humankind

The fundamentally new conception of the universe contained in the cosmological revolution of the sixteenth and seventeenth centuries inevitably had an impact on the Western view of humankind. Nowhere is this more evident than in the work of René Descartes (1596–1650), an extremely important figure in Western history. Descartes began by reflecting the doubt and uncertainty that seemed pervasive in the confusion of the seventeenth century and ended with a philosophy that dominated Western thought until the twentieth century.

René Descartes was born into a family of the French lower nobility. After a Jesuit education, he studied law at Poitiers but traveled to Paris to study by himself. As far as can be deduced, he spent much of this period absorbed in the skeptical works of Montaigne. Descartes volunteered for service in 1618 in the army of Maurice of Nassau at the beginning of the Thirty Years' War, but his motives seem to have been guided less by the desire for military action than for travel and leisure time to think. On the night of November 10, 1619, Descartes underwent what one historian has called an experience comparable to the "ecstatic illumination of the mystic." Having perceived in one night the outlines of a new rational-mathematical system, with a sense of divine approval he made a new commitment to mind, mathematics, and a mechanical universe. For the rest of his life, Descartes worked out the details of his vision.

The starting point for Descartes's new system was doubt, as he explained at the beginning of his most famous work, *Discourse on Method*, written in 1637:

▼ **Descartes.** René Descartes was one of the primary figures in the Scientific Revolution. Claiming to use reason as his sole guide to truth, Descartes posited a sharp distinction between mind and matter. The world of matter could be known by the mind, Descartes argued, since the universe was simply a great machine created by God and governed by physical laws.

> From my childhood I have been familiar with letters; and as I was given to believe that by their means a clear and assured knowledge can be acquired of all that is useful in life, I was extremely eager for instruction in them. As soon, however, as I had completed the course of study, at the close of which it is customary to be admitted into the order of the learned, I entirely changed my opinion. For I found myself entangled in so many doubts and errors that, as it seemed to me, the endeavor to instruct myself had served only to disclose to me more and more of my ignorance.[17]

Descartes decided to set aside all that he had learned and begin again. Having rejected the senses, since they easily deceived, one fact seemed to Descartes beyond doubt—his own existence:

> But I immediately became aware that while I was thus disposed to think that all was false, it was absolutely necessary that I who thus thought should be something; and noting that this truth *I think, therefore I am*, was so steadfast and so assured that the suppositions of the skeptics, to whatever extreme they might all be carried, could not avail to shake it, I concluded that I might without scruple accept it as being the first principle of the philosophy I was seeking.[18]

With this emphasis on the mind, Descartes asserted that he would accept only those things that his reason said were true.

From his first postulate, Descartes deduced two additional principles, the existence of God and the separation of mind and matter. Since he—an imperfect being—had conceived of the idea of perfection, it could only have come from a perfect being, i.e., God:

> And since it is no less contradictory that the more perfect should result from, and depend on, the less perfect than that something should proceed from nothing, it is equally impossible I should receive it from myself. Thus we are committed to the conclusion that it has been placed in me by a nature which is veritably more perfect than I am, and which has indeed within itself all the perfections of which I have any idea, that is to say, in a single word, that is God.[19]

Secondly, Descartes argued that since "the mind cannot be doubted but the body and material world can, the two must be radically different." From this came an absolute dualism between mind and body, or what has also been called Cartesian dualism.

According to Descartes, the universe contains two things, both of which God has created. One is thinking substance, what we call the mind. It is essentially spiritual and not composed of matter. Everything in the universe except the thinking substance or mind is extended substance, what we call matter. The material world is the most fundamental thing in the universe and displays two primary characteristics: extension (it occupies space) and motion (it moves). Using mind or human reason, the path to certain knowledge, and its best instrument, mathematics, humans can understand the material world because it is pure mechanism, a machine that is governed by its own physical laws because it was created by God—the great geometrician.

Descartes's conclusions about the nature of the universe and human beings had important implications. His separation of mind and matter allowed scientists to view matter as dead or inert, as something that was totally separate from themselves and could be investigated independently by reason. The split between mind and body led Westerners to equate their identity with mind and reason rather than with the whole organism. Descartes has rightly been called the father of modern ra-

The Father of Modern Rationalism
▼ ▼ ▼

René Descartes has long been viewed as the founder of modern rationalism and modern philosophy because he believed that human beings could understand the world—itself a mechanical system—by the same rational principles inherent in mathematical thinking. In his Discourse on Method, he elaborated upon his approach to discovering truth.

René Descartes, *Discourse on Method*

In place of the numerous precepts which have gone to constitute logic, I came to believe that the four following rules would be found sufficient, always provided I took the firm and unswerving resolve never in a single instance to fail in observing them.

The first was to accept nothing as true which I did not evidently know to be such, that is to say, scrupulously to avoid precipitance and prejudice, and in the judgments I passed to include nothing additional to what had presented itself to my mind so clearly and so distinctly that I could have no occasion for doubting it.

The second, to divide each of the difficulties I examined into as many parts as may be required for its adequate solution.

The third, to arrange my thoughts in order, beginning with things the simplest and easiest to know, so that I may then ascend little by little, as it were step by step, to the knowledge of the more complex, and in doing so, to assign an order of thought even to those objects which are not of themselves in any such order of precedence.

And the last, in all cases to make enumerations so complete, and reviews so general, that I should be assured of omitting nothing.

Those long chains of reasonings, each step simple and easy, which geometers are wont to employ in arriving even at the most difficult of their demonstrations, have led me to surmise that all the things we human beings are competent to know are interconnected in the same manner, and that none are so remote as to be beyond our reach or so hidden that we cannot discover them—that is, provided we abstain from accepting as true what is not thus related, i.e., keep always to the order required for their deduction one from another. And I had no great difficulty in determining what the objects are with which I should begin, for that I already knew, namely, that it was with the simplest and easiest. Bearing in mind, too, that of all those who in time past have sought for truth in the sciences, the mathematicians alone have been able to find any demonstrations, that is to say, any reasons which are certain and evident, I had no doubt that it must have been by a procedure of this kind that they had obtained them.

---

tionalism (see the box above). His books were placed on the papal Index of Forbidden Books and condemned by many Protestant theologians. The radical Cartesian split between mind and matter, and between mind and body, had devastating implications not only for traditional religious views of the universe, but for how Westerners viewed themselves, a perspective that would not be seriously questioned or challenged until the twentieth century.

▼ The Scientific Method

In the course of the Scientific Revolution, attention was also paid to the problem of establishing the proper means to examine and understand the physical realm. This creation of a scientific method was crucial to the evolution of science in the modern world.

Curiously enough, it was an Englishman with few scientific credentials who attempted to put forth a new method of acquiring knowledge that made an impact on the Royal Society in England in the seventeenth century and other European scientists in the eighteenth century. Francis Bacon (1561–1626), a lawyer and lord chancellor, rejected Copernicus and Kepler and misunderstood Galileo. And yet in his unfinished work, *The Great Instauration* (*The Great Restoration*), he called for his contemporaries "to commence a total reconstruction of sciences, arts, and all human knowledge, raised upon the proper foundations." According to Bacon, two attitudes had held people back from this project. Some men had foolishly continued to rely on the ancients, especially Aristotle: "And for its value and utility it must be plainly avowed that that wisdom which we have derived principally from the Greeks is but like the boyhood of knowledge, and has the characteristic property of boys: it can talk, but it cannot generate; for it is fruitful of controversies but barren of works." Equally harmful was the attitude that it was beyond "the powers of man" to understand what God had created in the world. Bacon did not doubt humans' ability to know the natural world, but believed that they had proceeded incorrectly: "The entire fabric of human reason which we employ in the inquisition of nature is badly put together and built up, and like some magnificent structure without foundation."

Bacon's new foundation—a correct scientific method—was to be built upon inductive principles. Rather than beginning with assumed first principles from which logical conclusions could be deduced, he urged scientists to proceed from the particular to the general. Carefully organized experiments and systematic, thorough observations would lead to the careful development of correct generalizations. Bacon's method—to seek knowledge by experiment and observation—has frequently been criticized for emphasizing the empirical, experimental side while lacking any foundation in mathematics and intuition.

Bacon was clear about what he believed his method could accomplish. His concern was more for practical than for pure science. He stated that "the true and lawful goal of the sciences is none other than this: that human life be endowed with new discoveries and power." He wanted science to contribute to the "mechanical arts" by creating devices that would benefit industry, agriculture, and trade. Bacon was prophetic when he said that "I am laboring to lay the foundation, not of any sect or doctrine, but of human utility and power." And how would this "human power" be used? To "conquer nature in action."[20] The control and domination of nature became a central proposition of modern science and the technology that accompanied it. Only in the twentieth century have some scientists raised the question of whether this assumption might not be at the heart of the twentieth-century ecological crisis.

René Descartes proposed a different approach to scientific methodology by emphasizing deduction and mathematical logic. As Descartes explained in *Discourse on Method*, each step in an argument should be as sharp and well founded as a mathematical proof:

These long chains of reasonings which geometers are accustomed to using to reach their most difficult demonstrations, had given me cause to imagine that everything which can be encompassed by man's knowledge is linked in the same way, and that provided only that one abstains from accepting any for true which is not true, and that one always keeps the right order for one thing to be deduced from that which precedes

it, there can be nothing so distant that one does not reach it eventually, or so hidden that one cannot discover it.[21]

Descartes believed then that one could start with self-evident truths, comparable to geometrical axioms, and deduce more complex conclusions. His emphasis on deduction and mathematical order complemented Bacon's stress on experiment and induction. It was Sir Isaac Newton who synthesized them into a single scientific methodology by uniting Bacon's empiricism with Descartes's rationalism. The scientific method, of course, was valuable in answering the question "how" something works, and its success in doing this gave others much confidence in the method. It did not attempt to deal with the question of "why" something happens or the purpose and meaning behind the world of nature. This allowed religion still to be important in the seventeenth century.

▼ Science and Religion in the Seventeenth Century

In Galileo's struggle with the inquisitorial Holy Office of the Catholic church, we see the beginning of the conflict between science and religion that has marked the history of modern Western civilization and ultimately led to much grief for the organized religions. Since time immemorial, theology had seemed to be the queen of the sciences. It was natural that the churches would continue to believe that religion was the final measure of everything. To the emerging scientists, however, it often seemed that theologians knew not of what they spoke. These "natural philosophers" then tried to draw lines between the knowledge of religion and the knowledge of "natural philosophy" or nature. Galileo had clearly felt that it was unnecessary to pit science against religion when he wrote that:

in discussions of physical problems we ought to begin not from the authority of scriptural passages, but from sense-experiences and necessary demonstrations; for the holy Bible and the phenomena of nature proceed alike from the divine word, the former as the dictate of the Holy Ghost and the latter as the observant executrix of God's commands. It is necessary for the Bible, in order to be accommodated to the understanding of every man, to speak many things which appear to differ from the absolute truth so far as the bare meaning of the words is concerned. But Nature, on the other hand, is inexorable and immutable; she never transgresses the laws imposed upon her, or cares a whit whether her abstruse reasons and methods of operation are understandable to men.[22]

To Galileo it made little sense for the church to determine the nature of physical reality on the basis of biblical texts that were subject to radically divergent interpretations. The church, however, decided otherwise in Galileo's case and lent its great authority to one scientific theory, the Ptolemaic-Aristotelian cosmology, no doubt because it fit so well with its own philosophical views of reality. But the church's decision had tremendous consequences, just as the rejection of Darwin's ideas did in the nineteenth century. For educated individuals, it established a dichotomy between scientific investigations and religious beliefs. As the scientific beliefs triumphed, it became almost inevitable that religious beliefs would suffer, leading to a growing secularization in European intellectual life, precisely what the church had hoped to combat by opposing Copernicanism. Many seventeenth-century intellectuals were both religious and scientific and believed that the implications of this split would be tragic. Some believed that the split was largely unnecessary while others felt the need to combine God, humans, and a mechanistic universe into a new philosophical synthesis. Three individuals—Spinoza, Comenius, and Pascal—illustrate some of the wide diversity in the response of European intellectuals to the implications of the cosmological revolution of the seventeenth century.

Benedict de Spinoza (1632–1677) was a Jewish philosopher who grew up in the relatively tolerant atmosphere of Amsterdam. He was excommunicated from the Amsterdam synagogue at the age of twenty-four for rejecting the tenets of Judaism. Ostracized by the local Jewish community and major Christian churches alike, Spinoza lived a quiet, independent life, earning a living by grinding optical lenses and refusing to accept an academic position in philosophy at the University of Heidelberg for fear of compromising his freedom of thought. Spinoza read a great deal of the new scientific literature and was influenced by Descartes.

Although he followed Descartes's rational approach to knowledge, Spinoza was unwilling to accept the implications of Descartes's ideas, especially the separation of mind and matter and the apparent separation of an infinite God from the finite world of matter. God was not simply creator of the universe, he was the universe. All that is is in God and nothing can be apart from God. This philosophy of pantheism (others have labeled it panentheism or monism) was set out in Spinoza's book, *Ethics Demonstrated in the Geometrical Manner*, which was not published until after his death.

To Spinoza, human beings are not "situated in nature as a kingdom within a kingdom," but are as much a part of God or nature or the universal order as other natural objects. The failure to understand God had led to many misconceptions; for one, that nature exists only for one's use:

> As they find in themselves and outside themselves many means which assist them not a little in their search for what is useful, for instance, eyes for seeing, teeth for chewing, herbs and animals for yielding food, the sun for giving light, the sea for breeding fish, they come to look on the whole of nature as a means for obtaining such conveniences.[23]

Furthermore, unable to find any other cause for the existence of these things, they attributed them to a creator-God who must be worshiped to gain their ends: "Hence also it follows, that everyone thought out for himself, according to his abilities, a different way of worshipping God, so that God might love him more than his fellows, and direct the whole course of nature for the satisfaction of his blind cupidity and insatiable avarice." Then, when nature appeared unfriendly in the form of storms, earthquakes, and diseases, "they declared that such things happen, because the gods are angry at some wrong done them by men, or at some fault committed in their worship," rather than realizing "that good and evil fortunes fall to the lot of pious and impious alike."[24] Likewise, human beings made moral condemnations of others since they failed to understand that human emotions, "passions of hatred, anger, envy and so, considered in themselves, follow from the same necessity and efficacy of nature" and "nothing comes to pass in nature in contravention to her universal laws." To explain human emotions, like everything else, we need to analyze them as we would the movements of planets: "I shall, therefore, treat of the nature and strength of my emotions according to the same method as I employed heretofore in my investigations concerning God and the mind. I shall consider human actions and desires in exactly the same manner as though I were concerned with lines, planes, and solids."[25] Everything has a rational explanation of which humans are capable. In using reason, people can find true happiness. Their real freedom comes when they understand the order and necessity of nature and achieve detachment from passing interests.

Spinoza's complex synthesis of God, humans, and the universe was not easily accepted by his contemporaries, and his pantheism was mistakenly condemned as "hideous atheism." Others were upset by his attitude toward morality since he viewed it as found in nature and known by reason, not revealed to people through the Bible. Even Spinoza declared that some would find strange his attempt to treat of human desires "in exactly the same manner as though I were concerned with lines, planes, and solids."

Of the seventeenth-century intellectuals that we might characterize as utopian thinkers, Johann Amos Comenius (1592–1671) perhaps best realized the dangers inherent in the separation of science and religion that was beginning to occur in his century. Comenius used the phrase "pansophia" or universal wisdom to describe the macrocosmic-microcosmic philosophy of Hermeticism: the connection between the inner world of humans and the outer world of nature. Comenius's pansophism was also a utopian fantasy; he dreamed of a revived Christian commonwealth that would begin a universal millennium on earth. By uniting science and religion, pansophism would show the way to a perfected society.

Like other intellectuals influenced by the Hermetic tradition, Comenius favored the establishment of learned societies that would further the goal of working toward a universal reformation of the whole world by the union of science and religion. When the Royal Society was established in England in 1662 (see The Scientific Societies later in the chapter), he hoped that this group would fulfill his goals. He dedicated a new edition of his book, *The Way of Light,* to the Royal Society expressing these hopes. But he also sounded a warning. If the members of the society did not envision ends beyond the cultivation of the natural sciences for themselves alone, their work might turn out to be a "Babylon turned upside down, building not towards heaven, but towards earth."[26] The Royal Society failed to heed his warning, and the separation of science and religion became an established fact of modern Western civilization.

Like Comenius, Blaise Pascal (1623–1662) sought to keep science and religion united; however, his religion was not a utopian Hermeticism but traditional Christianity. Pascal had a brief, but checkered career. He was for a short time a reader of Montaigne and a companion to freethinkers. He was an accomplished scientist and brilliant mathematician, combining the practical by inventing a calculating machine with the abstract by devising a theory of chance or probability and doing work on conic sections. After a profound mystical vision on the night of November 23, 1654, which assured him that God cared for the human soul, he devoted the rest of his life to religious matters. He planned to write an "Apology for the Christian Religion" but died before he could do so. He did leave a set of notes for the larger work, however, which in published form became known as *Pensées* or *The Thoughts.*

In the *Pensées,* Pascal tried to convert rationalists to Christianity by appealing both to their reason and their emotions. Humans were, he argued, frail creatures, often deceived by their senses, misled by reason, and battered by their emotions. And yet they were beings whose very nature involved thinking: "Man is but a reed, the weakest in nature; but he is a thinking reed. . . . Our whole dignity consists, therefore, in thought. By thought we must raise ourselves. . . . Let us endeavour, then, to think well; this is the beginning of morality."[27]

Pascal was determined to show that the Christian religion was not contrary to reason: "If we violate the principles of reason, our religion will be absurd, and it will be laughed at." Christianity, he felt, was the only religion that recognized people's true state of being as both vulnerable and great. To a Christian, a human being was both fallen and at the same time God's special creation. But it was not necessary to emphasize one at the expense of the other—to view humans as only rational or only hopeless. Thus, "Knowledge of God without knowledge of man's wretchedness leads to pride. Knowledge of man's wretchedness without knowledge of God leads to despair. Knowledge of Jesus Christ is the middle course, because by it we discover both God and our wretched state." Pascal even had an answer for skeptics in his famous wager. God is a reasonable bet; it is worthwhile to assume that God exists. If he does, then we win all; if he does not, we lose nothing.

Despite his background as a scientist and mathematician, Pascal refused to rely on the scientist's world of order and rationality to attract people to God: "If we submit everything to reason, there will be no mystery and no supernatural element in our religion." In the new cosmology of the seventeenth century, "finite man," Pascal believed, was lost in the new infinite world, a realization that frightened him: "The eternal silence of those infinite spaces strikes me with terror" (see the box on p. 587). The world of nature, then, could never reveal God: "Because they have failed to contemplate these infinites, men have rashly plunged into the examination of nature, as though they bore some proportion to her. . . . Their assumption is as infinite as their object." A Christian could only rely on a God who through Jesus cared for human beings. In the final analysis, after providing reasonable arguments for Christianity, Pascal came to rest on faith. Reason, he believed, could take people only so far: "The heart has its reasons of which the reason knows nothing." As a Christian, faith was the final step: "The heart feels God, not the reason. This is what constitutes faith: God experienced by the heart, not by the reason."[28]

In retrospect, it is obvious that Pascal failed to achieve his goal. Increasingly, the gap between science and traditional religion grew wider as Europe continued

Pascal: "What Is a Man in the Infinite?"
▼ ▼ ▼

Perhaps no intellectual in the seventeenth century gave greater expression to the uncertainties generated by the cosmological revolution than Blaise Pascal. Himself a scientist, Pascal's mystical vision of God's presence caused him to pursue religious truths with a passion. His work, the Pensées, consisted of notes for a larger, unfinished work justifying the Christian religion. In this selection, Pascal presents his musings on the human place in an infinite world.

Blaise Pascal, *Pensées*

Let man then contemplate the whole of nature in her full and exalted majesty. Let him turn his eyes from the lowly objects which surround him. Let him gaze on that brilliant light set like an eternal lamp to illumine the Universe; let the earth seem to him a dot compared with the vast orbit described by the sun, and let him wonder at the fact that this vast orbit itself is no more than a very small dot compared with that described by the stars in their revolutions around the firmament. But if our vision stops here, let the imagination pass on; it will exhaust its powers of thinking long before nature ceases to supply it with material for thought. All this visible world is no more than an imperceptible speck in nature's ample bosom. No idea approaches it. We may extend our conceptions beyond all imaginable space, yet produce only atoms in comparison with the reality of things. It is an infinite sphere, the center of which is everywhere, the circumference nowhere. In short, it is the greatest perceptible mark of God's almighty power that our imagination should lose itself in that thought.

Returning to himself, let man consider what he is compared with all existence; let him think of himself as lost in his remote corner of nature; and from this little dungeon in which he finds himself lodged—I mean the Universe—let him learn to set a true value on the earth, its kingdoms, and cities, and upon himself. What is a man in the infinite? . . .

For, after all, what is a man in nature? A nothing in comparison with the infinite, an absolute in comparison with nothing, a central point between nothing and all. Infinitely far from understanding these extremes, the end of things and their beginning are hopelessly hidden from him in an impenetrable secret. He is equally incapable of seeing the nothingness from which he came, and the infinite in which he is engulfed. What else then will he perceive but some appearance of the middle of things, in an eternal despair of knowing either their principle or their purpose? All things emerge from nothing and are borne onwards to infinity. Who can follow this marvelous process? The Author of these wonders understands them. None but He can.

---

along its path of secularization. Of course, traditional religions were not eliminated, nor is there any evidence that churches had yet lost their numbers. That would happen later. Nevertheless, more and more of the intellectual, social, and political elites began to act on the basis of secular rather than religious assumptions.

▼ The Spread of Scientific Knowledge

In the course of the seventeenth century, scientific learning and investigation began to increase dramatically. Major universities in Europe established new chairs of science, especially in medicine. Royal and princely patronage of individual scientists became an international phenomenon. The king of Denmark constructed an astronomical observatory for Tycho Brahe; Emperor Rudolf II hired Tycho Brahe and Johannes Kepler as imperial mathematicians; the grand duke of Tuscany appointed Galileo to a similar post. Of greater importance to the work of science, however, was the creation of new learned societies and journals that enabled the new scientists to communicate their ideas to each other and to disseminate them to a wider, literate public.

The Scientific Societies

The first of these scientific societies appeared in Italy and included the Academy of Experiments, founded in Florence in 1657 by two of Galileo's pupils under the patronage of the Medicean grand duke of Tuscany. Its laboratory facilities made possible research carried out along the new experimental lines. This Florentine

Academy was short-lived, however, and came to an end when its Medici supporters discontinued their funding in 1667.

Ultimately of more significance were the scientific societies of England and France. The English Royal Society evolved out of informal gatherings of scientists at London and Oxford in the 1640s, although it did not receive a formal charter from King Charles II until 1662. The French Royal Academy of Sciences also arose out of informal scientific meetings in Paris during the 1650s. In 1666, urged on by his minister Colbert, Louis XIV bestowed upon the group a formal recognition. The French

▼ **Louis XIV and Colbert Visit the Academy of Sciences.** In the seventeenth century, individual scientists received royal and princely patronage and a number of learned societies were established. The Academy of Experiments was established in Florence and the Royal Society was founded in England. In France, Louis XIV, urged on by his minister Colbert, gave formal recognition to the French Academy in 1666. In this illustration, Louis XIV and Colbert are shown visiting the French Royal Academy of Sciences.

Academy received abundant state support and remained under government control; its members were appointed and paid salaries by the state. In contrast, the Royal Society of England received little government encouragement, and its fellows simply co-opted new members.

Early on, both the English and French scientific societies formally emphasized the practical value of scientific research. The Royal Society created a committee to investigate technological improvements for industry while the French Academy collected tools and machines. This concern with the practical benefits of science proved short-lived, however, as both societies came to focus their primary interest on theoretical work in mechanics and astronomy. The construction of observatories at Paris in 1667 and at Greenwich, England, in 1675 greatly facilitated research in astronomy by both groups. The French Academy, however, since it was controlled by the state, was forced by the war minister of France, the marquis de Louvois, to continue its practical work to benefit both the "king and the state." The French example was especially important as a model for the scientific societies established in neighboring Germany. German princes and city governments encouraged the foundation of small-scale scientific societies of their own. Most of them, such as the Scientific Academy created in 1700 by the elector of Brandenburg, as well as the scientific academies established in most European countries in the eighteenth century, were sponsored by governments and were mainly devoted to the betterment of the state. While both the English and French societies made useful contributions to scientific knowledge in the second half of the seventeenth century, their true significance arose from their example that science should proceed as a cooperative venture.

Scientific journals furthered this concept of cooperation. The French *Journal des Savants,* published weekly beginning in 1665, printed results of experiments as well as general scientific knowledge. Its format appealed to both scientists and the educated public interested in the new science. The *Philosophical Transactions* of the Royal Society, however, also initiated in 1665, published papers of its members and learned correspondence and was aimed at practicing scientists. It became a prototype for the scholarly journals of later learned and academic societies and a crucial instrument for circulating news of scientific and academic activities.

Science and Society

The importance of science in the history of modern Western civilization is usually taken for granted. No

CAMERAM STELLATAM.

▼ **The Royal Observatory at Greenwich.** Although both the French and the English scientific societies initially stressed the practical value of scientific research, their interests soon shifted to theoretical work in mechanics and astronomy. To better facilitate their astronomical investigations, both the English and the French constructed observatories, such as the one pictured here, which was built at Greenwich, England, in 1675. The royal astronomer works at the table while his two assistants are shown making observations.

doubt the Industrial Revolution of the late eighteenth and nineteenth centuries provided tangible proof of the effectiveness of science and ensured its victory over Western minds. But how did science become such an integral part of Western culture in the seventeenth and early eighteenth centuries? Recent research has stressed that one cannot simply assert that people perceived that science was a rationally superior system. Two important social factors, however, might help to explain the relatively rapid acceptance of the new science.

It has been argued that the literate mercantile and propertied elites of Europe were soon attracted to a new science that offered new ways to exploit resources for profit. Some of the early scientists made it easier for these groups to accept the new ideas when they showed how they could be applied directly to specific industrial and technological needs. Galileo, for example, consciously sought an alliance between science and the material interests of the educated elite when he assured his listeners that the science of mechanics would be quite useful "when it becomes necessary to build bridges or other structures over water, something occurring mainly in affairs of great importance." At the same time, Galileo stressed that science was fit for the "minds of the wise" and not for "the shallow minds of the common people." This made science part of the high culture of

Europe's wealthy elites at a time when that culture was being increasingly separated from the popular culture of the lower classes (see Chapter 18). This merger of scientists with the literate and propertied elites occurred first in England and later in France and the Low Countries.

It has also been argued that the new scientific conception of the natural world was used by political interests to bolster social stability. One scholar has recently argued that "no single event in the history of early modern Europe more profoundly shaped the integration of the new science into Western culture than did the English Revolution (1640–1660)."[29] Fed by their millenarian expectations that the end of the world would come and usher in a thousand-year reign of the saints, Puritan reformers felt it was important to reform and renew their society. They seized on the new science as a socially useful instrument to accomplish this goal. The Puritan Revolution's role in the acceptance of science, however, stemmed even more from the reaction to the radicalism spawned by the revolutionary ferment. The upheavals of the Puritan Revolution gave rise to groups, such as the Levellers, Diggers, and Ranters, who advocated not only radical political ideas, but also a new radical science based on Paracelsus and the natural magic associated with the Hermetic tradition. The chaplain of the New Model Army said that the radicals wanted "the philosophy of Hermes, revived by the Paracelsian schools." The propertied and educated elites responded vigorously to these challenges to the established order by supporting the new mechanistic science and appealing to the material benefits of science. Hence, the founders of the Royal Society were men who wanted to pursue an experimental science that would remain detached from radical reforms of church and state. Although willing to make changes, they now viewed those changes in terms of an increase in food production and commerce. By the eighteenth century, the Newtonian world-machine had been readily accepted, and Newtonian science would soon be applied to trade and industry by a mercantile and landed elite that believed that they "could retain a social order that primarily rewarded and enriched themselves while still improving the human condition."

The Scientific Revolution represents a major turning point in modern Western civilization. In the Scientific Revolution, the Western world overthrew the medieval, Ptolemaic-Aristotelian worldview and arrived at a new conception of the universe: the sun at the center, the planets as material bodies revolving around the sun in elliptical orbits, and an infinite rather than finite world. With the changes in the conception of "heaven" came changes in the conception of "earth." The work of Bacon and Descartes left Europeans with the separation of mind and matter and the belief that by using only reason they could, in fact, understand and dominate the world of nature. The development of a scientific method furthered the work of scientists while the creation of scientific societies and learned journals spread its results. Although traditional churches stubbornly resisted the new ideas and a few intellectuals pointed to some inherent flaws, nothing was able to halt the replacement of the traditional ways of thinking by new ways of thinking that created a more fundamental break with the past than that represented by the breakup of Christian unity in the Reformation.

The Scientific Revolution forced Europeans to change their conception of themselves. At first, some were appalled and even frightened by its implications. Before humans on earth had been at the center of the universe. Now the earth was only a tiny planet revolving around a sun that was itself only a speck in a boundless universe. Most people remained optimistic despite the apparent blow to human dignity. After all, had Newton not demonstrated that the universe was a great machine governed by natural laws? Newton had found one—the universal law of gravitation. Could others not find other laws? Were there not natural laws governing every aspect of human endeavor that could be found by the new scientific method? Thus, the Scientific Revolution leads us logically to the age of the Enlightenment of the eighteenth century.

Notes

▼ ▼ ▼

1. Quoted in Alan G. R. Smith, *Science and Society in the Sixteenth and Seventeenth Centuries* (London, 1972), p. 59.

2. Edward MacCurdy, *The Notebooks of Leonardo da Vinci* (London, 1948), 1:634.

3. Ibid., p. 636.

4. Frances Yates, *Giordano Bruno and the Hermetic Tradition* (New York, 1964), p. 448.

5. Ibid., p. 450.

6. Quoted in Smith, *Science and Society in the Sixteenth and Seventeenth Centuries*, p. 97.

7. Logan P. Smith, *Life and Letters of Sir Henry Wotton* (Oxford, 1907), 1: 486–87.

8. Quoted in John H. Randall, *The Making of the Modern Mind* (Boston, 1926), p. 234.

9. Quoted in Smith, *Science and Society in the Sixteenth and Seventeenth Centuries*, p. 124.

10. Quoted in Betty J. Dobbs, *The Foundations of Newton's Alchemy* (Cambridge, 1975), pp. 13–14.

11. Jolande Jacobi, ed., *Paracelsus: Selected Writings* (New York, 1965), pp. 5–6.

12. Ibid., p. 21.

13. Quoted in Londa Schiebinger, *The Mind Has No Sex? Women in the Origins of Modern Science* (Cambridge, Mass., 1989), pp. 52–53.

14. Ibid., p. 85.

15. Galen, *On the Usefulness of the Parts of the Body*, trans. Margaret May (Ithaca, N.Y., 1968), 2: 628–29.

16. Quoted in Phyllis Stock, *Better Than Rubies: A History of Women's Education* (New York, 1978), p. 16.

17. René Descartes, *Philosophical Writings*, ed. and trans. Norman K. Smith (New York, 1958), p. 95.

18. Ibid., pp. 118–19.

19. Ibid., p. 120.

20. Francis Bacon, *The Great Instauration,* trans. Jerry Weinberger (Arlington Heights, Ill., 1989), pp. (in order of quotations) 2, 8, 2, 16, 21.

21. Descartes, *Discourse on Method*, in *Philosophical Writings*, p. 75.

22. Stillman Drake, ed. and trans., *Discoveries and Opinions of Galileo* (New York, 1957), p. 182.

23. Benedict de Spinoza, *Ethics*, trans. R. H. M. Elwes (New York, 1955), pp. 75–76.

24. Ibid., p. 76.

25. Benedict de Spinoza, *Letters*, quoted in Randall, *The Making of the Modern Mind*, p. 247.

26. John Amos Comenius, *The Way of Light*, trans. E. T. Campagnac (Liverpool, 1938), p. 51.

27. Blaise Pascal, *The Pensées*, trans. J. M. Cohen (Harmondsworth, 1961), p. 100.

28. Ibid., pp. (in order of quotations) 31, 45, 31, 52–53, 164, 165.

29. Margaret C. Jacob, *The Cultural Meaning of the Scientific Revolution* (New York, 1988), p. 73.

Suggestions for Further Reading
▼ ▼ ▼

Three general surveys of the entire Scientific Revolution are A. G. R. Smith, *Science and Society in the Sixteenth and Seventeenth Centuries* (London, 1972); M. Boas, *The Scientific Renaissance: 1450–1630* (London, 1962); and H. Butterfield, *The Origins of Modern Science* (New York, 1962). A more detailed and technical introduction can be found in A. R. Hall, *The Revolution in Science, 1500–1750* (London, 1983). Also of much value is A. G. Debus, *Man and Nature in the Renaissance* (Cambridge, 1978), which covers the period from the mid-fifteenth through the mid-seventeenth centuries. The importance of mathematics to the Scientific Revolution is brought out in P. L. Rose, *The Italian Renaissance of Mathematics: Studies on Humanists and Mathematicians from Petrarch to Galileo* (Geneva, 1975). On the relationship of magic to the beginnings of the Scientific Revolution, see the pioneering works by F. Yates, *Giordano Bruno and the Hermetic Tradition* (New York, 1969), and *The Rosicrucian Enlightenment* (London, 1975). Some criticism of this approach is provided in R. S. Westman and J. E. McGuire, eds., *Hermeticism and the Scientific Revolution* (Los Angeles, 1977). An important book on magic in the early modern period is

K. Thomas, *Religion and the Decline of Magic* (London, 1971).

A good introduction to the transformation from the late medieval to the early modern worldview is A. Koyré, *From the Closed World to the Infinite Universe* (New York, 1958). Also still of value is the older work by A. Koestler, *The Sleepwalkers: A History of Man's Changing Vision of the Universe* (New York, 1959). On the important figures of the revolution in astronomy, see E. Rosen, *Copernicus and the Scientific Revolution* (New York, 1984); C. Morphet, *Galileo and Copernican Astronomy* (London, 1977); S. Drake, *Galileo* (New York, 1980); M. Casper, *Johannes Kepler*, trans. C. D. Hellman (London, 1959), the standard biography; and F. Manuel, *A Portrait of Isaac Newton* (Cambridge, Mass., 1968), a massive work. On Newton's relationship to alchemy, see the invaluable study by B. J. Dobbs, *The Foundations of Newton's Alchemy* (Cambridge, 1975).

The worldview of Paracelsus and his followers can be examined in W. Pagel, *Paracelsus: An Introduction to Philosophical Medicine in the Era of the Renaissance* (New York, 1958); and A. G. Debus, *The Chemical Philosophy: Paracelsian Science and Medicine in the Sixteenth and

Seventeenth Centuries, 2 vols. (New York, 1977). The standard biography of Vesalius is C. D. O'Malley, *Andreas Vesalius of Brussels, 1514–1564* (Berkeley, 1964). The work of Harvey is discussed in G. Whitteridge, *William Harvey and the Circulation of the Blood* (London, 1971). A good general account of the development of medicine can be found in W. P. D. Wightman, *The Emergence of Scientific Medicine* (Edinburgh, 1971).

The importance of Francis Bacon in the early development of science is underscored in P. Rossi, *Francis Bacon: From Magic to Science* (Chicago, 1968); and C. Webster, *The Great Instauration: Science, Medicine, and Reform, 1620–1660* (London, 1975). A good introduction to the work of Descartes can be found in A. Kenny, *Descartes* (New York, 1968). The standard biography of Spinoza in English is S. Hampshire, *Spinoza* (New York, 1961).

For a general history of the development of scientific academies, see the older work by M. Ornstein, *The Role of Scientific Societies in the Seventeenth Century* (Chicago, 1928). Individual societies are examined in R. Hahn, *The Anatomy of a Scientific Institution: The Paris Academy of Sciences, 1666–1803* (Berkeley, 1971); and M. Purver, *The Royal Society, Concept and Creation* (London, 1967).

On the subject of women and early modern science, see the comprehensive and highly informative work by L. Schiebinger, *The Mind Has No Sex? Women in the Origins of Modern Science* (Cambridge, Mass., 1989). The social and political context for the triumph of science in the seventeenth and eighteenth centuries is examined in M. Jacobs, *The Cultural Meaning of the Scientific Revolution* (New York, 1988), and *The Newtonians and the English Revolution, 1689–1720* (Ithaca, N.Y., 1976).

Chapter 18

The Eighteenth Century: An Age of Enlightenment

▼ ▼ ▼ ▼ ▼

T he earth-shattering work of the "natural philosophers" in the Scientific Revolution had affected only a relatively small number of Europe's educated elite. In the eighteenth century, this changed dramatically as a group of intellectuals known as the philosophes popularized the ideas of the Scientific Revolution and used them to undertake a dramatic reexamination of all aspects of life. The widespread impact of the

philosophes' ideas on their society has caused historians ever since to call the eighteenth century an age of Enlightenment.

For most of the philosophes, "enlightenment" included the rejection of traditional Christianity. The religious wars and intolerance of the sixteenth and seventeenth centuries had created an environment in which intellectuals had become so disgusted with religious fanaticism that they were open to the new ideas of the Scientific Revolution. While the great scientists of the seventeenth century believed that their work exalted God, the intellectuals of the eighteenth century read their conclusions a different way and increasingly turned their backs on their Christian heritage. Consequently, European intellectual life in the eighteenth century was marked by the emergence of the secularization that has characterized the modern Western mentality. While some historians have argued that this secularism first arose in the Renaissance, it never developed then to the same extent that it did in the eighteenth century. Ironically, at the same time that reason and materialism were beginning to replace faith and worship, a great outburst of religious

sensibility manifested itself in music and art. Merely to mention the name of Johann Sebastian Bach is to remind us that the growing secularization of the eighteenth century had not yet captured the hearts and minds of all European intellectuals and artists.

▼ The Enlightenment

In 1784, the German philosopher Immanuel Kant defined the Enlightenment as "man's leaving his self-caused immaturity." Whereas earlier periods had been handicapped by the inability to "use one's intelligence without the guidance of another," Kant proclaimed as the motto of the Enlightenment: "Dare to Know!: Have the courage to use your own intelligence!" The eighteenth-century Enlightenment was a movement of intellectuals who dared to know. They were greatly impressed with the accomplishments of the Scientific Revolution, and when they used the word reason—one of their favorite words—they were advocating the application of the scientific method to the understanding of all life. All institutions and all systems of thought were subject to the rational, scientific way of thinking if people would only free themselves from the shackles of past, worthless traditions, especially religious ones. If Isaac Newton could discover the natural laws regulating the world of nature, they too by using reason could find the laws that governed human society. This belief in turn led them to hope that they could make progress toward a better society than the one they had inherited. Reason, natural law, hope, progress—these were common words in the heady atmosphere of the eighteenth century. But the philosophes were not naive optimists. Many of them realized that the ignorance and suffering of their society were not easily overcome and that progress would be slow and would exact a price.

The Paths to Enlightenment

Many philosophes saw themselves as the heirs of the pagan philosophers of antiquity and the Italian humanists of the Renaissance who had revived the world of classical antiquity. To the philosophes, the Middle Ages had been a period of intellectual darkness, when a society dominated by the dogmatic Catholic church allowed faith to obscure and diminish human reason. Closer to their own period, however, the philosophes were especially influenced by the revolutionary thinkers of the seventeenth century. What were the major intellectual changes, then, that culminated in the intellectual movement of the Enlightenment?

THE POPULARIZATION OF SCIENCE Although the philosophes of the eighteenth century were much influenced by the scientific ideas of the seventeenth century, they did not always acquire this knowledge directly from the original sources. After all, Newton's *Principia* was not an easy book to read or comprehend. The spread of scientific ideas to ever-widening circles of educated Europeans was accomplished not so much by scientists themselves as by popularizers. The greatest of them all, and especially important as the direct link between the Scientific Revolution of the seventeenth century and the philosophes of the eighteenth, was Bernard de Fontenelle (1657–1757), secretary of the French Royal Academy of Science from 1691 to 1741.

Although Fontenelle neither performed any scientific experiments nor made any scientific discoveries, he possessed a deep knowledge of all the scientific work of earlier centuries and his own time. Moreover, he was able to communicate that body of scientific knowledge in a clear and even witty fashion that appealed to his upper-class audiences in a meaningful way. One of his most successful books, the *Plurality of Worlds*, was actually presented in the form of an intimate conversation between a lady aristocrat and her lover who are engaged in conversation under the stars. What are they discuss-

ing? "Tell me," she exclaims, "about these stars of yours." Her lover proceeds to tell her of the tremendous advances in cosmology after the foolish errors of their forebears:

> There came on the scene a certain German, one Copernicus, who made short work of all those various circles, all those solid skies, which the ancients had pictured to themselves.

▼ The Popularization of Science: Fontenelle and the *Plurality of Worlds*.

The ideas of the Scientific Revolution often reached the educated circles of Europe through popularizers, not through the works of the scientists themselves. The most important of the popularizers was Bernard de Fontenelle who, while not a scientist himself, had much knowledge of scientific matters. One of his most popular works, the *Plurality of Worlds*, was set in the form of a dialogue between a lady and her lover.

The former he abolished; the latter, he broke in pieces. Fired with the noble zeal of a true astronomer, he took the earth and spun it very far away from the center of the universe, where it had been installed, and in that center he put the sun, which had a far better title to the honour.[1]

In the course of two evenings under the stars, the lady learned the basic fundamentals of the new mechanistic universe, which, as presented in Fontenelle's summary of Newton, resembled a watch. So too did scores of the educated elite of Europe. What bliss it was to learn the "truth" in such lighthearted fashion.

Thanks to Fontenelle, science was no longer the monopoly of experts, but part of literature. He was especially fond of downplaying the religious backgrounds of the seventeenth-century scientists. Himself a skeptic, Fontenelle portrayed the churches as enemies of scientific progress, adding to the growing skepticism of religion at the end of the seventeenth century.

SKEPTICISM   Although the Reformation had attempted to restore religion as the central focus of people's lives, it was perhaps inevitable that the dogmatic controversies, religious intolerance, and religious warfare engendered by it would open the door to the questioning of religious truths and values. The overthrow of medieval cosmology and the advent of scientific ideas and rational explanations in the seventeenth century likewise affected the belief of educated men and women in the traditional teachings of Christianity. This development of skepticism toward Christian beliefs did not, however, occur in any widespread fashion in the seventeenth century. Even the great scientists, such as Kepler, Galileo, and Newton, had pursued their work in a spirit of exalting God, not undermining Christianity. But as scientific knowledge spread, Christianity was affected ever more detrimentally. Skepticism about religion and the growing secularization of thought were especially evident in the work of Pierre Bayle (1647–1706).

This French precursor of the philosophes was the son of a Huguenot minister who converted briefly to Catholicism before reverting back to Protestantism. He remained a French Protestant while becoming a leading critic of traditional religious attitudes. Bayle attacked superstition, religious intolerance, and dogmatism. In his works, he made two major points. First of all, he argued that Christian religion and morality were not necessarily related:

> Morals and religion, far from being inseparable, are completely independent of each other. A man can be moral

without being religious. An atheist who lives a virtuous life is not a creature of wonder, something outside the natural order, a freak. There is nothing more extraordinary about an atheist living a virtuous life, than there is about a Christian leading a wicked one.[2]

Secondly, the idea of compelling people to believe a particular set of religious ideas (as Louis XIV was doing in Bayle's contemporary France) was wrong. It simply created hypocrites and in itself was contrary to what religion should be about. Individual conscience should determine one's actions. Bayle argued for complete religious toleration, maintaining that a multiplicity of religions would benefit rather than harm the state.

Bayle was one of a select group of intellectuals, including Hobbes and Spinoza (see Chapter 17), who believed that the new rational principles of textual criticism should be applied to the Bible as well as secular documents. In his most famous work, *Historical and Critical Dictionary,* Bayle demonstrated the results of his own efforts by a famous article on the Israelite King David. Undermining the traditional picture of the heroic David, he portrayed him as a sensual, treacherous, cruel, and basically evil man. Bayle's *Dictionary,* while purporting to be a biographical compendium, was primarily an instrument for his attacks on traditional religious practices and heroes. It was well known to eighteenth-century philosophes, and one critic regarded it as the "Bible of the eighteenth century."

THE IMPACT OF TRAVEL LITERATURE   Skepticism about Christianity as well as European culture itself was nourished by travel reports. In the course of the seventeenth century, traders, missionaries, medical men, and navigators began to publish an increasing number of travel books that gave accounts of many different cultures. By the end of the seventeenth century, this travel literature began to make an impact on the minds of educated Europeans. The discovery of highly developed civilizations like those of the Far East with different customs forced Europeans to evaluate their own civilization relative to others. What had seemed to be practices grounded in reason now appeared to be matters of custom. The missionary author of *On the Ceremonies of the Chinese* concluded: "We, too, deceive ourselves, because the prejudices of our childhood prevent us from realizing that the majority of human actions are indifferent in themselves, and that they only derive their significance from the meaning the various races of people arbitrarily attached to them when they were first instituted."[3] This development of cultural relativism was a healthy antidote to European parochialism.

Cultural relativism was accompanied by religious skepticism. As these travel accounts made clear, the Christian perception of God was merely one of many. Some people were devastated by this revelation: "Some complete their demoralization by extensive travel, and lose whatever shreds of religion remained to them. Every day they see a new religion, new customs, new rites."[4]

THE LEGACY OF LOCKE AND NEWTON   The intellectual inspiration for the Enlightenment came primarily from two Englishmen, Isaac Newton and John Locke, acknowledged by the philosophes as two great minds. Newton was frequently singled out for praise as the "greatest and rarest genius that ever rose for the ornament and instruction of the species." Enchanted by the grand design of the Newtonian world-machine, the intellectuals of the Enlightenment were convinced that by following Newton's rules of reasoning they could discover the natural laws that governed politics, economics, justice, religion, and the arts. The world and everything in it was like a giant machine.

In the eyes of the philosophes, only the philosopher John Locke came close to Newton's genius. Although Locke's political ideas had an enormous impact on the Western world in the eighteenth century, it was his theory of knowledge that especially influenced the philosophes. In his *Essay Concerning Human Understanding,* written in 1690, Locke denied Descartes's belief in innate ideas. Instead, argued Locke, every person was born with a *tabula rasa,* a blank mind:

> Let us then suppose the mind to be, as we say, white paper, void of all characters, without any ideas. How comes it to be furnished? Whence comes it by that vast store which the busy and boundless fancy of man has painted on it with an almost endless variety? Whence has it all the materials of reason and knowledge? To this I answer, in one word, from experience. . . . Our observation, employed either about external sensible objects or about the internal operations of our minds perceived and reflected on by ourselves, is that which supplies our understanding with all the materials of thinking.[5]

Our knowledge, then, is derived from our environment, not from heredity; from reason, not from faith. By denying innate ideas, Locke's philosophy implied that people were molded by their environment, by the experiences that they received through their senses from their surrounding world. By changing the environment and subjecting people to proper influences, they could be changed and a new society created. Evil was not innate in human beings, but a product of bad education, rotten

institutions, and inherited prejudices. And how should the environment be changed? Newton had already paved the way by showing how reason enabled enlightened people to discover the natural laws to which all institutions should conform. No wonder the philosophes were enamored of Newton and Locke. Taken together, their ideas seemed to offer the hope of a "brave new world" built on reason.

The Philosophes and Their Ideas

The intellectuals of the Enlightenment were known by the French name of philosophes although they were not all French and few were philosophers in the strict sense of the term. They were literary people, professors, journalists, statesmen, economists, political scientists, and, above all, social reformers. They came from both the nobility and the middle class, and a few even stemmed from lower-middle-class origins. Although it was a truly international and cosmopolitan movement, the Enlightenment also enhanced the dominant role being played by French culture; Paris was its recognized capital. Most of the leaders of the Enlightenment were French, although the French philosophes themselves for a long time idolized England as the home of freedom of philosophy. The French philosophes, in turn, affected intellectuals elsewhere and created a movement that touched the entire Western world, including the British colonies in America.

Although the philosophes faced different political circumstances depending upon the country in which they lived, they shared common bonds as part of a truly international movement. Although they were called philosophers, philosophy to them meant only effective criticism. The role of philosophy was to change the world, not just discuss it. As one writer said, the philosophe is one who "applies himself to the study of society with the purpose of making his kind better and happier." To the philosophes, rationalism did not mean the creation of a grandiose system of thought to explain all things. Reason was scientific method, and it meant an appeal to facts, to experience, to reasonableness. A spirit of rational criticism was to be applied to everything, including religion and politics. Traditional religion, in fact, was especially attacked for its miracles and revelations as well as its dogmas and intolerance.

The philosophes aggressively pursued a secular view of life since their focus was not on an afterlife, but on this world and how it could be improved and enjoyed. The philosophes were not simplistic in their appeal to reason, and some even balanced it with the power of passions.

Diderot, one of the most famous of the French philosophes (see Diderot later in the chapter), wrote: "People impute to the passions all of men's pains, and forget that they are also the source of all his pleasures. It is an element of man's constitution of which we can say neither too many favorable, nor too many unfavorable things. . . . It is only the passions, and the great passions, that can raise the soul to great things." Some philosophes attacked Christianity for its antipathy toward beneficent passions, especially human sensuality. To stifle it was to smother a crucial part of human nature.

The philosophes' call for freedom of expression is a reminder that their work was done in an atmosphere of censorship. The philosophes were not free to write whatever they chose. State censors decided what could be published, although standards fluctuated wildly at times, while protests from any number of government bodies could result in the seizure of books and the imprisonment of their authors, publishers, and sellers.

The philosophes found ways to circumvent state censorship. Some published under pseudonyms or anonymously or abroad, especially in Holland. The use of double meanings, such as talking about the Persians when they meant the French, became standard procedure for many. Books were also published and circulated secretly or in manuscript form to avoid censors. As frequently happens with attempted censorship, the government's announcement that a book had been burned often made the book more desirable and more popular.

Although the philosophes constituted a kind of "family circle" bound together by common intellectual bonds, they often disagreed as well. Spanning almost an entire century, the Enlightenment evolved over time with each succeeding generation becoming more radical as it built upon the contributions of the previous one. A few people, however, dominated the landscape completely, and we might best begin our survey of the ideas of the philosophes by looking at the three French giants—Montesquieu, Voltaire, and Diderot.

MONTESQUIEU Charles de Secondat, the baron de Montesquieu (1689–1755), came from the French nobility. He received a classical education and then studied law at the University of Bordeaux. Like almost all of the philosophes, he became interested in science and even conducted experiments on the effect of temperature changes on animal tissues. His own estate, as well as his marriage to a wealthy Protestant heiress, enabled him to live a life dedicated to travel, study, and writing. In his first work published in 1721, the *Persian Letters*, he

The Separation of Powers
▼ ▼ ▼

The Enlightenment affected the "new world" of America as much as it did the "old world" of Europe. American philosophes, such as Benjamin Franklin, James Madison, and Thomas Jefferson, were well aware of the ideas of European Enlightenment thinkers. This selection from Montesquieu's The Spirit of the Laws enunciates the "separation of powers" doctrine. Although Montesquieu had misread the English political system, his ideas were nevertheless incorporated into the American constitution.

Montesquieu, *The Spirit of the Laws*

Of the Constitution of England

In every government there are three sorts of power: the legislative; the executive in respect to things dependent on the law of nations; and the executive in regard to matters that depend on the civil law.

By virtue of the first, the prince or magistrate enacts temporary or perpetual laws, and amends or abrogates those that have been already enacted. By the second, he makes peace or war, sends or receives embassies, establishes the public security, and provides against invasions. By the third, he punishes criminals, or determines the disputes that arise between individuals. The latter we shall call the judiciary power, and the other simply the executive power of the state.

The political liberty of the subject is a tranquility of mind arising from the opinion each person has of his safety. In order to have this liberty, it is requisite the government be so constituted as one man need not be afraid of another.

When the legislative and executive powers are united in the same person, or in the same body of magistrates, there can be no liberty; because apprehensions may arise, lest the same monarch or senate should enact tyrannical laws, to execute them in a tyrannical manner.

Again, there is no liberty, if the judiciary power be not separated from the legislative and executive. Were it joined with the legislative, the life and liberty of the subject would be exposed to arbitrary control; for the judge would be then the legislator. Were it joined to the executive power, the judge might behave with violence and oppression.

There would be an end of everything, were the same man or the same body, whether of the nobles or of the people, to exercise those three powers, that of enacting laws, that of executing the public resolutions, and of trying the causes of individuals.

---

used the format of two Persians supposedly traveling in Western Europe and sending their impressions back home, to enable him to criticize French institutions, especially the Catholic church and the French monarchy. Much of the program of the French Enlightenment is contained in this work: the attack on traditional religion, the advocacy of religious toleration, the denunciation of slavery, and the use of reason to liberate human beings from their prejudices.

The fame of the *Persian Letters* brought Montesquieu into contact with the leading intellectuals of his age. To enhance his own knowledge, he traveled abroad for a number of years. In England, he was made a member of the Royal Society and initiated into the society of Freemasons. Everywhere he went, he was welcomed as a leading French intellectual. After his return to France, he settled down to manage his estates but still continued to write and visit the salons of Paris (see The Social Environment of the Philosophes later in the chapter).

From this last stage of his life came his famous work, *The Spirit of the Laws*, published in 1748.

This treatise was a comparative study of governments in which Montesquieu attempted to apply the scientific method to the social and political arena to ascertain the "natural laws" governing the social relationships of human beings. It has aptly been called a "pioneering work in political sociology." *The Spirit of the Laws* revealed Montesquieu as a relativist in an age of absolute thinkers. When other philosophes propounded their natural laws, they treated them as applicable everywhere and in every situation. To Montesquieu, the forms of political and social institutions varied since they depended upon conditions unique to different countries. Climate, soil, the size of the state, and the customs and traditions developed over the course of a state's history all determined what kind of government a nation would have.

Montesquieu distinguished three basic kinds of governments: republics, suitable for small states and depen-

dent on civic spirit; despotism, apt for large states and dependent on fear; and monarchy, appropriate for moderate-size states and dependent on the sense of honor of the leading class and respect for law. Montesquieu used England as an example of the last category, and it was his praise and analysis of England's constitution that led to his most far-reaching and lasting contribution to political thought—the importance of checks and balances created by means of a separation of powers (see the box on p. 599). He believed that England's system, with its separate executive, legislative, and judicial powers that served to limit and control each other, provided the greatest freedom and security for a state. In large part Montesquieu misread the English situation

▼ **Voltaire and Frederick II of Prussia.** François-Marie Arouet, better known as Voltaire, achieved his first success as a playwright. A philosophe, Voltaire was well known for his criticism of traditional religion and his support of religious toleration. Voltaire also supported deism, which posited a mechanical universe created by a God who had no direct involvement with his creation. This engraving shows Voltaire with one of his admirers, Frederick II, the king of Prussia.

and insisted on a separation of powers because he wanted the nobility of France (of which he was a member) to play an active role in the running of the French government. The translation of his work into English two years after publication ensured its being read by American philosophes, such as Benjamin Franklin, James Madison, John Adams, Alexander Hamilton, and Thomas Jefferson, who incorporated its principles into the American constitution (see Chapter 20).

VOLTAIRE   The greatest figure of the Enlightenment was François-Marie Arouet, known simply as Voltaire (1694–1778). Son of a prosperous middle-class family from Paris, Voltaire received a classical education typical of Jesuit schools. Although he studied law, he wished to be a writer and achieved his first success as a playwright. By his mid-twenties, Voltaire had been hailed as the successor to Racine (see Chapter 16) for his tragedy *Oedipe* and his epic *Henriade* on his favorite king, Henry IV. His wit and clever repartee made him a darling of the Paris salons but also involved him in a quarrel with a dissolute nobleman that led to Voltaire's imprisonment and voluntary exile to England.

Well received in English literary and social circles, the young playwright was much impressed by England. His *Philosophic Letters on the English*, written in 1733, expressed a deep admiration of English life, especially its respect for merchants, scientists, and literary men, its freedom of the press, its political freedom, and its religious toleration. In judging the English religious situation, he made the famous remark that "If there were just one religion in England, despotism would threaten, if there were two religions, they would cut each other's throats, but there are thirty religions, and they live together peacefully and happily." Although he clearly exaggerated the freedoms England possessed, by indirection Voltaire had managed to criticize many of the ills oppressing France, especially royal absolutism and the lack of religious toleration and freedom of thought. He had left France a playwright; he came back a philosophe.

Upon his return to France, Voltaire's reputation as the author of the *Philosophic Letters* made it necessary for him to live in semiseclusion on the estate at Cirey of Madame de Châtelet, his mistress. Although he was eventually accepted at the court of Louis XV, his alienation of Louis's mistress forced him to go wandering again. After a brief sojourn as a distinguished guest of King Frederick the Great of Prussia (see Chapter 19), he eventually settled on a magnificent estate at Ferney. Located in France near the Swiss border, it gave Voltaire the freedom to write what he wished. By this time,

The Attack on Religious Intolerance
▼ ▼ ▼

Although Voltaire's ideas on religion were in no way original, his lucid prose, biting satire, and clever wit caused his attacks to be widely read and all the more influential. These two selections present different sides of Voltaire's attack on religious intolerance. The first is from his straightforward treatise, The Ignorant Philosopher, *while the second is from his only real literary masterpiece, the novel* Candide, *where he uses humor to make the same fundamental point about religious intolerance.*

Voltaire, *The Ignorant Philosopher*

The contagion of fanaticism then still subsists. . . . The author of the Treatise upon Toleration has not mentioned the shocking executions wherein so many unhappy victims perished in the valleys of Piedmont. He has passed over in silence the massacre of six hundred inhabitants of Valtelina, men, women, and children, who were murdered by the Catholics in the month of September, 1620. I will not say it was with the consent and assistance of the archbishop of Milan, Charles Borome, who was made a saint. Some passionate writers have averred this fact, which I am very far from believing; but I say, there is scarce any city or borough in Europe, where blood has not been spilt for religious quarrels; I say, that the human species has been perceptibly diminished, because women and girls were massacred as well as men; I say, that Europe would have had a third larger population, if there had been no theological disputes. In fine, I say, that so far from forgetting these abominable times, we should frequently take a view of them, to inspire an eternal horror for them; and that it is for our age to make reparation by toleration, for this long collection of crimes, which has taken place through the want of toleration, during sixteen barbarous centuries.

Let it not then be said, that there are no traces left of that shocking fanaticism, of the want of toleration; they are still everywhere to be met with, even in those countries that are esteemed the most humane. The Lutheran and Calvinist preachers, were they masters, would, perhaps, be as little inclined to pity, as obdurate, as insolent as they upbraid their antagonists with being.

Voltaire, *Candide*

At last he [Candide] approached a man who had just been addressing a big audience for a whole hour on the subject of charity. The orator peered at him and said:

"What is your business here? Do you support the Good Old Cause?"

"There is no effect without a cause," replied Candide modestly. "All things are necessarily connected and arranged for the best. It was my fate to be driven from Lady Cunégonde's presence and made to run the gauntlet, and now I have to beg my bread until I can earn it. Things could not have happened otherwise."

"Do you believe that the Pope is Antichrist, my friend?" said the minister.

"I have never heard anyone say so," replied Candide; "but whether he is or he isn't, I want some food."

"You don't deserve to eat," said the other. "Be off with you, you villain, you wretch! Don't come near me again or you'll suffer for it."

The minister's wife looked out of the window at that moment, and seeing a man who was not sure that the Pope was Antichrist, emptied over his head a pot full of urine, which shows to what lengths ladies are driven by religious zeal.

---

through his writings, inheritance, and clever investments, Voltaire had become wealthy and now had the leisure to write an almost endless stream of pamphlets, novels, plays, letters, and histories.

Although he touched on all of the themes of importance to the philosophes, he was especially well known for his criticism of traditional religion and his strong attachment to the ideal of religious toleration (see the box above). He lent his prestige and skills as a po-

lemicist to fight cases of intolerance in France. The most famous incident was the Calas affair. Jean Calas was a Protestant from Toulouse who was accused of murdering his own son to stop him from becoming a Catholic. Tortured to confess his guilt, Calas died shortly thereafter. An angry and indignant Voltaire published devastating broadsides that aroused public opinion and forced a retrial in which Calas was exonerated when it was proved that his son had actually committed suicide. The

family was paid an indemnity, and Voltaire's appeals for toleration appeared all the more reasonable. In 1763, he penned his *Treatise on Toleration* in which he argued that religious toleration had created no problems for England and Holland and reminded governments that "all men are brothers under God." As he grew older, Voltaire became ever more strident in his denunciations. "Crush the infamous thing," he thundered repeatedly—the infamous thing being religious fanaticism, intolerance, and superstition.

Throughout his life, Voltaire championed not only religious tolerance, but also deism, a religious outlook shared by most other philosophes. Deism was built upon the Newtonian world-machine, which implied the existence of a mechanic (God) who had created the universe. Voltaire said: "In the opinion that there is a God, there are difficulties, but in the contrary opinion there are absurdities." To Voltaire and most other philosophes, God had no direct involvement in the world he had created and which he allowed to run according to its own natural laws. God did not extend grace or answer prayers as Christians liked to believe. Jesus might be a "good fellow," as Voltaire called him, but he was not divine as Christianity claimed. Deism proved to be a halfway house between belief in religion and disbelief and satisfied most philosophes. Voltaire feared atheism, feeling that it posed a threat to social stability among the masses. But deism also proved unsatisfactory. While accepting the idea that God had begun the world-machine and then had withdrawn, allowing it to operate according to its own natural laws, Voltaire expected that everyone would continue to live according to the moral teachings of Christianity. The subsequent history of Western civilization would show that the removal of God from an active role in the world was for many people simply the first step to his total elimination.

DIDEROT Denis Diderot (1713–1784) was the son of a skilled craftsman from eastern France. He received a Jesuit education and went on to the University of Paris to fulfill his father's hopes that he would be a lawyer or pursue a career in the church. Diderot did neither. Instead he became a free-lance writer so that he could be free to study and read in many subjects and languages. For the rest of his life, Diderot remained dedicated to his independence and was always in love with new ideas. He was especially known for his conversations; as one of his friends remarked: "His discussion was always animated, perfectly sincere, subtle without obscurity, varied in its forms, brilliant in imagination, and fertile in ideas. I have experienced no greater intellectual pleasure."[6]

Diderot was probably the most versatile of all the philosophes. His range of interests was enormous and was reflected in the variety of literature he wrote. His works on the blind and deaf, full of sound psychological observations, led some authors to call him "one of the founders of modern psychology." His profound interest in science led to a work published in 1753 in which he clearly foreshadowed the nineteenth-century theory of organic evolution. His novels ranged from the licentious *The Indiscreet Jewels* to his famous *Rameau's Nephew*, which analyzed an alienated man constantly at war with his society. His plays, such as *The Natural Son* and *The Father of the Family*, represent Diderot's attempt to move away from the traditional neoclassicism of the French theater to a more realistic treatment of the lives of the lower and middle classes. His essays on art created "modern art criticism in France," according to one historian. Diderot's own literary works as well as his essays on drama and art possess a common thread since he was one of the first European writers to see art and literature in social terms. Both, he believed, should serve to teach moral lessons that would improve society. They could, in fact, do this even better than the church: "I am not a Capuchin [monk], yet I would hasten the coming of the day when painting and sculpture, more decent and moral, will think of contributing, together with the other arts, to inspire virtue and purify our manners." Unfortunately, this desire to teach lessons resulted in stilted characters who never came alive on the stage or in his novels.

Diderot's numerous essays reflected typical Enlightened interests. One of his favorite topics was Christianity, which he condemned as fanatical and unreasonable. As he grew older, his literary attacks on Christianity grew more vicious. Of all religions, Christianity, he averred was the worst, "the most absurd and the most atrocious in its dogma" (see the box on p. 603). This progression reflected his own transformation from deism to atheism, ending with an essentially materialistic conception of life: "This world is only a mass of molecules. There is a law of necessity that works without design, without effort, without intelligence, and without progress."

Diderot's most famous contribution to the Enlightenment was the *Encyclopedia, or Classified Dictionary of the Sciences, Arts, and Trades*, a twenty-eight volume compendium of knowledge that he edited and referred to as the "great work of his life." It appeared sporadically since state censors periodically suppressed its publication for "tending to destroy royal authority, to establish the spirit of independence and revolt, . . . and to raise the foundations of error, moral corruption, and irreligion."

Diderot Questions Christian Sexual Standards
▼ ▼ ▼

Denis Diderot was one of the bolder thinkers of the Enlightenment. He moved from outspoken criticism of the Christian religion to outright atheism. Although best remembered for the Encyclopedia, he was the author of many works that he considered too advanced and withheld from publication. In his Supplement to the Voyage of Bouganville, he constructed a dialogue between Orou, a Tahitian who symbolizes the wisdom of a philosophe, and a chaplain who defends Christian sexual mores. The dialogue gave Diderot the opportunity to criticize the practice of sexual chastity and monogamy.

Denis Diderot, *Supplement to the Voyage of Bouganville*

[Orou] "You are young and healthy [speaking to the chaplain] and you have just had a good supper. He who sleeps alone, sleeps badly; at night a man needs a woman at his side. Here is my wife and here are my daughters. Choose whichever one pleases you most, but if you would like to do me a favor, you will give your preference to my youngest girl, who has not yet had any children. . . ."

The chaplain replied that his religion, his holy orders, his moral standards and his sense of decency all prevented him from accepting Orou's invitation.

Orou answered: "I don't know what this thing is that you call religion, but I can only have a low opinion of it because it forbids you to partake of an innocent pleasure to which Nature, the sovereign mistress of us all, invites everybody. It seems to prevent you from bringing one of your fellow creatures into the world, from doing a favor asked of by a father, a mother and their children, from repaying the kindness of a host, and from enriching a nation by giving it an additional citizen. . . . Look at the distress you have caused to appear on the faces of these four women—they are afraid you have noticed some defect in them that arouses your distaste. . . ."

The Chaplain: "You don't understand—it's not that. They are all four of them equally beautiful. But there is my religion! My holy orders!. . . . [God] spoke to our ancestors and gave them laws; he prescribed to them the way in which he wishes to be honored; he ordained that certain actions are good and others he forbade them to do as being evil."

Orou: "I see. And one of these evil actions which he has forbidden is that of a man who goes to bed with a woman or girl. But in that case, why did he make two sexes?"

The Chaplain: "In order that they might come together—but only when certain conditions are satisfied and only after certain initial ceremonies have been performed. By virtue of these ceremonies one man belongs to one woman and only to her; one woman belongs to one man and only to him." Orou: "For their whole lives?"

The Chaplain: "For their whole lives. . . ."

Orou: "I find these strange precepts contrary to nature, and contrary to reason. . . . Furthermore, your laws seem to me to be contrary to the general order of things. For in truth is there anything so senseless as a precept that forbids us to heed the changing impulses that are inherent in our being, or commands that require a degree of constancy which is not possible, that violate the liberty of both male and female by chaining them perpetually to one another? . . . I don't know what your great workman [God] is, but I am very happy that he never spoke to our forefathers, and I hope that he never speaks to our children, for if he does, he may tell them the same foolishness, and they may be foolish enough to believe it. . . ."

These charges by the censors remind us how important the *Encyclopedia* was to the eighteenth century. Its purpose, according to Diderot, was to "change the general way of thinking." It did precisely that in becoming a major weapon of the philosophes' crusade against the old French society. The contributors included many philosophes who expressed their major concerns. They attacked religious superstition and advocated toleration as well as a program for social, legal, and political improvements that would lead to a society that was more cosmopolitan, more tolerant, more humane, and more reasonable. In later editions, the price of the *Encyclopedia* was drastically reduced, dramatically increasing its sales and making it available to doctors, clergymen, teachers, lawyers, and even military officers, thus furthering the spread of the ideas of the Enlightenment.

Despite the enormous output and incredible variety of his literary works, Diderot wrote no masterpiece. While

important as a suggestive thinker, he was ill suited to systematic thought. As he reflected in old age: "I am not conscious of having made use of half my powers; I have only fiddle-faddled."

TOWARD A NEW "SCIENCE OF MAN" The Enlightenment belief that Newton's scientific methods could be used to discover the natural laws underlying all areas of human life led to the emergence in the eighteenth century of what the philosophes called a "science of man" or what we would call the social sciences. Philosophes in a number of areas, such as economics and justice, arrived at natural laws that they believed governed human actions. If these "natural laws" seem less than universal to us, it reminds us how much the philosophes were people of their times reacting to the conditions they faced. Nevertheless, their efforts did result in establishing their disciplines on a rational basis and at least laying the foundations for the modern social sciences.

That a "science of man" was possible was a strong belief of the Scottish philosopher David Hume (1711–1776). An important figure in the history of philosophy, Hume has also been called "a pioneering social scientist." In his *Treatise on Human Nature*, which he subtitled "An Attempt to Introduce the Experimental Method of Reasoning into Moral Subjects," Hume argued that observation and reflection, grounded in "systematized common sense," made conceivable a "science of man." Careful examination of the experiences that constituted human life would lead to the knowledge of human nature that would make possible "a science, which will not be inferior in certainty, and will be much superior in utility, to any other of human comprehension."

In Montesquieu's analysis of governmental forms in *The Spirit of the Laws*, we have already seen the beginnings of a comparative method in politics that led toward a science of political sociology. The Physiocrats played a similar role in economics, and they and Adam Smith have been viewed as founders of the modern discipline of economics. The leader of the Physiocrats was François Quesnay (1694–1774), a highly successful French court physician.

Quesnay and the Physiocrats felt that they were the Isaac Newtons of economics and claimed they would discover the natural economic laws that governed human society because they were "susceptible of demonstration as severe and incontestable as those of geometry and algebra." Their first principle was that land constituted the only source of wealth and that wealth itself could be increased only by agriculture since all other economic activities were unproductive and sterile. As Quesnay said, "It is agriculture which furnishes all the material of industry and commerce." To the Physiocrats, agriculture included the exploitation of natural resources, especially mining. Even the state's revenues should come from a single tax on the land rather than the hodgepodge of inequitable taxes and privileges currently in place. In stressing the economic primacy of agricultural production, the Physiocrats were rejecting the mercantilist emphasis on the significance of money—that is, gold and silver—as the primary determinants of wealth (see Chapter 16).

Their second major "natural law" of economics also represented a repudiation of mercantilism, specifically, its emphasis on a controlled economy for the benefit of the state. Instead the Physiocrats stressed that the existence of the natural economic forces of supply and demand made it imperative that individuals should be left free to pursue their own economic self-interest. In doing so, all of society would ultimately benefit. Consequently, they argued that the state should in no way interrupt the free play of natural economic forces by government regulations of the economy, but leave it alone, a doctrine that subsequently became known by its French name, *laissez-faire* (to let alone).

The best statement of laissez-faire was made in 1776 by a Scottish philosopher, Adam Smith (1723–1790), when he published his famous work, *Inquiry into the Nature and Causes of the Wealth of Nations*, known simply as *The Wealth of Nations*. In the process of enunciating three of his basic principles of economics, Smith presented a vigorous attack on mercantilism. First, he condemned the mercantilist use of protective tariffs to protect home industries. A tailor, he argued, does not try to make his own shoes, nor does a shoemaker try to make his own clothes. Following this line of reasoning, if one country can supply another country with a product cheaper than the latter can make it, it is better to purchase than to produce it. Each nation, then, should produce what it did best without the artificial barriers of tariffs. To Adam Smith, free trade was a fundamental economic principle. Smith's second principle was his labor theory of value. Like the Physiocrats, he claimed that gold and silver were not the source of a nation's true wealth; but, unlike the Physiocrats, he did not believe that soil was either. Rather labor—the labor of individual farmers, craftsmen, and merchants—constituted the true wealth of a nation. Finally, like the Physiocrats, Smith believed that the state should not interfere in economic matters; indeed, he gave to government only three basic functions: it should protect society from in-

vasion (army); defend individuals from injustice and oppression (police); and keep up certain public works, such as roads and canals that private individuals could not afford. Thus, in Smith's view the state should be a kind of "passive policeman" that remains out of the lives of individuals.

In the seventeenth century, the mercantilists had elevated the state over the individual. In creating their new human science of economics, the Physiocrats and Adam Smith reversed priorities, emphasizing the economic liberty of the individual and laying the foundation for what became known in the nineteenth century as economic liberalism.

Some philosophes also believed that there were natural laws of justice. They were horrified by the unjust and antiquated laws of their times and sought a new science to make the punishment of crime both effective and civilized. The most notable effort was made by the Italian philosophe, Cesare Beccaria (1738–1794), who wrote *An Essay on Crimes and Punishment* in 1764 proclaiming three fundamental principles of justice.

Beccaria argued first that punishments should fit the crime. The aim of punishment should be "to prevent the criminal from doing further injury to society, and to prevent others from committing the like offence." Therefore, "such punishments . . . ought to be chosen, as will make the strongest and most lasting impressions on the minds of others, with the least torment to the body of the criminal." Second, justice needs to act quickly so that crime and punishment are associated together in people's minds. And finally, Beccaria argued, "Crimes are more effectually prevented by the certainty than the severity of punishment."[7] To Beccaria, severe punishments simply lead to more crimes, since men will do everything to avoid the punishment due the first if it is severe.

Beccaria was opposed to the use of both torture and capital punishment. Torture, he argued, assumes that pain is a test of truth as if truth resides in the body of a mutilated prisoner. Capital punishment was spectacular, but failed to stop others from committing crimes. Imprisonment, the deprivation of freedom, made a far more lasting impression. Moreover, capital punishment was harmful to society because it set an example of barbarism: "Is it not absurd, that the laws, which detest and punish homicide, should, in order to prevent murder, publicly commit murder themselves?"

THE LATER ENLIGHTENMENT By the late 1760s, a new generation of philosophes who had grown up with the worldview of the Enlightenment began to move beyond

Chronology
▼ ▼ ▼
Works of the Philosophes

Montesquieu, *Persian Letters*	1721
Voltaire, *Philosophic Letters on the English*	1733
Hume, *Treatise on Human Nature*	1739–1740
Montesquieu, *The Spirit of the Laws*	1748
Voltaire, *The Age of Louis XIV*	1751
Diderot, *The Encyclopedia*	1751–1765
Rousseau, *The Social Contract, Emile*	1762
Voltaire, *Treatise on Toleration*	1763
Beccaria, *An Essay on Crimes and Punishment*	1764
Holbach, *System of Nature*	1770
Smith, *The Wealth of Nations*	1776
Gibbon, *Decline and Fall of the Roman Empire*	1776–1788
Condorcet, *The Progress of the Human Mind*	1794

their predecessors' beliefs. Baron Paul d'Holbach (1723–1789), a wealthy German aristocrat who settled in Paris, preached a doctrine of strict atheism and materialism. In his *System of Nature* written in 1770, he argued that everything in the universe consisted of matter in motion. Human beings were simply machines; theology, revelation, and God were all products of the human mind and its myth-making capacity and were unnecessary to live moral lives. People needed only reason to live in this world: "Let us persuade men to be just, beneficent, moderate, sociable; not because the gods demand it, but because they must please men. Let us advise them to abstain from vice and crimes; not because they will be punished in the other world, but because they will suffer for it in this."[8] Except for the atheistic Diderot, Holbach shocked almost all of his fellow philosophes with his materialistic determinism and uncompromising atheism. Most intellectuals remained more comfortable with deism and feared the effect of atheism on society.

Marie-Jean de Condorcet (1743–1794), another French philosophe, made an exaggerated claim for optimism that appears utopian in comparison with his predecessors' cautious hopes for gradual progress. Condorcet was a victim of the turmoil of the French Revolution and wrote his chief work, *The Progress of the Human Mind*, while in hiding during the Reign of Terror (see Chapter

20). His survey of human history convinced him that humans had progressed through nine stages of history. Now, with the spread of science and reason, humankind was about to enter the tenth stage, one of perfection, in which people will see that "there is no limit to the perfecting of the powers of man; that human perfectibility is in reality indefinite, that the progress of this perfectibility . . . has no other limit than the duration of the globe upon which nature has placed us." This prophet of humankind's perfection committed suicide shortly after composing this work in order to avoid the guillotine.

No one was more critical of the work of his predecessors than Jean-Jacques Rousseau (1712–1778). He was born in the city of Geneva, the son of a watchmaker. Almost entirely self-educated, he spent a wandering existence as a youth holding various jobs in France and Italy. He went back to school for a while to study music

▼ **Jean-Jacques Rousseau.** By the late 1760s a new generation of philosophes arose who began to move beyond and even to criticize the beliefs of their predecessors. Jean-Jacques Rousseau was perhaps the most critical philosophe of the late Enlightenment. Rousseau considered civilization itself to be an evil and blamed private property for the rise of civilization.

and the classics (he could afford to do so after becoming the paid lover of an older woman). Eventually, he made his way to Paris where he became a friend of Diderot and was introduced into the circles of the philosophes. He never really liked the social life of the cities, however, and especially detested the artificial conventions prevailing in Parisian society. He frequently withdrew into long periods of solitude.

Rousseau's political beliefs were presented in two major works. In his *Discourse on the Origins of the Inequality of Mankind,* Rousseau began with humans in their primitive condition (or state of nature—see Chapter 16) where they were happy. There were no laws, no judges; all people were equal. But what had gone wrong? Civilization had corrupted them, but how had this happened?:

> The first man who, having enclosed a piece of ground, thought of saying, This is mine, and found people simple enough to believe him, was the true founder of civil society. How many crimes, wars, murders; how much misery and horror the human race would have been spared if someone had pulled up the stakes and filled in the ditch, and cried to his fellow men: "Beware of listening to this impostor. You are lost if you forget that the fruits of the earth belong to everyone and that the earth itself belongs to no one!"[9]

Private property was the beginning of inequality and civilization; private property was the cause of crimes, wars, and murders. People adopted laws and governors in order to preserve their property. In so doing, they rushed headlong not to liberty but into chains. "What then is to be done? Must societies be totally abolished? . . . Must we return again to the forest to live among bears?" No, civilized humans could not return to the forests and live like wild animals; they could "no longer subsist on plants or acorns or live without laws and magistrates." Government was an evil, but a necessary one.

In his celebrated treatise *The Social Contract,* published in 1762, Rousseau used the concept of the social contract to try to harmonize the liberty of the individual with the institution of government (see the box on p. 607). An entire society agreed to be governed by its general will. Each individual might have a particular will contrary to the general will, but if the individual put his particular will (self-interest) above the general will, he should be forced to abide by the general will. "This means nothing less than that he will be forced to be free," said Rousseau, because the general will was not only political in nature but also ethical; it represented what the entire community ought to do, that which was its highest good. Thus freedom was achieved in being

A Social Contract
▼ ▼ ▼

Although Jean-Jacques Rousseau was one of the French philosophes, he has also been called "the father of romanticism." His political ideas have proved extremely controversial. While some have hailed him as the prophet of democracy, others have labeled him an apologist for totalitarianism. This selection is taken from one of his most famous books, The Social Contract.

Jean-Jacques Rousseau, *The Social Contract*

Book 1, Chapter 6: The Social Pact

"How to find a form of association which will defend the person and goods of each member with the collective force of all, and under which each individual, while uniting himself with the others, obeys no one but himself, and remains as free as before." This is the fundamental problem to which the social contract holds the solution. . . .

Chapter 7: The Sovereign

Despite their common interest, subjects will not be bound by their commitment unless means are found to guarantee their fidelity.

For every individual as a man may have a private will contrary to, or different from, the general will that he has as a citizen. His private interest may he speak with a very different voice from that of the public interest; his absolute and naturally independent existence may make him regard what he owes to the common cause as a gratuitous contribution, the loss of which would be less painful for others than the payment is onerous for him; and fancying that the artificial person which constitutes the state is a mere rational entity, he might seek to enjoy the rights of a citizen without doing the duties of a subject. The growth of this kind of injustice would bring about the ruin of the body politic.

Hence, in order that the social pact shall not be an empty formula, it is tacitly implied in that commitment—which alone can give force to all others—that whoever refused to obey the general will shall be constrained to do so by the whole body, which means nothing other than that he shall be forced to be free; for this is the condition which, by giving each citizen to the nation, secures him against all personal dependence, it is the condition which shapes both the design and the working of the political machine, and which alone bestows justice on civil contracts—without it, such contracts would be absurd, tyrannical and liable to the grossest abuse.

---

forced to follow what was best for all people. To Rousseau, since everybody was responsible for framing the general will, the power of legislation could never be delegated to a parliamentary body:

> Thus the people's deputies are not and could not be its representatives; they are merely its agents; and they cannot decide anything finally. Any law which the people has not ratified in person is void; it is not law at all. The English people believes itself to be free; it is gravely mistaken; it is free only during the election of Members of Parliament; as soon as the Members are elected, the people is enslaved; it is nothing.[10]

This is an extreme, idealistic statement, but it is the ultimate statement of participatory democracy. Perhaps Rousseau was thinking of his native city of Geneva, a community small enough that it could conform to these strict rules of absolute democracy. But we do not really know. *The Social Contract* has evoked contradictory interpretations ever since the outbreak of the French Revolution. It was used by the more radical revolutionaries in the second stage of the French Revolution to justify democratic politics, while others have viewed Rousseau's emphasis on a coercive general will ("forced to be free") as leading to a totalitarian system. Rousseau himself said, "Those who boast that they understand the whole of it are cleverer than I am."

Another influential treatise by Rousseau also appeared in 1762. Entitled *Emile*, it is one of the Enlightenment's most important works on education. Written in the form of a novel, the work was really a general treatise "on the education of the natural man." Rousseau began with the premise that the child was an evolving personality, not a small adult. During the years from five to twelve, the child went through a prerational stage with the senses of prime importance. Consequently, the child learned by doing, by a direct observation of nature. From twelve to sixteen, a young person was open to more abstract concepts; this was the time when education in morality would take hold. Seventeen to nineteen was the proper time for training the reasoning faculty and revealing God. Rousseau favored a deistic, but basically profound, spirituality. His fundamental concern was that education should encourage rather than restrict children's natural instincts. Life had taught Rousseau the importance of the promptings of the heart, and what he sought was a balance between heart and mind, between sentiment and reason. This emphasis on heart and sentiment made him a precursor of the intellectual movement called Romanticism that dominated Europe at the beginning of the nineteenth century.

The Social Environment of the Philosophes

The social background of the philosophes varied considerably, from the aristocratic Montesquieu to the lower-middle-class Diderot and Rousseau. The Enlightenment was not the preserve of any one class, although it obviously had its greatest appeal to the aristocracy and upper middle classes of the major cities. The common people, especially the peasants, were little affected by the Enlightenment.

Of great importance to the Enlightenment was the spread of its ideas to the literate elite of European society. While the publication and sale of books and treatises were important to this process, equally important was the salon. Salons came into being in the seventeenth century but rose to new heights in the eighteenth. The salons were the elegant drawing rooms of the wealthy class's great urban houses where invited philosophes and guests gathered together and engaged in witty, sparkling conversations often centered on the new ideas of the philosophes. In France's rigid hierarchical society, the salons were important in bringing together writers and artists with aristocrats, government officials, and wealthy bourgeoisie.

As hostesses of the salons, women found themselves in a position to affect the decisions of kings, sway political opinion, and influence literary and artistic taste. Salons provided havens for people and views unwelcome in the royal court. When the *Encyclopedia* was suppressed by the French authorities, Marie-Thérèse de Geoffrin (1699–1777), the daughter of a valet and a wealthy bourgeois widow, welcomed the encyclopedists to her salon and offered financial assistance to complete the work in secret.

Mme. Geoffrin was not without rivals, however. The marquise du Deffand (1697–1780) had abandoned her husband in the provinces and established herself in Paris where her ornate drawing room attracted many of the Enlightenment's great figures, including Montesquieu, Hume, and Voltaire. In 1754, after she began to go blind, she was joined as a hostess by her illegitimate niece, Julie de Lespinasse (1733–1776). For the next ten years, their salon became the most brilliant in Europe until they quarreled and separated.

Although run by women, the reputation of a salon depended upon the stature of the males a hostess was able to attract (see the box on p. 609). Despite this male domination, however, both French and foreign observers complained that females exerted undue influence in French political affairs. While exaggerated, this perception led to the decline of salons during the French Revolution. The salons were also criticized by some philos-

▼ **The Salon of Madame Geoffrin.** An important factor in the development of the Enlightenment was the spread of Enlightenment ideas to the literate elites of European society. Salons were an important part of this process. Madame Geoffrin, who presided over one of the most well known Parisian salons, is shown here, the third figure from the right in the front row.

The Salon: Can Men and Women Be Friends without Sex?

▼ ▼ ▼

The salon was established in the seventeenth century by aristocratic women who sought conversation with men as intellectual equals without the demands of sexual love. These "precious women," who sought to gain moral prestige over their male suitors by their chastity, dominated the French salon in the early seventeenth century. But in the late seventeenth and eighteenth centuries, the females who organized the salons were well known for their sexual affairs and marriages with the great men invited to their salons. It was now taken for granted "that relations between women and men, however intellectual or artistic they might appear, could not remain platonic." The first two selections are from the novel The Great Cyrus by Mlle. de Scudéry, who maintained one of the most famous literary salons. She applauded platonic love and scorned marriage. The third selection is from a nostalgic letter of Abbé Galiani to his former salon hostess, Mme. Necker, and describes an eighteenth-century salon.

Mlle. de Scudéry, *The Great Cyrus*

Among us, love is not a simple passion as it is elsewhere; it is one of the requirements for good breeding. Every man must be in love. Every lady must be loved. No one among us is indifferent. Anyone capable of such hardness of heart would be reproached as for a crime; such liberty is so shameful that those who are not in love at least pretend to be. Custom does not oblige ladies to love but merely to allow themselves to be loved, and they put their pride in making illustrious conquests and in never losing those whom they have brought under their rule; yet they are severe, for the honor of our beauties consists in keeping the slaves they have made by the sheer power of their attractions and not by according favors; so that, by this custom, to be a lover is almost necessarily to be unhappy. . . . Yet it is not forbidden to reward a lover's perseverance by a totally pure affection . . . whatever can render them more lovable and loving is allowed, provided it does not shock that purity or modesty which, despite their gallantry, is these ladies' supreme virtue.

Mlle. de Scudéry, *The Great Cyrus*

"Then, said Tisandre [to Sapho—the name under which Mlle de Scudéry portrayed herself] "you can hardly regard marriage as desirable." "It is true," replied Sapho, "that I consider it a lengthy slavery." "So you think all men are tyrants?" "I think they may all become so . . . I know of course that there are some very worthy men who deserve all my esteem and could even acquire some friendship from me; but again, as soon as I think of them as husbands, I see them as masters so likely to turn into tyrants that I cannot help hating them there and then and thank the gods for giving me an inclination totally opposed to marriage."

Abbé Galiani, Letter to Madame Necker

Not a Friday passes but I visit you in spirit. I arrive. I find you putting the finishing touches to your clothes. I sit at your feet. . . . Dinner is announced. We come out. The others eat meat. I abstain. I eat a lot of that green Scotch cod which I love. I give myself indigestion while admiring Abbé Morellet's skill at carving a young turkey. We get up from table. Coffee is served. Everyone talks at once. The Abbé Raynal agrees with me that Boston has severed its links with England forever and the same time Creutz and Marmontel agree that Grétry is the Pergolese of France. M. Necker thinks everything is perfect, bows his head, and goes away. That is how I spend my Fridays.

---

ophes for their superficiality, to which some wealthy men responded by organizing salons exclusively for serious discussion of ideas and for men only. The most famous was that of Baron d'Holbach whose five-hour discussions were, according to Holbach himself, "the most free, the most animated, and most instructive conversation that it was ever possible to hear."

The salon served an important role in making possible conversation and sociability between upper-class men and women as well as spreading the ideas of the Enlightenment. But there were also other means to spread Enlightenment ideas. Coffeehouses, cafes, reading clubs, and public lending libraries created by the state were gathering places to exchange ideas. Secret societies were also developed. The most famous was the Freemasons, established in London in 1717, France and Italy in 1726, and Prussia in 1744, where Frederick II himself was a grand master. It was no secret that the Freemasons were sympathetic to the ideas of the philosophes.

▼ Culture and Society in an Age of Enlightenment

The intellectual adventure fostered by the philosophes was accompanied by both traditional practices and important changes in the eighteenth-century world of culture and society.

Innovations in Art, Music, and Literature

The eighteenth century began with Baroque and neoclassical principles everywhere in evidence (see Chapters 15 and 16). But the philosophes' emphasis on freedom from rules and the need to allow the free play of the artistic imagination underscored the rapid change in the arts in the eighteenth century. Yet some things remained unchanged. Neoclassicism continued to maintain its strong appeal, especially in architecture, and the late eighteenth century even witnessed another classical revival that appealed to the French revolutionary and Napoleonic eras at the end of the century.

ROCOCO Although the Baroque and neoclassical styles that had dominated the seventeenth century continued into the eighteenth century, by the 1730s a new style affecting decoration and architecture known as Rococo had spread all over Europe. Though a French invention and enormously popular in Germany, Rococo truly became an international style.

Unlike the Baroque, which stressed grandeur, power, and movement, Rococo emphasized grace, charm, and gentle action. Rococo rejected strict geometrical patterns and had a fondness for curves; it liked to follow the wandering lines of natural objects, such as seashells and flowers. It made much use of interlaced designs colored in gold with delicate contours and graceful curves. Highly secular, its lightness and charm spoke of the pursuit of pleasure, happiness, and love.

Some of Rococo's appeal is evident already in the work of Antoine Watteau (1684–1721), whose lyrical views of aristocratic life, refined, sensual, civilized, with gentlemen and ladies in elegant dress, revealed a world of upper-class pleasure and joy. Underneath that exterior, however, was an element of sadness as the artist revealed the fragility and transitory nature of pleasure, love, and life.

Another aspect of Rococo was the sense of enchantment and exuberance, especially evident in the work of Giovanni Battista Tiepolo (1696–1770). Much of Tiepolo's painting came to adorn the walls and ceilings of churches and palaces. His masterpiece is the ceiling of the Bishop's Palace at Würzburg, a massive scene representing the four continents. Tiepolo's work reminds us that Rococo decorative work could easily be used with Baroque architecture.

The palace of Versailles had made an enormous impact on Europe. "Keeping up with the Bourbons" became important as the Austrian emperor, the Swedish king, German princes and prince-bishops, Italian

▼ **Antoine Watteau, *The Pilgrimage to Cythera.*** A French invention, the Rococo style spread all over Europe by the 1730s. Rococo emphasized grace and charm over grandeur and power. Antoine Watteau was one of the most gifted painters in eighteenth-century France. His portrayal of aristocratic life reveals a world of elegance, wealth, and pleasure. Yet it is a world also tinged with a sadness created by the realization of the transient nature of life.

princes, and even a Russian tsar built grandiose palaces. While imitating Versailles's size, they were not so much modeled after the French classical style of Versailles as they were after the seventeenth-century Italian Baroque, as modified by a series of brilliant German and Austrian sculptor-architects. This Baroque-Rococo architectural style of the eighteenth century was conceived as a total work of art in which building, sculptural figures, and wall and ceiling paintings were blended into a harmonious whole. This style was used in both palaces and ecclesiastical buildings, and often the same architects did both. This is evident in the work of one of the greatest architects of the eighteenth century, Balthasar Neumann (1687–1753).

Neumann's two masterpieces are the pilgrimage church of the Vierzehnheiligen (The Fourteen Saints) in southern Germany and the Bishop's Palace known as the Residenz, the residential palace of the Schönborn

▼ **Vierzehnheiligen, Exterior View.** The eighteenth century was marked by a Baroque-Rococo style of architecture, a style in which the building, sculptural figures, and ceiling and wall paintings were blended together to create a harmonious whole. Both palaces and ecclesiastical buildings were constructed in this style, and one of the most prominent architects of the eighteenth century, Balthasar Neumann, used it to design some of the most beautiful buildings of the century. Pictured here is the exterior of his pilgrimage church of the Vierzehnheiligen (The Fourteen Saints), located in southern Germany.

▼ **Vierzehnheiligen, Interior View.** Pictured here is the interior of the Vierzehnheiligen, the pilgrimage church designed by Balthasar Neumann. As this illustration shows, the Baroque-Rococo style of architecture created lavish buildings in which secular and spiritual elements became easily interchangeable. Elaborate detail, blazing light, rich colors, and opulent decoration are blended together to create a work of stunning beauty.

prince-bishop of Würzburg. Secular and spiritual become easily interchangeable as lavish and fanciful ornament, light, bright colors, and elaborate and rich detail greet us in both buildings. An even more stunning example of Rococo is evident in the pilgrimage church of the Wies in southern Bavaria, designed by Domenikus Zimmermann (1685–1766). The pilgrim in search of holiness is struck by an incredible richness of detail. Persuaded by joy rather than fear, the believer is lifted toward heaven on a cloud of rapture.

MUSIC   The eighteenth century was one of the greatest in the history of European music. Important to musicians in that century, as in previous centuries, was patronage, whether it came from princes, well-endowed ecclesiastics, or aristocrats. The many individual princes, archbishops, and bishops, each with his own court, provided the patronage that made Italy and Germany the musical leaders of Europe.

In the first half of the eighteenth century, two composers—Bach and Handel—stand out as musical geniuses. Johann Sebastian Bach (1685–1750) came from a family of musicians. Bach held the post of organist and music director at a number of small German courts before becoming director of church music at the church of St. Thomas in Leipzig in 1723. There Bach composed his Mass in B Minor, his St. Matthew's Passion, and the cantatas and motets that have established his reputation as one of the greatest composers of all time. Like the architect Balthasar Neumann, Bach could move with ease from the religious to the secular. His secular music reflects, in fact, a boisterous spirit; his Coffee Cantata was a dialogue between father and daughter over the daughter's desire to drink the new beverage. Bach had no problem adding religious texts to the secular music he had composed in princely courts to make it church music. Above all for Bach, music was a means to worship God; in his own words, his task in life was to make "well-ordered music in the honor of God."

The other great musical giant of the early eighteenth century, George Frederick Handel (1685–1759) was, like Bach, born in Saxony in Germany and in the same year. Unlike Bach, however, he was profoundly secular in temperament. He began his career by writing operas in the Italian manner and thereafter remained faithful to the Italian Baroque style. In 1712 he moved to England and remained there the rest of his life. Although patronized by the English royal court, Handel wrote music for large public audiences and was not adverse to writing huge, unusual-sounding pieces. The band for his Fireworks Music, for example, was supposed to be accom-

panied by 101 cannon. Although he wrote much secular music, it is ironic that the worldly Handel is probably best known for his religious music. He had no problem moving from Italian operas to religious oratorios when they proved to be in greater demand from his English public. An oratorio was an extended musical composition on a religious subject, usually taken from a biblical story. Handel's oratorio known as the *Messiah* has been called "one of those rare works that appeal immediately to everyone, and yet is indisputably a masterpiece of the highest order."[11]

To many music historians, Bach and Handel were not great innovators, but great clarifiers who perfected the Baroque musical style with its monumental and elaborate musical structures. Two geniuses of the second half of the eighteenth century—Haydn and Mozart—are viewed as innovators who wrote music called Classical rather than Baroque. Their renown caused the musical center of Europe to shift from Italy to the Austrian Empire.

Franz Joseph Haydn (1732–1809) spent most of his adult life as musical director for the wealthy Hungarian princes, the Esterhazy brothers. Haydn was incredibly prolific, composing 104 symphonies in addition to string quartets, concerti, songs, oratorios, and masses. His visits to England in 1790 and 1794 introduced him to another world where musicians wrote for public concerts rather than princely patrons. This "liberty," as he called it, induced him to write his two great oratorios, *The Creation* and *The Seasons*, both of which were dedicated to the common people.

Wolfgang Amadeus Mozart (1756–1791) was truly a child prodigy who gave his first harpsichord concert at six and wrote his first opera at twelve. He, too, sought a patron, but his discontent with the overly demanding archbishop of Salzburg forced him to move to Vienna where his failure to find a permanent patron made his life miserable. Nevertheless, he wrote music prolifically and passionately: string quartets, sonatas, symphonies, concerti, and operas. *The Marriage of Figaro, The Magic Flute,* and *Don Giovanni* are three of the world's greatest operas. Mozart composed with an ease of melody and a blend of grace, precision, and emotion that arguably no one has ever excelled. Haydn remarked to Mozart's father that "your son is the greatest composer known to me either in person or by reputation."

THE DEVELOPMENT OF THE NOVEL   Literary historians credit the eighteenth century with the decisive steps in the development of the novel. The novel was not a completely new literary genre but grew out of the medieval romances and the picaresque stories of the sixteenth century, such as Cervantes's *Don Quixote*. It is the English who are credited with establishing the "modern novel as the chief vehicle" for fiction writing. With no established rules, the novel was open to much experimentation. It also proved especially attractive to women readers and women writers.

Samuel Richardson (1689–1761) was a printer by trade who did not turn to writing until his fifties. His first novel, *Pamela: or, Virtue Rewarded,* focused on a servant girl's resistance to numerous seduction attempts by her master. Finally, by reading the girl's letters describing her feelings about his efforts, the master realizes that she has a good mind as well as body and marries her. Virtue is rewarded. *Pamela* won Richardson a large audience as he appealed to the growing cult of sensibility of the eighteenth century—the taste for the sentimental and emotional. Samuel Johnson, another great English writer of the century and an even greater wit, remarked, "If you were to read Richardson for the story . . . you would hang yourself. But you must read him for the sentiment."

Reacting against the moral seriousness of Richardson, Henry Fielding (1707–1754) wrote novels about people without scruples who survived by their wits. His best work was *The History of Tom Jones, A Foundling,* a lengthy novel about the numerous adventures of a young scoundrel. Fielding presented scenes of English life from the hovels of London to the country houses of the aristocracy. In a number of hilarious episodes, he described characters akin to real types in English society. Although he emphasized action rather than inner feeling, Fielding did his own moralizing by attacking the hypocrisy of his age.

THE WRITING OF HISTORY   The philosophes were responsible for creating a "revolution" in the writing of history. Their secular orientation caused them to eliminate the role of God in history and freed them to concentrate on events themselves and search for causal relationships within a natural world. Earlier, the humanist historians of the Renaissance had also placed their histories in purely secular settings, but not with the same intensity and complete removal of God. While the humanists had deemphasized Christian presuppositions in favor of humans, Voltaire and other philosophe-historians eliminated those presuppositions altogether.

The philosophe-historians also broadened the scope of history from the humanists' preoccupation with politics. Politics still predominated in the work of Enlightenment historians, but they also paid attention to economic, social, intellectual, and cultural developments.

As Voltaire explained in his masterpiece, *The Age of Louis XIV*: "It is not merely the life of Louis XIV that we propose to write; we have a wider aim in view. We shall endeavour to depict for posterity, not the actions of a single man, but the spirit of men in the most enlightened age the world has ever seen."[12] In seeking to describe the "totality of past human experience," Voltaire initiated the modern ideal of social history.

The weaknesses of these philosophe-historians stemmed from their preoccupations as philosophes. Following the ideals of the classics that dominated their minds, the philosophes sought to instruct as well as entertain. Their goal was to help civilize their age, and history could play a role by revealing its lessons according to their vision. Their emphasis on science and reason and their dislike of Christianity made them less than sympathetic to the period we call the Middle Ages. This is particularly noticeable in the other great masterpiece of eighteenth-century historiography, Edward Gibbon's *Decline and Fall of the Roman Empire*. Although Gibbon thought that the decline of Rome had many causes, he could not help blaming Christianity as one of the major ones. Gibbon's work reminds us that history in the eighteenth century was written to prove a point and remained a branch of literature rather than a social science.

High Culture

Historians and cultural anthropologists have grown accustomed to distinguishing between a civilization's high and popular culture. By high culture is usually meant the literary and artistic culture of the educated and wealthy ruling classes; by popular culture is meant the written and unwritten culture of the masses, most of which is passed down orally. By the eighteenth century, European high culture consisted of an ever-expanding and evolving world. There existed a learned culture of theologians, scientists, philosophers, intellectuals, poets, and dramatists, for whom Latin remained a truly international language. Their work was supported by a wealthy and literate lay group, the most important of whom were the landed aristocracy and the wealthier upper classes in the cities. European high culture was noticeably cosmopolitan. In addition to Latin, French had become an international language of the cultural elites. This high culture of Europe's elite was institutionally expressed in the salons, the universities, and the academies.

Especially noticeable in the eighteenth century was an expansion of both the reading public and publishing.

Samuel Johnson and the English Periodical
▼ ▼ ▼

*T*he periodical became a regular feature of upper-class English society in the eighteenth century. Samuel Johnson (1709–1784), one of England's great men of letters, contributed pieces to several of them. This selection is taken from one of Johnson's weekly essays that was published in the Weekly Gazette *under the name of* The Idler.

Samuel Johnson, "Robbery of Time," *The Idler,* no. 14, Saturday, July 15, 1758

When Diogenes received a visit in his tub from Alexander the Great, and was asked, according to the ancient forms of royal courtesy, what petition he had to offer; "I have nothing," said he, "to ask, but that you would remove to the other side, that you may not, by intercepting the sunshine, take from me what you cannot give me."

Such was the demand of Diogenes from the greatest monarch of the earth; which those who have less power than Alexander may, with yet more propriety, apply to themselves. He that does much good may be allowed to do sometimes a little harm. But if the opportunities of beneficence be denied by fortune, innocence should at least be vigilantly preserved.

It is well known that time once past never returns; and that the moment which is lost is lost forever. Time therefore ought, above all other kinds of property, to be free from invasion; and yet there is no man who does not claim the power of wasting that time which is the right of others.

This usurpation is so general that a very small part of the year is spent by choice; scarcely anything is done when it is intended, or obtained when it is desired. Life is continually ravaged by invaders; one steals away an hour, and another a day; one conceals the robbery by hurrying us into business, another by lulling us with amusement; the depredation is continued through a thousand vicissitudes of tumult and tranquillity, till, having lost all, we can lose no more. . . .

If we will have the kindness of others, we must endure their follies. He who cannot persuade himself to withdraw from society must be content to pay a tribute of his time to a multitude of tyrants; to the loiterer, who makes appointments which he never keeps; to the consulter, who asks advice which he never takes; to the boaster, who blusters only to be praised; to the complainer, who whines only to be pitied; to the projector, whose happiness is to entertain his friends with expectations which all but himself know to be vain; to the economist, who tells of bargains and settlements; to the politician, who predicts the fate of battles and breach of alliances; to the usurer, who compares the different funds; and to the talker, who talks only because he loves to be talking.

A recent study of French publishing, for example, reveals that while French publishers issued 300 titles in 1750, about 1,600 were being published yearly in the 1780s. While many of these titles were still geared for small groups of the educated elite, many were also directed to the new reading public of the middle classes, which included women and even urban artisans. The growth of publishing houses made it possible for authors to make money from their works and be less dependent on wealthy patrons. Of course, the increase in publishing does not necessarily mean that the significance and quality of what was being read were improving, as the best-seller in eighteenth-century England, Bishop Sherlock's *Letter from the Lord Bishop of London to the Clergy and People of London on the Occasion of the Late Earthquakes,* would indicate.

An important aspect of the growth of publishing and reading in the eighteenth century was the development of magazines for the general public (see the box above). Great Britain, an important center for the new magazines, saw 25 periodicals published in 1700, 103 in 1760, and 158 in 1780. Although short-lived, the best known was Joseph Addison's and Richard Steele's *Spectator,* begun in 1711. Its goal was "to enliven Morality with wit, and to temper Wit with Morality. . . . To bring Philosophy out of the closets and libraries, schools and colleges, to dwell in clubs and assemblies, at tea-tables and coffeehouses." In keeping with one of the chief intellectual goals of the philosophes, the *Spectator* wished to instruct and entertain at the same time. The *Spectator* with its praise of family, marriage, and courtesy also had a strong appeal to women.

Along with magazines came daily newspapers. The first was printed in London in 1702, but by 1780 thirty-seven other English towns had their own newspapers. Filled with news and special features, they were relatively cheap and were provided free in coffeehouses. Books, too, received wider circulation through the development of public libraries in the cities as well as private circulating libraries, which offered books for rental.

EDUCATION AND UNIVERSITIES   By the eighteenth century, Europe was home to a large number of privately endowed secondary schools, such as the grammar and public school in England, the gymnasium in German-speaking lands, and the collège in France and Spain. In many countries these secondary schools were often dominated by religious orders, especially by the Jesuits who had made education an important part of their philosophy.

These schools tended to be elitist, designed to meet the needs of the children of the upper classes of society. Some scholarships were provided for poor children if they were sponsored by local clerics or nobles. But their lot was not easy, and poor students who completed their studies usually went into the ranks of the lower clergy. Basically then, European secondary schools reinforced the class hierarchy of Europe rather than creating avenues for social mobility. In fact, most of the philosophes reinforced the belief that education should function to keep people in their own social class. Baron d'Holbach said, "Education should teach princes to reign, the ruling classes to distinguish themselves by their merit and virtue, the rich to use their riches well, the poor to live by honest industry."

The curriculum of these secondary schools still largely concentrated on the Greek and Latin classics with little attention paid to mathematics, the sciences, and modern languages. Complaints from philosophe-reformers, as well as from merchants and other middle-class people who wanted their sons to have a more practical education, led to the development of new schools designed to provide a broader education. In England, "dissenting academies," created to educate the non-Anglican segment of the population, offered a broader curriculum than the public and grammar schools. In Germany, the first *Realschule* was opened in Berlin in 1747 and offered modern languages, geography, and bookkeeping to prepare boys for careers in business. New schools of this kind were also created for upper-class girls although they placed most of their emphasis on religion and domestic skills.

The most common complaint about universities, especially from the philosophes, was the old-fashioned curriculum that focused on the classics and Aristotelian philosophy and left out training in the sciences and modern languages. Before the end of the century, this criticism led to reforms that introduced new ideas in the areas of physics, astronomy, and even mathematics into the universities. It is significant, however, that very few of the important scientific discoveries of the eighteenth century occurred in the universities. Most universities, with the exceptions of Edinburgh, Leiden, Vienna, Halle, and Göttingen, produced little intellectual growth and scholarship.

▼ **Library of Göttingen University.** The universities of the seventeenth and eighteenth centuries tended to cling to an old-fashioned curriculum emphasizing the classics and Aristotelian philosophy. Many philosophes argued that the universities should include training in modern languages and science. A reform program was begun before the end of the eighteenth century that allowed new ideas in physics, astronomy, and mathematics to become part of the university curriculum. The University of Göttingen, whose library is pictured here, was one of the universities that placed emphasis on the new physical sciences.

Halle and Göttingen were notable exceptions to this rule, especially in view of the fact that they were new universities. At the University of Halle in Prussia, the philosopher Christian Thomasius (1655–1728) was particularly important in creating a more lively and functional education. He revived theology and philosophy and steered these subjects away from medieval scholasticism. The University of Göttingen in Hanover, founded in 1737, placed its emphasis on the physical sciences. Although a new institution, it had the greatest university library in Europe by the end of the century.

Law, Crime, and Punishment

The legal profession in eighteenth-century Europe was divided into two major branches. Barristers sat atop the legal hierarchy while attorneys constituted a lower group. In England, barristers were usually men of aristocratic background who followed their university studies by apprenticing at the Inns of Court in London. Organized into a corporate group officially recognized by the state, only barristers could appear in court on behalf of their clients. Attorneys, on the other hand, dealt with clients' business outside the courtroom. Becoming an attorney required no university training, but simply a five-year apprenticeship to a regular attorney. Standards were generally lax, and it was not until the end of the century that English attorneys began to become more respectable and gain some prestige.

By the eighteenth century, most European states had developed a hierarchy of courts to deal with civil and criminal cases. With the exception of England, judicial torture remained an important means for obtaining evidence before a trial until the end of the century. Courts used the rack, thumbscrews, and other instruments to obtain confessions in criminal case. Seventeenth century legal reforms, however, led to the gradual demise of judicial torture. France was the last European state to abolish it in 1780.

Most crimes in the eighteenth century fell into four broad categories: violent crimes such as murder; crimes against property; crimes against the government, such as smuggling; and begging or public vagrancy. The eighteenth century seems to have witnessed a decline in crimes of violence while there was a noticeable increase in theft and other crimes against property, especially in the cities. Particularly in rural areas, the unplanned violence of desperate people that had been a prominent feature of the seventeenth century was replaced by "semi-professional vagabonds" who were primarily interested in theft.

Punishments for crimes were often cruel and even spectacular. Public spectacle was a basic part of traditional punishment because of the need to deter potential offenders in an age when a state's police arm was too weak to assure the capture of criminals. Although nobles were executed by simple beheading, lower-class criminals condemned to death were tortured, broken on the wheel, or drawn and quartered (see the box on p. 617). The death penalty was still commonly used in property

▼ **Cruel and Unusual Punishments.** Judicial torture remained a means of obtaining evidence in the eighteenth century. To obtain confessions, courts used the rack and thumbscrews as well as other horrific devices. Punishments for crimes were also often cruel. In this picture, a guilty person is being branded on the hand.

The Punishment of Crime
▼ ▼ ▼

Torture and capital punishment remained common features of European judicial systems well into the eighteenth century. Public spectacles were especially gruesome as this excerpt from the Nocturnal Spectator *of Restif de la Bretonne demonstrates.*

Restif de la Bretonne, *Nocturnal Spectator*

The Broken Man

I went home by way of rue Saint-Antoine and the Place de Grève. Three murderers had been broken on the wheel there, the day before. I had not expected to see any such spectacle, one that I had never dared to witness. But as I crossed the square I caught sight of a poor wretch, pale, half dead, wracked by the pains of the interrogation inflicted on him twenty hours earlier; he was stumbling down from the Hôtel de Ville supported by the executioner and the confessor. These two men, so completely different, inspired an inexpressible emotion in me! I watched the latter embrace a miserable man consumed by fever, filthy as the dungeons he came from, swarming with vermin! And I said to myself, "O Religion, here is your greatest glory! . . ."

I saw a horrible sight, even though the torture had been mitigated. . . . The wretch had revealed his accomplices. He was garroted before he was put to the wheel. A winch set under the scaffold tightened a noose around the victim's neck and he was strangled; for a long while the confessor and the hangman felt his heart to see whether the artery still pulsed, and the hideous blows were dealt only after it beat no longer. . . . I left, with my hair standing on end in horror.

---

as well as criminal cases. By 1800, the English listed over two hundred crimes that were subject to the death penalty. In addition to executions, European states resorted to forced labor in mines, forts, and navies. England also sent criminals as indentured servants to colonies in the New World and, after the American Revolution, to Australia.

By the end of the eighteenth century, a growing sentiment against executions and torture led to a decline in both corporal and capital punishment. A new type of prison, in which criminals were placed in cells and subjected to discipline and regular work to rehabilitate them, began to replace the public spectacle of barbarous punishments.

Medicine

In the eighteenth century, medicine was practiced by a hierarchy of practitioners. At the top stood the physicians, who were university graduates and enjoyed a high social status. Despite the scientific advances of the seventeenth and eighteenth centuries, however, university medical education was still largely conducted in Latin and was based primarily on Galen's work. New methods emphasizing clinical experience did begin to be introduced at the University of Leiden, which replaced Padua as the foremost medical school of Europe in the first half of the seventeenth century, only to be surpassed in the last half of the seventeenth century by Vienna. A graduate with a doctorate in medicine from a university needed to receive a license before he could be a practicing member of the physicians' elitist corporate body. In England the Royal College of Physicians licensed only one hundred physicians in the early eighteenth century. Only officially licensed physicians could hold regular medical consultations with patients and receive payments, already regarded in the eighteenth century as outrageously high.

Below the physicians were the surgeons, who were still known as barber-surgeons well into the eighteenth century from their original dual occupation. Their primary functions were to bleed patients and perform surgery; the latter was often done in a crude fashion since it was performed without painkillers and in filthy conditions because there was no understanding of bacteria and infection. Bleeding was widely believed to be efficacious as this doctor reported in 1799:

> Bleeding is proper at the beginning of all inflammatory fevers, as pleurisies. . . . It is likewise proper in all topical inflammations, as those of the intestines, womb, bladder, stomach, kidnies, throat, eyes, etc. as also in the asthma, sciatic pains, coughs, head-aches, rheumatisms, the apoplexy, epilepsy, and bloody flux. After falls, blows, bruises, or

any violent hurt received either externally or internally, bleeding is necessary.[13]

The surgeons underwent significant changes in the course of the eighteenth century. In the 1740s, they began to separate themselves from the barbers and organize their own guilds. At the same time, they started to undergo additional training by dissecting corpses and doing a more systematic study of anatomy. As they became more effective, the distinction between physicians and surgeons began to break down, and surgeons came to examine patients in a fashion similar to physicians by the end of the century. Moreover, surgeons also began to be licensed. In England the Royal College of Surgeons required clinical experience before granting the license.

Other medical practitioners, such as apothecaries, midwives, and faith healers, primarily served the common people in the eighteenth century. Although their primary function was to provide herbs and potions as recommended by physicians, apothecaries or pharmacists also acted independently in diagnosing illnesses and selling remedies. In the course of the eighteenth century, midwives were supplanted more and more by male doctors in the delivery of babies. However, the tradition of faith healing, so prominent in medieval medicine, continued to be practiced, especially in the rural areas of Europe.

Hospitals in the eighteenth century seemed more a problem than an aid in dealing with disease and illness. That conditions were bad is evident in this description by the philosophe Denis Diderot, who characterized the Hôtel-Dieu in Paris, France's "biggest, roomiest, and richest" hospital, in these words:

> Imagine a long series of communicating wards filled with sufferers of every kind of disease who are sometimes packed three, four, five or even six into a bed, the living alongside the dead and dying, the air polluted by this mass of unhealthy bodies, passing pestilential germs of their afflictions from one to the other, and the spectacle of suffering and agony on every hand. That is the Hôtel-Dieu.
>
> The result is that many of these poor wretches come out with diseases they did not have when they went in, and often pass them on to the people they go back to live with. Others are half-cured and spend the rest of their days in an invalidism as hard to bear as the illness itself; and the rest perish, except for the fortunate few whose strong constitutions enable them to survive.[14]

Despite appeals, reform efforts for hospitals in the eighteenth century remained in an infantile stage.

Popular Culture

Popular culture refers to the often unwritten and unofficial culture passed down orally that was fundamental to the lives of most people. The distinguishing characteristic of popular culture is its collective and public nature. Group activity was especially common in the festival, a broad name used to cover a variety of celebrations: family festivals, such as weddings; community festivals in Catholic Europe that celebrated the feastday of the local patron saint; annual festivals, such as Christmas and Easter that go back to medieval Christianity; and Carnival, the most spectacular form of festival, which was celebrated in the Mediterranean world of Spain, Italy, and France as well as in Germany and Austria. All of these festivals shared common characteristics. While having a spiritual function, they were celebrated in a secular fashion. They were special occasions on which people ate, drank, and celebrated to excess. In traditional societies, festival was a time to waste since the rest of the year was a time of thrift; it was a time of play since much of the rest of the year was a time of unrelieved work. As the poet Thomas Gray in 1739 said of Carnival in Turin: "This Carnival lasts only from Christmas to Lent; one half of the remaining part of the year is passed in remembering the last, the other in expecting the future Carnival."[15]

"The example par excellence of the festival" was Carnival, which started in January and lasted until Lent began, traditionally the forty-day period of fasting and purification leading up to Easter. Carnival was a time of great indulgence, just the reverse of Lent when people were expected to abstain from meat, sex, and most recreations. A heavy consumption of food, especially meat and other delicacies, and heavy drinking were the norm: "they drink as if they were never to drink more." Carnival was a time of intense sexual activity as well. Songs with double meanings could be sung publicly at this time of year whereas otherwise they would be considered offensive to the community. A float of Florentine "keymakers," for example, sang this ditty to the ladies: "Our tools are fine, new and useful; We always carry them with us; They are good for anything, If you want to touch them, you can." Finally, it was a time of aggression, a time to release pent-up feelings. Most often this took the form of verbal aggression since people could openly insult other people and were even allowed to criticize their social superiors and authorities. But other acts of violence were also permitted. People pelted each other with apples, eggs, flour, and pig's bladders filled with water.

This limited and sanctioned violence also led to unplanned violence. All contemporaries observed that Carnival was a time when the incidence of murder increased dramatically.

Evident in Carnival was the idea of a "world turned upside down" when the normal order of things was reversed. Peasants became kings, women wore men's clothes, men wore women's clothes, and people were free to express their sexual or violent emotions. Social anthropologists have speculated that the purpose of these traditional "rituals of reversal" was to create their opposite, to strengthen the established order: "By making the low high and the high low, they reaffirm the hierarchical principle."[16] While this may be true, it would be foolish to assume that it always worked. There are numerous examples of Carnival events developing into riots in which public authorities were killed.

The same sense of community evident in festival was also present in the chief gathering places of the common people, the local taverns or cabarets. Taverns were supposedly for travelers but functioned more frequently as a regular gathering place for neighborhood men to talk, play games, conduct small business matters, and, of course, to drink. In some countries, the favorite drinks of poor people, such as gin in England and vodka in Russia, proved devastating as poor people regularly drank themselves into oblivion. Gin was cheap; the classic sign in English taverns, "Drunk for a penny, dead drunk for two pence," was literally true. In England the consumption of gin rose from two to five million gallons from 1714 to 1733 and only declined when complaints finally led to strict laws to restrict sales in the 1750s. Of course, the rich drank too. Samuel Johnson remarked once, "All the decent people in Lichfield got drunk every night and were not the worse thought of." But unlike the poor, the rich drank port and brandy, usually in large quantities.

This difference in drinking habits between rich and poor reminds us of the ever-widening separation between the elite and poor in the eighteenth century. In 1500, popular culture was for everyone; a second culture for the elite, it was the only culture for the rest of society. But between 1500 and 1800, the nobility, clergy, and bourgeoisie had abandoned popular culture to the lower classes. This was, of course, a gradual process, and in abandoning the popular festivals, the upper classes were also abandoning the popular worldview as well. The new scientific outlook had brought a new mental world for the upper classes, and they now viewed such things as witchcraft, faith healing, fortune telling, and

prophecy as the beliefs of "such as are of the weakest judgment and reason, as women, children, and ignorant and superstitious persons."

Despite this growing gulf between elite and common people, there were still some forms of entertainment that occasionally brought them together. Most common were the urban fairs, a product of what some historians now call the "commercialization of leisure," or the attempt by businessmen to turn leisure activities into a good investment. The three fairs in Paris provided entertainment—farcical theater, magic shows, circus performers, or freak shows—as well as food booths and popular wares for purchase. Both the privileged and unprivileged classes were still attracted to boxing matches and horse races as well as the bloodier spectacles of bullbaiting, bearbaiting, and cockfighting.

Popular culture had always included a vast array of traditional songs and stories that were passed down from generation to generation. But popular culture was not entirely based on an oral tradition; there existed a popular literature as well. So-called chapbooks, printed on cheap paper, were short brochures sold by itinerant peddlers to the lower classes. They contained both spiritual and secular material; lives of saints and inspirational stories competed with crude satires and adventure stories. Another kind of popular literature in the eighteenth century was the almanac, which combined the traditional astrological charts and herbal remedies with information on history and how to write letters.

It is apparent from the chapbooks and almanacs that popular culture did not have to remain primarily oral. Its ability to change was dependent upon the growth of literacy. There is still considerable uncertainty about literacy in early modern Europe because of the difficulty in measuring it. Some reasonable estimates based on studies in France indicate that literacy rates for men increased from 29 percent in the late seventeenth century to 47 percent in the late eighteenth century; for women, the increase was from 14 to 27 percent during the same period. Of course, certain groups were more likely to be literate than others. Upper-class elites as well as the upper middle classes in the cities were mostly all literate. However, the figures also indicate dramatic increases for lower-middle-class artisans in urban areas. Recent research in the city of Marseilles, for example, indicates an increase in literacy for male artisans and workers from 28 percent in 1710 to 85 percent in 1789 while rates for women remained at 15 percent. Peasants, who constituted as much as 75 percent of the French population, remained largely illiterate.

The development of literacy was closely connected to primary education. In Catholic Europe, primary education was largely a matter of local community effort, leading to little real growth. Only in the Habsburg Austrian Empire was there created a system of state-supported primary schools (*Volkschulen*). Although attendance was supposedly compulsory, a 1781 census revealed that only one in four school-age children was actually attending.

The emphasis of the Protestant reformers on reading the Bible had led Protestant states to take greater interest in primary education. Some places, especially the Swiss cantons, Scotland, and the German states of Saxony and Prussia, witnessed the emergence of universal primary schools that provided a modicum of education for the masses. An edict of the Prussian king Frederick II (see Chapter 19) in 1763 made the schooling of children compulsory. But effective systems of primary education were hindered by the attitudes of the ruling classes, who feared the consequences of any education beyond teaching the lower classes the virtues of hard work and deference to their superiors. Hannah More, a conservative evangelical educator made clear the philosophy of her charity school for poor children: "My plan of instruction is extremely simple and limited. They learn on weekdays such coarse work as may fit them for servants. I allow of no writing for the poor. My object is to train up the lower classes in habits of industry and piety."

▼ Religion and the Churches

The music of Bach and the pilgrimage and monastic churches of southern Germany and Austria make us cognizant of a curious fact. While much of the great art and music of the time was religious, the thought of the time was antireligious as life became increasingly secularized and men of reason attacked the established churches. And yet most Europeans were still Christians. Except for governments, churches remained the most important institutions in people's lives. Even many of those most critical of the churches accepted that society could not function without religious faith.

The Institutional Church

In the eighteenth century, the established Catholic and Protestant churches were basically conservative institutions that upheld society's hierarchical structure, privileged classes, and traditions. Although churches experienced change because of new state policies, they did not sustain any dramatic internal changes. Whether in Catholic or Protestant countries, the parish church run by priest or pastor remained the center of religious practice. In addition to providing religious services, the parish church kept records of births, deaths, and marriages, provided charity for the poor, supervised whatever primary education there was, and cared for orphans.

CHURCH-STATE RELATIONS Early on, the Protestant Reformation had solved the problem of the relationship between church and state by establishing the principle of state control over the churches. In the eighteenth century, Protestant state churches flourished throughout Europe: Lutheranism in Scandinavia and the north German states; Anglicanism in England; and Calvinism (or Reformed churches) in Scotland, the United Provinces, and some of the Swiss cantons and German states. There were also Protestant minorities in other European countries.

In 1700, the Catholic church still exercised much power in Catholic European states: Spain, Portugal, France, Italy, the Habsburg Empire, Poland, and most of southern Germany. Only Catholics were allowed to hold political office while in some countries, such as France and Austria, Protestants had no civil rights as well. The church continued to possess enormous wealth. In Spain, 3,000 monastic institutions housing 100,000 men and women controlled enormous landed estates.

The Catholic church remained hierarchically structured. In most Catholic countries, the highest clerics, such as bishops, archbishops, abbots, and abbesses, were members of the upper class, especially members of the landed nobility who received enormous revenues from their landed estates and tithes from the faithful. A wide gulf existed between the upper and lower clergy. While the French bishop of Strasbourg, for example, received 100,000 livres a year, parish priests were paid only 500.

In the eighteenth century, the governments of many Catholic states began to seek greater authority over the churches in their countries. This "nationalization" of the Catholic church was not entirely new. Louis XIV had already achieved a certain amount of control over the Catholic church in France in the seventeenth century. Other Catholic rulers now achieved similar results in the eighteenth century. One of the best examples of the changing relations between church and state in Catholic countries can be found in Spain, known above all for its dedication to Catholicism. The Bourbon kings, especially Charles III (1759–1788), continued to appoint Spanish bishops, forbade the publication of papal bulls without royal consent, and established control over the Inquisition by eliminating its more arbitrary features.

For Catholic countries, "nationalization" meant controlling the papacy and in turn the chief papal agents, the Society of Jesus. The Jesuits had proved extremely successful, perhaps too successful for their own good. They had created special enclaves, virtually states-within-states, in the French, Spanish, and Portuguese colonies in the New World. Through their excellent secondary schools, they directed the education of the sons of Catholic aristocrats. As advisers to Catholic rulers, they exercised considerable political influence. The high profile they achieved through their successes led to a wide range of enemies, both religious, from groups within the Catholic church who envied their importance, and political, from government ministers who viewed them as belonging to an international network hostile to the interests of individual states. A series of actions soon undermined Jesuit power. The Portuguese monarch and his adviser Pombal destroyed the powerful Jesuit state in Paraguay and then in 1759 expelled the Jesuits from Portugal and confiscated their property. The Portuguese expulsion was but the beginning of a series of attacks from political interests and enemies of the Jesuits from within the Catholic church itself. In 1764, they were expelled from France and three years later from Spain and the Spanish colonies. In 1773, when Spain and France demanded that the entire society be dissolved, Pope Clement XIV reluctantly complied. The dissolution of the Jesuit order, the pillar of Catholic fanaticism and strength, was yet another victory for Catholic governments determined to win control over their churches.

The end of the Jesuits was paralleled by a decline in papal power. Already by the mid-eighteenth century, the papacy played a minor role in diplomacy and international affairs. The nationalization of the churches by the states meant the loss of the papacy's power to appoint high clerical officials. In addition, a number of aristocratic bishops and archbishops became increasingly less reverent toward papal power. As one bishop remarked: "The Pope has his rights and we have ours."

Another aspect of state control over the Catholic church involved the regulation and suppression of monastic orders. The most radical program was carried out in the Austrian Empire where the Empress Maria Theresa (1745–1780) and later Emperor Joseph II (1780–1790) had already curtailed the Catholic church's power (see Chapter 19). By the Edict on Idle Institutions in 1782, Joseph II suppressed all the contemplative monastic orders, allowing only those that provided charitable or educational services to survive. The number of monks in the Austrian Empire was cut in half while the confiscated monastic properties were used to extend education. Joseph II's attempts to modernize even religious practices by cutting down on pilgrimages and the observation of saints' days backfired, however, for it cost him the support of the peasants who resented this interference in their personal religious life.

TOLERATION AND RELIGIOUS MINORITIES   One of the chief battle cries of the philosophes had been a call for religious toleration. Out of political necessity, a certain level of tolerance of different creeds had occurred in the

▼ **The Coronation Procession of Louis XV.** Although their power had declined significantly, churches continued to play a role in the eighteenth century. This painting by Pierre-Denis Martin shows the procession after the coronation of King Louis XV at Reims cathedral in 1722. Royalty was still conferred by the church through the traditional sacramental ceremony of coronation.

seventeenth century in such places as Germany after the Thirty Years' War and France after the divisive religious wars. But many rulers still found it difficult to accept. Louis XIV had turned back the clock in France at the end of the seventeenth century, insisting on religious uniformity and suppressing the rights of the Huguenots (see Chapter 16). Even devout rulers, such as Maria Theresa of Austria, continued to believe that there was only one path to salvation; it was the true duty of a ruler not to allow subjects to be condemned to hell by being heretics. Catholic minorities in Protestant countries and Protestant minorities in Catholic countries did not enjoy full civil or political rights. Persecution of heretics continued; the last burning of a heretic took place in 1781.

Nevertheless, some progress was made toward the principle of religious toleration. In England, the late seventeenth-century laws against Protestant Dissenters (from the Anglican church) were repealed or enforced loosely or not at all. No ruler was more interested in the philosophes' call for religious toleration than Joseph II of Austria. His Toleration Patent of 1781, while recognizing Catholicism's public practice, granted Lutherans, Calvinists, and Greek Orthodox the right to worship privately. In all other ways, all subjects were now equal: "Non-Catholics are in future admitted under dispensation to buy houses and real property, to practice as master craftsmen, to take up academic appointments and posts in public service, and are not to be required to take the oath in any form contrary to their religious tenets."[17]

TOLERATION AND THE JEWS   The Jews remained the despised religious minority of Europe. The largest number of Jews (known as the Ashkenazic Jews) lived in Eastern Europe. Except in relatively tolerant Poland, Jews were restricted in their movements, forbidden to own land or hold many jobs, forced to pay burdensome special taxes, and also subject to periodic outbursts of popular wrath. The resulting pogroms in which Jewish communities were looted and massacred made Jewish existence precarious and dependent upon the favor of their territorial rulers.

Another major group was the Sephardic Jews who had been expelled from Spain in the fifteenth century. Although many had migrated to Turkish lands, some of them had settled in cities, such as Amsterdam, Venice, London, and Frankfurt, where they were relatively free to participate in the banking and commercial activities that Jews had practiced since the Middle Ages. The highly successful ones came to provide valuable services to rulers, especially in central Europe where they were known as the court Jews. But even these Jews were insecure since their religion set them apart from the Christian majority and served as a catalyst to social resentment.

Some Enlightenment thinkers in the eighteenth century favored a new acceptance of Jews. They argued that Jews and Muslims were all human and deserved the full rights of citizenship despite their religion. But some philosophes, especially Holbach and Voltaire, made no attempt to hide their hostility and ridiculed Jewish customs. Many Europeans favored the assimilation of the Jews into the mainstream of society, but only by the conversion of Jews to Christianity as the basic solution to the "Jewish problem." This, of course, was not acceptable to most Jews.

The Austrian emperor Joseph II attempted to adopt a new policy toward the Jews, although it too was limited. It freed Jews from nuisance taxes and allowed them more freedom of movement and job opportunities, but they were still restricted from owning land and worshiping in public. At the same time, Joseph II encouraged Jews to learn German and work toward greater assimilation into Austrian society. Joseph's policy was but a small step in the liberation of the Jews as it took a moderate position between toleration and assimilation. The real emancipation of the Jews awaited the French Revolution and nineteenth-century developments.

Popular Religion in the Eighteenth Century

Despite the rise of skepticism and the intellectuals' belief in deism and natural religion, it would appear that religious devotion remained strong in the eighteenth century. Catholic popular piety continued to be strong while within Protestantism the desire for more direct spiritual experience actually led to religious revivalism, especially in Germany and England.

CATHOLIC PIETY   It is difficult to assess precisely the religiosity of Europe's Catholics. The Catholic parish church remained an important center of life for the entire community. How many people went to church regularly cannot be known exactly, but it has been established that 90 to 95 percent of Catholic populations did go to mass on Easter Sunday, one of the church's most special celebrations. Confraternities, which were organizations of lay people dedicated to good works and acts of piety, were especially popular with townspeople. Consecrated to a patron saint, each confraternity honored that saint by holy processions in which members proudly wore their special robes.

Catholic religiosity proved highly selective, however. Despite the Reformation, much popular devotion was still directed to an externalized form of worship focusing on prayers to saints, pilgrimages, and devotion to relics and images. The latter bothered many clergymen who felt that their parishioners were "more superstitious than devout," as one Catholic priest remarked. Many common people continued to fear witches and relied on the intervention of the saints and Virgin Mary to save them from personal disasters caused by the devil. Although more moderate and learned Catholics denounced this behavior as superstitious and wished to make Catholicism more rational, these practices were not confined to the lower classes. When the son of the Emperor Charles VI died shortly after birth, the emperor made a pilgrimage to the shrine of the Virgin Mary at Mariazell in Austria where he placed an image of the Christ child weighing as much as his dead son while praying for another male heir.

Nevertheless, recent research in France has indicated some decline in popular religious practices, especially in the most outward manifestations of faith. Religious phrases, for example, were increasingly dropped from the preambles to wills in the course of the eighteenth century. This was especially true for middle-class businessmen and professionals as well as many urban wage earners. To some historians, this evidence indicates a growing secularization on the eve of the French Revolution and the nineteenth century. Scholars doubt, however, whether this was as widespread in other parts of Europe.

PROTESTANT REVIVALISM   After the initial century of religious fervor that created Protestantism in the sixteenth century, Protestant churches in the seventeenth century had settled down into well-established patterns controlled by state authorities and served by a well-educated clergy. Protestant churches became bureaucratized and bereft of religious enthusiasm. In Germany and England, where rationalism and deism had become influential and moved some theologians to a more "rational" Christianity, the desire of ordinary Protestant churchgoers for greater depths of religious experience led to new and dynamic religious movements.

Pietism in Germany was a response to this desire for a deeper personal devotion to God. Begun in the seventeenth century by a group of German clerics who wished their religion to be more personal and transformative of daily experience, Pietism was spread by the teachings of Count Nikolaus von Zinzendorf (1700–1760). To Zinzendorf and his Moravian Brethren, as his sect was called, it was the mystical dimensions—the personal experience of God—in one's life that constituted true religious experience. He was utterly opposed to what he perceived as the rationalistic approach of orthodox Lutheran clergy who were being educated in new "rational" ideas. As Zinzendorf commented, "He who wishes to comprehend God with his mind becomes an atheist." To temper their mysticism, the Moravian Brethren followed a collective discipline akin to that of monasticism. Other Pietists, especially at the University of Halle and in other small German states, downplayed Zinzendorf's mystical element in favor of infusing civil life with Christian spirit and good works. In the eighteenth century, Pietism added an element of liveliness to an orthodox Lutheranism that was threatening to stagnate.

After the civil wars of the seventeenth century, England too had arrived at a respectable, uniform, and complacent state church. While local Anglican parish rectors were under the control of neighboring landholding nobles and reflected their social prejudices, higher members of the clergy—the bishops—were appointed by the crown, most often for political reasons. A pillar of the establishment, the Anglican church seemed to offer little spiritual excitement, especially to the masses of people. The other dissenting Protestant groups—the Puritans, Quakers, Baptists—were relatively subdued while the growth of deism seemed to challenge Christianity itself. The desire for deep spiritual experience seemed unmet until the advent of John Wesley (1703–1791).

An ordained Anglican minister, John Wesley took religion very seriously and experienced a deep spiritual crisis, finally relieved only by the ministrations of a German Pietist. In the process, he underwent a mystical experience: "I felt I did trust in Christ alone for salvation; and an assurance was given me, that He had taken away my sins, even mine, and saved me from the law of sin and death. I felt my heart strangely warmed." To Wesley, "the gift of God's grace" assured him of salvation and led him, despite opposition from the Anglican church, which criticized this emotional mysticism or religious enthusiasm as superstitious nonsense, to become a missionary to the English people, to bring the "glad tidings" of salvation to all people. To Wesley, all could be saved by experiencing God and opening the doors to his grace.

In taking the Gospel to the people, Wesley preached to the masses in open fields, appealing especially to the lower classes neglected by the socially elitist Anglican church. He tried, he said, "to lower religion to the level of the lowest people's capacities." Wesley's charismatic

The Conversion Experience in Wesley's Methodism

▼ ▼ ▼

After his own conversion experience, John Wesley traveled extensively to bring the "glad tidings" of Christ to other people. It has been estimated that he preached over 40,000 sermons, some of them to audiences numbering 20,000 listeners. Wesley gave his message wherever people gathered—in the streets, hospitals, private houses, and even pubs. In this selection from his journal, Wesley describes how emotional and even violent conversion experiences could be.

The Works of the Reverend John Wesley

Sunday, May 20 [1759], being with Mr. B—11 at Everton, I was much fatigued, and did not rise: but Mr. B. did, and observed several fainting and crying out, while Mr. Berridge was preaching: afterwards at Church, I heard many cry out, especially children, whose agonies were amazing: one of the eldest, a girl of ten or twelve years old, was full in my view, in violent contortions of body, and weeping aloud, I think incessantly, during the whole service. . . . The Church was equally crowded in the afternoon, the windows being filled within and without, and even the outside of the pulpit to the very top; so that Mr. B. seemed almost stifled by their breath; yet feeble and sickly as he is, he was continually strengthened, and his voice, for the most part, distinguishable, in the midst of all the outcries. I believe there were present three times more men than women, a great part of whom came from far; thirty of them having set out at two in the morning, from a place thirteen miles off. The text was, *Having a form of godliness, but denying the power thereof.* When the power of religion began to be spoken of, the presence of God really filled the place: and while poor sinners felt the sentence of death in their souls, what sounds of distress did I hear! The greatest number of them who cried or fell, were men: but some women, and several children, felt the power of the same almighty Spirit, and seemed just sinking into hell. This occasioned a mixture of several sounds; some shrieking, some roaring aloud. The most general was a loud breathing, like that of people half strangled and gasping for life: and indeed almost all the cries were like those of human creatures, dying in bitter anguish. Great numbers wept without any noise: others fell down as death: some sinking in silence; some with extreme noise and violent agitation. I stood on the pew-seat, as did a young man in the opposite pew, an able-bodied, fresh, healthy countryman: but in a moment, while he seemed to think of nothing less, down he dropped with a violence inconceivable. The adjoining pews seemed to shake with his fall: I heard afterwards the stamping of his feet; ready to break the boards, as he lay in strong convulsions, at the bottom of the pew. Among several that were struck down in the next pew, was a girl, who was as violently seized as he. . . . Among the children who felt the arrows of the Almighty, I saw a sturdy boy, about eight years old, who roared above his fellows, and seemed in his agony to struggle with the strength of a grown man. His face was as red as scarlet: and almost all on whom God laid his hand, turned either very red or almost black. . . .

The violent struggling of many in the abovementioned churches, has broken several pews and benches. Yet it is common for people to remain unaffected there, and afterwards to drop down in their way home. Some have been found lying as dead on the road: others, in Mr. B.'s garden; not being able to walk from the Church to his house, though it is not two hundred yards. . . .

preaching often provoked highly charged and even violent conversion experiences (see the box above). Afterward, converts were organized into so-called Methodist societies or chapels in which they could aid each other in doing the good works that Wesley considered a component of salvation. A Central Methodist Conference supervised new lay preachers from Methodist circles. Controlled by Wesley, it enabled him to dominate the evangelical movement he had created. Although Wesley sought to keep Methodism within the Anglican church, after his death it became a separate and independent sect.

John Wesley's Methodism gave lower-class and even some middle-class English people a sense of purpose and community. Emphasizing the virtues of hard work and sobriety, it encouraged patterns of behavior that made people successful and content with spiritual rather than political equality. Indeed, some historians have argued that Methodism insulated the English lower classes from the political radicalism generated in the French revolutionary era of the 1790s. Although this view is an exaggeration, Methodism does represent an important revival of Christianity and proved that the need for spiritual experience had not been expunged by the eighteenth-century search for reason.

One prominent historian of the eighteenth century has appropriately characterized it as a century of change and tradition. Highly influenced by the new worldview created by the Scientific Revolution and especially the ideas of Locke and Newton, the philosophes hoped that they could create a new society by using reason to discover the natural laws that governed it. Like the Christian humanists of the fifteenth and sixteenth centuries,

they believed that education could create better human beings and a better human society. By attacking traditional religion as the enemy and creating the new "sciences of man" in economics, politics, justice, and education, the philosophes laid the foundation for a modern worldview based on rationalism and secularism.

But it was also an age of tradition. While secular thought and rational ideas began to pervade the mental world of the ruling elites, most people in eighteenth-century Europe still lived by seemingly eternal verities and practices—God, religious worship, and farming. The most brilliant architecture and music of the age were religious. And yet, the forces of secularization were too strong to stop. In the midst of intellectual change, economic, political, and social transformations of great purport were taking shape that by the end of the eighteenth century were to lead to both political and industrial revolutions. It is time now to examine the political, economic, and social traditions and changes of the century.

Notes

1. Quoted in Paul Hazard, *The European Mind, 1680–1715* (New York, 1963), pp. 304–5.

2. Quoted in Alan G. R. Smith, *Science and Society in the Sixteenth and Seventeenth Centuries* (London, 1972), pp. 174–75.

3. Quoted in Hazard, *The European Mind*, p. 11.

4. Ibid., p. 12.

5. John Locke, *An Essay Concerning Human Understanding* (New York, 1964), pp. 89–90.

6. Quoted in Frederick Artz, *The Enlightenment in France* (Kent, Ohio, 1968), p. 103.

7. Cesare Beccaria, *An Essay on Crimes and Punishments*, trans. E. D. Ingraham (Philadelphia, 1819), pp. 59–60, 93–94.

8. Baron d'Holbach, *Common Sense*, as quoted in Frank E. Manuel, ed., *The Enlightenment* (Englewood Cliffs, N.J., 1965), p. 62.

9. Jean-Jacques Rousseau, *A Discourse on Inequality*, trans. Maurice Cranston (Harmondsworth, 1984), p. 109.

10. Jean-Jacques Rousseau, *The Social Contract*, trans. Maurice Cranston (Harmondsworth, 1968), p. 141.

11. Kenneth Clark, *Civilisation* (New York, 1969), p. 231.

12. Voltaire, *The Age of Louis XIV*, trans. Martyn P. Pollack (New York, 1961), p. 1.

13. Quoted in Lester S. King, *The Medical World of the Eighteenth Century* (Chicago, 1958), pp. 318–19.

14. Quoted in Rene Sand, *The Advance to Social Medicine* (London, 1952), pp. 86–87.

15. Quoted in Peter Burke, *Popular Culture in Early Modern Europe* (New York, 1978), p. 179.

16. Quotations (in order of appearance) are from ibid., pp. 183, 186, 201.

17. Quoted in C. A. Macartney, *The Habsburg and Hohenzollern Dynasties in the Seventeenth and Eighteenth Centuries* (New York, 1970), p. 157.

Suggestions for Further Reading
▼ ▼ ▼

Two sound, comprehensive surveys of eighteenth-century Europe are I. Woloch, *Eighteenth-Century Europe* (New York, 1982); and M. S. Anderson, *Europe in the Eighteenth Century* (London, 1987).

A good, brief introduction to the Enlightenment can be found in N. Hampson, *A Cultural History of the Enlightenment* (New York, 1968). A more detailed synthesis can be found in P. Gay, *The Enlightenment: An Interpretation*, 2 vols. (New York, 1966–69). Two older works still of value are by P. Hazard, *The European Mind, 1680–1715* (New York, 1963), and *European Thought in the Eighteenth Century* (New York, 1963). For a short, popular survey on the French philosophes, see F. Artz, *The Enlightenment in France* (Kent, Ohio, 1968). Studies on the major Enlightenment intellectuals include R. Shackleton, *Montesquieu, A Critical Biography* (London, 1961); T. Besterman, *Voltaire* (London, 1969); A. Wilson, *Diderot* (New York, 1972); and R. Grimsley, *Jean-Jacques Rousseau* (Cardiff, 1961). Specialized studies on various aspects of the Enlightenment include F. Venturi, *Utopia and Reform in the Enlightenment* (Cambridge, 1971); F. Manuel, *The Eighteenth Century Confronts the Gods* (New York, 1967); M. C. Jacob, *The Radical Enlightenment: Pantheists, Freemasons and Republicans* (London, 1981); H. Chisack, *The Limits of Reform in the Enlightenment: Attitudes toward the Education of the Lower Classes in Eighteenth-Century France* (Princeton, N.J., 1980); and R. Darnton, *The Business of Enlightenment: A Publishing History of the Encyclopédie, 1775–1800* (Cambridge, Mass., 1979). On the role of women in the salon, see P. Quennell, ed., *Affairs of the Mind: The Salon in Europe and America from the 18th to the 20th Century* (Washington, D.C., 1980); and S. I. Spencer, ed., *French Women and the Age of Enlightenment* (Bloomington, Ind., 1984).

Two readable general surveys on the arts and literature are M. Levy, *Rococo to Revolution* (London, 1966); and H. Honour, *Neo-classicism* (Harmondsworth, 1968). On the development of the novel in England, see I. Watt, *The Rise of the Novel: Studies in Defoe, Richardson, and Fielding* (Berkeley, 1957). On one aspect of eighteenth-century education, see C. Bailey, *French Secondary Education, 1763–1790* (Philadelphia, 1978). The development of the attorney and barrister are examined in R. Robson, *The Attorney in Eighteenth Century England* (Cambridge, 1959); and L. Berlanstein, *The Barristers of Toulouse in the Eighteenth Century* (Baltimore, 1975). Different facets of crime and punishment are examined in the important works by M. Foucault, *Discipline and Punish: The Birth of the Prison* (New York, 1977); and J. Langbein, *Torture and the Law of Proof* (Chicago, 1977). On the medical profession, see L. King, *The Medical World of the Eighteenth Century* (Chicago, 1958); and M. Foucault, *The Birth of the Clinic* (New York, 1975).

Important studies on popular culture include P. Burke, *Popular Culture in Early Modern Europe* (New York, 1978); and R. Darnton, *The Great Cat Massacre and Other Episodes in French Cultural History* (New York, 1984). Recreational activities are covered in R. Malcolmson, *Popular Recreation in English Society, 1700–1850* (Cambridge, 1973); and R. Isherwood, *Farce and Fantasy: Popular Entertainment in Eighteenth-Century Paris* (New York, 1986). One approach to the popular literature of the lower classes can be found in B. Capp, *English Almanacs, 1500–1800: Astrology and the Popular Press* (Ithaca, N.Y., 1979).

A good introduction to the religious history of the eighteenth century can be found in G. R. Cragg, *The Church and the Age of Reason, 1648–1789* (London, 1966). A very informative regional study is T. Tacket, *Priest and Parish in Eighteenth-Century France* (Princeton, N.J., 1977). The problem of religious toleration is examined in C. H. O'Brien, *Ideas of Religious Toleration at the Time of Joseph II* (Philadelphia, 1969); and A. Hertzberg, *The French Enlightenment and the Jews* (New York, 1968).

Chapter 19

The Eighteenth Century: European States, International Wars, and Social Change

▼▼▼▼▼

Historians have often defined the eighteenth century chronologically as spanning the years from 1715 to 1789. Politically this makes sense since 1715 marks the end of the age of Louis XIV while 1789 was the year in which the French Revolution erupted. This period has often been portrayed as the final phase of Europe's old order, before the violent upheaval and reordering of society associated with the French Revolution. Europe's old order, still largely agrarian, dominated by kings and landed aristocrats, and grounded in privileges for nobles, clergy, towns, and provinces, seemed to continue a basic pattern that had prevailed in Europe since medieval times. Recent scholarship, however, has tended to undermine the idea of uniformity in the eighteenth century, especially in France and England. Just as a new intellectual order based on rationalism and secularism was emerging from the intellectual revolution of the Scientific Revolution and Enlightenment, demographic, economic, and social patterns were beginning to change in ways that represent the emergence of a modern new order.

In the eighteenth century, the process of centralization that had characterized the growth of states since the Middle Ages continued as most European states enlarged their bureaucratic machinery and consolidated their governments in order to collect the revenues and build the manpower they needed to compete militarily with the other European states. International competition continued to be the favorite pastime of eighteenth-century rulers. Within the European

Frederick the Great
of Prussia ▼

Maria Theresa
of Austria ▼

Catherine the Great
of Russia ▼

William Pitt the Younger
Becomes Prime Minister
of Britain ▼

•••••••• 1700 ••••••••••• 1725 ••••••••••• 1750 ••••••••••• 1775 ••••••••••• 1800 •••••••••

▲
Britain Enters
Spanish American Markets

▲
War of
Austrian Succession

▲
Seven Years'
War

▲
Quaker Criticism
of Slave Trade

state system, the nations that would dominate Europe until World War I—Britain, France, Austria, Prussia, and Russia—emerged as the five great powers of Europe. Their rivalries led to major wars, which some have called the first "world wars" since they were fought outside as well as inside Europe. In the midst of this state building and war making, dramatic demographic, economic, and social changes heralded the emergence of a radical transformation in the way Europeans would raise food and produce goods.

▼ The European States

Most European states in the eighteenth century were ruled by monarchs. Although individuals or factional parties often vied for influence over the monarch, few of those involved questioned either the moral or practical superiority of hereditary monarchy as the best form of government, especially in the large and successful states. As Catherine II wrote in 1764, "The Russian Empire is so large that apart from the Autocratic Sovereign every other form of government is harmful to it, because all others are slower in their execution and contain a great multitude of various horrors, which lead to the disintegration of power and strength more than that of one Sovereign."[1] States where hereditary monarchy was not strong, such as in the United Provinces, Sweden, and Poland, suffered decline or even worse. The lack of a strong monarchy led to Poland's partitioning by Austria, Prussia, and Russia in the course of the eighteenth century (see Poland later in the chapter).

The seventeenth-century justification for strong monarchy on the basis of divine right continued into the succeeding century, but in a diminished way as the eighteenth century became increasingly secularized. Although divine-right assumptions died hard, they were gradually superseded by influential utilitarian arguments. These were well expressed by the Prussian king Frederick II when he attempted to explain the services a monarch must provide for his people:

> These services consisted in the maintenance of the laws; a strict execution of justice; an employment of his whole powers to prevent any corruption of manners; and defending the state against its enemies. It is the duty of this magistrate to pay attention to agriculture; it should be his care that provisions for the nation should be in abundance, and that commerce and industry should be encouraged. He is a perpetual sentinel, who must watch the acts and the conduct of the enemies of the state. . . . If he be the first general, the first minister of the realm, it is not that he should remain the shadow of authority, but that he should fulfill the duties of such titles. He is only the first servant of the state.[2]

This utilitarian argument was reinforced by the praises of the philosophes.

Enlightened Politics?

There is no doubt that Enlightenment thought had some impact on the political development of European states in the eighteenth century. Closely associated with the Enlightenment idea of natural laws was the belief in natural rights, which were thought to be inalienable privileges that ought not to be withheld from any person. These natural rights included equality before the law, freedom of religious worship, freedom of speech and press, and the right to assemble, hold property, and pursue happiness. The American Declaration of Independence summarized the Enlightenment concept of natural rights in its opening paragraph: "We hold these truths to be self-evident, that all men are created equal; that they are endowed by their creator with certain unalienable rights; that among these are life, liberty and the pursuit of happiness."

But how were these natural rights to be established and preserved? Montesquieu had argued for constitutional guarantees achieved by a separation of powers in *The Spirit of the Laws*. Rousseau had advocated a democratic society as the ideal path to maintain people's natural rights. Most philosophes, however, did not trust the "people." "It must please the animals," Voltaire said, "when they see how foolishly men behave." In the opinion of the philosophes, most people needed the direction provided by an enlightened ruler. What, however, made rulers enlightened? They must allow religious toleration, freedom of speech and press, and the rights of private property. They must foster the arts, sciences, and education. Above all, they must not be arbitrary in their rule; they must obey the laws and enforce them fairly for all subjects. To Voltaire, only strong monarchs seemed capable of overcoming vested interests and effecting the reforms society needed. Reforms then should come from above—from the rulers—rather than from below—from the people. The philosophes were only too well aware of the power monarchs possessed and thought it unlikely that they would voluntarily relinquish it. Distrustful of the masses, the philosophes believed that absolute rulers, swayed by enlightened principles, were the best hope of reforming their societies.

The extent to which rulers actually did so is a frequently discussed issue in the political history of the eighteenth century. Many historians once assumed that a new type of monarchy emerged in the later eighteenth century, which they called "enlightened despotism" or "enlightened absolutism." Monarchs such as Frederick II of Prussia, Catherine the Great of Russia, and Joseph II of Austria supposedly followed the advice of the philosophes and ruled by enlightened principles, creating a path to modern nationhood. Recent scholarship, however, has questioned the usefulness of the concept of "enlightened absolutism." We can best determine the extent to which it can be applied by surveying the development of the European states in the eighteenth century and then making a judgment about the "enlightened absolutism" of the later eighteenth century.

The Atlantic Seaboard States

As a result of overseas voyages in the sixteenth century, the European economic axis began to shift from the Mediterranean to the Atlantic seaboard. In the seventeenth century, the English and Dutch expanded as Spain and Portugal declined. By the eighteenth century, Dutch power had waned, and it was left to the English and French to build the commercial empires that presaged the growth of a true global economy.

FRANCE   In the eighteenth century, France experienced an economic revival while the movement of the Enlightenment gained strength. The French monarchy, however, was not overly influenced by the philosophes and resisted reforms while the French aristocracy grew stronger.

Louis XIV had left France with enlarged territories but also an enormous debt, an unhappy populace, and his five-year-old great-grandson as his successor. The governing of France fell into the hands first of the regent, the duke of Orléans, whose good intentions were undermined by his drunken and immoral behavior, and later of Cardinal Fleury, the king's minister. France remained largely at peace as commerce and trade doubled and industry was promoted. Even the budget was balanced, at least for one year in 1738. Louis XV (1715–1774) then decided to rule alone, but his secrecy, deviousness, spendthrift ways, boredom with government affairs, and willingness to allow his mistresses to influence affairs of state undermined the monarchy's prestige. The loss of an empire in the Seven Years' War, accompanied by burdensome taxes, an ever-mounting public debt, more hungry people, and a court life at Versailles that remained frivolous and carefree forced even Louis to realize the growing disgust with his monarchy. "Things will last my time at any rate," he remarked myopically and prophetically.

Perhaps all might not have been in vain if Louis had been succeeded by a competent king. But the new king, the nineteen-year-old grandson who became Louis XVI (1774–1792), was obese, lacking in energy, and unable to stay awake during government business (see the box on p. 631). Unsure of himself, he proved ever indecisive and allowed himself to be swayed by his shallow wife, the Austrian Marie Antoinette. Neither Louis nor Marie Antoinette seemed able to fathom the depths of despair and discontent that soon led to violent revolution (see Chapter 20).

GREAT BRITAIN   The success of the Glorious Revolution in England had prevented absolutism without clearly inaugurating constitutional monarchy. The eighteenth-century British political system was characterized by a sharing of power between king and Parliament, with Parliament gradually gaining the upper hand. (The United Kingdom of Great Britain came into existence in 1707 when the governments of England and Scotland were united; the term *British* came into use to refer to both English and Scots.) The king chose ministers responsible to himself who set policy and guided Parlia-

The French King's Bedtime

▼ ▼ ▼

Louis XIV had used court etiquette to magnify the dignity of kingship. During the reign of Louis XVI (1774–1792), however, court etiquette degenerated to ludicrous depths. This excerpt from the Memoirs of Comtesse de Boigne describes the king's coucher, the formal ceremony in which the king retired for the night.

Comtesse de Boigne, Memoirs

The king [Louis XVI] went to his *coucher*. The so-called *coucher* took place every evening at half past nine. The gentlemen of the court assembled in the bedroom of Louis XIV (but Louis XVI did not sleep there). I believe that all those who had been presented at court were permitted to attend.

The king came in from an adjoining room, followed by his domestic staff. His hair was in curlers, and he was not wearing his decorations. Without paying attention to anybody, he stepped behind the handrail surrounding the bed, and the chaplain on duty was given the prayer book and a tall taperstand with two candles by one of the valets. He then joined the king behind the handrail, handed him the book, and held the taperstand during the king's prayer, which was short. The king then went to the part of the room where the courtiers were, and the chaplain gave the taperstand back to the first valet who, in turn, took it over to a person indicated by the king. This person held it as long as the *coucher* lasted. This distinction was very much sought after. . . .

The king had his coat, vest, and finally shirt removed. He was naked to the waist, scratching and rubbing himself as if alone, though he was in the presence of the whole court and often a number of distinguished foreigners.

The first valet handed the nightshirt to the most qualified person. . . . If it was a person with whom the king was on familiar terms, he often played little tricks before donning it, missed it, passed it, and ran away, accompanying this charming nonsense with hearty laughter, making those who were sincerely attached to him suffer. Having donned the nightshirt, he put on his robe and three valets unfastened the belt and the knee buckles of his trousers, which fell down to his feet. Thus attired, hardly able to walk so absurdly encumbered, he began to make the round of the circle.

The duration of this reception was by no means fixed; sometimes it lasted only a few minutes, sometimes almost an hour; it depended on who was there. . . . When the king had enough, he dragged himself backward to an easy chair which had been pushed to the middle of the room and fell heavily into it, raising both legs. Two pages on their knees seized his shoes, took them off, and dropped them on the floor with a thump, which was part of the etiquette. When he heard it, the doorman opened the door and said, "This way, gentlemen." Everybody left, and the ceremony was over. However, the person who held the taperstand was permitted to stay if he had anything special to say to the king. This explains the high price attached to this strange favor.

---

ment; Parliament had the power to make laws, levy taxes, pass the budget, and indirectly influence the king's ministers. The eighteenth-century British Parliament was dominated by a landed aristocracy that historians usually divide into two groups: an upper aristocracy or the peers who sat in the House of Lords and served as lord lieutenants controlling the appointment of the justices of the peace; and the landed gentry, lesser nobles who sat in the House of Commons and served as justices of the peace in the counties. There is much historical debate over whether it makes sense to distinguish between the aristocracies since the two groups had much in common. Both were landowners with similar economic interests, and they frequently intermarried.

Although the British monarchy was faced with a powerful aristocracy that monopolized Parliament and held most of the important governing posts locally (as justices of the peace in the counties) and nationally, it still exercised considerable power. Because the aristocracy was divided by factional struggles based on family rivalries, the kings could use their power of patronage by awarding titles, government posts, and positions in the church and household staff to win supporters among the aristocratic factions.

What enabled the British system of political patronage to work was the structure of parliamentary elections. The deputies to the House of Commons were chosen from the boroughs and counties but not by popular voting and hardly in any equitable fashion. Of the almost five hundred deputies in the House of Commons, about four hundred were chosen from the boroughs. The number of delegates from each borough, however, was determined by past history rather than population so one borough could have six people choosing two representatives while new cities like Manchester had none despite their growing populations. Who could vote also varied wildly, enabling wealthy landed aristocrats to gain support by patronage and bribery, giving rise to a number of "pocket boroughs" controlled by a single person (hence "in his pocket"). The duke of Newcastle, for example, controlled the representatives from seven boroughs. It has been estimated that out of 405 borough deputies, 293 were chosen by fewer than 500 voters. This control of borough deputies was also true of county delegates, two from each of England's forty counties. Although elected by holders of property worth at least forty shillings a year, the members of the leading landed gentry families were elected over and over again. In the Parliament of 1761, for example, over 50 percent of the members of the House of Commons were related to the upper aristocracy. Parliament then was an institution largely dominated by the landed aristocracy, but their factional struggles enabled the monarchy still to exercise some power by its control of patronage.

Since the ministers were responsible for exercising the king's patronage, who became his chief ministers took on great political significance. In 1714, a new dynasty—the Hanoverians—was established when the last Stuart ruler, Queen Anne (1702–1714), died without an heir. The crown was offered to the Protestant rulers of the German state of Hanover. Both George I (1714–1727) and George II (1727–1760) relied on Robert Walpole as their chief or prime minister and the duke of Newcastle as their main dispenser of patronage, putting the latter at the center of British politics. Since the first Hanoverian king did not speak English and neither the first nor the second George had much familiarity with the British system, the chief ministers were allowed to handle Parliament and dispense patronage. Many historians feel that this exercise of ministerial power was an important step in the development of the modern cabinet system in British government.

Robert Walpole served as prime minister from 1721 to 1742 and pursued a peaceful foreign policy to avoid new

▼ **The British House of Commons.** The British political system in the eighteenth century was characterized by a sharing of power between the king and Parliament. Parliament was divided into a House of Lords and a House of Commons. This painting shows the House of Commons in session in 1793 during a debate concerning the possibility of war with France. William Pitt is addressing the House.

land taxes. But new forces were emerging in eighteenth-century Britain as growing trade and industry led an ever-increasing middle class to favor expansion of trade and world empire. The exponents of empire found a spokesman in William Pitt the Elder, who became prime minister in 1757 and furthered imperial ambitions by acquiring Canada and India in the Seven Years' War (see The Seven Years' War later in the chapter).

Despite his successes, however, Pitt the Elder was dismissed by the new king George III (1760–1820) in 1761 and replaced by the king's favorite, Lord Bute. Although characterized as a rather stupid person, George III was not the tyrant he is often portrayed as being. Determined to strengthen monarchical authority, his desire to wield the power of patronage personally led to the ouster of Pitt. At the same time, however, the spread of the ideas of the Enlightenment through a growing number of newspapers and an expanding reading public increased public clamor for the reform of both patronage and the electoral system. The saga of John Wilkes soon enlarged the public outcry.

An ambitious middle-class member of the House of Commons, John Wilkes was an outspoken journalist who publicly criticized the king's ministers. Arrested and soon released, Wilkes was expelled from his seat in Parliament. When he persevered and won another parliamentary seat from the county of Middlesex near London, he was again denied the right to take his place in Parliament. The cause of John Wilkes quickly became identified with liberty, and the slogan "Wilkes and Liberty" was frequently used by his supporters who came from two major social groups: the common people of London, who had no voting rights, and a middle element of voting freeholders, such as guild masters and small merchants in London and the surrounding counties. The cry for liberty soon spilled over into calls for the reform of Parliament and the removal of parliamentary privileges. In 1780, the House of Commons affirmed that "the influence of the crown has increased, is increasing, and ought to be diminished." At the same time, criticism at home was exacerbated by criticism abroad, especially by the American colonists whose discontent with the British system had led to rebellion and separation (see Chapter 20). Although minor reforms of the patronage system were made in 1782, King George III managed to avoid more drastic change by appointing William Pitt the Younger (1759–1806), son of William Pitt the Elder, as prime minister in 1783. Supported by the merchants, industrial classes, and the king, who used patronage to gain support for Pitt in the House of Commons, the latter managed to stay in power through

Chronology
▼ ▼ ▼

The European States: The Atlantic Seaboard States

France	
Louis XV	1715–1774
Louis XVI	1774–1792
Great Britain	
The Stuarts	
Queen Anne	1702–1714
The Hanoverians	
George I	1714–1727
George II	1727–1760
Robert Walpole	1721–1742
William Pitt the Elder	1757–1761
George III	1760–1820
William Pitt the Younger	1783–1801

the French revolutionary and Napoleonic eras. George III, however, remained an uncertain supporter because of periodic bouts of insanity (he once thought a tree in Windsor Park was the king of Prussia). With Pitt's successes, serious reform of the corrupt parliamentary system was avoided for another generation.

THE DUTCH REPUBLIC   After its century in the sun, the Dutch Republic or United Netherlands suffered a decline in economic prosperity. Both local and national political affairs were dominated by the municipal oligarchies that governed the Dutch Republic's towns. In the eighteenth century, the struggle continued between these oligarchs (or regents as they were called from their governing positions) and the house of Orange, who as stadholders headed the executive branch of government. The regents sought to reduce the power of the Orangists but soon became divided when Dutch burghers who called themselves the Patriots (artisans, merchants, shopkeepers) began to agitate for democratic reforms that would open up the municipal councils to greater participation than that of the oligarchs. The success of the Patriots, however, led to foreign interference when the Prussian king sent troops to protect his sister, wife of the Orangist stadholder. The Patriots were crushed, and both Orangists and regents reestablished the old system. The intervention by Prussia serves to remind us of the growing power of the central European states.

Absolutism in Central and Eastern Europe

Of the five major European states, three were located in central and eastern Europe and came to play an increasingly important role in European international politics.

PRUSSIA   Two able Prussian kings in the eighteenth century, Frederick William I and Frederick II, further developed the two major institutions—the army and the bureaucracy—that were the backbone of Prussia. Frederick William I (1713–1740) promoted the evolution of Prussia's highly efficient civil bureaucracy by establishing the General Directory. Its supervision of military, police, economic, and financial affairs made it the chief administrative agent of the central government. Since Prussia's disjointed territories could hardly have been maintained without a centralized administrative machine, Frederick William strove to maintain a highly efficient bureaucracy of civil service workers. It became a special kind of organization with its own code in which the supreme values were obedience, honor, and service to the king as the highest duty. As Frederick William asserted: "One must serve the king with life and limb, with goods and chattels, with honor and conscience, and surrender everything except salvation. The latter is reserved for God. But everything else must be mine."[3] For his part, Frederick William kept a close personal watch over his officials to ensure the performance of their duties. As the Saxon minister at Berlin related:

> Every day His Majesty gives new proofs of his justice. Walking recently at Potsdam at six in the morning, he saw a post-coach arrive with several passengers who knocked for a long time at the post-house which was still closed. The King, seeing that no one opened the door, joined them in knocking and even knocked in some window-panes. The master of the post then opened the door and scolded the travelers, for no one recognized the King. But His Majesty let himself be known by giving the official some good blows of his cane and drove him from his house and his job after apologizing to the travelers for his laziness. Examples of this sort, of which I could relate several others, make everybody alert and exact.[4]

Close, personal supervision of the bureaucracy became a hallmark of the eighteenth-century Prussian rulers.

Under Frederick William I, the rigid class stratification that had emerged in seventeenth-century Brandenburg-Prussia was continued. The nobility or landed aristocracy known as Junkers, who owned large estates with many serfs, continued to play a dominating role in the Prussian state. The Junkers held a complete monopoly over the officer corps of the Prussian army, which Frederick William assiduously and passionately continued to expand. By the end of his reign, the army had grown from 45,000 to 83,000 men. Though tenth in physical size and thirteenth in population in Europe, Prussia had the fourth largest army after France, Russia, and Austria.

While nobles served as officers, rank-and-file soldiers were usually peasants who served a long number of years. Discipline in the army was extremely rigid and even cruel—so cruel, in fact, that desertion was common. The king advised his generals not to take troops through a forest on maneuvers because it offered too good an opportunity for running away. Frederick William believed that the nobles were naturally the best officers because they were used to commanding peasants on their estates. Moreover, by using nobles as officers, Frederick William ensured a close bond between the nobility and the army and, in turn, the loyalty of the nobility to the absolute monarch.

As officers, the Junker nobility became imbued with a sense of service to the king or state. All the virtues of the Prussian nobility were, in effect, military virtues: duty, obedience, sacrifice. At the same time, because of its size and reputation as one of the best armies in Europe, the Prussian army was the most important institution in the state. "Prussian militarism" became synonymous with the extreme exaltation of military virtues. Indeed, one Prussian minister remarked around 1800 that "Prussia was not a country with an army, but an army with a country which served as headquarters and food magazine."[5]

The remaining classes in Prussia were considerably less important than the nobility. The peasants were born on their lords' estates and spent most of the rest of their lives there or in the army. They had few real rights and even needed their Junker's permission before they could marry. For the middle class, the only opportunity for any social prestige was in the Prussian civil service where the ideal of loyal service to the state became a hallmark of the middle-class official. Frederick William allowed and even encouraged men of nonnoble birth to serve in important administrative posts. When he died in 1740, only three of his eighteen privy councillors were of noble birth.

Frederick the Great (1740–1786) was one of the best educated and most cultured monarchs in the eighteenth century. He was well versed in Enlightenment thought and even invited Voltaire to live at his court for several years. His intellectual interests were despised by his father who forced his intelligent son to prepare for a career in ruling (see the box on p. 635). A believer in the king as the "first servant of the state," Frederick the Great

Frederick the Great and His Father

▼ ▼ ▼

As a young man, the future Frederick the Great was quite different from his strict and austere father, Frederick William I. Possessing a high regard for French culture, poetry, and flute playing, Frederick resisted his father's wishes that he immerse himself in governmental and military affairs. Eventually, Frederick capitulated to his father's will and accepted the need to master affairs of state. These letters, written when Frederick was sixteen, illustrate the difficulties in their relationship.

Frederick to His Father, Frederick William I (September 11, 1728)

I have not ventured for a long time to present myself before my dear papa, partly because I was advised against it, but chiefly because I anticipated an even worse reception than usual and feared to vex my dear papa still further by the favor I have now to ask; so I have preferred to put it in writing.

I beg my dear papa that he will be kindly disposed toward me. I do assure him that after long examination of my conscience I do not find the slightest thing with which to reproach myself; but if, against my wish and will, I have vexed my dear papa, I hereby beg most humbly for forgiveness, and hope that my dear papa will give over the fearful hate which has appeared so plainly in his whole behavior and to which I cannot accustom myself. I have always thought hitherto that I had a kind father, but now I see the contrary. However, I will take courage and hope that my dear papa will think this all over and take me again into his favor. Meantime I assure him that I will never, my life long, willingly fail him, and in spite of his disfavor I am still, with most dutiful and childlike respect, my dear papa's

Most obedient and faithful servant and son,
Frederick

Frederick William to His Son Frederick

A bad, obstinate boy, who does not love his father; for when one does one's best, and especially when one loves one's father, one does what he wishes not only when he is standing by but when he is not there to see. Moreover you know very well that I cannot stand an effeminate fellow who has no manly tastes, who cannot ride or shoot (to his shame be it said!), is untidy about his person, and wears his hair curled like a fool instead of cutting it; and that I have condemned all these things a thousand times, and yet there is no sign of improvement. For the rest, haughty, offish as a country lout, conversing with none but a favored few instead of being affable and popular, grimacing like a fool, and never following my wishes out of love for me but only when forced into it, caring for nothing but to have his own way, and thinking nothing else is of any importance. This is my answer.

Frederick William

---

became a conscientious ruler who made few innovations in the administration of the state. His diligence in overseeing its operation, however, made the Prussian bureaucracy well known for both its efficiency and honesty.

For a time, Frederick seemed quite willing to follow the philosophes' recommendations for reform. He established a single code of laws for his territories that eliminated the use of torture except in treason and murder cases. He also granted a limited freedom of speech and press as well as complete religious toleration, no difficult task since he had no strong religious convictions anyway. Although Frederick was well aware of the philosophes' condemnation of serfdom, he was too dependent on the Prussian nobility to interfere with it or with the hierarchical structure of Prussian society. In fact, Frederick II

was a social conservative who made Prussian society even more aristocratic than it had been before. Frederick reversed his father's policy of allowing commoners to have power in the civil service and reserved the higher positions in the bureaucracy for members of the nobility. The upper ranks of the bureaucracy came close to constituting a hereditary caste over time.

Like his predecessors, Frederick the Great took a great interest in military affairs and enlarged the Prussian army (to 200,000 men). Unlike his predecessors, he had no objection to using it. Frederick did not hesitate to take advantage of a succession crisis in the Habsburg monarchy to seize the Austrian province of Silesia for Prussia. This act led to Austria's bitter hostility to Prussia and Frederick's engagement in two major wars, the War of the Austrian Succession and the Seven Years' War (see Wars and Diplomacy later in the chapter). Although the latter war left his country exhausted, Frederick succeeded in keeping Silesia. After the wars, the first partition of Poland with Austria and Russia in 1772 gave him the Polish territory between Prussia and Brandenburg and created greater unity for the scattered lands of Prussia. By the end of his reign, Prussia was recognized as a great European power.

THE AUSTRIAN EMPIRE   The Austrian Empire had become one of the great European states by the beginning of the eighteenth century. The city of Vienna, center of the Habsburg monarchy, was filled with magnificent palaces and churches built in the Baroque style and became the music capital of Europe. And yet Austria, by its very nature as a sprawling empire composed of many different nationalities, languages, religions, and cultures, found it difficult to provide common laws and administrative centralization for its people.

Empress Maria Theresa (1740–1780), however, stunned by the loss of Austrian Silesia to Prussia in the War of the Austrian Succession, resolved to reform her empire in preparation for the seemingly inevitable next conflict with rival Prussia. Although Maria Theresa was forced to accept the privileges of the Hungarian nobility and the right of her Hungarian subjects to have their own laws, she did abolish the Austrian and Bohemian chancelleries and replaced them with departments of foreign affairs, justice, war, commerce, and internal affairs that functioned for both territories. Maria Theresa also curtailed the role of the diets or provincial assemblies in taxation and local administration. Now clergy

and nobles were forced to pay property and income taxes to royal officials rather than the diets. The Austrian and Bohemian lands were divided into ten provinces and subdivided into districts, all administered by royal officials rather than representatives of the diets. Although the new system was not used in Hungary and the Austrian possessions in Italy and the Netherlands, the rest of the Austrian Empire was becoming more centralized and more bureaucratic. But these administrative reforms were done for practical reasons—to strengthen the power of the Habsburg state—and were accompanied by an enlargement and modernization of the armed forces. Maria Theresa remained staunchly Catholic and conservative and was not open to the wider reform calls of the philosophes. But her successor was.

From 1765 to 1780, Maria Theresa had allowed her son Joseph II to share rule with her, although Joseph felt restrained by his mother's lack of interest in the reform ideas of the Enlightenment that greatly appealed to him. When he achieved sole power in 1780, he was determined to make changes; at the same time, he carried on his mother's chief goal of enhancing Habsburg power within the monarchy and Europe. Joseph II was an earnest man who believed in the need to sweep away anything standing in the path of reason. As Joseph expressed it: "I have made Philosophy the lawmaker of my empire, her logical applications are going to transform Austria."

Joseph's reform program was far-reaching. He abolished serfdom and tried to give the peasants hereditary rights to their holdings. An exponent of the Physiocratic ideas (see Chapter 18), he abandoned economic restraints by eliminating internal trade barriers, ending

▼ **Frederick II.** Frederick II was one of the most cultured and well-educated European monarchs. Not adverse to using the military, Frederick took part in both the War of the Austrian Succession and the Seven Years' War. He is seen here returning from military maneuvers on a white horse, surrounded by his generals. Behind him on a black horse is his son, the future Frederick William II.

monopolies, and removing guild restrictions. A new penal code was instituted that abrogated the death penalty and established the principle of equality of all before the law. Joseph produced drastic religious reforms as well, including complete religious toleration and restrictions on the Catholic church. Altogether, Joseph II issued 6,000 decrees and 11,000 laws in his effort to transform Austria.

Joseph's reform program proved overwhelming for Austria, however. He alienated the nobility by freeing the serfs and alienated the church by his attacks on the monastic establishment. Even the serfs were unhappy, unable to comprehend the drastic changes inherent in Joseph's policies. His attempt to rationalize the administration of the empire by imposing German as the official bureaucratic language alienated the non-German nationalities. As Joseph complained, there were not enough people for the kind of bureaucracy he needed. He realized his failure when he wrote his own epitaph for his gravestone: "Here lies Joseph II who was unfortunate in everything that he undertook." Although his immediate successor, Leopold II (1790–1792), tried to hold the line, he too recognized that he could not rule without the support of the aristocrats and began to retrench. But it was the Emperor Francis II (1792–1835), frightened by the revolutionary terror in France (see Chapter 20), who ensured the undoing of most of Joseph's enlightened efforts.

RUSSIA   Peter the Great was followed by a series of six weak successors who were made and unmade by the palace guard. Only one of these, Elizabeth (1741–1762), Peter's daughter, reigned longer than ten years. She in turn was succeeded by her nephew Peter III (1762), whose German wife Catherine learned Russian and won the favor of the palace guard. Peter was murdered by a faction of nobles, and Catherine II the Great (1762–1796) emerged as autocrat of all the Russias.

Catherine was an intelligent woman who was familiar with the works of the philosophes. Voltaire and Diderot were among her correspondents. It is possible that like Joseph II she wished to reform Russia along the lines of Enlightenment ideas, but she was always shrewd enough to realize that her success depended upon the support of the palace guard and the gentry class from which it stemmed. She could not afford to alienate the Russian nobility.

Initially, Catherine seemed eager to pursue reform. She called for the election of an assembly in 1767 to debate the details of a new law code. In her *Instruction*, written as a guide to the deliberations, Catherine questioned the institution of serfdom, torture, and capital

▼ **Maria Theresa and Her Family.** Maria Theresa governed the vast possessions of the Austrian Empire from 1740 to 1780. In order to prepare for a conflict with Prussia, she attempted to reform her empire by streamlining its administration and restricting the power of local and provincial estates. Administrative reforms enabled Maria Theresa to enlarge and modernize the empire's armed forces.

punishment and even advocated the principle of the equality of all people in the eyes of the law (see the box on p. 638). But one and one-half years of negotiation produced little real change.

In fact, Catherine's subsequent policies had the effect of strengthening the hands of the landholding class at the expense of all others, especially the Russian serfs. In order to reorganize local government, Catherine divided Russia into fifty provinces, each of which in turn was subdivided into districts whose ruling officials were chosen by the nobles. In this way, the local nobility became responsible for the day-to-day governing of Russia. Moreover, the gentry were now formed into corporate groups with special legal privileges, including the right to trial by peers and exemption from personal taxation and corporal punishment. These rights were formalized in 1785 by a Charter of the Nobility.

Catherine's policy of favoring the landed nobility led to even worse conditions for the Russian peasantry. In 1767, serfs were forbidden to appeal to the state against

The Proposals of Catherine II for a New Law Code

▼ ▼ ▼

Catherine II the Great of Russia appeared for a while to be an enlightened ruler. In 1767, she convened a legislative commission to prepare a new code of laws for Russia. In her famous Instruction, she gave the delegates a detailed guide to the principles they should follow. Although the guidelines were obviously culled from the liberal ideas of the philosophes, the commission itself accomplished nothing, and Catherine's Instruction was soon forgotten.

Catherine II, Proposals for a New Law Code

13. What is the true End of Monarchy? Not to deprive People of their natural Liberty; but to correct their Actions, in order to attain the supreme good.

33. The Laws ought to be so framed, as to secure the Safety of every Citizen as much as possible.

34. The Equality of the Citizens consists in this; that they should all be subject to the same Laws.

38. A Man ought to form in his own Mind an exact and clear Idea of what Liberty is. Liberty is the Right of doing whatsoever the Laws allow: And if any one Citizen could do what the Laws forbid, there would be no more Liberty; because others would have an equal Power of doing the same.

123. The Usage of Torture is contrary to all the Dictates of Nature and Reason; even Mankind itself cries out against it, and demands loudly the total Abolition of it.

180. That Law, therefore, is highly beneficial to the Community where it is established, which ordains that every Man shall be judged by his Peers and Equals. For when the Fate of a Citizen is in Question, all Prejudices arising from the Difference of Rank or Fortune should be stifled; because they ought to have no Influence between the Judges and the Parties accused.

194. No Man ought to be looked upon as guilty, before he has received his judicial Sentence; nor can the Laws deprive him of their Protection, before it is proved that he has forfeited all Right to it. What Right therefore can Power give to any to inflict Punishment upon a Citizen at a Time, when it is yet dubious, whether he is Innocent or guilty?

270. It is highly necessary that the Law should prescribe a Rule to the Lords, for a more judicious Method of raising their Revenues; and oblige them to levy such a Tax, as tends least to separate the Peasant from His House and Family; this would be the Means by which Agriculture would become more extensive, and Population be more increased in the Empire.

---

their masters. Peasant unrest had frequently led to peasant rebellion in the Middle Ages, the Reformation, and seventeenth-century Europe and did so now in eighteenth-century Russia. The attempt of the Russian government to impose restrictions upon free peasants in the border districts of the Russian empire soon led to a full-scale revolt that spread to the Volga valley. It was intensified by the support of the Cossacks, independent tribes of fierce warriors who had at times fought for the Russians against the Turks but who now resisted the government's attempt to absorb them into the empire.

The elements of discontent were welded into a mass revolt by an illiterate Cossack, Emelyan Pugachev. Beginning in 1773, Pugachev's rebellion spread across southern Russia from the Urals to the Volga River. Initially successful, Pugachev won the support of many peasants when he issued a manifesto in July 1774, freeing all peasants from oppressive taxes and military service. Encouraged to seize their landlords' estates by Pugachev, the peasants responded by killing over 1,500 estate owners and their families. The rebellion soon faltered, however, as government forces became more effective. Betrayed by his own subordinates, Pugachev was captured, tortured, and executed. The rebellion collapsed completely, and Catherine responded by even greater repression of the peasantry. Not only was all rural reform dropped, but Catherine denounced and treated as treasonous any suggestion of agrarian reform. Serfdom was expanded into newer parts of the empire while parcels of crown land, on which peasants had received better treatment, were given to nobles to gain their support. There, too, the peasants were reduced to serfdom.

Above all, Catherine proved a worthy successor to Peter the Great in her policies of territorial expansion westward (into Poland) and southward (to the Black Sea). Russia spread southward by defeating the Turks. In the Treaty of Kuchuk-Kainarji in 1774, the Russians gained some land, the privilege of protecting Greek Orthodox Christians in the Ottoman Empire, and the right to sail in Turkish waters. Russian expansion westward occurred at the expense of neighboring Poland. In the three partitions of Poland, Russia gained about 50 percent of Polish territory.

POLAND   Poland was an excellent example of why a strong monarchy was needed in early modern Europe. The failure to develop the machinery of state building because of the excessive powers of the aristocracy proved disastrous. The Polish king was elected by the Polish nobles and forced to accept drastic limitations upon his power, including limited revenues, a small bureaucracy, and a standing army of no more than 20,000 soldiers. For Polish nobles, these limitations eliminated an absolute king; for Poland's powerful neighbors, they were an invitation to meddle in its affairs.

The total destruction of the Polish state in the eighteenth century arose out of the rivalries of its three great neighbors, Austria, Russia, and Prussia. To avoid war,

the leaders of these powers decided to compensate themselves by dividing Poland. A secret memorandum from Maria Theresa to the other two powers demonstrates well the spirit in which these negotiations were undertaken:

> His Majesty the King of Prussia and Her Majesty the Empress of All the Russias have rights and pretensions to certain districts in Poland, as we [Austria], have; in order to prevent any difficulties that might arise in this connection, we declare . . . that whatever the extent of our respective pretensions, the acquisitions . . . should be perfectly equal; that the portion of one should not exceed that of another, and that . . . we should, in the case of need, mutually and in good faith aid each other, in order to facilitate our success.[6]

To maintain the balance of power in central and eastern Europe, the three great powers cynically agreed to the acquisition of roughly equal territories at Poland's expense.

In 1772, Poland lost about 30 percent of its land and 50 percent of its population. Austria gained the agricul-

▼ **Map 19.1** The Partitions of Poland.

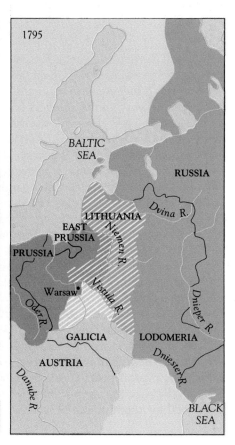

The European States: Absolutism in Central and Eastern Europe

Prussia	
Frederick William I	1713–1740
Frederick II the Great	1740–1786
The Austrian Empire	
Maria Theresa	1740–1780
Joseph II	1780–1790
Leopold I	1790–1792
Francis II	1792–1835
Russia	
Elizabeth	1741–1762
Peter III	1762
Catherine II the Great	1762–1796
Pugachev's Rebellion	1773–1775
Charter of the Nobility	1785
Poland	
First Partition	1772
Second Partition	1793
Third Partition	1795

turally rich district of Galicia, Russia achieved the largest slice of land in eastern Poland, and Prussia acquired West Prussia, the smallest but most valuable territory since it united two of the chief sections of Prussia.

The remaining Polish state was supposedly independent; in truth it was dominated by the Russians who even kept troops on Polish territory. After an effort by the Poles in 1791 to establish a stronger state under a hereditary monarchy, the Russians gained the support of Austria and Prussia and intervened militarily in May 1792. In the following year, a second partition of Polish territory was made by Russia and Prussia. Finally, after a heroic but hopeless rebellion in 1794–1795 under the General Thaddeus Kosciuszko, the remaining Polish state was obliterated by Austria, Prussia, and Russia in the third partition of Poland (1795). Many historians have pointed to Poland's demise as a cogent example of the importance of building a strong, absolutist state to survive in the seventeenth and eighteenth centuries. While true, the partition of Poland also serves to remind us that the cynical politics associated with the name of Machiavelli were becoming Europe's norm. It did not augur well for the future of European civilization.

The Mediterranean World

At the beginning of the eighteenth century, Spain experienced a change of dynasties from the Habsburgs to the Bourbons. Bourbon rule temporarily rejuvenated Spain and at least provided an opportunity to centralize the institutions of the state. Under Philip V (1700–1746), the laws, administrative institutions, and language of Castile were established in the other Spanish kingdoms, making the king of Castile truly the king of Spain. Moreover, French-style ministries replaced the old conciliar system of government, and officials similar to French intendants were introduced into the various Spanish provinces.

Since the Treaty of Utrecht in 1713 had taken the Italian territories and Netherlands away from Spain, the latter now had fewer administrative problems and less drain on its already overtaxed economic resources. In the second half of the eighteenth century, especially during the reign of Charles III (1759–1788), the Catholic church was also brought under control when the king banished the Jesuits and circumscribed the activities of the Inquisition. The landed aristocracy continued to exercise substantial power throughout the eighteenth century, however.

Portugal had experienced decline since the glorious days of empire in the sixteenth century. Nevertheless, during the long ministry of the marquis of Pombal (1699–1782), who served as chief minister to a series of Portuguese kings, the nobility and Catholic church were curtailed and the Portuguese empire temporarily revived. After Pombal was removed from office, the nobility and church regained much of their power.

After the Treaty of Utrecht, Austria had replaced Spain as the dominant force in Italy in the eighteenth century. The duchy of Milan, Sardinia, and the kingdom of Naples were all surrendered to the Habsburg emperors while Sicily was given to the northern Italian state of Savoy, which was slowly emerging as a state with "an appetite for territorial expansion." In 1734, the Bourbons of Spain reestablished control over Naples and Sicily while the remaining independent states of Italy, such as Venice and Genoa, grew increasingly impotent in international affairs.

Scandinavia

In the seventeenth century, Sweden had become the dominant power in northern Europe, but after the Battle of Poltava in 1709, Swedish power declined rapidly. Following the death of the powerful Charles XII in 1718, the Swedish nobility, using the Swedish Diet as its instrument, gained control of public life and reduced the monarchy to puppet status. But the division of the nobility into pro-French and pro-Russian factions eventually enabled King Gustavus III (1771–1792) to reassert the power of the monarchy. Gustavus proved to be one of the "most enlightened monarchs of his age." By decree, he established freedom of religion, speech, and press while instituting a new code of justice that eliminated the use of torture. Moreover, his economic reforms smacked of laissez-faire: he reduced tariffs, abolished tolls, and encouraged trade and agriculture. However, incensed at these reforms and their loss of power, a group of nobles assassinated the king in 1792, although they proved unable to fully restore the rule of the aristocracy.

Denmark also saw an attempt at enlightened reforms by King Christian VII (1766–1808) and his chief minister, John Frederick Struensee. Aristocratic opposition stymied his efforts, however, and led to Struensee's death in 1772.

Enlightened Politics Revisited

The subject of enlightened absolutism revolves around the relationship between "an intellectual movement and the actual practice of government." The ideas of the Enlightenment did have an impact on rulers in the second half of the eighteenth century. Some of the smaller states made the clearest efforts to institute enlightened reforms. Leopold I (1745–1790) of Tuscany, for example, abolished serfdom, encouraged trade and industry, reformed the penal code, abolished the Inquisition, and even toyed with the idea of granting a constitution that would allow his subjects to share governing power. While only Leopold dreamed of challenging the principle of political and social inequality on which all European society was based, almost every European ruler in the second half of the eighteenth century pursued some enlightened reforms, be they reform of laws, the development of secondary education, or religious tolerance.

Few rulers, however, felt compelled to make the state an experimental lab for a set of political principles. Of the three major rulers most closely associated traditionally with enlightened absolutism—Joseph II, Frederick II, and Catherine the Great—only Joseph II sought truly radical changes based on Enlightenment ideas. Both Frederick and Catherine liked to be cast as disciples of the Enlightenment, expressed interest in enlightened re-

Chronology ▼▼▼ The European States: The Mediterranean World and Scandinavia	
Spain	
Philip V, the First Bourbon King	1700–1746
Charles III	1759–1788
Portugal	
Marquis of Pombal	1699–1782
Sweden	
Charles XII	1697–1718
Gustavus III	1771–1792
Denmark	
Christian VII	1766–1808

forms, and even attempted some. But the policies of neither seemed seriously affected by Enlightenment thought. Necessities of state and maintenance of the existing system took precedence over reform. Indeed, many historians feel that Joseph, Frederick, and Catherine were all primarily guided by a concern for the power and well-being of their states and that their policies were not all that different from those of their predecessors. Perhaps their greatest success was in strengthening their administrative systems and creating an ideal of state service that separated the ruler and the ruling dynasty from the state. In the final analysis, however, the heightened state power was used to create armies and wage wars to gain more power. Despite their desire for reforms, enlightened rulers were not able to rise above their predecessors' goals. Nevertheless, in their desire to build stronger state systems, these rulers did pursue such enlightened reforms as legal reform, religious toleration, and the extension of education since these served to create more satisfied subjects and strengthened the state in significant ways.

It would be foolish, however, to overlook the fact that the ability of enlightened rulers to make reforms was also limited by political and social realities. Everywhere in Europe the hereditary aristocracy was still the most powerful class in society. Enlightened reforms were often limited to those administrative and judicial reforms that did not seriously undermine the powerful interests of the European nobility. Although aristocrats might join the populace in opposing monarchical extension of centralizing power, as the chief beneficiaries of a system based on traditional rights and privileges for their class, they were certainly not willing to support a political ideology that trumpeted the principal of equal rights for all.

▼ Wars and Diplomacy

Regardless of the philosophes' denunciations of war as a foolish waste of life and resources in stupid quarrels of no value to humankind, the rivalry among states that led to costly struggles remained unchanged in the European world of the eighteenth century. Although the European state system emerged in the seventeenth century, its implications were more fully realized in the eighteenth century. This system of self-governing, individual states was grounded largely in the amoral and potentially anarchic principle of self-interest. Since international relations were based upon considerations of power, the eighteenth-century concept of a "balance of power" was predicated on how to counterbalance the power of one state by another in order to prevent any one power from dominating the others. This balance of power, however, did not imply a desire for peace. Large armies created to defend a state's security were often used for offensive purposes as well. As Frederick the Great of Prussia remarked, "the fundamental rule of governments is the principle of extending their territories." Nevertheless, there were limits to the use of force in eighteenth-century Europe. No doubt technical considerations restricted the extent of warfare (see European Armies and Warfare later in the chapter), but a lack of the ideological fury that had made the religious wars of the sixteenth and seventeenth centuries so destructive also made compromises easier and the use of diplomacy more regular.

The system of modern diplomacy that had emerged in the Italian Renaissance was more fully developed by the eighteenth century. Parallel to the expansion of standing armies was the development of diplomatic machinery. Virtually every state now possessed a foreign ministry staffed by specialists who employed clerks and maintained archives while ambassadors resided in permanent embassies in the capital cities of the European states. Because most regular ambassadors were aristocrats, they formed a European community of sorts. Nevertheless, their interests remained those of their states, and they were quite prepared to lie if necessary, especially when preparing for war. As Frederick once said, "the safety and greater good of the state demands that treaties should be broken under certain circumstances."

The diplomacy of the eighteenth century still focused primarily on dynastic interests or the desire of ruling families to provide for their dependents and extend their dynastic holdings. But the eighteenth century also saw the emergence of the concept of "reason of state," on the basis of which a ruler such as Frederick II and a minister such as William Pitt the Elder looked beyond dynastic interests to the long-term future of their states.

International rivalry and the continuing centralization of the European states were closely related. The need for taxes to support large armies and navies created its own imperative for more efficient and effective control of power in the hands of bureaucrats who could collect taxes and organize states for the task of winning wars. At the same time, the development of large standing armies ensured that political disputes would periodically be resolved by armed conflict rather than diplomacy.

For a while, however, it seemed that Europe preferred peace. For two and one-half decades after the Peace of Utrecht, European states arranged alliances and met in international congresses that enabled them to maintain an apparent balance of power and keep the peace. There were problems, especially as competition for empire led to serious rivalry among the maritime states. But international cooperation seemed reasonably sure—at least until 1740 when the first of the two major conflicts of the mid-century erupted over the succession to the Austrian throne.

The War of the Austrian Succession (1740–1748)

Unable to produce a male heir to the Austrian throne, the Habsburg emperor Charles VI (1711–1740) so feared the consequences of the succession of his daughter Maria Theresa that he spent much of his reign negotiating the Pragmatic Sanction by which different European powers agreed to recognize his daughter as his legal heir.

Charles, however, failed to count on the faithlessness and duplicity of Europe's rulers. After his death, the Pragmatic Sanction was conveniently pushed aside, especially by Frederick II who had just succeeded to the throne of Prussia. The new Prussian ruler took advantage of the new queen to invade Austrian Silesia. At the same time, the ruler of the south German state of Bavaria seized some Habsburg territory and had himself chosen as the new Holy Roman emperor. The vulnerability of Maria Theresa encouraged France to enter the war against its traditional enemy Austria; in turn, Maria Theresa made an alliance with Great Britain who feared French hegemony over continental affairs. All too quickly, the Austrian succession had produced a worldwide conflagration. The war was fought not only in Europe where Prussia seized Silesia, and France occupied the Austrian Netherlands, but in the Far East where France took Madras in India from the British and in North America where the British captured the French fortress of Louisbourg at the entrance to the St. Lawrence River. By 1748, all parties were exhausted and agreed to stop. The peace treaty of Aix-la-Chapelle guaranteed the return of all occupied territories to their original owners except for Silesia. Prussia's refusal to return Silesia guaranteed another war, at least between the two hostile central European powers of Prussia and Austria.

The Seven Years' War (1756–1763)

Maria Theresa refused to accept the loss of Silesia and prepared for its return by rebuilding her army while working diplomatically to separate Prussia from its chief ally, France. In 1756, Austria achieved what was soon labeled a diplomatic revolution. Bourbon-Habsburg rivalry had been a fact of European diplomacy since the late sixteenth century. But two new rivalries made this old one seem superfluous: Britain and France over colonial empires, and Austria and Prussia over Silesia. France now abandoned Prussia and allied with Austria. Russia, who saw Prussia as a major hindrance to Russian goals in central Europe, joined the new alliance. In turn, Great Britain allied with Prussia. This diplomatic revolution of 1756 now led to another worldwide war.

There were three major areas of conflict: Europe, India, and North America. Europe witnessed the clash of the two major alliances: the British and Prussians against the Austrians, Russians, and French. With his superb army and military prowess, Frederick the Great was able for some time to defeat the Austrian, French, and Russian armies. He won a spectacular victory at the Battle of Rossbach in Saxony (1757) over the combined French-Austrian forces that far outnumbered his own troops.

▼ **Map 19.2** The Seven Years' War.

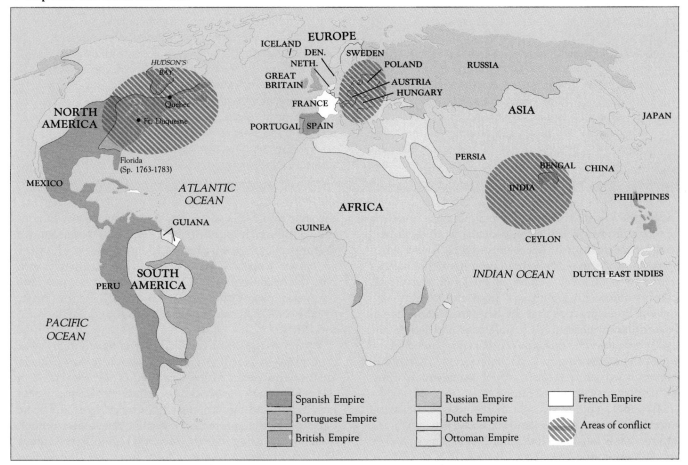

British Victory in India

▼ ▼ ▼

The Seven Years' War was fought in three major areas of the world: Europe, India, and North America. After the War of the Austrian Succession, the French and British continued to maneuver for advantage in India. The success of the British in defeating the French was due to Robert Clive, who, in this excerpt from one of his letters, describes his famous victory at Plassey, north of Calcutta (June 23, 1757). This battle demonstrated the inability of native Indian soldiers to compete with Europeans and signified the beginning of British control in Bengal. Clive claimed to have 1,000 Europeans, 2,000 Sepoys, and eight pieces of cannon available for this battle.

Robert Clive, Account of His Victory at Plassey

At daybreak we discovered the nabob's army moving towards us, consisting, as we since found, of about fifteen thousand horse and thirty-five thousand foot, with upwards of forty pieces of cannon. They approached apace, and by six began to attack with a number of heavy cannon, supported by the whole army, and continued to play on us very briskly for several hours, during which our situation was of the utmost service to us, being lodged in a large grove with good mud banks. To succeed in an attempt on their cannon was next to impossible, as they were planted in a manner round us and at considerable distances from each other. We therefore remained quiet in our post, in expectation of a successful attack upon their camp at night. About noon the enemy drew off their artillery and retired to their camp. . . .

On finding them make no great effort to dislodge us, we proceeded to take possession of one or two more eminences lying very near an angle of their camp, from whence, and an adjacent eminence in their possession, they kept a smart fire of musketry upon us. They made several attempts to bring out their cannon, but our advanced fieldpieces played so warmly and so well upon them that they were always driven back. Their horse exposing themselves a good deal on this occasion, many of them were killed, and among the rest four or five officers of the first distinction; by which the whole army being visibly dispirited and thrown into some confusion, we were encouraged to storm both the eminence and the angle of their camp, which were carried at the same instant, with little or no loss; though the latter was defended (exclusively of blacks) by forty French and two pieces of cannon; and the former by a large body of blacks, both horse and foot. On this a general rout ensued, and we pursued the enemy six miles, passing upwards of forty pieces of cannon they had abandoned, with an infinite number of carts and carriages filled with baggage of all kinds. . . . It is computed there are killed of the enemy about five hundred. Our loss amounted to only twenty-two killed and fifty wounded, and those chiefly blacks.

Under attack from three different directions, however, the forces of Frederick II were gradually worn down and faced utter defeat until they were saved by Russia when the death of Tsarina Elizabeth brought her nephew Peter III to power. A great admirer of Frederick the Great, Peter withdrew Russian troops from the conflict and from the Prussian lands that the Russians had occupied. His withdrawal guaranteed a stalemate and led to the desire for peace. The European conflict was ended by the Peace of Hubertusburg in 1763. All occupied territories were returned while Austria officially recognized Prussia's permanent control of Silesia.

The Anglo-French struggle in the rest of the world had more decisive results. Known as the Great War for Empire, it was fought in India and North America. The French had returned Madras to Britain after the War of the Austrian Succession, but jockeying for power continued as French and British policies were both founded on support of opposing native Indian princes. The British under Robert Clive (1725–1774) ultimately won out, not because they had better forces but because they were more persistent (see the box above). By the Treaty of Paris in 1763, the French withdrew and left India to the British.

By far, the greatest conflicts of the Seven Years' War took place in North America. There were two primary areas of contention. One consisted of the waterways of the Gulf of St. Lawrence, protected by the fortress of Louisbourg and by forts near the Great Lakes and Lake Champlain that protected French Quebec and French traders. The other was the unsettled Ohio River valley. The French began to move down from the Great Lakes and up from their forts on the Mississippi and establish forts from the Appalachians to the Mississippi River. To British settlers in the thirteen colonies, French activity threatened to cut off this vast area for their exploitation. The French were able to gain the support of the Indians; as traders and not settlers, they were viewed by the natives with less hostility than the British.

Despite initial French successes, British fortunes were revived by the efforts of William Pitt the Elder who was convinced that the destruction of the French colonial empire was a necessary prerequisite for the creation of Britain's own colonial empire. Pitt's policy focused on making a minimal effort in Europe while concentrating resources on the colonial war, especially through use of the British navy. Although French troops were greater in number, the ability of the French to use them in the New World was contingent upon naval support. The defeat of French fleets in major naval battles in 1759 gave the British an advantage since the French could no longer easily reinforce their garrisons. A series of British victories soon followed. In 1758, Forts Louisbourg and Duquesne were captured; in 1759, British forces under General Wolfe defeated the French under General Montcalm on the Plains of Abraham outside Quebec. Both generals died in the battle. The British went on to seize Montreal, the Great Lakes area, and the Ohio valley. The French were forced to make peace. By the Treaty of Paris, they ceded Canada and the lands east of the Mississippi to Britain. Their ally Spain transferred

Chronology
▼ ▼ ▼
The Mid-Century Wars

War of the Austrian Succession	1740–1748
Peace of Aix-la-Chapelle	1748
The Seven Years' War	1756–1763
Diplomatic Revolution	1756
Battle of Rossbach	1757
British Capture of Forts Duquesne and Louisbourg	1758
Battle of Quebec	1759
Peace of Hubertusburg	1763
Peace of Paris	1763

Spanish Florida to British control; in return, the French gave their Louisiana territory to the Spanish. By 1763, Great Britain had become the world's greatest colonial power.

European Armies and Warfare

The professional standing army, initiated in the seventeenth century, became a standard feature of eighteenth-century Europe. Especially noticeable was the increase in the size of armies as the development of absolutist states was paralleled by the growth of ever-larger armies. From 1740 to 1780, the French army grew

▼ **The Death of Wolfe.** The Seven Years' War was fought by the great powers of Europe in Europe, India, and North America. Despite initial French successes in North America, the British went on to win the war, and in the Treaty of Paris, the French ceded Canada and their lands east of the Mississippi to Britain. This painting by Benjamin West presents a heroic rendering of the death of General Wolfe, the British commander who defeated the French forces at the Battle of Quebec.

from 190,000 to 300,000 men; the Prussian from 83,000 to 200,000; the Austrian from 108,000 to 282,000; and the Russian from 130,000 to 290,000.

The composition of these armies reflected the hierarchical structure of European society and the great chasm that separated the upper and lower classes. Officers were primarily from the landed aristocracy, which had for centuries regarded military activity as one of its major functions. Prussia made military service compulsory for its nobles and forced the teenaged sons of aristocrats to attend a military academy in Berlin for training as officers. Middle-class individuals were largely kept out of the higher ranks of the officer corps while being admitted to the middle ranks. A prejudice against commoners in the officer corps remained a regular feature of military life in the eighteenth century.

Rank-and-file soldiers came mostly from the lower classes of society. Some states, such as Prussia and Russia, conscripted able-bodied peasants. But many states realized that this was counterproductive since they could not afford to waste agricultural manpower. For that reason, eighteenth-century armies were partially composed of foreign troops, many from Switzerland or the petty German states. Of the great powers, Britain alone had no regular standing army and relied on mercenaries, evident in its use of German troops in America. Most troops in European armies, especially the French and Austrian, were natives who enlisted voluntarily for six-year terms. Some were not exactly volunteers; often vagabonds and the unemployed were pressed into service. Most, however, came from the lower classes—peasants and also artisans from the cities—who saw the military as an opportunity to escape from hard times or personal problems.

The maritime powers, such as Britain and the Dutch Republic, regarded navies as more important than armies. In the second half of the eighteenth century, the British possessed 174 warships manned by 80,000 sailors. Conditions on these ships were often poor. Diseases such as scurvy and yellow fever were rampant, and crews were frequently press-ganged into duty.

The dramatic increase in the size of armies and navies did not necessarily result in more destructive warfare in eighteenth-century Europe. For one thing, warfare was no longer driven by ideological reasons as had been true of the religious wars of the sixteenth and seventeenth century. By their very nature, ideological wars are often violent and destructive. Moreover, since the larger armies depended upon increased taxes, rulers regarded the wanton destruction of civilian life as foolish. Finally, the costliness of eighteenth-century armies as well as the technology and tactical traditions of the age created a system of warfare based on limited objectives.

Generals were extremely reluctant to risk the destruction of their armies in pitched battles. Clever and elaborate maneuvers, rather than direct confrontation, became the norm. A system of formalities accepted by all sides allowed defeated opponents to withdraw without being captured or destroyed. This mentality also encouraged the construction of vast fortresses to secure major roads and the enormous quantities of supplies needed by eighteenth-century armies. With its own set patterns of tactics, siege warfare often became, as one French critic said disgustingly, "the art of surrendering strongholds honorably after certain conventional formalities."

▼ Economic and Social Change

The economic depression that had characterized the seventeenth century began to end in the early eighteenth century. Rapid population growth, economic expansion in banking and trade, an agricultural revolution (at least in Britain), and the beginnings of a new pattern of industrialization characterized the economic patterns of the eighteenth century.

Growth of the European Population

The cycles of population growth and decline that had characterized Europe since the Middle Ages came to an end in the eighteenth century. Despite regional variations, Europe's population began to grow around 1750 and continued a "slow but irreversible upward movement." It has been estimated that the total European population was around 120 million in 1700, expanded to 140 million by 1750, and then grew to 190 million by 1790; thus, the growth rate in the second half of the century was double that of the first half. Individual states also experienced rapid growth from 1700 to 1790: Russia's population went from 14 million to 28 million; France from 20 to 26 or 27 million; Spain from 6 to 10 million; Brandenburg-Prussia from 1.5 to 5.5 million (over half of this came from territorial acquisition); and Britain from 5 or 6 to 9 million. These increases occurred during the same time that several million Europeans were going abroad as colonists.

Historical demographers are not sure of the causes of this population growth. Enough statistical studies have been done, however, to show that a falling death rate was perhaps most important, especially the decline in infant mortality rates. One study of several French parishes reveals that in the first part of the century the mortality rate for infants under one year was 29 percent and the rate for all children from birth to nineteen years was 51 percent, compared to 20 and 42 percent, respectively, in the 1780s. Although the percentage of decrease seems small, it is statistically significant enough to cause a noticeable increase in population.

But why the decline in the death rate? Historians are not sure. Certainly, it was not from improved health care since little change occurred in that area until the end of the eighteenth century. No doubt, more plentiful food and better transportation of available food supplies led to some improvement in diet and relief from devastating famines. Also of great significance was the lowering of death rates brought by the ending of bubonic plague. The last great outbreak in western Europe occurred in 1720 in southern France. Nevertheless, despite the increase in population, death was still a ubiquitous feature of everyday life. Other diseases, such as typhus, smallpox, influenza, and dysentery, were rampant, especially due to poor hygienic conditions—little bathing, dirty clothes, and no systematic elimination of human wastes. Despite the improved transportation, famine and hunger could still be devastating. As a small textile merchant in Germany wrote in 1770: "And the misery grew so much that poor people could only hope for spring when they could find roots and herbs. And I had to cook that sort of stuff."[7]

Family, Marriage, and Birthrate Patterns

Detailed examination of parish registers has enabled historians to piece together some generalizations about family, marriage, and birthrate patterns in the eighteenth century.

The family, rather than the individual, was still at the heart of Europe's social organization. For the most part, people still thought of the family in traditional terms, as a patriarchal institution with the husband dominating his wife and children. Especially among the upper classes there was still a concern for the family as a "house," an association whose collective interests were more important than those of the individuals who made it up. Parents (especially the fathers) still generally selected marriage partners for their children based on the interests of the family. One French noble responded to his son's request about his upcoming marriage: "Mind your own business."

Generally, lower-class women breast-fed their own children since it provided the best nourishment. Moreover, since there were strong taboos in various parts of Europe against sexual intercourse while one was breast-feeding, mothers might also avoid another immediate pregnancy; if the infant died, they could then have another child. Lower-class women, however, also served as wet nurses for children of the aristocratic and upper middle classes. Mothers from these higher social strata considered breast-feeding undignified and hired wet nurses

▼ **The Practice of Infanticide.** Despite the creation of new foundling homes, infanticide remained one of the solutions to the problem of too many children. This engraving recounts the story of one infanticide in Germany. Top left: the infant is discovered, smothered under a mattress. Bottom left: the mother is taken from prison to be executed. Right: a large crowd observes the execution of the mother for her crime.

instead. Even urban mothers, the wives of artisans, for economic reasons sent their babies to wet nurses in the countryside if they could, making the practice widespread in the eighteenth century.

In the second half of the eighteenth century, traditional attitudes began to alter, especially in western Europe. The impact of Enlightenment thought, such as Rousseau's *Emile,* and the increasing survival of more infants led to new attitudes toward children. Childhood was more and more viewed as a phase in human development. One result was a shift to dressing children in more comfortable clothes appropriate to their age rather than dressing them in clothes modeled after adult styles. Shops for children's clothes appeared for the first time. There were also attacks on primogeniture or the practice of treating the first son as the favorite. All children, it was argued, deserve their parents' attention. Appeals for women to breast-feed their own children rather than use wet nurses soon followed. In England, games and toys specifically for children now appeared. The jigsaw puzzle was invented in the 1760s, and books, such as *Little Pretty Pocket-Book* (1744), aimed to please as well as teach children. These changes, however, were limited mostly to the upper classes of western European society and did not extend to the peasants. For most Europeans,

children were still a source of considerable anxiety. They represented more mouths to feed and in times of economic crisis proved such a liability that infanticide was practiced and foundling homes were overcrowded.

Despite being punishable by death, infanticide remained a solution to the problem of too many children. So many children were being "accidentally" suffocated while in their parents' bed that in Austria in 1784 a law was issued that forbade parents to place children under five years old in bed with them. More common than infanticide was the placement of unwanted children in foundling homes or hospitals, which became a favorite charity of the rich in eighteenth-century Europe. The largest of its kind, located in St. Petersburg, Russia, was founded by members of the nobility. By the end of the century, it was taking in 5,000 new babies a year and caring for 25,000 children at one time.

But severe problems arose as the system became overburdened. One historian has estimated that in the 1770s one-third of all babies born in Paris were taken to foundling institutions by parents or desperate unmarried mothers, creating serious overcrowding. Foundling institutions often proved fatal for infants. Mortality rates ranged from 50 to as high as 90 percent (in a sense making foundling homes a legalized form of infanticide).

▼ **Women at the Foundling Hospital, London.** During the second half of the eighteenth century, traditional attitudes toward children began to change among the upper classes. Nevertheless, children were still a source of much anxiety to most Europeans. Increasingly, parents placed unwanted children in foundling homes built by members of the wealthy classes. This engraving shows babies being brought by their mothers to the gates of a new foundling hospital in London built by Captain Thomas Coram.

Those who survived were usually sent to miserable jobs. The suffering of poor children was one of the blackest pages of eighteenth-century European history.

In most of Europe, newly married couples established their own households independent of their parents. This nuclear family, which had its beginning in the Middle Ages, had become a common European pattern. In order to save what they needed to create their own households, both men and women (outside of the aristocracy) married quite late; the average age for men in northwestern Europe was between twenty-seven and twenty-eight; for women between twenty-five and twenty-seven.

Late marriages imposed limits on the birthrate; in fact, they might be viewed as a natural form of birth control. But was this limitation offset by the number of babies born illegitimately? It would appear from the low illegitimacy rate of 1 percent in some places in France, and 5 percent in some English parishes, that it was not, at least in the first half of the eighteenth century. After 1750, however, illegitimacy appears to have increased. Studies in Germany, for example, show that rates of illegitimacy increased from 2 percent in 1700 to 5 percent in 1760 and to 10 percent in 1800, followed by an even more dramatic increase in the early nineteenth century.

For married couples, the first child usually appeared within one year of marriage, while additional children came at intervals of two or three years, producing an average number of five births per family. It would appear then that the birthrate had the potential of creating a significant increase in population. This possibility was restricted, however, since 40 to 60 percent of European women of childbearing age (between fifteen and forty-four) were not married at any given time. Moreover, by the end of the eighteenth century, especially among the upper classes in France and Britain, birth control techniques were being used to limit the number of children. Figures for the French aristocracy indicate that the average number of children declined from six in the period from 1650–1700 to three from 1700 to 1750 and to two between 1750 and 1780. These figures are even more significant when one considers that aristocrats married at ages younger than the rest of the population. Coitus interruptus remained the most commonly used form of birth control.

Among the working classes, whether peasants or urban workers, the contributions of women and children to the "family economy" were often crucial. In urban areas, both male and female children either helped in the handicraft manufacturing done in the home or were sent out to work as household servants. In rural areas, children worked on the land or helped in the activities of cottage industry. Married women grew vegetables in small plots, tended livestock, and sold eggs, vegetables, and milk. Wives of propertyless agricultural workers labored in the fields or as textile workers, spinning or knitting. In the cities, wives of artisans helped their husbands at their crafts or worked as seamstresses. The wives of unskilled workers labored as laundresses and cleaners for the rich or as peddlers of food or used clothing to the lower classes. But the family economy was often precarious. Bad harvests in the countryside or a downturn in employment in the cities often reduced people to utter poverty and a life of begging (see The Problem of Poverty later in the chapter).

An Agricultural Revolution?

Did improvements in agricultural practices and methods in the eighteenth century lead to an agricultural revolution? The topic is much debated. Some historians have noted the beginning of agrarian changes already in the seventeenth century, especially in the Low Countries. Others, however, have questioned the use of the term, arguing that significant changes occurred only in England and noting that even there the upward trend in agricultural production was not maintained after 1750.

Eighteenth-century agriculture was characterized by increases in food production that can be attributed to four interrelated factors: more land under cultivation, increased yields per acre, healthier and more abundant livestock, and an improved climate. Climatologists believe that the "little ice age" of the seventeenth century declined in the eighteenth, especially evident in the moderate summers that provided more ideal growing conditions.

The increase in the amount of land under cultivation was made possible by abandoning the old open field system in which part of the land was left to lie fallow to renew it. New crops, such as alfalfa, turnips, and clover, which stored nitrogen in their roots and helped to restore the soil's fertility, were planted in England, parts of France, and the Low Countries. The new crops provided winter fodder for livestock, enabling landlords to maintain an ever-larger number of animals; some enterprising landlords also engaged in scientific breeding and produced stronger and more productive strains of animals.

The increase in livestock enlarged the amount of meat in the European diet and affected the food production by making available larger amounts of animal ma-

Propaganda for the New Agriculture
▼ ▼ ▼

Enthusiastic supporters of the new English agricultural practices went to the continent to examine less efficient kinds of farming. One of these Englishmen, Arthur Young, wrote an account of his travels in which he blamed the low yields of French farmers on two causes: the old system of allowing part of the land to lie fallow and the small size of the farms. The latter factor was especially important to English aristocratic landholders who wished to justify the enclosure movement. This selection is taken from Young's account.

Arthur Young, Travels during the Years 1787, 1788, and 1789 . . . in the Kingdom of France

The Englishman, in eleven years, gets three bushels more of wheat than the Frenchman. He gets three crops of barley, tares, or beans, which produce nearly twice as many bushels per acre, as what the three French crops of spring corn produce. And he farther gets, at the same time, three crops of turnips and two of clover, the turnips worth 40s. the acre, and the clover 60s. That is 121 for both. What an enormous superiority. More wheat; almost double of the spring corn; and above 20s. per acre per annum in turnips and clover. But farther; the Englishman's land, by means of the manure arising from the consumption of the turnips and clover is in a constant state of improvement, while the Frenchman's farm is stationary.

The great populousness of France, I attribute very much to the division of the lands into small properties, which takes place in that country to a degree of which we have in England but little conception. . . . It has been said to me in France, "Would you leave uncultivated lands wastes, rather than let them be cultivated in small portions, through a fear of population?" I certainly would not: I would, on the contrary, encourage their culture; but I would prohibit the division of small farms, which is as mischievous to cultivation, as it is sure to be distressing to the people. . . . Go to districts where the properties are minutely divided, and you will find (at least I have done it) universally, great distress, and even misery, and probably very bad agriculture. Go to others, where such sub-division has not taken place, and you will find a better cultivation, and infinitely less misery. When you are engaged in this political tour, finish it by seeing England, and I will show you a set of peasants well clothed, well nourished, tolerably drunken from superfluity, well-lodged, and at their ease.

---

nure that helped to fertilize fields and produce better yields per acre. Increased yields were also encouraged by landed aristocrats who shared in the scientific experimentation of the age. Jethro Tull (1674–1741) in England discovered that using a hoe to keep the soil loose allowed air and moisture to reach plants and enabled them to grow better. He also used a drill to plant seeds in rows instead of scattering them by hand, a method that had lost much seed to the birds. The eighteenth century witnessed greater yields of vegetables, including two important American crops, the potato and maize (Indian) corn. Both had been brought to Europe from America in the sixteenth century although it was not until after 1700 that they were grown in quantity. The potato became a staple in Germany, the Low Countries, and especially Ireland, where repression by English landlords forced large numbers of poor peasants to survive on small pieces of marginal land. The potato took relatively little effort to produce in large quantities. High in car-

bohydrates and calories, rich in vitamins A and C, it could be easily stored for winter use.

The new agriculture was considered best suited to large-scale farmers who could make better use of the new techniques. Consequently, a change in landholding accompanied the increase in food production. The end of the open field system led to the demise of the cooperative farming of the village community. Instead, land was enclosed into bigger units by large landowners or yeomen farmers. In England, where small landholders resisted this process, Parliament, dominated by the landed aristocracy, enacted legislation by which agricultural lands could be legally enclosed. As a result of these enclosure acts, England gradually became a land of large estates while many small farmers were forced to become tenant farmers working 100–500 acre farms for land or as paid wage laborers. While some historians have emphasized the advantages of enclosures in enabling large landowners to practice new agricultural techniques and increase food production, the enclosure movement and new agricultural practices also effectively destroyed the traditional patterns of English village life.

In the eighteenth century, it was primarily the English who adopted the new techniques that have been characterized as an agricultural revolution (see the box on p. 650). This early modernization of English agriculture with its noticeable increase in productivity made possible the feeding of an expanding population about to enter a new world of industrialization and urbanization.

Finance and Industry

The decline in the available supply of gold and silver in the seventeenth century had created a chronic shortage of money that undermined the efforts of governments to meet their needs. The creation of new public and private banks and the acceptance of paper notes made possible an expansion of credit in the eighteenth century.

Perhaps the best example of this process can be observed in England where the Bank of England was founded in 1694. Unlike other banks accustomed to receiving deposits and exchanging foreign currencies, the Bank of England also made loans. In return for lending money to the government, the bank was allowed to issue paper "bank notes" backed by its credit. These soon became negotiable and created a paper substitute for gold and silver currency. In addition, the creation of government bonds earning regular interest, backed up by the Bank of England and the London financial community, created the notion of a public or "national debt" distinct from the monarch's personal debts. This process meant that capital could be raised in ever-greater quantities for financing larger armies and other government undertakings.

These new financial institutions and methods were not risk-free, however. In both Britain and France in the early eighteenth century, speculators provided opportunities for people to invest in colonial trading companies. The French company under John Law was also tied to his attempt to create a national bank and paper currency for France. When people went overboard and drove the price of the stock to incredibly high levels, the bubble burst. Law's company and bank went bankrupt, leading to a loss of confidence in paper money that prevented the formation of a French national bank. Consequently, French public finance developed slowly in the eighteenth century.

This was not the case in Britain, however. Despite crises, the development of public confidence in the new financial institutions enabled the British government to borrow large sums of money at relatively low rates of interest, giving it a distinct advantage in the struggle with France. According to a contemporary observer, Britain's public credit was "the permanent miracle of her policy, which has inspired both astonishment and fear in the States of Europe."[8] Despite Britain's growing importance in finance, however, the Dutch Republic remained the leader in Europe's financial life, and Amsterdam continued to be the center of international finance until London replaced it in the nineteenth century. One observer noted in 1769:

> If ten or twelve businessmen of Amsterdam of the first rank meet for a banking operation, they can in a moment send circulating throughout Europe over two hundred million florins in paper money, which is preferred to cash. There is no Sovereign who could do as much. . . . This credit is a power which the ten or twelve businessmen will be able to exert over all the States of Europe, in complete independence of any authority.[9]

The decline of Dutch trade, industry, and power meant that Dutch capitalists were inclined to lend money abroad because of fewer opportunities at home. Such investments, of course, did not directly benefit the United Provinces.

The most important product of European industry in the eighteenth century was textiles. Seventy-five percent of Britain's exports in the early eighteenth century were woolen cloth. France, too, was a leader in the production of woolen cloth while other major states emulated both France and Britain by encouraging the development of their own textile industries.

Most textiles were still produced by traditional methods. In cities that were textile centers, master artisans in their guild workshops used timeworn methods to produce their finished goods, while urban craft guilds still attempted to restrict handicraft production to the cities.

But a shift in textile production to the countryside had also begun to occur; it was already evident in Flanders and England by the sixteenth century and was spreading elsewhere by the eighteenth century. In France, not until 1762 did a royal edict strip urban guilds of their manufacturing monopoly and allow rural industries to expand. Industrial production in the countryside was done by the "putting-out" or "domestic" system in which a merchant-capitalist entrepreneur bought the raw materials, mostly wool and flax, and "put them out" to rural workers who spun the raw material into yarn and then wove it into cloth on simple looms. Capitalist-entrepreneurs sold the finished product, made a profit, and used it to manufacture more. This system became known as the "cottage industry," since spinners and weavers did their work on spinning wheels and looms in their own cottages. Cottage industry was truly a family enterprise since women and children could spin while men wove on the looms, enabling rural people to earn incomes that supplemented their pitiful wages as agricultural laborers.

The cottage system utilized traditional methods of manufacturing and in the eighteenth century was expanded to many areas of rural Europe. But significant changes in industrial production also began to occur in the second half of the century, pushed along by the introduction of cotton, originally imported from India. The importation of raw cotton from slave plantations encouraged the production of cotton cloth in Europe where a profitable market developed because of the growing demand for lightweight cotton clothes that were less expensive than linens and woolens. But the traditional methods of the cottage industry proved incapable of keeping up with the growing demand, leading English cloth entrepreneurs to develop new methods and new machines. The flying shuttle sped up the process of weaving on a loom, thereby increasing the need for large quantities of yarn. In response, Richard Arkwright (1732–1792) invented a "water frame," powered by horse or water, which turned out yarn much faster than cottage spinning wheels. This abundance of yarn, in turn, led to the development of mechanized looms, invented in the 1780s but not widely adopted until the early nineteenth century. By that time Britain was in the throes of an industrial revolution, but already at the end of the eighteenth century, rural workers, perceiving that the new machines threatened their traditional livelihood, had begun to call for their destruction (see the box on p. 653).

Mercantile Empires and Worldwide Trade

While bankers and industrialists came to dominate the nineteenth century economically, in the eighteenth century merchants and traders still reigned supreme. Intra-European trade still dominated total trade figures as wheat, timber, and naval stores from the Baltic, wines from France, wool and fruit from Spain, and silk from Italy were exchanged along with a host of other products. But the eighteenth century witnessed only a slight increase in this trade while overseas trade boomed. From 1716 to 1789, total French exports quadrupled while intra-European trade, which constituted 75 percent of these exports in 1716, constituted only 50 percent of the total in 1789. This increase in overseas trade has led some historians to speak of the emergence of a truly global economy in the eighteenth century. By the beginning of that century, Spain, Portugal, and the Dutch Republic, which had earlier monopolized overseas trade, found themselves increasingly overshadowed by France and Britain. The rivalry between these two great western European powers was especially evident in the Americas and the Far East.

COLONIAL EMPIRES   Both the French and British colonial empires in the New World consisted of large parts of

▼ **French Port of Dieppe.** Overseas trade experienced considerable expansion during the eighteenth century. Between 1716 and 1789, total French exports quadrupled while overseas trade expanded from 25 to 50 percent of the total volume of trade. Seen here is the port of Dieppe, typical of several ports along the French coast from which a regular trade was carried on with French colonies in the New World. Rebuilt after it had been bombarded during the War of the League of Augsburg in 1694, Dieppe was a modern town in the eighteenth century.

The Beginnings of Mechanized Industry: The Attack on New Machines

▼ ▼ ▼

Already by the end of the eighteenth century, mechanization was beginning to bring changes to the traditional cottage industry of textile manufacturing. Rural workers who depended on the extra wages made in their own homes often reacted by attacking the machinery that threatened their livelihoods. This selection is a petition that English wool workers published in their local newspapers asking that machines no longer be used to prepare wool for spinning.

The Leeds Woolen Workers' Petition (1786)

To the Merchants, Clothiers and all such as wish well to the Staple Manufactory of this Nation.

The Humble ADDRESS and PETITION of Thousands, who labour in the Cloth Manufactory.

SHEWETH, That the Scribbling-Machines have thrown thousands of your petitioners out of employ, whereby they are brought into great distress, and are not able to procure a maintenance for their families, and deprived them of the opportunity of bringing up their children to labour: We have therefore to request, that prejudice and self-interest may be laid aside, and that you may pay that attention to the following facts, which the nature of the case requires.

The number of Scribbling-Machines extending about seventeen miles southwest of LEEDS, exceed all belief, being no less than *one hundred and seventy!* and as each machine will do as much work in twelve hours, as ten men can in that time do by hand, (speaking within bounds) and they working night-and day, one machine will do as much work in one day as would otherwise employ twenty men.

As we do not mean to assert any thing but what we can prove to be true, we allow four men to be employed at each machine twelve hours, working night and day, will take eight men in twenty-four hours; so that, upon a moderate computation twelve men are thrown out of employ for every single machine used in scribbling; and as it may be supposed the number of machines in all the other quarters together, nearly equal those in the South-West, full four thousand men are left to shift for a living how they can, and must of course fall to the Parish, if not time relieved. Allowing one boy to be bound apprentice from each family out of work, eight thousand hands are deprived of the opportunity of getting a livelihood.

We therefore hope, that the feelings of humanity will lead those who have it in their power to prevent the use of those machines, to give every discouragement they can to what has a tendency so prejudicial to their fellow-creatures. . . .

We wish to propose a few queries to those who would plead for the further continuance of these machines:

How are those men, thus thrown out of employ to provide for their families; and what are they to put their children apprentice to, that the rising generation may have something to keep them at work, in order that they may not be like vagabonds strolling about in idleness? Some day, Begin and learn some other business.—Suppose we do, who will maintain our families, whilst we undertake the arduous task; and when we have learned it, how do we know we shall be any better for all our pains; for by the time we have served our second apprenticeship, another machine may arise, which may take away that business also. . . .

But what are our children to do; are they to be brought up in idleness? Indeed as things are, it is no wonder to hear of so many executions; for our parts, though we may be thought illiterate men, our conceptions are, that bringing children up to industry, and keeping them employed, is the way to keep them from falling into those crimes, which an idle habit naturally leads to.

---

the West Indies and the North American continent. In the former, the British held Barbados, Jamaica, and Bermuda while the French possessed Saint Dominique, Martinique, and Guadeloupe. On these tropical islands both the British and the French had developed plantation economies, worked by African slaves, which produced tobacco, cotton, coffee, and sugar, all products increasingly in demand in Europe.

On the North American continent, the French and British colonies were structured in different ways. French North America (Canada and Louisiana) was run autocratically as a vast trading area, valuable for the acquisition of fur, leather, fish, and timber. However, the inability of the French state to get its people to emigrate to these North American possessions left them thinly populated.

British North America had come to consist of thirteen colonies on the eastern coast of the present United States. They were thickly populated, containing about 1.5 million people by 1750, and were also prosperous. Supposedly run by the British Board of Trade, the Royal Council, and Parliament, these thirteen colonies had legislatures that tended to act independently. Merchants in such port cities as Boston, Philadelphia, New York, and Charleston resented and resisted regulation from the British government.

Both the North American and West Indian colonies of Britain and France were assigned roles in keeping with mercantilist theory. They provided raw materials for the mother country while buying the latter's manufactured goods. Navigation acts regulated what could be taken from and sold to the colonies. Theoretically, the system was supposed to provide a balance of trade favorable to the mother country.

British and French rivalry was also evident in the Spanish and Portuguese colonial empires in Latin America. The decline of Spain and Portugal had led these two states to depend even more on resources from their colonies, and they imposed strict mercantilist rules on them to keep others out. Spain, for example, tried to limit all trade with its colonies to Spanish ships. But the British and French were too powerful to be excluded. The British cajoled the Portuguese into allowing them into the lucrative Brazilian trade. The French, however, were the first to break into the Spanish Latin American market when the French Bourbons became kings of Spain. Britain's entry into Spanish American markets first came in 1713, when Britain was granted the privilege, known as the *asiento*, of transporting 4,500 slaves a year into Spanish Latin America.

The same was true in the Far East as Britain and France competed for trade in India and the East Indies where the valuable products remained tea, spices, cotton, hard woods, and luxury goods. The rivalry between France and Britain was played out by their state-backed national trading companies. In the course of the eighteenth century, the British defeated the French, and by the mid-nineteenth century they had assumed control of the entire Indian subcontinent.

GLOBAL TRADE   To justify the term *global economy*, historians have usually pointed to the patterns of trade that interlocked Europe, Africa, the Far East, and the American continents. One such pattern of triangular trade involved British merchant ships, which carried British manufactured goods to Africa, where they were traded for a cargo of slaves, which were then shipped to Virginia and paid for by tobacco, which in turn was shipped back to England where it was processed and then sold in Germany for cash.

▼ **The Sale of Slaves.** In the eighteenth century, the sale of slaves was one of the more profitable trading enterprises. While the use of slaves in the New World had begun as far back as the sixteenth century, the slave trade was greatly expanded in the eighteenth century due to the need for labor on sugar, tobacco, rice, and cotton plantations. This engraving shows the sale of slaves in the French West Indian possession of Martinique.

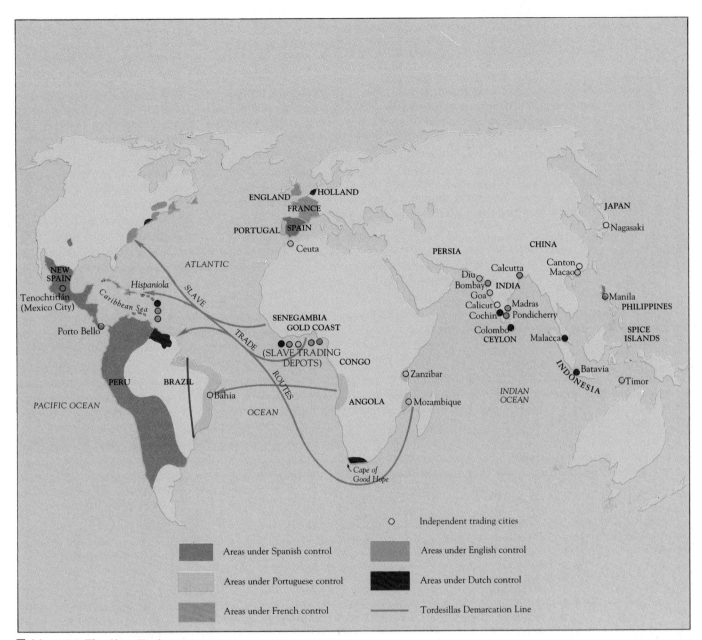

▼ **Map 19.3** The Slave Trade.

Of all the goods traded in the eighteenth century, perhaps the most profitable and certainly the most infamous were African slaves. Of course, the slave trade was not new; the Spanish and Portuguese had introduced black slaves into America in the sixteenth century. But the need for slaves in the lucrative plantation production of sugar, tobacco, rice, and cotton made the eighteenth century the high point of the Atlantic slave trade. It has been estimated that of the total 9,300,000 slaves transported from Africa, almost two-thirds were taken in the eighteenth century. Between 75,000 and 90,000 Afri-

cans were transported annually, 50 percent in British ships, with the rest divided among French, Dutch, Portuguese, Danish, and American ships.

Slaving ships sailed from a European port to the African coast where Europeans had established bases where merchants could trade manufactured goods, rum, and brandy for blacks captured by African middlemen. The captives were then closely packed into cargo ships, 300 to 450 per ship, and chained in holds without sanitary facilities or space in which to stand up for a voyage to America that took at least a hundred days (see the box

The Atlantic Slave Trade
▼▼▼

One of the most odious practices of early modern Western society was the Atlantic slave trade, which reached its height in the eighteenth century. Blacks were transported in densely packed cargo ships from the western coast of Africa to the Americas to work as slaves in the plantation economy. Not until late in the eighteenth century did a rising chorus of voices raise serious objections to this trade in human beings. This excerpt presents a criticism of the slave trade from an anonymous French writer.

Diary of a Citizen

As soon as the ships have lowered their anchors off the coast of Guinea, the price at which the captains have decided to buy the captives is announced to the Negroes who buy prisoners from various princes and sell them to the Europeans. Presents are sent to the sovereign who rules over that particular part of the coast, and permission to trade is given. Immediately the slaves are brought by inhuman brokers like so many victims dragged to a sacrifice. White men who covet that portion of the human race receive them in a little house they have erected on the shore, where they have entrenched themselves with two pieces of cannon and twenty guards. As soon as the bargain is concluded, the Negro is put in chains and led aboard the vessel, where he meets his fellow sufferers. Here sinister reflections come to his mind; everything shocks and frightens him and his uncertain destiny gives rise to the greatest anxiety. . . .

The vessel sets sail for the Antilles, and the Negroes are chained in a hold of the ship, a kind of lugubrious prison where the light of day does not penetrate, but into which air is introduced by means of a pump. Twice a day some disgusting food is distributed to them. Their consuming sorrow and the sad state to which they are reduced would make them commit suicide if they were not deprived of all the means for an attempt upon their lives. Without any kind of clothing it would be difficult to conceal from the watchful eyes of the sailors in charge any instrument apt to alleviate their despair. The fear of a revolt, such as sometimes happens on the voyage from Guinea, is the basis of a common concern and produces as many guards as there are men in the crew. The slightest noise or a secret conversation among two Negroes is punished with utmost severity. All in all, the voyage is made in a continuous state of alarm on the part of the white men, who fear a revolt, and in a cruel state of uncertainty on the part of the Negroes, who do not know the fate awaiting them.

When the vessel arrives at a port in the Antilles, they are taken to a warehouse where they are displayed, like any merchandise, to the eyes of buyers. The plantation owner pays according to the age, strength, and health of the Negro he is buying. He has him taken to his plantation, and there he is delivered to an overseer who then and there becomes his tormentor. In order to domesticate him, the Negro is granted a few days of rest in his new place, but soon he is given a hoe and a sickle and made to join a work gang. Then he ceases to wonder about his fate; he understands that only labor is demanded of him. But he does not know yet how excessive this labor will be. As a matter of fact, his work begins at dawn and does not end before nightfall; it is interrupted for only two hours at dinnertime. The food a full-grown Negro is given each week consists of two pounds of salt beef or cod and two pots of tapioca meal. . . . A Negro of twelve or thirteen years or under is given only one pot of meal and one pound of beef or cod. In place of food some planters give their Negroes the liberty of working for themselves every Saturday; others are even less generous and grant them this liberty only on Sundays and holidays.

above). Mortality rates averaged 10 percent except when longer journeys due to storms or adverse winds resulted in even higher death rates.

Once the human cargoes arrived in the New World, they immediately entered the plantation economy, in which the "sugar factories," as the sugar plantations in the Caribbean were called, played an especially valuable role. By the last two decades of the eighteenth century, the British colony of Jamaica, one of Britain's most important, was producing 50,000 tons of sugar annually with the slave labor of 200,000 blacks. The French colony of Saint Dominique (later Haiti) had 500,000 slaves working on 3,000 plantations at the same time. This colony produced 100,000 tons of sugar a year but at the expense of a high death rate from the brutal treatment of the slaves. It is not surprising that Saint Dominique saw the first successful slave uprising in 1793.

Despite a rising chorus of humanitarian sentiments from the philosophes, the use of black slaves remained acceptable to Western society. By and large, Europeans continued to view blacks as inferior beings fit primarily for slave labor. Not until the Society of Friends or Quakers began to criticize slavery in the 1770s and exclude from their church any member adhering to slave trafficking, did European sentiment against slavery begin to build. Even then it was not until the radical stage of the French Revolution in the 1790s that the French abolished slavery. The British followed suit in 1808. Despite the elimination of the African source, slavery continued in the newly formed United States until the Civil War of the 1860s.

▼ The Social Order of the Eighteenth Century

The pattern of Europe's social organization, first established in the Middle Ages, continued well into the eighteenth century. Social status was still largely determined not by wealth and economic standing but by the division into the traditional "orders" or "estates" determined by heredity and quality. This divinely sanctioned division of society into traditional orders was supported by Christian teaching, which emphasized the need to fulfill the responsibilities of one's estate. Inequality was part of that scheme and could not be eliminated. In the eighteenth century, this emphasis on a fixed order was expressed in secular terms as well. One observer wrote in 1747 that "a reasonable man is always happy if he has what is necessary for him according to his condition [his place in the social order], that is to say, if he has the protection of the laws, and can live as his father lived before him: so that one of the essential things to the good of a nation is being governed in one constant and uniform manner."[10]

Although Enlightenment intellectuals attacked these traditional distinctions, they did not die easily. In the Prussian law code of 1794, marriage between noble males and middle-class females was forbidden without a government dispensation. In cities, sumptuary legislation designated what dress different urban groups should wear so as to keep them separate. Even without government regulation, however, different social groups remained easily distinguished everywhere in Europe by the distinctive, traditional clothes they wore. Such social conservatism was reinforced by society's ongoing preoccupation with local and regional differences. Local rivalries and local grievances greatly outweighed any loyalty to the larger state. Even local dialects continued to separate people. A French magistrate at Riom was unable to question a young itinerant from a town only fifteen miles away because "the speech of Courpière differs considerably from that of Riom."

Nevertheless, some forces of change were at work in this traditional society. The ideas of the Enlightenment made headway as reformers argued that the idea of an unchanging social order based on privilege was hostile to the progress of society. Moreover, especially in some cities, the old structures were more difficult to maintain as new economic structures, especially the growth of larger industries, brought new social contrasts that destroyed the old order. Despite these forces of change, however, it would take the revolutionary upheavals at the end of the eighteenth century before the old order would finally begin to disintegrate.

The Peasants

Since society was still mostly rural in the eighteenth century, the peasantry constituted the largest social group, making up as much as 85 percent of Europe's population. There were rather wide differences, however, between peasants from area to area. The most important distinction—at least legally—was between the free peasant and the serf. Peasants in Britain, northern Italy, the Low Countries, Spain, most of France, and some areas of western Germany shared freedom despite numerous regional and local differences. Legally free peasants, however, were not exempt from burdens. Some free peasants in Andalusia in Spain, southern Italy, Sicily, and Portugal lived in a poverty more desperate than that of many serfs in Russia and eastern Germany. In France, 40 percent of free peasants owned little or no land whatever by 1789. As the century progressed and new agricultural methods developed, small peasant proprietors were often unable to compete in efficiency with large estates.

Small peasant proprietors or tenant farmers in western Europe were also not free from compulsory services. Most owed tithes, often one-third of their crops. Although tithes were intended for parish priests, in France only 10 percent of the priests received them. Instead they wound up in the hands of towns and aristocratic landowners. Moreover, peasants could still owe a variety of dues and fees. Local aristocrats claimed hunting rights on peasant land and had monopolies over the flour mills, community ovens, and wine and oil presses needed by the peasants. Hunting rights, dues, fees, and tithes were all deeply resented.

Eastern Europe continued to be dominated by large landed estates owned by powerful lords and worked by serfs. Serfdom had come late to the east having largely been imposed in the sixteenth and seventeenth centuries. Peasants in eastern Germany were bound to the lord's estate, had to provide labor services on the lord's land, and could not marry or move without permission and payment of a tax. By the eighteenth century, the landlord also possessed legal jurisdiction, giving him control over the administration of justice. Only in the Habsburg empire had a ruler attempted to improve the lot of the peasants through a series of reforms. In Russia, peasants were not attached to the land but to the landlord and thus existed in a condition approaching slavery. In 1762, landowners were given the right to transfer their serfs from one estate to another. Unlike the rest of Europe and with the exception of the clergy and a small merchant class, eighteenth-century Russia was largely a society of landlords and serfs. Although eastern Europe, especially Poland, Russia, and some Habsburg provinces, experienced revolts by desperate peasants, they were easily crushed.

The local villages in which they dwelt remained the centers of peasants' social lives. Villages, especially in western Europe, maintained public order, provided poor relief, a village church, and sometimes a schoolmaster, collected taxes for the central government, maintained roads and bridges, and established common procedures for sowing, ploughing, and harvesting crops. But villages were often dominated by richer peasants and proved highly resistant to innovations, such as new crops and agricultural practices.

The diet of the peasants in the eighteenth century did not vary much from that of the Middle Ages. Dark bread, made of roughly ground wheat and rye flour, remained the basic staple. It was quite nourishing and high in vitamins, minerals, and even proteins since the bran and germ were not ground out. Peasants drank water, wine, and beer and ate soups and gruel made of grains and vegetables. Especially popular were peas and beans, eaten fresh in summer but dried and used in soups and stews in winter. The new foods of the eighteenth century, potatoes and American corn, added important elements to the peasant diet. Of course, when harvests were bad, hunger and famine became the peasants' lot in life, making them even more susceptible to the ravages of disease.

The Nobility

The nobles, who constituted about 2 or 3 percent of the European population, played a dominating role in society. Being born a noble automatically guaranteed a place at the top of the social order with all of its attendant special privileges and rights. The legal privileges of the nobility included judgment by their peers, immunity from severe punishment, exemption from many forms of taxation, and rights of jurisdiction. Especially in central and eastern Europe, the rights of landlords over their serfs were overwhelming. In Poland until 1768, the nobility even possessed the right of life or death over their serfs. Other aristocratic privileges included the sole right to carry a sword, occupy a special pew in church, and possess a monopoly on hunting rights.

In many countries, nobles were self-conscious about their unique style of life that set them apart from the rest of society. This did not mean, however, that they were unwilling to bend the conventions of that lifestyle if there were profits to be made. For example, nobles by convention were expected to live off the yields of their estates. But although nobles almost everywhere talked about trade as being beneath their dignity, many were not averse to mercantile endeavors. Many were also only too eager to profit from industries based on the exploitation of raw materials found on their estates; as a result, many nobles were involved in mining, metallurgy, and glassmaking. Their diet also set them off from the rest of society. Aristocrats consumed enormous quantities of meat and fish dishes accompanied by cheeses, nuts, and a variety of sweets.

Nobles also played important roles in military and government affairs. Since medieval times, landed aristocrats had functioned as military officers. While monarchs found it impossible to exclude commoners from the ranks of officers, the tradition remained that nobles made the most natural and hence the best officers. Moreover, the eighteenth-century nobility played a significant role in the administrative machinery of state. In some countries, such as Prussia, the entire bureaucracy reflected aristocratic values. Moreover, in most of Europe, the landholding nobility controlled much of the local government in their districts.

The nobility or landowning class was not a homogeneous social group. Landlords in England leased their land to tenant farmers while those in eastern Europe used the labor services of serfs. Nobles in Russia and Prussia served the state while those in Spain and Italy had few official functions. Differences in wealth, education, and political power also led to differences within countries as well. In France, where there were about 350,000 nobles, only 4,000 noble families were allowed access to the court. The gap between rich and poor nobles could be enormous. According to figures for the poll tax in France, the richest nobles were assessed 2,000 livres a year while some nobles, because of their depressed economic state, paid only 6. Both groups were legally nobles. In Poland, where the legal nobility constituted 10 to 15 percent of the population or about 750,000 people, most were poor and owned little or no land. While these nobles had special pews in church and wore special dress, they were often as poor as the peasants. As the century progressed, these poor nobles increasingly sank into the ranks of the unprivileged masses of the population. It has been estimated that the number of European nobles declined by one-third between 1750 and 1815.

Although the nobles clung to their privileged status and struggled to keep others out, almost everywhere the possession of money made it possible to enter the ranks of the nobility. Rights of nobility were frequently attached to certain lands so purchasing the lands made one a noble; the acquisition of government offices also often conferred noble status.

THE ARISTOCRATIC WAY OF LIFE: THE COUNTRY HOUSE
The Comte Charles-Maurice de Talleyrand-Périgord, the arch-survivor of the French revolutionary era, once commented that "no one who did not live before the Revolution" could know the real sweetness of living. Of course, he spoke not for the peasants whose labor maintained the system, but for the landed aristocrats. For them the eighteenth century was a final century of "sweetness" before the Industrial Revolution and bourgeois society diminished their privileged way of life.

In so many ways, the court of Louis XIV had provided a model for other European monarchs who built palaces and encouraged the development of a court society as a center of culture. As at Versailles, these courts were peopled by members of the aristocracy whose income from rents or officeholding enabled them to participate in this lifestyle. This court society, whether in France, Spain, or Germany, manifested common characteristics: participation in intrigues for the king's or prince's favor, serene walks in formal gardens, and duels to maintain one's honor. Hierarchy and status were all important. A complex mixture of family heritage, title, and wealth determined the position one occupied in this society.

The majority of aristocratic landowners, however, remained on their country estates and did not participate in court society; their large houses continued to give witness to their domination of the surrounding countryside. This was especially true in England where the court of the Hanoverian kings (Georges I–III from 1714 to 1820) made little impact on the behavior of upper-class society. English landed aristocrats invested much time, energy, and money in their rural estates, giving the English country house an important role in English social life. One American observer remarked: "Scarcely any persons who hold a leading place in the circles of their society live in London. They have houses in London, in which they stay while Parliament sits, and occasionally visit at other seasons; but their homes are in the country."[11]

After the seventeenth century, the English referred to their country homes, regardless of size, not as chateaus or villas but merely houses. Although there was much variety in country houses, many in the eighteenth century were built in the Georgian style named after the Hanoverian kings. This style was greatly influenced by the classical serenity and sedateness of the sixteenth-century Venetian architect, Andrea Palladio, who had specialized in the design of country villas. The Georgian country house combined elegance with domesticity, and its interior was often characterized as possessing a comfort of home that combined visual delight and usefulness.

The country house also fulfilled a newfound desire for greater privacy. Domestic etiquette militated against unannounced visits, and the rooms were designed to serve specialized purposes while their arrangement ensured more privacy. The central entrance hall contained a large staircase to the upstairs and also led to the common rooms of the downstairs. The entrance hall, whose coats of arms and suits of armor still reflected its medieval ancestry, now also provided the setting for the ceremonial arrival and departure of guests on formal occasions. The lower floors of the country house held a series of common rooms for public activities. The largest was the drawing room (larger houses possessed two), which contained musical instruments and was used for dances or card games, a favorite pastime. Other common rooms included a formal dining room, informal breakfast room, library, study, gallery, billiard room, and a conservatory. The downstairs common rooms were used for dining, entertaining, and leisure. Upstairs rooms consisted of bedrooms for husbands and wives, sons, and daughters. These were used not only for sleeping but also for private activities, such as playing for the children and sewing, writing, and reading for wives. This arrangement reflected the new desire for privacy and to some extent the growing awareness of individuality. "Going upstairs" literally meant leaving the company of others in the downstairs common rooms to be alone in the privacy of the bedroom. This eighteenth-century desire for privacy also meant keeping servants at a distance. They were now housed in their own wing of rooms and alerted to their employers' desire for assistance by a new invention— long-distance cords connected to bells in the servants' quarters.

Although the arrangement of the eighteenth-century Georgian house originally reflected male interests, the influence of women was increasingly evident by the second half of the eighteenth century. Already in the seventeenth century, it had become customary for the sexes to separate after dinner; while the men preoccupied themselves with brandy and cigars in the dining room, women would exit into a "withdrawing room" for their own conversation. In the course of the eighteenth century, the drawing room became a larger, more feminine room with comfortable furniture grouped casually in front of fireplaces to create a cozy atmosphere.

THE ARISTOCRATIC WAY OF LIFE: THE GRAND TOUR   One characteristic of the high culture of the Enlightenment was its cosmopolitanism, reinforced by education in the Latin classics and the use of French as an international language. Travel was another manifestation of the En-

lightenment's cosmopolitanism and interest in new vistas. One important aspect of eighteenth-century travel was the Grand Tour in which the sons of aristocrats completed their educations by making a tour of Europe's major cities. The English aristocracy in particular regarded the Grand Tour as crucial to their education. The great-aunt of Thomas Coke wrote to him upon his completion of school: "Sir, I understand you have left Eton and probably intend to go to one of those Schools of Vice, the Universities. If, however, you choose to travel I will give you 500 pounds [about $12,500] per annum."[12] Coke was no fool and went on the Grand Tour, along with many others. In one peak year alone, 40,000 Englishmen were traveling in Europe.

Travel was not easy in the eighteenth century. Crossing the English Channel could be difficult in rough seas and might take anywhere from three to twelve hours. The trip from France to Italy could be done by sea, where the traveler faced the danger of pirates, or overland by sedan chair over the Alps, where narrow passes made travel an adventure in terror. Inns, especially in Germany, were populated by thieves and the ubiquitous bed bugs. The English were particularly known for spending vast sums of money during their travels, as one observer recounted: "The French usually travel to save money, so that they sometimes leave the places where they sojourn worse off than they found them. The English, on the other hand, come over with plenty of cash, plenty of gear, and servants to wait on them. They throw their money about like lords."[13]

▼ **Visit to the Art Collections.** The Grand Tour was the final step in the education of young aristocrats and consisted of a visit to Europe's major cities. Young aristocrats were usually accompanied by tutors and spent part of their time studying museum collections and antiquities. Florence was one of their favorite Italian destinations. This painting by Johann Zoffany shows some of the treasures of the Medici collection in the Tribuna of the Uffizi in Florence. This collection in the Uffizi art gallery was visited by all connoisseurs on the Grand Tour. In the center of the room are pieces of classical sculpture while the works of such great European artists as Raphael and Rubens adorn the walls.

Since the trip's purpose was educational, young Englishmen in particular were usually accompanied by a tutor who ensured that his charges spent time looking at museum collections of natural history and antiquities. But tutors were not able to stop young men from also pursuing wine, women, and song. After crossing the Channel, English visitors went to Paris for a cram course on how to act sophisticated. They then went on to Italy, where their favorite destinations were Florence, Venice, and Rome. In Florence, the studious and ambitious studied art in the Uffizi Gallery. The less ambitious followed a less vigorous routine, according to the poet Thomas Gray, since they "get up at twelve o'clock, breakfast till three, dine till five, sleep till six, drinking cooling liquors till eight, go to the bridge till ten, sup till two, and so sleep till twelve again." In Venice, where sophisticated prostitutes had flourished since Renaissance times, the chief attraction for young English males was women. As Samuel Johnson remarked, "If a young man is wild, and must run after women and bad company, it is better this should be done abroad." Rome was another "great object of our pilgrimage," where travelers visited the "modern" sights, such as Saint Peter's and, above all, the ancient ruins. To a generation raised on a classical education, souvenirs of ruins and Piranesi's etchings of classical ruins were required purchases. The accidental rediscovery of the ancient Roman towns of Herculaneum and Pompeii made them a popular eighteenth-century tourist attraction.

The Inhabitants of Towns and Cities

There was a significant difference between the social importance of towns in eastern and western Europe. In eastern Europe, cities were generally smaller and had little real autonomy. In western Europe, they were larger and frequently were accustomed to municipal self-government and municipal privileges that even so-called absolute monarchs had to respect, although in many places the latter had managed to undermine urban governments.

Except in the Dutch Republic, Britain, and parts of Italy, townspeople were still a distinct minority of the total population. At the end of the eighteenth century, about one-sixth of the French population lived in towns of 2,000 or more. The biggest city in Europe was London with its 1,000,000 inhabitants while Paris numbered between 550,000 and 600,000. Altogether, Europe had at least twenty cities in twelve countries with populations over 100,000, including Naples, Lisbon, Moscow, St. Petersburg, Vienna, Amsterdam, Berlin, Rome, and Madrid.

Although urban dwellers were vastly outnumbered by rural inhabitants, towns played an important role in Western culture. The contrasts between a large city with its education, culture, and material consumption and the surrounding, often poverty-stricken countryside were striking, evident in this British traveler's account of Russia's St. Petersburg in 1741:

> The country about Petersburg has full as wild and desert a look as any in the Indies; you need not go above 200 paces out of the town to find yourself in a wild wood of firs, and such a low, marshy, boggy country that you would think God when he created the rest of the world for the use of mankind had created this for an inaccessible retreat for all sorts of wild beasts.[14]

Peasants often resented the prosperity of towns and their exploitation of the countryside to serve urban interests. Palermo in Sicily used one-third of the island's food production while paying only one-tenth of the taxes. Towns lived off the countryside not by buying, but by using tithes, rents, and dues to acquire peasant produce.

Many cities in western and even central Europe had a long tradition of patrician oligarchies that continued to control their communities by dominating town and city councils. In Zürich half of the seats on the ruling Great Council were controlled by thirteen families while Venice, Frankfurt, Nuremberg, Strasbourg, Amsterdam, and Venice all had closed patrician elites who ran their cities. In some towns in Spain, France, and parts of Germany and Italy, nobles with residences in both town and country dominated their urban societies.

Despite their domination, patricians and nobles constituted only a small minority of the urban population. Just below the patricians stood an upper crust of the middle classes: nonnoble officeholders, financiers and bankers, merchants, wealthy rentiers who lived off their investments, and important professionals, including lawyers. Another large urban group was the petty bourgeoisie or lower middle class made up of master artisans, shopkeepers, and small traders. Below them were the laborers or working classes. Much urban industry was still done in small guild workshops by masters, journeymen, and apprentices. Apprentices who acquired the proper skills became journeymen before entering the ranks of the masters, but increasingly in the eighteenth century guilds became closed oligarchies as membership was restricted to the relatives of masters. Many skilled artisans were then often forced to become low-paid workers. Urban communities also had a large group of unskilled workers who served as servants, maids, and cooks at pitifully low wages. One study of a preindustrial French city found that two married workers with one child received a family income of 380 livres while needing to spend 336 livres on basic necessities, leaving very little for extra expenses.

Despite an end to the ravages of plague, eighteenth-century cities still experienced high death rates, especially among children, because of unsanitary living conditions, polluted water, and a lack of sewerage facilities. One observer compared the stench of Hamburg to an open sewer that could be smelled for miles around. Overcrowding also exacerbated urban problems as cities continued to grow from an influx of rural immigrants. But cities proved no paradise for them as unskilled workers found few employment opportunities. The result was a serious problem of poverty in the eighteenth century.

THE PROBLEM OF POVERTY   Poverty was a highly visible problem in the eighteenth century both in cities and the countryside (see the box on p. 663). In Venice licensed beggars made up 3 to 5 percent of the population while unlicensed beggars may have constituted as much as 13 to 15 percent. Beggars in Bologna, Italy were estimated at 25 percent of the population while in Mainz figures

indicate that 30 percent of the people were beggars or prostitutes. Prostitution was often an alternative to begging. It has been estimated that in France and Britain by the end of the century 10 percent of the people were dependent on charity or begging for food.

Earlier in Europe the poor had been viewed as blessed children of God; the duty of Christians was to assist them. A change of attitude that had begun in the latter part of the sixteenth century became even more apparent in the eighteenth century. Charity to poor beggars, it was argued, simply encouraged their idleness and led them to vice and crime. A French official stated: "Beggary is the apprenticeship of crime; it begins by creating a love of idleness which will always be the greatest political and moral evil. In this state the beggar does not long resist the temptation to steal."[15] While private charitable institutions such as the religious Order of Saint Vincent de Paul and the Sisters of Charity had been founded to help such people, they were soon overwhelmed by the increased numbers of indigent in the eighteenth century.

Although some "enlightened" officials argued that the state needed to become involved in the problem, mixed feelings prevented concerted action. Since the sixteenth century, vagrancy and begging had been considered crimes. In the eighteenth century, French authorities attempted to round up vagrants and beggars and incarcerate them for eighteen months to act as a deter-

▼ **A Market in Turin.** Except in Britain, the Dutch Republic, and parts of Italy, the inhabitants of towns were still a distinct minority in Europe in the eighteenth century. Although towns and cities were dominated by wealthy patrician elites, they were also scene to a remarkable diversity of social groups of varying incomes. This variety is evident in this view of a market square in the Italian city of Turin.

Poverty in France
▼ ▼ ▼

Unlike the British, who had a system of public-supported poor relief, the French responded to poverty with ad hoc policies when conditions became acute. This selection is taken from an intendant's report to the controller-general at Paris describing his suggestions for a program to relieve the grain shortages expected for the winter months.

M. de la Bourdonnaye, Intendant of Bordeaux, to the Controller-General, September 30, 1708

Having searched for the means of helping the people of Agen in this cruel situation and having conferred with His Eminence, the Bishop, it seems to us that three things are absolutely necessary if the people are not to starve during the winter.

Most of the inhabitants do not have seed to plant their fields. However, we decided that we would be going too far if we furnished it, because those who have seed would also apply [for more]. Moreover, we are persuaded that all the inhabitants will make strenuous efforts to find some seed, since they have every reason to expect prices to remain high next year. . . .

But this project will come to nothing if the collectors of the taille continue to be as strict in the exercise of their functions as they have been of late and continue to employ troops [to force collection]. Those inhabitants who have seed grain would sell it to be freed from an oppressive garrison, while those who must buy seed, since they had none left from their harvest and have scraped together a little money for this purchase, would prefer to give up that money [for taxes] when put under police constraint. To avoid this, I feel it is absolutely necessary that you order the receivers-general to reduce their operations during this winter, at least with respect to the poor. . . .

We are planning to import wheat for this region from Languedoc and Quercy, and we are confident that there will be enough. But there are two things to be feared: one is the greed of the merchants. When they see that general misery has put them in control of prices, they will raise them to the point where the calamity is almost as great as if there were no provisions at all. The other fear is that the artisans and the lowest classes, when they find themselves at the mercy of the merchants, will cause disorders and riots. As a protective measure, it would seem wise to establish two small storehouses. . . . Ten thousand ecus [30,000 livres] would be sufficient for each. . . .

A third point demanding our attention is the support of beggars among the poor, as well as of those who have no other resources than their wages. Since there will be very little work, these people will soon be reduced to starvation. We should establish public workshops to provide work as was done in 1693 and 1694. I should choose the most useful kind of work, located where there are the greatest number of poor. In this manner, we should rid ourselves of those who do not want to work and assure the others of a moderate subsistence. For these workshops, we would need about 40,000 livres, or altogether 100,000 livres. The receiver-general of the taille of Agen could advance this sum. The 60,000 livres for the storehouses he would get back very soon. I shall await your orders on all of the above.

Marginal Comments by the Controller-General

Operations for the collection of the taille are to be suspended. The two storehouses are to be established; great care must be taken to put them to good use. The interest on the advances will be paid by the king. His Majesty has agreed to the establishment of the public workshops for the able-bodied poor and is willing to spend up to 40,000 livres on them this winter.

---

rent. They accomplished little, however, since the basic problem was socioeconomic. These people had no work. In the 1770s the French tried to use public works projects, such as road building, to give people jobs, but not enough funds were available to accomplish much. The problem of poverty remained as another serious blemish on the quality of eighteenth-century life.

Everywhere in Europe at the beginning of the eighteenth century, the old order remained strong. Nobles, clerics, towns, provinces all had privileges, some medieval in origin, others the result of the attempt of monarchies in the sixteenth and seventeenth centuries to gain financial support from their subjects. Everywhere in the eighteenth century, monarchs sought to enlarge their bureaucracies to raise taxes to support the new large standing armies that had originated in the seventeenth century. The existence of these armies guaranteed wars. The existence of five great powers, with two of them (France and Britain) in conflict in the Far East and the New World, initiated a new scale of conflict; the Seven Years' War could legitimately be viewed as the first world war. While the wars changed little on the European continent, British victories brought the emergence of Great Britain as the world's greatest naval and colonial power. Everywhere in Europe, increased demands for taxes to support these conflicts led to attacks on the privileged orders and a desire for change not met by the ruling monarchs.

At the same time, sustained population growth, dramatic changes in finance, trade, and industry, and the growth of poverty created tensions that undermined the traditional foundations of the old order. The inability of that old order to deal meaningfully with these changes led to a revolutionary outburst at the end of the eighteenth century that brought the beginning of the end for that old order.

Notes
▼ ▼ ▼

1. Quoted in Paul Dukes, *The Making of Russian Absolutism, 1613–1801* (London, 1982), pp. 144–45.
2. Frederick II, *Forms of Government,* in Eugen Weber, *The Western Tradition* (Lexington, Mass., 1972), pp. 538, 544.
3. Quoted in Reinhold A. Dorwart, *The Administrative Reforms of Frederick William I of Prussia* (Cambridge, Mass., 1953), p. 36.
4. Quoted in Sidney B. Fay, *The Rise of Brandenburg-Prussia to 1786,* rev. Klaus Epstein (New York, 1964), p. 92.
5. Quoted in Hans Rosenberg, *Bureaucracy, Aristocracy, and Autocracy: The Prussian Experience, 1660–1815* (Cambridge, Mass., 1958), p. 40.
6. Quoted in Herbert Kaplan, *The First Partition of Poland* (New York, 1962), p. 167.
7. Quoted in W. Abel, "Die Landwirtschaft 1648–1800," in *Handbuch der deutschen Wirtschafts-und*

Sozialgeschichte, eds. H. Aubin and W. Zorn (Stuttgart, 1971), 1: 524–25.
8. Quoted in Fernand Braudel, *Civilization and Capitalism* (London, 1981–84), 3: 378.
9. Quoted in ibid., 3: 245.
10. Abbé le Blanc, *Letters on the English and French Nations* (London, 1747), 2: 404–5.
11. Quoted in Witold Rybczynski, *Home: A Short History of an Idea* (New York, 1986), p. 105.
12. Quoted in Peter Gay, *Age of Enlightenment* (New York, 1966), p. 87.
13. Quoted in Paul Hazard, *The European Mind, 1680–1715* (Cleveland, 1963), pp. 6–7.
14. *Oxford Slavonic Papers,* New Series (1982), 15: 76.
15. Quoted in Jeffrey Kaplow, *The Names of Kings: The Parisian Laboring Poor in the Eighteenth Century* (New York, 1972), p. 134.

Suggestions for Further Reading
▼ ▼ ▼

For a good introduction to the political history of the eighteenth century, see the relevant chapters in the general works by Woloch and Anderson listed in Chapter 18. See also G. Treasure, *The Making of Modern Europe, 1648–1780* (London, 1985); W. Doyle, *The Old European Order, 1660–1800* (Oxford, 1978); O. Hufton, *Europe: Privilege and Protest, 1730–1789* (London, 1980); and E. N. Williams, *The Ancien Régime in Europe: Government and Society in the Major States, 1648–1789* (New York, 1970). On the theory of enlightened absolutism, see L. Krieger, *An Essay on the Theory of Enlightened Despotism* (Chicago, 1970). For a brief study of its practice, see J. Gagliardo, *Enlightened Despotism* (New York, 1967). Good histories of individual states include W. A. Speck, *Stability and Strife: England, 1714–1760* (Cambridge, Mass., 1977); J. B. Owen, *The Eighteenth Century, 1714–1815* (London, 1975), also on England; P. R. Campbell, *The Ancien Régime in France* (Oxford, 1988); E. Wangermann, *The Austrian Achievement, 1700–1800* (London, 1973); R. Vierhaus,

Germany in the Age of Absolutism (Cambridge, 1988); W. N. Hargreaves-Mawdsley, Eighteenth-Century Spain, 1700–1788: A Political, Diplomatic, and Institutional History (London, 1978); S. B. Fay, The Rise of Brandenburg-Prussia to 1786 (New York, 1964); and P. Dukes, The Making of Russian Absolutism, 1613–1801 (London, 1982). Good biographies of some of Europe's monarchs include R. Asprey, Frederick the Great, The Magnificent Enigma (New York, 1986); I. de Madariaga, Russia in the Age of Catherine the Great (New Haven, Conn., 1981); the first volume of a new major work on Joseph II by D. Deales, Joseph II (Cambridge, 1987); and J. Brooke, King George III (London, 1972).

The warfare of this period is examined in J. Childs, Armies and Warfare in Europe, 1648–1789 (Manchester, 1982). On the social composition of European armies, see A. Corvisier, Armies and Society in Europe, 1494–1789 (Bloomington, Ind., 1978). For a study of one army, see C. Duffy, The Army of Frederick the Great (London, 1974). The impact of war on economic life is examined in M. Gutmann, War and Rural Life in the Early Modern Low Countries (Princeton, N.J., 1980).

A good introduction to European population can be found in M. W. Flinn, The European Demographic System, 1500–1820 (Brighton, 1981). Although historians now disagree with many of his conclusions, still worthwhile is the pioneering study of childhood by P. Aries, Centuries of Childhood: A Social History of Family Life (New York, 1965). One of the best works on family and marriage patterns is L. Stone, The Family, Sex, and Marriage in England, 1500–1800 (New York, 1977). An innovative work is A. MacFarlane, Origins of English Individualism: The Family, Property and Social Transition (Oxford, 1978).

A different perspective on economic history can be found in F. Braudel's Capitalism and Material Life, 1400–1800 (New York, 1973). P. G. M. Dickson, The Financial Revolution in England: A Study in the Development of Public Credit, 1688–1756 (London, 1967) is a detailed, specialized study on matters of finance. The subject of mercantile empires and worldwide trade is covered in J. H. Parry, Trade and Dominion: European Overseas Empires in the Eighteenth Century (London,

1971); D. K. Fieldhouse, The Colonial Empires (New York, 1971); and R. Davis, The Rise of the Atlantic Economies (Ithaca, N.Y., 1973). On the problem of slavery, see M. Craton, Sinews of Empire: A Short History of British Slavery (New York, 1974). On England's agricultural revolution, see J. D. Chambers and G. E. Mingay, The Agricultural Revolution, 1750–1880 (London, 1966). Eighteenth-century cottage industry and the beginnings of industrialization are examined in the early chapters of D. Landes, The Unbound Prometheus: Technological Change and Industrial Development in Western Europe from 1750 to the Present (New York, 1969).

For an introduction to the social order of the eighteenth century, see G. Rudé, Europe in the Eighteenth Century: Aristocracy and the Bourgeois Challenge (London, 1972); P. Goubert, The Ancien Régime (New York, 1973); and P. Laslett, The World We Have Lost, 3d ed. (New York, 1984). Two works by J. Blum are valuable on the peasantry, The End of the Old Order in Rural Europe (Princeton, N.J., 1978); and Lord and Peasant in Russia from the Ninth to the Nineteenth Century (Princeton, N.J., 1961). Also of much interest is E. Le Roy Ladurie, The Peasants of Languedoc (Urbana, Ill., 1974). On the European nobility, see the specialized studies of R. Forster, The Nobility of Toulouse in the Eighteenth Century (Baltimore, 1960); R. E. Jones, The Emancipation of the Russian Nobility, 1762–1785 (Princeton, N.J., 1973); and G. E. Mingay, The Gentry: The Rise and Fall of a Ruling Class (London, 1976). Studies of urban communities include F. L. Ford, Strasbourg in Transition, 1648–1789 (Cambridge, Mass., 1958); M. Walker, German Home Towns: Community, State, and General Estate, 1648–1871 (Ithaca, N.Y., 1971); G. Rudé, Hanoverian London, 1714–1808 (Berkeley, 1971); and G. L. Soliday, A Community in Conflict: Frankfurt Society in the Seventeenth and Early Eighteenth Centuries (Hanover, N.H., 1974). On the lower urban classes, see J. Kaplow, The Names of Kings: The Parisian Laboring Poor in the Eighteenth Century (New York, 1972). There is no better work on the problem of poverty than O. Hufton, The Poor of Eighteenth-Century France (Oxford, 1974).

Chapter 20

A Revolution in Politics: The Era of the French Revolution and Napoleon

▼▼▼▼▼

Historians have long assumed that the modern history of Europe began with two major transformations—the French Revolution and the Industrial Revolution (on the latter, see Chapter 21). Accordingly, the French Revolution has been portrayed as the major turning point in European political and social history when the institutions of the "old regime" were destroyed and a new order was created based on individual rights, representative institutions, and a concept of loyalty to the nation rather than the monarch. This perspective does have certain limitations, however.

Some historians have emphasized that France was only one of a number of areas in the Western world where the assumptions of the old order were challenged. Although they have used the phrase "democratic revolution" to refer to the upheavals of the late eighteenth and early nineteenth centuries, it is probably more appropriate to speak not of a "democratic movement," but of a liberal movement to extend political rights and power to the bourgeoisie "possessing capital," namely, those besides the aristocracy who were literate and had become wealthy through capitalist enterprises in trade, industry, and finance. The years preceding and accompanying the French Revolution included attempts at reform and revolt in the North American colonies, Britain, the Dutch Republic, some Swiss cities, and the Austrian Netherlands. The success of the American and French revolutions makes them the center of attention for this chapter.

American Declaration of Independence ▼

American Independence ▼

Ratification of the American Constitution ▼

•••••••• 1775 ••••••••••• 1785 ••••••••••• 1795 ••••••••••• 1805 ••••••••••• 1815 ••••••••

▲ Formation of the National Assembly

▲ Reign of Terror

▲ Constitution of 1795

▲ Napoleon Becomes Emperor

▲ Battle of Waterloo

It would be a mistake to assume that all of the decadent privileges that characterized the old European regime were destroyed in 1789. The revolutionary upheaval of the era, especially in France, did create new liberal and national political ideals, summarized in the French revolutionary slogan, "Liberty, Equality, and Fraternity," that transformed France and were then spread to other European countries through the conquests of Napoleon. After Napoleon's defeat, however, the forces of reaction did their best to restore the old order and resist pressures for reform.

▼ The Beginnings of the Revolutionary Era: The American Revolution

The revolutionary era began in North America when the thirteen British colonies along the eastern seaboard revolted against their mother country. Despite their differences, the colonists found ways to create a new government based on liberal principles that made an impact on the "old world" European states.

Reorganization, Resistance, and Rebellion

The immediate causes of the American Revolution stemmed from Britain's response to its victory over France in the Seven Years' War, known as the French and Indian War in America. British imperial policies toward their American colonies changed dramatically after 1763. The western lands of the Ohio and Mississippi valleys, surrendered to the British by the French, appeared to land-hungry Americans as an ideal territory for expansion. The British, however, feared conflict with the numerous Indian tribes settled there and forbade white purchases of land west of the Appalachians; fur-

thermore, they decided to enforce this policy by sending a standing army of 10,000 men to the colonies, a totally unprecedented peacetime act in the eyes of the colonists. It was also expensive. In the course of the French and Indian War (1756–1763), British policymakers realized that the Americans, in return for the British defense of the colonies from the French and their Indian allies, had contributed relatively little to the war's expenses while the British national debt had reached staggering proportions. While Americans were paying an average of one shilling a year in taxes, annual taxes per person in Britain had reached twenty-six shillings. It seemed only fair that the Americans should assume some of the costs of the North American army.

A new regulation of colonial trade appeared to be the most obvious means of obtaining new revenues from the colonies. Although helpful, it failed to raise more than £30,000, only one-tenth of the annual cost of the British army in America. In 1765, Parliament resorted to a Stamp Act, which levied a direct tax on legal documents, newspapers, almanacs, pamphlets, dice, and playing cards. The tax seemed perfectly reasonable to Parliament. It would raise another £60,000 annually and was set at a rate lower than the stamp tax in effect in Britain. The colonists, however, responded with fury. Riots against designated tax collectors and stamp offices were accompanied by boycotts of British goods. British exports to America dropped 14 percent from 1764 to 1765. Reluctantly, Parliament caved in to the pressure and repealed the Stamp Act, not, however, without asserting uncompromisingly its right to make laws "to bind the colonies and the people of America in all cases whatsoever."

The immediate crisis had ended, but the fundamental cause of the dispute had not been resolved. In the course of the eighteenth century, significant differences had arisen between the American and British political worlds. Both peoples shared the same property requirement for voting—voters had to possess a property that could be rented for at least forty shillings a year—but it resulted in a disparity in the number of voters in the two countries. In Britain fewer than one in five adult males had the right to vote. In the colonies, where a radically different economic structure led to an enormous group of independent farmers, the property requirement allowed over 50 percent of adult males to vote.

While both the British and Americans had representative governments, different systems had evolved. Representation in Britain was indirect; the members of Parliament did not speak for local interests but for the entire kingdom. In the colonies direct representation meant that representatives should reside in and own property in the communities electing them; hence, they should represent the interests of their local districts.

This divergence in political systems was paralleled by conflicting conceptions of empire. The British envisioned a single empire with Parliament as the supreme authority throughout; as one parliamentarian argued, "in sovereignty there are no gradations." All the people in the empire, including the American colonists, were consequently represented indirectly by members of Parliament, whether they were from the colonies or not. Colonial assemblies in the British perspective were only committees that made "temporary by-laws"; the real authority to make laws for the empire resided in London.

In view of Britain's "benign neglect" of its colonies, the Americans had been relatively free to develop their own peculiar view of the British Empire. To them, the British Empire was composed of self-regulating parts. While they conceded that as British subjects they owed allegiance to the king and that Parliament had the right to make laws for the peace and prosperity of the whole realm, they argued, nevertheless, that neither king nor Parliament had any right to interfere in the internal affairs of the colonies since they had their own representative assemblies. American colonists were especially defensive about property and believed strongly that no tax could be levied without the consent of an assembly whose members actually represented the people. At the Stamp Act Congress, where moderate representatives from nine colonies reassured the British that they "owe Allegiance to the Crown of Great-Britain" and "all due Subordination to that August Body the Parliament," it was nevertheless argued that the Stamp Act violated the "inherent Rights and Liberties" of Englishmen. No taxes could be imposed upon them "but with their own Consent, given personally, or by their Representatives." And importantly, "the People of these Colonies are not, and from their local Circumstances cannot be, Represented in the House of Commons in Great-Britain."[1]

By the 1760s, the American colonists had developed a sense of a common national identity. It was not unusual for American travelers to Britain in the eighteenth century to see British society as old and decadent compared to the youthfulness and vitality of their own. This sense of superiority made Americans resentful of British actions that seemed to treat them like children. Resentment eventually led to a desire for independence.

The respite gained by the resolution of the Stamp Act crisis proved short-lived. The Townsend Acts of 1767, which attempted to raise new revenues indirectly by imposing tariffs on a number of goods imported to the colonies, simply created another political storm. It, too, was once again resolved by concessions, but the struggle set off by the Tea Act of 1773 finally led to war.

The Tea Act was an attempt to help the financially hard-pressed East India Company by allowing it to go around American wholesalers and sell its tea directly to distributors. Wholesale merchants denounced this tea "monopoly" as the first step in Parliament's subjugation of colonial businesses. Although exaggerated, the argument seemed convincing to Americans grown suspicious of British motives. Some Americans—mistakenly—had even arrived at a sinister interpretation of ultimate British motives. Thomas Jefferson wrote in 1774 that "a series of oppressions, begun at a distinguished period and pursued unalterably through every change of ministers, too plainly proves a deliberate and systematical plan of reducing us to slavery."

In Boston, protest took a destructive turn when 150 Americans dressed as Indians unloaded the East India Company's tea into Boston harbor. Parliament responded vigorously with the Coercive Acts, which the colonists labeled the "Intolerable Acts." These closed the port of Boston until compensation for the destroyed tea was paid, restricted town meetings, and strengthened the power of the royal governor of Massachusetts. Designed to punish radical Massachusetts as an example to the other colonies, the Coercive Acts backfired. Many British politicians continued to believe that most Americans were completely loyal to the empire and that the problems in America came from a small number of radicals. But this was a mistake; colonial assemblies everywhere denounced the British action. The colonies' desire to take collective action led to the First Continental Congress, which met at Philadelphia in September 1774. The more militant members refused to compromise and urged colonists to "take up arms and organize militias." When the British army under General Gage attempted to stop rebel mobilization in Massachusetts,

The Argument for Independence
▼ ▼ ▼

On July 2, 1776, the Second Continental Congress adopted a resolution declaring the independence of the American colonies. Two days later the delegates approved the Declaration of Independence, which gave the reasons for their action. Its principal author was Thomas Jefferson who basically restated John Locke's theory of revolution (see Chapter 16).

The Declaration of Independence

When in the course of human events it becomes necessary for one people to dissolve the political bands which have connected them with another, and to assume among the Powers of the earth, the separate and equal station to which the Laws of Nature and of Nature's God entitle them, a decent respect to the opinions of mankind requires that they should declare the causes which impel them to the separation.

We hold these truths to be self-evident, that all men are created equal, that they are endowed by their Creator with certain unalienable Rights, that among these are Life, Liberty and the pursuit of Happiness. That to secure these rights, Governments are instituted among Men, deriving their just powers from the consent of the governed, That whenever any Form of Government becomes destructive of these ends, it is the Right of the People to alter or to abolish it and to institute new Government, laying its foundation on such principles and organizing its powers in such form, as to them shall seem most likely to effect their Safety and Happiness. Prudence, indeed, will dictate that Governments long established should not be changed for light and transient causes; and accordingly all experience hath shown, that mankind are more disposed to suffer, while evils are sufferable, than to right themselves by abolishing the forms to which they are accustomed. But when a long train of abuses and usurpations, pursuing invariably the same Object evinces a design to reduce them under absolute Despotism, it is their right, it is their duty, to throw off such Government, and to provide new Guards for their future security.—Such has been the patient sufferance of these Colonies; and such is now the necessity which constrains them to alter their former Systems of Government. The history of the present King of Great Britain is a history of repeated injuries and usurpations, all having in direct object the establishment of an absolute Tyranny over these States.

fighting erupted at Lexington and Concord between colonists and redcoats in April 1775.

The War for Independence

Despite the outbreak of hostilities, the colonists did not rush headlong into rebellion and war. It was more than a year after Lexington and Concord before the decision was made to declare their independence from the British Empire. An important factor in mobilizing public pressure for that decision came from *Common Sense*, a pamphlet published in January 1776 by Thomas Paine, a recently arrived English political radical. Within three months, it had sold 120,000 copies. Paine's pamphlet argued that it was ridiculous for "a continent to be perpetually governed by an island." From a practical point of view, Paine also pointed out that other countries, such as France and Spain, which were only too eager to strike at the British Empire, would never provide military aid for the colonies to resist Britain unless they were an independent power. On July 4, 1776, the Second Continental Congress approved a Declaration of Independence written by Thomas Jefferson (see the box above). A stirring political document, the Declaration of Independence affirmed the Enlightenment's natural rights of "life, liberty, and the pursuit of happiness" and declared the colonies to be "free and independent states absolved from all allegiance to the British crown." The war for American independence had formally begun.

The war against Great Britain was a great gamble. Britain was a strong European military power with enormous financial resources; by 1778 Britain had sent 50,000 regular British troops and 30,000 German mercenaries to America. The Second Continental Congress had authorized the formation of a Continental Army under George Washington as commander-in-chief. Washington, who had had political experience in Virginia and military experience in the French and Indian War, was a good choice for the job. As a southerner, he brought balance to an effort that up to now had been led by New Englanders. Nevertheless, compared to the British forces, the Continental Army consisted of undisciplined amateurs whose terms of service were usually very brief. The colonies also had militia units, but they likewise tended to be unreliable. Although 400,000 men served in the Continental Army and the militias during the course of the war, Washington never had more than 20,000 troops available for any single battle. The Americans did possess one advantage, however; they did not always fight the kind of eighteenth-century warfare to which the British were accustomed. Instead, the Americans periodically adopted the guerilla type of warfare that they had learned from their encounters with the Indians. A British officer complained, "Never had the British army so ungenerous an opponent. They send their riflemen five or six at a time, who conceal themselves behind trees, etc. until an opportunity presents itself of taking a shot at our advance sentries, which done they immediately retreat. What an unfair method of carrying on a war."[2]

Complicating the war effort were the internal divisions within the colonies. Fought for independence, the revolutionary war was also a civil war, pitting family members and neighbors against one another. The Loyalists, who may have numbered between 15 to 30 percent of the population, questioned whether British policies justified the rebellion. The Loyalists were strongest in New York and Pennsylvania and tended to be wealthy, older, and politically moderate.

Since probably 50 percent of the colonial population were apathetic at the beginning of the struggle, the patriots, like the Loyalists, constituted a minority of the population. The patriots, however, managed to win over many of the uncommitted, either by persuasion or by force. Committees of Safety harassed and jailed Loyalists, insulted their families, and seized and destroyed their property. There were rich patriots as well; George Washington owned an estate with 15,000 acres and 150 slaves. But the rich patriots joined an extensive coalition that included farmers and artisans. The wide social spectrum in this coalition had an impact on representative governments in the states after the war. The right to vote was often broadened; Pennsylvania, for example, dropped all property qualifications for voting. Fewer wealthy people were chosen for political offices. In the northern states, for example, the number of very wealthy individuals in the assemblies dropped from 36 to 12 percent while the number of people with small holdings increased dramatically from 17 to 62 percent.

Of great importance to the colonies' cause was their support by foreign countries who were eager to gain revenge for their defeats in earlier wars at the hands of the British. The French were particularly generous in sup-

▼ **Washington Reviews His Army.** George Washington was given charge of the Continental Army authorized by the Second Continental Congress. Although inferior to the British forces, the American soldiers did have some advantage in that they followed the guerilla type of warfare used by the native Americans, a style of fighting to which the British were unaccustomed. With the support and aid of other European powers, the Americans finally gained their independence in 1783. This painting shows Washington reviewing the Western Army at Fort Cumberland, Maryland.

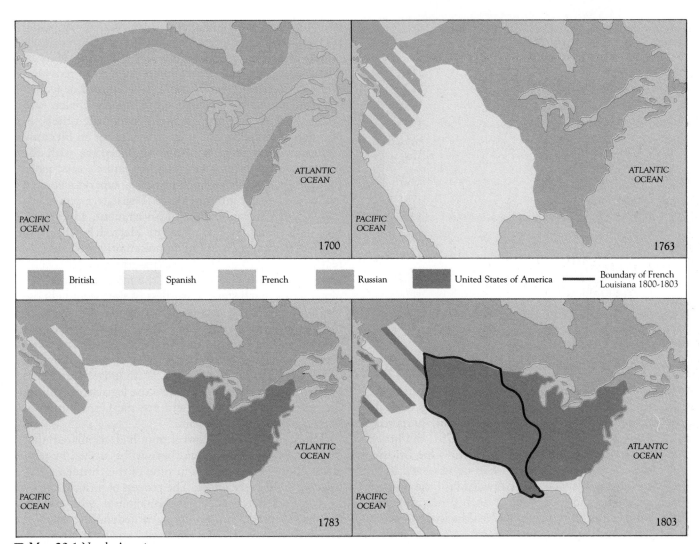

▪ British	░ Spanish	▫ French	▪ Russian	▪ United States of America

━━━ Boundary of French Louisiana 1800-1803

▼ **Map 20.1** North America.

plying arms and money to the rebels from the beginning of the war. French officers and soldiers also served in Washington's army. Uncertain of the military outcome, however, France was at first unwilling to recognize the new republic. The defeat of the British at Saratoga in October 1777 finally led the French to grant diplomatic recognition to the American state. When Spain in 1779 and the Dutch Republic in 1780 entered the war against Great Britain, and Russia formed the League of Armed Neutrality in 1780 to protect neutral shipping from British attacks, the British were faced with war against much of Europe as well as the Americans. Despite having won most of the battles, the British were in danger of losing the war. When the army of General Cornwallis was forced to surrender to a combined American and French army and French fleet under Washington at Yorktown in

1781, the British decided to call it quits. After extensive negotiations, complicated by French and Spanish aims that often conflicted with American desires, the Treaty of Paris was signed in 1783. It recognized the independence of the American colonies and surprisingly granted the Americans control of the western territory from the Appalachians to the Mississippi River. By playing off the mutual fears of the European powers, the Americans had cleverly gained a peace settlement that stunned the Europeans. The Americans were off to a good start but soon showed signs of political disintegration.

Toward a New Nation

Although the thirteen American colonies agreed to "hang together" to gain their independence from the

British, a fear of concentrated power and concern for their own interests caused them to have little enthusiasm for establishing a united nation with a strong central government. The Articles of Confederation, proposed in 1777 but not completely ratified until 1781, did little to provide for a strong central government. One British official described the scene well when he observed that the American people would stay divided "till the end of time, suspicious and distrustful of each other, divided and subdivided into little commonwealths with no center of union and no common interests."

The Articles of Confederation provided the "United States" with weak central government from 1781 to 1789; some historians view these years as a "critical period" in the history of the new nation. A series of economic, political, and international problems soon led to a movement for a different form of national government. In the summer of 1787, fifty-five delegates attended a convention in Philadelphia that was authorized by the Confederation Congress "for the sole and express purpose of revising the Articles of Confederation." The convention's delegates—wealthy, politically experienced, well educated and nationalistically inclined—rejected revision and decided to devise a new constitution.

The proposed Constitution created a central government distinct from and superior to the governments of the individual states. The national government was given the power to levy taxes, raise a national army, regulate domestic and foreign trade, and create a national currency. While states were not eliminated, their powers were noticeably diminished. Following Montesquieu's principle of a "separation of powers" to provide a system of "checks and balances," the central or federal government was divided into three branches, each with some power to check the functioning of the others. A president, elected by the indirect system of an Electoral College, would serve as the chief executive with the power to execute laws, veto the legislature's acts, make judicial and executive appointments, supervise foreign affairs, and direct military forces. Legislative power was vested in the second branch of government, a bicameral legislature composed of a Senate elected by the state legislatures and a House of Representatives elected directly by the people. The legislative structure was a compromise between delegates from the most and least populous states. Each state, regardless of size, would choose two senators, while the number of representatives to the House would be determined by population. The federal judiciary embodied in a Supreme Court and other courts "as deemed necessary" by Congress, provided the third branch of government. With judges nominated by the executive and approved by the legislative branch, the federal judiciary would enforce the Constitution as the "supreme law of the land."

The constitutional convention had stipulated that the new Constitution would have to be ratified by popularly chosen conventions in nine of the thirteen states before it would take effect. The process of ratification led to fierce debates between the Federalists, who favored the new Constitution, and the Antifederalists, who believed that the Constitution would create another tyranny by destroying the power of the states. One delegate at the Massachusetts convention expressed his fear that "these lawyers, and men of learning, and moneyed men, that talk so finely, and gloss over matters so smoothly, to make us poor illiterate people swallow down the pill, expect to get into Congress themselves." Once they have done so, "they expect to be managers of this Constitution and get all the power and all the money into their own hands." The well-organized Federalists won the debate but certainly not because of a massive outpouring of public support. The public remained largely passive; only one-fourth of the eligible voters bothered to choose the delegates to the state conventions.

The margin of victory for the Federalists had been quite slim. Important to their success had been a promise to add a Bill of Rights to the Constitution as the new government's first piece of business. Accordingly, in March of 1789, the new Congress enacted the first ten

amendments to the Constitution, ever since known as the Bill of Rights. These guaranteed freedom of religion, speech, press, petition, and assembly, as well as the right to bear arms, be protected against unreasonable searches and arrests, trial by jury, due process of law, and the protection of property rights. Although many had their origins in English law, others were derived from the natural rights philosophy of the eighteenth-century philosophies and American experience. Is it any wonder that many European intellectuals saw the American Revolution as the embodiment of the Enlightenment's political dreams?

The Impact of the American Revolution on Europe

The year 1789 witnessed two far-reaching events, the beginning of a new United States of America and the eruption of the French Revolution. Was there a connection between the two great revolutions of the last half of the eighteenth century?

There is no doubt that the American Revolution had an important impact on Europeans. Books, newspapers, and magazines provided a newly developing reading public with numerous accounts of American events. To many in Europe, it seemed to portend an era of significant changes, including new arrangements in international politics. The Venetian ambassador to Paris astutely observed in 1783 that "if only the union of the [American] provinces is preserved, it is reasonable to expect that, with the favorable effects of time, and of European arts and sciences, it will become the most formidable power in the world."[3] But the American Revolution also meant far more than that. It proved to many Europeans that the liberal political ideas of the Enlightenment were not merely the vapid utterances of intellectuals. The rights of man, ideas of liberty and equality, popular sovereignty, freedom of religion, thought, and press, and the separation of powers were not merely utopian ideals. The Americans had created a new social contract, embodied it in a written constitution, and made concepts of liberty and representative government a reality. The premises of the Enlightenment seemed confirmed; a new age and a better world could be achieved. As a Swiss philosophe expressed it, "I am tempted to believe that North America is the country where reason and humanity will develop more rapidly than anywhere else."[4]

Returning soldiers were an important source of information about America for Europeans, especially the hundreds of French officers who had served in the American war. One of them, the aristocrat marquis de Lafayette, had volunteered for service in America in order to "strike a blow against England," France's old enemy. Closely associated with Washington, Lafayette returned to France with ideas of individual liberties and notions of republicanism and popular sovereignty. He became a member of the Society of Thirty, a club composed of people from the Paris salons. These "lovers of liberty" were influential in the early stages of the French Revolution. The Declaration of the Rights of Man and Citizen (see The Destruction of the Old Regime later in the chapter) showed unmistakable signs of the influence of the American Declaration of Independence as well as the constitutions of American state governments. Yet, for all of its obvious impact, the American Revolution proved in the long run to be far less important to Europe than the French Revolution. The French Revolution was more complex, more violent, and far more radical with its attempt to reconstruct both a new political and a new social order. The French Revolution provided a model of revolution for Europe and much of the rest of the world; to many it has remained the political movement that truly inaugurated the modern political world.

▼ The French Revolution

Although we associate events like the French Revolution with sudden changes, the causes of such events involve long-range problems as well as immediate, precipitating forces. Revolutions, as has been repeatedly shown, are not necessarily the result of economic collapse and masses of impoverished people hungering for change. In fact, in the fifty years before 1789, France had experienced a period of economic growth due to an expansion of foreign trade and an increase in industrial production. The causes of the French Revolution must be found in a multifaceted examination of French society and its problems in the late eighteenth century.

Background to the French Revolution

Although France experienced an increase in economic growth in the eighteenth century, its wealth was not evenly distributed. The long-range or indirect causes of the French Revolution must first be sought in the condition of French society. Before the Revolution, France was a society grounded in the inequality of rights or the idea of privilege. Its population of 27 million was divided, as it had been since the Middle Ages, into three orders or estates.

The first estate consisted of the clergy and numbered about 130,000 people who owned approximately 10 percent of the land. Clergy were exempt from the *taille*, France's chief tax, although the church had agreed to pay a "voluntary" contribution every five years to the state. Clergy were also radically divided, since the higher clergy, stemming from aristocratic families, shared the interests of the nobility while the parish priests were often poor and from the class of commoners.

The second estate was the nobility, composed of from 120,000 to 350,000 people who nevertheless owned about 25 to 30 percent of the land. Under Louis XV and Louis XVI, the nobility had continued to play an important and even crucial role in French society, holding many of the leading positions in the government, the military, the law courts, and the higher church offices. Much heavy industry in France was controlled by nobles, either through investment or by ownership of mining and metallurgical enterprises. The French nobility was also divided. The nobility of the robe was derived from officeholding, a position that had often opened the doors for commoners to receive noble status. These nobles now dominated the royal law courts and important administrative offices. The nobility of the sword claimed to be descendants of the original medieval nobility. The nobles as a whole sought to expand their power at the expense of the monarchy—to defend liberty by resisting the arbitrary actions of monarchy, as some nobles asserted—and to maintain their monopolistic control over positions in the military, church, and government. In 1781, in reaction to the ambitions of aristocrats newly arrived from the bourgeoisie, the Ségur Law attempted to limit the sale of military officerships to fourth-generation nobles, thus excluding newly enrolled members of the nobility.

Although there were many poor nobles, on the whole the fortunes of the wealthy aristocrats outstripped those of most others in French society. Generally, the nobles tended to marry within their own ranks making the nobility a fairly closed group. Although their privileges varied from region to region, the very possession of privileges remained a hallmark of the nobility. Common to all were tax exemptions, especially from the *taille*.

The third estate, or the commoners of society, constituted the overwhelming majority of the French population. They were divided by vast differences in occupation, level of education, and wealth. The peasants who alone constituted 75 to 80 percent of the total population were by far the largest segment of the third estate. They owned about 35 to 40 percent of the land, although their landholdings varied from area to area and

over half had no or little land on which to survive. Serfdom no longer existed on any large scale in France, but French peasants still had seigneurial obligations to their local landlords. These "relics of feudalism," survivals from an earlier age, had continued and even been reaffirmed in the eighteenth century as a result of aristocratic strength. These obligations included the payment of fees for the use of village facilities, such as the flour mill, community oven, and winepress, as well as tithes to the clergy. The nobility also maintained the right to hunt on peasants' land. Peasants resented these obligations as well as the attempt of noble landowners in the eighteenth century to enclose open fields and divide village common lands since enclosure eliminated the open pastures that poor peasants used for their livestock.

Another part of the third estate consisted of skilled craftsmen, shopkeepers, and other wage earners in the cities. Although the eighteenth century had been a period of rapid urban growth, 90 percent of French towns had fewer than 10,000 inhabitants while only nine cities had more than 50,000. In the eighteenth century, a rise in consumer prices greater than the increase in wages left these urban groups with a noticeable decline in purchasing power. In Paris, for example, income lagged behind food prices and especially behind a 140 percent rise in rents for working people in skilled and unskilled trades. The economic discontent of this segment of the third estate and often simply their struggle for survival led them to play an important role in the Revolution, especially in the city of Paris. Insubordination, one observer noted, "has been visible among the people for some years now and above all among craftsmen." One historian has charted the ups and downs of revolutionary riots in Paris by showing their correlation to changes in bread prices. Sudden increases in the price of bread, which constituted three-fourths of an ordinary person's diet and cost one-third to one-half of his or her income, immediately affected public order. People expected bread prices to be controlled. They grew desperate when prices rose, and their only recourse was mob action to try to change the situation. The towns and cities were also home to large groups of unskilled workers. One magistrate complained that "misery . . . has thrown into the towns people who overburden them with their uselessness, and who find nothing to do, because there is not enough for the people who live there."[5]

About 8 percent or 2.3 million people constituted the bourgeoisie or middle class who owned about 20 to 25 percent of the land. This group included merchants, industrialists, and bankers who controlled the resources of trade, manufacturing, and finance and benefited from

the economic prosperity after 1730. The bourgeoisie also included professional people—lawyers, holders of public offices, doctors, and writers. Many members of the bourgeoisie sought security and status in the purchase of land. They had their own set of grievances because they were often excluded from the social and political privileges monopolized by the nobles. These resentments of the middle class were for a long time assumed to be a major cause of the French Revolution. But although these tensions existed, the situation was not simply the case of a unified bourgeoisie against a unified noble class. As is evident, neither group was monolithic. Nobles were separated by vast differences in wealth and importance. A similar gulf separated wealthy financiers from local lawyers in French provincial towns.

Remarkable similarities existed at the upper levels of society between the wealthier bourgeoisie and the nobility. It was still possible for wealthy middle-class individuals to enter the ranks of the nobility by obtaining public offices and entering the nobility of the robe. In fact, between 1774 and 1789, the not insignificant number of 2,500 wealthy bourgeoisie entered the ranks of the nobility. Over the century as a whole, 6,500 new noble families were created. In addition, as we saw in Chapter 19, the aristocrats were also participating in capitalist activities on their landed estates, such as mining, metallurgy, and glassmaking, and even investing in foreign trade. Viewed in terms of economic function, many members of the bourgeoisie and nobility formed a single class. Finally, the new and critical ideas of the Enlightenment proved attractive to both aristocrats and bourgeoisie. Members of both groups shared a common world of liberal political thought. The old view that the French Revolution was the result of the conflict between two rising, rigid orders, the bourgeoisie and nobility, has been enlarged and revised. Both aristocratic and bourgeois elites, long accustomed to a new socioeconomic reality based on wealth and economic achievement, were increasingly frustrated by a monarchical system resting on privileges and on an old and rigid social order based on the concept of estates. The opposition of these elites to the old order led them ultimately to drastic action against the monarchical regime, although they soon split over the problem of how far to proceed in the elimination of traditional privileges. In a real sense, the Revolution had its origins in political grievances.

While the long-range causes of the French Revolution, then, can be found in part in the growing frustration over the inability of the French monarchy to deal with new social realities and problems, other factors were also present. The failure of the French monarchy was exacerbated by specific problems in the 1780s. Despite economic expansion for fifty years, the French economy experienced periodic crises. Bad harvests in 1787 and 1788 and the beginnings of a manufacturing depression resulted in food shortages, rising prices for food and other necessities, and unemployment in the cities. The number of poor, estimated by some at almost one-third of the population, reached crisis proportions on the eve of the Revolution. An English traveler noted the misery of the poor in the countryside: "All the country girls and women are without shoes or stockings; and the ploughmen at their work have neither sabots nor stockings to their feet. This is a poverty that strikes at the root of national prosperity."[6]

Increased criticism of existing privileges as well as social and political institutions also characterized the eighteenth century. Although the *philosophes* did not advocate revolution, their ideas were widely circulated among the literate bourgeois and noble elites of France. Historians have debated the importance of the ideas of the *philosophes* in precipitating the French Revolution, but there is no doubt that the public statements of revolutionary leaders were often reflections of those ideas.

The French Parlements often frustrated efforts at reform. Responsible for registering royal decrees, these thirteen law courts could block royal edicts by not registering them. Although Louis XIV had forced them into submission, the Parlements had gained new strength in the eighteenth century as they and their noble judges assumed the role of defenders of "liberty" against the arbitrary power of the monarchy. As noble defenders, however, they often pushed their own interests as well, especially by blocking new taxes. This last point reminds us that one of the fundamental problems facing the monarchy was financial.

The immediate cause of the French Revolution was the near collapse of government finances. French governmental expenditures continued to grow due to costly wars and royal extravagance. Since the government responded by borrowing, by 1788 the interest on the debt alone constituted half of the government's spending. The king's finance ministry wrestled with the problem but met with resistance. In 1786, Charles de Calonne, the controller-general of finance, proposed a complete revamping of the fiscal and administrative system of the state. To gain support, Calonne adjourned an Assembly of Notables early in 1787. This gathering of nobles, prelates, and magistrates refused to cooperate, and the government's attempt to go it alone brought further disaster. On the verge of a complete financial collapse, the government was finally forced to call a meeting of the

Estates-General, the French parliamentary body that had not met since 1614. By calling the Estates-General, the government was virtually admitting that the crown could not govern without the assistance of some representative assembly.

The Estates-General consisted of representatives from the three orders of French society. In the elections for the Estates-General, the government had ruled that the Third Estate should get double representation (it did, after all, constitute 97 percent of the population). Consequently, while both the first estate (the clergy) and the second (the nobility) had about 300 delegates each, the commoners had almost 600 representatives. Two-thirds of the latter were people with legal training while three-fourths were from towns with over 2,000 inhabitants, giving the Third Estate a particularly strong legal and urban representation. Of the 282 representatives of the nobility, about 90 were liberal minded, urban oriented, and interested in the enlightened ideas of the century; one-half of them were under forty years of age. The activists of the Third Estate and reform-minded individuals among the first and second estates had common ties in their youthfulness, urban background, and hostility to privilege. The *cahiers de doléances* or statements of grievances, which were drafted during the elections to the Estates-General, advocated a regular constitutional government that would abolish the fiscal privileges of the church and nobility as the major way to regenerate France.

The Estates-General opened at Versailles on May 5, 1789. It was troubled from the start with the problem of whether voting should be by order or by head (each delegate having one vote). The Parlement of Paris, consisting of nobles of the robe, had advocated voting by order according to the form used in 1614. Each order would vote separately; each would have veto power over the other two, thus guaranteeing aristocratic control over reforms. But opposition to the Parlement of Paris's proposal had arisen from a group calling themselves the patriots or "lovers of liberty." Although they claimed to be the nation, they consisted primarily of bourgeoisie and nobles. One group of patriots known as the Society of Thirty drew most of its members from the salons of Paris. They were mostly nobles. Some of them had been directly influenced by the American Revolution, and all had been affected by the ideas of the Enlightenment and favored reforms made in the light of reason and usefulness.

The failure of the government to lead at the opening of the Estates-General created an opportunity for the Third Estate to push its demands for voting by head.

Since it had double representation, with the assistance of liberal nobles and clerics, it could turn the three estates into a single-chamber legislature that would reform France in its own way. One representative, Abbé Sieyès, issued a pamphlet in which he asked, "What is the third estate? Everything. What has it been thus far in the political order? Nothing. What does it demand? To become something." Sieyès's sentiment, however, was not representative of the general feeling in 1789. Most delegates still desired to make changes within a framework of respect for the authority of the king; revival or reform did not mean the overthrow of traditional institutions. When the first estate declared in favor of voting by order, the Third Estate felt compelled to respond in a significant fashion. On June 17, 1789, the Third Estate voted to constitute itself a "National Assembly" and decided to draw up a constitution. This declaration of June 17 stands as the first step in the French Revolution since the Third Estate had no legal right to act as the National Assembly. This revolution, largely the work of the lawyers of the Third Estate, was soon in jeopardy, however, as the king sided with the first estate and threatened to dissolve the Estates-General. Louis XVI now prepared to use force. The revolution of the lawyers appeared doomed.

The intervention of the common people, however, in a series of urban and rural uprisings in July and August of 1789 saved the Third Estate from the king's attempted counterrevolution. From now on, the common people would be used by both revolutionary and counterrevolutionary politicians and mobilized to support their interests. The common people had their own interests as well and would use the name of the Third Estate to wage a war on the rich, claiming the existence of an aristocratic plot to destroy the Estates-General and retain its privileges. This war was not what the deputies of the Third Estate had planned.

The most famous of the urban risings was the fall of the Bastille (see the box on p. 677). The king's attempt to take defensive measures by increasing the number of troops to secure the arsenals in Paris and guard the roads to Versailles served not to intimidate but rather to inflame public opinion. Increased mob activity in Paris led Parisian leaders to form a Permanent Committee to keep order. Needing arms, they organized a popular force to capture the Invalides, a royal armory, and on July 14 attacked the Bastille, another royal armory. But the Bastille had also been a state prison, and though it now contained only seven prisoners, its fall quickly became a popular symbol of triumph over despotism. Paris was abandoned to the insurgents, and Louis XVI was soon

The Fall of the Bastille
▼ ▼ ▼

On July 14, 1789, Parisian crowds in search of weapons attacked and captured the royal armory known as the Bastille. It had also been a state prison, and its fall marked the triumph of "liberty" over despotism. This intervention of the Parisian populace saved the Third Estate from Louis XVI's attempted counterrevolution.

A Parisian Newspaper Account of the Fall of the Bastille

First, the people tried to enter this fortress by the Rue St.—Antoine, this fortress, which no one has ever penetrated against the wishes of this frightful despotism and where the monster still resided. The treacherous governor had put out a flag of peace. So a confident advance was made; a detachment of French Guards, with perhaps five to six thousand armed bourgeois, penetrated the Bastille's outer courtyards, but as soon as some six hundred persons had passed over the first drawbridge, the bridge was raised and artillery fire mowed down several French Guards and some soldiers; the cannon fired on the town, and the people took fright; a large number of individuals were killed or wounded; but then they rallied and took shelter from the fire; . . . meanwhile, they tried to locate some cannon; they attacked from the water's edge through the gardens of the arsenal, and from there made an orderly siege; they advanced from various directions, beneath a ceaseless round of fire. It was a terrible scene. . . . The fighting grew steadily more intense; the citizens had become hardened to the fire; from all directions they clambered onto the roofs or broke into the rooms; as soon as an enemy appeared among the turrets on the tower, he was fixed in the sights of a hundred guns and mown down in an instant; meanwhile cannon fire was hurriedly directed against the second drawbridge, which it pierced, breaking the chains; in vain did the cannon on the tower reply, for most people were sheltered from it; the fury was at its height; people bravely faced death and every danger; women, in their eagerness, helped us to the utmost; even the children, after the discharge of fire from the fortress, ran here and there picking up the bullets and shot; [and so the Bastille fell and the governor, De Launay, was captured]. . . . Serene and blessed liberty, for the first time, has at last been introduced into this abode of horrors, this frightful refuge of monstrous despotism and its crimes.

Meanwhile, they get ready to march; they leave amidst an enormous crowd; the applause, the outbursts of joy, the insults, the oaths hurled at the treacherous prisoners of war; everything is confused; cries of vengeance and of pleasure issue from every heart; the conquerors, glorious and covered in honour, carry their arms and the spoils of the conquered, the flags of victory, the militia mingling with the soldiers of the fatherland, the victory laurels offered them from every side, all this created a frightening and splendid spectacle. On arriving at the square, the people, anxious to avenge themselves, allowed neither De Launay nor the other officers to reach the place of trial; they seized them from the hands of their conquerors, and trampled them underfoot one after the other. De Launay was struck by a thousand blows, his head was cut off and hoisted on the end of a pike with blood streaming down all sides. . . . This glorious day must amaze our enemies, and finally usher in for us the triumph of justice and liberty. In the evening, there were celebrations.

---

informed that the royal troops were unreliable. Louis's acceptance of that reality signaled the collapse of royal authority; Louis XVI could no longer enforce his will. The king then confirmed the appointment of the marquis de Lafayette as commander of a newly created citizens' militia known as the National Guard. The fall of the Bastille had saved the National Assembly.

At the same time, independently of what was going on in Paris, popular revolutions broke out in numerous cities. In Nantes, crowds seized the chief citadels, after which Permanent Committees and National Guards were created to maintain order. This collapse of royal authority in the cities was paralleled by peasant revolutions in the countryside.

A growing resentment of the entire seigneurial system with its fees and obligations, greatly exacerbated by the economic and fiscal activities of the great estate holders—whether noble or bourgeois—in the difficult decade of the 1780s, created the conditions for a popular uprising. The fall of the Bastille and the king's apparent

▼ **Storming of the Bastille.** Fearing that the First and Second Estates would block their desire for reforms, members of the Third Estate voted to constitute themselves a "National Assembly" on June 17, 1789. Louis XVI planned to use force to dissolve the Estates-General, but a number of rural and urban uprisings by the common people prevented this action. The fall of the Bastille, pictured here in an anonymous painting, is perhaps the most famous of the urban risings. The Parisians had attacked the Bastille in an attempt to acquire arms.

capitulation to the demands of the Third Estate now led peasants to take matters into their own hands. From July 19 to August 3, peasant rebellions occurred in five major areas of France. Patterns varied. In some places, peasants simply forced their lay and ecclesiastical lords to renounce dues and tithes; elsewhere they burned charters listing their obligations. The peasants were not acting in blind fury; they knew what they were doing. Many also believed they had the support of the king for their actions. As a contemporary chronicler wrote: "For several weeks, news went from village to village. They announced that the Estates-General was going to abolish tithes, quitrents and dues, that the King agreed but that the peasants had to support the public authorities by going themselves to demand the destruction of titles."[7]

The agrarian revolts served as a backdrop to the Great Fear, a vast panic that spread like wildfire through France between July 20 and August 6. The fear of invasion by foreign troops, aided by a supposed aristocratic plot, encouraged the formation of more citizens' militias and permanent committees. The greatest impact of the agrarian revolts and Great Fear was on the National Assembly meeting in Versailles. We will now examine its attempt to reform France.

The Destruction of the Old Regime

One of the first acts of the National Assembly (sometimes called the Constituent Assembly) was to destroy the relics of feudalism or aristocratic privileges. To some deputies, this was necessary to calm the peasants and restore order in the countryside, although many urban bourgeoisie were willing to abolish feudalism as a matter of principle. On the "night of 4 August," 1789, the National Assembly in an astonishing session voted to abolish seigneurial rights as well as the fiscal privileges of nobles, clergy, towns, and provinces.

On August 26, the assembly provided the ideological foundation for its actions and an educational device for the nation by adopting the Declaration of the Rights of Man and the Citizen (see the box on p. 680). This charter of basic liberties reflected the ideas of the major philosophes of the French Enlightenment and also owed much to the American Declaration of Independence and American state constitutions. The declaration began with a ringing affirmation of "the natural and imprescriptible rights of man" to "liberty, property, security and resistance to oppression." It went on to affirm the

destruction of aristocratic privileges by proclaiming an end to exemptions from taxation, freedom and equal rights for all men, and access to public office based on talent. The monarchy was restricted, and all citizens were to have the right to take part in the legislative process. Freedom of speech and press were coupled with the outlawing of arbitrary arrests.

In the meantime, Louis XVI had remained inactive at Versailles. He did refuse, however, to promulgate the decrees on the abolition of feudalism and the Declaration of Rights. Early in October, a Parisian crowd, initiated by several thousand women but soon taken over and led by Lafayette's National Guard, marched to Versailles and forced the king to accept the constitutional decrees and to change his residence to Paris. It was neither the first nor the last occasion when Parisian crowds would affect national politics. The king was virtually a prisoner in Paris, and the National Assembly, now meet-

▼ **Session of August 4, 1789.** The National Constituent Assembly destroyed many of the aristocratic privileges that still existed in France. During its session of August 4, 1789, the Assembly voted to abolish not only the fiscal privileges of the

nobility, clergy, towns, and provinces, but seigneurial rights as well. As seen in this contemporary rendering of the event, the Third Estate applauded while members of the First and Second Estates offered to give up their privileges.

Declaration of the Rights of Man and the Citizen

▼ ▼ ▼

One of the important documents of the French Revolution, the Declaration of the Rights of Man and the Citizen, was adopted in August 1789 by the National Assembly. The declaration affirmed that "men are born and remain free and equal in rights," that governments must protect these natural rights, and that political power is derived from the people.

Declaration of the Rights of Man and the Citizen

The representatives of the French people, organized as a national assembly, considering that ignorance, neglect, and scorn of the rights of man are the sole causes of public misfortunes and of corruption of governments, have resolved to display in a solemn declaration the natural, inalienable, and sacred rights of man, so that this declaration, constantly in the presence of all members of society, will continually remind them of their rights and their duties. . . . Consequently, the National Assembly recognizes and declares, in the presence and under the auspices of the Supreme Being, the following rights of man and citizen:

1. Men are born and remain free and equal in rights; social distinctions can be established only for the common benefit.

2. The aim of every political association is the conservation of the natural and imprescriptible rights of man; these rights are liberty, property, security, and resistance to oppression.

3. The source of all sovereignty is located in essence in the nation; no body, no individual can exercise authority which does not emanate from it expressly.

4. Liberty consists in being able to do anything that does not harm another person. . . .

6. The law is the expression of the general will; all citizens have the right to concur personally or through their representatives in its formation; it must be the same for all, whether it protects or punishes. All citizens being equal in its eyes are equally admissible to all honors, positions, and public employments, according to their capabilities and without other distinctions than those of their virtues and talents.

7. No man can be accused, arrested, or detained except in cases determined by the law, and according to the forms which it has prescribed. . . .

10. No one may be disturbed because of his opinions, even religious, provided that their public demonstration does not disturb the public order established by law.

11. The free communication of thoughts and opinions is one of the most precious rights of man: every citizen can therefore freely speak, write, and print. . . .

12. The guaranteeing of the rights of man and citizen necessitates a public force; this force is therefore instituted for the advantage of all, and not for the private use of those to whom it is entrusted. . . .

14. Citizens have the right to determine for themselves or through their representatives the need for taxation of the public, to consent to it freely, to investigate its use, and to determine its rate, basis, collection, and duration.

15. Society has the right to demand an accounting of his administration from every public agent.

16. Any society in which guarantees of rights are not assured nor the separation of powers determined has no constitution.

17. Property being an inviolable and sacred right, no one may be deprived of it unless public necessity, legally determined, clearly requires such action, and then only on condition of a just and prior indemnity.

The Declaration of the Rights of Woman and the Female Citizen
▼ ▼ ▼

Olympe de Gouges was a butcher's daughter who wrote plays and pamphlets. She argued that the Declaration of the Rights of Man and the Citizen did not apply to women and composed her own Declaration of the Rights of Woman. She became the principal spokeswoman for the cause of political rights for women in the early stages of the French Revolution.

The Declaration of the Rights of Woman and the Female Citizen (1791)

Mothers, daughters, sisters and representatives of the nation demand to be constituted into a national assembly. Believing that ignorance, omission, or scorn for the rights of woman are the only causes of public misfortunes and of the corruption of governments, the women have resolved to set forth in a solemn declaration the natural, inalienable, and sacred rights of woman in order that this declaration, constantly exposed before all the members of the society, will ceaselessly remind them of their rights and duties. . . .

Consequently, the sex that is as superior in beauty as it is in courage during the sufferings of maternity recognizes and declares in the presence and under the auspices of the Supreme Being, the following Rights of Woman and of Female Citizens.

1. Woman is born free and lives equal to man in her rights. Social distinctions can be based only on the common utility.

2. The purpose of any political association is the conservation of the natural and imprescriptible rights of woman and man; these rights are liberty, property, security, and especially resistance to oppression.

3. The principle of all sovereignty rests essentially with the nation, which is nothing but the union of woman and man; no body and no individual can exercise any authority which does not come expressly from it [the nation].

4. Liberty and justice consist of restoring all that belongs to others; thus, the only limits on the exercise of the natural rights of woman are perpetual male tyranny; these limits are to be reformed by the laws of nature and reason.

6. The law must be the expression of the general will; all female and male citizens must contribute either personally or through their representatives to its formation; it must be the same for all: male and female citizens, being equal in the eyes of the law, must be equally admitted to all honors, positions, and public employment according to their capacity and without other distinctions besides those of their virtues and talents.

7. No woman is an exception; she is accused, arrested, and detained in cases determined by law. Women, like men, obey this rigorous law.

10. No one is to be disquieted for his very basic opinions; woman has the right to mount the scaffold; she must equally have the right to mount the rostrum, provided that her demonstrations do not disturb the legally established public order.

11. The free communication of thoughts and opinions is one of the most precious rights of woman, since that liberty assured the recognition of children by their fathers. . . .

12. The guarantee of the rights of woman and the female citizen implies a major benefit; this guarantee must be instituted for the advantage of all, and not for the particular benefit of those to whom it is entrusted.

14. Female and male citizens have the right to verify, either by themselves or through their representatives, the necessity of the public contribution. This can only apply to women if they are granted an equal share, not only of wealth, but also of public administration, and in the determination of the proportion, the base, the collection, and the duration of the tax.

15. The collectivity of women, joined for tax purposes to the aggregate of men, has the right to demand an accounting of his administration from any public agent.

16. No society has a constitution without the guarantee of rights and the separation of powers; the constitution is null if the majority of individuals comprising the nation have not cooperated in drafting it.

17. Property belongs to both sexes whether united or separate; for each it is an inviolable and sacred right; no one can be deprived of it, since it is the true patrimony of nature, unless the legally determined public need obviously dictates it, and then only with a just and prior indemnity.

▼ **Women Return the King to Paris.** Louis XVI refused to accept either the decrees abolishing feudalism or the Declaration of the Rights of Man and the Citizen. A Parisian crowd, formed under the impetus of several thousand women led by the Marquis de Lafayette's National Guard, marched to Versailles and coerced Louis XVI into accepting the new constitutional decrees and changing his residence to Paris. For the first time, a Parisian crowd had affected national politics. Pictured here is the crowd of women returning in triumph to Paris.

ing in Paris, would also feel the influence of Parisian insurrectionary politics.

Because the Catholic church was viewed as an important pillar of the old order, reforms soon overtook it. Because of the need for money, most of the lands of the church were confiscated, and assignats, a form of paper money, were issued based on the collateral of the newly nationalized church property. The church was also secularized. In July 1790, a new Civil Constitution of the Clergy was put into effect. Both bishops and priests were to be elected by the people and paid by the state. All clergy were also required to swear an oath of allegiance to the Civil Constitution. Since the pope forbade it, only 54 percent of the French parish clergy took the oath while the majority of bishops refused. This was an important development because the Catholic church, still an important institution in the life of the French people, now became an enemy of the Revolution. This has often been viewed as a serious tactical blunder on the part of the National Assembly for it gave counterrevolution a popular base from which to operate.

By 1791, the National Assembly had finally completed a new constitution that established a limited, constitutional monarchy. There was still a monarch (now called king of the French), but he enjoyed few

powers not subject to review by the new Legislative Assembly. The Legislative Assembly, in which sovereign power was vested, was to sit for two years and consist of 745 representatives chosen by an indirect system of election that preserved power in the hands of the more affluent members of society. A differentiation was made between active and passive citizens. While all had the same civil rights, only active citizens (those men over the age of twenty-five paying in taxes the equivalent of three days' unskilled labor) could vote. There were probably 4.3 million active citizens in 1790. These citizens did not elect the members of the Legislative Assembly directly, but voted for electors (those men paying taxes equal in value to ten days' labor). This relatively small group of 50,000 electors chose the deputies. To qualify as a deputy, one had to pay at least a "silver mark" in taxes, an amount equivalent to fifty-four days' labor.

The National Assembly also undertook an administrative restructuring of France. It abolished all the old local and provincial divisions and divided France into eighty-three departments, roughly equal in size and population. In turn, departments were divided into districts and communes, all supervised by elected councils and officials who oversaw financial, administrative, judicial, and ecclesiastical institutions within their domains. Although both bourgeoisie and aristocrats were eligible for offices based on property qualifications, few nobles were elected, leaving local and departmental governments in the hands of the bourgeoisie, especially lawyers of various types.

By 1791, France had moved into a revolutionary reordering of the old regime that had been achieved by a revolutionary consensus that was largely the work of the wealthier bourgeoisie. This consensus, however, faced growing opposition by mid-1791 from clerics against the Civil Constitution of the Clergy, lower classes hurt by the rise in the cost of living resulting from the inflation of the assignats, peasants who remained opposed to dues that had still not been abandoned, and political clubs offering more radical solutions to France's problems. Most famous were the Jacobins. The Jacobins first emerged as a gathering of more radical deputies at the beginning of the Revolution, especially during the events of the night of 4 August. After October 1789, they occupied the former Jacobin convent in Paris. Jacobin clubs also formed in the provinces where they served primarily as discussion groups. Eventually, they joined together in an extensive correspondence network and, by spring 1790, were seeking affiliation with the Parisian club. One year later, there were 900 Jacobin clubs in France associated with its Parisian center. Members were usually the elite of their local societies, but they also included artisans and tradesmen.

In addition, by mid-1791, the government was still facing severe financial difficulties due to massive tax evasion. Despite all of their problems, however, the bourgeois politicians in charge remained relatively unified on the basis of their trust in the king. But Louis XVI disastrously undercut them. Quite upset with the whole turn of revolutionary events, he sought to flee France in June 1791 and almost succeeded before being recognized, captured, and brought back to Paris. While radicals called for the king to be deposed, the members of the National Assembly, fearful of the popular forces in Paris calling for a republic, chose to ignore the king's flight and pretended that he had been kidnapped. In this unsettled situation, with a discredited and seemingly disloyal monarch, the new Legislative Assembly held its first session in October 1791.

The composition of the Legislative Assembly tended to be quite different from that of the National Assembly. The clerics and nobles were largely gone. Most of the representatives were men of property; many were law-

yers. Although lacking national reputations, most had gained experience in the new revolutionary politics and prominence in their local areas through the National Guard, the Jacobin clubs, and the many elective offices spawned by the administrative reordering of France. The king made what seemed to be a genuine effort to work with the new Legislative Assembly, but France's relations with the rest of Europe soon led to Louis's downfall.

Over a period of time, some European countries had become concerned about the French example and feared that revolution would spread to their countries. On August 27, 1791, Emperor Leopold of Austria and King Frederick William II of Prussia issued the Declaration of Pillnitz, which invited other European monarchs to take "the most effectual means . . . to put the king of France in a state to strengthen, in the most perfect liberty, the bases of a monarchical government equally becoming to the rights of sovereigns and to the wellbeing of the French Nation."[8] But European monarchs were too suspicious of each other to undertake such a plan, and in any case French enthusiasm for war led the Legislative

▼ **Map 20.2** Reorganization of France by the National Assembly. (*Left:* French Provinces and Regions before 1789; *Right:* French Departments after 1789)

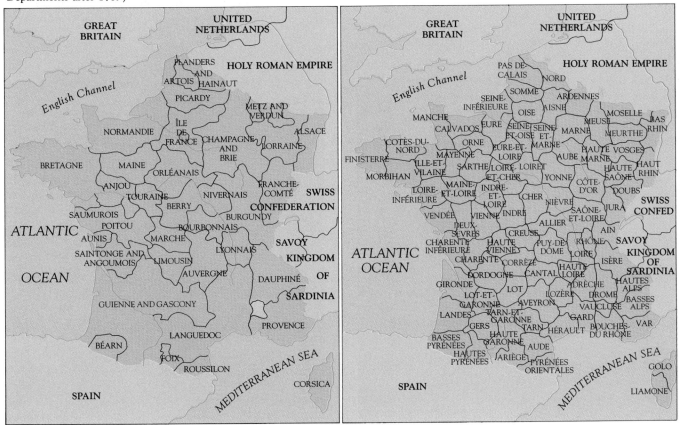

Assembly to declare war on Austria on April 20, 1792. But why take such a step in view of its obvious dangers? Practically everyone in France wanted war. Reactionaries hoped that a preoccupation with war would cool off the Revolution; French defeat, which seemed likely in view of the army's disintegration, might even lead to the restoration of the old regime. Leftists hoped that war would consolidate the Revolution at home and spread it to all of Europe.

The French fared badly in the initial fighting, and loud recriminations were soon heard in Paris. A frantic search for scapegoats began; as one observer noted, "Everywhere you hear the cry that the king is betraying us, the generals are betraying us, that nobody is to be trusted; . . . that Paris will be taken in six weeks by the Austrians . . . we are on a volcano ready to spout flames."[9] Defeats in war coupled with economic shortages in the spring reinvigorated popular groups that had been dormant since the previous summer and led to renewed political demonstrations, especially against the king. Radical Parisian political groups, declaring themselves an insurrectionary commune, organized a mob attack on the royal palace and Legislative Assembly in August 1792, took the king captive, and forced the Legislative Assembly to suspend the monarchy and call for a National Convention, chosen on the basis of universal male suffrage, to decide on the future form of government. The French Revolution was about to enter a more radical stage as power passed from the assembly to the new Paris Commune composed of many who proudly called themselves the sansculottes, ordinary patriots without fine clothes. While it has become customary to equate the more radical sansculottes with working people or the poor, many were merchants and better-off artisans who were often the elite of their neighborhoods and trades.

▼ **Sansculottes.** The sansculottes identified themselves as ordinary patriots without fine clothes. Composed of workers, merchants, and artisans, and often more radical than the members of the Legislative Assembly, sansculottes were members of the Paris Commune that dominated the political scene before the National Convention of 1792.

The Radical Revolution

Before the National Convention met, the Paris Commune dominated the political scene. Led by the newly appointed minister of justice, Georges Danton, the sansculottes sought revenge on those who had aided the king and resisted the popular will. Thousands of presumed traitors were arrested and then massacred as ordinary Parisian tradesmen and artisans solved the problem of overcrowded prisons by mass executions of their inmates. In September 1792, the newly elected National Convention began its sessions. Although it was called to draft a new constitution, it also acted as the sovereign ruling body of France.

Socially the composition of the National Convention was similar to its predecessors. Dominated by lawyers, professionals, and property owners, it also possessed for the first time a handful of artisans. Two-thirds of the deputies were under forty-five, and almost all had had political experience as a result of the Revolution. Almost all were also intensely distrustful of the king and his activities. It was therefore no surprise that the convention's first major step on September 21 was to abolish the monarchy and establish a republic. But that was about as far as members of the convention could agree, and the National Convention soon split into factions over the fate of the king. The two most important were the Girondins and the Mountain. Both were members of the Jacobin club.

Representing primarily the provinces, the Girondins came to fear the radical mobs in Paris and were disposed to keep the king alive as a hedge against future eventualities. The Mountain, on the other hand, represented the interests of the city of Paris and owed much of its strength to the radical and popular elements in the city, although the members of the Mountain themselves were middle class. The Mountain won out at the beginning of 1793 when they passed a decree condemning Louis XVI to death, although by a very narrow margin. On January 21, 1793, the king was executed and the destruction of the old regime was complete. There could be no turning back. But the execution of the king produced new challenges by creating new enemies for the Revolution both at home and abroad while strengthening those who were already its enemies.

Factional disputes between Girondins and the Mountain were only one part of France's domestic crisis in 1792 and 1793. Within Paris the local government known as the Commune, which possessed a number of leaders from the working classes, favored radical change and put constant pressure on the National Convention,

▼ **Execution of the King.** In 1792, after economic shortages and defeats in war, Louis XVI was taken captive and a National Convention was called to draft a new constitution. The convention abolished the monarchy and established a republic. The National Convention soon split, however, over what to do about the king. The Girondins favored keeping him alive, while the Mountain desired his death. In 1793, the Mountain won out, and on January 21 of that year, Louis XVI was executed.

pushing it to ever more radical positions. As one man warned his fellow deputies, "Never forget that you were sent here by the sansculottes."[10] At the end of May and the beginning of June 1793, the Commune organized a demonstration, invaded the National Convention, and forced the arrest of the Girondins, thus leaving the Mountain in control of the convention. The National Convention itself still did not rule all France. The authority of the convention was repudiated in western France, particularly in the department of the Vendée, by peasants who revolted against the new military draft (see The Levy-in-Mass later in the chapter). The Vendéan rebellion soon escalated into a full-blown counterrevolutionary appeal: "Long live the king and our good priests. We want our king, our priests and the old regime." Some of France's major provincial cities, including Lyons and Marseilles, also began to break away from central authority. Arguing as Marseilles did that "it is time for the anarchy of a few men of blood to stop,"[11] these cities favored a decentralized republic to free themselves of the ascendancy of Paris. In no way did they favor breaking up the "indivisible Republic."

Domestic turmoil was paralleled by a foreign crisis. By the beginning of 1793, after the king had been executed, most of Europe—an informal coalition of Austria, Prussia, Spain, Portugal, Britain, the Dutch Republic, and even Russia—was pitted against France. Carried away by initial successes and their own rhetoric, the French welcomed the struggle. Danton exclaimed to the convention: "They threaten you with kings! You have thrown down your gauntlet to them, and this gauntlet is a king's head, the signal of their coming death."[12] Grossly overextended, the French armies began to experience reverses, and by late spring some members of the anti-French coalition were poised for an invasion of France. If successful, both the Revolution and the revolutionaries would be destroyed and the old regime reestablished. The Revolution had reached a decisive moment.

To meet these crises, the program of the National Convention became one of curbing anarchy and counterrevolution at home while attempting to win the war by a great national mobilization. To administer the government, the convention gave broad powers to an executive committee known as the Committee of Public Safety, which was dominated initially by Danton. Maximilien Robespierre eventually became one of its most important members. For a twelve-month period, from 1793 to 1794, virtually the same twelve members were reelected and gave the country the leadership it needed to weather the domestic and foreign crises of 1793.

THE LEVY-IN-MASS   To meet the foreign crisis and save the republic from its foreign enemies, the Committee of Public Safety decreed a universal mobilization of the nation on August 23, 1793:

> Young men will fight, young men are called to conquer. Married men will forge arms, transport military baggage and guns and will prepare food supplies. Women, who at long last are to take their rightful place in the revolution and follow their true destiny, will forget their futile tasks: their delicate hands will work at making clothes for soldiers; they will make tents and they will extend their tender care to shelters where the defenders of the Patrie will receive the help that their wounds require. Children will make lint of old cloth. It is for them that we are fighting: children, those beings destined to gather all the fruits of the revolution, will raise their pure hands toward the skies. And old men, performing their missions again, as of yore, will be guided to the public squares of the cities where they will kindle the courage of young warriors and preach the doctrines of hate for kings and the unity of the Republic.[13]

In less than a year, the French revolutionary government had raised an army of 650,000; by September 1794, it numbered 1,169,000. The Republic's army was the largest ever seen in European history. It now pushed the allies back across the Rhine and even conquered the Austrian Netherlands. By May 1795, the anti-French coalition of 1793 was breaking up.

Historians have focused on the importance of the French revolutionary army as an important step in the creation of modern nationalism. Previously, wars had been fought between governments or ruling dynasties by relatively small armies of professional soldiers. Although innocent civilians had suffered in those struggles, the new French army was the creation of a "people's" government; its wars were now "people's" wars. The entire nation was to be involved in the war. But when dynastic wars became people's wars, warfare increased in ferocity and lack of restraint. Carnage was appalling at times. The wars of the French revolutionary era opened the door to the total war of the modern world.

THE COMMITTEE OF PUBLIC SAFETY AND THE REIGN OF TERROR   To meet the domestic crisis, the National Convention and the Committee of Public Safety established the "Reign of Terror." Revolutionary courts were instituted to protect the revolutionary Republic from its internal enemies, those "who either by their conduct, their contacts, their words or their writings, showed themselves to be supporters of tyranny or enemies of liberty," or those "who have not constantly manifested their attachment to the revolution."[14] Victims of the Terror ranged from royalists, such as Queen Marie Antoinette, to former revolutionary Girondins, and even to thousands of peasants. Many victims were figures who had opposed the radical activities of the sansculottes. In the course of nine months, 16,000 people were officially killed under the blade of the guillotine, the latter a revolutionary device for the quick and efficient separation of heads from bodies. But the true number of the Terror's victims was probably closer to 30,000. The bulk of the Terror's executions took place in the Vendée and in cities such as Lyons and Marseilles, places that had been in open rebellion against the authority of the National Convention.

Military force in the form of Revolutionary Armies was used to bring recalcitrant cities and districts back under the control of the National Convention. Marseilles fell to a Revolutionary Army in August. Starving Lyons surrendered early in October after two months of bombardment and resistance. Since Lyons was France's second city after Paris and had defied the National Convention during a time when the Republic was in peril, the Committee of Public Safety decided to make an example of it. By April 1794, 1,880 citizens of

Lyons had been executed. When guillotining proved too slow, cannon fire and grape shot were used to blow condemned men into open graves. A German observed:

> . . . whole ranges of houses, always the most handsome, burnt. The churches, convents, and all the dwellings of the former patricians were in ruins. When I came to the guillotine, the blood of those who had been executed a few hours beforehand was still running in the street . . . I said to a group of sansculottes that it would be decent to clear away all this human blood. Why should it be cleared? one of them said to me. It's the blood of aristocrats and rebels. The dogs should lick it up.[15]

In the Vendée, Revolutionary Armies were also brutal in defeating the rebel armies. After destroying one army on December 12, the commander of the Revolutionary Army ordered that no quarter be given: "The road to Laval is strewn with corpses. Women, priests, monks, children, all have been put to death. I have spared nobody." The Terror in the Vendée was the most destructive. Forty-two percent of the death sentences during the Terror were passed in territories affected by the Vendée

rebellion. Perhaps the most notorious act of violence occurred in Nantes where victims were executed by sinking them in barges in the Loire River.

Contrary to popular opinion, the Terror demonstrated no class prejudice. Estimates are that the nobles constituted 8 percent of its victims, the middle classes, 25, the clergy, 6, and the peasant and laboring classes, 60. To the Committee of Public Safety, this bloodletting was only a temporary expedient. Once the war and domestic emergency were over, then would follow "the republic of virtue" in which the Declaration of the Rights of Man and of the Citizen would be fully established. Although theoretically a republic, the French government during the Terror was led by a group of twelve men who ordered the execution of people as enemies of the Republic. But how did they justify this? Saint-Just, one of the younger members of the Committee of Public Safety explained their rationalization in a speech to the convention: "Since the French people has manifested its will, everything opposed to it is outside the sovereign. Whatever is outside the sovereign is an enemy."[16] Clearly, Saint-Just was referring to Rousseau's concept of the general will,

▼ **Map 20.3** French Conquests During the Revolutionary Wars.

Robespierre and Revolutionary Government

▼ ▼ ▼

In its time of troubles, the National Convention, under the direction of the Committee of Public Safety, instituted a Reign of Terror to preserve the Revolution from its internal enemies. In this selection, Maximilien Robespierre, one of the committee's leading members, tries to justify the violence to which these believers in republican liberty resorted.

Robespierre, Speech on Revolutionary Government

The theory of revolutionary government is as new as the Revolution that created it. It is as pointless to seek its origins in the books of the political theorists, who failed to foresee this revolution, as in the laws of the tyrants, who are happy enough to abuse their exercise of authority without seeking out its legal justification. And so this phrase is for the aristocracy a mere subject of terror or a term of slander, for tyrants an outrage and for many an enigma. It behooves us to explain it to all in order that we may rally good citizens, at least, in support of the principles governing the public interest.

It is the function of government to guide the moral and physical energies of the nation toward the purposes for which it was established.

The object of constitutional government is to preserve the Republic; the object of revolutionary government is to establish it.

Revolution is the war waged by liberty against its enemies; a constitution is that which crowns the edifice of freedom once victory has been won and the nation is at peace.

The revolutionary government has to summon extraordinary activity to its aid precisely because it is at war. It is subjected to less binding and less uniform regulations, because the circumstances in which it finds itself are tempestuous and shifting above all because it is compelled to deploy, swiftly and incessantly, new resources to meet new and pressing dangers.

The principal concern of constitutional government is civil liberty; that of revolutionary government, public liberty. Under a constitutional government little more is required than to protect the individual against abuses by the state, whereas revolutionary government is obliged to defend the state itself against the factions that assail it from every quarter.

To good citizens revolutionary government owes the full protection of the state; to the enemies of the people it owes only death.

---

but it is equally apparent that these twelve men, in the name of the Republic, had taken to themselves the right to ascertain the sovereign will of the French people (see the box above) and to kill their enemies as "outside the sovereign."

Along with the Terror, the Committee of Public Safety took other steps to control France. By spring 1793, they were sending "representatives on mission" as agents of the central government to all departments to explain the war emergency measures and to implement the laws dealing with the wartime emergency.

The committee also attempted to provide some economic controls, especially since members of the more radical working class were advocating them. They established a system of requisitions for food supplies to the cities enforced by the forays of Revolutionary Armies into the countryside. The Law of the General Maximum established price controls on goods declared of first necessity ranging from food and drink to fuel and clothing. The controls failed to work very well since the government lacked the machinery to enforce them.

The National Convention also pursued a policy of dechristianization. The word "saint" was removed from street names, churches were pillaged and closed by Revolutionary Armies, and priests were encouraged to marry. In Paris, the cathedral of Notre Dame was designated a Temple of Reason (see the box on p. 689); in November 1793, a public ceremony dedicated to the worship of reason was held in the former cathedral in which patriotic maidens adorned in white dresses paraded before a temple of reason where the high altar once stood. At the end of the ceremony, a female figure personifying Liberty rose out of the temple. As Robespierre came to realize, dechristianization backfired because

Dechristianization

▼ ▼ ▼

The phenomenon of dechristianization produced some unusual spectacles during the radical stage of the French Revolution. This selection from the minutes of the National Convention describes how the cathedral of Notre Dame was put to new use as a Temple of Reason.

The Temple of Reason

A member puts in the form of a motion the demand of the citizens of Paris that the metropolitan cathedral [Notre Dame] be henceforth the Temple of Reason.

A member requests that the goddess of Reason place herself at the side of the president.

The attorney of the Commune conducts her to the desk. The president and the secretaries give her the fraternal kiss in the midst of applause.

She sits at the side of the president.

A member demands that the National Convention march in a body, in the midst of the People, to the Temple of Reason, to sing the hymn of Liberty there.

This proposal is passed.

The Convention marches with the People to the Temple of Reason in the midst of general enthusiasm and joyful acclamations.

Having entered the Temple of Reason, they sing the following hymn:

Descend, O Liberty, daughter of Nature:
The People have recaptured their immortal power;
Over the pompous remains of age-old imposture
Their hands raise thine altar.
Come, vanquisher of kings, Europe gazes upon you;
Come, vanquish the false gods.
Thou, holy Liberty, come dwell in this temple;
Be the goddess of the French.
Thy countenance rejoices the most savage mountain,
Amid the rocks harvests grow:
Embellished by thy hands, the harshest coast,
Embedded in ice, smiles.
Thou doublest pleasures, virtues, genius;
Under thy holy standards, man is always victorious;
Before knowing thee he does not know life;
He is created by thy glance.
All kings make war on the sovereign People;
Let them henceforth fall at thy feet, O goddess;
Soon on the coffins of the world's tyrants
The world's peoples will swear peace.
Warrior liberators, powerful, brave race,
Armed with a human sword, sanctify terror;
Brought down by your blows, may the last slave
Follow the last king to the grave.

France was still overwhelmingly Catholic. Dechristianization, in fact, created more enemies than friends.

By the Law of 14 Frimaire (passed on December 4, 1793—see the next section for the new calendar), the Committee of Public Safety sought to centralize the administration of France more effectively and to exercise greater control in order to check the excesses of the Reign of Terror. The activities of both the representatives on mission and the Revolutionary Armies were scrutinized more carefully, and the campaign against Christianity was also dampened. Finally, in 1794, the Committee of Public Safety turned against its radical Parisian supporters, executed the leaders of the revolutionary Paris Commune, and turned it into a docile tool. This might have been a good idea for the sake of order, but in suppressing the people who had been its chief supporters, the National Convention alienated an important group. At the same time, the French had been successful against their foreign foes. The military successes meant that there was less need now for the Terror. But the Terror continued since Robespierre, who had become a figure of power and authority, became obsessed with purifying the body politic of all the corrupt. Only then could the Republic of Virtue follow. Many deputies in the National Convention were fearful, however, that they were not safe while Robespierre was free to act. An anti-Robespierre coalition in the National Convention, eager now to destroy Robespierre before he destroyed them, gathered enough votes to condemn him. Robespierre was guillotined on July 28, 1794, beginning a reaction that brought an end to this radical stage of the French Revolution.

The National Convention and its Committee of Public Safety had accomplished a great deal. By creating a

▼ **Robespierre.** While the Committee of Public Safety was originally dominated by Georges Danton, Maximilien Robespierre eventually came to exercise much control over the body. Robespierre and the Committee worked to centralize the administration of France and curb the excesses of the Reign of Terror. However, since Robespierre became obsessed with the idea of purifying the body politic and established a Republic of Virtue, he continued the use of the Terror. Fear of Robespierre led many in the National Convention to condemn him, and on July 28, 1794, Robespierre was executed.

nation-in-arms, they preserved the French Revolution and prevented it from being destroyed by its foreign enemies, who, if they had been successful, would have reestablished the old monarchical order. Domestically, the Revolution had also been saved from the forces of counterrevolution. The committee's tactics, however, provided an example for the use of violence in domestic politics that has continued to bedevil the Western world until this day.

THE REORDERING OF DAILY LIVES: THE REVOLUTIONARY CALENDAR There was no more visible symbol of the French Revolution's attempt to radically reorder the structure of daily life than its adoption of a new repub-

lican calendar on October 5, 1793. In part, this was simply another manifestation of the dechristianization that became popular with some radical leaders in 1793. Years would no longer be numbered from the birth of Christ but from September 22, 1792, the day the French Republic was proclaimed. Thus, at the time the calendar was adopted, the French were already living in year two. The calendar contained twelve months; each month consisted of three ten-day weeks (*décades*) with the tenth day of each week a rest-day (*décadi*). This eliminated Sundays and Sunday worship services and served to end the ordering of French lives by a Christian calendar that emphasized Sundays, saints' days, and church holidays and festivals. The latter were to be replaced by revolutionary festivals. Especially important were the five days (six in leap years) left over in the calendar at the end of the year. These days were to form a half-week of festivals to celebrate the revolutionary virtues—Virtue, Intelligence, Labor, Opinion, and Rewards. The sixth extra day in a leap year would be a special festival day when Frenchmen would "come from all parts of the Republic to celebrate liberty and equality, to cement by their embraces the national fraternity." Of course, ending church holidays also reduced the number of nonworking holidays from fifty-six to thirty-two, a goal long recommended by eighteenth-century economic theorists.

The anti-Christian purpose of the calendar was reinforced in the naming of the months and days of the year. Fabre d'Eglantine, secretary of the National Convention's Committee on Public Instruction, was assigned the task of preparing the new calendar. He made clear the anti-Christian principles that he followed in naming the months and days:

> The priests had assigned to each day of the year the commemoration of some pretended saint. This list of names had no method, and no usefulness; it was a catalogue of lies, dupery, and charlatanism. We have come to the conclusion that, after expelling this crowd of saints from its calendar, the nation ought to put in their places all those things which constitute its real wealth—the worthy objects, not of its cult, but of its culture: the useful products of the ground, the utensils we use in its cultivation, and the domesticated animals, which are doubtless much more precious to the eye of reason than beatified skeletons disinterred from Roman catacombs.[17]

Accordingly, the months were given names that were supposed to evoke the seasons, the temperature, or the state of the vegetation: Vendémiaire (harvest—the first month of thirty days beginning September 22), Brumaire (mist), Frimaire (frost), Nivôse (snow), Pluviôse (rain), Ventôse (wind), Germinal (seeding), Floréal (flowering), Prairial (meadows), Messidor (wheat harvest), Thermidor (heat), and Fructidor (ripening). Names were also devised for each day of the year. The tenth day of each *décade* was named after an agricultural implement; each fifth day after a domestic animal; the rest received names of herbs, flowers, vegetables, minerals, and other natural phenomena. Hence, a typical week would consist of Snowday, Iceday, Honeyday, Waxday, Dogday, Strawday, Petroleumday, Coalday, Resinday, and Flailday. Since France was still largely an agricultural society, Fabre reasoned that his calendar would teach rural economy to French children.

The new calendar faced intense popular opposition, and the revolutionary government relied primarily on coercion to win its acceptance. Property leases were to be dated only by using the new "calendar of liberty." Journalists were commanded to use republican dates in their newspaper articles. But the *décadi* failed to dethrone Sunday as a day of rest, despite penalties for nonobservance and the government's attempt to make it more attractive by holding communal celebrations. One government official reported:

> Sundays and Catholic holidays, even if there are ten in a row, have for some time been celebrated with as much pomp and splendor as before. The same cannot be said of *décadi*, which is observed by only a small handful of citizens. The first to disobey the law are the wives of public officials, who dress up on the holidays of the old calendar and abstain from work more religiously than anyone else.[18]

The government could hardly expect peasants to follow the new calendar when government officials were ignoring it. Napoleon later perceived that the revolutionary calendar was politically unpopular, and he simply abandoned it on January 1, 1806.

In addition to its anti-Christian function, the revolutionary calendar had also served to commemorate the Revolution as a new historical beginning, a radical discontinuity in time. Revolutionary upheavals often project millenarian expectations, the hope that a new age is dawning. The revolutionary dream of a new order presupposed the creation of a new human being freed from the old order and its symbols, a new citizen surrounded by a framework of new habits. Restructuring time itself offered the opportunity to forge new habits and create a lasting new order. The abandonment of the revolutionary calendar in 1806 by Napoleon signaled the abandonment of many of the revolutionary ideals. It would take another eight years and a series of devastating wars before the French people could accept that their brave new world of the Revolution was merely a chimera.

The Role of Women in the French Revolution

There had long been a tradition of laboring women involved in violent mass protests. Women had participated in peasant revolts for centuries and were prominent in the most common form of "crowd action" in the eighteenth century, the food riots, in which people attempted to keep bread prices at a fair level. Women also participated in the first mass protests against the introduction of machines in the late eighteenth century.

From its beginning stages, the French Revolution witnessed female participation in the crowd riots and demonstrations that played such an important role in determining the course of events. While present in the storming of the Bastille on July 14, 1789, women were even more prominent in the "October Days" of the same year. On October 5, after marching to the Hôtel de Ville, the city hall, to demand bread, crowds of Parisian women numbering in the thousands and described by one eyewitness as "detachments of women coming up from every direction, armed with broomsticks, lances, pitchforks, swords, pistols and muskets," set off for Versailles to confront the king and the National Assembly. After meeting with a delegation of these women, Louis XVI promised them provisions for Paris, thinking that this would end the protest. But the women's action had forced the Parisian National Guard under Lafayette to follow their lead and march to Versailles. The crowd now insisted that the royal family return to Paris. On October 6, the king complied. As a goodwill gesture, he brought along wagonloads of flour from the palace stores, escorted by women armed with pikes singing, "We are bringing back the baker, the baker's wife, and the baker's boy" (the king, queen, and their son).

From the "October Days" through 1795, women participated in a variety of activities on behalf of the Revolution. They demonstrated for bread and price controls, issued a "Declaration of the Rights of Woman and the Female Citizen" (see the box on p. 681), joined more violent groups that seized food, petitioned for the right to carry arms ("We are citizens, and we cannot be indifferent to the fate of the fatherland"), and, as spectators at sessions of revolutionary clubs and the National Convention, made the members and deputies aware of their demands. When on Sunday, February 25, 1793, a group of women appealed formally to the National Convention for lower bread prices, the convention reacted by adjourning until Tuesday. The women responded bitterly by accosting the deputies: "We are adjourned until Tuesday; but as for us, we adjourn ourselves until Monday. When our children ask us for milk, we don't adjourn them until the day after tomorrow."[19] In 1793, two women—an actress and a chocolate manufacturer—founded the Society for Revolutionary Republican Women. Composed largely of working-class women, this Parisian group viewed themselves as a "family of sisters" and vowed "to rush to the defense of the Fatherland."

Despite the importance of women to the revolutionary cause, male revolutionaries reacted disdainfully to female participation in political activity. In the radical phase of the Revolution, the Paris Commune outlawed women's clubs and forbade women to be present at its meetings. One of its members explained why:

> It is horrible, it is contrary to all laws of nature for a woman to want to make herself a man. The Council must recall that some time ago these denatured women, these viragos, wandered through the markets with the red cap to sully that badge of liberty and wanted to force all women to take off the modest headdress that is appropriate for them [the bonnet]. . . . Is it the place of women to propose motions? Is it the place of women to place themselves at the head of our armies?[20]

Most men—whether radical or conservative—agreed that women's place was in the home and not in military or political affairs, a position solidified by the classification of women as legal incompetents in Napoleon's Civil Code (see Domestic Policies later in the chapter).

Reaction and the Directory

After the death of Robespierre on July 28, 1794, a reaction set in called the Thermidorean Reaction, named after the month of Thermidor. The Terror came to a halt. The National Convention reduced the power of the Committee of Public Safety, closed the Jacobin club, and made attempts to provide better protection for the National Convention against the Parisian mobs. Churches were allowed to reopen for public worship while a decree of February 21, 1795, gave freedom of worship to all cults. Economic regulation was dropped in favor of laissez-faire policies, another clear indication that moderate forces were again gaining control of the Revolution. In addition, a new constitution was created in August 1795 that reflected this more conservative republicanism or a desire for a stability that did not sacrifice the ideals of 1789.

To avoid the dangers of another single legislative assembly, the Constitution of 1795 established a national legislative assembly consisting of two chambers: a lower house known as the Council of 500 whose function was to initiate legislation and an upper house of 250 mem-

Chronology
▼ ▼ ▼
The French Revolution

1789	
Meeting of Estates-General	May 5
Formation of National Assembly	June 17
Fall of the Bastille	July 14
Great Fear	Summer
Abolition of Feudalism	August 4
Declaration of the Rights of Man and of the Citizen	August 26
March to Versailles; the King's Return to Paris	October 5–6
1790	
Civil Constitution of the Clergy	July 12
1791	
Flight of the King	June 20–21
Declaration of Pillnitz	August 27
1792	
France Declares War on Austria	April 20
Attack on the Royal Palace	August 10
Abolition of Monarchy	September 21
1793	
Execution of the King	January 21
Levy-in-Mass	August 23
1794	
Execution of Robespierre	July 28
1795	
Constitution of 1795 Is Adopted—the Directory	August 22

bers, the Council of Elders, composed of married or widowed members over forty, which accepted or rejected the proposed laws. The 750 members of the two legislative bodies were chosen by electors who had to be owners or renters of property worth between 100 and 200 days' labor, a requirement that limited the number to 30,000, an even smaller base than that provided in the Constitution of 1791. The electors were chosen by the active citizens, now defined as all male taxpayers over twenty-one. The Council of Elders elected five directors from a list presented by the Council of 500 to act as the executive authority or Directory. To ensure some continuity from the old order to the new, the members of the National Convention ruled that two-thirds of the new members of the National Assembly must be chosen from their ranks. This produced disturbances in Paris and an insurrection at the beginning of October that was dispersed after fierce combat by an army contingent under the artillery general Napoleon Bonaparte. This would be the last time the city of Paris would attempt to impose its wishes on the central government. Even more significant and ominous was this use of the army, which made it clear that the Directory from its beginnings had to rely upon the military for survival.

The period of the Revolution under the government of the Directory was an era of stagnation, corruption, and graft, a materialistic reaction to the sufferings and sacrifices that had been demanded in the Reign of Terror and the Republic of Virtue. Speculators made fortunes in property by taking advantage of the government's severe monetary problems. Elaborate fashions, which had gone out of style because of their identification with the nobility, were worn again. Gambling and roulette became popular once more.

The government of the Directory was faced with political enemies from both the left and the right of the political spectrum. On the right, royalists who desired the restoration of the monarchy continued their agitation; some still toyed with violent means. On the left, Jacobin hopes of power were revived by continuing economic problems, especially the total collapse in value of the assignats. Some radicals even went beyond earlier goals, especially Gracchus Babeuf who raised the question "What is the French Revolution? An open war between patricians and plebeians, between rich and poor." Babeuf wanted to abolish private property and eliminate private enterprise. His Conspiracy of Equals was crushed in 1796, and he was executed in 1797.

New elections in 1797 created even more uncertainty and instability. Battered by the left and right, unable to find a definitive solution to the country's economic problems, and still carrying on the wars left from the Committee of Public Safety, the Directory increasingly relied on the military to maintain its power. This led to a coup d'etat in 1799 in which the successful and popular general Napoleon Bonaparte was able to seize power.

▼ The Age of Napoleon (1799–1815)

Napoleon dominated both French and European history from 1799 to 1815. The coup d'etat that brought him to power occurred exactly ten years after the outbreak of the French Revolution. In a sense, Napoleon brought the Revolution to an end in 1799, but Napo-

▼ **Napoleon as a Young Officer.** Napoleon had risen quickly through the military ranks, being promoted to brigadier general at the age of 25. In 1799, Napoleon Bonaparte led a coup d'etat and overthrew the government of the Directory. A new form of the republic was created after Napoleon seized power. In 1804, France returned to a monarchical form of government when Napoleon had himself crowned Emperor Napoleon I. This painting of Napoleon by the Romantic painter Baron Gros presents an idealized, heroic image of the young Napoleon.

leon was also a child of the Revolution; he called himself the son of the Revolution. The French Revolution had made possible his rise first in the military and then to supreme power in France. Even beyond this, Napoleon had once said, "I am the revolution," and he never ceased to remind Frenchmen that they owed to him the preservation of all that was beneficial in the revolutionary program.

The Rise of Napoleon

Napoleon was born in 1769 in Corsica shortly after the island had been annexed to France. The son of a minor noble, Napoleon was sent to France to study in one of the new military schools. When the Revolution

Napoleon and Psychological Warfare

▼ ▼ ▼

In 1796, at the age of twenty-seven, Napoleon Bonaparte was given command of the French army in Italy where he won a series of stunning victories. His use of speed, deception, and surprise to overwhelm his opponents is well known. In this selection from a proclamation to his troops in Italy, Napoleon also appears as a master of psychological warfare.

Napoleon Bonaparte, Proclamation to French Troops in Italy (April 26, 1796)

Soldiers:

In a fortnight you have won six victories, taken twenty-one standards, fifty-five pieces of artillery, several strong positions, and conquered the richest part of Piedmont [in northern Italy]; you have captured 15,000 prisoners and killed or wounded more than 10,000 men. . . . You have won battles without cannon, crossed rivers without bridges, made forced marches without shoes, camped without brandy and often without bread. Soldiers of liberty, only republican troops could have endured what you have endured. Soldiers, you have our thanks! The grateful Patrie [nation] will owe its prosperity to you. . . .

The two armies which but recently attacked you with audacity are fleeing before you in terror; the wicked men who laughed at your misery and rejoiced at the thought of the triumphs of your enemies are confounded and trembling.

But, soldiers, as yet you have done nothing compared with what remains to be done. . . . Undoubtedly the greatest obstacles have been overcome; but you still have battles to fight, cities to capture, rivers to cross. Is there one among you whose courage is abating? No. . . . All of you are consumed with a desire to extend the glory of the French people; all of you long to humiliate those arrogant kings who dare to contemplate placing us in fetters; all of you desire to dictate a glorious peace, one which will indemnify the Patrie for the immense sacrifices it has made; all of you wish to be able to say with pride as you return to your villages, "I was with the victorious army of Italy!"

---

broke out in 1789, Napoleon was a lieutenant and not well regarded by his fellow officers since he was short, spoke with an Italian accent, and had little money. He spent his time pondering military tactics and studying the works of such philosophes as Voltaire and Adam Smith. Although his dream seems to have been to free his native Corsica from French rule, the Revolution and the European war that followed broadened his sights and gave him new opportunities.

Napoleon rose quickly through the ranks. In 1792, he became a captain and in the following year achieved a reputation as an astute artillery commander. In 1794, at the age of only twenty-five, he was made a brigadier general by the Committee of Public Safety. In the next year he defended the National Convention against the Parisian mob and in 1796 was placed in command of the French armies in Italy (see the box above) where he won a series of victories and dictated peace to the Austrians in 1797. He returned to France as a conquering hero and was given command of an army in training to invade England. But Napoleon believed that the French were unready for such an invasion and proposed instead to strike indirectly at Britain by taking Egypt and threatening India, a major source of British wealth. By 1799, Napoleon's army in Egypt had been cut off from supplies because of British control of the seas. Seeing no future in certain defeat, Napoleon did not hesitate to abandon his army and return to Paris where he participated in the coup d'etat that ultimately led to his virtual dictatorship of France. He was only thirty years old at the time.

What kind of man was Napoleon? Usually labeled a genius, he was a person of many talents. Highly temperamental, he was either talkative or silent depending on his mood. A product of the Enlightenment and French Revolution, he believed himself free from conventional ideas and moral scruples. He had an exaggerated faith in his own destiny that grew more pronounced and more mystical as the years passed by (see the box on p. 695). He was a man of remarkable intellectual ability and impressed those he came into contact with as well as himself. Aware of his own special gifts, he was often contemptuous of his fellow human beings. With his ability to comprehend complex problems quickly and make rapid decisions, Napoleon inspired confidence in others.

The Man of Destiny
▼ ▼ ▼

N*apoleon possessed an overwhelming sense of his own importance. Among the images he fostered, especially as his successes multiplied and his megalomaniacal tendencies intensified, were those of the man of destiny and the great man who masters luck.*

Selections from Napoleon

When a deplorable weakness and ceaseless vacillations become manifest in supreme councils; when, yielding in turn to the influences of opposing parties, making shift from day to day, and marching with uncertain pace, a government has proved the full measure of its impotence; when even the most moderate citizens are forced to admit that the State is no longer governed; when, in fine, the administration adds to its nullity at home the gravest guilt it can acquire in the eyes of a proud nation—I mean its humiliation abroad—then a vague unrest spreads through the social body, the instinct of self-preservation is stirred, and the nation casts a sweeping eye over itself, as if to seek a man who can save it.

This guardian angel a great nation harbors in its bosom at all times; yet sometimes he is late in making his appearance. Indeed, it is not enough for him to exist: he also must be known. He must know himself. Until then, all endeavors are in vain, all schemes collapse. The inertia of the masses protects the nominal government, and despite its ineptitude and weakness the efforts of its enemies fail. But let that impatiently awaited savior give a sudden sign of his existence, and the people's instinct will divine him and call upon him. The obstacles are smoothed before his steps, and a whole great nation, flying to see him pass, will seem to be saying: "Here is the man!"

A consecutive series of great actions never is the result of chance and luck; it always is the product of planning and genius. Great men are rarely known to fail in their most perilous enterprises. . . . Is it because they are lucky that they become great? No, but being great, they have been able to master luck.

Although a consummate opportunist, he was, or at least seemed to be, what many French people were seeking after a decade of unrest.

With the coup d'etat of 1799, a new form of the republic was proclaimed with a constitution that established a bicameral legislative assembly elected indirectly to reduce the role of elections. Executive power in the new government was vested in the hands of three consuls although as Article 42 of the constitution said, "The decision of the First Consul shall suffice." As first consul, Napoleon directly controlled the entire executive authority of government. He had overwhelming influence over the legislature, appointed members of the bureaucracy, controlled the army, and conducted foreign affairs. In 1802, Napoleon was made consul for life and in 1804 returned France to monarchy when he had himself crowned as Emperor Napoleon I. This step undoubtedly satisfied his enormous ego but also stabilized the regime and provided a permanency not possible in the consulate. The revolutionary era that had begun with an attempt to limit arbitrary government had ended with a government far more autocratic than the monarchy of the old regime. As his reign progressed and the demands of war increased, Napoleon's regime became ever more dictatorial.

Domestic Policies

Napoleon often claimed that he had preserved the gains of the Revolution for the French people. The ideal of republican liberty had, of course, been destroyed by Napoleon's thinly disguised autocracy. But were revolutionary ideals maintained in other ways? An examination of his domestic policies will enable us to judge the truth or falsehood of Napoleon's assertion.

In 1801, Napoleon established peace with the oldest and most implacable enemy of the Revolution, the Catholic church. Napoleon himself was devoid of any personal faith; he was an eighteenth-century rationalist who regarded religion at most as a convenience. In Egypt, he called himself a Muslim; in France, a Catholic. But Napoleon saw the necessity to come to terms with the Catholic church in order to stabilize his regime. In 1800, Napoleon had declared to the clergy of Milan:

"It is my firm intention that the Christian, Catholic, and Roman religion shall be preserved in its entirety, No society can exist without morality; there is no good morality without religion. It is religion alone, therefore, that gives to the State a firm and durable support."[21] Soon after making this statement, Napoleon opened negotiations with Pope Pius VII to reestablish the Catholic church in France.

Both sides gained from the Concordat that Napoleon arranged with the pope in 1801. Although the pope gained the right to depose French bishops, this gave him little real control over the French Catholic church since the state was left with the right to nominate bishops. The Catholic church was also permitted to hold processions again and reopen the seminaries. But Napoleon gained more than the pope. Just by signing the Concordat, the pope acknowledged the accomplishments of the Revolution. Moreover, the pope agreed not to raise the question of the church lands confiscated in the Revolution. Contrary to the pope's wishes, Catholicism was not reestablished as the state religion; Napoleon was only willing to recognize Catholicism as the religion of a majority of the French people. The clergy would be paid by the state, but to avoid the appearance of a state church, Protestant ministers were also put on the state payroll. As a result of the Concordat, the Catholic church was no longer an enemy of the French government. At the same time the agreement reassured those who had acquired church lands during the Revolution that they would not be stripped of them, an assurance that obviously made them supporters of the Napoleonic regime.

Before the Revolution, France did not have a single set of laws, but rather virtually 300 different legal systems. During the Revolution, efforts were made to prepare a codification of laws for the entire nation, but it remained for Napoleon to bring the work to completion in the famous Civil Code. This preserved most of the revolutionary gains by recognizing the principle of the equality of all citizens before the law, the right of the individual to choose his profession, religious toleration, and the abolition of serfdom and feudalism. Property rights continued to be carefully protected while the interests of employers were safeguarded by outlawing trade unions and strikes. The Civil Code clearly reflected the revolutionary aspirations for a uniform legal system, legal equality, and protection of property and individuals.

Napoleon also worked on rationalizing the bureaucratic structure of France by developing a powerful, centralized administrative machine. During the Revolution, the National Assembly had divided France into eighty-three departments and replaced the provincial estates, nobles, and intendants with self-governing assemblies. Napoleon kept the departments but eliminated the locally elected assemblies and instituted new officials, the most important of which were the prefects. As the central government's agents, appointed by the first consul (Napoleon), the prefects were responsible for supervising all aspects of local government. Yet they were not

▼ **Napoleon Creates a New Nobility.** One of Napoleon's domestic policies involved the creation of a new nobility. The new aristocracy was based on merit and talent. The highest officials in the military and civil government were given titles. Service to the state was the primary criterion for the granting of a title. Only twenty-two percent of the nobility of the old regime became part of Napoleon's new aristocracy.

local men and their careers depended on the central government. This centralization of power in the central government represented a radical break with revolutionary practices.

As part of Napoleon's overhaul of the administrative system, tax collection became systematic and efficient (which it had never been under the old regime). Taxes were now collected by professional collectors employed by the state who dealt directly with each individual taxpayer. No tax exemptions due to birth, status, or special arrangement were granted. In principle these changes had been introduced in 1789, but not until Napoleon did they actually work. In 1802, the first consul proclaimed a balanced budget.

Administrative centralization required a bureaucracy of capable officials, and Napoleon worked hard to develop one. Early on, the regime showed its preference for experts and cared little whether that expertise had been acquired in royal or revolutionary bureaucracies. Promotion, whether in civil or military offices, was to be based not on rank or birth but only on demonstrated abilities. This was, of course, what many bourgeoisie had wanted before the Revolution. Napoleon, however, also created a new aristocracy based on merit in the state service. Napoleon created 3,263 nobles between 1808 and 1814; nearly 60 percent were military officers while the remainder came from the upper ranks of the civil service and other state and local officials. Socially, only 22 percent of Napoleon's aristocracy came from the nobility of the old regime; almost 60 percent were bourgeois in origin.

In his domestic policies, then, Napoleon both destroyed and preserved aspects of the Revolution. Liberty had been replaced by an initially benevolent despotism that grew increasingly arbitrary as the demands of war overwhelmed Napoleon and the French. While equality was preserved in the law code and the opening of careers to talent, the creation of a new aristocracy, the strong protection accorded to property rights, and the practices associated with conscription make it clear that a loss of equality accompanied the loss of liberty.

Napoleon's Empire and the European Response

When Napoleon became consul in 1799, France was at war with a second European coalition of Russia, Great Britain, and Austria. Napoleon realized the need for a pause. He remarked to a Prussian diplomat "that the French Revolution is not finished so long as the scourge of war lasts . . . I want peace, as much to settle the present French government, as to save the world from chaos."[22] The peace he sought was achieved at Amiens in March 1802 and left France with new frontiers and a number of client territories from the North Sea to the Adriatic. But the peace did not last, and war was renewed in 1803 with Britain, who was soon joined by Austria, Russia, and Prussia in the Third Coalition. In a series of battles at Ulm, Austerlitz, Jena, and Eylau from 1805 to 1807, Napoleon's Grand Army defeated the continental members of the coalition, giving Napoleon the opportunity to create a new European order. The Grand Empire was composed of three major parts: the French empire, a series of dependent states, and allied states. The French empire, the inner core of the Grand Empire, consisted of an enlarged France extending to the Rhine in the east and including the western half of Italy north of Rome. Dependent states were kingdoms under the rule of Napoleon's relatives; these came to include Spain, Holland, the kingdom of Italy, the Swiss Republic, the Grand Duchy of Warsaw, and the Confederation of the Rhine, the latter a union of all German states except Austria and Prussia. Allied states were those defeated by Napoleon and forced to join his struggle against Britain and included Prussia, Austria, Russia, and Sweden. Although the internal structure of the Grand Empire varied outside its inner core, Napoleon considered himself leader of the whole: "Europe cannot be at rest except under a single head who will have kings for his officers, who will distribute his kingdom to his lieutenants."

Within his empire, Napoleon demanded obedience, in part because he needed a common front against the British and in part because his growing egotism required obedience to his will. But as a child of the Enlightenment and Revolution, Napoleon also sought acceptance everywhere of certain revolutionary principles, including legal equality, religious toleration, and economic freedom. As he explained to his brother Jerome after he had made him king of the new German state of Westphalia:

> What the peoples of Germany desire most impatiently is that talented commoners should have the same right to your esteem and to public employments as the nobles, that any trace of serfdom and of an intermediate hierarchy between the sovereign and the lowest class of the people should be completely abolished. The benefits of the Code Napoléon, the publicity of judicial procedure, the creation of juries must be so many distinguishing marks of your monarchy. . . . What nation would wish to return under the arbitrary Prussian government once it had tasted the benefits of a wise and liberal administration? The peoples of Germany, the peoples of France, of Italy, of Spain all desire equality and liberal

ideas. I have guided the affairs of Europe for many years now, and I have had occasion to convince myself that the buzzing of the privileged classes is contrary to the general opinion. Be a constitutional king."

In the inner core and dependent states of his Grand Empire, Napoleon tried to destroy the old order. Nobility and clergy everywhere in these states lost their special privileges. He decreed equality of opportunity with offices open to talent, equality before the law, and religious toleration. This spread of French revolutionary principles was an important factor in the development of liberal traditions in these countries. The nature of these reforms have led some historians to view Napoleon as the last of the enlightened absolutists.

Like Hitler two hundred years later, Napoleon hoped that his Grand Empire would last for centuries; like Hitler's empire, it collapsed almost as rapidly as it had been formed. Two major reasons help to explain this, the survival of Great Britain and the force of nationalism. Britain's survival was primarily due to its seapower. As long as Britain ruled the waves, it was almost invulnerable to military attack. Although Napoleon contemplated an invasion of England and even collected ships for it, he could not overcome the British navy's decisive defeat of a combined French-Spanish fleet at Trafalgar in 1805. Napoleon then turned to his Continental System to defeat Britain. Put into effect between 1806 and 1808, it attempted to prevent British goods from reaching the European continent in order to weaken Britain

▼ **Map 20.4** Napoleon's Empire.

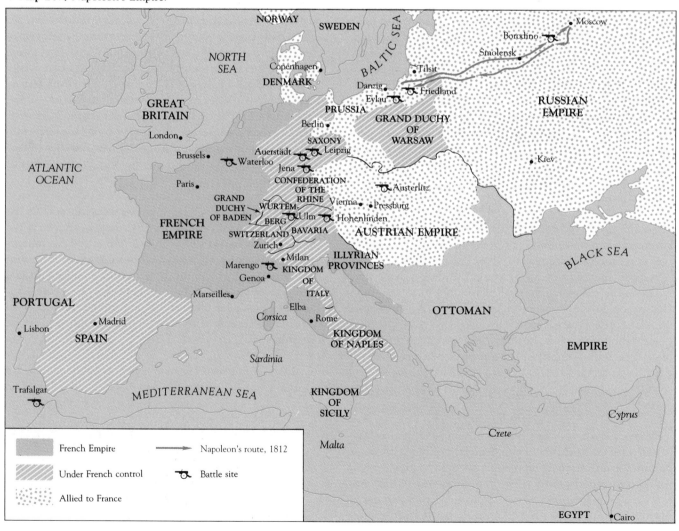

Napoleon as First Consul	1799–1804
Concordat with Catholic Church	1801
Peace of Amiens	1802
Emperor Napoleon I	1804–1815
Battles of Austerlitz; Trafalgar; Ulm	1805
Battle of Jena	1806
Continental System Established	1806
Battle of Eylau	1807
Invasion of Russia	1812
War of Liberation	1813–1814
Exile to Elba	1814
Battle of Waterloo; Exile to Saint Helena	1815
Death of Napoleon	1821

economically and destroy its capacity to wage war. But the Continental System failed. Allied states resented the ever-tightening French economic hegemony; some began to cheat and others to resist, thereby opening the door to British collaboration. New markets in the Levant and in Latin America also provided compensation for the British. Indeed, by 1809–1810 British overseas exports were at near-record highs.

A second important factor in the defeat of Napoleon was nationalism. This political creed had arisen during the French Revolution in the French people's emphasis on brotherhood (fraternité) and solidarity against other peoples. Nationalism involved the unique cultural identity of a people based on common language, religion, and national symbols. The spirit of French nationalism had made possible the mass armies of the revolutionary and Napoleonic eras. But Napoleon's spread of the principles of the French Revolution beyond France inadvertently brought a spread of nationalism as well. The French aroused nationalism in two ways: by making themselves hated oppressors and thus arousing the patriotism of others in opposition to French nationalism, and by showing the people of Europe what nationalism was and what a nation in arms could do. It was a lesson not lost on other peoples and rulers. A Spanish uprising against Napoleon's rule, aided by British support, kept a French force of 200,000 pinned down for years.

The beginning of Napoleon's downfall came in 1812 with his invasion of Russia. The latter's defection from

the Continental System left Napoleon with little choice. Although aware of the risks in invading such a large country, he also knew that if the Russians were allowed to challenge the Continental System unopposed, others would soon follow suit. Only 30,000 out of his original invading army of 600,000 managed to arrive back in Poland in January 1813. This military disaster then led to a war of liberation all over Europe, culminating in Napoleon's defeat in April 1814. He was allowed to play ruler on the island of Elba, off the coast of Tuscany, while the Bourbon monarchy was restored in the person of Louis XVIII, brother of the executed king. But Napoleon's escape from Elba and return to Paris gave him one last period of rule from March to June 1815. At the Battle of Waterloo, Napoleon's One Hundred Days ended in bloody defeat. Exiled to the forsaken rock of Saint Helena, only his memory would continue to haunt French political life.

The revolutionary era of the late eighteenth century witnessed a dramatic political transformation. Revolutionary upheavals, beginning in North America and continuing in France, produced movements for political liberty and equality. The documents created by these revolutions, the Declaration of Independence and the Declaration of the Rights of Man and the Citizen, embodied the fundamental ideas of the Enlightenment and created a liberal political agenda based on a belief in popular sovereignty—the people are the source of political power—and the principles of liberty and equality. Liberty, frequently limited in practice, meant, in theory, freedom from arbitrary power as well as the freedom to think, write, and worship as one chose. Equality meant equality in rights and equality of opportunity based on talent rather than birth. In practice, equality remained limited; those who owned property had greater opportunities for voting and officeholding while there was certainly no equality between men and women.

The leaders of France's liberal revolution, achieved between 1789 and 1791, were men of property, both bourgeois and noble, but they were assisted by commoners, both sansculottes and peasants. Yet the liberal revolution, despite the hopes of the men of property, was not the end of the Revolution. The decision of the revolutionaries to go to war "revolutionized the Revolution," opening the door to a more radical, democratic, and violent stage. The excesses of the Reign of Terror, however, led to a reaction, first under the Directory and then Napoleon, when men of property willingly forswore liberty to preserve property and the opening of careers to talent. Napoleon, while diminishing freedom by establishing order and centralizing the government, shrewdly preserved equality of rights and the opening of careers to talent and integrated the bourgeoisie and old nobility into a new elite of property owners. For despite the antiaristocratic revolutionary rhetoric and the loss of their privileges, nobles remained important landowners. While the nobles lost some of their lands during the Revolution, they were still the largest proprietors in the early 1800s. The great gainers from the redistribution of clerical and noble property, however, had been the bourgeoisie, who also gained dramatically when important government and military positions were opened to men of talent. After 1800, an elite group of property owners, both noble and middle class, dominated French society.

The French Revolution created a modern revolutionary concept. No one had foreseen or consciously planned the upheaval that began in 1789, but after 1789 "revolutionaries" knew that the proper use of mass uprisings could produce the overthrow of unwanted governments. The French Revolution became the classical political and social model for revolution. At the same time, the liberal and national political ideals created by the Revolution and spread to Europe by Napoleon's conquests dominated the political landscape of the nineteenth and early twentieth centuries. Until the Communist Revolution in 1917, few would have questioned the belief that it was "the greatest revolution in the history of the world." A new European era had begun and Europe would never again be the same.

Notes
▼ ▼ ▼

1. Quoted in Edmund and Helen Morgan, *The Stamp Act Crisis* (New York, 1963), pp. 142–43.

2. Quoted in Stephan Thernstrom, *A History of the American People* (New York, 1984), 1: 152.

3. Quoted in R. R. Palmer, *The Age of the Democratic Revolutions* (Princeton, N.J., 1959), 1: 239.

4. Quoted in ibid., p. 242.

5. Quoted in O. J. Hufton, "Towards an Understanding of the Poor of Eighteenth Century France," in J. F. Bosher, ed., *French Government and Society: 1500–1850* (London, 1973), p. 152.

6. Arthur Young, *Travels in France during the Years 1787, 1788 and 1789* (Cambridge, 1929), p. 23.

7. Quoted in D. M. G. Sutherland, *France 1789–1815: Revolution and Counter-Revolution* (New York, 1986), p. 74.

8. Quoted in William Doyle, *The Oxford History of the French Revolution* (Oxford, 1989), p. 156.

9. Quoted in ibid., p. 184.

10. Quoted in J. Hardman, ed., *French Revolution Documents* (Oxford, 1973), 2: 23.

11. Quoted in W. Scott, *Terror and Repression in Revolutionary Marseilles* (London, 1973), p. 84.

12. Quoted in H. Morse Stephens, *The Principal Speeches of the Statesmen and Orators of the French Revolution* (Oxford, 1892), 2: 189.

13. Quoted in Leo Gershoy, *The Era of the French Revolution* (Princeton, N.J., 1957), p. 157.

14. Quoted in J. M. Thompson, *French Revolution Documents* (Oxford, 1933), pp. 258–59.

15. Quoted in Doyle, *The Oxford History of the French Revolution*, p. 254.

16. Quoted in R. R. Palmer, *Twelve Who Ruled* (New York, 1965), p. 75.

17. Quoted in J. M. Thompson, *Leaders of the French Revolution* (New York, 1967), pp. 157–58.

18. Quoted in François Furet and Mona Ozouf, *A Critical Dictionary of the French Revolution*, trans. Arthur Goldhammer (Cambridge, Mass., 1989), p. 545.

19. Quoted in Darline Gay Levy, Harriet Branson Applewhite, and Mary Durham Johnson, eds., *Women in Revolutionary Paris, 1789–1795* (Urbana, Ill., 1979), p. 132.

20. Ibid., pp. 219–20.

21. Quoted in Felix Markham, *Napoleon* (New York, 1963), pp. 92–93.

22. Quoted in Doyle, *The Oxford History of the French Revolution*, p. 381.

23. Quoted in J. Christopher Herold, ed., *The Mind of Napoleon* (New York, 1955), pp. 74–75.

Suggestions for Further Reading

▼ ▼ ▼

A well-written, up-to-date introduction to the French Revolution can be found in W. Doyle, *The Oxford History of the French Revolution* (Oxford, 1989). Also valuable is J. F. Bosher, *The French Revolution* (New York, 1988). For the entire revolutionary and Napoleonic eras, the best general survey is D. M. G. Sutherland, *France 1789–1815: Revolution and Counter-Revolution* (New York, 1985). Although controversial, the massive and beautifully written work by S. Schama, *Citizens* (New York, 1989), makes exciting reading. A different approach to the French Revolution can be found in E. Kennedy, *A Cultural History of the French Revolution* (New Haven, Conn., 1989). Two comprehensive reference works are S. F. Scott and B. Rothaus, eds., *Historical Dictionary of the French Revolution*, 2 vols. (Westport, Conn., 1985); and F. Furet and M. Ozouf, *A Critical Dictionary of the French Revolution*, trans. A. Goldhammer (Cambridge, Mass., 1989).

The origins of the French Revolution are examined in the classic work by G. Lefebvre, *The Coming of the French Revolution* (Princeton, N.J., 1947), although his interpretive framework has been superseded by new work. On the latter, see especially W. Doyle, *Origins of the French Revolution* (Oxford, 1988). On the early years of the Revolution, see J. Egret, *The French Pre-Revolution, 1787–88* (Chicago, 1977); M. Kennedy, *The Jacobin Clubs in the French Revolution: The First Years* (Princeton, N.J., 1982); and N. Hampson, *Prelude to Terror* (Oxford, 1988). Important works on the radical stage of the French Revolution include N. Hampson, *The Terror in the French Revolution* (London, 1981); A. Soboul, *The Sans-Culottes* (New York, 1972); R. R. Palmer, *Twelve Who Ruled* (New York, 1965); D. Jordan, *The King's Trial* (Berkeley, 1979); and R. Cobb, *The People's Armies* (London, 1987). For a biography of Robespierre, one of the leading figures of this period, see N. Hampson, *The Life and Opinions of Maximilien Robespierre* (London, 1974). The importance of the revolutionary wars in the radical stage of the Revolution is underscored in T. C. W. Blanning, *The Origins of the French Revolutionary Wars* (London, 1986). Also valuable is J. P. Bertaud, *The Army of the French Revolution: From Citizen-Soldiers to Instruments of Power* (Princeton, N.J., 1988). The importance of the popular revolutionary crowds is examined in the classic work by G. Rudé, *The Crowd in the French Revolution* (Oxford, 1959). On the Directory, see M. Lyons, *France under the Directory* (Cambridge, 1975); and R. B. Rose, *Gracchus Babeuf*

(Stanford, 1978). Interesting regional studies include W. Scott, *Terror and Repression in Revolutionary Marseilles* (London, 1973); and M. Lyons, *Revolution in Toulouse: An Essay on Provincial Terrorism* (Berne, 1978).

The religious history of the French Revolution is covered in J. McManners, *The French Revolution and the Church* (London, 1969). The relationship between religion and counterrevolution is examined in C. Tilly, *The Vendée* (Cambridge, Mass., 1964); and D. M. G. Sutherland, *The Chouans* (Oxford, 1982). On the Great Fear, there is the classic work by G. Lefebvre, *The Great Fear of 1789: Rural Panic in Revolutionary France* (London, 1973). Two recent works that take rather different approaches to the French Revolution are W. H. Sewell, *Work and Revolution in France* (Cambridge, 1980); and P. Higonnet, *Class, Ideology and the Rights of Nobles during the French Revolution* (Oxford, 1981). On the role of women in revolutionary Paris, there is much to be found in the collection of documents edited by D. G. Levy, H. B. Applewhite, and M. D. Johnson, *Women in Revolutionary Paris, 1789–1795* (Urbana, Ill., 1979).

The best, brief biography of Napoleon is F. Markham, *Napoleon* (New York, 1963). Also valuable are J. M. Thompson, *Napoleon Bonaparte* (Oxford, 1963); and P. Geyl, *Napoleon, For and Against* (New Haven, Conn., 1963), a study of biographical writings on the French leader. A good, recent treatment is L. Bergeron, *France under Napoleon* (Princeton, N.J., 1981). On Napoleon's military campaigns, see D. Chandler, *The Campaigns of Napoleon* (London, 1966).

A good, brief survey of the revolutionary era in America can be found in E. S. Morgan, *Birth of the Republic, 1763–1789*, rev. ed. (New York, 1977). The importance of ideology is treated in B. Bailyn, *The Ideological Origins of the American Revolution* (Cambridge, 1966), while G. Wood, *The Creation of the American Republic, 1776–1787* (New York, 1972) examines the transformation of both politics and ideology. A comparative study that puts the American Revolution into a larger context is R. R. Palmer, *The Age of the Democratic Revolutions: A Political History of Europe and America, 1760–1800*, 2 vols. (Princeton, N.J., 1959–64). A more recent comparative study is the stimulating work by P. Higonnet, *Sister Republics: Origins of the French and American Revolutions* (Cambridge, Mass., 1988).

Chapter 21

The Industrial Revolution and Its Impact on European Society

▼▼▼▼▼

The French Revolution dramatically and quickly altered the political structure of France while the Napoleonic conquests spread many of the revolutionary principles in an equally rapid and stunning fashion to other parts of Europe. During the late eighteenth and early nineteenth centuries, another revolution—an industrial one—was transforming the economic and social structure of Europe, although in a less dramatic and rapid fashion.

The use of machinery to produce goods, one of the characteristics of the Industrial Revolution, was not entirely new. Beginning in the Middle Ages, Europeans had developed innovative tools that harnessed the power of wind and water to manufacture articles for consumption. Wind and water power, however, were neither sufficient nor  reliable enough to create a self-sustaining system of manufacturing. Most products were still made by hand. The period of the Industrial Revolution witnessed a quantum leap in industrial production. New sources of energy and power, especially coal and steam, replaced wind and water to create labor-saving machines that dramatically decreased the use of human and animal labor and, at the same time, increased the level of productivity. In turn, power machinery called for new ways of organizing human labor in order to maximize the benefits and profits from the new machines; factories replaced shop and home workrooms. During the Industrial Revolution, Europe experienced a shift from a traditional, labor-intensive economy based on agriculture and handicrafts to a more capital-intensive economy

Luddites

Factory
Act

People's
Charter

Chadwick's *Report*
on Cities

▼   ▼   ▼   ▼

•••••••••• 1770 ••••••••••• 1790 •••••••••• 1810 ••••••••• 1830 •••••••••• 1850 ••••••••

▲   ▲   ▲   ▲   ▲

Watt's
Steam Engine

Cartwright's
Power Loom

Stephenson's
Rocket

Coke-blast Iron
in Rhineland

Great Exhibition
in Britain

based on manufacturing by machines, specialized labor, and industrial factories.

Although it took decades for the Industrial Revolution to spread, it was truly revolutionary in the way it fundamentally changed Europeans, their society, their relationship to other peoples, and the world itself. The development of large factories encouraged mass movements of people from the countryside to urban areas where impersonal coexistence replaced the traditional intimacy of rural life. Higher levels of productivity led to a search for new sources of raw materials, new consumption patterns, and a revolution in transportation that allowed raw materials and finished products to be moved quickly around the world. The creation of a wealthy industrial middle class and a huge industrial working class (or proletariat) substantially transformed traditional social relationships. Finally, the Industrial Revolution fundamentally altered how the Western world related to nature, ultimately creating an environmental crisis that in the twentieth century has finally been recognized as a danger to human existence itself.

▼ The Industrial Revolution in Great Britain

Although a phenomenon like the Industrial Revolution evolved out of antecedents that occurred over a long period of time, historians generally agree that it had its beginnings in Britain in the 1780s. By 1850, the Industrial Revolution had made Great Britain the wealthiest country in the world; by that time it had also spread to the Continent and the New World. By the end of the nineteenth century, both Germany and the United States would surpass Britain in industrial production.

Origins

A number of factors or conditions coalesced in Britain to produce the first Industrial Revolution. One of these was the agricultural revolution of the eighteenth century. The changes in the methods of farming and stock breeding that characterized this agricultural transformation led to a significant increase in food production. British agriculture could now feed more people at lower prices with less labor. Unlike the rest of Europe, even ordinary British families did not have to use most of their income to buy food, giving them the potential to purchase manufactured goods. At the same time, a rapid growth of population in the second half of the eighteenth century provided a pool of surplus labor for the new factories of the emerging British industry. Rural workers in cottage industries also provided a potential labor force for industrial enterprises.

Britain had a ready supply of capital for investment in the new industrial machines and the factories that were needed to house them. In addition to profits from trade and cottage industry, Britain possessed an effective central bank and well-developed, flexible credit facilities. Nowhere in Europe were people so accustomed to paper instruments to facilitate capital transactions. Many early factory owners were merchants and entrepreneurs who had profited from eighteenth-century cottage industry. Of 110 cotton spinning mills created in the area known as the Midlands between 1769 and 1800, 62 were established by hosiers, drapers, mercers, and others involved in some fashion in the cottage textile industry. But capital alone is only part of the story. Britain had a fair number of individuals who were interested in making profits if the opportunity presented itself (see the box on p. 704). The British were a people, as one historian has said, "fascinated by wealth and commerce, collectively

The Traits of the British Industrial Entrepreneur
▼▼▼

Richard Arkwright (1732–1792), creator of a spinning frame and founder of cotton factories, was a good example of the successful entrepreneur in the early Industrial Revolution in Britain. In this selection, Edward Baines, who wrote The History of the Cotton Manufacture in Great Britain *in 1835, discusses the traits that explain the success of Arkwright and presumably other British entrepreneurs.*

Edward Baines, *The History of the Cotton Manufacture in Great Britain*

Richard Arkwright rose by the force of his natural talents from a very humble condition in society. He was born at Preston on the 23rd of December, 1732, of poor parents: being the youngest of thirteen children, his parents could only afford to give him an education of the humblest kind, and he was scarcely able to write. He was brought up to the trade of a barber at Kirkham and Preston, and established himself in that business at Bolton in the year 1760. Having become possessed of a chemical process for dyeing human hair, which in that day (when wigs were universal) was of considerable value, he travelled about collecting hair, and again disposing of it when dyed. In 1761, he married a wife from Leigh, and the connexions he thus formed in that town are supposed to have afterwards brought him acquainted with Highs's experiments in making spinning machines. He himself manifested a strong bent for experiments in mathematics, which he is stated to have followed with so much devotedness as to have neglected his business and injured his circumstances. His natural disposition was ardent, enterprising, and stubbornly persevering: his mind was as coarse as it was bold and active, and his manners were rough and unpleasing. . . .

The most marked traits in the character of Arkwright were his wonderful ardour, energy, and perseverance. He commonly laboured in his multifarious concerns from five o'clock in the morning till nine at night; and when considerably more than fifty years of age,—feeling that the defects of his education placed him under great difficulty and inconvenience in conducting his correspondence, and in the general management of his business,—he encroached upon his sleep, in order to gain an hour each day to learn English grammar, and another hour to improve his writing and orthography [spelling]! He was impatient of whatever interfered with his favorite pursuits; and the fact is too strikingly characteristic not to be mentioned, that he separated from his wife not many years after their marriage, because she, convinced that he would starve his family [because of the impractical nature of his schemes], broke some of his experimental models of machinery. Arkwright was a severe economist of time; and, that he might not waste a moment, he generally travelled with four horses, and at a very rapid speed. His concerns in Derbyshire, Lancashire, and Scotland were so extensive and numerous, as to [show] at once his astonishing power of transacting business and his all-grasping spirit. In many of these he had partners, but he generally managed in such a way, that, whoever lost, he himself was a gainer.

and individually." These early industrial entrepreneurs faced considerable financial hazards, however. Fortunes were made and easily lost. The structure of early firms was open and fluid. An individual or family proprietorship was the usual mode of operation, but entrepreneurs also brought in friends to help them. They just as easily jettisoned them. John Marshall, who made money in flax spinning, threw out his partners: "As they could neither of them be of any further use, I released them from the firm and took the whole upon myself."[1]

Britain was richly supplied with important mineral resources, such as coal and iron ore, needed in the manufacturing process. Britain was also a small country, and the relatively short distances made transportation readily accessible. In addition to nature's provision of abundant rivers, from the mid-seventeenth century onward, both private and public investment poured into the construction of new roads, bridges, and, beginning in the 1750s and 1760s, canals. By 1780, roads, rivers, and canals linked the major industrial centers of the North, the Midlands, London, and the Atlantic. Unlike the continental countries, Britain possessed no internal customs barriers to hinder domestic trade.

Britain's government also played a significant role in the process of industrialization. Parliament added to the favorable business climate by providing a stable government and passing laws that protected private property. Moreover, Britain was remarkable for the freedom it provided for private enterprise. There were fewer restrictions on private entrepreneurs than in any other European state.

Finally, a supply of markets gave British industrialists a ready outlet for their manufactured goods. British exports quadrupled from 1660 to 1760. In the course of its eighteenth-century wars and conquests, Great Britain had developed a vast colonial empire at the expense of its leading continental rivals, the Dutch Republic and France. Britain also possessed a well-developed merchant marine that was able to transport goods to any place in the world. A crucial factor in Britain's successful industrialization was the ability to produce cheaply those articles most in demand abroad. And the best markets abroad were not in Europe, where countries protected their own incipient industries, but in the Americas, Africa, and the Far East, where people wanted sturdy, inexpensive clothes rather than costly, highly finished, luxury items. Britain's machine-produced textiles fulfilled that demand. Nor should we overlook the British domestic market. Britain had the highest standard of living in Europe and a rapidly growing population. As Daniel Defoe noted already in 1728:

> For the rest, we see their Houses and Lodgings tolerably furnished, at least stuff'd well with useful and necessary household Goods: Even those we call poor People, Journeymen, working and Pains-staking People do thus; they lye warm, live in Plenty, work hard, and [need] know no Want.

These are the People that carry off the Gross of your Consumption; 'tis for these your Markets are kept open late on Saturday nights; because they usually receive their Week's Wages late . . . in a Word, these are the Life of our whole Commerce, and all by their Multitude: Their Numbers are not Hundreds or Thousands, or Hundreds of Thousands, but Millions; . . . by their Wages they are able to live plentifully, and it is by their expensive, generous, free way of living, that the Home Consumption is rais'd to such a Bulk, as well of our own, as of foreign Production.[2]

It was the demand from both domestic and foreign markets and the inability of the old system to fulfill it that led entrepreneurs to seek and accept the new methods of manufacturing that a series of inventions provided. In so doing, these individuals produced the Industrial Revolution.

Technological Changes and New Forms of Industrial Organization

It was in the cotton textile industry in the 1770s and 1780s that the first major step was taken toward the Industrial Revolution with the creation of the modern factory.

THE COTTON INDUSTRY Already in the eighteenth century, Great Britain had surged ahead in the production of cheap cotton goods using the traditional methods of cottage industry. The development of the flying shuttle had sped the process of weaving on a loom and enabled weavers to double their output. This, however, created short-

▼ **A British Colliery.** While the Industrial Revolution grew out of many prior conditions, it is generally thought to have begun in Britain in the 1780s. Building upon the agricultural revolution of the eighteenth century, rich natural resources, abundant capital for investment, and a supply of markets, Britain was well prepared for industrialization. Britain also had an ample supply of coal. By the 1830s and 1840s, the development of coal mines led to a landscape of coal-mining machinery and smoke-belching chimneys in parts of Britain. Seen here is the Percy Colliery in Northumberland in 1839.

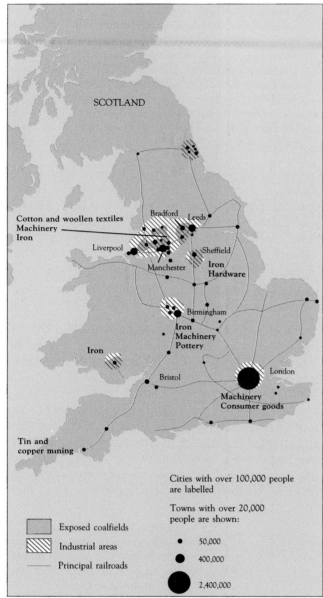

SCOTLAND

Cotton and woollen textiles
Machinery
Iron

Bradford
Leeds

Liverpool

Sheffield

Manchester

Iron
Hardware

Birmingham

Iron
Machinery
Pottery

Iron

London

Bristol

Machinery
Consumer goods

Tin and
copper mining

Cities with over 100,000 people
are labelled

Towns with over 20,000
people are shown:

☐ Exposed coalfields

▨ Industrial areas

— Principal railroads

• 50,000

● 400,000

⬤ 2,400,000

▼ **Map 21.1** England in the Industrial Revolution.

ages of yarn until James Hargreaves's spinning jenny, perfected by 1768, allowed spinners to produce yarn in greater quantities. Richard Arkwright's water frame spinning machine, powered by water or horse, and Samuel Crompton's so-called mule, which combined aspects of the water frame and spinning jenny, increased yarn production even more. Edmund Cartwright's power loom, invented in 1787, allowed the weaving of cloth to catch up with the spinning of yarn. Even then, early power looms were grossly inefficient, enabling cottage,

hand-loom weavers to continue to prosper, at least until the mid-1820s. After that they were gradually replaced by the new machines. In 1813, there were 2,400 power looms in operation in Great Britain, 14,150 in 1820, 100,000 in 1833, and 250,000 by 1850. In the 1820s, there were still 250,000 hand-loom weavers in Britain; by 1860, only 3,000 were left.

The water frame, Crompton's mule, and power looms presented new opportunities to entrepreneurs. It was much more efficient to bring workers to the machines and organize their labor collectively in factories located next to rivers and streams, the sources of power for many of these early machines, than to leave the workers dispersed in their cottages. The concentration of labor in the new factories also brought the laborers and their families to live in the new towns that rapidly grew up around the factories.

The early devices used to speed up the processes of spinning and weaving were the products of weavers and spinners, in effect, of craftsmen tinkerers. But the subsequent expansion of the cotton industry and the ongoing demand for even more cotton goods created additional pressure for new and more complicated technology. The invention that pushed the cotton industry to even greater heights of productivity was the steam engine.

THE STEAM ENGINE   The invention of the steam engine played a major role in the Industrial Revolution. It revolutionized the production of cotton goods and caused the factory system to spread to other areas of production, thereby creating whole new industries. The steam engine secured the triumph of the Industrial Revolution.

As in much of the Industrial Revolution, one kind of change forced other changes. In many ways the steam engine was the result of the need for more efficient pumps to eliminate water seepage from deep mines. Deep coal mines were in turn the result of Britain's need and desire to find new sources of energy to replace wood. By the early eighteenth century, the British were acutely aware of a growing shortage of timber, used in heating, building homes and ships, and in enormous quantities to produce the charcoal utilized in the smelting of iron ore to produce pig iron. The discovery at the beginning of the eighteenth century of new processes for smelting iron ore with coal and coke (see the next section) led to more intensive mining of coal by digging deeper and deeper mines. But as mines were dug below the water table, they filled with water. An early solution to the problem was the use of mechanical pumps powered by horses walking in circles. In one coal mine in Warwickshire, for example, 500 horses were used to lift the water from the mine, bucket by bucket. The need for more efficient pumps led Thomas Newcomen to develop a steam pump or, as it was called, an "atmospheric engine" that was first used in 1712. While better than horses, it still proved inefficient.

In the 1760s, a Scottish engineer, James Watt (1736–1819), was asked to repair a Newcomen engine. Instead he added a separate condenser and steam pump and transformed Newcomen's machine into a genuine steam engine. Power was derived not from air pressure as in Newcomen's atmospheric engine, but from steam itself. Much more efficient, Watt's engine could pump water three times as quickly. Initially, it possessed one major liability, however; as a contemporary noted in 1778: "the vast consumption of fuel in these engines is an immense drawback on the profit of our mines, for every fire-engine of magnitude consumes £3000 worth of coals per annum. This heavy tax amounts almost to a prohibition."[3] As steam engines were made more efficient, however, they also became cheaper to use.

In 1782, James Watt enlarged the possibilities of the steam engine when he developed a rotary engine that could turn a shaft and thus drive machinery. Steam power could now be applied to spinning and weaving cotton, and before long cotton mills using steam engines were multiplying across Britain. By 1850, seven-eighths of the power available to the cotton industry for all of Britain came from steam. Since steam engines were fired by coal, they did not need to be located near rivers; entrepreneurs now had greater flexibility in their choice of location.

The new boost given to cotton textile production by technological changes became readily apparent. In 1760, Britain had imported 2.5 million pounds of raw cotton, which was farmed out to cottage industries. All work was done by hand either in workers' homes or in the small shops of master weavers. In 1787, the British imported 22 million pounds of cotton; most of it was spun on machines, some powered by water in large mills. By 1840, 366 million tons of cotton—now Britain's most important product in value—were imported. By 1840, although there were still some hand-loom weavers, most cotton industry employees worked in factories. The price of yarn was but one-twentieth of what it had been. The cheapest labor in India could not compete in quality or quantity with Britain. British cotton goods sold everywhere in the world. And in Britain itself, cheap cotton cloth made it possible for millions of poor people to wear undergarments, long a preserve of the rich who alone could afford the underwear made with expensive linen

▼ **A Boulton and Watt Steam Engine.** The steam engine was a crucial factor in the growth and spread of the Industrial Revolution. Encouraged by his business partner, Matthew Boulton, James Watt developed the first genuine steam engine. Pictured here is a typical Boulton and Watt engine. Steam pressure in the cylinder on the left drives the beam upwards and sets the fly-wheel in motion. The steam engine was eventually applied to the spinning and weaving of cotton and allowed for greater flexibility in the location of an industry.

cloth. New work clothing that was tough, comfortable to the skin, and yet cheap and easily washable became common. Even the rich liked the colorful patterns of cotton prints and their light weight for summer use.

The steam engine proved invaluable to Britain's Industrial Revolution. In 1800, engines were generating 10,000 horsepower; by 1850, 500,000 in stationary engines and 790,000 in mobile engines, the last largely in locomotives (see A Revolution in Transportation later in the chapter). Unlike horses, the steam engine was a tireless source of power and depended for fuel on a substance—namely, coal—that seemed then to be unlimited in quantity. The popular saying that "Steam is an Englishman" had real significance by 1850. The steam engine also replaced waterpower in such places as flour and sugar mills. Just as the need for more coal had helped lead to the steam engine, so the success of the steam engine led to a need for more coal and an expansion in coal production; between 1815 and 1850, the output of coal quadrupled. In turn, new processes using coal furthered the development of an iron industry.

THE IRON INDUSTRY The British iron industry was radically transformed during the Industrial Revolution. Britain had large resources of iron ore, but at the beginning of the eighteenth century, the basic process of producing iron had altered little since the Middle Ages and still depended heavily on charcoal. In the early eighteenth century, new methods of smelting iron ore to produce cast iron were devised based on the use of coke derived from coal. A better quality of iron was still not possible, however, until the 1780s when Henry Cort developed a system called puddling, in which coke was used to burn away impurities in pig iron and produce an iron of high quality. A boom then ensued in the British iron industry. In 1740, Britain produced 17,000 tons of iron; in the 1780s, almost 70,000 tons; by the 1840s, over 2 million tons; and by 1852, almost 3 million tons, more than the rest of the world combined.

The development of the iron industry was in many ways a response to the demands for the new machines. The high-quality wrought iron produced by the Cort process made it the most widely used metal until the production of cheaper steel in the 1860s. The growing supply of less costly metal encouraged the growth of machinery in other industries, most noticeably in new means of transportation.

A REVOLUTION IN TRANSPORTATION The eighteenth century had witnessed an expansion of transportation facilities in Britain as entrepreneurs realized the need for more efficient means of moving resources and goods. Turnpike trusts provided new roads, and between 1760 and 1830 a network of canals was built. Both roads and canals were soon overtaken by a new form of transportation that dazzled people by its promises. To many economic historians, railroads were the "most important single factor in promoting European economic progress in the 1830s and 1840s." Again, Britain was the leader in the revolution.

The beginnings of railways can be found in mining operations in Germany as early as 1500 and in British coal mines after 1600 where small handcarts filled with coal were pushed along parallel wooden rails. The rails reduced friction, enabling horses to haul more substantial loads. By 1700, some entrepreneurs began to replace wooden rails with cast-iron rails, and by the early nineteenth century, railways—still dependent on horsepower—were common in British mining and industrial districts. The development of the steam engine brought a radical transformation to railways.

In 1804, Richard Trevithick pioneered the first steam-powered locomotive on an industrial rail-line in south Wales. It pulled ten tons of ore and seventy people at five miles per hour. Better locomotives soon followed.

Those engines built by George Stephenson and his son proved superior, and it was in their workshops in Newcastle upon Tyne that the locomotives for the first modern railways in Britain were built. George Stephenson's *Rocket* was used on the first public railway line, which opened in 1830, extending thirty-two miles from Liverpool to Manchester. *Rocket* sped along at sixteen miles per hour. Within twenty years, locomotives had reached fifty miles per hour, an incredible speed to contemporary passengers. During the same period, new companies were formed to build additional railroads as the infant industry proved to be not only technically but financially successful. In 1840, Britain had almost 2,000 miles of railroads; by 1850, 6,000 miles of railroad track crisscrossed much of the country.

The railroad was an important contribution to the success and maturing of the Industrial Revolution. The demands of railroads for coal and iron furthered the growth of those industries. British supremacy in civil and mechanical engineering, so evident after 1840, was in large part based upon the skills acquired in railway building. The huge capital demands necessary for railway construction encouraged a whole new group of middle-class investors to plough their money into joint-stock companies (see Limitations to Industrialization later in the chapter). Railway construction created new job opportunities, especially for farm laborers and peasants who had long been accustomed to finding work outside their local villages. Perhaps most importantly, a cheaper and faster means of transportation had a rippling effect on the growth of an industrial economy. By reducing the price of goods, larger markets were created; increased sales meant more factories and more machinery, thereby reinforcing the self-sustaining aspect of the Industrial Revolution that marked a fundamental break with the traditional European economy. The great productivity of the Industrial Revolution enabled entrepreneurs to reinvest their profits in new capital equipment, further expanding the productive capacity of the economy. Continuous, even rapid, self-sustaining economic growth came to be seen as a fundamental characteristic of the new industrial economy.

The railroad was the perfect symbol of this aspect of the Industrial Revolution. The ability to transport goods and people at dramatic speeds also provided visible confirmation of a new sense of power. When railway engineers pierced mountains with tunnels and spanned chasms with breathtaking bridges, contemporaries experienced a sense of power over nature not felt before in Western civilization.

THE INDUSTRIAL FACTORY   Initially the product of the new cotton industry, the factory became the chief means of organizing labor for the new machines. As the workplace shifted from the artisan's shop and the peasant's cottage to the factory, the latter was not viewed as just a larger work unit. Employers hired workers who no longer owned the means of production but simply provided the hands to run the machines. Wages formed the basis of their economic relationship, but discipline formed the foundation of their functional relationship.

From its beginning, the factory system demanded a new type of discipline from its employees. For factory owners, the purchase of machinery necessitated its constant use. Workers were forced to work regular hours and in shifts to keep the machines producing at a steady pace for maximum output. This represented a massive adjustment for early factory laborers.

Pre-industrial labor was not accustomed to a "timed" format. Agricultural labor had always functioned on the basis of irregular hours; hectic work at harvest time might be followed by periods of inactivity. Even in the burgeoning cottage industry of the eighteenth century, weavers and spinners who worked at home might fulfill their weekly quotas by working around the clock for two or three days, followed by a leisurely pace until the next week's demands forced another work spurt.

Factory owners, therefore, faced a formidable task. They had to create a system of work discipline in which employees became accustomed to working regular, unvarying hours during which they performed a set number of tasks over and over again as efficiently as possible. One early industrialist said that his aim was "to make such machines of the men as cannot err." Such work, of course, tended to be repetitive and boring, and factory owners resorted to tough methods to accomplish their goals. Factory regulations were minute and detailed (see the box on p. 710). Adult workers were fined for a wide variety of minor infractions, such as being a few minutes late for work, and dismissed for more serious misdoings, especially drunkenness. The latter was viewed as particularly offensive because it set a bad example for younger workers and also courted disaster in the midst of dangerous machinery. Employers found that dismissals and fines worked well for adult employees; in a time when great population growth had produced large masses of unskilled labor, dismissal meant disaster. Children were less likely to understand the implications of dismissal so they were sometimes disciplined more directly—by beating.

The efforts of factory owners in the early Industrial Revolution to impose a new set of values were frequently reinforced by the new evangelical churches. Methodism, in particular, emphasized that people reborn in Christ

▼ **Inside an Early Cotton Factory.**
The development of the factory changed the relationship between workers and employers. Workers were encouraged to adjust to a new system of discipline that forced them to work regular hours and in shifts. Since the early factory workers were not used to such a system, owners often resorted to tough methods to achieve the required discipline. This engraving depicts the inside of an early textile factory.

Discipline in the New Factories

▼ ▼ ▼

Workers in the new factories of the Industrial Revolution had been accustomed to a lifestyle free of overseers. Unlike the cottages, where workers spun thread and wove cloth in their own rhythm and time, the factories demanded a new, rigorous discipline geared to the requirements of the machines. This selection is taken from a set of rules for a factory in Berlin in 1844. They were typical of company rules everywhere the factory system had been established.

The Foundry and Engineering Works of the Royal Overseas Trading Company, Factory Rules

In every large works, and in the co-ordination of any large number of workmen, good order and harmony must be looked upon as the fundamentals of success, and therefore the following rules shall be strictly observed.

1. The normal working day begins at all seasons at 6 A.M. precisely and ends, after the usual break of half an hour for breakfast, an hour for dinner and half an hour for tea, at 7 P.M., and it shall be strictly observed. . . .
Workers arriving 2 minutes late shall lose half an hour's wages; whoever is more than 2 minutes late may not start work until after the next break, or at least shall lose his wages until then. Any disputes about the correct time shall be settled by the clock mounted above the gatekeeper's lodge. . . .

3. No workman, whether employed by time or piece, may leave before the end of the working day, without having first received permission from the overseer and having given his name to the gatekeeper. Omission of these two actions shall lead to a fine of ten silver groschen [pennies] payable to the sick fund.

4. Repeated irregular arrival at work shall lead to dismissal. This shall also apply to those who are found idling by an official or overseer, and refused to obey their order to resume work. . . .

6. No worker may leave his place of work otherwise than for reasons connected with his work.

7. All conversation with fellow-workers is prohibited; if any worker requires information about his work, he must turn to the overseer, or to the particular fellow-worker designated for the purpose.

8. Smoking in the workshops or in the yard is prohibited during working hours; anyone caught smoking shall be fined five silver groschen for the sick fund for every such offence. . . .

10. Natural functions must be performed at the appropriate places, and whoever is found soiling walls, fences, squares, etc., and similarly, whoever is found washing his face and hands in the workshop and not in the places assigned for the purpose, shall be fined five silver groschen for the sick fund. . . .

12. It goes without saying that all overseers and officials of the firm shall be obeyed without question, and shall be treated with due deference. Disobedience will be punished by dismissal.

13. Immediate dismissal shall also be the fate of anyone found drunk in any of the workshops. . . .

14. Every workman is obliged to report to his superiors any acts of dishonesty or embezzlement on the part of his fellow workmen. If he omits to do so, and it is shown after subsequent discovery of a misdemeanour that he knew about it at the time, he shall be liable to be taken to court as an accessory after the fact and the wage due to him shall be retained as punishment.

---

must forgo immoderation and follow a disciplined path. Laziness and wasteful habits were sinful. The acceptance of hardship in this life paved the way for the joys of the next. Evangelical values paralleled the efforts of the new factory owners to instill their own middle-class values of hard work, discipline, and thrift upon laborers. In one crucial sense the early industrialists proved successful. As the nineteenth century progressed, the second and third generations of workers came to view a regular working week as a natural way of life. It was, of course, an attitude that made possible Britain's incredible economic growth in that century.

The Great Exhibition: Britain in 1851

In 1851, the British organized the world's first industrial fair. It was housed at Kensington in London in the Crystal Palace, an enormous structure made entirely of glass and iron, a tribute to British engineering skills. Covering nineteen acres, the Crystal Palace contained 100,000 exhibits that showed the wide variety of products created by the Industrial Revolution. Six million people visited the fair in six months. While most of them were Britons, who had traveled to London by train, foreign visitors were also prominent. The Great Exhibition displayed Britain's wealth to the world; it was a gigantic symbol of British success. Even trees were brought inside the Crystal Palace as a visible symbol of how the Industrial Revolution had achieved human domination over nature. Prince Albert, Queen Victoria's husband, expressed the sentiments of the age when he described the exhibition as a sign that "man is approaching a more complete fulfilment of that great and sacred mission which he has to perform in this world . . . to conquer nature to his use." Not content with that, however, he also connected British success to divine will: "In promoting [the progress of the human race], we are accomplishing the will of the great and blessed God."[4]

By the year of the Great Exhibition, Great Britain had become the world's first and richest industrial nation. Britain was the "workshop, banker, and trader of the world." It produced one-half of the world's coal and manufactured goods; its cotton industry alone in 1851 was equal in size to the industries of all other European countries combined. The quantity of goods produced was growing at three times the rate it had achieved in 1780. No doubt, Britain's certainty about its mission in the world in the nineteenth century was grounded in its incredible material success story.

▼ The Spread of Industrialization

Beginning first in Great Britain, industrialization spread to the continental countries of Europe and the United States at different times and speeds during the nineteenth century. First to be industrialized on the Continent were Belgium, France, and the German states and in North America, the new nation of the United States. Not until after 1850 did the Industrial Revolution spread to the rest of Europe and other parts of the world.

Limitations to Industrialization

In 1815, Belgium, France, and the German states were still largely agrarian. During the eighteenth century, some of the continental countries had experienced developments similar to that of Britain. They, too, had population growth, made agricultural improvements, expanded their cottage industries, and witnessed growth in

▼ **Opening of the Great Exhibition.** The British organized the world's first industrial fair in 1851. Over 100,000 exhibits were housed within the Crystal Palace, an enormous structure made of glass and iron and covering nineteen acres. The Great Exhibition was a symbol of the success of Great Britain, which had become the world's first and richest industrial nation. Seen here is Queen Victoria at the opening of the Exhibition, surrounded by visitors from all over the world.

foreign trade. But while Britain's economy began to move into new industrial directions in the 1770s and 1780s, continental countries lagged behind because they did not share some of the advantages that had made Britain's Industrial Revolution possible. Lack of good roads and problems with river transit made transportation difficult. Toll stations on important rivers and customs barriers along state boundaries increased the costs and prices of goods. Guild restrictions were also more prevalent, creating restrictions that pioneer industrialists in Britain did not have to face. Finally, adherence to traditional patterns of business life, such as a dislike of competition, a high regard for family security coupled with an unwillingness to take risks in investment, and an excessive worship of thriftiness, left continental entrepreneurs with less enterprising attitudes.

One additional factor also affected most of the Continent between 1790 and 1812: the upheavals associated with the wars of the French revolutionary and Napoleonic eras. Disruption of regular communications between Britain and the Continent made it difficult for continental countries to keep up with the new British technology. Moreover, the wars wreaked havoc with trade, caused much physical destruction and loss of manpower, weakened currencies, and created political and social instability. Napoleon's Continental System helped to ruin a number of hitherto prosperous ports. The elimination of European markets for British textiles did bring a revival to the woolen industry in France and Belgium and stimulated textile manufacturing along the Rhine and in Silesia. After 1815, however, when cheap British goods again flooded European markets, the European textile industry suffered.

In the long run, the revolutionary and Napoleonic wars created an additional hurdle to rapid industrialization by widening the gap between British and continental industrial machinery. By 1815, after Napoleon had finally been defeated and normal communication between Britain and the Continent had been restored, British industrial equipment had grown larger and become more expensive. As a result, self-financed family enterprises were either unable or unwilling to raise the

▼ **Map 21.2** The Industrialization of Continental Europe by 1850.

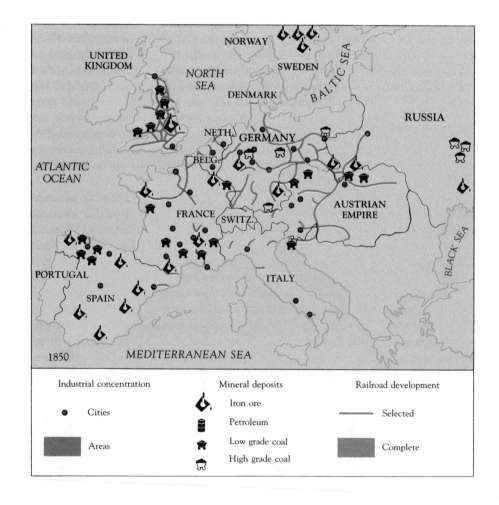

amount of capital necessary to modernize by investing in the latest equipment. Instead, most entrepreneurs in France, Belgium, and Germany initially chose to invest in used machines and less productive mills. Consequently, industrialization on the Continent faced numerous hurdles, and as it proceeded in earnest after 1815, it did so along lines that were somewhat different from Britain's.

Lack of technical knowledge was a first major obstacle to industrialization. But the continental countries possessed an advantage here; they could simply borrow British techniques and practices. Of course, the British tried to prevent that. Until 1825, British artisans were prohibited from leaving the country; until 1842, the export of important machinery and machine parts, especially for textile production, was forbidden. Nevertheless, the British were not able to control this situation by legislation. Already by 1825, there were at least 2,000 skilled British mechanics on the Continent, and British equipment, whether legally or illegally, was also being sold abroad.

Although many Britons who went abroad to sell their skills were simply skilled mechanics, a number of them were accomplished entrepreneurs who had managerial as well as technical skills. John Cockerill, for example, was an aggressive businessman who established a highly profitable industrial plant at Seraing near Liège in southern Belgium in 1817. Encouraged by the Belgian government, Cockerill thought nothing of pirating the innovations of other British industrialists to further his own factories. Aware of their importance, British technicians abroad were often contentious and arrogant, arousing the anger of continental industrialists. Fritz Harkort, who initiated the engineering industry in Germany, exclaimed once that he could scarcely wait for Germans to be trained "so that the Englishmen could all be whipped out: we must even now tread softly with them, for they're only too quick to speak of quitting if one does so little as not look at them in a friendly fashion."[5]

Gradually, the Continent achieved technological independence as local people learned all the skills they could from their British teachers. By the 1840s, a new generation of skilled mechanics from Belgium and France was spreading their knowledge east and south, playing the same role that the British had earlier. More importantly, however, continental countries, especially France and the German states, began to establish a wide range of technical schools to train engineers and mechanics.

That government played an important role in this regard brings us to a second difference between British and continental industrialization. Governments on much of the Continent were accustomed to play a significant role in economic affairs. Furthering the development of industrialization was a logical extension of that attitude. Hence governments provided for the costs of technical education; awarded grants to inventors and foreign entrepreneurs; exempted foreign industrial equipment from import duties; and, in some places, even financed factories. Of equal, if not greater importance in the long run, governments actively bore much of the cost of building roads and canals, deepening and widening river channels, and constructing railroads. By 1850, a network of iron rails had spread across Europe, although only Germany and Belgium had completed major parts of their systems by that time. Although the real impact of the railroad on European markets was not felt until after 1850, railroad construction itself in the 1830s and 1840s gave great impetus to the metalworking and engineering industries. In fact, by the 1840s, railroad construction had become the "most important single stimulus to industrial growth in western Europe."

Governments on the Continent also worked to further industrialization by tariff protection. After 1815, cheap British goods flooded continental markets. The French responded with high tariffs to protect their fledgling industries. The most systematic exposition for the use of tariffs, however, was made by a German writer, Friedrich List, who emigrated to America and returned to Germany as a United States consul. In his *National System of Political Economy*, written in 1844, List advocated a rapid and large-scale program of industrialization as the surest path to develop a nation's strength. To assure that path to industrialization, he felt that a nation must use protective tariffs. If countries followed the British policy of free trade, then cheaper British goods would inundate national markets and destroy infant industries before they had a chance to grow. Germany, he insisted, could not compete with Britain without protective tariffs.

A third significant difference between British and continental industrialization was the role of the joint-stock investment bank on the Continent. This development mobilized the savings of thousands of small and large investors, creating a supply of capital that could then be ploughed back into industry. Continental banks had been mostly merchant or private banks, but in the 1830s two Belgian banks, the Société Générale and the Banque de Belgique, took a new path. By accepting savings from many depositors, they developed large capital resources that they invested on a large scale in railroads, mining, and heavy industry. These investments were especially important to the Belgian coal industry, which became the largest on the Continent in the 1840s. Shareholders in these joint-stock corporations had limited liability; they could only be held responsible for the amount of their investment.

These new practices emerged in France and German-speaking lands as well in the 1850s with the establishment of the Crédit Mobilier in France, the Darmstadt Bank in Germany, and the Kreditanstalt in Austria. They, too, took in savings of small investors and bought shares in the new industries. The French consul in Leipzig noted their significance: "every town and state [in Germany]," he pointed out, "however small it may be, wants its bank and its Crédit Mobilier." These investments proved invaluable to continental industrialization. By starting with less expensive machines, the British had been able to industrialize largely through the private capital of successful individuals who reinvested their profits. On the Continent advanced industrial machines necessitated large amounts of capital; joint-stock industrial banks provided it.

Centers of Continental Industrialization

The Industrial Revolution on the Continent occurred in three major centers between 1815 and 1850—Belgium, France, and the German states. Here, too, cotton played an important role, although it was not as significant as heavy industry. France was the continental leader in the manufacture of cotton goods but still lagged far behind Great Britain. In 1849, France used 64,000 tons of raw cotton, Belgium, 11,000, and Germany, 20,000, while Britain utilized 286,000 tons. Continental cotton factories were older, used less efficient machines, and had less productive labor. In general, continental technology in the cotton industry was a generation behind Great Britain. But that is not the whole story. With its cheap coal and scarce water, Belgium gravitated toward the use of the steam engine as the major source of power and invested in the new machines. By the mid-1840s, Belgium had the most modern cotton-manufacturing system on the Continent.

Two significant differences characterize the development of cotton manufacturing on the Continent and in Britain. Unlike Britain, where cotton manufacturing was mostly centered in Lancashire and the Glasgow area, cotton mills in France, Germany, and to a lesser degree, Belgium, were dispersed in many regions. Noticeable, too, was the mixture of old and new. The old techniques of the cottage system, such as the use of hand looms, held on much longer. In the French district of

Normandy, for example, in 1849 eighty-three mills were still driven by hand or animal power.

The use of traditional methods alongside the new methods in cotton manufacturing left the continental countries making use of the new steam engine primarily in mining and metallurgy rather than in textile manufacturing. At first, almost all of the steam engines on the Continent came from Britain; not until the 1820s was a domestic machine industry developed.

In Britain, the Industrial Revolution had been built upon the cotton industry; on the Continent, it was the iron and coal of heavy industry that led the way. As in textiles, however, heavy industry on the Continent before 1850 was a mixture of old and new. New techniques, such as coke-smelted iron and puddling furnaces, were combined with the expansion of old-type charcoal blast furnaces. Before 1850, Germany lagged significantly behind both Belgium and France in heavy industry, and most German iron manufacturing remained based on old techniques. Not until the 1840s was coke-blast iron produced in the Rhineland. At that time, no one had yet realized the treasure of coal buried in the Ruhr valley. A German official wrote in 1852, "It is clearly not to be expected that Germany will ever be able to reach the level of production of coal and iron currently attained in England. This is implicit in our far more limited resource endowment." Little did he realize that although continental Europe was about a generation behind Britain in industrial development at mid-century, after 1850 an incredibly rapid growth in continental industry would demonstrate that Britain was not, after all, destined to remain the world's greatest industrial nation.

The Industrial Revolution in the United States

In 1800, society in the United States was agrarian. There were no cities over 100,000, and six out of every seven American workers were farmers. By 1860, however, the population had grown from 5 to 30 million people, larger than Great Britain. Almost half of them lived west of the Appalachian Mountains. There were now thirty-four instead of sixteen states, and nine American cities had over 100,000 in population. Only 50 percent of American workers were farmers. From 1800 to the eve of the Civil War, the United States had experienced an industrial revolution and the urbanization that accompanied it.

The initial application of machinery to production was accomplished—as in continental Europe—by borrowing from Great Britain. A British immigrant, Samuel

Slater, established the first textile factory using water-powered spinning machines in Rhode Island in 1790. By 1813, factories with power looms copied from British versions were being established. Soon thereafter, however, Americans began to equal or surpass British technical inventions. The Harpers Ferry arsenal, for example, built muskets with interchangeable parts. Because all the individual parts of a musket were identical (e.g., all triggers were the same), the final product could be put together quickly and easily; this enabled Americans to avoid the more costly system in which skilled craftsmen fitted together individual parts made separately. The so-called American system reduced costs and revolutionized production by saving labor, important to a society that had few skilled artisans.

Unlike Britain, the United States was a large country. The lack of a good system of internal transportation seemed to limit American economic development by making the transport of goods prohibitively expensive. This was gradually remedied, however. Thousands of miles of roads and canals were built linking east and west. The steamboat facilitated transportation on the Great Lakes, Atlantic coastal waters, and rivers. It was especially important to the Mississippi valley; by 1860, a thousand steamboats plied that river (see the box on p. 716). Most important of all in the development of an American transportation system was the railroad. Beginning with 100 miles in 1830, by 1860 there were over 27,000 miles of railroad track covering the United States. This transportation revolution turned the United States into a single massive market for the manufactured goods of the Northeast, the early center of American industrialization.

Labor for the growing number of factories in this area came primarily from rural New England. The United States did not possess a large number of craftsmen, but it did have a rapidly expanding farm population; its size in the Northeast soon outstripped the available farmland. While some of this excess population, especially men, went West, others, mostly women, found work in the new textile and shoe factories of New England. Indeed, women made up more than 80 percent of the laboring force in the large textile factories. In Massachusetts mill towns, company boarding houses provided rooms for large numbers of young women who worked for several years before marriage. Outside Massachusetts, factory owners sought entire families including children to work in their mills; one mill owner ran this advertisement in a newspaper in Utica, New York: "Wanted: A few sober and industrious families of at least five children each, over the age of eight years, are wanted at the Cotton Factory in Whitestown. Widows with large families would do well to attend this notice." When a decline in rural births threatened to dry up this labor pool in the 1830s and 1840s, European immigrants, especially poor and unskilled Irish, English, Scottish, and Welsh, appeared in large numbers to replace American women and children in the factories.

Women, children, and these immigrants had one thing in common as employees; they were largely unskilled laborers. Unskilled labor pushed American industrialization into a capital-intensive pattern. Factory

▼ **Samuel Slater's Cotton Mill.** While beginning the nineteenth century as an agrarian society, the United States quickly entered the industrial era. Samuel Slater, whose cotton mill at Pawtucket, Rhode Island is pictured here, was the first American to apply machinery to production. Initially, Americans copied from the British, but they soon began to equal or surpass British technical innovations. By the last third of the nineteenth century, American industrial production outstripped that of all Europe.

"S–t–e–a–m–boat a–coming'!"

▼ ▼ ▼

Steamboats and railroads were crucial elements in a transportation revolution that enabled industrialists to expand markets by shipping goods cheaply and efficiently. At the same time, these marvels of technology aroused a sense of power and excitement that was an important aspect of the triumph of industrialization. The American novelist Mark Twain captured this sense of excitement in this selection from Life on the Mississippi.

Mark Twain, *Life on the Mississippi*

After all these years I can picture that old time to myself now, just as it was then: the white town drowsing in the sunshine of a summer's morning; the streets empty, or pretty nearly so; one or two clerks sitting in front of the Water street stores, with their splint-bottomed chairs tilted back against the walls, chins on breasts, hats slouched over their faces, asleep; . . . two or three lonely little freight piles scattered about the "levee"; a pile of "skids" on the slope of the stone-paved wharf, and the fragrant town drunkard asleep in the shadow of them; . . . the great Mississippi, the majestic, the magnificent Mississippi, rolling its mile-wide along, shining in the sun; the dense forest away on the other side; the "point" above the town, and the "point" below, bounding the river-glimpse and turning it into a sort of sea, and withal a very still and brilliant and lonely one. Presently a film of dark smoke appears above on those remote "points"; instantly a negro drayman, famous for his quick eye and prodigious voice, lifts up to cry, "S–t–e–a–m–boat a–coming'!" and the scene changes! The town drunkard stirs, the clerks wake up, a furious clatter of drays follows, every house and store pours out a human contribution, and all in a twinkling the dead town [Hannibal, Missouri] is alive and moving.

Drays, carts, men, boys, all go hurrying from many quarters to a common center, the wharf. Assembled there, the people fasten their eyes upon the coming boat as upon a wonder they are seeing for the first time. And the boat is rather a handsome sight, too. She is long and sharp and trim and pretty; she has two tall, fancy-topped chimneys, with a gilded device of some kind swung between them; a fanciful pilot-house, all glass and "gin-ger bread," perched on top of the "texas" deck behind them; the paddle-boxes are gorgeous with a picture or with gilded rays above the boat's name; the boiler deck, the hurricane deck, and the texas deck are fenced and ornamented with clean white railings; there is a flag gallantly flying from the jack-staff; the furnace doors are open and the fires glaring bravely; the upper decks are black with passengers; the captain stands by the big bell, calm, imposing, the envy of all; great volumes of the blackest smoke are rolling and tumbling out of the chimneys—a husbanded grandeur created with a bit of pitch pine just before arriving at a town; the crew are grouped on the forecastle; the broad stage is run far out over the port bow, and an envied deck-hand stands picturesquely on the end of it with a coil of rope in his hand; the pent steam is screaming through the gauge-cocks; the captain lifts his hand, a bell rings, the wheels stop; then they turn back, churning the water to foam, and the steam is at rest. Then such a scramble as there is to get aboard, and to get ashore, and to take in freight and to discharge freight, all at one and the same time; and such a yelling and cursing as the mates facilitate it all with! Ten minutes later the steamer is under way again, with no flag on the jack-staff and no black smoke issuing from the chimneys. After ten more minutes the town is dead again, and the town drunkard asleep by the skids once more.

owners invested heavily in machines that could produce in quantity at the hands of untrained workers. In Britain, the pace of mechanization was never as rapid because Britain's supply of skilled craftsmen made it more profitable to pursue a labor-intensive economy.

By 1860, the United States was well on its way to being an industrial nation. In the Northeast, the most industrialized section of the country, per capita income was 40 percent higher than the national average. Diets, it has been argued, were better and more varied; machine-made clothing was more abundant. Nevertheless, despite a growing belief in a myth of social mobility based upon equality of economic opportunity, the reality was that the richest 10 percent of the population in the cities held 70 to 80 percent of the wealth compared to 50 percent in 1800. Nevertheless, American historians generally argue that while the rich got richer, the poor, as a result of experiencing an increase in their purchasing power, did not get poorer.

▼ The Social Impact of the Industrial Revolution

Eventually, the Industrial Revolution revolutionized the social life of Europe and the world. Although much of Europe remained bound by its traditional ways, already in the first half of the nineteenth century, the social impact of the Industrial Revolution was being felt and future avenues of growth were becoming apparent. Vast changes in the number of people and where they lived were already dramatically evident.

Population Growth

Population increases had already begun in the eighteenth century, but they became dramatic in the nineteenth century. They were also easier to discern because record keeping became more accurate. Governments in the nineteenth century began to take periodic censuses and systematically collect precise data on births, deaths, and marriages. In Britain, for example, the first census was taken in 1801, and a systematic registration of births, deaths, and marriages was begun in 1836. In 1750, the total European population stood at an estimated 140 million; by 1800, it had increased to 187 million, and by 1850 the population had almost doubled since 1750 to 266 million.

This population explosion cannot be explained by a higher birthrate for birthrates were declining after 1790. Between 1790 and 1850, Germany's birthrate dropped from 40 per thousand to 36.1; Great Britain's from 35.4 to 32.6, and France's from 32.5 to 26.7. The key to the expansion of population was the decline in death rates evident throughout Europe. Historians believe now that two major causes explain this decline. There was a drop in the number of deaths from famines, epidemics, and war. Major epidemic diseases, in particular, such as plague and smallpox declined noticeably, although small-scale epidemics continued. There was also a decline in the ordinary death rate as a general increase in the food supply, already evident in the agricultural revolution of Britain in the late eighteenth century, spread to more areas. More food enabled a greater number of people to be better fed and therefore more resistant to disease. Famine largely disappeared from western Europe, although there were dramatic exceptions in isolated areas, Ireland being the most significant.

In those areas where industrialization proceeded in the nineteenth century, a change occurred in the composition of the population. By 1850, the proportion of the active population involved in manufacturing, mining, or building had risen to 48 percent in Britain, 37 percent in Belgium, and 27 percent in France. But the actual areas of industrialization in 1850 were minimal, concentrated in northern and central England, northern France, Belgium, and sections of western and eastern Germany. As one author has commented, "they were islands in an agricultural sea."

This minimal industrialization, in light of the growing population, meant severe congestion in the countryside where a growing population divided the same amount of land into ever-smaller plots and also created an ever-larger mass of landless peasants. Overpopulation, especially noticeable in parts of France, northern Spain, southern Germany, Sweden, and Ireland, magnified the already existing problem of rural poverty. In Ireland, it produced the century's greatest catastrophe.

Ireland was one of the most backward and oppressed areas in western Europe. The mostly Catholic peasant population rented land from mostly absentee British Protestant landlords whose primary concern was collecting their rents. Irish peasants lived in mud hovels in desperate poverty. The cultivation of the potato, a nutritious and relatively easy food to grow that produced three times as much food per acre as grain, gave Irish peasants a basic staple that enabled them to survive and even expand in numbers. As only an acre or two of potatoes was sufficient to feed a family, Irish men and women married earlier than elsewhere and started having children earlier as well. This led to significant growth in the population. Between 1781 and 1845, the Irish population doubled from 4 to 8 million. Probably half of this population depended on the potato for survival. In the summer of 1845, the potato crop in Ireland was struck by blight due to a fungus that turned the potato black. Between 1845 and 1851, the Great Famine decimated the Irish population (see the box on p. 718). Over 1 million died of starvation and disease while almost 2 million emigrated to the United States and Britain. Of all the European nations, only Ireland had a declining population in the nineteenth century. But other countries, too, faced problems of dire poverty and declining standards of living as populations exploded. Some historians, in fact, have argued that without industrialization and the improvements it brought in the

The Great Irish Famine

▼ ▼ ▼

T he Great Irish Famine was one of the nineteenth century's worst natural catastrophes. Overly dependent on a single crop, the Irish were decimated by the potato blight. In this selection, an Irish nationalist reported what he had witnessed in Galway in 1847.

John Mitchel, The Last Conquest of Ireland

In the depth of winter we travelled to Galway, through the very centre of that fertile island, and saw sights that will never wholly leave the eyes that beheld them—cowering wretches, almost naked in the savage weather, prowling in turnip-fields, and endeavouring to grub up roots which had been left, but running to hide as the mail-coach rolled by;—very large fields where small farms had been "consolidated," showing dark bars of fresh mould running through them where the ditches had been levelled;—groups and families, sitting or wandering on the high-road, with failing steps and dim patient eyes, gazing hopelessly into infinite darkness; before them, around them, above them, nothing but darkness and despair;—parties of tall brawny men, once the flower of Meath and Galway, stalking by with a fierce but vacant scowl; as if they knew that all this ought not to be, but knew not whom to blame, saw none whom they could rend in their wrath; . . . . Around those farmhouses which were still inhabited were to be seen hardly any stacks of grain; the poor-rate collector, the rent agent, the county-cess collector had carried it off; and sometimes I could see in front of the cottages little children leaning against a fence when the sun shone out—for they could not stand—their limbs fleshless, their bodies half naked, their faces bloated yet wrinkled, and of a pale greenish hue,—children who would never, it was too plain, grow up to be men and women.

---

standard of living other countries might have faced "Irish disasters."

The flight of so many Irish to America reminds us that the traditional safety valve for overpopulation has always been emigration. Between 1821 and 1850, the number of emigrants from Europe averaged about 110,000 a year. Most of these emigrants came from places like Ireland and southern Germany, where peasant life had been reduced to marginal existence. Times of agrarian crisis resulted in great waves of emigration. Bad harvests in Europe in 1846–1847 (such as the catastrophe in Ireland) produced massive numbers of emigrants. In addition to the estimated 1,600,000 from Ireland, for example, 935,000 people left Germany between 1847 and 1854. More often than emigration, however, the rural masses sought a solution to their poverty by moving to towns and cities within their own countries to find work. It should not astonish us then that the first half of the nineteenth century was a period of rapid urbanization.

Urbanization

Although it was not until the twentieth century that the Western world became a predominantly urban society, cities and towns had already grown dramatically in the first half of the nineteenth century, a phenomenon related to industrialization. Cities had traditionally been centers for princely courts, government and military offices, churches, and commerce. By 1850, especially in Great Britain and Belgium, they were rapidly becoming places for manufacturing and industry. With the steam engine, entrepreneurs could locate their manufacturing plants in urban centers where they had ready access to transportation facilities and unemployed people from the country looking for work.

In 1800, Great Britain had one major city, London, with a population of 1 million, and six cities between 50,000 and 100,000. Fifty years later, London's population had swelled to 2,363,000 while there were nine cities over 100,000 and eighteen cities with populations between 50,000 and 100,000. All together, these twenty-eight cities accounted for 5.7 million or one-fifth of the total British population. When the populations of cities under 50,000 are added to this total, we realize that over 50 percent of the British population lived in towns and cities by 1850. Britain was forced to become a food importer rather than exporter as the number of people involved in agriculture declined to 20 percent of the population.

Urban populations also grew on the Continent, but less dramatically. Paris had 547,000 inhabitants in 1800, but there were only two other French cities with

100,000: Lyons and Marseilles. In 1851, Paris had grown to 1 million while Lyons and Marseilles were still under 200,000. German and Austrian lands had only three cities with over 100,000 inhabitants (Vienna had 247,000) in 1800; fifty years later, there were only five while Vienna had grown to 440,000. As these figures show, urbanization did not proceed as rapidly here as in Britain; of course, neither had industrialization. Even in Belgium, the most heavily industrialized country on the Continent, almost 50 percent of the male work force was still engaged in agriculture by mid-century.

URBAN LIVING CONDITIONS IN THE EARLY INDUSTRIAL REVOLUTION   The dramatic growth of cities in the first half of the nineteenth century produced miserable living conditions for many of the inhabitants. Of course, this had been true for centuries in European cities, but the rapid urbanization associated with the Industrial Revolution intensified the problems in the first half of the nineteenth century and made these appalling living conditions all the more apparent. City authorities of whatever kind either felt little responsibility for these conditions or more frequently did not have the skills to cope with the complex, new problems produced by such rapidly growing populations. City authorities might also often be factory owners who possessed little or no tradition of public service or public responsibility.

Wealthy, middle-class inhabitants, as usual, insulated themselves as best they could, often living in suburbs or the outer ring of the city where they could have individual houses and gardens. In the inner ring of the city stood the small row houses, some with gardens, of the artisans and lower middle class. Finally, located in the center of most industrial towns were the row houses of the industrial workers. This report on working-class housing in the British city of Birmingham in 1843 gives an idea of the general conditions they faced:

> The courts [of working-class row houses] are extremely numerous; . . . a very large portion of the poorer classes of the inhabitants reside in them. . . . The courts vary in the number of the houses which they contain, from four to twenty, and most of these houses are three stories high, and built, as it is termed, back to back. There is a wash-house, an ash-pit, and a privy at the end, or on one side of the court, and not unfrequently one or more pigsties and heaps of manure. Generally speaking, the privies in the old courts are in a most filthy condition. Many which we have inspected were in a state which renders it impossible for us to conceive how they could be used; they were without doors and overflowing with filth.

The people who lived in such houses were actually the fortunate; the truly unfortunate were those forced to live in cellars. As one reformer asked, "how can a hole underground of from 12 to 15 feet square admit of ventilation so as to fit it for a human habitation?" Rooms were not large and were frequently overcrowded, as this government report of 1838 revealed: "I entered several of the tenements. In one of them, on the ground floor, I found six persons occupying a very small room, two in

▼ **The City of Sheffield.** Cities and towns grew dramatically in the first half of the nineteenth century, largely as a result of industrialization. Cities in Britain expanded substantially. London's population exceeded 2 million by 1850. Countries on the Continent, however, which lagged behind Britain in industrial development, experienced less rapid urban growth. The dominant presence of factories in some British cities in the nineteenth century is evident in this view of Sheffield in 1858.

bed, ill with fever. In the room above this were two more persons in one bed ill with fever." Another report said: "There were 63 families where there were at least five persons to one bed; and there were some in which even six were packed in one bed, lying at the top and bottom—children and adults."[6]

Sanitary conditions in these towns were appalling. Due to the lack of municipal direction, sewers and open drains were common on city streets: "In the centre of this street is a gutter, into which potato parings, the refuse of animal and vegetable matters of all kinds, the dirty water from the washing of clothes and of the houses, are all poured, and there they stagnate and putrefy."[7] Unable to deal with human excrement, cities in the new industrial era smelled horrible and were extraordinarily unhealthy. Towns and cities were fundamentally death traps. As deaths outnumbered births in most large cities in the first half of the nineteenth century, only a constant influx of people from the country kept them alive and growing.

Added to the deterioration of urban life was the adulteration of food. Consumers were defrauded in appalling ways: alum was added to make bread look white and hence more expensive; beer and milk were watered down; and red lead despite its poisonous qualities was substituted for pepper. The government refused to intervene; a parliamentary committee stated that "more benefit is likely to result from the effects of a free competition . . . than can be expected to result from any regulations." It was not until 1875 that an effective Food and Drugs Act was passed in Britain.

Our knowledge of the pathetic conditions in the early industrial cities is largely derived from an abundance of social investigations. Such investigations began in France in the 1820s. In Britain the Poor Law Commissioners produced detailed reports, which culminated in the publication in 1842 of Edwin Chadwick's *Report on the Sanitary Conditions of the Labouring Population.* Chadwick and other reformers were often struck by the physically and morally debilitating effects of urban industrial life on the poor. They observed, for example, that young working-class men were considerably shorter and scrawnier than the sons of middle-class families and much more subject to disease. They were especially alarmed by what they considered the moral consequences of such living conditions: prostitution, crime, and sexual immoralities, all of which they saw as the effect of such squalid lives.

To many of the well-to-do middle classes, this situation presented a clear danger to society. Were not these masses of workers, sunk in crime, disease, and immorality, a potential threat to their own well-being? Might not the masses be organized and used by unscrupulous demagogues to overthrow the established order? One of the most eloquent British reformers of the 1830s and 1840s, James Kay-Shuttleworth, described them as "volcanic

▼ **Slums of Industrial London.** Industrialization and rapid urban growth produced dreadful living conditions in many nineteenth-century cities. The unskilled laborers suffered most in the area of housing, with five or six people often crowded into one small room. Filled with garbage and human waste, cities often smelled terrible and were extremely unhealthy. This drawing by Gutave Doré shows a London slum district overshadowed by rail viaducts.

elements, by whose explosive violence the structure of society may be destroyed." Another observer spoke more contemptuously in 1850:

> They live precisely like brutes, to gratify . . . the appetites of their uncultivated bodies, and then die, to go they have never thought, cared, or wondered whither. . . . Brought up in the darkness of barbarism, they have no idea that it is possible for them to attain any higher condition; they are not even sentient enough to desire to change their situation. . . . they eat, drink, breed, work and die; and . . . the richer and more intelligent classes are obliged to guard them with police.[8]

Some observers were less arrogant, however, and wondered if the workers could be held responsible for their fate.

One of the best of a new breed of urban reformers was Edwin Chadwick (1800–1890). With a background in law, Chadwick became obsessed with eliminating the poverty and squalor of the metropolitan areas. He became a civil servant and was soon appointed to a number of government investigatory commissions. As secretary of the Poor Law Commission, he initiated a passionate search for detailed facts about the living conditions of the working classes. After three years of investigation, Chadwick summarized the results in his *Report on the Condition of the Labouring Population of Great Britain*. In it he concluded that "the various forms of epidemic, endemic, and other disease" were directly caused by the "atmospheric impurities produced by decomposing animal and vegetable substances, by damp and filth, and close overcrowded dwellings [prevailing] amongst the population in every part of the kingdom." Such conditions, he argued, could be eliminated. As to the means: "The primary and most important measures, and at the same time the most practicable, and within the recognized province of public administration, are drainage, the removal of all refuse of habitations, streets, and roads, and the improvement of the supplies of water."[9] In other words, Chadwick was advocating a system of modern sanitary reforms consisting of efficient sewers and a supply of piped water. Six years after his report and largely due to his efforts, Britain's first Public Health Act created a National Board of Health empowered to form local boards that would establish modern sanitary systems.

New Social Classes: The Industrial Middle Class

The rise of industrial capitalism produced a new middle-class group. The bourgeois or middle class was not new; it had existed since the emergence of cities in the Middle Ages. Originally, the bourgeois was the burgher or town dweller, whether active as a merchant, official, artisan, lawyer, or man of letters, who enjoyed a special set of rights from the charter of his town. As wealthy townspeople bought land, the original meaning of the word *bourgeois* became lost, and the term came to include people involved in commerce, industry, and banking as well as professionals, such as lawyers, teachers, physicians, and government officials at varying levels. At the lower end of the economic scale were master craftsmen and shopkeepers.

Lest we make the industrial middle class too much of an abstraction, we need to look at who the new industrial entrepreneurs actually were. These were the people who constructed the factories, purchased the machines, and figured out where the markets were. Their qualities included resourcefulness, single-mindedness, resolution, initiative, vision, ambition, and often, of course, greed. As Jedediah Strutt, the cotton manufacturer said, "Getting of money . . . is the main business of the life of men."

But this was not an easy task. The early industrial entrepreneurs were called upon to superintend an enormous array of functions that are handled today by teams of managers; they raised capital, determined markets, set company objectives, organized the factory and its labor, and trained supervisors who could act for them. The opportunities for making money were great, but the risks were also tremendous. The cotton trade, for example, which was so important to the early Industrial Revolution, was intensely competitive. A feeling of security came only from constant expansion, requiring that early entrepreneurs reinvest most of their initial profits. Fear of bankruptcy was constant, especially among small firms. Furthermore, most early industrial enterprises were small. Even by the 1840s, in Britain only 10 percent of industrial firms employed more than 5,000 workers. Forty-three percent had fewer than 100 workers. As entrepreneurs went bankrupt, new people could enter the race for profits, especially since the initial outlay was not gigantic. In 1816, only one mill in five in the important industrial city of Manchester was in the hands of its original owners.

The social origins of industrial entrepreneurs were incredibly diverse. Many of the most successful came from a mercantile background. Three London merchants, for example, founded a successful ironworks in Wales that owned eight steam engines and employed 5,000 men. In Britain, land and domestic industry were often interdependent. Joshua Fielden, for example, earned enough from running a family sheep farm while working looms in the farmhouse to acquire sufficient capital to establish

a factory. Intelligent, clever, and ambitious apprentices who had learned their trades well could also strike it rich. William Radcliffe's family engaged in agriculture and spinning and weaving at home; he learned quickly how to succeed:

> Availing myself of the improvements that came out while I was in my teens . . . with my little savings and a practical knowledge of every process from the cotton bag to the piece of cloth . . . I was ready to commence business for myself and by the year 1789 I was well established and employed many hands both in spinning and weaving as a master manufacturer.[10]

By 1801, Radcliffe was operating a factory employing 1,000 workers.

Members of dissenting religious minorities were often prominent among the early industrial leaders of Britain. The Darbys and Lloyds who were iron manufacturers, the Barclays and Lloyds who were bankers, and the Trumans and Perkins who were brewers were all Quakers. These were expensive trades and depended upon the financial support that co-religionists in religious minorities provided for each other. Most historians believe that a major reason for the prominence of these religious minorities was that they lacked other opportunities. Legally excluded from many public offices, they directed their ambitions into the new industrial capitalism.

It is interesting to note that in Britain in particular aristocrats also became entrepreneurs. The Lambtons in Northumberland, the Curwens in Cumberland, the Norfolks in Yorkshire, and the Dudleys in Staffordshire all invested in mining enterprises. This close relationship between land and industry helped Britain to assume the leadership role in the early Industrial Revolution.

By 1850, in Britain at least, the kind of traditional entrepreneurship that had created the Industrial Revolution was declining and being replaced by a new business aristocracy. This new generation of entrepreneurs stemmed from the professional and industrial middle classes, especially as sons inherited the successful businesses established by their fathers. It must not be forgotten, however, that even after 1850 a large number of small businesses existed in Britain and some were still created by people from humble backgrounds. Indeed, it was not until the 1890s that the age of large-scale corporate capitalism began (see Chapter 24).

Increasingly, the new industrial entrepreneurs—the bankers and owners of factories and mines—came to amass much wealth and play an important role alongside the traditional landed elites of their societies. The Industrial Revolution began at a time when the pre-industrial agrarian world was still largely dominated by landed elites. As the new bourgeoisie bought great estates and acquired social respectability, they also sought political power, and in the course of the nineteenth century, their wealthiest members would merge with those old elites.

New Social Classes: The Industrial Workers

The industrial middle class sought to reduce the barriers between themselves and the landed elite, but it is clear that they tried at the same time to separate themselves from the laboring classes below them. The working class was actually a mixture of different groups in the first half of the nineteenth century. In the course of the nineteenth century, factory workers would form an industrial proletariat, but in the first half of that century, they by no means constituted a majority of the working class in any major city, even in Britain. According to the 1851 census in Britain, while there were 1.8 million agricultural laborers and 1 million domestic servants, there were only 811,000 workers in the cotton and woolen industries. Even one-third of these were still working in small workshops or in their own homes.

Within the cities, artisans or craftsmen remained the largest group of urban workers during the first half of the nineteenth century. They worked in numerous small industries, such as shoemaking, glovemaking, bookbinding, printing, and bricklaying. Some craftsmen formed a kind of aristocracy of labor, especially those employed in such luxury trades as coachbuilding and clockmaking who earned higher wages than others. Artisans were not factory workers; they were traditionally organized in guilds where they passed on their skills to apprentices. But guilds increasingly lost their power, especially in industrialized countries. Fearful of losing out to the new factories that manufactured goods more cheaply, artisans tended to support movements against industrialization. Industrialists welcomed the decline of skilled craftsmen, as one perceptive old tailor realized in telling his life story:

> It is upwards of 30 years since I first went to work at the tailoring trade in London. . . . I continued working for the honourable trade and belonging to the Society [for tailors] for about 15 years. My weekly earnings then averaged £1 16s. a week while I was at work, and for several years I was seldom out of work . . . no one could have been happier than I was. . . . But then, with my sight defective . . . I could get no employment at the honourable trade, and that was the ruin of me entirely; for working there, of course, I got "scratched"

from the trade society, and so lost all hope of being provided for by them in my helplessness. The workshop . . . was about seven feet square, and so low, that as you [sat] on the floor you could touch the ceiling with the tip of your finger. In this place seven of us worked. [The master] paid little more than half the regular wages, and employed such men as myself—only those who couldn't get anything better to do. . . . I don't think my wages there averaged above 12s a week. . . . I am convinced I lost my eyesight by working in that cheap shop. . . . It is by the ruin of such men as me that these masters are enabled to undersell the better shops. . . . That's the way, sir, the cheap clothes is produced, by making blind beggars of the workmen, like myself, and throwing us on the parish in our old age.[11]

Servants also formed another large group of urban workers, especially in major cities like London and Paris. Many were women from the countryside who became utterly dependent upon their upper- and middle-class employers.

WORKING CONDITIONS FOR THE INDUSTRIAL WORKING CLASS   Industrial workers were not the largest working-class group in the first half of the nineteenth century, but they soon would be, and it is appropriate to look at the working conditions they faced. The pathetic living conditions of the industrial working classes were matched by equally wretched working conditions. We have already observed the psychological traumas workers experienced from their employers' efforts to break old pre-industrial work patterns and create a well-disciplined labor force. But what were the physical conditions of the factories?

There is no question that in the early decades of the Industrial Revolution "places of work," as early factories were called, were dreadful. Work hours ranged from twelve to sixteen hours a day, six days a week, with a half hour for lunch and dinner. There was no security of employment and no minimum wage. The worst conditions were in the cotton mills where temperatures were especially debilitating. One report noted that "in the cotton-spinning work, these creatures are kept, fourteen hours in each day, locked up, summer and winter, in a heat of from eighty to eighty-four degrees." Mills were also dirty, dusty, and unhealthy:

Not only is there not a breath of sweet air in these truly infernal scenes, but . . . there is the abominable and pernicious stink of the gas to assist in the murderous effects of the heat. In addition to the noxious effluvia of the gas, mixed with the steam, there are the dust, and what is called cotton-flyings or fuz, which the unfortunate creatures have to inhale; and . . . the notorious fact is that well constitutioned men are rendered old and past labour at forty years of age, and that children are rendered decrepit and deformed, and thousands upon thousands of them slaughtered by consumptions, before they arrive at the age of sixteen.[12]

Thus ran a report on working conditions in the cotton industry in 1824.

Conditions in the coal mines were also harsh. The introduction of steam power into the coal mines meant only that steam-powered engines mechanically lifted coal to the top. Inside the mines, men still bore the burden of digging the coal out while horses, mules, women, and children hauled coal carts on rails to the lift. Dangerous conditions abounded in coal mines; cave-ins, explosions, and gas fumes (called "bad air") were a way of life. The cramped conditions in mines with tunnels not exceeding three or four feet in height, and their constant dampness resulted in deformed bodies and ruined lungs.

Both children and women were employed in large numbers in early factories and mines. Children had been an important part of the family economy in pre-

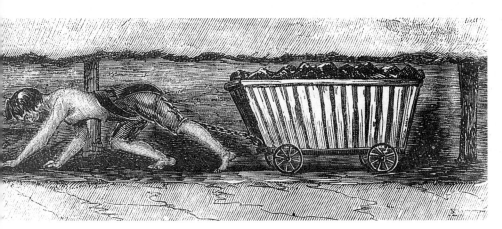

▼ **Women in the Mines.** Both women and children were often employed in the early factories and mines of the nineteenth century. However, even though women worked in industry, traditional female working patterns were not greatly altered. Many women continued to work as domestic servants and in agriculture, while the majority of married women continued to work inside their homes.

Child Labor: Discipline in the Textile Mills

▼ ▼ ▼

Child labor was certainly not new, but in the early Industrial Revolution it was exploited more systematically. These selections are taken from the Report of Sadler's Committee, which was commissioned in 1832 to inquire into the condition of child factory workers.

How They Kept the Children Awake

It is a very frequent thing at Mr. Marshall's [at Shrewsbury] where the least children were employed (for there were plenty working at six years of age), for Mr. Horseman to start the mill earlier in the morning than he formerly did; and provided a child should be drowsy, the overlooker walks round the room with a stick in his hand, and he touches that child on the shoulder, and says, "Come here." In a corner of the room there is an iron cistern; it is filled with water; he takes this boy, and takes him up by the legs, and dips him over head in the cistern, and sends him to work for the remainder of the day. . . .

What means were taken to keep the children to their work?—Sometimes they would tap them over the head, or nip them over the nose, or give them a pinch of snuff, or throw water in their faces, or pull them off where they were, and job them about to keep them waking.

The Sadistic Overlooker

Samuel Downe, age 29, factory worker living near Leeds; at the age of about ten began work at Mr.

Marshall's mill at Shrewsbury, where the customary hours when work was brisk were generally 5 A.M. to 8 P.M., sometimes from 5:30 A.M. to 8 or 9:

What means were taken to keep the children awake and vigilant, especially at the termination of such a day's labour as you have described?—There was generally a blow or a box, or a tap with a strap, or sometimes the hand.

Have you yourself been strapped?—Yes, most severely, till I could not bear to sit upon a chair without having pillows, and through that I left. I was strapped both on my own legs, and then I was put upon a man's back, and then strapped and buckled with two straps to an iron pillar, and flogged, and all by one overlooker; after that he took a piece of tow, and twisted it in the shape of a cord, and put it in my mouth, and tied it behind my head.

He gagged you?—Yes; and then he ordered me to run round a part of the machinery where he was overlooker, and he stood at one end, and every time I came there he struck me with a stick, which I believe was an ash plant, and which he generally carried in his hand, and sometimes he hit me, and sometimes he did not; and one of the men in the room came and begged me off, and that he let me go, and not beat me any more, and consequently he did.

You have been beaten with extraordinary severity?—Yes, I was beaten so that I had not power to cry at all, or hardly speak at one time. What age were you at that time?—Between 10 and 11.

---

industrial times, working in the fields or carding and spinning wool at home with the growth of cottage industry. In the Industrial Revolution, however, child labor was exploited more than ever and in a considerably more systematic fashion (see the boxes on pp. 724–725). The owners of cotton factories appreciated certain features of child labor. Children had a particular delicate touch as spinners of cotton. Their smaller size made it easier for them to move under machines to gather loose cotton. Moreover, children were more easily broken to factory work. Above all, children represented a cheap supply of labor. In 1821, 49 percent of the British people were under twenty years of age. Hence children made up a particularly abundant supply of labor, and they were

paid only about one-sixth or one-third of what a man was paid. In the cotton factories in 1838, children under eighteen made up 29 percent of the total work force; children as young as seven worked twelve to fifteen hours per day six days a week in cotton mills.

Especially terrible in the early Industrial Revolution was the use of so-called pauper apprentices. These were orphans or children abandoned by their parents who had wound up in the care of local parishes. To save on their upkeep, parish officials found it convenient to apprentice them to factory owners looking for a cheap source of labor. These children worked for long hours, were strictly disciplined, received inadequate food and recreation, and in large numbers frequently became deformed

Child Labor: The Mines
▼ ▼ ▼

After examining conditions in British coal mines, a government official commented that "the hardest labour in the worst room in the worst-conducted factory is less hard, less cruel, and less demoralizing than the labour in the best of coal-mines." Yet it was not until 1842 that legislation was passed eliminating the labor of boys under ten from the mines. This selection is taken from a government report on the mines in Lancashire.

The Black Holes of Worsley

Examination of Thomas Gibson and George Bryan, witnesses from the coal mines at Worsley:

Have you worked from a boy in a coal mine?— (Both) Yes.

What had you to do then?—Thrutching the basket and drawing. It is done by little boys; one draws the basket and the other pushes it behind. Is that hard labour?—Yes, very hard labour.

For how many hours a day did you work?—Nearly nine hours regularly; sometimes twelve; I have worked about thirteen. We used to go in at six in the morning, and took a bit of bread and cheese in our pocket, and stopped two or three minutes; and some days nothing at all to eat.

How was it that sometimes you had nothing to eat?—We were over-burdened. I had only a mother, and she had nothing to give me. I was sometimes half starved. . . .

Do they work in the same way now exactly?—Yes, they do; they have nothing more than a bit of bread and cheese in their pocket, and sometimes can't eat it all, owing to the dust and damp and badness of air; and sometimes it is as hot as an oven; sometimes I have seen it so hot as to melt a candle.

What are the usual wages of a boy of eight?—They used to get 3d or 4d a day. Now a man's wages is divided into eight eighths; and when a boy is eight years old he gets one of those eighths; at eleven, two eighths; at thirteen, three eighths; at fifteen, four eighths; at twenty, man's wages.

What are the wages of a man?—About 15s if he is in full employment, but often not more than 10s, and out of that he has to get his tools and candles. He consumes about four candles in nine hours' work, in some places six; 6d per pound, and twenty-four candles to the pound.

Were you ever beaten as a child?—Yes, many a score of times; both kicks and thumps.

Are many girls employed in the pits?—Yes, a vast of those. They do the same kind of work as the boys till they get above 14 years of age, when they get the wages of half a man, and never get more, and continue at the same work for many years.

Did they ever fight together?—Yes, many days together. Both boys and girls; sometimes they are very loving with one another.

---

from being kept too long in unusual positions. Although economic liberals and some industrialists were against all state intervention in economic matters, Parliament eventually remedied some of the worst ills of child abuse in factories and mines (see Efforts at Change: Reformers and Government later in the chapter). The legislation of the 1830s and 1840s, however, primarily affected child labor in textile factories and mines. It did not touch the use of children in small workshops or the nonfactory trades that were not protected. As these trades were in competition with the new factories, conditions there were often even worse. Pottery works, for example, were not investigated until the 1860s when it was found that 17 percent of the workers were under

eleven years of age. One investigator reported what he found:

> The boys were kept in constant motion throughout the day, each carrying from thirty to fifty dozen of moulds into the stoves, and remaining . . . long enough to take the dried earthenware away. The distance thus run by a boy in the course of a day . . . was estimated at seven miles. From the very nature of this exhausting occupation children were rendered pale, weak and unhealthy. In the depth of winter, with the thermometer in the open air sometimes below zero, boys, with little clothing but rags, might be seen running to and fro on errands or to their dinners with the perspiration on their foreheads, "after labouring for hours like little slaves." The

inevitable result of such transitions of temperature were consumption, asthma, and acute inflammation.[13]

Little wonder that child labor legislation included pottery works in 1864.

By 1830, women and children made up two-thirds of the cotton industry's labor. However, as the number of children employed declined under the Factory Act of 1833, their places were taken by women, who came to dominate the labor forces of the early factories. Women made up 50 percent of the labor force in textile (cotton and woolen) factories before 1870. They were mostly unskilled labor and were paid half or less of what men received. Excessive working hours for women were outlawed in 1844, but only in textile factories and mines; not until 1867 were they outlawed in craft workshops.

The employment of children and women in large part represents a continuation of a pre-industrial kinship pattern. Cottage industry had always involved the efforts of the entire family, and it seemed perfectly natural to continue this pattern. Men migrating from the countryside to industrial towns and cities took their wives and children with them into the factory or into the mines. Of 136 employees in Robert Peel's factory at Bury in 1801, 95 belonged to twenty-six families. The impetus for this family work often came from the family itself. The factory owner Jedediah Strutt was opposed to child labor under ten but was forced by parents to take children as young as seven.

The employment of large numbers of women in factories did not produce a significant transformation in female working patterns, as was once assumed. Studies of urban households in France and Britain, for example, have revealed that throughout the nineteenth century traditional types of female labor still predominated in the women's work world. In 1851, fully 40 percent of the female work force in Britain consisted of domestic servants. In France, the largest group of female workers, 40 percent, worked in agriculture. In addition, only 20 percent of female workers labored in Britain's factories, only 10 percent in France. Regional and local studies have also indicated that most of the workers were single women. Few married women worked outside their homes.

The Factory Acts that limited the work hours of children and women also began to break up the traditional kinship pattern of work and led to a new pattern based on a separation of work and home. Men came to be expected to be responsible for the primary work obligations while women assumed daily control of the family and performed low-paying jobs such as laundry work that could be done in the home. Domestic industry made it possible for women to continue their contributions to family survival.

Historians have also reminded us that if the treatment of children in the mines and factories seems particularly cruel and harsh, contemporary treatment of children in general was often brutal. Beatings, for example, had long been regarded, even by dedicated churchmen and churchwomen, as the best way to discipline children.

Standards of Living

One of the most heated debates on the Industrial Revolution concerns the standard of living. Most historians assume that in the long run the Industrial Revolution increased living standards dramatically in the form of higher per capita incomes and greater consumer choices. But did the first generation of industrial workers experience a decline in their living standards and suffer unnecessarily? Some historians have argued that early industrialization required huge profits to be reinvested in new and ever more expensive equipment, thus justifying lower wages and higher profits. Others have questioned that argument, pointing out that initial investments in early machinery were not necessarily large nor did they need to be. What certainly did occur in the first half of the nineteenth century was a widening gap between rich and poor. One estimate, based on income tax returns in Britain, is that the wealthiest 1 percent of the population increased its share of the national product from 25 percent in 1801 to 35 percent in 1848.

Wages, prices, and consumption patterns are some of the criteria used for measuring the standard of living. Between 1780 and 1850, as far as we can determine from the available evidence, both wages and prices fluctuated widely. Most historians believe that during the Napoleonic wars the increase in prices outstripped wages. Between 1815 and 1830, a price fall was accompanied by a slight increase in wages. But from 1830 to the late 1840s, real wages seem to have improved although regional variations make generalizations dangerous.

When we look at consumption patterns, we find that in Britain in 1850 tea, sugar, and coffee were still semiluxuries consumed primarily by the upper and middle classes and better-off artisans. Meat consumption per capita was less in 1840 than in 1780. On the other hand, a mass market had developed in the cheap cotton goods so important to the Industrial Revolution. As a final note on the question of the standard of living, some historians who take a positive view of the early Industrial Revolution have questioned what would have happened to Britain's growing population without the Industrial Revolution. Would it have gone the way of Ireland's in the Great Hunger of the mid-nineteenth century? No one really knows.

No doubt the periodic crises of overproduction that haunted industrialization from its beginnings caused even further economic hardship. Short-term economic depressions brought high unemployment and increased social tensions. Unemployment figures could be astronomical. During one of these economic depressions in 1842, for example, 60 percent of the factory employees in Bolton were laid off. Cyclical depressions were particularly devastating in towns whose prosperity rested on one industry.

Overall we can say that some evidence exists for an increase in real wages for the working classes between 1790 and 1850, especially in the 1840s. But can standards of living be assessed only in terms of prices, wages, and consumption patterns? No doubt those meant little to people who faced dreadful housing, adulterated food, public health hazards, and the psychological traumas associated with a complete change in work habits and way of life. The real gainers in the early Industrial Revolution were the middle and upper classes—and some skilled workers whose jobs were not eliminated by the new machines. But industrial workers themselves would have to wait until the second half of the nineteenth century until they reaped the benefits of industrialization.

Efforts at Change: The Workers

Before long, workers looked to the formation of labor organizations to gain decent wages and working conditions. The British government, reacting against the radicalism of the French revolutionary working classes, had passed a series of Combination Acts in 1799 and 1800 outlawing associations of workmen. The legislation failed to prevent the formation of trade unions, however. Similar to the craft societies of earlier times, these new associations were formed by skilled workers in a number of new industries, including the cotton spinners, ironworkers, coal miners, and shipwrights. These unions served two purposes. One was to preserve their own workers' position by limiting entry into their trade; another was to gain benefits from the employers. These early trade unions had limited goals. They favored a working-class struggle against employers, but only to win improvements for the members of their own trades.

Some trade unions were even willing to strike to gain their goals. Bitter strikes were carried out by hand-loom weavers in Glasgow in 1813, cotton spinners in Manchester in 1818, and miners in Northumberland and Durham in 1810. Such blatant illegal activity caused Parliament to repeal the Combination Acts in 1824, accepting the argument of some members that the acts themselves had so alienated workers that they had formed unions. Unions were now tolerated, but other legislation enabled authorities to keep close watch over their activities.

▼ **Membership Card in an Early Trade Union.** Skilled workers in a number of new industries formed trade unions in an attempt to gain higher wages and better working conditions. The trade union also served to protect the position of its members by limiting entry into the trade. In their attempts to gain benefits for their members, trade unions were even willing to go on strike. Pictured here is a membership card issued to the West of Scotland Power Loom Female Weavers Society in 1833.

In the 1820s and 1830s, the union movement began to focus on the creation of national unions. One of the leaders in this effort was a well-known cotton magnate and social reformer, Robert Owen (1771–1858). Owen came to believe in the creation of voluntary associations that would demonstrate to others the benefits of cooperative rather than competitive living (see Chapter 22 on the utopian socialists). Although Owen's ideas were not directed specifically to trade unionists, his ideas had great appeal to some of their leaders. Under Owen's direction, plans emerged for a Grand National Consolidated Trades Union, which was formed in February 1834. As a national federation of trade unions, its primary purpose was to coordinate a general strike for the eight-hour working day. Rhetoric, however, soon outpaced reality, and by the summer of the same year, the lack of real working-class support led to its total collapse. Afterward, the union movement reverted to trade unions for individual crafts. The largest and most successful was the Amalgamated Society of Engineers, formed in 1850. Its provision of generous unemployment benefits in return for a small weekly payment was precisely the kind of practical gains these trade unions sought. Larger goals would have to wait.

Trade unionism was not the only type of collective action by workers in the early decades of the Industrial Revolution. The Luddites were skilled craftsmen in the Midlands and northern England who in 1812 attacked the machines that they believed threatened their livelihoods. These attacks failed to stop the industrial mechanization of Britain and have been viewed as utterly naive. Some historians, however, have also seen them as an intense eruption of feeling against unrestrained industrial capitalism. The inability of 12,000 troops to find the culprits provides stunning evidence of the local support they received in their areas.

A much more meaningful expression of the attempts of British workers to improve their condition developed in the movement known as Chartism. It was the first "important political movement of working men organized during the nineteenth century." Its aim was to achieve political democracy. A People's Charter was drawn up in 1838 that demanded universal male suffrage, payment of the members of Parliament, and annual sessions of Parliament (see the box on p. 729). Two national petitions incorporating these points, affixed with millions of signatures, were presented to Parliament in 1839 and 1842. Both were rejected by the members of Parliament who were not at all ready for political democracy. As one member said, universal suffrage would be "fatal to all the purposes for which government ex-

ists" and was "utterly incompatible with the very existence of civilization." After 1843, Chartism as a movement had largely played itself out. It had never really posed a serious threat to the British establishment, but it had not been a total failure either. Its true significance stemmed from its ability to arouse and organize millions of working-class men and women, to give them a sense of working-class consciousness that they had not really possessed before. This political education of working people was important to the ultimate acceptance of all the points of the People's Charter in the future.

Efforts at Change: Reformers and Government

Efforts to improve the worst conditions of the industrial factory system also came from outside the ranks of the working classes. From its beginning the Industrial Revolution had been the source of much criticism. Romantic poets like William Wordsworth (see Chapter 22) decried the destruction of the natural world:

I grieve, when on the darker side
Of this great change I look; and there behold
Such outrage done to nature as compels
The indignant power to justify herself.

Reform-minded men, be they factory owners who felt twinges of Christian conscience or social reformers in Parliament, campaigned against the evils of the industrial factory, especially condemning the abuse of children. One hoped for the day "that these little ones should once more see the rising and setting of the sun."

As it became apparent that the increase in wealth generated by the Industrial Revolution was accompanied by ever-increasing numbers of poor people, more and more efforts were made to document and deal with the problems. As reports from civic-minded citizens and parliamentary commissions intensified and demonstrated the extent of poverty, degradation, and suffering, reform efforts began to succeed.

The first success was achieved in a series of Factory Acts passed between 1802 and 1819 that limited labor for children between the ages of nine and sixteen to twelve hours a day; it was forbidden to employ children under nine years old. Moreover, the laws stipulated that children were to receive instruction in reading and arithmetic during working hours. But these acts applied only to cotton mills, not to factories or mines where some of the worst abuses were taking place. Just as important, no provision was made for enforcing the acts through a system of inspection.

The Political Demands of the Chartist Movement
▼ ▼ ▼

In the late 1830s and early 1840s, working-class protest centered on achieving a clear set of political goals, particularly universal male suffrage, as the means to achieve economic and social improvements. This selection is taken from one of the national petitions presented to Parliament by the Chartist movement. Although the petition failed, Chartism helped to arouse and organize millions of workers.

National Petition (1839)

To the Honourable the Commons of the United Kingdom of Great Britain and Ireland, in Parliament assembled, the Petition of the undersigned, their suffering countrymen, HUMBLY SHEWETH,—

The energies of a mighty kingdom have been wasted in building up the power of selfish and ignorant men, and its resources squandered for their aggrandisement. The good of a part has been advanced at the sacrifice of the good of the nation. The few have governed for the interest of the few, while the interests of the many have been sottishly neglected, or insolently . . . trampled upon. . . . We come before your honourable house to tell you, with all humility, that this state of things must not be permitted to continue. That it cannot long continue, without very seriously endangering the stability of the throne, and the peace of the kingdom, and that if, by God's help, and all lawful and constitutional appliances, an end can be put to it, we are fully resolved that it shall speedily come to an end. . . . Required, as we are universally, to support and obey the laws, nature and reason entitle us to demand that in the making of the laws the universal voice shall be implicitly listened to. We perform the duties of freemen; we must have the privileges of freemen. Therefore, we demand universal suffrage. The suffrage, to be exempt from the corruption of the wealthy and the violence of the powerful, must be secret. . . . To public safety, as well as public confidence, frequent elections are essential. Therefore, we demand annual parliaments. With power to choose, and freedom in choosing, the range of our choice must be unrestricted. We are compelled, by the existing laws, to take for our representatives men who are incapable of appreciating our difficulties, or have little sympathy with them; merchants who have retired from trade and no longer feel its harassings; proprietors of land who are alike ignorant of its evils and its cure; lawyers by whom the notoriety of the senate is courted only as a means of obtaining notice in the courts. . . . We demand that in the future election of members of your . . . house, the approbation of the constituency shall be the sole qualification, and that to every representative so chosen, shall be assigned out of the public taxes, a fair and adequate remuneration for the time which he is called upon to devote to the public service. . . . Universal suffrage will, and it alone can, bring true and lasting peace to the nation; we firmly believe that it will also bring prosperity. May it therefore please your honourable house, to take this our petition into your most serious consideration, and to use your utmost endeavours, by all constitutional means, to have a law passed, granting to every male of lawful age, sane mind, and unconvicted of crime, the right of voting for members of parliament, and directing all future elections of members of parliament to be in the way of secret ballot, and ordaining that the duration of parliament, so chosen, shall in no case exceed one year, and abolishing all property qualifications in the members, and providing for their due remuneration while in attendance on their parliamentary duties.

In the reform-minded decades of the 1830s and 1840s, new legislation was passed. The Factory Act of 1833 strengthened earlier labor legislation. All textile factories were now included. Children between nine and thirteen could work only eight hours a day; those between thirteen and eighteen, twelve hours. Inspection was to be enforced. Another piece of legislation in 1833 required that children between nine and thirteen have at least two hours of elementary education during the working day. In 1847, the Ten Hours Act reduced the work day for children between thirteen and eighteen to ten hours. Women were also now included in the ten-hour limitation. It was not until 1842 that a Coal Mines Act eliminated the employment of boys under ten and women in mines. Eventually, men too would benefit from the move to restrict factory hours.

The Industrial Revolution became one of the major forces of change in the nineteenth century as it led Western civilization into the industrial era that has characterized the modern world. Beginning in Britain, its spread to the Continent and the new American nation ensured its growth and domination of the Western world.

The Industrial Revolution seemed to prove to Europeans the underlying assumption of the Scientific Revolution of the seventeenth century—that human beings were capable of dominating nature. By rationally manipulating the material environment for human benefit, people could create new levels of material prosperity and produce machines not dreamed of in their wildest imaginings. Lost in the excitement of the Industrial Revolution were the voices that pointed to the dehumanization of the work force and the alienation from one's work, one's associates, one's self, and the natural world.

The Industrial Revolution also transformed the social world of Europe. The creation of an industrial proletariat produced a whole new force for change. The development of a wealthy industrial middle class presented a challenge to the long-term hegemony of landed wealth. While that wealth had been threatened by the fortunes of commerce, it had never been overturned. But the new bourgeoisie was more demanding. How, in some places, this new industrial bourgeoisie came to play a larger role in the affairs of state will become evident in the next chapter.

Notes

▼ ▼ ▼

1. Quoted in W. Gorden Rimmer, *Marshall's of Leeds, Flax-Spinners 1788–1886* (Cambridge, 1960), p. 40.

2. Daniel Defoe, *A Plan of the English Commerce* (Oxford, 1928), pp. 76–77.

3. Quoted in David Landes, *The Unbound Prometheus: Technological Change and Industrial Development in Western Europe from 1750 to the Present* (Cambridge, 1969), pp. 99–100.

4. Quoted in Albert Tucker, *A History of English Civilization* (New York, 1972), p. 583.

5. Quoted in Landes, *The Unbound Prometheus*, pp. 149–50.

6. Quotations can be found in E. Royston Pike, *Human Documents of the Industrial Revolution in Britain* (London, 1966), pp. (in order of quotations) 320, 313, 314, 343.

7. Ibid., p. 315.

8. Quoted in A. J. Donajgrodzi, ed., *Social Control in Nineteenth Century Britain* (London, 1977), p. 141.

9. Quoted in Pike, *Human Documents of the Industrial Revolution in Britain*, pp. 343–44.

10. Quoted in Eric J. Evans, *The Forging of the Modern State: Early Industrial Britain, 1783–1870* (London, 1983), p. 113.

11. Henry Mayhew, *London Labour and the London Poor* (London, 1851), 1: 342–43.

12. Quoted in Pike, *Human Documents of the Industrial Revolution in Britain*, pp. 60–61.

13. Quoted in Evans, *The Forging of the Modern State*, p. 124.

Suggestions for Further Reading

▼ ▼ ▼

The well-written work by D. Landes, *The Unbound Prometheus: Technological Change and Industrial Development in Western Europe from 1750 to the Present* (Cambridge, 1969) is still the best introduction to the Industrial Revolution. Although more technical, also of value are C. Trebilcock, *The Industrialization of the Continental Powers, 1780–1914* (London, 1981); and S. Pollard, *Peaceful Conquest: The Industrialization of Europe, 1760–1970* (Oxford, 1981). A volume in the Fontana Economic History of Europe edited by C. M. Cipolla, *The Industrial Revolution* (London, 1973) is also valuable. Although older and dated, T. S. Ashton, *The Industrial Revolution, 1760–1830* (New York, 1948), still provides an interesting introduction to the Industrial Revolution in Britain. Much better, however, are P. Mathias, *The First Industrial Nation: An Economic History of Britain, 1700–1914*, 2d. ed. (New York, 1983); and P. Deane, *The First Industrial Revolution* (Cambridge, 1965). For a discussion of the areas in Europe that lagged behind in the industrialization process, see I. T. Behrend and G. Rankl, *The European Periphery and Industrialization, 1780–1914* (Cambridge, 1982).

Given the importance of Great Britain in the Industrial Revolution, a number of books are available for placing the Industrial Revolution in Britain into a broader context. See E. J. Evans, *The Forging of the Modern State: Early Industrial Britain, 1783–1870* (London, 1983); S. Checkland, *British Public Policy, 1776–1939: An Economic, Social and Political Perspective* (Cambridge, 1983); H. Perkin, *The Origins of Modern English Society, 1780–1880* (London, 1969); and E. J. Hobsbawm, *Industry and Empire* (London, 1968).

The early industrialization of the United States is examined in P. Temin, *Causal Factors in American Economic Growth in the Nineteenth Century* (London, 1975); and D. C. North, *The Economic Growth of the United States, 1790–1860* (New York, 1961), although the latter's stress on the importance of regional specialization to economic growth has been questioned. On the economic ties between Great Britain and the United States, see D. Jeremy, *Transatlantic Industrial Revolution: The Diffusion of Textile Technology between Britain and America, 1790–1830* (Cambridge, Mass., 1981).

A general discussion of population growth in Europe can be found in T. McKeown, *The Modern Rise of Population* (London, 1976), although it has been criticized for its emphasis on nutrition and hygiene as the two major causes of that growth. For an examination of urban growth, see the older but classic work of A. F. Weber, *The Growth of Cities in the Nineteenth Century: A Study in Statistics* (Ithaca, N.Y., 1963); and the more recent work by A. R. Sutcliffe, *Towards the Planned City: Germany, Britain, the United States and France, 1780–1914* (Oxford, 1981). C. Woodham Smith, *The Great Hunger* (New York, 1962) is a well-written account of the great Irish tragedy. Many of the works cited above have much information on the social impact of the Industrial Revolution, but additional material is available in C. Morazé, *The Triumph of the Middle Classes* (London, 1966); F. Crouzet, *The First Industrialists: The Problems of Origins* (Cambridge, 1985), on British entrepreneurs; and E. Gauldie, *Cruel Habitations, A History of Working-Class Housing, 1790–1918* (London, 1974). G. Himmelfarb, *The Idea of Poverty: England in the Early Industrial Age* (New York, 1984) traces the concepts of poverty and poor from the mid-eighteenth century to the mid-nineteenth century. A valuable work on female labor patterns is L. A. Tilly and J. W. Scott, *Women, Work, and Family* (New York, 1978).

Chapter 22

Reaction, Revolution, and Romanticism, 1815–1850

▼ ▼ ▼ ▼ ▼

The forces of upheaval unleashed during the French revolutionary and Napoleonic eras were temporarily quieted in 1815 as monarchs sought to restore stability by reestablishing much of the old order to a Europe ravaged by war. Kings and landed and bureaucratic elites regained their control over domestic governments while internationally the forces of conservatism attempted to maintain the new status quo; some states even used military force to intervene in the internal affairs of other countries in their desire to crush revolutions.

But the European world had been changed, and it would not readily go back to the old system. New ideologies of change, especially liberalism and nationalism, products of the revolutionary upheaval initiated in France, had become too powerful to be contained forever. Not content with the status quo, the forces of change called forth revolts and revolutions that periodically shook Europe in the 1820s and 1830s and culminated in the widespread revolutions of 1848. Some of the revolutions and revolutionaries were successful; most were not. Although the old order had prevailed in many ways, everywhere it was apparent by 1850 that it would not endure. This perception was reinforced by the changes wrought by the Industrial Revolution. Together the forces unleashed by the dual revolutions—the French Revolution and the Industrial Revolution—made it impossible to return to prerevolutionary Europe. While these two revolutions initiated what historians like to call the modern European world, it will also be apparent

| Congress of Vienna ▼ | Revolutions in France, Belgium, Poland, Italy ▼ | Reform Bill in Britain ▼ | Revolutions in France, Germany, Austrian Empire ▼ |

•••••••• 1810 •••••••••••• 1820 •••••••••• 1830 ••••••••••• 1840 ••••••••••• 1850 ••••••••

| ▲ Shelley, *Prometheus Unbound* | ▲ Beethoven, Ninth Symphony | ▲ London Police | ▲ Friedrich, *Man and Woman Gazing at the Moon* | ▲ Tristan, Worker's Union |

that much of the old still remained in the midst of the new.

▼ The Conservative Order, 1815–1830

The immediate response to the defeat of Napoleon was the desire to contain revolution and the revolutionary forces by restoring much of the old order. But the triumphant rulers were not naive and realized that they could not return to 1789.

The Peace Settlement

In March 1814, even before Napoleon had been defeated, his four major enemies—Great Britain, Austria, Prussia, and Russia—had agreed to remain united, not only to defeat France but to ensure peace after the war. After Napoleon's defeat, this Quadruple Alliance restored the Bourbon monarchy to France in the person of Louis XVIII and concluded the first Treaty of Paris with the conquered nation. It was a lenient treaty. The Bourbons had not been responsible for France's revolutionary upheaval, and there was little need to burden the government of Louis XVIII unnecessarily. Not only were the French allowed to keep the territories they had acquired by 1792 (some parts of Germany and the Austrian Netherlands), but they paid no indemnity as well. Since the Treaty of Paris did not deal with the problems created by Napoleon's rearrangement of the map of Europe, the great powers agreed to meet at a congress in Vienna in September 1814 to arrange a final peace settlement.

Although all the powers were invited to attend the congress, important decisions were closely guarded by the representatives of the four great powers. The skillful maneuvering of the French representative, the clever Prince Talleyrand, enabled the defeated power, France, to actually participate in some of the decisions. Above all, however, the congress was dominated by the Austrian foreign minister, Prince Klemens von Metternich

(1773–1859). An experienced diplomat, Metternich's public demeanor reflected the conceit and self-assurance of the comments that he recorded in his memoirs in 1819: "There is a wide sweep about my mind. I am always above and beyond the preoccupation of most public men; I cover a ground much vaster than they can see. I cannot keep myself from saying about twenty times a day: 'How right I am, and how wrong they are.'"[1]

Metternich claimed that he was guided at Vienna by the principle of legitimacy. To reestablish peace and stability in Europe, he considered it necessary to restore the legitimate monarchs who would preserve traditional institutions. This had already been done in the restoration of the Bourbons in France, but the principle of legitimacy was in fact largely ignored elsewhere and completely overshadowed by more practical considerations of power. The congress's treatment of Poland, to which Russia, Austria, and Prussia all had claims, illustrates this approach. Prussia and Austria were allowed to keep some Polish territory. A new, nominally independent Polish kingdom, about three-quarters of the size of the duchy of Warsaw, was established with the Romanov dynasty of Russia as its hereditary monarchs. Although the Russian tsar Alexander I (1801–1825) voluntarily granted the new kingdom a constitution guaranteeing its independence, Poland's foreign policy (and Poland) remained under Russian control. Prussia was compensated for its loss of Polish lands by receiving two-fifths of Saxony, the Napoleonic German kingdom of Westphalia, and the left bank of the Rhine. In turn, Austria was compensated for its loss of the Austrian Netherlands by being given control of the northern provinces of Italy called Lombardy and Venetia. In making these territorial rearrangements, the powers at Vienna believed they were following the familiar eighteenth-century practice of maintaining a balance of power or equilibrium among the great powers. Essentially, this meant a balance of political and military forces that guaranteed the independence of the great powers by ensuring that no one country could dominate Europe. To balance Russian gains, Prussia and Austria had been strengthened. According to Metternich, this arrangement had clearly avoided a great danger: "Prussia and Austria are completing their systems of defence; united, the two monarchies form an unconquerable barrier against the enterprises of any conquering prince who might perhaps once again occupy the throne of France or that of Russia."[2]

It was considerations of the balance of power that dictated the allied treatment of France. France had not been overly weakened so that it could remain a great power. Nevertheless, the fear that France might again upset the European peace remained strong enough that the great powers attempted to establish major defensive barriers against possible French expansion. To the north of France, they created a new enlarged kingdom of the Netherlands composed of the former Dutch Republic and the Austrian Netherlands (Belgium) under a new ruler, King William I of the House of Orange. To the southeast, Piedmont (officially styled the kingdom of Sardinia) was enlarged. Prussia was strengthened on France's eastern frontier by giving it control of the territory along the left bank of the Rhine. The British at least expected Prussia to be the major bulwark against French expansion in central Europe, but the Congress of Vienna also created a new league of German states, the Germanic Confederation, to replace the Napoleonic Confederation of the Rhine.

Napoleon's escape from Elba and his One Hundred Days in the midst of the Congress of Vienna, delayed the negotiations but did not significantly alter the overall agreement. It was decided, however, to punish the French people for their enthusiastic response to Napoleon's return. By the second Treaty of Paris, France's borders were returned to those of 1790, and it was forced to pay an indemnity and accept an army of occupation for five years.

The Vienna peace settlement of 1815 has sometimes been criticized for its failure to recognize the liberal and national forces unleashed by the French revolutionary and Napoleonic eras. Containing these revolutionary forces was precisely what the diplomats at Vienna hoped to achieve. Their transfers of territories and peoples to the victors to create a new balance of power, with little or no regard for the wishes of the peoples themselves, was in accord with long-standing traditions of European diplomacy. One could hardly expect Metternich, foreign minister of the Austrian Empire, a dynastic state composed of many different peoples, to espouse a principle of self-determination for European nationalities. Whatever its weaknesses, the Congress of Vienna has received credit for establishing a European order that managed to avoid a general European conflict for almost a century.

The Ideology of Conservatism

The peace arrangements of 1815 were but the beginning of a conservative reaction determined to contain the liberal and nationalist forces unleashed by the French Revolution. Metternich and his kind were representatives of the ideology known as conservatism (see the box on p. 736). As a modern political philosophy, conservatism dates from 1790 when Edmund Burke wrote his *Reflections on the Revolution in France* in reaction to the French Revolution, especially its radical

▼ **The Congress of Vienna.** Following the defeat of Napoleon, the states of Europe met at a congress in Vienna to arrange a final peace settlement. Seen here is a group portrait of the negotiators. Despite the number of states represented at the congress, the most important decisions were reached by the four major enemies of Napoleon—Great Britain, Austria, Prussia, and Russia.

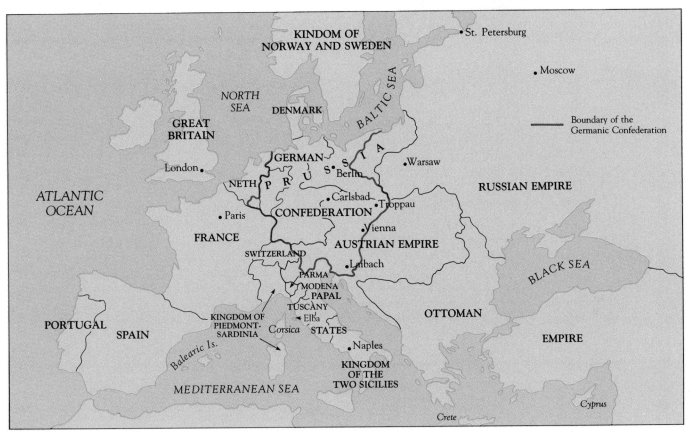

▼ **Map 22.1** Europe in 1815.

republican and democratic ideas. Those people labeled conservatives, however, did not always agree on all principles.

Edmund Burke (1729–1797)enunciated the principles of an evolutionary conservatism. In his *Reflections on the Revolution in France*, Burke maintained that society was a contract, but "the state ought not to be considered as nothing better than a partnership agreement in a trade of pepper and coffee, to be taken up for a temporary interest and to be dissolved by the fancy of the parties." The state was a partnership but one "not only between those who are living, but between those who are living, those who are dead and those who are to be born." No one generation therefore has the right to destroy this partnership; instead, each generation has the duty to preserve and transmit it to the next. Indeed, "changing the state as often as there are floating fancies, . . . no one generation could link with the other." Burke opposed the violent overthrow of a government by revolution, but he did not reject the possibility of change. Sudden change was unacceptable, but that did not eliminate gradual or evolutionary improvements. As Burke said, "a disposition to preserve and an ability to improve, taken together, would be my standard of a statesman." [3]

Burke's conservatism, however, was not the only kind. The Frenchman Joseph de Maistre (1753–1821) was the most influential spokesman for a counterrevolutionary and authoritarian conservatism. De Maistre espoused an unequivocal restoration of hereditary monarchy. He went beyond Burke's pragmatic justification for monarchy as a social cement needed to hold society together to a defense of monarchy as a divinely sanctioned institution. Only absolute monarchy could guarantee "order in society" and avoid the chaos generated by movements like the French Revolution. De Maistre even took his defense of absolutism to the absurd point of justifying love for and obedience to an unjust ruler: "We find ourselves in a realm whose sovereign has proclaimed his laws. . . . Some appear hard and even unjust." What should we do? "Since we start with the supposition that the master exists and that we must serve him absolutely, is it not better to serve him, whatever his nature, with love than without it?" [4]

The Voice of Conservatism: Metternich of Austria

▼ ▼ ▼

There was no greater symbol of conservatism in the first half of the nineteenth century than Prince Klemens von Metternich of Austria. Metternich played a crucial role at the Congress of Vienna and worked tirelessly for thirty years to repress the "revolutionary seed," as he called it, that had been spread to Europe by the "military despotism of Bonaparte."

Klemens von Metternich, Memoirs

We are convinced that society can no longer be saved without strong and vigorous resolutions on the part of the Governments still free in their opinions and actions.

We are also convinced that this may be, if the Governments face the truth, if they free themselves from all illusion, if they join their ranks and take their stand on a line of correct, unambiguous, and frankly announced principles.

By this course the monarchs will fulfil the duties imposed upon them by Him who, by entrusting them with power, has charged them to watch over the maintenance of justice, and the rights of all, to avoid the paths of error, and tread firmly in the way of truth. . . .

If the same elements of destruction which are now throwing society into convulsions have existed in all ages—for every age has seen immoral and ambitious men, hypocrites, men of heated imaginations, wrong motives, and wild projects—yet ours, by the single fact of the liberty of the press, possesses more than any preceding age the means of contact, seduction, and attraction whereby to act on these different classes of men.

We are certainly not alone in questioning if society can exist with the liberty of the press, a scourge unknown to the world before the latter half of the seventeenth century, and restrained until the end of the eighteenth, with scarcely any exceptions but England—a part of Europe separated from the continent by the sea, as well as by her language and by her peculiar manners.

The first principle to be followed by the monarchs, united as they are by the coincidence of their desires and opinions, should be that of maintaining the stability of political institutions against the disorganized excitement which has taken possession of men's minds; the immutability of principles against the madness of their interpretation; and respect for laws actually in force against a desire for their destruction. . . .

The first and greatest concern for the immense majority of every nation is the stability of the laws, and their uninterrupted action—never their change. Therefore, let the Governments govern, let them maintain the groundwork of their institutions, both ancient and modern; for if it is at all times dangerous to touch them, it certainly would not now, in the general confusion, be wise to do so. . . .

Let them maintain religious principles in all their purity, and not allow the faith to be attacked and morality interpreted according to the social contract or the visions of foolish sectarians.

Let them suppress Secret Societies, that gangrene of society. . . .

To every great State determined to survive the storm there still remain many chances of salvation, and a strong union between the States on the principles we have announced will overcome the storm itself.

Despite their differences, most conservatives held to a general body of beliefs. They favored obedience to political authority, believed that organized religion was crucial to social order, hated revolutionary upheavals, and were unwilling to accept either the liberal demands for civil liberties and representative governments or the nationalistic aspirations generated by the French revolutionary era. The community took precedence over individual rights; society must be organized and ordered, and tradition remained the best guide for order. After 1815, the political philosophy of conservatism was supported by hereditary monarchs, government bureaucracies, landowning aristocracies, and revived churches, be they Protestant or Catholic. Although not unopposed, both internationally and domestically the conservative forces appeared dominant after 1815.

The Conservative Domination:
The Concert of Europe

The conservative order that European diplomats were constructing at Vienna must have seemed fragile when the French people responded with enthusiasm to Napoleon after his escape from Elba. The great powers' fear of revolution and war led them to develop the Concert of Europe as a means to maintain the new status quo they had constructed. This Concert of Europe grew out of the reaffirmation of the Quadruple Alliance in November 1815. Great Britain, Russia, Prussia, and Austria renewed their commitment against any attempted restoration of Bonapartist power and agreed to meet periodically in conferences to discuss their common interests and examine measures that "will be judged most salutary for the repose and prosperity of peoples, and for the maintenance of peace in Europe."

In accordance with the agreement for periodic meetings, four congresses were held between 1818 and 1822. The first congress, held in 1818 at Aix-la-Chapelle, was by far the most congenial. "Never have I known a prettier little congress," said Metternich. The four great powers agreed to withdraw their army of occupation from France and add France to the Concert of Europe. The Quadruple Alliance became a Quintuple Alliance.

The next congress proved far less pleasant and produced the first fissure in the ranks of the allies. This session at Troppau was called in the autumn of 1820 to deal with the outbreak of revolution in Spain and Italy. The revolt in Spain was directed against Ferdinand VII, the Bourbon king who had been restored to the throne in 1814. In southern Italy, the restoration of another Bourbon, Ferdinand I as king of Naples and Sicily, was accompanied by the return of the nobility and clergy to their privileged positions. Army officers and businessmen led a rebellion that soon spread to the northern Italian kingdom of Piedmont.

Metternich was especially disturbed by the revolts in Italy since he saw them as a threat to Austria's domination of the peninsula. At Troppau, he proposed a protocol that established the principle of intervention. It read:

> States which have undergone a change of Government due to revolution, the results of which threaten other states, *ipso facto* cease to be members of the European Alliance, and remain excluded from it until their situation gives guarantees for legal order and stability. If, owing to such situations, immediate danger threatens other states, the Powers bind themselves, by peaceful means, or if need be by arms, to bring back the guilty state into the bosom of the Great Alliance.[5]

The principle of intervention meant the right of the great powers to send armies into countries where there were revolutions to restore legitimate monarchs to their thrones. Britain refused to agree to the principle, argu-

ing that it had never been the intention of the Quadruple Alliance to interfere in the internal affairs of other states. In Britain's eyes, only revolutionary outbursts threatening the peace of Europe necessitated armed intervention. Ignoring the British response, Austria, Prussia, and Russia met in a third congress at Laibach in January 1821 and authorized the sending of Austrian troops to Naples. These forces crushed the revolt, restored Ferdinand I to the throne, and then moved north to suppress the rebels in Sardinia. At the fourth postwar conference, held at Verona in October 1822, the same three powers authorized France to invade Spain to crush the revolt against Ferdinand VII. In the spring of 1823, French forces restored the Bourbon monarch. By this time, the split between Britain and the more conserva-

▼ **Metternich.** Prince Klemens von Metternich, the foreign minister of Austria, played a major role in the attempt to maintain the new conservative order after 1815. Metternich espoused the principle of intervention, which maintained the right of the great powers to intervene militarily in other countries in order to crush revolutionary movements against legitimate rulers. Metternich was forced to flee abroad during the early stages of the 1848 revolution in the Austrian Empire.

tive powers of central and eastern Europe had become irreversible.

The policy of intervention had succeeded in defeating revolutionary movements in Spain and Italy and in restoring legitimate (and conservative) monarchs to their thrones. It had been done at a price, however. The Concert of Europe had broken down when the British rejected Metternich's principle of intervention. And although the British had failed to thwart allied intervention in Spain and Italy, they were successful in keeping the continental powers from interfering with the revolutions in Latin America.

THE REVOLT OF LATIN AMERICA   While much of North America had been freed of European domination in the eighteenth century by the American Revolution, Latin America remained in the hands of the Spanish and Portuguese. Napoleon's continental wars at the beginning of the nineteenth century, however, soon had repercussions in Latin America. When the Bourbon monarchy of Spain was toppled by Bonaparte, Spanish authority in its colonial empire was weakened. By 1810, the disintegration of royal power in Argentina had led to that nation's

independence. In Venezuela a bitter struggle for independence was led by Simón Bolivar, hailed as the Liberator. His forces freed Colombia in 1819 and Venezuela in 1821. A second liberator was José de San Martin who liberated Chile in 1817 and then, in 1821, moved on to Lima, Peru, the center of Spanish authority. He was soon joined by Bolivar who assumed the task of crushing the last significant Spanish army in 1824. Mexico and the Central American provinces also achieved their freedom, and by 1825, after Portugal had recognized the independence of Brazil, almost all of Latin America had been freed of colonial domination.

In the early 1820s, only one major threat remained to the newly independent Latin American states. Flushed by their success in crushing rebellions in Spain and Italy, the victorious continental powers favored the use of troops to restore Spanish control in Latin America. This time British opposition to intervention prevailed. Eager to gain access to an entire continent for investment and trade, the British proposed joint action with the United States against European interference in Latin America. Distrustful of British motives, President James Monroe acted alone in 1823, guaranteeing the independence of

▼ **Map 22.2** Latin America in the First Half of the Nineteenth Century. (*Left:* Independent Nations by 1828; *Right:* Independent Nations by 1845)

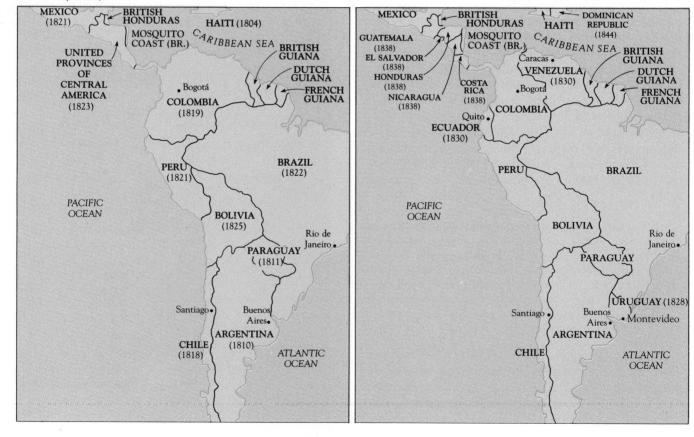

the new Latin American nations and warning against any further European intervention in the New World in the famous Monroe Doctrine. Actually more important to Latin American independence than American words was Britain's navy. It stood between Latin America and any European invasion force, and it was unlikely that any of the continental powers would challenge British naval power.

THE GREEK REVOLT, 1821–1832   The principle of intervention proved to be a double-edged sword. Designed to prevent revolution, it could also be used to support revolution if the great powers found it in their interest to do so. Despite their differences in the congresses, Great Britain, France, and Russia found cause for cooperation.

The Ottoman Empire had long been in control of much of southeastern Europe. By the beginning of the nineteenth century, however, when the Turkish empire was in decline and authority over its outlying territories in southeastern Europe waned, European governments began to take an active interest in its disintegration. This "Eastern Question," as it came to be called, troubled European diplomats throughout the nineteenth century. Russia's proximity to the Ottoman Empire and the religious bonds between the Russians and the Greek Orthodox Christians in Turkish-dominated southeastern Europe naturally gave it special opportunities to enlarge its sphere of influence. Other European powers feared Russian ambitions and had their own interest in the apparent demise of the Ottoman Empire. Austria craved more land in the Balkans, a desire that inevitably meant conflict with Russia, while France and Britain were interested in commercial opportunities and naval bases in the eastern Mediterranean.

In 1821, the Greeks revolted against their Turkish masters. Although subject to Muslim control for four hundred years, they had been allowed to maintain their language and their Greek Orthodox faith. A revival of Greek national sentiment at the beginning of the nineteenth century added to the growing desire for "the liberation of the fatherland from the terrible yoke of Turkish oppression." Initial reaction to the Greek revolt by the European powers was negative since this appeared to be simply another revolt against established authority that should be crushed. But the Greek revolt was soon transformed into a noble cause by an outpouring of European sentiment for the Greeks' struggle. Liberals rallied to the cause of Greek freedom, arguing that Greek democracy was being reborn. Romantic poets and artists (see Romanticism later in the chapter) also publicized the cause of Greek independence.

▼ **The Greek Struggle for Freedom: Eugène Delacroix,** *Greece Expiring on the Ruins of Missolonghi.* The Greek revolt against the Ottoman Empire brought a massive outpouring of European sentiment for the Greeks. Romantic artists and poets were especially eager to publicize the struggle of the Greeks for independence. In this painting, the French painter Delacroix personified Greece as a majestic, defenseless woman appealing for aid against the victorious Turk seen in the background. Delacroix's painting was done soon after the fall of the Greek fortress of Missolonghi to the Turks.

Despite the public ground swell, mutual fears and other interests kept the European powers from intervening until 1827 when a combined British and French fleet went to Greece and defeated a large Turkish fleet. In 1828, Russia declared war on Turkey and invaded its European provinces of Moldavia and Wallachia. By the Treaty of Adrianople in 1829, which ended the Russian-

Turkish war, the Russians received a protectorate over the two provinces. By the same treaty, the Turks agreed to allow Russia, France, and Britain to decide the fate of Greece. In 1830, the three powers declared Greece an independent kingdom, and two years later a new royal dynasty was established in the hands of a son of the Bavarian king.

The Greek revolt made a deep impression on Europeans. It was the first successful revolt against the status quo and represented a victory for both the liberal and national forces that the great powers were trying so hard to repress. But to keep this in perspective, we need to remember that the European powers did not quite see it that way. They had given the Greeks a German king, and the revolution had been successful only because the great powers themselves supported it. Until 1830 the Greek revolt had been the only successful one; the conservative domination was still largely intact.

The Conservative Domination: The European States

Between 1815 and 1830, the conservative domination of Europe evident in the Concert of Europe was also apparent in domestic affairs.

GREAT BRITAIN   In 1815, Great Britain was governed by the aristocratic landowning classes that dominated both houses of Parliament. Suffrage for elections to the House of Commons, controlled by the landed gentry, was restricted and unequal, especially in light of the changing distribution of the British population due to the Industrial Revolution. New, large industrial cities such as Birmingham and Manchester, for example, had no representatives as landowners used pocket and rotten boroughs (see Chapter 19) to control seats in the House of Commons. Although the monarchy was not yet powerless, in practice the power of the crown was largely in the hands of the ruling party in Parliament.

Within Parliament there were two parties, the Tories and Whigs. Although both of them were still dominated by members of the landed classes, the Whigs were beginning to receive support from the new moneyed interests generated by industrialization. Tory ministers largely dominated the government until 1830 and had little desire to change the existing political and electoral system. Tory leadership during the Napoleonic wars made them wary of radicalism and reform movements, an attitude that governed their activities after 1815.

Popular discontent grew apace after 1815 because of severe economic difficulties. The Tory government's response to falling agricultural prices was the Corn Law of 1815, a measure that placed extraordinarily high tariffs on foreign grain. While beneficial to the landowners, subsequent high prices for bread made conditions for the working classes more difficult. Mass protest meetings took a nasty turn when a squadron of cavalry attacked a crowd of 60,000 demonstrators at St. Peter's Fields in Manchester in 1819. The death of eleven people, called the Peterloo Massacre by government detractors, led Parliament to even more repressive measures. The government restricted large public meetings and the circulation of pamphlets and journals among the poor. Before further repression could lead to greater violence, the Tory ministry was broadened by the addition of men who believed that some concessions to change rather than sheer repression might best avoid revolution. By making minor reforms in the 1820s, the Tories managed to avoid meeting the demands for electoral reforms—at least until 1830 (see Reform in Great Britain later in the chapter).

FRANCE   In 1814, the Bourbon family was restored to the throne of France in the person of Louis XVIII (1814–1824). Louis was clever enough to realize that the restored monarchy had to accept the constructive work of the revolutionary and Napoleonic eras or face disaster. Consequently, the constitutional Charter of 1814 maintained Napoleon's Concordat with the pope and accepted Napoleon's Civil Code with its recognition of the principle of equality before the law (see Chapter 20). The property rights of those who had purchased confiscated lands during the Revolution were preserved. The Charter of 1814 also established a bicameral (two-house) legislature with a Chamber of Peers chosen by the king and a Chamber of Deputies chosen by an electorate restricted to slightly less than 100,000 wealthy people.

Louis's grudging moderation, however, was opposed by liberals anxious to extend the revolutionary reforms and a group of ultraroyalists who criticized the king's willingness to compromise and retain so many features of the Napoleonic era. The ultras hoped to return to a monarchical system dominated by a privileged landed aristocracy and to restore the Catholic church to its former position of influence.

The initiative passed to the ultraroyalists in 1824 when Louis XVIII died and was succeeded by his brother, the count of Artois, who became Charles X (1824–1830). Charles had been the leader of the ultraroyalists and was determined to restore the old regime as far as possible. In 1825, an indemnity was granted to aristocrats whose lands had been confiscated during the Revolution. Moreover, the king pursued a religious policy that encouraged the church to reestablish control over France's educational system. Public outrage, fed by liberal newspapers, forced the king to compromise in 1827

and even to accept the principle of ministerial responsibility—that the ministers of the king were responsible to the legislature. But in 1829 he violated his commitment. A protest by the deputies led the king to dissolve the legislature in 1830 and call for new elections. France was on the brink of another revolution.

ITALY AND SPAIN   Italy in 1815 was one of the most backward countries in Europe. The typical Italian was a poverty-stricken illiterate peasant who cared little about the change from French to Austrian control of Italy in 1815. A small, educated middle class in the cities of northern Italy, however, who had benefited from Napoleon's changes, objected to the restoration of despotic governments controlled by Austria. Italy was still divided into a number of states; as Metternich contemptuously noted, Italy was only a "geographical expression." The Congress of Vienna had established nine states, including Piedmont in the north ruled by the house of Savoy; the kingdom of the Two Sicilies (Naples and Sicily); the Papal States; a handful of small duchies ruled by relatives of the Austrian emperor; and the important northern provinces of Lombardy and Venetia that were now part of the Austrian Empire.

Italy was largely under Austrian domination while all the states had extremely reactionary governments eager to smother any liberal or nationalist sentiment. The

▼ **The Revolution of 1830.** In 1830, the forces of change began to undo the conservative domination of Europe. In France, the reactionary Charles X was overthrown and replaced by the constitutional monarch Louis-Philippe, a liberal and former revolutionary soldier. In this painting by Gustave Wappers, Louis-Philippe is shown riding to the Hôtel de Ville, preceded by a man holding the French revolutionary tricolor flag, which had not been seen in France since 1815.

crushing of attempts at revolt in the kingdom of the Two Sicilies and Piedmont in 1821 discouraged opposition, although nationalistic secret societies known as the Carbonari—the charcoal burners—continued to conspire and plan for revolution.

In Spain, another Bourbon dynasty had been restored in the person of Ferdinand VII in 1814. Ferdinand (1814–1833) had agreed to observe the liberal constitution of 1812, which allowed for the functioning of an elected parliamentary assembly known as the Cortes. But the king soon reneged on his promises, tore up the constitution, dissolved the Cortes, and persecuted its members. Economic crisis and government despotism, inefficiency, and corruption soon led a combined group of army officers, upper-middle-class merchants, and liberal intellectuals to revolt. The king capitulated in March 1820 and promised once again to restore the constitution and the Cortes.

Metternich's policy of intervention came to Ferdinand's rescue. In April 1823, a French army moved into Spain and forced the revolutionary government to flee Madrid. By August of that year, the king had been restored to his throne. Ignoring French advice to adopt moderate policies, Ferdinand VII tortured to death, imprisoned, or exiled the supporters of a constitutional system. Intervention had succeeded.

CENTRAL EUROPE: THE GERMANIC CONFEDERATION AND THE AUSTRIAN EMPIRE After 1815 the forces of reaction were particularly successful in central Europe. The Habsburg empire and its chief agent, Prince Klemens von Metternich, played an important role. Metternich boasted: "You see in me the chief Minister of Police in Europe. I keep an eye on everything. My contacts are such that nothing escapes me."[6] Metternich's spies were everywhere, searching for evidence of liberal or nationalist plots. Metternich worried too much in 1815. Although both liberalism and nationalism emerged in Germany and the Austrian Empire, they were initially weak as central Europe tended to remain dominated by aristocratic landowning classes and autocratic, centralized monarchies. Real opposition to the conservative order came from a relatively small group of army officers, merchants, students, teachers, and liberal nobles. Since the Industrial Revolution did not emerge until the 1830s and 1840s, there was no substantial industrial middle class to take on the liberal cause (see Liberalism later in the chapter).

The Vienna settlement in 1815 recognized the existence of thirty-eight sovereign states in what had once been the Holy Roman Empire. Austria and Prussia were the two great powers although their non-German territory was not included in the confederation. The other states varied considerably in size from the large south German kingdom of Bavaria to the small principality of Schaumburg-Lippe. Together these states formed the Germanic Confederation, but the confederation had little real power. It had no real executive, and its only central organ was the federal diet, which needed the consent of all member states to take action, making it virtually powerless. The purpose of the Germanic Confederation was not to govern Germany but to provide a common defense against France or Russia. However, it also came to serve as Metternich's instrument to repress revolutionary movements in Germany.

Initially, Germans who favored the creation of liberal principles and German unity looked to Prussia for leadership. During the Napoleonic era, King Frederick William III (1797–1840), following the advice of his two chief ministers, Baron Heinrich von Stein and Baron Karl von Hardenberg, instituted political and institutional reforms in response to Prussia's defeat at the hands of Napoleon. Hardenberg told the king in 1806: "Your Majesty! We must do from above what the French have done from below." The reforms included the abolition of serfdom, fewer restrictions on the ability of the nobility to go into trade, municipal self-government through town councils, enlargement of primary and secondary schools, and universal military conscription to create a national army. The reforms, however, did not include the creation of a legislative assembly or representative government as Stein and Hardenberg wished. After 1815 Frederick William grew more reactionary and was content to follow Metternich's lead. While reforms had made Prussia strong and efficient, it remained largely an absolutist state with little interest in German unity.

Liberal and national movements in Germany seemed largely limited to university professors and students. The latter began to organize *Burschenschaften* or student societies dedicated to fostering the goal of a free, united Germany (see the box on p. 743). Their ideas and their motto, "Honor, Liberty, Fatherland" were in part inspired by Friedrich Ludwig Jahn, who had organized gymnastic societies during the Napoleonic wars to foster the regeneration of German youth. Jahn was a noisy nationalist who encouraged Germans to pursue their Teutonic heritage and inspired his followers to disrupt the lectures of professors whose views were not nationalistic.

From 1817 to 1819, the *Burschenschaften* pursued a variety of activities that alarmed German governments.

University Students and German Unity

▼ ▼ ▼

In the early nineteenth century, German nationalism was largely supported by university students and professors. Especially important were the Burschenschaften, student societies that espoused the cause of German unity. In this selection, the liberal Heinrich von Gagern explains to his father the purpose of the Burschenschaften.

Heinrich von Gagern, Letter to His Father

It is very hard to explain the spirit of the student movement to you, but I shall try, even though I can only give you a few characteristics. . . . It speaks to the better youth, the man of heart and spirit and love for all that is good, and gives him nourishment and being. For the average student of the past, the university years were a time to enjoy life, and to make a sharp break with his own background in defiance of the philistine world, which seemed to him somehow to foreshadow the tomb. Their pleasures, their organizations, and their talk were determined by their *status* as students, and their university obligation was only to avoid failing the examination and scraping by adequately—bread-and-butter learning. They were satisfied with themselves if they thought they could pass the examination. There are still many of those nowadays, indeed the majority over-all. But at several universities, and especially here, another group —in my eyes a better one—has managed to get the upper hand in the sense that it sets the mood. I prefer really not to call it a mood; rather, it is something that presses hard and tried to spread its ideas. . . .

Those who share in this spirit have then quite another tendency in their student life, Love of Fatherland is their guiding principle. Their purpose is to make a better future for the Fatherland, each as best he can, to spread national consciousness, or to use the much ridiculed and maligned Germanic expression, more folkishness, and to work for better constitutions. . . .

We want more sense of community among the several states of Germany, greater unity in their policies and in their principles of government; no separate policy for each state, but the nearest possible relations with one another; above all, we want Germany to be considered *one* land and the German people *one* people. In the forms of our student comradeship we show how we want to approach this as nearly as possible in the real world. Regional fraternities are forbidden, and we live in a German comradeship, one people in spirit, as we want it for all Germany in reality. We give our selves the freest of constitutions, just as we should like Germany to have the freest possible one, insofar as that is suitable for the German people. We want a constitution for the people that fits in with the spirit of the times and with the people's own level of enlightenment, rather than what each prince gives his people according to what he likes and what serves his private interest. Above all, we want the princes to understand and to follow the principle that they exist for the country and not the country for them. In fact, the prevailing view is that the constitution should not come from the individual states at all. The main principles of the German constitution should apply to all states in common, and should be expressed by the German federal assembly. This constitution should deal not only with the absolute necessities, like fiscal administration and justice, general administration and church and military affairs and so on; this constitution ought to be extended to the education of the young, at least at the upper age levels, and to many other such things.

An aide wrote to Metternich that "of all the evils affecting Germany today, even including the licentiousness of the press, this student nuisance is the greatest, the most urgent and the most threatening."[7] At an assembly held at the Wartburg Castle in 1817, marking the three-hundredth anniversary of Luther's Ninety-Five Theses, the crowd burned books written by conservative authors. When a deranged student assassinated a reactionary playwright, Metternich had the diet of the Germanic Confederation draw up the Karlsbad Decrees of 1819. These closed the *Burschenschaften*, provided for censorship of the press, and placed the universities under close supervision and control. Thereafter, except for a minor flurry of activity from 1830 to 1832, Metternich and the cooperative German rulers maintained the conservative status quo.

The Austrian Empire was a multinational state, a collection of different peoples under the Habsburg emperor who provided a common bond. Eleven peoples of different national origin constituted the empire, including Germans, Czechs, Magyars (Hungarians), Slovaks, Romanians, Slovenes, Poles, Serbians, and Italians. The Germans, though only a quarter of the population, were

▼ **Portrait of Nicholas I.** Tsar Nicholas I was a reactionary ruler who sought to prevent rebellion in Russia by strengthening the government bureaucracy, increasing censorship, and suppressing individual freedom by the use of political police. Nicholas's fear of revolution made him willing to send Russian troops to crush revolutions in other European states. One of his enemies remarked about his facial characteristics: "The sharply retreating forehead and the lower jaw were expressive of iron will and feeble intelligence."

economically the most advanced and played a leading role in governing Austria. Since Austria was predominantly agricultural, the landed nobility continued to be the most important class and held most of the important positions as army officers, diplomats, ministers, and civil servants. Essentially, the Austrian Empire was held together by the dynasty, the imperial civil service, the imperial army, and the Catholic church. But its national groups, especially the Hungarians, with their increasing desire for autonomy acted as forces to break the Austrian Empire apart.

It was Metternich who managed to hold it all together after 1815. His antipathy to liberalism and nationalism was understandably grounded in the realization that these forces threatened to tear the empire apart. The growing liberal belief that each national group had the right to its own system of government could only mean disaster for the multinational Austrian Empire. Metternich however, realized the need for some change and hoped to establish a central parliament with deputies from the different nationalities making up the empire. But he was never permitted to do so by Emperor Francis II (1806–1835) who resisted all change. Thus, the Austrian Empire largely stagnated while the forces of liberalism and nationalism grew. Metternich had not prevented an explosion in Austria; he only postponed it until 1848.

RUSSIA   At the beginning of the nineteenth century, Russia was overwhelmingly rural, agricultural, and autocratic. The Russian tsar was still regarded as a divine-right monarch with unlimited power although the extent of the Russian empire made the claim impractical. Most of the Russian land remained in the control of a class of noble landlords who monopolized the civil service and army officer corps. The land was tilled by serfs, the most exploited lower class in Europe.

In 1801, Alexander I (1801–1825) came to the Russian throne after a group of aristocrats assassinated his detested father, Tsar Paul I (1796–1801). Alexander had been raised in the tradition and ideas of the Enlightenment and gave every appearance of being liberal minded. But his liberalism was always conditioned by the autocratic tradition of the tsars. As one adviser said, "He would have willingly agreed that every man should be free, on the condition that he should voluntarily do only what the Emperor wished."

Initially, however, Alexander seemed willing to make reforms. With the aid of his liberal adviser, Michael Speransky, he relaxed censorship, permitted the sale of foreign books, and reformed the educational system. Substantial changes, however, such as the granting of a constitution and the freeing of the serfs never materialized in the face of opposition from the nobility. Then, too, Alexander himself gradually moved away from his reforming tendencies. No doubt, the struggle against Napoleon contributed to his abandonment of liberal reforms, but after the defeat of Napoleon, Alexander's reactionary tendencies blossomed as he became engrossed in religious mysticism. Now the government reverted to strict and arbitrary censorship. Soon opposition arose to Alexander from a group of secret societies.

One of these groups, known as the Northern Union, was composed of young aristocrats who had served in the Napoleonic wars and had become aware of the world outside Russia as well as intellectuals alienated by the censorship and lack of academic freedom in Russian universities. The Northern Union favored the establishment of a constitutional monarchy and the abolition of serfdom. The sudden death of Alexander in 1825 offered them their opportunity.

Although Alexander's brother Constantine was the legal heir to the throne, he had renounced his claims in favor of his brother Nicholas. As Nicholas was known to be more conservative than Constantine, the military leaders of the Northern Union rebelled against his accession. This so-called Decembrist Revolt was soon crushed by troops loyal to Nicholas and its leaders executed.

The revolt transformed Nicholas I (1825–1855) from a conservative into a reactionary determined to avoid another rebellion. Under Nicholas both the bureaucracy and the secret police were strengthened. Constituting the Third Section of the tsar's chancellery, the political police were given sweeping powers over much of Russian life. They deported suspicious or dangerous persons, maintained close surveillance of foreigners in Russia, and gave regular reports to the tsar on public opinion.

Matching Nicholas's fear of revolution at home was his fear of revolution abroad. There would be no revolution in Russia during the rest of his reign; if he could help it, there would be none in Europe either. Contemporaries called him the Policeman of Europe because of his willingness to use Russian troops to crush revolutions.

▼ The Ideologies of Change

Although the conservative forces were in the ascendancy from 1815 to 1830, powerful movements for change were also at work. These depended on ideas embodied in a series of political philosophies or ideologies that came into their own in the first half of the nineteenth century. They continue to affect the entire world.

Liberalism

One of the most prominent ideologies of the nineteenth century was liberalism. Liberalism owed much to the Enlightenment of the eighteenth century and the American and French revolutions at the end of that century. In addition, liberalism became increasingly important as the Industrial Revolution progressed since the developing industrial middle class largely adopted it as its own. There were divergencies of opinion among people classified as liberals, but all began with a common denominator, a conviction that people should be as free from restraint as possible. This opinion is evident in both economic and political liberalism.

ECONOMIC LIBERALISM   Also called classical economics, economic liberalism is based on the primary tenet of laissez-faire, whose principal exponent had been Adam Smith, author of the *Wealth of Nations* (see Chapter 18). Laissez-faire meant that the state should not interrupt the free play of natural economic forces, especially supply and demand. According to Smith, government should not interfere with the economic liberty of the individual and should restrict itself to only three primary functions: defense of the country, police protection of individuals, and the construction and maintenance of public works too expensive for individuals to undertake. In Smith's view, if individuals were allowed economic liberty, ultimately they would bring about the maximum good for the maximum number and benefit the general welfare of society.

The arguments against government intervention in economic matters were greatly strengthened by Thomas Malthus (1766–1834). In his major work, *Essay on the Principles of Population*, Malthus assailed the ideas of human progress and perfectibility propagated by Enlightenment thinkers. The laws of nature, he argued, made progress impossible. According to Malthus, population, when unchecked, increases in a geometric ratio while the food supply correspondingly increases only in an arithmetic ratio. The result will be severe overpopulation and ultimately starvation for the human race if this growth is not held in check. According to Malthus, two checks operate to hold the population in balance with the food supply. One is the voluntary limiting of the birthrate by moral restraint—by chastity and late marriages. Malthus did not expect much of this voluntary check and postulated yet another, more effective one. Nature, he argued, imposes the second: "unwholesome occupations, severe labor and exposure to the seasons, extreme poverty, bad nursing of children, great towns, excesses of all kinds, the whole train of common disease, and epidemics, wars, plague and famine." Malthus's ideas justified the policies of many industrialists who could not fail to notice his arguments. Misery and poverty were simply the inevitable result of the law of nature; no government or individual should interfere with its operation.

The ideas of Thomas Malthus were further developed by David Ricardo (1772–1823). In his *Principles of Political Economy*, written in 1817, Ricardo developed his famous "iron law of wages." Following Malthus, Ricardo argued that an increase in population means a greater supply of labor; a greater supply of labor causes wages to fall below the subsistence level. The result is misery and starvation, which then reduce the population. Consequently, wages rise above the subsistence level again, which in turn encourages workers to have larger families as the cycle is repeated. According to Ricardo, raising wages arbitrarily would be pointless since it would accomplish little but this vicious cycle. Nature is harsh, but attempting to change the laws of nature through the charity of employers or legislation by the state would merely make the situation worse. An editorial in an 1848 newspaper expressed what some members of the industrial middle class were only too happy to hear: "Suffering and evil are nature's admonitions; they cannot be got rid of; and the impatient attempts of benevolence to banish them from the world by legislation . . . have always been productive of more evil than good."

If economic liberalism was of little comfort to the working classes, it did offer a reward for those laborers who helped themselves. By hard work and thriftiness, an ordinary worker could become a foreman and perhaps even a factory owner. Dr. Samuel Smiles made a fortune with a little book on all the capitalistic virtues. Entitled *Self-Help*, it expounded on how the proverbs of all nations— "No pain no gains," "No sweat no sweet," "A penny saved is a penny gained"—contained the essence of what people must do to be successful entrepreneurs (see the box on p. 747).

POLITICAL LIBERALISM   In political as in economic liberalism, liberals stressed that people should be free from restraint. One French liberal proclaimed "The liberty of the individual is the object of all human associations. This liberty is the peaceful enjoyment of private independence, the right to pursue our own ends unimpeded, so long as they do not interfere with the equally legitimate activities of others."

The emphasis on liberty was directly connected to liberal ideas on power. Since power was seen as the ability by people to control the behavior of others, there needed to be limits on the exercise of power so that humans could be free. Politically, liberals came to hold a common set of beliefs. Chief among them was the protection of civil liberties or the basic rights of all people, which included equality before the law, freedom of assembly, speech, and press, and freedom from arbitrary arrest. All of these freedoms should be guaranteed by a written document, such as the American Bill of Rights or the French Declaration of the Rights of Man and the Citizen. In addition to religious toleration for all, most liberals advocated separation of church and state. The right of peaceful opposition to the government in and out of parliament and the making of laws by a representative assembly (legislature) elected by qualified voters constituted two other liberal demands. Many liberals believed, then, in a constitutional monarchy or constitutional state with limits on the powers of government in order to prevent despotism, and in written constitutions that would also help to guarantee these rights.

Many liberals also advocated ministerial responsibility or a system in which ministers of the king were responsible to the legislature rather than to the king, giving the legislative branch a check upon the power of the executive. Liberals in the first half of the nineteenth century also believed in a limited suffrage. While all people were entitled to equal civil rights, they should not have equal political rights. The right to vote and hold office would be open only to men who met certain property qualifications. As a political philosophy, liberalism was tied to middle-class, and especially industrial, middle-class men who favored the extension of voting rights so that they could share power with the landowning classes. They had little desire to let the lower classes share that power. Liberals were not democrats.

Nationalism

Nationalism can be defined as a state of mind rising out of an awareness of being part of a community that has common institutions, traditions, language, and customs. This community is called a "nation," and the primary political loyalty of individuals would be to the nation rather than to a dynasty or city-state or other political unit. Nationalism did not become a popular force for change until the French Revolution, and even then nationalism was not so much political as cultural with its emphasis upon the uniqueness of a particular nationality. People began to undertake the study of their

Self-Help

▼ ▼ ▼

S amuel Smiles (1812–1904) was a writer who made his fortune espousing the belief of middle-class economic liberals that people succeed through "individual industry, energy, and uprightness." This selection is taken from Self-Help, first published in 1859. His most popular book, it was translated into seventeen languages.

Samuel Smiles, *Self-Help*

"Heaven helps those who help themselves," is a well-worn maxim, embodying in a small compass the results of vast human experience. The spirit of self-help is the root of all genuine growth in the individual; and, exhibited in the lives of many, it constitutes the true source of national vigor and strength. Help from without is often enfeebling in its effects, but help from within invariably invigorates. Whatever is done for men or classes, to a certain extent takes away the stimulus and necessity of doing for themselves; and where men are subjected to overguidance and over-government, the inevitable tendency is to render them comparatively helpless. . . .

National progress is the sum of individual industry, energy, and uprightness, as national decay is of individual idleness, selfishness, and vice. What we are accustomed to decry as great social evils, will, for the most part, be found to be only the outgrowth of our own perverted life; and though we may endeavour to cut them down and extirpate them by means of law, they will only spring up again with fresh luxuriance in some other form, unless the individual conditions of human life and character are radically improved. If this view be correct, then it follows that the highest patriotism and philanthropy consist, not so much in altering laws and modifying institutions, as in helping and stimulating men to elevate and improve themselves by their own free and independent action as individuals. . . .

Many popular books have been written for the purpose of communicating to the public the grand secret of making money. But there is no secret whatever about it, as the proverbs of every nation abundantly testify. . . . "Take care of the pennies and the pounds will take care of themselves."—"A penny saved is a penny gained."—"Diligence is the mother of good-luck."—"No pains no gains."—"No sweat no sweet."—"Sloth, the Key of poverty."—"Work, and thou shalt have." "He who will not work, neither shall he eat."—"The world is his, who has patience and industry."—"It is too late to spare when all is spent."—"Better go to bed supperless than rise in debt."—"The morning hour has gold in its mouth."—"Credit keeps the crown of the causeway." Such are specimens of the proverbial philosophy, embodying the hoarded experience of many generations, as to the best means of thriving in the world. They were current in people's mouths long before books were invented; and like other popular proverbs, they were the first codes of popular morals. Moreover they have stood the test of time and the experience of every day still bears witness to their accuracy, force, and soundness.

---

language, history, literature, art, and folklore to understand the spirit of their nation.

This cultural idea of nationality usually came before the wish for political unity; cultural nationalism evolved into political nationalism. The latter advocated that governments should coincide with nationalities. Thus, a disunited people such as the Germans wanted national unity in a German nation-state with one central government. Subject peoples, such as the Hungarians, wanted national self-determination or the right to establish their own autonomy rather than be subject to a German minority in a multinational empire.

Nationalism threatened to upset the existing political order, both internationally and nationally, making nationalism fundamentally radical. A united Germany or united Italy would upset the balance of power established in 1815. By the same token, an independent Hungarian state would mean the breakup of the Austrian Empire. Fear of such dramatic change makes it evident why conservatives tried so hard to repress nationalism.

At the same time, in the first half of the nineteenth century, nationalism found a firm ally in liberalism. Most liberals believed that freedom could only be realized by

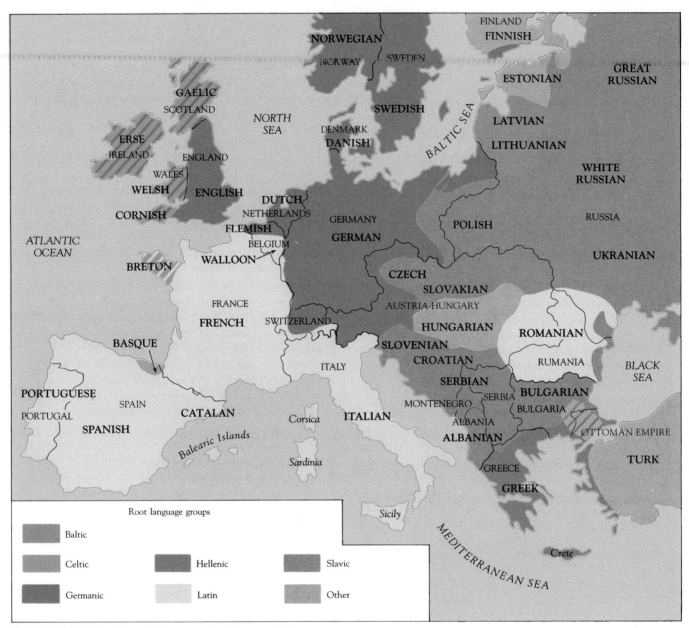

▼ **Map 22.3** Nationalism in Europe in the Nineteenth Century.

nationalities who ruled themselves. Each people should have its own country; no state should try to dominate others. One British liberal said, "it is in general a necessary condition of free institutions that the boundaries of governments should coincide in the main with those of nationalities." The combination of liberalism with nationalism also gave a cosmopolitan dimension to nationalism. Young Italy, Young Germany, Young Switzerland, all were parts of a wider Young Europe movement (see Italy later in the chapter). Supporting an uprising in

Genoa in 1834 was an invasion army of young Italians, Swiss, Poles, and Germans.

In its German expression, nationalism took a turn that was hardly cosmopolitan and foreshadowed an aggressive kind of nationalism that was popular in the second half of the nineteenth century. An important contribution to German nationalism came from the famous philosopher, Georg Wilhelm Friedrich Hegel (1770–1831). Aspects of Hegel's philosophy of history eventually made their way into German nationalistic thought.

One of these was his emphasis on the nation, which he envisioned as the direct manifestation of the "world-spirit" or "divine idea" operating in history. Since Hegel believed that this spirit of history was progressing toward an ideal of freedom, he implied that individuals could only find their true freedom or meaning by identifying fully with the nation. Moreover, Hegel stressed that the Germanic nation would play a special role as the final "world historical people" in the realization of freedom or the spiritual liberation of humanity. As a philosopher, Hegel did not derive a specific political program from his philosophical system. But others did, and what they stressed was the role of the state and a belief in the peculiar historical destiny of Germany; both became an integral part of German nationalism in the second half of the nineteenth century.

Early Socialism

In the first half of the nineteenth century, the pitiful conditions found in the slums, mines, and factories of the Industrial Revolution gave rise to another ideology for change known as socialism. The term eventually became associated with a Marxist analysis of human society (see Chapter 23), but early socialism was largely the product of political theorists or intellectuals who wanted to introduce equality into social conditions and believed that human cooperation was superior to the competition that characterized early industrial capitalism. To later Marxists, their ideas seemed impractical dreams, and they contemptuously labeled them utopian socialists. The term has remained to this day.

The early socialists accepted the Enlightenment belief that people by nature are not evil and are capable of a higher moral development if they live in a suitable environment. The economic system of their day, which they believed had brought wealth to some and misery to others, was incapable of providing this environment. The utopian socialists were against private property and the competitive spirit of early industrial capitalism. By eliminating them and creating new systems of social organization, they thought that a better environment for humanity could be achieved. Early socialists proposed a variety of ways to accomplish that task.

One approach, set out in the teachings of the Frenchman Henri de Saint-Simon (1760–1825), was the organization of all society into a cooperative community. Two elites, the intellectual leaders and the industrial managers, would use industrial and scientific technology to coordinate society for the benefit of all. In the process, government would vanish, no longer needed in the new society.

Another group of early socialists rejected Saint-Simon's collectivist approach in favor of creating voluntary associations that would demonstrate the advantages of cooperative living. Charles Fourier (1772–1838) offered a concrete scheme for this kind of approach. To Fourier, the competitive industrial system was failing to satisfy human passions or instincts and actually repressed them. He proposed instead the creation of small model communities called phalansteries. These were self-contained cooperatives, each consisting ideally of 1,620 people. Communally housed, the inhabitants of the phalanstery would live and work together for the mutual

▼ **Charles Fourier, *Plan of a Phalanstery.*** Charles Fourier believed that voluntary associations could be used to encourage cooperative rather than competitive living patterns. This sketch by Fourier is his plan for a phalanstery, a self-contained model community of about 1600 people who would live and work together for the common good of the group. This early socialist scheme of Fourier was attacked by others as an impractical or utopian fantasy.

benefit of its members. Work assignments would be rotated frequently to relieve workers of nonattractive tasks. Unable to gain financial backing for his phalansteries, Fourier's plan remained untested, although his followers did set up a number of communities in the United States.

Robert Owen (1771–1858), the British cotton manufacturer, also believed that humans would reveal their true natural goodness if they lived in a cooperative environment. At New Lanark in Scotland, he was successful in transforming a squalid factory town into a flourishing, healthy community. But when he attempted to create a self-contained cooperative community at New Harmony, Indiana, in the United States in the 1820s, internal bickering within the community eventually destroyed his dream.

The Frenchman Louis Blanc (1813–1882) offered yet another early socialist approach to a better society, based on the idea that government had a responsibility for the welfare of its citizens. In *The Organization of Work*, he maintained that social problems could be solved by government assistance. Denouncing competition as the main cause of the economic evils of his day, he called for the creation of social workshops that would produce goods for current markets. These would be financed by the state and owned and operated by the workers. By the gradual spread of such workshops, he believed, a cooperative rather than competitive foundation could be created for the entire economic life of the nation.

In their plans for the reconstruction of society, utopian socialists included schemes to change the roles of women and the relations between men and women. Saint-Simon's cooperative society included a recognition of equality between men and women, and his movement attracted a group of women who published a newspaper dedicated to the emancipation of women. Fourier's cooperative model communities were supposed to provide the same educational and job opportunities for men and women. Collective living would also entail both male and female responsibilities for child care and housecleaning.

One female utopian socialist, Flora Tristan (1803–1844), even attempted to foster a "utopian synthesis of socialism and feminism." She traveled through France preaching the need for the liberation of women. Her *Worker's Union*, published in 1843, advocated the application of Fourier's ideas to reconstruct both family and work:

> Workers, be sure of it. If you have enough equity and justice to inscribe into your Charter the few points I have just outlined, this declaration of the rights of women will soon pass into custom, from custom into law, and before twenty-five years pass you will then see inscribed in front of the book of laws which will govern French society: THE ABSOLUTE EQUALITY of man and woman. Then, my brothers, and only then, will human unity be constituted.[8]

She envisioned this absolute equality as the only hope to free the working class and transform civilization.

Flora Tristan, like the other utopian socialists, was largely ignored by her contemporaries. Although criticized for their impracticality, the utopian socialists at least laid the groundwork for later attacks on capitalism that would have a far-reaching result. Further industrialization would have to occur before those changes could be realized. In the first half of the nineteenth century, socialism remained merely a fringe movement compared to liberalism and nationalism.

▼ Revolution and Reform, 1830–1850

Beginning in 1830, the forces of change began to break through the conservative domination of Europe, more successfully in some places than in others. Finally, in 1848 a wave of revolutionary fervor moved through Europe, causing liberals and nationalists everywhere to think that they were on the verge of creating a new order.

Another French Revolution

The new elections Charles X had called in 1830 produced another victory for the liberal forces; at this point the king decided to seize the initiative. He believed that concessions had brought the downfall of Louis XVI during the first French Revolution. He was determined not to go in that direction: "I have either got to mount a horse or a death-cart." On July 26, 1830, Charles issued a set of edicts (July Ordinances) that imposed a rigid censorship on the press, dissolved the legislative assembly, and reduced the electorate in preparation for new elections. This unilateral revocation of the Charter of 1814 produced an immediate rebellion—the July Revolution. Barricades went up in Paris as a provisional government led by a group of moderate, propertied liberals was hastily formed and appealed to Louis-Philippe, the duke of Orléans, a cousin of Charles X, to become the constitutional king of France. Charles X fled to Britain; a new monarchy had been born.

THE BOURGEOIS MONARCHY OF LOUIS-PHILIPPE Louis-Philippe (1830–1848) was soon called the bourgeois monarch since political support for his rule came from the upper middle class. Louis-Philippe even dressed in a conventional business suit rather than a royal uniform. Constitutional changes were also made to favor the interests of the upper bourgeoisie. The Charter of 1814 was reinstated. Financial qualifications for voting were reduced, yet they were sufficiently high that the number of voters only increased from 100,000 to barely 200,000, thus guaranteeing that only the wealthiest people would vote.

The bourgeois monarchy represented the stopping place for political progress to the upper middle class. To the lesser bourgeoisie and the Parisian working class, who had helped to overthrow Charles X in 1830, it was a severe disappointment because they had been completely excluded from political power. The rapid expansion of French industry in the 1830s and 1840s led to the emergence of an industrial working class concentrated in certain urban regions. Terrible working and living conditions and the periodic economic crises that created high levels of unemployment led to worker unrest and sporadic outbursts of violence. In 1831 and 1834, government troops were used to crush working-class disturbances in Lyons, center of the silk industry. These insurrections witnessed an emerging alliance between workers and radical advocates of a republic. The government's response—repression and strict censorship of the press—worked temporarily to curb further overt resistance.

Even in the legislature—the Chamber of Deputies—there were differences of opinion about the bourgeois monarchy and the direction in which it should grow. Two groups rapidly emerged, although both were composed of upper-middle-class representatives. The Party of Movement was led by Adolphe Thiers who wished France to pursue an active foreign policy, adopt the practice of ministerial responsibility, and extend the suffrage, although only in a limited way. Thiers was no democrat. The Party of Resistance was led by François Guizot who believed that France had finally reached the "perfect form" of government and needed no further institutional changes. After 1840, the Party of Resistance dominated

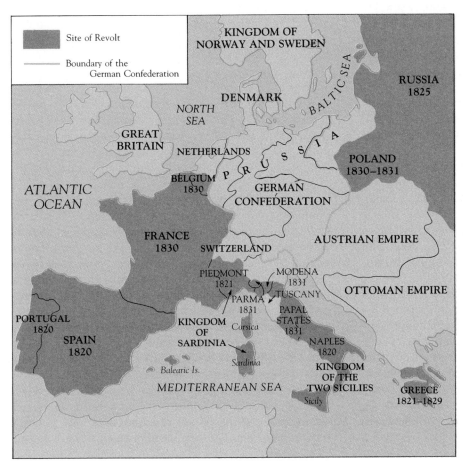

▼ **Map 22.4** European Revolts in the 1820s and 1830s.

the Chamber of Deputies. Guizot cooperated with Louis-Philippe in suppressing ministerial responsibility and pursuing a policy favoring the interests of the wealthier manufacturers and tradesmen. The government's unwillingness to allow any reform of the electoral system or to deal with either republican demands for greater political representation or working-class demands for improved social conditions led to growing frustration and revolutionary stirrings. They finally erupted in 1848.

Revolutionary Outbursts in Belgium, Poland, and Italy

Supporters of liberalism played a primary role in the July Revolution in France, but nationalism was the crucial force in three other revolutionary outbursts in 1830. The Austrian Netherlands or what came to be known as Belgium had been annexed to the Dutch Republic in 1815 to create a larger state to act as a barrier to French aggression. The combination of two states with different languages, traditions, and religions was never really acceptable to the Belgians, nor did they appreciate the absolutist rule of the king, William of Orange, and his Dutch administrators. The success of the July Revolution in France precipitated a student riot that soon turned into an uprising that spread throughout Belgium as the forces of William of Orange proved unable to crush the popular upheaval.

Since the Belgian revolt clearly meant the disruption of the Vienna agreement of 1815, Russia, Prussia, and Austria seemed eager to help King William with armed force. France and Britain opposed this intervention and managed to arrange a conference in December 1830 that created an independent, neutral Belgium under the collective guarantees of the great powers. Leopold of Saxe-Coburg, a minor German prince, was designated to be the new king while a Belgian national congress established a constitutional monarchy for the new state. The cooperation of the great powers had assured the success of the Belgian nationalistic revolution.

The revolutionary scenarios in Poland and Italy were much less successful. The July Revolution in France led Italian secret societies to revolt against reactionary governments in Modena, Parma, and the Papal States. Their only hope for success was to obtain support from the new government of Louis-Philippe in order to counter Austrian intervention. The new French ruler refused. Metternich then sent Austrian troops to the three Italian states, crushed the insurrections, and restored the deposed rulers.

Poland, too, had a nationalist uprising in 1830. Although Poland had been granted a liberal constitution by Tsar Alexander I, Russian interference in Polish affairs grew increasingly burdensome. After the accession of the reactionary Nicholas I to the Russian throne, tension increased until in November 1830 a combined group of junior army officers and university students led a revolt in Warsaw. Leadership of the revolution was soon taken over by Polish landed aristocrats. Their factional divisions and lack of support from the mass of Polish peasants, however, made them incapable of standing up to Russian forces. Hoped-for support from France and Britain, where liberals advocated backing the Polish uprising, failed to materialize as the governments of those countries refused to get involved. By September 1831, the revolt was crushed, and an oppressive Russian military dictatorship was established over Poland.

Reform in Great Britain

In 1830, new parliamentary elections brought the Whigs to power in Britain. At the same time, the successful July Revolution in France served to catalyze change in Britain. The Industrial Revolution had led to an expanding group of industrial leaders who objected to their exclusion from political power by the corrupt British electoral system. The Whigs, though also members of the landed classes, realized that concessions to reform were superior to revolution; the demands of the wealthy industrial middle class could no longer be ignored. In 1830, the Whigs introduced an election reform bill that was enacted in 1832 after an intense struggle (see the box on p. 753).

The Reform Bill gave explicit recognition to the changes wrought in British life by the Industrial Revolution. It disfranchised fifty-six rotten boroughs and enfranchised forty-two new towns and cities and reapportioned others. This gave the new industrial urban communities some voice in government. A property qualification (of £ 10 annual rent) for voting was retained, however, so the number of voters only increased from 478,000 to 814,000, a figure that still meant that only one in every thirty people was represented in Parliament. Thus, the Reform Bill of 1832 primarily benefited the upper middle class; the lower middle class, artisans, and industrial workers still had no vote. Moreover, the change did not significantly alter the composition of the House of Commons. One political leader noted that the Commons chosen in the first elec-

The Voice of Reform: Macaulay on the Reform Bill of 1832
▼ ▼ ▼

Thomas Babington Macaulay (1800–1859) was a historian and Whig member of Parliament. This selection is an excerpt from his speech given in Parliament in support of the Reform Bill of 1832, which extended the right to vote to the industrial middle classes of Britain. His argument was very simple: it is better to reform than to have a political revolution.

Thomas Babington Macaulay, Speech of March 2, 1831

My hon. friend the member of the University of Oxford tells us that, if we pass this law, England will soon be a Republic. The reformed House of Commons will, according to him, before it has sat ten years, depose the King, and expel the Lords from their House. Sir, if my hon. friend could prove this, he would have succeeded in bringing an argument for democracy infinitely stronger than any that is to be found in the works of Paine. His proposition is, in fact, this—that our monarchical and aristocratical institutions have no hold on the public mind of England; that these institutions are regarded with aversion by a decided majority of the middle class . . . . Now, sir, if I were convinced that the great body of the middle class in England look with aversion on monarchy and aristocracy, I should be forced, much against my will, to come to this conclusion, that monarchical and aristocratical institutions are unsuited to this country. Monarchy and aristocracy, valuable and useful as I think them, are still valuable and useful as means, and not as ends. The end of government is the happiness of the people; and I do not conceive that, in a country like this, the happiness of the people can be promoted by a form of government in which the middle classes place no confidence, and which exists only because the middle classes have no organ by which to make their senti-ments known. But, sir, I am fully convinced that the middle classes sincerely wish to uphold the royal prerogatives, and the constitutional rights of the Peers. . . .

But let us know our interest and our duty better. Turn where we may—within, around—the voice of great events is proclaiming to us, "Reform, that you may preserve." Now, therefore, while everything at home and abroad forebodes ruin to those who persist in a hopeless struggle against the spirit of the age; now, while the crash of the proudest throne of the Continent is still resounding in our ears; . . . now, while the heart of England is still sound; now, while the old feelings and the old associations retain a power and a charm which may too soon pass away; now, in this your accepted time; now, in this your day of salvation, take counsel, not of prejudice, not of party spirit, not of the ignominious pride of a fatal consistency, but of history, of reason, of the ages which are past, of the signs of this most portentous time. Pronounce in a manner worthy of the expectation with which this great debate has been anticipated, and of the long remembrance which it will leave behind. Renew the youth of the State. Save property divided against itself. Save the multitude, endangered by their own ungovernable passions. Save the aristocracy, endangered by its own unpopular power. Save the greatest, and fairest, and most highly civilised community that ever existed, from calamities which may in a few days sweep away all the rich heritage of so many ages of wisdom and glory. The danger is terrible. The time is short. If this Bill should be rejected, I pray to God that none of those who concur in rejecting it may ever remember their votes with unavailing regret, amidst the wreck of laws, the confusion of ranks, the spoliation of property, and the dissolution of social order.

tion after the Reform Bill seemed "to be very much like every other parliament." Nevertheless, a significant step had been taken. The "monied, manufacturing, and educated elite" had been "hitched" to the landed interest in ruling Britain. At the same time, the Reform Bill established a precedent that would lead to electoral re-form bills in the second half of the nineteenth century that would extend the right to vote to significantly larger numbers of Britons.

The 1830s and 1840s witnessed considerable reform legislation. The aristocratic landowning class was usually (but not always) the driving force for legislation that halted some of the worst abuses in the industrial system by instituting government regulation of working conditions in the factories and mines. Opposed to such legislation because of their belief in economic liberalism, the industrialists and manufacturers now in Parliament were usually (but not always) the driving forces for legislation that favored the principles of economic liberalism. The Poor Law of 1834 was based on the theory that giving aid to the poor and unemployed only increased their laziness and the number of paupers. The Poor Law of 1834 tried to remedy this by making paupers so wretched they would choose to work. Those unable to support themselves were crowded together in workhouses where living and working conditions were intentionally miserable so that people would be encouraged to find profitable employment.

Another piece of liberal legislation involved the repeal of the Corn Laws. This was primarily the work of the manufacturers Richard Cobden and John Bright who formed the Anti-Corn Law Association in 1838 to help workers by lowering bread prices. But this also aided the industrial middle classes who, as economic liberals, favored the principles of free trade. Repeal came in 1846 when some Tories were converted to free trade principles.

The year 1848, which witnessed revolutions in most of Europe, ended without a major crisis in Britain. On the Continent, middle-class liberals and nationalists took direction of the revolutionary forces. In Britain, however, the middle class had been largely satisfied by the Reform Act of 1832 and the repeal of the Corn Laws in 1846. The British working classes were discontented, but would have to wait until the second half of the nineteenth century to begin to achieve their goals.

The Growth of the United States

The American Constitution, ratified in 1789, committed the United States to two of the major forces of the first half of the nineteenth century, liberalism and nationalism. Initially, this constitutional commitment to national unity was challenged by divisions over the power of the federal government vis-à-vis the individual states. Bitter conflict erupted between the Federalists and the Republicans. Led by Alexander Hamilton (1757–1804), the Federalists favored a financial program that would establish a strong central government. The Republicans, guided by Thomas Jefferson (1743–1826) and James Madison (1751–1836), feared centralization and its consequences for popular liberties. These divisions were intensified by European rivalries as the

Federalists were pro-British and the Republicans pro-French. The successful conclusion of the War of 1812 brought an end to the Federalists, who had opposed the war, while the surge of national feeling generated by the war served to heal the nation's divisions.

Another strong force for national unity came from the Supreme Court while John Marshall (1755–1835) was chief justice from 1801 to 1835. Marshall made the Supreme Court into an important national institution by asserting the right of the Court to overrule an act of Congress if the Court found it to be in violation of the Constitution. Under Marshall, the Supreme Court contributed further to establishing the supremacy of the national government by curbing the actions of state courts and legislatures.

The election of Andrew Jackson (1767–1845) as president in 1828 opened a new era in American politics. Jacksonian democracy introduced a mass democratic politics. The electorate was expanded by dropping traditional property qualifications; by the 1830s suffrage had been extended to almost all adult white males. During the period from 1815 to 1850, the traditional liberal belief in the improvement of human beings was also given concrete expression. Americans developed detention schools for juvenile delinquents and new penal institutions, both motivated by the liberal belief that the right kind of environment would rehabilitate those in need of it. The abolitionist or national antislavery movement that developed in the 1830s also stemmed from liberal convictions. The American Anti-Slavery Society, established by William Lloyd Garrison (1805–1879) in 1833, already had 250,000 members by 1838.

By 1850, Europeans had become well aware of the growth of the American republic. Between 1830 and 1850, a wide variety of European political writers visited and examined the United States. The general thrust of their collective wisdom was that the United States was emerging as a world power. The French critic Sainte-Beuve wrote in 1847 that: "Russia is still barbarous, but she is great. . . . The other youthful people is America . . . the future of the world is there, between these two great worlds." Sainte-Beuve had the right idea even if he was somewhat premature.

The Revolutions of 1848

Europe had experienced two waves of revolution, one in the early 1820s and another in 1830–1831. And yet, despite successes in France, Belgium, and Greece, the conservative order continued to dominate much of Europe. Revolutions in Spain, Italy, Germany, Russia, and

Poland had all failed. Oftentimes liberal forces depended almost exclusively on junior army officers, liberal nobles, writers, university students, professors, and adventurers. But the forces of liberalism and nationalism, first generated by the French Revolution, continued to grow as the second great revolution—the Industrial Revolution—expanded and brought new groups of people who wanted change. In 1848, these forces of change erupted once more. As usual, revolution in France provided the spark for other countries, and soon most of central and southern Europe was ablaze with revolutionary fires. Tsar Nicholas I of Russia lamented to Queen Victoria in April 1848, "What remains standing in Europe? Great Britain and Russia."

YET ANOTHER FRENCH REVOLUTION   Numerous signs of trouble preceded the revolution. A severe industrial and agricultural depression beginning in 1846 brought untold hardship to the lower middle class, workers, and peasants. One-third of the workers in Paris were unemployed by the end of 1847. Scandals, graft, and corruption were rife while the government's persistent refusal to extend the suffrage angered the disfranchised members of the middle class. Even members of the upper middle class were discontented with the colorless reign of Louis-Philippe.

As Louis-Philippe's government continued to refuse to make changes, opposition grew. Radical republicans and socialists, joined by the upper middle class under the leadership of Adolphe Thiers, agitated for the dismissal of Guizot. Since they were forbidden by law to stage political rallies, they used the political banquet to call for reforms. Almost seventy such banquets were held in France during the winter of 1847–1848; a grand, culminating banquet was planned for Paris on February 22. When the government forbade it, people came anyway; students and workers threw up barricades in Paris. Although Louis-Philippe called out the National Guard, many of its bourgeois members joined the opposition. The king now proposed reform, but unable to form another ministry, he abdicated on February 24 and fled to Britain. A provisional government was established by a group of moderate and radical republicans; the latter even included the socialist Louis Blanc. The provisional government ordered that representatives be elected by universal manhood suffrage for a Constituent Assembly to draw up a new constitution.

The provisional government also established national workshops under the influence of Louis Blanc. As Blanc envisioned them, the workshops were supposed to be cooperative factories run by the workers. In fact, the work-

shops became unemployment compensation units or public works, except that they provided little work beyond leaf raking and ditch digging. The cost of the program became increasingly burdensome to the government.

The result was an growing split between the moderate republicans, who had the support of most of France, and the radical republicans, whose main support came from the Parisian working class. In the elections for the National Assembly, 500 seats went to moderate republicans and 300 to avowed monarchists while the radicals gained only 100. From March to June, the number of unemployed enrolled in the national workshops rose from 10,000 to almost 120,000, emptying the treasury and frightening the moderates who responded by closing the workshops on June 21. The workers refused to accept this decision and poured into the streets. Four days of bitter and bloody fighting by government forces crushed the working-class revolt, described by some as a "class struggle, a sort of servile war." Thousands were killed, and 11,000 prisoners were deported to the French colony of Algeria in northern Africa. These "June days" produced a legacy of hate. They had aspects of class warfare as the propertied classes became convinced that they had barely averted an attempt by the working class to destroy the social order. To many Europeans, the "June days" appeared to be a struggle of the bourgeoisie against the working class.

The new constitution, ratified on November 4, 1848, established a republic (Second Republic) with a unicameral (one-house) legislature of 750 elected by universal male suffrage for three years and a president, also elected by universal male suffrage, for four years. In the elections for the presidency held in December 1848, four republicans who had been associated with the early months of the Second Republic were resoundingly defeated by Charles Louis Napoleon Bonaparte.

How could a virtual unknown who had been arrested twice and sent into exile once be chosen president by a landslide? People considered him inept with none of his uncle's ability. And yet the name of Bonaparte had obviously worked its magic. The Napoleonic revival had been going on for years as romanticists glorified his legend. One old veteran said: "Why shouldn't I vote for this gentleman. I, whose nose was frozen near Moscow." Perhaps just as important, the French were tired of revolution, and Louis Napoleon had posed as a defender of order. The large number of rural and urban masses who voted for Napoleon saw him as a man of the people. Since they had been excluded from political life since 1815, what better choice did they have? Within four years President Napoleon had become Emperor Napo-

Revolutionary Excitement: Carl Schurz and the Revolution of 1848 in Germany

▼▼▼

The excitement with which German liberals and nationalists received the news of the February Revolution in France and their own expectations for Germany are well captured in this selection from the Reminiscences of Carl Schurz (1829–1906). Schurz made his way to America after the failure of the German revolution and eventually became a United States senator.

Carl Schurz, *Reminiscences*

One morning, toward the end of February, 1848, I sat quietly in my attic-chamber, working hard at my tragedy of "Ulrich von Hutten," [a sixteenth-century German humanist and knight] when suddenly a friend rushed breathlessly into the room, exclaiming: "What, you sitting here! Do you not know what has happened?"

"No; what?"

"The French have driven away Louis Philippe and proclaimed the republic."

I threw down my pen—and that was the end of "Ulrich von Hutten." I never touched the manuscript again. We tore down the stairs, into the street, to the market-square, the accustomed meeting-place for all the student societies after their midday dinner. Although it was still forenoon, the market was already crowded with young men talking excitedly. There was no shouting, no noise, only agitated conversation. What did we want there? This probably no one knew. But since the French had driven away Louis Philippe and proclaimed the republic, something of course must happen here, too. . . . We were dominated by a vague feeling as if a great outbreak of elemental forces had begun, as if an earthquake was impending of which we had felt the first shock, and we instinctively crowded together. . . .

The next morning there were the usual lectures to be attended. But how profitless! The voice of the professor sounded like a monotonous drone coming from far away. What he had to say did not seem to concern us. The pen that should have taken notes remained idle. At last we closed with a sigh the notebook and went away, impelled by a feeling that now we had something more important to do—to devote ourselves to the affairs of the fatherland. And this we did by seeking as quickly as possible again the company of our friends, in order to discuss what had happened and what was to come. In these conversations, excited as they were, certain ideas and catchwords worked themselves to the surface, which expressed more or less the feelings of the people. Now had arrived in Germany the day for the establishment of "German Unity," and the founding of a great, powerful national German Empire. In the first line the convocation of a national parliament. Then the demands for civil rights and liberties, free speech, free press, the right of free assembly, equality before the law, a freely elected representation of the people with legislative power, responsibility of ministers, self-government of the communes, the right of the people to carry arms, the formation of a civic guard with elective officers, and so on—in short, that which was called a "constitutional form of government on a broad democratic basis." Republican ideas were at first only sparingly expressed. But the word democracy was soon on all tongues, and many, too, thought it a matter of course that if the princes should try to withhold from the people the rights and liberties demanded, force would take the place of mere petition. Of course the regeneration of the fatherland must, if possible, be accomplished by peaceable means . . . . Like many of my friends, I was dominated by the feeling that at last the great opportunity had arrived for giving to the German people the liberty which was their birthright and to the German fatherland its unity and greatness, and that it was now the first duty of every German to do and to sacrifice everything for this sacred object.

---

leon (see Chapter 23). The French had once again made their journey from republican chaos to authoritarian order, a pattern that was becoming all too common in French history.

CENTRAL EUROPE   There were rural and urban tensions in central Europe (just as in France) due to an agricultural depression beginning in 1845. But what seems to have caused the upheaval here was news of the revolution in Paris in February 1848 (see the box above). By early March 1848, handicraft workers in Germany were destroying the machines and factories that they blamed for depriving them of their jobs; peasants looted and burned the manor houses of the nobility. Many German rulers promised constitutions, a free press, jury trials and other liberal reforms. In Prussia concessions were also made to appease the revolutionaries. King Frederick William IV (1840–1861) agreed to abolish censorship, establish a new constitution, and work for a united Germany. The latter promise had its counterpart throughout all the German states as governments allowed elections by universal male suffrage for deputies to an all-German parliament. Its purpose was to fulfill a liberal dream—the preparation of a constitution for a new united Germany.

This Frankfurt Assembly was dominated by a university-educated middle class, including civil servants, lawyers, professors, teachers, jurists, and physicians. From its beginning, the assembly claimed to be a government for all Germany, a pretension unacceptable to the German states themselves. Moreover, one especially troublesome problem arose as deliberations over the new Germany ensued. What should be the nature of the new German state? Supporters of a *Grossdeutsch* ("Big German") solution wished to include the German provinces of Austria. The *Kleindeutsch* ("Small German") supporters favored the inclusion only of Prussia and the other German states with the Prussian king as emperor. This, of course, would leave many Germans (in Austria) outside a German state. The problem was solved by the Austrians who withdrew from the assem-

bly, leaving the victory to the *Kleindeutsch* solution. In March 1849, the Frankfurt Assembly elected Frederick William IV of Prussia as "emperor of the Germans." But he contemptuously refused the crown as a "diadem moulded out of the dirt and dregs of revolution, disloyalty and treason." By this time Frederick William IV had regained control of the situation in Prussia and ordered the Prussian delegates home.

The Frankfurt Assembly soon disbanded. Although some members spoke of using force, they had no real means of compelling the German rulers to accept the constitution they had drawn up. The attempt of the German liberals at Frankfurt to create a German state had failed, and leadership for unification would now pass to the Prussian military monarchy (see Chapter 23).

The Austrian Empire also had its social, political, and nationalist grievances and needed only the news of the revolution in Paris to encourage it to erupt in flames in March 1848. The Hungarian liberal gentry under Louis Kossuth agitated for "commonwealth" status; they were willing to keep the Habsburg monarch, but wanted their own legislature. In March, demonstrations in Budapest, Prague, and Vienna led to Metternich's dismissal. The arch-symbol of the conservative order fled abroad. In Vienna, revolutionary forces, carefully guided by the educated and propertied classes, took control of the capital and insisted upon the summoning of a constituent assembly to draw up a liberal constitution. Hungary was granted its wish for its own legislature, a separate national army, and control over its foreign policy and bud-

▼ **Austrian Students in the Revolutionary Civic Guard.** In 1848, revolutionary fervor swept through Europe and toppled governments in France, central Europe, and Italy. In the Austrian Empire, students joined the revolutionary civic guard in taking control of Vienna and forcing the Austrian emperor to call a constitutent assembly to draft a liberal constitution. However, divisions between radical and moderate revolutionaries enabled the emperor and his officials to crush the revolution.

The Voice of Italian Nationalism: Giuseppe Mazzini and Young Italy
▼ ▼ ▼

After the failure of the uprisings in Italy in 1830–1831, Giuseppe Mazzini emerged as the leader of the Italian risorgimento—the movement for Italian nationhood. In 1831, he founded an organization known as Young Italy whose goal was the creation of a united Italian republic. This selection is excerpted from the oath that the members of Young Italy were required to take.

Giuseppe Mazzini, The Young Italy Oath

Young Italy is a brotherhood of Italians who believe in a law of Progress and Duty, and are convinced that Italy is destined to become one nation,—convinced also that she possesses sufficient strength within herself to become one, and that the ill success of her former efforts is to be attributed not to the weakness, but to the misdirection of the revolutionary elements within her,—that the secret of force lies in constancy and unity of effort. They join this association in the firm intent of consecrating both thought and action to the great aim of reconstituting Italy as one independent sovereign nation of free men and equals. . . .

Each member will, upon his initiation into the association of Young Italy, pronounce the following form of oath, in the presence of the initiator:

In the name of God and of Italy;

In the name of all the martyrs of the holy Italian cause who have fallen beneath foreign and domestic tyranny;

By the duties which bind me to the land wherein God has placed me, and to the brothers whom God has given me;

By the love—innate in all men—I bear to the country that gave my mother birth, and will be the home of my children. . . .

By the sufferings of the millions,—

I, . . . believing in the mission intrusted by God to Italy, and the duty of every Italian to strive to attempt its fulfillment; convinced that where God has ordained that a nation shall be, He has given the requisite power to create it; that the people are the depositaries of that power, and that in its right direction for the people, and by the people, lies the secret of victory; convinced that virtue consists in action and sacrifice, and strength in union and constancy of purpose: I give my name to Young Italy, an association of men holding the same faith, and swear:

To dedicate myself wholly and forever to the endeavor with them to constitute Italy one free, independent, republican nation; to promote by every means in my power—whether by written or spoken word, or by action—the education of my Italian brothers towards the aim of Young Italy; towards association, the sole means of its accomplishment, and to virtue, which alone can render the conquest lasting; to abstain from enrolling myself in any other association from this time forth; to obey all the instructions, in conformity with the spirit of Young Italy, given me by those who represent with me the union of my Italian brothers; and to keep the secret of these instructions, even at the cost of my life; to assist my brothers of the association both by action and counsel—NOW AND FOREVER.

---

get. Allegiance to the Habsburg dynasty was now Hungary's only tie to the Austrian Empire. In Bohemia, the Czechs began to demand their own government as well.

Although Emperor Ferdinand I and Austrian officials had made concessions to appease the revolutionaries, they awaited an opportunity to reestablish their firm control. As in the German states, they were increasingly encouraged by the divisions between radical and moderate revolutionaries and played upon the middle-class fear of a working-class social revolution. Their first success came in June 1848 when a military force under General Windischgrätz ruthlessly suppressed the Czech rebels in Prague. In October the death of the minister for war at the hands of a Viennese mob gave Windischgrätz the pretext for an attack on Vienna. By the end of the month, radical rebels there had been crushed. In December the feebleminded Ferdinand I agreed to abdicate in favor of his nephew, Francis Joseph I (1848–1916), who worked vigorously to restore the imperial government in Hungary. The Austrian armies, however, were unable to defeat Kossuth's forces, and it was only through the intervention of Nicholas I, who sent a Russian army of 140,000 men to aid the Austrians, that the Hungarian revolution was finally crushed in 1849. The revolutions in Austria had also failed. Autocratic government was restored; emperor and propertied classes remained in control while the numerous nationalities remained subject to the Austrian government.

ITALY   The failure of the revolutionary uprisings in Italy in 1830–1831 had served to discredit the secret societies that had fomented them and encouraged the Italian movement for unification to take a new direction. The leadership of Italy's *risorgimento* ("Resurgence") passed into the hands of Giuseppe Mazzini (1805–1872), a dedicated Italian nationalist who founded an organization known as Young Italy in 1831 (see the box on p. 758). With its membership limited to men under forty years old, this group set as its goal the creation of a united Italian republic. In his work, *The Duties of Man,* Mazzini urged Italians to dedicate their lives to the Italian nation: "O my Brother! love your Country. Our Country is our home." And yet to Mazzini love of country represented but one stage towards the higher responsibility of loving humanity: "You are men before you are either citizens or fathers."

Mazzini's dreams seemed on the verge of fulfillment when Italy rose in revolt in 1848. Beginning in Sicily, rebellions spread northward through the Italian states as ruler after ruler granted a constitution to his people. Citizens in the two provinces of Lombardy and Venetia also rebelled against their Austrian overlords. The Venetians declared a republic in Venice. The king of the northern Italian state of Piedmont, Charles Albert (1831–1849), took up the call and assumed the leadership for a war of liberation from Austrian domination. His invasion of Lombardy proved unsuccessful, however, and by 1849 the Austrians had reestablished complete control over Lombardy and Venetia.

Counterrevolutionary forces also prevailed throughout Italy. French forces helped Pope Pius IX regain control of Rome. Elsewhere Italian rulers managed to regain control on their own. Only Piedmont managed to keep its liberal constitution. Despite the lack of success, revolutionaries in Italy had learned two valuable lessons. Only Piedmont could be relied upon for leadership in the cause of Italian unity and even then, without foreign help, Italy could not succeed in throwing off Austrian domination. Both lessons proved helpful in achieving Italian unification (see Chapter 23).

▼ **Map 22.5** The Revolutions of 1848–1849.

Reaction, Reform, and Revolution: The European States, 1815–1850

Great Britain	
Corn Law	1815
Peterloo Massacre	1819
Reform Act	1832
Poor Law	1834
Formation of Anti-Corn Law Association	1838
Repeal of Corn Laws	1846

France	
Louis XVIII	1814–1824
Constitutional Charter	1814
Charles X	1824–1830
July Revolution	1830
Louis-Philippe	1830–1848
Abdication of Louis-Philippe; Formation of Provisional Government	1848 (February 22–24)
Formation of National Workshops	1848 (February 26)
June Days: Workers' Revolt in Paris	1848 (June)
Establishment of Second Republic	1848 (November)
Election of Louis Napoleon as French President	1848 (December)

Low Countries	
Union of Netherlands and Belgium	1815
Belgian Revolt	1830

Germany	
Germanic Confederation Established	1815
Frederick William III of Prussia	1797–1840
Burschenschaften at the Wartburg	1817
Karlsbad Decrees	1819

Frederick William IV of Prussia	1840–1861
Revolution in Germany	1848
Frankfurt Assembly	1848–1849

The Austrian Empire	
Emperor Francis II	1806–1835
Emperor Ferdinand I	1835–1848
Revolt in Austrian Empire; Metternich Dismissed	1848 (March)
Austrian Forces under General Windischgrätz Crush Czech Rebels	1848 (June)
Viennese Rebels Crushed	1848 (October)
Abdication of Ferdinand I	1848 (December)
Francis Joseph I	1848–1916
Defeat of Hungarians with Help of Russian Troops	1849

Italy	
Crushing of Revolts in Southern Italy and Sardinia	1821
Aborted Revolutions in Modena, Parma, and Papal States	1830
Revolutions in Italy	1848
King Charles Albert of Piedmont	1831—1849
Charles Albert Attacks Austrians	1848
Austrians Reestablish Control in Lombardy and Venetia	1849

Russia	
Tsar Paul I	1796–1801
Tsar Alexander I	1801–1825
Decembrist Revolt	1825
Tsar Nicholas I	1825–1855
Polish Uprising	1830
Suppression of Polish Revolt	1831

Throughout Europe in 1848, popular revolts had initiated revolutionary upheavals that had produced the formation of liberal constitutions and liberal governments. But how could so many immediate successes in 1848 be followed by so many disasters only months later? Two reasons stand out. The unity of the revolutionaries had made the revolutions possible, but divisions soon shattered their ranks. Except in France, moderate liberals from the propertied classes failed to extend suffrage to the working classes who had helped to achieve the revolutions. But as radicals pushed for universal male suffrage, liberals everywhere pulled back. Concerned about their property and security, they rallied to the old ruling classes for the sake of order and out of fear of social revolution by the working classes. All too soon, established governments were back in power.

In 1848, nationalities everywhere had also revolted in pursuit of self-government. But here too, frightfully little was achieved as divisions among nationalities proved utterly disastrous. Though the Hungarians demanded autonomy from the Austrians, at the same time they refused the same to their minorities—the Slovenes, Croats, and Serbs. Instead of joining together against the old empire, minorities fought each other. No wonder that one Czech could remark in April 1848: "If the Austrian state had not already existed for so long, it would have been in the interests of Europe, indeed of humanity itself, to endeavour to create it as soon as possible."[9] The Austrians began the successful recovery of the Hungarian provinces when they began to play off Hungary's rebellious minority nationalities against the Hungarians.

▼ The Emergence of an Ordered Society

Everywhere in Europe, the revolutionary upheavals of the late eighteenth and early nineteenth centuries made the ruling elite nervous about social disorder and the potential dangers to their lives and property. At the same time, the influx of large numbers of people from the countryside into rapidly growing cities had led to horrible living conditions, poverty, unemployment, and great social dissatisfaction. The first half of the nineteenth century witnessed a significant increase in crime rates, especially against property, in Britain, France, and Germany. The rise in incidences of pickpocketing, burglary, shoplifting, and embezzlement may in part have reflected the increased desperation of the poor, but it also provoked a severe reaction against crimes of property by middle-class urban inhabitants who feared the threat the urban poor posed to their security and possessions.

Several kinds of organizations already existed to defend the propertied classes from criminals and social misfits. Some European countries, including Prussia, Sardinia, and Spain, had created gendarmes after the French model of 1791. These were essentially military police recruited from ex-soldiers who were employed mainly in the countryside to keep order. During the French revolutionary era, citizen militias (known as the National Guard in France) had also come into existence. Strongly distrusted by reactionary governments, however, they were either disbanded or closely supervised. Finally, military forces were also enlisted for domestic use in times of serious popular disorder.

The Development of New Police Forces

The first major contribution of the nineteenth century to the development of a disciplined or ordered society in Europe was a regular system of police. A number of European states established civilian police forces—a group of well-trained law enforcement officers who were to preserve property and lives, maintain domestic order, investigate crime, and arrest offenders. It was hoped that their very presence would prevent crime. The new police forces were not readily welcomed, especially in countries where the memory of oppressive acts carried out by political and secret police still lingered. The function of the new police—to protect citizens—eventually made them acceptable, and by the end of the nineteenth century many Europeans viewed them approvingly.

This new approach to policing made its first appearance in France in 1828 when Louis-Maurice Debelleyme, the prefect of Paris, proclaimed as his goal: "The essential object of our municipal police is the safety of the inhabitants of Paris. Safety by day and night, free traffic movement, clean streets, the supervision of and precaution against accidents, the maintenance of order in public places, the seeking out of offences and their perpetrators."[10] In March 1829, the new policemen, known as *serjents,* became visible on Paris streets. They were dressed in blue uniforms to make them easily recognizable by all citizens. They were also lightly armed with a white cane during the day and a saber at night, underscoring the fact that they made up a civilian, not a military body. Initially, there were not many of the new policemen. Paris had 85 by August of 1829 and only 500 in 1850. Before the end of the century, their number had increased to 4,000.

Britain, fearful of the powers exercised by military or secret police in authoritarian continental European states, had long resisted the creation of a professional police force. Instead, Britain depended upon a system of unpaid constables recruited by local authorities. Often these local constables were incapable of keeping order, preventing crimes, or apprehending criminals. Such jobs could also be dangerous and involve incidents like the one reported by a man passing by a local pub in 1827:

> I saw Thomas Franklin [constable of the village of Leighton Buzzard] coming out backwards. John Brandon . . . was opposite and close to the constable. I saw the said John Brandon strike the said constable twice "bang full in the face" the blows knocked the constable down on his back. John Brandon fell down with him. Sarah Adams . . . got on top of the constable and jostled his head against the ground . . . . The constable appeared very much hurt and his face was all over blood.[11]

The failure of the local constables led to a new approach. Between September 1829 and May 1830, 3,000 uniformed policemen appeared on the streets of London. They came to be known as bobbies after Sir Robert Peel, who had introduced the legislation that created the force. The Municipal Corporations Act of 1835 spread the new police into provincial boroughs while counties were permitted to establish police forces in 1839. By 1856, the new police had become obligatory for all local authorities.

As is evident from the first instruction book for the new policemen, the primary goal of the new British police was to prevent crime: "Officers and police constables should endeavour to distinguish themselves by such vigilance and activity as may render it impossible for any one to commit a crime within that portion of the town under their charge."[12] The municipal authorities soon found, however, that the police were also useful for imposing order on working-class urban inhabitants. On Sundays they were called upon to clean up after Saturday night's drinking bouts. As demands for better pay and treatment led to improved working conditions, British policemen began to develop a sense of professionalism (see the box on p. 763).

Police systems were reorganized throughout the Western world during the nineteenth century. Reformers followed first the French and then the British as their models, but local traditions were often important in shaping a nation's system. After the revolutions of 1848 in Germany, a state-financed police force called the *Schutzmannschaft,* modeled after the London police, was created for the city of Berlin. The *Schutzmannschaft* began as a civilian body, but already by 1851 the force had become organized more along military lines and was used for political purposes. Although their work in providing

▼ **The London Police.** Revolutionary upheavals in the late eighteenth and early nineteenth centuries led European ruling elites to seek new ways to create an ordered society. One result was the development of civilian police forces that would be responsible for preserving property, arresting criminals, and maintaining domestic order. This early photograph shows a group of London policemen who came to be known as bobbies after Sir Robert Peel, the man who was responsible for introducing the legislation that initiated the London police force.

The New British Police: "We Are Not Treated as Men"
▼ ▼ ▼

The new British police forces, created first in London in 1829, were generally well established throughout a good part of Britain by the 1840s. As professionalism arose in the ranks of the forces, so too did demands for better pay and treatment. In these two selections, police constables make clear their demands and complaints.

Petition for Higher Pay by a Group of Third-Class Constables (1848)

Men joining the Police service as 3rd Class Constables and having a wife and 3 children to support on joining, are not able properly to do so on the pay of 16/8d. Most of the married men on joining are somewhat in debt, and are unable to extricate themselves on account of rent to pay and articles to buy which are necessary for support of wife and children. We beg leave to state that a married man having a wife and 2 children to support on joining, that it is as much as he can do upon 16/8d per week, and having to remain upon that sum for the first 12 to 18 months.

Complaints from Constables of D Division of the London Metropolitan Police

We are not treated as men but as slaves we englishmen do not like to be terrorised by a set of Irish sergeants who are only lenient to their own countrymen we the D division of Paddington are nearly all ruled by these Irish Sergeants after we have done our night-Duty may we not have the privilege of going to Church or staying at home to Suit our own inclination when we are ordered by the Superintendent to go to church in our uniform on wednesday we do not object to the going to church we like to go but we do not like to be ordered there and when we go on duty Sunday nights we are asked like so many schoolboys have we been to church should we say no let reason be what it may it does not matter we are forthwith ordered from Paddington to Marylebone lane the next night—about 2 hours before we go to Duty that is 2 miles from many of our homes being tired with our walk there and back we must either loiter about the streets or in some public house and there we do not want to go for we cannot spare our trifling wages to spend them there but there is no other choice left—for us to make our time out to go on Duty at proper time on Day we are ordered there for that offence another Man may faultlessly commit—the crime of sitting 4 minutes during the night—then we must be ordered there another to Shew his old clothes before they are given in even we must go to the expense of having them put in repair we have indeed for all these frightful crimes to walk 3 or 4 miles and then be wasting our time that makes our night 3 hours longer than they ought to be another thing we want to know who has the money that is deducted out of our wages for fines and many of us will be obliged to give up the duty unless we can have fair play as to the stationing of us on our beats why cannot we follow round that may all and each of us go over every beat and not for the Sergeants to put their favourites on the good beats and the others kept back their favourites are not the best policemen but those that will spend the most with them at the public house there are a great many of these things to try our temper.

---

welfare services for the city made them more acceptable to the citizens, the Berlin police exercised considerably more power than their British counterparts. Their military nature was reinforced by their weaponry, which included swords, pistols, and brass knuckles. One observer noted that "A German policeman on patrol is armed as if for war."[13]

While the new policemen alleviated some of the fears about the increase in crime, contemporary reformers approached the problem in other ways. Some of them believed that the increase in crime was related to the dramatic increase in poverty. As one commented in 1816: "Poverty, misery are the parents of crime." Relief for the poverty-stricken became a major concern. Strongly influenced by the middle-class belief that unemployment was the result of sheer laziness, European states passed Poor Laws that attempted to force paupers to find work on their own or enter workhouses designed to make people so utterly uncomfortable they would choose to reenter the labor market.

Meanwhile, another group of reformers was arguing that poor laws failed to address the real problem, which was that poverty was a result of the moral degeneracy of the lower-classes, increasingly labeled the "dangerous classes" because of their threat to middle-class society. This belief led one group of secular reformers to form institutes for the instruction of the working classes in the applied sciences in order to make them more productive members of society. The London Mechanics' Institute, established in Britain, and the Society for the Diffusion of Useful Knowledge in the Field of Natural Sciences, Technical Science, and Political Economy, founded in Germany, are but two examples of this approach to the "dangerous classes."

Organized religion took a different approach. British evangelicals created Sunday Schools to improve the morals of working children while in Germany evangelical Protestants established nurseries for orphans and homeless children, women's societies to care for the sick and poor, and prison societies that prepared women to work in prisons. The Catholic church attempted the same kind of work through a revival of its religious orders; dedicated priests and nuns used spiritual instruction and recreation to turn young male workers away from the moral vices of gambling and drinking and female workers from lives of prostitution.

The Reform of Prisons

The increase in crimes led to a rise in arrests. By the 1820s, in most countries the indiscriminate use of capital punishment, even for crimes against property, was being increasingly viewed as ineffective and replaced by imprisonment. Although the British had shipped people convicted for serious offenses to their colonial territory of Australia, that practice began to slow down in the late 1830s when the colonists loudly objected. Incarceration, then, was the only alternative. Prisons served to isolate criminals from society, but a growing number of reformers questioned their purpose and effectiveness, especially when prisoners were subjected to harsh and even humiliating work as punishment. By the 1830s, European governments were seeking ways to reform their penal systems. Motivated by the desire not just to punish, but to rehabilitate and transform criminals into new persons, the British and French in the early 1830s sent missions to the United States to examine how the two different systems then used in American prisons accomplished this goal. At the Auburn Prison in New York, for example, prisoners were separated at night but worked together in the same workshop during the day. At Walnut Street Prison in Philadelphia, prisoners were separated into individual cells.

After examining the American prisons, both the French and British constructed prisons on the Walnut Street model with separate cells that isolated prisoners from one another. At Petite Roquette in France and Pentonville in Britain, prisoners wore leather masks while they exercised and sat in separate stalls when in chapel. Solitary confinement, it was believed, forced prisoners back on their own consciences, led to greater remorse, and increased the possibility that they would change their evil ways. One supporter of the separate-cell system noted how:

> a few months in the solitary cell renders a prisoner strangely impressible. The chaplain can then make the brawny navvy cry like a child; he can work on his feelings in almost any way he pleases; he can, so to speak, photograph his thoughts, wishes and opinions on his patient's mind, and fill his mouth with his own phrases and language.[14]

As prison populations increased, however, solitary confinement proved expensive and less feasible. The French even returned to their custom of sending prisoners to French Guiana to handle the overload.

Prison reform and police forces were geared toward one primary end, the creation of a more disciplined society. Disturbed by the upheavals associated with revolutions and the social discontent wrought by industrialization and urbanization, the ruling elites sought to impose some order upon society. Even many radical working-class activists, who were often the object of police activity, welcomed the domestication and discipline that the new system imposed.

▼ Romanticism

At the end of the eighteenth century, a new intellectual movement was developing to challenge the ideas of the Enlightenment. Although some historians have argued that Romanticism was more a "mood" than a movement, it revolutionized painting, literature, and music in the first half of the nineteenth century. Romanticism was a reaction against the Enlightenment's preoccupation with reason in discovering truth. While the romantics, especially the early romantics, by no means disparaged reason, they tried to balance its use by stressing the importance of feeling, emotion, and imagination as sources of knowing. As one German romantic put it,

"It was my heart that counselled me to do it, and my heart cannot err." Romanticism manifested itself in a remarkable variety of ways, evident in a survey of its major characteristics and some of its major figures.

The Characteristics of Romanticism

Although European in scope, Romanticism had its roots in Germany and can be said to have had its beginnings in the *Sturm und Drang* ("Storm and Stress") literary movement of the 1770s. German poets rejected classicism's adherence to strict discipline and form as artificial and favored more "natural" compositions in which people were moved by inner forces rather than the external events that impinged on them. For romantic writers, this meant an emphasis on emotion and sentiment and the belief that these inner feelings were only understandable to the person experiencing them. An important model for romantics was the tragic figure in *The Sorrows of the Young Werther,* a novel by the great German writer, Johann Wolfgang von Goethe (1749–1832), who later rejected Romanticism in favor of classicism. Werther was a romantic figure who sought freedom in order to fulfill himself. Misunderstood and rejected by society, he continued to believe in his own worth through his inner feelings, but his deep love for a girl who did not love him finally led him to commit suicide.

The romantic preoccupation with sentiment and the suffering that deepens it was easily exaggerated in less talented writers than Goethe. After Goethe's *Sorrows of the Young Werther,* numerous novels and plays appeared whose plots revolved around young maidens tragically carried off at an early age (twenty-three was most common) by disease (usually tuberculosis, at that time a drawn-out disease that was usually fatal) to the sorrow and sadness of their male lovers.

Individualism was another important characteristic of Romanticism. The Enlightenment concern with the universal in human nature, the common qualities of all people, was superseded by the romantics' interest in the uniqueness of each person. This urge to achieve self-realization was aptly portrayed in Goethe's *Faust,* the story of the scholar whose love of life and inability to find truth through the path of reason persuades him to seek fulfillment by turning to occult forces.

The desire of romantics to follow their inner drives to achieve self-realization also led them to rebel against middle-class conventions. Long hair, beards, and outra-

▼ **Neo-Gothic Revival (British Houses of Parliament).** The romantic movement of the first half of the nineteenth century led, among other things, to a revival of medieval Gothic architecture that left European cities bedecked with neo-Gothic buildings. After the Houses of Parliament in London burned down in 1834, they were replaced with the new buildings of neo-Gothic design seen in this photograph.

geous clothes served to reinforce the individualism that young romantics were trying to express. Rejection of contemporary modes of thought could take other directions as well. In his novel *Lucinde,* the German writer and critic, Friedrich Schlegel (1772–1829), presented a portrait of a free and "innocent" girl who followed the demands of her heart by advocating the so-called "natural" practice of free love. But the revolt against convention combined with sentimental suffering could also lead the romantics to disorderly lives and bizarre behavior. Charlotte Stieglitz stabbed herself in the hope that her husband's sorrow would make him a better poet. It failed to work.

Sentiment and individualism came together in the romantics' stress on the heroic. The romantic hero was the solitary genius who was ready to defy the world and sacrifice his life for a great cause. However, in the hands of the British writer, Thomas Carlyle (1795–1881), the romantic hero did not destroy himself in ineffective protests against society, but transformed society instead. In his historical works, Carlyle stressed that the course of history was largely determined by the deeds of such heroes.

Many romantics adhered to a belief in the organic evolution of political and social institutions. States and societies, like individual organisms, they thought, evolved through time. Each people had its own *Geist* or spirit that made it unique. This *Volksgeist* (national spirit) was reflected in governments, culture, traditions, and institutions and was passed on from generation to generation. This perspective inspired romantics to study history because they saw it as a way to understand how a nationality came to be what it was. In the process, the romantics spawned a historical renaissance. Governments supported the publication of collections of documents; historical societies flourished. One period of history—the Middle Ages—was singled out for special attention because it was the age in which European states had begun their existence. It was also seen as an age of faith and religious emotion rather than reason. No doubt, the romantic reverence for history contributed to the age's fascination with nationalism.

This historical mindedness was furthered in many ways. In Germany, the Grimm brothers collected and published their nation's fairy tales, as did Hans Christian Andersen in Denmark. The revival of medieval Gothic architecture left European countrysides adorned with pseudo-medieval castles and cities bedecked with grandiose neo-Gothic cathedrals, city halls, parliamentary buildings, and even railway stations.

Literature, too, reflected this historical consciousness. The novels of Walter Scott (1771–1832) became European best-sellers in the first half of the nineteenth century. Scott had a background in law but was raised on old tales of Scottish history. He first made his mark as a writer of verse romances, but it was his historical novels that brought him even greater attention. *Ivanhoe*, in which he tried to evoke the clash between Saxon and Norman knights in medieval England, became one of his most popular. On the Continent, Alexandre Dumas (1802–1870) likewise gained fame for his historical evocations. Most famous was *The Three Musketeers* with its vivid portrayal of swashbuckling adventurers in seventeenth-century France.

To some historians, the romantic vogue for the past, especially the Middle Ages, represents a nostalgia for a simpler time, for a society envisioned by the romantics themselves as an organic community in which people were secure in knowing their rightful place in life. Many romantics were especially critical of the emerging industrialization and were convinced that it would cause people to become alienated from their inner selves and the natural world around them.

To the historical mindedness of the romantics could be added a love of the exotic and unfamiliar, be it in the past, distant places, or the supernatural. In an exaggerated form, this preoccupation gave rise to so-called Gothic literature, chillingly evident in Mary Shelley's *Frankenstein* and the American Edgar Allen Poe's short stories of horror (see the box on p. 767). Some romantics even sought the unusual in their own lives by seeking extraordinary states of experience in dreams, nightmares, supernatural possession, frenzies, and suicidal depression or in drug-induced, altered states of consciousness by experimenting with cocaine, opium, and hashish.

Romantic Poets and the Love of Nature

To the romantics, poetry ranked above all other literary forms because it was viewed as the direct expression of one's soul. The romantic poets were viewed as seers who could reveal the invisible world to others. Their incredible sense of drama made some of them the most colorful figures of their era, living intense but short lives. Percy Bysshe Shelley (1792–1822), expelled from school for advocating atheism, set out to reform the world. His *Prometheus Unbound*, completed in 1820, is a portrait of the revolt of human beings against the laws and customs that oppress them. He drowned in a storm in the Mediterranean. Lord Byron (1788–1824) dramatized himself as the melancholy romantic hero that he had described in his work, *Childe Harold's Pilgrimage*. He participated in the movement for Greek independence and died in Greece fighting the Turks.

Romantic poetry gave full expression to one of the most important characteristics of Romanticism: love of nature, especially evident in William Wordsworth (1770–1850), the foremost romantic prophet of nature. He spent days wandering through British forests, often hiking as much as forty miles a day. Like other romantics, he was fascinated by the different moods of nature:

From Nature doth emotion come, and moods
Of calmness equally are Nature's gift:
This is her glory; these two attributes
Are sister horns that constitute her strength. [15]

Gothic Literature: Edgar Allan Poe
▼ ▼ ▼

American writers and poets made significant contributions to the movement of Romanticism. Although Edgar Allan Poe (1809–1849) was influenced by the German romantic school of mystery and horror, many literary historians give him the credit for pioneering the modern short story. This selection from the conclusion of "The Fall of the House of Usher" gives a sense of the nature of so-called Gothic literature.

Edgar Allan Poe, "The Fall of the House of Usher"

No sooner had these syllables passed my lips, than—as if a shield of brass had indeed, at the moment, fallen heavily upon a floor of silver—I became aware of a distinct, hollow, metallic, and clangorous, yet apparently muffled, reverberation. Complete unnerved, I leaped to my feet; but the measured rocking movement of Usher was undisturbed. I rushed to the chair in which he sat. His eyes were bent fixedly before him, and throughout his whole countenance there reigned a stony rigidity. But, as I placed my hand upon his shoulder, there came a strong shudder over his whole person; a sickly smile quivered about his lips; and I saw that he spoke in a low, hurried, and gibbering murmur, as if unconscious of my presence. Bending closely over him, I at length drank in the hideous import of his words.

"Not hear it?—yes, I hear it, and *have* heard it. Long-long-long-many minutes, many hours, many days, have I heard it—yet I dared not—oh, pity me, miserable wretch that I am!—I dared not—I *dared* not speak! *We have put her living in the tomb!* Said I not that my senses were acute? I *now* tell you that I heard her first feeble movements in the hollow coffin. I heard them—many, many days ago—yet I dared not—*I dared not speak!* And now—to-night—. . . the rending of her coffin, and the grating of the iron hinges of her prison, and her struggles within the coppered archway of the vault! Oh whither shall I fly? Will she not be here anon? Is she not hurrying to upbraid me for my haste? Have I not heard her footstep on the stair? Do I not distinguish that heavy and horrible beating of her heart? MADMAN!"—here he sprang furiously to his feet, and shrieked out his syllables, as if in the effort he were giving up his soul—"MADMAN! I TELL YOU THAT SHE NOW STANDS WITHOUT THE DOOR!"

As if in the superhuman energy of his utterance there had been found the potency of a spell, the huge antique panels to which the speaker pointed threw slowly back, upon the instant, their ponderous and ebony jaws. It was the work of the rushing gust—but then without those doors there DID stand the lofty and enshrouded figure of the lady Madeline of Usher. There was blood upon her white robes, and the evidence of some bitter struggle upon every portion of her emaciated frame. For a moment she remained trembling and reeling to and fro upon the threshold, then, with a low moaning cry, fell heavily inward upon the person of her brother, and in her violent and now final death-agonies, bore him to the floor a corpse, and a victim to the terrors he had anticipated.

But Wordsworth's admiration of nature went beyond a simple observation of streams and trees. His experience of nature was almost mystical as he claimed to receive "authentic tidings of invisible things":

> One impulse from a vernal wood
> May teach you more of man,
> Of Moral Evil and of good,
> Than all the sages can.[16]

To Wordsworth, nature contained a mysterious force that the poet could perceive and learn from. Nature served as a mirror into which humans could look to learn about themselves. Nature was, in fact, alive and sacred:

> To every natural form, rock, fruit or flower,
> Even the loose stones that cover the high-way,
> I gave a moral life, I saw them feel,
> Or link'd them to some feeling: the great mass
> Lay bedded in a quickening soul, and all
> That I beheld, respired with inward meaning.[17]

Other romantics carried this worship of nature further into pantheism by identifying the great force in nature with God. The romantics would have nothing to do with the deist god of the Enlightenment, the creator of the world-machine, far removed from his creation. As the German romantic poet Friedrich Novalis said, "Anyone seeking God will find him anywhere."

William Blake and the Romantic Attack on Science
▼ ▼ ▼

William Blake (1757–1827) was a British poet, painter, and graphic artist who combined all of these vocations to produce visually stunning books. He was a religious mystic, and much of his poetic and artistic work was an attempt to give visible form to his profound visionary experiences. In this selection from his poem Milton, he expressed his deep distrust of "the Reasoning Power in Man" and materialistic science.

William Blake, Milton

The Negation is the Spectre; the Reasoning Power in
    Man
This is a false body: an Incrustation over my Immortal
Spirit; a Selfhood, which must be put off and
    annihilated away
To cleanse the Face of my Spirit by Self-examination.
To bathe in the Waters of Life; to wash off the Not
    Human
I come in Self-annihilation and the grandeur of
    Inspiration
To cast off Rational Demonstration by Faith in the
    Saviour
To cast off the rotten rags of Memory by Inspiration
To cast off Bacon, Locke and Newton [three English
    forerunners of science] from Albion's [usually
    ancient name of Britain] covering
To take off his filthy garments, & clothe him with
    Imagination
To cast aside from Poetry, all that is not Inspiration
That it no longer shall dare to mock with the aspersion
    of Madness
Cast on the Inspired, by the tame high finisher of paltry
    Blots,

Indefinite, or paltry Rhymes; or paltry Harmonies,
Who creeps into State Government like a catterpiller to
    destroy
To cast off the idiot Questioner who is always
    questioning,
But never capable of answering; who sits with a sly
    grin
Silent plotting when to question, like a thief in a cave;
Who publishes doubt & calls it knowledge; whose
    Science is Despair,
Whose pretence to knowledge is Envy, whose whole
    Science is
To destroy the wisdom of ages to gratify ravenous Envy
That rages round him like a Wolf day & night without
    rest
He smiles with condescension; he talks of Benevolence
    & Virtue
And those who act with Benevolence & Virtue, they
    murder time on time
These are the destroyers of Jerusalem, these are the
    murderers
Of Jesus, who deny the Faith & mock at Eternal Life:
Who pretend to Poetry that they may destroy
    Imagination;
By imitation of Nature's Images drawn from
    Remembrance
These are the Sexual Garments, the Abomination of
    Desolation
Hiding the Human Lineaments as with an Ark &
    Curtains
Which Jesus rent: & now shall wholly purge away with
    Fire
Till Generation is swallowed up in Regeneration.

The worship of nature also led Wordsworth and other romantic poets to a critique of the mechanistic materialism of eighteenth-century science, which, they believed, had reduced nature to a mere object of study, to simply a cold abstraction (see the box above). Against that view of the natural world, Wordsworth offered his own vivid and concrete experience. To him the scientists' dry, mathematical approach left no room for the imagination and even worse none for the human soul. The poet who left to the world "one single moral precept, one single affecting sentiment," Wordsworth said, did more for the world than scientists who were soon forgotten.

Romanticism in Art and Music

Like the literary arts, the visual arts were also deeply affected by Romanticism. Although they varied widely in what they produced, romantic artists shared at least two fundamental characteristics. All artistic expression to them was a reflection of the artist's inner feelings; a painting should mirror the artist's vision of the world and be the instrument of his own imagination. Moreover, romantic artists deliberately rejected the principles of classicism. Beauty was not a timeless thing; its expression depended on one's culture and one's age. The romantics abandoned classical restraint for warmth, emotion, and movement. Through an examination of three painters, we can see how Romanticism influenced the visual arts.

Caspar David Friedrich's (1774–1840) early life experiences left him with a lifelong preoccupation with God and nature. Friedrich painted many landscapes but with an interest that transcended the mere presentation of natural details. His portrayal of mountains shrouded in mist, gnarled trees bathed in moonlight, and the stark ruins of monasteries surrounded by withered trees all conveyed a feeling of mystery and mysticism. For Friedrich, nature was a manifestation of divine life. As in *Man and Woman Gazing at the Moon,* he liked to depict one or two solitary figures gazing upon the grandeur of a natural scene with their backs to the viewer. Not only were his human figures dwarfed by the overwhelming presence of nature, but they expressed the human yearning for infinity, the desire to lose oneself in the universe. To Friedrich, the artistic process depended upon the use of an unrestricted imagination that could only be achieved through inner vision. He advised artists: "Shut your physical eye and look first at your picture with your spiritual eye, then bring to the light of day what you have seen in the darkness."

Another artist who dwelled on nature and made landscape his major subject, although with less spiritual intensity, was the Briton Joseph Malford William Turner (1775–1851). Turner was an incredibly prolific artist who produced over 20,000 paintings, drawings, and watercolors. Turner's concern with nature manifested itself in innumerable landscapes and seascapes, sunrises and sunsets. He, however, did not idealize nature or reproduce it with realistic accuracy. He sought instead to convey its moods by using a skilled interplay of light and color to suggest natural effects. In allowing his objects to melt into their surroundings, he anticipated the Impressionist painters of the last half of the nineteenth century (see Chapter 25).

Eugène Delacroix (1798–1863) was one of the most famous French exponents of the romantic school of painting. Largely self-taught, Delacroix's paintings exhibited two primary characteristics, a fascination with the exotic and a passion for color. Both are visible in his *Women of Algiers.* Significant for its use of light and its patches of interrelated color, this portrayal of the world of harem concubines in exotic north Africa was actually somewhat scandalous to the early nineteenth century. In Delacroix, theatricality and movement combined with a daring use of color. Many of his works reflect his own belief that "a painting should be a feast to the eye."

To many romantics, music was the most romantic of the arts since it enabled the composer to probe deeply into human emotions. One romantic writer noted:

It has been rightly said that the object of music is the awakening of emotion. No other art can so sublimely arouse human sentiments in the innermost heart of man. No other art

▼ Caspar David Friedrich, *Man and Woman Gazing at the Moon.* Romantic artists rejected classical restraint in favor of emotion and sentiment. Moreover, they believed that artistic expression should be a reflection of an artist's inner feelings. The German artist Caspar David Friedrich sought to express in painting his own mystical view of nature. "The divine is everywhere," he once wrote, "even in a grain of sand." In this painting, two solitary wanderers are shown from the back gazing at the moon. Overwhelmed by the all-pervasive presence of nature, the two figures express the human longing for infinity.

can paint to the eyes of the soul the splendours of nature, the delights of contemplation, the character of nations, the tumult of their passions, and the languour of their sufferings as music can.[18]

Although music historians have called the eighteenth century an age of classicism and the nineteenth the era of Romanticism, there was much carryover of classical forms from one century to the next, especially in the use of the sonata, string quartet, and symphony. One of the greatest composers of all time, Ludwig van Beethoven, served as a bridge between classicism and Romanticism.

Beethoven (1770–1827) was born in Bonn (Germany) where he played for a while as an organist at the court of the elector of Cologne. He soon made his way to Vienna, then the musical capital of Europe, where he studied briefly under Mozart. Beginning in 1792, Vienna became his permanent residence although he was barely tolerated by Viennese society because of his unruly manner and repulsive appearance. During his first major period of composing from 1792 to 1802, his work was still largely within the classical framework of the eighteenth century, and his style differed little from that of Mozart and Haydn. But with this Third Symphony, the *Eroica,* originally intended for Napoleon, Beethoven broke through to the elements of Romanticism in his use of uncontrolled rhythms to create dramatic struggle and uplifted resolutions. E. T. A. Hoffman, a contemporary composer and writer, said, "Beethoven's music opens the flood gates of fear, of terror, of horror, of pain, and arouses that longing for the eternal which is the essence of Romanticism. He is thus a pure Romantic composer"[19] Beethoven went on to write a vast quantity of works including symphonies, piano and violin sonatas, concerti, masses, an opera, and a cycle of songs. In the midst of this productivity and growing fame, Beethoven was more and more burdened by his growing deafness, which intensified noticeably after 1800. To the composer Richard Wagner (see Chapter 23), this was a distinct advantage. "Undisturbed by the bustle of life," he wrote, Beethoven "only heard the harmonies of his soul." One of the most moving pieces of music of all time, the chorale finale of his Ninth Symphony, was composed when Beethoven was totally deaf.

The Revival of Religion in the Age of Romanticism

Catholicism experienced a revival after the Napoleonic era. In the eighteenth century, Catholicism had lost its attraction for many of the educated elite as even the European nobility flirted with the ideas of the Enlightenment. The restoration of the nobility, however, brought them to a new appreciation for the Catholic faith as a force for order in society, an appreciation greatly reinforced by the movement of Romanticism. The attraction of romantics to the Middle Ages and their emphasis on emotion led them to their own widespread revival of Christianity. This revival took many forms. Some romantics condemned irreligion as a cause

▼ **Eugène Delacroix,** *Women of Algiers.* Also characteristic of Romanticism was its love of the exotic and unfamiliar. In his *Women of Algiers,* Delacroix reflected this fascination with the exotic in his portrayal of harem concubines from Morocco. At the same time, Delacroix's painting reflects his preoccupation with light and color.

of civilization's disintegration while others stressed the otherworldly side of Christianity and reawakened a genuine interest in mysticism.

Catholicism particularly benefited from this romantic enthusiasm for religion. Especially among German romantics, there were many conversions to the Catholic faith. One of the most popular expressions of this romantic revival of Catholicism was found in the work of the Frenchman François-René de Chateaubriand (1768–1848). His book, *Genius of Christianity*, published in 1802, was soon labeled the "Bible of Romanticism." His defense of Catholicism was based not upon historical, theological, or even rational grounds, but largely upon romantic sentiment. As a faith, Catholicism echoed the harmony of all things. Its liturgy contained the divine mysteries that mirrored the universe. Its cathedrals brought one into the very presence of God; according to Chateaubriand: "You could not enter a Gothic church without feeling a kind of awe and a vague sentiment of the Divinity . . . every thing in a Gothic church reminds you of the labyrinths of a wood; every thing excites a feeling of religious awe, of mystery, and of the Divinity."[20]

Protestantism also experienced a revival. That revival or Awakening as it was called had already begun in the eighteenth century with the enthusiastic emotional experiences of Methodism in Britain and Pietism in Germany (see Chapter 18). Methodist missionaries from England and Scotland carried their messages of sin and redemption to liberal Protestant churches in France and Switzerland, winning converts to their strongly evangelical message. Germany, too, witnessed a Protestant Awakening as enthusiastic evangelical preachers found that their messages of hellfire and their methods of emotional conversion found a ready response among people alienated by the highly educated establishment clergy of the state churches.

In 1815, a conservative order had been reestablished throughout Europe, and the cooperation of the great powers, embodied in the Concert of Europe, tried to ensure its durability. But the revolutionary waves of the early 1820s and the early 1830s made it clear that the ideologies of liberalism and nationalism, unleashed by the French Revolution and now reinforced by the spread of the Industrial Revolution, were still alive and active. They faced enormous difficulties, however, as failed revolutions in Poland, Russia, Italy, and Germany all testify. At the same time, reform legislation in Britain and successful revolutions in Greece, France, and Belgium demonstrated the continuing strength of these forces of change. In 1848, they erupted once more all across Europe. And once more they failed. But not all was lost. Both liberalism and nationalism would succeed in the second half of the nineteenth century but in ways not foreseen by the idealistic liberals and nationalists who, when they manned the barricades in 1848, were utterly convinced that their time had come.

Notes

1. Quoted in Charles Breunig, *The Age of Revolution and Reaction, 1789–1850* (New York, 1970), p. 119.

2. Quoted in M. S. Anderson, *The Ascendancy of Europe, 1815–1914*, 2d ed. (London, 1985), p. 1.

3. Quotations from Burke can be found in Peter Viereck, *Conservatism* (Princeton, N.J., 1956), pp. 27, 114.

4. Quoted in ibid., p. 51.

5. Quoted in René Albrecht-Carrié, *The Concert of Europe* (New York, 1968), p. 48.

6. Quoted in G. de Berthier de Sauvigny, *Metternich and His Times* (London, 1962), p. 105.

7. Quoted in Donald E. Emerson, *Metternich and the Political Police* (The Hague, 1968), p. 110.

8. Quoted in S. Joan Moon, "Feminism and Socialism: The Utopian Synthesis of Flora Tristan," in Marilyn J. Boxer and Jean H. Quataert, eds., *Socialist Women* (New York, 1978), p. 38.

9. Quoted in Stanley Z. Pech, *The Czech Revolution of 1848* (Chapel Hill, N.C., 1969), p. 82.

10. Quoted in Clive Emsley, *Policing and Its Context, 1750–1870* (New York, 1984), p. 58.

11. Quoted in Clive Emsley, *Crime and Society in England, 1750–1900* (London, 1987), p. 173.

12. Quoted in Emsley, *Policing and Its Context, 1750–1870*, p. 66.

13. Quoted in ibid., p. 102.

14. Quoted in Emsley, *Crime and Society in England, 1750–1900*, p. 226.

15. William Wordsworth, *The Prelude* (Harmondsworth, 1971), p. 489.

16. William Wordsworth, "The Tables Turned," *Poems of Wordsworth*, ed. Matthew Arnold (London, 1963). p. 138.

17. Wordsworth, *The Prelude*, p. 109.

18. Quoted in H.G. Schenk, *The Mind of the European Romantics* (Garden City, N.Y., 1969), p. 205.

19. Quoted in Siegbert Prawer, ed., *The Romantic Period in Germany* (London, 1970), p. 285.

20. Quoted in John B. Halsted, ed., *Romanticism* (New York, 1969), p. 156.

Suggestions for Further Reading
▼ ▼ ▼

For a good, up-to-date survey of the entire nineteenth century, see R. Gildea, *Barricades and Borders: Europe 1800–1914* (Oxford, 1987) in the Short Oxford History of the Modern World series. Also valuable is M. S. Anderson, *The Ascendancy of Europe, 1815–1914*, 2d ed. (London, 1985). For surveys of the period covered in this chapter, see C. Breunig, *The Age of Revolution and Reaction, 1789–1850*, 2d ed. (New York, 1979); and J. Droz, *Europe between Revolutions, 1815–1848* (London, 1967). There are also some useful books on individual countries that cover more than the subject of this chapter. These include R. Magraw, *France, 1815–1914: The Bourgeois Century* (London, 1983); H. Seton-Watson, *The Russian Empire, 1801–1917* (Oxford, 1967); H. Holborn, *A History of Modern Germany*, vol. 2, *1648–1840* (New York, 1964); C. A. Macartney, *The Habsburg Empire, 1790–1918* (London, 1971); S. J. Woolf, *A History of Italy, 1700–1860* (London, 1979); and N. Gash, *Aristocracy and People: Britain 1815–1865* (London, 1979).

On the peace settlement of 1814–1815, there is the older work by H. Nicolson, *The Congress of Vienna, 1814–15* (New York, 1946). A concise summary of the international events of the entire nineteenth century can be found in R. Bullen and F. R. Bridge, *The Great Powers and the European States System, 1815–1914* (London, 1980). For the period covered in this chapter, see A. Sked, ed., *Europe's Balance of Power, 1815–1848* London, 1979). On the man whose conservative policies dominated this era, see the brief but good biography by A. Palmer, *Metternich* (New York, 1972). Also useful is D. E. Emerson, *Metternich and the Political Police* (The Hague, 1968). On the revolutions in Europe in 1830, see C. Church, *Europe in 1830: Revolution and Political Change* (Chapel Hill, N.C., 1983). The standard work on the revolution of 1830 in France is D. Pinkney, *The French Revolution of 1830* (Princeton, N.J., 1972), while D. Porch, *Army and Revolution: France 1815–48* (London, 1979), examines republican sentiment in the

army. On Great Britain's reform legislation, see M. Brock, *Great Reform Act* (London, 1973); and D. C. Moore, *The Politics of Deference: A Study of the Mid-Nineteenth Century English Political System* (New York, 1976). The Greek revolt is examined in detail in D. Dakin, *The Greek Struggle for Independence, 1821–33* (Berkeley, 1973). Revolt in Russia is covered in M. Raeff, *The Decembrist Movement* (Englewood Cliffs, N.J., 1966). On the role of the political police in the Russia of Nicholas I, see S. Monas, *The Third Section: Police and Society in Russia under Nicholas I* (Cambridge, Mass., 1961).

The best introduction to the revolutions of 1848 is P. Stearns, *1848: The Revolutionary Tide in Europe* (New York, 1974). Good accounts of the revolutions in individual countries include G. Duveau, *1848: The Making of a Revolution* (New York, 1967); R. J. Rath, *The Viennese Revolution of 1848* (Austin, Tex., 1957); I Deák, *The Lawful Revolution: Louis Kossuth and the Hungarians, 1848–49* (New York, 1979); P. Brock, *The Slovak National Awakening* (Toronto, 1976); R. Stadelmann, *Social and Political History of the German 1848 Revolution* (Athens, Ohio, 1975); and P. Ginsborg, *Daniele Manin and the Venetian Revolution of 1848–9* (New York, 1979). An important book on France's relations to the European revolutions of 1848 is L. C. Jennings, *France and Europe in 1848: A Study of French Foreign Affairs in Time of Crisis* (Oxford, 1973).

Good introductions to the major ideologies of the first half of the nineteenth century including both analysis and readings from the major figures can be found in H. Kohn, *Nationalism* (Princeton, N.J., 1955); J. S. Schapiro, *Liberalism: Its Meaning and History* (Princeton, N.J., 1958); and P. Viereck, *Conservatism* (Princeton, N.J., 1956). For a general survey, see R. Stromberg, *An Intellectual History of Modern Europe*, 3d ed. (Englewood Cliffs, N.J., 1981). An excellent work on French utopian socialism is F. Manuel, *The Prophets of Paris* (New York, 1962).

On changes in the treatment of crime and punishment, see M. Foucault, *Discipline and Punish: The Birth of the Prison* (New York, 1977). The new policemen are examined in C. Emsley, *Policing and Its Context, 1750–1870* (New York, 1984). Also useful on crime, policemen, and prisons are J. J. Tobias, *Nineteenth-Century Crime Prevention and Punishment* (Newton Abbott, 1972); G. Wright, *Between the Guillotine and Liberty: Two Centuries of the Crime Problem in France* (New York, 1983); M. Ignatieff, *A Just Measure of Pain: The Penitentiary in the Industrial Revolution, 1750–1850* (New York, 1978); and C. Emsley, *Crime and Society in England, 1750–1900* (London, 1987). The religious approach to solving the problem of the dangerous classes can be studied in T. Laqueur, *Religion and Respectability: Sunday Schools and Working-Class Culture, 1780–1850* (New Haven, Conn., 1976).

G. L. Mosse, *The Culture of Western Europe: The Nineteenth and Twentieth Centuries* (Chicago, 1961), remains a good introduction to the cultural history of Europe. A beautifully illustrated introduction to Romanticism can be found in H. Honour, *Romanticism* (New York, 1979). There is an interesting analysis of the ideas of the romantics in H. G. Schenk, *The Mind of the European Romantics* (Garden City, N.Y., 1969). There is an excellent collection of writings by romantics in J. B. Halsted, ed., *Romanticism* (New York, 1969). On German romanticism, see S. Prawer, ed., *The Romantic Period in Germany* (London, 1970). On Wordsworth and English Romanticism, see J. Wordsworth, *William Wordsworth and the Age of English Romanticism* (New Brunswick, N.J., 1987).

Chapter 23

An Age of Nationalism and Realism, 1850–1871

▼ ▼ ▼ ▼ ▼

A cross the Continent, the revolutions of 1848 had failed. The forces of liberalism and nationalism appeared to have been decisively defeated as authoritarian governments reestablished their control almost everywhere in Europe by 1850. And yet within twenty-five years, many of the goals sought by the liberals and nationalists during the first half of the nineteenth century seemed to have been achieved. National unity became a reality in Italy and Germany while many European states were governed by constitutional monarchies, even though the constitutional-parliamentary features were frequently facades.

All the same, these goals were not achieved by liberal and nationalist leaders but by a new generation of conservative leaders who were proud of being practitioners of *realpolitik*, a "politics of reality." One reaction to the failure of the revolutions of 1848 had been a new toughness of mind in which people prided themselves on being realistic in their handling of power. The new conservative leaders used armies and power politics to achieve their foreign policy goals. And they did not hesitate to manipulate liberal means to achieve conservative ends at home. Nationalism had failed as a revolutionary movement in 1848–1849; tied to conservatism, national unification was now used to avert revolution.

During the period from 1850 to 1871, international relations changed dramatically. Between 1815 and 1850, the statesmen of Europe, reacting to the upheaval of the French revolutionary and Napoleonic eras, had sought to settle their major

•••••••• 1850 ••••••••••• 1855 ••••••••••• 1860 ••••••••••• 1865 ••••••••••• 1870 ••••••••••

▲ Marx and Engels, *The Communist Manifesto*   ▲ ▲ Flaubert, *Madame Bovary*   Darwin, *On the Origins of Species*   ▲ Emancipation of the Russian Serfs

differences by diplomacy, fearful that war might once more unleash revolutionary forces. After 1850 a new generation of statesmen was no longer motivated by the fears of 1815 and did not hesitate to use war to achieve their ends. The new attitude eventually had dire consequences for the peace of Europe.

▼ The France of Napoleon III

After 1850 a new generation of conservative leaders came to power in Europe. Foremost among them was Napoleon III (1852–1870) of France who taught his contemporaries how authoritarian governments could use liberal and nationalistic forces to bolster their own power. It was a lesson others quickly learned.

Louis Napoleon: Toward the Second Empire

Even after his election as the president of the French Republic, many of his contemporaries dismissed Napoleon "the Small" as a nonentity whose success was due only to his name. But physical appearances can be deceiving. Louis Napoleon was a clever politician who was especially astute at understanding the popular forces of his day. Some historians think that as a Bonaparte, Louis Napoleon believed it his mission to govern France. Apparently, as he told a friend shortly after the election, the presidency of the Republic was only the beginning of this quest: "We are not at the summit yet. This is only a stop on the way, a terrace where we may rest a moment to gaze at the horizon."

Louis Napoleon was a patient man, however. For three years he persevered in winning the support of the French people while using governmental favors to gain the loyalty of the army and the Catholic church. He faced considerable opposition from the National Assembly, which had a conservative-monarchist majority after elections in May of 1849. When the assembly voted to deprive three million men of the right to vote, Louis Napoleon achieved even more popular favor by posing as the savior of universal male suffrage. When the assembly rejected his proposal to revise the constitution and allow him to stand again for reelection, Louis resorted to a coup d'etat. On December 1, 1851, troops loyal to the president seized the major administrative buildings and arrested opposition leaders. After restoring universal male suffrage, Louis Napoleon asked the French people to restructure the government by electing him president for ten years (see the box on p. 776). By an overwhelming majority, 7.5 million "yes" votes to 640,000 "no" votes, they agreed. A year later, on November 21, 1852, Louis Napoleon returned to the people to ask for the restoration of the Empire. This time 97 percent responded affirmatively, and on December 2, 1852, Louis Napoleon assumed the title of Napoleon III (the first Napoleon had abdicated in favor of his son, Napoleon II, on April 6, 1814). The Second Empire had begun.

The Second Napoleonic Empire

The government of Napoleon III was clearly authoritarian in a Bonapartist sense. Louis Napoleon had asked, "Since France has carried on for fifty years only by virtue of the administrative, military, judicial, religious and financial organization of the Consulate and Empire, why should she not also adopt the political institutions of that period?"[1] As chief of state, Napoleon III controlled the armed forces, police, and civil service. Only he could introduce legislation and declare war. His ministers had no collective responsibility and were answerable only to the emperor. The Legislative Corps gave an appearance of representative government since its members were elected by universal male suffrage for six-year terms. But they could neither initiate legislation nor affect the budget. Moreover, only government candidates were allowed complete freedom to campaign and were supposedly selected from "men enjoying public es-

Louis Napoleon Appeals to the People

▼ ▼ ▼

After his coup d'etat on December 2, 1851, Louis Napoleon asked the French people to approve his actions. By making this appeal, the clever politician was demonstrating how universal male suffrage, considered a democratic and hence revolutionary device, could be used to bolster a basically authoritarian regime. It was a lesson eagerly learned by other conservative rulers in the second half of the nineteenth century. This selection is from Louis Napoleon's proclamation to the French people in 1851.

Louis Napoleon, Proclamation to the People (1851)

Frenchmen! The present situation cannot last much longer. Each passing day increases the danger to the country. The [National] Assembly, which ought to be the firmest supporter of order, has become a center of conspiracies . . . it attacks the authority that I hold directly from the people; it encourages all evil passions; it jeopardizes the peace of France: I have dissolved it and I make the whole people judge between it and me. . . .

I therefore make a loyal appeal to the whole nation, and I say to you: If you wish to continue this state of uneasiness which degrades us and makes our future uncertain, choose another in my place, for I no longer wish an authority which is powerless to do good, makes me responsible for acts I cannot prevent, and chains me to the helm when I see the vessel speeding toward the abyss.

If, on the contrary, you still have confidence in me, give me the means to accomplish the great mission that I hold from you. This mission consists in bringing to a close the era of revolutions by satisfying the legitimate wants of the people and by protecting them against subversive passions. It consists, especially, in creating institutions that may survive men and that may be at length foundations on which something durable can be established.

Persuaded that the instability of authority and the preponderance of a single Assembly are permanent causes of trouble and discord, I submit to you the following fundamental bases of a constitution which the Assemblies will develop later.

1. A responsible chief elected for ten years.
2. Ministers dependent upon the executive power alone.
3. A Council of State composed of the most distinguished men to prepare the laws and discuss them before the legislative body.
4. A legislative body to discuss and vote the laws, elected by universal [male] suffrage. . . .

This system, created by the First Consul [Napoleon I] at the beginning of the century, has already given France calm and prosperity; it will guarantee them to her again.

Such is my profound conviction. If you share it, declare that fact by your votes. If, on the contrary, you prefer a government without force, monarchical or republican, borrowed from I know not what past or from which chimerical future, reply in the negative. . . .

If I do not obtain a majority of your votes, I shall then convoke a new assembly, and I shall resign to it the mandate that I received from you. But if you believe that the cause of which my name is the symbol, that is, France regenerated by the revolution of 1789 and organized by the Emperor, is forever yours, proclaim it by sanctioning the powers that I ask from you. Then France and Europe will be saved from anarchy, obstacles will be removed, rivalries will disappear, for all will respect the decree of Providence in the decision of the people.

---

teem, concerned more with the interests of the country than with the strife of parties, sympathetic towards the suffering of the labouring classes."[2]

The first five years of Napoleon III's reign were a spectacular success as he reaped the benefits of worldwide economic prosperity, although the government's economic policies also contributed to French economic renewal. In light of the loss of political freedom, Napoleon realized the importance of diverting "the attention of the French from politics to economics." He believed in using the resources of government to encourage the national economy and took many steps to expand industrial growth. He promoted the expansion of credit by backing the formation of new investment banks, which provided long-term loans for industrial, commercial, and agricultural expansion. Government subsidies were used to foster the rapid construction of railroads as well as harbors, roads, and canals. The major French railway lines were completed during Napoleon's reign while industrial expansion was evident in the tripling of iron production. In his concern to reduce tensions and improve the social welfare of the nation, Napoleon provided hospitals and free medicine for the workers, and advocated better housing for the working class.

In the midst of this economic expansion, Napoleon III undertook a vast reconstruction of the city of Paris. Under the direction of Baron Haussmann, the medieval Paris of narrow streets and old city walls was destroyed and replaced by a modern Paris of broad boulevards, spacious buildings, circular plazas, public squares, an underground sewage system, a new public water supply, and gaslights. The new Paris served a military as well as aesthetic purpose. Broad streets made it more difficult for would-be insurrectionists to throw up barricades and easier for troops to move rapidly through the city in the event of revolts.

Napoleon III took a great interest in public opinion. Freedom of speech was, of course, not permitted in the authoritarian empire. Freedom of assembly was limited and newspapers were regularly censored. Nevertheless, Napoleon's desire to know the mood of his people led him to request regular reports on public opinion from his subordinates. In the 1860s, as opposition to some of Napoleon's policies began to mount, his sensitivity to the change in the public mood led him to undertake new policies liberalizing his regime. As a result, historians speak of the "liberal empire" for the latter part of the 1860s.

Opposition to Napoleon came from a variety of sources. His attempt to move toward free trade by lowering tariffs on foreign goods, especially those of the British, angered French manufacturers. Then, too, the financial crash of 1857, a silkworm disease, and the devastation of French vineyards by plant lice, although beyond his control, caused severe damage to the French economy. Retrenchment in government spending proved unpopular as well. To shore up his regime, Napoleon III reached out to the working class by legalizing trade unions and granting them the right to strike. He also began to liberalize the political process.

The Legislative Corps had been closely controlled during the 1850s. In the 1860s, opposition candidates were allowed greater freedom to campaign, and the Leg-

▼ **Emperor Napoleon III.** On December 2, 1852, Louis Napoleon took the title of Napoleon III and then proceeded to create an authoritarian monarchy. As opposition to his policies intensified in the 1860s, Napoleon III began to liberalize his government's policies. However, a disastrous military defeat at the hands of Prussia in 1870–1871 brought the collapse of his regime.

islative Corps was permitted more say in affairs of state, including debate over the budget. Historians do not agree about the ultimate aim and potential of Napoleon's liberalization, although it did serve initially to strengthen the hands of the government. In another plebiscite in May 1870, on whether to accept a new constitution that might have inaugurated a parliamentary regime, the French people gave Napoleon another resounding victory. This triumph was short-lived, however. Foreign policy failures had led to growing criticism, and war with Prussia in 1870 turned out to be the death blow for Napoleon III's regime (see The Franco-Prussian War, 1870–1871 later in the chapter).

Foreign Policy: The Crimean War

As heir to the Napoleonic Empire, Napoleon III was motivated by the desire to free France from the restrictions of the peace settlements of 1814–1815 and to make France the chief arbiter of Europe. Although his foreign policy ultimately led to disaster and his own undoing, Napoleon had initial success in the Crimean War (1854–1856).

The Crimean War was another chapter in the story of the so-called Eastern Question, or who would be the chief beneficiaries of the disintegration of the Turkish or Ottoman Empire. War had erupted between the Russians and Turks in 1853 when the Russians demanded the right to protect Christian shrines in Palestine, a privilege that had already been extended to the French. When the Turks refused, the Russians invaded Turkish Moldavia and Walachia. Failure to resolve the problem by negotiations led the Turks to declare war on Russia on October 4, 1853. In the following year, on March 28, Great Britain and France declared war on Russia.

Why did Britain and France take such a step? The British feared the expansion of Russian power into the eastern Mediterranean as a threat to their own sea power there, although some British statesmen also viewed Russia as the foremost threat to the European balance of power because of its aggressive designs on its neighbors. In his desire to undo the settlement of 1815, Napoleon had no doubt realized that Russia, as the chief supporter of those treaties, was his main obstacle. Although the Russian tsar, Nicholas I, hoped for Austrian support (since Russian troops had saved the Austrian Empire in 1849), the Austrians remained neutral. As the Austrian prime minister remarked, "We will astonish the world by our ingratitude." At least the Russians were, but Austria did not want to become a Russian protectorate and very likely had its own designs in the Balkans. Problems among the Balkan Slavs would only serve to inflame the Slavic minorities in the Austrian Empire.

The Crimean War was poorly planned and poorly fought. Britain and France decided on an attack on Russia's Crimean peninsula in the Black Sea. After a long siege and at a terrible cost in manpower for both sides, the main Russian fortress of Sevastopol fell in September 1855, six months after the death of Tsar Nicholas I. His successor, Alexander II, soon sued for peace. By the Treaty of Paris, signed in March 1856, Russia was forced to give up Bessarabia at the mouth of the Danube and accept the neutrality of the Black Sea. In addition, the Danubian principalities of Moldavia and Walachia were placed under the protection of all the great powers.

The Crimean War broke up long-standing European power relationships and effectively destroyed the Concert of Europe. Austria and Russia, the two chief powers maintaining the status quo in the first half of the nineteenth century, were now enemies because of Austria's unwillingness to support Russia in the war. Russia, defeated, humiliated, and weakened by the obvious failure of its serf-armies, withdrew from European affairs for the next two decades to set its house in order and await a better opportunity to undo the Treaty of Paris. Great Britain, disillusioned by its role in the war, also pulled back from continental affairs. Austria, paying the price for its neutrality, was now without friends among the great powers. Not until the 1870s were new combinations formed to replace those that had disappeared, but in the meantime the European international situation remained fluid. Those willing to pursue the "politics of reality" found themselves presented with a situation rife with opportunity. It was this new international situation that made possible the unification of Italy and Germany.

Only Louis Napoleon seemed to have gained in prestige from the Crimean War. His experiences in the war had taught him that he was not the military genius his uncle had been, but he became well aware of the explosive power of the forces of nationalism and determined upon pursuing a foreign policy that would champion the cause of national movements. Some historians have argued that Napoleon believed ardently in the cause of national liberation. Be that as it may, as the liberator of national peoples, Napoleon III envisioned France as the natural leader of free European states. His policy proved to be a disaster as we can observe by examining the movements for unification in Italy and Germany.

▼ National Unification: Italy and Germany

The breakdown of the Concert of Europe opened the way for the Italians and the Germans to establish national states. Their successful unifications transformed the power structure of the Continent. Well into the twentieth century, Europe would still be dealing with the consequences.

The Unification of Italy

The Italians were the first people to benefit from the breakdown of the Concert of Europe. In 1850, Austria was still the dominant power on the Italian peninsula. Austria controlled the prosperous northern provinces of Lombardy and Venetia while Modena and Tuscany were ruled by members of Austria's house of Habsburg. Moreover, the Papal States governed by the pope, the other petty Italian states, and even the Bourbon kingdom of the Two Sicilies looked to the Austrians to maintain the status quo.

Although a minority, Italian liberals and nationalists had tried earnestly to achieve unification in the first half of the nineteenth century. Some had favored the *risorgimento* movement led by Giuseppe Mazzini, which favored a republican Italy; others looked to a confederation of Italian states under the direction of the pope. Neither of those alternatives was feasible after the defeats of 1849. A growing number of advocates of Italian unification now focused on the northern Italian state of Piedmont as their best hope to achieve their goal. As one observed, "To defeat cannons and soldiers, cannons and soldiers are needed. Arms are needed, and not Mazzinian pratings. Piedmont has soldiers and cannons. Therefore I am Piedmontese. By ancient custom, inclination and duty, Piedmont these days is a monarchy. Therefore I am not a republican."[3]

The royal house of Savoy ruled the kingdom of Piedmont, which also included the island of Sardinia. Although soundly defeated by the Austrians in 1848–1849, Piedmont under King Charles Albert had made a valiant effort; it seemed reasonable that it would now assume the leading role in the cause of national unity. It was, however, doubtful that the little state could supply the leadership needed until the new king, Victor Emmanuel II (1849–1878), named Count Camillo di Cavour (1810–1861) as his prime minister in 1852.

Cavour was a liberal-minded nobleman who had made a fortune in agriculture and went on to make even more money in banking, railroads, and shipping. He admired the British, especially their parliamentary system, industrial techniques, and economic liberalism. Cavour was a moderate who favored constitutional government. While he might have wanted Italian unification, he had no preconceived notions about how to obtain it. He was a consummate politician with the ability to persuade others of the rightness of his own convictions. After becoming prime minister in 1852, he pursued a policy of economic expansion, encouraging the building of roads, canals, and railroads and fostering business enterprise by expanding credit and stimulating investment in new industries. The growth in the Piedmontese economy and the subsequent increase in government revenues enabled Cavour to pour money into equipping a large army.

Cavour had no illusions about Piedmont's military strength and was only too well aware that he could not challenge Austrian strength directly. He would need the French. In 1858, Cavour came to an agreement with Napoleon III. The emperor agreed to become an ally of Piedmont in driving the Austrians out of Italy provided that the war could be justified "in the eyes of the public opinion of France and Europe." Once the Austrians were driven out, Italy would be reorganized. Piedmont would be extended into the kingdom of Upper Italy by adding Lombardy, Venetia, Parma, Modena, and part of the Papal States to its territory. In compensation for its efforts, France would receive the Piedmontese provinces of Nice and Savoy. A kingdom of Central Italy would be created for Napoleon III's cousin, Prince Napoleon, who would be married to the younger daughter of King Victor Emmanuel. This agreement between Napoleon and Cavour seemed to assure the French ruler of the opportunity to control Italy. Confident that the Austrians would be driven out of Italy, Cavour provoked the Austrians into invading Piedmont in April 1859, thus fulfilling Napoleon's demand that the war be justified "in the eyes of the public opinion of France and Europe."

In the initial stages of fighting, it was mostly French armies that defeated the Austrians in two major battles. It was also the French who made peace with Austria on July 11, 1859, without informing their Italian ally. Why had Napoleon withdrawn so hastily? For one thing, he realized that, despite two losses, the Austrian army had not yet been defeated; the struggle might be longer and more costly than he had anticipated. Moreover, the Prussians were mobilizing in support of Austria, and Napoleon III had no desire to take on two enemies at once. As a result of Napoleon's peace with Austria, Piedmont received only Lombardy; Austria remained in control of Venetia. Cavour was furious with the French perfidy, but events in northern Italy now turned in his favor. Soon after the war with Austria had begun, some northern Italian states, namely Parma, Modena, Tuscany, and part of the Papal States, had been taken over by nationalists. In plebiscites held in 1860, these states agreed to join Piedmont. Napoleon, in return for Nice and Savoy, agreed to the annexations.

Italian unification might have stopped here since there is little indication that Cavour envisioned uniting all of Italy in the spring of 1860. But the forces of ro-

Garibaldi and Romantic Nationalism

▼ ▼ ▼

Giuseppe Garibaldi was one of the more colorful figures involved in the unification of Italy. Accompanied by only a thousand of his famous "Red Shirts," the Italian soldier of fortune left Genoa on the night of May 5, 1860, for an invasion of the kingdom of the Two Sicilies. The ragged band entered Palermo, the chief city on the island of Sicily, on May 31. This selection is taken from an account by a correspondent for The Times of London, the Hungarian-born Nandor Eber.

The Times, June 13, 1860

Palermo, May 31—Anyone in search of violent emotions cannot do better than set off at once for Palermo. However blasé he may be, or however milk-and-water his blood, I promise it will be stirred up. He will be carried away by the tide of popular feeling. . . .

In the afternoon Garibaldi made a tour of inspection round the town. I was there, but find it really impossible to give you a faint idea of the manner in which he was received everywhere. It was one of those triumphs which seem to be almost too much for a man. . . . The popular idol, Garibaldi, in his red flannel shirt, with a loose colored handkerchief round his neck, and his worn "wide-awake," [a soft-brimmed felt hat] was walking on foot among those cheering, laughing, crying, mad thousands; and all his few followers could do was to prevent him from being bodily carried off the ground. The people threw themselves forward to kiss his hands, or, at least, to touch the hem of his garment, as if it contained the panacea for all their past and perhaps coming suffering. Children were brought up, and mothers asked on their knees for his blessing; and all this while the object of this idolatry was calm and smiling as when in the deadliest fire, taking up the children and kissing them, trying to quiet the crowd, stopping at every moment to hear a long complaint of houses burned and property sacked by the retreating soldiers, giving good advice, comforting, and promising that all damages should be paid for. . . .

One might write volumes of horrors on the vandalism already committed, for every one of the hundred ruins has its story of brutality and inhumanity. . . . In these small houses a dense population is crowded together even in ordinary times. A shell falling on one, and crushing and burying the inmates, was sufficient to make people abandon the neighboring one and take refuge a little further on, shutting themselves up in the cellars. When the Royalists retired they set fire to those of the houses which had escaped the shells, and numbers were thus burned alive in their hiding places. . . .

If you can stand the exhalation, try and go inside the ruins, for it is only there that you will see what the thing means and you will not have to search long before you stumble over the remains of a human body, a leg sticking out here, an arm there, a black face staring at you a little further on. You are startled by a rustle. You look round and see half a dozen gorged rats scampering off in all directions, or you see a dog trying to make his escape over the ruins. . . . I only wonder that the sight of these scenes does not convert every man in the town into a tiger and every woman into a fury. But these people have been so long ground down and demoralized that their nature seems to have lost the power of reaction.

---

mantic republican nationalism forced Cavour to act. Giuseppe Garibaldi (1807–1882) was a dedicated Italian patriot who had supported Mazzini and the republican cause of Young Italy. While in exile in Latin America, he had gained much experience in guerrilla warfare, which he put to good use in the Italian revolutionary struggles of 1848–1849. In 1859, he became involved in the fighting against Austria. Garibaldi was a nuisance to Cavour, and the Piedmontese prime minister diverted his energies by encouraging him to move on to southern Italy where a revolt had broken out against the Bourbon king of the Two Sicilies. With his thousand Red Shirts, as his volunteers were called because of their distinctive dress, Garibaldi landed in Sicily on May 11, 1860.

Although greatly outnumbered, Garibaldi's daring tactics won the day (see the box above). By the end of July 1860, most of Sicily had been pacified under Garibaldi's control. In August Garibaldi and his forces crossed over to the mainland and began a victorious march up the Italian peninsula. Naples, and with it the kingdom of the Two Sicilies, fell in early September. At this point Cavour reentered the scene. Aware that Garibaldi planned to march on Rome, Cavour feared that such a move would bring war with France as the defender of papal interests. Moreover, Garibaldi and his men favored a democratic republicanism; Cavour did not and acted quickly to preempt Garibaldi. The Piedmontese army invaded the Papal States (although bypassing Rome) and moved into the kingdom of Naples. Ever the patriot, Garibaldi chose to yield to Cavour's fait accompli rather than provoke a civil war and retired to his farm. Plebiscites in the Papal States and the kingdom of the Two Sicilies resulted in overwhelming support for union with Piedmont. On March 17, 1861, a new kingdom of Italy was proclaimed under a centralized government subordinated to the control of Piedmont and King Victor Emmanuel II (1861–1878) of the house of Savoy. Worn out by his efforts, Cavour died three months later.

Despite the proclamation of a new kingdom, the task of unification was not yet complete since Venetia in the north was still held by Austria and Rome was under

▼ **Garibaldi Arrives in Sicily.** The dream of Italian nationalists for a united Italian state finally became a reality by 1870. The northern Italian state of Piedmont played a crucial role in that process. Also important, however, was Giuseppe Garibaldi, a determined Italian patriot. Garibaldi is shown here arriving in Sicily on May 11, 1860, with his band of Red Shirts.

▼ **Map 23.1** The Unification of Italy.

SWITZERLAND

SAVOY

FRANCE

PIEDMONT

LOMBARDY

Magenta • • Milan • Solferino

VENETIA

• Venice

AUSTRIAN EMPIRE

PARMA

Genoa •

MODENA

ROMAGNA

OTTOMAN EMPIRE

KINGDOM OF SARDINIA

CORSICA

Florence •

MARCHES

TUSCANY

UMBRIA

PAPAL

STATES

• Rome

ADRIATIC SEA

SARDINIA

MEDITERRANEAN SEA

• Naples

KINGDOM

OF THE

Palermo •

Messina •

TWO SICILIES

Kingdom of Sardinia: Before 1859

To Kingdom of Sardinia: 1859

To Kingdom of Sardinia: 1860

To Kingdom of Italy: 1866, 1870

papal control, supported by French troops. To attack either one meant war with a major European state, which the Italian army was not prepared to handle. It was the Prussian army that indirectly completed the task of Italian unification. In the Austro-Prussian War of 1866 (see The Austro-Prussian War, 1866 later in the chapter), the new Italian state became an ally of Prussia. Although the Italian army was defeated by the Austrians, Prussia's victory left the Italians with Venetia. In 1870, the Franco-Prussian War (see The Franco-Prussian War, 1870–1871 later in the chapter) resulted in the withdrawal of French troops from Rome. The Italian army then annexed the city on September 20, 1870, and Rome became the new capital of the united Italian state.

The Unification of Germany

After the failure of the Frankfurt Assembly to achieve German unification in 1848–1849, German nationalists focused on Austria and Prussia as the only two states powerful enough to dominate German affairs. Austria had long controlled the existing Germanic Confederation, but Prussian power had grown, strongly reinforced by economic expansion in the 1850s. Industrial growth made rapid strides in Germany, especially within the *Zollverein,* a German customs union that had been formed in 1834 under Prussian leadership. By eliminating tolls on rivers and roads among member states, the *Zollverein* had stimulated trade and added to the prosperity of its member states. By 1853, all the German states except Austria had joined the Prussian-dominated customs union. Although Austria attempted to create its own customs union with the south German states, it was

rapidly being excluded from a new Germany based on common economic ties. Prussia benefited the most from this development, as even middle-class liberals began to find some good things in the Prussian state. In 1859, for example, a group of Hanoverian liberals formed the German *Nationalverein,* which advocated constitutional reforms and a united Germany. It looked openly to Prussia to bring about this unification.

In 1848, Prussia had created a constitution that at least had the appearance of constitutional monarchy as it had established a bicameral legislature with the lower house elected by universal male suffrage. However, the voting population was divided into three classes determined by the amount of taxes they paid, a system that allowed the biggest taxpayers to gain the most seats. Unintentionally this system allowed the rising middle classes, who were growing as a result of continuing industrialization, largely to control the lower house by 1859. Their desire for a real parliamentary system was counteracted, however, by the strength of the king's executive power because royal ministers were responsible to the king alone. Nevertheless, the parliament had been granted important legislative and taxation powers upon which it could build.

In 1861, King Frederick William IV died and was succeeded by his brother William. King William I (1861–1888) had definite ideas about the Prussian army because of his own military training. He and his advisers believed that the army was in dire need of change if Prussia was to remain a great power. Working closely with Albrecht von Roon as minister for war and Helmuth von Moltke as chief of the army general staff, the king planned to double the size of the army, diminish the role of the *Landwehr,* the popular militia reserves that had first been formed to fight Napoleon in 1806, and institute three years of compulsory military service for all young men.

Middle-class liberals in the parliament, while willing to have reform, feared compulsory military service because they believed the government would use it to inculcate obedience to the monarchy and strengthen the influence of the conservative-military clique in Prussia. The liberals were powerful enough to reject the new military budget submitted to parliament in March 1862. William I, unwilling to rule by military force, in his frustration appointed a new prime minister, Count Otto von Bismarck (1815–1898). Bismarck, regarded even by the king as too conservative, came to determine the course of modern German history. Until 1890, he dominated both German and European politics.

Otto von Bismarck was born into the Junker class, the traditional, landowning aristocracy of Prussia, to which he remained loyal for the rest of his life. "I was born and raised as an aristocrat," he once said. As a university student, Bismarck indulged heartily in wine, women, and song, yet managed to read widely in German history. After earning a law degree, he embarked upon a career in the Prussian civil service but soon tired of bureaucratic, administrative routine and retired to manage his country estates. Comparing the civil servant to a musician in an orchestra, he responded, "But I want to play the tune the way it sounds good to me or not at all . . . . My pride bids me command rather than obey."[4] In 1847, desirous of more excitement and power than he could find in the country, he reentered public life. Four years later, he began to build a base of diplomatic experience as the Prussian delegate to the diet (parliament) of the Germanic Confederation. This, combined with his experience as Prussian ambassador to Russia and later to France, gave him opportunities to acquire a wide knowledge of European affairs and to learn how to assess the character of rulers.

Because Bismarck succeeded in guiding Prussia's unification of Germany, it is often assumed that he had determined upon a course of action that led precisely to that goal. That is hardly the case. Bismarck was a consummate politician and opportunist. He was not a political gambler, but a moderate who waged war only when all other diplomatic alternatives had been exhausted and when he was reasonably sure that all the military and diplomatic advantages were on his side. Nor was he doctrinaire. Although loyal to the Junkers, the Prussian king, and Lutheranism, he was capable of transcending them all in favor of a broader perspective, although there is no doubt that he came to see the German empire, which he had helped to create, as the primary focus of his efforts. Bismarck has often been portrayed as the ultimate realist, the foremost nineteenth-century practitioner of *realpolitik*—the "politics of reality." His ability to manipulate people and power makes that claim justified, but unlike Hitler in the twentieth century, Bismarck also recognized the limitations of power. When he perceived that the advantages to be won from war "no longer justified the risks involved," he became an ardent defender of peace.

In 1862, the immediate problem facing Bismarck was domestic Prussian politics. Bismarck resubmitted the army appropriations bill to parliament along with a passionate appeal to his liberal opponents: "Germany does not look to Prussia's liberalism but to her power. . . . Not by speeches and majorities will the great questions of the day be decided—that was the mistake of 1848–1849—but by iron and blood."[5] His opponents were not impressed and rejected the bill once again. Bismarck went ahead, collected the taxes, and reorganized the army anyway, blaming the liberals for causing the breakdown of constitutional government. From 1862 to 1866, Bismarck governed Prussia by simply ignoring parliament. Unwilling to revolt and unable to force people not to pay their taxes, parliament did nothing. In the meantime, opposition to his domestic policy determined Bismarck upon an active foreign policy, which led in 1864 to his first war.

THE DANISH WAR, 1864   In the three wars that he waged, Bismarck's victories were as much diplomatic and political as they were military. Before war was declared, Bismarck always saw to it that Prussia would be fighting only one power and that that opponent was isolated diplomatically. He knew enough Prussian history to realize that Frederick the Great had almost been crushed by a mighty coalition in the eighteenth century (see Chapter 19).

The Danish War arose over the duchies of Schleswig and Holstein. In 1863, contrary to international treaty, the Danish government moved to incorporate the two duchies into Denmark. German nationalists were outraged since both duchies had large German populations and were regarded as German states. The diet of the Germanic Confederation urged its member states to send troops against Denmark, but Bismarck did not care to subject Prussian policy to the Austrian-dominated German diet. Instead, he persuaded the Austrians to join Prussia in declaring war on Denmark on February 1, 1864. The Danes were quickly defeated and surrendered Schleswig and Holstein to the victors. Austria and Prussia then agreed to divide the administration of the two duchies; Prussia took Schleswig while Austria administered Holstein. The plan was Bismarck's. By this time Bismarck had come to the realization that the ability of Prussia to expand its power by dominating the northern, largely Protestant part of the Germanic Confederation had to mean the exclusion of Austria from German affairs or, less likely, Austria's willingness to accept Prussian domination of Germany. The joint administration of the two duchies offered plenty of opportunities to create friction with Austria and provide a reason for war if it came to that. While he pursued negotiations with Austria, at the same time he laid the foundations for the isolation of Austria.

THE AUSTRO-PRUSSIAN WAR, 1866   Bismarck had no problem gaining Russia's agreement to remain neutral in the event of an Austro-Prussian war because Prussia had been the only great power to support Russia's repression of a Polish revolt in 1863. A thornier problem was Napoleon III, but Bismarck was able to buy his neutrality by

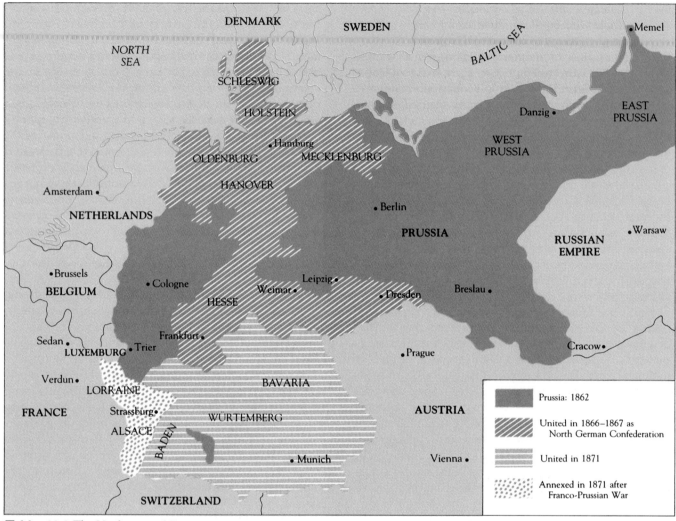

▼ **Map 23.2** The Unification of Germany

Legend:
- Prussia: 1862
- United in 1866–1867 as North German Confederation
- United in 1871
- Annexed in 1871 after Franco-Prussian War

vague promises of territory in the Rhineland in return for France's neutrality in the event of an Austro-Prussian conflict. Finally, Bismarck made an alliance with the new Italian state and promised it Venetia in the event of Austrian defeat.

With the Austrians isolated, Bismarck used the joint occupation of Schleswig-Holstein to goad the Austrians into a war on June 14, 1866. Many Europeans, including Napoleon III, expected a quick Austrian victory, but they overlooked the effectiveness of the Prussian military reforms of the 1860s. The Prussian breech-loading needle gun had a much faster rate of fire than the Austrian muzzle-loader, and a superior network of railroads enabled the Prussians to mass troops quickly. At König-grätz (or Sadowa) on July 3, the Austrian army was decisively defeated. Looking ahead, Bismarck refused to

create a hostile enemy by burdening Austria with a harsh peace as the Prussian king wanted. Austria lost no territory except Venetia to Italy but was excluded from German affairs. The German states north of the Main River were organized into a North German Confederation controlled by Prussia. The south German states, largely Catholic, remained independent but were coerced into signing military agreements with Prussia. In addition to Schleswig and Holstein, Prussia annexed Hanover, Hesse-Cassel, and the free city of Frankfurt because they had openly sided with Austria.

The Austrian War was a rather decisive turning point in Prussian domestic affairs. After the war, Bismarck asked the Prussian parliament to pass a bill of indemnity, legalizing retroactively the taxes Bismarck had collected illegally since 1862. Most liberals did so, having become enthusiastic supporters of Bismarck's achievements. With his victory over Austria and the creation of the North German Confederation, Bismarck had proven Napoleon III's dictum that nationalism and authoritarian government could be combined. In splitting liberalism and nationalism, the two major forces of change in the early nineteenth century, Bismarck made nationalism itself into an antirevolutionary force.

He showed the same flexibility in the creation of a new constitution for the North German Confederation. Each German state kept its own local government, but the king of Prussia was head of the confederation while the chancellor (Bismarck) was responsible directly to the king. Both the army and foreign policy remained in the hands of the king and his chancellor. Parliament consisted of two bodies: a Bundesrat, or federal council composed of delegates nominated by the states, and a lower house, the Reichstag, elected by universal male suffrage. Like Napoleon, Bismarck believed that the peasants and artisans who made up most of the population were conservative at heart and could be used to overcome the advantages of the liberals. He had not counted on the industrial proletariat whose growth in the years ahead would provide him with some of his most vehement opposition (see Chapter 24).

THE FRANCO-PRUSSIAN WAR, 1870–1871 Bismarck and William I had achieved a major goal by 1866. Prussia now dominated all of northern Germany, and Austria had been excluded from any significant role in German affairs. In effect, Prussian militaristic and counterrevolutionary conservatism had triumphed. At the same time, unsettled business led to new international complications and further change. Bismarck realized that France would never be content with a strong German state to its east because of the potential threat to French security. At the same time, after a series of setbacks, Napoleon III needed a diplomatic triumph to offset his serious domestic problems. The French were not happy with the turn of events in Germany and looked for opportunities to humiliate the Prussians.

After a successful revolution had deposed Queen Isabella II, the throne of Spain was offered to Prince Leopold of Hohenzollern-Sigmaringen, a distant relative of the Hohenzollern king of Prussia. Bismarck welcomed this possibility for the same reason that the French objected to it. By placing Leopold on the throne of Spain, France would be virtually encircled by members of the Hohenzollern dynasty. French objections caused King William I to force his relative to withdraw his candidacy. Bismarck was disappointed with the king's actions, but

at this point the French overreached themselves. Not content with their diplomatic victory, they pushed William I to make a formal apology to France and promise never to allow Leopold to be a candidate again. When Bismarck received a telegraph from the king informing him of the French request, Bismarck edited it to make it appear even more insulting to the French, knowing that the French would probably declare war over the issue (see the box on p. 786). Through diplomacy, Bismarck had already made it virtually certain that no other European power would interfere in a war between France and Prussia. The French reacted as Bismarck expected they would and declared war on Prussia on July 15, 1870. The French prime minister remarked, "We go to war with a light heart."

Unfortunately for the French, a "light heart" was not enough. They had barely started their military reorganization and proved no match for the better led and organized Prussian forces. The south German states honored

▼ The Unification of Germany: Anton von Werner, *Proclamation of the German Empire.* Under Prussian leadership, a new German empire was proclaimed on January 18, 1871, in the Hall of Mirrors in the palace at Versailles. King William of Prussia became Emperor William I of the Second German Empire. Otto von Bismarck, the man who had been so instrumental in creating the new German state, is shown here, resplendently attired in his white uniform, standing at the foot of the throne.

Bismarck "Goads" France into War

▼ ▼ ▼

After his meeting with the French ambassador at Ems, King William I of Prussia sent a telegraph to Bismarck with a report of their discussions. By editing the telegraph from King William I before he released it to the press, Bismarck made it sound as if the Prussian king had treated the ambassador in a demeaning fashion. Six days later, Napoleon III declared war on Prussia.

The Abeken [Privy Councillor] Text, Ems, July 13, 1870

To the Federal Chancellor, Count Bismarck. His Majesty the King writes to me:

"M. Benedetti intercepted me on the Promenade in order to demand of me most insistently that I should authorize him to telegraph immediately to Paris that I shall obligate myself for all future time never again to give my approval to the candidacy of the Hohenzollerns should it be renewed. I refused to agree to this, the last time somewhat severely, informing him that one dare not and cannot assume such obligations à *tout jamais* [forever]. Naturally, I informed him that I had received no news as yet, and since he had been informed earlier than I by way of Paris and Madrid, he could easily understand why my government was once again out of the matter."

Since then His Majesty has received a dispatch from the Prince [father of the Hohenzollern candidate for the Spanish throne]. As His Majesty has informed Count Benedetti that he was expecting news from the Prince, His Majesty himself, in view of the above-mentioned demand and in consonance with the advice of Count Eulenburg and myself, decided not to receive the French envoy again but to inform him through an adjutant that His Majesty had now received from the Prince confirmation of the news which Benedetti had already received from Paris, and that he had nothing further to say to the Ambassador. His Majesty leaves it to the judgment of Your Excellency whether or not to communicate at once the new demand by Benedetti and its rejection to our ambassadors and to the press.

Bismarck's Edited Version

After the reports of the renunciation by the hereditary Prince of Hohenzollern had been officially transmitted by the Royal Government of Spain to the Imperial Government of France, the French Ambassador presented to His Majesty the King at Ems the demand to authorize him to telegraph to Paris that His Majesty the King would obligate himself for all future time never again to give his approval to the candidacy of the Hohenzollerns should it be renewed.

His Majesty the King thereupon refused to receive the French envoy again and informed him through an adjutant that His Majesty had nothing further to say to the Ambassador.

---

their military alliances with Prussia and joined the war effort against the French. The Prussian armies advanced into France, and at Sedan, on September 2, 1870, an entire French army and Napoleon III himself were captured. Although the Second French Empire collapsed, the war was not yet over. After four months of bitter resistance, Paris finally capitulated on January 28, 1871, and an official peace treaty was signed in May. France had to pay an indemnity of five billion francs (about one billion dollars) and give up the provinces of Alsace and Lorraine to the new German state. The latter demand rankled the French and left them burning for revenge.

Even before the war had ended, the south German states had agreed to enter the North German Confederation. On January 18, 1871, in the Hall of Mirrors in Louis XIV's palace at Versailles, William I was proclaimed kaiser or emperor of the Second German Empire (the first was the medieval Holy Roman Empire). German unity had been achieved by the Prussian monarchy and the Prussian army. In a real sense, Germany had been merged into Prussia, not Prussia into Germany. German liberals also rejoiced. They had dreamed of unity and freedom, but the achievement of unity now seemed much more important. One old liberal proclaimed:

> I cannot shake off the impression of this hour. I am no devotee of Mars; I feel more attached to the goddess of beauty and the mother of graces than to the powerful god of war, but the trophies of war exercise a magic charm even upon the

King William I of Prussia	1861–1888
Bismarck Becomes Minister-President of Prussia	1862
The Danish War	1864
The Austro-Prussian War	1866
Battle of Königgrätz	1866 (July 3)
The Franco-Prussian War	1870–1871
Battle of Sedan	1870 (September 2)
Fall of Paris	1871 (January 28)
German Empire Is Proclaimed	1871 (January 18)

child of peace. One's view is involuntarily chained and one's spirit goes along with the boundless row of men who acclaim the god of the moment—success.[6]

The Prussian leadership of German unification meant the triumph of authoritarian, militaristic values over liberal, constitutional sentiments in the development of the new German state. With its industrial resources and military might, the new state had become the strongest power on the Continent. A new European balance of power was at hand.

▼ Nationalism and Reform: The National State in Mid-Century

While European affairs were dominated by the unification of Italy and Germany, other states were also undergoing transformations. War, civil war, and changing political alignments served as catalysts for domestic reforms.

The Austrian Empire

After the Habsburgs had crushed the revolutions of 1848–1849, they restored centralized, autocratic government to the empire. What seemed to be the only lasting result of the revolution of 1848 was the act of emancipation of September 7, 1848, that freed the serfs and eliminated all compulsory labor services. Nevertheless, the development of industrialization after 1850, especially in Vienna and the provinces of Bohemia and Galicia, served to bring some economic and social change to the empire in the form of an urban proletariat, labor unrest, and a new industrial middle class.

In 1851, the revolutionary constitutions were abolished, and a system of centralized autocracy was imposed on the empire. Under the leadership of Alexander von Bach (1813–1893), local privileges were subordinated to a unified system of administration, law, and taxation implemented by German-speaking officials. Hungary was subjected to the rule of military officers while the Catholic church was declared the state church and given control of education. The Bach regime, according to one critic, was composed of "a standing army of soldiers, a sitting army of officials, a kneeling army of priests, and a creeping army of denunciators." Change soon came, however, impelled by severe economic troubles and defeat in war. Failure in war usually had severe internal consequences for European states after 1789, and Austria was no exception. After Austria's defeat in the Italian war in 1859, the Emperor Francis Joseph (1848–1916) attempted to establish an imperial parliament (*Reichsrat*) with a nominated upper house and an elected lower house of representatives. Although the system was supposed to provide representation for the nationalities of the empire, the complicated formula used for elections ensured the election of a German-speaking majority, serving once again to alienate the ethnic minorities, particularly the Hungarians.

Only when military disaster struck again did the Austrians deal with the fiercely nationalistic Hungarians. The result was the negotiated *Ausgleich*, or Compromise, of 1867, which created the dual monarchy of Austria-Hungary. Each part of the empire now had its constitution, its own bicameral legislature, its own governmental machinery for domestic affairs, and its own capital (Vienna for Austria and Budapest for Hungary). Holding the two states together were a single monarch (Francis Joseph was emperor of Austria and king of Hungary) and a common army, foreign policy, and system of finances. In domestic affairs, the Hungarians had become an independent nation. The *Ausgleich* did not, however, satisfy the other nationalities that made up the multinational Austro-Hungarian Empire. The dual monarchy simply enabled the German-speaking Austrians and Hungarian Magyars to dominate the minorities, especially the Slavs, in their respective states. As the Hungarian nationalist Louis Kossuth remarked, "Dualism is the alliance of the conservative, reactionary and any apparently liberal elements in Hungary with those of the Austrian Germans who despise liberty, for the oppres-

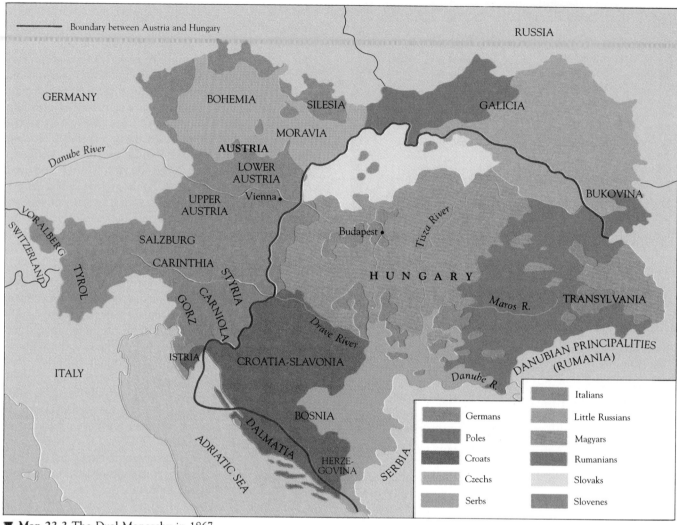

——— Boundary between Austria and Hungary

RUSSIA

GERMANY

BOHEMIA   SILESIA   GALICIA

MORAVIA

AUSTRIA

LOWER
AUSTRIA

UPPER   Vienna•
AUSTRIA

BUKOVINA

Danube River

SALZBURG

CARINTHIA

Budapest•   Tisza River

H U N G A R Y

VORALBERG

SWITZERLAND

TYROL

STYRIA

GORZ   CARNIOLA

Maros R.   TRANSYLVANIA

Drave River

ISTRIA

ITALY   CROATIA-SLAVONIA

DANUBIAN PRINCIPALITIES
(RUMANIA)

Danube R.

BOSNIA

ADRIATIC SEA   DALMATIA

HERZE-
GOVINA

SERBIA

	Germans		Italians
	Poles		Little Russians
	Croats		Magyars
	Czechs		Rumanians
	Serbs		Slovaks
			Slovenes

▼ **Map 23.3** The Dual Monarchy in 1867.

sion of the other nationalities and races."[7] The nationalities problem remained until the demise of the empire at the end of World War I.

Imperial Russia

The Russian imperial autocracy, based on soldiers, secret police, repression, and censorship, had withstood the revolutionary fervor of 1848 and even served as the "arsenal of autocracy" in crushing revolutions elsewhere in Europe. The defeat in the Crimean War at the hands of the British and French revealed the blatant deficiencies behind the facade of absolute power and make it clear even to staunch conservatives that Russia was falling hopelessly behind the western European powers. Tsar Alexander II (1855–1881), who came to power in the midst of the Crimean War, turned his energies to a se-

rious overhaul of the Russian system. Though called the Liberator because of his great reforms, Alexander II was no liberal but a thoughtful realist who knew reforms could not be postponed. Following the autocratic procedures of his predecessors, he attempted to impose those reforms upon the Russian people.

Serfdom was the most burdensome problem in tsarist Russia. The continuing subjugation of millions of peasants to the land and their landlords was an obviously corrupt and failing system. Reduced to antiquated methods of production based on serf labor, Russian landowners were economically pressed and unable to compete with foreign agriculture. Russian serfs, who formed the backbone of the Russian infantry, were uneducated and consequently increasingly unable to deal with the more complex machines and weapons of war. It was, after all, the failure of the serf-armies in the Crimean War that

Emancipation: Serfs and Slaves

▼ ▼ ▼

Although overall their histories have been quite different, the two great adversaries of the late twentieth century—the United States and the Soviet Union—shared a common feature in the 1860s. They were the only states in the Western world that still had large enslaved populations (the Russian serfs were virtually slaves). The leaders of both countries issued emancipation proclamations within two years of each other. The first excerpt is taken from the Imperial Decree of March 3, 1861, which freed the Russian serfs. The second excerpt is from Abraham Lincoln's Emancipation Proclamation, issued on January 1, 1863.

The Imperial Decree, March 3, 1861

By the grace of God, we, Alexander II, Emperor and Autocrat of all the Russias, King of Poland, Grand Duke of Finland, etc., to all our faithful subjects, make known:

Called by Divine Providence and by the sacred right of inheritance to the throne of our ancestors, we took a vow in our innermost heart to respond to the mission which is intrusted to us as to surround with our affection and our Imperial solicitude all our faithful subjects of every rank and of every condition, from the warrior, who nobly bears arms for the defence of the country to the humble artisan devoted to the works of industry; from the official in the career of the high offices of the State to the laborer whose plough furrows the soil. . . .

We thus came to the conviction that the work of a serious improvement of the condition of the peasants was a sacred inheritance bequeathed to us by our ancestors, a mission which, in the course of events, Divine Providence called upon us to fulfill. . . .

In virtue of the new dispositions above mentioned, the peasants attached to the soil will be invested within a term fixed by the law with all the rights of free cultivators. . . .

At the same time, they are granted the right of purchasing their close, and, with the consent of the proprietors, they may acquire in full property the arable lands and other appurtenances which are allotted to them as a permanent holding. By the acquisition in full property of the quantity of land fixed, the peasants are free from their obligations towards the proprietors for land thus purchased, and they enter definitely into the condition of free peasants—landholders.

The Emancipation Proclamation, January 1, 1863

Now therefore, I, Abraham Lincoln, President of the United States, by virtue of the power in me vested as Commander-in-Chief of the Army and Navy of the United States in time of actual armed rebellion against the authority and government of the United States, and as a fit and necessary war measure for suppressing such rebellion, do, on this 1st day of January, A.D. 1863, and in accordance with my purpose to do so, . . . order and designate as the States and parts of States wherein the people thereof, respectively, are this day in rebellion against the United States the following, to wit:

Arkansas, Texas, Louisiana, . . . Mississippi, Alabama, Florida, Georgia, South Carolina, North Carolina, and Virginia . . .

And by virtue of the power for the purpose aforesaid, I do order and declare that all persons held as slaves within said designated States and parts of States are, and henceforward shall be free; and that the Executive Government of the United States, including the military and naval authorities thereof, will recognize and maintain the freedom of said persons.

---

created the need for change in the first place. Then, too, peasant dissatisfaction still led to local peasant revolts that disrupted the countryside. Alexander II seemed to recognize the inevitable: "The existing order of serfdom," he told a group of Moscow nobles, "cannot remain unchanged. It is better to abolish serfdom from above than to wait until it is abolished from below."

On March 3, 1861, Alexander issued his emancipation edict (see the box above). Peasants were now free to own property, marry as they chose, and bring suits in the law courts. But the system of land redistribution instituted after emancipation was not that favorable to them. The government provided land for the peasants by purchasing it from the landlords, but the landowners

▼ **Russian Serfs: A Grandmother and Her Grandchild.**
Serfdom was a costly burden for tsarist Russia. Realizing the
need for change, Tsar Alexander II legally freed the serfs on
March 3, 1861. Nevertheless, Russian peasants remained
economically bound to the land, and emancipation of the serfs
did little to bring any real improvements for the peasants. Most
Russian peasants continued to follow traditional ways of life and
farming.

often chose to keep the best lands. The Russian peasants
soon found that they had inadequate amounts of good
arable land to support themselves, a situation worsened
by the rapidly increasing peasant population in the second half of the nineteenth century.

Nor were the peasants completely free. The state
compensated the landowners for the land given to the
peasants, but the peasants, in turn, were expected to
repay the state in long-term installments. To ensure that
the payments were made, peasants were subjected to the
authority of their *mir* or village commune, which was
collectively responsible for the land payments to the
government. In a very real sense, then, the village commune, not the individual peasants, owned the land the
peasants were purchasing. And since the village communes were responsible for the payments, they were reluctant to allow peasants to leave their land. Emancipation, then, led not to a free, landowning peasantry along
the Western model, but to an unhappy, land-starved
peasantry that largely followed the old ways of agricultural production. Comprehensive reforms that would
have freed the peasants completely and given them access to their own land were unfortunately left until the
early twentieth century.

Alexander II attempted other reforms, however.
In 1864, he instituted a system of zemstvos or local assemblies that provided a moderate degree of self-
government. Representatives to the zemstvos were to be
elected from the noble landowners, townspeople, and
peasants, but the property-based system of voting gave a
distinct advantage to the nobles. Zemstvos were given a
limited power to provide public services, such as education and famine relief, maintain roads and bridges, and
levy taxes to pay for these responsibilities, although government bureaucrats, fearful of such self-government,
often obstructed their efforts. As one official noted, "In
Russia reform can be carried out only by authority. We
have too much disturbance and too much divergence of
interests to expect anything good from the representation of those interests."[8] The hope of liberal nobles and
other social reformers that the zemstvos would be expanded into a national parliament remained unfulfilled.
The legal reforms of 1864, which created a regular system of local and provincial courts and a judicial code
that accepted the principle of equality before the law,
proved successful, however.

Even the autocratic tsar was unable to control the
forces he unleashed by his reform program. Reformers
wanted more and rapid change; conservatives opposed
what they perceived as the tsar's attempts to undermine
the basic institutions of Russian society. By 1870, Russia
was witnessing an increasing number of reform movements. One of the most popular stemmed from the radical writings of Alexander Herzen (1812–1870), a Russian exile living in London, whose slogan of "land and
freedom" epitomized his belief that the Russian peasant
must be the chief instrument for social reform. Following
Herzen's ideas, Russian students and intellectuals created a populist movement that supported a revolutionary
reordering of society based on peasant communal life.
The peasants' lack of interest in their form of revolution,

however, led some revolutionaries to resort to violent means to overthrow tsarist autocracy. One such group of radicals, known as the People's Will, succeeded in assassinating Alexander II in 1881. His son and successor, Alexander III, turned against reform and returned to the traditional methods of repression.

Great Britain

Like Russia, Britain also experienced no revolutionary disturbances during 1848, although for quite different reasons. The Reform Act of 1832 had opened the door to political representation for the industrial middle

▼ **Map 23.4** Europe in 1871.

German Empire
Austria-Hungary
Italy
France
Ottoman Empire

class, and in the 1860s the liberal parliamentary system of Britain demonstrated once more its ability to make both social and political reforms that enabled the country to remain stable and prosperous.

One of the reasons for Britain's stability was its continuing economic growth. The British had flaunted their wealth and satisfaction with their achievements to the world in the great Industrial Exhibition in 1851. Now middle-class prosperity was at last coupled with some improvements for the working classes as well. Real wages for laborers increased over 25 percent between 1850 and 1870. The British sense of national pride was well reflected in Queen Victoria (1837–1901), whose self-contentment and sense of moral respectability mirrored the attitudes of her age. The Victorian Age, as Britain during the reign of Queen Victoria has ever since been known, was characterized by a pious complacency.

Politically, this was an era of uneasy stability as the aristocratic and upper-middle-class representatives who dominated Parliament blurred party lines by their internal strife and shifting positions. The one political figure who stood out was Henry John Temple, Lord Palmerston (1784–1865), who was prime minister for most of the period from 1855 to 1865. Although a Whig, Palmerston was without strong party loyalty and found it easy to make political compromises. His primary interest was foreign policy, and his chauvinistic defense of British interests worldwide made him a popular figure with his countrymen. He did not, however, want to move beyond the status quo and became an obstacle to further reform, especially denouncing proposals to expand the franchise to new groups. By extending representation from one class to another, he said, "We should by such an arrangement increase the number of Bribeable Electors and overpower Intelligence and Property by Ignorance and Poverty."

After Palmerston's death in 1865, the movement for the extension of the franchise only intensified. One mass meeting even led to a riot in London's Hyde Park. Although the Whigs (now called the Liberals), who had been responsible for the Reform Act of 1832, talked about passing such reform legislation, it was actually the Tories (now called the Conservatives) who carried it through. The Tory leader in Parliament, Benjamin Disraeli (1804–1881), was apparently motivated by the desire to win over the newly enfranchised groups to the Conservative party, believing that the uneducated classes would defer to their social superiors when they voted. He knew that the Liberals, viewed as the party of reform, would dare not oppose the reform bill. The Reform Act of 1867 was an important step toward the

democratization of Britain. It extended the right to vote by lowering the required amount of taxes paid or income earned sufficiently that it by and large enfranchised many male urban workers. The number of voters increased from about one million to slightly over two million. Although Disraeli believed this would benefit the Conservatives, industrial workers helped to produce a huge Liberal victory in 1868.

The extension of the right to vote had an important by-product as it forced the Liberal and Conservative parties to organize carefully in order to manipulate the electorate. Party discipline intensified, and the rivalry between two well-established political parties, the Liberals and Conservatives, became a regular feature of parliamentary life. In large part this was due to the personal and political opposition of the two leaders of these parties, William Gladstone (1809–1898) and Disraeli.

The first Liberal administration of William Gladstone from 1868 to 1874 was responsible for a series of impressive reform acts. In fact, historians have called the first Gladstone ministry the apex of "classical British liberalism." Legislation and government orders opened civil service positions to competitive exams rather than patronage, dropped religious requirements for degrees at Oxford and Cambridge, introduced the secret ballot for voting, and abolished the purchase of military commissions. The Education Act of 1870 attempted to make elementary schools available for all children (see Chapter 25). These reforms were typically liberal. By eliminating abuses and enabling people with talent to compete fairly, they sought to strengthen the nation and its institutions.

The United States: Civil War and Reunion

While the Germans and Italians were fighting Austria and France to achieve national unity, some Americans were hoping to dissolve theirs. During its early existence, the young republic had shown a remarkable ability to resolve peacefully many issues that might have disrupted national unity. Slavery, however, proved to be an issue beyond compromise and led to a bitter and bloody civil war.

Like the North, the South had grown dramatically in population during the first half of the nineteenth century. But its development was quite different. Its cotton economy and social structure were based on the exploitation of enslaved black Africans and their descendants. The importance of cotton is evident from production figures. In 1810, the South produced a raw cotton crop of 178,000 bales worth $10 million. By 1860, it was generating 4.5 million bales of cotton with a value of $249 million. Ninety-three percent of southern cotton in 1850 was produced by a slave population that had grown dramatically in fifty years. Although new slave imports had been barred in 1808, there were 4 million Afro-American slaves in the South by 1860 compared to 1 million in 1800. The cotton economy and a plantation-based slavery were intimately related, and the attempt to maintain them in the course of the first half of the nineteenth century led the South to become increasingly defensive, monolithic, and isolated. At the same time, the growth of an abolitionist movement in the North challenged the southern order and created an "emotional chain reaction" that led to civil war.

The push of Americans westward was a major factor in bringing the issue of slavery to the forefront of Amer-ican politics. The issue had already arisen in the 1810s as new states were being created by the rush of settlers beyond the Mississippi. The free states of the North feared the creation of a slave state majority in the national government. The debate touched off by the desire of Missouri to obtain statehood as a slave state was only ended by the Missouri Compromise of 1820, which used the latitude 36°30' as a dividing line. All new states north of the line would be admitted as free states; those south of the line as slave states. The Missouri Compromise worked, at least until the addition of vast new territories in the Southwest after the Mexican War (1846–1848). If the line of the Missouri Compromise were extended to the Pacific Ocean, most of the new territory acquired by the United States in its war with Mexico would be open to slavery, a disquieting prospect

▼ **Map 23.5** The United States: The West and Civil War.

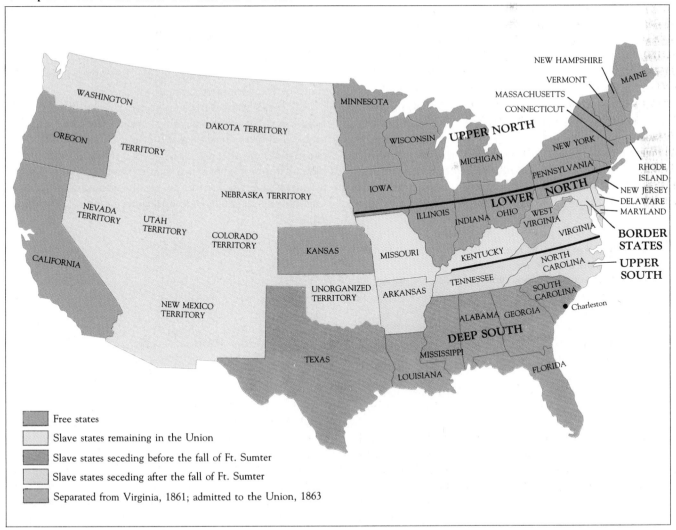

Free states

Slave states remaining in the Union

Slave states seceding before the fall of Ft. Sumter

Slave states seceding after the fall of Ft. Sumter

Separated from Virginia, 1861; admitted to the Union, 1863

to northern free states that feared the growth of southern power in the national government. It was time for another compromise.

The Compromise of 1850, which admitted California as a free state while allowing slavery in Utah and New Mexico if a majority of settlers favored it, was really an armistice, not a compromise. It had merely postponed, not solved this divisive issue. By the 1850s, the slavery question had caused the Whig party to become defunct while the Democrats were splitting along North-South lines. The Kansas-Nebraska Act of 1854, which effectively repealed the Missouri Compromise by allowing slavery in the Kansas-Nebraska territories to be determined by popular sovereignty, created a firestorm in the North and led to the creation of a new one-issue party. The Republicans were united by antislavery and were especially driven by the fear that the "slave power" of the South would attempt to spread the slave system throughout the country.

After 1854, polarization over the issue of slavery intensified. The outbreak of bloody conflict in Kansas between free staters and slave owners demonstrated that the issue was moving beyond the realm of compromise. Six more years of maneuvering only reinforced that point. When Abraham Lincoln, the man who had said in a speech in Illinois in 1858 that "this government cannot endure permanently half slave and half free," was elected president in November 1860, the die was cast. Lincoln carried only 2 of the 1,109 counties in the South; the Republicans were not even on the ballot in ten southern states. On December 20, 1860, a South Carolina convention voted to repeal ratification of the Constitution of the United States. In February 1861, six more southern states did the same, and a rival nation—the Confederate States of America—was formed. In March fighting erupted between North and South.

The American Civil War (1861–1865) was an extraordinarily bloody struggle, a clear foretaste of the total war to come in the twentieth century. Over 600,000 soldiers died, either in battle or from deadly infectious diseases spawned by filthy camp conditions. This figure exceeds the combined American casualties of World War I and World War II. The northern or Union forces enjoyed a formidable advantage in numbers of troops and material resources to fight the war; but to southerners, those assets were not decisive. To them, the Confederacy, after all, did not have to conquer the North, only defend the South from invasion. Many of the most promising young military officers were from the South, whose aristocratic landowning society had a far stronger military tradition than the business-oriented North. Southerners also believed that the dependence of manufacturers in the North and the European countries on southern raw cotton would lead to antiwar sentiment in the North and support abroad for the South.

All these southern calculations meant little in the long run. Over a period of four years, the Union states mobilized their superior assets and gradually wore down the South. As the war dragged on, it had the effect of radicalizing public opinion in the North. What began as a war to save the Union became a war against slavery. On January 1, 1863, Lincoln's Emancipation Proclama-

▼ **The Dead at Antietam.** Nation-building took many forms in the mid-nineteenth century. National unity in the United States dissolved over the issue of slavery and led to a bloody Civil War that restored the Union at a cost of 600,000 American lives. This photograph shows the Southern dead after the Battle of Antietam on September 17, 1862.

tion made most of the nation's slaves "forever free" (see the box on p. 789). The increasingly effective Union blockade of the South combined with a shortage of fighting men made the Confederate cause desperate by the end of 1864. The final push of Union troops under General Ulysses S. Grant forced General Robert E. Lee's army to surrender on April 9, 1865. Although the prob-

lems of reconstruction were ahead, the Union victory confirmed that the United States would be "one nation, indivisible." National unity, not particularism, had prevailed in the United States.

▼ Industrialization and the Marxist Response

Between 1850 and 1871, continental industrialization came of age. The innovations of the British Industrial Revolution—mechanized factory production, the use of coal, the steam engine, and the transportation revolution—all became regular features of economic expansion. Although marred periodically by economic depression (1857–1858) or recession (1866–1867), this was an age of considerable economic prosperity, particularly evident in the growth of domestic and foreign markets.

Industrialization on the Continent

The transformation of textile production from hand looms to power looms had largely been completed in Britain by the 1850s (for cotton) and 1860s (for wool). On the Continent, the period from 1850 to 1870 witnessed increased mechanization of the cotton and textile industries, although continental countries still remained behind Britain. By 1870, hand looms had virtually disappeared in Britain whereas in France there were still 200,000 of them compared to 80,000 power looms; in Germany, there were 125,000 hand looms to 57,000 power looms. However, this period of industrial expansion on the Continent was fueled not so much by textiles but by the growth of railroads, which, as one economic historian has noted, "displaced textiles as the drummer of industrial activity." Between 1850 and 1870, European railroad track mileage increased from 14,500 to almost 70,000. In turn, the railroad stimulated growth in both the iron and coal industries.

Between 1850 and 1870, continental iron industries made the transition from charcoal iron smelting to coke-blast smelting. In Prussia, for example, where charcoal was used to produce 82 percent of iron output in 1842, this figure had declined to 60 percent in 1852, and to only 12.3 percent by 1862. Despite the dramatic increases in the production of pig iron, the continental countries had not yet come close to surpassing British iron production. In 1870, the British iron industry produced one-half of the world's pig iron, four times as much as Germany and five times as much as France. In the middle decades of the nineteenth century, continen-

▼ **Opening of the Suez Canal.** Between 1850 and 1871, continental Europeans built railways, bridges, and canals as part of an ever-spreading process of industrialization. A French diplomat, Ferdinand de Lesseps, was the guiding force behind the construction of the Suez Canal, which provided a link between the Mediterranean and Red seas. Work on the canal began in 1859 and was completed ten years later. As seen here, an elaborate ceremony marked the opening of the canal. A French vessel led the first convoy of ships through the canal.

tal countries also witnessed a rapid conversion to the use of the steam engine in textile, mining, and metallurgical industries.

Although policies varied from country to country, continental governments took a more or less active role in passing laws and initiating actions that were favorable to the expansion of industry and commerce. While some countries exercised direct control over nationalized industries, such as Prussia's development of coal mines in the Saar region, others provided financial assistance to private companies to develop mines, ironworks, dockyards, and railways.

An important factor in the expansion of markets was the elimination of barriers to international trade. Essential international waterways were opened up by the elimination of restrictive tolls. The Danube River in 1857 and the Rhine in 1861, for example, were declared freeways for all ships. The negotiation of trade treaties in the 1860s reduced or eliminated protective tariffs throughout much of Western Europe.

Governments also played a role in first allowing and then encouraging the formation of joint-stock investment banks (see Chapter 21). These banks were crucial to continental industrial development since they mobilized enormous capital resources for investment. In the 1850s and 1860s, they were very important in the promotion of railway construction, although they were not always a safe investment. During a trip to Spain to examine possibilities for railroad construction, the locomotive manufacturer George Stephenson reported: "I have been a month in the country, but have not seen during the whole of that time enough people of the right sort to fill a single train."[9] His misgivings proved to be well-founded. In 1864, the Spanish banking system, which depended largely on investments in railway shares, collapsed.

During this ongoing process of industrialization between 1850 and 1870, capitalist factory owners remained largely free to hire labor on their own terms based on market forces. Increased mechanization of industry meant further displacement of skilled artisans by semiskilled workers. What the working classes needed were organizations that would fight for improved working conditions and reasonable wages, but the liberal bourgeoisie condemned them as criminal agencies that used strikes and pickets to threaten private property. This did not stop the gradual organization of trade unions in the 1860s, however, as conservative regimes sanctioned the creation of trade unions in order to gain popular support against liberals. Bismarck did so in Prussia in 1863, and Napoleon III did likewise in France in 1864. Even where they did form, however, trade unions tended to represent only a small part of the industrial working class, usually such select groups as engineers, shipbuilders, miners, and printers. Real change for the industrial proletariat would only come with the development of socialist parties and socialist trade unions. These emerged after 1870, but the theory that made them possible had already been developed by mid-century in the work of Karl Marx.

Marx and Marxism

Marxism made its first appearance in 1848 with the publication of a short treatise entitled *The Communist Manifesto,* written by two Germans, Karl Marx (1818–1883) and Friedrich Engels (1820–1895). Karl Marx was born into a relatively prosperous middle-class family in Trier in western Germany. He descended from a long line of Jewish rabbis although his father, a lawyer, had become a Protestant to keep his job. Marx enrolled at the University of Bonn in 1835, but a year later his carefree student ways led his father to send him to the more serious-minded University of Berlin, where he encountered the influence of Hegelian thought (see Chapter 22). After receiving a Ph.D. in philosophy, he planned to teach at a university. Unable to obtain a position because of his professed atheism, Marx decided upon a career in journalism and eventually became the editor of a liberal bourgeois newspaper in Cologne in 1842. After the newspaper was suppressed because of his radical views, Marx moved to Paris. There he met Friedrich Engels, who became his lifelong friend and financial patron.

Engels, the son of a wealthy German cotton manufacturer, had worked in Britain at one of his father's factories in Manchester. There he had acquired a firsthand knowledge of what he came to call the "wage slavery" of the British working classes, which he detailed in a damning indictment of industrial life entitled *The Conditions of the Working Class in England,* written in 1844. Engels would contribute his knowledge of actual working conditions as well as monetary assistance to the financially strapped Marx.

In 1847, Marx and Engels joined a tiny group of primarily German socialist revolutionaries known as the Communist League. By this time, both Marx and Engels were enthusiastic advocates of the radical working-class movement and agreed to draft a statement of their ideas for the league. The resulting *Communist Manifesto,* published in January 1848, appeared on the eve of the revolutions of 1848. One would think from its opening lines that the pamphlet alone had caused this revolutionary upheaval: "A spectre is haunting Europe—the spectre of Communism. All the Powers of Old Europe have entered into a holy alliance to exorcize this spectre: Pope and Czar, Metternich and Guizot, French Radicals and German police spies."[10] In fact, written in German, *The Communist Manifesto* was known to only a few of Marx's friends. Although its closing words—"The proletarians have nothing to lose but their chains. They have a world to win. WORKING MEN OF ALL COUNTRIES, UNITE!"—were clearly intended to rouse the working classes to action, they passed unnoticed in 1848. The work, however, became one of the most influential political treatises in modern European history. At the same time, it contained the substance of the basic economic and political ideas that Marx elaborated upon during the rest of his life.

Engels claimed that Marx's ideas were a synthesis of three major strands of thought: British classical economics, French political and social theory, and German idealist philosophy, namely, that of Hegel. What did each of these contribute to Marx's thought? Much of Marx's economic theory was derived from the British economists, especially the argument that the value of any product depended upon the amount of labor put into it. From this "labor theory of value," Marx developed a doctrine of surplus value. According to Marx, the

worker was given in wages only part of the real value of the product that his toil had created. The difference— the surplus value—was taken by the owners of the factories, the bourgeois capitalists. As workers never received in wages the equivalent of what they made, capitalism was threatened by an accumulation of goods that people could not afford to purchase. This led to economic depressions and depressions led to social revolution.

The influence of French political and social theory on Marx was ultimately derived from his knowledge of the French Revolution and the works of early French socialists. Marx questioned why the great French Revolution had failed to redistribute social wealth, but he did feel

▼ **Karl Marx.** Karl Marx was a radical journalist who joined with Friedrich Engels to write *The Communist Manifesto,* which proclaimed the ideas of a revolutionary socialism. After the failure of the 1848 revolution in Germany, Marx fled to Britain, where he continued to write and become involved in the work of the first International Working Men's Association.

that it had at least demonstrated that there could be a total reconstruction of human society by revolution.

The third influence stemmed from Marx's study of Hegel at the University of Berlin. From Hegel, Marx borrowed the idea of dialectic: everything evolves, and all change in history comes through the conflict of elements antagonistic to one another. But Marx differed from Hegel in one fundamental way. Hegel had said that the course of history was determined by Absolute Spirit or ideas manifested in historical forces. Marx said the course of history was determined by material forces. It is not ideas that determine social conditions but the way in which people make their living. From the "mode of production" or kind of economic system stemmed the class structure; from the class structure came the political and institutional structure of society and the beliefs people held. The state, political institutions, literature, art, and religion are all developed by the dominant class to maintain its position. Ideas did not precede actualities as Hegel would have it, but actualities—the material conditions—preceded the ideas. As Marx said, he found Hegel standing on his head and put him right side up. This dialectical materialism, as others called it, with its sense of inevitability inspired Marxism and raised it not to a level of science, as Marx thought, but to the level of a religious faith.

What, then, was the picture of historical development that Marx and Engels offered in *The Communist Manifesto*? They began their treatise with the statement that "the history of all hitherto existing society is the history of class struggles." Throughout history, then, oppressor and oppressed have "stood in constant opposition to one another." The agrarian economy of the Middle Ages gave rise to the landholding feudal class, but a change in the mode of production with the development of money, trade, and new production techniques resulted in the emergence of the bourgeoisie: "We see, therefore, how the modern bourgeoisie is itself the product of a long course of development, of a series of revolutions in the modes of production and of exchange." Each class produced an outlook appropriate to its own needs; religion, laws, and morals all reflected the ideology of these classes. As Marx and Engels stated: "What else does the history of ideas prove, than that intellectual production changes in character in proportion as material production is changed? The ruling ideas of each age have ever been the ideas of its ruling class." Likewise, government itself was but the instrument of the ruling class: "The executive of the modern State is but a committee for managing the common affairs of the whole bourgeoisie."[11]

Modern bourgeois society, then, emerged victorious out of the ruins of feudal society, but the class struggle continued: "Our epoch, the epoch of the bourgeoisie, possesses, however, this distinctive feature: it has simplified the class antagonism. Society as a whole is more and more splitting up into two great hostile camps, into two great classes directly facing each other: Bourgeoisie and Proletariat." But in their great struggle, the bourgeoisie would dig its own grave. In order to survive, the bourgeoisie needs constantly expanding markets all over the world. But they will never be sufficient. Because of surplus value, the "epidemic of overproduction" can never be solved, leading to ever more destructive crises or economic depressions. At the same time, the expansion of industrial capitalism will lead to an ever-larger proletariat. As a result of competition, the bourgeoisie will devour each other, and the lower middle class will sink into the ranks of the proletariat. Not only will the proletariat increase in numbers, but it will also become concentrated and organized. As the struggle intensifies, some of the bourgeoisie—"a portion of the bourgeois ideologists who have raised themselves to the level of comprehending theoretically the historical movement as a whole"—will go over to the proletariat and become its leaders, a role Marx and Engels clearly envisioned for themselves. Finally, the struggle between the bourgeoisie and proletariat would break into open revolution, "where the violent overthrow of the bourgeoisie lays the foundation for the sway of the proletariat." The fall of the bourgeoisie "and the victory of the proletariat are equally inevitable."[12] For a while the proletariat would form a dictatorship in order to organize the means of production. However, a classless society would be the end result since classes themselves arose from the economic differences that have been abolished; the state—itself an instrument of the bourgeois interests—would wither away (see the box on p. 799).

After the outbreak of revolution in 1848, Marx returned to Germany where he edited a new newspaper in Cologne, optimistic that the ideas of *The Communist Manifesto* were beginning to be fulfilled in a "colossal eruption of the revolutionary crater." The counterrevolution ended his hopes, and in August 1849, Marx was forced to return to Britain, where he spent the rest of his life in exile. At first life was not easy for Marx, whose income from Engels and newspaper articles was never sufficient for him and his family. Marx's last years, however, from 1869 to 1883, were quite comfortable due to an annuity from Engels. Marx continued his writing on political economy, especially his famous work, *Das Kapital (Capital)*. He only completed one volume. After his

The Classless Society
▼ ▼ ▼

In The Communist Manifesto, *Karl Marx and Friedrich Engels projected as the final end product of the struggle between the bourgeoisie and the proletariat the creation of a classless society. In this selection, they discuss the steps by which that classless society would be reached. Although Marx had criticized the utopian socialists for their lack of a scientific approach to the labor problem, his solution sounds equally utopian.*

Karl Marx and Friedrich Engels, *The Communist Manifesto*

We have seen above, that the first step in the revolution by the working class, is to raise the proletariat to the position of ruling class. . . . The proletariat will use its political supremacy to wrest, by degrees, all capital from the bourgeoisie, to centralize all instruments of production in the hands of the State, i.e., of the proletariat organized as the ruling class; and to increase the total of productive forces as rapidly as possible.

Of course, in the beginning, this cannot be effected except by means of despotic inroads on the rights of property, and on the conditions of bourgeois production; by means of measures, therefore, which appear economically insufficient and untenable, but which, in the course of the movement, outstrip themselves, necessitate further inroads upon the old social order, and are unavoidable as a means of entirely revolutionizing the mode of production.

These measures will of course be different in different countries.

Nevertheless, in the most advanced countries, the following will be pretty generally applicable:

1. Abolition of property in land and application of all rents of land to public purposes.
2. A heavy progressive or graduated income tax.
3. Abolition of all right of inheritance. . . .

5. Centralization of credit in the hands of the State, by means of a national bank with State capital and an exclusive monopoly.
6. Centralization of the means of communication and transport in the hands of the State.
7. Extension of factories and instruments of production owned by the State . . . .
8. Equal liability of all to labour. Establishment of industrial armies, especially for agriculture.
9. Combination of agriculture with manufacturing industries; gradual abolition of the distinction between town and country, by a more equable distribution of the population over the country.
10. Free education for all children in public schools. Abolition of children's factory labour in its present form. . . .

When, in the course of development, class distinctions have disappeared, and all production has been concentrated in the whole nation, the public power will lose its political character. Political power, properly so called, is merely the organized power of one class for oppressing another. If the proletariat during its contest with the bourgeoisie is compelled, by the force of circumstances, to organize itself as a class, if, by means of a revolution, it makes itself the ruling class, and, as such, sweeps away by force the old conditions of production, then it will, along with these conditions, have swept away the conditions for the existence of class antagonisms and of classes generally, and will thereby have abolished its own supremacy as a class.

In place of the old bourgeois society, with its classes and class antagonisms, we shall have an association, in which the free development of each is the condition for the free development of all.

---

death, the remaining volumes were edited by his friend Engels.

One of the reasons *Capital* was not finished was Marx's own preoccupation with organizing the working-class movement. In *The Communist Manifesto,* Marx had defined the communists as "the most advanced and res-olute section of the working-class parties of every country." Their advantage was their ability to understand "the line of march, the conditions, and the ultimate general results of the proletarian movement." Marx saw his role in this light and participated enthusiastically in the activities of the International Working Men's Association. Formed in 1864 by British and French trade unionists, this "First International" served as an umbrella organization for working-class interests. Marx was the dominant personality on the organization's General Council and devoted much time to its activities. He wrote in 1865: "Compared with my work on the book [i.e., *Capital*] the International Association takes up an enormous amount of time, because I am in fact in charge of the whole business."[13] Internal dissension within the ranks of the association soon damaged the organization. In 1871, Marx supported the Paris Commune as a genuine proletarian uprising (see Chapter 24), but British trade unionists did not want to be identified with the crimes of the Parisians. In 1872, Marx essentially ended the association by moving its headquarters to the United States. The First International had failed. Although it would be revived in 1889, the fate of socialism by that time was in the hands of national socialist parties (see Chapter 24).

▼ Cultural Life in an Age of Realism

Between 1850 and 1870, two major intellectual developments stand out: the expansion of scientific knowledge with its rapidly growing impact on the Western worldview; and the shift from Romanticism with its emphasis on the inner world of reality to Realism with its focus on the outer, material world.

A New Age of Science

By the mid-nineteenth century, as theoretical discoveries in science led to an increased number of derived practical benefits, science came to have a greater and greater impact on European life. The Scientific Revolution of the sixteenth and seventeenth centuries had fundamentally transformed the Western worldview and created a modern, rational approach to the study of natural phenomena. Even in the eighteenth century, however, these intellectual developments had remained the preserve of an educated elite and resulted in few practical benefits. Moreover, the technical advances of the early Industrial Revolution had depended little on pure science and much more on the practical experiments of technologically oriented amateur inventors. Advances in industrial technology, however, fed an interest in basic scientific research, which, in turn, in the 1830s and afterward resulted in a rash of basic scientific discoveries that were soon transformed into technological improvements that affected all Europeans.

Important to advances in all the sciences was the development of mathematics, especially mathematical statistics. The development of the steam engine was important in encouraging scientists to work out its theoretical foundations, a preoccupation that led to thermodynamics, the science of the relationship between heat and mechanical energy. The laws of thermodynamics were at the core of nineteenth-century physics. In biology, the Frenchman Louis Pasteur discovered the germ theory of disease, which had enormous practical applications in the development of modern, scientific medical practices (see A Revolution in Health Care later in the chapter). In chemistry, the Russian Dmitri Mendeleyev in the 1860s classified all the material elements then known on the basis of their atomic weights and provided the systematic foundation for the periodic law. The Briton Michael Faraday discovered the phenomenon of electromagnetic induction and put together a primitive generator that laid the foundation for the use of electricity, although it was not until the 1870s that economically efficient generators were built.

The steadily increasing and often dramatic material benefits generated by science and technology led Europeans to a growing faith in the benefits of science. Even ordinary people who did not understand the theoretical concepts of science were impressed by its accomplishments. The popularity of scientific and technological achievement produced a widespread acceptance of the scientific method, based on observation, experiment, and logical analysis, as the only path to objective truth and objective reality. This, in turn, undermined the faith of many people in religious revelation and truth. It is no accident that the nineteenth century was an age of increasing secularization, particularly evident in the growth of materialism or the belief that everything mental, spiritual, or ideal was simply an outgrowth of physical forces. Truth was to be found in the concrete material existence of human beings, not as romanticists imagined in revelations gained by feeling or intuitive flashes. The importance of materialism was strikingly evident in the most important scientific event of the nineteenth century, the development of the theory of organic evolution according to natural selection. On the theories of Charles Darwin could be built a picture of humans as material beings that were simply part of the natural world.

Charles Darwin and the Theory of Organic Evolution

The concept of evolution was not new when Darwin first postulated his theory in 1859. Until the early nineteenth century, most European intellectuals still believed that a divine power had created the world and its species. Humans, of course, occupied a special superior position because the Book of Genesis in the Bible stated: "Let us make man in our image and likeness and let him have dominion over all other things." By the beginning of the nineteenth century, however, people were questioning the biblical account; some had already posited an evolutionary theory. In 1809, the Frenchman Jean-Baptiste Lamarck had presented a theory of evolution that argued that plants and animals were different because of their effort to adjust to their environment. His assumption that they subsequently passed on their acquired characteristics was later rejected. Geologists had also been busy demonstrating that the earth underwent constant change and was far older than had been believed. They argued that it had evolved slowly over millions of years rather than the thousands of years postulated by theological analysis of the biblical account of creation. Despite the growth in evolutionary ideas, however, even by the mid-nineteenth century there was no widely accepted theory of evolution that explained things satisfactorily.

Charles Darwin (1809–1882), like many of the great scientists of the nineteenth century, was a scientific amateur. Born into an upper-middle-class family, he studied theology at Cambridge University while pursuing an intense side interest in geology and biology. In 1831, at the age of twenty-two, his hobby became his vocation when he accepted an appointment as a naturalist to study animals and plants on an official Royal Navy scientific expedition aboard the H.M.S. *Beagle*. Its purpose was to survey and study the land masses of South America and the South Pacific. Darwin's specific job was to study the structure of various forms of plant and animal life. He was able to observe animals on islands virtually untouched by external influence and compare them to animals on the mainland. As a result, Darwin came to discard the notion of a special creation and to believe that animals evolved over time and in response to their environment. When he returned to Britain, he eventually formulated an explanation for evolution in the principle of natural selection. Although he had arrived at his major ideas by 1838, he spent the next twenty years collecting data to demonstrate his theory precisely, finally presenting his ideas in print in 1859 in his celebrated book, *On the Origin of Species by Means of Natural Selection*.

The basic idea of this book was that nature's creatures—all plants and animals—had not been created anew by God, but had evolved over a long period of time from earlier and simpler forms of life, a principle known as organic evolution. Darwin was important in explaining how this natural process worked. He took the first step from Thomas Malthus's theory of population: in every species, "many more individuals of each species are born than can possibly survive." This results in a "struggle for existence." Darwin believed that, "As more individuals are produced than can possibly survive, there must in every case be a struggle for existence, either one individual with another of the same species, or with the individuals of distinct species, or with the physical conditions of life." Those who succeeded in this struggle for existence had adapted better to their environment, a process made possible by the appearance of "variants." Chance variations occurred in the process of inheritance, he thought, that enabled some organisms to be more adaptable to the environment than others, a process that Darwin called natural selection:

> Owing to this struggle [for existence], variations, however slight . . . , if they be in any degree profitable to the individuals of a species, in their infinitely complex relations to other organic beings and to their physical conditions of life, will tend to the preservation of such individuals, and will generally be inherited by the offspring.[14]

Those that were naturally selected for survival ("survival of the fit") survived. The unfit did not and became extinct. The fit who survived, in turn, propagated and passed on the variations that enabled them to survive until, from Darwin's point of view, a new separate species emerged. Darwin did not attempt to explain how variants first occurred and did not arrive at the modern explanation of mutations. This was not crucial to him; he was not concerned with how the fit arrived, but how they survived.

In *On the Origin of Species*, Darwin discussed plant and animal species only. He was not concerned with humans themselves and only later applied his theory of natural selection to humans. In *The Descent of Man*, published in 1871, he argued for the animal origins of human beings: "man is the co-descendant with other mammals of a common progenitor." Humans were not an exception to the rule governing other species (see the box on p. 802).

Although Darwin's ideas were eventually accepted, initially they were highly controversial. Some people objected to what they considered Darwin's debasement of humans; his theory, they claimed, made human beings ordinary products of nature rather than unique beings. The acceptance of Darwinism, one professor of geology at Cambridge declared, would "sink the human race into a lower grade of degradation than any into which it has

Darwin and the Descent of Man

▼ ▼ ▼

Although Darwin published his theory of organic evolution in 1859, it was not until 1871 that his book, The Descent of Man, appeared. In it, Darwin argued that human beings have also evolved from lower forms of life. The theory met with a firestorm of criticism, especially from clergymen. One described Darwin's theory as a "brutal philosophy—to wit, there is no God, and the ape is our Adam."

Charles Darwin, *The Descent of Man*

The main conclusion here arrived at, and now held by many naturalists who are well competent to form a sound judgment, is that man is descended from some less highly organised form. The grounds upon which this conclusion rests will never be shaken, for the close similarity between man and the lower animals in embryonic development, as well as in innumerable points of structure and constitution, both of high and of the most trifling importance,—the rudiments which he retains, and the abnormal reversions to which he is occasionally liable,—are facts which cannot be disputed. They have long been known, but until recently they told us nothing with respect to the origin of man. Now when viewed by the light of our knowledge of the whole organic world, their meaning is unmistakable. The great principle of evolution stands up clear and firm, when these groups of facts are considered in connection with others, such as the mutual affinities of the members of the same group, their geographical distribution in past and present times, and their geological succession. It is incredible that all these facts should speak falsely. He who is not content to look, like a savage, at the phenomena of nature as disconnected, cannot any longer believe that man is the work of a separate act of creation. He will be forced to admit that the close resemblance of the embryo of man to that, for instance, of a dog—the construction of his skull, limbs and whole frame on the same plan with that of other mammals, independently of the uses to which the parts may be put—the occasional reappearance of various structures, for instance of several muscles, which man does not normally possess . . .—and a crowd of analogous facts—all point in the plainest manner to the conclusion that man is the co-descendant with other mammals of a common progenitor. . . .

Man may be excused for feeling some pride at having risen, though not through his own exertions, to the very summit of the organic scale; and the fact of his having thus risen, instead of having been aboriginally placed there, may give him hope for a still higher destiny in the distant future. But we are not here concerned with hopes or fears, only with the truth as far as our reason permits us to discover it; and I have given the evidence to the best of my ability. We must, however, acknowledge, as it seems to me, that man with all his noble qualities, with sympathy which feels for the most debased, with benevolence which extends not only to other men but to the humblest living creature, with his god-like intellect which has penetrated into the movements and constitution of the solar system—with all these exalted powers—Man still bears in his bodily frame the indelible stamp of his lowly origin.

---

fallen since its written records tell of its history." Others were disturbed by the implications of life as a struggle for survival, of "nature red in tooth and claw." Was there a place in the Darwinian world for moral values? For those who believed in a rational order in the world, Darwin's theory seemed to eliminate purpose and design from the universe. Gradually, however, Darwin's theory was accepted by scientists and other intellectuals although Darwin was somewhat overly optimistic when he wrote in 1872 that "almost every scientist admits the principle of evolution." In the process of accepting Darwin's ideas, some people even tried to apply them to society, yet another example of science's increasing prestige.

Auguste Comte and Positivism

The impact of the materialistic frame of mind perhaps made it inevitable that a scientific approach would be applied to the realm of human activity. Marx himself presented his view of history as a class struggle grounded in the material conditions of life as a "scientific" work of analysis. The attempt to apply the methods of science systematically to the study of society was perhaps most evident in the work of the Frenchman Auguste Comte (1798–1857). His major work, entitled *System of Positive Philosophy,* was published between 1837 and 1842, but had its real impact after 1850. The title of the work gave rise to the philosophical system called positivism, which maintained that only scientifically established facts and observed phenomena are valid. It rejected idealist philosophies, such as Hegel's, which asserted that ideas constitute the ultimate reality.

Comte maintained that all human knowledge has passed through three major states: the theological, the metaphysical, and the scientific. In the theological era, events were explained as the actions of gods or spirits. The metaphysical age attempted to explain events by attributing them to abstract, transcendental forces. The third and final state, Comte's own age, was the scientific or "positive" age in which events would be explained by general laws discovered by the scientific method— observation, experiment, and logical reasoning. According to Comte, human beings had proceeded through history seeking knowledge first from religion, then philosophy, and now science. His scheme was simplistic but highly attractive to nineteenth-century intellectuals who sought a comprehensive synthesis of all human knowledge.

For the third stage, Comte created a system of "positive" knowledge based upon a hierarchy of all the sciences. Mathematics was the foundation on which the physical sciences, earth sciences, and biological sciences were built. At the top was sociology, the science of human society, which for Comte incorporated economics, anthropology, history, and social psychology. Consequently, some historians call Comte one of the "founders of the modern discipline" of sociology. Comte saw sociology's task as a difficult one. The discovery of the general laws of society would have to be based upon the collection and analysis of data on humans and their social environment. Although his schemes were often complex and dense, Comte played an important role in making science and materialism so popular in the mid-nineteenth century.

Realism in Literature and Art

The belief that the world should be viewed realistically, frequently expressed after 1850, was closely related to the materialistic outlook. Evident in the "politics of reality" of a Bismarck or Cavour, Realism became a movement in the literary and visual arts as well. The word *Realism* was first employed in 1850 to describe a new style of painting and soon spread to literature.

LITERATURE Realism has been more or less a component of literature throughout time, although the literary realists of the mid-nineteenth century were distinguished by their deliberate rejection of Romanticism. The literary realists wanted to deal with ordinary characters from actual life rather than romantic heroes in exotic settings. They also sought to avoid exaggerated and emotional language by using close observation and precise description, an approach that led them to eschew poetry in favor of prose and the novel. Realists often combined their interest in everyday life with a searching examination of social questions. Even then they tried not to preach but to allow their characters to speak for themselves. Although the French were preeminent in literary Realism, it proved to be international in scope.

The leading novelist of the 1850s and 1860s, the Frenchman Gustave Flaubert (1821–1880), perfected the realist novel. His *Madame Bovary* (1857) was a straightforward description of barren and sordid provincial life in France. Emma Bovary, a woman of some vitality, is trapped in a marriage to a drab provincial doctor. Impelled by the images of romantic love she has read about in novels, she seeks the same thing for herself in adulterous love affairs. Unfulfilled, she is ultimately driven to suicide, unrepentant to the end for her lifestyle. Flaubert's hatred of bourgeois society was evident in his portrayal of middle-class hypocrisy and smugness. *Madame Bovary* so offended French middle-class sensibilities that the author was prosecuted—unsuccessfully—for public obscenity.

William Thackeray (1811–1863) wrote the opening manifesto of the realist novel in Britain with his *Vanity Fair* in 1848. Subtitled *A Novel without a Hero,* Thackeray deliberately flaunted the romantic conventions. A novel, Thackeray said, should "convey as strongly as possible the sentiment of reality as opposed to a tragedy or poem, which may be heroical." One of Thackeray's fellow countrymen, Charles Dickens (1812–1870), became extraordinarily successful with his realistic novels focusing on the lower and middle classes in Britain's early industrial age. His descriptions of the urban poor and the brutalization of human life were vividly realistic. But Dickens also demonstrated an interesting facet of Realism—a streak of romantic imagery that permeated his descriptions of the sordid and commonplace. No-

Realism: Charles Dickens and an Image of Hell on Earth

▼ ▼ ▼

Charles Dickens was a highly successful English novelist. While he realistically portrayed the material, social, and psychological milieu of his time, an element of Romanticism still pervaded his novels. This is evident in this selection from The Old Curiosity Shop *in which his description of the English mill town of Birmingham takes on the imagery of Dante's Hell.*

Charles Dickens, *The Old Curiosity Shop*

A long suburb of red brick houses,—some with patches of garden ground, where coal-dust and factory smoke darkened the shrinking leaves, and coarse rank flowers; and where the struggling vegetation sickened and sank under the hot breath of kiln and furnace, making them by its presence seem yet more blighting and unwholesome than in the town itself,—a long, flat, straggling suburb passed, they came by slow degrees upon a cheerless region, where not a blade of grass was seen to grow; where not a bud put forth its promise in the spring; where nothing green could live but on the surface of the stagnant pools, which here and there lay idly sweltering by the black roadside.

Advancing more and more into the shadow of this mournful place, its dark depressing influence stole upon their spirits, and filled them with a dismal gloom. On every side, and as far as the eye could see into the heavy distance, tall chimneys, crowding on each other, and presenting that endless repetition of the same dull, ugly form, which is the horror of oppressive dreams, poured out their plague of smoke, obscured the light, and made foul the melancholy air. On mounds of ashes by the wayside, sheltered only by a few rough boards, or rotten pent-house roofs, strange engines spun and writhed like tortured creatures; clanking their iron chains, shrieking in their rapid whirl from time to time as though in torment unendurable, and making the ground tremble with their agonies. Dismantled houses here and there appeared, tottering to the earth, propped up by fragments of others that had fallen down, unroofed, windowless, blackened, desolate, but yet inhabited. Men, women, children, wan in their looks and ragged in attire, tended the engines, fed their tributary fires, begged upon the road, or scowled half-naked from the doorless houses. Then came more of the wrathful monsters, whose like they almost seemed to be in their wildness and their untamed air, screeching and turning to the right and left, with the same interminable perspective of brick towers, never ceasing in their black vomit, blasting all things living or inanimate, shutting out the face of day, and closing in on all these horrors with a dense dark cloud.

But night-time in this dreadful spot!—night, when the smoke was changed to fire; when every chimney spurted up its flame; and places, that had been dark vaults all day, now shone red-hot, with figures moving to and fro within their blazing jaws, and calling to one another with hoarse cries—night, when the noise of every strange machine was aggravated by the darkness; when the people near them looked wilder and more savage; when bands of unemployed labourers paraded in the roads, or clustered by torchlight round their leaders, who told them in stern language of their wrongs, and urged them on by frightful cries and threats; when maddened men, armed with sword and firebrand, spurning the tears and prayers of women who would restrain them, rushed forth on errands of terror and destruction, to work no ruin half so surely as their own—night, when carts came rumbling by, filled with rude coffins (for contagious disease and death had been busy with the living crops); or when orphans cried, and distracted women shrieked and followed in their wake—night, when some called for bread, and some for drink to drown their cares; and some with tears, and some with staggering feet, and so with bloodshot eyes, went brooding home—night, which, unlike the night that Heaven sends on earth, brought with it no peace, nor quiet, nor signs of blessed sleep—who shall tell the terrors of the night to that young wandering child!

where is this more evident than in *The Old Curiosity Shop* where his description of an industrial nightmare conjures up the imagery of Dante's Hell (see the box on p. 804).

ART   In the first half of the nineteenth century, Romanticism in art had been paralleled by the classical school of painting, but both were superseded by the new mood of the mid-nineteenth century. In art, too, Realism became dominant after 1850, although Romanticism was by no means dead. Realist art demonstrated three major characteristics: a desire to depict the everyday life of ordinary people, whether peasants, workers, or prostitutes; an attempt at photographic realism; and an interest in the natural environment. The French became leaders in realist painting.

Gustave Courbet (1819–1877) was the most famous artist of the realist school. In fact, the word *Realism* was first coined in 1850 to describe one of his paintings. Courbet reveled in a realistic portrayal of everyday life. His subjects were factory workers, peasants, and the wives of saloon keepers. "I have never seen either angels or goddesses, so I am not interested in painting them," he exclaimed. One of his famous works, *The Stonebreakers*, painted in 1849, shows two road workers engaged in the deadening work of breaking stones to build a road. This representation of human misery was a scandal to those who objected to his "cult of ugliness." To Courbet, no subject was too ordinary, too harsh, or too ugly to interest him.

Jean-François Millet (1814–1875) was preoccupied with scenes from rural life, especially peasants laboring in the fields, although his Realism still contained an element of romantic sentimentality. In *The Sower*, a peasant, energetically scattering seeds in a field, becomes a symbol of new life and the symbiotic relationship between humans and nature. Millet, too, was criticized by his contemporaries for crude subject matter and unorthodox technique. One critic wrote that Millet "trowels on top of his dishcloth of a canvas, without oil or turpentine, vast masonries of colored paint so dry that no varnish could quench its thirst." Millet made landscape and country life an important subject matter for French artists.

▼ A Revolution in Health Care

Perhaps no area of everyday life in the nineteenth century was more affected by the application of natural science than the field of medicine. Some improvements had already been made in the development of health services in the eighteenth century, but the nineteenth century was a time of revolutionary breakthroughs in the development of medical science.

The initial tentative steps toward a more scientific basis for medicine arose in Paris hospitals during the first half of the nineteenth century. Clinical observation, consisting of an active physical examination of patients,

▼ **Gustave Courbet, *The Stonebreakers*.** By 1850, Realism began to replace Romanticism as the most important European school of painting. Realism, largely developed by French painters, aimed at a lifelike portrayal of the daily activities of ordinary people. Gustave Courbet was the most famous of the realist artists. As is evident in *The Stonebreakers*, he sought to portray things as they really appear. He shows an old road builder and his young assistant in their tattered clothes, engrossed in their dreary work of breaking stones to construct a road.

▼ **Jean-François Millet, *The Sower*.** Jean-François Millet was another prominent French realist painter. Millet took a special interest in the daily activities of French peasants, although he tended to transform his peasants into heroic figures who dominated their environment. In *The Sower*, for example, the peasant scattering seed into the newly plowed fields, despite his rough clothes, appears as a powerful figure, symbolizing the union of humans with the earth.

was combined with the knowledge gained from detailed autopsies to create a new clinical medicine. Nevertheless, the major breakthrough toward a scientific medicine occurred with the discovery of microorganisms or germs as the agents causing disease. The germ theory of disease was largely the work of Louis Pasteur (1822–1895). Pasteur was not a doctor but a chemist who approached medical problems in a scientific fashion. In 1857, Pasteur went to Paris as director of scientific studies in the École Normale. In his experiments on fermentations, he soon proved that various microorganisms were responsible for the process of fermentation, thus launching the science of bacteriology.

Government and private industry soon perceived the inherent practical value of Pasteur's work. His examination of a disease threatening the wine industry led to the development in 1863 of a process—subsequently known as pasteurization—for heating a product to destroy the organisms causing spoilage. Additional research on the microorganisms responsible for diseases of the silkworm enabled Pasteur to save the lucrative French silk industry. In 1877, Pasteur turned his attention to human diseases. His desire to do more than simply identify disease-producing organisms led him in 1885 to a preventive vaccination against rabies. In the 1890s, the principle of vaccination was extended to diphtheria, typhoid fever, cholera, and plague, creating a modern immunological science.

Robert Koch (1843–1910) was another important figure in the development of the science of bacteriology. Koch had received a medical degree at the University of Göttingen in Germany. In 1879, his experiments with anthrax led him to discover the bacteria responsible for wound infections. Koch was also responsible for providing specific methodological postulates to determine whether a particular organism was the cause of a disease.

The work of Pasteur and Koch and the many others who followed them in isolating the specific bacteriological causes of numerous diseases had a far-reaching impact. By providing a rational means of treating and preventing infectious diseases, they transformed the medical world. Both the practice of surgery and public health experienced a renaissance.

Surgeons had already experienced a new professionalism by the end of the eighteenth century (see Chapter 18), but the discovery of germs and the introduction of anesthesia created a new environment for surgical operations. Traditionally, surgeons had mainly set broken bones, treated wounds, and amputated limbs, usually shattered in war. One major obstacle to more successful surgery was the inevitable postoperative infection, especially rampant in hospitals.

A Hungarian obstetrician, Ignaz P. Semmelweiss (1818–1865), was the first physician to recognize that a simple hand washing with a chlorine solution before working on patients prevented infection. Rejected by his colleagues for his belief, Semmelweiss was dismissed from the Vienna hospital where he worked and died, a broken man, in an insane asylum. Joseph Lister (1827–1912) has instead been credited with developing the antiseptic principle. Following the work of Pasteur, Lister perceived that bacteria might enter a wound and cause infection. His use of carbolic acid, a newly discovered disinfectant, proved remarkably effective in eliminating infections during surgery. Lister's discoveries dramatically transformed surgery wards as patients no

Anesthesia and Modern Surgery

▼ ▼ ▼

Modern scientific medicine became established in the nineteenth century. Important to the emergence of modern surgery was the development of anesthetic agents that would block the patient's pain and enable surgeons to complete their surgery without the haste that had characterized earlier operations. This document is an eyewitness account of the first successful use of ether anesthesia, which took place at the Massachusetts General Hospital in 1846.

The First Public Demonstration of Ether Anesthesia, October 16, 1846

The day arrived; the time appointed was noted on the dial, when the patient was led into the operating-room, and Dr. Warren and a board of the most eminent surgeons in the State were gathered around the sufferer. "All is ready—the stillness oppressive." It had been announced "that a test of some preparation was to be made for which the astonishing claim had been made that it would render the person operated upon free from pain." These are the words of Dr. Warren that broke the stillness.

Those present were incredulous, and, as Dr. Morton had not arrived at the time appointed and fifteen minutes had passed, Dr. Warren said, with significant meaning, "I presume he is otherwise engaged." This was followed with a "derisive laugh," and Dr. Warren grasped his knife and was about to proceed with the operation. At that moment Dr. Morton entered a side door, when Dr. Warren turned to him and in a strong voice said, "Well, sir, your patient is ready." In a few minutes he was ready for the surgeon's knife, when Dr. Morton said, "Your patient is ready, sir."

Here the most sublime scene ever witnessed in the operating-room was presented, when the patient placed himself voluntarily upon the table, which was to become the altar of future fame. Not that he did so for the purpose of advancing the science of medicine, nor for the good of his fellow-men, for the act itself was purely a personal and selfish one. He was about to assist in solving a new and important problem of therapeutics, whose benefits were to be given to the whole civilized world, yet wholly unconscious of the sublimity of the occasion or the art he was taking.

That was a supreme moment for a most wonderful discovery, and, had the patient died upon the operation, science would have waited long to discover the hypnotic effects of some other remedy of equal potency and safety, and it may be properly questioned whether chloroform would have come into use as it has at the present time.

The heroic bravery of the man who voluntarily placed himself upon the table, a subject for the surgeon's knife, should be recorded and his name enrolled upon parchment, which should be hung upon the walls of the surgical amphitheatre in which the operation was performed. His name was Gilbert Abbott.

The operation was for a congenital tumor on the left side of the neck, extending along the jaw to the maxillary gland and into the mouth, embracing a margin of the tongue. The operation was successful; and when the patient recovered he declared he had suffered no pain. Dr. Warren turned to those present and said, "Gentlemen, this is no humbug."

---

longer succumbed regularly to what was called "hospital gangrene."

The second great barrier to large-scale surgery stemmed from the inability to lessen the pain of the patient. Alcohol and opiates had been used for centuries during surgical operations, but even their use did not allow unhurried operative maneuvers. After experiments with numerous agents, sulfuric ether was first used successfully in an operation at the Massachusetts General Hospital in 1846 (see the box above). Within a year chloroform began to rival ether as an anesthetic agent.

Although the great discoveries of bacteriology came after the emergence of the first public health movement, they significantly furthered its development. Based on a principle of preventive, rather than curative, medicine, the public health movement in urban areas of the 1840s and 1850s was largely a response to the cholera epidemic (see Chapter 24). Robert Koch once called cholera, "our best ally" in furthering public hygiene. The prebacteriological hygiene movement focused on providing clean water, good sewage disposal, and less crowded housing conditions. Bacterial discoveries, however, led to even greater measures of preventive medicine, such as the pasteurization of milk, greater purification of water supplies, immunization against disease, and control of waterborne diseases. The public health movement also resulted in the government hiring medical doctors not just to treat people but to deal with issues of public health.

The new scientific developments also had an important impact on the training of doctors for professional careers in health care. Although there were a few medical schools at the beginning of the nineteenth century, most medical instruction was still done by a system of apprenticeship. In the course of the nineteenth century, virtually every Western country founded new medical schools, but attempts to impose uniform standards on them through certifying bodies met considerable resistance. Entrance requirements were virtually nonexistent, and degrees were granted after several months of lectures. Professional organizations founded around the mid-century, such as the British Medical Association in 1832, the American Medical Association in 1847, and the German Doctors' Society in 1872, attempted to el-

evate professional standards but achieved little until the end of the century. The establishment of the Johns Hopkins University School of Medicine in 1893, with its four-year graded curriculum, clinical training for advanced students, and use of laboratories for teaching purposes, provided a new model for medical training that finally became standard practice in the twentieth century.

During most of the nineteenth century, medical schools in Europe and America were closed to female students. When Harriet Hunt applied to Harvard Medical School, the male students drew up resolutions that prevented her admission:

> Resolved, that no woman of true delicacy would be willing in the presence of men to listen to the discussion of subjects that necessarily come under consideration of the students of medicine.
> Resolved, that we object to having the company of any female forced upon us, who is disposed to unsex herself, and to sacrifice her modesty by appearing with men in the lecture room.[15]

▼ **First Successful Use of Surgical Anesthesia.** Depicted in this scene is an artist's rendering of the first successful operation using ether as an anesthetic agent. The operation took place at the Massachusetts General Hospital in 1846 and was yet another of the many medical advances in the nineteenth century that helped to create modern scientific medicine.

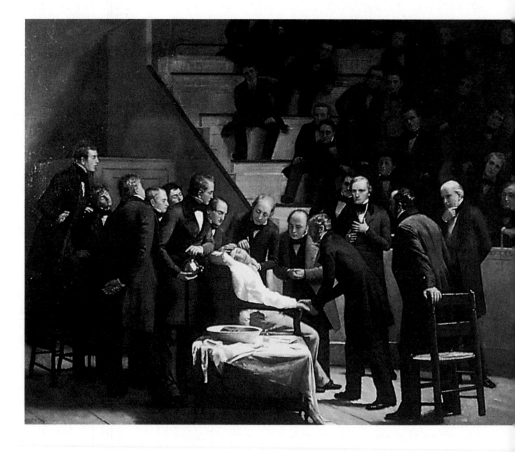

Elizabeth Blackwell (1821–1910) achieved the first major breakthrough for women in medicine. Although she had been admitted to the Geneva College of Medicine in New York by a mistake, Blackwell's perseverance and intelligence won her the respect of her fellow male students. She received her M.D. degree in 1849 and eventually established a clinic in New York City.

European women experienced difficulties similar to those of Elizabeth Blackwell. In Britain, Elizabeth Garret and Sophia Jex-Blake had to struggle for years before they were finally admitted to the practice of medicine. The unwillingness of medical schools to open their doors to women led to the formation of separate medical schools for women. The Female Medical College of Pennsylvania, established in 1850, was the first in the United States while the London School of Medicine for women was founded in 1874. But even after graduation from such institutions, women faced obstacles when they tried to practice as doctors. They were often refused licenses and hospitals often closed their doors to them. In Britain, Parliament finally capitulated to pressure and passed a bill in 1876 allowing women the right to take qualifying examinations. Soon women were entering medical schools in ever-larger numbers. By the 1890s, universities in Great Britain, Sweden, Denmark, Norway, Finland, Russia, and Belgium were admitting women to medical training and practice. Germany and Austria did not do so until after 1900. Even then, medical associations refused to accept women as equals in the medical profession. Women were not given full membership in the American Medical Association until 1915.

Between 1850 and 1871, the national state became the focus of people's loyalty. Wars, both foreign and civil, were fought to create unified nation-states. Political nationalism had emerged during the French revolutionary era and had become a powerful force of change during the first half of the nineteenth century, but its triumph came only after 1850. Tied initially to middle-class liberals, by the end of the nineteenth century it would have great appeal to the broad masses as well. In 1871, however, the political transformations stimulated by the force of nationalism were by no means complete. Significantly large minorities, especially in the polyglot empires controlled by the Austrians, Turks, and Russians, had not achieved the goal of their own national states. Moreover, the nationalism that had triumphed by 1871 was no longer the nationalism that had been closely identified with liberalism. Liberal nationalists had believed that unified nation-states would preserve individual rights and lead to a greater community of European peoples. But the new nationalism of the late nineteenth century, loud and chauvinistic, did not unify peoples, but divided them instead as the new national states became embroiled in bitter competition after 1871.

Europeans, however, were hardly aware of nationalism's dangers in 1871. The spread of industrialization and the wealth of scientific and technological achievements were sources of optimism, not pessimism. After the revolutionary and military upheavals of the mid-century decades, many Europeans undoubtedly believed that they stood on the verge of a new age of progress.

Notes

1. Quoted in Robert Gildea, *Barricades and Borders: Europe 1800–1914* (Oxford, 1987), p. 176.

2. Quoted in Maurice Agulhon, *The Republican Experiment, 1848–1852* (Cambridge, 1983), p. 177.

3. Quoted in Raymond Grew, *A Sterner Plan for Italian Unity: The Italian National Society in the Risorgimento* (Princeton, N.J., 1963), p. 10.

4. Quoted in Otto Pflanze, *Bismarck and the Development of Germany: The Period of Unification, 1815–1871* (Princeton, N.J., 1963), p. 60.

5. Louis L. Snyder, ed., *Documents of German History* (New Brunswick, N.J., 1958), p. 202.

6. Quoted in Pflanze, *Bismarck and the Development of Germany,* p. 327.

7. Quoted in György Szabad, *Hungarian Political Trends between the Revolution and the Compromise, 1849–1867* (Budapest, 1977), p. 163.

8. Quoted in George L. Yaney, *The Systematization of Russian Government, 1711–1905* (Champaign, Ill., 1973), p. 241.

9. Quoted in Rondo Cameron, "Crédit Mobilier and the Economic Development of Europe," *Journal of Political Economy* 61 (1953): 470.

10. Karl Marx and Friedrich Engels, *The Communist Manifesto* (Harmondsworth, 1967), p. 79.

11. Ibid., pp. (in order of quotations), 79, 81, 102, 82.

12. Ibid., pp. (in order of quotations), 80, 91, 94.

13. Quoted in David McLellan, *Karl Marx* (New York, 1975), p. 14.

14. Charles Darwin, *On the Origins of Species* (New York, 1872), 1: 77, 79.

15. Quoted in Albert Lyons and R. Joseph Petrucelli, *Medicine: An Illustrated History* (New York, 1978), p. 569.

Suggestions for Further Reading
▼ ▼ ▼

Two general surveys of the mid-century decades are N. Rich, *The Age of Nationalism and Reform, 1850–1890*, 2d ed. (New York, 1979); and J. A. S. Grenville, *Europe Reshaped, 1848–1878* (London, 1976). In addition to the books listed for individual countries in Chapter 22 that also cover the material of this chapter, see H. Holborn, *A History of Modern Germany*, vol. 3, *1840–1945* (New York, 1969); G. Craig, *Germany, 1866–1945* (Oxford, 1981); the two detailed volumes of T. Zeldin, *France, 1848–1945* (Oxford, 1973–77); A. J. May, *The Habsburg Monarchy, 1867–1914* (Cambridge, Mass., 1951); and D. Read, *England, 1868–1914* (London, 1979).

For a good introduction to the French Second Empire, see A. Plessis, *The Rise and Fall of the Second Empire, 1852–1871*, trans. J. Mandelbaum (New York, 1985). Napoleon's role can be examined in W. H. C. Smith, *Napoleon III* (New York, 1972). The Crimean War and its impact are examined in P. W. Schroeder, *Austria, Great Britain and the Crimean War: The Destruction of the European Concert* (Ithaca, N.Y., 1972).

The unification of Italy can best be examined in the works of D. M. Smith, *Victor Emmanuel, Cavour and the Risorgimento* (London, 1971); and *Cavour* (London, 1985). The unification of Germany can be pursued first in two good biographies of Bismarck, E. Crankshaw, *Bismarck* (New York, 1981); and G. O. Kent, *Bismarck and His Times* (Carbondale, Ill., 1978). See also the older, but clear surveys in W. M. Simon, *Germany in the Age of Bismarck* (New York, 1968); and W. N. Medlicott, *Bismarck and Modern Germany* (London, 1965). T. S. Hamerow, *The Social Foundations of German Unification, 1858–1871* (Princeton, N.J., 1969) is good on the political implications of social changes in Germany. Also valuable is O. Pflanze, *Bismarck and the Development of Germany: The Period of Unification, 1815–1871* (Princeton, N.J., 1963). A classic on the role of the Prussian military is G. Craig, *The Politics of*

the Prussian Army (New York, 1955). On the position of liberals in the unification of Germany, see J. J. Sheehan, *German Liberalism in the Nineteenth Century* (Chicago, 1978).

A reliable survey on the Austrian-Hungarian *Ausgleich* can be found in G. Szabad, *Hungarian Political Trends between the Revolution and the Compromise, 1849–1867* (Budapest, 1977). On the emancipation of the Russian serfs, see D. Field, *The End of Serfdom: Nobility and Bureaucracy in Russia, 1855–1861* (Cambridge, 1976); and T. Emmons, ed., *Emancipation of the Russian Serfs* (New York, 1970). On the 1867 Reform Act in Britain, see M. Cowling, *1867: Disraeli, Gladstone and Revolution* (London, 1967), while the evolution of British political parties in mid-century is examined in H. J. Hanham, *Elections and Party Management: Politics in the Time of Disraeli and Gladstone*, 2d ed. (London, 1978). On the southern slave economy in the United States, see the opposing views of R. W. Fogel and S. Engerman, *Time on the Cross: The Economics of American Negro Slavery* (Boston, 1974); and G. Wright, *The Political Economy of the Cotton South* (New York, 1978). On the background to the American Civil War, see D. Potter, *The Impending Crisis, 1845–1861* (New York, 1976); and M. Holt, *The Political Crisis of the 1850's* (New York, 1978). A good, brief biography of Lincoln is O. and L. Handlin, *Abraham Lincoln and the Union* (Boston, 1980). A good one-volume survey of the Civil War can be found in P. J. Parish, *The American Civil War* (New York, 1975).

In addition to the general works on economic development listed in Chapters 21 and 23, there are some specialized works on this period that are worthwhile. These include P. O'Brien, *The New Economic History of the Railways* (New York, 1977); W. O. Henderson, *The Rise of German Industrial Power, 1834–1914* (Berkeley, 1975); and F. Crouzet, *The Victorian Economy* (London, 1982). On Marx there is the standard work by D. McLellan, *Karl Marx: His Life and*

Thought (New York, 1974), but it can be supplemented by the interesting and comprehensive work by L. Kolakowski, *Main Currents of Marxism,* 3 vols. (Oxford, 1978).

For an introduction to the intellectual changes of the nineteenth century, see O. Chadwick, *The Secularization of the European Mind in the Nineteenth Century* (Cambridge, 1975). A detailed biography of Darwin can be found in R. W. Clark, *The Survival of Charles Darwin*

(New York, 1984). On Realism, there is a good introduction in L. Nochlin, *Realism* (Harmondsworth, 1971). Also valuable is F. W. J. Hemmings, *Culture and Society in France, 1848–1898* (London, 1971). For an introduction to the transformation of medical practices in the nineteenth century, see the appropriate chapters in E. H. Ackerknecht, *A Short History of Medicine,* rev. ed. (Baltimore, 1982); and A. S. Lyons and R. J. Petrucelli, *Medicine: An Illustrated History* (New York, 1978).

Chapter 24

Society and Politics in the "Age of Progress," 1871–1914

▼▼▼▼▼

During the fifty years before 1914, Europe witnessed a dynamic age of material prosperity. With new industries, new sources of energy, and new goods, a Second Industrial Revolution transformed the human environment, dazzled Europeans, and led them to believe that their material progress meant human progress. Scientific and technological achievements, many naively believed, would improve humanity's condition and solve all human problems. The doctrine of progress became an article of great faith.

This Second Industrial Revolution was also accompanied by political and social transformation. The national state had become the focus of Europeans' lives, and within the nation-state the growth of the middle class had led in many places to the triumph of liberal practices: constitutional states, parliaments, and principles of equality. The period after 1871 also witnessed the growth of political democracy in which universal male suffrage was used to elect parliamentary bodies with cabinets responsible to the legislature.

During the same period, social legislation to benefit the working classes also emerged. While workers turned to socialist parties and labor unions to push for improvements in their working and living conditions, they also used their newly acquired voting rights to push for social legislation that would benefit them. But social welfare measures also came from conservative governments that tried to divert workers away from socialism by making concessions to their demands for a better life.

Public Health Act
in Britain

Bell's Invention
of the Telephone

Britain's First
Public Power Station

Ten-Hour Industrial
Work Day

Creation of Women's
Social and Political Union

▼ ▼ ▼ ▼ ▼

••••••••• 1870 ••••••••••• 1880 •••••••••••• 1890 •••••••••••• 1900 •••••••••••• 1910 ••••••••••

▲ ▲ ▲ ▲ ▲

First Birth
Control Clinic

Germany's Social
Welfare Legislation

Separation of Church
and State in France

Social Democratic Party Becomes
Germany's Largest Party

▼ The Second Industrial Revolution

At the heart of Europe's belief in progress between 1871 and 1914 was the stunning material growth produced by what historians have called the Second Industrial Revolution. The first Industrial Revolution had given rise to textiles, railroads, iron, and coal. In the second revolution, steel, chemicals, electricity, and petroleum led the way to new industrial frontiers.

Technological Innovations and New Products

The first major change in industrial development between 1870 and 1914 was the substitution of steel for iron. The development of a steel industry began in the 1850s when a British engineer, Henry Bessemer, invented a converter furnace. It was not until the end of the 1870s, however, that the process was refined enough to produce large quantities of basic steel at a price cheaper than iron. New methods for rolling and shaping steel made it useful in the construction of lighter, smaller, and faster machines and engines, as well as railways, shipbuilding, and armaments. In 1860, Great Britain, France, Germany, and Belgium produced 125,000 tons of steel; by 1913, the total was 32 million tons. Whereas in the early 1870s Britain had produced twice as much steel as Germany, by 1910, German production was double that of Great Britain. Both had been surpassed by the United States in 1890.

Great Britain also fell behind in the new chemical industry. A change in the method of making soda enabled France and Germany to take the lead in producing the alkalies used in the textile, soap, and paper industries. German laboratories soon overtook the British in the development of new organic chemical compounds, such as artificial dyes. By 1900, German firms had cornered 90 percent of the market for dye stuffs, "imperial Germany's greatest industrial achievement." Germany also led in the development of photographic plates and film.

Electricity was a major new form of energy that proved to be of great value since it could be easily converted into other forms of energy, such as heat, light, and motion, and moved relatively effortlessly through space by means of transmitting wires. It was not until the 1870s that the first commercially practical generators of electrical current were developed. By 1881, Britain had its first public power station. By 1910, hydroelectric power stations and coal-fired steam-generating plants enabled entire districts to be tied into a single power distribution system that provided a common source of power for homes, shops, and industrial enterprises.

Electricity spawned a whole new series of inventions. The creation of the incandescent filament lamp by the American Thomas Edison and the Briton Joseph Swan opened homes and cities to illumination by electric lights. A revolution in communications was fostered when Alexander Graham Bell invented the telephone in 1876 and Guglielmo Marconi sent the first radio waves across the Atlantic in 1901. Although most electricity was initially used for lighting, it was eventually put to use in transportation. The first electric railway was installed in Berlin in 1879. By the 1880s, streetcars and subways had appeared in major European cities. Horse-drawn buses disappeared from London streets by 1911. Electricity also transformed the factory. Conveyor belts, cranes, machines, and machine tools could all be powered by electricity and located anywhere. In the first Industrial Revolution, coal had been the major source of energy. Countries without adequate coal supplies lagged behind in industrialization. Thanks to electricity, they could now enter the industrial age.

The development of the internal combustion engine had a similar effect. The first internal combustion engine, fired by gas and air, was produced in 1878. It proved unsuitable for widespread use as a source of power in transportation until the development of liquid fuels,

▼ **An Age of Progress.** Between 1871 and 1914, a Second
Industrial Revolution led many Europeans to believe that their
age was an age of progress in which most human problems
could be solved by scientific achievements. This illustration is
taken from a special issue of *The Illustrated London News*
celebrating the Diamond Jubilee of Queen Victoria in 1897.
On the left are scenes from 1837, when Victoria came to the
British throne; on the right are scenes from 1897. The vivid
contrast was used to underscore the magazine's conclusion:
"The most striking . . . evidence of progress during the reign is
the ever increasing speed which the discoveries of physical
science have forced into everyday life. Steam and electricity
have conquered time and space to a greater extent during the
last sixty years than all the preceding six hundred years
witnessed."

namely, petroleum and its distilled derivatives. An
oil-fired engine was made in 1897, and by 1902, the
Hamburg-Amerika Line had switched from coal to oil on
its new ocean liners. By the beginning of the twentieth
century, some naval fleets had been converted to oil
burners as well.

The development of the internal combustion engine
gave rise to the automobile and airplane. Gottlieb Daim-
ler's creation of a light engine in 1886 was the key to the
development of the automobile. In 1900, world production stood at 9,000 cars; by 1906, Americans had overtaken the initial lead of the French. It was an American,
Henry Ford, who revolutionized the car industry with
the mass production of the Model T. By 1916, Ford's
factories were producing 735,000 cars a year. In the
meantime an age of air transportation emerged with the
Zeppelin airship in 1900. In 1903, at Kitty Hawk, North
Carolina, the Wright brothers made the first flight in a
fixed-wing, gasoline-engine-powered plane. It took
World War I, however, to stimulate the aircraft industry,
and it was not until 1919 that the first regular passenger
air service was established. Despite the new sources of
energy in hydroelectricity, oil, gasoline, and gas, coal
remained the primary source of industrial energy at the
beginning of the twentieth century.

The Development of Markets

The growth of industrial production depended upon
the development of markets for the sale of manufactured
goods. The British in particular had actively sought markets abroad for their textiles. In 1820, 60 percent of
Britain's cotton cloth was sold outside the country; by
1880, 82 percent was exported. The British were especially active in developing markets in the Far East. In
1814, they sold 1 million yards of cloth to ports east of
Suez; by 1870, they were selling 1,402 million yards. But
in the second half of the nineteenth century, the British
experienced severe competition from Germany and the
United States, and even from India and Japan, in their
eastern markets.

After 1870, the best markets were already heavily
saturated, forcing Europeans to take a renewed look at
their domestic markets. As Europeans were the richest
consumers in the world, those markets offered abundant
possibilities. The dramatic population increases after
1870 (see Chapter 25) were accompanied by a steady rise
in national incomes. The leading industrialized nations,
Britain and Germany, doubled or tripled their national
incomes. Between 1850 and 1900, real wages had increased in Britain by two-thirds and in Germany by one-
third. A decline in the cost of food combined with lower
prices for manufactured goods because of reduced transportation costs made it easier for Europeans to buy consumer products. In the cities, new methods for retail
distribution, in particular the department store (see the
box on p. 815), were used to expand sales of a whole

The Department Store and the Beginnings of Mass Consumerism

▼ ▼ ▼

Domestic markets were especially important for the sale of the goods being turned out by Europe's increasing number of industrial plants. New techniques of mass marketing arose to encourage the sale of the new consumer goods. The Parisians pioneered in the development of the department store, and this selection is taken from a contemporary's account of the growth of these stores in the French capital city.

E. Lavasseur, On Parisian Department Stores, 1907

It was in the reign of Louis-Philippe that department stores for fashion goods and dresses, extending to material and other clothing began to be distinguished. The type was already one of the notable developments of the Second Empire; it became one of the most important ones of the Third Republic. These stores have increased in number and several of them have become extremely large. Combining in their different departments all articles of clothing, toilet articles, furniture and many other ranges of goods, it is their special object so to combine all commodities as to attract and satisfy customers who will find conveniently together an assortment of a mass of articles corresponding to all their various needs. They attract customers by permanent display, by free entry into the shops, by periodic exhibitions, by special sales, by fixed prices, and by their ability to deliver the goods purchased to customers' homes, in Paris and to the provinces. Turning themselves into direct intermediaries between the producer and the consumer, even producing sometimes some of their articles in their own workshops, buying at lowest prices because of their large orders and because they are in a position to profit from bargains, working with large sums, and selling to most of their customers for cash only, they can transmit these benefits in lowered selling prices.

They can even decide to sell at a loss, as an advertisement or to get rid of out-of-date fashions. Taking 5–6 percent on 100 million brings them in more than 20 per cent would bring to a firm doing a turnover of 50,000 francs.

The success of these department stores is only possible thanks to the volume of their business and this volume needs considerable capital and a very large turnover. Now capital, having become abundant, is freely combined nowadays in large enterprises, although French capital has the reputation of being more wary of the risks of industry than of State or railway securities. On the other hand, the large urban agglomerations, the ease with which goods can be transported by the railways, the diffusion of some comforts to strata below the middle classes, have all favoured these developments.

As example we may cite some figures relating to these stores, since they were brought to the notice of the public in the *Revue des Deux-Mondes*. . . .

Le Louvre, dating to the time of the extension of the rue de Rivoli under the Second Empire, did in 1893 a business of 120 million at a profit of 6.4 per cent. *Le Bon-Marché*, which was a small shop when Mr. Boucicaut entered it in 1852, already did a business of 20 million at the end of the Empire. During the republic its new buildings were erected; Mme. Boucicaut turned it by her will into a kind of co-operative society, with shares and an ingenious organization; turnover reached 150 million in 1893, leaving a profit of 5 per cent. . . .

According to the tax records of 1891, these stores in Paris, numbering 12, employed 1,708 persons and were rated on their site values at 2,159,000 francs; the largest had then 542 employees. These same stores had, in 1901, 9,784 employees; one of them over 2,000 and another over 1,600; their site value has doubled (4,089,000 francs).

new range of consumer goods made possible by the development of the steel and electrical industries. The desire to own sewing machines, clocks, bicycles, electric lights, and typewriters was rapidly generating a new consumer ethic that has been a crucial part of the modern economy.

Meanwhile, increased competition for foreign markets and the growing importance of domestic demand led to a reaction against free trade. To many industrial and political leaders, protective tariffs guaranteed domestic markets for the products of their own industries. Thus, after a decade of experimentation with free trade in the 1860s, Europeans returned to tariff protection. The Austro-Hungarian Empire was the first in 1874, followed by Russia in 1877, Germany in 1879, Italy in 1887, the United States in 1890, and France in 1892. Only Britain, Denmark, and the Netherlands refused to follow suit.

During this same period, cartels were being formed to decrease competition internally. In a cartel, independent enterprises worked together to control prices and fix production quotas, thereby restraining the kind of competition that led to reduced prices. Cartels were especially strong in Germany, where banks moved to protect their investments by eliminating the "anarchy of competition." German businessmen established cartels in potash, coal, steel, and chemicals. Founded in 1893, the Rhenish-Westphalian Coal Syndicate controlled 98 percent of Germany's coal production by 1904.

The formation of cartels was paralleled by a move toward ever-larger manufacturing plants, especially in the iron and steel, machinery, heavy electrical equipment, and chemical industries. Although evident in Britain, France, and Belgium, it was most pronounced in Germany. Between 1882 and 1907, the number of people working in German factories with over 1,000 employees rose from 205,000 to 879,000. This growth in the size of industrial plants led to pressure for greater efficiency in factory production at the same time that competition led to demands for greater economy. The result was a desire to streamline or rationalize production as much as possible. One way to accomplish this was by cutting labor costs through the mechanization of transport within plants, such as using electric cranes to move materials. More importantly, the development of precision tools enabled manufacturers to produce interchangeable parts, which in turn led to the creation of the assembly line for production. First used in the United States for small arms and clocks, the assembly line had moved to Europe by 1850. In the last half of the nineteenth century, it was primarily used in manufacturing nonmilitary goods, such as sewing machines, type-

writers, bicycles, and finally the automobile. Principles of scientific management were also introduced by 1900 to maximize workers' efficiency.

The emergence of protective tariffs and cartels was clearly a response to the growth of the multinational industrial system. Economic competition intensified the political rivalries of the age. The growth of the national state, which had seemed in the mid-nineteenth century to be the answer to old problems, now seemed to be creating new ones.

Economic Patterns

In the fifty years before World War I, the Second Industrial Revolution of Europe played a role in the emergence of basic economic patterns that characterized much of modern European economic life.

EUROPEAN TRENDS   Although we have described the period from 1871 to 1914 as an age of material property, recessions and crises were still very much a part of economic life. Although some historians have questioned the appropriateness of the title Great Depression for the period from 1873 to 1895, Europeans did witness a series of economic crises during those years. Prices, especially those of agricultural products, fell dramatically. Slumps in the business cycle reduced profits although economic recession occurred at different times in different countries. France and Britain, for example, sank into depression in the 1880s while Germany and the United States were recovering from their depression of the 1870s. After 1895, however, until World War I, Europe overall experienced an economic boom and achieved a level of prosperity that encouraged people later to look back to that era as *la belle époque*—a golden age in European civilization.

Between 1870 and 1914, Germany replaced Great Britain as the industrial leader of Europe. Already in the 1890s Germany's superiority was evident in new areas of manufacturing, such as organic chemicals and electrical equipment, and increasingly apparent in its ever-greater share of worldwide trade. Why had industrial leadership passed from Britain to Germany?

Britain's early lead in industrialization gave it an established industrial plant and made it more difficult to shift to the new techniques of the Second Industrial Revolution. As later entrants to the industrial age, the Germans could build the latest and most efficient industrial plant. British entrepreneurs made the situation worse by their tendency to be suspicious of innovations and their reluctance to invest in new plants and industries. As one manufacturer remarked: "One wants to be

thoroughly convinced of the superiority of a new method before condemning as useless a large plant that has hitherto done good service."[1] German managers, on the other hand, were accustomed to change, and the formation of large cartels encouraged German banks to provide enormous sums for investment. Then, too, unlike the Germans, the British were not willing to encourage formal scientific and technical education.

The struggle for economic (and political) supremacy between Great Britain and Germany should not cause us to overlook the other great polarization of the age. By 1900, Europe was divided into two economic zones. Great Britain, Belgium, France, the Netherlands, Germany, the western part of the Austro-Hungarian Empire, and northern Italy constituted an advanced industrialized core that had a high standard of living, decent systems of transportation, and relatively healthy and educated peoples. Another part of Europe, the backward and little industrialized area to the south and east, consisting of southern Italy, most of Austria-Hungary, Spain, Portugal, the Balkan kingdoms, and Russia, was still largely agricultural and relegated by the industrial countries to the function of providing food and raw materials. The presence of Romanian oil, Greek olive oil, and Serbian pigs and prunes in western Europe served as reminders of an economic division of Europe that continued well into the twentieth century. Some industrially backward countries of Europe, however, managed to use the export of their produce to boost themselves into the industrial age. Sweden's sale of timber and iron ore abroad, combined with hydroelectric power, gave it the resources to develop paper, steel, and cellulose industries.

SCIENCE AND TECHNOLOGY   Already by 1850, research in the basic sciences was rapidly being translated into new industrial techniques. Between 1870 and 1914, the union of science and technology grew closer. Newer fields of industrial activity, such as organic chemistry and electrical engineering, required more scientific knowledge than the commonsense tinkering once employed by amateur inventors. Companies began to invest capital in laboratory equipment for their own research or hired scientific consultants for advice.

Nowhere was the relationship between science and technology more apparent than in Germany. In 1899, German technical high schools were allowed to award doctorate degrees, and by 1900, they were turning out 3,000 to 4,000 graduates a year. Many of these graduates made their way into industrial firms. Some large firms, such as the Badische Anilin und Soda Fabrike, even established their own schools to train scientists. By 1907, 77 percent of salaried managers in Germany had had the benefit of some kind of higher education.

AGRICULTURAL CRISIS   European agriculture experienced a difficult time after 1870. An abundance of grain and lower costs of transportation caused the prices of farm commodities to plummet. Some countries responded with tariff barriers against lower priced foodstuffs. Where agricultural labor was scarce and hence expensive, as in Britain and Germany, landowners introduced machines for threshing and harvesting. The slump in grain prices also led some countries to specialize in other food products. Denmark, for example, exported eggs, butter, and cheese while sugar beets predominated in Bohemia and northern France, fruit in Mediterranean countries, and wine in Spain and Italy. This age also witnessed the introduction of chemical fertilizers. While large estates could make these adjustments easily, individual small farmers could not afford them and created farm cooperatives that provided capital for making improvements and purchasing tools and fertilizer.

TOWARD A WORLD ECONOMY   The economic developments of the late nineteenth century, combined with the transportation revolution that saw the growth of marine transport and railroads, not only played a role in the new imperialism in the last half of the nineteenth century (see Chapter 25), but also fostered a true world economy. By 1900, Europeans were receiving beef and wool from Argentina and Australia, coffee from Brazil, nitrates from Chile, iron ore from Algeria, and sugar from Java. European capital was also invested abroad to develop railways, mines, electrical power plants, and banks. High rates of return, such as 11.3 percent on Latin American banking shares that were floated in London, provided plenty of incentive. Of course, foreign countries also provided markets for the surplus manufactured goods of Europe. With its capital, industries, and military might, Europe dominated the world economy by the beginning of the twentieth century.

▼ Cities and Social Structure in an Age of Mass Society

The new urban and industrial world created by the rapid economic and social changes of the nineteenth century has led historians to speak of the emergence of a mass society by the late nineteenth century. A mass society meant new forms of expression for the lower classes as they benefited from the extension of voting rights, an improved standard of living, and compulsory

elementary education. However, mass society also made possible the development of organizations that manipulated and controlled the populations of the European nation-states. Governments fostered national loyalty and created mass armies by conscription. Big businesses imposed rational systems of discipline and organization upon their working-class employees. A mass press swayed popular opinion by flamboyant journalistic practices. To understand this mass society, we must examine the urban environment in which it lived and the structure of the social classes that made it up.

Transformation of the Urban Environment

By far one of the most important consequences of industrialization and the population explosion of the nineteenth century was urbanization. In the course of the nineteenth century, urban dwellers came to make up an ever-increasing percentage of the European population. In 1800, they constituted 40 percent of the population in Britain, 25 percent in France and Germany,

and only 10 percent in eastern Europe. By 1914, urban inhabitants had increased to 80 percent of the population in Britain, 45 percent in France, 60 percent in Germany, and 30 percent in eastern Europe. The size of cities also expanded dramatically, especially in industrialized countries. In 1800, there were 21 European cities with populations over 100,000; by 1900, there were 147. Between 1800 and 1900, London's population grew from 960,000 to 6,500,000 and Berlin's from 172,000 to 2,700,000. These statistics demonstrate what one observer noted in 1899: "the most remarkable social phenomenon of the present century is the concentration of population in cities."

Urban populations grew faster than the general population primarily because of the vast migration from rural areas to cities. Often this was due to negative factors. People were driven by sheer economic necessity—unemployment, land hunger, and physical want—from the countryside to the cities. Urban centers offered something positive as well, usually mass employment in factories and later in service trades and professions. But

▼ **Map 24.1** The Industrial Regions of Europe by 1914.

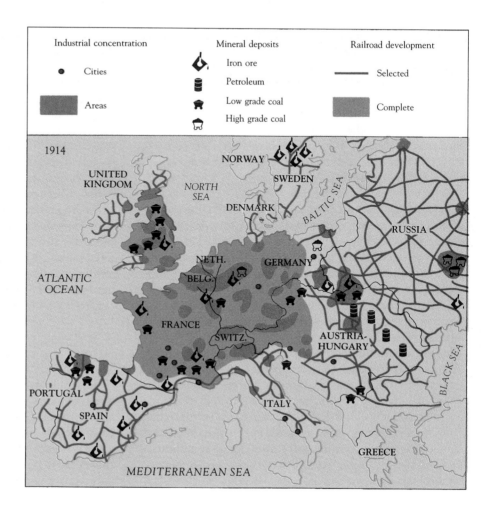

▼ **The City at Night.** Industrialization and the population explosion of the nineteenth century fostered the growth of cities. At the same time, technological innovations enabled cities to develop pure water and sewerage systems that dramatically improved living conditions in European cities. Gas lighting and later electricity also transformed the nighttime environment of Europe's cities, as is evident in this painting of Liverpool.

cities also grew faster in the second half of the nineteenth century because health and living conditions in them were improving.

PUBLIC HEALTH AND HOUSING   Throughout the Middle Ages, cities had been important centers of commerce, small industry, church and government offices, and culture, but these medieval cities had also been characterized by filth and disease. Early industrial cities had only magnified the squalor. Well into the mid-nineteenth century, urban death rates outstripped birth rates, and only the influx of large numbers of rural emigrants ensured urban growth. Between 1850 and 1914, however, the environment of the cities improved dramatically as urban reformers and city officials used new technology to improve the urban landscape.

When cholera swept across Europe in the 1830s and 1840s, it proved especially devastating to people living in working-class urban areas. But it also affected middle-class urban dwellers, who often, though incorrectly, believed that dirt caused disease. Consequently, public health and housing became important issues to city dwellers, and they began to put pressure on city governments to clean up the filthy environment.

In the 1840s, a number of urban reformers, such as Edwin Chadwick in England (see Chapter 21) and Rudolf Virchow and Solomon Neumann in Germany, had pointed to filthy living conditions as the primary cause of epidemic diseases and urged sanitary reforms to correct the problem. The efforts of Chadwick led to Britain's first Public Health Act in 1848. The Melun Act in France in 1851 and laws in German states achieved similar purposes. These and later legislative acts created Boards of Health that brought governmental action to bear on public health issues. Urban medical officers and building inspectors were authorized to inspect dwellings for public health hazards. New building regulations made it more difficult for private contractors to build shoddy housing. The Public Health Act of 1875 in Britain, for example, prohibited the construction of new buildings without running water and an internal drainage system. For the first time in Western history, the role of municipal governments had been expanded to include detailed regulations for the improvement of the living conditions of urban dwellers. German municipal administration in particular became a model for other European cities. By 1900, German municipal bureaucracies regularly hired university graduates with specialized medical and scientific knowledge to provide their cities with professional and technocratic management.

Essential to the public health of the modern European city was the ability to bring clean water to it and to expel sewage from it. The accomplishment of those two tasks was a major engineering feat in the last half of the nineteenth century. The problem of fresh water was solved by a system of dams and reservoirs that stored the water and aqueducts and tunnels that carried it from the countryside to the city and into individual dwellings. By the second half of the nineteenth century, regular private baths became accessible to many people as gas heaters in the 1860s and later electric heaters made hot baths possible. Even the shower had appeared by the 1880s. The treatment of sewage was also improved by building mammoth underground pipes that carried raw sewage far from the city for disposal. In the late 1860s, a number of German cities began to construct sewer systems. Frankfurt began its program after a lengthy public campaign enlivened by the slogan "from the toilet to the river in half an hour." London devised a system of five enormous sewers that discharged their loads twelve miles from the city where it was chemically treated. Unfortunately, in many places new underground sewers simply continued to discharge their raw sewage into what soon became highly polluted lakes and rivers. Nevertheless, the development of pure water and sewerage systems dramatically improved the public health of European cities by 1914.

Middle-class reformers who denounced the unsanitary living conditions of the working class also focused on their housing needs. Overcrowded, disease-ridden slums were viewed as dangerous not only to physical health, but to the political and moral health of the entire nation. V. A. Huber, the foremost early German housing reformer, wrote in 1861: "Certainly it would not be too much to say that the home is the communal embodiment of family life. Thus the purity of the dwelling is almost as important for the family as is the cleanliness of the body for the individual."[2] To Huber, good housing was a prerequisite for stable family life, and without stable family life one of the "stabilising elements of society" would be dissolved, much to society's detriment.

Early efforts to attack the housing problem emphasized the middle-class, liberal belief in the efficacy of private enterprise. Reformers such as Huber believed that the construction of model dwellings renting at a reasonable price would force other private landlords to elevate their housing standards. A fine example of this approach was the work of Octavia Hill, granddaughter of a celebrated social reformer (see the box on p. 821). With the financial assistance of a friend, she rehabilitated some old dwellings and constructed new ones to create housing for 3,500 tenants.

Other wealthy reformer-philanthropists took a different approach to the housing problem. In 1887, Lord Leverhulme began construction of a model village called Port Sunlight outside Liverpool for the workers at his soap factory. Port Sunlight offered pleasant living conditions in the belief that good housing would ensure a healthy and happy work force. Yet another approach was the garden city. At the end of the nineteenth century, Ebenezer Howard founded the British garden city movement that advocated the construction of new towns separated from each other by open country that would provide the recreational areas, fresh air, and sense of community that would encourage healthy family life. Letchward Garden City, started in 1903, was the first concrete result of Howard's theory.

As the number and size of cities continued to mushroom, governments by the 1880s came to the conclusion—although reluctantly—that private enterprise could not solve the housing crisis. In 1890, a British Housing Act empowered local town councils to construct cheap housing for the working classes. London and Liverpool were the first communities to take advantage of their new powers. Similar activity had been set in motion in Germany by 1900. In France in 1894 the government took a lesser step by providing easy credit for private contractors to build working-class housing. Everywhere, however, these lukewarm measures failed to do much to meet the real housing needs of the working classes. In Britain, for example, only 5 percent of all dwellings erected between 1890 and 1914 were constructed by municipalities under the Housing Act of 1890. Nevertheless, by the start of World War I, the need for planning had been recognized, and after the war municipal governments moved into housing construction on a large scale. In housing, as in so many other areas of life in the late nineteenth and early twentieth centuries, the liberal principle that the government that governs least governs best had simply proven untrue. More and more, governments were stepping into areas of activity that they would never have touched earlier.

URBAN RECONSTRUCTION Housing was but one area of urban reconstruction in the fifty years before World War I. As urban populations expanded in the nineteenth

The Housing Venture of Octavia Hill

▼ ▼ ▼

Octavia Hill was a practical-minded British housing reformer who believed that workers and their families were entitled to happy homes. At the same time, she was convinced that the poor needed guidance and encouragement, not charity. In this selection, she describes her housing venture.

Octavia Hill, *Homes of the London Poor*

About four years ago I was put in possession of three houses in one of the worst courts of Marylebone. Six other houses were bought subsequently. All were crowded with inmates.

The first thing to be done was to put them in decent tenantable order. The set last purchased was a row of cottages facing a bit of desolate ground, occupied with wretched, dilapidated cow-sheds, manure heaps, old timber, and rubbish of every description. The houses were in a most deplorable condition—the plaster was dropping from the walls; on one staircase a pail was placed to catch the rain that fell through the roof. All the staircases were perfectly dark; the banisters were gone, having been burnt as firewood by tenants. The grates, with large holes in them, were falling forward into the rooms. The washhouse, full of lumber belonging to the landlord, was locked up; thus the inhabitants had to wash clothes, as well as to cook, eat and sleep in their small rooms. The dust-bin, standing in the front part of the houses, was accessible to the whole neighbourhood, and boys often dragged from it quantities of unseemly objects and spread them over the court. The state of the drainage was in keeping with everything else. The pavement of the backyard was all broken up, and great puddles stood in it, so that the damp crept up the outer walls. . . .

As soon as I entered into possession, each family had an opportunity of doing better: those who would not pay, or who led clearly immoral lives, were ejected. The rooms they vacated were cleansed; the tenants who showed signs of improvement moved into them, and thus, in turn, an opportunity was obtained for having each room distempered and papered. The drains were put in order, a large slate cistern was fixed, the washhouse was cleared of its lumber, and thrown open on stated days to each tenant in turn. The roof, the plaster, the woodwork were repaired; the staircase walls were distempered; new grates were fixed; the layers of paper and rag (black with age) were torn from the windows, and glass was put in; out of 192 panes only eight were found unbroken. The yard and footpath were paved.

The rooms, as a rule, were re-let at the same prices at which they had been let before; but tenants with large families were counselled to take two rooms, and for these much less was charged than if let singly: this plan I continue to pursue. In-coming tenants are not allowed to take a decidedly insufficient quantity of room, and no sub-letting is permitted. . . .

The pecuniary result has been very satisfactory. Five per cent has been paid on all the capital invested. A fund for the repayment of capital is accumulating. A liberal allowance has been made for repairs. . . .

My tenants are mostly of a class far below that of mechanics. They are, indeed, of the very poor. And yet, although the gifts they have received have been next to nothing, none of the families who have passed under my care during the whole four years have continued in what is called "distress," except such as have been unwilling to exert themselves. Those who will not exert the necessary self-control cannot avail themselves of the means of livelihood held out to them. But, for those who are willing, some small assistance in the form of work has, from time to time, been provided—not much, but sufficient to keep them from want or despair.

▼ **The Reconstruction of Paris.** In the second half of the nineteenth century, urban reconstruction projects transformed the appearance of many European cities. Perhaps most famous was the reconstruction of Paris during the reign of Emperor Napoleon III. As can be seen in this illustration, a congested section of old Paris is being torn down to make way for the wide boulevards and open spaces that characterized the new Paris.

century, the older layout in which the city was confined to a compact area enclosed by defensive walls seemed restrictive and utterly useless. In the second half of the nineteenth century, many of the old defensive walls—worthless anyway from a military standpoint—were pulled down, and the areas converted into parks and boulevards. In Vienna, for example, the great boulevards of the Ringstrasse replaced the old medieval walls. While the broad streets served a military purpose—the rapid deployment of troops to crush civil disturbances—they also offered magnificent views of the city hall, the university, and the parliament building, all powerful symbols of middle-class social values.

Like Vienna, many European urban centers were redesigned during the second half of the nineteenth century. The reconstruction of Paris after 1850 by Emperor Napoleon III was perhaps the most famous project and provided a model for other urban centers. The old residential districts located in the central city, many of them working-class slums, were pulled down and replaced with town halls, government office buildings, retail stores, including the new department stores, museums, cafes, and theaters, all of which provided for the shopping and recreational pleasures of the middle classes.

As cities expanded and entire groups of people were displaced from urban centers by reconstruction, city populations spilled over into the neighboring villages and countrysides, which were soon incorporated into the cities. The construction of streetcars and commuter trains by the turn of the century enabled both working-class and middle-class populations to live in their own suburban neighborhoods far removed from their places of work. Cheap, modern transportation essentially separated home and work for many Europeans.

The Social Structure of Mass Society

Historians generally agree that between 1871 and 1914 the average person enjoyed an increasing standard of living. The real wages of British workers, for example, probably doubled between 1871 and 1910. We should not allow this increase in the standard of living to mislead us, however. Great poverty did remain in Western society, and the gap between the rich and poor was enormous by 1914. In the western and central European countries most affected by industrialization, the richest 20 percent of the population received between 50 and 60 percent of the national income. This meant that while the upper and middle classes received almost three-fifths of the wealth, the remaining 80 percent of the population received only two-fifths. It would, however, be equally misleading to portray European society as split simply into rich and poor. Between the small group of the elite at the top and the large number of very poor at the bottom, there existed many different groups of varying wealth.

THE ELITE At the top of European society stood a wealthy elite, constituting but 5 percent of the population while controlling between 30 and 40 percent of its wealth. This nineteenth-century elite was an amalgamation of the traditional landed aristocracy that had dominated European society for centuries and the wealthy upper middle class. In the course of the nineteenth century, aristocrats coalesced with the most successful industrialists, bankers, and merchants to form a new elite. The growth of big business had created this group of wealthy plutocrats while aristocrats, whose income from landed estates declined, invested in railway shares, public utilities, government bonds, and even businesses, sometimes on their own estates. Gradually, the greatest fortunes shifted into the hands of the upper middle class. In Great Britain, for example, landed aristocrats constituted 73 percent of the country's millionaires in mid-century while the commercial and financial magnates made up 14 percent. By the period 1900–1914, landowners had declined to 27 percent. The wealthiest person in Germany was not an aristocrat, but Bertha Krupp, granddaughter of Alfred Krupp and heiress to the business dynasty left by her father Friedrich, who committed suicide in 1902 over a homosexual scandal.

Increasingly, aristocrats and plutocrats fused as the wealthy upper middle class purchased landed estates to join the aristocrats in the pleasures of country living while the aristocrats bought lavish town houses for part-time urban life. Common bonds were also created when the sons of wealthy middle-class families were admitted to the elite schools dominated by the children of the aristocracy. At Oxford, the landed upper class made up 40 percent of the student body in 1870, but only 15 percent in 1910, while undergraduates from business families went from 7 to 21 percent during the same period. This educated elite, whether aristocratic or middle class in background, assumed leadership roles in government bureaucracies and military hierarchies. Marriage also served to unite the two groups. Daughters of tycoons gained titles while aristocratic heirs gained new sources of cash. Wealth American heiresses were in special demand. When Consuelo Vanderbilt married the duke of Marlborough, the new duchess brought £2 million (approximately $10 million) to her husband.

It would be misleading, however, to assume that the alliance of the wealthy business elite and traditional aristocrats was always harmonious. In Germany class lines were sometimes well drawn, especially if they were complicated by anti-Semitism. Albert Ballin, the wealthy director of the Hamburg-Amerika luxury liners, may have been close to Emperor William II, who entertained him on a regular basis, but the Prussian aristocracy never fully accepted Ballin because of his Jewish origins. Although the upper middle class was allowed into the bureaucracy of the German empire, the diplomatic corps remained the preserve of nobles.

THE MIDDLE CLASSES The middle classes consisted of a variety of groups. Below the upper middle class was a middle level that included such traditional groups as professionals in law, medicine, and the civil service as well as moderately well-to-do industrialists and merchants. The industrial expansion of the nineteenth century also added new groups to the middle middle class. These included business managers and new professionals, such as the engineers, architects, accountants, and chemists who formed professional associations as the symbols of their newfound importance. Beneath this solid and comfortable middle middle class was a lower middle class of small shopkeepers, traders, manufacturers, and prosperous peasants. Their chief preoccupation was the provision of goods and services for the classes above them.

Standing between the lower middle class and the lower classes were new groups of white-collar workers who were the product of the Second Industrial Revolution. They were the traveling salesmen, bookkeepers, bank tellers, telephone operators, department store salespeople, and secretaries. Although largely propertyless and often little better paid than skilled laborers, these white-collar workers were often committed to middle-class ideals and optimistic about improving their status. Some even achieved professional standing and middle-class status.

The moderately prosperous and successful middle classes shared a certain style of life, one whose values tended to dominate much of nineteenth-century society.

The members of the middle class were especially active in preaching their worldview to their children and to the upper and lower classes of their society. This was especially evident in Victorian Britain, often considered a model of middle-class society. It was the European middle classes who accepted and promulgated the importance of progress and science. They believed in hard work, which they viewed as the primary human good, open to everyone and guaranteed to have positive results. Knowledge was important as a functional instrument for personal gain. They were also regular churchgoers who believed in the good conduct associated with traditional Christian morality. The middle class was concerned with propriety, the right way of doing things, which gave rise to an incessant number of books aimed at the middle-class market with such titles as *The Habits of Good Society* or *Don't: A Manual of Mistakes and Improprieties More or Less Prevalent in Conduct and Speech.*

THE WORKING CLASSES The working classes of European society constituted almost 80 percent of the European population. Many of them were landholding peasants, agricultural laborers, and sharecroppers, especially in eastern Europe. This was less true, however, in western and central Europe. About 10 percent of the British population worked in agriculture, while in Germany the figure was 25 percent.

Although the experiences of peasants were very different from those of the urban working classes, the two groups were drawing closer together by the end of the nineteenth century. Many prosperous, landowning peasants shared the values of the middle class. Military con-

scription brought peasants into contact with the other groups of mass society while state-run elementary schools forced the children of peasants to speak the national dialect and accept national loyalties.

There was no such thing as a homogeneous urban working class. The elite of the working class included, first of all, skilled artisans in such traditional handicraft trades as cabinetmaking, printing, and the making of jewelry. As the production of more items was mechanized in the course of the nineteenth century, these highly skilled workers found their economic security threatened. Printers, for example, were replaced by automatic typesetting machines operated by semiskilled workers. The Second Industrial Revolution, however, also brought new entrants into the group of highly skilled workers, such as machine-tool specialists, shipbuilders, and metal workers. Many of the skilled workers attempted to pattern themselves after the middle class by seeking good housing and educating their children.

Semiskilled laborers, who included such people as carpenters, bricklayers, and many factory workers, earned wages that were about two-thirds of those of highly skilled workers. At the bottom of the working-class hierarchy stood the largest group of workers, the unskilled laborers. They included day laborers, who worked irregularly for very low wages, and large numbers of domestic servants. One out of every seven employed persons in Great Britain in 1900 was a domestic servant. Most of them were women.

Urban workers did experience a real betterment in the material conditions of their lives after 1871. For one thing, urban improvements meant better living condi-

▼ **Working-Class Housing in London.** Although urban workers experienced some improvements in the material conditions of their lives after 1871, working-class housing remained drab and depressing. This 1912 photograph of working-class housing in the East End of London shows rows of similar-looking buildings on treeless streets. Most often, these buildings had no gardens and no green areas.

tions. A rise in real wages, accompanied by a decline in many consumer costs, especially in the 1880s and 1890s, made it possible for workers to buy more than just food and housing. French workers in 1900, for example, spent 60 percent of their income on food, down from 75 percent in 1870. Workers' budgets now provided money for more clothes and even leisure at the same time that strikes and labor agitation were providing ten-hour days and Saturday afternoons off. The combination of more income and more free time produced whole new patterns of mass leisure (see Chapter 25).

▼ The "Woman Question": Female Experiences

The "woman question" was the term used to identify the debate over the role of women in society. In the nineteenth century, the "woman question" was really a series of "women's questions": Did women have a right to work? Did they have the right to own property? What should be the extent of their political rights? Such questions were important in view of women's position in society. Excluded from citizenship and defined by family and household roles, women remained legally inferior and economically dependent. In the course of the nineteenth century, women struggled to change their status.

Women and Work

During the course of the nineteenth century, considerable controversy erupted over a woman's "right to work." Working-class organizations tended to reinforce the underlying ideology of domesticity; women should remain at home to bear and nurture children and should not be allowed in the industrial work force. Working-class men argued that keeping women out of industrial work would ensure the moral and physical well-being of families. In reality, keeping women out of the industrial work force simply made it easier to exploit them when they needed income to supplement their husbands' wages or to support their families when their husbands were unemployed. The desperate need to work at times forced women to do marginal work at home or labor as pieceworkers in sweatshops. "Sweating" referred to the subcontracting of piecework usually, but not exclusively, in the tailoring trades; it was done at home since it required few skills or equipment. Pieceworkers were poorly paid and worked long hours. The poorest paid jobs for the cheapest goods were called "slop work." In this description of the room of a London slopper, we see how precarious her position was:

> I then directed my steps to the neighborhood of Drurylane, to see a poor woman who lived in an attic on one of the closest courts in that quarter. On the table was a quarter of an ounce of tea. Observing my eye to rest upon it, she told me it was all she took. "Sugar," she said, "I broke myself of long ago; I couldn't afford it. A cup of tea, a piece of bread, and an onion is generally all I have for my dinner, and sometimes I haven't even an onion, and then I sops my bread."[3]

Excluded from factories and in need of income, many women had no choice but to work for the pitiful wages of the sweated industries.

NEW JOB OPPORTUNITIES The Second Industrial Revolution had an enormous impact on the position of women in the labor market. Although the growth of heavy industry in the mining, metallurgy, engineering, chemicals, and electrical sectors meant fewer jobs for women in manufacturing, the development of larger industrial plants and the expansion of government services created a wide number of service or white-collar jobs. The increased demand for white-collar workers at relatively low wages coupled with a shortage of male workers led employers to hire women. Big businesses and retail shops needed clerks, typists, secretaries, file clerks, and sales clerks. The expansion of government services created opportunities for women to be secretaries and telephone operators and to take jobs in health and social services. Compulsory education necessitated more teachers while the development of modern hospital services opened the way for an increase in nurses.

Many of the new white-collar jobs were by no means exciting. Their work was routine and, except for teaching and nursing, required few skills beyond basic literacy. Although there was little hope for advancement, these jobs had distinct advantages to the daughters of the middle classes and especially the upward-aspiring working classes. For some middle-class women, the new jobs offered freedom from the domestic patterns expected of them. Most of them, however, were filled by working-class females who saw them as an opportunity to escape from the "dirty" work of the lower-class world. Studies in France and Britain indicate that the increase in white-collar jobs did not lead to a rise in the size of the female labor force, but only a shift from industrial jobs to the white-collar sector of the economy.

PROSTITUTION Despite new job opportunities, many lower-class women were forced to become prostitutes to survive. The influx of rural, working-class girls into the cities in search of new opportunities often left them highly vulnerable. Employment was unstable and wages were low. No longer protected by family or village community and church, some girls faced only one grim alternative—prostitution. In Paris, London, and many other large cities with transient populations, thousands of prostitutes plied their trade. One journalist estimated that in 1885 there were 60,000 prostitutes in London. Most prostitutes were active for a short time, usually from late teens through early twenties. Many eventually rejoined the regular work force or married when they could.

In most European countries, prostitution was licensed and regulated by government and municipal authorities. Although the British government provided minimal regulation of prostitution, it did attempt to enforce the Contagious Diseases Acts in the 1870s and 1880s by giving authorities the right to examine prostitutes for venereal disease. Those prostitutes with the disease were confined for some time to special institutions called lock hospitals, where they were given moral instruction. Opposition to the Contagious Diseases Acts by middle-class female reformers, who objected to laws that punished women and not men who suffered from venereal disease, led to the repeal of the acts in 1886.

Marriage, Family, and Children

Many women in the nineteenth century aspired to the ideal of femininity popularized by writers and poets. Alfred Lord Tennyson's *The Princess* expressed it well:

Man for the field and woman for the hearth:
Man for the sword and for the needle she:
Man with the head and woman with the heart:
Man to command and woman to obey;
All else confusion.

Historians have pointed out that this traditional characterization of the sexes, based on gender-defined social roles, was virtually elevated to the status of universal male and female attributes in the nineteenth century, largely due to the impact of the Industrial Revolution on the family. As the chief family wage earners, men worked outside the home while women were left with the care of the family for which they were paid nothing. Of course, the ideal did not always match reality, especially for the lower classes, where the need for supplemental income drove women to do "sweated" work.

For most women, marriage was viewed as the only honorable and available career throughout most of the nineteenth century. While the middle class glorified the ideal of domesticity (see the box on p. 827), for most women marriage was a matter of economic necessity. The lack of meaningful work and the lower wages paid to women made it difficult for single women to earn a living. Since retiring to convents as in the past was no longer an option, many spinsters, who could not find sufficiently remunerative work, entered domestic service as live-in servants. Most women chose instead to marry, which was reflected in the increase in marriage rates and a decline in illegitimacy rates in the course of the nineteenth century.

Birthrates also dropped significantly in the nineteenth century. The most significant development in the modern family was the decline in the number of offspring born to the average woman. The change was not necessarily due to new technology. Although the invention of the vulcanization of rubber in the 1840s made possible the production of condoms and diaphragms, they were not widely used as effective contraceptive devices until the era of World War I. Some historians maintain that the change in attitude that led parents to limit the number of offspring deliberately was more important than the method used. While some historians attribute increased birth control to more widespread use of coitus interruptus, or male withdrawal before ejaculation, others have emphasized female control of family size through abortion and even infanticide or abandonment. That a change in attitude occurred was apparent in the development of a movement to increase awareness of birth control methods. Authorities prosecuted those who spread information about contraception for "depraving public morals," but were unable to stop them. In 1882 in Amsterdam, Dr. Aletta Jacob founded Europe's first birth control clinic. Initially, "family planning" was the suggestion of reformers who thought that the problem of poverty could be solved by reducing the number of children among the lower classes. In fact, the practice spread quickly among the propertied classes, rather than among the impoverished, a good reminder that considerable differences still remained between middle-class and working-class families.

THE MIDDLE-CLASS FAMILY The family was the central institution of middle-class life. Men provided the family income while women focused on household and child care. The use of domestic servants in many middle-class homes, made possible by an abundant supply of cheap labor, reduced the amount of time middle-class women

Advice to Women: Be Dependent

▼ ▼ ▼

Industrialization had a strong impact on middle-class women as gender-based social roles became the norm. Men worked outside the home to support the family while women provided for the needs of their children and husband at home. In this selection, one woman gives advice to middle-class women on their proper role and behavior.

Elizabeth Poole Sanford, *Woman in Her Social and Domestic Character*

The changes wrought by Time are many. It influences the opinions of men as familiarity does their feelings; it has a tendency to do away with superstition, and to reduce every thing to its real worth.

It is thus that the sentiment for woman has undergone a change. The romantic passion which once almost deified her is on the decline; and it is by intrinsic qualities that she must now inspire respect. She is no longer the queen of song and the star of chivalry. But if there is less of enthusiasm entertained for her, the sentiment is more rational, and, perhaps, equally sincere; for it is in relation to happiness that she is chiefly appreciated.

And in this respect it is, we must confess, that she is most useful and most important. Domestic life is the chief source of her influence; and the greatest debt society can owe to her is domestic comfort: for happiness is almost an element of virtue; and nothing conduces more to improve the character of men than domestic peace. A woman may make a man's home delightful, and may thus increase his motives for virtuous exertion. She may refine and tranquillize his mind,—may turn away his anger or allay his grief. Her smile may be the happy influence to gladden his heart, and to disperse the cloud that gathers on his brow. And in proportion to her endeavors to make those around her happy, she will be esteemed and loved. She will secure by her excellence that interest and that regard which she might formerly claim as the privilege of her sex, and will really merit the deference which was then conceded to her as a matter of course. . . .

Perhaps one of the first secrets of her influence is adaptation to the tastes, and sympathy in the feelings, of those around her. This holds true in lesser as well as in graver points. It is in the former, indeed, that the absence of interest in a companion is frequently most disappointing. Where want of congeniality impairs domestic comfort, the fault is generally chargeable on the female side. It is for woman, not for man, to make the sacrifice, especially in indifferent matters. She must, in a certain degree, be plastic herself if she would mould others. . . .

Nothing is so likely to conciliate the affections of the other sex as a feeling that woman looks to them for support and guidance. In proportion as men are themselves superior, they are accessible to this appeal. On the contrary, they never feel interested in one who seems disposed rather to offer than to ask assistance. There is, indeed, something unfeminine in independence. It is contrary to nature, and therefore it offends. We do not like to see a woman affecting tremors, but still less do we like to see her acting the amazon. A really sensible woman feels her dependence. She does what she can; but she is conscious of inferiority, and therefore grateful for support. She knows that she is the weaker vessel, and that as such she should receive honor. In this view, her weakness is an attraction, not a blemish.

In every thing, therefore, that women attempt, they should show their consciousness of dependence. If they are learners, let them evince a teachable spirit; if they give an opinion, let them do it in an unassuming manner. There is something so unpleasant in female self-sufficiency that it not unfrequently deters instead of persuading, and prevents the adoption of advice which the judgment even approves.

---

had to spend on household work. At the same time, by reducing the number of children in the family, mothers could devote more time to child care and domestic leisure. The idea that leisure should be used for constructive purposes supported and encouraged the cult of middle-class domesticity.

The middle-class family fostered an ideal of togetherness. The Victorians created the family Christmas with its yule log, Christmas tree, songs, and exchange of gifts. In the United States, Fourth of July celebrations changed from drunken revels to family picnics by the 1850s. The education of middle-class females in domes-

▼ **A Middle-Class Family.** Nineteenth-century middle-class moralists considered the family the fundamental pillar of a healthy society. The family was a crucial institution in middle-class life, and togetherness constituted one of the important ideals of the middle-class family. This painting by William P. Frith, entitled *Many Happy Returns of the Day,* shows a family birthday celebration for a little girl in which grandparents, parents, and children take part. The servant at the left holds the presents for the little girl.

tic crafts, singing, and piano playing prepared them for their function of providing a proper environment for home recreation.

The new domestic ideal had an impact on child raising and children's play. Eighteenth-century Enlightenment thought had encouraged a new view of children as unique beings, not small adults, which had carried over into the nineteenth century. They were entitled to a long childhood involved in activities with other children their own age. The early environment in which they were raised, it was thought, would determine how they turned out. And mothers were seen as the most important force in protecting them from the harmful influences of the adult world. New children's games and toys, including mass-produced dolls for girls, appeared in middle-class homes. The middle-class emphasis on the functional value of knowledge was also evident in these games. One advice manual maintained that young children should learn checkers because it "calls forth the resources of the mind in the most gentle, as well as the most successful manner."

Since the sons of the middle-class family were intended to follow careers like their father's, they were isolated and kept in school until the age of sixteen or seventeen. Sport was used in the schools to "toughen" boys up while their leisure activities centered around

both national military concerns and character building. This combination was especially evident in the establishment of the Boy Scouts in Britain in 1908. Boy Scouts provided organized recreation for boys between twelve and eighteen in which adventure was combined with the discipline of earning merit badges and ranks in such a way as to instill ideals of patriotism and self-sacrifice. Many men viewed such activities as a corrective to the possible dangers that female domination of the home posed for male development. As one scout leader wrote, "The REAL Boy Scout is not a sissy. [He] adores his mother [but] is not hitched to [her] apron strings." There was little organized recreational activity of this type for girls, although Robert Baden-Powell, the founder of the Boy Scouts, did encourage his sister to establish a girls' division as an afterthought. Its goal is evident from Agnes Baden-Powell's comment that "you do not want to make tomboys of refined girls, yet you want to attract, and thus raise, the slum girl from the gutter. The main object is to give them all the ability to be better mothers and Guides to the next generation."[4] Despite her comment, most organizations of this kind were for middle-class children, although some reformers tried to establish boys' clubs for working-class youths to reform them.

The new ideal of the middle-class woman as nurturing mother and wife who "determined the atmosphere of the household" through her character, not her work, frequently did not correspond to reality. Recent research indicates that in France, Germany, and even mid-Victorian Britain, relatively few families could actually afford to hire a host of servants. More often, middle-class families had one servant, usually a young working-class or country girl not used to middle-class lifestyles. Women, then, were often forced to work quite hard to maintain the expected appearance of the well-ordered household. A German housekeeping manual makes this evident:

> If often happens that even high-ranking ladies help at home with housework, and particularly with kitchen chores, scrubbing, etc., so that, above all the hands have good cause to become very rough, hard, and calloused. When these ladies appear in society, they are extremely upset at having such rough-looking hands. In order to perform the hardest and most ordinary chores . . . and, at the same time, to keep a soft hand like those fine ladies who have no heavier work to do than embroidering and sewing, always keep a piece of fresh bacon, rub your hands with it just before bedtime, and you will fully achieve your goal. You will, as a result, have the inconvenience of having to sleep with gloves on, in order not to soil the bed.[5]

Many middle-class wives, then, were caught in a no-win situation. Often for the sake of the advancement of her husband's career, she was expected to maintain in public the image of the "idle" wife, freed from demeaning physical labor and able to pass her days in ornamental pursuits. In truth, it was frequently the middle-class woman who paid the price for this facade in a life of unpaid work, carefully managing the family budget and participating in housework that could never be done by simply one servant girl. As one historian has argued, the reality of many middle-class women's lives was that "what appears at first glance to be idleness is revealed, on closer examination, to be difficult and tiresome work."

THE WORKING-CLASS FAMILY   Hard work was, of course, standard fare for women in working-class families. Daughters in working-class families were expected to work until they married; even after marriage, they often did piecework at home to help support the family. For the children of the working classes, childhood was over by the age of nine or ten when they became apprentices or were employed in odd jobs.

Between 1890 and 1914, however, family patterns among the working class began to change. High-paying jobs in heavy industry and improvements in the standard of living made it possible for working-class families to depend on the income of husbands and the wages of grown children. By the early twentieth century, some working-class mothers could afford to stay at home, following the pattern of middle-class women. At the same time, new consumer products, such as sewing machines, clocks, bicycles, and cast-iron stoves, created a new mass consumer society whose focus was on higher levels of consumption.

These working-class families also followed the middle classes in limiting the size of their families. Children began to be viewed as dependents rather than wage earners as child labor laws and compulsory education took children out of the work force and into schools. Improvements in public health as well as advances in medicine and a better diet resulted in a decline in infant mortality rates for the lower classes, especially noticeable in the cities after 1890, and made it easier for working-class families to choose to have fewer children. At the same time, strikes and labor agitation (see Trade Unions later in the chapter) led to laws that reduced work hours to ten per day by 1900 and eliminated work on Saturday afternoons, which enabled working-class parents to devote more attention to their children and develop more emotional ties with them. Even working-class fathers became involved in their children's lives.

One observer in the French town of Belleville in the 1890s noted that "the workingman's love for his children borders on being an obsession."[6] Interest in educating children as a way to improve their future also grew.

The Rise of the Feminist Movement

Modern European feminism had its beginnings during the social upheaval of the French Revolution when some women advocated equality for women based on the doctrine of natural rights. Mary Wollstonecraft (1759–1797), who gave expression to this thinking in her book, *Vindication of the Rights of Woman*, is often viewed as the first modern feminist.

In the 1830s, a number of women in the United States and Europe, who worked together in several reform movements, became frustrated by the apparent prejudices against females. They sought improvements for women by focusing on specific goals. Family and marriage law were especially singled out since it was difficult for women to secure divorces and property laws gave husbands almost complete control over the property of their wives. These early efforts were not overly successful, however. For example, women did not gain the right to their own property until 1870 in Britain, 1900 in Germany, and 1907 in France.

Custody and property rights were only a beginning for the women's movement, however. Some middle- and upper-middle-class women gained access to higher education while others sought entry into occupations dominated by men. The first to fall was teaching. As medical training was largely closed to women, they sought alternatives in the development of nursing. A nursing pioneer in Germany was the upper-class spinster Amalie Sieveking (1794–1859), who founded the Female Association for the Care of the Poor and Sick in Hamburg. As she explained: "To me, at least as important were the benefits which [work with the poor] seemed to promise for those of my sisters who would join me in such a work of charity. The higher interests of my sex were close to my heart."[7] Sieveking's work was followed by the more famous British nurse, Florence Nightingale, whose efforts during the Crimean War (1854–1856), combined with those of Clara Barton in the American Civil War (1861–1865), transformed nursing into a profession of trained, middle-class "women in white."

By the 1840s and 1850s, the movement for women's rights had entered the political arena with the call for equal political rights. Many feminists believed that the right to vote was the key to all other reforms to improve

Advice to Women: Be Independent

▼ ▼ ▼

Although a majority of women probably followed the nineteenth-century middle-class ideal of women as keepers of the household and nurturers of husband and children, an increasing number of women fought for the rights of women. This selection is taken from Act III of Henrik Ibsen's A Doll's House (1879), in which the character Nora Helmer declares her independence from her husband's control.

Henrik Ibsen: A Doll's House

NORA: (Pause) Does anything strike you as we sit here?

HELMER: What should strike me?

NORA: We've been married eight years; does it not strike you that this is the first time we two, you and I, man and wife, have talked together seriously?

HELMER: Seriously? What do you mean, seriously?

NORA: For eight whole years, and more—ever since the day we first met—we have never exchanged one serious word about serious things. . . .

HELMER: Why, my dearest Nora, what have you to do with serious things?

NORA: There we have it! You have never understood me. I've had great injustice done to me, Torvald; first by father, then by you.

HELMER: What! Your father and me? We, who have loved you more than all the world?

NORA (Shaking her head): You have never loved me. You just found it amusing to think you were in love with me.

HELMER: Nora! What a thing to say!

NORA: Yes, it's true, Torvald. When I was living at home with father, he told me his opinions and mine were the same. If I had different opinions, I said nothing about them, because he would not have liked it. He used to call me his doll-child and played with me as I played with my dolls. Then I came to live in your house.

HELMER: What a way to speak of our marriage!

NORA (Undisturbed): I mean that I passed from father's hands into yours. You arranged everything to your taste and I got the same tastes as you; or pretended to—I don't know which—both, perhaps; sometimes one, sometimes the other. When I look back on it now, I seem to have been living here like a beggar, on hand-outs. I lived by performing tricks for you, Torvald. But that was how you wanted it. You and father have done me a great wrong. It is your fault that my life has come to naught.

HELMER: Why, Nora, how unreasonable and ungrateful! Haven't you been happy here?

NORA: No, never. I thought I was, but I never was.

HELMER: Not—not happy! . . .

NORA: I must stand quite alone if I am ever to know myself and my surroundings; so I cannot stay with you.

HELMER: Nora! Nora!

NORA: I am going at once. I daresay [my friend] Christina will take me in for tonight.

HELMER: You are mad! I shall not allow it! I forbid it!

NORA: It's no use your forbidding me anything now. I shall take with me only what belongs to me; from you I will accept nothing, either now or later.

HELMER: This is madness!

NORA: Tomorrow I shall go home—I mean to what was my home. It will be easier for me to find a job there.

HELMER: On, in your blind inexperience—

NORA: I must try to gain experience, Torvald.

HELMER: Forsake your home, your husband, your children! And you don't consider what the world will say.

NORA: I can't pay attention to that. I only know that I must do it.

HELMER: This is monstrous! Can you forsake your holiest duties?

NORA: What do you consider my holiest duties?

HELMER: Need I tell you that? Your duties to your husband and children.

NORA: I have other duties equally sacred.

HELMER: Impossible! What do you mean?

NORA: My duties toward myself.

HELMER: Before all else you are a wife and a mother.

NORA: That I no longer believe. Before all else I believe I am a human being just as much as you are—or at least that I should try to become one. I know that most people agree with you, Torvald, and that they say so in books. But I can no longer be satisfied with what most people say and what is in books. I must think things out for myself and try to get clear about them.

the position of women. This movement was strongest in Great Britain and the United States, both countries that had been influenced by the natural rights tradition of the Enlightenment. It was not as strong in Germany because of that country's authoritarian structure nor in France where feminists were unable to organize mass rallies in support of women's rights. Suffragists had one basic aim, the right of women to full citizenship in the nation-state (see the box on p. 830).

The British women's movement was the most vocal and active in Europe, but divided over tactics. The liberal Millicent Fawcett (1847–1929) organized a moderate group who believed that women must demonstrate that they would use political power responsibly if they wanted Parliament to grant them the right to vote. Another group, however, favored a more radical approach. Emmeline Pankhurst (1858–1928) and her daughters, Christabel and Sylvia, founded the Women's Social and Political Union in 1903, which enrolled mostly middle- and upper-class women. Pankhurst's organization realized the value of the media and used unusual publicity stunts to call attention to its demands. Derisively labeled suffragettes by male politicians, they pelted government officials with eggs, chained themselves to lampposts, smashed the windows of department stores on fashionable shopping streets, burned railroad cars, and went on hunger strikes in jail. In 1913, Emily Davison accepted martyrdom for the cause when she threw herself in front of the king's horse at the Epsom Derby horse race.

Before World War I, the demands for women's rights were being heard throughout Europe and the United States. Only in Norway and some American states did women actually receive the right to vote before 1914. It would take the dramatic upheaval of World War I before male-dominated governments capitulated on this basic issue (see Chapter 26).

▼ The Socialist Movement

A commonly heard phrase in the second half of the nineteenth century was the "social question," which referred to the debate over class relations and the condition of the poor. The most important response to this "social question" came from the socialist movement.

In 1872, Karl Marx and Friedrich Engels had allowed the International Working Men's Association or First International to wither away (see Chapter 23). A Second International was not formed until 1889, six years after Marx's death. By that time the workingmen's movement had undergone a significant growth and

▼ **The Arrest of Suffragettes.** The nineteenth century witnessed the development of a strong movement for women's rights. For many feminists, the right to vote came to represent the key to making other reforms that would benefit women. In Britain, so-called suffragettes attracted attention to their cause by unusual publicity stunts. This photograph shows the arrest of suffragettes after a demonstration near Buckingham Palace, the London residence of the royal family.

transformation with rise of socialist parties and trade unions, most of which were Marxist in orientation.

The Socialist Parties

The growth of socialist parties after the demise of the First International was rapid and widespread. Most important was the formation of a socialist party in Germany. Ferdinand Lassalle had founded a German Workingman's Association in 1863 that advocated the nonrevolutionary use of political action to make gains for the working classes. After his death, his followers joined with advocates of Marxism to form the German Social Democratic party (SPD) in 1875. Under the direction of its two Marxist leaders, Wilhelm Liebknecht and August Bebel, the SPD espoused revolutionary Marxist rhetoric while organizing itself as a mass political party competing in elections for the Reichstag. Once in the Reichstag, SPD delegates worked to achieve legislation to improve the condition of the working class. As August Bebel explained, "Pure negation would not be accepted by the voters. The masses demand that something should be done for today irrespective of what will happen on the morrow."[8] Despite government efforts to destroy it (see The New Germany later in the chapter), the German Social Democratic party continued to grow. In 1890, it received 1.5 million votes and thirty-five seats in the Reichstag. When it received 4

▼ **The Social Democratic Party in Germany.** The German Social Democratic party was formed in 1875. Although Social Democrats preached revolutionary Marxist rhetoric, they also organized themselves as a mass political organization and competed for seats in the Reichstag, the German parliament. Once in the Reichstag, Social Democrats introduced legislation to benefit the workers. Shown here is a session of the Social Democratic party in Berlin on November 14, 1892.

million votes in the 1912 elections, it became the largest single party in Germany, although it still refused for ideological reasons to participate in a coalition government.

Socialist parties emerged in other European states, although not with the kind of success achieved by the German Social Democrats. France had a variety of socialist parties, including a Marxist one. The leader of French socialism, Jean Jaurès, was an independent socialist who looked to the French revolutionary tradition rather than Marxism to justify revolutionary socialism. In 1905, the French socialist parties succeeded in unifying themselves into a single mostly Marxist-oriented socialist party. Social Democratic parties on the German model were founded in Belgium, Austria, Hungary, Bulgaria, Poland, Romania, and the Netherlands before 1900. A Marxist Social Democratic Labor party had also been organized in Russia by 1898.

As the socialist parties grew, agitation for an international organization that would strengthen their position against international capitalism also grew. In 1889, leaders of the various socialist parties formed the Second International. Significantly, while the First International had been formed by individuals and had been highly centralized, the Second International was created by representatives of national working-class parties and was organized as a loose association of national groups. It was not until 1900 that a permanent executive was established for the organization. While the Second Inter-

national took some coordinated actions—May Day (May 1), for example, was made an international labor day to be marked by strikes and mass labor demonstrations—differences often wreaked havoc at the congresses of the organization. Two issues proved particularly divisive: revisionism and nationalism.

Under the impact of government persecution, the ideology of the German Social Democratic party became increasingly revolutionary. In 1891, the Erfurt Program of the party had reaffirmed an almost pure Marxian platform that accepted the imminent collapse of capitalism and the need for socialist ownership of the means of production. The party's guiding light, August Bebel, confided to another socialist that "Every night I go to sleep with the thought that the last hour of bourgeois society strikes soon." In fact, already at Erfurt, Bebel had said, "I am convinced that the fulfillment of our aims is so close, that there are few in this hall who will not live to see the day."[9] But a severe challenge to this orthodox Marxist position arose in the form of revisionism.

Most prominent among the revisionists was Eduard Bernstein(1850–1932), a member of the German Social Democratic party who had spent years in exile in Britain where he had been influenced by moderate English socialism and the British parliamentary system. In 1899, Bernstein challenged Marxist orthodoxy with a book entitled *Evolutionary Socialism* in which he argued that some of Marx's ideas had turned out to be quite wrong (see the box on p. 833). The capitalist system had not broken down, nor, said Bernstein, did its collapse seem near. Contrary to Marx's assertion, the middle class was not declining but actually growing larger. At the same time, the proletariat was not sinking further down, but its lot was actually improving as workers experienced a higher standard of living. Due to this reality, Bernstein abandoned Marx's emphasis on the class struggle and revolution. The workers, he asserted, must continue to organize in mass political parties and even work together with the other progressive elements in a nation to gain reform. With the extension of the right to vote, workers were in a better position than ever to achieve their aims by democratic channels. Evolution by democratic means, not revolution, would achieve the desired goal of socialism. German and French socialist leaders, as well as the Second International, condemned revisionism as heresy and opportunism. But many socialist parties, including the German Social Democrats, while spouting revolutionary slogans, continued to practice Bernstein's revisionist, gradualist approach.

A second divisive issue for international socialism was nationalism. Karl Marx and Friedrich Engels had said

The Voice of Evolutionary Socialism: Eduard Bernstein

▼ ▼ ▼

T*he German Marxist Eduard Bernstein was regarded as the foremost late nineteenth-century theorist of Marxist revisionism. In his book,* Evolutionary Socialism, *Bernstein argued that Marx had made some fundamental mistakes and that socialists needed to stress cooperation and evolution rather than class conflict and revolution.*

Eduard Bernstein, *Evolutionary Socialism*

It has been maintained in a certain quarter that the practical deductions from my treatises would be the abandonment of the conquest of political power by the proletariat organised politically and economically. That is quite an arbitrary deduction, the accuracy of which I altogether deny.

I set myself against the notion that we have to expect shortly a collapse of the bourgeois economy, and that social democracy should be induced by the prospect of such an imminent, great, social catastrophe to adapt its tactics to that assumption. That I maintain most emphatically.

The adherents of this theory of a catastrophe, base it especially on the conclusions of the *Communist Manifesto*. This is a mistake in every respect.

The theory which the *Communist Manifesto* sets forth of the evolution of modern society was correct as far as it characterised the general tendencies of that evolution. But it was mistaken in several special deductions, above all in the estimate of the time the evolution would take. . . . But it is evident that if social evolution takes a much greater period of time than was assumed, it must also take upon itself forms and lead to forms that were not foreseen and could not be foreseen then.

Social conditions have not developed to such an acute opposition of things and classes as is depicted in the *Manifesto*. It is not only useless, it is the greatest folly to attempt to conceal this from ourselves. The number of members of the possessing classes is to-day not smaller but larger. The enormous increase of social wealth is not accompanied by a decreasing number of large capitalists but by an increasing number of capitalists of all degrees. The middle classes change their character but they do not disappear from the social scale. . . .

In all advanced countries we see the privileges of the capitalist bourgeoisie yielding step by step to democratic organisations. Under the influence of this, and driven by the movement of the working classes which is daily becoming stronger, a social reaction has set in against the exploiting tendencies of capital, a counteraction which, although it still proceeds timidly and feebly, yet does exist, and is always drawing more departments of economic life under its influence. Factory legislation, the democratising of local government, and the extension of its area of work, the freeing of trade unions and systems of co-operative trading from legal restrictions, the consideration of standard conditions of labour in the work undertaken by public authorities—all these characterise this phase of the evolution.

But the more the political organisations of modern nations are democratised the more the needs and opportunities of great political catastrophes are diminished. . . . But is the conquest of political power by the proletariat simply to be by a political catastrophe? Is it to be the appropriation and utilisation of the power of the State by the proletariat exclusively against the whole non-proletarian world? . . .

No one has questioned the necessity for the working classes to gain the control of government. The point at issue is between the theory of a social cataclysm and the question whether, with the given social development in Germany and the present advanced state of its working classes in the towns and the country, a sudden catastrophe would be desirable in the interest of the social democracy. I have denied it and deny it again, because in my judgment a greater security for lasting success lies in a steady advance than in the possibilities offered by a catastrophic crash.

that "the working men have no country" and that "national differences and antagonisms between peoples are daily more and more vanishing, owing to the development of the bourgeoisie."[10] They proved drastically wrong. Congresses of the Second International passed resolutions in 1907 and 1910 advocating joint action by workers of different countries to avert war, but no real machinery was provided to implement them. In truth, socialist parties varied from country to country and remained tied to national concerns and issues. Socialist leaders always worried that in the end national loyalties might outweigh class loyalties among the masses. When World War I came in 1914, not only the working-class masses, but even many of their socialist party leaders, supported the war efforts of their national governments. Nationalism had proved a much more powerful force than socialism, an observation not lost on a young Austrian named Adolf Hitler who fought in World War I.

Trade Unions

Another force working for evolutionary rather than revolutionary socialism and at the same time an expression of a nationalistically oriented socialism was the development of trade unions. Trade unions were not new since they had a history dating back to the Late Middle Ages. The modern trade union, however, was a product of the Industrial Revolution. Initially, European governments tried to suppress the development of trade unions. The Le Chapelier Law in France in 1791 and the Combination Laws of 1799 and 1800 in Great Britain prohibited the formation of trade unions. But prohibitions seemed counterproductive, and European nations found themselves allowing workers to form trade unions while still seeking to prohibit them from such overt action as strikes.

In Great Britain trade unions were legalized with the repeal of the Combination Laws in 1824 and 1825, although the unions did not receive the right to strike. Failure to achieve national trade union organizations over the next two decades led to a reversion to the practice of forming trade unions for skilled workers in specialized crafts, such as the Amalgamated Society of Engineers, formed in 1850. These New Model unions, as they have been called, worked to better their members' wages and improve working conditions by peaceful negotiations with employers. Self-help, in the form of unemployment benefits collected from members' own contributions, was typical of their activity. They avoided political activity and strikes. But New Model unions,

mostly of "elite" skilled craftsmen, were of little help to the masses of unskilled and semiskilled workers in factory industries. Attempts to organize them did not come until the last two decades of the nineteenth century after unions had won the right to strike in the 1870s. Strikes proved necessary to achieve the goals of these workers. A walkout by female workers in the match industry in 1888 and dock workers in London the following year led to the establishment of trade union organizations for both groups. By 1900, there were two million workers in British trade unions, and by the outbreak of World War I, between three and four million workers, less than one-fifth of the total work force, were collectively organized.

Trade unions failed to develop as quickly on the Continent as they had in Britain. In France, the trade union movement was from the beginning closely tied to the socialist ideology. As there were a number of French socialist parties, the socialist trade unions remained badly splintered. Not until 1895 did French unions create a national organization called the General Confederation of Labor. Its decentralization and failure to include some of the more important individual unions, however, left it a weak and ineffective movement.

German trade unions, also closely attached to political parties, were first formed in the 1860s. Although there were liberal trade unions comprised of skilled craftsmen and Catholic or Christian trade unions, the largest German trade unions were those of the socialists. By 1899, even the latter had accepted the practice of collective bargaining with employers. As strikes and collective bargaining achieved successes, German workers were increasingly inclined to forgo revolution for gradual improvements. By 1914, its three million members made the German trade union movement the second largest in Europe after Great Britain's. Almost 85 percent of these three million belonged to socialist unions.

Trade unions in the rest of Europe had varying degrees of success. In the Low Countries, Switzerland, and Austria-Hungary, they followed the German model. Despite local successes, governments prevented them from operating well at a national level. Like the French, the Spanish and Italian trade unions tended toward ideology and divisiveness. Trade unions were prohibited in both Russia and eastern Europe until World War I. Perhaps most successful were the Scandinavian trade unions, which were closely allied with Social Democratic political parties. By the beginning of World War I, they had made considerable progress in bettering both the living and working conditions of the laboring classes.

Anarchism

Despite the revolutionary rhetoric, socialist parties and trade unions gradually became less radical in pursuing their goals. Indeed, this lack of revolutionary fervor drove some people from Marxian socialism into anarchism, a movement that was especially prominent in less industrialized and less democratic countries. The growth of universal male suffrage in Great Britain, France, and Germany had led workers there to believe that they could acquire tangible benefits by elections, not by revolution. These democratic channels were not open in other countries where revolutionary violence seemed the only alternative.

Initially, anarchism was not a violent movement. Early anarchists, such as Pierre-Joseph Proudhon, believed that people were inherently good but corrupted by the state and society. True freedom could only by accomplished by elimination of the state and all existing social institutions. Voluntary cooperation of people in small communities would eliminate the need for the state. Only then could people use their freedom to cooperate toward common ends.

In the second half of the nineteenth century, anarchists in Spain, Portugal, Italy, and Russia advocated radical means to accomplish this goal. The Russian Michael Bakunin, for example, believed that small groups of well-trained, fanatical revolutionaries could perpetrate so much violence that the state and all its institutions would disintegrate. To revolutionary anarchists, that would usher in the anarchist Golden Age. As one Russian anarchist wrote shortly before his execution:

> Slavery, poverty, weakness, and ignorance—the eternal fetters of man—will be broken. Man will be at the center of nature. The earth and its products will serve everyone dutifully. Weapons will cease to be a measure of strength and gold a measure of wealth; the strong will be those who are bold and daring in the conquest of nature, and riches will be the things that are useful. Such a world is called "Anarchy." It will have no castles, no place for masters and slaves. Life will be open to all. Everyone will take what he needs—this is the anarchist ideal. And when it comes about, men will live wisely and well. The masses must take part in the construction of this paradise on earth.[11]

After Bakunin's death in 1876, anarchist revolutionaries used assassinations as their primary instrument of terror. The list of victims of anarchist assassins at the turn of the century included a Russian tsar (1881), a president of the French Republic (1894), the king of Italy (1900), and a president of the United States (1901). Despite anarchist hopes, these states did not collapse.

▼ The National State: Domestic Politics

Throughout much of Europe by 1871, the national state had become the focus of people's loyalties and the arena for political activity. Only in Russia, eastern Europe, Austria-Hungary, and Ireland did national groups still struggle for independence and political unity. Within the major European states, domestic politics focused on five major themes: the achievement of liberal practices (constitutions, parliaments, and individual liberties); the growth of political democracy through universal male suffrage; the organization of mass political parties as a result of a widened electorate; the rise of socialist, working-class parties; and the enactment of social welfare measures to meet the demands of the working classes. These developments varied in expression from place to place. In general, western European states (France and Britain) and, to a lesser degree, Mediterranean states (Spain and Italy) had the greatest success with the growth of parliamentary governments. Central European states (Germany, Austria-Hungary) had the trappings of parliamentary government with their legislative bodies and elections by universal male suffrage, but authoritarian forces, especially powerful monarchies and conservative social groups, remained strong. In eastern Europe, especially Russia, the old system of autocracy was barely touched by the winds of change.

Great Britain

By the end of the first liberal ministry of William Gladstone in 1874, Great Britain had a functioning two-party parliamentary system. For fifty years the Liberals and Conservatives alternated in power at regular intervals. Liberals and Conservatives, however, shared one common feature. Both were dominated by a ruling class comprised of a coalition of aristocratic landowners frequently involved in industrial and financial activities and upper-middle-class businessmen. Three major developments preoccupied British domestic politics until 1914: the growth of political democracy; social welfare legislation for the workers; and the Irish question.

The cause of political democracy was pushed along by the expansion of suffrage. Much advanced by the Re-

▼ **William Gladstone in His Later Years.** The first Liberal ministry of William Gladstone had been responsible for a series of significant liberal reforms. During his second ministry, Gladstone and the Liberals expanded the right to vote by enfranchising agricultural workers. Gladstone had much less political success when he tried to solve the problem of Ireland.

After 1911, the House of Lords became largely a debating society. Also in 1911, the payment of salaries to members of the House of Commons further democratized that institution by at least opening the door to people other than the wealthy. By the beginning of World War I, the British system of gradual reform through parliamentary institutions had become the way of British political life. Political democracy became well entrenched and was soon accompanied by social welfare measures for the working class.

Some social legislation had already been passed during the Conservative ministry of Benjamin Disraeli between 1874 and 1880. In 1875, trade unions had been given the right to strike, and a work week limited to fifty-six hours had been established for factory workers. But there was little other significant reform. While workers were enjoying better wages and living standards, those improvements were relative to the miseries of the first half of the nineteenth century. Considerable suffering still remained. Neither Liberals nor Conservatives were moved to accommodate the working class with significant social reforms until they were forced to do so by the pressure of two new working class organizations: trade unions and the Labor party.

Trade unions began to advocate more radical change of the economic system, calling for "collective ownership and control over production, distribution and exchange." At the same time, there was a movement for laborers among a group of intellectuals known as the Fabian Socialists, which included the playwright George Bernard Shaw, the novelist H. G. Wells, and the social reformers Beatrice and Sidney Webb. The program of the Fabians stressed the need for the workingman to use his right to vote to capture the House of Commons and pass legislation that would benefit the laboring class. Much of the socialism of the Fabians was to be applied at the local level, as in the creation of city-owned water works and power plants. Neither the Fabian socialists nor the British trade unions were Marxist oriented. They did not advocate class struggle and revolution but evolution by democratic means toward a socialist state. In 1900, representatives of the trade unions and Fabian Socialists coalesced to form the Labour party. Initially, they were not too successful, but by 1906 they had managed to elect twenty-nine members to the House of Commons.

The Liberals, who won control of the House of Commons in that year and held the government from 1906 to 1914, perceived that they would have to create a program of social welfare or lose the support of the workers. The policy of reform was especially advanced by David

form Act of 1867 (see Chapter 23), the right to vote was further extended during the second ministry of William Gladstone (1880–1885) with the passage of the Reform Act of 1884. It gave the vote to all men who paid regular rents or taxes, thus largely enfranchising the agricultural workers, a group previously excluded. The following year, a Redistribution Act (1885) eliminated historic boroughs and counties and established constituencies with approximately equal populations and one representative each.

Before World War I, the role of the House of Lords, composed of hereditary aristocrats, was also transformed. A Parliamentary Act in 1911 restricted the ability of the House of Lords to impede legislation enacted by the

A Parliamentary Debate on Old Age Pensions
▼ ▼ ▼

After the new British Labour party succeeded in electing twenty-nine of its candidates to the House of Commons in 1906, the ruling Liberals realized the need to provide a program of social legislation if they wished to keep working-class support. In 1908, they introduced a bill providing for old age pensions to be paid by the state to those seventy or older. These excerpts are taken from the parliamentary debate over the bill.

A Labour View on Old Age Pensions

After all, who are these old men and women? Let me appeal to the noble Lord the Member of Marylebone [Lord Robert Cecil]. They are the veterans of industry, people of almost endless toil, who have fought for and won the industrial and commercial supremacy of Great Britain. Is their lot and end to be the Bastille of the everlasting slur of pauperism? We claim these pensions as a right. Ruskin, I think, read you a little homily on the subject—"Even a laborer serves his country with his spade and shovel as the statesman does with his pen, or the soldier with his sword." He has a right to some consideration from the State. Here in a country rich beyond description there are people poverty-stricken beyond description. There can be no earthly excuse for the condition of things which exists in this country today. If it be necessary to have a strong Army and Navy to protect the wealth of the nation, do not let us forget that it is the veterans of industry who have created that wealth; and let us accept this as an installment to bring decency and comfort to our aged men and women.

A Bishop's View on the Subject

We are going forward tonight and saying: "Let us help them [those of seventy years of age], let us give to them something which will ease their later years, and if a few have not deserved well, we will at any rate with large-heartedness forget those who were weak and deal largely and generously with this matter before us, for all these men or women of seventy naturally appeal to the pity and sympathy of our hearts." But when I look beyond and ask whether it is conceivable that we may begin so to hold out the thought that men may be able to receive from the State that which in olden days they won by their own strong labors, self-denial, and thrift, then I am apprehensive lest we should, in attempting to do a good, do a great and grievous wrong, robbing ourselves and our children of that which is the best inheritance, the inheritance of a sturdy, strong, self-reliant manhood, that will take upon itself the responsibilities of life and be equal, therefore, to the responsibilities of Empire. I think none of us can shut our eyes to the fact that there are among us people who are very ready to shirk responsibility, and I, for one, would feel that the whole system and condition of English life had lost its meaning and value if once we should act in such fashion as to remove responsibility, and the sense of responsibility, from the people of this country. We are in this world for responsibility; through responsibility we grow and rise to the height of character which Divine Providence intended us to reach. Let us not, by any action of ours, weaken that which is the best thing we can preserve, the character of the population, for out of that, and out of that alone, will spring the strength and the stability of the nation.

Lloyd George (1863-1945), a brilliant young orator from Wales who had been deeply moved by the misery of Welsh coal miners. The Liberals abandoned the classical principles of laissez-faire and voted for a series of social reforms. The National Insurance Act of 1911 provided benefits for workers in case of sickness and unemployment, to be paid for by compulsory contributions from workers, employers, and the state. Additional legislation provided a small pension for those over seventy (see the box above) and compensation for those injured in accidents while at work. To pay for the new program, Lloyd George increased the tax burden on the wealthy classes. While the benefits of the program and tax increases were both modest, they were the first hesitant steps toward the future British welfare state.

A third problem—the Irish question—proved more difficult to solve. The Irish had long been subject to British rule. An Act of Union had brought the English

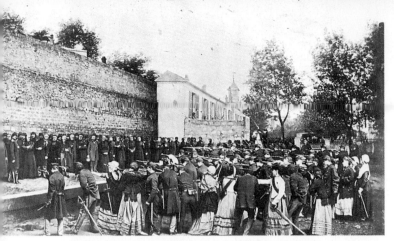

▼ **Revolutionary Violence in the Commune.** Defeat in war brought the collapse of Napoleon III's Second Empire in 1871. The authority of the newly-created National Assembly was soon challenged by the Commune, an independent republican government in Paris. The attempt by the National Assembly to crush the Commune led to vicious fighting and brutal reprisals. This photograph shows the execution of 62 hostages by the forces of the Commune.

and Irish parliaments together in 1801, while largely Catholic Ireland had its own official Protestant church—the Church of Ireland. Irish discontent was intense in the nineteenth century. Like other unfree ethnic groups in Europe, the Irish developed a sense of national self-consciousness. They detested the Protestant establishment and the absentee British landlords and their burdensome rents.

William Gladstone was the first British politician to attempt to alleviate Irish discontent. In 1869, Parliament ended the domination of the Church of Ireland by eliminating its official church status and stripping it of half of its property. The Land Law of 1870 accomplished little, however, and as evictions of Irish tenants increased in the 1870s, the Irish peasants responded with terrorist acts. The government reacted in turn with more coercion. In 1881, when Gladstone pushed a Land Act through Parliament that met most of the Irish demands, it was already too late. By this time Irish Catholics wanted only independence. Although Liberals introduced home rule bills that would have given Ireland self-government in 1886 and 1893, they failed to win a majority vote. Only after the Irish representatives in Parliament supported the Liberal reforms against the House of Lords did the Liberals finally enact a Home Rule Act in 1914. But an explosive situation in Ireland itself created more problems. Irish Protestants in northern Ireland, especially in the province of Ulster, wanted no part of an Irish Catholic state. The outbreak of World War I enabled the government to sidestep the poten-

tially explosive issue and to suspend Irish home rule for the duration of the war. Failure to deal decisively with the issue simply led to more problems later.

Between 1815 and 1914, Britain made the shift from classical liberalism to political democracy. The transition was not as smooth as has sometimes been claimed, however. The Irish question, for example, resulted in considerable violence on both sides. The growth of parliamentary democracy also served to make increasing numbers of British aware of the gross financial and social inequalities existing in their country. Especially among the working classes, this awareness led to more determined and even violent action in the form of direct action or strikes in 1911 and 1912. Serious tensions remained in the British system, and World War I would make them all the more obvious.

France

The defeat of the French armies and the capture of Napoleon III at Sedan on September 2–3, 1870, brought the downfall of the Second Empire. Republicans established a provisional government and continued the war with Germany but were forced to surrender by January 28, 1871. Wanting to make peace only with a properly constituted government, the victorious Otto von Bismarck insisted that the French establish a government chosen by universal male suffrage. The French people rejected the republicans who wanted to renew the war and overwhelmingly favored the monarchists who won 400 of the 630 seats in the new National Assembly.

After the National Assembly decided to establish itself at Versailles, radical republicans in Paris, feeling betrayed by the conservative National Assembly, created an independent republican government in Paris known as the Commune on March 26 (see the box on p. 839). Although Karl Marx in London proclaimed the Commune's action as the beginning of the proletarian socialist revolution, the radical lower-middle-class and working-class supporters of the Commune were inspired more by the revolutionary ideals of 1789 and 1848 than by Marxist theory. The National Assembly determined to crush the revolutionary Commune. Vicious fighting in April and May finally ended in a government victory when government troops in the last week of May massacred thousands of the Commune's defenders. Estimates are that 20,000 were shot; another 10,000 were shipped overseas to the French penal colony of New Caledonia. The horrors of the suppression of the Commune left a legacy of hatred that continued to plague French politics

Parisian Violence

▼ ▼ ▼

In March 1871, an insurrection erupted in Paris when the National Assembly attempted to disarm the Parisian National Guard. When troops were sent to seize guns that had been moved earlier to the hills of Montmartre, fighting broke out. Georges Clemenceau, the mayor of Montmartre, wrote a description of the day's events. Two generals had been taken prisoner by the National Guard and shot before Clemenceau could arrive to prevent it. This excerpt describes what happened next. Eight days after the events described here, the Parisians established the Commune.

Georges Clemenceau, How the Uprising Began, March 18, 1871

We had hardly turned the corner of the wall when a man ran up and said that the Generals had just been shot. We did not stop to answer him but ran even faster. He did not seem very sure of his facts, anyhow, and seemed to be repeating a rumor rather than something he had seen for himself.

The *Buttes* [hills of Montmartre] were covered with armed National Guards. We made our way into this crowd. My sash called everybody's attention to me, and I at once became the object of the most hostile demonstrations. They reproached me for having conspired with the Government to have the guns taken away, they accused me of betraying the National Guard, they insulted me.

Keeping between Mayer and Sabourdy, who were both fairly well-known in the *arrondissement* [district] and were my only safeguard, I continued on my way without answering.

As we went on, I heard people saying, "It's all over! Justice has been done! The traitors are punished! If anybody doesn't like it, we'll do the same to him! It's too late!" . . . It was no longer possible to doubt the assassination of the Generals, for everyone was repeating the news with somber enthusiasm. . . .

Suddenly there was a great noise, and the mob which filled the courtyard of no. 6 burst into the street, in the grip of a kind of frenzy.

There were chasseurs, soldiers of the line, National Guards, women and children. They were all shrieking like wild beasts, without realizing what they were doing. I observed then that pathological phenomenon which could be called blood lust. A breath of madness seemed to have passed over this mob. From the top of a wall children were waving indescribable trophies, women with streaming hair and all disheveled twisted their bare arms and uttered raucous cries, bereft of any sense. I saw some of them weeping and shouting louder than the others. Men were dancing about and jostling one another in a kind of frenzied fury. It was one of those nervous phenomena so frequent in the Middle Ages, and occasionally occurring still among masses of human beings under the stress of some powerful emotion.

Suddenly a piece of artillery, drawn by four horses, arrived in front of the house. The confusion increased, if that was possible. Men clad in ill-matched uniforms, riding on the horses, swore and shouted. I saw one woman jump onto one of the horses. She was waving her bonnet and yelling, "Down with the traitors!"—a cry the crowd repeated and repeated.

The situation was becoming more and more dangerous for me. The mob looked at me in crazed defiance, shouting its cry of "Down with the traitors!" Several fists were raised.

I could do nothing more in this place. I had not been able to prevent the crime. It remained for me to look after the fate of the prisoners whom I had just seen go by, and to stop any misfortune befalling my prisoners at the Mairie, against whom there was very great hostility.

---

for decades. The split between the middle and working classes, begun in the revolutionary hostilities of 1848–1849, had widened immensely.

Although a majority of the members of the monarchist-dominated National Assembly wished to restore a monarchy to France, inability to agree on who should be king caused the monarchists to miss their opportunity and led to a improvised constitution in 1875 that established a republican form of government as the least divisive compromise. This constitution established a bicameral legislature with an upper house or Senate elected indirectly and a lower house or Chamber of Deputies chosen by universal male suffrage. The powers of the president, chosen by the legislature for seven years as executive of the government, were not completely defined as many expected that his place would soon be taken by a king. But the Constitution of 1875, intended only as a stopgap measure, solidified the republic—the Third Republic—that lasted sixty-five years. New elections in 1876 and 1877 strengthened the hands of the republicans who managed by 1879 to create ministerial responsibility and establish the power of the Chamber of Deputies. The prime minister or premier and his ministers were now responsible not to the president, but to the Chamber of Deputies. France failed, however, to develop a strong parliamentary system on the British model because the existence of a dozen political parties forced a premier to depend upon a coalition of parties to stay in power. The Third Republic was notorious for its changes of government. Between 1875 and 1914, there were no fewer than fifty cabinet changes; during the same period, the British had nine. But figures can be misleading. Despite the numerous changes, the same politicians tended to appear in almost every cabinet. Moreover, since France was by and large a nation of small businessmen and farmers, the numerous political parties appealed to similar constituencies and reflected only minor differences.

Nevertheless, the position of the Third Republic remained precarious after 1875 because monarchists, Catholic clergy, and professional army officers remained its enemies. The government's moderation gradually encouraged more and more middle-class and peasant support. This did not prevent two major crises for the republic in the 1880s and 1890s.

The first of these crises actually served to strengthen the republican government. General Georges Boulanger (1837–1891) was a popular military officer who attracted the public attention of all those discontented with the Third Republic: the monarchists, Bonapartists, aristocrats, and nationalists who favored a war of revenge against Germany. Boulanger appeared as the strong man on horseback, the savior of France. By 1889, just when his strength had grown to the point where many expected a coup d'etat, he lost his nerve and fled France, a completely discredited man. In the long run, the Boulanger crisis served to rally support for the resilient republic.

Perhaps the strongest indication of the fragile nature of the democratic structure of France and an expression of a renewed anti-Semitism in the late nineteenth century was the Dreyfus affair. Alfred Dreyfus, a Jew, was a captain in the French general staff, who was found guilty by a secret military court early in 1895 of selling army secrets and condemned to life imprisonment on Devil's Island. Evidence soon emerged that pointed to his innocence. Another officer, a Catholic aristocrat, was more obviously the traitor, but the army, a stronghold of aristocratic and Catholic officers, refused a new trial. Republican leaders insisted, however, after a wave of immense public outrage. Although the new trial failed to set aside the guilty verdict, the government pardoned Dreyfus in 1899, and in 1906, he was finally fully exonerated.

One result of his whole sorry affair was a change in government. Moderate republicans lost control of the government to radical republicans who were determined to make greater progress toward a more democratic society by breaking the power of the republic's enemies, especially the army and the Catholic church. The army was purged of all high-ranking officers who had antirepublican reputations while a civilian official, the minister for war, was now placed in charge of all promotions to the rank of general. Most of the Catholic religious orders that had controlled many French schools were forced to leave France. Moreover, church and state were officially separated in 1905.

These changes ended the political threat from the right to the Third Republic, which by now commanded the loyalty of most French people. Nevertheless, problems remained. As a nation of small businessmen and farmers, the French fell far behind Great Britain, Germany, and the United States in industrial activity. Moreover, a surge of industrialization after 1896 left the nation with the realization that little had been done to appease the discontent of the French working classes who were suffering from abysmal working conditions. Since only a quarter of the French wage earners worked in industry, there was little pressure for labor legislation from the French parliament. This made the use of strikes more appealing to the working classes. The brutal government repression of labor walkouts in 1911 only further alienated the working classes.

The Mediterranean Powers: Spain and Italy

Both Italy and Spain possessed trappings of constitutional government similar to those of Britain and France, but there were significant differences. In Spain and Italy, the kings could still exercise some power as a result of their control of the army led by conservative generals loyal to the monarch. Although both possessed parliaments, a relatively small conservative social group controlled each country because the middle classes re-

mained relatively small. While each country possessed some industrialized areas, both were still largely agricultural. Workers in both countries were poorly treated, and their desire for change led them to radical movements that were not opposed to the use of violence.

SPAIN   Between the 1850s and 1875, Spain had experienced considerable instability as governments proved unable to meet the demands of the most influential groups: the army, the Catholic church, big business, and regional interests. In 1875, a new constitution under King Alfonso XII (1874–1885) established a parliamentary government dominated by two political groups, the Conservatives and Liberals, whose members stemmed from the same small social group of great landowners allied with a few wealthy industrialists. Because suffrage was limited to the propertied classes, Liberals and Conservatives alternated in power but followed basically the same conservative policies.

Spain's defeat in the Spanish-American War in 1898 and the loss of Cuba and the Philippines to the United States increased the discontent with the status quo, which was manifested in a call for political and social reforms from a group of young intellectuals known as the Generation of 1898. In response, both Liberals and Conservatives attempted to enlarge the electorate and win over the masses in support of their policies. Attempted reforms, however, did little to allay the unrest while the growth of industrialization in some areas resulted in more workers being attracted to the radical solutions of socialism and anarchism. Violence erupted in July 1909, when the masses in Barcelona seized the city, destroyed churches and convents, and were then in turn brutally suppressed by military forces. "The army," one astute Spanish politician had said, "will remain for long, perhaps forever, the robust supporter of the social order, and an invincible dyke against the illegal attempts of the proletariat, which will accomplish nothing by violence but the useless shedding of its own blood."[12] The revolt and its repression revealed the strong strain of violence underlying Spanish political life. It also made clear that it was not easy to reform Spain because the Catholic church, large landowners, and the army remained tied to a conservative social order. Dictatorship or revolution seemed the only alternatives available to Spain on the eve of the First World War.

THE NEW ITALIAN STATE   Italy had emerged by 1870 as a geographically united state with pretensions to great power status. Its internal weaknesses, however, gave that claim a particularly hollow ring. Newly unified, it had little tradition of centralized government; local loyalties and rivalries remained paramount to most Italians.

Italy suffered a lack of a sense of community due to sectional differences. The south was a conspicuously poverty-stricken area populated by large landowners and an immense number of landless peasants who looked upon the northern Italians as foreigners. In great contrast, the north was becoming industrialized and modern. The attitude of the Catholic church also divided the new nation. Pope Pius IX (1846–1878) refused to accept the loss of his temporal power and declared himself a prisoner in the Vatican. Catholics, who made up most of the population, were forbidden to vote in national elections or participate in the new government. Although ignored by many Italians, the opposition of the Catholic church was an ongoing source of embarrassment to the new government.

Economically, Italy had severe problems as well. Lack of natural resources and a highly illiterate population hindered economic development in most parts of the country. There was, however, considerable industrial growth in the north where hydroelectricity could be used to power electrical, textile, and chemical industries. Between 1896 and 1914, northern Italy experienced rapid industrialization. The growth of industry, in turn, gave rise to a labor movement and the formation of the Italian Socialist party in 1892. Chronic turmoil plagued the relationship between industry and labor. Workers tended to identify with the politics of violence and revolution, while industrialists and landowners favored repressive reaction.

Perhaps all of these problems might have been dealt with more easily if Italy had had a strong national government, but that was not the case. United Italy began as a liberal constitutional monarchy with a Chamber of Deputies elected by a restricted suffrage. Universal male suffrage was granted in 1912. But the ability of the government to function well was weakened by the practice known as *trasformismo* or transformism. This was a system in which old political groups were transformed into new government coalitions by political and economic bribery. The system led to extensive corruption and weak government since it militated against any kind of party coherence and organization. A certain amount of stability was achieved, however, from 1903 to 1914 when Giovanni Giolitti served intermittently as prime minister and emerged as the dominant political figure. His devious means, however, served in the long run to make Italian politics even more corrupt.

Italy also had a problem of imperialistic pretensions. To preserve its status as a great power, it maintained a

large army and navy, which it could not really afford, to pursue imperialistic goals. In 1896 Italy became the first European power to lose to an African state, Ethiopia, a disgrace that led later to the costly (but successful) attempt to compensate by conquering Libya in 1911 and 1912.

The New Germany

Despite unification, important divisions remained in German society that could not simply be papered over by the force of nationalism. These divisions were already evident in the new German constitution that provided for a federal system with a bicameral legislature. The Bundesrat or upper house represented the twenty-five states that made up Germany. Individual states, such as Bavaria and Prussia, kept their own kings, their own post offices, and even their own armies in peacetime. The lower house of the German parliament, known as the Reichstag, was elected on the basis of universal male suffrage, but it did not have ministerial responsibility. Ministers of government, the most important of which was the chancellor, were responsible not to the parliament, but to the emperor. The emperor also commanded the armed forces and controlled foreign policy and internal administration. While the creation of a parliament elected by universal male suffrage presented opportunities for the growth of a real political democracy, it failed to develop in Germany before World War I. The army and Bismarck were two major reasons why it did not.

The German (largely Prussian) army viewed itself as the defender of monarchy and aristocracy and sought to escape any control by the Reichstag by operating under a general staff responsible only to the emperor. Prussian military tradition was strong, and military officers took steps to ensure the loyalty of their subordinates to the emperor. While that was easy as long as Junker landowners were officers, the growth of the army made it necessary to turn to the middle class for officers. But extreme care was taken to choose only sons "of honorable bourgeois families in whom the love for King and Fatherland, a warm heart for the soldier's calling, and Christian morality are planted and nurtured."

The policies of Bismarck, who served as chancellor of the new German state until 1890, often served to prevent the growth of more democratic institutions. Although the lack of ministerial responsibility in the constitution meant that Bismarck was not required to achieve a parliamentary majority, he thought it necessary to do so, especially since a Reichstag majority was necessary for military appropriations bills. Initially, until 1878, Bismarck found this majority by working with the National Liberals, whose admiration for the revered hero of German unification made them willing to work with Bismarck, especially to achieve greater centralization of Germany through common codes of criminal and commercial law. The National Liberals also joined Bismarck in his attack on the Catholic church, the so-called *Kulturkampf* or "struggle for civilization." Like Bismarck, middle-class liberals distrusted Catholic loyalty to the new Germany, especially when the Center party, organized by Catholics in 1870, voted against legislation it considered harmful to the church's interests. Bismarck's strong-arm tactics against Catholic clergy and Catholic institutions proved counterproductive, however, and Bismarck welcomed an opportunity in 1878 to abandon the attack on Catholicism by making an abrupt shift in policy.

In 1878, Bismarck decided to abandon his coalition with the National Liberals and ally himself with the Catholic Center party, the Conservatives (largely the party of the Prussian landowners), and the right wing of the National Liberals. Three factors explain this shift. First, Bismarck realized the failure of *Kulturkampf* and no longer wished to continue a losing cause. Second, Bismarck, contrary to liberal wishes, abandoned free trade and came to support a policy of protective tariffs favored by both the Prussian landowners and upper-middle-class industrialists. The landowners wished to protect their production against the cheap grain being imported from America and Russia while the economic depression that began in 1873 had persuaded German industrialists that British manufactured goods should be kept out by high tariffs. Bismarck's tariff policy received the support of the Catholic Center party, the Conservatives, because they were the party of the landowners, and the right wing of the National Liberals, who were upper-middle-class businessmen.

Bismarck's third reason for abandoning his alliance with the National Liberals stemmed from his desire to persecute the socialists. When the Social Democratic party elected twelve deputies in 1877, Bismarck grew alarmed. He genuinely believed that the socialists' antinationalistic, anticapitalistic, and antimonarchical stance represented a danger to the empire. In 1878, Bismarck got parliament to pass a stringent antisocialist law that outlawed the Social Democratic party and limited socialist meetings and publications, although socialist candidates were still permitted to run for the Reichstag. In addition to repressive measures, Bismarck also attempted to woo workers away from socialism by enacting

social welfare legislation. Between 1883 and 1889, the Reichstag passed laws that created sickness, accident, and disability benefits as well as old age pensions paid for by compulsory contributions from workers, employers, and the state. Bismarck's social security system was the most progressive the world had yet seen, although even his system left much to be desired as the Social Democrats pointed out. A full pension, for example, was payable only at age seventy after forty-eight years of contributions. In the event of a male worker's death, no benefits were paid to his widow or children.

Both the repressive and social welfare measures failed to stop the growth of socialism, however. The Social Democratic party continued to grow. In his frustration, Bismarck planned yet more repressive measures in 1890, but before he could carry them out, the new emperor, William II (1888–1918), eager to pursue his own policies, cashiered the aged chancellor.

THE GERMAN EMPIRE UNDER WILLIAM II The new imperial Germany begun by Bismarck in 1871 continued as an "authoritarian, conservative, military-bureaucratic power state" during the reign of Emperor William II (1888–1918). Unstable and aggressive, the emperor was inclined to tactless remarks, as when he told the soldiers of a Berlin regiment that they must be prepared to shoot their fathers and mothers if he ordered them to do so. A small group of about twenty powerful men joined William in setting government policy.

By 1914, Germany had become the strongest military and industrial power on the Continent. New social configurations had emerged as over 50 percent of German workers had jobs in industry while only 30 percent of the work force was still in agriculture. Urban centers had mushroomed in number and size. The rapid changes in Wilhelmine Germany helped to produce a society torn between modernization and traditionalism.

The growth of industrialization led to even greater expansion for the Social Democratic party. Despite the enactment of new welfare legislation to favor the working classes, William II was no more successful than Bismarck in slowing the growth of the Social Democrats. By 1912, it had become the largest single party in the Reichstag. At the same time, the party increasingly became less revolutionary and more revisionist in its outlook. Nevertheless, its growth frightened the middle and upper classes who blamed labor for their own problems.

With the expansion of industry and cities came demands for more political participation and growing sentiment for reforms that would produce greater democratization. Conservative forces, especially the landowning

nobility and representatives of heavy industry, two of the powerful ruling groups in Wilhelmine Germany, tried to block it by supporting William II's activist foreign policy of finding Germany's "place in the sun." Expansionism would divert people from further democratization.

The tensions in German society created by the conflict between modernization and traditionalism were also manifested in a new, radicalized, right-wing politics. A number of nationalist pressure groups arose to support nationalistic goals. Antisocialist and antiliberal, such groups as the Pan-German League stressed strong German nationalism and advocated imperialism as a tool to overcome social divisions and unite all classes. They were also anti-Semitic and denounced Jews as the destroyers of the national community. Traditional conservatives, frightened by the growth of the socialists, often made common cause with these radical right-wing groups, giving them respectability. After Germany's defeat in World War I, Nazism would emerge out of this radical right-wing politics (see Chapter 27).

Austria-Hungary

After the creation of the dual monarchy of Austria-Hungary in 1867, the Austrian part received a constitution that theoretically recognized the equality of the nationalities and established a parliamentary system with the principle of ministerial responsibility. In truth, although ethnic Germans made up only one-third of Austria's population, they dominated the parliament. Moreover, the Emperor Francis Joseph (1848–1916) largely ignored ministerial responsibility by personally appointing and dismissing his ministers and ruling by decree when parliament was not in session.

The problem of the various nationalities remained a difficult one. The German minority that governed Austria felt increasingly threatened by the Czechs, Poles, and other Slavic groups within the empire. The difficulties in dealing with this problem were especially evident from 1879 to 1893 when Count Edward von Taaffe served as prime minister. Taaffe attempted to "muddle through" by relying on a coalition of German conservatives, Czechs, and Poles to maintain a majority in parliament. But his concessions to national minorities, such as allowing the Slavic languages as well as German to be used in education and administration, served to antagonize the German-speaking Austrian bureaucracy and aristocracy, two of the basic pillars of the empire. Opposition to Taaffe's policies brought his downfall in 1893, but no solution to the nationalities problem. While the dissatisfied non-German groups demanded

concessions, the ruling Austrian Germans resisted change. The granting of universal male suffrage in 1907 served only to exacerbate the problem when nationalities that had played no role in the government now agitated in the parliament for autonomy. This led prime ministers after 1900 to ignore the parliament and rely increasingly on imperial emergency decrees to govern.

The threat the nationalities posed to the position of the dominant German minority in Austria also produced a backlash in the form of virulent German nationalism. As Austria industrialized in the 1870s and 1880s, two working-class parties came into existence, and both were strongly influenced by nationalism. The Social Democrats, although a Marxist party, supported the Austrian government, fearful that the autonomy of the different nationalities would hinder industrial development and prevent improvements for workers. Even more nationalistic, however, were the Christian Socialists.

The Christian Socialists combined agitation for workers with a virulent anti-Semitism. They were most powerful in Vienna where they were led by Karl Lueger, mayor of Vienna from 1897 to 1910. Imperial Vienna at the turn of the century was a brilliant center of European culture, but it was also the home of an insidious German nationalism that blamed Jews for the corruption of German culture. It was in Vienna from 1907 to 1913 that Adolf Hitler later claimed to have found his worldview, one that was largely based on a violent German nationalism and a rabid anti-Semitism.

Unlike Austria, Hungary had a working parliamentary system, but one controlled by the great Magyar landowners who dominated both the Hungarian peasantry and the other ethnic groups in Hungary. The Hungarians attempted to solve their nationalities problem by systematic Magyarization. The Magyar language was imposed upon all schools and was the only language that could be used by government and military officials.

While subjugating their nationalities, the ruling Magyars developed a movement for complete separation from Austria. When they demanded in 1903 that the Hungarian army be separated from the imperial army, Emperor Francis Joseph (as king of Hungary) responded quickly and forcefully. He threatened to impose universal male suffrage upon Hungary, a move that would challenge Magyar domination of the minorities. Hungarian leaders fell into line, and the new Hungarian parliamentary leader, Count Istvàn Tisza, cooperated in maintaining the dual monarchy. Magyar rule in Hungary, he realized, was inextricably bound up with the Dual Empire; its death would only harm the rule of the Magyar landowning class.

On the eve of World War I, the Austro-Hungarian Empire was as far away as ever from solving its minorities problem. Some imperial leaders even came to believe that only a policy of expansion could unify the nationalities and save the empire. World War I would prove what an illogical and fundamentally stupid idea that was.

Imperial Russia

The assassination of Alexander II in 1881 convinced his son and successor, Alexander III (1881–1894), that reform had been a mistake, and he quickly instituted what he said were "exceptional measures." The powers of the secret police were expanded. Advocates of constitutional monarchy and social reform, along with revolutionary groups, were persecuted. Entire districts of Russia were placed under martial law if the government suspected the inhabitants of treason. The powers of the zemstvos, created by the reforms of Alexander II, were sharply curtailed. When Alexander III died, his weak son and successor, Nicholas II (1894–1917), began his rule with his father's conviction that the absolute power of the tsars should be preserved: "I shall maintain the principle of autocracy just as firmly and unflinchingly as did my unforgettable father."[13] But conditions were changing, especially with the growth of industrialization, and the tsar's approach was not realistic in view of the new circumstances he faced.

THE DRIVE TO INDUSTRIALIZATION   Industrialization came late to Russia. It was realized after the fiasco of the Crimean War that Russia could not remain a great power without industrial development. Although it had the natural resources for industry—especially coal, iron, and oil—Russia did not have a very large middle class to provide the necessary capital and skills. Consequently, Russia came to depend on foreign capital for its industrial development. By 1900, over 50 percent of the capital in Russian industrial firms had come from abroad; in mining, 90 percent. The state led the way in subsidizing railway companies to build railroads, an absolute necessity if Russia were to grow industrially. In 1860, 1,250 miles of railroad track had been laid; by 1880, there were 15,500 miles.

Russia's initial industrialization was slowed by economic depression in the 1880s, but another massive surge of industrialism began in the 1890s under the guiding hand of Sergei Witte, the minister for finance from 1892 to 1903. A disciple of the economic nationalist Friedrich List (see Chapter 21), Count Witte saw indus-

trial growth as crucial to Russia's national strength. Believing that railroads were a very powerful weapon in economic development, Witte pushed the government toward a program of massive railroad construction. By 1900, 35,000 miles of railroads, including the 5,000-mile trans-Siberian line between Moscow and Vladivostok on the Pacific Ocean, had been built. As a follower of List, Witte also encouraged a system of protective tariffs to help Russian industry and persuaded the tsar that foreign capital was the only way Russian industrial development could quickly advance. Witte's program made possible the rapid growth of a modern steel and coal industry in the Ukraine, making Russia by 1900, the fourth largest producer of steel behind the United States, Germany, and Great Britain. At the same time, Russia was turning out half of the world's production of oil.

With industrialization came factories, an industrial working class, industrial suburbs around St. Petersburg and Moscow, and the pitiful working and living conditions that were common to the beginnings of industrialization everywhere. Socialist thought and socialist parties were developed, although repression in Russia soon forced them to go underground and become revolutionary. The Marxist Social Democratic party, for example, held its first congress in Minsk in 1898, but the arrest of its leaders caused the next one to be held in Brussels in 1903, attended by Russian emigres. The Social Revolutionaries worked to overthrow the tsarist autocracy and establish peasant socialism. Having no other outlet for opposition to the regime, they advocated political terrorism, attempting to assassinate government officials and members of the ruling dynasty. The growing opposition to the tsarist regime finally exploded into revolution in 1905.

THE REVOLUTION OF 1905   As elsewhere in Europe in the nineteenth century, defeat in war led to political upheaval at home. Like other European powers, Russia pursued imperialistic policies in the late nineteenth century, which led to territorial expansion to the south and east. In the east, Russian designs on northern Korea were countered by Japanese ambitions. Japan made a surprise attack on the Russian Far Eastern fleet at Port Arthur on February 8, 1904. Much to the astonishment of many Europeans who could not believe that an Asian state was militarily superior to a great European power, the Russians were defeated and sued for peace in 1905.

In the midst of the war, the growing discontent of increased numbers of Russians rapidly led to upheaval. A middle class of business and professional people longed

▼ **"Bloody Sunday."** After the defeat of Russia by Japan in 1905, the growing discontent of many Russians led to demonstrations against the tsarist regime. When a peaceful procession of workers outside the Winter Palace in St. Petersburg was fired upon by tsarist troops, a revolution broke out.

for liberal institutions and a liberal political system. Nationalities were dissatisfied with their domination by an ethnic Russian population that constituted only 45 percent of the empire's total population. Peasants were still suffering from lack of land, and laborers felt oppressed by their working and living conditions in Russia's large cities. The breakdown of the transport system caused by the Russo-Japanese War led to food shortages in the major cities of Russia. As a result, on January 9, 1905, a massive procession of workers went to the Winter Palace in St. Petersburg to present a petition of grievances to the tsar (see the box on p. 846). Troops foolishly opened fire on the peaceful demonstration, killing hundreds and launching a revolution. This "Bloody Sunday" incited workers to call strikes and form unions while zemstvos demanded the formation of parliamentary government, ethnic groups revolted, and peasants burned the houses of landowners. After a general strike in October 1905, the government capitulated. Count Witte had advised the tsar to divide his opponents: "It is not on the extremists that the existence and integrity of the state depend. As long as the government has support in the broad strata of society, a peaceful solution to the crisis is still possible."[14] Nicholas II issued the October Manifesto, in which he granted civil liberties and agreed to create a Duma or legislative assembly elected directly by a broad franchise. This satisfied the middle-class moderates who now supported the government's repression of a workers' uprising in Moscow at the end of 1905.

But real constitutional monarchy proved short-lived. Under Peter Stolypin, who served as the tsar's chief ad-

Russian Workers Appeal to the Tsar
▼ ▼ ▼

On January 9, 1905, a massive procession of workers led by an Orthodox priest loyal to the tsar, Father George Gapon, carried a petition to present to the tsar at his imperial palace in St. Petersburg. Although the tsar was not even there, government officials ordered troops to fire on the crowd. "Bloody Sunday," as it was called, precipitated the Revolution of 1905. This selection is an excerpt from the petition that was never presented.

George Gapon and Ivan Vasimov, Petition to the Tsar

Sovereign!

We, the workers and the inhabitants of various social strata of the city of St. Petersburg, our wives, children, and helpless old parents, have come to you, Sovereign, to seek justice and protection. We are impoverished; our employers oppress us, overburden us with work, insult us, consider us inhuman, and treat us as slaves who must suffer a bitter fate in silence. Though we have suffered, they push us deeper and deeper into a gulf of misery, disfranchisement, and ignorance. Despotism and arbitrariness strangle us and we are gasping for breath. Sovereign, we have no strength left. We have reached the limit of endurance. We have reached that terrible moment when death is preferable to the continuance of unbearable sufferings.

And so we left our work and informed our employers that we shall not resume work until they meet our demands. We do not demand much; we only want what is indispensable to life and without which life is nothing but hard labor and eternal suffering. Our first request was that our employers discuss our needs jointly with us. But they refused to do this; they even denied us the right to speak about our needs, saying that the law does not give us such a right. Also unlawful were our requests to reduce the working day to eight hours, to set wages jointly with us; to examine our disputes with lower echelons of factory administration; to increase the wages of unskilled workers and women to one ruble [about $1.00] per day; to abolish overtime work; to provide medical care without insult. . . .

Sovereign, there are thousands of us here; outwardly we resemble human beings, but in reality neither we nor the Russian people as a whole enjoy any human right, have any right to speak, to think, to assemble, to discuss our needs, or to take measures to improve our conditions. They have enslaved us and they did it under the protection of your officials, with their aid and with their cooperation. They imprison and send into exile any one of us who has the courage to speak on behalf of the interests of the working class and of the people. . . . All the workers and the peasants are at the mercy of bureaucratic administrators consisting of embezzlers of public funds and thieves who not only disregard the interests of the people but also scorn these interests. . . . The people are deprived of the opportunity to express their wishes and their demands and to participate in determining taxes and expenditures. The workers are deprived of the opportunity to organize themselves in unions to protect their interests.

Sovereign! Is all this compatible with God's laws, by the grace of which you reign? And is it possible to live under such laws? Wouldn't it be better for all of us if we, the toiling people of all Russia, died? . . . Sovereign, these are the problems that we face and these are the reasons that we have gathered before the walls of your palace. Here we seek our last salvation. Do not refuse to come to the aid of your people.

---

viser from late 1906 until his assassination in 1911, important agrarian reforms dissolved the village ownership of land and opened the door to private ownership by enterprising peasants. Nicholas II, however, was no friend of reform. Already by 1907, the tsar had curtailed the power of the Duma, and after Stolypin's murder he fell back on the army and bureaucracy to rule Russia. World War I would give revolutionary forces another chance to undo the tsarist regime, and this time they would not fail.

The Balkans and the Ottoman Empire

Like the Austro-Hungarian Empire, the Ottoman Empire was severely troubled by the nationalist aspirations of its subject peoples, especially in the Balkans.

Great Britain	
Ministry of Benjamin Disraeli	1874–1880
Trade Unions Receive Right to Strike	1875
Second Ministry of William Gladstone	1880–1885
Irish Land Act	1881
Reform Act	1884
Redistribution Act	1885
Formation of Labor Party	1900
Liberal Ministry	1906–1914
Restriction of Power of the House of Lords	1911
National Insurance Act	1911
Home Rule Act for Ireland	1914
France	
Surrender of French Provisional Government to Germany	1871 (January 28)
Paris Commune	1871 (March-May)
Republican Constitution (Third Republic	1875
Boulanger Is Discredited	1889
The Dreyfus Affair	1895–1899
Spain	
King Alfonso XII	1874–1885
New Constitution	1875
Defeat in Spanish-American War	1898
Violence in Barcelona	1909

Italy	
Foundation of Italian Socialist Party	1892
Defeat by Ethiopia	1896
Ministries of Giovanni Giolitti	1903–1914
Universal Male Suffrage	1912
Germany	
Bismarck as Chancellor	1871–1890
Antisocialist Law	1878
Social Welfare Legislation	1883–1889
Emperor William II	1888–1918
Social Democratic Party Becomes Largest Party in Reichstag	1912
Austria-Hungary	
Emperor Francis Joseph	1848–1916
Count Edward Taaffe as Prime Minister	1879–1893
Universal Male Suffrage in Austria	1907
Imperial Russia	
Tsar Alexander III	1881–1894
Tsar Nicholas II	1894–1917
Count Witte as Minister of Finance	1892–1903
First Congress of Social Democratic Party	1898
Russo-Japanese War	1904–1905
Revolution	1905
Reforms of Peter Stolypin	1906–1911

Corruption and inefficiency had so weakened the Ottoman Empire that only the interference of the great European powers, who were fearful of each other's designs on the Turkish territories, kept it alive.

In the course of the nineteenth century, the Balkan provinces of the empire gradually gained their freedom, although the rivalry in the region between Austria and Russia complicated the process. Serbia had received a large degree of autonomy already in 1829, although it was still a province of the Ottoman Empire until 1878. Greece was made an independent kingdom in 1830 after its successful revolt. By the Treaty of Adrianople in 1829, Russia received a protectorate over the principalities of Moldavia and Walachia, but was forced to give them up after the Crimean War. In 1861, Moldavia and Walachia were merged into the state of Romania. Not until Russia's defeat of Turkey in 1878, however, was Romania recognized as completely independent, as was Serbia at the same time. Although freed from Turkish rule, Montenegro was placed under an Austrian protectorate while Bulgaria achieved autonomous status under Russian protection. Despite these gains, by 1878 the forces of Balkan nationalism were by no means stilled. A series of wars in the region at the beginning of the twentieth century would serve as the prelude to World War I.

The Lesser States of Europe

Switzerland had been an independent, self-governing confederation of cantons since 1648. Although the cantons were divided linguistically (German, French, and Italian) and religiously (Catholic and Protestant), their desire to remain independent and neutral enabled them to compromise and to develop a national tradition. A combination of universal free elementary education, a strong tradition of craftsmanship, and the development of hydroelectricity in the 1880s encouraged the emergence of a modern industrial system. By 1914, the Swiss had achieved a relatively high standard of living and a stable political democracy.

Belgium had achieved its independence in 1830. Growing industrialization led to the emergence of trade unionists and socialists who joined together to form the Belgian Labor party and agitate for electoral reform. The threat of a general strike in 1893 brought the introduction of universal manhood suffrage, but only in a very restricted fashion. Belgium did not achieve full universal suffrage until after World War I. The Netherlands also evolved toward political democracy but did not achieve universal male suffrage until 1917 because of bitter divisions between Catholics and Calvinists.

The Scandinavian nations made remarkable progress toward a modern industrial economy and political democracy between 1871 and 1914. In Sweden, 80 percent of the people were engaged in agriculture in 1850. But the development of Sweden's manufacturing, mining, and handicraft industries transformed the country. By 1910, less than 50 percent of the population still worked the land. Sweden also groped toward democratic institutions and granted universal male suffrage in 1909. Although Norway had been subjected to Swedish rule in 1815, the union was peacefully dissolved in 1905. Norway rapidly developed a highly democratic system and became the first European nation to extend voting rights to women. Denmark resisted political liberalization dur-

ing most of the nineteenth century and did not achieve political democracy until World War I.

The United States

Four years of bloody civil war had preserved American national unity. The old South had been destroyed; one-fifth of its adult white male population had been killed, and four million black slaves had been freed. Although Reconstruction (1865–1877) was meant to create a new southern order, it largely failed.

For a while at least, a program of radical change was attempted. Slavery was abolished by the Thirteenth Amendment to the Constitution in 1865 while the Fourteenth and Fifteenth Amendments extended citizenship to blacks and guaranteed them the right to vote. Radical Reconstruction in the early 1870s tried to create a new South based on a principle of the equality of black and white people, but it was soon mostly undone. Militia organizations, such as the Ku Klux Klan, used violence to discourage blacks from voting. A new system of sharecropping made blacks once again economically dependent on white landowners. New state laws stripped blacks of their right to vote. By the end of the 1870s, supporters of white supremacy were back in power everywhere in the South.

Between 1860 and World War I, the United States made the shift from an agrarian to a mighty industrial nation. American heavy industry stood unchallenged in 1900. In that year, the Carnegie Steel Company alone produced more steel than Great Britain's entire steel industry. Industrialization also led to urbanization. While established cities, such as New York, Philadelphia, and Boston, grew even larger, other moderate-size cities, such as Pittsburgh, grew by leaps and bounds because of industrialization. While 20 percent of Americans lived in cities in 1860, over 40 percent did in 1900. Four-fifths of the population growth in cities came from migration. Eight to ten million Americans moved from rural areas into the cities, and fourteen million foreigners came from abroad.

By 1900, the United States had become the world's richest nation and greatest industrial power. Yet serious questions remained about the quality of American life. In 1890, the richest 9 percent of Americans owned an incredible 71 percent of all the wealth. Labor unrest over unsafe working conditions, strict work discipline, and periodic cycles of devastating unemployment led workers to organize. By the turn of the century, one national organization, the American Federation of Labor, emerged as labor's dominant voice. Its lack of real power, however, is reflected in its membership figures. In 1900, it constituted but 8.4 percent of the American industrial labor force.

During the so-called Progressive Era after 1900, the reform of many features of American life became a primary issue. Efforts to improve living conditions in the cities included attempts to eliminate corrupt machine politics. At the state level, reforming governors sought to achieve clean government by introducing elements of direct democracy, such as direct primaries for selecting nominees for public office. State governments also enacted economic and social legislation, such as laws that governed hours, wages, and working conditions, especially for women and children. The realization that state laws were ineffective in dealing with nationwide problems, however, led to a progressive movement at the national level.

National progressivism was evident in the administrations of both Theodore Roosevelt and Woodrow Wilson. Under Roosevelt (1901–1909), a Meat Inspection Act and Pure Food and Drug Act provided for a limited degree of federal regulation of corrupt industrial practices. Roosevelt's expressed principle, "We draw the line against misconduct, not against wealth," guaranteed that public protection would have to be within limits tolerable to big corporations. Wilson (1913–1921) was responsible for the creation of a graduated federal income tax and a Federal Reserve System that permitted the federal government to play a role in important economic decisions formerly made by bankers. Like European nations, the United States was moving slowly into policies that extended the functions of the state.

Between 1871 and 1914, the national state began to expand its functions beyond all previous limits. Fearful of the growth of socialism and trade unions, governments attempted to appease the working masses by adopting such social insurance measures as protection against accident, illness, and old age. These social welfare measures were narrow in scope and limited in benefits before 1914. Moreover, they failed to halt the growth of socialism. Nevertheless, they signaled a new direction for state action to benefit the mass of its citizens. The enactment of public health and housing measures, designed to curb the worst ills of urban living, were yet another indication of how state power could be used to benefit the people.

This extension of state functions took place in an atmosphere of increased national loyalty. After 1871, nation-states increasingly sought to solidify the social order and win the active loyalty and support of their citizens by deliberately cultivating national feelings. Yet this policy contained potentially great dangers. Nations had discovered once again that imperialistic adventures and military successes could arouse nationalistic passions and smother domestic political unrest. But they also found—belatedly in 1914—that nationalistic feelings could also lead to intense international rivalries that made war almost inevitable.

Notes

▼ ▼ ▼

1. Quoted in David Landes, *The Unbound Prometheus: Technological Change and Industrial Development in Western Europe from 1750 to the Present* (Cambridge, 1969), p. 353.

2. Quoted in Nicholas Bullock and James Read, *The Movement for Housing Reform in Germany and France, 1840–1914* (Cambridge, 1985), p. 42.

3. Quoted in Barbara Franzoi, ". . . with the wolf always at the door. . . . Women's Work in Domestic Industry and Germany," in Marilyn J. Boxer and Jean H. Quataert, eds., *Connecting Spheres: Women in the Western World, 1500 to the Present* (New York, 1987), p. 151.

4. Quoted in Gary Cross, *A Social History of Leisure since 1600* (State College, Pa., 1990), pp. (in order of quotations) 116, 119.

5. Quoted in Sibylle Meyer, "The Tiresome Work of Conspicuous Leisure: On the Domestic Duties of the Wives of Civil Servants in the German Empire (1871–1918)," in Boxer and Quataert, *Connecting Spheres*, p. 161.

6. Quoted in Lenard R. Berlanstein, *The Working People of Paris, 1871–1914* (Baltimore, 1984), p. 141.

7. Quoted in Catherine M. Prelinger, "Prelude to Consciousness: Amalie Sieveking and the Female

Association for the Care of the Poor and the Sick," in John C. Fout, ed., *German Women in the Nineteenth Century: A Social History* (New York, 1984), p. 119.

8. Quoted in W. L. Guttsman, *The German Social Democratic Party, 1875–1933* (London, 1981), p. 63.

9. Quoted in Leslie Derfler, *Socialism since Marx: A Century of the European Left* (New York, 1973), p. 58.

10. Karl Marx and Friedrich Engels, *The Communist Manifesto* (Harmondsworth, 1967), p. 102.

11. Quoted in Paul Avrich, *The Russian Anarchists* (Princeton, N.J., 1971), p. 67.

12. Quoted in Stanley G. Payne, *Politics and the Military in Modern Spain* (Stanford, 1967), p. 60.

13. Quoted in Shmuel Galai, *The Liberation Movement in Russia, 1900–1905* (Cambridge, 1973), p. 26.

14. Quoted in Geoffrey A. Hosking, *The Russian Constitutional Experiment, 1907–1914* (Cambridge, 1973), p. 5.

Suggestions for Further Reading
▼ ▼ ▼

In addition to the general works on the nineteenth century and individual European countries cited in Chapters 22 and 23, two more specialized works on the subject matter of this chapter are available in N. Stone, *Europe Transformed, 1878–1919* (London, 1983); and J. B. Joll, *Europe since 1870: An International History* (London, 1973).

The subject of the Second Industrial Revolution is well covered in D. Landes, *The Unbound Prometheus*, cited in Chapter 21. For a fundamental survey of European industrialization, see A. S. Milward and S. B. Saul, *The Development of the Economies of Continental Europe, 1850–1914* (Cambridge, Mass., 1977); while Britain can be examined in A. L. Levine, *Industrial Retardation in Britain, 1880–1914* (New York, 1967); and Germany in W. Henderson, *The Rise of German Industrial Power* (Berkeley, 1975). An examination of the business cycles of the period can be found in A. Lewis, *Growth and Fluctuations, 1870–1913* (London, 1978). For an introduction to the development of mass consumerism in Britain, see W. H. Fraser, *The Coming of the Mass Market, 1850–1914* (Hamden, Conn., 1981). The impact of the new technology on European thought is imaginatively discussed in S. Kern, *The Culture of Time and Space, 1880–1918* (Cambridge, Mass., 1983).

For a good introduction to housing reform on the Continent, see N. Bullock and J. Read, *The Movement for Housing Reform in Germany and France, 1840–1914* (Cambridge, 1985). Working-class housing in Paris during its reconstruction is the subject of A. L. Shapiro, *Housing the Poor of Paris, 1850–1902* (Madison, Wis., 1985). E. Gauldie, *Cruel Habitations* (London, 1974) is a good account of working-class housing in Britain. D. Owen, *The Government of Victorian London, 1855–1889* (Cambridge, Mass., 1982) examines how the city of London confronted urban development. The

reconstruction of Paris is discussed in D. Pinkney, *Napoleon III and the Rebuilding of Paris* (Princeton, N.J., 1958).

An interesting work on aristocratic life is G. D. Philips, *The Diehards: Aristocratic Society and Politics in Edwardian England* (Cambridge, 1979). The argument for the continuing importance of the aristocracy is presented in the provocative book by A. Mayer, *Persistence of the Old Regime: Europe to the Great War* (New York, 1981). On the working classes, see L. Berlanstein, *The Working People of Paris, 1871–1914* (Baltimore, 1984). The transformation of the French peasants into good French citizens is examined in E. Weber, *Peasants into Frenchmen: The Modernization of Rural France, 1870–1914* (Stanford, 1976).

There are good overviews of women's experiences in the nineteenth century in B. S. Anderson and J. P. Zinsser, *A History of Their Own*, vol. 2 (New York, 1988); and M. J. Boxer and J. H. Quataert, eds., *Connecting Spheres: Women in the Western World, 1500 to the Present* (New York, 1987). The world of women's work is examined in L. A. Tilly and J. W. Scott, *Women, Work, and Family* (New York, 1978). Important studies of middle-class women include P. Branca, *Silent Sisterhood: Middle Class Women in the Victorian Home* (London, 1975); and B. G. Smith, *Ladies of the Leisure Class: The Bourgeoises of Northern France in the Nineteenth Century* (Princeton, N.J., 1981). Prostitution is discussed in J. R. Walkowitz, *Prostitution and Victorian Society: Women, Class, and the State* (Cambridge, 1980). The rise of feminism is examined in J. Rendall, *The Origins of Modern Feminism: Women in Britain, France and the United States* (London, 1985). On the family and children, see M. Mitterauer and R. Sieder, *The European Family* (Chicago, 1982); and the controversial E. Shorter, *The Making of the Modern Family* (New York, 1975). The treatment of children is examined in G. Behlmer, *Child Abuse and Moral Reform in England, 1870–1908* (Stanford, 1982).

For an introduction to international socialism, see J. Joll, *The Second International, 1889–1914*, 2d ed. (New York, 1975); and L. Derfler, *Socialism since Marx: A Century of the European Left* (New York, 1973). On the emergence of German social democracy, there is W. L. Guttsman, *The German Social Democratic Party, 1875–1933* (London, 1981); and V. Lidtke, *The Outlawed Party: Social Democracy in Germany, 1878–1890* (Princeton, N.J., 1966). Eduard Bernstein's revisionism is examined in P. Gay, *The Dilemma of Democratic Socialism: Eduard Bernstein's Challenge to Marx* (New York, 1952). On the French socialists, there is a "classic" biography by H. Goldberg, *The Life of Jean Jaurès* (Madison, Wis., 1962). There is a good introduction to anarchism in G. Woodcock, *Anarchism: A History of Libertarian Ideas and Movements* (Cleveland, Ohio, 1962).

The domestic politics of the period can be examined in the general works on individual countries listed in the bibliographies for Chapters 22 and 23. There are also specialized works on aspects of each country's history. The importance of Fabian Socialism in England is discussed in A. H. McBriar, *Fabian Socialism and English Politics, 1884–1918* (Cambridge, 1962); while the beginnings of the Labor party are examined in H. Pelling, *The Origins of the Labour Party*, 2d ed. (Oxford, 1965). On the problem of English industrial decline, see M. J. Wiener, *English Culture and the Decline of the Industrial Spirit, 1850–1980* (Cambridge, 1981). The Irish problem is covered in O. MacDonagh, *States of Mind: A Study of Anglo-Irish Conflict, 1780–1980* (London, 1983). For a detailed examination of French history from 1871 to 1914, see J. M. Mayeur and M. Reberioux, *The Third Republic from Its Origins to the Great War, 1871–1914* (Cambridge, 1984). On the Paris Commune, see R. Tombs, *The War against Paris, 1871* (Cambridge, 1981). On Italy, see C. Seton-Watson, *Italy from Liberalism to Fascism* (London, 1967). An important aspect of Spanish history is examined in S. G. Payne, *Politics and the Military in Modern Spain* (Stanford, 1967). There is a good introduction to the political world of Wilhelmine Germany in J. C. G. Röhl, *Germany without Bismarck* (Berkeley, 1965). An important study on right-wing German politics is G. Eley, *Reshaping the German Right: Radical Nationalism and Political Change after Bismarck* (New Haven, Conn., 1980). K. H. Jarausch, *Students, Society, and Politics in Imperial Germany: The Rise of Academic Illiberalism* (Princeton, N.J., 1982) examines the reaction of universities to the danger of socialism. The best, one-volume biography in English on Emperor William II is M. Balfour, *The Kaiser and His Times* (London, 1964). On the nationalities problem in the Austro-Hungarian Empire, see R. Kann, *The Multinational Empire, Nationalism and National Reform in the Habsburg Monarchy, 1848–1918*, 2 vols. (New York, 1950). On aspects of Russian history, see H. Rogger, *Russia in the Age of Modernization and Revolution, 1881–1917* (London, 1983); and T. H. Von Laue, *Sergei Witte and the Industrialization of Russia* (New York, 1963). On the United States, see D. Cashman, *America in the Gilded Age: From the Death of Lincoln to the Rise of Theodore Roosevelt* (New York, 1984); and J. W. Chambers, *The Tyranny of Change: America in the Progressive Era, 1900–1917* (New York, 1980).

Chapter 25

Imperialism, International Rivalry, and Culture in the "Age of Progress," 1871–1914

▼▼▼▼▼

Many Europeans saw the period between 1871 and 1914 as an age of material and human progress. It was also a time of great tension, however, as imperialist adventures, international rivalries, and cultural uncertainties disturbed the apparent calm. After 1870, Europeans engaged in a great race for colonies that did not end until Africa had been divided among the powers and much of Asia had been incorporated into their spheres of influence. This competition for lands abroad greatly intensified existing antagonisms among European states.

Ultimately, Europeans proved incapable of finding constructive ways to cope with their international rivalries. The development of two large alliance systems—the Triple Alliance and the Triple Entente—may have served to preserve the peace, but at the same time the development of a balance of power based on these alliances led to the creation of mass conscript armies and enormous military establishments that served to exacerbate the tensions among the major powers. These tensions were only finally released when Europeans rushed headlong into the catastrophic carnage of World War I.

The cultural life of Europe between 1871 and 1914 reflected similar dynamic tensions. The advent of mass education created more well-informed citizens, but it also made it easier for governments to stir up the masses by nationalistic appeals through the new mass journalism. At the same time, despite the appearance of progress, European philosophers, writers, and artists were creating modern cultural expressions that ques-

| Congress of Berlin | Triple Alliance (Germany, Austria, Italy) | Open Door Policy in China | Boxer Rebellion | Triple Entente (France, Britain, Russia) |

•••••••••• 1870 ••••••••••• 1880 ••••••••••• 1890 ••••••••••• 1900 ••••••••••• 1910 ••••••••••

| Emergence of Mass Newspapers | Cézanne, *Woman with Coffee Pot* | Freud, *The Interpretation of Dreams* | Einstein's Special Theory of Relativity | Picasso's First Cubist Painting |

tioned traditional ideas and values and increasingly provoked a crisis of confidence. Before 1914, many intellectuals had a sense of unease about the direction society was headed, accompanied by a feeling of imminent catastrophe. They proved remarkably prophetic.

▼ The Expansion of Europe

Europeans had begun to explore the world in the fifteenth century, but even as late as 1870 they had not yet completely penetrated North America, South America, and Australia. In Asia and Africa, they had mostly established trading posts. Between 1870 and 1914, however, Western civilization expanded into the rest of the Americas and Australia while all of Africa was divided into European colonies and spheres of influence were created in much of Asia. Two major events explain this remarkable expansion: the migration of many Europeans to other parts of the world due to population growth and the revival of imperialism.

Population Increase and Demographic Transformation

The European population increased dramatically between 1850 and 1910, rising from 270 million to over 460 million by 1910. Between 1850 and 1880, noticeable jumps in the number of inhabitants occurred in Germany, Britain, the Scandinavian countries, the Low Countries, and Russia while France remained static and the Mediterranean countries and Austria-Hungary grew slowly. After 1880, this pattern changed. The rate of population growth remained static in France and relatively slow in the Mediterranean countries and Great Britain. Scandinavia, the Netherlands, Belgium, Germany, and Austria grew faster while eastern Europe, especially Romania, Bulgaria, Greece, Serbia, and above all Russia, experienced a population explosion (see Table 1).

Between 1850 and 1880, the main cause of population increase was a rising birth rate, at least in western Europe. Industrialization in northwestern Europe created greater employment possibilities, which encouraged earlier marriages and consequently higher birth rates. Death rates remained high during this period. In some areas, especially backward southern and eastern Europe, death rates almost canceled out high birth rates. Large cities had particularly hazardous environments because of the lack of sanitation and overcrowded conditions. In Germany, for example, in 1880, the life expectancy of males in rural Hanover was 43.1, but in the moderate-

Table 1 ▼ European Populations, 1851–1911

	1851	1881	1911
England and Wales	17,928,000	25,974,000	36,070,000
Scotland	2,889,000	3,736,000	4,761,000
Ireland	6,552,000	5,175,000	4,390,000
France	35,783,000	37,406,000	39,192,000
Germany	33,413,000	45,234,000	64,926,000
Belgium	4,530,000	5,520,000	7,424,000
Netherlands	3,309,000	4,013,000	5,858,000
Denmark	1,415,000	1,969,000	2,757,000
Norway	1,490,000	1,819,000	2,392,000
Sweden	3,471,000	4,169,000	5,522,000
Spain	15,455,000	16,622,000	19,927,000
Portugal	3,844,000	4,551,000	5,958,000
Italy	24,351,000	28,460,000	34,671,000
Switzerland	2,393,000	2,846,000	3,753,000
Austria	17,535,000	22,144,000	28,572,000
Hungary	18,192,000	15,739,000	20,886,000
Russia	68,500,000	97,700,000	160,700,000
Romania		4,600,000	7,000,000
Bulgaria		2,800,000	4,338,000
Greece		1,679,000	2,632,000
Serbia		1,700,000	2,912,000

Source: B. R. Mitchell, *European Historical Statistics, 1750–1970* (1975).

▼ **Map 25.1** Population Growth in Europe

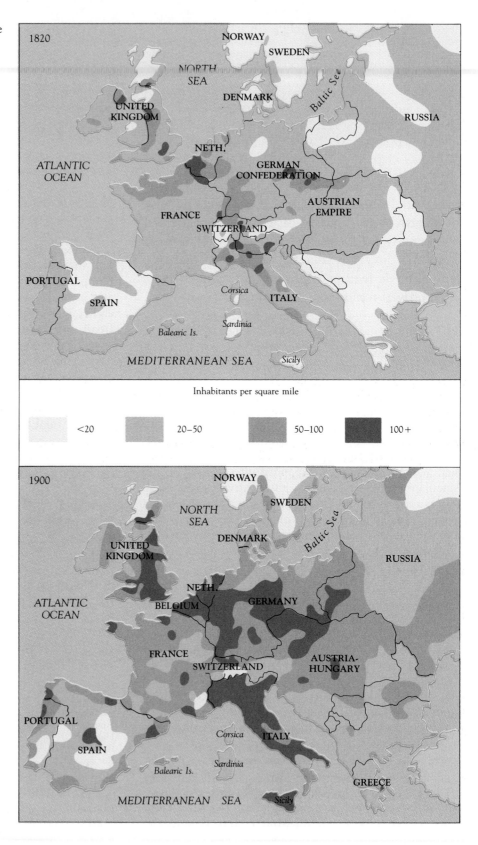

sized industrial town of Düsseldorf, it was 36.7 and in Berlin, 29.9.

After 1880, a noticeable decline in death rates largely explains the increase in population. Although the causes of this decline have been debated, two major factors—medical discoveries and environmental conditions—stand out. Some historians have stressed the importance of improvements in medical science. Smallpox vaccinations, for example, were made compulsory in many European countries by the mid-1850s, although smallpox fatalities accounted for only a small percentage of deaths. More important were such infectious diseases as diarrhea, dysentery, typhoid fever, and cholera, which were spread through contaminated water supplies and improper elimination of sewage. The improvement of the urban environment in the last half of the nineteenth century greatly decreased fatalities from these diseases. Improved nutrition also made a significant difference in the health of the population. The increase in agricultural productivity combined with improvements in transportation facilitated the shipment of food supplies from areas of surplus to regions with poor harvests. Better nutrition and food hygiene were especially instrumental in the decline of infant mortality by 1900. The pasteurization of milk reduced intestinal disorders that had been a major cause of infant deaths.

Although high birth rates continued to be noticeable in economically backward eastern and southern Europe, the general trend for the rest of Europe was a decline in birth rates, especially in France, Scandinavia, the Low Countries, and Great Britain, and to a lesser extent in Germany. Birth rates fell more in cities than in rural areas and more among the upper and middle classes than among the lower classes. This decline in birth rates, coupled with falling death rates, affected the composition of populations. In France, for example, the proportion of the population under fifteen was 22.5 percent in 1910, while in Germany it was 34.1 percent. These figures had great significance in an age of mass armies.

Although marriages still occurred later in western than eastern Europe, the delay in marriage was no longer the chief cause of the falling birth rates. The decline in infant mortality rates meant that couples felt free to have fewer children because there was less need to worry about their early death. Most importantly, however, increased prosperity led to a voluntary limitation of children by birth control as families sought to improve their standard of living. Factory acts in Europe gradually eliminated child labor, which made children less of an asset and more of an economic liability.

Migrations

Although growing agricultural and industrial prosperity supported an increase in European population, it could not do so indefinitely, especially in areas that had little industrialization and a severe problem of rural overpopulation. Some of the excess labor from underdeveloped areas migrated to the industrial regions of Europe. By 1913, over 400,000 Poles were working in the heavily industrialized Ruhr region of western Germany while thousands of Italian laborers had migrated to France. The industrialized regions of Europe, however, were not able to absorb the entire surplus population of heavily agricultural regions like southern Italy, Spain, Hungary, and Romania. A booming American economy after 1898 and cheap shipping fares after 1900 led to mass emigration from southern and eastern Europe to America at the beginning of the twentieth century. In 1880, the average number of annual departures from Europe was around 500,000, but between 1906 and 1910 it increased to 1,300,000, many of them from southern and eastern Europe. Altogether between 1846 and 1932, probably 60 million Europeans left Europe, half of them bound for the United States and most of the rest for Canada or Latin America (see Table 2).

It was not only economic motives that caused people to leave eastern Europe. Migrants from Austria and Hungary, for example, were not the dominant nationalities, the Germans and Magyars, but mostly their oppressed minorities, such as Poles, Slovaks, Serbs, Croats, Romanians, and Jews. Between 1880 and 1914, 3,500,000 Poles from Russia, Austria, and Germany went to the United States. Jews constituted 40 percent of the Russian emigrants to the United States between 1900 and 1913 and almost 12 percent of all emigrants to the United States during the first five years of the twentieth century.

▼ The New Imperialism

Beginning in the 1880s, European states began an intense scramble for overseas territory. This revival of imperialism, or the "new imperialism" as some have called it, led Europeans to carve up Asia and Africa. Imperialism was not a new phenomenon. Since the crusades of the Middle Ages and the overseas expansion between 1500 and 1800, when Europeans established colonies in North and South America and trading posts around Africa and the Indian Ocean, Europeans had shown a marked proclivity for the domination of less technologically oriented, non-European peoples. Nevertheless, the imperialism of the late nineteenth century was different from the earlier European imperialism. It occurred after a period in which Europeans had reacted against imperial expansion. Between 1775 and 1875, Europeans had lost more colonial territory than they acquired as many Europeans had actually come to regard colonies as expensive and useless. The new imperialism was also more rapid and resulted in greater and deeper penetrations into non-European societies. Finally, most of the new imperialism was directed toward the domination of Africa and Asia, two civilizations that had been largely ignored earlier.

Causes of the New Imperialism

Why did Europeans begin their mad scramble for colonies after 1880? Although historians disagree, they have advanced a number of factors to explain the rapid spread of imperialism.

The existence of competitive nation-states after 1870 was undoubtedly a major determinant in the growth of this new imperialism. As European affairs grew tense, heightened competition led European states to acquire colonies abroad that provided ports and coaling stations for their navies. Colonies were also a source of international prestige. Once the scramble for colonies began, failure to enter the race was perceived as a sign of weakness, totally unacceptable to an aspiring great power. Nationalistically oriented intellectuals reinforced these

national aspirations when they argued that nations could not be great without colonies. The German historian Heinrich von Treitschke, for example, maintained that "all great nations in the fullness of their strength have desired to set their mark upon barbarian lands and those who fail to participate in this great rivalry will play a pitiable role in time to come."[1]

Treitschke's comments are a reminder that late nineteenth-century imperialism was closely tied to nationalism, Social Darwinism, and racism. After the unification of Italy and Germany in 1871, nationalism entered a new stage of development. In the first half of the nineteenth century, nationalism had been closely identified with liberals who had pursued both individual rights and national unification and independence. Liberal nationalists maintained that unified, independent nation-states could best preserve individual rights. The new nationalism of the late nineteenth century, tied to conservatism, was loud and chauvinistic. As one exponent expressed it, "a true nationalist places his country above everything"; he believes in the "exclusive pursuit of national policies" and "the steady increase in national power—for a nation declines when it loses military might."

Then, too, imperialism was tied to Social Darwinism and racism (see The Impact of Darwin: Social Darwinism and Racism later in the chapter). Social Darwinists believed that in the struggle between nations, the fit are victorious and survive. Superior races must dominate inferior races by military force to show how strong and virile they are. As the British professor of mathematics,

Table 2 ▼ European Emigration, 1876–1910 (Average Annual Emigration to Non-European Countries per 100,000 Population)

	1876–80	1881–5	1886–90	1891–5	1896–1900	1901–5	1906–10
Europe	94	196	213	185	147	271	322
Ireland	650	1,422	1,322	988	759	743	662
Great Britain	102	174	162	119	88	127	172
Denmark	157	380	401	338	117	292	275
Norway	432	1,105	819	597	312	903	746
Sweden	301	705	759	587	249	496	347
Germany	108	379	207	163	47	50	44
Belgium			86	50	23	57	69
Netherlands	32	136	111	76	25	45	58
France	8	14	49	14	13	12	12
Spain		280	437	434	446	391	758
Portugal	258	356	423	609	417	464	694
Italy	396	542	754	842	974	1,706	1,938
Austria	48	90	114	182	182	355	469
Hungary		92	156	134	205	437	616
Russia	6	13	42	47	32	63	67

Source: Robert Gildea, *Barricades and Borders: Europe, 1800–1914* (Oxford, 1987), p. 283.

Karl Pearson, arrogantly argued in 1900: "The path of progress is strewn with the wrecks of nations; traces are everywhere to be seen of the [slaughtered remains] of inferior races. . . . Yet these dead people are, in very truth, the stepping stones on which mankind has arisen to the higher intellectual and deeper emotional life of today."[2] Others were equally blunt. One Briton wrote: "To the development of the White Man, the Black Man and the Yellow must ever remain inferior, and as the former raised itself higher and yet higher, so did these latter seem to shrink out of humanity and appear nearer and nearer to the brutes."[3]

Some historians have emphasized an economic motivation for imperialism. There was a great demand for natural resources and products not found in Western countries, such as rubber, oil, and tin. Instead of just trading for these products, European investors advocated direct control of the areas where the raw materials were found. The large surpluses of capital that were being accumulated by bankers and industrialists often encouraged them to seek higher rates of profit in underdeveloped areas. All of these factors combined to create an economic imperialism whereby European finance dominated the economic activity of a large part of the world. This economic imperialism, however, was not necessarily the same thing as colonial expansion. Businessmen invested where it was most profitable, not necessarily where their own countries had colonial empires. For example, less than 10 percent of French foreign investments before 1914 went to French colonies; most of the rest went to Latin American and European countries. It should also be remembered that much of the colonial territory that was acquired was mere wasteland from the point of view of industrialized Europe and cost more to administer than it produced economically. Only the search for national prestige could justify such losses.

Followers of Karl Marx were especially eager to argue that imperialism was economically motivated because they associated imperialism with the ultimate demise of the capitalist system. Marx had hinted at this argument, but it was one of his followers, the Russian Vladimir Lenin (see Chapter 26), who in *Imperialism, the Highest Stage of World Capitalism* developed the idea that capitalism led to imperialism. According to Lenin, as the capitalist system concentrated more wealth in ever-fewer hands, it exhausted the possibility of investment at home, thus compelling capitalists to invest abroad, establish colonies, and exploit small, weak nations. The only cure for imperialism, then, was the destruction of capitalism.

Some Europeans took a more religious-humanitarian approach to imperialism when they argued that Europeans had a moral responsibility to civilize ignorant peoples. This notion of the "white man's burden" (see the box on p. 858) helped at least the more idealistic individuals to rationalize imperialism in their own minds. Nevertheless, the belief that the superiority of their civilization obligated them to impose modern industry, cities, and new medicines on supposedly primitive nonwhites—even if the native peoples had to be killed in the process—was yet another form of racism.

The Creation of Empires

Whatever the reasons for the new imperialism, it had a dramatic effect on Africa and Asia as European powers competed for control of these two continents.

AFRICA Europeans controlled relatively little of the African continent before 1880. During the Napoleonic wars, the British had established themselves in south Africa by taking control of Capetown, originally founded by the Dutch. After the wars, the British encouraged settlers to come to what they called Cape Colony where they created a new administrative system that used English as the official language. British policies disgusted the Boers or Afrikaners, as the descendants of the Dutch colonists were called, and led them in 1835 to migrate north on the Great Trek to the region between the Orange and Vaal rivers (later known as the Orange Free State) and north of the Vaal River (the Transvaal). Hostilities between the British and the Boers continued, however. In 1877, the British governor of Cape Colony seized the Transvaal, but a Boer revolt led the British government to recognize Transvaal as the independent South African Republic. These struggles between the British and the Boers did not prevent either white group from massacring and subjugating the Zulu and Xhosa peoples of south Africa.

In the 1880s, British policy in south Africa was largely determined by Cecil Rhodes (1853–1902). Rhodes founded both diamond and gold companies that monopolized production of these precious commodities and enabled him to establish power over a territory north of Transvaal that he named Rhodesia after himself. The imperialist ambitions of Rhodes brought his downfall in 1896 when the British government forced him to resign as prime minister of Rhodesia after he conspired to overthrow the Boer government of the South African Re-

The White Man's Burden
▼ ▼ ▼

One of the justifications for European imperialism was the misguided, arrogant, and racist notion that superior white peoples had the moral responsibility to raise ignorant native peoples to a higher level of civilization. The British poet Rudyard Kipling (1865–1936) captured this notion in his poem, The White Man's Burden.

Rudyard Kipling, *The White Man's Burden*

Take up the White Man's burden—
Send forth the best ye breed—
Go bind your sons to exile
To serve your captives' needs;
To wait in heavy harness,
On fluttered folk and wild—
Your new-caught sullen peoples,
Half-devil and half-child.

Take up the White Man's burden—
In patience to abide,
To veil the threat of terror
And check the show of pride;
By open speech and simple,
An hundred times made plain
To seek another's profit,
And work another's gain.

Take up the White Man's burden—
The savage wars of peace—
Fill full the mouth of Famine
And bid the sickness cease;
And when your goal is nearest
The end for others sought,
Watch sloth and heathen Folly
Bring all your hopes to nought.

Take up the White Man's burden—
No tawdry rule of kings,
But toil of serf and sweeper—
The tale of common things.
The ports ye shall not enter,
The roads ye shall not read,
Go mark them with your living,
And mark them with your dead.

Take up the White Man's burden—
And reap his old reward:
The blame of those ye better,
The hate of those ye guard—
The cry of hosts ye humour
(Ah, slowly!) toward the light:—
'Why brought he us from bondage,
Our loved Egyptian night?'

Take up the White Man's burden—
Ye dare not stoop to less—
Nor call too loud on Freedom
To cloke your weariness;
By all ye cry or whisper,
By all you leave or do,
The silent, sullen peoples
Shall weigh your gods and you.

Take up the White Man's burden—
Have done with childish days—
The lightly proferred laurel,
The easy, ungrudged praise.
Comes now, to search your manhood
Through all the thankless years,
Cold, edged with dear-bought wisdom,
The judgment of your peers!

---

public without British approval. Although the British government had hoped to avoid war with the Boers, it could not stop extremists on both sides from precipitating such action. The Boer War dragged on from 1899 to 1902 when the Boers were overwhelmed by the larger British army. British policy toward the defeated Boers was remarkably conciliatory. Transvaal and the Orange Free State had representative governments by 1907, and in 1910, a Union of South Africa was created. Like Canada, Australia, and New Zealand, it became a fully self-governing dominion within the British Empire.

Before 1880, the only other European settlements in Africa had been made by the French and Portuguese. The Portuguese had held on to their settlements in An-

The Black Man's Burden
▼ ▼ ▼

The Western justification of imperialism that was based on a sense of moral responsibility, evident in Rudyard Kipling's poem, was often hypocritical. Edward Morel, a British journalist who spent time in the Congo, pointed out the destructive effects of Western imperialism on native Africans in his book, The Black Man's Burden.

Edward Morel, The Black Man's Burden

It is [the Africans] who carry the "Black man's burden." They have not withered away before the white man's occupation. Indeed . . . Africa has ultimately absorbed within itself every Caucasian and, for that matter, every Semitic invader, too. In hewing out for himself a fixed abode in Africa, the white man has massacred the African in heaps. The African has survived, and it is well for the white settlers that he has. . . .

What the partial occupation of his soil by the white man has failed to do; what the mapping out of European political "spheres of influence" has failed to do; what the Maxim [machine gun] and the rifle, the slave gang, labour in the bowels of the earth and the lash, have failed to do; what imported measles, small-pox and syphilis have failed to do; whatever the overseas slave trade failed to do; the power of modern capitalistic exploitation, assisted by modern engines of destruction, may yet succeed in accomplishing.

For from the evils of the latter, scientifically applied and enforced, there is no escape for the African. Its destructive effects are not spasmodic: they are permanent. In its permanence resides its fatal consequences. It kills not the body merely, but the soul. It breaks the spirit. It attacks the African at every turn, from every point of vantage. It wrecks his polity, uproots him from the land, invades his family life, destroys his natural pursuits and occupations, claims his whole time, enslaves him in his own home. . . .

In Africa, especially in tropical Africa, which a capitalistic imperialism threatens and has, in part, already devastated, man is incapable of reacting against unnatural conditions. In those regions man is engaged in a perpetual struggle against disease and an exhausting climate, which tells heavily upon child-bearing; and there is no scientific machinery for saving the weaker members of the community. The African of the tropics is capable of tremendous physical labours. But he cannot accommodate himself to the European system of monotonous, uninterrupted labour, with its long and regular hours, involving, moreover, as it frequently does, severance from natural surroundings and nostalgia, the condition of melancholy resulting from separation from home, a malady to which the African is specially prone. Climatic conditions forbid it. When the system is forced upon him, the tropical African droops and dies.

Nor is violent physical opposition to abuse and injustice henceforth possible for the African in any part of Africa. His chances of effective resistance have been steadily dwindling with the increasing perfectibility in the killing power of modern armament. . . .

Thus the African is really helpless against the material gods of the white man, as embodied in the trinity of imperialism, capitalistic exploitation, and militarism. . . .

To reduce all the varied and picturesque and stimulating episodes in savage life to a dull routine of endless toil for uncomprehended ends, to dislocate social ties and disrupt social ties and disrupt social institutions; to stifle nascent desires and crush mental development; to graft upon primitive passions the annihilating evils of scientific slavery, and the bestial imaginings of civilized man, unrestrained by convention or law; in fine, to kill the soul in a people—this is a crime which transcends physical murder.

gola on the west coast and Mozambique on the east coast. The French had started the conquest of Algeria in Muslim north Africa in 1830, although it was not until 1879 that French civilian rule was established there. By the next year, 1880, the European scramble for possession of Africa began in earnest. Before 1900, the French had added the huge area of French West Africa and Tunisia to their African empire. In 1912, they created a protectorate over much of Morocco; the rest was left to Spain.

The British took an active interest in Egypt after the Suez Canal was opened by the French in 1869. Since they believed that the canal was essential to their lifeline to India, the British sought to exercise as much control as possible over the canal area. Egypt was a well-established state with an autonomous Muslim government, but that did not stop the British from landing an expeditionary force in Egypt in 1882. Although they asserted that their occupation was only temporary, they soon established a protectorate over Egypt. From Egypt, the British moved south into Sudan and seized it after narrowly averting a war with France. Not to be undone, Italy joined in the imperialist scramble. The humiliating defeat of the Italians by the Ethiopians in 1896 only led the Italians to try again in 1911 by invading and seizing Turkish Tripoli, which the Italians renamed Libya.

Central Africa was also added to the list of European colonies. Popular interest in the forbiddingly dense tropical jungles of central Africa was first aroused in the 1860s and 1870s by explorers, such as the Scottish missionary David Livingstone and the British-American journalist Henry M. Stanley. But the real driving force for the colonization of central Africa was King Leopold II (1865–1909) of Belgium, who had rushed enthusiastically into pursuit of empire in Africa: "To open to civilization," he said, "the only part of our globe where it has not yet penetrated, to pierce the darkness which envelops whole populations, is a crusade, if I may say so,

▼ **Map 25.2** Africa in 1914.

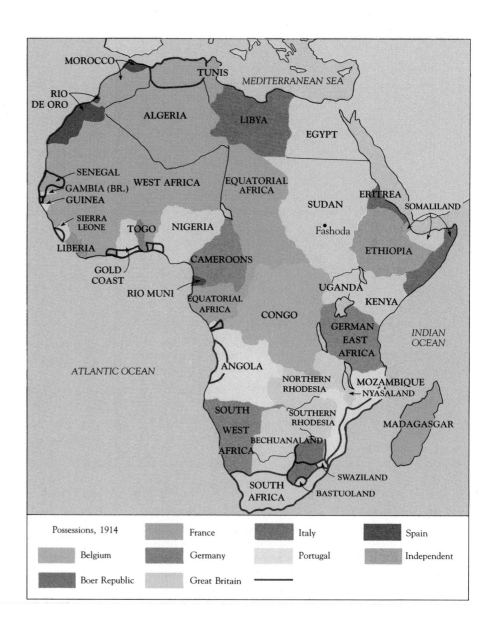

a crusade worthy of this century of progress." Profit, however, was more important to Leopold than progress. In 1876, he created the International Association for the Exploration and Civilization of Central Africa and engaged Henry Stanley to establish Belgian settlements in the Congo. Alarmed by Leopold's actions, the French also moved into the territory north of the Congo River.

Between 1884 and 1900, most of the rest of Africa was carved up by the European powers. Germany also entered the ranks of the imperialist powers at this time. Initially, Bismarck had downplayed the significance of colonies but as domestic political pressures for a German empire increased, Bismarck became a political convert to colonialism. As he expressed it, "All this colonial business is a sham, but we need it for the elections." The Germans established colonies in Southwest Africa, the Cameroons, Togoland, and East Africa.

By 1914, Britain, France, Germany, Belgium, Spain, and Portugal had divided Africa. Only Liberia, founded by emancipated American slaves, and Ethiopia remained free states. Despite the humanitarian rationalizations about the "white man's burden," Africa had been conquered by European states determined to create colonial empires (see the box on p. 859). Any native people who dared to resist (with the exception of the Ethiopians) was simply devastated by the superior military force of the Europeans. At the Battle of Omdurman in 1898, when the native Muslims in the Sudan tried to stop a British expedition armed with the recently developed machine gun, a typical massacre of natives occurred. One observer noted: "It was not a battle but an execution. . . . The bodies were not in heaps—bodies hardly ever are; but they spread evenly over acres and acres. Some lay very composedly with their slippers placed under their heads for a last pillow; some knelt, cut short in the middle of a last prayer. Others were torn to pieces."[4] The battle casualties at Omdurman tell the story of the one-sided conflicts between Europeans and native Africans: 28 British deaths to 11,000 Muslim tribesmen. Military superiority was frequently accompanied by brutality in the handling of blacks. Nor did Europeans hesitate to deceive the natives to gain their way. One south African king, Lo Bengula, informed Queen Victoria about how he had been cheated:

> Some time ago a party of men came to my country, the principal one appearing to be a man called Rudd. They asked me for a place to dig for gold, and said they would give me certain things for the right to do so. I told them to bring what they could give and I would show them what I would give. A document was written and presented to me for signature. I asked what it contained, and was told that in it were my

words and the words of those men. I put my hand to it. About three months afterwards I heard from other sources that I had given by that document the right to all the minerals of my country.[5]

ASIA   Although Asia had been open to Western influence since the sixteenth century, not much of its immense territory had fallen under direct European control. The Dutch were established in the East Indies and the Spanish in the Philippines while the French and Portuguese had trading posts on the Indian coast. China, Japan, Korea, and Southeast Asia had largely managed to exclude westerners. The British and the Russians, however, had acquired the most Asian territory.

Britain's interest in the Far East dated back to the seventeenth century, but it was not until the explorations of Australia by Captain James Cook between 1768 and 1771 that Britain took an active interest. By the 1780s, Britain had begun to use Australia as a penal colony to relieve overcrowded British prisons. The availability of land for grazing sheep and the discovery of gold led, however, to an influx of free settlers who slaughtered many of the native inhabitants. In 1850, the British government granted the various Australian colonies virtually complete self-government, and fifty years later, on January 1, 1901, all the colonies were unified into a Commonwealth of Australia. Nearby New Zealand, which the British had declared a colony in 1840, was also granted dominion status in 1907.

The British East India Company (see Chapter 18) had been responsible for subjugating much of India. In 1858, however, after a revolt of the sepoys or native troops of the East India Company's army had been defeated, the British Parliament transferred the company's powers directly to the government in London. In 1876, the title Empress of India was bestowed upon Queen Victoria.

Russian expansion in Asia was a logical outgrowth of its traditional territorial aggrandizement. Russian explorers had penetrated the wilderness of Siberia in the seventeenth century and reached the Pacific coast in 1637. In the eighteenth century, Russians established a claim on Alaska, which was later sold to the United States in 1867. Gradually, Russian settlers moved into cold and forbidding Siberia. Altogether 7 million Russians settled in Siberia between 1800 and 1914; by 1914, 90 percent of the Siberian population were Slavs, not Asiatics.

In the nineteenth century, the Russians also moved south, attracted by warmer lands and the crumbling Ottoman Empire. By 1830, the Russians had established control over the entire northern coast of the Black Sea

▼ **British Tourists in Asia.** After 1870, European states engaged in an intense struggle for overseas territory and did not stop until Africa and Asia had been carved up into colonies or spheres of influence. Western imperialistic attitudes were often based upon an assumption of cultural superiority. Westerners, as is evident in this photograph of British tourists in front of an Indian temple, often seemed to take for granted their superiority over native peoples.

and then pressed on into central Asia, securing the trans-Caspian area by 1881 and Turkestan in 1885. These advances brought the Russians to the borders of Persia and Afghanistan where the British also had interests because of their desire to protect their holdings in India. In 1907, the Russians and British agreed to make Afghanistan a buffer state between Russian Turkestan and British India and divide Persia into two spheres of influence. Halted by the British in their expansion to the south, the Russians moved east in Asia. The Russian occupation of Manchuria and their attempt to move into Korea brought war with the new imperialist power, Japan (see Japan later in the chapter). After losing the Russo-Japanese War in 1905, the Russians agreed to a Japanese protectorate in Korea, and their Asian expansion was brought to a temporary halt.

The thrust of imperialism after 1880 led Westerners to move into new areas of Asia hitherto largely free of Western influence. By the nineteenth century, the ruling Manchu dynasty of the Chinese empire was showing signs of decline. In 1842, the British had obtained (through war) the island of Hong Kong and trading rights in a number of Chinese cities. Other Western nations soon rushed in to gain similar trading privileges. Chinese attempts to resist this encroachment of foreigners led to military defeats and new demands. Only rivalry among the great powers themselves prevented the complete dismemberment of the Chinese empire. Instead, Britain, France, Germany, Russia, the United States, and Japan established spheres of influence and long-term leases of Chinese territory. In 1899, urged along by the American Secretary of State John Hay, they agreed to an "open door" policy in which one country would not restrict the commerce of the other countries in their own spheres of influence.

Japan avoided Western intrusion until 1853–1854 when American naval forces under Commodore Matthew Perry forced the Japanese to grant the United States trading and diplomatic privileges. Japan, however, managed to avoid China's fate. Korea had also largely excluded Westerners. The fate of Korea was determined first by the struggle between China and Japan in 1894–1895 and later between Japan and Russia in 1904–1905. Japan's victories gave it a clear superiority, and in 1910 Japan formally annexed Korea.

In Southeast Asia, Britain established control over Burma and the Malay States while France played an active role in subjugating Indochina. The city of Saigon was occupied in 1858, and four years later Cochin China was taken. In the 1880s, the French extended "protection" over Cambodia, Annam, Tonkin, and Laos and organized them into a Union of French Indochina. Only

Siam (Thailand) remained free as a buffer state because of British-French rivalry.

The Pacific islands were also the scene of great power competition and witnessed the entry of the United States onto the imperialist stage. The Samoan Islands became the first important American colony; the Hawaiian Islands were the next to fall. Soon after Americans had made Pearl Harbor into a naval station in 1887, American settlers gained control of the sugar industry on the islands. When Hawaiian natives tried to reassert their authority, the United States Marines were brought in to "protect" American lives. Hawaii was annexed by the United States in 1898 during the era of American nationalistic fervor generated by the Spanish-American War. The American defeat of Spain encouraged Americans to extend their empire by acquiring Cuba, Puerto Rico, Guam, and the Philippine Islands. Although the Filipinos hoped for independence, the Americans refused to grant it. As President William McKinley said, the United States had the duty "to educate the Filipinos and uplift and Christianize them," a remarkable statement in view of the fact that most of them had been Roman Catholics for centuries. It took three years and 60,000 troops to pacify the Philippines and establish American control. Not until 1946 did the Filipinos receive complete independence.

Native Responses to Imperialism

When Europeans imposed their culture upon peoples they considered inferior, how did the conquered native peoples respond? Initial attempts to expel the foreigners only led to devastating defeats at the hands of Westerners, whose industrial technology gave them modern weapons of war with which to crush the natives. Accustomed to rule by small elites, most native peoples simply accepted their new governors, making Western rule relatively easy. Natives subsequently adjusted to foreign rule in different ways. Traditionalists sought to maintain their cultural traditions while modernizers believed that adoption of Western ways would enable them to reform their societies and subsequently challenge Western rule. Most people probably stood somewhere between these two extremes.

Despite Western domination, movements for change soon arose, led by a few strong-willed figures who usually had the benefit of Western knowledge or good insight into Western ways. These native leaders were especially resentful of Western attitudes of superiority and demanded human dignity for the indigenous people. They also adopted the West's own ideologies for change. Lib-

eralism, with its doctrine of civil rights and political self-determination, and nationalism, with its emphasis on the right of peoples to have their own nations, were used to foster independence movements wherever native people suffered under foreign oppression. Three eventually powerful Asian nations—China, Japan, and India—present different approaches to the question of how native populations responded to foreign rule.

CHINA   The humiliation of China by the Western powers led to much antiforeign violence, but this lawlessness was only used as an excuse by Westerners to extort further concessions from the Chinese. A major outburst of violence against foreigners occurred in the Boxer Rebellion in 1900–1901. Boxers was the popular name given to the Chinese who belonged to a secret organization called the Society of Harmonious Fists, whose aim was to push foreigners out of China. The Boxers murdered foreign missionaries, Chinese who had converted to Christianity, railroad workers, foreign businessmen, and even the German envoy to Peking. Response to the killings was immediate and overwhelming. An allied army consisting of British, French, German, Russian, American, and Japanese troops attacked Peking, restored order, and demanded more concessions from the Chinese government. The imperial government was so weakened that the forces of the revolutionary leader Sun Yat-sen (1866–1925), who adopted a program of "nationalism, democracy, and socialism," overthrew the Manchu dynasty in 1912. The new Republic of China remained weak and ineffective, and China's travails were far from over.

JAPAN   In the late 1850s and early 1860s, it looked as if Japan would follow China's fate and be carved up into spheres of influence by aggressive Western powers. A remarkably rapid transformation, however, produced a very different result. Before 1868, the shogun, a powerful hereditary military governor assisted by a warrior nobility known as the samurai, exercised real power in Japan. The emperor's functions had become primarily religious. After the shogun's concessions to the Western nations, antiforeign sentiment led to a samurai revolt in 1867 and the restoration of the emperor as the rightful head of the government. The new emperor was the astute, dynamic, young Mutsuhito (1867–1912), who called his reign the Meiji (Enlightened Government) and inaugurated a remarkable transformation of Japan that has since been known as the Meiji Restoration.

Recognizing the obvious military and industrial superiority of the West, the new emperor and his advisers

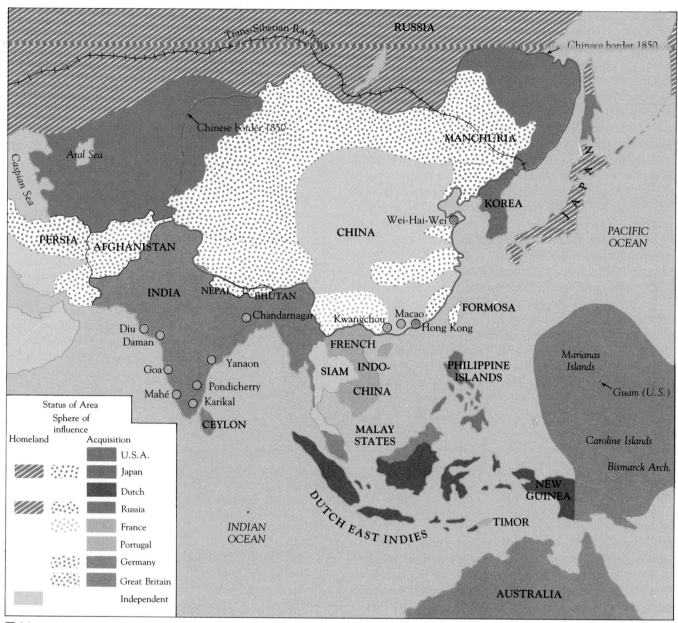

Status of Area

Sphere of influence

Homeland	Acquisition	
		U.S.A.
		Japan
		Dutch
		Russia
		France
		Portugal
		Germany
		Great Britain
		Independent

▼ **Map 25.3** Asia in 1914.

decided to modernize Japan by absorbing and adopting Western methods. Thousands of young Japanese were sent abroad to receive Western educations, especially in the social and natural sciences. A German-style army and a British-style navy were adopted. The Japanese copied the industrial and financial methods of the United States and developed a modern commercial and industrial system. A highly centralized administrative system copied from the French replaced the old feudal system. Initially, the Japanese adopted the French principles of social and legal equality, but by 1890 they had created an authoritarian political system that largely rejected democracy.

In its imitation of the West, Japan also developed a powerful military state. Universal military conscription was introduced in 1872, and a modern peacetime army of 240,000 was eventually established. The Japanese avidly pursued the Western imperialistic model. They de-

feated China in 1894–1895, annexed some Chinese territory, and established their own sphere of influence in China. After they had defeated the Russians in 1905, the Japanese were left in control of Korea. The Japanese had proven that an Eastern power could play the "white man's" imperialistic game and provided a potent example to native peoples in other regions of Asia and Africa.

INDIA The British had been in control of India since the mid-nineteenth century. After crushing what the natives called the Great Rebellion (the British called it a mutiny), the British ruled India directly. Parliament had overall supervision while a small, all-white civil service directed affairs in India. This meant that 3,500 British officials ruled almost 300 million people.

No doubt, British rule bestowed a number of benefits upon India. The British put an end to the internal wars that had ravaged India for centuries and created a unified state through their centralized bureaucracy. They also brought Western technology—railroads, banks, mines, industry, medical knowledge, and hospitals. The British introduced Western-style secondary schools and colleges where the Indian upper classes were educated so that they could serve as trained subordinates in the government and army.

The Indians, however, had many complaints about British rule. Extreme poverty was a way of life for most Indians; almost two-thirds of the population were malnourished in 1901. British industrialization brought little improvement for the masses. British manufactured goods destroyed native industries while Indian wealth was used to pay British officials and a large army. The system of education served only the elite, upper-class Indians, and it was only conducted in the rulers' English language while 90 percent of the population remained illiterate. Even for the newly educated upper classes who benefited the most from their Western educations, British rule was degrading. The best jobs and the best housing were reserved for Britons. Despite their education, the Indians were never considered equals of the British whose racial attitudes were made quite clear by Lord Kitchener, one of Britain's foremost military commanders of India, when he said: "It is this consciousness of the inherent superiority of the European which has won for us India. However well educated and clever a native may be, and however brave he may prove himself, I believe that no rank we can bestow on him would cause him to be considered an equal of the British officer."[6] Such smug racial attitudes made it difficult for British rule, no matter how beneficent, ever to be ultimately accepted and

Chronology
▼ ▼ ▼
The New Imperialism: Asia

Britain Obtains Hong Kong and Trading Rights from Chinese Government	1842
Australian Colonies Receive Self-Government	1850
Mission of Commodore Perry to Japan	1853–1854
Great Rebellion in India	1858
French Occupy Saigon	1859
Overthrow of the Shogun in Japan	1867
Emperor Mutsuhito and the Meiji Restoration	1867–1912
Queen Victoria Is Made Empress of India	1876
Russians in Central Asia (Trans-Caspian Area)	1881
Formation of Indian National Congress	1883
Russians in Turkestan	1885
Japanese Defeat of China	1894–1895
Spanish-American War; United States Annexes Philippines	1898
"Open Door" Policy in China	1899
Boxer Rebellion in China	1900–1901
Commonwealth of Australia	1901
Commonwealth of New Zealand	1907
Russian-British Agreement over Afghanistan and Persia	1907
Japan Annexes Korea	1910
Overthrow of Manchu Dynasty in China	1912

led to the rise of an Indian nationalist movement. By 1883, when the Indian National Congress was formed, moderate, educated Indians began to seek some self-government. Within another twenty years, radical demands for complete independence were being expressed. One of the major hurdles to the independence movement, however, came from Indians themselves. The Hindu majority was often bitterly opposed by the Muslim and Sikh religious minorities. These divisions, however, did not stop the movement for national independence.

▼ International Rivalry and the Coming of War

Between 1871 and 1914, Europeans experienced a long period of peace. There were wars (including wars of conquest in the non-Western world), but none involved the great powers. There were, however, a series of crises that might easily have led to general war. Until 1890, Bismarck of Germany exercised a restraining influence on Europeans. He realized that the emergence in 1871 of a unified Germany as the most powerful state on the Continent had upset the balance of power established at Vienna in 1815. Bismarck knew that Germany's success frightened Europeans, and he feared the creation of an anti-German coalition. The preservation of peace would best maintain the new status quo and preserve the new German state. As leader of the powerful German state and an astute diplomat, Bismarck dominated the European international scene until 1890.

The Bismarckian System

Bismarck was well aware that the French constituted Germany's greatest threat. The loss of Alsace-Lorraine to the Germans in the Franco-Prussian War ensured French desire for revenge. Bismarck understood that if France became allied with others, it would pose a real danger to Germany. His first move was to seek the cooperation of the traditionally conservative powers, Austria-Hungary and Russia. By 1873, he had concluded several treaties with them that created the first Three Emperors' League. The three powers agreed to suppress subversive activities at home and consult together if other powers threatened the European peace. The league failed to work very well, however, primarily because of Russian-Austrian rivalry in eastern Europe, specifically, in the Balkans.

The problem in the Balkans was yet another extension of the "Eastern Question" (see Chapter 22). The disintegration of the Turkish or Ottoman Empire had troubled Europeans for some time. Both Russia and Austria had designs on the Balkans. For Russia, the Balkans provided the shortest overland route to Istanbul and the Straits. Austria viewed the Balkans as fertile ground for Austrian expansion, which some Austrian leaders saw as the only way to circumvent the nationalities problem. Both Britain and France feared the extension of Russian power into the Mediterranean and Middle East. Although Germany had no real interests in the Balkans, Bismarck was fearful of the consequences of a war between Russia and Austria over the Balkans and served as a restraining influence on both powers. Events in the Balkans, however, precipitated a new crisis.

In 1876, the Balkan states of Serbia and Montenegro declared war on Turkey. Both were defeated, but Russia, with Austrian approval, attacked and defeated the Turks. By the Treaty of San Stefano in 1878, a large Bulgarian state, extending from the Danube in the north to the Aegean Sea in the south, was created. As Bulgaria was viewed as a Russian satellite, this Russian success caused the other great powers to call for a congress of European powers to discuss a revision of the treaty.

The Congress of Berlin, which met in the summer of 1878, was dominated by Bismarck. The congress effectively demolished the Treaty of San Stefano, much to Russia's humiliation. The new Bulgarian state was considerably reduced while the rest of the territory was returned to Turkish control. The three Balkan states of Serbia, Montenegro, and Romania, until then nominally under Turkish control, were recognized as independent. The other Balkan territories of Bosnia and Herzegovina were placed under Austrian protection; Austria could occupy but not annex them. Although the Germans received no territory, they felt they had at least preserved the peace among the great powers.

The Russians, however, resented the Germans' failure to prevent their diplomatic setback at Berlin. The Three Emperors' League was demolished. Fearful of a possible anti-German alliance between France, Russia, and possibly even Austria, Bismarck made a defensive alliance with Austria in 1879. Both powers agreed to support each other in the event of an attack by Russia. In 1882, this German-Austrian alliance was enlarged with the entrance of Italy, angry with the French over conflicting colonial ambitions in north Africa. The Triple Alliance of 1882 committed the three powers to support the existing political and social order while providing a defensive alliance against France or "two or more great powers not members of the alliance." Although the three powers agreed to a five-year term for the treaty, it was renewed regularly and became a regular feature of European international politics until World War I.

In the midst of his alliance making, Bismarck had not forgotten Russia and sought to reestablish the Three Emperors' League as the "only system offering the maximum stability for the peace of Europe." Austria, Germany, and Russia joined together once more in 1881. Again, however, the Three Emperors' League floundered on the shoals of Austrian-Russian hostility over the Balkans, and the league collapsed in 1886. Bismarck was still eager to maintain a good relationship with Russia, especially to prevent a French-Russian alliance that would

threaten Germany with the possibility of a two-front war. In the Reinsurance Treaty of 1887, Germany and Russia pledged to remain neutral if the other became involved in a war with a third power, unless it was an aggressive war by Germany against France or Russia against Austria. At the same time, Bismarck tried to remain on good terms with Great Britain.

The Bismarckian system of alliances, geared to preserving peace and the status quo, had worked. Whether it would have continued to work in the face of Russian, Italian, French, and Austrian desires to change the status quo for their own gains is problematic. Even in Germany there was growing criticism of Bismarck's policy and increased talk about the need for expansion if Germany were to remain a great state. These forces for chauvinistic nationalism were encouraged when William II cashiered Bismarck in 1890 and assumed direction of Germany's foreign policy.

New Directions and New Crises

At the end of the nineteenth century and beginning of the twentieth, diplomatic activity was still largely the preserve of aristocrats who were guided by the eighteenth- and nineteenth-century concepts of balance of power, reason of state, and the concert of Europe. But the manipulation of national interests by the secret negotiations of aristocratic diplomats was increasingly threatened by mass interest in national affairs. The growth of nationalism and mass politics led to an increased emphasis on national competition. Politicians found that an appeal to nationalism carried great weight with the masses of people and could easily be reinforced by the use of mass communications. The growth of literacy after 1870 (see Mass Education later in the chapter) made possible mass-circulation newspapers that fostered jingoistic feelings and encouraged the desire for national prestige. Imperialism, as we have seen, was impelled not only by industrial and commercial interests, but to a great extent by public clamor for national greatness. Driven by popular excitement, diplomats found themselves increasingly directed by events rather than by rational calculations, and they were forced to seek short-term successes regardless of their long-term consequences.

Bismarck's alliances had served to bring the European powers into an interlocking system in which no one state could be certain of much support if it chose to initiate a war of aggression. After 1890, a new European diplomacy unfolded in which Europe became divided into two opposing camps that became more and more inflexible and unwilling to compromise.

After Bismarck's dismissal, Emperor William II embarked upon an activist foreign policy dedicated to enhancing German power by finding, as he put it, Germany's rightful "place in the sun." One of his changes in Bismarck's foreign policy was to drop the Reinsurance Treaty with Russia, which he viewed as being at odds with Germany's alliance with Austria. Although William II tried to remain friendly with Russia, the ending of the alliance achieved what Bismarck had feared: it brought France and Russia together. Long isolated by Bismarck's policies, republican France leapt at the chance to draw closer to tsarist Russia, and in 1894 the two powers concluded a military alliance.

The attitude of the British now became crucial. Secure in its vast empire, the British had long pursued a policy of "splendid isolation" toward the Continent. The British were startled, however, when many Europeans condemned their activity in the Boer War (1899–1902) in south Africa. Fearful of an anti-British continental alliance, they saw the weakness of "splendid isolation" and sought an alliance with a continental power. Initially, neither France nor Russia seemed a logical choice. Britain's traditional enmity with France had only intensified because of their imperialistic rivalries in Africa and Asia. Likewise, British and Russian imperialistic interests had frequently collided.

Germany, therefore, seemed the most likely potential ally. Certainly, there were both Britons and Germans

▼ **The Kaiser and the Krupps.** After 1890, Emperor William of Germany established an activist foreign policy for Germany that tended to increase tensions in Europe. The close connection between the imperialist state and armaments manufacturers is evident in this photograph. Emperor William II is shown visiting the Krupp works in 1912. The Krupp industrial empire was one of the largest in the world.

The Emperor's "Big Mouth"

▼ ▼ ▼

Emperor William II's world policy, which was aimed at finding Germany's "place in the sun," created considerable ill will and unrest among other European states, especially Britain. Moreover, the emperor had the unfortunate tendency to stir up trouble by his often tactless public remarks. In this 1908 interview, for example, William II intended to strengthen Germany's ties with Britain. His words had just the opposite effect and raised a storm of protest in both Britain and Germany.

Daily Telegraph Interview, October 28, 1908

As I have said, his Majesty honoured me with a long conversation, and spoke with impulsive and unusual frankness. "You English," he said, "are mad, mad, mad as March hares. What has come over you that you are so completely given over to suspicions quite unworthy of a great nation? What more can I do than I have done? I declared with all the emphasis at my command, in my speech at Guildhall, that my heart is set upon peace, and that it is one of my dearest wishes to live on the best of terms with England. Have I ever been false to my word? Falsehood and prevarication are alien to my nature. My actions ought to speak for themselves, but you listen not to them but to those who misinterpret and distort them. That is a personal insult which I feel and resent. To be forever misjudged, to have my repeated offers of friendship weighed and scrutinized with jealous, mistrustful eyes, taxes my patience severely. I have said time after time that I am a friend of England, and your Press—or, at least, a considerable section of it—bids the people of England to refuse my proffered hand, and insinuates that the other holds a dagger. How can I convince a nation against its will?"

"I repeat," continued his Majesty, "that I am a friend of England, but you make things difficult for me. My task is not of the easiest. The prevailing sentiment among large sections of the middle and lower classes of my own people is not friendly to England. I am, therefore, so to speak, in a minority in my own land, but it is a minority of the best elements as it is in England with respect to Germany. That is another reason why I resent your refusal to accept my pledged word that I am the friend of England. I strive without ceasing to improve relations, and you retort that I am your arch-enemy. You make it hard for me. Why is it? . . ."

"But, you will say, what of the German Navy? Surely, that is a menace to England! Against whom but England are my squadrons being prepared? If England is not in the minds of those Germans who are bent on creating a powerful fleet, why is Germany asked to consent to such new and heavy burdens of taxation? My answer is clear. Germany is a young and growing Empire. She has a world-wide commerce, which is rapidly expanding, and to which the legitimate ambition of patriotic Germans refuses to assign any bounds. Germany must have a powerful fleet to protect that commerce, and her manifold interests in even the most distant seas. She expects those interests to go on growing, and she must be able to champion them manfully in any quarter of the globe. Germany looks ahead. Her horizons stretch far away. She must be prepared for any eventualities in the Far East. Who can foresee what may take place in the Pacific in the days to come, days not so distant as some believe, but days, at any rate, for which all European Powers with Far Eastern interests ought steadily to prepare? Look at the accomplished rise of Japan; think of the possible national awakening of China; and then judge of the vast problems of the Pacific. Only those Powers which have great navies will be listened to with respect, when the future of the Pacific comes to be solved; and, if for that reason only, Germany must have a powerful fleet. It may even be that England herself will be glad that Germany has a fleet when they speak together on the same side in the great debates of the future."

who believed that their common German heritage (Anglo-Saxons from Germany had settled in Britain in the Early Middle Ages) made them "natural allies." But Britain was not particularly popular in Germany, nor did the British especially like the Germans. Industrial and commercial rivalry had created much ill feeling while William II's imperial posturing and grabbing for colonies made the British suspicious of Germany's ultimate aims (see the box on p. 868). Especially worrisome to the British was the German construction of a large navy, especially the number of battleships advocated by the persistent Admiral von Tirpitz, secretary of the German navy. The British now turned to their traditional enemy, France, and in 1904 concluded the Entente Cordiale by which the two settled all of their outstanding colonial disputes.

German response to the Entente was swift, creating what has been called the First Moroccan Crisis in 1905. The Germans chose to oppose French designs on Morocco in order to humiliate them and drive a wedge between the two new allies—Britain and France. Refusing to compromise, the Germans insisted upon an international conference to settle the problem. Germany's foolish saber rattling had the opposite effect of what had been intended and succeeded only in uniting Russia, France, Great Britain, and even the United States against Germany. The conference at Algeciras, Spain, in January 1906 awarded control of Morocco to France. Germany came out of the conference with nothing.

The First Moroccan Crisis of 1905–1906 had important repercussions. France and Britain drew closer together as both began to view Germany as a real threat to European peace. German leaders, on the other hand, began to speak of sinister plots to encircle Germany and hinder its emergence as a world power. Russia, too, grew more and more suspicious of the Germans and signed an agreement in 1907 with Great Britain. By that year, Europe's division into two major blocs—the Triple Alliance of Germany, Austria-Hungary, and Italy and the Triple Entente, as the loose confederation of Russia, France, and Great Britain was called—grew increasingly rigid at the same time that the problems in the Balkans were heating up.

Three forces were now working against any peaceful resolution of the region's difficult problems. The forces of nationalism continued to grow as Slavic peoples gained their freedom from Turkish overlordship and saw Austrian expansion as the new danger to their national aspirations. At the same time, Austrian and Russian rivalry in the Balkans only intensified. Finally, while Bismarck had labored to make Germany a mediator be-

Three Emperors' League	1873
Serbia and Montenegro Attack the Turks	1876
Treaty of San Stefano	1878
Congress of Berlin	1878
Defensive Alliance: Germany and Austria	1879
Renewal of Three Emperors' League	1881
Triple Alliance: Germany, Austria, and Italy	1882
Collapse of Three Emperors' League	1886
Reinsurance Treaty: Germany and Russia	1887
Military Alliance: Russia and France	1894
Entente Cordiale: France and Britain	1904
First Moroccan Crisis	1905–1906
Triple Entente: France, Britain, and Russia	1907
First Balkan War	1912
Second Balkan War	1913

tween Austria-Hungary and Russia, under Emperor William II, Germany became the chief advocate for maintaining the Ottoman Empire. No longer a mediator but a participant in Balkan affairs, Germany added a potentially dangerous element to the situation. A new series of crises between 1908 and 1913 over the struggle for the control of the remnants of the Ottoman Empire in the Balkans set the stage for World War I.

CRISES IN THE BALKANS, 1908–1913 The Bosnian Crisis of 1908–1909 began a chain of events that eventually went out of control. Since 1878, Bosnia and Herzegovina had been under the protection of Austria, but in 1908, Austria took the drastic step of annexing these two Slavic-speaking territories. Serbia became outraged at this action because it dashed the Serbians' hopes of creating a large Serbian kingdom that would include most of the south Slavs. This was why the Austrians had annexed Bosnia and Herzegovina. To the Austrians, a large Serbia would be a threat to the unity of the Austro-Hungarian Empire with its large Slavic population. The Russians, as protectors of their fellow Slavs and with their own desire to increase their authority in the Balkans, supported the Serbs and opposed the Austrian action. Backed by the Russians, the Serbs prepared for war against Austria. At this point William II intervened and demanded that the Russians accept Austria's annexation of Bosnia and Herzegovina or face war with Germany. Weakened from their defeat in the Russo-Japanese War in 1904–1905, the Russians were afraid to risk war and backed down. Humiliated, the Russians vowed revenge.

European attention returned to the Balkans in 1912 when Serbia, Bulgaria, Montenegro, and Greece organized a Balkan League and defeated the Turks in the First Balkan War. When the victorious allies were unable to agree on how to divide the conquered Turkish provinces of Macedonia and Albania, a second Balkan War erupted in 1913. Greece, Serbia, Romania, and Turkey attacked and defeated Bulgaria. As a result, Bulgaria obtained only a small part of Macedonia, and most of the rest was divided between Serbia and Greece. Yet Serbia's aspirations remained unfulfilled. The two Balkan wars left the inhabitants embittered and created more tensions among the great powers.

One of Serbia's major ambitions had been to acquire Albanian territory that would give it a port on the Adriatic. At the London Conference arranged by Austria at the end of the two Balkan wars, the Austrians had blocked Serbia's wishes by creating an independent Albania. The Germans, as Austrian allies, had supported this move. In their frustration, Serbian nationalists increasingly portrayed the Austrians as evil monsters who were keeping the Serbs from becoming a great nation. As Serbia's chief supporters, the Russians were also upset by the turn of events in the Balkans. A feeling had grown among Russian leaders that they could not back down again in the event of a confrontation with Austria or Germany in the Balkans. One Russian military journal even stated early in 1914: "We are preparing for a war in the west. The whole nation must accustom itself to the idea that we arm ourselves for a war of annihilation against the Germans." Moreover, as a result of the Balkan wars, both Russia and Austria expressed discontent that their supposed friends and allies, Great Britain and Germany, had not done enough to support them.

▼ **Map 25.4a** The Balkans in 1878.

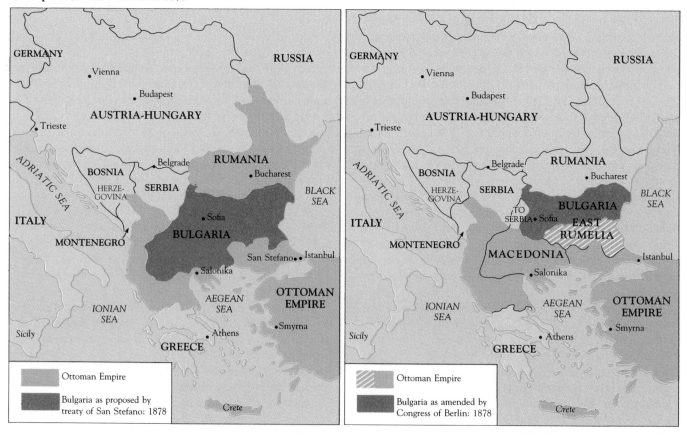

This made the British and Germans more determined to support their allies in order to avoid endangering their alliances with them.

Austria-Hungary had achieved another of its aims, but it was still convinced that Serbia was a mortal threat to its empire and must at some point be crushed. Meanwhile, the French and Russian governments renewed their alliance and promised each other that they would not back down at the next crisis. Britain drew closer to France. By the beginning of 1914, two armed camps viewed each other with suspicion. An American in Europe observed, "The whole of Germany is charged with electricity. Everybody's nerves are tense. It only needs a spark to set the whole thing off." The German ambassador to France noted at the same time that "peace remains at the mercy of an accident." The European "age of progress" was about to come to an inglorious and bloody end.

▼ Intellectual and Cultural Developments: Toward the Modern Consciousness

Before 1914, most Europeans continued to believe in the values and ideals that had been generated by the Scientific Revolution and the Enlightenment. Reason,

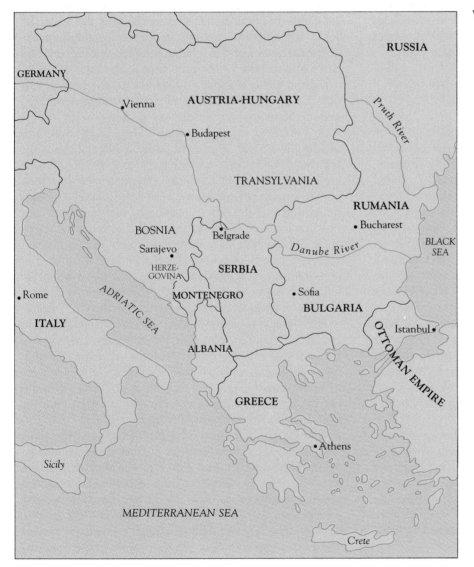

▼ **Map 25.4b.** The Balkans in 1913.

science, and progress were still important words in the European vocabulary. The ability of human beings to improve themselves and achieve a better society seemed to be well demonstrated by a rising standard of living, urban improvements, and mass education. Such products of modern technology as electric lights, phonographs, and automobiles reinforced the popular prestige of science and the belief in the ability of the human mind to comprehend the universe through the use of reason. Between 1870 and 1914, however, a dramatic transformation in the realm of ideas and culture challenged many of these assumptions. A new view of the physical universe, a flight to the irrational, alternative views of human nature, and radically innovative forms of literary and artistic expression shattered old beliefs and opened the way to a modern consciousness. Although the real impact of many of these ideas was not felt until after World War I, they served to provoke a sense of confusion and anxiety before 1914 that would become even more pronounced after the war.

Developments in the Sciences: The Emergence of a New Physics

Science was one of the chief pillars underlying the optimistic and rationalistic view of the world that many Westerners shared in the nineteenth century. Supposedly based on hard facts and cold reason, science offered a certainty of belief in the orderliness of nature that was comforting to many people for whom traditional religious beliefs no longer had much meaning. This faith in science's ability to explain the world was reflected in an introductory paragraph in the University of Chicago's catalog in 1893: "It seems probable that most of the grand underlying principles in the physical sciences have been firmly established and that further advances are to be sought chiefly in the rigorous application of these principles to all the phenomena which come under our notice." Many naively believed that the application of already known scientific laws would give humanity a complete understanding of the physical world and an accurate picture of reality. The new physics dramatically altered that perspective.

Throughout much of the nineteenth century, Westerners adhered to the mechanical conception of the universe postulated by the classical physics of Isaac Newton. In this perspective, the universe was viewed as a giant machine in which time, space, and matter were objective realities that existed independently of those observing them. Matter was thought to be composed of indivisible and solid material bodies called atoms.

These views were first seriously questioned at the end of the nineteenth century. Some scientists had discovered that certain elements such as radium and polonium spontaneously gave off rays or radiation that apparently came from within the atom itself. Atoms were not simply hard, material bodies but small worlds containing such subatomic particles as electrons and protons that behaved in seemingly random and inexplicable fashion. Inquiry into the disintegrative process within atoms became a central theme of the new physics.

Building upon this work, in 1900 a Berlin physicist, Max Planck (1858–1947), disclosed a discovery that he believed was "as important as that of Newton." Planck rejected the belief that a heated body radiates energy in a steady stream but maintained instead that it did so discontinuously, in irregular packets of energy that he called "quanta." The quantum theory raised fundamental questions about the subatomic realm of the atom. By 1900, the old view of atoms as the basic building blocks of the material world was being seriously questioned, and the world of Newtonian physics was in trouble.

Albert Einstein (1879–1955), a German-born patent officer working in Switzerland, pushed these new theories of thermodynamics into new terrain. In 1905, Einstein published a paper entitled "The Electro-dynamics of Moving Bodies" that contained his special theory of relativity. According to relativity theory, space and time are not absolute, but relative to the observer, and both are interwoven into what Einstein called a four-dimensional space-time continuum. Neither space nor time had an existence independent of human experience. As Einstein later explained simply to a journalist: "It was formerly believed that if all material things disappeared out of the universe, time and space would be left. According to the relativity theory, however, time and space disappear together with the things."[7] Moreover, matter and energy reflected the relatively of time and space. Einstein concluded that matter was nothing but another form of energy. His epochal formula $E = mc^2$—that each particle of matter is equivalent to its mass times the square of the velocity of light—was the key theory explaining the vast energies contained within the atom. It led to the atomic age.

Like many geniuses throughout the ages, Einstein soon learned that new ideas are not readily acceptable to people accustomed to old patterns. His work threatened the long-accepted Newtonian celestial mechanics and was not well received initially. When Einstein applied for a position at the University of Bern in 1907, he was immediately rejected. Both Planck's quantum theory and Einstein's theories of relativity were known only to a relatively small group of scientists. A total eclipse of the sun in May 1919, however, which provided calculations derived from the observation of the planet Mercury, confirmed Einstein's general theory of relativity and opened the scientific and intellectual world to his ideas. The 1920s would become the "heroic age" of physics.

Flight to the Irrational

Intellectually, the period from 1871 to 1914 witnessed a combination of contradictory developments. Thanks to the influence of science, confidence in human reason and progress still remained a dominant thread of thought. At the same time, however, a small group of intellectuals attacked optimistic progress, dethroned reason, and glorified the irrational. Although these thinkers and writers were a distinct minority, the destructiveness of World War I made their ideas even more appealing after 1918 when it seemed that they had been proven right.

Friedrich Nietzsche (1844–1900) was one of the intellectuals who glorified the irrational. According to Nietzsche, Western bourgeois society was decadent and incapable of any real cultural creativity, primarily because of an excessive emphasis on the rational faculty at the expense of emotions, passions, and instincts. Reason, claimed Nietzsche, actually played little role in human life because humans were at the mercy of irrational life forces.

Nietzsche believed that Christianity shouldered much of the blame for Western civilization's enfeeblement. The "slave morality" of Christianity, he believed, had obliterated the human impulse for life and had crushed the human will:

> I call Christianity the one great curse, the one enormous and innermost perversion, . . . I call it the one immortal blemish of mankind. . . . Christianity has taken the side of everything weak, base, ill-constituted, it has made an ideal out of opposition to the preservative instincts of strong life. . . . Christianity is called the religion of pity.—Pity stands in antithesis to the basic emotions which enhance the energy of the feeling of life: it has a depressive effect. One loses force when one pities.[8]

According to Nietzsche, Christianity crushed spontaneous human instincts and inculcated weakness and humility.

How, then, could Western society be renewed? Nietzsche first called for the need to recognize that "God is dead." Europeans, said Nietzsche, had killed God, and it

▼ **Friedrich Nietzsche.** Between 1871 and 1914, two contradictory impulses were evident in European intellectual life. Although many thinkers maintained their confidence in human reason and progress, other intellectuals downplayed reason and glorified irrational instincts. Friedrich Nietzsche was a German philosopher who claimed that irrational life forces, not reason, determined the lives of human beings. Nietzsche proclaimed the "death of God" and the arrival of the "Superman."

was no longer possible to believe in some kind of cosmic order. Eliminating God and hence Christian morality had liberated human beings and made it possible to create a higher kind of being Nietzsche called the superman: "I teach you the Superman. Man is something that is to be surpassed."[9] Superior intellectuals must free themselves from the ordinary thinking of the masses, "the slaves, or the populace, or the herd, or whatever name you care to give them." Beyond good and evil, the supermen would create their own values, embrace life passionately, and lead the masses: "It is necessary for higher man to declare war upon the masses." Nietzsche rejected and condemned political democracy, social reform, and universal suffrage.

Another popular revolutionary against reason in the 1890s was Henri Bergson (1859–1941), a French Jewish philosopher whose lectures at the University of Paris made him one of the most important influences in French thought in the early twentieth century. Bergson accepted rational, scientific thought as a practical instrument for providing useful knowledge, but, according to Bergson, it was incapable of arriving at truth or ultimate reality. To him, reality was the "life force" that suffused all things; it could not be divided into analyzable parts. Reality was a whole that could only be grasped intuitively and experienced directly. When we analyze it, we have merely a description, no longer the reality we have experienced.

Georges Sorel (1847–1922), a French political theorist, combined Bergson's and Nietzsche's ideas on the limits of rational thinking with his own passionate interest in revolutionary socialism. Sorel understood the political potential of the nonrational. He criticized Marxism for being an apocalyptical religion, not a scientific system, and advocated violent action as the only sure way to achieve the aims of socialism. To destroy capitalist society, he recommended the use of the general strike, envisioning it as a mythic image that had the power to inspire workers to take violent, heroic action against the capitalist order. Sorel also came to believe in the need for a small elite ruling body for the new socialist society since the masses were incapable of ruling themselves.

Sigmund Freud and the Emergence of Psychoanalysis

The two contradictory trends between 1871 and 1914, the glorification of science and reason and the praise of the irrational, came together in the work of Sigmund Freud. Although poets and mystics had revealed a world of unconscious and irrational behavior, many scientifically oriented intellectuals under the impact of Enlightenment thought continued to believe that human beings responded to conscious motives in a rational fashion. At the end of the nineteenth century and beginning of the twentieth, the Viennese doctor Sigmund Freud put forth a series of theories that undermined optimism about the rational nature of the human mind. Freud's thought, like the new physics and the irrationalism of Nietzsche, added to the uncertainties of the age.

Sigmund Freud (1856–1939) had studied medicine at the University of Vienna where he received a medical degree in 1881. Freud first came to his discovery of the unconscious or subconscious realms of human beings while working with patients who had nervous disorders. He said, "Anyone who wanted to make a living from the treatment of nervous patients must clearly be able to do something to help them. My therapeutic arsenal contained only two weapons: electrotherapy and hypnotism."[10] Freud found electrotherapy worthless, but was fascinated by the results of hypnosis. He found that patients who had been hypnotized often revealed information about their past lives that cured them of hysteria when they were confronted with this information upon awakening. Freud was impressed by what appeared to be an empirically verifiable unconscious level of human existence. He spent the rest of his life studying the unconscious and its relationship to the conscious mind. His major ideas were published in 1900 in *The Interpretation of Dreams*, which contained the basic foundation of what came to be known as psychoanalysis.

According to Freud, human behavior was strongly determined by the unconscious, by past experiences and internal forces of which people were largely oblivious. To explore the contents of the unconscious, Freud relied not only on hypnosis but also on free-thought associations in which the patient spoke freely of thoughts so that the doctor could enter his or her unconscious. Dreams were another entry into the unconscious, but they were dressed in an elaborate code that needed to be deciphered if the contents were to be properly understood.

But why did some experiences whose power continued to influence one's life remain unconscious? According to Freud, this was repression (see the box on p. 876), a process by which painful and unsettling experiences were blotted from conscious awareness but still continued to influence behavior since they had become part of the unconscious. To explain how repression worked, Freud developed an elaborate theory of the inner life of human beings.

According to Freud, a human being's inner life was a battleground of three contending forces: the id, ego, and superego. The id was the center of unconscious drives and was ruled by what Freud termed the pleasure principle. As creatures of desire, human beings directed their energy toward pleasure and away from pain. The id contained all kinds of lustful drives and desires, crude appetites and impulses, loves and hates. The ego was the seat of reason and hence the coordinator of the inner life. It was governed by the reality principle. Although humans were dominated by the pleasure principle, a true pursuit of pleasure was not feasible. The reality principle meant that people rejected pleasure for the sake of life in society; reality thwarted the unlimited pursuit of pleasure. The superego was the locus of conscience and represented the inhibitions and moral values that society in general and parents in particular imposed upon people. The superego served to force the ego to curb the unacceptable pressures of the id.

The human being was thus a battleground between id, ego, and superego. Ego and superego exerted restraining influences on the unconscious id and repressed or kept out of consciousness what they wanted to. The most important repressions, according to Freud, were sexual, and he went on to develop a theory of infantile sexual drives embodied in the Oedipus complex (Electra complex for females) or the infant's craving for exclusive possession of the parent of the opposite sex.

To Freud, the inner life of humans was not a pretty picture. Repression began in childhood, and psychoanalysis was accomplished through a dialogue between psychotherapist and patient in which the therapist probed deeply into memory in order to retrace the chain of repression all the way back to its childhood origins. By making the conscious mind aware of the unconscious and its repressed contents, the patient's psychic conflict was resolved.

Freud, Marx, and Darwin have often been linked together as the three intellectual giants of the nineteenth century. Like the theories of Marx and Darwin, many of Freud's ideas have been shown to be wrong in many details. Like them, nevertheless, he is still regarded as an important figure because of the impact his theories have had. Many historians still accept Freud's judgment of himself: "I have the distinct feeling that I have touched on one of the great secrets of nature."

The Impact of Darwin: Social Darwinism and Racism

In the second half of the nineteenth century, scientific theories were sometimes wrongly applied to achieve other ends. The application of Darwin's principle of organic evolution to the social order came to be known as Social Darwinism. The most popular exponent of Social Darwinism was the British philosopher Herbert Spencer (1820–1893). Using Darwin's terminology, Spencer argued that societies were organisms that evolved through time from a struggle with their environment. Progress came from "the struggle for survival," as the "fit"—the

▼ **Sigmund Freud.** Sigmund Freud was one of the intellectual giants of the nineteenth century. His belief that unconscious forces strongly determined human behavior created the foundation for twentieth-century psychoanalysis.

strong—moved forward while the weak fell by the wayside. As Spencer expressed it in 1896 in his book *Social Statics*:

> Pervading all Nature we may see at work a stern discipline which is a little cruel that it may be very kind. . . . Meanwhile, the well-being of existing humanity and the unfolding of it into this ultimate perfection, are both secured by the same beneficial though severe discipline to which the animate creation at large is subject. It seems hard that an unskillfulness, which with all his efforts he cannot overcome, should entail hunger upon the artisan. It seems hard that a laborer, incapacitated by sickness from competing with his stronger fellows, should have to bear the resulting privations. It seems hard that widows and orphans should be left to struggle for life or death. Nevertheless, when regarded not separately but in connection with the interests of universal

Freed and the Concept of Repression

▼ ▼ ▼

Freud's psychoanalytical theories resulted from his attempt to understand the world of the unconscious. This excerpt is taken from a lecture given in 1909 in which Freud describes how he arrived at his theory of the role of repression. Although Freud valued science and reason, his theories of the unconscious produced a new image of the human being as governed less by reason than by irrational forces.

Sigmund Freud, *Five Lectures on Psychoanalysis*

I did not abandon it [his technique of encouraging patients to reveal forgotten experiences], however, before the observations I made during my use of it afforded me decisive evidence. I found confirmation of the fact that the forgotten memories were not lost. They were in the patient's possession and were ready to emerge in association to what was still known by him; but there was some force that prevented them from becoming conscious and compelled them to remain unconscious. The existence of this force could be assumed with certainty, since one became aware of an effort corresponding to it if, in opposition to it, one tried to introduce the unconscious memories into the patient's consciousness. The force which was maintaining the pathological condition became apparent in the form of resistance on the part of the patient.

It was on this idea of resistance, then, that I based my view of the course of psychical events in hysteria. In order to effect a recovery, it had proved necessary to remove these resistances. Starting out from the mechanism of cure, it now became possible to construct quite definite ideas of the origin of the illness.

The same forces which, in the form of resistance, were now offering opposition to the forgotten material's being made conscious, must formerly have brought about the forgetting and must have pushed the pathogenic experiences in question out of consciousness. I gave the name of "repression" to this hypothetical process, and I considered that it was proved by the undeniable existence of resistance.

The further question could then be raised as to what these forces were and what the determinants were of the repression in which we now recognized the pathogenic mechanism of hysteria. A comparative study of the pathogenic situations which we had come to know through the cathartic procedure made it possible to answer this question. All these experiences had involved the emergence of a wishful impulse which was in sharp contrast to the subject's other wishes and which proved incompatible with the ethical and aesthetic standards of his personality. There had been a short conflict, and the end of this internal struggle was that the idea which had appeared before consciousness as the vehicle of this irreconcilable wish fell a victim to repression, was pushed out of consciousness with all its attached memories, and was forgotten. Thus the incompatibility of the wish in question with the patient's ego was the motive for the repression; the subject's ethical and other standards were the repressing forces. An acceptance of the incompatible wishful impulse or a prolongation of the conflict would have produced a high degree of unpleasure; this unpleasure was avoided by means of repression, which was thus revealed as one of the devices serving to protect the mental personality.

---

humanity, these harsh fatalities are seen to be full of beneficence—the same beneficence which brings to early graves the children of diseased parents, and singles out the intemperate and the debilitated as the victims of an epidemic.[11]

The state, then, should not intervene in this natural process. Some prominent businessmen used Social Darwinism to explain their success in the competitive business world. The strong and fit, the able and energetic

had risen to the top; the stupid and lazy had fallen by the wayside.

Darwin's ideas were also applied to human society in an even more radical way by rabid nationalists and racists. In their pursuit of national greatness, extreme nationalists argued that individual needs must be subordinated to those of the nation and often insisted that nations, too, were engaged in a "struggle for existence" in which only the fittest survived. The German general Friedrich von Bernhardi gave war a Darwinist interpretation in his book, *Germany and the Next War*, published in 1907. He argued that:

> War is a biological necessity of the first importance, a regulative element in the life of mankind which cannot be dispensed with, since without it an unhealthy development will follow, which excludes every advancement of the race, and therefore all real civilization. "War is the father of all things." The sages of antiquity long before Darwin recognized this.[12]

Numerous nationalist organizations preached the same doctrine as Bernhardi. The Nationalist Association of Italy, for example, founded in 1910, declared that "we must teach Italy the value of international struggle. But international struggle is war? Well, then, let there be war! And nationalism will arouse the will for a victorious war, . . . the only way to national redemption."[13]

Although certainly not new to Western society, racism, too, was dramatically revived and strengthened by new biological arguments. Darwinian concepts were used throughout the Western world to justify the new imperialism of the late nineteenth century. Perhaps nowhere was the combination of extreme nationalism and racism more evident and more dangerous than in Germany where racist nationalism was expressed in volkish thought. The concept of the *Volk* (nation, people, or race) had been an underlying idea in German history since the beginning of the nineteenth century. Volkish thought combined a belief in the superiority of German culture with the sense of a universal mission for the German people. One of the chief propagandists for German volkish ideology at the turn of the century was Houston Stewart Chamberlain (1855–1927), a Briton who became a German citizen. His book, *The Foundations of the Nineteenth Century*, published in 1899, made a special impact on Germany. Modern-day Germans, according to Chamberlain, were the only pure successors of the Aryans who were portrayed as the true and original creators of Western culture. The Aryan race, under German leadership, must be prepared to fight for Western civilization and save it from the destructive assaults of such lower races as Jews, Negroes, and Orientals. Increasingly, Jews were singled out by German volkish nationalists as the racial enemy in biological terms and as parasites who wanted to destroy the Aryan race.

ANTI-SEMITISM   Anti-Semitism was not new to European civilization. Since the Middle Ages, Jews had been portrayed as the murderers of Christ and subjected to mob violence; their rights had been restricted, and they had been physically separated from Christians in quarters known as ghettos.

In the nineteenth century, as a result of the ideals of the Enlightenment and the French Revolution, Jews were increasingly granted legal equality in many European countries. The French revolutionary decrees of 1790 and 1791 emancipated the Jews and admitted them to full citizenship. They were not completely accepted, however, and anti-Semitism remained a fact of French life. In 1805, Napoleon consolidated their position as citizens, but followed this in 1808 with an "Infamous Decree" that placed restrictions on Jewish moneylending and on the movement of Jews within France.

This ambivalence toward the Jews was apparent throughout Europe. In Prussia, for example, Jews were emancipated in 1812 but still restricted. They could not hold government offices or take advanced degrees in universities. After the revolutions of 1848, emancipation became a fact of life for Jews throughout western and central Europe. For many Jews, emancipation enabled them to leave the ghetto and become assimilated as hundreds of thousands of Jews entered what had been the closed worlds of parliaments and universities. "A Jew could leave his Jewishness" behind as the career of Benjamin Disraeli, who became prime minister of Great Britain, demonstrated. Many Jews became eminently successful as bankers, lawyers, scientists, scholars, journalists, and stage performers. In 1880, for example, Jews made up 10 percent of the population of the city of Vienna, Austria, but 39 percent of its medical students and 23 percent of its law students.

These achievements represent only one side of the picture, however. When right-wing mobs yelled "Death to the Jews" during the Dreyfus trial, they illustrated the continuing strength of anti-Semitism in France. In Germany and Austria during the 1880s and 1890s, conservatives founded right-wing anti-Semitic parties, such as Adolf Stöcker's Christian Social Workers and Karl Lueger's Christian Socialists. These parties used anti-Semitism to win the votes of traditional lower-middle-class groups who felt threatened by the new economic forces of the times. These German anti-Semitic parties were based on race. In medieval times Jews could convert to Christianity and escape from their religion. To modern racial anti-Semites, Jews were racially stained; this could not be altered by conversion. One could not be both German and Jew. Hermann Ahlwardt, an anti-Semitic member of the German Reichstag, made this clear in a speech to that body: "The Jew is no German. . . . A Jew who was born in Germany does not thereby become a German; he is still a Jew. Therefore it is imperative that we realize that Jewish racial characteristics differ so greatly from ours that a common life of Jews and

The Voice of Zionism: Theodor Herzl and the Jewish State

▼ ▼ ▼

The Austrian Jewish journalist Theodor Herzl wrote The Jewish State *in the summer of 1895 in Paris while he was covering the Dreyfus case for his Vienna newspaper. In several weeks, during a period of feverish composition, he set out to analyze the fundamental causes of anti-Semitism and devise a solution to the "Jewish problem." In this selection, he discusses two of his major conclusions.*

Theodor Herzl, *The Jewish State*

I do not intend to arouse sympathetic emotions on our behalf. That would be a foolish, futile, and un-dignified proceeding. I shall content myself with putting the following questions to the Jews: Is it true that, in countries where we live in perceptible numbers, the position of Jewish lawyers, doctors, technicians, teachers, and employees of all descriptions becomes daily more intolerable? True, that the Jewish middle classes are seriously threatened? True, that the passions of the mob are incited against our wealthy people? True, that our poor endure greater sufferings than any other proletariat?

I think that this external pressure makes itself felt everywhere. In our economically upper classes it causes discomfort, in our middle classes continual and grave anxieties, in our lower classes absolute despair.

Everything tends, in fact, to one and the same conclusion, which is clearly enunciated in that classic Berlin phrase: "Juden 'raus!" (Out with the Jews!)

I shall now put the Jewish Question in the curtest possible form: Are we to "get out" now? And if so, to what place?

Or, may we yet remain? And if so, how long?

Let us first settle the point of staying where we are. Can we hope for better days, can we possess our souls in patience, can we wait in pious resignation till the princes and peoples of this earth are more mercifully disposed towards us? I say that we cannot hope for a change in the current of feeling. And why not? Were we as near to the hearts of princes as are their other subjects, even so they could not protect us. They would only feed popular hatred of Jews by showing us too much favour. By "too much," I really mean less than is claimed as a right by every ordinary citizen, or by every race. The nations in whose midst Jews live are all, either covertly or openly, Anti-Semitic. . . .

The whole plan is in its essence perfectly simple, as it must necessarily be if it is to come within the comprehension of all.

Let the sovereignty be granted us over a portion of the globe large enough to satisfy the rightful requirements of a nation; the rest we shall manage for ourselves.

The creation of a new State is neither ridiculous nor impossible. We have in our day witnessed the process in connection with nations which were not in the bulk of the middle class, but poorer, less educated, and consequently weaker than ourselves. The Governments of all countries scourged by Anti-Semitism will be keenly interested in assisting us to obtain the sovereignty we want. . . .

Palestine is our ever-memorable historic home. The very name of Palestine would attract our people with a force of marvellous potency. Supposing his Majesty the Sultan were to give us Palestine, we could in return undertake to regulate the whole finances of Turkey. We should there form a portion of the rampart of Europe against Asia, an outpost of civilisation as opposed to barbarism. We should as a neutral State remain in contact with all Europe, which would have to guarantee our existence. The sanctuaries of Christendom would be safeguarded by assigning to them an extra-territorial status such as is well known to the law of nations. We should form a guard of honour about these sanctuaries, answering for the fulfillment of this duty with our existence. This guard of honour would be the great symbol of the solution of the Jewish Question after eighteen centuries of Jewish suffering.

Germans under the same laws is quite impossible because the Germans will perish."[14] After 1898, the political strength of the German anti-Semitic parties began to decline.

The worst treatment of Jews in the last two decades of the nineteenth century and the first decade of the twentieth occurred in eastern Europe where 72 percent of the entire world Jewish population lived. In Romania, Jews were not allowed to hold office or vote. Anti-Semitism was a regular part of tsarist Russian life. Russian Jews were admitted to secondary schools and universities only under a quota system and were forced to live in certain regions of the country. Persecutions and pogroms were widespread. Between 1903 and 1906, pogroms took place in almost 700 Russian towns and villages, mostly in the Ukraine region. Hundreds of thousands of Jews decided to emigrate to escape the persecution. Between 1881 and 1899, an average of 23,000 Jews left Russia each year. Many of them went to the United States, although some (probably about 25,000) moved to Palestine, which soon became the focus for a Jewish nationalist movement called Zionism.

The emancipation of the nineteenth century had presented vast opportunities to some Jews, but dilemmas to others. What was the price of citizenship? Did emancipation mean full assimilation and did assimilation mean the disruption of traditional Jewish life? Many paid the price willingly, but others questioned its value and advocated a different answer, a return to Palestine. For many Jews, Palestine had long been the land of their dreams. During the nineteenth century, as nationalist ideas spread and Italians, Poles, Irish, Greeks, and others sought national emancipation so too did the idea of national independence capture the imagination of some Jews. A key figure in the growth of political Zionism was Theodor Herzl (1860–1904). Herzl had received a law degree in Vienna where he became a journalist for a Viennese newspaper. He was shocked into action on behalf of Jews when he covered the Dreyfus trial as a correspondent for his newspaper in Paris. In 1896, he published a book called *The Jewish State* (see the box on p. 878) in which he straightforwardly advocated that "The Jews who wish it will have their state." Financial support for the development of yishuvs or settlements in Palestine came from wealthy Jewish banking families, especially from Baron Edmond James de Rothschild, called "Father of the Yishuv" for his contributions. Rothschild and others like him wanted a refuge in Palestine for persecuted Jews, not a political Jewish state. Even settlements were difficult because Palestine was then part of the Ottoman Empire and Turkish authori-

ties were opposed to Jewish immigration. In 1891, one Jewish essayist pointed to the problems this would create:

> We abroad are accustomed to believe that Erez Israel [the land of Israel] is almost totally desolate at present . . . but in reality it is not so. . . . Arabs, especially those in towns, see and understand our activities and aims in the country but keep quiet and pretend as if they did not know, . . . and they try to exploit us, too, and profit from the new guests while laughing at us in their hearts. But if the time comes and our people make such progress as to displace the people of the country . . . they will not lightly surrender the place.[15]

Despite the warnings, however, the First Zionist Congress, which met in Switzerland in 1897, proclaimed as its aim the creation of a "home in Palestine secured by public law" for the Jewish people. In 1900, 1,000 Jews migrated to Palestine. And although 3,000 Jews went annually to Palestine between 1904 and 1914, the Zionist dream remained just that on the eve of World War I.

The Attack on Christianity and the Response of the Churches

The growth of scientific thinking as well as the forces of modernization presented new challenges to the Christian churches. Although the churches experienced defections among Europe's educated elite, they remained strong at a popular level and in some places even showed remarkable institutional strength.

Industrialization and urbanization had an adverse effect on the churches. The mass migration of people from the countryside to the city meant a change from the close-knit, traditional ties of the village in which the church had been a key force to new urban patterns of social life from which the churches were often excluded. The established Christian churches had a weak hold on workers. For one thing, new churches were rarely built in working-class neighborhoods. Although workers were not atheists, as is sometimes claimed, they tended to develop their own culture in which organized religion played little role.

The political movements of the late nineteenth century were also hostile to the established Christian churches. Beginning during the eighteenth-century Enlightenment and continuing well into the nineteenth century, European governments, especially in predominantly Catholic countries, had imposed controls over church courts, religious orders, and appointments of the clergy. But after the failure of the revolutions of 1848, governments were eager to use the churches' aid in re-establishing order and therefore relaxed these controls. Education was given back to the Catholic church in France, Roman Catholicism was made "the only religion of the Spanish nation," and the jurisdiction of Catholic church courts over marriage was restored in Austria. In France, the murder of the archbishop of Paris by the Paris Commune of 1871 served as an impetus to return people temporarily to organized religion. As the British Catholic Cardinal Manning wrote to the British prime minister, "My belief is that society without Christianity is the Commune. What hope can you give me?"[16]

Eventually, however, the close union of state authorities with established churches produced a backlash in the form of anticlericalism, especially by the liberal nation-states of the late nineteenth century. As one example, in the 1880s the French republican government substituted civic training for religious instruction in order to undermine the Catholic church's control of education. In 1901, Catholic teaching orders were outlawed, and four years later, in 1905, church and state were completely separated.

Science became one of the chief threats to all the Christian churches and even to religion itself in the nineteenth century. Darwin's theory of evolution, accepted by ever-larger numbers of educated Europeans, seemed to contradict the doctrine of divine creation. By suppressing Darwin's books and forbidding the teaching of the evolutionary hypothesis, the churches often caused even more educated people to reject established religions.

The social sciences proved just as dangerous as science to the Christian churches. From their studies of ancient societies, anthropologists concluded that modern religions, including Christianity, were based on early myths, cults, and superstitions. Sociologists placed more and more faith in mechanistic evolution as the key to all social progress and increasingly criticized religion for being detrimental to that progress. Intellectuals such as Nietzsche and psychologists denounced religion as an illusion created by human beings who were afraid of the threatening world around them.

The scientific spirit encouraged a number of biblical scholars to apply critical principles to the Bible, leading to the so-called higher criticism. One of its leading exponents was Ernst Renan (1823–1892), a French Catholic scholar. In his *Life of Jesus*, published in 1863, Renan questioned the historical accuracy of the Bible and presented a radically different picture of Jesus Christ. He saw Christ not as the son of God, but as a human being whose value lay in the example he

provided by his life and teaching. To Renan, Christ's belief in his own divinity was merely the result of hallucinations.

One response of the Christian churches to these attacks was the outright rejection of modern ideas and forces. Protestant fundamentalist sects were especially important in maintaining a literal interpretation of the Bible. The Catholic church under Pope Pius IX (1846–1878) also took a rigid stand against modern ideas. In 1864, Pope Pius issued a papal encyclical called the *Syllabus of Errors* in which he stated that it is "an error to believe that the Roman Pontiff can and ought to reconcile himself to, and agree with, progress, liberalism, and modern civilization." He condemned nationalism, socialism, religious toleration, lay-controlled education, and freedom of speech and press. At the First Vatican Council in 1870, Pius IX championed the doctrine of papal infallibility, which stated that the pope, when speaking *ex cathedra*—that is, officially—on matters of faith and morals, could not err in his pronouncements.

Rejection of the new was not the churches' only response, however. A religious movement called Modernism included an attempt by the churches to reinterpret Christianity in the light of new developments. The modernists viewed the Bible as a book of useful moral ideas, encouraged Christians to become involved in social reforms, and insisted that the churches must provide a greater sense of community. The Catholic church condemned Modernism in 1907 and drove it underground by the beginning of the World War I. In Protestant churches, modernists competed with fundamentalists and had more success.

Yet another response of the Christian churches to modern ideas was compromise, an approach especially evident in the Catholic church during the pontificate of Leo XIII (1878–1903). Pope Leo permitted the teaching of evolution as a hypothesis in Catholic schools and allowed Catholics to take part in the politics of liberal nation-states. In 1892, he urged French Catholics to accept the French Republic. He also responded to the challenges of modernization in the economic and social spheres. In his encyclical *De Rerum Novarum*, issued in 1891, he upheld the individual's right to private property but at the same time criticized "naked" capitalism for the poverty and degradation in which it had left the working classes. Much in socialism, he declared, was Christian in principle, but he condemned Marxian socialism for its materialistic and antireligious foundations. The pope recommended that Catholics form socialist parties and labor unions of their own. Despite his new thoughts, Leo XIII still clung to a conservative, hierarchical social order organized according to corporate groups that would cooperate on the basis of Christian principles. A number of young, radical priests rejected this conservative approach. By accepting class conflict and advocating use of the strike, they hoped to spread the Gospel among poor workers. Jules Lemire organized meetings of Christian democratic priests in France while Romolo Murri founded workers' groups in central Italy after 1900. Before his death in 1903, Pope Leo XIII insisted that these radical priests cease their efforts.

Other steps were taken to win support for Christianity among the working-class poor and to restore religious practice among the urban working classes. These efforts were not strong among mainstream churches because their parish systems were not prepared to cope with the flood of urban immigrants. Sects of evangelical missionaries were more successful, especially the Salvation Army founded in London in 1865 by William Booth, the first "general" of the army. The Salvation Army established food centers, shelters where the homeless could sleep, and "rescue homes" for women, but for a larger purpose as Booth admitted: "it is primarily and mainly for the sake of saving the soul that I seek the salvation of the body."[17] The Salvation Army moved to Paris in the 1880s, but was not well received by French Protestants who considered its revivalist-style meetings vulgar.

Literature and the Arts: Toward Modernism

The revolution in physics and psychology was paralleled by a revolution in literature and the arts. Before 1914, writers and artists were rebelling against the traditional literary and artistic styles that had dominated European cultural life since the Renaissance. The changes that they produced have since been called Modernism.

LITERATURE: NATURALISM AND SYMBOLISM Throughout much of the late nineteenth century, literature was dominated by Naturalism. Naturalists accepted the material world as real and felt that literature should be realistic. By addressing social problems, writers could contribute to an objective understanding of the world. Although Naturalism was a continuation of Realism, it lacked the underlying note of liberal optimism about people and society that had still been prevalent in the 1850s. The Naturalists were pessimistic about Europe's future. They doubted the existence of free will and portrayed characters caught in the grip of forces beyond their control.

The novels of the French writer, Émile Zola (1840–1902), provide a good example of Naturalism. Against a backdrop of the urban slums and coal fields of northern France, Zola showed how alcoholism and different environments affected people's lives. The materialistic science of his age had an important influence on Zola. He had read Darwin's Origin of Species and had been impressed by its emphasis on the struggle for survival and the importance of environment and heredity. These themes were central to his Rougon-Macquart, a twenty-volume series of novels on the "natural and social history of a family." Zola maintained that the artist must analyze and dissect life as a biologist would a living organism. He said, "I have simply done on living bodies the work of analysis which surgeons perform on corpses."

The last half of the nineteenth century was a golden age for Russian literature. The nineteenth-century realistic novel reached its high point in the works of Leo Tolstoy (1828–1910) and Fyodor Dostoevsky (1821–1881). Tolstoy's greatest work was War and Peace, a lengthy novel played out against the historical background of Napoleon's invasion of Russia in 1812. It is realistic in its vivid descriptions of military life and character portrayal. Each person is delineated clearly and analyzed psychologically. Upon a great landscape, Tolstoy imposed a fatalistic view of history that ultimately proved irrelevant in the face of life's enduring values of human love and trust.

Fyodor Dostoevsky combined narrative skill and acute psychological and moral observation with profound insights into human nature. Dostoevsky maintained that the major problem of his age was a loss of spiritual belief. Western people were attempting to gain salvation through the construction of a materialistic paradise built only by human reason and human will. Dostoevsky feared that the failure to incorporate spirit would result in total tyranny. His own life experiences led him to believe that only through suffering and faith could the human soul be purified, views that are evident in his best-known works, Crime and Punishment and The Brothers Karamazov.

At the turn of the century, a new group of writers, known as the Symbolists, reacted against Realism. Primarily interested in writing poetry, the Symbolists believed that an objective knowledge of the world was impossible. The external world was not real but only a collection of symbols that reflected the true reality of the individual human mind. Art, they believed, should function for its own sake instead of serving, criticizing, or seeking to understand society. In the works of the symbolist poets, W. B. Yeats and Rainer Maria Rilke,

Symbolist Poetry: Art for Art's Sake

▼ ▼ ▼

The Symbolist movement was an important foundation for Modernism. The Symbolists believed that the working of the mind was the proper study of literature. Arthur Rimbaud was one of Symbolism's leading practitioners in France. Although his verses seem to have little real meaning, they were not meant to describe the external world precisely, but to enchant the mind. Art was not meant for the masses, but only for "art's sake." Rimbaud wrote, "By the alchemy of the words, I noted the inexpressible. I fixed giddiness."

Arthur Rimbaud, *The Drunken Boat*

As I floated down impassable rivers,
I felt the boatmen no longer guiding me:
After them came redskins who with war cries
Nailed them naked to the painted poles.

I was oblivious to the crew,
I who bore Flemish wheat and English cotton.
When the racket was finished with my boatmen,
The waters let me drift my own free way.

In the tide's furious pounding,
I, the other winter, emptier than children's minds,
I sailed! And the unmoored peninsulas
Have not suffered more triumphant turmoils.

The tempest blessed my maritime watches.
Lighter than a cork I danced on the waves,
Those eternal rollers of victims,
Ten nights, without regretting the lantern-foolish eye!

Sweeter than the bite of sour apples to a child,
The green water seeped through my wooden hull,
Rinsed me of blue wine stains and vomit,
Broke apart grappling iron and rudder.

And then I bathed myself in the poetry
Of the star-sprayed milk-white sea,
Devouring the azure greens; where, pale
And ravished, a pensive drowned one sometimes floats;

Where, suddenly staining the blueness, frenzies
And slow rhythms in the blazing of day,
Stronger than alcohol, vaster than our lyres,
The russet bitterness of love ferments. . . .

I have dreamed of the green night bedazzled with snow,
A kiss climbing slowly to the eyes of the sea,
The flow of unforgettable sap,
And the yellow-blue waking of singing phosphorous!

Long months I have followed, like maddened cattle,
The surge assaulting the rocks
Without dreaming that the Virgin's luminous feet
Could force a muzzle on the panting ocean!

I have struck against the shares of incredible Floridas
Mixing panther-eyed flowers like human skins!
Rainbows stretched like bridle reins
Under the ocean's horizon, toward sea-green troops!

I have seen the fermenting of monstrous marshes,
Nets where a whole Leviathan rots in the reeds!
The waters collapsing in the middle of the calm,
And horizons plunging toward the abyss!

Glaciers, silver suns, waves of pearl, charcoal skies,
Hideous beaches at the bottom of brown gulfs
Where giant serpents devoured by vermin
Tumble from twisted trees with black perfumes!

I would have liked to show the children those dolphins
On the blue waves, those golden singing fish.
—The froth of flowers lulled my voyagings,
Ineffable winds gave me wings by the moment. . . .

poetry ceased to be part of popular culture because only through a knowledge of the poet's personal language could one hope to understand what the poet was saying (see the box on p. 882). Symbolism began in France and its founder, Stéphane Mallarmé (1842–1898), attempted to summarize its poetic theory in one sentence: "It is not description which can unveil the efficacy and beauty of monuments, seas, or the human face in all their maturity and native state, but rather evocation, allusion, suggestion."

THE ARTS   The period from 1871 to 1914 was one of the most fertile in the history of art and witnessed three major movements, Impressionism, Post-Impressionism, and abstract painting.

Since the Renaissance, the task of artists had been to represent reality as accurately as possible. By the late nineteenth century, artists sought new forms of expression. The preamble to modern painting can be found in Impressionism, a movement that originated in France in the 1870s when a group of artists rejected the studios and museums and went out into the countryside to paint nature directly. Camille Pissarro (1830–1903), one of Impressionism's founders, expressed what they sought:

> Precise drawing is dry and hampers the impression of the whole, it destroys all sensations. Do not define too closely the outlines of things; it is the brush stroke of the right value and color which should produce the drawing. . . . The eye should not be fixed on one point, but should take in everything, while observing the reflections which the colors produce on their surroundings. Work at the same time upon sky, water, branches, ground, keeping everything going on an equal basis and unceasingly rework until you have got it. . . . Don't proceed according to rules and principles, but paint what you observe and feel. Paint generously and unhesitatingly, for it is best not to lose the first impression.[18]

Above all, said, Pissarro, "Don't be timid in front of nature: one must be bold, at the risk of being deceived, and making mistakes. One must have only one master—nature; she is the one always to be consulted."

Pissarro's suggestions are visibly portrayed in the work of Claude Monet (1840–1926). He was especially enchanted with water and painted many pictures in which he sought to capture the interplay of light, water, and atmosphere, especially evident in Impression, Sunrise. But the Impressionists did not just paint scenes from nature. Streets and cabarets, rivers, and busy boulevards—wherever people congregated for work and leisure—formed their subject matter.

By the 1880s, a new movement known as Post-Impressionism arose in France but soon spread to other European countries. Post-Impressionism retained the Impressionist emphasis upon light and color but revolutionized it even further by paying more attention to structure and form. Post-Impressionists sought to use both color and line to express inner feelings and produce a personal statement of reality rather than an imitation of objects. Impressionist paintings had retained a sense of realism, but the Post-Impressionists shifted from objective reality to subjective reality and, in so doing, began to withdraw from the artist's traditional task of depicting the external world. Post-Impressionists were the real forerunners of modern art.

Paul Cézanne (1839–1906) was one of the most important Post-Impressionists. Initially, he was influenced by the Impressionists but soon rejected their work. In his paintings, such as *Woman with Coffee Pot*, Cézanne sought to express visually the underlying structure and form of everything he painted. The geometric shapes

▼ **Claude Monet, *Impression, Sunrise*.** Impressionism was a movement in painting that originated in France and is often considered the precursor to modern painting. Impressionists rejected "rules and principles" and sought to paint what they observed and felt in order "not to lose the first impression." As is evident in *Impression, Sunrise*, Monet sought to capture his impression of the fleeting moments of sunrise through the simple interplay of light, water, and atmosphere.

▼ **Paul Cézanne, *Woman with Coffee Pot*.** Post-Impressionism began to replace Impressionism in the 1880s, especially in France. Post-Impressionists sought above all to express their inner feelings and capture on canvas their own vision of reality. In *Woman with Coffee Pot*, Paul Cézanne tried to relate the geometric shapes of his central female figure to the geometric shapes of the coffee pot and the rectangles of the door panels.

(cylinders and triangles) of the human form are related to the geometric shapes (cylinders and rectangles) of the other objects in the picture. As Cézanne explained to one young painter: "You must see in nature the cylinder, the sphere, and the cone."

Like Cézanne, Paul Gauguin (1848–1903) was first influenced by the Impressionists, but later turned away from them, calling them superficial. Gauguin sought a deeper reality in the world of the unconscious and primitive life. His rejection of modern civilization and search for paradise in such places as Tahiti resulted in his almost neoprimitive and mystical paintings of Tahitians. As in

The Day of the Gods, Gauguin used shape and large areas of flat color to create intense images.

Another famous Post-Impressionist was the tortured and tragic figure, Vincent van Gogh (1853–1890). For van Gogh, art was a spiritual experience. He was especially interested in color and believed that it could act as its own form of language. Van Gogh maintained that artists should paint what they feel. In his *Starry Night*, he painted a sky alive with whirling stars that overwhelmed the huddled buildings in the village below.

By the beginning of the twentieth century, the belief that the task of art was to represent "reality" had lost much of its meaning. By that time, the new psychology and the new physics had made it evident that many people were not sure what constituted reality anyway. Then, too, the growth of photography gave artists another reason to reject visual realism. First invented in the 1830s, photography became popular and widespread after George Eastman created the first Kodak camera in 1888 for the mass market. What was the point of an artist doing what the camera did better? Unlike the camera, which could only mirror reality, artists could create reality. As in literature, so also in modern art, individual consciousness became the source of meaning. As one artist expressed it: "Each [artist] should follow where the pulse of his own heart leads. . . . Our pounding heart drives us down, deep down to the source of all. What springs from this source, whether it may be called dream, idea or phantasy—must be taken seriously."[19] Between 1905 and 1914, this search for individual expression produced a great variety of painting schools that had their greatest impact after World War I.

Henri Matisse (1869–1954) was the leading figure in a group of painters called the Fauvists—the "wild beasts"—by the critics. Their program, evident in Matisse's 1905 *Portrait with Green Stripe*, was to depict emotions by using colors that were not related to the natural colors of the subject. Criticized for this work, Matisse responded: "I did not create a woman, I made a painting."

By 1905, one of the most important figures in modern art was just beginning his career. Pablo Picasso (1881–1973) was from Spain but settled in Paris in 1904. Picasso was extremely flexible and painted in a remarkable variety of styles. He was instrumental in the development of a new style called cubism that used geometric designs as visual stimuli to recreate reality in the viewer's mind. Picasso's 1907 work *Les Demoiselles d'Avignon* has been called the first cubist painting.

The modern artist's flight from "visual reality" reached a high point in 1910 with the beginning of abstract painting. A Russian who worked in Germany, Vasily Kandinsky (1866–1944), was one of the founders of abstract expressionism. As is evident in his Painting with White Border Kandinsky sought to avoid representation altogether. He believed that art should speak directly to the soul. To do so, it must avoid any reference to visual reality and concentrate on color.

Modernism in the arts revolutionized architecture and architectural practices. A new principle known as functionalism motivated this revolution. Functionalism meant that buildings, like the products of machines, should be "functional" or useful, fulfilling the purpose for which they were constructed. Art and engineering were to be unified, and all unnecessary ornamentation was to be stripped away.

The United States was a leader in these pioneering architectural designs. Unprecedented urban growth and the absence of restrictive architectural traditions allowed for new building methods, especially in the relatively "new city" of Chicago. The Chicago school of the

▼ **Vincent Van Gogh, *The Starry Night*.** The Dutch painter Vincent Van Gogh was a major figure among the Post-Impressionists. His career was brief; all of his artistic activity occurred in a ten-year span of time. His originality and power of expression made a strong impact upon his artistic successors. In *The Starry Night*, Van Gogh's subjective vision was given full play as the dynamic swirling forms of the heavens above overwhelmed the village below. The heavens seem alive with a mysterious spiritual force.

In Europe, the Germans took the lead in modern architectural design. Most outstanding was Walter Gropius (1883–1969), who anticipated much modern building with his Fagus factory building in Alfeld, Germany, built between 1911 and 1914. This unornamented steel box with walls of windows reflected Gropius's belief that "the sensibility of the artist must be combined with the knowledge of the technician to create new forms in architecture and design."

MUSIC Until the mid-nineteenth century, the classical-Romantic tradition, based on the tonal harmony of the seven-note scale with major and minor keys, dominated the musical world. Richard Wagner (1813–1883) made the first significant departure from this tradition with his "musical dramas." In his operas, such as *Parsifal* and *Tristan and Isolde*, music was combined with poetry and visual effects to produce a total artistic experience. Wagner also experimented with musical moods and even departed from strict tonality in his compositions.

▼ **Henri Matisse, *Portrait with a Green Stripe.*** By 1900, art was no longer considered a means of representing reality as artists sought to create reality by examining the depths of their inner consciousness. One group of painters known as the Fauvists sought to express emotions by the use of colors starkly different from the natural colors of the subject. In his *Portrait with a Green Stripe*, Henri Matisse used startling green, black, and purple hues to describe the human face. While recognizable, it is certainly not one that would be encountered in everyday life.

▼ **Pablo Picasso, *Les Demoiselles D'Avignon.*** Pablo Picasso, a major pioneer and activist of modern art, began his career in Paris at the beginning of the twentieth century. Picasso experimented with a remarkable variety of modern styles. His *Les Demoiselles D'Avignon* was the first great example of Cubism, which one art historian has called "the first style of this century to break radically with the past." Geometric shapes replace traditional forms, forcing the viewer to recreate reality in his or her own mind.

1890s, led by Louis H. Sullivan (1856–1924), used reinforced concrete, steel frames, and electric elevators to build skyscrapers virtually free of external ornamentation. One of Sullivan's most successful pupils was Frank Lloyd Wright (1869–1959), who became known for innovative designs in domestic architecture. Wright's private houses, built chiefly for wealthy patrons, featured geometric structures with long lines, overhanging roofs, and severe planes of brick and stone. The interiors were open spaced and included cathedral ceilings and built-in furniture and lighting fixtures. Wright pioneered the modern American house.

At the beginning of the twentieth century, developments in music paralleled those in painting. Expressionism in music was a Russian creation, the product of the composer Igor Stravinsky (1882–1971) and the Ballet Russe, the dancing company of Sergei Diaghilev (1872–1929). Together they revolutionized the world of music with Stravinsky's ballet, *The Rite of Spring*. When it was performed in Paris in 1913, the savage and primitive sounds and beats of the music and dance caused a near riot from an audience outraged at its audacity.

▼ Education and Leisure in an Age of Mass Society

Between 1871 and 1914, Europe witnessed the emergence of a mass society. Trade unions and political parties gave an economic and political voice to many workers. Mass conscription created mass armies and possibilities for warfare on a scale never before imagined. The masses became a major force in Western society as mass education and mass leisure created new forms of popular culture.

Mass Education

Mass education was a product of the "mass society" of the late nineteenth and early twentieth centuries. Being "educated" in the early nineteenth century meant attending a secondary school or possibly even a university.

▼ **Walter Gropius, Fagus Factory Building.** Walter Gropius was one of Europe's pioneers in modern architecture. His Fagus Factory Building in Alfeld, Germany, a simple steel structure with walls of windows, expressed the basic principle of modern architectural functionalism, the belief that buildings should be useful and devoid of all unnecessary ornamentation. Gropius's building established a model for many modern buildings.

Secondary schools, such as the *Gymnasien* in Germany and the public schools (which were really private boarding schools) in Britain, mostly emphasized a classical

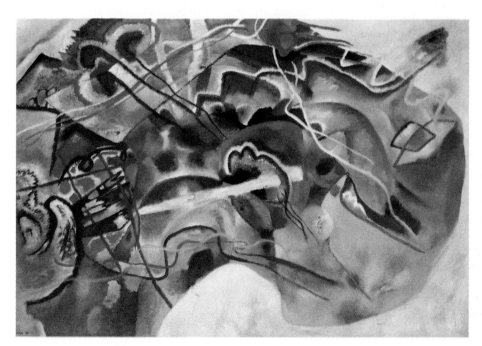

▼ **Vasily Kandinsky, *Painting with White Border*.** The attempt of modern artists to reject the principle of visual reality reached its high point with Abstract Expressionism. One of its founders was the Russian Vasily Kandinsky, who sought to eliminate representation altogether by focusing on color and avoiding any resemblance to visual reality. In *Painting with White Border*, Kandinsky used color "to send light into the darkness of men's hearts." He believed that color could, like music, fulfill a spiritual goal of appealing directly to the human being.

education based on the study of Greek and Latin. Secondary and university education were primarily for the elite, the sons of government officials, nobles, or the wealthier middle class. By the 1830s and 1840s, a lesser system of secondary education, such as the *Realschule* in Germany, had come into being for the children of the lower middle class and rich peasants. After 1850, secondary education was expanded as more middle-class families sought employment in public service and the professions or entry into elite scientific and technical schools. Existing secondary schools also placed more emphasis on practical and scientific education by adding foreign languages and natural sciences to their curriculum.

At the beginning of the nineteenth century, European states showed little interest in primary education. In Catholic countries after the upheavals of the French revolutionary era, teaching orders of nuns and lay brothers dominated most primary schools. Only in the German states was there a state-run system for elementary education. In Prussia, primary education had already become compulsory in the eighteenth century.

In 1833, the French government instructed local governments to establish an elementary school for both boys and girls, thus creating a system of state-run, secular schools. Attendance, however, was not required. In the United States, state governments (except in the southern states) had already established both primary and secondary schools. By 1860, 60 percent of the white children in the northeastern United States were enrolled in an educational institution. In England, elementary education was mostly left to the Church of England and to the Nonconformists (Protestants who did not belong to the Church of England). Both Anglican and Nonconformist elementary schools were financed by voluntary subscription.

Although government officials considered primary schools to be guarantors of "social stability," primary school teachers were not highly regarded. Most were from peasant or artisan backgrounds with minimal training. Salaries depended on local community support, and teachers were often forced to supplement their meager incomes with other work. Attendance at primary schools was also irregular. In rural society, children were still expected to work in the fields. In industrializing countries like Britain and France, both employers and parents were eager to maintain the practice of child labor. Even this irregular system of elementary education, however, stimulated a growth in literacy in Europe.

In the decades after 1870, the functions of the state were extended to include the development of mass education in state-run systems. Between 1870 and 1914, most Western governments began to offer at least primary education to both boys and girls between the ages of six and twelve. In most countries it was not optional. Austria had decreed free, compulsory elementary education in 1869. In France, a law of March 29, 1882, made primary education compulsory for all children between six and thirteen. The British Parliament at first was unwilling to go that far but did pass a compromise Education Act in 1870 that provided public support for church schools while subjecting them to government inspection. In 1880, elementary education was made compulsory in Britain, but it was not until 1902 that an act of Parliament brought all elementary schools under county and town control. States also assumed responsibility for better training of teachers by establishing teacher-training schools.

By the beginning of the twentieth century, many European states, especially in northern and western Europe, had provided state-financed primary schools, salaried and trained teachers, and free, compulsory mass elementary education. In 1900, Germany spent 12 percent of its national budget on public education while Britain spent 10 percent and France 8 percent. States in southern and eastern Europe offered much less. Spain, for example, spent only 1.5 percent of its budget on education.

Why did European states make this commitment to mass education? Liberals believed that education was important to personal and social improvement and also sought, as in France, to supplant Catholic education with moral and civic training based on secular values. Even conservatives, however, were attracted to mass education as a means of improving the quality of military recruits and training people in social discipline. In 1875, a German military journal stated: "We in Germany consider education to be one of the principal ways of promoting the strength of the nation and above all military strength."[20]

Another incentive for mass education came from industrialization. In the early Industrial Revolution, unskilled labor was sufficient to meet factory needs, but the new firms of the Second Industrial Revolution demanded skilled labor. Diversification of the economic and social structure provided incentives to learn new skills. Both boys and girls with an elementary education had new possibilities of jobs beyond their villages or small towns, including white-collar jobs in railways, new metro stations, post offices, banking and shipping firms, teaching, and nursing. To industrialists, then, mass education furnished the trained workers they needed.

Nevertheless, the chief motive for mass education was political. On the one hand, the increase in suffrage created the need for a more educated electorate. Even more important, however, mass compulsory education instilled patriotism and nationalized the masses, providing an opportunity for even greater national integration. As people lost their ties to local regions and even to religion, nationalism supplied a new faith. The use of a single national language created greater national unity than did loyalty to a ruler, but in some countries this process was complicated by the existence of large national minorities. In the polyglot empires, such as Austria-Hungary and Russia, ethnic minorities strove to hold on to their languages since these defined their nationalities. In Russian Poland, for example, the attempt by Russian authorities to impose the Russian language on Polish elementary schools led to the creation of underground schools where local clerks, priests, children of local gentry, and, above all, women taught Polish. A Polish primer, written by Konrad Prósszynski in 1872, had sold 750,000 copies by 1906.

A nation's motives for universal elementary education largely determined what was taught in the elementary schools. Obviously, indoctrination in national values took on great importance. At the core of the academic curriculum were reading, writing, arithmetic, national history, especially geared to a patriotic view, geography, literature, and some singing and drawing. The education of boys and girls varied, however. Where possible, the sexes were separated. Girls did less math and no science but concentrated on such domestic skills as sewing, washing, ironing, and cooking, all prerequisites for providing a good home for husband and children. Boys were taught some practical skills, such as carpentry, and even some military drill. Most of the elementary schools also inculcated the middle-class virtues of hard work, thrift, sobriety, cleanliness, and respect for the family. For most students, elementary education led to apprenticeship and a job.

The development of compulsory elementary education created a demand for teachers, and most of them were female. In the United States, for example, females constituted two-thirds of all teachers by the 1880s. Many men viewed the teaching of children as an extension of women's "natural role" as nurturers of children. Moreover, females were paid lower salaries, in itself a considerable incentive for governments to encourage the establishment of teacher-training institutes for women. The first female colleges were really teacher-training schools. In Britain, the women's colleges of Queen's and Bedford were established in the 1840s to provide teacher

▼ **A Women's College.** Women were largely excluded from male-dominated universities before 1900. Consequently, the demand of women for higher education led to the foundation of women's colleges, most of which were primarily teacher-training schools. This photograph shows a group of women in an astronomy class at Vassar College in the United States in 1878. Maria Mitchell, a famous woman astronomer, was head of the department.

training for middle-class spinsters who needed to work. A pioneer in the development of female education was Barbara Bodichon (1827–1891), who established her own school in which girls were trained not only for domesticity, but also for economic independence. It was not until the beginning of the twentieth century that women were permitted to enter the male-dominated universities. In France, 3 percent of university students in 1902 were women; by 1914, their number had increased to 10 percent of the total.

The most immediate result of mass education was an increase in literacy. Compulsory elementary education and the growth of literacy were directly related. In Germany, Great Britain, France, and the Scandinavian countries, adult illiteracy was virtually eliminated by 1900. Where there was less schooling, the story is very different. Adult illiteracy rates were 79 percent in Serbia, 78 percent in Romania, 72 percent in Bulgaria, and 79 percent in Russia. These were all countries where little had been invested in compulsory mass education. The growth of literacy, in turn, was important in the development of a new mass culture, one of whose prominent features was the emergence of new forms of mass leisure.

Mass Leisure

In the pre-industrial centuries, play or leisure activities had been closely connected to work patterns based on the seasonal or daily cycles typical of agricultural and even artisanal life. The process of industrialization in the nineteenth century had an enormous impact upon that traditional pattern. The factory imposed new work patterns that were determined by the rhythms of machines and clocks and removed work time completely from the family environment of farms and workshops. Work and leisure became opposites as leisure was viewed as what people do for fun after work. In fact, the new leisure hours created by the industrial system—evening hours after work, weekends, and later a week or two in the summer—largely determined the contours of the new mass leisure.

At the same time, the influx of rural people into industrial towns eventually caused the demise of traditional village culture, especially the fairs and festivals that had formed such an important part of that culture. Industrial progress, of course, demanded that such traditional celebrations as Whitsuntide, which had occasioned thirteen days of games and drinking, be eliminated or reduced. In fact, Whitsuntide had been reduced by the 1870s to a single one-day holiday.

New technology and business practices also determined the forms of the new mass leisure. The new technology created novel experiences for leisure, such as the Ferris wheel at amusement parks, while the mechanized urban transportation systems of the 1880s meant that even the working classes were no longer dependent on neighborhood bars, but could make their way to athletic events, amusement parks, and dance halls. Likewise, railroads could take people to the beaches on weekends.

The commercialization of leisure had come first from the upper and middle classes. Their desire for leisure created new forms of tourism, urban entertainment districts, and amusing fads to while away the time. But the increase in real wages after 1860 in the advanced industrial countries opened the way to commercial leisure for the lower classes. An increase in real wages enabled working classes to enjoy middle-class pleasures, which included not only such unhealthy items as sugar and cigarettes, but also tickets to music halls, amusement parks, and beach excursions.

BACKGROUND TO MASS LEISURE: RATIONAL RECREATION
The new mass leisure did not arrive overnight. Much leisure in the nineteenth century, especially in the middle-class environment, remained a product of the family home. Also important was the development of what social historians have called "rational recreation." After the 1830s, a number of middle-class reformers, fearful of the urban working masses (the "dangerous classes"), believed that there was a need for forms of recreation that would instill in the lower classes the middle-class values of self-control, individualism, family, and, above all, respectability. Some upper- and middle-class reformers hoped as well to create a new sense of community for all classes while improving the individual. One avenue for such activity came from social clubs. In Britain, beginning in the 1850s, Henry Solly's Working Men's Social Clubs joined education with entertainment by providing cards and games and leisure activities for adult men. So, too, did the Young Men's Christian Association (YMCA) established in London in 1844.

The movement for "rational" recreation also led to new urban services, especially public libraries, museums, and public parks. Peel Park, created in Manchester in 1846, provided a model for others. Often the establishment of these new services depended on philanthropy. The wealthy American industrialist Andrew Carnegie explained his generosity: "How a man spends his time at work may be taken for granted but how he spends his hours of recreation is really the key to his progress in all the virtues."[21] To justify the creation of public parks, the British Parliament explained that open places set aside for the pleasure of the "humbler classes, would assist to wean them from low and debasing pleasure."

Historians are divided about the effect these activities had on the working classes. One of the chief purposes of "rational recreation" was to bring social classes together, but this was hardly achieved. Recreational activities continued to divide along class lines. The upper and middle classes continued to go to their own exclusive beach resorts. And when the custom of promenade concerts, which provided live orchestra entertainment, open to all classes of people, was first brought to Britain from Germany, one British observer's comment made clear the class division: "Can an Englishman imagine the inhabitants of the filthy cellars, alleys and courts of our towns, or the peasants of our villages, sitting in Kensington or other gardens, mixed up with the gentry of our metropolis and the officers of our army? The idea seems to us preposterous."[22]

FORMS OF THE NEW MASS LEISURE   The dramatic increase in literacy after 1871 made possible the rise of mass newspapers, such as the *Evening News* (1881) and *Daily Mail* (1896) in London, which sold millions of copies a day. Known as the "yellow press" in the United States, these newspapers shared some common characteristics. They were written in an easily understood style and tended to be extremely sensational. Unlike eighteenth-century newspapers that were full of serious editorials and lengthy political analysis, these tabloids provided lurid details of crimes, jingoistic diatribes, gossip, and sports news. There were other forms of cheap literature as well. Specialty magazines, such as *Family Herald* for the entire family, and women's magazines began in the 1860s. Pulp fiction for adults included the extremely popular westerns with their innumerable variations on conflicts between cowboys and Indians.

Music and dance halls appeared in the last half of the nineteenth century. The first music hall in London was constructed in 1849 for a lower-class audience. As is evident from one Londoner's observation, the music hall was primarily for males:

> [It was a] popular place of Saturday night resort with working men, as at them they can combine the drinking of the Saturday night glass and the smoking of the Saturday night pipe, with the seeing and hearing of a variety of entertainments, ranging from magnificent ballets and marvelous scenic illusions to inferior tumbling, and from well-given operatic selections to the most idiotic of the so-called comic songs of the Jolly Dogs Class.[23]

By the 1880s, there were five hundred music halls in London. Promoters gradually made them more respectable and broadened their fare to entice both women and children to attend the programs. The new dance halls, which were all the rage by 1900, were more strictly oriented toward adults. Contemporaries were often shocked by the sight of young people engaged in sexually suggestive dancing.

The upper and middle classes had created the first market for tourism, but as wages increased and workers were given paid vacations, tourism, too, became another form of mass leisure. Thomas Cook (1808–1892) was a British pioneer of mass tourism. Secretary to a British

▼ **Middle Classes at the Beach.** By the beginning of the twentieth century, changing work and leisure patterns created a new mass leisure. The upper and middle classes created the first market for tourism, although it too became another form of mass leisure as wages increased and workers received paid vacations. This photograph shows primarily the middle classes enjoying a British beach at the beginning of the twentieth century.

temperance group, Cook had accepted responsibility for organizing a railroad trip to temperance gatherings in 1841. This experience led him to offer trips on a regular basis after he found that by renting special trains, lowering prices, and increasing the number of passengers, he could make substantial profits. In 1867, he offered tours to Paris and by the 1880s to Switzerland. Of course, overseas tours were for the rich, but through their savings clubs even British factory workers were able to take weekend excursions by the turn of the century.

By the late nineteenth century, team sports had also developed into yet another important form of mass leisure. Sports were by no means a new activity. Landed elites had long had sporting clubs and activities that enabled them to display their privilege and status. The lower classes also had their sporting contests. In middle-class minds, these were usually associated with drunkenness, gambling, and excessive rowdiness. Attempts by educational and religious reformers in the nineteenth century to "purify" the games of the poor and make them respectable led to the creation of modern sporting contests.

The new team sports of the late nineteenth century exhibited certain characteristics. Unlike the old rural games, they were no longer chaotic and spontaneous activities, but became strictly organized with sets of rules and officials to enforce them. These rules were the products of organized athletic groups, such as the English Football Association (1863) and the American Bowling Congress (1895).

The Fight Song: Sports in the English Public School
▼ ▼ ▼

In the second half of the nineteenth century, organized sports were often placed at the center of the curriculum in English public schools. These sports were not just for leisure, but were intended to instill character, strength, and teamwork. This "fight song" was written by H. B. Tristam for the soccer team at Loretto School.

H. B. Tristam, *Going Strong*

Sing Football the grandest of sports in the world,
And you know it yourself if your pluck's never curled,
If you've gritted your teeth and gone hard to the last,
And sworn that you'll never let anyone past.

Chorus
Keeping close upon the ball—we drive it through them
   all,

And again we go rushing along, along, along;
O the tackle and the run, and the matches we have
   won,
From the start to the finish going strong, strong, strong,
   going strong!

If you live to be a hundred you'll never forget
How they hacked in the scrum, how you payed back
   the debt;
The joy of the swing when you tackled your man,
The lust of the fray when the battle began.

Long hence when you look with a quivering eye
On the little white tassel you value so high;
You'll think of the matches you've played in and won,
And you'll long for the days that are over and done.

The new sports were not just for leisure or fun, but like other forms of middle-class "rational recreation," they were intended to provide excellent training for people, especially youth. Not only could they develop individual skills, but they could also acquire a sense of teamwork useful for military service. These characteristics were already evident in the British public schools in the 1850s and 1860s when organized sports were placed at the center of the curriculum in such schools as Harrow, Uppingham, and Loretto (see the box above). At Loretto, for example, education was supposed to instill "First—Character. Second—Physique. Third—Intelligence. Fourth—Manners. Fifth—Information."

The new team sports rapidly became professionalized. In Britain, soccer had its Football Association in 1863 and rugby its Rugby Football Union in 1871. In the United States, the first National Association to recognize professional baseball players was formed in 1863. By 1900, the National League and American League had a complete monopoly over professional baseball. The development of urban transportation systems made possible the construction of stadiums where thousands could attend, making mass spectator sports a big business. In 1872, 2,000 people watched the British Soccer Cup finals. By 1885, the crowd had increased to 10,000 and by 1901 to 100,000. Professional teams became objects of mass adulation by crowds of urbanites who compensated for their lost sense of identity in mass urban areas by developing these new loyalties. Spectator sports even reflected class differences. Upper-class soccer teams in Britain viewed working-class teams as vicious and prone to "money-grubbing, tricks, sensational displays, and utter rottenness."

The sports cult of the late nineteenth century was mostly male oriented. Many men believed that females were not particularly suited for "vigorous physical activity," although it was permissible for middle-class women to indulge in such easy sports as croquet and lawn tennis. Eventually, some athletics crept into women's colleges and girls' public schools in England.

The new forms of popular leisure were standardized forms of amusement that drew mass audiences. Although some argued that they were important for improving people, in truth, they mostly served to provide entertainment and distract people from the realities of their work lives. Much of mass leisure was secular. Churches found that they had to compete with popular amusements for people's attention on Sundays. The new mass leisure also represented a significant change from earlier forms of popular culture. Festivals and fairs had been based on an ethos of active community participation, whereas the new forms of mass leisure were standardized for largely passive mass audiences. Amusement parks and professional sports teams were, after all, big businesses organized to make profits.

Some historians have questioned whether the new mass leisure—standardized, organized for profit, and largely spectator oriented—was a real substitute for the popular culture of previous eras that had involved the active participation of people in the life of their village communities. In view of the multibillion dollar mass entertainment markets of the twentieth century, the question, while worthwhile, may also be largely irrelevant.

What many Europeans liked to call their "age of progress" between 1871 and 1914 was also an era of anxiety. Frenzied imperialist expansion had created vast European empires and spheres of influence around the globe. This feverish competition for colonies, however, had markedly increased the existing antagonisms among the European states. At the same time, the Western treatment of native peoples as racial inferiors caused educated, non-Western elites in these colonies to initiate movements for national independence. Before these movements could be successful, however, the power that Europeans had achieved through their mass armies and technological superiority had to be weakened. The Europeans inadvertently accomplished this task for their colonial subjects by demolishing their own civilization on the battlegrounds of Europe in World War I and World War II.

The cultural revolutions before 1914 had also produced anxiety and a crisis of confidence in European civilization. A brilliant minority of intellectuals had created a modern consciousness that questioned most Europeans' optimistic faith in reason, the rational structure of nature, and the certainty of progress. The devastating experiences of World War I turned this culture of uncertainty into a way of life after 1918.

Notes

▼ ▼ ▼

1. Quoted in G. H. Nadel and P. Curtis, eds., *Imperialism and Colonialism* (New York, 1964), p. 94.

2. Karl Pearson, *National Life from the Standpoint of Science* (London, 1905), p. 184.

3. Quoted in John Ellis, *The Social History of the Machine Gun* (New York, 1975), p. 80.

4. Quoted in ibid., p. 86.

5. Quoted in Louis L. Snyder, ed., *The Imperialism Reader* (Princeton, N.J., 1962), p. 220.

6. Quoted in K. M. Panikkar, *Asia and Western Dominance* (London, 1959), p. 116.

7. Quoted in Arthur E. E. McKenzie, *The Major Achievements of Science* (New York, 1960), 1: 310.

8. Friedrich Nietzsche, *Twilight of the Idols and The Anti-Christ*, trans. R. J. Hollingdale (New York, 1972), pp. 117–18.

9. Friedrich Nietzsche, *Thus Spake Zarathustra*, in *The Philosophy of Nietzsche* (New York, 1954), p. 6.

10. Sigmund Freud, *Autobiography* (New York, 1935), p. 25.

11. Herbert Spencer, *Social Statics* (New York, 1896), pp. 146–50.

12. Friedrich von Bernhardi, *Germany and the Next War*, trans. Allen H. Powles (New York, 1914), pp. 18–19.

13. Quoted in Edward R. Tannenbaum, *1900: The Generation before the Great War* (Garden City, N.Y., 1976), p. 337.

14. Quoted in Paul Massing, *Rehearsal for Destruction: A Study of Political Anti-Semitism in Imperial Germany* (New York, 1949), p. 147.

15. Quoted in Abba Eban, *Heritage: Civilization and the Jews* (New York, 1984), p. 249.

16. Quoted in Owen Chadwick, *The Secularization of the European Mind in the Nineteenth Century* (Cambridge, 1975), p. 125.

17. William Booth, *In Darkest England and the Way Out* (London, 1890), p. 45.

18. Quoted in John Rewald, *The History of Impressionism* (New York, 1961), pp. 456–58.

19. Paul Klee, *On Modern Art*, trans. Paul Findlay (London, 1948), p. 51.

20. Quoted in Robert Gildea, *Barricades and Borders: Europe, 1800–1914* (Oxford, 1987), p. 249.

21. Quoted in Gary Cross, *A Social History of Leisure since 1600* (State College, Pa., 1990), p. 97.

22. Quoted in Gildea, *Barricades and Borders*, pp. 113–14.

23. Quoted in Cross, *A Social History of Leisure since 1600*, p. 130.

Suggestions for Further Reading
▼ ▼ ▼

Demographic problems are examined in T. McKeown, *The Modern Rise of Population* (New York, 1976). On European emigration, see C. Erickson, *Emigration from Europe, 1815–1914* (Cambridge, 1976). For broad perspectives on imperialism, see the works by T. Smith, *The Pattern of Imperialism* (Cambridge, 1981); and P. Darby, *Three Faces of Imperialism: British and American Approaches to Asia and Africa, 1870–1970* (New Haven, Conn., 1987). Different aspects of imperialism are covered in R. Robinson and J. Gallagher, *Africa and the Victorians*, 2d ed. (New York, 1981); P. Gifford and W. R. Louis, eds., *France and Britain in Africa* (New Haven, Conn., 1971); and W. Baumgart, *Imperialism: The Idea and Reality of British and French Colonial Expansion, 1880–1914* (London, 1982). British-Indian relations are examined in J. M. Brown, *Modern India: The Origins of an Asian Democracy* (New York, 1981).

Two fundamental works on the diplomatic history of the period are W. L. Langer, *European Alliances and Alignments*, 2d ed. (New York, 1966), and *The Diplomacy of Imperialism*, 2d ed. (New York, 1965). Also valuable are S. R. Williamson, *The Politics of Grand Strategy: Britain and France Prepare for War, 1904–1914* (Cambridge, Mass., 1969); G. Kennan, *The Decline of Bismarck's European Order: Franco-Prussian Relations, 1875–1890* (Princeton, N.J., 1979); and the masterful study by P. Kennedy, *The Rise of Anglo-German Antagonism, 1860–1914* (London, 1982).

A well-regarded study of Freud is P. Gay, *Freud: A Life for Our Time* (New York, 1988). Also see R. Clark, *Freud: The Man and the Cause* (New York, 1980). Nietzsche is examined in W. Kaufmann, *Nietzsche: Philosopher, Psychologist, Antichrist* 4th ed. (Princeton, N.J., 1974); and J. P. Stern, *The Mind of Nietzsche* (Oxford, 1980). On the impact of Nietzsche, see R. H. Thomas, *Nietzsche in German Politics and Society, 1890–1918* (Dover, N.H., 1983). On Bergson, see A. E. Pilkington, *Henri Bergson and His Influence* (Cambridge, 1976). The basic study on Sorel is J. J. Roth, *The Cult of Violence: Sorel and the Sorelians* (Berkeley, 1980). The best introduction to social theory is H. S. Hughes, *Consciousness and Society: The Reorientation of European Social Thought, 1890–1930* (New York, 1979). Very valuable on modern art are J. Rewald, *The History of Impressionism* 4th ed. (New York, 1973), and *Post-Impressionism*, 3d ed. (New York, 1962). On literature, see R. Pascal, *From Naturalism to Expressionism: German Literature and Society, 1880–1918*

(New York, 1973). The intellectual climate of Vienna is examined in C. E. Schorske, *Fin de Siècle Vienna: Politics and Culture* (New York, 1980).

The subject of modern anti-Semitism is covered in J. Katz, *From Prejudice to Destruction* (Cambridge, Mass., 1980), which argues that modern anti-Semitism stems from traditional Christian anti-Semitism. European racism is analyzed in G. L. Mosse, *Toward the Final Solution* (New York, 1980); while German anti-Semitism as a political force is examined in P. J. Pulzer, *The Rise of Political Anti-Semitism in Germany and Austria* (New York, 1964). Anti-Semitism in France is the subject of S. Wilson, *Ideology and Experience: Anti-Semitism in France at the Time of the Dreyfus Affair* (Rutherford, N.J., 1982). The problems of Jews in Russia are examined in J. Frankel, *Prophecy and Politics: Socialism, Nationalism and the Russian Jews, 1862–1917* (Cambridge, 1981). On Zionism, see D. Vital, *The Origins of Zionism* (Oxford, 1975).

A good introduction to the challenge scientific movements presented to the established churches is J. W. Burrow, *Evolution and Society: A Study in Victorian Social Theory* (London, 1966). A useful study on the impact of Darwinian thought on religion is J. Moore, *The Post-Darwinian Controversies: A Study of the Protestant Struggle to Come to Terms with Darwin in Great Britain and America, 1870–1900* (Cambridge, 1979). Studies of the popular religion of the period include T. A. Kselman, *Miracles and Prophesies in Nineteenth-Century France* (New Brunswick, N.J., 1983); and J. Sperber, *Popular Catholicism in Nineteenth-Century Germany* (Princeton, N.J., 1984).

On various aspects of education, see M. J. Maynes, *Schooling in Western Europe: A Social History* (Albany, N.Y., 1985); J. S. Hurt, *Elementary Schooling and the Working Classes, 1860–1918* (London, 1979); and J. C. McClelland, *Autocrats and Academics: Education, Culture and Society in Tsarist Russia* (Chicago, 1978). A concise and well-presented survey of leisure patterns is G. Cross, *A Social History of Leisure since 1600* (State College, Pa., 1990). A more specialized study is P. Bailey, *Leisure and Class in Victorian England* (London, 1978). On sport, see T. Mason, *Association Football and English Society, 1863–1915* (Brighton, England, 1980). On the expansion of reading material, see A. J. Lee, *The Origins of the Popular Press in Britain, 1855–1914* (London, 1978).

Chapter 26

The Beginning of the Twentieth-Century Crisis: War and Revolution

▼▼▼▼▼

World War I (1914–1918) was one of the dominant events of the twentieth century. It devastated the prewar economic, social, and political order of Europe while its uncertain outcome served to prepare the way for an even more destructive war. Overwhelmed by the size of its battles, the extent of its casualties, and the effects of its impact on all facets of European life, contemporaries referred to it simply as the "Great War."

The Great War was all the more disturbing to Europeans because it came after a period that many believed to have been an age of progress. There had been international crises before 1914, but somehow Europeans had managed to avoid serious and prolonged military confrontations. When smaller European states had gone to war, as in the Balkans in 1912 and 1913, the great European powers had shown the ability to keep the conflict localized. Material prosperity and a fervid belief in scientific and technological progress had convinced many people that Europe stood on the verge of creating the utopia that humans had dreamed of for centuries. The historian Arnold Toynbee expressed what the pre–World War I era had meant to his generation:

> [it was expected] that life throughout the World would become more rational, more humane, and more democratic and that, slowly, but surely, political democracy would produce greater social justice. We had also expected that the progress of science and technology would make mankind richer, and that this increasing wealth would gradually spread from a minority to a majority. We had expected that all this would happen peacefully. In fact we thought that mankind's course was set for an earthly paradise.[1]

Assassination of Archduke Francis Ferdinand ▼	Battle of Verdun ▼	United States Enters the War ▼	Surrender of Germany ▼	Paris Peace Conference ▼
•••••••• 1915 •••••••••	• 1916 •••••••••••	1917 ••••••••••	1918 •••••••••	1919 ••••••••

Ministry of Munitions in Britain ▲   Complete Mobilization for Total War in Germany ▲   The Bolshevik Revolution ▲   Civil War in Russia ▲

After 1918, it was no longer possible to maintain naive illusions about the progress of Western civilization. As World War I was followed by the destructiveness of World War II and the mass murder machines of totalitarian regimes, it became all too apparent that instead of a utopia, European civilization had become a nightmare. World War I and the revolutions it spawned can properly be seen as the first stage in the crisis of the twentieth century.

▼ The Road to World War I

On June 28, 1914, the heir to the Austrian throne, the Archduke Francis Ferdinand, was assassinated in the Bosnian city of Sarajevo. Although this event precipitated the confrontation between Austria and Serbia that led to World War I, war was by no means a foregone conclusion. Previous assassinations of European leaders had not usually led to war, and European statesmen had managed before on a number of occasions to localize such conflicts. Although the decisions that European statesmen made during this crisis were crucial in leading to war, there were also long-range, underlying forces that were propelling Europeans toward armed conflict.

Nationalism and Internal Dissent

In the first half of the nineteenth century, liberals had maintained that the organization of European states along national lines would lead to a peaceful Europe based on a sense of international fraternity. They had been very wrong. The system of nation-states that had emerged in Europe in the last half of the nineteenth century led not to cooperation but to competition. Rivalries over colonial and commercial interests intensified during an era of frenzied imperialist expansion while the division of Europe's great powers into two loose alliances (Germany, Austria, and Italy and France, Great Britain, and Russia) only added to the tensions. The series of crises that tested these alliances in the 1900s and early 1910s had left European states with a dangerous lesson. Those governments that had exercised restraint in order to avoid war wound up being publicly humiliated, while those that went to the brink of war to maintain their national interests had often been praised for having preserved national honor. In either case, by 1914, the major European states had come to believe that their allies were important and that their security depended on supporting those allies, even when they took foolish risks.

Diplomacy based on brinkmanship was especially frightening in view of the nature of the European state system. Each nation-state regarded itself as sovereign, subject to no higher interest or authority. Each state was motivated by its own self-interest and success. As Emperor William II of Germany remarked, "In questions of honor and vital interests, you don't consult others." Such attitudes made war an ever-present possibility, particularly since most statesmen considered war an acceptable way to preserve the power of their national states.

The growth of nationalism in the nineteenth century had yet another serious consequence. Not all ethnic groups had achieved the goal of nationhood. Slavic minorities in the Balkans and the polyglot Habsburg empire, for example, still dreamed of creating their own national states. So did the Irish in the British Empire and the Poles in the Russian Empire.

National aspirations, however, were not the only source of internal strife at the beginning of the twentieth century. Socialist labor movements had grown more powerful and were increasingly inclined to use strikes, even violent ones, to achieve their goals. Some conservative leaders, alarmed at the increase in labor strife and class division, even feared that European nations were on the verge of revolution. Did these statesmen opt for war in 1914 because they believed that "prosecuting an active foreign policy," as some Austrian leaders expressed it, would smother "internal troubles"? Some historians have argued that the desire to suppress internal disorder may have encouraged some leaders to take the plunge into war in 1914.

Militarism

The growth of large mass armies after 1900 not only heightened the existing tensions in Europe, but made it inevitable that if war did come it would be highly destructive. Conscription had been established as a regular practice in most Western countries before 1914 (the United States and Britain were major exceptions). European military machines had doubled in size between 1890 and 1914. With its 1.3 million men, the Russian army had grown to be the largest, while the French and Germans were not far behind with 900,000 each. The British, Italian, and Austrian armies numbered between 250,000 and 500,000 soldiers. Most European land armies were filled with peasants, since many young, urban working-class males were unable to pass the physical examinations required for military service.

Militarism, however, involved more than just large armies. As armies grew, so too did the influence of military leaders who drew up vast and complex plans for quickly mobilizing millions of men and enormous quantities of supplies in the event of war. Fearful that changes in these plans would cause chaos in the armed forces, military leaders insisted that their plans could not be altered. In the crises during the summer of 1914, the generals' lack of flexibility forced European political leaders to make decisions for military instead of political reasons.

The Outbreak of War: The Summer of 1914

Militarism, nationalism, and the desire to stifle internal dissent may all have played a role in the coming of World War I, but the decisions made by European leaders in the summer of 1914 directly precipitated the conflict. It was another crisis in the Balkans that forced this predicament upon European statesmen.

As we have seen, states in southeastern Europe had struggled to free themselves of Turkish rule in the course of the nineteenth and early twentieth centuries. But the rivalry between Austria-Hungary and Russia for domination of these new states created serious tensions in the region. The crises of 1908 to 1913 had only intensified the antagonisms. By 1914, Serbia, supported by Russia, was determined to create a large, independent Slavic state in the Balkans, while Austria, which had its own Slavic minorities to contend with, was equally set on preventing that possibility. Many Europeans perceived the inherent dangers in this combination of Serbian am-

▼ **Apprehension of an Assassin.** World War I was precipitated by the assassination of the Archduke Francis Ferdinand, heir to the Austrian throne, on June 28, 1914. His assassin was Gavrillo Princip, an eighteen-year-old Bosnian activist who favored the creation of a pan-Slavic kingdom at Austria's expense. As shown here, he was arrested soon after killing Franz Ferdinand and his wife.

bition bolstered by Russian hatred of Austria and Austrian conviction that Serbia's success meant the end of its empire. The British ambassador to Vienna wrote in 1913:

> Serbia will some day set Europe by the ears, and bring about a universal war on the Continent. . . . I cannot tell you how exasperated people are getting here at the continual worry which that little country causes to Austria under encouragement from Russia. . . . It will be lucky if Europe succeeds in avoiding war as a result of the present crisis. The next time a Serbian crisis arises. . . , I feel sure that Austria-Hungary will refuse to admit of any Russian interference in the dispute and that she will proceed to settle her differences with her little neighbor by herself.[2]

It was against this backdrop of mutual distrust and hatred between Austria-Hungary and Russia, on the one hand, and Austria-Hungary and Serbia, on the other, that the events of the summer of 1914 were played out.

The assassination of the Austrian Archduke Francis Ferdinand and his wife Sophia on June 28, 1914, was carried out by a Bosnian activist who worked for the Black Hand, a Serbian terrorist organization dedicated to the creation of a pan-Slavic kingdom. Although the Austrian government did not know whether the Serbian government had been directly involved in the archduke's assassination, it saw an opportunity to "render Serbia innocuous once and for all by a display of force," as the Austrian foreign minister put it. Fearful of Russian intervention on Serbia's behalf, Austrian leaders sought the backing of their German allies. Emperor William II and his chancellor, Theobald von Bethmann-Hollweg, responded with the infamous "blank check," their assurance that Austria-Hungary could rely on Germany's "full support," even if "matters went to the length of a war between Austria-Hungary and Russia." Much historical debate has focused on this "blank check" extended to the Austrians. Did the Germans realize that an Austrian-Serbian war could lead to a wider war? If so,

▼ **Map 26.1** Europe in 1914.

"You Have to Bear the Responsibility for War or Peace"

▼ ▼ ▼

After Austria declared war on Serbia on July 28, 1914, Russian support of Serbia and German support of Austria threatened to escalate the conflict in the Balkans into a wider war. As we can see in these last-minute telegrams between the Russians and Germans, neither side was able to accept the other's line of reasoning.

Communications between Berlin and St. Petersburg on the Eve of World War I

Emperor William II to Tsar Nicholas II, July 28, 10:45 P.M.

I have heard with the greatest anxiety of the impression which is caused by the action of Austria-Hungary against Servia [Serbia]. The inscrupulous agitation which has been going on for years in Servia, has led to the revolting crime of which Archduke Franz Ferdinand has become a victim. The spirit which made the Servians murder their own King and his consort still dominates that country. Doubtless You will agree with me that both of us, You as well as I, and all other sovereigns, have a common interest to insist that all those who are responsible for this horrible murder shall suffer their deserved punishment. . . .

> Your most sincere and devoted friend and cousin
> (Signed)   Wilhelm

Tsar Nicholas II to Emperor William II, July 29, 1:00 P.M.

I am glad that you are back in Germany. In this serious moment I ask You earnestly to help me. An ignominious war has been declared against a weak country and in Russia the indignation which I full share is tremendous. I fear that very soon I shall be unable to resist the pressure exercised upon me and that I shall be forced to take measures which will lead to war. To prevent a calamity as a European war would be, I urge You in the name of our old friendship to do all in Your power to restrain Your ally from going too far.

> (Signed)   Nicolas

Emperor William II to Tsar Nicholas II, July 29, 6:30 P.M.

I have received Your telegram and I share Your desire for the conservation of peace. However: I cannot—as I told You in my first telegram—consider the action of Austria-Hungary as an "ignominious war." Austria-

Hungary knows from experience that the promises of Servia as long as they are merely on paper are entirely unreliable. . . . I believe that a direct understanding is possible and desirable between Your Government and Vienna, an understanding which I—as I have already telegraphed you—my Government endeavours to aid with all possible effort. Naturally military measures by Russia, which might be construed as a menace by Austria-Hungary, would accelerate a calamity which both of us desire to avoid and would undermine my position as mediator which—upon Your appeal to my friendship and aid—I willingly accepted.

> (Signed)   Wilhelm

Emperor William II to Tsar Nicholas II, July 30, 1:00 A.M.

My Ambassador has instructions to direct the attention of Your Government to the dangers and serious consequences of a mobilisation. I have told You the same in my last telegram. Austria-Hungary has mobilised only against Servia, and only a part of her army. If Russia, as seems to be the case, according to Your advice and that of Your Government, mobilises against Austria-Hungary, the part of the mediator with which You have entrusted me in such friendly manner and which I have accepted upon Your express desire, is threatened if not made impossible. The entire weight of decision now rests upon Your shoulders, You have to bear the responsibility for war or peace.

> (Signed)   Wilhelm

German Chancellor to German Ambassador at St. Petersburg, July 31, URGENT

In spite of negotiations still pending and although we have up to this hour made no preparations for mobilisation, Russia has mobilised her entire army and navy, hence also against us. On account of these Russian measures, we have been forced, for the safety of the country, to proclaim the threatening state of war, which does not yet imply mobilisation. Mobilisation, however, is bound to follow if Russia does not stop every measure of war against us and against Austria-Hungary within 12 hours, and notifies us definitely to this effect. Please to communicate this at once to M. Sasonof and wire hour of communication.

did they actually want one? Historians are still seriously divided on the answers to these questions.

Strengthened by German support, Austrian leaders issued an ultimatum to Serbia on July 23. Austrian leaders made their demands so extreme that Serbia had little choice but to reject some of them in order to preserve its sovereignty. Austria then declared war on Serbia on July 28. Although both Germany and Austria had hoped to keep the war limited to Serbia and Austria in order to ensure Austria's success in the Balkans, these hopes soon vanished.

Still smarting from its humiliation in the Bosnian crisis of 1908, Russia was determined to support Serbia's cause. On July 28, Tsar Nicholas II ordered partial mobilization of the Russian army against Austria. At this point, the rigidity of the military war plans played havoc with diplomatic and political decisions. The Russian General Staff informed the Tsar that their mobilization plans were based on a war against both Germany and Austria simultaneously. They could not execute partial mobilization without creating chaos in the army. Consequently, the Russian government ordered full mobilization of the Russian army on July 29, knowing that the Germans would consider this an act of war against them (see the box on p. 900). Germany responded to Russian mobilization with its own ultimatum that the Russians must halt their mobilization within twelve hours. When the Russians ignored it, Germany declared war on Russia on August 1.

At this stage of the conflict, German war plans determined whether or not France would become involved in the war. Under the guidance of General Alfred von Schlieffen, chief of staff from 1891 to 1905, the German General Staff had devised a military plan based on the assumption of a two-front war with France and Russia, since the two powers had formed a military alliance in 1894. The Schlieffen Plan called for a minimal troop deployment against Russia while most of the German army would make a rapid invasion of western France by way of neutral Belgium. After the planned quick defeat of the French, the German army expected to redeploy to the east against Russia. Under the Schlieffen Plan, Germany could not mobilize its troops solely against Russia and therefore declared war on France on August 3 after it had issued an ultimatum to Belgium on August 2 demanding the right of German troops to pass through Belgian territory. On August 4, Great Britain declared war on Germany, officially over this violation of Belgian neutrality, but in fact over the British desire to maintain its world power. As one British diplomat argued, if Germany and Austria were to win the war, "what would be the position of a friendless England?" By August 4, all the great powers of Europe were at war.

▼ The War

Before 1914, many political leaders had become convinced that war involved so many political and economic risks that it was not worth fighting. Others had believed that "rational" diplomats could control any situation and prevent the outbreak of war. At the beginning of August 1914, both of these prewar illusions were shattered, but the new illusions that replaced them soon proved to be equally foolish.

1914–1915: Illusions and Stalemate

Europeans went to war in 1914 with remarkable enthusiasm (see the box on p. 902). Government propaganda had been successful in stirring up national antagonisms before the war. Now in August of 1914, the urgent pleas of governments for defense against aggressors fell on receptive ears in every belligerent nation. Most people seemed genuinely convinced that their na-

▼ **The Excitement of War.** World War I was greeted with incredible enthusiasm. Each of the major belligerents was convinced of the rightness of its nation's cause. Everywhere in Europe, jubilant civilians sent their troops off to war with joyous fervor. Their belief that the soldiers would be home by Christmas proved to be a pathetic illusion.

The Excitement of War

▼ ▼ ▼

The incredible outpouring of patriotic enthusiasm that greeted the declaration of war at the beginning of August 1914 demonstrated the power that nationalistic feeling had attained at the beginning of the twentieth century. Many Europeans seemingly believed that the war had given them a higher purpose, a renewed dedication to the greatness of their nation. This selection is taken from the autobiography of Stefan Zweig, an Austrian writer who captured well the orgiastic celebration of war in Vienna in 1914.

Stefan Zweig, *The World of Yesterday*

The next morning I was in Austria. In every station placards had been put up announcing general mobilization. The trains were filled with fresh recruits, banners were flying, music sounded, and in Vienna I found the entire city in a tumult. . . . There were parades in the street, flags, ribbons, and music burst forth everywhere, young recruits were marching triumphantly, their faces lighting up at the cheering. . . .

And to be truthful, I must acknowledge that there was a majestic, rapturous, and even seductive something in this first outbreak of the people from which one could escape only with difficulty. And in spite of all my hatred and aversion for war, I should not like to have missed the memory of those days. As never before, thousands and hundreds of thousands felt what they should have felt in peace time, that they belonged together. A city of two million, a country of nearly fifty million, in that hour felt that they were participating in world history, in a moment which would never recur, and that each one was called upon to cast his infinitesimal self into the glowing mass, there to be purified of all selfishness. All differences of class, rank, and language were flooded over at that moment by the rushing feeling of fraternity. Strangers spoke to one another in the streets, people who had avoided each other for years shook hands, everywhere one saw excited faces. Each individual experienced an exaltation of his ego, he was no longer the isolated person of former times, he had been incorporated into the mass, he was part of the people, and his person, his hitherto unnoticed person, had been given meaning. . . .

What did the great mass know of war in 1914, after nearly half a century of peace? They did not know war, they had hardly given it a thought. It had become legendary, and distance had made it seem romantic and heroic. They still saw it in the perspective of their school readers and of paintings in museums; brilliant cavalry attacks in glittering uniforms, the fatal shot always straight through the heart, the entire campaign a resounding march of victory—"We'll be home at Christmas," the recruits shouted laughingly to their mothers in August of 1914. . . . A rapid excursion into the romantic, a wild, manly adventure—that is how the war of 1914 was painted in the imagination of the simple man, and the young people were honestly afraid that they might miss this most wonderful and exciting experience of their lives; that is why they hurried and thronged to the colors, and that is why they shouted and sang in the trains that carried them to the slaughter; wildly and feverishly the red wave of blood coursed through the veins of the entire nation.

---

tion's cause was just. Even domestic differences were temporarily shelved in the midst of war fever. Socialists had long derided "imperialist war" as a blow against the common interests that united the working classes of all countries. Nationalism, however, proved more powerful than working-class solidarity in the summer of 1914 as socialist parties everywhere dropped plans for strikes and workers expressed their readiness to fight for their country. The German Social Democrats, for example, decided that it was imperative to "safeguard the culture and independence of our own country."

A new set of illusions fed the enthusiasm for war. Almost everyone in August 1914 believed that the war would be over in a few weeks. People were reminded that all European wars since 1815 had, in fact, ended in a matter of weeks, conveniently overlooking the American Civil War (1861–1865), which was the "real prototype" for World War I. The illusion of a short war was also bolstered by another illusion, the belief that in an age of modern industry war could not be supported for more than a few months without destroying a nation's economy. Both the soldiers who exuberantly boarded the trains for the war front in August 1914 and the jubilant citizens who bombarded them with flowers when they departed believed that the warriors would be home by Christmas.

Then, too, war held a fatal attraction for many people. To some, war was an exhilarating release from humdrum bourgeois existence, from a "world grown old and cold and weary," as one poet wrote. To some, war meant a glorious adventure, as a young German student wrote to his parents: "My dear ones, be proud that you live in such a time and in such a nation and that you . . . have the privilege of sending those you love into so glorious a battle."[3] And finally there were those who believed that the war would have a redemptive effect, that millions would abandon their petty preoccupations with material life, ridding the nation of selfishness and providing a national rebirth based on self-sacrifice, heroism, and nobility. All of these illusions about war died painful deaths on the battlefields of World War I.

German hopes for a quick end to the war rested upon a military gamble. The Schlieffen Plan had called for the

German army to make a vast encircling movement through Belgium into northern France that would sweep around Paris and encircle most of the French army. German troops crossed into Belgium on August 4 and by the first week of September had reached the Marne River, only twenty miles from Paris. The Germans seemed on the verge of success, but an unexpected counterattack by British and French forces under the French commander General Joseph Joffre stopped them at the First Battle of the Marne (September 6–10). The German troops fell back, but the exhausted French army was unable to pursue its advantage. The war quickly turned into a stalemate as neither the Germans nor French could dislodge each other from the trenches they had begun to dig for shelter. Two lines of trenches soon extended from the English Channel to the frontiers of Switzerland. The Western Front had become bogged down in a trench warfare that kept both sides immobilized in virtually the same positions for four years.

In contrast to the West, the war in the East was marked by much more mobility, although the cost in

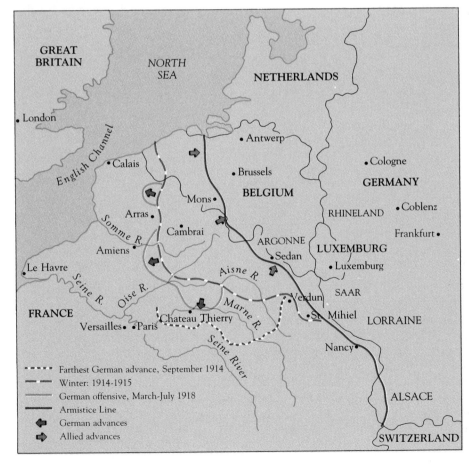

▼ **Map 26.2** The Western Front, 1914–1918.

lives was equally enormous. At the beginning of the war, the Russian army moved into eastern Germany but was decisively defeated at the Battles of Tannenberg on August 30 and the Masurian Lakes on September 15. These battles established the military reputations of the commanding general, Paul von Hindenburg, and his chief of staff, General Erich Ludendorff. The Russians were no longer a threat to German territory.

The Austrians, Germany's allies, fared less well initially. They had been defeated by the Russians in Galicia and thrown out of Serbia as well. To make matters worse, the Italians betrayed the Germans and Austrians and entered the war on the Allied side by attacking Austria in May 1915. By this time, the Germans had come to the aid of the Austrians. A German-Austrian army defeated and routed the Russian army in Galicia and pushed the Russians back three hundred miles into their own territory. Russian casualties stood at 2.5 million killed, captured, or wounded; the Russians had almost been knocked out of the war. Buoyed by their success, the Germans and Austrians, joined by the Bulgarians in September 1915, attacked and eliminated Serbia from the war.

1916–1917: *The Great Slaughter*

The successes in the East enabled the Germans to move back to the offensive in the West. The early

▼ **Map 26.3** The Eastern Front, 1914–1918.

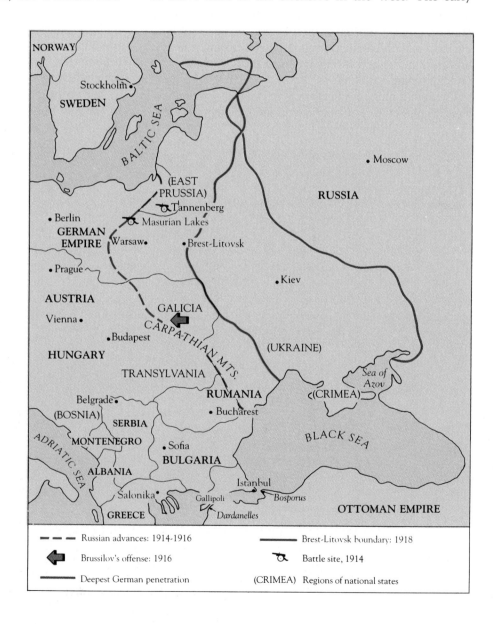

trenches dug in 1914 had by now become elaborate systems of defense. Both lines of trenches were protected by barbed wire entanglements three to five feet high and thirty yards wide, concrete machine-gun nests, and mortar batteries, supported further back by heavy artillery. Troops lived in holes in the ground, separated from each other by a "no man's land."

The unexpected development of trench warfare baffled military leaders who had been trained to fight wars of movement and maneuver. But they were under heavy pressure from public outcries for action. The only plan generals could devise was to attempt a breakthrough by throwing masses of men against enemy lines that had first been battered by artillery barrages. Once the decisive breakthrough had been achieved, they thought, they could then return to the war of movement that they knew best. Periodically, the high command on either side would order an offensive that would begin with an artillery barrage to flatten the enemy's barbed wire and leave the enemy in a state of shock. After "softening up" the enemy in this fashion, a mass of soldiers would climb out of their trenches with fixed bayonets and hope to work their way toward the enemy trenches. The attacks rarely worked, since the machine gun put hordes of men advancing unprotected across open fields at a severe disadvantage. In 1916 and 1917, millions of young men were sacrificed in the search for the elusive breakthrough. In the German offensive at Verdun in 1916, the British campaign on the Somme in 1916, and the French attack in the Champagne in 1917, the senseless-

ness of trench warfare became all too obvious. In ten months at Verdun, 700,000 men lost their lives over a few miles of terrain.

DAILY LIFE IN THE TRENCHES Warfare in the trenches of the Western Front produced unimaginable horrors (see the box on p. 906). Many participants commented on the fog of confusion that hung over the battlefields. When an attacking force entered "no man's land," the combination of noise, machine-gun fire, bombardment, and terror often caused soldiers to lose their sense of direction; they went forward only because they were carried on by the momentum of the soldiers beside them. Rarely were battles as orderly as they were portrayed on military maps and in civilian newspapers.

Battlefields were hellish landscapes of barbed wire, shell holes, mud, and injured and dying men. The introduction of poison gas in 1915 produced new forms of injuries, as one British writer described:

> I wish those people who write so glibly about this being a holy war could see a case of mustard gas . . . could see the poor things burnt and blistered all over with great mustard-coloured suppurating blisters with blind eyes all sticky . . . and stuck together, and always fighting for breath, with voices a mere whisper, saying that their throats are closing and they know they will choke.[4]

Soldiers in the trenches also lived with the persistent presence of death. Since combat went on for months,

▼ **The Destruction at Verdun.** In 1916, the German high command decided to take the offensive against the French fortifications at Verdun, which was 125 miles east of Paris. The ferocious Battle of Verdun cost 700,000 lives and resulted in an exchange of only a few miles of land. As seen in the photograph, the city of Verdun, subjected to massive artillery shelling, was severely damaged. The population of Verdun dropped from 15,000 to 3,000 in the course of the battle.

The Reality of War: Trench Warfare

▼ ▼ ▼

T he romantic illusion about the excitement and adventure of war that filled the minds of so many young men who marched off to battle (see the box on p. 902) quickly disintegrated after a short time in the trenches on the Western Front. This description of trench warfare is taken from the most famous novel that emerged from World War I, Erich Maria Remarque's All Quiet on the Western Front, written in 1929. Remarque had fought in the trenches in France.

Erich Maria Remarque, *All Quiet on the Western Front*

We wake up in the middle of the night. The earth booms. Heavy fire is falling on us. We crouch into corners. We distinguish shells of every calibre.

Each man lays hold of his things and looks again every minute to reassure himself that they are still there. The dug-out heaves, the night roars and flashes. We look at each other in the momentary flashes of light, and with pale faces and pressed lips shake our heads.

Every man is aware of the heavy shells tearing down the parapet, rooting up the embankment and demolishing the upper layers of concrete. . . . Already by morning a few of the recruits are green and vomiting. They are too inexperienced. . . .

The bombardment does not diminish. It is falling in the rear too. As far as one can see it spouts fountains of mud and iron. A wide belt is being raked.

The attack does not come, but the bombardment continues. Slowly we become mute. Hardly a man speaks. We cannot make ourselves understood.

Our trench is almost gone. At many places it is only eighteen inches high, it is broken by holes, and craters, and mountains of earth. A shell lands square in front of our post. At once it is dark. We are buried and must dig ourselves out. . . .

Towards morning, while it is still dark, there is some excitement. Through the entrance rushes in a swarm of fleeing rats that try to storm the walls. Torches light up the confusion. Everyone yells and curses and slaughters. The madness and despair of many hours unloads itself in this outburst. Faces are distorted, arms strike out, the beasts scream; we just stop in time to avoid attacking one another. . . .

Suddenly it howls and flashes terrifically, the dug-out cracks in all its joints under a direct hit, fortu-

nately only a light one that the concrete blocks are able to withstand. It rings metallically, the walls reel, rifles, helmets, earth, mud, and dust fly everywhere. Sulphur fumes pour in. . . . The recruit starts to rave again and two others follow suit. One jumps up and rushes out, we have trouble with the other two. I start after the one who escapes and wonder whether to shoot him in the leg—then it shrieks again, I fling myself down and when I stand up the wall of the trench is plastered with smoking splinters, lumps of flesh, and bits of uniform. I scramble back.

The first recruit seems actually to have gone insane. He butts his head against the wall like a goat. We must try tonight to take him to the rear. Meanwhile we bind him, but so that in case of attack he can be released.

Suddenly the nearer explosions cease. The shelling continues but it has lifted and falls behind us, our trench is free. We seize the hand-grenades, pitch them out in front of the dug-out and jump after them. The bombardment has stopped and a heavy barrage now falls behind us. The attack has come.

No one would believe that in this howling waste there could still be men; but steel helmets now appear on all sides out of the trench, and fifty yards from us a machine-gun is already in position and barking.

The wire-entanglements are torn to pieces. Yet they offer some obstacle. We see the storm-troops coming. Our artillery opens fire. Machine-guns rattle, rifles crack. The charge works its way across. Haie and Kropp begin with the hand-grenades. They throw as fast as they can, others pass them, the handles with the strings already pulled. Haie throws seventy-five yards, Kropp sixty, it has been measured, the distance is important. The enemy as they run cannot do much before they are within forty yards.

We recognize the distorted faces, the smooth helmets: they are French. They have already suffered heavily when they reach the remants of the barbed-wire entanglements. A whole line has gone down before our machine-guns; then we have a lot of stoppages and they come nearer.

I see one of them, his face upturned, fall into a wire cradle. His body collapses, his hands remain suspended as though he were praying. Then his body drops clean away and only his hands with the stumps of his arms, shot off, now hang in the wire.

soldiers had to carry on in the midst of countless bodies of dead men or the remains of men dismembered by artillery barrages. Many soldiers remembered the stench of decomposing bodies and the swarms of rats that grew fat in the trenches.

Soldiers on the Western Front did not spend all of their time on the front line or in combat when they were on the front line. Out of every month an infantryman spent one week in the front-line trenches, one week in the reserve lines, and the remaining two weeks somewhere behind the lines. Daily routine in the trenches was predictable. Thirty minutes before sunrise, troops had to "stand to" or be combat ready to repel any attack. If no attack were forthcoming that day, the day's routine consisted of breakfast followed by inspection, sentry duty, repair work on the trenches, care of personal items, or whiling away the time as best they could. Soldiers often recalled the boredom of life in the dreary, lice-ridden, wet and muddy or dry and dusty trenches.

At many places along the opposing lines of trenches, a "live and let live" system evolved based on the realization that neither side was going to dislodge the other anyway. The "live and let live" system resulted in such unspoken agreements as not to shell the latrines or open fire during breakfast. Some parties even worked out

▼ **Impact of the Machine Gun.** The development of trench warfare on the Western Front stymied military leaders who had expected to fight a war based on movement and maneuver. Their efforts to effect a breakthrough by sending masses of men against enemy lines was the height of folly in view of the machine gun. Masses of men advancing across open land made magnificent targets.

▼ **The Horrors of War.** The slaughter of millions of men in the trenches of World War I created unimaginable horrors for the participants. For the sake of survival, many soldiers learned to harden themselves against the stench of decomposing bodies and the sight of bodies horribly dismembered by artillery barrages.

agreements to make noise before minor raids so that the other side could withdraw to protective bunkers.

On both sides, troops produced their own humorous magazines to help pass the time and fulfill the need to laugh in the midst of their daily madness. The British trench magazine, the *B. E. F. Times*, devoted one of its issues to defining military terms. A typical definition "DUDS—These are of two kinds. A shell on impact failing to explode is called a dud. They are unhappily not as plentiful as the other kind, which often draws a big salary and explodes for no reason. These are plentiful away from the fighting areas."[5] Soldiers' songs also captured a mixture of the sentimental and the frivolous (see the box on p. 908).

The Widening of the War

As another response to the stalemate on the Western Front, both sides sought to gain new allies who might provide a winning advantage. The Turkish or Ottoman Empire had already come into the war on Germany's side in August 1914. Russia, Great Britain, and France declared war on Turkey in November. Although the Allies attempted to open a Balkan front by landing forces at

The Songs of World War I

▼ ▼ ▼

W hether on the march, in bars, in trains, and even in
the trenches, the soldiers of World War I spent time
singing. The songs sung by soldiers of different nationalities varied considerably. A German favorite, The Watch
on the Rhine, focused on heroism and patriotism. British
war songs often partook of black humor, as in The Old
Barbed Wire. An American favorite was the rousing
Over There, written by the professional songwriter
George M. Cohan.

From *The Watch on the Rhine*

There sounds a call like thunder's roar,
Like the crash of swords, like the surge of waves.
To the Rhine, the Rhine, the German Rhine!
Who will the stream's defender be?
   Dear Fatherland, rest quietly
   Sure stands and true the Watch,
   The Watch on the Rhine.

To heaven he gazes.
Spirits of heroes look down.
He vows with proud battle-desire:
O Rhine! You will stay as German as my breast!
   Dear Fatherland, etc.
Even if my heart breaks in death,
You will never be French.
As you are rich in water
Germany is rich in hero's blood.
   Dear Fatherland, etc.

So long as a drop of blood still glows,
So long a hand the dagger can draw,
So long an arm the rifle can hold—
Never will an enemy touch your shore.
   Dear Fatherland, etc.

From *The Old Barbed Wire*

If you want to find the old battalion,
I know where they are,
I know where they are.

If you want to find a battalion,
I know where they are,
They're hanging on the old barbed wire.
I've seen 'em, I've seen 'em,
Hanging on the old barbed wire,
I've seen 'em,
Hanging on the old barbed wire.

George M. Cohan, *Over There*

Over There
Over There
Send the word
Send the word
Over There
That the boys are coming
The drums rum-tuming everywhere.
Over There
Say a prayer
Send the word
Send the word
To Beware.
It will be over.
We're coming over
And we won't come back
Till it's over
Over There.

Johnnie get your gun
   get your gun
   get your gun
Back in town to run
Home to run Home to run
Hear them calling you and me
Every son of liberty
Hurry right away
Don't delay go today
Make your Daddy glad
To have had such a lad
Tell your sweetheart not to pine
To be proud their boy's in line.

Gallipoli, southwest of Constantinople, in April 1915, the entry of Bulgaria into the war on the side of the Central Powers (as Germany, Austria-Hungary, and Turkey were called) and a disastrous campaign at Gallipoli caused them to withdraw. The Italians, as we have seen, also entered the war on the Allied side after France and Britain promised to further their acquisition of Austrian territory. In the long run, however, Italian military incompetence forced the Allies to come to the assistance of Italy.

By 1917, the war that had originated in Europe had truly become a world conflict. In the Middle East, a British officer who came to be known as Lawrence of Arabia incited Arab princes to revolt in 1917 against their Turkish overlords. In 1918, British forces from Egypt destroyed the rest of the Ottoman Empire in the Middle East. For their Middle East campaigns, the British mobilized forces from India, Australia, and New Zealand. The Allies also took advantage of Germany's preoccupations in Europe and lack of naval strength to seize German colonies in the rest of the world.

ENTRY OF THE UNITED STATES   At first, the United States tried to remain neutral in the Great War, but it became more difficult to do so as the war dragged on. Although there was considerable sentiment for the British side in the conflict, the immediate cause of American involvement grew out of the naval conflict between Germany and Great Britain. Only once did the German and British naval forces engage in direct battle—at the Battle of Jutland on May 31, 1916, when the two fleets fought to a standstill. But Britain used its superior naval power to maximum effect by creating a naval blockade of Germany. Germany retaliated by imposing a counterblockade enforced by the use of unrestricted submarine warfare. At the beginning of 1915, the German government declared the area around the British Isles a war zone and threatened to torpedo any ship caught in it. Strong American protests over the German sinking of passenger liners, especially the British ship *Lusitania* on May 7, 1915, when over a hundred Americans lost their lives, forced the German government to suspend unrestricted submarine warfare in September 1915 to avoid further antagonizing the Americans.

In January 1917, however, eager to break the deadlock in the war, the Germans decided on another military gamble by returning to unrestricted submarine warfare. German naval officers convinced Emperor William II that the use of unrestricted submarine warfare could starve the British into submission within five months. When the emperor expressed his concern about the

Americans, he was told not to worry. The Americans, the chief of the German Naval Staff said, were "disorganized and undisciplined." The British would starve before the Americans could act. And even if the Americans did intervene, Admiral Holtzendorff assured the emperor, "I give your Majesty my word as an officer, that not one American will land on the continent."

The return to unrestricted submarine warfare brought the United States into the war on April 6, 1917. Although American troops did not arrive in large numbers in Europe until 1918, the entry of the United States into the war in 1917 gave the Allied powers a psychological boost when they needed it. The year 1917 was not a good year for them. Allied offensives on the Western Front were disastrously defeated. The Italian armies were smashed in October, and in November 1917 the Bolshevik Revolution in Russia led to Russia's withdrawal from the war (see The Russian Revolution later in the chapter). The cause of the Central Powers looked favorable, although war weariness in Turkey, Bulgaria, Austria-Hungary, and Germany was beginning to take its toll. The home front was rapidly becoming a cause for as much concern as the war front.

The Home Front: The Impact of Total War

The prolongation of World War I made it a total war that affected the lives of all citizens, however remote they might be from the battlefields. World War I transformed the governments, economics, and societies of the European belligerents in fundamental ways. The need to organize masses of men and matériel for years of combat (Germany alone had 5.5 million men in active units in 1916) led to increased centralization of government powers, economic regimentation, and manipulation of public opinion to keep the war effort going.

TOTAL WAR: POLITICAL CENTRALIZATION AND ECONOMIC REGIMENTATION   As we have seen, the outbreak of World War I was greeted with a rush of patriotism; even socialists joined enthusiastically into the fray. As the war dragged on, governments realized, however, that more than patriotism would be needed. Since the war was expected to be short, little thought had been given to economic problems and long-term wartime needs. Governments had to respond quickly, however, when the war machines failed to achieve their knockout blows and made ever-greater demands for men and matériel.

The extension of government power was a logical outgrowth of these needs. Most European countries had already devised some system of mass conscription or mil-

itary draft. It was now carried to unprecedented heights as countries mobilized tens of millions of young men for that elusive breakthrough to victory. Even countries that continued to rely on volunteers (Great Britain had the largest volunteer army in modern history—one million men—in 1914 and 1915) were forced to resort to conscription, especially to ensure that skilled laborers did not enlist but remained in factories that were important to the production of munitions. In 1916, despite widespread resistance to this extension of government power, compulsory military service was introduced in Great Britain.

Throughout Europe, wartime governments expanded their powers over their economies. Free-market capitalistic systems were temporarily shelved as governments experimented with price, wage, and rent controls, the rationing of food supplies and materials, the regulation of imports and exports, and the nationalization of transportation systems and industries. Some governments even moved toward compulsory labor employment. In effect, in order to mobilize the entire resources of their nations for the war effort, European nations had moved toward planned economies directed by government agencies. Under total war mobilization, the distinction between soldiers at war and civilians at home was narrowed. In the view of political leaders, all citizens constituted a national army dedicated to victory. As the American president Woodrow Wilson expressed it, the men and women "who remain to till the soil and man the factories are no less a part of the army than the men beneath the battle flags."

Not all European nations made the shift to total war equally well. Germany had the most success in developing a planned economy. At the beginning of the war, Walter Rathenau, head of the German General Electric Company, was asked by the government to use his business methods to organize a War Raw Materials Board that would allocate strategic raw materials to build the products that were most needed. Rathenau made it possible for the German war machine to be effectively supplied. The Germans were much less successful with the rationing of food, however. Even before the war, Germany had had to import about 20 percent of its food supply. The British blockade of Germany and a decline in farm labor made food shortages inevitable. Daily food rations in Germany were cut from 1,350 calories in 1916 to 1,000 by 1917, barely adequate for survival. As a result of a poor potato harvest in the winter of 1916–1917, turnips became the basic staple for the poor. It has been estimated that 750,000 German civilians died of hunger during World War I.

The German war government was eventually consolidated under military authority. The two popular military heroes of the war, General Paul von Hindenburg, chief of the General Staff, and Erich Ludendorff, deputy chief of staff, came to control the government by 1916 and virtually became the military dictators of Germany. In 1916, Hindenburg and Ludendorff decreed a system of complete mobilization for total war. In the Auxiliary Service Law of December 2, 1916, they required all male noncombatants between the ages of seventeen and sixty to work only in jobs deemed crucial for the war effort.

Germany, of course, had already possessed a rather authoritarian political system before the war began. France and England did not, but even in those countries the power of the central government was dramatically

▼ **The Leaders of Germany.** In the course of the war, the power of central governments was greatly enlarged in order to meet the demands of total war. In Germany, the two military heroes of the war, Paul von Hindenburg and Erich Ludendorf, became the virtual military dictators of Germany by 1916. The two are shown here (Hindenburg on the left) with Emperor William II, whose power declined as the war dragged on.

increased. At first, Great Britain tried to fight the war by continuing its liberal tradition of limited government interference in economic matters. The pressure of circumstances, however, forced the British government to take a more active role in economic matters. The need to ensure an adequate production of munitions led to the creation in July 1915 of a Ministry of Munitions under the dynamic leader, David Lloyd George. The Ministry of Munitions took numerous steps to ensure that private industry would produce war matériel at limited profits. It developed a vast bureaucracy, which expanded from 20 to 65,000 clerks to oversee munitions plants. Beginning in 1915, it was given the power to take over plants manufacturing war goods that did not cooperate with the government. The British government also rationed food supplies and imposed rent controls.

The French were less successful than the British and Germans in establishing a strong war government during much of the war. For one thing, the French faced a difficult obstacle in organizing a total war economy. German occupation of northeastern France cost the nation 75 percent of its coal production and almost 80 percent of its steel-making capacity. Then, too, the relationship between civil and military authorities in France was extraordinarily strained. For the first three years of the war, military and civil authorities struggled over who would oversee the conduct of the war. Not until the end of 1917 did the French war government find a strong leader in Georges Clemenceau. Declaring that "war is too important to be left to generals," Clemenceau established clear civilian control of a total war government.

The three other major belligerents—Russia, Austria-Hungary, and Italy—had much less success than Great Britain, Germany, and France in mobilizing for total war. The autocratic empires of Russia and Austria-Hungary had backward economies that proved incapable of turning out the quantity of war matériel needed to fight a modern war. The Russians, for example, conscripted millions of men but could arm only one-fourth of them. Unarmed Russian soldiers were sent into battle anyway and advised to pick up rifles from their dead colleagues. The multinational nature of the Russian and Austro-Hungarian empires also precluded the kind of internal cohesion necessary to fight a prolonged total war. Italy, too, had neither the public enthusiasm of its people nor the industrial resources to wage a successful total war.

PUBLIC ORDER AND PUBLIC OPINION   As the Great War dragged on and both casualties and privations worsened, internal dissatisfaction replaced the patriotic enthusiasm

that had marked the early stages of World War I. By 1916, there were numerous signs that civilian morale was beginning to crack under the pressure of total war.

For one thing, strike activity increased dramatically. The first two years of the war witnessed only a few scattered strikes. By 1916, however, social tranquility was dissipating. In Germany in 1916, 50,000 workers carried out a three-day work stoppage in Berlin to protest the arrest of a radical socialist leader. In both France and Britain, the number of strikes increased significantly. Even worse was the violence that erupted in Ireland when members of the Irish Republican Brotherhood and Citizens Army occupied government buildings in Dublin on Easter Sunday (April 24), 1916. British forces crushed the Easter Rebellion in a week of bloody fighting and then condemned its leaders to death.

Internal opposition to the war came from two major sources in 1916 and 1917, liberals and socialists. Liberals in both Germany and Britain sponsored peace resolutions calling for a negotiated peace without any territorial acquisitions. They were largely ignored. Socialists in Germany and Austria also called for negotiated settlements. By 1917, war morale had so deteriorated that more dramatic protests took place. Mutinies in the Italian and French armies were put down with difficulty. Czech leaders in the Austrian Empire openly called for an independent democratic Czech state. In April 1917, 200,000 workers in Berlin went out on strike for a week to protest the reduction of bread rations. Only the threat of military force and prison brought them back to their jobs. Despite the strains, all of the belligerent countries except Russia survived the war in 1917 and fought on.

War governments also fought back against the growing opposition to the war. Authoritarian regimes, such as those of Germany, Russia, and Austria-Hungary, had always relied on force to subdue their populations. Under the pressures of the war, however, even parliamentary regimes resorted to an expansion of police powers to stifle internal dissent. The British Parliament passed a Defence of the Realm Act (DORA) at the very beginning of the war that allowed the public authorities to arrest dissenters as traitors. The act was later extended to authorize public officials to censor newspapers by deleting objectional material and even to suspend newspaper publication. In France, government authorities had initially been lenient about public opposition to the war. But by 1917, they began to fear that open opposition to the war might weaken the French will to fight. When Georges Clemenceau became premier near the end of 1917, the lenient French policies came to an end, and basic civil liberties were suppressed for the duration of

Daddy, what did __YOU__ do in the Great War?

▼ **British Recruiting Poster.** As the war persisted month after month and year after year, governments found themselves hard pressed to maintain the morale of the civilian populations. Wartime governments resorted to active propaganda campaigns to generate enthusiasm for the war. In this British recruiting poster, the government tried to shame men into volunteering for military service. By 1916, the British were forced to adopt compulsory military service.

the war. When a former premier publicly advocated a negotiated peace, Clemenceau's government had him sentenced to prison for two years for treason. The editor of an antiwar newspaper was even executed on a charge of treason. Clemenceau also punished journalists who wrote negative war reports by having them drafted.

Wartime governments made active use of propaganda to arouse enthusiasm for the war. At the beginning,

public officials needed to do little to achieve this goal. The British and French, for example, exaggerated German atrocities in Belgium and found that their citizens were only too willing to believe these accounts. But as the war progressed and morale sagged, governments were forced to devise new techniques to stimulate declining enthusiasm. In one British recruiting poster, for example, a small daughter asked her father, "Daddy, what did YOU do in the Great War?" while her younger brother played with toy soldiers and cannon.

THE SOCIAL IMPACT OF TOTAL WAR   Total war made a significant impact on European society, most visibly by bringing an end to unemployment. The withdrawal of millions of men from the labor market to fight, combined with the heightened demand for wartime products, led to jobs for everyone able to work.

The cause of labor also benefited from the war. The enthusiastic patriotism of workers was soon rewarded with a greater acceptance of trade unions. In order to guarantee worker cooperation, war governments in Britain, France, and Germany not only sought union cooperation but also for the first time allowed trade unions to participate in making important government decisions on labor matters. In return, unions cooperated on wage limits and production schedules. In Britain, for example, the government agreed to limit profits in war industries and gave trade unions representation on the National Labour Advisory Committee while unions in turn agreed to renounce the use of strikes and resort only to arbitration during the course of the war. In Germany, the government pursued a policy of "war socialism" in which trade union representatives were added to labor committees in factories and also to regional farm and labor committees. Two benefits emerged for labor out of these cooperative practices. They opened the way to the collective bargaining practices that became more widespread after World War I and increased the prestige of trade unions, enabling them to attract more members.

World War I also created new roles for women. Since so many men went off to fight at the front, women were called upon to take over jobs and responsibilities that had not been available to them before. These included certain clerical jobs that only small numbers of women had held earlier. In Britain, for example, the number of women who worked in banking rose from 9,500 to almost 64,000 in the course of the war, while the number of women in commerce rose from a half million to almost one million. Overall, the number of women employed in Britain who held new jobs or replaced men rose by 1,345,000. Women were also now employed in jobs that

had been considered beyond the "capacity of women." These included such occupations as chimney sweeps, truck drivers, farm laborers, and, above all, factory workers in heavy industry. In France, 684,000 women worked in armaments plants for the first time; in Britain, the figure was 920,000. Thirty-eight percent of the workers in the Krupp Armaments works in Germany in 1918 were women.

Male resistance, however, often made it difficult for women to enter these new jobs, especially in heavy industry. One Englishwoman who worked in a munitions factory recalled her experience: "I could quite see it was hard on the men to have women coming into all their pet jobs and in some cases doing them a good deal better. I sympathized with the way they were torn between not wanting the women to undercut them, and yet hating them to earn as much."[6] While male workers expressed concern that the employment of females at lower wages would depress their own wages, women began to demand equal pay legislation. The French government passed a law in July 1915 that enacted a minimum wage for women homeworkers in textiles, an industry that had grown dramatically because of the need for military uniforms. Later in 1917 the government decreed that men and women should receive equal rates for piecework. Despite the noticeable increase in women's wages that resulted from government regulations, women's industrial wages still were not equal to men's wages by the end of the war.

Even worse, women had achieved little real security about their place in the work force. Both men and women seemed to expect that many of the new jobs for women were only temporary, an expectation quite evident in the British poem, "War Girls," written in 1916:

> There's the girl who clips your ticket for the train,
> And the girl who speeds the lift from floor to floor,
> There's the girl who does a milk-round in the rain,
> And the girl who calls for orders at your door.
> Strong, sensible, and fit,
> They're out to show their grit,
> And tackle jobs with energy and knack.
> No longer caged and penned up,
> They're going to keep their end up
> Till the khaki soldier boys come marching back.[7]

At the end of the war, governments moved quickly to remove women from the jobs they had encouraged them to take earlier. By 1919, there were 650,000 unemployed women in Britain while wages for women who were still employed were also lowered. The work benefits for women from World War I seemed to be short-lived.

Nevertheless, in some countries the role played by women in the wartime economies did have a positive impact on the women's movement for social and political emancipation. The most obvious gain was the right to vote that was given to women in Germany and Austria immediately after the war (in Britain already in January 1918). Contemporary media, however, tended to focus on the more noticeable, yet in some ways more superficial, social emancipation of upper- and middle-class women. In ever-larger numbers, these young

▼ **Women Workers in a German Munitions Factory.** World War I created new job opportunities for women. They were now employed in jobs that had earlier been considered beyond their capacity. As seen in this picture, this included factory work in heavy industry. These German women are performing a variety of tasks in a shell factory. Between 1913 and 1917, the total female labor force in metal work increased from five to twenty-eight percent of the total labor force.

women took jobs, had their own apartments, and showed their new independence by smoking in public, wearing shorter dresses, cosmetics, and new hair styles.

In one sense, World War I had been a great social leveler. Death in battle did not distinguish between classes. Although all social classes suffered casualties in battle, two groups were especially hard-hit. Junior officers who led the charges across the "no man's land" that separated the lines of trenches experienced death rates that were three times higher than regular casualty rates. Many of these junior officers were members of the aristocracy (see the box on p. 915). The unskilled workers and peasants who made up the masses of soldiers mowed down by machine guns also suffered heavy casualties. The fortunate ones were the skilled laborers who gained exemptions from military service because they were needed at home to train workers in the war industries.

The burst of patriotic enthusiasm that marked the beginning of the war deceived many into believing that the war was creating a new sense of community that meant the end of the class conflict that had marked European society at the end of the nineteenth and beginning of the twentieth centuries. David Lloyd George, who became the British prime minister in 1916, wrote in September 1914 that "all classes, high and low, are shedding themselves of selfishness. . . . It is bringing a new outlook to all classes. . . . We can see for the first time the fundamental things that matter in life, and that have been obscured from our vision by the . . . growth of prosperity."[8] Lloyd George's optimistic opinion proved to be quite misguided, however. The Great War did not eliminate the class conflict that had characterized pre-1914 Europe, and this became increasingly apparent as the war progressed.

Certainly, the economic impact of the war was felt unevenly. One group of people who especially benefited were the owners of the large industries manufacturing the weapons of war. Despite public outrage, governments rarely limited the enormous profits made by the industrial barons. In fact, in the name of efficiency, wartime governments tended to favor large industries when scarce raw materials were allocated. Small firms considered less essential to the war effort even had to shut down because of a lack of resources.

Growing inflation also caused inequities. The combination of full employment and high demand for scarce consumer goods caused prices to climb. Many skilled workers were able to earn wages that enabled them to keep up with the inflation, but this was not true for unskilled workers and workers in nonessential industries. Only in Great Britain did the wages of workers outstrip prices. Everywhere else in Europe, people experienced a loss of purchasing power.

Many middle-class people were especially hard-hit by inflation. They included both those who lived on fixed incomes, such as retired people on pensions, and professional people, such as clerks, lesser civil servants, teachers, small shopkeepers, and clergymen, who received stable incomes at a time when prices were rising. By the end of the war, many of them were actually doing less well economically than skilled workers. Their discontent would find expression after the war.

▼ War and Revolution

By 1917, total war was creating serious domestic turmoil in all of the European belligerent states. Most countries were able to prop up their regimes and convince their peoples to continue the war for another year. Others, however, were reaching a point of near collapse. In Austria, for example, a government minister warned that "if the monarchs of the Central Powers cannot make peace in the coming months, it will be made for them by their peoples." In 1917, however, Russia was the only belligerent that actually experienced the kind of complete collapse that others were predicting might happen throughout Europe. Out of Russia's collapse came the Russian Revolution, whose impact would be widely felt in Europe for decades to come.

The Russian Revolution

After the Revolution of 1905 had failed to bring any substantial changes to Russia, Tsar Nicholas II fell back on the army and bureaucracy as the basic props for his autocratic regime. Perhaps Russia could have survived this way, as some have argued, but World War I magnified Russia's problems and put the tsarist government to a test that it could not meet.

Russia was unprepared both militarily and technologically for the total war of World War I. Competent military leadership was lacking. Even worse, the tsar, alone of all European monarchs, insisted upon taking personal charge of the armed forces despite his obvious lack of ability and training for such an awesome burden. Russian industry was unable to produce the weapons needed for the army. Ill-led and ill-armed, Russian armies suffered incredible losses. Between 1914 and 1916, two million soldiers had been killed while another four to six million had been wounded or captured. By 1917, the Russian will to fight had vanished.

The Reality of War: War and the Family
▼ ▼ ▼

John Mott was a captain in the British army. He came from an aristocratic family with a strong military tradition. He married Muriel Backhouse in 1907, and they had three sons before he was called up for service in World War I. These excerpts are taken from four of Mott's letters to his wife and a letter informing Mott's wife of her husband's death during the Gallipoli campaign. The human experience of World War I was made up of millions of stories like that of John Mott and his family.

One Family's War

1 July [1915]

My darling Childie,

I hope you got home safely. I have been promised that I shall know the ship we go on tomorrow. But it will be no good writing to Gibraltar as we should get there before the letter. Try Malta as that goes over land. If you get overdrawn go and see Cox. Goodbye Darling. Don't worry I shall come back alright. Your devoted husband John F. Mott

13 July

Mediterranean field force,   Mudros
My darling Childie,

This island is very hot indeed but beastly windy. We have absolutely no news from the Front. Troops are pouring out now and I expect we shall be in it next week.

We have all gone through our little bout of diarrhea. I was not too bad and only had pains in my stomach otherwise I am very well indeed.

Everyone is standing the heat very well. The Brigadier has a tent but everybody else is out in the blazing sun.

31 July

My darling Childie,

I got more letters from you today dated 5th, 6th, 7th. I had no idea till I read the letter that they could do all that about writs. I would never have left things in such a muddle, I only hope you can get straight.

Yesterday I left here at 5:30 AM to go to the trenches with the Brigadier. We had an awful day, and I am not at all keen to go into that lot at all events. We sailed over in a trawler and had a long walk in the open under shrapnel fire. It was not very pleasant. Then we got to the communications trenches and had a mile and a half of them to go up. When we got to the fire trenches the stink was awful. Arms and legs of Turks sticking out of the trench parapets and lying dead all round. In one place the bottom of the trench was made up by dead Turks, but this has been abandoned as the place was too poisonous.

Our battle ships have been shelling very heavily so there may be an attack on. I must write to my mother tonight. All my love and kisses for ever Your loving husband John F. Mott

6 August

My darling Childie,

We are off today just as we stand up, with four days rations. I can't say where we are going but we shall see spots. I shall not get a chance to write again for a bit as we shall be on the move. I expect you have got a map of the place by now and perhaps you will hear where we have gone.

Very good to get away. All my love and kisses for ever

Your loving husband John F. Mott
Best love to all kids and baby

Pte A Thompson
6 Batt Y and L Red Cross Hospital

We landed on the 6th of Aug and took 2 hills and at daybreak on the 7th advanced across an open plain to the left of Salt Lake and got an awful shelling. We came to a small hill which was flat on top and it was about 2 hundred yards further on where the Capt was hit. They gave us it worse than ever when we got on there and I might have been happen 50 yds away when I saw the Capt and about 5 men fall badly hit. I could not say whether it was shrapnel or common shell but I think it was most probably shrapnel as they use that mostly. It was that thick that no one could get to the Capt at the time and I don't think he lived very long, well he could not the way they were hit and was afterwards buried when things had quietened down in the evening and a cross was put on his grave with an inscription and he got as good a burial as could be given out there. Well I think I have told you all I know about Capt Mott. I only wishe I could have given you better news, so I will close with Kind Regards
Yours Obediently,
Pte Thompson

The tsarist government was totally inadequate for the tasks that it faced in 1914. The surge of patriotic enthusiasm that greeted the outbreak of war was soon dissipated by a government that distrusted its own people. When leading industrialists formed committees to improve factory production, a government suspicious of their motives undermined their efforts. Although the middle classes and liberal aristocrats still hoped for a constitutional monarchy, they were sullen over the tsar's revocation of the political concessions made during the Revolution of 1905. Peasant discontent flourished as conditions worsened. The concentration of Russian industry in a few large cities made workers' frustrations all the more evident and dangerous. Even conservative aristocrats were appalled by the incompetent and inefficient bureaucracy that controlled the political and military system. In the meantime, Tsar Nicholas II was increasingly insulated from events by his wife Alexandra.

This German-born princess was a stubborn, willful, and ignorant woman who had fallen under the influence of Rasputin, a Siberian peasant who belonged to a religious sect that indulged in sexual orgies. To the tsarina, Rasputin was a holy man for he alone seemed able to stop the bleeding of her hemophiliac son Alexis. Rasputin's influence made him an important power behind the throne, and he did not hesitate to interfere in government affairs. As the leadership at the top stumbled its way through a series of military and economic disasters, the middle class, aristocrats, peasants, soldiers, and workers grew more and more disenchanted with the tsarist regime. Even conservative aristocrats who supported the monarchy felt the need to do something to reverse the deteriorating situation. For a start, they assassinated Rasputin in December 1916. By then it was too late to save the monarchy, and its fall came quickly at the beginning of March 1917.

THE MARCH REVOLUTION   At the beginning of March, a series of strikes broke out in the capital city of Petrograd (formerly St. Petersburg). Here the actions of working-class women helped to change the course of Russian history. In February of 1917, the government had introduced bread rationing in the capital city after the price of bread had skyrocketed. Many of the women who stood in the lines waiting for bread were also factory workers who had put in twelve-hour days. The number of women working in Petrograd factories had doubled since 1914. The Russian government had become aware of the volatile situation in the capital from a police report:

Mothers of families, exhausted by endless standing in line at stores, distraught over their half-starving and sick children, are today perhaps closer to revolution than [the liberal opposition leaders] and of course they are a great deal more dangerous because they are the combustible material for which only a single spark is needed to burst into flame.[9]

On March 8, a day celebrated since 1910 as International Women's Day, about ten thousand Petrograd women marched through the city demanding "Peace and Bread" and "Down with Autocracy." Soon the women were joined by other workers, and together they called for a general strike that succeeded in shutting down all the factories in the city on March 10. The tsarina wrote to Nicholas II at the battlefront that "This is a hooligan movement. If the weather were very cold they would all probably stay at home." Nicholas ordered the troops to disperse the crowds by shooting them if necessary. Initially, the troops did so, but soon significant numbers of the soldiers joined the demonstrators. The situation was out of the tsar's control. The Duma or legislative body, which the tsar had tried to dissolve, met anyway and on March 12 established a Provisional Government that urged the tsar to abdicate. He did so on March 15.

In just one week, the tsarist regime had fallen apart. It was not really overthrown since there had been no deliberate revolution. Even those who were conscious revolutionaries were caught by surprise at the rapidity of the monarchy's disintegration. Although no particular group had been responsible for the outburst, the moderate Constitutional Democrats were responsible for establishing the Provisional Government. They represented primarily a middle-class and liberal aristocratic minority. Their program consisted of a nineteenth-century liberal agenda: freedom of speech, religion, assembly, and civil liberties. Their determination to carry on the war to preserve Russia's honor was a major blunder since it satisfied neither the workers nor the peasants who above all wanted an end to the war.

The Provisional Government was also faced with another authority, the soviets, or councils of workers' and soldiers' deputies. The soviet of Petrograd had been formed in March 1917; at the same time soviets sprang up spontaneously in army units, factory towns, and rural areas. The soviets represented the more radical interests of the lower classes and were largely composed of socialists of different kinds. Most numerous were the Socialist Revolutionaries, who wished to establish peasant socialism by seizing the great landed estates and creating a rural democracy. Since the beginning of the twentieth century, the Socialist Revolutionaries had come to rely on the use of political terrorism to accomplish their goals. Since 1893, Russia had also had a Marxist Social Democratic party, which had divided in 1903 into two factions known as the Mensheviks and Bolsheviks. The Mensheviks wanted the Social Democrats to be a mass electoral socialist party based on a Western model. Like the Social Democrats of Germany, they were willing to cooperate temporarily in a parliamentary democracy while working toward the ultimate achievement of the socialist state.

The Bolsheviks were a small faction of Russian Social Democrats who had come under the leadership of Vladimir Ulianov, known to the world as V. I. Lenin (1870–1924). Born in 1870 to a middle-class family, Lenin received a legal education and became a lawyer. In 1887, he turned into a dedicated enemy of tsarist Russia when his older brother was executed for planning to assassinate the tsar. Lenin's search for a revolutionary faith led him to Marxism, and in 1894 he moved to St. Petersburg where he organized an illegal group known as the Union for the Liberation of the Working Class. Arrested for this activity, Lenin was shipped to Siberia. After his release, he chose to go into exile in Switzerland and eventually assumed the leadership of the Bolshevik wing of the Russian Social Democratic party.

Under Lenin's direction, the Bolsheviks became a party dedicated to violent revolution. He believed that only a violent revolution could destroy the capitalist system and that a "vanguard" of activists must form a small party of well-disciplined professional revolutionaries to accomplish the task. Between 1900 and 1917, Lenin spent most of his time in Switzerland. When the Provisional Government was formed in March 1917, he believed that an opportunity for the Bolsheviks to seize power had come. In April 1917, with the connivance of the German High Command, who hoped to create disorder in Russia, Lenin, his wife, and a small group of his followers were shipped to Russia in a "sealed train" by way of Finland.

Lenin's arrival in Russia opened a new stage of the Russian Revolution. In his "April Theses," issued on April 20, Lenin presented a blueprint for revolutionary action based on his own version of Marxist theory. According to Lenin, it was not necessary for Russia to experience a bourgeois revolution before it could move toward socialism, as orthodox Marxists had argued. Instead, Russia could move directly into socialism. In the "April Theses," Lenin maintained that the soviets of soldiers, workers, and peasants were ready-made instruments of power. The Bolsheviks must work toward gaining control of these groups and then use them to over-

throw the Provisional Government. At the same time, Bolshevik propaganda must seek mass support through promises geared to the needs of the people: an end to the war; redistribution of all land to the peasants; the transfer of factories and industries from capitalists to committees of workers; and the relegation of government power from the Provisional Government to the soviets. Three simple slogans summed up the Bolshevik program: "Peace, Land, Bread," "Worker Control of Production," and "All Power to the Soviets."

In late spring and early summer, while the Bolsheviks set about winning over the masses to their program and gaining a majority in the Petrograd and Moscow soviets, the Provisional Government struggled to gain control of Russia against almost overwhelming obstacles. Although the Provisional Government promised that a constitutional convention called for the fall of 1917 would confiscate and redistribute royal and monastic lands, the offer was meaningless since many peasants had already starting seizing lands on their own in March. The military situation was also deteriorating. The Petrograd soviet had issued its Army Order No. 1 in March to all Russian military forces, encouraging them to remove their officers and replace them with committees composed of "the elected representatives of the lower ranks" of the army. Army Order No. 1 led to the collapse of all discipline and created military chaos. When the Provisional Government attempted to initiate a new military offensive in July, the army simply dissolved as masses of peasant soldiers turned their backs on their officers and returned home to join their families in seizing lands.

THE BOLSHEVIK REVOLUTION   In July 1917, Lenin and the Bolsheviks attempted to overthrow the Provisional Government. The government was still strong enough to crush the rebellion, however, and Lenin was forced to flee to Finland. But the days of the Provisional Government were numbered. In July 1917, Alexander Kerensky, a Socialist Revolutionary, had become prime minister in the Provisional Government. In September, when General Lavr Kornilov attempted to march on Petrograd and seize power, Kerensky released Bolsheviks from prison and turned to the Petrograd soviet for help. Although General Kornilov's forces never reached Petrograd, Kerensky's action had strengthened the hands of the Petrograd soviet and had shown Lenin how weak the Provisional Government really was.

By the end of October, the Bolsheviks had achieved a slight majority in the Petrograd and Moscow soviets. The number of party members had also grown from

Ten Days That Shook the World: Lenin and the Bolshevik Seizure of Power

▼ ▼ ▼

John Reed was an American journalist who helped to found the American Communist Labor party. Accused of sedition, he fled the United States and went to Russia. In Ten Days That Shook the World, *Reed left an impassioned eyewitness account of the Russian Revolution. It is apparent from his comments that Reed considered Lenin the indispensable hero of the Bolshevik success.*

John Reed, *Ten Days That Shook the World*

It was just 8:40 when a thundering wave of cheers announced the entrance of the presidium, with Lenin—great Lenin—among them. A short, stocky figure, with a big head set down in his shoulders, bald and bulging. Little eyes, a snubbish nose, wide, generous mouth, and heavy chin; clean-shaven now, but already beginning to bristle with the well-known beard of his past and future. Dressed in shabby clothes, his trousers much too long for him. Unimpressive, to be the idol of a mob, loved and revered as perhaps few leaders in history have been. A strange popular leader—a leader purely by virtue of intellect; colourless, humourless, uncompromising and detached; without picturesque idiosyncrasies—but with the power of explaining profound ideas in simple terms, of analysing a concrete situation. And combined with shrewdness, the greatest intellectual audacity. . . .

Now Lenin, gripping the edge of the reading stand, letting his little winking eyes travel over the crowd as he stood there waiting, apparently oblivious to the long-rolling ovation, which lasted several minutes. When it finished, he said simply, "We shall now proceed to construct the Socialist order!" Again that overwhelming human roar.

"The first thing is the adoption of practical measures to realise peace. . . . We shall offer peace to the peoples of all the belligerent countries upon the basis of the Soviet terms—no annexations, no indemnities, and the right of self-determination of peoples. At the same time, according to our promise, we shall publish and repudiate the secret treaties. . . . The question of War and Peace is so clear that I think that I may, without preamble, read the project of a Proclamation to the Peoples of All the Belligerent Countries. . . ."

His great mouth, seeming to smile, opened wide as he spoke; his voice was hoarse—not unpleasantly so, but as if it had hardened that way after years and years of speaking—and went on monotonously, with the effect of being able to go forever. . . . For emphasis he bent forward slightly. No gestures. And before him, a thousand simple faces looking up in intent adoration.

[Reed then reproduces the full text of the Proclamation.]

When the grave thunder of applause had died away, Lenin spoke again: "We propose to the Congress to ratify this declaration. . . . This proposal of peace will meet with resistance on the part of the imperialist governments—we don't fool ourselves on that score. But we hope that revolution will soon break out in all the belligerent countries; that is why we address ourselves especially to the workers of France, England and Germany. . . .

"The revolution of November 6th and 7th," he ended, "has opened the era of the Social Revolution. . . . The labour movement, in the name of peace and Socialism, shall win, and fulfill its destiny. . . ."

There was something quiet and powerful in all this, which stirred the souls of men. It was understandable why people believed when Lenin spoke.

50,000 to 240,000. Lenin had become convinced from reports of unrest abroad that "we are on the threshold of a world proletarian revolution," and he tried to convince his fellow Bolsheviks that the time was ripe for the overthrow of the Provisional Government. Although he faced formidable opposition within the Bolshevik ranks, he managed to gain support for his policy. He was espe-cially fortunate to have the close cooperation of Leon Trotsky (1877–1940), a former Menshevik turned fervid revolutionary. Lenin and Trotsky organized a Military Revolutionary Committee within the Petrograd soviet to plot the overthrow of the government. On the night of November 6–7, Bolshevik forces seized the Winter Palace, seat of the Provisional Government. The

Provisional Government collapsed quickly with little bloodshed.

This coup d'etat had been timed to coincide with a meeting in Petrograd of the all-Russian Congress of Soviets representing local soviets from all over the country. Lenin nominally turned over the sovereignty of the Provisional Government to this Congress of Soviets. Real power, however, passed to a Council of People's Commissars, headed by Lenin (see the box on p. 918). One immediate problem that faced the Bolsheviks was the Constituent Assembly, which had been initiated by the Provisional Government and was scheduled to meet in January 1918. Elections to the assembly by universal male suffrage had produced a defeat for the Bolsheviks, who had only 225 delegates compared to the 420 garnered by the Socialist Revolutionaries. But no matter. Lenin simply broke the Constituent Assembly by force. "To hand over power," he said, "to the Constituent Assembly would again be compromising with malignant bourgeoisie." The Bolsheviks did not want majority rule, but the rule of the proletariat, exercised for them, of course, by the Bolsheviks, soon renamed the Communists.

But the Bolsheviks still had a long way to go. Lenin, ever the opportunist, realized the importance of winning mass support as quickly as possible by fulfilling Bolshevik promises. In his first law, Lenin declared the land nationalized and turned it over to local rural soviets. In effect, this action merely ratified the peasants' seizure of the land and assured the Bolsheviks of peasant support, especially against any attempt by the old landlords to restore their power. The demands of urban workers were also met when Lenin granted control of factories to committees of workers. To Lenin, however, this was merely a temporary expedient.

Lenin had also promised peace and that, he realized, was not an easy task because of the humiliating losses of Russian territory that it would entail. There was no real choice, however. On March 15, 1918, Lenin signed the Treaty of Brest-Litovsk with Germany and gave up eastern Poland, the Ukraine, Finland, and the Baltic provinces. To his critics, Lenin argued that it made no difference since the spread of socialist revolution throughout Europe would make the treaty largely irrelevant. In any case, he had promised peace to the Russian people, but real peace did not come for the country soon sank into civil war.

CIVIL WAR   There was great opposition to the new Bolshevik or Communist regime, not only from groups loyal to the tsar but also from bourgeois and aristocratic liberals and anti-Leninist socialists, including Mensheviks and Socialist Revolutionaries. In addition, thousands of Allied troops were eventually sent to different parts of Russia in the hope of bringing Russia back into the war.

Between 1918 and 1921, the Bolshevik (or Red) Army was forced to fight on many fronts. The first serious threat to the Bolsheviks came from Siberia where a White (anti-Bolshevik) force under Admiral Alexander Kolchak attacked westward and advanced almost to the Volga River before being stopped. Attacks also came from the Ukrainians in the southeast and from the Baltic regions. In mid-1919, White forces under General Anton Denikin, probably the most effective of the White generals, swept through the Ukraine and advanced almost to Moscow. At one point by late 1919, three separate White armies seemed to be closing in on the Bolsheviks, but were eventually pushed back. By 1920, the major White forces had been defeated, and the Ukraine retaken. The next year, the Communist regime regained control over the independent nationalist governments in the Caucasus: Georgia, Russian Armenia, and Azerbaijan.

▼ **Lenin Addresses a Crowd.** V. I. Lenin was the driving force behind the success of the Bolsheviks in seizing power in Russia and creating the Union of Soviet Socialist Republics (USSR). By 1921, after a hard fought Civil War, the Communists managed to retain their control of Russia. Lenin is seen addressing a rally in Moscow in 1917.

How had Lenin and the Bolsheviks triumphed over what seemed at one time to be overwhelming forces? For one thing, the Red Army became a well-disciplined and formidable fighting force, largely due to the organizational genius of Leon Trotsky. As commissar of war, Trotsky reinstated the draft and even recruited and gave commands to former tsarist army officers. Trotsky insisted on rigid discipline; soldiers who deserted or refused to obey orders were summarily executed. The Red Army also had the advantage of interior lines of defense and was able to move its troops rapidly from one battlefront to the other.

The disunity of the anti-Communist forces seriously weakened the efforts of the Whites. Political differences created distrust among the Whites and prevented them from cooperating effectively with each other. Some Whites, such as Admiral Kolchak, insisted on restoring the tsarist regime, while others understood that only a more liberal and democratic program had any chance of success. Since the White forces were forced to operate on the exterior fringes of the Russian empire, it was

difficult enough to achieve military cooperation. Political differences made it virtually impossible.

The lack of a common goal on the part of the Whites was paralleled by a single-minded sense of purpose on the part of the Communists. Inspired by their vision of a new socialist order, the Communists had the advantage of possessing that determination that comes from revolutionary fervor and revolutionary convictions.

The Communists also succeeded in translating their revolutionary faith into practical instruments of power. A policy of "war communism," for example, was used to ensure regular supplies for the Red Army. "War communism" included the nationalization of banks and most industries, the forcible requisition of grain from peasants, and the centralization of state administration under Bolshevik control. Another Bolshevik instrument was "revolutionary terror." Although the old tsarist secret police had been abolished, a new Red secret police—known as the Cheka—replaced it. The Red Terror instituted by the Cheka aimed at nothing less than the destruction of all those who opposed the new re-

▼ **Map 26.4** The Russian Revolution and Civil War.

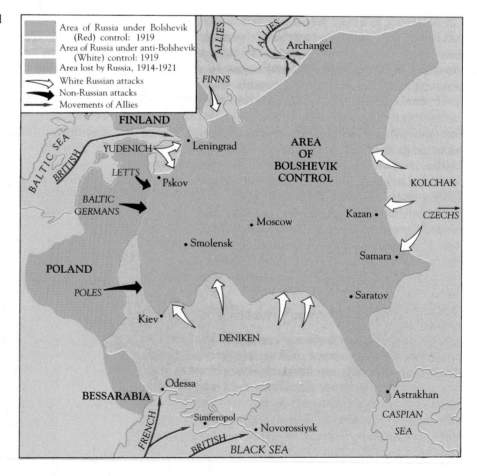

pitched battles, however, nor did they pursue a common strategy, although they did give material assistance to anti-Bolshevik forces. This intervention by the Allies enabled the Communist government to appeal to patriotic Russians to fight the attempts of foreigners to control their country. Allied interference was never substantial enough to make a military difference in the civil war, but it did serve indirectly to help the Bolshevik cause.

▼ **Trotsky as Leader of the Red Army.** Crucial to the success of the Communists in the Civil War was the Red Army. As commissar of war, Leon Trotsky, who had played an important role in the Bolshevik seizure of power, made the Red Army into a formidable fighting force. He is shown here (at the left) on one of his numerous journeys across Russia during the Civil War.

gime. "Class enemies"—the bourgeoisie—were especially singled out, at least according to a Cheka officer: "The first questions you should put to the accused person are: To what class does he belong, what is his origin, what was his education, and what is his profession? These should determine the fate of the accused." In practice, however, the Cheka promulgated terror against all classes, including the proletariat, if they opposed the new regime. The Red Terror added an element of fear to the Bolshevik regime.

Finally, the intervention of foreign armies enabled the Communists to appeal to the powerful force of Russian patriotism. Although the Allied powers had intervened initially in Russia to encourage the Russians to remain in the war, the end of the war on November 11, 1918, had made that purpose inconsequential. Nevertheless, Allied troops remained, and more were even sent as Allied countries did not hide their anti-Bolshevik feelings. At one point, over 100,000 foreign troops, mostly Japanese, British, American, and French were stationed on Russian soil. These forces rarely engaged in

By 1921, the Communists had succeeded in retaining control of Russia. In the course of the civil war, the Bolshevik regime had also transformed Russia into a bureaucratically centralized state dominated by a single party. It was also a state that was largely hostile to the Allied powers that had sought to assist the Bolsheviks' enemies in the civil war. To most historians, the Russian Revolution is unthinkable without the total war of World War I for only the collapse of Russia made it possible for a radical minority like the Bolsheviks to seize the reins of power. In turn, the Russian Revolution had an impact on the course of World War I.

The Last Year of the War

For Germany, the withdrawal of the Russians from the war in March 1918 offered renewed hope for a favorable end to the war. The victory over Russia persuaded Ludendorff and most German leaders to make one final military gamble—a grand offensive in the west to break the military stalemate. The German attack was launched in March and lasted into July. The German forces succeeded in advancing forty miles to the Marne River, within thirty-five miles of Paris. But an Allied counterattack, led by the French General Ferdinand Foch and supported by the arrival of 140,000 fresh American troops, defeated the Germans at the Second Battle of the Marne on July 18. Ludendorff's gamble had failed. Having used up his reserves, Ludendorff knew that defeat was now inevitable. With the arrival of 2 million more American troops on the Continent, Allied forces began making a steady advance toward Germany.

On September 29, 1918, General Ludendorff informed German leaders that the war was lost. Unwilling to place the burden of defeat on the army, Ludendorff demanded that the government sue for peace at once. When German officials discovered, however, that the Allies were unwilling to make peace with the autocratic imperial government, reforms were instituted to create a liberal government. But these constitutional reforms came too late for the exhausted and angry German people. On November 3, naval units in Kiel mutinied, and within days councils of workers and soldiers, German versions of the Russian soviets, were forming throughout northern Germany and taking over the supervision of civilian and military administrations. William II capitulated to public pressure and left the country on November 9, while the Socialists under Friedrich Ebert announced the establishment of a republic. Two days later, on November 11, 1918, the new German government agreed to an armistice. The war was over, but the revolutionary forces set in motion by the war were not yet exhausted.

Revolutionary Upheavals in Germany and Austria-Hungary

Like Russia, Germany and Austria-Hungary also experienced political revolution as a result of military defeat. In its early stage, the German November Revolution of 1918 was similar to the Russian Revolution of March 1917. War weariness had led to a popular upheaval that overthrew an autocratic monarchy and created a liberal, democratic republic. As in Russia, liberals and moderate socialists formed a new provisional government while workers' and soldiers' councils competed for ruling power. In Russia, the radical forces represented in these councils went on to overthrow the Provisional Government and establish a socialist state. In Germany, the radicals lost as moderate socialists remained in power in a democratic republic.

In November 1918, when Germany began to disintegrate in a convulsion of mutinies and mass demonstrations, only the Social Democrats were numerous and well organized enough to pick up the pieces. But the German Socialists had divided into two groups during the war. A majority of the Social Democrats still favored parliamentary democracy as a gradual approach to social democracy and the elimination of the capitalist system. A minority of German socialists, however, disgusted with the Social Democrats' support of the war, had formed an Independent Social Democratic Party in 1916. In 1918, the more radical members of the Independent Socialists favored an immediate social revolution carried out by the councils of soldiers, sailors, and workers. Led by Karl Liebknecht and Rosa Luxemburg, these radical, left-wing socialists formed the German Communist party in December 1918. In effect, two parallel governments were established in Germany: the parliamentary republic proclaimed by the majority Social Democrats and the revolutionary socialist republic declared by radicals.

Unlike Russia's Bolsheviks, Germany's radicals failed to achieve control of the government. By ending the war on November 11, the moderate socialists had removed a major source of dissatisfaction. When the radical socialists (now known as Communists) attempted to seize power in Berlin in January 1919, Friedrich Ebert and the moderate socialists called on the regular army and groups of antirevolutionary volunteers known as Free Corps to crush the rebels. The victorious forces brutally murdered Liebknecht and Luxemburg. A similar attempt at Communist revolution in the city of Munich in southern Germany was also crushed by the Free Corps and the regular army. The German republic had been saved, but only because the moderate socialists had relied on the traditional army—in effect, the same conservatives who had dominated the old imperial regime. Moreover, this "second revolution" of January 1919, bloodily crushed by the republican government, created a deep fear of communism among the German middle classes. All too soon, this fear would be cleverly manipulated by a politician named Adolf Hitler.

Austria-Hungary, too, experienced disintegration and revolution. In 1914, when it attacked Serbia, the imperial regime had tried to crush the nationalistic forces that it believed were destroying the empire. By 1918, those same nationalistic forces had brought the complete breakup of the Austro-Hungarian Empire. As war weariness took hold of the empire, ethnic minorities increasingly sought to achieve national independence. This desire was further encouraged by Allied war aims that included calls for the independence of the subject peoples. By the time the war ended, the Austro-Hungarian Empire had been replaced by the independent republics of Austria, Hungary, and Czechoslovakia and the large South Slav monarchical state called Yugoslavia. Other regions clamored to join Italy, Romania, and a reconstituted Poland. Rivalries among the nations that succeeded Austria-Hungary would weaken eastern Europe for the next seventy years. Ethnic pride and national statehood proved far more important to these states than class differences. Only in Hungary was there an attempt at social revolution when Béla Kun established a communist state. It was crushed after a brief five-month existence.

▼ The Peace Settlement

In January 1919, the delegations of twenty-seven victorious Allied nations gathered in Paris to conclude a final settlement of the Great War. Some delegates believed that this conference would avoid the mistakes made at Vienna in 1815 (see Chapter 22) by aristocrats who rearranged the map of Europe to meet the selfish desires of the great powers. Harold Nicolson, one of the British delegates, expressed what he believed this conference would achieve instead: "We were journeying to Paris not merely to liquidate the war, but to found a New Order in Europe. We were preparing not Peace only, but

Eternal Peace. There was about us the halo of some divine mission. . . . For we were bent on doing great, permanent and noble things."[10]

National expectations, however, made Nicolson's quest for "eternal peace" a difficult one. Over a period of years, the reasons for fighting World War I had been transformed from selfish national interests to idealistic principles. At the end of 1917, after they had taken over the Russian government, Lenin and the Bolsheviks had publicly revealed the contents of secret wartime treaties found in the archives of the Russian foreign ministry. The Bolshevik action made it clear that European nations had gone to war primarily to achieve territorial gains. But the American president Woodrow Wilson attempted at the beginning of 1918 to shift the discussion of war aims to a higher ground. Wilson outlined "Fourteen Points" to the American Congress that he believed justified the enormous military struggle then being waged. Later, Wilson spelled out additional steps for a truly just and lasting peace. Wilson's proposals included "open covenants of peace, openly arrived at" instead of secret diplomacy; the reduction of national armaments to a "point consistent with domestic safety"; and the self-determination of people so that "all well-defined national aspirations shall be accorded the utmost satisfaction." Wilson characterized World War I as a people's war waged against "absolutism and militarism," two scourges of liberty that could only be eliminated by creating democratic governments and a "general association of nations" that would guarantee the "political independence and territorial integrity to great and small states alike" (see the box on p. 924). As the spokesman for a new world order based on democracy and international cooperation, Wilson was enthusiastically cheered by many Europeans when he arrived in Europe for the peace conference.

Wilson soon found, however, that other states at the Paris Peace Conference were guided by considerably more pragmatic motives. The secret treaties and agreements, for example, that had been made before the war could not be totally ignored, even if they did conflict with the principle of self-determination enunciated by Wilson.

National interests also complicated the deliberations of the Paris Peace Conference. David Lloyd George, prime minister of Great Britain, had won a decisive electoral victory in December of 1918 on a platform of making the Germans pay for this dreadful war. Public opinion had been inflamed during the war by a government propaganda campaign that portrayed the Germans as beasts. With the war over, the influence of that propa-

The Voice of Peacemaking: Woodrow Wilson

▼ ▼ ▼

"We are fighting for the liberty, the self-government, and the undictated development of all peoples. . . ."

When the Allied powers met at Paris in January 1919, it soon became apparent that the victors had differences of opinion on the kind of peace they expected. These excerpts are from the speeches of Woodrow Wilson in which the American president presented his idealistic goals for a peace based on justice and reconciliation.

Woodrow Wilson, May 26, 1917

We are fighting for the liberty, the self-government, and the undictated development of all peoples, and every feature of the settlement that concludes this war must be conceived and executed for that purpose. Wrongs must first be righted and then adequate safeguards must be created to prevent their being committed again. . . .

No people must be forced under sovereignty under which it does not wish to live. No territory must change hands except for the purpose of securing those who inhabit it a fair chance of life and liberty. No indemnities must be insisted on except those that constitute payment for manifest wrongs done. No readjustments of power must be made except such as will tend to secure the future peace of the world and the future welfare and happiness of its peoples.

And then the free peoples of the world must draw together in some common covenant, some genuine and practical cooperation that will in effect combine their force to secure peace and justice in the dealings of nations with one another.

April 6, 1918

We are ready, whenever the final reckoning is made, to be just to the German people, deal fairly with the German power, as with all others. There can be no difference between peoples in the final judgment, if it is indeed to be a righteous judgment. To propose anything but justice, even-handed and dispassionate justice, to Germany at any time, whatever the outcome of the war, would be to renounce and dishonor our own cause. For we ask nothing that we are not willing to accord.

January 3, 1919

Our task at Paris is to organize the friendship of the world, to see to it that all the moral forces that make for right and justice and liberty are united and are given a vital organization to which the peoples of the world will readily and gladly respond. In other words, our task is no less colossal than this, to set up a new international psychology, to have a new atmosphere.

---

ganda continued to be felt as many British believed that only a total victory over Germany could ever compensate for the terrible losses of the war.

France's approach to peace was primarily determined by considerations of national security. To Georges Clemenceau, the feisty premier of France who had led his country to victory, the French people had borne the brunt of German aggression. They deserved revenge and security against future German aggression (see the box on p. 925). The French knew that Germany's larger population (60 million to 40 million) posed a long-term threat to France. Clemenceau wanted a demilitarized Germany, vast German reparations to pay for the costs of the war, and a separate Rhineland as a buffer state between France and Germany, demands that Wilson viewed as vindictive and contrary to the principle of national self-determination.

Yet another consideration affected the negotiations at Paris, namely, the fear that Bolshevik revolution would spread from Russia to other European countries. This concern led the Allies to enlarge and strengthen such eastern European states as Poland, Czechoslovakia, and Romania at the expense of both Germany and Bolshevik Russia.

Although twenty-seven nations were represented at the Paris Peace Conference, the most important decisions were made by Woodrow Wilson, Georges Clemenceau, and David Lloyd George. Italy was considered one of the so-called Big Four powers, but played a much less important role than the other three countries. Germany, of course, was not invited to attend and Russia could not because of its civil war.

In view of the many conflicting demands at Versailles, it was inevitable that the Big Three would quarrel. Wil-

The Voice of Peacemaking: Georges Clemenceau
▼ ▼ ▼

"For the catastrophe of 1914 the Germans are responsible."

The French leader Georges Clemenceau had a vision of peacemaking quite different from that of Woodrow Wilson. The French sought revenge and security. In this selection from his book Grandeur and Misery of Victory, *Clemenceau revealed his fundamental dislike and distrust of Germany.*

Georges Clemenceau, *Grandeur and Misery of Victory*

War and peace, with their strong contrasts, alternate against a common background. For the catastrophe of 1914 the Germans are responsible. Only a professional liar would deny this. . . .

What after all is this war, prepared, undertaken, and waged by the German people, who flung aside every scruple of conscience to let it loose, hoping for a peace of enslavement under the yoke of a militarism, destructive of all human dignity? It is simply the continuance, the recrudescence, of those never-ending acts of violence by which the first savage tribes carried out their depredations with all the resources of barbarism. . . .

I have sometimes penetrated into the sacred cave of the Germanic cult, which is, as every one knows, the *Bierhaus* [beer hall]. A great aisle of massive humanity where there accumulate, amid the fumes of tobacco and beer, the popular rumblings of a nationalism upheld by the sonorous brasses blaring to the heavens the supreme voice of Germany, *Deutschland über alles! Germany above everything!* Men, women, and children, all petrified in reverence before the divine stoneware pot, brows furrowed with irrepressible power, eyes lost in a dream of infinity, mouths twisted by the intensity of will-power, drink in long draughts the celestial hope of vague expectations. These only remain to be realized presently when the chief marked out by Destiny shall have given the word. There you have the ultimate framework of an old but childish race.

---

son was determined to create a League of Nations to prevent future wars. Clemenceau and Lloyd George were equally determined to punish Germany. In the end, only compromise made it possible to achieve a peace settlement. Wilson's wish that the creation of an international peacekeeping organization be the first order of business was granted, and already on January 25, 1919, the conference adopted the principle of a League of Nations. The details of its structure were left for later sessions, and Wilson willingly agreed to make compromises on territorial arrangements to guarantee the establishment of the league, believing that a functioning league could later rectify bad arrangements. Clemenceau also compromised to obtain some guarantees for French security. He renounced France's desire for a separate Rhineland and instead accepted a defensive alliance with Great Britain and the United States. Both states pledged to help France if it were attacked by Germany.

The final peace settlement of Paris consisted of five separate treaties with the defeated nations—Germany, Austria, Hungary, Bulgaria, and Turkey. The Treaty of Versailles with Germany, signed on June 28, 1919, was by far the most important. The Germans considered it a harsh peace, conveniently overlooking that the Treaty of Brest-Litovsk that they had imposed on Bolshevik Russia was even more severe. The Germans were particularly unhappy with Article 231, the so-called War Guilt Clause, which declared Germany (and Austria) responsible for starting the war and ordered Germany to pay reparations for all the damage to which the Allied governments and their people were subjected as a result of the war "imposed upon them by the aggression of Germany and her allies." Reparations were a logical con-

▼ **The Big Four at Paris.** Shown here are the Big Four at the Paris Peace Conference: Lloyd George of Britain, Orlando of Italy, Clemenceau of France, and Wilson of the United States. Although Italy was considered one of the Big Four powers, Britain, France, and the United States (the Big Three) made the major decisions at the peace conference.

▼ **Map 26.5** Europe in 1919.

sequence of the wartime promises that Allied leaders had made to their people that the Germans would pay for the war effort.

The military and territorial provisions of the treaty also rankled Germans, although they were by no means as harsh as the Germans claimed. Germany had to lower its army to 100,000 men, reduce its navy, and eliminate its air force. German territorial losses included the cession of Alsace and Lorraine to France and sections of Prussia to the new Polish state. German land west and as far as thirty miles east of the Rhine was established as a demilitarized zone and stripped of all armaments or fortifications to serve as a barrier to any future German military moves westward against France. Outraged by the "dictated peace," the new German government vowed to resist rather than accept the treaty, but it had no real alternative. Rejection meant a renewal of the war, and as the army pointed out, that was no longer possible.

The separate peace treaties made with the other Central Powers (Austria, Hungary, Bulgaria, and Turkey) extensively redrew the map of eastern Europe. Many of

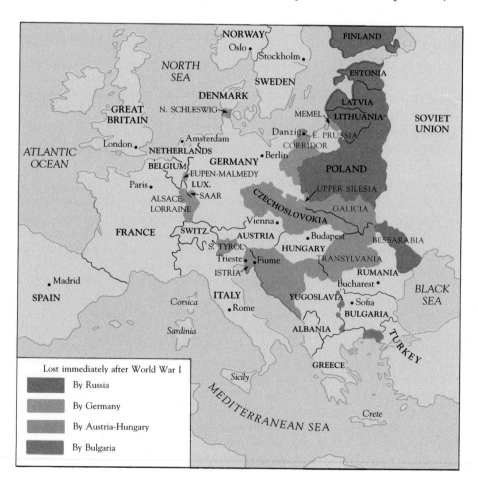

Lost immediately after World War I
By Russia
By Germany
By Austria-Hungary
By Bulgaria

The Path to War	**1914**
Assassination of Archduke Francis Ferdinand	June 28
Austria's Ultimatum to Serbia	July 23
Austrian Declares War on Serbia	July 28
Russian Mobilizes	July 29
German Ultimatum to Russia	July 31
Germany Declares War on Russia	August 1
Germany Declares War on France	August 3
German Troops Invade Belgium	August 4
Great Britain Declares War on Germany	August 4
The War	**1914**
Battle of Tannenberg	August 26–30
First Battle of the Marne	September 6–10
Battle of Masurian Lakes	September 15
Russia, Great Britain, and France Declare War on Ottoman Empire	November
	1915
Battle of Gallipoli Begins	April 25
Italy Declares War on Austria-Hungary	May 23
Entry of Bulgaria into the War	October

	1916
Battle of Verdun	February 21–December 18
Battle of Jutland	May 31
The Somme Offensive	July 1–November 19
	1917
Germany Returns to Unrestricted Submarine Warfare	January
United States Enters the War	April 6
The Champagne Offensive	April 16–29
	1918
Last German Offensive	March 21–July 18
Second Battle of the Marne	July 18
Allied Counteroffensive	July 18–November 10
Armistice between Allies and Germany	November 11
	1919
Paris Peace Conference Begins	January 18
Peace of Versailles	June 28

these changes merely ratified what the war had already accomplished. The empires that had controlled eastern Europe for centuries had been destroyed or weakened, and a number of new states appeared on the map of Europe.

Both the German and Russian empires lost considerable territory in eastern Europe while the Austro-Hungarian Empire disappeared altogether. New nation-states emerged from the lands of these three empires: Finland, Latvia, Estonia, Lithuania, Poland, Czechoslovakia, Austria, and Hungary. Territorial rearrangements were also made in the Balkans. Romania acquired additional lands from Russia, Hungary, and Bulgaria. Serbia formed the nucleus of a new South Slav state, called Yugoslavia, which combined Serbs, Croats, and Slovenes. Although the Paris Peace Conference was sup-

posedly guided by the principle of self-determination, the mixtures of peoples in eastern Europe made it impossible to draw boundaries along neat ethnic lines. Compromises had to be made, sometimes to satisfy the national interest of the victors. France, for example, had lost Russia as its major ally on Germany's eastern border and wanted to strengthen and expand Poland, Czechoslovakia, Yugoslavia, and Romania as much as possible so that those states could serve as barriers against Germany and Communist Russia. As a result of compromises, virtually every eastern Europe state was left with a minorities problem that could lead to future conflicts. Germans in Poland and Czechoslovakia, Hungarians in Romania, and Turks in Hungary all became sources of later conflict. Moreover, the new map of eastern Europe was based upon the temporary collapse of power in both

Germany and Russia. Since neither country accepted the new eastern frontiers, it seemed only a matter of time before a resurgent Germany or Russia would make changes.

Yet another centuries-old empire—the Ottoman Empire—was dismembered by the peace settlement after the war. To gain Arab support against the Turks during the war, the Western allies had promised to recognize the independence of Arab states in the Middle Eastern lands of the Turkish empire. But the imperialist habits of Western nations died hard. After the war, France took control of Lebanon and Syria while Britain received Iraq and Palestine. Officially, both acquisitions were called mandates. Since Woodrow Wilson had opposed the outright annexation of colonial territories by the Allies, the peace settlement had created a system of mandates whereby a nation officially administered a territory on behalf of the League of Nations. The system of mandates could not hide the fact that the principle of national self-determination at the Paris Peace Conference was largely for Europeans.

The peace settlement negotiated at Paris soon came under attack, not only by the defeated Central Powers, but by others who felt that the peacemakers had been shortsighted. The famous British economist John Maynard Keynes, for example, condemned the preoccupation with frontiers at the expense of economic issues that left Europe "inefficient, unemployed, disorganized." Despite the criticisms, the peace settlement was a sensible one. Self-determination had served reasonably well as a central organizing principle while the establishment of the League of Nations gave some hope that future conflicts could be resolved peacefully. And yet, within twenty years after the signing of the peace treaties, Europe was again engaged in deadly conflict. As some historians have suggested, perhaps the cause of the failure of the peace of 1919 was less in its structure than in its lack of enforcement.

Successful enforcement of the peace necessitated the active involvement of its principal architects, especially in assisting the new German state to develop a peaceful and democratic republic. The failure of the American Senate to ratify the Treaty of Versailles, however, meant that the United States never joined the League of Nations. In addition, the American Senate also rejected Wilson's defensive alliance with Great Britain and France. Already by the end of 1919, America was retreating into isolationism.

This retreat had dire consequences. American withdrawal from the defensive alliance with Britain and France led Britain to withdraw as well. By removing itself from European affairs, the United States forced France to stand alone facing its old enemy, leading the embittered nation to take strong actions against Germany that only intensified German resentment. By the end of 1919, it appeared that the peace of 1919 was already beginning to unravel.

World War I shattered the liberal, rational society of late nineteenth- and early twentieth-century Europe. The incredible destruction and the death of almost 10 million people undermined the whole idea of progress. New propaganda techniques had manipulated entire populations into sustaining their involvement in a meaningless slaughter.

World War I was a total war and involved a mobilization of resources and populations and increased government centralization of power over the lives of its citizens. Civil liberties, such as freedom of the press, speech, assembly, and movement, were circumscribed in the name of national security. Governments' need to plan the production and distribution of goods and to ration consumer goods restricted economic freedom. Although the late nineteenth and early twentieth centuries had witnessed the extension of government authority into such areas as mass education, social welfare legislation, and mass conscription, World War I made the practice of strong central authority a way of life.

Finally, World War I ended the age of European hegemony over world affairs. In 1917, the Russian Revolution laid the foundation for the creation of a new Soviet power, and the United States entered the war. The termination of the European age was not evident to all, however, for it was clouded by two developments—American isolationism and the withdrawal of the Soviets from world affairs while they nurtured the growth of their own socialist system. Although these developments were only temporary, they created a political vacuum in Europe that all too soon was filled by the revival of German power.

Notes

▼ ▼ ▼

1. Arnold Toynbee, *Surviving the Future* (New York, 1971), pp. 106–107.

2. Quoted in Joachim Remak, "1914—The Third Balkan War: Origins Reconsidered," *Journal of Modern History* 43 (1971): 364–65.

3. Quoted in Robert G. L. Waite, *Vanguard of Nazism* (New York, 1969), p. 22.

4. Quoted in J. M. Winter, *The Experience of World War I* (New York, 1989), p. 142.

5. Quoted in ibid., p. 137.

6. Quoted in Gail Braybon, *Women Workers in the First World War: The British Experience* (London, 1981), p. 79.

7. Quoted in Catherine W. Reilly, ed., *Scars upon My Heart: Women's Poetry and Verse of the First World War* (London, 1981), p. 90.

8. Quoted in Robert Paxton, *Europe in the Twentieth Century*, 2d ed. (New York, 1985), p. 110.

9. Quoted in William M. Mandel, *Soviet Women* (Garden City, N.Y., 1975), p. 43.

10. Harold Nicolson, *Peacemaking, 1919* (Boston and New York, 1933), pp. 31–32.

Suggestions for Further Reading

The historical literature on the causes of World War I is enormous. A good starting point is the work by J. Joll, *The Origins of the First World War* (London, 1984). Also useful is J. Remak, *The Origins of World War I, 1871–1914* (New York, 1967). The belief that Germany was primarily responsible for the war was argued vigorously by the German scholar F. Fischer, *Germany's Aims in the First World War* (New York, 1967); *World Power or Decline: The Controversy over Germany's Aims in World War I* (New York, 1974); and *War of Illusions: German Policies from 1911 to 1914* (New York, 1975). The role of each great power has been reassessed in a series of books on the causes of World War I. They include V. R. Berghahn, *Germany and the Approach of War in 1914* (London, 1973); Z. S. Steiner, *Britain and the Origins of the First World War* (New York, 1977); R. Bosworth, *Italy and the Approach of the First World War* (New York, 1983); J. F. Keiger, *France and the Origins of the First World War* (New York, 1984); and D. C. B. Lieven, *Russia and the Origins of the First World War* (New York, 1984). The domestic origins of the war are probed in A. Mayer, *The Persistence of the Old Regime* (New York, 1981).

There are two good recent accounts of World War I in B. E. Schmitt and H. C. Vedeler, *The World in the Crucible, 1914–1919* (New York, 1984); and the lavishly illustrated book by J. M. Winter, *The Experience of World War I* (New York, 1989). For an account of the military operations of the war, see the classic work by B. H. Liddell-Hart, *History of the First World War* (Boston,

1970). A good study of the Eastern Front is N. Stone, *The Eastern Front, 1914–1917* (London, 1975). On war as redemption, see R. Stromberg, *Redemption by War: The Intellectuals and 1914* (Lawrence, Kans., 1982). The nature of trench warfare is examined in T. Ashworth, *Trench Warfare, 1914–1918: The Live and Let-Live System* (London, 1980). The use of poison gas is examined in L. F. Haber, *The Poisonous Cloud: Chemical Warfare in the First World War* (Oxford, 1985). On the morale of soldiers in World War I, see J. Keegan, *The Face of Battle* (London, 1975). The war at sea is examined in R. Hough, *The Great War at Sea, 1914–18* (Oxford, 1983). In *The Great War and Modern Memory* (London, 1975), Paul Fussell attempted to show how British writers described their war experiences. Although scholars do not always agree with her conclusions, B. Tuchman's *The Guns of August* (New York, 1962) is a magnificently written account of the opening days of the war. For an interesting perspective on World War I and the beginnings of the modern world, see M. Eksteins, *Rites of Spring, The Great War and the Birth of the Modern Age* (Boston, 1989).

For a good account of the economic consequences for the European states at war, see G. Hardach, *The First World War, 1914–1918* (Princeton, N.J., 1966). On the role of women in World War I, see G. Braybon, *Women Workers in the First World War: The British Experience* (London, 1981); and J. M. Winter and R. M. Wall, eds., *The Upheaval of War: Family, Work and Welfare in Europe, 1914–1918* (Cambridge, 1988). Labor unrest and class conflict are examined in J. J. Becker, *The Great War and the French People* (Leamington Spa, 1985); and B. Waites, *A Class Society at War* (Leamington Spa, 1987).

A good introduction to the Russian Revolution can be found in S. Fitzpatrick, *The Russian Revolution, 1917–1932* (New York, 1982); and R. V. Daniels, *Red October* (New York, 1967). On Lenin, see R. W. Clark, *Lenin* (New York, 1988); and the valuable work by A. B. Ulam, *The Bolsheviks* (New York, 1965). The role of workers in the events of the Russian Revolution is examined in D. Koenker, *Moscow Workers and the 1917 Revolution* (Princeton, N. J., 1981). On Allied intervention in the civil war, see M. Kettle, *Russia and the Allies, 1917–1920* (Minneapolis, 1981). There is now a comprehensive study of the Russian civil war in W. B. Lincoln, *Red Victory: A History of the Russian Civil War* (New York, 1989). On the revolutions in Germany and Austria-Hungary, see F. L. Carsten, *Revolution in Central Europe* (Berkeley, 1972); and A. J. Ryder, *The German Revolution of 1918* (Cambridge, 1967).

The role of war aims in the shaping of the peace settlement is examined in V. H. Rothwell, *British War Aims and Peace Diplomacy, 1914–1918* (Oxford, 1971); and D. R. Stevenson, *French War Aims against Germany, 1914–1919* (New York, 1982). The fear of Bolshevism as a factor at the Paris Peace Conference is argued in A. Mayer, *The Politics and Diplomacy of Peacemaking: Containment and Counter-Revolution at Versailles, 1918–1919* (New York, 1967).

Chapter 27

The Futile Search for a New Stability: Europe between the Wars, 1919–1939

▼▼▼▼▼

Only twenty years after the Treaty of Versailles, Europeans were again at war. Yet, in the 1920s, many people continued to assume that Europe and the world were about to enter a new era of international peace, economic growth, and political democracy. In all of these areas, the optimistic hopes of the 1920s failed to be realized. After 1919, numerous efforts were made to create conditions for peace. The League of Nations, conceived as a new instrument to provide for collective security, failed to be effective. Attempts to achieve peace by means of treaties that renounced the use of war did not succeed because the treaties lacked any means of enforcement. Having realized that the arms race before World War I had helped lead to war, almost everyone favored disarmament

agreements, but no one could agree on any substantive proposals. These efforts at collective security in the 1920s proved unable to halt aggression in the 1930s.

Internally, Europe was faced with severe economic problems after World War I. The European economy did not begin to recover from the war until 1922, and even then it was beset by serious problems, such as Germany's payment of reparations, Allied war debts to the United States, and, most devastating of all, the Great Depression that began at the end of 1929.

In 1919, there was cause for considerable optimism in regard to political developments, despite the success of the Russian Revolution and the fear that communism would spread to other European states. Overall, political democracy seemed well established in 1919. Four major nations—Great Britain, France, Germany, and

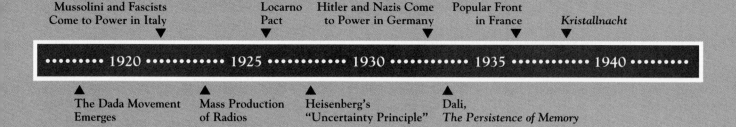

Mussolini and Fascists
Come to Power in Italy

Locarno
Pact

Hitler and Nazis Come
to Power in Germany

Popular Front
in France

Kristallnacht

▼ 1920 ••••••••• 1925 ••••••••• 1930 ••••••••• 1935 ••••••••• 1940 •••••••••

The Dada Movement
Emerges

Mass Production
of Radios

Heisenberg's
"Uncertainty Principle"

Dali,
The Persistence of Memory

Italy—as well as a host of minor ones maintained democratic forms of government. These democracies, however, were plagued by many problems, and by the 1930s a number of authoritarian regimes had replaced democratic governments.

▼ An Uncertain Peace: The Search for Security

The peace settlement at the end of World War I had tried to fulfill the nineteenth-century dream of nationalism by the creation of boundaries and new states. From its inception, however, this peace settlement had left nations unhappy. Conflicts over disputed border regions between Germany and Poland, Poland and Lithuania, Poland and Czechoslovakia, Austria and Hungary, and Italy and Yugoslavia poisoned mutual relations in eastern Europe for years. Many Germans viewed the Peace of Versailles as a dictated peace and vowed to seek its revision.

The American president Woodrow Wilson had recognized that the peace treaties contained unwise provisions that could serve as new causes for conflicts and had placed many of his hopes for the future in the League of Nations. The league, however, was not particularly effective in maintaining the peace. The failure of the United States to join the league and the subsequent American retreat into isolationism undermined the effectiveness of the league from its beginning. Moreover, the league could only use economic sanctions to halt aggression. The French attempt to strengthen the league's effectiveness as an instrument of collective security by creating some kind of international army was rejected by nations that feared giving up any of their sovereignty to a larger international body.

The weakness of the League of Nations and the failure of both the United States and Great Britain to honor their defensive military alliances with France left France embittered and alone. Before World War I, France's alliance with Russia had served to threaten Germany with the possibility of a two-front war. But Communist Russia was now a hostile power. To compensate, France built a network of alliances in eastern Europe with Poland and the members of the so-called Little Entente (Czechoslovakia, Romania, Yugoslavia). While these alliances looked good on paper as a way to contain Germany and maintain the new status quo, they overlooked the fundamental military weaknesses of those nations. Poland and the Little Entente states were no real substitutes for powerful Russia.

The French Policy of Coercion, 1919–1924

France's search for security between 1919 and 1924 was founded primarily upon a strict enforcement of the Treaty of Versailles. This tough policy toward Germany began with the issue of reparations, or the payments that the Germans were supposed to make to compensate for the "damage done to the civilian population of the Allied and Associated Powers and to their property," as the treaty asserted. Behind reparations lay some straightforward political and economic calculations. The Allied governments needed to raise vast sums of money to reconstruct their war-damaged economies. France, above all, needed to rebuild railroads, bridges, and industrial plants as well as to restore battle-devastated farmlands. Moreover, the Allied governments had war loans to repay. The Allies had received large loans from the United States and expected that after the war the United States would cancel all or part of the debts. The United States refused. To the Allied governments, especially France, reparations from defeated Germany seemed an intelligent and even just way to alleviate postwar financial burdens. From the Allied perspective, shouldn't the Germans, who had caused the war, pay for the damages?

In April 1921, the Allied Reparations Commission settled on a sum of 132 billion marks ($33 billion) for German reparations, payable in annual installments of

2.5 billion (gold) marks. Allied threats to occupy the Ruhr valley, Germany's chief industrial and mining center, led the new German republic to accept the reparations settlement and make its first payment in 1921. By the following year, however, faced with rising inflation and domestic turmoil, the German position on reparations had changed. The German government announced that it was unable to pay more and asked for a moratorium on reparation payments while a commission of experts drew up a more realistic program.

Outraged by what they considered to be Germany's unilateral dissolution of the peace settlement, the French, under Raymond Poincaré and the conservative National Bloc that dominated the government, took a tough stand against Germany. With the cooperation of its Belgian allies, the French government sent troops to

▼ **The Effects of Inflation.** Germany experienced a number of serious economic problems after the war. The inflationary pressures that had begun in Germany at the end of World War I intensified during the French occupation of the Ruhr. By the early 1920s, the value of the German mark had fallen precipitously. This photograph shows a German housewife using the worthless currency to light a fire in her cooking stove.

occupy the Ruhr valley. French aims were clear. Since the Germans would not pay reparations, the French would collect reparations in kind by operating and using the Ruhr mines and factories. Moreover, the French hoped to hold the occupied Ruhr industries as "productive pledges" that would not be returned to German control until the German government promised to fulfill its reparations responsibilities under the Treaty of Versailles.

Both Germany and France suffered from the French occupation of the Ruhr. The German government adopted a policy of passive resistance to French occupation that was largely financed by printing more paper money. This only intensified the inflationary pressures that had already begun in Germany by the end of the war. The German mark became worthless. Economic disaster fueled political upheavals as Communists staged uprisings in October, and Adolf Hitler's band of Nazis attempted to seize power in Munich in 1923 (see Hitler and Nazi Germany later in the chapter). But the French were hardly victorious. The cost of the French occupation was not offset by the gains; Poincaré's need to raise taxes early in 1924 caused his government to fall in May. Meanwhile, pressure from the United States and Great Britain against the French policy forced the French to agree to a new conference of experts to reassess the reparations problem. By the time the conference did its work in 1924, both France and Germany were opting to pursue a more conciliatory approach toward each other.

The Hopeful Years, 1924–1929

The formation of liberal-socialist governments in both Great Britain and France opened the door to conciliatory approaches to Germany and the reparations problem. At the same time, a new German government led by Gustav Stresemann (1878–1929) ended the policy of passive resistance and committed Germany to carry out the provisions of the Treaty of Versailles while seeking a new settlement of the reparations question.

In August 1924, an international commission produced a new plan for reparations. Named the Dawes Plan after the American banker who chaired the commission, it reduced reparations and stabilized Germany's payments on the basis of its ability to pay. The Dawes Plan also granted an initial $200 million loan for German recovery, which opened the door to heavy American investments in Europe that helped create a new era of European prosperity between 1924 and 1929.

A new era of European diplomacy accompanied the new economic stability. A spirit of international cooperation was fostered by the foreign ministers of Germany and France, Gustav Stresemann and Aristide Briand (1862–1932), who concluded the Treaty of Locarno in 1925. This guaranteed Germany's new western borders with France and Belgium. Britain and Italy agreed to intervene if either Germany or France violated these frontiers. Although Germany's new eastern borders with Poland were conspicuously absent from the agreement, the Locarno pact was viewed by many as the beginning of a new era of European peace. On the day after the pact was concluded, the headlines in the *New York Times* ran "France and Germany Ban War Forever," while the London *Times* declared, "Peace at Last."[1]

Germany's entry into the League of Nations in March 1926 soon reinforced the new spirit of conciliation engendered at Locarno. Two years later, similar optimistic attitudes prevailed in the Kellogg-Briand pact, drafted by the American secretary of state Frank B. Kellogg and the French foreign minister Aristide Briand. Sixty-three nations signed this accord, in which they pledged "to renounce war as an instrument of national policy." Nothing was said, however, about what would be done if anyone violated the treaty.

The spirit of Locarno was based on little real substance. Germany lacked the military power to alter its western borders even if it wanted to. Pious promises to renounce war without mechanisms to enforce them were virtually worthless. And the issue of disarmament soon proved that even the spirit of Locarno could not bring nations to cut back on their weapons. The League of Nations Covenant had suggested the "reduction of national armaments to the lowest point consistent with national safety." Germany, of course, had been disarmed with the expectation that other states would do likewise. Numerous disarmament conferences, however, failed to achieve anything substantial as states proved unwilling to trust their security to anyone but their own military forces. When a World Disarmament Conference finally met in Geneva in 1932, the issue was already dead.

One other hopeful sign of the years between 1924 and 1929 was the new coexistence of the West with Soviet Russia. By the beginning of 1924, Soviet hopes for communist revolutions in Western states had largely dissipated. In turn, these states had realized by then that the Bolshevik regime could no longer be ousted. Weimar Germany had already established full diplomatic relations with Soviet Russia in 1922, and in 1924 Britain, France, Italy, and other small European states did likewise. Nevertheless, Western powers remained highly suspicious of Soviet intentions, especially when the Soviet Union continued to support the propaganda activities of the Comintern, or Communist International, a worldwide organization of pro-Soviet Marxist parties originally formed in 1919 by Lenin to foster world revolution.

The Great Depression

After World War I, most European states began to dismantle the wartime agencies that had regulated their economies in the hope of returning to the liberal ideal of a private-enterprise, market economy largely free of state intervention. But the war had vastly strengthened business cartels and labor unions, and any postwar economy had to include some form of government regulation of these powerful organizations. Moreover, the war had a powerful effect on the postwar international economy. Reparations and war debts, as we have seen, created a cycle of payments from Germany to Britain and France and from France and Great Britain to the United States that came to depend on the American loans to Germany in the second half of the 1920s. Thus, the prosperity between 1924 and 1929 was at best a fragile one, and the dream of returning to the liberal ideal of a self-regulating market economy was merely an illusion. What destroyed the concept altogether was the Great Depression.

Two factors played a major role in the coming of the Great Depression: a downturn in domestic economies and an international financial crisis created by the collapse of the American stock market in 1929. Already in the mid-1920s, prices for agricultural goods were beginning to decline rapidly due to overproduction of basic commodities, such as wheat. In 1925, states in central and eastern Europe began to impose tariffs to close their markets to other countries' goods. An increase in the use of oil and hydroelectricity led to a slump in the coal industry even before 1929.

In addition to these domestic economic troubles, much of the European prosperity between 1924 and 1929 had been built upon American bank loans to Germany. Twenty-three billion marks had been invested in German municipal bonds and German industries since 1924. Already in 1928 and 1929, American investors had begun to pull money out of Germany in order to invest in the booming New York stock market. The crash of the American stock market in October 1929 led panicky American investors to withdraw even more of their funds from Germany and other European markets. The withdrawal of funds seriously weakened the banks of Germany and other central European states. The Credit-Anstalt, Vienna's most prestigious bank, collapsed on May 31, 1931. By that time, trade was slowing down,

The Great Depression: Unemployed and Homeless in Germany

▼ ▼ ▼

In 1932, Germany had six million unemployed workers, many of them wandering about Germany aimlessly, begging for food and seeking shelter in city lodging houses for the homeless. The Great Depression was an important factor in the rise to power of Adolf Hitler and the Nazis. This selection presents a description of unemployed homeless in 1932.

Heinrich Hauser, "With Germany's Unemployed"
An almost unbroken chain of homeless men extends the whole length of the great Hamburg-Berlin highway. . . . All the highways in Germany over which I have traveled this year presented the same aspect. . . .

Most of the hikers paid no attention to me. They walked separately or in small groups, with their eyes on the ground. And they had the queer, stumbling gait of barefooted people, for their shoes were slung over their shoulders. Some of them were guild members,—carpenters . . . milkmen . . . and bricklayers . . . but they were in a minority. Far more numerous were those whom one could assign to no special profession or craft—unskilled young people, for the most part, who had been unable to find a place for themselves in any city or town in Germany, and who had never had a job and never expected to have one. There was something else that had never been seen before—whole families that had piled all their goods into baby carriages and wheelbarrows that they were pushing along as they plodded forward in dumb despair. It was a whole nation on the march.

I saw them—and this was the strongest impression that the year 1932 left with me—I saw them, gathered into groups of fifty or a hundred men, attacking fields of potatoes. I saw them digging up the potatoes and throwing them into sacks while the farmer who owned the field watched them in despair and the local policeman looked on gloomily from the distance. I saw them staggering toward the lights of the city as night fell, with their sacks on their backs. What did it remind me of? Of the War, of the worst periods of starvation in 1917 and 1918, but even then people paid for the potatoes. . . .

I saw that the individual can know what is happening only by personal experience. I know what it is to be a tramp. I know what cold and hunger are. . . . But there are two things that I have only recently experienced—begging and spending the night in a municipal lodging house.

I entered the huge Berlin municipal lodging house in a northern quarter of the city. . . .

Distribution of spoons, distribution of enameled-ware bowls with the words "Property of the City of Berlin" written on their sides. Then the meal itself. A big kettle is carried in. Men with yellow smocks have brought it in and men with yellow smocks ladle out the food. These men, too, are homeless and they have been expressly picked by the establishment and given free food and lodging and a little pocket money in exchange for their work about the house.

Where have I seen this kind of food distribution before? In a prison that I once helped to guard in the winter of 1919 during the German civil war. There was the same hunger then, the same trembling, anxious expectation of rations. Now the men are standing in a long row, dressed in their plain nightshirts that reach to the ground, and the noise of their shuffling feet is like the noise of big wild animals walking up and down the stone floor of their cages before feeding time. The men lean far over the kettle so that the warm steam from the food envelops them and they hold out their bowls as if begging and whisper to the attendant, "Give me a real helping. Give me a little more." A piece of bread is handed out with every bowl.

My next recollection is sitting at a table in another room on a crowded bench that is like a seat in a fourth-class railway carriage. Hundreds of hungry mouths make an enormous noise eating their food. The men sit bent over their food like animals who feel that someone is going to take it away from them. They hold their bowl with their left arm part way around it, so that nobody can take it away, and they also protect it with their other elbow and with their head and mouth, while they move the spoon as fast as they can between their mouth and the bowl.

industrialists were cutting back production, and unemployment was increasing as the ripple effects of international bank failures had a devastating impact on domestic economies.

Economic depression was by no means a new phenomenon in European history. But the depth of the economic downturn after 1929 fully justifies the label Great Depression. During 1932, the worst year of the depression, one British worker in four was unemployed, while 6 million or 40 percent of the German labor force were out of work. Between 1929 and 1932, industrial production plummeted almost 50 percent in the United States and over 40 percent in Germany. The unemployed and homeless filled the streets of the cities throughout the advanced industrial countries (see the box on p. 936).

Governments seemed powerless to deal with the crisis. The classical liberal remedy for depression, a deflationary policy of balanced budgets, which involved cutting costs by lowering wages and raising tariffs to exclude other countries' goods from home markets, only served to worsen the economic crisis and create even greater mass discontent. This, in turn, led to serious political repercussions. Increased government activity in the economy was one reaction, even in countries like the United States that had a strong laissez-faire tradition. Another effect was a renewed interest in Marxist doctrines since Marx had predicted that capitalism would destroy itself through overproduction. Communism took on new popularity, especially with workers and intellectuals. Finally, the Great Depression increased the attractiveness of facile dictatorial solutions, especially from a new movement known as fascism. Everywhere in Europe, democracy seemed on the defensive in the 1930s. We can best understand the full impact of the depression on Europe by examining the domestic scene in Western states between the two world wars.

▼ The Democratic States

According to Woodrow Wilson, World War I had been fought to make the world safe for democracy. In 1919, there seemed to be some justification for his claim. Four major European states and a host of minor ones had functioning political democracies. In a number of states, universal male suffrage had even been replaced by universal suffrage as male politicians rewarded women for their contributions to World War I by granting them the right to vote (except in Italy, France, and Spain where women had to wait until the end of World War II). In the 1920s, Europe seemed to be returning to the political trends of the prewar era—the broadening of parliamentary regimes and the fostering of individual liberties. But it was not an easy process; four years of total war and four years of postwar turmoil made the "return to normalcy" a difficult and troublesome affair.

Great Britain

After World War I, Great Britain went through a period of painful readjustment and serious economic difficulties. During the war, Britain had lost many of the markets for its industrial products, especially to the United States and Japan. The postwar decline of such staple industries as coal, steel, and textiles led to a rise in unemployment, which reached the two-million mark in 1921. The Liberal government of David Lloyd George proved unable either to change this situation or to meet

▼ **The Great Depression: Bread-lines in Paris.** The Great Depression devastated the European economy and led to serious political repercussions. Because of its more balanced economy, France did not feel the effects of the depression as quickly as other European countries. However, by 1931, even France was experiencing lines of unemployed people at free-food centers.

the demands of the working class for better housing and an improved standard of living.

By 1923, British politics experienced a major transformation when the Labour party surged ahead of the Liberals as the second most powerful party in Britain after the Conservatives. In fact, after the elections of November 1923, a Labour-Liberal coalition enabled Ramsay MacDonald (1866–1937) to become the first Labour prime minister of Britain. His tenure, however, was brief and not particularly innovative. Dependent on Liberal support, MacDonald rejected any extreme social or economic experimentation. No doubt, his moderation made the Labour party acceptable to many of the British who had previously feared that a Labour government would nationalize "everything." MacDonald's government lasted only ten months, however, as the Conservative party's charge that MacDonald's government was friendly toward communism proved to be a highly successful campaign tactic.

Under the direction of Stanley Baldwin (1867–1947) as prime minister, the Conservatives guided Britain during an era of renewed prosperity from 1925 to 1929. This prosperity, however, was relatively superficial. British exports in the 1920s never compensated for the overseas investments lost during the war, and even in these so-called prosperous years, unemployment remained at a startling 10 percent level. Coal miners were especially affected by the decline of the antiquated and inefficient British coal mines, which also suffered from a world glut of coal. Attempts by mine owners to lower coal miners' wages only led to a national strike (the General Strike of 1926) by miners and sympathetic trade unions. The Trades Union Congress soon accepted a compromise settlement, but many miners who refused to accept the settlement were eventually forced back to work at lower wages for longer hours.

In 1929, the Conservatives were defeated, and a second Labour government came back into power just as the Great Depression was beginning. Although Labour had now become the largest party in Britain, it still depended on the Liberals for a majority in Parliament. Attempts to deal with the effects of the depression by an increase in unemployment benefits led to budget deficits and a banking crisis. Responding to investors' demands, the Labour government prepared to cut unemployment benefits, a move that split the Labour party and brought the collapse of the Labour government.

The Labour government was replaced in 1931 by the National Government, a coalition of all three parties. Although MacDonald remained as prime minister until 1935, the Conservatives played a leading role in the coalition government, and in 1935, Stanley Baldwin once more replaced MacDonald as prime minister. The National Government claimed credit for bringing Britain out of the worst stages of the depression, primarily by using the traditional policies of balanced budgets and protective tariffs. Historians argue, however, that the general upswing of the business cycle more than anything else helped to revive the British economy. By 1935, industrial production exceeded the predepression level of 1929, and by 1936, unemployment had dropped to 1.6 million after reaching a depression high of 3 million in 1932 (see the box on p. 939).

British politicians largely ignored the new ideas of a Cambridge economist, John Maynard Keynes (1883–1946). In 1936, Keynes published his *General Theory of Employment, Interest, and Money.* Contrary to the traditional view that depressions should be left to work themselves out through the self-regulatory mechanisms of a free economy, Keynes argued that unemployment stemmed not from overproduction but from a decline in demand, and that demand could be increased by public works, financed, if necessary, through deficit spending to stimulate production. These policies, however, could only be accomplished by government intervention in the economy, and Britain's political leaders were unwilling to go that far in the 1930s.

France

After the defeat of Germany and the demobilization of the German army, France had become the strongest power on the European continent. Its biggest problem involved the reconstruction of the devastated areas of northern and eastern France. The conservative National Bloc government, led by Raymond Poincaré (1860–1934), sought to use German reparations for this purpose. Tying French economic stability to German reparations resulted in Poincaré's hard-line policy toward Germany and the Ruhr invasion. When Poincaré's conservative government was forced to raise taxes in 1924 to pay for the cost of the Ruhr fiasco, his National Bloc was voted out of power and replaced by the so-called Cartel of the Left.

The Cartel of the Left was a coalition government formed by two French parties of the left, the Radicals and Socialists. These two leftist parties shared beliefs in antimilitarism, anticlericalism, and the importance of education. But despite their title, the Radicals were a democratic party of small property owners while the Socialists were nominally committed to Marxist socialism. Although they cooperated to win elections, their differ-

The Struggles of a Democracy: Unemployment and Slums in Great Britain
▼ ▼ ▼

During the 1920s and 1930s, Britain struggled with the problems of economic depression. Unemployment was widespread, especially after the onset of the Great Depression. Even after Britain began to recover in the late 1930s, many Britons still lived in wretched conditions. These selections reflect Britain's economic and social problems.

Men without Work: A Report Made to the Pilgrim Trust, 1938

A week's notice may end half a lifetime's service, with no prospects, if he is elderly, but the dole, followed by a still further reduction in his means of livelihood when the old age pension comes. We take as an example a shoe laster from Leicester, who had worked thirty-seven years with one firm. "When I heard the new manager going through and saying: "The whole of this side of this room, this room, and this room is to be stopped, I knew it would be uphill work to get something." He went on to describe to us how he had not been able to bring himself to tell his wife the bad news when he got home, how she had noticed that something was wrong, how confident she had been that he would get work elsewhere, but how he had known that the chances were heavily against him. For months and indeed often for years such men go on looking for work, and the same is true of many casual labourers. There were in the sample old men who have not a remote chance of working again but yet make it a practice to stand every morning at six o'clock at the works gates in the hope that perhaps they may catch the foreman's eye.

George Orwell, "A Woman in the Slums" from *The Road to Wigan Pier*, 1937

As we moved slowly through the outskirts of the town we passed row after row of little grey slum houses. . . . At the back of one of the houses a young woman was kneeling on the stones, poking a stick up the leaden waste-pipe which ran from the sink inside, and which I suppose was blocked. . . . She had a round pale face, the usual exhausted face of the slum girl who is twenty-five and looks forty, thanks to miscarriages and drudgery; and it wore, for the second in which I saw it, the most desolate, hopeless expression I have ever seen. It struck me then that we are mistaken when we say that "It isn't the same for them as it would be for us," and that people bred in the slums can imagine nothing but the slums. For what I saw in her face was not the ignorant suffering of an animal. She knew well enough what was happening to her— understood as well as I did how dreadful a destiny it was to be kneeling there in the bitter cold, on the slimy stones of a slum backyard, poking a stick up a foul drain-pipe.

---

ences on economic and financial issues made their efforts to solve France's financial problems between 1924 and 1926 largely futile. The failure of the Cartel of the Left led to the return of Raymond Poincaré, whose government from 1926 to 1929 stabilized the French economy during a period of relative prosperity.

France did not feel the effects of the depression as soon as other countries because of its more balanced economy. The French population was almost evenly divided between urban and agricultural pursuits while a slight majority of industrial plants were small enterprises employing five workers or less. Even large industrialists were more conservative and invested little in foreign goods. It was not until 1932 that France began to feel the full effects of the Great Depression, and economic instability soon had political repercussions. During a nineteen-month period in 1932 and 1933, six different cabinets were formed as France faced political chaos. During the same time, French Fascist groups, adhering to far-right policies similar to those of the Fascists in Italy and the Nazis in Germany (see Fascist Italy and Hitler and Nazi Germany later in the chapter), marched through French streets in a number of demonstrations. The February riots of 1934, caused by a number of French Fascist leagues, frightened many into believing that the Fascists intended to seize power. These fears began to drive the leftist parties together despite their other differences and led in 1936 to the formation of the Popular Front.

The first Popular Front government was formed in June 1936 and was a coalition of the Communists, Socialists, and Radicals. The Socialist leader, Léon Blum

(1872–1950), served as prime minister. The Popular Front succeeded in initiating a program for workers that some have called the French New Deal. It consisted of the right of collective bargaining, a forty-hour work week, two-week paid vacations, and minimum wages. The Popular Front's policies, however, failed to solve the problems of the depression. In 1938, French Industrial production was still below the levels of 1929. Although the French Popular Front survived in name until 1938, it was for all intents and purposes dead before then. By 1938, the French were experiencing a serious decline of confidence in their political system that left them unprepared to deal with their aggressive Nazi enemy to the east.

The Scandinavian Example

The Scandinavian democracies were particularly successful in coping with the Great Depression. Socialist parties had grown steadily in the late nineteenth and early twentieth centuries and between the wars came to head the governments of Sweden, Denmark, Norway, and Finland. These Social Democratic governments encouraged the development of rural and industrial cooperative enterprises. Ninety percent of the Danish milk industry, for example, was organized on a cooperative basis by 1933. Privately owned and managed, Scandina-

vian cooperatives seemed to avoid the pitfalls of either communist or purely capitalist economic systems.

Social Democratic governments also greatly expanded social services. Not only did Scandinavian governments increase old age pensions and unemployment insurance, but they also provided such novel forms of assistance as subsidized housing, free prenatal care, maternity allowances, and annual paid vacations for workers. To achieve their social welfare states, the Scandinavian governments required high taxes and large bureaucracies, but these did not prevent both private and cooperative enterprises from prospering. Indeed between 1900 and 1939, Sweden experienced a greater rise in real wages than any other European country.

The United States

After Germany, no Western nation was more affected by the Great Depression than the United States. The full force of the depression had struck the United States by 1932. In that year industrial production fell to 50 percent of what it had been in 1929. By 1933, there were 15 million unemployed. Under these circumstances, the Democrat Franklin Delano Roosevelt (1882–1945) was able to win a landslide electoral victory in 1932.

Roosevelt did not favor either socialism or government ownership of industry to correct America's economic ills. A believer in free enterprise, he realized, however, that capitalism would have to be reformed in order to "save it." Following the example of the American experience during World War I, he and his advisers pursued a policy of active government intervention in the economy that came to be known as the New Deal.

Initially, the New Deal attempted to restore prosperity by creating the National Recovery Administration (NRA), which required government, labor, and industrial leaders to work out regulations for each industry. Declared unconstitutional by the Supreme Court in 1935, the NRA was soon superseded by other efforts collectively known as the Second New Deal. These included a stepped-up program of public works, such as the Works Progress Administration (WPA) established in 1935. This government organization employed between two and three million people who worked at building bridges, roads, post offices, and airports. The Roosevelt administration was also responsible for social legislation that launched the American welfare state. In 1935, the Social Security Act created a system of old age pensions and unemployment insurance. Moreover, the National

Labor Relations Act of 1935 encouraged the rapid growth of labor unions.

No doubt, the New Deal provided some social reform measures that perhaps averted the possibility of social revolution in the United States. It did not, however, solve the unemployment problems of the Great Depression. In May 1937, during what was considered a period of full recovery, American unemployment still stood at 7 million. A recession the following year increased that number to 11 million. Only World War II and the subsequent growth of armaments industries brought American workers back to full employment.

▼ The Retreat from Democracy: The Authoritarian and Totalitarian States

The apparent triumph of liberal democracy in 1919 proved extremely short-lived. By 1939, only two major states, France and Great Britain, and a host of minor ones, the Low Countries, the Scandinavian states, Switzerland, and Czechoslovakia, remained democratic. Italy and Germany had succumbed to the political movement called fascism while Soviet Russia under Stalin moved toward a repressive totalitarian state. A host of other European states, especially in eastern Europe, adopted authoritarian structures of different kinds. The crisis of European civilization, inaugurated in the total war of World War I, seemed only to be worsening with new assaults on individual liberties.

The dictatorial regimes between the wars assumed both old and new forms. Dictatorship was by no means a new phenomenon, but the modern totalitarian state was. The totalitarian regimes, whose best examples can be found in Stalinist Russia and Nazi Germany, extended the functions and power of the central state far beyond what they had been in the past. The immediate origins of totalitarianism can be found in the total warfare of World War I when governments, even in the democratic states, exercised controls over economic, political, and personal freedom in order to achieve victory.

The modern totalitarian state might have begun as an old-fashioned political dictatorship, but it soon moved beyond the ideal of passive obedience expected in a traditional dictatorship or authoritarian monarchy. The new "total states" expected the active loyalty and commitment of citizens to the regime's goals. They used modern mass propaganda techniques and high-speed modern communications to conquer the minds and hearts of their subjects. The total state aimed to control not only the economic, political, and social aspects of life, but the intellectual and cultural as well. But that control also had a purpose: the active involvement of the masses in the achievement of the regime's goals, whether they be war, a socialist state, or a thousand-year Reich.

The modern totalitarian state was to be led by a single leader and a single party. It ruthlessly rejected the liberal ideal of limited government power and constitutional guarantees of individual freedoms. Indeed, individual freedom was to be subordinated to the collective will of the masses, organized and determined for them by a leader or leaders. Modern technology also gave total states unprecedented police controls to enforce their wishes on their subjects.

Totalitarianism is an abstract term, and no state followed all its theoretical implications. The fascist states—Italy and Nazi Germany—as well as Stalin's Communist Russia have all been labeled totalitarian, although their regimes exhibited significant differences and met with varying degrees of success.

At the same time, there were a number of other states in Europe that were not totalitarian but did possess conservative authoritarian governments. These states adopted some of the trappings of totalitarian states, especially their wide police powers, but their greatest concern was not the creation of a mass movement aimed at the establishment of a new kind of society, but rather the defense of the existing social order. Consequently, the authoritarian states tended to limit the participation of the masses and were content with passive obedience rather than active involvement in the goals of the regime.

Fascist Italy

In the early 1920s, in the wake of economic turmoil, political disorder, and the general insecurity and fear stemming from World War I, Benito Mussolini burst upon the Italian scene with a movement that he called the *Fascio di Combattimento* (League of Combat). It was the beginning of the first fascist movement in Europe.

THE BIRTH OF FASCISM   As a new European state after 1870, Italy faced a number of serious problems that were only magnified when Italy became a belligerent in World War I. The war's cost in lives and money was enormous. An estimated 700,000 Italian soldiers died, and the treasury reckoned the cost of war at 148 billion lire, twice the sum of all government expenditures between 1861 and 1913. Italy did gain some territory, namely, Trieste, and a new northern border that included the formerly Austrian South Tyrol area. Italy's demands for Fiume and Dalmatia on the Adriatic coast were rejected, however, which gave rise to the myth that Italy had been cheated of its just rewards by the other victors. The war created untold domestic confusion. Inflation undermined middle-class security. Demobilization of the troops created high unemployment and huge groups of dissatisfied veterans. The government, which continued to be characterized by parliamentary paralysis due to the politicians' reliance on tactical and often unprincipled maneuvering to maintain their grip on power, was unable to deal effectively with these problems.

Benito Mussolini (1883–1945) was an unruly and rebellious child who ultimately received a diploma as an elementary school teacher. After an unsuccessful stint as a teacher, Mussolini became a socialist and gradually became well known in Italian socialist circles. In 1912, he obtained the important position of editor of *Avanti* (*Forward*), the official socialist daily newspaper. After editorially switching his position from ardent neutrality, the socialist position, to intervention in World War I, he was expelled from the socialist party.

In 1919, Mussolini laid the foundations for a new political movement that came to be called fascism after the name of his group, the *Fascio di Combattimento*. Mussolini's small group received little attention and were themselves unclear about their beliefs. In elections held in November 1919, the Fascists won no delegates, and Mussolini reflected bitterly that fascism had "come to a dead end." But political stalemate in Italy's parliamentary system and strong nationalist sentiment saved Mussolini and the Fascists.

The new parliament elected in November quickly proved to be incapable of governing Italy. Three major parties, the socialists, liberals, and popolari (or Christian Democrats, a new Catholic party formed in January 1919), and numerous small ones were unable to form an effective governmental coalition. The socialists, who had now become the largest party, spoke theoretically of the need for revolution, which alarmed conservatives who quickly associated them with bolsheviks or communists. Thousands of industrial and agricultural strikes in 1919 and 1920 created a climate of class warfare and continual violence. Mussolini realized the advantages of capitalizing on the fear created by these conditions and shifted quickly from leftist to rightist politics. The rewards were immediate as Mussolini's Fascist movement began to gain support from middle-class industrialists fearful of working-class agitation and large landowners

who objected to the agricultural strikes. Mussolini also perceived that Italians were angry over the failure of Italy to receive more fruits of victory in the form of territorial acquisitions after World War I. Mussolini realized then that anticommunism, antistrike activity, and nationalist rhetoric combined with the use of brute force might help him obtain what he had been unable to achieve in free elections.

In 1920 and 1921, bands of armed Fascists called *squadristi* were formed and turned loose in attacks on socialist offices and newspapers. Strikes by trade unionists and socialist workers and peasant leagues were broken up by force. At the same time, Mussolini entered into a political alliance with the liberals under then Prime Minister Giovanni Giolitti. No doubt, Giolitti and the liberals believed that the Fascists could be used to crush socialism temporarily and then be dropped. In this game of mutual deceit, Mussolini soon proved to be the more skillful player. By allying with the government coalition, he gained respectability and a free hand for his *squadristi* violence. Mussolini's efforts were rewarded with success when the Fascists won thirty-five parliamentary seats, or 7 percent of the total, in the election of May 1921. Mussolini's Fascist movement had gained a new lease on life.

Crucial to Mussolini's plans was the use of violence. By 1921, the black-shirted Fascist squads numbered 200,000 and had become a regular feature of Italian life. World War I veterans and students were especially attracted to the *squadristi* and relished the opportunity to use unrestrained violence. Administering large doses of castor oil to unwilling victims became one of their favorite tactics.

Mussolini and the Fascists believed that these terrorist tactics would eventually achieve political victory. They deliberately created conditions of disorder knowing that fascism would flourish in such an environment. Fascists construed themselves as the party of order and drew the bulk of their support from the middle and upper classes; white-collar workers, professionals and civil servants, landowners, merchants and artisans, and students made up almost 60 percent of the membership of the Fascist party. The middle-class fear of socialism, communist revolution, and disorder made the Fascists attractive.

With the further deterioration of the Italian political situation, Mussolini and the Fascists were emboldened to plan a march on Rome in order to seize power. In a speech in Naples to Fascist blackshirts, Mussolini exclaimed on October 24, 1922: ". . . either we are allowed to govern, or we will seize power by marching on Rome" to "take by the throat the miserable political

The Voice of Italian Fascism
▼ ▼ ▼

Mussolini at first seemed uncertain about how to react to the storm of criticism provoked by the Matteotti murder. Finally, he seized the initiative and in a defiant speech to parliament on January 3, 1925, made clear his intentions to "make the nation fascist."

Mussolini: Speech of January 3, 1925

But, Gentlemen [members of parliament], what butterflies are we chasing?. . . Very well, then. I declare here before this assembly and before the Italian people that I alone take the political, moral, and historical responsibility for all that has happened. . . . If Fascism means nothing but castor oil and the cudgel and not a superb passion of the best Italian youth, it is my fault! If Fascism is a criminal association, if all acts of violence are the result of a given historical, political, and moral climate, mine is the responsibility for it, because it was I who created this historical, political, and moral climate with a propaganda which lasted from the intervention to this day. . . .

It is clear that the Aventine secession [those deputies who withdrew from parliament to protest Matteotti's murder] has had profound repercussions throughout the country. Well, then a moment comes when we must say: Enough! When two irreducible elements clash, the solution is force. There has never been another solution in history and never will be.

Now I dare say the problem will be solved. Fascism, as a Government and Party, is at top efficiency. Gentlemen, you have been laboring under an illusion! You thought Fascism was through because I held it down, that the Party was dead because I chastened it and I was cruel enough to say so. But it will not be necessary [to unleash the Fascists] . . . because the Government is strong enough to break the Aventine secession completely and finally.

Italy wants peace, tranquillity, calm in which to work; we will give it to her, by means of love if possible, by force if necessary. Rest assured that within the next 48 hours the entire situation will be clarified. Everyone must realize that what I am planning to do is not one man's whim, it is not a lust for power, it is not ignoble passion, but solely the expression of a boundless and mighty love of Country. [Loud, prolonged, and repeated applause—cries of Viva Mussolini!]

---

class that governs us."[2] Bold words, but in truth the planned march on Rome was really a calculated bluff to frighten the government into giving them power. The bluff worked, and the government capitulated even before the march occurred. On October 29, 1922, King Victor Emmanuel III (1900–1946) made Mussolini prime minister of Italy. Twenty-four hours later, the Fascist blackshirts were allowed to march into Rome in order to create the "myth" that they had gained power by an armed insurrection after a civil war.

MUSSOLINI AND THE ITALIAN FASCIST STATE Since the Fascists constituted but a small minority in parliament, the new prime minister was forced to move slowly. Mussolini also had to balance two conflicting interests. The rural Fascists were eager to assume complete power, but the traditional institutions, such as the industrialists, the landowners, the Catholic church, and the military, wanted a period of domestic tranquillity. In the summer of 1923, Mussolini began to prepare for a national election that would consolidate the power of his Fascist government and give him a more secure base from which to govern. In July 1923, parliament enacted the Acerbo Law, which stipulated that any party winning at least 25 percent of the votes in the next national election would automatically be allotted two-thirds of the seats in parliament. The national elections that were subsequently held on April 6, 1924, constituted an enormous victory for the Fascists. They won 65 percent of the votes and garnered 374 seats out of a total of 535 in parliament. Although the elections were conducted in an atmosphere of Fascist fraud, force, and intimidation, the size of the victory indicated the growing popularity of Mussolini and his Fascists.

With this victory, Mussolini moved faster to consolidate his power. A campaign of intimidation of opposition deputies reached its high point with the assassination of the socialist deputy Giacomo Matteotti in June of 1924. Mussolini was severely challenged for his assumed complicity in the murder of Matteotti. The public outcry even caused numerous Italian political leaders to predict in December 1924 that Mussolini would have to resign.

▼ **Mussolini and Hitler.** By 1926, Mussolini and the Italian Fascists had created the institutional framework for the first fascist state in Europe. By the 1930s, Fascist Italy was being increasingly overshadowed by yet another fascist state, Nazi Germany. Benito Mussolini met Adolf Hitler, creator of Germany's fascist dictatorship, at Venice in June 1914.

At the beginning of 1925, yielding to the demands of extremists within his own Fascist party for decisive action and a "second wave" of Fascist change, Mussolini counterattacked. To save himself, Mussolini now pushed to establish a full dictatorship. This may have been Mussolini's ultimate intention anyway, but the Matteotti crisis forced him to make his move at this time. In a speech to parliament on January 3, Mussolini accepted responsibility for all Fascist violence and vowed to establish a new tranquillity (see the box on p. 943).

By 1926, Mussolini had established the institutional framework for his Fascist dictatorship. Press laws gave the government the right to suspend any publications that fostered disrespect for the Catholic church, monarchy, or the state. The prime minister was made "Head of Government" with the power to legislate by decree. A police law empowered the police to arrest and confine anybody for both nonpolitical and political crimes without due process of the law. The government was given the power to dissolve political and cultural associations. In 1926, all antifascist parties were outlawed. A secret police, known as the OVRA, was also established. By the end of 1926, Mussolini ruled Italy as *Il Duce*, the leader.

Mussolini conceived of the Fascist state as totalitarian: "Fascism is totalitarian, and the Fascist State, the synthesis and unity of all values, interprets, develops and gives strength to the whole life of the people."[3] Mussolini did try to create a totalitarian apparatus for police surveillance and for controlling mass communications, but this machinery was not all that effective. Police activities in Italy were never as repressive, efficient, or savage as those of Nazi Germany. Likewise, the Italian Fascists' attempt to exercise control over all forms of mass media, including newspapers, radio, and cinema, in order to use propaganda as an instrument to integrate the masses into the state failed to achieve its major goals. Most commonly, Fascist propaganda was disseminated through simple slogans, such as "Mussolini is always right," plastered on walls all over Italy.

Mussolini and the Fascists also attempted to mold Italians into a single-minded community by pursuing a Fascist educational policy and developing Fascist organizations. In 1939, Giuseppe Bottai, minister of education, proposed a new School Charter whose basic aim was "the will to substitute, both in principle and practice, for the bourgeois schools a people's school, which will really be for everyone and which will really meet the needs of everyone, that is the needs of the State."[4] Bottai hoped to make the educational system an instrument to create the "new Fascist man," but his reforms were never implemented, primarily because the middle class resisted any alterations in the traditional paths of upward mobility.

Since the secondary schools maintained considerable freedom from Fascist control, the regime relied more and more on the activities of Fascist youth organizations known as the Young Fascists to indoctrinate the young people of the nation in Fascist ideals. By 1939, about 6,800,000 children, teenagers, and young adults of both sexes, or 66 percent of the population between eight and eighteen, were enrolled in some kind of Fascist youth group. Activities for these groups included unpopular Saturday afternoon marching drills and calisthenics, seaside and mountain summer camps, and youth contests. An underlying motif for all of these activities was the

Fascist insistence on militarization. Beginning in the 1930s, all male groups were given some kind of premilitary exercises to develop discipline and provide training for war. Results were mixed. Italian teenagers, who liked neither military training nor routine discipline of any kind, simply refused to attend Fascist youth meetings on a regular basis.

The Fascist organizations hoped to create a new Italian, who would be hard-working, physically fit, disciplined, intellectually sharp, and martially inclined; this ideal was symbolized by the phrase, "book and musket—the perfect Fascist." In practice, the Fascists largely reinforced traditional social attitudes in Italy, as is evident in their policies regarding women. The Fascists portrayed the family as the pillar of the state and women as the basic foundation of the family. "Woman into the home" became the Fascist slogan. Women were to be homemakers and baby producers, "their natural and fundamental mission in life," according to Mussolini, for population growth was viewed as an indicator of national strength. To Mussolini, female emancipation was "unfascist." Employment outside the home was an impediment distracting women from conception. "It forms an independence and consequent physical and moral habits contrary to child bearing."[5] A practical consideration also underlay the Fascist attitude toward women. Working women would compete with males for jobs in the depression economy of the 1930s. Eliminating women from the market reduced male unemployment figures.

The Fascists translated their attitude toward women into law by a series of enactments in the 1930s that aimed at encouraging larger families by offering supplementary pay, loans, prizes, and subsidies for families with many offspring. Gold medals were given to mothers of many children. A national holiday of "the Mother and the Child" was held on December 24, at which prizes for fertility were awarded. Also in the 1930s decrees were passed that set quotas on the employment of women, but they were not overly successful in accomplishing their goal.

Despite the instruments of repression, the use of propaganda, and the creation of numerous Fascist organizations, Mussolini never really achieved the degree of totalitarian control accomplished in Hitler's Germany or Stalin's Soviet Union. Mussolini and the Fascist party never really destroyed the old power structure. Some institutions, including the armed forces and monarchy, were never absorbed into the Fascist state and mostly managed to maintain their independence. Mussolini had boasted that he would help workers and peasants, but instead he generally allied himself with the interests of the industrialists and large landowners at the expense of the lower classes.

Even more indicative of Mussolini's compromise with the traditional institutions of Italy was his attempt to gain the support of the Catholic church. In the Lateran Accords of February 1929, Mussolini's regime recognized the sovereign independence of a small enclave of 109 acres within Rome, known as Vatican City, which had remained in the church's possession since unification in 1870; in return, the papacy recognized the Italian state. The Lateran Accords also guaranteed the church a large grant of money and recognized Catholicism as the "sole religion of the state." In return, the Catholic church urged Italians to support the Fascist regime.

In all areas of Italian life under Mussolini and the Fascists, there was a noticeable dichotomy between Fascist ideals and practice. The Italian Fascists promised much but actually delivered considerably less, and they were soon overshadowed by a much more powerful fascist movement to the north.

Hitler and Nazi Germany

In 1923, a small, south German rightist party, known as the Nazis, led by an obscure Austrian rabble-rouser named Adolf Hitler, created a stir with the Beer Hall Putsch, an attempt to seize power in southern Germany in conscious imitation of Mussolini's march on Rome in 1922. Although it failed, the putsch projected Adolf Hitler and the Nazis into national prominence. Within ten years, Hitler and the Nazis had taken over complete power.

WEIMAR GERMANY AND THE RISE OF THE NAZIS   After the Imperial Germany of William II had come to an end with Germany's defeat in World War I, a German democratic state known as the Weimar Republic had been established. From its beginnings, the Weimar Republic was plagued by a series of problems. The Republic had no truly outstanding political leaders. Even its more able leaders, such as Friedrich Ebert, who served as president, and Gustav Stresemann, the foreign minister and chancellor, died in the 1920s. When Ebert died in 1925, Paul von Hindenburg, the World War I military hero, was elected president. Hindenburg was a traditional military man, monarchist in sentiment, who at heart was not in favor of the Republic. The young Republic also suffered politically from attempted uprisings and attacks from both the left and right.

Another of the Republic's problems was its inability to change the basic structure of Germany. The government never really controlled the army, which operated as a state within a state. This independence was true of other institutions as well. Hostile judges, teachers, and bureaucrats remained in office and used their positions to undermine democracy from within. At the same time, important groups of landed aristocrats and leaders of powerful business cartels refused to accept the overthrow of the imperial regime and remained hostile to the Weimar Republic.

The Weimar Republic also faced serious economic difficulties. Germany experienced runaway inflation in 1922 and 1923 with serious social effects. Widows, orphans, the retired elderly, army officers, teachers, civil servants, and others who lived on fixed incomes all watched their monthly stipends become worthless or their lifetime savings disappear. Their economic losses increasingly pushed the middle class to the rightist parties that were hostile to the Republic. To make matters worse, after a period of prosperity from 1924 to 1929, Germany faced the Great Depression. Unemployment increased to 3 million in March 1930 and 4.38 million by December of the same year. The depression paved the way for social discontent, fear, and extremist parties. The political, economic, and social problems of the Weimar Republic provided an environment in which Adolf Hitler and the Nazis were able to rise to power.

Born on April 20, 1889, Adolf Hitler was the son of an Austrian customs official. He was a total failure in secondary school and eventually made his way to Vienna to become an artist. Rejected by the Vienna Academy of Fine Arts and supported by an inheritance and orphan's pension, Hitler stayed on in Vienna to live the bohemian lifestyle of an artist. In his autobiography, *Mein Kampf,* Hitler characterized his years in Vienna from 1908 to 1913 as an important formative period in his life: "In this period there took shape within me a world picture and a philosophy which became the granite foundation of all my acts. In addition to what I then created, I have had to learn little, and I have had to alter nothing."[6]

Hitler experienced four major influences in Vienna. Georg von Schönerer, the leader of the Austrian Pan-German movement, was an extreme German nationalist who urged the union of all Germans in one national state. Karl Lueger was mayor of Vienna and leader of the anti-Semitic Christian Social party. Hitler called him "the greatest German mayor of all time" and especially admired his demagogic methods and leadership of a mass party that was formed with the aid of

emotional slogans. Much of Hitler's early anti-Semitism was imbibed from an ex-Catholic monk named Adolf Lanz who called himself Lanz von Liebenfels. Hitler was an avid reader of *Ostara,* a periodical published by Liebenfels in which he propagated his racial beliefs that the German Aryans were exalted beings destined to rule the earth. Liebenfels characterized the Jews and other allegedly inferior races as "animal-men" who must someday be eliminated by sterilization, deportation, forced labor, and even "direct liquidation." Finally, Hitler was also strongly influenced by Richard Wagner's operas, which he attended frequently in Vienna. Hitler absorbed Wagner's ideal of the true artist as a social outcast from the bourgeois world who is subject to his own rhythms. Wagner's music also spoke of a boundless will to power and a need to dominate.

In Vienna, then, Hitler established the basic ideas of an ideology from which he never deviated for the rest of his life. At the core of Hitler's ideas was racism, especially anti-Semitism (see the box on p. 947). His hatred of the Jews lasted to the very end of his life. Hitler had also become an extreme German nationalist who had learned from the mass politics of Vienna how political parties could effectively use propaganda and terror. Finally, in his Viennese years, Hitler also came to a firm belief in the need for struggle, which he saw as the "granite foundation of the world." Hitler emphasized a crude Social Darwinism (see Chapter 23); the world was a brutal place filled with constant struggle in which only the fit survived.

In 1913, Hitler moved to Munich, still without purpose and with no real future in sight. World War I saved him: "Overpowered by stormy enthusiasm, I fell down on my knees and thanked Heaven from an overflowing heart for granting me the good fortune of being permitted to live at this time."[7] As a dispatch runner on the Western Front, Hitler distinguished himself by his brave acts. At the end of the war, finding again that his life had no purpose or meaning, he returned to Munich and decided to enter politics and found, at last, his true profession.

As a Munich politician from 1919 to 1923, Hitler accomplished a great deal. He joined the obscure German Worker's Party, one of a number of right-wing extreme nationalist parties in Munich. By the summer of 1921, Hitler had assumed total control over the party, which he renamed the National Socialist German Workers' Party (NSDAP), or Nazi for short. His idea was that the party's name would distinguish the Nazis from the socialist parties while gaining support from both working-class and nationalist circles. Hitler worked as-

Adolf Hitler's Hatred of the Jews
▼ ▼ ▼

A believer in Aryan racial supremacy, Adolf Hitler viewed the Jews as the archenemies of the Aryans. Hitler believed that the first task of a true Aryan state would be the elimination of the Jewish threat. This is why Hitler's political career both began and ended with a warning against the Jews. In this excerpt from his autobiography, Mein Kampf, *Hitler describes how he came to be an anti-Semite when he lived in Vienna in his early twenties.*

Adolf Hitler, *Mein Kampf*

My views with regard to anti-Semitism thus succumbed to the passage of time, and this was my greatest transformation of all. . . .

Once, as I was strolling through the Inner City [of Vienna], I suddenly encountered an apparition in a black caftan and black hair locks. Is this a Jew? was my first thought.

For, to be sure, they had not looked like that in Linz. I observed the man furtively and cautiously, but the longer I stared at this foreign face, scrutinizing feature for feature, the more my first question assumed a new form:

Is this a German?

As always in such cases, I now began to try to relieve my doubts by books. For a few pennies I bought the first anti-Semitic pamphlets of my life. . . .

Yet I could no longer very well doubt that the objects of my study were not Germans of a special religion, but a people in themselves; for since I had begun to concern myself with this question and to take cognizance of the Jews, Vienna appeared to me in a different light than before. Wherever I went, I began to see Jews, and the more I saw, the more sharply they became distinguished in my eyes from the rest of humanity. . . .

In a short time I was made more thoughtful than ever by my slowly rising insight into the type of activity carried on by the Jews in certain fields.

Was there any form of filth or profligacy, particularly in cultural life, without at least one Jew involved in it? . . .

Sometimes I stood there thunderstruck.

I didn't know what to be more amazed at: the agility of their tongues or their virtuosity at lying.

Gradually I began to hate them.

---

siduously to develop the party into a mass political movement with flags, party badges, uniforms, its own newspaper, and its own police force or party militia known as the SA, the *Sturmabteilung,* or Storm Troops. The SA was used to defend the party in meeting halls and to break up the meetings of other parties. It added an element of force and terror to the growing Nazi movement. Hitler's own oratorical skills were largely responsible for attracting an increasing number of followers. By 1923, the party had grown from its early hundreds into a membership of 55,000 with 15,000 SA members.

In its early years, the Nazi party had been only one of many radical right-wing political groups in southern Germany. By 1923, it had become the strongest. When it appeared that the Weimar Republic was on the verge of collapse in the fall of 1923, the Nazis and other right-wing leaders in the south German state of Bavaria decided to march on Berlin to overthrow the Weimar government. When his fellow conspirators reneged, Hitler and the Nazis decided to act on their own by staging an armed uprising in Munich on November 8. The so-called Beer Hall Putsch was quickly crushed. Hitler was arrested, put on trial for treason, and sentenced to prison for five years, a lenient sentence indeed from sympathetic right-wing judges.

THE NAZI SEIZURE OF POWER   The Beer Hall Putsch and Hitler's imprisonment proved to be a major turning point in his career. He now saw clearly the need for a change in tactics. The Nazis could not come to power by overthrowing the Weimar Republic, but would have to use constitutional means to gain power. This implied the formation of a mass political party that would actively compete for votes with the other political parties. Rather than discouraging him, Hitler's trial and imprisonment reinforced his faith in himself and in his mission.

Hitler occupied himself in prison with the writing of *Mein Kampf* (*My Struggle*), an autobiographical account of his movement and its underlying ideology. Extreme

German nationalism, virulent anti-Semitism, and vicious anti-communism are linked together by a Social Darwinian theory of struggle that stresses the right of superior nations to *Lebensraum* (living space) through expansion and the right of superior individuals to secure authoritarian leadership over the masses. The only originality in *Mein Kampf*, as historians have pointed out, is in Hitler's analysis of mass propaganda, mass psychology, and the mass organization of peoples. What is perhaps most remarkable about *Mein Kampf* is its elaboration of a series of ideas that directed Hitler's actions once he took power. That others refused to take Hitler and his ideas seriously was one of his greatest advantages.

When Hitler was released, the Nazi party was in shambles, and he set about to reestablish his sole control over the party and organize it for the lawful takeover of power. Hitler's position on leadership in the party was quite clear. There was to be no discussion of ideas in the party, and the party was to follow the *Führerprinzip*, the leadership principle, which entailed nothing less than a single-minded party under one leader. As Hitler expressed it: "A good National Socialist is one who would let himself be killed for his Führer at any time."[8]

The late 1920s were a period of building and waiting. These were years of relative prosperity for Germany, and, as Hitler perceived, they were not conducive to the growth of extremist parties. He declared, however, that the prosperity would not last and that his time would come. In the meantime, Hitler worked to establish a highly structured party that could compete in elections and attract new recruits when another time of troubles arose. He reorganized the Nazi party on a regional basis and expanded it to all parts of Germany. By 1929, the Nazi party had a national party organization. It also grew from 27,000 members in 1925 to 178,000 by the end of 1929. Especially noticeable was the youthfulness of the regional, district, and branch leaders of the Nazi organization. Many were between the ages of twenty-five and thirty and were fiercely committed to Hitler because he gave them the kind of active politics they sought. Rather than democratic debate, they wanted brawls in beer halls, enthusiastic speeches, and comradeship in the building of a new Germany. One new, young Nazi member expressed his excitement about the party:

> For me this was the start of a completely new life. There was only one thing in the world for me and that was service in the movement. All my thoughts were centred on the movement. I could talk only politics. I was no longer aware of anything else. At the time I was a promising athlete; I was very keen on sport, and it was going to be my career. But I had to give this up too. My only interest was agitation and propaganda.[9]

Such youthful enthusiasm gave the Nazi movement an aura of a "young man's movement" and a sense of dynamism that the other parties could not match. In 1931, almost 40 percent of Nazi party members were under thirty.

By 1929, the Nazi party had also made a significant shift in strategy. Between 1925 and 1927, Hitler and the Nazis had pursued an urban strategy geared toward winning workers from the Socialists and Communists. But failure in the 1928 elections, when the Nazis gained only 2.6 percent of the vote and twelve seats in the Reichstag or German parliament, convinced Hitler of the need for a change. By 1929, the party began to pursue middle-class and lower-middle-class votes in small towns and rural areas, especially in northern, central, and eastern Germany. By the end of 1929, the Nazis had successfully made their shift to the new strategy. The end of 1929 was the beginning of the depression and the beginning of Hitler's real success.

Germany's economic difficulties made possible the Nazi rise to power. Unemployment rose dramatically, from 4.35 million in 1931 to 6 million by the winter of 1932. The economic and psychological impact of the Great Depression made the extremist parties more attractive. Already in the Reichstag elections of September 1930, the Nazis polled 18 percent of the vote and gained 107 seats in the Reichstag, making the Nazi party one of the largest parties.

By 1930, Chancellor Heinrich Brüning (1885–1970) had found it impossible to form a working parliamentary majority in the Reichstag and relied on the use of emergency decrees by President Hindenburg to rule. In a real sense, then, parliamentary democracy was already dying in 1930, three years before Hitler destroyed it.

Hitler's quest for power from late 1930 to early 1933 depended on the political maneuvering around President Hindenburg. Nevertheless, the elections from 1930 through 1932 were indirectly responsible for the Nazi rise to power since they showed the importance of the Nazi party. The party itself grew dramatically during this period, from 289,000 members in September 1930 to 800,000 by 1932. The SA also rose to 500,000 members.

The Nazis proved very effective in developing modern electioneering techniques. They crossed Germany in whirlwind campaigns by car, train, and airplane. His "Hitler Over Germany" campaign by airplane saw Hitler speaking in fifty cities in fifteen days. The Nazis were successful in presenting two fundamentally different approaches to the German voters. In their election campaigns, party members pitched their themes to the needs and fears of different social groups. In working-class districts, for example, the Nazis attacked international high finance, while in middle-class neighborhoods, they exploited fears of a Communist revolution and its threat to private property. At the same time that the Nazis made blatant appeals to class interests, they were denouncing conflicts of interest and maintaining that they stood above classes and parties. Hitler, in particular, claimed to stand above all differences and promised to create a new Germany free of class differences and party infighting. His appeal to national pride, national honor, and traditional militarism struck chords of emotion in his listeners.

Elections, however, proved to have their limits. In the elections of July 1932, the Nazis won 230 seats, making them the largest party in the Reichstag. But four months later, in November, they declined to 196 seats. It became apparent to many Nazis that they would not gain power simply by the ballot box. Hitler saw clearly, however, that the Reichstag after 1930 was not all that important, since the government ruled by decree with the support of President Hindenburg. Increasingly, the right-wing elites of Germany, the industrial magnates, landed aristocrats, military establishment, and higher bureaucrats, came to see Hitler as the man who had the mass support to establish a right-wing, authoritarian regime that would save Germany and their privileged positions from a Communist takeover. Under pressure, President Hindenburg agreed to allow Hitler to become chancellor (on January 30, 1933) and create a new government, but with supposed safeguards. There would be only three Nazis in the cabinet and Franz von Papen (1878–1969), who had served as chancellor and done so

much to win over Hindenburg to the arrangements, would serve as vice-chancellor. To those who reproached von Papen for giving power to Hitler, he responded: "What do you want? I have Hindenburg's trust. Within two months, we will have pushed Hitler so far into a corner that he will squeak."[10]

Within those two months, Hitler basically laid the foundations for the Nazis' complete control over Germany. One of Hitler's important cohorts, Hermann Göring (1893–1946), had been made minister of the interior and hence head of the police of the Prussian state, the largest of the federal states in Germany. He used his power to purge the police of non-Nazis and to establish an auxiliary police force composed of SA members. This action legitimized Nazi terror. On the day after a fire broke out in the Reichstag building (February 27), supposedly set by the Communists, Hitler was also able to convince President Hindenburg to issue a decree that gave the government emergency powers. It suspended all basic rights of citizens for the full duration of the emergency, thus enabling the Nazis to arrest and imprison anyone without redress. Although Hitler promised to return to the "normal order of things" when the Communist danger was past, in reality this decree provided the legal basis for the creation of a police state.

The crowning step of Hitler's "legal seizure" of power came after the Nazis had gained 288 Reichstag seats in the elections of March 5, 1933. Since they still did not possess an absolute majority, on March 23 the Nazis sought the passage of an Enabling Act, which would empower the government to dispense with constitutional forms for four years while it issued laws that would deal with the country's problems. Since it was to be an

▼ **Hitler and the Blood Flag Ritual.** In the development of his mass political movement, Adolf Hitler used ritualistic ceremonies as a means of binding party members to his own person. Hitler is shown here touching the "blood flag," which had supposedly been stained with the blood of Nazis killed during the Beer Hall Putsch, to a SS banner while the SS standard-bearer made a "blood oath" of allegiance: "I vow to remain true to my Führer, Adolf Hitler. I bind myself to carry out all orders conscientiously and without reluctance. Standards and flags shall be sacred to me."

amendment to the Weimar constitution, the Nazis needed and obtained a two-thirds vote to pass it. Only the Social Democrats had the courage to oppose Hitler. The Enabling Act provided the legal basis for Hitler's subsequent acts. He no longer needed either the Reichstag or President Hindenburg. In effect, Hitler became a dictator appointed by the parliamentary body itself.

With their new source of power, the Nazis acted quickly to enforce *Gleichschaltung,* or the coordination of all institutions under Nazi control. The civil service was purged of Jews and democratic elements, concentration camps were established for opponents of the new regime, the autonomy of the federal states was eliminated, trade unions were dissolved and swallowed up by a gigantic Labor Front, and all political parties except the Nazis were abolished. By the end of the summer of 1933, within seven months of being appointed chancellor, Hitler and the Nazis had established the foundations for a totalitarian state.

Why had this seizure of power been so quick and easy? The Nazis were not only ruthless in their use of force, but had also been ready to seize power. The depression had weakened what little faith the Germans had in their democratic state. But negative factors alone cannot explain the Nazi success. To many Germans, the Nazis offered a national awakening. "Germany Awake," one of the many Nazi slogans, had a powerful appeal to a people psychologically crushed by their defeat in World War I. The Nazis presented a strong image of a dynamic new Germany that was above parties and above classes.

By the end of 1933, there were only two sources of potential danger to Hitler's authority: the armed forces and the SA within his own party. The SA spoke of the need for a "second revolution" and the replacement of the regular army by the SA. Neither the army nor Hitler favored such a possibility. Hitler solved both problems simultaneously on June 30, 1934, by a purge of the SA leadership in return for the support of the army in allowing Hitler to succeed Hindenburg when the president died. When Hindenburg died on August 2, 1934, the office of Reich president was abolished, and Hitler became sole ruler of Germany. Public officials and soldiers were all required to take a personal oath of loyalty to Hitler as the "Führer of the German Reich and people." On August 19, 1934, Hitler held a plebiscite in which 85 percent of the German people indicated their approval of the new order. The Third Reich had begun.

THE NAZI STATE, 1933–1939   Having smashed the parliamentary state, Hitler now felt the real task was at hand: to develop the "total state." Hitler's aims had not been simply power for power's sake or a tyranny based on personal power. Hitler had larger ideological goals. The development of an Aryan racial state that would dominate Europe and possibly the world for generations to come required a massive movement in which the German people would be actively involved, not passively cowed by force. Hitler stated:

> We must develop organizations in which an individual's entire life can take place. Then every activity and every need of every individual will be regulated by the collectivity represented by the party. There is no longer any arbitrary will, there are no longer any free realms in which the individual belongs to himself. . . . The time of personal happiness is over.[11]

▼ **The Nazi Mass Spectacle.** Hitler and the Nazis made a clever use of mass spectacles to rally the German people behind the Nazi regime. These mass demonstrations evoked intense enthusiasm, as is evident at the Bückeberg near Hamelin when Hitler arrived for the Harvest Festival in 1937. Almost one million people were present for the celebration.

Propaganda and Mass Meetings in Nazi Germany
▼ ▼ ▼

Propaganda and mass rallies were two of the chief instruments that Hitler used to prepare the German people for the tasks he set before them. In the first selection, taken from Mein Kampf, Hitler explains the psychological importance of mass meetings in creating support for a political movement. In the second excerpt, taken from his speech to a crowd at Nuremberg, he describes the kind of mystical bond he hoped to create through his mass rallies.

Adolf Hitler, Mein Kampf

The mass meeting is also necessary for the reason that in it the individual, who at first, while becoming a supporter of a young movement, feels lonely and easily succumbs to the fear of being alone, for the first time gets the picture of a larger community, which in most people has a strengthening, encouraging effect. . . . When from his little workshop or big factory, in which he feels very small, he steps for the first time into a mass meeting and has thousands and thousands of people of the same opinions around him, when, as a seeker, he is swept away by three or four thousand others into the mighty effect of suggestive intoxication and enthusiasm, when the visible success and agreement of thousands confirm to him the rightness of the new doctrine and for the first time arouse doubt in the truth of his previous conviction—then he himself has succumbed to the magic influence of what we designate as "mass suggestion." The will, the longing, and also the power of thousands are accumulated in every individual. The man who enters such a meeting doubting and wavering leaves it inwardly reinforced: he has become a link in the community.

Adolf Hitler, Speech at the Nuremberg Party Rally, 1936

Do we not feel once again in this hour the miracle that brought us together? Once you heard the voice of a man, and it struck deep into your hearts; it awakened you, and you followed this voice. Year after year you went after it, though him who had spoken you never even saw. You heard only a voice, and you followed it. When we meet each other here, the wonder of our coming together fills us all. Not everyone of you sees me, and I do not see everyone of you. But I feel you, and you feel me. It is the belief in our people that has made us small men great, that has made us poor men rich, that has made brave and courageous men out of us wavering, spiritless, timid folk; this belief made us see our road when we were astray; it joined us together into one whole! . . . You come, that . . . you may, once in a while, gain the feeling that now we are together; we are with him and he with us, and we are now Germany!

The Nazis pursued the creation of this totalitarian state in a variety of ways.

Mass demonstrations and spectacles were employed to integrate the German nation into a collective fellowship and to mobilize it as an instrument for Hitler's policies (see the box above). These mass demonstrations, especially the Nuremberg party rallies that were held every September and the Harvest Festivals celebrated at the Bückeberg near Hamelin every fall, combined the symbolism of a religious service with the merriment of a popular amusement. They had great appeal and usually evoked mass enthusiasm and excitement. Even foreigners were frequently affected by the passions aroused by these mass demonstrations.

The state apparatus of Hitler's "total state" offers some confusing features. One usually thinks of Nazi Germany as having an all-powerful government that maintained absolute control and order. In truth, Nazi Germany was the scene of almost constant personal and institutional conflict, which resulted in administrative chaos. In matters such as foreign policy, education, and economics, parallel government and party bureaucracies competed with each other over spheres of influence. Incessant struggle characterized relationships within the party, within the state, and between party and state. Why this "authoritarian anarchy," as one observer called it, existed is a source of much controversy. One group of historians has assumed that Hitler's aversion to making decisions resulted in the chaos that subverted his own authority and made him a "weak dictator." Another group believes that Hitler's style of leadership created his regime's administrative chaos, but maintains that Hitler deliberately created this institutional confusion. By fostering rivalry within the party and between party and state, he would be the final decision maker and absolute ruler.

In the economic sphere, Hitler and the Nazis also established control, but industry was not nationalized as the left wing of the Nazi party wanted. Hitler felt that it was irrelevant who owned the means of production so long as the owners recognized their master. Although the regime pursued the use of public works projects and "pump-priming" grants to private construction firms to foster employment and end the depression, there is little doubt that rearmament was a far more important contributor to solving the unemployment problem. Unemployment, which had stood at 6 million in 1932, dropped to 2.6 million in 1934 and less than 500,000 in 1937. The regime claimed full credit for solving Germany's economic woes, and this was an important factor in leading many Germans to accept the new regime, despite its excesses.

The German Labor Front under Robert Ley regulated the world of labor. The Labor Front was a single, state-controlled union. To control all laborers, it used the workbook. Every salaried worker had to have one in order to hold a job. Only by submitting to the policies of the Nazi-controlled Labor Front could a worker obtain and retain a workbook. The Labor Front also sponsored activities to keep the workers happy (see Mass Leisure later in the chapter).

For those who needed coercion, the Nazi total state had its instruments of terror and repression. Until 1934, the SA had been most visible in terrorizing the people, but after the June 30 purge, the SS took over that function in a much more systematic fashion. Originally created as Hitler's personal bodyguard, the SS, under the direction of Heinrich Himmler (1900–1945), came to control all of the regular and secret police forces. Himmler and the SS functioned on the basis of two principles: terror and ideology. Terror included the instruments of repression and murder: the secret police, criminal police, concentration camps, and later the execution squads and death camps for the extermination of the Jews (see Chapter 28). For Himmler, the SS was a crusading order whose primary goal was to further the Aryan master race. SS members, who constituted a carefully chosen elite, were thoroughly indoctrinated in racial ideology.

Other institutions, such as the Catholic and Protestant churches, primary and secondary schools, and universities, were also brought under the control of the Nazi totalitarian state. Nazi professional organizations and leagues were formed for civil servants, teachers, women, farmers, doctors, and lawyers. These groups were inspired by a sound principle perverted to other ends. Common flags, uniforms, meetings, and indoctrination gave a sense of identity to individuals, a sense of belonging and human warmth, but one that was cultivated to produce inhuman brutality.

Since the early indoctrination of the nation's youth would create the foundation for a strong totalitarian state for the future, youth organizations, the *Hitler Jugend* (Hitler Youth) and its female counterpart, the *Bund deutscher Mädel* (League of German Maidens), were given special attention. The oath required of Hitler Youth members demonstrates the degree of dedication expected of youth in the Nazi state: "In the presence of

▼ Anti-Semitism in Nazi Germany.
At the core of Hitler's ideology was an intense anti-Semitism. Soon after their seizure of power, Hitler and the Nazis began to translate their anti-Semitic ideas into anti-Semitic policies. This photograph shows one example of Nazi action against the Jews. Two women clean up some of the debris the morning after *Kristallnacht,* the night of shattered glass.

this blood banner, which represents our Führer, I swear to devote all my energies and my strength to the savior of our country, Adolf Hitler. I am willing and ready to give up my life for him, so help me God."

The Nazi total state was intended to be an Aryan racial state. From its beginning, the Nazi party reflected the strong anti-Semitic beliefs of Adolf Hitler. Once in power, it did not take long for the Nazis to translate anti-Semitic ideas into anti-Semitic policies. Already on April 1, 1933, the new Nazi government initiated a two-day boycott of Jewish businesses. A series of laws soon followed that excluded "non-Aryans" (defined as anyone "descended from non-Aryans, especially Jewish parents or grandparents") from the legal professions, civil service, judgeships, the medical profession, teaching positions, cultural and entertainment enterprises, and the press.

In 1935, the Nazis unleashed another stage of anti-Jewish activity when new racial laws were announced in September at the annual party rally in Nuremberg. These "Nuremberg laws" excluded German Jews from German citizenship and forbade marriages and extramarital relations between Jews and German citizens. The "Nuremberg laws" essentially separated Jews from the Germans politically, socially, and legally and were the natural extension of Hitler's stress upon the creation of a pure Aryan race.

Another, considerably more violent phase of anti-Jewish activity took place in 1938 and 1939, initiated on November 9–10, 1938, the infamous *Kristallnacht,* or night of shattered glass. The assassination of a third secretary in the German embassy in Paris became the occasion for a Nazi-led destructive rampage against the Jews in which synagogues were burned, 7,000 Jewish businesses were destroyed, and at least one hundred Jews were killed. Moreover, 20,000 Jewish males were rounded up and sent to concentration camps. *Kristallnacht* also led to further drastic steps. Jews were barred from all public buildings and prohibited from owning, managing, or working in any retail store. Finally, under the direction of the SS, Jews were encouraged to "emigrate from Germany." After the outbreak of World War II, the policy of emigration was replaced by a more gruesome one.

The creation of the Nazi total state also had an impact on women. The Nazi attitude toward women was largely determined by ideological considerations. Women played a crucial role in the Aryan racial state as bearers of the children who would bring about the triumph of the Aryan race. To the Nazis, the differences between men and women were quite natural. Men were

Chronology

▼ ▼ ▼

Fascist Italy and Nazi Germany

Fascist Italy	
Creation of *Fascio di Combattimento*	1919
Squadristi Violence	1920–1921
Fascists Win Thirty-five Seats in Parliament	1921
Mussolini Is Made Prime Minister	1922 (October 29)
Acerbo Law	1923
Electoral Victory for Fascists	1924
Establishment of Fascist Dictatorship	1925–1926
Lateran Accords with Catholic Church	1929
Fascist School Charter	1939
Nazi Germany	
Hitler as Munich Politician	1919–1923
Beer Hall Putsch	1923
Election of Hindenburg as President	1925
Nazis Win 107 Seats in Reichstag	1930 (September)
Hitler Is Made Chancellor	1933 (January 30)
Reichstag Fire	1933 (February 27)
Enabling Act	1933 (March 23)
Purge of the SA	1934 (June 30)
Hindenburg Dies; Hitler as Sole Ruler	1934 (August 2)
Nuremberg Laws	1935
Kristallnacht	1938 (November 9–10)

warriors and political leaders while women were destined to be wives and mothers. By maintaining this clear distinction, each could best serve to "maintain the whole community."

Nazi ideas determined employment opportunities for women. The Nazis hoped to drive women out of certain areas of the labor market. This included heavy industry or other jobs that might hinder women from bearing healthy children, as well as certain professions, including university teaching, medicine, and law, which were

considered inappropriate for women, especially married women. The Nazis encouraged women to pursue professional occupations that had direct practical application, such as social work and nursing. In addition to restrictive legislation against females, the Nazi regime pushed its campaign against working women with such poster slogans as "Get ahold of pots and pans and broom and you'll sooner find a groom!" Nazi policy toward female workers remained inconsistent, however. Especially after the rearmament boom and increased conscription of males for military service produced a labor shortage, the government encouraged women to work, even in areas previously dominated by males.

Authoritarianism in Eastern Europe

Nowhere had the map of Europe been more drastically altered by World War I than in eastern Europe. The new states of Austria, Poland, Czechoslovakia, and Yugoslavia (known as the kingdom of the Serbs, Croats, and Slovenes until 1929) adopted parliamentary systems while the preexisting kingdoms of Romania and Bulgaria gained new parliamentary constitutions in 1920. Greece became a republic in 1924. Hungary's government was parliamentary in form, but controlled by its landed aristocrats. At the beginning of the 1920s, political democracy seemed well established, but almost everywhere in eastern Europe, parliamentary governments soon gave way to authoritarian regimes.

Several problems helped to create this situation. Eastern European states had little tradition of liberalism or parliamentary politics and no substantial middle class to support them. Then, too, these states were largely rural and agrarian in character. While many of the peasants were largely illiterate, much of the land was still dominated by large landowners who feared the growth of agrarian peasant parties with their schemes for land redistribution. Ethnic conflicts also threatened to tear these countries apart. Fearful of land reform, communist agrarian upheaval, and ethnic conflict, powerful landowners, the churches, and even some members of the small middle class looked to authoritarian governments to maintain the old system.

Already in the 1920s, some eastern European states began to move away from political democracy toward authoritarian structures. Poland established an authoritarian regime in 1926 when Marshal Joseph Pilsudski created a military dictatorship. King Alexander I (1921–1934) abolished the constitution and imposed a royal dictatorship on Yugoslavia in 1929. King Boris III

(1918–1943) created an authoritarian regime in Bulgaria in 1923.

During the 1930s, all of the remaining parliamentary regimes (except Czechoslovakia) succumbed to authoritarianism. No doubt, the Great Depression was a crucial factor in this development. The collapse of farm prices worldwide in the late 1920s adversely affected a region so agrarian as eastern Europe. Eastern European states were increasingly attracted to the authoritarian examples of Fascist Italy and Nazi Germany, which in turn gave rise to the growth of their own fascist parties.

Although Admiral Miklós Horthy had ruled Hungary as "regent" since 1919, the appointment of General Julius Gömbös as prime minister in 1932 brought Hungary even closer to Italy and Germany. In Austria, the Christian Socialist chancellor Engelbert Dollfuss used the armed forces to crush the Social Democrats and create his own brand of fascist state, a Christian Corporate State. Romania witnessed the development of a strong fascist movement led by Corneliu Codreanu. Known as the Legion of the Archangel Michael, it possessed its own paramilitary squad called the Iron Guard. As Codreanu's fascist movement grew and became Romania's third largest political party, King Carol II (1930–1940) responded in 1938 by ending parliamentary rule, crushing the leadership of the legion, and imposing authoritarian rule. At the beginning of World War II, General Ian Antonescu seized power and established his own military dictatorship in Romania. In Greece, General John Metaxas imposed a dictatorship in 1936. The new Baltic republics of Lithuania, Latvia, and Estonia also succumbed to dictatorial governments after brief experiments with democracy.

Only Czechoslovakia, with its substantial middle class, liberal tradition, and strong industrial base, maintained its political democracy. Thomas Masaryk, an able and fair leader while serving as president from 1918 to 1935, was able to maintain an uneasy but stable alliance of reformist socialists, agrarians, and Catholics.

The Iberian Peninsula

Parliamentary regimes in both Spain and Portugal also failed to survive. Both countries were largely agrarian, illiterate, and dominated by powerful landlords and Catholic clergy.

Spain's parliamentary monarchy was unable to deal with the social tensions generated by the industrial boom and inflation that accompanied World War I. Supported by King Alfonso XIII (1886–1931), General Miguel Primo de Rivera led a successful military coup in

September 1923 and created a personal dictatorship that lasted until 1930. But a faltering economy because of the Great Depression led to the collapse of de Rivera's regime in January 1930 as well as a widespread lack of support for the monarchy. King Alfonso XIII left Spain in 1931, and a new Spanish Republic was instituted, governed by a coalition of democrats and reformist socialists. Political turmoil ensued as control of the government passed from leftists to rightists until a Popular Front, an antifascist coalition composed of democrats, socialists, and the revolutionary left, took over in 1936. The Popular Front was unacceptable, however, to senior army officers. Led by General Francisco Franco (1892–1975), Spanish military forces revolted against the government and inaugurated a brutal and bloody civil war that lasted three years.

Foreign intervention complicated the Spanish Civil War. Franco's forces were aided by arms, money, and men from the fascist regimes of Italy and Germany while the Popular Front was assisted by 40,000 foreign volunteers and trucks, planes, tanks, and military advisers from the Soviet Union. Gradually, Franco's forces wore down the Popular Front, and after the capture of Madrid on March 28, 1939, the Spanish Civil War finally came to an end.

General Francisco Franco soon established a dictatorship that lasted until his death in 1975. It was not a fascist government. The fascist movement in Spain, known as the Falange and led by José Antonio Primo de Rivera, son of the former dictator, contributed little to Franco's success and played a minor role in the new regime. Franco's regime, which favored large landowners, businessmen, and the Catholic clergy, was yet another example of a traditional, conservative, authoritarian regime.

In 1910, the Portuguese had overthrown their monarchy and established a republic. Severe inflation after World War I, however, undermined support for the republic and helped to intensify political instability. In 1926, a group of army officers seized power, and by the early 1930s, the military junta's finance minister, Antonio Salazar (1889–1970), had become the strong man of the regime. Salazar controlled the Portuguese government for the next forty years.

Soviet Russia

The civil war in Russia had come to an end by the beginning of 1921. It had taken an enormous toll of life, but the Red Terror and the victories of the Red Army had guaranteed the survival of the Communist regime.

During the civil war, Lenin had pursued a policy of "war communism." Under this policy of expedience, the government had nationalized banks, mines, factories, and businesses that employed more than ten workers. The government had also assumed the right to requisition the produce of peasants. War communism worked during the civil war, but once the war was over, peasants began to sabotage the program by hoarding food. Added to this problem was drought, which caused the great famine between 1920 and 1922 that claimed as many as 5 million lives. Industrial collapse paralleled the agricultural disaster. By 1921, industrial output was only 20 percent of its 1913 levels. Russia was exhausted. As Leon Trotsky said, "the collapse of the productive forces surpassed anything of the kind that history had ever seen. The country, and the government with it, were at the very edge of the abyss."[12]

THE NEW ECONOMIC POLICY   In March 1921, Lenin pulled Russia back from the abyss by aborting war communism in favor of his New Economic Policy (NEP). Lenin's New Economic Policy was a modified version of the old capitalist system. Forced requisitioning of food from the peasants was halted as peasants were now allowed to sell their produce openly. Retail stores as well as small industries that employed fewer than twenty employees could now operate under private ownership, although heavy industry, banking, and mines remained in the hands of the government. Already by 1922, a revived market and good harvest had brought an end to famine; Soviet agriculture climbed to 75 percent of its prewar level. Industry, especially state-owned heavy industry, fared less well and continued to stagnate. Only coal production had reached prewar levels by 1926. Overall, the NEP had saved Communist Russia from complete economic disaster even though Lenin and other leading Communists intended it to be only a temporary, tactical retreat from the goals of communism.

Between 1922 and 1924, Lenin suffered a series of strokes that finally led to his death on January 21, 1924. Although Communist party rule theoretically rested on a principle of collective leadership, in fact, Lenin had provided an example of one-man rule. Lenin's death inaugurated a struggle for power among the members of the Politburo, the institution that had become the leading organ of the party.

In 1924, the Politburo of seven members was severely divided over the future direction of Soviet Russia. The Left, led by Leon Trotsky, wanted to end the NEP and launch Russia on the path of rapid industrialization, primarily at the expense of the peasantry. This same group

wanted to carry the revolution on, believing that the survival of the Russian Revolution ultimately depended on the spread of communism abroad. Another group in the Politburo, called the Right, rejected the cause of world revolution and wanted instead to concentrate on constructing a socialist state in Russia. This group also favored a continuation of Lenin's NEP because it believed that too rapid industrialization would harm the living standards of the Soviet peasantry.

These ideological divisions were underscored by an intense personal rivalry between Leon Trotsky and Joseph Stalin. Trotsky had been a key figure in the success of the Bolshevik Revolution and the Red Army. In 1924, he held the post of commissar of war and was the leading spokesman for the Left in the Politburo. Joseph Stalin (1879–1953) had joined the Bolsheviks in 1903 and had come to Lenin's attention after he had staged a daring bank robbery to obtain funds for the Bolshevik cause. Stalin, who was neither a dynamic speaker nor a forceful writer, was content to hold the dull bureaucratic job of party general secretary while other Politburo members held party positions that enabled them to display their brilliant oratorical abilities. He was a good organizer, and the other members of the Politburo soon found that the position of party secretary was really the most important in the party hierarchy. The general secretary appointed the regional, district, city, and town party secretaries. In 1922, for example, Stalin had made

some 10,000 appointments, many of them trusted followers whose holding of key positions proved valuable in the struggle for power. Although Stalin at first refused to support either the Left or Right in the Politburo, he finally came to favor the goal of "socialism in one country" rather than world revolution.

Stalin used his post as party general secretary to gain complete control of the Communist party. Trotsky was expelled from the party in 1927. Eventually, he made his way to Mexico where he was murdered in 1940, no doubt on Stalin's orders. By 1929, Stalin had succeeded in eliminating the Old Bolsheviks of the revolutionary era from the Politburo and establishing a dictatorship so powerful that the Russian tsars of old would have been envious.

THE STALIN ERA, 1929–1939   The Stalinist era marked the beginning of an economic, social, and political revolution that was more sweeping in its results than the revolutions of 1917. Stalin made a significant shift in economic policy in 1928 when he launched his first five-year plan. Its real goal was nothing less than the transformation of Russia from an agricultural into an industrial country virtually overnight. Instead of consumer goods, the first five-year plan emphasized maximum production of capital goods and armaments and succeeded in quadrupling the production of heavy machinery and doubling oil production. Europe's largest electrical

▼ **Russian Agricultural Workers in the 1930s.** The rapid industrialization of Stalin's Russia was paralleled by the collectivization of agriculture. By 1934, most of Russia's family farms had been collectivized. The process of collectivization included "production meetings" in the fields to encourage higher levels of agricultural production.

The Formation of Collective Farms
▼ ▼ ▼

Accompanying the rapid industrialization of the Soviet Union was the collectivization of agriculture, a feat that involved nothing less than transforming Russia's 26 million family farms into 250,000 collective farms (kolkhozes). This selection provides a firsthand account of how the process worked.

Max Belov, *The History of a Collective Farm*

General collectivization in our village was brought about in the following manner: Two representatives of the [Communist] Party arrived in the village. All the inhabitants were summoned by the ringing of the church bell to a meeting at which the policy of general collectivization was announced. . . . The upshot was that although the meeting lasted two days, from the viewpoint of the Party representatives nothing was accomplished.

After this setback the Party representatives divided the village into two sections and worked each one separately. Two more officials were sent to reinforce the first two. A meeting of our section of the village was held in a stable which had previously belonged to a kulak. The meeting dragged on until dark. Suddenly someone threw a brick at the lamp, and in the dark the peasants began to beat the Party representatives who jumped out the window and escaped from the village barely alive. The following day seven people were arrested. The militia was called in and stayed in the village until the peasants, realizing their helplessness, calmed down. . . .

By the end of 1930 there were two kolkhozes in our village. Though at first these collectives embraced at most only 70 percent of the peasant households, in the months that followed they gradually absorbed more and more of them.

In these kolkhozes the great bulk of the land was held and worked communally, but each peasant household owned a house of some sort, a small plot of ground and perhaps some livestock. All the members of the kolkhoz were required to work on the kolkhoz a certain number of days each month; the rest of the time they were allowed to work on their own holdings. They derived their income partly from what they grew on their garden strips and partly from their work in the kolkhoz.

When the harvest was over, and after the farm had met its obligations to the state and to various special funds (for insurance, seed, etc.) and had sold on the market whatever undesignated produce was left, the remaining produce and the farm's monetary income were divided among the kolkhoz members according to the number of "labor days" each one had contributed to the farm's work. . . . It was in 1930 that the kolkhoz members first received their portions out of the "communal kettle." After they had received their earnings, at the rate of 1 kilogram of grain and 55 kopecks per labor day, one of them remarked, "You will live, but you will be very, very thin."

In the spring of 1931 a tractor worked the fields of the kolkhoz for the first time. The tractor was "capable of plowing every kind of hard soil and virgin sod," as Party representatives told us at the meeting in celebration of its arrival. The peasants did not then know that these "steel horses" would carry away a good part of the harvest in return for their work. . . .

By late 1932 more than 80 percent of the peasant households . . . had been collectivized. . . . That year the peasants harvested a good crop and had hopes that the calculations would work out to their advantage and would help strengthen them economically. These hopes were in vain. The kolkhoz workers received only 200 grams of flour per labor day for the first half of the year; the remaining grain, including the seed fund, was taken by the government. The peasants were told that industrialization of the country, then in full swing, demanded grain and sacrifices from them.

---

power station was also built during this period. Between 1928 and 1937, during the first two five-year plans, steel production increased from 4 to 18 million tons per year while hard coal output went from 36 to 128 million tons. The annual growth rate of the Soviet Union was between 14 and 20 percent a year, a phenomenal accomplishment. At the same time, new industrial cities, located near iron ore and coal deposits, sprang up overnight in the Urals and Siberia.

The social and political costs of industrialization were enormous. Little provision was made for absorbing the expanded labor force into the cities. While the indus-

Eastern Europe

Boris III Establishes Authoritarian Regime in Bulgaria	1923
Pilsudski Creates a Military Dictatorship in Poland	1926
Alexander I Creates Royal Dictatorship in Yugoslavia	1929
Gömbös Is Made Prime Minister in Hungary	1932
Dictatorship of General Metaxas in Greece	1936
Carol II Crushes Iron Guard and Imposes Authoritarian Rule in Romania	1938

Spain

Dictatorship of Primo de Rivera	1923–1930
Creation of Spanish Republic	1931
Spanish Civil War	1936–1939

The Soviet Union

New Economic Policy Begins	1921
Death of Lenin	1924
Trotsky Is Expelled from the Communist Party	1927
First Five-Year Plan Begins	1928
Stalin's Dictatorship Is Established	1929
Stalin's Purge	1936–1938

achievement, typified by the Stakhanov cult. Alexei Stakhanov was a coal miner who mined 102 tons of coal in one shift and exceeded the norm by 1,300 percent. He was held up as an example to others.

Rapid industrialization was accompanied by an equally rapid collectivization of agriculture. Almost all of the Bolsheviks had been appalled by one result of Lenin's New Economic Policy, the growth of a class of well-to-do peasant proprietors known as kulaks who employed wage labor. Of the 26 million peasant households in 1929, 2 million were kulaks. It seemed an anomaly to have this capitalist group in the midst of a communist society. To rectify this, Stalin inaugurated a policy of collectivization of agriculture even before he initiated the first five-year plan. Its goal was to eliminate private farms and push people into collective farms (see the box on p. 957). One of its major aims was to stimulate industrial growth through profits from the rural economy.

Initially, Stalin planned to collectivize only the wealthier kulaks, but strong resistance to his plans from peasants who hoarded crops and killed livestock led him to step up the program. By 1930, 10 million peasant households had been collectivized; by 1934, Russia's 26 million family farms had been collectivized into 250,000 units. This was done at tremendous cost, since the hoarding of food and the slaughter of livestock produced widespread famine. Stalin himself is supposed to have told Winston Churchill during World War II that 10 million peasants died in the artificially created famines of 1932 and 1933. The only concession Stalin made to the peasants was that each collective farm worker was allowed to have one tiny, privately owned garden plot.

There were additional costs to Stalin's program of rapid industrialization, however. To achieve his goals, Stalin strengthened the party bureaucracy under his control. Those who resisted were sent into forced labor camps in Siberia. Stalin's desire for sole control of decision making also led to purges of the Old Bolsheviks. Between 1936 and 1938, the most prominent Old Bolsheviks were put on trial and condemned to death. During this same time, Stalin undertook a purge of army officers, diplomats, union officials, party members, intellectuals, and numerous ordinary citizens. Estimates are that 8 million Russians were arrested; millions were sent to Siberian forced labor camps, from which they never returned. The Stalinist blood bath made what some Western intellectuals had hailed as the "New Civilization" much less attractive by the late 1930s.

The Stalin era also reversed much of the permissive social legislation of the early 1920s. Advocating complete equality of rights for women, the Communists had

trial labor force increased by millions between 1932 and 1940, total investment in housing actually declined after 1929, with the result that millions of workers and their families lived in pitiful conditions. Real wages in industry also declined by 43 percent between 1928 and 1940 while strict laws limited workers' freedom of movement. To inspire and pacify the workers, government propaganda stressed the need for sacrifice to create the new socialist state. Soviet labor policy stressed high levels of

made divorce and abortion easy to obtain while also encouraging women to work outside the home and liberate themselves sexually. After Stalin came to power, the family was praised as a miniature collective in which parents were responsible for inculcating values of duty, discipline, and hard work. Abortion was outlawed while divorced fathers who did not support their children were fined heavily. The new divorce law of June 1936 imposed fines for repeated divorces. This return of social conservatism was paralleled by official encouragement of Soviet patriotism. Even the tsars were rehabilitated as Russian heroes.

▼ Mass Culture and Mass Leisure between the Wars

Technological innovations continued to have profound effects upon European society. Nowhere is this more evident than in mass culture and mass leisure. The mass distribution of commercialized popular forms of entertainment had a profound effect on European society.

Radio and Movies

A series of technological inventions in the late nineteenth century had prepared the way for a revolution in mass communications. Especially important was Marconi's discovery of "wireless" radio waves. But it was not until June 16, 1920, that a radio broadcast (of a concert by soprano Nellie Melba from London) for a mass audience was attempted. Permanent broadcasting facilities were then constructed in the United States, Europe, and Japan during 1921 and 1922, while mass production of radios (receiving sets) also began. In 1926, when the British Broadcasting Corporation (BBC) was made into a public corporation, there were 2,200,000 radios in Great Britain. By the end of the 1930s there were 9 million. Although broadcasting networks in the United States were privately owned and financed by advertising, those in Europe were usually controlled by the government.

The technical foundation for motion pictures had already been developed in the 1890s when short moving pictures were produced as novelties for music halls. Shortly before World War I, full-length features, such as the Italian film *Quo Vadis* and the American film *Birth of a Nation* became available and made it apparent that cinema had created a new form of mass entertainment. By 1939, about 40 percent of adults in the more advanced industrial countries were attending a movie once

a week. That figure increased to 60 percent by the end of World War II.

Mass forms of communication and entertainment were, of course, not new. But the increased size of audiences and the ability of radio and cinema, unlike the printed word, to provide an immediate mass experience did add new dimensions to mass culture. Of course, radio and movies could be used for political purposes. Hitler had said, "without motor-cars, sound films, and wireless, no victory of National Socialism." Radio seemed to offer great opportunities for reaching the masses, especially when it became apparent that the emotional harangues of an Adolf Hitler had just as much impact on people when heard on radio as in person. The Nazi regime encouraged radio listening by urging manufacturers to produce cheap radios that could be bought on installment plans. The Nazis also erected loudspeaker pillars in the streets to encourage communal radio listening, especially to radio broadcasts of mass meetings.

Film, too, had propaganda potential, a possibility not lost on Joseph Goebbels (1897–1945), the propaganda minister of Nazi Germany. Believing that film constituted one of the "most modern and scientific means of influencing the masses," Goebbels created a special film section in his Propaganda Ministry and encouraged the production of both documentaries and popular feature films that carried the Nazi message. *The Triumph of the Will,* for example, was a documentary of the 1934 Nuremberg party rally that conveyed forcefully to viewers the power of National Socialism. Both Fascist Italy and Nazi Germany controlled and exploited the content of newsreels.

Mass Leisure

Mass leisure activities had developed at the turn of the century, but new work patterns after World War I dramatically expanded the amount of free time available to take advantage of them. By 1920, the eight-hour day had become the norm for many office and factory workers in northern and western Europe.

Professional sporting events for mass audiences became an especially important aspect of mass leisure. Attendance at association football (soccer) games increased dramatically while the creation of the World Cup contest in 1930 added to the nationalistic rivalries that began to surround such mass sporting events. Increased attendance also made the 1920s and 1930s a great era of stadium building. The Germans built a stadium in Berlin for the 1936 Olympics that seated 140,000 people. Strahav Stadium in Prague held

240,000 spectators for gymnastics and track meets. As the popularity of mass spectator sports grew, so too did the amount of money spent on betting.

Travel opportunities also added new dimensions to mass leisure activities. The military use of aircraft during World War I helped to improve planes and make civilian air travel a reality. The first regular international air mail service began in 1919, and regular passenger service soon followed. Although air travel remained the preserve of the wealthy or the adventurous, trains, buses, and private cars made excursions to beaches or holiday resorts more and more popular and affordable. Beaches, such as the one at Brighton in Great Britain, were increasingly mobbed by crowds of people from all social classes.

Mass leisure provided totalitarian regimes with new ways to control their populations. Mussolini's Italy created the *Dopolavoro* (Afterwork) as a vast national recreation agency. The *Dopolavoro* was responsible for establishing clubhouses with libraries, radios, and athletic facilities in virtually every town and village. In some places, they included auditoriums for plays and films and travel agencies that arranged tours, cruises, and resort vacations on the Adriatic at reduced rates. *Dopolavoro* groups introduced many Italians to various facets of mass culture and mass leisure with activities such as band concerts, movies, choral groups, roller skating, and ballroom dancing. Essentially the *Dopolavoro* enabled the Italian government to provide, but also to supervise, recreational activities. By doing so, the state placed new rules and regulations on previously spontaneous activities, thus breaking down old group solidarities and enabling these groups to be guided by the goals of the state.

The Nazi regime adopted a program similar to the *Dopolavoro* in its *Kraft durch Freude* (Strength through Joy). The purpose of the *Kraft durch Freude* was to coordinate the free time of the working class by offering a variety of leisure time activities, including concerts, operas, films, guided tours, and sporting events (see the box on p. 961). Especially popular were the inexpensive vacations, essentially the modern package tour. This could be a cruise to Scandinavia or the Mediterranean or, more likely for workers, a shorter trip to different sites in Germany. Only 130,000 workers took cruises in 1938, compared with the 7 million who took short trips.

More and more, mass culture and mass leisure had the consequence of expanding the homogeneity of national populations, a process that had begun in the nineteenth century with the development of the national state. Local popular culture was increasingly replaced by national and even international culture as new forms of mass production and consumption brought similar styles of clothing and fashion to people throughout Europe.

▼ Cultural and Intellectual Trends in the Interwar Years

The artistic and intellectual innovations of the pre–World War I period, which had shocked many Europe-

▼ **New Patterns of Recreation: The Ford Model T.** Mass leisure activities expanded between the wars as new work patterns increased the free time available to members of the working class. For the middle classes, mass-produced automobiles, such as the American Ford Model T, made possible a new freedom of movement.

Mass Leisure: Strength through Joy
▼ ▼ ▼

*I n November 1933, the German Labor Front estab-
lished an organization called Kraft durch Freude
(Strength through Joy), whose purpose was to organize the
leisure time of workers in the interests of the Nazi regime.
These excerpts are taken from the reports of the Social
Democratic party's contact men in Germany and give a
fairly accurate account of the attitudes of the German
workers toward the Kraft durch Freude (KdF) program.*

The SOPADE [Social Democratic Party in Exile] Reports

Central Germany, April 1939

While Beauty of Labor [another Labor Front organi-
zation] makes no impressions whatsoever . . .
Strength through Joy is not without impact. However, workers' wages are only barely sufficient for essentials and nobody can afford a trip to Madeira, 150
Reichsmarks per person—300 RM with the wife.
Even the shorter trips produce so many additional
expenses that they often double the cost. But some
people like them nonetheless. Anybody who has
never made a trip in his life and sees the sea for the
first time is much impressed. The effect is: "The Nazis
have done some good things after all." The enthusiasm is, however, greater on the first trip. On the
second, many are put off by the crowds.

Berlin, February 1938

Strength through Joy is very popular. The events appeal to the yearning of the little man who wants an
opportunity to get out and about himself and to take
part in the pleasures of the "top people." It is a clever
appeal to the petty bourgeois inclinations of the un-
political workers. For such a man it really means
something to have been on a trip to Scandinavia, or
even if he only went to the Black Forest or the Harz
Mountains, he imagines that he has thereby climbed
up a rung on the social ladder.

Bavaria, April 1939

On the group tours there is a sharp social differentiation. The "top people" only go on big trips where
there will be a more select clientele. The big mass
trips are for the proletariat. People now look for
places where there are no KdF visitors. "Not visited
by KdF" is now a particular asset for summer vacations. A landlord in a mountain village in Upper
Bavaria wrote in his prospectus: "Not visited by KdF
tourists." The Labor Front, which was sent the prospectus by someone, took the landlord to court. He
had to withdraw the prospectus and was not allowed
to receive summer guests. Nevertheless, information
about summer Pensions [boardinghouses] which are
not used by KdF is becoming more and more widespread.

---

ans, had been the preserve primarily of a small group of
avant-garde artists and intellectuals. In the 1920s and
1930s, they became more widespread as artists and intellectuals continued to work out the implications of the
ideas developed before 1914. In effect, prewar "outsiders" became "insiders." But what made the prewar avant-
garde culture acceptable in the 1920s and the 1930s?
Perhaps the most important factor was the impact of
World War I.

The optimistic liberal-rationalist clichés that many
Europeans had taken for granted before 1914 seemed
hopelessly outdated in 1918. Four years of devastating
war left many Europeans with a profound sense of despair
and disillusionment. World War I indicated to many
people that something was dreadfully wrong with West-

ern values. In his *Decline of the West,* the German writer
Oswald Spengler (1880–1936) reflected the disillusionment when he emphasized the decadence of Western
civilization and posited its collapse. To many people, the
experiences of World War I seemed to confirm the prewar avant-garde belief that human beings were really
violent and irrational animals who were incapable of
creating a sane and rational world. The Great Depression of the late 1920s and early 1930s, as well as the
growth of fascist movements based on violence and the
degradation of individual rights, only added to the uncertainties generated by World War I. The crisis of confidence in Western civilization indeed ran deep and was
well captured in the words of the French poet Paul
Valéry in the early 1920s:

The storm has died away, and still we are restless, uneasy, as if the storm were about to break. Almost all the affairs of men remain in a terrible uncertainty. We think of what has disappeared, and we are almost destroyed by what has been destroyed; we do not know what will be born, and we fear the future. . . . Doubt and disorder are in us and with us. There is no thinking man, however shrewd or learned he may be, who can hope to dominate this anxiety, to escape from this impression of darkness.[13]

Political, economic, and social uncertainties were paralleled by intellectual uncertainties, which were quite evident in the cultural and intellectual achievements of the interwar years.

Art and Music

Postwar artistic trends were largely a working out of the implications of prewar developments. Abstract Expressionism, for example, became ever more popular as many pioneering artists of the early twentieth century matured between the two world wars. In addition, prewar fascination with the absurd and the unconscious contents of the mind seemed even more appropriate after the nightmare landscapes of World War I battlefronts. This gave rise to both the Dada movement and Surrealism.

Dadaism attempted to enshrine the purposelessness of life (see the box on p. 964). Revolted by the insanity of life, the Dadaists tried to give it expression by creating anti-art. The 1918 Berlin Dada Manifesto maintained that "Dada is the international expression of our times, the great rebellion of artistic movements." In the hands of Kurt Schwitters (1887–1948), however, Dada represented a form of cultural rebirth that liberated people from conformity. By taking pieces of junk (wire, string, rags, scraps of newspaper, nails, washers) and assembling them into collages, Schwitters believed that he was transforming the refuse of his culture into art. "I am a painter, I nail my pictures together," he once stated.

Perhaps more important as an artistic movement was Surrealism, which sought a reality beyond the material, sensible world and found it in the world of the unconscious through the portrayal of fantasies, dreams, or nightmares. Employing logic to portray the illogical, the Surrealists created disturbing and evocative images. The Spaniard Salvador Dali (1904–1989) became the high priest of Surrealism and in his mature phase became a master of representational Surrealism. In *The Persistence of Memory*, Dali portrayed recognizable objects that have nevertheless been divorced from their normal context. By placing these objects into unrecognizable relationships, Dali created a disturbing world in which the irrational had become tangible.

The move to functionalism in modern architecture also became more widespread in the 1920s and 1930s. Especially important in the spread of functionalism was the Bauhaus school of art, architecture, and design, founded in 1919 at Weimar, Germany, by the Berlin architect Walter Gropius (see Chapter 25). The Bauhaus teaching staff consisted of architects, artists, and designers who worked together to blend the study of fine arts

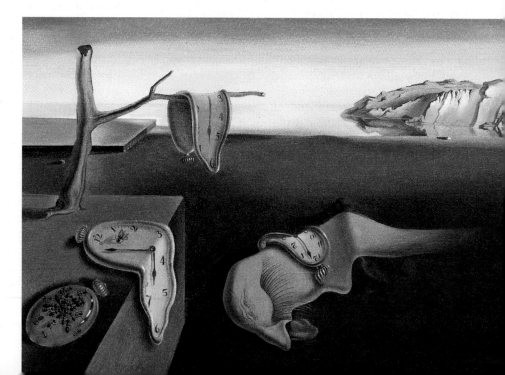

▼ **Salvador Dali,** *The Persistence of Memory.* Surrealism was another important artistic movement between the wars. Influenced by the theories of Freudian psychology, surrealists sought to reveal the world of the unconscious, or the "greater reality" that they believed existed beyond the world of physical appearances. Salvador Dali sought to portray the world of dreams by painting recognizable objects in unrecognizable relationships.

(painting and sculpture) with the applied arts (printing, weaving, and furniture making). Gropius urged his followers to foster a new union of arts and crafts to create the buildings and objects of the future.

Important to the development of artistic expression between the wars was the search for a new popular audience. To attract a wider audience, artists and musicians began to involve themselves in the new mass culture. The German Kurt Weill, for example, had been a struggling composer of classical music before he turned to the use of jazz rhythms and other popular musical idioms for *The Threepenny Opera.* Some artists even regarded art as a means to transform society and located their studios in poor, working-class neighborhoods. Walter Gropius envisioned the Bauhaus as a means to "achieve the reunion of all forms and creative work" and thereby create a new civilization. Theater proved especially attractive as postwar artists sought to make an impact on popular audiences. The German director Erwin Piscator began his directing career by offering plays to workers on picket lines. Piscator hoped to reach workers by experimental drama with political messages. Like many other artists, however, he became frustrated by his failure to achieve a mass audience.

The postwar acceptance of modern art forms was by no means universal. Many traditionalists denounced what they considered the degeneracy and decadence in the arts. Nowhere was this more evident than in the totalitarian states of Nazi Germany and the Soviet Union.

In the 1920s, Weimar Germany was one of the chief European centers for modern arts and sciences. Hitler and the Nazis rejected modern art as "degenerate" or "Jewish" art. In an address at the premiere of the Great German Art Exhibition in the newly opened House of German Art in July 1937, Hitler proclaimed:

> The people regarded this art [modern art] as the outcome of an impudent and unashamed arrogance or of a simply shocking lack of skill; it felt that . . . these achievements which might have been produced by untalented children of from eight to ten years old—could never be valued as an expression of our own times or of the German future.[14]

Hitler and the Nazis believed that they had laid the foundation for a new and genuine German art, which would glorify the strong, the healthy, and the heroic— all of which were supposedly attributes of the Aryan race. The new German art was actually the old nineteenth-century genre art with its emphasis on realistic scenes of everyday life.

▼ **Kurt Schwitters,** *Picture with Light Center.* To a great extent, trends in postwar painting were largely a continuation of prewar developments. But the horrors of World War I reinforced prewar preoccupations with the absurd and gave rise to two new movements, Dada and Surrealism. Kurt Schwitters became identified with the Dada movement when he began to create his collages. He wrote in 1928: "Fundamentally, I cannot understand why one is not able to use in a picture, exactly in the same way as commercially made color . . . all the old junk which piles up in closets or the rubbish heaps." Schwitters brought together postage stamps, old handbills, streetcar tickets, newspaper scraps, and pieces of cardboard to form his works of art.

So, too, was the art produced by the school of "socialist realism" in the Soviet Union. After the bold experimentalism of the 1920s, the Stalinist era imposed a stifling uniformity on artistic creativity. Like German painting, Soviet painting was expected to focus on a nineteenth-century pictorial style aimed at realistic presentation. Both the new German art and "socialist re-

The Voice of Dadaism

▼ ▼ ▼

The Dadaists attempted to give expression to what they saw as the meaninglessness and absurdity of life. In this excerpt, Tristan Tzara (1896–1945), a Romanian-French poet and one of the founders of Dadaism, expressed the Dadaist contempt for the Western tradition.

Tristan Tzara, "Lecture on Dada," 1922

I know that you have come here today to hear explanations. Well, don't expect to hear any explanations about Dada. You explain to me why you exist. You haven't the faintest idea. . . .

The acts of life have no beginning or end. Everything happens in a completely idiotic way. That is why everything is alike. Simplicity is called Dada. . . .

The beginnings of Dada were not the beginnings of an art, but of a disgust. Disgust with the magnificence of philosophers who for 3000 years have been explaining everything to us (what for?), disgust with the pretensions of these artists—God's-representatives-on-earth, . . . disgust with a false form of domination and restriction *en masse*, that accentuates rather than appeases man's instinct of domination, disgust with . . . the false prophets who are nothing but a front for the interests of money, pride, disease.

Dada is a state of mind. . . . Dada applies itself to everything, and yet it is nothing, it is the point where the yes and the no and all the opposites meet, not solemnly in the castles of human philosophies, but very simply at street corners, like dogs and grasshoppers.

Like everything in life, Dada is useless.

Dada is without pretension, as life should be.

---

alism" were intended to inculcate social values useful to the ruling regimes.

At the beginning of the twentieth century, a revolution in music parallel to the revolution in art had begun with the work of Igor Stravinsky (see Chapter 25). But Stravinsky still wrote music in a definite key. In 1924, the Viennese composer Arnold Schönberg (1874–1951) released a piano suite in which he used a scale composed of twelve notes independent of any tonal key. His atonal music, which grew out of a quarter century of experimentation, was closely akin to abstract painting. Whereas the latter arranged colors and lines without reference to concrete images, so atonal music organized sounds without making recognizable harmonies. Resistance to modern music was even greater than to modern painting, and it did not begin to win favor until after World War II.

Literature

The interest in the unconscious, evident in Surrealism, was also apparent in the new literary techniques that emerged in the 1920s. One of its most apparent manifestations was in the "stream of consciousness" technique in which the writer presented an interior monologue or a report of the innermost thoughts of each character. The most famous example of this genre was written by the Irish exile James Joyce (1882–1941). His *Ulysses*, published in 1922, told the story of one day in the life of ordinary people in Dublin by following the flow of their inner dialogue. Disconnected ramblings and veiled allusions pervade Joyce's work.

The German writer Hermann Hesse (1877–1962) dealt with the unconscious in a considerably different fashion. His novels reflected the influence of both Carl Jung's psychological theories (see the next section) and Eastern religions and focused among other things on the spiritual loneliness of modern human beings in a mechanized urban society. *Demian* was a psychoanalytic study of incest while *Steppenwolf* mirrored the psychological confusion of modern existence. Hesse's novels made a large impact on German youth in the 1920s. He won the Nobel Prize for literature in 1946.

Intellectual Trends: Physics and Psychology

The prewar revolution in physics initiated by Max Planck and Albert Einstein continued in the interwar period. In fact, Ernest Rutherford (1871–1937), one of the physicists responsible for demonstrating that the atom could be split, dubbed the 1920s the "heroic age of physics." By the early 1940s, seven subatomic particles had been distinguished, and a sufficient understanding of the potential of the atom had been achieved to lay the foundations for the development of the atomic bomb.

The new picture of the universe that was unfolding continued to undermine the old scientific certainties of classical physics. Classical physics had rested on the fundamental belief that all phenomena could be predicted if they could be completely understood; thus, the weather could be accurately predicted if we only knew everything about the wind, sun, and water. In 1927, the German physicist Werner Heisenberg (1901–1976) upset this belief when he posited the "uncertainty principle." In essence, Heisenberg argued that no one could determine the path of an electron because the very act of observing the electron with light affected the electron's location. The "uncertainty principle" was more than an explanation for the path of an electron, however; it was a new worldview. Heisenberg shattered confidence in predictability and dared to propose that uncertainty was at the bottom of all physical laws.

Few nonscientists understood the implications of Heisenberg's work, but another newly emerging scientific field had greater popular impact. The full importance of Sigmund Freud's thought was not felt until after World War I. The 1920s witnessed a worldwide acceptance of his ideas. Freudian terms, such as unconscious, repression, id, ego, and Oedipus complex, entered the popular vocabulary. Popularization of Freud's ideas led to the widespread misconception that an uninhibited sex life was necessary for a healthy mental life. Despite such misconceptions, psychoanalysis did develop into a major profession, especially in the United States. But Freud's ideas did not go unchallenged, even by his own pupils. One of the most prominent challenges came from Carl Jung.

A disciple of Freud, Carl Jung (1856–1961) came to believe that Freud's theories were too narrow and based on Freud's own personal biases. Jung's study of dreams—his own and others—led him to diverge sharply from Freud. Whereas for Freud the unconscious was the seat of repressed desires or appetites, for Jung, it was an opening to deep spiritual needs and ever-greater vistas for humans. Two concepts were particularly important to his theories: the process of individuation and collective unconscious.

Jung believed that a person's dreams are linked together in some arrangement or pattern, which he called "the process of individuation." Only by examining one's dreams over a long period of time could a person see the pattern. He or she would then be able to understand the process of psychic growth or individuation as the mature personality emerges. The organizing center of the mind from which all this came was the "self," the whole psyche, rather than the ego. The general function of dreams, then, was to bring people back to the center, thereby restoring their psychological balance.

Jung viewed the unconscious as twofold: a "personal unconscious" and a "collective unconscious," which existed at a deeper level of the unconscious. The collective unconscious was the repository of memories that all human beings share and consisted of archetypes, mental forms or images that appear in dreams. The archetypes are not derived from the individual's experience, how-

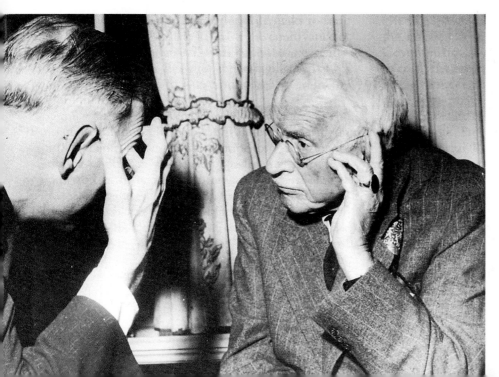

▼ **Carl Jung.** Although a disciple of Sigmund Freud, Carl Jung broke with his master over the understanding of the nature of the unconscious. In his numerous writings, Jung developed elaborate theories on the individuation process and the concept of a collective unconscious. He is shown here at the age of 85 with one of his followers.

ever, but from the biological, prehistoric, and unconscious development of mind. They are common to all people and have a special energy that creates myths, religions, and philosophies. To Jung, the archetypes proved that mind was only in part personal or individual because their origin was buried so far in the past that they seemed to have no human source. Their function was to bring the original mind of humans into a new, higher state of consciousness.

The devastation wrought by World War I destroyed the liberal optimism of the prewar era. Yet many in the 1920s still hoped that the progress of Western civilization, so seemingly evident before 1914, could somehow be restored. These hopes proved largely unfounded as plans for economic reconstruction gave way to inflation and to an even more devastating Great Depression at the

end of the 1920s. Likewise, confidence in political democracy was soon shattered by the rise of authoritarian governments that not only restricted individual freedoms, but in the cases of Italy, Germany, and the Soviet Union, sought even greater control over the lives of their subjects in order to manipulate and guide them to achieve the goals of their totalitarian regimes. For many people, despite the loss of personal freedom, these mass movements at least offered some sense of security in a world that seemed fraught with uncertainties.

But the seeming security of these mass movements gave rise to even greater uncertainties as Europeans, after a brief twenty-year interlude of peace, once again plunged into war, this time on a scale even more horrendous than that of World War I. The twentieth-century crisis, begun in 1914, seemed only to be worsening in 1939.

Notes

▼ ▼ ▼

1. Quoted in Robert Paxton, *Europe in the Twentieth Century*, 2d ed. (San Diego, 1985), p. 237.
2. Quoted in Denis Mack Smith, *Mussolini* (New York, 1982), p. 51.
3. Benito Mussolini, "The Doctrine of Fascism," in Adrian Lyttleton, ed., *Italian Fascisms from Pareto to Gentile* (London, 1973), p. 42.
4. Quoted in Edward Tannenbaum, *The Fascist Experience: Italian Society and Culture, 1922–1945* (New York, 1972), p. 170.
5. Quoted in Alexander De Grand, "Women under Italian Fascism," *Historical Journal* 19 (1976): 958–59.
6. Adolf Hitler, *Mein Kampf*, trans. Ralph Manheim (Boston, 1943), p. 22.
7. Ibid., p. 161.

8. Quoted in Joachim Fest, *Hitler*, trans. Richard and Clara Winston (New York, 1974), p. 241.
9. Quoted in Jeremy Noakes and Geoffrey Pridham, eds., *Nazism, 1919–1945* (Exeter, 1983), 1: 50–51.
10. Quoted in Jackson Spielvogel, *Hitler and Nazi Germany: A History* (Englewood Cliffs, N.J., 1988), p. 67.
11. Quoted in Fest, *Hitler*, p. 418.
12. Irving Howe, ed., *The Basic Writings of Trotsky* (London, 1963), p. 162.
13. Paul Valéry, *Variety*, trans. Malcolm Cowley (New York, 1927), pp. 27–28.
14. Norman H. Baynes, ed., *The Speeches of Adolf Hitler, 1922–1939* (Oxford, 1942), 1: 591.

Suggestions for Further Reading

▼ ▼ ▼

For a general introduction to the interwar period, see R. J. Sontag, *A Broken World, 1919–39* (New York, 1971). On European security issues after the Peace of Paris, see S. Marks, *The Illusion of Peace: Europe's International Relations, 1918–1933* (New York, 1976). The Locarno agreements have been well examined in J. Jacobson, *Locarno Diplomacy* (Princeton, N.J., 1972).

The important role of French diplomacy in the 1920s is examined in J. M. Hughes, *To the Maginot Line: The Politics of French Military Preparations in the 1920s* (Cambridge, Mass., 1971); and J. Néré, *The Foreign Policy of France from 1914 to 1945* (London, 1975). On German foreign policy, see the older but valuable work of H. W. Gatzke, *Stresemann and the Rearmament of*

Germany (Baltimore, Md., 1965). Russian foreign policy is examined in A. B. Ulam, *Expansion and Coexistence: The History of Soviet Foreign Policy, 1917–1943*, 2d ed. (New York, 1974). The best study on the problem of reparations is now M. Trachtenberg, *Reparations in World Politics* (New York, 1980), which paints a more positive view of French policies. S. A. Schuker, *The End of French Predominance in Europe: The Financial Crisis of 1924 and the Adoption of the Dawes Plan* (Chapel Hill, N.C., 1976) demonstrates the importance of economic factors, such as international bankers, in European security problems. The "return to normalcy" after the war is analyzed in C. S. Maier, *Recasting Bourgeois Europe: Stabilization in France, Germany, and Italy in the Decade after World War I* (Princeton, N.J., 1975). Also valuable is D. P. Silverman, *Reconstructing Europe after the Great War* (Cambridge, Mass., 1982). On the Great Depression, see C. P. Kindleberger, *The World in Depression, 1929–39*, rev. ed. (Berkeley, 1986). On Keynes and his new economic theories, see R. Skidelsky, *John Maynard Keynes: A Biography* (New York, 1986).

The best biography of Mussolini is now D. Mack Smith, *Mussolini* (New York, 1982). Two brief, but excellent surveys of Fascist Italy are A. Cassels, *Fascist Italy*, 2d ed. (Arlington Heights, Ill., 1985); and A. De Grand, *Italian Fascism* (Lincoln, Neb., 1982). An excellent reference guide for all aspects of Fascist Italy is P. Cannistraro, ed., *Historical Dictionary of Fascist Italy* (Westport, Conn., 1982). The best work on the rise of Fascism is A. Lyttleton, *Seizure of Power* (New York, 1973), which covers the period from 1919 to 1929. Of the recent regional studies, the best is P. Corner, *Fascism in Ferrara, 1915–1925* (London, 1975). On propaganda and other aspects of cultural life in Fascist Italy, see E. R. Tannenbaum, *The Fascist Experience: Italian Society and Culture, 1922–1945* (New York, 1972).

Two brief but sound surveys of Nazi Germany are J. Spielvogel, *Hitler and Nazi Germany: A History* (Englewood Cliffs, N.J., 1988); and J. Bendersky, *A History of Nazi Germany* (Chicago, 1985). A more detailed examination can be found in K. Bracher, *The German Dictatorship: The Origins, Structure, and Effects of National Socialism* (New York, 1970). The best biographies of Hitler are A. Bullock, *Hitler: A Study in Tyranny* (New York, 1964); and J. Fest, *Hitler*, trans. R. and C. Winston (New York, 1974). A good sociological analysis of the Nazi party can be found in M. Kater, *The Nazi Party: A Social Profile of Members and Leaders, 1919–1945* (Cambridge, Mass., 1983). A good regional study of the Nazi party's rise to power is W. S. Allen's "classic" *The Nazi Seizure of Power: The Experience of a Single German Town*, rev. ed. (New York, 1984). On the SA, see P. Merkl, *The Making of a Stormtrooper* (Princeton, N.J., 1980). The relationship between German big business and Hitler is well covered in H. A. Turner, *German Big Business and the Rise of Hitler* (New York, 1985). On the Nazi administration of the state, see M. Broszat, *The Hitler State: The Foundations and Development of the Internal Structure of the Third Reich* (New York, 1981). A brief perspective on Germany's economic recovery can be found in R. J. Overy, *The Nazi Economic Recovery, 1932–1938* (London, 1982). Basic studies of the SS include R. Koehl, *The Black Corps: The Structure and Power Struggles of the Nazi SS* (Madison, Wis., 1983); and H. Krausnick and M. Broszat, *Anatomy of the SS State* (London, 1970). An insightful book about the responses of ordinary Germans to the Third Reich is D. Peukert, *Inside Nazi Germany: Conformity, Opposition, and Racism in Everyday Life*, trans. R. Deveson (New Haven, Conn., 1987). On women, see J. Stephenson, *Women in Nazi Society* (London, 1975); and C. Koonz, *Mothers in the Fatherland: Women, the Family, and Nazi Politics* (New York, 1987). The Hitler Youth is examined in H. W. Koch, *The Hitler Youth* (New York, 1976). The books on the Holocaust cited in Chapter 28 contain background information on Nazi anti-Jewish policies between 1933 and 1939. The importance of racial ideology in Nazi Germany is evident in R. Proctor, *Racial Hygiene: Medicine Under the Nazis* (Cambridge, Mass., 1988). In addition to these, see K. A. Schleunes, *The Twisted Road to Auschwitz: Nazi Policy towards German Jews, 1933–1939* (Chicago, 1970); and S. Gordon, *Hitler, Germans and the "Jewish Question"* (Princeton, N.J., 1984).

For a general study of other fascist movements, see F. L. Carsten, *The Rise of Fascism*, 2d ed. (Berkeley, 1980). For a general interpretation of fascism, see S. G. Payne, *Fascism: Comparison and Definition* (Madison, Wis., 1980). Starting points for the study of eastern Europe are J. Rothschild, *East Central Europe between the Two World Wars* (New York, 1974); and B. Jelavich, *History of the Balkans*, vol. 2: *The Twentieth Century* (New York, 1983). On Franco, see J. W. D. Trythall, *El Caudillo: A Political Biography* (New York, 1970). On the Spanish Civil War, see S. G. Payne, *The Spanish Revolution* (New York, 1970); and H. Thomas, *The Spanish Civil War*, rev. ed. (New York, 1977).

On Russia in the 1920s, see S. F. Cohen, *Bukharin and the Bolshevik Revolution: A Political Biography, 1888–1938* (New York, 1973). The collectivization of agriculture is examined in R. W. Davies, *The Socialist Offensive: The Collectivization of Soviet Agriculture, 1929–30* (Cambridge,

Mass., 1980); while the impact of that collectivization on the Russian peasants is discussed in R. W. Davies, *The Soviet Collective Farm, 1929–1930* (Cambridge, Mass., 1980). Industrialization is covered in H. Kuromiya, *Stalin's Industrial Revolution: Politics and Workers, 1928–1932* (New York, 1988). Stalin's purges are examined in R. Conquest, *The Great Terror: Stalin's Purge of the Thirties,* rev. ed. (New York, 1973). For a biography of Stalin, see I. Deutscher, *Stalin,* 2d ed. (New York, 1967); and the more recent R. H. McNeal, *Stalin: Man and Ruler* (New York, 1988).

The use of cinema for propaganda purposes is well examined in D. Welch, *Propaganda and the German Cinema* (New York, 1985). The organization of leisure time in Fascist Italy is thoughtfully examined in V. De Grazia, *The Culture of Consent: Mass Organization of Leisure in Fascist Italy* (New York, 1981). On the cultural and intellectual environment of Weimar Germany, see W. Laqueur, *Weimar: A Cultural History* (New York, 1974); and P. Gay, *Weimar Culture: The Outsider as Insider* (New York, 1968). For a study of Carl Jung, see G. Wehr, *Jung: A Biography* (New York, 1987).

Chapter 28

The Deepening of the European Crisis: World War II

▼▼▼▼▼

On February 3, 1933, only four days after he had been appointed chancellor of Germany, Adolf Hitler met secretly with Germany's leading generals. He revealed to them his desire to create a new domestic unity that would enable Germany to rearm and prepare for the conquest of *Lebensraum* ("living space") in the east. Even before he had consolidated his power, Adolf Hitler had a clear vision of his goals. Their implementation meant another European war. World War II was clearly Hitler's war. Although other countries may have helped to make the war possible by not resisting Hitler's Germany earlier, it was Nazi Germany's actions that made World War II inevitable.

World War II was also more, however, than just Hitler's war. This chapter will focus on the European theater of war, but both European and American armies were also involved in fighting around the world. World War II consisted of two conflicts: one provoked by the ambitions of Germany in Europe; the other by the ambitions of Japan in Asia. By 1941, with the involvement of the United States in both wars, the two had merged into one global conflict.

Although World War I has been described as a total war, World War II was even more so, and was fought on a scale unprecedented in history. The entire populations of warring countries were involved: as combatants; as workers in wartime industries; as civilians who suffered invasion, occupation, and aerial bombing; or as victims of persecution and mass extermination. The world had never witnessed such widespread human-made death and destruction.

●●●●●●●● 1935 ●●●●●●●●●● 1940 ●●●●●●●●●● 1943 ●●●●●●●● 1944 ●●●●●●●● 1945 ●●●●●●●

▼ Prelude to War, 1933–1939

Only twenty years after the war to end war, Europe plunged back into the nightmare of total war. The efforts at collective security in the 1920s—the League of Nations, the attempts at disarmament, the pacts and treaties—all proved meaningless in view of the growth of Nazi Germany and its deliberate scrapping of the postwar settlement in the 1930s. Still weary from the last war, France and Great Britain refused to accept the possibility of another war. The Soviet Union had turned in on itself, while the United States had withdrawn into its traditional isolationism. Finally, the small successor states to Austria-Hungary were too weak to oppose Germany. The power vacuum in the heart of Europe encouraged a revived and militarized Germany to acquire the living space that Hitler claimed Germany needed for its rightful place in the world.

The Role of Hitler

World War II in Europe had its beginnings in the ideas of Adolf Hitler, who believed that only the Aryans were capable of building a great civilization. But to Hitler, the Germans (the leading group of Aryans) were threatened from the east by a large mass of inferior peoples, the Slavs, who had learned to use German weapons and technology. Germany needed more land to support a larger population and be a great power. Hitler was a firm believer in the doctrine of Lebensraum (living space), espoused by Karl Haushofer, a professor of geography at the University of Munich. The doctrine of Lebensraum maintained that a nation's power depended upon the amount and kind of land it occupied. Already in the 1920s, in the second volume of Mein Kampf, Hitler had indicated where a National Socialist regime would find this land: "And so we National Socialists . . . take up where we broke off six hundred years ago. We stop the endless German movement to the south and west, and turn our gaze toward the land in the east. . . .

If we speak of soil in Europe today, we can primarily have in mind only Russia and her vassal border states."[1]

In Hitler's view, the Russian Revolution had created the conditions for Germany's acquisition of land to its east. Imperial Russia had only been strong because of its German leadership. The seizure of power by the Bolsheviks (who, in Hitler's mind, were Jewish) had left Russia weak and vulnerable. Once it had been conquered, the land of Russia could be resettled by German peasants while the Slavic population could be used as slave labor to build the Aryan racial state that would dominate Europe for a thousand years. Hitler's conclusion was apparent: Germany must prepare for its inevitable war with the Soviet Union. Hitler's ideas were by no means secret. He had spelled them out in Mein Kampf, a book readily available to anyone who wished to read it (see the box on p. 972).

Hitler and the Nazis were neither the first Europeans not the first Germans to undertake European conquest and world power. Certainly, a number of elite circles in Germany before World War I had argued that Germany needed to annex lands to its south, east, and west if it wished to compete with the large states and remain a great power. The defeat in World War I destroyed this dream of world power, but the traditional conservative elites in the German military and the Foreign Office supported Hitler's foreign policy until 1937, largely because it accorded with their own desires for German expansion. But, as they realized too late, Nazi policy went far beyond previous German goals. Hitler's desire to create an Aryan racial empire led to slave labor and even mass extermination on a scale that would have been incomprehensible to previous generations of Germans.

Although Hitler had defined his goals, he had no prearranged timetable for achieving them. During his rise to power, he had demonstrated the ability to be both ideologue and opportunist. After 1933, a combination of military and diplomatic situations, organizational chaos in the administration of Germany, and economic pres-

Hitler's Foreign Policy Goals
▼ ▼ ▼

Adolf Hitler was a firm believer in the geopolitical doctrine of Lebensraum, which advocated that nations must find sufficient living space to be strong. This idea was evident in Mein Kampf, but it was explained in even more detail in a treatise that Hitler wrote in 1928. It was not published in his lifetime.

Hitler's Secret Book, 1928

I have already dealt with Germany's various foreign policy possibilities in this book. Nevertheless I shall once more briefly present the possible foreign policy goals so that they may yield a basis for the critical examination of the relations of these individual foreign policy aims to those of other European states.

(1) Germany can renounce setting a foreign policy goal altogether. This means that in reality she can decide for anything and need be committed to nothing at all. . . . [Hitler rejects this alternative.]
(2) Germany desires to effect the sustenance of the German people by peaceful economic means, as up to now. Accordingly even in the future she will participate most decisively in world industry, export and trade. . . . From a folkish standpoint setting this foreign policy aim is calamitous, and it is madness from the point of view of power politics.
(3) Germany establishes the restoration of the borders of the year 1914 as her foreign policy aim. This goal is insufficient from a national standpoint, unsatisfactory from a military point of view, impossible from a folkish standpoint with its eye on the future, and mad from the viewpoint of its consequences. . . .
(4) Germany decides to go over to [her future aim] a clear, far-seeing territorial policy. Thereby she abandons all attempts at world-industry and world-trade and instead concentrates all her strength in order, through the allotment of sufficient living space for the next hundred years to our people, also to prescribe a path of life. Since this territory can be only in the East, the obligation to be a naval power also recedes into the background. Germany tries anew to champion her interests through the formation of a decisive power on land.

This aim is equally in keeping with the highest national as well as folkish requirements. It likewise presupposes great military power means for its execution, but does not necessarily bring Germany into conflict with all European great powers. As surely as France here will remain Germany's enemy, just as little does the nature of such a political aim contain a reason for England, and especially for Italy, to maintain the enmity of the World War.

sures, especially after 1936, caused Hitler periodically to take steps that seemed to contradict the foreign policy goals of *Mein Kampf.* But he always returned to his basic ideological plans for racial supremacy and empire. He was certain of one thing: only he had the ability to accomplish these goals, and his fears for his health pushed him to fulfill his mission as quickly as possible. His impatience would become a major cause of his own undoing.

The "Diplomatic Revolution," 1933–1936

Between 1933 and 1936, Hitler and Nazi Germany achieved a "diplomatic revolution" in Europe. When Hitler become chancellor of Germany on January 30, 1933, Germany's position in Europe seemed weak. The Versailles treaty had created a demilitarized zone on Germany's western border that would allow the French to move into the heavily industrialized parts of Germany in the event of war. To Germany's east, the smaller states, such as Poland and Czechoslovakia, had defensive treaties with France. The Versailles treaty had also limited Germany's army to 100,000 troops with no air or naval forces.

The Germans were not without advantages, however. Germany was the second most populous European state after the Soviet Union and still possessed a great industrial capacity. Hitler was also well aware that Great Britain and France, dismayed by the costs and losses of World War I, wanted to avoid another war. Hitler knew that the French posed a threat to an unarmed Germany, but he believed that if he could keep the French from acting unilaterally against Germany in his first years, he could remove the restrictions imposed on Germany by Versailles and restore its strength.

Hitler's ability to rearm Germany and fulfill his expansionist policies depended initially upon his ability to convince others that his intentions were peaceful. Posing as the man of peace in his public speeches, Hitler emphasized that Germany wished only to revise the unfair provisions of Versailles by peaceful means and achieve Germany's rightful place among the European states. During his first two years in office, Hitler pursued a prudent foreign policy without unnecessary risks. His dramatic action in October 1933, when he withdrew Germany from the Geneva Disarmament Conference and the League of Nations, was done primarily for domestic political reasons, to give the Germans the feeling that their country was no longer dominated by other European states.

By the beginning of 1935, Hitler had become convinced that Germany could break some of the provisions of the Treaty of Versailles without serious British and French opposition. Hitler had come to believe, based on their responses to his early actions, that both states wanted to maintain the international status quo, but without using force. Consequently, Hitler decided to announce publicly what had been going on secretly for some time—Germany's military rearmament. On March 9, 1935, Hitler announced the creation of a new air force

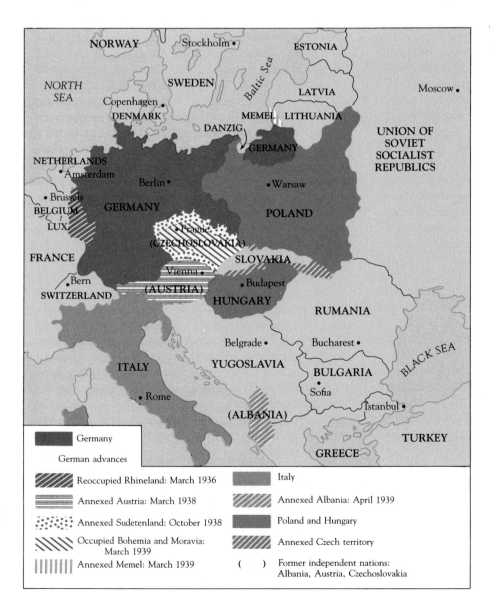

▼ **Map 28.1** Changes in Central Europe, 1936–Summer, 1939.

and, one week later, the introduction of a military draft that would expand Germany's army from 100,000 to 550,000 troops.

Hitler's unilateral repudiation of the Versailles treaty brought a swift reaction as France, Great Britain, and Italy condemned Germany's action and warned against future aggressive steps. But nothing concrete was done. Even worse, Britain subsequently moved toward an open acceptance of Germany's right to rearm when it agreed to the Anglo-German Naval Pact on June 18, 1935. This treaty allowed Germany to build a navy that would be 35 percent of the size of the British navy, with parity in submarines. The British were starting a policy of appeasement, based on the belief that if European states satisfied the reasonable demands of dissatisfied powers, the latter would be content and stability and peace would be achieved in Europe. British appeasement was grounded in large part upon Britain's desire to avoid another war, but it was also fostered by those British statesmen who believed that Nazi Germany offered a powerful bulwark against Soviet Communism.

On March 7, 1936, buoyed by his conviction that the Western democracies had no intention of using force to maintain the Treaty of Versailles, Hitler sent German troops into the demilitarized Rhineland. According to the Versailles treaty, the French had the right to use force against any violation of the demilitarized Rhineland. But France would not act without British support, and the British viewed the occupation of German territory by German troops as another reasonable action by a dissatisfied power. The London *Times* noted that the Germans were only "going into their own back garden." To Hitler, the French and British response only reinforced his growing conviction that they were weak nations unwilling to use force to defend the old order.

Meanwhile, Hitler gained new allies. In October 1935, Benito Mussolini had committed Fascist Italy to imperial expansion by invading Ethiopia. Angered by French and British opposition to his invasion, Mussolini welcomed Hitler's support and began to draw closer to the German dictator he had once called a buffoon. The joint intervention in 1936 of Germany and Italy on behalf of General Francisco Franco in the Spanish Civil War also drew the two nations closer together. In October 1936, Mussolini and Hitler concluded an agreement that recognized their common political and economic interests, and one month later, Mussolini referred publicly to the new Rome-Berlin Axis. Also in November 1936, Germany and Japan (the rising military power in the Far East), concluded the Anti-Comintern Pact and agreed to maintain a common front against communism.

By the end of 1936, Hitler and Nazi Germany had achieved a "diplomatic revolution" in Europe. The Treaty of Versailles had been virtually scrapped and Germany was once more a "World Power," as Hitler proclaimed. Hitler had demonstrated a great deal of diplomatic skill in taking advantage of Europeans' burning desire for peace. He had used the tactic of peaceful revision as skillfully as he had used the tactic of legality in his pursuit of power in Germany. By the end of 1936, Nazi power had increased enough that Hitler could initiate an even more daring foreign policy. As Hitler perceived, if the Western states were so afraid of war that they resisted its use when they were strong and Germany was weak, then they would be even more reluctant to do so now that Germany was strong. Although many Europeans still wanted to believe Hitler's own protestations of peace, his moves had actually made war more possible.

The Path to War, 1937–1939

On November 5, 1937, at a secret conference in Berlin with his military leaders, Adolf Hitler revealed his future aims. Germany's ultimate goal, he assured his audience, must be the conquest of living space in the east. Although this might mean war with France and Great Britain, Germany had no alternative if the basic needs of the German people were to be met. First, however, Germany must deal with Austria and Czechoslovakia and secure its eastern and southern flanks.

By the end of 1937, Hitler was convinced that neither the French nor the British would provide much opposition to his plans. The new British prime minister, Neville Chamberlain (1869–1940), was a strong advocate of appeasement and believed that the survival of the British Empire depended upon an accommodation with Germany. Chamberlain had made it known to Hitler in November 1937 that he would not oppose changes in central Europe provided that they were executed peacefully.

Hitler decided to move first on Austria. Hitler had failed miserably in 1934 when he tried to help the Austrian Nazi party seize power. He was more successful in 1938. By threatening Austria with invasion, Hitler coerced the Austrian chancellor, Kurt von Schuschnigg (1897–1977), into putting Austrian Nazis in charge of the government. The new government promptly invited German troops to enter Austria and assist in maintaining law and order. One day later, on March 13, 1938, after his triumphal return to his native land, Hitler formally annexed Austria to Germany. Great Britain's ready acknowledgment of Hitler's action only increased the German dictator's contempt for Western weakness.

The annexation of Austria improved Germany's strategic position in central Europe and put Germany in position for Hitler's next objective—the destruction of Czechoslovakia. On May 30, 1938, Hitler had already told his generals that it was his "unalterable decision to smash Czechoslovakia by military action in the near future."[2] This goal might have seemed unrealistic since democratic Czechoslovakia was quite prepared to defend itself and was well supported by pacts with France and Soviet Russia. Nevertheless, Hitler believed that France and Britain would not use force to defend Czechoslovakia.

In the meantime, Hitler had stepped up his demands on the Czechs. Initially, the Germans had asked for autonomy for the Sudetenland, the mountainous northwestern border area of Czechoslovakia that was home to three million ethnic Germans. As Hitler knew, the Sudetenland also contained Czechoslovakia's most important frontier defenses and considerable industrial resources as well. But on September 15, 1938, Hitler demanded the cession of the Sudetenland to Germany and expressed his willingness to risk "world war" to achieve his objective. War was not necessary, however, as appeasement triumphed once again. On September 29, at the hastily arranged Munich Conference, the British, French, Germans, and Italians (neither the Czechs nor the Russians were invited) reached an agreement that essentially met all of Hitler's demands. German troops were allowed to occupy the Sudetenland as the Czechs, abandoned by their Western allies, stood by helplessly. The Munich Conference was the high point of Western appeasement of Hitler. When Chamberlain returned to England from Munich, he boasted that the Munich agreement meant "peace in our times." Hitler had promised Chamberlain that he had made his last demand; all other European problems could be settled by negotiation. Like many German politicians, Chamberlain had believed Hitler's assurances (see the box on p. 976).

In fact, Munich confirmed Hitler's perception that the Western democracies were weak and would not fight. Increasingly, Hitler was convinced of his own infallibility, and he had by no means been satisfied at Munich. Already at the end of October 1938, Hitler told his generals to prepare for the final liquidation of the Czechoslovakian state. Using the internal disorder that he had deliberately fostered as a pretext, Hitler occupied the Czech lands (Bohemia and Moravia) while the Slovaks, with Hitler's encouragement, declared their independence of the Czechs and become a puppet state (Slovakia) of Nazi Germany. On the evening of March 15, 1939, Hitler triumphantly declared in Prague that he would be known as the greatest German of them all.

At last, the Western states reacted vigorously to Hitler's threat. After all, the Czechs were not Germans crying for reunion with Germany. Hitler's naked aggression made clear that his promises were utterly worthless. When Hitler began to demand the return of Danzig

▼ **The Munich Conference.** At a conference in Munich at the end of September 1938, the British and French capitulated to Hitler's demands and agreed to the German occupation of Czechoslovakia's Sudetenland area. The Munich Conference represents the high point of the West's appeasement of Hitler. Seen here are the chief participants in the conference: Chamberlain, Daladier (premier of France), Hitler, and Mussolini.

The Munich Conference

▼ ▼ ▼

At the Munich Conference, the leaders of France and Great Britain capitulated to Hitler's demands on Czechoslovakia. While the British prime minister, Neville Chamberlain, defended his actions at Munich as necessary for peace, another British statesman, Winston Churchill, characterized the settlement at Munich as "a disaster of the first magnitude."

Winston Churchill, Speech to the House of Commons, October 5, 1938

I will begin by saying what everybody would like to ignore or forget but which must nevertheless be stated, namely, that we have sustained a total and unmitigated defeat, and that France has suffered even more than we have. . . . The utmost my right honorable Friend the Prime Minister . . . has been able to gain for Czechoslovakia and in the matters which were in dispute has been that the German dictator, instead of snatching his victuals from the table, has been content to have them served to him course by course. . . . And I will say this, that I believe the Czechs, left to themselves and told they were going to get no help from the Western Powers, would have been able to make better terms than they have got. . . .

We are in the presence of a disaster of the first magnitude which has befallen Great Britain and France. Do not let us blind ourselves to that. . . .

And do not suppose that this is the end. This is only the beginning of the reckoning. This is only the first sip, the first foretaste of a bitter cup which will be proffered to us year by year unless by a supreme recovery of moral health and martial vigor, we arise again and take our stand for freedom as in the olden time.

Neville Chamberlain, Speech to the House of Commons, October 6, 1938

That is my answer to those who say that we should have told Germany weeks ago that, if her army crossed the border of Czechoslovakia, we should be at war with her. We had no treaty obligations and no legal obligations to Czechoslovakia. . . . When we were convinced, as we become convinced, that nothing any longer would keep the Sudetenland within the Czechoslovakian State, we urged the Czech Government as strongly as we could to agree to the cession of territory, and to agree promptly. . . . It was a hard decision for anyone who loved his country to take, but to accuse us of having by that advice betrayed the Czechoslovakian State is simply preposterous. What we did was to save her from annihilation and give her a chance of new life as a new State, which involves the loss of territory and fortifications, but may perhaps enable her to enjoy in the future and develop a national existence under a neutrality and security comparable to that which we see in Switzerland today. Therefore, I think the Government deserve the approval of this House for their conduct of affairs in this recent crisis which has saved Czechoslovakia from destruction and Europe from Armageddon.

(which had been made a free city by the Treaty of Versailles to serve as a seaport for Poland) to Germany, Britain recognized the danger and offered to protect Poland in the event of war. At the same time, both France and Britain realized that only the Soviet Union was powerful enough to help contain Nazi aggression, and began political and military negotiations with Joseph Stalin and the Soviets. The West's distrust of Soviet Communism, however, made an alliance unlikely.

Meanwhile, Hitler pressed on in the belief that the West would not really fight over Poland. He ordered his generals to prepare for the invasion of Poland on September 1, 1939. To preclude an alliance between the West and the Soviet Union, which would create the danger of a two-front war, Hitler, ever the opportunist, negotiated his own nonaggression pact with Stalin and shocked the world with its announcement on August 23, 1939. A secret protocol to the treaty created German and Soviet spheres of influence in eastern Europe: Finland, the Baltic states (Estonia, Latvia, and Lithuania), and eastern Poland would go to the Soviet Union while Germany would acquire western Poland. The treaty with the Soviet Union gave Hitler the freedom to attack Poland. He told his generals: "Now Poland is in the position in which I wanted her . . . I am only afraid that at the last moment some swine or other will yet submit to me a plan for mediation."[3] He need not have worried. On September 1, German forces invaded Poland; two days later, Britain and France declared war on Germany. Europe was again at war.

▼ The Course of World War II

Nine days before he attacked Poland, Hitler made clear to his generals what was expected of them: "When starting and waging a war it is not right that matters, but victory. Close your hearts to pity. Act brutally. Eighty million people must obtain what is their right . . . . The wholesale destruction of Poland is the military objective. Speed is the main thing. Pursuit until complete annihilation."[4] Hitler's remarks set the tone for what became the most destructive war in human history.

▼ **Hitler Declares War.** Adolf Hitler believed that Germany's living space must be gained by conquest in the east. This policy meant war. Hitler's nonaggression pact with Soviet Russia on August 23, 1939, paved the way for his invasion of Poland on September 1. On that day, Hitler spoke to the German Reichstag and announced the outbreak of war.

Chronology
▼ ▼ ▼
Prelude to War, 1933–1939

Hitler Becomes Chancellor	January 30, 1933
Germany Withdraws from League of Nations and Geneva Disarmament Conference	October 1933
Hitler Announces a German Air Force	March 9, 1935
Hitler Announces Military Conscription	March 16, 1935
Anglo-German Naval Pact	June 18, 1935
Mussolini Invades Ethiopia	October 1935
Hitler Occupies Demilitarized Rhineland	March 7, 1936
Mussolini and Hitler Intervene in Spanish Civil War	1936
Rome-Berlin Axis	October 1936
Anti-Comintern Pact (Japan and Germany)	November 1936
Japan Invades China	1937
Germany Annexes Austria	March 13, 1938
Munich Conference: Germany Occupies Sudetenland	September 29, 1938
Germany Occupies the Rest of Czechoslovakia	March 1939
German-Soviet Nonaggression Pact	August 23, 1939
Germany Invades Poland	September 1, 1939
Britain and France Declare War on Germany	September 3, 1939

Victory and Stalemate

Using *Blitzkrieg,* or "lightning war," Hitler stunned Europe with the speed and efficiency of the German attack. Armored columns or panzer divisions (a panzer division was a strike force of about three hundred tanks and accompanying forces and supplies) supported by airplanes broke quickly through Polish lines and encircled the bewildered Polish troops. Conventional infantry units then moved in to hold the newly conquered territory. Within four weeks, Poland had surrendered. On September 28, 1939, Germany and the Soviet Union officially divided Poland between them.

Although Hitler's hopes to avoid a war with the West were dashed when France and Britain declared war on

September 3, he was confident that he could control the situation. Expecting another war of attrition and economic blockade, Britain and France refused to go on the offensive. After a winter of waiting (called the "phony war"), Hitler resumed the war on April 9, 1940, with another *Blitzkrieg* against Denmark and Norway. One month later, on May 10, the Germans launched their attack on the Netherlands, Belgium, and France. The main assault through Luxembourg and the Ardennes forest, completely unexpected by the French and British forces, enabled German panzer divisions to break through the weak French defensive positions there and race across northern France, splitting the Allied armies and trapping French troops and the entire British army on the beaches of Dunkirk. Only by heroic efforts did

▼ **German Troops in Paris.** On May 10, 1940, Hitler launched his attack on the Netherlands, Belgium, and France. Overwhelmed by the speed and audacity of the German attack, the French capitulated on June 22. This photograph shows German troops marching in Paris with the Arc de Triomphe in the background.

the British succeed in achieving a gigantic evacuation of 330,000 Allied (mostly British) troops.

On June 5, the Germans launched another offensive into southern France. Five days later, Mussolini, believing that the war was over and eager to grab some of the spoils, declared war on France and invaded from the south. The French capitulated on June 22. German armies occupied about three-fifths of France while the French hero of World War I, Marshal Henri Pétain (1856–1951) established an authoritarian regime (known as Vichy France) over the remainder. Germany was now in control of western and central Europe, but Britain had still not been defeated.

German victories in Denmark and Norway coincided with a change of government in Great Britain. On May 10, 1940, Winston Churchill (1874–1965), a longtime advocate for a hard-line policy toward Nazi Germany, replaced the apostle of appeasement, Neville Chamberlain. Churchill proved to be an inspiring leader who rallied the British people with stirring speeches and stubborn determination. Hitler hoped that the British could be persuaded to make peace so that he could fulfill his long-awaited opportunity to gain living space in the east. The British refused, and Hitler was forced to prepare for an invasion of Britain, a prospect that he faced with little confidence.

As Hitler realized, an amphibious invasion of Britain would only be possible if Germany gained control of the air. At the beginning of August 1940, the *Luftwaffe* (the German air force) launched a major offensive against British air and naval bases, harbors, communication centers, and war industries. The British fought back doggedly, supported by an effective radar system that gave them early warning of German attacks. Moreover, the Ultra intelligence operation, which had broken German military codes, gave the British air force information about the specific targets of German air attacks. Nevertheless, the British air force suffered critical losses by the end of August and was probably saved by Hitler's change of strategy. In September, in retaliation for a British attack on Berlin, Hitler ordered a shift from military targets to massive bombing of British cities to break British morale. The British rebuilt their air strength quickly and were soon inflicting major losses on *Luftwaffe* bombers. By the end of September, Germany had lost the Battle of Britain, and the invasion of Britain had to be postponed.

At this point, Hitler pursued the possibility of a Mediterranean strategy, which would involve capturing Egypt and the Suez Canal and closing the Mediterranean to British ships, thereby shutting off Britain's supply of

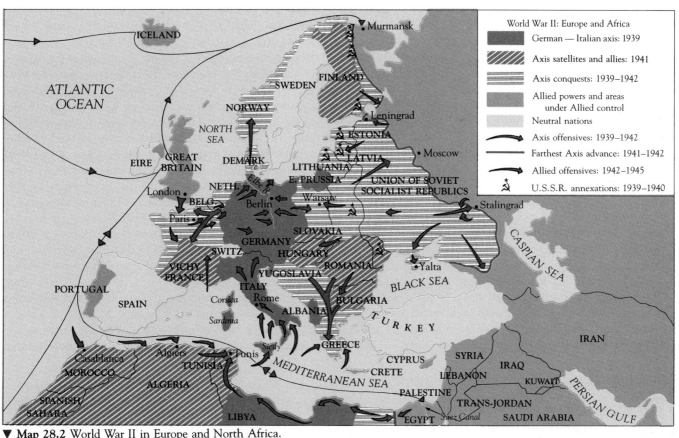

▼ **Map 28.2** World War II in Europe and North Africa.

oil. Hitler's commitment to the Mediterranean was never wholehearted, however. His initial plan was to let the Italians defeat the British in North Africa, but this strategy failed when the British routed the Italian army. Although Hitler then sent German troops to the north African theater of war, his primary concern lay elsewhere: he had already reached the decision to fulfill his lifetime obsession with the acquisition of living space in the east.

Already at the end of July 1940, Hitler had told his army leaders to begin preparations for the invasion of the Soviet Union. Although he had no desire for a two-front war, Hitler became convinced that Britain was remaining in the war only because it expected Russian support. If Russia were smashed, Britain's last hope would be eliminated. Moreover, Hitler had convinced himself that the Soviet Union, with its Jewish-Bolshevik leadership and a pitiful army, could be defeated quickly and decisively. Although the invasion of the Soviet Union was scheduled for spring 1941, the attack was delayed because of problems in the Balkans. Hitler had already obtained the political cooperation of Hungary, Bulgaria,

and Romania. Mussolini's disastrous invasion of Greece in October 1940 exposed Hitler's southern flank to British air bases in Greece. To secure his Balkan flank, German troops seized both Yugoslavia and Greece in April. Now reassured, Hitler turned to the east and invaded the Soviet Union on June 22, 1941, in the belief that the Russians could still be decisively defeated before winter set in.

The massive attack stretched out along an 1,800-mile front. German troops advanced rapidly, capturing two million Russian soldiers. By November, one German army group had swept through the Ukraine, while a second was besieging Leningrad; a third approached within twenty-five miles of Moscow, the Russian capital. An early Russian winter and unexpected Russian resistance, however, brought a halt to the German advance. For the first time in the war, German armies had been stopped. A counterattack in December 1941 by a Soviet army supposedly exhausted by Nazi victories brought an ominous ending to the year for the Germans. By that time, another of Hitler's decisions—the declaration of war on the United States—had probably made his defeat inevitable and turned another European conflict into a global war.

THE WAR IN ASIA   The war in Asia arose from the ambitions of Japan, whose rise to the status of world power had been swift. Japan had defeated China in 1895, Russia in 1905, and had taken over many of Germany's eastern and Pacific colonies in World War I. By 1933, the Japanese empire included Korea, Formosa (now Taiwan), Manchuria, and the Marshall, Caroline, and Mariana Islands in the Pacific.

By the early 1930s, Japan was experiencing severe internal tensions. Its population had exploded from 30 million in 1870 to 80 million by 1937. Much of Japan's ability to feed its population and to pay for industrial raw materials depended upon the manufacture of heavy industrial goods (especially ships) and textiles. But in the 1930s, Western nations created tariff barriers to protect their own economies from the effects of the depression. Japan was devastated, both economically and politically.

Although political power had been concentrated in the hands of the emperor and his cabinet, Japan had also experienced a slow growth of political democracy with universal male suffrage in 1924 and the emergence of mass political parties. The economic crises of the 1930s stifled this democratic growth. Right-wing patriotic societies allied themselves with the army and navy to push a program of expansion at the expense of China and Russia, while the navy hoped to make Japan self-sufficient in raw materials by conquering British Malaya and the Dutch East Indies. In 1935, Japan began to build a modern naval fleet, and after 1936 the armed forces exercised much control over the government.

The war in Asia began in July 1937 when Japanese troops invaded northern China. Moreover, Japanese naval expansion brought the Japanese into conflict with the European imperial powers—Britain (in India, Burma, Malaya), France (in Indochina), and the Netherlands (in Indonesia)—as well as with the other rising power in the Pacific, the United States. When the Japanese occupied Indochina in July 1941, the Americans responded by cutting off sales of vital scrap iron and oil to Japan. Japan's military leaders decided to preempt any further American response by attacking the American

▼ **Map 28.3** World War II in Asia and the Pacific.

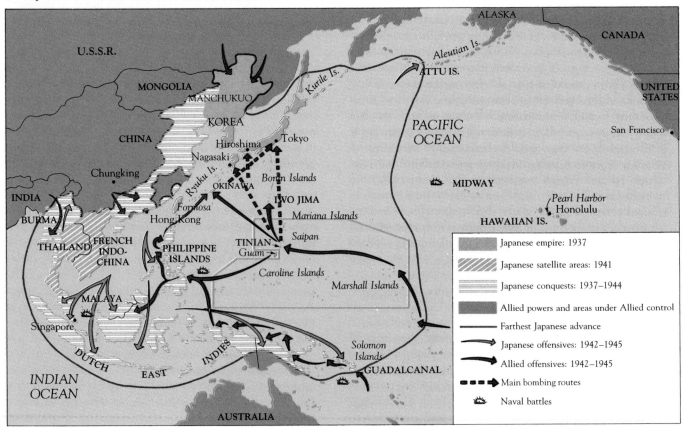

naval fleet at Pearl Harbor on December 7, 1941. The United States declared war on Japan the next day. Three days later, Hitler declared war on the United States, although he was by no means required to do so by his loose alliance with Japan. This action enabled President Roosevelt to overcome strong American isolationist sentiment and to bring the United States into the European conflict. The simultaneous involvement of the United States in both the European and Asian theaters made World War II a single, truly world war.

The Turning Point of the War, 1942–1943

The entry of the United States into the war created a coalition (the Grand Alliance) that ultimately defeated the Axis powers (Germany, Italy, Japan). Nevertheless, the three major Allies, Britain, the United States, and the Soviet Union, had to overcome mutual suspicions before they could operate as an effective alliance. Two factors aided that process. First, Hitler's declaration of war on the United States made it easier for the United States to accept the British and Russian contention that the defeat of Germany should be the first priority of the United States. For that reason, the United States, under its Lend-Lease program, sent large amounts of military aid, including $50 billion worth of trucks, planes, and other arms, to the British and Soviets. Also important to the alliance was the tacit agreement of the three chief Allies to stress military operations while ignoring political differences and larger strategic issues concerning any postwar settlement. At the beginning of 1943, the Allies agreed to fight until the Axis powers surrendered unconditionally. Although this principle of unconditional surrender might have discouraged dissident Germans and Japanese from overthrowing their governments in order to arrange a negotiated peace, it also had the effect of cementing the Grand Alliance by making it nearly impossible for Hitler to divide his foes.

Defeat, however, was far from Hitler's mind at the beginning of 1942. As Japanese forces advanced into Southeast Asia and the Pacific after crippling the American naval fleet at Pearl Harbor, Hitler and his European allies continued the war in Europe against Britain and the Soviet Union. Until the fall of 1942, it appeared that the Germans might still prevail on the battlefield. Reinforcements in North Africa enabled the Afrika Korps under General Erwin Rommel to break through the British defenses in Egypt and advance toward Alexandria. The Germans were also continuing their success in the Battle of the North Atlantic as their submarines continued to attack Allied ships carrying supplies to

▼ **The Air War.** Air power played a major role in the battles of World War II. Because of his stretched-out supply lines in north Africa, the German general Erwin Rommel was forced to rely heavily on transport aircraft to keep his forces supplied.

Great Britain. In the spring of 1942, a renewed German offensive in Russia led to the capture of the entire Crimea, causing Hitler to boast in August 1942:

> As the next step, we are going to advance south of the Caucasus and then help the rebels in Iran and Iraq against the English. Another thrust will be directed along the Caspian Sea toward Afghanistan and India. Then the English will run out of oil. In two years we'll be on the borders of India. Twenty to thirty elite German divisions will do. Then the British Empire will collapse.[5]

But this would be Hitler's last optimistic outburst. By the fall of 1942, the war had turned against the Germans.

In North Africa, British forces had stopped Rommel's troops at El Alamein in the summer of 1942 and then

A German Soldier at Stalingrad

▼ ▼ ▼

The Russian victory at Stalingrad was a major turning point in World War II. This excerpt comes from the diary of a German soldier who fought and died in the Battle of Stalingrad. His dreams of victory and a return home with medals are soon dashed by the realities of Russian resistance.

Diary of a German Soldier

Today, after we'd had a bath, the company commander told us that if our future operations are as successful, we'll soon reach the Volga, take Stalingrad and then the war will inevitably soon be over. Perhaps we'll be home by Christmas.

July 29. The company commander says the Russian troops are completely broken, and cannot hold out any longer. To reach the Volga and take Stalingrad is not so difficult for us. The Führer knows where the Russians' weak point is. Victory is not far away. . . .

August 10. The Führer's orders were read out to us. He expects victory of us. We are all convinced that they can't stop us.

August 12. This morning outstanding soldiers were presented with decorations. . . . Will I really go back to Elsa without a decoration? I believe that for Stalingrad the Führer will decorate even me. . . .

September 4. We are being sent northward along the front towards Stalingrad. We marched all night and by dawn had reached Voroponovo Station. We can already see the smoking town. It's a happy thought that the end of the war is getting nearer. That's what everyone is saying. . . .

September 8. Two days of non-stop fighting. The Russians are defending themselves with insane stubbornness. Our regiment has lost many men. . . .

September 16. Our battalion, plus tanks, is attacking the [grain storage] elevator, from which smoke is pouring—the grain in it is burning, the Russians seem to have set light to it themselves. Barbarism. The battalion is suffering heavy losses. . . .

October 10. The Russians are so close to us that our planes cannot bomb them. We are preparing for a decisive attack. The Führer has ordered the whole of Stalingrad to be taken as rapidly as possible. . . .

October 22. Our regiment has failed to break into the factory. We have lost many men; every time you move you have to jump over bodies. . . .

November 10. A letter from Elsa today. Everyone expects us home for Christmas. In Germany everyone believes we already hold Stalingrad. How wrong they are. If they could only see what Stalingrad has done to our army. . . .

November 21. The Russians have gone over to the offensive along the whole front. Fierce fighting is going on. So, there it is—the Volga, victory and soon home to our families! We shall obviously be seeing them next in the other world.

November 29. We are encircled. It was announced this morning that the Führer has said: "The army can trust me to do everything necessary to ensure supplies and rapidly break the encirclement."

December 3. We are on hunger rations and waiting for the rescue that the Führer promised. . . .

December 14. Everybody is racked with hunger. Frozen potatoes are the best meal, but to get them out of the ice-covered ground under fire from Russian bullets is not so easy. . . .

December 26. The horses have already been eaten. I would eat a cat; they say its meat is also tasty. The soldiers look like corpses or lunatics, looking for something to put in their mouths. They no longer take cover from Russian shells; they haven't the strength to walk, run away and hide. A curse on this war!

forced them back across the desert. In November 1942, British and American forces invaded French North Africa and forced the German and Italian troops to surrender in May 1943. By that time, new detection devices had enabled the Allies to destroy increasing numbers of German submarines in the shipping war in the Atlantic. On the Eastern Front, the turning point of the war occurred at Stalingrad. After the capture of the Crimea, Hitler's generals wanted him to concentrate on the capture of the Caucasus and its oil fields, but Hitler decided that Stalingrad, a major industrial center on the Volga, should be taken first. Between November 1942 and February 1943, German troops were stopped, then encircled, and finally forced to surrender on February 2, 1943 (see the box on p. 982). The entire German Sixth Army of 300,000 men was lost. By February 1943, German forces in Russia were back to their positions of June 1942. By the spring of 1943, even Hitler knew that the Germans would not defeat the Soviet Union.

The tide of battle in the Far East also turned dramatically in 1942. In the Battle of the Coral Sea on May 7–8, 1942, American naval forces stopped the Japanese advance and temporarily relieved Australia of the threat of invasion. On June 4, at the Battle of Midway Island, American planes destroyed all four of the attacking Japanese aircraft carriers and established American naval superiority in the Pacific. After a series of bitter engagements in the waters near the Solomon Islands from August to November, Japanese fortunes began to fade.

The Last Years of the War

By the beginning of 1943, the tide of battle had turned against Germany, Italy, and Japan. After the Axis forces had surrendered in Tunisia on May 13, 1943, the Allies crossed the Mediterranean and carried the war to Italy, an area that Winston Churchill had called the "soft underbelly" of Europe. After taking Sicily, Allied troops began the invasion of mainland Italy in September. In the meantime, after the ouster and arrest of Benito Mussolini, a new Italian government offered to surrender to Allied forces. But Musso-

lini was liberated by the Germans in a daring raid and then set up as the head of a puppet German state in northern Italy while German troops moved in and occupied much of Italy. The new defensive lines established by the Germans in the hills south of Rome were so effective that the Allied advance up the Italian peninsula was a painstaking affair accompanied by heavy casualties. Rome did not fall to the Allies until June 4, 1944. By that time, the Italian war had assumed a secondary role anyway as the Allies opened their long-awaited "second front" in western Europe.

Since the autumn of 1943, the Allies had been planning a cross-channel invasion of France from Britain. A series of Allied deceptions managed to trick the Germans into believing that the invasion would come on the flat plains of northern France. Instead, the Allies, under the direction of the American general, Dwight D. Eisenhower (1890–1969), landed five assault divisions on the Normandy beaches on June 6 in history's greatest naval invasion. An initially indecisive German response enabled the Allied forces to establish a beachhead. Within three months, they had landed two million men and a half-million vehicles that pushed inland and broke through German defensive lines.

After the breakout, Allied troops moved south and east and liberated Paris by the end of August. Supply problems as well as a last-minute, desperate (and unsuccessful) offensive by German troops in the Battle of the

▼ **Crossing the Rhine.** After landing at Normandy, Allied forces liberated France and prepared to move into Germany. Makeshift bridges enabled the Allies to cross the Rhine in some areas and advance deeper into Germany. By this time, Allied forces had a massive superiority over the Germans in both men and equipment.

Germany and the Soviet Union Divide Poland	October 1939
Blitzkrieg against Denmark and Norway	April 1940
Blitzkrieg against Belgium, Netherlands, and France	May 1940
Churchill Becomes British Prime Minister	May 10, 1940
France Surrenders	June 22, 1940
Battle of Britain	Fall 1940
Nazi Seizure of Yugoslavia and Greece	April 1941
Germany Invades the Soviet Union	June 22, 1941
Japanese Attack on Pearl Harbor	December 7, 1941
Battle of the Coral Sea	May 7–8, 1942
Battle of Midway Island	June 4, 1942
Allied Invasion of North Africa	November 1942
German Surrender at Stalingrad	February 2, 1943
Axis Forces Surrender in North Africa	May 1943
Battle of Kursk	July 5–12, 1943
Invasion of Mainland Italy	September 1943
Allied Invasion of France	June 6, 1944
Hitler Commits Suicide	April 30, 1945
Surrender of Germany	May 7, 1945
Atomic Bomb Dropped on Hiroshima	August 6, 1945
Japan Surrenders	August 14, 1945

Bulge slowed the Allied advance. Nevertheless, by March 1945, Allied armies had crossed the Rhine River and advanced further into Germany. At the end of April, Allied forces in northern Germany moved toward the Elbe River where they finally linked up with the Russians.

The Russians had come a long way since the Battle of Stalingrad in 1943. In the summer of 1943, Hitler's generals had urged him to build an East Wall based on river barriers to halt the Russians. Instead, Hitler gambled on taking the offensive by making use of newly developed heavy tanks. German forces were soundly defeated by the Russians at the Battle of Kursk (July 5–12), the

greatest tank battle of World War II. The Germans lost eighteen of their best panzer divisions. Soviet forces now began a relentless advance westward. The Soviets had reoccupied the Ukraine by the end of 1943 and lifted the siege of Leningrad and moved into the Baltic states by the beginning of 1944. Advancing along a northern front, Soviet troops occupied Warsaw in January 1945 and entered Berlin in April. Meanwhile, soviet troops swept along a southern front through Hungary, Romania, and Bulgaria.

In January 1945, Adolf Hitler had moved into a bunker fifty-five feet under Berlin to direct the final stages of the war. Hitler continued to arrange his armies on worn-out battle maps as if it still made a difference. In his final political testament, Hitler, consistent to the end in his rabid anti-Semitism, blamed the Jews for the war: "Above all I charge the leaders of the nation and those under them to scrupulous observance of the laws of race and to merciless opposition to the universal poisoner of all peoples, international Jewry."[6] Hitler committed suicide on April 30, two days after Mussolini had been shot by partisan Italian forces. On May 7, German commanders surrendered. The war in Europe was over.

The war in Asia continued. Beginning in 1943, American forces had gone on the offensive and advanced their way, slowly at times, across the Pacific. American forces took an increasing toll of enemy resources, especially at sea and in the air. When President Harry Truman (Roosevelt had died on April 12, 1945) and his advisers become convinced that American troops might suffer heavy casualties in the invasion of the Japanese homeland, they made the decision to drop the newly developed atomic bomb on Hiroshima and Nagasaki. The Japanese surrendered unconditionally on August 14. World War II, in which 17 million men died in battle and perhaps 18 million civilians perished as well (some estimate total losses at 50 million), was finally over.

▼ The Nazi New Order

After the German victories in Europe, Nazi propagandists created glowing images of a new European order based on "equal chances" for all nations and an integrated economic community. This was not Hitler's conception of a European New Order. He saw the Europe he had conquered simply as subject to German domination. Only the Germans, he once said, "can really organize Europe."

The Nazi Empire

The Nazi empire stretched across continental Europe from the English Channel in the west to the outskirts of Moscow in the east. In no way was this empire organized systematically or governed efficiently. Some states—Spain, Portugal, Switzerland, Sweden, and Turkey—remained neutral and outside the empire. Germany's allies—Italy, Romania, Bulgaria, Hungary, and Finland—kept their independence, but found themselves increasingly restricted by the Germans as the war progressed. The remainder of Europe was largely organized in one of two ways. Some areas, such as western Poland, were directly annexed by Nazi Germany and made into German provinces. Most of occupied Europe was administered by German military or civilian officials, combined with different degrees of indirect control from collaborationist regimes. Competing lines of authority by different offices in occupied Europe made German occupation inefficient.

Racial considerations played an important role in how conquered peoples were treated. German civil administrations were established in Norway, Denmark, and the Netherlands because the Nazis considered their peoples to be Aryan or racially akin to the Germans and hence worthy of more lenient treatment. "Inferior" Latin peoples, such as the occupied French, were given military administrations. By 1943, however, as Nazi losses continued to multiply, all the occupied territories of northern and western Europe were ruthlessly exploited for material goods and manpower for Germany's war needs.

Because the conquered lands in the east contained the living space for German expansion and were populated in Nazi eyes by racially inferior Slavic peoples, Nazi administration there was considerably more ruthless. Hitler's racial ideology and his plans for an Aryan racial empire were so important to him that he and the Nazis began to implement their racial program soon after the conquest of Poland. Heinrich Himmler, a strong believer in Nazi racial ideology and the leader of the SS, was put in charge of German resettlement plans in the east. Himmler's task was to evacuate the inferior Slavic peoples and replace them with Germans, a policy first applied to the new German provinces created from the lands of western Poland. One million Poles were uprooted and dumped in southern Poland. Hundreds of thousands of ethnic Germans (descendants of Germans who had migrated years ago from Germany to different parts of southern and eastern Europe) were encouraged to colonize the designated areas in Poland. By 1942, two million ethnic Germans had been settled in Poland.

The invasion of the Soviet Union inflated Nazi visions of German colonization in the east. Hitler spoke to his intimate circle of a colossal project of social engineering after the war, in which Poles, Ukrainians, and Russians would become slave labor while German peasants settled on the abandoned lands and Germanized them (see the box on p. 986). Nazis involved in this kind of planning were well aware of the human costs. Himmler told a gathering of SS officers that although the destruction of 30 million Slavs was a prerequisite for German plans in the east, "Whether nations live in prosperity or starve to death interests me only insofar as we need them as slaves for our culture. Otherwise it is of no interest."[7]

Economically, the Nazi New Order meant the ruthless exploitation of conquered Europe's resources. In eastern Europe, economic exploitation was direct and severe. The Germans seized raw materials, machines, and food, leaving only enough to maintain local peoples at a bare subsistence level. Although the Germans adopted legal formalities in their economic exploitation of western Europe, military supplies and important raw materials were taken outright. Nazi policies created drastic shortages of food, clothing, and shelter. Many Europeans suffered severely.

Labor shortages in Germany led to a policy of ruthless mobilization of foreign labor for Germany. After the invasion of Russia, the 4 million Russian prisoners of war captured by the Germans became a chief source of heavy labor, but it was wasted by allowing 3 million of them to die from neglect. In 1942, a special office was created to recruit labor for German farms and industries. By the summer of 1944, 7 million foreign workers were laboring in Germany and constituted 20 percent of Germany's labor force. At the same time, another 7 million workers were supplying forced labor in their own countries on farms, in industries, and even in military camps. Forced labor, however, often proved counterproductive because it created economic chaos in occupied countries and disrupted industrial production that could have helped Germany. Even worse for the Germans, the brutal character of Germany's recruitment policies often led more and more people to resist the Nazi occupation forces.

Resistance Movements

German policies toward conquered peoples quickly led to the emergence of resistance movements throughout Europe, especially in the east, where brutality toward the native peoples produced a strong reaction. In

Hitler's Plans for a New Order in the East
▼ ▼ ▼

Hitler's nightly monologues to his postdinner guests, which were recorded by the Führer's private secretary, Martin Bormann, reveal much about the New Order he wished to create. On the evening of October 17, 1941, he expressed his views on what the Germans would do with their newly conquered territories in the east.

Hitler's Secret Conversations, October 17, 1941

In comparison with the beauties accumulated in Central Germany, the new territories in the East seem to us like a desert. . . . This Russian desert, we shall populate it. . . . We'll take away its character of an Asiatic steppe, we'll Europeanise it. With this object, we have undertaken the construction of roads that will lead to the southernmost point of the Crimea and to the Caucasus. These roads will be studded along their whole length with German towns, and around these towns our colonists will settle.

As for the two or three million men whom we need to accomplish this task, we'll find them quicker than we think. They'll come from Germany, Scandinavia, the Western countries and America. I shall no longer be here to see all that, but in twenty years the Ukraine will already be a home for twenty million inhabitants besides the natives. In three hundred years, the country will be one of the loveliest gardens in the world.

As for the natives, we'll have to screen them carefully. The Jew, that destroyer, we shall drive out. . . . We shan't settle in the Russian towns, and we'll let them fall to pieces without intervening. And, above all, no remorse on this subject! We're not going to play at children's nurses; we're absolutely without obligations as far as these people are concerned. To struggle against the hovels, chase away the fleas, provide German teachers, bring out newspapers—very little of that for us! We'll confine ourselves, perhaps, to setting up a radio transmitter, under our control. For the rest, let them know just enough to understand our highway signs, so that they won't get themselves run over by our vehicles. . . . There's only one duty: to Germanise this country by the immigration of Germans, and to look upon the natives as Redskins. If these people had defeated us, Heaven have mercy! But we don't hate them. That sentiment is unknown to us. We are guided only by reason. . . .

All those who have the feeling for Europe can join in our work.

In this business I shall go straight ahead, cold-bloodedly. What they may think about me, at this juncture, is to me a matter of complete indifference. I don't see why a German who eats a piece of bread should torment himself with the idea that the soil that produces this bread has been won by the sword.

---

the Ukraine and Baltic states, for example, Germans were hailed as liberators from communist rule, but Hitler's policies of treating Slavic peoples as subhumans only drove those peoples to support and join guerrilla forces.

Resistance movements were formed throughout Europe. Active resisters committed acts of sabotage against German installations, assassinated German officials, spread anti-German newspapers, wrote anti-German sentiments on walls, and spied on German military positions for the Allies. Some anti-Nazi groups from occupied countries, such as the Free French movement under Charles de Gaulle, created governments-in-exile in London. In some countries, resistance groups even grew strong enough to take on the Germans in pitched battles. In Yugoslavia, for example, Josip Broz, known as Tito (1892–1980), led a band of guerrillas against Ger-

man occupation forces. By 1944, his partisan army numbered 250,000.

After the invasion of Russia in 1941, Communists throughout Europe assumed leadership roles in underground resistance movements. This sometimes led to conflict with other local resistance groups who feared the postwar consequences of Communist power. Charles de Gaulle's Free French movement, for example, thwarted the attempt of French Communists to dominate the major French resistance groups.

Germany, too, had its resistance movements, although the increased control of the SS over everyday life made resistance both dangerous and ineffectual. The White Rose movement involved an attempt by a small group of students and one professor at the University of Munich to distribute pamphlets denouncing the Nazi regime as lawless, criminal, and godless. Its members were caught, arrested, and promptly executed. Likewise, Communist resistance groups were mostly crushed by the Gestapo.

Only one plot against Hitler and the Nazi regime came remotely close to success. It was the work primarily of a group of military officers and conservative politicians who were appalled at Hitler's war mongering and sickened by the wartime atrocities he had encouraged. One of their number, Colonel Count Claus von Stauffenberg (1907–1944), believed that only the elimination of Hitler would bring the overthrow of the Nazi regime. On July 20, 1944, a bomb planted by Stauffenberg in Hitler's East Prussian headquarters exploded, but failed to kill the dictator. The plot was then quickly uncovered and crushed. Five thousand people were executed and Hitler remained in control of Germany.

The Holocaust

There was no more terrifying aspect of the Nazi New Order than the deliberate attempt to exterminate the Jewish people of Europe. Racial struggle was a key element in Hitler's ideology and meant to him a clearly defined conflict of opposites: the Aryans, creators of human cultural development, against the Jews, parasites who were trying to destroy the Aryans. At a meeting of the Nazi party in 1922, Hitler proclaimed: "There can be no compromise—there are only two possibilities: either victory of the Aryan or annihilation of the Aryan and the victory of the Jew."[8] Although Hitler later toned down his anti-Semitic message when his party sought mass electoral victories, anti-Semitism was a recurring theme in Nazism and resulted in a wave of legislative acts against the Jews between 1933 and 1939.

By the beginning of 1939, Nazi policy focused on promoting the "emigration" of German Jews from Germany. At the same time, Hitler had given ominous warnings about the future of European Jewry. When he addressed the German Reichstag on January 30, 1939, he stated:

> I have often been a prophet in life and was generally laughed at. During my struggle for power, the Jews primarily received with laughter my prophecies that I would someday assume the leadership of the state and thereby of the entire Volk and then, among many other things, achieve a solution of the Jewish problem. . . . Today I will be a prophet again: if international finance Jewry within Europe and abroad should succeed once more in plunging the peoples into a world war, then the consequence will be not the Bolshevization of the world and therewith a victory of Jewry, but on the contrary, the destruction of the Jewish race in Europe.[9]

At the time, emigration was still the favored policy. Once the war began in September 1939, the so-called Jewish problem took on new dimensions. For a while there was discussion of the Madagascar Plan, which

▼ **Tito and the Partisan Resistance.** The brutality of German occupation forces quickly led to the emergence of resistance movements in Nazi-occupied Europe. In some places, resistance movements grew strong enough to challenge the Germans to pitched battles. Tito (foreground right), leader of the outlawed Communist party of Yugoslavia, was the leader of a band of partisans who waged guerrilla warfare against German occupation forces. When the odds turned against them, they retreated to hideouts in the rugged mountain areas of Yugoslavia.

aspired to the mass shipment of Jews to the African island of Madagascar. When war contingencies made this plan impractical, an even more drastic policy was conceived.

Heinrich Himmler and the SS organization closely shared Adolf Hitler's racial ideology. The SS was given responsibility for what the Nazis called their Final Solution to the Jewish problem, that is, the annihilation of the Jewish people. Reinhard Heydrich (1904–1942), head of the SS's Security Service, was given administrative responsibility for the Final Solution. After the defeat of Poland, Heydrich ordered the special strike forces (*Einsatzgruppen*) that he had created to round up all Polish Jews and concentrate them in ghettos established in a number of Polish cities.

In June 1941, the *Einsatzgruppen* were given new responsibilities as mobile killing units. These SS death squads followed the regular army's advance into Russia. Their job was to round up Jews in their villages and execute and bury them in mass graves, often giant pits dug by the victims themselves before they were shot. The leader of one these death squads described the mode of operation:

> The unit selected for this task would enter a village or city and order the prominent Jewish citizens to call together all

▼ The Holocaust: The Extermination Camp at Auschwitz.

After his initial successes in the east, Hitler set in motion the machinery for the physical annihilation of Europe's Jewish people. Shown here is the arrival at Auschwitz, a major extermination camp, of yet another shipment of Jews. In the background are the chimneys of the crematoria. This photograph was made by a SS guard in 1944.

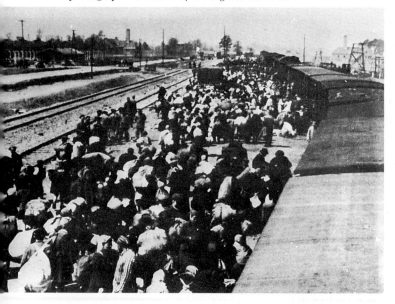

Jews for the purpose of resettlement. They were requested to hand over their valuables to the leaders of the unit, and shortly before the execution to surrender their outer clothing. The men, women, and children were led to a place of execution which in most cases was located next to a more deeply excavated anti-tank ditch. Then they were shot, kneeling or standing, and the corpses thrown into the ditch.[10]

Such regular killing created morale problems among the SS executioners. During a visit to Minsk in the Soviet Union, SS leader Himmler tried to build morale by pointing out that: "He would not like it if Germans did such a thing gladly. But their conscience was in no way impaired, for they were soldiers who had to carry out every order unconditionally. He alone had responsibility before God and Hitler for everything that was happening, . . . and he was acting from a deep understanding of the necessity for this operation."[11]

Although it has been estimated that as many as one million Jews were killed by the *Einsatzgruppen*, this approach to solving the Jewish problem was soon perceived as inadequate. Instead, the Nazis opted for the systematic annihilation of the European Jewish population in specially built death camps. The plan was basically simple. Jews from countries occupied by Germany (or sympathetic to Germany) would be rounded up, packed like cattle into freight trains, and shipped to Poland, where six extermination centers were built for this purpose. The largest and most infamous was Auschwitz-Birkenau. Technical assistance for the construction of the camps was provided by experts from the T-4 program, which had been responsible for the extermination of 80,000 alleged racially unfit, mental and physical defectives in Germany between 1938 and 1941. Based on their experiences, medical technicians had chosen Zyklon B (the commercial name for hydrogen cyanide) as the most effective gas for quickly killing large numbers of people in gas chambers designed to look like shower rooms to facilitate the cooperation of the victims. After gassing, the corpses would be burned in specially built crematoria.

By the spring of 1942, the death camps were in operation. Although initial priority was given to the elimination of the ghettos in Poland, by the summer of 1942, Jews were also being shipped from France, Belgium, and Holland. In 1943, there were shipments of Jews from the capital cities of Berlin, Vienna, and Prague and from Greece, southern France, Italy, and Denmark. Even as the Allies were making important advances in 1944, Jews were being shipped from Greece and Hungary. These shipments depended on the cooperation of Ger-

The Holocaust: The Camp Commandant and the Camp Victims
▼ ▼ ▼

The systematic annihilation of millions of men, women, and children in extermination camps makes the Holocaust one of the most horrifying events in history. The first document is taken from an account by Rudolf Höss, commandant of the extermination camp at Auschwitz-Birkenau. In the second document, a French doctor explains what happened to the victims at one of the crematoria described by Höss.

Commandant Höss Describes the Equipment

The two large crematoria, Nos. I and II, were built during the winter of 1942–43. . . . They each . . . could cremate c. 2,000 corpses within twenty-four hours. . . . Crematoria I and II both had underground undressing and gassing rooms which could be completely ventilated. The corpses were brought up to the ovens on the floor above by lift. The gas chambers could hold c. 3,000 people.

The firm of Topf had calculated that the two smaller crematoria, III and IV, would each be able to cremate 1,500 corpses within twenty-four hours. However, owing to the wartime shortage of materials, the builders were obliged to economise and so the undressing rooms and gassing rooms were built above ground and the ovens were of a less solid construction. But it soon became apparent that the flimsy construction of these two four-retort ovens was not up to the demands made on it. No. III ceased operating altogether after a short time and later was no longer used. No. IV had to be repeatedly shut down since after a short period in operation of 4–6 weeks, the ovens and chimneys had burnt out. The victims of the gassing were mainly burnt in pits behind crematorium IV.

The largest number of people gassed and cremated within twenty-four hours was somewhat over 9,000.

A French Doctor Describes the Victims

It is mid-day, when a long line of women, children, and old people enter the yard. The senior official in charge . . . climbs on a bench to tell them that they are going to have a bath and that afterwards they will get a drink of hot coffee. They all undress in the yard. . . . The doors are opened and an indescribable jostling begins. The first people to enter the gas chamber begin to draw back. They sense the death which awaits them. The SS men put an end to this pushing and shoving with blows from their rifle butts beating the heads of the horrified women who are desperately hugging their children. The massive oak double doors are shut. For two endless minutes one can hear banging on the walls and screams which are no longer human. And then—not a sound. Five minutes later the doors are opened. The corpses, squashed together and distorted, fall out like a waterfall. . . . The bodies which are still warm pass through the hands of the hairdresser who cuts their hair and the dentist who pulls out their gold teeth . . . One more transport has just been processed through No. IV crematorium.

many's Transport Ministry, and despite desperate military needs, the Final Solution had priority in using railroad cars for the transportation of Jews to death camps. Even the military argument that Jews could be used to produce armaments was overridden by the demands of extermination.

A harrowing experience awaited the Jews when they arrived at one of the six death camps. Rudolf Höss, commandant at Auschwitz-Birkenau, described it:

> We had two SS doctors on duty at Auschwitz to examine the incoming transports of prisoners. The prisoners would be marched by one of the doctors who would make spot decisions as they walked by. Those who were fit for work were sent into the camp. Others were sent immediately to the extermination plants. Children of tender years were invariably exterminated since by reason of their youth they were unable to work. . . . at Auschwitz we endeavored to fool the victims into thinking that they were to go through a delousing process. Of course, frequently they realized our true intentions and we sometimes had riots and difficulties due to that fact. [12]

About 30 percent of the arrivals at Auschwitz were sent to a labor camp, while the remainder went to the gas chambers (see the box above). After they had been gassed, the bodies were burned in the crematoria. The victims' goods and even their bodies were used for economic gain. Female hair was cut off, collected, and turned into mattresses or cloth. Some inmates were also subjected to cruel and painful "medical" experiments. The Germans killed between 5 and 6 million Jews, over 3 million of them in the death camps. Virtually 90 percent of the Jewish populations of Poland, the Baltic countries, and Germany were exterminated. Overall, the Holocaust was responsible for the death of nearly two out of every three European Jews.

The Nazis were also responsible for another Holocaust, the death by shooting, starvation, or overwork of at least another 9 to 10 million people. Because the Nazis also considered the Gypsies of Europe (like the Jews) a race containing alien blood, they were systematically rounded up for extermination. About 40 percent of Europe's one million Gypsies were killed in the death camps. The leading elements of the "subhuman" Slavic peoples—the clergy, intelligentsia, civil leaders, judges, and lawyers—were arrested and deliberately killed. Probably an additional 4 million Poles, Ukrainians, and Belorussians lost their lives as slave laborers for Nazi Germany. Finally, probably at least 3–4 million Soviet prisoners of war were killed in captivity.

▼ The Home Front

World War II was even more of a total war than World War I. Fighting was much more widespread and covered most of the world. Economic mobilization was more extensive; so too was the mobilization of women. The number of civilians killed was far higher. Almost 20 million were killed from the strategic bombing of civilian populations, mass extermination policies, and reprisals by invading armies.

The Mobilization of Peoples: Four Examples

The home fronts of the major Western countries varied considerably, based on local circumstances. The British mobilized their resources more thoroughly than their allies or even Germany. By the summer of 1944, 55 percent of the British people were in the armed forces or civilian "war work." The British were especially determined to make use of women. Most women under forty years of age were called upon to do war work of some kind. By 1944, women held almost 50 percent of the civil service positions while the number of women in agriculture doubled as "Land Girls" performed agricultural labor usually undertaken by men.

The government encouraged a "Dig for Victory" campaign to increase food production. Fields normally reserved for athletic events were turned over to citizens to plant gardens in "Grow Your Own Food" campaigns. Even with 1.4 million garden allotments in 1943, Britain still faced a shortage of food as German submarines continued to sink hundreds of British merchant vessels. Food rationing, with its weekly allotments of bacon, sugar, fats, and eggs, intensified during the war as the British became accustomed to a diet dominated by bread and potatoes. For many British people, hours after work were spent in such wartime activities as "Dig for Vic-

▼ **Women in the Factories.** Although only the Soviet Union used women in combat positions, the number of women working in industry increased dramatically in most belligerent countries. British women, dressed in slacks for industrial work, are shown here building the barrage balloons that were used around British cities to defend them against air raid attacks.

tory," the Civil Defence, or Home Guard. The latter had been founded in 1940 to fight off German invaders. Even elderly people were expected to help manufacture airplane parts in their homes.

During the war, the British placed much emphasis on a planned economy. In 1942, the government created a ministry for fuel and power to control the coal industry and a ministry for production to oversee supplies for the armed forces. Although controls and bureaucratic "red tape" became unpopular, especially with businessmen, most British citizens seemed to accept that total war required unusual governmental dominance over people's lives. The British did make substantial gains in manufacturing war materials. Tank production quadrupled between 1940 and 1942. Production of aircraft grew from 8,000 in 1939 to 26,000 in 1943 and 1944, although there was considerable scandal over the inflation of the production figures by building such obsolescent planes as the Whitley bombers. Indeed, some historians have argued that British wartime success helped maintain antiquated enterprises and inefficient industrial practices, contributing to the decline of Britain after the war.

World War II had an enormous impact on the Soviet Union. Known to the Soviets as the Great Patriotic War, the German-Soviet war witnessed the greatest land campaign in history as well as incredible barbarism. To Nazi Germany, it was a war of enslavement and extermination that called for ruthless measures. Two out of every five persons killed in World War II were Soviet citizens.

The shift to a war footing required little administrative adjustment in the Soviet Union. As the central authority, the dictator Joseph Stalin simply created a system of "super-centralization," by which he directed military and political affairs. All civil and military organizations were subjected to the control of the Communist party and Soviet police.

The initial defeats of the Soviet Union led to drastic emergency mobilization measures that affected the civilian population. Leningrad, for example, experienced 900 days of siege, during which its inhabitants faced starvation. As the German army made its rapid advance into Soviet territory, the factories in the western part of the Soviet Union were dismantled and shipped to the interior—to the Urals, western Siberia, and the Volga region. Machines were placed on the bare ground, and walls went up around them as workers began their work. The Kharkov Tank Factory produced its first 25 T-34 tanks only ten weeks after the plant had been rebuilt.

This widespread military, industrial, and economic mobilization created yet another Industrial Revolution for the Soviet Union. Stalin labeled it a "battle of machines," and the Soviets won, producing 78,000 tanks and 98,000 artillery pieces. Fifty-five percent of Soviet national income went for war materials compared to 15 percent in 1940. As a result of the emphasis on military goods, Soviet citizens experienced incredible shortages of both food and housing. Civilian food consumption fell by 40 percent during the war while in the Volga area, the Urals, and Siberia, workers lived in dugouts or dilapidated barracks.

Soviet women played a major role in the war effort. Women and girls were enlisted for work in industries, mines, and railroads. Women constituted between 26 and 35 percent of the laborers in mines and 48 percent in the oil industry. Overall, the number of women working in industry increased almost 60 percent. Soviet women were also expected to dig antitank ditches and work as air-raid wardens. In addition, the Soviet Union was the only country in World War II to use women as combatants. Soviet women functioned as snipers and also as aircrews in bomber squadrons. The female pilots who helped to defeat the Germans at Stalingrad were known as the "Night Witches."

Soviet peasants were asked to bear enormous burdens. They supplied the manpower for 60 percent of the military forces. At the same time, the Soviet peasantry was expected to feed the Red Army and the general population under very difficult circumstances. The German occupation in the early months of the war resulted in the loss of 47 percent of the country's grain-producing regions. Because military needs overshadowed everything else, mechanized farm equipment such as tractors and trucks was requisitioned to carry guns. As a result, women and children were literally harnessed to do the plowing while peasants worked long hours on collective farms for no payment. Although new land was opened in the Urals, Siberia, and Soviet Asia, a shortage of labor hindered the effort to expand agricultural production. In 1943, the Soviet harvest was only 60 percent of its 1940 figure, which meant extreme hardship and poverty for the population. The small private farm plots of Soviet peasants were also subject to compulsory production for the state.

Total mobilization produced victory for the Soviet Union. Stalin and the Communist party had quickly realized after the start of the German invasion that the Soviet people would not fight for communist ideology, but would do battle to preserve "Mother Russia." Government propaganda played on patriotic feelings. In a speech in November 1941, on the anniversary of the Bolshevik Revolution, Stalin rallied the Soviet people by speaking of the country's past heroes, including the famous tsars of Imperial Russia.

The home front in the United States was quite different from those of its two chief wartime allies, largely because the United States faced no threat of war in its own territory. The American home front was disorderly, yet productive in the long run. Although the mobilization of the economy and labor force was slow to develop, eventually the United States became the arsenal of the Allied powers, producing the military equipment they needed. The mobilization of the United States also had a great impact on American social and economic developments.

The American economy was never fully mobilized. In 1941, industries were reluctant to convert to full-time war operations because they feared too much production would flood postwar markets and create another depression. Unemployment did not decrease significantly in the United States until mid-1943, a situation that affected the use of women in industrial jobs. Seventy-one percent of American women over eighteen years of age remained at home, in part due to male attitudes concerning women's traditional place in the home, but also because the services of women were not seriously needed. During the high point of war production in the United States in November 1943, the country was constructing six ships a day and $6 billion worth of war-related goods a month. Within a year many small factories were being shut down because of overproduction.

The mobilization of the American economy produced social problems. The construction of new factories created boom towns where thousands came to work but then faced a shortage of houses, health facilities, and schools. The dramatic expansion of small towns into large cities often brought a breakdown in traditional social mores, especially evident in the growth of teenage prostitution. Economic mobilization also led to considerable internal migration. Sixteen million men and women became members of the armed services, while another 16 million moved around the country. The latter were either wives and sweethearts of servicemen or workers looking for jobs. One million blacks from rural areas in the south, for example, went to urban areas in the north and northwest, especially the Pacific Coast. One social by-product of internal migration was an increase in racial tensions. The migration of blacks brought them to areas where they had not been present before. The one million blacks who joined the armed services, only to be segregated into their own battle units, became deeply resentful. At the same time, the blacks who found industrial jobs were often given the lowest paid, menial tasks.

Japanese-Americans were treated even more shabbily. On the West Coast, 110,000 Japanese-Americans, 65 percent of whom had been born in the United States, were removed to camps encircled by barbed wire and made to take loyalty oaths. Although public officials claimed this policy was necessary for security reasons, no similar treatment of German-Americans or Italian-Americans ever took place. The racism inherent in this treatment of Japanese-Americans was evident when the California governor, Culbert Olson, said: "You know, when I look out at a group of Americans of German or Italian descent, I can tell whether they're loyal or not. I can tell how they think and even perhaps what they are thinking. But it is impossible for me to do this with inscrutable orientals, and particularly the Japanese."[13]

In August 1914, Germans had enthusiastically cheered their soldiers marching off to war. In September 1939, the streets were quiet. Many Germans were apathetic or, even worse for the Nazi regime, had a foreboding of disaster. Hitler was very aware of the importance of the home front. He believed that the collapse of the home front in World War I had caused Germany's defeat, and in his determination to avoid a repetition of that experience, he adopted economic policies that may indeed have cost Germany the war.

To maintain the morale of the home front during the first two years of the war, Hitler refused to cut consumer goods production or increase the production of armaments. Blitzkrieg allowed the Germans to win quick victories, after which they could plunder the food and raw materials of conquered countries in order to avoid diverting resources away from the civilian economy. After German defeats on the Russian front and the American entry into the war, the economic situation changed. Early in 1942, Hitler finally ordered a massive increase in armaments production and the size of the army. Hitler's personal architect, Albert Speer, was made minister for armaments and munitions in 1942. By eliminating waste and rationalizing procedures, Speer was able to triple the production of armaments between 1942 and 1943 despite the intense Allied air raids. Speer's urgent plea for a total mobilization of resources for the war effort went unheeded, however. Hitler, fearful of civilian morale problems that would undermine the home front, refused any dramatic cuts in the production of consumer goods. A total mobilization of the economy was not implemented until 1944, when schools, theaters, and

The Bombing of Civilians
▼ ▼ ▼

The home front became a battlefront when civilian populations became the targets of mass bombing raids. Many people believed that mass bombing could effectively weaken the morale of the people and shorten the war. Rarely did it achieve its goal. In these selections, British, German, and Japanese civilians relate their experiences during bombing raids.

London, 1940

Early last evening, the noise was terrible. My husband and Mr. P. were trying to play chess in the kitchen. I was playing draughts with Kenneth in the cupboard. . . . Presently I heard a stifled voice "Mummy! I don't know what's become of my glasses." "I should think they are tied up in my wool." My knitting had disappeared and wool seemed to be everywhere! We heard a whistle, a bang which shook the house, and an explosion. . . . Well, we straightened out, decided draughts and chess were no use under the circumstances, and waited for a lull so we could have a pot of tea.

Hamburg, 1943

As the many fires broke through the roofs of the burning buildings, a column of heated air rose more than two and a half miles high and one and a half miles in diameter. . . . This column was turbulent, and it was fed from its base by in-rushing cooler ground-surface air. One and one and half miles from the fires this draught increased the wind velocity from eleven to thirty-three miles per hour. At the edge of the area the velocities must have been appreciably greater, as trees three feet in diameter were uprooted. In a short time the temperature reached ignition point for all combustibles, and the entire area was ablaze. In such fires complete burn-out occurred; that is, no trace of combustible material remained, and only after two days were the areas cool enough to approach.

Hiroshima, August 6, 1945

I heard the airplane; I looked up at the sky, it was a sunny day, the sky was blue. . . . Then I saw something drop—and pow!—a big explosion knocked me down. Then I was unconscious—I don't know for how long. Then I was conscious but I couldn't see anything. . . . Then I see people moving away and I just follow them. It is not light like it was before, it is more like evening. I look around; houses are all flat! . . . I follow the people to the river. I couldn't hear anything, my ears are blocked up. I am thinking—a bomb has dropped! . . . I didn't know my hands were burned, nor my face. . . . My eyes were swollen and felt closed up.

---

cafes were closed and Speer was finally permitted to use all remaining resources for the production of a few basic military items. By that time, it was in vain. Total war mobilization was too little and too late in July 1944 to save Germany from defeat.

The war produced a reversal in Nazi attitudes toward women. Nazi resistance to female employment declined as the war progressed and more and more men were called up for military service. Nazi magazines now proclaimed: "We see the woman as the eternal mother of our people, but also as the working and fighting comrade of the man."[14] But the number of women working in industry, agriculture, commerce, and domestic service increased only slightly. The total number of employed women in September 1944 was 14.9 million compared to 14.6 in May 1939. Many women, especially those of the middle class, resisted regular employment, particularly in factories. Even the introduction of labor conscription for women in January 1943 failed to achieve much as women found ingenious ways to avoid the regulations.

The Frontline Civilians: The Bombing of Cities

Bombing was used in World War II in a variety of ways: against nonhuman military targets; against enemy troops, in conjunction with land forces; and indiscriminately against civilian populations. The latter made World War II as devastating for civilians as for frontline soldiers (see the box above). A small number of bombing raids in the last year of World War I had given rise to the argument, crystallized in 1930 by the Italian general Giulio Douhet, that the public outcry created by the bombing of civilian populations would be an effective way to coerce governments into making peace. Consequently, European air forces began to develop long-range bombers in the 1930s.

The first sustained use of civilian bombing contradicted Douhet's theory. Beginning in early September 1940, the German *Luftwaffe* subjected London and many other British cities and towns to nightly air raids, making the Blitz (as the British called the German air raids) a national experience. Londoners took the first heavy blows, and it was their maintenance of morale that set the standard for the rest of the British population. One British woman expressed well what many others apparently felt:

> It was a beautiful summer night, so warm it was incredible, and made more beautiful than ever by the red glow from the East, where the docks were burning. We stood and stared for a minute, and I tried to fix the scene in my mind, because one day this will be history, and I shall be one of those who actually saw it. I wasn't frightened any more.[15]

But London morale was helped by the fact that German raids were widely dispersed over a very large city. Smaller communities were more directly affected by the devastation. On November 14, 1940, for example, the *Luftwaffe* destroyed hundreds of shops and a hundred acres of the city center of Coventry. The destruction of smaller

cities did produce morale problems as wild rumors of social collapse spread quickly in these communities. Nevertheless, morale was soon restored. War production in these areas, in any case, seems to have been little affected by the raids.

The British failed to learn from their own experience, however, and soon proceeded with the bombing of Germany. Churchill and his advisers believed that destroying German communities would break civilian morale and bring victory. Major bombing raids began in 1942 under the direction of Arthur Harris, the wartime leader of the British air force's Bomber Command, which was rearmed with four-engine heavy bombers capable of taking the war into the center of occupied Europe. On May 31, 1942, Cologne became the first German city to be subjected to an attack by a thousand bombers.

The entry of the Americans into the war produced a new bombing strategy. American planes flew daytime missions aimed at the precision bombing of transportation facilities and war industries, while the British Bomber Command continued nighttime saturation bombing of all German cities with populations over 100,000. Bombing raids added an element of terror to circumstances already made difficult by growing shortages of food, clothing, and fuel. Germans especially feared the incendiary bombs that created firestorms that swept destructive paths through the cities. Four raids on Hamburg in August 1943 produced temperatures of 1,800 degrees Fahrenheit, obliterated half the city's

▼ **Total War: The Destruction of Cologne.** In the 1930s, a number of military theorists had argued that the bombing of civilian populations might be an effective way to coerce nations into making peace. In the course of World War II, Allied bombing raids on German targets became a daily occurrence. Many German cities, as this photograph of Cologne demonstrates, were left in ruins.

buildings, and killed 50,000 civilians. The ferocious bombing of Dresden from February 13 to 15, 1945, created a firestorm that may have killed as many as 100,000 inhabitants and refugees. Even some Allied leaders began to criticize what they saw as the unnecessary terror bombing of German cities. Urban dwellers become accustomed to living in air-raid shelters, usually cellars in businesses or houses. Occupants of shelters could be crushed to death if the shelters were hit directly or die by suffocation from the effects of high-explosive bombs. Not until 1943 did Nazi leaders begin to evacuate women and children to rural areas. This evacuation policy, however, created its own problems since people in country villages were often hostile to the urban newcomers.

Germany suffered enormously from the Allied bombing raids. Millions of buildings were destroyed, and possibly half a million civilians died from the raids. Nevertheless, it is highly unlikely that Allied bombing sapped the morale of the German people. Instead, Germans, whether pro-Nazi or anti-Nazi, fought on stubbornly, often driven simply by a desire to live. Nor did the bombing destroy Germany's industrial capacity. The Allied Strategic Bombing survey revealed that the production of war materials actually increased between 1942 and 1944. Even in 1944 and 1945, Allied raids cut German production of armaments by only 7 percent. Nevertheless, the widespread destruction of transportation systems and fuel supplies made it extremely difficult for the new materials to reach the German military. The destruction of German cities from the air did accomplish one major goal. There would be no stab-in-the-back myth after World War II as there had been after World War I. The loss of the war could not be blamed on the collapse of the home front. Many Germans understood that the home front had been a battlefront, and they had lost on their front just as the soldiers had on theirs.

In Japan, the bombing of civilians reached a new level with the use of the first atomic bomb. Japan was especially vulnerable to air raids because its air force had been virtually destroyed in the course of the war, and its crowded cities were built of flimsy materials. Attacks on Japanese cities by the new American B-29 Superfortresses, the biggest bombers of the war, had begun on November 24, 1944. By the summer of 1945, many of Japan's industries had been destroyed along with one-fourth of its dwellings. After the Japanese government decreed the mobilization of all people between the ages of thirteen and sixty into a People's Volunteer Corps, President Truman and his advisers decided that Japanese fanaticism might mean a million American casualties.

▼ **Hiroshima.** The most devastating destruction of civilians came near the end of World War II when the United States dropped atomic bombs on the Japanese cities of Hiroshima and Nagasaki. This general panoramic view of Hiroshima after the bombing shows the incredible devastation produced by the atomic bomb.

This was the official reason for Truman's decision to drop the atomic bomb on Hiroshima and Nagasaki. The destruction was incredible. Of 76,000 buildings near the hypocenter of the explosion in Hiroshima, 70,000 were flattened, while 140,000 of the city's 400,000 inhabitants died by the end of 1945. By the end of 1950, another 50,000 had perished from the effects of radiation.

▼ The Aftermath of the War: The Emergence of the Cold War

The total victory of the Allies in World War II was not followed by a real peace, but by the beginnings of a new conflict known as the Cold War that dominated European and world politics until the end of the 1980s. The origins of the Cold War stemmed from the military, political, and ideological differences, especially between the Soviet Union and the United States, that became apparent at the Allied war conferences held in the last years of the war. Although Allied leaders were mostly preoccupied with how to end the war, they also were strongly motivated by differing, and often conflicting, visions of postwar Europe.

The Conferences at Teheran, Yalta, and Potsdam

Stalin, Roosevelt, and Churchill, the leaders of the Big Three of the Grand Alliance, met at Teheran (the capital of Iran) in November 1943 to decide the future course of the war. Their major tactical decision concerned the final assault on Germany. Churchill had wanted British and American forces to follow up their north African and Italian campaigns by an indirect attack on Germany through the Balkans. Although an extremely difficult route, this would give the Western Allies a better position in postwar central Europe. Stalin and Roosevelt, however, overruled Churchill and argued successfully for an American-British invasion of the Continent through France, which they scheduled for the spring of 1944. The acceptance of this plan had important consequences. It meant that Soviet and British-American forces would meet in defeated Germany along a north-south dividing line and that, most likely, Eastern Europe would be liberated by Soviet forces. The Allies also agreed to a partition of postwar Germany until denazification could take place, but differences over questions like the frontiers of Poland were carefully set aside. Roosevelt was pleased with the accord with Stalin. Harry Hopkins, one of Roosevelt's advisers at the conference, remarked:

> We really believed in our hearts that this was the dawn of the new day. . . . We were absolutely certain that we had won

the first great victory of the peace—and by "we," I mean *all* of us, the whole civilized human race. The Russians had proved that they could be reasonable and farseeing and there wasn't any doubt in the minds of the President or any of us that we could live with them and get along with them peacefully for as far into the future as any of us could imagine.[16]

Winston Churchill was more cautious about future relations with the Soviets. Although overruled at the Teheran Conference, in October of 1944, Churchill met with Stalin in Moscow and was able to pin him down to a more specific determination of postwar spheres of influence. The agreement between Churchill and Stalin, written on a scrap of paper, assigned the various Allies a certain percentage of political influence in a given area on the basis of past historical roles. The Soviet Union received 90 percent influence in Romania and Bulgaria, while Britain obtained 90 percent influence in Greece. Eastern European countries that had a strong tradition of Western ties, such as Yugoslavia and Hungary, were divided "fifty-fifty." Churchill perceived how callous this division of sovereign countries might seem from a distance. He remarked to Stalin, "Might it not be thought rather cynical if it seemed we had disposed of these issues, so fateful to millions of people, in such an offhand manner? Let us burn the paper." Stalin, not worrying what others might think, simply replied, "No, you keep it."[17]

By the time of the conference at Yalta in southern Russia in February 1945, the defeat of Germany was a

▼ **The Victorious Allied Leaders at Yalta.** Even before World War II ended, the leaders of the Big Three of the Grand Alliance, Churchill, Roosevelt, and Stalin (shown from left to right), met in wartime conferences to plan the final assault on Germany and negotiate the outlines of the postwar settlement. At the Yalta meeting (February 5–11, 1945), the three leaders concentrated on postwar issues. The American president, who died two months later, was already a worn-out man at Yalta.

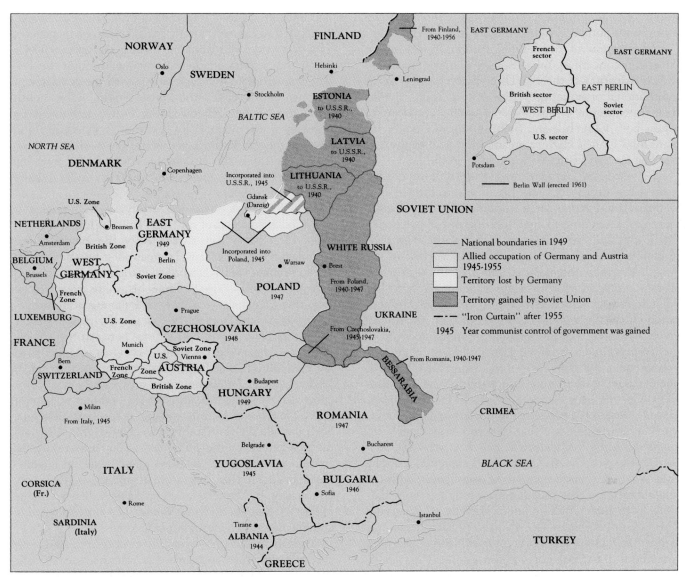

▼ **Map 28.4** Territorial Changes after World War II.

foregone conclusion. The Western powers, which had earlier believed that the Soviets were in a weak position, were now faced with the reality of 11 million Red Army soldiers taking possession of eastern and much of central Europe. Stalin was still operating under the notion of spheres of influence. He was deeply suspicious of the Western powers and desired a buffer to protect the Soviet Union from possible future Western aggression. At the same time, however, Stalin was eager to obtain economically important resources and strategic military positions. Roosevelt by this time was moving away from the notion of spheres of influence to the more Wilsonian ideal of self-determination. He called for "the end of the

system of unilateral action, exclusive alliances, and spheres of influence." The Grand Alliance approved a "Declaration on Liberated Europe." This was a pledge to assist liberated European nations in the creation of "democratic institutions of their own choice." Liberated countries were to hold free elections to determine their political systems.

At Yalta, Roosevelt sought Russian military help against Japan. The atomic bomb was not yet assured, and American military planners feared the possible loss of as many as one million men in amphibious assaults on the Japanese home islands. Roosevelt therefore agreed to Stalin's price for military assistance against Japan: possession of Sakhalin and the Kuril Islands as well as two warm water ports and railroad rights in Manchuria.

The creation of the United Nations was a major American concern at Yalta. Roosevelt hoped to ensure the participation of the Big Three powers in a postwar international organization before difficult issues divided them into hostile camps. After a number of compromises, both Churchill and Stalin accepted Roosevelt's plans for a United Nations organization and set the first meeting for San Francisco in April of 1945.

The issues of Germany and Eastern Europe were treated less decisively. The Big Three reaffirmed that Germany must surrender unconditionally and created four occupation zones. Churchill, over the objections of the Soviets and Americans, insisted that the French be given one occupation zone, carved out of the British and American zones. German reparations were set at $20 billion. A compromise was also worked out in regard to Poland. It was agreed that a provisional government would be established with members of both the Lublin Poles, who were Polish Communists living in exile in the Soviet Union, and the London Poles, who were non-Communists exiled in Britain. Stalin also agreed to free elections in the future to determine a new government. But the issue of free elections in Eastern Europe caused a serious rift between the Soviets and the Americans. The principle was that Eastern European governments would be freely elected, but they were also supposed to be pro-Soviet. As Churchill expressed it: "The Poles will have their future in their owns hands, with the single limitation that they must honestly follow in harmony with their allies, a policy friendly to Russia."[18] This attempt to reconcile two irreconcilable goals was doomed to failure, as soon became evident at the next conference of the Big Three powers.

Even before the conference at Potsdam took place in July 1945, Western relations with the Soviets were deteriorating rapidly. The Grand Alliance had been one of necessity in which ideological incompatibility had been subordinated to the pragmatic concerns of the war. The Allied powers' only common aim was the defeat of Nazism. Once this aim had all but been accomplished, the many differences that antagonized East-West relations came to the surface. Each side committed acts that the other viewed as unbecoming of "allies."

From the perspective of the Soviets, the United States' termination of Lend-Lease aid before the war was over and its failure to respond to the Soviet request for a $6 billion loan for reconstruction exposed the Western desire to keep the Soviet state weak. On the American side, the Soviet Union's failure to fulfill its

Yalta pledge on the "Declaration on Liberated Europe" as applied to Eastern Europe set a dangerous precedent. This was evident in Romania as early as February 1945, when the Soviets engineered a coup, ousting the Radescu government and replacing it with the government of Petra Groza, called the "Little Stalin." One month later, the Soviets sabotaged the Polish settlement by arresting the London Poles and their sympathizers and placing the Soviet-backed Lublin Poles in power. To the Americans, the Russians seemed to be asserting control of Eastern European countries under puppet communist regimes.

The Potsdam Conference of July 1945 consequently began under a cloud of mistrust. Roosevelt had died on April 12 and had been succeeded by the somewhat less flexible president, Harry Truman. During the conference, Truman received word that the atomic bomb had been successfully tested. Some historians have argued that this knowledge resulted in Truman's stiffened resolve against the Soviets. Whatever the reasons, there was a new coldness in the relations between the Soviets and Americans. At Potsdam, Truman demanded free elections throughout Eastern Europe. Stalin responded: "A freely elected government in any of these East European countries would be anti-Soviet, and that we cannot allow."[19] After a bitterly fought and devastating war, Stalin sought absolute military security. To him, it could only be gained by the presence of communist states in Eastern Europe. Free elections might result in governments hostile to the Soviets. By the middle of 1945, only an invasion by Western forces could undo developments in Eastern Europe, and after the world's most destructive conflict had ended, few people favored such a policy.

The Soviets did not view their actions as dangerous expansionism but as legitimate security maneuvers. Was it not the West that had attacked the East? When Stalin sought help against the Nazis in the 1930s, had not the West turned a deaf ear? But there was little sympathy from the West for Soviet fears and even less trust in Stalin. When the American secretary of state James Byrnes proposed a twenty-five year disarmament of Germany, the Soviet Union rejected it. In the West, many saw this as proof of Stalin's plans to expand in central Europe and create a communist East German state. When Byrnes responded by announcing that American troops would be needed in Europe for an indefinite time and made moves that foreshadowed the creation of an independent West Germany, the Soviets saw this as a direct threat to Soviet security in Europe.

As the war slowly receded into the past, the reality of conflicting ideologies had reappeared. Many in the West

Emergence of the Cold War: Churchill and Stalin

▼ ▼ ▼

Less than a year after the end of World War II, the major Allies that had fought together to destroy Hitler's Germany had divided into two hostile camps. These excerpts, taken from Winston Churchill's speech to an American audience on March 5, 1946, and Joseph Stalin's reply to Churchill only nine days later, reveal the divisions in the Western world that marked the beginning of the Cold War.

Churchill's Speech at Fulton, Missouri, March 5, 1946

From Stettin in the Baltic to Trieste in the Adriatic, an iron curtain has descended across the continent. Behind that line lie all the capitals of the ancient states of central and eastern Europe. Warsaw, Berlin, Prague, Vienna, Budapest, Belgrade, Bucharest, and Sofia, all these famous cities and the populations around them lie in the Soviet sphere and all are subject, in one form or another, not only to Soviet influence but to a very high and increasing measure of control from Moscow. . . .

The Russian-dominated Polish Government has been encouraged to make enormous and wrongful inroads upon Germany, and mass expulsions of millions of Germans on a scale grievous and undreamed of are now taking place. The Communist parties, which were very small in all these eastern states of Europe, have been raised to preeminence and power far beyond their numbers and are seeking everywhere to obtain totalitarian control. Police governments are prevailing in nearly every case, and so far, except in Czechoslovakia, there is no true democracy. . . . Whatever conclusions may be drawn from these facts—and facts they are—this is certainly not the liberated Europe we fought to build up. Nor is it one which contains the essentials of permanent peace.

Stalin's Reply to Churchill, March 14, 1946

In substance, Mr. Churchill now stands in the position of a firebrand of war. And Mr. Churchill is not alone here. He has friends not only in England but also in the United States of America.

In this respect, one is reminded remarkably of Hitler and his friends. Hitler began to set war loose by announcing his racial theory, declaring that only people speaking the German language represent a fully valuable nation. Mr. Churchill begins to set war loose, also by a racial theory, maintaining that only nations speaking the English language are fully valuable nations, called upon to decide the destinies of the entire world.

The German racial theory brought Hitler and his friends to the conclusion that the Germans, as the only fully valuable nation, must rule over other nations. The English racial theory brings Mr. Churchill and his friends to the conclusion that nations speaking the English language, being the only fully valuable nations, should rule over the remaining nations of the world.

interpreted Soviet policy as part of a worldwide communist conspiracy. The Soviets, on the other hand, viewed Western, especially American, policy as nothing less than global capitalist expansionism or, in Leninist terms, as nothing less than economic imperialism. Molotov, the Russian foreign minister, referred to the Americans as "insatiable imperialists" and "war-mongering groups of adventurers."[20] In March 1946, in a speech to an American audience, the former British prime minister, Winston Churchill, declared that "an iron curtain" had "descended across the continent," dividing Germany and Europe into two hostile camps. Stalin branded Churchill's speech a "call to war with the Soviet Union" (see the box above). Only months after the world's most devastating conflict had ended, the world seemed once again bitterly divided. Would the twentieth-century crisis of Western civilization never end?

Between 1933 and 1939, Europeans watched as Adolf Hitler rebuilt Germany into a great military power. For Hitler, military power was an absolute prerequisite for the creation of a German racial empire that would dominate Europe and the world for generations to come. If Hitler had been successful, the Nazi New Order, built upon authoritarianism, racial extermination, and the brutal oppression of peoples, would have meant a triumph of barbarism and the end of freedom and equality, which, however imperfectly realized, had become important ideals in Western civilization.

The Nazis lost, but only after tremendous sacrifices and costs. Much of European civilization lay in ruins. Europeans, who had been accustomed to dominating the world at the beginning of the twentieth century, now watched helplessly at mid-century as the two new superpowers created by their two world wars took control of their destinies. Even before the last battles had been fought, the United States and the Soviet Union had arrived at different visions of the postwar European world. No sooner had the war ended than their differences created a new and potentially even more devastating conflict known as the Cold War. Yet even though Europeans seemed merely pawns in the struggle between the two superpowers, they managed to stage a remarkable recovery of their own civilization.

Notes
▼ ▼ ▼

1. Adolf Hitler, *Mein Kampf,* trans. Ralph Manheim (Boston, 1971), p. 654.

2. *Documents on German Foreign Policy* (London, 1956), Series D, 2: 358.

3. Ibid., 7: 204.

4. Quoted in Norman Rich, *Hitler's War Aims* (New York, 1973), 1: 129.

5. Albert Speer, *Spandau,* trans. Richard and Clara Winston (New York, 1976), p. 50.

6. *Nazi Conspiracy and Aggression* (Washington, D.C., 1946), 6: 262.

7. International Military Tribunal, *Trial of the Major War Criminals* (Nuremberg, 1947–49), 22: 480.

8. Adolf Hitler, *My New Order,* ed. Raoul de Roussy de Sales (New York, 1941), pp. 21–22.

9. Quoted in Lucy Dawidowicz, *The War against the Jews* (New York, 1975), p. 106.

10. *Nazi Conspiracy and Aggression,* 5: 341–42.

11. Quoted in Raul Hilberg, *The Destruction of the European Jews,* rev. ed. (New York, 1985), 1: 332–33.

12. *Nazi Conspiracy and Aggression,* 6: 789.

13. Quoted in John Campbell, *The Experience of World War II* (New York, 1989), p. 170.

14. Quoted in Claudia Koonz, "Mothers in the Fatherland: Women in Nazi Germany," in Renate Bridenthal and Claudia Koonz, eds., *Becoming Visible: Women in European History* (Boston, 1977), p. 466.

15. Quoted in Campbell, *The Experience of World War II,* p. 177.

16. Quoted in Robert E. Sherwood, *Roosevelt and Hopkins: An Intimate History* (New York, 1948), p. 870.

17. Quoted in Walter Laqueur, *Europe since Hitler,* rev. ed. (New York, 1982), p. 102.

18. Quoted in Norman Graebner, *Cold War Diplomacy, 1945–1960* (Princeton, N.J., 1962), p. 117.

19. Quoted in ibid.

20. Quoted in Wilfried Loth, *The Division of the World, 1941–1955* (New York, 1988), p. 81.

Suggestions for Further Reading
▼ ▼ ▼

The basic study of Germany's foreign policy from 1933 to 1939 can be found in G. Weinberg, *The Foreign Policy of Hitler's Germany: Diplomatic Revolution in Europe, 1933–36* (Chicago, 1970) and *The Foreign Policy of Hitler's Germany: Starting World War II, 1937–1939* (Chicago, 1980). Additional works on foreign policy include W. Carr, *Arms, Autarchy and Aggression: A Study in German Foreign Policy, 1933–1939* (New York, 1973); and K. Hildebrandt, *The Foreign Policy of the Third Reich,* trans. A. Fothergill (London, 1973). The ideological background of Nazi imperialism is examined in W. Smith, *The Ideological Origins of Nazi Imperialism* (New York, 1986). For a detailed account of the immediate events leading to World War II, see D. C. Watt, *How War Came: The Immediate Origins of the Second World War 1938–1939* (New York, 1989).

Hitler's war aims and the importance of ideology to those aims are examined in N. Rich, *Hitler's War Aims,* vol. 1, *Ideology, the Nazi State and the Course of Expansion* (New York, 1973), and vol. 2, *The Establishment of the New Order* (New York, 1974). General works on World War II include M. K. Dziewanowski, *War at Any Price: World War II in Europe, 1939–1945* (Englewood Cliffs, N.J., 1987); P. Calvocoressi and G. Wint, *Total War: Causes and Courses of the Second World War* (New York, 1979); J. Campbell, *The Experience of World War II* (New York, 1989); and E. Mandel, *The Meaning of the Second World War* (London, 1986). On Hitler as a military leader, see R. Lewin, *Hitler's Mistakes* (New York, 1986). The Eastern Front is covered in J. Erickson, *Stalin's War with Germany*, vol. 1, *The Road to Stalingrad;* vol. 2, *The Road to Berlin* (London, 1973, 1985); A. Seaton, *The Russo-German War, 1941–45* (London, 1971); and O. Bartov, *The Eastern Front, 1941–45: German Troops and the Barbarisation of Warfare* (London, 1986). On the war in Italy, see J. Strawson, *The Italian Campaign* (London, 1987). The second front in Europe is examined in C. D'Este, *Decision in Normandy* (London, 1983). See also S. E. Ambrose, *Eisenhower: The Solider* (London, 1984). On the war at sea, see D. MacIntyre, *Battle of the Atlantic, 1939–1945* (London, 1970).

A standard work on the German New Order in Russia is A. Dallin, *German Rule in Russia, 1941–1945*, rev. ed. (London, 1981). On Poland, see J. T. Gross, *Polish Society under German Occupation* (Princeton, N. J., 1981). On foreign labor, see E. Homze, *Foreign Labor in Nazi Germany* (Princeton, N.J., 1967). Resistance movements in Europe are covered in M. R. D. Foot, *Resistance: An Analysis of European Resistance to Nazism* (London, 1976). A fundamental study on resistance in Germany is P. Hoffmann, *The History of the German Resistance, 1933–1945*, trans. R. Barry (Cambridge, Mass., 1977). On the White Rose, see A. E. Dumbach and J. Newborn, *Shattering the German Night: The Story of the White Rose* (Boston, 1986).

The best studies of the Holocaust include R. Hilberg, *The Destruction of the European Jews*, rev. ed., 3 vols. (New York, 1985); L. Dawidowicz, *The War against the Jews* (New York, 1975); and M. Gilbert, *The Holocaust: The History of the Jews of Europe during the Second World War* (New York, 1985). There is a good overview of the scholarship on the Holocaust in M. Marrus, *The Holocaust in History* (New York, 1987). The role of Hitler in the Holocaust has been well examined in G. Fleming, *Hitler and the Final Solution* (Berkeley, 1984). On the extermination camps, see K. G. Feig, *Hitler's Death Camps: The Sanity of Madness* (New York, 1981). On the problem of what the Allied countries

knew about the Holocaust, see D. Wyman, *The Abandonment of the Jews: America and the Holocaust* (New York, 1984); W. Laqueur, *The Terrible Secret* (Boston, 1980); and M. Gilbert, *Auschwitz and the Allies* (New York, 1981). The other holocaust is examined in R. C. Lukas, *Forgotten Holocaust: The Poles under German Occupation, 1939–44* (Lexington, Ky., 1986); and B. Wytwycky, *The Other Holocaust* (Washington, D.C., 1980).

General studies on the impact of total war include J. Costello, *Love, Sex and War: Changing Values, 1939–1945* (London, 1985); A. Marwick, *War and Social Change in the Twentieth Century: A Comparative Study of Britain, France, Germany, Russia and the United States* (London, 1974); A. S. Milward, *War, Economy and Society, 1939–1945* (London, 1977); and M. R. Marrus, *The Unwanted: European Refugees in the Twentieth Century* (New York, 1985). On the home front in Germany, see E. R. Beck, *Under the Bombs: The German Home Front, 1942–1945* (Lexington, Ky., 1986); M. G. Steinert, *Hitler's War and the Germans* (Athens, Ohio, 1977); I. Kershaw, *The "Hitler Myth": Image and Reality in the Third Reich* (Oxford, 1987); J. Stephenson, *The Nazi Organisation of Women* (London, 1981); and L. J. Rupp, *Mobilizing Women for War: German and American Propaganda, 1939–1945* (Princeton, N.J., 1978). On the home front in Britain, see A. Marwick, *The Home Front* (London, 1976). The Soviet Union during the war is examined in M. Harrison, *Soviet Planning in Peace and War, 1938–1945* (Cambridge, 1985). On the American home front, see G. Perrett, *Days of Sadness, Years of Triumph: The American People, 1939–1945* (New York, 1973).

On the destruction of Germany by bombing raids, see H. Rumpf, *The Bombing of Germany* (London, 1963). The German bombing of Britain is covered in T. Harrisson, *Living through the Blitz* (London, 1985). On Hiroshima, see A. Chisholm, *Faces of Hiroshima* (London, 1985).

On the emergence of the Cold War, see W. Loth, *The Division of the World, 1941–1955* (New York, 1988), and the more extensive list of references at the end of Chapter 29. On the wartime summit conferences, see H. Feis, *Churchill, Roosevelt, Stalin: The War They Waged and the Peace They Sought*, 2d ed. (Princeton, N.J., 1967); and D. Clemens, *Yalta* (New York, 1970). The impact of the atomic bomb on Truman's relationship to Stalin is discussed in M. Sherwin, *A World Destroyed: The Atomic Bomb and the Grand Alliance* (New York, 1975).

Chapter 29

The Postwar Western World

▼▼▼▼▼

In 1945, Europe lay in ruins. Some Europeans questioned whether Europe had the will to regain its former prosperity and importance. Winston Churchill wrote: "What is Europe now? A rubble heap, a charnel house, a breeding ground of pestilence and hate."[1] There was ample justification for his pessimism. Almost 40 million people (both soldiers and civilians) had been killed over the last six years. All across Europe, great cities had been reduced to rubble. Millions of Europeans faced starvation as grain harvests were only 50 percent of what they had been in 1939. Transportation systems were paralyzed. In Germany alone, 50 percent of the railroad tracks were not usable. Untold millions of people had been displaced by the war. Eleven million prisoners of war had to be repatriated while fifteen million Germans and East Europeans were driven out of countries where they were no longer wanted. Despite the chaos, however, Europe was soon on the road to a remarkable recovery. Already by 1948, Europe's industrial and agricultural output (except in Germany and Italy) had almost reached prewar levels.

World War II, however, had cost Europe more than physical destruction. European supremacy in world affairs had also been destroyed. After 1945, the colonial empires of the European nations rapidly disintegrated while Europe's place in the world radically changed. As the Cold War conflict between the world's two superpowers—the United States and the Soviet Union—intensified, the European nations were divided into two armed camps dependent upon one or the other of these two major powers. The United

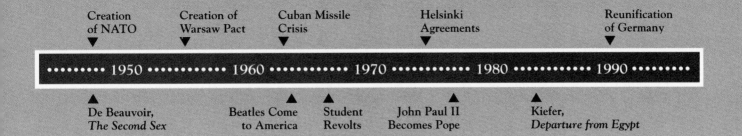

Creation of NATO ▼

Creation of Warsaw Pact ▼

Cuban Missile Crisis ▼

Helsinki Agreements ▼

Reunification of Germany ▼

•••••••• 1950 ••••••••• 1960 ••••••••• 1970 ••••••••• 1980 ••••••••• 1990 •••••••

▲ De Beauvoir, *The Second Sex*

▲ Beatles Come to America

▲ Student Revolts

▲ John Paul II Becomes Pope

▲ Kiefer, *Departure from Egypt*

States and the Soviet Union, whose rivalry raised the specter of nuclear war, seemed to hold the survival of Europe and the world in their hands. As the danger of nuclear war reached its peak in the Cuban missile crisis in 1962, the immediate possibility of thermonuclear destruction opened the door to a search for compromise. By the end of the 1980s, this trend had accelerated sufficiently that many political observers were speaking of a post–Cold War world.

▼ From Cold War to Post–Cold War: International Relations since 1945

Even before World War II had ended, the two major Allied powers—the United States and the Soviet Union—had begun to disagree on the nature of the postwar European world. Unity had been maintained during the war because of the urgent need to defeat the Axis powers, but once they were defeated, the differences between American and Soviet institutions and ideologies again surged to the front. Stalin had never overcome his fear of capitalist superiority while Western leaders still had serious misgivings about communism.

The Development of the Cold War

There has been considerable historical debate about who was most responsible for the beginning of the Cold War. No doubt, both the United States and the Soviet Union took steps at the end of the war that were unwise or might have been avoided. Both nations, however, were working within a framework conditioned by the past. Ultimately, the rivalry between the two superpowers stemmed from their different historical perspectives and their irreconcilable political ambitions. Intense competition for political and military supremacy had

long been a regular feature of Western civilization. The United States and the Soviet Union were the heirs of that European tradition of power politics, and it should not surprise us that two such different systems would seek to extend their way of life to the rest of the world. Because of its need to feel secure on its western border, the Soviet Union was not prepared to give up the advantages it had gained in Eastern Europe from Germany's defeat. But neither were American leaders willing to give up the power and prestige the United States had gained throughout the world. Suspicious of each other's motives, the United States and Soviet Union soon raised their mutual fears to a level of intense competition. Between 1945 and 1949, a number of events seemed to entangle the two countries in continual conflict.

Eastern Europe was the first area of disagreement. The United States and Great Britain had championed self-determination and democratic freedom for the liberated nations of Eastern Europe. Stalin, however, fearful that the Eastern European nations would return to traditional anti-Soviet attitudes if they were permitted free elections, opposed the West's plans. Having liberated Eastern Europe from the Nazis, the Red Army proceeded to install pro-Soviet governing regimes in Poland, Romania, Bulgaria, and Hungary. Although these pro-Soviet governments ensured Stalin's desire for a buffer zone against the West, to the local populations and their sympathizers in the West, they meant an expansion of Stalin's empire. Only another war could change this situation, and few people advocated another armed conflict.

A civil war in Greece created another arena for confrontation between the superpowers. The Communist People's Liberation Army backed by the Soviet Union and the anticommunist forces supported by the British were fighting each other for control of Greece in 1946. But continued postwar economic problems caused the British to withdraw from the active role they had been playing in both Greece and Turkey. President Harry S. Truman of the United States, alarmed by British weak-

The Truman Doctrine
▼▼▼

By 1947, the battlelines had been clearly drawn in the Cold War. This selection is taken from a speech by President Harry S. Truman to the American Congress in which he justified his request for aid to Greece and Turkey. Truman expressed the urgent need to contain the expansion of communism.

President Harry S. Truman Addresses Congress, March 12, 1947

The peoples of a number of countries of the world have recently had totalitarian regimes forced upon them against their will. The Government of the United States has made frequent protests against coercion and intimidation, in violation of the Yalta agreement, in Poland, Rumania, and Bulgaria. I must also state that in a number of other countries there have been similar developments.

At the present moment in world history nearly every nation must choose between alternative ways of life. The choice is too often not a free one.

One way of life is based upon the will of the majority, and is distinguished by free institutions, representative government, free elections, guaranties of individual liberty, freedom of speech and religion, and freedom from political oppression.

The second way of life is based upon the will of a minority forcibly imposed upon the majority. It relies upon terror and oppression, a controlled press and radio, fixed elections, and the suppression of personal freedoms.

I believe that it must be the policy of the United States to support free peoples who are resisting attempted subjugation by armed minorities or by outside pressures.

I believe that we must assist free people to work out their own destinies in their own way.

I believe that our help should be primarily through economic and financial aid which is essential to economic stability and orderly political processes. . . . I therefore ask the Congress for assistance to Greece and Turkey in the amount of $400,000,000.

---

ness and the possibility of Soviet expansion into the eastern Mediterranean, responded with the Truman Doctrine (see the box above). According to the president, "It must be the policy of the United States to support free peoples who are resisting attempted subjugation by armed minorities or by outside pressures." This statement was made to the American Congress in March 1947 when Truman requested $400 million in aid for the defense of Greece and Turkey. If the Soviets were not stopped in Greece, the Truman argument ran, then the United States would have to face the spread of communism throughout the free world. As Dean Acheson, the American secretary of state explained, "Like apples in a barrel infected by disease, the corruption of Greece would infect Iran and all the East . . . likewise Africa . . . Italy . . . France. . . . Not since Rome and Carthage had there been such a polarization of power on this earth."[2]

The proclamation of the Truman Doctrine was soon followed in June 1947 by the European Recovery Program, better known as the Marshall Plan. Intended to rebuild prosperity and stability, this program included $13 billion for the economic recovery of war-torn Europe. Underlying it was the belief that communist aggression fed off economic turmoil. From the Soviet perspective, the Marshall Plan was nothing less than capitalist imperialism, a thinly veiled attempt to buy the support of the smaller European countries, which in return would be expected to submit to economic exploitation by the United States. A Soviet spokesman described the United States as the "main force in the imperialist camp," whose ultimate goal was "the strengthening of imperialism, preparation for a new imperialist war, a struggle against socialism and democracy, and the support of reactionary and anti-democratic, profascist regimes and movements." According to the Soviet view, the Marshall Plan aimed at "the construction of a bloc of states bound by obligations to the USA, and to guarantee the American loans in return for the relinquishing by the European states of their economic and later also their political independence."[3] The Soviets, however, were in no position to compete financially with the United States and could do little to counter the Marshall Plan.

The fate of Germany also became a source of heated contention between East and West. Besides denazification and a "temporary" partitioning of Germany (and Berlin) into four occupied zones, the Allied powers had agreed on little else with regard to the conquered nation. The Soviets, hardest hit by the war, took reparations from Germany in the form of booty. The technology-starved Soviets dismantled and removed to Russia 380 factories from the western zones of Berlin before transferring their control to the Western powers. By the summer of 1946, 200 chemical, paper, and textile factories in the Soviets' East German zone had likewise been shipped to the Soviet Union. At the same time, the German Communist party was reestablished under the control of Walter Ulbricht (1893–1973) and was soon in charge of the political reconstruction of the Soviet zone in eastern Germany.

Although the foreign ministers of the four occupying powers (the United States, Soviet Union, Britain, and France) kept meeting to arrive at a final peace treaty with Germany, they moved further and further apart. At the same time, the British, French, and Americans gradually began to merge their zones economically and, by February 1948, were making plans for the unification of these three Western sections of Germany and the formal creation of a West German federal government. The Soviets responded with a blockade of West Berlin that

allowed neither trucks nor trains to enter the three Western zones of Berlin. The Russians hoped to secure economic control of all Berlin and force the Western powers to stop the creation of a separate West German state.

The Western powers were faced with a dilemma. Direct military confrontation seemed dangerous. American troops were severely outnumbered, and no one wished to risk World War III. Therefore, an attempt to break through the blockade with tanks and trucks was ruled out. The solution was the Berlin Air Lift. At its peak, 13,000 tons of supplies were flown daily to Berlin. The Soviets, also not wanting war, did not interfere and finally lifted the blockade in May 1949. The blockade of Berlin had severely increased tensions between the United States and the Soviet Union and brought the separation of Germany into two states. The West German Federal Republic was formally created in September 1949, and a month later, a separate German Democratic Republic was established in East Germany.

In that same year, the Cold War spread from Europe to the rest of the world. The victory of the Chinese Communists in 1949 in the Chinese civil war created a new Communist regime and only intensified American fears about the spread of communism. The Soviet Union

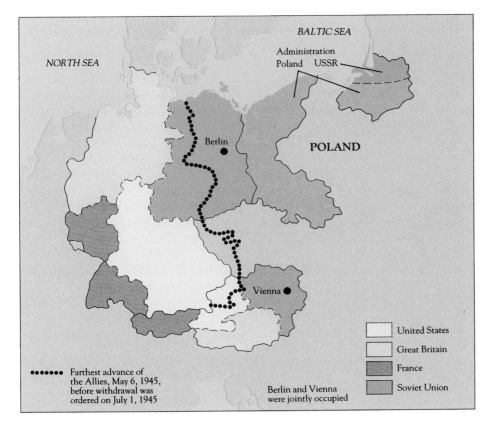

▼ **Map 29.1** Occupied Germany and Austria.

also detonated its first atomic bomb in 1949, and all too soon both powers were involved in an escalating arms race that resulted in the construction of ever more destructive nuclear weapons. Soon the search for security took the form of mutual deterrence or the belief that an arsenal of nuclear weapons prevented war by assuring that even if one nation launched its nuclear weapons in a preemptive first strike, the other nation would still be able to respond and devastate the attacker.

The search for security in the new world of the Cold War also led to the creation of military alliances. The North Atlantic Treaty Organization (NATO) was formed in April 1949 when Belgium, Luxemburg, the Netherlands, France, Britain, Italy, Denmark, Norway, Portugal, and Iceland signed a treaty with the United States and Canada. All the powers agreed to provide mutual assistance if any one of them was attacked. A few years later West Germany, Greece, and Turkey joined NATO.

The Eastern European states soon followed suit. In 1949, they had already formed the Council for Mutual Economic Assistance (COMECON) for economic cooperation. But in 1955, Albania, Bulgaria, Czechoslovakia, East Germany, Hungary, Poland, Romania, and the Soviet Union organized a formal military alliance in the Warsaw Pact. Once again, Europe was tragically divided into hostile alliance systems.

A system of military alliances spread to the rest of the world after the United States became involved in the Korean War in 1950. Korea had been liberated from the Japanese in 1945, but was soon divided into two parts. The land north of the thirty-eighth parallel became the Democratic People's Republic (North Korea) and was supported by the Soviet Union. The Republic of Korea (South Korea) received aid from the United States. In 1950, perhaps with Stalin's approval, North Korean forces invaded South Korea. The Americans, perceiving this as yet another example of communist aggression and expansion, gained the support of the United Nations (see The United Nations later in the chapter) and intervened by sending American troops to turn back the invasion. Although the United Nations forces (mostly Americans and South Koreans) under the com-

▼ **Map 29.2** The New European Alliance Systems.

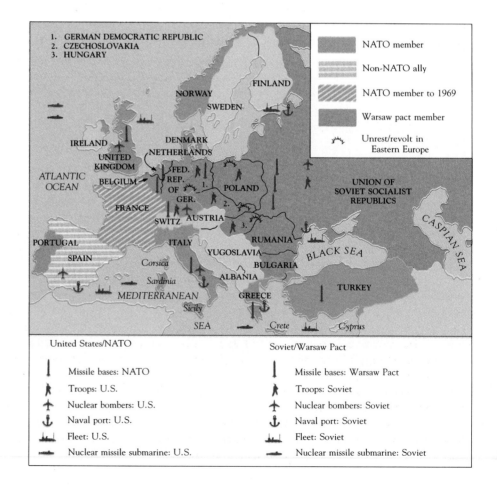

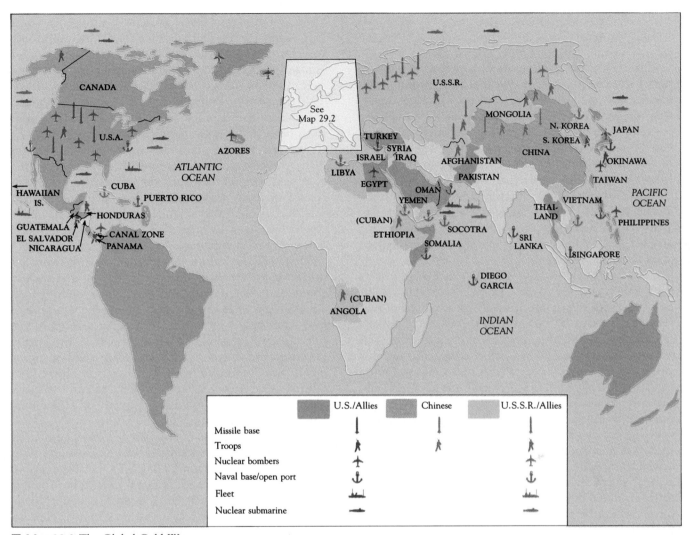

▼ Map 29.3 The Global Cold War.

mand of General Douglas MacArthur pushed the North Koreans back toward the Chinese border, Mao Zedong (1893–1976), the leader of Communist China, then sent Chinese forces into the fray and forced MacArthur's troops to retreat back to South Korea. Believing that the Chinese were simply the puppets of Moscow, American policymakers created an image of communism as a monolithic force directed by the Soviet Union. After two more years of inconclusive fighting, an uneasy truce was reached in 1953 and the division of Korea reaffirmed. To many Americans, the policy of containing communism had succeeded in Asia, just as it had earlier in Europe.

The Korean experience seemed to confirm American fears of communist expansion and reinforced American determination to contain Soviet power. As President Dwight D. Eisenhower (1890–1969) expressed it: "The freedom we cherish and defend in Europe and in the Americas is no different from the freedom that is imperiled in Asia." As a result, American military alliances were extended around the world. The Central Treaty Organization (CENTO) of Turkey, Iraq, Iran, Pakistan, Britain, and the United States was intended to prevent the Soviet Union from expanding at the expense of its southern neighbors. To stem Soviet aggression in the Far East, the United States, Britain, France, Pakistan, Thailand, the Philippines, Australia, and New Zealand formed the Southeast Asia Treaty Organization (SEATO). By the mid-1950s, the United States found itself allied militarily with forty-two states around the world.

The Cuban Missile Crisis and the Move toward Détente

The Cold War confrontation between the United States and the Soviet Union reached frightening levels in 1962 during the Cuban missile crisis. In 1959, a left-wing revolutionary named Fidel Castro (b. 1927) had overthrown the Cuban dictator Fulgencio Batista and established a Soviet-supported totalitarian regime. After the utter failure of a United States-supported attempt (the "Bay of Pigs" incident) to overthrow Castro's regime in 1961, the Soviet Union decided to place nuclear missiles in Cuba. The United States was not prepared to allow nuclear weapons to be within such close striking distance of the American mainland, despite the fact that it had placed nuclear weapons in Turkey within easy range of the Soviet Union. The Soviet leader, Nikita Khrushchev (see The Soviet Union: From Stalin to Gorbachev later in the chapter), was quick to point out that "your rockets are in Turkey. You are worried by Cuba . . . because it is 90 miles from the American coast. But Turkey is next to us."[4] When American intelligence discovered that a Soviet fleet carrying missiles was heading to Cuba, President John F. Kennedy (1917–1963) decided to blockade Cuba and prevent the fleet from reaching its destination. This approach to the problem had the benefit of delaying confrontation and giving each side time to find a peaceful solution. Khrushchev agreed to turn back the fleet if Kennedy pledged not to invade Cuba. In a conciliatory letter to Kennedy, Khrushchev wrote, "We and you ought not to pull on the ends of the rope in which you have tied the knot of war, because the more the two of us pull, the tighter that knot will be tied. And a moment may come when that knot will be tied too tight that even he who tied it will not have the strength to untie it. . . . Let us not only relax the forces pulling on the ends of the rope, let us take measures to untie that knot. We are ready for this."[5]

The intense feeling that the world might have been annihilated in a few days had a profound influence on both sides. A hotline communications system between Moscow and Washington was installed in 1963 to expedite rapid communications between the two superpowers in a time of crisis. In the same year, the two powers agreed to ban nuclear tests in the atmosphere, a step that at least served to lessen the tensions between the two nations.

By that time, the United States had also been drawn into a new confrontation that had an important impact on the Cold War—the Vietnam War. After Vietnamese forces had defeated their French colonial masters in 1954, Vietnam had been divided. A strongly nationalistic regime in the north under Ho Chi Minh (1890–1969) received Soviet aid, while American sponsors worked to establish a democratic regime in South Vietnam. In 1964, under President Lyndon Johnson (1908–1973), increasing numbers of American troops were sent to Vietnam to keep the Communist regime of the north from uniting the entire country under its control. Although nationalism played a powerful role in this conflict, American policymakers saw the conflict in terms of a domino theory concerning the spread of communism. If the Communists succeeded in Vietnam, the argument was that all the other countries in the Far East freeing themselves from colonial domination would fall (like dominoes) to communism.

Despite their massive superiority in equipment and firepower, American forces failed to prevail over the persistence of the North Vietnamese. The mounting destruction and increasing brutalization of the war, brought into American homes every evening on television, also turned American public opinion against the war. Finally, President Richard Nixon (b. 1913) reached an agreement with North Vietnam in 1973 that allowed the United States to withdraw its forces. Within two years, Vietnam had been forcibly reunited by Communist armies from the North.

Despite the success of the North Vietnamese Communists, the domino theory proved unfounded. A noisy rupture between Communist China and the Soviet Union put an end to the idea of a monolithic communism directed by Moscow. Under President Nixon, American relations with China were resumed. New nations in Southeast Asia also managed to avoid Communist governments. Above all, Vietnam helped to show the limitations of American power. By the end of the Vietnam War, a new era in American-Soviet relations—known as détente—had begun to emerge.

Détente meant a reduction of tensions between the Soviet Union and the United States. An appropriate symbol of détente was the Antiballistic Missiles (ABM) Treaty in 1972. Despite some lessening of tensions after the Cuban missile crisis, both the Soviet Union and the United States had continued to expand their nuclear arsenals. In the 1960s, both nations sought to extend the destructive power of their missiles by arming them with multiple warheads. By 1970, Americans had developed the capacity to arm their inter-continental ballistic missiles (ICBMs) with "multiple independently targeted re-entry vehicles" (MIRVs) that enabled one missile to hit ten different targets. The Soviet Union soon followed suit. Between 1968 and 1972, both sides had also developed antiballistic missiles (ABMs), whose purpose was to hit and destroy incoming missiles. In the 1972 ABM Treaty, the two nations agreed to limit their antiballistic missile systems.

In 1975, the Helsinki Agreements provided yet another example of reduced tensions between the superpowers. Signed by the United States, Canada, and all European nations, these accords recognized all borders in central and eastern Europe that had been established since the end of World War II, thereby acknowledging the Soviet sphere of influence in Eastern Europe. The Helsinki Agreements also committed the signatory powers to recognize and protect the human rights of their citizens.

This protection of human rights became one of the major foreign policy goals of the next American president, Jimmy Carter (b. 1924). Although hopes ran high for détente, the Soviet invasion of Afghanistan in 1979, undertaken to restore a pro-Soviet regime, hardened relations between the United States and the Soviet Union. President Carter canceled American participation in the 1980 Olympic Games held in Moscow and placed an embargo on the shipment of American grain to the Soviet Union.

The early administration of President Ronald Reagan (b. 1911) witnessed a return to the harsh rhetoric, if not all of the harsh practices, of the Cold War. Calling the Soviet Union an "evil empire," Reagan began a military buildup that stimulated a renewed arms race. In 1982, the Reagan administration introduced the nuclear-tipped cruise missile, whose ability to fly at low altitudes made it difficult to detect. President Reagan also became an ardent proponent of the Strategic Defense Initiative (SDI), nicknamed "Star Wars." Its purpose was to create a space shield that could destroy incoming missiles. By providing military support to the Afghan insurgents, the Reagan administration helped to maintain a Vietnam-like war in Afghanistan that the Soviet Union could not win. Like the Vietnam War, the war in Afghanistan demonstrated that the power of a superpower was actually limited in the face of strong nationalist, guerrilla-type opposition.

The accession of Mikhail Gorbachev to power in the Soviet Union (see The Gorbachev Era later in the chapter) in 1985 eventually brought a dramatic end to the Cold War. Gorbachev initiated a plan for arms limitation that led in 1987 to an agreement with the United States to eliminate intermediate-range nuclear weapons (the INF Treaty). Both sides had incentives to dampen the expensive arms race. Gorbachev hoped to make extensive economic and internal reforms while the United

▼ **Gorbachev and Reagan.** The willingness of Mikhail Gorbachev and Ronald Reagan to dampen the arms race was a significant factor in ending the Cold War confrontation between the United States and the Soviet Union. Reagan and Gorbachev are shown standing before St. Basil's Cathedral during Reagan's visit to Moscow in 1988.

States had serious deficit problems. During the Reagan years, the United States had moved from being a creditor nation to the world's biggest debtor nation. By 1990, both countries were becoming aware that their large military budgets made it difficult for them to solve their serious social problems.

The years 1989 and 1990 will surely be remembered as crucial years in the ending of the Cold War. The postwar settlements that had become the norm in central and eastern Europe came unstuck as a mostly peaceful revolutionary upheaval swept through Eastern Europe. Gorbachev's policy of allowing greater autonomy for the Communist regimes of Eastern Europe meant that the Soviet Union would no longer militarily support Communist governments that were faced with internal revolt. The unwillingness of the Soviet regime to use force to maintain the status quo, as it had in Hungary in 1956 and in Czechoslovakia in 1968, opened the door to the overthrow of the Communist regimes (see Eastern Europe: From Soviet Satellites to Sovereign Nations later in the chapter). The reunification of Germany on October 3, 1990, also destroyed one of the most prominent symbols of the Cold War era. Increasingly throughout 1990, the military role of NATO was also being seriously questioned. There is, of course, always the danger that if the Gorbachev revolution fails and right-wing neo-Stalinists take over in the Soviet Union, the Cold War could resume. By the fall of 1990, most of the world's people were hoping instead that a new, truly post–Cold War era had begun. American and Soviet cooperation after the Iraqi invasion of Kuwait in August 1990 seemed to support these hopes.

▼ Europe since 1945: Recovery and Renewal

At the height of Nazi success in 1942, a new era of barbarism seemed to challenge the very existence of European civilization. But Europeans made a remarkable recovery, and within a few years after the defeat of Germany and Italy, economic revival brought a renewed growth to European society. Major differences, however, remained between Western and Eastern Europe.

The Soviet Union: From Stalin to Gorbachev

World War II devastated the Soviet Union. To create a new industrial base, Stalin returned to the method that had proved effective in the 1930s—the acquisition of development capital from Soviet labor. Working hard for little pay, poor housing, and precious few consumer goods, Soviet laborers were expected to produce goods for export with little in return for themselves. The incoming capital from abroad could then be used to purchase machinery and Western technology. The loss of millions of men in the war meant that much of this tremendous work load fell upon Soviet women. Almost 40 percent of heavy manual labor was performed by women.

Although this policy was successful in promoting economic growth in heavy industry, primarily for the benefit of the military, consumer goods were scarce. While the development of thermonuclear weapons in 1953, MIG fighters from 1950 to 1953, and the first space satellite (*Sputnik*) in 1957 elevated the Soviet state's reputation as a world power abroad, domestically the Russian people were shortchanged. Heavy industry grew at a rate three times that of personal consumption. Moreover, the housing shortage was acute. A British military attaché in Moscow reported that "all houses, practically without exception, show lights from every window after dark. This seems to indicate that every room is both a living room by day and a bedroom by night. There is no place in overcrowded Moscow for the luxury of eating and sleeping in separate rooms."[6]

Stalin demanded a dogmatic superpatriotism from all Soviets, but found that contact with Western ways during the war had shaken many people's belief in the superiority of the Soviet system. Returning Russian soldiers brought back stories of the prosperity of the West, and the obvious disparity between the Western and Soviet systems led to a "crisis of faith" for many young Communists. Partly for this reason, Stalin imprisoned

Khrushchev Denounces Stalin
▼ ▼ ▼

Three years after the death of Stalin, the new Soviet premier, Nikita Khrushchev, addressed the Twentieth Congress of the Communist Party and denounced the former Soviet dictator for his crimes. This denunciation was the beginning of a policy of destalinization.

Nikita Khrushchev Addresses the Twentieth Party Congress, February 1956

Comrades, . . . quite a lot has been said about the cult of the individual and about its harmful consequences. . . . The cult of the person of Stalin . . . became at a certain specific stage the source of a whole series of exceedingly serious and grave perversions of Party principles, of Party democracy, of revolutionary legality.

Stalin absolutely did not tolerate collegiality in leadership and in work and . . . practiced brutal violence, not only toward everything which opposed him, but also toward that which seemed to his capricious and despotic character, contrary to his concepts.

Stalin abandoned the method of ideological struggle for that of administrative violence, mass repressions and terror. . . . Arbitrary behavior by one person encouraged and permitted arbitrariness in others. Mass arrests and deportations of many thousands of people, execution without trial and without normal investigation created conditions of insecurity, fear and even desperation.

Stalin showed in a whole series of cases his intolerance, his brutality and his abuse of power. . . . He often chose the path of repression and annihilation, not only against actual enemies, but also against individuals who had not committed any crimes against the Party and the Soviet government. . . .

Many Party, Soviet and economic activists who were branded in 1937–8 as "enemies" were actually never enemies, spies, wreckers and so on, but were always honest communists; they were only so stigmatised, and often, no longer able to bear barbaric tortures, they charged themselves (at the order of the investigative judges-falsifiers) with all kinds of grave and unlikely crimes.

This was the result of the abuse of power by Stalin, who began to use mass terror against the Party cadres. . . . Stalin put the Party and the NKVD [the secret police] up to the use of mass terror when the exploiting classes had been liquidated in our country and when there were no serious reasons for the use of extraordinary mass terror. The terror was directed . . . against the honest workers of the Party and the Soviet state. . . .

Stalin was a very distrustful man, sickly suspicious. . . . Everywhere and in everything he saw "enemies," "two-facers" and "spies." Possessing unlimited power, he indulged in great wilfulness and choked a person morally and physically. A situation was created where one could not express one's own will. When Stalin said that one or another would be arrested, it was necessary to accept on faith that he was an "enemy of the people." What proofs were offered? The confession of the arrested. . . . How is it possible that a person confesses to crimes that he had not committed? Only in one way—because of application of physical methods of pressuring him, tortures, bringing him to a state of unconsciousness, deprivation of his judgement, taking away of his human dignity.

---

many soldiers, who were simply shipped from German concentration camps to Soviet concentration camps. Stalin believed that Western influence was a threat to Communist orthodoxy. In 1946, government decrees subordinated all forms of literary and scientific expression to the political needs of the state. Along with the anti-intellectual campaign came political terror. A new series of purges seemed imminent in 1953 when a number of Jewish doctors were implicated in a spurious plot to kill high-level party officials. Only Stalin's death on March 5, 1953, prevented more bloodletting.

A new collective leadership succeeded Stalin until Nikita Khrushchev (1894–1971) emerged as the chief Soviet policymaker. Khrushchev had been responsible for ending the system of forced-labor camps, a regular feature of Stalinist Russia. At the Twentieth Congress of the Communist Party in 1956, Khrushchev condemned Stalin for his "administrative violence, mass repression, and terror" (see the box on p. 1011).

Once in power, Khrushchev continued and even extended the early policies of the collective leadership that had replaced Stalin. The intellectual thaw continued as Khrushchev stated that "readers should be given the chance to make their own judgments" regarding the acceptability of controversial literature, and that "police measures shouldn't be used."[7] He allowed the publication in 1962 of Alexander Solzhenitsyn's *A Day in the Life of Ivan Denisovich,* a grim portrayal of the horrors of Russia's forced-labor camps. Most importantly, Khrushchev extended the process of destalinization. Khrushchev's revelations about Stalin at the Twentieth Congress created turmoil in Communist ranks everywhere and encouraged rebellions in Soviet satellite countries in Eastern Europe—rebellions that were then crushed by the Red Army (see Eastern Europe: From Soviet Satellites to Sovereign Nations later in the chapter).

Economically, Khrushchev tried to place more emphasis on consumer goods. Likewise, he encouraged the decentralization of agriculture by allowing more local decision making with less interference from Moscow. Khrushchev's attempts to increase agricultural output by growing corn and cultivating vast lands east of the Ural Mountains proved less successful and damaged his reputation within the party. These failures, combined with increased military spending, hurt the Soviet economy. The industrial growth rate, which had soared in the early 1950s, now declined dramatically from 13 percent in 1953 to 7.5 percent in 1964.

Khrushchev's personality also did not endear him to the higher Soviet officials who frowned at his tendency to crack jokes and play the clown. Nor were the higher members of the party bureaucracy pleased when Khrushchev tried to curb their privileges. Foreign policy failures caused additional damage to Khrushchev's reputation among his colleagues. His rash plan to place missiles in Cuba was the final straw. While he was away on vacation in 1964, a special meeting of the Soviet Politburo voted him out of office (because of "ill-health") and forced him into retirement. Although a group of leaders succeeded him, real power came into the hands of Leonid Brezhnev (1906–1982), the "trusted" supporter of Khrushchev who had engineered his downfall.

The Brezhnev years were relatively calm ones for the Soviet Union. Brezhnev benefited from the more relaxed atmosphere associated with détente. The Soviets had reached a rough parity with the United States in nuclear arms and enjoyed a sense of external security that seemed to allow for a relaxation of authoritarian rule. The regime permitted more access to Western styles of music, dress, and art, although dissenters were still punished. Andrei Sakharov, for example, who had played an important role in the development of the Soviet hydrogen bomb, was placed under house arrest for his defense of human rights.

In his economic policies, Brezhnev continued to emphasize heavy industry. Overall industrial growth declined, although the Soviet production of iron, steel, coal, and cement surpassed that of the United States. Two problems bedeviled the Soviet economy. The government's insistence on vigorous central planning led to a huge, complex bureaucracy that discouraged efficiency and reduced productivity. Moreover, the Soviet system, based on guaranteed employment and a lack of incentives, bred apathy, complacency, absenteeism, and drunkenness.

Agricultural problems added to Soviet economic woes. Collective farmers also lacked incentives. Many preferred working their own small private plots to laboring in the collective work brigades. To make matters worse, bad harvests in the mid-1970s, caused by a series of droughts, heavy rains, and early frosts, forced the Soviet government to buy grain from the West, particularly the United States. To their chagrin, the Soviets were increasingly dependent on capitalist countries.

Despite the underlying problems, higher living standards for the Soviet elite—the scientists, managers, and technicians—created a sense of confidence and optimism in the 1970s. This confidence began to wane, however, by the end of the decade, especially when Soviet fears of a growing anti-communist fundamentalist Islamic government in Afghanistan led to the Soviet quagmire in Afghanistan. Brezhnev declined noticeably after 1975 because of frequent illness. Although he was succeeded briefly by two older, ailing members of the Soviet leadership, a new era was about to begin.

THE GORBACHEV ERA   In 1985, Mikhail Gorbachev (b. 1931), a young, vigorous, and progressive politician, took over the reins of Soviet power. Born of the peasantry and educated during the reform years of Khrushchev, Gorbachev seemed intent on taking earlier reforms to their logical conclusions. By the 1980s, Soviet economic problems were obvious. Rigid, centralized planning led to mismanagement and stifled innovation. Although the Soviets still excelled in space exploration, they fell behind the West in high technology, especially in the development and production of computers for private and public use. Most noticeable to the Soviet people was the actual decline in the standard of living. In February 1986, at the Twenty-Seventh Congress of the Communist Party, Gorbachev made clear the need for changes in Soviet society: "The practical actions of the Party and state agencies lag behind the demands of the times and of life itself. . . . Problems grow faster than they are solved. Sluggishness, ossification in the forms, and methods of management decrease the dynamism of work. . . . Stagnation begins to show up in the life of society."[8] Thus, from the start, Gorbachev preached the need for radical reforms.

The cornerstone of Gorbachev's radical reforms was *perestroika* or "restructuring." At first this meant only a reordering of economic policy as Gorbachev called for the beginning of a market economy with limited free enterprise and some private property. But Gorbachev perceived that in the Soviet system, the economic sphere was intimately tied to the social and political spheres. Attempts to reform the economy without political or social reform would be doomed to failure.

One of the most important instruments of *perestroika* was *glasnost* or "openness." Soviet citizens and officials were encouraged to discuss openly the strengths and weaknesses of the Soviet Union. This policy could be seen in *Pravda,* the official newspaper of the Communist party, where increased coverage was given to such disasters as the nuclear accident at Chernobyl in 1986 and collisions of ships in the Black Sea. Soon this type of reporting was extended to include reports of official corruption, sloppy factory work, and protests against government policy. The arts also benefited from the new policy as previously banned works were now published, and motion pictures began to show negative aspects of Soviet life. Music based on Western styles, such as jazz and rock, began to be performed openly.

Political reforms have been equally revolutionary. In June 1987, the principle of two-candidate elections was introduced, whereas before voters were presented with only one candidate. Though multiparty elections have not been introduced as of 1990, their implementation appears almost inevitable. Most dissidents, including Andrei Sakharov, who had spent years in internal exile, were released. The revolutionary nature of Gorbachev's political reforms can perhaps be seen most clearly in Sakharov's rise from dissident to an elected member of the Congress of People's Deputies in March of 1989. As a leader of the dissident deputies, Sakharov called for the end of the Communist monopoly of power, and on the day he died, December 11, 1989, urged the creation of a new noncommunist party.

Gorbachev has also pushed for greater powers for the office of president, previously only a titular post. This is a consequence of the dissociation of the state and the Communist party. Hitherto, the position of first secretary of the party was the most important post in the Soviet Union, but as the Communist party becomes less closely associated with the state, the powers of this office will diminish correspondingly. Increasing the powers of the presidency may well be Gorbachev's way of attempting to secure his political survival if the Communist party does indeed fall.

At the Communist party conference in 1988, Gorbachev called for the creation of a new Soviet parliament. This parliament convened in 1989, the first such meeting in Russia since 1918. Gorbachev consolidated power in 1989 by convincing 110 full and alternate members of the Central Committee of the Communist party to resign "voluntarily." The party congress of July 1990 saw Gorbachev attempting to maintain power against the stiff opposition of party hard-liners such as Yegor Ligachev, who wished to slow or stop reforms, and liberals such as Boris Yeltsin, who wanted more and faster reforms.

Gorbachev made it clear that the Communist monopoly of power in the Soviet Union was ending and that the party must prepare itself accordingly if it hopes to remain a political force in the coming democracy. He emphatically stated that reform must go forward: "There is no way to bring yesterday back. . . . No dictatorship, if someone has this crazy idea in his head, can resolve anything."[9] On July 10, 1990, Gorbachev won reelection as general secretary of the party. On July 12, Boris Yeltsin, the main opposition from the liberals, resigned from the Communist party and announced his intention to form the Democratic Platform into an opposition party, moving the Soviet Union in the direction of a multiparty system.

CRISIS IN THE SOVIET REPUBLICS: ETHNIC VIOLENCE AND INDEPENDENCE MOVEMENTS   One of Gorbachev's most serious problems stems from the character of the Soviet Union. The Union of Soviet Socialist Republics is a truly multiethnic country, containing 92 nationalities and 112 recognized languages. Previously, the iron hand of the Communist party, centered in Moscow, kept a lid on the centuries-old ethnic tensions that have periodically erupted. As Gorbachev released this iron grip, tensions resurfaced, a by-product of *glasnost* that Gorbachev had not anticipated. Ethnic groups took advantage of the new openness to protest what they perceived to be ethnically motivated slights. As violence has erupted, the Soviet army, in disrepair since Afghanistan, has had difficulty controlling the situation. In some cases, independence movements and ethnic causes have become linked, as in Azerbaijan where the National Front became the spokesgroup for the Muslim Azerbaijanis in their conflict with Christian Armenians.

The period 1988 to 1990 also witnessed the appearance of nationalist movements throughout the republics of the Soviet Union. Many are motivated by ethnic concerns, with calls for sovereignty of the republics and independence from the Russian-based rule centered in Moscow. These movements sprang up first in Georgia late in 1988 and later in Latvia, Estonia, Moldavia, Uzbekistan, Azerbaijan, and most dramatically in Lithuania.

In December of 1989, the Communist party of Lithuania declared itself independent of the Communist party of the Soviet Union. A leading force in this independence movement was the nationalist Lithuanian Restructuring Movement or "Popular Front for Perestroika," commonly known as *Sajudis,* led by Vytautas Landsbergis. *Sajudis* also favored a more radical policy of independence for Lithuania. Gorbachev made it clear that he supported self-determination, but not secession, which he believed would be detrimental to the Soviet Union. Nevertheless, on March 11, 1990, the Lithuanian Supreme Council unilaterally declared Lithuania independent. Its formal name was now the Lithuanian Republic; the adjectives Soviet and Socialist had been dropped. On March 15, the Soviet Congress of People's Deputies, though recognizing a general right to secede from the Union of Soviet Socialist Republics, declared the Lithuanian declaration null and void; the congress stated that proper procedures must be established and followed before secession will be acceptable. Although Soviet resistance had made immediate independence for Lithuania less likely, Lithuanians seem intent on pursuing their goal.

Eastern Europe: From Soviet Satellites to Sovereign Nations

The political structure of Eastern Europe after World War II was, for the most part, the creation of Joseph Stalin. Communist governments were established by force or subterfuge in most of the countries "liberated" by the Soviet army. The new Communist governments generally fell into two categories, those run by "Little Stalins" and those led by national Communists. The "Little Stalins" ruled as virtual dictators and generally followed the dictates of the Soviets. The national Communists believed in the merits of communism but also cherished national sovereignty and had no desire to follow the wishes of their Soviet "protector" at all times. Nevertheless, whenever they tried to act independently of the Soviet Union, they were forced to retreat. Only at the end of the 1980s did Gorbachev's policies make possible radical changes in Eastern Europe.

POLAND Stalin had installed a pro-Soviet Communist regime in "liberated" Poland. In 1956, after the circulation of Khrushchev's denunciation of Stalin, protests—especially by workers—erupted in Poland. In response, the Polish Communist party adopted a series of reforms in October 1956 and elected Wladyslaw Gomulka (1905–1982) as first secretary. Gomulka declared that Poland had the right to follow its own socialist path. Fearful of Soviet armed response, however, the Poles compromised. Poland pledged to remain loyal to the Warsaw Pact, while the Soviets agreed to allow Poland to follow its own path to socialism. The Catholic church, an extremely important institution to many Poles, was also permitted to administer its own affairs.

This compromise enabled Poland to achieve a certain stability for the next decade, but economic problems brought the ouster of Gomulka in 1971. His replacement, Edward Gierek, attempted to solve Poland's economic problems by borrowing heavily from the West. But in 1980, when he announced huge increases in food prices in an effort to pay off part of the Western debt, workers' protests erupted once again. This time, however, the revolutionary demands of the workers led directly to the rise of the independent labor movement called Solidarity. Led by Lech Walesa (b. 1943), Solidarity represented 10 million of Poland's 35 million people. Almost instantaneously, Solidarity became a tremendous force for change and a threat to the government's monopoly of power. With the support of the workers, many intellectuals, and the Catholic church, Solidarity was able to win a series of concessions. The Polish government seemed powerless to stop the flow of concessions until December 1981, when it arrested Walesa and other Solidarity leaders, outlawed the union, and imposed military rule under General Wojciech Jaruzelski (b. 1923).

But martial rule did not solve Poland's serious economic problems. In 1988, new demonstrations broke out. After much maneuvering and negotiating with Solidarity, the Polish regime finally consented to elections that led to even greater strength for Solidarity. Bowing to the inevitable, Jaruzelski's regime allowed the

Solidarity-led coalition in the lower house of the new legislature to elect Tadeusz Mazowiecki, a leading member of Solidarity, as prime minister. The Communist monopoly of power in Poland had come to an end after forty-five years. In April 1990, it was decided that a new president would be freely elected by the populace by the end of the year.

YUGOSLAVIA   Most of the initial Communist governments set up by Joseph Stalin after the war were run by "Little Stalins." Yugoslavia, however, was the first to be led by a national Communist and to assert its independence from the Soviet Union. During World War II, Josip Broz, known as Tito, leader of the Communist resistance movement, seemed to be a loyal Stalinist. After the war, however, he moved toward the establishment of an independent Communist state in Yugoslavia. This alienated him from Stalin and created a potential ally for the West in the Cold War. But Tito was not about to be a capitalist pawn either. Communist Yugoslavia became a neutral force in Eastern Europe and the world for the remainder of Tito's rule.

In 1958, the Yugoslav party congress asserted that Yugoslav Communists did not see themselves as deviating from communism, only Stalinism. They considered their way closer to the Marxist-Leninist ideal. This included a more decentralized economic and political system in which workers could manage themselves and local communes could exercise some political power. By the 1970s, however, Tito became concerned that decentralization had gone too far in creating too much power at the local level and encouraging regionalism. As a result, he purged thousands of local Communist leaders who seemed more concerned with local affairs than national concerns.

After Tito's death in 1980, no strong leader emerged as Tito's responsibilities passed to a collective state presidency and the presidium of the League of Communists of Yugoslavia (LCY). At the end of the 1980s, Yugoslavia was caught up in the reform movements sweeping through Eastern Europe. On January 20, 1990, the League of Communists called for an end to authoritarian socialism and proposed the creation of a pluralistic political system with freedom of speech and other civil liberties, free elections, an independent judiciary, and a mixed economy with equal status for private property. But divisions between radical Slovenes who wanted a loose federation and Serbians who wanted to retain the centralized system caused the collapse of the party congress, and hence the Communist party. New parties quickly emerged. In multiparty elections held in the states of Slovenia and Croatia in April and May of 1990 (the first multiparty elections in Yugoslavia in fifty-one years), the Communists fared poorly. Yugoslavia seemed on its way to a pluralistic political system, although ethnic minorities problems could still wreak havoc with a peaceful transition to a new era.

HUNGARY   The developments in Poland in 1956 inspired national Communists in Hungary to seek the same kinds of reforms and independence. Intense debates eventually resulted in the ouster of the ruling Stalinist and the selection of Imry Nagy (1896–1958) as the new Hungarian leader. Internal dissent, however, was not simply directed against the Soviets, but against communism in general, which was viewed as a creation of the Soviets, not the Hungarians. The Stalinist secret police had also bred much terror and hatred. This dissatisfaction, combined with economic difficulties, created a situation ripe for revolt. In order to quell the rising rebellion, Nagy declared Hungary a free nation on November 1, 1956. He promised free elections, and the mood of the country made it clear that this could mean the end of Communist rule in Hungary. But Khrushchev was in no position at home to allow a member of the Communist flock to leave. Just three days after Nagy's declaration, the Red Army attacked Budapest (see the box on p. 1016). The Soviets reestablished control over the country while János Kádár (1912–1989), a cabinet minister who had appeared liberal, replaced Nagy and worked with the Soviets to squash the revolt.

Remaining in power for over thirty years, Kádár enacted the most far-reaching economic reforms in Eastern Europe. In the early 1980s, he legalized small private enterprises, such as retail stores, restaurants, and artisan shops. His economic reforms were termed "Communism with a capitalist facelift." Hungary moved slowly away from its strict adherence to Soviet dominance and even established fairly friendly relations with the West. Multicandidate elections with at least two candidates for each office were held for the first time on June 8, 1985.

As the 1980s progressed, however, the economy sagged, and Kádár fell from power in 1988. By 1989, the Hungarian Communist government was aware of the growing dissatisfaction and began to undertake reforms. The more important new political parties united to form an opposition Round Table, whose negotiations with the Communists led to an agreement that Hungary would become a democratic republic. The Hungarian Communist party changed its name to the Hungarian Socialist party in order to have a greater chance of success in the new elections scheduled for March 25, 1990. The party

Soviet Repression in Eastern Europe: Hungary, 1956

▼ ▼ ▼

Developments in Poland in 1956 inspired the Communist leaders of Hungary to begin to remove their country from Soviet control. But there were limits to Khrushchev's tolerance, and he sent Soviet troops to crush Hungary's movement for independence. The first selection is a statement by the Soviet government justifying the use of Soviet troops, while the second is a brief and tragic final statement from Imry Nagy, the Hungarian leader.

Statement of the Soviet Government, October 30, 1956

The Soviet Government regards it as indispensable to make a statement in connection with the events in Hungary.

The course of the events has shown that the working people of Hungary, who have achieved great progress on the basis of their people's democratic order, correctly raise the question of the necessity of eliminating serious shortcomings in the field of economic building, the further raising of the material well-being of the population, and the struggle against bureaucratic excesses in the state apparatus.

However, this just and progressive movement of the working people was soon joined by forces of black reaction and counterrevolution, which are trying to take advantage of the discontent of part of the working people to undermine the foundations of the people's democratic order in Hungary and to restore the old landlord and capitalist order.

The Soviet Government and all the Soviet people deeply regret that the development of events in Hungary has led to bloodshed. On the request of the Hungarian People's Government the Soviet Government consented to the entry into Budapest of the Soviet Army units to assist the Hungarian People's Army and the Hungarian authorities to establish order in the town.

The Last Message of Imry Nagy, November 4, 1956

This fight is the fight for freedom by the Hungarian people against the Russian intervention, and it is possible that I shall only be able to stay at my post for one or two hours. The whole world will see how the Russian armed forces, contrary to all treaties and conventions, are crushing the resistance of the Hungarian people. They will also see how they are kidnapping the Prime Minister of a country which is a Member of the United Nations, taking him from the capital, and therefore it cannot be doubted at all that this is the most brutal form of intervention. I should like in these last moments to ask the leaders of the revolution, if they can, to leave the country. I ask that all that I have said in my broadcast, and what we have agreed on with the revolutionary leaders during meetings in Parliament, should be put in a memorandum, and the leaders should turn to all the peoples of the world for help and explain that today it is Hungary and tomorrow, or the day after tomorrow, it will be the turn of other countries because the imperialism of Moscow does not know borders, and is only trying to play for time.

---

came in fourth, however, a clear repudiation of communism. By the summer of 1990, Hungary seemed committed to democratic government and the institution of a free market economy.

CZECHOSLOVAKIA The developments in Poland and Hungary in 1956 did not generate similar revolts in Czechoslovakia. The "Little Stalin," Antonin Novotny (1904–1975), placed in power in 1952 by Stalin himself, remained firmly in control. By the late 1960s, however, Novotny had alienated many members of his own party and was particularly resented by Czechoslovakia's writers, such as the playwright Vaclav Havel (b. 1936).

A writers' rebellion late in 1967, in fact, led to Novotny's resignation. In January 1968, Alexander Dubcek (b. 1921) was elected first secretary of the Communist party and soon introduced a number of reforms, including freedom of speech and press, freedom to travel abroad, and a relaxation of secret police activities. Dubcek hoped to create "communism with a human face." A period of euphoria erupted that came to be known as the "Prague Spring."

It proved to be short-lived. This euphoria had led many to call for more far-reaching reforms, including neutrality and withdrawal from the Soviet bloc. To forestall the spreading of this "spring" fever, the Red Army invaded Czechoslovakia in August of 1968 and crushed the reform movement. Gustav Husák (b. 1913), a committed nonreformist, replaced Dubcek, crushed his reforms, and maintained the old order until the end of 1987.

In 1988, dissident movements once again resurfaced. Government attempts to suppress mass demonstrations in Prague and other Czechoslovakian cities in 1988 and 1989 only led to more and larger demonstrations. By November 1989, crowds as large as 500,000, which included many students, were forming in Prague. A new opposition group, the Civic Forum, emerged and was officially recognized on November 17. The Czechoslovakian Federal Assembly now voted to delete the constitutional articles giving the Communists the leading role in politics. In December 1989, as demonstrations continued, the Communist government, lacking any real support, collapsed. President Husák resigned and at the end of December was replaced by Vaclav Havel, the dissident playwright who had played such an important role in bringing the Communist government down. In January 1990, Havel declared amnesty for some 30,000 political prisoners. He also set out on a goodwill tour to various Western countries in which he proved to be an eloquent spokesman for Czech democracy and a new order in Europe.

ROMANIA   By 1948, with Soviet assistance, a Communist People's Democratic Front had assumed complete power in Romania. In 1965, leadership of the Communist government passed into the hands of Nicolae Ceaus-

▼ **President Vaclav Havel of Czechoslovakia and the American Congress, 1990.** The upheaval in Czechoslovakia in 1988 and 1989 brought an end to the Communist government in that country. In December of 1989, Vaclav Havel, a dissident playwright who had been instrumental in bringing the Communist government down, became the new president of Czechoslovakia. During a visit to the United States in February 1990, Havel spoke to the American Congress. His speech received an enthusiastic reception, and he is shown here surrounded by members of Congress after his speech.

escu (1918–1989), who with his wife Elena established a rigid and dictatorial regime. Ceausescu ruled Romania with an iron grip, using a secret police force—the Securitate—as his personal weapon against any dissent. Nevertheless, opposition to his regime grew as Ceausescu rejected the reforms in Eastern Europe promoted by Gorbachev. Economic difficulties also developed from

▼ **Soviet Tanks in Czechoslovakia, 1968.** Alexander Dubcek, the new first secretary of the Communist party, tried to liberalize communist rule in Czechoslovakia in 1968. Feeling threatened by Dubcek's far-reaching reforms, the Soviet Union sent Red Army forces into Czechoslovakia and crushed the reform movement. Shown are Soviet tanks in the capital city of Prague.

Ceausescu's extreme measures to reduce Romania's external debt. Although he was successful in reducing foreign debt, the sharp drop in living standards that resulted from those hardship measures angered many. Despite food shortages and the rationing of bread, flour, and sugar, Ceausescu stated that the exporting of such goods would not cease. Ceausescu's plan for rapid urbanization, especially a rural systematization program that called for the bulldozing of entire villages, further incited the populace.

A small incident became the spark that ignited heretofore suppressed flames of discontent. The ruthless crushing of a demonstration in Timisoara in December 1989 led to other mass demonstrations. After the dictator was booed at a mass rally on December 21, the army refused to support any more repression. Ceausescu and his wife were captured on December 22 and tried and executed on Christmas Day, 1989.

Leadership now passed into the hands of a hastily formed National Salvation Front led by Ion Iliescu (b. 1930), a former Communist who had studied in Moscow with Gorbachev and worked with Ceausescu until they had a falling out. Although the National Salvation Front was the solid victor in elections in the spring of 1990, questions remain about the new government's commitment to democracy, especially since antigovernment demonstrations have been met with Ceausescu-like repression.

BULGARIA In Bulgaria, too, Soviet cooperation after the war enabled the local Communist party to assume control of the country. In 1954, Todor Zhivkov (b. 1911) became the leader of the Bulgarian Communist party and hence leader of the nation. Not until the late 1980s did a number of small opposition groups begin to emerge. In October of 1989, antigovernment demonstrations were held in the capital city of Sofia. On November 10, 1989, Zhivkov was unexpectedly relieved of his post as general secretary of the Communist party, a position he had held for thirty-five years. He was replaced by the minister for foreign affairs, Peter Mladenov (b. 1936), who immediately pledged political and economic reforms with special attention to environmental concerns. In December the central committee recommended the elimination of the constitutional provision according the Communist party the leading role in government. Free elections were slated for the second half of 1990. On February 23, 1990, the Bulgarian Communist party voted to change its name to the Bulgarian Socialist party. Despite antigovernment demonstrations,

the new Socialist party managed to retain control of the government.

EAST GERMANY The ruling Communist government in East Germany, led by Walter Ulbricht, consolidated its position in the early 1950s and became a faithful Soviet

Chronology

▼ ▼ ▼

The Soviet Union and Satellite States in Eastern Europe

Death of Stalin	1953
Workers' Revolt Crushed in East Germany	1953
Zhivkov as Leader of Bulgarian Communist Party	1954
Khrushchev's Denunciation of Stalin	1956
Attempt at Reforms in Poland	1956
Hungarian Revolt is Crushed	1956
Berlin Wall is Built	1961
Breshnev Era	1964–1982
Ceausescu Takes Power in Romania	1965
Soviets Crush "Prague Spring" in Czechoslovakia	1968
Emergence of Solidarity in Poland	1980
Gorbachev Comes to Power in Soviet Union	1985
Multicandidate Elections in Hungary	1985
Collapse of Communist Government in Czechoslovakia	1989
Zhivkov Replaced by Mladenov in Bulgaria	1989
East German Communist Government Collapses	1989
Execution of Ceausescu in Romania	1989
	1990
Lithuania Declares Independence	March 11
East German Elections-Victory of Christian Democrats	March 18
Hungarian Elections	March 25
Multiparty Elections in Yugoslavia	April–May
Union of Currencies-West and East Germany	July 1
Gorbachev Reelected as General Secretary of Communist Party	July 10
Reunification of Germany	October 3

satellite. Industry was nationalized and agriculture collectivized. After a workers' revolt in 1953 was crushed by Soviet tanks, a steady flight of East Germans to West Germany ensued, primarily through the city of Berlin. This exodus of mostly skilled laborers created economic problems and led the East German government to build the infamous Berlin Wall in 1961 separating West from East Berlin, as well as equally fearsome barriers along the entire border with West Germany.

After building the Wall, East Germany succeeded in developing the strongest economy among the Soviet Union's Eastern European satellites. In 1971, Walter Ulbricht was succeeded by Erich Honecker (b. 1912), a party hard-liner who was deeply committed to the ideological battle against détente. Propaganda increased, and the use of the *Stasi*, the secret police, became a hallmark of Honecker's virtual dictatorship. Honecker ruled with an iron fist for the next eighteen years.

In 1988, however, popular unrest, partly fueled by the continual economic slump of the 1980s (which affected most of Eastern Europe) as well as the ongoing oppressiveness of Honecker's regime, caused another mass exodus of East German refugees. Violent repression as well as Honecker's refusal to institute reforms only led to a larger exodus and mass demonstrations against the regime in the summer and fall of 1989. By the beginning of November 1989, the Communist government had fallen into complete disarray. Capitulating to popular pressure on November 9, it opened the entire border with the West. Hundreds of thousands of Germans swarmed across the border, mostly to visit and return.

The Berlin Wall, long the symbol of the Cold War, became the site of a massive celebration. By December, new political parties had emerged, and on March 18, 1990, in East Germany's first free elections ever, the Christian Democrats won almost 50 percent of the vote. The Christian Democrats supported rapid monetary unification followed shortly by political unification with West Germany. On July 1, 1990, the economies of West and East Germany were united with the West German deutsche mark becoming the official currency of the two countries. Political reunification was achieved on October 3, 1990. What had seemed almost impossible at the beginning of 1989 had become a reality by the end of 1990. Developments in Germany reinforced the belief that the Cold War was truly over.

Western Europe: Domestic Politics

With the economic aid of the Marshall Plan, Western European countries recovered relatively rapidly from the devastation of World War II. Between 1950 and the late 1970s, industrial production in Western Europe increased dramatically. The European states had mixed economies that combined private enterprise with varying degrees of public ownership of banks, key industries, public utilities, and transportation systems. Social welfare programs—in the form of health services, housing, and educational opportunities—were also widely extended. Despite adverse economic trends in the 1970s, especially after the dramatic increase in the price of oil in 1973, the economies of the Western European states

▼ **And the Wall Came Tumbling Down.** The Berlin Wall, long a symbol of Europe's Cold War divisions, became the site of massive celebrations after the East German government opened its border with the West. Later, the East German government began to dismantle the wall. This photograph shows children playing on a pile of Berlin Wall rubble in front of the Reichstag building.

De Gaulle Calls for French Autonomy
▼ ▼ ▼

In the 1960s, the French president Charles de Gaulle sought to maintain France's independence from both the Soviet Union and the United States. In this 1966 speech, de Gaulle denounced those who were trying to subordinate France to international organizations.

A Speech of Charles de Gaulle, 1966

It is true that, among our contemporaries, there are many minds . . . who have envisaged that our country renounce its independence under the cover of one or another international group. Having thus handed over to foreign bodies the responsibility for our destiny, our leaders would . . . have nothing more to do than "plead France's case."

Thus some—exulting in the dream of the international—wanted to see our country itself, as they placed themselves, under the obedience of Moscow. Thus others—invoking either the supranational myth, or the danger from the East, or the advantage that the Atlantic West could derive from unifying its economy, or even the imposing utility of world arbitration—maintained that France should allow her policy to be dissolved in a tailor-made Europe, her defense in NATO, her monetary concepts in the Washington Fund, her personality in the United Nations.

Certainly, it is a good thing that such institutions exist, and it is only in our interest to belong to them; but if we had listened to their extreme apostles, these organs in which, as everyone knows, the political protection, military protection, economic power and multiform aid of the United States predominate—these organs would have been for us only a cover for our submission to American hegemony. Thus, France would disappear swept away by illusion.

---

had recovered by the beginning of the 1980s. Western Europeans have been full participants in the technological growth of the age and seem quite capable of standing up to American and Japanese economic competition.

Politically, Western Europe has also become accustomed to political democracy. Even Spain and Portugal, which had maintained their prewar dictatorial regimes until the mid-1970s, established democratic systems in the late 1970s. Overall, Socialist parties, such as the Labour party in Britain and the Social Democrats in West Germany, have fared poorly. Western European Communist parties have declined drastically. During the mid-1970s, a new variety of communism called Eurocommunism briefly emerged as Communist parties tried to work within the democratic system as mass movements committed to better government. But by the 1980s, internal political developments in Western Europe and events within the communist world itself had combined to undermine the Eurocommunist experiment.

FRANCE: FROM DE GAULLE TO MITTERAND   The history of France for nearly a quarter century after the war was dominated by one man—Charles de Gaulle (1890–1970). During the war, de Gaulle had assumed leadership of all resistance groups and played an important role in ensuring the establishment of a French provisional government after the war. The creation of the Fourth Republic, with a return to a parliamentary system based on parties that de Gaulle considered weak, led him to withdraw from politics. Eventually, he formed the "French Popular Movement," a decidedly rightist organization. It blamed the parties for France's political mess and called for an even stronger presidency, a goal that de Gaulle finally achieved in 1958.

The fragile political stability of the Fourth Republic had been badly shaken by the Algerian crisis. The French army had suffered defeat in Indochina in 1954 and was determined to defeat Algerian demands for independence. But a strong antiwar movement among French intellectuals and church leaders led to bitter divisions within France that brought the downfall of the Fourth Republic and a call for the return of de Gaulle.

In 1958, de Gaulle immediately drafted a new constitution for the Fifth Republic that greatly enhanced the power of the office of president. As the new president, de Gaulle sought to return France to a position of great power (see the box above). He believed that playing a pivotal role in the Cold War might enhance France's stature. For that reason, he pulled France out of the NATO high command. He increased French prestige

among the Third World countries by consenting to Algerian independence despite strenuous opposition from the army. With an eye toward achieving the status of a world power, de Gaulle invested heavily in the nuclear arms race. France exploded its first nuclear bomb in 1960.

Although the cost of the nuclear program increased the defense budget, de Gaulle did not neglect the French economy. Economic decision making was centralized, a reflection of the overall centralization undertaken by the Gaullist government. From 1958 to 1968, the French gross national product experienced an annual increase of 5.5 percent, faster than that of the United States. By the end of de Gaulle's era, France was a major industrial producer and exporter, particularly in such areas as automobiles and armaments.

Despite his successes, de Gaulle did not really achieve his ambitious goals of world power. Although his successors maintained that France was the "third nuclear power" after the United States and the Soviet Union, in truth France was too small for such global ambitions. A tired and discouraged Charles de Gaulle resigned from office in April 1969 and died within a year.

The worsening of France's economic situation in the 1970s brought a shift to the left politically. By 1981, the Socialists had become the dominant party in the National Assembly, and the Socialist leader, François Mitterand (b. 1916), was elected president. His first concern was with France's economic difficulties. In 1982, Mitterand froze prices and wages in the hope of reducing the huge budget deficit and high inflation. Mitterand also passed a number of liberal measures to aid workers: an increased minimum wage, expanded social benefits, a mandatory fifth week of paid vacation for salaried workers, a thirty-nine-hour work week, higher taxes for the rich, and nationalization of major banks. Mitterand's administrative reforms included both centralization (nationalization of banks and industry) and decentralization (granting local governments greater powers). In the 1988 presidential election, Mitterand won a second seven-year term.

WEST GERMANY   As a result of the pressures of the Cold War, the unification of the three Western zones into the West German Federal Republic became a reality in 1949. Konrad Adenauer (1876–1967), the leader of the Christian Democratic Union (CDU) who served as chancellor from 1949 to 1963, became the "founding hero" of the Federal Republic. Adenauer sought respect for Germany by cooperating with the United States and the other Western European nations. The beginning of the Korean War in June of 1950 had unexpected repercussions for West Germany. The fear that South Korea might fall to the Communist forces of the north led many Germans and westerners to worry about the security of West Germany and led to calls for the rearmament of West Germany. Although many people, concerned

▼ **De Gaulle and Adenauer.** While the postwar world was dividing into opposing Cold War camps, old enemies were becoming reconciled. The meeting of French president Charles de Gaulle and the German chancellor Konrad Adenauer in 1962 was an important step in beginning a friendly relationship between France and Germany.

about a revival of German militarism, condemned this proposal, Cold War tensions were decisive. West Germany rearmed in 1955 and became a member of NATO.

Adenauer's chancellorship is largely associated with the resurrection of the West German economy, often referred to as the "economic miracle." It was largely guided by the minister of finance, Ludwig Erhard. Although West Germany had only 75 percent of the population and 52 percent of the territory of prewar Germany, by 1955 the West German gross national product exceeded that of prewar Germany. Real wages doubled from 1950 to 1965 even though work hours were cut by 20 percent.

After the Adenauer era, German voters moved politically from the center-right politics of the Christian Democrats to center-left politics, and in 1969, the Social Democrats became the leading party. By forming a ruling coalition with the small Free Democratic party (FPD), the Social Democrats remained in power until 1982. The first Social Democratic chancellor was Willy Brandt (b. 1913). Brandt was especially successful with his "opening toward the east" (known as *Ostpolitik*), for which he received the Nobel Peace Prize in 1972. On March 19, 1971, Brandt met with Walter Ulbricht, the East German leader, and worked out the details of a Basic Treaty that was signed in 1972. This agreement did not establish full diplomatic relations with East Germany, but did call for "good neighborly" relations. As a result, it led to greater cultural, personal, and economic contacts between West and East Germany. Despite this success, the discovery of an East German spy among Brandt's advisers caused his resignation in 1974.

His successor, Helmut Schmidt (b. 1918), was more of a technocrat than a reform-minded socialist and concentrated primarily on the economic problems largely brought about by high oil prices between 1973 and 1975. Schmidt was successful in eliminating a deficit of 10 billion marks in three years. In 1982, when the coalition of Schmidt's Social Democrats with the Free Democrats fell apart over the reduction of social welfare expenditures, the Free Democrats joined with the Christian Democratic Union of Helmut Kohl (b. 1930) to form a new government. As the two German states approached unification in 1990, Kohl remained in power and became the leading candidate to become the first chancellor of a reunified German state.

Throughout its postwar existence, West Germany has been troubled by its Nazi past. The surviving major Nazi leaders had been tried and condemned as war criminals at the Nuremberg war crimes trials in 1945 and 1946. As part of the denazification of Germany, the victorious Allies continued war crimes trials of lesser officials, but these diminished as the Cold War produced a shift in attitudes. By 1950, German courts had begun to take over the war crimes trials, and the German legal machine has persisted in prosecuting cases. The West German government has also made payments to Israel and to Holocaust survivors and their relatives in order to make some restitution for the crimes of the Nazi era. The German president Richard von Weizsäcker has been especially eloquent in reminding Germans of their responsibility "for the unspeakable sorrow that occurred in the name of Germany."

GREAT BRITAIN The end of World War II left Britain with massive economic problems. In elections held immediately after the war, the Labour party overwhelmingly defeated Churchill's Conservative party. The Labour party had promised far-reaching reforms, particularly in the area of social welfare, and in a country with a tremendous shortage of consumer goods and housing, its platform was quite appealing. The new Labour government proceeded to enact the reforms that created the modern welfare state. Clement Attlee (1883–1967), the new prime minister, was a pragmatic reformer and certainly not the leftist revolutionary that Churchill had warned against in the election campaign.

The establishment of the British welfare state began with the nationalization of the Bank of England, the coal and steel industries, public transportation, and public utilities, such as electricity and gas. In the area of social welfare, the new government enacted the National Insurance Act and the National Health Service Act in 1946. The insurance act established a comprehensive social security program and nationalized medical insurance, thereby enabling the state to subsidize the unemployed, the sick, and the aged. The health act created a system of socialized medicine that forced doctors and dentists to work with state hospitals, although private practices could be maintained. This was an especially costly measure for the state, but within a few years 90 percent of the medical profession was participating. The British welfare state became the norm for most European states after the war.

The cost of building a welfare state at home forced the British to reduce expenses abroad. This meant the dismantling of the British Empire and the reduction of military aid to such countries as Greece and Turkey. Not a belief in the morality of self-determination, but economic necessity brought an end to the British Empire.

Continuing economic problems, however, brought the Conservatives back into power from 1951 to 1964.

Although they favored private enterprise, the Conservatives accepted the welfare state and even extended it when they undertook an ambitious construction program to improve British housing.

Between 1964 and 1979, Conservatives and Labour alternated in power. Both parties had to face seemingly intractable problems. While separatist movements in Scotland and Wales were overcome, fighting between Catholics and Protestants in Northern Ireland was not so easily settled. Violence increased as the Irish Republican Army (IRA) staged a series of dramatic terrorist acts in response to the suspension of Northern Ireland's parliament in 1972 and the establishment of direct rule by London. The problems in Northern Ireland have not yet been solved. Nor was either party able to deal with Britain's ailing economy. Failure to modernize made British industry less and less competitive. Moreover, Britain was hampered by frequent labor strikes, many of them caused by conflicts between rival labor unions.

In 1979, after Britain's economic problems had seemed to worsen during five years under a Labour government, the Conservatives returned to power under Margaret Thatcher (b. 1925). She became the first woman prime minister in British history. Thatcher pledged to lower taxes, reduce government bureaucracy, limit social welfare, restrict union power, and end inflation. The "Iron Lady," as she was called, did break the power of the labor unions. While she did not eliminate the basic components of the social welfare system, she did use austerity measures to control inflation. "Thatcherism," as her economic policy was termed, improved the British economic situation but at a price. The south of England, for example, prospered, but the old industrial areas of the Midlands and north declined and were beset by high unemployment, poverty, and even violence. Cutbacks in education seriously undermined the quality of British education, long regarded as one of the world's finest.

In the area of foreign policy, Thatcher, like Ronald Reagan in the United States, took a hard-line approach against communism. She oversaw a large military buildup aimed at replacing older technology and reestablishing Britain as a world policeman. In 1982, when Argentina attempted to take control of the Falkland Islands (one of Britain's few remaining colonial outposts) 300 miles off its coast, the British successfully rebuked the Argentines, although at great economic cost and the loss of 255 lives. The Falklands War, however, did generate much popular patriotic support for Thatcher.

Margaret Thatcher dominated British politics in the 1980s. The Labour party, beset by divisions between its moderate and radical wings, offered little effective opposition. Only in 1990 did Labour's fortunes seem to revive when Thatcher's government attempted to replace local property taxes with a flat-rate tax payable by every adult to his or her local authority. While Thatcher argued that this would make local government more responsive to its electors, many argued that this was nothing more than a poll tax that would enable the rich to pay the same rate as the poor. In 1990, after antitax riots broke out, Thatcher's once remarkable popularity fell to all-time lows. At the end of November, a revolt within her own party caused Thatcher to resign as prime minister.

ITALY   After the war, Italy faced a period of heavy reconstruction. No other Western country, except Germany, sustained more physical destruction. The monarchy was abolished when 54 percent of Italian voters rejected the royal house, and in June 1946, Italy became a democratic republic.

In the first postwar parliamentary elections held in April 1948, the Christian Democrats, still allied with the Catholic church, emerged as the leading political party. Alcide de Gasperi (1881–1954) became prime minister from 1948 to 1953, an unusually long span of time for an Italian government. Like prefascist governments, postwar Italian coalitions, largely dominated by the Christian Democrats, remained notorious for their instability and short lives. Although the Italian Communist party is one of Italy's three largest parties, it has been largely excluded from all of these government coalitions, although it managed to gain power in a number of provinces and municipalities in the 1960s and 1970s. The Christian Democrats have been able to maintain control by keeping the support of the upper and middle classes and the southern peasantry. In the 1980s, Italian politics continued to be marked by numerous changes of government and prime ministers.

The Marshall Plan helped to stabilize the postwar Italian economy. By 1957, worker income had risen far above 1939 levels. As in other Western welfare states, the Italian economy combined private enterprise with government management, particularly of heavy industry. The major economic problem continued to be the backwardness of southern Italy. In the 1960s millions of Italians from the south migrated to the more prosperous north.

Western Europe: The Move toward Unity

As we have seen, the divisions created by the Cold War led the nations of Western Europe to form the North Atlantic Treaty Organization in 1949. But mili-

tary unity was not the only kind of unity fostered in Europe after 1945. The destructiveness of two world wars caused many thoughtful Europeans to consider the need for some form of European unity. National feeling was still too powerful, however, for European nations to give up their political sovereignty. Consequently, the desire for unity was forced to focus primarily on the economic arena, not the political.

In 1951, France, West Germany, the Benelux countries (Belgium, Netherlands, and Luxemburg), and Italy formed the European Coal and Steel Community (ECSC). Its purpose was to create a common market for coal and steel products among the six nations by eliminating tariffs and other trade barriers. The success of the ECSC encouraged these six nations to proceed further, and in 1957 they created the European Atomic Energy Community (EURATOM) to further European research on the peaceful uses of nuclear energy.

In the same year, these six nations created the European Economic Community (EEC), also known as the Common Market. The Common Market eliminated customs barriers for the six member nations and created a large free-trade area protected from the rest of the world by a common external tariff. By promoting free trade, the Common Market also encouraged cooperation and standardization in many aspects of the six nations' economies. All the member nations benefited economically. The Common Market was expanded in 1973 when

▼ **Map 29.4** European Economic and Political Developments.

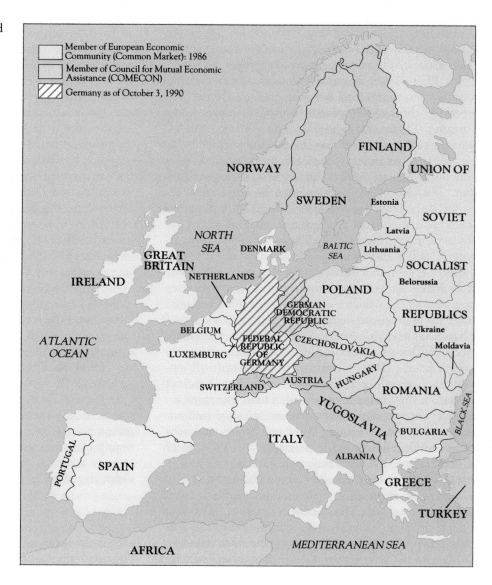

Great Britain, Ireland, and Denmark gained membership in what its members now began to call the European Community (EC). By 1986, three additional members—Spain, Portugal, and Greece—had been added.

The economic integration of the members of the European Community led to cooperative efforts in international and political affairs as well. The foreign ministers of the twelve members consult frequently and provide a common front for negotiations on important issues. Nevertheless, the European Community is still primarily an economic union, not a political one. By 1990, the European Community comprised 320 million people and constituted the world's largest single trading entity, transacting almost one-fourth of the world's commerce. Full economic integration for the European Community is projected by the end of 1992.

▼ Thought and Culture in the Postwar Era: New and Old Directions

Intellectually and culturally, the postwar era has been marked by much diversity. Although many trends represent a continuation of prewar modern developments, new directions have also led some to speak of a postmodern cultural world.

Recent Trends in Art, Music, and Literature

Modern art continued to prevail at exhibitions and museums. For the most part, the United States dominated the art world, much as it did the world of popular culture (see Popular Culture and the Americanization of the World later in the chapter). American art, often vibrantly colored and filled with activity, reflected the energy and exuberance of postwar America. After 1945, New York City became the artistic center of the Western world. The Guggenheim Museum, the Museum of Modern Art, and the Whitney Museum of American art, together with New York's numerous art galleries, promoted modern art and helped determine artistic tastes not only in New York and the United States, but throughout much of the world.

Abstractionism, especially Abstract Expressionism, emerged as the artistic mainstream (see Chapters 25 and 27). American exuberance in Abstract Expressionism is evident in the enormous canvases of Jackson Pollock (1912–1956). In such works as *Lavender Mist* (1950), paint seems to explode, assaulting the viewer with emotion and movement. Pollock's swirling forms and seemingly chaotic patterns broke all conventions of form and structure. His drip paintings, with their total abstraction, were extremely influential with other artists, although the public was initially quite hostile to his work. Pollock also introduced the technique of painting with the canvas laid on the floor or hung on a wall rather than placed on an easel. Significantly, paint itself was more the subject of his work than any preconceived representation.

The early 1960s saw the emergence of Pop Art, which took images of popular culture and transformed them into works of fine art. Andy Warhol (1930–1987), who began his career as an advertising illustrator, was the most famous of the pop artists. Warhol adapted images from commercial art, such as the Campbell soup cans, and photographs of such celebrities as Marilyn Monroe. Derived from mass culture, these works were mass pro-

▼ **Jackson Pollock Does a Painting.** American artists dominated the art world for many decades after the end of World War II. Abstract Expressionism remained at the center of the artistic mainstream. One of its best known practitioners was the American Jackson Pollock, who achieved his ideal of total abstraction by his drip paintings. He is shown here at work in his Long Island studio. Pollock found it easier to cover his large canvases with exploding patterns of color by putting them on the floor.

duced and deliberately "of the moment," expressing the fleeting whims of popular culture.

In the 1980s, styles have emerged that some have referred to as Postmodern. Although as yet ill-defined, Postmodernism tends to move away from the futurism or "cutting edge" qualities of Modernism. Instead it favors "utilizing tradition," whether that includes more

styles of painting or elevating traditional craftsmanship to the level of fine art. Weavers, potters, glassmakers, metalsmiths, and furniture makers have gained respect as artists.

Another response to Modernism can be seen in a return to realism in the arts. Some extreme realists paint or sculpt with such minute attention to realistic detail that their paintings appear to be photographs and their sculptures living human beings. Their subjects are often ordinary individuals, stuck in ordinary lives. These works are often pessimistic and cynical.

Abstract Expressionism, however, continues to proliferate. Anselm Kiefer, born in Germany in 1945, combines aspects of Abstract Expressionism, collage, and German Expressionism to create works that are stark and haunting. His *Departure from Egypt* (1984) is a meditation on Jewish history and its descent into the horrors of Nazism. Kiefer's international stature reflects a movement away from American dominance in the fine arts, a trend that gained momentum in the 1980s.

Classical music also witnessed a continuation of prewar developments. Some composers, the neoclassicists, remained closely tied to nineteenth-century romantic music, although they occasionally used some twentieth-century developments, such as atonality and dissonance. Their style was strongly reminiscent of Stravinsky (see Chapter 25).

The major musical trend since the war, however, has been serialism. Inspired mostly by the twelve tone music of Schönberg (see Chapter 27), serialism is a compositional procedure where an order of succession is set for specific values: pitch (for tones of the tempered scale); loudness (for dynamic levels); and units of time (for rhythm). By predetermining the order of succession, the composer restricts his or her intuitive freedom as the work to some extent creates itself. However, the mechanism the composer initially creates could generate unanticipated musical events, thereby creating new and exciting compositions. Serialist composition diminishes the role of intuition and emotion in favor of intellect and mathematical precision. The first recognized serialist was the Frenchman Olivier Messiaen (b. 1908). Significantly, Messiaen was influenced in part by Indian and Greek music, plain chant, folk music, and birdsongs. Most critics have respected serialism, although the public has been largely indifferent, if not hostile, to it. An offshoot of serialism that has won popular support, but not the same critical favor, is minimalism. Like serialism, this style uses repeated patterns and series and steady pulsation with gradual changes occurring over time. But whereas serialism is often atonal, minimalism is usually tonal and more harmonic.

The most significant new trend in postwar literature has been called the "Theater of the Absurd." This new convention in drama began in France in the 1950s, although its most famous proponent was the Irishman Samuel Beckett (1906–1990), who lived in France. In Beckett's *Waiting for Godot* (1952), it is readily apparent that the action on stage is not realistic. Two men wait incessantly for the appearance of someone, with whom they may or may not have an appointment. No background information on the two men is provided. During the course of the play, nothing seems to be happening. The audience is never told if the action in front of them is a dream, an allegory, or purely symbolic. As in lyric poetry, images in absurdist literature are presented as metaphors for aspects of human existence, involving states of mind and complex feelings. Unlike traditional theater, suspense is not maintained by having the audience wonder, "what is going to happen next?" but simply, "what is happening now?"

The Theater of the Absurd reflected its time. The postwar period was a time of disillusionment with fixed ideological beliefs in politics or religion. The same disillusionment that inspired Sartre's and Camus's existentialism (see The Philosophical Dilemma: Existentialism later in the chapter), with its sense of the world's meaninglessness, underscored the desolate worldview of absurdist drama and literature. This can be seen in Günter Grass's *Tin Drum*, published in 1959, which reflected postwar Germany's preoccupation with the seeming incomprehensibility of Nazi Germany.

The Theater of the Absurd also questioned the ability of language to reflect reality accurately. Beckett's play *Act without Words* contains no dialogue. In another play, Beckett used a beam of light and a buzzing sound as "words" of the discourse. The Czech playwright, Vaclav Havel, in his *Memorandum* (1966), examined the language and mechanics of bureaucracy. The plot revolved around the introduction of an artificial language that is imposed on people in the hope of fostering more efficient communication. Because no one can understand the new language, communication breaks down and, therefore, so do human relationships. The artificial language is finally eliminated, only to be replaced by an equally incomprehensible language imposed from above. The overt critique of Communist bureaucracy and the absurdity of imposing artificial systems with the hope of recreating society along ideological lines did little for Havel's position in Communist Czechoslovakia.

Postwar Science and Technology

Since the Scientific Revolution of the seventeenth century and the Industrial Revolution of the nineteenth century, science and technology have played increasingly important roles in Western civilization. Many of the scientific and technological achievements since

▼ **Anselm Kiefer, *Departure for Egypt*.** Although Western artists experimented with a variety of modern and even postmodern styles in the 1970s and 1980s, Abstract Expressionism continued its popularity. The German artist Anselm Kiefer used the tradition of Abstract Expressionism to create haunting images that reflect the horrors of Germany's Nazi past.

World War II have revolutionized people's lives. When American astronauts walked on the moon, millions watched the event on their televisions in the privacy of their living rooms.

Before World War II, theoretical science and technology were largely separated. Pure science was the domain of university professors who were quite far removed from the practical technological concerns of technicians and engineers. "Pure" scientists were rarely concerned with the practical usefulness of their research. But during World War II, university scientists were recruited to work for their governments and develop new weapons and practical instruments of war. British physicists played a crucial role in the development of an improved radar system in 1940 that helped to defeat the German air force in the Battle of Britain. German scientists converted coal to gasoline to keep the German war machine moving and created self-propelled rockets as well as jet airplanes to keep Hitler's hopes alive for a miraculous turnaround in the war. The computer, too, was a wartime creation. The British mathematician Alan Turing designed a primitive computer to assist British intelligence in breaking the secret codes of German ciphering machines. The most famous result of wartime scientific research was the creation of the atomic bomb by a team of American and European scientists who worked under the guidance of the physicist J. Robert Oppenheimer. Obviously, most wartime devices were created for destructive purposes, but merely to mention computers and jet airplanes demonstrates that they could easily be adapted for peacetime uses.

The sponsorship of research by governments and the military during World War II created a new model for science that some have labeled "Big Science." Science had become very complex. Only large organizations with teams of scientists, huge laboratories, and complex equipment could undertake such large-scale projects. Such facilities were so expensive, however, that they could only be provided by governments and large corporations. Because of its postwar prosperity, the United States was able to lead in the development of Big Science. Almost 75 percent of all scientific research funds in the United States came from the government in 1965. Unwilling to lag behind, especially in military developments, the Soviet Union was also forced to provide large outlays for scientific and technological research. In fact, the defense establishments of the United States and the Soviet Union generated much of postwar scientific research. One-fourth of trained scientists and engineers after 1945 were utilized in the creation of new weapons systems. Universities found their research agendas increasingly determined by government funding for military-related projects.

There was no more stunning example of how Big Science operated than in the space race of the 1960s. The announcement by the Russians in 1957 that they had sent the first space satellite—*Sputnik I*—into orbit around the earth, caused the United States to launch a gigantic project to land a manned spacecraft on the moon within a decade. Massive government funds financed the scientific research and technological advances that achieved this goal in 1969.

The postwar alliance of science and technology led to an accelerated rate of change that became a fact of life in Western society. But the underlying assumption of this alliance—that scientific knowledge gave human beings the ability to manipulate the environment for their benefit—was questioned by some in the 1960s and 1970s who believed that some technological advances had far-reaching side effects damaging to the environment. The chemical fertilizers, for example, that were touted for producing larger crops, wreaked havoc with the ecological balance of streams, rivers, and woodlands. *Small Is Beautiful*, written by the British economist E. F. Schumacher (1911–1977), was a fundamental critique of the dangers of Big Science (see the box on p. 1029). The widespread proliferation of fouled beaches and dying forests and lakes promised to make environmentalism one of the important issues of the 1990s.

After World War II, a number of physicists continued to explore the implications of Einstein's revolution in physics and raised fundamental questions about the nature of reality. To some physicists, quantum and relativity theory described the universe as a complicated web of relations in which there were no isolated building blocks. Thus, the universe was not a "collection of physical objects," but a complicated web of relations between "various parts of a unified whole." Moreover, this web of relations that is the universe also included the human observer. Human beings could not be objective observers of objects detached from themselves because the very act of observation made them participants in the process itself. These speculations implied that the old Newtonian conception of the universe as a machine was an outdated tool for understanding the nature of the universe.

The Philosophical Dilemma: Existentialism

In the twentieth century, philosophy divided itself into two major schools of thought. In Great Britain and the United States, logical positivism (or logical empiri-

Small Is Beautiful: The Limits of Modern Technology
▼ ▼ ▼

Although the alliance of science and technology has produced an amazing array of achievements in the postwar world, some voices have been raised in criticism of the sometimes destructive aspects of Big Science. In 1975, in his book Small Is Beautiful, *the British economist E. F. Schumacher examined the effects modern industrial technology has had on the earth's resources.*

E. F. Schumacher, *Small Is Beautiful*

Is it not evident that our current methods of production are already eating into the very substance of industrial man? To many people this is not at all evident. Now that we have solved the problem of production, they say, have we ever had it so good? Are we not better fed, better clothed, and better housed than ever before—and better educated? Of course we are: most, but by no means all, of us: in the rich countries. But this is not what I mean by "substance." The substance of man cannot be measured by Gross National Product. Perhaps it cannot be measured at all, except for certain symptoms of loss. However, this is not the place to go into the statistics of these symptoms, such as crime, drug addiction, vandalism, mental breakdown, rebellion, and so forth. Statistics never prove anything.

I started by saying that one of the most fateful errors of our age is the belief that the problem of production has been solved. This illusion, I suggested, is mainly due to our inability to recognize that the modern industrial system, with all its intellectual sophistication, consumes the very basis on which it has been erected. To use the language of the economist, it lives on irreplaceable capital which it cheerfully treats as income. I specified three categories of such capital: fossil fuels, the tolerance margins of nature, and the human substance. Even if some readers should refuse to accept all three parts of my argument, I suggest that any one of them suffices to make my case.

And what is my case? Simply that our most important task is to get off our present collision course. And who is there to tackle such a task? I think every one of us. . . . To talk about the future is useful only if it leads to action *now.* And what can we do *now,* while we are still in the position of "never having had it so good"? To say the least . . . we must thoroughly understand the problem and begin to see the possibility of evolving a new life-style, with new methods of production and new patterns of consumption: a life-style designed for permanence. To give only three preliminary examples: in agriculture and horticulture, we can interest ourselves in the perfection of production methods which are biologically sound, build up soil fertility, and produce health, beauty and permanence. Productivity will then look after itself. In industry, we can interest ourselves in the evolution of small-scale technology, relatively nonviolent technology, "technology with a human face," so that people have a chance to enjoy themselves while they are working, instead of working solely for their pay packet and hoping, usually forlornly, for enjoyment solely during their leisure time.

cism) became dominant in university circles. Logical empiricism rejected as senseless the emphasis of traditional philosophy on such issues as God, happiness, and the meaning of freedom. Largely based on the teachings of the Austrian philosopher Ludwig Wittgenstein (1889–1951), logical positivism concentrated on logic and a theory of knowledge. Impressed by the methods and achievements of modern science, it turned to mathematics and linguistics for its models. It was concerned with criticizing what people believe by analyzing what they say and how they know.

On the Continent, the philosophical doctrine of existentialism continued philosophy's traditional concern with moral questions and the immediate problems of life and existence. Although it had antecedents before the twentieth century, existentialism (especially in its atheistic form) was largely born of the desperation caused by two world wars and the breakdown of traditional values. Existentialism reflected the anxieties of the twentieth century and became especially well known after World War II through the works of two Frenchmen, Jean-Paul Sartre (1905–1980) and Albert Camus (1913–1960).

The beginning point of the existentialism of Sartre and Camus was the absence of God in the universe. While the death of God was tragic, it meant that humans had no preordained destiny and were utterly alone

According to Camus, then, the world was absurd and without meaning; humans, too, are without meaning and purpose. Reduced to despair and depression, humans have but one ground of hope—themselves.

While the world might be absurd, Camus argued, it could not be absurd unless people judged it to be so. People are unique in the world, and their kind of being is quite different from that of all others. In the words of Sartre, human "existence precedes essence." Humans are beings who first exist, and then afterward define themselves. They determine what they will be. According to Sartre: "Man is nothing else but what he makes of himself. Such is the first principle of existentialism." People then must take full responsibility for what they are. They create their values and give their lives mean-

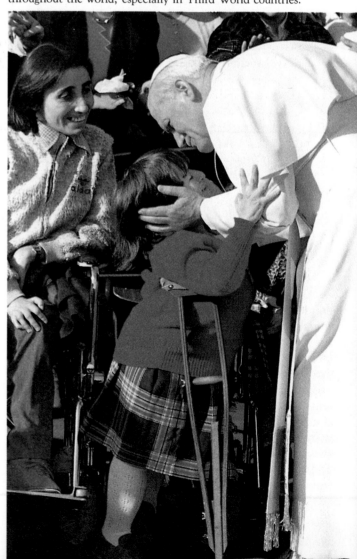

▼ **Pope John Paul II.** The travels of Pope John Paul II have helped to strengthen the presence of the Catholic church throughout the world, especially in Third World countries.

▼ **Sartre and De Beauvoir.** Jean-Paul Sartre and Simone de Beauvoir were two of the leading intellectuals in twentieth-century Europe. Sartre and de Beauvoir had a lifelong relationship that lasted until his death in 1980. Both were actively involved in the existentialist movement. De Beauvoir also played a crucial role in the emergence of the postwar women's liberation movement.

in the universe with no future and no hope. As Camus expressed it:

> A world that can be explained even with bad reasons is a familiar world. But, on the other hand, in a universe suddenly divested of illusions and lights, man feels an alien, a stranger. His exile is without remedy since he is deprived of the memory of a lost home or the hope of a promised land. This divorce between man and his life, the actor and his setting, is properly the feeling of absurdity.[10]

The Pope Denounces the Arms Race

▼ ▼ ▼

Pope John XXIII was a caring man who anguished over the world's social, economic, and political problems. In a papal letter entitled Pacem in Terris (Peace on Earth), *he argued for an end to the arms race.*

Pope John XXIII, *Pacem in Terris*, 1963

It is with deep sorrow that We note the enormous stocks of armaments that have been and still are being made in more economically developed countries, with a vast outlay of intellectual and economic resources. And so it happens that, while the people of these countries are loaded with heavy burdens, other countries as a result are deprived of the collaboration they need in order to make economic and social progress.

The production of arms is allegedly justified on the grounds that in present-day conditions peace cannot be preserved without an equal balance of armaments. And so, if one country increases its armaments, others feel the need to do the same; and if one country is equipped with nuclear weapons, other countries must produce their own, equally destructive.

Consequently, people live in constant fear lest the storm that every moment threatens should break upon them with dreadful violence. And with good reason, for the arms of war are ready at hand. . . . And one must bear in mind that, even though the monstrous power of modern weapons acts as a deterrent, it is to be feared that the mere continuance of nuclear tests, undertaken with war in mind will prove a serious hazard for life on earth.

Justice, then, right reason and humanity urgently demand that the arms race should cease; that the stockpiles which exist in various countries should be reduced equally and simultaneously by the parties concerned; that nuclear weapons should be banned; and that a general agreement should eventually be reached about progressive disarmament and an effective method of control. . . .

All must realize that there is no hope of putting an end to the building up of armaments, nor of reducing the present stocks, nor, still less, of abolishing them altogether, unless the process is complete and thorough and unless it proceeds from inner conviction: unless, that is, everyone sincerely co-operates to banish the fear and anxious expectation of war with which men are oppressed. If this is to come about, the fundamental principle on which our present peace depends must be replaced by another, which declares that the true and solid peace of nations consists not in equality of arms but in mutual trust alone. We believe that this can be brought to pass, and We consider that it is something which reason requires, that it is eminently desirable in itself and that it will prove to be the source of many benefits.

---

ing. And this can only be done by their involvement in life. Only through a person's acts can one determine his or her values. According to Sartre: "I may say that I like so-and-so well enough to sacrifice a certain amount of money for him, but I may say so only if I've done it."

Existentialism, therefore, involved an ethics of action, of involvement in life. But people could not define themselves without their involvement with others. Thus, existentialism's ethical message was just as important as its philosophy of being. Essentially, the message of existentialism was one of authenticity. Individuals true to themselves refused to be depersonalized by their society. As one author noted, "Existentialism is the struggle to discover the human person in a depersonalized age."

The Revival of Religion

Existentialism was one response to the despair generated by the apparent collapse of civilized values in the twentieth century. The revival of religion has been another. Ever since the Enlightenment of the eighteenth century, Christianity and religion had been on the defensive. But a number of religious thinkers and leaders attempted to bring new life to Christianity in the twentieth century. Despite the attempts of the Communist world to build an atheistic society and the West to build a secular society, religion continued to play an important role in the lives of many people.

One expression of this religious revival was the attempt by such theologians as the Lutheran Karl Barth

(1886–1968) to infuse traditional Christian teachings with new life. In his numerous writings, Barth attempted to reinterpret the religious insights of the Reformation era for the modern world. To Barth, the sinful and hence imperfect nature of human beings meant that humans could know religious truth not through reason, but only through the grace of God.

In the Catholic church, attempts at religious renewal came from two charismatic popes—John XXIII and John Paul II. Pope John XXIII (1881–1963) reigned as pope for only a short time (1958–1963), but sparked a dramatic revival of Catholicism when he summoned the twenty-first ecumenical council of the Catholic church. Known as Vatican Council II, it liberalized a number of Catholic practices. The mass was henceforth to be celebrated in the vernacular languages rather than Latin. New avenues of communication with other Christian faiths were also opened for the first time since the Reformation (see the box on p. 1031).

John Paul II (b. 1920), who had been the archbishop of Cracow in Poland before his elevation to the papacy in 1978, was the first non-Italian to be elected pope since the sixteenth century. Although he reasserted traditional Catholic teaching on such issues as papal authority, birth control, and clerical celibacy, John Paul's numerous travels around the world helped strengthen the Catholic church throughout the non-Western world. A strong believer in social justice, the charismatic John Paul II has been a powerful figure in reminding Europeans of their spiritual heritage and the need to temper the pursuit of materialism with spiritual concerns.

▼ The Creation of a New Society

During the postwar era, Western society has witnessed remarkably rapid change. Such products of new technologies as computers, television, jet planes, contraceptive devices, and new surgical techniques have all dramatically and quickly altered the pace and nature of human life.

Social Changes

The rapid changes in postwar society, fueled by scientific advances and rapid economic growth, have led many to view it as a new society. Called a technocratic society by some and the consumer society by others, postwar Western society has been characterized by a changing social structure and new movements for change.

SOCIAL STRUCTURE The structure of European society was altered after 1945. Especially noticeable were the changes in the middle class. Such traditional middle-class groups as businesspeople and professionals in law, medicine, and the universities were greatly augmented by a new breed of managers and technicians, as large corporations and government agencies employed increasing numbers of white-collar supervisory and administrative personnel. Whether in Eastern or Western Europe, the new managers and experts were not very different from each other. Everywhere their positions depended upon specialized skills acquired from some form of higher education. Everywhere they focused on the practical and efficient administration of their organizations. Since their positions usually depended upon their skills, they took steps to ensure that their own children would be educated.

Changes have also occurred among the traditional lower classes. Especially noticeable was the dramatic shift of people from rural to urban areas. After 1945, the number of peasants in most European countries dropped by 50 percent. While the size of the industrial working class stabilized or declined, making up slightly less than 50 percent of laborers in highly industrialized countries, there was a dramatic increase in the number of white-collar service employees. At the same time, a substantial increase in their real wages enabled the working classes to aspire to the consumption patterns of the middle class, leading to what some observers have called the "consumer society." Buying on the installment plan, which was introduced in the 1930s, became widespread in the 1950s and gave workers a chance to imitate the middle class by buying such products as televisions, washing machines, refrigerators, vacuum cleaners, and stereos. But the most visible symbol of mass consumerism was the automobile. Before World War II, cars were reserved mostly for the European upper classes. In 1948, there were 5 million cars in all of Europe, but by 1957, the number had tripled. By the 1960s, there were almost 45 million cars.

Rising incomes, combined with decreased working hours, created an even greater market for mass leisure activities. Between 1900 and 1980, the work week was reduced from sixty hours to forty hours. All aspects of popular culture—music, sports, media—became commercialized (see Popular Culture later in the chapter). Another very visible symbol of mass consumerism was the growth of mass travel and tourism. Before World War II, mostly the upper and middle classes enjoyed travel for pleasure. After the war, the combination of more vacation time and automobiles made it possible for many

1968: The Year of Student Revolts
▼ ▼ ▼

The outburst of student upheavals in the late 1960s reached its high point in 1968. These two very different selections illustrate some of the issues that prompted university students to occupy campus buildings and demand reforms.

A Student Manifesto in Search of a Real and Human Educational Alternative (University of British Columbia), June 1968

Today we as students are witnessing a deepening crisis within our society. We are intensely aware, in a way perhaps not possible for the older generation, that humanity stands on the edge of a new era. Because we are young, we have insights into the present and visions of the future that our parents do not have. Tasks of an immense gravity wait solution in our generation. We have inherited these tasks from our parents. We do not blame them so much for that . . . but we do blame them for being unwilling to admit that there are problems or for saying that it is we who have visited these problems on ourselves because of our perversity, ungratefulness and unwillingness to listen to "reason."

Much of the burden of solving the problems of the new era rests on the university. We have been taught to look to it for leadership. While we know that part of the reason for the university is to render direct services to the community, we are alarmed at its servility to industry and government as to what and how

it teaches. We are scandalized that the university fails to realize its role in renewing and vivifying those intellectual and moral energies necessary to create a new society—one in which a sense of personal dignity and human community can be preserved.

Student Inscriptions on the Walls of Paris, May and June 1968

The dream is the reality.
May 1968. World revolution is the order of the day.
I decree a state of permanent happiness.
To be free in 1968 is to take part.
Take the trip every day of your life.
Make love, not war.
No exams.
The mind travels farther than the heart but it doesn't go as far.
Run, comrade, the old are behind you!
Don't make a revolution in the image of your confused and hide-bound university.
Exam = servility, social promotion, hierarchic society.
Love each other.
SEX. It's good, said Mao, but not too often.
Alcohol kills. Take LSD.
Are you consumers or participants?
Professors, you are as old as your culture; your modernism is only the modernization of the police.
Live in the present.
Revolution, I love you.
Long live direct democracy!

---

members of the middle class and even workers to go to beaches, ski resorts, and mountain retreats. Moreover, as packaged tours with their lower travel rates and low-budget rooms became widely available, possibilities for travel abroad to other continents increased.

EDUCATION AND STUDENT REVOLT   Before World War II, higher education had largely remained the preserve of Europe's wealthier classes. Even in 1950, for example, only 3 or 4 percent of West European young people were enrolled in some form of higher education. Moreover, European higher education still largely centered on the liberal arts, pure science, and preparation for the professions of law and medicine.

Much of this changed after World War II as European universities experienced an influx of more students from the middle and even lower classes. The curriculum also expanded as such applied disciplines as computer science and business administration were introduced. Enrollments grew dramatically; in France, 4.5 percent of young people went to a university in 1950. By 1965, the figure had increased to 14.5 percent. Enrollments in European universities more than tripled between 1940 and 1960.

But there were problems. Overcrowded classrooms and lack of attention from professors led to student discontent. Moreover, despite changes in the curriculum, students often felt that the universities were not providing a really modern education. This discontent led to an outburst of student revolts in the late 1960s (see the box on p. 1033). In part, these protests were an extension of the large-scale disruptions in American universities in the mid-1960s, which were often sparked by student opposition to the Vietnam War. Perhaps the most famous student revolt occurred in France in 1968. It erupted at the University of Nanterre outside Paris but soon spread to the Sorbonne, the main campus of the University of Paris. French students demanded curriculum changes and a greater voice in the administration of the university. Students took over buildings and then expanded the scale of their protests when they invited workers to support them. Half of France's work force went on strike in May 1968. After the Gaullist government instituted a hefty wage hike, the workers returned to work and the police repressed the remaining student protesters.

The high point of the student protest movement was reached in 1968, although scattered incidents lasted into the early 1970s. There were several reasons for the student radicalism. Some students were genuinely motivated by the desire to reform the university. Others were protesting the Vietnam War, which they viewed as a product of Western imperialism. They also attacked other aspects of Western society, such as its materialism, and expressed concern about becoming cogs in the large and impersonal bureaucratic jungles of the modern world. For many students, the calls for democratic decision making within the universities were a reflection of their deeper concerns about the direction of Western society. Although student revolts fizzled out in the

1970s, the larger issues they raised have been increasingly revived in the late 1980s.

New (and Old) Patterns: Women in the Postwar World

After World War II, the trend toward earlier marriage continued. In Sweden, the average age of first marriage dropped from twenty-six in the 1940s to twenty-three in 1970. Although birthrates rose immediately after World War II, they have mostly declined since the war as both contraceptive devices and abortion have become widely available. It is estimated that mothers need to average 2.1 children in order to ensure a natural replacement of a country's population. In many European countries, the population stopped growing in the 1960s, and the trend has worsened since then. By 1990, fertility rates were down drastically; among the twelve nations of the European Community, the average number of children per mother was 1.58. No doubt, the trend toward early marriage and smaller families contributed to the changes in the character of women's employment in both Europe and the United States as women experienced considerably more years when they were not involved in rearing children.

The most important development was the increased number of married women in the work force. At the beginning of the twentieth century, even working-class wives tended to stay at home if they could afford to do so. In the postwar period, this was no longer the case. In the United States, for example, in 1900, married women made up about 15 percent of the female labor force; by

▼ **Student Revolts in Paris, 1968.** The discontent of university students exploded in the late 1960s in a series of student revolts. Perhaps best known was the student revolt in Paris in 1968. This photograph depicts one of the many violent confrontations between helmeted anti-riot policemen and rioting students.

1970, their number had increased to 62 percent. The percentage of married women in the female labor force in Sweden increased from 47 to 66 percent between 1963 and 1975. Figures for the Soviet Union and its satellites were even higher. In 1970, 92.5 percent of all women in the Soviet Union held jobs compared to around 50 percent in France and West Germany. The industrial development of the Soviet Union relied on female labor.

But the increased number of women in the work force has not changed some old patterns. Working-class women in particular still earn salaries lower than those of men for equal work. Women still tend to enter traditionally female jobs. As one Swedish woman guidance counselor remarked in 1975: "Every girl now thinks in terms of a job. This is progress. They want children, but they don't pin their hopes on marriage. They don't intend to be housewives for some future husband. But there has been no change in their vocational choices."[11] A 1980 study of twenty-five European nations revealed that women still made up over 80 percent of the typists, nurses, tailors, and dressmakers in their countries. Many European women also still faced the double burden of earning income on one hand and raising a family and maintaining the household on the other. Such inequalities led increasing numbers of women to rebel.

THE FEMINIST MOVEMENT: THE SEARCH FOR LIBERATION
The participation of women in World War I and II helped them achieve one of the major aims of the nineteenth-century feminist movement—the right to vote. Already after World War I, many governments acknowledged the contributions of women to the war effort by granting them the right to vote. Sweden, Great Britain, Germany, Poland, Hungary, Austria, and Czechoslovakia did so in 1918, followed by the United States in 1920. Women in France and Italy did not obtain the right to vote until 1945. After World War II, European women tended to fall back into the traditional roles expected of them, and little was heard of feminist concerns. But by the late 1960s, women began to assert their rights again and speak as feminists. Along with the student upheavals of the late 1960s came renewed interest in feminism, or the women's liberation movement as it was now called. Increasingly women protested that the acquisition of political and legal equality had not brought true equality with men:

We are economically oppressed: in jobs we do full work for half pay, in the home we do unpaid work full time. We are commercially exploited by advertisement, television and the

▼ **WOMANPOWER.** In the late 1960s, as women began once again to assert their rights, a revived women's liberation movement emerged. Feminists in the women's liberation movement maintained that women themselves must alter the conditions of their lives. This sign in a women's liberation parade shows that some women believed that it was time for "womanpower."

press; legally we often have only the status of children. We are brought up to feel inadequate, educated to narrower horizons than men. This is our specific oppression as women. It is as women that we are, therefore, organizing.[12]

These were the words of a British Women's Liberation Workshop in 1969.

Of great importance to the emergence of the postwar women's liberation movement was the work of Simone de Beauvoir (1908–1986). Born into a Catholic middle-class family and educated at the Sorbonne in Paris, she supported herself as a teacher and later as a novelist and writer. She established a lifelong relationship (but not marriage) with Jean-Paul Sartre. Her involvement in the existentialist movement—the leading intellectual movement of its time—led to her involvement in political causes. De Beauvoir believed that she lived a "liberated" life for a twentieth-century European woman, but for all her freedom, she still came to perceive that as a woman she faced limits that men did not. In 1949, she published her highly influential work, *The Second Sex,* in which she argued that as a result of male-dominated societies, women had been defined by their differences from men and consequently received second-class status: "What peculiarly signalizes the situation of woman is that she—a free and autonomous being like all human creatures—nevertheless finds herself living in a world where men compel her to assume the status of the Other."[13] De Beauvoir took an active role in the French women's movement of the 1970s, and her book was a

The Voice of the Women's Liberation Movement

▼ ▼ ▼

S imone de Beauvoir was an important figure in the emergence of the postwar women's liberation movement. This excerpt is taken from her influential book, The Second Sex, in which she argued that women have been forced into a position subordinate to men.

Simone de Beauvoir, The Second Sex

Now, woman has always been man's dependent, if not his slave; the two sexes have never shared the world in equality. And even today woman is heavily handicapped, though her situation is beginning to change. Almost nowhere is her legal status the same as man's, and frequently it is much to her disadvantage. Even when her rights are legally recognized in the abstract, long-standing custom prevents their full expression in the mores. In the economic sphere men and women can almost be said to make up two castes; other things being equal, the former hold the better jobs, get higher wages, and have more opportunity for success than their new competitors. In industry and politics men have a great many more positions and they monopolize the most important posts. In addition to all this, they enjoy a traditional prestige that the education of children tends in every way to support, for the present enshrines the past—and in the past all history has been made by men. At the present time, when women are beginning to take part in the affairs of the world, it is still a world that belongs to men—they have no doubt of it at all and women have scarcely any. To decline to be the Other, to refuse to be a party to a deal—this would be for women to renounce all the advantages conferred upon them by their alliance with the superior caste. Man-the-sovereign will provide woman-the-liege with material protection and will undertake the moral justification of her existence; thus she can evade at once both economic risk and the metaphysical risk of a liberty in which ends and aims must be contrived without assistance. Indeed, along with the ethical urge of each individual to affirm his subjective existence, there is also the temptation to forgo liberty and become a thing. This is an inauspicious road, for he who takes it—passive, lost, ruined—becomes henceforth the creature of another's will, frustrated in his transcendence and deprived of every value. But it is an easy road; on it one avoids the strain involved in undertaking an authentic existence. When man makes of woman the *Other*, he may, then, expect her to manifest deep-seated tendencies toward complicity. Thus, woman may fail to lay claim to the status of subject because she lacks definite resources, because she feels the necessary bond that ties her to man regardless of reciprocity, and because she is often very well pleased with her role as the *Other*.

Now, what peculiarly signalizes the situation of woman is that she—a free and autonomous being like all human creatures—nevertheless finds herself living in a world where men compel her to assume the status of the Other.

---

major influence on both the American and European women's movements (see the box above).

Feminists in the women's liberation movement came to believe that women themselves must transform the fundamental conditions of their lives. They did so in a variety of ways. First, in the 1960s and 1970s, they formed numerous "consciousness-raising" groups to further awareness of women's issues. Women also sought and gained a measure of control over their own bodies by seeking to overturn the illegality of both contraception and abortion. In the 1960s and 1970s, hundreds of thousands of European women worked to repeal the laws that outlawed contraception and abortion and began to meet with success. A French law in 1968 permitted the sale of contraceptive devices. In 1979, another French law legalized abortion. Even in Catholic countries, where the church remained strongly opposed to abortion, legislation allowing contraception and abortion was passed in the 1970s and 1980s. In the 1980s, the women's liberation movement concentrated on developing new cultural attitudes through the new academic field of "women's studies" and affecting the political and natural environment by allying with the antinuclear and ecological movements.

Popular Culture

Popular culture in the twentieth century, especially since World War II, has played an important role in helping Western people define themselves. If on one level popular culture is but the history of the superficial and transient whims of mass taste, on another level "it is a history of how modern society has created images of itself and expressed its fantasies, its fears, its ambitions."[14]

The history of popular culture is also the history of the economic system that supports it, for it is this system that manufactures, distributes, and sells the images that people consume as popular culture. As popular culture and its economic support system become increasingly intertwined, industries of leisure emerge. As one historian of popular culture has argued, "industrial societies turn the provision of leisure into a commercial activity, in which their citizens are sold entertainment, recreation, pleasure, and appearance as commodities that differ from the goods at the drugstore only in the way they are used."[15] Modern popular culture therefore is inextricably tied to the mass consumer society in which it has emerged. This consumer-oriented aspect of popular culture delineates it clearly from the folk culture of preceding centuries, for folk culture is something people make while popular culture is something people buy.

POPULAR CULTURE AND THE AMERICANIZATION OF THE WORLD The United States has been the most influential force in shaping popular culture in the West and, to a lesser degree, the entire world. Through movies, music, advertising, and television, the United States has spread its particular form of consumerism and the American Dream to millions around the world. Already in 1923 the New York *Morning Post* noted that "the film is to America what the flag was once to Britain. By its means Uncle Sam may hope some day . . . to Americanize the world."[16] In movies, television, and popular music, the impact of American popular culture on the Western world is apparent.

In the years immediately following the war, motion pictures continued to be the primary vehicle for the diffusion of American popular culture. The emergence of *film noir*—films with a darker outlook—was a characteristic of the period. The heroes, often private detectives, were not the typical good guys in white hats of the past, but characters who had a nasty side and often broke the law themselves. They were troubled individuals, sometimes by the war, more often by women. Women in *film noir* were usually portrayed as independent and highly sexual and were often linked to betrayal and murder. This darker side of male-female relationships stood in contrast to the light screwball comedies that had proliferated in the 1930s.

In the 1950s, Cold War tensions and the "bomb" found expression in a rash of spy movies and nuclear war films. In the 1960s, the film industry sagged as television prospered. In the late 1960s, youth-oriented films, such as *The Graduate* and *Easy Rider,* appealed to the eighteen to twenty-five year olds to whom Hollywood increasingly geared its films. Also popular were films that presented antiestablishment figures as heroes, such as *Bonnie and Clyde.* This was a clear reflection of the antiestablishment sentiment that was pervasive at this time in both the United States and Europe. These films mixed the reality of historical figures with contemporary social sentiment. From the mid-1970s throughout the 1980s, Hollywood concentrated on "blockbusting," the practice of spending huge sums on a few, big star films, often with tremendous special effects. All this was done to ensure huge box office hits. In this way one film could make or break a studio's year.

Although American films dominated both European and American markets (40 percent of Hollywood's income in the 1960s came from the European market), the existence of a profitable art-house circuit in America and Europe enabled European filmmakers to make films whose themes and avant-garde methods were quite different from those of Hollywood. Italy and Sweden, for example, developed a tradition of "national cinema" that reflected "specific cultural traits in a mode in which they could be successfully exported." The 1957 film *The Seventh Seal,* by the Swedish director Ingmar Bergman, was a good example of the successful European art film. Bergman's films caused him to be viewed as "an artist of comparable stature to a novelist or playwright." So too were François Truffaut in France and Federico Fellini in Italy; such directors gloried in experimenting with subject matter and technique and produced films dealing with more complex and daring themes than Hollywood would attempt.

Although developed in the 1930s, television did not become readily available until the late 1940s. By 1954, there were 32 million sets in the United States as television became the centerpiece of middle-class life. It has been said that television was perfect for the suburban home, the "nuclear family's bunker," as it was "a piece of furniture that did something." Early television borrowed heavily from radio. Like radio, it was based in New York.

In 1951, however, when the two most popular shows were "I Love Lucy" and "Dragnet," both based in Hollywood, television studios relocated to the West Coast.

In the 1960s, as television spread around the world, American networks unloaded their products on Europe and the Third World at extraordinarily low prices. For instance, the British Broadcasting Corporation (BBC) could buy American programs for one-tenth the cost per viewer of producing its own. The establishment of quota systems prevented American television from completely inundating these countries. Nevertheless, American shows have remained popular in Europe with the result that many Europeans base their understanding of American life on such programs as "Dallas" and "Dynasty."

Unlike the United States, television and radio in Europe have largely been controlled by the state. The BBC model strongly influenced German broadcasting after the war. In France, de Gaulle saw state control of television as an important counterbalance to the opposition French press. In the Communist countries of Eastern Europe and the Soviet Union, state control was even more pervasive. In the 1980s, however, there has been an increasing trend toward commercial television in Western Europe. As communism began to loosen its grip in Eastern Europe, calls for freedom of press and speech have been extended to mass media. In July of 1990, Gorbachev announced that independent television and radio productions would be allowed in the Soviet Union for the first time.

The United States has dominated popular music since the end of World War II. Jazz, blues, rhythm and blues, rap, and rock and roll have been by far the most popular music forms in the Western world—and much of the non-Western world—during this time. All of them originated in the United States, and all are rooted in African American musical innovations. These forms later spread to the rest of the world, inspiring local artists who then transformed the music in their own way. Often these transformed models then returned to the United States to inspire American artists. This was certainly the case with rock and roll. Through the 1950s, American figures such as Chuck Berry, Little Richard, and Elvis Presley inspired the Beatles and other British performers, who then led an "invasion" of the United States in the 1960s, creating a sensation and in part sparking new rockers in America. Rock music itself developed in the 1950s. In 1952, white disc jockeys began playing rhythm and blues and traditional blues music performed by African-Americans to young white audiences. The music was popular with this audience, and record companies began recording watered-down white cover versions of this music. It was not until such individuals as Elvis Presley mixed white "folkabilly" with rhythm and blues that rock and roll became popular with the larger white audience.

The period from 1967 to 1973 was probably the true golden age of rock. During this brief period, much experimentation in rock music took place, as it did in society in general. Straightforward rock and roll competed with a new hybrid blues rock, created in part by British performers such as the Rolling Stones, who were in turn inspired by African-American blues artists. Many musicians also experimented with non-Western musical sounds, such as Indian sitars. The one-world philosophy of the 1960s was expressed musically in this way. The popular music of the 1960s was also noted for

▼ **The Beatles in Concert.** Popular music has played a significant role in the impact of American popular culture on the postwar Western world. Although rock and roll originated in the United States, it also inspired musical groups in Europe as well. This was certainly true of Britain's Beatles, who created a sensation among young people when they came to the United States in the 1960s. Shown here are the Beatles during a performance on "The Ed Sullivan Show."

its social conscience. It was against the Vietnam War and materialism and promoted "peace and love" as alternatives to the prevailing "establishment" culture.

The same migration of a musical form from the United States to Britain and back to the United States occurred when the early punk movement in New York, which failed to make an immediate impact in the United States, spread to Britain in the mid-1970s. The more influential British punk movement of 1976–1979 was also fueled by an economic crisis that had resulted in large numbers of unemployed and undereducated young people. However, the punk movement was not simply a proletarian movement. Many of its supporters, performers, and promoters were British art school graduates who applied a leftist political philosophy and avant-garde experimentation to the movement. Punk rockers rejected most social conventions and preached anarchy and rebellion. They often wore tattered clothes and clothespins in their cheeks, symbolizing their rejection of a materialistic and degenerate culture. Musically, punk was extremely primitive in structure and performance, with noise and distortion elevated to art. Pure punk was short-lived, partly because its intense energy quickly burned out (as did many of its performers) and partly because, as ex-punk Mick Hucknall stated, "the biggest mistake of the punks was that they rejected music." However, offshoots of punk proliferated through the 1980s and continue to influence the rock and roll scene.

The social consciousness of popular music, so prevalent in the 1960s, also began to reappear in the late 1980s. Benefit concerts such as Live Aid, a high-technology affair staged simultaneously in London and Philadelphia, were held for the benefit of famine victims in Africa. At the same time, non-Western musical forms and sounds, heavy on rhythm and exotic tunings, began to influence Western pop music. The increasingly shrinking world, brought on by advancements in mass media technology, has led to a reemergence of the one-world philosophy of the 1960s. Some see this melding of world cultures as a positive step toward world unity, while others warn that it could lead to the watering down of cultural diversity and therefore the loss of unique forms of art.

SPORTS In the postwar years, sports have become a major product of both popular culture and the leisure industry. The development of satellite television and various electronic breakthroughs helped make sports a global phenomenon. Olympic Games could now be broadcast across the globe from anywhere in the world. Sports became a cheap form of entertainment for the consumer as fans did not have to leave their homes to enjoy athletic competitions. In fact, some sports organizations initially resisted television fearing that it would hurt ticket sales. However, the tremendous revenues possible from television contracts overcame this hesitation.

Television has also helped some sports, such as American football, to expand. Long a poor cousin of baseball, the suitability of American football to television programming and technology made it a perfect "telesport." By the mid-1960s, the National Football League had an exclusive contract with CBS for $14 million. By the end of the 1980s, football's television contract passed the $1 billion mark. As sports television revenue has escalated, many sports now receive the bulk of their yearly revenue from television contracts. The Olympics, for example, are now funded primarily by American television. These contracts are paid for by advertising sponsors, mostly for products to be consumed along with the sport: beer, soda, and snack foods. The 1984 Los Angeles Olympic Games were dubbed "the Corporate Games" and were the most financially successful in history. Whereas other Olympic contests have left massive debts, the Los Angeles Olympic Games turned a profit.

Sports have become big politics as well as big business. The politicization of sports has been one of the most significant trends in sports during the second half of the twentieth century. Football (soccer) remains the dominant world sport and has become more than ever a vehicle for nationalist sentiment and expression. The World Cup is the most watched event on television. Although the sport can be a positive outlet for national and local pride, all too often it has been marred by violence as nationalistic energies have overcome rational behavior. Events in Britain in particular have been marred by fan violence as extreme hooligans have rioted at matches.

The most telling example of the potent mix of politics and sport continues to be the Olympic Games. When the Soviets entered Olympic competition in 1952, the Olympics began to take on Cold War implications and became known as the "war without weapons." The Soviets saw the Olympics as a way to stimulate nationalist spirit, as well as to promote the Communist system as the best path for social progress. The Soviets have led the Olympics in terms of total medals won since 1956. The nature of the Olympics, with their daily medal count by nation and elaborate ceremonies and rituals such as the playing of the national anthem of the winning athletes and the parade of nations, virtually ensured the politicization of the games originally intended to foster international cooperation through friendly competition.

The political nature of the games found expression in other ways as well. In 1956, six nations withdrew from the games to protest the Soviet crushing of the Hungarian uprising. In 1972, twenty-seven African nations threatened to pull out of the Munich Olympics because of apartheid in South Africa. Also at the Munich Games, the Palestinian terrorist group Black September seized eleven Israeli athletes as hostages, all of whom died in a confrontation at an airport. The United States led a boycott of the 1980 Moscow Games to protest the Soviet invasion of Afghanistan, and the Soviets responded by boycotting the Los Angeles Games in 1984.

POPULAR CULTURE: TOWARD A NEW GLOBALISM Media critic and theorist Marshall McLuhan predicted in the 1960s that advancements in mass communications technology, such as satellites and electronics, would eventually lead to a shrinking of the world, a lessening of cultural distinctions, and a breaking down of cultural barriers, all of which would in time transform the world into a single "global village." McLuhan was quite optimistic about these developments, and his ideas became quite popular at the time. Many critics have since argued that McLuhan was too utopian about the benefits of technological progress and maintain that the mass media that these technological breakthroughs created are still controlled by a small number of multinational corporations that "colonize the rest of the world, sometimes benignly, sometimes not." They argue that this has allowed Western popular culture to disrupt the traditional cultures of Third World countries and inculcate new patterns of behavior as well as new desires and new dissatisfactions.

Cultural contacts, however, often move in two directions. While the world has been "Americanized" to a great extent, formerly unfamiliar ways of life and styles of music have also come into the world of the West. This has expanded the horizons of Westerners and led to the creation of new cultural hybrids in music, philosophy, and religion. There is some truth in the "global village" image, for increasingly in the late 1980s the one-world vision of the late 1960s has reemerged in popular culture. This was evident in the benefit concerts, for example, as well as in the increasing concern for such global issues as the destruction of the rain forests in South America. This emergence of a global culture has been part of the new globalism in the postwar world.

▼ A New Globalism

In large part, the new globalism that has come to characterize the postwar world has been a product of Western expansion. For better or worse, non-Western peoples have been forced to modernize. This has basically meant that these peoples have had to adjust to the continuing imposition of Western institutions, technology, and even attitudes upon their societies. The work of combining Western and non-Western ways to construct modern states began with the process of decolonization after World War II.

Decolonization

World War I had initiated nationalistic movements against colonial rule, but World War II greatly accelerated this process. The colonial empires of the Western nations in the Far East had already been overrun by the Japanese during the war. Moreover, colonial soldiers who had fought on behalf of the Allies were well aware that Allied war aims included the principle of self-determination for the peoples of the world. Equally important to the process of decolonization after the war, the power of the European states had been destroyed by the exhaustive struggles of World War II. The greatest colonial empire builder, Great Britain, no longer had the energy or wealth to maintain its colonial empire after the war and quickly sought to let its colonies go. Given the combination of circumstances, a rush of decolonization swept through the world. Between 1947 and 1962, almost every colony gained independence and achieved statehood. While some colonial powers willingly relinquished their control, others, especially the French, had to be driven out by national wars of liberation. Decolonization created a new world as the non-Western states ended the long-held ascendancy of the Western nations.

In Asia, the United States began the process of decolonization in 1946 when it granted independence to the Philippines. Britain soon followed suit with its oldest and largest nonwhite possession—India. The conflict between India's Hindu and Muslim populations was solved by forming two states, a mostly Hindu India and a predominantly Muslim Pakistan in 1947. In 1948, Britain granted independence to Ceylon (modern Sri Lanka) and Burma. When the Dutch failed to reestablish control over the Dutch East Indies, Indonesia emerged as an independent nation in 1949. The French effort to remain in Indochina led to a bitter defeat in

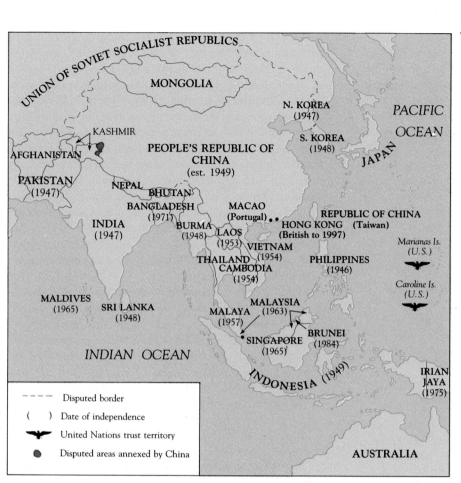

▼ **Map 29.5** Asia After World War II.

1954 by the forces of Ho Chi Minh, the Communist and nationalist leader of the Vietnamese. In the midst of the decolonization of Asia, a civil war between the Nationalist Chinese under Chiang Kai-Shek (1887–1975) and the Communists under Mao Zedong was being vigorously fought. Mao's victory in 1949 led to the creation of a powerful Communist state in Asia.

In the Middle East and northern Africa, Arab nationalism was a powerful factor in ending colonial empires. Although some Arab states had already become independent before the end of World War II, they were joined by other free Arab states, not without considerable bloodshed and complications, however. When the British left Palestine in 1947, the United Nations voted to create both an Arab and a Jewish state. When the Arabs attempted to destroy the new Israeli state, Israel's victories secured its existence. But the problem of the Palestinian refugees, supported by existing Arab states, created an Arab-Israeli conflict that has lasted to this day. In northern Africa, Arab nationalists in Algeria fought a bitter war of liberation with their French masters until Charles de Gaulle accepted the inevitable and granted Algerian independence in 1962.

Decolonization in Africa south of the Sahara took place less turbulently. Ghana proclaimed its independence in 1957, and by 1960, almost all French and British possessions in Africa had gained their freedom. In 1960, the Belgians freed the Congo (modern Zaire). The Portuguese held on stubbornly but were also driven out of Africa by 1975. Nevertheless, the continuing economic presence of European states in black Africa led radicals to accuse Europeans of "neocolonial" attitudes.

Although expectations ran high in the new states, they soon found themselves beset with problems of extreme poverty and antagonistic tribal groups that had little loyalty to the new nations. Under the new globalism, the world's nations soon divided into three levels. The "First World" consisted of the advanced industrial countries, basically by the 1960s Japan and the states of Western Europe and North America. The "Second World" comprised the Soviet Union and its satellites while most of the rest of the world's nations are known collectively as the "Third World." Their status as "backward" nations led many Third World countries to modernize by pursuing Western technology and industrialization. The gulf between the "developed" and "less developed" nations of the world, however, offers a major challenge to global stability in the decade ahead.

The United Nations

The United Nations has been one of the most visible symbols of the new postwar globalism. It was founded in 1945 in San Francisco when Allied representatives worked out a plan for the new organization. President Roosevelt had been especially anxious to create a new international organization to help maintain the peace after the war. At the Yalta Conference in February 1945, Stalin had agreed to join. In the original charter of the organization, its members pledged:

> to save succeeding generations from the scourge of war, which twice in our lifetime has brought untold sorrow to mankind, and to reaffirm faith in fundamental human rights, in the dignity and worth of the human person, in the equal rights of men and women and of nations large and small, and . . . to promote social progress and better standards of life in larger freedom.[17]

The United Nations, then, has two chief goals: peace and human dignity.

The General Assembly of the United Nations is composed of representatives of all members and is empowered to discuss any question of importance to the organization and to recommend action to be taken. The day-to-day administrative business of the United Nations is supervised by the secretary-general, whose offices are located at the permanent headquarters in New York City. The most important organ of the United Nations is the Security Council. It is composed of five permanent members—the United States, the Soviet Union, Great Britain, France, and China—and ten members chosen by the General Assembly. The Security Council decides what actions the United Nations should take to settle international disputes, but since each of the permanent members can veto the council's decision, a stalemate has frequently resulted.

A number of specialized agencies function under the auspices of the United Nations. These include the United Nations Educational, Scientific, and Cultural Organization (UNESCO), the World Health Organization (WHO), and the United Nations International Children's Emergency Fund (UNICEF). All of these have been successful in providing assistance for the world's economic and social problems. The United Nations has also performed a valuable service in organizing international conferences on such important issues as population growth and the environment.

The United Nations has also managed to provide peacekeeping military forces drawn from neutral member states to settle conflicts. Until recently, however, the fundamental weakness of the United Nations has been that throughout its history it has been subject to the whims of the two superpowers, whose rivalry in the Cold

▼ **Map 29.6** The Middle East After World War II.

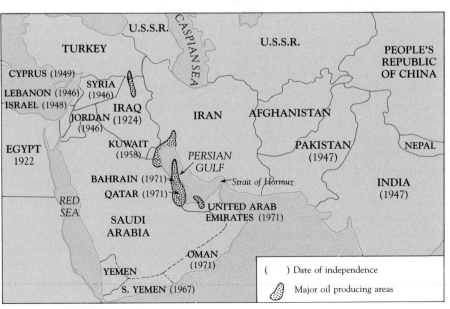

War was often played out at the organization's expense. The United Nations had little success, for example, in reducing the arms race between the United States and the Soviet Union. Nevertheless, the United Nations remains important in keeping alive a vision of international order and peace.

At the end of World War II, a new conflict erupted in the Western world as the two new superpowers, the United States and the Soviet Union, competed for political domination. Europeans, whether they wanted to or not, were forced to become supporters of one side or the other. But this ideological division also spread to the rest of the world as the United States fought in Korea and Vietnam to prevent the spread of communism, while the Soviet Union used its armies to prop up pro-Soviet regimes in Eastern Europe and Afghanistan.

But at the end of the 1980s, profound changes in the Soviet Union, initiated by Mikhail Gorbachev, brought an apparent end to the Cold War. The rapid collapse of Communist governments in Eastern Europe was clearly due to Gorbachev's reversal of Soviet postwar policy as he decided not to interfere in the internal turmoils of the Soviet satellites. Almost everywhere in Eastern Europe, Communist regimes gave way to popular demands for political reforms and restructuring.

In addition to the Cold War conflict, the postwar era has also been characterized by a new globalism, evident in popular culture as well as political, economic, and social developments around the world. World War II had

▼ **Map 29.7** Africa After World War II.

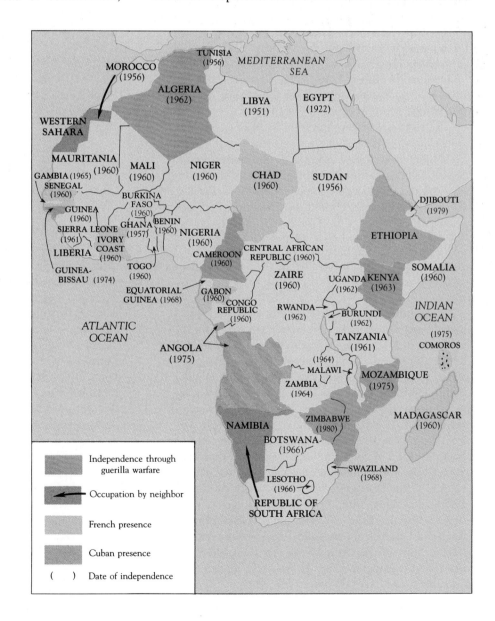

been a truly global conflict that ushered in a new global era. After the war, the colonial empires of the European states were largely dissolved, and the liberated territories of Africa, Asia, and the Middle East emerged as sovereign states. By the late 1980s, the approximately 160 sovereign states of the world had become an emerging global community. But the differences among the members of this global community are immense. An enormous economic gulf separates the "advanced industrial nations" from the "less developed" countries. More and more, however, the world's states have become aware of the fragile interdependence that connects them all.

Notes
▼ ▼ ▼

1. Quoted in Walter Laqueur, *Europe since Hitler*, rev. ed. (New York, 1982), p. 118.
2. Quoted in Joseph M. Jones, *The Fifteen Weeks (February 21–June 5, 1947)*, 2d ed. (New York, 1964), pp. 140–41.
3. Quoted in Wilfried Loth, *The Division of the World, 1941–1955* (New York, 1988), pp. 160–61.
4. Quoted in Peter Lane, *Europe since 1945: An Introduction* (Totowa, N.J., 1985), p. 248.
5. Quoted in Robert F. Kennedy, *Thirteen Days: A Memoir of the Cuban Missile Crisis* (New York, 1969), pp. 89–90.
6. R. Hilton, *Military Attaché in Moscow* (London, 1949), p. 41.
7. Nikita Khrushchev, *Khrushchev Remembers*, trans. Strobe Talbott (Boston, 1970), p. 77.
8. Mikhail Gorbachev, "Report to the 27th Party Congress," February 25, 1986, in *Current Soviet Policies* 9 (1986): 10.

9. *Philadelphia Inquirer*, July 11, 1990, p. 1a.
10. Quoted in Henry Grosshans, *The Search for Modern Europe* (Boston, 1970), p. 421.
11. Quoted in Hilda Scott, *Sweden's 'Right to be Human'—Sex-Role Equality: The Goal and the Reality* (London, 1982), p. 125.
12. Quoted in Marsha Rowe et al., *Spare Rib Reader* (Harmondsworth, 1982), p. 574.
13. Simone de Beauvoir, *The Second Sex*, trans. H. M. Parshley (New York, 1961), p. xxviii.
14. Richard Maltby, ed., *Passing Parade: A History of Popular Culture in the Twentieth Century* (New York, 1989), p. 8.
15. Ibid.
16. Quoted in ibid., p. 11.
17. "The Charter of the United Nations," *Yearbook of the United Nations* (New York, 1983), p. 1325.

Suggestions for Further Reading
▼ ▼ ▼

Three introductory surveys on postwar Europe are P. Lane, *Europe Since 1945: An Introduction* (Totowa, N.J., 1985); J. R. Wegs, *Europe Since 1945: A Concise History*, 2d ed. (New York, 1984); and W. Laqueur, *Europe Since Hitler*, rev. ed. (New York, 1982). There is a detailed literature on the Cold War. Two general accounts are R. B. Levering, *The Cold War, 1945–1972* (Arlington Heights, Ill., 1982); and B. A. Weisberger, *Cold War, Cold Peace: The United States and Russia Since 1945* (New York, 1984). The following works maintain that the Soviet Union was chiefly responsible for the Cold War: H. Feis, *From Trust to Terror: The Onset of the Cold War, 1945–1950* (New York, 1970); and A. Ulam, *The Rivals: America and Russia Since World War II* (New York, 1971). Revisionist studies on the Cold War have emphasized the responsibility of the United States for the Cold War, especially its global aspects. These works include J. and G. Kolko, *The Limits of Power: The World and United States Foreign Policy, 1945–1954* (New York, 1972); W. LaFeber, *America, Russia and the Cold War, 1945–1966*, 2d ed. (New York, 1972); and M. Sherwin, *A World Destroyed: The Atomic Bomb and the Grand Alliance* (New York, 1975). For a critique of the revisionist studies, see R. L. Maddox, *The New Left and the Origins of the Cold War* (Princeton, N. J., 1973). There is a detailed analysis of American-Soviet relations in the 1970s and 1980s in R. Garthoff, *Détente and Confrontation: American-Soviet Relations From Nixon to Reagan* (Washington, D. C., 1985). On the end of the Cold War, see B. Denitch, *The End of the Cold War* (Minneapolis, Minn., 1990); W. G. Hyland, *The Cold War is Over* (New York, 1990); and W. Laqueur, *Soviet Union 2000: Reform or Revolution?* (New York, 1990). For important studies of Soviet foreign policy, see A. B. Ulam, *Expansion and Coexistence: Soviet Foreign Policy 1917–1973*, 2d ed. (New York, 1974), and *Dangerous Relations: The Soviet Union in World Politics,*

1970–1982 (New York, 1983). The effects of the Cold War on Germany are examined in J. H. Backer, *The Decision to Divide Germany: American Foreign Policy in Transition* (Durham, N. Car., 1978). On atomic diplomacy in the Cold War, see G. F. Herken, *The Winning Weapon: The Atomic Bomb in the Cold War, 1945–1950* (New York, 1981). For a good introduction to the arms race, see E. M. Bottome, *The Balance of Terror: A Guide to the Arms Race,* rev. ed. (Boston, 1986). On the Cuban Missile Crisis, see R. A. Chayes, *The Cuban Missile Crisis* (New York, 1974). For a good account of the Vietnam War, see S. Karnow, *Vietnam: A History* (New York, 1983).

For a general view of Soviet society, see D. K. Shipler, *Russia: Broken Idols, Solemn Dreams* (New York, 1983). On the Khrushchev years, see E. Crankshaw, *Khrushchev: A Career* (New York, 1966). Recent problems in the Soviet Union are analyzed in A. Brown and M. Kaser, *Soviet Policy for the 1980s* (London, 1983). For a general study of the Soviet satellites in Eastern Europe, see A. Brown and J. Gary, *Culture and Political Changes in Communist States* (London, 1977); and S. Fischer-Galati, *Eastern Europe in the 1980s* (London, 1981). On the Soviet Union's actions against Czechoslovakia in 1968, see J. Valenta, *Intervention in Czechoslovakia in 1968* (Baltimore, 1979). The unique path of Yugoslavia is examined in L. J. Cohen and P. Warwick, *Political Cohesion in a Fragile Mosaic: The Yugoslav Experience* (Boulder, Colo., 1983). On Romania, see L. S. Graham, *Rumania: A Developing Socialist State* (Boulder, Colo., 1978). On Hungary, see B. Kovrig, *The Hungarian People's Republic* (Baltimore, 1970). The Solidarity movement in Poland is examined in T. G. Ash, *The Polish Revolution: Solidarity* (New York, 1984). On East Germany, see C. B. Scharf, *Politics and Change in East Germany* (Boulder, Colo., 1984).

The rebuilding of postwar Europe is examined in A. S. Milward, *The Reconstruction of Western Europe, 1945–51* (Berkeley, 1984). On the building of common institutions in Western Europe, see J. Lodge, *Institutions and Policies of the European Community* (New York, 1983). For a survey of West Germany, see M. Balfour, *West Germany: A Contemporary History* (London, 1983). France under de Gaulle is examined in P. Williams and M. Harrison, *Politics and Society in de Gaulle's Republic* (New York, 1971). On Britain, see C. J. Bartlett, *A History of Post-War Britain* (London, 1977); and A. Sampson, *The Changing Anatomy of Britain* (New York, 1982). On Italy, see J. LaPalombara, *Democracy, Italian Style* (New Haven, Conn., 1987).

For a general view of postwar thought, see R. N. Stromberg, *European Intellectual History Since 1789,* 4th ed. (Englewood Cliffs, N. J. 1986). Also valuable is D. LaCapra and S. L. Kaplan, eds., *Modern European Intellectual History: Reappraisals and New Perspectives* (Ithaca, N. Y., 1982). A physicist's view of science is contained in J. Ziman, *The Force of Knowledge: The Scientific Dimension of Society* (Cambridge, 1976). A physicist's view of a new conception of reality is D. Bohm, *Wholeness and the Implicate Order* (Boston, 1980). The space race is examined in W. A. McDougall, *The Heavens and the Earth: A Political History of the Space Age* (New York, 1984). For background on logical positivism, see A. Janik and S. Toulmin, *Wittgenstein's Vienna* (New York, 1973). A classic work on existentialism is W. Barrett, *Irrational Man* (Garden City, New York, 1962).

For a survey of contemporary Western society, see A. Sampson, *The New Europeans* (New York, 1968). The changing role of women is examined in E. Sullerot, *Women, Society and Change* (New York, 1971); and A. Cherlin, *Marriage, Divorce, Remarriage* (Cambridge, Mass., 1981). On the women's liberation movement, see D. Bouchier, *The Feminist Challenge: The Movement for Women's Liberation in Britain and the United States* (New York, 1983). The student revolts of the late 1960s are put into a broader context in L. S. Feuer, *The Conflict of Generations* (New York, 1969). There is an excellent survey of twentieth-century popular culture in R. Maltby, ed., *Passing Parade: A History of Popular Culture in the Twentieth Century* (Oxford, 1989). Also valuable is D. Horne, *The Public Culture: The Triumph of Industrialism* (London, 1986). On film and the media, see L. May, *Screening Out the Past: The Birth of Mass Culture and the Motion Picture Industry* (New York, 1980); E. A. Rhodes, *A History of the Cinema from the Silents to the Seventies* (Harmondsworth, 1978); and F. Wheen, *Television* (London, 1985). On popular music, see P. Eberly, *Music in the Air* (New York, 1982). Sport is examined in A. Guttmann, *From Ritual to Record: The Nature of Modern Sports* (New York, 1978); and R. Mandell, *Sport: A Cultural History* (New York, 1984). On the "global village" idea, see M. McLuhan, *Understanding Media: The Extensions of Man* (London, 1964).

On decolonization after World War II, see R. von Albertini, *Decolonization* (New York, 1971); A. Mazrui and M. Tidy, *Nationalism and New States in Africa* (London, 1984); J. Talbott, *The War without a Name: France in Algeria, 1954–1962* (New York, 1980); D. K. Shipler, *Arab and Jew: Wounded Spirits in a Promised Land* (New York, 1986). On the problems of the Third World, see P. Harrison, *Inside the Third World,* 2d ed. (New York, 1984). On the United Nations, see H. G. Nicholas, *The United Nations as a Political Institution* (New York, 1967).

Chapter 30

Epilogue: Toward A Global Civilization

▼▼▼▼▼

I ncreasingly, more and more people are becoming aware of the political and economic interdependence of the world's nations as well as the global nature of our contemporary problems. On the threshold of the twenty-first century, human beings are coming to understand that destructive forces generated in one part of the world soon affect the entire world. Nuclear proliferation makes nuclear war an ever-present possibility; nuclear war would mean radioactive fallout for the entire planet. Smokestack pollution in one nation can produce acid rain in another. Oil spills and dumping of wastes in the ocean have an impact on the shores of many nations. The consumption of drugs in the world's wealthy nations affects the stability of both wealthy and less developed nations. As food, water, energy, and natural resources crises proliferate, solutions by one nation often affect other nations. The new globalism includes the recognition that the challenges that seem to threaten human existence at the end of the twentieth century are global challenges. As a Soviet physicist and an American engineer jointly concluded: "The emergence of global problems and the recognition of their importance is perhaps the greatest accomplishment of contemporary thought."[1]

▼ The Emergence of New Global Visions

The authors of a report on the impact of population growth in South Asia concluded that the only way to avoid disaster in that region was to build a new global economic order:

In summary, the only feasible solution to the world food situation requires:

1. A global approach to the problem. . . .
3. A balanced economic development for all regions. . . .
5. Worldwide diversification of industry, leading to a truly global economic system.

Only a proper combination of these measures can lead to a solution. Omission of any one measure will surely lead to disaster. But the strains on the global food production capacity would be lessened if the eating habits in the affluent part of the world would change, becoming less wasteful.[2]

At the same time, some Western political thinkers have argued that we need to let go of practices that have evolved over the course of Western civilization, but no longer serve much purpose. Above all, war has been singled out as an issue that the current generation must seek to change. According to the Soviet and American editors of *Breakthrough-Emerging New Thinking:* "War, indiscriminate and brutal, which destroys the fragile civil processes it is designed to protect, wastes and ravages everything in its path, and twice in our century has decimated a generation of young men. . . . War is the issue for this generation, and global thinking is the challenge."[3]

As the heirs of Western civilization have become aware that the problems humans face are global—not national—they have responded to this challenge in several ways. One approach has been to develop grass-roots social movements, including environmental, women's and men's liberation, human potential, appropriate-technology, and nonviolence movements. Hazel Henderson, a British-born economist, has been especially active in founding public interest groups. She believes that citizen groups can be an important force for greater global unity and justice. In *Creating Alternative Futures,* she explained: "These aroused citizens are by no means all mindless young technophobes or radicals. Well-dressed, clean-shaven, middle-class businessmen and their suburban wives comprise the major forces in California fighting against nuclear power. Hundreds of thousands of middle-class mothers are bringing massive pressure to ban commercials and violent programs from children's television."[4] "Think globally, act locally" is frequently the slogan of these grass-roots groups.

Related to the emergence of these social movements is the growth of nongovernmental organizations (NGOs). The American educator Elise Boulding has been especially active in encouraging and publicizing the existence of these groups. According to Boulding,

NGOs are an important instrument in the cultivation of global perspectives:

Since NGOs by definition are identified with interests that transcend national boundaries, we expect all NGOs to define problems in global terms, to take account of human interests and needs as they are found in all parts of the planet. Because they have neither armies nor large bureaucracies at their command, we assume that they will utilize the power of shared values and concerns, rather than the power of political dominance to carry out aims. . . . Since they are emergent structures, we may also assume that they will reflect new perceptions of planetary society, and of appropriate social roles for individuals and groups. In short, we might look to them for new definitions of problems based on global frames of reference, and new ways of thinking and working.[5]

NGOs are often represented at the United Nations and include professional, business, and cooperative organizations; foundations; religious, peace, and disarmament groups; youth and women's organizations; environmental and human rights groups; and research institutes. The number of international NGOs increased from 176 in 1910 to 18,000 in 1988.

Some international NGOs have sections in both NATO and Warsaw Pact states, a reminder that the Communist countries are participating in the new global thinking. While this new sociopolitical thought began to emerge in the Soviet Union in the 1970s, it was Mikhail Gorbachev who implemented it in the 1980s in his policies for *glasnost* (openness) and *perestroika* (restructuring). In his book *Perestroika,* Gorbachev stated:

Thereby, an altogether different situation has emerged. A way of thinking and a way of acting, based on the use of force in world politics, have formed over centuries, even millennia. It seems they have taken root as something unshakable. Today, they have lost all reasonable grounds. . . . For the first time in history, basing international politics on moral and ethical norms that are common to all humankind, as well as humanizing interstate relations, has become a vital requirement. . . .

There is a great thirst for mutual understanding and mutual communication in the world. It is felt among politicians, it is gaining momentum . . . . among the public at large. And if the Russian word "perestroika" has easily entered the international lexicon, this is due to more than just interest in what is going on in the Soviet Union. Now the whole world needs restructuring, . . . a fundamental change.

People feel and understand this. They have to find their bearings, to understand the problems besetting mankind, to realize how they should live in the future. The restructuring is a must for a world overflowing with nuclear weapons; for a world ridden with serious economic and ecological problems; for a world laden with poverty, backwardness and disease; for a human race now facing the urgent need of ensuring its own survival.[6]

Gorbachev's thinking was clearly based on the recognition of an interdependent world.

Another source for global thinking in the West has come from the Western tradition's own spiritual perspective. As might be expected, a number of religious leaders have urged the West not to overlook its spiritual heritage as it searches for solutions to its problems. Somewhat more surprisingly, some secular figures, including Vaclav Havel, the president of Czechoslovakia, have also found inspiration in the West's spiritual tradition. In a speech to the American Congress on February 21, 1990, Havel declared:

> For this reason, the salvation of this human world lies nowhere else than in the human heart, in the human power to reflect, in human meekness and in human responsibility.
>
> Without a global revolution in the sphere of human consciousness, nothing will change for the better in the sphere of our being as humans, and the catastrophe toward which this world is headed—be it ecological, social, demographic or a general breakdown of civilization—will be unavoidable. . . .
>
> In other words, we still don't know how to put morality ahead of politics, science and economics. We are still incapable of understanding that the only genuine backbone of all our actions, if they are to be moral, is responsibility.
>
> Responsibility to something higher than my family, my country, my company, my success—responsibility to the order of being where all our actions are indelibly recorded and where and only where they will be properly judged.
>
> The interpreter or mediator between us and this higher authority is what is traditionally referred to as human conscience.[7]

Many lessons can be learned from the history of Western civilization, but one of them is especially clear. Lack of involvement in the affairs of one's society leads to powerlessness. An understanding of our Western heritage and its lessons might well give us the wisdom not to continue to repeat the mistakes of the past. For we are all creators of history and upon us depends the future of Western and indeed world civilization.

▼ **The Earth.** For many people in the West as in the rest of the world, the view of Earth from outer space fostered an important image of global unity. The American astronaut Russell Schweickart wrote: "From where you see it, the thing is a whole, and it is so beautiful." In a similar reaction, Yuri Gagarin, a Soviet cosmonaut, remarked: "What strikes me, is not only the beauty of the continents . . . but their closeness to one another . . . their essential unity."

Notes

▼ ▼ ▼

1. Sergei Kapitza and Martin Hellman, "A Message to the Scientific Community," in Anatoly Gromyko and Martin Hellman, eds., *Breakthrough—Emerging New Thinking: Soviet and Western Scholars Issue a Challenge to Build a World beyond War* (New York, 1988), p. xii.

2. Mihajlo Mesarovic and Eduard Pestel, *Mankind at the Turning Point: The Second Report to the Club of Rome* (New York, 1974), p. 127.

3. Gromyko and Hellman, eds., *Breakthrough*, p. 2.

4. Hazel Henderson, *Creating Alternative Futures* (New York, 1978), p. 356.

5. Elise Boulding, *Women in the Twentieth Century World* (New York, 1977), pp. 186–187.

6. Mikhail Gorbachev, *Perestroika* (New York, 1987), pp. 141, 253–254.

7. Vaclav Havel, *The Washington Post*, February 22, 1990, p. A28d.

Index

▼ ▼ ▼

Illustration Credits (*continued*)

▼ ▼ ▼

lin(West), Photo: Jorg P. Anders; **457**(Bottom Left) Jean Clouet, *Francis I, Musée du Louvre*, © Photo R. M. N.; **457**(Top Right) Alte Pinakothek Munich; **461** Hans Asper, *Zwingli*, Kunstmuseum Winterthur; **463** Reproduced by Courtesy of the Trustees of the British Museum; **468** The Bettmann Archive; **472** Oeffentliche Kunstsammlung Basel, Kunstmuseum: Colorphoto Hans Hinz; **477** Titian, *The Council of Trent*, Musée du Louvre, © Photo R. M. N.

Chapter 15

Page 482 Museés Royaux des Beaux-Arts de Belgique, Bruxelles(Photo by G. Cussac); **485** Musées Royaux des Beaux-Arts de Belgique, Bruxelles (Photo by G. Cussac); **489** National Maritime Museum Greenwich; **491** Francois Dubois D'Amiens, *The St. Bartholomew's Day Massacre*, Musée Cantonal des Beaux-Arts, Lausanne; **494** Derechos Reservados, © Museo del Prado, Madrid; **496** Private Collection; **499** Herzog Anton Ulrich-Museum, Braunschweig; **502** Herzog Anton Ulrich-Museum, Braunschweig; **509** The National Galleries of Scotland, By permission of the Earl of Rosebery; **511** Kunsthistorisches Museum, Vienna; **514**(Left) Scala/Art Resource, N.Y.; **514**(Right) Peter Paul Rubens, *The Landing of Marie de Medicis at Marseilles*, Musée du Louvre, © Photo R. M. N.; **515** Laocoon, El Greco, National Gallery of Art, Washington: Samuel H. Kress Collection; **516** Courtesy of James R. Spencer; **518** The National Portrait Gallery, London.

Chapter 16

Page 522 Hyacinthe Rigaud, *Louis XIV*, Musée du Louvre, © Photo R.M.N.; **525** Reproduced by Courtesy of the Trustees, The National Gallery, London; **527** Hyacinthe Rigaud, *Louis XIV*, Musée du Louvre, © Photo R. M. N.; **531** Courtesy of James R. Spencer; **532** Courtesy of James R. Spencer; **540** The Bettmann Archive; **542** Dumesnil, *Queen Christina of Sweden with Descartes*, Musee du Louvre, © Photo R. M. N.; **547** Courtesy of Jackson Spielvogel; **553** H. v. Schuylenburgh, *Head Office of the Dutch East India Company at Hugly in Bengal, 1665*, Rijksmuseum, Amsterdam; **555** Nicholas Poussin, *Landscape with the Burial of Phocion*, Musée du Louvre, © Photo R. M. N.; **556** Rembrandt, *The Syndics of the Cloth Guild*, Rijksmuseum, Amsterdam.

Chapter 17

Page 562 Bibliothèque Nationale, Paris; **566** Courtesy of the Lilly Library, Indiana University, Bloomington, Indiana; **567** Courtesy of the Lilly Library, Indiana University, Bloomington, Indiana; **569** Deutsches Museum, Munich; **571** Biblioteca Nazionale Centrale, Firenze; **575** National Portrait Gallery, London; **577** Metsys, *Paracelus*, Musée du Louvre, © Photo R. M. N.; **578** Reproduced by Courtesy of the Trustees of the British Museum; **582** Historical Pictures Service, Chicago; **588** Bibliothèque Nationale, Paris; **589** Reproduced by permission of the Trustees of the Science Museum(neg. 4534).

Chapter 18

Page 594 Giraudon/Art Resource, N.Y. Detail from *First Reading of Voltaire's "L'Orphelin de Chine"* at the Salon of Mme Geoffrin, 1725, by Lemmonier; **596** By permission of the Houghton Library, Harvard University; **600** Bibliothèque Nationale, Paris; **606** Allan Ramsay; *Jean-Jaques Rousseau*; National Gallery of Scotland; **608** Giraudon/Art Resource, N.Y. *First Reading of Voltaire's "L'Orphelin de Chine" at the Salon of Mme Geoffrin, 1725*, by Lemmonier; **610** Antoine Watteau, *The Pilgrimage to Cythera*, Mussee du Louvre, © Photo R. M. N.; **611** (Top and Bottom) Courtesy of James R. Spencer; **615** Germanisches Nationalmuseum; **616** Guildhall Library, City of London; **621** Pierre Deni-Martin, *Procession after Louis XV's Coronation at Rheims*, Musee National des Chateau de Versailles, © Photo R. M. N.

Chapter 19

Page 628 Detail from Benjamin West's *The Death of General Wolfe*, Transfer from the Canadian War Memorial, 1921, Gift of the Second Duke of Westminster, Eaton Hall, Cheshire, 1918, National Gallery of Canada, Ottawa; **632** National Portrait Gallery, London; **636** Staatliche Schlosser und Garten, Potsdam; **637** Kunsthistorisches Museum, Vienna; **645** Benjamin West, *The Death of General Wolfe*, Transfer from the Canadian War Memorial, 1921, Gift of the second Duke of Westminster, Eaton Hall, Cheshire, 1918, National Gallery of Canada, Ottawa; **647** Germanisches Nationalmuseum; **648** Reproduced by Courtesy of the Trustees of the British Museum; **652** Joseph Vernet, *Port of Dieppe*, Depot du Louvre au Musee de la Marine, © Photo R. M. N.; **654** Bibliothèque Nationale, Paris; **660** The Royal Collection, Copyright Reserved to Her Majesty Queen Elizabeth II; **662** Giovanni Michele Graneri, *Market in Piazza San Carlo, 1752*, Museo Civico di Torino.

Chapter 20

Page 666 Anonymous, *The Fall of the Bastille*, Musee National des Chateau de Versailles, © Photo R. M. N.; **670** Kemmelmeyer, *Washington Reviewing the Western Army at Fort Cumberland, Maryland*, The Metropolitan Museum of Art, Gift of Edgar William and Bernice Chrysler Garbisch, 1963(63.201.2); **678** Anonymous, *Fall of the Bastille*, Musee National des Chateau de Versailles, © Photo R. M. N.; **679** Bibliothèque Nationale, Paris; **682** The Mansell Collection; **684**(Left and Right) Bibliothèque Nationale, Paris; **685** *Execution of Louis XVI, 21 January 1793*, Musee Carnavalet, ·Paris/Bridgeman Art Library; **690** Giraudon/Art Resource, N.Y.; **693** Antoine Jean Gros, *Napoleon Crossing the Bridge at Arcola*, Musee du Louvre, © Photo R. M. N.; **696** Lauros-Giraudon/Art Resource, N.Y.

Chapter 21

Page 702 Courtesy of Sheffield City Museums; **705** Reproduced by permission of the Trustees of the Science Museum(neg. 385/54); **707** Reproduced by permission of the Trustees of the Science Museum(neg. 607/56); **709** Reproduced from the Collections of the Library of Congress; **711** Reproduced by Courtesy of the Trustees of the Victoria and Albert Museum; **715** Courtesy of the Rhode Island Historical Society; **719** Courtesy of Sheffield City Museums; **720** Gustave Dore, *Over London by Rail*, from *London, A Pilgrimage*; Billy Rose Theatre Collection, The New York Public Library at Lincoln Center; Astor, Lenox, and Tilden Foundations; **723** Bettmann/Hulton; **727** The Mansell Collection.

Chapter 22

Page 732 Lauros-Giraudon/Art Resource, N.Y.; **734** Isabey, *The Congress of Vienna*, Departement des Arts Graphiques, Musee du Louvre, © Photo R. M. N.; **737** Austrian Information Service; **739** Bordeaux Musee des Beaux-Arts; **741** Lauros-Giraudon/Art Resource, N.Y.; **744** Reproduced by Courtesy of the Trustees of the British Museum; **749** Bibliothèque Nationale, Paris; **757** Historisches Museum der Stadt Wien; **762** The Mansell Collection; **765** Parliament Square, Syndication International; **769** Caspar David Friedrich, *Man and Woman Gazing at the Moon*, Nationalgalerie SMPK Berlin, Photo: Jorg P. Anders, © Bildarchiv Preussischer Kulturbesitz, Berlin; **770** Eugene Delacroix, *Women of Algiers*, Musee du Louvre, © Photo R. M. N.

Chapter 23

Page 774 Civica Raccolta Stampe Achille Bertarelli, Castello Sforzesco, Milano; **777** Flandrin, *Napoleon III*, Musee National des Chateau de Versailles, © Photo R. M. N.; **781** Civica Raccolta Stampe Achille Bertarelli, Castello Sforzesco, Milano; **785** *Proclamation of the German Empire at Versailles, 1871*, Anton von Werner, Photo © Bildarchiv Preussischer